Features

Visit us on the Web at
http://www.census.gov/statab/www/

ACKNOWLEDGMENTS

Lars B. Johanson, Chief, Statistical Compendia Branch, was responsible for the technical supervision and coordination of this volume. Assisting in the research and analytical phases of assigned sections and in the development aspects of new tables were **Rosemary E. Clark**, **Richard P. Kersey**, **Jean F. Mullin**, and **Michael Sellner**. **Catherine Lavender** provided primary editorial assistance. Other editorial assistance was rendered by **Susan Antroinen** and **Barbara Shugart**.

Maps were designed and produced by **Connie Beard** and **Jessica Dobrowolski** of the Cartographic Products Management Branch within the Geography Division.

Catherine M. Raymond, **Patricia Edwards**, **Linda Chen**, and **Diane Oliff-Michael** of the Administrative and Customer Services Division, **Walter C. Odom**, Chief, provided publications and printing management, graphics design and composition, and editorial review for print and electronic media. General direction and production management were provided by **Wanda Cevis**, Chief, Publications Services Branch.

The cooperation of many contributors to this volume is gratefully acknowledged. The source note below each table credits the various government and private sector agencies that have collaborated in furnishing the information for the *Statistical Abstract*.

Statistical Abstract
of the United States: 2008

Issued October 2007

HA
202
.S8
2008

U.S. Department of Commerce
Carlos M. Gutierrez,
Secretary

Vacant,
Deputy Secretary

Economics and Statistics
Administration
Cynthia A. Glassman,
Under Secretary for Economic Affairs

U.S. CENSUS BUREAU
Charles Louis Kincannon,
Director

SUGGESTED CITATION

U.S. Census Bureau,
*Statistical Abstract of the
United States: 2008*
(127th Edition)
Washington, DC,
2007

ECONOMICS
AND STATISTICS
ADMINISTRATION

Economics
and Statistics
Administration

Cynthia A. Glassman,
Under Secretary
for Economic Affairs

U.S. CENSUS BUREAU

Charles Louis Kincannon,
Director

Preston Jay Waite,
Deputy Director and
Chief Operating Officer

Ted A. Johnson, Associate Director
for Administration
and Chief Financial Officer

Walter C. Odom, Chief, Administrative
and Customer Services Division

NATIONAL BIBLIOGRAPHY OF U.S. GOVERNMENT PUBLICATIONS

Statistical Abstract of the United States : 2008.—127 ed.
  Includes index.
  ISBN 978-0-16-078736-2
  ISSN 0081-4741
  1. United States—Statistics. I. United States. Census Bureau.

HA 202.S8 2008
317.3

Library of Congress Card No. 0418089

http://purl.access.gpo.gov/GPO/LPS2878

For sale by the Superintendent of Documents, U.S. Government Printing Office
Internet: bookstore.gpo.gov   Phone: toll free (866) 512-1800;   DC area (202) 512-1800
Fax: (202) 512-2104 Mail: Stop IDCC, Washington, DC 20402-0001

ISBN 978-0-16-079581-7

Preface

The *Statistical Abstract of the United States,* published since 1878, is the standard summary of statistics on the social, political, and economic organization of the United States. It is designed to serve as a convenient volume for statistical reference and as a guide to other statistical publications and sources. The latter function is served by the introductory text to each section, the source note appearing below each table, and Appendix I, which comprises the Guide to Sources of Statistics, the Guide to State Statistical Abstracts, and the Guide to Foreign Statistical Abstracts.

This volume includes a selection of data from many statistical sources, both government and private. Publications cited as sources usually contain additional statistical detail and more comprehensive discussions of definitions and concepts. Data not available in publications issued by the contributing agency but obtained from the Internet or unpublished records are identified in the source notes. More information on the subjects covered in the tables so noted may generally be obtained from the source.

Except as indicated, figures are for the United States as presently constituted. Although emphasis in the *Statistical Abstract* is primarily given to national data, many tables present data for regions and individual states and a smaller number for metropolitan areas and cities. Appendix II, Metropolitan and Micropolitan Statistical Areas: Concepts, Components, and Population, presents explanatory text, a complete current listing and population data for metropolitan and micropolitan areas defined as of December 2005. Statistics for the Commonwealth of Puerto Rico and for island areas of the United States are included in many state tables and are supplemented by information in Section 29. Additional information for states, cities, counties, metropolitan areas, and other small units,

as well as more historical data are available in various supplements to the *Abstract* (see inside back cover).

Statistics in this edition are generally for the most recent year or period available by summer 2007. Each year over 1,400 tables and charts are reviewed and evaluated; new tables and charts of current interest are added, continuing series are updated, and less timely data are condensed or eliminated. Text notes and appendices are revised as appropriate. In addition, three special features—*Historical Statistics, State Rankings,* and *USA Statistics in Brief*—can be found on our Web site: <http://www.census.gov /compendia/statab/>.

Changes in this edition—This year we have introduced 64 new tables covering a wide range of subject areas. These cover a variety of topics including: grandparents living with children, selected cosmetic plastic surgery procedures, average out-of-pocket expenses for undergraduates, workplace violence, tribal gaming revenue, Internet service providers, wildland fires, and tobacco consumption by country and sex. For a complete list of new tables, see section titled "New Tables," p. xi.

In addition to the above new tables, there are other changes to note for this edition. The title for Section 2, "Vital Statistics," has been changed to "Births, Deaths, Marriages, and Divorces"; Section 13, "Income, Expenditures, and Wealth," has been changed to "Income, Expenditures, Poverty, and Wealth"; and Section 26, "Arts, Entertainment, and Recreation," has been changed to "Arts, Recreation, and Travel."

Statistical Abstract on other media— The *Abstract* is available on the Internet and on CD-ROM. Both versions contain the same material as the book, except for a few copyrighted tables for which we did not receive permission to release in these

formats. Our Internet site <http://www .census.gov/compendia/statab/> contains this 2008 edition plus selected earlier editions in Adobe Acrobat .pdf format. Spreadsheet files for each table in the book are also available on the Web site and CD-ROM (free distribution of single copies on request). In many cases, the spreadsheet files show more years and/or subject/geographical detail.

Statistics for states and metropolitan areas—Extensive data for states and metropolitan areas of the United States can be found in the *State and Metropolitan Area Data Book: 2006*. This publication minus some data items, as well as selected rankings of the states and metropolitan areas, is available on our Internet site at <http: //www.census.gov/compendia/smadb>.

Statistics for counties and cities— Extensive data for counties can be found in the *County and City Data Book: 2007*. It features 175 data items covering everything from age and agriculture to retail trade and water use for all states and counties with U.S. totals for comparison. Also included are approximately 80 data items for cities with populations of 25,000 or more. Six tables present nearly 80 additional data items from the 2005 American Community Survey for 242 incorporated places with populations of 100,000 or more.

This publication is available on our Internet site at <http://www.census.gov

/compendia/ccdb> (tentative). For a database with over 6,000 county items, check out USA Counties at <http://censtats .census.gov/usa/usa.shtml>.

Limitations of the data—The contents of this volume were taken from many sources. All data from censuses and surveys or from administrative records are subject to error arising from a number of factors: Sampling variability (for statistics based on samples), reporting errors in the data for individual units, incomplete coverage, nonresponse, imputations, and processing error. (See also Appendix III, p. 907.) The Census Bureau cannot accept the responsibility for the accuracy or limitations of the data presented here, other than those for which it collects. The responsibility for selection of the material and for proper presentation, however, rests with the Census Bureau.

For additional information on data presented—Please consult the source publications available in local libraries or write to the agency indicated in the source notes. Write to the Census Bureau only if it is cited as the source.

Suggestions and comments—Users of the Statistical Abstract and its supplements (see inside back cover) are urged to make their data needs known for consideration in planning future editions. Suggestions and comments for improving coverage and presentation of data should be sent to the Director, U.S. Census Bureau, Washington, DC 20233.

Contents

[Numbers following subjects are page numbers]

New Tables

xii   New Tables

Guide to Tabular Presentation

Example of Table Structure

Table 521. **Seizure Statistics for Intellectual Property Rights (IPR): 2002 to 2006**

[In thousands (98,990 represents 98,990,000). Customs and Border Protection (CBP) is dedicated to protecting against the importation of goods which infringe/violate Intellectual Property Rights (IPR) by devoting substantial resources toward identifying and seizing shipments of infringing articles]

Item	2002	2003	2004	2005	2006
Number of IPR Seizures	5,793	6,500	7,255	8,022	14,675
Total domestic value in U.S. dollars of IPR Seizures ($1,000)[1].	98,990	94,019	138,768	93,235	155,369
Selected IPR commodities seized by value ($1,000):					
Footwear	(NA)	2,555	2,049	8,941	63,446
Wearing apparel	9,295	13,889	51,737	16,100	24,321
Handbags/wallets/backpacks	2,927	11,458	23,190	14,955	14,750
Cigarettes	37,580	41,720	24,161	9,649	(NA)
Consumer electronics [2]	5,307	3,780	8,880	8,794	7,057
Toys/electronic games	2,151	1,511	3,971	8,569	(NA)
Watches/parts.	3,919	3,384	2,543	3,071	(NA)
All others	6,154	5,697	13,184	13,550	13,060

NA Not available.   [1] Domestic value is the cost of the seized goods, plus the costs of shipping and importing the goods into the U.S. and an amount for profit.   [2] Consumer electronics includes cell phones and accessories, radios, and music on CD or tape.

Source: U.S. Department of Homeland Security, Customs and Border Protection, Import, Commercial Enforcement, Intellectual Property Rights, Seizure Statistics <www.cbp.gov/xp/cgov/import/commercial_enforcement/ipr/seizure/> (accessed 7 June 2007).

Headnotes immediately below table titles provide information important for correct interpretation or evaluation of the table as a whole or for a major segment of it.

Footnotes below the bottom rule of tables give information relating to specific items or figures within the table.

Unit indicators show the *specified quantities* in which data items are presented. They are used for two primary reasons. Sometimes data are not available in absolute form and are estimates (as in the case of many surveys). In other cases we round the numbers in order to save space to show more data, as in the case above.

EXAMPLES OF UNIT INDICATOR INTERPRETATION FROM TABLE

Year	Item	Unit Indicator	Number shown	Multiplier
2002	Value of seizures	$ Thousands	98,990	1,000

To Determine the Figure it is Necessary to Multiply the Number Shown by the Unit Indicator:

Value of seizures by Customs and Border Patrol – 98,990 x $1,000 = $98,990,000 (almost $99 million)

When a table presents data with more than one unit indicator, they are found in the headnotes and column headings (Tables 2 and 26), spanner (Table 39), stub (Table 25), or unit column (Table 130). When the data in a table are shown in the same unit indicator, it is shown in boldface as the first part of the headnote (Table 2). If no unit indicator is shown, data presented are in absolute form (Table 1).

Vertical rules are used to separate independent sections of a table (Table 1), or in tables where the stub is continued into one or more additional columns (Table 2).

Averages—An average is a single number or value that is often used to represent the "typical value" of a group of numbers. It is regarded as a measure of "location" or "central tendency" of a group of numbers.

The *arithmetic mean* is the type of average used most frequently. It is derived by summing the individual item values of a particular group and dividing the total by the number of items. The arithmetic mean is often referred to as simply the "mean" or "average."

The *median* of a group of numbers is the middle number or value when each item in the group is arranged according to size (lowest to highest or visa versa); it generally has the same number of items above it as well as below it. If there is an even number of items in the group, the median is taken to be the average of the two middle numbers.

Per capita (or per person) quantities—a per capita figure represents an average computed for every person in a specified group (or population). It is derived by taking the total for an item (such as income, taxes, or retail sales) and dividing it by

the number of persons in the specified population.

Index numbers—An index number is the measure of difference or change, usually expressed as a percent, relating one quantity (the variable) of a specified kind to another quantity of the same kind. Index numbers are widely used to express changes in prices over periods of time, but may also be used to express differences between related subjects for a single point in time.

To compute a price index, a base year or period is selected. The base year price (of the commodity or service) is then designated as the base or reference price to which the prices for other years or periods are related. Many price indexes use the year 1982 as the base year; in tables this is shown as "1982 = 100." A method of expressing the price relationship is: The price of a set of one or more items for a related year (e.g. 1990) **divided by** the price of the same set of items for the base year (e.g. 1982). The result multiplied by 100 provides the index number. When 100 is subtracted from the index number, the result equals the percent change in price from the base year.

Average annual percent change—Unless otherwise stated in the *Abstract* (as in Section 1, Population), average annual percent change is computed by use of a *compound interest formula*. This formula assumes that the rate of change is constant throughout a specified compounding period (1 year for average annual rates of change). The formula is similar to that used to compute the balance of a savings account that receives compound interest. According to this formula, at the end of a compounding period the amount of accrued change (e.g., school enrollment or bank interest) is added to the amount that existed at the beginning of the period. As a result, over time (e.g., with each year or quarter), the same rate of change is applied to a larger and larger figure.

The *exponential formula*, which is based on continuous compounding, is often used to measure population change. It is preferred by population experts, because they view population and population-related subjects as changing without interruption, ever ongoing. Both exponential and compound interest formulas assume a constant rate of change. The former, however, applies the amount of change continuously to the base rather than at the end of each compounding

period. When the average annual rates are small (e.g., less than 5 percent) both formulas give virtually the same results. For an explanation of these two formulas as they relate to population, see U.S. Census Bureau, *The Methods and Materials of Demography*, Vol. 2, 3d printing (rev.), 1975, pp. 372–381.

Current and constant dollars—Statistics in some tables in a number of sections are expressed in both current and constant dollars (see, e.g., Table 659 in Section 13, Income, Expenditures, Poverty, and Wealth). Current dollar figures reflect actual prices or costs prevailing during the specified year(s). Constant dollar figures are estimates representing an effort to remove the effects of price changes from statistical series reported in dollar terms. In general, constant dollar series are derived by dividing current dollar estimates by the appropriate price index for the appropriate period (e.g., the Consumer Price Index). The result is a series as it would presumably exist if prices were the same throughout, as in the base year—in other words, as if the dollar had constant purchasing power. Any changes in this constant dollar series would reflect only changes in real volume of output, income, expenditures, or other measure.

Explanation of Symbols

The following symbols, used in the tables throughout this book, are explained in condensed form in footnotes to the tables where they appear:

– Represents zero or rounds to less than half the unit of measurement shown.

B Base figure too small to meet statistical standards for reliability of a derived figure.

D Figure withheld to avoid disclosure pertaining to a specific organization or individual.

NA Data not enumerated, tabulated, or otherwise available separately.

S Figure does not meet publication standards for reasons other than that covered by symbol B, above.

X Figure not applicable because column heading and stub line make entry impossible, absurd, or meaningless.

Z Entry would amount to less than half the unit of measurement shown.

In many tables, details will not add to the totals shown because of rounding.

Telephone & Internet Contacts

To help *Abstract* users find more data and information about statistical publications, we are issuing this list of contacts for federal agencies with major statistical programs. The intent is to give a single, first-contact point-of-entry for users of statistics. These agencies will provide general information on their statistical programs and publications, as well as specific information on how to order their publications. We are also including the Internet (World Wide Web) addresses for many of these agencies. These URLs were current in July 2007.

Executive Office of the President
Office of Management and Budget
Administrator
Office of Information and Regulatory
 Affairs
Office of Management and Budget
725 17th Street, NW
Washington, DC 20503
Information: 202-395-3080
Internet address:
 http://www.whitehouse.gov/omb

Department of Agriculture
Economic Research Service
Information Center
U.S. Department of Agriculture
1800 M Street, NW
Washington, DC 20036-5831
Information and Publications:
 202-694-5050
Internet address:
 http://www.ers.usda.gov/

National Agricultural Statistics Service
National Agricultural Statistics Service
USDA-NASS
1400 Independence Ave., SW
Washington, DC 20250
Information hotline: 1-800-727-9540
Internet address:
 http://www.nass.usda.gov/

Department of Commerce
U.S. Census Bureau
Customer Services Branch
U.S. Census Bureau
4600 Silver Hill Road
Washington, DC 20233
Information and Publications:
1-800-923-8282
Internet address:
 http://www.census.gov/

Bureau of Economic Analysis
Bureau of Economic Analysis
1441 L Street, NW
Washington, DC 20230
Information and Publications:
202-606-9900
Internet address: http://www.bea.gov/

Department of Commerce—Con.
International Trade Administration
International Trade Administration
1401 Constitution Ave., NW
U.S. Department of Commerce
Washington, DC 20230
Information: 1-800-872-8723
Internet address: http://trade.gov/

National Oceanic and Atmospheric Administration
National Oceanic and Atmospheric
 Administration Central Library
U.S. Department of Commerce
1315 East-West Highway
SSMC3, 2nd Floor
Silver Spring, MD 20910
Library: 301-713-2600 x.124
Internet address:
 http://www.lib.noaa.gov/

Department of Defense
Department of Defense
Directorate for Public Inquiry and
 Analysis
Office of the Assistant Secretary of
 Defense, Public Affairs
Room 3A750
1400 Defense Pentagon
Washington, DC 20301-1400
Information: 703-428-0711
Internet address:
 http://www.defenselink.mil

Department of Education
National Library of Education
U.S. Department of Education
400 Maryland Avenue, SW
Washington, DC 20202
Education Information and Statistics:
1-800-872-5327
Education Publications: 1-877-433-7827
Internet address: http://www.ed.gov/

Department of Energy
Energy Information Administration
National Energy Information Center
Energy Information Administration
1000 Independence Ave., SW
Washington, DC 20585
Information and Publications:
202-586-8800
Internet address:
 http://www.eia.doe.gov/

Department of Health and Human Services

Health Resources and Services Administration
HRSA Information Center
P.O. Box 2910
Merrifield, VA 22116
Information Center: 1-888-275-4772
Internet address: http://www.hrsa.gov/

Substance Abuse and Mental Health Services Administration
Substance Abuse and Mental Health Services Administration
1 Choke Cherry Road
Rockville, MD 20857
Information: 240-276-2130
Publications: 1-877-726-4727
Internet address:
http://www.samhsa.gov/

Centers for Disease Control and Prevention
Public Inquiries/MASO
1600 Clifton Road
Atlanta, GA 30333
Public Inquiries: 1-800-311-3435
Internet address: http://www.cdc.gov/

Centers for Medicare and Medicaid Services (CMS)
U.S. Department of Health and Human Services
7500 Security Boulevard
Baltimore, MD 21244
1-877-267-2323
Internet address:
http://www.cms.hhs.gov/

National Center for Health Statistics
National Center for Health Statistics
3311 Toledo Road
Hyattsville, MD 20782
1-800-232-4636
Internet address:
http://www.cdc.gov/nchs

Department of Homeland Security

Office of Public Affairs
245 Murray Lane, NW
Washington, DC 20258
Information and Publications:
202-282-8010
Internet address: http://www.dhs.gov

Department of Housing and Urban Development

Office of the Assistant Secretary for Community Planning and Development
451 7th St., SW
Washington, DC 20410
Information: 202-708-1112
Publications: 1-800-767-7468
Internet address: http://www.hud.gov/

Department of the Interior

U.S. Geological Survey
USGS National Center
12201 Sunrise Valley Drive
Reston, VA 20192
Information and Publications:
1-888-275-8747
Internet address for minerals:
http://minerals.usgs.gov/
Internet address for other materials:
http://ask.usgs.gov/

Department of Justice

Bureau of Justice Statistics
Statistics Division
810 7th Street, NW
Washington, DC 20531
Information and Publications:
1-800-851-3420
Datasets and Codebooks: 1-800-999-0960
Internet address:
http://www.ojp.usdoj.gov/bjs/

National Criminal Justice Reference Service
P.O. Box 6000
Rockville, MD 20849-6000
Publications: 1-800-851-3420
Internet address: http://www.ncjrs.gov/

Federal Bureau of Investigation
Federal Bureau of Investigation
J. Edgar Hoover Building
935 Pennsylvania Avenue, NW
Washington, DC 20535-0001
Information: 202-324-3000
Internet address: http://www.fbi.gov/

Department of Labor

Bureau of Labor Statistics
Office of Publications and Special Studies Services
Bureau of Labor Statistics
Postal Square Building
2 Mass. Ave., NE
Washington, DC 20212-0001
Information and Publications:
202-691-5200
Internet address: http://www.bls.gov/

Employment and Training Administration
U.S. Department of Labor
Francis Perkins Building
200 Constitution Ave., NW
Washington, DC 20210
Information and Publications:
1-877-872-5627
Internet address: http://www.doleta.gov/

Department of Transportation

Federal Aviation Administration

Federal Aviation Administration
800 Independence Ave., SW
Washington, DC 20591
Information and Publications:
1-866-835-5322
Internet address: http://www.faa.gov/

Bureau of Transportation Statistics

Bureau of Transportation Statistics
1200 New Jersey Avenue, SE
Washington, DC 20590
Products and Statistical Information:
1-800-853-1351
Internet address: http://www.bts.gov/

Federal Highway Administration

Office of Public Affairs
U.S. Department of Transportation
1200 New Jersey Avenue, SE
Washington, DC 20590
Information: 1-202-366-0660
Internet address:
http://www.fhwa.dot.gov/

National Highway Traffic Safety Administration

Office of Public & Consumer Affairs
1200 New Jersey Avenue, SE—West
Building
Washington, DC 20590
Information and Publications:
1-888-327-4236
Internet address:
http://www.nhtsa.dot.gov/

Department of the Treasury

Internal Revenue Service

Statistics of Income Division
Internal Revenue Service
P. O. Box 2608
Washington, DC 20013-2608
Information and Publications:
202-874-0410
Internet address:
http://www.irs.gov/taxstats/

Department of Veterans Affairs

Department of Veterans Affairs
Office of Public Affairs
810 Vermont Ave., NW
Washington, DC 20420
Information: 202-273-6000
Internet address: http://www.va.gov/

Independent Agencies

Administrative Office of the U.S. Courts

Office of Public Affairs
Washington, DC 20544
Information: 202-502-2600
Internet address:
http://www.uscourts.gov/

Board of Governors of the Federal Reserve System

Division of Research and Statistics
Federal Reserve Board
20th & Constitution Avenue, NW
Washington, DC 20551
Information: 202-452-3000
Publications: 202-452-3245
Internet address:
http://www.federalreserve.gov/

Environmental Protection Agency

Environmental Protection Agency
Ariel Rios Building
1200 Pennsylvania Ave., NW
Washington, DC 20460
Publications: 202-564-4355
Internet address: http://www.epa.gov/

National Science Foundation

Office of Legislation and Public Affairs
National Science Foundation
4201 Wilson Boulevard
Arlington, Virginia 22230
Information: 703-292-5111
Publications: 703-292-8134
Internet address: http://www.nsf.gov/

Securities and Exchange Commission

Office of Public Affairs
Securities and Exchange Commission
100 F Street, NE
Washington, DC 20549
Information: 202-942-8088
Publications: 202-551-4040
Internet address: http://www.sec.gov/

Social Security Administration

Social Security Administration
Office of Public Inquiries
6401 Security Boulevard
Baltimore, MD 21235
Information and Publications:
1-800-772-1213
Internet address:
http://www.socialsecurity.gov/

Population

This section presents statistics on the growth, distribution, and characteristics of the U.S. population. The principal source of these data is the U.S. Census Bureau, which conducts a decennial census of population, a monthly population survey, a program of population estimates and projections, and a number of other periodic surveys relating to population characteristics.

Decennial censuses—The U.S. Constitution provides for a census of the population every 10 years, primarily to establish a basis for apportionment of members of the House of Representatives among the states. For over a century after the first census in 1790, the census organization was a temporary one, created only for each decennial census. In 1902, the Census Bureau was established as a permanent federal agency, responsible for enumerating the population and also for compiling statistics on other population and housing characteristics.

Historically, the enumeration of the population has been a complete (100 percent) count. That is, an attempt is made to account for every person, for each person's residence, and for other characteristics (sex, age, family relationships, etc.). Since the 1940 census, in addition to the complete count information, some data have been obtained from representative samples of the population. In the 1990 and 2000 censuses, variable sampling rates were employed. For most of the country, 1 in every 6 households (about 17 percent) received the long form or sample questionnaire; in governmental units estimated to have fewer than 2,500 inhabitants, every other household (50 percent) received the sample questionnaire to enhance the reliability of sample data for small areas. Exact agreement is not to be expected between sample data and the 100-percent count. Sample data may be used with confidence where large numbers are involved and assumed to indicate trends and relationships where small numbers are involved.

Current Population Survey (CPS)—This is a monthly nationwide survey of a scientifically selected sample representing the noninstitutionalized civilian population. The sample is located in 824 areas with coverage in every state and the District of Columbia and is subject to sampling error. At the present time, about 60,000 occupied households are eligible for interview every month; of these, about 8 percent are, for various reasons, unavailable for interview.

While the primary purpose of the CPS is to obtain monthly statistics on the labor force, it also serves as a vehicle for inquiries on other subjects. Using CPS data, the Census Bureau issues a series of publications under the general title of *Current Population Reports*, which cover population characteristics (P20), consumer income (P60), special studies (P23), and other topics.

Estimates of population characteristics based on the CPS will not agree with the counts from the census because the CPS and the census use different procedures for collecting and processing the data for racial groups, the Hispanic population, and other topics. Caution should also be used when comparing estimates for various years because of the periodic introduction of changes into the CPS. Beginning in January 1994, a number of changes were introduced into the CPS that effect all data comparisons with prior years. These changes included the results of a major redesign of the survey questionnaire and collection methodology and the introduction of 1990 census population controls, adjusted for the estimated undercount. Beginning with the 2001 CPS Annual Demographic Supplement, the independent estimates used as control totals for the CPS are based on civilian population benchmarks consistent with Census 2000. In March 2002, the sample size of the Annual Demographic Supplement was increased to approximately 78,000. In 2003 the name of the March supplement was changed to Annual Social

U.S. Census Bureau, Statistical Abstract of the United States: 2008

and Economic Supplement. These changes in population controls had relatively little impact on derived measures such as means, medians, and percent distribution, but did have a significant impact on levels.

American Community Survey (ACS)—This is a nationwide survey to obtain data about demographic, social, economic, and housing information of people, households, and housing units. The survey collects the same type of information that has been collected every 10 years from the long-form questionnaire of the census, which the American Community Survey will replace. The estimates are limited to the household population and exclude the population living in institutions, college dormitories, and other group quarters.

Population estimates and projections—Estimates of the United States population are derived by updating the resident population enumerated in Census 2000 with information on the components of population change: births, deaths, and net international migration. The April 1, 2000, population used in these estimates reflects modifications to the Census 2000 population as documented in the Count Question Resolution program.

Registered births and deaths are estimated from data supplied by the National Center for Health Statistics. The net international migration component consists of three parts: (1) net migration of the foreign born, (2) emigration of natives, and (3) net movement from Puerto Rico to the United States (50 states and DC). Data from the American Community Survey are used to estimate the annual net migration of the foreign-born population. Estimates of native emigration and net movement between Puerto Rico and the United States are derived from the Demographic Analysis and Population Estimates (DAPE) project (see Population Division Working Paper Series, No. 63 and No. 64).

Estimates for state and county areas are based on the same components of change data and sources as the national estimates with the addition of net internal migration. School enrollment statistics from state departments of education and parochial school systems, federal income

tax returns from the Internal Revenue Service, group quarters data from the Federal-State Cooperative Program, and Medicare data from the Centers for Medicare and Medicaid Services are also included.

The population by age for April 1, 1990, (shown in Table 7) reflects modifications to the 1990 census data counts. The review of detailed 1990 information indicated that respondents tended to report age as of the date of completion of the questionnaire, not as of April 1, 1990. In addition, there may have been a tendency for respondents to round up their age if they were close to having a birthday. A detailed explanation of the age modification procedure appears in 1990 Census of Population and Housing, Data Paper Listing CPH-L74.

Population estimates and projections are available on the Census Bureau Internet site <http://www.census.gov>. These estimates and projections are consistent with official decennial census figures with no adjustment for estimated net census coverage. However, the categories for these estimates and projections by race have been modified and are not comparable to the census race categories (see section below under "Race"). For details on methodology, see the sources cited below the individual tables.

Immigration—Immigration (migration *to* a country) is one component of international migration; the other component is emigration (migration *from* a country). In its simplest form, international migration is defined as any movement across a national border. In the United States, federal statistics on international migration are produced primarily by the U.S. Census Bureau and the Office of Immigration Statistics (located in the U.S. Department of Homeland Security).

The Census Bureau collects data used to estimate international migration through its decennial censuses and numerous surveys of the U.S. population.

The Office of Immigration Statistics publishes immigration data in annual flow reports and the *Yearbook of Immigration Statistics*. Data for these publications are collected from several administrative data sources including the DS-230 Application for Immigrant Visa and Alien Registration

(U.S. Department of State) for new arrivals, and the I-485 Application to Register Permanent Residence or Adjust Status (U.S. Citizenship and Immigration Services—USCIS) for persons adjusting immigrant status.

An immigrant, or legal permanent resident, is a foreign national who has been granted lawful permanent residence in the United States. New arrivals are foreign nationals living abroad who apply for an immigrant visa at a consular office of the Department of State, while individuals adjusting status are already living in the United States and file an application for adjustment of status to lawful permanent residence with USCIS. Individuals adjusting status include refugees, asylees, and various classes of nonimmigrants, such as temporary workers, foreign students, and certain undocumented immigrants. A nonimmigrant is a foreign national who enters the United States temporarily for a specific purpose. A refugee is an alien outside the United States who is unable or unwilling to return to his or her country of origin because of persecution or a well founded fear of persecution. Asylees must meet the same criteria as refugees, but are located in the United States or at a port of entry. After 1 year of residence, refugees and asylees are eligible to adjust to legal permanent resident status.

U.S. immigration law gives preferential immigration status to persons with a close family relationship with a U.S. citizen or legal permanent resident, persons with needed job skills, persons who qualify as refugees or asylees, and persons who are from countries with relatively low levels of immigration to the United States. Immigration to the United States can be divided into two general categories: (1) those subject to the annual worldwide limitation and (2) those exempt from it. Numerical limits are imposed on visas issued and not on admissions. The maximum number of visas available under the preference categories in 2006 was 369,949—226,000 for family-sponsored immigrants and 143,949 for employment-based immigrants. Those exempt from the worldwide limitation include immediate relatives of U.S. citizens, refugees and asylees adjusting to permanent residence, and other various classes of special immigrants (see Table 47).

Metropolitan and micropolitan areas—The U.S. Office of Management and Budget (OMB) defines metropolitan and micropolitan statistical areas according to published standards that are applied to Census Bureau data. The general concept of a metropolitan or micropolitan statistical area is that of a core area containing a substantial population nucleus, together with adjacent communities having a high degree of economic and social integration with that core. Currently defined metropolitan and micropolitan statistical areas are based on application of 2000 standards to 2000 decennial census data as updated by application of those standards to more recent Census Bureau population estimates. The term "metropolitan area" (MA) was adopted in 1990 and referred collectively to metropolitan statistical areas (MSAs), consolidated metropolitan statistical areas (CMSAs), and primary metropolitan statistical areas (PMSAs). The term "core-based statistical area" (CBSA) became effective in 2003 and refers collectively to metropolitan and micropolitan statistical areas.

Over time, new statistical areas are created and the components of others change. Because of historical changes in geographic definitions, users must be cautious in comparing data for these statistical areas from different dates. For descriptive details and a list of titles and components of metropolitan and micropolitan statistical areas, see Appendix II.

Urban and rural—For Census 2000, the Census Bureau classified as urban all territory, population, and housing units located within urbanized areas (UAs) and urban clusters (UCs). A UA consists of densely settled territory that contains 50,000 or more people, while a UC consists of densely settled territory with at least 2,500 people but fewer than 50,000 people. (UCs are a new type of geographic entity for Census 2000.) From the 1950 census through the 1990 census, the urban population consisted of all people living in UAs and most places outside of UAs with a census population of 2,500 or more.

U.S. Census Bureau, Statistical Abstract of the United States: 2008

UAs and UCs encompass territory that generally consists of:

- A cluster of one or more block groups or census blocks each of which has a population density of at least 1,000 people per square mile at the time.
- Surrounding block groups and census blocks each of which has a population density of at least 500 people per square mile at the time.
- Less densely settled blocks that form enclaves or indentations, or are used to connect discontiguous areas with qualifying densities.

They also may include an airport located adjacent to qualifying densely settled area if it has an annual enplanement (aircraft boarding) of at least 10,000 people.

"Rural" for Census 2000 consists of all territory, population, and housing units located outside of UAs and UCs. Prior to Census 2000, rural consisted of all territory, population, and housing outside of UAs and outside of other places designated as "urban." For Census 2000, many more geographic entities, including metropolitan areas, counties, county subdivisions, and places, contain both urban and rural territory, population, and housing units.

Residence—In determining residence, the Census Bureau counts each person as an inhabitant of a usual place of residence (i.e., the place where one lives and sleeps most of the time). While this place is not necessarily a person's legal residence or voting residence, the use of these different bases of classification would produce the same results in the vast majority of cases.

Race—For the 1990 census, the Census Bureau collected and published racial statistics as outlined in Statistical Policy Directive No. 15 issued by the OMB. This directive provided standards on ethnic and racial categories for statistical reporting to be used by all federal agencies. According to the directive, the basic racial categories were American Indian or Alaska Native, Asian or Pacific Islander, Black, and White. (The directive identified Hispanic origin as an ethnicity.) The question on race for Census 2000 was different from the one for the 1990 census in

several ways. Most significantly, respondents were given the option of selecting one or more race categories to indicate their racial identities. Because of these changes, the Census 2000 data on race are not directly comparable with data from the 1990 census or earlier censuses. Caution must be used when interpreting changes in the racial composition of the United States population over time. Census 2000 adheres to the federal standards for collecting and presenting data on race and ethnicity as established by the OMB in October 1997. Starting with Census 2000, the OMB requires federal agencies to use a minimum of five race categories: White, Black or African American, American Indian or Alaska Native, Asian, and Native Hawaiian or Other Pacific Islander. Additionally, to collect data on individuals of mixed race parentage, respondents were allowed to select one or more races. For respondents unable to identify with any of these five race categories, the OMB approved and included a sixth category— "Some other race" on the Census 2000 questionnaire. The Census 2000 question on race included 15 separate response categories and three areas where respondents could write in a more specific race group. The response categories and write-in answers can be combined to create the five minimum OMB race categories plus "Some other race." People who responded to the question on race by indicating only one race are referred to as the *race alone* population, or the group that reported only one race category. Six categories make up this population: White alone, Black or African American alone, American Indian and Alaska Native alone, Asian alone, Native Hawaiian and Other Pacific Islander alone, and Some other race alone. Individuals who chose more than one of the six race categories are referred to as the *Two or More Races* population, or as the group that reported more than one race. Additionally, respondents who reported one race together with those who reported the same race plus one or more other races are combined to create the *race alone or in combination* categories. For example, the *White alone or in combination group* consists of those respondents who reported only White or who reported White combined with one or more other race

groups, such as "White and Black or African American," or "White and Asian and American Indian and Alaska Native." Another way to think of the group who reported White alone or in combination is as the total number of people who identified entirely or partially as White. This group is also described as people who reported White, whether or not they reported any other race.

The *alone or in combination* categories are tallies of *responses* rather than *respondents*. That is, the alone or in combination categories are not mutually exclusive. Individuals who reported two races were counted in two separate and distinct alone or in combination race categories, while those who reported three races were counted in three categories, and so on. Consequently, the sum of all alone or in combination categories equals the number of races reported (i.e., responses) which exceeds the total population.

The concept of race, as used by the Census Bureau, reflects self-identification by people according to the race or races with which they most closely identify. These categories are sociopolitical constructs and should not be interpreted as being scientific or anthropological in nature. Furthermore, the race categories include both racial and national-origin groups. Additionally, data are available for the American Indian and Alaska Native tribes. A detailed explanation of race can be found at <http://www.census.gov/prod/cen2000/doc/sf1.pdf>.

Data for the population by race for April 1, 2000, (shown in Tables 6, 8, and 9) are modified counts and are not comparable to Census 2000 race categories. These numbers were computed using Census 2000 data by race that had been modified to be consistent with the 1997 OMB's "Revisions to the Standards for the Classification of Federal Data on Race and Ethnicity," (Federal Register Notice, Vol. 62, No 210, October 1997). A detailed explanation of the race modification procedure appears on the Census Web page <http://www.census.gov/popest/archives/files/MRSF-01-US1.html>.

In the CPS and other household sample surveys in which data are obtained through personal interview, respondents are asked to classify their race as: (1) White; (2) Black, African American, or Negro; (3) American Indian or Alaska Native; (4) Asian; (5) Native Hawaiian or Other Pacific Islander. Beginning January 2003, respondents were allowed to report more than one race to indicate their mixed racial heritage.

Hispanic population—The Census Bureau collected data on the Hispanic-origin population in the 2000 census by using a self-identification question. Persons of Spanish/Hispanic/Latino origin are those who classified themselves in one of the specific Hispanic origin categories listed on the questionnaire—Mexican, Puerto Rican, Cuban, as well as those who indicated that they were of Other Spanish/ Hispanic/Latino origin. Persons of Other Spanish/Hispanic/Latino origin are those whose origins are from Spain, the Spanish-speaking countries of Central or South America, or the Dominican Republic.

In the CPS, information on Hispanic persons is gathered by using a self-identification question. Based on a two-part question, the respondents are first asked whether or not they are of Hispanic, Spanish, or Latino origin and based on their response are further classified into the following categories: Mexican or Mexican American or Chicano; Puerto Rican; Cuban; Central or South American; or Other Hispanic, Spanish, or Latino origin group.

Traditional and current data collection and classification treat race and Hispanic origin as two separate and distinct concepts in accordance with guidelines from the OMB. Race and Hispanic origin are two separate concepts in the federal statistical system. People who are Hispanic may be any race and people in each race group may be either Hispanic or Not Hispanic. Also, each person has two attributes, their race (or races) and whether or not they are Hispanic. The overlap of race and Hispanic origin is the main comparability issue. For example, Black Hispanics (Hispanic Blacks) are included in both the number of Blacks and in the number of Hispanics. For further information, see Census Web page <http://www.census.gov/population/www/socdemo/compraceho.html>.

U.S. Census Bureau, Statistical Abstract of the United States: 2008

Foreign-born and native populations—The Census Bureau separates the U.S. resident population into two groups based on whether or not a person was a U.S. citizen or U.S. national at the time of birth. Anyone born in the United States, Puerto Rico, or a U.S. Island Area (such as Guam) or born abroad to a U.S. citizen parent is a U.S. citizen at the time of birth and consequently included in the *native population.* The term *foreign-born population* refers to anyone who is not a U.S. citizen or U.S. national at birth. This includes naturalized U.S. citizens, legal permanent resident aliens (immigrants), temporary migrants (such as foreign students), humanitarian migrants (such as refugees), and people illegally present in the United States. The Census Bureau provides a variety of demographic, social, economic, geographic, and housing information on the foreign-born population in the United States at <http://www.census.gov/population/www/socdemo/foreign.html>.

Mobility status—The U.S. population is classified according to mobility status on the basis of a comparison between the place of residence of each individual at the time of the survey or census and the place of residence at a specified earlier date. Nonmovers are all persons who were living in the same house or apartment at the end of the period as at the beginning of the period. Movers are all persons who were living in a different house or apartment at the end of the period than at the beginning of the period. Movers are further classified as to whether they were living in the same or different county, state, region, or were movers from abroad. Movers from abroad include all persons, either U.S. citizens or noncitizens, whose place of residence was outside the United States (including Puerto Rico, other U.S. Island Area, or a foreign country) at the beginning of the period.

Living arrangements—Living arrangements refer to residency in households or in group quarters. A "household" comprises all persons who occupy a "housing unit," that is, a house, an apartment or other group of rooms, or a single room that constitutes "separate living quarters." A household includes the related family members and all the unrelated persons, if any, such as lodgers, foster children, wards, or employees who share the housing unit. A person living alone or a group of unrelated persons sharing the same housing unit is also counted as a household. See text, Section 20, Construction and Housing, for definition of housing unit.

All persons not living in housing units are classified as living in group quarters. These individuals may be institutionalized, e.g., under care or custody in juvenile facilities, jails, correctional centers, hospitals, or nursing homes; or they may be residents in noninstitutional group quarters such as college dormitories, group homes, or military barracks.

Householder—The householder is the person in whose name the home is owned or rented. If a home is owned or rented jointly by a married couple, either the husband or the wife may be listed first.

Family—The term family refers to a group of two or more persons related by birth, marriage, or adoption and residing together in a household. A family includes among its members the householder.

Subfamily—A subfamily consists of a married couple and their children, if any, or one parent with one or more never married children under 18 years old living in a household. Subfamilies are divided into "related" and "unrelated" subfamilies. A related subfamily is related to, but does not include, the householder or the spouse of the householder. Members of a related subfamily are also members of the family with whom they live. The number of related subfamilies, therefore, is not included in the count of families. An unrelated subfamily may include persons such as guests, lodgers, or resident employees and their spouses and/or children; none of whom is related to the householder.

Married couple—A married couple is defined as a husband and wife living together in the same household, with or without children and other relatives.

Statistical reliability—For a discussion of statistical collection and estimation, sampling procedures, and measures of statistical reliability applicable to Census Bureau data, see Appendix III.

6 Population

Table 1. **Population and Area: 1790 to 2000**

[Area figures represent area on indicated date including in some cases considerable areas not then organized or settled, and not covered by the census. Area data include Alaska beginning in 1870 and Hawaii beginning in 1900. Total area figures for 1790 to 1970 have been recalculated on the basis of the remeasurement of states and counties for the 1980 census, but not on the basis of the 1990 census. The land and water area figures for past censuses have not been adjusted and are not strictly comparable with the total area data for comparable dates because the land areas were derived from different base data, and these values are known to have changed with the construction of reservoirs, draining of lakes, etc. Density figures are based on land area measurements as reported in earlier censuses]

| Census date | Resident population | | | | Area (square miles) | | |
| | Number | Per square mile of land area | Increase over preceding census | | Total | Land | Water [1] |
			Number	Percent			
1790 (Aug. 2)	3,929,214	4.5	(X)	(X)	891,364	864,746	24,065
1800 (Aug. 4)	5,308,483	6.1	1,379,269	35.1	891,364	864,746	24,065
1810 (Aug. 6)	7,239,881	4.3	1,931,398	36.4	1,722,685	1,681,828	34,175
1820 (Aug. 7)	9,638,453	5.5	2,398,572	33.1	1,792,552	1,749,462	38,544
1830 (June 1)	12,866,020	7.4	3,227,567	33.5	1,792,552	1,749,462	38,544
1840 (June 1)	17,069,453	9.8	4,203,433	32.7	1,792,552	1,749,462	38,544
1850 (June 1)	23,191,876	7.9	6,122,423	35.9	2,991,655	2,940,042	52,705
1860 (June 1)	31,443,321	10.6	8,251,445	35.6	3,021,295	2,969,640	52,747
1870 (June 1)	[2]39,818,449	[2]11.2	8,375,128	26.6	3,612,299	3,540,705	68,082
1880 (June 1)	50,189,209	14.2	10,370,760	26.0	3,612,299	3,540,705	68,082
1890 (June 1)	62,979,766	17.8	12,790,557	25.5	3,612,299	3,540,705	68,082
1900 (June 1)	76,212,168	21.5	13,232,402	21.0	3,618,770	3,547,314	67,901
1910 (Apr. 15)	92,228,496	26.0	16,016,328	21.0	3,618,770	3,547,045	68,170
1920 (Jan. 1)	106,021,537	29.9	13,793,041	15.0	3,618,770	3,546,931	68,284
1930 (Apr. 1)	123,202,624	34.7	17,181,087	16.2	3,618,770	3,554,608	60,607
1940 (Apr. 1)	132,164,569	37.2	8,961,945	7.3	3,618,770	3,554,608	60,607
1950 (Apr. 1)	151,325,798	42.6	19,161,229	14.5	3,618,770	3,552,206	63,005
1960 (Apr. 1)	179,323,175	50.6	27,997,377	18.5	3,618,770	3,540,911	74,212
1970 (Apr. 1)	203,302,031	57.5	23,978,856	13.4	3,618,770	3,536,855	78,444
1980 (Apr. 1)	[3]226,542,199	64.0	23,240,168	11.4	3,618,770	3,539,289	79,481
1990 (Apr. 1)	[4]248,718,302	70.3	22,176,103	9.8	[5]3,717,796	3,536,278	[5]181,518
2000 (Apr. 1)	[6]281,424,603	79.6	32,706,301	13.1	3,794,083	3,537,438	256,645

X Not applicable.   [1] Data for 1790 to 1980 cover inland water only. Data for 1990 comprise Great Lakes, inland, and coastal water. Data for 2000 comprise Great Lakes, inland, territorial, and coastal water.   [2] Revised to include adjustments for underenumeration in southern states; unrevised number is 38,558,371 (10.9 per square mile).   [3] Total population count has been revised since the 1980 census publications. Numbers by age, race, Hispanic origin, and sex have not been corrected.   [4] The April 1, 1990, census count includes count question resolution corrections processed through December 1997, and does not include adjustments for census coverage errors.   [5] Data reflect corrections made after publication of the results.   [6] Reflects modifications to the Census 2000 population as documented in the Count Question Resolution program.

Source: U.S. Census Bureau, 2000 Census of Population and Housing, *Population and Housing Counts*, Series PHC-3-1, United States Summary; *Notes and Errata, 2000* SF/01-ER ; <http://www.census.gov/prod/cen2000/notes/errata.pdf>; *Areas of the United States: 1940*; Area data for 1990: unpublished data from TIGER®; and Davis, Warren; personal correspondence; U.S. Census Bureau; 23 June 2006.

Table 2. **Population: 1960 to 2006**

[In thousands, except percent (180,671 represents 180,671,000). Estimates as of July 1. Total population includes Armed Forces abroad; civilian population excludes Armed Forces. For basis of estimates, see text of this section]

| Year | Total | | Resident population | Civilian population | Year | Total | | Resident population | Civilian population |
	Population	Percent change [1]				Population	Percent change [1]		
1960	180,671	1.60	179,979	178,140	1984	236,348	0.87	235,825	234,110
1961	183,691	1.67	182,992	181,143	1985	238,466	0.90	237,924	236,219
1962	186,538	1.55	185,771	183,677	1986	240,651	0.92	240,133	238,412
1963	189,242	1.45	188,483	186,493	1987	242,804	0.89	242,289	240,550
1964	191,889	1.40	191,141	189,141	1988	245,021	0.91	244,499	242,817
1965	194,303	1.26	193,526	191,605	1989	247,342	0.95	246,819	245,131
1966	196,560	1.16	195,576	193,420	1990	250,132	1.13	249,623	247,983
1967	198,712	1.09	197,457	195,264	1991	253,493	1.34	252,981	251,370
1968	200,706	1.00	199,399	197,113	1992	256,894	1.34	256,514	254,929
1969	202,677	0.98	201,385	199,145	1993	260,255	1.31	259,919	258,446
1970	205,052	1.17	203,984	201,895	1994	263,436	1.22	263,126	261,714
1971	207,661	1.27	206,827	204,866	1995	266,557	1.18	266,278	264,927
1972	209,896	1.08	209,284	207,511	1996	269,667	1.17	269,394	268,108
1973	211,909	0.96	211,357	209,600	1997	272,912	1.20	272,647	271,394
1974	213,854	0.92	213,342	211,636	1998	276,115	1.17	275,854	274,633
1975	215,973	0.99	215,465	213,789	1999	279,295	1.15	279,040	277,841
1976	218,035	0.95	217,563	215,894	2000	282,430	1.12	282,217	280,972
1977	220,239	1.01	219,760	218,106	2001	285,454	1.07	285,226	283,990
1978	222,585	1.06	222,095	220,467	2002	288,427	1.04	288,126	286,859
1979	225,055	1.11	224,567	222,969	2003	291,289	0.99	290,796	289,576
1980	227,726	1.19	227,225	225,621	2004	294,056	0.95	293,638	292,377
1981	229,966	0.98	229,466	227,818	2005	296,940	0.98	296,507	295,316
1982	232,188	0.97	231,664	229,995	2006	299,801	0.96	299,398	298,219
1983	234,307	0.91	233,792	232,097					

[1] Percent change from immediate preceding year.

Source: U.S. Census Bureau, 1960 to 1979: *Current Population Reports* P25-802 and P25-917; 1980 to 1989: "Monthly Estimates of the United States Population: April 1, 1980, to July 1, 1999, with Short-Term Projections to November 1, 2000"; published 2 January 2001; <http://www.census.gov/popest/archives/1990s/nat-total.txt>; 1990 to 1999: "national intercensal estimates (1990–2000)"; published 13 August 2004; <http://www.census.gov/popest/archives/EST90INTERCENSAL/US-EST90INT-datasets.html>; 2000 to 2006: "Monthly Population Estimates for the United States: April 1, 2000, to May 1, 2007"; published 1 June 2007 <http://www.census.gov/popest/national/tables/NA-EST2006-01.xls>.

Table 3. Resident Population Projections: 2007 to 2050

[300,913 represents 300,913,000. As of July 1. The projections are based on assumptions about future childbearing, mortality, and migration. The level of childbearing among women is assumed to remain close to present levels, with differences by race and Hispanic origin diminishing over time. Mortality is assumed to decline gradually with less variation by race and Hispanic origin than at present. International migration is assumed to vary over time and decrease generally relative to the size of the population]

Year	Number (1,000)	Percent change [1]	Year	Number (1,000)	Percent change [1]	Year	Number (1,000)	Percent change [1]
2007	300,913	0.9	2022	341,195	0.8	2037	383,537	0.7
2008	303,598	0.9	2023	343,921	0.8	2038	386,348	0.7
2009	306,272	0.9	2024	346,669	0.8	2039	389,151	0.7
2010	308,936	0.9	2025	349,439	0.8	2040	391,946	0.7
2011.	311,601	0.9	2026	352,229	0.8	2041	394,734	0.7
2012	314,281	0.9	2027	355,035	0.9	2042	397,519	0.7
2013	316,971	0.9	2028	357,862	0.8	2043	400,301	0.7
2014	319,668	0.9	2029	360,711	0.8	2044	403,081	0.7
2015	322,366	0.8	2030	363,584	0.8	2045	405,862	0.7
2016	325,063	0.8	2031	366,466	0.8	2046	408,646	0.7
2017	327,756	0.8	2032	369,336	0.8	2047	411,435	0.7
2018	330,444	0.8	2033	372,196	0.8	2048	414,230	0.7
2019	333,127	0.8	2034	375,046	0.8	2049	417,035	0.7
2020	335,805	0.8	2035	377,886	0.8	2050	419,854	0.7
2021	338,490	0.8	2036	380,716	0.7			

[1] Percent change from immediate preceding year. 2007, change from 2006.

Source: U.S. Census Bureau, "U.S. Interim Projections by Age, Sex, Race, and Hispanic Origin"; published 18 March 2004; <http://www.census.gov/ipc/www/usinterimproj/>.

Table 4. Components of Population Change: 2000 to 2006

[In thousands (281,425 represents 281,425,000), except as indicated. Resident population]

Period	Population as of beginning of period	Net increase Total	Net increase Percent [1]	Births	Deaths	Net international migration [2]	Population as of end of period
April 1, 2000 to July 1, 2000 [3] . . .	281,425	792	0.3	989	561	364	282,217
July 1, 2000 to July 1, 2001	282,217	3,009	1.1	4,047	2,419	1,381	285,226
July 1, 2001 to July 1, 2002	285,226	2,900	1.0	4,007	2,430	1,323	288,126
July 1, 2002 to July 1, 2003	288,126	2,670	0.9	4,053	2,423	1,040	290,796
July 1, 2003 to July 1, 2004	290,796	2,842	1.0	4,113	2,450	1,179	293,638
July 1, 2004 to July 1, 2005	293,638	2,869	1.0	4,126	2,415	1,158	296,507
July 1, 2005 to July 1, 2006	296,507	2,891	1.0	4,152	2,465	1,204	299,398

[1] Percent of population at beginning of period. [2] Includes net migration of the foreign-born, emigration of natives, net movement from Puerto Rico to the United States, and Armed Forces movement. [3] The April 1, 2000, Population Estimates base reflects changes to the Census 2000 population from the Count Question Resolution program and geographic program revisions.

Source: U.S. Census Bureau, "Population, Population change and estimated components of population change: April 1, 2000 to July 1, 2006"; Release data: December 22, 2006; <http://www.census.gov/popest/national/files/NSTEST2006ALLDATA.csv>.

Table 5. Components of Population Change by Race and Hispanic Origin: 2000 to 2006

[In thousands (17,974 represents 17,974,000). Resident population. Covers period April 1, 2000, to July 1, 2006. The April 1, 2000, Population Estimates base reflects changes to the Census 2000 population from the Count Question Resolution program and geographic program revisions]

Race and Hispanic origin	Net increase	Natural increase Total	Natural increase Births	Natural increase Deaths	Net international migration [1]
Total	**17,974**	**10,324**	**25,487**	**15,162**	**7,650**
One race.	17,153	9,596	24,664	15,068	7,557
White	11,640	6,487	19,410	12,923	5,152
Black or African American	2,638	2,064	3,890	1,827	574
American Indian and Alaska Native	239	180	252	72	59
Asian	2,570	827	1,066	240	1,743
Native Hawaiian and Other Pacific Islander	66	38	45	8	29
Two or more races	821	728	822	94	93
Race alone or in combination: [2]					
White	12,389	7,169	20,170	13,001	5,220
Black or African American	3,136	2,531	4,383	1,853	605
American Indian and Alaska Native	273	197	322	124	76
Asian	2,900	1,098	1,367	268	1,802
Native Hawaiian and Other Pacific Islander	101	58	76	19	43
Hispanic or Latino [3]	9,015	5,017	5,704	687	3,998
White alone, not Hispanic or Latino	3,167	1,804	14,083	12,279	1,363

[1] See footnote 2, Table 4. [2] In combination with one or more other races. The sum of the five race groups adds to more than the total population because individuals may report more than one race. [3] Persons of Hispanic origin may be any race.

Source: U.S. Census Bureau, "Table 5: Cumulative Estimates of the Components of Population Change by Race and Hispanic or Latino Origin for the United States: April 1, 2000 to July 1, 2006 (NC-EST2006-05)" Release Date: May 17, 2007; <http://www.census.gov/popest/national/asrh/NC-EST2006-compchg.html>.

8   Population

Table 6. Resident Population by Sex, Race, and Hispanic-Origin Status: 2000 to 2006

[281,425 represents 281,425,000. As of July, except as noted. Data shown are modified race counts; see text, this section]

Characteristic	Number (1,000)					Percent change, 2000 to 2006
	2000 [1] (April 1)	2003	2004	2005	2006	
BOTH SEXES						
Total	281,425	290,796	293,638	296,507	299,398	6.4
One race	277,527	286,488	289,195	291,928	294,680	6.2
White	228,107	234,191	236,036	237,885	239,746	5.1
Black or African American	35,705	37,045	37,473	37,905	38,343	7.4
American Indian and Alaska Native	2,664	2,786	2,825	2,864	2,903	9.0
Asian	10,589	11,970	12,354	12,757	13,159	24.3
Native Hawaiian and Other Pacific Islander	463	496	507	517	529	14.3
Two or more races	3,898	4,308	4,443	4,579	4,719	21.1
Race alone or in combination: [2]						
White	231,436	237,894	239,864	241,837	243,825	5.4
Black or African American	37,105	38,695	39,204	39,719	40,241	8.5
American Indian and Alaska Native	4,225	4,364	4,409	4,453	4,498	6.5
Asian	12,007	13,551	13,990	14,448	14,907	24.2
Native Hawaiian and Other Pacific Islander	907	959	975	991	1,008	11.1
Not Hispanic or Latino	246,118	250,790	252,227	253,635	255,077	3.6
One race	242,712	247,043	248,368	249,662	250,987	3.4
White	195,577	197,219	197,749	198,235	198,744	1.6
Black or African American	34,314	35,538	35,922	36,302	36,690	6.9
American Indian and Alaska Native	2,097	2,179	2,205	2,232	2,259	7.7
Asian	10,357	11,718	12,094	12,487	12,882	24.4
Native Hawaiian and Other Pacific Islander	367	390	398	405	412	12.3
Two or more races	3,406	3,747	3,859	3,973	4,090	20.1
Race alone or in combination: [2]						
White	198,477	200,428	201,060	201,651	202,266	1.9
Black or African American	35,499	36,932	37,385	37,835	38,294	7.9
American Indian and Alaska Native	3,456	3,543	3,572	3,600	3,629	5.0
Asian	11,632	13,135	13,560	14,002	14,446	24.2
Native Hawaiian and Other Pacific Islander	752	790	801	813	824	9.7
Hispanic or Latino	35,306	40,006	41,411	42,872	44,321	25.5
One race	34,815	39,445	40,827	42,266	43,693	25.5
White	32,530	36,971	38,288	39,650	41,002	26.0
Black or African American	1,391	1,508	1,551	1,603	1,653	18.8
American Indian and Alaska Native	566	608	619	632	644	13.7
Asian	232	253	260	269	278	19.5
Native Hawaiian and Other Pacific Islander	95	105	109	113	116	22.0
Two or more races	491	561	583	606	628	27.8
Race alone or in combination: [2]						
White	32,959	37,466	38,803	40,187	41,559	26.1
Black or African American	1,606	1,763	1,819	1,884	1,947	21.2
American Indian and Alaska Native	770	822	837	853	869	12.9
Asian	375	415	430	445	461	22.9
Native Hawaiian and Other Pacific Islander	155	169	174	178	183	18.2
MALE						
Total	138,056	142,938	144,467	145,974	147,512	6.8
One race	136,146	140,820	142,281	143,718	145,186	6.6
White	112,478	115,748	116,775	117,776	118,797	5.6
Black or African American	16,972	17,628	17,847	18,061	18,285	7.7
American Indian and Alaska Native	1,333	1,395	1,415	1,434	1,454	9.1
Asian	5,128	5,798	5,987	6,183	6,380	24.4
Native Hawaiian and Other Pacific Islander	235	252	258	263	269	14.5
Two or more races	1,910	2,117	2,186	2,255	2,327	21.8
Race alone or in combination: [2]						
White	114,116	117,575	118,665	119,729	120,815	5.9
Black or African American	17,644	18,426	18,687	18,944	19,210	8.9
American Indian and Alaska Native	2,088	2,158	2,181	2,203	2,226	6.6
Asian	5,834	6,587	6,803	7,028	7,253	24.3
Native Hawaiian and Other Pacific Islander	456	482	490	498	507	11.1
Not Hispanic or Latino	119,894	122,291	123,078	123,813	124,587	3.9
Hispanic or Latino	18,162	20,647	21,390	22,161	22,925	26.2
FEMALE						
Total	143,368	147,858	149,171	150,534	151,886	5.9
One race	141,381	145,668	146,914	148,210	149,494	5.7
White	115,628	118,443	119,261	120,110	120,949	4.6
Black or African American	18,733	19,418	19,626	19,843	20,058	7.1
American Indian and Alaska Native	1,331	1,392	1,410	1,429	1,448	8.8
Asian	5,461	6,172	6,368	6,573	6,779	24.1
Native Hawaiian and Other Pacific Islander	227	244	249	254	260	14.2
Two or more races	1,987	2,191	2,256	2,324	2,392	20.4
Race alone or in combination: [2]						
White	117,321	120,320	121,199	122,108	123,010	4.8
Black or African American	19,461	20,269	20,517	20,775	21,031	8.1
American Indian and Alaska Native	2,137	2,207	2,228	2,250	2,272	6.3
Asian	6,173	6,964	7,186	7,420	7,654	24.0
Native Hawaiian and Other Pacific Islander	451	477	485	493	501	11.1
Not Hispanic or Latino	126,224	128,499	129,150	129,822	130,490	3.4
Hispanic or Latino	17,144	19,359	20,021	20,711	21,396	24.8

[1] See footnote 3, Table 7.   [2] In combination with one or more other races. The sum of the five race groups adds to more than the total population because individuals may report more than one race.

Source: U.S. Census Bureau, "Table 3: Annual Estimates of the Population by Sex, Race and Hispanic or Latino Origin for the United States: April 1, 2000 to July 1, 2006"; Release Date: May 17, 2007; <http://www.census.gov/popest/national/asrh/NC-EST2006/NC-EST2006-03.xls>.

U.S. Census Bureau, Statistical Abstract of the United States: 2008

Table 7. Resident Population by Age and Sex: 1980 to 2006

[In thousands, except as indicated (226,546,000). 1980, 1990, and 2000 data are enumerated population as of April 1; data for other years are estimated population as of July 1. Excludes Armed Forces overseas. For definition of median, see Guide to Tabular Presentation]

Age group	1980[1]			1990[2]			1995, total	2000[3]			2001, total	2002, total	2003, total	2004, total	2005, total	2006		
	Total	Male	Female	Total	Male	Female		Total	Male	Female						Total	Male	Female
Total	226,546	110,053	116,493	248,791	121,284	127,507	266,278	281,425	138,056	143,368	285,226	288,126	290,796	293,638	296,507	299,398	147,512	151,886
Under 5 years	16,348	8,362	7,986	18,765	9,603	9,162	19,627	19,176	9,811	9,365	19,354	19,544	19,783	20,070	20,315	20,418	10,442	9,976
5 to 9 years	16,700	8,539	8,161	18,042	9,236	8,806	19,438	20,550	10,523	10,026	20,241	19,990	19,774	19,624	19,558	19,710	10,077	9,633
10 to 14 years	18,242	9,316	8,926	17,067	8,742	8,325	19,207	20,528	10,520	10,008	20,898	21,121	21,212	21,143	20,879	20,627	10,563	10,065
15 to 19 years	21,168	10,755	10,413	17,893	9,178	8,714	18,374	20,219	10,391	9,828	20,317	20,384	20,497	20,737	21,063	21,324	10,935	10,389
20 to 24 years	21,319	10,663	10,655	19,143	9,749	9,394	18,300	18,963	9,688	9,275	19,823	20,350	20,709	20,957	21,053	21,111	10,910	10,201
25 to 29 years	19,521	9,705	9,816	21,336	10,708	10,629	19,680	19,382	9,799	9,583	18,957	18,937	19,113	19,539	20,054	20,709	10,584	10,125
30 to 34 years	17,561	8,677	8,884	21,838	10,866	10,973	22,372	20,511	10,322	10,189	20,745	20,831	20,717	20,467	20,090	19,706	9,980	9,726
35 to 39 years	13,965	6,862	7,104	19,851	9,837	10,014	22,492	22,707	11,319	11,388	22,289	21,849	21,403	21,047	21,006	21,186	10,650	10,536
40 to 44 years	11,669	5,708	5,961	17,593	8,679	8,914	20,219	22,442	11,130	11,313	22,850	22,954	22,985	23,050	22,860	22,481	11,200	11,281
45 to 49 years	11,090	5,388	5,702	13,747	6,741	7,006	17,624	20,093	9,890	10,203	20,713	21,281	21,766	22,121	22,486	22,798	11,262	11,536
50 to 54 years	11,710	5,621	6,089	11,315	5,494	5,821	13,856	17,586	8,608	8,978	18,665	18,701	19,043	19,498	20,001	20,481	10,028	10,453
55 to 59 years	11,615	5,482	6,133	10,489	5,009	5,480	11,182	13,469	6,509	6,961	13,935	15,086	15,725	16,487	17,353	18,224	8,845	9,379
60 to 64 years	10,088	4,670	5,418	10,627	4,947	5,679	10,138	10,806	5,137	5,669	11,106	11,504	12,113	12,589	13,002	13,362	6,379	6,984
65 to 74 years	15,581	6,757	8,824	18,048	7,908	10,140	18,866	18,391	8,303	10,088	18,324	18,286	18,355	18,480	18,650	18,917	8,670	10,247
75 to 84 years	7,729	2,867	4,862	10,014	3,745	6,268	11,222	12,361	4,879	7,482	12,591	12,761	12,887	12,981	13,060	13,047	5,298	7,748
85 years and over	2,240	682	1,559	3,022	841	2,181	3,681	4,240	1,227	3,013	4,418	4,547	4,716	4,848	5,077	5,297	1,688	3,609
5 to 13 years	31,159	15,923	15,237	31,839	16,301	15,538	34,825	37,026	18,964	18,062	37,091	36,996	36,788	36,390	36,123	36,078	18,461	17,617
14 to 17 years	16,247	8,298	7,950	13,345	6,860	6,485	15,013	16,093	8,285	7,808	16,190	16,365	16,514	16,834	17,096	17,240	8,832	8,408
18 to 24 years	30,022	15,054	14,969	26,961	13,744	13,217	25,482	27,141	13,873	13,268	27,999	28,484	28,889	29,236	29,333	29,455	15,192	14,263
18 years and over	162,791	77,473	85,321	184,841	88,519	96,322	196,814	209,130	100,996	108,133	212,591	215,220	217,711	220,344	222,973	225,663	109,777	115,885
55 years and over	47,253	20,458	26,796	52,200	22,450	29,748	55,089	59,267	26,055	33,212	60,374	62,184	63,796	65,386	67,142	68,847	30,881	37,966
65 years and over	25,550	10,306	15,245	31,084	12,494	18,589	33,769	34,992	14,410	20,582	35,333	35,594	35,958	36,309	36,787	37,260	15,657	21,603
75 years and over	9,969	3,549	6,421	13,036	4,586	8,449	14,903	16,601	6,106	10,495	17,008	17,308	17,603	17,829	18,137	18,344	6,987	11,357
Median age (years)	30.0	28.8	31.3	32.8	31.6	34.0	34.2	35.3	34.0	36.5	35.5	35.7	35.9	36.0	36.2	36.4	35.1	37.7

[1] Total population count has been revised since the 1980 census publications. The April 1, 1990, estimates base (248,790,925) includes count resolution corrections processed through August 1997. It generally does not include adjustments for census coverage errors. However, it includes adjustments estimated for the 1995 Test Census in various localities in California, New Jersey, and Louisiana; and the 1998 census dress rehearsals in localities in California and Wisconsin. These adjustments amounted to a total of 81,052 persons. [3] The April 1, 2000, population estimates base reflects changes to the Census 2000 population from the Count Question Resolution program and geographic program revisions. [2] The data shown have been modified from the official 1990 census counts. See text of this section for explanation. Numbers by age and sex have not been corrected.

Source: U.S. Census Bureau, Current Population Reports, P25-1095; "Table US-EST90INT-04 - Intercensal Estimates of the United States Resident Population by Age Groups and Sex, 1990-2000: Selected Months"; published 13 September 2002; <http://www.census.gov/popest/archives/EST90INTERCENSAL/US-EST90INT-04.html>; and "Table 1: Annual Estimates of the Population by Five-Year Age Groups and Sex for the United States: April 1, 2000 to July 1, 2006"; Release date: May 17, 2007; <http://www.census.gov/popest/national/asrh/NC-EST2006/NC-EST2006-01.xls>.

Table 8. **Resident Population by Race, Hispanic Origin, and Age: 2000 and 2006**

[In thousands (281,425 represents 281,425,000); except as indicated. 2000, as of April and 2006, as of July. For definition of median, see Guide to Tabular Presentation]

Age group	Total		White alone		Black or African American alone		American Indian, Alaska Native alone		Asian alone		Native Hawaiian, Other Pacific Islander alone		Two or more races		Hispanic or Latino origin [2]		Not Hispanic or Latino White alone	
	2000[1]	2006	2000[1]	2006	2000[1]	2006	2000[1]	2006	2000[1]	2006	2000[1]	2006	2000[1]	2006	2000[1]	2006	2000[1]	2006
Total	281,425	299,398	228,107	239,746	35,705	38,343	2,664	2,903	10,589	13,159	463	529	3,898	4,719	35,306	44,321	195,577	198,744
Under 5 years	19,176	20,418	14,657	15,549	2,925	3,073	233	203	708	890	41	38	613	665	3,718	4,705	11,288	11,162
5 to 9 years	20,550	19,710	15,688	15,044	3,320	2,967	258	226	716	807	44	40	524	627	3,624	4,091	12,392	11,291
10 to 14 years	20,528	20,627	15,843	15,721	3,221	3,246	264	253	715	814	42	45	443	548	3,163	3,942	12,961	12,125
15 to 19 years	20,219	21,324	15,745	16,357	3,024	3,359	251	272	776	818	44	45	380	472	3,172	3,623	12,836	13,049
20 to 24 years	18,963	21,111	14,826	16,395	2,729	3,096	218	264	848	906	46	47	297	403	3,409	4,163	11,681	12,938
25 to 29 years	19,382	20,709	15,217	16,092	2,645	2,899	204	236	1,019	1,098	42	51	254	333	3,385	3,929	12,077	12,236
30 to 34 years	20,511	19,706	16,349	15,279	2,710	2,624	202	208	980	1,283	39	45	231	267	3,125	3,532	13,451	11,622
35 to 39 years	22,707	21,186	18,372	16,736	2,910	2,738	217	206	937	1,217	38	42	233	247	2,825	3,127	15,753	13,455
40 to 44 years	22,442	22,481	18,346	18,027	2,772	2,875	202	215	870	1,088	27	40	219	236	2,304	2,825	16,213	15,125
45 to 49 years	20,093	22,798	16,615	18,570	2,330	2,781	169	206	770	978	21	35	183	226	1,775	2,557	14,973	16,200
50 to 54 years	17,586	20,481	14,794	16,887	1,846	2,338	135	174	641	863	15	29	149	191	1,361	1,960	13,530	15,072
55 to 59 years	13,469	18,224	11,479	15,275	1,332	1,903	95	142	443	725	11	23	106	157	960	1,500	10,582	13,883
60 to 64 years	10,806	13,362	9,214	11,371	1,082	1,275	70	96	350	497	8	16	78	109	750	1,040	8,511	10,400
65 to 69 years	9,534	10,376	8,238	8,839	895	992	52	69	279	385	6	12	61	78	599	777	7,675	8,113
70 to 74 years	8,858	8,541	7,799	7,339	742	789	38	50	224	297	4	8	49	58	477	599	7,348	6,777
75 to 79 years	7,416	7,381	6,634	6,481	557	590	27	36	159	225	2	6	36	44	327	463	6,325	6,045
80 to 84 years	4,945	5,666	4,466	5,041	350	417	15	24	90	150	1	4	22	30	180	306	4,296	4,752
85 to 89 years	2,790	3,341	2,525	3,001	200	231	8	13	43	78	1	2	12	17	98	158	2,432	2,851
90 to 94 years	1,113	1,457	1,007	1,306	82	105	3	6	15	32	–	1	4	8	39	69	970	1,240
95 to 99 years	287	425	254	375	27	36	1	2	4	9	–	–	1	3	11	23	243	353
100 years and over	50	74	41	62	7	9	–	1	1	2	–	–	–	1	3	5	39	57
5 to 13 years	37,026	36,078	28,381	27,519	5,923	5,528	471	425	1,288	1,459	78	76	885	1,071	6,186	7,255	22,754	20,880
14 to 17 years	16,093	17,240	12,523	13,167	2,426	2,763	205	220	590	654	33	37	315	400	2,438	3,006	10,290	10,424
18 to 24 years	27,141	29,455	21,197	22,831	3,944	4,377	315	370	1,178	1,232	64	65	444	580	4,744	5,146	16,827	18,098
16 years and over	217,151	234,316	178,790	190,130	25,633	28,360	1,857	2,166	8,304	10,487	328	396	2,237	2,778	24,204	30,818	156,352	161,562
18 years and over	209,130	225,663	172,546	183,511	24,431	26,978	1,755	2,055	8,003	10,157	311	378	2,084	2,584	22,964	29,355	151,245	156,279
16 to 64 years	182,159	197,055	147,826	157,686	22,773	25,192	1,713	1,964	7,489	9,310	305	363	2,051	2,540	22,471	28,419	127,023	131,374
55 years and over	59,267	68,847	51,656	59,089	5,274	6,345	310	439	1,608	2,398	48	71	371	504	3,444	4,939	48,422	54,471
65 years and over	34,992	37,260	30,964	32,444	2,860	3,168	144	202	815	1,177	23	33	186	238	1,734	2,399	29,329	30,188
75 years and over	16,601	18,344	14,927	16,265	1,223	1,387	55	82	312	495	8	13	77	102	657	1,024	14,306	15,298
85 years and over	4,240	5,297	3,827	4,743	316	380	13	22	63	121	2	3	18	28	151	256	3,685	4,501
Median age (years)	35.3	36.4	36.6	37.8	30.0	31.0	27.7	29.9	32.5	34.9	26.8	29.7	19.8	20.6	25.8	27.4	38.6	40.5

– Represents or rounds to zero.   [1] April 1, 2000, population estimates base reflects changes to the Census 2000 population from the Count Question Resolution program and geographic program revisions.   [2] Persons of Hispanic origin may be of any race.

Source: U.S. Census Bureau, "Annual Estimates of the Resident Population by Race, Age and Sex for the United States: April 1, 2000 to July 1, 2006"; Release Date: May 17, 2007; <http://www.census.gov/popest/national/asrh/NC-EST2006-asrh.html>.

Table 9. **Resident Population by Race, Hispanic Origin, and Single Years of Age: 2006**

[In thousands, except as indicated (299,398 represents 299,398,000). As of July 1. For derivation of estimates, see text of this section]

Age	Total	Race						Hispanic or Latino origin [1]	Not-Hispanic or Latino White alone
		White alone	Black or African American alone	American Indian, Alaska Native alone	Asian alone	Native Hawaiian and Other Pacific Islander alone	Two or more races		
Total	299,398	239,746	38,343	2,903	13,159	529	4,719	44,321	198,744
Under 5 years old. . .	20,418	15,549	3,073	203	890	38	665	4,705	11,162
Under 1 year old. .	4,130	3,131	628	42	181	8	139	971	2,234
1 year old	4,108	3,111	629	41	182	8	137	976	2,209
2 years old	4,104	3,129	612	41	180	8	134	947	2,246
3 years old	4,054	3,101	599	40	177	7	129	917	2,239
4 years old	4,022	3,077	605	39	169	7	125	893	2,234
5 to 9 years old . . .	19,710	15,044	2,967	226	807	40	627	4,091	11,291
5 years old	4,080	3,117	621	39	172	7	124	880	2,288
6 years old	3,928	2,999	588	45	157	8	130	832	2,237
7 years old	3,885	2,965	579	47	155	9	129	797	2,242
8 years old	3,896	2,969	588	47	159	9	124	792	2,249
9 years old	3,922	2,994	591	47	163	8	119	790	2,275
10 to 14 years old . .	20,627	15,721	3,246	253	814	45	548	3,942	12,125
10 years old.	4,005	3,063	604	48	166	9	116	797	2,336
11 years old.	4,070	3,106	631	48	163	9	113	797	2,380
12 years old.	4,104	3,122	652	50	162	9	109	787	2,404
13 years old.	4,188	3,184	676	52	162	9	106	784	2,469
14 years old.	4,260	3,246	684	54	162	9	104	778	2,536
15 to 19 years old . .	21,324	16,357	3,359	272	818	45	472	3,623	13,049
15 years old.	4,328	3,303	697	55	162	9	102	765	2,605
16 years old.	4,406	3,366	710	56	165	9	100	756	2,676
17 years old.	4,247	3,253	672	54	165	9	94	708	2,607
18 years old.	4,188	3,224	649	54	164	9	89	700	2,583
19 years old.	4,155	3,212	632	53	162	9	87	694	2,577
20 to 24 years old . .	21,111	16,395	3,096	264	906	47	403	3,752	12,938
20 years old.	4,193	3,249	629	53	168	9	85	702	2,605
21 years old.	4,228	3,285	625	53	173	9	83	719	2,624
22 years old.	4,165	3,233	611	52	179	9	80	736	2,555
23 years old.	4,244	3,300	615	53	187	9	79	779	2,580
24 years old.	4,282	3,329	616	51	198	10	77	816	2,574
25 to 29 years old . .	20,709	16,092	2,899	236	1,098	51	333	4,163	12,236
25 years old.	4,330	3,366	617	51	211	10	75	834	2,595
26 years old.	4,319	3,352	618	50	217	11	71	856	2,559
27 years old.	4,114	3,193	580	47	219	10	66	827	2,428
28 years old.	4,000	3,114	548	45	221	10	62	825	2,349
29 years old.	3,946	3,067	536	45	230	10	59	821	2,305
30 to 34 years old . .	19,706	15,279	2,624	208	1,283	45	267	3,929	11,622
30 years old.	3,849	2,986	515	43	241	10	56	813	2,230
31 years old.	3,959	3,071	525	42	257	9	55	810	2,317
32 years old.	3,844	2,977	508	41	257	9	52	776	2,254
33 years old.	3,934	3,040	528	41	264	9	52	771	2,323
34 years old.	4,119	3,205	547	42	265	9	53	760	2,498
35 to 39 years old . .	21,186	16,736	2,738	206	1,217	42	247	3,532	13,455
35 years old.	4,347	3,412	570	43	259	9	54	752	2,714
36 years old.	4,429	3,489	574	43	261	9	53	751	2,791
37 years old.	4,185	3,313	530	41	245	8	49	695	2,667
38 years old.	4,107	3,247	533	40	234	8	46	680	2,614
39 years old.	4,116	3,275	531	40	218	8	45	653	2,669
40 to 44 years old . .	22,481	18,027	2,875	215	1,088	40	236	3,127	15,125
40 years old.	4,232	3,360	557	41	220	8	46	654	2,753
41 years old.	4,519	3,602	592	44	225	8	48	659	2,990
42 years old.	4,584	3,678	584	44	222	8	48	633	3,091
43 years old.	4,567	3,676	574	43	218	8	47	601	3,119
44 years old.	4,579	3,711	568	43	203	8	47	580	3,172
45 to 49 years old . .	22,798	18,570	2,781	206	978	35	226	2,557	16,200
45 years old.	4,623	3,761	567	43	199	7	47	555	3,246
46 years old.	4,703	3,806	590	44	208	8	47	559	3,288
47 years old.	4,509	3,672	552	41	193	7	45	504	3,205
48 years old.	4,509	3,684	540	40	193	7	44	479	3,241
49 years old.	4,453	3,647	532	39	186	6	43	460	3,220

See footnote at end of table.

U.S. Census Bureau, Statistical Abstract of the United States: 2008

Table 9. **Resident Population by Race, Hispanic Origin, and Single Years of Age: 2006**—Con.

[In thousands, except as indicated (299,398 represents 299,398,000). **As of July 1.** For derivation of estimates, see text of this section]

Age	Total	White alone	Black or African American alone	American Indian, Alaska Native alone	Asian alone	Native Hawaiian and Other Pacific Islander alone	Two or more races	Hispanic or Latino origin [1]	Not-Hispanic or Latino White alone
50 to 54 years old ..	20,481	16,887	2,338	174	863	29	191	1,960	15,072
50 years old.	4,279	3,505	505	37	184	6	41	436	3,101
51 years old.	4,296	3,524	504	37	184	6	41	427	3,129
52 years old.	4,106	3,388	469	35	171	6	38	390	3,027
53 years old.	3,967	3,286	440	33	166	5	37	365	2,948
54 years old.	3,832	3,183	420	31	158	5	34	341	2,867
55 to 59 years old ..	18,224	15,275	1,903	142	725	23	157	1,500	13,883
55 years old.	3,729	3,093	416	30	152	5	33	330	2,787
56 years old.	3,712	3,066	416	30	161	5	33	327	2,763
57 years old.	3,562	2,974	379	28	146	5	31	295	2,700
58 years old.	3,526	2,972	355	27	138	4	30	281	2,711
59 years old.	3,696	3,170	336	27	128	4	31	267	2,922
60 to 64 years old ..	13,362	11,371	1,275	96	497	16	109	1,040	10,400
60 years old.	2,748	2,317	272	21	110	4	24	235	2,099
61 years old.	2,733	2,309	271	20	106	3	23	223	2,100
62 years old.	2,682	2,285	254	19	99	3	22	207	2,092
63 years old.	2,768	2,381	251	19	92	3	22	196	2,198
64 years old.	2,432	2,079	226	17	89	3	19	179	1,911
65 to 69 years old ..	10,376	8,839	992	69	385	12	78	777	8,113
65 years old.	2,249	1,914	215	16	84	3	18	169	1,756
66 years old.	2,177	1,844	216	15	83	3	17	167	1,687
67 years old.	2,059	1,759	193	14	76	2	15	154	1,615
68 years old.	2,010	1,716	190	13	73	2	15	148	1,578
69 years old.	1,880	1,606	178	12	69	2	13	138	1,476
70 to 74 years old ..	8,541	7,339	789	50	297	8	58	599	6,777
70 years old.	1,833	1,566	175	11	66	2	13	133	1,441
71 years old.	1,822	1,559	173	11	64	2	12	132	1,435
72 years old.	1,650	1,415	154	10	58	2	11	117	1,306
73 years old.	1,637	1,409	149	9	57	2	11	111	1,305
74 years old.	1,600	1,390	138	9	52	1	10	107	1,289
75 to 79 years old ..	7,381	6,481	590	36	225	6	44	463	6,045
75 years old.	1,566	1,370	127	8	50	1	10	103	1,273
76 years old.	1,569	1,369	131	8	50	1	9	103	1,273
77 years old.	1,455	1,278	116	7	44	1	9	92	1,192
78 years old.	1,427	1,259	111	7	42	1	8	86	1,177
79 years old.	1,363	1,205	105	6	38	1	8	78	1,131
80 to 84 years old .	5,666	5,041	417	24	150	4	30	306	4,752
80 years old.	1,279	1,131	99	6	35	1	7	73	1,062
81 years old.	1,237	1,097	94	5	34	1	7	68	1,033
82 years old.	1,142	1,019	82	5	30	1	6	61	961
83 years old.	1,039	927	75	4	27	1	5	54	875
84 years old.	968	867	68	4	24	1	5	49	821
85 to 89 years old ..	3,341	3,001	231	13	78	2	17	158	2,851
90 to 94 years old ..	1,457	1,306	105	6	32	1	8	69	1,240
95 to 99 years old ..	425	375	36	2	9	–	3	23	353
100 years old and over.	74	62	9	1	2	–	1	5	57
Median age (years). .	36.4	37.8	31.0	29.9	34.9	29.7	20.6	27.4	40.5

– Represents or rounds to zero. [1] Persons of Hispanic origin may be any race.

Source: U.S. Census Bureau, "Monthly Population Estimates by Age, Sex, Race, and Hispanic Origin for the United States: April 1, 2000 to July 1, 2006"; Release Date: May 17, 2007; <http://www.census.gov/popest/national/asrh/2006natres.html>.

Population 13

Table 10. Resident Population Projections by Sex and Age: 2010 to 2050

[In thousands, except as indicated (308,936 represents 308,936,000). As of July 1. For assumptions, see Table 3. For definition of median, see Table 3. For definition of median, see Guide to Tabular Presentation]

Age	2010 Total	2010 Male	2010 Female	2015 Total	2015 Male	2015 Female	2020	2025	2030	2035	2040	2045	2050	Pct. 2010	Pct. 2015	Pct. 2020	Pct. 2025	Pct. 2050
Total	308,936	151,815	157,121	322,366	158,489	163,877	335,805	349,439	363,584	377,886	391,946	405,862	419,854	100.0	100.0	100.0	100.0	100.0
Under 5 years	21,426	10,947	10,479	22,358	11,423	10,935	22,932	23,518	24,272	25,262	26,299	27,233	28,080	6.9	6.9	6.8	6.7	6.7
5 to 9 years	20,706	10,575	10,131	21,623	11,044	10,579	22,564	23,163	23,790	24,562	25,550	26,586	27,521	6.7	6.7	6.7	6.6	6.6
10 to 14 years	19,767	10,109	9,658	20,984	10,718	10,265	21,914	22,888	23,539	24,186	24,953	25,938	26,974	6.4	6.5	6.5	6.5	6.4
15 to 19 years	21,336	10,938	10,398	20,243	10,366	9,877	21,478	22,052	23,136	24,182	24,897	25,534	26,572	6.9	6.3	6.4	6.3	6.3
20 to 24 years	21,676	11,075	10,602	21,810	11,137	10,673	20,751	22,457	22,810	24,227	25,024	25,690	26,297	7.0	6.8	6.2	6.4	6.3
25 to 29 years	21,375	10,868	10,507	22,195	11,269	10,926	22,361	21,390	22,125	23,503	24,731	25,808	26,327	6.9	6.9	6.7	6.1	6.3
30 to 34 years	20,271	10,238	10,034	21,858	11,075	10,783	22,704	22,955	23,399	23,943	24,101	25,223	26,477	6.6	6.8	6.8	6.6	6.3
35 to 39 years	20,137	10,091	10,046	20,543	10,337	10,206	22,143	23,046	23,277	23,605	23,747	24,376	26,300	6.5	6.4	6.6	6.6	6.3
40 to 44 years	20,984	10,462	10,523	20,250	10,108	10,142	20,673	22,305	23,605	23,350	23,350	24,101	25,496	6.8	6.3	6.2	6.4	6.1
45 to 49 years	22,654	11,190	11,464	20,926	10,387	10,539	20,219	20,678	23,352	23,669	22,907	23,001	24,466	7.3	6.5	6.0	5.9	5.8
50 to 54 years	22,173	10,874	11,299	22,376	10,992	11,383	20,702	20,043	20,550	22,234	23,234	23,641	24,376	7.2	6.9	6.2	5.7	5.8
55 to 59 years	19,507	9,456	10,051	21,649	10,532	11,117	21,876	20,291	19,702	20,241	21,910	22,916	22,917	6.3	6.7	6.5	5.8	5.5
60 to 64 years	16,678	7,982	8,696	18,761	8,985	9,776	20,856	21,128	19,676	19,156	19,719	21,370	23,337	5.4	5.8	6.2	6.0	5.6
65 to 69 years	12,172	5,686	6,486	15,621	7,336	8,285	17,618	19,647	19,980	18,683	18,237	18,829	22,384	3.9	4.8	5.2	5.6	5.3
70 to 74 years	9,097	4,111	4,987	10,987	4,988	5,998	14,161	16,041	19,968	18,350	17,233	16,879	20,444	2.9	3.4	4.2	4.6	4.9
75 to 79 years	7,186	3,066	4,120	7,761	3,351	4,409	9,450	12,268	13,989	15,764	16,192	15,449	17,499	2.3	2.4	2.8	3.5	4.2
80 to 84 years	5,665	2,206	3,459	5,600	2,226	3,374	6,134	7,557	9,914	11,414	12,978	15,304	12,835	1.8	1.7	1.8	2.2	3.1
85 to 89 years	3,713	1,274	2,439	3,857	1,363	2,494	3,897	4,353	5,451	7,259	8,476	9,768	10,254	1.2	1.2	1.2	1.2	2.4
90 to 94 years	1,727	510	1,218	2,069	629	1,440	2,221	2,312	2,651	3,395	4,621	5,510	6,473	0.6	0.6	0.7	0.7	1.5
95 to 99 years	569	137	432	723	185	537	909	1,018	1,102	1,310	1,731	2,430	2,984	0.2	0.2	0.3	0.3	0.7
100 years and over	114	21	93	173	35	138	241	327	399	467	581	790	1,150	(Z)	0.1	0.1	0.1	0.3
5 to 13 years	36,439	18,618	17,821	38,418	19,621	18,796	40,148	41,501	42,627	43,922	45,536	47,379	49,138	11.8	11.9	12.0	11.9	11.7
14 to 17 years	16,566	8,492	8,074	16,243	8,313	7,930	17,220	18,079	18,809	19,311	19,847	20,505	21,330	5.4	5.0	5.1	5.2	5.1
18 to 24 years	30,481	15,587	14,894	30,000	15,331	14,669	29,339	30,980	32,533	33,924	34,841	35,763	36,895	9.9	9.3	8.7	8.9	8.8
16 years and over	242,936	118,082	124,854	253,361	123,235	130,126	264,085	275,339	287,281	299,051	310,182	320,974	331,940	78.6	78.6	78.6	78.8	79.1
18 years and over	234,504	113,758	120,746	245,347	119,132	126,216	255,505	266,341	277,877	289,391	300,264	310,746	321,305	75.9	76.1	76.1	76.2	76.5
16 to 64 years	202,693	101,071	101,622	206,570	103,120	103,450	209,453	211,815	215,828	222,410	230,132	238,015	245,234	65.6	64.1	62.4	60.6	58.4
55 years and over	76,429	34,450	41,980	87,201	39,632	47,569	97,363	104,944	110,831	116,039	121,679	127,245	132,427	24.7	27.1	29.0	30.0	31.5
65 years and over	40,244	17,011	23,233	46,791	20,115	26,676	54,632	63,524	71,453	76,641	80,050	82,959	86,706	13.0	14.5	16.3	18.2	20.7
75 years and over	18,974	7,211	11,762	20,182	7,790	12,393	22,853	27,836	33,506	39,609	44,580	47,251	48,763	6.1	6.3	6.8	8.0	11.6
85 years and over	6,123	1,942	4,182	6,822	2,213	4,609	7,269	8,011	9,603	12,430	15,409	18,498	20,861	2.0	2.1	2.2	2.3	5.0
Median age (years)	37.0	35.6	38.4	37.4	36.0	38.8	38.0	38.5	39.0	39.2	39.1	39.1	39.1	(X)	(X)	(X)	(X)	(X)

X Not applicable.   Z Less than 0.05 percent.

Source: U.S. Census Bureau, "U.S. Interim Projections by Age, Sex, Race, and Hispanic Origin"; published March 2004; <http://www.census.gov/ipc/www/usinterimproj/>.

U.S. Census Bureau, Statistical Abstract of the United States: 2008

Table 11. Resident Population by Race, Hispanic-Origin Status, and Age—Projections: 2010 and 2015

[In thousands (308,936 represents 308,936,000), except as indicated. As of July 1. For definition of median, see Guide to Tabular Presentation. Projections are based on middle series of assumptions; see headnote, Table 3]

Age group	Total 2010	Total 2015	White alone 2010	White alone 2015	Black alone 2010	Black alone 2015	Asian alone 2010	Asian alone 2015	All other races[1] 2010	All other races[1] 2015	Hispanic origin[2] 2010	Hispanic origin[2] 2015	White alone, not of Hispanic origin 2010	White alone, not of Hispanic origin 2015
Total	308,936	322,366	244,995	252,850	40,454	42,927	14,241	16,099	9,246	10,489	47,756	53,647	201,112	203,649
Under 5 years	21,426	22,358	15,995	16,556	3,332	3,498	919	987	1,181	1,318	4,824	5,201	11,647	11,884
5 to 9 years	20,706	21,623	15,639	16,114	3,127	3,347	888	976	1,052	1,186	4,515	4,927	11,553	11,668
10 to 14 years	19,767	20,984	15,049	15,799	2,976	3,163	834	963	909	1,059	4,057	4,660	11,361	11,577
15 to 19 years	21,336	20,243	16,203	15,341	3,396	3,043	886	937	851	922	4,162	4,338	12,401	11,390
20 to 24 years	21,676	21,810	16,591	16,473	3,357	3,451	943	1,020	785	866	3,927	4,472	12,992	12,380
25 to 29 years	21,375	22,195	16,495	16,890	3,130	3,413	1,041	1,093	709	799	3,878	4,162	12,919	13,069
30 to 34 years	20,271	21,858	15,654	16,727	2,856	3,180	1,166	1,231	595	720	3,973	4,035	11,977	13,004
35 to 39 years	20,137	20,543	15,597	15,758	2,701	2,880	1,319	1,303	520	601	3,769	4,052	12,096	12,009
40 to 44 years	20,984	20,250	16,566	15,616	2,724	2,697	1,208	1,414	486	486	3,343	3,799	13,466	12,088
45 to 49 years	22,654	20,926	18,213	16,473	2,844	2,685	1,105	1,282	492	486	2,939	3,342	15,489	13,374
50 to 54 years	22,173	22,376	18,066	17,966	2,657	2,768	997	1,154	453	487	2,371	2,916	15,870	15,264
55 to 59 years	19,507	21,649	16,102	17,637	2,176	2,546	857	1,023	372	444	1,806	2,331	14,431	15,479
60 to 64 years	16,679	18,761	14,004	15,484	1,674	2,044	706	873	295	359	1,365	1,755	12,736	13,860
65 to 69 years	12,172	15,621	10,357	13,125	1,127	1,518	489	701	199	278	941	1,301	9,477	11,918
70 to 74 years	9,097	10,987	7,767	9,363	838	979	355	463	138	181	694	870	7,117	8,552
75 to 79 years	7,186	7,761	6,226	6,641	622	688	244	313	94	119	510	617	5,747	6,065
80 to 84 years	5,665	5,600	5,005	4,861	440	471	158	194	61	74	359	423	4,666	4,464
85 to 89 years	3,713	3,857	3,321	3,404	274	303	83	108	34	42	204	268	3,128	3,152
90 to 94 years	1,727	2,069	1,546	1,839	136	165	31	46	14	19	84	128	1,467	1,718
95 to 99 years	569	723	503	636	53	68	8	13	4	6	28	41	476	598
100 years and over . .	114	173	98	147	14	22	1	2	1	2	6	10	92	138
5 to 13 years	36,439	38,418	27,613	28,744	5,491	5,885	1,550	1,747	1,786	2,041	7,760	8,670	20,580	20,909
14 to 17 years	16,566	16,243	12,589	12,301	2,597	2,430	695	742	685	770	3,291	3,513	9,586	9,108
18 to 24 years	30,481	30,000	23,280	22,682	4,768	4,689	1,307	1,408	1,125	1,221	5,611	6,214	18,142	16,998
16 years and over . . .	242,936	253,361	195,194	201,321	30,383	32,319	11,427	12,988	5,933	6,733	33,541	37,977	164,179	166,259
18 years and over . . .	234,504	245,347	188,799	195,250	29,034	31,114	11,077	12,623	5,594	6,361	31,881	36,263	159,300	161,747
16 to 64 years	202,693	206,570	160,372	161,303	26,877	28,106	10,056	11,147	5,387	6,013	30,715	34,321	132,007	129,655
55 years and over . . .	76,429	87,201	64,928	73,139	7,355	8,802	2,934	3,737	1,213	1,523	5,997	7,742	59,339	65,942
65 years and over . . .	40,244	46,791	34,821	40,018	3,505	4,212	1,371	1,841	546	720	2,826	3,656	32,171	36,604
75 years and over . . .	18,974	20,182	16,698	17,529	1,540	1,716	527	676	209	261	1,191	1,485	15,577	16,134
85 years and over . . .	6,123	6,822	5,467	6,027	478	558	125	169	54	69	322	446	5,163	5,606
Median age (yrs.) . . .	37.0	37.4	38.6	38.9	31.5	32.4	36.7	38.3	24.0	24.4	28.1	28.8	41.3	42.1

[1] Includes 2 or more races.   [2] Persons of Hispanic origin may be any race.

Source: U.S. Census Bureau, "U.S. Interim Projections by Age, Sex, Race, and Hispanic Origin"; published March 2004; <http://www.census.gov/ipc/www/usinterimproj/>.

Population   15

Figure 1.1
Center of Population: 1790 to 2000

[Prior to 1960, excludes Alaska and Hawaii. The median center is located at the intersection of two median lines, a north-south line constructed so that half of the nation's population lives east and half lives west of it, and an east-west line selected so that half of the nation's population lives north and half lives south of it. The mean center of population is that point at which an imaginary, flat, weightless, and rigid map of the United States would balance if weights of identical value were placed on it so that each weight represented the location of one person on the date of the census]

Year	Median center		Mean center		
	Latitude-N	Longitude	Latitude-N	Longitude-W	Approximate location
1790 (August 2)	(NA)	(NA)	39 16 30	76 11 12	In Kent County, MD, 23 miles E of Baltimore MD
1850 (June 1). .	(NA)	(NA)	38 59 00	81 19 00	In Wirt County, WV, 23 miles SE of Parkersburg, WV[1]
1900 (June 1). .	40 03 32	84 49 01	39 09 36	85 48 54	In Bartholomew County, IN, 6 miles SE of Columbus, IN
1950 (April 1) . .	40 00 12	84 56 51	38 50 21	88 09 33	In Richland County, IL, 8 miles NNW of Olney, IL
1960 (April 1) . .	39 56 25	85 16 60	38 35 58	89 12 35	In Clinton County, IL, 6.5 miles NW of Centralia, IL
1970 (April 1)	39 47 43	85 31 43	38 27 47	89 42 22	In St. Clair County, IL, 5.3 miles ESE of Mascoutah, IL
1980 (April 1) . .	39 18 60	86 08 15	38 08 13	90 34 26	In Jefferson County, MO, .25 mile W of DeSoto, MO
1990 (April 1). .	38 57 55	86 31 53	37 52 20	91 12 55	In Crawford County, MO, 10 miles SE of Steelville, MO
2000 (April 1) . .	38 45 23	86 55 51	37 41 49	91 48 34	In Phelps County, MO, 3 miles E of Edgar Springs, MO

NA Not available.   [1]West Virginia was set off from Virginia, Dec. 31, 1862, and admitted as a state, June 19, 1863.

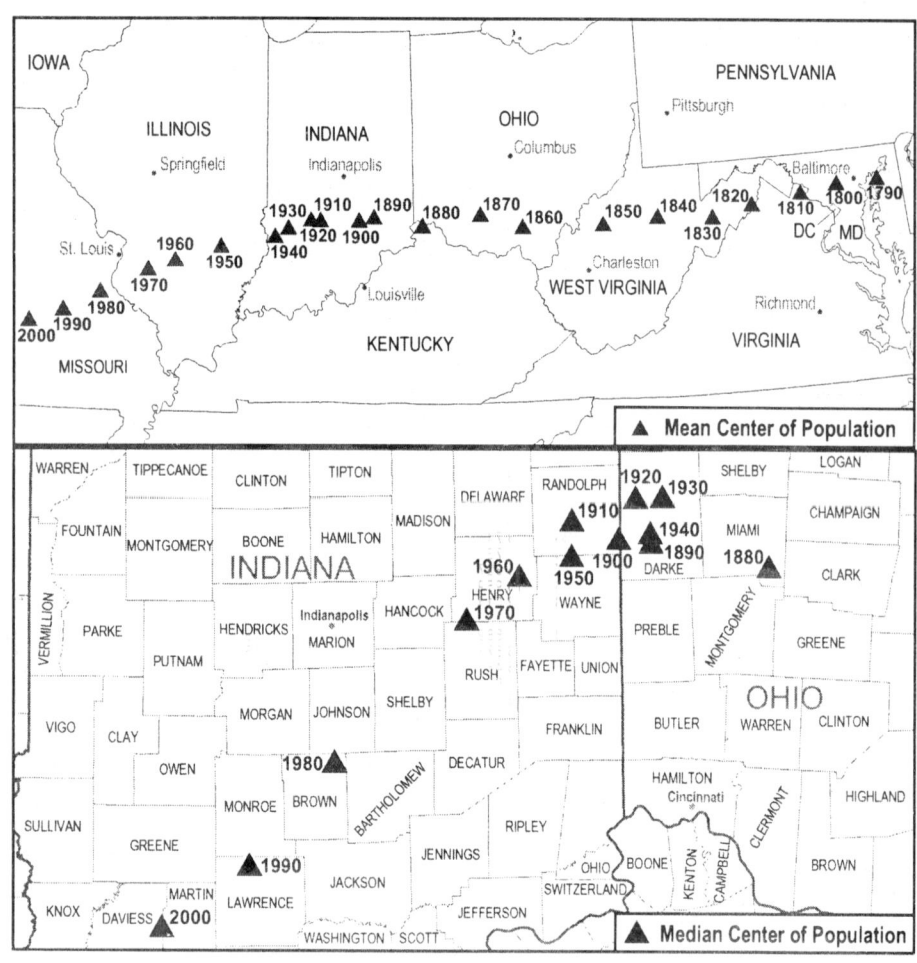

U.S. Census Bureau, Statistical Abstract of the United States: 2008

Table 12. **Resident Population—States: 1980 to 2006**

[In thousands (226,546 represents 226,546,000). 1980, 1990, and 2000 data as of April 1, data for other years as of July 1. Insofar as possible, population shown for all years is that of present area of state. See Appendix III]

State	1980 [1]	1990 [2]	1995	2000 [3]	2002	2003	2004	2005	2006
United States	226,546	248,791	266,278	281,425	288,126	290,796	293,638	296,507	299,398
Alabama.	3,894	4,040	4,297	4,447	4,478	4,495	4,517	4,548	4,599
Alaska	402	550	604	627	641	648	657	663	670
Arizona.	2,718	3,665	4,432	5,131	5,445	5,582	5,746	5,953	6,166
Arkansas	2,286	2,351	2,535	2,673	2,706	2,724	2,747	2,776	2,811
California	23,668	29,811	31,697	33,872	35,025	35,466	35,841	36,154	36,458
Colorado.	2,890	3,294	3,827	4,302	4,500	4,546	4,599	4,663	4,753
Connecticut.	3,108	3,287	3,324	3,406	3,458	3,482	3,494	3,501	3,505
Delaware	594	666	730	784	806	817	829	842	853
District of Columbia	638	607	581	572	579	577	580	582	582
Florida.	9,746	12,938	14,538	15,983	16,682	16,982	17,367	17,768	18,090
Georgia	5.463	6,478	7,328	8,187	8,598	8,750	8,935	9,133	9,364
Hawaii	965	1,108	1,197	1,212	1,233	1,246	1,259	1,273	1,285
Idaho.	944	1,007	1,177	1,294	1,344	1,367	1,395	1,429	1,466
Illinois	11,427	11,431	12,008	12,420	12,595	12,650	12,714	12,765	12,832
Indiana.	5,490	5,544	5,851	6,081	6,155	6,192	6,223	6,266	6,314
Iowa	2,914	2,777	2,867	2,926	2,935	2,942	2,954	2,966	2,982
Kansas.	2,364	2,478	2,601	2,689	2,715	2,727	2,738	2,748	2,764
Kentucky	3,661	3,687	3,887	4,042	4,089	4,114	4,140	4,173	4,206
Louisiana	4,206	4,222	4,379	4,469	4,471	4,481	4,496	4,507	4,288
Maine.	1,125	1,228	1,243	1,275	1,297	1,307	1,314	1,318	1,322
Maryland	4,217	4,781	5,070	5,297	5,441	5,507	5,553	5,590	5,616
Massachusetts.	5,737	6,016	6,141	6,349	6,431	6,440	6,436	6,433	6,437
Michigan.	9,262	9,295	9,676	9,938	10,038	10,068	10,093	10,101	10,096
Minnesota.	4,076	4,376	4,660	4,919	5,025	5,059	5,094	5,127	5,167
Mississippi	2,521	2,575	2,723	2,845	2,863	2,874	2,893	2,908	2,911
Missouri	4,917	5,117	5,378	5,597	5,680	5,712	5,753	5,798	5,843
Montana.	787	799	877	902	910	917	926	935	945
Nebraska	1,570	1,578	1,657	1,711	1,727	1,737	1,747	1,758	1,768
Nevada	800	1,202	1,582	1,998	2,169	2,241	2,332	2,412	2,496
New Hampshire	921	1,109	1,158	1,236	1,274	1,286	1,298	1,307	1,315
New Jersey.	7,365	7,748	8,083	8,414	8,578	8,633	8,676	8,703	8,725
New Mexico	1,303	1,515	1,720	1,819	1,855	1,878	1,901	1,926	1,955
New York	17,558	17,991	18,524	18,977	19,168	19,238	19,292	19,316	19,306
North Carolina	5,882	6,632	7,345	8,046	8,313	8,416	8,531	8,672	8,857
North Dakota.	653	639	648	642	634	633	636	635	636
Ohio	10,798	10,847	11,203	11,353	11,415	11,438	11,461	11,471	11,478
Oklahoma	3,025	3,146	3,308	3,451	3,488	3,504	3,523	3,543	3,579
Oregon	2,633	2,842	3,184	3,421	3,524	3,561	3,589	3,639	3,701
Pennsylvania	11,864	11,883	12,198	12,281	12,322	12,351	12,377	12,405	12,441
Rhode Island.	947	1,003	1,017	1,048	1,069	1,075	1,079	1,074	1,068
South Carolina.	3,122	3,486	3,749	4,012	4,101	4,142	4,195	4,247	4,321
South Dakota	691	696	738	755	760	764	770	775	782
Tennessee	4,591	4,877	5,327	5,689	5,788	5,834	5,886	5,956	6,039
Texas.	14,229	16,986	18,959	20,852	21,762	22,134	22,518	22,929	23,508
Utah	1,461	1,723	2,014	2,233	2,326	2,356	2,422	2,490	2,550
Vermont	511	563	589	609	616	619	621	622	624
Virginia.	5,347	6,189	6,671	7,079	7,286	7,376	7,472	7,564	7,643
Washington.	4,132	4,867	5,481	5,894	6,070	6,130	6,206	6,292	6,396
West Virginia	1,950	1,793	1,824	1,808	1,804	1,809	1,811	1,814	1,818
Wisconsin	4,706	4,892	5,185	5,364	5,439	5,467	5,499	5,528	5,557
Wyoming	470	454	485	494	499	501	506	509	515

[1] See footnote 3, Table 1.   [2] The April 1, 1990, census counts include corrections processed through August 1997, results of special censuses and test censuses, and do not include adjustments for census coverage errors.   [3] Reflects modifications to the Census 2000 population as documented in the Count Question Resolution program and geographic program revisions.

Source: U.S. Census Bureau, Current Population Reports, P25-1106; "Table CO-EST2001-12-00 - Time Series of Intercensal State Populaton Estimates: April 1, 1990 to April 1, 2000"; published 11 April 2002; <http://www.census.gov/popest/archives /2000s/vintage2001/CO-EST2001-12/CO-EST2001-12-00.html>; and "Table 1: Annual Estimates of the Population for the United States, Regions, and States, and for Puerto Rico: April 1, 2000 to July 1, 2006 (NST-EST2006-01)"; published 22 December 2006; <http://www.census.gov/popest/states/NST-ann-est.html>.

Table 13. State Population—Rank, Percent Change, and Population Density: 1980 to 2006

[As of April 1, except 2006, as of July 1. Insofar as possible, population shown for all years is that of present area of state. For area figures of states, see Table 348. Minus sign (–) indicates decrease. See Appendix III]

State	Rank				Percent change			Population per square mile of land area [1]		
	1980	1990	2000	2006	1980– 1990	1990– 2000	2000– 2006	1990	2000	2006
United States.....	(X)	(X)	(X)	(X)	9.8	13.1	6.4	70.3	79.6	84.6
Alabama	22	22	23	23	3.8	10.1	3.4	79.6	87.6	90.6
Alaska	50	49	48	47	36.9	14.0	6.9	1.0	1.1	1.2
Arizona.	29	24	20	16	34.8	40.0	20.2	32.3	45.2	54.3
Arkansas.	33	33	33	32	2.8	13.7	5.1	45.1	51.3	54.0
California.	1	1	1	1	26.0	13.6	7.6	191.1	217.2	233.8
Colorado.	28	26	24	22	14.0	30.6	10.5	31.8	41.5	45.8
Connecticut	25	27	29	29	5.8	3.6	2.9	678.5	702.9	723.4
Delaware.	47	46	45	45	12.1	17.6	8.9	341.0	401.1	436.9
District of Columbia. . .	(X)	(X)	(X)	(X)	–4.9	–5.7	1.7	9,884.4	9,316.4	9,471.2
Florida	7	4	4	4	32.7	23.5	13.2	239.9	296.4	335.5
Georgia	13	11	10	9	18.6	26.4	14.4	111.9	141.4	161.7
Hawaii	39	41	42	42	14.9	9.3	6.1	172.6	188.6	200.2
Idaho	41	42	39	39	6.7	28.5	13.3	12.2	15.6	17.7
Illinois.	5	6	5	5	(Z)	8.7	3.3	205.6	223.4	230.9
Indiana	12	14	14	15	1.0	9.7	3.8	154.6	169.5	176.0
Iowa.	27	30	30	30	–4.7	5.4	1.9	49.7	52.4	53.4
Kansas	32	32	32	33	4.8	8.5	2.8	30.3	32.9	33.8
Kentucky	23	23	25	26	0.7	9.6	4.1	92.8	101.7	105.9
Louisiana	19	21	22	25	0.4	5.9	–4.1	96.9	102.6	98.4
Maine	38	38	40	40	9.2	3.8	3.7	39.8	41.3	42.8
Maryland.	18	19	19	19	13.4	10.8	6.0	489.1	541.9	574.6
Massachusetts	11	13	13	13	4.9	5.5	1.4	767.4	809.8	821.1
Michigan	8	8	8	8	0.4	6.9	1.6	163.6	175.0	177.7
Minnesota	21	20	21	21	7.4	12.4	5.0	55.0	61.8	64.9
Mississippi.	31	31	31	31	2.2	10.5	2.3	54.9	60.6	62.0
Missouri	15	15	17	18	4.1	9.4	4.4	74.3	81.2	84.8
Montana	44	44	44	44	1.6	12.9	4.7	5.5	6.2	6.5
Nebraska	35	36	38	38	0.5	8.4	3.3	20.5	22.3	23.0
Nevada.	43	39	35	35	50.1	66.3	24.9	10.9	18.2	22.7
New Hampshire	42	40	41	41	20.5	11.4	6.4	123.7	137.8	146.6
New Jersey	9	9	9	11	5.2	8.6	3.7	1,044.5	1,134.4	1,176.2
New Mexico.	37	37	36	36	16.3	20.1	7.5	12.5	15.0	16.1
New York	2	2	3	3	2.5	5.5	1.7	381.0	401.9	408.9
North Carolina	10	10	11	10	12.8	21.3	10.1	136.2	165.2	181.8
North Dakota	46	47	47	48	–2.1	0.5	–1.0	9.3	9.3	9.2
Ohio.	6	7	7	7	0.5	4.7	1.1	264.9	277.3	280.3
Oklahoma	26	28	27	28	4.0	9.7	3.7	45.8	50.3	52.1
Oregon	30	29	28	27	7.9	20.4	8.2	29.6	35.6	38.6
Pennsylvania	4	5	6	6	0.2	3.4	1.3	265.1	274.0	277.6
Rhode Island	40	43	43	43	5.9	4.5	1.8	960.3	1,003.2	1,021.7
South Carolina	24	25	26	24	11.7	15.1	7.7	115.8	133.2	143.5
South Dakota	45	45	46	46	0.8	8.5	3.6	9.2	9.9	10.3
Tennessee.	17	17	16	17	6.2	16.7	6.1	118.3	138.0	146.5
Texas	3	3	2	2	19.4	22.8	12.7	64.9	79.6	89.8
Utah.	36	35	34	34	17.9	29.6	14.2	21.0	27.2	31.0
Vermont	48	48	49	49	10.0	8.2	2.5	60.8	65.8	67.5
Virginia	14	12	12	12	15.8	14.4	8.0	156.3	178.8	193.0
Washington	20	18	15	14	17.8	21.1	8.5	73.1	88.6	96.1
West Virginia	34	34	37	37	–8.0	0.8	0.6	74.5	75.1	75.5
Wisconsin	16	16	18	20	4.0	9.6	3.6	90.1	98.8	102.3
Wyoming.	49	50	50	50	–3.4	8.9	4.3	4.7	5.1	5.3

X Not applicable.   Z Less than 0.05 percent.   [1] Persons per square mile were calculated on the basis of land area data from the 2000 census.

Source: U.S. Census Bureau, Current Population Reports, P25-1106; "ST-99-3 State Population Estimates: Annual Time Series, July 1, 1990 to July 1, 1999"; published 29 December 1999; <http://www.census.gov/population/estimates/state /st-99-3.txt>; *Population Change and Distribution: 1990 to 2000, Census 2000 Brief*, (C2KBR/01-2), April 2001; and "Table 3: Estimates of Population Change for the United States, Regions, States, and Puerto Rico and Region and State Rankings: July 1, 2005 to July 1, 2006"; <http://www.census.gov/popest/states/tables/NST-EST2006-03.xls> and "Table 1: Annual Estimates of the Population for the United States, Regions, and States and for Puerto Rico: April 1, 2000 to July 1, 2006"; <http://www.census.gov /popest/states/tables/NST-EST2006-01.xls>; both released December 22, 2006.

Table 14. State Resident Population—Projections: 2010 to 2030

[As of July 1. These projections were produced in correspondence with the U.S. interim projections released in March 2004 (see Table 3). They were developed for each of the 50 states and the District of Columbia by age and sex for the years 2000 to 2030, based on Census 2000 results. These projections differ from forecasts in that they represent the results of the mathematical projection model given that current state-specific trends in fertility, mortality, internal migration, and international migration continue. The projections to 2006 have been superseded by population estimates which are shown in Table 12. Minus sign (–) indicates decrease]

State	Number (1,000)					Change, 2000–2030		Rank	
	2010	2015	2020	2025	2030	Number (1,000)	Percent	Total population, 2030	Percent change, 2000–2030
United States....	308,936	322,366	335,805	349,439	363,584	82,163	29.2	(X)	(X)
Alabama.........	4,596	4,663	4,729	4,800	4,874	427	9.6	24	35
Alaska..........	694	733	774	821	868	241	38.4	46	12
Arizona.........	6,637	7,495	8,456	9,532	10,712	5,582	108.8	10	2
Arkansas........	2,875	2,969	3,060	3,151	3,240	567	21.2	32	21
California........	38,067	40,123	42,207	44,305	46,445	12,573	37.1	1	13
Colorado........	4,832	5,049	5,279	5,523	5,792	1,491	34.7	22	14
Connecticut.....	3,577	3,635	3,676	3,691	3,689	283	8.3	30	38
Delaware........	884	927	963	991	1,013	229	29.2	45	18
District of Columbia..	530	506	481	455	433	–139	–24.2	(X)	(X)
Florida.........	19,252	21,204	23,407	25,912	28,686	12,703	79.5	3	3
Georgia	9,589	10,231	10,844	11,439	12,018	3,831	46.8	8	8
Hawaii	1,341	1,386	1,412	1,439	1,466	255	21.0	41	22
Idaho	1,517	1,630	1,741	1,853	1,970	676	52.2	37	6
Illinois..........	12,917	13,097	13,237	13,341	13,433	1,014	8.2	5	39
Indiana	6,392	6,518	6,627	6,721	6,810	730	12.0	18	31
Iowa...........	3,010	3,026	3,020	2,993	2,955	29	1.0	34	48
Kansas.........	2,805	2,853	2,891	2,919	2,940	252	9.4	35	36
Kentucky........	4,265	4,351	4,424	4,490	4,555	513	12.7	27	30
Louisiana	4,613	4,674	4,719	4,762	4,803	334	7.5	26	41
Maine..........	1,357	1,389	1,409	1,414	1,411	136	10.7	42	32
Maryland........	5,905	6,208	6,498	6,763	7,022	1,726	32.6	16	16
Massachusetts.....	6,649	6,759	6,856	6,939	7,012	663	10.4	17	33
Michigan........	10,429	10,599	10,696	10,714	10,694	756	7.6	11	40
Minnesota........	5,421	5,668	5,901	6,109	6,306	1,387	28.2	20	20
Mississippi........	2,971	3,014	3,045	3,069	3,092	248	8.7	33	37
Missouri	5,922	6,070	6,200	6,315	6,430	835	14.9	19	27
Montana	969	999	1,023	1,037	1,045	143	15.8	44	25
Nebraska	1,769	1,789	1,803	1,813	1,820	109	6.4	38	42
Nevada	2,691	3,058	3,452	3,863	4,282	2,284	114.3	28	1
New Hampshire	1,386	1,457	1,525	1,586	1,646	411	33.2	40	15
New Jersey	9,018	9,256	9,462	9,637	9,802	1,388	16.5	13	24
New Mexico.......	1,980	2,042	2,084	2,107	2,100	281	15.4	36	26
New York	19,444	19,547	19,577	19,540	19,477	501	2.6	4	46
North Carolina	9,346	10,011	10,709	11,449	12,228	4,178	51.9	7	7
North Dakota	637	635	630	621	607	–36	–5.5	49	50
Ohio...........	11,576	11,635	11,644	11,606	11,551	197	1.7	9	47
Oklahoma	3,592	3,662	3,736	3,821	3,913	463	13.4	29	29
Oregon.........	3,791	4,013	4,260	4,536	4,834	1,413	41.3	25	10
Pennsylvania......	12,584	12,711	12,787	12,802	12,768	487	4.0	6	45
Rhode Island	1,117	1,140	1,154	1,158	1,153	105	10.0	43	34
South Carolina.....	4,447	4,642	4,823	4,990	5,149	1,137	28.3	23	19
South Dakota......	786	797	802	802	800	46	6.0	47	43
Tennessee........	6,231	6,502	6,781	7,073	7,381	1,691	29.7	15	17
Texas..........	24,649	26,586	28,635	30,865	33,318	12,466	59.8	2	4
Utah...........	2,595	2,783	2,990	3,226	3,485	1,252	56.1	31	5
Vermont	653	673	691	703	712	103	16.9	48	23
Virginia.........	8,010	8,467	8,917	9,364	9,825	2,747	38.8	12	11
Washington	6,542	6,951	7,432	7,996	8,625	2,731	46.3	14	9
West Virginia	1,829	1,823	1,801	1,766	1,720	–88	–4.9	39	49
Wisconsin........	5,727	5,883	6,005	6,088	6,151	787	14.7	21	28
Wyoming........	520	528	531	529	523	29	5.9	50	44

X Not applicable.

Source: U.S. Census Bureau, "Table A1: Interim Projections of the Total Population for the United States and States: April 1, 2000 to July 1, 2030"; published 21 April 2005; <http://www.census.gov/population/www/projections/projectionsagesex.html>.

Population 19

Table 15. **State Resident Population—Components of Change: 2000 to 2006**

[Covers period April 1, 2000, to July 1, 2006. Minus sign (–) indicates net decrease or net outflow]

State	Numeric population change [1]	Births	Deaths	Natural increase (births minus deaths)	Net internal migration	Net international migration
United States	17,973,882	25,486,569	15,162,197	10,324,372	(X)	7,649,510
Alabama.	151,679	375,808	287,990	87,818	42,641	30,537
Alaska	43,122	63,170	19,342	43,828	–3,436	4,654
Arizona.	1,035,686	564,062	266,134	297,928	541,283	204,661
Arkansas	137,474	237,755	175,236	62,519	55,141	26,467
California	2,585,896	3,375,297	1,465,929	1,909,368	–950,592	1,724,790
Colorado.	451,362	425,394	181,115	244,279	80,057	133,930
Connecticut.	99,207	256,735	185,987	70,748	–53,125	92,635
Delaware	69,876	69,846	44,173	25,673	33,419	13,394
District of Columbia	9,471	48,355	35,525	12,830	–60,644	24,795
Florida	2,107,064	1,338,458	1,056,111	282,347	1,221,540	642,188
Georgia	1,177,125	849,414	410,475	438,939	378,258	228,415
Hawaii	73,961	110,926	54,675	56,251	–9,275	31,092
Idaho	172,509	135,942	63,465	72,477	83,870	17,266
Illinois	412,323	1,138,398	656,599	481,799	–473,713	402,257
Indiana.	233,003	541,506	344,778	196,728	–17,818	68,935
Iowa	55,703	239,348	173,795	65,553	–41,489	36,142
Kansas.	75,251	246,484	152,585	93,899	–65,589	44,847
Kentucky	163,789	345,318	246,797	98,521	44,188	30,889
Louisiana	–181,190	410,364	265,009	145,355	–330,492	22,244
Maine.	46,651	86,331	78,414	7,917	36,792	5,616
Maryland	319,221	464,251	275,093	189,158	–13,017	129,730
Massachusetts.	88,088	499,440	349,448	149,992	–289,967	200,155
Michigan.	157,163	816,225	543,921	272,304	–239,349	151,435
Minnesota.	247,609	432,306	236,211	196,095	–26,574	86,925
Mississippi	65,884	266,971	177,467	89,504	–25,280	10,896
Missouri	246,030	480,763	343,199	137,564	37,638	50,450
Montana.	42,437	70,509	52,472	18,037	24,944	2,092
Nebraska	57,066	160,471	94,590	65,881	–31,457	26,224
Nevada	497,272	210,950	107,795	103,155	318,182	80,482
New Hampshire	79,109	90,680	62,189	28,491	40,531	13,718
New Jersey.	310,213	705,812	451,046	254,766	–277,900	357,111
New Mexico	135,553	174,378	89,316	85,062	22,887	32,967
New York	329,362	1,576,125	974,346	601,779	–1,242,869	820,388
North Carolina	810,014	749,959	456,198	293,761	347,005	180,986
North Dakota.	–6,333	49,881	36,748	13,133	–21,149	3,664
Ohio	124,861	938,169	675,165	263,004	–237,819	92,101
Oklahoma.	128,558	317,771	220,169	97,602	–4,799	41,665
Oregon.	279,322	284,655	191,461	93,194	108,748	88,976
Pennsylvania.	159,567	902,068	806,419	95,649	–27,718	126,007
Rhode Island.	19,291	79,147	60,604	18,543	–18,742	23,086
South Carolina.	309,433	349,748	234,424	115,324	167,070	40,168
South Dakota	27,075	68,615	43,865	24,750	470	4,333
Tennessee	349,541	493,881	351,615	142,266	160,166	59,385
Texas.	2,655,993	2,351,909	962,634	1,389,275	451,910	801,576
Utah	316,865	308,460	82,192	226,268	–17,709	60,944
Vermont	15,081	40,670	31,805	8,865	2,822	5,295
Virginia.	563,854	633,794	357,755	276,039	124,544	151,748
Washington	501,658	503,819	281,861	221,958	129,809	157,950
West Virginia	10,120	130,202	131,811	–1,609	12,772	4,419
Wisconsin	192,791	434,966	290,915	144,051	9,224	56,557
Wyoming	21,222	41,063	25,329	15,734	4,611	2,323

X Not applicable.   [1] The estimated components of population change will not sum to the numerical population change due to the process of controlling to national totals.

Source: U.S. Census Bureau, "Table 4: Cumulative Estimates of the Components of Population Change for the United States, Regions, and States: April 1, 2000 to July 1, 2006 (NST-EST2006-04);" published 22 December 2006; <http://www.census.gov /popest/states/NST-comp-chg.html>.

Table 16. **Resident Population by Age and State: 2006**

[In thousands, except percent (299,398 represents 299,398,000). As of July. Includes Armed Forces stationed in area]

State	Total	Under 5 years	5 to 17 years	18 to 24 years	25 to 34 years	35 to 44 years	45 to 54 years	55 to 64 years	65 to 74 years	75 to 84 years	85 years and over	Percent 65 years and over
U.S.	299,398	20,418	53,318	29,455	40,416	43,667	43,278	31,587	18,917	13,047	5,297	12.5
AL.	4,599	299	815	448	602	638	666	516	327	209	80	13.4
AK.	670	50	132	72	97	99	109	67	28	14	4	6.8
AZ.	6,166	480	1,148	588	899	853	789	619	403	282	105	12.8
AR.	2,811	193	498	267	378	381	387	316	203	132	55	13.9
CA.	36,458	2,678	6,855	3,784	5,257	5,511	5,015	3,427	2,002	1,374	555	10.8
CO.	4,753	341	828	459	721	719	718	490	256	160	61	10.0
CT.	3,505	203	615	320	408	546	550	392	225	169	76	13.4
DE.	853	57	147	83	109	125	123	95	60	40	15	13.4
DC.	582	35	80	72	104	85	75	60	36	25	11	12.3
FL.	18,090	1,123	2,899	1,595	2,285	2,583	2,528	2,040	1,451	1,124	463	16.8
GA.	9,364	702	1,753	915	1,375	1,456	1,315	935	504	295	113	9.8
HI	1,285	87	211	125	178	180	182	143	85	67	27	14.0
ID	1,466	113	281	149	204	194	203	153	89	57	23	11.5
IL.	12,832	888	2,328	1,282	1,791	1,868	1,845	1,296	770	537	227	12.0
IN	6,314	431	1,147	616	850	894	924	668	399	274	111	12.4
IA	2,982	192	518	312	360	400	442	322	205	155	75	14.6
KS.	2,764	194	502	293	355	375	403	284	171	127	60	12.9
KY.	4,206	276	724	384	585	607	619	474	286	182	69	12.8
LA.	4,288	301	789	455	560	581	622	455	277	179	68	12.2
ME.	1,322	70	211	116	152	195	218	168	98	67	27	14.6
MD.	5,616	368	992	533	732	871	858	610	342	223	86	11.6
MA.	6,437	388	1,061	633	830	993	972	705	410	309	137	13.3
MI	10,096	638	1,840	983	1,273	1,462	1,531	1,108	640	447	175	12.5
MN.	5,167	345	912	520	676	759	791	536	310	216	102	12.1
MS.	2,911	209	550	304	380	391	407	307	191	122	50	12.4
MO	5,843	387	1,030	569	768	818	857	635	395	270	114	13.3
MT.	945	58	160	95	112	121	153	116	67	45	19	13.8
NE.	1,768	128	317	189	227	236	256	181	112	83	39	13.3
NV.	2,496	184	451	213	379	376	341	274	158	92	28	11.1
NH.	1,315	74	224	120	155	208	218	154	83	56	23	12.4
NJ	8,725	559	1,530	764	1,084	1,388	1,329	942	559	402	167	12.9
NM.	1,955	142	367	205	257	259	274	209	128	83	31	12.4
NY.	19,306	1,220	3,294	1,939	2,529	2,894	2,818	2,088	1,265	886	372	13.1
NC.	8,857	611	1,544	835	1,220	1,329	1,266	975	575	366	136	12.2
ND.	636	40	105	82	75	79	96	66	43	33	17	14.6
OH.	11,478	735	2,035	1,097	1,459	1,622	1,738	1,260	767	548	217	13.4
OK.	3,579	255	639	369	481	472	503	387	246	162	66	13.2
OR.	3,701	231	626	340	520	513	557	436	241	167	71	12.9
PA	12,441	725	2,080	1,199	1,454	1,771	1,916	1,411	887	703	295	15.2
RI	1,068	62	175	116	132	158	160	116	67	56	25	13.9
SC.	4,321	283	756	423	568	612	621	504	299	185	69	12.8
SD.	782	55	140	83	95	100	114	83	52	40	19	14.2
TN.	6,039	398	1,044	549	839	877	877	686	414	257	98	12.7
TX.	23,508	1,925	4,569	2,449	3,474	3,420	3,168	2,168	1,242	790	303	9.9
UT.	2,550	248	543	319	409	311	294	200	119	78	29	8.8
VT.	624	33	101	62	71	90	104	79	43	29	12	13.3
VA	7,643	509	1,298	747	1,048	1,179	1,141	834	475	301	112	11.6
WA	6,396	408	1,118	607	896	947	972	709	379	252	107	11.5
WV	1,818	105	284	163	233	245	279	230	144	99	36	15.3
WI	5,557	349	964	561	703	806	853	597	356	256	111	13.0
WY	515	34	88	54	67	66	83	60	33	21	8	12.2

Source: U.S. Census Bureau, "Age and Sex for States and for Puerto Rico: April 1, 2000 to July 1, 2006"; Release Date: May 17, 2007; <http://www.census.gov/popest/states/asrh/SC-EST2006-02.html>.

Population 21

Table 17. Resident Population by Age and State—Projections: 2010 and 2015

[As of July 1. 74,432 represents 74,432,000. These projections were produced in correspondence with the U.S. interim projections released in March 2004 (see Tables 3 and 10). They were developed for each of the 50 states and the District of Columbia by age and sex for the years 2000 to 2030, based on Census 2000 results. These projections differ from forecasts in that they represent the results of the mathematical projection model given that current state-specific trends in fertility, mortality, internal migration and international migration continue. The projections to 2006 have been superseded by population estimates which are shown in Table 16]

State	Population (1,000)										Percent of population, 2015	
	Under 18 years old		18 to 44 years old		45 to 64 years old		65 to 74 years old		75 years old and over		Under 18 years old	65 years old and over
	2010	2015	2010	2015	2010	2015	2010	2015	2010	2015		
U.S.	74,432	77,018	113,248	114,845	81,012	83,711	21,270	26,608	18,974	20,182	23.9	14.5
AL	1,092	1,089	1,605	1,575	1,251	1,259	354	427	295	312	23.4	15.9
AK	184	199	270	280	184	178	35	49	21	26	27.2	10.2
AZ	1,688	1,892	2,349	2,529	1,678	1,892	516	711	406	470	25.2	15.8
AR	703	721	996	998	765	782	227	274	185	194	24.3	15.8
CA	9,497	9,820	14,787	15,240	9,391	9,835	2,333	2,972	2,060	2,256	24.5	13.0
CO	1,189	1,256	1,863	1,886	1,263	1,280	282	369	235	258	24.9	12.4
CT	814	807	1,257	1,251	990	1,001	253	308	262	270	22.2	15.9
DE	202	210	309	305	249	264	68	87	57	61	22.6	16.0
DC	114	112	237	225	118	108	32	34	29	27	22.1	12.2
FL	4,086	4,455	6,315	6,614	5,431	6,002	1,773	2,345	1,646	1,789	21.0	19.5
GA	2,502	2,679	3,724	3,822	2,382	2,543	564	723	417	464	26.2	11.6
HI	316	330	477	479	357	350	101	131	90	96	23.8	16.3
ID	400	427	554	583	381	400	99	129	82	91	26.2	13.5
IL	3,197	3,215	4,842	4,798	3,277	3,307	826	979	774	799	24.5	13.6
IN	1,596	1,614	2,328	2,333	1,656	1,664	425	508	386	398	24.8	13.9
IA	711	707	1,049	1,031	800	794	217	259	233	236	23.4	16.3
KS	699	708	1,004	1,001	727	724	185	225	190	194	24.8	14.7
KY	1,002	1,007	1,540	1,526	1,165	1,181	309	376	249	262	23.1	14.6
LA	1,172	1,176	1,665	1,642	1,194	1,192	313	379	270	285	25.2	14.2
ME	269	269	462	455	413	415	110	142	102	108	19.3	18.0
MD	1,406	1,487	2,212	2,283	1,568	1,601	386	478	332	359	23.9	13.5
MA	1,484	1,474	2,440	2,402	1,817	1,857	454	567	454	458	21.8	15.2
MI	2,487	2,479	3,822	3,799	2,785	2,814	699	852	635	654	23.4	14.2
MN	1,290	1,349	2,027	2,069	1,433	1,475	343	429	327	346	23.8	13.7
MS	759	753	1,052	1,028	781	801	209	254	170	179	25.0	14.4
MO	1,411	1,436	2,111	2,123	1,578	1,589	432	518	390	404	23.7	15.2
MT	212	216	324	326	287	284	77	100	68	74	21.6	17.4
NE	446	454	619	608	460	455	119	145	125	126	25.4	15.2
NV	665	752	961	1,033	735	851	199	264	131	158	24.6	13.8
NH	304	313	494	508	408	418	97	129	82	88	21.5	14.9
NJ	2,088	2,104	3,252	3,239	2,446	2,528	632	760	600	625	22.7	15.0
NM	479	485	669	654	553	560	153	201	126	142	23.7	16.8
NY	4,421	4,353	7,227	7,077	5,144	5,173	1,346	1,589	1,306	1,354	22.3	15.1
NC	2,269	2,438	3,471	3,586	2,445	2,611	641	810	520	565	24.4	13.7
ND	142	139	223	219	174	169	46	56	51	51	21.8	17.0
OH	2,744	2,723	4,123	4,054	3,121	3,093	816	980	771	786	23.4	15.2
OK	895	915	1,264	1,260	938	933	266	316	229	238	25.0	15.1
OR	863	916	1,412	1,470	1,022	1,036	263	348	231	242	22.8	14.7
PA	2,748	2,741	4,385	4,334	3,496	3,487	960	1,159	997	990	21.6	16.9
RI	249	248	410	412	300	304	76	94	82	81	21.8	15.4
SC	1,036	1,061	1,579	1,581	1,226	1,271	343	439	263	290	22.9	15.7
SD	194	196	269	264	209	209	55	67	60	61	24.6	16.1
TN	1,479	1,539	2,249	2,275	1,673	1,720	461	570	368	399	23.7	14.9
TX	6,785	7,376	9,417	9,848	5,859	6,248	1,426	1,826	1,162	1,287	27.7	11.7
UT	819	872	1,021	1,073	520	556	127	162	108	119	31.3	10.1
VT	132	132	232	235	195	193	50	67	43	46	19.6	16.9
VA	1,880	1,982	2,997	3,085	2,139	2,207	554	703	441	490	23.4	14.1
WA	1,488	1,561	2,481	2,591	1,777	1,833	429	567	367	399	22.5	13.9
WV	382	373	618	595	536	525	156	190	136	140	20.4	18.1
WI	1,319	1,343	2,076	2,067	1,561	1,591	392	487	380	395	22.8	15.0
WY	116	115	177	174	154	150	40	52	33	37	21.9	16.8

Source: U.S. Census Bureau, "File 2. Annual projections by 5-year and selected age groups by sex;" published 21 April 2005; <http://www.census.gov/population/www/projections/projectionsagesex.html>.

Table 18. Resident Population by Race, Hispanic or Latino Origin, and State: 2006

[In thousands (299,398 represents 299,398,000). As of July. Persons of Hispanic or Latino origin may be any race. Due to the complexities associated with the production of detailed characteristics' estimates at the state level, the values of the estimates at lower levels of geography may not necessarily sum to estimates at higher levels of geography]

| State | Total population | One race | | | | | Two or more races | Hispanic or Latino origin | Non-Hispanic White alone |
		White alone	Black or African American alone	American Indian/Alaska Native alone	Asian alone	Native Hawaiian and Other Pacific Islander alone			
U.S....	299,398	239,746	38,343	2,903	13,159	529	4,719	44,321	198,744
AL........	4,599	3,277	1,212	24	42	2	43	114	3,175
AK........	670	474	25	103	31	4	33	38	445
AZ........	6,166	5,381	232	294	147	12	101	1,803	3,680
AR........	2,811	2,280	442	22	29	3	35	141	2,149
CA........	36,458	28,044	2,445	421	4,511	153	884	13,074	15,723
CO........	4,753	4,283	196	55	126	7	87	934	3,410
CT........	3,505	2,966	358	12	118	3	47	392	2,622
DE........	853	636	178	3	24	(Z)	12	54	589
DC........	582	223	329	2	19	1	8	48	184
FL........	18,090	14,504	2,864	80	397	15	229	3,646	11,093
GA........	9,364	6,159	2,800	31	261	7	106	703	5,518
HI........	1,285	367	32	6	514	117	249	100	317
ID........	1,466	1,397	10	21	16	2	22	139	1,266
IL........	12,832	10,170	1,928	41	541	8	143	1,887	8,373
IN........	6,314	5,575	563	19	84	3	70	301	5,296
IA........	2,982	2,820	73	11	47	1	29	115	2,714
KS........	2,764	2,462	165	27	61	2	47	237	2,241
KY........	4,206	3,793	317	10	42	2	42	86	3,716
LA........	4,288	2,802	1,358	27	60	2	39	124	2,694
ME........	1,322	1,278	11	8	11	(Z)	13	14	1,266
MD........	5,616	3,574	1,657	19	278	4	85	337	3,282
MA........	6,437	5,569	447	19	314	5	84	511	5,150
MI........	10,096	8,199	1,444	61	237	4	150	393	7,846
MN........	5,167	4,616	231	60	181	3	76	196	4,440
MS........	2,911	1,772	1,081	14	22	1	21	53	1,726
MO........	5,843	4,975	673	28	83	4	79	164	4,826
MT........	945	858	4	61	6	1	15	24	838
NE........	1,768	1,623	78	17	29	1	20	130	1,501
NV........	2,496	2,038	196	35	150	12	64	610	1,469
NH........	1,315	1,260	14	3	24	1	13	30	1,233
NJ........	8,725	6,665	1,265	28	648	7	112	1,365	5,458
NM........	1,955	1,654	49	191	26	3	32	861	836
NY........	19,306	14,220	3,353	105	1,326	19	283	3,139	11,677
NC........	8,857	6,558	1,921	111	164	6	96	594	6,015
ND........	636	584	5	34	5	(Z)	7	11	575
OH........	11,478	9,748	1,377	28	177	4	145	268	9,514
OK........	3,579	2,804	279	288	60	3	145	247	2,581
OR........	3,701	3,348	69	51	134	10	88	379	2,996
PA........	12,441	10,660	1,336	24	293	5	122	527	10,216
RI........	1,068	947	67	7	29	1	16	118	850
SC........	4,321	2,959	1,253	17	50	2	40	151	2,827
SD........	782	691	7	67	6	(Z)	11	17	677
TN........	6,039	4,856	1,020	19	80	3	62	195	4,681
TX........	23,508	19,453	2,805	163	788	27	272	8,385	11,351
UT........	2,550	2,384	26	34	50	19	38	286	2,114
VT........	624	603	4	2	7	(Z)	7	7	597
VA........	7,643	5,605	1,520	26	363	6	123	480	5,175
WA........	6,396	5,421	228	104	422	30	191	581	4,895
WV........	1,818	1,726	60	4	12	1	16	17	1,710
WI........	5,557	5,000	332	52	111	2	59	259	4,761
WY........	515	486	5	13	4	(Z)	7	36	454

Z Less than 500.

Source: U.S. Census Bureau, "SC-EST2006-6RACE: Annual State Population Estimates with Sex, 6 Race Groups (5 Race Alone Groups and One Group with Two or more Race Groups) and Hispanic Origin: April 1, 2000 to July 1, 2006"; Release Date: May 17, 2007; <http://www.census.gov/popest/states/asrh/files/SCEST20066RACEALL.csv>.

U.S. Census Bureau, Statistical Abstract of the United States: 2008

Table 19. Resident Population by Region, Race, and Hispanic Origin: 2000

[As of April (281,422 represents 281,422,000). For composition of regions, see map, inside front cover]

Race and Hispanic origin	Population (1,000)					Percent distribution				
	United States	North-east	Midwest	South	West	United States	North-east	Mid-west	South	West
Total population	281,422	53,594	64,393	100,237	63,198	100.0	19.0	22.9	35.6	22.5
One race.	274,596	52,366	63,370	98,390	60,470	100.0	19.1	23.1	35.8	22.0
White	211,461	41,534	53,834	72,819	43,274	100.0	19.6	25.5	34.4	20.5
Black or African American . . .	34,658	6,100	6,500	18,982	3,077	100.0	17.6	18.8	54.8	8.9
American Indian and Alaska Native	2,476	163	399	726	1,188	100.0	6.6	16.1	29.3	48.0
Asian	10,243	2,119	1,198	1,922	5,004	100.0	20.7	11.7	18.8	48.8
Asian Indian	1,679	554	293	441	391	100.0	33.0	17.5	26.3	23.3
Chinese	2,433	692	212	343	1,186	100.0	28.4	8.7	14.1	48.8
Filipino	1,850	202	151	245	1,253	100.0	10.9	8.2	13.2	67.7
Japanese	797	76	63	77	580	100.0	9.6	7.9	9.7	72.8
Korean.	1,077	246	132	224	474	100.0	22.9	12.3	20.8	44.0
Vietnamese.	1,123	115	107	336	564	100.0	10.3	9.5	29.9	50.3
Other Asian [1]	1,285	233	239	257	556	100.0	18.2	18.6	20.0	43.2
Native Hawaiian and Other Pacific Islander. . . .	399	21	22	51	304	100.0	5.2	5.6	12.8	76.3
Native Hawaiian.	141	4	6	12	118	100.0	3.2	4.1	8.9	83.8
Guamanian or Chamorro. .	58	5	5	15	34	100.0	7.9	7.9	25.1	59.1
Samoan	91	4	5	9	73	100.0	4.2	5.6	9.7	80.5
Other Pacific Islander [2] . .	109	8	7	15	79	100.0	7.3	6.4	14.0	72.2
Some other race	15,359	2,430	1,417	3,889	7,623	100.0	15.8	9.2	25.3	49.6
Two or more races	6,826	1,228	1,022	1,847	2,728	100.0	18.0	15.0	27.1	40.0
Hispanic or Latino [3].	35,306	5,254	3,125	11,587	15,341	100.0	14.9	8.8	32.8	43.5
Mexican.	20,641	479	2,200	6,548	11,413	100.0	2.3	10.7	31.7	55.3
Puerto Rican	3,406	2,075	325	759	247	100.0	60.9	9.6	22.3	7.2
Cuban.	1,242	169	45	921	106	100.0	13.6	3.6	74.2	8.5
Other Hispanic or Latino. . . .	10,017	2,531	554	3,358	3,574	100.0	25.3	5.5	33.5	35.7
Not Hispanic or Latino	246,116	48,340	61,268	88,650	47,857	100.0	19.6	24.9	36.0	19.4
White alone	194,553	39,327	52,386	65,928	36,912	100.0	20.2	26.9	33.9	19.0

[1] Other Asian alone, or two or more Asian categories.   [2] Other Pacific Islander alone, or two or more Native Hawaiian and Other Pacific Islander categories.   [3] Persons of Hispanic origin may be any race.

Source: U.S. Census Bureau, "Demographic Profiles: Census 2000"; <http://www.census.gov/Press-Release/www/2001/demoprofile.html>.

Table 20. Large Metropolitan Statistical Areas—Population: 1990 to 2006

[1990 and 2000, as of April 1; beginning 2004 as of July 1 (658 represents 658,000). Covers metropolitan statistical areas with 250,000 and over population in 2006, as defined by the U.S. Office of Management and Budget as of December 2005. All geographic boundaries for 2000 to 2006 population estimates are defined as of January 1, 2006. For definitions and components of all metropolitan and micropolitan areas, see Appendix II. Minus sign (–) indicates decrease]

Metropolitan statistical area	Number (1,000)					Percent change		Rank, 2006
	1990	2000, estimates base [1]	2004	2005	2006	1990 to 2000	2000 to 2006 [1]	
Akron, OH.	658	695	701	701	701	5.7	0.9	70
Albany-Schenectady-Troy, NY	810	826	844	847	851	2.0	3.0	57
Albuquerque, NM	599	730	780	798	817	21.7	11.9	61
Allentown-Bethlehem-Easton, PA-NJ	687	740	779	790	800	7.8	8.1	62
Anchorage, AK	266	320	346	352	359	20.1	12.4	137
Ann Arbor, MI	283	323	339	342	344	14.1	6.6	141
Asheville, NC.	308	369	387	392	398	19.9	7.8	125
Atlanta-Sandy Springs-Marietta, GA.	3,069	4,248	4,822	4,972	5,138	38.4	21.0	9
Atlantic City, NJ	224	253	268	270	272	12.6	7.6	164
Augusta-Richmond County, GA-SC	436	500	515	518	523	14.7	4.7	95
Austin-Round Rock, TX.	846	1,250	1,411	1,455	1,514	47.7	21.1	37
Bakersfield, CA	545	662	734	757	780	21.4	17.9	65
Baltimore-Towson, MD	2,382	2,553	2,642	2,651	2,658	7.2	4.1	20
Baton Rouge, LA	624	706	726	731	767	13.2	8.6	67
Beaumont-Port Arthur, TX	361	385	383	383	380	6.6	-1.4	130
Birmingham-Hoover, AL.	957	1,051	1,080	1,088	1,100	10.0	4.6	47
Boise City-Nampa, ID	320	465	525	545	568	45.4	22.1	87
Boston-Cambridge-Quincy, MA-NH	4,134	4,392	4,449	4,449	4,455	6.2	1.4	11
Boulder, CO [2]	209	270	279	280	282	29.1	4.6	160
Bridgeport-Stamford-Norwalk, CT	828	883	901	901	900	6.6	2.0	54
Brownsville-Harlingen, TX	260	335	371	379	388	28.9	15.7	127
Buffalo-Niagara Falls, NY.	1,189	1,170	1,152	1,145	1,138	-1.6	-2.8	46
Canton-Massillon, OH	394	407	410	410	410	3.3	0.7	117
Cape Coral-Fort Myers, FL.	335	441	514	544	571	31.6	29.6	86
Charleston, WV.	308	310	307	306	306	0.6	-1.3	151
Charleston-North Charleston, SC	507	549	582	592	603	8.3	9.9	81
Charlotte-Gastonia-Concord, NC-SC	1,025	1,330	1,473	1,521	1,583	29.8	19.0	36
Chattanooga, TN-GA	433	477	488	492	497	10.0	4.2	99
Chicago-Naperville-Joliet, IL-IN-WI	8,182	9,099	9,394	9,447	9,506	11.2	4.5	3
Cincinnati-Middletown, OH-KY-IN	1,845	2,010	2,075	2,091	2,104	8.9	4.7	25

See footnotes at end of table.

24   Population

[1990 and 2000, as of April 1; beginning 2004 as of July 1 (658 represents 658,000). Covers metropolitan statistical areas with 250,000 and over population in 2006, as defined by the U.S. Office of Management and Budget as of December 2005. All geographic boundaries for 2000 to 2006 population estimates are defined as of January 1, 2006. For definitions and components of all metropolitan and micropolitan areas, see Appendix II. Minus sign (–) indicates decrease]

Metropolitan statistical area	Number (1,000)				Percent change		Rank, 2006
	1990	2000, estimates base [1]	2004	2005	2006	1990 to 2000	2000 to 2006 [1]	

Metropolitan statistical area	1990	2000, estimates base [1]	2004	2005	2006	1990 to 2000	2000 to 2006 [1]	Rank, 2006
Cleveland-Elyria-Mentor, OH	2,102	2,148	2,134	2,125	2,114	2.2	-1.6	24
Colorado Springs, CO	409	537	579	587	599	31.3	11.5	83
Columbia, SC	549	647	685	691	704	17.9	8.7	69
Columbus, GA-AL	266	282	281	282	289	5.7	2.5	156
Columbus, OH	1,405	1,613	1,689	1,707	1,726	14.8	7.0	32
Corpus Christi, TX	368	403	409	413	416	9.7	3.1	114
Dallas-Fort Worth-Arlington, TX	3,989	5,162	5,695	5,823	6,004	29.4	16.3	4
Davenport-Moline-Rock Island, IA-IL	368	376	375	376	377	2.1	0.3	131
Dayton, OH	844	848	844	841	839	0.5	-1.1	59
Deltona-Daytona Beach-Ormond Beach, FL	371	443	478	488	497	19.6	12.0	100
Denver-Aurora, CO [2]	1,667	2,179	2,326	2,362	2,409	30.7	10.5	21
Des Moines-West Des Moines, IA	416	481	513	523	534	15.6	11.0	92
Detroit-Warren-Livonia, MI	4,249	4,453	4,484	4,479	4,469	4.8	0.4	10
Duluth, MN-WI	269	275	276	275	274	2.3	-0.5	163
Durham, NC	345	424	450	456	464	23.7	9.6	104
El Paso, TX	592	680	712	721	736	14.9	8.3	68
Erie, PA	276	281	281	280	280	1.9	-0.4	161
Eugene-Springfield, OR	283	323	331	334	338	14.2	4.6	143
Evansville, IN-KY	325	343	348	349	350	5.5	2.2	139
Fayetteville, NC	298	337	345	340	341	13.1	1.4	142
Fayetteville-Springdale-Rogers, AR-MO	239	347	392	407	421	44.9	21.3	111
Flint, MI	430	436	443	443	442	1.3	1.3	108
Fort Collins-Loveland, CO	186	251	269	272	276	35.1	9.8	162
Fort Smith, AR-OK	234	273	282	284	289	16.7	5.7	157
Fort Wayne, IN	354	390	401	404	408	10.1	4.6	118
Fresno, CA	667	799	865	878	892	19.8	11.6	56
Grand Rapids-Wyoming, MI	646	740	766	770	774	14.6	4.5	66
Green Bay, WI	244	282	295	297	299	16.0	5.8	153
Greensboro-High Point, NC	540	643	665	674	685	19.1	6.5	73
Greenville, SC	472	560	583	591	602	18.6	7.5	82
Hagerstown-Martinsburg, MD-WV	193	223	244	251	258	15.6	15.6	169
Harrisburg-Carlisle, PA	474	509	518	521	525	7.3	3.2	94
Hartford-West Hartford-East Hartford, CT	1,124	1,149	1,181	1,186	1,189	2.2	3.5	44
Hickory-Lenoir-Morganton, NC	292	342	353	356	360	16.9	5.3	136
Holland-Grand Haven, MI	188	238	253	255	258	26.9	8.1	168
Honolulu, HI	836	876	898	905	910	4.8	3.8	53
Houston-Sugar Land-Baytown, TX	3,767	4,715	5,233	5,353	5,540	25.2	17.5	6
Huntington-Ashland, WV-KY-OH	288	289	286	285	285	0.2	-1.1	158
Huntsville, AL	293	343	363	369	377	16.8	10.0	132
Indianapolis-Carmel, IN	1,294	1,525	1,617	1,640	1,666	17.8	9.2	33
Jackson, MS	447	497	515	521	529	11.2	6.5	93
Jacksonville, FL	925	1,123	1,222	1,248	1,278	21.4	13.8	40
Kalamazoo-Portage, MI	293	315	318	319	320	7.3	1.5	147
Kansas City, MO-KS	1,637	1,836	1,926	1,945	1,967	12.2	7.1	28
Killeen-Temple-Fort Hood, TX	269	331	345	350	351	23.0	6.2	138
Kingsport-Bristol-Bristol, TN-VA	276	298	300	301	302	8.3	1.3	152
Knoxville, TN	535	616	647	656	667	15.2	8.3	77
Lafayette, LA	209	239	245	247	254	14.5	6.5	171
Lakeland, FL	405	484	524	542	562	19.4	16.1	88
Lancaster, PA	423	471	486	490	494	11.3	5.1	101
Lansing-East Lansing, MI	433	448	455	455	454	3.5	1.4	106
Las Vegas-Paradise, NV	741	1,376	1,648	1,709	1,778	85.6	29.2	31
Lexington-Fayette, KY	348	408	424	430	437	17.2	6.9	110
Lincoln, NE	229	267	278	281	284	16.5	6.4	159
Little Rock-North Little Rock, AR	535	611	635	643	653	14.1	6.9	79
Los Angeles-Long Beach-Santa Ana, CA	11,274	12,366	12,902	12,934	12,950	9.7	4.7	2
Louisville-Jefferson County, KY-IN	1,056	1,162	1,201	1,210	1,222	10.0	5.1	42
Lubbock, TX	230	250	258	259	261	8.6	4.7	167
Madison, WI	432	502	531	537	543	16.1	8.2	90
Manchester-Nashua, NH	336	381	398	401	403	13.4	5.8	121
McAllen-Edinburg-Mission, TX	384	569	657	679	701	48.5	23.0	71
Memphis, TN-MS-AR	1,067	1,205	1,245	1,257	1,275	12.9	5.8	41
Miami-Fort Lauderdale-Miami Beach, FL	4,056	5,008	5,351	5,425	5,464	23.5	9.1	7
Milwaukee-Waukesha-West Allis, WI	1,432	1,501	1,511	1,509	1,510	4.8	0.6	38
Minneapolis-St. Paul-Bloomington, MN-WI	2,539	2,969	3,112	3,141	3,175	16.9	6.9	16
Mobile, AL	379	400	399	400	404	5.6	1.1	120
Modesto, CA	371	447	497	505	512	20.6	14.6	97
Montgomery, AL	305	347	353	356	362	13.6	4.4	135
Naples-Marco Island, FL	152	251	297	308	315	65.3	25.2	150
Nashville-Davidson–Murfreesboro, TN	1,048	1,312	1,394	1,421	1,455	25.1	10.9	39
New Haven-Milford, CT	804	824	843	845	845	2.5	2.6	58
New Orleans-Metairie-Kenner, LA	1,264	1,317	1,314	1,314	1,025	4.1	-22.2	50

See footnotes at end of table.

U.S. Census Bureau, Statistical Abstract of the United States: 2008

Table 20. Large Metropolitan Statistical Areas—Population: 1990 to 2006—Con.

[1990 and 2000, as of April 1; beginning 2004 as of July 1 (658 represents 658,000). Covers metropolitan statistical areas with 250,000 and over population in 2006, as defined by the U.S. Office of Management and Budget as of December 2005. All geographic boundaries for 2000 to 2006 population estimates are defined as of January 1, 2006. For definitions and components of all metropolitan and micropolitan areas, see Appendix II. Minus sign (–) indicates decrease]

Metropolitan statistical area	Number (1,000)					Percent change		Rank, 2006
	1990	2000, estimates base [1]	2004	2005	2006	1990 to 2000	2000 to 2006 [1]	
New York-Northern New Jersey-Long Island, NY-NJ-PA	16,846	18,323	18,766	18,814	18,819	8.8	2.7	1
Norwich-New London, CT	255	259	266	264	263	1.6	1.6	166
Ocala, FL	195	259	291	303	316	32.9	22.1	149
Ogden-Clearfield, UT	352	443	477	486	498	25.8	12.4	98
Oklahoma City, OK	971	1,095	1,141	1,155	1,172	12.8	7.0	45
Omaha-Council Bluffs, NE-IA	686	767	802	813	823	11.8	7.2	60
Orlando-Kissimmee, FL	1,225	1,645	1,861	1,931	1,985	34.3	20.7	27
Oxnard-Thousand Oaks-Ventura, CA	669	753	796	796	800	12.6	6.2	63
Palm Bay-Melbourne-Titusville, FL	399	476	518	529	534	19.4	12.2	91
Pensacola-Ferry Pass-Brent, FL	344	412	434	438	440	19.7	6.8	109
Peoria, IL	359	367	367	368	370	2.3	0.9	133
Philadelphia-Camden-Wilmington, PA-NJ-DE-MD	5,436	5,687	5,788	5,806	5,827	4.6	2.5	5
Phoenix-Mesa-Scottsdale, AZ	2,238	3,252	3,720	3,879	4,039	45.3	24.2	13
Pittsburgh, PA	2,468	2,431	2,395	2,382	2,371	-1.5	-2.5	22
Portland-South Portland-Biddeford, ME	441	488	511	513	514	10.5	5.4	96
Portland-Vancouver-Beaverton, OR-WA	1,524	1,928	2,062	2,097	2,138	26.5	10.9	23
Port St. Lucie-Fort Pierce, FL	251	319	365	379	392	27.2	22.8	126
Poughkeepsie-Newburgh-Middletown, NY	567	622	662	667	672	9.6	8.0	76
Providence-New Bedford-Fall River, RI-MA	1,510	1,583	1,626	1,619	1,613	4.8	1.9	35
Provo-Orem, UT	269	377	443	461	474	39.9	25.9	102
Raleigh-Cary, NC	544	797	915	952	995	46.5	24.8	51
Reading, PA	337	374	391	396	401	11.0	7.4	122
Reno-Sparks, NV	257	343	384	394	401	33.3	16.8	123
Richmond, VA	949	1,097	1,155	1,173	1,194	15.6	8.8	43
Riverside-San Bernardino-Ontario, CA	2,589	3,255	3,783	3,910	4,026	25.7	23.7	14
Roanoke, VA	269	288	291	292	295	7.4	2.4	155
Rochester, NY	1,002	1,038	1,040	1,037	1,035	3.5	-0.2	49
Rockford, IL	284	320	337	342	348	12.9	8.8	140
Sacramento-Arden-Arcade-Roseville, CA	1,481	1,797	2,014	2,042	2,067	21.3	15.0	26
St. Louis, MO-IL [3]	2,581	2,699	2,766	2,782	2,796	4.6	3.6	18
Salem, OR	278	347	370	376	385	24.9	10.8	129
Salinas, CA	356	402	415	412	410	13.0	2.1	116
Salt Lake City, UT	768	969	1,020	1,047	1,068	26.1	10.2	48
San Antonio, TX	1,408	1,712	1,851	1,888	1,942	21.6	13.5	29
San Diego-Carlsbad-San Marcos, CA	2,498	2,814	2,934	2,937	2,941	12.6	4.5	17
San Francisco-Oakland-Fremont, CA	3,684	4,124	4,149	4,158	4,180	11.9	1.4	12
San Jose-Sunnyvale-Santa Clara, CA	1,534	1,736	1,742	1,761	1,787	13.1	3.0	30
San Luis Obispo-Paso Robles, CA	217	247	254	256	257	13.6	4.2	170
Santa Barbara-Santa Maria, CA	370	399	402	401	400	8.0	0.2	124
Santa Rosa-Petaluma, CA	388	459	468	467	467	18.1	1.8	103
Sarasota-Bradenton-Venice, FL	489	590	651	671	683	20.5	15.7	74
Savannah, GA	258	293	310	313	320	13.6	9.1	146
Scranton-Wilkes-Barre, PA	575	561	551	551	551	-2.6	-1.7	89
Seattle-Tacoma-Bellevue, WA	2,559	3,044	3,169	3,208	3,263	18.9	7.2	15
Shreveport-Bossier City, LA	360	376	380	382	387	4.5	2.9	128
South Bend-Mishawaka, IN-MI	297	317	317	318	318	6.8	0.4	148
Spartanburg, SC	227	254	264	267	271	11.9	6.8	165
Spokane, WA	361	418	435	440	447	15.7	6.9	107
Springfield, MA	673	680	686	686	686	1.0	0.9	72
Springfield, MO	299	368	391	398	407	23.3	10.5	119
Stockton, CA	481	564	649	665	673	17.3	19.4	75
Syracuse, NY	660	650	653	650	650	-1.5	(-Z)	80
Tallahassee, FL	259	320	330	333	337	23.6	5.1	144
Tampa-St. Petersburg-Clearwater, FL	2,068	2,396	2,584	2,647	2,698	15.9	12.6	19
Toledo, OH	654	659	657	656	654	0.8	-0.8	78
Trenton-Ewing, NJ	326	351	364	366	368	7.7	4.8	134
Tucson, AZ	667	844	906	925	946	26.5	12.2	52
Tulsa, OK	761	860	880	886	898	12.9	4.4	55
Utica-Rome, NY	317	300	298	298	297	-5.3	-0.9	154
Vallejo-Fairfield, CA	339	395	411	411	412	16.2	4.4	115
Virginia Beach-Norfolk-Newport News, VA-NC	1,451	1,577	1,638	1,642	1,649	8.7	4.6	34
Visalia-Porterville, CA	312	368	401	411	420	18.0	14.1	112
Washington-Arlington-Alexandria, DC-VA-MD-WV	4,122	4,796	5,179	5,252	5,290	16.3	10.3	8
Wichita, KS	511	571	584	587	592	11.7	3.7	84
Wilmington, NC	200	275	303	315	326	37.2	18.8	145
Winston-Salem, NC	361	422	441	448	457	16.7	8.2	105
Worcester, MA	710	750	778	782	785	5.8	4.7	64
York-Hanover, PA	340	382	401	408	416	12.4	9.1	113
Youngstown-Warren-Boardman, OH-PA	614	603	595	591	587	-1.7	-2.7	85

Z Less than 0.05 percent.   [1] The April 1, 2000, estimates base reflects changes to the Census 2000 population resulting from legal boundary updates as of January 1 of the estimates year, other geographic program changes, and Count Question Resolution actions.   [2] Broomfield County, CO, was formed from parts of Adams, Boulder, Jefferson, and Weld Counties, CO, on November 15, 2001, and is coextensive with Broomfield city. For purposes of defining and presenting data for metropolitan statistical areas, Broomfield city is treated as if it were a county at the time of the 1990 and 2000 censuses.   [3] The portion of Sullivan city in Crawford County, Missouri, is legally part of the St. Louis, MO-IL MSA. Data shown here do not include this area.

Source: U.S. Census Bureau, "Table 1: Annual Estimates of the Population of Metropolitan and Micropolitan Statistical Areas: April 1, 2000 to July 1, 2006 (CBSA-EST2006-01)"; published 5 April 2007; <http://www.census.gov/population/www/estimates/CBSA-est2006-annual.html>.

Table 21. **50 Largest Metropolitan Statistical Areas—Population Change: 2000 to 2006**

[Covers period April 1, 2000, to July 1, 2006 (890 represents 890,000). Covers metropolitan statistical areas as defined by the U.S. Office of Management and Budget as of December 2005. All geographic boundaries for 2000 to 2006 population estimates are defined as of January 1, 2006. For definitions and components of all metropolitan and micropolitan areas, see Appendix II. Minus sign (–) indicates decrease or outmigration]

Metropolitan statistical area	Number (1,000)							Percent change
	Total change [1]	Natural increase			Net migration			
		Total	Births	Deaths	Total	Interna- tional	Internal migration	
Atlanta-Sandy Springs-Marietta, GA	890	295	469	174	455	178	277	21.0
Austin-Round Rock, TX	264	101	143	42	166	58	108	21.1
Baltimore-Towson, MD	105	67	214	147	17	32	–15	4.1
Birmingham-Hoover, AL	49	24	93	69	26	9	17	4.6
Boston-Cambridge-Quincy, MA-NH	63	130	354	224	–102	164	–265	1.4
Buffalo-Niagara Falls, NY	–33	4	81	77	–32	10	–42	–2.8
Charlotte-Gastonia-Concord, NC-SC	253	76	142	65	181	42	139	19.0
Chicago-Naperville-Joliet, IL-IN-WI	407	447	883	437	–44	377	–421	4.5
Cincinnati-Middletown, OH-KY-IN	95	73	183	110	2	17	–15	4.7
Cleveland-Elyria-Mentor, OH	–34	34	168	134	–69	24	–93	–1.6
Columbus, OH	113	79	158	79	35	30	5	7.0
Dallas-Fort Worth-Arlington, TX	842	402	607	205	455	286	168	16.3
Denver-Aurora, CO [2]	229	144	231	87	91	91	(Z)	10.5
Detroit-Warren-Livonia, MI	16	129	374	244	–103	89	–192	0.4
Hartford-West Hartford-East Hartford, CT	40	20	83	63	24	25	–1	3.5
Houston-Sugar Land-Baytown, TX	825	361	548	188	406	259	146	17.5
Indianapolis-Carmel, IN	141	77	156	79	65	21	44	9.2
Jacksonville, FL	155	43	107	64	116	11	105	13.8
Kansas City, MO-KS	131	84	179	96	48	28	20	7.1
Las Vegas-Paradise, NV	402	82	155	73	324	64	260	29.2
Los Angeles-Long Beach-Santa Ana, CA	585	764	1,243	480	–140	798	–938	4.7
Louisville-Jefferson County, KY-IN	60	32	100	68	29	12	17	5.1
Memphis, TN-MS-AR	70	54	121	66	19	13	6	5.8
Miami-Fort Lauderdale-Miami Beach, FL	456	138	438	300	327	409	–82	9.1
Milwaukee-Waukesha-West Allis, WI	9	52	134	82	–38	23	–61	0.6
Minneapolis-St. Paul-Bloomington, MN-WI	206	164	283	119	49	72	–22	6.9
Nashville-Davidson–Murfreesboro, TN	143	57	125	68	91	25	66	10.9
New Orleans-Metairie-Kenner, LA	–292	39	118	79	–323	10	–333	–22.2
New York-Northern New Jersey-Long Island, NY-NJ-PA	495	724	1,618	894	–380	1,068	–1,447	2.7
Oklahoma City, OK	77	46	107	62	35	20	15	7.0
Orlando-Kissimmee, FL	340	74	160	86	269	62	206	20.7
Philadelphia-Camden-Wilmington, PA-NJ-DE-MD . . .	140	132	469	337	25	93	–68	2.5
Phoenix-Mesa-Scottsdale, AZ	787	226	383	157	563	165	398	24.2
Pittsburgh, PA	–60	–21	157	178	–32	16	–48	–2.5
Portland-Vancouver-Beaverton, OR-WA	210	83	176	93	133	68	65	10.9
Providence-New Bedford-Fall River, RI-MA	30	28	121	92	7	28	–22	1.9
Richmond, VA	97	34	95	61	67	13	54	8.8
Riverside-San Bernardino-Ontario, CA	771	209	366	157	570	95	475	23.7
Rochester, NY	–2	20	76	56	–16	13	–29	–0.2
Sacramento–Arden-Arcade–Roseville, CA	270	85	173	88	190	62	128	15.0
St. Louis, MO-IL [3]	98	67	227	160	3	27	–23	3.6
Salt Lake City, UT	99	89	124	35	–1	39	–40	10.2
San Antonio, TX	231	102	184	82	134	29	104	13.5
San Diego-Carlsbad-San Marcos, CA	128	159	282	124	–20	99	–120	4.5
San Francisco-Oakland-Fremont, CA	56	171	353	182	–105	245	–350	1.4
San Jose-Sunnyvale-Santa Clara, CA	51	119	175	56	–65	159	–224	3.0
Seattle-Tacoma-Bellevue, WA	220	126	257	131	92	102	–10	7.2
Tampa-St. Petersburg-Clearwater, FL	302	10	190	180	299	57	242	12.6
Virginia Beach-Norfolk-Newport News, VA-NC	73	71	148	77	6	–2	7	4.6
Washington-Arlington-Alexandria, DC-VA-MD-WV . .	494	288	478	190	159	239	–80	10.3

Z Less than 500.   [1] The estimated components of population change will not sum to the total population change due to the process of controlling to national totals.   [2] Broomfield County, CO, was formed from parts of Adams, Boulder, Jefferson, and Weld Counties, CO, on November 15, 2001, and is coextensive with Broomfield city. For purposes of defining and presenting data for metropolitan statistical areas, Broomfield city is treated as if it were a county at the time of the 2000 census.   [3] The portion of Sullivan city in Crawford County, Missouri, is legally part of the St. Louis, MO-IL MSA. Data shown here do not include this area.

Source: U.S. Census Bureau, "Table 9: Cumulative Estimates of the Components of Population Change for Metropolitan and Micropolitan Statistical Areas: April 1, 2000 to July 1, 2006 (CBSA-EST2006-09)"; published 5 April 2007; <http://www.census.gov/population/www/estimates/CBSA-est2006-comp-chg.html>.

Table 22. Metropolitan Statistical Areas With More Than 750,000 Persons in 2006—Population by Race and Hispanic Origin: 2006

[In thousands (851 represents 851,000). As of July 1. Covers metropolitan statistical areas as defined by the U.S. Office of Management and Budget as of December 2005. All geographic boundaries are defined as of January 1, 2006. For definitions and components of all metropolitan and micropolitan areas, see Appendix II]

Metropolitan statistical area	Total persons	White alone	Black or African American alone	American Indian and Alaska Native alone	Asian alone	Native Hawaiian and Other Pacific Islander alone	Two or more races	Hispanic or Latino origin [1]
Albany-Schenectady-Troy, NY	851	749	62	2	25	(Z)	12	26
Albuquerque, NM	817	710	26	49	15	1	15	358
Allentown-Bethlehem-Easton, PA-NJ	800	736	35	2	19	(Z)	8	81
Atlanta-Sandy Springs-Marietta, GA	5,138	3,235	1,609	17	210	4	63	470
Austin-Round Rock, TX	1,514	1,294	120	10	67	2	21	448
Bakersfield, CA	780	668	49	13	32	2	15	352
Baltimore-Towson, MD	2,658	1,749	764	8	99	1	37	76
Baton Rouge, LA	767	468	279	2	12	(Z)	5	17
Birmingham-Hoover, AL	1,100	767	309	3	11	(Z)	8	31
Boston-Cambridge-Quincy, MA-NH	4,455	3,779	343	12	262	3	57	335
Bridgeport-Stamford-Norwalk, CT	900	752	97	3	38	1	10	131
Buffalo-Niagara Falls, NY	1,138	958	140	8	19	(Z)	13	37
Charlotte-Gastonia-Concord, NC-SC	1,583	1,145	371	8	41	1	17	127
Chicago-Naperville-Joliet, IL-IN-WI	9,506	7,135	1,733	33	493	8	105	1,829
Cincinnati-Middletown, OH-KY-IN	2,104	1,790	252	4	35	1	22	34
Cleveland-Elyria-Mentor, OH	2,114	1,625	420	5	38	1	25	81
Columbus, OH	1,726	1,394	246	5	53	1	27	46
Dallas-Fort Worth-Arlington, TX	6,004	4,727	868	41	281	8	79	1,590
Dayton, OH	839	687	124	2	14	(Z)	12	13
Denver-Aurora, CO	2,409	2,115	138	24	83	4	45	528
Detroit-Warren-Livonia, MI	4,469	3,220	1,030	15	142	2	60	157
Fresno, CA	892	726	51	17	80	2	17	425
Grand Rapids-Wyoming, MI	774	682	62	4	14	1	12	60
Hartford-West Hartford-East Hartford, CT	1,189	999	131	3	38	1	16	125
Honolulu, HI	910	227	29	4	410	78	161	63
Houston-Sugar Land-Baytown, TX	5,540	4,166	962	31	313	6	61	1,824
Indianapolis-Carmel, IN	1,666	1,367	245	5	29	1	20	73
Jacksonville, FL	1,278	929	288	5	37	1	19	67
Kansas City, MO-KS	1,967	1,642	242	10	39	2	31	132
Las Vegas-Paradise, NV	1,778	1,395	182	17	125	10	49	483
Los Angeles-Long Beach-Santa Ana, CA	12,950	9,749	1,012	122	1,785	45	237	5,694
Louisville-Jefferson County, KY-IN	1,222	1,025	163	3	16	1	14	30
Memphis, TN-MS-AR	1,275	657	580	4	22	1	11	43
Miami-Fort Lauderdale-Miami Beach, FL	5,464	4,114	1,146	21	117	6	60	2,093
Milwaukee-Waukesha-West Allis, WI	1,510	1,191	250	9	39	1	20	120
Minneapolis-St. Paul-Bloomington, MN-WI	3,175	2,726	210	25	157	2	56	141
Nashville-Davidson–Murfreesboro, TN	1,455	1,180	223	5	29	1	17	72
New Haven-Milford, CT	845	694	108	3	28	1	12	104
New Orleans-Metairie-Kenner, LA	1,025	665	317	5	27	(Z)	11	58
New York-Northern New Jersey-Long Island, NY-NJ-PA	18,819	13,006	3,696	90	1,736	22	269	3,985
Oklahoma City, OK	1,172	929	127	46	35	1	36	105
Omaha-Council Bluffs, NE-IA	823	725	65	5	16	1	11	59
Orlando-Kissimmee, FL	1,985	1,553	317	9	72	2	31	438
Oxnard-Thousand Oaks-Ventura, CA	800	700	17	9	53	2	18	292
Philadelphia-Camden-Wilmington, PA-NJ-DE-MD	5,827	4,260	1,229	15	249	3	71	361
Phoenix-Mesa-Scottsdale, AZ	4,039	3,578	181	94	112	9	66	1,210
Pittsburgh, PA	2,371	2,111	198	4	34	1	23	23
Portland-Vancouver-Beaverton, OR-WA	2,138	1,877	63	20	116	7	55	208
Providence-New Bedford-Fall River, RI-MA	1,613	1,453	88	8	39	2	23	143
Raleigh-Cary, NC	995	740	201	5	36	1	12	83
Richmond, VA	1,194	783	361	5	30	1	14	42
Riverside-San Bernardino-Ontario, CA	4,026	3,313	322	56	228	15	92	1,774
Rochester, NY	1,035	875	118	3	23	(Z)	15	50
Sacramento–Arden-Arcade–Roseville, CA	2,067	1,568	156	24	230	13	75	372
St. Louis, MO-IL [2]	2,796	2,193	511	8	51	1	32	55
Salt Lake City, UT	1,068	981	16	10	31	13	17	158
San Antonio, TX	1,942	1,730	129	19	35	3	26	1,021
San Diego-Carlsbad-San Marcos, CA	2,941	2,347	162	28	304	16	85	886
San Francisco-Oakland-Fremont, CA	4,180	2,696	382	27	911	30	134	836
San Jose-Sunnyvale-Santa Clara, CA	1,787	1,142	50	14	529	8	45	474
Seattle-Tacoma-Bellevue, WA	3,263	2,571	181	38	339	21	114	229
Tampa-St. Petersburg-Clearwater, FL	2,698	2,267	311	12	69	2	36	371
Tucson, AZ	946	840	32	32	23	2	17	308
Tulsa, OK	898	700	81	66	13	1	38	60
Virginia Beach-Norfolk-Newport News, VA-NC	1,649	1,029	527	7	51	2	34	61
Washington-Arlington-Alexandria, DC-VA-MD-WV	5,290	3,301	1,421	20	444	5	101	609
Worcester, MA	785	714	29	2	29	1	9	62

Z Less than 500.   [1] Persons of Hispanic origin may be any race.   [2] The portion of Sullivan city in Crawford County, Missouri, is legally part of the St. Louis, MO-IL MSA. Data shown here do not include this area.

Source: U.S. Census Bureau, USA Counties; <http://censtats.census.gov/usa/usa.shtml>; accessed 22 August 2007.

28   Population

Table 23. **Metropolitan Statistical Areas With More Than 750,000 Persons in 2006—Population by Age: 2006**

[In thousands (851 represents 851,000). **As of July 1.** Covers metropolitan statistical areas as defined by the U.S. Office of Management and Budget as of December 2005. All geographic boundaries are defined as of January 1, 2006. For definitions and components of all metropolitan and micropolitan areas, see Appendix II]

Metropolitan statistical area	Number (1,000)						Percent under 18 years	Percent 65 years and over
	Total	Under 18 years	18 to 44 years	45 to 64 years	65 to 74 years	75 years and over		
Albany-Schenectady-Troy, NY	851	184	327	225	54	60	21.6	13.5
Albuquerque, NM	817	205	311	205	50	46	25.2	11.7
Allentown-Bethlehem-Easton, PA-NJ	800	180	290	212	54	63	22.5	14.7
Atlanta-Sandy Springs-Marietta, GA.	5,138	1,369	2,110	1,249	235	175	26.6	8.0
Austin-Round Rock, TX.	1,514	384	685	331	62	51	25.4	7.5
Bakersfield, CA	780	232	325	155	37	32	29.7	8.8
Baltimore-Towson, MD	2,658	638	997	703	165	155	24.0	12.0
Baton Rouge, LA	767	193	309	186	42	36	25.2	10.2
Birmingham-Hoover, AL.	1,100	268	405	288	72	67	24.4	12.7
Boston-Cambridge-Quincy, MA-NH	4,455	1,009	1,716	1,169	278	283	22.6	12.6
Bridgeport-Stamford-Norwalk, CT	900	227	312	245	58	59	25.2	13.0
Buffalo-Niagara Falls, NY.	1,138	254	402	306	81	94	22.3	15.4
Charlotte-Gastonia-Concord, NC-SC	1,583	406	635	392	82	68	25.7	9.5
Chicago-Naperville-Joliet, IL-IN-WI	9,506	2,479	3,676	2,324	530	497	26.1	10.8
Cincinnati-Middletown, OH-KY-IN	2,104	532	788	537	127	120	25.3	11.8
Cleveland-Elyria-Mentor, OH	2,114	512	722	577	147	157	24.2	14.4
Columbus, OH.	1,726	435	699	417	94	81	25.2	10.1
Dallas-Fort Worth-Arlington, TX.	6,004	1,664	2,492	1,365	272	211	27.7	8.1
Dayton, OH.	839	197	303	222	60	57	23.5	14.0
Denver-Aurora, CO.	2,409	614	955	615	122	103	25.5	9.3
Detroit-Warren-Livonia, MI	4,469	1,139	1,605	1,192	266	267	25.5	11.9
Fresno, CA	892	269	354	182	43	43	30.2	9.6
Grand Rapids-Wyoming, MI	774	206	298	188	42	41	26.6	10.6
Hartford-West Hartford-East Hartford, CT	1,189	268	436	322	77	85	22.6	13.6
Honolulu, HI	910	210	348	221	61	70	23.1	14.4
Houston-Sugar Land-Baytown, TX.	5,540	1,562	2,222	1,313	252	191	28.2	8.0
Indianapolis-Carmel, IN.	1,666	440	642	409	92	83	26.4	10.5
Jacksonville, FL.	1,278	317	481	338	79	63	24.8	11.1
Kansas City, MO-KS.	1,967	506	735	504	114	108	25.7	11.3
Las Vegas-Paradise, NV	1,778	461	709	422	107	78	26.0	10.4
Los Angeles-Long Beach-Santa Ana, CA	12,950	3,471	5,172	2,970	694	643	26.8	10.3
Louisville-Jefferson County, KY-IN.	1,222	296	447	328	78	73	24.2	12.3
Memphis, TN-MS-AR	1,275	351	477	319	69	58	27.5	10.0
Miami-Fort Lauderdale-Miami Beach, FL.	5,464	1,273	1,962	1,364	397	467	23.3	15.8
Milwaukee-Waukesha-West Allis, WI	1,510	384	542	398	92	94	25.4	12.3
Minneapolis-St. Paul-Bloomington, MN-WI	3,175	808	1,238	817	162	150	25.4	9.8
Nashville-Davidson—Murfreesboro, TN	1,455	356	577	370	83	68	24.5	10.4
New Haven-Milford, CT	845	195	315	219	53	63	23.1	13.7
New Orleans-Metairie-Kenner, LA	1,025	249	357	287	69	63	24.3	12.8
New York-Northern New Jersey-Long Island, NY-NJ-PA	18,819	4,519	7,131	4,772	1,214	1,182	24.0	12.7
Oklahoma City, OK.	1,172	294	455	288	72	63	25.0	11.6
Omaha-Council Bluffs, NE-IA	823	218	316	200	46	43	26.5	10.8
Orlando-Kissimmee, FL.	1,985	477	775	483	131	120	24.0	12.6
Oxnard-Thousand Oaks-Ventura, CA	800	213	299	201	46	41	26.6	10.9
Philadelphia-Camden-Wilmington, PA-NJ-DE-MD	5,827	1,416	2,136	1,520	371	384	24.3	13.0
Phoenix-Mesa-Scottsdale, AZ.	4,039	1,095	1,596	892	232	223	27.1	11.3
Pittsburgh, PA	2,371	499	794	673	182	223	21.0	17.1
Portland-Vancouver-Beaverton, OR-WA	2,138	520	828	569	115	107	24.3	10.4
Providence-New Bedford-Fall River, RI-MA	1,613	363	613	415	101	120	22.5	13.7
Raleigh-Cary, NC	995	255	418	242	45	35	25.6	8.1
Richmond, VA	1,194	283	460	314	71	66	23.7	11.4
Riverside-San Bernardino-Ontario, CA	4,026	1,152	1,676	808	197	193	28.6	9.7
Rochester, NY	1,035	239	384	275	66	71	23.1	13.2
Sacramento-Arden-Arcade-Roseville, CA	2,067	517	827	488	120	116	25.0	11.4
St. Louis, MO-IL [1]	2,796	686	1,020	734	179	177	24.5	12.7
Salt Lake City, UT	1,068	317	434	228	47	41	29.7	8.3
San Antonio, TX	1,942	531	759	444	108	100	27.4	10.7
San Diego-Carlsbad-San Marcos, CA	2,941	745	1,207	662	157	170	25.3	11.1
San Francisco-Oakland-Fremont, CA.	4,180	934	1,617	1,117	257	255	22.3	12.2
San Jose-Sunnyvale-Santa Clara, CA	1,787	448	715	438	101	86	25.1	10.4
Seattle-Tacoma-Bellevue, WA.	3,263	762	1,285	881	175	161	23.3	10.3
Tampa-St. Petersburg-Clearwater, FL.	2,698	587	942	705	214	249	21.8	17.2
Tucson, AZ	946	228	349	231	67	71	24.1	14.6
Tulsa, OK	898	231	327	230	58	52	25.7	12.2
Virginia Beach-Norfolk-Newport News, VA-NC	1,649	419	653	397	95	85	25.4	10.9
Washington-Arlington-Alexandria, DC-VA-MD-WV.	5,290	1,301	2,104	1,378	283	224	24.6	9.6
Worcester, MA.	785	188	298	203	45	51	24.0	12.2

[1] The portion of Sullivan city in Crawford County, Missouri, is legally part of the St. Louis, MO-IL MSA. Data shown here do not include this area.

Source: U.S. Census Bureau, USA Counties; <http://censtats.census.gov/usa/usa.shtml>; accessed 22 August 2007.

Table 24. Population by Core-Based Statistical Area Status and State: 2000 to 2006

[2000, as of April 1; beginning 2005, as of July 1 (262,114 represents 262,114,000). Covers core-based statistical areas (metropolitan and micropolitan statistical areas) as defined by the U.S. Office of Management and Budget as of December 2005. All geographic boundaries for 2000 to 2006 population estimates are defined as of January 1, 2006. For definitions and components of all metropolitan and micropolitan areas, see Appendix II. Minus sign (–) indicates decrease]

State	Core-based statistical area (metropolitan and micropolitan) population						Population outside core-based statistical area					
	Number (1,000)			Percent of total		Percent change, 2000–2006	Number (1,000)			Percent of total		Percent change, 2000–2006
	2000 [1]	2005	2006	2000	2006	2006	2000 [1]	2005	2006	2000	2006	2006
U.S.	262,114	277,027	279,848	93.1	93.5	6.8	19,310	19,480	19,551	6.9	6.5	1.2
AL.	3,945	4,058	4,109	88.7	89.3	4.2	503	490	490	11.3	10.7	-2.4
AK.	461	496	503	73.6	75.1	9.1	166	167	167	26.4	24.9	0.7
AZ.	4,944	5,755	5,964	96.4	96.7	20.6	187	198	203	3.6	3.3	8.7
AR.	2,082	2,189	2,224	77.9	79.1	6.8	591	587	587	22.1	20.9	-0.6
CA.	33,628	35,895	36,195	99.3	99.3	7.6	243	259	262	0.7	0.7	7.7
CO	[2]3,922	4,270	4,356	91.2	91.6	11.1	380	393	397	8.8	8.4	4.4
CT.	3,406	3,501	3,505	100.0	100.0	2.9	–	–	–	–	–	–
DE.	784	842	853	100.0	100.0	8.9	–	–	–	–	–	–
DC	572	582	582	100.0	100.0	1.7	–	–	–	–	–	–
FL.	15,620	17,377	17,692	97.7	97.8	13.3	363	392	398	2.3	2.2	9.8
GA	7,411	8,315	8,534	90.5	91.1	15.1	776	818	830	9.5	8.9	7.0
HI	1,211	1,273	1,285	100.0	100.0	6.1	–	–	–	–	–	-18.4
ID	1,103	1,232	1,267	85.2	86.4	14.9	191	198	200	14.8	13.6	4.5
IL	11,796	12,150	12,218	95.0	95.2	3.6	624	615	614	5.0	4.8	-1.6
IN	5,715	5,899	5,946	94.0	94.2	4.1	366	367	367	6.0	5.8	0.4
IA	2,090	2,148	2,167	71.4	72.7	3.7	836	818	816	28.6	27.3	-2.5
KS.	2,248	2,330	2,349	83.6	85.0	4.5	440	418	415	16.4	15.0	-5.9
KY.	3,036	3,155	3,184	75.1	75.7	4.9	1,006	1,017	1,022	24.9	24.3	1.6
LA.	4,156	4,201	3,979	93.0	92.8	-4.3	312	307	309	7.0	7.2	-1.1
ME	893	929	931	70.0	70.4	4.2	382	389	391	30.0	29.6	2.4
MD	5,218	5,508	5,533	98.5	98.5	6.0	79	82	82	1.5	1.5	4.6
MA	6,325	6,408	6,411	99.6	99.6	1.4	25	26	26	0.4	0.4	5.1
MI	9,153	9,305	9,302	92.1	92.1	1.6	785	796	794	7.9	7.9	1.1
MN	4,266	4,470	4,510	86.7	87.3	5.7	654	657	657	13.3	12.7	0.5
MS	2,196	2,263	2,263	77.2	77.8	3.0	648	645	647	22.8	22.2	-0.2
MO	4,810	5,001	5,043	85.9	86.3	4.8	787	797	800	14.1	13.7	1.7
MT	574	606	615	63.7	65.1	7.1	328	329	330	36.3	34.9	0.6
NE.	1,339	1,401	1,415	78.2	80.0	5.7	373	357	354	21.8	20.0	-5.1
NV.	1,950	2,365	2,447	97.6	98.0	25.5	48	48	49	2.4	2.0	1.5
NH	1,192	1,260	1,267	96.5	96.4	6.3	44	47	47	3.5	3.6	8.7
NJ	8,414	8,703	8,725	100.0	100.0	3.7	–	–	–	–	–	–
NM	1,737	1,847	1,876	95.5	96.0	8.0	82	79	78	4.5	4.0	-5.0
NY.	18,547	18,883	18,873	97.7	97.8	1.8	430	432	433	2.3	2.2	0.6
NC	7,352	7,957	8,135	91.4	91.9	10.7	695	716	722	8.6	8.1	3.9
ND	435	439	442	67.7	69.6	1.8	208	196	194	32.3	30.4	-6.8
OH	10,849	10,959	10,966	95.6	95.5	1.1	504	511	512	4.4	4.5	1.6
OK	2,891	2,984	3,018	83.8	84.3	4.4	560	560	561	16.2	15.7	0.3
OR	3,281	3,498	3,559	95.9	96.2	8.5	140	141	142	4.1	3.8	1.0
PA	11,899	12,021	12,056	96.9	96.9	1.3	382	384	385	3.1	3.1	0.6
RI	1,048	1,074	1,068	100.0	100.0	1.8	–	–	–	–	–	–
SC.	3,735	3,973	4,046	93.1	93.6	8.3	277	274	275	6.9	6.4	-0.7
SD.	527	553	560	69.8	71.6	6.2	228	222	222	30.2	28.4	-2.4
TN.	5,080	5,332	5,412	89.3	89.6	6.5	610	623	627	10.7	10.4	2.9
TX.	19,465	21,518	22,090	93.4	94.0	13.5	1,386	1,411	1,418	6.6	6.0	2.2
UT.	2,107	2,362	2,420	94.4	94.9	14.8	126	128	130	5.6	5.1	3.5
VT.	449	459	460	73.8	73.7	2.3	159	164	164	26.2	26.3	3.0
VA.	6,269	6,741	6,814	88.6	89.2	8.7	810	823	829	11.4	10.8	2.3
WA	5,678	6,067	6,168	96.3	96.4	8.6	216	225	227	3.7	3.6	5.3
WV	1,348	1,361	1,366	74.5	75.1	1.3	461	453	453	25.5	24.9	-1.7
WI.	4,604	4,750	4,777	85.8	86.0	3.7	759	778	779	14.2	14.0	2.7
WY	352	364	368	71.3	71.5	4.6	142	145	147	28.7	28.5	3.4

– Represents or rounds to zero. [1] The April 1, 2000, estimates base reflects changes to the Census 2000 population resulting from legal boundary updates as of January 1 of the estimates year, other geographic program changes, and the Count Question Resolution program. [2] Includes Broomfield city.

Source: U.S. Census Bureau, "Annual Estimates of the Population for Counties: April 1, 2000 to July 1, 2006 (CO-EST2006-01)"; published 22 March 2007; <http://www.census.gov/popest/counties/CO-EST2006-01.html>; and unpublished data.

Table 25. **Population in Coastal Counties: 1980 to 2006**

[Population as of April 1, except as indicated (3,537 represents 3,537,000). Areas as defined by U.S. National Oceanic and Atmospheric Administration, 1992. Covers 673 counties and equivalent areas with at least 15 percent of their land area either in a coastal watershed (drainage area) or in a coastal cataloging unit (a coastal area between watersheds). See Appendix III]

| Year | Total | Counties in coastal regions | | | | | Balance of United States |
		Total	Atlantic	Gulf of Mexico	Great Lakes	Pacific	
Land area, 2000 (1,000 sq. mi.)	3,537	889	148	115	115	511	2,649
POPULATION							
1980 (mil.)	226.5	119.8	53.7	13.1	26.0	27.0	106.7
1990 (mil.)	248.7	133.4	59.0	15.2	25.9	33.2	115.3
2000 (mil.)	281.4	148.3	65.2	18.0	27.3	37.8	133.1
2006 (July 1) (mil.)	299.4	156.1	68.6	19.7	27.5	40.4	143.3
1980 (percent)	100	53	24	6	11	12	47
1990 (percent)	100	54	24	6	10	13	46
2000 (percent)	100	53	23	6	10	13	47
2006 (July 1) (percent)	100	52	23	7	9	13	48

Source: U.S. Census Bureau, 1980 Census of Population, Vol. 1, Chapter A (PC80-1-A-1), *U.S. Summary*; 1990 Census of Population and Housing (CPH1); and unpublished data.

Table 26. **States with Coastal Counties—Population, Housing Units, Establishments, and Employees by Coastal Region and State: 2000 to 2006**

[281,425 represents 281,425,000. Population and housing as of July 1, except 2000 as of April 1. See headnote, Table 25. Minus sign (–) indicates decrease]

| Coastal region and state | Population | | | | | Housing units | | | Private nonfarm [3]— | |
| | 2000 [1] (1,000) | 2006 | | Percent change, 2000– 2006 | Per square mile, 2006 [2] | Number | | Percent change, 2000– 2005 | Estab- lish- ments, 2005 (1,000) | Employ- ees, 2005 (1,000) |
		Num- ber (1,000)	Percent of state total			2000 [1] (1,000)	2005 (1,000)			
United States, total . .	281,425	299,398	(X)	6.4	85	115,904	124,522	7.4	7,500	116,317
Interior U.S.	133,103	143,296	(X)	7.7	54	55,918	60,796	8.7	3,494	55,346
Coastal counties, total . .	148,321	156,102	(X)	5.2	176	59,986	63,726	6.2	4,006	60,971
Atlantic.	65,198	68,575	(X)	5.2	464	26,821	28,368	5.8	1,866	27,683
Maine	1,184	1,231	93.1	4.0	61	599	631	5.2	39	468
New Hampshire	1,007	1,076	81.8	6.9	256	432	463	7.2	32	449
Massachusetts	6,125	6,212	96.5	1.4	940	2,531	2,595	2.5	170	2,903
Rhode Island	1,048	1,068	100.0	1.8	1,022	440	448	1.8	30	441
Connecticut	3,406	3,505	100.0	2.9	723	1,386	1,423	2.7	93	1,526
New York	13,573	13,925	72.1	2.6	1,796	5,285	5,409	2.3	392	5,425
New Jersey	8,312	8,614	98.7	3.6	1,220	3,269	3,399	4.0	239	3,536
Pennsylvania	5,750	5,908	47.5	2.8	858	2,334	2,418	3.6	144	2,542
Delaware.	784	853	100.0	8.9	437	343	375	9.3	25	393
Maryland.	4,865	5,146	91.6	5.8	679	1,970	2,081	5.7	126	1,967
District of Columbia	572	582	100.0	1.7	9,471	275	278	1.1	20	440
Virginia	4,794	5,191	67.9	8.3	373	1,912	2,091	9.4	132	2,161
North Carolina	1,985	2,076	23.4	4.6	106	905	991	9.6	48	634
South Carolina	1,653	1,790	41.4	8.3	118	750	835	11.3	46	613
Georgia.	822	880	9.4	7.1	73	346	374	8.2	20	271
Florida	9,320	10,518	58.1	12.9	562	4,043	4,557	12.7	310	3,915
Gulf of Mexico	18,003	19,682	(X)	9.3	172	7,718	8,571	11.1	454	6,656
Florida	6,249	7,122	39.4	14.0	226	3,074	3,500	13.8	185	2,310
Georgia.	95	99	1.1	4.5	62	40	43	6.7	2	31
Alabama	712	743	16.1	4.2	85	319	346	8.5	17	253
Mississippi	588	589	20.2	0.1	87	246	267	8.2	12	175
Louisiana	3,510	3,325	77.6	–5.2	129	1,439	1,516	5.3	82	1,284
Texas	6,850	7,604	33.2	13.9	194	2,599	2,900	11.6	156	2,603
Great Lakes	27,324	27,452	(X)	0.5	238	11,405	11,884	4.2	665	11,216
New York	3,650	3,606	18.7	–1.2	168	1,586	1,616	1.9	83	1,373
Pennsylvania	281	280	2.2	–0.4	349	114	117	2.3	7	118
Ohio	4,418	4,377	38.1	–0.9	415	1,869	1,932	3.3	110	1,876
Michigan	8,859	9,003	89.2	1.6	176	3,782	3,997	5.7	214	3,396
Indiana	1,378	1,425	22.6	3.4	350	556	591	6.4	33	582
Illinois	6,021	6,002	46.8	–0.3	4,308	2,322	2,390	2.9	150	2,643
Wisconsin	2,469	2,514	45.2	1.8	163	1,055	1,114	5.7	62	1,133
Minnesota	248	246	4.8	–0.8	23	121	126	4.4	7	95
Pacific	37,796	40,392	(X)	6.9	79	14,042	14,903	6.1	1,020	15,415
Washington	4,587	4,987	78.0	8.7	202	1,919	2,084	8.6	141	1,889
Oregon	1,808	1,905	51.5	5.4	91	794	837	5.5	59	796
California.	29,650	31,646	86.8	6.7	407	10,650	11,259	5.7	771	12,044
Alaska	530	569	84.9	7.4	1	219	231	5.6	17	200
Hawaii	1,212	1,285	100.0	6.1	200	461	491	6.6	32	486

X Not applicable.   [1] Reflects modifications to the Census 2000 population as documented in the Count Question Resolution program and geographic program revisions.   [2] Calculated on the basis of land area data from the 2000 census.   [3] Covers establishments with payroll. Excludes most government employees, railroad employees, self-employed persons. Employees are for the week including March 12.

Source: U.S. Census Bureau, USA Counties; <http://censtats.census.gov/usa/usa.shtml>; accessed 1 August 2007; and "County Business Patterns," <http://www.census.gov/epcd/cbp/view/cbpview.html>.

Population   31

[In thousands, except as indicated (223 represents 223,000). As of April 1, except 2005 and 2006 as of July 1. Beginning 2005 data refer to boundaries in effect on January 1, 2006; 1990 and 2000 data, boundaries in effect on January 1, 2000; Minus sign (−) indicates decrease. See Appendix III]

Incorporated place	Number (1,000)				Percent change		Rank, 2006
	1990	2000 [1]	2005	2006	1990 to 2000 [1]	2000 to 2006 [2]	
Akron, OH	223	217	211	210	−2.7	−3.4	92
Albuquerque, NM	387	449	494	505	15.9	12.6	33
Amarillo, TX	158	174	183	186	10.0	6.9	119
Anaheim, CA	267	328	333	334	23.0	1.7	54
Anchorage, AK	226	260	275	279	15.0	7.1	65
Arlington, TX [3]	262	333	363	367	27.1	10.2	49
Arlington, VA [3]	171	189	200	200	10.9	5.5	99
Atlanta, GA	394	416	476	486	5.8	16.8	34
Augusta-Richmond County, GA [4]	186	195	189	189	4.8	−3.0	116
Aurora, CO	222	276	297	304	24.6	10.0	59
Aurora, IL	100	143	169	171	42.6	19.1	132
Austin, TX	497	657	691	710	32.1	7.6	16
Bakersfield, CA	188	247	296	308	31.4	26.7	58
Baltimore, MD	736	651	636	631	−11.5	−3.0	19
Baton Rouge, LA	223	228	221	230	2.2	0.7	79
Birmingham, AL	266	243	231	229	−8.7	−5.4	80
Boise City, ID	142	186	199	199	30.8	1.9	102
Boston, MA	575	589	597	591	2.5	0.3	22
Brownsville, TX	114	140	168	172	22.6	21.3	130
Buffalo, NY	328	293	279	276	−10.8	−5.7	66
Cape Coral, FL	75	102	140	151	36.1	47.8	150
Chandler, AZ	91	177	232	241	94.7	35.9	76
Charlotte, NC	428	541	616	630	26.4	11.2	20
Chattanooga, TN	153	156	155	155	1.8	−0.7	144
Chesapeake, VA	152	199	218	221	31.1	10.7	84
Chicago, IL	2,783	2,896	2,843	2,833	4.1	−2.2	3
Chula Vista, CA	135	174	211	213	28.3	22.6	89
Cincinnati, OH	365	331	331	332	−9.1	0.3	56
Cleveland, OH	506	478	451	444	−5.5	−6.9	40
Colorado Springs, CO	282	361	369	372	28.0	3.1	48
Columbus, GA	[4]179	[4]186	186	189	[4]4.0	1.3	117
Columbus, OH	639	711	730	733	11.3	3.0	15
Corona, CA	76	125	149	150	64.0	17.5	153
Corpus Christi, TX	258	277	283	285	7.4	2.8	63
Dallas, TX	1,007	1,189	1,216	1,233	18.1	3.7	9
Dayton, OH	182	166	158	157	−8.9	−5.7	143
Denver, CO	468	555	559	567	18.6	2.4	26
Des Moines, IA	193	199	194	194	2.8	−2.5	111
Detroit, MI	1,028	951	883	871	−7.5	−8.4	11
Durham, NC	149	187	205	209	25.5	11.3	93
El Paso, TX	516	564	598	609	9.3	8.1	21
Fayetteville, NC	117	121	169	168	3.4	−4.0	136
Fontana, CA	88	129	164	170	46.7	31.1	133
Fort Lauderdale, FL	150	152	185	186	1.6	8.9	118
Fort Wayne, IN	206	206	247	249	−0.1	−0.6	70
Fort Worth, TX	449	535	623	653	19.1	20.7	18
Fremont, CA	173	203	201	202	17.3	−0.8	97
Fresno, CA	355	428	461	467	20.3	8.8	36
Garden Grove, CA	144	165	166	166	15.0	0.7	139
Garland, TX	181	216	216	218	19.3	1.0	86
Gilbert, AZ	30	110	178	192	265.6	73.9	115
Glendale, AZ	151	219	243	247	45.0	12.7	72
Glendale, CA	180	195	200	199	8.3	2.3	100
Grand Prairie, TX	100	127	144	154	27.4	21.0	148
Grand Rapids, MI	189	198	194	193	4.7	−2.4	112
Greensboro, NC	192	224	233	237	16.9	4.6	77
Henderson, NV	65	175	232	241	169.4	37.2	75
Hialeah, FL	188	226	221	217	20.5	−4.1	87
Honolulu, HI [3]	376	372	377	377	−1.2	1.5	46
Houston, TX	1,697	1,954	2,118	2,144	15.1	8.8	4
Huntington Beach, CA	181	190	195	194	4.7	2.5	109
Huntsville, AL	161	158	166	168	−1.7	5.5	135
Indianapolis, IN [4]	732	782	783	786	6.9	0.5	13
Irvine, CA	111	143	187	194	28.4	34.6	110
Irving, TX	155	192	194	196	23.5	2.3	108
Jackson, MS	197	184	177	177	−6.3	−4.1	126
Jacksonville, FL	635	736	783	795	15.8	8.0	12
Jersey City, NJ	229	240	239	242	4.8	0.7	73
Kansas City, MO	435	442	444	447	1.5	1.3	39
Knoxville, TN	174	174	181	182	−0.1	4.0	123
Laredo, TX	126	177	209	215	40.1	21.3	88
Las Vegas, NV	259	478	545	553	84.7	15.1	28
Lexington-Fayette, KY	225	261	268	271	15.6	3.9	68
Lincoln, NE	193	226	239	241	17.0	6.5	74
Little Rock, AR	177	183	184	184	3.4	0.7	121
Long Beach, CA	430	462	474	472	7.4	2.4	35
Los Angeles, CA	3,486	3,695	3,847	3,849	6.0	4.2	2
Louisville-Jefferson County, KY [4]	[5]269	[5]256	556	554	[5]−4.7	0.6	27
Lubbock, TX	187	200	210	212	6.9	6.2	90
Madison, WI	191	208	222	223	9.0	6.8	82

See footnotes at end of table.

U.S. Census Bureau, Statistical Abstract of the United States: 2008

Table 27. Incorporated Places With 150,000 or More Inhabitants in 2006—Population: 1990 to 2006—Con.

[In thousands, except as indicated (223 represents 223,000). As of April 1, except 2005 and 2006 as of July 1. Beginning 2005 data refer to boundaries in effect on January 1, 2006; 1990 and 2000 data, boundaries in effect on January 1, 2000; Minus sign (−) indicates decrease. See Appendix III]

Incorporated place	Number (1,000)				Percent change		Rank, 2006
	1990	2000 [1]	2005	2006	1990 to 2000 [1]	2000 to 2006 [2]	
Memphis, TN	664	650	670	671	−2.1	−8.1	17
Mesa, AZ	291	396	442	448	36.2	12.5	38
Miami, FL	359	362	387	404	1.0	11.5	43
Milwaukee, WI	629	597	576	573	−5.1	−4.0	25
Minneapolis, MN	368	383	373	373	3.9	−2.6	47
Mobile, AL	198	199	191	193	0.3	−3.2	114
Modesto, CA	166	189	207	206	13.5	9.0	95
Montgomery, AL	191	202	199	202	5.6	0.1	96
Moreno Valley, CA	119	142	178	184	19.9	28.9	122
Nashville-Davidson, TN [4]	488	546	548	552	11.7	1.2	29
New Orleans, LA	497	485	452	223	−2.5	−53.9	83
New York, NY	7,323	8,008	8,214	8,214	9.4	2.6	1
Newark, NJ	275	274	280	281	−0.6	3.3	64
Newport News, VA	171	180	179	178	5.1	−1.3	125
Norfolk, VA	261	234	231	229	−10.3	−2.3	81
North Las Vegas, NV	48	115	177	198	140.8	71.1	105
Oakland, CA	372	399	396	397	7.4	−0.6	44
Oceanside, CA	128	161	166	166	25.8	3.0	140
Oklahoma City, OK	445	506	531	538	13.8	6.2	30
Omaha, NE	373	390	414	420	4.6	7.2	42
Ontario, CA	135	158	173	173	17.0	9.7	129
Orlando, FL	166	186	213	220	12.0	14.5	85
Overland Park, KS	111	149	165	167	34.3	11.6	138
Oxnard, CA	142	170	184	184	19.6	8.1	120
Pembroke Pines, FL	65	137	151	150	110.0	9.1	154
Philadelphia, PA	1,586	1,518	1,456	1,448	−4.3	−4.6	6
Phoenix, AZ	989	1,321	1,470	1,513	33.6	14.5	5
Pittsburgh, PA	370	335	316	313	−9.6	−6.5	57
Plano, TX	128	222	251	255	73.5	14.9	69
Pomona, CA	132	149	154	154	13.0	4.3	146
Portland, OR	486	529	533	537	8.9	1.5	31
Providence, RI	161	174	177	175	7.8	0.9	128
Raleigh, NC	221	276	343	356	24.9	25.0	51
Rancho Cucamonga, CA	101	128	169	171	26.0	33.6	131
Reno, NV	139	180	206	210	29.8	14.8	91
Richmond, VA	203	198	193	193	−2.4	−2.6	113
Riverside, CA	227	255	290	294	12.6	14.9	61
Rochester, NY	230	220	210	208	−4.4	−5.3	94
Rockford, IL	144	150	154	155	4.3	2.6	145
Sacramento, CA	370	407	452	454	10.0	11.5	37
Salem, OR	109	137	149	152	25.8	11.1	149
Salt Lake City, UT	160	182	178	179	13.6	−1.6	124
San Antonio, TX	998	1,145	1,264	1,297	14.7	11.8	7
San Bernardino, CA	171	185	199	199	8.3	7.0	101
San Diego, CA	1,111	1,223	1,257	1,257	10.1	2.7	8
San Francisco, CA	724	777	741	744	7.3	−4.2	14
San Jose, CA	783	895	916	930	14.2	3.9	10
Santa Ana, CA	294	338	341	340	14.8	0.6	53
Santa Clarita, CA	123	151	168	168	22.8	11.1	137
Santa Rosa, CA	121	148	154	154	22.0	3.9	147
Scottsdale, AZ	130	203	228	231	55.8	14.1	78
Seattle, WA	516	563	576	582	9.1	3.4	23
Shreveport, LA	199	200	198	200	0.6	−0.3	98
Spokane, WA	178	196	198	198	9.8	0.6	103
Springfield, MA	157	152	151	151	−3.1	−0.6	151
Springfield, MO	141	152	150	151	7.4	−0.8	152
St. Louis, MO	397	348	353	347	−12.2	−0.3	52
St. Paul, MN	272	287	275	274	5.5	−4.6	67
St. Petersburg, FL	240	248	248	248	3.3	−0.1	71
Stockton, CA	212	244	287	290	15.0	19.0	62
Tacoma, WA	177	194	196	197	9.1	1.5	107
Tallahassee, FL	126	151	157	159	19.5	4.4	141
Tampa, FL	280	303	326	333	8.4	9.7	55
Tempe, AZ	142	159	167	170	11.7	7.0	134
Toledo, OH	333	314	302	298	−5.8	−4.9	60
Tucson, AZ	418	487	516	519	16.4	6.5	32
Tulsa, OK	367	393	381	383	7.0	−2.6	45
Vancouver, WA	104	144	158	159	38.0	10.6	142
Virginia Beach, VA	393	425	437	436	8.2	2.4	41
Washington, DC	607	572	582	582	−5.7	1.7	24
Wichita, KS	311	344	355	358	10.7	1.8	50
Winston-Salem, NC	168	186	194	197	10.6	6.0	106
Worcester, MA	170	173	176	175	1.8	1.6	127
Yonkers, NY	188	196	198	198	4.2	0.9	104

[1] As tabulated. [2] Based on the April 1, 2000, population estimates base which reflects changes to the Census 2000 population from the Count Question Resolution program and geographic program revisions. [3] The population shown is for the census designated place (CDP). [4] Represents the portion of a consolidated city that is not within one or more separately incorporated places. [5] Data are for the incorporated place of Louisville city before consolidation of the city and county governments.

Source: U.S. Census Bureau, 2000 Census of Population and Housing, *Population and Housing Unit Counts* PHC-3; and "Table 1: Annual Estimates of the Population for Incorporated Places Over 100,000, Ranked by July 1, 2006 Population: April 1, 2000 to July 1, 2006"; Release Date: June 28, 2007; <http://www.census.gov/popest/cities/tables/SUB-EST2006-01.xls>.

Population   33

Table 28. Incorporated Places by Population Size: 1990 to 2006

[152.9 represents 152,900,000. See Appendix III]

Population size	Number of incorporated places				Population (mil.)				Percent of total			
	1990	2000	2005	2006	1990	2000 [1]	2005	2006	1990	2000 [1]	2005	2006
Total	19,262	19,475	19,475	19,475	152.9	176.6	184.5	186.1	100.0	100.0	100.0	100.0
1,000,000 or more....	8	9	9	9	20.0	23.0	23.7	23.8	13.0	13.0	12.8	12.8
500,000 to 999,999 ...	15	21	23	24	10.1	13.5	14.8	15.4	6.6	7.7	8.0	8.3
250,000 to 499,999 ...	41	38	38	36	14.2	13.7	13.7	12.9	9.3	7.8	7.4	6.9
100,000 to 249,999 ...	131	176	183	189	19.1	26.1	27.8	28.8	12.5	14.8	15.1	15.5
50,000 to 99,999.....	309	371	414	421	21.2	25.5	28.7	29.2	13.9	14.4	15.6	15.7
25,000 to 49,999.....	567	655	677	681	20.0	23.0	23.6	23.7	13.0	13.0	12.8	12.7
10,000 to 24,999.....	1,290	1,450	1,493	1,501	20.3	22.9	23.5	23.7	13.3	13.0	12.7	12.7
Under 10,000........	16,901	16,755	16,638	16,614	28.2	28.9	28.7	28.7	18.4	16.4	15.6	15.4

[1] The April 1, 2000, population estimates base reflects modifications to the Census 2000 population as documented in the Count Question Resolution program and geographic program revisions.

Source: U.S. Census Bureau, *1990 Census of Population and Housing, Population and Housing Unit Counts* (CPH-2-1); and "SUB-EST2006: Subcounty Population Estimates, April 1, 2000 to July 1, 2006" Release Date: June 28, 2007; <http://www.census.gov/popest /cities/files/SUB-EST2006-IP.csv>.

Table 29. Urban and Rural Population by State: 1990 and 2000

[222,361 represents 222,361,000. As of April 1. Resident population. For urban definitions; see text, this section]

State	Urban population				Rural popu-lation, 2000 (1,000)	State	Urban population				Rural popu-lation, 2000 (1,000)
	1990		2000, current definition				1990		2000, current definition		
	Former defini-tion (per-cent)	Current defini-tion (per-cent)	Number (1,000)	Percent			Former defini-tion (per-cent)	Current defini-tion (per-cent)	Number (1,000)	Percent	
US, total ..	75.2	78.0	222,361	79.0	59,061	MS......	47.1	49.1	1,387	48.8	1,457
						MO	68.7	69.6	3,883	69.4	1,712
						MT......	52.5	56.4	488	54.1	414
AL......	60.4	56.8	2,466	55.4	1,981	NE......	66.1	67.2	1,194	69.8	518
AK......	67.5	61.0	411	65.6	216	NV......	88.3	87.4	1,829	91.5	170
AZ......	87.5	86.5	4,524	88.2	607	NH......	51.0	57.2	732	59.3	503
AR......	53.5	52.0	1,404	52.5	1,269	NJ......	89.4	93.5	7,939	94.4	475
CA......	92.6	93.7	31,990	94.4	1,882	NM.....	73.0	75.0	1,364	75.0	456
CO......	82.4	83.8	3,633	84.5	668	NY......	84.3	87.4	16,603	87.5	2,374
CT......	79.1	87.0	2,988	87.7	418	NC......	50.4	57.8	4,849	60.2	3,200
DE......	73.0	79.2	628	80.1	156	ND......	53.3	53.4	359	55.9	283
DC......	100.0	100.0	572	100.0	–						
FL......	84.8	88.0	14,270	89.3	1,712	OH......	74.1	77.5	8,782	77.4	2,571
						OK......	67.7	65.2	2,255	65.3	1,196
GA......	63.2	68.7	5,864	71.6	2,322	OR......	70.5	74.9	2,694	78.7	727
HI	89.0	90.5	1,108	91.5	103	PA......	68.9	76.8	9,464	77.1	2,817
ID	57.4	62.2	859	66.4	434	RI	86.0	89.9	953	90.9	95
IL......	84.6	86.4	10,910	87.8	1,510	SC......	54.6	61.5	2,427	60.5	1,585
IN	64.9	69.1	4,304	70.8	1,776	SD......	50.0	50.3	391	51.9	363
IA	60.6	59.4	1,787	61.1	1,139	TN......	60.9	62.7	3,620	63.6	2,069
KS	69.1	69.5	1,921	71.4	768	TX......	80.3	81.2	17,204	82.5	3,648
KY.....	51.8	55.9	2,254	55.8	1,788	UT......	87.0	86.8	1,970	88.2	263
LA	68.1	72.9	3,246	72.6	1,223						
ME.....	44.6	42.6	513	40.2	762	VT......	32.2	40.2	232	38.2	376
						VA......	69.4	71.5	5,170	73.0	1,909
MD.....	81.3	85.0	4,559	86.1	738	WA.....	76.4	79.9	4,831	82.0	1,063
MA.....	84.3	90.5	5,801	91.4	548	WV.....	36.1	46.9	833	46.1	976
MI	70.5	75.2	7,419	74.7	2,519	WI	65.7	67.3	3,664	68.3	1,700
MN.....	69.9	69.0	3,490	70.9	1,429	WY	65.0	67.1	321	65.1	172

– Represents zero.

Source: U.S. Census Bureau. 2000 Census of Population and Housing, *Population and Housing Unit Counts* PHC-3.

Table 30. Mobility Status of the Population by Selected Characteristics: 1981 to 2006

[As of March (221,641 represents 221,641,000). For persons 1 year old and over. Based on comparison of place of residence in immediate prior year and year shown. Excludes members of the Armed Forces except those living off post or with their families on post. Based on Current Population Survey, Annual Social and Economic Supplement; see text of this section and Appendix III. For composition of regions, see map, inside front cover]

Mobility period and characteristic	Total (1,000)	Non-movers	Movers (different house in United States)					Movers from abroad
			Total	Same county	Different county			
					Total	Same state	Different state	
1981	221,641	83	17	10	6	3	3	1
1991	244,884	83	16	10	6	3	3	1
2001	275,611	86	14	8	6	3	3	1
2006, total	289,781	86	13	9	5	3	2	–
1 to 4 years old	16,310	79	20	14	6	4	3	1
5 to 9 years old	19,626	84	15	10	5	3	2	–
10 to 14 years old	20,651	88	12	8	4	2	2	–
15 to 19 years old	20,916	86	13	9	4	3	2	–
20 to 24 years old	20,393	71	28	17	10	6	4	1
25 to 29 years old	20,138	72	26	17	9	5	4	1
30 to 44 years old	62,464	85	15	9	5	3	2	1
45 to 64 years old	73,777	93	7	4	3	2	1	–
65 to 74 years old	18,554	95	4	2	2	1	1	–
75 to 84 years old	12,962	97	3	2	1	1	–	–
85 years old and over	3,989	96	4	3	2	1	1	–
Northeast	53,452	90	9	6	3	2	1	–
Midwest	64,244	87	12	8	4	3	2	–
South	104,862	85	14	8	6	3	3	1
West	67,223	84	16	11	5	3	2	1
Persons 16 years and over	228,862	87	13	8	5	3	2	–
Civilian labor force	149,668	85	14	9	5	3	2	–
Employed	142,147	86	14	9	5	3	2	–
Unemployed	7,521	76	24	14	10	5	5	1
Armed Forces	887	64	30	13	17	6	12	5
Not in labor force	78,307	90	10	6	4	2	2	–
Employed civilians, 16 years and over	142,147	86	14	9	5	3	2	–
Management, business, and financial	20,781	88	12	7	5	3	2	–
Professional	28,795	87	12	8	5	3	2	–
Service	23,522	83	16	11	5	3	2	1
Sales	16,450	85	15	10	5	3	2	–
Office and administrative support	19,360	87	13	9	4	3	1	–
Farming, fishing, and forestry	885	86	12	9	3	2	1	2
Construction and extraction	9,168	81	17	12	5	4	2	1
Installation, maintenance, and repair	5,178	87	12	7	5	3	2	–
Production	9,395	85	14	10	5	3	1	–
Transportation and material moving	8,612	84	15	11	5	3	2	–
Tenure:								
Owner-occupied units	206,136	93	7	4	3	2	1	–
Renter-occupied units	83,646	70	29	19	10	5	4	1

– Represents or rounds to zero.

Source: U.S. Census Bureau, "Geographical Mobility: 2005 to 2006, Detailed Tables"; <http://www.census.gov/population/www/socdemo/migrate.html>.

Table 31. Movers by Type of Move and Reason for Moving: 2006

[As of March (39,837 represents 39,837,000). For persons 1 year old and over. Based on comparison of place of residence in 2005 and 2006. Excludes members of the Armed Forces except those living off post or with their families on post. Based on Current Population Survey, Annual Social and Economic Supplement; see text of this section and Appendix III]

Reason for move	All movers	Intra-county	Inter-county	From abroad	Reason for move	All movers	Intra-county	Inter-county	From abroad
Total (1,000)	39,837	24,851	13,690	1,296	Housing-related reasons	46.2	59.1	26.3	6.9
PERCENT DISTRIBUTION					Wanted to own home/ not rent	8.6	10.6	5.7	0.5
Total	100.0	100.0	100.0	100.0	New/better house/				
Family-related reasons	27.7	27.7	27.5	28.7	apartment	17.8	24.4	7.4	1.3
Change in marital status	6.0	6.2	5.7	4.8	Better neighborhood/				
To establish own					less crime	4.4	4.6	4.3	0.6
household	8.5	10.5	5.5	1.5	Cheaper housing	6.2	7.6	3.9	2.0
Other family reasons	13.2	11.0	16.2	22.4	Other housing	9.2	11.9	5.0	2.5
Work-related reasons	18.4	8.7	32.8	52.2	Other reasons	7.8	4.4	13.4	12.2
New job/job transfer	8.7	2.2	19.3	23.3	Attend/leave college	2.7	1.3	4.8	7.7
To look for work/lost job	1.6	0.6	2.3	12.8	Change of climate	0.4	0.1	1.1	0.4
Closer to work/					Health reasons	1.3	1.0	1.9	0.8
easier commute	3.6	3.0	5.1	0.2	Natural disaster	1.7	0.6	3.7	–
Retired	0.4	–	1.2	0.2	Other reason	1.7	1.5	2.0	3.3
Other job-related reason	4.0	2.9	4.9	15.7					

– Represents or rounds to zero.

Source: U.S. Census Bureau, "Geographic Mobility: 2005 to 2006, Detailed Tables"; <http://www.census.gov/population/www/socdemo/migrate.html>.

Population   35

Table 32. **Mobility Status of Households by Household Income: 2006**

[As of March (114,401 represents 114,401,000). Covers householders 15 years old and over. Based on comparison of place of residence in 2005 and 2006. Excludes members of the Armed Forces except those living off post or with their families on post. Based on Current Population Survey, Annual Social and Economic Supplement; see text of this section and Appendix III]

Household income in **2005**	Total (1,000)	Non-movers	Percent distribution						Movers from abroad
			Movers (different house in United States)						
			Total	Same county	Different county				
					Total	Same state	Different state		
Householders, 15 years and over. . .	114,401	87	13	8	5	3	2	–
Less than $5,000	3,733	78	21	13	7	4	3	1
$5,000 to $9,999.	5,669	83	16	11	5	3	2	–
$10,000 to $14,999	7,332	84	15	10	5	3	2	–
$15,000 to $24,999	14,141	84	15	11	5	3	2	–
$25,000 to $34,999	13,035	85	15	10	5	3	2	–
$35,000 to $49,999	17,005	86	14	9	5	3	2	–
$50,000 to $74,999	17,491	87	13	8	5	3	2	–
$75,000 and over	35,993	91	9	5	4	2	1	–

– Represents or rounds to zero.

Source: U.S. Census Bureau, "Geographical Mobility: 2005 to 2006, Detailed Tables"; <http://www.census.gov/population/www/socdemo/migrate.html>.

Table 33. **Mobility Status of Resident Population by State: 2005**

[In percent, except as indicated (284,367 represents 284,367,000). Based on comparison of place of residence in 2004 and 2005. The American Community Survey universe is limited to the household population and excludes the population living in institutions, college dormitories, and other group quarters. Based on a sample and subject to sampling variability; see text, this section and Appendix III]

State	Population 1 year old and over [1] (1,000)	Same house in 2004	Different house in United States in 2004		State	Population 1 year old and over [1] (1,000)	Same house in 2004	Different house in United States in 2004	
			Same county	Different county				Same county	Different county
U.S. . .	284,367	83.9	9.9	5.6					
AL	4,383	83.8	10.3	5.5	MO	5,561	83.4	9.5	6.9
AK	633	81.3	10.5	7.7	MT	900	81.5	11.2	7.0
AZ	5,735	78.0	14.3	6.7	NE	1,682	83.9	9.8	5.8
AR	2,664	81.4	11.2	7.0	NV	2,346	78.4	13.9	6.8
CA	34,738	83.7	11.1	4.3	NH	1,260	86.3	7.4	5.9
CO	4,488	79.7	10.7	8.8	NJ	8,403	88.3	6.7	4.3
CT	3,356	88.1	7.4	3.8	NM	1,864	81.6	11.3	6.3
DE	810	83.8	10.4	5.0	NY	18,417	88.6	7.3	3.4
DC	506	81.4	9.9	7.4	NC	8,300	83.0	10.0	6.5
FL	17,159	81.4	11.0	6.8	ND	602	84.9	9.2	5.4
GA	8,679	81.7	9.3	8.5	OH	11,014	84.9	10.2	4.6
HI	1,219	85.3	9.0	4.6	OK	3,387	81.1	11.2	7.4
ID	1,375	79.6	11.4	8.5	OR	3,512	79.3	12.1	8.0
IL	12,261	85.4	9.8	4.3	PA	11,839	87.9	7.5	4.2
IN	6,015	84.3	10.1	5.2	RI	1,019	88.4	6.8	4.2
IA	2,826	84.4	9.4	5.9	SC	4,061	84.4	8.7	6.4
KS	2,626	81.9	11.1	6.5	SD	735	83.4	9.0	7.3
KY	4,006	84.1	9.9	5.6	TN	5,730	83.0	10.7	6.0
LA	4,329	83.9	10.0	5.8	TX	21,896	80.9	11.9	6.3
ME	1,270	85.5	8.9	5.4	UT	2,378	80.0	13.0	6.4
MD	5,385	85.1	7.9	6.3	VT	597	85.4	8.8	5.4
MA	6,103	86.3	8.6	4.3	VA	7,233	84.0	6.9	8.4
MI	9,736	85.8	9.4	4.3	WA	6,069	79.9	12.5	6.7
MN	4,923	85.6	7.5	6.4	WV	1,754	88.1	7.3	4.4
MS	2,787	83.5	9.7	6.6	WI	5,310	85.2	9.5	5.0
					WY	489	81.7	10.8	7.2

[1] Includes persons moving from abroad, not shown separately.

Source: U.S. Census Bureau, 2005 American Community Survey; B07003. Residence 1 Year Ago by Sex; using American FactFinder®; <http://factfinder.census.gov/>; (31 July 2007).

Table 34. **Persons 65 Years Old and Over—Characteristics by Sex: 1990 to 2006**

[As of March, except as noted (29.6 represents 29,600,000). Covers civilian noninstitutional population. Excludes members of Armed Forces except those living off post or with their families on post. Data for 1990 are based on 1980 census population controls; 2000 data based on 1990 census population controls; beginning 2005, data based on 2000 census population controls and an expanded sample of households. Based on Current Population Survey; see text of this section and Appendix III]

Characteristic	Total				Male				Female			
	1990	2000	2005	2006	1990	2000	2005	2006	1990	2000	2005	2006
Total (million)	**29.6**	**32.6**	**35.2**	**35.5**	**12.3**	**13.9**	**15.1**	**15.2**	**17.2**	**18.7**	**20.0**	**20.3**
PERCENT DISTRIBUTION												
Marital status:												
Never married	4.6	3.9	4.1	3.6	4.2	4.2	4.4	3.8	4.9	3.6	3.9	3.6
Married	56.1	57.2	57.7	57.8	76.5	75.2	74.9	75.0	41.4	43.8	44.7	44.9
Spouse present	54.1	54.6	54.8	54.7	74.2	72.6	71.7	71.9	39.7	41.3	42.0	41.9
Spouse absent	2.0	2.6	2.9	3.0	2.3	2.6	3.2	3.1	1.7	2.5	2.7	3.0
Widowed	34.2	32.1	30.3	29.9	14.2	14.4	13.7	13.1	48.6	45.3	42.9	42.4
Divorced	5.0	6.7	7.9	8.7	5.0	6.1	7.0	8.1	5.1	7.2	8.5	9.1
Educational attainment:												
Less than ninth grade	28.5	16.7	13.4	13.0	30.0	17.8	13.2	13.0	27.5	15.9	13.5	12.9
Completed 9th to 12th grade, but no high school diploma	[1]16.1	13.8	12.7	11.9	[1]15.7	12.7	11.9	11.0	[1]16.4	14.7	13.3	12.5
High school graduate	[2]32.9	35.9	36.3	36.7	[2]29.0	30.4	31.6	32.9	[2]35.6	39.9	39.9	39.5
Some college or associate's degree . .	[3]10.9	18.0	18.7	19.0	[3]10.8	17.8	18.4	17.4	[3]11.0	18.2	19.0	20.2
Bachelor's or advanced degree	[4]11.6	15.6	18.9	19.5	[4]14.5	21.4	24.9	25.6	[4]9.5	11.4	14.3	14.9
Labor force participation: [5]												
Employed	11.5	12.4	14.5	15.0	15.9	16.9	19.1	19.8	8.4	9.1	11.1	11.4
Unemployed	0.4	0.4	0.5	0.4	0.5	0.6	0.7	0.6	0.3	0.3	0.4	0.3
Not in labor force	88.1	87.2	84.9	84.6	83.6	82.5	80.2	79.7	91.3	90.6	88.5	88.3
Percent below poverty level [6]	11.4	9.7	9.8	10.1	7.8	6.9	7.0	7.3	13.9	11.8	11.9	12.3

[1] Represents those who completed 1 to 3 years of high school.   [2] Represents those who completed 4 years of high school.
[3] Represents those who completed 1 to 3 years of college.   [4] Represents those who completed 4 years of college or more.
[5] Annual averages of monthly figures. Source: U.S. Bureau of Labor Statistics, *Employment and Earnings*, January issues. See footnote 2, Table 569.   [6] Poverty status based on income in preceding year.

Source: Except as noted, U.S. Census Bureau, *Current Population Reports*, P20-546, and earlier reports; "Educational Attainment"; <http://www.census.gov/population/www/socdemo/educ-attn.html>; "Families and Living Arrangements"; <http://www.census.gov/population/www/socdemo/hh-fam.html>; and "Detailed Poverty Tabulations from the CPS"; <http://www.census.gov/hhes/www/poverty/detailedpovtabs.html>.

Table 35. **Persons 65 Years Old and Over—Living Arrangements and Disability Status: 2005**

[In thousands (34,761 represents 34,761,000), except as indicated. The American Community Survey universe is limited to the household population and excludes the population living in institutions, college dormitories, and other group quarters. Based on a sample and subject to sampling variability; see text of this section and Appendix III]

Relationship by household type	Number	Percent distri- bution	Type of disability	Total	65 to 74 years old	75 years old and over
Total	**34,761**	**100.0**	**Persons with a disability**	**14,064**	**5,556**	**8,508**
In family households	23,553	67.8				
Householder	12,205	35.1	With a sensory disability	5,707	1,871	3,836
Spouse	8,620	24.8	With a physical disability	10,712	4,286	6,426
Parent	1,571	4.5	With a mental disability	3,988	1,329	2,659
Other relatives	1,026	3.0	With a self-care disability	3,358	1,061	2,297
Nonrelatives	130	0.4	With a go-outside-home disability	5,778	1,636	4,142
In nonfamily households	11,208	32.2				
Householder	10,799	31.1				
Living alone	10,299	29.6				
Not living alone	500	1.4				
Nonrelatives	409	1.2				

Source: U.S. Census Bureau, 2005 American Community Survey; B09017. Relationship by Household Type (Including Living Alone) for the Population 65 Years and Over; B18002. Sex by Age by Disability Status for the Civilian Noninstitutionalized Population 5 Years and Over; B18003. Sex by Age by Sensory Disability for the Civilian Noninstitutionalized Population 5 Years and Over; B18004. Sex by Age by Physical Disability for the Civilian Noninstitutionalized Population 5 Years and Over; B18005. Sex by Age by Mental Disability for the Civilian Noninstitutionalized Population 5 Years and Over; B18006. Sex by Age by Self-Care Disability for the Civilian Noninstitutionalized Population 5 Years and Over; B18007. Sex by Age by Go-Outside-Home Disability for the Civilian Noninstitutionalized Population 16 Years and Over; using American FactFinder®; <http://factfinder.census.gov/>; (23 August 2006).

Table 36. **Selected Characteristics of Racial Groups and Hispanic/Latino Population: 2005**

[In thousands (188,951 represents 188,951,000), **except as indicated**. The American Community Survey universe is limited to the household population and excludes the population living in institutions, college dormitories, and other group quarters. Based on a sample and subject to sampling variability; see text of this section and Appendix III. For definition of median, see Guide to Tabular Presentation]

Characteristic	Total population	White alone	Black or African American alone	American Indian and Alaska Native alone	Asian alone
EDUCATIONAL ATTAINMENT					
Persons 25 years old and over, total	**188,951**	**146,653**	**20,518**	**1,406**	**8,520**
Less than 9th grade	11,793	7,295	1,174	119	692
9th to 12th grade, no diploma	17,989	12,414	2,942	213	538
High school graduate (includes equivalency).	55,857	43,931	6,751	438	1,429
Some college, no degree	37,985	30,024	4,575	324	1,076
Associate's degree.	13,960	11,048	1,527	119	602
Bachelor's degree	32,536	26,538	2,343	128	2,488
Graduate degree	18,831	15,402	1,206	63	1,695
Percent high school graduate or higher	84.2	86.6	79.9	76.3	85.6
Percent bachelor's degree or higher	27.2	28.6	17.3	13.6	49.1
OCCUPATION					
Employed civilian population, 16 years old and over, total	**136,459**	**105,449**	**14,375**	**951**	**6,067**
Management, professional, and related occupations	46,515	37,889	3,775	248	2,850
Management, business, and financial operations occupations	18,612	15,559	1,334	99	912
Professional and related occupations	27,903	22,329	2,441	149	1,938
Service occupations	22,224	15,344	3,451	202	933
Sales and office occupations	35,352	27,739	3,822	218	1,414
Farming, fishing, and forestry occupations	930	686	44	11	11
Construction, extraction, and maintenance occupations	13,631	10,954	909	128	219
Construction and extraction occupations	8,705	6,929	515	90	94
Installation, maintenance, and repair occupations	4,926	4,025	394	39	125
Production, transportation, and material moving occupations	17,808	12,837	2,373	143	640
Production occupations	9,416	6,796	1,083	75	456
Transportation and material moving occupations	8,392	6,041	1,290	68	184
FAMILY INCOME IN THE PAST 12 MONTHS					
Total families	**74,341**	**57,460**	**8,528**	**568**	**2,997**
Less than $10,000	3,947	2,217	1,122	61	128
$10,000 to $19,999	6,282	4,038	1,281	82	204
$20,000 to $29,999	7,615	5,360	1,205	81	233
$30,000 to $39,999	7,751	5,776	1,011	69	241
$40,000 to $49,999	7,411	5,756	828	56	247
$50,000 to $59,999	6,761	5,403	666	48	230
$60,000 to $74,999	8,829	7,174	785	57	343
$75,000 to $99,999	10,255	8,496	812	59	445
$100,000 to $124,999.	6,225	5,245	404	28	333
$125,000 to $149,999.	3,315	2,806	193	12	199
$150,000 to $199,999.	3,048	2,607	146	8	211
$200,000 or more	2,901	2,581	76	7	184
Median family income in the past 12 months (dol.). . .	55,832	60,310	36,075	38,558	69,159
POVERTY STATUS IN THE PAST 12 MONTHS [2]					
Persons below poverty level	38,231	22,371	8,889	593	1,429
Percent below poverty level	13.3	10.4	25.6	25.4	11.5
Families below poverty level	7,605	4,319	1,941	120	266
Percent below poverty level	10.2	7.5	22.8	21.2	8.9
HOUSING TENURE					
Total householders	**111,091**	**86,765**	**13,141**	**836**	**4,067**
Owner-occupied	74,319	62,497	6,014	468	2,402
Renter-occupied	36,772	24,267	7,127	368	1,664

See footnotes at end of table.

U.S. Census Bureau, Statistical Abstract of the United States: 2008

Table 36. **Selected Characteristics of Racial Groups and Hispanic/Latino Population: 2005**—Con.

[See headnote, page 38]

Characteristic	Native Hawaiian and Other Pacific Islander alone	Some other race alone	Two or more races	Hispanic/ Latino [1]	White alone, not Hispanic or Latino
EDUCATIONAL ATTAINMENT					
Persons 25 years old and over, total	**237**	**9,389**	**2,230**	**22,663**	**134,106**
Less than 9th grade	15	2,371	127	5,442	4,323
9th to 12th grade, no diploma	25	1,629	228	3,748	10,414
High school graduate (includes equivalency)	89	2,621	597	6,118	40,629
Some college, no degree	53	1,367	565	3,417	28,148
Associate's degree	19	461	184	1,170	10,385
Bachelor's degree	26	676	338	1,888	25,393
Graduate degree	11	263	190	880	14,814
Percent high school graduate or higher	83.1	57.4	84.1	59.5	89.0
Percent bachelor's degree or higher	15.4	10.0	23.7	12.2	30.0
OCCUPATION					
Employed civilian population, 16 years old and over, total	**187**	**7,617**	**1,813**	**17,938**	**95,716**
Management, professional, and related occupations	43	1,161	548	3,127	36,059
Management, business, and financial operations occupations	19	481	208	1,296	14,800
Professional and related occupations	24	680	340	1,831	21,259
Service occupations	42	1,883	369	4,235	13,116
Sales and office occupations	55	1,609	494	3,871	25,634
Farming, fishing, and forestry occupations	1	167	8	408	453
Construction, extraction, and maintenance occupations	18	1,236	167	2,935	9,327
Construction and extraction occupations	12	956	110	2,273	5,660
Installation, maintenance, and repair occupations	6	280	57	662	3,666
Production, transportation, and material moving occupations	27	1,561	226	3,361	11,128
Production occupations	12	887	107	1,863	5,861
Transportation and material moving occupations	16	674	120	1,498	5,267
FAMILY INCOME IN THE PAST 12 MONTHS					
Total families	**85**	**3,825**	**878**	**9,092**	**52,495**
Less than $10,000	5	339	75	800	1,793
$10,000 to $19,999	9	570	98	1,345	3,307
$20,000 to $29,999	9	627	100	1,432	4,596
$30,000 to $39,999	10	540	105	1,232	5,118
$40,000 to $49,999	9	431	85	1,015	5,201
$50,000 to $59,999	8	328	78	760	4,996
$60,000 to $74,999	11	362	97	860	6,704
$75,000 to $99,999	12	329	103	811	8,044
$100,000 to $124,999	7	152	57	394	5,020
$125,000 to $149,999	4	71	31	193	2,691
$150,000 to $199,999	2	47	26	140	2,519
$200,000 or more	2	30	22	110	2,504
Median family income in the past 12 months (dol.) . . .	50,641	36,588	46,897	37,387	62,300
POVERTY STATUS IN THE PAST 12 MONTHS [2]					
Persons below poverty level	69	3,910	970	9,316	17,374
Percent below poverty level	17.6	22.7	17.6	22.4	9.0
Families below poverty level	14	807	138	1,865	3,329
Percent below poverty level	16.1	21.1	15.7	20.5	6.3
HOUSING TENURE					
Total householders	**117**	**4,791**	**1,375**	**11,723**	**80,273**
Owner-occupied	53	2,154	730	5,664	59,178
Renter-occupied	63	2,637	645	6,059	21,095

[1] Persons of Hispanic/Latino origin may be of any race.   [2] For explanation of poverty level, see text, Section 13.

Source: U.S. Census Bureau, 2005 American Community Survey; B15002. Sex by Educational Attainment for the Population 25 Years and Over. B24010. Sex by Occupation for the Employed Civilian Population 16 Years and Over. B19101. Family Income in the Past 12 Months (In 2005 Inflation-Adjusted Dollars), B19113. Median Family Income in the Past 12 Months (In 2005 Inflation-Adjusted Dollars), B17001. Poverty Status in the Past 12 Months by Sex by Age, B17010. Poverty Status in the Past 12 Months of Families by Family Type by Presence of Related Children Under 18 Years by Age of Related Children, B25003. Tenure; using American FactFinder; <http://factfinder.census.gov/>; (accessed: 21 March 2007).

Table 37. American Indian and Alaska Native Population by Tribe: 2000

[As of April. This table shows data for American Indian and Alaska Native tribes alone or in combination of tribes or races. Respondents who identified themselves as American Indian or Alaska Native were asked to report their enrolled or principal tribe. Therefore, data shown here reflect the written tribal entries reported on the questionnaire. Some of the entries (for example, Iroquois, Sioux, Colorado River, and Flathead) represent nations or reservations. The information on tribe is based on self-identification and includes federally or state-recognized tribes, as well as bands and clans]

American Indian and Alaska Native tribe	Number	American Indian and Alaska Native tribe	Number
Total persons [1]	**4,119,301**	Osage	15,897
Apache	96,833	Ottawa	10,677
Blackfeet	85,750	Paiute	13,532
Cherokee	729,533	Pima	11,493
Cheyenne	18,204	Potawatomi	25,595
Chickasaw	38,351	Pueblo	74,085
Chippewa	149,669	Puget Sound Salish	14,631
Choctaw	158,774	Seminole	27,431
Colville	9,393	Shoshone	12,026
Comanche	19,376	Sioux	153,360
Cree	7,734	Tohono O'odham	20,087
Creek	71,310	United Houma Nation	8,713
Crow	13,394	Ute	10,385
Delaware	16,341	Yakama	10,851
Iroquois	80,822	Yaqui	22,412
Kiowa	12,242	Yuman	8,976
Latin American Indian	180,940	Alaskan Athabascan	18,838
Lumbee	57,868	Aleut	10,548
Menominee	9,840	Eskimo	54,761
Navajo	298,197	Tlingit-Haida	22,365

[1] Includes other tribes not shown separately.

Source: U.S. Census Bureau, *The American Indian and Alaska Native Population: 2000*, Census 2000 Brief (C2KBR/01-15), February 2002.

Table 38. Population Living on Selected Reservations and Trust Lands: 2000

[As of April. OTSA = Oklahoma Tribal Statistical Area; SDAISA = State Designated American Indian Statistical Area; ANRC = Alaska Native Regional Corporation]

Reservation, Trust Land, or Other Area	Total population	American Indian and Alaska Native population alone	American Indian and Alaska Native population alone or in combination with one or more races
Navajo Nation Reservation and Off-Reservation Trust Land, AZ–NM–UT	180,462	173,987	175,228
Cherokee OTSA, OK	462,327	76,041	104,482
Creek OTSA, OK	704,565	51,296	77,253
Lumbee SDAISA, NC	474,100	58,238	62,327
Choctaw OTSA, OK	224,472	29,521	39,984
Cook Inlet ANRC, AK	364,205	24,923	35,972
Chickasaw OTSA, OK	277,416	22,946	32,372
Calista ANRC, AK	23,032	19,617	20,353
United Houma Nation SDAISA, LA	839,880	11,019	15,305
Sealaska ANRC, AK	71,507	11,320	15,059
Pine Ridge Reservation and Off-Reservation Trust Land, SD–NE	15,521	14,304	14,484
Doyon ANRC, AK	97,190	11,182	14,128
Kiowa-Comanche-Apache-Fort Sill Apache OTSA, OK	193,260	9,675	13,045
Fort Apache Reservation, AZ	12,429	11,702	11,854
Citizen Potawatomi Nation-Absentee Shawnee OTSA, OK	106,624	6,733	10,617
Gila River Reservation, AZ	11,257	10,353	10,578
Cheyenne-Arapaho OTSA, OK	157,869	7,402	10,310
Tohono O'odham Reservation and Off-Reservation Trust Land, AZ	10,787	9,718	9,794
Osage Reservation, OK	44,437	6,410	9,209
Rosebud Reservation and Off-Reservation Trust Land, SD	10,469	9,040	9,165
San Carlos Reservation, AZ	9,385	8,921	9,065
Blackfeet Reservation and Off-Reservation Trust Land, MT	10,100	8,507	8,684
Yakama Reservation and Off-Reservation Trust Land, WA	31,799	7,411	8,193
Turtle Mountain Reservation and Off-Reservation Trust Land, MT–ND–SD	8,331	8,009	8,043
Flathead Reservation, MT	26,172	6,999	7,883
Zuni Reservation and Off-Reservation Trust Land, NM–AZ	7,758	7,426	7,466
Bering Straits ANRC, AK	9,196	6,915	7,274
Sac and Fox OTSA, OK	55,690	5,334	7,232
Eastern Cherokee Reservation, NC	8,092	6,665	6,898
Wind River Reservation and Off-Reservation Trust Land, WY	23,250	6,544	6,864
Hopi Reservation and Off-Reservation Trust Land, AZ	6,946	6,573	6,633
Fort Peck Reservation and Off-Reservation Trust Land, MT	10,321	6,391	6,577
Cheyenne River Reservation and Off-Reservation Trust Land, SD	8,470	6,249	6,346
NANA ANRC, AK	7,208	5,944	6,181
Standing Rock Reservation, SD–ND	8,250	5,964	6,054
Bristol Bay ANRC, AK	7,892	5,336	5,749
Arctic Slope ANRC, AK	7,385	5,541	5,453
Crow Reservation and Off-Reservation Trust Land, MT	6,894	5,155	5,275
Red Lake Reservation, MN	5,162	5,071	5,087

Source: U.S. Census Bureau, 2000 Census of Population and Housing, *Profiles of General Demographic Characteristics*. See also <http://factfinder.census.gov/home/aian/index.html>.

Table 39. **Social and Economic Characteristics of the Hispanic Population: 2006**

[As of March, except labor force status, annual average (43,168 represents 43,168,000). Excludes members of the Armed Forces except those living off post or with their families on post. Based on Current Population Survey; see text of this section and Appendix III]

Characteristic	Number (1,000)					Percent distribution				
	His-panic, total [1]	Mexi-can	Puerto Rican	Cuban	Central, South Ameri-can	His-panic, total [1]	Mexi-can	Puerto Rican	Cuban	Central, South Ameri-can
Total persons	43,168	28,323	3,704	1,584	7,414	100.0	100.0	100.0	100.0	100.0
Under 5 years	4,596	3,324	345	116	599	10.6	11.7	9.3	7.3	8.1
5 to 14 years old.	7,931	5,571	667	206	1,115	18.3	19.7	18.0	13.0	15.0
15 to 44 years old	21,457	14,106	1,759	648	4,020	49.7	49.8	47.5	41.0	54.2
45 to 64 years old	6,868	4,105	687	327	1,324	15.9	14.5	18.6	20.7	17.8
65 years old and over	2,315	1,216	247	286	355	5.4	4.3	6.7	18.1	4.8
EDUCATIONAL ATTAINMENT										
Persons 25 years old and over.	23,499	14,621	2,052	1,094	4,512	100.0	100.0	100.0	100.0	100.0
High school graduate or more	13,932	7,760	1,483	820	2,894	59.3	53.1	72.3	74.9	64.1
Bachelor's degree or more	2,907	1,238	310	267	836	12.4	8.5	15.1	24.4	18.5
LABOR FORCE STATUS [2]										
Civilians 16 years old and over.	30,103	19,036	2,600	1,326	(NA)	100.0	100.0	100.0	100.0	(NA)
Civilian labor force.	20,694	13,158	1,599	807	(NA)	68.7	69.1	61.5	60.9	(NA)
Employed.	19,613	12,477	1,484	778	(NA)	65.2	65.5	57.1	58.7	(NA)
Unemployed . . . . ·3· .	1,081	681	115	29	(NA)	3.6	3.6	4.4	2.2	(NA)
Unemployment rate [3]	5.2	5.2	7.2	3.6	(NA)	(X)	(X)	(X)	(X)	(X)
Male	4.8	4.7	7.2	3.3	(NA)	(X)	(X)	(X)	(X)	(X)
Female	5.9	6.0	7.2	3.9	(NA)	(X)	(X)	(X)	(X)	(X)
Not in labor force	9,409	5,877	1,001	519	(NA)	31.3	30.9	38.5	39.1	(NA)
HOUSEHOLDS										
Total	12,519	7,702	1,239	587	2,274	100.0	100.0	100.0	100.0	100.0
Family households . . . . ·,·	9,862	6,239	900	429	1,808	78.8	81.0	72.6	73.1	79.5
Married-couple families [4]	6,642	4,371	480	324	1,136	53.1	56.8	38.7	55.2	50.0
Male householder, no spouse present	969	598	85	27	218	7.7	7.8	6.9	4.6	9.6
Female householder, no spouse present	2,252	1,271	334	78	454	18.0	16.5	27.0	13.3	20.0
Nonfamily households	2,657	1,463	339	158	466	21.2	19.0	27.4	26.9	20.5
Male householder	1,480	880	154	75	262	11.8	11.4	12.4	12.8	11.5
Female householder.	1,177	583	185	83	204	9.4	7.6	14.9	14.1	9.0
Size:										
One person	1,954	1,048	271	132	311	15.6	13.6	21.9	22.5	13.7
Two people.	2,771	1,547	321	197	501	22.1	20.1	26.0	33.5	22.0
Three people	2,443	1,439	243	95	535	19.5	18.7	19.7	16.1	23.5
Four people	2,534	1,600	235	109	477	20.2	20.8	19.0	18.6	21.0
Five people	1,606	1,131	116	29	277	12.8	14.7	9.4	4.9	12.2
Six people	723	544	33	17	112	5.8	7.1	2.7	2.9	4.9
Seven people or more	488	393	18	9	60	3.9	5.1	1.5	1.5	2.6
FAMILY INCOME IN 2005										
Total families [5]	9,868	6,244	901	429	1,782	100.0	100.0	100.0	100.0	100.0
Less than $5,000	388	253	51	11	56	4.0	4.1	5.7	2.4	3.2
$5,000 to $14,999 . . . . ·.	1,060	702	134	34	144	10.8	11.2	15.0	7.9	8.1
$15,000 to $24,999	1,613	1,106	126	54	264	16.4	17.7	14.0	12.4	14.8
$25,000 to $34,999	1,503	943	129	68	295	15.2	15.1	14.3	15.9	16.5
$35,000 to $49,999	1,713	1,123	124	62	321	17.4	18.0	13.7	14.5	18.0
$50,000 to $74,999	1,800	1,112	159	78	354	18.2	17.8	17.7	18.3	19.9
$75,000 and over	1,792	1,005	177	123	346	18.2	16.1	19.6	28.6	19.4
POVERTY STATUS IN 2005										
Families below poverty level [6]	1,948	1,376	211	39	255	19.7	22.0	23.5	9.1	14.3
Persons below poverty level [6]	9,368	6,711	932	169	1,201	21.8	23.8	25.3	10.7	16.3
HOUSEHOLD TENURE										
Total occupied units	12,519	7,702	1,239	587	2,242	100.0	100.0	100.0	100.0	100.0
Owner-occupied ,[7]	6,103	3,911	490	368	845	48.8	50.8	39.6	62.7	37.7
Renter-occupied	6,416	3,791	749	219	1,397	51.2	49.2	60.4	37.3	62.3

NA Not available.   X Not applicable.   [1] Includes other Hispanic groups not shown separately.   [2] Source: U.S. Bureau of Labor Statistics, *Employment and Earnings*, January 2007.   [3] Total unemployment as percent of civilian labor force.   [4] In married-couple families, Hispanic origin refers to the householder.   [5] Includes families in group quarters.   [6] For explanation of poverty level, see text, Section 13.   [7] Includes no cash rent.

Source: Except as noted, U.S. Census Bureau, "Educational Attainment"; <http://www.census.gov/population/www/socdemo /educ-attn.html>; "Families and Living Arrangements"; <http://www.census.gov/population/www/socdemo/hh-fam.html>; "Detailed Income Tabulations from the CPS"; <http://www.census.gov/hhes/www/income/dinctabs.html>; "Detailed Poverty Tabulations from the CPS"; <http://www.census.gov/hhes/www/poverty/detailedpovtabs.html>, and unpublished data.

Population   41

Table 40. Native and Foreign-Born Population by State: 2005

[252,688 represents 252,688,000. The American Community Survey universe is limited to the household population and excludes the population living in institutions, college dormitories, and other group quarters. Based on a sample and subject to sampling variability; see text of this section and Appendix III]

State	Native popu- lation (1,000)	Foreign-born population Number (1,000)	Percent of total popu- lation	Percent entered 2000 or later	State	Native popu- lation (1,000)	Foreign-born population Number (1,000)	Percent of total popu- lation	Percent entered 2000 or later
U.S., total ..	252,688	35,690	12.4	22.2					
					MO	5,438	194	3.4	30.9
AL	4,322	121	2.7	38.1	MT	894	17	1.8	19.2
AK	607	34	5.4	17.1	NE	1,611	96	5.6	31.2
AZ	4,987	843	14.5	28.4	NV	1,968	413	17.4	22.5
AR	2,600	101	3.7	31.6	NH	1,200	72	5.7	25.9
CA	25,667	9,611	27.2	17.3					
					NJ	6,859	1,663	19.5	21.0
CO	4,102	460	10.1	28.1	NM	1,719	169	8.9	26.4
CT	2,971	423	12.5	22.3	NY	14,658	3,997	21.4	17.3
DE	756	63	7.7	32.0	NC	7,850	561	6.7	34.9
DC	447	68	13.1	25.4	ND	598	12	2.0	27.9
FL	14,170	3,213	18.5	22.7					
					OH	10,768	387	3.5	27.6
GA	8,026	795	9.0	31.9	OK	3,278	156	4.5	28.4
HI	1,026	212	17.2	17.8	OR	3,216	345	9.7	26.8
ID	1,319	76	5.5	27.6	PA	11,375	604	5.0	25.3
IL	10,745	1,695	13.6	20.6	RI	902	131	12.6	20.3
IN	5,851	242	4.0	34.3					
					SC	3,943	171	4.2	40.9
IA	2,759	103	3.6	28.0	SD	729	17	2.3	44.0
KS	2,509	154	5.8	29.6	TN	5,587	223	3.8	37.5
KY	3,960	99	2.4	35.3	TX	18,728	3,543	15.9	23.8
LA	4,268	122	2.8	19.4	UT	2,234	193	7.9	28.3
ME	1,245	39	3.0	17.2					
					VT	580	22	3.6	19.1
MD	4,820	641	11.7	28.5	VA	6,609	724	9.9	25.7
MA	5,292	891	14.4	24.0	WA	5,396	750	12.2	26.2
MI	9,260	606	6.1	26.6	WV	1,752	19	1.1	18.9
MN	4,673	317	6.3	28.0	WI	5,148	227	4.2	26.7
MS	2,781	43	1.5	33.4	WY	484	11	2.3	16.8

Source: U.S. Census Bureau, 2005 American Community Survey; B05002. Place of Birth by Citizenship Status; and B05005. Year of Entry by Citizenship Status; using American FactFinder; <http://factfinder.census.gov/>; (accessed: 15 December 2006).

Table 41. Nativity and Place of Birth of Resident Population—25 Largest Cities: 2005

[678 represents 678,000. The American Community Survey universe is limited to the household population and excludes the population living in institutions, college dormitories, and other group quarters. Based on a sample and subject to sampling variability; see text of this section and Appendix III]

City	Total population (1,000)	Native population Total (1,000)	Born in United States (1,000)	Born outside United States (1,000)	Foreign-born population Total Number (1,000)	Percent of total population	Entered 2000 or later Number (1,000)	Percent of foreign- born population
Austin, TX	678	555	548	7	123	18.2	40	32.1
Baltimore, MD	608	574	571	4	34	5.6	15	43.5
Charlotte, NC	602	522	517	5	80	13.2	31	39.0
Chicago, IL	2,702	2,112	2,069	43	590	21.9	121	20.5
Columbus, OH	694	631	625	6	63	9.1	27	42.8
Dallas, TX	1,145	832	825	7	313	27.3	95	30.3
Denver, CO	545	442	436	6	103	18.9	33	31.8
Detroit, MI	836	784	778	6	52	6.3	16	30.2
El Paso, TX	583	433	422	11	151	25.9	24	15.9
Fort Worth, TX	605	499	492	7	106	17.5	28	26.0
Houston, TX	1,941	1,377	1,360	17	564	29.1	142	25.3
Indianapolis, IN [1]	765	714	708	6	51	6.7	21	40.0
Jacksonville, FL	769	709	694	14	60	7.8	12	20.5
Las Vegas, NV	539	431	424	7	108	20.0	26	24.1
Los Angeles, CA	3,731	2,226	2,193	33	1,505	40.3	258	17.2
Louisville-Jefferson County, KY [1]	548	522	518	4	26	4.7	9	33.7
Memphis, TN	642	606	603	2	36	5.7	16	44.1
Milwaukee, WI	557	504	496	8	53	9.5	14	26.6
New York, NY	7,956	5,040	4,717	323	2,916	36.6	497	17.0
Philadelphia, PA	1,406	1,250	1,208	43	156	11.1	53	33.7
Phoenix, AZ	1,378	1,067	1,051	16	311	22.6	97	31.2
San Antonio, TX	1,202	1,033	1,007	26	169	14.0	44	26.1
San Diego, CA	1,208	889	866	23	319	26.4	63	19.9
San Francisco, CA	719	462	452	10	258	35.8	39	15.1
San Jose, CA	887	551	540	12	336	37.9	55	16.3

[1] Represents the portion of a consolidated city that is not within one or more separately incorporated places.

Source: U.S. Census Bureau, 2005 American Community Survey; B05002. Place of Birth by Citizenship Status; and B05005. Year of Entry by Citizenship Status; using American FactFinder; ; (accessed: 15 December 2006).

U.S. Census Bureau, Statistical Abstract of the United States: 2008

Table 42. **Native and Foreign-Born Populations by Selected Characteristics: 2006**

[In thousands (293,834 represents 293,834,000). **As of March.** The foreign-born population includes anyone who is not a U.S. citizen at birth. This includes legal permanent residents (immigrants), temporary migrants (such as students), humanitarian migrants (such as refugees), and persons illegally present in the United States. Based on Current Population Survey, Annual Social and Economic Supplement which includes the civilian noninstitutional population plus Armed Forces living off post or with their families on post; see text, this section, and Appendix III]

Characteristic	Total population	Native population	Foreign-born population			
			Total	Natural-ized citizen	Not U.S. citizen	Year of entry: 2000 to March 2006
Total	293,834	258,175	35,659	13,884	21,775	8,927
Under 5 years old	20,363	20,044	319	43	276	319
5 to 14 years old	40,277	38,509	1,769	223	1,545	1,083
15 to 24 years old	41,309	36,945	4,365	905	3,460	2,044
25 to 34 years old	39,481	31,529	7,952	1,740	6,212	2,867
35 to 44 years old	43,121	35,187	7,935	3,035	4,899	1,455
45 to 54 years old	42,797	37,064	5,733	2,927	2,807	621
55 to 64 years old	30,980	27,337	3,644	2,204	1,439	310
65 to 74 years old	18,554	16,330	2,224	1,516	708	149
75 to 84 years old	12,962	11,617	1,345	1,011	334	60
85 years old and over	3,989	3,615	374	279	95	18
Median age (years)	36.3	35.6	39.3	48.3	34.0	28.1
Male	144,188	126,177	18,010	6,593	11,417	4,758
Female	149,647	131,998	17,649	7,291	10,358	4,169
MARITAL STATUS						
Persons 15 years old and over	233,194	199,622	33,571	13,617	19,954	7,524
Married	122,875	102,111	20,763	8,933	11,829	4,015
Widowed	13,935	12,399	1,536	982	554	139
Divorced	22,817	20,761	2,056	1,170	886	235
Separated	4,964	3,983	981	350	631	159
Never married	68,602	60,368	8,235	2,182	6,053	2,977
EDUCATIONAL ATTAINMENT						
Persons 25 years old and over	191,884	162,678	29,206	12,712	16,494	5,480
Not high school graduate	27,896	18,569	9,327	2,714	6,613	1,800
High school graduate/some college	110,269	98,513	11,756	5,649	6,107	1,992
Bachelor's degree	35,153	30,108	5,045	2,752	2,293	1,064
Advanced degree	18,567	15,489	3,078	1,598	1,480	624
EARNINGS IN 2005 [1]						
Persons 15 yrs old and over with earnings	104,851	88,223	16,628	6,988	9,641	3,277
Under $15,000	8,429	6,281	2,149	540	1,609	638
$15,000 to $24,999	19,381	14,970	4,411	1,285	3,125	1,202
$25,000 to $34,999	19,897	16,693	3,204	1,304	1,900	573
$35,000 to $49,999	22,389	19,801	2,588	1,317	1,272	372
$50,000 to $74,999	19,262	17,013	2,250	1,330	919	293
$75,000 and over	15,492	13,465	2,027	1,211	816	199
Median earnings (dollars) [2]	36,911	38,371	30,177	38,072	25,269	22,113
HOUSEHOLD SIZE [3]						
Total households	114,384	99,579	14,806	6,990	7,815	2,510
One person	30,453	27,887	2,566	1,389	1,177	408
Two persons	37,775	34,075	3,700	2,057	1,642	630
Three persons	18,924	16,101	2,823	1,241	1,582	557
Four persons	15,998	13,152	2,846	1,173	1,673	506
Five persons	7,306	5,655	1,651	693	958	220
Six persons	2,562	1,837	725	289	436	107
Seven persons or more	1,366	871	495	147	348	82
INCOME IN 2005 [3]						
Total family households	77,418	65,902	11,516	5,371	6,145	1,815
Under $15,000	6,944	5,686	1,259	440	819	285
$15,000 to $24,999	7,765	6,181	1,584	549	1,036	327
$25,000 to $34,999	8,296	6,780	1,516	585	931	311
$35,000 to $49,999	11,302	9,529	1,773	781	993	243
$50,000 to $74,999	15,753	13,607	2,146	1,046	1,100	313
$75,000 and over	27,358	24,119	3,239	1,972	1,267	336
Median income (dollars) [2]	56,194	58,028	46,307	56,913	38,531	34,238

[1] Covers only year-round full-time workers. [2] For definition of median, see Guide to Tabular Presentation. [3] Based on citizenship of householder.

Source: U.S. Census Bureau, unpublished data.

U.S. Census Bureau, Statistical Abstract of the United States: 2008

Table 43. **Foreign-Born Population—Selected Characteristics by Region of Origin: 2006**

[In thousands (35,659 represents 35,659,000). As of March. The term foreign-born refers to anyone who is not a U.S. citizen at birth. This includes naturalized U.S. citizens, legal permanent residents (immigrants), temporary migrants (such as foreign students), humanitarian migrants (such as refugees), and persons illegally present in the United States. Based on Current Population Survey, Annual Social and Economic Supplement; see text, this section and Appendix III]

Characteristic	Total foreign-born	Europe	Asia	Latin America Total	Carib-bean	Central America [1]	South America	Other areas
Total	35,659	4,340	9,239	19,280	3,169	13,703	2,408	2,799
Under 5 years old.	319	16	91	166	18	143	5	46
5 to 14 years old	1,769	153	387	1,076	129	821	126	152
15 to 24 years old	4,365	327	919	2,774	306	2,160	307	345
25 to 34 years old	7,952	550	1,885	4,962	488	3,979	494	556
35 to 44 years old	7,935	741	2,105	4,467	698	3,238	530	622
45 to 54 years old	5,733	620	1,679	2,919	600	1,862	458	516
55 to 64 years old	3,644	714	1,147	1,512	406	832	274	270
65 to 74 years old	2,224	617	618	841	272	416	153	148
75 to 84 years old	1,345	455	344	432	191	191	52	113
85 years old and over.	374	147	65	131	61	61	9	31
EDUCATIONAL ATTAINMENT								
Persons 25 years old and over . . .	29,206	3,844	7,842	15,264	2,716	10,579	1,969	2,256
Less than ninth grade	6,118	367	677	4,887	441	4,265	180	188
Ninth to twelfth grade (no diploma) . . .	3,209	159	361	2,531	314	2,038	179	158
High school graduate	7,282	1,098	1,664	4,039	893	2,559	586	481
Some college or associate's degree . . .	4,474	770	1,170	1,987	523	1,055	409	547
Bachelor's degree	5,045	831	2,384	1,295	363	512	419	536
Advanced degree	3,078	618	1,586	527	181	150	196	347
High school graduate or more.	19,879	3,317	6,804	7,847	1,960	4,276	1,610	1,911
Bachelor's degree or more.	8,123	1,449	3,970	1,821	545	662	615	883
INCOME IN 2005								
Total family households	11,516	1,467	3,019	6,111	1,098	4,282	731	919
Under $15,000.	1,259	80	243	853	124	678	52	83
$15,000 to $24,999	1,584	132	262	1,102	178	833	91	87
$25,000 to $34,999	1,516	153	201	1,034	181	752	101	127
$35,000 to $49,999	1,773	206	346	1,112	174	811	126	109
$50,000 to $74,999	2,146	327	583	1,078	206	732	139	158
$75,000 and over.	3,239	570	1,383	932	234	476	222	354
Median income (dol.) [2]	46,307	61,337	68,094	35,734	40,200	32,669	49,495	56,865
POVERTY STATUS IN 2005 [3]								
Persons below poverty level	5,870	402	1,107	3,991	466	3,286	239	370
Persons above poverty level	29,751	3,934	8,130	15,258	2,701	10,390	2,166	2,429

[1] Includes Mexico.   [2] For definition of median, see Guide to Tabular Presentation.   [3] Persons for whom poverty status is determined. Excludes unrelated individuals under 15 years old.

Source: U.S. Census Bureau, unpublished data.

Table 44. **Foreign-Born Population by Place of Birth and Citizenship Status: 2005**

[In thousands, except percent (35,689 represents 35,689,000). The term foreign-born refers to anyone who is not a U.S. citizen at birth. This includes naturalized U.S. citizens, legal permanent residents (immigrants), temporary migrants (such as foreign students), humanitarian migrants (such as refugees), and persons illegally present in the United States. The survey universe is limited to the household population and excludes the population living in institutions, college dormitories, and other group quarters. Based on a sample and subject to sampling variability; see text, this section and Appendix III]

Region	Foreign-born population, total	Naturalized citizen	Not U.S. citizen Number	Percent of foreign-born
Total	35,689	14,968	20,722	58
Latin America	19,019	5,834	13,185	69
Caribbean.	3,144	1,699	1,445	46
Central America	13,444	3,168	10,276	76
Mexico	10,970	2,446	8,524	78
Other Central America	2,474	722	1,752	71
South America.	2,431	967	1,464	60
Asia	9,534	5,369	4,165	44
Europe	4,870	2,841	2,029	42
Africa.	1,252	(NA)	(NA)	(NA)
Northern America.	829	(NA)	(NA)	(NA)
Oceania	185	(NA)	(NA)	(NA)

NA Not available.

Source: U.S. Census Bureau, 2005 American Community Survey; C05006. Place of Birth for the Foreign-Born Population; and B05007. Place of Birth by Year of Entry by Citizenship Status for The Foreign-Born Population, using America's FactFinder®; <http://factfinder.census.gov>; (accessed: 20 December 2006).

Table 45. **Persons Obtaining Legal Permanent Resident Status: 1901 to 2006**

[8,795 represents 8,795,000. For fiscal years ending in year shown; see text, Section 8. Rates based on Census Bureau estimates as of July 1 for resident population through 1929 and for total population thereafter (excluding Alaska and Hawaii prior to 1959)]

Period	Number (1,000)	Rate [1]	Year	Number (1,000)	Rate [1]
1901 to 1910	8,795	10.4	1990	1,536	6.1
1911 to 1920	5,736	5.7	1991	1,827	7.2
1921 to 1930	4,107	3.5	1992	973	3.8
			1993	904	3.5
1931 to 1940	528	0.4	1994	804	3.1
1941 to 1950	1,035	0.7	1995	720	2.7
			1996	916	3.4
1951 to 1960	2,515	1.5	1997	798	2.9
1961 to 1970	3,322	1.7	1998	653	2.4
			1999	645	2.3
1971 to 1980	4,399	2.0	2000	841	3.0
1981 to 1990	7,256	3.0	2001	1,059	3.7
			2002	1,059	3.7
1991 to 2000	9,081	3.4	2003	704	2.4
2001 to 2006	6,168	3.5	2004	958	3.3
			2006	1,266	4.2

[1] Annual rate per 1,000 U.S. population. Rate computed by dividing sum of annual immigration totals by sum of annual U.S. population totals for same number of years.

Source: U.S. Department of Homeland Security, Office of Immigration Statistics, *2006 Yearbook of Immigration Statistics*. See also <http://www.dhs.gov/ximgtn/statistics/publications/yearbook.shtm>.

Table 46. **Estimated Unauthorized Immigrants by Selected States and Countries of Origin: 2000 and 2005**

[8,460 represents 8,460,000. As of January. Unauthorized immigrants refers to foreign-born persons who entered the United States without inspection or who were admitted temporarily and stayed past the date they were required to leave. Unauthorized aliens who have applied for but have not yet received approval to lawfully remain in the United States are considered to be unauthorized. These estimates were calculated using a "residual method," whereby estimates of the legally resident foreign-born population were subtracted from the total foreign-born population in order to derive the unauthorized immigrant population. All of these component populations were resident in the United States on January 1, 2005, and entered during the 1980–2004 period. Persons who entered the United States prior to 1980 were assumed to be legally resident. Estimates of the legally resident foreign-born were based primarily on administrative data of the Department of Homeland Security, while estimates of the total foreign-born population were obtained from the American Community Survey of the U.S. Census Bureau. Estimates for 2000 are based on the same methodology, assumptions, and definitions with the exception that data from Census 2000 were used to estimate the foreign-born population in 2000 that entered the United States from January 1, 1980, through December 31, 1999]

State	2000 (1,000)	2005 (1,000)	Country	2000 (1,000)	2005 (1,000)
United States, total	8,460	10,500	Total	8,460	10,500
California	2,510	2,770	Mexico	4,680	5,970
Texas	1,090	1,360	El Salvador	430	470
Florida	800	850	Guatemala	290	370
New York	540	560	India	120	280
Illinois	440	520	China	190	230
Arizona	330	480	Korea	180	210
Georgia	220	470	Philippines	200	210
New Jersey	350	380	Honduras	160	180
North Carolina	260	360	Brazil	100	170
Nevada	170	240	Vietnam	160	160
Other states	1,750	2,510	Other countries	1,950	2,250

Source: U.S. Department of Homeland Security, Office of Immigration Statistics, "Estimates of the Unauthorized Immigrant Population Residing in the United States: January 2005"; published August 2006; <http://www.dhs.gov/xlibrary/assets/statistics /publications/ILLPE2005.pdf>.

Table 47. Persons Obtaining Legal Permanent Resident Status by Class of Admission: 2000 to 2006

[For years ending **September 30**. For definition of immigrants, see text of this section]

Class of admission	2000	2002	2003	2004	2005	2006
Total	841,002	1,059,356	703,542	957,883	1,122,373	1,266,264
New arrivals.	407,279	384,289	358,333	373,962	384,071	447,016
Adjustments.	433,723	675,067	345,209	583,921	738,302	819,248
Family-sponsored preferences.	235,092	186,880	158,796	214,355	212,970	222,229
Unmarried sons/daughters of U.S. citizens and their children	27,635	23,517	21,471	26,380	24,729	25,432
Spouses, unmarried sons/daughters of alien residents and their children	124,540	84,785	53,195	93,609	100,139	112,051
Married sons/daughters of U.S. citizens [1].	22,804	21,041	27,287	28,695	22,953	21,491
Brothers or sisters of U.S. citizens [1]	60,113	57,537	56,843	65,671	65,149	63,255
Employment-based preferences	106,642	173,814	81,727	155,330	246,878	159,081
Priority workers [1]	27,566	34,168	14,453	31,291	64,731	36,960
Professionals with advanced degrees or aliens of exceptional ability [1]	20,255	44,316	15,406	32,534	42,597	21,911
Skilled workers, professionals, unskilled workers [1]	49,589	88,002	46,415	85,969	129,070	89,922
Special immigrants [1]	9,014	7,186	5,389	5,407	10,134	9,539
Employment creation (investors) [1]	218	142	64	129	346	749
Immediate relatives of U.S. citizens	346,350	483,676	331,286	417,815	436,231	580,483
Spouses	196,405	293,219	183,796	252,193	259,144	339,843
Children [2]	82,638	96,941	77,948	88,088	94,974	120,199
Parents	67,307	93,516	69,542	77,534	82,113	120,441
Refugees	56,091	115,601	34,362	61,013	112,676	99,609
Asylees.	6,837	10,197	10,402	10,217	30,286	116,845
Diversity [3]	50,920	42,820	46,335	50,084	46,234	44,471
Cancellation of removal	12,154	23,642	28,990	32,702	20,785	29,516
Parolees	3,162	6,018	4,196	7,121	7,715	4,569
Nicaraguan Adjustment and Central American Relief Act (NACARA)	20,364	9,307	2,498	2,292	1,155	661
Haitian Refugee Immigration Fairness Act (HRIFA) . . .	435	5,345	1,406	2,451	2,820	3,375
Other	2,955	2,056	3,544	4,503	4,623	5,425

[1] Includes spouses and children.   [2] Includes orphans.   [3] Includes categories of immigrants admitted under three laws intended to diversify immigration: P.L. 99-603, P.L. 100-658, and P.L. 101-649.

Source: U.S. Dept. of Homeland Security, Office of Immigration Statistics, *2006 Yearbook of Immigration Statistics*. See also <http://www.dhs.gov/ximgtn/statistics/publications/yearbook.shtm>.

Table 48. Persons Obtaining Legal Permanent Resident Status by Selected Country of Birth and Selected Characteristics: 2005

[For year ending September 30]

Age, marital status, class of admission	Total [1]	Mexico	India	China	Philip- pines	Cuba	Viet- nam	Domini- can Republic	Korea
Total	1,122,373	161,445	84,681	69,967	60,748	36,261	32,784	27,504	26,562
Under 18 years.	231,527	34,021	11,343	16,636	12,870	5,451	5,891	10,218	6,831
18 to 24 years	139,345	24,879	7,070	5,374	6,172	3,371	4,747	4,614	1,940
25 to 34 years	295,638	43,909	33,247	13,250	14,594	8,731	9,036	4,234	5,074
35 to 44 years	225,049	30,741	15,026	16,144	11,152	9,054	6,292	3,932	6,957
45 to 54 years	117,663	13,269	8,355	9,360	6,911	4,140	3,884	2,219	3,641
55 to 64 years	63,343	7,714	5,677	4,636	5,139	2,797	1,897	1,232	1,062
65 years and over	49,789	6,909	3,958	4,566	3,908	2,717	1,037	1,055	1,057
Unknown	19	3	5	1	2	–	–	–	–
Single	421,335	59,421	19,292	23,250	23,884	14,078	13,087	18,445	9,627
Married	650,829	97,044	62,709	44,309	34,328	16,646	18,064	8,177	16,032
Other	45,594	4,589	2,490	2,302	2,456	5,270	1,481	816	854
Unknown	4,615	391	190	106	80	267	.152	66	49
Family-sponsored preferences. . . .	212,970	65,369	15,256	17,082	14,975	1,478	12,220	15,813	1,997
Employment-based preferences. . . .	246,877	16,347	47,705	20,626	18,332	18	304	444	15,929
Immediate relatives of U.S. citizens	436,231	72,435	19,108	26,852	27,157	1,759	11,379	11,134	8,598
Diversity programs.	46,234	11	60	32	6	371	5	6	8
Refugee and asylee adjustments	142,962	240	2,331	5,335	85	32,555	5,818	49	7
Other	37,099	7,043	221	40	193	80	3,058	58	23

– Represents zero.   [1] Includes other countries not shown separately.

Source: U.S. Department of Homeland Security, Office of Immigration Statistics, "Profiles on Legal Permanent Residents: 2005"; published 27 October 2006; <http://www.dhs.gov/ximgtn/statistics/data/DSLPR05c.shtm>.

[In thousands (7,256.0 represents 7,256,000). For years ending Sept. 30. Persons by country prior to 1996 are unrevised]

Country of birth	1981–1990, total	1991–2000, total	2001–2005, total	2006	Country of birth	1981–1990, total	1991–2000, total	2001–2005, total	2006
All countries [1]	7,256.0	9,080.5	4,902.1	1,266.3	Philippines	495.3	505.3	267.8	74.6
Europe [1]	705.6	1,309.1	758.1	164.3	Syria	20.6	26.1	12.9	2.9
Albania	(NA)	26.2	21.3	7.9	Taiwan	(6)	106.3	47.0	8.1
Armenia	(X)	[2]26.6	9.3	6.3	Thailand	64.4	48.4	21.3	11.8
Belarus	(X)	[2]28.9	13.4	3.1	Turkey	20.9	26.3	18.1	4.9
Bosnia and Herzegovina	(X)	[2]38.8	79.7	3.8	Vietnam	401.4	420.8	155.4	30.7
Bulgaria	(NA)	23.1	21.7	4.8	Africa [1]	192.3	382.5	314.0	117.4
France	23.1	27.4	18.7	4.3	Egypt	31.4	46.7	26.8	10.5
Germany	70.1	67.6	40.1	8.4	Ethiopia	27.2	49.3	38.2	16.2
Ireland	32.8	58.9	7.5	1.9	Ghana	14.9	35.6	24.5	9.4
Italy	32.9	22.5	12.7	3.2	Nigeria	35.3	67.2	44.2	13.5
Poland	97.4	169.5	64.7	17.1	Somalia	(NA)	20.1	19.7	9.5
Portugal	40.0	22.7	5.9	1.4	Oceania	(NA)	47.9	28.5	7.4
Romania	38.9	57.5	26.8	7.1	North America [1]	3,125.0	3,910.1	1,746.6	414.1
Russia	(X)	[2]127.8	90.5	13.2	Canada	119.2	137.2	89.9	18.2
Serbia and Montenegro [3, 4]	19.2	25.8	28.1	5.9	Mexico	1,653.3	2,250.5	876.8	173.8
Soviet Union [3]	84.0	[2]103.8	10.0	6.2	Cuba	159.2	178.7	121.6	45.6
Ukraine	(X)	[2]141.0	90.7	17.1	Dominican Republic	251.8	340.8	127.9	38.1
United Kingdom	142.1	[2]135.6	78.8	17.2	Haiti	140.2	181.7	88.3	22.2
Uzbekistan	(X)	[2]22.9	10.7	4.0	Jamaica	213.8	173.4	76.3	25.0
Asia [1]	2,817.4	2,890.2	1,667.3	422.3	Trinidad and Tobago	39.5	63.2	28.4	8.9
Bangladesh	15.2	66.0	36.8	14.6	El Salvador	214.6	217.3	141.5	31.8
Cambodia	116.6	18.5	15.1	5.8	Guatemala	87.9	103.0	79.8	24.1
China [5]	[6]388.8	424.4	283.4	87.3	Honduras	49.5	66.7	30.2	8.2
Hong Kong	63.0	74.0	25.6	3.3	Nicaragua	44.1	94.6	41.7	4.1
India	261.9	383.0	345.9	61.4	Panama	29.0	24.0	7.9	2.4
Iran	154.8	112.5	54.9	13.9	South America [1]	455.9	539.3	372.9	138.0
Iraq	19.6	40.7	20.2	4.3	Argentina	25.7	24.3	22.0	7.3
Israel	36.3	31.9	20.2	5.9	Brazil	23.7	52.2	52.4	17.9
Japan [7]	43.2	61.4	40.3	8.3	Colombia	124.4	130.8	94.5	43.2
Jordan [7]	32.6	39.7	18.6	4.0	Ecuador	56.0	76.3	47.5	17.5
Korea	338.8	171.1	100.0	24.4	Guyana	95.4	73.8	40.7	9.6
Laos	145.6	43.5	5.9	2.9	Peru	64.4	105.6	59.9	21.7
Lebanon	41.6	43.4	19.6	4.1	Venezuela	17.9	29.9	31.3	11.3
Pakistan	61.3	124.5	66.5	17.4					

NA Not available.   X Not applicable.   [1] Includes countries not shown separately.   [2] Covers years 1992–2000.   [3] Prior to 1992, data include independent republics; beginning in 1992, data are for unknown republic only.   [4] Yugoslavia (unknown republic) prior to February 7, 2003.   [5] See footnote 2, Table 1298.   [6] Data for Taiwan included with China.   [7] Prior to 2003, includes Palestine; beginning in 2003, Palestine included in Unknown.

Source: U.S. Department of Homeland Security, Office of Immigration Statistics, *2006 Yearbook of Immigration Statistics*. See also <http://www.dhs.gov/ximgtn/statistics/publications/yearbook.shtm>.

Table 50. **Refugee Arrivals and Individuals Granted Asylum by Country of Birth: 1991 to 2006**

[For years ending September 30]

Country of birth	1991–2000, total	2001–2005, total	2006	Country of birth	1991–2000, total	2001–2005, total	2006
Total [1]	1,016,820	492,735	216,454	India	2,538	7,514	6,841
Europe [1]	425,047	207,187	35,689	Iran	24,251	18,625	6,316
Albania	3,250	2,048	3,542	Iraq	22,488	11,604	2,540
Armenia	1,794	1,731	4,585	Laos	37,203	1,621	1,628
Azerbaijan	[2]10,566	2,577	1,761	Pakistan	1,649	2,530	2,408
Belarus	[2]21,592	5,803	1,202	Thailand	22,716	2,010	5,539
Bosnia and Herzegovina	[2]37,251	77,439	2,744	Vietnam	206,530	27,419	1,832
Croatia	1,786	8,804	407	Africa [1]	51,469	65,601	44,808
Germany	1,294	4,746	271	Ethiopia [5]	17,829	9,322	7,595
Kazakhstan	[2]3,799	2,384	560	Kenya	1,438	2,049	3,412
Moldova	[2]10,150	6,086	1,971	Liberia	3,836	8,448	4,989
Poland	7,451	245	49	Sierra Leone	272	3,993	2,260
Romania	15,682	539	362	Somalia	16,737	17,819	9,045
Russia	[2]54,488	19,467	4,146	Sudan	5,174	10,803	4,711
Serbia and Montenegro [3, 4]	6,242	18,900	3,194	Oceania	291	153	678
Soviet Union [3]	117,783	4,579	605	North America [1]	183,251	113,632	51,031
Ukraine	[2]96,974	42,426	5,934	Cuba	142,571	103,525	40,985
Uzbekistan	[2]17,991	3,770	1,700	El Salvador	4,072	1,395	878
Asia [1]	350,702	97,388	67,011	Haiti	9,354	3,623	6,101
Afghanistan	9,711	7,478	2,534	Nicaragua	22,468	1,142	303
Cambodia	6,358	553	426	South America [1]	5,840	8,124	16,857
China	7,577	8,506	27,454	Colombia	1,129	2,702	12,591
				Peru	2,500	2,473	1,644

[1] Includes other countries and unknown, not shown separately.   [2] Covers years 1992–2000.   [3] Prior to 1992, data include independent republics; beginning in 1992, data are for unknown republic only.   [4] Yugoslavia (unknown republic) prior to February 7, 2003.   [5] Prior to 1993, data include Eritrea.

Source: U.S. Department of Homeland Security, Office of Immigration Statistics, *2006 Yearbook of Immigration Statistics*. See also <http://www.dhs.gov/ximgtn/statistics/publications/yearbook.shtm>.

Population   47

Table 51. **Population by Selected Ancestry Group and Region: 2005**

[In thousands (288,378 represents 288,378,000). Covers single and multiple ancestries. Ancestry refers to a person's ethnic origin or descent, roots, or heritage; or the place of birth of the person, the person's parents, or ancestors before their arrival in the United States. The American Community Survey universe is limited to the household population and excludes the population living in institutions, college dormitories, and other group quarters. Based on a sample and subject to sampling variability; see text, this section and Appendix III. For composition of regions, see map, inside front cover]

Ancestry group	Total (1,000)	North-east	Mid-west	South	West	Ancestry group	Total (1,000)	North-east	Mid-west	South	West
Total population [1]	**288,378**	**18**	**22**	**36**	**23**	Irish	34,669	26	25	31	18
Afghan	70	17	5	31	46	Israeli	126	39	9	22	30
Albanian	151	60	23	12	5	Italian	17,235	45	17	21	16
American.	20,536	11	20	55	14	Latvian	88	34	25	20	21
Arab [1]	1,400	25	25	27	22	Lithuanian	712	39	29	18	14
Egyptian	179	40	11	25	25	Northern European .	196	13	21	23	43
Jordanian	54	18	29	23	30	Norwegian.	4,601	6	49	12	33
Lebanese.	464	23	28	30	19	Pennsylvania					
Moroccan.	62	34	11	39	17	German.	324	57	23	12	8
Palestinian	66	12	26	33	29	Polish.	9,771	33	38	17	12
Syrian	155	39	20	21	20	Portuguese	1,379	47	3	13	37
Arab	264	18	34	26	22	Romanian	453	27	26	20	27
Armenian	421	22	9	8	60	Russian	3,010	37	17	21	25
Assyrian/						Scandinavian.	572	9	31	17	43
Chaldean/Syriac . .	72	4	55	3	38	Scotch-Irish	5,289	15	18	46	21
Australian	90	21	14	26	39	Scottish	5,859	17	20	36	26
Austrian	781	30	24	22	24	Serbian.	169	18	47	15	20
Basque.	60	7	4	8	82	Slavic	137	31	26	22	21
Belgian	382	11	55	18	16	Slovak	819	45	34	14	8
Brazilian	304	52	4	33	11	Slovene	173	16	58	12	15
British.	1,284	16	17	40	28	Subsaharan					
Bulgarian.	90	22	26	25	26	African [1]	2,263	24	18	43	16
Cajun	117	3	4	87	6	Cape Verdean . .	81	85	2	8	5
Canadian	714	27	17	27	29	Ethiopian	128	9	16	39	36
Celtic	59	20	13	37	30	Ghanian	61	42	12	36	11
Croatian	401	25	40	14	21	Nigerian.	200	26	15	43	16
Czech.	1,556	12	45	25	17	Somalian	74	9	59	16	16
Czechoslovakian . .	327	24	33	24	19	South African . . .	53	18	12	41	29
Danish	1,434	9	33	14	45	African	1,459	21	18	47	14
Dutch	5,079	16	35	27	21	Swedish	4,260	14	39	16	31
Eastern European. .	357	45	13	21	21	Swiss	1,017	16	35	20	30
English	27,762	17	21	37	24	Turkish	165	35	15	28	22
European	2,527	13	20	32	35	Ukrainian	963	42	20	17	21
Finnish	646	12	47	13	29	Welsh.	1,928	20	23	29	28
French (except						West Indian [1, 2]	2,233	49	4	42	4
Basque)	9,530	25	24	32	20	British West					
French						Indian	93	71	2	24	3
Canadian.	2,266	41	21	23	15	Dutch West					
German	49,179	16	39	25	19	Indian	58	4	8	76	12
Greek	1,291	34	24	23	19	Haitian.	694	44	2	52	2
Guyanese	205	75	3	20	3	Jamaican.	843	50	5	41	4
Hungarian	1,522	32	31	20	17	Trinidadian and					
Icelander.	51	6	25	18	51	Tobagonian. . . .	153	64	3	30	4
Iranian	378	13	9	25	53	West Indian . . .	260	66	3	26	5
						Yugoslavian.	372	19	33	21	27

[1] Includes other groups not shown separately.   [2] Excludes Hispanic-origin groups.

Source: U.S. Census Bureau, 2005 American Community Survey: B04006. People Reporting Ancestry; using American FactFinder; <http://factfinder.census.gov/>; (accessed: 20 December 2006).

Table 52. **Languages Spoken at Home by Language: 2005**

[**268,111 represents 268,111,000**. The American Community Survey universe is limited to the household population and excludes the population living in institutions, college dormitories, and other group quarters. Based on a sample and subject to sampling variability; see text of this section and Appendix III]

Language	Number (1,000)	Language	Number (1,000)
Total population 5 yrs. old and over . .	**268,111**	Other Indic languages.	586
Speak only English.	216,176	Other Indo-European languages	385
Spanish or Spanish Creole.	32,184	Chinese	2,300
French (incl. Patois, Cajun)	1,383	Japanese	458
French Creole	549	Korean	984
Italian.	802	Mon-Khmer, Cambodian	189
Portuguese or Portuguese Creole	662	Hmong.	174
German	1,120	Thai.	130
Yiddish	137	Laotian.	152
Other West Germanic languages.	275	Vietnamese	1,142
Scandinavian languages	129	Other Asian languages	544
Greek	324	Tagalog	1,377
Russian	812	Other Pacific Island languages	319
Polish.	608	Navajo	173
Serbo-Croatian	271	Other Native North American languages. . .	207
Other Slavic languages	316		
Armenian	203	Hungarian	99
Persian.	326	Arabic	687
Gujarathi.	276	Hebrew	190
Hindi	462	African languages	582
Urdu	303	Other and unspecified languages	114

Source: U.S. Census Bureau, 2005 American Community Survey: C16001. Language Spoken at Home by Ability to Speak English for the Population 5 Years and Over; using American FactFinder; <http://factfinder.census.gov/>; (accessed: 3 January 2007).

Table 53. Language Spoken at Home by State: 2005

[268,111 represents 268,111,000. The American Community Survey universe is limited to the household population and excludes the population living in institutions, college dormitories, and other group quarters. Based on a sample and subject to sampling variability; see text, this section and Appendix III]

State	Population 5 years and over (1,000)	English only (1,000)	Language other than English — Number (1,000)	Language other than English — Percent of population 5 years and over	State	Population 5 years and over (1,000)	English only (1,000)	Language other than English — Number (1,000)	Language other than English — Percent of population 5 years and over
U.S.. .	268,111	216,176	51,935	19.4	MO	5,253	4,973	280	5.3
AL.	4,150	3,978	173	4.2	MT.	857	821	36	4.2
AK.	593	512	80	13.6	NE.	1,584	1,441	143	9.0
AZ.	5,370	3,900	1,470	27.4	NV.	2,208	1,630	579	26.2
AR.	2,515	2,366	149	5.9	NH.	1,199	1,095	104	8.7
CA.	32,599	18,808	13,791	42.3	NJ.	7,940	5,765	2,175	27.4
CO.	4,224	3,506	718	17.0	NM.	1,756	1,122	634	36.1
CT.	3,184	2,579	604	19.0	NY.	17,408	12,496	4,912	28.2
DE.	763	675	88	11.5	NC.	7,810	7,088	722	9.2
DC.	477	403	75	15.7	ND.	573	541	33	5.7
FL.	16,270	12,142	4,128	25.4	OH.	10,420	9,784	636	6.1
GA.	8,126	7,184	941	11.6	OK.	3,188	2,932	257	8.1
HI	1,148	873	275	24.0	OR.	3,334	2,870	464	13.9
ID	1,290	1,165	125	9.7	PA.	11,254	10,226	1,027	9.1
IL.	11,541	9,064	2,477	21.5	RI	969	772	197	20.3
IN	5,663	5,252	411	7.3	SC.	3,836	3,611	225	5.9
IA	2,679	2,514	165	6.2	SD.	692	650	42	6.0
KS.	2,475	2,242	233	9.4	TN	5,422	5,119	303	5.6
KY.	3,787	3,639	148	3.9	TX	20,404	13,557	6,847	33.6
LA.	4,071	3,729	342	8.4	UT.	2,191	1,887	304	13.9
ME.	1,217	1,125	92	7.6	VT.	570	541	29	5.1
MD.	5,080	4,344	735	14.5	VA.	6,827	5,962	865	12.7
MA.	5,788	4,612	1,176	20.3	WA	5,751	4,831	920	16.0
MI	9,214	8,396	818	8.9	WV	1,673	1,636	37	2.2
MN.	4,653	4,215	437	9.4	WI	5,036	4,631	405	8.0
MS.	2,614	2,534	80	3.1	WY	464	437	27	5.9

Source: U.S. Census Bureau, 2005 American Community Survey; C16005. Nativity by Language Spoken at Home by Ability to Speak English for the Population 5 Years and Over; using American FactFinder; <http://factfinder.census.gov/>; (accessed 3 January 2007).

Table 54. Language Spoken at Home—25 Largest Cities: 2005

[622 represents 622,000. The American Community Survey universe is limited to the household population and excludes the population living in institutions, college dormitories, and other group quarters. Based on a sample and subject to sampling variability; see text, this section and Appendix III]

City	Population 5 years and over (1,000)	English only (1,000)	Language other than English, total [1] — Number (1,000)	Language other than English, total [1] — Percent of population 5 years and over	Language other than English, total [1] — Speak English less than "very well" (1,000)	Spanish (1,000)	Other Indo-European languages (1,000)	Asian and Pacific Island languages (1,000)
Austin, TX.	622	416	206	33.2	88	163	16	24
Baltimore, MD	561	516	45	8.0	16	17	14	7
Charlotte, NC	551	457	94	17.0	49	54	21	14
Chicago, IL	2,486	1,557	929	37.4	459	646	180	77
Columbus, OH.	633	556	77	12.1	32	24	17	18
Dallas, TX.	1,033	579	453	43.9	258	400	21	22
Denver, CO.	494	340	154	31.1	78	124	14	10
Detroit, MI.	774	697	77	9.9	44	44	11	4
El Paso, TX.	527	141	386	73.2	149	376	6	4
Fort Worth, TX.	547	381	166	30.4	88	140	8	16
Houston, TX	1,768	938	830	46.9	453	679	59	72
Indianapolis, IN [2]	699	631	68	9.8	36	45	13	8
Jacksonville, FL.	706	630	76	10.8	29	33	21	19
Las Vegas, NV	496	344	152	30.7	79	118	14	17
Los Angeles, CA	3,444	1,349	2,095	60.8	1,079	1,526	232	289
Louisville-Jefferson County, KY [2]	508	477	31	6.0	13	15	10	5
Memphis, TN.	589	540	49	8.3	24	30	6	8
Milwaukee, WI.	509	412	96	18.9	44	66	12	14
New York, NY	7,367	3,873	3,494	47.4	1,669	1,809	971	549
Philadelphia, PA.	1,297	1,039	258	19.9	118	121	70	52
Phoenix, AZ	1,257	791	465	37.0	242	408	24	15
San Antonio, TX.	1,101	607	494	44.8	179	465	13	14
San Diego, CA.	1,115	705	410	36.8	193	231	45	121
San Francisco, CA	679	367	312	46.0	163	80	42	185
San Jose, CA	814	366	447	55.0	209	189	52	196

[1] Includes other language groups not shown separately. [2] Represents the portion of a consolidated city that is not within one or more separately incorporated places.

Source: U.S. Census Bureau, 2005 American Community Survey; B16005. Nativity by Language Spoken at Home by Ability to Speak English for the Population 5 Years and Over; using American FactFinder; <http://factfinder.census.gov/>; (accessed 4 January 2007).

Population   49

Table 55. Marital Status of the Population by Sex, Race, and Hispanic Origin: 1990 to 2006

[In millions, except percent (181.8 represents 181,800,000). As of March. Persons 18 years old and over. Excludes members of Armed Forces except those living off post or with their families on post. Beginning 2005 population controls based on Census 2000 and an expanded sample of households. Based on Current Population Survey, see text of this section, and Appendix III]

Marital status, race, and Hispanic origin	Total				Male				Female			
	1990	2000	2005	2006	1990	2000	2005	2006	1990	2000	2005	2006
Total [1]	181.8	201.8	217.2	219.7	86.9	96.9	104.8	106.3	95.0	104.9	112.3	113.4
Never married	40.4	48.2	53.9	55.3	22.4	26.1	29.6	30.3	17.9	22.1	24.3	25.0
Married [2]	112.6	120.1	127.4	127.7	55.8	59.6	63.3	63.6	56.7	60.4	64.0	64.1
Widowed	13.8	13.7	13.8	13.9	2.3	2.6	2.7	2.6	11.5	11.1	11.1	11.3
Divorced	15.1	19.8	22.1	22.8	6.3	8.5	9.2	9.7	8.8	11.3	12.9	13.1
Percent of total	100.0	100.0	100.0	100.0	100.0	100.0	100.0	100.0	100.0	100.0	100.0	100.0
Never married	22.2	23.9	24.8	25.2	25.8	27.0	28.2	28.6	18.9	21.1	21.6	22.0
Married [2]	61.9	59.5	58.6	58.1	64.3	61.5	60.4	59.9	59.7	57.6	56.9	56.5
Widowed	7.6	6.8	6.4	6.3	2.7	2.7	2.6	2.5	12.1	10.5	9.9	9.9
Divorced	8.3	9.8	10.2	10.4	7.2	8.8	8.8	9.1	9.3	10.8	11.5	11.6
White, total [3]	155.5	168.1	177.5	179.2	74.8	81.6	86.6	87.6	80.6	86.6	90.9	91.6
Never married	31.6	36.0	39.7	40.5	18.0	20.3	22.6	23.1	13.6	15.7	17.0	17.4
Married [2]	99.5	104.1	108.3	108.6	49.5	51.8	54.0	54.3	49.9	52.2	54.2	54.3
Widowed	11.7	11.5	11.5	11.5	1.9	2.2	2.3	2.2	9.8	9.3	9.2	9.4
Divorced	12.6	16.5	18.1	18.5	5.4	7.2	7.6	8.0	7.3	9.3	10.4	10.5
Percent of total	100.0	100.0	100.0	100.0	100.0	100.0	100.0	100.0	100.0	100.0	100.0	100.0
Never married	20.3	21.4	22.3	22.6	24.1	24.9	26.1	26.3	16.9	18.1	18.7	19.0
Married [2]	64.0	62.0	61.0	60.6	66.2	63.5	62.4	62.0	61.9	60.3	59.7	59.2
Widowed	7.5	6.8	6.5	6.4	2.6	2.7	2.6	2.5	12.2	10.8	10.2	10.2
Divorced	8.1	9.8	10.2	10.3	7.2	8.8	8.8	9.1	9.0	10.7	11.5	11.5
Black, total [3]	20.3	24.0	25.2	25.6	9.1	10.7	11.2	11.5	11.2	13.3	13.9	14.1
Never married	7.1	9.5	10.2	10.5	3.5	4.3	4.7	4.9	3.6	5.1	5.5	5.6
Married [2]	9.3	10.1	10.3	10.3	4.5	5.0	5.0	5.1	4.8	5.1	5.2	5.2
Widowed	1.7	1.7	1.7	1.8	0.3	0.3	0.3	0.3	1.4	1.4	1.4	1.4
Divorced	2.1	2.8	2.9	3.1	0.8	1.1	1.1	1.2	1.3	1.7	1.8	1.9
Percent of total	100.0	100.0	100.0	100.0	100.0	100.0	100.0	100.0	100.0	100.0	100.0	100.0
Never married	35.1	39.4	40.6	40.8	38.4	40.2	42.0	42.5	32.5	38.3	39.5	39.5
Married [2]	45.8	42.1	41.0	40.1	49.2	46.7	45.5	44.4	43.0	38.3	37.4	36.7
Widowed	8.5	7.0	6.6	6.9	3.7	2.8	2.7	2.9	12.4	10.5	10.0	10.1
Divorced	10.6	11.5	11.7	12.1	8.8	10.3	9.8	10.2	12.0	12.8	13.3	13.7
Asian, total [3]	(NA)	(NA)	9.4	9.7	(NA)	(NA)	4.5	4.6	(NA)	(NA)	4.9	5.1
Never married	(NA)	(NA)	2.3	2.6	(NA)	(NA)	1.3	1.5	(NA)	(NA)	1.0	1.1
Married [2]	(NA)	(NA)	6.2	6.2	(NA)	(NA)	2.9	2.9	(NA)	(NA)	3.3	3.3
Widowed	(NA)	(NA)	0.4	0.4	(NA)	(NA)	0.1	0.1	(NA)	(NA)	0.3	0.3
Divorced	(NA)	(NA)	0.5	0.5	(NA)	(NA)	0.2	0.2	(NA)	(NA)	0.3	0.3
Percent of total	100.0	100.0	100.0	100.0	100.0	100.0	100.0	100.0	100.0	100.0	100.0	100.0
Never married	(NA)	(NA)	24.8	26.8	(NA)	(NA)	29.7	31.6	(NA)	(NA)	20.3	22.5
Married [2]	(NA)	(NA)	65.6	64.3	(NA)	(NA)	64.7	63.2	(NA)	(NA)	66.5	65.2
Widowed	(NA)	(NA)	4.3	4.0	(NA)	(NA)	1.3	1.2	(NA)	(NA)	6.7	6.6
Divorced	(NA)	(NA)	5.3	4.9	(NA)	(NA)	4.1	4.0	(NA)	(NA)	6.4	5.8
Hispanic, total [4]	13.6	21.1	27.5	28.3	6.7	10.4	14.1	14.6	6.8	10.7	13.4	13.7
Never married	3.7	5.9	8.6	8.5	2.2	3.4	5.2	5.1	1.5	2.5	3.4	3.4
Married [2]	8.4	12.7	15.6	16.6	4.1	6.2	7.8	8.4	4.3	6.5	7.8	8.2
Widowed	0.5	0.9	1.0	1.0	0.1	0.2	0.2	0.2	0.4	0.7	0.8	0.8
Divorced	1.0	1.6	2.2	2.2	0.4	0.7	0.9	0.9	0.6	1.0	1.3	1.3
Percent of total	100.0	100.0	100.0	100.0	100.0	100.0	100.0	100.0	100.0	100.0	100.0	100.0
Never married	27.2	28.0	31.3	30.1	32.1	32.3	36.7	35.1	22.5	23.4	25.6	24.7
Married [2]	61.7	60.2	57.0	58.4	60.9	59.7	55.6	57.4	62.4	60.7	58.7	59.6
Widowed	4.0	4.2	3.7	3.6	1.5	1.6	1.5	1.3	6.5	6.5	6.1	5.9
Divorced	7.0	7.6	7.9	7.9	5.5	6.4	6.3	6.2	8.5	9.3	9.7	9.8
Non-Hispanic White, total [3,4]	(NA)	(NA)	151.9	152.9	(NA)	(NA)	73.4	74.0	(NA)	(NA)	78.5	78.9
Never married	(NA)	(NA)	31.8	32.8	(NA)	(NA)	17.8	18.3	(NA)	(NA)	13.9	14.4
Married [2]	(NA)	(NA)	93.5	93.1	(NA)	(NA)	46.6	46.5	(NA)	(NA)	47.0	46.6
Widowed	(NA)	(NA)	10.6	10.6	(NA)	(NA)	2.1	2.1	(NA)	(NA)	8.5	8.6
Divorced	(NA)	(NA)	16.0	16.5	(NA)	(NA)	6.8	7.2	(NA)	(NA)	9.2	9.3
Percent of total	100.0	100.0	100.0	100.0	100.0	100.0	100.0	100.0	100.0	100.0	100.0	100.0
Never married	(NA)	(NA)	20.9	21.4	(NA)	(NA)	24.3	24.8	(NA)	(NA)	17.7	18.3
Married [2]	(NA)	(NA)	61.5	60.8	(NA)	(NA)	63.5	62.8	(NA)	(NA)	59.7	59.1
Widowed	(NA)	(NA)	6.9	6.9	(NA)	(NA)	2.8	2.7	(NA)	(NA)	10.8	10.9
Divorced	(NA)	(NA)	10.6	10.8	(NA)	(NA)	9.3	9.7	(NA)	(NA)	11.7	11.8

NA Not available. [1] Includes persons of other races, not shown separately. [2] Includes persons who are married with spouse present, married with spouse absent, and separated. [3] 2005 and 2006 data represent persons who selected this race group only and exclude persons reporting more than one race. The CPS in 1990 and 2000 only allowed respondents to report one race group. See also comments on race in the text for this section. [4] Hispanic persons may be any race.

Source: U.S. Census Bureau, *Current Population Reports*, P20-537, and earlier reports; and "Families and Living Arrangements"; <http://www.census.gov/population/www/socdemo/hh-fam.html>.

Table 56. Marital Status of the Population by Sex and Age: 2006

[As of March (106,256 represents 106,256,000). Excludes members of Armed Forces except those living off post or with their families on post. Population controls based on Census 2000 and an expanded sample of households. Based on Current Population Survey, see text, this section, and Appendix III]

Sex and age	Number of persons (1,000)					Percent distribution				
	Total	Never married	Married [1]	Widowed	Divorced	Total	Never married	Married [1]	Widowed	Divorced
Male	**106,256**	**30,345**	**63,632**	**2,623**	**9,654**	**100.0**	**28.6**	**59.9**	**2.5**	**9.1**
18 to 19 years old	3,795	3,710	83	2	2	100.0	97.8	2.1	–	–
20 to 24 years old	10,305	8,931	1,282	13	80	100.0	86.7	12.5	0.1	0.8
25 to 29 years old	10,185	5,843	4,021	9	312	100.0	57.4	39.5	0.1	3.1
30 to 34 years old	9,639	3,223	5,849	12	555	100.0	33.4	60.6	0.1	5.8
35 to 39 years old	10,305	2,396	6,914	21	973	100.0	23.3	67.1	0.2	9.4
40 to 44 years old	11,039	2,045	7,575	62	1,356	100.0	18.5	68.6	0.6	12.3
45 to 54 years old	20,957	2,594	15,030	196	3,137	100.0	12.4	71.7	0.9	15.0
55 to 64 years old	14,856	1,030	11,497	323	2,005	100.0	6.9	77.4	2.2	13.5
65 to 74 years old	8,518	350	6,681	621	867	100.0	4.1	78.5	7.3	10.2
75 years old and over . . .	6,657	223	4,700	1,365	368	100.0	3.3	70.6	20.5	5.5
Female	**113,443**	**24,994**	**64,062**	**11,284**	**13,104**	**100.0**	**22.0**	**56.5**	**9.9**	**11.6**
18 to 19 years old	3,766	3,565	184	5	13	100.0	94.7	4.8	0.1	0.3
20 to 24 years old	10,075	7,589	2,317	17	152	100.0	75.3	23.0	0.2	1.5
25 to 29 years old	9,953	4,289	5,096	43	526	100.0	43.1	51.3	0.4	5.3
30 to 34 years old	9,700	2,327	6,543	52	778	100.0	24.0	67.5	0.5	8.0
35 to 39 years old	10,450	1,741	7,261	114	1,334	100.0	16.7	69.5	1.1	12.8
40 to 44 years old	11,295	1,476	7,855	201	1,764	100.0	13.1	69.6	1.8	15.6
45 to 54 years old	21,818	2,246	15,051	702	3,817	100.0	10.3	69.0	3.2	17.5
55 to 64 years old	16,100	1,041	10,651	1,540	2,868	100.0	6.5	66.2	9.6	17.8
65 to 74 years old	10,022	391	5,765	2,631	1,235	100.0	3.9	57.5	26.3	12.3
75 years old and over . . .	10,265	330	3,339	5,979	618	100.0	3.2	32.6	58.2	6.0

– Represents or rounds to zero.   [1] Includes persons who are married with spouse present, married with spouse absent, and separated.

Source: U.S. Census Bureau, "America's Families and Living Arrangements: 2006, Table A1. Marital Status of People 15 Years and Over, by Age, Sex, Personal Earnings, Race, and Hispanic Origin, 2006"; published 27 March 2007; <http://www.census.gov/population/www/socdemo/hh-fam/cps2006.html>.

Table 57. Living Arrangements of Persons 15 Years Old and Over by Selected Characteristics: 2006

[In thousands (233,039 represents 233,039,000). As of March. See headnote, Table 56]

Living arrangement	Total	15 to 19 years old	20 to 24 years old	25 to 34 years old	35 to 44 years old	45 to 54 years old	55 to 64 years old	65 to 74 years old	75 years old and over
Total [1] **. . . . .**	**233,039**	**20,901**	**20,380**	**39,476**	**43,089**	**42,775**	**30,956**	**18,540**	**16,921**
Alone	30,453	134	1,456	3,751	3,886	5,246	5,244	4,295	6,442
With spouse	119,055	237	3,163	19,781	27,463	28,016	20,978	11,842	7,574
With other persons	83,531	20,530	15,761	15,944	11,740	9,513	4,734	2,403	2,905
White [2]	189,500	16,106	15,933	30,862	34,472	35,112	26,155	15,895	14,968
Alone	24,794	67	1,081	2,815	3,022	4,151	4,260	3,629	5,769
With spouse	102,573	205	2,776	16,709	23,070	23,979	18,383	10,521	6,928
With other persons	62,133	15,834	12,076	11,338	8,380	6,982	3,512	1,745	2,271
Black [2]	27,680	3,228	2,875	5,155	5,353	4,987	3,075	1,699	1,308
Alone	4,298	50	283	629	663	866	754	530	523
With spouse	8,442	18	210	1,410	2,148	2,210	1,407	707	332
With other persons	14,940	3,160	2,382	3,116	2,542	1,911	914	462	453
Asian [2]	10,180	758	870	2,248	2,218	1,775	1,193	658	460
Alone	793	10	65	219	111	105	120	71	92
With spouse	5,784	9	78	1,138	1,696	1,319	868	446	232
With other persons	3,603	739	727	891	411	351	205	141	136
Hispanic origin [3]	30,613	3,510	3,628	7,850	6,450	4,396	2,466	1,366	946
Alone	1,954	9	120	360	315	346	308	252	244
With spouse	14,356	87	871	4,105	3,890	2,776	1,421	798	407
With other persons	14,303	3,414	2,637	3,385	2,245	1,274	737	316	295
Non-Hispanic White [2, 3] .	161,116	12,879	12,656	23,619	28,457	30,996	23,845	14,604	14,060
Alone	22,990	58	974	2,489	2,727	3,844	3,970	3,394	5,533
With spouse	89,081	119	1,977	12,882	19,402	21,350	17,047	9,762	6,541
With other persons	49,045	12,702	9,705	8,248	6,328	5,802	2,828	1,448	1,986

[1] Includes other races and persons not of Hispanic origin, not shown separately.   [2] See footnote 3, Table 55.   [3] Persons of Hispanic origin may be any race.

Source: U.S. Census Bureau, "America's Families and Living Arrangements: 2006, Table A2. Family Status and Household Relationship of People 15 Years and Over, by Marital Status, Age, Sex, Race, and Hispanic Origin: 2006"; published 30 March 2007; <http://www.census.gov/population/www/socdemo/hh-fam/cps2006.html>.

Table 58. Households, Families, Subfamilies, and Married Couples: 1980 to 2006

[In thousands, except as indicated (80,776 represents 80,776,000). As of March. Excludes members of Armed Forces except those living off post or with their families on post. Beginning 2004, population controls based on Census 2000 and an expanded sample of households. Based on Current Population Survey, see text of this section, and Appendix III. Minus sign (−) indicates decrease]

Type of unit	1980	1990	1995	2000	2004	2005	2006	Percent change 1980–1990	1990–2000	2000–2006
Households	80,776	93,347	98,990	104,705	112,000	113,343	114,384	16	12	9
Persons per household . . .	2.76	2.63	2.65	2.62	2.57	2.57	2.57	(X)	(X)	(X)
White [1]	70,766	80,163	83,737	87,671	91,962	92,880	93,588	13	9	7
Black [1]	8,586	10,486	11,655	12,849	13,629	13,809	14,002	22	23	9
Hispanic [2]	3,684	5,933	7,735	9,319	11,182	12,178	12,519	61	57	34
Family households	59,550	66,090	69,305	72,025	76,217	76,858	77,402	11	9	7
Married couple	49,112	52,317	53,858	55,311	57,719	57,975	58,179	7	6	5
Male householder [3]	1,733	2,884	3,226	4,028	4,716	4,901	5,130	66	40	27
Female householder [3] . . .	8,705	10,890	12,220	12,687	13,781	13,981	14,093	25	17	11
Nonfamily households	21,226	27,257	29,686	32,680	35,783	36,485	36,982	28	20	13
Male householder	8,807	11,606	13,190	14,641	16,136	16,543	16,753	32	26	13
Female householder	12,419	15,651	16,496	18,039	19,647	19,942	20,230	26	15	11
One person	18,296	22,999	24,732	26,724	29,586	30,137	30,453	26	16	14
Families	59,550	66,090	69,305	72,025	76,217	76,858	77,402	11	9	7
Persons per family	3.29	3.17	3.19	3.17	3.13	3.13	3.13	(X)	(X)	(X)
With own children [4]	31,022	32,289	34,296	34,605	35,944	36,211	36,466	4	7	5
Without own children [4]	28,528	33,801	35,009	37,420	40,273	40,647	40,936	18	11	9
Married couple	49,112	52,317	53,858	55,311	57,719	57,975	58,179	7	6	5
With own children [4]	24,961	24,537	25,241	25,248	25,793	25,919	25,982	−2	3	3
Without own children [4]	24,151	27,780	28,617	30,062	31,926	32,056	32,197	15	8	7
Male householder [3]	1,733	2,884	3,226	4,028	4,716	4,901	5,130	66	40	27
With own children [4]	616	1,153	1,440	1,786	1,931	2,021	2,095	87	55	17
Without own children [4]	1,117	1,731	1,786	2,242	2,786	2,880	3,035	55	30	35
Female householder [3]	8,705	10,890	12,220	12,687	13,781	13,981	14,093	25	17	11
With own children [4]	5,445	6,599	7,615	7,571	8,221	8,270	8,389	21	15	11
Without own children [4]	3,261	4,290	4,606	5,116	5,560	5,711	5,703	32	19	11
Unrelated subfamilies	360	534	674	571	509	515	504	48	7	−12
Married couple	20	68	64	37	42	62	36	(B)	(B)	(B)
Male reference persons [3] . .	36	45	59	57	61	61	59	(B)	(B)	(B)
Female reference persons [3] . .	304	421	550	477	406	392	409	39	13	−14
Related subfamilies	1,150	2,403	2,878	2,984	3,309	3,427	3,265	109	24	9
Married couple	582	871	1,015	1,149	1,303	1,336	1,312	50	32	14
Father-child [3]	54	153	195	201	296	387	347	(B)	31	73
Mother-child [3]	512	1,378	1,668	1,634	1,710	1,704	1,606	169	19	−2
Married couples	49,714	53,256	54,937	56,497	59,064	59,373	59,528	7	6	5
With own household	49,112	52,317	53,858	55,311	57,719	57,975	58,179	7	6	5
Without own household	602	939	1,079	1,186	1,345	1,398	1,348	56	26	14
Percent without	1.2	1.8	2.0	2.1	2.3	2.4	2.3	(X)	(X)	(X)

B Not shown; base less than 75,000.   X Not applicable.   [1] Beginning with the 2003 Current Population Survey (CPS), respondents could choose more than one race. Beginning 2004, data shown represent persons who selected this race group only and exclude persons reporting more than one race. The CPS prior to 2003 only allowed respondents to report one race group. See also comments on race in the text for this section.   [2] Persons of Hispanic origin may be any race.   [3] No spouse present.   [4] Under 18 years old.

Source: U.S. Census Bureau, "Families and Living Arrangements"; <http://www.census.gov/population/www/socdemo/hh-fam.html>.

Table 59. Married Couples by Race and Hispanic Origin of Spouses: 1980 to 2006

[In thousands (49,714 represents 49,714,000). As of March. Persons 15 years old and over. Persons of Hispanic origin may be any race. Based on Current Population Survey; see headnote, Table 58 and Appendix III]

Race and origin of spouses	1980	1990	2000	2006
Married couples, total [1]	**49,714**	**53,256**	**56,497**	**59,528**
Interracial married couples, total	651	964	1,464	2,274
White/Black [2]	167	211	363	403
Black husband/White wife	122	150	268	286
White husband/Black wife	45	61	95	117
White [2]/other race [3]	450	720	1,051	1,763
Black [2]/other race [3]	34	33	50	108
HISPANIC ORIGIN				
Hispanic/Hispanic	1,906	3,085	4,739	6,065
Hispanic/other origin (not Hispanic)	891	1,193	1,743	2,226
All other couples (not of Hispanic origin)	46,917	48,979	50,015	51,236

[1] Includes other married couples not shown separately.   [2] See footnote 1, Table 58.   [3] "Other race" is any race other than White or Black, such as American Indian, Japanese, Chinese, etc. This total excludes combinations of other races by other races.

Source: U.S. Census Bureau, Table MS-3. Interracial Married Couples: 1980 to 2002; published 15 September 2004; <http://www.census.gov/population/www/socdemo/hh-fam.html>; and unpublished data.

Table 60. **Households and Persons Per Household by Type of Household: 1990 to 2006**

[As of March (93,347 represents 93,347,000). See headnote, Table 58]

Type of household	Households						Persons per household		
	Number (1,000)			Percent distribution					
	1990	2000	2006	1990	2000	2006	1990	2000	2006
Total households	93,347	104,705	114,384	100	100	100	2.63	2.62	2.57
Family households	66,090	72,025	77,402	71	69	68	3.22	3.24	3.20
Married couple family.	52,317	55,311	58,179	56	53	51	3.25	3.26	3.21
Male householder, no spouse present.	2,884	4,028	5,130	3	4	4	3.04	3.16	3.14
Female householder, no spouse present . . .	10,890	12,687	14,093	12	12	12	3.10	3.17	3.16
Nonfamily households.	27,257	32,680	36,982	29	31	32	1.22	1.25	1.25
Living alone	22,999	26,724	30,453	25	26	27	1.00	1.00	1.00
Male householder	11,606	14,641	16,753	12	14	15	1.33	1.34	1.34
Living alone	9,049	11,181	13,061	10	11	11	1.00	1.00	1.00
Female householder	15,651	18,039	20,230	17	17	18	1.14	1.17	1.18
Living alone	13,950	15,543	17,392	15	15	15	1.00	1.00	1.00

Source: U.S. Census Bureau, Current Population Reports, P20-537 and earlier reports; and "America's Families and Living Arrangements: 2006"; published 30 March 2007; <http://www.census.gov/population/www/socdemo/hh-fam/cps2006.html>.

Table 61. **Households by Age of Householder and Size of Household: 1990 to 2006**

[In millions (93.3 represents 93,300,000). As of March. Based on Current Population Survey; see headnote, Table 58]

Age of householder and size of household				2006					
	1990	2000	2005	Total [1]	White [2]	Black [2]	Asian [2]	His-panic [3]	Non-Hispanic White [3]
Total.	93.3	104.7	113.3	114.4	93.6	14.0	4.3	12.5	82.0
Age of householder:									
15 to 24 years old	5.1	5.9	6.7	6.8	5.1	1.1	0.3	1.2	4.0
25 to 29 years old	9.4	8.5	9.2	9.2	7.2	1.3	0.4	1.6	5.7
30 to 34 years old	11.0	10.1	10.1	9.9	7.6	1.4	0.5	1.7	6.1
35 to 44 years old	20.6	24.0	23.2	23.0	18.4	3.0	1.1	3.2	15.4
45 to 54 years old	14.5	20.9	23.4	23.7	19.4	3.0	0.8	2.3	17.3
55 to 64 years old	12.5	13.6	17.5	18.3	15.3	2.0	0.6	1.2	14.1
65 to 74 years old	11.7	11.3	11.5	11.7	10.0	1.2	0.3	0.7	9.3
75 years old and over . . .	8.4	10.4	11.6	11.8	10.5	0.9	0.2	0.6	10.0
One person	23.0	26.7	30.1	30.5	24.8	4.3	0.8	2.0	23.0
Male	9.0	11.2	12.8	13.1	10.7	1.8	0.3	1.0	9.7
Female.	14.0	15.5	17.3	17.4	14.1	2.5	0.4	0.9	13.3
Two persons	30.1	34.7	37.4	37.8	31.9	3.9	1.2	2.8	29.3
Three persons	16.1	17.2	18.3	18.9	15.1	2.6	0.8	2.4	12.8
Four persons	14.5	15.3	16.4	16.0	13.0	1.7	0.9	2.5	10.7
Five persons	6.2	7.0	7.2	7.3	5.9	0.8	0.3	1.6	4.4
Six persons	2.1	2.4	2.5	2.6	1.9	0.4	0.1	0.7	1.3
Seven persons or more. . . .	1.3	1.4	1.4	1.4	1.0	0.2	0.1	0.5	0.5

[1] Includes other races, not shown separately.   [2] Beginning with the 2003 Current Population Survey (CPS), respondents could choose more than one race. 2006 data represent persons who selected this race group only and exclude persons reporting more than one race. The CPS in prior years only allowed respondents to report one race group. See also comments on race in the text for this section.   [3] Hispanic persons may be any race.

Source: U.S. Census Bureau, Current Population Reports, P20-537, and earlier reports; and "America's Families and Living Arrangements: 2006"; published 30 March 2007; <http://www.census.gov/population/www/socdemo/hh-fam/cps2006.html>.

Table 62. **Unmarried-Partner Households by Sex of Partners: 2005**

[The American Community Survey universe is limited to the household population and excludes the population living in institutions, college dormitories, and other group quarters. Based on a sample and subject to sampling variability; see text, this section and Appendix III]

Item	Number
Total households.	111,090,617
Unmarried-partner households.	5,966,106
Male householder and male partner	413,095
Male householder and female partner	2,660,434
Female householder and female partner	363,848
Female householder and male partner.	2,528,729
All other households	105,124,511

Source: U.S. Census Bureau, 2005 American Community Survey; B11009. Unmarried-Partner Households and Household Type by Sex of Partner; using American FactFinder; <http://factfinder.census.gov/>; (accessed: 4 January 2007).

Table 63. Family Groups With Children Under 18 Years Old by Race and Hispanic Origin: 1990 to 2006

[In thousands. As of March (34,670 represents 34,670,000). Family groups comprise family households, related subfamilies, and unrelated subfamilies. Excludes members of Armed Forces except those living off post or with their families on post. Beginning 2005, population controls based on Census 2000 and an expanded sample of households. Based on Current Population Survey, see text of this section, and Appendix III]

Race and Hispanic origin of householder or reference person	1990	2000	2005	2006 Total	Family house- holds	Subfamilies Total	Related	Unrelated
All races, total [1]	34,670	37,496	39,317	39,374	36,466	2,908	2,425	483
Two-parent family groups	24,921	25,771	26,482	26,469	25,982	486	472	14
One-parent family groups	9,749	11,725	12,835	12,905	10,484	2,421	1,953	468
Maintained by mother	8,398	9,681	10,366	10,404	8,389	2,015	1,606	409
Maintained by father	1,351	2,044	2,469	2,501	2,095	406	347	59
White, total [2]	28,294	30,079	30,960	30,947	28,937	2,010	1,616	394
Two-parent family groups	21,905	22,241	22,319	22,404	22,010	394	383	11
One-parent family groups	6,389	7,838	8,641	8,542	6,927	1,616	1,233	383
Maintained by mother	5,310	6,216	6,747	6,628	5,283	1,346	1,009	337
Maintained by father	1,079	1,622	1,894	1,914	1,644	270	224	46
Black, total [2]	5,087	5,530	5,495	5,609	4,967	642	588	54
Two-parent family groups	2,006	2,135	2,065	2,051	2,021	30	29	1
One-parent family groups	3,081	3,396	3,430	3,558	2,947	612	559	53
Maintained by mother	2,860	3,060	3,037	3,143	2,639	505	460	45
Maintained by father	221	335	393	415	308	107	99	8
Asian, total [2]	(NA)	1,469	1,757	1,716	1,609	107	101	6
Two-parent family groups	(NA)	1,184	1,472	1,431	1,389	41	39	2
One-parent family groups	(NA)	285	285	286	220	65	61	4
Maintained by mother	(NA)	236	222	219	164	55	52	3
Maintained by father	(NA)	49	63	67	56	10	9	1
Hispanic, total [3]	3,429	5,503	6,752	6,905	6,119	786	687	99
Two-parent family groups	2,289	3,625	4,346	4,524	4,334	190	182	8
One-parent family groups	1,140	1,877	2,406	2,380	1,785	596	505	91
Maintained by mother	1,003	1,565	1,964	1,957	1,470	487	410	77
Maintained by father	138	313	442	423	315	109	95	14
Non-Hispanic White, total [2, 3] . . .	(NA)	24,847	24,730	24,579	23,290	1,289	987	302
Two-parent family groups	(NA)	18,750	18,253	18,148	17,934	214	212	2
One-parent family groups	(NA)	6,096	6,476	6,432	5,357	1,076	776	300
Maintained by mother	(NA)	4,766	4,984	4,899	3,997	903	636	267
Maintained by father	(NA)	1,331	1,492	1,532	1,360	173	140	33

NA Not available. [1] Includes other races, not shown separately. [2] Beginning with the 2003 Current Population Survey (CPS), respondents could choose more than one race. Beginning 2005, data represent persons who selected this race group only and exclude persons reporting more than one race. The CPS prior to 2003 allowed respondents to report only one race group. See also comments on race in the text for this section. [3] Hispanic persons may be any race.

Source: U.S. Census Bureau, Current Population Reports, P20-537, and earlier reports; and "Families and Living Arrangements"; <http://www.census.gov/population/www/socdemo/hh-fam.html>.

Table 64. Parents and Children in Stay-At-Home Parent Family Groups: 1995 to 2006

[In thousands (22,973 represents 22,973,000). Family groups with children include those families that maintain their own household (family households with own children); those that live in the home of a relative (related subfamilies); and those that live in the home of a nonrelative (unrelated subfamilies). Stay-at-home family groups are married-couple family groups with children under 15 where one parent is in the labor force all of the previous year and their spouse is out of the labor force for the entire year with the reason 'taking care of home and family.' Only married couples with children under 15 are included. Based on Current Population Survey; see Appendix III]

Year	Married-couple family groups with children under 15 years old			Children under 15 years old in married-couple family groups		
	Total	With stay-at-home mothers	With stay-at-home fathers	Total in married-couple family groups	With stay-at-home mothers	With stay-at-home fathers
1995	22,973	4,440	64	41,008	9,106	125
1996	22,808	4,633	49	40,739	9,693	115
1997	22,779	4,617	71	40,798	9,788	140
1998	22,881	4,555	90	41,038	9,432	196
1999	22,754	4,731	71	41,003	9,796	143
2000	22,953	4,785	93	41,860	10,087	180
2001	22,922	4,934	81	41,862	10,194	148
2002	23,339	5,206	106	41,802	10,573	189
2003	23,209	5,388	98	41,654	11,028	175
2004	23,160	5,571	147	41,409	11,205	268
2005	23,305	5,584	142	41,111	11,224	247
2006	23,232	5,646	159	41,259	11,372	283

Source: U.S. Census Bureau, Table SHP-1. Parents and Children in Stay-At-Home Parent Family Groups: 1994 to Present; published 27 March 2007; <http://www.census.gov/population/www/socdemo/hh-fam.html>.

Table 65. **Children Under 18 Years Old by Presence of Parents: 1990 to 2006**

[As of **March (64,137 represents 64,137,000)**. Excludes persons under 18 years old who maintained households or family groups. Based on Current Population Survey; see headnote, Table 58]

Race Hispanic origin, and year	Number (1,000)	Both parents	Percent living with— Mother only Total	Divorced	Married, spouse absent	Never married	Widowed	Father only	Neither parent
ALL RACES [1]									
1990	64,137	72.5	21.6	8.0	5.3	6.8	1.5	3.1	2.8
2000	72,012	69.1	22.4	7.9	4.5	9.2	1.0	4.2	4.2
2005	73,494	67.3	23.4	7.9	4.6	10.1	0.8	4.8	4.5
2006	73,664	67.4	23.3	7.8	4.5	10.1	0.8	4.7	4.6
WHITE [2]									
1990	51,390	79.0	16.2	(NA)	(NA)	(NA)	(NA)	3.0	1.8
2000	56,455	75.3	17.3	(NA)	(NA)	(NA)	(NA)	4.3	3.1
2005	56,234	73.5	18.4	7.9	4.0	5.8	0.7	4.7	3.4
2006	56,332	73.8	17.9	7.7	3.7	5.8	0.7	4.6	3.6
BLACK [2]									
1990	10,018	37.7	51.2	(NA)	(NA)	(NA)	(NA)	3.5	7.5
2000	11,412	37.6	49.0	(NA)	(NA)	(NA)	(NA)	4.2	9.2
2005	11,293	35.0	50.2	8.7	8.1	32.0	1.3	5.0	9.8
2006	11,225	34.6	51.2	9.1	9.0	31.7	1.4	4.8	9.4
ASIAN [2]									
2005	2,843	83.6	10.2	4.0	2.3	2.7	1.3	3.6	2.5
2006	2,869	83.8	9.7	3.4	2.9	2.8	0.6	3.6	3.0
HISPANIC [3]									
1990	7,174	66.8	27.1	(NA)	(NA)	(NA)	(NA)	2.9	3.2
2000	11,613	65.1	25.1	(NA)	(NA)	(NA)	(NA)	4.4	5.4
2005	14,241	64.7	25.4	6.1	7.1	11.4	0.8	4.8	5.2
2006	14,697	65.9	25.0	6.3	6.5	11.4	0.8	4.1	5.0
NON-HISPANIC WHITE [2,3]									
2005	43,106	75.9	16.4	8.5	3.1	4.2	0.7	4.8	2.9
2006	42,744	75.9	16.0	8.2	2.8	4.2	0.7	4.8	3.2

NA Not available.   [1] Includes other races not shown separately.   [2] Beginning with the 2003 Current Population Survey (CPS), respondents could choose more than one race. Beginning 2005, data represent persons who selected this race group only and exclude persons reporting more than one race. The CPS prior to 2003 allowed respondents to report only one race group. See also comments on race in the text for this section.   [3] Hispanic persons may be any race.

Source: U.S. Census Bureau, "Families and Living Arrangements"; <http://www.census.gov/population/www/socdemo/hh-fam.html>.

Table 66. **Grandparents Living With Grandchildren by Race and Sex: 2005**

[**5,743 represents 5,743,000.** The American Community Survey universe is limited to the household population and excludes the population living in institutions, college dormitories, and other group quarters. Based on a sample and subject to sampling variability; see text, this section and Appendix III]

Race, Hispanic origin, and sex	Grandparents living with grandchildren, total [1]	Grandparents responsible for grandchildren Total	30 to 59 years old	60 years old and over
Grandparents living with own grandchildren under 18 years old (1,000)	**5,743**	**2,459**	**1,677**	**782**
PERCENT DISTRIBUTION				
Total	100.0	100.0	100.0	100.0
White alone	59.3	60.4	60.1	60.9
Black or African American alone	21.0	25.5	25.3	26.0
American Indian and Alaska Native alone	1.6	2.2	2.2	2.0
Asian alone	6.8	2.8	2.1	4.3
Native Hawaiian and Other Pacific Islander alone	0.3	0.2	0.3	0.2
Some other race alone	9.7	7.5	8.4	5.4
Two or more races	1.4	1.5	1.6	1.2
Hispanic or Latino [2]	22.2	18.1	19.9	14.4
White alone, not Hispanic or Latino	47.5	50.4	49.4	52.6
Male	36.0	37.2	35.5	40.9
Female	64.0	62.8	64.5	59.1

[1] Covers both grandchildren living in grandparent's home and grandparents living in grandchildren's home.   [2] Persons of Hispanic origin may be of any race.

Source: U.S. Census Bureau, American Community Survey 2005, Subject Table S1002; using American FactFinder®; <http://factfinder.census.gov/>; (accessed: 3 August 2007).

Population   55

Table 67. Families by Number of Own Children Under 18 Years Old: 1990 to 2006

[As of March (66,090 represents 66,090,000). Based on Current Population Survey; see headnote, Table 63]

Race, Hispanic origin, and year	Number of families (1,000)					Percent distribution				
	Total	No children	One child	Two children	Three or more children	Total	No children	One child	Two children	Three or more children
ALL FAMILIES [1]										
1990	66,090	33,801	13,530	12,263	6,496	100	51	20	19	10
2000	72,025	37,420	14,311	13,215	7,080	100	52	20	18	10
2005	76,858	40,647	15,069	13,741	7,400	100	53	20	18	10
2006, total	77,402	40,936	15,528	13,664	7,275	100	53	20	18	9
Married couple	58,179	32,197	10,031	10,336	5,615	100	55	17	18	10
Male householder [2]	5,130	3,035	1,313	588	194	100	59	26	11	4
Female householder [2]	14,093	5,703	4,184	2,739	1,466	100	40	30	19	10
WHITE FAMILIES [3]										
1990	56,590	29,872	11,186	10,342	5,191	100	53	20	18	9
2000	60,251	32,144	11,496	10,918	5,693	100	53	19	18	9
2005	63,079	34,255	11,872	11,127	5,825	100	54	19	18	9
2006, total	63,401	34,465	12,150	10,988	5,799	100	54	19	17	9
Married couple	50,363	28,352	8,405	8,795	4,811	100	56	17	17	10
Male householder [2]	3,903	2,259	1,041	461	142	100	58	27	12	4
Female householder [2]	9,136	3,853	2,704	1,732	846	100	42	30	19	9
BLACK FAMILIES [3]										
1990	7,470	3,093	1,894	1,433	1,049	100	41	25	19	14
2000	8,664	3,882	2,101	1,624	1,058	100	45	24	19	12
2005	8,902	4,077	2,059	1,641	1,125	100	46	23	18	13
2006, total	9,047	4,080	2,298	1,659	1,011	100	45	25	18	11
Married couple	4,126	2,105	879	693	449	100	51	21	17	11
Male householder [2]	805	497	187	89	32	100	62	23	11	4
Female householder [2]	4,117	1,478	1,232	876	530	100	36	30	21	13
ASIAN FAMILIES [3]										
2005	3,142	1,535	730	646	230	100	49	23	21	7
2006, total	3,208	1,599	681	717	211	100	50	21	22	7
Married couple	2,590	1,201	535	660	194	100	46	21	25	7
Male householder [2]	235	179	32	17	7	100	76	14	7	3
Female householder [2]	383	219	114	39	11	100	57	30	10	3
HISPANIC FAMILIES [4]										
1990	4,840	1,790	1,095	1,036	919	100	37	23	21	19
2000	7,561	2,747	1,791	1,693	1,330	100	36	24	22	18
2005	9,521	3,528	2,130	2,163	1,699	100	37	22	23	18
2006, total	9,862	3,743	2,249	2,206	1,664	100	38	23	22	17
Married couple	6,642	2,307	1,415	1,643	1,276	100	35	21	25	19
Male householder [2]	969	654	186	90	38	100	67	19	9	4
Female householder [2]	2,252	782	648	472	350	100	35	29	21	16
NON-HISPANIC WHITE FAMILIES [3,4]										
2005	54,257	30,965	9,924	9,151	4,217	100	57	18	17	8
2006, total	54,257	30,967	10,113	8,942	4,235	100	57	19	16	8
Married couple	44,116	26,182	7,086	7,257	3,591	100	59	16	16	8
Male householder [2]	3,003	1,644	877	377	106	100	55	29	13	4
Female householder [2]	7,138	3,141	2,150	1,308	539	100	44	30	18	8

[1] Includes other races, not shown separately. [2] No spouse present. [3] Beginning with the 2003 Current Population Survey (CPS), respondents could choose more than one race. Beginning 2005, data represent persons who selected this race group only and exclude persons reporting more than one race. The CPS prior to 2003 only allowed respondents to report one race group. See also comments on race in the text for this section. [4] Hispanic persons may be any race.

Source: U.S. Census Bureau, Current Population Reports, P20-537 and earlier reports; and "Families and Living Arrangements"; <http://www.census.gov/population/www/socdemo/hh-fam.html>.

Table 68. Families by Size and Presence of Children: 1990 to 2006

[As of March (66,090 represents 66,090,000). See headnote, Table 63]

Characteristic	Number (1,000)				Percent distribution			
	1990	2000	2005	2006	1990	2000	2005	2006
Total	66,090	72,025	76,858	77,402	100	100	100	100
Size of family:								
Two persons	27,606	31,455	34,022	34,454	42	44	44	45
Three persons	15,353	16,073	17,163	17,525	23	22	22	23
Four persons	14,026	14,496	15,512	15,075	21	20	20	19
Five persons	5,938	6,526	6,639	6,863	9	9	9	9
Six persons	1,997	2,226	2,274	2,307	3	3	3	3
Seven or more persons	1,170	1,249	1,247	1,179	2	2	2	2
Own children under age 6:								
None	50,905	57,039	61,000	61,400	77	79	79	79
One	10,304	10,454	10,851	11,180	16	15	14	14
Two or more	4,882	4,533	5,008	4,822	7	6	7	6

Source: U.S. Census Bureau, Current Population Reports, P20-537 and earlier reports; and "Families and Living Arrangements"; <http://www.census.gov/population/www/socdemo/hh-fam.html>.

Table 69. Families by Type, Race, and Hispanic Origin: 2006

[In thousands (77,402 represents 77,402,000). As of March. Excludes members of Armed Forces except those living off post or with their families on post. Population controls based on Census 2000 and an expanded sample of households. Based on Current Population Survey, see text of this section and Appendix III]

Characteristic	All families	Married couple families						Female family householder [4]						Male family householder, [4] all races
		All races [1]	White [2]	Black [2]	Asian [2]	Hispanic [3]	Non-Hispanic White [2,3]	All races [1]	White [2]	Black [2]	Asian [2]	Hispanic [3]	Non-Hispanic White [2,3]	
All families	**77,402**	**58,179**	**50,363**	**4,126**	**2,590**	**6,642**	**44,116**	**14,093**	**9,136**	**4,117**	**383**	**2,252**	**7,138**	**5,130**
Age of householder:														
Under 25 years old	3,696	1,416	1,235	106	33	363	901	1,424	885	433	41	279	642	857
25 to 34 years old	13,496	9,405	8,007	671	473	1,892	6,228	2,970	1,705	1,066	78	561	1,212	1,122
35 to 44 years old	18,064	13,365	11,257	1,021	817	1,872	9,496	3,599	2,341	1,085	67	637	1,771	1,099
45 to 54 years old	17,462	13,572	11,689	1,067	568	1,324	10,437	2,825	1,897	754	89	403	1,545	1,065
55 to 64 years old	12,447	10,460	9,165	727	409	635	8,571	1,488	996	388	68	204	818	498
65 to 74 years old	7,109	6,009	5,380	369	176	352	5,047	863	604	213	27	89	520	238
75 years old and over	5,127	3,953	3,630	164	114	203	3,435	924	708	179	13	78	630	251
Without own children under 18	40,936	32,197	28,352	2,105	1,201	2,307	26,182	5,703	3,853	1,478	219	782	3,141	3,035
With own children under 18	36,466	25,982	22,010	2,021	1,389	4,334	17,934	8,389	5,283	2,639	164	1,470	3,997	2,095
One own child under 18	15,528	10,031	8,405	879	535	1,415	7,086	4,184	2,704	1,232	114	648	2,150	1,313
Two own children under 18	13,664	10,336	8,795	693	660	1,643	7,257	2,739	1,732	876	39	472	1,308	588
Three or more own children under 18	7,275	5,615	4,811	449	194	1,276	3,591	1,466	846	530	11	350	539	194
Average per family with own children under 18	1.82	1.88	1.89	1.91	1.81	2.01	1.85	1.71	1.65	1.85	1.44	1.79	1.59	1.48
Age of own children:														
Of any age	47,201	31,997	27,057	2,514	1,740	4,960	22,393	12,154	7,932	3,545	271	1,943	6,220	3,051
Under 25 years	42,085	29,750	25,204	2,326	1,579	4,708	20,776	9,781	6,203	3,015	214	1,679	4,739	2,554
Under 12 years	26,501	19,264	16,358	1,422	1,074	3,505	13,057	5,818	3,591	1,909	102	1,085	2,635	1,419
Under 6 years	16,002	11,984	10,209	851	648	2,335	8,011	3,224	1,954	1,083	55	601	1,424	793
Under 3 years	9,401	7,151	6,122	487	368	1,365	4,843	1,768	1,113	539	38	343	810	482
Under 1 year	3,336	2,549	2,219	161	111	442	1,812	584	363	175	12	106	273	203
Members 65 years and older:														
Without members 65 and older	61,991	46,096	39,662	3,426	2,077	5,831	34,187	11,707	7,426	3,572	306	1,962	5,703	4,187
With members 65 years and older	15,411	12,083	10,700	699	513	811	9,929	2,386	1,710	544	78	289	1,434	943
Marital status of householder:														
Married, spouse present	58,179	58,179	50,363	4,126	2,590	6,642	44,116	(X)	(X)	(X)	(X)	(X)	(X)	(X)
Married, spouse absent	2,724	(X)	(X)	(X)	(X)	(X)	(X)	2,052	1,298	615	67	488	867	673
Separated	1,853	(X)	(X)	(X)	(X)	(X)	(X)	1,514	942	492	22	365	626	340
Other	871	(X)	(X)	(X)	(X)	(X)	(X)	538	356	123	45	123	241	333
Widowed	2,669	(X)	(X)	(X)	(X)	(X)	(X)	2,234	1,646	476	62	255	1,399	435
Divorced	6,500	(X)	(X)	(X)	(X)	(X)	(X)	4,915	3,751	911	112	614	3,204	1,585
Never married	7,329	(X)	(X)	(X)	(X)	(X)	(X)	4,892	2,441	2,115	142	895	1,667	2,438

X Not applicable. [1] Includes other races not shown separately. [2] Beginning with the 2003 Current Population Survey (CPS), respondents could choose more than one race. Data represent persons who selected this race group only and exclude persons reporting more than one race. See also comments on race in the text for this section. [3] Persons of Hispanic origin may be any race. [4] No spouse present.

Source: U.S. Census Bureau, "America's Families and Living Arrangements: 2006"; published 27 March 2007; <http://www.census.gov/population/www/socdemo/hh-fam/cps2006.html>.

Population 57

Table 70. Family Households With Own Children Under Age 18 by Type of Family, 1990 to 2006, and by Age of Householder, 2006

[As of March (32,289 represents 32,289,000). Excludes members of Armed Forces except those living off post or with their families on post. Population controls for 2006 based on Census 2000 and an expanded sample of households. Based on Current Population Survey, see text of this section and Appendix III]

Family type	1990	2000	2006						
			Total	15 to 24 years old	25 to 34 years old	35 to 44 years old	45 to 54 years old	55 to 64 years old	65 years old and over
NUMBER (1,000)									
Family households with children......	32,289	34,605	36,466	2,003	10,370	14,662	8,001	1,225	205
Married couple...................	24,537	25,248	25,982	860	7,038	10,865	6,132	947	141
Male householder [1]...............	1,153	1,786	2,095	161	597	738	491	87	21
Female householder [1].............	6,599	7,571	8,389	981	2,737	3,059	1,378	192	43
HOUSEHOLDS WITH CHILDREN, AS A PERCENT OF ALL FAMILY HOUSEHOLDS BY TYPE									
Family households with children, total..	49	48	47	54	77	81	46	10	2
Married couple...................	47	46	45	61	75	81	45	9	1
Male householder [1]...............	40	44	41	19	53	67	46	17	4
Female householder [1].............	61	60	59	69	92	85	49	13	2

[1] No spouse present.

Source: U.S. Census Bureau, Current Population Reports, P20-537 and earlier reports; and "America's Families and Living Arrangements: 2006"; published 27 March 2007; <http://www.census.gov/population/www/socdemo/hh-fam/cps2006.html>.

Table 71. Nonfamily Households by Sex and Age of Householder: 2006

[In thousands (16,752 represents 16,752,000). As of March. See headnote, Table 70]

Item	Male householder					Female householder				
	Total	15 to 24 yrs. old	25 to 44 yrs. old	45 to 64 yrs. old	65 yrs. old and over	Total	15 to 24 yrs. old	25 to 44 yrs. old	45 to 64 yrs. old	65 yrs. old and over
Total...........	16,753	1,615	6,373	5,586	3,180	20,230	1,485	4,203	6,502	8,043
One person (living alone)..	13,061	826	4,572	4,717	2,947	17,392	765	3,066	5,774	7,789
Nonrelatives present	3,691	789	1,801	869	233	2,838	720	1,137	728	254
Never married.........	8,386	1,523	4,528	1,889	446	6,567	1,411	2,956	1,697	502
Married [1].............	1,615	56	539	696	322	1,213	44	258	532	378
Widowed.............	1,777	11	42	277	1,448	7,114	7	124	1,141	5,841
Divorced.............	4,975	25	1,263	2,723	963	5,336	23	863	3,129	1,321

[1] No spouse present.

Source: U.S. Census Bureau, "America's Families and Living Arrangements: 2006"; published 27 March 2007; <http://www.census.gov/population/www/socdemo/hh-fam/cps2006.html>.

Table 72. Persons Living Alone by Sex and Age: 1990 to 2006

[As of March (22,999 represents 22,999,000). Excludes members of Armed Forces except those living off post or with their families on post. Beginning 2005, population controls based on Census 2000 and an expanded sample of households. Based on Current Population Survey, see text of this section and Appendix III]

Sex and age	Number of persons (1,000)					Percent distribution				
	1990	1995	2000	2005	2006	1990	1995	2000	2005	2006
Both sexes	22,999	24,732	26,724	30,137	30,453	100	100	100	100	100
15 to 24 years old	1,210	1,196	1,144	1,521	1,590	5	5	4	5	5
25 to 34 years old	3,972	3,653	3,848	3,836	3,751	17	15	14	13	12
35 to 44 years old	3,138	3,663	4,109	3,988	3,886	14	15	15	13	13
45 to 64 years old	5,502	6,377	7,842	10,180	10,490	24	26	29	34	34
65 to 74 years old	4,350	4,374	4,091	4,222	4,295	19	18	15	14	14
75 years old and over......	4,825	5,470	5,692	6,391	6,442	21	22	21	21	21
Male...............	9,049	10,140	11,181	12,808	13,061	39	41	42	42	43
15 to 24 years old	674	623	556	759	826	3	3	2	3	3
25 to 34 years old	2,395	2,213	2,279	2,181	2,219	10	9	9	7	7
35 to 44 years old	1,836	2,263	2,569	2,335	2,353	8	9	10	8	8
45 to 64 years old	2,203	2,787	3,422	4,620	4,717	10	11	13	15	15
65 to 74 years old	1,042	1,134	1,108	1,361	1,436	5	5	4	5	5
75 years old and over......	901	1,120	1,247	1,551	1,511	4	5	5	5	5
Female.............	13,950	14,592	15,543	17,330	17,392	61	59	58	58	57
15 to 24 years old	536	572	588	762	765	2	2	2	3	3
25 to 34 years old	1,578	1,440	1,568	1,655	1,532	7	6	6	5	5
35 to 44 years old	1,303	1,399	1,540	1,654	1,534	6	6	6	5	5
45 to 64 years old	3,300	3,589	4,420	5,559	5,774	14	15	17	18	19
65 to 74 years old	3,309	3,240	2,983	2,860	2,859	14	13	11	10	9
75 years old and over......	3,924	4,351	4,444	4,838	4,930	17	18	17	16	16

Source: U.S. Census Bureau, Current Population Reports, P20-553 and earlier reports; and "Families and Living Arrangements"; <http://www.census.gov/population/www/socdemo/hh-fam.html>.

58   Population

Table 73. Population in Group Quarters by State: 2000 to 2006

[In thousands (7,780 represents 7,780,000). 2000, as of April; beginning 2005, as of July. For definition of group quarters, see text, this section]

State	2000	2005	2006	State	2000	2005	2006	State	2000	2005	2006
				IA	104	104	104	NC	254	271	271
U.S.	7,780	8,059	8,066	KS	82	82	82	ND	24	26	28
				KY	115	115	115				
AL	115	115	115	LA	136	134	122	OH	299	308	308
AK	19	23	23	ME	35	37	37	OK	112	111	111
AZ	110	110	110					OR	77	80	80
AR	74	78	78	MD	134	141	142	PA	433	456	456
CA	820	855	863	MA	221	216	216	RI	39	43	43
				MI	250	255	255				
CO	103	103	103	MN	136	142	142	SC	135	140	143
CT	108	113	113	MS	95	96	94	SD	28	29	30
DE	25	25	25					TN	148	152	152
DC	36	35	35	MO	164	167	167	TX	561	594	594
FL	389	410	412	MT	25	25	25	UT	40	43	43
				NE	51	52	52				
GA	234	267	273	NV	34	33	33	VT	21	21	21
HI	36	38	38	NH	36	37	37	VA	231	235	235
ID	31	34	34					WA	136	143	141
IL	322	324	324	NJ	195	196	198	WV	43	46	46
IN	178	179	179	NM	36	41	41	WI	156	160	160
				NY	581	603	603	WY	14	14	14

[1] The April 1, 2000, Population Estimates base reflects changes to the Census 2000 population from the Count Question Resolution program and geographic program revisions.

Source: U.S. Census Bureau, "Annual County Population Estimates and Estimated Components of Change: April 1, 2000 to July 1, 2006" Release date: March 22, 2007 <http://www.census.gov/popest/counties/files/CO-EST2006-ALLDATA.csv>.

Table 74. Self-Described Religious Identification of Adult Population: 1990 and 2001

[In thousands (175,440 represents 175,440,000). The American Religious Identification Survey (ARIS) 2001 was based on a random digit-dialed telephone survey of 50,281 American residential households in the continental U.S.A. (48 states). Respondents were asked to describe themselves in terms of religion with an open-ended question. Interviewers did not prompt or offer a suggested list of potential answers. Moreover, the self-description of respondents was not based on whether established religious bodies, institutions, churches, mosques, or synagogues considered them to be members. Quite the contrary, the survey sought to determine whether the respondents themselves regarded themselves as adherents of a religious community. Subjective rather than objective standards of religious identification were tapped by the surveys]

Religious group	1990	2001	Religious group	1990	2001
Adult population, total [1]	175,440	207,980	Fundamentalist	27	61
			Salvation Army	27	25
Total Christian	151,496	159,506	Independent Christian Church	25	71
Catholic	46,004	50,873			
Baptist	33,964	33,830	Total other religions	5,853	7,740
Protestant—no denomination supplied	17,214	4,647	Jewish	3,137	2,831
Methodist/Wesleyan	14,174	14,150	Muslim/Islamic	527	1,104
Lutheran	9,110	9,580	Buddhist	401	1,082
Christian—no denomination supplied	8,073	14,150	Unitarian/Universalist	502	629
Presbyterian	4,985	5,596	Hindu	227	766
Pentecostal/Charismatic	3,191	4,407	Native American	47	103
Episcopalian/Anglican	3,042	3,451	Scientologist	45	55
Mormon/Latter-Day Saints	2,487	2,787	Bahá'i	28	84
Churches of Christ	1,769	2,593	Taoist	23	40
Jehovah's Witness	1,381	1,331	New Age	20	68
Seventh-Day Adventist	668	724	Eckankar	18	26
Assemblies of God	660	1,106	Rastafarian	14	11
Holiness/Holy	610	569	Sikh	13	57
Congregational/United Church of Christ	599	1,378	Wiccan	8	134
Church of the Nazarene	549	544	Deity	6	49
Church of God	531	944	Druid	(NA)	33
Orthodox (Eastern)	502	645	Santeria	(NA)	22
Evangelical [2]	242	1,032	Pagan	(NA)	140
Mennonite	235	346	Spiritualist	(NA)	116
Christian Science	214	194	Ethical Culture	(NA)	4
Church of the Brethren	206	358	Other unclassified	837	386
Born Again [2]	204	56			
Nondenominational [2]	195	2,489	No religion specified, total	14,331	29,481
Disciples of Christ	144	492	Atheist	(NA)	902
Reformed/Dutch Reform	161	289	Agnostic	1,186	991
Apostolic/New Apostolic	117	254	Humanist	29	49
Quaker	67	217	Secular	(NA)	53
Full Gospel	51	168	No religion	13,116	27,486
Christian Reform	40	79			
Foursquare Gospel	28	70	Refused to reply to question	4,031	11,246

NA Not available. [1] Refers to the total number of adults in all fifty states. All other figures are based on projections from surveys conducted in the continental United States (48 states). [2] Because of the subjective nature of replies to open-ended questions, these categories are the most unstable as they do not refer to clearly identifiable denominations as much as underlying feelings about religion. Thus they may be the most subject to fluctuation over time.

Source: 1990 data, Barry A. Kosmin and Seymour P. Lachman, "One Nation Under God: Religion in Contemporary American Society", 1993; 2001 data, Barry A. Kosmin and Ariela Keysar, Institute for the Study of Secularism in Society and Culture, Trinity College, Hartford, CT, <http://www.trincoll.edu/secularisminstitute/> (copyright).

Population 59

Table 75. Religious Bodies—Selected Data

[**Membership data: 2,500 represents 2,500,000.** Includes the self-reported membership of religious bodies with 750,000 or more as reported to the *Yearbook of American and Canadian Churches*. Groups may be excluded if they do not supply information. The data are not standardized so comparisons between groups are difficult. The definition of "church member" is determined by the religious body]

Religious body	Year reported	Churches reported	Membership (1,000)
African Methodist Episcopal Church.	1999	4,174	2,500
African Methodist Episcopal Zion Church	2005	3,260	1,440
American Baptist Churches in the USA	2005	5,740	1,397
Assemblies of God.	2005	12,298	2,831
Baptist Bible Fellowship International	1997	4,500	1,200
Catholic Church.	2005	18,992	69,135
Christian Churches and Churches of Christ.	1988	5,579	1,072
Christian Methodist Episcopal Church	2005	3,320	850
Church of God in Christ.	1991	15,300	5,500
Church of God (Cleveland, Tennessee)	2005	6,587	1,013
Church of Jesus Christ of Latter-day Saints.	2005	12,753	5,691
Churches of Christ	2005	15,000	1,639
Episcopal Church.	2004	7,200	2,248
Evangelical Lutheran Church in America.	2005	10,549	4,851
Greek Orthodox Archdiocese of America	2005	566	1,500
Jehovah's Witnesses	2005	12,384	1,046
Lutheran Church—Missouri Synod.	2005	6,144	2,441
National Baptist Convention of America Inc	2000	(NA)	3,500
National Baptist Convention, U.S.A., Inc.	2004	9,000	5,000
National Missionary Baptist Convention of America.	1992	(NA)	2,500
Orthodox Church in America.	2004	737	1,064
Pentecostal Assemblies of the World, Inc	1998	1,750	1,500
Presbyterian Church (U.S.A.)	2005	10,960	3,099
Progressive National Baptist Convention, Inc.	1995	2,000	2,500
Seventh Day Adventist Church	2005	4,750	965
Southern Baptist Convention	2005	43,669	16,270
United Church of Christ.	2005	5,567	1,224
United Methodist Church	2004	34,660	8,075

NA Not available.

Source: National Council of Churches USA, New York, NY, *2007 Yearbook of American & Canadian Churches*, annual (copyright). (For more church-related information visit <http://www.ncccusa.org> or call 888-870-3325).

Table 76. Christian Church Adherents, 2000, and Jewish Population, 2004—States

[**133,377 represents 133,377,000.** Christian church adherents were defined as "all members, including full members, their children and the estimated number of other regular participants who are not considered as communicant, confirmed or full members." The Jewish population includes Jews who define themselves as Jewish by religion as well as those who define themselves as Jewish in cultural terms. Data on Jewish population are based primarily on a compilation of individual estimates made by local Jewish federations. Additionally, most large communities have completed Jewish demographic surveys from which the Jewish population can be determined]

State	Christian adherents 2000		Jewish population 2004		State	Christian adherents 2000		Jewish population 2004	
	Number (1,000)	Percent of population [1]	Number (1,000)	Percent of population [1]		Number (1,000)	Percent of population [1]	Number (1,000)	Percent of population [1]
U.S.	133,377	47.4	6,452	2.2	MO	2,813	50.3	59	1.0
AL	2,418	54.4	9	0.2	MT	401	44.4	1	0.1
AK	210	33.6	3	0.5	NE	995	58.2	7	0.4
AZ	1,946	37.9	106	1.8	NV	604	30.2	70	2.9
AR	1,516	56.7	2	0.1	NH	571	46.2	10	0.8
CA	14,328	42.3	1,194	3.3	NJ	4,262	50.7	480	5.5
CO	1,604	37.3	79	1.7	NM	1,041	57.2	11	0.6
CT	1,828	53.7	112	3.2	NY	9,569	50.4	1,618	8.4
DE	299	38.2	14	1.6	NC	3,598	44.7	26	0.3
DC	331	57.8	28	5.1	ND	468	72.9	(Z)	0.1
FL	5,904	36.9	653	3.7	OH	4,912	43.3	145	1.3
GA	3,528	43.1	127	1.4	OK	2,079	60.3	5	0.1
HI	431	35.6	7	0.5	OR	1,029	30.1	32	0.9
ID	624	48.3	1	0.1	PA	6,751	55.0	285	2.3
IL	6,457	52.0	279	2.2	RI	646	61.7	19	1.7
IN	2,578	42.4	17	0.3	SC	1,874	46.7	11	(Z)
IA	1,698	58.0	6	0.2	SD	510	67.6	(Z)	(Z)
KS	1,307	48.6	18	0.7	TN	2,867	50.4	19	0.3
KY	2,141	53.0	11	0.3	TX	11,316	54.3	131	0.6
LA	2,599	58.2	16	0.4	UT	1,659	74.3	4	0.2
ME	450	35.3	10	0.8	VT	230	37.8	6	0.9
MD	2,012	38.0	235	4.2	VA	2,807	39.7	98	1.3
MA	3,725	58.7	275	4.3	WA	1,872	31.8	43	0.7
MI	3,970	39.9	88	0.9	WV	646	35.7	2	0.1
MN	2,974	60.5	47	0.9	WI	3,198	59.6	28	0.5
MS	1,549	54.5	1	0.1	WY	229	46.4	(Z)	0.1

Z Fewer than 500 or .05 percent. [1] Based on U.S. Census Bureau data for resident population enumerated as of April 1, 2000, and estimated as of July 1, 2004.

Source: Christian church adherents—Dale E. Jones, Sherri Doty, Clifford Grammich, James E. Horsch, Richard Houseal, John P. Marcum, Kenneth M. Sanchagrin, and Richard H. Taylor, *Religious Congregations and Membership in the United States: 2000*, Glenmary Research Center, Nashville, TN <www.glenmary.org/grc>, 2002 (copyright); Jewish population—American Jewish Committee, New York, NY, *American Jewish Year Book* (copyright).

60 Population

Section 2
Births, Deaths, Marriages, and Divorces

This section presents vital statistics data on births, deaths, abortions, fetal deaths, fertility, life expectancy, marriages, and divorces. Vital statistics are compiled for the country as a whole by the National Center for Health Statistics (NCHS) and published in its annual report, *Vital Statistics of the United States,* in certain reports of the *Vital and Health Statistics* series, and in the *National Vital Statistics Reports.* Reports in this field are also issued by the various state bureaus of vital statistics. Data on fertility, on age of persons at first marriage, and on marital status and marital history are compiled by the U.S. Census Bureau from its Current Population Survey (CPS; see text, Section 1) and published in *Current Population Reports,* P20 Series. Data on abortions are published by the Alan Guttmacher Institute, New York, NY, in selected issues of *Perspectives on Sexual and Reproductive Health* online at <www.guttmacher.org /sections/abortion.php>.

Registration of vital events—The registration of births, deaths, fetal deaths, and other vital events in the United States is primarily a state and local function. The civil laws of every state provide for a continuous and permanent birth- and death-registration system. Many states also provide for marriage- and divorce-registration systems. Vital events occurring to U.S. residents outside the United States are not included in the data.

Births and deaths—The live-birth, death, and fetal-death statistics prepared by NCHS are based on vital records filed in the registration offices of all states, New York City, and the District of Columbia. The annual collection of death statistics on a national basis began in 1900 with a national death-registration area of ten states and the District of Columbia; a similar annual collection of birth statistics for a national birth-registration area began in 1915, also with ten reporting states and the District of Columbia. Since 1933, the birth- and death-registration areas have comprised the entire United

States, including Alaska (beginning 1959) and Hawaii (beginning 1960). National statistics on fetal deaths were first compiled for 1918 and annually since 1922.

Prior to 1951, birth statistics came from a complete count of records received in the Public Health Service (now received in NCHS). From 1951 through 1971, they were based on a 50-percent sample of all registered births (except for a complete count in 1955 and a 20- to 50-percent sample in 1967). Beginning in 1972, they have been based on a complete count for states participating in the Vital Statistics Cooperative Program (VSCP) (for details, see the technical appendix in *Vital Statistics of the United States*) and on a 50-percent sample of all other areas. Beginning in 1986, all reporting areas participated in the VSCP. Mortality data have been based on a complete count of records for each area (except for a 50-percent sample in 1972). Beginning in 1970, births to and deaths of nonresident aliens of the United States and U.S. citizens outside the United States have been excluded from the data. Fetal deaths and deaths among Armed Forces abroad are excluded. Data based on samples are subject to sampling error; for details, see annual issues of *Vital Statistics of the United States.*

Mortality statistics by cause of death are compiled in accordance with World Health Organization regulations according to the *International Classification of Diseases* (ICD). The ICD is revised approximately every 10 years. The tenth revision of the ICD was employed beginning in 1999. Deaths for prior years were classified according to the revision of the ICD in use at the time. Each revision of the ICD introduces a number of discontinuities in mortality statistics; for a discussion of those between the ninth and tenth revisions of the ICD, see *National Vital Statistics Reports,* Vol. 49, Nos. 2 and 8. Preliminary mortality data are based on a percentage of death records weighted up to the total number of deaths reported for the given

U.S. Census Bureau, Statistical Abstract of the United States: 2008

year; for a discussion of preliminary data, see *National Vital Statistics Reports*, Vol. 49, No. 3. Information on tests of statistical significance, differences between death rates, and standard errors can also be found in the reports mentioned above.

Some of the tables present age-adjusted death rates in addition to crude death rates. Age-adjusted death rates shown in this section were prepared using the direct method, in which age-specific death rates for a population of interest are applied to a standard population distributed by age. Age adjustment eliminates the differences in observed rates between points in time or among compared population groups that result from age differences in population composition.

Fertility and life expectancy—The total fertility rate, defined as the number of births that 1,000 women would have in their lifetime if, at each year of age, they experienced the birth rates occurring in the specified year, is compiled and published by NCHS. Other data relating to social and medical factors that affect fertility rates, such as contraceptive use and birth expectations, are collected and made available by both NCHS and the Census Bureau. NCHS figures are based on information in birth and fetal death certificates and on the periodic National Surveys of Family Growth; Census Bureau data are based on decennial censuses and the CPS.

Data on life expectancy, the average remaining lifetime in years for persons who attain a given age, are computed and published by NCHS. For details, see *National Vital Statistics Reports*, Vol. 52, No. 3.

Marriage and divorce—In 1957 and 1958 respectively, the National Office of Vital Statistics established marriage- and divorce-registration areas. Beginning in 1957, the marriage-registration area comprised 30 states, plus Alaska, Hawaii, Puerto Rico, and the Virgin Islands; it currently includes 42 states and the District of Columbia. The divorce-registration area, starting in 1958 with 14 states, Alaska, Hawaii, and the Virgin Islands, currently includes a total of 31 states and

the Virgin Islands. Procedures for estimating the number of marriages and divorces in the registration states are discussed in *Vital Statistics of the United States*, Vol. III—Marriage and Divorce. Total counts of events for registration and nonregistration states are gathered by collecting already summarized data on marriages and divorces reported by state offices of vital statistics and by county offices of registration. The collection and publication of detailed marriage and divorce statistics was suspended beginning in January 1996. For additional information, contact the National Center for Health Statistics online at <http://www.cdc.gov/nchs/datawh/datasite/frnotice.htm>.

Vital statistics rates—Except as noted, vital statistics rates computed by NCHS are based on decennial census population figures as of April 1 for 1960, 1970, 1980, 1990, and 2000; and on midyear population figures for other years, as estimated by the Census Bureau (see text, Section 1).

Race—Data by race for births, deaths, marriages, and divorces from NCHS are based on information contained in the certificates of registration. The Census Bureau's Current Population Survey obtains information on race by asking respondents to classify their race as (1) White, (2) Black, (3) American Indian or Alaska Native, (4) Native Hawaiian or Other Pacific Islander, and (5) Asian.

Beginning with the 1989 data year, NCHS is tabulating its birth data primarily by race of the mother. In 1988 and prior years, births were tabulated by race of the child, which was determined from the race of the parents as entered on the birth certificate.

Trend data by race shown in this section are by race of mother beginning with the 1980 data. Hispanic origin of the mother is reported and tabulated independently of race. Thus, persons of Hispanic origin may be any race. In 1994, 91 percent of women of Hispanic origin were reported as White.

Statistical reliability—For a discussion of statistical collection, estimation, and sampling procedures and measures of reliability applicable to data from NCHS and the Census Bureau, see Appendix III.

Table 77. **Live Births, Deaths, Marriages, and Divorces: 1960 to 2006**

[**4,258 represents 4,258,000**. Beginning 1970, excludes births to, and deaths of, nonresidents of the United States. See Appendix III]

Year	Number					Rate per 1,000 population				
		Deaths					Deaths			
	Births (1,000)	Total (1,000)	Infant [1] (1,000)	Marriages [2] (1,000)	Divorces [3] (1,000)	Births	Total	Infant [1]	Marriages [2]	Divorces [3]
1960	4,258	1,712	111	1,523	393	23.7	9.5	26.0	8.5	2.2
1965	3,760	1,828	93	1,800	479	19.4	9.4	24.7	9.3	2.5
1970	3,731	1,921	75	2,159	708	18.4	9.5	20.0	10.6	3.5
1971	3,556	1,928	68	2,190	773	17.2	9.3	19.1	10.6	3.7
1972	3,258	1,964	60	2,282	845	15.6	9.4	18.5	10.9	4.0
1973	3,137	1,973	56	2,284	915	14.8	9.3	17.7	10.8	4.3
1974	3,160	1,934	53	2,230	977	14.8	9.1	16.7	10.5	4.6
1975	3,144	1,893	51	2,153	1,036	14.6	8.8	16.1	10.0	4.8
1976	3,168	1,909	48	2,155	1,083	14.6	8.8	15.2	9.9	5.0
1977	3,327	1,900	47	2,178	1,091	15.1	8.6	14.1	9.9	5.0
1978	3,333	1,928	46	2,282	1,130	15.0	8.7	13.8	10.3	5.1
1979	3,494	1,914	46	2,331	1,181	15.6	8.5	13.1	10.4	5.3
1980	3,612	1,990	46	2,390	1,189	15.9	8.8	12.6	10.6	5.2
1981	3,629	1,978	43	2,422	1,213	15.8	8.6	11.9	10.6	5.3
1982	3,681	1,975	42	2,456	1,170	15.9	8.5	11.5	10.6	5.1
1983	3,639	2,019	41	2,446	1,158	15.6	8.6	11.2	10.5	5.0
1984	3,669	2,039	40	2,477	1,169	15.6	8.6	10.8	10.5	5.0
1985	3,761	2,086	40	2,413	1,190	15.8	8.8	10.6	10.1	5.0
1986	3,757	2,105	39	2,407	1,178	15.6	8.8	10.4	10.0	4.9
1987	3,809	2,123	38	2,403	1,166	15.7	8.8	10.1	9.9	4.8
1988	3,910	2,168	39	2,396	1,167	16.0	8.9	10.0	9.8	4.8
1989	4,041	2,150	40	2,403	1,157	16.4	8.7	9.8	9.7	4.7
1990	4,158	2,148	38	2,443	1,182	16.7	8.6	9.2	9.8	4.7
1991	4,111	2,170	37	2,371	1,187	16.2	8.6	8.9	9.4	4.7
1992	4,065	2,176	35	2,362	1,215	15.8	8.5	8.5	9.3	4.8
1993	4,000	2,269	33	2,334	1,187	15.4	8.8	8.4	9.0	4.6
1994	3,953	2,279	31	2,362	1,191	15.0	8.8	8.0	9.1	4.6
1995	3,900	2,312	30	2,336	1,169	14.6	8.7	7.6	8.9	4.4
1996	3,891	2,315	28	2,344	1,150	14.4	8.6	7.3	8.8	4.3
1997 [4] . . .	3,881	2,314	28	2,384	1,163	14.2	8.5	7.2	8.9	4.3
1998 [4] . . .	3,942	2,337	28	2,244	1,135	14.3	8.5	7.2	8.4	4.2
1999 [4] . . .	3,959	2,391	28	2,358	(NA)	14.2	8.6	7.1	8.6	4.1
2000 [4] . . .	4,059	2,403	28	2,329	(NA)	14.4	8.5	6.9	8.3	4.1
2001 [4] . . .	4,026	2,416	28	2,345	(NA)	14.1	8.5	6.8	8.2	4.0
2002 [5] . . .	4,022	2,443	28	2,254	(NA)	13.9	8.5	7.0	7.8	3.9
2003 [5] . . .	4,090	2,448	28	2,245	(NA)	14.1	8.4	6.9	7.7	3.8
2004 [5] . . .	4,112	2,398	28	2,279	(NA)	14.0	8.2	6.8	7.8	3.7
2005 [5,6] . .	4,143	2,432	28	2,249	(NA)	14.0	8.2	6.8	[7]7.6	3.6
2006 [5,6] . .	4,269	2,416	28	[7]2.160	(NA)	14.3	8.1	6.6	[7]7.3	3.6

NA Not available.   [1] Infants under 1 year, excluding fetal deaths; rates per 1,000 registered live births.   [2] Includes estimates for some states through 1965 and also for 1976 and 1977, and marriage licenses for some states for all years except 1973 and 1975. Beginning 1978, includes nonlicensed marriages in California.   [3] Includes reported annulments and some estimated state figures for all years.   [4] Divorce rate excludes data for California, Colorado, Indiana, and Louisiana; population for this rate also excludes these states.   [5] Divorce rates exclude data for California, Georgia, Hawaii, Indiana, Louisiana, and Minnesota in 2005 and 2006; California, Georgia, Hawaii, Indiana, and Louisiana in 2004; California, Hawaii, Indiana, Louisiana, and Oklahoma in 2003; and California, Indiana, and Oklahoma in 2002. Populations for these rates also exclude these states.   [6] Provisional data. Includes nonresidents of the United States.   [7] Excludes Louisiana.

Source: U.S. National Center for Health Statistics, *Vital Statistics of the United States, annual;* and *National Vital Statistics Reports (NVSR)*. See also <http://www.cdc.gov/nchs/births.htm>.

Table 78. **Live Births, Birth Rates, and Fertility Rates by Hispanic Origin Status: 1990 to 2005**

[**4,093 represents 4,093,000**. Represents registered births. Excludes births to nonresidents of the United States. Data are based on Hispanic origin and race of mother. Persons of Hispanic origin may be any race. See Appendix III]

Hispanic origin status and race of mother	Number of births (1,000)				Birth rate per 1,000 population				Fertility rate [2]			
	1990 [1]	2000	2004	2005, prel.	1990 [1]	2000	2004	2005, prel.	1990 [1]	2000	2004	2005, prel.
Total [3]	4,093	4,059	4,112	4,140	16.7	14.4	14.0	14.0	71.0	65.9	66.3	66.7
Hispanic origin	595	816	946	983	26.7	23.1	22.9	23.0	107.7	95.9	97.8	99.1
Mexican	386	582	678	(NA)	28.7	25.0	24.9	(NA)	118.9	105.1	106.8	(NA)
Puerto Rican	59	58	61	(NA)	21.6	18.1	16.1	(NA)	82.9	73.5	68.4	(NA)
Cuban	11	13	15	(NA)	10.9	9.7	9.3	(NA)	52.6	49.3	53.2	(NA)
Central and South American [4] . . .	83	113	144	(NA)	27.5	21.8	22.2	(NA)	102.7	85.1	89.3	(NA)
Other and unknown Hispanic .	56	49	49	(NA)	([4])	([4])	([4])	(NA)	([4])	([4])	([4])	(NA)
Non-Hispanic [5]	3,457	3,200	3,133	(NA)	15.7	13.2	12.5	(NA)	67.1	61.1	60.5	(NA)
White	2,627	2,363	2,297	2,285	14.4	12.2	11.6	11.5	62.8	58.5	58.4	58.4
Black	662	604	579	584	23.0	17.3	15.8	15.7	89.0	71.4	67.0	67.2

NA Not available.   [1] Excludes data for New Hampshire and Oklahoma, which did not report Hispanic origin.   [2] Live births per 1,000 women age 15 to 44 years in specified group.   [3] Includes Hispanic origin status not stated.   [4] Rates for the Central and South American population include other and unknown Hispanic.   [5] Includes other races not shown separately.

Source: U.S. National Center for Health Statistics, *National Vital Statistics Reports (NVSR)*, Volume 55, Number 1, September 29, 2006, and Volume 55, Number 11, December 28, 2006.

U.S. Census Bureau, Statistical Abstract of the United States: 2008

Table 79. Births and Birth Rates by Race, Sex, and Age: 1980 to 2005

[Births in thousands (3,612 represents 3,612,000). Births by race of mother. Excludes births to nonresidents of the United States. For population bases used to derive these data, see text this section, and Appendix III]

Item	1980	1985	1990	1995	1999	2000	2001	2002	2003	2004	2005, prel.
Live births [1]	3,612	3,761	4,158	3,900	3,959	4,059	4,026	4,022	4,090	4,112	4,140
White	2,936	3,038	3,290	3,099	3,133	3,194	3,178	3,175	3,226	3,223	3,232
Black	568	582	684	603	606	623	606	594	600	616	633
American Indian, Eskimo, Aleut	29	34	39	37	41	42	42	42	43	44	45
Asian or Pacific Islander	74	105	142	160	182	201	200	211	221	229	231
Male	1,853	1,928	2,129	1,996	2,027	2,077	2,058	2,058	2,094	2,105	(NA)
Female	1,760	1,833	2,029	1,903	1,933	1,982	1,968	1,964	1,996	2,007	(NA)
Males per 100 females	105	105	105	105	105	105	105	105	105	105	(NA)
Age of mother:											
Under 20 years old	562	478	533	512	485	478	454	433	421	422	421
20 to 24 years old	1,226	1,141	1,094	966	982	1,018	1,022	1,022	1,032	1,034	1,040
25 to 29 years old	1,108	1,201	1,277	1,064	1,078	1,088	1,058	1,060	1,086	1,104	1,132
30 to 34 years old	550	696	886	905	892	929	943	951	976	966	952
35 to 39 years old	141	214	318	384	434	452	452	454	468	476	483
40 to 44 years old	(NA)	(NA)	(NA)	(NA)	83	90	93	96	101	104	105
45 to 49 years old	(NA)	(NA)	(NA)	(NA)	4	4	5	5	6	6	7
Mean age of mother at first birth (years)	22.7	23.7	24.2	24.5	(NA)	24.9	25.0	25.1	25.2	25.2	(NA)
Birth rate per 1,000 population	15.9	15.8	16.7	14.6	14.2	14.4	14.1	13.9	14.1	14.0	14.0
White	15.1	15.0	15.8	14.1	13.7	13.9	13.7	13.5	13.6	13.5	(NA)
Black	21.3	20.4	22.4	17.8	16.8	17.0	16.3	15.7	15.7	16.0	(NA)
American Indian, Eskimo, Aleut	20.7	19.8	18.9	15.3	14.2	14.0	13.7	13.8	13.8	14.0	14.2
Asian or Pacific Islander	19.9	18.7	19.0	16.7	15.9	17.1	16.4	16.5	16.8	16.8	16.5
Age of mother:											
10 to 14 years old	1.1	1.2	1.4	1.3	0.9	0.9	0.8	0.7	0.6	0.7	0.7
15 to 19 years old	53.0	51.0	59.9	56.0	48.8	47.7	45.3	43.0	41.6	41.1	40.4
20 to 24 years old	115.1	108.3	116.5	107.5	107.9	109.7	106.2	103.6	102.6	101.7	102.2
25 to 29 years old	112.9	111.0	120.2	108.8	111.2	113.5	113.4	113.6	115.6	115.5	115.6
30 to 34 years old	61.9	69.1	80.8	81.1	87.1	91.2	91.9	91.5	95.1	95.3	95.9
35 to 39 years old	19.8	24.0	31.7	34.0	37.8	39.7	40.6	41.4	43.8	45.4	46.3
40 to 44 years old	3.9	4.0	5.5	6.6	7.4	8.0	8.1	8.3	8.7	8.9	9.1
45 to 49 years old [2]	0.2	0.2	0.2	0.3	0.4	0.5	0.5	0.5	0.5	0.5	0.6
Fertility rate per 1,000 women [3]	68.4	66.2	70.9	64.6	64.4	65.9	65.3	64.8	66.1	66.3	66.7
White [3]	65.6	64.1	68.3	63.6	64.0	65.3	65.0	64.8	66.1	66.1	(NA)
Black [3]	84.9	78.8	84.8	71.0	68.5	70.0	67.6	65.8	66.3	67.6	(NA)
American Indian, Eskimo, Aleut [3]	82.7	78.6	76.2	63.0	59.0	58.7	58.1	58.0	58.4	58.9	59.9
Asian or Pacific Islander [3]	73.2	68.4	69.6	62.6	60.9	65.8	64.2	64.1	66.3	67.1	66.6

NA Not available.   [1] Includes other races not shown separately.   [2] Beginning 1999, rates computed by relating births to women aged 45 to 54 years old to women 45 to 49 years old.   [3] Number of live births per 1,000 women, 15 to 44 years old in specified group.

Source: U.S. National Center for Health Statistics, *National Vital Statistics Reports (NVSR)*, Volume 55, Number 1, September 29, 2006; Volume 55, Number 11, December 28, 2006; and prior reports.

Table 80. Births and Birth Rates by Plurality of Birth and Race and Hispanic-Origin Status of Mother: 1990 to 2004

[Persons of Hispanic origin may be of any race. See headnote, Table 78. See Appendix III]

Birth order	1990 [1]	1995	2000	2002	2003	2004
All births, total number [2]	4,158,212	3,899,589	4,058,814	4,021,726	4,089,950	4,112,052
Twin births	93,865	96,736	118,916	125,134	128,665	132,219
Triplet and higher order multiple births	3,028	4,973	7,325	7,401	7,663	7,275
Multiple birth rate [3]	23.3	26.1	31.1	33.0	33.3	33.9
Twin birth rate [4]	22.6	24.8	29.3	31.1	31.5	32.2
Triplet and higher order multiple birth rate [5]	72.8	127.5	180.5	184.0	187.4	176.9
Non-Hispanic White births, total number	2,626,500	2,382,638	2,362,968	2,298,156	2,321,904	2,296,683
Twin births	60,210	62,370	76,018	79,949	81,691	83,346
Triplet and higher order multiple births	2,358	4,050	5,821	5,754	5,922	5,590
Multiple birth rate [3]	23.8	27.9	34.6	37.3	37.7	38.7
Twin birth rate [4]	22.9	26.2	32.2	34.8	35.2	36.3
Non-Hispanic Black births, total number	661,701	587,741	604,346	578,033	576,033	578,772
Twin births	17,646	16,622	20,173	20,064	20,010	20,605
Triplet and higher order multiple births	306	340	498	591	631	577
Multiple birth rate [3]	27.1	28.9	34.2	35.7	35.8	36.6
Twin birth rate [4]	26.7	28.3	33.4	34.7	34.7	35.6
Hispanic births, total number	595,073	679,768	815,868	876,642	912,329	946,349
Twin births	10,713	12,685	16,470	18,128	19,472	20,351
Triplet and higher order multiple births	235	355	659	737	784	723
Multiple birth rate [3]	18.4	19.2	21.0	21.5	22.2	22.3
Twin birth rate [4]	18.0	18.7	20.2	20.7	21.3	21.5

[1] Data by Hispanic-origin status exclude data for New Hampshire and Oklahoma, which did not report Hispanic origin.   [2] Includes other races not shown separately.   [3] Number of live births in all multiple deliveries per 1,000 live births.   [4] Number of live births in twin deliveries per 1,000 live births.   [5] Number of live births in triplet and other higher-order deliveries per 100,000 live births.

Source: U.S. National Center for Health Statistics. *National Vital Statistics Reports (NVSR)*, Vol. 55. Number 1. September 29, 2006.

64   Births, Deaths, Marriages, and Divorces

Table 81. **Live Births by State and Island Areas: 2005**

[Number of births, except rate. Registered births. Excludes births to nonresidents of the United States. By race and Hispanic origin of mother. Data are preliminary. See Appendix III]

State and island area	All races [1]	White	Black	Asian or Pacific Islander	American Indian, Eskimo, Aleut	Hispanic [2]	Birth rate [3]	Fertility rate [4]
United States	**4,140,419**	**3,231,783**	**632,625**	**231,244**	**44,767**	**982,862**	**14.0**	**66.7**
Alabama.	60,447	41,247	18,137	873	189	3,987	13.3	63.5
Alaska.	10,463	6,537	424	776	2,726	780	15.8	75.4
Arizona.	96,231	83,163	3,648	2,959	6,460	42,883	16.2	79.2
Arkansas	39,196	30,798	7,470	687	241	4,037	14.1	69.1
California	549,626	445,665	32,410	68,458	3,093	283,600	15.2	71.4
Colorado.	68,963	62,875	3,123	2,390	575	21,798	14.8	68.8
Connecticut.	41,717	33,985	5,279	2,239	213	8,005	11.9	58.7
Delaware	11,648	8,199	2,911	500	38	1,654	13.8	65.1
District of Columbia	7,893	2,425	5,268	193	7	1,086	14.3	59.2
Florida	226,280	161,497	56,520	7,564	698	60,082	12.7	65.6
Georgia	142,256	91,165	45,818	5,005	268	22,001	15.7	70.0
Hawaii	17,925	5,044	487	12,311	83	2,792	14.1	72.9
Idaho	23,062	22,112	146	392	412	3,493	16.1	77.4
Illinois	179,061	138,991	30,733	9,052	284	43,449	14.0	66.4
Indiana.	87,282	75,808	9,885	1,442	147	8,054	13.9	67.3
Iowa	39,312	36,605	1,507	946	254	3,117	13.3	65.4
Kansas.	39,893	35,123	3,125	1,214	431	6,127	14.5	70.4
Kentucky	56,385	50,398	5,085	818	84	2,509	13.5	64.7
Louisiana	61,005	35,498	24,109	1,034	364	1,947	13.5	62.6
Maine.	14,113	13,508	265	226	114	183	10.7	53.6
Maryland	74,986	43,326	26,491	4,979	189	8,689	13.4	62.8
Massachusetts.	76,920	62,453	8,805	5,485	177	10,119	12.0	56.1
Michigan.	127,799	100,142	22,480	4,446	731	8,614	12.6	61.0
Minnesota.	70,969	57,827	6,897	4,776	1,469	5,515	13.8	65.0
Mississippi	42,398	23,047	18,660	408	283	1,170	14.5	67.8
Missouri	78,619	64,730	11,686	1,760	443	4,275	13.6	65.0
Montana.	11,602	9,931	62	119	1,490	397	12.4	63.3
Nebraska	26,148	23,236	1,719	696	497	3,858	14.9	72.1
Nevada	37,258	30,665	3,206	2,900	486	14,056	15.4	74.5
New Hampshire	14,426	13,578	233	586	29	523	11.0	53.4
New Jersey.	113,700	82,617	19,967	10,938	178	27,952	13.0	63.8
New Mexico	28,834	24,120	538	460	3,716	15,825	15.0	72.8
New York	246,354	170,026	54,358	21,297	674	57,436	12.8	60.3
North Carolina	123,118	89,650	28,441	3,342	1,685	19,529	14.2	67.2
North Dakota.	8,393	7,196	130	106	961	180	13.2	65.3
Ohio	148,916	120,914	24,233	3,475	294	6,098	13.0	63.2
Oklahoma.	51,746	39,991	4,817	1,087	5,852	6,273	14.6	70.8
Oregon.	45,937	41,576	1,010	2,503	848	9,175	12.6	61.6
Pennsylvania	145,584	116,580	22,886	5,754	364	12,189	11.7	58.8
Rhode Island.	12,680	10,691	1,286	557	146	2,559	11.8	55.6
South Carolina.	57,728	36,109	20,376	1,027	215	4,994	13.6	64.5
South Dakota.	11,457	9,263	143	111	1,940	392	14.8	73.4
Tennessee	81,743	61,405	18,484	1,696	157	7,005	13.7	64.9
Texas.	385,963	327,419	44,088	13,559	896	191,492	16.9	77.7
Utah	51,554	48,930	484	1,500	640	7,565	20.9	90.4
Vermont	6,475	6,273	78	110	14	73	10.4	51.0
Virginia.	104,592	74,351	22,916	7,163	161	13,064	13.8	65.2
Washington.	82,705	67,921	4,228	8,474	2,082	15,019	13.2	62.1
West Virginia	20,838	19,936	708	177	16	174	11.5	58.8
Wisconsin	70,978	60,466	6,796	2,599	1,116	6,240	12.8	61.7
Wyoming	7,239	6,771	63	70	335	829	14.2	71.3
Puerto Rico	50,572	45,635	4,927	10	(NA)	(NA)	12.9	59.4
Virgin Islands	1,599	373	1,163	1	62	331	14.7	71.5
Guam	3,187	278	31	2,874	4	57	18.9	85.0
American Samoa	1,720	2	(NA)	1,718	(NA)	(NA)	27.6	125.5
Northern Marianas	1,332	19	1	1,312	(NA)	(NA)	16.6	41.3

NA Not available.   [1] Includes persons of non-Hispanic origin not shown separately.   [2] Persons of Hispanic origin may be any race.   [3] Per 1,000 estimated population.   [4] Number of births per 1,000 women age 15 to 44 years estimated.

Source: U.S. National Center for Health Statistics, *National Vital Statistics Reports (NVSR)*, Volume 55, Number 11, December 28, 2006.

Births, Deaths, Marriages, and Divorces   65

Table 82. **Total Fertility Rate by Race and Hispanic Origin: 1980 to 2005**

[Based on race of mother. Excludes births to nonresidents of United States. The *total fertility rate* is the number of births that 1,000 women would have in their lifetime if, at each year of age, they experienced the birth rates occurring in the specified year. A total fertility rate of 2,110 represents "replacement level" fertility for the total population under current mortality conditions (assuming no net immigration). See Appendix III]

Race and Hispanic origin	1980	1990	1995	2000	2002	2003	2004	2005 [1]
Total [2]	1,840	2,081	1,978	2,056	2,013	2,043	2,046	2,054
White	1,773	2,003	1,955	2,051	2,028	2,061	2,055	(NA)
Black	2,177	2,480	2,128	2,129	1,991	1,999	2,033	(NA)
American Indian, Eskimo, Aleut. . .	2,165	2,185	1,879	1,773	1,735	1,732	1,735	1,749
Asian or Pacific Islander	1,954	2,003	1,796	1,892	1,820	1,873	1,898	1,890
Hispanic [3]	(NA)	2,960	2,799	2,730	2,718	2,786	2,825	2,877

NA Not available. [1] Preliminary data. [2] For 1980 and 1990, includes births to races not shown separately. Beginning 1995, unknown race of mother is imputed. [3] Persons of Hispanic origin may be any race.

Source: U.S. National Center for Health Statistics, *National Vital Statistics Reports (NVSR)*, Volume 55, Number 1, September 29, 2006, and Volume 55, Number 11, December 28, 2006.

Table 83. **Teenagers—Births and Birth Rates by Age, Race and Hispanic Origin: 1990 to 2005**

[Birth rates per 1,000 women in specified group, see text, this section. Based on race and Hispanic origin of mother]

Age, race, and Hispanic origin	Number of births					Birth rate				
	1990	1995	2000	2004	2005 [1]	1990	1995	2000	2004	2005 [1]
All races, total	[2]521,826	499,873	468,990	415,262	414,406	59.9	56.0	47.7	41.1	40.4
15 to 17 years old.	183,327	192,508	157,209	133,980	133,138	37.5	35.5	26.9	22.1	21.4
18 and 19 years old	338,499	307,365	311,781	281,282	281,269	88.6	87.7	78.1	70.0	69.9
White	354,482	349,635	333,013	297,133	295,277	50.8	49.5	43.2	37.7	37.0
Black	151,613	133,694	118,954	102,793	103,733	112.8	94.4	77.4	63.3	61.9
American Indian, Eskimo, Aleut.	(NA)	7,764	8,055	7,704	7,799	81.1	72.9	58.3	52.5	52.7
Asian or Pacific Islander. . .	(NA)	8,780	8,968	7,632	7,597	26.4	25.5	20.5	17.3	16.9
Hispanic [3]	(NA)	118,449	129,469	133,044	136,550	100.3	99.3	87.3	82.6	81.5
Non-Hispanic White.	(NA)	230,024	204,056	168,795	165,276	42.5	39.3	32.6	26.7	26.0
Non-Hispanic Black.	(NA)	130,907	116,019	97,290	96,761	116.2	97.2	79.2	63.1	60.9

NA Not available. [1] Preliminary data. [2] Includes races other than White and Black not shown separately [3] Persons of Hispanic origin may be any race.

Source: U.S. National Center for Health Statistics, *National Vital Statistics Reports (NVSR)*, Volume 55, Number 1, September 29, 2006, and Volume 55, Number 11, December 28, 2006.

Table 84. **Births to Unmarried Women by Race, Hispanic Origin, and Age of Mother: 1990 to 2005**

[1,165 represents 1,165,000. Excludes births to nonresidents of United States. Persons of Hispanic origin may be any race. Marital status is inferred from a comparison of the child's and parents' surnames on the birth certificate for those states that do not report on marital status. No estimates included for misstatements on birth records or failures to register births. Based on race and Hispanic origin of mother. See also Appendix III]

Race and age of mother	Number (1,000)					Percent distribution				Birth rate [1]			
	1990	1995	2000	2004	2005, prel.	1990	1995	2000	2004	1990	1995	2000	2004
Total live births [2]	1,165	1,254	1,347	1,470	1,525	100.0	100.0	100.0	100.0	43.8	44.3	44.1	46.1
White	670	785	866	983	(NA)	57.5	62.6	64.3	66.9	32.9	37.0	38.2	41.6
Black	455	421	427	424	(NA)	39.1	33.6	31.7	28.8	90.5	74.5	70.5	67.2
American Indian, Eskimo, Aleut.	(NA)	(NA)	(NA)	27	(NA)	(NA)	(NA)	(NA)	1.9	(NA)	(NA)	(NA)	(NA)
Asian or Pacific Islander. .	(NA)	(NA)	(NA)	35	(NA)	(NA)	(NA)	(NA)	2.4	(NA)	(NA)	20.9	23.6
Hispanic	[3]219	278	348	440	(NA)	[3]18.8	22.1	25.8	29.9	[3]89.6	88.8	87.3	95.7
Non-Hispanic White.	[3]443	504	522	563	(NA)	[3]38.0	40.2	38.7	38.3	[3]24.4	28.1	28.0	29.4
Non-Hispanic Black.	(NA)	(NA)	415	401	(NA)	(NA)	(NA)	30.8	27.3	(NA)	(NA)	(NA)	(NA)
Under 15 years	11	11	8	7	7	0.9	0.9	0.6	0.4	(NA)	(NA)	(NA)	(NA)
15 to 19 years	350	376	369	342	343	30.0	30.0	27.4	23.3	42.5	43.8	39.0	34.7
20 to 24 years	404	432	504	566	(NA)	34.7	34.5	37.4	38.5	65.1	68.7	72.2	72.5
25 to 29 years	230	229	255	308	(NA)	19.7	18.2	18.9	20.9	56.0	54.3	58.5	68.6
30 to 34 years	118	133	130	155	(NA)	10.1	10.6	9.7	10.6	37.6	38.9	39.3	47.0
35 to 39 years	44	60	65	72	(NA)	3.8	4.8	4.8	4.9	17.3	19.3	19.7	23.5
40 years and over.	9	13	16	20	(NA)	0.7	1.0	1.2	1.4	3.6	4.7	5.0	6.0

NA Not available. [1] Rate per 1,000 unmarried women (never-married, widowed, and divorced) estimated as of July 1. Total rate and rates by race/Hispanic origin cover women 15 to 44 years old. Rate for unmarried women 40 years and over relate births to women 40 years and over to unmarried women 40 to 44 years old. [2] Includes races other than White and Black not shown separately. [3] Excludes data for New Hampshire and Oklahoma, which did not report Hispanic origin.

Source: U.S. National Center for Health Statistics, *National Vital Statistics Reports (NVSR)*, Volume 55, Number 1, September 29, 2006, and Volume 55, Number 11, December 28, 2006.

Table 85. Births to Teens and Unmarried Mothers, and Births with Low Birth Weight, by Race and Hispanic Origin: 1990 to 2005

[Represents registered births. Excludes births to nonresidents of the United States. Data are based on race and Hispanic origin of mother. See Appendix III]

Race and Hispanic origin	1990	1995	2000	2002	2003	2004	2005, prel.
Percent of births to teenage mothers ...	**12.8**	**13.1**	**11.8**	**10.8**	**10.3**	**10.3**	**10.2**
White................................	10.9	11.5	10.6	9.8	9.4	9.3	9.2
Black................................	23.1	23.1	19.7	18.0	17.3	17.1	16.8
American Indian, Eskimo, Aleut	19.5	21.4	19.7	18.5	18.2	17.9	17.7
Asian or Pacific Islander	5.7	5.6	4.5	3.8	3.5	3.4	3.3
Hispanic origin [1]	16.8	17.9	16.2	14.9	14.3	14.3	14.1
Mexican...........................	17.7	18.8	17.0	15.9	15.3	15.3	(NA)
Puerto Rican......................	21.7	23.5	20.0	17.8	17.9	17.6	(NA)
Cuban	7.7	7.7	7.5	8.1	7.9	7.8	(NA)
Central and South American............	9.0	10.6	9.9	8.5	8.3	8.4	(NA)
Percent of births to unmarried mothers ..	**26.6**	**32.2**	**33.2**	**34.0**	**34.6**	**35.8**	**36.8**
White................................	16.9	25.3	27.1	28.5	29.4	30.5	(NA)
Black................................	66.7	69.9	68.5	68.2	68.2	68.8	(NA)
American Indian, Eskimo, Aleut	53.6	57.2	58.4	59.7	61.3	62.3	63.3
Asian or Pacific Islander	13.2	16.3	14.8	14.9	15.0	15.5	16.2
Hispanic origin [1]	36.7	40.8	42.7	43.5	45.0	46.4	47.9
Mexican...........................	33.3	38.1	40.7	42.1	43.7	45.2	(NA)
Puerto Rican......................	55.9	60.0	59.6	59.1	59.8	61.0	(NA)
Cuban	18.2	23.8	27.3	29.8	31.4	33.2	(NA)
Central and South American............	41.2	44.1	44.7	44.8	46.0	47.6	(NA)
Percent of births with low birth weight [2]	**7.0**	**7.3**	**7.6**	**7.8**	**7.9**	**8.1**	**8.2**
White................................	5.7	6.2	6.5	6.8	6.9	7.1	(NA)
Black................................	13.3	13.1	13.0	13.3	13.4	13.4	(NA)
American Indian, Eskimo, Aleut	6.1	6.6	6.8	7.2	7.4	7.5	7.4
Asian or Pacific Islander	(NA)	6.9	7.3	7.8	7.8	7.9	8.0
Hispanic origin [1]	6.1	6.3	6.4	6.5	6.7	6.8	6.9
Mexican...........................	5.5	5.8	6.0	6.2	6.3	6.4	(NA)
Puerto Rican......................	9.0	9.4	9.3	9.7	10.0	9.8	(NA)
Cuban	5.7	6.5	6.5	6.5	7.0	7.7	(NA)
Central and South American............	5.8	6.2	6.3	6.5	6.7	6.7	(NA)

NA Not available.   [1] Hispanic persons may be any race. Includes other types, not shown separately.   [2] Births less than 2,500 grams (5 lb.-8 oz.).

Source: U.S. National Center for Health Statistics, *National Vital Statistics Reports (NVSR)*, Volume 55, Number 1, September 29, 2006, and Volume 55, Number 11, December 28, 2006.

Table 86. Births by Race, Hispanic-Origin Status and Method of Delivery: 1990 to 2004

[In thousands (4,111 represents 4,111,000), except rate. 1990 excludes data for Oklahoma, which did not report method of delivery on the birth certificate. Persons of Hispanic origin may be any race. See Appendix III]

Method of delivery	1990	2000	2003	2004					
				Total [1]	White	Black	Hispanic	Non-Hispanic White	Non-Hispanic Black
Births, total	**4,111**	**4,059**	**4,090**	**4,112**	**3,223**	**616**	**946**	**2,297**	**579**
Vaginal	3,111	3,108	2,950	2,903	2,283	424	679	1,618	398
After previous caesarean ...	84	90	52	46	35	8	10	25	7
Caesarean deliveries........	914	924	1,119	1,190	925	189	263	668	178
Primary	575	578	684	740	571	120	149	426	113
Repeat	339	346	435	450	354	69	115	242	65
Not stated	85	27	21	19	15	3	4	11	2
Caesarean delivery rate [2].....	22.7	22.9	27.5	29.1	(NA)	(NA)	28.0	29.2	31.0
Primary [3]	16.0	16.1	19.1	20.6	(NA)	(NA)	18.2	21.1	22.5
Rate of vaginal birth after previous caesarean [4] ...	19.9	20.6	10.6	9.2	(NA)	(NA)	8.3	9.3	10.1

NA Not available.   [1] Includes other races not shown separately.   [2] Caesarean rates are the number of caesarean deliveries per 100 total deliveries for specified category.   [3] Number of primary caesareans per 100 live births to women who have not had a previous caesarean.   [4] Number of vaginal births after previous caesarean delivery per 100 live births to women with a previous cesarean delivery.

Source: U.S. National Center for Health Statistics. *National Vital Statistics Reports (NVSR)*, Volume 55, Number 1, September 29, 2006.

Births, Deaths, Marriages, and Divorces   67

[Represents registered births. Excludes births to nonresidents of the United States. Based on 100 percent of births in all states and the District of Columbia. 2005 data are preliminary and based on a substantial proportion of vital records for that year. See Appendix III]

State and island area	Births to teenage mothers, percent of total [1]			Births to unmarried women, percent of total			Percent of births with low birth weight [2]		
	2000	2004	2005	2000	2004	2005	2000	2004	2005
United States	11.8	10.3	10.2	33.2	35.8	36.8	7.6	8.1	8.2
Alabama	15.7	13.9	13.1	34.3	36.2	35.7	9.7	10.4	10.7
Alaska	11.8	10.5	10.0	33.0	34.6	36.0	5.6	6.0	6.1
Arizona	14.3	12.7	12.5	39.3	42.2	43.1	7.0	7.2	6.9
Arkansas	17.3	15.1	14.6	35.7	38.8	40.2	8.6	9.3	8.9
California	10.6	9.3	9.2	32.7	34.4	35.7	6.2	6.7	6.9
Colorado	11.7	10.0	9.8	25.0	27.5	27.1	8.4	9.0	9.2
Connecticut	7.8	6.9	6.8	29.3	30.6	32.2	7.4	7.8	8.0
Delaware	12.3	10.6	10.7	37.9	42.3	44.3	8.6	9.0	9.5
District of Columbia	14.2	11.2	10.8	60.3	55.9	55.5	11.9	11.1	11.1
Florida	12.6	10.9	10.9	38.2	41.4	42.8	8.0	8.5	8.7
Georgia	13.9	11.9	11.8	37.0	39.2	40.3	8.6	9.3	9.4
Hawaii	10.3	8.0	8.3	32.2	33.4	36.2	7.5	7.9	8.2
Idaho	11.6	9.2	8.8	21.6	22.6	22.9	6.7	6.8	6.7
Illinois	11.4	9.9	9.7	34.5	36.3	37.1	7.9	8.4	8.5
Indiana	12.5	11.0	11.0	34.7	38.8	40.2	7.4	8.1	8.3
Iowa	10.0	8.5	8.5	28.0	31.0	32.5	6.1	7.0	7.2
Kansas	12.0	10.2	10.3	29.0	33.0	34.2	6.9	7.3	7.2
Kentucky	14.1	12.2	12.1	31.0	35.0	35.6	8.2	8.8	9.1
Louisiana	17.0	14.7	13.6	45.6	49.1	47.6	10.3	10.9	11.3
Maine	9.4	8.0	8.0	31.0	34.1	35.0	6.0	6.4	6.8
Maryland	9.9	8.5	8.5	34.6	35.7	37.0	8.6	9.3	9.1
Massachusetts	6.6	5.9	6.0	26.5	28.5	30.1	7.1	7.8	7.9
Michigan	10.5	9.6	9.4	33.3	35.7	35.8	7.9	8.3	8.3
Minnesota	8.3	7.1	6.8	25.8	29.0	29.7	6.1	6.5	6.5
Mississippi	18.8	15.7	15.6	46.0	48.3	49.5	10.7	11.6	11.8
Missouri	13.1	11.4	11.1	34.6	37.0	37.8	7.6	8.3	8.1
Montana	11.6	10.6	10.4	30.8	34.3	34.5	6.2	7.6	6.6
Nebraska	10.2	8.7	8.3	27.2	30.2	30.9	6.8	7.0	7.0
Nevada	12.7	11.0	10.6	36.4	39.7	40.7	7.2	8.0	8.3
New Hampshire	6.8	5.8	5.9	24.7	26.4	27.3	6.3	6.8	7.0
New Jersey	7.1	6.1	6.1	28.9	30.1	31.5	7.7	8.3	8.2
New Mexico	17.4	15.7	15.8	45.6	48.8	50.8	8.0	8.1	8.5
New York	8.2	6.9	7.0	36.6	37.8	38.7	7.7	8.2	8.3
North Carolina	13.0	11.6	11.5	33.3	36.9	38.4	8.8	9.0	9.2
North Dakota	9.2	7.7	7.9	28.3	29.9	32.2	6.4	6.6	6.4
Ohio	12.1	10.4	10.6	34.6	37.4	38.9	7.9	8.5	8.7
Oklahoma	15.9	13.6	13.1	34.3	38.4	39.1	7.5	8.0	8.0
Oregon	11.3	8.9	8.8	30.1	32.5	33.2	5.6	6.0	6.1
Pennsylvania	9.9	9.0	9.0	32.7	35.2	36.3	7.7	8.2	8.2
Rhode Island	10.2	9.2	8.9	35.5	37.3	37.8	7.2	8.0	7.7
South Carolina	15.3	13.4	13.2	39.8	41.9	43.6	9.7	10.2	10.2
South Dakota	11.6	10.0	9.5	33.5	35.1	36.2	6.2	6.9	6.6
Tennessee	14.7	12.9	13.4	34.5	38.2	40.2	9.2	9.2	9.5
Texas	15.3	13.7	13.5	30.5	36.0	37.6	7.4	8.0	8.3
Utah	8.9	6.4	6.0	17.3	17.5	16.9	6.6	6.7	6.8
Vermont	8.0	7.1	6.7	28.1	32.3	32.3	6.1	6.4	6.2
Virginia	9.9	8.6	8.5	29.9	31.0	32.2	7.9	8.3	8.2
Washington	10.2	8.4	8.3	28.2	30.4	30.9	5.6	6.2	6.1
West Virginia	15.9	12.0	11.9	31.7	34.8	36.5	8.3	9.3	9.5
Wisconsin	10.2	8.7	8.6	29.3	31.3	32.5	6.5	7.0	7.0
Wyoming	13.5	12.0	11.1	28.8	31.7	32.8	8.3	8.6	8.6
Puerto Rico	(NA)	18.2	18.1	49.7	55.3	56.6	10.8	11.5	12.9
Virgin Islands	(NA)	14.5	14.1	66.7	68.2	71.6	9.1	11.4	11.2
Guam	(NA)	12.7	13.5	54.8	56.7	59.8	7.6	8.5	8.5
American Samoa	(NA)	7.6	5.8	35.5	36.6	34.1	2.7	3.3	3.8
Northern Marianas	(NA)	8.5	7.1	(NA)	56.1	56.0	8.9	7.6	7.6

NA Not available. [1] Defined as mothers who are 19 years of age or younger. [2] Less than 2,500 grams (5 pounds-8 ounces).

Source: U.S. National Center for Health Statistics, *National Vital Statistics Reports (NVSR)*.

Table 88. **Women Who Have Had a Child in the Last Year by Age: 1990 to 2006**

[3,913 represents 3,913,000. As of June. See headnote, Table 89]

Age of mother	Women who had a child in last year (1,000)			Total births per 1,000 women			First births per 1,000 women		
	1990	2000	2006	1990	2000	2006	1990	2000	2006
Total	3,913	3,934	3,974	67.0	64.6	64.4	26.4	26.7	25.1
15 to 29 years old	2,568	2,432	2,399	90.8	85.9	79.0	43.2	43.1	37.1
15 to 19 years old	338	586	417	39.8	59.7	40.6	30.1	38.7	23.7
20 to 24 years old	1,038	850	935	113.4	91.8	92.8	51.8	47.1	47.9
25 to 29 years old	1,192	996	1,046	112.1	107.9	104.6	46.2	43.7	40.1
30 to 44 years old	1,346	1,502	1,576	44.7	46.1	50.3	10.6	12.5	13.5
30 to 34 years old	892	871	888	80.4	87.9	92.0	21.9	27.5	28.7
35 to 39 years old	377	506	579	37.3	45.1	55.4	6.5	9.6	11.6
40 to 44 years old	77	125	109	8.6	10.9	9.7	1.2	2.3	2.3

Source: U.S. Census Bureau, *Current Population Reports*, P20-543RV and unpublished data.

Table 89. **Women Who Had a Child in the Last Year by Selected Characteristics: 1990 to 2006**

[58,381 represents 58,381,000. As of June. Covers civilian noninstitutional population. Since the number of women who had a birth during the 12-month period was tabulated and not the actual numbers of births, some small underestimation of fertility for this period may exist due to the omission of: (1) Multiple births, (2) Two or more live births spaced within the 12-month period (the woman is counted only once), (3) Women who had births in the period and who did not survive to the survey date, (4) Women who were in institutions and therefore not in the survey universe. These losses may be somewhat offset by the inclusion in the CPS of births to immigrants who did not have their children born in the United States and births to nonresident women. These births would not have been recorded in the vital registration system. Based on Current Population Survey (CPS); see Appendix III]

Characteristic	Total women (1,000)	Percent childless	Women who had a child in the last year			
			Total births		First births	
			Number (1,000)	Per 1,000 women	Number (1,000)	Per 1,000 women
1990	58,381	41.6	3,913	67.0	1,540	26.4
2000	60,873	42.8	3,934	64.6	1,626	26.7
2006, total [1]	61,683	45.1	3,974	64.4	1,551	25.1
15 to 19 years old.	10,269	93.3	417	40.6	243	23.7
20 to 24 years old.	10,079	68.6	935	92.8	483	47.9
25 to 29 years old.	10,004	45.6	1,046	104.6	401	40.1
30 to 34 years old.	9,647	26.2	888	92.0	277	28.7
35 to 39 years old.	10,450	18.9	579	55.4	121	11.6
40 to 44 years old.	11,235	20.4	109	9.7	26	2.3
White alone	47,846	45.6	3,155	65.9	1,216	25.4
White alone, non-Hispanic.	38,532	47.5	2,383	61.8	923	24.0
Black alone	8,896	41.4	513	57.7	201	22.6
Asian alone	3,145	47.7	178	56.6	75	23.8
Hispanic [2]	10,099	38.1	830	82.2	309	30.6
Married, husband present	26,499	18.6	2,469	93.2	886	33.4
Married, husband absent [3]	2,534	24.5	148	58.4	32	12.6
Widowed or divorced	4,920	21.3	129	26.2	41	8.3
Never married	27,730	76.6	1,228	44.3	592	21.3
Educational attainment:						
Not a high school graduate	13,377	61.4	867	64.8	293	21.9
High school, 4 years	15,420	33.6	989	64.1	392	25.4
Some college, no degree	12,760	48.2	713	55.9	252	19.7
Associate's degree	5,155	33.5	335	65.0	126	24.4
Bachelor's degree	10,771	44.2	746	69.3	332	30.8
Graduate or professional degree	4,199	43.1	324	77.2	156	37.2
Labor force status:						
Employed	39,961	44.5	2,054	51.4	914	22.9
Unemployed.	2,728	54.0	167	61.2	61	22.4
Not in labor force.	18,994	45.2	1,754	92.3	576	30.3
Family income:						
Under $10,000	3,878	39.4	337	86.9	110	28.4
$10,000 to $19,999	4,984	41.4	386	77.4	122	24.5
$20,000 to $24,999	2,903	41.7	223	76.8	81	27.9
$25,000 to $29,999	2,989	44.7	185	61.9	93	31.1
$30,000 to $34,999	3,236	42.8	202	62.4	78	24.1
$35,000 to $49,999	7,571	44.6	484	63.9	216	28.5
$50,000 to $74,999	10,724	45.0	705	65.7	277	25.8
$75,000 and over	15,421	47.9	949	61.5	387	25.1

[1] Includes women of other races and women with family income not reported, not shown separately. [2] Persons of Hispanic origin may be any race. [3] Includes separated women.

Source: U.S. Census Bureau, *Current Population Reports*, P20-543RV and unpublished data.

Table 90. **Women Who Have Had a Child in the Last Year by Age and Labor Force Status: 1990 to 2006**

[3,913 represents 3,913,000. See headnote, Table 89. See Appendix III]

Year	Total, 15 to 44 years old			15 to 29 years old			30 to 44 years old		
	Number (1,000)	In the labor force		Number (1,000)	In the labor force		Number (1,000)	In the labor force	
		Number (1,000)	Percent		Number (1,000)	Percent		Number (1,000)	Percent
1990	3,913	2,068	53	2,568	1,275	50	1,346	793	59
1995	3,696	2,034	55	2,252	1,150	51	1,444	884	61
1998	3,671	2,155	59	2,274	1,275	56	1,397	880	63
2000	3,934	2,170	55	2,432	1,304	54	1,502	866	58
2002	3,766	2,056	55	2,318	1,175	51	1,448	881	61
2004	3,746	2,045	55	2,205	(NA)	(NA)	1,542	(NA)	59
2006	3,974	2,221	56	2,399	1,273	53	1,576	948	60

NA Not available.

Source: U.S. Census Bureau, *Current Population Reports*, P20-555; and earlier reports and unpublished data.

Births, Deaths, Marriages, and Divorces 69

Table 91. Persons Who Have Ever Had Sexual Contact by Selected Characteristics: 2002

[In percent except as indicated (61,147 represents 61,147,000). Based on the National Survey of Family Growth, see Appendix III]

Characteristic	Number (1,000)	Number of opposite-sex partners in lifetime							Any same-sex sexual contact[2]
		Any	One	Two	3 to 6	7 to 14	15 or more	Median number[1]	
Males, 15 to 44 years old[3]	61,147	90.3	12.8	8.1	27.5	19.3	22.6	5.4	6.0
15 to 19 years old	10,208	61.6	23.0	9.2	20.7	6.2	2.5	1.9	4.5
20 to 24 years old	9,883	91.1	15.9	11.7	33.5	14.1	15.9	3.8	5.5
25 to 44 years old	41,056	97.3	9.6	7.0	27.8	23.7	29.2	6.7	6.5
25 to 29 years old	9,226	95.2	10.0	8.8	29.4	23.2	23.8	5.9	5.7
30 to 34 years old	10,138	97.2	10.7	6.9	28.5	21.9	29.2	6.4	(NA)
35 to 39 years old	10,557	98.2	8.9	7.0	28.0	25.5	28.8	6.9	(NA)
40 to 44 years old	11,135	98.2	8.8	5.4	25.6	24.2	34.2	8.2	(NA)
White only, non-Hispanic	38,738	90.3	13.4	8.3	27.1	19.2	22.3	5.3	(NA)
Black only, non-Hispanic	6,940	91.8	5.8	5.9	24.1	22.2	33.8	8.3	(NA)
Hispanic or Latino origin	10,188	91.8	13.7	8.6	32.8	18.6	18.1	4.5	(NA)
Currently married	25,808	100.0	15.4	8.5	30.5	22.3	23.3	5.2	3.4
Currently cohabiting	5,653	100.0	4.7	6.4	34.1	26.6	28.3	6.6	5.3
Never married, not cohabiting	25,412	76.8	13.9	8.7	24.0	13.8	16.4	4.3	8.6
Formerly married, not cohabiting	4,274	100.0	0.7	3.6	22.5	24.6	48.6	11.9	7.1
Females, 15 to 44 years old[3]	61,561	91.4	22.5	10.8	32.6	16.3	9.2	3.3	11.2
15 to 19 years old	9,834	62.2	27.2	9.0	19.1	5.0	1.9	1.4	10.6
20 to 24 years old	9,840	91.1	24.6	13.0	32.2	14.4	6.9	2.8	14.2
25 to 44 years old	41,887	98.4	20.9	10.7	36.0	19.4	11.4	3.8	10.7
25 to 29 years old	9,249	97.5	22.5	11.7	31.3	20.1	11.9	3.5	14.1
30 to 34 years old	10,272	98.0	20.5	9.4	38.8	18.0	11.3	3.8	(NA)
35 to 39 years old	10,853	98.9	20.2	11.2	35.8	20.5	11.2	3.9	(NA)
40 to 44 years old	11,512	98.6	20.4	10.5	37.4	19.1	11.2	3.8	(NA)
White only, non-Hispanic	39,498	92.1	21.0	10.6	32.1	18.2	10.2	3.6	(NA)
Black only, non-Hispanic	8,250	92.4	12.4	8.4	44.8	18.0	8.8	4.1	(NA)
Hispanic or Latino origin	9,107	89.5	34.6	14.9	27.2	8.2	4.6	1.7	(NA)
Currently married	28,327	100.0	30.8	12.2	34.0	15.6	7.4	2.7	7.2
Currently cohabiting	5,570	100.0	13.7	12.2	39.2	20.4	14.5	4.3	17.6
Never married, not cohabiting	21,568	75.4	18.3	9.4	27.7	12.8	7.2	3.1	13.5
Formerly married, not cohabiting	6,096	100.0	6.5	8.1	37.8	28.5	19.1	5.6	16.3

NA Not available. [1] Excludes those who have never had sexual intercourse with a person of the opposite sex. For definition of median, see Guide to Tabular Presentation. [2] Same-sex sexual contact was measured using significantly different questions for males and females. [3] Includes person of other or multiple race and origin groups, not shown separately.

Source: U.S. National Center for Health Statistics, *Advance Data*, No. 362; "Sexual Behavior and Selected Health Measures: Men and Women 15–44 Years of Age, United States, 2002," September 15, 2005, and unpublished data.

Table 92. Males and Females Who Have Had Sexual Contact in Last 12 Months by Number and Sex of Partners: 2002

[In percent except as indicated (61,147 represents 61,147,000). Based on the National Survey of Family Growth, see Appendix III]

Sex and age	Number (1,000)	Total	No partners in last 12 months	Percent distribution					Number of partners not ascertained
				One partner		Two or more partners			
				Same sex[1]	Opposite sex	Same sex only[1]	Opposite sex only	Both same and opposite sex[1]	
Males 15 to 44 years old	61,147	100.0	14.8	0.7	62.2	0.9	17.6	1.0	2.6
15 to 19 years old	10,208	100.0	45.1	0.8	29.7	(S)	21.8	0.9	1.4
20 to 24 years old	9,883	100.0	14.2	0.4	48.8	0.9	30.9	1.5	3.2
25 to 44 years old	41,056	100.0	7.4	0.7	73.6	1.1	13.4	1.0	2.8
25 to 29 years old	9,226	100.0	10.0	0.5	66.6	0.9	18.4	1.1	2.5
30 to 34 years old	10,138	100.0	5.6	0.9	74.3	1.0	14.5	1.3	2.4
35 to 39 years old	10,557	100.0	7.1	0.9	76.5	1.2	11.4	0.5	2.5
40 to 44 years old	11,135	100.0	7.0	0.7	75.9	1.3	10.1	1.0	3.8
Females 15 to 44 years old	61,561	100.0	13.9	1.1	66.8	0.2	12.7	3.1	2.2
15 to 19 years old	9,834	100.0	42.9	1.7	30.5	(S)	16.8	5.8	2.1
20 to 24 years old	9,840	100.0	12.5	0.4	58.9	(S)	21.1	4.8	1.9
25 to 44 years old	41,887	100.0	7.4	1.1	77.2	0.2	9.8	2.0	2.2
25 to 29 years old	9,249	100.0	6.1	0.5	74.1	0.4	14.1	2.8	2.0
30 to 34 years old	10,272	100.0	7.1	0.5	78.5	(S)	9.7	2.1	1.9
35 to 39 years old	10,853	100.0	7.3	1.8	76.8	(S)	9.4	2.5	2.0
40 to 44 years old	11,512	100.0	9.0	1.4	78.8	(S)	6.7	0.9	3.0

S Does not meet standards for reliability or precision. [1] Same-sex sexual contact was measured using significantly different questions for males and females.

Source: U.S. National Center for Health Statistics, *Advance Data*, No. 362; "Sexual Behavior and Selected Health Measures: Men and Women 15–44 years of Age, United States, 2002," September 15, 2005.

Table 93. Contraceptive Use by Women, 15 to 44 Years of Age, Who Have Ever Had Sexual Intercourse: 1982 to 2002

[46,684 represents 46,684,000. Based on the National Survey of Family Growth, see Appendix III]

Contraceptive status and method	1982	1995	2002 Total [1]	2002 White only, Non-Hispanic	2002 Black only, Non-Hispanic	2002 Hispanic [2]
Women who have had sexual intercourse (1,000)...	46,684	53,800	54,190	34,999	7,403	7,887
PERCENT DISTRIBUTION						
Ever used any method	94.8	98.2	98.2	98.8	97.3	96.5
Female sterilization	22.3	23.4	20.7	19.2	26.9	24.1
Male sterilization	10.1	14.6	13.0	16.7	5.0	4.4
Pill	76.3	82.2	82.3	87.0	79.8	68.5
Norplant implant	(X)	2.1	2.1	1.4	3.3	4.0
1-month injectable (Lunelle ™)	(X)	(X)	0.9	0.5	1.0	3.1
3-month injectable (Depo-Provera ™)	(X)	4.5	16.8	13.6	23.3	24.3
Emergency contraception	(X)	0.8	4.2	4.2	4.1	3.8
Contraceptive patch	(X)	(X)	0.9	0.7	1.4	1.1
Today™	(X)	12.0	7.3	8.8	6.3	2.7
Intrauterine device	18.4	10.0	5.8	4.7	5.4	10.0
Diaphragm	17.1	15.2	8.5	10.4	6.9	3.4
Condom	51.8	82.0	89.7	92.2	91.8	78.2
Female condom	(X)	1.2	1.9	1.2	5.4	1.4
Periodic abstinence—calendar rhythm	17.0	24.3	16.2	16.6	13.7	16.2
Periodic abstinence—natural family planning	2.3	4.2	3.5	3.6	1.7	4.7
Withdrawal	24.5	40.6	56.1	59.7	50.5	47.2
Foam alone	24.9	18.3	12.1	12.5	15.5	8.2
Jelly/cream alone	5.8	9.1	7.3	7.7	9.6	3.4
Suppository/insert	9.7	10.6	7.5	7.9	8.8	4.5
Other methods	9.3	0.3	1.0	0.8	1.3	1.3

X Not applicable.   [1] Includes other races, not shown separately.   [2] Persons of Hispanic origin may be any race.

Source: U.S. National Center for Health Statistics, *Advance Data*, Number 350, "Use of Contraception and Use of Family Planning Services in the United States: 1982–2002," December 10, 2004.

Table 94. Select Family Planning and Medical Service Use by Women, 15 to 44 Years of Age: 2002

[61,561 represents 61,561,000. Based on the National Survey of Family Growth, see Appendix III]

Characteristic	Number (1,000)	Family planning services: At least one family planning service	Family planning services: Birth control method	Family planning services: Birth control checkup or test	Medical services: At least one medical service	Medical services: Pregnancy test	Medical services: Pap smear	Medical services: Pelvic exam	Medical services: Counseling/ test/ treatment for STD [1]
All women [2]	61,561	41.7	33.9	23.6	69.1	19.7	64.4	59.7	12.6
15 to 19 years old	9,834	39.9	31.1	22.0	40.6	18.3	34.6	27.0	15.2
15 to 17 years old	5,819	31.8	22.2	15.8	28.0	11.4	23.2	17.9	11.1
18 to 19 years old	4,016	51.6	43.9	31.0	58.9	28.2	51.2	40.2	21.1
20 to 24 years old	9,840	63.3	54.0	35.7	75.7	31.5	69.7	60.6	22.3
25 to 29 years old	9,249	55.4	46.3	30.2	75.9	30.2	70.7	66.0	16.6
30 to 34 years old	10,272	47.0	39.1	27.2	78.1	22.2	72.7	69.7	12.2
35 to 39 years old	10,853	30.5	23.9	18.6	71.5	13.6	68.3	65.9	6.9
40 to 44 years old	11,512	19.5	14.0	10.8	71.8	5.9	69.4	67.0	4.4
Currently married	28,327	39.5	31.5	21.3	77.2	21.1	73.1	69.8	8.1
Currently cohabiting	5,570	50.4	43.2	30.2	77.2	31.0	72.2	64.7	20.3
Never married, not cohabiting	21,568	44.4	36.4	25.4	55.8	16.5	50.7	43.9	15.9
Formerly married, not cohabiting	6,096	34.5	28.0	22.0	71.0	14.1	66.0	64.0	14.4
White only, Non-Hispanic	39,940	43.1	36.4	25.4	70.1	17.3	66.1	63.2	11.8
Black only, Non-Hispanic	8,250	39.4	30.6	21.8	74.4	23.7	69.1	58.1	15.7
Hispanic [3]	9,107	39.7	28.9	20.6	63.4	24.3	57.1	48.5	12.5

[1] STD stands for sexually transmitted disease.   [2] Includes other races, not shown separately.   [3] Persons of Hispanic origin may be any race.

Source: U.S. National Center for Health Statistics, *Advance Data*, Number 350, "Use of Contraception and Use of Family Planning Services in the United States: 1982–2002," December 10, 2004.

Table 95. Current Contraceptive Use by Women, 15 to 44 Years of Age: 1995 and 2002

[In percent, except total (60,201 represents 60,201,000). Based on the National Survey of Family Growth; see Appendix III]

Contraceptive status and method	All women, 1995	2002 All women	Age 15 to 19 years old	20 to 24 years old	25 to 29 years old	30 to 34 years old	35 to 39 years old	40 to 44 years old	Race/ethnicity White only, Non-Hispanic	Black only, Non-Hispanic	Hispanic [3]	Marital status Never married, not cohabiting	Currently married	Formerly married, not cohabiting
All women (1,000)	60,201	61,561	9,834	9,840	9,249	10,272	10,853	11,512	39,498	8,250	9,107	21,568	28,327	6,096
PERCENT DISTRIBUTION														
Using contraception (contraceptors) [4]	64.2	61.9	31.5	60.7	68.0	69.0	70.8	69.1	64.6	57.6	59.0	44.0	72.9	64.4
Female sterilization	17.8	16.7	–	2.2	10.3	19.0	29.2	34.7	15.4	22.6	19.9	4.4	21.7	35.3
Male sterilization.	7.0	5.7	–	0.5	2.8	6.4	10.0	12.7	7.6	1.3	2.6	0.4	11.2	2.2
Pill.	17.3	18.9	16.7	31.9	25.6	21.8	13.2	7.6	22.2	13.1	13.0	21.8	17.2	12.3
Implant, Lunelle (™) . . .	0.9	0.8	0.4	0.9	1.7	0.9	0.5	0.2	0.5	0.6	1.8	0.4	1.0	0.5
3-month injectable (Depo-Provera (™) . . .	1.9	3.3	4.4	6.1	4.4	2.9	1.5	1.1	2.7	5.4	4.3	4.2	2.2	1.7
Intrauterine device (IUD) . .	0.5	1.3	0.1	1.1	2.5	2.2	1.0	0.8	1.0	0.8	3.2	0.2	1.9	1.9
Diaphragm.	1.2	0.2	–	0.1	0.3	0.1	–	0.4	0.2	0.1	–	0.2	0.2	–
Condom.	13.1	11.1	8.5	14.0	14.0	11.8	11.1	8.0	10.7	11.4	10.9	10.3	12.0	8.0
Periodic abstinence—calendar rhythm	1.3	0.7	–	0.8	0.3	0.9	1.1	1.2	0.8	0.3	0.6	0.2	1.3	0.3
Periodic abstinence—natural family planning . . .	0.2	0.2	0.8	–	0.4	0.2	0.3	0.4	0.3	0.1	0.3	0.0	0.4	–
Withdrawal.	2.0	2.5	0.8	3.1	5.3	2.6	2.4	1.0	2.6	1.5	2.2	1.6	3.0	1.3
Other methods [5]	1.1	0.6	0.6	0.2	0.4	0.4	0.5	1.1	0.7	0.5	0.3	0.2	0.7	0.9
Not using contraception.	35.8	38.1	68.5	39.3	32.0	30.8	29.2	30.9	35.4	42.4	41.0	56.0	27.1	35.6
Surgically sterile-female (noncontraceptive)	3.0	1.5	–	–	0.4	0.9	2.1	4.9	1.6	1.6	0.9	0.4	2.1	3.0
Nonsurgically sterile-female or male [6]	1.7	1.6	0.7	0.7	0.9	1.4	1.2	4.4	1.7	1.4	1.7	1.0	2.0	2.5
Pregnant or postpartum . . .	4.6	5.3	3.5	9.5	8.4	6.9	3.8	0.8	4.7	5.7	6.9	2.3	7.5	2.2
Seeking pregnancy	4.0	4.2	1.2	2.8	5.5	7.0	5.1	3.3	4.0	4.3	5.2	0.8	6.9	2.0
Other nonuse	22.5	25.5	63.1	26.3	16.9	14.6	16.9	17.6	23.6	29.5	26.4	51.4	8.6	26.0
Never had intercourse or no intercourse in 3 months before inter . . .	17.1	18.1	56.2	17.9	8.9	7.6	9.1	10.8	17.0	19.0	18.7	42.9	2.3	17.7
Had intercour . . in 3 months before inter . . .	5.2	7.4	6.9	8.4	8.0	7.0	7.7	6.7	6.5	10.4	7.7	8.5	6.3	8.2
All other nonus	0.2	–	–	–	–	–	0.1	0.1	0.1	0.1	–	–	–	0.1

– Represents or rounds to zero. [1] Includes other races, not shown separately. [2] Includes women who are currently cohabiting, not shown separately. [3] Persons of Hispanic origin may be any race. [4] Percents m . . . . to . . . total who were using contraception because more than one method could have been used in the month of interview. [5] Includes implants, injectables, morning-after pill, suppository, Today (™) sponge, and less fr . . . . . . used methods. [6] Persons sterile from illness, accident, or congenital conditions.

Source: U.S. National Center for Health Statistics, Advance Data, Number 350, "Use of Contraception and Use of Family Planning Services in the United States: 1982–2002," December 10, 2004.

Table 96. Abortions—Number, Rate, and Ratio by Race: 1980 to 2003

[53,048 represents 53,048,000]

Year	All races Women 15 to 44 years old (1,000)	All races Abortions Number (1,000)	All races Abortions Rate per 1,000 women	All races Abortions Ratio per 1,000 live births [1]	White Women 15 to 44 years old (1,000)	White Abortions Number (1,000)	White Abortions Rate per 1,000 women	White Abortions Ratio per 1,000 live births [1]	Black and other Women 15 to 44 years old (1,000)	Black and other Abortions Number (1,000)	Black and other Abortions Rate per 1,000 women	Black and other Abortions Ratio per 1,000 live births [1]
1980...	53,048	1,554	29.3	428	44,942	1,094	24.3	376	8,106	460	56.5	642
1985...	56,754	1,589	28.0	422	47,512	1,076	22.6	360	9,242	513	55.5	659
1986 [2]..	57,483	1,574	27.4	416	48,010	1,045	21.8	350	9,473	529	55.9	661
1987...	57,964	1,559	27.1	405	48,288	1,017	21.1	338	9,676	542	56.0	648
1988...	58,192	1,591	27.3	401	48,325	1,026	21.2	333	9,867	565	57.3	638
1989 [2]..	58,365	1,567	26.8	380	48,104	1,006	20.9	309	10,261	561	54.7	650
1990 [2]..	58,700	1,609	27.4	389	48,224	1,039	21.5	318	10,476	570	54.4	655
1991...	59,305	1,557	26.2	379	48,560	982	20.2	303	10,745	574	53.5	661
1992...	59,417	1,529	25.7	380	48,435	943	19.5	298	10,982	585	53.3	681
1993 [2]..	59,712	1,495	25.0	376	48,497	908	18.7	290	11,215	587	52.4	698
1994 [2]..	60,020	1,423	23.7	362	48,592	856	17.6	275	11,429	567	49.6	696
1995...	60,368	1,359	22.5	350	48,719	817	16.8	265	11,648	542	46.6	684
1996...	60,704	1,360	22.4	349	48,837	797	16.3	258	11,867	563	47.5	699
1997 [2]..	61,041	1,335	21.9	341	48,942	777	15.9	251	12,099	558	46.1	684
1998 [2]..	61,326	1,319	21.5	334	49,012	762	15.5	244	12,313	557	45.2	678
1999...	61,475	1,315	21.4	327	48,974	743	15.2	234	12,501	572	45.8	674
2000...	61,631	1,313	21.3	324	48,936	733	15.0	230	12,695	580	45.7	676
2001 [2]..	61,673	1,303	21.1	325	48,868	723	14.8	229	12,805	579	45.3	686
2002 [2]..	62,044	1,293	20.8	319	48,998	719	14.7	225	13,046	574	44.0	672
2003 [2]..	61,911	1,287	20.8	313	48,782	715	14.7	221	13,129	572	43.6	654

[1] Live births are those which occurred from July 1 of year shown through June 30 of the following year (to match time of conception with abortions). Births are classified by race of child 1980–1988, and by race of mother after 1988.   [2] Total numbers of abortions in 1986, 1989, 1990, 1993, 1994, 1997, and 1998 have been estimated by interpolation. Data for 2001 through 2003 have been estimated using trends in Centers for Disease Control data.

Source: 1980–1988, S.K. Henshaw and J. Van Vort, eds., *Abortion Factbook, 1992 Edition: Readings, Trends, and State and Local Data to 1988*, The Alan Guttmacher Institute, New York, NY, 1992 (copyright); 1989–2000, L.B. Finer and S.K. Henshaw, "Abortion Incidence and Services in the United States in 2000," *Perspectives on Sexual and Reproductive Health*, 35:6; 2001–2003, L.B. Finer and S.K. Henshaw, "Estimates of U.S. abortion incidence in 2001–2003", New York: Guttmacher Institute, 2006, <http://www.guttmacher.org/pubs/2006/08/03/ab_incidence.pdf>; and unpublished data from Guttmacher Institute.

Table 97. Abortions by Selected Characteristics: 1990 to 2003

[1,609 represents 1,609,000. Number of abortions from surveys conducted by source; characteristics from the U.S. Centers for Disease Control's (CDC) annual abortion surveillance summaries, with adjustments for changes in states reporting data to the CDC each year]

Characteristic	Number (1,000) 1990	Number (1,000) 2000	Number (1,000) 2003	Percent distribution 1990	Percent distribution 2000	Percent distribution 2003	Abortion ratio [1] 1990	Abortion ratio [1] 2000	Abortion ratio [1] 2003
Total abortions	1,609	1,313	1,287	100	100	100	280	245	238
Age of woman:									
Less than 15 years old	13	9	8	1	1	1	515	512	537
15 to 19 years old	351	235	212	22	18	17	403	339	337
20 to 24 years old	532	430	430	33	33	33	328	296	293
25 to 29 years old	360	303	294	22	23	23	224	220	211
30 to 34 years old	216	190	196	13	15	15	196	169	167
35 to 39 years old	108	110	108	7	8	8	249	195	186
40 years old and over.	29	37	40	2	3	3	354	276	268
Race of woman:									
White.	1,039	733	715	65	56	56	241	187	181
Black and other.	570	580	572	35	44	44	396	403	395
Marital status of woman:									
Married	341	246	229	21	19	18	104	84	79
Unmarried	1,268	1,067	1,058	79	81	82	516	443	422
Number of prior live births:									
None.	780	533	517	49	41	40	316	248	239
One.	396	361	354	25	28	28	230	216	210
Two.	280	260	253	17	20	20	292	278	268
Three	102	104	106	6	8	8	279	285	283
Four or more.	50	56	56	3	4	4	223	250	246
Number of prior induced abortions:									
None.	891	699	693	55	53	54	(NA)	(NA)	(NA)
One.	443	355	343	28	27	27	(NA)	(NA)	(NA)
Two or more	275	259	251	17	20	19	(NA)	(NA)	(NA)
Weeks of gestation:									
Less than 9 weeks.	825	757	790	51	58	61	(NA)	(NA)	(NA)
9 to 10 weeks	416	266	230	26	20	18	(NA)	(NA)	(NA)
11 to 12 weeks	195	138	124	12	11	10	(NA)	(NA)	(NA)
13 weeks or more	173	153	143	11	12	11	(NA)	(NA)	(NA)

NA Not available.   [1] Number of abortions per 1,000 abortions and live births. Live births are those which occurred from July 1 of year shown through June 30 of the following year (to match time of conception with abortions).

Source: L.B. Finer and S.K. Henshaw, "Estimates of U.S. abortion incidence in 2001–2003", New York: Guttmacher Institute, 2006, <http://www.guttmacher.org/pubs/2006/08/03/ab_incidence.pdf> and unpublished data, from Guttmacher Institute.

Table 98. Expectation of Life at Birth, 1970 to 2004, and Projections, 2010 and 2015

[In years. Excludes deaths of nonresidents of the United States. See Appendix III]

Year	Total			White			Black		
	Total	Male	Female	Total	Male	Female	Total	Male	Female
1970.........	70.8	67.1	74.7	71.7	68.0	75.6	64.1	60.0	68.3
1975.........	72.6	68.8	76.6	73.4	69.5	77.3	66.8	62.4	71.3
1980.........	73.7	70.0	77.4	74.4	70.7	78.1	68.1	63.8	72.5
1981.........	74.1	70.4	77.8	74.8	71.1	78.4	68.9	64.5	73.2
1982.........	74.5	70.8	78.1	75.1	71.5	78.7	69.4	65.1	73.6
1983.........	74.6	71.0	78.1	75.2	71.6	78.7	69.4	65.2	73.5
1984.........	74.7	71.1	78.2	75.3	71.8	78.7	69.5	65.3	73.6
1985.........	74.7	71.1	78.2	75.3	71.8	78.7	69.3	65.0	73.4
1986.........	74.7	71.2	78.2	75.4	71.9	78.8	69.1	64.8	73.4
1987.........	74.9	71.4	78.3	75.6	72.1	78.9	69.1	64.7	73.4
1988.........	74.9	71.4	78.3	75.6	72.2	78.9	68.9	64.4	73.2
1989.........	75.1	71.7	78.5	75.9	72.5	79.2	68.8	64.3	73.3
1990.........	75.4	71.8	78.8	76.1	72.7	79.4	69.1	64.5	73.6
1991.........	75.5	72.0	78.9	76.3	72.9	79.6	69.3	64.6	73.8
1992.........	75.8	72.3	79.1	76.5	73.2	79.8	69.6	65.0	73.9
1993.........	75.5	72.2	78.8	76.3	73.1	79.5	69.2	64.6	73.7
1994.........	75.7	72.4	79.0	76.5	73.3	79.6	69.5	64.9	73.9
1995.........	75.8	72.5	78.9	76.5	73.4	79.6	69.6	65.2	73.9
1996.........	76.1	73.1	79.1	76.8	73.9	79.7	70.2	66.1	74.2
1997.........	76.5	73.6	79.4	77.2	74.3	79.9	71.1	67.2	74.7
1998.........	76.7	73.8	79.5	77.3	74.5	80.0	71.3	67.6	74.8
1999.........	76.7	73.9	79.4	77.3	74.6	79.9	71.4	67.8	74.7
2000.........	77.0	74.3	79.7	77.6	74.9	80.1	71.9	68.3	75.2
2001.........	77.2	74.4	79.8	77.7	75.0	80.2	72.2	68.6	75.5
2002.........	77.3	74.5	79.9	77.7	75.1	80.3	72.3	68.8	75.6
2003.........	77.4	74.7	80.0	77.9	75.3	80.4	72.6	68.9	75.9
2004	77.8	75.2	80.4	78.3	75.7	80.8	73.1	69.5	76.3
Projections [1]:									
2010	78.5	75.6	81.4	79.0	76.1	81.8	74.5	70.9	77.8
2015	79.2	76.2	82.2	80.9	78.0	83.8	75.5	71.9	78.9

[1] Based on middle mortality assumptions; for details, see source. Source: U.S. Census Bureau, Population Division Working Paper No. 38.

Source: Except as noted, U.S. National Center for Health Statistics, *National Vital Statistics Reports*, Vol. 55, No. 19, August 21, 2007.

Table 99. Average Number of Years of Life Remaining by Sex and Age: 1979 to 2003

[Excludes deaths of nonresidents of the United States. See Appendix III]

Age (years)	Total			Male			Female		
	1979–81	1989–91	2003	1979–81	1989–91	2003	1979–81	1989–91	2003
0	73.9	75.4	77.4	70.1	71.8	74.7	77.6	78.8	80.0
1	73.8	75.1	77.0	70.1	71.6	74.3	77.5	78.5	79.5
5	70.0	71.2	73.1	66.3	67.7	70.4	73.7	74.6	75.6
10	65.1	66.3	68.1	61.4	62.8	65.5	68.8	69.7	70.6
15	60.2	61.4	63.2	56.5	57.9	60.5	63.8	64.7	65.7
20	55.5	56.6	58.4	51.9	53.3	55.8	59.0	59.9	60.8
25	50.8	51.9	53.6	47.4	48.7	51.2	54.2	55.0	56.0
30	46.1	47.2	48.9	42.8	44.1	46.5	49.3	50.2	51.1
35	41.4	42.6	44.1	38.2	39.6	41.8	44.5	45.4	46.3
40	36.8	38.0	39.5	33.6	35.1	37.2	39.8	40.7	41.5
45	32.3	33.4	34.9	29.2	30.7	32.8	35.2	36.0	36.9
50	27.9	29.0	30.5	25.0	26.4	28.5	30.7	31.4	32.3
55	23.9	24.8	26.2	21.1	22.3	24.3	26.4	27.1	27.9
60	20.0	20.9	22.2	17.5	18.5	20.4	22.3	22.9	23.7
65	16.5	17.3	18.4	14.2	15.1	16.8	18.4	19.0	19.7
70	13.3	14.0	14.8	11.4	12.1	13.4	14.8	15.4	15.9
75	10.5	11.0	11.7	8.9	9.4	10.5	11.6	12.1	12.5
80	8.0	8.4	8.9	6.8	7.1	7.9	8.7	9.1	9.5
85	6.0	6.2	6.6	5.1	5.3	5.9	6.4	6.7	7.0
90	4.4	4.5	4.8	3.9	3.9	4.3	4.7	4.7	5.0
95	3.3	3.3	3.5	3.0	2.9	3.1	3.5	3.4	3.5
100	2.7	2.5	2.5	2.5	2.3	2.2	2.8	2.5	2.5

Source: U.S. National Center for Health Statistics, *National Vital Statistics Reports*, Vol. 54, No. 14, April 19, 2006.

Table 100. Selected Life Table Values: 1979 to 2004

[See Appendix III]

Age and sex	Total								White								Black							
	1979–1981	1985	1990	1995	2000	2002	2003	2004	1979–1981	1985	1990	1995	2000	2002	2003	2004	1979–1981	1985	1990	1995	2000	2002	2003	2004
AVERAGE EXPECTATION OF LIFE IN YEARS																								
At birth: Male	70.1	71.1	71.8	72.5	74.3	74.5	74.7	75.2	70.8	71.8	72.7	73.4	74.9	75.1	75.3	75.7	64.1	65.0	64.5	65.2	68.3	68.8	68.9	69.5
Female	77.6	78.2	78.8	78.9	79.7	79.9	80.0	80.4	78.2	78.7	79.4	79.6	80.1	80.3	80.4	80.8	72.9	73.4	73.6	73.9	75.2	75.6	75.9	76.3
Age 20: Male	51.9	52.6	53.3	53.8	55.3	55.6	55.8	56.2	52.5	53.2	54.0	54.5	55.8	56.1	56.2	56.6	46.4	47.1	46.7	47.3	50.0	50.5	50.6	51.2
Female	59.0	59.3	59.8	59.9	60.5	60.7	60.8	61.2	59.4	59.8	60.3	60.5	60.9	61.0	61.1	61.5	54.9	55.2	55.3	55.5	56.6	57.0	57.2	57.7
Age 40: Male	33.6	34.2	35.1	35.6	36.7	37.0	37.2	37.6	34.0	34.7	35.6	36.1	37.1	37.4	37.6	37.9	29.5	29.8	30.1	30.6	32.3	32.8	32.9	33.4
Female	39.8	40.0	40.6	40.7	41.2	41.4	41.5	41.9	40.2	40.4	41.0	41.0	41.5	41.6	41.8	42.1	36.3	36.4	36.8	37.0	37.8	38.1	38.4	38.8
Age 50: Male	25.0	25.5	26.4	27.0	27.9	28.3	28.5	28.8	25.3	25.8	26.7	27.3	28.2	28.5	28.7	29.1	22.0	22.1	22.5	23.1	24.2	24.6	24.7	25.1
Female	30.7	30.8	31.3	31.4	32.0	32.2	32.3	32.7	31.0	31.1	31.6	31.7	32.2	32.4	32.5	32.9	27.8	27.8	28.2	28.5	29.1	29.5	29.8	30.1
Age 65: Male	14.2	14.5	15.1	15.6	16.2	16.6	16.8	17.1	14.3	14.5	15.2	15.7	16.3	16.6	16.8	17.2	13.3	13.0	13.2	13.7	14.2	14.6	14.8	15.2
Female	18.4	18.5	18.9	18.9	19.3	19.5	19.7	20.0	18.6	18.7	19.1	19.0	19.4	19.5	19.7	20.0	17.1	16.9	17.2	17.2	17.7	18.0	18.3	18.6
EXPECTED DEATHS PER 1,000 ALIVE AT SPECIFIED AGE [2]																								
At birth: Male	13.9	12.0	10.3	8.3	7.5	7.6	7.6	7.5	12.3	10.6	8.6	7.0	6.2	6.4	6.4	6.2	23.0	19.9	19.7	16.2	15.6	15.4	15.6	15.3
Female	11.2	9.4	8.2	6.8	6.2	6.3	6.1	6.1	9.7	8.0	6.6	5.6	5.1	5.1	5.1	5.1	19.3	16.5	16.3	13.8	12.7	13.2	12.4	12.4
Age 20: Male	1.8	1.5	1.6	(NA)	1.3	1.4	1.3	1.3	1.8	1.4	1.4	(NA)	1.2	1.3	1.2	1.2	2.2	1.9	2.7	(NA)	2.0	2.1	1.9	1.8
Female	0.6	0.5	0.5	(NA)	0.4	0.5	0.4	0.5	0.6	0.5	0.5	(NA)	0.4	0.4	0.5	0.4	0.7	0.6	0.7	(NA)	0.6	0.6	0.6	0.6
Age 40: Male	3.0	2.8	3.1	(NA)	2.6	2.7	2.6	2.4	2.6	2.5	2.7	(NA)	2.4	2.5	2.4	2.3	6.9	6.5	7.1	(NA)	4.6	4.3	4.3	3.9
Female	1.6	1.4	1.4	(NA)	1.5	1.5	1.5	1.5	1.4	1.3	1.2	(NA)	1.3	1.4	1.4	1.3	3.2	2.9	3.1	(NA)	2.8	2.6	2.7	2.6
Age 50: Male	7.8	6.8	6.2	(NA)	5.7	5.7	5.7	5.6	7.1	6.2	5.6	(NA)	5.2	5.2	5.2	5.2	14.9	13.3	12.8	(NA)	11.2	10.4	10.5	10.1
Female	4.2	3.8	3.5	(NA)	3.3	3.2	3.3	3.2	3.8	3.5	3.2	(NA)	2.9	2.8	2.9	2.9	7.7	6.8	6.6	(NA)	6.2	6.2	6.1	5.9
Age 65: Male	28.2	26.1	22.9	(NA)	20.0	18.9	18.5	17.8	27.4	25.2	23.0	(NA)	19.2	18.2	17.8	17.1	38.5	28.5	36.8	(NA)	29.6	29.3	29.1	28.4
Female	14.3	14.1	13.5	(NA)	12.7	12.1	11.9	11.5	13.6	13.5	12.8	(NA)	12.2	11.7	11.4	11.0	21.6	21.4	21.4	(NA)	18.2	17.8	17.7	16.9
NUMBER SURVIVING TO SPECIFIED AGE PER 1,000 BORN ALIVE																								
Age 20: Male	973	977	979	981	984	984	985	985	975	979	981	981	986	986	986	987	961	966	963	967	973	974	974	974
Female	982	985	986	987	989	989	989	989	984	986	988	987	990	991	991	991	972	976	976	978	981	981	982	982
Age 40: Male	933	941	938	940	953	954	954	955	940	946	946	940	958	958	958	959	885	897	880	885	918	920	923	925
Female	965	970	971	971	975	975	975	976	969	973	975	971	978	978	978	978	941	948	944	944	955	957	958	958
Age 50: Male	890	902	899	899	917	918	918	921	901	911	912	899	925	925	925	927	801	820	801	803	855	862	864	869
Female	941	948	950	950	954	954	954	954	947	953	957	950	960	959	959	959	896	908	904	902	915	918	919	921
Age 65: Male	706	727	741	750	779	786	787	792	724	744	760	750	794	799	800	805	551	571	571	581	640	657	659	668
Female	835	844	851	855	863	867	867	870	848	855	864	855	874	876	877	879	733	746	751	758	780	785	786	792

NA Not available.   [1] Includes other races not shown separately.   [2] See footnote 1, Table 101.

Source: U.S. National Center for Health Statistics, U.S. Life Tables and Actuarial Tables, 1979–81; Vital Statistics of the United States, annual, and unpublished data.

Table 101. Expectation of Life and Expected Deaths by Race, Sex, and Age: 2004

[See Appendix III]

Age (years)	Expectation of life in years					Expected deaths per 1,000 alive at specified age [2]				
	Total [1]	White Male	White Female	Black Male	Black Female	Total [1]	White Male	White Female	Black Male	Black Female
At birth	77.8	75.7	80.8	69.5	76.3	5.66	6.22	5.07	15.25	12.37
1	77.4	75.2	80.2	69.6	76.3	0.44	0.46	0.42	0.76	0.66
2	76.4	74.2	79.2	68.6	75.3	0.27	0.30	0.23	0.47	0.41
3	75.4	73.2	78.2	67.7	74.3	0.20	0.22	0.18	0.40	0.30
4	74.4	72.2	77.3	66.7	73.4	0.17	0.20	0.15	0.31	0.25
5	73.5	71.3	76.3	65.7	72.4	0.15	0.17	0.13	0.28	0.24
6	72.5	70.3	75.3	64.7	71.4	0.15	0.17	0.12	0.26	0.21
7	71.5	69.3	74.3	63.8	70.4	0.14	0.16	0.12	0.24	0.19
8	70.5	68.3	73.3	62.8	69.4	0.13	0.14	0.11	0.21	0.18
9	69.5	67.3	72.3	61.8	68.4	0.11	0.12	0.10	0.17	0.18
10	68.5	66.3	71.3	60.8	67.5	0.09	0.10	0.09	0.15	0.18
11	67.5	65.3	70.3	59.8	66.5	0.10	0.10	0.10	0.16	0.19
12	66.5	64.3	69.3	58.8	65.5	0.14	0.15	0.12	0.22	0.21
13	65.5	63.3	68.3	57.8	64.5	0.22	0.26	0.17	0.35	0.24
14	64.6	62.4	67.3	56.9	63.5	0.33	0.41	0.23	0.55	0.27
15	63.6	61.4	66.4	55.9	62.5	0.45	0.56	0.31	0.77	0.31
16	62.6	60.4	65.4	54.9	61.5	0.57	0.75	0.38	1.00	0.36
17	61.6	59.5	64.4	54.0	60.6	0.67	0.90	0.43	1.23	0.41
18	60.7	58.5	63.4	53.0	59.6	0.74	1.02	0.45	1.44	0.46
19	59.7	57.6	62.5	52.1	58.6	0.79	1.11	0.45	1.63	0.51
20	58.8	56.6	61.5	51.2	57.7	0.83	1.20	0.44	1.82	0.56
21	57.8	55.7	60.5	50.3	56.7	0.88	1.28	0.44	2.00	0.62
22	56.9	54.8	59.5	49.4	55.7	0.90	1.33	0.44	2.15	0.68
23	55.9	53.8	58.6	48.5	54.8	0.91	1.34	0.44	2.25	0.73
24	55.0	52.9	57.6	47.6	53.8	0.90	1.31	0.45	2.31	0.77
25	54.0	52.0	56.6	46.7	52.8	0.88	1.28	0.46	2.37	0.83
26	53.1	51.1	55.7	45.8	51.9	0.87	1.24	0.47	2.42	0.89
27	52.1	50.1	54.7	44.9	50.9	0.86	1.22	0.48	2.46	0.95
28	51.2	49.2	53.7	44.0	50.0	0.87	1.21	0.50	2.49	1.01
29	50.2	48.2	52.7	43.2	49.0	0.88	1.21	0.53	2.50	1.07
30	49.3	47.3	51.8	42.3	48.1	0.90	1.23	0.56	2.51	1.13
31	48.3	46.3	50.8	41.4	47.1	0.93	1.25	0.59	2.53	1.21
32	47.4	45.4	49.8	40.5	46.2	0.97	1.29	0.64	2.57	1.29
33	46.4	44.5	48.8	39.6	45.2	1.02	1.35	0.68	2.64	1.37
34	45.5	43.5	47.9	38.7	44.3	1.09	1.43	0.74	2.74	1.47
35	44.5	42.6	46.9	37.8	43.4	1.17	1.53	0.81	2.86	1.58
36	43.6	41.6	46.0	36.9	42.4	1.27	1.64	0.88	3.01	1.70
37	42.7	40.7	45.0	36.0	41.5	1.38	1.78	0.97	3.20	1.87
38	41.7	39.8	44.0	35.1	40.6	1.52	1.94	1.08	3.41	2.10
39	40.8	38.9	43.1	34.2	39.7	1.66	2.12	1.19	3.66	2.35
40	39.9	37.9	42.1	33.4	38.8	1.81	2.30	1.31	3.91	2.62
41	38.9	37.0	41.2	32.5	37.9	1.96	2.49	1.42	4.19	2.88
42	38.0	36.1	40.2	31.6	37.0	2.12	2.69	1.55	4.56	3.14
43	37.1	35.2	39.3	30.8	36.1	2.31	2.93	1.69	5.04	3.42
44	36.2	34.3	38.4	29.9	35.2	2.53	3.20	1.85	5.63	3.71
45	35.3	33.4	37.4	29.1	34.3	2.76	3.48	2.03	6.27	4.02
46	34.4	32.5	36.5	28.3	33.5	3.00	3.78	2.21	6.93	4.34
47	33.5	31.7	35.6	27.5	32.6	3.25	4.11	2.39	7.64	4.69
48	32.6	30.8	34.7	26.7	31.8	3.50	4.45	2.56	8.39	5.06
49	31.7	29.9	33.8	25.9	30.9	3.76	4.81	2.72	9.19	5.45
50	30.9	29.1	32.9	25.1	30.1	4.05	5.22	2.89	10.06	5.87
51	30.0	28.2	32.0	24.4	29.3	4.36	5.66	3.09	11.01	6.33
52	29.1	27.4	31.1	23.6	28.5	4.70	6.09	3.34	11.93	6.78
53	28.3	26.5	30.2	22.9	27.6	5.06	6.52	3.64	12.81	7.24
54	27.4	25.7	29.3	22.2	26.8	5.44	6.94	3.99	13.65	7.70
55	26.6	24.9	28.4	21.5	26.0	5.85	7.37	4.37	14.54	8.20
56	25.8	24.1	27.5	20.8	25.3	6.30	7.86	4.79	15.53	8.77
57	24.9	23.3	26.6	20.1	24.5	6.81	8.44	5.24	16.61	9.40
58	24.1	22.5	25.8	19.5	23.7	7.43	9.17	5.76	17.78	10.11
59	23.3	21.7	24.9	18.8	22.9	8.15	10.06	6.34	19.07	10.89
60	22.5	20.9	24.1	18.2	22.2	9.01	11.11	7.03	20.50	11.77
61	21.7	20.1	23.2	17.5	21.4	9.97	12.28	7.80	22.06	12.74
62	20.9	19.3	22.4	16.9	20.7	10.96	13.50	8.61	23.69	13.76
63	20.2	18.6	21.6	16.3	20.0	11.93	14.69	9.39	25.29	14.79
64	19.4	17.9	20.8	15.7	19.3	12.89	15.86	10.17	26.84	15.83
65	18.7	17.2	20.0	15.2	18.6	13.94	17.14	11.04	28.38	16.91
70	15.2	13.7	16.2	12.4	15.3	21.64	26.43	17.54	39.00	24.37
75	11.9	10.7	12.8	9.9	12.2	34.03	41.84	27.93	56.86	36.69
80	9.1	8.1	9.7	8.0	9.6	54.40	66.48	2.1	79.37	54.76

[1] Includes other races not shown separately. [2] Based on the proportion of the cohort who are alive at the beginning of the indicated age who will die before reaching the age shown plus 1. For example, out of every 1,000 people alive and exactly 50 years old at the beginning of the period, between 4 and 5 (4.05) will die before reaching their 51st birthdays.

Source: U.S. National Center for Health Statistics, unpublished data.

[1,990 represents 1,990,000. Rates are per 1,000 population for specified groups. Excludes deaths of nonresidents of the United States and fetal deaths. For explanation of age adjustment, see text, this section. The standard population for age adjustment is the projected year 2000 population of the United States. See Appendix III. Data for Hispanic origin and specified races other than White and Black should be interpreted with caution because of inconsistencies between reporting Hispanic origin and race on death certificates and censuses and surveys]

Sex, race, and Hispanic origin	1980	1990	1995	1997	1998	1999	2000	2001	2002	2003	2004
Deaths [1] (1,000)	**1,990**	**2,148**	**2,312**	**2,314**	**2,337**	**2,391**	**2,403**	**2,416**	**2,443**	**2,448**	**2,398**
Male [1] (1,000)	1,075	1,113	1,173	1,154	1,157	1,175	1,178	1,183	1,199	1,202	1,182
Female [1] (1,000)	915	1,035	1,139	1,160	1,180	1,216	1,226	1,233	1,244	1,246	1,216
White (1,000)	1,739	1,853	1,987	1,996	2,016	2,061	2,071	2,080	2,103	2,104	2,057
Male (1,000)	934	951	997	987	990	1,005	1,007	1,011	1,025	1,026	1,007
Female (1,000)	805	902	990	1,010	1,026	1,056	1,064	1,068	1,077	1,078	1,049
Black (1,000)	233	265	286	277	278	285	286	288	290	291	287
Male (1,000)	130	145	154	144	143	146	145	146	147	148	146
Female (1,000)	103	120	132	132	135	139	141	142	143	143	141
Asian or Pacific Islander (1,000)	11	21	28	31	32	34	35	37	38	40	41
Male (1,000)	7	12	16	17	18	18	19	20	20	21	21
Female (1,000)	4	9	12	14	14	15	16	17	18	19	19
American Indian, Eskimo, Aleut (1,000)	7	8	10	11	11	11	11	12	12	13	13
Male (1,000)	4	5	6	6	6	6	6	6	7	7	7
Female (1,000)	3	4	4	5	5	5	5	6	6	6	6
Hispanic origin [2] (1,000)	(NA)	(NA)	(NA)	95	98	104	107	113	117	122	122
Male (1,000)	(NA)	(NA)	(NA)	54	56	58	60	63	66	68	69
Female (1,000)	(NA)	(NA)	(NA)	41	43	46	47	50	51	54	54
Non-Hispanic, White (1,000)	(NA)	(NA)	(NA)	1,895	1,913	1,953	1,960	1,963	1,982	1,979	1,933
Male (1,000)	(NA)	(NA)	(NA)	930	932	945	945	946	958	956	938
Female (1,000)	(NA)	(NA)	(NA)	966	981	1,008	1,015	1,017	1,024	1,023	995
Death rates [1]	**8.8**	**8.6**	**8.7**	**8.5**	**8.5**	**8.6**	**8.5**	**8.5**	**8.5**	**8.4**	**8.2**
Male [1]	9.8	9.2	9.0	8.6	8.6	8.6	8.5	8.5	8.5	8.4	8.2
Female [1]	7.9	8.1	8.4	8.3	8.4	8.5	8.6	8.5	8.5	8.4	8.2
White	8.9	8.9	9.0	8.9	8.9	9.0	9.0	9.0	9.0	8.9	8.6
Male	9.8	9.3	9.3	8.9	8.9	9.1	8.9	8.8	8.8	8.8	8.5
Female	8.1	8.5	8.9	8.9	8.9	9.2	9.1	9.1	9.1	9.0	8.7
Black	8.8	8.7	8.5	7.9	7.8	7.9	7.8	7.7	7.7	7.6	7.4
Male	10.3	10.1	9.8	8.7	8.5	8.8	8.3	8.2	8.2	8.1	7.9
Female	7.3	7.5	7.6	7.2	7.2	7.6	7.3	7.3	7.2	7.2	7.0
Asian or Pacific Islander	3.0	2.8	2.9	2.9	2.9	3.0	3.0	3.0	3.0	3.0	3.0
Male	3.8	3.3	3.4	3.4	3.4	3.3	3.3	3.4	3.3	3.3	3.2
Female	2.2	2.3	2.5	2.5	2.5	2.6	2.6	2.7	2.7	2.8	2.7
American Indian, Eskimo, Aleut	4.9	4.0	4.1	4.0	4.0	4.0	3.8	3.9	4.0	4.2	4.2
Male	6.0	4.8	4.6	4.6	4.4	4.3	4.2	4.2	4.4	4.6	4.5
Female	3.8	3.3	3.6	3.5	3.5	3.7	3.5	3.6	3.7	3.9	3.8
Hispanic origin [2]	(NA)	(NA)	(NA)	3.1	3.0	3.1	3.0	3.1	3.0	3.1	3.0
Male	(NA)	4.1	(NA)	3.4	3.3	3.7	3.3	3.3	3.3	3.3	3.2
Female	(NA)	2.9	(NA)	2.7	2.7	2.9	2.7	2.8	2.7	2.8	2.7
Non-Hispanic, White	(NA)	(NA)	(NA)	9.7	9.7	9.9	9.9	9.9	10.0	9.9	9.7
Male	(NA)	9.9	(NA)	9.7	9.7	9.8	9.8	9.8	9.8	9.8	9.6
Female	(NA)	9.0	(NA)	9.6	9.8	10.0	10.1	10.1	10.1	10.1	9.8
Age-adjusted death rates [1]	**10.4**	**9.4**	**9.2**	**8.8**	**8.7**	**8.8**	**8.7**	**8.5**	**8.5**	**8.3**	**8.0**
Male [1]	13.5	12.0	11.5	10.9	10.7	10.7	10.5	10.3	10.1	9.9	9.6
Female [1]	8.2	7.5	7.5	7.3	7.2	7.3	7.3	7.2	7.2	7.1	6.8
White	10.1	9.1	8.9	8.6	8.5	8.5	8.5	8.4	8.3	8.2	7.9
Male	13.2	11.7	11.1	10.6	10.4	10.4	10.3	10.1	9.9	9.7	9.4
Female	8.0	7.3	7.3	7.1	7.1	7.2	7.2	7.1	7.0	6.9	6.7
Black	13.1	12.5	12.2	11.4	11.3	11.4	11.2	11.0	10.8	10.7	10.3
Male	17.0	16.4	15.8	14.6	14.3	14.3	14.0	13.8	13.4	13.2	12.7
Female	10.3	9.8	9.7	9.2	9.2	9.3	9.3	9.1	9.0	8.9	8.6
Asian or Pacific Islander	5.9	5.8	6.2	5.3	5.2	5.2	5.1	4.9	4.7	4.7	4.4
Male	7.9	7.2	7.9	6.6	6.5	6.4	6.2	6.0	5.8	5.6	5.3
Female	4.3	4.7	4.9	4.3	4.3	4.3	4.2	4.1	4.0	3.9	3.8
American Indian, Eskimo, Aleut	8.7	7.2	7.2	7.7	7.7	7.8	7.1	6.9	6.8	6.9	6.5
Male	11.1	9.2	8.6	9.7	9.4	9.3	8.4	8.0	7.9	8.0	7.6
Female	6.6	5.6	5.9	6.3	6.4	6.7	6.0	5.9	5.8	5.9	5.6
Hispanic origin [2]	(NA)	(NA)	(NA)	6.7	6.7	6.8	6.7	6.6	6.3	6.2	5.9
Male	(NA)	8.9	(NA)	8.4	8.3	8.3	8.2	8.0	7.7	7.5	7.1
Female	(NA)	5.4	(NA)	5.4	5.4	5.6	5.5	5.4	5.2	5.2	4.9
Non-Hispanic, White	(NA)	(NA)	(NA)	8.6	8.5	8.6	8.6	8.4	8.4	8.3	8.0
Male	(NA)	11.7	(NA)	10.6	10.5	10.5	10.4	10.1	10.0	9.8	9.5
Female	(NA)	7.3	(NA)	7.1	7.1	7.2	7.2	7.1	7.1	7.0	6.8

NA Not available.   [1] Includes other races, not shown separately.   [2] Persons of Hispanic origin may be any race.

Source: U.S. National Center for Health Statistics, *Vital Statistics of the United States*, annual; and *National Vital Statistics Reports*, Vol. 55, No. 19, August 21, 2007.

Table 103. **Death Rates by Age, Sex, and Race: 1950 to 2004**

[Rates per 100,000 population. See headnote, Table 102 and Appendix III]

Characteristic	All ages [1]	Under 1 year	1–4 years	5–14 years	15–24 years	25–34 years	35–44 years	45–54 years	55–64 years	65–74 years	75–84 years	85 years and over
MALE												
1950	1,106	3,728	152	71	168	217	429	1,067	2,395	4,931	10,426	21,636
1960	1,105	3,059	120	56	152	188	373	992	2,310	4,914	10,178	21,186
1970	1,090	2,410	93	51	189	215	403	959	2,283	4,874	10,010	17,822
1980	977	1,429	73	37	172	196	299	767	1,815	4,105	8,817	18,801
1990	918	1,083	52	29	147	204	310	610	1,553	3,492	7,889	18,057
2000	853	807	36	21	115	139	255	543	1,231	2,980	6,973	17,501
2001	846	750	37	20	117	144	260	545	1,193	2,912	6,833	16,745
2002	847	762	35	20	117	142	258	548	1,184	2,855	6,761	16,255
2003	840	777	35	20	117	141	255	552	1,166	2,772	6,642	15,794
2004	818	754	32	19	115	140	244	544	1,129	2,645	6,394	15,031
White:												
1990	931	896	46	26	131	176	268	549	1,467	3,398	7,845	18,268
2000	888	668	33	20	106	124	234	497	1,163	2,906	6,933	17,716
2003	878	659	32	18	109	129	238	509	1,102	2,707	6,621	16,038
2004	854	632	29	18	108	127	229	504	1,066	2,584	6,385	15,251
Black:												
1990	1,008	2,112	86	41	252	431	700	1,261	2,618	4,946	9,130	16,955
2000	834	1,568	55	28	181	261	453	1,018	2,080	4,254	8,486	16,791
2003	814	1,410	54	27	171	256	427	991	2,011	3,981	8,067	14,903
2004	793	1,414	49	26	164	252	397	955	1,961	3,818	7,710	14,453
Asian or Pacific Islander [2]:												
1990	334	605	45	21	76	80	131	287	789	2,041	5,009	12,446
2000	333	529	23	13	55	55	105	250	642	1,661	4,328	12,125
2003	330	497	25	15	56	54	96	243	566	1,473	4,041	10,392
2004	321	443	21	15	54	51	91	242	545	1,363	3,766	10,118
American Indian, Eskimo, Aleut [2]:												
1990	476	1,057	77	33	220	256	365	620	1,211	2,462	5,389	11,244
2000	416	700	45	20	136	179	295	520	1,090	2,478	5,351	10,726
2003	458	912	57	29	153	185	338	584	1,058	2,237	4,644	9,584
2004	454	1,076	55	24	136	189	321	543	1,067	2,197	4,584	7,924
FEMALE												
1950	824	2,855	127	49	89	143	290	642	1,405	3,333	8,400	19,195
1960	809	2,321	98	37	61	107	229	527	1,196	2,872	7,633	19,008
1970	808	1,864	75	32	68	102	231	517	1,099	2,580	6,678	15,518
1980	785	1,142	55	24	58	76	159	413	934	2,145	5,440	14,747
1990	812	856	41	19	49	74	138	343	879	1,991	4,883	14,274
2000	855	663	29	15	43	64	143	313	772	1,921	4,815	14,719
2001	850	614	30	15	43	66	148	317	754	1,891	4,761	14,430
2002	848	625	27	15	44	64	149	317	738	1,865	4,758	14,210
2003	843	619	28	14	44	65	149	318	733	1,823	4,676	14,063
2004	815	613	27	14	44	64	144	314	707	1,761	4,522	13,280
White:												
1990	847	690	36	18	46	62	117	309	823	1,924	4,839	14,401
2000	912	551	26	14	41	55	126	281	731	1,868	4,785	14,891
2003	902	521	26	13	43	58	133	287	694	1,781	4,672	14,241
2004	872	514	24	13	42	57	130	285	672	1,724	4,514	13,451
Black:												
1990	748	1,736	68	28	69	160	299	639	1,453	2,866	5,688	13,310
2000	733	1,280	45	20	58	122	272	588	1,227	2,690	5,697	13,941
2003	718	1,132	40	19	54	114	270	582	1,179	2,487	5,386	13,617
2004	700	1,150	41	21	54	112	256	564	1,129	2,386	5,300	12,897
Asian or Pacific Islander [2]:												
1990	234	518	32	13	29	38	70	183	483	1,089	3,128	10,254
2000	262	434	20	12	22	28	66	156	391	996	2,882	9,052
2003	279	428	20	12	29	30	58	151	359	990	2,682	8,329
2004	275	392	22	10	24	27	54	146	340	933	2,558	8,126
American Indian, Eskimo, Aleut [2]:												
1990	330	689	38	26	69	102	156	381	806	1,679	3,073	8,201
2000	346	492	40	18	59	85	172	285	772	1,900	3,850	9,118
2003	388	676	43	18	62	89	196	364	785	1,711	3,834	7,920
2004	380	715	53	20	65	103	192	340	704	1,701	3,533	7,094

[1] Figures for age not stated are included in "All ages" but not distributed among age groups. [2] The death rates for specified races other than White and Black should be interpreted with caution because of inconsistencies between reporting race on death certificates and censuses and surveys.

Source: U.S. National Center for Health Statistics, *Vital Statistics of the United States*, annual; and *National Vital Statistics Reports*, Vol. 55, No. 19, August 21, 2007; and prior reports.

Table 104. Age-Adjusted Death Rates by Sex, Race, and Hispanic Origin: 1960 to 2004

[Age-adjusted rates per 100,000 population; see headnote, Table 102. Populations enumerated as of April 1 for census years and estimated as of July 1 for all other years. Beginning 1970, excludes deaths of nonresidents of the United States. Data for Hispanic origin and specified races other than White and Black should be interpreted with caution because of inconsistencies reporting race on death certificates and on censuses and surveys. See Appendix III]

Sex, race, and Hispanic origin	1960	1970	1980	1990	1995	2000	2001	2002	2003	2004
ALL RACES [1]										
Total	1,339	1,223	1,039	939	919	869	855	845	833	801
Male	1,609	1,542	1,348	1,203	1,150	1,054	1,029	1,014	994	956
Female.	1,105	971	818	751	748	731	722	715	706	679
WHITE										
Total	1,311	1,193	1,013	910	890	850	837	829	817	786
Male	1,586	1,514	1,318	1,166	1,113	1,029	1,006	993	974	937
Female.	1,074	944	796	729	727	715	707	701	693	667
BLACK										
Total	1,578	1,518	1,315	1,250	1,225	1,121	1,101	1,083	1,066	1,027
Male	1,811	1,874	1,698	1,645	1,582	1,404	1,375	1,341	1,319	1,269
Female.	1,370	1,229	1,033	975	970	928	913	902	886	855
ASIAN OR PACIFIC ISLANDER										
Total	(NA)	(NA)	590	582	616	506	492	474	466	444
Male	(NA)	(NA)	787	716	788	624	597	578	563	535
Female.	(NA)	(NA)	426	469	488	417	412	396	393	376
AMERICAN INDIAN, ESKIMO, ALEUT										
Total	(NA)	(NA)	867	716	717	709	687	677	685	650
Male	(NA)	(NA)	1,112	916	864	842	799	794	797	758
Female.	(NA)	(NA)	662	562	593	605	594	581	592	558
HISPANIC ORIGIN [2]										
Total	(NA)	(NA)	(NA)	(NA)	(NA)	666	659	629	621	587
Male	(NA)	(NA)	(NA)	886	(NA)	818	803	767	748	707
Female.	(NA)	(NA)	(NA)	537	(NA)	546	544	518	516	486
NON-HISPANIC, WHITE										
Total	(NA)	(NA)	(NA)	(NA)	(NA)	856	843	838	826	797
Male	(NA)	(NA)	(NA)	1,171	(NA)	1,035	1,013	1,002	984	949
Female.	(NA)	(NA)	(NA)	735	(NA)	722	714	710	702	678

NA Not available. [1] For 1960 to 1990 includes deaths among races not shown separately. [2] Persons of Hispanic origin may be any race.

Source: U.S. National Center for Health Statistics, *Vital Statistics of the United States*, annual and *National Vital Statistics Reports*, Vol. 55, No. 19, August 21, 2007.

Table 105. Death Rates by Hispanic Origin Status, Sex, and Age: 1990 to 2004

[Rates per 100,000 population. Rates are based on populations enumerated as of April 1 for census years and estimated as of July 1 for all other years. Excludes deaths of nonresidents of the United States. Data for Hispanic origin should be interpreted with caution because of inconsistencies between reporting Hispanic origin and race on death certificates and censuses and surveys]

Age	Hispanic male			Hispanic female			Non-Hispanic White male			Non-Hispanic White female		
	1990	2000	2004	1990	2000	2004	1990	2000	2004	1990	2000	2004
Age-adjusted [1]	886	818	707	537	546	486	1,171	1,035	949	735	722	678
Crude	412	331	321	285	275	270	986	979	957	904	1,007	978
Under 1 year	922	637	637	747	554	535	865	659	625	655	531	501
1 to 4 years	54	32	30	42	28	24	44	32	29	34	24	24
5 to 14 years	26	18	17	17	13	12	26	20	18	18	14	13
15 to 24 years	159	108	115	41	32	32	123	104	105	46	43	44
25 to 34 years	234	120	109	63	43	41	165	123	131	61	57	60
35 to 44 years	342	211	184	109	101	88	257	234	236	117	128	136
45 to 54 years	534	439	418	253	224	208	545	498	511	312	285	293
55 to 64 years	1,124	966	874	608	548	511	1,480	1,171	1,076	835	742	684
65 to 74 years	2,368	2,288	1,994	1,454	1,423	1,297	3,435	2,931	2,618	1,940	1,891	1,752
75 to 84 years	5,369	5,395	4,792	3,351	3,625	3,330	7,920	6,978	6,462	4,887	4,819	4,571
85 years and over . . .	12,272	13,086	9,933	10,099	11,203	9,253	18,505	17,853	15,489	14,533	14,972	13,610

[1] See headnote, Table 102.

Source: U.S. National Center for Health Statistics. *Vital Statistics of the United States*, annual and *National Vital Statistics Reports*, Vol. 55, No. 19. August 21, 2007.

Births, Deaths, Marriages, and Divorces 79

Table 106. **Deaths and Death Rates by State and Island Areas: 1990 to 2005**

[2,148 represents 2,148,000. By state of residence. Except as noted, excludes deaths of nonresidents of the United States. Caution should be used in comparing death rates by state; rates are affected by the population composition of the area. For explanation of age adjustment, see Table 102. See also Appendix III]

State and island area	Number of deaths (1,000)						Crude rate per 1,000 population [2]						Age adjusted rate, 2004
	1990	1995	2000	2003	2004	2005 [1]	1990	1995	2000	2003	2004	2005 [1]	
United States . . .	2,148	2,312	2,403	2,448	2,398	2,432	8.6	8.7	8.5	8.4	8.2	8.2	8.0
Alabama	39	42	45	47	46	47	9.7	10.0	10.1	10.4	10.2	10.4	9.9
Alaska	2	3	3	3	3	3	4.0	4.2	4.6	4.9	4.7	4.4	7.5
Arizona	29	35	41	43	43	46	7.9	8.4	7.9	7.8	7.5	7.7	7.6
Arkansas	25	27	28	28	28	28	10.5	10.8	10.6	10.2	10.0	10.2	9.2
California	214	224	230	239	233	232	7.2	7.1	6.8	6.7	6.5	6.4	7.2
Colorado	22	25	27	30	28	30	6.6	6.7	6.3	6.5	6.2	6.3	7.4
Connecticut	28	29	30	30	29	30	8.4	9.0	8.8	8.5	8.4	8.4	7.1
Delaware	6	6	7	7	7	7	8.7	8.8	8.8	8.6	8.6	8.8	8.2
District of Columbia .	7	7	6	6	5	5	12.0	12.4	10.5	9.9	9.9	9.3	9.7
Florida	134	153	164	169	169	170	10.4	10.8	10.3	9.9	9.7	9.6	7.6
Georgia	52	58	64	66	66	66	8.0	8.1	7.8	7.7	7.5	7.2	9.2
Hawaii	7	8	8	9	9	9	6.1	6.4	6.8	7.1	7.2	7.2	6.2
Idaho	7	9	10	10	10	11	7.4	7.3	7.4	7.6	7.2	7.5	7.5
Illinois	103	108	107	105	103	103	9.0	9.2	8.6	8.3	8.1	8.1	8.0
Indiana	50	53	55	56	54	55	8.9	9.2	9.1	9.0	8.7	8.8	8.5
Iowa	27	28	28	28	27	28	9.7	9.9	9.6	9.5	9.1	9.4	7.3
Kansas	22	24	25	25	24	25	9.0	9.3	9.2	9.0	8.7	9.0	7.9
Kentucky	35	37	40	40	39	40	9.5	9.6	9.8	9.8	9.3	9.7	9.4
Louisiana	38	40	41	43	42	42	8.9	9.1	9.2	9.5	9.3	9.3	9.9
Maine	11	12	12	13	12	13	9.0	9.5	9.7	9.6	9.4	9.7	8.1
Maryland	38	42	44	44	43	44	8.0	8.3	8.3	8.1	7.8	7.9	8.1
Massachusetts	53	55	57	56	55	53	8.8	9.1	8.9	8.8	8.5	8.3	7.4
Michigan	79	84	87	87	85	87	8.5	8.8	8.7	8.6	8.4	8.6	8.1
Minnesota	35	38	38	38	37	37	7.9	8.1	7.7	7.4	7.3	7.3	6.9
Mississippi	25	27	29	28	28	29	9.8	10.0	10.1	9.9	9.6	10.1	10.0
Missouri	50	54	55	56	54	55	9.8	10.2	9.8	9.7	9.4	9.4	8.7
Montana	7	8	8	8	8	8	8.6	8.8	9.0	9.2	8.7	9.0	7.8
Nebraska	15	15	15	15	15	15	9.4	9.3	8.8	8.9	8.4	8.5	7.5
Nevada	9	13	15	18	18	19	7.8	8.2	7.6	8.0	7.7	7.7	8.8
New Hampshire	8	9	10	10	10	10	7.7	8.0	7.8	7.5	7.8	7.6	7.6
New Jersey	70	74	75	74	71	72	9.1	9.3	8.9	8.5	8.2	8.3	7.5
New Mexico	11	13	13	15	14	15	7.0	7.4	7.4	7.9	7.5	7.7	7.8
New York	169	168	158	156	153	154	9.4	9.3	8.3	8.1	7.9	8.0	7.3
North Carolina	57	65	72	73	72	75	8.6	9.0	8.9	8.7	8.5	8.6	8.7
North Dakota	6	6	6	6	6	6	8.9	9.3	9.1	9.6	8.8	9.1	7.0
Ohio	99	106	108	109	106	108	9.1	9.5	9.5	9.5	9.3	9.4	8.5
Oklahoma	30	33	35	36	34	36	9.7	10.0	10.2	10.2	9.8	10.2	9.5
Oregon	25	28	30	31	30	31	8.8	9.0	8.6	8.7	8.4	8.6	7.8
Pennsylvania	122	128	131	130	128	128	10.3	10.6	10.7	10.5	10.3	10.4	8.1
Rhode Island	10	10	10	10	10	10	9.5	9.8	9.6	9.3	9.0	9.4	7.4
South Carolina	30	34	37	38	37	37	8.5	9.1	9.2	9.2	8.9	8.8	9.0
South Dakota	6	7	7	7	7	7	9.1	9.5	9.3	9.3	8.9	9.1	7.5
Tennessee	46	51	55	57	56	57	9.5	9.8	9.7	9.8	9.5	9.6	9.5
Texas	125	138	150	155	153	155	7.4	7.4	7.2	7.0	6.8	6.8	8.4
Utah	9	11	12	13	13	13	5.3	5.6	5.5	5.7	5.6	5.4	7.6
Vermont	5	5	5	5	5	5	8.2	8.5	8.4	8.3	8.0	7.9	7.3
Virginia	48	53	56	58	57	58	7.8	8.0	8.0	7.9	7.6	7.6	8.1
Washington	37	41	44	46	45	46	7.6	7.5	7.5	7.5	7.2	7.3	7.4
West Virginia	19	20	21	21	21	21	10.8	11.1	11.7	11.8	11.5	11.4	9.7
Wisconsin	43	45	46	46	46	47	8.7	8.8	8.7	8.4	8.3	8.4	7.5
Wyoming	3	4	4	4	4	4	7.1	7.7	7.9	8.3	7.8	8.0	7.9
Puerto Rico	26	30	28	28	29	29	7.3	8.1	7.2	7.3	7.4	(NA)	7.9
Virgin Islands	(Z)	1	1	1	1	(NA)	4.6	5.8	5.3	5.8	5.8	(NA)	6.9
Guam	1	1	1	1	1	(NA)	3.9	4.1	4.2	4.2	4.1	(NA)	6.9
American Samoa .	(NA)	(NA)	(Z)	(Z)	(NA)	(NA)	(NA)	(NA)	3.3	4.4	4.9	(NA)	13.5
Northern Marianas	(NA)	(NA)	(Z)	(Z)	(NA)	(NA)	(NA)	(NA)	1.9	1.9	2.1	(NA)	11.6

NA Not available.   Z Less than 500.   [1] Provisional data. Includes nonresidents of the United States.   [2] Rates based on enumerated resident population as of April 1 for 1990 and 2000; estimated resident population as of July 1 for all other years.

Source: U.S. National Center for Health Statistics, *Vital Statistics of the United States*, annual; and *National Vital Statistics Reports*, Vol. 54, No. 20, July 21, 2006; Vol. 55, No. 19, August 21, 2007; and prior reports.

Table 107. Fetal and Infant Deaths: 1990 to 2003

[See Appendix III]

Year	Fetal deaths			Infant deaths		Fetal mortality rate [3]			Perinatal mortality rate	
	Total [1]	20 to 27 weeks [2]	28 weeks or more [2]	Less than 7 days	Less than 28 days	Total [1]	20 to 27 weeks [2]	28 weeks or more [2]	Definition I [4]	Definition II [5]
1990 ...	31,386	13,427	17,959	19,439	23,591	7.49	3.22	4.30	8.95	13.12
1995 ...	27,294	13,043	14,251	15,483	19,186	6.95	3.33	3.64	7.60	11.84
1996 ...	27,069	12,990	14,079	14,947	18,556	6.91	3.33	3.60	7.43	11.64
1997 ...	26,486	12,800	13,686	14,827	18,507	6.78	3.29	3.51	7.32	11.51
1998 ...	26,702	13,229	13,473	15,061	18,915	6.73	3.35	3.41	7.21	11.50
1999 ...	26,884	13,457	13,427	14,874	18,700	6.74	3.39	3.38	7.12	11.44
2000 ...	27,003	13,497	13,506	14,893	18,733	6.61	3.31	3.32	6.97	11.19
2001 ...	26,373	13,122	13,251	14,622	18,275	6.51	3.25	3.28	6.90	11.02
2002 ...	25,943	13,072	12,871	15,020	18,791	6.41	3.24	3.19	6.91	11.05
2003 ...	25,653	13,168	12,485	15,152	18,935	6.23	3.21	3.04	6.74	10.83

[1] Fetal deaths with stated or presumed gestation of 20 weeks or more. [2] Not stated gestational age proportionally distributed. [3] Rate is number of fetal deaths in specified group per 1,000 live births and fetal deaths. [4] Infant deaths of less than 7 days and fetal deaths with stated or presumed period of gestation of 28 weeks or more, per 1,000 live births and fetal deaths. [5] Infant deaths of less than 28 days and fetal deaths with stated or presumed period of gestation of 20 weeks or more per 1,000 live births and fetal deaths.

Source: U.S. National Center for Health Statistics, *National Vital Statistics Reports*, Vol. 55, No. 6, February 21, 2007.

Table 108. Infant, Neonatal, and Maternal Mortality Rates by Race: 1980 to 2004

[Deaths per 1,000 live births, except as noted. Excludes deaths of nonresidents of U.S. Infant and maternal deaths are based on race of the decedent. Fetal deaths and live births are based on race of mother. See also Appendix III]

Race and year	Infant mortality [1]	Neonatal mortality [1]		Post-neonatal mortality [1]	Fetal mortality rate [2]	Late fetal mortality rate [3]	Perinatal mortality rate [4]	Maternal mortality rate [5]
		Under 28 days	Under 7 days					
ALL RACES								
1980	12.6	8.5	7.1	4.1	9.1	6.2	13.2	9.2
1990	9.2	5.8	4.8	3.4	7.5	4.3	9.1	8.2
1995	7.6	4.9	4.0	2.7	7.0	3.6	7.6	7.1
2000	6.9	4.6	3.7	2.3	6.6	3.3	7.0	9.8
2001	6.8	4.5	3.6	2.3	6.5	3.3	6.9	9.9
2002	7.0	4.7	3.7	2.3	6.4	3.2	6.9	8.9
2003	6.9	4.6	3.7	2.2	6.2	3.0	6.7	[6]12.1
2004	6.8	4.5	3.6	2.3	(NA)	(NA)	(NA)	[6]13.1
WHITE								
1980	10.9	7.4	6.1	3.5	8.1	5.7	11.8	6.7
1990	7.6	4.8	3.9	2.8	6.4	3.8	7.7	5.4
1995	6.3	4.1	3.3	2.2	5.9	3.3	6.5	4.2
2000	5.7	3.8	3.0	1.9	5.6	2.9	5.9	7.5
2001	5.7	3.8	3.0	1.9	5.5	2.9	5.9	7.2
2002	5.8	3.9	3.1	1.9	5.5	2.8	5.9	6.0
2003	5.7	3.9	3.1	1.8	5.2	2.7	5.8	[6]8.7
2004	5.7	3.8	3.0	1.9	(NA)	(NA)	(NA)	[6]9.3
BLACK								
1980	22.2	14.6	12.3	7.6	14.7	9.1	21.3	21.5
1990	18.0	11.6	9.7	6.4	13.3	6.7	16.4	22.4
1995	15.1	9.8	8.2	5.3	12.7	5.7	13.8	22.1
2000	14.1	9.4	7.6	4.7	12.4	5.4	13.0	22.0
2001	14.0	9.2	7.6	4.8	12.1	5.3	12.8	24.7
2002	14.4	9.5	7.8	4.8	11.9	5.2	12.8	24.9
2003	14.0	9.4	7.5	4.6	12.0	5.1	12.4	[6]30.5
2004	13.8	9.1	7.3	4.7	(NA)	(NA)	(NA)	[6]34.7

NA Not available. [1] Infant (under 1 year of age), neonatal (under 28 days), early neonatal (under 7 days), and postneonatal (28 days-11 months). [2] Number of fetal deaths of 20 weeks or more gestation per 1,000 live births plus fetal deaths. [3] Number of fetal deaths of 28 weeks or more gestation (late fetal deaths) per 1,000 live births plus fetal deaths. [4] Number of late fetal deaths plus infant deaths within 7 days of birth per 1,000 live births plus late fetal deaths. [5] Per 100,000 live births from deliveries and complications of pregnancy, childbirth, and the puerperium. Beginning 2000, deaths are classified according to the tenth revision of the *International Classification of Diseases*; earlier years classified according to the revision in use at the time; see text, this section. [6] Increase partially reflects the use of a separate item on the death certificate on pregnancy status by an increasing number of states.

Source: U.S. National Center for Health Statistics, *Health, United States 2006*; *National Vital Statistics Report*, Vol. 55, No. 19, August 21, 2007; and unpublished data.

U.S. Census Bureau, Statistical Abstract of the United States: 2008

Table 109. Infant Mortality Rates by Race—States: 1980 to 2004

[Deaths per 1,000 live births, by place of residence. Represents deaths of infants under 1 year old, exclusive of fetal deaths. Excludes deaths of nonresidents of the United States. See headnote, Table 108 and Appendix III]

State	Total [1]				White				Black			
	1980	1990	2000	2004	1980	1990	2000	2004	1980	1990	2000	2004
United States	12.6	9.2	6.9	6.8	10.9	7.6	5.7	5.7	22.2	18.0	14.1	13.8
Alabama.	15.1	10.8	9.4	8.7	11.6	8.1	6.6	6.8	21.6	16.0	15.4	13.3
Alaska	12.3	10.5	6.8	6.7	9.4	7.6	5.8	5.5	19.5	(B)	(B)	(B)
Arizona.	12.4	8.8	6.7	6.7	11.8	7.8	6.2	6.5	18.4	20.6	17.6	12.0
Arkansas	12.7	9.2	8.4	8.3	10.3	8.4	7.0	7.1	20.0	13.9	13.7	13.4
California	11.1	7.9	5.4	5.2	10.6	7.0	5.1	4.9	18.0	16.8	12.9	12.4
Colorado.	10.1	8.8	6.2	6.3	9.8	7.8	5.6	6.0	19.1	19.4	19.5	14.7
Connecticut.	11.2	7.9	6.6	5.5	10.2	6.3	5.6	4.5	19.1	17.6	14.4	12.9
Delaware	13.9	10.1	9.2	8.6	9.8	9.7	7.9	6.5	27.9	20.1	14.8	15.5
District of Columbia	25.0	20.7	12.0	12.0	17.8	(B)	(B)	(B)	26.7	24.6	16.1	14.7
Florida	14.6	9.6	7.0	7.1	11.8	6.7	5.4	5.6	22.8	16.8	12.6	11.8
Georgia	14.5	12.4	8.5	8.5	10.8	7.4	5.9	6.1	21.0	18.3	13.9	13.9
Hawaii	10.3	6.7	8.1	5.7	11.6	6.1	6.5	5.2	(B)	(B)	(B)	(B)
Idaho	10.7	8.7	7.5	6.2	10.7	8.6	7.5	6.1	(NA)	(B)	(B)	(B)
Illinois	14.8	10.7	8.5	7.5	11.7	7.9	6.6	6.0	26.3	22.4	17.1	15.7
Indiana.	11.9	9.6	7.8	8.0	10.5	7.9	6.9	7.0	23.4	17.4	15.8	16.9
Iowa	11.8	8.1	6.5	5.1	11.5	7.9	6.0	4.8	27.2	21.9	21.1	(B)
Kansas.	10.4	8.4	6.8	7.2	9.5	8.0	6.4	6.5	20.6	17.7	12.2	16.5
Kentucky	12.9	8.5	7.2	6.8	12.0	8.2	6.7	6.3	22.0	14.3	12.7	12.6
Louisiana	14.3	11.1	9.0	10.5	10.5	8.1	5.9	7.7	20.6	16.7	13.3	14.8
Maine.	9.2	6.2	4.9	5.7	9.4	6.7	4.8	5.5	(B)	(B)	(B)	(B)
Maryland	14.0	9.5	7.6	8.4	11.6	6.8	4.8	5.7	20.4	17.1	13.2	14.0
Massachusetts.	10.5	7.0	4.6	4.8	10.1	6.1	4.0	4.4	16.8	11.9	9.9	9.2
Michigan.	12.8	10.7	8.2	7.6	10.6	7.4	6.0	5.5	24.2	21.6	18.2	17.5
Minnesota.	10.0	7.3	5.6	4.7	9.6	6.7	4.8	4.2	20.0	23.7	14.6	9.2
Mississippi	17.0	12.1	10.7	9.8	11.1	7.4	6.8	6.2	23.7	16.2	15.3	14.6
Missouri	12.4	9.4	7.2	7.5	11.1	7.9	5.9	6.4	20.7	18.2	14.7	14.7
Montana	12.4	9.0	6.1	4.5	11.8	6.0	5.5	4.2	(NA)	(B)	(B)	(B)
Nebraska	11.5	8.3	7.3	6.6	10.7	6.9	6.4	5.9	25.2	18.9	20.3	16.5
Nevada	10.7	8.4	6.5	6.4	10.0	8.2	6.0	5.3	20.6	14.2	12.7	18.6
New Hampshire	9.9	7.1	5.7	5.6	9.9	6.0	5.5	5.3	22.5	(B)	(B)	(B)
New Jersey.	12.5	9.0	6.3	5.7	10.3	6.4	5.0	4.8	21.9	18.4	13.6	10.7
New Mexico	11.5	9.0	6.6	6.3	11.3	7.6	6.3	5.8	23.1	(B)	(B)	(B)
New York	12.5	9.6	6.4	6.1	10.8	7.4	5.4	5.0	20.0	18.1	10.9	10.9
North Carolina	14.5	10.6	8.6	8.8	12.1	8.0	6.3	6.3	20.0	16.5	15.7	16.8
North Dakota.	12.1	8.0	8.1	5.6	11.7	7.2	7.5	5.1	27.5	(B)	(B)	(B)
Ohio	12.8	9.8	7.6	7.7	11.2	7.8	6.3	6.1	23.0	19.5	15.4	16.3
Oklahoma.	12.7	9.2	8.5	8.0	12.1	9.1	7.9	7.1	21.8	14.3	16.9	17.2
Oregon.	12.2	8.3	5.6	5.5	12.2	7.0	5.5	5.3	15.9	(B)	(B)	(B)
Pennsylvania.	13.2	9.6	7.1	7.3	11.9	7.4	5.8	6.2	23.1	20.5	15.7	13.5
Rhode Island.	11.0	8.1	6.3	5.3	10.9	7.0	5.9	5.0	(B)	(B)	(B)	(B)
South Carolina.	15.6	11.7	8.7	9.3	10.8	8.1	5.4	6.8	22.9	17.3	14.8	14.1
South Dakota	10.9	10.1	5.5	8.2	9.0	8.0	4.3	7.0	(NA)	(B)	(B)	(B)
Tennessee	13.5	10.3	9.1	8.6	11.9	7.3	6.8	6.7	19.3	17.9	18.0	16.0
Texas.	12.2	8.1	5.7	6.3	11.2	6.7	5.1	5.6	18.8	14.7	11.4	12.7
Utah	10.4	7.5	5.2	5.2	10.5	6.0	5.1	5.2	27.3	(B)	(B)	(B)
Vermont	10.7	6.4	6.0	4.6	10.7	5.9	6.1	4.7	(B)	(B)	(B)	(B)
Virginia.	13.6	10.2	6.9	7.5	11.9	7.4	5.4	5.8	19.8	19.5	12.4	14.2
Washington.	11.8	7.8	5.2	5.5	11.5	7.3	4.9	5.4	16.4	20.6	9.4	10.6
West Virginia.	11.8	9.9	7.6	7.6	11.4	8.1	7.4	7.4	21.5	(B)	(B)	(B)
Wisconsin.	10.3	8.2	6.6	6.0	9.7	7.7	5.5	4.6	18.5	19.0	17.2	19.4
Wyoming	9.8	8.6	6.7	8.8	9.3	7.5	6.5	8.3	25.9	(B)	(B)	(B)
Puerto Rico	(NA)	(NA)	9.7	8.0	(NA)	(NA)	10.2	8.6	(NA)	(NA)	(B)	(B)
Virgin Islands	(NA)	(NA)	13.4	(B)	(NA)	(NA)	(B)	(B)	(B)	(B)	(B)	(B)
Guam	(NA)	(NA)	5.8	11.7	(NA)	(NA)	(B)	(B)	(B)	(B)	(B)	(B)
American Samoa	(NA)	(NA)	(B)	15.2	(B)	(B)	(B)	(B)	(B)	(B)	(B)	(B)
Northern Marianas . . .	(NA)	(NA)	(B)	(B)	(B)	(B)	(B)	(B)	(B)	(B)	(B)	(B)

B Base figure too small to meet statistical standards for reliability.   NA Not available.   [1] Includes other races, not shown separately.

Source: U.S. National Center for Health Statistics, *Vital Statistics of the United States*, annual; and *National Vital Statistics Reports*, Vol. 55, No. 19, August 21, 2007; and earlier reports.

Table 110. **Age-Adjusted Death Rates by Major Causes: 1960 to 2004**

[Rates per 100,000 population; see headnote, Table 102. Beginning 1999, deaths classified according to tenth revision of International Classification of Diseases; for earlier years, causes of death were classified according to the revisions then in use. Changes in classification of causes of death due to these revisions may result in discontinuities in cause-of-death trends. See Appendix III]

Year	Diseases of heart	Malignant neo-plasms (cancer)	Cere-bro-vascular diseases	Chronic lower respira-tory diseases	Acci-dents [1]	Diabetes mellitus	Influenza and pneu-monia	Nephritis, nephrotic syndrome, and nephrosis	Septi-cemia	Intentional self harm (suicide)
1960	559.0	193.9	177.9	12.5	63.1	22.5	53.7	10.6	1.2	12.5
1961	545.3	193.4	173.1	12.6	60.6	22.1	43.4	10.0	1.2	12.2
1962	556.9	193.3	174.0	14.2	62.9	22.6	47.1	9.6	1.3	12.8
1963	563.4	194.7	173.9	16.5	64.0	23.1	55.6	9.2	1.5	13.0
1964	543.3	193.6	167.0	16.3	64.1	22.5	45.4	8.9	1.5	12.7
1965	542.5	195.6	166.4	18.3	65.8	22.9	46.8	8.3	1.5	13.0
1966	541.2	196.5	165.8	19.2	67.6	23.6	47.9	7.9	1.6	12.7
1967	524.7	197.3	159.3	19.2	66.2	23.4	42.2	7.3	1.6	12.5
1968	531.0	198.8	162.5	20.7	65.5	25.3	52.8	6.1	1.7	12.4
1969	516.8	198.5	155.4	20.9	64.9	25.1	47.9	6.0	1.7	12.7
1970	492.7	198.6	147.7	21.3	62.2	24.3	41.7	5.5	2.0	13.1
1971	492.9	199.3	147.6	21.8	60.3	23.9	38.4	5.2	2.2	13.1
1972	490.2	200.3	147.3	22.8	60.2	23.7	41.3	5.2	2.4	13.3
1973	482.0	200.0	145.2	23.6	59.3	23.0	41.2	5.0	2.6	13.1
1974	458.8	201.5	136.8	23.2	52.7	22.1	35.5	4.7	3.0	13.2
1975	431.2	200.1	123.5	23.7	50.8	20.3	34.9	4.7	3.1	13.6
1976	426.9	202.5	117.4	24.9	48.7	19.5	38.8	4.9	3.5	13.2
1977	413.7	203.5	110.4	24.7	48.8	18.2	31.0	4.8	3.8	13.7
1978	409.9	204.9	103.7	26.3	48.9	18.3	34.5	4.8	4.2	12.9
1979	401.6	204.0	97.1	25.5	46.5	17.5	26.1	8.6	4.3	12.6
1980	412.1	207.9	96.4	28.3	46.4	18.1	31.4	9.1	5.0	12.2
1981	397.0	206.4	89.5	29.0	43.4	17.6	30.0	9.1	5.4	12.3
1982	389.0	208.3	84.2	29.1	40.1	17.2	26.5	9.4	5.9	12.5
1983	388.9	209.1	81.2	31.6	39.1	17.6	29.8	9.6	6.7	12.4
1984	378.8	210.8	78.7	32.4	38.8	17.2	30.6	10.0	7.4	12.6
1985	375.0	211.3	76.6	34.5	38.5	17.4	34.5	10.4	8.3	12.5
1986	365.1	211.5	73.1	34.8	38.6	17.2	34.8	10.4	9.0	13.0
1987	355.9	211.7	71.6	35.0	38.2	17.4	33.8	10.4	9.3	12.8
1988	352.5	212.5	70.6	36.5	38.9	18.0	37.3	10.4	9.7	12.5
1989	332.0	214.2	66.9	36.6	37.7	20.5	35.9	9.6	8.8	12.3
1990	321.8	216.0	65.3	37.2	36.3	20.7	36.8	9.3	8.6	12.5
1991	312.5	215.2	62.9	37.9	34.7	20.7	34.7	9.3	8.6	12.3
1992	304.0	213.5	61.5	37.7	33.2	20.7	32.8	9.4	8.4	12.0
1993	308.1	213.5	62.7	40.7	34.2	21.9	35.0	9.7	8.6	12.1
1994	297.5	211.7	62.6	40.3	34.2	22.6	33.6	9.4	8.3	11.9
1995	293.4	209.9	63.1	40.1	34.4	23.2	33.4	9.5	8.4	11.8
1996	285.7	206.7	62.5	40.6	34.5	23.8	32.9	9.6	8.4	11.5
1997	277.7	203.4	61.1	41.1	34.2	23.7	33.3	9.8	8.6	11.2
1998	267.4	202.1	62.8	43.8	35.6	24.2	24.2	9.8	8.9	11.1
1999	266.5	200.8	61.6	45.4	35.3	25.0	23.5	13.0	11.3	10.5
2000	257.6	199.6	60.9	44.2	34.9	25.0	23.7	13.5	11.3	10.4
2001	247.8	196.0	57.9	43.7	35.7	25.3	22.0	14.0	11.4	10.7
2002	240.8	193.5	56.2	43.5	36.9	25.4	22.6	14.2	11.7	10.9
2003	232.3	190.1	53.5	43.3	37.3	25.3	22.0	14.4	11.6	10.8
2004	217.0	185.8	50.0	41.1	37.7	24.5	19.8	14.2	11.2	10.9

[1] Unintentional injuries.

Source: U.S. National Center for Health Statistics, *Vital Statistics of the United States*, annual; *Health, United States, 2006*; and *National Vital Statistics Reports (NVSR)*, Vol. 55, No. 19, August 21, 2007; and unpublished data.

Table 111. **Deaths and Death Rates by Selected Causes: 2003 and 2004**

[**Rates per 100,000 population.** Figures are weighted data rounded to the nearest individual, so categories may not add to total or subtotal. Excludes deaths of nonresidents of the United States. Deaths classified according to tenth revision of International Classification of Diseases. See also Appendix III]

Cause of death	2003 Number	2003 Rate	2003 Age-adjusted rate [1]	2004 Number	2004 Rate	2004 Age-adjusted rate [1]
All causes [2]	**2,448,288**	**841.9**	**832.7**	**2,397,615**	**816.5**	**800.8**
Major cardiovascular diseases [2]	902,443	310.3	306.1	861,190	293.3	286.5
Diseases of heart	685,089	235.6	232.3	652,486	222.2	217.0
Acute rheumatic fever and chronic rheumatic heart disease	3,624	1.2	1.2	3,254	1.1	1.1
Hypertensive heart disease	28,345	9.7	9.6	28,585	9.7	9.5
Hypertensive heart and renal disease	3,108	1.1	1.1	3,046	1.0	1.0
Ischemic heart disease	480,028	165.1	162.9	451,326	153.7	150.2
Acute myocardial infarction	170,564	58.7	57.9	156,816	53.4	52.2
Essential (primary) hypertension and hypertensive renal disease	21,940	7.5	7.4	23,076	7.9	7.7
Cerebrovascular diseases	157,689	54.2	53.5	150,074	51.1	50.0
Atherosclerosis	13,053	4.5	4.4	11,861	4.0	3.9
Malignant neoplasms [2]	556,902	191.5	190.1	553,888	188.6	185.8
Malignant neoplasms of lip, oral cavity, and pharynx . .	7,778	2.7	2.6	7,826	2.7	2.6
Malignant neoplasms of esophagus	12,860	4.4	4.4	13,023	4.4	4.3
Malignant neoplasms of stomach	12,110	4.2	4.1	11,859	4.0	4.0
Malignant neoplasms of colon, rectum, and anus	55,958	19.2	19.1	53,772	18.3	18.0
Malignant neoplasms of liver and intrahepatic bile ducts . .	14,706	5.1	5.0	15,321	5.2	5.1
Malignant neoplasms of pancreas	30,777	10.6	10.5	31,772	10.8	10.6
Malignant neoplasms of trachea, bronchus, and lung . .	158,086	54.4	54.1	158,091	53.8	53.2
Malignant melanoma of skin	7,818	2.7	2.7	7,952	2.7	2.7
Malignant neoplasm of breast	42,000	14.4	14.2	41,316	14.1	13.8
Malignant neoplasm of ovary	14,657	5.0	5.0	14,716	5.0	4.9
Malignant neoplasm of prostate	29,554	10.2	10.1	29,004	9.9	9.8
Malignant neoplasms of kidney and renal pelvis	12,286	4.2	4.2	12,313	4.2	4.1
Malignant neoplasms of bladder	12,483	4.3	4.3	13,030	4.4	4.4
Malignant neoplasms of meninges, brain, and other parts of central nervous system	12,901	4.4	4.4	12,829	4.4	4.3
Malignant neoplasms of lymphoid, hematopoietic, and related tissue [2] . .	55,679	19.1	19.1	54,645	18.6	18.4
Non-Hodgkins' lymphoma	21,475	7.4	7.3	20,938	7.1	7.0
Leukemia	21,535	7.4	7.4	21,395	7.3	7.2
Accidents (unintentional injuries) [2]	109,227	37.6	37.3	112,012	38.1	37.7
Motor vehicle accidents	44,757	15.4	15.3	44,933	15.3	15.2
Falls	17,229	5.9	5.9	18,807	6.4	6.3
Accidental drowning and submersion	3,306	1.1	1.1	3,308	1.1	1.1
Accidental exposure to smoke, fire, and flames	3,369	1.2	1.2	3,229	1.1	1.1
Accidental poisoning and exposure to noxious substances	19,457	6.7	6.7	20,950	7.1	7.1
Chronic lower respiratory diseases	126,382	43.5	43.3	121,987	41.5	41.1
Emphysema	14,861	5.1	5.1	13,639	4.6	4.6
Asthma	4,099	1.4	1.4	3,816	1.3	1.3
Other chronic lower respiratory diseases	106,572	36.6	36.5	103,759	35.3	35.0
Influenza and pneumonia [2]	65,163	22.4	22.0	59,664	20.3	19.8
Pneumonia	63,371	21.8	21.4	58,564	19.9	19.4
Septicemia	34,069	11.7	11.6	33,373	11.4	11.2
Human immunodeficiency virus (HIV) disease	13,658	4.7	4.7	13,063	4.4	4.5
Anemias	4,594	1.6	1.6	4,575	1.6	1.6
Diabetes mellitus	74,219	25.5	25.3	73,138	24.9	24.5
Parkinson's disease	17,997	6.2	6.2	17,989	6.1	6.1
Alzheimer's disease	63,457	21.8	21.4	65,965	22.5	21.8
Chronic liver disease and cirrhosis	27,503	9.5	9.3	27,013	9.2	9.0
Cholelithiasis and other disorders of gallbladder	2,948	1.0	1.0	3,086	1.1	1.0
Nephritis, nephrotic syndrome, and nephrosis [2]	42,453	14.6	14.4	42,480	14.5	14.2
Renal failure	41,737	14.4	14.2	41,732	14.2	13.9
Intentional self-harm (suicide)	31,484	10.8	10.8	32,439	11.0	10.9
Assault (homicide)	17,732	6.1	6.0	17,357	5.9	5.9
Events of undetermined intent	5,072	1.7	1.7	4,976	1.7	1.7
Injury by firearms [3]	30,136	10.4	10.3	29,569	10.1	10.0
Drug-induced deaths [3]	28,723	9.9	9.9	30,711	10.5	10.4
Alcohol-induced deaths [3]	20,687	7.1	7.0	21,081	7.2	7.0
Injury at work	5,025	2.2	2.2	5,157	1.8	2.2

[1] See headnote, Table 102.   [2] Includes other causes not shown separately.   [3] Included in selected categories.

Source: U.S. National Center for Health Statistics, *Vital Statistics of the United States,* annual; *National Vital Statistics Reports (NSVR),* Vol. 54, No. 13, April 19, 2006, and Vol. 55, No 19, August 21, 2007.

Table 112. **Deaths by Age and Selected Causes: 2004**

[Deaths are classified according to the Tenth Revision of the International Classification of Diseases. See Appendix III]

Cause of death	All ages [1]	Under 1 year	1 to 4 years	5 to 14 years	15 to 24 years	25 to 34 years	35 to 44 years	45 to 54 years	55 to 64 years	65 to 74 years	75 to 84 years	85 years and over
All causes [2]	2,397,615	27,936	4,785	6,834	33,421	40,868	85,362	177,697	264,697	399,666	684,230	671,773
Septicemia	33,373	271	84	66	135	328	846	2,251	3,745	5,983	10,586	9,075
Human immunodeficiency virus (HIV) disease	13,063	3	4	25	191	1,468	4,826	4,422	1,562	436	106	16
Malignant neoplasms [2]	553,888	74	399	1,019	1,709	3,633	14,723	49,520	96,956	139,417	166,085	80,345
Malignant neoplasm of esophagus	13,023	–	–	–	5	36	291	1,423	2,991	3,554	3,467	1,256
Malignant neoplasms of colon, rectum, and anus	53,772	–	–	1	54	279	1,326	4,273	8,208	11,954	16,714	10,963
Malignant neoplasm of liver and intrahepatic bile ducts	15,321	1	–	16	43	84	380	2,348	3,123	3,670	4,059	1,575
Malignant neoplasm of pancreas	31,772	–	22	–	11	62	521	2,641	5,756	8,178	9,853	4,749
Malignant neoplasm of trachea, bronchus, and lung	158,091	2	4	4	23	147	2,426	12,448	31,086	49,029	48,464	14,455
Malignant neoplasm of breast	41,316	–	–	–	11	396	2,511	6,232	8,474	8,285	9,371	6,036
Malignant neoplasm of ovary	14,716	2	4	2	23	94	454	1,654	2,794	3,693	4,165	1,831
Malignant neoplasm of prostate	29,004	–	–	–	29	–	–	434	2,044	5,711	11,993	8,792
Malignant neoplasm of bladder	13,030	–	1	–	1	2	23	545	1,452	2,753	4,847	3,299
Malignant neoplasms of lymphoid, hematopoietic and related tissue [2]	54,645	25	122	359	645	822	1,514	3,741	7,491	12,588	18,132	9,206
Non-Hodgkins lymphoma	20,938	1	2	41	144	256	543	1,538	2,866	4,820	7,080	3,647
Leukemia	21,395	23	120	312	435	416	713	1,367	2,688	4,694	6,797	3,830
In situ neoplasms, benign neoplasms, and neoplasms of uncertain or unknown behavior	13,580	71	53	84	110	173	318	698	1,310	2,343	4,644	3,774
Diabetes mellitus	73,138	1	8	37	161	599	2,026	5,567	10,780	16,093	22,945	14,918
Parkinson's disease	17,989	–	–	–	1	2	8	64	349	2,214	8,752	6,598
Alzheimer's disease	65,965	–	–	–	–	–	7	101	542	3,641	21,882	39,790
Major cardiovascular diseases [2]	861,190	564	234	336	1,333	4,006	16,138	46,153	77,984	128,816	264,037	321,544
Diseases of heart [2]	652,486	421	187	245	1,038	3,163	12,925	37,556	63,613	99,999	195,379	237,924
Hypertensive heart disease	28,585	–	–	2	44	302	1,317	3,265	3,885	4,001	6,398	9,368
Ischemic heart diseases	451,326	13	10	17	125	1,092	7,132	24,923	46,002	73,102	139,128	159,756
Acute myocardial infarction	156,816	3	–	5	51	447	2,838	10,084	18,758	28,327	48,037	48,252
Essential (primary) hypertension and hypertensive renal disease	23,076	2	–	–	21	103	348	1,138	1,839	3,152	6,819	9,648
Cerebrovascular diseases	150,074	127	41	77	211	567	2,361	6,181	9,966	19,901	50,092	60,545
Influenza and pneumonia	59,664	273	119	82	185	303	891	1,897	3,154	6,382	18,066	28,312
Chronic lower respiratory diseases [2]	121,987	35	48	120	179	255	887	3,511	11,754	28,390	47,568	29,239
Emphysema	13,639	3	2	3	3	10	80	413	1,583	3,793	5,324	2,427
Pneumonitis due to solids and liquids	16,780	12	9	11	39	68	159	394	743	1,767	5,564	8,014
Chronic liver disease and cirrhosis	27,013	9	1	1	19	309	2,799	7,496	6,569	5,119	3,733	957
Nephritis, nephrotic syndrome, and nephrosis [2]	42,480	174	14	21	87	246	801	2,067	3,963	7,119	14,058	13,928
Renal failure	41,732	165	9	18	79	223	767	2,009	3,883	6,997	13,830	13,750
Certain conditions originating in the perinatal period	14,213	14,079	61	37	11	10	6	–	–	–	–	1
Accidents (unintentional injuries) [2]	112,012	1,052	1,641	2,666	15,449	13,032	16,471	16,942	9,651	8,116	13,457	13,447
Motor vehicle accidents	44,933	143	635	1,653	10,987	7,036	6,663	6,276	4,093	2,974	3,180	1,267
Falls	18,807	23	47	37	241	320	659	1,184	1,393	2,255	5,682	6,962
Accidental poisoning and exposure to noxious substances	20,950	13	18	55	2,259	3,641	6,444	6,033	1,577	421	315	165
Intentional self-harm (suicide)	32,439	(X)	(X)	285	4,316	5,074	6,638	6,906	4,011	2,279	2,120	799
By discharge of firearms	16,750	(X)	(X)	59	2,104	2,283	2,868	3,349	2,328	1,631	1,588	537
By other and unspecified means and their sequelae	15,689	(X)	(X)	226	2,212	2,791	3,770	3,557	1,683	648	532	262
Assault (homicide)	17,357	325	377	329	5,085	4,495	2,984	2,008	879	446	289	104

– Represents zero.   X Not applicable.   [1] Includes persons with age not stated, not shown separately.   [2] Includes other causes, not shown separately.

Source: U.S. National Center for Health Statistics. *National Vital Statistics Reports*, Vol. 55, No. 19, August 21, 2007.

Births, Deaths, Marriages, and Divorces   85

Table 113. Deaths and Death Rates by Leading Causes of Death and Age: 2004

[Rates per 100,000 population in specified group. Data are based on the tenth revision of the International Classification of Diseases (ICD). Numbers are based on weighted data rounded to the nearest individual, so categories may not add to totals. See Appendix III]

Age and cause of death	Number	Rate	Age and cause of death	Number	Rate
ALL AGES [1]			**35 TO 44 YEARS**		
All causes	**2,397,615**	**816.5**	**All causes**	**85,362**	**193.5**
Diseases of heart	652,486	222.2	Accidents	16,471	37.3
Malignant neoplasms	553,888	188.6	Malignant neoplasms	14,723	33.4
Cerebrovascular diseases	150,074	51.1	Diseases of heart	12,925	29.3
Chronic lower respiratory diseases	121,987	41.5	Intentional self-harm (suicide)	6,638	15.0
Accidents (unintentional injuries)	112,012	38.1	Human immunodeficiency virus (HIV)		
Diabetes mellitus	73,138	24.9	disease	4,826	10.9
Alzheimer's disease	65,965	22.5	Assault (homicide)	2,984	6.8
Influenza and pneumonia	59,664	20.3	Chronic liver disease and cirrhosis	2,799	6.3
Nephritis, nephrotic syndrome, and			Cerebrovascular diseases	2,361	5.4
nephrosis	42,480	14.5	Diabetes mellitus	2,026	4.6
Septicemia	33,373	11.4	Chronic lower respiratory diseases	887	2.0
			45 TO 54 YEARS		
1 TO 4 YEARS			**All causes**	**177,697**	**427.0**
			Malignant neoplasms	49,520	119.0
All causes	**4,785**	**29.9**	Diseases of heart	37,556	90.2
Accidents (unintentional injuries)	1,641	10.3	Accidents	16,942	40.7
Congenital malformations,			Chronic liver disease and cirrhosis	7,496	18.0
deformations, and chromosomal			Intentional self-harm (suicide)	6,906	16.6
abnormalities	569	3.6	Cerebrovascular diseases	6,181	14.9
Malignant neoplasms	399	2.5	Diabetes mellitus	5,567	13.4
Assault (homicide)	377	2.4	Human immunodeficiency virus (HIV)		
Diseases of heart	187	1.2	disease	4,422	10.6
Influenza and pneumonia	119	0.7	Chronic lower respiratory diseases	3,511	8.4
Septicemia	84	0.5	Viral hepatitis	2,226	5.3
Certain conditions originating in the			**55 TO 64 YEARS**		
perinatal period [2]	61	0.4	**All causes**	**264,697**	**910.3**
In situ neoplasms [2]	53	0.3	Malignant neoplasms	96,956	333.4
Chronic lower respiratory diseases	48	0.3	Diseases of heart	63,613	218.8
			Chronic lower respiratory diseases	11,754	40.4
5 TO 14 YEARS			Diabetes mellitus	10,780	37.1
			Cerebrovascular diseases	9,966	34.3
All causes	**6,834**	**16.8**	Accidents (unintentional injuries)	9,651	33.2
Accidents (unintentional injuries)	2,666	6.5	Chronic liver disease and cirrhosis	6,569	22.6
Malignant neoplasms	1,019	2.5	Intentional self-harm (suicide)	4,011	13.8
Congenital malformations,			Nephritis, nephrotic syndrome, and		
deformations, and chromosomal			nephrosis	3,963	13.6
abnormalities	389	1.0	Septicemia	3,745	12.9
Assault (homicide)	329	0.8	**65 TO 74 YEARS**		
Intentional self-harm (suicide)	285	0.7	**All causes**	**399,666**	**2,164.6**
Diseases of heart	245	0.6	Malignant neoplasms	139,417	755.1
Chronic lower respiratory diseases	120	0.3	Diseases of heart	99,999	541.6
In situ neoplasms [2]	84	0.2	Chronic lower respiratory diseases	28,390	153.8
Influenza and pneumonia	82	0.2	Cerebrovascular diseases	19,901	107.8
Cerebrovascular diseases	77	0.2	Diabetes mellitus	16,093	87.2
			Accidents (unintentional injuries)	8,116	44.0
15 TO 24 YEARS			Nephritis, nephrotic syndrome, and		
			nephrosis	7,119	38.6
All causes	**33,421**	**80.1**	Influenza and pneumonia	6,382	34.6
Accidents (unintentional injuries)	15,449	37.0	Septicemia	5,983	32.4
Assault (homicide)	5,085	11.2	Chronic liver disease and cirrhosis	5,119	27.7
Intentional self-harm (suicide)	4,316	10.3	**75 TO 84 YEARS**		
Malignant neoplasms	1,709	4.1	**All causes**	**684,230**	**5,275.1**
Diseases of heart	1,038	2.5	Diseases of heart	195,379	1,506.3
Congenital malformations,			Malignant neoplasms	166,085	1,280.4
deformations, and chromosomal			Cerebrovascular diseases	50,092	386.2
abnormalities	483	1.2	Chronic lower respiratory diseases	47,568	366.7
Cerebrovascular diseases	211	0.5	Diabetes mellitus	22,945	176.9
Human immunodeficiency virus (HIV)			Alzheimer's disease	21,882	168.7
disease	191	0.5	Influenza and pneumonia	18,066	139.3
Influenza and pneumonia	185	0.4	Nephritis, nephrotic syndrome, and		
Chronic lower respiratory diseases	179	0.4	nephrosis	14,058	108.4
			Accidents (unintentional injuries)	13,457	103.7
25 TO 34 YEARS			Septicemia	10,586	81.6
			85 YEARS AND OVER		
All causes	**40,868**	**102.1**	**All causes**	**671,773**	**13,823.5**
Accidents	13,032	32.6	Diseases of heart	237,924	4,895.9
Intentional self-harm (suicide)	5,074	12.7	Malignant neoplasms	80,345	1,653.3
Assault (homicide)	4,495	11.2	Cerebrovascular diseases	60,545	1,245.9
Malignant neoplasms	3,633	9.1	Alzheimer's disease	39,790	818.8
Diseases of heart	3,163	7.9	Chronic lower respiratory diseases	29,239	601.7
Human immunodeficiency virus (HIV)			Influenza and pneumonia	28,312	582.6
disease	1,468	3.7	Diabetes mellitus	14,918	307.0
Diabetes mellitus	599	1.5	Nephritis, nephrotic syndrome, and		
Cerebrovascular diseases	567	1.4	nephrosis	13,928	286.6
Congenital malformations,			Accidents (unintentional injuries)	13,447	276.7
deformations, and chromosomal			Septicemia	9,075	186.7
abnormalities	420	1.0			
Chronic liver disease and cirrhosis	309	0.8			

[1] Includes deaths under 1 year of age. [2] Includes benign neoplasms and neoplasms of uncertain or unknown behavior.

Source: U.S. National Center for Health Statistics, *National Vital Statistics Reports*, Vol. 55, No. 19, August 21, 2007.

[Deaths per 100,000 resident population estimated as of July 1. By place of residence. Excludes nonresidents of the United States. Causes of death classified according to tenth revisions of International Classification of Diseases. See Appendix III]

State and island areas	Total	Diseases of heart	Malignant neoplasms (cancer)	Cerebrovascular diseases	Chronic lower respiratory diseases	Accidents Total	Accidents Motor vehicle accidents	Diabetes mellitus	Alzheimer's disease	Influenza and pneumonia	Nephritis, nephrotic syndrome, and nephrosis
U.S.	816.5	222.2	188.6	51.1	41.5	38.1	15.3	24.9	22.5	20.3	14.5
AL......	1,018.1	282.0	215.4	65.9	52.1	53.0	27.8	32.0	30.6	21.9	23.2
AK......	465.5	89.9	111.1	26.2	21.2	49.7	18.2	14.2	7.3	6.4	3.5
AZ......	752.1	183.5	167.4	42.6	42.1	48.2	19.6	20.8	29.2	19.3	11.0
AR......	1,000.1	273.7	229.0	70.8	51.9	51.1	28.3	30.4	22.6	27.6	20.4
CA......	647.8	181.1	149.6	47.0	34.9	29.6	12.3	19.8	19.4	20.4	6.6
CO	615.2	132.1	134.7	35.6	41.3	39.3	15.2	15.1	19.8	13.8	8.8
CT......	836.7	224.6	204.8	46.7	40.9	36.0	9.6	21.9	19.5	24.8	17.2
DE......	860.2	242.7	220.0	42.2	41.5	35.4	17.0	25.3	18.7	17.5	15.4
DC	985.3	278.9	208.1	39.4	29.8	39.6	8.3	40.5	21.5	16.4	14.3
FL......	971.5	271.1	229.0	55.8	51.6	47.3	18.9	27.6	24.8	17.5	12.9
GA	745.4	187.5	162.1	46.0	35.4	41.5	17.0	18.4	19.4	17.5	16.5
HI	715.1	194.6	165.3	56.5	24.3	30.9	11.2	15.4	13.5	18.7	13.0
ID	719.7	175.8	159.8	51.1	41.1	42.6	17.9	24.7	26.4	15.7	7.8
IL	807.6	222.5	191.0	51.0	37.1	32.5	11.9	24.1	20.4	21.9	18.4
IN	869.1	234.6	201.2	55.4	50.4	38.4	16.1	26.8	24.9	18.2	19.9
IA	910.4	247.1	214.6	66.3	52.4	37.5	14.1	23.7	32.8	30.1	9.0
KS......	870.7	221.1	194.2	58.9	48.1	41.8	18.3	25.2	28.1	20.5	20.3
KY......	932.1	252.4	220.9	56.4	54.6	54.5	23.9	28.8	23.7	23.3	19.9
LA......	934.8	240.3	208.9	55.1	35.8	50.9	22.6	38.0	28.1	20.2	24.6
ME	944.6	223.8	237.2	60.8	58.2	36.4	13.7	29.0	38.9	23.4	20.0
MD	777.8	204.1	182.9	48.9	34.4	25.4	12.1	25.5	16.3	20.0	12.6
MA	849.5	215.4	207.9	50.7	40.1	21.3	8.3	20.7	26.1	30.5	19.5
MI	842.2	245.5	194.3	52.3	42.0	32.8	12.9	29.2	22.1	19.4	14.9
MN	726.0	154.7	178.3	49.8	36.1	36.6	12.8	22.2	24.1	14.7	13.1
MS	960.1	285.3	206.1	56.9	46.5	58.7	31.5	22.9	21.7	21.9	22.8
MO	937.5	269.3	216.3	60.9	47.5	47.4	19.3	25.4	24.0	24.1	18.8
MT	873.3	198.3	201.4	52.2	62.4	57.7	26.0	25.6	24.6	17.8	11.7
NE......	838.9	213.9	187.2	56.0	46.6	42.5	16.1	22.6	26.3	19.9	16.2
NV......	767.9	201.0	176.4	44.1	48.3	43.7	18.1	12.4	12.5	17.2	18.2
NH	778.1	203.1	196.5	45.1	46.2	34.2	12.7	24.1	25.5	20.9	12.5
NJ......	820.5	236.4	197.8	43.5	34.8	26.7	8.9	29.8	19.7	18.2	18.7
NM	751.2	171.5	159.5	37.9	39.6	64.3	25.2	31.0	17.2	16.2	11.9
NY......	794.1	272.9	187.8	36.0	35.3	23.6	8.2	20.4	10.3	28.6	12.4
NC	847.5	206.1	192.9	58.0	42.4	47.1	19.8	26.4	25.6	19.7	17.2
ND	882.9	231.7	199.4	74.9	43.0	43.2	18.4	32.9	49.3	23.3	8.7
OH	927.5	253.8	217.6	56.7	51.5	36.9	12.1	31.5	25.5	19.2	16.5
OK	978.6	293.3	206.3	62.0	56.3	55.3	21.7	32.3	24.6	23.0	16.0
OR	843.3	187.1	201.3	64.8	49.5	40.2	13.9	29.9	35.1	15.5	8.6
PA......	1,028.8	293.7	237.2	62.8	48.2	41.9	12.9	28.8	26.4	23.7	24.7
RI	904.0	274.7	223.8	48.3	42.8	27.6	9.2	25.9	26.2	24.1	12.1
SC......	887.9	218.7	198.9	63.0	42.7	49.9	24.6	27.8	29.7	18.3	19.5
SD......	886.4	231.3	201.7	60.8	50.7	54.0	24.5	29.7	31.5	23.2	11.9
TN......	946.1	254.8	213.3	62.4	50.6	53.5	23.5	31.9	27.4	26.6	11.5
TX......	679.7	178.7	150.9	43.8	32.9	37.0	17.2	24.2	19.3	14.3	11.4
UT......	558.0	123.1	102.3	33.1	24.9	29.2	13.4	20.3	15.7	16.1	9.8
VT......	803.8	207.4	195.0	48.6	47.6	40.7	13.4	24.1	27.8	13.8	9.2
VA......	758.1	191.5	179.4	50.8	36.6	35.3	13.6	21.5	19.8	19.4	16.7
WA	721.7	171.6	177.1	52.3	41.1	37.7	10.8	24.3	36.0	11.9	5.6
WV	1,145.4	312.6	258.6	64.9	67.5	61.1	22.8	46.3	27.2	26.1	24.8
WI	827.7	216.2	197.1	55.7	42.0	41.8	14.8	23.8	25.8	20.7	16.8
WY	780.8	187.6	172.7	42.2	60.8	18.0	23.9	21.7	20.7	21.5	8.9
PR	742.3	154.7	123.7	41.7	28.9	28.3	13.4	69.8	29.9	26.8	23.6
VI	575.5	156.3	112.2	46.0	(S)	25.7	(S)	32.2	(S)	(S)	(S)
GU....	411.2	130.7	67.4	23.5	12.0	31.9	(S)	16.3	(S)	(S)	13.2
AS....	493.9	77.7	62.2	39.7	(S)	(S)	(S)	48.4	(S)	(S)	(S)
MP....	209.6	29.4	28.1	(S)	(S)	28.1	(S)	(S)	(S)	(S)	(S)

S Figure does not meet standards of reliability or precision.

Source: U.S. National Center for Health Statistics, *National Vital Statistics Reports*, Vol. 55, No. 19, August 21, 2007.

U.S. Census Bureau, *Statistical Abstract of the United States: 2008*

Table 115. **Death Rates from Heart Disease by Selected Characteristics: 1980 to 2004**

[Rates per 100,000 population. See headnote, Tables 102 and 110. See Appendix III]

Characteristic	1980	1985	1990	1995	2000	2001	2002	2003	2004
Total, age adjusted	**412.1**	**375.0**	**321.8**	**293.4**	**257.6**	**247.8**	**240.8**	**232.3**	**217.0**
Total, crude	**336.0**	**324.1**	**289.5**	**277.0**	**252.6**	**245.8**	**241.7**	**235.6**	**222.2**
Under 1 year	22.8	25.0	20.1	17.4	13.0	11.9	12.4	11.0	10.3
1 to 4 years	2.6	2.2	1.9	1.6	1.2	1.5	1.1	1.2	1.2
5 to 14 years	0.9	1.0	0.9	0.8	0.7	0.7	0.6	0.6	0.6
15 to 24 years	2.9	2.8	2.5	2.8	2.6	2.5	2.5	2.7	2.5
25 to 34 years	8.3	8.3	7.6	8.2	7.4	8.0	7.9	8.2	7.9
35 to 44 years	44.6	38.1	31.4	31.8	29.2	29.6	30.5	30.7	29.3
45 to 54 years	180.2	153.8	120.5	109.6	94.2	92.9	93.7	92.5	90.2
55 to 64 years	494.1	443.0	367.3	320.1	261.2	246.9	241.5	233.2	218.8
65 to 74 years	1,218.6	1,089.8	894.3	795.4	665.6	635.1	615.9	585.0	541.6
75 to 84 years	2,993.1	2,693.1	2,295.7	2,050.5	1,780.3	1,725.7	1,677.2	1,611.1	1,506.3
85 years and over	7,777.1	7,384.1	6,739.9	6,391.5	5,926.1	5,664.2	5,446.8	5,278.4	4,895.9
Male, age adjusted	**538.9**	**488.0**	**412.4**	**371.0**	**320.0**	**305.4**	**297.4**	**286.6**	**267.9**
White	539.6	487.3	409.2	367.0	316.7	301.8	294.1	282.9	264.6
Black	561.4	533.9	485.4	451.3	392.5	384.5	371.0	364.3	342.1
American Indian, Alaska Native . . .	320.5	280.5	264.1	256.4	222.2	200.7	201.2	203.2	182.7
Asian, Pacific Islander	286.9	258.9	220.7	214.5	185.5	169.8	169.8	158.3	146.5
Hispanic origin [1]	(NA)	296.6	270.0	260.8	238.2	232.6	219.8	206.8	193.9
Non-Hispanic, White [1]	(NA)	480.4	413.6	369.1	319.9	304.8	297.7	286.9	268.7
Male, crude	**368.6**	**344.1**	**297.6**	**278.5**	**249.8**	**242.5**	**240.7**	**235.0**	**222.8**
Under 1 year	25.5	27.8	21.9	17.7	13.3	11.8	12.9	12.1	10.9
1 to 4 years	2.8	2.2	1.9	1.7	1.4	1.5	1.1	1.1	1.1
5 to 14 years	1.0	0.9	0.9	0.8	0.8	0.7	0.7	0.7	0.6
15 to 24 years	3.7	3.5	3.1	3.5	3.2	3.2	3.3	3.4	3.2
25 to 34 years	11.4	11.6	10.3	11.0	9.6	10.3	10.5	10.5	10.5
35 to 44 years	68.7	58.6	48.1	46.9	41.4	41.7	43.1	42.8	40.9
45 to 54 years	282.6	237.8	183.0	166.1	140.2	136.4	138.4	136.2	132.3
55 to 64 years	746.8	659.1	537.3	460.1	371.7	349.8	343.4	331.7	312.8
65 to 74 years	1,728.0	1,535.8	1,250.0	1,095.3	898.3	851.3	827.1	785.3	723.8
75 to 84 years	3,834.3	3,496.9	2,968.2	2,622.9	2,248.1	2,177.3	2,110.1	2,030.3	1,893.6
85 years and over	8,752.7	8,251.8	7,418.4	6,993.5	6,430.0	6,040.5	5,823.5	5,621.5	5,239.3
Female, age adjusted	**320.8**	**294.5**	**257.0**	**236.6**	**210.9**	**203.9**	**197.2**	**190.3**	**177.3**
White	315.9	289.1	250.9	230.8	205.6	198.7	192.1	185.4	172.9
Black	378.6	357.7	327.5	304.0	277.6	269.8	263.2	253.8	236.5
American Indian, Alaska Native . . .	175.4	170.0	153.1	164.8	143.6	127.0	123.6	127.5	119.9
Asian, Pacific Islander	132.3	149.4	149.2	137.6	115.7	112.9	108.1	104.2	96.1
Hispanic origin [1]	(NA)	195.9	177.2	173.8	163.7	161.0	149.7	145.8	130.0
Non-Hispanic, White [1]	(NA)	287.2	252.6	231.5	206.8	200.0	193.7	187.1	175.1
Female, crude	**305.1**	**305.2**	**281.8**	**275.5**	**255.3**	**249.0**	**242.7**	**236.2**	**221.6**
Under 1 year	20.0	22.0	18.3	17.0	12.5	12.0	11.8	9.8	9.7
1 to 4 years	2.5	2.2	1.9	1.5	1.0	1.4	1.0	1.3	1.2
5 to 14 years	0.9	1.0	0.8	0.7	0.5	0.7	0.6	0.5	0.6
15 to 24 years	2.1	2.1	1.8	2.1	2.1	1.8	1.7	2.1	1.7
25 to 34 years	5.3	5.0	5.0	5.4	5.2	5.6	5.2	5.7	5.2
35 to 44 years	21.4	18.3	15.1	17.0	17.2	17.6	18.0	18.6	17.7
45 to 54 years	84.5	74.4	61.0	55.4	49.8	50.7	50.6	50.2	49.6
55 to 64 years	272.1	252.1	215.7	192.6	159.3	151.8	147.2	141.9	131.5
65 to 74 years	828.6	746.1	616.8	554.9	474.0	455.9	440.1	417.5	388.6
75 to 84 years	2,497.0	2,220.4	1,893.8	1,692.7	1,475.1	1,428.9	1,389.7	1,331.1	1,245.6
85 years and over	7,350.5	7,037.6	6,478.1	6,159.6	5,720.9	5,506.8	5,283.3	5,126.7	4,741.5

NA Not available.   [1] Persons of Hispanic origin may be any race. Data for 1985 to 1995 exclude data from states lacking an Hispanic-origin item on their death certificates.

Source: U.S. National Center for Health Statistics, *Health, United States, 2006.*

Table 116. **Death Rates from Cerebrovascular Diseases by Sex and Age: 1990 to 2004**

[Rates per 100,000 population. See headnote, Tables 102 and 110. See Appendix III]

Age	Total				Male				Female			
	1990	1995	2000	2004	1990	1995	2000	2004	1990	1995	2000	2004
All ages, age adjusted	**65.3**	**63.1**	**60.9**	**50.0**	**68.5**	**65.9**	**62.4**	**50.4**	**62.6**	**60.5**	**59.1**	**48.9**
All ages, crude . .	**57.8**	**59.2**	**59.6**	**51.1**	**46.7**	**47.2**	**46.9**	**40.7**	**68.4**	**70.7**	**71.8**	**61.2**
Under 1 year	3.8	5.9	3.3	3.1	4.4	6.4	3.8	3.4	3.1	5.3	2.7	2.8
1 to 4 years	0.3	0.4	0.3	0.3	0.3	0.4	(B)	0.3	0.3	0.3	0.4	(B)
5 to 14 years	0.2	0.2	0.2	0.2	0.2	0.2	0.2	0.2	0.2	0.1	0.2	0.2
15 to 24 years	0.6	0.5	0.5	0.5	0.7	0.5	0.5	0.5	0.6	0.4	0.5	0.5
25 to 34 years	2.2	1.7	1.5	1.4	2.1	1.8	1.5	1.4	2.2	1.6	1.5	1.4
35 to 44 years	6.4	6.5	5.8	5.4	6.8	7.0	5.8	5.6	6.1	6.0	5.7	5.1
45 to 54 years	18.7	17.4	16.0	14.9	20.5	19.5	17.5	16.7	17.0	15.3	14.5	13.1
55 to 64 years	47.9	45.6	41.0	34.3	54.3	52.7	47.2	39.5	42.2	39.1	35.3	29.5
65 to 74 years	144.2	136.2	128.6	107.8	166.6	154.7	145.0	121.1	126.7	121.4	115.1	96.6
75 to 84 years	498.0	477.1	461.3	386.2	551.1	517.7	490.8	402.9	466.2	451.8	442.1	374.9
85 years and over . .	1,628.9	1,607.2	1,589.2	1,245.9	1,528.5	1,522.1	1,484.3	1,118.1	1,667.6	1,640.0	1,632.0	1,303.4

B Base figure too small to meet statistical standards for reliability.

Source: U.S. National Center for Health Statistics, *Health, United States, 2006.*

Table 117. **Death Rates from Malignant Neoplasms, by Selected Characteristics: 1990 to 2004**

[Rates per 100,000 population. Beginning 2000, cause of death is coded according to ICD-10; for explanation, see text, this section. For explanation of age adjustment, see headnote, Table 102. See Appendix III]

Characteristic	1990	1995	2000	2001	2002	2003	2004
Total, age adjusted	216.0	209.9	199.6	196.0	193.5	190.1	185.8
Total, crude	203.2	202.2	196.5	194.4	193.2	191.5	188.6
Under 1 year.	2.3	1.8	2.4	1.6	1.8	1.9	1.8
1 to 4 years.	3.5	3.1	2.7	2.7	2.6	2.5	2.5
5 to 14 years.	3.1	2.7	2.5	2.5	2.6	2.6	2.5
15 to 24 years	4.9	4.5	4.4	4.3	4.3	4.0	4.1
25 to 34 years	12.6	11.6	9.8	10.1	9.7	9.4	9.1
35 to 44 years	43.3	40.1	36.6	36.8	35.8	35.0	33.4
45 to 54 years	158.9	140.4	127.5	126.5	123.8	122.2	119.0
55 to 64 years	449.6	412.3	366.7	356.5	351.1	343.0	333.4
65 to 74 years	872.3	863.3	816.3	802.8	792.1	770.3	755.1
75 to 84 years	1,348.5	1,355.4	1,335.6	1,315.8	1,311.9	1,302.5	1,280.4
85 years and over	1,752.9	1,797.7	1,819.4	1,765.6	1,723.9	1,698.2	1,653.3
AGE-ADJUSTED RATES							
Male	280.4	267.5	248.9	243.7	238.9	233.3	227.7
Female.	175.7	173.6	167.6	164.7	163.1	160.9	157.4
White male	272.2	260.6	243.9	239.2	235.2	230.1	224.4
Black male	397.9	374.3	340.3	330.9	319.6	308.8	301.2
American Indian, Alaska Native male	145.8	169.0	155.8	155.3	141.9	139.9	147.1
Asian, Pacific Islander male	172.5	164.3	150.8	147.0	137.9	137.2	136.3
Hispanic male, [1]	174.7	180.9	171.7	168.2	161.4	156.5	151.2
Non-Hispanic, White male, [1]	276.7	263.5	247.7	243.1	239.6	234.6	229.2
White female	174.0	172.1	166.9	163.9	162.4	160.2	157.0
Black female	205.9	203.8	193.8	191.3	190.3	187.7	182.5
American Indian, Alaska Native female. . . .	106.9	117.7	108.3	114.1	112.9	105.6	108.6
Asian, Pacific Islander female.	103.0	107.4	100.7	99.3	95.9	96.7	92.0
Hispanic female, [1]	111.9	110.8	110.8	108.6	106.1	105.9	101.4
Non-Hispanic, White female, [1]	177.5	174.7	170.0	167.2	165.9	163.8	160.9
DEATH RATES FOR MALIGNANT NEOPLASM OF BREASTS FOR FEMALES							
All ages, age adjusted	33.3	30.5	26.8	26.0	25.6	25.3	24.4
All ages, crude	34.0	32.2	29.2	28.6	28.3	28.2	27.5
Under 25 years	(B)	(B)	(B)	(B)	(B)	(B)	(B)
25 to 34 years	2.9	2.6	2.3	2.4	2.1	2.1	2.0
35 to 44 years	17.8	14.9	12.4	12.4	12.0	12.2	11.3
45 to 54 years	45.4	41.0	33.0	32.8	31.4	30.4	29.3
55 to 64 years	78.6	69.4	59.3	57.5	56.2	56.6	55.8
65 to 74 years	111.7	102.8	88.3	85.8	84.4	82.6	81.6
75 to 84 years	146.3	140.1	128.9	125.8	125.9	123.7	119.5
85 years and over	196.8	200.2	205.7	188.9	191.5	189.4	178.6
DEATH RATES FOR MALIGNANT NEOPLASM OF TRACHEA, BRONCHUS, AND LUNG							
All ages, age adjusted	59.3	58.4	56.1	55.3	54.9	54.1	53.2
All ages, crude	56.8	56.8	55.3	54.8	57.7	54.4	53.8
Under 25 years	(Z)	(Z)	(Z)	(Z)	(Z)	(Z)	(Z)
25 to 34 years	0.7	0.6	0.5	0.4	0.4	0.4	0.4
35 to 44 years	6.8	6.0	6.1	6.2	6.0	5.6	5.5
45 to 54 years	46.8	37.5	31.6	30.7	30.3	30.3	29.9
55 to 64 years	160.6	141.6	122.4	117.7	115.3	111.0	106.9
65 to 74 years	288.4	295.4	284.2	279.7	275.0	269.3	265.5
75 to 84 years	333.3	358.9	370.8	371.4	377.6	377.8	373.6
85 years and over	242.5	279.9	302.1	302.7	297.2	298.9	297.5

B Base figure too small to meet statistical standards for reliability of a derived figure.   Z Less than 0.05.   [1] Data for 1990 and 1995 exclude data from states lacking an Hispanic-origin item on their death certificates. See text, this section. Persons of Hispanic origin may be any race.

Source: U.S. National Center for Health Statistics, *Health, United States, 2006.*

Births, Deaths, Marriages, and Divorces   89

Table 118. **Death Rates From Suicide, by Selected Characteristics: 1990 to 2004**

[Rates per 100,000 population. Beginning 2000, cause of death is coded according to ICD-10; for explanation, see text this section. For explanation of age adjustment, see headnote, Table 102. See Appendix III]

Characteristic	1990	1995	2000	2001	2002	2003	2004
All ages, age adjusted	12.5	11.8	10.4	10.7	10.9	10.8	10.9
All ages, crude	12.4	11.7	10.4	10.8	11.0	10.8	11.0
Under 1 year.	(X)	(X)	(X)	(X)	(X)	(X)	(X)
1 to 4 years.	(X)	(X)	(X)	(X)	(X)	(X)	(X)
5 to 14 years.	0.8	0.9	0.7	0.7	0.6	0.6	0.7
15 to 24 years	13.2	13.0	10.2	9.9	9.9	9.7	10.3
25 to 34 years	15.2	15.0	12.0	12.8	12.6	12.7	12.7
35 to 44 years	15.3	15.1	14.5	14.7	15.3	14.9	15.0
45 to 54 years	14.8	14.4	14.4	15.2	15.7	15.9	16.6
55 to 64 years	16.0	13.2	12.1	13.1	13.6	13.8	13.8
65 to 74 years	17.9	15.7	12.5	13.3	13.5	12.7	12.3
75 to 84 years	24.9	20.6	17.6	17.4	17.7	16.4	16.3
85 years and over	22.2	21.3	19.6	17.5	18.0	16.9	16.4
AGE ADJUSTED							
Male	21.5	20.3	17.7	18.2	18.4	18.0	18.0
Female.	4.8	4.3	4.0	4.0	4.2	4.2	4.5
White male	22.8	21.6	19.1	19.6	20.0	19.6	19.6
Black male	12.8	12.4	10.0	9.8	9.8	9.2	9.6
American Indian, Alaska Native male . . .	20.1	17.4	16.0	17.4	16.4	16.6	18.7
Asian, Pacific Islander male	9.6	9.6	8.6	8.4	8.0	8.5	8.4
Hispanic male [1]	13.7	12.7	10.3	10.1	9.9	9.7	9.8
Non-Hispanic, White male [1]	23.5	22.3	20.2	21.0	21.4	21.0	21.0
White female	5.2	4.7	4.3	4.5	4.7	4.6	5.0
Black female	2.4	2.0	1.8	1.8	1.6	1.9	1.8
American Indian, Alaska Native female. . .	3.6	3.9	3.8	4.0	4.1	3.5	5.9
Asian, Pacific Islander female.	4.1	4.1	2.8	2.9	3.0	3.1	3.5
Hispanic female [1]	2.3	2.0	1.7	1.6	1.8	1.7	2.0
Non-Hispanic, White female [1]	5.4	4.9	4.7	4.9	5.1	5.0	5.4

X Not applicable.   [1] Data for 1990 and 1995 exclude data from states lacking an Hispanic-origin item on their death certificates. Persons of Hispanic origin may be any race.

Source: U.S. National Center for Health Statistics, *Health, United States, 2006.*

Table 119. **Death Rates from Human Immunodeficiency Virus (HIV) Disease by Selected Characteristics: 1990 to 2004**

[Rates per 100,000 population. Beginning 2000, cause of death is coded according to ICD 10; for explanation, see text this section. For explanation of age adjustment, see headnote, Table 102. See Appendix III]

Characteristic	1990	1995	2000	2001	2002	2003	2004
All ages, age adjusted	10.2	16.2	5.2	5.0	4.9	4.7	4.5
All ages, crude	10.1	16.2	5.1	5.0	4.9	4.7	4.4
Under 1 year.	2.7	1.5	(B)	(B)	(B)	(B)	(B)
1 to 4 years.	0.8	1.3	(B)	(B)	(B)	(B)	(B)
5 to 14 years.	0.2	0.5	0.1	0.1	0.1	0.1	0.1
15 to 24 years	1.5	1.7	0.5	0.6	0.4	0.4	0.5
25 to 34 years	19.7	28.3	6.1	5.3	4.6	4.0	3.7
35 to 44 years	27.4	44.2	13.1	13.0	12.7	12.0	10.9
45 to 54 years	15.2	26.0	11.0	10.5	11.2	10.9	10.6
55 to 64 years	6.2	10.9	5.1	5.2	5.1	5.4	5.4
65 to 74 years	2.0	3.6	2.2	2.1	2.2	2.4	2.4
75 to 84 years	0.7	0.7	0.7	0.7	0.8	0.7	0.8
85 years and over	(B)	(B)	(B)	(B)	(B)	(B)	(B)
AGE ADJUSTED							
Male	18.5	27.3	7.9	7.5	7.4	7.1	6.6
Female.	2.2	5.3	2.5	2.5	2.5	2.4	2.4
White male	15.7	20.4	4.6	4.4	4.3	4.2	3.8
Black male	46.3	89.0	35.1	33.8	33.3	31.3	29.2
American Indian, Alaska Native male . . .	3.3	10.5	3.5	4.2	3.4	3.5	4.3
Asian or Pacific Islander male.	4.3	6.0	1.2	1.2	1.5	1.1	1.2
Hispanic male [1]	28.8	40.8	10.6	9.7	9.1	9.2	8.2
Non-Hispanic, White male [1]	14.1	17.9	3.8	3.6	3.5	3.4	3.1
White female	1.1	2.5	1.0	0.9	0.9	0.9	0.9
Black female	10.1	24.4	13.2	13.4	13.4	12.8	13.0
American Indian, Alaska Native female. . .	(B)	2.5	1.0	(B)	(B)	1.5	1.5
Asian or Pacific Islander female	(B)	0.6	0.2	(B)	(B)	(B)	(B)
Hispanic female [1]	3.8	8.8	2.9	2.7	2.6	2.7	2.4
Non-Hispanic, White female [1]	0.7	1.7	0.7	0.6	0.6	0.6	0.6

B Base figure too small to meet statistical standards for reliability of a derived figure.   [1] Data for 1990 and 1995 exclude data from states lacking an Hispanic-origin item on their death certificates. Persons of Hispanic origin may be any race.

Source: U.S. National Center for Health Statistics, *Health, United States, 2006.*

90   Births, Deaths, Marriages, and Divorces

Table 120. Deaths—Life Years Lost and Mortality Costs by Age, Sex, and Cause: 2000 and 2003

[2,403 represents 2,403,000. **Life years lost:** Number of years person would have lived in absence of death. **Mortality cost:** value of lifetime earnings lost by persons who die prematurely]

Characteristic	Number of deaths (1,000)	Life years lost [1]		Mortality cost [2]	
		Total (1,000)	Per death	Total (mil. dol.)	Per death (dol.)
2000, total	**2,403**	**38,843**	**16.2**	**431,992**	**179,772**
Under 5 years old	33	2,522	76.4	30,421	921,471
5 to 14 years old	7	513	69.2	8,331	1,123,778
15 to 24 years old	31	1,835	58.6	43,039	1,374,751
25 to 44 years old	130	5,604	43.1	144,409	1,108,713
45 to 64 years old	346	10,555	30.5	168,201	486,146
65 years old and over	1,855	17,815	9.6	37,591	20,265
Heart disease	711	8,917	12.5	72,224	101,623
Cancer	553	10,028	18.1	107,501	194,367
Cerebrovascular diseases	168	1,934	11.5	12,103	72,187
Accidents and adverse effects	98	3,303	33.8	69,429	709,801
Other	874	14,661	16.8	170,736	195,408
Male	**1,177**	**20,415**	**17.3**	**316,850**	**269,135**
Under 5 years old	19	1,373	74.0	19,287	1,040,197
5 to 14 years old	4	295	67.0	5,540	1,258,796
15 to 24 years old	23	1,319	57.2	34,230	1,483,692
25 to 44 years old	85	3,549	41.7	107,638	1,263,555
45 to 64 years old	244	6,098	25.0	123,301	505,917
65 years old and over	802	7,781	9.7	26,853	33,467
Heart disease	345	4,709	13.7	56,883	164,989
Cancer	286	5,333	18.6	75,819	265,036
Cerebrovascular diseases	65	777	12.0	7,861	121,377
Accidents and adverse effects	64	2,259	35.4	55,756	874,831
Other	418	7,336	17.6	120,531	288,386
Female	**1,226**	**18,428**	**15.0**	**115,142**	**93,939**
Under 5 years old	14	1,149	79.4	11,134	769,356
5 to 14 years old	3	218	72.4	2,791	926,495
15 to 24 years old	8	516	62.6	8,809	1,069,584
25 to 44 years old	45	2,054	45.6	36,770	815,994
45 to 64 years old	102	4,457	43.6	44,899	439,031
65 years old and over	1,053	10,034	9.5	10,738	10,201
Heart disease	366	4,208	11.5	15,341	41,923
Cancer	267	4,695	17.6	31,681	118,653
Cerebrovascular diseases	103	1,157	11.2	4,241	41,223
Accidents and adverse effects	34	1,044	30.6	13,673	401,183
Other	456	7,325	16.1	50,205	110,150
2003, total	**2,448**	**40,981**	**16.7**	**504,771**	**206,202**
Under 5 years old	33	2,541	77.0	32,985	999,855
5 to 14 years old	7	484	69.7	8,475	1,218,780
15 to 24 years old	34	1,984	59.1	49,677	1,479,889
25 to 44 years old	131	5,704	43.6	159,174	1,217,287
45 to 64 years old	380	11,844	31.1	212,026	557,387
65 years old and over	1,863	18,423	9.9	42,434	22,774
Heart disease	685	9,012	13.2	83,917	122,497
Cancer	557	10,423	18.7	125,039	224,531
Cerebrovascular diseases	158	1,900	12.1	13,540	85,866
Accidents and adverse effects	109	3,674	33.6	82,926	759,387
Other	939	15,972	17.0	199,349	212,273
Male	**1,202**	**21,527**	**17.9**	**362,464**	**301,628**
Under 5 years old	19	1,399	74.7	20,651	1,102,705
5 to 14 years old	4	280	67.4	5,551	1,337,603
15 to 24 years old	25	1,423	57.7	38,891	1,576,464
25 to 44 years old	85	3,596	42.3	116,188	1,366,327
45 to 64 years old	267	6,846	25.6	152,458	570,697
65 years old and over	802	7,982	10.0	28,724	35,817
Heart disease	336	4,788	14.2	64,744	192,653
Cancer	288	5,553	19.3	86,717	301,119
Cerebrovascular diseases	61	771	12.6	8,662	141,022
Accidents and adverse effects	70	2,479	35.2	65,032	922,944
Other	446	7,936	17.8	137,308	308,034
Female	**1,246**	**19,454**	**15.6**	**142,307**	**114,188**
Under 5 years old	14	1,141	80.0	12,334	864,798
5 to 14 years old	3	205	72.9	2,924	1,042,919
15 to 24 years old	9	561	63.0	10,786	1,212,134
25 to 44 years old	46	2,108	46.1	42,985	940,105
45 to 64 years old	113	4,997	44.1	59,568	525,990
65 years old and over	1,061	10,442	9.8	13,710	12,918
Heart disease	349	4,224	12.1	19,173	54,939
Cancer	269	4,870	18.1	38,322	142,510
Cerebrovascular diseases	96	1,129	11.7	4,878	50,670
Accidents and adverse effects	39	1,195	30.9	17,893	461,895
Other	493	8,036	16.3	62,041	125,752

[1] Based on life expectancy at year of death. [2] Cost estimates based on the person's age, sex, life expectancy at the time of death, labor force participation rates, annual earnings, value of homemaking services, and a 3 percent discount rate by which to convert to present worth the potential aggregate earnings lost over the years.

Source: Wendy Max and Dorothy Rice, Institute for Health and Aging, University of California, San Francisco, CA, unpublished data.

Births, Deaths, Marriages, and Divorces **91**

Table 121. **Marriages and Divorces—Number and Rate by State: 1990 to 2005**

[**2,443.5 represents 2,443,500.** By place of occurence. See Appendix III]

State	Marriages [1] Number (1,000) 1990	2000	2005	Rate per 1,000 population [2] 1990	2000	2005	Divorces [3] Number (1,000) 1990	2000	2005	Rate per 1,000 population [2] 1990	2000	2005
U.S. [4]	2,443.5	2,329.0	2,230.0	9.8	8.3	7.5	1,182.0	(NA)	(NA)	4.7	4.1	3.6
Alabama	43.1	45.0	43.3	10.6	10.3	9.5	25.3	23.5	22.1	6.1	5.4	4.9
Alaska	5.7	5.6	5.5	10.2	8.9	8.3	2.9	2.7	3.9	5.5	4.4	5.8
Arizona [5]	36.8	38.7	37.5	10.0	7.9	6.3	25.1	21.6	24.5	6.9	4.4	4.1
Arkansas	36.0	41.1	35.1	15.3	16.0	12.6	16.8	17.9	16.6	6.9	6.9	6.0
California	237.1	196.9	227.9	7.9	5.9	6.3	128.0	(NA)	(NA)	4.3	(NA)	(NA)
Colorado	32.4	35.6	29.7	9.8	8.6	6.4	18.4	(NA)	20.5	5.5	(NA)	4.4
Connecticut	26.0	19.4	19.2	7.9	5.9	5.5	10.3	6.5	9.4	3.2	2.0	2.7
Delaware	5.6	5.1	4.7	8.4	6.7	5.5	3.0	3.2	3.3	4.4	4.2	3.9
District of Columbia	5.0	2.8	2.4	8.2	5.4	4.2	2.7	1.5	1.1	4.5	3.0	2.0
Florida	141.8	141.9	158.8	10.9	9.3	8.9	81.7	81.9	81.3	6.3	5.3	4.6
Georgia	66.8	56.0	62.9	10.3	7.1	6.9	35.7	30.7	(NA)	5.5	3.9	(NA)
Hawaii	18.3	25.0	28.6	16.4	21.2	22.5	5.2	4.6	(NA)	4.6	3.9	(NA)
Idaho	14.1	14.0	15.1	13.9	11.0	10.5	6.6	6.9	7.0	6.5	5.4	4.9
Illinois	100.6	85.5	74.1	8.8	7.0	5.8	44.3	39.1	32.4	3.8	3.2	2.5
Indiana	53.2	34.5	48.5	9.6	5.8	7.7	(NA)	(NA)	(NA)	(NA)	(NA)	(NA)
Iowa	24.9	20.3	20.4	9.0	7.0	6.9	11.1	9.4	8.1	3.9	3.3	2.7
Kansas	22.7	22.2	19.1	9.2	8.3	7.0	12.6	10.6	8.6	5.0	4.0	3.1
Kentucky	49.8	39.7	36.8	13.5	10.0	8.8	21.8	21.6	18.9	5.8	5.4	4.5
Louisiana	40.4	40.5	36.6	9.6	9.3	8.1	(NA)	(NA)	(NA)	(NA)	(NA)	(NA)
Maine	11.9	10.5	10.5	9.7	8.3	7.9	5.3	5.8	4.7	4.3	4.6	3.5
Maryland	46.3	40.0	37.6	9.7	7.7	6.7	16.1	17.0	17.1	3.4	3.3	3.1
Massachusetts	47.7	37.0	39.1	7.9	6.0	6.1	16.8	18.6	14.3	2.8	3.0	2.2
Michigan	76.1	66.4	61.5	8.2	6.7	6.1	40.2	39.4	34.7	4.3	4.0	3.4
Minnesota	33.7	33.4	30.3	7.7	6.9	5.9	15.4	14.8	(NA)	3.5	3.1	(NA)
Mississippi	24.3	19.7	17.2	9.4	7.1	5.9	14.4	14.4	13.0	5.5	5.2	4.5
Missouri	49.1	43.7	47.0	9.6	7.9	8.1	26.4	26.5	21.0	5.1	4.8	3.6
Montana	6.9	6.6	6.8	8.6	7.4	7.3	4.1	2.1	3.5	5.1	2.4	3.8
Nebraska	12.6	13.0	12.3	8.0	7.8	7.0	6.5	6.4	6.0	4.0	3.8	3.4
Nevada	120.6	144.3	147.3	99.0	76.7	61.0	13.3	18.1	18.6	11.4	9.6	7.7
New Hampshire	10.5	11.6	9.5	9.5	9.5	7.3	5.3	7.1	4.4	4.7	5.8	3.3
New Jersey	58.7	50.4	43.9	7.6	6.1	5.0	23.6	25.6	25.3	3.0	3.1	2.9
New Mexico [5]	13.3	14.5	12.8	8.8	8.3	6.7	7.7	9.2	8.8	4.9	5.3	4.6
New York [5]	154.8	162.0	135.6	8.6	8.9	7.0	57.9	62.8	53.5	3.2	3.4	2.8
North Carolina	51.9	65.6	58.6	7.8	8.5	6.8	34.0	36.9	32.7	5.1	4.8	3.8
North Dakota	4.8	4.6	4.1	7.5	7.3	6.5	2.3	2.0	1.5	3.6	3.2	2.4
Ohio	98.1	88.5	76.3	9.0	7.9	6.6	51.0	49.3	41.7	4.7	4.4	3.6
Oklahoma	33.2	15.6	25.8	10.6	4.6	7.3	24.9	12.4	20.0	7.7	3.7	5.6
Oregon	25.3	26.0	26.8	8.9	7.8	7.4	15.9	16.7	15.5	5.5	5.0	4.3
Pennsylvania	84.9	73.2	58.4	7.1	6.1	4.7	40.1	37.9	29.1	3.3	3.2	2.3
Rhode Island	8.1	8.0	7.5	8.1	8.0	7.0	3.8	3.1	3.1	3.7	3.1	2.9
South Carolina	55.8	42.7	35.4	15.9	10.9	8.3	16.1	14.4	12.4	4.5	3.7	2.9
South Dakota	7.7	7.1	6.5	11.1	9.6	8.4	2.6	2.7	2.4	3.7	3.6	3.0
Tennessee	68.0	88.2	61.3	13.9	15.9	10.3	32.3	33.8	27.6	6.5	6.1	4.6
Texas	178.6	196.4	169.3	10.5	9.6	7.4	94.0	85.2	74.0	5.5	4.2	3.2
Utah	19.4	24.1	21.4	11.2	11.1	8.6	8.8	9.7	10.0	5.1	4.5	4.0
Vermont	6.1	6.1	5.5	10.9	10.2	8.9	2.6	5.1	2.1	4.5	8.6	3.3
Virginia	71.0	62.4	62.1	11.4	9.0	8.2	27.3	30.2	29.1	4.4	4.3	3.9
Washington	46.6	40.9	41.5	9.5	7.0	6.6	28.8	27.2	25.3	5.9	4.7	4.0
West Virginia	13.0	15.7	13.5	7.2	8.7	7.4	9.7	9.3	9.2	5.3	5.2	5.1
Wisconsin	38.9	36.1	33.9	7.9	6.8	6.1	17.8	17.6	16.5	3.6	3.3	3.0
Wyoming	4.9	4.9	4.8	10.7	10.3	9.4	3.1	2.8	2.7	6.6	5.9	5.3

NA Not available. [1] Data are counts of marriages performed, except as noted. [2] Based on total population residing in area; population enumerated as of April 1 for 1990 and 2000; estimated as of July 1 for all other years. [3] Includes annulments. [4] U.S. total for the number of divorces is an estimate which includes states not reporting. Beginning 2000, divorce rates based solely on the combined counts and populations for reporting states and the District of Columbia. [5] Some figures for marriages are marriage licenses issued.

Source: U.S. National Center for Health Statistics, *Vital Statistics of the United States,* annual; and *National Vital Statistics Reports,* Vol. 54. No. 20, July 21, 2006, and prior reports.

Section 3
Health and Nutrition

This section presents statistics on health expenditures and insurance coverage, including Medicare and Medicaid, medical personnel, hospitals, nursing homes and other care facilities, injuries, diseases, disability status, nutritional intake of the population, and food consumption. Summary statistics showing recent trends on health care and discussions of selected health issues are published annually by the U.S. National Center for Health Statistics (NCHS) in *Health, United States*. Data on national health expenditures, medical costs, and insurance coverage are compiled by the U.S. Centers for Medicare & Medicaid Services (CMS) (formerly Health Care Financing Administration), and appear on the CMS Web site at <http://www.cms.hhs.gov /NationalHealthExpendData/> and in the annual *Medicare and Medicaid Statistical Supplement* to the *Health Care Financing Review*. Statistics on health insurance are also collected by NCHS and are published in Series 10 of *Vital and Health Statistics*. U.S. Census Bureau also publishes data on utilization of insurance coverage. Statistics on hospitals are published annually by the Health Forum, L.L.C., an American Hospital Association (AHA) company, in *AHA Hospital Statistics*. Primary source for data on nutrition is the annual *Food Consumption, Prices, and Expenditures*, issued by the U.S. Department of Agriculture. NCHS also conducts periodic surveys of nutrient levels in the population, including estimates of food and nutrient intake, overweight and obesity, hypercholesterolemia, hypertension, and clinical signs of malnutrition.

National health expenditures—CMS compiles estimates of national health expenditures (NHE) to measure spending for health care in the United States. The NHE accounts are structured to show spending by type of expenditure (i.e., hospital care, physician and clinical care, dental care, and other professional care; home health care; retail sales of prescription drugs; other medical nondurables;

vision products and other medical durables; nursing home care and other personal health expenditures; plus other health expenditures such as public health activities, administration, and the net cost of private health insurance; plus medical sector investment, the sum of noncommercial medical research and capital formation in medical sector structures and equipment; and by source of funding (e.g., private health insurance, out-of-pocket payments, and a range of public programs including Medicare, Medicaid, and those operated by the U.S. Department of Veterans Affairs (VA)).

Data used to estimate health expenditures come from existing sources, which are tabulated for other purposes. The type of expenditure estimates rely upon statistics produced by such groups as the AHA, the Census Bureau, and the U.S. Department of Health and Human Services (HHS). Source of funding estimates are constructed using administrative and statistical records from the Medicare and Medicaid programs, the U.S. Department of Defense and VA medical programs, the Social Security Administration, Census Bureau's *Governmental Finances*, state and local governments, other HHS agencies, and other nongovernment sources.

Medicare, Medicaid and SCHIP—Since July 1966, the federal Medicare program has provided two coordinated plans for nearly all people age 65 and over: (1) a hospital insurance plan, which covers hospital and related services and (2) a voluntary supplementary medical insurance plan, financed partially by monthly premiums paid by participants, which partly covers physicians' and related medical services. Such insurance also applies, since July 1973, to disabled beneficiaries of any age after 24 months of entitlement to cash benefits under the social security or railroad retirement programs and to persons with end stage renal disease. On January 1, 2006, Medicare began to provide coverage for prescription drugs as

mandated by the Medicare Prescription Drug, Improvement, and Modernization Act of 2003 (MMA). This benefit is available on a voluntary basis to everyone with Medicare, and beneficiaries pay a monthly premium to enroll in one of Medicare's prescription drug plans.

Medicaid is a health insurance program for certain low-income people. These include: certain low-income families with children; aged, blind, or disabled people on supplemental security income; certain low-income pregnant women and children; and people who have very high medical bills. Medicaid is funded and administered through a state/federal partnership. Although there are broad federal requirements for Medicaid, states have a wide degree of flexibility to design their program. Congress created the State Children's Health Insurance Program (SCHIP) to address the growing problem of children without health insurance. SCHIP was designed as a federal/state partnership, similar to Medicaid, with the goal of expanding health insurance to children whose families earn too much money to be eligible for Medicaid, but not enough money to purchase private insurance.

Health resources—Hospital statistics based on data from AHA's yearly survey are published annually in *AHA Hospital Statistics* and cover all hospitals accepted for registration by the Association. To be accepted for registration, a hospital must meet certain requirements relating to number of beds, construction, equipment, medical and nursing staff, patient care, clinical records, surgical and obstetrical facilities, diagnostic and treatment facilities, laboratory services, etc. Data obtained from NCHS cover all U.S. hospitals that meet certain criteria for inclusion. The criteria are published in *Vital and Health Statistics* reports, Series 13.

Statistics on the demographic characteristics of persons employed in the health occupations are compiled by the U.S. Bureau of Labor Statistics and reported in *Employment and Earnings* (monthly) (see Table 598, Section 12, Labor Force, Employment, and Earnings). Data based on surveys of health personnel and utilization of health facilities providing long-term care, ambulatory care, emergency room care, and hospital care are presented in NCHS Series 13, *Data on Health Resources Utilization and Advance Data from Vital and Health Statistics.* Statistics on patient visits to health care providers, as reported in health interviews, appear in NCHS Series 10, *National Health Interview Survey Data.*

The CMS's *Health Care Financing Review* and its annual *Medicare and Medicaid Statistical Supplement* present data for hospitals and nursing homes as well as extended care facilities and home health agencies. These data are based on records of the Medicare program and differ from those of other sources because they are limited to facilities meeting federal eligibility standards for participation in Medicare.

Disability and illness—General health statistics, including morbidity, disability, injuries, preventive care, and findings from physiological testing are collected by NCHS in its National Health Interview Survey and its National Health and Nutrition Examination Surveys and appear in *Vital and Health Statistics,* Series 10 and 11, respectively. The Department of Labor compiles statistics on occupational injuries (see Section 12, Labor Force, Employment, and Earnings). Annual incidence data on notifiable diseases are compiled by the Public Health Service (PHS) at its Centers for Disease Control and Prevention in Atlanta, Georgia, and are published as a supplement to its *Morbidity and Mortality Weekly Report.* The list of diseases is revised annually and includes those which, by mutual agreement of the states and PHS, are communicable diseases of national importance.

Nutrition—Statistics on annual per capita consumption of food and its nutrient value are estimated by the Department of Agriculture. Data are available online at <http://www.ers.usda.gov/data/foodconsumption>. NCHS collects physical examination data to assess the population's nutritional status, including growth, overweight/obesity, nutritional deficiencies, and prevalence of nutrition-related conditions, such as hypertension, hypercholesterolemia, and diabetes.

Figure 3.1
Number of Retail Drug Prescriptions Sales: 1995 to 2006

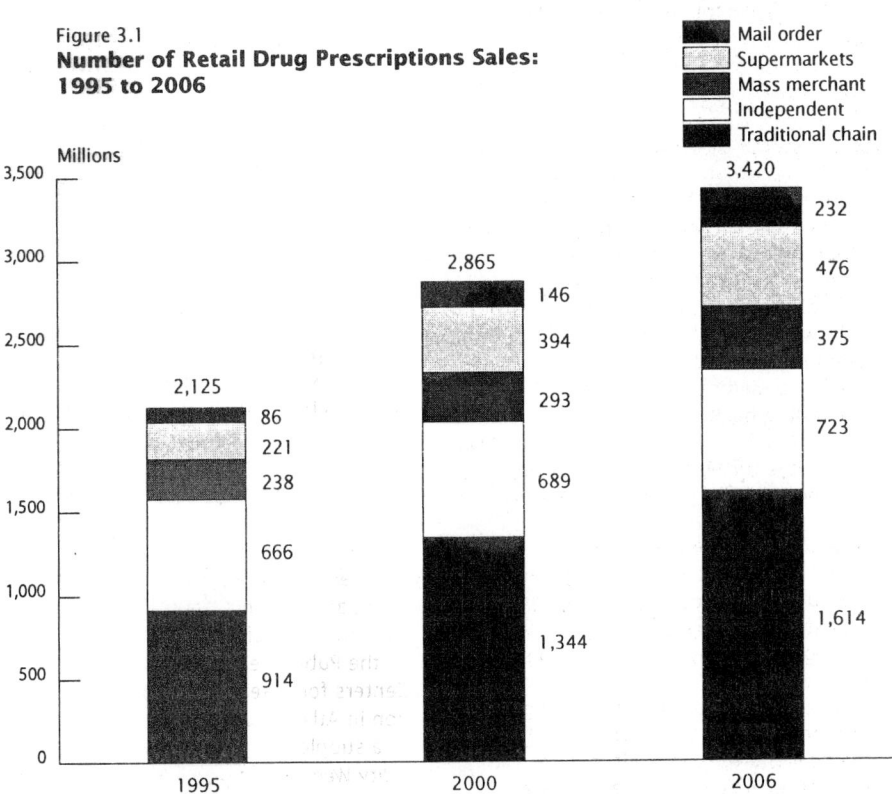

Source: Chart prepared by U.S. Census Bureau. For data, see Table 130.

U.S. Census Bureau, Statistical Abstract of the United States: 2008

Table 122. National Health Expenditures—Summary, 1960 to 2005, and Projections, 2006 to 2016

[In billions of dollars (28 represents $28,000,000,000). Excludes Puerto Rico and island areas]

Year	Total expenditures [1]	Private expenditures			Public expenditures			Health services and supplies				
		Total [2]	Out-of-pocket	Insurance	Total	Federal	State and local	Total [3]	Hospital care	Physician and clinical services	Prescription drugs	Nursing home care
1960	28	21	13	6	7	3	4	25	9	5	3	1
1961	29	22	13	6	7	3	4	26	10	6	3	1
1962	32	24	14	7	8	4	4	29	11	6	3	1
1963	35	26	15	8	9	4	5	31	12	7	3	1
1964	39	29	17	9	10	4	5	34	13	8	3	1
1965	42	32	18	10	10	5	6	37	14	8	4	1
1966	46	32	18	10	14	8	6	41	16	9	4	2
1967	52	33	18	10	19	12	7	47	18	10	4	2
1968	59	37	21	12	22	14	8	53	21	11	5	3
1969	66	41	23	13	25	16	9	59	24	12	5	3
1970	75	47	25	15	28	18	10	67	28	14	5	4
1971	83	51	26	18	32	21	12	74	31	16	6	5
1972	93	57	29	21	36	23	13	83	34	17	6	5
1973	103	63	32	23	40	25	15	93	38	19	7	6
1974	117	69	34	26	48	30	17	106	45	22	7	7
1975	133	77	37	30	56	36	20	121	52	25	8	8
1976	152	89	41	37	63	43	20	139	60	28	9	10
1977	173	102	45	45	71	47	23	159	67	33	9	12
1978	195	114	48	52	80	54	26	179	76	35	10	14
1979	220	129	53	60	91	61	30	203	87	41	11	16
1980	254	148	59	69	106	72	35	234	101	47	12	19
1981	294	172	66	81	123	83	40	271	118	55	13	21
1982	331	195	72	94	136	92	44	305	134	61	15	23
1983	365	216	79	105	150	103	47	336	145	68	17	26
1984	402	239	87	119	163	113	50	372	155	77	20	29
1985	440	263	96	131	177	123	54	409	165	90	22	32
1986	472	278	104	136	194	133	61	440	177	100	24	34
1987	513	301	109	149	212	144	68	478	190	112	27	36
1988	574	344	119	175	230	155	75	535	207	127	31	40
1989	639	383	125	205	256	174	82	596	227	142	35	46
1990	714	427	136	234	287	194	93	667	252	158	40	53
1991	782	456	140	255	325	223	102	731	277	175	44	58
1992	849	485	143	275	364	253	111	794	300	190	48	62
1993	913	512	145	296	400	279	121	853	317	201	51	65
1994	962	526	143	308	436	304	132	900	330	210	54	68
1995	1,017	552	146	325	465	327	138	953	341	221	61	74
1996	1,069	580	152	343	488	348	140	1,003	352	229	69	80
1997	1,125	614	162	359	511	365	146	1,054	365	241	78	84
1998	1,191	663	175	385	528	372	156	1,112	376	256	89	90
1999	1,265	710	184	418	555	390	165	1,180	395	270	105	91
2000	1,353	757	193	455	596	417	179	1,264	417	289	121	95
2001	1,470	808	200	499	661	464	197	1,376	451	313	139	102
2002	1,603	881	211	551	722	509	213	1,499	489	338	158	106
2003	1,733	956	225	604	778	553	225	1,622	525	367	175	110
2004	1,859	1,021	236	651	838	601	237	1,739	567	394	190	115
2005	1,988	1,085	249	694	903	644	259	1,861	612	421	201	122
2006, proj.. . .	2,122	1,130	251	727	993	725	268	1,988	652	447	214	126
2007, proj.. . .	2,262	1,205	266	776	1,058	772	285	2,119	697	474	230	132
2008, proj.. . .	2,420	1,287	281	830	1,133	829	304	2,267	747	506	248	139
2009, proj.. . .	2,596	1,379	299	891	1,217	892	325	2,432	803	541	268	146
2010, proj.. . .	2,776	1,471	317	950	1,305	957	348	2,601	861	577	291	153
2011, proj.. . .	2,966	1,566	335	1,012	1,400	1,027	373	2,778	922	613	317	161
2012, proj.. . .	3,173	1,667	353	1,078	1,507	1,107	400	2,971	988	650	346	170
2013, proj.. . .	3,396	1,776	373	1,150	1,620	1,191	428	3,179	1,058	690	379	179
2014, proj.. . .	3,629	1,889	395	1,223	1,740	1,281	459	3,396	1,130	732	414	189
2015, proj.. . .	3,875	2,004	417	1,296	1,871	1,379	492	3,626	1,207	775	454	199
2016, proj.. . .	4,137	2,123	441	1,371	2,014	1,486	527	3,870	1,288	820	498	211

[1] Includes medical research and medical facilities construction, not shown separately.   [2] Includes other private expenditures, not shown separately.   [3] Includes other objects of expenditure, not shown separately.

Source: U. S. Centers for Medicare & Medicaid Services, Office of the Actuary, "National Health Expenditure Group"; <http://www.cms.hhs.gov/NationalHealthExpendData/>.

Table 123. **National Health Expenditures by Type: 1990 to 2005**

[In billions of dollars (714.0 represents $714,000,000,000), **except percent.** Excludes Puerto Rico and island areas]

Type of expenditure	1990	1995	2000	2001	2002	2003	2004	2005
Total	714.0	1,016.5	1,353.3	1,469.6	1,602.8	1,733.4	1,858.9	1,987.7
Annual percent change [1]	11.8	5.6	7.0	8.6	9.1	8.1	7.2	6.9
Percent of gross domestic product	12.3	13.7	13.8	14.5	15.3	15.8	15.9	16.0
Private expenditures	**427.3**	**551.7**	**757.1**	**808.5**	**880.7**	**955.8**	**1,020.9**	**1,085.0**
Health services and supplies	400.9	516.3	706.1	756.3	821.8	893.0	953.6	1,013.5
Out-of-pocket payments	136.1	146.3	192.9	200.0	211.3	224.5	235.8	249.4
Insurance premiums [2]	233.7	325.2	455.2	498.7	551.0	603.8	651.5	694.4
Other	31.1	44.8	58.0	57.6	59.5	64.7	66.4	69.8
Medical research	1.0	1.6	2.5	2.8	3.1	3.4	3.5	3.7
Medical structures and equipment [3]	25.4	33.8	48.5	49.4	55.9	59.3	63.8	67.7
Public expenditures	**286.7**	**464.8**	**596.1**	**661.1**	**722.1**	**777.7**	**838.0**	**902.7**
Percent federal of public	67.6	70.4	70.0	70.2	70.5	71.1	71.7	71.3
Health services and supplies	265.8	435.5	558.3	619.9	677.0	728.7	785.3	847.3
Medicare [4]	109.5	184.4	224.3	247.7	265.7	283.5	312.8	342.0
Public assistance medical payments [5] . .	78.7	150.3	207.5	233.2	258.4	281.9	303.2	324.9
Temporary disability insurance [6]	0.1	0.1	–	0.1	0.1	0.1	0.1	0.1
Workers' compensation (medical) [6]	17.4	21.7	24.9	28.1	30.1	31.4	32.1	33.5
Defense Dept. hospital, medical.	10.4	12.0	13.7	15.4	18.7	21.8	24.5	26.1
Maternal, child health programs.	1.7	2.2	2.7	2.7	2.7	2.7	2.7	2.6
Public health activities	20.0	31.0	43.4	46.8	52.4	52.8	52.5	56.6
Veterans' hospital, medical care.	10.8	14.6	18.9	20.9	22.6	26.3	27.7	30.2
Medical vocational rehabilitation.	0.3	0.4	0.4	0.4	0.5	0.5	0.5	0.5
State and local hospitals [7]	13.2	13.8	13.7	14.7	15.4	16.7	17.8	19.2
Other [8]	3.8	6.0	8.8	9.9	10.4	11.1	11.6	11.6
Medical research	11.7	16.8	23.1	26.0	29.5	32.4	34.8	36.3
Medical structures and equipment [3]	9.2	11.5	14.7	15.3	15.6	16.6	17.9	19.1

– Represents zero. [1] Change from immediate prior year. For explanation of average annual percent change, see Guide to Tabular Presentation. [2] Covers insurance benefits and amount retained by insurance companies for expenses, additions to reserves, and profits (net cost of insurance). [3] Represents expenditures for total medical sector acquisitions of structures and equipment including structures that house medical professionals' offices. [4] Represents expenditures for benefits and administrative cost from federal hospital and medical insurance trust funds under old-age, survivors, disability, and health insurance programs; see text, this section. [5] Payments made directly to suppliers of medical care (primarily Medicaid). [6] Includes medical benefits paid under public law by private insurance carriers, state governments, and self-insurers. [7] Expenditures not offset by other revenues. [8] Covers expenditures for Substance Abuse and Mental Health Services Administration, Indian Health Service; school health and other programs.

Source: U. S. Centers for Medicare & Medicaid Services, Office of the Actuary, "National Health Expenditure Group"; See also <http://www.cms.hhs.gov/NationalHealthExpendData/>.

Table 124. **National Health Expenditures by Object, 1990 to 2005, and Projections, 2006**

[In billions of dollars (714.0 represents $714,000,000,000). Excludes Puerto Rico and outlying areas]

Object of expenditure	1990	1995	2000	2001	2002	2003	2004	2005	2006, proj.
Total	714.0	1,016.5	1,353.3	1,469.6	1,602.8	1,733.4	1,858.9	1,987.7	2,122.5
Spent by—									
Consumers	369.8	471.5	648.1	698.7	762.3	828.4	887.2	943.8	978.0
Out-of-pocket	136.1	146.3	192.9	200.0	211.3	224.5	235.8	249.4	250.6
Private insurance.	233.7	325.2	455.2	498.7	551.0	603.8	651.5	694.4	727.4
Public	286.7	464.8	596.1	661.1	722.1	777.7	838.0	902.7	992.9
Other [1]	57.5	80.2	109.0	109.7	118.4	127.4	133.6	141.2	151.5
Spent for—									
Health services and supplies	666.7	952.8	1,264.4	1,376.2	1,498.8	1,621.7	1,738.9	1,860.9	1,987.7
Personal health care expenses	607.5	863.7	1,139.9	1,239.0	1,341.2	1,446.3	1,551.3	1,661.4	1,769.2
Hospital care.	251.6	340.7	417.0	451.4	488.6	525.4	566.9	611.6	651.8
Physician and clinical services	157.5	220.5	288.6	313.2	337.9	366.7	393.7	421.2	447.0
Dental services	31.5	44.5	62.0	67.5	73.3	76.9	81.5	86.6	92.8
Other professional services [2]	18.2	28.5	39.1	42.8	45.6	49.0	52.6	56.7	60.9
Home health care.	12.6	30.5	30.5	32.2	34.2	38.0	42.7	47.5	53.4
Prescription drugs	40.3	60.9	120.8	138.6	157.9	174.6	189.7	200.7	213.7
Other nondurable medical products .	22.5	25.7	30.2	30.3	30.9	32.3	32.8	34.1	36.3
Durable medical equipment [3]	11.2	15.3	19.3	19.6	20.8	22.4	23.1	24.0	25.2
Nursing home care	52.6	74.1	95.3	101.5	105.7	110.5	115.0	121.9	126.1
Other personal health care.	9.6	23.0	37.1	41.9	46.3	50.4	53.3	57.2	62.0
Public administration and net cost of private health insurance [4]	39.2	58.1	81.2	90.4	105.2	122.6	135.2	143.0	156.8
Public health activities	20.0	31.0	43.4	46.8	52.4	52.8	52.5	56.6	61.7
Medical research [5]	12.7	18.3	25.6	28.8	32.5	35.8	38.3	40.0	41.7
Medical structures and equipment [6]	34.7	45.4	63.2	64.7	71.5	75.9	81.7	86.8	93.1

[1] Includes nonpatient revenues, privately funded construction, and industrial inplant. [2] Includes services of registered and practical nurses in private duty, podiatrists, optometrists, physical therapists, clinical psychologists, chiropractors, naturopaths, and Christian Science practitioners. [3] Includes expenditures for eyeglasses, hearing aids, orthopedic appliances, artificial limbs, crutches, wheelchairs, etc. [4] Includes administrative expenses of federally financed health programs. [5] Research and development expenditures of drug companies and other manufacturers and providers of medical equipment and supplies are excluded from research expenditures, but are included in the expenditure class in which the product falls. [6] Represents expenditures for total medical sector acquisitions of structures and equipment including structures that house medical professionals' offices.

Source: U. S. Centers for Medicare & Medicaid Services, Office of the Actuary, "National Health Expenditure Group"; See also <http://www.cms.hhs.gov/NationalHealthExpendData/>.

Health and Nutrition 97

Table 125. Health Services and Supplies—Per Capita Consumer Expenditures by Object: 1990 to 2005

[In dollars, except percent. Based on U.S. Census Bureau estimates of total U.S. population as of July 1, excluding Armed Forces and federal employees abroad and civilian population of outlying areas. Excludes medical research, medical structures and equipment]

Object of expenditure	1990	1995	2000	2001	2002	2003	2004	2005
Total, national	**2,627**	**3,546**	**4,475**	**4,821**	**5,198**	**5,568**	**5,914**	**6,270**
Annual percent change [1]	10.6	4.7	6.1	7.7	7.8	7.1	6.2	6.0
Hospital care	991	1,268	1,476	1,581	1,695	1,804	1,928	2,061
Physician and clinical services	621	821	1,021	1,097	1,172	1,259	1,339	1,419
Dental services [2]	124	166	219	237	254	264	277	292
Other professional services [2]	72	106	138	150	158	168	179	191
Home health care	50	114	108	113	119	131	145	160
Prescription drugs	159	227	428	485	548	600	645	676
Other nondurable medical products	88	95	107	106	107	111	111	115
Durable medical equipment [2]	44	57	68	69	72	77	79	81
Nursing home care	207	276	337	356	367	379	391	411
Other personal health care	38	85	131	147	161	173	181	193
Public administration and net cost of private health insurance	155	216	287	317	365	421	460	482
Public health activities	79	115	153	164	182	181	179	191
Total, private consumer [3]	**1,457**	**1,754**	**2,294**	**2,448**	**2,644**	**2,844**	**3,017**	**3,180**
Hospital care	430	444	559	600	649	698	749	799
Physician and clinical services	384	492	598	640	687	737	783	828
Dental services [2]	120	158	209	223	239	248	260	274
Other professional services [2]	49	68	88	94	97	104	111	117
Home health care	20	39	44	39	35	34	35	37
Prescription drugs	130	178	330	370	411	441	469	492
Other nondurable medical products	86	91	102	101	102	105	105	108
Durable medical equipment [2]	36	43	52	51	51	53	55	56
Nursing home care	87	99	129	130	133	134	134	140
Net cost of private health insurance	115	144	184	201	241	289	317	329

[1] Change from immediate prior year. [2] See footnotes for corresponding objects in Table 124. [3] Represents out-of-pocket payments and private health insurance.

Source: U. S. Centers for Medicare and Medicaid Services, Office of the Actuary, "National Health Expenditure Group." See also <http://www.cms.hhs.gov/NationalHealthExpendData/>.

Table 126. Public Expenditures for Health Services and Supplies: 2005

[In millions of dollars (847,341 represents $847,341,000,000). Excludes Puerto Rico and island areas. Excludes medical research, medical structures, and equipment]

Type of selected service	Total [1]	Federal	State and local	Medicare [2] (OASDHI)	Public assistance [3]	Other health services		
						Veterans	Defense Dept. [4]	Workers' compensation [5]
Total [1]	**847,341**	**605,104**	**242,237**	**342,047**	**324,870**	**30,202**	**26,088**	**33,486**
Hospital care	347,071	279,360	67,711	180,307	109,830	19,354	13,954	6,510
Physician and clinical services	148,518	121,780	26,739	89,260	32,161	2,467	4,925	13,384
Prescription drugs	54,606	32,872	21,733	3,999	41,676	2,807	3,665	2,260
Nursing home care	75,937	52,012	23,925	19,175	53,802	2,960	–	–
Public administration and net cost of private health insurance	43,883	25,911	17,972	10,631	22,689	137	2,171	7,977
Public health activities	56,558	10,719	45,840	–	–	–	–	–

– Represents zero. [1] Includes other items not shown separately. [2] Covers hospital and medical insurance payments and administrative costs under old-age, survivors, disability, and health insurance program. [3] Covers Medicaid and other medical public assistance. Excludes funds paid into Medicare trust fund by states to cover premiums for public assistance recipients and medically indigent persons. [4] Includes care for retirees and military dependents. [5] Medical benefits.

Source: U. S. Centers for Medicare and Medicaid Services, Office of the Actuary, "National Health Expenditure Group." See also <http://www.cms.hhs.gov/NationalHealthExpendData/>.

Table 127. Personal Health Care—Third Party Payments and Private Consumer Expenditures, 1990 to 2005, and Projections, 2006

[In billions of dollars (607.5 represents $607,500,000,000), except percent. See headnote, Table 128]

Item	1990	1995	2000	2001	2002	2003	2004	2005	2006, proj.
Personal health care expenditures	607.5	863.7	1,139.9	1,239.0	1,341.2	1,446.3	1,551.3	1,661.4	1,769.2
Third party payments, total	**471.3**	**717.4**	**946.9**	**1,039.0**	**1,129.9**	**1,221.7**	**1,315.5**	**1,412.0**	**1,518.6**
Percent of personal health care	77.6	83.1	83.1	83.9	84.2	84.5	84.8	85.0	85.8
Private insurance payments	204.6	286.6	403.2	441.3	481.5	519.7	558.1	596.7	624.9
Public expenditures	236.2	386.7	486.8	541.4	590.2	638.6	692.4	746.9	820.6
Other [1]	30.5	44.1	56.9	56.3	58.2	63.4	65.0	68.4	73.1
Private consumer expenditures [2]	**340.7**	**432.9**	**596.1**	**641.3**	**692.8**	**744.2**	**793.9**	**846.1**	**875.5**
Percent met by private insurance	60.1	66.2	67.6	68.8	69.5	69.8	70.3	70.5	71.4
Hospital care	109.1	119.2	157.8	171.3	187.1	203.2	220.3	237.1	254.9
Percent met by private insurance	89.6	91.4	91.4	91.7	91.7	91.6	91.6	91.5	91.4
Physician and clinical services	97.5	132.1	169.0	182.6	198.0	214.7	230.1	245.8	259.6
Percent met by private insurance	69.0	80.3	80.9	81.6	82.2	82.6	82.7	82.7	83.0
Prescription drugs	33.0	47.8	93.2	105.5	118.6	128.6	137.8	146.1	129.7
Percent met by private insurance	32.2	51.1	64.1	65.7	65.9	65.4	65.3	65.2	68.9

[1] Includes nonpatient revenues and industrial inplant health services. [2] Includes expenditures not shown separately. Represents out-of-pocket payments and private health insurance benefits. Excludes net cost of insurance.

Source: U. S. Centers for Medicare and Medicaid Services, Office of the Actuary, "National Health Expenditure Group." See also <http://www.cms.hhs.gov/NationalHealthExpendData/>.

[In millions of dollars (1,661,372 represents $1,661,372,000,000). Excludes Puerto Rico and island areas. Covers all expenditures for health services and supplies, except net cost of insurance and administration, government public health activities, and administration for government and philanthropic agencies for fund-raising activities]

Object of expenditure	Total	Private payments					Public	Third party payments[2]
		Total	Consumer					
			Total	Out-of-pocket payments	Private health insurance	Other[1]		
Total...............	1,661,372	914,472	846,109	249,445	596,665	68,363	746,900	1,411,928
Hospital care............	611,566	264,495	237,134	20,102	217,032	27,361	347,071	591,464
Physician and clinical services	421,170	272,652	245,803	42,521	203,283	26,849	148,518	378,650
Dental services.............	86,635	81,437	81,383	38,304	43,079	54	5,198	48,331
Other professional services[3]	56,742	37,656	34,759	14,534	20,225	2,897	19,086	42,208
Home health care.........	47,451	11,997	10,900	5,120	5,780	1,097	35,454	42,331
Prescription drugs...........	200,716	146,110	146,110	50,906	95,204	–	54,606	149,810
Other nondurable medical products .	34,097	31,995	31,995	31,995	–	–	2,102	2,102
Durable medical equipment[3]	23,975	16,600	16,600	13,678	2,922	–	7,375	10,297
Nursing home care	121,862	45,925	41,425	32,286	9,139	4,501	75,937	89,577
Other personal health care	57,158	5,604	--	--	–	5,604	51,553	57,157

– Represents zero. [1] Includes nonpatient revenues and industrial inplant. [2] Covers private health insurance, other private payments (excluding out-of-pocket payments), and government. [3] See footnotes for corresponding items on Table 124.

Source: U. S. Centers for Medicare and Medicaid Services, Office of the Actuary "National Health Statistics Group"; see also <http://www.cms.hhs.gov/NationalHealthExpendData/>.

Table 129. Hospital Care, Physician and Clinical Service, Nursing Home Care, and Prescription Drug Expenditures by Source of Payment: 1990 to 2005

[In billions of dollars (251.6 represents $251,600,000,000). Excludes Puerto Rico and island areas]

Source of payment	1990	1995	2000	2001	2002	2003	2004	2005
Hospital care, total	251.6	340.7	417.0	451.4	488.6	525.4	566.9	611.6
Out-of-pocket payments............	11.3	10.4	13.6	14.2	15.5	17.0	18.6	20.1
Third-party payments............	240.2	330.3	403.5	437.2	473.1	508.4	548.3	591.5
Private health insurance	97.8	110.6	143.6	156.7	171.3	186.2	201.7	217.0
Other private funds	10.4	14.5	21.8	20.8	21.4	24.4	25.4	27.4
Public	132.0	205.2	238.1	259.7	280.3	297.8	321.2	347.1
Federal	101.7	166.0	192.9	210.9	227.2	241.8	261.2	279.4
State and local	30.3	39.2	45.2	48.9	53.2	56.0	60.0	67.7
Medicare [1]	67.8	106.9	125.5	137.6	146.7	153.8	166.7	180.3
Medicaid [2]	26.7	56.8	71.1	76.5	84.4	90.3	96.8	105.7
Physician and clinical services, total .	157.5	220.5	288.6	313.1	337.9	366.7	393.7	421.2
Out-of-pocket payments............	30.2	26.0	32.2	33.5	35.2	37.4	39.9	42.5
Third-party payments............	127.3	194.5	256.4	279.6	302.7	329.3	353.9	378.6
Private health insurance	67.3	106.1	136.8	149.1	162.7	177.2	190.2	203.3
Other private funds	11.3	17.6	22.2	23.2	24.4	26.1	26.2	26.8
Public	48.7	70.9	97.4	107.3	115.6	126.0	137.4	148.5
Federal	38.0	56.2	79.0	86.9	93.9	102.9	112.8	121.8
State and local	10.7	14.7	18.4	20.4	21.6	23.0	24.6	26.7
Medicare [1]	29.4	41.4	58.3	63.6	67.7	73.8	81.5	89.3
Medicaid [2]	7.0	14.8	19.1	21.6	23.8	25.4	27.8	29.9
Nursing home care, total	52.6	74.1	95.3	101.5	105.7	110.5	115.0	121.9
Out-of-pocket payments............	19.0	20.8	28.6	28.8	29.5	30.5	30.6	32.3
Third-party payments............	33.6	53.3	66.7	72.7	76.2	80.0	84.4	89.6
Private health insurance	2.9	5.8	7.9	8.1	8.6	8.7	8.6	9.1
Other private funds	3.8	5.0	4.5	4.0	4.0	4.2	4.2	4.5
Public	26.9	42.5	54.3	60.6	63.6	67.2	71.5	75.9
Federal	16.3	27.4	36.5	42.2	44.6	46.1	49.3	52.0
State and local	10.6	15.0	17.8	18.4	18.9	21.1	22.2	23.9
Medicare [1]	1.7	6.7	10.3	12.6	14.1	14.7	17.1	19.2
Medicaid [2]	24.1	34.1	42.0	45.8	47.1	49.7	51.5	53.5
Prescription drugs, total	40.3	60.9	120.8	138.6	157.9	174.6	189.7	200.7
Out-of-pocket payments............	22.4	23.3	33.4	36.2	40.0	44.4	47.9	50.9
Third-party payments............	17.9	37.5	87.4	102.4	117.9	130.2	141.8	149.8
Private health insurance	10.6	24.4	59.7	69.3	78.7	84.1	90.0	95.2
Other private funds	–	–	–	–	–	–	–	–
Public	7.3	13.1	27.6	33.0	39.2	46.1	51.8	54.6
Federal	3.2	6.6	15.8	19.2	23.1	27.7	31.4	32.9
State and local	4.0	6.5	11.8	13.8	16.2	18.4	20.4	21.7
Medicare [1]	0.2	0.7	2.1	2.4	2.4	2.4	3.3	4.0
Medicaid [2]	5.1	9.7	20.2	23.8	27.8	32.5	36.3	37.3

– Represents zero. [1] Medicare expenditures come from federal funds. [2] Medicaid expenditures come from federal, state, and local funds.

Source: U. S. Centers for Medicare and Medicaid Services, Office of the Actuary, "National Health Statistics Group"; see also <http://www.cms.hhs.gov/NationalHealthExpendData/>.

Health and Nutrition   99

Table 130.

Table 130. Retail Prescription Drug Sales: 1995 to 2006

[2,125 represents 2,125,000,000]

Sales outlet	Unit	1995	1999	2000	2001	2002	2003	2004	2005	2006
Number of prescriptions...	Mil...	2,125	2,707	2,865	3,009	3,139	3,215	3,274	3,279	3,420
Traditional chain	Mil..	914	1,246	1,344	1,415	1,474	1,494	1,510	1,527	1,614
Independent	Mil..	666	680	689	700	708	726	728	705	723
Mass merchant.	Mil..	238	289	293	314	339	345	353	359	375
Supermarkets	Mil..	221	357	394	418	444	462	470	465	476
Mail order	Mil..	86	134	146	161	174	189	214	223	232
Retail sales	Bil. dol...	72.2	125.8	145.6	164.1	182.7	203.1	221.0	232.0	249.8
Traditional chain	bil. dol.	28.8	53.8	61.2	67.7	75.9	85.4	90.6	94.5	102.8
Independent	bil. dol.	21.1	28.9	31.4	33.9	35.4	38.3	40.5	41.9	43.5
Mass merchant	bil. dol.	7.7	11.8	13.5	15.2	18.0	19.5	21.5	22.5	24.3
Supermarkets	bil. dol.	7.4	13.8	17.4	19.8	23.1	25.1	27.0	27.6	28.8
Mail order	bil. dol.	7.4	17.4	22.1	27.6	30.2	34.9	41.3	45.5	50.4
Average prices [1]										
All prescriptions	Dollars	30.01	42.42	45.79	50.06	55.37	59.52	63.59	64.86	68.26
Brand drugs	Dollars	40.22	60.66	65.29	69.75	77.49	85.57	95.86	101.71	111.02
Generic drugs	Dollars	14.84	18.16	19.33	21.72	24.89	27.69	28.71	29.82	32.23
Percentage of number of drug prescriptions by brand/generic mix:										
Brand drugs	Percent	59.8	57.1	57.6	59.0	57.9	55.0	51.9	48.7	45.7
Generic drugs	Percent	40.2	42.9	42.4	41.0	42.1	45.0	48.1	51.3	54.3

[1] Excludes mail order.

Source: National Association of Chain Drug Stores, Alexandria, VA, *NACDS Foundation Chain Pharmacy Industry Profile, 2006* (copyright); <http://www.nacds.org>.

Table 131. Prescription Drug Use in the Past Month by Sex, Age, Race, and Hispanic Origin: 1988–1994 and 1999–2002

[Data are based on National Health and Nutrition Examination Survey (NHANES), a sample of the civilian noninstitutionalized population]

Sex and age	Percent of population using at least one prescription drug in past month							
	All persons [1]		Not Hispanic or Latino [2]				Mexican [3]	
			White		Black or African American			
	1988–1994	1999–2002	1988–1994	1999–2002	1988–1994	1999–2002	1988–1994	1999–2002
Both sexes, age adjusted [4]...	39.1	45.3	41.1	48.9	36.9	40.1	31.7	31.7
Male	32.7	39.9	34.2	43.1	31.1	35.4	27.5	25.8
Female	45.0	50.4	47.6	54.5	41.4	43.8	36.0	37.8
Both sexes, crude	37.8	45.1	41.4	50.9	31.2	36.0	24.0	23.7
Male	30.6	38.7	33.5	43.9	25.5	30.8	20.1	18.8
Female	44.6	51.2	48.9	57.6	36.2	40.6	28.1	28.9
Under 18 years old	20.5	24.2	22.9	27.6	14.8	18.6	16.1	15.9
18 to 44 years old	31.3	35.9	34.3	41.3	27.8	28.5	21.1	19.2
45 to 64 years old	54.8	64.1	55.5	66.1	57.5	62.3	48.1	49.3
65 years old and over.	73.6	84.7	74.0	85.4	74.5	81.1	67.7	72.0
Male:								
Under 18 years old	20.4	26.2	22.3	30.6	15.5	19.8	16.3	16.2
18 to 44 years old	21.5	27.1	23.5	31.2	21.1	21.5	14.9	13.0
45 to 64 years old	47.2	55.6	48.1	57.4	48.2	54.0	43.8	36.4
65 years old and over	67.2	80.1	67.4	81.0	64.4	78.1	61.3	66.8
Female:								
Under 18 years old.	20.6	22.0	23.6	24.4	14.2	17.3	16.0	15.6
18 to 44 years old	40.7	44.6	44.7	51.7	33.4	34.2	28.1	26.2
45 to 64 years old	62.0	72.0	62.6	74.7	64.4	69.0	52.2	62.4
65 years old and over	78.3	88.1	78.8	88.8	81.3	83.1	73.0	76.3

[1] Includes persons of other races and Hispanic origins, not shown separately. [2] Starting with data year 1999, race-specific estimates are not comparable with estimates for earlier years, see footnote 3, Table 156. [3] Persons of Mexican origin may be of any race. [4] Age adjusted to the 2000 standard population using four age groups: Under 18, 18–44, 45–64, and 65 years and over. See text, Section 2.

Source: National Center for Health Statistics *Health, United States, 2005.* <http://www.cdc.gov/nchs/hus.htm>.

Table 132. Consumer Price Indexes of Medical Care Prices: 1980 to 2006

[1982–1984 = 100. Indexes are annual averages of monthly data based on components of consumer price index for all urban consumers; for explanation, see text, Section 14, and Appendix III]

Year	Medical care, total	Medical care services					Medical care commodities		Annual percent change [3]		
		Total [1]	Professional services			Hospital and related services	Total [2]	Prescription drugs and medical supplies	Medical care, total	Medical care services	Medical care commodities
			Total [1]	Physicians	Dental						
1980....	74.9	74.8	77.9	76.5	78.9	69.2	75.4	72.5	11.0	11.3	9.3
1985....	113.5	113.2	113.5	113.3	114.2	116.1	115.2	120.1	6.3	6.1	7.2
1990....	162.8	162.7	156.1	160.8	155.8	178.0	163.4	181.7	9.0	9.3	8.4
1995....	220.5	224.2	201.0	208.8	206.8	257.8	204.5	235.0	4.5	5.1	1.9
1999....	250.6	255.1	229.2	236.0	247.2	299.5	230.7	273.4	3.5	3.4	4.0
2000....	260.8	266.0	237.7	244.7	258.5	317.3	238.1	285.4	4.1	4.3	3.2
2001....	272.8	278.8	246.5	253.6	269.0	338.3	247.6	300.9	4.6	4.8	4.0
2002....	285.6	292.9	253.9	260.6	281.0	367.8	256.4	316.5	4.7	5.1	3.6
2003....	297.1	306.0	261.2	267.7	292.5	394.8	262.8	326.3	4.0	4.5	2.5
2004....	310.1	321.3	271.5	278.3	306.9	417.9	269.3	337.1	4.4	5.0	2.5
2005....	323.2	336.7	281.7	287.5	324.0	439.9	276.0	349.0	4.2	4.8	2.5
2006....	336.2	350.6	289.3	291.9	340.9	468.1	285.9	363.9	4.0	4.1	3.6

[1] Includes other services not shown separately. [2] Includes other commodities not shown separately. [3] Percent change from the immediate prior year.

Source: Bureau of Labor Statistics, CPI Detailed Report, monthly, and at <http://www.bls.gov/cpi/cpidr.htm>. See also Monthly Labor Review at <http://www.bls.gov/opub/mlr/welcome.htm>.

Table 133. Average Annual Expenditures Per Consumer Unit for Health Care: 1990 to 2005

[In dollars, except percent. See text, Section 13, and headnote, Table 664. Consumer Expenditures Survey (CE) has implemented multiple imputation of income data, starting with the publication of the 2004 tables. Because of income imputation, data for 2004 are not strictly comparable to data from previous years, especially for income tables. For more information go to <http://www.bls.gov/cex/csxann04.pdf>, page 4. For composition of regions, see map, inside front cover]

Item	Health care, total		Health insurance	Medical services	Drugs and medical supplies [1]	Percent distribution		
	Amount	Percent of total expenditures				Health insurance	Medical services	Drugs and medical supplies [1]
1990	1,480	5.2	581	562	337	39.3	38.0	22.8
1995	1,732	5.4	860	512	360	49.7	29.6	20.8
2000	2,066	5.4	983	568	515	47.6	27.5	24.9
2002	2,350	5.8	1,168	590	592	49.7	25.1	25.2
2003	2,416	5.9	1,252	591	574	51.8	24.5	23.8
2004	2,574	5.9	1,332	648	594	51.7	25.2	23.1
2005	2,664	5.7	1,361	677	626	51.1	25.4	23.5
Age of reference person:								
Under 25 years old	704	2.5	377	197	130	53.6	28.0	18.5
25 to 34 years old.......	1,522	3.4	822	399	300	54.0	26.2	19.7
35 to 44 years old.......	2,272	4.1	1,160	665	447	51.1	29.3	19.7
45 to 54 years old.......	2,672	4.8	1,283	771	618	48.0	28.9	23.1
55 to 64 years old.......	3,410	6.9	1,585	979	847	46.5	28.7	24.8
65 to 74 years old.......	4,176	10.8	2,352	733	1,090	56.3	17.6	26.1
75 years old and over	4,210	15.6	2,260	805	1,144	53.7	19.1	27.2
Race of reference person:								
White and other	2,829	5.9	1,431	726	673	50.6	25.7	23.8
Black	1,448	4.4	841	321	287	58.1	22.2	19.8
Origin of reference person:								
Hispanic	1,520	3.8	750	444	327	49.3	29.2	21.5
Non-Hispanic..........	2,800	5.9	1,433	705	662	51.2	25.2	23.6
Region of residence:								
Northeast	2,581	5.4	1,429	563	589	55.4	21.8	22.8
Midwest	2,841	6.3	1,409	755	677	49.6	26.6	23.8
South	2,606	6.1	1,353	600	653	51.9	23.0	25.1
West................	2,647	5.0	1,264	820	564	47.8	31.0	21.3
Size of consumer unit:								
One person	1,750	6.5	893	424	433	51.0	24.2	24.7
Two or more persons.....	3,042	5.6	1,554	782	705	51.1	25.7	23.2
Two persons.........	3,359	6.9	1,731	777	851	51.5	23.1	25.3
Three persons	2,815	5.1	1,442	727	646	51.2	25.8	22.9
Four persons	2,786	4.5	1,453	771	562	52.2	27.7	20.2
Five persons or more ...	2,718	4.3	1,291	904	523	47.5	33.3	19.2
Income before taxes:								
Quintiles of income:								
Lowest 20 percent.....	1,448	7.6	780	266	402	53.9	18.4	27.8
Second 20 percent	2,329	8.1	1,198	509	622	51.4	21.9	26.7
Third 20 percent	2,567	6.6	1,349	613	605	52.6	23.9	23.6
Fourth 20 percent	3,012	5.5	1,552	788	672	51.5	26.2	22.3
Highest 20 percent	3,962	4.4	1,924	1,208	830	48.6	30.5	20.9

[1] Includes prescription and nonprescription drugs.

Source: U.S. Bureau of Labor Statistics, Consumer Expenditure Survey, annual; <http://www.bls.gov/cex/>.

Health and Nutrition   101

Table 134. **Medicare Benefits by Type of Provider: 1990 to 2006**

[In millions of dollars (65,721 represents $65,721,000,000). For years ending Sept. 30. Distribution of benefits by type is estimated and subject to change. The Medicare program has two components: Hospital Insurance (HI) or Medicare Part A and Supplementary Medical Insurance (SMI) consisting of Medicare Part B and Part D. See text in this section for details]

Type of provider	1990	1995	2000	2002	2003	2004	2005	2006
Hospital insurance benefits, total (Part A).................	65,721	113,395	125,992	144,140	153,144	163,764	180,973	181,462
Inpatient hospital	57,012	81,095	86,561	102,299	108,576	114,386	121,796	119,120
Skilled nursing facility	2,761	8,684	10,269	14,814	14,934	16,665	18,648	19,236
Home health agency	3,295	15,715	4,880	4,782	4,938	5,211	5,867	5,923
Hospice	318	1,854	2,818	4,380	5,429	6,571	7,660	8,515
Managed care	2,335	6,047	21,463	17,865	19,267	20,932	27,001	28,668
Supplementary medical insurance benefits, total (Part B)........	41,498	63,490	88,876	108,068	119,455	131,357	148,410	158,021
Physician fee schedule	(NA)	31,110	35,958	44,217	47,486	52,224	57,256	57,980
Durable medical equipment	(NA)	3,576	4,577	6,132	7,429	7,685	7,809	8,190
Carrier lab [1]	(NA)	2,819	2,194	2,692	2,946	3,204	3,524	3,682
Other carrier [2]	(NA)	4,513	7,154	10,304	12,432	13,799	15,231	15,268
Hospital [3]	(NA)	8,448	8,516	13,474	14,692	16,930	19,490	22,118
Home health	(NA)	223	4,281	4,794	5,158	5,578	6,758	7,097
Intermediary lab [4]	(NA)	1,437	1,748	2,151	2,408	2,670	2,907	3,182
Other intermediary [5]	(NA)	5,110	6,099	8,251	9,700	10,459	11,699	13,290
Managed care	(NA)	6,253	18,348	16,052	17,203	18,809	23,735	27,213
Supplementary medical insurance benefits, total (Part D)[6]........	(X)	(X)	(X)	(X)	(X)	216	1,198	33,710

NA Not available.   X Not applicable.   [1] Lab services paid under the lab fee schedule performed in a physician's office lab or an independent lab.   [2] Includes free-standing ambulatory surgical centers' facility costs, ambulance, and supplies.   [3] Includes the hospital facility costs for Medicare Part B services which are predominantly in the outpatient department. The physician reimbursement associated with these services is included on the "Physician Fee Schedule" line.   [4] Lab fee services paid under the lab fee schedule performed in a hospital outpatient department.   [5] Includes ESRD (End Stage Renal Disease) free-standing dialysis facility payments and payments to rural health clinics, outpatient rehabilitation facilities, psychiatric hospitals, and federally qualified health centers.   [6] Benefits prior to 2006 are for transitional assistance to beneficiaries with low income. In 2006 and later, Part D provides subsidized access to drug insurance coverage on a voluntary basis for all beneficiaries and premium and cost-sharing subsidies for low-income enrollees.

Source: U.S. Centers for Medicare and Medicaid Services, unpublished data. See also <http://www.cms.hhs.gov/ReportsTrustFunds/>.

Table 135. **Medicare—Enrollment by State and Other Areas: 2000 to 2005**

[In thousands (39,620 represents 39,620,000) Hospital (HI) and/or supplementary medical insurance (SMI) enrollment as of July 1]

State and area	2000	2003	2004	2005	State and area	2000	2003	2004	2005
All areas	39,620	41,087	41,729	42,395					
U.S.	38,762	40,173	40,792	41,003	NE	254	257	259	259
					NV	240	271	286	294
AL	685	719	733	740	NH	170	180	183	185
AK	42	48	50	51	NJ	1,203	1,220	1,225	1,215
AZ	675	729	755	777	NM	234	250	257	261
AR	439	453	460	464	NY	2,715	2,763	2,775	2,758
CA	3,901	4,078	4,150	4,158	NC	1,133	1,205	1,235	1,255
CO	467	493	506	513	ND	103	103	103	103
CT	515	522	524	520	OH	1,701	1,727	1,739	1,731
DE	112	119	123	125	OK	508	521	529	531
DC	75	74	73	72	OR	489	513	527	532
FL	2,804	2,921	2,982	3,008	PA	2,095	2,110	2,118	2,108
GA	916	974	998	1,016	RI	172	172	173	171
HI	165	175	178	180	SC	568	606	624	637
ID	165	178	184	188	SD	119	122	123	123
IL	1,635	1,661	1,676	1,674	TN	829	872	891	903
IN	852	878	889	893	TX	2,265	2,390	2,451	2,491
IA	477	482	486	484	UT	206	220	227	231
KS	390	394	397	397	VT	89	93	94	95
KY	623	648	660	668	VA	893	946	967	981
LA	602	620	627	630	WA	736	775	799	807
ME	216	227	231	233	WV	338	347	351	351
MD	645	674	685	687	WI	783	804	814	818
MA	961	966	968	961	WY	65	69	70	70
MI	1,403	1,445	1,464	1,468					
MN	654	676	686	691	Outlying areas [1]	537	575	613	622
MS	419	437	446	449	Pending state				
MO	861	884	896	901	designation [2] ..	321	340	324	769
MT	137	142	145	146					

[1] Includes American Samoa, Federated States of Micronesia, Guam, Marshall Islands, Northern Marianas, Puerto Rico, Virgin Islands, and Wake Island.   [2] Includes foreign and other.

Source: U.S. Centers for Medicare and Medicaid Services, Medicare Enrollment Reports. See also <http://www.cms.hhs.gov/MedicareEnrpts/>.

Table 136. **Medicare Enrollees: 1980 to 2006**

[In millions (28.4 represents 28,400,000). As of July 1. Includes Puerto Rico and island areas and enrollees in foreign countries and unknown place of residence. SMI is Supplemental Medical Insurance. See headnote, Table 134]

Item	1980	1990	1995	2000	2003	2004	2005	2006
Total	28.4	34.3	37.6	39.7	41.2	41.9	42.6	43.2
Aged	25.5	31.0	33.2	34.3	35.0	35.4	35.8	36.3
Disabled	3.0	3.3	4.4	5.4	6.2	6.5	6.8	7.0
Hospital insurance, Part A	28.0	33.7	37.2	39.3	40.7	41.5	42.2	42.9
Aged	25.0	30.5	32.7	33.8	34.6	35.0	35.4	35.9
Disabled	3.0	3.3	4.4	5.4	6.2	6.5	6.8	7.0
SMI, Part B	27.3	32.6	35.6	37.3	38.6	39.1	39.7	40.3
Aged	24.6	29.6	31.7	32.6	33.2	33.5	33.8	34.1
Disabled	2.7	2.9	3.9	4.8	5.4	5.7	5.9	6.1
SMI, Part D	(X)	(X)	(X)	(X)	(X)	1.2	1.8	27.9
Medicare Advantage [1]	(X)	1.3	2.7	6.2	4.7	4.7	5.1	6.5

X Not applicable.   [1] Prior to 2004, Medicare Advantage was referred to as Medicare + Choice.

Source: U.S. Centers for Medicare and Medicaid Services, Office of the Actuary, CMS Statistics Medicare Enrollment and unpublished data. See also <http://www.cms.hhs.gov/statistics/enrollment/>.

Table 137. **Medicare Disbursements by Type of Beneficiary: 1990 to 2006**

[In millions of dollars (109,709 represents $109,709,000,000). For years ending September 30. Distribution of benefits by type is estimated and subject to change. SMI is Supplemental Medical Insurance. See headnote, Table 134]

Selected type of beneficiary	1990	1995	2000	2002	2003	2004	2005	2006
Total disbursements	109,709	180,096	219,276	256,856	277,846	301,488	336,877	380,433
HI, Part A disbursements [1]	66,687	114,883	130,284	148,031	153,792	166,998	184,142	184,901
Benefits	65,722	113,394	125,992	144,140	153,144	163,764	180,973	181,462
Aged	58,503	100,107	110,261	125,248	132,415	140,704	155,054	154,362
Disabled	7,218	13,288	15,731	18,892	20,729	23,060	25,919	27,100
SMI, Part B disbursements [1]	43,022	65,213	88,992	108,825	124,055	134,274	151,537	161,647
Benefits	41,498	63,490	88,875	108,068	119,455	131,357	148,410	158,021
Aged	36,837	54,830	76,340	91,667	100,505	109,890	123,666	131,268
Disabled	4,661	8,660	12,535	16,414	18,940	21,467	24,744	26,752
Part D Transitional Assistance	(X)	(X)	(X)	(X)	(X)	153	566	366
SMI, Part D disbursements [1]	(X)	(X)	(X)	(X)	(X)	216	1,198	33,884
Benefits	(X)	(X)	(X)	(X)	(X)	–	73	33,481
Transitional assistance benefit payments .	(X)	(X)	(X)	(X)	(X)	216	1,125	229

– Represents or rounds to zero.   X not applicable.   [1] Other types not shown separately.

Source: U.S. Centers for Medicare and Medicaid Services, Trustees Report and Trust Funds, and unpublished data. See also <http://www.cms.hhs.gov/ReportsTrustFunds/>.

Table 138. **Medicare Trust Funds: 1990 to 2006**

[In billions of dollars (126.3 represents $126,300,000,000). SMI is Supplemental Medical Insurance. See headnote, Table 134. Minus sign (–) indicates a decrease]

Type of trust fund	1990	1995	2000	2001	2002	2003	2004	2005	2006
TOTAL MEDICARE									
Total income	126.3	175.3	257.1	273.3	284.8	291.6	317.7	357.5	437.0
Total expenditures.	111.0	184.2	221.8	244.8	265.7	280.8	308.9	336.4	408.3
Assets, end of year	114.4	143.4	221.5	250.0	269.1	280.0	288.8	309.8	338.5
HOSPITAL INSURANCE (Part A)									
Net contribution income [1]	72.1	103.3	154.5	160.9	162.7	159.2	167.2	182.6	194.2
Interest received [2]	8.5	10.8	11.7	14.0	15.1	15.8	16.0	16.1	16.4
Benefit payments [3]	66.2	116.4	126.8	138.1	148.6	154.3	167.6	180.0	189.0
Assets, end of year	98.9	130.3	177.5	208.7	234.8	256.0	269.3	285.8	305.4
SMI (Part B)									
Net premium income	11.3	19.7	20.6	22.8	25.1	27.4	31.4	37.5	42.9
Transfers from general revenue	33.0	39.0	65.9	72.8	78.3	86.4	100.4	118.1	132.7
Interest received [2]	1.6	1.6	3.5	3.1	2.8	2.0	1.5	1.4	1.8
Benefit payments [3]	42.5	65.0	88.9	99.7	111.0	123.8	135.0	149.2	165.9
Assets, end of year	15.5	13.1	44.0	41.3	34.3	24.0	19.4	24.0	32.3
SMI (Part D)									
Net premium income	(X)	(X)	(X)	(X)	(X)	(X)	–	–	3.5
Transfers from general revenue [4]	(X)	(X)	(X)	(X)	(X)	(X)	0.4	1.1	39.2
Interest received	(X)	(X)	(X)	(X)	(X)	(X)	–	–	–
Benefit payments [4]	(X)	(X)	(X)	(X)	(X)	(X)	0.4	1.1	47.1
Assets, end of year	(X)	(X)	(X)	(X)	(X)	(X)	–	–	0.8

– Represents zero.   X Not Applicable.   [1] Includes income from taxation of benefits beginning in 1994. Includes premiums from aged ineligibles enrolled in HI.   [2] Includes recoveries of amounts reimbursed from the trust fund.   [3] Beginning 1998, monies transferred to the SMI trust fund for home health agency costs, as provided for by P.L. 105-33, are included in HI benefit payments but excluded from SMI benefit payments.   [4] These amounts for 2004 and 2005 include amounts transferred for transitional assistance for Part D of Medicare.

Source: U.S. Centers for Medicare and Medicaid Services, Annual Report of the Board of Trustees of the Federal Hospital Insurance Trust Fund and Annual Report of the Board of Trustees of the Federal Supplementary Medical Insurance Trust Fund. See also <http://www.cms.hhs.gov/ReportsTrustFunds/>.

Health and Nutrition   103

Table 139. Medicaid—Selected Characteristics of Persons Covered: 2005

[In thousands, **except percent (37,738 represents 37,738,000).** Represents number of persons as of March of following year who were enrolled at any time in year shown. Excludes unrelated individuals under age 15. Person did not have to receive medical care paid for by Medicaid in order to be counted. See head note, Table 548]

Poverty status	Total [1]	White alone [2]	Black alone [3]	Asian alone [4]	His-panic [5]	Under 18 years old	18–44 years old	45–64 years old	65 years old and over
Persons covered, total [6]..	**37,738**	**25,722**	**9,054**	**1,208**	**9,274**	**19,357**	**9,825**	**5,162**	**3,394**
Below poverty level........	15,730	9,644	4,929	370	4,034	8,493	4,143	2,074	1,021
Above poverty level........	22,008	16,078	4,125	838	5,240	10,864	5,681	3,088	2,373
Percent of population covered.............	12.9	10.9	24.6	9.6	21.6	26.4	8.9	7.0	9.6
Below poverty level........	42.6	38.8	53.8	26.4	43.1	65.9	29.1	33.4	28.3
Above poverty level........	8.6	7.6	14.9	7.5	15.6	18.0	5.9	4.6	7.4

[1] Includes other races not shown separately.   [2] White alone refers to people who reported White and did not report any other race category.   [3] Black alone refers to people who reported Black and did not report any other race category.   [4] Asian alone refers to people who reported Asian and did not report any other race category.   [5] Persons of Hispanic origin may be of any race.   [6] The estimates are revised from the originally published data.

Source: U.S. Census Bureau, Current Population Reports, P60-231, and Table HI02. Health Insurance Coverage Status and Type of Coverage by Selected Characteristics for People in the Poverty Universe: 2005; and Table HI03. Health Insurance Coverage Status and Type of Coverage by Selected Characteristics for Poor People in the Poverty Universe: 2005; <http://www.census.gov/hhes/www/hlthins/hlthin05.html>.

Table 140. Medicaid—Beneficiaries and Payments: 2000 to 2004

[For year ending September 30 (42,887 represents 42,887,000).

Basis of eligibility and type of service	Beneficiaries (1,000) [1]				Payments (mil. dol.)			
	2000	2002	2003	2004 [2]	2000	2002	2003	2004 [2]
Total	**42,887**	**49,755**	**51,971**	**55,078**	**168,443**	**213,491**	**233,206**	**257,722**
Age 65 and over	3,730	3,886	4,041	4,289	44,560	51,733	55,271	59,524
Blind/Disabled	6,890	7,414	7,669	7,912	72,772	91,889	102,014	111,473
Children	19,018	22,369	23,992	25,639	23,490	31,247	35,080	39,202
Adults	8,671	11,238	11,679	12,303	17,671	23,460	26,689	30,628
Foster Care Children.	761	816	839	845	3,309	4,282	4,791	5,006
Unknown	3,817	4,027	3,739	4,071	6,639	10,848	9,251	11,691
BCCA WOMEN [3]	(NA)	5	12	19	(NA)	33	110	197
Capitated care [4]	21,292	25,864	27,574	29,589	25,026	33,634	37,405	42.601
Clinic services	7,678	9,499	10,162	10,958	6,138	6,694	7,312	8,336
Dental services	5,922	7,886	8,510	9,000	1,413	2,309	2,595	2,867
Home health services	1,007	1,065	1,184	1,135	3,133	3,925	4,404	4,566
ICF/MR services [5]	119	117	114	114	9,376	10,681	10,861	11,141
Inpatient hospital services	4,913	5,051	5,217	5,408	24,131	29,127	31,549	34,816
Lab and X-ray services	11,439	14,067	14,687	15,630	1,292	2,157	2,365	2,699
Mental health facility services [6]...	100	99	105	116	1,769	2,122	2,143	2,326
Nursing facility services	1,706	1,766	1,091	1,710	34,528	39,282	40,381	42,060
Other care	9,022	10,959	11,742	12,409	14,755	19,877	21,809	24,946
Outpatient hospital services	13,170	14,861	15,511	15,781	7,082	8,471	9,252	10,196
Other practitioner services	4,758	5,571	5,746	5,767	664	842	882	946
PCCM services [8]	5,649	7,178	7,542	8,548	177	200	208	500
Prescribed drugs	20,325	24,424	26,075	27,528	19,898	28,408	33,714	39,476
Physician services	18,965	22,103	22,857	23,592	6,809	8,355	9,210	10,199
Personal support services [9]	4,559	5,688	6,022	6,167	11,629	15,363	17,245	18,497
Sterilizations	137	164	160	167	128	166	166	207
Unknown	74	73	88	81	496	1,879	1,702	1,345

NA Not available.   [1] Beneficiaries data do not add due to number of beneficiaries that are reported in more than one category.   [2] 2004 beneficiary data is not available for Tennessee; 2003 data is reported.   [3] Women-Breast and Cervical Cancer Assistance.   [4] HMO payments and prepaid health plans.   [5] Intermediate care facilities for mentally retarded.   [6] Inpatient mental health-aged and inpatient mental health-under 21.   [7] Includes beneficiaries of, and payments for, other care not shown separately.   [8] Primary Care Case Management Services.   [9] Includes personal care services, rehabilitative services, physical occupational targeted case management services, speech therapies, hospice services, nurse midwife services, nurse practitioner services, private duty nursing services, and religious nonmedical health care institutions.

Source: U.S. Centers for Medicare and Medicaid Services, Medicaid Program Statistics, Medicaid Statistical Information System; <http://www.cms.hhs.gov/MedicaidDataSourcesGenInfo/02MSISDATA.asp#TopOfPage>.

Table 141. Medicaid—Summary by State: 2000 and 2004

[(42,887 represents 42,887,000). For year ending September 30. See headnote, Table 140]

State	Beneficiaries [1] (1,000)		Payments [2] (mil. dol.)		State	Beneficiaries [1] (1,000)		Payments [2] (mil. dol.)	
	2000	2004	2000	2004		2000	2004	2000	2004
U.S.	42,887	55,078	168,443	257,722	MO	890	726	3,274	3,312
AL	619	118	2,393	905	MT	104	113	422	585
AK	96	808	473	3,857	NE	229	1,513	960	7,388
AZ	681	708	2,112	2,358	NV	138	78	516	477
AR	489	1,070	1,543	3,888	NH	97	244	651	1,346
CA	7,918	10,015	17,105	27,444	NJ	822	119	4,714	822
CO	381	503	1,809	2,399	NM	376	960	1,249	6,623
CT	420	501	2,839	3,696	NY	3,420	474	26,148	2,278
DE	115	158	529	1,269	NC	1,214	237	4,834	806
DC	139	157	793	800	ND	63	4,712	358	37,273
FL	2,373	2,952	7,433	12,834	OH	1,305	1,896	7,115	11,375
GA	1,369	1,929	3,624	6,944	OK	507	654	1,604	2,335
HI	194	218	600	862	OR	558	559	1,714	2,153
ID	131	383	594	2,206	PA	1,492	1,835	6,366	10,055
IL	1,519	206	7,807	990	RI	179	208	1,070	1,531
IN	706	2,032	2,977	10,796	SC	689	857	2,765	4,015
IA	314	946	1,477	4,343	SD	102	128	402	580
KS	263	365	1,227	1,860	TN [3]	1,568	1,730	3,491	6,945
KY	764	861	2,921	3,924	TX	2,633	3,604	9,277	13,214
LA	761	1,108	2,632	4,039	UT	225	307	960	1,356
ME	194	1,074	1,310	7,776	VT	139	732	480	3,574
MD	626	750	3,003	4,594	VA	627	149	2,479	744
MA	1,060	294	5,413	2,366	WA	896	1,109	2,435	4,930
MI	1,352	1,799	4,881	7,697	WV	342	896	1,394	4,314
MN	558	698	3,280	4,575	WI	577	377	2,968	2,020
MS	605	1,140	1,808	4,887	WY	46	68	215	363

[1] Persons who had payments made on their behalf at any time during the fiscal year. [2] Payments are for fiscal year and reflect federal and state contribution payments. Data exclude disproportionate share hospital payments. Disproportionate share hospitals receive higher medicaid reimbursement than other hospitals because they treat a disproportionate share of Medicaid patients. [3] 2004 beneficiary data are not available for Tennessee; 2003 data are reported.

Source: U.S. Centers for Medicare and Medicaid Services, "Medicaid, Program Statistics, Medicaid Statistical Information System." <http://www.cms.hhs.gov/MedicaidDataSourcesGenInfo/02MSISData.asp#TopOfPage>.

Table 142. State Children's Health Insurance Program (SCHIP)—Enrollment and Expenditures by State: 2000 and 2006

[(3,357.4 represents 3,357,400). For year ending September 30. This program provides health benefits coverage to children living in families whose incomes exceed the eligibility limits for Medicaid. Although it is generally targeted to families with incomes at or below 200 percent of the federal poverty level, each state may set its own income eligibility limits, within certain guidelines. States have three options: they may expand their Medicaid programs, develop a separate child health program that functions independently of Medicaid, or do a combination of both]

State	Enrollment [1] (1,000)		Expenditures [2] (mil. dol.)		State	Enrollment [1] (1,000)		Expenditures [2] (mil. dol.)	
	2000	2006	2000	2006		2000	2006	2000	2006
US	3,357.4	6,624.2	1,928.8	7,034.3	MO	72.8	106.6	41.2	106.4
AL	37.6	84.3	31.9	111.1	MT	8.3	17.3	4.3	21.8
AK	13.4	22.2	18.1	27.8	NE	11.4	45.0	6.1	29.9
AZ	59.6	96.7	29.4	95.8	NV	15.9	39.3	9.0	40.2
AR	1.9	3.4	1.5	60.4	NH	4.3	12.4	1.6	11.6
CA	484.4	1,391.4	187.3	1,801.1	NJ	89.0	120.9	46.9	190.6
CO	34.9	70.0	13.9	77.1	NM	8.0	25.2	3.4	23.8
CT	19.9	23.1	12.8	31.5	NY	769.5	688.4	401.0	505.4
DE	4.5	10.8	1.5	10.8	NC	103.6	248.0	65.5	271.9
DC	2.3	6.3	5.8	9.9	ND	2.6	6.3	1.8	14.1
FL	227.5	303.6	125.7	300.6	OH	118.3	218.5	53.1	236.1
GA	120.6	343.7	48.7	265.2	OK	57.7	116.0	51.3	105.0
HI	(Z)	22.0	0.4	19.3	OR	37.1	59.0	12.5	72.5
ID	12.4	24.7	7.5	23.0	PA	119.7	188.8	70.7	239.8
IL	62.5	316.8	32.7	312.1	RI	11.5	25.5	10.4	42.1
IN	44.4	133.7	53.7	106.3	SC	60.4	68.9	46.6	62.6
IA	20.0	49.6	15.5	64.2	SD	5.9	14.6	3.1	14.0
KS	26.3	48.9	12.8	67.2	TN	14.9	(NA)	41.7	(NA)
KY	55.6	64.9	60.0	98.3	TX	131.1	585.5	41.4	371.8
LA	50.0	142.4	25.3	122.4	UT	25.3	52.0	12.8	56.9
ME	22.7	31.1	11.4	33.1	VT	4.1	6.3	1.4	4.7
MD	93.1	136.0	92.2	212.4	VA	37.7	137.2	18.6	145.9
MA	113.0	190.6	44.2	233.5	WA	2.6	15.0	0.6	40.3
MI	55.4	118.5	36.2	95.5	WV	21.7	39.9	9.7	41.6
MN	(Z)	5.3	(Z)	39.4	WI	47.1	56.6	21.4	33.4
MS	12.2	83.4	21.1	124.2	WY	2.5	7.7	1.0	9.4

NA Not available. Z Less than 50 or $50,000. [1] Number of children ever enrolled during the year in SCHIP. [2] Expenditures for which states are entitled to federal reimbursement under Title XXI and which reconciles any advance of Title XXI federal funds made on the basis of estimates.

Source: U.S. Centers for Medicare & Medicaid Services, The State Children's Health Insurance Program, Annual Enrollment Report and the Statement of Expenditures for the SCHIP Program (CMS-21). See also <http://www.cms.hhs.gov/NationalSCHIPPolicy /SCHIPER/list.asp> and <http://www.cms.hhs.gov/medicaid/mbes/default.asp>.

Health and Nutrition 105

Table 143. **Medicaid Managed Care Enrollment by State and Other Areas: 1995 to 2006**

[For year ending June 30. (33,373 represents 33,373,000)]

State and other areas	Total enrollment [1] (1,000)	Managed care enrollment [2] Number (1,000)	Percent of total	State and other areas	Total enrollment [1] (1,000)	Managed care enrollment [2] Number (1,000)	Percent of total	State and other areas	Total enrollment [1] (1,000)	Managed care enrollment [2] Number (1,000)	Percent of total
1995	33,373	9,800	29.4	HI	203	163	80.0	NY......	4,209	2,572	61.1
2000	33,690	18,786	55.8	ID	172	140	81.4	NC......	1,300	843	64.9
2002	40,148	23,118	57.6	IL	1,929	140	7.3	ND......	54	30	55.6
2003	42,741	24,406	58.4	IN	839	605	72.1	OH......	1,749	698	39.9
2004	44,356	26,914	60.7	IA	330	285	86.5	OK......	556	478	85.9
2005	45,392	28,576	63.0	KS......	283	162	57.0	OR......	409	369	90.3
				KY......	707	653	92.4	PA	1,817	1,568	86.3
2006, total .	45,653	29,830	65.3	LA......	969	690	71.2	RI	181	119	65.8
U.S....	44,716	28,923	64.7	ME......	243	162	66.7	SC......	690	139	20.2
AL.....	786	498	63.3	MD.....	700	490	70.0	SD......	101	99	98.3
AK.....	101	–	–	MA.....	1,038	627	60.4	TN......	1,190	1,190	100.0
AZ.....	977	875	89.6	MI	1,523	1,293	84.9	TX......	2,768	1,897	68.6
AR.....	635	527	83.0	MN.....	584	371	63.7	UT.....	209	181	86.9
CA.....	6,509	3,276	50.3	MS.....	570	58	10.2	VT	133	86	64.7
CO.....	391	372	95.1	MO.....	830	826	99.5	VA.....	705	446	63.2
CT.....	396	299	75.6	MT.....	83	55	66.9	WA.....	990	858	86.6
DE.....	145	111	76.5	NE.....	210	170	80.9	WV.....	297	137	46.3
DC.....	138	93	67.8	NV.....	172	142	82.4	WI	863	403	46.7
FL.....	2,277	1,491	65.5	NH.....	112	84	74.9	WY	63	–	–
GA.....	1,322	1,291	97.7	NJ.....	858	596	69.4	PR	931	907	97.5
				NM.....	401	261	65.2	VI....	5	–	–

– Represents zero.   [1] The unduplicated Medicaid enrollment figures include individuals in state health care reform programs that expand eligibility beyond traditional Medicaid eligibility standards.   [2] The unduplicated managed care enrollment figures include enrollees receiving comprehensive and limited benefits.

Source: U.S. Centers for Medicare and Medicaid Services, *2006 Medicaid Managed Care Enrollment Report*; See also <http://www.cms.hhs.gov/MedicaidDataSourcesGenInfo/04MdManCrEnrllRep.asp>.

Table 144. **Health Maintenance Organizations (HMOs): 1990 to 2006**

[As of January 1 (33.0 represents 33,000,000). An HMO is a prepaid health plan delivering comprehensive care to members through designated providers, having a fixed periodic payment for health care services, and requiring members to be in a plan for a specified period of time (usually 1 year). A group HMO delivers health services through a physician group that is controlled by the HMO unit or contracts with one or more independent group practices to provide health services. An individual practice association (IPA) HMO contracts directly with physicians in independent practice, and/or contracts with one or more associations of physicians in independent practice, and/or contracts with one or more multispecialty group practices. Data are based on a census of HMOs]

Model type	Number of plans						Enrollment [1] (mil.)					
	1990	1995	2000	2004 [2]	2005 [4]	2006 [3,4]	1990	1995	2000	2004 [2]	2005 [4]	2006 [3,4]
Total ..	572	550	568	412	420	548	33.0	46.2	80.9	68.8	69.2	73.9
IPA	360	323	278	176	171	191	13.7	17.4	33.4	24.6	23.5	22.4
Group [5] ..	212	107	102	96	98	122	19.3	12.9	15.2	15.3	16.4	20.7
Mixed ..	(NA)	120	188	140	141	134	(NA)	15.9	32.3	28.9	29.0	25.5

NA Not available.   [1] 1990–1995 exclude enrollees participating in open-ended plans; beginning 1999, includes open-ended enrollment.   [2] Starting with 2004 data, Puerto Rico and Guam included in the total.   [3] 2006 data include "HMO Medicaid only" plans for the first time.   [4] 2005 and 2006 totals include plans that did not provide enough information to be classified as a model type.   [5] 2005 and 2006 data include data for "Network, Staff, and Group" type.

Source: HealthLeaders-InterStudy, Nashville, TN, *The Competitive Edge*, copyright). See also <http://www.interstudypublications.com/>.

Table 145. **Persons Enrolled in Health Maintenance Organizations (HMOs) by State: 2005 and 2006**

[As of January 1 (71,109 represents 71,109,000). Data are based on a census of health maintenance organizations]

State	Number 2006 (1,000)	Percent of population 2005	2006	State	Number 2006 (1,000)	Percent of population 2005	2006	State	Number 2006 (1,000)	Percent of population 2005	2006
US ...	71,109	22.8	23.8	KS	405	16.6	14.8	ND.....	2	0.4	0.4
AL	143	2.8	3.1	KY	260	10.2	6.2	OH.....	2,655	16.4	23.2
AK.....	–	–	–	LA	432	10.7	9.5	OK.....	250	7.1	7.0
AZ.....	2,031	16.4	34.2	ME	484	25.9	36.6	OR.....	904	16.2	24.8
AR.....	96	6.4	3.5	MD.....	1,632	28.0	29.1	PA.....	3,347	29.8	26.9
CA.....	17,775	49.1	49.2	MA.....	2,830	37.4	44.2	RI.....	270	25.9	25.0
CO.....	1,207	25.6	25.9	MI	2,688	26.3	26.6	SC.....	314	7.1	7.4
CT.....	1,100	36.1	31.3	MN.....	1,200	25.4	23.4	SD.....	58	7.9	7.5
DE.....	131	10.1	15.5	MS.....	23	0.1	0.8	TN.....	1,539	14.4	25.8
DC.....	305	42.2	55.4	MO.....	1,082	24.6	18.6	TX.....	2,766	11.8	12.1
FL.....	4,367	26.1	24.5	MT.....	68	8.1	7.3	UT.....	646	21.3	26.1
GA.....	1,397	16.4	15.4	NE.....	138	5.3	7.9	VT.....	153	16.1	24.5
HI.....	596	37.4	46.8	NV.....	597	25.2	24.7	VA.....	1,477	22.2	19.5
ID.....	42	2.9	2.9	NH.....	281	21.9	21.5	WA.....	1,149	18.1	18.3
IL.....	1,940	15.7	15.2	NJ.....	2,131	25.0	24.4	WV.....	161	8.1	8.9
IN.....	1,614	22.5	25.7	NM.....	458	24.3	23.7	WI.....	1,456	26.8	26.3
IA	342	10.9	11.5	NY.....	5,302	24.0	27.5	WY	10	2.1	2.0
				NC.....	854	10.5	9.8				

-- Represents zero.

Source: HealthLeaders-InterStudy, Nashville, TN, *The Competitive Edge*, copyright). See also <http://www.interstudypublications.com/>.

Table 146. Health Insurance Coverage Status by Selected Characteristics: 2004 and 2005

[(291,166 represents 291,166,000). Persons as of following year for coverage in the year shown. Government health insurance includes Medicare, Medicaid, and military plans. Based on Current Population Survey, Annual Social and Economic Supplement; see text, Section 1, and Appendix III]

Characteristic	Number (1,000)								Percent			
		Covered by private or government health insurance					Not covered by health insurance		Covered by private or government health insurance			Not covered by health insurance
			Private		Government							
	Total persons	Total [1]	Total	Group health [2]	Medicare	Medicaid			Total [1]	Private	Medicaid	
2004, total [3,4]	291,166	247,669	200,924	176,247	39,703	37,955	43,498		85.1	69.0	13.0	14.9
2005 [3]	293,834	249,020	201,167	176,924	40,177	38,104	44,815		84.7	68.5	13.0	15.3
Age:												
Under 18 years	73,985	65,935	48,686	45,039	538	19,723	8,050		89.1	65.8	26.7	10.9
Under 6 years	24,400	21,856	14,989	14,088	210	7,690	2,544		89.6	61.4	31.5	10.4
6 to 11 years	23,671	21,333	15,763	14,803	165	6,397	2,338		90.1	66.6	27.0	9.9
12 to 17 years	25,914	22,745	17,934	16,148	163	5,636	3,169		87.8	69.2	21.8	12.2
18 to 24 years	27,965	19,765	16,733	13,526	186	3,289	8,201		70.7	59.8	11.8	29.3
25 to 34 years	39,480	29,320	25,751	23,927	541	3,449	10,161		74.3	65.2	8.7	25.7
35 to 44 years	43,121	35,220	31,903	29,747	885	3,087	7,901		81.7	74.0	7.2	18.3
45 to 54 years	42,797	36,570	33,114	30,651	1,591	2,837	6,227		85.5	77.4	6.6	14.5
55 to 64 years	30,981	27,154	23,543	21,092	2,708	2,325	3,826		87.6	76.0	7.5	12.4
65 years and over	35,505	35,056	21,437	12,942	33,727	3,394	449		98.7	60.4	9.6	1.3
Sex: Male	144,188	120,022	98,463	87,659	17,492	17,164	24,166		83.2	68.3	11.9	16.8
Female	149,647	128,998	102,704	89,265	22,685	20,940	20,648		86.2	68.6	14.0	13.8
Race: White alone [5]	235,903	201,957	167,430	146,365	34,326	25,968	33,946		85.6	71.0	11.0	14.4
Black alone [5]	36,965	29,959	19,950	18,263	4,108	9,154	7,006		81.0	54.0	24.8	19.0
Asian alone [5]	12,599	10,438	9,006	7,968	1,103	1,211	2,161		82.8	71.5	9.6	17.2
Hispanic origin [6]	43,168	29,214	19,252	17,597	2,771	9,357	13,954		67.7	44.6	21.7	32.3
Household income:												
Less than $25,000	59,598	45,146	20,219	12,992	16,840	19,619	14,452		75.8	33.9	32.9	24.2
$25,000-$49,999	72,865	58,214	44,846	37,696	12,378	10,768	14,651		79.9	61.5	14.8	20.1
$50,000-$74,999	59,048	51,223	46,029	42,156	5,284	4,352	7,826		86.7	78.0	7.4	13.3
$75,000 or more	102,323	94,437	90,074	84,080	5,675	3,365	7,886		92.3	88.0	3.3	7.7
Persons below poverty	36,950	25,625	8,795	5,649	5,129	15,730	11,325		69.4	23.8	42.6	30.6

[1] Includes other government insurance, not shown separately. Persons with coverage counted only once in total, even though they may have been covered by more than one type of policy. [2] Related to employment of self or other family members. [3] The estimates are revised from the originally published data. [4] Estimates reflect results of follow-up verification questions. [5] Refers to people who reported specified race and did not report any other race category. [6] Persons of Hispanic origin may be any race.

Source: U.S. Census Bureau, Current Population Reports; P60-231, and Table HI01 Health Insurance Data, Health Insurance Coverage Status and Type of Coverage by Selected Characteristics: 2005. Table HI02. Health Insurance Coverage Status and Type of Coverage by Selected Characteristics for People in the Poverty Universe: 2005; published August 2006; <http://www.census.gov/hhes/www/hlthins/hlthin05.html>.

Table 147. Persons With and Without Health Insurance Coverage by State: 2005

[249,020 represents 249,020,000. Based on the Current Population Survey, Annual Social and Economic Supplement, see text, Section 1, and Appendix III]

State	Total persons covered (1,000)	Total persons not covered		Children not covered		State	Total persons covered (1,000)	Total persons not covered		Children not covered	
		Number (1,000)	Percent of total	Number (1,000)	Percent of total			Number (1,000)	Percent of total	Number (1,000)	Percent of total
U.S. [1]	249,020	44,815	15.3	8,050	10.9	MO	5,041	668	11.7	104	7.5
AL	3,867	657	14.5	49	4.5	MT	783	145	15.6	30	14.2
AK	545	113	17.2	16	8.4	NE	1,581	185	10.5	23	5.3
AZ	4,864	1,183	19.6	267	16.4	NV	2,030	418	17.1	93	14.3
AR	2,277	482	17.5	72	10.7	NH	1,175	126	9.7	16	5.3
CA	29,182	6,757	18.8	1,309	13.4	NJ	7,460	1,265	14.5	228	10.5
CO	3,869	772	16.6	163	13.7	NM	1,545	393	20.3	99	20.0
CT	3,106	381	10.9	64	7.7	NY	16,548	2,474	13.0	347	7.7
DE	742	103	12.2	23	11.9	NC	7,249	1,312	15.3	259	11.7
DC	468	71	13.2	7	6.3	ND	558	69	11.0	13	8.9
FL	14,270	3,616	20.2	731	18.1	OH	10,046	1,288	11.4	207	7.6
GA	7,391	1,654	18.3	260	11.0	OK	2,878	627	17.9	95	11.0
HI	1,169	110	8.6	16	5.3	OR	3,062	566	15.6	91	10.4
ID	1,229	213	14.8	45	11.4	PA	11,085	1,196	9.7	209	7.4
IL	10,878	1,730	13.7	329	10.1	RI	932	122	11.5	19	7.6
IN	5,308	832	13.6	158	9.8	SC	3,459	721	17.3	104	10.2
IA	2,668	241	8.3	34	5.0	SD	679	90	11.7	15	8.1
KS	2,417	278	10.3	43	6.2	TN	5,069	798	13.6	127	9.1
KY	3,554	498	12.3	67	6.7	TX	17,426	5,394	23.6	1,224	18.9
LA	3,363	725	17.7	89	8.4	UT	2,110	414	16.4	94	12.3
ME	1,185	136	10.3	21	7.7	VT	550	72	11.5	7	5.3
MD	4,823	746	13.4	115	8.3	VA	6,503	951	12.8	156	8.5
MA	5,745	583	9.2	63	4.2	WA	5,422	828	13.3	133	8.7
MI	8,949	1,033	10.3	128	5.0	WV	1,495	304	16.9	26	6.6
MN	4,722	408	7.9	73	5.9	WI	4,938	509	9.3	90	6.9
MS	2,370	483	16.9	85	11.3	WY	436	75	14.6	13	10.8

[1] The estimates are revised from the originally published data.
Source: U.S. Census Bureau, Current Population Reports; P60-231, and Table HI05. Health Insurance Coverage Status and Type of Coverage by State for All People: 2005 <http://www.census.gov/hhes/www/hlthins/hlthin05.html>.

Health and Nutrition 107

Table 148. People Without Health Insurance for the Entire Year by Selected Characteristics: 2004 and 2005

[In thousands, except as noted (291,166 represents 291,166,000). Based on the Current Population Survey; Annual Social and Economic Supplement (ASEC); see text, Section 1 and Appendix III]

Characteristic	2004			2005		
	Total persons	Uninsured persons		Total persons	Uninsured persons	
		Number	Percent distribution		Number	Percent distribution
Total [1, 2]	291,166	43,498	100.0	293,834	44,815	100.0
Under 18 years	73,791	7,721	17.8	73,985	8,050	18.0
18 to 24 years	28,008	8,247	19.0	27,965	8,201	18.3
25 to 34 years	39,310	9,766	22.5	39,480	10,161	22.7
35 to 44 years	43,351	7,904	18.2	43,121	7,901	17.6
45 to 64 years	71,497	9,405	21.6	73,778	10,053	22.4
65 years and over	35,209	454	1.0	35,505	449	1.0
Male	142,757	23,556	54.2	144,188	24,166	53.9
Female	148,409	19,941	45.8	149,647	20,648	46.1
White alone [3]	234,116	33,022	75.9	235,903	33,946	75.7
White alone or in combination	238,920	33,813	77.7	240,909	34,750	77.5
Black alone [3]	36,548	6,864	15.8	36,965	7,006	15.6
Black alone or in combination	38,179	7,103	16.3	38,729	7,239	16.2
Asian alone [3]	12,241	1,900	4.4	12,599	2,161	4.8
Asian alone or in combination	13,307	2,031	4.7	13,758	2,286	5.1
Hispanic [4]	41,840	13,313	30.6	43,168	13,954	31.1
White alone, not Hispanic	195,347	20,554	47.3	195,893	20,909	46.7

[1] Includes other races not shown separately. [2] The estimates are revised from the originally published data. [3] Refers to people who reported specified race and did not report any other race category. [4] Persons of Hispanic origin may be of any race.

Source: U.S. Census Bureau, Current Population Reports, P60-231, and Table HI01. *Health Insurance Coverage Status and Type of Coverage by Selected Characteristics: 2005*. See also <http://www.census.gov/hhes/www/hlthins/hlthin05.html>.

Table 149. Percent of Workers Participating in Health Care Benefit Programs and Percent of Participants Required to Contribute: 2006

[Based on National Compensation Survey, a sample survey of 10,370 private industry establishments of all sizes, representing about 103 million workers; see Appendix III. See also Table 634]

Characteristic	Percent of workers participating—				Single coverage medical care		Family coverage medical care	
	Medical care	Dental care	Vision care	Outpatient prescrip-tion drug coverage	Employee contri-butions required (percent)	Average monthly contri-bution [1] (dol.)	Employee contri-butions required (percent)	Average monthly contri-bution [1] (dol.)
Total	52	36	22	49	75	76.05	87	296.88
White-collar occupations	57	41	24	54	80	76.69	91	303.36
Blue-collar occupations	60	38	25	57	67	73.20	80	279.03
Service occupations	27	18	13	27	80	80.41	91	311.79
Full-time [2]	64	44	26	60	75	75.39	87	294.46
Part-time [2]	13	10	7	12	79	86.75	88	339.90
Union [3]	80	63	48	77	51	57.28	60	196.60
Nonunion	49	33	19	46	80	78.34	92	308.88

[1] The average is presented for all covered workers and excludes workers without the plan provision. Averages are for plans stating a flat monthly cost. [2] Employees are classified as working either a full-time or part-time schedule based on the definition used by each establishment. [3] Union workers are those whose wages are determined through collective bargaining.

Source: U.S. Bureau of Labor Statistics, *National Compensation Survey: Employee Benefits in Private Industry in the United States, March, 2006*. See also <http://www.bls.gov/ncs/ebs/sp/ebsm0004.pdf>.

Table 150. **Medical Care Benefits of Workers by Type and Amount of Employee Contribution: 2006**

[In percent. See headnote, Table 149]

Type and amount of contribution	Individual coverage				Type and amount of contribution	Family coverage			
	All employees	White-collar occupations	Blue-collar occupations	Service occupations		All employees	White-collar occupations,	Blue-collar occupations,	Service occupations
Total with contributory coverage	100	100	100	100	Total with contributory coverage	100	100	100	100
Flat monthly amount	76	76	77	72	Flat monthly amount	77	76	80	73
Less than $5.00	(Z)	(Z)	(Z)	1	Less than $25.00	1	1	1	1
$5.00–$9.99	1	1	1	1	$25.00–$49.99	3	2	3	5
$10.00–$14.99	2	1	2	2	$50.00–$74.99	2	2	3	1
$15.00–$19.99	2	1	2	3	$75.00–$99.99	3	4	3	3
$20.00–$29.99	5	6	5	4	$100.00–$124.99	3	3	4	2
$30.00–$39.99	7	7	8	5	$125.00–$149.99	4	4	5	2
$40.00–$49.99	7	7	7	9	$150.00–$174.99	5	5	6	4
$50.00–$59.99	9	9	10	6	$175.00–$199.99	6	6	7	6
$60.00–$69.99	8	8	8	8	$200.00–$224.99	6	5	5	8
$70.00–$79.99	6	6	7	6	$225.00–$249.99	4	4	5	3
$80.00–$89.99	7	7	6	7	$250.00–$274.99	5	6	4	3
$90.00–$99.99	5	5	5	3	$275.00–$299.99	4	4	4	3
$100.00–$124.99	8	8	8	6	$300.00–$324.99	4	4	5	3
$125.00 or more	9	10	9	11	$325.00–$349.99	2	3	2	3
					$350.00 or more	23	24	22	25
Composite rate [1]	1	1	(Z)	(Z)	Composite rate [1]	1	1	(Z)	(Z)
Varies [2]	5	5	4	5	Varies [2]	5	5	4	4
Flexible benefits [3]	1	1	1	1	Flexible benefits [3]	1	1	1	1
Percent of earnings	(Z)	(Z)	(Z)	1	Percent of earnings	(Z)	(Z)	(Z)	1
Exists, but unknown	15	14	15	20	Exists, but unknown	15	15	14	19
Other	2	1	2	1	Other	1	1	2	2

Z Less than 0.5 percent.   [1] A composite rate is a set contribution covering more than one benefit area; for example, health care and life insurance. Cost data for individual plans cannot be determined.   [2] Based on worker attributes. For example, employee contributions may vary based on earnings, length of service, or age.   [3] Amount varies by options selected under a cafeteria plan or employer–sponsored reimbursement account.

Source: U.S. Bureau of Labor Statistics, *National Compensation Survey: Employee Benefits in Private Industry in the United States, March, 2006.* See also <http://www.bls.gov/ncs/ebs/sp/ebsm0004.pdf>.

Table 151. **Annual Receipts/Revenue for Health Care Industries: 2000 to 2005**

[In millions of dollars (1,033,029 represents $1,033,029,000,000). Based on the North American Industry Classification System, 2002 (NAICS); see text, Section 15. All firms in NAICS 6211, 6212, 6213, and 6215 are defined as taxable. Estimates for the nonemployer portion are derived from administrative records data provided by other federal agencies. These data are available only at the total revenue level. See Appendix III]

Selected kind of business	2002 NAICS code	Total, all firms [1]			Taxable employer firms		
		2000	2004	2005	2000	2004	2005
Health care and social assistance	62	1,033,029	1,379,523	1,477,951	500,932	681,110	732,378
Ambulatory health care services [2]	621	419,402	568,247	611,544	376,095	512,426	551,755
Offices of physicians	6211	213,806	290,768	311,215	213,806	290,768	311,215
Offices of dentists	6212	60,931	78,871	83,889	60,931	78,871	83,889
Offices of other health practitioners	6213	32,037	42,917	45,312	32,037	42,917	45,312
Offices of chiropractors	62131	7,570	9,624	9,877	7,570	9,624	9,877
Offices of optometrists	62132	7,639	9,318	9,858	7,639	9,318	9,858
Offices of mental health practitioners	62133	3,516	3,854	4,062	3,516	3,854	4,062
Offices of PT/OT/speech therapy & audiology [3]	62134	8,486	13,396	14,368	8,486	13,396	14,368
Outpatient care centers	6214	(S)	63,557	69,445	(S)	29,176	32,473
Medical & diagnostic laboratories	6215	23,450	32,413	34,940	23,450	32,413	34,940
Home health care services	6216	26,841	38,311	43,227	16,879	25,477	29,475
Other ambulatory health care services	6219	15,565	21,410	23,516	9,421	12,804	14,451
Hospitals [2]	622	423,889	569,463	610,517	42,908	65,473	70,650
General medical & surgical hospitals	6221	397,526	533,848	572,816	36,926	54,275	58,715
Psychiatric & substance abuse hospitals	6222	13,422	13,363	13,602	2,189	2,002	2,007
Other specialty hospitals	6223	12,941	22,252	24,099	3,793	9,196	9,928
Nursing and residential care facilities [2]	623	112,706	138,068	146,629	66,245	80,827	86,017
Nursing care facilities	6231	67,238	79,961	84,291	49,816	58,738	61,981
Residential mental retardation/health facilities	6232	16,718	21,602	22,814	4,726	6,143	6,567
Residential mental retardation facilities	62321	11,570	14,703	15,594	3,297	4,298	4,569
Community care facilities for the elderly	6233	22,104	28,333	30,986	10,812	14,822	16,254
Continuing care retirement communities	623311	12,948	16,344	18,011	3,576	5,212	5,771
Homes for the elderly	623312	9,156	11,989	12,975	7,236	9,610	10,483
Other residential care facilities	6239	6,646	8,172	8,538	891	1,124	1,215
Social assistance [2]	624	77,032	103,745	109,261	15,684	22,384	23,956
Community food and housing, and emergency and other relief services	6242	12,281	16,593	18,796	46	101	113
Individual and family services	6241	37,311	50,177	51,737	3,824	6,295	6,894
Vocational rehabilitation services	6243	9,458	13,025	13,546	1,593	2,250	2,424
Child day care services	6244	17,982	23,950	25,182	10,221	13,738	14,525

S Figure does not meet publication standards.   [1] Includes taxable nonemployer firms, not shown separately.   [2] Includes other kinds of business not shown separately.   [3] Offices of physical, occupational, and speech therapists, and audiologists.

Source: U.S. Census Bureau, Current Business Reports, *Service Annual Survey, 2005.* <http://www.census.gov/econ/www/servmenu.html>.

Table 152. Receipts for Selected Health Service Industries by Source of Revenue: 2000 and 2005

[In millions of dollars (213,808 represents $213,808,000,000). Based on the 2002 North American Industry Classification System (NAICS), see text, Section 15. Based on a sample of taxable employer firms only and does not include nonemployer revenue. See Appendix III]

Source of revenue	Offices of physicians (NAICS 6211)		Offices of dentists (NAICS 6212)		Hospitals (NAICS 622)		Nursing and residential care facilities (NAICS 623)	
	2000	2005	2000	2005	2000	2005	2000	2005
Total.	213,808	311,215	59,463	83,559	423,889	610,517	112,678	146,334
Medicare.	51,030	76,916	(S)	616	137,322	186,556	13,130	23,315
Medicaid.	14,624	19,560	1,467	3,504	51,049	72,219	45,956	56,434
Other government [1].	2,123	4,105	(S)	(S)	21,918	35,725	8,041	12,404
Workers' compensation	7,833	8,107	(S)	114	4,673	6,326	(S)	(S)
Private insurance	102,472	151,075	31,321	42,599	153,428	230,003	6,400	6,532
Patient (out-of-pocket) . . . . [3].	23,977	30,890	26,675	36,002	22,525	33,048	[2]28,178	[2]35,591
Other patient care sources, n.e.c [3]. . .	7,695	11,714	(S)	724	10,404	15,880	3,563	2,835
Nonpatient care revenue	4,054	8,848	(S)	(S)	22,570	30,760	7,410	9,223

S Figure does not meet publication standards. [1] Veterans, National Institute of Health, Indian Affairs, etc. [2] Represents payment from patients and their families plus patients' assigned social security benefits. [3] n.e.c. represents not elsewhere classified.

Source: U.S. Census Bureau, Current Business Reports, *Service Annual Survey, 2005*. <http://www.census.gov/econ/www/servmenu.html>.

Table 153. Employment in the Health Service Industries: 1990 to 2006

[In thousands (9,296 represents 9,296,000). See headnote, Table 614. Based on the North American Industry Classification System 2002 code; see text, Section 15]

Industry	2002 NAICS code	1990	1995	2000	2002	2003	2004	2005	2006
Health care and social assistance [1]	62	9,296	11,278	12,718	13,556	13,893	14,190	14,536	14,920
Ambulatory health care services [1]	621	2,842	3,768	4,320	4,633	4,786	4,952	5,114	5,283
Offices of physicians	6211	1,278	1,540	1,840	1,968	2,003	2,048	2,094	2,154
Offices of dentists	6212	513	592	688	725	744	760	774	784
Offices of other health practitioners	6213	276	395	438	486	503	527	549	571
Medical and diagnostic laboratories	6215	129	146	162	175	182	190	198	202
Home health care services	6216	288	622	633	680	733	777	821	867
Hospitals [1]	622	3,513	3,734	3,954	4,160	4,245	4,285	4,345	4,427
General medical and surgical hospitals	6221	3,305	3,520	3,745	3,930	4,005	4,042	4,096	4,167
Psychiatric and substance abuse hospitals . .	6222	113	101	86	90	92	92	93	98
Other hospitals	6223	95	112	123	140	148	151	156	162
Nursing and residential care facilities [1]	623	1,856	2,308	2,583	2,743	2,786	2.818	2,855	2,901
Nursing care facilities.	6231	1,170	1,413	1,514	1,573	1,580	1,577	1,577	1,584

[1] Includes other industries not shown separately.

Source: U.S. Bureau of Labor Statistics, *Employment and Earnings*, March issues. See also <http://stats.bls.gov/ces/home.htm>.

Table 154. Active Physicians–2005 and Nurses–2004, by State

[As of December. Excludes doctors of osteopathy, physicians with addresses unknown, and inactive status. Includes all physicians not classified according to activity status]

State	Physicians Total	Physicians Rate [1]	Nurses Total	Nurses Rate [1]	State	Physicians Total	Physicians Rate [1]	Nurses Total	Nurses Rate [1]
United States. .	790,128	266	2,421,000	824	Missouri	13,965	241	57,400	997
Alabama.	9,786	215	36,500	807	Montana	2,084	223	7,900	852
Alaska	1,515	228	6,800	1,034	Nebraska	4,209	239	18,500	1,059
Arizona.	12,503	210	39,100	681	Nevada	4,519	187	14,100	604
Arkansas	5,619	202	20,100	731	New Hampshire	3,440	263	13,600	1,047
California	94,341	261	211,600	590	New Jersey	26,918	309	73,000	841
Colorado.	12,101	259	34,700	754	New Mexico	4,622	240	13,600	715
Connecticut.	12,780	365	32,700	935	New York	74,945	388	174,200	903
Delaware	2,090	248	8,600	1,036	North Carolina	21,972	253	76,800	899
District of Columbia .	4,483	770	11,600	2,093	North Dakota.	1,523	240	7,500	1,179
Florida	43,314	244	132,800	764	Ohio	30,096	262	112,800	985
Georgia	19,997	219	66,500	746	Oklahoma.	6,041	170	24,400	692
Hawaii	3,964	311	9 300	737	Oregon.	9,684	266	30.900	860
Idaho	2,429	170	8,800	631	Pennsylvania.	36,429	294	127,000	1,025
Illinois	34,826	273	113,800	895	Rhode Island.	3,866	360	11,400	1,056
Indiana.	13,448	215	54,600	877	South Carolina	9,769	230	30,700	731
Iowa	5,503	186	32,700	1,107	South Dakota	1,698	219	9,300	1,207
Kansas	6,070	221	24,900	911	Tennessee	15,683	263	54,300	921
Kentucky	9,608	230	37,600	908	Texas.	48,776	213	145,300	647
Louisiana	11,481	255	35,400	785	Utah	5,221	210	15,800	653
Maine.	3,520	267	15,100	1,148	Vermont	2,269	365	6,400	1,030
Maryland	23,128	414	47,100	847	Virginia.	20.461	270	56,700	758
Massachusetts.	29,343	456	75,400	1,177	Washington	16,707	266	48,400	780
Michigan.	24,387	241	85,000	841	West Virginia	4,190	231	16,000	883
Minnesota.	14,595	285	51,900	1,018	Wisconsin	14,093	255	51,700	939
Mississippi	5,168	178	24,000	827	Wyoming	949	187	4,100	810

[1] Per 100,000 resident population. Based on U.S. Census Bureau estimates as of July 1.

Source: Physicians: American Medical Association, Chicago, IL, *Physician Characteristics and Distribution in the U.S.*, annual (copyright); Nurses: U.S. Dept. of Health and Human Services, Health Resources and Services Administration, unpublished data.

Table 155. Physicians by Sex and Specialty: 1980 to 2005

[In thousands (467.7 represents 467,700). As of Dec. 31, except 1990 as of Jan. 1, and as noted. Includes Puerto Rico and island areas]

Activity	1980 Total	1980 Office-based	1990 Total	1990 Office-based	2000 Total	2000 Office-based	2005 Total	2005 Office-based
Doctors of medicine, total [1]	467.7	272.0	615.4	361.0	813.8	490.4	902.1	563.2
Place of medical education:								
U.S. medical graduates	370.0	226.2	483.7	286.2	616.8	376.5	661.3	426.3
International medical graduates [2]	97.7	45.8	131.8	74.8	197.0	113.9	228.7	137.0
Sex: Male	413.4	251.4	511.2	311.7	618.2	382.3	657.1	413.1
Female	54.3	20.6	104.2	49.2	195.5	108.1	244.9	150.1
Allergy/immunology	1.5	1.4	3.4	2.5	4.0	3.1	4.1	3.2
Anesthesiology	16.0	11.3	26.0	17.8	35.7	27.6	40.5	31.9
Cardiovascular diseases	9.8	6.7	15.9	10.7	21.0	16.3	22.3	17.5
Child psychiatry	3.3	2.0	4.3	2.6	6.2	4.3	7.2	5.4
Dermatology	5.7	4.4	7.6	6.0	9.7	8.0	10.6	8.8
Diagnostic radiology	7.0	4.2	15.4	9.8	21.1	14.6	24.2	17.6
Emergency medicine	5.7	3.4	14.2	8.4	23.1	14.5	29.1	20.2
Family practice	27.5	18.4	47.6	37.5	71.6	54.2	81.7	65.7
Gastroenterology	4.0	2.7	7.5	5.2	10.6	8.5	12.0	9.7
General practice	32.5	29.6	22.8	20.5	15.2	13.0	11.0	9.3
General surgery	34.0	22.4	38.4	24.5	36.7	24.5	38.0	26.2
Internal medicine	71.5	40.6	98.3	58.0	134.5	89.7	154.0	107.0
Neurology	5.7	3.3	9.2	5.6	12.3	8.6	14.3	10.4
Neurological surgery	3.3	2.5	4.4	3.1	5.0	3.7	5.4	4.2
Obstetrics and gynecology	26.3	19.5	33.7	25.5	40.2	31.7	42.6	34.7
Ophthalmology	13.0	10.6	16.1	13.1	18.1	15.6	18.9	16.6
Orthopedic surgery	14.0	10.7	19.1	14.2	22.3	17.4	24.1	19.1
Otolaryngology	6.6	5.3	8.1	6.4	9.4	7.6	9.9	8.2
Pathology	13.6	6.1	16.6	7.5	18.8	10.6	20.0	12.2
Pediatrics	29.5	18.2	41.9	27.1	63.9	43.2	74.1	53.1
Physical med./rehab.	2.1	1.0	4.1	2.2	6.5	4.3	7.7	5.6
Plastic surgery	3.0	2.4	4.6	3.8	6.2	5.3	7.0	6.0
Psychiatry	27.5	16.0	35.2	20.1	39.5	25.0	41.6	27.6
Pulmonary diseases	3.7	2.0	6.1	3.7	8.7	5.9	10.1	7.3
Radiology	11.7	7.8	8.5	6.1	8.7	6.7	8.8	7.0
Radiation oncology	1.6	1.0	2.8	2.0	3.9	3.0	4.4	3.5
Urological surgery	7.7	6.2	9.4	7.4	10.3	8.5	10.7	9.0
Doctors of Osteopathy [3]	18.8	(X)	30.9	(X)	44.9	(X)	56.5	29.5

X Not applicable. [1] Includes other activities and categories not shown. [2] International medical graduates received their medical education in schools outside the United States and Canada. [3] Total number of DOs as of June 1. This number includes all living DOs, including retired DOs, DOs in postdoctoral training and federally employed DOs. Data from American Osteopathic Association Fact Sheet, American Osteopathic Association, Chicago, IL. <http://www.osteopathic.org/index.cfm?PageID=aoaannualrprt>.
Source: Except as noted, American Medical Association, Chicago, IL, Physician Characteristics and Distribution in the U.S. annual (copyright).

Table 156. Percent Distribution of Number of Visits to Health Care Professionals by Selected Characteristics: 2000 and 2005

[Covers ambulatory visits to doctor's offices and emergency departments, and home health care visits during a 12-month period. Based on the National Health Interview Survey, a sample survey of the civilian noninstitutionalized population. See Appendix III]

Characteristic	None 2000	None 2005	1–3 visits 2000	1–3 visits 2005	4–9 visits 2000	4–9 visits 2005	10 or more visits 2000	10 or more visits 2005
All persons [1, 2]	16.6	15.6	45.4	46.2	24.7	24.6	13.3	13.7
AGE								
Under 18 years old	12.2	10.2	53.7	56.3	26.4	26.1	7.7	7.4
18 to 44 years old	23.2	23.1	45.3	46.0	19.2	18.8	12.2	12.1
45 to 64 years old	15.0	14.1	43.4	43.1	25.7	26.4	15.8	16.4
65 to 74 years old	9.0	6.0	34.5	34.8	34.4	35.1	22.1	24.1
75 years old and over	5.8	5.3	29.3	26.9	39.3	38.5	25.6	29.2
SEX [2]								
Male	21.5	20.4	46.0	46.9	22.4	21.9	10.1	10.8
Female	11.9	10.8	44.8	45.5	27.0	27.3	16.4	16.4
RACE [2, 3]								
Race alone:								
White	16.0	15.2	45.1	46.0	25.3	24.9	13.7	14.0
Black or African American	17.3	16.0	46.7	47.5	23.4	23.6	12.6	12.9
American Indian or Alaska Native	21.2	20.5	42.9	36.6	20.0	29.4	15.8	13.4
Asian	20.2	21.6	49.2	49.5	20.9	20.5	9.7	8.5
Two or more races	12.1	15.6	41.6	37.9	28.3	26.7	17.9	19.9
HISPANIC ORIGIN AND RACE [2, 3, 4]								
Hispanic or Latino	26.5	24.0	41.8	42.4	20.0	21.7	11.7	11.9
Mexican	30.7	26.7	40.9	41.7	18.0	20.5	10.4	11.1
Not Hispanic or Latino	15.2	13.9	45.9	46.8	25.3	25.2	13.6	14.0
White, non-Hispanic	14.5	13.1	45.4	46.7	26.0	25.7	14.1	14.6
Black, non-Hispanic	17.2	16.0	46.9	47.5	23.4	23.6	12.6	12.9

[1] Includes other categories not shown separately. [2] Estimates are age adjusted to the year 2000 standard using six age groups: Under 18 years, 18–44 years, 45–54 years, 55–64 years, 65–74 years, and 75 years and over. [3] Estimates by race and Hispanic origin are tabulated using the 1997 standards for federal data on race and ethnicity. Estimates for specific race groups are shown when they meet requirements for statistical reliability and confidentiality. The categories "White only," "Black or African American only," "American Indian and Alaska Native (AI/AN) only," and "Asian only" include persons who reported only one racial group; and the category "2 or more races" includes persons who reported more than one of the five racial groups in the 1997 standards or one of the five racial groups and "Some other race." [4] Persons of Hispanic or Latino origin may be of any race or combination of races.
Source: U.S. National Center for Health Statistics, Health, United States, annual. See also <www.cdc.gov/nchs/hus.htm>.

Table 157. **Ambulatory Care Visits to Physicians' Offices and Hospital Outpatient and Emergency Departments: 2005**

[1,169.3 represents 1,169,300,000. Based on the annual National Ambulatory Medical Care Survey and National Hospital Ambulatory Medical Care Survey and subject to sampling error; see source for details]

Characteristic	Number of visits (mil.)				Visits per 100 persons			
	Total	Physician offices	Outpatient dept.	Emergency dept.	Total	Physician offices	Outpatient dept.	Emergency dept.
Total	1,169.3	963.6	90.4	115.3	401.6	331.0	31.1	39.6
Age:								
Under 15 years old	206.2	160.6	21.1	24.5	339.9	264.7	34.8	40.4
15 to 24 years old.	99.7	70.6	10.4	18.7	243.0	172.1	25.4	45.5
25 to 44 years old.	256.7	201.6	21.8	33.2	313.0	245.9	26.6	40.5
45 to 64 years old.	328.6	283.2	23.2	22.2	454.2	[1]391.5	32.1	30.7
65 to 74 years old.	133.3	119.1	7.5	6.8	724.8	647.2	40.9	36.7
75 years old and over	144.9	128.6	6.3	10.0	865.1	767.7	37.9	59.5
Sex:								
Male.	491.6	403.3	35.1	53.2	345.1	283.1	24.7	37.4
Female	677.7	560.4	55.3	62.1	455.7	376.8	37.2	41.8
Race:								
White	984.4	832.0	66.2	86.2	420.4	355.3	28.3	36.8
Black/African American	134.9	88.9	20.8	25.2	369.2	243.4	56.8	69.0
Asian	37.6	33.3	2.2	2.2	298.2	263.6	17.3	17.2
Native Hawaiian/Other Pacific Islander	[1]4.5	[1]3.5	[1]0.4	[1]0.6	[1]881.9	[1]693.4	[1]68.4	[1]120.1
American Indian/Alaska Native	4.3	3.1	0.5	0.8	153.7	108.4	17.3	28.0
More than one race reported.	3.6	2.8	0.4	[1]0.4	79.2	62.4	8.4	[1]8.4
Primary source of payment:								
Private insurance	598.1	524.9	33.7	39.6	(X)	(X)	(X)	(X)
Medicare	241.4	212.7	12.7	16.0	(X)	(X)	(X)	(X)
Medicaid	167.4	108.6	30.2	28.7	(X)	(X)	(X)	(X)
Workers' compensation	12.6	9.9	0.8	1.9	(X)	(X)	(X)	(X)
Self pay	63.1	39.2	5.3	18.6	(X)	(X)	(X)	(X)
No charge	6.6	[1]4.4	[1]1.3	0.9	(X)	(X)	(X)	(X)
Other	21.6	17.6	1.8	2.2	(X)	(X)	(X)	(X)
Unknown.	58.5	46.4	4.6	7.5	(X)	(X)	(X)	(X)

X Not applicable.   [1] Figures do not meet standard of reliability or precision.

Source: U.S. National Center for Health Statistics, *Advance Data*, Nos. 386, 387, and 389; June 29, 2007; <http://www.cdc.gov/nchs/namcs.htm>.

Table 158. **Visits to Office-Based Physicians and Hospital Outpatient Departments by Diagnosis: 2000 and 2005**

[369.0 represents 369,000,000. See headnote, Table 157]

Leading diagnosis [1]	Number (mil.)		Rate per 1,000 persons [2]		Leading diagnosis [1]	Number (mil.)		Rate per 1,000 persons [2]	
	2000	2005	2000	2005		2000	2005	2000	2005
MALE					**FEMALE**				
All ages	369.0	438.4	2,760	3,078	All ages	537.8	615.6	3,829	4,140
					Under 15 years old [3].	75.4	82.9	2,556	2,798
Under 15 years old [3]	85.3	98.8	2,765	3,184	Routine infant or child				
Routine infant or child					health check.	17.5	19.1	593	644
health check	17.9	23.3	580	750	Acute respiratory infections [4]. .	8.1	8.8	276	297
Acute respiratory infections [4] . .	8.5	9.8	276	316	Otitis media and Eustachian				
Otitis media and Eustachian					tube disorders.	6.6	5.4	222	183
tube disorders.	7.1	6.9	231	221	Acute pharyngitis.	2.3	2.9	78	97
Asthma.	3.1	3.7	101	120	Unspecified viral and				
Attention deficit disorder	3.4	3.5	110	112	chlamydial infection	1.7	2.4	59	81
					15 to 44 years old [3]	194.8	196.4	3,199	3,183
15 to 44 years old [3]	98.9	108.0	1,660	1,762	Normal pregnancy	24.5	18.1	402	294
Acute respiratory infections [4] . .	3.6	4.4	60	72	Gynecological examination . . .	6.1	8.9	100	144
Spinal disorders	3.0	4.4	50	72	Complications of pregnancy,				
General medical examination. .	3.9	4.4	66	72	childbirth, & the puerperium. .	6.2	6.9	102	112
Arthropathies and related					Acute upper respiratory				
disorders	2.8	3.7	47	61	infections [4]	6.0	5.2	98	85
Rheumatism, excluding back . .	3.3	3.5	55	57	General medical examination. .	6.6	5.0	108	81
					45 to 64 years old [3]	141.0	180.3	4,511	4,847
45 to 64 years old [3]	96.5	126.0	3,294	3,588	Essential hypertension	8.3	10.7	264	288
Essential hypertension	6.8	10.8	233	307	Arthropathies and related				
Diabetes mellitus	5.8	6.9	199	198	disorders	6.6	10.4	212	280
Arthropathies and related					Malignant neoplasms	5.7	7.2	184	194
disorders	2.9	4.3	99	122	Gynecological examination . . .	3.1	6.2	100	168
Spinal disorders	3.1	4.0	106	113	Spinal disorders	4.1	5.7	130	153
Malignant neoplasms	2.7	3.7	93	105	65 years old and over [3]	126.6	156.0	6,736	7,731
65 years old and over [3]	88.2	105.5	6,340	7,050	Essential hypertension	11.8	13.2	628	653
Malignant neoplasms	7.1	7.9	507	525	Arthropathies and related				
Essential hypertension	6.6	7.5	478	500	disorders	6.3	9.3	333	459
Diabetes mellitus	4.8	4.5	344	300	Malignant neoplasms	5.9	8.2	312	408
Heart disease, excluding					Diabetes mellitus.	6.0	7.8	318	387
ischemic.	4.1	3.8	296	254	Heart disease, excluding				
Ischemic heart disease.	4.9	3.7	349	244	ischemic.	3.6	4.6	194	229

[1] Based on the International Classification of Diseases, 9th Revision, clinical modification, (ICD-9-CM).   [2] Based on U.S. Census Bureau estimated civilian population as of July 1.   [3] Includes other first-listed diagnoses, not shown separately.   [4] Excluding pharyngitis.

Source: U.S. National Center for Health Statistics, unpublished data. Nos. 387 and 389; June 29, 2007; <http://www.cdc.gov/nchs/namcs.htm>.

Table 159. Visits to Hospital Emergency Departments by Diagnosis: 2005

[53,213 represents 53,213,000. See headnote, Table 157]

Leading diagnosis [1]	Number (1,000)	Rate per 1,000 persons [2]	Leading diagnosis [1]	Number (1,000)	Rate per 1,000 persons [2]
MALE			**FEMALE**		
			All ages	**62,109**	**418**
All ages	**53,213**	**374**	Under 15 years old [3]	11,149	376
			Acute respiratory infections [4]	1,112	38
Under 15 years old [3]	13,349	430	Otitis media and Eustachian		
Acute upper respiratory infections [4]	1,326	43	tube disorders	877	30
Otitis media and Eustachian			Pyrexia of unknown origin	519	18
tube disorders	875	28	Contusions with intact skin surfaces	450	15
Contusions with intact skin surfaces	677	22	Unspecified viral and		
Pyrexia of unknown origin	647	21	chlamydial infection	440	15
Open wound of head	625	20	15 to 44 years old [3]	29,244	474
15 to 44 years old [3]	22,670	370	Abdominal pain	1,781	29
Open wound, excluding head	1,390	23	Complications of pregnancy,		
Contusions with intact skin surfaces	1,156	19	childbirth, and the puerperium	1,382	22
Chest pain	870	14	Contusions with intact skin surfaces	1,163	19
Spinal disorders	855	14	Sprains and strains of neck and back	942	15
Sprains and strains of neck and back	789	13	Chest pain	894	14
45 to 64 years old [3]	10,030	285	45 to 64 years old [3]	12,152	327
Chest pain	709	20	Chest pain	939	25
Open wound, excluding head	545	16	Abdominal pain	564	15
Abdominal pain	396	11	Contusion with intact skin surface	469	13
Spinal disorders	360	10	Spinal disorders	446	12
Cellulitis and abscess	354	10	Migraine	325	9
65 years old and over [3]	7,166	479	65 years old and over [3]	9,565	474
Heart disease, excluding ischemic	518	35	Chest pain	558	28
Chest pain	350	23	Contusion with intact skin surface	485	24
Pneumonia	266	18	Heart disease, excluding ischemic	465	23
Contusion with intact skin surface	223	15	Abdominal pain	409	20
Abdominal pain	205	14	Urinary tract infection, site not specified	331	16

[1] Based on the International Classification of Diseases, 9th Revision, Clinical Modification (ICD-9-CM).   [2] Based on U.S. Census Bureau estimated civilian noninstitutional population as of July 1.   [3] Includes other first-listed diagnoses, not shown separately.   [4] Excluding pharyngitis.

Source: U.S. National Center for Health Statistics, Advance Data, No. 386, June 29, 2007. <http://www.cdc.gov/nchs/namcs.htm>.

Table 160. Procedures for Inpatients Discharged From Short-Stay Hospitals: 1990 to 2005

[23,051 represents 23,051,000. Procedure categories are based on the International Classification of Diseases, Ninth Revision, Clinical Modification. See headnote, Table 167]

Sex and type of procedure	Number of procedures (1,000)				Rate per 1,000 population [1]			
	1990	1995	2000	2005	1990	1995	2000	2005
Surgical procedures, total [2]	**23,051**	**22,530**	**23,244**	**26,564**	**92.4**	**86.2**	**83.6**	**90.0**
Removal of coronary artery obstruction [3]	285	434	1,025	1,271	1.2	1.7	3.7	4.3
Cesarean section	945	785	855	1,262	3.8	3.0	3.1	4.3
Repair of current obstetric laceration	795	964	1,136	1,259	3.2	3.7	4.1	4.3
Cardiac catheterization	995	1,068	1,221	1,209	4.0	4.1	4.4	4.1
Reduction of fracture [4]	609	577	628	621	2.4	2.2	2.3	2.1
Male, total [2]	**8,538**	**8,388**	**8,689**	**10,371**	**70.6**	**65.9**	**63.9**	**71.5**
Removal of coronary artery obstruction [3]	200	285	655	874	1.7	2.2	4.8	6.0
Cardiac catheterization	620	660	732	742	5.1	5.2	5.4	5.1
Coronary artery bypass graft	286	423	371	321	2.4	3.3	2.7	2.2
Female, total [2]	**14,513**	**14,142**	**14,556**	**16,193**	**113.0**	**105.3**	**102.4**	**107.8**
Cesarean section	945	785	855	1,262	7.4	5.8	6.0	8.4
Repair of current obstetric laceration	795	964	1,136	1,259	6.2	7.2	8.0	8.4
Hysterectomy	591	583	633	575	4.6	4.3	4.5	3.8
Diagnostic and other nonsurgical procedures [5]	**17,455**	**17,278**	**16,737**	**18,387**	**70.0**	**66.1**	**60.2**	**62.3**
Angiocardiography and arteriography [6]	1,735	1,834	2,005	1,986	7.0	7.0	7.2	6.7
Respiratory therapy	1,164	1,127	991	1,160	4.7	4.3	3.6	3.9
Manual assisted delivery	750	866	898	1,022	3.0	3.3	3.2	3.5
Diagnostic ultrasound	1,608	1,181	886	884	6.4	4.5	3.2	3.0
Fetal electrocardiogram and fetal monitoring	1,377	935	750	828	5.6	3.6	2.7	2.8
Male, total [5]	**7,378**	**7,261**	**6,965**	**7,620**	**61.0**	**57.1**	**51.2**	**52.6**
Angiocardiography and arteriography [6]	1,051	1,076	1,157	1,125	8.7	8.5	8.5	7.8
Respiratory therapy	586	572	507	606	4.9	4.5	3.7	4.2
CAT scan [7]	736	473	345	378	6.1	3.7	2.5	2.6
Female, total [5]	**10,077**	**10,016**	**9,772**	**10,767**	**78.5**	**74.6**	**68.8**	**71.7**
Manual assisted delivery	750	866	898	1,022	5.9	6.5	6.3	6.8
Fetal EKG and fetal monitoring	1,377	935	750	828	10.8	7.0	5.5	5.5
Respiratory therapy	578	555	484	554	4.5	4.1	3.4	3.7

[1] Based on Census Bureau estimated civilian population as of July 1. Population estimates based on the 1990 census were used to calculate rates for 1990 through 2000. Population estimates based on the 2000 census were used to calculate rates for 2001 through 2005.   [2] Includes other types of surgical procedures not shown separately.   [3] Beginning 1996, includes separately coded "insertion of stent."   [4] Excluding skull, nose, and jaw.   [5] Includes other nonsurgical procedures not shown separately.   [6] Using contrast material.   [7] Computerized axial tomography.

Source: U.S. National Center for Health Statistics, Vital and Health Statistics, series 13; and unpublished data. <http://www.cdc.gov/nchs/products/pubs/pubd/series/ser.htm>.

Health and Nutrition   113

Table 161. **Selected Cosmetic Procedures: 2000 to 2006**

[In thousands (5,741.2 represents 5,741,200). As of December 31. Surveys were sent to board certified surgeons and physicians in the following specialities: plastic surgery, dermatology, and otolaryngology. The final data as reported by the American Society for Aesthetic Plastic Surgery (ASAPS) are projected to reflect nationwide statistics. Procedures are ranked by total number in the most current year]

Procedure	2000	2001	2002	2003	2004	2005	2006
Total all procedures	5,741.2	8,470.4	6,889.5	8,252.0	11,855.0	11,428.8	11,456.8
Total surgical procedures	1,429.0	1,609.6	1,620.7	1,819.5	2,120.0	2,131.0	1,922.8
Lipoplasty (liposuction)	376.6	385.4	372.8	384.6	478.3	455.5	403.7
Breast augmentation	203.3	216.8	249.6	280.4	334.1	364.6	383.9
Blepharoplasty (eyelid surgery)	212.1	246.3	229.1	267.6	290.3	231.5	210.0
Abdominoplasty (tummy tuck)	58.4	71.1	83.0	117.7	151.0	169.3	172.5
Breast reduction	90.0	114.9	125.6	147.2	144.4	160.5	145.8
Total nonsurgical procedures	4,311.2	6,860.8	5,268.8	6,432.5	9,735.0	9,297.7	9,534.0
Botox injection	1,096.6	1,600.3	1,658.7	2,272.1	2,837.3	3,294.8	3,181.6
Hyaluronic acid [1]	(X)	(X)	(X)	116.2	882.5	1,194.2	1,593.6
Laser hair removal	487.8	854.6	736.5	923.2	1,411.9	1,566.9	1,475.3
Microdermabrasion [2]	610.7	915.3	1,032.4	858.3	1,098.3	1,023.9	993.1
Laser skin resurfacing	116.9	122.6	72.5	127.5	589.7	475.7	576.5
Total female procedures	5,100.8	7,447.8	6,081.9	7,177.9	10,681.4	10,443.8	10,516.7
Total surgical procedures	1,211.9	1,363.2	1,407.7	1,559.4	1,887.3	1,918.1	1,730.5
Breast augmentation	203.3	216.8	249.6	280.4	334.1	364.6	383.9
Lipoplasty (liposuction)	317.9	307.3	316.5	323.0	416.6	402.9	350.4
Blepharoplasty (eyelid surgery)	180.0	204.8	192.8	216.8	249.3	198.1	182.4
Abdominoplasty (tummy tuck)	56.5	67.7	79.7	112.7	145.3	164.1	164.8
Breast reduction	90.0	114.9	125.6	147.2	144.4	160.5	145.8
Total nonsurgical procedures	3,887.9	6,083.1	4,674.2	5,618.6	8,794.1	8,525.7	8,786.2
Botox injection	971.1	1,379.9	1,424.9	1,963.0	2,525.4	2,990.7	2,881.1
Hyaluronic acid [1]	(X)	(X)	(X)	104.7	838.9	1,149.2	1,519.9
Laser hair removal	401.6	715.1	588.5	695.2	1,215.1	1,334.7	1,308.7
Microdermabrasion [2]	536.7	820.5	936.2	774.3	999.1	939.5	922.0
Sclerotherapy (spider veins)	513.8	530.5	291.1	431.3	479.2	548.0	541.3
Total male procedures	640.2	1,021.8	807.7	1,074.1	1,173.6	984.9	940.0
Total surgical procedures	217.1	246.4	213.1	260.1	232.7	212.9	192.3
Lipoplasty (liposuction)	58.7	78.0	56.3	61.6	61.6	52.5	53.3
Rhinoplasty (nose reshaping)	41.5	54.4	39.0	53.4	39.0	45.9	33.1
Blepharoplasty (eyelid surgery)	32.1	41.5	36.3	50.8	41.1	33.4	27.6
Gynecomastia (male breast reduction)	15.9	16.5	16.6	22.0	19.6	17.7	23.7
Facelift	10.3	11.8	11.1	13.6	11.8	13.0	14.1
Total nonsurgical procedures	423.2	777.7	594.6	814.0	932.6	772.0	747.7
Botox injection	125.5	220.4	233.8	309.1	311.9	304.1	300.5
Laser hair removal	86.2	139.5	147.9	228.0	196.8	232.2	166.6
Hyaluronic acid [1]	(X)	(X)	(X)	11.5	43.6	45.0	73.6
Microdermabrasion [2]	74.0	94.3	96.2	84.0	99.2	84.4	71.1
Laser skin resurfacing	13.0	17.5	4.2	11.0	69.4	43.1	48.5

X Not applicable.   [1] In 2003, the FDA has approved hyaluronan injections for filling soft tissue defects such as facial wrinkles.   [2] Procedure for reducing fine lines, "crow's feet," age spots, and acne scars.

Source: The American Society for Aesthetic Plastic Surgery, Statistics, annual. See also, <http://www.surgery.org/press/statistics.php> (copyright).

Table 162. **Organ Transplants and Grafts: 1990 to 2006**

[As of end of year. Based on reports of procurement programs and transplant centers in the United States, except as noted]

Procedure	Number of procedures						Number of centers		Number of people waiting, 2006	1-year patient survival rates, 2005 (percent)
	1990	1995	2000	2004	2005	2006	1990	2006		
Transplant: [1]										
Heart	2,095	2,342	2,172	2,015	2,125	2,192	148	135	2,698	87.7
Heart-lung	52	69	47	40	35	31	79	58	117	56.4
Lung	203	869	955	1,172	1,406	1,405	70	66	2,756	82.8
Liver	2,631	3,818	4,816	6,169	6,443	6,650	85	126	16,802	86.3
Kidney	9,358	10,957	13,258	16,004	16,481	17,094	232	248	72,355	98.0
Kidney-pancreas	459	915	910	881	903	924	(NA)	(NA)	2,318	95.5
Pancreas	60	103	420	602	541	463	84	144	1,676	94.2
Intestine	1	21	29	152	178	175	(NA)	45	235	82.4
Multiorgan	71	124	213	441	514	(NA)	(NA)	(NA)	(NA)	(NA)
Cornea grafts [2]	40,631	44,652	46,949	46,841	44,329	45,035	[3]107	[3]86	(NA)	(NA)
Bone grafts (1,000) . .	350	450	800	1,500	1,620	(NA)	30	64	(X)	(NA)
Skin grafts [4]	5,500	5,500	13,000	19,000	20,000	(NA)	25	45	(X)	(NA)

NA Not available.   X Not applicable.   [1] Kidney-pancreas and heart-lung transplants are each counted as one procedure. All other multiorgan transplants, excluding kidney-pancreas and heart-lung, are included in the multiorgan row. Based on the Organ Procurement and Transplant Network (OPTN) as of July 26, 2007. The data have been supplied by UNOS under contract with HHS. This work was supported in part by Health Resources and Services Administration contract 231-00-0015. The authors alone are responsible for the reporting and interpretation of these data. Data subject to change based on future data submission or correction.   [2] 1990–1992, number of procedures and eye banks include Canada. From 1993 on, the data is for the U.S. only.   [3] Eye banks.   [4] Procedure data are shown in terms of square feet.

Source: U.S. Department of Health and Human Services, Health Resources and Services Administration, Office of Special Programs, Division of Transplantation, Rockville, MD; United Network for Organ Sharing (UNOS), Richmond, VA; University Renal Research and Education Association, Ann Arbor, MI; American Association of Tissue Banks, McLean, VA; and Eye Bank Association of America, Washington, DC; and unpublished data. See also <http://www.optn.org/>.

Table 163. **Hospitals—Summary Characteristics: 1980 to 2005**

[For beds, (1,365 represents 1,365,000). Covers hospitals accepted for registration by the American Hospital Association; see text, this section. Short-term hospitals have an average patient stay of less than 30 days; long-term, an average stay of longer duration. Special hospitals include obstetrics and gynecology; eye, ear, nose, and throat; rehabilitation; orthopedic; and chronic and other special hospitals except psychiatric, tuberculosis, alcoholism, and chemical dependency hospitals]

Item	1980	1990	1995	2000	2001	2002	2003	2004	2005
Number:									
All hospitals	6,965	6,649	6,291	5,810	5,801	5,794	5,764	5,759	5,756
With 100 beds or more	3,755	3,620	3,376	3,102	3,084	3,032	3,007	2,972	2,942
Nonfederal [1]	6,606	6,312	5,992	5,565	5,558	5,554	5,525	5,520	5,530
Community hospitals [2]	5,830	5,384	5,194	4,915	4,908	4,927	4,895	4,919	4,936
Nongovernmental nonprofit	3,322	3,191	3,092	3,003	2,998	3,025	2,984	2,967	2,958
For profit	730	749	752	749	754	766	790	835	868
State and local government	1,778	1,444	1,350	1,163	1,156	1,136	1,121	1,117	1,110
Long-term general and special	157	131	112	131	136	124	126	108	115
Psychiatric	534	757	657	496	491	477	477	466	456
Tuberculosis	11	4	3	4	4	4	4	4	3
Federal	359	337	299	245	243	240	239	239	226
Beds (1,000) [3]:									
All hospitals	1,365	1,213	1,081	984	987	976	965	956	947
Rate per 1,000 population [4]	6.0	4.9	4.1	3.5	3.5	3.4	3.3	3.3	3.2
Beds per hospital	196	182	172	169	170	168	167	166	165
Nonfederal [1]	1,248	1,113	1,004	931	936	926	917	908	901
Community hospitals [2]	988	927	873	824	826	821	813	808	802
Rate per 1,000 population [4]	4.3	3.7	3.3	2.9	2.9	2.8	2.8	2.8	2.7
Nongovernmental nonprofit	692	657	610	583	585	582	575	567	561
For profit	87	102	106	110	109	108	110	112	114
State and local government	209	169	157	131	132	130	120	127	128
Long-term general and special	39	25	19	18	19	18	18	15	15
Psychiatric	215	158	110	87	89	85	85	86	82
Tuberculosis	2	(Z)	(Z)	(Z)	(Z)	(Z)	(Z)	(Z)	(Z)
Federal	117	98	78	53	53	50	47	58	46
Average daily census (1,000): [5]									
All hospitals	1,060	844	710	650	658	662	657	658	656
Community hospitals [2]	747	619	548	526	533	540	539	541	540
Nongovernmental nonprofit	542	455	393	382	385	391	389	388	388
For profit	57	54	55	61	63	64	65	68	68
State and local government	149	111	100	83	85	84	84	84	85
Expenses (bil. dol.): [6]									
All hospitals	91.9	234.9	320.3	395.4	426.8	462.2	498.1	533.8	570.5
Nonfederal [1]	84.0	219.6	300.0	371.5	399.3	432.5	467.2	499.0	533.7
Community hospitals [2]	76.9	203.7	285.6	356.6	383.7	416.6	450.1	481.2	551.7
Nongovernmental nonprofit	55.8	150.7	209.6	267.1	287.3	312.7	337.7	359.4	386.0
For profit	5.8	18.8	26.7	35.0	37.3	40.1	44.0	48.9	51.8
State and local government	15.2	34.2	49.3	54.5	59.1	63.8	68.4	72.8	77.9
Long-term general and special	1.2	2.7	2.2	2.8	3.3	3.6	3.6	3.6	3.6
Psychiatric	5.8	12.9	11.7	11.9	13.2	12.1	13.1	13.8	13.9
Tuberculosis	0.1	0.1	0.4	(Z)	(Z)	(Z)	(Z)	(Z)	(Z)
Federal	7.9	15.2	20.2	23.9	27.5	29.7	30.9	34.8	36.8
Personnel (1,000): [7]									
All hospitals	3,492	4,063	4,273	4,454	4,535	4,610	4,650	4,695	4,790
Nonfederal [1]	3,213	3,760	3,971	4,157	4,236	4,312	4,350	4,379	4,479
Community hospitals [2]	2,873	3,420	3,714	3,911	3,987	4,069	4,108	4,147	4,260
Nongovernmental nonprofit	2,086	2,533	2,702	2,919	2,971	3,039	3,058	3,076	3,154
For profit	189	273	343	378	379	380	391	405	421
State and local government	598	614	670	614	637	651	658	665	681
Long-term general and special	56	55	38	41	44	46	45	42	38
Psychiatric	275	280	215	200	201	193	194	185	182
Tuberculosis	3	1	1	1	1	1	1	1	1
Federal	279	303	301	297	299	299	300	315	311
Outpatient visits (mil.)	263.0	368.2	483.2	592.7	612.0	640.5	648.6	662.1	673.7
Emergency	82.0	92.8	99.9	106.9	109.8	114.2	115.1	116.9	118.9

Z Less than 500 beds or $50 million.   [1] Includes hospital units of institutions.   [2] Short-term (average length of stay less than 30 days) general and special (e.g., obstetrics and gynecology; eye, ear, nose and throat; rehabilitation etc. except psychiatric, tuberculosis, alcoholism, and chemical dependency). Excludes hospital units of institutions.   [3] Beginning 1990, number of beds at end of reporting period; prior years, average number in 12-month period.   [4] Based on Census Bureau estimated resident population as of July 1. 1980, 1990, and 2000 based on enumerated resident population as of April 1. Estimates reflect revisions based on the 2000 census of population.   [5] The average number of people served on an inpatient basis on a single day during the reporting period.   [6] Excludes new construction.   [7] Includes full-time equivalents of part-time personnel.

Source: Health Forum, An American Hospital Association Company, Chicago, IL, *AHA Hospital Statistics 2007 Edition*, and prior years (copyright). <http://www.healthforum.com/>.

U.S. Census Bureau, Statistical Abstract of the United States: 2008

Table 164. **Average Cost to Community Hospitals Per Patient: 1980 to 2005**

[In dollars, except percent. Covers nonfederal short-term general or special hospitals (excluding psychiatric or tuberculosis hospitals and hospital units of institutions). Total cost per patient based on total hospital expenses (payroll, employee benefits, professional fees, supplies, etc.). Data have been adjusted for outpatient visits]

Type of expense and hospital	1980	1990	1995	1999	2000	2001	2002	2003	2004	2005
Average cost per day, total	245	687	968	1,103	1,149	1,217	1,290	1,379	1,450	1,522
Annual percent change [1]	12.9	7.8	4.0	3.3	4.2	5.9	6.0	6.9	5.1	5.0
Nongovernmental nonprofit	246	692	994	1,140	1,182	1,255	1,329	1,429	1,501	1,585
For profit	257	752	947	999	1,057	1,121	1,181	1,264	1,362	1,412
State and local government	239	635	878	1,007	1,064	1,114	1,188	1,238	1,291	1,329
Average cost per stay, total	1,851	4,947	6,216	6,512	6,649	6,980	7,346	7,796	8,166	8,793
Nongovernmental nonprofit	1,902	5,001	6,279	6,608	6,717	7,052	7,458	7,905	8,266	8,670
For profit	1,676	4,727	5,425	5,350	5,642	5,972	6,161	6,590	7,139	7,351
State and local government	1,750	4,838	6,445	6,923	7,106	7,400	7,773	8,205	8,473	8,793

[1] Change from immediate prior year.

Source: Health Forum, An American Hospital Association Company, Chicago, IL, *AHA Hospital Statistics 2007 Edition*, and prior years (copyright); <http://www.healthforum.com/>.

Table 165. **Community Hospitals—States: 2000 and 2005**

[In thousands, (823.6 represents 823,600). For definition of community hospitals see footnote 2, Table 163]

State	Number of hospitals		Beds (1,000)		Patients admitted (1,000)		Average daily census [1] (1,000)		Outpatient visits (mil.)		Average cost per day (dol.)	
	2000	2005	2000	2005	2000	2005	2000	2005	2000	2005	2000	2005
United States	4,915	4,936	823.6	802.3	33,089	35,239	525.7	540.3	521.4	584.4	1,149	1,522
Alabama	108	109	16.4	15.5	680	706	9.8	9.9	8.0	7.5	980	1,198
Alaska	18	22	1.4	1.4	47	51	0.8	0.8	1.3	1.7	1,495	2,246
Arizona	61	67	10.9	11.8	539	665	6.8	8.0	5.3	6.8	1,311	1,769
Arkansas	83	85	9.8	9.4	368	380	5.7	5.5	4.4	5.0	908	1,238
California	389	357	72.7	70.2	3,315	3,434	47.8	50.0	44.9	49.0	1,438	1,994
Colorado	69	71	9.4	9.6	397	417	5.4	5.8	6.7	7.4	1,280	1,751
Connecticut	35	36	7.7	7.7	349	405	5.8	6.3	6.7	7.1	1,373	1,714
Delaware	5	6	1.8	2.0	83	104	1.4	1.7	1.5	1.9	1,311	1,715
District of Columbia	11	11	3.3	3.5	129	141	2.5	2.7	1.3	1.6	1,512	1,910
Florida	202	205	51.2	51.2	2,119	2,371	31.0	33.9	21.8	22.3	1,161	1,497
Georgia	151	149	23.9	25.0	863	961	15.0	17.0	11.2	13.8	978	1,202
Hawaii	21	25	3.1	3.0	100	114	2.3	2.3	2.5	1.9	1,088	1,310
Idaho	42	39	3.5	3.3	123	130	1.8	1.8	2.2	2.7	1,003	1,484
Illinois	196	191	37.3	34.5	1,531	1,583	22.4	22.6	25.1	28.7	1,278	1,637
Indiana	109	113	19.2	17.8	700	717	10.8	10.3	14.1	16.5	1,132	1,569
Iowa	115	116	11.8	10.8	360	363	6.8	6.4	9.2	10.1	740	1,036
Kansas	129	131	10.8	10.1	310	330	5.7	5.7	5.3	5.9	837	1,055
Kentucky	105	105	14.8	14.9	582	618	9.1	9.3	8.7	8.8	929	1,194
Louisiana	123	128	17.5	15.5	654	620	9.8	9.5	10.0	9.8	1,075	1,293
Maine	37	37	3.7	3.5	147	151	2.4	2.3	3.2	4.3	1,148	1,528
Maryland	49	50	11.2	11.4	587	680	8.2	8.7	6.0	6.8	1,315	1,831
Massachusetts	80	80	16.6	16.2	740	800	11.7	12.0	16.7	18.9	1,467	1,751
Michigan	146	146	26.1	26.2	1,106	1,198	16.9	17.6	24.9	26.1	1,211	1,460
Minnesota	135	133	16.7	16.0	571	635	11.2	11.0	7.3	9.4	932	1,300
Mississippi	95	94	13.6	12.8	425	414	8.0	7.3	3.7	4.1	719	1,021
Missouri	119	119	20.1	19.1	773	836	11.7	12.0	14.8	17.2	1,185	1,560
Montana	52	54	4.3	4.3	99	106	2.9	2.8	2.6	2.9	579	814
Nebraska	85	87	8.2	7.6	209	214	4.8	4.8	3.4	3.9	743	1,066
Nevada	22	32	3.8	4.7	199	241	2.7	3.5	2.2	2.6	1,285	1,685
New Hampshire	28	28	2.9	2.8	111	117	1.7	1.8	2.8	3.8	1,201	1,627
New Jersey	80	80	25.3	22.1	1,074	1,110	17.3	16.2	16.3	16.8	1,299	1,797
New Mexico	35	37	3.5	3.5	174	172	2.0	2.2	3.1	4.7	1,388	1,780
New York	215	203	66.4	63.1	2,416	2,538	52.1	50.1	46.4	51.5	1,118	1,539
North Carolina	113	115	23.1	23.3	971	1,013	16.0	16.7	12.4	16.8	1,061	1,320
North Dakota	42	40	3.9	3.5	89	87	2.3	2.1	1.7	1.9	747	898
Ohio	163	170	33.8	33.3	1,404	1,511	20.6	21.4	26.9	31.3	1,198	1,673
Oklahoma	108	110	11.1	10.8	429	457	6.2	6.4	4.7	5.4	1,031	1,332
Oregon	59	58	6.6	6.5	330	336	3.9	4.1	7.3	8.0	1,461	2,062
Pennsylvania	207	191	42.3	39.6	1,796	1,863	28.8	27.9	31.8	34.9	1,080	1,500
Rhode Island	11	11	2.4	2.4	119	127	1.7	1.9	2.1	2.5	1,313	1,719
South Carolina	63	63	11.5	11.5	495	528	8.0	8.4	7.8	5.8	1,101	1,465
South Dakota	48	52	4.3	4.3	99	102	2.8	2.8	1.7	1.6	476	733
Tennessee	121	130	20.6	20.6	737	829	11.5	13.1	10.3	11.7	1,078	1,234
Texas	403	415	55.9	58.2	2,367	2,509	33.1	36.0	29.4	32.3	1,274	1,636
Utah	42	43	4.3	4.6	194	223	2.4	2.6	4.5	4.8	1,375	1,823
Vermont	14	12	1.7	0.9	52	51	1.1	0.6	1.2	2.3	888	1,166
Virginia	88	87	16.9	17.5	727	780	11.4	12.3	9.5	13.2	1,057	1,394
Washington	84	86	11.1	11.0	505	543	6.6	6.8	9.6	10.0	1,511	2,143
West Virginia	57	57	8.0	7.2	288	292	4.8	4.5	5.2	6.1	844	1,113
Wisconsin	118	124	15.3	14.5	558	612	9.1	9.0	10.9	12.7	1,055	1,458
Wyoming	24	24	1.9	2.1	48	51	1.1	1.2	0.9	1.0	677	805

[1] The average number of people served on an inpatient basis on a single day during the reporting period.

Source: Health Forum, An American Hospital Association Company, Chicago, IL, *AHA Hospital Statistics 2007 Edition*, and prior years (copyright); <http://www.healthforum.com/>.

Table 166. Hospital Use Rates by Type of Hospital: 1980 to 2005

Type of hospital	1980	1990	1995	2000	2002	2003	2004	2005
Community hospitals: [1]								
Admissions per 1,000 population [2].......	159	125	116	117	120	120	119	119
Admissions per bed...............	37	34	35	40	42	43	43	44
Average length of stay (days) [3].........	7.6	7.2	6.5	5.8	5.7	5.7	5.6	5.6
Outpatient visits per admission	5.6	9.7	13.4	15.8	16.1	16.2	16.3	16.5
Outpatient visits per 1,000 population [2].....	890	1,207	1,556	1,852	1,932	1,937	1,946	1,976
Surgical operations (million [4])...........	18.8	21.9	23.2	26.1	27.6	27.1	27.4	27.5
Number per admission............	0.5	0.7	0.7	0.8	0.8	0.8	0.8	0.8
Nonfederal psychiatric:								
Admissions per 1,000 population [2].....	2.5	2.9	2.7	2.4	2.5	2.6	2.7	2.5
Days in hospital per 1,000 population [2].....	295	190	122	93	92	91	88	89

[1] Short term (average length of stay less than 30 days) general and special (e.g., obstetrics and gynecology; eye, ear, nose and throat; rehabilitation etc. except psychiatric, tuberculosis, alcoholism and chemical dependency). Excludes hospital units of institutions. [2] Based on U.S. Census Bureau estimated resident population as of July 1. Estimates reflect revisions based on the 2000 census of population. [3] Number of inpatient days divided by number of admissions. [4] 18.8 represents 18,800,000.

Source: Health Forum, An American Hospital Association Company, Chicago, IL, *AHA Hospital Statistics 2007 Edition*, and prior years (copyright); <http://www.healthforum.com/>.

Table 167. Hospital Utilization Rates by Sex: 1990 to 2005

[30,788 represents 30,788,000. Represents estimates of inpatients discharged from noninstitutional, short-stay hospitals, exclusive of federal hospitals. Excludes newborn infants. Based on sample data collected from the National Hospital Discharge Survey, a sample survey of hospital records of patients discharged in year shown; subject to sampling variability]

Item and sex	1990	1995	1999	2000	2001	2002	2003	2004	2005
Patients discharged (1,000).........	30,788	30,722	32,132	31,706	32,653	33,727	34,738	34,864	34,667
Patients discharged per 1,000 persons,									
total [1]...................	122	116	117	114	115	118	120	119	117
Male....................	100	94	95	92	93	95	98	97	96
Female..................	143	136	138	135	137	139	141	141	138
Days of care per 1,000 persons, total [1]..	784	620	581	560	562	572	578	574	562
Male....................	694	551	510	491	490	506	507	505	498
Female..................	869	686	649	627	631	635	646	641	624
Average stay (days)..............	6.4	5.4	5.0	4.9	4.9	4.9	4.8	4.8	4.8
Male....................	6.9	5.8	5.4	5.3	5.3	5.3	5.2	5.2	5.2
Female..................	6.1	5.0	4.7	4.6	4.6	4.6	4.6	4.5	4.5

[1] Rates are computed using Census Bureau estimates of the civilian population as of July 1. Rates for 1990–99 were based on population estimates adjusted for the net underenumeration in the 1990 census. Rates for 2000 and later were calculated using 2000-based postcensal estimates.

Source: U.S. National Center for Health Statistics, *Vital and Health Statistics*, Series 13; and unpublished data. <http://www.cdc.gov/nchs/products/pubs/pubd/series/ser.htm>.

Table 168. Hospital Utilization Measures for HIV Patients: 1990 to 2005

[HIV represents human immunodeficiency virus. See headnote, Table 167]

Measure of utilization	Unit	1990	1995	2000	2003	2004	2005
Number of patients discharged......	1,000....	146	249	173	207	204	185
Male......................	1,000....	114	183	115	136	132	113
Female....................	1,000....	32	66	58	71	73	72
Rate of patient discharges [1].......	Rate....	5.8	9.4	6.2	7.2	7.0	6.3
Number of days of care...........	1,000....	2,188	2,326	1,257	1,696	1,477	1,244
Male......................	1,000....	1,777	1,649	895	1,003	876	751
Female....................	1,000....	411	677	362	693	601	493
Rate of days of care [1]...........	Rate....	86.9	87.6	45.2	58.6	50.5	42.2
Average length of stay...........	Days....	14.9	9.3	7.3	8.2	7.2	6.7
Male......................	Days....	15.5	9.0	7.8	7.4	6.7	6.7
Female....................	Days....	12.9	10.3	6.3	9.7	8.3	6.8

[1] Per 10,000 population. Based on Census Bureau estimated civilian population as of July 1. Populations for 1990–99 were adjusted for the net underenumeration in the 1990 census. Populations for 2000 and later were 2000-based postcensal estimates.

Source: National Center for Health Statistics, *Vital and Health Statistics*, Series 13; and unpublished data; <http://www.cdc.gov/nchs/products/pubs/pubd/series/ser.htm>.

Table 169. **Hospital Discharges and Days of Care: 2002 and 2005**

[33,727 represents 33,727,000. See headnote, Table 167. For composition of regions, see map, inside front cover]

Age, race, and region	Discharges				Days of care per 1,000 persons [1]		Average stay (days)	
	Number (1,000)		Per 1,000 persons [1]					
	2002	2005	2002	2005	2002	2005	2002	2005
Total [2]	33,727	34,667	118	117	572	562	4.9	4.8
Age:								
Under 1 year old.	810	800	201	195	1,134	1,213	5.6	6.2
1 to 4 years old	713	696	46	43	159	136	3.5	3.2
5 to 14 years old	1,016	934	25	23	109	104	4.4	4.5
15 to 24 years old.	3,083	3,074	77	74	266	261	3.5	3.5
25 to 34 years old.	3,897	4,001	99	101	328	343	3.3	3.4
35 to 44 years old.	3,757	3,583	84	82	368	351	4.4	4.3
45 to 64 years old.	7,723	8,349	116	115	575	572	5.0	5.0
65 to 74 years old.	4,642	4,900	254	263	1,412	1,399	5.6	5.3
75 years old and over	8,085	8,328	467	459	2,795	2,594	6.0	5.7
Race:								
White	20,806	20,897	90	88	436	422	4.9	4.8
Black	3,995	4,109	109	109	584	584	5.3	5.4
Asian/Pacific Islander.	538	617	45	47	243	247	5.4	5.3
American Indian/Eskimo/ Aleut	173	104	63	37	330	169	5.2	4.6
Region:								
Northeast	6,990	7,192	129	132	727	710	5.6	5.4
Midwest	7,503	7,948	115	121	512	512	4.4	4.3
South	12,994	12,907	127	121	618	588	4.9	4.9
West.	6,239	6,621	96	98	430	451	4.5	4.6

[1] Rates were calculated using U.S. Census Bureau 2000-based postcensal estimates of the civilian population as of July 1.
[2] Includes other races not shown separately.

Source: U.S. National Center for Health Statistics, *Vital and Health Statistics*, Series 13; and unpublished data; <http://www.cdc.gov/nchs/products/pubs/pubd/series/ser.htm>.

Table 170. **Hospital Discharges and Days of Care by Sex: 2005**

[13,902 represents 13,902,000. Represents estimates of inpatients discharged from noninstitutional, short-stay hospitals, exclusive of federal hospitals. Excludes newborn infants. Diagnostic categories are based on the International Classification of Diseases, Ninth Revision, Clinical Modification. See headnote, Table 167]

Sex, age, and selected first-listed diagnosis [1]	Discharges		Days of care per 1,000 per- sons [2]	Aver- age stay (days)	Sex, age, and selected first-listed diagnosis [1]	Discharges		Days of care per 1,000 per- sons [2]	Aver- age stay (days)
	Num- ber (1,000)	Per 1,000 per- sons [2]				Num- ber (1,000)	Per 1,000 per- sons [2]		
Male					**Female**				
All ages [3, 4]	13,902	101.3	530.1	5.2	**All ages** [3, 4]	20,766	132.0	582.9	4.5
Under 18 years	1,550	41.2	200.6	4.9	Under 18 years	1,470	41.0	182.6	4.5
Injuries and poisoning	183	4.9	[5]24.0	[5]4.9	Injuries and poisoning	113	3.1	12.0	3.8
Pneumonia	108	2.9	9.0	3.1	Pneumonia	91	2.5	8.4	3.3
Asthma	103	2.7	6.3	2.3	Asthma	61	1.7	3.8	2.2
18–44 years.	2660	47.1	228.3	4.8	18–44 years.	7,410	133.1	434.2	3.3
Injuries and poisoning	452	8.0	36.7	4.6	Delivery	3,888	69.8	180.3	2.6
Serious mental illness [6] . .	344	6.1	[5]50.3	[5]8.3	Serious mental illness [6] . .	[5]381	[5]6.8	[5]45.6	[5]6.7
Alcohol and drug [7]	203	3.6	16.1	4.5	Injuries and poisoning	282	5.1	22.2	4.4
Diseases of heart	166	2.9	11.1	3.8	Alcohol and drug [7]	110	2.0	[5]9.9	[5]5.0
45–64 years.	4,076	114.9	577.3	5.0	45–64 years.	4,273	114.5	566.4	4.9
Diseases of heart	795	22.4	85.1	3.8	Diseases of heart	447	12.0	55.9	4.7
Injuries and poisoning	380	10.7	59.2	5.5	Injuries and poisoning	324	8.7	46.0	5.3
Malignant neoplasms [8] . . .	211	5.9	39.2	6.6	Malignant neoplasms	228	6.1	38.5	6.3
Serious mental illness [6] . .	167	4.7	41.2	8.8	Serious mental illness [6] . .	223	6.0	53.0	8.9
Alcohol and drug [7]	141	4.0	18.6	4.7	Pneumonia	126	3.4	18.0	5.3
65–74 years.	2,339	274.3	1,450.3	5.3	65–74 years.	2,561	253.3	1,354.9	5.3
Diseases of heart	545	63.9	280.8	4.4	Diseases of heart	435	43.0	191.1	4.4
Injuries and poisoning	165	19.4	119.1	6.2	Injuries and poisoning	187	18.5	114.3	6.2
Malignant neoplasms	158	18.6	126.7	6.8	Osteoarthritis.	179	17.7	67.4	3.8
Pneumonia	126	14.7	75.9	5.2	Malignant neoplasms	127	12.5	82.9	6.6
Cerebrovascular diseases .	109	12.8	58.9	4.6	Pneumonia	119	11.8	65.8	5.6
Osteoarthritis	108	12.6	48.0	3.8	Cerebrovascular diseases .	104	10.3	44.8	4.3
75 years old and over . .	3,276	476.0	2,745.4	5.8	75 years old and over . .	5,052	448.4	2,501.4	5.6
Diseases of heart	706	102.6	490.8	4.8	Diseases of heart	1,020	90.5	435.8	4.8
Pneumonia	247	35.8	208.7	5.8	Injuries and poisoning	517	45.9	249.3	5.4
Injuries and poisoning	221	32.1	197.2	6.1	Pneumonia	323	28.6	168.3	5.9
Cerebrovascular diseases .	167	24.2	132.4	5.5	Cerebrovascular diseases .	244	21.7	108.6	5.0
Malignant neoplasms	156	22.7	155.8	6.9	Malignant neoplasms	161	14.3	104.4	7.3

[1] The first-listed diagnosis is the one specified as the principal diagnosis or the first diagnosis listed on the face sheet or discharge summary of the medical record. It is usually the main cause of the hospitalization. The number of first-listed diagnoses is the same as the number of discharges. [2] Based on Census Bureau estimated civilian population as of July 1. [3] Estimates are age adjusted to the year 2000 standard population using six age groups: under 18 years, 18–44 years, 45–54 years, 55–64 years, 65–74 years, and 75 years and over. [4] Includes discharges with first-listed diagnoses not shown in table. [5] Estimates are considered unreliable. [6] These estimates are for nonfederal short-stay hospitals only and do not include serious mental illness discharges. from other types of facilities or programs such as the Department of Veterans Affairs or long-term hospitals. [7] Includes abuse, dependence, and withdrawal. These estimates are for nonfederal short-stay hospitals only and do not include alcohol and drug discharges from other types of facilities or or programs such as the Department of Veterans Affairs or day treatment programs.

Source: Centers for Disease Control and Prevention, National Center for Health Statistics, National Hospital Discharge Survey; <http://www.cdc.gov/nchs/about/major/hdasd/nhds.htm\>.

Table 171. Cancer—Estimated New Cases, 2007, and Survival Rates: 1987–1989 to 1996–2003

[1,445 represents 1,445,000. The 5-year relative survival rate, which is derived by adjusting the observed survival rate for expected mortality, represents the likelihood that a person will not die from causes directly related to their cancer within 5 years. Survival data shown are based on those patients diagnosed while residents of an area listed below during the time periods shown. Data are based on information collected as part of the National Cancer Institute's Surveillance, Epidemiology and End Results (SEER) program, a collection of population-based registries in five states (Connecticut, Hawaii, Iowa, New Mexico, Utah) and four metropolitan areas (Atlanta, Detroit, San Francisco-Oakland, and Seattle-Puget Sound)]

| Site | Estimated new cases,[1] 2007 (1,000) | | | 5-year relative survival rates (percent) | | | | | | | |
| | | | | White | | | | Black | | | |
	Total	Male	Female	1987–1989	1990–1992	1993–1995	1996–2003	1987–1989	1990–1992	1993–1995	1996–2003
All sites [2]	1,445	767	678	57.7	62.4	63.4	67.0	43.6	48.2	52.8	57.0
Lung.	213	115	99	13.8	14.5	15.1	15.7	11.2	10.8	13.0	12.5
Breast [3]	181	2	178	85.3	86.7	87.9	90.3	71.2	71.7	72.8	77.9
Colon and rectum	154	79	75	61.1	63.1	61.5	65.9	53.3	53.8	52.9	55.7
Colon	112	55	57	61.7	63.9	61.4	65.6	53.2	54.2	52.3	54.7
Rectum	41	24	18	59.6	61.2	61.7	66.4	53.5	52.2	54.8	58.4
Prostate	219	219	(X)	85.4	95.3	96.1	99.0	72.2	85.5	91.4	95.3
Bladder	67	50	17	81.4	81.9	82.2	81.3	63.3	64.7	61.8	65.0
Corpus uteri	39	(X)	39	85.7	87.2	86.5	86.9	59.2	57.0	62.0	62.4
Non-Hodgkin's lymphoma [4]	63	34	29	52.8	52.9	54.4	64.8	47.5	42.1	42.0	56.0
Oral cavity and pharynx	34	24	10	56.6	58.7	60.9	62.0	34.4	33.3	38.2	40.6
Leukemia [4]	44	25	19	45.5	48.0	49.3	50.8	36.9	37.4	42.0	40.3
Melanoma of skin	60	34	26	88.2	89.6	89.6	91.7	79.9	60.3	66.8	77.0
Pancreas	37	19	18	3.4	4.6	4.2	4.9	5.7	3.7	3.7	4.6
Kidney	51	32	20	58.5	62.1	63.1	65.5	55.8	57.6	58.6	65.5
Stomach	21	13	8	19.1	19.3	20.7	22.2	20.0	24.1	19.8	24.2
Ovary	22	(X)	22	39.9	42.5	42.7	44.7	35.3	37.8	42.8	37.5
Cervix uteri [5]	11	(X)	11	73.6	71.9	74.6	74.3	58.2	58.6	64.0	65.8

X Not applicable.   [1] Estimates provided by American Cancer Society (<www.cancer.org>) are based on rates from the National Cancer Institute's SEER program.   [2] Includes other sites not shown separately.   [3] Survival rates for female only.   [4] All types combined.   [5] Invasive cancer only.

Source: U.S. National Institutes of Health, National Cancer Institute; <http://seer.cancer.gov/csr/1975_2004/>.

Table 172. Cancer—Estimated New Cases and Deaths by State: 2007

[In thousands (1,444.9 represents 1,444,900). Excludes basal and squamous cell skin cancers and in situ carcinomas except urinary bladder]

| State | New cases [1] | | | Deaths | | | State | New cases [1] | | | Deaths | | |
	Total [2]	Female breast	Lung & bronchus	Total [2]	Female breast	Lung & bronchus		Total [2]	Female breast	Lung & bronchus	Total [2]	Female breast	Lung & bronchus
U.S.	1,444.9	213.4	178.5	559.7	160.4	40.5							
AL	20.6	3.9	2.8	9.7	3.2	0.7	MO	29.9	5.4	3.7	12.6	4.1	0.9
AK	2.5	0.3	0.3	0.8	0.2	0.1	MT	4.9	0.7	0.6	1.9	0.5	0.1
AZ	26.3	3.7	3.2	10.1	2.9	0.7	NE	8.7	1.2	1.2	3.3	0.9	0.2
AR	14.1	2.4	1.8	6.2	2.2	0.4	NV	11.0	1.8	1.2	4.7	1.3	0.3
CA	151.3	17.9	19.8	54.9	13.2	4.1	NH	7.1	1.0	0.9	2.6	0.7	0.2
							NJ	49.4	6.3	6.1	17.1	4.4	1.4
CO	19.2	2.1	2.7	6.7	1.7	0.5	NM	8.0	0.9	1.1	3.3	0.7	0.2
CT	19.8	2.7	2.5	7.0	1.9	0.5	NY	101.0	13.4	12.6	35.3	9.5	2.7
DE	4.5	0.8	0.6	1.8	0.6	0.1	NC	38.2	6.3	4.9	16.9	5.2	1.2
DC	2.5	0.4	0.3	1.0	0.3	0.1	ND	3.3	0.4	0.4	1.2	0.4	0.1
FL	106.6	17.5	11.7	40.4	12.4	2.7							
							OH	59.2	9.8	6.7	24.6	7.3	1.8
GA	35.4	5.8	4.5	15.0	4.5	1.1	OK	17.2	3.2	2.2	7.4	2.4	0.5
HI	6.0	0.7	0.8	2.3	0.5	0.1	OR	18.6	2.5	2.5	7.4	2.1	0.5
ID	6.1	0.8	0.8	2.4	0.6	0.2	PA	75.1	10.5	8.9	29.1	7.8	2.5
IL	62.0	9.6	7.0	23.9	6.7	1.7	RI	6.4	0.9	0.7	2.4	0.6	0.1
IN	30.0	5.2	3.6	12.7	3.8	0.9							
							SC	21.4	3.5	2.6	8.9	2.8	0.6
IA	16.5	2.3	2.0	6.5	1.8	0.4	SD	4.0	0.5	0.5	1.6	0.4	0.1
KS	12.8	1.9	1.8	5.3	1.5	0.4	TN	28.4	5.1	3.7	12.9	4.3	0.9
KY	22.9	4.5	2.6	9.4	3.5	0.6	TX	91.0	13.5	12.1	34.2	9.9	2.5
LA	22.5	3.5	2.8	9.6	3.0	0.7	UT	7.7	0.6	0.9	2.7	0.5	0.2
ME	8.3	1.4	1.0	3.2	1.0	0.2							
							VT	3.5	0.4	0.4	1.2	0.4	0.1
MD	26.4	4.1	3.6	10.2	2.9	0.8	VA	35.1	5.4	4.6	13.7	4.3	1.1
MA	34.9	5.1	4.3	13.2	3.6	0.9	WA	31.1	4.0	4.1	11.4	3.2	0.8
MI	54.4	8.2	5.9	19.2	5.8	1.3	WV	10.5	2.1	1.2	4.6	1.5	0.3
MN	25.4	3.2	3.2	9.4	2.5	0.6	WI	28.1	3.9	3.3	10.9	2.9	0.8
MS	12.5	2.2	1.6	6.0	2.0	0.5	WY	2.3	0.3	0.3	1.0	0.3	0.1

[1] Estimates are offered as a rough guide and should be interpreted with caution.   [2] Includes other types of cancer, not shown separately.

Source: American Cancer Society, Inc., Atlanta, Georgia, *Cancer Facts and Figures—2007* (copyright); <http://www.cancer.org/docroot/STT/stt_0.asp>.

Health and Nutrition 119

Table 173. Selected Notifiable Diseases—Cases Reported: 1980 to 2005

[190.9 represents 190,900. Figures should be interpreted with caution. Although reporting of some of these diseases is incomplete, the figures are of value in indicating trends of disease incidence. Includes cases imported from outside the United States]

Disease	1980	1990	1995	2000	2001	2002	2003	2004	2005
AIDS [1]	(2)	41,595	71,547	40,758	41,868	42,745	44,232	44,108	41,120
Botulism [3]	89	92	97	138	155	118	129	133	135
Brucellosis (undulant fever)	183	85	98	87	136	125	104	114	120
Chickenpox (Varicella) [4] (1,000)	190.9	173.1	120.6	27.4	22.5	22.8	20.9	32.9	32.2
Coccidoidomycosis	(2)	(2)	(2)	2,867	3,922	4,968	4,870	6,449	6,542
Cholera	9	6	23	5	3	2	2	5	8
Cryptosporidiosis [5]	(2)	(2)	(NA)	3,128	3,785	3,016	3,506	3,577	5,659
Domestic arboviral diseases [5]									
West Nile									
Neuroinvasie	(2)	(2)	(2)	(2)	(2)	2,840	2,866	1,142	1,309
Nonneuroinvasie	(2)	(2)	(2)	(2)	(2)	(2)	(2)	(2)	1,691
Enterohemorrhagic Escherichia coli 0157:H7	(2)	(2)	2,139	4,528	3,287	3,840	2,671	2,544	2,621
Giardiasis	(2)	(2)	(2)	(2)	(2)	21,206	19,709	20,636	19,733
Haemophilus influenza	(2)	(2)	1,180	1,398	1,597	1,743	2,013	2,085	2,304
Hansen disease (Leprosy)	223	198	144	91	79	96	95	105	87
Hepatitis: A (infectious) (1,000)	29.1	31.4	31.6	13.4	10.6	8.8	7.7	5.7	4.5
B (serum) (1,000)	19.0	21.1	10.8	8.0	7.8	8.0	7.5	6.2	5.1
C/Non-A, non-B (1,000) [6]	(2)	2.6	4.6	3,197	3,976	1,835	1,102	720	652
Legionellosis	(2)	1,370	1,241	1,127	1,168	1,321	2,232	2,093	2,301
Lyme disease	(2)	(2)	11,700	17,730	17,029	23,763	21,273	19,804	23,305
Malaria	2,062	1,292	1,419	1,560	1,544	1,430	1,402	1,458	1,494
Measles (1,000)	13.5	27.8	0.3	0.1	0.1	–	0.1	–	–
Meningococcal infections	2,840	2,451	3,243	2,256	2,333	1,814	1,756	1,361	1,245
Mumps (1,000)	8.6	5.3	0.9	0.3	0.3	0.3	0.2	0.3	0.3
Pertussis [7] (1,000)	1.7	4.6	5.1	7.9	7.6	9.8	11.6	25.8	25.6
Plague	18	2	9	6	2	2	1	3	8
Psittacosis	124	113	64	17	25	18	12	12	16
Rabies, animal	6,421	4,826	7,811	6,934	7,150	7,609	6,846	6,345	5,915
Rabies, human	–	1	5	4	1	3	2	7	2
Rocky Mountain spotted fever	1,163	651	590	495	695	1,104	1,091	1,713	1,936
Rubella [8]	3,904	1,125	128	176	23	18	7	10	11
Salmonellosis [9] (1,000)	33.7	48.6	46.0	39.6	40.5	44.3	43.7	42.2	45.3
Shigellosis [10] (1,000)	19.0	27.1	32.1	22.9	20.2	23.5	23.6	14.6	16.2
Streptococcal disease, invasive, Group A	(2)	(2)	(2)	3,144	3,750	4,720	5,872	4,395	4,715
Streptococcus pneumoniae, invasive:									
Drug-resistant	(2)	(2)	(2)	4,533	2,896	2,546	2,356	2,590	2,996
Age less than 5 years	(2)	(2)	(2)	(2)	498	513	845	1,162	1,495
Tetanus	95	64	41	35	37	25	20	34	27
Toxic-shock syndrome	(2)	322	191	135	127	109	133	95	90
Trichinosis	131	129	29	16	22	14	6	5	16
Tuberculosis [11] (1,000)	27.7	25.7	22.9	16.4	16.0	15.1	14.9	14.5	14.1
Typhoid fever	510	552	369	377	368	321	356	322	324
Sexually transmitted diseases:									
Chlamydia (1,000)	(2)	(2)	478	702	783	835	877	929	976
Gonorrhea (1,000)	1,004	690	393	359	362	352	335	330	340
Syphilis (1,000)	69	134	69	32	32	34	34	33	33

– Represents zero. [1] Acquired immunodeficiency syndrome was not a notifiable disease until 1984. Figures are shown for years in which cases were reported to the CDC. Beginning 1995, based on revised classification system and expanded surveillance case definition. [2] Disease was not notifiable. [3] Includes foodborne, infant, wound, and unspecified cases. [4] Chickenpox was taken off the nationally notifiable list in 1991 but many states continue to report. [5] The national surveillance case definitions for the arboviral diseases were revised in 2005, and nonneuroinvasive arboviral diseases were added to the list of nationally notifiable infectious diseases. [6] Includes some persons positive for antibody to hepatitis C virus. [7] Whooping cough. [8] German measles. Excludes rubella, congenital syndrome. [9] Excludes typhoid fever. [10] Bacillary dysentery. [11] Newly reported active cases.

Source: U.S. Centers for Disease Control and Prevention, Atlanta, GA, *Summary of Notifiable Diseases, United States, 2005, Morbidity and Mortality Weekly Report*, Vol. 54, No. 53, March 30, 2007. <http://www.cdc.gov/mmwr/PDF/wk/mm5453.pdf>.

Table 174. AIDS, Syphilis, and Tuberculosis Cases Reported by State: 2005

State	AIDS	Syphilis	Tuberculosis	State	AIDS	Syphilis	Tuberculosis	State	AIDS	Syphilis	Tuberculosis
U.S.	41,120	33,278	14,097	KS	110	88	60	ND	10	1	6
				KY	267	129	124	OH	796	502	260
AL	523	551	216	LA	976	1,237	257	OK	284	159	144
AK	29	22	59	ME	22	6	17	OR	220	109	103
AZ	645	792	281	MD	1,596	1,005	283	PA	1,524	712	325
AR	242	231	114	MA	716	398	265	RI	90	64	47
CA	4,117	5,340	2,904	MI	829	488	246	SC	621	549	261
CO	364	144	101	MN	223	206	199	SD	19	4	16
CT	674	166	95	MS	390	371	103	TN	851	916	298
DE	177	35	26	MO	384	372	108	TX	3,152	4,287	1,535
DC	708	365	56	MT	20	7	10	UT	66	50	29
FL	5,055	2,888	1,094	NE	49	18	35	VT	7	1	8
GA	2,396	1,924	505	NV	296	343	112	VA	649	655	355
HI	110	57	112	NH	37	33	4	WA	486	359	256
ID	26	54	23	NJ	1,276	813	485	WV	76	18	28
IL	1,938	1,608	596	NM	139	183	39	WI	125	138	78
IN	414	288	146	NY	6,350	3,851	1,289	WY	6	1	–
IA	95	28	55	NC	945	712	329				

– Represents zero. [1] Includes cases among persons with unknown state of residence.

Source: U.S. Centers for Disease Control and Prevention, Atlanta, GA, *Summary of Notifiable Diseases, United States, 2005, Morbidity and Mortality Weekly Report*, Vol. 54, No. 53, March 30, 2007; <http://www.cdc.gov/mmwr/PDF/wk/mm5453.pdf>.

Table 175. **Reported AIDS Cases for Adults and Adolescents by Transmission Category and Sex: 2005**

[**Provisional.** For cases reported in the year shown. Includes Puerto Rico, Virgin Islands, Guam, and U.S. Pacific Islands. Acquired immunodeficiency syndrome (AIDS) is a specific group of diseases or conditions which are indicative of severe immunosuppression related to infection with the human immunodeficiency virus (HIV). Data are subject to retrospective changes and may differ from those data in Table 173]

Transmission category	2005			Cumulative through 2005[1]		
	Total	Male	Female	Total	Male	Female
Persons 13 years old and over, total . . .	41,900	30,956	10,944	946,578	764,808	181,769
Male-to-male sexual contact.	14,819	14,819	(X)	416,232	416,232	(X)
Injection drug use.	6,215	4,168	2,047	225,210	159,676	65,534
Male-to-male sexual contact and injection drug use	1,742	1,742	(X)	62,940	62,940	(X)
Hemophilia/coagulation disorder	79	68	11	5,482	5,142	340
High-risk heterosexual contact	8,028	3,110	4,918	126,405	46,533	79,872
Sex with injection drug user	1,140	389	751	36,681	11,371	25,310
Sex with bisexual male	223	(X)	223	4,876	(X)	4,876
Sex with person with hemophilia	16	3	13	574	81	493
Sex with HIV-infected transfusion recipient. . .	40	13	27	1,296	529	767
Sex with HIV-infected person, risk factor not specified.	6,609	2,705	3,904	82,978	34,552	48,426
Receipt of blood transfusion, blood components, or tissue.	160	73	87	9,334	5,190	4,144
Other/risk not reported or identified	10,857	6,976	3,881	100,975	69,095	31,879

X Not applicable. [1] Includes persons with a diagnosis of AIDS, reported from the beginning of the epidemic through 2005. Cumulative total includes persons with characteristics unknown.

Source: U.S. Centers for Disease Control and Prevention, Atlanta, GA, *HIV/AIDS Surveillance Report, 2005*, Volume 17. <http://www.cdc.gov/hiv/topics/surveillance/resources/reports/2005report/default.htm> (accessed 20 December 2006).

Table 176. **Estimated Numbers of Persons Living With Acquired Immunodeficiency Syndrome (AIDS) by Year and Selected Characteristics: 2000 to 2005**

[These numbers do not represent reported case counts. Rather, these numbers are point estimates, which result from adjustments of reported case counts. The reported case counts are adjusted for reporting delays and for redistribution of cases in persons initially reported without an identified risk factor. The estimates do not include adjustment for incomplete reporting. See the Commentary section in the 2005 report. See headnote, Table 175]

Age and characteristic	2000	2002	2003	2004	2005
Total [1, 2]	320,177	363,496	386,310	408,875	433,760
AGE AS OF END OF YEAR					
Less than 13 years old	2,843	2,303	1,998	1,670	1,393
13 and 14 years old	513	689	753	802	793
15 to 24 years old	4,944	5,419	6,056	6,729	7,562
25 to 34 years old	54,473	48,408	46,822	45,530	44,497
35 to 44 years old	143,920	151,292	155,309	157,579	158,856
45 to 54 years old	85,445	107,040	119,335	132,051	145,946
55 to 64 years old	22,089	30,249	35,935	42,213	49,809
65 years old and over.	5,950	7,851	9,304	11,009	13,018
RACE/ETHNICITY					
White, not Hispanic.	119,420	130,510	136,501	142,884	149,658
Black, not Hispanic.	132,090	152,536	163,683	174,363	185,988
Hispanic	63,894	63,871	68,388	72,723	78,054
Asian/Pacific Islander	2,612	3,158	3,532	3,891	4,276
American Indian/Alaska Native	1,099	1,266	1,378	1,481	1,581
TRANSMISSION CATEGORY MALE ADULT/ADOLESCENT					
Males 13 years old and over, total	248,726	272,553	288,509	304,500	322,125
Male-to-male sexual contact.	142,069	159,143	169,479	180,061	191,362
Injection drug use.	57,778	58,089	59,909	61,582	63,864
Male-to-male sexual contact and injection drug use . . .	22,603	24,030	24,678	25,307	25,961
High-risk heterosexual contact	22,568	27,531	30,593	33,571	36,784
Other [3]	3,708	3,760	3,849	3,979	4,154
FEMALE ADULT/ADOLESCENT					
Females 13 years old and over, total	67,601	76,930	83,224	89,313	95,959
Injection drug use.	26,656	28,176	29,230	30,232	31,521
Heterosexual contact	39,121	46,743	51,844	56,760	61,938
Other [3]	1,824	2,012	2,149	2,321	2,500
CHILD (LESS THAN 13 YEARS OLD AT DIAGNOSIS)					
Total	3,848	3,763	3,775	3,766	3,787
Perinatal	3,706	3,631	3,648	3,640	3,661
Other [4]	142	132	127	126	126

[1] Includes persons of unknown or multiple race and of unknown sex. Because column totals were calculated independently of the values for the subpopulations, the values in each column may not sum to the column total. [2] Persons who reported multiple racial categories or whose race was unknown are included in the total numbers. [3] Includes hemophilia, blood transfusion, perinatal, and risk not reported or not identified. [4] Includes hemophilia, blood transfusion, and risk not reported or not identified.

Source: U.S. Centers for Disease Control and Prevention, Atlanta, GA, *HIV/AIDS Surveillance Report, 2005*, Volume 17; <http://www.cdc.gov/hiv/topics/surveillance/resources/reports/2005report/default.htm> (revised June 2007).

Health and Nutrition   121

Table 177. Children Immunized Against Specified Diseases: 1995 to 2005

[In percent. Covers civilian noninstitutionalized population ages 19 months to 35 months. Based on estimates from the National Immunization Survey. The health care providers of the children are contacted to verify and/or complete vaccination information. Results are based on race/ethnic status of the child]

Vaccination	1995, total	2000, total	2005 [1]					
			Total	White, non-Hispanic	Black, non-Hispanic	Hispanic [2]	American Indian/ Alaska Native [3]	Asian [3]
Diphtheria-tetanus-pertussis (DTP) diphtheria-tetanus:								
3+ doses	95.0	94.0	96.1	96.1	95.2	96.3	90.7	96.8
4+ doses	79.0	82.0	85.7	87.1	84.0	83.6	(NA)	88.8
Polio: 3+ doses	88.0	90.0	91.7	91.4	91.0	92.3	(NA)	92.9
Measles, mumps, rubella vaccine	90.0	91.0	91.5	91.4	91.9	91.1	89.7	91.9
Hib: 3+ doses [4]	92.0	93.0	93.9	94.2	92.9	94.2	87.9	89.3
Hepatitis B: 3+ doses	68.0	90.0	92.9	93.1	92.7	92.7	90.1	92.7
Varicella [5]	(NA)	68.0	87.9	86.1	90.6	89.2	82.2	91.9
PCV: 3+ doses [6]	(X)	(X)	82.8	83.2	79.6	83.5	(NA)	78.7
4+ DTP/3+ polio/1+ MCV [7]	76.0	78.0	83.1	84.0	81.4	81.8	(NA)	85.7
4+ DTP/3+ polio/1+ MCV/3+ Hib	74.0	76.0	82.4	83.6	80.5	81.2	(NA)	82.3
4+ DTP/3+ polio/1+ MCV/3+ Hib/3+ HepB	55.1	72.8	80.8	82.1	79.3	78.8	(NA)	80.5

NA Not available. X Not Applicable. [1] Children were born between February 2002 and July 2004. [2] Children of Hispanic ethnicity may be any race. [3] Non-Hispanic. [4] Haemophilus influenzae type B. [5] Data collection for varicella (chicken pox) began in July 1996. [6] PCV = Pneumococcal conjugate vaccine. [7] MCV = Measles containing vaccine.

Source: U.S. Centers for Disease Control and Prevention, Atlanta, GA, National Immunization Program, Data and Statistics, "Immunization Coverage in the U.S."; <http://www.cdc.gov/vaccines/stats-surv/imz-coverage.htm#nis>.

Table 178. Learning Disability or Attention Deficit Hyperactivity Disorder for Children 3–17 Years of Age by Selected Characteristics: 2005

[In thousands, except percent (61,192 represents 61,192,000). Learning Disability is based on the question, "Has a representative from a school or a health professional ever told you that (child's name) has a learning disability?" Attention Deficit Hyperactivity Disorder is based on the question, "Has a doctor or health professional ever told you that (child's name) had Attention Hyperactivity Disorder or Attention Deficit Disorder?"]

Selected characteristic	Total	Ever told had—			
		Learning disability		Attention deficit hyperactivity disorder	
		Number	Percent	Number	Percent
Total [1,2]	61,192	4,244	6.9	3,998	6.5
SEX [2]					
Male	31,235	2,711	8.7	2,854	9.1
Female.	29,957	1,534	5.1	1,143	3.8
AGE					
3 to 4 years old	8,119	125	1.5	[4]60	[4]0.7
5 to 11 years old	27,766	1,791	6.5	1,682	6.1
12 to 17 years old	25,307	2,329	9.2	2,256	8.9
RACE					
Race alone [2,3]	59,480	4,104	6.9	3,842	6.4
White	47,287	3,233	6.8	3,123	6.6
Black or African American.	9,355	774	8.2	634	6.8
American Indian or Alaska Native.	510	[4]37	[4]7.4	[4]40	[4]8.2
Asian	2,219	[4]48	[4]2.1	[4]44	[4]2.0
Native Hawaiian or Other Pacific Islander . . .	109	(B)	(B)	–	–
Two or more races [2,5]	1,712	141	9.0	156	9.1
HISPANIC ORIGIN AND RACE: [2,6]					
Hispanic or Latino	11,600	807	7.1	533	4.7
Mexican or Mexican American.	7,967	505	6.5	327	4.2
Not Hispanic or Latino.	49,592	3,438	6.9	3,465	6.9
White, single race	36,546	2,525	6.8	2,680	7.2
Black or African American, single race	9,038	744	8.2	616	6.9

– Represents zero. B Base figure too small to meet statistical standards for reliability of a derived figure. [1] Includes other races not shown separately. [2] Estimates are age-adjusted to the 2000 projected U.S. standard population using age groups 3-4 years, 5-11 years, and 12-17 years. [3] Refers to persons who indicated only a single race group. [4] Figures do not meet standard of reliability or precision. [5] Refers to all persons who indicated more than one race group. [6] Persons of Hispanic or Latino origin may be any race or combination of races.

Source: U.S. National Center for Health Statistics, Vital and Health Statistics, Series 10, Number 231, Summary Health Statistics for U.S. Children: National Health Interview Survey, 2005; <http://www.cdc.gov/nchs/data/series/sr_10/sr10_231.pdf>.

Table 179. **Asthma Incidence Among Children Under 18 Years of Age by Selected Characteristics: 2005**

[In thousands, except percent (73,376 represents 73,376,000). Based on the National Health Interview Survey, a sample survey of the civilian noninstitutionalized population; see Appendix III]

Selected characteristic	Total	Ever told had asthma		Had asthma attack in past 12 months	
		Number	Percent	Number	Percent
Total [1, 2]	73,376	9,287	12.7	6,531	8.9
SEX [2]					
Male	37,511	5,481	14.7	3,745	10.0
Female	35,865	3,806	10.6	2,786	7.8
AGE					
0 to 4 years old	20,303	1,741	8.6	1,371	6.8
5 to 11 years old	27,766	3,715	13.4	2,742	9.9
12 to 17 years old	25,307	3,830	15.2	2,417	9.6
RACE					
Race alone: [2, 3]	71,242	8,932	12.6	6,263	8.8
White	56,761	6,558	11.6	4,519	8.0
Black or African American	11,152	1,949	17.5	1,467	13.2
American Indian or Alaska Native	591	112	20.1	[4]81	[4]14.0
Asian	2,621	278	10.5	171	6.5
Native Hawaiian or Other Pacific Islander . . .	117	[4]34	[4]33.3	(B)	[4]29.2
Two or more races [2, 5]	2,133	355	17.3	268	13.0
HISPANIC ORIGIN AND RACE [2, 6]					
Hispanic or Latino	14,423	1,780	12.6	1,237	8.7
Mexican or Mexican American	9,953	1,058	10.8	736	7.5
Not Hispanic or Latino	58,953	7,507	12.7	5,294	9.0
White, single race	43,429	4,963	11.4	3,432	7.9
Black or African American, single race	10,741	1,859	17.4	1,401	13.1

B Figure too small to meet statistical standards for reliability of a derived figure. [1] Includes other races not shown separately. [2] Estimates are age-adjusted to the 2000 projected U.S. standard population using age groups 3-4 years, 5-11 years, and 12-17 years. [3] Refers to persons who indicated only a single race group. [4] Figures do not meet standard of reliability or precision. [5] Refers to all persons who indicated more than one race group. [6] Persons of Hispanic or Latino origin may be any race or combination of races.

Source: U.S. National Center for Health Statistics, *Vital and Health Statistics, Series 10, Number 231, Summary Health Statistics for U.S. Children: National Health Interview Survey, 2005;* <http://www.cdc.gov/nchs/data/series/sr_10/sr10_231.pdf>.

Table 180. **Number of Persons with a Disability by Age Group and by State: 2005**

[In thousands (39,736 represents 39,736,000). Based on data from American Community Survey (ACS). See text, Section 1 and Appendix III]

State	Total	5 to 15 years [1]	16 to 64 years [2]	65 years and over [3]	State	Total	5 to 15 years [1]	16 to 64 years [2]	65 years and over [3]
U.S. . . .	39,736	2,887	22,789	14,062	MO	907	59	536	312
AL	826	58	494	274	MT	142	10	81	51
AK	86	7	59	20	NE	221	16	121	84
AZ	749	57	425	267	NV	262	20	148	95
AR	532	40	314	178	NH	167	15	95	56
CA	4,122	284	2,357	1,482	NJ	950	63	501	386
CO	497	36	297	164	NM	297	18	179	100
CT	402	29	218	155	NY	2,433	169	1,343	921
DE	112	10	64	38	NC	1,275	94	757	424
DC	67	5	39	23	ND	81	5	41	35
FL	2,567	161	1,324	1,082	OH	1,668	130	966	572
GA	1,161	81	723	357	OK	604	35	361	208
HI	145	7	77	61	OR	533	35	312	187
ID	201	14	117	69	PA	1,787	130	973	684
IL	1,464	115	797	552	RI	155	14	87	55
IN	879	72	511	297	SC	660	41	402	217
IA	382	25	209	148	SD	98	5	53	40
KS	352	22	197	133	TN	1,012	63	623	326
KY	801	55	505	241	TX	2,885	253	1,681	951
LA	737	61	443	233	UT	273	26	168	79
ME	218	18	130	70	VT	91	7	53	31
MD	647	58	364	226	VA	930	69	532	329
MA	784	61	426	297	WA	889	61	544	283
MI	1,438	118	835	485	WV	390	20	236	133
MN	569	44	321	204	WI	668	51	377	240
MS	548	35	330	183	WY	72	5	43	24

[1] Persons aged 5–15 were classified as having a disability if they reported any one of the four conditions; sensory, physical, mental, or self-care disability. [2] Persons aged 16–64 were classified as having a disability if they reported any one of the six conditions; sensory, physical, mental, self-care disability, go-outside-home, or employment disability. [3] Persons 65 years and over were classified as having a disability if they reported any one of the five conditions; sensory, physical, mental, self-care disability, or go-outside-home disability.

Source: U.S. Census Bureau, "American Factfinder®, 2005 American Community Survey, Summary Table, Sex by Age by Disability Status for the Civilian Noninstitutionalized Population 5 Years and Over"; <http://www.factfinder.census.gov/>.

U.S. Census Bureau, Statistical Abstract of the United States: 2008

Table 181. **Persons With Limitation of Activity Caused by Chronic Conditions: 2000 to 2005**

[In percent. Limitation of activity is assessed by asking respondents a series of questions about limitations in their ability to perform activities usual for their age group because of a physical, mental, or emotional problem. Based on the National Health Interview Survey, a sample survey of the civilian noninstitutionalized population; see Appendix III]

Characteristic	2000	2003	2004	2005	Characteristic	2000	2003	2004	2005
Total [1,2]	11.7	12.1	11.9	11.7	Male [2]	11.7	11.9	11.8	11.7
Under 18 years old	6.0	6.9	7.0	7.0	Female [2]	11.5	12.2	11.9	11.6
18 to 44 years old	5.8	6.0	6.0	5.7					
45 to 54 years old	12.4	13.0	12.5	11.9	White, non-Hispanic [2]	11.5	11.8	12.1	11.5
55 to 64 years old	19.7	21.1	19.9	19.9	Black, non-Hispanic [2]	14.3	15.3	15.3	14.1
65 to 74 years old	26.1	26.3	25.5	25.2	Hispanic [2,3]	10.3	10.2	10.2	10.5
75 years and over	45.1	44.0	43.9	43.5	Mexican	10.4	10.1	10.1	11.4

[1] Includes all other races not shown separately.   [2] Estimates for all persons are age adjusted to the year 2000 standard using six age groups: Under 18 years old, 18–44 years old, 45–54 years old, 55–64 years old, 65–74 years old, and 75 years old and over.   [3] Persons of Hispanic origin may be any race.

Source: U.S. National Center for Health Statistics, *Health, United States*, annual; <http://www.cdc.gov/nchs/hus.htm>.

Table 182. **Persons 65 Years Old and Over With Limitation of Activity Caused by Chronic Conditions: 2000 to 2005**

[In percent. Covers noninstitutionalized persons 65 years old and over. To determine activities of daily living (ADL) limitations respondents were asked "Because of a physical, mental, or emotional problem, does (this person) need the help of other persons with personal care needs, such as eating, bathing, dressing, or getting around inside this home?" Instrumental activities of daily living (IADL) were determined by asking respondents "Because of a physical, mental, or emotional problem, does (this person) need the help of other persons in handling routine needs, such as everyday household chores, doing necessary business, shopping, or getting around for other purposes?" See also headnote, Table 181]

Characteristic	Percent with ADL limitation				Percent with IADL limitation			
	2000	2003	2004	2005	2000	2003	2004	2005
Total [1,2]	6.3	6.4	6.1	6.2	12.7	12.2	11.5	12.0
65 to 74 years old	3.3	3.1	2.9	3.2	6.6	6.5	5.5	6.4
75 years old and over	9.5	9.9	9.5	9.4	19.3	18.4	18.1	18.3
Male [2]	5.1	5.2	4.8	4.6	9.2	8.6	8.4	8.1
Female [2]	7.0	7.2	6.9	7.2	15.1	14.6	13.6	14.8
Not Hispanic or Latino [2]	6.1	6.1	5.8	5.9	12.6	12.1	11.3	11.8
White	5.7	5.7	5.5	5.4	12.1	11.4	10.7	11.2
Black or African American	10.1	10.4	8.7	10.1	19.1	19.0	17.1	17.7
Hispanic or Latino [2,3]	8.6	10.3	10.4	10.7	13.4	13.8	14.8	16.9
Mexican	9.4	9.8	10.7	12.0	16.3	15.1	15.3	19.6

[1] Includes other races not shown separately.   [2] Estimates are age adjusted to the year 2000 standard using two age groups: 65–74 years old and 75 years old and over.   [3] Persons of Hispanic origin may be any race.

Source: U.S. National Center for Health Statistics, *Health, United States*, annual; <http://www.cdc.gov/nchs/hus.htm>.

Table 183. **Nursing Homes—Selected Characteristics: 2004**

[Beds: 1,730 represents 1,730,000. Covers licensed and/or certified nursing homes in the conterminous United States that had three or more beds. Based on the 2004 National Nursing Home Survey, a two-stage survey sample of nursing homes and their residents. Subject to sampling variability.]

Characteristic	Nursing homes	Beds			Current residents		Full-time equivalent employees [2]	
		Number (1,000)	Per nursing home	Number (1,000)	Occupancy rate [1]	Number (1,000)	Rate per 100 beds
Total	16,100	1,730	107.6	1,492	86.3	1,053	60.9
Ownership:							
Proprietary	9,900	1,074	108.6	918	85.5	615	57.2
Voluntary nonprofit	5,000	504	101.6	440	87.4	326	64.6
Government and other	1,200	152	123.6	134	87.9	113	74.1
Certification:							
Medicare and medicaid certified	14,100	1,600	113.5	1,380	86.2	972	60.8
Medicare only	[3]700	33	50.6	28	85.0	20	59.7
Medicaid only	1,100	76	69.0	68	89.1	41	53.7
Not certified	[3]200	21	90.4	17	78.3	20	95.7
Bed size:							
Fewer than 50 beds	2,200	76	33.8	62	82.1	43	56.6
50–99 beds	6,000	455	75.7	423	92.9	254	55.8
100–199 beds	6,800	903	132.0	789	87.3	563	62.4
200 beds or more	1,000	296	298.2	219	73.9	193	65.3
Region:							
Northeast	2,800	382	136.0	331	86.8	263	68.9
Midwest	5,300	527	99.4	448	85.1	286	54.2
South	5,400	586	108.2	502	85.6	353	60.3
West	2,600	236	92.1	211	89.5	151	64.1
Affiliation:							
Chain	8,700	939	107.9	812	86.5	540	57.4
Independent	7,400	791	107.2	680	86.0	514	65.0

[1] Number of residents divided by number of available beds multiplied by 100.   [2] Includes only those employees providing direct health-related services to residents. Includes nurses, nurses' aides, orderlies, dental hygienists, physical therapists, speech pathologists, and/or audiologists, dieticians or nutritionists, podiatrists, and social workers.   [3] Figure does not meet standards of reliability or precision.
Source: U.S. National Center for Health Statistics; *National Nursing Home Survey*; see also <http://www.cdc.gov/nchs/about/major/nnhsd/Facilitytables.htm>.

Table 184. **Injury and Poisoning Episodes and Conditions by Age and Sex: 2005**

[33,202 represents 33,202,000. Covers all medically attended injuries and poisonings occurring during the 5-week period prior to the survey interview. Age adjustment is used to adjust for differences in the age distribution of populations being compared. There may be more than one condition per episode. Based on the National Health Interview Survey, a sample survey of the civilian noninstitutionalized population; see Appendix III]

External cause and nature of injury	Both sexes							Male, total	Female, total
	Total	Total, age-adjusted [1]	Under 12 years old	12 to 21 years old	22 to 44 years old	45 to 64 years old	65 years old and over		
EPISODES									
Number (1,000)	33,202	(X)	4,851	6,155	9,303	7,899	4,994	17,750	15,451
Annual rate per 1,000 population, total [2]	114.0	114.1	100.6	148.3	98.9	109.3	142.5	124.6	103.9
Fall	40.5	40.6	47.5	32.4	23.2	40.5	87.2	35.1	45.7
Struck by or against a person or an object	14.4	14.5	14.4	34.8	12.3	7.7	[4]9.5	18.6	10.4
Transportation [3]	13.2	13.2	[4]13.5	16.0	14.4	12.0	[4]8.6	15.3	11.2
Overexertion	15.4	15.2	[4]2.4	21.2	19.0	19.2	[4]8.7	16.9	13.9
Cutting, piercing instruments.	7.8	7.7	[4]4.7	[4]4.4	8.9	10.2	[4]8.1	11.7	[4]4.1
Poisoning [5]	1.8	1.8	[4]3.2	[4]1.2	[4]1.0	[4]2.9	[4]0.9	[4]1.8	[4]1.9
CONDITIONS									
Annual rate per 1,000 population, total [2]	146.6	146.7	111.0	180.4	132.5	142.2	202.3	152.6	140.8
Sprains/strains	42.0	41.8	13.7	63.9	47.0	45.2	35.4	39.5	44.5
Open wounds	20.0	20.1	31.9	17.5	15.7	16.9	24.5	26.6	13.7
Fractures	24.1	24.1	20.2	27.9	15.7	22.7	50.3	25.2	23.0
Contusions	24.4	24.4	15.7	29.8	20.8	24.1	39.8	23.7	25.0

X Not applicable.   [1] Data were age-adjusted using the 2000 standard population.   [2] Includes other items not shown separately.   [3] Includes the categories "Motor vehicle traffic"; "Pedal cycle, other"; "Pedestrian, other"; and "Transport, other."   [4] Figure does not meet standard of reliability or precision.   [5] Poisoning episodes are assumed to have a single condition resulting from the episode.

Source: U.S. National Center for Health Statistics, unpublished data. See also <http://www.cdc.gov/nchs/injury.htm>.

Table 185. **Injuries Associated With Selected Consumer Products: 2005**

[Estimates calculated from a representative sample of hospitals with emergency treatment departments in the United States. Data are estimates of the number of emergency-room-treated cases nationwide associated with various products. Product involvement does not necessarily mean the product caused the accident. Products were selected from the U.S. Consumer Product Safety Commission's National Electronic Injury Surveillance System (NEISS)]

Product	Number	Product	Number
Home workshop equipment:		Stairs or steps	1,104,071
Saws (hand or power)	95,448	Ceilings and walls	308,518
Hammers	34,105	Other doors [2]	307,713
Household packaging and containers:		Home entertainment equipment:	
Household containers and packaging	207,680	Televisions	51,091
Bottles and jars	73,916	Personal use items:	
Housewares:		Footwear	115,944
Knives	429,021	Wheelchairs	103,055
Tableware and flatware	97,559	Crutches, canes, walkers	81,205
Drinking glasses	74,018	Yard and garden equipment:	
Home furnishing		Lawn mowers	84,316
Beds	505,826	Sports and recreation equipment:	
Chairs	302,328	Bicycles	494,712
Tables [1]	298,949	Skateboards	112,544
Household cabinets, racks, and shelves . .	245,555	Trampolines	108,029
Home structures, construction:		Playground climbing equipment	80,312
Floors or flooring materials	1,114,816	Swimming pools	79,823

[1] Excludes baby-changing and television tables or stands.   [2] Excludes glass doors and garage doors.

Source: National Safety Council, Itasca, IL, *Injury Facts, Annual* (copyright); <http://www.nsc.org/lrs/statstop.htm>.

Table 186. **Costs of Unintentional Injuries: 2005**

[625.5 represents $625,500,000,000. Covers costs of deaths or disabling injuries together with vehicle accidents and fires]

Cost	Amount (bil. dol.)					Percent distribution				
	Total [1]	Motor vehicle	Work	Home	Other	Total [1]	Motor vehicle	Work	Home	Other
Total	625.5	247.7	160.4	142.3	96.3	1.00	1.00	1.00	1.00	1.00
Wage and productivity losses [2]	318.2	88.0	80.0	90.6	64.0	50.9	35.5	49.9	63.7	66.5
Medical expense	118.8	34.3	31.3	33.5	21.6	19.0	13.8	19.5	23.5	22.4
Administrative expenses [3]	117.4	81.9	34.4	7.0	6.9	18.8	33.1	21.4	4.9	7.2
Motor vehicle damage	41.3	41.3	1.7	(NA)	(NA)	6.6	16.7	1.1	(NA)	(NA)
Employer uninsured cost [4]	19.1	2.2	10.7	4.2	2.4	3.1	0.9	6.7	3.0	2.5
Fire loss	10.7	(NA)	2.3	7.0	1.4	1.7	(NA)	1.4	4.9	1.5

NA Not available.   [1] Excludes duplication between work and motor vehicle ($21.2 billion in 2005).   [2] Actual loss of wages and household production, and the present value of future earnings lost.   [3] Home and other costs may include costs of administering medical treatment claims for some motor-vehicle injuries filed through health insurance plans.   [4] Estimate of the uninsured costs incurred by employers, representing the money value of time lost by noninjured workers.

Source National Safety Council, Itasca, IL, *Injury Facts, Annual* (copyright); <http://www.nsc.org/lrs/statstop.htm>.

Table 187. **Persons 18 Years and Over With Selected Diseases and Conditions by Selected Characteristics: 2005**

[In thousands (217,774 represents 217,774,000). Based on National Health Interview Survey, a sample survey of the civilian noninstitutionalized population; see Appendix III]

Selected characteristic	Total persons	Diabetes [1,2]	Ulcers [1]	Kidney disease [3,4]	Liver disease [3]	Arthritis diagnosis [5]	Chronic joint symptoms [6]
Total [7,8]	217,774	16,186	15,104	3,791	2,965	46,941	58,863
SEX [8]							
Male	104,919	7,896	6,913	1,736	1,571	18,260	25,967
Female	112,855	8,290	8,190	2,055	1,395	28,681	32,896
AGE							
18 to 44 years old	110,431	2,640	4,787	931	738	8,624	17,161
45 to 64 years old	72,296	7,595	6,008	1,305	1,721	20,780	25,426
65 to 74 years old	18,446	3,421	2,100	675	321	8,609	8,313
75 years old and over.....	16,600	2,529	2,209	880	185	8,927	7,963
RACE							
Race alone [8,9]	215,349	15,982	14,916	3,696	2,912	46,288	58,006
White...................	180,477	12,886	13,042	2,967	2,484	40,351	50,803
Black or African American ...	24,817	2,513	1,327	570	314	4,718	5,593
American Indian or Alaska Native	1,469	116	148	[10]38	[10]33	310	420
Asian..................	8,155	437	349	[10]104	[10]81	868	1,138
Native Hawaiian or other Pacific Islander	431	(B)	(B)	(B)	–	[10](B)	53
Two or more races [8,11] ...	2,425	204	188	[10]95	[10]53	653	857
HISPANIC ORIGIN AND RACE [8,12]							
Hispanic or Latino	27,770	1,898	1,311	563	386	3,194	4,729
Mexican or Mexican American	17,163	1,242	745	351	213	1,677	2,631

– Represents zero. B Figure too small to meet statistical standards for reliability of a derived figure. [1] Respondents were asked if they had ever been told by a health professional that they had an ulcer or diabetes. A person may be represented in more than one column. [2] Excludes borderline diabetes. [3] Respondents were asked if they had been told in the last 12 months by a health professional that they had weak or failing kidneys or any kind of liver condition. [4] Excludes kidney stones, bladder infections, or incontinence. [5] Respondents were asked if they had ever been told by a health professional that they had some form of arthritis, rheumatoid arthritis, gout, lupus, or fibromyalgia. [6] Respondents with joint symptoms that began more than 3 months ago prior to interview. Excludes back and neck. [7] Total includes other races not shown separately. [8] Estimates are age adjusted to the year 2000 standards using four age groups: 18–44 years, 45–64 years, 65–74 years, and 75 years and over. [9] Refers to persons who indicated only a single race group. [10] Figures do not meet standard of reliability or precision. [11] Refers to all persons who indicated more than one race group. [12] Persons of Hispanic or Latino origin may be of any race or combination of races.

Source: U.S. National Center for Health Statistics, *Vital and Health Statistics, Series 10, Number 232, Summary Health Statistics for U.S. Adults: National Health Interview Survey, 2005;* <http://www.cdc.gov/nchs/data/series/sr10/sr10232.pdf>.

Table 188. **Persons 18 Years of Age and Over with Selected Circulatory Diseases by Selected Characteristics: 2005**

[In thousands (217,774 represents 217,774,000). In separate questions, respondents were asked if they had ever been told by a doctor or other health professional that they had: hypertension (or high blood pressure); coronary heart disease, angina (or angina pectoris); heart attack (or myocardial infarction); any other heart condition or disease not already mentioned; or a stroke. A person may be represented in more than one column. Based on National Health Interview Survey, a sample survey of the civilian noninstitutionalized population; see Appendix III]

Characteristic	Total persons	Heart disease — All types [1]	Heart disease — Coronary [2]	Hypertension [3]	Stroke
Total [4,5]	217,774	25,583	14,088	48,759	5,166
SEX [5]					
Male	104,919	12,538	7,903	22,171	2,239
Female	112,855	13,045	6,185	26,588	2,926
AGE					
18 to 44 years old	110,431	4,763	1,089	8,067	401
45 to 64 years old	72,296	9,822	5,316	22,521	1,558
65 to 74 years old	18,446	4,927	3,480	9,127	1,144
75 years old and over.....	16,600	6,071	4,203	9,044	2,063
RACE					
Race alone [5,6]	215,349	25,264	13,929	48,258	5,078
White...................	180,477	22,366	12,325	39,414	4,213
Black or African American ...	24,817	2,258	1,311	7,097	706
American Indian or Alaska Native	1,469	163	[7]42	308	[7]37
Asian..................	8,155	445	231	1,372	118
Native Hawaiian or Other Pacific Islander	431	(B)	(B)	(B)	(B)
Two or more races [5,8] ...	2,425	318	158	501	[7]88
HISPANIC ORIGIN AND RACE [5,9]					
Hispanic or Latino	27,770	1,596	1,028	3,964	347
Mexican or Mexican American	17,163	846	512	2,194	233

B Figure too small to meet statistical standards for reliability of a derived figure. [1] Heart disease includes coronary heart disease, angina pectoris, heart attack, or any other heart condition or disease. [2] Coronary heart disease includes coronary heart disease, angina pectoris, or heart attack. [3] Persons had to have been told on two or more different visits that they had hypertension, or high blood pressure, to be classified as hypertensive. [4] Includes other races not shown separately. [5] See footnote 8, Table 187. [6] Refers to persons who indicated only a single race group. [7] Figures do not meet standard of reliability or precision. [8] Refers to all persons who indicated more than one race group. [9] Persons of Hispanic or Latino origin may be any race or combination of races.

Source: U.S. National Center for Health Statistics, *Vital and Health Statistics, Series 10, Number 232, Summary Health Statistics for U.S. Adults: National Health Interview Survey, 2005;* <http://www.cdc.gov/nchs/data/series/sr10/sr10232.pdf>.

Table 189. **Selected Respiratory Diseases Among Persons 18 Years of Age and Over by Selected Characteristics: 2005**

[In thousands (217,774 represents 217,774,000). Respondents were asked in two separate questions if they had ever been told by a doctor or other health professional that they had emphysema or asthma. Respondents who had been told they had asthma were asked if they still had asthma. Respondents were asked in three separate questions if they had been told by a doctor or other health professional in the past 12 months that they had hay fever, sinusitis, or bronchitis. Based on the National Health Interview Survey, a sample survey of the civilian noninstitutionalized population; see Appendix III]

Selected characteristic	Total persons	Emphy-sema	Asthma Ever	Asthma Still	Hay fever	Sinusitis	Chronic bronchitis
Total [2, 3]	217,774	3,791	23,334	15,697	18,651	29,517	8,912
SEX [3]							
Male	104,919	2,061	9,148	5,348	7,983	10,170	2,886
Female	112,855	1,730	14,186	10,349	10,668	19,346	6,026
AGE							
18 to 44 years old........	110,431	341	12,322	7,746	8,566	12,875	3,504
45 to 64 years old........	72,296	1,430	7,555	5,281	7,750	11,831	3,544
65 to 74 years old........	18,446	1,070	2,011	1,600	1,438	2,683	1,026
75 years old and over	16,600	951	1,445	1,070	897	2,126	838
RACE							
Race alone: [3, 4]	215,349	3,725	22,964	15,425	18,481	29,115	8,744
White	180,477	3,503	19,174	12,895	16,225	24,996	7,511
Black or African American..	24,817	180	2,899	2,048	1,502	3,292	1,063
American Indian or Alaska Native.	1,469	(B)	120	[5]85	[5]122	193	[5]56
Asian	8,155	[5]24	626	337	569	509	[5]96
Native Hawaiian or other Pacific Islander.	431	(B)	(B)	[5]59	(B)	(B)	(B)
Two or more races [3, 6].....	2,425	[5]66	370	271	170	401	168
HISPANIC ORIGIN AND RACE [3, 7]							
Hispanic or Latino..........	27,770	132	2,097	1,386	1,846	2,242	666
Mexican or Mexican American.	17,163	[5]66	1,028	664	1,039	1,138	327
Not Hispanic or Latino......	190,004	3,659	21,237	14,311	16,805	27,275	8,247
White, single race	154,325	3,377	17,248	11,626	14,460	22,942	6,889
Black or African American, single race ...	24,186	180	2,810	1,993	1,486	3,220	1,049

B Figure too small to meet statistical standards for reliability of a derived figure. [1] A person may be represented in more than one column. [2] Total includes other races not shown separately. [3] See footnote 8, Table 187. [4] Refers to persons who indicated only a single race group. [5] Figure does not meet standard of reliability or precision. [6] Refers to all persons who indicated more than one race group. [7] Persons of Hispanic or Latino origin may be any race or combination of races.
Source: U.S. National Center for Health Statistics, *Vital and Health Statistics, Series 10, Number 232, Summary Health Statistics for U.S. Adult: National Health Interview Survey, 2005;* <http://www.cdc.gov/nchs/data/series/sr10/sr10232.pdf>.

Table 190. **Persons 18 Years of Age and Over With Migraines and Pains in the Neck, Lower Back, Face or Jaw, by Selected Characteristics: 2005**

[In thousands (217,774 represents 217,774,000). Based on National Health Interview Survey, a sample survey of the civilian noninstitutionalized population, Appendix III]

Selected characteristic	Total persons	Migraine and pain [1] Migraine or severe headache [2]	Pain in neck [3]	Pain in lower back [3]	Pain in face or jaw [3]
Total [4, 5]	217,774	32,826	32,294	61,965	9,639
SEX [5]					
Male..................	104,919	9,857	13,022	27,502	2,818
Female...............	112,855	22,970	19,271	34,463	6,821
AGE					
18 to 44 years old........	110,431	20,281	14,076	27,632	4,981
45 to 64 years old........	72,296	10,319	13,018	22,784	3,439
65 to 74 years old........	18,446	1,366	2,906	5,909	687
75 years old and over	16,600	860	2,293	5,640	532
RACE					
Race alone [5, 6]	215,349	32,242	31,699	61,096	9,428
White	180,477	27,461	27,745	52,561	8,144
Black or African American. ..	24,817	3,621	2,954	6,303	964
American Indian or Alaska Native.	1,469	235	170	433	[7]88
Asian	8,155	864	757	1,599	227
Native Hawaiian or other Pacific Islander.	431	[7]60	(B)	(B)	(B)
Two or more races [5, 8]	2,425	585	594	869	211
HISPANIC ORIGIN AND RACE [5, 9]					
Hispanic or Latino	27,770	4,319	3,492	6,983	923
Mexican or Mexican American.	17,163	2,506	1,853	3,984	566

B Figure too small to meet statistical standards for reliability of a derived figure. [1] A person may be represented in more than one column. [2] Respondents were asked, "During the past 3 months, did you have a severe headache or migraine?" Respondents were instructed to report pain that had lasted a whole day or more and, conversely, not to report fleeting or minor aches or pains. [3] Respondents were asked, "During the past 3 months, did you have a neck pain; or low back pain; or facial ache or pain in the jaw muscles or the joint in front of the ear?" Respondents were instructed to report pain that had lasted a whole day or more and, conversely, not to report fleeting or minor aches or pains. [4] Total includes other races not shown separately. [5] See footnote 8, Table 187. [6] Refers to persons who indicated only a single race group. [7] Figure does not meet standard of reliability or precision. [8] Refers to all persons who indicated more than one race group. [9] Persons of Hispanic or Latino origin may be any race or combination of races.
Source U.S. National Center for Health Statistics, *Vital and Health Statistics, Series 10, Number 232, Summary Health Statistics for U.S. Adults: National Health Interview Survey, 2005;* <http://www.cdc.gov/nchs/data/series/sr10/sr10232.pdf>.

Health 127

Table 191. Use of Mammography for Women 40 Years Old and Over by Patient Characteristics: 1990 to 2005

[Percent of women having a mammogram within the past 2 years. Covers civilian noninstitutional population. Based on National Health Interview Survey; see Appendix III]

Characteristic	1990	2000 [1]	2005 [2]	Characteristic	1990	2000 [1]	2005 [2]
Total [3]	51.4	70.4	66.8	Years of school completed:			
40 to 49 years old	55.1	64.3	63.5	No high school diploma or GED	36.4	57.7	52.8
50 years old and over	49.7	73.6	68.4	High school diploma or GED	52.7	69.7	64.9
50 to 64 years old	56.0	78.7	71.8	Some college or more	62.8	76.2	72.7
65 years old and over	43.4	67.9	63.8				
White, non-Hispanic	52.7	72.2	68.4	Poverty status: [5]			
Black, non-Hispanic	46.0	67.9	65.2	Below poverty	28.7	54.8	48.5
Hispanic origin [4]	45.2	61.2	58.8	At or above poverty	54.8	72.1	68.8

[1] Adjusted data—data for 2000 have been reweighted using the 2000 census population controls. [2] Data for 2005 are weighted using 2000 census population controls. [3] Includes other races not shown separately and unknown education level and poverty status. [4] Persons of Hispanic origin may be any race. [5] For explanation of poverty level, see text, Section 13.

Source: U.S. National Center for Health Statistics, *Health, United States*, annual. See also <http://www.cdc.gov/nchs/hus.htm>.

Table 192. Current Cigarette Smoking: 1990 to 2005

[In percent. Prior to 1992, a current smoker is a person who has smoked at least 100 cigarettes and who now smokes. Beginning 1995, definition includes persons who smoke only "some days." Excludes unknown smoking status. Based on National Health Interview Survey; for details, see Appendix III]

Sex, age, and race	1990 [1]	1995 [1]	2000	2005	Sex, age, and race	1990 [1]	1995 [1]	2000	2005
Total smokers, age-adjusted [2]	25.3	24.6	23.1	20.8	Black, total	32.5	28.5	26.1	26.5
					18 to 24 years	21.3	[3]14.6	20.8	21.6
Male	28.0	26.5	25.2	23.4	25 to 34 years	33.8	25.1	23.3	29.8
Female	22.9	22.7	21.1	18.3	35 to 44 years	42.0	36.3	30.8	23.3
					45 to 64 years	36.7	33.9	32.2	32.4
White male	27.6	26.2	25.5	23.3	65 years and over	21.5	28.5	14.2	16.8
Black male	32.8	29.4	25.7	25.9	Female, total	22.8	22.6	21.0	18.1
White female	23.5	23.4	22.0	19.1	18 to 24 years	22.5	21.8	25.1	20.7
Black female	20.8	23.5	20.7	17.1	25 to 34 years	28.2	26.4	22.5	21.5
					35 to 44 years	24.8	27.1	26.2	21.3
Total smokers	25.5	24.7	23.2	20.9	45 to 64 years	24.8	24.0	21.6	18.8
					65 years and over	11.5	11.5	9.3	8.3
Male, total	28.4	27.0	25.7	23.9	White, total	23.4	23.1	21.6	18.7
18 to 24 years	26.6	27.8	28.5	28.0	18 to 24 years	25.4	24.9	28.7	22.6
25 to 34 years	31.6	29.5	29.0	27.7	25 to 34 years	28.5	27.3	25.1	23.1
35 to 44 years	34.5	31.5	30.2	26.0	35 to 44 years	25.0	27.0	26.6	22.2
45 to 64 years	29.3	27.1	26.4	25.2	45 to 64 years	25.4	24.3	21.4	18.9
65 years and over	14.6	14.9	10.2	8.9	65 years and over	11.5	11.7	9.1	8.4
White, total	28.0	26.6	25.8	23.6	Black, total	21.2	23.5	20.8	17.3
18 to 24 years	27.4	28.4	30.9	29.7	18 to 24 years	[3]10.0	[3]8.8	14.2	14.2
25 to 34 years	31.6	29.9	29.9	27.7	25 to 34 years	29.1	26.7	15.5	16.9
35 to 44 years	33.5	31.2	30.6	26.3	35 to 44 years	25.5	31.9	30.2	19.0
45 to 64 years	28.7	26.3	25.8	24.5	45 to 64 years	22.6	27.5	25.6	21.0
65 years and over	13.7	14.1	9.8	7.9	65 years and over	11.1	13.3	10.2	10.0

[1] Data prior to 1997 are not strictly comparable with data for later years due to the 1997 questionnaire redesign. [2] Estimates are age adjusted to the year 2000 standard using five age groups: 18–24 years, 25–34 years, 35–44 years, 45–64 years, 65 years and over. [3] Data have a relative standard error of 20 to 30 percent.

Source: U.S. National Center for Health Statistics, *Health, United States*, annual. See also <http://www.cdc.gov/nchs/hus.htm>.

Table 193. Current Cigarette Smoking by Sex and State: 2005

[In percent. Current cigarette smoking is defined as persons 18 years and older who reported having smoked 100 or more cigarettes during their lifetime and who currently smoke every day or some days. Based on the Behavioral Risk Factor Surveillance System, a telephone survey of health behaviors of the civilian, noninstitutionalized U.S. population, 18 years old and over; for details, see source]

State	Total	Male	Female	State	Total	Male	Female	State	Total	Male	Female
U.S. [1]	20.6	22.1	19.2	KS	17.8	18.9	16.8	ND	20.0	21.5	18.6
				KY	28.7	30.6	26.9	OH	22.3	21.9	22.8
AL	24.8	29.5	20.5	LA	22.6	24.6	20.6	OK	25.1	26.5	23.8
AK	25.0	27.9	22.0	ME	20.9	22.4	19.5	OR	18.5	20.6	16.5
AZ	20.4	22.0	18.8	MD	19.0	19.7	18.4	PA	23.7	25.0	22.5
AR	23.5	25.2	21.9	MA	18.1	18.1	18.0	RI	19.8	19.4	20.1
CA	15.2	19.2	11.3	MI	22.1	24.1	20.2	SC	22.6	25.3	20.1
CO	19.9	21.6	18.1	MN	20.0	21.0	19.1	SD	19.8	20.4	19.2
CT	16.5	16.9	16.2	MS	23.7	25.9	21.7	TN	26.8	29.3	24.5
DE	20.7	22.5	19.0	MO	23.4	24.9	22.1	TX	20.0	23.3	16.8
DC	20.1	22.9	17.6	MT	19.2	19.3	19.1	UT	11.5	13.7	9.3
FL	21.6	24.8	18.7	NE	21.3	23.4	19.2	VT	19.3	21.6	17.0
GA	22.2	25.0	19.4	NV	23.1	25.2	20.9	VA	20.6	21.5	19.7
HI	17.1	19.3	15.0	NH	20.5	20.4	20.5	WA	17.6	19.1	16.1
ID	17.9	19.7	16.2	NJ	18.1	19.6	16.8	WV	26.6	27.4	26.0
IL	19.9	21.2	18.7	NM	21.5	24.4	18.8	WI	20.8	22.1	19.5
IN	27.3	29.7	25.1	NY	20.5	23.0	18.2	WY	21.3	20.5	22.1
IA	20.4	21.8	19.1	NC	22.7	25.6	19.9				

[1] Represents median value among the states and DC. For definition of median, see Guide to Tabular Presentations.

Source: U.S. Centers for Disease Control and Prevention, Atlanta, GA, *Morbidity and Mortality Weekly Report*, Vol. 55, No. 42, accessed 8 June 2007; <http://www.cdc.gov/mmwr>.

Table 194. **Substance Abuse Treatment Facilities and Clients: 1995 to 2006**

[As of October 2 (1995); as of October 1 (1997–2000), as of March 29 (2002), and as of March 31 (2003–2006). Based on the Uniform Facility Data Set (UFDS)/National Survey of Substance Abuse Treatment Services (N-SSATS) survey, a census of all known facilities that provide substance abuse treatment in the United States and associated jurisdictions. Selected missing data for responding facilities were imputed]

Primary focus	Number	Primary focus	Number	Type of care and type of problem	Number of clients
FACILITIES		CLIENTS		**2006, total** [1]	**1,130,881**
1995	10,746	1995	1,009,127	Outpatient rehabilitation . . .	996,336
1997	10,860	1997	929,086	Outpatient detoxification. . .	12,579
1998	13,455	1998	1,038,378	24-hour rehabilitation	110,259
1999	15,239	2000	1,000,896	24-hour detoxification	11,707
2000	13,428	2002	1,136,287		
2002	13,720	2003	1,092,546		
2003	13,623	2004	1,072,251	**2006, total** [1]	**1,122,555**
2004	13,454	2005	1,081,049	Drug only	394,294
2005	13,371			Alcohol only.	207,193
2006, total	**13,771**	**2006, total**	**1,130,881**	Both alcohol & drug.	521,068
Substance abuse treatment services	8,577	Substance abuse treatment services	771,962		
Mental health services. . .	1,050	Mental health services. . .	52,586		
General health care	223	General health care	16,256	Total with a drug problem [2]	915,362
Both substance abuse and mental health.	3,715	Both substance abuse and mental health.	279,757	Total with an alcohol problem [3]	728,261
Other	206	Other	10,320		

[1] Excludes clients at facilities that did not provide data on type of substance abuse problem treated.   [2] The sum of clients with a drug problem and clients with both diagnoses.   [3] The sum of clients with an alcohol problem and clients with both diagnoses.

Source: U.S. Substance Abuse and Mental Health Services Administration, *Uniform Facility Data Set (UFDS): Annual surveys for 1995–1999 and 2000–2006*; <http://oas.samhsa.gov/oasftp.cfm#Data>.

Table 195. **Drug Use by Type of Drug and Age Group: 2002 and 2005**

[In percent. Data comes from the National Survey on Drug Use and Health (NSDUH). Current users are those who used drugs at least once within month prior to this study. Based on a representative sample of the U.S. population age 12 and older, including persons living in households and in some group quarters such as dormitories and homeless shelters. Estimates are based on computer-assisted interviews of about 68,000 respondents. Subject to sampling variability; see source]

Age and type of drug	Ever used 2002	Ever used 2005	Current user 2002	Current user 2005	Age and type of drug	Ever used 2002	Ever used 2005	Current user 2002	Current user 2005
12 YEARS OLD AND OVER					**18 TO 25 YEARS OLD**				
Any illicit drug [1]	46.0	46.1	8.3	8.1	Any illicit drug [1]	59.8	59.2	20.2	20.1
Marijuana and hashish	40.4	40.1	6.2	6.0	Marijuana and hashish	53.8	52.4	17.3	16.6
Cocaine	14.4	13.8	0.9	1.0	Cocaine	15.4	15.1	2.0	2.6
Crack	3.6	3.3	0.2	0.3	Hallucinogens	24.2	21.0	1.9	1.5
Heroin	1.6	1.5	0.1	0.1	Inhalants	15.7	13.3	0.5	0.5
Hallucinogens	14.6	13.9	0.5	0.4	Any psychotherapeutic [2] . . .	27.7	30.3	5.4	6.3
LSD	10.4	9.2	–	–	Alcohol	86.7	85.7	60.5	60.9
PCP	3.2	2.7	–	–	"Binge" alcohol use [3]	(NA)	(NA)	40.9	41.9
Inhalants	9.7	9.4	0.3	0.3	Cigarettes	71.2	67.3	40.8	39.0
Any psychotherapeutic [2] . . .	19.8	20.0	2.6	2.6	Smokeless tobacco	23.7	20.8	4.8	5.1
Pain relievers	12.6	13.4	1.9	1.9	Cigars	45.6	43.2	11.0	12.0
Tranquilizers	8.2	8.7	0.8	0.7	**26 TO 34 YEARS OLD**				
Stimulants	9.0	7.8	0.5	0.4	Any illicit drug [1]	58.3	56.7	10.5	11.0
Methamphetamine	5.3	4.3	0.3	0.2	Marijuana and hashish	52.2	49.8	7.7	8.6
Sedatives	4.2	3.7	0.2	0.1	Cocaine	17.6	15.9	1.2	1.3
Alcohol	83.1	82.9	51.0	51.8	Hallucinogens	20.6	20.8	0.5	0.5
"Binge" alcohol use [3]	(NA)	(NA)	22.9	22.7	Inhalants	14.1	14.1	0.1	0.2
Cigarettes	69.1	66.6	26.0	24.9	Any psychotherapeutic [2] . . .	24.4	24.8	3.6	3.5
Smokeless tobacco	19.9	18.4	3.3	3.2	**35 YEARS OLD AND OVER**				
Cigars	37.4	36.3	5.4	5.6	Any illicit drug	42.7	43.9	4.6	4.5
Pipe tobacco	17.0	15.8	0.8	0.9	Marijuana and hashish	38.0	39.0	3.1	3.0
12 to 17 YEARS OLD					Cocaine	15.4	15.1	0.6	0.6
Any illicit drug [1]	30.9	27.7	11.6	9.9	Hallucinogens	12.6	12.4	0.1	0.1
Marijuana and hashish	20.6	17.4	8.2	6.8	Inhalants	7.2	7.2	0.1	0.1
Cocaine	2.7	2.3	0.6	0.6	Any psychotherapeutic [2] . . .	18.0	18.1	1.6	1.5
Hallucinogens	5.7	3.9	1.0	0.8	**26 YEARS OLD AND OVER**				
Inhalants	10.5	10.5	1.2	1.2	Alcohol	88.0	88.2	53.9	55.1
Any psychotherapeutic [2] . . .	13.7	11.9	4.0	3.3	"Binge" alcohol use [3]	(NA)	(NA)	21.4	21.0
Alcohol	43.4	40.6	17.6	16.5	Cigarettes	73.7	71.9	25.2	24.3
"Binge" alcohol use [3]	(NA)	(NA)	10.7	9.9	Smokeless tobacco	20.9	19.5	3.2	3.0
Cigarettes	33.3	26.7	13.0	10.8	Cigars	39.0	38.1	4.6	4.7
Smokeless tobacco	8.0	7.1	2.0	2.1					
Cigars	16.3	14.1	4.5	4.2					

– Represents or rounds to zero.   NA Not available.   [1] Illicit drugs include marijuana/hashish, cocaine (including crack), heroin, hallucinogens, inhalants, or prescription-type psychotherapeutics used nonmedically.   [2] Nonmedical use of prescription-type psychotherapeutics includes the nonmedical use of pain relievers, tranquilizers, stimulants, or sedatives and does not include over-the-counter drugs.   [3] Binge alcohol use is defined as drinking five or more drinks on the same occasion (i.e., at the same time or within a couple of hours of each other) on at least 1 day in the past 30 days. Heavy alcohol use is defined as drinking five or more drinks on the same occasion on each of 5 or more days in the past 30 days; all heavy alcohol users are also binge alcohol users.

Source: U.S. Substance Abuse and Mental Health Services Administration, National Survey on Drug Use and Health, 2002 and 2005; <http://oas.samhsa.gov/nhsda.htm>.

U.S. Census Bureau, Statistical Abstract of the United States: 2008

Table 196. **Estimated Use of Selected Drugs by State: 2004–2005**

[19,396 represents 19,396,000. Data in this table cover a 2-year period. Data is based on the National Survey on Drug Use and Health (NSDUH). Current users are those persons 12 years old and over who used drugs at least once within month prior to this study. Based on national sample of respondents (see also headnote, Table 195). The state estimates were produced by combining the prevalence rate based on the state sample data and the prevalence rate based on a national regression model applied to local-area county and census block group/tract-level estimates from the state (i.e., a survey-weighted hierarchical Bayes estimation approach). The parameters of the regression model are estimated from the entire national sample. For comparison purposes, the data shown here display estimates for all 50 states and the District of Columbia utilizing the modeled estimates for all 51 areas]

State	Estimated current users (1,000)					Current users as percent of population				
	Any illicit drug [1]	Mari-juana	Any illicit drug other than mari-juana [1]	Ciga-rettes	Binge alcohol [2]	Any illicit drug [1]	Mari-juana	Any illicit drug other than mari-juana [1]	Ciga-rettes	Binge alcohol [2]
U.S....	19,396	14,602	8,605	60,209	54,906	8.0	6.0	3.6	24.9	22.7
AL........	275	184	149	1,017	718	7.3	4.9	4.0	27.1	19.1
AK........	63	52	22	127	112	12.2	10.1	4.2	24.6	21.8
AZ........	345	251	163	1,069	1,134	7.3	5.3	3.5	22.7	24.1
AR........	173	125	96	636	437	7.6	5.5	4.2	28.0	19.2
CA........	2,575	1,951	1,017	5,323	5,828	8.9	6.7	3.5	18.3	20.0
CO........	375	284	168	850	914	9.9	7.5	4.5	22.6	24.3
CT........	262	220	110	671	751	9.0	7.6	3.8	23.1	25.8
DE........	58	43	27	178	143	8.3	6.2	3.8	25.7	20.6
DC........	44	34	17	118	127	9.5	7.3	3.7	25.4	27.5
FL........	1,216	863	578	3,559	3,153	8.3	5.9	3.9	24.3	21.5
GA........	539	404	228	1,772	1,404	7.5	5.6	3.2	24.7	19.6
HI	86	63	33	199	221	8.4	6.2	3.2	19.5	21.7
ID	80	58	39	268	252	7.0	5.1	3.5	23.4	22.1
IL	780	582	325	2,816	2,736	7.5	5.6	3.1	27.0	26.3
IN	378	263	200	1,431	1,126	7.4	5.1	3.9	28.0	22.0
IA	146	105	73	638	691	5.9	4.2	2.9	25.7	27.9
KS........	161	118	80	618	585	7.2	5.3	3.6	27.6	26.2
KY........	288	210	137	1,081	753	8.4	6.1	4.0	31.5	21.9
LA........	299	202	147	1,020	880	8.2	5.5	4.0	27.9	24.1
ME........	107	97	36	300	237	9.5	8.6	3.2	26.6	21.0
MD........	301	233	139	1,032	913	6.6	5.1	3.0	22.6	20.0
MA........	503	407	212	1,242	1,405	9.4	7.6	4.0	23.1	26.2
MI........	730	561	311	2,356	2,059	8.7	6.7	3.7	28.1	24.6
MN........	349	297	132	1,064	1,168	8.2	7.0	3.1	25.0	27.4
MS........	157	113	75	626	465	6.7	4.8	3.2	26.6	19.8
MO	366	265	175	1,429	1,164	7.7	5.5	3.7	29.9	24.4
MT........	77	64	29	213	224	9.8	8.2	3.7	27.1	28.5
NE........	93	72	43	352	391	6.5	5.0	3.0	24.5	27.2
NV........	161	118	76	514	435	8.3	6.1	3.9	26.6	22.5
NH........	98	84	35	254	262	8.9	7.6	3.2	23.0	23.7
NJ	517	368	232	1,588	1,533	7.2	5.1	3.2	22.1	21.4
NM........	139	104	62	370	333	8.9	6.6	3.9	23.6	21.3
NY........	1,478	1,162	560	3,926	3,681	9.2	7.3	3.5	24.5	23.0
NC........	511	395	254	1,882	1,446	7.3	5.7	3.6	26.9	20.7
ND........	33	25	15	139	168	6.2	4.7	2.8	26.1	31.5
OH........	743	570	311	2,674	2,172	7.8	6.0	3.3	28.2	22.9
OK........	233	149	114	835	617	8.1	5.2	4.0	29.0	21.4
OR........	291	253	114	762	626	9.6	8.4	3.8	25.2	20.7
PA........	823	636	338	2,802	2,569	7.9	6.1	3.3	26.9	24.7
RI	97	81	37	224	253	10.7	8.9	4.1	24.8	28.0
SC........	253	189	120	994	699	7.3	5.5	3.5	28.7	20.2
SD........	41	32	17	166	172	6.5	5.0	2.8	26.2	27.2
TN........	394	288	194	1,458	876	8.0	5.9	3.9	29.6	17.8
TX........	1,213	834	642	4,508	4,308	6.8	4.7	3.6	25.1	24.0
UT........	142	91	79	361	308	7.6	4.8	4.2	19.1	16.3
VT........	57	49	21	136	127	10.7	9.0	3.9	25.4	23.6
VA........	411	297	207	1,506	1,363	6.8	4.9	3.4	24.8	22.4
WA	438	364	184	1,244	1,126	8.5	7.0	3.6	24.0	21.7
WV........	119	90	61	500	289	7.7	5.8	4.0	32.4	18.7
WI	346	278	155	1,252	1,450	7.5	6.0	3.3	27.1	31.4
WY........	32	24	16	109	102	7.6	5.7	3.6	25.5	23.9

[1] Illicit drugs include marijuana/hashish, cocaine (including crack), heroin, hallucinogens, inhalants, or prescription-type psychotherapeutics used nonmedically. Illicit drugs other than marijuana include cocaine (including crack), heroin, hallucinogens, inhalants, or prescription-type psychotherapeutics used nonmedically. [2] Binge alcohol use is defined as drinking five or more drinks on the same occasion (i.e., at the same time or within a couple of hours of each other) on at least 1 day in the past 30 days.

Source: U.S. Substance Abuse and Mental Health Services Administration, *National Survey on Drug Use and Health, 2004 and 2005*; <http://www.oas.samhsa.gov/nhsda.htm>.

Table 197. Cumulative Percent Distribution of Population by Height and Sex: 2003-2004

[Data are based on National Health and Nutrition Examination Survey (NHANES), a sample of the civilian noninstitutional population. For this survey, the respondent participates in an interview and a physical examination. For persons 20 years old and over. Height was measured without shoes. Based on sample and subject to sampling variability; see source]

Height	Males						Females					
	20-29 years	30-39 years	40-49 years	50-59 years	60-69 years	70-79 years	20-29 years	30-39 years	40-49 years	50-59 years	60-69 years	70-79 years
Percent under—												
4'10"	–	–	–	–	–	–	(B)	(B)	(B)	(B)	(B)	(B)
4'11"	–	–	–	(B)	–	(B)	(B)	(B)	(B)	(B)	3.2	5.1
5'	–	(B)	–	(B)	–	(B)	3.7	3.9	5.9	9.0	4.8	11.4
5'1"	–	(B)	(B)	(B)	(B)	(B)	8.2	10.0	12.3	14.5	11.8	24.6
5'2"	–	(B)	(B)	(B)	(B)	(B)	14.7	16.3	21.8	20.9	20.6	38.5
5'3"	(B)	2.5	(B)	(B)	(B)	(B)	29.8	26.7	32.1	33.3	35.4	55.9
5'4"	(B)	5.3	2.2	(B)	2.8	6.6	45.2	42.1	46.2	52.0	51.1	68.9
5'5"	5.4	9.2	3.4	(B)	6.5	13.8	57.8	60.9	60.2	63.9	66.7	86.5
5'6"	10.3	13.7	8.3	12.1	11.1	24.3	74.2	75.6	72.0	76.7	80.8	93.3
5'7"	15.2	20.0	15.2	18.2	20.1	33.3	84.5	86.5	84.2	87.4	89.0	96.8
5'8"	23.0	31.1	25.1	26.7	32.2	45.4	94.3	92.4	89.7	93.3	94.5	100.0
5'9"	33.9	43.4	38.0	41.7	44.7	56.7	97.5	96.6	95.9	97.8	96.0	100.0
5'10"	45.0	59.8	51.1	53.9	55.9	68.1	98.4	98.9	98.5	99.0	97.0	100.0
5'11"	60.9	72.3	63.9	67.6	68.6	84.7	99.4	99.4	100.0	99.5	98.9	100.0
6'	72.3	80.2	75.7	78.0	81.3	89.0	99.6	99.8	100.0	99.8	99.4	100.0
6'1"	85.1	87.8	86.1	85.0	89.1	94.5	99.6	99.8	100.0	100.0	100.0	100.0
6'2"	92.1	93.1	96.4	93.6	95.1	97.5	100.0	100.0	100.0	100.0	100.0	100.0
6'3"	95.7	97.3	98.4	96.8	98.0	98.7	100.0	100.0	100.0	100.0	100.0	100.0
6'4"	97.5	98.4	99.3	99.5	99.2	100.0	100.0	100.0	100.0	100.0	100.0	100.0
6'5"	98.8	99.5	99.3	99.5	99.8	100.0	100.0	100.0	100.0	100.0	100.0	100.0
6'6"	99.5	100.0	100.0	99.5	100.0	100.0	100.0	100.0	100.0	100.0	100.0	100.0

– Represents zero.   B Base figure too small to meet statistical standards of reliability of a derived figure.

Source: U.S. National Center for Health Statistics, unpublished data. See also <http://www.cdc.gov/nchs/nhanes.htm>.

Table 198. Cumulative Percent Distribution of Population by Weight and Sex: 2003-2004

[See headnote, Table 197. Data are based on National Health and Nutrition Examination Survey (NHANES). Weight was measured without shoes. Pregnant females were excluded from the analyses. Based on sample and subject to sampling variability; see source]

Weight	Males						Females					
	20-29 years	30-39 years	40-49 years	50-59 years	60-69 years	70-79 years	20-29 years	30-39 years	40-49 years	50-59 years	60-69 years	70-79 years
Percent under—												
100 lbs	(B)	(B)	–	–	(B)	(B)	2.2	(B)	(B)	(B)	(B)	(B)
110 lbs	(B)	(B)	(B)	–	(B)	(B)	6.2	(B)	(B)	(B)	(B)	(B)
120 lbs	(B)	(B)	(B)	–	(B)	(B)	17.6	10.8	10.5	10.2	5.8	9.2
130 lbs	5.7	(B)	2.2	(B)	(B)	(B)	30.6	22.8	15.5	18.1	12.9	18.7
140 lbs	10.6	6.9	3.8	(B)	5.1	9.6	47.5	34.1	26.7	24.8	22.4	31.2
150 lbs	15.0	12.4	6.7	7.6	9.2	18.1	57.9	44.0	36.5	35.0	32.7	47.1
160 lbs	26.9	23.7	13.3	14.5	14.2	27.1	66.8	55.4	48.5	47.7	46.2	59.0
170 lbs	36.7	35.5	20.0	25.3	22.9	37.9	72.8	62.8	56.3	58.8	59.7	70.9
180 lbs	49.8	46.5	31.2	38.9	31.0	49.0	78.1	72.8	64.2	66.5	69.2	82.0
190 lbs	61.4	52.4	43.2	46.4	44.1	57.2	82.0	79.1	71.5	72.7	76.1	86.7
200 lbs	69.2	61.7	54.4	57.7	52.7	67.3	86.7	81.6	78.0	79.8	81.9	89.1
210 lbs	76.1	69.6	66.7	66.6	62.6	76.6	89.4	86.8	83.9	83.5	86.1	91.8
220 lbs	79.5	76.8	77.3	74.7	73.3	86.6	90.3	89.0	86.1	86.9	90.6	95.4
230 lbs	83.9	85.8	82.6	81.7	79.4	89.4	92.1	91.2	89.9	88.8	93.4	96.7
240 lbs	86.8	91.5	87.7	86.9	85.4	92.0	93.5	92.7	92.2	91.9	94.6	98.5
250 lbs	90.7	92.7	92.0	92.1	88.6	94.8	94.4	93.9	94.6	93.2	97.1	98.5
260 lbs	93.4	94.3	95.3	92.9	92.2	95.8	95.3	95.0	95.6	95.9	97.6	99.3
270 lbs	94.9	94.8	95.8	93.5	94.6	98.0	96.6	96.7	95.9	96.9	99.1	99.8
280 lbs	96.0	95.9	97.0	96.5	95.5	98.2	98.3	97.7	96.5	97.7	99.2	99.8
290 lbs	96.6	96.1	97.4	97.1	97.5	99.5	98.9	98.2	97.5	97.7	99.3	99.8
300 lbs	96.9	97.6	98.0	98.2	97.5	100.0	99.1	98.7	97.7	98.7	99.6	100.0
320 lbs	98.0	99.5	98.8	99.7	98.2	100.0	100.0	98.9	98.9	98.7	99.8	100.0
340 lbs	98.7	99.6	99.4	99.7	99.1	100.0	100.0	99.8	99.3	99.5	99.8	100.0
360 lbs	99.2	99.6	99.9	100.0	99.4	100.0	100.0	99.8	100.0	99.5	100.0	100.0
380 lbs	99.2	99.7	100.0	100.0	100.0	100.0	100.0	100.0	100.0	99.5	100.0	100.0
400 lbs	99.2	99.9	100.0	100.0	100.0	100.0	100.0	100.0	100.0	100.0	100.0	100.0
420 lbs	99.2	99.9	100.0	100.0	100.0	100.0	100.0	100.0	100.0	100.0	100.0	100.0
440 lbs	99.7	100.0	100.0	100.0	100.0	100.0	100.0	100.0	100.0	100.0	100.0	100.0

– Represents zero.   B Base figure too small to meet statistical standards of reliability of a derived figure.

Source: U.S. National Center for Health Statistics, unpublished data; <http://www.cdc.gov/nchs/nhanes.htm>.

Health and Nutrition   131

Table 199. Age-Adjusted Percent Distributions of Body Mass Index (BMI) Among Persons 18 Years Old and Over by Selected Characteristics: 2003–2004

[See headnote, Table 197. Body Mass Index (BMI) is a measure that adjusts body weight for height. It is calculated as weight in kilograms divided by height in meters squared. For both men and women, underweight is indicated by a BMI under 18.5; healthy weight is indicated by a BMI greater than or equal to 18.5 and less than 25.0; overweight is greater than or equal to 25.0 and less than 30.0; obesity is indicated by a BMI greater than or equal to 30.0. BMI is calculated from the measurement of the participant's weight and height during the examination. Based on the National Health and Nutrition Examination Survey (NHANES)]

Selected characteristic	Under-weight	Healthy weight	Above healthy weight		
			Total	Overweight	Obese
Total [1] (age-adjusted)	**1.8**	**32.9**	**65.3**	**33.7**	**31.6**
Total [1] (crude)	**1.8**	**32.6**	**65.6**	**33.8**	**31.8**
Age: [2]					
18 to 44 years old	2.7	38.0	59.3	29.5	29.8
45 to 64 years old	(B)	26.0	73.1	37.2	35.9
65 to 74 years old	(B)	25.5	74.0	39.4	34.6
75 years old and over	0.8	33.3	65.9	42.4	23.5
Sex:					
Male	1.5	28.5	69.9	39.2	30.7
Female	2.0	36.6	61.5	28.7	32.8
Race/ethnicity and sex:					
Not Hispanic or Latino:					
White, male	1.5	27.8	70.7	39.6	31.1
White, female	2.2	39.2	58.6	28.4	30.2
Black alone or African American, male	(B)	31.3	67.0	33.7	33.3
Black alone or African American, female....	(B)	18.3	80.3	27.3	53.0
Mexican or Mexican American, male	(B)	26.3	73.4	42.0	31.4
Mexican or Mexican American, female	(B)	27.2	72.1	32.6	39.5
Education: [3]					
Less than a high school diploma	1.4	31.0	67.6	34.5	33.1
High school diploma or GED	(B)	27.2	71.8	36.6	35.2
Some college, bachelor's degree, or higher ...	1.3	31.7	66.9	35.0	32.0

B Base figure too small to meet statistical standards for reliability of a derived figure.   [1] Total includes other race/ethnicities not shown separately and persons with unknown race/ethnicity.   [2] Estimates for age groups are not age adjusted.   [3] Education is shown only for persons 25 years old and over.

Source: U.S. National Center for Health Statistics, unpublished data; <http://www.cdc.gov/nchs/nhanes.htm>.

Table 200. Percentage of Adults Engaging in Leisure-Time, Transportation-Related and Household-Related Physical Activity: 2005

[In percent. Covers persons 18 years old and over. Based on responses to questions about physical activity in prior month from the Behavioral Risk Factor Surveillance System. Estimates are age-adjusted to the year 2000 standard population. Based on a survey sample of approximately 350,000 persons in 50 states and the District of Columbia in 2005. Leisure-time physical activity is exercise, sports, recreation, or hobbies that are not associated with activities as part of one's regular job duties, household, or transportation. Transportation physical activity is walking, biking or wheeling (for wheelchair users), or similar activities to and from places such as: work, school, place of worship, and stores. Household physical activity includes, but is not limited to, activities such as sweeping floors, scrubbing, washing windows, and raking the lawn]

Characteristic	Persons who meet recommended activity [1]	Persons not meeting recommended activity [2]	Persons who are physically inactive [3]	Characteristic	Persons who meet recommended activity [1]	Persons not meeting recommended activity [2]	Persons who are physically inactive [3]
Total	**48.3**	**51.7**	**25.1**	30 to 44 years old ...	50.3	49.7	24.3
				45 to 64 years old ...	45.8	54.2	27.3
Male	49.9	50.1	22.9	65 to 74 years old ...	41.2	58.8	31.7
Female	47.0	53.0	27.1	75 years old and over	31.8	68.2	41.8
White, non-Hispanic ...	50.9	49.1	21.4				
Black, non-Hispanic. ...	40.2	59.8	32.8	School years completed:			
Hispanic	42.1	57.9	37.4	Less than 12 years ...	37.2	62.8	45.4
Other	46.2	53.8	25.5	12 years	45.6	54.4	31.4
				Some college (13 to 15 years)	49.2	50.8	22.5
Males:				College (16 or more years)	54.2	45.8	13.8
18 to 29 years old ...	58.5	41.5	18.8				
30 to 44 years old ...	50.1	49.9	21.0	Household income:			
45 to 64 years old ...	46.6	53.4	24.6	Less than $10,000. ...	36.9	63.1	44.6
65 to 74 years old ...	47.7	52.3	26.0	$10,000 to $19,999 ..	38.7	61.3	39.8
75 years old and over	40.3	59.7	32.0	$20,000 to $34,999 ..	45.3	54.7	30.6
				$35,000 to $49,999 ..	49.1	50.9	22.9
Females:				$50,000 and over ...	55.0	45.0	15.0
18 to 29 years old ...	52.1	47.9	23.2				

[1] Recommended activity is physical activity at least 5 times a week for 30 minutes/time or vigorous physical activity for 20 minutes at a time at least 3 times/week.   [2] Persons whose reported physical activity does not meet recommended level or report no leisure-time, transportation-related, or household-related physical activity.   [3] Persons with no reported physical activity.

Source: U.S. National Center for Chronic Disease Prevention and Health Promotion, unpublished data; <http://www.cdc.gov/nccdphp/dnpa>.

Table 201. **High School Students Engaged in Physical Activity by Sex, Race, and Hispanic Origin: 2005**

[In percent. For students in grades 9 to 12. Based on the Youth Risk Behavior Survey, a school-based survey and subject to sampling error; for details see source]

| Characteristic | Met currently recommended levels of physical activity [1] | Met previously recommended levels of physical activity [2] | No vigorous or moderate physical activity [3] | Enrolled in physical education class | | | Played on a sports team | Watched three or more hours/day of TV |
				Total	Attended daily	Exercised 20 minutes or more per class [4]		
All students	35.8	68.7	9.6	54.2	33.0	84.0	56.0	37.2
Male.	43.8	75.8	7.9	60.0	37.1	87.2	61.8	38.0
Grade 9	42.8	78.4	7.2	72.8	46.5	86.3	64.7	42.4
Grade 10	46.8	77.8	7.5	65.4	39.0	88.0	63.4	42.7
Grade 11	43.8	74.2	8.4	51.1	33.5	87.5	61.0	34.1
Grade 12	41.9	71.9	8.4	45.9	26.1	87.3	57.3	30.3
Female	27.8	61.5	11.3	48.3	29.0	80.3	50.2	36.3
Grade 9	30.8	68.4	8.2	70.3	43.1	80.3	56.1	42.4
Grade 10	30.0	63.0	10.3	53.0	31.5	81.0	52.3	37.4
Grade 11	25.1	60.7	12.4	32.9	19.4	79.5	48.9	31.7
Grade 12	24.0	51.7	15.2	32.0	18.8	79.7	41.3	32.4
White, non-Hispanic . .	38.7	70.2	8.1	52.1	31.7	86.3	57.8	29.2
Male	46.9	77.0	6.9	58.1	36.7	89.3	61.5	30.2
Female	30.2	63.3	9.3	46.1	26.6	82.5	53.9	28.1
Black, non-Hispanic. . .	29.5	62.0	14.4	55.8	34.4	78.7	53.7	64.1
Male	38.2	71.7	10.2	61.7	37.5	83.8	64.6	63.5
Female	21.3	53.1	18.2	50.5	31.6	73.1	43.6	64.5
Hispanic	32.9	69.4	10.6	61.5	38.3	81.6	53.0	45.8
Male	39.0	76.0	8.9	65.9	38.1	85.0	62.0	45.8
Female	26.5	62.6	12.3	57.1	38.6	77.5	43.8	45.8

[1] Were physically active doing any kind of physical activity that increased their heart rate and made them breathe hard some of the time for a total of at least 60 minutes/day for at least 5 or more days out of the 7 days preceding the survey. [2] Participated in at least 20 minutes of vigorous physical activity on at least 3 or more days of the 7 days preceding the survey and/or at least 30 minutes of moderate physical activity (physical activity that did not make them sweat and breathe hard) on a least 5 or more days of the 7 days preceding the survey. [3] During the seven days preceding the survey. [4] For students enrolled in physical education classes.

Source: U.S. Centers for Disease Control and Prevention, Atlanta, GA, Youth Risk Behavior Surveillance—United States, 2005, *Morbidity and Mortality Weekly Report*, Vol. 55, No. SS-1, June 9, 2006. See also <http://www.cdc.gov/mmwr/preview/mmwrhtml /ss5505a1.htm>.

Table 202. **Households and Persons Having Problems With Access to Food: 2000 to 2005**

[106,043 represents 106,043,000. Food secure means that a household had access at all times to enough food for an active healthy life for all household members with no need for recourse to socially unacceptable food sources or extraordinary coping behaviors to meet their basic food needs. Food-insecure households had limited or uncertain ability to acquire acceptable foods in socially acceptable ways. Households with very low food security (a subset of food-insecure households) were those in which food intake of one or more household members was reduced and normal eating patterns disrupted due to inadequate resources for food. The severity of food insecurity in households is measured through a series of questions about experiences and behaviors known to characterize households that are having difficulty meeting basic food needs. These experiences and behaviors generally occur in an ordered sequence as the severity of food insecurity increases. As resources become more constrained, adults in typical households first worry about having enough food, then they stretch household resources and juggle other necessities, then decrease the quality and variety of household members' diets, then decrease the frequency and quantity of adults' food intake, and finally decrease the frequency and quantity of children's food intake. All questions refer to the previous 12 months and include a qualifying phrase reminding respondents to report only those occurrences that resulted from inadequate financial resources. Restrictions to food intake due to dieting or busy schedules are excluded. The omission of homeless persons may be a cause of underreporting. Data are from the Food Security Supplement to the Current Population Survey (CPS); for details about the CPS, see text, Section 1, and Appendix III]

| Household food security level | Number (1,000) | | | | | Percent distribution | | | | |
	2000	2002	2003	2004	2005	2000	2002	2003	2004	2005
Households, total	106,043	108,601	112,214	112,967	114,437	100.0	100.0	100.0	100.0	100.0
Food secure	94,942	96,543	99,631	99,473	101,851	89.5	88.9	88.8	88.1	89.0
Food insecure	11,101	12,058	12,583	13,494	12,586	10.5	11.1	11.2	11.9	11.0
With low food security [1]	7,786	8,259	8,663	9,045	8,158	7.3	7.6	7.7	8.0	7.1
With very low food security [2] . . .	3,315	3,799	3,920	4,449	4,428	3.1	3.5	3.5	3.9	3.9
With very low food security among children [3]	255	265	207	274	270	0.7	0.7	0.5	0.7	0.7
Adult members	201,922	206,493	213,441	215,564	217,897	100.0	100.0	100.0	100.0	100.0
In food-secure households	181,586	184,718	190,451	191,236	195,172	89.9	89.5	89.2	88.7	89.6
In food-insecure households	20,336	21,775	22,990	24,328	22,725	10.1	10.5	10.8	11.3	10.4
With low food security	14,763	15,486	16,358	16,946	15,146	7.3	7.5	7.7	7.9	7.0
With very low food security [2] . . .	5,573	6,289	6,632	7,382	7,579	2.8	3.0	3.1	3.4	3.5
Child members	71,763	72,542	72,969	73,039	73,604	100.0	100.0	100.0	100.0	100.0
In food-secure households	58,867	59,415	59,704	59,171	61,201	82.0	81.9	81.8	81.0	83.1
In food-insecure households	12,896	13,127	13,265	13,868	12,403	18.0	18.1	18.2	19.0	16.9
With low food security among adults or children	12,334	12,560	12,845	13,323	11,797	17.2	17.3	17.6	18.2	16.0
With very low food security among children [3]	562	567	420	545	606	0.8	0.8	0.6	0.7	0.8

[1] Prior to 2006, USDA described these households as food insecure without hunger. [2] Food intake of one or more members in these households was reduced and normal eating patterns disrupted at some time during the year because of the household's food insecurity. Prior to 2006, USDA described these households as food insecure with hunger. [3] Food intake of one or more children in these households was reduced and their normal eating patterns were disrupted at some time during the year because of the household's food insecurity. Prior to 2006, USDA described these households as food insecure with hunger among children. Percent distribution of households with very low food security among children excludes households with no child from the denominator.

Source: U.S. Dept. of Agriculture, Economic Research Service, *Household Food Security in the United States, 2005*, Economic Research Report Number 29; November 2006; <http://www.ers.usda.gov/publications/err29/>.

Health and Nutrition 133

Table 203. **Per Capita Consumption of Selected Beverages by Type: 1980 to 2005**

[In gallons. See headnote, Table 205. Per capita consumption uses U.S. resident population, July 1, for all beverages except coffee, tea, and fruit juices which use U.S. total population, July 1. Data for 2004 and preceding years have been revised]

Commodity	1980	1985	1990	1995	2000	2002	2003	2004	2005
Nonalcoholic	105.5	125.4	134.3	138.1	150.9	149.4	150.8	152.6	152.6
Milk (plain and flavored)	27.6	26.7	25.7	23.9	22.5	21.9	21.6	21.2	21.0
Whole	17.0	14.3	10.5	8.6	8.1	7.7	7.6	7.3	6.9
Reduced-fat, light, and skim	10.5	12.3	15.2	15.3	14.4	14.2	13.9	13.9	14.0
Tea	7.3	7.1	6.9	7.9	7.8	7.8	7.5	7.9	7.9
Coffee	26.7	27.4	26.8	20.2	26.3	23.6	24.2	24.6	24.2
Bottled water	2.7	5.1	8.8	11.6	16.7	20.1	21.6	23.2	25.4
Carbonated soft drinks	33.6	41.2	47.1	50.6	53.2	52.8	52.5	52.3	51.5
Diet	(NA)	10.4	14.0	13.8	13.8	14.4	15.0	15.8	16.0
Regular	(NA)	30.8	33.1	36.8	39.4	38.4	37.4	36.5	35.5
Fruit juices	7.6	7.7	6.6	8.1	9.0	8.1	8.6	8.6	8.2
Fruit drinks, cocktails, and ades	(NA)	10.2	12.3	15.0	14.8	14.6	14.5	14.3	13.9
Canned iced tea	(NA)	(NA)	0.1	0.7	(NA)	(NA)	(NA)	(NA)	(NA)
Vegetable juices	(NA)	(NA)	(NA)	(NA)	0.5	0.5	0.5	0.5	0.5
Alcoholic	28.3	28.0	27.5	24.7	25.0	25.2	25.1	25.2	25.0
Beer	24.3	23.8	23.9	21.8	21.7	21.8	21.6	21.6	21.3
Wine [1]	2.1	2.4	2.0	1.7	2.0	2.1	2.2	2.3	2.4
Distilled spirits	2.0	1.8	1.5	1.2	1.3	1.3	1.3	1.4	1.4

NA Not available. [1] Beginning 1983, includes wine coolers.

Source: U.S. Department of Agriculture, Economic Research Service, *Food Consumption, Prices, and Expenditures, 1970–1997*; Food Consumption (Per Capita) Data System; <http://www.ers.usda.gov/data/foodconsumption/>.

Table 204. **Nutrition—Nutrients in Foods Available for Civilian Consumption Per Capita Per Day: 1970 to 2004**

[Computed by the Center for Nutrition Policy and Promotion (CNPP). Based on Economic Research Service (ERS) estimates of per capita quantities of food available for consumption from "Food Consumption, Prices, and, Expenditures," on imputed consumption data for foods no longer reported by ERS, and on CNPP estimates of quantities of produce from home gardens. Food supply estimates do not reflect loss of food or nutrients from further marketing or home processing. Enrichment and fortification levels of iron, zinc, thiamin, riboflavin, niacin, folate, vitamin A, vitamin B_6, vitamin B_{12}, and Vitamin C are included]

Nutrient	Unit	1970–79	1980–89	1990–99	2000	2004
Food energy	Kilocalories	3,200	3,400	3,600	3,900	3,900
Carbohydrate	Grams	396	420	481	497	481
Fiber	Grams	20	21	24	25	25
Protein	Grams	98	101	109	113	113
Total fat [1]	Grams	144	151	151	173	179
Saturated	Grams	49	50	48	54	56
Monounsaturated	Grams	58	61	64	77	79
Polyunsaturated	Grams	27	31	31	36	37
Cholesterol	Milligrams	440	420	400	420	430
Vitamin A	Micrograms RAE [2]	1,260	1,230	1,270	1,250	1,080
Carotene	Micrograms	580	620	750	720	680
Vitamin E	Milligrams a-TE [3]	13.9	15.6	16.8	20.0	21.0
Vitamin C	Milligrams	112	119	127	130	119
Thiamin	Milligrams	2.3	2.6	3.0	3.0	2.9
Riboflavin	Milligrams	2.5	2.8	2.9	2.9	2.9
Niacin	Milligrams	25	29	32	33	33
Vitamin B_6	Milligrams	2.0	2.2	2.4	2.5	2.4
Folate [4]	Micrograms DFE [5]	343	386	517	925	898
Vitamin B_{12}	Micrograms	8.9	8.1	7.9	8.2	8.2
Calcium	Milligrams	940	940	980	980	970
Phosphorus	Milligrams	1,530	1,580	1,690	1,720	1,710
Magnesium	Milligrams	340	360	390	400	400
Iron	Milligrams	16.7	19.9	23.1	23.7	23.4
Zinc	Milligrams	13.4	14.3	15.3	15.4	15.4
Copper	Milligrams	1.7	1.8	2.0	2.1	2.1
Potassium	Milligrams	3,610	3,640	3,850	3,920	3,820
Sodium [6]	Milligrams	1,270	1,260	1,290	1,280	1,240
Selenium	Micrograms	129.5	139.1	162.6	178.9	189.7

[1] Includes other types of fat not shown separately. [2] Retinol activity equivalents. [3] Alpha-Tocopherol equivalents. [4] Reflects new terminology from Institute of Medicine's Dietary Reference Intakes reports. [5] Dietary Folate Equivalents (DFE). [6] Does not include amount from processed foods; underestimates actual availability.

Source: U.S. Department of Agriculture, Center for Nutrition Policy and Promotion, *Nutrient Content of the U.S. Food Supply, 1909–2004*, (released 15 March 2007). Data also published by Economic Research Service in *Food Consumption, Prices, and Expenditures*, annual. See also <http://www.usda.gov/cnpp/>.

Table 205. **Per Capita Consumption of Major Food Commodities: 1980 to 2005**

[In pounds, retail weight, except as indicated. Consumption represents the residual after exports, nonfood use and ending stocks are subtracted from the sum of beginning stocks, domestic production, and imports. Based on Census Bureau estimated resident population]

Commodity	Unit	1980	1990	1995	2000	2003	2004	2005
Red meat, total (boneless, trimmed weight) [1, 2]	Pounds . . .	126.4	112.2	113.6	113.7	111.6	112.0	110.0
Beef	Pounds . . .	72.1	63.9	63.5	64.5	61.9	62.9	62.4
Veal	Pounds . . .	1.3	0.9	0.8	0.5	0.5	0.4	0.4
Lamb and mutton	Pounds . . .	1.0	1.0	0.9	0.8	0.8	0.8	0.8
Pork . . . . [2]	Pounds . . .	52.1	46.4	48.4	47.8	48.4	47.8	46.5
Poultry (boneless, trimmed weight) [2]	Pounds . . .	40.8	56.2	62.1	67.9	71.2	72.7	73.6
Chicken	Pounds . . .	32.7	42.4	48.2	54.2	57.5	59.2	60.4
Turkey	Pounds . . .	8.1	13.8	13.9	13.7	13.7	13.4	13.1
Fish and shellfish (boneless, trimmed weight) . . .	Pounds . . .	12.4	14.9	14.8	15.2	16.3	16.5	16.1
Eggs	Number . .	271	234	232	251	254	256	254
Shell	Number . .	236	186	172	178	182	180	175
Processed	Number . .	35	48	60	73	72	76	79
Dairy products, total [3]	Pounds . . .	543.1	568.0	576.2	592.2	588.8	591.8	600.5
Fluid milk products [4]	Gallons . . .	27.9	26.2	24.6	23.2	22.5	22.3	22.0
Beverage milks	Gallons . . .	27.6	25.7	23.9	22.5	21.6	21.2	21.0
Plain whole milk	Gallons . . .	16.5	10.2	8.3	7.7	7.2	6.9	6.6
Plain reduced-fat milk (2%)	Gallons . . .	6.3	9.1	8.0	7.1	6.9	6.9	6.9
Reduced fat milk (1%) and skim milk	Gallons . . .	3.1	4.9	6.1	6.1	5.6	5.5	5.6
Flavored whole milk	Gallons . . .	0.6	0.3	0.3	0.4	0.4	0.3	0.3
Flavored milks other than whole	Gallons . . .	0.6	0.8	0.8	1.0	1.2	1.4	1.4
Buttermilk	Gallons . . .	0.5	0.4	0.3	0.3	0.2	0.2	0.2
Yogurt (excl. frozen)	1/2 pints . .	4.6	7.8	11.4	12.0	15.2	17.0	15.9
Fluid cream products [5]	1/2 pints . .	10.5	14.3	15.6	18.3	22.2	23.5	24.3
Cream [6]	1/2 pints . .	6.3	8.7	9.4	11.6	13.9	14.8	15.1
Sour cream and dips	1/2 pints . .	3.4	4.7	5.4	6.1	7.5	7.9	8.3
Condensed and evaporated milks	Pounds . . .	7.0	7.9	6.8	5.8	5.9	5.5	5.8
Whole milk	Pounds . . .	3.8	3.1	2.3	2.0	2.6	2.2	2.2
Skim milk	Pounds . . .	3.3	4.8	4.5	3.8	3.3	3.2	3.6
Cheese [7] . . . . [8] . .	Pounds . . .	17.5	24.6	26.9	29.8	30.4	31.3	31.4
American [8]	Pounds . . .	9.6	11.1	11.7	12.7	12.5	12.9	12.7
Cheddar	Pounds . . .	6.8	9.0	9.0	9.7	9.2	10.3	10.1
Italian [8]	Pounds . . .	4.4	9.0	10.3	12.1	12.6	12.9	13.3
Mozzarella	Pounds . . .	3.0	6.9	8.0	9.3	9.6	9.9	10.2
Other [8]	Pounds . . .	3.3	4.3	5.0	4.8	5.1	5.3	5.4
Swiss	Pounds . . .	1.3	1.4	1.1	1.0	1.2	1.2	1.2
Cream and Neufchatel	Pounds . . .	0.9	1.6	2.2	2.3	2.4	2.3	2.3
Cottage cheese, total	Pounds . . .	4.5	3.4	2.7	2.6	2.7	2.6	2.6
Lowfat	Pounds . . .	0.8	1.2	1.2	1.3	1.3	1.3	1.3
Frozen dairy products	Pounds . . .	26.4	28.5	29.0	28.0	27.1	26.4	24.1
Ice cream	Pounds . . .	17.5	15.8	15.5	16.7	16.4	15.4	15.4
Lowfat ice cream	Pounds . . .	7.1	7.7	7.4	7.3	7.5	7.8	5.9
Sherbet	Pounds . . .	1.2	1.2	1.3	1.2	1.2	1.2	0.9
Frozen yogurt	Pounds . . .	(NA)	2.8	3.4	2.0	1.4	1.8	1.3
Fats and oils:								
Total, fat content only	Pounds . . .	56.9	62.3	64.2	82.3	88.0	87.5	85.5
Butter (product weight)	Pounds . . .	4.5	4.4	4.4	4.5	4.5	4.6	4.6
Margarine (product weight)	Pounds . . .	11.3	10.9	9.1	7.5	5.3	5.3	4.0
Lard (direct use, ...	Pounds . . .	2.3	0.9	0.4	0.8	1.3	0.7	1.5
Edible beef tallow (direct use)	Pounds . . .	1.1	0.6	2.7	4.0	3.8	4.0	3.8
Shortening	Pounds . . .	18.2	22.2	22.2	31.6	32.8	32.6	29.1
Salad and cooking oils	Pounds . . .	21.2	25.2	26.5	34.8	40.8	40.8	42.7
Other edible fats and oils	Pounds . . .	1.5	1.2	1.6	1.5	1.5	1.5	1.5
Flour and cereal products [9]	Pounds . . .	144.9	181.0	188.7	199.2	193.1	191.5	192.3
Wheat flour	Pounds . . .	116.9	135.9	140.0	146.3	136.7	134.3	134.1
Rice, milled	Pounds . . .	9.5	15.8	17.1	18.9	20.3	20.4	21.0
Corn products	Pounds . . .	12.9	21.4	24.9	28.4	30.3	30.9	31.4
Oat products	Pounds . . .	3.9	6.5	5.5	4.4	4.7	4.7	4.6
Caloric sweeteners, total [10]	Pounds . . .	120.2	132.4	144.1	148.8	141.4	141.0	141.6
Sugar, refined cane and beet	Pounds . . .	83.6	64.4	64.9	65.5	60.9	61.5	62.8
Corn sweeteners [11]	Pounds . . .	35.3	66.8	77.9	81.8	79.1	78.1	77.4
High-fructose corn syrup	Pounds . . .	19.0	49.6	57.6	62.6	60.8	59.2	59.0
Other:								
Cocoa beans	Pounds . . .	3.4	5.4	4.5	5.9	5.3	6.0	6.5
Coffee (green beans)	Pounds . . .	10.3	10.3	7.9	10.3	9.5	9.6	9.5
Peanuts (shelled)	Pounds . . .	5.1	6.1	5.7	5.9	6.4	6.7	6.6
Tree nuts (shelled)	Pounds . . .	1.8	2.5	1.9	2.6	3.5	3.6	2.7

NA Not available. [1] Excludes edible offals.[2] Excludes shipments to Puerto Rico and the other U.S. possessions. [3] Milk-equivalent, milk-fat basis. Includes butter. [4] Fluid milk figures are aggregates of commercial sales and milk produced and consumed on farms. [5] Includes eggnog, not shown separately. [6] Heavy cream, light cream, and half-and-half. [7] Excludes full-skim American, cottage, pot, and baker's cheese. [8] Includes other cheeses not shown separately. [9] Includes rye flour and barley products not shown separately. Excludes quantities used in alcoholic beverages. [10] Dry weight. Includes edible syrups (maple, molasses, etc.) and honey not shown separately. [11] Includes glucose and dextrose not shown separately.

Source: U.S. Department of Agriculture, Economic Research Service, *Food Consumption, Prices, and Expenditures, Food Availability (Per Capita) Data System;* <http://www.ers.usda.gov/data/foodconsumption/>.

Health and Nutrition 135

Table 206. Per Capita Utilization of Selected Commercially Produced Fruits and Vegetables: 1980 to 2005

[In pounds, farm weight. Domestic food use of fresh fruits and vegetables reflects the fresh-market share of commodity production plus imports and minus exports]

Commodity	1980	1990	1995	2000	2001	2002	2003	2004	2005
Fruits and vegetables, total [1] ...	**608.5**	**659.3**	**690.9**	**711.2**	**684.2**	**684.9**	**702.0**	**693.8**	**688.6**
Fruits, total	270.6	274.2	284.7	289.2	272.3	273.8	281.8	272.1	273.2
Fresh fruits	106.5	117.0	123.5	128.7	126.0	127.0	128.2	127.9	126.0
Noncitrus	80.5	95.6	99.6	105.2	102.1	103.6	104.3	105.2	104.4
Apples	19.4	19.8	18.9	17.6	15.8	16.2	17.1	19.0	17.1
Bananas...............	20.8	24.3	27.1	28.4	26.6	26.8	26.1	25.7	25.1
Cantaloupes	5.8	9.2	9.0	11.1	11.2	11.1	10.8	10.0	10.1
Grapes.................	4.0	7.9	7.5	7.5	7.5	8.5	7.7	7.9	8.7
Peaches and nectarines	7.1	5.5	5.3	5.3	5.2	5.2	5.2	5.1	4.8
Pears...................	2.6	3.3	3.4	3.4	3.3	3.1	3.1	3.0	2.9
Pineapples	1.5	2.0	1.9	3.2	3.2	3.8	4.4	4.4	4.9
Plums and prunes	1.5	1.5	0.9	1.2	1.3	1.3	1.2	1.1	1.1
Strawberries	2.0	3.2	4.1	4.9	4.2	4.6	5.3	5.5	5.8
Watermelons..............	10.7	13.3	15.2	13.8	15.0	14.0	13.5	13.0	13.8
Other [2]................	5.1	5.4	6.3	8.7	9.0	9.1	9.8	10.5	10.0
Fresh citrus	26.1	21.4	23.8	23.5	23.9	23.4	23.9	22.7	21.6
Oranges...............	14.3	12.4	11.8	11.7	11.9	11.7	11.9	10.8	11.4
Grapefruit..............	7.3	4.4	6.0	5.1	4.8	4.6	4.1	4.1	2.6
Other [3]...............	4.5	4.6	6.0	6.7	7.2	7.0	8.0	7.8	7.6
Processed fruits	164.1	157.3	161.2	160.4	146.2	146.8	153.6	144.2	147.2
Frozen fruits [4]..............	3.3	4.3	5.2	4.2	7.1	4.1	5.5	4.9	5.4
Dried fruits [5]...............	11.3	12.2	12.8	10.5	9.9	10.5	9.9	9.3	10.4
Canned fruits [6].............	24.8	21.2	17.5	17.7	17.8	16.9	17.4	17.0	16.8
Fruit juices [7]..............	123.9	119.3	125.5	127.7	111.3	115.2	120.5	112.4	114.1
Vegetables, total	337.9	385.1	406.2	422.0	411.9	411.1	420.1	421.7	415.4
Fresh vegetables	151.4	170.2	180.9	198.7	195.7	194.7	199.1	202.4	198.6
Asparagus (all uses)	0.3	0.6	0.6	1.0	0.9	1.0	1.0	1.1	1.2
Broccoli................	1.4	3.4	4.3	5.9	5.4	5.3	5.5	5.9	5.6
Cabbage	8.0	8.3	8.1	8.9	8.8	8.3	7.5	8.3	8.1
Carrots	6.2	8.3	11.2	9.2	9.4	8.4	8.8	8.8	8.7
Cauliflower	1.1	2.2	1.6	1.7	1.5	1.4	1.6	1.6	1.5
Celery (all uses)	7.4	7.2	6.9	6.3	6.4	6.3	6.3	6.2	6.1
Corn	6.5	6.7	7.8	9.0	9.2	9.0	9.5	9.2	8.9
Cucumbers	3.9	4.7	5.6	6.4	6.3	6.5	6.0	6.5	6.5
Head lettuce..............	25.6	27.7	22.2	23.5	23.0	22.5	22.2	21.2	20.3
Mushrooms	1.2	2.0	2.0	2.6	2.6	2.6	2.6	2.6	2.6
Onions	11.4	15.1	17.8	18.9	18.5	19.3	19.5	21.6	21.2
Snap beans	1.3	1.1	1.6	2.0	2.2	2.1	2.0	1.9	1.8
Bell peppers (all uses)	2.9	4.5	6.2	7.0	6.9	6.8	6.9	7.0	6.6
Potatoes	51.1	46.7	49.2	47.1	46.6	44.3	46.8	45.8	43.1
Sweet potatoes (all uses)	4.4	4.4	4.2	4.2	4.4	3.8	4.7	4.6	4.5
Tomatoes................	12.8	15.5	16.8	19.0	19.2	20.3	19.5	20.1	20.6
Other fresh vegetables [8]........	6.0	11.8	14.7	26.1	24.6	26.8	28.7	30.1	31.3
Processed vegetables	186.5	214.9	225.3	223.3	216.2	216.4	221.0	219.3	216.8
Selected vegetables for freezing [9]..	51.5	66.8	78.8	79.3	78.6	76.7	78.3	78.2	75.3
Selected vegetables for canning [10]..	102.5	110.4	108.0	103.2	97.3	100.7	101.5	103.4	105.3
Vegetables for dehydrating [11]...	10.5	14.6	14.5	17.3	15.8	15.8	17.3	15.3	14.1
Potatoes for chips	16.5	16.4	16.4	15.9	17.6	16.5	17.3	16.5	16.0
Pulses [12]...............	5.4	6.7	7.5	7.6	6.9	6.7	6.6	6.0	6.1

[1] Excludes wine grapes. [2] Apricots, avocados, cherries, cranberries, kiwifruit, mangoes, papayas, and honeydew melons. [3] Lemons, limes, tangerines, and tangelos. [4] Apples, apricots, blackberries, blueberries, boysenberries, cherries, loganberries, peaches, plums, prunes, raspberries, and strawberries. [5] Apples, apricots, dates, figs, peaches, pears, prunes, and raisins. [6] Apples, apricots, cherries, olives, peaches, pears, pineapples, plums, and prunes. [7] Apple, cranberry, grape, grapefruit, lemon, lime, orange, pineapple, and prunes. [8] Artichokes, brussels sprouts, eggplant, escarole, endive, garlic, romaine, leaf lettuce, radishes, spinach, and squash. Beginning 2000, includes collard greens, kale, mustard greens, okra, pumpkin, and turnip greens. [9] Asparagus, snap beans, lima beans, broccoli, carrots, cauliflower, sweet corn, green peas, potatoes, spinach, and miscellaneous vegetables. [10] Asparagus, snap beans, beets, cabbage, carrots, chili peppers, sweet corn, cucumbers for pickling, green peas, lima beans, mushrooms, spinach, and tomatoes. [11] Onions and potatoes. [12] Dry peas, lentils, and dry edible beans.

Source: U.S. Department of Agriculture, Economic Research Service, *Food Consumption, Prices, and Expenditures, Food Availability (Per Capita) Data System;* <http://www.ers.usda.gov/data/foodconsumption/>.

Section 4
Education

This section presents data primarily concerning formal education as a whole, at various levels, and for public and private schools. Data shown relate to the school-age population and school enrollment, educational attainment, education personnel, and financial aspects of education. In addition, data are shown for charter schools, security measures used in schools, computer usage in schools, distance education, and adult education. The chief sources are the decennial census of population and the Current Population Survey (CPS), both conducted by the U.S. Census Bureau (see text, Section 1, Population); annual, biennial, and other periodic surveys conducted by the National Center for Education Statistics (NCES), a part of the U.S. Department of Education; and surveys conducted by the National Education Association.

The censuses of population have included data on school enrollment since 1840 and on educational attainment since 1940. The CPS has reported on school enrollment annually since 1945 and on educational attainment periodically since 1947.

The NCES is continuing the pattern of statistical studies and surveys conducted by the U.S. Office of Education since 1870. The annual *Digest of Education Statistics* provides summary data on pupils, staff, finances, including government expenditures, and organization at the elementary, secondary, and higher education levels. It is also a primary source for detailed information on federal funds for education, projections of enrollment, graduates, and teachers. *The Condition of Education,* issued annually, presents a summary of information on education of particular interest to policymakers. NCES also conducts special studies periodically.

The census of governments, conducted by the Census Bureau every 5 years (for the years ending in "2" and "7"), provides data on school district finances and state and local government expenditures for education. Reports published by the Bureau of Labor Statistics contain data relating civilian labor force experience to educational attainment (see also Tables 574, 601, and 609 in Section 12, Labor Force, Employment, and Earnings).

Types and sources of data—The statistics in this section are of two general types. One type, exemplified by data from the Census Bureau, is based on direct interviews with individuals to obtain information about their own and their family members' education. Data of this type relate to school enrollment and level of education attained, classified by age, sex, and other characteristics of the population. The school enrollment statistics reflect attendance or enrollment in any regular school within a given period; educational attainment statistics reflect the highest grade completed by an individual, or beginning 1992, the highest diploma or degree received.

Beginning in 2001, the CPS used Census 2000 population controls. From 1994 to 2000, the CPS used 1990 census population controls plus adjustment for undercount. Also the survey changed from paper to computer-assisted technology. For years 1981 through 1993, 1980 census population controls were used; 1971 through 1980, 1970 census population controls had been used. These changes had little impact on summary measures (e.g., medians) and proportional measures (e.g., enrollment rates); however, use of the controls may have significant impact on absolute numbers.

The second type, generally exemplified by data from the NCES and the National Education Association, is based on reports from administrators of educational institutions and of state and local agencies having jurisdiction over education. Data of this type relate to enrollment, attendance, staff, and finances for the nation, individual states, and local areas.

U.S. Census Bureau, Statistical Abstract of the United States: 2008

Unlike the NCES, the Census Bureau does not regularly include specialized vocational, trade, business, or correspondence schools in its surveys. The NCES includes nursery schools and kindergartens that are part of regular grade schools in their enrollment figures. The Census Bureau includes all nursery schools and kindergartens. At the higher education level, the statistics of both agencies are concerned with institutions granting degrees or offering work acceptable for degree-credit, such as junior colleges.

School attendance—All states require that children attend school. While state laws vary as to the ages and circumstances of compulsory attendance, generally they require that formal schooling begin by age 6 and continue to age 16.

Schools—The NCES defines a school as "a division of the school system consisting of students composing one or more grade groups or other identifiable groups, organized as one unit with one or more teachers to give instruction of a defined type, and housed in a school plant of one or more buildings. More than one school may be housed in one school plant, as is the case when the elementary and secondary programs are housed in the same school plant."

Regular schools are those which advance a person toward a diploma or degree. They include public and private nursery schools, kindergartens, graded schools, colleges, universities, and professional schools.

Public schools are schools controlled and supported by local, state, or federal governmental agencies; private schools are those controlled and supported mainly by religious organizations or by private persons or organizations.

The Census Bureau defines *elementary* schools as including grades 1 through 8; *high* schools as including grades 9 through 12; and *colleges* as including junior or community colleges, regular 4-year colleges, and universities and graduate or professional schools. Statistics reported by the NCES and the National Education Association by type of organization, such as elementary level and secondary level, may not be strictly comparable with those from the Census Bureau because the grades included at the two levels vary, depending on the level assigned to the middle or junior high school by the local school systems.

School year—Except as otherwise indicated in the tables, data refer to the school year which, for elementary and secondary schools, generally begins in September of the preceding year and ends in June of the year stated. For the most part, statistics concerning school finances are for a 12-month period, usually July 1 to June 30. Enrollment data generally refer to a specific point in time, such as fall, as indicated in the tables.

Statistical reliability—For a discussion of statistical collection, estimation, and sampling procedures and measures of statistical reliability applicable to the Census Bureau and the NCES data, see Appendix III.

Table 207. **School Enrollment: 1980 to 2016**

[In thousands (58,305 represents 58,305,000). As of fall]

Year	All levels			Pre-K through grade 8		Grades 9 through 12		College [1]	
	Total	Public	Private	Public	Private	Public	Private	Public	Private
1980	58,305	50,335	7,971	27,647	3,992	13,231	1,339	9,457	2,640
1985	57,226	48,901	8,325	27,034	4,195	12,388	1,362	9,479	2,768
1986	57,709	49,467	8,242	27,420	4,116	12,333	1,336	9,714	2,790
1987	58,253	49,982	8,272	27,933	4,232	12,076	1,247	9,973	2,793
1988	58,485	50,349	8,136	28,501	4,036	11,687	1,206	10,161	2,894
1989	59,279	51,120	8,159	29,152	4,035	11,390	1,163	10,578	2,961
1990	60,269	52,061	8,208	29,878	4,084	11,338	1,150	10,845	2,974
1991	62,087	53,357	8,730	30,506	4,518	11,541	1,163	11,310	3,049
1992	62,987	54,208	8,779	31,088	4,528	11,735	1,148	11,385	3,103
1993	63,438	54,654	8,784	31,504	4,536	11,961	1,132	11,189	3,116
1994	64,177	55,245	8,932	31,898	4,624	12,213	1,162	11,134	3,145
1995	65,020	55,933	9,087	32,341	4,721	12,500	1,197	11,092	3,169
1996	65,913	56,733	9,180	32,764	4,720	12,847	1,213	11,121	3,247
1997	66,573	57,323	9,250	33,073	4,726	13,054	1,218	11,196	3,306
1998	67,034	57,677	9,357	33,346	4,748	13,193	1,240	11,138	3,369
1999	67,667	58,166	9,501	33,488	4,765	13,369	1,254	11,309	3,482
2000	68,685	58,956	9,729	33,688	4,878	13,515	1,292	11,753	3,560
2001	69,920	59,905	10,014	33,938	4,993	13,734	1,326	12,233	3,695
2002	71,015	60,935	10,080	34,116	4,886	14,067	1,334	12,752	3,860
2003	71,540	61,397	10,143	34,202	4,761	14,338	1,338	12,857	4,043
2004 . . . . `2`. . .	72,200	61,775	10,425	34,178	4,773	14,617	1,360	12,980	4,292
2005, proj. [2]. . .	72,626	62,050	10,577	34,174	4,736	14,853	1,376	13,022	4,466
2006, proj.. . . .	73,196	62,622	10,574	34,387	4,779	14,983	1,375	13,252	4,420
2007, proj.. . . .	73,720	63,067	10,653	34,592	4,784	15,018	1,368	13,457	4,501
2008, proj.. . . .	74,230	63,490	10,740	34,873	4,805	14,939	1,348	13,677	4,587
2009, proj.. . . .	74,753	63,924	10,830	35,195	4,834	14,834	1,324	13,895	4,672
2010, proj.. . . .	75,319	64,388	10,930	35,581	4,873	14,722	1,304	14,085	4,754
2011, proj.. . . .	75,963	64,922	11,040	35,994	4,921	14,659	1,284	14,269	4,836
2012, proj.. . . .	76,712	65,546	11,166	36,397	4,975	14,696	1,270	14,453	4,921
2013, proj.. . . .	77,534	66,231	11,303	36,841	5,032	14,739	1,261	14,651	5,010
2014, proj.. . . .	78,430	66,981	11,449	37,271	5,088	14,864	1,262	14,846	5,098
2015, proj.. . . .	79,339	67,748	11,591	37,578	5,133	15,155	1,281	15,015	5,177
2016, proj.. . . .	80,223	68,486	11,737	37,917	5,179	15,382	1,301	15,186	5,256

[1] Data beginning 1996 based on new classification system. See footnote 1, Table 271.   [2] Pre-K through 12 are projections; college data are actual.

Source: U.S. National Center for Education Statistics, *Digest of Education Statistics*, annual, and *Projections of Education Statistics*, annual.

Table 208. **School Expenditures by Type of Control and Level of Instruction in Constant (2004–2005) Dollars: 1980 to 2005**

[In millions of dollars (395,259 represents $395,259,000,000). For school years ending in year shown. Data shown reflect historical revisions. Total expenditures for public elementary and secondary schools include current expenditures, interest on school debt and capital outlay. Data deflated by the Consumer Price Index, for all urban consumers, on a school year basis (supplied by the National Center for Education Statistics). See also Appendix III. Based on survey of state education agencies; see source for details]

Year		Elementary and secondary schools			Colleges and universities [2]		
	Total	Total	Public	Private [1]	Total	Public	Private
1980	395,259	254,727	236,949	17,778	140,531	93,257	47,275
1985	433,800	270,772	248,299	22,474	163,028	105,689	57,338
1986	456,846	285,027	261,774	23,253	171,819	111,322	60,497
1987	484,195	301,929	277,285	24,644	182,266	116,590	65,676
1988	499,387	311,095	285,777	25,318	188,292	120,205	68,086
1989	527,102	331,177	305,237	25,940	195,925	124,870	71,053
1990	552,280	348,993	321,215	27,778	203,287	129,486	73,801
1991	565,867	356,753	328,411	28,342	209,114	133,067	76,047
1992	579,681	363,049	334,339	28,711	216,632	137,099	79,532
1993	591,620	369,376	340,190	29,186	222,244	140,644	81,601
1994	604,582	377,317	347,820	29,498	227,264	143,306	83,959
1995	618,593	385,403	355,580	29,823	233,190	147,158	86,032
1996	630,937	394,608	364,335	30,274	236,329	148,297	88,031
1997	650,024	408,879	377,757	31,123	241,144	151,968	89,176
1998	676,106	428,576	396,221	32,355	247,530	157,446	90,085
1999	703,483	448,104	414,552	33,552	255,379	163,728	91,651
2000	735,238	467,123	432,361	34,762	268,115	172,480	95,635
2001	771,858	486,983	449,759	37,223	284,875	186,495	98,380
2002	809,811	507,828	468,348	39,480	301,983	197,333	104,650
2003	837,438	518,742	478,848	39,895	318,695	207,253	111,442
2004	854,887	528,605	488,123	40,483	326,282	211,240	115,043
2005	878,300	536,900	495,800	41,100	341,400	218,300	123,100

[1] Estimated.   [2] Data beginning 1996 based on new classification system. See footnote 1, Table 271.

Source: U.S. National Center for Education Statistics, *Digest of Education Statistics*, annual.

Table 209. **School Enrollment, Faculty, Graduates, and Finances—Projections:**
2006 to 2012

[As of fall, except as indicated (55,524 represents 55,524,000)]

Item	Unit	2006	2007	2008	2009	2010	2011	2012
ELEMENTARY AND SECONDARY SCHOOLS								
School enrollment, total.	1,000. . .	55,524	55,762	55,966	56,186	56,480	56,857	57,338
Pre-kindergarten through grade 8 . .	1,000. . .	39,166	39,376	39,678	40,028	40,454	40,915	41,372
Grades 9 through 12	1,000. . .	16,358	16,386	16,287	16,158	16,025	15,943	15,966
Public.	1,000. . .	49,370	49,610	49,812	50,028	50,303	50,653	51,093
Pre-kindergarten through grade 8 .	1,000. . .	34,387	34,592	34,873	35,195	35,581	35,994	36,397
Grades 9 through 12	1,000. . .	14,983	15,018	14,939	14,834	14,722	14,659	14,696
Private	1,000. . .	6,155	6,152	6,154	6,158	6,177	6,204	6,245
Pre-kindergarten through grade 8 .	1,000. . .	4,779	4,784	4,805	4,834	4,873	4,921	4,975
Grades 9 through 12	1,000. . .	1,375	1,368	1,348	1,324	1,304	1,284	1,270
Classroom teachers, total FTE [1]	1,000. . .	3,637	3,679	3,725	3,770	3,812	3,857	3,913
Public	1,000. . .	3,177	3,213	3,252	3,289	3,325	3,363	3,410
Private	1,000. . .	460	466	473	480	487	494	502
High school graduates, total [2].	1,000. . .	3,240	3,303	3,330	3,304	3,275	3,231	3,223
Public	1,000. . .	2,929	2,988	3,012	2,995	2,970	2,933	2,927
Public schools: [2]								
Average daily attendance (ADA) . . .	1,000. . .	45,927	46,151	46,339	46,540	46,796	47,121	47,530
Current dollars: [3]								
Current school expenditure	Bil. dol. .	474.8	495.7	519.0	543.3	(NA)	(NA)	(NA)
Per pupil in fall enrollment	Dollar . .	9,618	9,992	10,418	10,859	(NA)	(NA)	(NA)
Constant (2004–2005) dollars: [3, 4]								
Current school expenditure	Bil. dol. .	451.0	461.9	474.3	487.3	(NA)	(NA)	(NA)
Per pupil in fall enrollment	Dollar . .	9,136	9,311	9,521	9,739	(NA)	(NA)	(NA)
HIGHER EDUCATION								
Enrollment, total.	1,000. . .	17,672	17,958	18,264	18,567	18,839	19,105	19,374
Male.	1,000. . .	7,470	7,574	7,685	7,793	7,884	7,967	8,035
Full-time.	1,000. . .	4,836	4,919	5,009	5,096	5,170	5,231	5,276
Part-time	1,000. . .	2,634	2,654	2,676	2,697	2,715	2,736	2,759
Female	1,000. . .	10,202	10,385	10,579	10,774	10,955	11,139	11,339
Full-time.	1,000. . .	6,146	6,314	6,487	6,660	6,826	6,991	7,166
Part-time	1,000. . .	4,056	4,070	4,092	4,114	4,129	4,148	4,173
Public	1,000. . .	13,252	13,457	13,677	13,895	14,085	14,269	14,453
Four-year institutions	1,000. . .	6,930	7,054	7,186	7,318	7,444	7,566	7,685
Two-year institutions	1,000. . .	6,322	6,403	6,492	6,577	6,642	6,704	6,768
Private	1,000. . .	4,420	4,501	4,587	4,672	4,754	4,836	4,921
Four-year institutions	1,000. . .	4,115	4,190	4,268	4,347	4,424	4,501	4,580
Two-year institutions	1,000. . .	305	311	318	325	330	335	340
Undergraduate	1,000. . .	15,136	15,386	15,659	15,929	16,162	16,376	16,576
Graduate.	1,000. . .	2,195	2,224	2,251	2,277	2,308	2,351	2,407
First-time professional	1,000. . .	341	348	355	361	369	378	390
Full-time equivalent	1,000. . .	13,383	13,647	13,925	14,201	14,451	14,692	14,930
Public	1,000. . .	9,607	9,792	9,988	10,182	10,354	10,518	10,677
2-year	1,000. . .	3,772	3,838	3,909	3,976	4,028	4,078	4,129
4-year	1,000. . .	5,835	5,954	6,080	6,206	6,326	6,439	6,548
Private.	1,000. . .	3,776	3,855	3,937	4,019	4,097	4,175	4,253
2-year	1,000. . .	279	285	292	299	304	308	313
4-year	1,000. . .	3,497	3,570	3,645	3,720	3,794	3,866	3,940
Degrees conferred, total [2]	1,000. . .	2,951	3,019	3,093	3,154	3,197	3,240	3,285
Associate's	1,000. . .	689	699	714	724	730	735	740
Bachelor's	1,000. . .	1,506	1,544	1,585	1,622	1,649	1,673	1,697
Master's	1,000. . .	614	631	647	659	667	679	692
Doctoral	1,000. . .	55	55	56	56	57	58	60
First-professional	1,000. . .	88	89	91	93	94	95	96

NA Not available.   [1] Full-time equivalent.   [2] For school year ending in June the following year.   [3] Limited financial projections are shown due to the uncertain behavior of inflation over the long term.   [4] Based on the Consumer Price Index (CPI) for all urban consumers, U.S. Bureau of Labor Statistics. CPI adjusted to a school year basis by NCES.

Source: U.S. National Center for Education Statistics, *Projections of Education Statistics to 2016*, NCES 2007-038. See Internet site <http://www.nces.ed.gov/surveys/AnnualReports/>.

Table 210. Federal Funds for Education and Related Programs: 2004 to 2006

[In millions of dollars (132,420.7 represents $132,420,700,000), except percent. For fiscal years ending in September. Figures represent on-budget funds]

Level, agency, and program	2004	2005	2006[1]
Total, all programs	132,420.7	146,005.3	166,134.5
Percent of federal budget outlays	5.8	5.9	6.3
Elementary/secondary education programs	62,653.2	68,969.8	70,748.6
Department of Education[2]	33,689.4	37,477.6	39,770.5
Grants for the disadvantaged	12,486.3	14,635.6	14,655.5
School improvement programs	7,459.8	7,918.1	8,154.5
Indian education	114.4	121.9	126.1
Special education	9,749.4	10,940.3	11,462.6
Vocational and adult education	1,945.2	1,967.1	2,069.9
Education reform—Goals 2000	50.8	-35.0	-64.2
Department of Agriculture[2]	11,725.3	12,577.3	13,419.8
Child nutrition programs	[3]11,206.4	[3]11,901.9	[3]12,660.8
Agricultural Marketing Service—commodities[4]	171.0	399.3	465.0
Special milk program[3]	(3)	(3)	(3)
Department of Defense[2]	1,642.1	1,786.3	1,932.8
Overseas dependents schools	959.3	1,060.9	1,212.0
Section VI schools	390.1	410.2	401.3
Department of Health and Human Services	7,727.5	8,003.3	8,007.1
Head Start	6,774.4	6,842.3	6,875.8
Social security student benefits[6]	953.0	1,161.0	1,131.3
Department of the Interior[2]	0.5	0.5	0.6
Mineral Leasing Act and other funds	983.3	938.5	881.2
Indian Education	150.1	140.0	133.4
Department of Justice	832.2	797.5	746.8
Inmate programs	482.5	554.5	600.6
Department of Labor	478.5	554.5	600.6
Job Corps.	5,675.0	5,654.0	4,203.0
Department of Veterans Affairs.	1,438.0	1,521.0	1,725.0
Vocational rehab for disabled veterans	551.0	1,815.0	1,725.0
Other agencies and programs	551.0	1,815.0	208.1
Other agencies and programs	176.7	162.9	
Higher education programs[2]	32,433.0	38,591.1	57,381.5
Department of Education[2]	25,341.0	31,420.0	49,953.5
Student financial assistance	14,968.6	15,209.5	14,093.0
Federal Family Education Loans[7]	4,661.6	10,777.5	26,297.0
Department of Agriculture	93.8	62.0	82.9
Department of Commerce[8]	4.0	—	
Department of Defense	1,780.3	1,858.3	1,925.4
Tuition assistance for military personnel	594.4	608.1	636.6
Service academies[8]	286.2	300.8	293.6
Senior ROTC	525.2	537.5	566.7

Level, agency, and program	2004	2005	2006[1]
Professional development education	374.5	411.9	428.5
Department of Health and Human Services[2]	1,535.3	1,433.5	1,275.8
Health professions training programs.	698.3	581.7	420.4
National Health Service Corps scholarships.	45.0	45.0	40.0
National Institutes of Health training grants[9]	740.5	756.0	760.8
Department of Homeland Security[6]	41.1	36.4	41.5
Department of the Interior.	246.2	249.2	255.6
Shared revenues, Mineral Leasing Act and other receipts—estimated education share	142.9	146.0	149.9
Indian programs.	103.9	103.5	105.7
Department of State.	399.6	424.0	411.0
Department of Transportation.	66.0	73.0	72.0
Department of Veterans Affairs[2]	2,294.0	2,478.6	2,801.5
Post-Vietnam veterans	1.0	1.1	0.9
All-volunteer-force educational assistance.	1,942.8	2,071.0	2,351.3
Other agencies and programs	631.7	556.0	562.3
National Endowment for the Humanities	29.8	29.5	29.0
National Science Foundation	566.0	490.0	496.0
Other education programs[2]	6,576.8	6,908.7	7,186.7
Department of Education[2]	3,437.8	3,538.9	3,721.3
Administration.	525.2	548.8	531.1
Rehabilitative services and handicapped research	2,894.0	2,973.3	3,168.7
Department of Agriculture	462.1	468.6	473.4
Department of Health and Human Services	310.0	313.0	315.0
Department of Homeland Security[6]	205.4	278.2	316.0
Department of Justice	25.2	26.1	26.7
Department of State.	90.4	109.3	114.3
Other agencies and programs[2]	2,045.0	2,173.4	2,219.0
Agency for International Development	536.0	574.0	554.0
Library of Congress	402.0	430.0	424.0
National Endowment for the Arts.	1.6	2.5	2.5
National Endowment for the Humanities.	94.9	88.0	88.0
Research programs at universities and related institutions[2]	30,757.7	31,535.7	30,817.8
Department of Education[2]	652.9	819.9	552.3
Department of Agriculture	2,513.4	2,880.8	2,312.7
Department of Defense	4,331.5	4,216.5	4,024.4
Department of Energy.			
Department of Health and Human Services	15,838.0	16,121.7	16,220.1
National Aeronautics and Space Administration.	2,758.6	2,867.2	3,010.6
National Science Foundation.	3,617.0	3,521.7	3,610.9

– Represents or rounds to zero. [1] Estimated except U.S. Department of Education, which are actual data reports. [2] Includes other programs and agencies, not shown separately. [3] The Special Milk Program is included in the Child Nutrition Program. [4] Purchased under Section 32 of the Act of August 1935 for use in child nutrition programs. [5] Program provides for the education of dependents of federal employees residing on federal property where free public education is unavailable in the nearby community. [6] The U.S. Department of Homeland Security was created on January 24, 2003, under public law (107–296). [7] Includes Federal Direct Loans. [8] Instructional costs only including academics, audiovisual, academic computer center, faculty training, military training, physical education, and libraries. [9] Includes alcohol, drug abuse, and mental health training programs.

Source: U.S. National Center for Education Statistics, Digest of Education Statistics, annual.

Table 211. School Enrollment by Age: 1970 to 2005

[As of October (60,357 represents 60,357,000). Covers civilian noninstitutional population enrolled in nursery school and above. Based on Current Population Survey, see text, Section 1, and Appendix III]

Age	1970	1980	1985	1990	1995	2000	2002	2003	2004	2005
ENROLLMENT (1,000)										
Total, 3 to 34 years old	60,357	57,348	58,013	60,588	66,939	69,560	71,003	72,116	72,418	72,768
3 and 4 years old	1,461	2,280	2,801	3,292	4,042	4,097	4,187	4,590	4,552	4,383
5 and 6 years old	7,000	5,853	6,697	7,207	7,901	7,648	7,353	7,309	7,561	7,486
7 to 13 years old	28,943	23,751	22,849	25,016	27,003	28,296	28,525	28,184	28,006	27,936
14 and 15 years old	7,869	7,282	7,362	6,555	7,651	7,885	8,022	8,329	8,327	8,375
16 and 17 years old	6,927	7,129	6,654	6,098	6,997	7,341	7,669	8,177	8,086	8,472
18 and 19 years old	3,322	3,788	3,716	4,044	4,274	4,926	5,007	4,856	4,961	5,109
20 and 21 years old	1,949	2,515	2,708	2,852	3,025	3,314	3,696	3,684	3,904	4,069
22 to 24 years old	1,410	1,931	2,068	2,231	2,545	2,731	3,003	3,397	3,221	3,254
25 to 29 years old	1,011	1,714	1,942	2,013	2,216	2,030	2,196	2,212	2,479	2,340
30 to 34 years old	466	1,105	1,218	1,281	1,284	1,292	1,345	1,378	1,321	1,344
35 years old and over	(NA)	1,290	1,766	2,439	2,830	2,653	3,043	2,797	3,042	3,013
ENROLLMENT RATE										
Total, 3 to 34 years old	56.4	49.7	48.3	50.2	53.7	55.8	56.1	56.2	56.2	56.5
3 and 4 years old	20.5	36.7	38.9	44.4	48.7	52.1	54.5	55.1	54.0	53.6
5 and 6 years old	89.5	95.7	96.1	96.5	96.0	95.6	95.2	94.5	95.4	95.4
7 to 13 years old	99.2	99.3	99.2	99.6	98.9	98.2	98.3	98.3	98.4	98.6
14 and 15 years old	98.1	98.2	98.1	99.0	98.9	98.7	98.4	97.5	98.5	98.0
16 and 17 years old	90.0	89.0	91.7	92.5	93.6	92.8	94.3	94.9	94.5	95.1
18 and 19 years old	47.7	46.4	51.6	57.3	59.4	61.2	63.3	64.5	64.4	67.6
20 and 21 years old	31.9	31.0	35.3	39.7	44.9	44.1	47.8	48.3	48.9	48.7
22 to 24 years old	14.9	16.3	16.9	21.0	23.2	24.6	25.6	27.8	26.3	27.3
25 to 29 years old	7.5	9.3	9.2	9.7	11.6	11.4	12.1	11.8	13.0	11.9
30 to 34 years old	4.2	6.4	6.1	5.8	6.0	6.7	6.6	6.8	6.6	6.9
35 years old and over	(NA)	1.4	1.6	2.1	2.2	1.9	2.1	1.9	2.0	2.0

NA Not available.

Source: U.S. Census Bureau, Current Population Reports, PPL-148; and earlier PPL and P-20 reports; and data published on the Internet. See Internet site <http://www.census.gov/population/www/socdemo/school.html>.

Table 212. School Enrollment by Race, Hispanic Origin, and Age: 1980 to 2005

[(47,673 represents 47,673,000). See headnote, Table 211]

Age	White [1]			Black [1]			Hispanic origin [2]		
	1980	1990	2005	1980	1990	2005	1980	1990	2005
ENROLLMENT (1,000)									
Total, 3 to 34 years old	47,673	48,899	55,715	8,251	8,854	10,885	4,263	6,073	12,502
3 and 4 years old	1,844	2,700	3,380	371	452	655	172	249	773
5 and 6 years old	4,781	5,750	5,707	904	1,129	1,144	491	835	1,532
7 to 13 years old	19,585	20,076	21,310	3,598	3,832	4,317	2,009	2,794	5,394
14 and 15 years old	6,038	5,265	6,429	1,088	1,023	1,321	568	739	1,431
16 and 17 years old	5,937	4,858	6,520	1,047	962	1,281	454	592	1,357
18 and 19 years old	3,199	3,271	4,006	494	596	707	226	329	681
20 and 21 years old	2,206	2,402	3,262	242	305	430	111	213	447
22 to 24 years old	1,669	1,781	2,411	196	274	475	93	121	419
25 to 29 years old	1,473	1,706	1,740	187	162	307	84	130	310
30 to 34 years old	942	1,090	950	124	119	248	54	72	158
35 years old and over	1,104	2,096	2,299	186	238	499	(NA)	145	307
ENROLLMENT RATE									
Total, 3 to 34 years old	48.9	49.5	55.9	53.9	51.9	58.4	49.8	47.4	50.9
3 and 4 years old	36.3	44.9	54.2	38.2	41.6	52.2	28.5	29.8	43.0
5 and 6 years old	95.8	96.5	95.3	95.4	96.3	95.9	94.5	94.8	93.8
7 to 13 years old	99.2	99.6	98.6	99.4	99.8	98.6	99.2	99.4	97.6
14 and 15 years old	98.3	99.1	98.3	97.9	99.2	95.8	94.3	99.0	97.3
16 and 17 years old	88.6	92.5	95.4	90.6	91.7	93.1	81.8	85.4	92.6
18 and 19 years old	46.3	57.1	68.0	45.7	55.2	62.8	37.8	44.1	54.3
20 and 21 years old	31.9	41.0	49.3	23.4	28.4	37.6	19.5	27.2	30.0
22 to 24 years old	16.4	20.2	26.0	13.6	20.0	28.0	11.7	9.9	19.5
25 to 29 years old	9.2	9.9	11.3	8.8	6.1	11.7	6.9	6.3	7.8
30 to 34 years old	6.3	5.9	6.2	6.8	4.4	10.0	5.1	3.6	4.2
35 years old and over	1.3	2.1	1.8	1.8	2.1	3.1	(NA)	2.1	2.0

NA Not available. [1] 2005 for persons who selected this race group only. See footnote 2, Table 217. [2] Persons of Hispanic origin may be of any race.

Source: U.S. Census Bureau, Current Population Reports, PPL-148; and earlier PPL and P-20 reports; and data published on the Internet. See Internet site <http://www.census.gov/population/www/socdemo/school.html>.

Table 213. **Enrollment in Public and Private Schools: 1970 to 2005**

[In millions (52.2 represents 52,200,000), except percent. As of October. For civilian noninstitutional population. For 1970 to 1985, persons 3 to 34 years old; **beginning 1988**, for 3 years old and over. For enrollment 35 years old and over, see Table 211. Based on the Current Population Survey; see text, Section 1]

Year	Public						Private					
	Total	Nursery	Kindergarten	Elementary	High school	College	Total	Nursery	Kindergarten	Elementary	High school	College
1970	52.2	0.3	2.6	30.0	13.5	5.7	8.1	0.8	0.5	3.9	1.2	1.7
1975	52.8	0.6	2.9	27.2	14.5	7.7	8.2	1.2	0.5	3.3	1.2	2.0
1980	(NA)	0.6	2.7	24.4	(NA)	(NA)	(NA)	1.4	0.5	3.1	(NA)	(NA)
1985 [1]	49.0	0.9	3.2	23.8	12.8	8.4	9.0	1.6	0.6	3.1	1.2	2.5
1988	52.2	0.9	3.4	25.5	12.2	10.3	8.9	1.8	0.5	2.8	1.0	2.8
1989	52.5	0.9	3.3	25.9	12.1	10.3	8.9	1.9	0.6	2.7	0.8	2.9
1990	53.8	1.2	3.3	26.6	11.9	10.7	9.2	2.2	0.6	2.7	0.9	2.9
1991	54.5	1.1	3.5	26.6	12.2	11.1	9.4	1.8	0.6	3.0	1.0	3.0
1992	55.0	1.1	3.5	27.1	12.3	11.1	9.4	1.8	0.6	3.1	1.0	3.0
1993	56.0	1.2	3.5	27.7	12.6	10.9	9.4	1.8	0.7	2.9	1.0	3.0
1994	58.6	1.9	3.3	28.1	13.5	11.7	10.7	2.3	0.6	3.4	1.1	3.3
1995	58.7	2.0	3.2	28.4	13.7	11.4	11.1	2.4	0.7	3.4	1.2	3.3
1996	59.5	1.9	3.4	28.1	14.1	12.0	10.8	2.3	0.7	3.4	1.2	3.2
1997	61.6	2.3	3.3	29.3	14.6	12.1	10.5	2.2	0.7	3.1	1.2	3.3
1998	60.8	2.3	3.1	29.1	14.3	12.0	11.3	2.3	0.7	3.4	1.2	3.6
1999	60.8	2.3	3.2	29.2	14.4	11.7	11.4	2.3	0.7	3.6	1.3	3.5
2000	61.2	2.2	3.2	29.4	14.4	12.0	11.0	2.2	0.7	3.5	1.3	3.3
2001	62.4	2.2	3.1	29.8	14.8	12.4	10.8	2.1	0.6	3.4	1.2	3.5
2002	62.8	2.2	3.0	29.7	15.1	12.8	11.3	2.2	0.6	3.5	1.3	3.7
2003	63.8	2.6	3.1	29.2	15.8	13.1	11.1	2.4	0.6	3.4	1.3	3.5
2004	64.3	2.5	3.4	29.2	15.5	13.7	11.3	2.3	0.6	3.4	1.3	3.7
2005	64.2	2.5	3.3	29.0	15.8	13.4	11.5	2.1	0.6	3.4	1.4	4.0
Percent White:												
1970.	84.5	59.5	84.4	83.1	85.6	90.7	93.4	91.1	88.2	94.1	96.1	92.8
1980.	(NA)	68.2	80.7	80.9	(NA)	(NA)	(NA)	89.0	87.0	90.7	(NA)	(NA)
1990.	79.8	71.7	78.3	78.9	79.2	84.1	87.4	89.6	83.2	88.2	89.4	85.0
2000.	77.0	69.4	77.3	76.7	78.0	78.0	83.5	84.9	82.8	85.9	84.6	79.8
2002.	76.6	71.8	75.3	76.5	77.9	76.2	83.8	83.6	87.5	84.1	86.4	82.1
2003 [2]	75.6	74.7	76.4	75.0	75.6	77.1	82.3	84.3	80.3	83.8	86.0	79.0
2004 [2] . . . ,	75.2	68.5	75.2	75.0	75.4	76.7	82.4	82.7	82.1	85.1	88.0	77.8
2005 [2]	75.7	71.3	78.0	75.2	76.0	76.7	81.4	83.6	79.0	83.0	83.6	78.4

NA Not available. [1] Beginning 1988, based on a revised edit and tabulation package. [2] Beginning 2003, for persons who selected this race group only. See footnote 2, Table 217.

Source: U.S. Census Bureau, Current Population Reports, PPL-148; and earlier PPL and P-20 reports; and data published on the Internet. See Internet site <http://www.census.gov/population/www/socdemo/school.html>.

Table 214. **School Enrollment by Sex and Level: 1970 to 2005**

[In millions (60.4 represents 60,400,000). As of Oct. For the civilian noninstitutional population. **1970–1979**, for persons 3 to 34 years old; **beginning 1980**, 3 years old and over. Elementary includes kindergarten and grades 1–8; high school, grades 9–12; and college, 2-year and 4-year colleges, universities, and graduate and professional schools. Data for college represent degree-credit enrollment. See headnote, Table 211]

Year	All levels [1]			Elementary			High school			College		
	Total	Male	Female	Total	Male	Female	Total	Male	Female	Total	Male	Female
1970	60.4	31.4	28.9	37.1	19.0	18.1	14.7	7.4	7.3	7.4	4.4	3.0
1980	58.6	29.6	29.1	30.6	15.8	14.9	14.6	7.0	7.3	11.4	5.4	6.0
1985 [2]	59.8	30.0	29.7	30.7	15.7	15.0	14.1	7.2	6.9	12.5	5.9	6.6
1987 [2]	60.6	30.7	29.9	31.6	16.3	15.3	13.8	7.0	6.8	12.7	6.0	6.7
1988	61.1	30.7	30.5	32.2	16.6	15.6	13.2	6.7	6.4	13.1	5.9	7.2
1989	61.5	30.8	30.7	32.5	16.7	15.8	12.9	6.6	6.3	13.2	6.0	7.2
1990	63.0	31.5	31.5	33.2	17.1	16.0	12.8	6.5	6.4	13.6	6.2	7.4
1991	63.9	32.1	31.8	33.8	17.3	16.4	13.1	6.8	6.4	14.1	6.4	7.6
1992	64.6	32.2	32.3	34.3	17.7	16.6	13.3	6.8	6.5	14.0	6.2	7.8
1993	65.4	32.9	32.5	34.8	17.9	16.9	13.6	7.0	6.6	13.9	6.3	7.6
1994	69.3	34.6	34.7	35.4	18.2	17.2	14.6	7.4	7.2	15.0	6.8	8.2
1995	69.8	35.0	34.8	35.7	18.3	17.4	15.0	7.7	7.3	14.7	6.7	8.0
1996	70.3	35.1	35.2	35.5	18.3	17.3	15.3	7.9	7.4	15.2	6.8	8.4
1997	72.0	35.9	36.2	36.3	18.7	17.6	15.8	8.0	7.7	15.4	6.8	8.6
1998	72.1	36.0	36.1	36.4	18.7	17.7	15.6	7.9	7.6	15.5	6.9	8.6
1999	72.4	36.3	36.1	36.7	18.8	17.9	15.9	8.2	7.7	15.2	7.0	8.2
2000	72.2	35.8	36.4	36.7	18.9	17.9	15.8	8.1	7.7	15.3	6.7	8.6
2001	73.1	36.3	36.9	36.9	19.0	17.9	16.1	8.2	7.8	15.9	6.9	9.0
2002	74.0	36.8	37.3	36.7	18.9	17.8	16.4	8.3	8.0	16.5	7.2	9.3
2003	74.9	37.3	37.6	36.3	18.7	17.6	17.1	8.6	8.4	16.6	7.3	9.3
2004	75.5	37.4	38.0	36.5	19.0	17.6	16.8	8.4	8.4	17.4	7.6	9.8
2005	75.8	37.4	38.4	36.4	18.6	17.7	17.4	8.9	8.5	17.5	7.5	9.9

[1] Includes nursery schools, not shown separately. [2] Data beginning 1987, based on a revised edit and tabulation package.

Source: U.S. Census Bureau, Current Population Reports, PPL-148; and earlier PPL and P-20 reports; and data published on the Internet. See Internet site <http://www.census.gov/population/www/socdemo/school.html>.

Education 143

Table 215. **School Enrollment by Control and Level: 1980 to 2005**

[In thousands (58,305 represents 58,305,000). As of fall. Data below college level are for regular day schools and exclude subcollegiate departments of colleges, federal schools, and home-schooled children. College data include degree-credit and non-degree-credit enrollment. Based on survey of state education agencies; see source for details. For more projections, see Tables 207 and 209]

Control of school and level	1980	1990	1995	1999	2000	2001	2002	2003	2004	2005, proj.
Total	58,305	60,269	65,020	67,667	68,685	69,920	71,015	71,540	72,200	72,626
Public.	50,335	52,061	55,933	58,166	58,956	59,905	60,935	61,397	61,775	62,050
Private	7,971	8,208	9,087	9,501	9,729	10,014	10,080	10,143	10,425	10,577
Pre-kindergarten through 8 . .	31,639	33,962	37,062	38,253	38,566	38,931	39,002	38,964	38,951	38,910
Public	27,647	29,878	32,341	33,488	33,688	33,938	34,116	34,202	34,178	34,174
Private	3,992	4,084	4,721	4,765	4,878	4,993	4,886	4,761	4,773	4,736
Grades 9 through 12	14,570	12,488	13,697	14,623	14,807	15,061	15,402	15,676	15,977	16,229
Public	13,231	11,338	12,500	13,369	13,515	13,734	14,067	14,338	14,617	14,853
Private	1,339	1,150	1,197	1,254	1,292	1,326	1,334	1,338	1,360	1,376
College [1]	12,097	13,819	14,261	14,791	15,312	15,928	16,612	16,900	17,272	[2]17,487
Public	9,457	10,845	11,092	11,309	11,753	12,233	12,752	12,857	12,980	[2]13,022
Private	2,640	2,974	3,169	3,482	3,560	3,695	3,860	4,043	4,292	[2]4,466
Not-for-profit	2,528	2,760	2,929	3,052	3,109	3,167	3,265	3,341	3,412	[2]3,455
For profit	112	214	240	430	450	528	594	703	880	[2]1,011

[1] Data beginning 1999, reflects new classification system. See footnote 1, Table 271.   [2] Actual data.

Source: U.S. National Center for Education Statistics, *Digest of Education Statistics,* annual, and *Projections of Education Statistics,* annual.

Table 216. **Students Who Are Foreign Born or Who Have Foreign-Born Parents: 2005**

[In thousands (49,792 represents 49,792,000), except percent. As of October. Covers civilian noninstitutional population enrolled in elementary school and above. Based on Current Population Survey, see text, Section 1 and Appendix III]

Characteristic	All students	Students with at least one foreign-born parent					
		Total		Foreign-born student		Native student	
		Number	Percent	Number	Percent	Number	Percent
ELEMENTARY AND HIGH SCHOOL							
Total [1]	49,792	10,980	22.1	2,495	5.0	8,485	17.0
White [2]	37,949	7,636	20.1	1,694	4.5	5,941	15.7
White, non-Hispanic.	29,505	2,209	7.5	420	1.4	1,789	6.1
Black [2]	7,829	1,047	13.4	310	4.0	737	9.4
Asian [2, 3]	1,870	1,746	93.4	442	23.6	1,304	69.7
Hispanic [4]	9,267	5,847	63.1	1,374	14.8	4,472	48.3
COLLEGE, 1 TO 4 YEARS							
Total [1]	14,169	3,151	22.2	1,528	10.8	1,623	11.5
White [2]	10,932	1,846	16.9	783	7.2	1,063	9.7
White, non-Hispanic.	9,418	877	9.3	373	4.0	504	5.4
Black [2]	1,972	416	21.1	254	12.9	163	8.2
Asian [2, 3]	795	743	93.5	440	55.3	303	38.2
Hispanic [4]	1,671	1,071	64.1	455	27.2	615	36.8
GRADUATE SCHOOL							
Total [1]	3,304	890	26.9	525	15.9	364	11.0
White [2]	2,534	467	18.4	236	9.3	231	9.1
White, non-Hispanic.	2,297	288	12.5	137	5.9	151	6.6
Black [2]	326	45	13.7	32	9.8	13	3.9
Asian [2, 3]	389	351	90.1	251	64.4	100	25.7
Hispanic [4]	271	191	70.4	102	37.7	88	32.7

[1] Includes other races, not shown separately.   [2] For persons who selected this race group only. See footnote 2, Table 217.   [3] Data are for Asians only; excludes Pacific Islanders.   [4] Persons of Hispanic origin may be of any race.

Source: U.S. Census Bureau, Current Population Survey, unpublished data. See Internet site <http://www.census.gov/population/www/socdemo/school.html>.

Table 217. Educational Attainment by Race and Hispanic Origin: 1960 to 2006

[In percent. For persons 25 years old and over. 1960, 1970, and 1980 as of April 1 and based on sample data from the censuses of population. Other years as of March and based on the Current Population Survey; see text, Section 1, and Appendix III. See Table 218 for data by sex]

Year	Total [1]	White [2]	Black [2]	Asian and Pacific Islander [2]	Hispanic [3] Total [4]	Mexican	Puerto Rican	Cuban
HIGH SCHOOL GRADUATE OR MORE [5]								
1960	41.1	43.2	20.1	(NA)	(NA)	(NA)	(NA)	(NA)
1970	52.3	54.5	31.4	(NA)	32.1	24.2	23.4	43.9
1980	66.5	68.8	51.2	(NA)	44.0	37.6	40.1	55.3
1990	77.6	79.1	66.2	80.4	50.8	44.1	55.5	63.5
1995	81.7	83.0	73.8	(NA)	53.4	46.5	61.3	64.7
2000	84.1	84.9	78.5	85.7	57.0	51.0	64.3	73.0
2003	84.6	85.1	80.0	[6]87.6	57.0	50.9	69.7	70.8
2004	85.2	85.8	80.6	86.8	58.4	51.9	71.8	72.1
2005	85.2	85.7	81.1	87.6	58.5	52.2	72.3	73.5
2006	85.5	86.1	80.7	87.4	59.3	53.1	72.3	74.9
COLLEGE GRADUATE OR MORE [5]								
1960	7.7	8.1	3.1	(NA)	(NA)	(NA)	(NA)	(NA)
1970	10.7	11.3	4.4	(NA)	4.5	2.5	2.2	11.1
1980	16.2	17.1	8.4	(NA)	7.6	4.9	5.6	16.2
1990	21.3	22.0	11.3	39.9	9.2	5.4	9.7	20.2
1995	23.0	24.0	13.2	(NA)	9.3	6.5	10.7	19.4
2000	25.6	26.1	16.5	43.9	10.6	6.9	13.0	23.0
2003	27.2	27.6	17.3	[6]49.8	11.4	7.8	12.3	21.6
2004	27.7	28.2	17.6	49.4	12.1	7.9	14.0	24.0
2005	27.6	28.0	17.6	50.1	12.0	8.3	13.8	24.7
2006	28.0	28.4	18.5	49.7	12.4	8.5	15.1	24.4

NA Not available. [1] Includes other races, not shown separately. [2] Beginning 2003, for persons who selected this race group only. The 2003 Current Population Survey (CPS) allowed respondents to choose more than one race. Beginning 2003, data represent persons who selected this race group only and exclude persons reporting more than one race. The CPS in prior years only allowed respondents to report one race group. See also comments on race in the text for Section 1. [3] Persons of Hispanic origin may be of any race. [4] Includes persons of other Hispanic origin, not shown separately. [5] Through 1990, completed 4 years of high school or more and 4 years of college or more. [6] Starting in 2003, data are for Asians only, excludes Pacific Islanders.

Source: U.S. Census Bureau, U.S. Census of Population, 1960, 1970, and 1980, Vol. 1; and Current Population Reports P20-550 and earlier reports; and data published on the Internet. See Internet site <http://www.census.gov/population/www/socdemo/educ-attn.html>.

Table 218. Educational Attainment by Race, Hispanic Origin, and Sex: 1960 to 2006

[In percent. See Table 217 for headnote and totals for both sexes]

Year	All races [1] Male	Female	White [2] Male	Female	Black [2] Male	Female	Asian and Pacific Islander [2] Male	Female	Hispanic [3] Male	Female
HIGH SCHOOL GRADUATE OR MORE [4]										
1960	39.5	42.5	41.6	44.7	18.2	21.8	(NA)	(NA)	(NA)	(NA)
1970	51.9	52.8	54.0	55.0	30.1	32.5	(NA)	(NA)	37.9	34.2
1980	67.3	65.8	69.6	68.1	50.8	51.5	(NA)	(NA)	67.3	65.8
1990	77.7	77.5	79.1	79.0	65.8	66.5	84.0	77.2	50.3	51.3
1995	81.7	81.6	83.0	83.0	73.4	74.1	(NA)	(NA)	52.9	53.8
2000	84.2	84.0	84.8	85.0	78.7	78.3	[5]88.2	[5]83.4	56.6	57.5
2003	84.1	85.0	84.5	85.7	79.6	80.3	[5]89.5	[5]86.0	56.3	57.8
2004	84.8	85.4	85.3	86.3	80.4	80.8	88.7	85.0	57.3	59.5
2005	84.9	85.5	85.2	86.2	81.0	81.2	90.4	85.2	57.9	59.1
2006	85.0	85.9	85.5	86.7	80.1	81.2	89.6	85.5	58.5	60.1
COLLEGE GRADUATE OR MORE [4]										
1960	9.7	5.8	10.3	6.0	2.8	3.3	(NA)	(NA)	(NA)	(NA)
1970	13.5	8.1	14.4	8.4	4.2	4.6	(NA)	(NA)	7.8	4.3
1980	20.1	12.8	21.3	13.3	8.4	8.3	(NA)	(NA)	9.4	6.0
1990	24.4	18.4	25.3	19.0	11.9	10.8	44.9	35.4	9.8	8.7
1995	26.0	20.2	27.2	21.0	13.6	12.9	(NA)	(NA)	10.1	8.4
2000	27.8	23.6	28.5	23.9	16.3	16.7	47.6	40.7	10.7	10.6
2003	28.9	25.7	29.4	25.9	16.7	17.8	[5]53.9	[5]46.1	11.2	11.6
2004	29.4	26.1	30.0	26.4	16.6	18.5	53.7	45.6	11.8	12.3
2005	28.9	26.5	29.4	26.8	16.0	18.8	54.0	46.8	11.8	12.1
2006	29.2	26.9	29.7	27.1	17.2	19.4	52.5	47.1	11.9	12.9

NA Not available. [1] Includes other races, not shown separately. [2] Beginning 2003, for persons who selected this race group only. See footnote 2, Table 217. [3] Persons of Hispanic origin may be of any race. [4] Through 1990, completed 4 years of high school or more and 4 years of college or more. [5] Starting in 2003, data are for Asians only, excludes Pacific Islanders.

Source: U.S. Census Bureau, U.S. Census of Population, 1960, 1970, and 1980, Vol. 1; and Current Population Reports P20-550 and earlier reports; and data published on the Internet. See Internet site <http://www.census.gov/population/www/socdemo/educ-attn.html>.

Table 219. **Educational Attainment by Selected Characteristic: 2006**

[For persons 25 years old and over (191,884 represents 191,884,000). As of March. Based on the Current Population Survey; see text, Section 1, and Appendix III. For composition of regions, see map inside front cover]

Characteristic	Population (1,000)	Percent of population—highest level					
		Not a high school graduate	High school graduate	Some college, but no degree	Associate's degree [1]	Bachelor's degree	Advanced degree
Total persons	**191,884**	**14.5**	**31.7**	**17.0**	**8.7**	**18.3**	**9.7**
Age:							
25 to 34 years old	39,480	13.0	28.6	19.1	9.3	21.8	8.1
35 to 44 years old	43,121	11.9	30.5	16.8	9.8	21.1	10.0
45 to 54 years old	42,797	11.4	31.5	17.4	10.3	19.0	10.4
55 to 64 years old	30,981	12.7	32.0	17.6	8.5	16.7	12.4
65 to 74 years old	18,554	21.1	37.3	14.7	5.7	12.5	8.8
75 years old or over.	16,951	28.9	36.1	12.9	4.5	10.8	6.7
Sex:							
Male	92,233	15.0	31.9	16.3	7.7	18.5	10.7
Female	99,651	14.1	31.6	17.7	9.7	18.1	8.8
Race:							
White [2]	157,566	13.9	31.8	16.9	9.0	18.6	9.8
Black [2]	21,600	19.3	35.6	19.0	7.7	12.6	5.8
Other	12,718	14.7	23.9	14.2	7.6	24.6	14.9
Hispanic origin:							
Hispanic	23,499	40.7	28.4	12.7	5.9	8.8	3.6
Non-Hispanic	168,385	10.9	32.2	17.6	9.1	19.6	10.5
Region:							
Northeast.	36,282	13.0	33.9	12.9	7.7	19.8	12.7
Midwest.	42,603	10.9	35.0	17.7	9.7	17.8	8.9
South	69,458	16.9	32.1	16.8	8.5	17.2	8.6
West	43,541	15.7	26.1	20.0	9.1	19.5	9.6
Marital status:							
Never married.	31,603	15.2	30.3	17.7	7.8	20.5	8.5
Married spouse present	115,673	12.0	30.8	16.6	9.2	20.1	11.3
Married spouse absent [3]	3,545	29.6	29.6	14.2	6.1	12.7	7.8
Separated	4,648	25.0	35.2	17.0	8.2	9.5	5.1
Widowed	13,892	29.3	38.0	13.1	5.5	9.0	5.1
Divorced	22,523	13.0	34.3	20.6	10.2	14.6	7.2
Civilian labor force status:							
Employed	122,740	9.6	29.6	17.7	10.1	21.4	11.7
Unemployed.	5,132	20.1	34.3	18.6	8.5	14.1	4.4
Not in the labor force	63,282	23.9	35.8	15.3	6.1	12.7	6.1

[1] Includes vocational degrees.   [2] For persons who selected this race group only. See footnote 2, Table 217.   [3] Excludes those separated.

Source: U.S. Census Bureau, Current Population Survey. See Internet site <http://www.census.gov/population/www/socdemo/educ-attn.html>.

Table 220. **Mean Earnings by Highest Degree Earned: 2005**

[In dollars. For persons 18 years old and over with earnings. Persons as of March the following year. Based on Current Population Survey; see text, Section 1, and Appendix III. For definition of mean, see Guide to Tabular Presentation]

Characteristic	Total persons	Mean earnings by level of highest degree (dol.)							
		Not a high school graduate	High school graduate only	Some college, no degree	Associate's	Bachelor's	Master's	Professional	Doctorate
All persons [1] . . .	**39,579**	**19,915**	**29,448**	**31,421**	**37,990**	**54,689**	**67,898**	**119,009**	**92,863**
Age:									
25 to 34 years old. . . .	34,004	20,355	26,820	30,473	33,011	44,960	48,185	75,600	62,268
35 to 44 years old. . . .	45,373	22,516	32,637	39,124	41,110	60,297	72,098	126,520	97,109
45 to 54 years old. . . .	49,486	24,416	35,209	41,068	42,936	66,776	79,555	137,115	117,324
55 to 64 years old. . . .	46,561	25,071	33,424	41,005	42,532	56,142	69,981	129,956	87,125
65 years old and over .	35,879	16,995	24,847	26,672	34,303	49,050	62,322	100,847	85,854
Sex:									
Male.	48,034	23,222	35,248	38,768	46,201	67,980	86,667	139,773	105,163
Female	29,897	14,294	22,208	24,086	30,912	40,684	49,573	82,268	66,411
White [2]	40,717	20,264	30,569	32,191	38,788	55,785	69,112	122,975	93,412
Male.	49,611	23,556	36,753	39,849	47,534	69,852	89,207	142,879	105,657
Female	30,125	14,086	22,590	24,248	31,005	40,344	49,281	84,125	66,728
Black [2]	30,472	17,216	23,904	27,291	33,198	47,101	56,057	100,030	79,087
Male.	34,165	19,890	27,360	31,919	38,441	52,070	64,000	(B)	(B)
Female	27,314	14,300	20,449	23,798	29,722	43,516	50,831	76,298	(B)
Hispanic [3]	27,760	19,294	25,659	28,539	33,053	45,933	62,449	83,239	99,774
Male.	31,008	21,632	29,471	33,288	38,764	54,700	74,365	91,546	(B)
Female	22,887	14,365	19,864	23,073	27,673	37,003	50,314	(B)	(B)

B Base figure too small to meet statistical standards for reliability of a derived figure.   [1] Includes other races, not shown separately.   [2] For persons who selected this race group only. See footnote 2, Table 217.   [3] Persons of Hispanic origin may be of any race.

Source: U.S. Census Bureau, Current Population Survey. See Internet site <http://www.census.gov/population/www/socdemo/educ-attn.html>.

Table 221. Educational Attainment by State: 1990 to 2006

[In percent. As of March, except 1990 as of April. For persons 25 years old and over. Based on the 1990 Census of Population and the Current Population Survey; see text, Section 1, and Appendix III]

State	1990 High school graduate or more	1990 Bachelor's degree or more	1998 High school graduate or more	1998 Bachelor's degree or more	2000 High school graduate or more	2000 Bachelor's degree or more	2006 High school graduate or more	2006 Bachelor's degree or more
United States ...	75.2	20.3	82.8	24.4	84.1	25.6	85.5	28.0
Alabama	66.9	15.7	78.8	20.6	77.5	20.4	82.1	20.8
Alaska	86.6	23.0	90.6	24.2	90.4	28.1	92.0	27.7
Arizona	78.7	20.3	81.9	21.9	85.1	24.6	83.1	24.5
Arkansas	66.3	13.3	76.8	16.2	81.7	18.4	82.5	19.0
California	76.2	23.4	80.1	26.4	81.2	27.5	80.8	29.8
Colorado	84.4	27.0	89.6	34.0	89.7	34.6	90.0	36.4
Connecticut	79.2	27.2	83.7	31.4	88.2	31.6	88.4	36.0
Delaware	77.5	21.4	85.2	25.1	86.1	24.0	86.0	26.2
District of Columbia	73.1	33.3	83.8	36.5	83.2	38.3	83.3	49.1
Florida	74.4	18.3	81.9	22.5	84.0	22.8	86.7	27.2
Georgia	70.9	19.3	80.0	20.7	82.6	23.1	84.2	28.1
Hawaii	80.1	22.9	84.6	24.0	87.4	26.3	88.7	32.3
Idaho	79.7	17.7	82.7	20.3	86.2	20.0	88.9	25.1
Illinois	76.2	21.0	84.2	25.8	85.5	27.1	87.6	31.2
Indiana	75.6	15.6	83.5	17.7	84.6	17.1	88.2	21.9
Iowa	80.1	16.9	87.7	20.3	89.7	25.5	90.4	24.7
Kansas	81.3	21.1	89.2	28.5	88.1	27.3	90.2	31.6
Kentucky	64.6	13.6	77.9	20.1	78.7	20.5	79.9	20.2
Louisiana	68.3	16.1	78.6	19.5	80.8	22.5	79.7	21.2
Maine	78.8	18.8	86.7	19.2	89.3	24.1	89.3	26.9
Maryland	78.4	26.5	84.7	31.8	85.7	32.3	87.2	35.7
Massachusetts	80.0	27.2	85.6	31.0	85.1	32.7	89.9	40.4
Michigan	76.8	17.4	85.4	22.1	86.2	23.0	89.7	26.1
Minnesota	82.4	21.8	89.4	31.0	90.8	31.2	93.0	33.5
Mississippi	64.3	14.7	77.3	19.5	80.3	18.7	81.1	21.1
Missouri	73.9	17.8	82.9	22.4	86.6	26.2	87.1	24.3
Montana	81.0	19.8	89.1	23.9	89.6	23.8	91.4	25.1
Nebraska	81.8	18.9	87.7	20.9	90.4	24.6	91.0	27.2
Nevada	78.8	15.3	89.1	20.6	82.8	19.3	85.6	20.8
New Hampshire	82.2	24.4	84.0	26.6	88.1	30.1	91.6	32.1
New Jersey	76.7	24.9	86.5	30.1	87.3	30.1	86.7	35.6
New Mexico	75.1	20.4	79.6	23.1	82.2	23.6	81.8	26.7
New York	74.8	23.1	81.5	26.8	82.5	28.7	85.1	32.2
North Carolina	70.0	17.4	81.4	23.3	79.2	23.2	84.2	25.6
North Dakota	76.7	18.1	84.3	22.5	85.5	22.6	88.7	28.7
Ohio	75.7	17.0	86.2	21.5	87.0	24.6	88.1	23.3
Oklahoma	74.6	17.8	84.6	20.5	86.1	22.5	87.5	22.9
Oregon	81.5	20.6	85.5	27.7	88.1	27.2	89.7	28.3
Pennsylvania	74.7	17.9	84.1	22.1	85.7	24.3	87.5	26.6
Rhode Island	72.0	21.3	80.7	27.8	81.3	26.4	84.0	30.9
South Carolina	68.3	16.6	78.6	21.3	83.0	19.0	83.1	22.6
South Dakota	77.1	17.2	86.3	21.8	91.8	25.7	89.9	25.3
Tennessee	67.1	16.0	76.9	16.9	79.9	22.0	80.7	22.0
Texas	72.1	20.3	78.3	23.3	79.2	23.9	78.7	25.5
Utah	85.1	22.3	89.3	27.6	90.7	26.4	91.2	27.0
Vermont	80.8	24.3	86.7	27.1	90.0	28.8	91.0	34.0
Virginia	75.2	24.5	82.6	30.3	86.6	31.9	86.5	32.1
Washington	83.8	22.9	92.0	28.1	91.8	28.6	91.1	31.4
West Virginia	66.0	12.3	76.4	16.3	77.1	15.3	81.5	15.9
Wisconsin	78.6	17.7	88.0	22.3	86.7	23.8	91.1	24.6
Wyoming	83.0	18.8	90.0	19.8	90.0	20.6	91.1	20.8

Source: U.S. Census Bureau, 1990 Census of Population, CPH-L-96, and Current Population Reports, P20-550, and earlier reports; and data published on the Internet. See Internet site <http://www.census.gov/population/www/socdemo/educ-attn.html>.

U.S. Census Bureau, Statistical Abstract of the United States: 2008

Table 222. **Children's Involvement in Home Literacy Activities: 1993 and 2005**

[In percent, except number of children (8,579 represents 8,579,000). For children 3 to 5 years old not yet enrolled in kindergarten who participated in activities with a family member. Based on the School Readiness Early Childhood Program Participation Surveys of the National Household Education Surveys Program; see source and Appendix III. See also Tables 225]

Characteristic	Children (1,000)		Read to [1]		Told a story [1]		Taught letters, words, or numbers [1]		Visited a library [2]	
	1993	2005	1993	2005	1993	2005	1993	2005	1993	2005
Total.................	8,579	9,066	78	86	43	54	58	77	38	42
Age:										
3 years old................	3,889	4,070	79	86	46	54	57	75	34	40
4 years old................	3,713	3,873	78	85	41	53	58	77	41	44
5 years old................	976	1,123	76	86	36	55	58	80	38	46
Race/ethnicity:										
White, non-Hispanic.........	5,902	5,177	85	92	44	53	58	76	42	45
Black, non-Hispanic	1,271	1,233	66	78	39	54	63	81	29	44
Hispanic..................	1,026	1,822	58	72	38	50	54	74	26	32
Other....................	381	834	73	88	50	64	59	82	43	48
Mother's home language: [3]										
English	7,805	7,618	81	89	44	55	58	78	39	45
Not English................	603	1,245	42	66	36	45	52	69	26	29
Mother's highest education: [3]										
Less than high school.........	1,036	886	60	64	37	39	56	70	22	23
High school...............	3,268	2,687	76	82	41	51	56	78	31	33
Vocational ed or some college ...	2,624	2,461	83	88	45	57	60	79	44	45
College degree	912	1,832	90	92	48	56	56	75	55	52
Graduate/professional training or degree.................	569	997	90	94	50	64	60	76	59	60

[1] Three or more times in the past week.　[2] At least once in the past month.　[3] Excludes children with no mother in the household and no female guardian.

Source: U.S. National Center for Education Statistsics, Statistical Brief, NCES 2000-026, November 1999; and the Early Childhood Program Participation Survey, National Household Education Surveys Program, 2005, unpublished data. See Internet site <http://nces.ed.gov/nhes>.

Table 223. **Children Who Speak a Language Other Than English at Home: 2000 to 2004**

[In percent, except as indicated. For children 5 to 17 years old (9.5 represents 9,500,000). Based on the American Community Survey; see text Section 1, and Appendix III]

Characteristic	2000	2001	2002	2003	2004
Children who speak another language at home (mil.).......	**9.5**	**9.8**	**9.8**	**9.9**	**10.0**
Percent of children 5 to 17 years old	18.1	18.5	18.5	18.6	18.9
Race and Hispanic origin:					
White alone, non-Hispanic.....................	5.7	5.7	5.6	5.1	5.3
Black alone, non-Hispanic.....................	4.4	4.5	4.5	5.0	4.7
American Indian and Alaska Native alone	19.9	23.8	22.5	20.8	17.0
Asian alone	68.4	67.9	65.8	64.5	63.4
Native Hawaiian and Other Pacific Islander alone	36.2	42.9	39.2	34.2	32.6
Two or more races..........................	18.2	17.9	17.2	15.2	13.4
Hispanic [1]	68.6	68.7	67.8	67.6	67.4
Region: [2]					
Northeast................................	19.1	18.7	18.4	19.0	19.0
Midwest.................................	9.5	9.9	10.0	9.9	10.5
South...................................	14.6	15.1	15.4	15.7	15.6
West....................................	31.0	31.1	31.3	31.0	31.4
Living in linguistically isolated household [3] (mil.)...........	2.4	2.6	2.6	2.8	2.8
Percent of children 5 to 17 years old..............	4.6	4.9	4.9	5.3	5.5
Children who speak another language at home and have difficulty speaking English [4] (mil.).........	**2.9**	**2.8**	**2.8**	**2.9**	**2.8**
Percent of children 5 to 17 years old	5.5	5.4	5.3	5.4	5.2
Race and Hispanic origin:					
White alone, non-Hispanic.....................	1.3	1.4	1.3	1.4	1.3
Black alone, non-Hispanic.....................	1.2	1.0	1.2	1.3	1.2
American Indian and Alaska Native alone	4.6	4.5	4.2	3.9	3.1
Asian alone	20.4	21.1	19.3	17.9	16.9
Native Hawaiian and Other Pacific Islander alone	10.2	8.8	9.2	5.9	7.1
Two or more races...........................	4.3	3.9	3.9	3.4	2.5
Hispanic [1]	22.8	21.3	20.5	20.9	19.7
Region: [2]					
Northeast	5.0	5.1	5.0	5.5	4.8
Midwest	2.8	2.9	3.0	3.2	3.2
South...................................	4.4	4.1	4.3	4.7	4.4
West....................................	10.0	9.7	9.0	8.7	8.8

[1] Persons of Hispanic origin may be of any race.　[2] For composition of regions, see map, inside front cover.　[3] No person in the household aged 14 or over speaks English at least "very well."　[4] Children who speak English less than "very well."

Source: Federal Interagency Forum on Child and Family Statistics, *America's Children: Key National Indicators of Well-Being, 2006.* See Internet site <http://www.childstats.gov/>.

Table 224. **Preprimary School Enrollment—Summary: 1970 to 2005**

[As of October. **Civilian noninstitutional population (10,949 represents 10,949,000).** Includes public and nonpublic nursery school and kindergarten programs. Excludes 5-year olds enrolled in elementary school. Based on Current Population Survey; see text, Section 1, and Appendix III]

Item	1970	1975	1980	1985	1990	1995	2000	2004	2005
NUMBER OF CHILDREN (1,000)									
Population, 3 to 5 years old	10,949	10,183	9,284	10,733	11,207	12,518	11,858	12,362	12,134
Total enrolled [1]	4,104	4,954	4,878	5,865	6,659	7,739	7,592	7,968	7,801
Nursery	1,094	1,745	1,981	2,477	3,378	4,331	4,326	4,672	4,529
Public.	332	570	628	846	1,202	1,950	2,146	2,429	2,409
Private	762	1,174	1,353	1,631	2,177	2,381	2,180	2,244	2,120
Kindergarten	3,010	3,211	2,897	3,388	3,281	3,408	3,266	3,296	3,272
Public.	2,498	2,682	2,438	2,847	2,767	2,799	2,701	2,813	2,804
Private	511	528	459	541	513	608	565	485	468
White [2].	3,443	4,105	3,994	4,757	5,389	6,144	5,861	5,976	6,025
Black [2].	586	731	725	919	964	1,236	1,265	1,332	1,148
Hispanic [3]	(NA)	(NA)	370	496	642	1,040	1,155	1,438	1,494
3 years old	454	683	857	1,035	1,205	1,489	1,540	1,583	1,715
4 years old	1,007	1,418	1,423	1,765	2,086	2,553	2,556	2,969	2,668
5 years old	2,643	2,852	2,598	3,065	3,367	3,697	3,496	3,417	3,418
ENROLLMENT RATE									
Total enrolled [1]	37.5	48.6	52.5	54.6	59.4	61.8	64.0	64.4	64.3
White [2].	37.8	48.6	52.7	54.7	59.7	63.0	63.2	63.8	65.1
Black [2].	34.9	48.1	51.8	55.8	57.8	58.9	68.5	67.0	62.0
Hispanic [3].	(NA)	(NA)	43.3	43.3	49.0	51.1	52.6	55.6	56.1
3 years old	12.9	21.5	27.3	28.8	32.6	35.9	39.2	38.7	41.3
4 years old	27.8	40.5	46.3	49.1	56.0	61.6	64.9	68.4	66.2
5 years old	69.3	81.3	84.7	86.5	88.8	87.5	87.6	86.9	86.4

NA Not available.   [1] Includes races not shown separately.   [2] Beginning 2003, for persons who selected this race group only. See footnote 2, Table 217.   [3] Persons of Hispanic origin may be of any race. The method of identifying Hispanic children was changed in 1980 from allocation based on status of mother to status reported for each child. The number of Hispanic children using the new method is larger.

Source: U.S. Census Bureau, Current Population Reports, PPL-148; and earlier PPL and P-20 reports; and data published on the Internet. See Internet site <http://www.census.gov/population/www/socdemo/school.html>.

Table 225. **Children's School Readiness Skills: 1993 and 2005**

[In percent. For children 3 to 5 years old not yet enrolled in kindergarden. Based on the School Readiness Surveys of the National Household Education Survey Program; see source for details. See also Table 222]

Characteristic	Recognizes all letters		Counts to 20 or higher		Writes name		Reads or pretends to read storybooks		Has 3 to 4 skills	
	1993	2005	1993	2005	1993	2005	1993	2005	1993	2005
Total	21	26	52	61	50	59	72	70	35	42
Age:										
3 years old.	11	16	37	46	22	32	66	67	15	24
4 years old.	28	31	62	71	70	78	75	73	49	55
5 years old.	36	44	78	81	84	91	81	72	65	66
Sex:										
Male	19	26	49	59	47	57	68	70	32	40
Female	23	26	56	64	53	60	76	71	39	45
Race/ethnicity:										
White, non-Hispanic.	23	29	56	65	52	60	76	75	39	47
Black, non-Hispanic	18	24	53	69	45	61	63	67	31	44
Hispanic	10	16	32	42	42	51	59	55	22	26
Other	22	31	49	65	52	63	70	79	36	48
Mother's employment status: [1]										
Employed	23	28	57	65	52	62	75	72	39	46
Unemployed.	17	18	41	49	46	53	67	61	29	32
Not in the labor force	18	24	49	57	47	55	68	69	32	39
Family type:										
Two parents	22	27	54	63	51	59	74	72	37	44
None or one parent	18	22	49	56	47	57	65	65	31	36
Poverty status: [2]										
Above threshold	24	29	57	64	53	61	74	75	40	47
Below threshold	12	14	41	49	41	52	64	54	23	26

[1] Excludes children with no mother in the household and no female guardian.   [2] Children are considered poor if they lived in households with incomes below the poverty threshold which is a dollar amount determined by the federal government to meet the household's need, given its size and composition.

Source: U.S. Department of Education, U.S. National Center for Education Statistics. *Home Literacy Activities and Signs of Children's Emerging Literacy,* 1993. NCES 2000-026, November 1999; and the Early Childhood Program Participation Survey, National Household Education Surveys Program, 2005, unpublished data. See Internet site <http://nces.ed.gov/nhes>.

Table 226. Type of School Attended By Student and Household Characteristics: 1993 and 2003

[In percent, except total in thousands (33,900 represent 33,900,000. For students in grades 1 to 12. Includes homeschooled students enrolled in public or private school 9 or more hours per week. Based on the Parent and Family Involvement Survey of the National Household Education Survey Program; see source and Appendix III for details]

Characteristic	Public — Assigned 1993	Public — Assigned 2003	Public — Chosen 1993	Public — Chosen 2003	Private — Church-related 1993	Private — Church-related 2003	Private — Not church-related 1993	Private — Not church-related 2003
Total students (1,000)	33,900	35,300	4,700	7,400	3,200	4,000	700	1,100
Percent distribution	79.9	73.9	11.0	15.4	7.5	8.4	1.6	2.4
Grade level:								
1 to 5	78.6	71.6	11.6	16.6	8.3	9.7	1.5	2.1
6 to 8	81.3	75.0	9.9	14.5	7.4	7.9	1.5	2.5
9 to 12	80.6	76.0	11.2	14.4	6.5	6.9	1.8	2.6
Race/ethnicity:								
White, non-Hispanic	81.0	74.7	8.6	12.9	8.6	9.7	1.8	2.7
Black, non-Hispanic	77.2	68.1	18.6	24.0	3.4	5.7	0.8	2.2
Other, non-Hispanic	73.0	70.1	14.9	19.3	9.0	7.2	3.1	3.4
Hispanic [1]	79.2	77.9	13.7	15.1	6.4	6.2	0.7	0.8
Family type:								
Two-parent household	80.1	73.6	9.3	14.1	8.8	9.7	1.8	2.6
One-parent household	78.9	74.5	15.2	18.3	4.8	5.3	1.1	1.9
Nonparent guardians	83.7	74.7	13.5	20.0	2.1	3.7	0.7	1.5
Parents' education:								
Less than high school	83.6	77.6	13.7	19.7	2.4	2.1	0.2	0.6
High school diploma or equivalent	83.5	79.3	11.4	15.8	4.6	3.7	0.5	1.2
Some college, including vocational/technical	79.8	75.8	11.1	15.8	7.7	6.7	1.4	1.7
Bachelor's degree	75.8	69.0	9.2	13.7	12.5	14.5	2.6	2.8
Graduate/professional degree	72.7	66.2	9.8	14.1	13.1	14.1	4.4	5.6
Region: [2]								
Northeast	77.8	73.5	9.3	11.6	10.5	11.0	2.4	3.9
South	82.0	75.9	10.9	15.8	5.4	6.3	1.7	2.1
Midwest	79.6	71.6	10.4	14.4	9.2	12.1	0.8	1.9
West	78.7	73.6	13.4	18.6	6.5	5.8	1.5	2.0

[1] Persons of Hispanic origin may be of any race.   [2] For composition of regions see map, inside front cover.

Source: U.S. National Center for Education Statistics, *Condition of Education, 2004*, NCES 2004-077, June 2004.

Table 227. Public Charter and Traditional Schools—Selected Characteristics: 2004–2005

[47,694 represents 47,694,000. A public charter school is a public school that, in accordance with an enabling state statute, has been granted a charter exempting it from selected state and local rules and regulations. Schools open as public charter schools during 2003–04 and still open in the 2004–05 school year were surveyed]

Characteristic	All schools — Traditional	All schools — Public charter	Elementary — Traditional	Elementary — Public charter	Secondary — Traditional	Secondary — Public charter	Combined — Traditional	Combined — Public charter
Number of schools	90,001	3,294	64,188	1,735	21,412	898	4,373	660
Enrollment (1,000)	47,694	887	30,713	474	15,698	186	1,275	227
PERCENT DISTRIBUTION OF STUDENTS								
Race/ethnicity	100.0	100.0	100.0	100.0	100.0	100.0	100.0	100.0
White, non-Hispanic	57.7	41.5	55.7	39.0	61.3	38.7	59.6	49.2
Black, non-Hispanic	16.8	30.9	17.3	35.3	15.6	27.0	19.6	24.8
Hispanic [1]	19.2	21.6	20.7	20.4	16.7	27.1	15.4	19.6
Asian/Pacific Islander	4.5	3.3	4.5	3.3	4.8	3.6	2.5	3.0
American Indian/Alaska Native	1.2	1.5	1.2	1.1	1.2	2.3	2.4	1.6
Other	0.6	1.2	0.6	0.9	0.4	1.2	0.5	1.8
PERCENT DISTRIBUTION OF SCHOOLS								
Size of enrollment	100.0	100.0	100.0	100.0	100.0	100.0	100.0	100.0
Less than 300 students	30.9	70.9	26.8	67.4	35.3	81.5	68.9	65.6
300 to 599 students	38.2	20.1	45.7	23.3	19.9	13.9	16.9	20.3
600 to 999 students	20.8	6.1	22.7	7.3	17.6	2.2	8.8	8.0
1,000 students or more	10.1	2.9	4.7	2.0	27.3	2.3	5.4	6.1
Percent minority enrollment	100.0	100.0	100.0	100.0	100.0	100.0	100.0	100.0
Less than 10.0	27.8	9.8	26.4	9.1	33.4	9.4	19.9	12.2
10.0 to 24.9	18.9	18.5	19.0	18.9	18.9	16.5	18.0	20.3
25.0 to 49.9	19.0	18.4	19.0	17.7	18.3	16.9	21.0	22.1
50.0 to 74.9	13.0	13.9	12.9	11.3	11.8	17.4	19.0	15.8
75.0 or more	21.4	39.4	22.6	43.0	17.7	39.8	22.1	29.6
Percent of students eligible for free or reduced-price lunch [2]	100.0	100.0	100.0	100.0	100.0	100.0	100.0	100.0
Less than 15.0	16.7	32.6	20.1	34.5	8.5	28.5	22.8	32.1
15.0 to 29.9	19.2	11.2	14.6	11.0	17.8	10.9	9.1	12.2
30.0 to 49.9	16.6	14.0	16.5	13.6	25.8	14.3	14.1	14.5
50.0 to 74.9	20.4	18.1	23.7	17.9	28.5	20.7	23.7	15.5
75.0 or more	27.2	24.2	25.0	23.0	19.3	25.6	30.3	25.6

[1] Persons of Hispanic origin may be of any race.   [2] Excludes data for schools not providing information on eligibility for free or reduced-price lunch.

Source: U.S. National Center for Education Statistics, Common Core of Data, "Public Elementary/Secondary School Universe Survey," 2004–05, unpublished data.

Table 228. Students Who are Homeschooled by Selected Characteristics: 2003

[As of spring. (50,707 represents 50,707,000). For students 5 to 17 with a grade equivalent of K–12. Homeschoolers are students whose parents reported them to be schooled at home instead of a public or private school. Excludes students who were enrolled in school for more than 25 hours a week or were homeschooled due to a temporary illness. Based on the Parent and Family Involvement Survey of the National Household Education Surveys Program; see source and Appendix III for details]

Characteristic	Number of students			Percent distribution		
	Total (1,000)	Home-schooled (1,000)	Percent home-schooled	All students	Home-schooled	Nonhome-schooled
Total	50,707	1,096	2.2	100.0	100.0	100.0
Grade equivalent: [1]						
K–5	24,269	472	1.9	47.9	43.3	48.0
Kindergarten.	3,643	98	2.7	7.2	9.0	7.2
Grades 1 to 3	12,098	214	1.8	23.9	19.7	24.0
Grades 4 to 5	8,528	160	1.9	16.8	14.7	16.9
Grades 6 to 8.	12,472	302	2.4	24.6	27.8	24.5
Grades 9 to 12.	13,958	315	2.3	27.5	28.9	27.5
Sex:						
Male.	25,819	569	2.2	50.9	51.9	50.9
Female	24,888	527	2.1	49.1	48.1	49.1
Race/ethnicity:						
White, non-Hispanic	31,584	843	2.7	62.3	77.0	62.0
Black, non-Hispanic.	7,985	103	1.3	15.7	9.4	15.9
Hispanic [2]	8,075	59	0.7	15.9	5.3	16.2
Other	3,063	91	3.0	6.0	8.3	6.0
Number of children in the household:						
One child	8,005	110	1.4	15.8	10.1	16.0
Two children	20,510	306	1.5	40.4	28.0	40.8
Three or more children.	22,192	679	3.1	43.8	62.0	43.3
Number of parents in the household:						
Two parents.	35,936	886	2.5	70.9	80.8	70.7
One parent	13,260	196	1.5	26.2	17.9	26.3
Nonparental guardians	1,511	14	0.9	3.0	1.3	3.0
Parents' participation in the labor force:						
Two parents—one in labor force	10,545	594	5.6	20.8	54.2	20.1
Two parents—both in labor force	25,108	274	1.1	49.5	25.0	50.1
One parent in labor force	12,045	174	1.4	23.8	15.9	23.9
No parent in labor force	3,008	54	1.8	5.9	4.9	6.0
Household income:						
$25,000 or less	12,375	283	2.3	24.4	25.8	24.4
$25,001 to 50,000.	13,220	311	2.4	26.1	28.4	26.0
$50,001 to 75,000.	10,944	264	2.4	21.6	24.1	21.6
$75,001 or more	14,167	238	1.7	27.9	21.7	28.0
Parents' highest educational attainment:						
High school diploma or less	16,106	269	1.7	31.8	24.5	31.9
Voc/tech degree or some college	16,068	338	2.1	31.7	30.8	31.7
Bachelor's degree	9,798	274	2.8	19.3	25.0	19.2
Graduate/professional school	8,734	215	2.5	17.2	19.6	17.2

[1] Excludes those ungraded. [2] Persons of Hispanic origin may be of any race.

Source: U.S. National Center for Education Statistics, "Parent and Family Involvement in Education Survey", 2003 National Household Education Surveys Program, unpublished data. See also <http://nces.ed.gov/nhes>.

Table 229. Public Elementary and Secondary Schools by Type and Size of School: 2004–2005

[Enrollment in thousands (48,582 represents 48,582,000). Data reported by schools, rather than school districts. Based on the Common Core of Data Survey; see source for details]

Enrollment size of school	Number of schools					Enrollment [1]				
	Total	Elementary [2]	Secondary [3]	Combined [4]	Other [5]	Total	Elementary [2]	Secondary [3]	Combined [4]	Other [5]
Total	96,513	65,984	23,445	5,572	1,512	48,582	31,161	15,876	1,502	42
PERCENT										
Total	100.00	100.00	100.00	100.00	100.00	100.00	100.00	100.00	100.00	100.00
Under 100 students.	11.03	6.20	17.81	41.68	51.19	0.96	0.65	1.08	5.88	16.18
100 to 199 students	9.69	8.59	11.11	16.97	24.91	2.78	2.75	2.27	8.29	24.28
200 to 299 students	11.56	12.85	8.20	9.80	8.53	5.61	6.87	2.86	8.07	15.27
300 to 399 students	13.53	15.96	7.82	7.35	9.56	9.09	11.78	3.81	8.57	23.33
400 to 499 students	13.20	16.23	6.06	5.78	3.75	11.37	15.35	3.81	8.62	11.65
500 to 599 students	10.80	13.06	5.76	4.23	1.37	11.35	15.05	4.44	7.72	5.15
600 to 699 students	8.14	9.49	5.36	3.38	–	10.11	12.93	4.87	7.33	–
700 to 799 students	5.56	6.24	4.36	2.23	0.34	7.96	9.82	4.57	5.57	1.78
800 to 999 students	6.60	6.68	7.24	3.08	0.34	11.25	12.47	9.08	9.17	2.34
1,000 to 1,499 students . . .	5.96	4.08	12.25	2.96	–	13.66	10.02	21.00	11.91	–
1,500 to 1,999 students . . .	2.16	0.49	7.23	1.57	–	7.12	1.74	17.51	9.06	–
2,000 to 2,999 students . . .	1.43	0.10	5.53	0.64	–	6.46	0.51	18.29	5.08	–
3,000 or more students . . .	0.33	0.01	1.28	0.34	–	2.27	0.05	6.42	4.73	–
Average enrollment [1] . . .	521	474	713	298	143	521	474	713	298	143

– Represents zero. [1] Exclude data for schools not reporting enrollment. [2] Includes schools beginning with grade 6 or below and with no grade higher than 8. [3] Includes schools with no grade lower than 7. [4] Includes schools beginning with grade 6 or below and ending with grade 9 or above. [5] Includes special education, alternative, and other schools not classified by grade span.

Source: U.S. National Center for Education Statistics, *Digest of Education Statistics,* annual.

Table 230. **Public Elementary and Secondary Schools—Summary: 1980 to 2005**

[For school year ending in year shown, except as indicated (48,041 represents 48,041,000). Data are estimates]

Item	Unit	1980	1985	1990	1995	2000	2004	2005
School districts, total	Number. .	16,044	15,812	15,552	14,947	15,403	15,789	15,746
ENROLLMENT								
Population 5–17 years old [1]	1,000. . . .	48,041	44,787	44,949	48,855	52,811	53,303	53,225
Percent of resident population . . .	Percent . .	21.4	19.0	18.2	18.6	18.8	18.1	17.9
Fall enrollment [2]	1,000. . . .	41,778	39,354	40,527	43,898	46,577	48,092	48,370
Percent of population								
5–17 years old	Percent . .	87.0	87.9	90.2	89.9	88.2	90.2	90.9
Elementary [3]	1,000. . . .	24,397	23,830	26,253	28,148	29,243	29,595	29,612
Secondary [4]	1,000. . . .	17,381	15,524	14,274	15,750	17,334	18,497	18,758
Average daily attendance (ADA)	1,000. . . .	38,411	36,530	37,573	40,792	43,313	45,149	45,503
High school graduates	1,000. . . .	2,762	2,424	2,327	2,282	2,544	2,766	2,803
INSTRUCTIONAL STAFF								
Total [5]	1,000. . . .	2,521	2,473	2,685	2,919	3,273	3,459	3,503
Classroom teachers	1,000. . . .	2,211	2,175	2,362	2,565	2,891	3,035	3,066
Average salaries:								
Instructional staff	Dollar . . .	16,715	24,666	32,638	38,349	43,837	48,398	49,377
Classroom teachers	Dollar . . .	15,970	23,600	31,367	36,675	41,807	46,704	47,674
REVENUES								
Revenue receipts	Mil. dol. . .	97,635	141,013	208,656	273,255	369,754	456,265	477,408
Federal	Mil. dol. . .	9,020	9,533	13,184	18,764	26,346	39,863	43,025
State	Mil. dol. . .	47,929	69,107	100,787	129,958	183,986	217,294	227,310
Local	Mil. dol. . .	40,686	62,373	94,685	124,533	159,421	199,108	207,072
EXPENDITURES								
Total	Mil. dol.. .	96,105	139,382	209,698	276,584	374,782	470,517	493,352
Current expenditures								
(day schools)	Mil. dol. . .	85,661	127,230	186,583	242,995	320,954	401,095	418,925
Other current expenditures [6]	Mil. dol. . .	1,859	2,109	3,341	5,564	6,618	8,368	8,287
Capital outlay	Mil. dol. . .	6,504	7,529	16,012	21,646	37,552	46,815	50,827
Interest on school debt	Mil. dol. . .	2,081	2,514	3,762	6,379	9,659	14,239	15,313
In current dollars:								
Revenue receipts per pupil								
enrolled	Dollar . . .	2,337	3,583	5,149	6,225	7,939	9,487	9,870
Current expenditures per pupil								
enrolled	Dollar . . .	2,050	3,233	4,604	5,535	6,891	8,340	8,661
In constant (2005) dollars: [7]								
Revenue receipts per pupil								
enrolled	Dollar . . .	5,773	6,492	7,771	7,934	8,989	9,773	9,870
Current expenditures per pupil								
enrolled	Dollar . . .	5,065	5,858	6,949	7,055	7,802	8,591	8,661

[1] Estimated resident population as of July 1 of the previous year, except 1980, 1990, and 2000 population enumerated as of April 1. Estimates reflect revisions based on the 2000 Census of Population.   [2] Fall enrollment of the previous year.   [3] Kindergarten through grade 6.   [4] Grades 7 through 12.   [5] Full-time equivalent.   [6] Current expenses for summer schools, adult education, post-high school vocational education, personnel retraining, etc., when operated by local school districts and not part of regular public elementary and secondary day-school program.   [7] Compiled by U.S. Census Bureau. Deflated by the Consumer Price Index, all urban consumers (for school year July through June) supplied by U.S. National Center for Education Statistics.

Source: Except as noted, National Education Association, Washington, DC, Estimates of School Statistics Database (copyright).

Table 231. **Public Elementary and Secondary School Enrollment by Grade: 1980 to 2004**

[In thousands (40,877 represents 40,877,000). As of fall of year. Based on survey of state education agencies; see source for details]

Grade	1980	1985	1990	1995	1997	1998	1999	2000	2001	2002	2003	2004
Pupils enrolled	40,877	39,422	41,217	44,840	46,127	46,539	46,857	47,204	47,672	48,183	48,540	48,795
Pre-kindergarten to 8 [1] . . .	27,647	27,034	29,878	32,341	33,073	33,346	33,488	33,688	33,938	34,116	34,202	34,178
Pre-K and Kindergarten . .	2,689	2,992	3,610	4,173	4,198	4,172	4,148	4,158	4,244	4,349	4,453	4,534
First	2,894	3,239	3,499	3,671	3,755	3,727	3,684	3,636	3,614	3,594	3,613	3,663
Second	2,800	2,941	3,327	3,507	3,689	3,681	3,656	3,634	3,593	3,565	3,544	3,560
Third	2,893	2,895	3,297	3,445	3,597	3,696	3,691	3,676	3,653	3,623	3,611	3,580
Fourth	3,107	2,771	3,248	3,431	3,507	3,592	3,686	3,711	3,695	3,669	3,619	3,612
Fifth	3,130	2,776	3,197	3,438	3,458	3,520	3,604	3,707	3,727	3,711	3,685	3,635
Sixth	3,038	2,789	3,110	3,395	3,492	3,497	3,564	3,663	3,769	3,788	3,772	3,735
Seventh	3,085	2,938	3,067	3,422	3,520	3,530	3,541	3,629	3,720	3,821	3,841	3,818
Eighth	3,086	2,982	2,979	3,356	3,415	3,480	3,497	3,538	3,616	3,709	3,809	3,825
Grades 9 to 12 [1]	13,231	12,388	11,338	12,500	13,054	13,193	13,369	13,515	13,734	14,067	14,338	14,617
Ninth	3,377	3,439	3,169	3,704	3,819	3,856	3,935	3,963	4,012	4,105	4,190	4,281
Tenth	3,368	3,230	2,896	3,237	3,376	3,382	3,415	3,491	3,528	3,584	3,675	3,750
Eleventh	3,195	2,866	2,612	2,826	2,972	3,021	3,034	3,083	3,174	3,229	3,277	3,369
Twelfth	2,925	2,550	2,381	2,487	2,673	2,722	2,782	2,803	2,863	2,990	3,046	3,094

[1] Includes unclassified students, not shown separately.

Source: U.S. National Center for Education Statistics, Digest of Education Statistics, annual.

Table 232. Public Elementary and Secondary Schools and Enrollment—States: 2004–2005

[For schools with membership (48,795 represents 48,795,000). Based on the Common Core of Data Program; see source for details]

State	Total number of schools with member-ship	Total number of students (1,000)	Regular Number of schools	Regular Percent of students	Special education [1] Number of schools	Special education Percent of students	Vocational education [2] Number of schools	Vocational education Percent of students	Alternative education [3] Number of schools	Alternative education Percent of students
Total	93,295	48,795	86,487	98.1	1,635	0.4	326	0.4	4,847	1.1
Alabama	1,386	730	1,337	99.6	21	0.2	1	(Z)	27	0.3
Alaska	497	133	471	97.6	4	0.4	1	0.2	21	1.7
Arizona........	1,976	1,043	1,823	94.6	11	0.1	84	4.2	58	1.2
Arkansas........	1,130	463	1,121	99.8	4	(Z)	–	–	5	0.1
California.......	9,373	6,442	8,046	96.8	129	0.5	–	–	1,198	2.8
Colorado.......	1,679	766	1,598	98.6	8	0.1	4	(Z)	69	1.3
Connecticut.....	1,095	577	1,011	97.0	31	0.6	17	1.9	36	0.5
Delaware.......	198	119	173	92.9	13	1.2	5	4.9	7	1.0
District of Columbia......	214	77	189	91.7	14	4.9	2	1.3	9	2.1
Florida	3,498	2,639	3,200	98.7	111	0.5	19	0.1	168	0.7
Georgia	2,069	1,553	2,037	99.6	8	0.1	–	–	24	0.4
Hawaii	285	183	281	99.9	3	0.1	–	–	1	0.1
Idaho	662	256	593	98.1	5	0.1	–	–	64	1.8
Illinois.........	4,245	2,098	3,888	98.4	229	1.3	–	–	128	0.4
Indiana	1,913	1,021	1,855	99.6	26	0.2	–	–	32	0.3
Iowa..........	1,524	478	1,440	98.9	10	0.2	–	–	74	0.9
Kansas........	1,400	469	1,400	100.0	–	–	–	–	–	–
Kentucky.......	1,368	675	1,224	98.9	8	0.1	–	–	136	1.1
Louisiana......	1,510	724	1,362	97.8	36	0.2	–	–	112	2.0
Maine.........	655	199	652	100.0	3	(Z)	–	–	–	–
Maryland.......	1,372	866	1,267	97.0	44	0.8	10	1.0	51	1.2
Massachusetts...	1,872	976	1,806	96.3	1	(Z)	39	3.4	26	0.3
Michigan.......	3,901	1,751	3,495	96.8	168	1.5	13	0.1	225	1.6
Minnesota......	2,214	839	1,623	96.5	246	1.4	1	(Z)	344	2.1
Mississippi......	896	495	896	100.0	–	–	–	–	–	–
Missouri.......	2,257	905	2,183	99.6	13	0.2	–	–	61	0.2
Montana	852	147	847	99.9	2	(Z)	–	–	3	0.1
Nebraska	1,203	286	1,163	99.3	40	0.7	–	–	–	–
Nevada........	556	400	516	99.0	5	0.1	1	(Z)	34	1.0
New Hampshire ..	477	207	477	100.0	–	–	–	–	–	–
New Jersey.....	2,440	1,393	2,311	97.7	75	0.7	54	1.6	–	–
New Mexico.....	834	326	757	97.7	16	0.3	2	0.2	59	1.8
New York	4,470	2,836	4,290	97.3	65	0.7	25	1.1	90	0.8
North Carolina ...	2,283	1,386	2,190	99.4	21	0.2	1	(Z)	71	0.4
North Dakota....	511	101	511	100.0	–	–	–	–	–	–
Ohio..........	3,862	1,840	3,838	99.9	13	0.1	8	(Z)	3	(Z)
Oklahoma	1,787	629	1,787	100.0	–	–	–	–	–	–
Oregon........	1,208	552	1,173	99.0	2	(Z)	–	–	33	1.0
Pennsylvania	3,189	1,828	3,149	98.3	12	1.0	16	0.7	12	0.1
Rhode Island	334	156	320	97.9	4	0.1	3	0.9	7	1.1
South Carolina...	1,101	704	1,079	99.6	10	0.1	–	–	12	0.3
South Dakota....	713	123	688	99.2	2	(Z)	–	–	23	0.8
Tennessee......	1,671	941	1,621	99.4	16	0.2	7	0.3	27	0.2
Texas	7,941	4,405	6,967	98.3	3	(Z)	–	–	971	1.7
Utah..........	915	504	767	98.1	41	0.6	2	(Z)	105	1.3
Vermont	361	98	316	98.0	43	1.9	–	–	2	(Z)
Virginia........	1,861	1,205	1,827	99.6	11	(Z)	–	–	23	0.3
Washington	2,203	1,020	1,854	96.3	97	0.4	7	0.1	245	3.2
West Virginia	752	280	721	99.6	7	0.1	3	(Z)	21	0.3
Wisconsin	2,206	865	2,000	96.7	4	(Z)	1	(Z)	201	3.3
Wyoming.......	376	85	347	98.1	–	–	–	–	29	1.9

– Represents zero.   Z Less than 0.05 percent.   [1] Focuses on special education with materials and instructional approaches adapted to meet the students' needs.   [2] Focuses on vocational, technical, or career education and provides education and training in at least one semi-skilled or technical occupation.   [3] Addresses the needs of students that typically cannot be met in the regular school setting and provides nontraditional education.

Source: U.S. National Center for Education Statistics, *Public Elementary and Secondary Staff, Schools and School Districts: School Year 2004–05*, NCES 2007-309, November 2006.

Table 233. Selected Statistics for the Largest Public School Districts: 2005-2006

[For the 50 largest districts by enrollment size. Based on reports from state education agencies in the spring 2006. Data from the Common Core Data Program; see source for details. School district boundaries are not necessarily the same as city or county boundaries]

School district	City	County	Number of students [1]	Number of full-time equivalent (FTE) teachers	Number of 2004-05 completers [2]	Number of schools
New York City Public Schools, NY......	New York	New York	1,014,058	70,889	41,322	1,408
Los Angeles Unified, CA	Los Angeles	Los Angeles	727,319	34,961	29,741	808
Puerto Rico Department of Education, PR	San Juan	San Juan	563,490	42,036	30,371	1,523
City of Chicago, IL	Chicago	Cook	420,982	27,039	16,866	633
Dade County, FL	Miami	Miami-Dade	362,070	20,606	18,702	394
Clark County, NV	Las Vegas	Clark	294,131	14,862	10,314	314
Broward County, FL	Fort Lauderdale	Broward	271,630	15,717	14,436	285
Houston Independent School District, TX	Houston	Harris	210,292	12,082	8,476	312
Hillsborough County, FL	Tampa	Hillsborough	193,757	10,924	9,614	261
Philadelphia City School District, PA	Philadelphia	Philadelphia	184,560	10,060	10,819	270
Hawaii Department of Education, HI	Honolulu	Honolulu	182,818	11,226	11,014	285
Orange County, FL...............	Orlando	Orange	175,609	10,737	9,434	211
Palm Beach County, FL............	West Palm Beach	Palm Beach	174,935	10,084	9,523	236
Fairfax County, VA	Falls Church	Fairfax	163,753	13,090	11,570	207
Dallas Independent School District, TX...	Dallas	Dallas	161,244	10,324	6,832	255
Gwinnett County, GA	Lawrenceville	Gwinnett	144,598	9,801	7,045	122
Montgomery County, MD	Rockville	Montgomery	139,398	9,371	9,351	199
Prince George's County Public Schools, MD	Upper Marlboro	Prince George's	133,325	8,395	7,947	205
Detroit City, MI.................	Detroit	Wayne	133,255	7,187	5,673	235
San Diego Unified, CA	San Diego	San Diego	132,482	7,332	6,653	219
Duval County, FL	Jacksonville	Duval	126,662	7,526	6,276	182
Charlotte-Mecklenburg, NC	Charlotte	Mecklenburg	124,005	8,616	5,836	142
Wake County, NC................	Raleigh	Wake	120,996	8,179	6,659	138
Memphis City School District, TN	Memphis	Shelby	120,275	7,085	5,946	194
Pinellas County, FL..............	Largo	Pinellas	112,174	6,799	5,949	173
Baltimore County, MD.............	Baltimore	Baltimore	107,043	7,388	7,238	168
Cobb County, GA................	Marietta	Cobb	106,724	7,065	6,354	110
DeKalb County, GA	Decatur	De Kalb	102,310	6,858	5,199	148
Jefferson County, KY	Louisville	Jefferson	98,537	5,780	5,194	172
Albuquerque, NM	Albuquerque	Bernalillo	94,022	6,139	4,650	169
Long Beach Unified, CA	Long Beach	Los Angeles	93,589	4,298	4,956	90
Milwaukee, WI..................	Milwaukee	Milwaukee	92,395	5,420	3,915	235
Polk County, FL.................	Bartow	Polk	89,443	6,046	4,380	153
Baltimore City, MD...............	Baltimore	Baltimore City	87,643	5,666	4,145	197
Jefferson County, CO	Golden	Jefferson	86,332	4,785	5,651	162
Cypress-Fairbanks Independent School District, TX	Houston	Harris	86,256	5,521	4,622	75
Austin Independent School District, TX...	Austin	Travis	81,155	5,630	3,746	124
Fulton County, GA	Atlanta	Fulton	81,100	5,634	4,291	95
Fort Worth Independent School District, TX	Fort Worth	Tarrant	80,336	4,794	3,608	147
Fresno Unified, CA...............	Fresno	Fresno	79,046	3,737	4,022	106
Northside Independent School District, TX	San Antonio	Bexar	78,711	4,867	4,238	95
Jordan, UT	Sandy	Salt Lake	77,110	3,120	4,922	92
Lee County School District, FL	Fort Myers	Lee	75,634	4,322	3,728	101
Brevard County, FL..............	Viera	Brevard	75,233	4,489	4,493	117
Mesa Unified District, AZ	Mesa	Maricopa	74,626	3,805	4,391	89
Virginia Beach City Public Schools, VA...	Virginia Beach	Va. Beach City	74,303	5,647	4,778	88
Anne Arundel County, MD	Annapolis	Anne Arundel	73,565	4,754	4,861	121
Nashville-Davidson, TN	Nashville	Davidson	72,713	4,951	3,390	132
Denver County, CO	Denver	Denver	72,312	3,974	2,849	148
Guilford County Schools, NC	Greensboro	Guilford	68,951	4,621	4,087	111

[1] Number of students receiving educational services from the school district. [2] Includes high school diploma recipients and other completers (for example certificates of attendance) but does not include high school equivalents (GEDs).

Source: U.S. Department of Education, National Center for Education Statistics. Common Core of Data (CCD), "Local Education Agency Universe Survey," 2005_06, Version 1a.

Table 234. **Public Elementary and Secondary School Enrollment by State: 1980 to 2004**

[In thousands (27,647 represents 27,647,000), **except rate. As of fall**. Includes unclassified students. Based on survey of state education agencies; see source for details]

State	Enrollment Prekindergarten through grade 8				Enrollment Grades 9 through 12				Enrollment rate [1]			
	1980	1990	2000	2004, est.	1980	1990	2000	2004, est.	1980	1990	2000	2004, est.
United States...	27,647	29,878	33,688	34,178	13,231	11,338	13,515	14,617	86.2	91.2	88.8	91.7
Alabama.........	528	527	539	522	231	195	201	208	87.6	93.2	89.6	91.3
Alaska	60	85	94	92	26	29	39	41	94.0	97.4	93.4	95.8
Arizona.........	357	479	641	722	157	161	237	321	88.9	93.3	88.4	95.0
Arkansas........	310	314	318	328	138	123	132	135	90.3	95.8	90.2	94.3
California........	2,730	3,615	4,408	4,508	1,347	1,336	1,733	1,934	87.1	92.6	90.5	92.7
Colorado........	374	420	517	541	172	154	208	225	92.2	94.6	89.7	91.5
Connecticut......	364	347	406	404	168	122	156	173	83.3	90.2	90.7	92.3
Delaware........	62	73	81	84	37	27	34	35	79.5	87.2	80.3	84.6
District of Columbia.......	71	61	54	57	29	19	15	20	91.8	100.6	84.0	103.1
Florida	1,042	1,370	1,760	1,858	468	492	675	782	84.4	92.6	89.7	90.7
Georgia	742	849	1,060	1,118	327	303	385	435	86.8	93.7	91.4	93.9
Hawaii.........	110	123	132	129	55	49	52	54	83.4	87.4	84.8	87.2
Idaho..........	144	160	170	178	59	61	75	78	95.4	96.9	90.3	95.2
Illinois..........	1,335	1,310	1,474	1,484	649	512	575	614	82.6	86.9	86.4	89.4
Indiana.........	708	676	703	720	347	279	286	301	88.0	90.4	85.8	87.2
Iowa...........	351	345	334	324	183	139	161	154	88.4	92.1	91.3	95.7
Kansas.........	283	320	323	321	133	117	147	148	88.7	92.5	90.0	94.4
Kentucky........	464	459	471	486	206	177	194	189	83.7	90.5	91.4	94.4
Louisiana	544	586	547	534	234	199	197	191	80.2	88.1	82.6	86.3
Maine..........	153	155	146	136	70	60	61	63	91.6	96.5	90.3	92.6
Maryland........	493	527	609	597	258	188	244	268	83.9	89.1	84.9	84.9
Massachusetts....	676	604	703	682	346	230	273	293	88.6	88.8	88.5	91.1
Michigan........	1,227	1,145	1,222	1,211	570	440	498	539	86.9	90.3	89.5	93.0
Minnesota.......	482	546	578	558	272	211	277	280	87.2	91.3	89.5	92.3
Mississippi.......	330	372	364	361	147	131	134	134	79.6	91.3	87.5	91.4
Missouri	567	588	645	629	277	228	268	277	83.8	86.5	86.5	89.2
Montana	106	111	105	99	50	42	50	48	92.9	94.1	89.1	94.0
Nebraska........	189	198	195	195	91	76	91	91	86.6	88.7	86.2	91.2
Nevada.........	101	150	251	289	49	51	90	111	93.4	98.6	91.8	92.3
New Hampshire ...	112	126	147	140	55	46	61	67	85.3	89.1	89.1	89.1
New Jersey......	820	784	968	976	426	306	346	417	81.5	85.9	85.9	88.5
New Mexico......	186	208	225	228	85	94	95	98	89.5	94.4	85.0	90.5
New York	1,838	1,828	2,029	1,943	1,033	770	853	893	80.8	86.6	83.6	85.5
North Carolina	786	783	945	986	343	304	348	400	90.1	94.8	90.4	91.3
North Dakota	77	85	72	67	40	33	37	33	85.9	92.6	90.9	96.9
Ohio...........	1,312	1,258	1,294	1,267	645	514	541	573	84.8	88.0	86.1	89.8
Oklahoma	399	425	445	453	179	154	178	177	92.9	95.1	95.4	101.7
Oregon	319	340	379	377	145	132	167	176	88.5	90.6	87.5	88.3
Pennsylvania.....	1,231	1,172	1,258	1,235	678	496	556	593	80.4	83.5	82.8	86.5
Rhode Island	98	102	114	107	51	37	44	49	80.1	87.5	85.6	85.9
South Carolina....	426	452	493	504	193	170	184	199	88.1	93.9	90.9	94.4
South Dakota.....	86	95	88	84	42	34	41	39	87.4	89.9	85.3	88.0
Tennessee.......	602	598	668	671	252	226	241	270	87.8	93.5	88.8	93.5
Texas..........	2,049	2,511	2,943	3,184	851	872	1,117	1,221	92.4	98.4	94.9	99.5
Utah...........	250	325	333	355	93	122	148	148	98.2	97.8	94.5	98.9
Vermont	66	71	70	66	29	25	32	32	87.9	94.3	90.5	94.7
Virginia.........	703	728	816	840	307	270	329	365	90.7	94.2	89.5	92.1
Washington......	515	613	694	695	242	227	310	325	91.7	94.1	89.8	92.8
West Virginia	270	224	201	198	113	98	85	83	92.6	95.7	95.6	98.6
Wisconsin	528	566	595	578	303	232	285	287	82.1	86.1	86.0	89.0
Wyoming........	70	71	60	57	28	27	30	27	97.3	97.7	92.7	98.2

[1] Percent of persons 5–17 years old. Based on enumerated resident population as of April 1, 1980, and 1990, and estimated resident population as of July 1 for 2000 and 2002.

Source: U.S. National Center for Education Statistics, *Digest of Education Statistics*, annual.

Education 155

Table 235. Public Schools Reporting Incidents of Crime, by Incident Type and Selected School Characteristic: 2003–04

[For school year. Includes incidents that happen in school buildings, on schools grounds, on school buses, and at places that hold school-sponsored events or activities. Based on sample; see source for details]

School characteristic	Total number of schools	Percent of schools with—				Rate per 1,000 students			
		Violent incidents [1]	Serious violent incidents [2]	Theft [3]	Other incidents [4]	Violent incidents [1]	Serious violent incidents [2]	Theft [3]	Other incidents [4]
All public schools	**80,454**	**81**	**18**	**46**	**64**	**33.3**	**1.2**	**4.3**	**8.1**
Level: [5]									
Primary.	48,765	74	13	30	51	28.2	0.8	1.6	3.5
Middle.	14,493	94	24	63	83	52.7	1.6	5.5	10.7
High school	10,829	96	29	84	93	27.5	1.4	8.1	14.5
Combined	6,367	85	24	67	73	29.7	1.4	6.2	10.9
Enrollment size:									
Less than 300	18,990	69	15	40	51	36.4	2.1	4.7	7.1
300 to 499.	23,522	80	15	34	60	33.9	0.9	2.5	5.2
500 to 999.	29,007	86	18	49	67	33.5	1.0	3.5	6.7
1,000 or more	8,935	98	36	81	93	31.6	1.5	6.6	12.7
Percent minority enrollment: [6]									
Less than 5 percent	17,078	74	16	43	58	27.1	0.9	4.4	7.2
5 to 20 percent.	19,732	77	14	46	63	24.7	0.8	4.5	7.4
20 to 50 percent	17,685	85	19	45	65	32.0	1.0	4.4	7.7
50 percent or more	24,267	88	24	49	68	43.4	1.8	4.1	9.5

[1] Violent incidents include rape, sexual battery other than rape, physical attack or fight with or without a weapon, threat of physical attack with or without a weapon, and robbery with or without a weapon. [2] Serious violent incidents include rape, sexual battery other than rape, physical attack or fight with a weapon, threat of physical attack with a weapon, and robbery with or without a weapon. [3] Theft or larceny (taking things worth over $10 without personal confrontation). Includes pocket picking, stealing purse or backpack (if left unattended or no force was used to take from owner), theft from motor vehicles, etc. [4] Other incidents include possession of a firearm or explosive device, possession of knife or sharp object, distribution of illegal drugs, possession or use of alcohol or illegal drugs, and vandalism. [5] Primary schools are defined as schools in which the lowest grade is not higher than grade 3 and the highest grade is not higher than grade 8. Middle schools are defined as schools in which the lowest grade is not lower than grade 4 and the highest grade is not higher than grade 9. High schools are defined as schools in which the lowest grade is not lower than grade 9 and the highest grade is not higher than grade 12. Combined schools include all other combination of grades, including K–12 schools. [6] These estimates exclude data from Tennessee because schools in this state did not report estimates of student race.

Source: U.S. National Center for Education Statistics, *Crime, Violence, Discipline, and Safety in U.S. Public Schools 2003–04*, NCES 2007-302rev, December 2006.

Table 236. Public Schools Reporting Selected Types of Disciplinary Problems Occurring at School, by Selected School Characteristics: 2003–04

[For school year. "At school" includes activities that happen in school buildings, on school grounds, on school buses, and at places that hold school-sponsored events or activities. Based on sample; see source for details]

School characteristic	Happens daily or at least once a day						Happens at all	
	Student racial tensions	Student bullying	Student sexual harassment of other students [1]	Student verbal abuse of teachers	Wide-spread disorder in class-rooms	Student acts of disrespect for teachers	Undesirable gang activities [2]	Undesirable cult or extremist group activities [3]
All public schools	**2**	**27**	**4**	**11**	**3**	**19**	**17**	**3**
Level: [4]								
Primary.	1	24	2	7	2	14	8	1
Middle.	5	42	9	18	6	32	31	6
High school	3	21	6	17	4	26	41	13
Combined	2	23	4	14	3	25	11	2
Enrollment size:								
Less than 300	1	23	2	7	3	14	7	2
300 to 499.	1	27	3	8	2	17	10	1
500 to 999.	3	28	4	12	3	21	18	3
1,000 or more	6	30	8	23	7	34	49	13
Percent minority enrollment: [5]								
Less than 5 percent	1	25	3	6	1	14	3	2
5 to 20 percent.	2	27	3	6	1	14	10	3
20 to 50 percent	3	28	4	12	3	19	20	6
50 percent or more	2	27	5	17	6	29	30	3

[1] Sexual harassment includes "unsolicited, offensive behavior that inappropriately asserts sexuality over another person. This behavior may be verbal or nonverbal." [2] Gang includes an "ongoing loosely organized association of three or more persons, whether formal or informal, that has a common name, signs, symbols, or colors, whose members engage, either individually or collectively in violent or other forms of illegal behavior." [3] Cult or extremist group includes "a group that espouses radical beliefs and practices, which may include a religious component, that are widely seen as threatening the basic values and cultural norms of society at large." [4] Primary schools are defined as schools in which the lowest grade is not higher than grade 3 and the highest grade is not higher than grade 8. Middle schools are defined as schools in which the lowest grade level is not lower than grade 4 and the highest grade is not higher than grade 9. High schools are defined as schools in which the lowest grade is not lower than grade 9 and the highest grade is not higher than grade 12. Combined schools include all other combinations of grades, including K–12 schools. [5] These estimates exclude data from Tennessee because schools in this state did not report estimates of student race.

Source: U.S. National Center for Education Statistics. *Crime, Violence, Discipline, and Safety in U.S. Public Schools 2003–04*, NCES 2007-302rev, December 2006.

Table 237. **Students Who Reported Carrying a Weapon: 1995 to 2005**

[In percent. For students in grades 9 to 12. Percentages are based on students who reported carrying a weapon at least one day during the previous thirty days. Weapons are such things as guns, knives, and clubs. Based on the Youth Risk Behavior Surveillance System. See source for details. See also <http://www.cdc.gov/HealthyYouth/yrbs/index.htm>]

Student Characteristics	Anywhere					On school property				
	1995	1999	2001	2003	2005	1995	1999	2001	2003	2005
Total	20.0	17.3	17.4	17.1	18.5	9.8	6.9	6.4	6.1	6.5
Sex:										
Male	31.1	28.6	29.3	26.9	29.8	14.3	11.0	10.2	8.9	10.2
Female	8.3	6.0	6.2	6.7	7.1	4.9	2.8	2.9	3.1	2.6
Race/ethnicity:										
White, non-Hispanic	18.9	16.4	17.9	16.7	18.7	9.0	6.4	6.1	5.5	6.1
Black, non-Hispanic	21.8	17.2	15.2	17.3	16.4	10.3	5.0	6.3	6.9	5.1
Hispanic [1]	24.7	18.7	16.5	16.5	19.0	14.1	7.9	6.4	6.0	8.2
Asian, non-Hispanic	[2]	13.0	10.6	11.6	7.0	[2]	6.5	7.2	[3]6.6	[3]2.8
American Indian, non-Hispanic ...	32.0	21.8	31.2	[3]29.3	[3]25.6	[3]13.0	[3]11.6	16.4	[3]12.9	7.2
Pacific Islander, non-Hispanic. ...	[2]	25.3	17.4	[3]16.3	[3]20.0	[2]	9.3	[3]10.0	[3]4.9	[3]15.4
More than one race	[2]	22.2	25.2	29.8	26.7	[2]	11.4	13.2	[3]13.3	11.9
Grade:										
9th	22.6	17.6	19.8	18.0	19.9	10.7	7.2	6.7	5.3	6.4
10th	21.1	18.7	16.7	15.9	19.4	10.4	6.6	6.7	6.0	6.9
11th...................	20.3	16.1	16.8	18.2	17.1	10.2	7.0	6.1	6.6	5.9
12th	16.1	15.9	15.1	15.5	16.9	7.6	6.2	6.1	6.4	6.7

[1] Persons of Hispanic origin may be of any race   [2] The response categories for race/ethnicity changed in 1999 making comparisons of some categories with earlier years problematic.   [3] Data should be interpreted with caution.

Source: U.S. National Center for Education Statistics and U.S. Bureau of Justice Statistics, *Indicators of School Crime and Safety: 2006*, December 2006, NCES 2007-003.

Table 238. **Public Schools Using Selected Safety and Security Measures, by School Characteristics: 2003–04**

[In percent. Based on survey of prinicpals or persons knowledgeable about discipline issues at the school. Refers only to those times during normal school hours or when school activities or events were in session. Based on the School Survey on Crime and Safety and subject to sampling error; for details see source]

Measure	All public schools	School level [1]				Enrollment size			
		Primary	Middle	High school	Combined	Less than 300 students	300 to 499 students	500 to 999 students	1,000 or more students
Limited access during school hours:									
Buildings (locked or monitored doors)	83.0	84.0	86.7	78.9	73.3	77.7	85.8	84.2	82.6
Grounds (locked or monitored gates)	36.2	36.8	35.7	38.3	28.9	30.4	34.1	37.3	50.4
Visitor requirements:									
Sign-in or check-in........	98.3	98.0	99.6	98.4	97.2	94.2	99.8	99.4	99.6
Pass through metal detectors	0.9	0.3	1.8	2.6	(S)	(S)	[2]0.3	1.3	3.1
Required to wear badges or picture IDs:									
Students	6.4	2.6	11.3	16.1	7.5	[2]1.8	4.6	6.7	19.6
Faculty and staff	48.0	51.6	50.0	41.3	26.7	29.5	50.3	54.9	58.7
Metal detector checks on students:									
Random checks	5.6	2.5	10.0	13.0	(S)	[2]3.3	3.6	6.1	13.7
Require to pass through daily	1.1	(S)	2.1	3.7	(S)	(S)	[2]0.7	1.2	3.1
Sweeps and technology:									
Random dog sniffs to check for drugs [3]	21.3	4.6	39.7	58.6	43.5	18.9	15.9	21.4	39.9
Random sweeps for contraband [3, 4]	12.8	4.9	23.5	28.2	23.4	13.8	8.3	12.4	23.9
Use security cameras to monitor school [3]	36.0	28.5	41.8	60.3	39.1	26.1	35.0	37.5	54.8
Require clear book bags or ban book bags	6.2	3.2	12.7	9.0	[2]8.9	2.7	5.6	8.4	7.7

S Reporting standards not met.   [1] Primary schools are defined as schools in which the lowest grade is not higher than grade 3 and the highest grade is not higher than grade 8. Middle schools are defined as schools in which the lowest grade is not lower than grade 4 and the highest grade is not higher than grade 9. High schools are defined as schools in which the lowest grade is not lower than grade 9. Combined schools include all other combinations of grades, including K–12 schools. [2] Interpret with caution.   [3] One or more.   [4] For example, drugs or weapons. Does not include dog sniffs.

Source: U.S. National Center for Education Statistics and U.S. Bureau of Justice Statistics, *Indicators of School Crime and Safety: 2006*, December 2006, NCES 2007-003

Education   157

Table 239. School Enrollment Below Postsecondary—Summary by Sex, Race, and Hispanic Origin: 2005

[In thousands (58,307 represents 58,307,000), except percent and rate. As of October. Covers civilian noninstitutional population enrolled in nursery school through high school. Based on Current Population Survey, see text, Section 1 and Appendix III]

Characteristic	Total			Race and Hispanic origin				
				White [2]				
	Number [1]	Male	Female	Total	Non-Hispanic	Black [2]	Asian [2]	Hispanic [3]
All students	**58,307**	**29,847**	**28,460**	**44,547**	**34,623**	**9,086**	**2,193**	**10,868**
Nursery	4,603	2,351	2,252	3,542	2,810	719	185	797
Full day	2,317	1,191	1,126	1,585	1,197	569	73	428
Part day	2,286	1,160	1,127	1,957	1,613	150	112	369
Kindergarten	3,912	2,004	1,909	3,056	2,308	538	138	804
Elementary	32,438	16,626	15,813	24,652	18,858	5,106	1,228	6,330
High school	17,354	8,868	8,486	13,296	10,647	2,723	642	2,937
Students in public schools	50,835	26,117	24,718	38,346	29,048	8,367	1,912	10,141
Nursery	2,480	1,251	1,229	1,767	1,211	542	80	601
Full day	1,330	666	665	827	531	427	29	323
Part day	1,149	585	564	940	680	115	51	278
Kindergarten	3,349	1,726	1,623	2,611	1,936	486	99	725
Elementary	29,072	14,959	14,113	21,858	16,335	4,747	1,137	5,991
High school	15,934	8,181	7,753	12,109	9,566	2,592	596	2,824
Population 15 to 17 years old	13,204	6,645	6,559	10,131	8,150	2,085	457	2,202
Percent below modal grade [4]	29.4	32.9	25.8	28.5	28.0	36.3	18.7	30.3
Students, 10th to 12th grade	11,494	5,843	5,651	8,855	7,228	1,763	424	1,814
Annual dropout rate	3.5	4.0	3.2	3.1	2.7	6.9	1.4	4.7
Population 18 to 24 years old	27,854	14,076	13,778	21,777	17,293	3,964	1,145	4,897
Dropouts	11.3	13.2	9.4	11.3	7.0	12.9	3.1	27.3
High school graduates	82.9	79.4	86.5	83.3	87.8	79.2	93.7	66.0
Enrolled in college	38.9	35.3	42.5	39.0	42.8	32.7	60.6	24.8

[1] Includes other races, not shown separately. [2] For persons who selected this race group only. See footnote 2, Table 217. [3] Persons of Hispanic origin may be of any race. [4] The modal grade is the grade most common for a given age.

Source: U.S. Census Bureau, Current Population Survey, unpublished data. See Internet site <http://www.census.gov/population/www/socdemo/school.html>.

Table 240. Elementary and Secondary Schools—Teachers, Enrollment, and Pupil-Teacher Ratio: 1970 to 2004

[In thousands (2,292 represents 2,292,000), except ratios. As of fall. Data are for full-time equivalent teachers. Based on surveys of state education agencies and private schools; see source for details]

Year	Teachers			Enrollment			Pupil-teacher ratio		
	Total	Public	Private	Total	Public	Private	Total	Public	Private
1970	2,292	2,059	233	51,257	45,894	5,363	22.4	22.3	23.0
1975	2,453	2,198	255	49,819	44,819	5,000	20.3	20.4	19.6
1977	2,488	2,209	279	48,717	43,577	5,140	19.6	19.7	18.4
1978	2,479	2,207	272	47,637	42,551	5,086	19.2	19.3	18.7
1979	2,461	2,185	276	46,651	41,651	5,000	19.0	19.1	18.1
1980	2,485	2,184	301	46,208	40,877	5,331	18.6	18.7	17.7
1981	2,440	2,127	313	45,544	40,044	5,500	18.7	18.8	17.6
1982	2,458	2,133	325	45,166	39,566	5,600	18.4	18.6	17.2
1983	2,476	2,139	337	44,967	39,252	5,715	18.2	18.4	17.0
1984	2,508	2,168	340	44,908	39,208	5,700	17.9	18.1	16.8
1985	2,549	2,206	343	44,979	39,422	5,557	17.6	17.9	16.2
1986	2,592	2,244	348	45,205	39,753	5,452	17.4	17.7	15.7
1987	2,631	2,279	352	45,487	40,008	5,479	17.3	17.6	15.6
1988	2,668	2,323	345	45,430	40,189	5,242	17.0	17.3	15.2
1989	2,713	2,357	356	46,141	40,543	5,599	17.0	17.2	15.7
1990	2,759	2,398	361	46,865	41,217	5,648	17.0	17.2	15.6
1991	2,797	2,432	365	47,728	42,047	5,681	17.1	17.3	15.6
1992	2,827	2,459	368	48,500	42,823	5,677	17.2	17.4	15.4
1993	2,874	2,504	370	49,133	43,465	5,668	17.1	17.4	15.3
1994	2,925	2,552	373	49,898	44,111	5,787	17.1	17.3	15.5
1995	2,974	2,598	376	50,759	44,840	5,918	17.1	17.3	15.7
1996	3,051	2,667	384	51,544	45,611	5,933	16.9	17.1	15.5
1997	3,138	2,746	391	52,071	46,127	5,944	16.6	16.8	15.2
1998	3,230	2,830	400	52,525	46,539	5,988	16.3	16.4	15.0
1999	3,319	2,911	408	52,876	46,857	6,018	15.9	16.1	14.7
2000	3,366	2,941	424	53,373	47,204	6,169	15.9	16.0	14.5
2001	3,440	3,000	441	53,992	47,672	6,320	15.7	15.9	14.3
2002	3,476	3,034	442	54,403	48,183	6,220	15.7	15.9	14.1
2003	3,490	3,049	441	54,639	48,540	6,099	15.7	15.9	13.8
2004	3,537	3,091	447	54,946	48,795	6,151	15.5	15.8	13.8

Source: U.S. National Center for Education Statistics, Digest of Education Statistics, annual.

Table 241. Public Elementary and Secondary School Teachers—Selected Characteristics: 2004–2005

[For school year (449 represents 449,000). Based on the 2004–2005 Teacher Follow-up Survey, a component of the School and Staffing Survey, and subject to sampling error; for details, see source Web site at <http://nces.ed.gov/surveys/sass/>. Excludes prekindergarten teachers. See Table 257 for similar data on private school teachers]

Characteristic	Unit	Age				Sex		Race/ethnicity		
		Under 30 years old	30 to 39 years old	40 to 49 years old	Over 50 years old	Male	Fe-male	White [1]	Black [1]	His-panic
Total teachers [2]	1,000 . . .	449	769	750	976	723	2,220	2,502	216	124
Highest degree held:										
Bachelor's	Percent. .	80.9	57.1	44.9	37.6	2.4	0.7	49.7	53.7	67.9
Master's.	Percent. .	17.7	38.8	48.8	49.4	51.8	50.9	43.2	38.7	22.1
Education specialist	Percent. .	0.6	3.4	5.5	9.6	38.8	42.6	5.5	5.8	7.6
Doctorate	Percent. .	(X)	0.3	0.5	1.3	6.5	5.3	0.6	1.2	0.2
Full-time teaching experience:										
Less than 3 years	Percent. .	26.2	4.3	2.5	0.8	5.5	6.2	5.7	6.5	9.8
3 to 9 years	Percent. .	73.3	56.7	19.3	8.8	35.9	33.1	31.9	47.3	40.0
10 to 20 years	Percent. .	0.5	39.0	47.5	25.4	26.7	32.1	31.6	20.3	37.8
20 years or more	Percent. .	(X)	(X)	30.7	65.0	31.9	28.6	30.9	26.0	12.4
Full-time teachers	1,000 . . .	411	706	687	902	687	2,018	2,284	207	120
Earned income	Dollars . .	37,510	43,288	48,392	54,577	50,823	46,328	47,710	45,981	45,941
Salary	Dollars . .	37,093	42,607	47,662	53,590	49,207	45,865	46,864	45,672	45,646

X Not applicable. [1] Non-Hispanic. [2] Includes teachers with no degrees and associates degrees, not shown separately.

Source: U.S. National Center for Education Statistics, "Teacher Follow-up Survey, 2004–05," unpublished data.

Table 242. Public Elementary and Secondary Schools—Number and Average Salary of Classroom Teachers, 1990 to 2005, and by State, 2005

[Estimates for school year ending in June of year shown (2,362 represents 2,362,000). Schools classified by type of organization rather than by grade-group; elementary includes kindergarten]

Year and state	Teachers [1] (1,000)			Avg. salary ($1,000)			Year and state	Teachers [1] (1,000)			Avg. salary ($1,000)		
	Total	Ele-men-tary	Sec-ond-ary	All teach-ers	Ele-men-tary	Sec-ond-ary		Total	Ele-men-tary	Sec-ond-ary	All teach-ers	Ele-men-tary	Sec-ond-ary
1990 . . .	2,362	1,390	972	31.4	30.8	32.0	MD. . . .	56.2	32.9	23.3	52.3	52.0	52.7
1995 . . .	2,565	1,517	1,048	36.7	36.1	37.5	MA.	66.8	26.6	40.1	54.7	54.7	54.7
1997 . . .	2,671	1,586	1,086	38.4	38.0	39.2	MI	96.8	47.3	49.4	57.0	57.0	57.0
1998 . . .	2,746	1,630	1,116	39.4	39.0	39.9	MN.	52.2	26.4	25.8	46.9	47.6	46.2
1999 . . .	2,814	1,650	1,164	40.5	40.1	41.3	MS.	30.7	18.7	12.0	36.6	36.6	36.6
2000 . . .	2,891	1,696	1,195	41.8	41.3	42.5	MO.	64.8	33.1	31.6	39.1	39.2	39.0
2001 . . .	2,947	1,735	1,213	43.4	42.9	44.0	MT.	10.2	6.8	3.4	38.5	38.5	38.5
2002 . . .	2,992	1,751	1,240	44.6	44.1	45.2	NE.	20.7	13.2	7.4	39.5	39.5	39.5
2003 . . .	3,022	1,764	1,259	45.7	45.4	46.0	NV.	20.6	12.3	8.3	43.4	42.9	44.1
2004 . . .	3,035	1,769	1,266	46.7	46.4	47.0	NH.	15.3	10.5	4.8	43.9	43.9	43.9
2005,							NJ.	109.6	42.3	67.3	56.7	56.7	56.7
U.S. . . .	3,066	1,788	1,278	47.7	47.4	48.0	NM.	21.7	15.3	6.4	39.4	38.9	40.5
AL.	46.5	26.7	19.8	38.2	37.8	38.6	NY.	223.0	110.0	113.0	56.2	55.5	56.9
AK.	7.9	5.3	2.6	52.4	52.1	53.1	NC.	90.7	64.1	26.6	43.3	43.3	43.3
AZ.	45.9	29.8	16.1	42.9	42.9	42.9	ND.	7.7	5.2	2.5	36.7	37.0	36.1
AR.	32.7	16.0	16.8	40.5	40.5	40.5	OH.	114.1	77.4	36.8	48.7	48.8	48.6
CA.	298.1	218.9	79.2	57.9	57.9	57.9	OK.	40.4	20.5	19.9	37.9	37.0	38.8
CO.	45.2	22.4	22.8	43.9	44.0	43.8	OR.	27.9	18.2	9.6	48.3	48.2	48.6
CT.	42.5	29.2	13.4	57.7	57.3	58.7	PA.	119.9	61.3	58.6	53.3	53.3	53.3
DE.	8.0	3.9	4.1	50.6	51.0	50.2	RI.	14.2	8.7	5.5	53.5	53.5	53.5
DC.	5.0	3.6	1.5	58.5	58.5	58.5	SC.	46.2	32.4	13.7	42.2	40.0	40.8
FL.	158.0	79.7	78.3	41.6	41.6	41.6	SD.	8.9	6.3	2.7	34.0	34.1	33.8
GA.	104.8	63.5	41.3	46.5	46.0	47.4	TN.	59.2	42.6	16.6	42.1	41.7	43.0
HI	11.4	6.0	5.3	46.1	46.1	46.1	TX.	294.5	151.6	142.9	41.0	40.6	41.5
ID.	14.2	7.2	7.0	42.1	42.1	42.1	UT.	21.0	11.8	9.2	39.5	40.0	40.0
IL.	131.8	88.5	43.3	55.4	53.0	60.4	VT.	8.7	4.5	4.3	44.5	44.6	44.4
IN	60.5	32.4	28.0	46.6	46.6	46.5	VA.	98.9	58.2	40.7	42.8	42.8	42.8
IA	34.7	16.5	18.2	39.3	39.3	39.3	WA.	53.3	29.2	24.1	45.7	45.8	45.6
KS.	32.8	16.1	16.7	39.3	39.3	39.3	WV.	19.8	14.1	5.7	38.4	38.2	38.9
KY.	40.1	30.7	9.4	40.5	40.4	40.8	WI	60.1	41.3	18.9	44.3	44.1	44.7
LA.	48.8	34.2	14.6	39.0	39.0	39.0	WY	6.6	3.2	3.4	40.5	40.6	40.4
ME.	16.7	11.2	5.5	39.6	40.0	38.7							

[1] Full-time equivalent.

Source: National Education Association, Washington, DC, Estimates of School Statistics Database (copyright).

Education 159

Table 243. Teacher Stayers, Movers, and Leavers, by Sector: 1988–89 and 2004–05

[2,386.5 represents 2,386,500. Data compare the teaching status of teacher between one school year and the prior year. Stayers are teachers who were teaching in the same school in both years. Movers are teachers who were still teaching in the current school year but in a different school. Leavers are teachers who left the teaching profession. Based on the School and Staffing Survey; see source for details]

Characteristics	Public				Private			
	Total [1]	Stayers	Movers	Leavers	Total [1]	Stayers	Movers	Leavers
NUMBER (1,000)								
1988–89	2,386.5	2,065.8	188.4	132.3	311.9	242.5	29.7	39.7
2004–05	3,214.9	2,684.2	261.1	269.6	465.3	374.6	27.6	63.1
PERCENT DISTRIBUTION								
Total, 2004–05	100.0	83.5	8.1	8.4	100.0	80.5	5.9	13.6
Age:								
Less than 30 years old	100.0	76.3	14.7	9.0	100.0	68.1	11.8	20.1
30 to 39 years old	100.0	84.2	9.0	6.8	100.0	80.6	5.2	14.2
40 to 49 years old	100.0	87.6	7.1	5.3	100.0	84.3	5.0	10.7
50 years old or more	100.0	83.7	4.5	11.8	100.0	84.7	3.8	[2]11.5
Sex:								
Male	100.0	83.9	8.3	7.7	100.0	80.5	5.2	14.2
Female	100.0	83.4	8.1	8.6	100.0	80.5	6.1	13.4
Race/ethnicity:								
White, non-Hispanic	100.0	83.9	7.9	8.2	100.0	81.3	5.7	13.0
Black, non-Hispanic	100.0	79.3	9.7	11.0	100.0	67.8	9.2	[2]23.0
Hispanic, single or more than one race	100.0	80.6	10.1	9.3	100.0	70.3	7.6	22.1
Asian, Native Hawaiian, or Other Pacific Islander, non-Hispanic	100.0	81.8	7.9	[2]10.3	100.0	89.7	2.7	7.6
American Indian/Alaska Native, non-Hispanic	100.0	93.1	5.0	1.9	100.0	65.5	[2]18.5	[2]16.0
More than one race, non-Hispanic . . .	100.0	88.1	6.6	[2]5.3	100.0	65.8	[2]13.4	[2]20.8
Full-time teaching experience:								
No full-time teaching experience	100.0	63.3	17.1	19.6	100.0	73.6	4.0	22.3
1 to 3 years experience	100.0	77.1	14.8	8.1	100.0	71.0	10.1	18.9
4 to 9 years experience	100.0	82.7	9.4	7.9	100.0	77.2	6.7	16.1
10 to 19 years experience	100.0	88.2	6.3	5.5	100.0	88.3	3.8	7.8
20 years or more experience	100.0	84.9	3.9	11.2	100.0	89.7	3.3	7.0
Main assignment field:								
Early childhood/general elementary . . .	100.0	84.5	7.4	8.1	100.0	81.1	6.8	12.2
Special education	100.0	78.9	11.1	10.0	100.0	72.2	[2]7.4	20.4
Arts/music	100.0	84.7	9.3	6.0	100.0	77.6	4.4	18.0
English/language arts	100.0	83.2	9.0	7.8	100.0	81.1	5.6	13.3
Mathematics	100.0	84.6	8.6	6.8	100.0	83.8	5.4	10.7
Natural sciences	100.0	88.5	5.6	5.9	100.0	84.0	5.9	10.1
Social sciences	100.0	85.6	6.0	8.4	100.0	81.8	4.8	13.4
Other	100.0	81.3	8.0	10.7	100.0	79.2	5.3	15.5

[1] Total teachers prior school year.   [2] Interpret data with caution. The standard error for this estimate is equal to 50 percent.

Source: U.S. National Center for Education Statistics, *Teacher Attrition and Mobility: Results for the 2004–05 Teacher Follow-up Survey* NCES 2007-307, January 2007.

Table 244. Public and Private School Teachers Who Moved to a Different School or Left Teaching, by Reason: 2004–05

[In percent. Movers are teachers who were still teaching in the current school year but had moved to a different school after the 2003–04 school year. Leavers are teachers who left the teaching profession after the 2003–04 school year. Based on the School and Staffing Survey; see source for details]

Reason for moving	Movers		Reason for leaving	Leavers	
	Public	Private		Public	Private
New school is closer to home.	26.2	22.8	Changed residence	11.2	17.4
Better safety and benefits	16.5	46.4	Pregnancy or child rearing	18.7	24.6
Higher job security	19.1	33.4	Health.	11.8	13.2
Opportunity for a better teaching assignment. .	38.1	33.1	Retirement.	31.4	10.2
Dissatisfaction with workplace conditions at previous school	32.7	21.4	School staffing action [1]	14.6	17.7
Dissatisfaction with support from administrators at previous school.	37.2	27.0	Better salary or benefits	14.2	21.8
Dissatisfaction with changes in job description or responsibilities	18.3	17.5	To pursue a position other than that of a K–12 teacher	25.3	29.5
Laid off or involuntarily transferred.	18.7	19.2	To take courses to improve career opportunities within the field of education. .	8.9	9.8
Did not have enough autonomy over classroom at previous school	10.4	7.6	To take courses to improve career opportunities outside the field of education .	5.3	7.3
Dissatisfaction with opportunities for professional development at previous school .	12.8	19.7	Dissatisfied with teaching as a career	14.6	10.8
Other dissatisfaction with previous school. . . .	31.2	29.7	Dissatisfied with previous school or teaching assignment.	16.0	18.1
			Other family or personal reasons	20.4	30.6

[1] For example reduction in force, lay-off, school closing, school reorganization, reassignment.

Source: U.S. National Center for Education Statistics, *Teacher Attrition and Mobility: Results for the 2004–05 Teacher Follow-up Survey,* NCES 2007-307, January 2007.

160   Education

Table 245. Average Salary and Wages Paid in Public School Systems: 1985 to 2006

[In dollars. For school year ending in year shown. Data reported by a stratified sample of school systems enrolling 300 or more pupils. Data represent unweighted means of average salaries paid school personnel reported by each school system]

Position	1985	1990	1995	2000	2002	2003	2004	2005	2006
ANNUAL SALARY									
Central-office administrators:									
Superintendent (contract salary)...	56,954	75,425	90,198	112,158	121,794	126,268	125,609	128,770	134,436
Deputy/assoc. superintendent	52,877	69,623	81,266	97,251	107,458	112,104	113,790	116,186	122,078
Assistant superintendent........	48,003	62,698	75,236	88,913	96,627	98,623	100,808	103,212	106,492
Administrators for—									
Finance and business........	40,344	52,354	61,323	73,499	80,132	81,451	82,269	83,678	86,390
Instructional services	43,452	56,359	66,767	79,023	82,418	84,640	84,866	88,950	91,094
Public relations/information	35,287	44,926	53,263	60,655	67,170	67,298	70,291	70,502	72,378
Staff personnel services	44,182	56,344	65,819	76,608	83,035	85,041	86,333	86,966	90,097
Technology	(X)	(X)	(X)	(X)	72,962	73,931	76,139	76,308	78,249
Subject area supervisors........	34,422	45,929	54,534	63,103	66,351	66,582	67,098	68,714	71,984
School building administrators:									
Principals:									
Elementary..............	36,452	48,431	58,589	69,407	73,114	75,291	75,144	76,182	79,496
Junior high/middle	39,650	52,163	62,311	73,877	78,176	80,708	80,060	81,514	84,685
Senior high..............	42,094	55,722	66,596	79,839	83,944	86,452	86,160	86,938	90,260
Assistant principals:									
Elementary..............	30,496	40,916	48,491	56,419	60,672	62,230	62,213	63,140	65,770
Junior high/middle	33,793	44,570	52,942	60,842	64,375	67,288	66,360	67,600	70,268
Senior high..............	35,491	46,486	55,556	64,811	67,822	70,847	70,495	71,401	73,622
Classroom teachers..........	23,587	31,278	37,264	42,213	43,802	45,026	45,646	45,884	48,160
Auxiliary professional personnel:									
Counselors................	27,593	35,979	42,486	48,195	50,022	51,706	52,303	52,500	53,744
Librarians.................	24,981	33,469	40,418	46,732	48,741	49,611	50,403	50,720	53,331
School nurses..............	19,944	26,090	31,066	35,540	38,221	39,165	40,201	40,520	41,746
Secretarial/clerical personnel:									
Central office:									
Secretaries	15,343	20,238	23,935	28,405	30,039	31,295	31,830	32,716	34,132
Accounting/payroll clerks......	15,421	20,088	24,042	28,498	30,551	32,154	32,632	33,217	34,812
Typists/data entry clerks	12,481	16,125	18,674	22,853	24,840	25,793	25,318	26,214	26,899
School building level:									
Secretaries	12,504	16,184	19,170	22,630	24,041	24,853	24,964	25,381	26,396
Library clerks.............	9,911	12,152	14,381	16,509	18,104	18,170	18,427	18,443	19,125
HOURLY WAGE RATE									
Other support personnel:									
Teacher aides:									
Instructional	5.80	7.43	8.77	10.00	10.68	10.93	11.22	11.35	11.77
Noninstructional...........	5.60	7.08	8.29	9.77	10.42	10.98	11.08	11.23	11.75
Custodians................	6.90	8.54	10.05	11.35	11.96	12.40	12.47	12.61	13.20
Cafeteria workers	5.42	6.77	7.89	9.02	9.71	9.98	10.18	10.33	10.70
Bus drivers...............	7.27	9.21	10.69	12.48	13.49	13.85	13.79	14.18	14.81

X Not applicable.

Source: Educational Research Service, Arlington, VA, *National Survey of Salaries and Wages in Public Schools,* annual. (All rights reserved. Copyright.)

Table 246. Public School Employment: 1990 and 2004

[In thousands (3,181 represents 3,181,000). Covers all public elementary-secondary school districts with 100 or more full-time employees]

Occupation	1990					2004				
	Total	Male	Female	White [1]	Black [1]	Total	Male	Female	White [1]	Black [1]
All occupations	3,181	914	2,267	2,502	463	4,499	1,170	3,329	3,424	582
Officials, administrators	43	28	15	37	4	61	30	31	50	7
Principals and assistant										
principals.................	90	56	34	70	13	122	57	65	91	20
Classroom teachers [2]	1,746	468	1,278	1,469	192	2,467	608	1,859	2,033	230
Elementary schools	875	128	747	722	103	1,246	173	1,073	1,019	109
Secondary schools	662	304	358	570	66	921	374	547	769	85
Other professional staff	227	58	170	187	30	373	76	297	300	42
Teachers' aides [3]	324	54	270	208	69	472	58	414	308	90
Clerical, secretarial staff.......	226	5	221	181	24	298	10	288	217	35
Service workers [4]	524	245	279	348	129	707	331	376	425	158

[1] Excludes individuals of Hispanic origin. [2] Includes other classroom teachers, not shown separately. [3] Includes technicians. [4] Includes craftworkers and laborers.

Source: U.S. Equal Employment Opportunity Commission, *Elementary-Secondary Staff Information (EEO-5),* biennial.

Table 247. Finances of Public Elementary and Secondary School Systems by Enrollment-Size Group: 2004–2005

[In millions of dollars (488,453 represents $488,453,000,000). Data are based on annual survey. For details, see source. See also Appendix III]

Item	All school systems	School systems with enrollment of—						
		50,000 or more	25,000 to 49,999	15,000 to 24,999	7,500 to 14,999	5,000 to 7,499	3,000 to 4,999	Under 3,000
General revenue	488,453	102,922	57,684	44,573	69,482	44,043	57,891	111,858
From federal sources	44,355	11,207	5,428	3,784	5,758	3,092	4,170	10,916
Through state	40,836	10,591	5,076	3,577	5,207	2,851	3,877	9,658
Child nutrition programs	8,464	2,261	1,135	832	1,152	655	855	1,574
Direct	3,519	616	351	208	551	242	293	1,258
From state sources [1]	229,526	46,210	28,451	22,900	33,582	19,593	25,451	53,337
General formula assistance	156,034	28,675	19,324	16,377	23,495	13,488	17,398	37,277
Compensatory programs	5,686	1,114	1,455	644	912	419	438	703
Special education	14,738	3,795	1,540	1,063	1,849	1,148	1,746	3,597
From local sources	214,572	45,505	23,805	17,888	30,142	21,358	28,270	47,604
Taxes	144,292	23,815	15,889	12,433	21,751	15,591	20,468	34,346
Contributions from parent government	37,070	15,930	3,619	2,290	3,962	3,010	3,966	4,294
From other local governments	5,170	577	705	364	456	389	740	1,940
Current charges	12,542	1,996	1,356	1,214	1,880	1,138	1,536	3,421
School lunch	6,505	942	712	671	1,049	683	885	1,563
Other	15,498	3,187	2,237	1,588	2,093	1,230	1,561	3,604
General expenditure	496,982	105,940	59,097	46,231	70,987	44,595	57,817	112,315
Current spending	427,167	89,920	49,654	38,800	60,751	38,681	50,323	99,038
By function: Instruction	258,338	55,636	29,957	23,564	36,948	23,624	30,593	58,016
Support services	146,328	29,430	16,993	13,051	20,643	13,162	17,252	35,797
Other current spending	22,502	4,854	2,703	2,185	3,160	1,895	2,478	5,226
By object:								
Total salaries and wages	261,339	55,100	31,243	24,485	37,730	23,842	30,818	58,122
Total employee benefits	82,102	17,036	9,008	7,502	12,061	7,690	9,950	18,855
Other	83,727	17,784	9,403	6,813	10,960	7,149	9,556	22,062
Capital outlay	54,222	12,799	7,505	6,023	7,870	4,370	5,610	10,046
Interest on debt	12,765	2,866	1,589	1,227	1,899	1,154	1,566	2,465
Payments to other governments	2,828	355	350	182	468	390	317	766
Debt outstanding	297,482	64,757	37,840	29,207	43,366	27,086	36,915	58,312
Long-term	288,519	63,183	37,016	28,526	41,909	26,262	35,748	55,875
Short-term	8,963	1,574	824	681	1,456	824	1,167	2,437
Long-term debt issued	57,791	11,099	8,303	7,020	9,194	5,273	7,284	9,617
Long-term debt retired	33,894	6,357	4,389	3,487	5,244	3,324	4,668	6,426

[1] Includes other sources, not shown separately.
Source: U.S. Census Bureau, *Public Education Finances, 2005*, April 2007. See Internet site <http://www.census.gov/govs/www/school.html>.

Table 248. Per Pupil Amounts of Finances of Public Elementary and Secondary School Systems by Enrollment-Size Group: 2004–2005

[In dollars, except as indicated (48,080 represents 48,080,000). Data are based on annual survey. For details, see source. See also Appendix III]

Item	All school systems	School systems with enrollment of—						
		50,000 or more	25,000 to 49,999	15,000 to 24,999	7,500 to 14,999	5,000 to 7,499	3,000 to 4,999	Under 3,000
Fall enrollment (1,000)	48,080	10,165	6,093	4,902	7,093	4,324	5,575	9,928
General revenue	10,159	10,125	9,467	9,093	9,796	10,186	10,384	11,267
From federal sources	923	1,102	891	772	812	715	748	1,100
From state sources [1]	4,774	4,546	4,670	4,672	4,734	4,531	4,565	5,373
General formula assistance	3,245	2,821	3,171	3,341	3,312	3,119	3,121	3,755
Special education	307	373	253	217	261	266	313	362
From local sources [1]	4,463	4,477	3,907	3,649	4,249	4,940	5,071	4,795
Taxes	3,001	2,343	2,608	2,536	3,066	3,606	3,671	3,460
Contributions from parent government	771	1,567	594	467	559	696	711	433
Current charges	261	196	223	248	265	263	275	345
School lunch	135	93	117	137	148	158	159	157
General expenditure [1]	10,153	10,199	9,526	9,280	9,850	10,138	10,201	11,119
Current spending	8,701	8,623	7,976	7,764	8,407	8,770	8,857	9,781
By function: Instruction	5,303	5,378	4,847	4,767	5,153	5,382	5,414	5,783
Support services	3,043	2,895	2,789	2,662	2,910	3,044	3,094	3,606
By object:								
Total salaries and wages	5,435	5,421	5,128	4,995	5,319	5,514	5,528	5,855
Total employee benefits	1,708	1,676	1,478	1,530	1,700	1,778	1,785	1,899
Capital outlay	1,128	1,259	1,232	1,229	1,110	1,011	1,006	1,012
Interest on debt	265	282	261	250	268	267	281	248
Debt outstanding	6,187	6,371	6,210	5,958	6,114	6,264	6,621	5,874
Long-term	6,001	6,216	6,075	5,819	5,908	6,074	6,412	5,628

[1] Includes other sources of revenue and expenditures, not shown separately.
Source: U.S. Census Bureau, *Public Education Finances, 2005*, April 2007. See Internet site <http://www.census.gov/govs/www/school.html>.

Table 249. Public Elementary and Secondary Estimated Finances, 1980 to 2005, and by State, 2005

[In millions of dollars (101,724 represents $101,724,000,000), except as noted. For school years ending in June of year shown]

Year and state	Receipts Total	Revenue receipts Total	Source Federal	Source State	Source Local	Non-revenue receipts [1]	Expenditures Total [2]	Per capita [3] (dol.)	Current expenditures Elementary and secondary day schools	Average per pupil in ADA [4] Amount (dol.)	Rank
1980	101,724	97,635	9,020	47,929	40,686	4,089	96,105	427	85,661	2,230	(X)
1985	146,976	141,013	9,533	69,107	62,373	5,963	139,382	591	127,230	3,483	(X)
1990	218,126	208,656	13,184	100,787	94,685	9,469	209,698	850	186,583	4,966	(X)
1995	288,501	273,255	18,764	129,958	124,533	15,246	276,584	1,051	242,995	5,957	(X)
1998	349,787	324,429	21,668	159,596	143,164	25,359	330,952	1,214	285,213	6,666	(X)
1999	370,735	345,901	23,583	170,606	151,711	24,835	350,539	1,271	301,380	7,011	(X)
2000	390,861	369,754	26,346	183,986	159,421	21,106	374,782	1,343	320,954	7,410	(X)
2001	426,200	397,255	28,300	198,802	170,152	28,946	404,271	1,432	344,033	7,859	(X)
2002	449,039	416,891	32,213	206,112	178,565	32,148	427,577	1,499	363,551	8,210	(X)
2003	472,400	436,621	35,995	214,564	186,063	35,779	450,302	1,563	385,389	8,619	(X)
2004	490,219	456,265	39,863	217,294	199,108	33,954	470,517	1,618	401,095	8,884	(X)
2005, total. . . .	**515,583**	**477,408**	**43,025**	**227,310**	**207,072**	**38,175**	**493,352**	**1,680**	**418,925**	**9,207**	**(X)**
Alabama	6,286	5,825	679	3,253	1,892	461	5,810	1,286	5,138	7,300	43
Alaska	1,466	1,305	164	829	312	161	1,440	2,192	1,335	11,588	7
Arizona	7,574	7,522	582	3,855	3,085	52	6,621	1,152	5,399	5,699	49
Arkansas	3,766	3,704	418	1,920	1,365	62	3,279	1,194	2,804	7,011	47
California	67,453	61,373	7,283	37,191	16,899	6,080	63,450	1,770	50,211	8,237	33
Colorado	7,981	6,689	466	2,898	3,325	1,292	7,628	1,659	6,392	8,990	26
Connecticut	7,677	7,665	460	3,008	4,197	13	7,677	2,197	6,856	12,519	4
Delaware	1,625	1,419	142	894	383	206	1,572	1,897	1,312	11,955	6
District of Columbia	876	876	129	–	746	–	1,145	1,976	939	16,550	(X)
Florida	24,542	22,821	2,380	9,533	10,908	1,722	23,869	1,374	18,888	7,668	41
Georgia	15,239	14,597	1,410	6,333	6,854	642	15,849	1,774	13,797	9,535	22
Hawaii	2,239	2,163	239	1,873	51	76	1,792	1,423	1,582	9,340	24
Idaho	1,730	1,672	160	1,004	508	58	1,797	1,288	1,686	7,173	45
Illinois	22,206	19,874	1,609	5,680	12,585	2,332	22,117	1,740	19,564	10,348	14
Indiana	12,231	11,279	739	5,326	5,214	952	10,686	1,717	8,904	9,545	21
Iowa	4,849	4,478	316	2,064	2,098	371	4,286	1,451	3,640	8,024	36
Kansas	4,747	4,227	357	2,363	1,507	520	4,302	1,571	3,604	8,596	29
Kentucky	5,466	5,459	647	3,192	1,620	8	5,506	1,330	5,035	8,775	28
Louisiana	6,909	6,050	841	2,869	2,339	859	6,436	1,431	5,543	8,273	32
Maine	2,356	2,214	212	902	1,099	142	2,356	1,793	2,137	11,566	8
Maryland . . . : . .	9,649	9,368	674	3,846	4,848	281	9,011	1,623	8,036	9,781	18
Massachusetts . . .	12,982	12,981	769	5,651	6,561	1	12,991	2,019	11,396	12,457	5
Michigan	20,579	20,228	1,489	12,937	5,802	351	19,287	1,911	16,859	10,301	15
Minnesota	9,864	8,725	592	6,067	2,065	1,139	9,762	1,916	7,749	9,888	17
Mississippi	3,728	3,600	542	1,951	1,107	128	3,548	1,226	3,130	6,901	48
Missouri	9,263	8,335	753	2,813	4,769	929	7,720	1,342	6,605	8,034	35
Montana	1,318	1,291	157	608	526	27	1,237	1,335	1,177	9,112	25
Nebraska	2,368	2,349	210	851	1,288	19	2,337	1,338	2,159	8,328	31
Nevada	4,605	3,390	257	918	2,216	1,215	3,442	1,476	2,688	7,184	44
New Hampshire . .	2,326	2,192	127	871	1,194	134	2,171	1,673	1,976	10,473	12
New Jersey	19,394	19,388	631	7,313	11,445	5	19,272	2,221	18,614	13,740	1
New Mexico	3,179	3,017	501	2,116	400	162	3,158	1,662	2,657	10,172	16
New York	40,050	39,500	2,600	17,900	19,000	550	40,962	2,123	36,345	12,764	3
North Carolina . . .	10,888	9,966	1,113	6,361	2,492	922	10,923	1,280	9,942	7,852	39
North Dakota	939	897	134	311	452	42	906	1,424	733	8,011	37
Ohio	22,970	19,712	1,236	9,063	9,413	3,257	20,101	1,754	17,649	10,684	11
Oklahoma	4,952	4,621	634	2,466	1,521	330	4,558	1,294	4,161	7,087	46
Oregon	5,402	4,990	506	2,450	2,034	412	5,133	1,430	4,331	8,871	27
Pennsylvania	20,254	20,025	1,660	7,126	11,239	230	21,163	1,710	17,495	9,654	20
Rhode Island	1,535	1,535	53	563	919	–	1,787	1,656	1,709	11,306	9
South Carolina . . .	7,932	6,280	662	2,837	2,781	1,652	6,751	1,609	5,469	8,542	30
South Dakota	1,142	1,062	180	356	526	80	1,052	1,365	917	7,928	38
Tennessee	7,034	6,663	809	3,051	2,803	371	6,767	1,150	6,365	7,346	42
Texas	43,316	37,029	4,259	13,327	19,442	6,287	39,599	1,759	32,045	7,823	40
Utah	3,543	3,209	325	1,756	1,128	334	3,098	1,279	2,486	5,574	50
Vermont	1,276	1,255	95	1,091	70	20	1,260	2,029	1,111	13,488	2
Virginia	13,037	12,186	850	4,894	6,442	850	13,002	1,740	10,517	9,434	23
Washington	9,947	9,097	876	5,629	2,591	850	10,057	1,621	7,848	8,231	34
West Virginia	3,087	2,826	352	1,696	779	261	3,063	1,691	2,644	9,749	19
Wisconsin	10,735	9,448	640	4,916	3,892	1,287	10,587	1,925	8,479	10,384	13
Wyoming	1,073	1,032	107	586	339	41	1,034	2,045	869	11,157	10

– Represents or rounds to zero. X Not applicable. [1] Amount received by local education agencies from the sales of bonds and real property and equipment, loans, and proceeds from insurance adjustments. [2] Includes interest on school debt and other current expenditures not shown separately. [3] Based on U.S. Census Bureau estimated resident population, as of July 1, the previous year, except 1980, 1990, and 2000 population enumerated as of April 1. [4] Average daily attendance.

Source: National Education Association, Washington, DC, Estimates of School Statistics Database (copyright).

Education   163

Table 250. **Public Schools With Broadband and Wireless Connections: 2000 to 2005**

[In percent. As of fall. Excludes special education, vocational education, and alternative schools. Based on the Fast Response Survey System and subject to sampling error; see source for details]

School characteristic	Percent of schools with Internet access using broadband connections				Percent using any type of wireless Internet connection		Percent of instructional rooms with wireless Internet connections	
	2000	2002	2003	2005	2002	2005	2002	2005
Total [1]	80	94	95	97	23	45	15	15
Instructional level:								
Elementary	77	93	94	97	20	45	13	16
Secondary	89	98	97	99	33	48	19	14
Size of enrollment:								
Less than 300	67	90	90	94	17	40	12	14
300 to 999	83	94	96	98	23	46	14	16
1,000 or more	90	100	100	100	37	56	19	12
Percent minority enrollment: [2]								
Less than 6 percent	76	92	90	96	21	37	14	14
6 to 20 percent	82	91	96	97	23	51	13	19
21 to 49 percent.	84	96	98	98	25	45	15	11
50 percent or more	81	95	97	97	23	46	16	16
Percent of students eligible for free or reduced-price lunch:								
Less than 35 percent	81	93	95	98	24	46	15	16
35 to 49 percent.	82	96	96	95	25	45	15	16
50 to 74 percent.	79	93	96	97	23	47	17	12
75 percent or more	75	95	93	98	20	44	11	16

[1] Includes combined schools.   [2] Percent minority enrollment was not available for 9 schools in 2000, 15 schools in 2002, 28 schools in 2003 and 20 schools in 2005.

Source: U.S. National Center for Education Statistics, "Internet Access in U.S. Public Schools and Classrooms: 1994–2005," NCES 2007-020, November 2006.

Table 251. **Public Schools Providing Hand-held Computers to Students or Teachers for Instructional Purposes, by School Characteristics: 2002 to 2005**

[In percent. As of fall. Excludes special education, vocational education, and alternative schools. Based on the Fast Response Survey System and subject to sampling error; see source for details]

Characteristic	2002	2003	2005		
			Total	Teachers	Students
All public schools [1]	7	10	19	17	8
Instructional level:					
Elementary	6	9	19	18	8
Secondary.	10	14	17	15	9
School size:					
Less than 300	8	5	17	16	6
300 to 999.	6	11	20	19	9
1,000 or more	12	21	15	12	8
Percent minority enrollment: [2]					
Less than 6 percent	9	9	21	20	9
6 to 20 percent.	7	10	16	14	8
21 to 49 percent.	5	10	16	12	11
50 percent or more	7	12	23	22	6
Percent of students eligible for free or reduced-price lunch:					
Less than 35 percent.	9	10	16	14	9
35 to 49 percent.	5	10	18	17	8
50 to 74 percent.	7	9	23	22	8
75 percent or more	5	11	21	19	6

[1] Includes combined schools.   [2] Percent minority enrollment was not available for 15 schools in 2002, 28 schools in 2003, and 20 schools in 2005.

Source: U.S. National Center for Education Statistics, "Internet Access in U.S. Public Schools and Classrooms: 1994–2005," NCES 2007-020, November 2006.

Table 252. Computers for Student Instruction in Elementary and Secondary Schools: 2005–2006

[54,848 represents 54,848,000. Market Data Retrieval collects student use computer information in elementary and secondary schools nationwide through a comprehensive annual technology survey that utilizes mail, telephone, and Internet data methods]

Level	Total schools	Total enroll-ment (1,000)	Number of com-puters [1] (1,000)	Students per computer	Schools with a wireless network (per-cent)	Schools with distance learning programs for students (per-cent) [2]	Schools with laptop com-puters (per-cent) [3]	Schools with high speed Internet access (per-cent) [4]	Schools with video-stream-ing (per-cent)
U.S. total......	114,749	54,848	14,165	3.9	54.2	19.1	59.7	84.3	43.4
Public schools, total ...	91,977	49,567	12,914	3.8	54.4	20.3	60.0	85.7	45.0
Elementary	53,245	23,805	5,612	4.2	49.1	11.2	55.4	85.0	41.3
Middle/junior high ...	14,310	9,376	2,503	3.7	61.6	15.6	66.2	85.8	53.2
Senior high	17,282	14,028	4,067	3.4	64.0	43.8	67.9	87.5	50.4
K to 12/other	7,140	2,358	733	3.2	54.7	43.2	61.7	85.9	41.0
Catholic schools, total ..	7,673	2,481	554	4.5	51.0	7.1	60.3	74.0	29.7
Elementary	6,326	1,797	358	5.0	46.5	3.8	57.9	71.6	27.3
Secondary.......	1,179	621	179	3.5	67.7	20.8	70.0	83.8	38.8
K to 12/other	168	63	17	3.8	73.1	7.7	65.4	73.1	38.5
Other private schools, total.............	15,099	2,800	697	4.0	52.1	6.5	50.1	66.4	24.1
Elementary	7,426	1,171	283	4.1	52.9	2.0	51.4	67.6	26.5
Secondary.......	1,274	265	77	3.4	67.5	18.1	54.2	68.7	24.1
K to 12/other	6,399	1,363	338	4.0	47.1	9.5	47.4	64.2	20.8

[1] Includes estimates for schools not reporting number of computers.   [2] Distance learning programs as determined by respondents.   [3] For student instruction.   [4] Statistics based on responses to those indicating type of Internet connection. High speed includes Internet connection types: T1, T3, and cable modem.

Source: Market Data Retrieval, Shelton, CT, unpublished data (copyright).

Table 253. Computer and Internet Use by Children and Adolescents: 2003

[For persons 5 to 17 years old (53,561 represents 53,561,000). As of September. Based on the Current Population Survey; see source and Appendix III for details]

User characteristic	Number of children (1,000)	Percent using computers at school	Percent using computers at home	Home use activity (percent)					
				Word process-ing	Connect to the Internet	E-mail	Complete school assign-ments	Play games [1]	
Total..................	53,561	84.5	68.6	33.4	46.6	32.9	49.2	56.9	
Age: 5 to 7 years old	11,785	72.2	59.3	9.6	23.3	7.7	16.6	51.7	
8 to 10 years old	11,849	86.3	66.1	23.5	38.2	19.5	42.7	58.0	
11 to 14 years old............	17,173	89.0	72.0	42.7	54.8	40.9	61.8	61.0	
15 to 17 years old............	12,753	87.9	75.0	51.9	64.7	57.7	68.1	55.4	
Sex: Male..................	27,422	84.2	68.0	31.2	45.5	30.2	47.5	57.8	
Female..................	26,139	84.7	69.3	35.6	47.7	35.7	50.9	56.0	
Race/ethnicity:									
White alone, non-Hispanic	32,279	86.6	79.6	40.1	56.9	41.1	56.6	67.3	
Black alone, non-Hispanic	8,048	82.6	47.2	20.5	28.0	18.6	35.9	39.1	
Hispanic	9,503	79.7	48.3	20.2	27.2	17.1	34.4	37.8	
Other	3,731	82.1	71.4	35.9	46.4	32.6	50.8	54.7	
Parent educational attainment:									
Less than high school credential ...	10,001	77.9	43.7	17.7	24.2	16.3	29.5	34.6	
High school credential	15,270	84.1	61.4	26.9	39.9	28.2	43.7	50.6	
Some college...............	14,384	86.8	75.4	35.5	51.9	35.7	54.1	63.4	
Bachelor's degree.............	9,410	86.9	86.5	47.4	62.9	45.2	63.2	73.0	
Graduate education............	4,495	87.6	89.5	53.8	67.9	50.5	66.0	73.6	
Household language:									
Spanish-only	2,680	75.3	33.6	12.7	14.3	9.0	24.1	26.7	
Not Spanish-only	50,881	84.9	70.5	34.4	48.3	34.1	50.5	58.5	
Family income:									
Under $20,000..............	16,459	81.3	51.7	23.1	30.7	21.7	36.2	41.2	
20,000 to 34,999	8,615	81.9	55.7	22.9	33.3	23.2	38.2	45.4	
35,000 to 49,999	6,993	85.9	72.2	33.2	46.7	32.2	50.5	60.5	
50,000 to 74,999	9,053	86.0	80.5	38.6	56.7	39.2	57.6	67.1	
75,000 or more...............	12,441	88.5	89.3	50.5	69.3	50.1	67.0	76.4	

[1] Includes other home activities, not shown separately.

Source: U.S. National Center for Education Statistics, CPS October (Education) Supplement, October 2003, special tabulation.

Education 165

[**For the school year.** Distance education courses are for-credit classes offered to students enrolled in the district where the teacher and student were in different locations. They could be delivered via audio, video, Internet, or other computer technologies. Reasons for districts providing these courses include offering courses not otherwise available, offering Advanced Placement courses, addressing growing populations and space limitations, reducing scheduling conflicts for students, and permitting students who failed a course to take the course again. Excludes such things as virtual field trips, online homework, or a course delivered mainly by written correspondence. Based on the Fast Response Survey System and subject to sampling error; see source for details]

District characteristic	Number of districts		Enrollments in distance education courses							
	Total	With students enrolled in distance education courses	Total [1]	Curriculum						High school level
				English/language arts	Social studies/social sciences	Computer sciences	Natural/physical sciences	Math	Foreign language	
All public school districts [2]..	15,040	5,480	327,670	61,590	74,570	11,660	38,920	49,210	39,090	222,090
District enrollment size:										
Less than 2,500	11,080	4,060	117,730	21,480	25,550	3,060	12,900	15,060	22,300	74,160
2,500 to 9,999	3,100	1,010	85,640	15,810	18,950	1,970	11,090	13,480	9,290	44,780
10,000 or more.	820	410	124,300	24,300	30,070	6,630	14,930	20,670	7,500	103,150
Region: [3]										
Northeast	3,040	640	42,070	6,060	8,280	3,020	4,830	4,730	5,300	17,420
South	1,750	790	59,010	10,240	12,490	1,420	5,400	8,920	11,120	50,410
Midwest	5,390	2,500	108,140	21,250	21,500	2,750	14,270	17,040	14,250	60,560
West.	4,850	1,540	118,450	24,040	32,290	4,470	14,420	18,520	8,410	93,700
Poverty concentration: [4]										
Less than 10 percent.	4,850	1,620	77,380	15,300	17,350	2,140	6,900	10,590	9,600	57,320
10 to 19 percent	5,330	2,220	97,300	18,370	23,820	3,000	10,720	15,030	10,600	77,810
20 percent or more	3,690	1,560	93,280	17,800	22,770	6,290	11,800	14,150	15,330	83,100

[1] Includes other curriculum not shown separately. [2] Includes districts and enrollments where enrollment size and poverty concentration were not known. [3] For composition or regions, see map inside front cover. [4] Percentage of children in the district ages 5 to 17 in families living below the poverty level.

Source: U.S. National Center for Education Statistics, *Distance Education Courses for Public Elementary and Secondary School Students: 2002–03* NCES 2005-010, March 2005.

Table 255. **Children and Youth With Disabilities Served by Selected Programs: 1995 to 2005**

[In thousands (5,078.8 represents 5,078,800). As of Fall. For children and youth ages 6 to 21 served under the Individuals with Disabilities Education Act (IDEA) Part B. Includes outlying areas]

Disability	1995	1999	2000	2001	2002	2003	2004	2005
Total	5,078.8	5,677.9	5,773.9	5,861.4	5,959.1	6,045.4	6,116.4	6,109.6
Specific learning disabilities	2,601.8	2,867.7	2,881.6	2,878.3	2,878.6	2,867.1	2,839.3	2,780.2
Speech or language impairments. . .	1,026.9	1,087.8	1,093.4	1,093.2	1,110.9	1,128.1	1,149.6	1,157.2
Mental retardation.	585.6	614.3	613.4	605.0	591.7	582.6	567.6	545.5
Emotional disturbance	439.2	469.8	474.3	477.8	482.0	484.5	484.5	472.4
Multiple disabilities	94.5	113.0	122.9	128.7	130.8	132.7	133.4	133.9
Hearing impairments	68.0	71.4	70.8	71.2	72.0	72.0	72.6	72.4
Orthopedic impairments	63.2	71.4	73.0	73.7	74.0	68.2	65.4	63.1
Other health impairments	134.2	255.3	294.0	341.3	393.0	452.7	512.2	561.0
Visual impairments	25.5	26.4	26.0	25.8	26.1	25.9	26.1	26.0
Autism	29.1	66.0	79.6	98.6	118.8	141.1	166.5	193.6
Deaf-blind	1.4	1.7	1.3	1.6	1.6	1.7	1.7	1.6
Traumatic brain injury	9.6	13.9	14.9	20.8	21.5	22.5	23.3	23.5
Developmental delay [1]	(X)	19.3	28.6	45.3	58.3	66.3	74.4	79.1

X Not applicable. [1] States had the option of reporting children ages 3 to 9 under developmental delay beginning 1997.

Source: U.S. Department of Education, Office of Special Education Programs, Data Analysis System (DANS). See Internet site <http://www.ideadata.org/index.html>.

Table 256. **Private Schools: 2003–2004**

[5,123 represents 5,123,000. Based on the Private School Survey, conducted every 2 years; see source for details. For composition of regions, see map, inside front cover]

Characteristic	Schools				Students (1,000)				Teachers (1,000) [1]			
	Number	Elementary	Secondary	Combined	Total	Elementary	Secondary	Combined	Total	Elementary	Secondary	Combined
Total.........	**28,384**	**17,197**	**2,694**	**8,494**	**5,123**	**2,694**	**845**	**1,583**	**425**	**199**	**68**	**158**
School type:												
Catholic........	7,919	6,539	1,096	284	2,365	1,659	610	97	153	101	43	9
Parochial......	4,074	3,852	171	51	1,097	1,006	75	17	67	60	6	1
Diocesan......	2,947	2,367	504	76	909	593	291	25	57	36	19	2
Private	897	319	420	157	359	60	244	55	28	5	18	5
Other religious....	13,659	7,278	758	5,623	1,836	734	117	984	163	63	11	88
Conservative Christian ..	5,060	1,838	195	3,026	774	216	25	533	65	18	2	45
Affiliated	3,398	2,110	329	959	553	264	61	229	51	24	6	22
Unaffiliated.	5,201	3,330	234	1,637	508	255	31	222	47	22	3	22
Nonsectarian.....	6,806	3,380	840	2,587	922	301	118	502	110	35	14	61
Regular.......	2,963	1,606	320	1,036	603	179	87	337	67	19	10	38
Special emphasis.....	2,392	1,550	303	539	214	109	21	84	25	13	3	9
Special education.....	1,451	223	217	1,011	105	14	10	81	18	3	2	14
Program emphasis:												
Regular elem/sec..	22,896	14,709	1,981	6,206	4,639	2,511	784	1,345	365	177	61	127
Montessori	1,318	1,195	(B)	118	83	72	(B)	10	10	9	(B)	1
Special program emphasis	961	465	126	369	170	59	28	84	18	6	3	9
Special education..	1,634	272	233	1,129	115	16	11	88	20	3	2	15
Vocational/tech ...	(B)	(B)	(B)	(B)	(B)	(B)	(B)	(B)	(B)	(B)	(B)	(B)
Alternative.......	1,454	443	343	668	110	32	21	57	12	4	2	6
Early childhood ...	116	112	(X)	(B)	5	4	(X)	(B)	(Z)	(Z)	(X)	(B)
Size:												
Less than 50.....	8,741	5,053	654	3,033	224	129	16	79	33	17	3	13
50 to 149	8,206	5,190	605	2,411	760	490	55	215	81	48	7	27
150 to 299	6,324	4,465	424	1,435	1,352	953	92	307	106	66	9	31
300 to 499	3,000	1,823	399	778	1,154	699	155	300	85	44	13	27
500 to 749	1,298	562	278	458	777	328	169	281	55	18	12	25
750 or more	816	103	334	378	856	95	358	403	64	5	24	35
Region:												
Northeast	6,558	4,035	844	1,679	1,273	683	296	294	111	50	25	36
Midwest	7,226	5,169	644	1,413	1,271	818	233	220	94	56	17	21
South..........	8,820	4,467	573	3,780	1,612	657	160	795	143	54	13	76
West	5,780	3,526	633	1,621	967	537	155	275	77	38	12	26

B Does not meet standard of reliability or precision. X Not applicable. Z Less than 500. [1] Full-time equivalents.

Source: U.S. National Center for Education Statistics, *Characteristics of Private Schools in the United States: Results from the 2003–2004 Private School Universe Survey,* NCES 2006-319, March 2006. See Internet site <http://nces.ed.gov/surveys/pss/>.

Table 257. **Private Elementary and Secondary School Teachers— Selected Characteristics: 2004–2005**

[For school year (63 represents 63,000). Based on the 2004–2005 Teacher Follow-up Survey, a component of the School and Staffing Survey, and subject to sampling error; for details, see source Web site at <http://nces.ed.gov/surveys/sass/>. Excludes prekindergarten teachers. See Table 241 for similar data on public school teachers]

Characteristic	Unit	Age				Sex		Race/ethnicity		
		Under 30 years old	30 to 39 years old	40 to 49 years old	50 years old and over	Male	Female	White [1]	Black [1]	Hispanic
Total teachers [2]....	1,000 ...	**63**	**91**	**100**	**148**	**90**	**312**	**359**	**13**	**13**
Highest degree held:										
Bachelor's........	Percent..	78.2	64.4	58.2	49.1	4.4	8.1	58.4	66.4	78.3
Master's........	Percent..	13.6	22.1	29.2	38.0	55.5	60.5	30.2	13.6	12.6
Education specialist..	Percent..	(X)	1.1	2.4	4.0	33.3	27.0	2.3	3.7	0.0
Doctorate	Percent..	(X)	2.1	3.1	3.7	1.3	2.6	2.2	0.0	3.3
Full-time teaching experience:										
Less than 3 years ...	Percent..	24.3	6.7	4.0	1.5	9.6	6.1	6.4	10.4	8.9
3 to 9 years.......	Percent..	75.7	60.4	33.3	12.5	35.4	39.3	38.2	51.2	32.6
10 to 20 years	Percent..	(X)	32.8	43.6	25.8	23.4	29.1	28.3	8.1	36.0
20 years or more ...	Percent..	(X)	(X)	19.1	60.2	31.7	25.6	27.1	30.3	22.5
Full-time teachers..	1,000 ..	55	73	74	125	68	259	292	12	9
Earned income.....	Dollars ..	30,455	33,200	36,413	40,448	42,618	34,577	36,212	29,414	44,844
Salary	Dollars ..	29,489	32,335	35,325	39,391	40,981	33,737	35,164	28,919	43,414

X Not applicable. [1] Non-Hispanic. [2] Includes teachers with no degrees and associate's degrees, not shown separately.

Source: U.S. National Center for Education Statistics, "Teacher Follow-up Survey, 2004–05," unpublished data.

Table 258. SAT Scores and Characteristics of College-Bound Seniors: 1967 to 2006

[For school year ending in year shown. Data are for the SAT I: Reasoning Tests. SAT I: Reasoning Test replaced the SAT in March 1994. Scores between the two tests have been equated to the same 200–800 scale and are thus comparable. Scores for 1995 and prior years have been recentered and revised]

Type of test and characteristic	Unit	1967	1970	1975	1980	1985	1990	1995	2000	2005	2006
AVERAGE TEST SCORES [1]											
Verbal, total [2]	Point....	543	537	512	502	509	500	504	505	508	503
Male	Point....	540	536	515	506	514	505	505	507	513	505
Female	Point....	545	538	509	498	503	496	502	504	505	502
Math, total [2]	Point....	516	512	498	492	500	501	506	514	520	518
Male	Point....	535	531	518	515	522	521	525	533	538	536
Female	Point....	495	493	479	473	480	483	490	498	504	502
Writing	Point....	(X)	(X)	(X)	(X)	(X)	(X)	(X)	(X)	(X)	497
Male	Point....	(X)	(X)	(X)	(X)	(X)	(X)	(X)	(X)	(X)	491
Female	Point....	(X)	(X)	(X)	(X)	(X)	(X)	(X)	(X)	(X)	502
PARTICIPANTS											
Total [3]	1,000 ...	(NA)	(NA)	996	922	977	1,026	1,068	1,260	1,476	1,466
Male	Percent..	(NA)	(NA)	49.9	48.2	48.3	47.8	46.4	46.2	46.5	46.4
White	Percent..	(NA)	(NA)	86.0	82.1	81.0	73.0	69.2	66.4	62.3	62.1
Black	Percent..	(NA)	(NA)	7.9	9.1	7.5	10.0	10.7	11.2	11.6	11.3
Obtaining scores [1] of—											
600 or above:											
Verbal	Percent..	(NA)	(NA)	(NA)	(NA)	(NA)	20.3	21.9	21.1	22.5	21.4
Math	Percent..	(NA)	(NA)	(NA)	(NA)	(NA)	20.4	23.4	24.2	26.5	25.8
Writing	Percent..	(X)	(X)	(X)	(X)	(X)	(X)	(X)	(X)	(X)	18.9
Below 400:											
Verbal	Percent..	(NA)	(NA)	(NA)	(NA)	(NA)	17.3	16.4	15.9	15.5	16.6
Math	Percent..	(NA)	(NA)	(NA)	(NA)	(NA)	15.8	16.0	14.7	13.8	14.3
Writing	Percent..	(X)	(X)	(X)	(X)	(X)	(X)	(X)	(X)	(X)	17.8

NA Not available. X Not applicable. [1] Minimum score, 200; maximum score, 800. [2] 1967 and 1970 are estimates based on total number of persons taking SAT. For 2006, critical reading based on 1,377,000 test takers. [3] 996 represents 996,000.

Source: The College Board, New York, NY, *College Bound Seniors*. Copyright 1967 to 2007. Reproduced with permission. All rights reserved. See Internet site <http://www.collegeboard.com/>.

Table 259. ACT Program Scores and Characteristics of College-Bound Students: 1970 to 2006

[For academic year ending in year shown. Except as indicated, test scores and characteristics of college-bound students. Through 1980, data based on 10 percent sample; thereafter, based on all ACT tested graduating seniors]

Type of test and characteristic	Unit	1970	1975	1980	1985	1990 [1]	1995 [1]	2000 [1]	2004 [1]	2005 [1]	2006 [1]
TEST SCORES [2]											
Composite	Point....	19.9	18.6	18.5	18.6	20.6	20.8	21.0	20.9	20.9	21.1
Male	Point....	20.3	19.5	19.3	19.4	21.0	21.0	21.2	21.0	21.1	21.2
Female	Point....	19.4	17.8	17.9	17.9	20.3	20.7	20.9	20.9	20.9	21.0
English	Point....	18.5	17.7	17.9	18.1	20.5	20.2	20.5	20.4	20.4	20.6
Male	Point....	17.6	17.1	17.3	17.6	20.1	19.8	20.0	19.9	20.0	20.1
Female	Point....	19.4	18.3	18.3	18.6	20.9	20.6	20.9	20.8	20.8	21.0
Math	Point....	20.0	17.6	17.4	17.2	19.9	20.2	20.7	20.7	20.7	20.8
Male	Point....	21.1	19.3	18.9	18.6	20.7	20.9	21.4	21.3	21.3	21.5
Female	Point....	18.8	16.2	16.2	16.0	19.3	19.7	20.2	20.2	20.2	20.3
Reading [3]	Point....	19.7	17.4	17.2	17.4	(NA)	21.3	21.4	21.3	21.3	21.4
Male	Point....	20.3	18.7	18.2	18.3	(NA)	21.1	21.2	21.1	21.0	21.1
Female	Point....	19.0	16.4	16.4	16.6	(NA)	21.4	21.5	21.5	21.5	21.6
Science reasoning [4]	Point....	20.8	21.1	21.1	21.2	(NA)	21.0	21.0	20.9	20.9	20.9
Male	Point....	21.6	22.4	22.4	22.6	(NA)	21.6	21.6	21.3	21.4	21.2
Female	Point....	20.0	20.0	20.0	20.0	(NA)	20.5	20.6	20.5	20.5	21.0
PARTICIPANTS [5]											
Total [6]	1,000 ...	788	714	822	739	817	945	1,065	1,171	1,186	1,206
Male	Percent..	52	46	45	46	46	44	43	44	44	44
White	Percent..	(NA)	77	83	82	79	75	76	72	71	70
Black	Percent..	4	7	8	8	9	10	11	12	13	13
Obtaining composite scores of—[7]											
27 or above	Percent..	14	14	13	14	12	13	14	14	14	14
18 or below	Percent..	21	33	33	32	35	34	32	34	34	33

NA Not available. [1] Beginning 1990, not comparable with previous years because a new version of the ACT was introduced. Estimated average composite scores for prior years: 1989, 20.6; 1988, 1987, and 1986, 20.8. [2] Minimum score, 1; maximum score, 36. [3] Prior to 1990, social studies; data not comparable with previous years. [4] Prior to 1990, natural sciences; data not comparable with previous years. [5] Beginning 1985, data are for seniors who graduated in year shown and had taken the ACT in their junior or senior years. Data by race are for those responding to the race question. [6] 788 represents 788,000. [7] Prior to 1990, 26 or above and 15 or below.

Source: ACT, Inc., Iowa City, IA, *High School Profile Report*, annual.

Table 260. **Proficiency Levels on Selected NAEP Tests for Students in Public Schools, by State: 2005**

[Represents percent of public school students scoring at or above basic and proficient levels. Basic denotes mastery of the knowledge and skills that are fundamental for proficient work at a given grade level. Proficient represents solid academic performance. Students reaching this level demonstrated competency over challenging subject matter. For more detail see <http://www.nagb.org/pubs/pubs.html>. Based on the National Assessment of Educational Progress (NAEP) tests which are administered to a representative sample of students in public schools, private schools, and Department of Defense schools. Data shown here are for public school students only]

State	Grade 4 Math		Grade 8 Math		Grade 4 Reading		Grade 8 Reading	
	At or above basic	At or above proficient	At or above basic	At or above proficient	At or above basic	At or above proficient	At or above basic	At or above proficient
U.S. average	79	35	68	28	62	30	71	29
Alabama	66	21	53	15	53	22	63	22
Alaska	77	34	69	29	58	27	70	26
Arizona	70	28	64	26	52	24	65	23
Arkansas	78	34	64	22	63	30	69	26
California	71	28	57	22	50	21	60	21
Colorado	81	39	70	32	69	37	75	32
Connecticut	84	42	70	35	71	38	74	34
Delaware	84	36	72	30	73	34	80	30
District of Columbia	45	10	31	7	33	11	45	12
Florida	82	37	65	26	65	30	66	25
Georgia	76	30	62	23	58	26	67	25
Hawaii	73	27	56	18	53	23	58	18
Idaho	86	40	73	30	69	33	76	32
Illinois	74	32	68	29	62	29	75	31
Indiana	84	38	74	30	64	30	73	28
Iowa	85	37	75	34	67	33	79	34
Kansas	88	47	77	34	66	32	78	35
Kentucky	75	26	64	23	65	31	75	31
Louisiana	74	24	59	16	53	20	64	20
Maine	84	39	74	30	71	35	81	38
Maryland	79	38	66	30	65	32	69	30
Massachusetts	91	49	80	43	78	44	83	44
Michigan	79	38	68	29	63	32	73	28
Minnesota	88	47	79	43	71	38	80	37
Mississippi	69	19	52	14	48	18	60	18
Missouri	79	31	68	26	67	33	76	31
Montana	85	38	80	36	71	36	82	37
Nebraska	80	36	75	35	68	34	80	35
Nevada	72	26	60	21	52	21	63	22
New Hampshire	89	47	77	35	74	39	80	38
New Jersey	86	45	74	36	68	37	80	38
New Mexico	65	19	53	14	51	20	62	19
New York	81	36	70	31	69	33	75	33
North Carolina	83	40	72	32	62	29	69	27
North Dakota	89	40	81	35	72	35	83	37
Ohio	84	43	74	33	69	34	78	36
Oklahoma	79	29	63	21	60	25	72	25
Oregon	80	37	72	34	62	29	74	33
Pennsylvania	82	41	72	31	69	36	77	36
Rhode Island	76	31	63	24	62	30	71	29
South Carolina	81	36	71	30	57	26	67	25
South Dakota	86	41	80	36	70	33	82	35
Tennessee	74	28	61	21	59	27	71	26
Texas	87	40	72	31	64	29	69	26
Utah	83	37	71	30	68	34	73	29
Vermont	87	44	78	38	72	39	79	37
Virginia	83	39	75	33	72	37	78	36
Washington	84	42	75	36	70	36	75	34
West Virginia	75	25	60	18	61	26	67	22
Wisconsin	84	40	76	36	67	33	77	35
Wyoming	87	43	76	29	71	34	81	36

Source: U.S. Department of Education, National Center for Education Statistics, National Assessment of Educational Progress (NAEP), 2005 Mathematics and Reading Assessments. See Internet site <http://nces.ed.gov/nationsreportcard/> (accessed 15 March 2006).

Education 169

Table 261. Public High Schools Offering Dual Credit and Exam-Based Courses and Course Enrollments: 2002–2003

[For the school year. Includes public schools with a grade of 11 or 12. Excludes schools with the highest grade lower than 11, special education, vocational, and alternative/other schools. Based on the Fast Response Survey System and subject to sampling error; for details, see source]

School characteristic	Number of high schools	Schools offering—			Enrollments in—		
		Dual credit courses [1]	AP courses [2]	IB courses [3]	Dual credit courses [1]	AP courses [2]	IB courses [3]
All public high schools [4] . . .	16,500	11,700	11,000	390	1,162.0	1,795.4	165.1
Enrollment size:							
Fewer than 500	7,400	4,700	3,000	(B)	185.3	81.1	(B)
500 to 1,199	5,000	3,700	4,100	70	335.1	481.0	24.8
1,200 or more	4,100	3,300	3,900	290	641.6	1,233.3	140.2
Region: [5]							
Northeast	2,800	1,600	2,300	30	144.8	390.9	(NA)
Southeast	3,500	2,400	2,400	170	194.0	386.1	65.8
Central	5,200	4,100	2,800	50	333.9	319.3	(NA)
West	5,100	3,600	3,500	150	489.4	699.1	66.4
Percent minority enrollment:							
Less than 6 percent	5,600	4,300	3,300	(Z)	317.4	267.1	(Z)
6 to 20 percent	3,800	3,000	2,600	90	380.9	463.8	16.7
21 to 49 percent.	3,200	2,300	2,400	150	228.9	528.5	64.3
50 percent or more	3,600	2,100	2,500	150	231.4	497.7	84.1

B Base too small to meet statistical standards for reliability of a derived figure.   NA Not available.   Z Rounds to zero.   [1] Courses where students can earn both secondary and postsecondary credit.   [2] Advanced Placement courses follow the content and curricular goals developed by the College Board.   [3] International baccalaureate courses compose a 2-year liberal arts curriculum that leads to a diploma and meets requirements established by the International Baccalaureate program.   [4] Includes schools whose minority enrollment was not available.   [5] For compositions of regions, see map inside front cover.

Source: U.S. National Center for Education Statistics, *Dual Credit and Exam-Based Courses in U.S. Public High Schools: 2002–03* NCES 2005-009, April 2005.

Table 262. Foreign Language Enrollment in Public High Schools: 1970 to 2000

[In thousands (13,301.9 represents 13,301,900), except percent. As of fall, for grades 9 through 12]

Language	1970	1974	1978	1982	1985	1990	1994	2000
Total enrollment	13,301.9	13,648.9	13,941.4	12,879.3	12,466.5	11,099.6	11,847.5	13,457.8
Enrolled in all foreign languages. . . .	3,779.3	3,294.5	3,200.1	2,909.8	4,028.9	4,256.9	5,001.9	5,899.4
Percent of all students	28.4	24.1	23.0	22.6	32.3	38.4	42.2	43.8
Enrolled in modern foreign languages [1] . . .	3,514.1	3,127.3	3,048.3	2,740.2	3,852.0	4,093.0	4,813.0	5,721.9
Spanish	1,810.8	1,678.1	1,631.4	1,562.8	2,334.4	2,611.4	3,219.8	4,057.6
French	1,230.7	977.9	856.0	858.0	1,133.7	1,089.4	1,105.9	1,075.4
German	410.5	393.0	330.6	266.9	312.2	295.4	326.0	283.3
Italian	27.3	40.2	45.5	44.1	47.3	40.4	43.8	64.1
Japanese	(NA)	(NA)	(NA)	6.2	8.6	24.1	42.3	50.9
Russian	20.2	15.1	8.8	5.7	6.4	16.5	16.4	10.6
Percent of all students [1]	26.4	22.9	21.9	21.3	30.9	36.9	40.6	42.5
Spanish	13.6	12.3	11.7	12.1	18.7	23.5	27.2	30.2
French.	9.3	7.2	6.1	6.7	9.1	9.8	9.3	8.0
German	3.1	2.9	2.4	2.1	2.5	2.7	2.8	2.1
Italian	0.2	0.3	0.3	0.3	0.4	0.4	0.4	0.5
Japanese.	(NA)	(NA)	(NA)	0.1	0.1	0.2	0.4	0.4
Russian	0.2	0.1	0.1	(Z)	0.1	0.2	0.1	0.1

NA Not available.   Z Less than 0.05 percent.   [1] Includes other foreign languages, not shown separately.

Source: The American Council on the Teaching of Foreign Languages, Alexandria, VA, *Foreign Language Enrollments in Public Secondary Schools, fall 1994 and fall 2000.*

Table 263. Public High School Graduates by State: 1980 to 2005

[In thousands (2,747.7 represents 2,747,700). For school year ending in year shown]

State	1980	1990	2000	2005, proj.	State	1980	1990	2000	2005, proj.
United States . . .	2,747.7	2,320.3	2,553.8	2,801.2	Missouri.	62.3	49.0	52.8	57.0
Alabama	45.2	40.5	37.8	36.9	Montana	12.1	9.4	10.9	10.3
Alaska	5.2	5.4	6.6	7.2	Nebraska	22.4	17.7	20.1	19.7
Arizona	28.6	32.1	38.3	62.4	Nevada	8.5	9.5	14.6	17.9
Arkansas	29.1	26.5	27.3	26.6	New Hampshire	11.7	10.8	11.8	13.8
California	249.2	236.3	309.9	355.7					
Colorado	36.8	33.0	38.9	44.1	New Jersey	94.6	69.8	74.4	89.3
Connecticut	37.7	27.9	31.6	35.8	New Mexico	18.4	14.9	18.0	17.8
Delaware	7.6	5.6	6.1	6.8	New York	204.1	143.3	141.7	149.2
District of Columbia . . .	5.0	3.6	2.7	2.9	North Carolina	70.9	64.8	62.1	74.0
Florida	87.3	88.9	106.7	136.5	North Dakota	9.9	7.7	8.6	7.6
Georgia	61.6	56.6	62.6	71.1	Ohio	144.2	114.5	111.7	118.4
Hawaii	11.5	10.3	10.4	10.5	Oklahoma	39.3	35.6	37.6	36.3
Idaho	13.2	12.0	16.2	16.1	Oregon	29.9	25.5	30.2	32.3
Illinois	135.6	108.1	111.8	121.0	Pennsylvania	146.5	110.5	114.0	124.7
Indiana	73.1	60.0	57.0	57.4	Rhode Island	10.9	7.8	8.5	9.9
Iowa	43.4	31.8	33.9	33.2	South Carolina	38.7	32.5	31.6	32.6
Kansas	30.9	25.4	29.1	29.7	South Dakota	10.7	7.7	9.3	8.6
Kentucky	41.2	38.0	36.8	36.9	Tennessee	49.8	46.1	41.6	44.6
Louisiana	46.3	36.1	38.4	35.9	Texas	171.4	172.5	212.9	241.0
Maine	15.4	13.8	12.2	13.3	Utah	20.0	21.2	32.5	29.2
Maryland	54.3	41.6	47.8	54.2	Vermont	6.7	6.1	6.7	7.2
Massachusetts	73.8	55.9	53.0	59.1	Virginia	66.6	60.6	65.6	74.5
Michigan	124.3	93.8	97.7	103.3	Washington	50.4	45.9	57.6	61.1
Minnesota	64.9	49.1	57.4	58.4	West Virginia	23.4	21.9	19.4	17.0
Mississippi	27.6	25.2	24.2	23.4	Wisconsin	69.3	52.0	58.5	63.6
					Wyoming	6.1	5.8	6.5	5.5

Source: U.S. National Center for Education Statistics, Digest of Education Statistics, annual.

Table 264. High School Dropouts by Race and Hispanic Origin: 1975 to 2005

[In percent. As of October]

Item	1975	1980	1985	1990 [1]	1995	1999	2000	2001	2002	2003	2004	2005
EVENT DROPOUTS [2]												
Total [3]	5.8	6.0	5.2	4.5	5.4	4.7	4.5	4.7	3.3	3.8	4.4	3.6
White [4]	5.4	5.6	4.8	3.9	5.1	4.4	4.3	4.6	3.0	3.7	4.2	3.1
Male	5.0	6.4	4.9	4.1	5.4	4.1	4.7	5.3	3.0	3.9	4.9	3.4
Female	5.8	4.9	4.7	3.8	4.8	4.7	4.0	3.8	3.0	3.4	3.5	2.7
Black [4]	8.7	8.3	7.7	7.7	6.1	6.0	5.6	5.7	4.4	4.5	5.2	6.9
Male	8.3	8.0	8.3	6.9	7.9	5.2	7.6	6.1	5.1	4.1	4.8	7.5
Female	9.0	8.5	7.2	8.6	4.4	6.8	3.8	5.4	3.8	4.9	5.7	6.2
Hispanic [5]	10.9	11.5	9.7	7.7	11.6	7.1	6.8	8.1	5.3	6.5	8.0	4.7
Male	10.1	16.9	9.3	7.6	10.9	6.9	7.1	7.6	6.2	7.7	11.5	5.6
Female	11.6	6.9	9.8	7.7	12.5	7.3	6.5	8.7	4.4	5.4	4.6	3.9
STATUS DROPOUTS [6]												
Total [3]	15.6	15.6	13.9	14.4	13.9	13.1	12.4	13.0	12.3	11.8	12.1	11.3
White [4]	13.9	14.4	13.5	14.1	13.6	12.8	12.2	13.4	12.2	11.6	11.9	11.3
Male	13.5	15.7	14.7	15.4	14.3	13.9	13.5	15.3	13.7	13.3	13.7	13.2
Female	14.2	13.2	12.3	12.8	13.0	11.8	10.9	11.4	10.6	9.8	10.0	9.4
Black [4]	27.3	23.5	17.6	16.4	14.4	16.0	15.3	13.8	14.6	14.2	15.1	12.9
Male	27.8	26.0	18.8	18.6	14.2	16.3	17.4	16.9	16.9	16.7	17.9	14.8
Female	26.9	21.5	16.6	14.5	14.6	15.7	13.5	11.0	12.5	12.0	12.7	11.2
Hispanic [5]	34.9	40.3	31.5	37.7	34.7	33.9	32.3	31.7	30.1	28.4	28.0	27.3
Male	32.6	42.6	35.8	40.3	34.2	36.4	36.8	37.1	33.8	31.7	33.5	32.1
Female	36.8	38.1	27.0	35.0	35.4	31.1	27.3	25.5	25.6	24.7	21.7	21.8

[1] Beginning 1990, reflects new editing procedures for cases with missing data on school enrollment. [2] Percent of students who drop out in a single year without completing high school. For grades 10 to 12. [3] Includes other races, not shown separately. [4] Beginning 2003, for persons who selected this race group only. See footnote 2, Table 217. [5] Persons of Hispanic origin may be of any race. [6] Percent of the population who have not completed high school and are not enrolled, regardless of when they dropped out. For persons 18 to 24 years old.

Source: U.S. Census Bureau, Current Population Reports, PPL-148; and earlier PPL and P-20 reports; and data published on the Internet. See Internet site <http://www.census.gov/population/www/socdemo/school.html>.

Table 265. High School Dropouts by Age, Race, and Hispanic Origin: 1980 to 2005

[As of October (5,212 represents 5,212,000). For persons 14 to 24 years old. See Table 267 for definition of dropouts]

Age and race	Number of dropouts (1,000)					Percent of population				
	1980	1990	1995	2000	2005	1980	1990	1995	2000	2005
Total dropouts [1,2] . . .	5,212	3,854	3,963	3,883	3,597	12.0	10.1	9.9	9.1	7.9
16 to 17 years.	709	418	406	460	303	8.8	6.3	5.4	5.8	3.4
18 to 21 years.	2,578	1,921	1,980	2,005	1,669	15.8	13.4	14.2	12.9	10.5
22 to 24 years.	1,798	1,458	1,491	1,310	1,485	15.2	13.8	13.6	11.8	12.4
White [2,3]	4,169	3,127	3,098	3,065	2,785	11.3	10.1	9.7	9.1	7.9
16 to 17 years.	619	334	314	366	223	9.2	6.4	5.4	5.8	3.3
18 to 21 years.	2,032	1,516	1,530	1,558	1,299	14.7	13.1	13.8	12.6	10.4
22 to 24 years.	1,416	1,235	1,181	1,040	1,167	14.0	14.0	13.4	11.7	12.6
Black [2,3]	934	611	605	705	616	16.0	10.9	10.0	10.9	9.2
16 to 17 years.	80	73	70	84	64	6.9	6.9	5.8	7.0	4.7
18 to 21 years.	486	345	328	383	281	23.0	16.0	15.8	16.0	12.4
22 to 24 years.	346	185	194	232	231	24.0	13.5	12.5	14.3	13.6
Hispanic [2,4]	919	1,122	1,355	1,499	1,467	29.5	26.8	24.7	23.5	18.6
16 to 17 years.	92	89	94	121	93	16.6	12.9	10.7	11.0	6.3
18 to 21 years.	470	502	652	733	672	40.3	32.9	29.9	30.0	24.5
22 to 24 years.	323	523	598	602	663	40.6	42.8	37.4	35.5	30.8

[1] Includes other groups not shown separately. [2] Includes persons 14 to 15 years, not shown separately. [3] For 2005, for persons who selected this race group only. See footnote 2, Table 217. [4] Persons of Hispanic origin may be of any race.

Source: U.S. Census Bureau, Current Population Reports, PPL-148; and earlier PPL and P-20 reports; and data published on the Internet. See Internet site <http://www.census.gov/population/www/socdemo/school.html>.

Table 266. Enrollment Status by Race, Hispanic Origin, and Sex: 1975 and 2005

[As of October (15,693 represents 15,693,000). For persons 18 to 21 years old. For the civilian noninstitutional population. Based on the Current Population Survey; see text, Section 1, and Appendix III]

Characteristic	Total persons 18 to 21 years old (1,000)		Percent distribution							
			Enrolled in high school		High school graduates				Not high school graduates	
					Total		In college			
	1975	2005	1975	2005	1975	2005	1975	2005	1975	2005
Total [1]	15,693	15,916	5.7	9.4	78.0	80.1	33.5	48.2	16.3	10.6
White [2]	13,448	12,510	4.7	8.8	80.6	80.7	34.6	49.1	14.7	10.5
Black [2]	1,997	2,271	12.5	12.7	60.4	74.9	24.9	37.4	27.0	12.4
Hispanic [3]	899	2,745	12.0	10.8	57.2	64.5	24.4	30.1	30.8	24.7
Male [1]	7,584	8,184	7.4	11.8	76.6	75.7	35.4	43.4	15.9	12.5
White [2]	6,545	6,460	6.2	11.0	79.7	76.6	36.9	43.8	14.1	12.4
Black [2]	911	1,132	15.9	17.8	55.0	68.2	23.9	33.0	29.0	14.1
Hispanic [3]	416	1,453	17.3	12.5	54.6	58.4	25.2	24.5	27.9	29.0
Female [1]	8,109	7,732	4.2	6.8	79.2	84.6	31.8	53.3	16.6	8.6
White [2]	6,903	6,051	3.2	6.5	81.4	85.0	32.4	54.8	15.3	8.5
Black [2]	1,085	1,130	9.7	7.7	65.0	81.7	25.8	41.7	25.4	10.5
Hispanic [3]	484	1,294	7.6	8.8	59.3	71.3	23.6	36.2	33.1	19.9

[1] Includes other races not shown separately. [2] For 2005, for persons who selected this race group only. See footnote 2, Table 217. [3] Persons of Hispanic origin may be of any race.

Source: U.S. Census Bureau, Current Population Reports, PPL-148; and earlier PPL and P-20 reports; and data published on the Internet. See Internet site <http://www.census.gov/population/www/socdemo/school.html>.

Table 267. Employment Status of High School Graduates and School Dropouts: 1980 to 2005

[In thousands (11,622 represents 11,622,000), except percent. As of October. For civilian noninstitutional population 16 to 24 years old. Based on Current Population Survey; see text, Section 1, and Appendix III]

Employment status, sex, and race	Graduates [1]				Dropouts [3]			
	1980	1990	2000 [2]	2005 [2]	1980	1990	2000 [2]	2005 [2]
Civilian population	11,622	8,370	7,351	7,068	5,254	3,800	3,776	3,458
In labor force	9,795	7,107	6,195	5,736	3,549	2,506	2,612	2,378
Percent of population	84.3	84.9	84.3	81.1	67.5	66.0	69.2	68.8
Employed	8,567	6,279	5,632	5,101	2,651	1,993	2,150	1,968
Percent of labor force	87.5	88.3	90.9	88.9	74.7	79.5	82.3	82.8
Unemployed	1,228	828	563	634	898	513	463	410
Unemployment rate, total [4]	12.5	11.7	9.1	11.1	25.3	20.5	17.7	17.3
Male	13.5	11.1	9.3	10.7	23.5	18.8	16.3	15.3
Female	11.5	12.3	8.8	11.5	28.7	23.5	20.3	21.2
White [5]	10.8	9.0	7.2	9.4	21.6	17.0	15.0	14.4
Black [5]	26.1	26.0	18.1	18.3	43.2	43.3	33.2	34.3
Not in labor force	1,827	1,262	1,156	1,332	1,705	1,294	1,163	1,080
Percent of population	15.7	15.1	15.7	18.8	32.5	34.0	30.8	31.2

[1] For persons not enrolled in college who have completed 4 years of high school only. [2] Data not strictly comparable with data for earlier years. See text, this section, and February 2000 and 2005 issues of Employment and Earnings. [3] For persons not in regular school and who have not completed the 12th grade nor received a general equivalency degree. [4] Includes other races not shown separately. [5] For 2005, for persons who selected this race group only. See footnote 2, Table 217.

Source: U.S. Bureau of Labor Statistics, Bulletin 2307; News, USDL 06-514, March 24, 2006; and unpublished data. See Internet site <http://www.bls.gov/news.release/hsgec.toc.htm>.

Table 268. General Educational Development (GED) Credentials Issued: 1975 to 2004

[GEDs issued in thousands (340 represents 340,000). For the 50 states and DC]

Year	GEDs issued	Percent distribution by age of test taker				
		19 years old or under	20 to 24 years old	25 to 29 years old	30 to 34 years old	35 years old and over
1975	340	33	26	14	9	18
1980	479	37	27	13	8	15
1985	413	32	26	15	10	16
1990	410	36	25	13	10	15
1995	504	38	25	13	9	15
2000	487	45	25	11	7	13
2001	648	41	26	11	8	14
2002	330	49	25	10	6	11
2003	387	47	26	10	7	11
2004	406	46	26	11	6	10

Source: U.S. National Center for Education Statistics, *Digest of Education Statistics*, annual.

Table 269. College Enrollment of Recent High School Completers: 1970 to 2005

[2,758 represents 2,758,000. For persons 16 to 24 years old who graduated from high school in the preceding 12 months. Includes persons receiving GEDs. Based on surveys and subject to sampling error; data will not agree with data in other tables]

Year	Number of high school completers (1,000)						Percent enrolled in college [5]					
	Total [1]	Male	Female	White [2]	Black [2, 3]	His-panic [3, 4]	Total [1]	Male	Female	White [2]	Black [2, 3]	His-panic [3, 4]
1970 . . .	2,758	1,343	1,415	2,461	(NA)	(NA)	51.7	55.2	48.5	52.0	(NA)	(NA)
1975 . . .	3,185	1,513	1,672	2,701	302	132	50.7	52.6	49.0	51.1	41.7	58.0
1980 . . .	3,088	1,498	1,589	2,554	350	130	49.3	46.7	51.8	49.8	42.7	52.3
1985 . . .	2,668	1,287	1,381	2,104	332	141	57.7	58.6	56.8	60.1	42.2	51.0
1990 . . .	2,362	1,173	1,189	1,819	331	121	60.1	58.0	62.2	63.0	46.8	42.7
1992 . . .	2,397	1,216	1,180	1,724	354	198	61.9	60.0	63.8	64.3	48.2	55.0
1993 . . .	2,342	1,120	1,223	1,719	304	201	62.6	59.9	65.2	62.9	55.6	62.2
1994 . . .	2,517	1,244	1,273	1,915	316	178	61.9	60.6	63.2	64.5	50.8	49.1
1995 . . .	2,599	1,238	1,361	1,861	349	288	61.9	62.6	61.3	64.3	51.2	53.7
1996 . . .	2,660	1,297	1,363	1,875	406	227	65.0	60.1	69.7	67.4	56.0	50.8
1997 . . .	2,769	1,354	1,415	1,909	384	336	67.0	63.6	70.3	68.2	58.5	65.6
1998 . . .	2,810	1,452	1,358	1,980	386	314	65.6	62.4	69.1	68.5	61.9	47.4
1999 . . .	2,897	1,474	1,423	1,978	436	329	62.9	61.4	64.4	66.3	58.9	42.3
2000 . . .	2,756	1,251	1,505	1,938	393	300	63.3	59.9	66.2	65.7	54.9	52.9
2001 . . .	2,549	1,277	1,273	1,834	381	241	61.8	60.1	63.5	64.3	55.0	51.7
2002 . . .	2,796	1,412	1,384	1,903	382	344	65.2	62.1	68.4	69.1	59.4	53.6
2003 . . .	2,677	1,306	1,372	1,832	327	314	63.9	61.2	66.5	66.2	57.5	58.6
2004 . . .	2,752	1,327	1,425	1,854	398	286	66.7	61.4	71.5	68.8	62.5	61.8
2005 . . .	2,675	1,262	1,414	1,799	345	390	68.6	66.5	70.4	73.2	55.7	54.0

NA Not available. [1] Includes other races, not shown separately. [2] Beginning 2003, for persons of this race group only. See footnote 2, Table 217. [3] Due to small sample size, data are subject to relatively large sampling errors. [4] Persons of Hispanic origin may be of any race. [5] As of October.

Source: U.S. National Center for Education Statistics, *Digest of Education Statistics*, annual.

Table 270. College Enrollment by Sex and Attendance Status: 1983 to 2005

[As of fall. In thousands (12,465 represents 12,465,000)]

Sex and age	1983		1988		1993		1998 [1]		2005 [1]	
	Total	Part-time	Total	Part-time	Total	Part-time	Total	Part-time	Total	Part-time
Total	12,465	5,204	13,055	5,619	14,305	8,128	14,507	5,944	17,487	6,690
Male	6,024	2,264	6,002	2,340	6,427	3,891	6,369	2,436	7,456	2,653
14 to 17 years old	102	16	55	5	83	72	45	5	78	16
18 to 19 years old	1,256	158	1,290	132	1,224	1,086	1,535	296	1,585	243
20 to 21 years old	1,241	205	1,243	216	1,294	1,084	1,374	245	1,764	360
22 to 24 years old	1,158	382	1,106	378	1,260	868	1,127	350	1,376	415
25 to 29 years old	1,115	624	875	485	950	386	908	485	1,066	544
30 to 34 years old	570	384	617	456	661	177	463	322	509	311
35 years old and over. . .	583	494	816	668	955	216	917	733	1,078	764
Female	6,441	2,940	7,053	3,278	7,877	4,237	8,138	3,508	10,032	4,038
14 to 17 years old	142	16	115	17	93	87	74	21	97	22
18 to 19 years old	1,496	179	1,536	195	1,416	1,244	1,847	292	2,076	314
20 to 21 years old	1,125	204	1,278	218	1,414	1,135	1,437	295	1,964	388
22 to 24 years old	884	378	932	403	1,263	770	1,250	463	1,671	542
25 to 29 years old	947	658	932	633	1,058	369	1,083	617	1,390	739
30 to 34 years old	721	553	698	499	811	236	732	506	803	514
35 years old and over. . .	1,126	953	1,563	1,313	1,824	397	1,715	1,315	2,031	1,519

[1] In this table, data beginning in 1998 reflect the new classification of institutions. See footnote 1, Table 271.

Source: U.S. National Center for Education Statistics, *Digest of Education Statistics*, annual.

Table 271. **Higher Education—Institutions and Enrollment 1980 to 2005**

[As of fall (686 represents 686,000). Covers universities, colleges, professional schools, junior, and teachers colleges, both publicly and privately controlled, regular session. Includes estimates for institutions not reporting. See also Appendix III]

Item	Unit	1980	1985	1990	1995	2000	2002	2003	2004	2005
ALL INSTITUTIONS										
Number of institutions [1]	Number ..	3,231	3,340	3,559	3,706	4,182	4,168	4,236	4,216	4,276
4-year	Number...	1,957	2,029	2,141	2,244	2,450	2,466	2,530	2,533	2,582
2-year	Number...	1,274	1,311	1,418	1,462	1,732	1,702	1,706	1,683	1,694
Instructional staff—										
(lecturer or above) [2]	1,000	686	715	817	932	(NA)	(NA)	1,175	(NA)	1,290
Percent full-time	Percent ...	66	64	61	59	(NA)	(NA)	54	(NA)	52
Total enrollment [3, 4]	1,000	12,097	12,247	13,819	14,262	15,312	16,612	16,900	17,272	17,487
Male	1,000	5,874	5,818	6,284	6,343	6,722	7,202	7,256	7,387	7,456
Female	1,000	6,223	6,429	7,535	7,919	8,591	9,410	9,645	9,885	10,032
4-year institutions	1,000	7,571	7,716	8,579	8,769	9,364	10,082	10,408	10,726	10,999
2-year institutions	1,000	4,526	4,531	5,240	5,493	5,948	6,529	6,493	6,546	6,488
Full-time	1,000	7,098	7,075	7,821	8,129	9,010	9,946	10,312	10,610	10,797
Part-time	1,000	4,999	5,172	5,998	6,133	6,303	6,665	6,589	6,662	6,690
Public	1,000	9,457	9,479	10,845	11,092	11,753	12,752	12,857	12,980	13,022
Private	1,000	2,640	2,768	2,974	3,169	3,560	3,860	4,043	4,292	4,466
Not-for-profit	1,000	2,528	2,572	2,760	2,929	3,109	3,265	3,341	3,412	3,455
For profit	1,000	112	196	213	240	450	594	703	880	1,011
Undergraduate [4]	1,000	10,475	10,597	11,959	12,232	13,155	14,257	14,474	14,781	14,964
Men	1,000	5,000	4,962	5,380	5,401	5,778	6,192	6,224	6,340	6,409
Women	1,000	5,475	5,635	6,579	6,831	7,377	8,065	8,250	8,441	8,555
First-time freshmen	1,000	2,588	2,292	2,257	2,169	2,428	2,571	2,605	2,630	2,657
First professional	1,000	278	274	273	298	307	319	329	335	337
Men	1,000	199	180	167	174	164	163	166	168	170
Women	1,000	78	94	107	124	143	156	163	166	167
Graduate [4]	1,000	1,343	1,376	1,586	1,732	1,850	2,036	2,098	2,157	2,186
Men	1,000	675	677	737	768	780	847	865	879	877
Women	1,000	670	700	849	965	1,071	1,189	1,233	1,278	1,309
2-YEAR INSTITUTIONS										
Number of institutions [1, 5]	Number ..	1,274	1,311	1,418	1,462	1,732	1,702	1,706	1,683	1,694
Public	Number...	945	932	972	1,047	1,076	1,081	1,086	1,061	1,053
Private	Number...	329	379	446	415	656	621	620	622	641
Instructional staff—										
(lecturer or above) [2]	1,000	192	211	(NA)	285	(NA)	(NA)	359	(NA)	373
Enrollment [3, 4]	1,000	4,526	4,531	5,240	5,493	5,948	6,529	6,493	6,546	6,488
Public	1,000	4,329	4,270	4,996	5,278	5,697	6,270	6,208	6,244	6,184
Private	1,000	198	261	244	215	251	259	285	302	304
Male	1,000	2,047	2,002	2,233	2,329	2,559	2,753	2,689	2,698	2,680
Female	1,000	2,479	2,529	3,007	3,164	3,390	3,776	3,804	3,848	3,808

NA Not available. [1] Number of institutions includes count of branch campuses. Due to revised survey procedures, data beginning 1990 are not comparable with previous years. Beginning 1996 (2000 for this table), data reflect a new classification of institutions; this classification includes some additional, primarily 2-year, colleges and excludes a few institutions that did not award degrees. Includes institutions that were eligible to participate in Title IV federal financial aid programs. [2] Due to revised survey methods, data beginning 1990 not comparable with previous years. [3] Branch campuses counted according to actual status, e.g., 2-year branch in 2-year category. [4] Includes unclassified students. (Students taking courses for credit, but are not candidates for degrees.) [5] Includes schools accredited by the National Association of Trade and Technical Schools. See footnote 1 for information pertaining to data beginning 2000.

Source: U.S. National Center for Education Statistics, *Digest of Education Statistics*, annual; and unpublished data.

Table 272. College Enrollment by Selected Characteristics: 1990 to 2005

[In thousands (13,818.6 represents 13,818,600). As of fall. Nonresident alien students are not distributed among racial/ethnic groups]

Characteristic	1990	1995	2000 [1]	2001 [1]	2002 [1]	2003 [1]	2004 [1]	2005 [1]
Total..........	13,818.6	14,261.8	15,312.3	15,928.0	16,611.7	16,900.5	17,272.0	17,487.5
Male...........	6,283.9	6,342.5	6,721.8	6,960.8	7,202.1	7,255.6	7,387.3	7,455.9
Female.........	7,534.7	7,919.2	8,590.5	8,967.2	9,409.6	9,644.9	9,884.8	10,031.6
Public.........	10,844.7	11,092.4	11,752.8	12,233.2	12,752.0	12,857.1	12,980.1	13,021.8
Private........	2,973.9	3,169.4	3,559.5	3,694.8	3,859.7	4,043.4	4,291.9	4,465.6
2-year.........	5,240.1	5,492.5	5,948.4	6,250.6	6,529.4	6,492.9	6,545.9	6,488.1
4-year.........	8,578.6	8,769.3	9,363.9	9,677.4	10,082.3	10,407.6	10,726.2	10,999.4
Undergraduate.......	11,959.2	12,232.0	13,155.4	13,715.6	14,257.1	14,473.9	14,780.6	14,964.0
Graduate	1,586.2	1,732.0	1,850.3	1,903.7	2,035.7	2,097.5	2,156.9	2,186.5
First professional	273.4	297.6	306.6	308.6	319.0	329.1	334.5	337.0
White [2]	10,722.5	10,311.2	10,462.1	10,774.5	11,140.2	11,275.4	11,422.8	11,495.4
Male	4,861.0	4,594.1	4,634.6	4,762.3	4,897.9	4,927.9	4,988.0	5,007.2
Female.........	5,861.5	5,717.2	5,827.5	6,012.2	6,242.3	6,347.5	6,434.8	6,488.2
Public.........	8,385.4	7,945.4	7,963.4	8,214.0	8,490.5	8,531.4	8,546.3	8,518.2
Private........	2,337.0	2,365.9	2,498.7	2,560.5	2,649.8	2,744.1	2,876.5	2,977.3
2-year.........	3,954.3	3,794.0	3,804.1	3,955.7	4,086.5	4,076.7	4,063.8	3,998.6
4-year.........	6,768.1	6,517.2	6,658.0	6,818.8	7,053.8	7,198.7	7,359.0	7,496.9
Undergraduate.......	9,272.6	8,805.6	8,983.5	9,278.7	9,564.9	9,662.5	9,771.3	9,828.6
Graduate	1,228.4	1,282.3	1,258.5	1,275.1	1,348.0	1,378.6	1,413.3	1,428.7
First professional	221.5	223.3	220.1	220.8	227.4	234.3	238.2	238.1
Black [2]	1,247.0	1,473.7	1,730.3	1,850.4	1,978.7	2,068.9	2,164.7	2,214.6
Male	484.7	555.9	635.3	672.4	708.6	730.6	758.4	774.1
Female.........	762.3	917.8	1,095.0	1,178.0	1,270.2	1,338.2	1,406.3	1,440.4
Public.........	976.4	1,160.6	1,319.2	1,397.1	1,487.2	1,533.5	1,574.6	1,580.4
Private........	270.6	313.0	411.1	453.3	491.6	535.3	590.1	634.2
2-year.........	524.3	621.5	734.9	795.7	859.1	879.9	905.8	901.1
4-year.........	722.8	852.2	995.4	1,054.7	1,119.7	1,189.0	1,258.9	1,313.4
Undergraduate.......	1,147.2	1,333.6	1,548.9	1,657.1	1763.8	1,838.2	1,918.5	1,955.4
Graduate	83.9	118.6	157.9	169.4	189.6	204.9	220.4	233.2
First professional	15.9	21.4	23.5	23.9	25.3	25.8	25.9	26.0
Hispanic	782.4	1,093.8	1,461.8	1,560.6	1,661.7	1,716.0	1,809.6	1,882.0
Male	353.9	480.2	627.1	664.2	699.0	709.1	745.1	774.6
Female.........	428.5	613.7	834.7	896.4	962.7	1,006.9	1,064.5	1,107.3
Public.........	671.4	937.1	1,229.3	1,308.8	1,388.7	1,414.6	1,477.4	1,525.6
Private........	111.0	156.8	232.5	251.8	273.1	301.4	332.2	356.4
2-year.........	424.2	608.4	843.9	904.3	958.9	932.6	972.4	981.5
4-year.........	358.2	485.5	617.9	656.3	702.9	783.4	837.2	900.5
Undergraduate.......	724.6	1,012.0	1,351.0	1,444.4	1,533.3	1,579.6	1,666.9	1,733.6
Graduate	47.2	68.0	95.4	100.5	112.3	119.5	125.8	130.7
First professional	10.7	13.8	15.4	15.6	16.1	16.9	17.0	17.7
American Indian/ Alaska Native	102.8	131.3	151.2	158.2	165.9	172.7	176.1	176.3
Male	43.1	54.8	61.4	63.6	65.7	67.1	68.6	68.4
Female.........	59.7	76.5	89.7	94.5	100.2	105.6	107.5	107.9
Public.........	90.4	113.8	127.3	133.6	140.0	144.3	144.4	143.0
Private........	12.4	17.5	23.9	24.6	25.9	28.3	31.8	33.3
2-year.........	54.9	65.6	74.7	78.2	81.3	82.2	82.2	80.7
4-year.........	47.9	65.7	76.5	80.0	84.6	90.4	93.9	95.6
Undergraduate.......	95.5	120.7	138.5	144.8	151.7	157.8	160.3	160.4
Graduate	6.2	8.5	10.3	11.2	11.9	12.5	13.4	13.4
First professional	1.1	2.1	2.3	2.1	2.2	2.3	2.4	2.5
Asian/ Pacific Islander	572.4	797.4	978.2	1,019.0	1,074.2	1,075.7	1,108.7	1,134.4
Male	294.9	393.3	465.9	480.8	503.9	498.1	511.6	522.0
Female.........	277.5	404.1	512.3	538.3	570.2	577.6	597.1	612.4
Public.........	461.0	638.0	770.5	806.1	851.6	845.2	866.1	881.9
Private........	111.5	159.4	207.7	213.0	222.6	230.5	242.6	252.4
2-year.........	215.2	314.9	401.9	417.5	441.0	425.3	430.7	434.4
4-year.........	357.2	482.4	576.3	601.6	633.1	650.4	678.0	700.0
Undergraduate.......	500.5	692.2	845.5	883.9	927.4	922.7	949.9	971.4
Graduate	53.2	75.6	95.8	97.4	107.1	111.7	115.9	118.4
First professional	18.7	29.6	36.8	37.7	39.6	41.3	42.9	44.6
Nonresident alien ...	391.5	454.4	528.7	565.3	590.9	591.8	590.2	584.8
Male	246.3	264.3	297.3	317.4	327.0	322.7	315.6	309.5
Female.........	145.2	190.1	231.4	247.8	263.9	269.2	274.6	275.3
Public.........	260.0	297.5	343.1	373.6	394.1	388.0	371.4	372.8
Private........	131.4	156.9	185.6	191.6	196.8	203.9	218.8	212.0
2-year.........	67.1	88.1	89.0	99.2	102.6	96.2	90.9	91.8
4-year.........	324.3	366.2	439.7	466.1	488.3	495.6	499.2	493.1
Undergraduate.......	218.7	267.6	288.0	306.7	316.0	313.0	313.8	314.7
Graduate	167.3	179.5	232.3	250.1	266.6	270.4	268.1	262.1
First professional	5.4	7.3	8.4	8.4	8.3	8.4	8.2	8.1

[1] In this table, data beginning 2000 reflect a new classification of institutions; see footnote 1, Table 271.   [2] Non-Hispanic.

Source: U.S. National Center for Education Statistics, *Digest of Education Statistics,* annual.

Education 175

Table 273. Degree-Granting Institutions, Number and Enrollment by State: 2005

[17,487 represents 17,487,000. Number of institutions beginning in academic year. Opening fall enrollment of resident and extension students attending full-time or part-time. Excludes students taking courses for credit by mail, radio, or TV, and students in branches of U.S. institutions operated in foreign countries. See Appendix III]

State	Number of institutions[1]	Enrollment (1,000) Total	Male	Female	Public	Private	Full-time	White[2]	Minority enrollment Total[3]	Black[2]	Hispanic	Nonresident alien
United States..	**4,276**	**17,487**	**7,456**	**10,032**	**13,022**	**4,466**	**10,797**	**11,495**	**5,407**	**2,215**	**1,882**	**585**
Alabama	66	256	106	150	228	28	170	166	84	75	4	6
Alaska.	8	30	12	18	29	1	13	22	8	1	1	1
Arizona	76	546	223	322	321	225	353	347	172	49	86	26
Arkansas	48	143	58	85	128	15	94	108	33	26	3	3
California	408	2,400	1,057	1,343	2,008	392	1,222	1,034	1,291	186	632	74
Colorado	78	303	132	170	235	68	180	231	65	16	34	6
Connecticut	44	175	72	102	112	63	111	127	41	19	14	6
Delaware	10	52	20	31	39	13	33	37	14	10	2	1
District of Columbia	15	105	42	62	6	99	62	50	48	36	5	7
Florida.	169	873	359	514	649	224	495	493	348	155	160	31
Georgia	132	427	172	255	342	85	282	256	159	131	11	12
Hawaii.	23	67	28	39	50	17	40	18	44	2	2	5
Idaho	14	78	35	43	60	17	53	69	7	1	4	2
Illinois	172	833	357	476	555	278	486	543	266	119	96	24
Indiana	100	361	162	200	267	94	251	299	49	30	10	13
Iowa	65	228	98	130	149	79	149	197	24	12	6	7
Kansas	62	192	85	107	170	21	113	156	30	11	9	6
Kentucky.	76	245	105	140	202	43	153	213	28	21	3	4
Louisiana.	90	198	79	119	181	17	147	123	68	60	4	6
Maine	30	66	26	39	48	18	41	60	4	1	1	1
Maryland	58	314	128	187	256	58	169	181	121	87	12	12
Massachusetts . . .	121	443	188	256	188	255	305	321	96	35	27	26
Michigan	104	627	267	360	506	121	364	478	127	83	18	22
Minnesota	109	362	152	210	241	121	229	300	53	24	8	9
Mississippi.	41	150	58	93	136	15	115	87	62	59	1	2
Missouri.	128	374	158	216	218	157	226	296	69	47	11	9
Montana	23	48	22	26	43	5	36	41	6	(Z)	1	1
Nebraska.	39	121	54	67	93	28	80	105	13	5	4	3
Nevada	23	111	48	62	100	11	53	70	38	9	16	3
New Hampshire . .	26	70	29	41	41	29	48	63	5	1	2	2
New Jersey	59	380	163	217	304	75	228	227	138	54	51	15
New Mexico	42	131	53	78	121	10	69	57	72	4	54	3
New York.	308	1,152	482	670	626	526	811	699	384	160	130	69
North Carolina . . .	128	484	194	291	397	88	309	326	147	117	12	12
North Dakota	22	49	24	26	43	7	37	43	5	1	(Z)	2
Ohio	200	616	265	352	453	163	417	496	102	75	12	17
Oklahoma	57	208	90	118	179	29	135	146	52	19	7	9
Oregon	60	200	89	111	164	36	121	163	32	5	11	6
Pennsylvania	259	692	300	392	380	312	502	546	123	71	21	23
Rhode Island	14	81	35	46	40	41	59	65	14	5	5	3
South Carolina . . .	64	210	82	128	175	36	142	142	65	58	3	3
South Dakota	24	49	21	28	38	11	33	43	5	1	1	1
Tennessee.	98	283	117	166	200	83	204	211	67	55	5	6
Texas	213	1,241	536	705	1,081	159	695	645	547	153	325	48
Utah	31	201	102	99	149	52	122	175	20	2	10	6
Vermont	25	40	18	22	24	16	29	36	3	1	1	1
Virginia	107	439	186	253	349	90	269	300	128	85	17	11
Washington	80	348	152	196	297	52	216	264	74	15	20	10
West Virginia	44	100	43	56	85	14	74	89	8	5	1	2
Wisconsin	68	335	143	192	269	66	215	288	40	17	10	7
Wyoming	10	35	16	19	33	3	20	32	3	(Z)	2	1
U.S. military[4] . .	5	15	13	3	15	(X)	15	12	3	1	1	(Z)

X Not applicable.   Z Fewer than 500.   [1] Branch campuses counted as separate institutions.   [2] Non-Hispanic.   [3] Includes other races not shown separately.   [4] Service schools.

Source: U.S. National Center for Education Statistics, *Digest of Education Statistics*, annual.

Table 274. **College Enrollment by Sex, Age, Race, and Hispanic Origin: 1980 to 2005**

[In thousands (11,387 represents 11,387,000). As of October for the civilian noninstitutional population, 14 years old and over. Based on the Current Population Survey; see text, Section 1, and Appendix III]

Characteristic	1980	1985	1990 [1]	1995	1999	2000	2001	2002	2003	2004	2005
Total [2]	11,387	12,524	13,621	14,715	15,203	15,314	15,873	16,497	16,638	17,383	17,472
Male [3]	5,430	5,906	6,192	6,703	6,956	6,682	6,875	7,240	7,318	7,575	7,539
18 to 24 years old	3,604	3,749	3,922	4,089	4,397	4,342	4,437	4,629	4,697	4,866	4,972
25 to 34 years old	1,325	1,464	1,412	1,561	1,458	1,361	1,476	1,460	1,590	1,604	1,486
35 years old and over . .	405	561	772	985	1,024	918	908	1,071	970	1,033	1,019
Female [3]	5,957	6,618	7,429	8,013	8,247	8,631	8,998	9,258	9,319	9,808	9,933
18 to 24 years old	3,625	3,788	4,042	4,452	4,863	5,109	5,192	5,404	5,667	5,742	5,859
25 to 34 years old	1,378	1,599	1,749	1,788	1,637	1,846	1,946	1,946	1,904	2,091	2,115
35 years old and over . .	802	1,100	1,546	1,684	1,675	1,589	1,776	1,797	1,660	1,850	1,838
White [3, 4]	9,925	10,781	11,488	12,021	12,053	11,999	12,208	12,781	12,870	13,381	13,467
18 to 24 years old	6,334	6,500	6,635	7,011	7,446	7,566	7,548	7,921	8,150	8,354	8,499
25 to 34 years old	2,328	2,604	2,698	2,686	2,345	2,339	2,469	2,515	2,545	2,748	2,647
35 years old and over . .	1,051	1,448	2,023	2,208	2,174	1,978	2,103	2,236	2,075	2,143	2,206
Male	4,804	5,103	5,235	5,535	5,562	5,311	5,383	5,719	5,714	5,944	5,844
Female	5,121	5,679	6,253	6,486	6,491	6,689	6,826	7,062	7,155	7,438	7,624
Black [3, 4]	1,163	1,263	1,393	1,772	1,998	2,164	2,230	2,278	2,144	2,301	2,297
18 to 24 years old	688	734	894	988	1,146	1,216	1,206	1,227	1,225	1,238	1,229
25 to 34 years old	289	295	258	426	453	567	562	542	503	522	520
35 years old and over . .	156	213	207	334	354	361	429	454	388	502	448
Male	476	552	587	710	833	815	781	802	798	776	864
Female	686	712	807	1,062	1,164	1,349	1,449	1,476	1,346	1,525	1,435
Hispanic origin [3, 5]	443	580	748	1,207	1,307	1,426	1,700	1,656	1,714	1,975	1,942
18 to 24 years old	315	375	435	745	740	899	1,035	979	1,115	1,223	1,216
25 to 34 years old	118	189	168	250	334	309	392	414	380	460	438
35 years old and over . .	(NA)	(NA)	130	193	226	195	260	249	207	271	257
Male	222	279	364	568	568	619	731	705	703	852	804
Female	221	299	384	639	739	807	969	951	1,011	1,123	1,139

NA Not available.   [1] Beginning 1990, based on a revised edit and tabulation package.   [2] Includes other races not shown separately.   [3] Includes persons 14 to 17 years old, not shown separately.   [4] Beginning 2003, for persons who selected this race group only. See footnote 2, Table 217.   [5] Persons of Hispanic origin may be of any race.

Source: U.S. Census Bureau, *Current Population Reports*, PPL-148; and earlier PPL and P-20 reports. See Internet site <http://www.census.gov/population/www/socdemo/school.html>.

Table 275. **Foreign (Nonimmigrant) Student Enrollment in College: 1976 to 2006**

[In thousands (179 represents 179,000). For fall of the previous year]

Region of origin	1976	1980	1985	1990	1995	1997	1998	1999	2000	2001	2002	2003	2004	2005	2006
All regions . . .	179	286	342	387	453	458	481	491	515	548	583	586	573	565	565
Africa	25	36	40	25	21	22	23	26	30	34	38	40	38	36	36
Nigeria	11	16	18	4	2	2	2	3	4	4	4	6	6	6	6
Asia [1, 2]	97	165	200	245	292	291	308	308	315	339	363	367	356	356	346
China: Taiwan . . .	11	18	23	31	36	30	31	31	29	29	29	28	26	26	28
Hong Kong	12	10	10	11	13	11	10	9	8	8	8	8	7	7	8
India	10	9	15	26	34	31	34	37	42	55	67	75	80	80	77
Indonesia	1	2	7	9	12	12	13	12	11	12	12	10	9	8	8
Iran	20	51	17	7	3	2	2	2	2	2	2	2	2	2	2
Japan	7	12	13	30	45	46	47	46	47	46	47	46	41	42	39
Malaysia	2	4	22	14	14	15	15	12	9	8	7	7	6	6	6
Saudi Arabia	3	10	8	4	4	4	5	5	5	5	6	4	4	3	3
South Korea	3	5	16	22	34	37	43	39	41	46	49	52	52	53	59
Thailand	7	7	7	7	11	13	15	12	11	11	12	10	9	9	9
Europe [3]	14	23	33	46	65	68	72	74	78	81	82	78	74	72	85
Latin America [1, 4] . . .	30	42	49	48	47	50	51	55	62	64	68	69	66	68	65
Mexico	5	6	6	7	9	9	10	10	11	11	13	13	13	13	14
Venezuela	5	10	10	3	4	5	5	5	5	5	6	5	6	5	5
North America	10	16	16	19	23	24	23	23	24	26	27	27	28	29	29
Canada	10	15	15	18	23	23	22	23	24	25	27	27	27	28	28
Oceania	3	4	4	4	4	4	4	4	5	5	5	5	5	4	5

[1] Includes countries not shown separately.   [2] Beginning 2006, excludes Cyprus and Turkey.   [3] Beginning 2006, includes Cyprus and Turkey.   [4] Includes Central America, Caribbean, and South America.

Source: Institute of International Education, New York, NY, *Open Doors Report on International Educational Exchange*, annual (copyright).

Table 276. College Enrollment—Summary by Sex, Race, and Hispanic Origin: 2005

[In thousands (17,472 represents 17,472,000), except percent. As of October. Covers civilian noninstitutional population 15 years old and over enrolled in colleges and graduate schools. Based on Current Population Survey, see text, Section 1, and Appendix III]

Characteristic	Total			Race and Hispanic origin				
				White [2]				
	Number [1]	Male	Female	Total	Non-Hispanic	Black [2]	Asian [2]	Hispanic [3]
Total enrollment	**17,472**	**7,539**	**9,933**	**13,466**	**11,714**	**2,299**	**1,184**	**1,941**
15 to 17 years old	182	62	119	116	94	31	22	32
18 to 19 years old	3,727	1,676	2,052	2,972	2,619	451	188	405
20 to 21 years old	3,945	1,877	2,067	3,177	2,769	397	271	420
22 to 24 years old	3,162	1,420	1,742	2,350	2,006	447	232	388
25 to 29 years old	2,291	924	1,367	1,708	1,445	292	225	288
30 to 34 years old	1,309	562	748	939	807	228	113	150
35 years old and over	2,858	1,019	1,838	2,206	1,978	446	130	255
Type of school:								
2-year	4,327	1,866	2,462	3,230	2,663	702	223	641
15 to 19 years old	1,259	570	689	979	807	163	62	199
20 to 24 years old	1,436	686	750	1,066	854	218	91	236
25 years old and over. . .	1,631	611	1,020	1,186	1,004	319	69	204
4-year	9,841	4,324	5,517	7,702	6,754	1,271	572	1,029
15 to 19 years old	2,643	1,167	1,476	2,102	1,899	319	148	238
20 to 24 years old	5,000	2,329	2,671	3,954	3,465	563	317	515
25 years old and over. . .	2,200	829	1,374	1,646	1,392	387	103	277
Graduate school	3,304	1,349	1,954	2,534	2,297	326	389	271
15 to 24 years old	678	283	394	514	463	63	95	57
25 to 34 years old	1,458	662	796	1,084	965	115	224	130
35 years old and over. . .	1,169	403	763	937	869	145	72	82
Public	13,435	5,733	7,702	10,303	8,852	1,800	904	1,625
2-year	3,890	1,672	2,218	2,921	2,389	612	204	604
4-year	7,402	3,212	4,190	5,751	4,974	967	448	853
Graduate	2,143	849	1,294	1,631	1,489	221	252	168
Percent of students:								
Employed full-time.	17.9	17.1	18.6	18.0	18.4	18.8	15.8	16.1
Employed part-time	25.4	23.3	27.2	22.6	29.1	15.4	21.9	18.6

[1] Includes other races, not shown separately.   [2] For persons who selected this race group only. See footnote 2, Table 217.
[3] Persons of Hispanic origin may be of any race.

Source: U.S. Census Bureau, unpublished data. See Internet site <http://www.census.gov/population/www/socdemo/school.html>.

Table 277. Higher Education Enrollments in Foreign Languages: 1970 to 2002

[As of fall (1,111.5 represents 1,111,500). For credit enrollment]

Enrollment	1970	1977	1980	1983	1986	1990	1995	1998	2002
Registrations [1] (1,000).	**1,111.5**	**933.5**	**924.8**	**966.0**	**1,003.2**	**1,184.1**	**1,138.8**	**1,193.8**	**1,397.3**
By selected language (1,000):									
Spanish	389.2	376.7	379.4	386.2	411.3	533.9	606.3	656.6	746.3
French	359.3	246.1	248.4	270.1	275.3	272.5	205.4	199.1	202.0
German	202.6	135.4	126.9	128.2	121.0	133.3	96.3	89.0	91.1
Italian	34.2	33.3	34.8	38.7	40.9	49.7	43.8	49.3	63.9
American Sign Language	(X)	(X)	(X)	(X)	(X)	1.6	4.3	11.4	60.8
Japanese	6.6	10.7	11.5	16.1	23.5	45.7	44.7	43.1	52.2
Chinese	6.2	9.8	11.4	13.2	16.9	19.5	26.5	28.5	34.2
Latin.	27.6	24.4	25.0	24.2	25.0	28.2	25.9	26.1	29.8
Russian	36.2	27.8	24.0	30.4	34.0	44.6	24.7	23.8	23.9
Hebrew.	16.6	19.4	19.4	18.2	15.6	13.0	13.1	15.8	22.8
Ancient Greek	16.7	25.8	22.1	19.4	17.6	16.4	16.3	16.4	20.4
Arabic.	1.3	3.1	3.5	3.4	3.4	3.5	4.4	5.5	10.6
Portuguese	5.1	5.0	4.9	4.4	5.1	6.2	6.5	6.9	8.4
Korean	0.1	0.2	0.4	0.7	0.9	2.3	3.3	4.5	5.2
Index (1965 = 100).	107.3	90.1	89.3	93.2	96.8	114.3	109.9	115.2	134.9

X Not applicable.   [1] Includes other foreign languages, not shown separately.

Source: Association of Departments of Foreign Languages, New York, NY, ADFL Bulletin, Vol. 35, No. 2-3, Winter-Spring 2004 (copyright). For 1970 to 1998, consult prior ADFL Bulletins.

Table 278. College Freshmen—Summary Characteristics: 1970 to 2006

[In percent, except as indicated (12.8 represents $12,800). As of fall for first-time full-time freshmen in 4-year colleges and universities. Based on sample survey and subject to sampling error; see source]

Characteristic	1970	1980	1985	1990	1995	2000	2004	2005	2006
Sex: Male	52.1	48.8	48.9	46.9	45.6	45.2	44.9	45.0	45.1
Female	47.9	51.2	51.1	53.1	54.4	54.8	55.1	55.0	54.9
Applied to three or more colleges	(NA)	31.5	35.4	42.9	44.4	52.5	52.8	55.4	56.5
Average grade in high school:									
A– to A+	19.6	26.6	28.7	29.4	36.1	42.9	47.5	46.6	46.0
B– to B+	62.5	58.2	57.1	57.0	54.2	50.5	47.6	48.0	49.4
C to C+	17.7	14.9	14.0	13.4	9.6	6.5	5.0	5.4	4.6
D	0.3	0.2	0.2	0.2	0.1	0.1	0.1	0.1	0.1
Political orientation:									
Liberal	35.7	21.0	22.4	24.6	22.9	24.8	26.1	27.1	28.4
Middle of the road	43.4	57.0	53.1	51.7	51.3	51.9	46.4	45.0	43.3
Conservative	17.3	19.0	21.3	20.6	21.8	18.9	21.9	22.6	23.9
Probable field of study:									
Arts and humanities	(NA)	10.5	10.1	10.5	11.2	12.1	12.0	12.8	13.1
Biological sciences	(NA)	4.5	4.5	4.9	8.3	6.6	7.7	7.6	8.3
Business	(NA)	21.2	24.6	21.1	15.4	16.7	16.0	17.4	17.9
Education	(NA)	8.4	6.9	10.3	10.1	11.0	9.6	9.9	9.5
Engineering	(NA)	11.2	11.0	9.7	8.1	8.7	9.6	8.3	8.0
Physical science	(NA)	3.2	3.2	2.8	3.1	2.6	3.0	3.1	3.1
Social science	(NA)	8.2	9.4	11.0	9.9	10.0	10.3	10.7	11.2
Professional	(NA)	15.5	13.1	13.0	16.5	11.6	15.1	14.6	13.0
Technical	(NA)	3.1	2.4	1.1	1.2	2.1	1.5	1.2	1.1
Data processing/computer programming	(NA)	1.7	1.7	0.7	0.8	1.5	0.6	0.5	0.5
Other [1]	(NA)	14.0	15.1	15.8	16.0	17.9	15.0	14.1	14.2
Communications	(NA)	2.4	2.8	2.9	1.8	2.7	1.9	2.0	2.2
Computer science	(NA)	2.6	2.4	1.7	2.2	3.7	1.4	1.1	1.1
Personal objectives—very important or essential:									
Being very well off financially	36.2	62.5	69.2	72.3	72.8	73.4	73.6	74.5	73.4
Developing a meaningful philosophy of life	79.1	62.5	46.9	45.9	45.4	42.4	42.1	45.0	46.3
Keeping up to date with political affairs	57.2	45.2	(NA)	46.6	32.3	28.1	34.3	36.4	37.2
Attitudes—agree or strongly agree:									
Capital punishment should be abolished	59.4	34.8	27.6	23.1	22.0	31.2	33.2	33.3	34.5
Legalize marijuana	40.6	37.1	21.4	18.8	33.4	34.2	37.2	37.7	37.1
There is too much concern for the rights of criminals	50.7	65.0	(NA)	65.1	73.2	66.5	58.1	57.9	55.9
Abortion should be legalized	85.7	53.7	56.4	65.5	59.9	53.9	53.9	55.2	56.8
Median family income ($1,000)	12.8	24.5	37.3	46.6	54.8	64.4	71.9	73.2	76.2

NA Not available.   [1] Includes other fields, not shown separately.

Source: The Higher Education Research Institute, University of California, Los Angeles, CA, *The American Freshman: National Norms*, annual.

Table 279. Students Reported Disability Status by Selected Characteristic: 2003–2004

[(19,054 represents 19,054,000). Disabled students reported that they had one or more of the following conditions: a specific learning disability, a visual handicap, hard of hearing, deafness, a speech disability, an orthopedic handicap, or a health impairment. Based on the 2003–2004 National Postsecondary Student-Aid Study; see source for details. Includes Puerto Rico. See also Appendix III]

Student characteristic	Undergraduate			Graduate and first-professional		
	All students	Disabled students	Nondisabled students	All students	Disabled students	Nondisabled students
Total students (1,000)	19,054	2,156	16,897	2,826	189	2,637
PERCENT DISTRIBUTION						
Total	100.0	100.0	100.0	100.0	100.0	100.0
Age:						
15 to 23 years old	56.8	45.8	58.2	11.2	8.5	11.4
24 to 29 years old	17.3	15.5	17.5	39.6	33.9	40.0
30 years or older	25.9	38.7	24.3	49.2	57.6	48.6
Sex:						
Male	42.4	42.1	42.4	41.9	38.0	42.2
Female	57.6	57.9	57.6	58.1	62.0	57.8
Race/ethnicity of student:						
White, non-Hispanic	63.1	65.1	62.9	68.3	67.0	68.4
Black, non-Hispanic	14.0	13.2	14.1	9.6	12.5	9.3
Hispanic	12.7	12.3	12.8	7.7	7.9	7.6
Asian/Pacific Islander	5.9	3.8	6.2	11.0	5.9	11.3
American Indian/Alaska Native	0.9	1.2	0.9	0.6	0.4	0.6
Other	3.3	4.4	3.2	2.9	6.3	2.7
Attendance status:						
Full-time, full-year	38.6	33.5	39.2	32.7	28.9	32.9
Part-time or part-year	61.4	66.5	60.8	67.3	71.1	67.1
Student housing status:						
On-campus	13.8	10.7	14.2	(NA)	(NA)	(NA)
Off-campus	55.2	61.5	54.4	(NA)	(NA)	(NA)
With parents or relatives	31.0	27.7	31.4	(NA)	(NA)	(NA)
Dependency status:						
Dependent	49.7	39.4	51.0	(NA)	(NA)	(NA)
Independent, unmarried	15.2	19.5	14.7	47.5	48.1	47.5
Independent, married	7.9	9.1	7.8	18.8	15.7	19.0
Independent with dependents	27.1	32.0	26.5	33.7	36.2	33.6

NA Not available.
Source: U.S. National Center for Education Statistics, *Digest of Education Statistics, 2005*.

Education   179

Table 280. Average Total Price of Attendance of Undergraduate Education: 2003–2004

[In dollars. Excludes students attending more than one institution. Price of attendance includes tuition and fees, books and supplies, room and board, transportation, and personal and other expenses allowed for federal cost of attendance budgets. Based on the 2003–2004 National Postsecondary Student-Aid Study; see source for details. Includes Puerto Rico. See also Appendix III]

Student characteristic	All institutions[1]	Public 2-year	Public 4-year Non-doctorate	Public 4-year Doctorate	Private not-for-profit 4-year Non-doctorate	Private not-for-profit 4-year Doctorate	Private for-profit
Total	11,300	6,100	10,800	13,100	19,400	26,800	14,900
Age: [2]							
18 years or younger	13,500	6,900	12,300	14,800	24,900	30,800	16,500
19 to 23 years	13,200	6,600	11,700	13,900	23,500	29,300	15,200
24 to 29 years	9,500	6,100	9,400	11,200	14,900	17,200	14,700
30 to 39 years	8,600	5,900	9,100	9,800	12,900	14,000	14,600
40 years or older	7,500	5,200	8,400	8,700	11,600	13,300	14,300
Sex:							
Male	11,600	6,100	11,000	13,200	19,400	27,100	16,200
Female	11,000	6,200	10,700	13,000	19,400	26,500	14,000
Race:							
One race:							
White	11,600	6,200	10,900	13,100	20,500	27,500	15,100
Black or African American	10,500	6,300	10,200	13,400	16,700	23,500	14,100
Asian	12,500	6,600	11,200	14,500	22,800	31,300	17,400
American Indian/Alaska Native	9,100	5,800	10,300	11,000	18,600	(S)	13,600
Native Hawaiian or other Pacific Islander	9,500	4,900	(S)	13,800	(S)	(S)	17,400
Other race	11,700	7,100	11,300	12,500	19,600	26,800	15,700
More than one race	11,400	6,100	11,100	13,300	19,500	29,600	15,800
Hispanic or Latino [3]	9,900	5,800	10,300	11,900	16,000	21,400	14,600
Attendance pattern:							
Full-time, full-year	17,200	10,500	13,700	15,900	25,400	32,300	20,300
Full-time, part-year	9,800	5,700	7,500	9,000	15,600	20,200	12,800
Part-time, full-year	8,700	6,500	9,200	11,100	14,400	18,500	13,800
Part-time, part-year	4,200	3,200	4,400	5,200	6,700	8,800	8,500

S Data do not meet publication standards.   [1] Includes public less-than-2-year and private not-for-profit less-than-4-year. [2] As of December 31, 2003.   [3] Persons of Hispanic origin may be of any race.

Source: U.S. National Center for Education Statistics, "Student Financing of Undergraduate Education 2003–04" NCES 2006-186 (released August 23, 2006). See Internet site <http://nces.ed.gov/surveys/npsas/>.

Table 281. Average Amount of Aid Received by Aided Undergraduates: 2003–2004

[In dollars, except percent. Excludes students attending more than one institution. Types of financial aid are grants, loans, and work study. Based on the 2003–2004 National Postsecondary Student-Aid Study; see source for details. Includes Puerto Rico. See also Appendix III]

Student characteristic	Percent of undergraduates receiving aid	All institutions[1]	Public 2-year	Public 4-year Non-doctorate	Public 4-year Doctorate	Private not-for-profit 4-year Non-doctorate	Private not-for-profit 4-year Doctorate	Private for-profit
Total	63.2	7,400	3,200	6,700	8,100	12,100	15,000	8,800
Age: [2]								
18 years or younger	65.5	8,300	3,400	6,800	7,900	15,000	16,900	10,400
19 to 23 years	63.9	8,300	3,200	6,900	8,100	14,600	16,000	9,000
24 to 29 years	66.8	6,800	3,500	6,600	8,700	9,700	11,500	8,700
30 to 39 years	63.3	5,800	3,200	6,800	7,600	7,800	8,300	8,400
40 years or older	53.9	5,000	2,600	6,000	6,600	6,600	7,800	8,300
Sex:								
Male	60.6	7,600	3,100	6,700	8,100	12,100	14,700	10,000
Female	65.2	7,200	3,200	6,800	8,100	12,100	15,200	8,000
Race:								
One race:								
White	61.5	7,500	3,100	6,600	7,800	12,900	14,700	8,900
Black or African American	75.8	7,200	3,500	7,700	10,000	11,000	15,900	8,300
Asian	51.6	8,000	3,100	6,800	8,200	13,200	17,500	10,900
American Indian/Alaska Native	67.4	6,400	3,300	7,100	7,400	12,700	(S)	8,800
Native Hawaiian or other Pacific Islander	51.3	7,400	2,600	(S)	6,700	(S)	(S)	11,800
Other race	66.4	8,000	3,700	7,500	8,000	13,200	17,600	9,700
More than one race	61.9	7,200	3,700	5,800	7,100	13,300	12,900	10,100
Hispanic or Latino [3]	63.2	6,600	2,900	6,400	7,600	8,500	13,700	8,400
Attendance pattern:								
Full-time, full-year	76.2	9,900	4,900	8,000	9,100	15,400	17,600	11,100
Full-time, part-year	66.2	5,900	2,700	4,300	5,200	8,300	10,300	7,800
Part-time, full-year	60.5	5,400	3,000	5,700	7,500	8,500	10,600	8,900
Part-time, part-year	40.5	3,000	1,500	2,900	3,800	4,900	6,100	5,500

S Data do not meet publication standards.   [1] Includes public less-than-2-year and private not-for-profit less-than-4-year. [2] As of December 31, 2003.   [3] Persons of Hispanic origin may be of any race.

Source: U.S. National Center for Education Statistics, "Student Financing of Undergraduate Education 2003–04" NCES 2006-186 (released August 23, 2006). See Internet site <http://nces.ed.gov/surveys/npsas/>.

Table 282. **Average Out-of-Pocket Net Price of Attendance for Undergraduates: 2003–2004**

[In dollars. Excludes students attending more than one institution. Net Price of attendance is the price that students pay to receive postsecondary education after taking financial aid into account. Based on net tuition and net price for all students. Based on the 2003-2004 National Postsecondary Student-Aid Study; see source for details. Includes Puerto Rico. See also Appendix III]

Student characteristic	All institutions [1]	Public 2-year	Public 4-year		Private not-for-profit 4-year		Private for-profit
			Non-doctorate	Doctorate	Non-doctorate	Doctorate	
Total	6,600	4,700	6,300	7,500	9,100	14,700	7,000
Age: [2]							
18 years or younger..................	8,000	5,300	7,300	9,000	11,100	16,800	7,300
19 to 23 years	7,800	5,100	7,000	8,400	10,800	16,400	7,300
24 to 29 years	5,100	4,200	4,900	4,700	6,800	7,800	6,800
30 to 39 years	5,000	4,300	4,600	4,600	6,300	7,700	6,900
40 years or older..................	4,800	4,100	4,900	4,800	6,500	7,900	7,000
Sex:							
Male	6,900	4,800	6,500	7,800	9,400	15,500	7,200
Female	6,400	4,600	6,000	7,300	8,800	14,100	7,000
Race:							
One race:							
White.	7,000	4,800	6,500	7,900	9,600	16,000	7,300
Black or African American	5,100	4,100	4,600	5,100	7,000	9,400	6,500
Asian	8,200	5,600	7,300	9,200	13,200	18,300	8,300
American Indian/Alaska Native	4,800	4,000	5,200	5,400	6,200	(S)	5,900
Native Hawaiian or other Pacific Islander . . .	5,800	4,100	(S)	9,000	(S)	(S)	6,500
Other race	7,000	5,200	7,000	7,500	9,100	16,500	6,500
More than one race	6,400	4,500	6,000	7,700	8,100	14,800	7,300
Hispanic or Latino [3]	5,800	4,500	5,600	6,100	8,700	9,500	7,000
Attendance pattern:							
Full-time, full-year.	9,500	7,400	7,600	8,900	11,200	17,500	10,100
Full-time, part-year.	5,900	4,400	4,800	5,900	8,600	12,600	5,900
Part-time, full-year.	5,500	4,900	5,600	6,000	7,200	10,000	5,900
Part-time, part-year.	3,000	2,700	3,200	3,600	3,600	5,000	3,800

S Date do not meet publication standards.   [1] Includes public less-than-2-year and private not-for-profit less-than-4-year.
[2] As of December 31, 2003.   [3] Persons of Hispanic origin may be of any race.

Source: U.S. National Center for Education Statistics, "Student Financing of Undergraduate Education 2003–04" NCES 2006-186 (released August 23, 2006). See Internet site <http://nces.ed.gov/surveys/npsas/>.

Table 283. **Higher Education Price Indexes: 1970 to 2007**

[1983 = 100. For years ending June 30. Reflects prices paid by colleges and universities. Minus sign (–) indicates decrease]

Item and year	Index, total	Personnel compensation					Contracted services, supplies, and equipment		
		Faculty salaries	Administrative salaries	Clerical salaries	Service employee salaries	Fringe benefits	Miscellaneous services	Supplies and materials	Utilities
INDEXES									
1970	39.5	(NA)	(NA)	(NA)	(NA)	24.7	(NA)	37.6	16.3
1980	77.5	(NA)	(NA)	(NA)	(NA)	72.6	(NA)	84.6	64.1
1990	140.8	(NA)	(NA)	(NA)	(NA)	171.4	(NA)	119.6	90.1
2000	196.9	(NA)	(NA)	(NA)	(NA)	254.8	(NA)	145.0	104.9
2001	206.5	214.5	229.2	197.7	182.6	261.7	199.8	130.4	140.7
2002	215.0	222.7	236.4	205.4	189.6	277.1	205.8	130.6	149.4
2003	221.2	229.4	255.7	211.1	193.9	292.3	209.5	129.0	127.0
2004	231.5	234.2	263.3	217.1	197.6	312.8	216.4	133.8	174.6
2005	239.8	240.7	274.0	223.4	201.4	327.2	222.7	140.2	190.1
2006	251.8	248.2	287.7	229.5	205.5	343.7	228.8	151.9	241.8
2007	260.3	257.6	299.2	237.7	213.6	360.8	238.3	162.2	223.5
ANNUAL PERCENT CHANGE [1]									
1970	6.7	(NA)	(NA)	(NA)	(NA)	(NA)	(NA)	(NA)	(NA)
1980	9.9	(NA)	(NA)	(NA)	(NA)	12.6	(NA)	18.0	27.4
1990	6.0	(NA)	(NA)	(NA)	(NA)	7.9	(NA)	5.5	5.6
2000	4.1	(NA)	(NA)	(NA)	(NA)	6.5	(NA)	-0.1	4.4
2001	4.9	(NA)	(NA)	(NA)	(NA)	2.7	(NA)	6.0	34.1
2002	4.1	3.8	3.1	3.9	3.8	5.9	3.0	0.1	6.2
2003	2.9	3.0	8.2	2.8	2.3	5.5	1.8	-1.2	-15.0
2004	4.6	2.1	3.0	2.8	1.9	7.0	3.3	3.7	37.5
2005	3.6	2.8	4.1	2.9	1.9	4.6	2.9	4.8	8.9
2006	5.0	3.1	5.0	2.7	2.0	5.0	2.7	8.3	27.2
2007	3.4	3.8	4.0	3.6	4.0	5.0	4.2	6.8	-7.6

NA Not available.   [1] Percent change from the immediate prior year.

Source: The Commonfund Institute, Wilton, CT, (copyright). See Internet site <http://www.commonfund.org>.

Table 284. Federal Student Financial Assistance: 1995 to 2007

[For award years July 1 of year shown to the following June 30 (35,477 represents ($35,477,000,000). Funds utilized exclude operating costs, etc., and represent funds given to students]

Type of assistance	1995	2000	2003	2004	2005	2006, est.	2007, est.
FUNDS UTILIZED (mil. dol.)							
Total	35,477	44,007	62,275	69,053	72,634	77,395	82,199
Federal Pell Grants..................	5,472	7,956	12,707	13,149	12,693	12,746	12,986
Academic Competitiveness Grants/SMART [2] Grants....	(X)	(X)	(X)	(X)	(X)	790	850
Federal Supplemental Educational Opportunity Grant ...	764	907	1,064	1,065	1,084	975	976
Federal Work-Study	764	939	1,106	1,082	1,050	1,172	1,172
Federal Perkins Loan	1,029	1,144	1,638	1,651	1,593	1,135	133
Federal Direct Student Loan (FDSL)	8,296	10,348	11,969	12,840	12,930	13,874	15,158
Federal Family Education Loans (FFEL)...........	19,152	22,712	33,791	39,266	43,284	46,703	50,924
NUMBER OF AWARDS (1,000)							
Total	13,667	15,043	19,414	20,777	21,317	22,380	22,649
Federal Pell Grants..................	3,612	3,899	5,139	5,308	5,167	5,213	5,272
Academic Competitiveness Grants/SMART [2] Grants....	(X)	(X)	(X)	(X)	(X)	535	600
Federal Supplemental Educational Opportunity Grant ...	1,083	1,175	1,389	1,408	1,419	1,274	1,274
Federal Work-Study	702	713	764	762	710	810	810
Federal Perkins Loan	688	639	756	748	727	524	61
Federal Direct Student Loan (FDSL)	2,339	2,739	2,937	3,001	2,971	3,092	3,222
Federal Family Education Loans (FFEL)...........	5,243	5,878	8,429	9,550	10,323	10,932	11,410
AVERAGE AWARD (dol.)							
Total	2,596	2,925	3,208	3,324	3,407	3,458	3,629
Federal Pell Grants..................	1,515	2,041	2,473	2,477	2,456	2,445	2,463
Academic Competitiveness Grants/SMART [2] Grants....	(X)	(X)	(X)	(X)	(X)	1,477	1,417
Federal Supplemental Educational Opportunity Grant ...	705	772	766	759	764	766	766
Federal Work-Study	1,088	1,318	1,447	1,419	1,478	1,447	1,447
Federal Perkins Loan	1,496	1,790	2,166	2,206	2,190	2,166	2,180
Federal Direct Student Loan (FDSL)	3,547	3,778	4,075	4,279	4,352	4,487	4,705
Federal Family Education Loans (FFEL)...........	3,653	3,864	4,009	4,112	4,193	4,272	4,463
COHORT DEFAULT RATE [1]							
Federal Perkins Loan	12.6	9.9	8.3	8.1	8.1	(NA)	(NA)

NA Not available.   X Not applicable.   [1] As of June 30. Represents the percent of borrowers entering repayment status in year shown who defaulted in the following year.   [2] National Science and Mathematics Access to Retain Talent.
Source: U.S. Dept. of Education, Office of Postsecondary Education, unpublished data.

Table 285. State and Local Financial Support for Higher Education by State: 2005–2006

[For 2005–2006 fiscal year, except as indicated (10,189.8 represents 10,189,800). Data for the 50 states]

State	FTE enrollment [1] (1,000)	Educational appropriations per FTE [2] (dol.)	Appropriations for higher ed. as a percent of state and local tax revenue [3] 2004–2005	State	FTE enrollment [1] (1,000)	Educational appropriations per FTE [2] (dol.)	Appropriations for higher ed. as a percent of state and local tax revenue [3] 2004–2005
Total...	10,189.8	6,325	7.1	MO	170.7	5,846	5.9
				MT......	35.4	4,409	5.8
AL	181.0	5,617	9.0	NE......	72.6	6,999	10.3
AK	18.8	12,097	10.0	NV......	60.9	8,919	6.4
AZ	219.5	6,316	7.8	NH......	31.7	3,193	2.3
AR	101.3	5,899	9.0	NJ......	228.1	8,145	5.5
CA	1,662.1	6,586	8.1	NM.....	79.5	9,299	14.2
CO	158.9	3,364	3.7	NY......	501.8	7,784	6.9
CT	73.6	9,503	4.7	NC......	338.6	7,522	10.9
DE	31.3	6,632	6.5	ND......	35.9	4,683	10.1
FL	532.7	5,641	5.0	OH......	381.9	4,690	6.1
GA	292.7	7,824	8.7	OK......	134.9	5,638	7.7
HI	35.3	10,893	9.3	OR......	126.4	4,466	5.5
ID	44.6	7,303	8.6	PA......	327.2	5,660	4.9
IL	385.3	6,689	7.2	RI	28.1	6,413	4.8
IN	218.7	5,390	7.3	SC......	144.0	5,822	7.8
IA	112.3	5,809	8.3	SD......	29.3	4,499	6.5
KS	127.6	5,792	9.8	TN......	170.4	6,275	7.1
KY	144.3	6,753	9.2	TX......	820.8	6,276	7.9
LA	170.8	5,583	11.6	UT......	104.3	5,941	9.5
ME	35.2	6,096	5.9	VT......	18.9	3,030	3.8
MD	192.6	6,427	6.0	VA......	265.6	5,223	5.3
MA	139.9	8,372	4.0	WA......	213.1	6,437	6.4
MI	377.7	5,799	7.3	WV	71.7	4,181	9.0
MN	189.0	5,907	6.6	WI	212.2	6,226	8.0
MS	117.7	5,053	11.1	WY	22.5	13,425	15.7

[1] Full-time equivalent. Includes degree enrollment and enrollment in public postsecondary programs resulting in a certificate or other formal recognition. Includes summer sessions. Excludes medical enrollments.   [2] State and local appropriations for general operating expenses of public postsecondary education. Includes state-funded financial aid to students attending in-state public institutions. Excludes sums for research, agricultural extension, and teaching hospitals and medical schools.   [3] Includes state and local appropriations for public and independent postsecondary education (including sums for research, agricultural extension, and teaching hospitals and medical schools).
Source: State Higher Education Executive Officers, Boulder, CO (copyright). See Internet site <http://www.sheeo.org>.

182   Education

Table 286. Institutions of Higher Education—Charges: 1985 to 2006

[In dollars. Estimated. For the entire academic year ending in year shown. Figures are average charges per full-time equivalent student. Room and board are based on full-time students]

Academic control and year	Tuition and required fees [1]				Board rates [2]				Dormitory charges			
	All institutions	2-yr. colleges	4-yr. colleges	Other 4-yr. schools	All institutions	2-yr. colleges	4-yr. colleges	Other 4-yr. schools	All institutions	2-yr. colleges	4-yr. colleges	Other 4-yr. schools
Public:												
1985	971	584	1,386	1,117	1,241	1,302	1,276	1,201	1,196	921	1,237	1,200
1990	1,356	756	2,035	1,608	1,635	1,581	1,728	1,561	1,513	962	1,561	1,554
1995	2,057	1,192	2,977	2,499	1,949	1,712	2,108	1,866	1,959	1,232	1,992	2,044
2000	2,506	1,338	3,768	3,091	2,364	1,834	2,628	2,239	2,440	1,549	2,516	2,521
2002	2,700	1,380	4,273	3,409	2,598	2,036	2,835	2,504	2,723	1,722	2,838	2,801
2003	2,903	1,483	4,686	3,668	2,669	2,164	2,895	2,580	2,930	1,954	3,023	3,032
2004	3,319	1,702	5,363	4,141	2,823	2,233	3,084	2,724	3,107	2,086	3,232	3,198
2005	3,629	1,849	5,939	4,512	2,931	2,353	3,222	2,809	3,304	2,174	3,427	3,413
2006, prel. . . .	3,874	1,935	6,399	4,765	3,035	2,306	3,372	2,899	3,545	2,251	3,654	3,672
Private:												
1985	5,315	3,485	6,843	5,135	1,462	1,294	1,647	1,405	1,426	1,424	1,753	1,309
1990	8,147	5,196	10,348	7,778	1,948	1,811	2,339	1,823	1,923	1,663	2,411	1,774
1995	11,111	6,914	14,537	10,653	2,509	2,023	3,035	2,362	2,587	2,233	3,469	2,347
2000	14,081	8,235	19,307	13,361	2,882	2,922	3,157	2,790	3,224	2,808	4,070	2,976
2002	15,742	10,076	21,176	14,923	3,104	2,633	3,462	2,996	3,567	3,116	4,478	3,301
2003	16,383	10,651	22,716	15,416	3,206	3,870	3,602	3,071	3,752	3,232	4,724	3,478
2004	17,327	11,546	24,128	16,298	3,364	4,432	3,778	3,222	3,945	3,581	4,979	3,647
2005	18,154	12,122	25,643	17,050	3,485	3,728	3,855	3,370	4,171	4,243	5,263	3,854
2006, prel. . . .	18,862	12,450	26,954	17,702	3,647	4,726	4,039	3,517	4,380	3,994	5,517	4,063

[1] For in-state students.   [2] Beginning 1990, rates reflect 20 meals per week, rather than meals served 7 days a week.
Source: U.S. National Center for Education Statistics, *Digest of Education Statistics,* annual.

Table 287. Voluntary Financial Support of Higher Education: 1990 to 2006

[For school years ending in years shown (9,800 represents $9,800,000,000). Voluntary support, as defined in Gift Reporting Standards, excludes income from endowment and other invested funds as well as all support received from federal, state, and local governments and their agencies and contract research]

Item	Unit	1990	1995	2000	2002	2003	2004	2005	2006
Estimated support, total	Mil. dol. . .	9,800	12,750	23,200	23,900	23,900	24,400	25,600	28,000
Individuals	Mil. dol. . .	4,770	6,540	12,220	11,300	11,300	11,150	11,900	14,100
Alumni	Mil. dol. . .	2,540	3,600	6,800	5,900	6,600	6,700	7,100	8,400
Business corporations	Mil. dol. . .	2,170	2,560	4,150	4,370	4,250	4,400	4,400	4,600
Foundations	Mil. dol. . .	1,920	2,460	5,080	6,300	6,600	6,200	7,000	7,100
Fundraising consortia and other organizations	Mil. dol. . . .	700	940	1,380	1,570	1,540	1,550	1,730	1,825
Religious organizations	Mil. dol. . . .	240	250	370	360	360	350	370	375
Current operations	Mil. dol. . . .	5,440	7,230	11,270	12,400	12,900	13,600	14,200	15,000
Capital purposes	Mil. dol. . . .	4,360	5,520	11,930	11,500	11,000	10,800	11,400	13,000
Support per student	Dollars . . .	709	894	1,515	1,439	1,371	1,352	1,476	1,585
In 2005–2006 dollars	Dollars . . .	1,094	1,183	1,774	1,612	1,549	1,508	1,523	1,585
Expenditures, higher education.	Bil. dol. . .	105.59	144.16	203.32	228.91	248.23	258.85	336.68	343.66
Expenditures per student	Dollars . . .	7,641	10,108	13,278	13,780	14,237	14,341	19,405	19,455
In 2005–2006 dollars	Dollars . . .	15,031	16,971	18,104	18,937	19,160	19,290	20,031	19,455
Institutions reporting support . . .	Number . . .	1,056	1,086	945	955	954	971	997	1,014
Total support reported	Mil. dol. . .	8,214	10,992	19,419	19,824	19,823	19,630	20,953	23,475
Private 4-year institutions	Mil. dol. . . .	5,072	6,500	11,047	10,953	10,318	10,695	11,011	12,857
Public 4-year institutions.	Mil. dol. . . .	3,056	4,382	8,254	8,754	9,400	8,802	9,780	10,421
2-year colleges	Mil. dol. . . .	85	110	117	117	105	133	163	197

Source: Council for Aid to Education, New York, NY, *Voluntary Support of Education,* annual.

Table 288. Average Salaries for College Faculty Members: 2005 to 2007

[In thousands of dollars (66.9 represents $66,900). For academic year ending in year shown. Figures are for 9 months teaching for full-time faculty members in 2-year and 4-year institutions with ranks. Fringe benefits averaged in 2005, $17,966 in public institutions and $21,332 in private institutions; in 2006, $18,677 in public institutions and $22,170 in private institutions; and in 2007, $19,746 in public institutions and $23,040 in private institutions]

Type of control and academic rank	2005	2006	2007	Type of control and academic rank	2005	2006	2007
Public: All ranks.	66.9	68.4	71.4	Private: [1] All ranks	79.3	81.5	84.2
Professor	88.5	91.4	95.6	Professor	108.2	111.8	116.2
Associate professor	64.4	66.3	69.2	Associate professor	71.0	73.3	75.7
Assistant professor.	54.3	55.9	58.5	Assistant professor	59.4	61.0	62.9
Instructor	39.4	40.1	41.8	Instructor	42.2	44.5	45.6

[1] Excludes church-related colleges and universities.

Source: American Association of University Professors, Washington, DC, *AAUP Annual Report on the Economic Status of the Profession.*

U.S. Census Bureau, Statistical Abstract of the United States: 2008

Table 289. **Employees in Higher Education Institutions by Sex and Occupation: 1991 to 2005**

[In thousands (2,545.2 represents 2,545,200). As of fall. Based on complete census taken every other year; see source]

Year and status		Professional staff									Nonpro-fessional staff, total
		Total	Executive, administrative, and managerial		Faculty [1]		Research/instruction assistants		Other		
	Total	Total	Male	Female	Male	Female	Male	Female	Male	Female	
1991, total	2,545.2	1,595.5	85.4	59.3	525.6	300.7	119.1	78.6	165.4	261.3	949.8
Full-time	1,812.9	1,031.8	82.9	56.2	366.2	169.4	–	–	142.2	214.8	781.1
Part-time....	732.3	563.7	2.5	3.1	159.4	131.2	119.1	78.6	23.2	46.4	168.7
1997, total [2] ...	2,752.5	1,835.9	81.9	69.4	587.4	402.4	125.9	96.9	187.6	284.4	916.6
Full-time	1,828.5	1,104.8	78.9	65.6	363.9	204.8	–	–	159.3	232.3	723.7
Part-time....	924.0	731.1	3.0	3.8	223.5	197.6	125.9	96.9	28.3	52.1	192.9
2005, total	3,379.1	2,459.9	95.2	101.1	714.5	576.0	167.5	149.6	262.8	393.2	919.2
Full-time	2,179.9	1,432.1	92.9	97.2	401.5	274.1	–	–	231.4	335.0	747.8
Part-time....	1,199.2	1,027.8	2.4	3.9	312.9	301.9	167.5	149.6	31.4	58.2	171.4

– Represents zero. [1] Instruction and research. [2] In this table, 1997 data reflect the new classification of institutions. See footnote 1, Table 271.

Source: U.S. National Center for Education Statistics, *Digest of Education Statistics*, annual.

Table 290. **Faculty in Institutions of Higher Education: 1980 to 2005**

[In thousands (686 represents 686,000), except percent. As of fall. Based on complete census taken every other year; see source]

Year		Employment status		Control		Level		Percent		
	Total	Full-time	Part-time	Public	Private	4-Year	2-Year or less	Part-time	Public	2-Year or less
1980 [1]	686	450	236	495	191	494	192	34	72	28
1985 [1]	715	459	256	503	212	504	211	36	70	30
1991 [2]	826	536	291	581	245	591	235	35	70	28
1993	915	546	370	650	265	626	290	40	71	32
1995	932	551	381	657	275	647	285	41	70	31
1997 [3]	990	569	421	695	295	683	307	43	70	31
1999 [3]	1,028	591	437	713	315	714	314	43	69	31
2001 [3]	1,113	618	495	771	342	764	349	44	69	31
2003 [3]	1,175	632	543	793	382	816	359	46	67	31
2005 [3]	1,290	676	615	841	449	917	373	48	65	29

[1] Estimated on the basis of enrollment. [2] Data beginning 1991 not comparable to prior years. [3] In this table, data beginning in 1997 reflect the new classification of institutions. See footnote 1, Table 271.

Source: U.S. National Center for Education Statistics, *Digest of Education Statistics*, annual.

Table 291. **Salary Offers to Candidates for Degrees: 2004 to 2006**

[In dollars. Data are average beginning salaries based on offers made by business, industrial, government, nonprofit, and educational employers to graduating students. Data from representative colleges throughout the United States]

Field of study	Bachelor's			Master's [1]			Doctoral		
	2004	2005	2006	2004	2005	2006	2004	2005	2006
Accounting...........	41,058	42,940	44,928	43,042	45,992	47,003	(NA)	(NA)	(NA)
Business administration/ management [2]	38,254	39,480	41,155	[3]44,807	[3]50,513	[3]47,824	[3]75,125	[3]66,500	[3]81,438
Marketing............	34,712	36,409	37,191	[3]65,000	[3]47,000	[3]38,000	(NA)	(NA)	(NA)
Engineering:									
Civil...............	42,056	43,774	46,084	48,852	48,619	50,953	[3]53,067	[3]59,216	[3]63,100
Chemical	52,539	53,639	56,269	[3]53,920	62,845	[3]59,008	[3]72,613	[3]73,317	75,659
Computer..........	51,297	52,242	53,096	[3]63,563	58,631	66,545	(NA)	[3]69,625	[3]74,750
Electrical	51,124	51,773	53,300	63,413	64,781	66,687	73,674	[3]75,066	81,297
Mechanical	48,578	50,175	51,808	58,298	60,223	61,234	[3]68,003	69,757	[3]69,034
Nuclear [4]	[3]47,914	[3]51,225	[3]54,616	[3]66,350	[3]59,059	[3]53,798	(NA)	(NA)	(NA)
Petroleum..........	[3]58,518	62,236	[3]67,069	[3]71,332	[3]65,000	[3]68,833	(NA)	(NA)	(NA)
Engineering technology..	43,425	45,790	48,514	(NA)	(NA)	(NA)	(NA)	(NA)	(NA)
Chemistry	37,618	38,635	39,804	[3]59,043	(NA)	[3]51,136	60,986	[3]55,874	68,458
Mathematics.........	43,567	[3]43,304	44,672	[3]37,805	[3]34,500	[3]51,767	[3]49,254	[3]55,047	[3]63,952
Physics	[3]38,945	[3]44,700	[3]45,120	[3]37,440	[3]62,500	[3]52,333	[3]54,729	[3]54,897	[3]72,357
Humanities......	30,626	31,565	[3]31,183	[3]33,049	[3]35,212	[3]40,952	[3]47,500	[3]43,728	[3]48,938
Social sciences [5]	31,698	31,621	32,134	[3]35,174	[3]40,575	[3]42,220	[3]42,727	[3]46,838	[3]48,487
Computer science	49,036	50,664	50,744	60,457	64,840	71,165	[3]74,598	[3]84,025	[3]76,630

NA Not available. [1] Candidates with 1 year or less of full-time nonmilitary employment. [2] For master's degree, offers are after nontechnical undergraduate degree. [3] Fewer than 50 offers reported. [4] Includes engineering physics. [5] Excludes economics.

Source: National Association of Colleges and Employers, Bethlehem, PA (copyright). Reprinted with permission from Fall 2004, 2005, and 2006 Salary Survey. All rights reserved.

Table 292. **Earned Degrees Conferred by Level and Sex: 1960 to 2005**

[In thousands (477 represents 477,000), except percent. Based on survey; see Appendix III]

Year ending	All degrees Total	All degrees Percent male	Associate's Male	Associate's Female	Bachelor's Male	Bachelor's Female	Master's Male	Master's Female	First professional Male	First professional Female	Doctoral Male	Doctoral Female
1960 [1]	477	65.8	(NA)	(NA)	254	138	51	24	(NA)	(NA)	9	1
1970	1,271	59.2	117	89	451	341	126	83	33	2	26	4
1975	1,666	56.0	191	169	505	418	162	131	49	7	27	7
1980	1,731	51.1	184	217	474	456	151	147	53	17	23	10
1985	1,828	49.3	203	252	483	497	143	143	50	25	22	11
1988	1,835	48.0	190	245	477	518	145	154	45	25	23	12
1989	1,873	47.3	186	250	483	535	149	161	45	26	23	13
1990	1,940	46.6	191	264	492	560	154	171	44	27	24	14
1991	2,025	45.8	199	283	504	590	156	181	44	28	25	15
1992	2,108	45.6	207	297	521	616	162	191	45	29	26	15
1993	2,167	45.5	212	303	533	632	169	200	45	30	26	16
1994	2,206	45.1	215	315	532	637	176	211	45	31	27	17
1995	2,218	44.9	218	321	526	634	179	219	45	31	27	18
1996 [2]	2,248	44.2	220	336	522	642	179	227	45	32	27	18
1997 [2]	2,288	43.6	224	347	521	652	181	238	46	33	27	19
1998 [2]	2,298	43.2	218	341	520	664	184	246	45	34	27	19
1999 [2]	2,323	42.7	218	342	519	682	186	254	44	34	25	19
2000 [2]	2,385	42.6	225	340	530	708	192	265	44	36	25	20
2001 [2]	2,416	42.4	232	347	532	712	194	274	43	37	25	20
2002 [2]	2,494	42.2	238	357	550	742	199	283	43	38	24	20
2003 [2]	2,621	42.1	253	380	573	775	211	301	42	39	24	22
2004 [2]	2,755	41.8	260	405	595	804	230	329	42	41	25	23
2005 [2]	2,850	41.6	268	429	613	826	234	341	44	43	27	26

NA Not available. [1] First-professional degrees are included with bachelor's degrees. [2] Data beginning in 1996 reflect the new classification of institutions. See footnote 1, Table 271.

Source: U.S. National Center for Education Statistics, *Digest of Education Statistics*, annual.

Table 293. **Degrees Earned by Level and Race/Ethnicity: 1981 to 2005**

[For school year ending in year shown. Based on survey; see Appendix III]

Level of degree and race/ethnicity	Total 1981 [1]	Total 1985 [1]	Total 1990	Total 1995	Total 2000 [2]	Total 2005 [2]	Percent distribution 1981	Percent distribution 2005 [2]
Associate's degrees, total	410,174	429,815	455,102	539,691	564,933	696,660	100.0	100.0
White, non-Hispanic	339,167	355,343	376,816	420,656	408,772	475,513	82.7	68.3
Black, non-Hispanic	35,330	35,791	34,326	47,067	60,221	86,402	8.6	12.4
Hispanic	17,800	19,407	21,504	35,962	51,573	78,557	4.3	11.3
Asian or Pacific Islander	8,650	9,914	13,066	20,677	27,782	33,669	2.1	4.8
American Indian/Alaska Native	2,584	2,953	3,430	5,482	6,497	8,435	0.6	1.2
Nonresident alien	6,643	6,407	5,960	9,847	10,088	14,084	1.6	2.0
Bachelor's degrees, total	934,800	968,311	1,051,344	1,160,134	1,237,875	1,439,264	100.0	100.0
White, non-Hispanic	807,319	826,106	887,151	914,610	929,106	1,049,141	86.4	72.9
Black, non-Hispanic	60,673	57,473	61,046	87,236	108,013	136,122	6.5	9.5
Hispanic	21,832	25,874	32,829	54,230	75,059	101,124	2.3	7.0
Asian or Pacific Islander	18,794	25,395	39,230	60,502	77,912	97,209	2.0	6.8
American Indian/Alaska Native	3,593	4,246	4,390	6,610	8,719	10,307	0.4	0.7
Nonresident alien	22,589	29,217	26,698	36,946	39,066	45,361	2.4	3.2
Master's degrees, total	294,183	280,421	324,301	397,629	457,056	574,618	100.0	100.0
White, non-Hispanic	241,216	223,628	254,299	293,345	320,485	379,350	82.0	66.0
Black, non-Hispanic	17,133	13,939	15,336	24,166	35,874	54,482	5.8	9.5
Hispanic	6,461	6,864	7,892	12,905	19,253	31,485	2.2	5.5
Asian or Pacific Islander	6,282	7,782	10,439	16,847	23,218	32,783	2.1	5.7
American Indian/Alaska Native	1,034	1,256	1,090	1,621	2,246	3,295	0.4	0.6
Nonresident alien	22,057	26,952	35,245	48,745	55,980	73,223	7.5	12.7
Doctor's degrees, total	32,839	32,307	38,371	44,446	44,808	52,631	100.0	100.0
White, non-Hispanic	25,908	23,934	26,221	27,846	27,843	30,261	78.9	57.5
Black, non-Hispanic	1,265	1,154	1,149	1,667	2,246	3,056	3.9	5.8
Hispanic	456	677	780	984	1,305	1,824	1.4	3.5
Asian or Pacific Islander	877	1,106	1,225	2,689	2,420	2,911	2.7	5.5
American Indian/Alaska Native	130	119	98	130	160	237	0.4	0.5
Nonresident alien	4,203	5,317	8,898	11,130	10,834	14,342	12.8	27.3
First-professional degrees, total	71,340	71,057	70,988	75,800	80,057	87,289	100.0	100.0
White, non-Hispanic	64,551	63,219	60,487	59,402	59,637	63,429	90.5	72.7
Black, non-Hispanic	2,931	3,029	3,409	4,747	5,555	6,313	4.1	7.2
Hispanic	1,541	1,884	2,425	3,231	3,865	4,445	2.2	5.1
Asian or Pacific Islander	1,456	1,816	3,362	6,396	8,584	10,501	2.0	12.0
American Indian/Alaska Native	192	248	257	413	564	564	0.3	0.6
Nonresident alien	669	861	1,048	1,611	1,852	2,037	0.9	2.3

[1] Excludes some persons whose race/ethnicity was unknown and are slight undercounts of degrees awarded. [2] In this table, data beginning in 2000 reflect the new classification of institutions. See footnote 1, Table 271.

Source: U.S. National Center for Education Statistics, *Digest of Education Statistics*, annual.

Table 294. Degrees and Awards Earned Below Bachelor's by Field: 2005

[Covers associate's degrees and other awards based on postsecondary curriculums of less than 4 years in institutions of higher education. Based on survey; see Appendix III. See headnote, Table 295]

Field of study	Less than 1-year awards		1- to less than 4-year awards		Associate's degrees	
	Total	Women	Total	Women	Total	Women
Total	220,502	124,158	181,212	110,054	696,660	429,124
Agriculture and natural resources, total	3,044	907	1,759	669	6,404	2,395
Architecture and related services	162	74	171	116	583	346
Area, ethnic, cultural, and gender studies	352	257	105	77	115	77
Biological and biomedical sciences	36	32	20	16	1,709	1,161
Business, management, and marketing	25,827	17,629	17,573	13,454	96,067	65,805
Communications and communications						
technologies	1,120	586	1,249	533	6,061	2,768
Computer and information sciences	10,865	4,156	7,665	2,943	36,173	10,621
Construction trades	5,691	321	7,711	290	3,512	204
Education	2,976	2,647	1,882	1,735	13,329	11,141
Engineering and engineering technologies	7,677	1,236	7,141	933	35,989	5,236
English language and literature/letters	572	392	106	68	995	682
Family and consumer sciences	10,636	8,914	3,586	2,916	9,707	9,261
Foreign languages and literatures	687	538	391	344	1,234	1,037
Health professions and related sciences	86,875	69,372	77,668	67,736	122,520	105,423
Nursing	2,827	2,580	3,151	2,783	58,007	51,454
Legal professions and studies	1,799	1,563	2,793	2,402	9,885	8,930
Liberal arts and sciences, general studies,						
and humanities	322	227	2,799	1,868	240,131	152,286
Library science	196	179	53	41	108	97
Mathematics	14	7	6	2	807	278
Mechanics and repairers	14,305	1,084	21,842	859	13,619	718
Military technologies	190	60	–	–	355	52
Multi/interdisciplinary studies	513	294	412	316	13,888	8,010
Parks, recreation, leisure, and fitness	391	183	193	101	966	385
Personal and culinary services	6,172	4,610	9,934	7,918	16,311	7,408
Philosophy and religion	18	12	85	43	422	300
Physical sciences and science technologies	221	95	300	151	2,814	1,167
Precision production trades	5,071	260	4,888	224	2,039	162
Psychology	134	108	36	32	1,942	1,497
Public administration and social services	769	655	478	391	4,027	3,456
Security and protective services	19,675	4,717	5,575	1,574	23,749	10,389
Social sciences and history	263	138	180	73	6,533	4,342
Theology and religious vocations	59	35	438	240	581	311
Transportation and material moving	11,918	1,884	790	84	1,435	194
Visual and performing arts	1,952	986	3,363	1,905	22,650	12,985

– Represents zero.

Source: U.S. National Center for Education Statistics, *Digest of Education Statistics*, annual.

Table 295. Bachelor's Degrees Earned by Field: 1980 to 2005

[The new Classification of Instructional Programs was introduced in 2002–03. Data for previous years has been reclassified where necessary to conform to the new classifications. Based on survey; see Appendix III]

Field of study	1980	1990	2000	2003	2004	2005
Total	929,417	1,051,344	1,237,875	1,348,503	1,399,542	1,439,264
Agriculture and natural resources	22,802	12,900	24,238	23,294	22,835	23,002
Architecture and related services	9,132	9,364	8,462	9,054	8,838	9,237
Area, ethnic, cultural, and gender studies	2,840	4,447	6,212	6,629	7,181	7,569
Biological and biomedical sciences	46,190	37,204	63,005	60,072	61,509	64,611
Business	186,264	248,568	256,070	293,545	307,149	311,574
Communication, journalism, and related programs [1] .	28,616	51,572	57,058	69,792	73,002	75,238
Computer and information sciences	11,154	27,347	37,788	57,439	59,488	54,111
Education	118,038	105,112	108,034	105,790	106,278	105,451
Engineering and engineering technologies	69,387	82,480	73,419	77,267	78,227	79,743
English language and literature/letters	32,187	46,803	50,106	53,670	53,984	54,379
Family and consumer sciences/human sciences . . .	18,411	13,514	16,321	18,166	19,172	20,074
Foreign languages, literatures, and linguistics	12,480	13,133	15,886	16,901	17,754	18,386
Health professions and related clinical sciences	63,848	58,983	80,863	71,223	73,934	80,685
Legal professions and studies	683	1,632	1,969	2,466	2,841	3,161
Liberal arts and sciences, general studies, and						
humanities	23,196	27,985	36,104	40,221	42,106	43,751
Mathematics and statistics	11,378	14,276	11,418	12,493	13,327	14,351
Multi/interdisciplinary studies	11,457	16,557	28,561	28,757	29,162	30,243
Parks, recreation, leisure, and fitness studies	5,753	4,582	17,571	21,428	22,164	22,888
Philosophy and religious studies	7,069	7,034	8,535	10,344	11,152	11,584
Physical sciences and science technologies	23,407	16,056	18,331	17,940	17,983	18,905
Psychology	42,093	53,952	74,194	78,613	82,098	85,614
Public administration and social services	16,644	13,908	20,185	19,878	20,552	21,769
Security and protective services	15,015	15,354	24,877	26,189	28,175	30,723
Social sciences and history	103,662	118,083	127,101	143,218	150,357	156,892
Theology and religious vocations	6,170	5,185	6,789	7,926	8,126	9,284
Transportation and materials moving	213	2,387	3,395	4,567	4,824	4,904
Visual and performing arts	40,892	39,934	58,791	71,474	77,181	80,955
Other and unclassified	436	2,992	2,592	147	143	180

[1] Includes technologies.

Source: U.S. National Center for Education Statistics, *Digest of Education Statistics*, annual; and unpublished data.

Table 296. **Master's and Doctoral Degrees Earned by Field: 1980 to 2005**

[The new Classification of Instructional Programs was introduced in 2002–03. Data for previous years has been reclassified where necessary to conform to the new classifications. Based on survey; see Appendix III]

Field of study	1980	1990	2000	2003	2004	2005
MASTER'S DEGREES						
Total.	**298,081**	**324,301**	**457,056**	**512,645**	**558,940**	**574,618**
Agriculture and natural resources	3,976	3,382	4,360	4,492	4,783	4,746
Architecture and related services.	3,139	3,499	4,268	4,925	5,424	5,674
Area, ethnic, cultural, and gender studies	852	1,191	1,544	1,509	1,683	1,755
Biological and biomedical sciences	6,322	4,906	6,781	6,990	7,657	8,199
Business	55,008	76,676	111,532	127,545	139,347	142,617
Communication, journalism, and related programs [1] .	3,082	4,353	5,525	6,495	6,900	7,195
Computer and information sciences	3,647	9,677	14,990	19,503	20,143	18,416
Education	101,819	84,890	123,045	147,448	162,345	167,490
Engineering and engineering technologies	16,765	25,294	26,726	30,669	35,197	35,133
English language and literature/letters	6,026	6,317	7,022	7,413	7,956	8,468
Family and consumer sciences/human sciences . . .	2,690	1,679	1,882	1,610	1,794	1,827
Foreign languages, literatures, and linguistics	3,067	3,018	3,037	3,049	3,124	3,407
Health professions and related clinical sciences. . . .	15,374	20,406	42,593	42,715	44,939	46,703
Legal professions and studies	1,817	1,888	3,750	4,126	4,243	4,170
Liberal arts and sciences, general studies, and humanities	2,646	1,999	3,256	3,312	3,697	3,680
Library science	5,374	4,341	4,577	5,314	6,015	6,213
Mathematics and statistics	2,860	3,624	3,208	3,626	4,191	4,477
Multi/interdisciplinary studies	2,494	3,182	3,487	3,780	4,047	4,252
Parks, recreation, leisure, and fitness studies	647	529	2,322	2,978	3,199	3,740
Philosophy and religious studies	1,204	1,327	1,376	1,578	1,578	1,647
Physical sciences and science technologies	5,167	5,410	4,810	5,109	5,570	5,678
Psychology	9,938	10,730	15,740	17,123	17,898	18,830
Public administration and social services	17,560	17,399	25,594	25,894	28,250	29,552
Security and protective services	1,805	1,151	2,609	2,955	3,717	3,991
Social sciences and history	12,176	11,634	14,066	14,634	16,110	16,952
Theology and religious vocations.	3,872	4,941	5,534	5,099	5,486	5,815
Visual and performing arts	8,708	8,481	10,918	11,986	12,906	13,183
Other and unclassified	46	2,377	2,504	768	741	808
DOCTORAL DEGREES						
Total	**32,615**	**38,371**	**44,808**	**46,024**	**48,378**	**52,631**
Agriculture and natural resources	991	1,295	1,168	1,229	1,185	1,173
Architecture and related services.	79	103	129	152	173	179
Area, ethnic, cultural, and gender studies	151	125	205	186	209	189
Biological and biomedical sciences	3,527	3,837	5,180	5,003	5,242	5,578
Business	767	1,093	1,194	1,251	1,481	1,498
Communication, journalism, and related programs [1] .	193	272	357	398	426	468
Computer and information sciences	240	627	779	816	909	1,119
Education	7,314	6,503	6,409	6,835	7,088	7,681
Engineering and engineering technologies	2,546	5,030	5,421	5,333	5,981	6,601
English language and literature/letters	1,196	986	1,470	1,246	1,207	1,212
Family and consumer sciences/human sciences . . .	192	273	327	372	329	331
Foreign languages, literatures, and linguistics	857	816	1,086	1,042	1,031	1,027
Health professions and related clinical sciences. . . .	821	1,449	2,053	3,328	4,361	5,868
Legal professions and studies	40	111	74	105	119	98
Liberal arts and sciences, general studies, and humanities	192	63	83	78	95	109
Mathematics and statistics	724	917	1,075	1,007	1,060	1,176
Multi/interdisciplinary studies	318	442	792	899	876	983
Parks, recreation, leisure, and fitness studies	21	35	134	199	222	207
Philosophy and religious studies	374	445	598	662	595	586
Physical sciences and science technologies	3,044	4,116	3,963	3,858	3,815	4,114
Psychology	3,395	3,811	4,731	4,831	4,827	5,106
Public administration and social services	342	508	537	596	649	673
Security and protective services	18	38	52	72	54	94
Social sciences and history	3,230	3,010	4,095	3,850	3,811	3,819
Theology and religious vocations.	1,315	1,317	1,630	1,321	1,304	1,422
Visual and performing arts	655	849	1,127	1,293	1,282	1,278
Other and unclassified	73	300	139	62	47	42

[1] Includes technologies.

Source: U.S. National Center for Education Statistics, *Digest of Education Statistics,* annual; and unpublished data.

Table 297. **First Professional Degrees Earned in Selected Professions: 1970 to 2004**

[First professional degrees include degrees which require at least 6 years of college work for completion (including at least 2 years of preprofessional training). Based on survey; see Appendix III]

Type of degree and sex of recipient	1970	1975	1980	1985	1990	1995	2000	2002	2003	2004
Medicine (M.D.):										
Institutions conferring degrees.....	86	104	112	120	124	119	118	118	118	118
Degrees conferred, total.........	8,314	12,447	14,902	16,041	15,075	15,537	15,286	15,237	15,034	15,442
Percent to women	8.4	13.1	23.4	30.4	34.2	38.8	42.7	44.4	45.3	46.4
Dentistry (D.D.S. or D.M.D.):										
Institutions conferring degrees.....	48	52	58	59	57	53	54	53	53	53
Degrees conferred, total.........	3,718	4,773	5,258	5,339	4,100	3,897	4,250	4,239	4,344	4,335
Percent to women	0.9	3.1	13.3	20.7	30.9	36.4	40.1	38.5	38.9	41.6
Law (LL.B. or J.D.):										
Institutions conferring degrees.....	145	154	179	181	182	183	190	192	194	195
Degrees conferred, total.........	14,916	29,296	35,647	37,491	36,485	39,349	38,152	38,981	39,067	40,209
Percent to women	5.4	15.1	30.2	38.5	42.2	42.6	45.9	48.0	49.0	49.4
Theological (B.D., M.Div., M.H.L.):										
Institutions conferring degrees.....	(NA)	(NA)	(NA)	(NA)	(NA)	192	198	191	196	200
Degrees conferred, total.........	5,298	5,095	7,115	7,221	5,851	5,978	6,129	5,195	5,351	5,332
Percent to women	2.3	6.8	13.8	18.5	24.8	25.7	29.2	32.9	34.6	34.2

NA Not available.

Source: U.S. National Center for Education Statistics, *Digest of Education Statistics*, annual.

Table 298. **Participation in Adult Education: 2004–2005**

[In thousands (211,607 represents 211,607,000), except percent. For the civilian noninstitutional population 16 years old. Adult education includes enrollment in formal education activities in the previous 12 months. Excludes participants in only postsecondary degree, certificate, or diploma programs as full-time students. Based on the Adult Education Survey of the National Household Education Survey Program and subject to sampling error; see source and Appendix III for details]

Characteristic	Adult population (1,000)	Participants in adult education				
		Number taking adult education courses [1] (1,000)	Percent of total [1]	Type of course (percent)		
				College or university degree program	Work-related course	Personal interest course
Total, 2005.	211,607	93,939	44	4	27	21
Age:						
16 to 30 years old.............	48,544	25,040	52	8	25	23
31 to 40 years old.............	40,009	20,839	52	6	34	23
41 to 50 years old.............	45,662	21,983	48	3	36	20
51 to 65 years old.............	46,211	18,767	41	2	28	20
66 years old and over	31,181	7,310	23	–	5	19
Sex:						
Male............................	101,596	41,724	41	4	24	18
Female	110,011	52,216	47	4	29	24
Race/ethnicity:						
White, Non-Hispanic	146,614	66,909	46	4	29	22
Black, Non-Hispanic	23,467	10,878	46	4	27	24
Hispanic	26,101	9,824	38	4	17	15
Other	15,426	6,328	41	5	24	22
Educational attainment:						
Less than high school	31,017	6,851	22	–	4	11
High school diploma or GED......	64,334	20,955	33	2	17	16
Some college...............	58,545	30,070	51	6	31	25
Bachelor's degree or higher	57,711	36,063	62	7	46	29
Marital status:						
Married	132,008	58,748	45	3	29	21
Living with partner, unmarried	12,498	4,879	39	4	26	16
Separated/divorced/widowed......	30,170	10,874	36	2	20	19
Never married	36,930	19,439	53	8	23	26
Employment/occupation						
Employed	152,450	78,879	52	5	36	22
Professional or managerial	48,647	34,138	70	8	56	29
Services, sales, or support	65,289	31,609	48	5	31	22
Trades....................	38,514	13,132	34	2	19	13
Unemployed or not in labor force in past 12 months	59,157	15,060	25	1	4	20
Household income:						
$20,000 or less	34,670	9,552	28	2	11	16
$20,001 to $35,000............	35,839	12,866	36	4	18	17
$35,001 to $50,000............	33,376	14,122	42	2	23	22
$50,001 to $75,000............	47,114	22,494	48	5	33	21
$75,001 or more..............	60,607	34,904	58	5	39	27
Children under 10 in household:						
Yes	57,560	26,746	46	5	29	20
No	154,047	67,193	44	5	26	22

– Represents or rounds to zero. [1] Includes English as a Second Language, basic education skills, vocational or technical diploma programs, and apprenticeship programs each with a total participation rate of about 1 percent.

Source: U.S. Department of Education, National Center for Education Statistics, Adult Education Survey of the National Household Education Surveys Program 2005, unpublished data.

Section 5
Law Enforcement, Courts, and Prisons

This section presents data on crimes committed, victims of crimes, arrests, and data related to criminal violations and the criminal justice system. The major sources of these data are the Bureau of Justice Statistics (BJS), the Federal Bureau of Investigation (FBI), and the Administrative Office of the U.S. Courts. BJS issues many reports—see our Guide to Sources for a complete listing. The Federal Bureau of Investigation's major annual reports are *Crime in the United States, Law Enforcement Officers Killed and Assaulted,* annual, and *Hate Crimes,* annual, which present data on reported crimes as gathered from state and local law enforcement agencies.

Legal jurisdiction and law enforcement—Law enforcement is, for the most part, a function of state and local officers and agencies. The U.S. Constitution reserves general police powers to the states. By act of Congress, federal offenses include only offenses against the U.S. government and against or by its employees while engaged in their official duties and offenses which involve the crossing of state lines or an interference with interstate commerce. Excluding the military, there are 52 separate criminal law jurisdictions in the United States: one in each of the 50 states, one in the District of Columbia, and the federal jurisdiction. Each of these has its own criminal law and procedure and its own law enforcement agencies. While the systems of law enforcement are quite similar among the states, there are often substantial differences in the penalties for like offenses.

Law enforcement can be divided into three parts: Investigation of crimes and arrests of persons suspected of committing them; prosecution of those charged with crime; and the punishment or treatment of persons convicted of crime.

Crime—The U.S. Department of Justice administers two statistical programs to measure the magnitude, nature, and

impact of crime in the nation: the Uniform Crime Reporting (UCR) Program and the National Crime Victimization Survey (NCVS). Each of these programs produces valuable information about aspects of the nation's crime problem. Because the UCR and NCVS programs are conducted for different purposes, use different methods, and focus on somewhat different aspects of crime, the information they produce together provides a more comprehensive panorama of the nation's crime problem than either could produce alone.

Uniform Crime Reports (UCR)—The FBI's UCR Program, which began in 1929, collects information on the following crimes reported to law enforcement authorities—Part 1 offenses: murder and nonnegligent manslaughter, forcible rape, robbery, aggravated assault, burglary, larceny-theft, motor vehicle theft, and arson. Law enforcement agencies report arrest data for 21 additional crime categories—Part 2 offenses: for UCR definitions of criminal offenses (including those listed), please go to: <www.fbi.gov /ucr/05cius/about/offense_definitions.html>.

The UCR Program compiles data from monthly law enforcement reports or individual crime incident records transmitted directly to the FBI or to centralized state agencies that then report to the FBI. The Program thoroughly examines each report it receives for reasonableness, accuracy, and deviations that may indicate errors. Large variations in crime levels may indicate modified records procedures, incomplete reporting, or changes in a jurisdiction's boundaries. To identify any unusual fluctuations in an agency's crime counts, the Program compares monthly reports to previous submissions of the agency and with those for similar agencies.

The UCR Program presents crime counts for the nation as a whole, as well as for regions, states, counties, cities, towns, tribal law enforcement, and colleges and universities. This permits studies among

neighboring jurisdictions and among those with similar populations and other common characteristics.

The UCR Program annually publishes its findings in a preliminary release in the spring of the following calendar year, followed by a detailed annual report, *Crime in the United States*, issued in the fall. In addition to crime counts and trends, this report includes data on crimes cleared, persons arrested (age, sex, and race), law enforcement personnel (including the number of sworn officers killed or assaulted), and the characteristics of homicides (including age, sex, and race of victims and offenders; victim-offender relationships; weapons used; and circumstances surrounding the homicides). Other periodic reports are also available from the UCR Program.

National Crime Victimization Survey (NCVS)—A second perspective on crime is provided by this survey of the BJS. Details about the crimes come directly from the victims 12 years and older. No attempt is made to validate the information against police records or any other source.

The NCVS measures rape/sexual assault, robbery, assault, pocket-picking, purse snatching, burglary, and motor vehicle theft. The NCVS includes crimes reported to the police, as well as those not reported.

Police reporting rates (percent of victimizations) varied by type of crime. In 2005, for instance, 38 percent of rapes/sexual assaults were reported; 52 percent of robberies; 47 percent of assaults; 32 percent of personal thefts; 35 percent of pocket-pickings/purse snatchings; 56 percent of household burglaries; and 83 percent of motor vehicle thefts.

Murder and kidnaping are not covered. Commercial burglary and robbery were dropped from the program during 1977. The so-called victimless crimes, such as drunkenness, drug abuse, and prostitution, also are excluded, as are crimes for which it is difficult to identify knowledgeable respondents or to locate data records.

Crimes of which the victim may not be aware also cannot be measured effectively. Buying stolen property may fall into this category, as may some instances of embezzlement. Attempted crimes of many types probably are under recorded for this reason. Events in which the victim has shown a willingness to participate in illegal activity also are excluded.

In any encounter involving a personal crime, more than one criminal act can be committed against an individual. For example, a rape may be associated with a robbery, or a household offense, such as a burglary, can escalate into something more serious in the event of a personal confrontation. In classifying the survey-measured crimes, each criminal incident has been counted only once—by the most serious act that took place during the incident and ranked in accordance with the seriousness classification system used by the FBI. The order of seriousness for crimes against persons is as follows: rape, robbery, assault, and larceny. Personal crimes take precedence over household offenses.

A *victimization,* basic measure of the occurrence of crime, is a specific criminal act as it affects a single victim. The number of victimizations is determined by the number of victims of such acts. Victimization counts serve as key elements in computing rates of victimization. For crimes against persons, the rates are based on the total number of individuals age 12 and over or on a portion of that population sharing a particular characteristic or set of traits. As general indicators of the danger of having been victimized during the reference period, the rates are not sufficiently refined to represent true measures of risk for specific individuals or households.

An *incident* is a specific criminal act involving one or more victims; therefore the number of incidents of personal crimes is lower than that of victimizations.

Courts—Statistics on criminal offenses and the outcome of prosecutions are incomplete for the country as a whole, although data are available for many states individually.

U.S. Census Bureau, Statistical Abstract of the United States: 2009

Since 1982, through its National Judicial Reporting Program, the BJS has surveyed a nationally representative sample of 300 counties every 2 years and collected detailed information on demographic characteristics of felons, conviction offenses, type of sentences, sentence lengths, and time from arrest to conviction and sentencing.

The bulk of civil and criminal litigation in the country is commenced and determined in the various state courts. Only when the U.S. Constitution and acts of Congress specifically confer jurisdiction upon the federal courts may civil or criminal litigation be heard and decided by them. Generally, the federal courts have jurisdiction over the following types of cases: suits or proceedings by or against the United States; civil actions between private parties arising under the Constitution, laws, or treaties of the United States; civil actions between private litigants who are citizens of different states; civil cases involving admiralty, maritime, or private jurisdiction; and all matters in bankruptcy.

There are several types of courts with varying degrees of legal jurisdiction. These jurisdictions include original, appellate, general, and limited or special. A court of original jurisdiction is one having the authority initially to try a case and pass judgment on the law and the facts; a court of appellate jurisdiction is one with the legal authority to review cases and hear appeals; a court of general jurisdiction is a trial court of unlimited original jurisdiction in civil and/or criminal cases, also called a "major trial court"; a court of limited or special jurisdiction is a trial court with legal authority over only a particular class of cases, such as probate, juvenile, or traffic cases.

The 94 federal courts of original jurisdiction are known as the U.S. district courts. One or more of these courts is established in every state and one each in the District of Columbia, Puerto Rico, the Virgin Islands, the Northern Mariana Islands, and Guam. Appeals from the district courts are taken to intermediate appellate courts of which there are 13, known as U.S. courts of appeals and the United States Court of Appeals for the Federal Circuit. The Supreme Court of the United States is the final and highest appellate court in the federal system of courts.

Juvenile offenders—For statistical purposes, the FBI and most states classify as juvenile offenders persons under the age of 18 years who have committed a crime or crimes.

Delinquency cases are all cases of youths referred to a juvenile court for violation of a law or ordinance or for seriously "antisocial" conduct. Several types of facilities are available for those adjudicated delinquents, ranging from the short-term physically unrestricted environment to the long-term very restrictive atmosphere.

Prisoners and jail inmates—BJS started to collect annual data in 1979 on prisoners in federal and state prisons and reformatories. Adults convicted of criminal activity may be given a prison or jail sentence. A *prison* is a confinement facility having custodial authority over adults sentenced to confinement of more than 1 year. A *jail* is a facility, usually operated by a local law enforcement agency, holding persons detained pending adjudication and/or persons committed after adjudication to 1 year or less.

Data on inmates in local jails were collected by the BJS for the first time in 1970. Since then, BJS has conducted censuses of facilities and inmates every 5 to 6 years. In 1984, BJS initiated an annual survey of jails conducted in noncensus years.

Statistical reliability—For discussion of statistical collection, estimation and sampling procedures, and measures of statistical reliability pertaining to the National Crime Victimization Survey and Uniform Crime Reporting Program, see Appendix III.

U.S. Census Bureau, Statistical Abstract of the United States: 2008

Table 299. **Crimes and Crime Rates by Type of Offense: 1980 to 2005**

[(1,345 represents 1,345,000). Data include offenses actually reported to law enforcement and also offense estimations for nonreporting and partially reporting agencies within each state. Rates are based on Census Bureau estimated resident populations of July 1; 1980, 1990, and 2000 enumerated as of April 1. See source for details. For definitions of types of crimes, go to <http://www.fbi.gov/ucr/05cius/about/offense_definitions.html>]

Item and year	Violent crime					Property crime			
	Total	Murder [1]	Forcible rape	Robbery	Aggravated assault	Total	Burglary	Larceny/ theft	Motor vehicle theft
Number of offenses (1,000):									
1980	1,345	23	83	566	673	12,064	3,795	7,137	1,132
1985	1,328	19	88	498	723	11,103	3,073	6,926	1,103
1990	1,820	23	103	639	1,055	12,655	3,074	7,946	1,636
1991	1,912	25	107	688	1,093	12,961	3,157	8,142	1,662
1992	1,932	24	109	672	1,127	12,506	2,980	7,915	1,611
1993	1,926	25	106	660	1,136	12,219	2,835	7,821	1,563
1994	1,858	23	102	619	1,113	12,132	2,713	7,880	1,539
1995	1,799	22	97	581	1,099	12,064	2,594	7,998	1,472
1996	1,689	20	96	536	1,037	11,805	2,506	7,905	1,394
1997	1,636	18	96	499	1,023	11,558	2,461	7,744	1,354
1998	1,534	17	93	447	977	10,952	2,333	7,376	1,243
1999	1,426	16	89	409	912	10,208	2,101	6,956	1,152
2000 [2]	1,425	16	90	408	912	10,183	2,051	6,972	1,160
2001 [2]	1,439	16	91	424	909	10,437	2,117	7,092	1,228
2002	1,424	16	95	421	891	10,455	2,151	7,057	1,247
2003 [3]	1,384	17	94	414	859	10,443	2,155	7,027	1,261
2004 [3]	1,360	16	95	401	847	10,319	2,144	6,937	1,238
2005	1,391	17	94	417	863	10,166	2,154	6,777	1,235
Rate per 100,000 population:									
1980	597	10	37	251	299	5,353	1,684	3,167	502
1985	558	8	37	209	304	4,666	1,292	2,911	464
1990	730	9	41	256	423	5,073	1,232	3,185	656
1991	758	10	42	273	433	5,140	1,252	3,229	659
1992	758	9	43	264	442	4,904	1,168	3,104	632
1993	747	10	41	256	441	4,740	1,100	3,034	606
1994	714	9	39	238	428	4,660	1,042	3,027	591
1995	685	8	37	221	418	4,591	987	3,043	560
1996	637	7	36	202	391	4,451	945	2,980	526
1997	611	7	36	186	382	4,316	919	2,892	506
1998	568	6	35	166	361	4,053	863	2,730	460
1999	523	6	33	150	334	3,744	770	2,551	423
2000 [2]	507	6	32	145	324	3,618	729	2,477	412
2001 [2]	505	6	32	149	319	3,658	742	2,486	431
2002	494	6	33	146	310	3,631	747	2,451	433
2003 [3]	476	6	32	143	295	3,591	741	2,417	434
2004 [3]	463	6	32	137	289	3,514	730	2,362	422
2005	469	6	32	141	291	3,430	727	2,286	417

[1] Includes nonnegligent manslaughter. [2] The murder and nonnegligent homicides that occurred as a result of the events of September 11, 2001, were not included in this table. [3] The 2004 crime figures have been adjusted.

Source: U.S. Department of Justice, Federal Bureau of Investigation. *Crime in the United States*, annual. See also <http://www.fbi.gov/ucr/05cius/>.

Table 300. **Crimes and Crime Rates by Type and Area: 2005**

[In thousands (1,391 represents 1,391,000), except rate. Rate per 100,000 population; based on Census Bureau estimated resident population as of July 1. See headnote, Table 299. For definitions of types of crimes, go to <http://www.fbi.gov/ucr/05cius/about/offense_definitions.html>]

Type of crime	United States		Metropolitan statistical areas [1]		Cities outside metropolitan areas		Nonmetropolitan counties	
	Total	Rate	Total	Rate	Total	Rate	Total	Rate
Violent crime	1,391	469	1,253	510	75	374	63	207
Murder and nonnegligent manslaughter	17	6	15	6	1	3	1	4
Forcible rape	94	32	78	32	8	39	8	25
Robbery	417	141	401	163	12	58	5	16
Aggravated assault	863	291	759	309	55	273	50	162
Property crime	10,166	3,430	8,844	3,599	801	3,998	520	1,700
Burglary	2,154	727	1,828	744	161	801	166	542
Larceny-theft	6,777	2,286	5,864	2,386	602	3,002	311	1,017
Motor vehicle theft	1,235	417	1,153	469	39	195	43	141

[1] For definition, see Appendix II.

Source: U.S. Department of Justice, Federal Bureau of Investigation. *Crime in the United States*, annual. See <http://www.fbi.gov/ucr/05cius/>.

Table 301. Crime Rates by State, 2004 and 2005, and by Type, 2005

[Rates per 100,000 population. Data include offenses actually reported to law enforcement and also offense estimations for nonreporting and partially reporting agencies within each state. Based on Census Bureau estimated resident population as of July 1. For definitions of types of crimes, go to<http://www.fbi.gov/ucr/05cius/about/offense_definitions.html>]

State	Violent crime						Property crime				
		2005						2005			
	2004, total [1]	Total	Mur- der [2]	Forc- ible rape	Rob- bery	Aggra- vated assault	2004, total	Total	Burglary	Lar- ceny/ theft	Motor vehicle theft
United States...	463	469	6	32	141	291	3,517	3,430	727	2,286	417
Alabama........	427	432	8	34	141	248	4,025	3,892	954	2,650	288
Alaska.........	632	632	5	81	81	465	3,383	3,613	623	2,599	391
Arizona........	504	513	8	34	144	327	5,341	4,838	948	2,965	924
Arkansas.......	502	528	7	43	91	387	4,013	4,058	1,085	2,711	262
California.......	528	526	7	26	176	317	3,419	3,323	693	1,917	713
Colorado.......	372	397	4	43	85	265	3,919	4,040	745	2,735	560
Connecticut......	289	275	3	20	113	139	2,627	2,558	437	1,824	297
Delaware.......	615	632	4	45	155	428	3,164	3,111	689	2,144	279
District of Columbia [3]......	1,369	1,459	35	30	672	721	4,859	4,747	650	2,695	1,402
Florida.........	712	708	5	37	169	497	4,180	4,008	926	2,658	423
Georgia	451	449	6	24	155	264	4,266	4,172	931	2,751	490
Hawaii	255	255	2	27	79	148	4,793	4,793	768	3,308	716
Idaho	247	257	2	40	19	195	2,794	2,698	564	1,932	202
Illinois [4]........	546	552	6	34	182	330	3,186	3,080	607	2,165	309
Indiana........	326	324	6	30	109	180	3,398	3,456	698	2,412	347
Iowa..........	288	291	1	28	39	223	2,905	2,834	606	2,043	185
Kansas........	378	387	4	38	65	280	3,974	3,787	689	2,758	340
Kentucky.......	245	267	5	34	88	140	2,538	2,531	634	1,686	211
Louisiana	640	594	10	31	118	435	4,410	3,683	871	2,495	318
Maine.........	104	112	1	25	24	62	2,410	2,413	479	1,833	102
Maryland.......	701	703	10	23	257	414	3,640	3,544	641	2,294	608
Massachusetts....	460	457	3	27	119	308	2,460	2,364	541	1,527	295
Michigan.......	492	552	6	51	132	363	3,058	3,091	697	1,918	477
Minnesota......	270	297	2	44	92	159	3,039	3,084	579	2,227	278
Mississippi......	295	278	7	39	82	149	3,479	3,260	920	2,084	257
Missouri	490	525	7	28	124	366	3,904	3,928	738	2,746	443
Montana	294	282	2	32	19	229	2,936	3,143	389	2,543	211
Nebraska	309	287	3	33	59	193	3,521	3,423	532	2,574	317
Nevada........	616	607	9	42	195	362	4,207	4,242	972	2,154	1,115
New Hampshire ...	170	132	1	31	27	72	2,040	1,796	317	1,377	102
New Jersey	356	355	5	14	152	184	2,429	2,333	447	1,568	318
New Mexico......	687	702	7	54	99	542	4,198	4,148	1,094	2,640	415
New York	440	446	5	19	183	240	2,199	2,109	353	1,570	186
North Carolina....	448	468	7	27	146	289	4,160	4,075	1,201	2,546	328
North Dakota....	88	98	1	24	7	66	1,917	1,978	312	1,500	166
Ohio..........	339	351	5	40	163	143	3,673	3,663	873	2,429	361
Oklahoma	501	509	5	42	91	371	4,242	4,042	1,006	2,644	392
Oregon........	299	287	2	35	68	182	4,631	4,400	759	3,112	529
Pennsylvania....	412	425	6	29	155	235	2,415	2,417	452	1,729	237
Rhode Island....	248	251	3	30	72	146	2,884	2,719	494	1,816	409
South Carolina....	790	761	7	43	132	579	4,505	4,339	1,001	2,954	384
South Dakota.....	171	176	2	47	19	108	1,934	1,776	324	1,344	108
Tennessee.......	698	753	7	36	167	542	4,307	4,276	1,027	2,828	421
Texas.........	541	530	6	37	157	330	4,494	4,332	962	2,962	409
Utah..........	233	227	2	37	44	143	4,086	3,869	606	2,919	344
Vermont	115	120	1	23	12	84	2,308	2,281	492	1,686	103
Virginia	276	283	6	23	99	155	2,677	2,638	392	2,035	211
Washington	344	346	3	45	92	206	4,849	4,893	960	3,150	784
West Virginia	282	273	4	18	45	206	2,506	2,625	621	1,794	210
Wisconsin	210	242	4	21	82	135	2,663	2,660	441	1,993	227
Wyoming........	230	230	3	24	15	188	3,334	3,155	476	2,534	145

[1] The 2004 data for violent crime have been revised.   [2] Includes nonnegligent manslaughter.   [3] Includes offenses reported by the Zoological Police and the Metro Transit Police.   [4] Limited data for 2004 were available for Illinois.

Source: U.S. Department of Justice, Federal Bureau of Investigation. *Crime in the United States*, annual. See <http://www.fbi.gov/ucr/05cius/>.

Table 302. Crime Rates by Type—Selected Large Cities: 2005

[Offenses known to the police per 100,000 population. Based on U.S. Census Bureau estimated resident population. For definitions of types of crimes, go to <http://www.fbi.gov/ucr/05cius/about/offense_definitions.html\>]

City ranked by population size, 2005	Violent crime					Property crime			
	Total	Murder	Forcible rape	Robbery	Aggra-vated assault	Total	Burglary	Larceny-theft	Motor vehicle theft
New York, NY	673	6.6	17.4	305	344	2,002	286	1,490	226
Los Angeles, CA [1]	821	12.6	28.5	356	423	3,030	584	1,704	742
Chicago, IL [2]	(NA)	15.6	(NA)	556	624	4,565	881	2,902	783
Houston,TX	1,173	16.3	42.6	544	570	5,887	1,346	3,543	998
Philadelphia, PA	1,467	25.6	69.5	684	688	4,102	744	2,583	775
Phoenix, AZ	729	15.0	36.4	289	389	6,365	1,109	3,583	1,673
Las Vegas MPD Jurisidiction, NV. .	744	11.3	48.1	273	412	4,838	1,121	2,161	1,557
San Diego, CA.	519	4.0	29.6	146	339	3,633	587	1,935	1,111
San Antonio,TX	637	6.8	47.2	171	412	6,445	1,143	4,826	475
Dallas,TX	1,254	16.4	45.7	559	633	7,230	1,818	4,252	1,160
San Jose, CA.	384	2.9	28.9	97	255	2,518	445	1,469	605
Honolulu, HI.	283	1.7	25.8	93	163	4,665	683	3,233	748
Detroit, MI [1]	2,361	41.4	65.5	758	1,497	6,004	1,700	1,932	2,373
Indianapolis, IN	993	13.5	65.8	409	505	6,258	1,443	3,691	1,124
Jacksonville, FL	830	11.4	23.8	283	511	5,472	1,131	3,720	621
San Francisco, CA	799	12.8	23.0	411	352	4,574	829	2,655	1,091
Columbus, OH	849	14.1	76.3	522	237	7,518	2,015	4,406	1,097
Austin,TX	490	3.8	45.0	171	270	6,013	1,051	4,594	368
Memphis,TN	1,861	20.3	59.1	658	1,124	8,372	2,336	4,813	1,223
Charlotte-Mecklenburg PD, NC . . .	1,172	12.6	47.7	539	572	6,880	1,888	3,944	1,048
Baltimore, MD	1,754	42.0	25.3	610	1,077	5,185	1,145	3,071	969
Louisville Metro, KY [1,3]	625	8.8	33.5	292	290	4,400	1,146	2,750	505
Fort Worth,TX	639	9.8	50.7	225	354	6,068	1,416	4,046	606
El Paso,TX [1].	435	2.3	50.0	74	309	3,284	358	2,493	433
Milwaukee, WI [1]	1,028	20.6	26.9	501	479	5,650	786	3,725	1,140
Seattle, WA	709	4.3	23.8	277	404	7,505	1,167	4,687	1,651
Boston, MA	1,318	12.9	47.2	467	791	4,441	798	2,811	831
Denver, CO [1]	788	10.5	56.0	253	468	5,996	1,300	3,278	1,418
Nashville,TN	1,612	17.1	61.8	438	1,096	6,426	1,158	4,649	619
Washington, DC	1,402	35.4	30.0	636	700	4,577	649	2,572	1,356
Portland, OR	714	3.7	60.1	210	440	6,966	1,133	4,773	1,060
Oklahoma City, OK	854	10.2	67.3	224	552	7,927	1,679	5,386	862
Tucson, AZ	953	10.4	71.4	318	553	5,912	969	3,710	1,233
Albuquerque, NM	952	10.8	58.1	234	649	6,164	1,171	4,220	774
Long Beach, CA.	709	8.8	21.7	292	386	2,815	616	1,419	780
New Orleans, LA [4]	(NA)	(NA)	(NA)	(NA)	(NA)	(NA)	(NA)	(NA)	(NA)
Fresno, CA [1].	846	10.6	32.3	277	526	5,544	905	3,492	1,148
Cleveland, OH	1,401	24.0	106.3	816	455	6,258	1,881	2,892	1,484
Sacramento, CA	1,151	11.4	37.2	441	661	5,703	1,277	2,912	1,514
Mesa, AZ	504	6.4	42.9	102	353	5,321	787	3,595	939
Kansas City, MO.	1,459	28.1	68.9	447	919	7,774	1,659	4,823	1,293
Virginia Beach, VA	255	4.3	22.4	139	89	2,996	497	2,331	169
Atlanta, GA	1,675	20.9	51.8	664	938	7,290	1,544	4,410	1,337
Omaha, NB	565	7.5	48.3	165	343	5,352	768	3,659	925
Oakland, CA	(NA)	(NA)	(NA)	(NA)	(NA)	(NA)	(NA)	(NA)	(NA)
Miami, FL	1,580	13.9	16.0	520	1,030	6,006	1,385	3,587	1,034
Tulsa, OK	1,293	15.0	78.4	284	916	6,513	1,706	3,842	965
Minneapolis, MN.	1,454	12.5	106.8	687	648	5,958	1,471	3,452	1,035
Colorado Springs, CO	477	3.2	66.5	117	291	5,235	979	3,782	474
Arlington,TX.	648	6.6	48.7	210	383	5,584	1,090	3,998	495
Wichita, KS	745	3.4	52.4	140	549	4,713	984	3,240	488
Saint Louis, MO	2,405	37.9	79.8	857	1,431	11,053	2,085	6,614	2,354
Santa Ana, CA	535	4.9	21.4	187	322	2,983	346	1,599	1,039
Anaheim, CA	481	3.0	24.1	165	289	2,831	574	1,648	609
Raleigh, NC.	617	5.7	26.5	229	356	3,773	915	2,554	304
Pittsburgh, PA	1,023	19.0	35.4	489	480	4,725	912	3,125	687
Tampa, FL.	1,431	6.1	63.8	353	1,008	6,161	1,493	3,818	849
Cincinnati, OH	1,189	25.1	104.7	738	321	7,156	1,731	4,484	941
Toledo, OH	1,221	9.2	58.7	444	709	7,745	2,327	4,369	1,048
Aurora, CO	620	9.5	75.4	218	318	4,974	836	3,211	927
Riverside, CA.	673	3.4	38.9	233	398	4,625	860	2,810	954
Corpus Christi, TX	717	2.8	75.9	168	470	7,044	1,175	5,552	317
Bakersfield, CA	597	11.2	15.7	185	385	5,751	1,311	3,511	930
Buffalo, NY	1,390	19.8	65.0	588	717	5,906	1,497	3,562	848
Stockton, CA	1,491	14.6	38.7	482	957	6,694	1,219	4,077	1,398
Newark, NJ	1,004	34.5	29.5	445	495	4,526	732	1,770	2,024
St. Paul, MN	877	8.6	78.9	279	510	4,913	1,250	2,785	878
Anchorage, AK.	736	5.8	81.1	139	510	4,116	646	2,987	483
Lexington, KY	550	5.6	54.8	214	276	3,844	810	2,757	278
St. Petersburg, FL	1,546	11.8	39.7	377	1,118	6,408	1,387	4,081	940
Mobile, AL [5]	466	14.0	29.6	239	184	5,744	1,534	3,761	449

NA Not available.   [1] Due to reporting changes or annexations, figures are not comparable to previous years.   [2] Forcible rape figures furnished by the state-level Uniform Crime Reporting (UCR) Program administered by the Illinois Department of State Police were not in accordance with national UCR guidelines. Therefore, the figures were excluded from the forcible rape and Violent Crime and Crime Index total categories.   [3] Louisville, KY, and Jefferson County, KY, Police Departments merged forming the Louisville Metro Police Department.   [4] Did not provide complete data for 12 months.   [5] Mobile, Alabama, population includes a redistribution of jurisdiction with the Mobile County Sheriff's Department.

Source: U.S. Department of Justice, Federal Bureau of Investigation, *Crime in the United States*, annual. See also <http://www.fbi.gov/ucr/05cius/>.

U.S. Census Bureau, Statistical Abstract of the United States: 2008

Table 303. **Murder Victims—Circumstances and Weapons Used or Cause of Death: 1990 to 2005**

[Based solely on police investigation. For definition of crimes, go to <http://www.fbi.gov/ucr/05cius/about/offensedefinitions.html>]

Characteristic	1990	2000	2004	2005	Characteristic	1990	2000	2004	2005
Murders, total. . . .	**20,273**	**13,230**	**14,249**	**14,860**	Other motives	19.4	20.2	18.9	19.1
Percent distribution. . . .	**100.0**	**100.0**	**100.0**	**100.0**	Unknown.	24.8	30.8	35.0	37.6
CIRCUMSTANCES					TYPE OF WEAPON				
Felonies, total	20.8	16.8	14.8	14.9	OR CAUSE OF DEATH				
Robbery	9.2	8.1	7.0	6.2	Guns	64.3	65.5	66.0	67.8
Narcotics	6.7	4.5	3.9	4.0	Handguns	49.8	51.2	51.3	50.5
Sex offenses	1.1	0.6	0.4	0.4	Cutting or stabbing	17.4	13.5	13.1	12.8
Other felonies.	3.7	3.7	3.4	4.0	Blunt objects [1]	5.4	4.7	4.7	4.1
Suspected felonies . . .	0.7	0.5	0.8	0.3	Personal weapons [2] . . .	5.5	7.0	6.6	6.0
Argument, total.	34.4	31.8	30.4	28.5	Strangulations,				
Property or money. . .	2.5	1.6	1.6	1.4	asphyxiations	2.0	2.0	1.9	1.4
Romantic triangle . . .	2.0	0.9	0.7	0.8	Fire	1.4	1.0	0.8	0.8
Other arguments. . . .	29.8	29.3	28.8	26.3	All other [3]	4.0	6.4	6.8	7.0

[1]. Refers to club, hammer, etc.   [2] Hands, fists, feet, etc.   [3] Includes poison, drowning, explosives, narcotics, and unknown.

Source: U.S. Department of Justice, Federal Bureau of Investigation, *Crime in the United States,* annual. See also <http://www.fbi.gov/ucr/05cius/>.

Table 304. **Murder Victims by Age, Sex, and Race: 2005**

Age	Total	Sex			Race			
		Male	Female	Unknown	White	Black	Other	Unknown
Murders, total.	**14,860**	**11,683**	**3,155**	**22**	**7,133**	**7,125**	**390**	**212**
Percent of total [1]	100.0	78.6	21.2	0.1	48.0	47.9	2.6	1.4
Under 18 years old [2].	1,446	1,019	422	5	716	670	35	25
18 years old and over [2].	13,153	10,474	2,677	2	6,302	6,370	350	131
Infant (under 1 year old)	182	104	73	5	115	53	4	10
1 to 4 years old	328	186	142	–	175	140	5	8
5 to 8 years old	75	38	37	–	38	32	4	1
9 to 12 years old	78	38	40	–	39	36	2	1
13 to 16 years old	456	365	91	–	208	237	10	1
17 to 19 years old	1,349	1,184	165	–	555	751	32	11
20 to 24 years old	2,834	2,460	374	–	1,110	1,606	93	25
25 to 29 years old	2,262	1,920	342	–	951	1,247	48	16
30 to 34 years old	1,649	1,341	308	–	736	860	36	17
35 to 39 years old	1,257	930	326	1	625	586	32	14
40 to 44 years old	1,194	874	320	–	636	504	38	16
45 to 49 years old	938	705	233	–	528	373	25	12
50 to 54 years old	708	543	164	1	403	277	19	9
55 to 59 years old	384	275	109	–	259	108	13	4
60 to 64 years old	272	192	80	–	175	81	11	5
65 to 69 years old	183	108	75	–	125	51	6	1
70 to 74 years old	159	96	63	–	117	38	4	–
75 years old and over	291	134	157	–	223	60	3	5
Age unknown	261	190	56	15	115	85	5	56

– Represents zero.   [1] Because of rounding, details may not equal total.   [2] Does not include unknown ages.

Source: U.S. Department of Justice, Federal Bureau of Investigation. *Crime in the United States,* annual. See <http://www.fbi.gov/ucr/05cius/>.

Law Enforcement, Courts, and Prisons **195**

Table 305. Homicide Trends: 1980 to 2004

[Not all agencies which report offense information to the FBI also submit supplemental data on homicides. To account for the total number of homicide victims, the data was weighted to match national and state estimates prepared by the FBI; hence, detail may not equal total]

Year	Number of victims Total	Male	Female	White	Black	Other	Rate [1] Total	Male	Female	White	Black	Other
1980	23,040	17.788	5,232	12,275	9,767	327	10.2	16.2	4.5	6.3	37.7	5.7
1985	18,976	14,079	4,880	10,590	7,891	399	8.0	12.2	4.0	5.2	27.6	5.5
1990	23,438	18,304	5,115	11,279	11,488	400	9.4	15.0	4.0	5.4	37.6	4.2
1992	23,760	18,513	5,217	11,229	11,777	573	9.3	14.9	4.0	5.3	37.2	5.4
1993	24,526	18,937	5,550	11,278	12,435	601	9.5	15.0	4.2	5.3	38.7	5.5
1994	23,326	18,294	5,007	10,773	11,856	526	9.0	14.4	3.8	5.0	36.4	4.6
1995	21,606	16,552	5,022	10,376	10,444	581	8.2	12.9	3.7	4.8	31.6	4.9
1996	19,645	15,153	4,469	9,483	9,476	512	7.4	11.7	3.3	4.3	28.3	4.1
1997	18,208	14,057	4,125	8,620	8,842	524	6.8	10.7	3.0	3.9	26.0	4.1
1998	16,974	12,753	4,139	8,389	7,931	393	6.3	9.7	3.0	3.8	23.0	2.9
1999	15,522	11,704	3,800	7,777	7,139	458	5.7	8.8	2.7	3.5	20.5	3.3
2000	15,586	11,818	3,733	7,560	7,425	399	5.5	8.6	2.6	3.3	20.5	2.7
2001	16,037	12,232	3,775	7,884	7,522	424	5.6	8.8	2.6	3.4	20.4	2.8
2002	16,204	12,410	3,764	7,784	7,758	437	5.6	8.8	2.6	3.3	20.8	2.7
2003	16,582	12,804	3,693	7,932	7,893	468	5.7	9.0	2.5	3.4	20.9	2.8
2004	16,137	12,556	3,541	7,939	7,557	417	5.5	8.7	2.4	3.3	19.7	2.4

[1] Rate is per 100,000 inhabitants.

Source: U.S. Department of Justice, Office of Justice Programs, Bureau of Justice Statistics, Homicide Trends in the United States, 1976–2004 See also: <http://www.ojp.usdoj.gov/bjs/homicide/hortmd.htm>.

Table 306. Homicide Victims by Race and Sex: 1980 to 2004

[Rates per 100,000 resident population in specified group. Excludes deaths to nonresidents of United States. Beginning 1999, deaths classified according to the tenth revision of the *International Classification of Diseases*; see text, Section 2, and footnote 3 in table]

Year	Homicide victims Total [1]	White Male	Female	Black Male	Female	Homicide rate [2] Total [1]	White Male	Female	Black Male	Female
1980	24,278	10,381	3,177	8,385	1,898	10.7	10.9	3.2	66.6	13.5
1985	19,893	8,122	3,041	6,616	1,666	8.3	8.2	2.9	48.4	11.0
1990	24,932	9,147	3,006	9,981	2,163	10.0	9.0	2.8	69.2	13.5
1992	25,488	9,456	3,012	10,131	2,187	10.0	9.1	2.8	67.5	13.1
1993	26,009	9,054	3,232	10,640	2,297	10.1	8.6	3.0	69.7	13.6
1994	24,926	9,055	2,921	10,083	2,124	9.6	8.5	2.6	65.1	12.4
1995	22,895	8,336	3,028	8,847	1,936	8.7	7.8	2.7	56.3	11.1
1996	20,971	7,570	2,747	8,183	1,800	7.9	7.0	2.5	51.5	10.2
1997	19,846	7,343	2,570	7,601	1,652	7.4	6.7	2.3	47.1	9.3
1998	18,272	6,707	2,534	6,873	1,547	6.8	6.1	2.2	42.1	8.0
1999 [3]	16,889	6,162	2,466	6,214	1,434	6.2	5.6	2.2	37.5	7.8
2000	16,765	5,925	2,414	6,482	1,385	6.1	5.3	2.1	38.6	7.5
2001	20,308	8,254	3,074	6,780	1,446	7.1	7.2	2.6	38.3	7.4
2002	17,638	6,282	2,403	6,896	1,391	6.1	5.4	2.0	38.4	7.0
2003	17,732	6,337	2,372	7,083	1,309	6.1	5.4	2.0	38.9	6.6
2004	17,357	6,302	2,341	6,873	1,296	5.9	5.3	1.9	37.1	6.4

[1] Includes races not shown separately. [2] Rate based on enumerated population figures as of April 1 for 1980, 1990, and 2000; estimated resident population as of July 1 for other years. [3] Effective with data for 1999, causes of death are classified by The Tenth Revision International Classification of Diseases (ICD-10), replacing the Ninth Revision (ICD-9) used for 1979–98 data. Breaks in the comparability of some cause-of-death statistics result from changes in category titles, changes in the structure and content of the classification, and changes in coding rules used to select the underlying cause of death. In ICD-9, the category Homicide also inludes death as a result of legal intervention. ICD-10 has two separate categories for these two causes of death. Some caution should be used in comparing data between 1998 and 1999.

Source: U.S. National Center for Health Statistics, *Vital Statistics of the United States*, annual; and *National Vital Statistics Reports (NVSR)* (formerly *Monthly Vital Statistics Report*); and unpublished data.

Table 307. Forcible Rape—Number and Rate: 1980 to 2005

[For definition of rape, go to <http://www.fbi.gov/ucr/05cius/about/offense_definitions.html>]

Item	1980	1990	1995	1999	2000	2001	2002	2003	2004 [1]	2005
NUMBER										
Total	82,990	102,560	97,460	89,411	90,186	90,863	95,235	93,883	95,809	93,934
By force	63,599	86,541	85,249	79,697	81,111	82,004	86,655	85,837	87,953	86,231
Attempt	19,391	16,019	12,211	9,714	9,075	8,859	8,580	8,046	7,856	7,703
RATE										
Per 100,000 population	36.8	41.1	37.1	32.8	32.0	31.8	33.1	32.3	32.4	31.7
Per 100,000 females	71.6	80.5	72.5	64.1	62.7	62.6	65.0	63.5	63.8	62.5

[1] Data have been revised.

Source: U.S. Department of Justice, Federal Bureau of Investigation, *Population-at-Risk Rates and Selected Crime Indicators*, annual. See also <http://www.fbi.gov/ucr/05cius/offenses/violent_crime/forcible_rape.html>.

Table 308. **Violence by Intimate Partners by Sex, 1995 to 2004, and by Type of Crime, 2004**

[Violent acts covered include murder, rape, sexual assault, robbery, and aggravated and simple assault. Intimate partners involve current spouses, former spouses, current boy/girlfriends, and former boy/girlfriends. Based on the National Criminal Victimization Survey; see text, this section, and Appendix III. For definitions, go to <http://www.ojp.usdoj.gov/bjs/intimate/definitions.htm>]

Year and type of crime	All persons		Female victims		Male victims	
	Number	Rate per 100,000 [1]	Number	Rate per 100,000 [1]	Number	Rate per 100,000 [1]
1995	1,063,520	493.0	953,700	855.8	109,820	105.3
1996	1,008,860	462.8	879,290	781.7	129,570	122.8
1997	953,780	432.7	848,480	747.3	105,300	98.5
1998	1,054,260	475.7	896,030	780.9	158,230	146.7
1999	783,120	347.7	672,330	578.4	110,790	101.6
2000	630,530	277.2	547,310	466.5	83,220	75.5
2001	693,321	301.4	589,692	497.1	103,629	92.8
2002	568,690	245.4	495,772	214.0	72,918	31.5
2003	521,760	218.0	437,990	183.0	83,750	35.0
2004, total	627,410	258.7	475,940	381.9	151,470	128.5
Murder	1,544	0.5	1,159	0.8	385	0.3
Rape or sexual assault	28,900	11.9	28,900	23.2	(B)	(B)
Robbery	64,340	19.2	46,620	37.4	17,720	15.0
Aggravated assault	97,000	30.9	74,820	60.0	22,180	18.8
Simple assault	437,170	134.3	325,600	261.3	111,570	94.6

B Base figure too small to meet statistical standards for reliability of derived figure. [1] Rates are the number of victimizations per 100,000 persons.

Source: U.S. Department of Justice, Office of Justice Programs, Bureau of Justice Statistics, Intimate Partner Violence, Series NCJ-210675, December 2006 and unpublished data; <http://www.ojp.usdoj.gov/bjs/intimate/ipv.htm>.

Table 309. **Robbery and Property Crimes by Type and Selected Characteristic: 1990 to 2005**

[(639 represents 639,000.) For definitions of types of crimes, go to <http://www.fbi.gov/ucr/05cius/about/offense_definitions.html>]

Characteristic of offenses	Number of offenses (1,000)				Rate per 100,000 population				Average value lost (dol.)	
	1990	2000	2004	2005	1990	2000	2004	2005	2004	2005
Robbery, total [1]	639	408	401	417	256.3	144.9	141.6	140.7	1,283	1,239
Type of crime:										
Street or highway	359	188	172	184	144.2	66.7	60.6	62.1	913	1,020
Commercial house	73	57	59	60	29.5	20.1	20.8	20.1	1,521	1,662
Gas station	18	12	11	12	7.1	4.1	3.8	4.0	1,698	1,104
Convenience store	39	26	25	24	15.6	9.3	8.7	8.0	642	677
Residence	62	50	56	59	25.1	17.7	19.6	20.0	1,444	1,332
Bank	9	9	10	9	3.8	3.1	3.4	3.0	4,153	4,113
Weapon used:										
Firearm	234	161	163	175	94.1	57.0	55.5	59.0	(NA)	(NA)
Knife or cutting instrument . . .	76	36	36	37	30.7	12.8	12.2	12.5	(NA)	(NA)
Other dangerous weapon	61	53	38	39	24.5	18.9	12.8	13.2	(NA)	(NA)
Strongarm	268	159	165	166	107.7	56.4	56.3	56.0	(NA)	(NA)
Burglary, total	3,074	2,050	2,144	2,154	1232.2	728.4	756.3	726.7	1,726	1,771
Forcible entry	2,150	1,297	1,310	1,310	864.5	460.7	462.1	440.0	(NA)	(NA)
Unlawful entry	678	615	701	701	272.8	218.7	247.2	237.5	(NA)	(NA)
Attempted forcible entry	245	138	133	133	98.7	49.0	47.0	45.2	(NA)	(NA)
Residence	2,033	1,335	1,409	1,417	817.4	474.3	497.0	477.9	1,737	1,813
Nonresidence	1,041	715	735	738	418.5	254.1	259.3	248.8	1,702	1,687
Occurred during the night	1,135	699	713	708	456.4	248.3	251.5	238.9	(NA)	(NA)
Occurred during the day	1,151	836	889	890	462.8	297.2	313.6	328.8	(NA)	(NA)
Larceny-theft, total	7,946	6,972	6,937	6,777	3185.1	2477.3	2446.5	2286.3	733	857
Pocket picking	81	36	30	29	32.4	12.7	10.5	9.8	350	346
Purse snatching	82	37	42	42	32.8	13.2	14.9	14.2	417	404
Shoplifting	1,291	959	1,009	939	519.1	340.7	355.9	317.0	155	184
From motor vehicles	1,744	1,754	1,758	1,751	701.3	623.3	620.1	590.6	702	704
Motor vehicle accessories	1,185	677	749	693	476.3	240.6	264.2	233.6	428	482
Bicycles	443	312	250	249	178.2	110.9	88.1	83.9	241	267
From buildings	1,118	914	861	852	449.4	324.6	303.7	287.3	1,114	1,738
From coin-operated machines . .	63	46	46	41	25.4	16.2	16.2	13.8	238	232
Other	1,940	2,232	2,191	2,182	780.0	793.0	772.8	736.1	1,052	1,137
Motor vehicles, total [2]	1,636	1,160	1,238	1,237	655.8	412.2	436.6	417.4	6,019	6,204
Automobiles	1,304	877	903	907	524.3	311.5	318.5	304.5	(NA)	(NA)
Trucks and buses	238	209	226	219	95.5	74.1	79.7	76.2	(NA)	(NA)

NA Not available. [1] Includes other crimes not shown separately. [2] Includes other types of motor vehicles not shown separately.

Source: U.S. Department of Justice, Federal Bureau of Investigation, Population-at-Risk Rates and Selected Crime Indicators, Crime in the United States, annual. See <http://www.fbi.gov/ucr/05cius/>.

Table 310. **Hate Crimes—Number of Incidents, Offenses, Victims, and Known Offenders by Bias Motivation: 2000 to 2005**

[The FBI collected statistics on hate crimes from 12,417 law enforcement agencies representing over 245 million inhabitants in 2005. Hate crime offenses cover incidents motivated by race, religion, sexual orientation, ethnicity/national origin, and disability]

Bias motivation	Incidents reported	Offenses	Victims[1]	Known offenders[2]
2000, Total	8,213	9,619	10,117	7,690
2003, Total	7,529	8,773	9,164	6,979
2004, Total	7,679	9,065	9,561	7,175
2005, Total	7,163	8,380	8,804	6,804
Race, total	3,919	4,691	4,895	3,913
Anti-White	828	935	975	963
Anti-Black	2,630	3,200	3,322	2,581
Anti-American Indian/Alaska native.	79	95	97	73
Anti-Asian/Pacific Islander	199	231	240	163
Anti-multiracial group	183	230	261	133
Ethnicity/national origin, total	944	1,144	1,228	1,115
Anti-Hispanic	522	660	722	691
Anti-other ethnicity/national origin.	422	484	506	424
Religion, total.	1,227	1,314	1,405	580
Anti-Jewish	848	900	977	364
Anti-Catholic	58	61	61	22
Anti-Protestant	57	58	58	32
Anti-Islamic	128	146	151	89
Anti-other religious group	93	102	106	54
Anti-multireligious group	39	42	47	18
Anti-atheism/agnosticism/etc.	4	5	5	1
Sexual orientation, total	1,017	1,171	1,213	1,138
Anti-male homosexual	621	713	743	715
Anti-female homosexual	155	180	186	146
Anti-homosexual.	195	228	233	237
Anti-heterosexual	21	23	23	18
Anti-bisexual	25	27	28	22
Disability, total	53	53	54	54
Anti-physical	21	21	21	21
Anti-mental	32	32	33	33
Multiple bias [3]	3	7	9	4

[1] The term "victim" may refer to a person, business, institution, or a society as a whole. [2] The term "known offender" does not imply that the identity of the suspect is known, but only that an attribute of the suspect is identified which distinguishes him/her from an unknown offender. [3] In a "multiple-bias incident" two conditions must be met: more than one offense type must occur in the incident and at least two offense types must be motivated by different biases.

Source: U.S. Department of Justice, Federal Bureau of Investigation, Uniform Crime Reports, *Hate Crime Statistics*, annual. See <http://www.fbi.gov/ucr/hc2005/>.

Table 311. **Hate Crimes Reported by State: 2005**

[(245,006 represents 245,006,000.) See headnote, Table 310]

State	Number of participating agencies	Population covered (1,000)	Agencies submitting incidents	Incidents reported	State	Number of participating agencies	Population covered (1,000)	Agencies submitting incidents	Incidents reported
United States . . .	12,417	245,006	2,037	7,163	Mississippi.	67	867	–	–
					Missouri	278	3,526	25	78
Alabama	32	455	–	–	Montana	108	935	25	65
Alaska	1	276	1	4	Nebraska	194	1,437	11	71
Arizona	78	4,203	26	138	Nevada	35	2,415	4	77
Arkansas	205	1,704	66	134	New Hampshire	140	1,019	23	32
California	725	36,132	252	1,379	New Jersey	513	8,718	216	738
Colorado	205	4,517	43	125	New Mexico	48	1,223	3	18
Connecticut	98	3,429	45	95	New York	302	7,869	43	249
Delaware.	53	844	11	45	North Carolina	436	8,458	41	89
District of Columbia. . .	2	551	2	48	North Dakota	71	569	8	12
Florida	492	17,744	95	231	Ohio.	443	8,702	60	176
Georgia	71	1,926	4	17	Oklahoma	297	3,548	33	41
Hawaii	(1)	(1)	(1)	(1)	Oregon	168	3,637	26	137
Idaho	106	1,426	16	33	Pennsylvania	916	11,565	36	118
Illinois.	66	5,047	50	168	Rhode Island	48	1,076	10	15
Indiana	142	3,933	18	54	South Carolina	446	4,254	50	98
Iowa.	225	2,935	19	37	South Dakota	95	533	7	9
Kansas	349	2,048	35	72	Tennessee.	455	5,963	68	128
Kentucky	321	3,745	22	44	Texas	997	22,840	79	264
Louisiana	133	3,248	10	17	Utah.	112	2,433	14	44
Maine	147	1,322	27	57	Vermont	75	602	17	32
Maryland	150	5,600	29	195	Virginia	395	7,517	68	295
					Washington	252	6,282	55	171
Massachusetts	267	5,665	83	371	West Virginia	349	1,680	17	47
Michigan	597	9,997	166	640	Wisconsin	359	5,290	20	46
Minnesota	302	4,923	55	206	Wyoming.	51	380	3	3

– Represents zero. [1] Did not report.

Source: U.S. Department of Justice, Federal Bureau of Investigation, Uniform Crime Reports, *Hate Crime Statistics*, annual. See <http://www.fbi.gov/ucr/hc2005/>.

198   Law Enforcement, Courts, and Prisons

[**(39,926 represents 39,926,000.)** Based on National Crime Victimization Survey; see text, this section, and Appendix III. For definitions of crimes, go to <http://www.ojp.usdoj.gov/bjs/abstract/cvus/definitions.htm>]

Type of crime	Number of victimizations (1,000)				Victimization rates [1]			
	1995	2000	2004	2005	1995	2000	2004	2005
All crimes, total	**39,926**	**25,893**	**24,061**	**23,441**	(X)	(X)	(X)	(X)
Personal crimes [2]	**10,436**	**6,597**	**5,407**	**5,401**	46.2	29.1	22.4	22.1
Crimes of violence	10,022	6,323	5,183	5,174	44.5	27.9	21.4	21.2
Completed violence	2,960	2,044	1,737	1,659	12.9	9.0	7.2	6.8
Attempted/threatened violence	7,061	4,279	2,446	3,515	31.6	18.9	14.3	14.4
Rape/sexual assault	363	261	210	192	1.6	1.2	0.9	0.8
Rape/attempted rape	252	147	101	130	1.1	0.6	0.4	0.5
Rape	153	92	59	69	0.7	0.4	0.2	0.3
Attempted rape	99	55	42	61	0.4	0.2	0.2	0.2
Sexual assault	112	114	109	62	0.5	0.5	0.5	0.3
Robbery	1,171	732	502	625	5.3	3.2	2.1	2.6
Completed/property taken	753	520	299	415	3.5	2.3	1.2	1.7
With injury	224	160	110	143	1.0	0.7	0.5	0.6
Without injury	529	360	189	272	2.4	1.6	0.8	1.1
Attempted to take property	418	212	203	210	1.8	0.9	0.8	0.9
With injury	84	66	71	65	0.4	0.3	0.3	0.3
Without injury	335	146	132	145	1.4	0.6	0.5	0.6
Assault	8,487	5,330	4,471	4,357	37.6	23.5	18.5	17.8
Aggravated	2,050	1,293	1,030	1,052	8.8	5.7	4.3	4.3
With injury	533	346	378	331	2.4	1.5	1.6	1.4
Threatened with weapon	1,517	946	652	723	6.4	4.2	2.7	3.0
Simple	6,437	4,038	3,441	3,305	28.9	17.8	14.2	13.5
With minor injury	1,426	989	898	795	6.0	4.4	3.7	3.3
Without injury	5,012	3,048	2,543	2,510	22.9	13.4	10.5	10.3
Personal theft [3]	414	274	224	227	1.7	1.2	0.9	0.9
Property crimes	**29,490**	**19,297**	**18,654**	**18,040**	279.5	178.1	161.1	154.0
Household burglary	5,004	3,444	3,428	3,456	47.4	31.8	29.6	29.5
Completed	4,232	2,909	2,909	2,900	40.0	26.9	25.1	24.8
Attempted forcible entry	773	534	518	556	7.4	4.9	4.5	4.7
Motor vehicle theft	1,717	937	1,015	978	16.2	8.6	8.8	8.4
Completed	1,163	642	779	775	10.8	5.9	6.7	6.6
Attempted	554	295	236	203	5.5	2.7	2.0	1.7
Theft	22,769	14,916	14,212	13,606	215.9	137.7	122.8	116.2
Completed [4]	21,857	14,300	13,584	13,116	207.6	132.0	117.3	112.0
Attempted	911	616	628	489	8.4	5.7	5.4	4.2

X Not applicable.   [1] Per 1,000 persons age 12 or older or per 1,000 households.   [2] The victimization survey cannot measure murder because of the inability to question the victim.   [3] Includes pocket picking, purse snatching, and attempted purse snatching.   [4] Includes thefts in which the amount taken was not ascertained.
Source: U.S. Department of Justice, Office of Justice Programs, Bureau of Justice Statistics, *Criminal Victimization, Series NCJ-215244, December 2006; Trends 1996–2004.* See also <http://www.ojp.usdoj.gov/bjs/abstract/cvusst.htm>.

Table 313. **Victimization Rates by Type of Crime and Characteristic of the Victim: 2005**

[**Rate per 1,000 persons age 12 years or older.** Based on National Crime Victimization Survey; see text, this section, and Appendix III. For definitions of crimes, go to <http://www.ojp.usdoj.gov/bjs/abstract/cvus/definitions.htm>]

Characteristic of the victim	All crimes	Crimes of violence						Purse snatching/ pocket picking [1]
		Total	Rape/ sexual assault	Robbery	Assault			
					Total	Aggra- vated	Simple	
Total	**22.1**	**21.2**	**0.8**	**2.6**	**17.8**	**4.3**	**13.5**	**0.9**
Male	26.3	25.5	[2]0.1	3.8	21.5	5.6	15.9	0.8
Female	18.1	17.1	1.4	1.4	14.3	3.1	11.2	1.0
12 to 15 years old	45.3	44.0	[2]1.2	3.5	39.3	8.7	30.6	[2]1.3
16 to 19 years old	45.8	44.2	3.2	7.0	33.9	9.7	24.2	[2]1.6
20 to 24 years old	48.4	46.9	[2]1.1	5.5	40.3	10.0	30.3	[2]1.5
25 to 34 years old	24.6	23.6	[2]0.7	3.1	19.9	4.7	15.2	1.0
35 to 49 years old	18.4	17.5	[2]0.6	1.9	15.0	3.2	11.8	1.0
50 to 64 years old	12.0	11.4	[2]0.6	1.4	9.3	2.4	7.0	[2]0.6
65 years old and over	2.8	2.4	[2]0	[2]0.6	1.9	[2]0.8	1.1	[2]0.4
White	20.9	20.1	0.6	2.2	17.2	3.8	13.4	0.9
Black	28.7	27.0	1.8	4.6	20.6	7.6	13.0	1.7
Other	14.1	13.9	[2]0.5	3.0	10.4	[2]2.5	7.9	[2]0.2
Hispanic	26.0	25.0	[2]1.1	4.0	19.9	5.9	14.0	[2]1.0
Non-Hispanic	21.5	20.6	0.7	2.4	17.5	4.1	13.4	0.9
Household income:								
Less than $7,500	40.9	37.7	[2]2.2	5.6	29.9	9.7	20.1	[2]3.2
$7,500–$14,999	28.1	26.5	[2]0.6	4.9	21.0	6.8	14.2	[2]1.6
$15,000–$24,999	31.2	30.1	[2]1.4	3.5	25.2	6.4	18.8	[2]1.1
$25,000–$34,999	27.1	26.1	1.7	2.8	21.6	5.2	16.4	[2]1.0
$35,000–$49,999	23.6	22.4	[2]0.9	2.5	19.0	4.3	14.7	[2]1.1
$50,000–$74,999	21.7	21.1	[2]0.5	1.8	18.8	4.3	14.5	[2]0.6
$75,000 or more	17.4	16.4	[2]0.6	2.1	13.7	2.6	11.1	1.0

– Rounds to zero.   [1] Formerly personal theft.   [2] Based on 10 or fewer sample cases.
Source: U.S. Department of Justice, Office of Justice Programs, Bureau of Justice Statistics, *Criminal Victimization,* annual; and Series NCJ-215244. See also <http://www.ojp.usdoj.gov/bjs/pub/pdf/cv05.pdf>.

Law Enforcement, Courts, and Prisons   **199**

Table 314. Fraud and Identity Theft Consumer Complaints by State: 2006

[Rate per 100,000 population. As of December 31. Based on Census Bureau population estimates. Federal Trade Commission (FTC) has developed and maintained a complaint data base called the Consumer Sentinel. This database collects information about consumer fraud and identity theft from the FTC and over 115 other organizations and makes it available to law enforcement. See appendices in the annual report for list of contributing organizations]

Consumer state	Fraud complaints		Identity theft victims		Consumer state	Fraud complaints		Identity theft victims	
	Number	Rate	Number	Rate		Number	Rate	Number	Rate
U.S.[1]	374,907	125.2	239,313	79.9	MO	7,331	125.5	3,753	64.2
AL	4,708	102.4	2,774	60.3	MT	1,289	136.5	434	45.9
AK	1,079	161.0	384	57.3	NE	1,968	111.3	868	49.1
AZ	9,222	149.6	9,113	147.8	NV	4,222	169.2	2,994	120.0
AR	2,428	86.4	1,537	54.7	NH	1,964	149.4	606	46.1
CA	49,070	134.6	41,396	113.5	NJ	11,284	129.3	6,394	73.3
CO	7,657	161.1	4,395	92.5	NM	2,406	123.1	1,621	82.9
CT	4,695	134.0	2,305	65.8	NY	21,129	109.4	16,452	85.2
DE	1,119	131.1	569	66.7	NC	10,300	116.3	5,748	64.9
DC	1,139	195.9	765	131.5	ND	544	85.6	189	29.7
FL	25,902	143.2	17,780	98.3	OH	14,241	124.1	6,878	59.9
GA	11,941	127.5	8,084	86.3	OK	3,711	103.7	2,254	63.0
HI	2,020	157.1	615	47.8	OR	5,583	150.9	2,815	76.1
ID	2,012	137.2	718	49.0	PA	16,242	130.6	8,080	64.9
IL	13,908	108.4	10,080	78.6	RI	1,153	108.0	615	57.6
IN	7,863	124.5	3,928	62.2	SC	4,841	112.0	2,408	55.7
IA	2,666	89.4	1,041	34.9	SD	618	79.0	236	30.2
KS	3,068	111.0	1,626	58.8	TN	6,871	113.8	3,700	61.3
KY	4,477	106.4	1,766	42.0	TX	25,425	108.2	26,006	110.6
LA	3,981	92.8	2,256	52.6	UT	4,563	178.9	1,577	61.8
ME	1,791	135.5	525	39.7	VT	718	115.1	178	28.5
MD	8,653	154.1	4,656	82.9	VA	12,039	157.5	5,137	67.2
MA	7,333	113.9	4,102	63.7	WA	10,451	163.4	5,336	83.4
MI	11,665	115.5	6,784	67.2	WV	2,058	113.2	715	39.3
MN	5,860	113.4	2,872	55.6	WI	6,724	121.0	2,536	45.6
MS	2,318	79.6	1,494	51.3	WY	657	127.6	218	42.3

[1] Data represent only complaints from consumers in states listed in this table.

Source: U.S. Federal Trade Commission, *Consumer Fraud and Identity Theft complaint data, January–December 2006*. Issued February 2007. See also <http://www.consumer.gov/sentinel/pubs/Top10Fraud2006.pdf>.

Table 315. Authorized Intercepts of Communication—Summary: 1980 to 2006

[Data for jurisdictions with statutes authorizing or approving interception of wire or oral communication]

Item	1980	1985	1990	1995	2000	2002	2003	2004	2005	2006
Jurisdictions:[1]										
With wiretap statutes	28	32	40	41	45	47	47	47	47	47
Reporting interceptions	22	22	25	19	26	20	24	20	23	24
Intercept applications authorized	564	784	872	1,156	1,266	1,358	1,442	1,710	1,773	1,839
Intercept installations[2]	524	722	812	1,024	1,139	1,273	1,367	1,633	1,694	1,714
Federal	79	235	321	527	472	490	576	723	624	461
State	445	487	491	497	667	783	791	910	1,070	1,253
Intercepted communications, average[3]	1,058	1,320	1,487	2,028	1,769	1,708	3,004	3,017	2,835	2,685
Incriminating average[3]	315	275	321	459	402	403	993	619	629	547
Persons arrested[4]	1,871	2,469	2,057	2,577	3,411	3,060	3,674	4,506	4,674	4,376
Convictions[4]	259	660	420	494	736	493	844	634	776	711
Major offense specified:										
Gambling	199	206	116	95	49	82	49	90	42	56
Drugs	282	434	520	732	894	1,052	1,104	1,308	1,433	1,473
Homicide and assault	13	25	21	30	72	58	80	48	82	119
Racketeering	(NA)	(NA)	(NA)	98	76	72	96	138	94	90
Other	70	119	215	201	175	94	113	126	122	101

NA Not available   [1] Jurisdictions include federal government, 44 states and the Virgin Islands, and the District of Columbia. [2] Based on the number of orders for which intercept devices were installed as reported by the prosecuting official. [3] Average per authorized installation. [4] Based on information received from intercepts installed in year shown; additional arrests/convictions will occur in subsequent years but are not shown here.

Source: Administrative Office of the U.S. Courts, *Report on Applications for Orders Authorizing or Approving the Interception of Wire, Oral, or Electronic Communications* (Wiretap Report), annual. See also <http://www.uscourts.gov/wiretap06/contents.html> (accessed April 2007).

Table 316. Victim-Offender Relationship in Crimes of Violence by Characteristics of the Criminal Incident: 2005

[In percent. Covers only crimes of violence. Based on National Crime Victimization Survey; see text, this section, and Appendix III. For definitions of crimes, go to <http://www.ojp.usdoj.gov/bjs/abstract/cvus/definitions.htm>]

Selected characteristics of incident	Rape/ sexual assault Total	Rape/ sexual assault	Robbery	Assault Total	Assault Aggra- vated [1]	Simple
Total	100.0	100.0	100.0	100.0	100.0	100.0
Victim/offender relationship: [2]						
Relatives	1.6	0.0	0.0	2.2	2.5	2.0
Well-known	11.3	21.3	2.9	13.8	14.4	13.4
Casual acquaintance . . .	10.2	23.4	1.3	12.8	13.7	12.2
Stranger	73.7	55.3	93.5	67.7	64.5	69.5
Time of day: [3]						
6 a.m. to 6 p.m.	52.6	35.4	38.6	55.4	48.0	57.7
6 p.m. to midnight	34.5	24.9	40.8	34.1	37.6	33.0
Midnight to 6 a.m.	10.1	35.2	15.2	8.2	12.5	6.9
Location of crime:						
At or near victim's home or lodging . . .	29.9	37.9	27.0	29.9	29.9	52.3
Friend's/relative's/neighbor's home	8.2	23.7	4.7	7.9	10.1	3.6
Commercial places	11.6	1.3	5.3	13.0	12.6	7.1
Parking lots/garages	8.2	0.0	12.0	8.0	7.1	14.8
School	12.3	7.8	5.0	13.5	7.2	9.8
Streets other than near victim's home . .	18.6	8.6	35.3	16.6	24.4	3.5
Other [4]	11.5	20.7	10.7	11.0	8.7	8.9
Victim's activity: [5]						
At work or traveling to or from work	20.1	12.3	14.9	(NA)	17.7	22.3
School	12.3	7.8	10.6	(NA)	7.4	14.4
Activities at home	23.6	45.0	16.4	(NA)	23.2	23.7
Shopping/errands	4.2	0.0	10.7	(NA)	3.6	3.5
Leisure activities away from home	22.3	29.1	21.7	(NA)	31.2	19.3
Traveling	10.3	4.3	20.0	(NA)	11.9	8.4
Other [6]	6.6	1.7	4.8	(NA)	4.9	7.7
Distance from victim's home: [7]						
Inside home or lodging	14.9	38.0	13.7	14.0	12.2	14.5
Near victim's home	17.7	1.5	16.2	18.7	19.1	18.5
1 mile or less	18.7	21.4	27.3	17.4	21.9	16.0
5 miles or less	24.9	14.3	20.2	26.1	24.1	26.7
50 miles or less	18.6	18.6	16.0	19.0	18.1	19.3
More than 50 miles	3.7	6.2	6.0	3.3	2.7	3.5
Weapons:						
No weapons present	67.4	84.6	38.5	70.8	7.2	90.2
Weapons present	24.3	6.5	48.3	21.7	92.8	–
Firearm	8.9	3.1	26.3	6.7	28.5	–
Other type of weapon [8] . . .	15.4	3.4	22.0	15.0	64.3	–

NA Not available. – Represents zero. [1] An aggravated assault is any assault in which an offender possesses or uses a weapon or inflicts serious injury. [2] Excludes "don't know" relationships. [3] Excludes "not known and not available" time of day. [4] Includes areas on public transportation or inside station, in apartment yard, park, field, playground, or other areas. [5] Excludes "don't know" and "not available" victim activity. [6] Includes sleeping. [7] Excludes "don't know" and "not available" distance from victim's home. [8] Includes knives, other sharp objects, blunt objects, and other types of weapons.

Source: U.S. Department of Justice, Office of Justice Programs, Bureau of Justice Statistics, *Criminal Victimization*, annual; and series NCJ-214644, September 2006. See also <http://www.ojp.usdoj.gov/bjs/abstract/cv05.htm>.

Table 317. Property Victimization Rates by Selected Household Characteristic: 2005

[Victimizations per 1,000 households. Based on National Crime Victimization Survey (NCVS); see text, this section and Appendix III. For definitions of crimes, go to<http://www.ojp.usdoj.gov/bjs/abstract/cvus/definitions.htm>]

Characteristic	Total	Burglary	Motor vehicle theft	Theft
Total	154.0	29.5	8.4	116.2
Race:				
White	155.7	28.6	7.6	119.6
Black	144.6	35.0	12.7	96.9
Other	122.8	23.3	9.9	89.5
Ethnicity:				
Hispanic	209.8	34.6	19.0	156.1
Non-Hispanic	147.9	29.0	7.1	111.8
Household income:				
Less than $7,500	200.6	55.1	9.4	136.0
$7,500 to $14,999	174.3	46.7	9.8	117.8
$15,000 to $24,999	170.4	41.7	12.4	116.3
$25,000 to $34,999	173.9	33.4	9.9	130.6
$35,000 to $49,999	159.9	30.2	6.6	123.0
$50,000 to $74,999	155.9	23.2	7.2	125.5
$75,000 or more	171.0	23.9	7.1	140.0
Residence:				
Urban	200.0	37.7	12.7	149.6
Suburban	141.4	24.7	7.7	109.0
Rural	125.1	29.4	4.6	91.1
Form of tenure:				
Home owned	136.5	25.3	6.1	105.1
Home rented	192.3	38.6	13.3	140.3

Source: U.S. Department of Justice, Office of Justice Programs, Bureau of Justice Statistics, *Criminal Victimization*, annual; and series NCJ-216444, September 2006. See also <http://www.ojp.usdoj.gov/bjs/abstract/cv05.htm>.

Law Enforcement, Courts, and Prisons   201

Table 318. **Persons Arrested by Charge and Selected Characteristics: 2005**

[In thousands (10,369.8 represents 10,369,800). Represents arrests (not charges) reported by approximately 10,970 agencies with a total 2005 population of approximately 218 million as estimated by FBI. Age and sex data are mandatory, while race data are optional and not always reported with arrest data; hence, two different total number of arrests. See source for details. For definitions of crimes, go to <http://www.fbi.gov/ucr/05cius/about/offensedefinitions.html>]

Offense	Total arrests	Male	Female	Total arrests	White	Black	American Indian or Alaska Native	Asian or Pacific Islander
Total	**10,369.8**	**7,897.5**	**2,472.3**	**10,189.7**	**7,117.0**	**2,830.8**	**135.9**	**106.0**
Serious crimes:								
Murder and nonnegligent manslaughter	10.3	9.2	1.1	10.1	5.0	4.9	0.1	0.1
Forcible rape	18.7	18.5	0.3	18.4	12.0	6.0	0.2	0.2
Robbery	85.3	75.8	9.5	84.8	35.8	47.7	0.5	0.8
Aggravated assault	331.5	262.6	68.9	329.2	208.3	113.1	4.3	3.6
Burglary.....................	220.4	188.3	32.0	217.9	151.8	62.0	2.2	1.9
Larceny/theft	854.9	525.1	329.7	846.2	586.4	236.6	11.3	11.9
Motor vehicle theft...........	108.3	89.3	19.0	107.6	67.6	37.5	1.1	1.4
Arson	12.0	10.0	2.0	11.8	9.0	2.5	0.1	0.1
Nonserious crimes:								
Other assaults	958.5	722.2	236.2	944.8	615.3	305.4	13.5	10.6
Forgery and counterfeiting	87.3	52.7	34.7	83.7	59.2	23.1	0.5	1.0
Fraud	231.7	126.3	105.4	217.7	149.6	65.4	1.2	1.4
Embezzlement	14.1	7.0	7.0	13.7	9.2	4.3	0.1	0.2
Stolen property—buying, receiving, possessing...................	99.2	79.8	19.3	97.1	62.2	33.2	0.7	0.9
Vandalism	206.4	170.9	35.5	203.6	152.6	45.8	3.1	2.1
Weapons; carrying, possessing, etc....	142.9	131.4	11.5	141.3	83.8	55.2	1.0	1.3
Prostitution and commercialized vice...	62.7	21.1	41.6	62.5	34.4	26.1	0.6	1.3
Sex offenses (except forcible rape and prostitution)	67.1	61.5	5.6	64.4	47.4	15.6	0.7	0.7
Drug abuse violations............	1,357.8	1,098.5	259.4	1,330.8	861.6	451.4	8.6	9.2
Gambling....................	8.1	7.4	0.7	8.1	2.1	5.7	–	0.2
Offenses against family and children...	93.2	70.4	22.7	89.2	61.1	25.8	1.7	0.5
Driving under the influence	997.3	805.5	191.9	976.8	864.0	88.7	13.7	10.5
Liquor laws..................	437.9	322.8	115.1	431.0	368.0	46.8	11.9	4.3
Drunkenness	412.9	349.8	63.1	399.1	334.2	53.7	9.0	2.2
Disorderly conduct.............	501.1	371.9	129.2	493.7	316.5	165.9	7.7	3.7
Vagrancy....................	24.4	19.2	5.1	24.4	14.5	9.4	0.4	0.1
Suspicion....................	2.7	2.3	0.4	2.7	1.8	0.9	–	–
Curfew and loitering law violations	104.1	72.4	31.7	103.9	64.9	36.9	0.9	1.2
Runaways....................	81.2	34.1	47.1	80.9	57.8	18.7	1.5	2.9
All other offenses (except traffic)	2,837.8	2,191.4	646.4	2,794.4	1,881.1	842.6	39.0	31.7

– Rounds to zero.

Source: U.S. Department of Justice, Federal Bureau of Investigation. Crime in the United States, annual. See <http://www.fbi.gov/ucr/05cius/arrests/index.html> (Release September 2006).

Table 319. **Juvenile Arrests for Selected Offenses: 1980 to 2005**

[169,439 represents 169,439,000. Juveniles are persons under 18 years of age]

Offense	1980	1990	1995	1999	2000	2001	2002	2003	2004	2005
Number of contributing agencies	8,178	10,765	10,037	9,502	9,904	10,281	10,946	11,368	11,437	11,778
Population covered (1,000) ...	169,439	204,543	206,762	195,324	204,965	215,380	220,157	219,562	222,147	230,176
NUMBER										
Violent crime, total	77,220	97,103	123,131	81,715	78,450	78,443	71,059	69,060	68,247	73,377
Murder	1,475	2,661	2,812	1,131	1,027	1,069	1,014	960	829	968
Forcible rape	3,668	4,971	4,556	3,544	3,402	3,504	3,553	3,195	3,186	3,088
Robbery	38,529	34,944	47,240	26,125	24,206	23,408	19,491	18,950	19,000	22,356
Aggravated assault.......	33,548	54,527	68,523	50,915	49,815	50,462	47,001	45,955	45,232	46,965
Weapon law violations	21,203	33,123	46,506	31,307	28,514	29,290	26,786	29,512	30,530	34,468
Drug abuse, total..........	86,685	66,300	149,236	138,774	146,594	146,758	133,557	134,746	135,056	137,809
Sale and manufacturing...	13,004	24,575	34,077	26,134	26,432	24,649	22,086	21,987	21,136	21,607
Heroin/cocaine	1,318	17,511	19,187	12,686	11,000	10,535	8,832	7,848	7,852	7,863
Marijuana	8,876	4,372	10,682	10,770	11,792	10,552	9,962	10,463	9,743	9,845
Synthetic narcotics	465	346	701	722	945	911	974	1,043	1,119	1,071
Dangerous nonnarcotic drugs	2,345	2,346	3,507	1,956	2,695	2,651	2,318	2,633	2,422	2,828
Possession	73,681	41,725	115,159	112,640	120,432	122,109	111,471	112,759	113,920	116,202
Heroin/cocaine	2,614	15,194	21,253	13,445	12,586	11,734	10,969	9,932	10,805	11,131
Marijuana	64,465	20,940	82,015	89,523	95,962	97,088	85,769	87,909	87,717	88,909
Synthetic narcotics	1,524	1,155	2,047	1,581	2,052	2,237	2,805	2,872	3,279	3,235
Dangerous nonnarcotic drugs	5,078	4,436	9,844	8,091	9,832	11,050	11,928	12,046	12,119	12,927

Source: U.S. Department of Justice, Federal Bureau of Investigation, *Crime in the United States*, annual, Person arrested. See also <http://www.fbi.gov/ucr/05cius/arrests/index.html> (Release September 2006).

202　Law Enforcement, Courts, and Prisons

Table 320. **Drug Use by Arrestees in Major U.S. Cities by Type of Drug and Sex: 2003**

[Percent testing positive. Based on data from the Arrestee Drug Abuse Monitoring Program]

City	Male				Female			
	Any drug [1]	Marijuana	Cocaine	Opiates	Any drug [1]	Marijuana	Cocaine	Opiates
Albuquerque, NM	70.3	41.6	35.0	11.2	70.0	29.4	38.1	13.8
Atlanta, GA	73.5	41.8	49.8	3.0	(NA)	(NA)	(NA)	(NA)
Chicago, IL	86.0	53.2	50.6	24.9	66.7	38.9	33.3	22.2
Cleveland, OH	74.9	48.9	39.0	5.4	72.4	27.2	52.7	6.7
Dallas, TX	63.8	39.1	32.7	6.9	(NA)	(NA)	(NA)	(NA)
Denver, CO	72.6	42.3	38.3	6.8	75.1	34.3	52.5	6.1
Indianapolis, IN	66.4	44.8	35.3	5.1	79.9	42.0	55.7	5.7
Las Vegas, NV	70.0	34.4	21.9	6.4	(NA)	(NA)	(NA)	(NA)
Los Angeles, CA.	68.9	40.7	23.5	2.0	63.0	29.6	25.9	0.0
New Orleans, LA	79.6	50.8	47.6	14.0	62.2	30.3	37.3	13.3
New York, NY	72.7	43.1	35.7	15.0	73.3	36.7	50.0	23.3
Oklahoma City, OK	73.5	54.9	24.6	3.0	78.4	43.3	35.3	5.6
Philadelphia, PA	68.8	45.8	30.3	11.5	(NA)	(NA)	(NA)	(NA)
Phoenix, AZ.	76.8	40.9	23.4	4.4	78.5	31.6	28.1	6.1
Portland, OR	72.7	38.4	29.7	15.0	84.4	35.2	39.6	22.0
Sacramento, CA.	81.1	49.2	21.6	6.9	(NA)	(NA)	(NA)	(NA)
San Antonio, TX	65.2	41.9	30.5	9.1	(NA)	(NA)	(NA)	(NA)
San Diego, CA.	71.2	41.0	10.3	5.1	72.6	29.1	15.2	8.7
San Jose, CA.	63.7	35.4	12.9	3.1	72.8	29.1	10.1	3.4
Seattle, WA	69.4	37.2	36.6	6.8	(NA)	(NA)	(NA)	(NA)
Tucson, AZ	76.4	44.1	42.5	4.2	73.2	29.0	40.0	9.7
Washington, D.C.	65.8	37.4	26.5	9.8	66.7	29.1	30.9	10.9

NA Not available. [1] Includes other drugs not shown separately.

Source: U.S. National Institute of Justice, *ADAM 2003 Annual Report on Drug Use Among Adult and Juvenile Arrestees*, June 2004. See also <http://www.ncjrs.org/drgswww.html#top>.

Table 321. **Drug Arrest Rates for Drug Abuse Violations, 1990 to 2005, and by Region, 2005**

[Rate per 100,000 inhabitants. Based on Census Bureau estimated resident population as of July 1, except 1990 and 2000, enumerated as of April 1. For composition of regions, see map, inside front cover]

Offense				2005				
					Region			
	1990	1995	2000	Total	North-east	Mid-west	South	West
Drug arrest rate, total	**435.3**	**564.7**	**587.1**	**600.9**	**489.2**	**431.1**	**646.0**	**684.3**
Sale and/or manufacture	139.0	140.7	122.7	109.9	115.9	78.9	125.6	99.9
Heroin or cocaine [1]	93.7	83.7	60.8	47.8	75.4	24.3	53.9	35.5
Marijuana	26.4	32.7	34.2	29.6	29.2	31.0	29.5	25.9
Synthetic or manufactured drugs ...	2.7	3.9	6.4	8.6	4.5	5.4	16.2	4.0
Other dangerous nonnarcotic drugs. . .	16.2	20.3	21.3	23.9	6.8	18.2	26.0	34.4
Possession	296.3	423.9	464.4	490.9	373.3	352.2	520.5	584.4
Heroin or cocaine [1]	144.4	157.4	138.7	131.5	122.5	61.9	145.8	154.8
Marijuana	104.9	192.7	244.4	228.9	206.0	207.7	288.9	167.9
Synthetic or manufactured drugs. . .	6.6	8.5	12.0	21.0	9.1	15.5	28.8	21.6
Other dangerous nonnarcotic drugs. . .	40.4	65.4	69.4	109.6	35.8	62.1	56.9	240.1

[1] Includes other derivatives such as morphine, heroin, and codeine.

Source: U.S. Department of Justice, Federal Bureau of Investigation, *Crime in the United States*, annual. See also <http://www.fbi.gov/ucr/05cius/arrests/index.html>; as of 17 February 2007.

Table 322. **Federal Drug Seizures by Type of Drug: 1990 to 2005**

[In pounds. For fiscal years ending in year shown. Reflects the combined drug seizure effort of the Drug Enforcement Administration, the Federal Bureau of Investigation, the U.S. Customs Services, and beginning October 1995, the U.S. Border Patrol within the jurisdiction of the United States as well as maritime seizures by the U.S. Coast Guard. Based on reports to the federal-wide Drug Seizure System, which eliminates duplicate reporting of a seizure involving more than one federal agency. Data have been revised for years through 2004]

Drug	1990	1995	1999	2000	2001	2002	2003	2004	2005
Total	464,583	1,574,890	2,568,899	2,888,169	2,922,543	2,649,756	2,956,580	3,047,047	2,821,890
Heroin.	1,704	2,971	2,727	3,341	4,358	6,859	5,920	4,078	4,294
Cocaine.	235,891	234,342	282,207	248,894	237,857	225,368	245,623	336,365	398,842
Cannabis.	226,988	1,337,577	2,283,965	2,635,934	2,680,328	2,417,529	2,705,037	2,706,604	2,418,754
Marijuana	219,249	1,305,701	2,282,287	2,611,947	2,679,898	2,417,343	2,703,664	2,706,031	2,417,936
Hashish	7,739	31,876	1,678	23,987	430	186	1,373	573	818

Source: U.S. Drug Enforcement Administration, unpublished data from federal-wide Drug Seizure System.

Table 323. **State and Local Government Expenditures Per Capita by Criminal Justice Function and State: 2004**

[In dollars]

State	Total justice system	Police protec- tion	Judicial and legal	Correc- tions	State	Total justice system	Police protec- tion	Judicial and legal	Correc- tions
Total.	542	237	112	192	Missouri	403	189	71	143
Alabama	375	170	73	131	Montana	429	181	91	157
Alaska	766	285	210	271	Nebraska	401	161	71	169
Arizona	571	247	120	205	Nevada.	663	302	127	234
Arkansas.	399	160	72	167	New Hampshire . . .	366	184	82	100
California.	776	311	200	265	New Jersey	648	309	130	209
Colorado.	507	239	87	181	New Mexico.	568	235	112	221
Connecticut	533	230	144	159	New York	760	358	154	248
Delaware.	638	243	151	244	North Carolina	403	189	58	155
District of Columbia .	1,139	744	100	295	North Dakota	320	134	93	93
Florida	597	288	105	204	Ohio.	509	219	129	161
Georgia	480	186	88	207	Oklahoma	401	165	70	166
Hawaii	512	209	178	125	Oregon.	533	231	90	212
Idaho	438	179	91	167	Pennsylvania	503	187	109	207
Illinois.	508	272	91	144	Rhode Island	526	263	113	150
Indiana	357	149	61	147	South Carolina	365	173	55	137
Iowa.	369	168	91	110	South Dakota.	337	159	73	105
Kansas	445	199	98	148	Tennessee.	399	185	79	135
Kentucky.	378	144	85	149	Texas	449	191	78	180
Louisiana	520	219	112	189	Utah.	474	194	110	169
Maine	350	158	69	123	Vermont	414	184	79	150
Maryland.	593	257	101	236	Virginia	480	205	85	190
Massachusetts	520	231	130	159	Washington	489	192	96	201
Michigan	539	223	109	207	West Virginia	319	120	81	118
Minnesota	469	225	108	136	Wisconsin	556	252	95	210
Mississippi.	363	177	62	124	Wyoming	670	273	137	260

Source: U.S. Department of Justice, Office of Justice Programs, Bureau of Justice Statistics, *Expenditures and Employment Statistics, Series NCJ 215648,* November 2006; <http://www.ojp.usdog.gov/bjs/eande.htm>.

Table 324. **Background Checks for Firearm Transfers: 1994 to 2005**

[In thousands (69,912 represents 69,912,000), except rates]

Inquiries and rejections	Total 1994– 2005 [1]	Interim period 1994– 1998 [2]	Permanent Brady							
			1998 [3, 4]	1999	2000	2001	2002	2003	2004	2005
Applications and rejections:										
Applications received.	69,912	12,740	893	8,621	7,699	7,958	7,806	7,831	8,084	8,278
Applications rejected	1,360	312	20	204	153	151	136	126	126	132
Rejection rate	1.9	2.4	2.2	2.4	2.0	1.9	1.7	1.6	1.6	1.6

[1] National totals from 1999 to 2005 combine Firearm Inquiry Statistics Program (FIST) estimates for state and local agencies with actual transactions and rejections reported by the FBI.   [2] For the interim period of March 1, 1994, through November 29,1998, covered handgun transfers (most of the applications) and purchases from licensed firearm dealers. See report.   [3] The period beginning November 30, 1998 (effective date for the Brady Handgun Violence Prevention Act, P.L. 103-159, 1993), covers the transfer of both handguns and long guns from a federal firearms licensee, as well as purchases from pawnshops and retail gun shops.   [4] For the period of November 30, 1998, to December 31, 1998, counts are from the National Instant Criminal Background Check Systems (NICS) Operations Report (November 30, 1998, to December 31, 1999). Counts may include multiple transactions for the same application. See report.

Source: U.S. Department of Justice, Office of Justice Programs, Bureau of Justice Statistics, Presale Handgun Checks, The Brady Interim Period 1994–1998, Series NCJ 175034, June 1999. Background Checks for Firearm Transfers, 2005, Series NCJ 214256, November 2006. See internet site <http://www.ojp.usdoj.gov/bjs/guns.htm>.

Table 325. **Law Enforcement Officers Killed and Assaulted: 1990 to 2005**

[Contains statistics on felonious and accidental deaths of duly sworn local, state, tribal, and federal law enforcement officers. For composition of regions, see map, inside front cover]

Item	1990	1995	1999	2000	2001 [1]	2002	2003	2004	2005
OFFICERS KILLED									
Total killed	132	133	107	134	218	131	133	139	122
Northeast	13	16	11	13	79	10	13	18	12
Midwest	20	19	17	32	26	22	20	25	23
South	68	63	56	67	68	64	66	66	58
West	23	32	22	19	38	28	31	24	24
Puerto Rico	8	2	1	3	7	7	3	5	5
Island areas, foreign countries.	–	1	–	–	–	–	–	1	–
Total feloniously killed	65	74	42	51	142	56	52	57	55
Firearms	56	63	41	47	61	51	45	54	50
Handgun	47	44	25	33	46	38	34	36	42
Rifle	8	14	11	10	11	10	10	13	3
Shotgun	1	5	5	4	4	3	1	5	5
Blunt instrument	–	–	–	–	1	–	1	–	–
Bomb	–	8	–	–	–	–	–	–	–
Knife/cutting instrument . . .	3	1	–	1	–	1	–	1	–
Personal weapons [3]	2	–	–	–	1	–	–	–	–
Vehicle	1	2	1	3	7	4	6	2	5
Other	3	–	–	–	72	–	–	–	–
Total accidentally killed	67	59	65	83	76	75	81	82	67
OFFICERS ASSAULTED									
Population covered(1,000) [2] . .	197,426	191,759	207,124	204,599	213,645	219,425	225,770	226,273	221,016
Number of—									
Reporting agencies	9,343	8,503	9,832	8,940	9,773	10,164	10,539	10,589	10,032
Officers employed	410,131	428,379	462,782	452,531	471,096	491,009	501,738	501,462	485,048
Total assaulted	72,091	57,762	55,971	58,398	57,463	59,526	58,600	59,692	57,546
Firearm	3,651	2,354	1,772	1,749	1,841	1,927	1,879	2,114	2,145
Knife/cutting instrument	1,647	1,356	999	1,015	1,168	1,061	1,084	1,123	1,059
Other dangerous weapon . . .	7,423	6,414	7,560	8,132	8,233	8,526	8,180	8,645	8,314
Personal weapons [3]	59,370	47,638	45,640	47,502	46,221	48,012	47,457	47,810	46,028

– Represents zero.   [1] The 72 felonious deaths that resulted from the events of September 11, 2001, are included in this table. [2] Represents the number of persons covered by agencies shown.   [3] Includes hands, fists, feet, etc.

Source: U.S. Department of Justice, Federal Bureau of Investigation, *Law Enforcement Officers Killed and Assaulted*, annual; <http://www.fbi.gov/ucr/killed/2005/>.

Table 326. **U.S. Supreme Court—Cases Filed and Disposition: 1980 to 2005**

[Statutory term of court begins first Monday in October]

Action	1980	1990	1995	2000	2001	2002	2003	2004	2005
Total cases on docket	5,144	6,316	7,565	8,965	9,176	9,406	8,882	8,588	9,608
Appellate cases on docket	2,749	2,351	2,456	2,305	2,210	2,190	2,058	2,041	2,025
From prior term	527	365	361	351	324	321	336	300	354
Docketed during present term	2,222	1,986	2,095	1,954	1,886	1,869	1,722	1,741	1,671
Cases acted upon	2,324	2,042	2,130	2,024	1,932	1,899	1,798	1,727	1,703
Granted review	167	114	92	85	82	83	74	69	63
Denied, dismissed, or withdrawn	1,999	1,802	1,945	1,842	1,751	1,727	1,641	1,529	1,554
Summarily decided	90	81	62	63	57	46	37	89	46
Cases not acted upon . . .	425	309	326	281	278	291	260	314	322
Pauper cases on docket	2,371	3,951	5,098	6,651	6,958	7,209	6,818	6,543	7,575
Cases acted upon [1]	2,027	3,436	4,514	5,736	6,139	6,488	6,036	5,815	6,533
Granted review	17	27	13	14	6	8	13	11	15
Denied, dismissed, or withdrawn	1,968	3,369	4,439	5,658	6,114	6,459	6,005	5,061	6,459
Summarily decided	32	28	55	61	13	17	13	737	58
Cases not acted upon	344	515	584	915	819	721	782	728	1,042
Original cases on docket	24	14	11	9	8	7	6	4	8
Cases disposed of during term	7	3	5	2	1	1	2	–	4
Total cases available for argument . . .	264	201	145	138	137	139	140	128	122
Cases disposed of	162	131	93	89	90	87	93	87	87
Cases argued	154	125	90	86	88	84	91	87	88
Cases dismissed or remanded without argument	8	6	3	3	2	3	2	–	1
Cases remaining	102	70	52	49	47	52	47	41	31
Cases decided by signed opinion	144	121	87	83	85	79	89	85	82
Cases decided by per curiam opinion.	8	4	3	4	3	5	2	2	5
Number of signed opinions.	123	112	75	77	76	71	73	74	69

– Represents zero.   [1] Includes cases granted review and carried over to next term, not shown separately.

Source: Office of the Clerk, Supreme Court of the United States, unpublished data.

U.S. Census Bureau, Statistical Abstract of the United States: 2008

Table 327. U.S. District Courts—Civil Cases Commenced and Pending: 2000 to 2006

[For years ending June 30]

Type of case	Cases commenced				Cases pending			
	2000	2004	2005	2006	2000	2004	2005	2006
Cases total [1]	**263,049**	**258,117**	**282,758**	**244,343**	**249,692**	**267,881**	**267,270**	**246,547**
Contract actions [1]	54,494	29,687	28,590	28,139	38,262	28,413	26,712	26,671
Recovery of overpayments [2] . . .	25,636	2,914	3,380	2,856	12,107	2,146	1,953	1,789
Real property actions	6,481	6,341	4,541	4,761	4,249	5,651	4,512	4,178
Tort actions	40,877	51,881	75,273	53,809	63,116	74,589	76,821	64,701
Personal injury [1]	36,867	45,948	52,215	49,834	59,232	68,928	72,716	60,569
Personal injury product liability [1]	15,349	29,089	35,615	32,515	31,772	42,886	46,575	34,280
Asbestos	7,893	1,208	1,628	8,709	4,949	2,528	1,073	856
Other personal injury	21,518	16,859	16,600	17,319	27,460	26,042	26,141	26,289
Personal property damage	4,010	5,933	23,058	3,975	3,884	5,661	4,105	4,132
Actions under statutes [1]	161,187	170,168	171,922	157,536	144,053	159,200	157,357	150,891
Civil rights [1]	41,226	40,118	36,724	33,417	44,259	43,431	40,596	38,384
Employment	21,404	19,670	17,998	14,851	24,456	22,964	21,344	18,591
Bankruptcy suits	3,378	3,982	3,428	3,193	2,555	2,684	2,650	2,565
Commerce (ICC rates, etc.) . . .	1,007	483	492	404	444	427	395	351
Environmental matters	894	999	726	874	1,355	2,282	1,193	1,148
Prisoner petitions	57,706	53,132	62,698	55,775	43,560	44,317	47,870	46,655
Forfeiture and penalty	2,246	2,112	2,214	2,318	1,772	2,017	2,156	2,309
Labor laws.	14,229	18,189	18,643	16,853	11,267	15,131	15,725	14,014
Protected property rights [3]	8,745	9,289	11,809	11,745	7,858	8,992	10,507	10,274
Securities commodities and exchanges	2,500	3,081	2,371	1,654	3,578	5,325	5,192	4,463
Social security laws.	14,365	15,935	16,066	14,052	13,667	14,853	15,420	14,202
Tax suits	938	1,291	1,348	1,498	1,068	1,158	1,222	1,331
Freedom of information	335	300	426	309	380	360	378	370

[1] Includes other types not shown separately. [2] Includes enforcement of judgments in student loan cases, and overpayments of veterans' benefits. [3] Includes copyright, patent, and trademark rights.

Source: Administrative Office of the U.S. Courts, *Statistical Tables for the Federal Judiciary*, annual; <http://www.uscourts.gov/>.

Table 328. Federal Prosecutions of Public Corruption: 1980 to 2005

[As of Dec. 31. Prosecution of persons who have corrupted public office in violation of Federal Criminal Statutes]

Prosecution Status	1980	1985	1990	1995	1998	1999	2000	2001	2002	2003	2004	2005
Total: [1] Charged	727	1,157	1,176	1,051	1,174	1,134	1,000	1,087	1,136	1,150	1,213	1,163
Convicted	602	997	1,084	878	1,014	1,065	938	920	1,011	868	1,020	1,027
Awaiting trial	213	256	300	323	340	329	327	437	413	412	419	451
Federal officials: Charged . .	123	563	615	527	442	480	441	502	478	479	424	445
Convicted	131	470	583	438	414	460	422	414	429	421	381	390
Awaiting trial	16	90	103	120	85	101	92	131	119	129	98	118
State officials: Charged. . . .	72	79	96	61	91	115	92	95	110	94	111	96
Convicted	51	66	79	61	58	80	91	61	132	87	81	94
Awaiting trial	28	20	28	23	37	44	37	75	50	38	48	51
Local officials: Charged . . .	247	248	257	236	277	237	211	224	299	259	268	309
Convicted	168	221	225	191	264	219	183	184	262	119	252	232
Awaiting trial	82	49	98	89	90	95	89	110	118	106	105	148
Others involved: Charged . .	285	267	208	227	364	302	256	266	249	318	410	313
Convicted	252	240	197	188	278	306	242	261	188	241	306	311
Awaiting trial	87	97	71	91	128	89	109	121	126	139	168	134

[1] Includes individuals who are neither public officials nor employees, but were involved with public officials or employees in violating the law, not shown separately.

Source: U.S. Department of Justice, Criminal Division, *Federal Prosecutions of Corrupt Public Officials,1970–1980* and *Report to Congress on the Activities and Operations of the Public Integrity Section*, annual; <http://www.usdoj.gov/criminal/pin/>.

Table 329. **U.S. District Courts—Offenders Convicted and Sentenced to Prison and Length of Sentence: 2000 and 2004**

Selected Most serious offense of conviction	Offenders convicted [1]		Offenders sentenced to prison [1, 2]		Mean length of sentence for incarceration (months) [3]	
	2000	2004	2000	2004	2000	2004
Total	68,156	74,782	50,451	58,106	56.7	59.7
Violent offenses [4]	2,557	2,569	2,360	2,402	86.5	96.2
Murder [5]	283	190	249	175	94.2	111.2
Negligent manslaughter	1	1	1	1	(B)	(B)
Assault	253	465	188	384	33.0	44.8
Property offenses.................	12,454	12,202	7,462	7,323	24.2	27.4
Fraudulent..................	10,396	10,403	6,272	6,267	22.5	25.8
Embezzlement	917	646	506	302	14.8	16.0
Fraud [6]	8,177	8,677	5,008	5,278	23.5	26.6
Forgery	86	73	41	44	19.1	20.0
Counterfeiting...............	1,216	1,007	717	643	20.8	24.1
Other [4]	2,058	1,799	1,190	1,056	33.2	36.7
Larceny [7]	1,394	1,307	689	695	27.3	31.3
Arson	158	165	134	136	71.8	75.2
Transportation of stolen property	272	166	200	115	33.4	35.0
Drug offenses [4]	24,206	24,472	22,352	22,744	75.5	83.6
Public-order offenses [4]	4,585	4,398	2,989	3,135	45.8	43.6
Regulatory..................	1,376	1,106	647	580	28.4	32.3
Other	3,209	3,292	2,342	2,555	46.5	46.2
Tax law violations [8]	655	425	355	265	18.5	26.5
Escape	487	415	447	380	19.2	18.7
Racketeering and extortion	951	844	778	651	81.5	70.9
Nonviolent sex offenses	475	724	429	692	47.1	57.0
Obscene material [9]	28	32	7	25	(B)	32.7
Weapon offenses [10]	4,196	8,082	3,834	7,518	91.4	84.3
Immigration offenses [10]	11,125	14,819	10,073	13,387	29.5	26.9
Misdemeanors [11]	8,961	8,240	1,356	1,597	10.4	5.6

B Base figures too small to meet statistical standards for reliability of a derived figure.   [1] Total may not equal the sum of individual sanctions.   [2] All sentences to incarceration, including split, mixed, life, and indeterminate sentences.   [3] Excludes sentences of life, death, and indeterminate sentences.   [4] Includes offenses not shown separately.   [5] Includes nonnegligent manslaughter.   [6] Excludes tax fraud.   [7] Excludes transportation of stolen property.   [8] Includes tax fraud.   [9] Denotes the mail or transport thereof.   [10] Beginning in 2001, "Weapon and Immigration"offenses became major offense categories. Previously these offenses were classified within "Public-order offenses."   [11] Includes misdemeanors, petty offenses, unknown offense levels, and drug possession.

Source: U.S. Department of Justice, Office of Justice Programs, Bureau of Justice Statistics, *Federal Criminal Justice Trends, 2003*, Series NCJ 205331, August 2006; <http://www.ojp.usdoj.gov/bjs/abstract/cfjs03.htm>. *Compendium of Federal Justice Statistics, 2004*, Series NCJ 213476, December 2006; <http://www.ojp.usdoj.gov/bjs/abstract/cfjs04.htm>.

Table 330. **Suspects Arrested for Federal Offenses and Booked by United States Marshals Service (USMS), by Offense: 1994 to 2004**

[Persons suspected of violating federal law may be arrested by any one of the many federal agencies empowered to make arrests, or by state or local authorities. Regardless of which agency makes the arrest, federal suspects are typically transferred to the custody of the U.S. Marshals Service for booking, processing, and detention. See Methodology for a listing of detailed offense categories under each major offense category]

Most serious offense	1994	1995	1996	1997	1998 [2]	1999 [1, 2]	2000 [2]	2001 [2]	2002 [2]	2003	2004
All offenses [3]	80,730	83,324	85,195	91,747	104,119	109,340	115,589	118,868	124,074	131,064	140,755
Violent offenses [4]	3,905	3,873	4,519	4,801	4,989	4,254	4,250	4,843	4,723	4,484	4,587
Property offenses	15,540	16,245	16,191	16,288	16,786	16,569	16,842	16,824	17,268	17,258	15,609
Fraudulent [5]	11,919	12,804	12,729	12,912	13,219	13,116	13,432	13,397	13,976	14,169	12,709
Other [6]	3,621	3,441	3,462	3,376	3,567	3,453	3,410	3,427	3,292	3,089	2,900
Drug offenses	23,268	23,768	24,682	26,843	30,012	31,867	32,630	33,589	33,730	34,217	32,980
Public-order offenses.....	11,596	10,336	9,578	9,324	9,234	9,841	10,063	9,156	8,772	8,591	8,618
Regulatory	530	697	656	749	775	752	621	687	524	425	335
Other	11,066	9,639	8,922	8,575	8,459	9,089	9,442	8,469	8,248	8,166	8,283
Weapon offenses [7]	3,885	3,724	3,131	3,235	3,539	4,268	5,203	6,007	7,488	9,416	9,936
Immigration offenses [7]	8,777	10,600	12,026	14,994	20,942	22,849	25,205	24,794	25,270	27,620	39,135
Supervision violations	12,719	13,498	13,304	13,995	15,157	15,603	17,133	18,978	21,777	23,605	23,399
Material witness	886	1,143	1,617	2,169	3,398	4,016	4,203	3,679	3,918	4,615	5,385
Unknown or indeterminable offenses	154	137	147	163	62	73	60	1,026	1,128	1,258	1,106

[1] Starting in 1999, and through the current year of data, nonviolent sex offenses were reclassified from "Violent offenses" to "Public-order offenses."   [2] Data for 1998 through 2002 are not directly comparable to 2003 and 2004 because of changes in the data processing methodology. See note 2 on page 24, chapter 1 of the 2004 Compendium of Federal Justice Statistics.   [3] Includes suspects whose offense category could not be determined.   [4] In this table "Violent offenses" may include nonnegligent manslaughter.   [5] Fraudulent property excludes tax fraud.   [6] Excludes fraudulent property and includes destruction of property and trespassing.   [7] Beginning in 2001, "Weapon" and "Immigration" offenses became major offense categories. Previously, theses offenses were classified within "Public-order offenses."

Source: U.S. Department of Justice, Office of Justice Programs, Bureau of Justice Statistics, *Federal Criminal Justice Trends, 2003*, Series NCJ 205331, August 2006; <http://www.ojp.usdoj.gov/bjs/abstract/fcjt03.htm> *Compendium of Federal Justice Statistics, 2004*, Series NCJ 213476, December 2006; <http://www.ojp.usdoj.gov/bjs/abstract/cfjs04.htm>.

Law Enforcement, Courts, and Prisons   **207**

Table 331. Suspects in Criminal Matters Investigated by U.S. Attorneys by Offense: 1994 to 2004

[The most serious offense investigated is based on the criminal lead charge as determined by the assistant U.S. attorney responsible for the criminal matter]

Most serious offense investigated	1994	1995	1996	1997	1998	1999[1]	2000	2001	2002	2003	2004
All offenses[2]	99,251	102,220	97,776	110,034	115,692	117,994	123,559	121,818	124,335	130,078	141,212
Violent offenses[3]	5,570	5,720	6,570	7,354	7,527	5,768	6,036	6,225	6,392	5,688	5,714
Property offenses	32,579	31,759	28,962	29,916	30,125	28,011	28,423	28,608	27,321	27,375	24,956
Fraudulent[4]	28,491	27,836	25,245	25,854	26,328	24,200	24,679	25,275	24,019	24,261	22,182
Other[5]	4,088	3,923	3,717	4,062	3,797	3,811	3,744	3,333	3,302	3,114	2,774
Drug offenses	29,311	31,686	30,227	34,027	36,355	37,313	38,959	37,944	38,150	37,416	37,501
Public-order offenses.....	19,143	19,036	18,918	22,857	21,244	22,816	24,180	23,980	23,472	23,717	21,277
Regulatory	5,059	5,371	5,154	5,423	6,541	6,332	5,737	5,411	4,738	5,366	4,959
Other[6]	14,084	13,665	13,764	17,434	14,703	16,484	18,443	18,569	18,734	18,351	16,318
Weapon offenses[6]	5,996	5,376	4,462	4,870	4,907	6,982	8,589	8,989	11,200	14,022	14,398
Immigration offenses[6]	5,526	7,256	7,122	9,366	14,114	15,539	16,495	15,378	16,699	20,341	35,858
Unknown or indeterminable offenses	1,126	1,387	1,515	1,644	1,420	1,565	877	694	1,101	1,519	1,508

[1] Starting in 1999 and through the current year of data, nonviolent sex offenses were reclassified from "Violent offenses" to "Public-order offenses." [2] Includes suspects whose offense category could not be determined. See Methodology for a listing of detailed offense categories within each major offense category. [3] In this table, "Violent offenses" may include nonnegligent manslaughter; "Fraudulent property" excludes tax fraud; and "Other nonfraudulent property" excludes fraudulent property and includes destruction of property and trespassing. [4] Fradulent property excludes tax fraud. [5] Excludes fraudulent property and includes destruction of property and trespassing. [6] Beginning in 2001, "Weapon" and "Immigration" offenses became major offense categories. Previously, theses offenses were classified within "Public-order offenses."

Source: U.S. Department of Justice, Office of Justice Programs, Bureau of Justice Statistics, *Federal Criminal Justice Trends,* 2003. Series NCJ 205331, August 2006. See also, <http://www.ojp.usdoj.gov/bjs/abstract/fcjt03.htm>. *Compendium of Federal Justice Statistics, 2004*, Series NCJ 213476, December 2006; <http://www.ojp.usdoj.gov/bjs/abstract/cfjs04.htm>.

Table 332. Criminal Appeals Filed, by Offense: 1994 to 2004

[Appeals were classified into the offense category that represents the offense of conviction. Offenses represent the statutory offense charged against a defendant in a criminal appeal]

Most serious offense of conviction	1994	1995	1996	1997	1998	1999[1]	2000	2001	2002	2003	2004
All offenses[2]	10,674	10,162	10,889	10,521	10,535	10,251	9,162	11,281	11,569	11,968	12,517
Violent offenses[3]	856	700	685	739	742	559	490	591	606	601	673
Property offenses	1,949	1,767	2,093	1,972	1,947	1,739	1,482	1,681	1,726	1,842	1,873
Fraudulent[4]	1,410	1,323	1,581	1,519	1,439	1,338	1,164	1,299	1,389	1,478	1,524
Other[5]	539	444	512	453	508	401	318	382	337	364	349
Drug offenses	5,102	4,499	5,099	4,750	4,845	4,513	3,843	4,529	4,689	4,565	4,678
Public-order offenses	1,037	886	985	1,050	878	954	827	1,024	876	894	955
Regulatory............	288	220	196	224	178	162	150	144	128	137	142
Other[6]	749	666	789	826	700	792	677	880	642	757	813
Weapon offenses[6]	1,141	1,034	1,183	1,135	982	1,070	872	1,266	1,386	1,681	2,024
Immigration offenses[6]	261	277	353	417	693	934	1,179	1,654	1,679	1,821	1,856
Unknown or indeterminable offenses	328	999	491	458	448	482	469	536	607	564	458

[1] Starting in 1999 and through the current data year, nonvioient sex offenses were reclassified from "Violent offenses" to "Public-order offenses." [2] Includes suspects whose offense category could not be determined. See Methodology for a listing of detailed offense categories within each major offense category. [3] In this table, "Violent offenses" may include nonnegligent manslaughter; "Fraudulent property" excludes tax fraud; and "Other nonfraudulent property" excludes fraudulent property and includes destruction of property and trespassing. [4] Fradulent property excludes tax fraud. [5] Excludes fraudulent property and includes destruction of property and trespassing. [6] Beginning in 2001, "Weapon" and "Immigration" offenses became major offense categories. Previously, theses offenses were classified within "Public-order offenses."

Source: U.S. Department of Justice, Office of Justice Programs, Bureau of Justice Statistics, *Federal Criminal Justice Trends,* 2003. Series NCJ 205331, August 2006. See also, <http://www.ojp.usdoj.gov/bjs/abstract/fcjt03.htm>. *Compendium of Federal Justice Statistics, 2004*, Series NCJ 213476, December 2006; <http://www.ojp.usdoj.gov/bjs/abstract/cfjs04.htm>.

Table 333. Delinquency Cases Disposed by Juvenile Courts by Reason for Referral: 1990 to 2004

[In thousands (1,336 represents 1,336,000), except rate. A delinquency offense is an act committed by a juvenile for which an adult could be prosecuted in a criminal court. Disposition of a case involves taking a definite action such as waiving the case to criminal court, dismissing the case, placing the youth on probation, placing the youth in a facility for delinquents, or such actions as fines, restitution, and community service. Data have been revised through 2004]

Reason for referral	1990	1995	1996	1997	1998	1999	2000	2001	2002	2003	2004
All delinquency offenses . .	**1,336**	**1,784**	**1,825**	**1,847**	**1,773**	**1,690**	**1,665**	**1,650**	**1,645**	**1,643**	**1,661**
Case rate [1]	52.1	62.2	62.7	62.6	59.4	55.9	54.2	53.1	52.5	52.2	52.6
Person offenses [2]	255	394	395	407	396	385	377	388	388	396	401
Criminal homicide	2	3	3	2	2	2	2	2	2	2	2
Forcible rape	4	6	5	5	5	4	4	5	4	5	4
Robbery	28	42	39	35	30	26	21	22	21	21	21
Aggravated assault	53	73	68	61	57	50	49	46	43	44	45
Property offenses [2]	785	900	887	854	778	698	668	631	629	616	603
Burglary	146	147	150	146	133	113	108	103	103	101	96
Larceny-theft	344	424	416	399	351	316	309	289	288	281	278
Motor vehicle theft	71	54	53	52	45	38	37	37	37	37	34
Arson	7	11	10	9	9	9	9	9	9	8	9
Drug law violations	71	163	182	188	187	186	194	201	191	189	194
Public order offenses [2]	224	329	363	399	412	421	426	430	437	443	463
Obstruction of justice	81	127	155	182	200	200	205	208	206	209	217
Disorderly conduct	55	90	89	91	87	93	96	100	110	112	122
Weapons offenses	31	47	45	45	43	40	38	37	35	38	41
Liquor law violations	17	16	18	19	23	24	28	27	28	28	29
Nonviolent sex offenses	11	9	11	11	11	12	13	14	14	14	14

[1] Number of cases disposed per 1,000 youth (ages 10 to 17) at risk of referral to juvenile court.   [2] Total include other offenses not shown.

Source: National Center for Juvenile Justice, Pittsburgh, PA, *Juvenile Court Statistics*, annual. See also <http://www.ojjdp.ncjrs.org/ojstatbb/index.html>.

Table 334. Delinquency Cases and Case Rates by Sex and Race: 1994 to 2004

[Data have been revised. See head note, Table 333]

Sex, race, and offense	Number of cases disposed			Case rate [1]		
	1994	2000	2004	1994	2000	2004
Male, total	**1,322,571**	**1,245,428**	**1,208,215**	**91.5**	**79.0**	**74.7**
Person	280,245	272,199	282,422	19.4	17.3	17.5
Property	688,371	498,786	438,814	47.6	31.6	27.1
Drugs	110,956	160,830	155,094	7.7	10.2	9.6
Public order	242,999	313,614	331,886	16.8	19.9	20.5
Female, total	**361,778**	**419,379**	**452,457**	**26.4**	**28.0**	**29.4**
Person	87,217	105,025	118,264	6.4	7.0	7.7
Property	190,567	169,160	164,368	13.9	11.3	10.7
Drugs	17,538	32,716	38,636	1.3	2.2	2.5
Public order	66,456	112,478	131,189	4.9	7.5	8.5
White, total	**1,127,439**	**1,149,134**	**1,096,480**	**50.2**	**47.6**	**44.6**
Person	216,643	236,646	234,653	9.7	9.8	9.6
Property	624,953	469,507	411,723	27.8	19.4	16.8
Drugs	79,775	145,604	146,201	3.6	6.0	6.0
Public order	206,069	297,377	303,904	9.2	12.3	12.4
Black, total	**505,952**	**467,457**	**513,801**	**118.5**	**96.7**	**99.7**
Person	141,071	130,503	154,955	33.0	27.0	30.1
Property	224,141	174,953	169,600	52.5	36.2	32.9
Drugs	46,621	43,628	42,421	10.9	9.0	8.2
Public order	94,119	118,373	146,825	22.0	24.5	28.5
Other races, total	**30,330**	**25,380**	**26,144**	**83.9**	**55.7**	**56.6**
Person	5,775	5,260	5,818	16.0	11.5	12.6
Property	17,068	12,100	11,068	47.2	26.6	23.9
Drugs	1,184	2,501	2,952	3.3	5.5	6.4
Public order	6,303	5,519	6,305	17.4	12.1	13.6

[1] Cases per 1,000 youth (ages 10 to 17).

Source: National Center for Juvenile Justice, Pittsburgh, PA, *Juvenile Court Statistics*, annual. See also <http://www.ojjdp.ncjrs.org/ojstatbb/index.html>.

Table 335. **Child Abuse and Neglect Cases Substantiated and Indicated—Victim Characteristics: 1990 to 2005**

[Based on reports alleging child abuse and neglect that were referred for investigation by the respective child protective services agency in each state. The reporting period may be either calendar or fiscal year. The majority of states provided duplicated counts. Also, varying number of states reported the various characteristics presented below. A substantiated case represents a type of investigation disposition that determines that there is sufficient evidence under state law to conclude that maltreatment occurred or that the child is at risk of maltreatment. An indicated case represents a type of disposition that concludes that there was a reason to suspect maltreatment had occurred]

ITEM	1990		2000		2004		2005	
	Number	Percent	Number	Percent	Number	Percent	Number	Percent
TYPES OF SUBSTANTIATED MALTREATMENT [1,2]								
Victims, total	690,658	(X)	864,837	116.5	876,937	113.3	899,454	113.1
Neglect.	338,770	49.1	517,118	59.8	518,519	59.1	564,765	62.8
Physical abuse	186,801	27.0	167,713	19.4	151,108	17.2	149,319	16.6
Sexual abuse	119,506	17.3	87,770	10.2	83,221	9.5	83,810	9.3
Emotional maltreatment.	45,621	6.6	66,965	7.7	61,157	7.0	63,497	7.1
Medical neglect	(NA)	(NA)	25,498	3.0	17,211	2.0	17,637	2.0
SEX OF VICTIM [3]								
Victims, total	742,519	100.0	864,837	100.0	876,937	100.0	899,454	100.0
Male	323,339	43.5	413,744	47.8	422,290	48.2	425,387	47.3
Female.	369,919	49.8	446,230	51.6	451,718	51.5	455,652	50.7
AGE OF VICTIM [3]								
Victims, total	731,282	100.0	864,837	100.0	876,937	100.0	899,454	100.0
1 year and younger	97,101	13.3	133,094	15.4	146,670	16.7	155,046	17.2
2 to 5 years old	172,791	23.6	205,790	23.8	218,600	24.9	222,067	24.7
6 to 9 years old	157,681	21.6	212,186	24.5	194,038	22.1	192,777	21.4
10 to 13 years old	135,130	18.5	176,071	20.4	177,416	20.2	171,531	19.1
14 to 17 years old	105,383	14.1	126,207	14.6	136,479	15.6	138,729	15.4
18 years old and over	4,880	0.7	992	0.1	475	0.1	471	0.1

NA Not available.   X Not applicable.   [1] Not all types of maltreatment are shown.   [2] A child may be a victim of more than one maltreatment. Therefore, the total for this item adds up to more than 100 percent.   [3] The increase in unknown age, sex, and race in 2005 is due to some states reporting summary data without breakdown of corresponding fields.

Source: U.S. Department of Health and Human Services, Administration for Children and Families, Statistics and Research, *Child Maltreatment 2005,* annual; <http://www.acf.hhs.gov/programs/cb/pubs/cm05/index.htm>.

Table 336. **Child Abuse and Neglect Cases Reported and Investigated by State: 2005**

[See headnote, Table 335]

State and outlying area	Population under 18 years old	Number of reports [1]	Number of children subject of an investigation [2]	Number of child victims [3]	State and outlying area	Population under 18 years old	Number of reports [1]	Number of children subject of an investigation [2]	Number of child victims [3]
Total [4] . .	74,502,089	1,915,641	3,529,172	899,454	MT	204,994	8,181	13,793	2,095
					NE	431,629	15,501	35,621	6,630
AL	1,089,753	18,318	27,378	9,029	NV	621,180	14,291	27,738	4,971
AK	188,324	4,273	6,813	2,693	NH	303,151	6,583	9,275	941
AZ	1,580,436	37,088	84,154	6,119	NJ	2,161,801	34,806	61,041	9,812
AR	675,622	23,120	46,950	8,124					
CA	9,701,862	228,012	434,589	95,314	NM	489,482	20,225	32,950	7,285
CO	1,180,525	26,950	41,166	9,406	NY	4,545,884	140,214	236,897	70,878
CT	835,006	30,030	45,064	11,419	NC	2,141,041	66,698	135,809	33,250
DE	195,879	5,799	13,878	1,960	ND	136,518	3,961	6,972	1,547
DC	112,837	4,958	11,950	2,840	OH	2,759,112	71,762	112,600	42,483
FL	4,067,877	148,004	334,293	130,633	OK	853,336	36,952	65,716	13,941
GA	2,362,722	74,165	174,409	47,158	OR	849,944	25,063	40,110	12,414
					PA	2,816,739	23,114	23,114	4,353
HI	299,852	2,733	5,426	2,762	RI	245,354	7,101	10,734	3,366
ID	374,180	6,499	9,646	1,912	SC	1,027,202	17,088	38,238	10,759
IL	3,241,039	66,305	146,091	29,325					
IN	1,602,847	37,860	57,752	19,062	SD	188,270	3,968	7,158	1,442
IA	670,801	24,536	38,038	14,016	TN	1,390,522	59,998	94,469	18,376
KS	674,285	14,146	21,240	2,775	TX	6,326,285	161,895	269,122	61,994
KY	980,160	47,960	75,625	19,474	UT	742,556	21,052	33,684	13,152
LA	1,147,651	26,901	44,630	12,366	VT	132,619	2,504	3,099	1,080
ME	277,336	5,396	9,241	3,349	VA	1,824,568	27,937	56,156	6,469
MD	1,402,961	(NA)	(NA)	14,603	WA	1,484,365	34,293	53,124	7,932
MA	1,458,036	38,669	79,909	35,887	WV	382,497	22,400	50,249	9,511
MI	2,524,274	65,174	173,806	24,603	WI	1,295,995	29,660	41,430	9,686
MN	1,229,578	18,843	27,682	8,499	WY	114,321	2,020	3,936	853
MS	748,544	15,745	24,648	6,154					
MO	1,378,232	55,217	82,252	8,945	PR	1,032,105	31,673	49,507	15,807

NA Not available.   [1] The number of investigations includes assessments. The number of investigations is based on the total number of investigations that received a disposition in 2005.   [2] The number of Children Subject of an Investigation or Assessment is based on the total number of children for whom an alleged maltreatment was substantiated, indicated, or assessed to have occurred or the child was at risk of occurrence.   [3] Victims are defined as children subject of a substantiated, indicated, or alternative response-victim maltreatment.   [4] Includes Puerto Rico and estimates for states that did not report.

Source: U.S. Department of Health and Human Services, Administration for Children and Families, Statistics and Research, *Child Maltreatment 2005,* annual; <http://www.acf.hhs.gov/programs/cb/pubs/cm05/index.htm>.

Table 337. Prisoners Under Jurisdiction of Federal or State Correctional Authorities—Summary by State: 1990 to 2005

[For years ending December 31. Minus sign (–) indicates decrease]

State	1990	2000	2004	2005, advance Total	2005, advance Percent change, 2004–2005	State	1990	2000	2004	2005, advance Total	2005, advance Percent change, 2004–2005
U.S.[1]	773,919	1,391,261	1,497,100	1,525,924	1.9	MN	3,176	6,238	8,758	9,281	6.0
						MS	8,375	20,241	20,983	20,515	-2.2
Federal	65,526	145,416	180,328	187,618	4.0	MO	14,943	27,543	31,081	30,823	-0.8
State	708,393	1,245,845	1,316,772	1,338,306	1.6	MT	1,425	3,105	3,164	3,509	10.9
						NE	2,403	3,895	4,130	4,455	7.9
AL	15,665	26,332	25,887	27,888	7.7	NV	5,322	10,063	11,365	11,782	3.7
AK[2]	2,622	4,173	4,554	4,812	5.7	NH	1,342	2,257	2,448	2,530	3.3
AZ[3]	14,261	26,510	32,515	33,471	2.9	NJ	21,128	29,784	26,757	27,359	2.2
AR	7,322	11,915	13,807	13,511	-2.1	NM	3,187	5,342	6,379	6,571	3.0
CA	97,309	163,001	166,556	170,676	2.5	NY	54,895	70,199	63,751	62,743	-1.6
CO[2]	7,671	16,833	20,293	21,456	5.7	NC	18,411	31,266	35,434	36,365	2.6
CT[2]	10,500	18,355	19,497	19,442	-0.3	ND	483	1,076	1,327	1,385	4.4
DE[2]	3,471	6,921	6,927	6,944	0.2	OH	31,822	45,833	44,806	45,854	2.3
DC[4,5]	9,947	7,456	(NA)	(NA)	(NA)	OK	12,285	23,181	24,508	24,826	1.3
FL[3]	44,387	71,319	85,533	89,768	5.0	OR	6,492	10,580	13,183	13,411	1.7
GA[3]	22,411	44,232	51,104	48,749	-4.6	PA	22,290	36,847	40,963	42,380	3.5
HI[2]	2,533	5,053	5,960	6,146	3.1	RI[2]	2,392	3,286	3,430	3,654	6.5
ID	1,961	5,535	6,375	6,818	6.9	SC	17,319	21,778	23,428	23,160	-1.1
IL	27,516	45,281	44,054	44,919	2.0	SD	1,341	2,616	3,095	3,463	11.9
IN	12,736	20,125	24,008	24,455	1.9	TN	10,388	22,166	25,884	26,369	1.9
IA[3]	3,967	7,955	8,525	8,737	2.5	TX	50,042	166,719	168,105	169,003	0.5
KS	5,775	8,344	8,966	9,068	1.1	UT	2,496	5,637	5,991	6,373	6.4
KY	9,023	14,919	17,814	19,662	10.4	VT[2]	1,049	1,697	1,968	2,078	5.6
LA	18,599	35,207	36,939	36,083	-2.3	VA	17,593	30,168	35,564	35,344	-0.6
ME	1,523	1,679	2,024	2,023	–	WA	7,995	14,915	16,614	17,382	4.6
MD	17,848	23,538	23,285	22,737	-2.4	WV	1,565	3,856	5,067	5,312	4.8
MA	8,345	10,722	10,144	10,701	5.5	WI	7,465	20,754	22,959	22,720	-1.0
MI	34,267	47,718	48,883	49,546	1.4	WY	1,110	1,680	1,980	2,047	3.4

– Rounds to zero. NA Not available. [1] U.S. total includes federal prisoners not distributed by state. This total includes all inmates held in public and private adult correctional facilities. [2] Includes both jail and prison inmates (state has combined jail and prison system). [3] Numbers are for custody rather than jurisdiction counts. [4] The transfer of responsibility for sentenced felons from the District of Columbia to the federal system was completed by the year end 2001. [5] The District of Columbia inmates sentenced to more than 1 year are now under the responsibility of the Bureau of Prisons.

Source: U.S. Department of Justice, Office of Justice Programs, Bureau of Justice Statistics, *Prisoners in 2005*, Series NCJ 215092; and earlier reports; <http://www.ojp.usdoj.gov/bjs/abstract/p05.htm/>.

Table 338. Adults on Probation, in Jail or Prison, or on Parole: 1980 to 2005

[As of December 31, except jail counts as of June 30]

Year	Total [1]	Supervision rate per 100,000 adults	Probation	Jail	Prison	Parole	Male	Female
1980	1,840,400	1.1	1,118,097	182,288	319,598	220,438	(NA)	(NA)
1985	3,011,500	1.7	1,968,712	254,986	487,593	300,203	2,606,000	405,500
1986	3,239,400	1.8	2,114,621	272,735	526,436	325,638	2,829,100	410,300
1987	3,459,600	1.9	2,247,158	294,092	562,814	355,505	3,021,000	438,600
1988	3,714,100	2.0	2,356,483	341,893	607,766	407,977	3,223,000	491,100
1989	4,055,600	2.2	2,522,125	393,303	683,367	456,803	3,501,600	554,000
1990	4,348,000	2.3	2,670,234	403,019	743,382	531,407	3,746,300	601,700
1991	4,535,600	2.4	2,728,472	424,129	792,535	590,442	3,913,000	622,600
1992	4,762,600	2.5	2,811,611	441,781	850,566	658,601	4,050,300	712,300
1993	4,944,000	2.6	2,903,061	455,500	909,381	676,100	4,215,800	728,200
1994	5,141,300	2.7	2,981,022	479,800	990,147	690,371	4,377,400	763,900
1995	5,342,900	2.8	3,077,861	507,044	1,078,542	679,421	4,513,000	822,100
1996	5,482,700	2.8	3,164,996	510,400	1,127,528	679,733	4,629,900	852,800
1997	5,725,800	2.9	3,296,513	557,974	1,176,564	694,787	4,825,300	900,500
1998	6,126,100	3.1	3,670,441	584,372	1,224,469	696,385	(NA)	(NA)
1999	6,331,400	3.1	3,779,922	596,485	1,287,172	714,457	(NA)	(NA)
2000	6,445,100	3.1	3,826,209	621,149	1,316,333	723,898	(NA)	(NA)
2001	6,581,700	3.1	3,931,731	631,240	1,330,007	732,333	(NA)	(NA)
2002	6,758,800	3.1	4,024,067	665,475	1,367,547	750,934	(NA)	(NA)
2003 [2,3]	6,924,500	3.2	4,120,012	691,301	1,390,279	769,925	(NA)	(NA)
2004 [3]	6,995,200	3.2	4,143,466	713,990	1,421,911	771,852	(NA)	(NA)
2005, advance	7,056,000	3.2	4,162,536	747,529	1,446,269	784,408	(NA)	(NA)

NA Not available. [1] Totals may not add due to individuals having multiple correctional statuses. [2] Due to changes in reporting, total probation and parole counts include estimated counts for Massachusetts, Pennsylvania, and Washington based on reporting methods comparable to 2004. [3] Revised data.

Source: U.S. Department of Justice, Office of Justice Programs, Bureau of Justice Statistics, *Correctional Populations in the United States*, annual; <http://www.ojp.usdoj.gov/bjs/correct.htm>.

Law Enforcement, Courts, and Prisons 211

Table 339. Jail Inmates by Sex, Race, and Hispanic Origin: 1990 to 2005

[As of June 30. Excludes federal and state prisons or other correctional institutions; institutions exclusively for juveniles; state-operated jails in Alaska, Connecticut, Delaware, Hawaii, Rhode Island, and Vermont; and other facilities which retain persons for less than 72 hours. Data based on the Annual Survey of Jails, a sample survey, and subject to sampling variability. Due to rounding, details may not add to total. 2000–2004 rated capacity subject to sampling error]

Characteristic	1990	1995	2000	2001	2002	2003	2004	2005
Total inmates [1,2]	405,320	507,044	621,149	631,240	665,475	691,301	713,990	747,529
Incarceration rate [3]	163	193	220	222	231	238	243	252
Rated capacity [4]	389,171	545,763	677,787	699,309	713,899	736,471	755,603	789,001
Male	365,821	448,000	543,120	551,007	581,411	602,781	626,407	646,807
Female.	37,148	51,300	70,414	72,621	76,817	81,650	87,583	93,963
Juveniles [5]	2,301	7,800	7,613	7,613	7,248	6,869	7,083	6,759
White, non-Hispanic	169,600	203,300	260,500	271,700	291,800	301,200	317,400	331,000
Black, non-Hispanic	172,300	220,600	256,300	256,200	264,900	271,000	275,400	290,500
Hispanic/Latino	58,100	74,400	94,100	93,000	98,000	106,600	108,300	111,900
Other [6]	5,400	8,800	10,200	10,300	10,800	12,500	12,900	13,000

[1] Total does not include offenders who were supervised outside of jail facilities. [2] Race/Hispanic origin data do not include the two or more race data. [3] Number of jail inmates per 100,000 residents. [4] Rated capacity is the number of beds or inmates assigned by a rating official to facilities within each jurisdiction. [5] Juveniles are persons held under the age of 18. Includes juveniles who were tried or awaiting trial as adults. [6] Includes American Indians, Alaska Natives, Asians, and Pacific Islanders.
Source: U.S. Department of Justice, Office of Justice Programs, Bureau of Justice Statistics, Jail Inmates, annual; beginning 1995, Prison and Jail Inmates at Midyear, Series NCJ 213133 annual; <http://www.ojp.usdoj.gov/bjs/jails.htm>.

Table 340. Federal and State Prisoners by Sex: 1980 to 2005

[Prisoners, as of December 31. Includes all persons under jurisdiction of federal and state authorities rather than those in the custody of such authorities. Represents inmates sentenced to maximum term of more than a year]

Year	Total [1]	Rate [2]	State	Male	Female	Year	Total [1]	Rate [2]	State	Male	Female
1980...	315,974	139	295,363	303,643	12,331	1995...	1,085,022	411	1,001,359	1,021,059	63,963
1985...	480,568	202	447,873	459,223	21,345	1996...	1,137,722	427	1,048,907	1,068,123	69,599
1986...	522,084	217	485,553	497,540	24,544	1997..	1,195,498	445	1,100,511	1,121,663	73,835
1987...	560,812	231	521,289	533,990	26,822	1998...	1,245,402	461	1,141,720	1,167,802	77,600
1988...	603,732	247	560,994	573,587	30,145	1999...	1,304,074	476	1,189,799	1,221,611	82,463
1989...	680,907	276	633,739	643,643	37,264	2000...	1,331,278	[3]470	1,204,323	1,246,234	85,044
1990...	739,980	297	689,577	699,416	40,564	2001...	1,345,217	470	1,208,708	1,260,033	85,184
1991...	789,610	313	732,914	745,808	43,802	2002...	1,380,516	476	1,237,476	1,291,450	89,066
1992...	846,277	332	780,571	799,776	46,501	2003...	1,408,361	482	1,256,442	1,315,790	92,571
1993...	932,074	359	857,675	878,037	54,037	2004...	1,433,728	486	1,274,591	1,337,730	95,998
1994...	1,016,691	389	936,896	956,566	60,125	2005...	1,461,132	491	1,294,959	1,362,530	98,602

[1] Includes federal. [2] Rate per 100,000 estimated population. Based on U.S. Census Bureau estimated resident population. [3] Decrease in incarceration rate from 1999 to 2000 due to use of new Census numbers.
Source: U.S. Department of Justice, Office of Justice Programs, Bureau of Justice Statistics, Prisoners in 2005, Series NCJ 215092, annual; <http://www.ojp.usdoj.gov/bjs/abstract/p05.htm>.

Table 341. Prisoners Under Sentence of Death by Characteristic: 1980 to 2005

[As of December 31. Excludes prisoners under sentence of death who remained within local correctional systems pending exhaustion of appellate process or who had not been committed to prison]

Characteristic	1980	1990	1995	1997	1998	1999	2000	2001	2002	2003	2004	2005
Total [1,2]	688	2,346	3,064	3,328	3,465	3,540	3,601	3,577	3,562	3,377	3,320	3,254
White	418	1,368	1,732	1,864	1,917	1,960	1,989	1,968	1,939	1,882	1,856	1,805
Black and other	270	978	1,332	1,464	1,548	1,580	1,612	1,609	1,623	1,495	1,464	1,440
Under 20 years	11	8	20	16	16	16	11	4	4	1	1	–
20 to 24 years	173	168	264	275	273	251	237	192	153	133	95	61
25 to 34 years	334	1,110	1,068	1,077	1,108	1,108	1,103	1,099	1,058	965	896	816
35 to 54 years	186	1,006	1,583	1,809	1,897	1,958	2,019	2,043	2,069	1,969	1,977	2,012
55 years and over.	10	64	119	151	171	194	223	243	273	306	345	365
Years of school completed:												
7 years or less	68	178	191	205	208	201	214	212	215	213	207	192
8 years	74	186	195	206	218	221	233	236	234	227	221	206
9 to 11 years	204	775	979	1,069	1,122	1,142	1,157	1,145	1,130	1,073	1,053	1,030
12 years	162	729	995	1,084	1,128	1,157	1,184	1,183	1,173	1,108	1,091	1,105
More than 12 years	43	209	272	288	301	307	315	304	294	270	262	256
Unknown	163	279	422	476	488	499	490	501	511	483	480	465
Marital status:												
Never married.	268	998	1,412	1,555	1,645	1,689	1,749	1,763	1,746	1,641	1,622	1,586
Married	229	632	718	740	752	731	739	716	709	684	658	649
Divorced [3]	217	726	924	1,033	1,068	1,107	1,105	1,102	1,102	1,049	1,034	1,019
Time elapsed since sentencing:												
Less than 12 months	185	231	287	262	293	259	208	151	147	137	117	122
12 to 47 months	389	753	784	844	816	800	786	734	609	495	421	399
48 to 71 months	102	438	423	456	482	499	507	476	468	451	388	299
72 months and over.	38	934	1,560	1,766	1,874	1,969	2,092	2,220	2,333	2,291	2,388	2,434
Legal status at arrest:												
Not under sentence	384	1,345	1,764	1,957	2,036	2,088	2,202	2,189	2,165	2,048	2,026	1,979
Parole or probation [4]	115	578	866	880	879	886	921	918	909	845	809	792
Prison or escaped	45	128	110	116	127	125	126	135	141	137	145	144
Unknown	170	305	314	375	423	428	344	339	342	344	334	339

– Represents zero. [1] Revisions to the total number of prisoners were not carried to the characteristics except for race. [2] Includes races not shown separately. [3] Includes persons married but separated, widows, widowers, and unknown. [4] Includes prisoners on mandatory conditional release, work release, other leave, AWOL or bail. Covers 28 prisoners in 1990, 33 in 1995, 30 in 1997, 26 in 1998, 21 in 1999 and 2000, and 17 in 2001, 2002, and 2003; 15 in 2004; and 14 in 2005.
Source: U.S. Department of Justice, Office of Justice Programs, Bureau of Justice Statistics, Capital Punishment 2005, Series NCJ 215083. See also <http://www.ojp.usdoj.gov/bjs/abstract/cp05.htm>.

Table 342. **Movement of Prisoners Under Sentence of Death: 1980 to 2005**

[Prisoners reported under sentence of death by civil authorities. The term "under sentence of death" begins when the court pronounces the first sentence of death for a capital offense]

Status	1980	1990	1995	1997	1998	1999	2000	2001	2002	2003	2004	2005
Under sentence of death, Jan. 1	595	2,243	2,905	3,242	3,328	3,465	3,540	3,601	3,577	3,562	3,377	3,320
Received death sentence [1]	203	244	310	256	285	272	214	155	159	144	125	128
White	125	147	168	146	145	157	122	89	83	92	75	70
Black	77	94	138	106	132	104	86	61	73	44	50	52
Dispositions other than executions . . .	101	108	105	89	93	112	76	109	108	267	129	134
Executions . . . . 1, 2 .	–	23	56	74	68	98	85	66	71	65	59	60
Under sentence of death, Dec. 31 [1], [2] .	688	2,356	3,054	3,335	3,452	3,527	3,593	3,581	3,557	3,374	3,314	3,254
White	425	1,375	1,730	1,876	1,906	1,948	1,990	1,969	1,931	1,878	1,850	1,805
Black	268	943	1,275	1,406	1,486	1,514	1,535	1,538	1,554	1,418	1,390	1,372

– Represents zero.   [1] Includes races other than White or Black.   [2] Revisions to total number of prisoners under death sentence not carried to this category.

Source: U.S. Department of Justice, Office of Justice Programs, Bureau of Justice Statistics, *Capital Punishment, Series NCJ 215083,* annual. See also <http://www.ojp.usdoj.gov/bjs/abstract/cp05.htm>.

Table 343. **Prisoners Executed Under Civil Authority by Sex and Race: 1930 to 2006**

[Excludes executions by military authorities. The Army (including the Air Force) carried out 160 (148 between 1942 and 1950; three each in 1954, 1955, and 1957; and one each in 1958, 1959, and 1961). Of the total, 106 were executed for murder (including 21 involving rape), 53 for rape, and one for desertion. The Navy carried out no executions during the period]

Year or period	Total [1]	Male	Female	White	Black	Executed for murder Total [1]	Executed for murder White	Executed for murder Black
All years, 1930–2006 . .	4,916	4,873	43	2,431	2,428	4,391	2,344	1,992
1930 to 1939	1,667	1,656	11	827	816	1,514	803	687
1940 to 1949 [2]	1,284	1,272	12	490	781	1,064	458	595
1950 to 1959 [2]	717	709	8	336	376	601	316	280
1960 to 1967	191	190	1	98	93	155	87	68
1968 to 1976	–	–	–	–	–	–	–	–
1977 to 2006	1,057	1,046	11	680	362	1,057	680	362
1985	18	18	–	11	7	18	11	7
1990	23	23	–	16	7	23	16	7
1991	14	14	–	7	7	14	7	7
1992	31	31	–	19	11	31	19	11
1993	38	38	–	23	14	38	23	14
1994	31	31	–	20	11	31	20	11
1995	56	56	–	33	22	56	33	22
1996	45	45	–	31	14	45	31	14
1997	74	74	–	45	27	74	45	27
1998	68	66	2	48	18	68	48	18
1999	98	98	–	61	33	98	61	33
2000	85	83	2	49	35	85	49	35
2001	66	63	3	48	17	66	48	17
2002	71	69	2	53	18	71	53	18
2003	65	65	–	44	20	65	44	20
2004	59	59	–	39	19	59	39	19
2005	60	59	1	41	19	60	41	19
2006	53	53	–	32	21	53	32	21

– Represents zero.   [1] Includes races other than White or Black.   [2] Includes 25 armed robbery, 20 kidnapping, 11 burglary, 8 espionage (6 in 1942 and 2 in 1953), and 6 aggravated assault.

Source: Through 1978, U.S. Law Enforcement Assistance Administration; thereafter, U.S. Department of Justice, Office of Justice Programs, Bureau of Justice Statistics, *Correctional Populations in the United States,* annual; <http://www.ojp.usdoj .gov/bjs/abstract/cp05.htm>and *Capital Punishment,* annual; <http://www.ojp.usdoj.gov/bjs/abstract/cp05.htm>.

Table 344. **Prisoners Executed Under Civil Authority by State: 1977 to 2006**

[Alaska, District of Columbia, Hawaii, Iowa, Maine, Massachusetts, Michigan, Minnesota, New York, North Dakota, Rhode Island, Vermont, West Virginia, and Wisconsin are jurisdictions without a death penalty]

State	1977 to 2006	2003	2004	2005	2006	State	1977 to 2006	2003	2004	2005	2006	State	1977 to 2006	2003	2004	2005	2006
U.S. . .	1,057	65	59	60	53	IL	12	–	–	–	–	OK . . .	83	14	6	4	4
						IN	17	2	–	5	1	OR . . .	2	–	–	–	–
AL . . .	35	3	2	4	1	KY . . .	2	–	–	–	–	PA . . .	3	–	–	–	–
AZ . . .	22	–	–	–	–	LA . . .	27	–	–	–	–	SC . . .	36	–	4	3	1
AR . . .	27	1	1	1	–	MD . . .	5	–	1	1	–	TN . . .	2	–	–	–	1
CA . . .	13	–	–	2	1	MS . . .	8	–	–	1	1	TX . . .	379	24	23	19	24
DE . . .	14	–	–	1	–	MO . . .	66	2	–	5	–	UT . . .	6	–	–	–	–
FL . . .	64	3	2	1	4	NE . . .	3	–	–	–	–	VA . . .	98	2	5	–	4
GA . . .	39	3	2	3	–	NV . . .	12	–	2	–	1	WA . . .	4	–	–	–	–
ID	1	–	–	–	–	NC . . .	43	7	4	5	4	WY . . .	1	–	–	–	–

– Represents zero.

Source: Through 1978, U.S. Law Enforcement Assistance Administration; thereafter, U.S. Department of Justice, Office of Justice Programs, Bureau of Justice Statistics, *Capital Punishment, Series NCJ 215083,* annual; <http://www.ojp.usdoj.gov/bjs/cp.htm>.

U.S. Census Bureau, Statistical Abstract of the United States: 2008

Table 345. Fire Losses—Total and Per Capita: 1980 to 2005

[5,579 represents $5,579,000,000. Includes allowance for uninsured and unreported losses but excludes losses to government property and forests. Represents incurred losses]

Year	Total (mil. dol.)	Per capita [1] (dol.)	Year	Total (mil. dol.)	Per capita [1] (dol.)	Year	Total (mil. dol.)	Per capita [1] (dol.)
1980	5,579	24.56	1990	9,495	38.07	1998	11,510	45.59
1983	6,320	27.20	1991	11,302	44.82	1999	12,428	45.58
1984	7,602	32.35	1992	13,588	53.28	2000	13,457	47.68
1985	7,753	32.70	1993	11,331	43.96	2001 [2] ...	17,118	60.04
1986	8,488	35.21	1994	12,778	49.08	2002	17,586	61.07
1987	8,504	34.96	1995	11,887	45.23	2003	21,129	72.66
1988	9,626	39.11	1996	12,544	47.29	2004 [3] ...	17,344	59.06
1989	9,514	38.33	1997	12,940	48.32	2005	20,706	69.86

[1] Based on U.S. Census Bureau estimated resident population as of July 1. Enumerated population as of April 1 for 1980, 1990, and 2000. [2] Does not include insured fire losses related to terrorism. [3] Data revised.

Source: Insurance Information Institute, New York, NY, The Fact Book, Property/Casualty Insurance Facts, annual (copyright) <http://www.iii.org/>.

Table 346. Fires—Number and Loss by Type and Property Use: 2001 to 2005

[1,734 represents 1,734,000 and property loss of 44,023 represents $44,023,000,000. Based on annual sample survey of fire departments. No adjustments were made for unreported fires and losses]

Type and property use	Number (1,000)				Direct property loss (mil. dol.) [1]			
	2001	2003	2004	2005	2001	2003	2004	2005
Fires, total	1,734	1,584	1,550	1,602	[2]44,023	12,367	9,794	10,672
Structure	521	520	526	511	42,314	8,678	8,314	9,193
Outside of structure [3]	75	66	69	78	86	162	108	93
Brush and rubbish	623	550	514	594	–	–	–	–
Vehicle	351	312	297	290	1,512	1,356	1,304	1,318
Other.	164	136	144	129	111	[4]2,171	68	68
Structure by property use:								
Public assembly	15	14	13	13	336	302	316	320
Educational	7	7	7	6	170	69	68	67
Institutional	7	7	6	8	27	28	25	40
Stores and offices.	26	25	24	23	34,155	721	586	687
Residential	396	402	411	396	5,643	6,074	5,948	6,875
1–2 family units [5]	295	297	302	287	4,652	5,052	4,948	5,781
Apartments	88	92	94	94	864	897	885	948
Other residential [6]	13	13	15	15	127	125	115	146
Storage [6]	34	32	32	30	930	675	748	590
Industry, utility, defense [7] ...	13	11	12	12	858	625	423	376
Special structures.	23	22	21	23	195	184	200	238

– Represents zero. [1] Direct property damage figures do not include indirect losses, like business interruption, and adjustments for inflation. [2] Includes $33.4 billion in property loss that occured due to the events of September 11, 2001. [3] Includes outside storage, crops, timber, etc. [4] Includes Southern California wildfires where there was an estimated $2.044 billion in property loss. [5] Includes mobile homes. [6] Includes hotels and motels, college dormitories, boarding houses, etc. [7] Data underreported as some incidents were handled by private fire brigades or fixed suppression systems which do not report.

Source: National Fire Protection Association, Quincy, MA, 2005 U.S. Fire Loss, NFPA Journal, November 2006, and prior issues (copyright 2006); <http://www.nfpa.org/index.asp>.

Table 347. Fires and Property Loss for Incendiary and Suspicious Fires and Civilian Fire Deaths and Injuries by Selected Property Type: 2001 to 2005

[521 represents 521,000. Based on sample survey of fire departments]

Characteristic	2001	2003	2004	2005	Characteristic	2001	2003	2004	2005
NUMBER (1,000)					CIVILIAN FIRE DEATHS				
					Deaths, total [3]	[4]6,196	3,925	3,900	3,675
Structure fires, total ..	521	520	526	511	Residential property.....	3,140	3,165	3,225	3,055
					One- and two-family dwellings	2,650	2,735	2,680	2,575
Structure fires that were intentionally set	46	38	37	32	Apartments.........	460	410	510	460
					Vehicles	485	475	550	520
PROPERTY LOSS [1] (mil. dol.)					CIVILIAN FIRE INJURIES				
					Injuries, total [3]	[5]21,100	18,125	17,785	17,925
Structure fires, total ..	[2]42,314	8,678	8,314	9,193	Residential property.....	15,575	14,075	14,175	13,825
					One- and two-family dwellings	11,400	10,000	10,500	10,300
Structure fires that were intentionally set	[2]34,453	692	714	664	Apartments.........	3,800	3,650	3,200	3,000
					Vehicles	1,875	1,500	1,500	1,650

[1] Direct property loss only. [2] Includes $33.44 billion in property loss due to the events of September 11, 2001. [3] Includes other not shown separately. [4] Includes 2,451 civilian deaths due to the events of September 11, 2001. [5] Includes 800 civilian injuries due to the events of September 11, 2001.

Source: National Fire Protection Association, Quincy, MA, 2005 U.S. Fire Loss, NFPA Journal, November 2006, and prior issues (copyright 2006); <http://www.nfpa.org/index.asp>.

Geography and Environment

This section presents a variety of information on the physical environment of the United States, starting with basic area measurement data and ending with climatic data for selected weather stations around the country. The subjects covered between those points are mostly concerned with environmental trends but include related subjects such as land use, water consumption, air pollutant emissions, toxic releases, oil spills, hazardous waste sites, municipal waste and recycling, threatened and endangered wildlife, and the environmental industry.

The information in this section is selected from a wide range of federal agencies that compile the data for various administrative or regulatory purposes, such as the Environmental Protection Agency (EPA), U.S. Geological Survey (USGS), National Oceanic and Atmospheric Administration (NOAA), Natural Resources Conservation Service (NRCS), and General Services Administration (GSA). New information on waste generation recycling and wetlands may be found in Tables 352 and 365.

Area—For the 2000 census, area measurements were calculated by computer based on the information contained in a single, consistent geographic database, the Topologically Integrated Geographic Encoding & Referencing system (TIGER®) database, rather than relying on historical, local, and manually calculated information. Information from the 2000 census may be found in Table 348.

Geography—The USGS conducts investigations, surveys, and research in the fields of geography, geology, topography, geographic information systems, mineralogy, hydrology, and geothermal energy resources as well as natural hazards. The USGS provides United States cartographic data through the Earth Sciences Information Center, water resources data through the *Water Resources of the United States* at <http://water.usgs.gov/pubs/>.

In a joint project with the U.S. Census Bureau, during the 1980s, the USGS provided the basic information on geographic features for input into a national geographic and cartographic database prepared by the Census Bureau, called TIGER® database. Since then, using a variety of sources, the Census Bureau has updated these features and their related attributes (names, descriptions, etc.) and inserted current information on the boundaries, names, and codes of legal and statistical geographic entities; very few of these updates added aerial water features. Maps prepared by the Census Bureau using the TIGER® database show the names and boundaries of entities and are available on a current basis.

An inventory of the nation's land resources by type of use/cover was conducted by the National Resources Inventory Conservation Services (NRCS) every 5 years beginning in 1977 through 1997. Beginning with the release of the 2001 estimates, this program shifted to become an annual release of land use data. The most recent survey results, which were published for the year 2003, covered all nonfederal land for the contiguous 48 states. Tables 350 to 353 provide results from the survey.

Environment —The principal federal agency responsible for pollution abatement and control activities is the Environmental Protection Agency (EPA). It is responsible for establishing and monitoring national air quality standards, water quality activities, solid and hazardous waste disposal, and control of toxic substances. Many of these series now appear in the Envirofacts portion of the EPA Web site at <http://www.epa.gov/enviro/>.

National Ambient Air Quality Standards (NAAQS) for suspended particulate matter, sulfur dioxide, photochemical oxidants, carbon monoxide, and nitrogen dioxide were originally set by the EPA in April 1971. Every 5 years, each of the NAAQS is

U.S. Census Bureau, Statistical Abstract of the United States: 2008

reviewed and revised to include any additional or new health or welfare data. The standard for photochemical oxidants, now called ozone, was revised in February 1979. Also, a new NAAQS for confining lead was promulgated in October 1978 and for suspended particulate matter in 1987. Table 359 gives some of the health-related standards for the six air pollutants having NAAQS. Data gathered from state networks are periodically submitted to EPA's National Aerometric Information Retrieval System (AIRS) for summarization in annual reports on the nationwide status and trends in air quality. For details, see *National Air Quality and Emissions Trends Report*. More current information on emissions may be found on the EPA Web site at <http://www.epa.gov/airtrends/index.html>.

The Toxics Release Inventory (TRI), published by the EPA, is a valuable source of information on nearly 650 chemicals that are being used, manufactured, treated, transported, or released into the environment. Sections 313 of the Emergency Planning and Community Right-to-Know Act (EPCRA) and 6607 of the Pollution Prevention Act (PPA), mandate that a publicly-accessible toxic chemical database be developed and maintained by EPA. This database, known as the TRI, contains information concerning waste management activities and the release of toxic chemicals by facilities that manufacture, process, or otherwise use said materials. Data on the release of these chemicals are collected from over 23,000 facilities and facilities added in 1998 that have the equivalent of 10 or more full-time employees and meet the established

thresholds for manufacturing, processing, or "other use" of listed chemicals. Facilities must report their releases and other waste management quantities. Since 1994 federal facilities have been required to report their data regardless of industry classification. In May 1997, EPA added seven new industry sectors that reported to the TRI for the first time in July 1999 for the 1998 reporting year. More current information on this program can be found at <http://www.epa.gov/tri/index.htm>.

Climate—NOAA, through the National Weather Service and the National Environmental Satellite, Data, and Information Service, is responsible for climate data. NOAA maintains about 11,600 weather stations, of which over 3,000 produce autographic precipitation records, about 600 take hourly readings of a series of weather elements, and the remainder record data once a day. These data are reported monthly in the Climatological Data and Storm Data, published monthly and annually in the Local Climatological Data (published by location for major cities).

The normal climatological temperatures, precipitation, and degree days listed in this publication are derived for comparative purposes and are averages for the 30-year period, 1971–2000. For stations that did not have continuous records for the entire 30 years from the same instrument site, the normals have been adjusted to provide representative values for the current location. The information in all other tables is based on data from the beginning of the record at that location through 2005.

216   Geography and Environment

Table 348. Land and Water Area of States and Other Entities: 2000

[One square mile = 2.59 square kilometers. Area is calculated from the specific boundary recorded for each entity in the U.S. Census Bureau's geographic TIGER® database]

State and other areas	Total area Sq. mi.	Total area Sq. km.	Land area Sq. mi.	Land area Sq. km.	Water area Total Sq. mi.	Water area Total Sq. km.	Inland (sq. mi.)	Coastal (sq. mi.)	Great Lakes (sq. mi.)	Territorial (sq. mi.)
Total........	3,803,290	9,850,521	3,541,479	9,172,430	261,811	678,090	79,018	42,241	60,251	77,777
United States ..	3,794,083	9,826,675	3,537,438	9,161,966	256,645	664,710	78,797	42,225	60,251	75,372
Alabama	52,419	135,765	50,744	131,426	1,675	4,338	956	519	–	200
Alaska.........	663,267	1,717,854	571,951	1,481,347	91,316	236,507	17,243	27,049	–	47,024
Arizona	113,998	295,254	113,635	294,312	364	942	364	–	–	–
Arkansas	53,179	137,732	52,068	134,856	1,110	2,876	1,110	–	–	–
California	163,696	423,970	155,959	403,933	7,736	20,037	2,674	222	–	4,841
Colorado	104,094	269,601	103,718	268,627	376	974	376	–	–	–
Connecticut	5,543	14,357	4,845	12,548	699	1,809	161	538	–	–
Delaware	2,489	6,447	1,954	5,060	536	1,388	72	371	–	93
District of Columbia	68	177	61	159	7	18	7	–	–	–
Florida........	65,755	170,304	53,927	139,670	11,828	30,634	4,672	1,311	–	5,845
Georgia	59,425	153,909	57,906	149,976	1,519	3,933	1,016	48	–	455
Hawaii	10,931	28,311	6,423	16,635	4,508	11,677	38	–	–	4,470
Idaho.........	83,570	216,446	82,747	214,314	823	2,131	823	–	–	–
Illinois	57,914	149,998	55,584	143,961	2,331	6,037	756	–	1,575	–
Indiana	36,418	94,321	35,867	92,895	551	1,427	316	–	235	–
Iowa	56,272	145,743	55,869	144,701	402	1,042	402	–	–	–
Kansas	82,277	213,096	81,815	211,900	462	1,197	462	–	–	–
Kentucky	40,409	104,659	39,728	102,896	681	1,763	681	–	–	–
Louisiana	51,840	134,264	43,562	112,825	8,278	21,440	4,154	1,935	–	2,189
Maine	35,385	91,646	30,862	79,931	4,523	11,715	2,264	613	–	1,647
Maryland	12,407	32,133	9,774	25,314	2,633	6,819	680	1,843	–	110
Massachusetts ...	10,555	27,336	7,840	20,306	2,715	7,031	423	977	–	1,314
Michigan	96,716	250,494	56,804	147,121	39,912	103,372	1,611	–	38,301	–
Minnesota	86,939	225,171	79,610	206,189	7,329	18,982	4,783	–	2,546	–
Mississippi	48,430	125,434	46,907	121,489	1,523	3,945	785	590	–	148
Missouri........	69,704	180,533	68,886	178,414	818	2,120	818	–	–	–
Montana.......	147,042	380,838	145,552	376,979	1,490	3,859	1,490	–	–	–
Nebraska	77,354	200,345	76,872	199,099	481	1,247	481	–	–	–
Nevada	110,561	286,351	109,826	284,448	735	1,903	735	–	–	–
New Hampshire...	9,350	24,216	8,968	23,227	382	989	314	–	–	68
New Jersey......	8,721	22,588	7,417	19,211	1,304	3,377	396	401	–	507
New Mexico	121,590	314,915	121,356	314,309	234	606	234	–	–	–
New York	54,556	141,299	47,214	122,283	7,342	19,016	1,895	981	3,988	479
North Carolina....	53,819	139,389	48,711	126,161	5,108	13,229	3,960	–	–	1,148
North Dakota	70,700	183,112	68,976	178,647	1,724	4,465	1,724	–	–	–
Ohio..........	44,825	116,096	40,948	106,056	3,877	10,040	378	–	3,499	–
Oklahoma.......	69,898	181,036	68,667	177,847	1,231	3,189	1,231	–	–	–
Oregon	98,381	254,805	95,997	248,631	2,384	6,174	1,050	80	–	1,254
Pennsylvania	46,055	119,283	44,817	116,075	1,239	3,208	490	–	749	–
Rhode Island	1,545	4,002	1,045	2,706	500	1,295	178	9	–	314
South Carolina ...	32,020	82,932	30,110	77,983	1,911	4,949	1,008	72	–	831
South Dakota	77,117	199,731	75,885	196,540	1,232	3,191	1,232	–	–	–
Tennessee	42,143	109,151	41,217	106,752	926	2,399	926	–	–	–
Texas	268,581	695,621	261,797	678,051	6,784	17,570	5,056	404	–	1,324
Utah	84,899	219,887	82,144	212,751	2,755	7,136	2,755	–	–	–
Vermont........	9,614	24,901	9,250	23,956	365	945	365	–	–	–
Virginia	42,774	110,785	39,594	102,548	3,180	8,237	1,006	1,728	–	446
Washington......	71,300	184,665	66,544	172,348	4,756	12,317	1,553	2,537	–	666
West Virginia.....	24,230	62,757	24,078	62,361	152	394	152	–	–	–
Wisconsin.......	65,498	169,639	54,310	140,663	11,188	28,976	1,830	–	9,358	–
Wyoming	97,814	253,336	97,100	251,489	713	1,847	713	–	–	–
Puerto Rico	5,325	13,790	3,425	8,870	1,900	4,921	(NA)	(NA)	(X)	(NA)
Island Areas:	3,866	10,014	600	1,554	3,266	8,460	(NA)	(NA)	(X)	(NA)
American Samoa ..	584	1,511	77	200	506	1,311	(NA)	(NA)	(X)	(NA)
Guam	571	1,478	210	544	361	934	(NA)	(NA)	(X)	(NA)
Northern Mariana Islands	1,975	5,114	179	464	1,796	4,651	(NA)	(NA)	(X)	(NA)
Virgin Islands of the U.S.	737	1,910	134	346	604	1,564	(NA)	(NA)	(X)	(NA)
U.S. minor outlying islands [1]	16	41	16	41	–	–	(NA)	(NA)	(X)	(NA)

– Represents or rounds to zero.   NA Not available.   X Not applicable.   [1] Baker, Howland, and Jarvis Islands; Johnston Atoll, Kingman Reef, Midway Islands, Navassa Island, Palmyra Atoll, and Wake Island.

Source: U.S. Census Bureau, 2000 Census of Population and Housing, *Summary Population and Housing Characteristics*, Series PHC-1, PHC-3, and unpublished data from the Census TIGER® data base.

Geography and Environment   217

Table 349. Total and Federally Owned Land by State: 2004

[(2,271,343 represents 2,271,343,000). As of September 30. See text, Section 8. Total land area figures are not comparable with those in Table 348]

State	Total (1,000 acres)	Not owned by federal government (1,000 acres)	Owned by federal government [1] Acres (1,000)	Per-cent	State	Total (1,000 acres)	Not owned by federal government (1,000 acres)	Owned by federal government [1] Acres (1,000)	Per-cent
United States ...	2,271,343	1,618,044	653,299	28.8	Mississippi	30,223	28,026	2,197	7.3
					Missouri	44,248	42,024	2,225	5.0
Alabama	32,678	32,164	514	1.6	Montana	93,271	65,361	27,910	29.9
Alaska	365,482	112,986	252,496	69.1	Nebraska	49,032	48,366	665	1.4
Arizona	72,688	37,755	34,933	48.1	Nevada	70,264	10,902	59,363	84.5
Arkansas	33,599	31,191	2,408	7.2	New Hampshire	5,769	4,993	776	13.4
California	100,207	54,813	45,393	45.3	New Jersey	4,813	4,665	148	3.1
Colorado	66,486	42,131	24,355	36.6	New Mexico	77,766	45,283	32,484	41.8
Connecticut	3,135	3,121	14	0.4	New York	30,681	30,447	234	0.8
Delaware	1,266	1,240	26	2.0	North Carolina	31,403	27,693	3,710	11.8
District of Columbia	39	29	10	24.7	North Dakota	44,452	43,267	1,186	2.7
Florida	34,721	31,862	2,859	8.2	Ohio	26,222	25,774	448	1.7
Georgia	37,295	35,886	1,409	3.8	Oklahoma	44,088	42,502	1,586	3.6
Hawaii	4,106	3,309	797	19.4	Oregon	61,599	28,883	32,716	53.1
Idaho	52,933	26,368	26,565	50.2	Pennsylvania	28,804	28,085	720	2.5
Illinois	35,795	35,153	642	1.8	Rhode Island	677	674	3	0.4
Indiana	23,158	22,695	463	2.0	South Carolina	19,374	18,813	561	2.9
Iowa	35,860	35,587	274	0.8	South Dakota	48,882	45,854	3,028	6.2
Kansas	52,511	51,879	631	1.2	Tennessee	26,728	25,862	866	3.2
Kentucky	25,512	24,134	1,379	5.4	Texas	168,218	165,087	3,130	1.9
Louisiana	28,868	27,393	1,475	5.1	Utah	52,697	22,425	30,272	57.4
Maine	19,848	19,639	208	1.1	Vermont	5,937	5,493	443	7.5
Maryland	6,319	6,141	179	2.8	Virginia	25,496	22,962	2,534	9.9
Massachusetts	5,035	4,941	94	1.9	Washington	42,694	29,744	12,950	30.3
Michigan	36,492	32,854	3,638	10.0	West Virginia	15,411	14,264	1,146	7.4
Minnesota	51,206	48,332	2,874	5.6	Wisconsin	35,011	33,039	1,972	5.6
					Wyoming	62,343	35,952	26,391	42.3

[1] Excludes trust properties.

Source: U.S. General Services Administration, *Federal Real Property Profile*, annual. For most recent report, see <http://www.gsa.gov/realpropertyprofile>.

Table 350. Land Cover/Use by Type: 1982 to 2003

[In millions of acres (1,937.7 represents 1,937,700,000), except percent. Excludes Alaska, Hawaii, and District of Columbia. For inventory-specific glossary of key terms, see http://www.nrcs.usda.gov/technical/NRI/glossaries.html]

Year	Total surface area	Nonfederal rural land Rural land, total [1]	Crop-land	Pasture land	Range-land	Forest land	Other rural land	Devel-oped land	Water areas	Fed-eral land
1982	1,937.7	1,417.2	420.4	131.4	414.5	402.6	48.3	72.8	48.6	399.1
1992	1,937.6	1,400.2	381.2	125.1	406.6	404.0	49.3	86.5	49.4	401.5
2003	1,937.7	1,377.3	367.9	117.0	405.1	405.6	50.2	108.1	50.4	401.9
Percent of total land										
1982	100.0	73.1	21.7	6.8	21.4	20.8	2.5	3.8	2.5	20.6
1992	100.0	72.3	19.7	6.5	21.0	20.9	2.5	4.5	2.5	20.7
2003	100.0	71.1	19.0	6.0	20.9	20.9	2.6	5.6	2.6	20.7

[1] Includes Conservation Reserve Program land not shown separately.

Source: U.S. Department of Agriculture, Natural Resources and Conservation Service, *2003 Annual National Resources Inventory*. See also <http://www.nrcs.usda.gov/technical/NRI/>.

Table 351. Developed Land by Type: 1982 to 2001

[In millions of acres (1,937.7 represents 1,937,700,000), except percent. See headnote, Table 350]

Year	Total surface area	Developed land, total	Developed land Large urban and built-up areas	Small built-up areas	Rural transporta-tion land
Land					
1982	1,937.7	72.8	46.9	4.7	21.2
1992	1,937.7	86.5	59.6	5.4	21.5
2001	1,937.7	106.3	77.6	6.7	22.0
Percent of total land					
1982	100.0	3.8	2.4	0.2	1.1
1992	100.0	4.5	3.1	0.3	1.1
2001	100.0	5.5	4.0	0.3	1.1

Source: U.S. Department of Agriculture, Natural Resources and Conservation Service, *National Resources Inventory 2001 Annual NRI, Urbanization and Development of Rural Land*, July 2003. See also <http://www.nrcs.usda.gov/technical/land/nri01/urban.pdf> (released July 2003).

[In thousands of acres (110,760 represents 110,760,000). Represents palustrine and estuarine wetlands; see source. For information on farm production regions, see source]

Farm production region	Total	Crop-land [1]	Forest land	Range-land	Other rural land	Developed land	Water area
Wetlands, total	110,760	16,730	65,440	7,740	15,800	1,590	3,460
Lake states	22,460	2,710	15,480	–	3,880	160	230
Southeast	22,360	940	16,010	970	3,460	420	560
Delta states	17,950	3,240	11,020	270	2,730	190	500
Northeast	14,150	1,250	10,890	–	1,550	240	220
Northern plains	7,640	3,020	210	2,870	1,090	80	370
Appalachian	7,460	400	6,080	–	570	110	300
Southern plains	5,590	970	2,350	970	520	230	550
Mountain	4,780	1,570	220	2,010	820	30	130
Corn belt	4,690	1,330	2,440	–	380	100	440
Pacific	3,680	1,300	740	650	800	30	160

– Represents or rounds to zero.   [1] Includes pastureland and Conservation Reserve Program (CRP) lands.

Source: U.S. Department of Agriculture, Natural Resources Conservation Service, *2003 Annual National Resources Inventory*. See also <http://www.nrcs.usda.gov/technical/NRI/>.

Table 353. **Land Cover/Use by State: 2003**

[In thousands of acres (1,937,664 represents 1,937,664,000), except percent. State-level results are preliminary. Data for 1997 and 2003 are not comparable. Excludes Alaska, District of Columbia, Hawaii, and Island Areas]

State	Total surface area	Crop-land	Range-land	Forest land	State	Total surface area	Crop-land	Range-land	Forest land
United States .	1,937,664	19.0	20.9	20.9					
					Montana	94,110	15.4	39.0	5.7
Alabama	33,424	7.5	0.2	64.4	Nebraska	49,510	39.5	46.6	1.6
Arizona	72,964	1.3	44.2	5.7	Nevada	70,763	0.9	11.7	0.4
Arkansas	34,037	22.1	0.1	44.1	New Hampshire .	5,941	2.1	–	65.6
California	101,510	9.3	17.5	13.7	New Jersey	5,216	10.1	–	30.8
					New Mexico	77,823	2.0	51.3	7.0
Colorado	66,625	12.5	37.2	4.9	New York	31,361	17.1	–	56.1
Connecticut	3,195	5.4	–	53.4	North Carolina . .	33,709	16.4	–	45.9
Delaware	1,534	29.8	–	22.2	North Dakota . . .	45,251	53.6	24.5	1.0
Florida	37,534	7.7	7.2	33.9	Ohio	26,445	42.5	0.0	27.3
Georgia	37,741	11.0	–	58.0	Oklahoma	44,738	20.1	31.6	16.5
Idaho	53,488	10.2	12.0	7.5	Oregon	62,161	6.0	15.1	20.5
Illinois	36,059	66.5	–	11.0	Pennsylvania . . .	28,995	17.7	–	53.9
Indiana	23,158	57.5	–	16.5	Rhode Island . . .	813	2.5	–	45.9
Iowa	36,017	70.8	–	6.4	South Carolina . .	19,939	11.9	–	56.0
Kansas	52,661	50.3	30.1	2.9	South Dakota . . .	49,358	34.6	44.7	1.0
Kentucky	25,863	21.2	–	40.6	Tennessee	26,974	17.6	0.0	44.3
Louisiana	31,377	17.3	0.9	42.5	Texas	171,052	14.9	56.2	6.2
Maine	20,966	1.8	–	84.0	Utah	54,339	3.1	19.6	3.5
Maryland	7,870	19.3	–	30.1	Vermont	6,154	9.5	–	67.1
Massachusetts . .	5,339	4.7	–	49.9	Virginia	27,087	10.6	–	48.7
Michigan	37,349	21.7	–	44.7	Washington	44,035	14.7	13.3	28.9
Minnesota	54,010	39.1	–	30.3	West Virginia . . .	15,508	5.3	–	68.1
Mississippi	30,527	16.3	–	54.9	Wisconsin	35,920	28.7	–	40.4
Missouri	44,614	30.7	0.2	28.1	Wyoming	62,603	3.5	44.0	1.5

– Represents zero.

Source: U.S. Department of Agriculture, Natural Resources and Conservation Service, Summary Report, 2003 Annual National Resources Inventory. See also <http://www.nrcs.usda.gov/technical/NRI/>.

Geography and Environment 219

Table 354. **Extreme and Mean Elevations by State and Other Areas**

[One foot = .305 meter]

State and other areas	Highest point Name	Elevation Feet	Meters	Lowest point Name	Elevation Feet	Meters	Approximate mean elevation Feet	Meters
U.S.	Mt. McKinley (AK)	20,320	6,198	Death Valley (CA). . . .	−282	−86	2,500	763
AL	Cheaha Mountain	2,407	734	Gulf of Mexico	(¹)	(¹)	500	153
AK	Mount McKinley	20,320	6,198	Pacific Ocean	(¹)	(¹)	1,900	580
AZ	Humphreys Peak.	12,633	3,853	Colorado River	70	21	4,100	1,251
AR	Magazine Mountain	2,753	840	Ouachita River	55	17	650	198
CA	Mount Whitney	14,494	4,419	Death Valley.	−282	−86	2,900	885
CO	Mt. Elbert.	14,433	4,402	Arikaree River.	3,315	1,011	6,800	2,074
CT	Mt. Frissell on south slope . .	2,380	726	Long Island Sound . . .	(¹)	(¹)	500	153
DE	Ebright Road [2]	448	137	Atlantic Ocean	(¹)	(¹)	60	18
DC	Tenleytown at Reno Reservoir.	410	125	Potomac River	1	(Z)	150	46
FL	Britton Hill	345	105	Atlantic Ocean	(¹)	(¹)	100	31
GA	Brasstown Bald.	4,784	1,459	Atlantic Ocean	(¹)	(¹)	600	183
HI	Pu'u Wekiu, Mauna Kea. . . .	13,796	4,208	Pacific Ocean	(¹)	(¹)	3,030	924
ID	Borah Peak	12,662	3,862	Snake River.	710	217	5,000	1,525
IL	Charles Mound	1,235	377	Mississippi River	279	85	600	183
IN	Hoosier Hill	1,257	383	Ohio River	320	98	700	214
IA	Hawkeye Point	1,670	509	Mississippi River	480	146	1,100	336
KS	Mount Sunflower	4,039	1,232	Verdigris River	679	207	2,000	610
KY	Black Mountain.	4,145	1,264	Mississippi River	257	78	750	229
LA	Driskill Mountain	535	163	New Orleans	−8	−2	100	31
ME.	Mount Katahdin	5,268	1,607	Atlantic Ocean	(¹)	(¹)	600	183
MD.	Hoye Crest.	3,360	1,025	Atlantic Ocean	(¹)	(¹)	350	107
MA.	Mount Greylock.	3,491	1,065	Atlantic Ocean	(¹)	(¹)	500	153
MI	Mount Arvon.	1,979	604	Lake Erie.	571	174	900	275
MN.	Eagle Mountain.	2,301	702	Lake Superior.	601	183	1,200	366
MS.	Woodall Mountain	806	246	Gulf of Mexico	(¹)	(¹)	300	92
MO	Taum Sauk Mountain	1,772	540	St. Francis River.	230	70	800	244
MT	Granite Peak	12,799	3,904	Kootenai River	1,800	549	3,400	1,037
NE.	Panorama Point	5,424	1,654	Missouri River.	840	256	2,600	793
NV.	Boundary Peak	13,140	4,007	Colorado River	479	146	5,500	1,678
NH	Mount Washington.	6,288	1,918	Atlantic Ocean	(¹)	(¹)	1,000	305
NJ	High Point	1,803	550	Atlantic Ocean	(¹)	(¹)	250	76
NM.	Wheeler Peak.	13,161	4,014	Red Bluff Reservoir . . .	2,842	867	5,700	1,739
NY.	Mount Marcy.	5,344	1,630	Atlantic Ocean	(¹)	(¹)	1,000	305
NC	Mount Mitchell	6,684	2,039	Atlantic Ocean	(¹)	(¹)	700	214
ND	White Butte	3,506	1,069	Red River of the North .	750	229	1,900	580
OH	Campbell Hill	1,550	473	Ohio River	455	139	850	259
OK	Black Mesa	4,973	1,517	Little River.	289	88	1,300	397
OR	Mount Hood	11,239	3,428	Pacific Ocean	(¹)	(¹)	3,300	1,007
PA	Mount Davis.	3,213	980	Delaware River.	(¹)	(¹)	1,100	336
RI	Jerimoth Hill	812	248	Atlantic Ocean	(¹)	(¹)	200	61
SC	Sassafras Mountain	3,560	1,086	Atlantic Ocean	(¹)	(¹)	350	107
SD	Harney Peak	7,242	2,209	Big Stone Lake.	966	295	2,200	671
TN	Clingmans Dome.	6,643	2,026	Mississippi River	178	54	900	275
TX	Guadalupe Peak	8,749	2,668	Gulf of Mexico	(¹)	(¹)	1,700	519
UT	Kings Peak	13,528	4,126	Beaverdam Wash	2,000	610	6,100	1,861
VT	Mount Mansfield	4,393	1,340	Lake Champlain	95	29	1,000	305
VA	Mount Rogers.	5,729	1,747	Atlantic Ocean	(¹)	(¹)	950	290
WA.	Mount Rainier.	14,411	4,395	Pacific Ocean	(¹)	(¹)	1,700	519
WV.	Spruce Knob	4,863	1,483	Potomac River	240	73	1,500	458
WI	Timms Hill	1,951	595	Lake Michigan	579	177	1,050	320
WY.	Gannett Peak.	13,804	4,210	Belle Fourche River. . . .	3,099	945	6,700	2,044
Puerto Rico.	Cerro de Punta	4,390	1,339	Atlantic Ocean	(¹)	(¹)	1,800	549
American Samoa . .	Lata Mountain	3,160	964	Pacific Ocean	(¹)	(¹)	1,300	397
Guam	Mount Lamlam	1,332	406	Pacific Ocean			330	101
U.S. Virgin Islands .	Crown Mountain	1,556	475	Atlantic Ocean	(¹)	(¹)	750	229

Z Less than 0.5 meter.   ¹ Sea level.   ² At DE-PA state line.

Source: U.S. Geological Survey, for highest and lowest points, "Elevations and Distances in the United States" at <http://erg.usgs.gov/isb/pubs/booklets/elvadist/elvadist.html> (released 29 April 2005). For mean elevations, *Elevations and Distances in the United States*, 1983 edition.

Table 355. U.S. Wetland Resources and Deepwater Habitats by Type: 1998 to 2004

[In thousands of acres (148,618.8 represents 148,618,800). Wetlands and deepwater habitats are defined separately because the term wetland does not include permanent water bodies. Deepwater habitats are permanently flooded land lying below the deepwater boundary of wetlands. Deepwater habitats include environments where surface water is permanent and often deep, so that water, rather than air, is the principal medium within which the dominant organisms live, whether or not they are attached to the substrate. As in wetlands, the dominant plants are hydrophytes; however, the substrates are considered nonsoil because the water is too deep to support emergent vegetation. In general terms, wetlands are lands where saturation with water is the dominant factor determining the nature of soil development and the types of plant and animal communities living in the soil and on its surface. The single feature that most wetlands share is soil or substrate that is at least periodically saturated with or covered by water. Wetlands are lands transitional between terrestrial and aquatic systems where the water table is usually at or near the surface or the land is covered by shallow water. For more information on wetlands, see the "Classification of Wetlands and Deepwater Habitats of the United States" at <http://www.fws.gov/nwi/PubsReports/ClassManual/classtitlepg.htm>]

Wetland or deepwater category	Estimated area, 1998	Estimated area, 2004	Change, 1998 to 2004
All wetlands and deepwater habitats, total	**148,618.8**	**149,058.5**	**439.7**
All deepwater habitats, total	41,046.6	41,304.5	247.9
Lacustrine [1]	16,610.5	16,773.4	162.9
Riverine [2]	6,765.5	6,813.3	47.7
Estuarine subtidal [3]	17,680.5	17,717.8	37.3
All wetlands, total	107,562.3	107,754.0	191.8
Intertidal wetlands [4]	5,328.7	5,300.3	-28.4
Marine intertidal	130.4	128.6	-1.9
Estuarine intertidal nonvegetated	594.1	600.0	5.9
Estuarine intertidal vegetated	4,604.2	4,571.7	-32.4
Freshwater wetlands	102,233.6	102,453.8	220.2
Freshwater nonvegetated	5,918.7	6,633.9	715.3
Freshwater vegetated [5]	96,414.9	95,819.8	-495.1
Freshwater emergent [5]	26,289.6	26,147.0	-142.6
Freshwater forested [6]	51,483.1	52,031.4	548.2
Freshwater shrub [7]	18,542.2	17,641.4	-900.8

[1] The lacustrine system includes deepwater habitats with all of the following characteristics: (1) situated in a topographic depression or a dammed river channel; (2) lacking trees, shrubs, persistent emergents, emergent mosses or lichens with greater than 30 percent coverage; (3) total area exceeds 20 acres (8 hectares). [2] The riverine system includes deepwater habitats contained within a channel, with the exception of habitats with water containing ocean derived salts in excess of 0.5 parts per thousand. [3] The estuarine system consists of deepwater tidal habitats and adjacent tidal wetlands that are usually semi-enclosed by land but have open, partly obstructed, or sporadic access to the open ocean, and in which ocean water is at least occasionally diluted by freshwater runoff from the land. Subtidal is where the substrate is continuously submerged by marine or estuarine waters. [4] Intertidal is where the substrate is exposed and flooded by tides. Intertidal includes the splash zone of coastal waters. [5] Emergent wetlands are characterized by erect, rooted, herbaceous hydrophytes, excluding mosses and lichens. This vegetation is present for most of the growing season in most years. These wetlands are usually dominated by perennial plants. [6] Forested wetlands are characterized by woody vegetation that is 20 feet tall or taller. [7] Shrub wetlands include areas dominated by woody vegetation less than 20 feet tall. The species include true shrubs, young trees, and trees or shrubs that are small or stunted because of environmental conditions.

Source: U.S. Fish and Wildlife Service, *Status and Trends of Wetlands in the Conterminous United States, 1998 to 2004*, December 2005. See also <http://wetlandsfws.er.usgs.gov/status_trends/national_reports/trends_2005_report.pdf>.

Table 356. Flows of Largest U.S. Rivers—Length Discharge, and Drainage Area

River	Location of mouth	Source stream (name and location)	Length (miles) [1]	Average discharge at mouth (1,000 cubic ft. per second)	Drainage area (1,000 sq. mi.)
Missouri	Missouri	Red Rock Creek, MT	2,540	76.2	529 [2]
Mississippi	Louisiana	Mississippi River, MN	2,340 [3]	593 [4]	1,150 [2, 5]
Yukon	Alaska	McNeil River, Canada	1,980	225	328 [2]
St. Lawrence	Canada	North River, MN	1,900	348	396 [2]
Rio Grande	Mexico-Texas	Rio Grande, CO	1,900	(7)	336
Arkansas	Arkansas	East Fork Arkansas River, CO	1,460	41	161
Colorado	Mexico	Colorado River, CO	1,450	(7)	246
Atchafalaya [6]	Louisiana	Tierra Blanca Creek, NM	1,420	58	95.1
Ohio	Illinois-Kentucky	Allegheny River, PA	1,310	281	203
Red	Louisiana	Tierra Blanca Creek, NM	1,290	56	93.2
Brazos	Texas	Blackwater Draw, NM	1,280	(7)	45.6
Columbia	Oregon-Washington	Columbia River, Canada	1,240	265	258 [2]
Snake	Washington	Snake River, WY	1,040	56.9	108
Platte	Nebraska	Grizzly Creek, CO	990	(7)	84.9
Pecos	Texas	Pecos River, NM	926	(7)	44.3
Canadian	Oklahoma	Canadian River, CO	906	(7)	46.9
Tennessee	Kentucky	Courthouse Creek, NC	886	68	40.9
Colorado (of Texas)	Texas	Colorado River, TX	862	(7)	42.3
North Canadian	Oklahoma	Corrumpa Creek, NM	800	(7)	17.6
Mobile	Alabama	Tickanetley Creek, GA	774	67.2	44.6
Kansas	Kansas	Arikaree River, CO	743	(7)	59.5
Kuskokwim	Alaska	South Fork Kuskokwim River, AK	724	67	48
Yellowstone	North Dakota	North Folk Yellowstone River, WY	692	(7)	70
Tanana	Alaska	Nabesna River, AK	659	41	44.5
Gila	Arizona	Middle Fork Gila River, NM	649	(7)	58.2
Porcupine	Alaska	Porcupine River, Canada	569	23	45.1
Susquehanna	Maryland	Hayden Creek, NY	447	38.2	27.2

[1] From source to mouth. [2] Drainage area includes both the United States and Canada. [3] The length from the source of the Missouri River to the Mississippi River and thence to the Gulf of Mexico is about 3,710 miles. [4] Includes about 167,000 cubic ft. per second diverted from the Mississippi into the Atchafalaya River but excludes the flow of the Red River. [5] Excludes the drainage areas of the Red and Atchafalaya Rivers. [6] In east-central Louisiana, the Red River flows into the Atchafalaya River, a distributary of the Mississippi River. Data on average discharge, length, and drainage area include the Red River, but exclude all water diverted into the Atchafalaya from the Mississippi River. [7] Less than 15,000 cubic feet per second.

Source: U.S. Geological Survey, *Largest Rivers in the United States*, <http://pubs.usgs.gov/of/1987/ofr87-242/>.

Geography and Environment **221**

Table 357. U.S. Water Withdrawals and Consumptive Use Per Day by End Use: 1940 to 2000

[In billions of gallons, except as indicated. (140 represents 140,000,000,000). Includes the District of Columbia, Puerto Rico and U.S. Virgin Islands. Withdrawal signifies water physically withdrawn from a source. Includes fresh and saline water; excludes water used for hydroelectric power]

Year	Total (bil. gal.)	Per capita [1] (gal.)	Irrigation (bil. gal.)	Public supply (bil. gal.) [2]	Rural (bil. gal.) [3]	Industrial and misc. [4] (bil. gal.)	Steam electric utilities (bil. gal.)
WITHDRAWALS							
1940	140	1,027	71	10	3.1	29	23
1950	180	1,185	89	14	3.6	37	40
1955	240	1,454	110	17	3.6	39	72
1960	270	1,500	110	21	3.6	38	100
1965	310	1,602	120	24	4.0	46	130
1970	370	1,815	130	27	4.5	47	170
1975	420	1,972	140	29	4.9	45	200
1980	440	1,953	150	34	5.6	45	210
1985	399	1,650	137	38	7.8	31	187
1990	408	1,620	137	41	7.9	30	195
1995	402	1,500	134	40	8.9	29	190
2000	408	1,430	137	43	9.2	23	196
CONSUMPTIVE USE							
1960	61	339	52	3.5	2.8	3.0	0.2
1965	77	403	66	5.2	3.2	3.4	0.4
1970	87	427	73	5.9	3.4	4.1	0.8
1975	96	451	80	6.7	3.4	4.2	1.9
1980	100	440	83	7.1	3.9	5.0	3.2
1985	92	380	74	(5)	9.2	6.1	6.2
1990	94	370	76	(5)	8.9	6.7	4.0
1995	100	374	81	(5)	9.9	4.8	3.7
2000	(NA)	(NA)	(NA)	(NA)	(NA)	(NA)	(NA)

NA Not available. [1] Based on U.S. Census Bureau resident population as of July 1. [2] Includes commercial water withdrawals. [3] Rural farm and nonfarm household and garden use, and water for farm stock and dairies. [4] For 1940 to 1960, includes manufacturing and mineral industries, rural commercial industries, air-conditioning, resorts, hotels, motels, military and other state and federal agencies, and miscellaneous; thereafter, includes manufacturing, mining and mineral processing, ordnance, construction, and miscellaneous. [5] Public supply consumptive use included in end-use categories.

Source: 1940–1960, U.S. Bureau of Domestic Business Development, based principally on committee prints, *Water Resources Activities in the United States,* for the Senate Committee on National Water Resources, U.S. Senate, thereafter, U.S. Geological Survey, *Estimated Use of Water in the United States in 2000,* circular 1268. See also <http://water.usgs.gov/pubs/circ/2004 /circ1268/> (released 12 March 2004).

Table 358. Oil Spills in U.S. Water—Number and Volume: 2000 to 2004

[Based on reported discharges into U.S. navigable waters, including territorial waters (extending 3 to 12 miles from the coastline), tributaries, the contiguous zone, onto shoreline, or into other waters that threaten the marine environment. U.S. Coast Guard polluting incident database]

Spill characteristic	Number of spills				Spill volume (gallons)			
	2000	2002	2003	2004	2000	2002	2003	2004
Total	8,354	4,497	4,192	3,897	1,431,370	638,882	401,140	1,416,714
Size of spill (gallons):								
1 to 100	8,058	4,269	3,975	3,677	39,355	35,728	32,881	31,150
101 to 1,000	219	176	169	170	78,779	62,331	59,661	60,387
1,001 to 3,000	37	34	19	34	67,529	60,706	33,722	66,152
3,001 to 5,000	12	2	12	2	45,512	7,686	44,630	7,840
5,001 to 10,000	16	5	11	4	112,415	37,340	77,366	26,739
10,001 to 50,000	6	8	6	5	108,400	186,065	152,880	86,430
50,001 to 100,000	4	2	–	1	266,380	144,126	–	58,036
100,001 to 1,000,000	2	1	–	4	713,000	104,900	–	1,079,981
1,000,000 and over	–	–	–	–	–	–	–	–
Waterbody:								
Atlantic Ocean	150	83	39	31	135,010	7,852	2,223	332,110
Pacific Ocean	623	103	118	143	36,301	8,336	3,003	345,276
Gulf of Mexico	1,838	733	801	908	112,069	106,465	49,617	31,935
Great Lakes	96	41	37	77	4,535	505	3,339	895
Lakes	32	16	24	6	349	881	175	93
Rivers and canals	1,816	1,415	1,501	1,426	663,404	227,898	165,022	163,841
Bays and sounds	1,248	804	688	569	49,783	46,399	107,419	35,797
Harbors	801	999	714	630	273,095	153,965	19,033	504,321
Other	1,750	303	270	107	156,824	86,581	51,308	2,447
Source:								
Tankship	111	55	38	35	608,176	4,753	4,450	636,834
Tankbarge	229	126	156	143	133,540	30,219	102,874	215,822
All other vessels	5,220	1,635	1,521	1,527	291,927	212,410	103,481	453,901
Facilities	1,054	1,219	1,083	1,099	311,604	198,718	78,202	42,675
Pipelines	25	–	1	1	17,021	–	14,952	15,000
All other nonvessels	566	67	56	37	45,136	2,153	361	12,781
Unknown	1,149	1,395	1,337	1,055	23,966	190,630	96,819	39,700

– Represents zero.

Source: U.S. Coast Guard, *Pollution Incidents In and Around U.S. Waters, A Spill/Release Compendium: 1969–2004* <http://www.uscg.mil/hq/g-m/nmc/response/stats/ac.htm>.

222 Geography and Environment

Table 359. National Ambient Air Pollutant Concentrations by Type of Pollutant: 1990 to 2005

[Data for 1990 through 2004 has been revised. Data represent annual composite averages of pollutant based on daily 24-hour averages of monitoring stations, except carbon monoxide is based on the second-highest, nonoverlapping, 8-hour average; ozone, the second-highest daily maximum 1-hour value or the fourth-highest maximum 8-hour value; and lead, the maximum quarterly average of ambient lead levels. Based on data from the Air Quality System. $\mu g/m^3$ = micrograms of pollutant per cubic meter of air; ppm = parts per million. Also see document at <http://www.epa.gov/airtrends/index.html>]

Pollutant	Unit	Monitoring stations, number	Air quality standard [1]	1990	1995	2000	2002	2003	2004	2005
Carbon monoxide	ppm	258	[2]9	6.0	4.7	3.5	3.0	2.8	2.6	2.4
Ozone	ppm	613	[3]0.12	0.110	0.112	0.101	0.106	0.101	0.091	0.097
Ozone	ppm	612	[4]0.08	0.085	0.088	0.080	0.086	0.080	0.074	0.078
Sulfur dioxide	ppm	310	0.03	0.0082	0.0056	0.0050	0.0044	0.0044	0.0042	0.0043
Particulates (PM-10)	$\mu g/m^3$	436	[5]150	78.1	65.8	60.0	58.0	60.0	53.1	56.3
Fine Particulates (PM-2.5)	$\mu g/m^3$	658	[6]15	(NA)	(NA)	13.6	12.7	12.3	11.9	12.9
Nitrogen dioxide	ppm	173	0.053	0.020	0.019	0.018	0.017	0.016	0.015	0.015
Lead	$\mu g/m^3$	47	[7]1.5	0.13	0.07	0.06	0.04	0.06	0.06	0.08

NA Not available. [1] Refers to the primary National Ambient Air Quality Standard. [2] Based on 8-hour standard of 9 ppm. [3] Based on 1-hour standard of .12 ppm. [4] Based on 8-hour standard of .08 ppm. [5] Based on 24-hour (daily) standard of 150mg/m³. The particulates (PM-10) standard replaced the previous standard for total suspended particulates in 1987. In 2006, EPA revoked the annual PM-10 standard. [6] The PM-2.5 national monitoring network was deployed in 1999. National trend data prior to that time is not available. [7] Based on 3-month standard of 1.5 µg/m³.

Source: U.S. Environmental Protection Agency, *National Emissions Inventory (NEI) Air Pollution Emissions Trends Data, 1970–2002*; released August 2005; <http://www.epa.gov/ttn/chief/trends/index.html#tables>.

Table 360. Selected National Air Pollutant Emissions: 1970 to 2005

[In thousands of tons (12,184 represents 12,184,000), except as indicated. Data throughout the table from 1970 to 2002 have been revised. 2003 through 2005 are new data. PM-10 is equal to or less than 10 microns in diameter; PM-2.5 is equal to or less than 2.5 microns effective diameter. Methodologies to estimate data for 1970 to 1980 period and 1985 to present emissions differ. Beginning with 1985, the methodology for more recent years is described in the document available at <http://www.epa.gov /ttn/chief/net/2002inventory.html>]

Year	PM-10	PM-10, fugitive dust [1]	PM-2.5	Sulfur dioxide	Nitrogen dioxide	Volatile organic compounds	Carbon monoxide	Lead (tons) [2]
1970	12,184	839	(NA)	(NA)	31,218	26,883	204,043	220,869
1975	6,987	569	(NA)	(NA)	28,043	26,337	188,398	159,659
1980	6,161	852	(NA)	(NA)	25,925	27,079	185,407	74,153
1985	3,588	37,736	(NA)	(NA)	23,307	25,757	176,844	22,890
1990	3,216	24,536	2,326	5,233	23,076	25,529	154,186	4,975
1995	3,054	22,765	2,203	4,726	18,619	24,956	126,777	3,929
1999	2,395	20,179	1,897	4,504	17,545	22,845	114,541	3,356
2000	2,319	20,642	1,821	4,681	16,347	22,598	114,467	(NA)
2001	2,362	20,573	1,840	4,382	15,932	21,549	106,262	(NA)
2002	2,340	16,095	1,308	1,795	14,728	21,186	114,592	1,640
2003	2,312	15,556	1,304	1,750	15,122	20,392	112,008	(NA)
2004	2,285	15,018	1,300	1,705	14,761	19,490	109,426	(NA)
2005	2,258	14,479	1,297	1,660	14,709	18,878	106,843	(NA)

NA Not available. [1] Sources such as agricultural tilling, construction, mining and quarrying, paved roads, unpaved roads, and wind erosion. [2] Beginning 1996, lead and lead compounds are inventoried through the hazardous air pollutants (HAPs) portion of the National Emission Inventory (NEI) every three years.

Source: U.S. Environmental Protection Agency, *National Emissions Inventory (NEI) Air Pollution Emissions Trends Data, 1970–2002*. See also <http://www.epa.gov/ttn/chief/trends/index.html#tables>; *Air and Radiation; Air Trends*. See also <http://www .epa.gov/airtrends/reports.html>.

Table 361. Selected Air Pollutant Emissions by Pollutant and Source: 2003

[In thousands of tons, except as indicated. See headnote, Table 360]

Source	PM-10 [1]	PM-2.5	Sulfur dioxide	Nitrogen dioxide	Volatile organic compounds	Carbon monoxide
Total emissions	**17,868**	**3,054**	**15,122**	**20,392**	**20,141**	**112,008**
Fuel combustion, stationary sources	529	284	13,192	7,169	1,730	5,463
Electric utilities	222	118	10,846	4,390	50	666
Industrial	241	115	1,795	2,072	154	1,263
Other fuel combustion	66	52	551	707	1,526	3,534
Residential						
Industrial processes	1,282	595	1,099	1,045	7,236	3,889
Chemical and allied product manufacturing	37	28	261	71	248	291
Metals processing	69	45	219	71	48	1,013
Petroleum and related industries	23	16	256	336	583	342
Other	854	258	332	431	437	503
Solvent utilization	8	6	–	7	4,297	5
Storage and transport	51	19	5	19	1,230	123
Waste disposal and recycling	240	224	26	110	393	1,613
Highway vehicles	198	142	240	7,750	4,458	60,744
Off highway [2]	304	283	463	4,218	3,007	24,111
Miscellaneous [3]	15,556	1,750	128	210	3,709	17,801

– Rounds to zero. [1] Represents both PM-10 and PM-10 fugitive dust; see Table 360. [2] Includes emissions from farm tractors and other farm machinery, construction equipment, industrial machinery, recreational marine vessels, and small general utility engines such as lawn mowers. [3] Includes emissions such as from forest fires and other kinds of burning, various agricultural activities, fugitive dust from paved and unpaved roads, and other construction and mining activities, and natural sources.

Source: U.S. Environmental Protection Agency, *National Emissions Inventory (NEI) Air Pollution Emissions Trends Data, 1970–2002*. See also <http://www.epa.gov/ttn/chief/trends/index.html#tables>; *Air and Radiation; Air Trends*. See also <http://www. epa.gov/airtrends/reports.html>.

Geography and Environment   223

Table 362. Emissions of Greenhouse Gases by Type and Source: 1990 to 2005

[In millions of metric tons (6,112.8 represents 6,112,800,000). Metric ton = 2,200 lbs. Emission estimates were mandated by Congress through Section 1605(a) of the Energy Policy Act of 1992 (Title XVI) Gases that contain carbon can be measured either in terms of the full molecular weight of the gas or just in terms of their carbon dioxide equivalent. Both measures are utilized below]

Type and source	1990	2000	2001	2002	2003	2004	2005 [1]
CARBON DIOXIDE EQUIVALENT							
Total emissions	6,112.8	6,945.4	6,831.0	6,886.3	6,946.9	7,104.6	7,147.2
Carbon dioxide, total	4,990.6	5,853.4	5,767.0	5,814.7	5,875.3	5,988.7	6,008.6
Energy use by sector							
Residential	953.7	1,171.9	1,161.1	1,186.4	1,214.0	1,213.9	1,253.8
Commercial	780.7	1,006.4	1,014.2	1,009.4	1,020.3	1,034.1	1,050.6
Industrial	1,683.6	1,778.0	1,702.8	1,684.8	1,688.0	1,736.0	1,682.3
Transportation	1,566.8	1,854.0	1,831.7	1,871.7	1,878.2	1,939.2	1,958.6
Energy adjustments	-82.6	-59.1	-44.1	-37.0	-27.5	-40.2	-42.1
Adjusted energy subtotal	4,902.3	5,751.1	5,665.7	5,715.2	5,773.0	5,883.0	5,903.2
Other sources							
CO_2 in natural gas	14.0	18.2	18.6	17.9	18.1	17.8	17.3
Cement production	33.3	41.3	41.5	43.0	43.2	45.7	45.9
Gas flaring	9.1	5.5	5.9	6.0	5.9	5.9	5.9
Other industrial	26.8	29.4	27.4	26.4	27.6	28.5	28.1
Waste combustion	5.1	7.9	8.0	6.2	7.5	7.7	8.3
Total other sources	88.3	102.3	101.3	99.5	102.3	105.7	105.4
Methane	701.7	611.2	597.7	600.2	602.2	606.5	611.9
Nitrous oxide	333.5	342.8	337.9	333.6	332.9	359.9	366.6
HFCs, PFCs, and SF_6 [2]	87.1	138.0	128.5	137.8	136.6	149.5	160.2
GAS							
Carbon dioxide	4,990.6	5,853.4	5,767.0	5,814.7	5,875.3	5,988.7	6,008.6
Methane, total	30.5	26.6	26.0	26.1	26.2	26.4	26.6
Nitrous oxide, total	1.1	1.2	1.1	1.1	1.1	1.2	1.2
HFCs, PFCs, and SF_6 [2]	(3)	(3)	(3)	(3)	(3)	(3)	(3)

[1] 2005 preliminary data. [2] Hyrdofluorocarbons, perfluorocarbons, and sulfur hexafluoride. [3] Mixture of gases. These gases cannot be summed in native units.

Source: US Energy Information Administration, *Emissions of Greenhouse Gases in the United States*, Series DOE/EIA-0573(2005), annual. See also <http://www.eia.doe.gov/oiaf/1605/ggrpt/index.html>.

Table 363. Municipal Solid Waste Generation, Recovery, Combustion, and Discards in the United States: 1980 to 2005

[In millions of tons (151.6 represents 151,600,000), except as indicated. Covers postconsumer residential and commercial solid wastes which comprise the major portion of typical municipal collections. Excludes mining, agricultural and industrial processing, demolition and construction wastes, sewage sludge, and junked autos and obsolete equipment wastes. Based on material-flows estimating procedure and wet weight as generated]

Item and material	1980	1990	2000	2002	2003	2004	2005
Waste generated	151.6	205.2	237.6	235.5	240.4	247.3	245.7
Per person per day (lb.)	3.7	4.5	4.6	4.5	4.5	4.6	4.5
Materials recovered	14.5	33.2	69.1	70.5	74.8	77.7	79.0
Per person per day (lb.)	0.35	0.7	1.4	1.3	1.4	1.5	1.5
Combustion for energy recovery	2.7	29.7	33.7	33.4	33.7	34.1	33.4
Per person per day (lb.)	0.06	0.7	0.7	0.6	0.6	0.6	0.6
Discards to landfill, other disposal	123.4	142.3	134.8	131.7	131.9	135.5	133.3
Per person per day (lb.)	3.0	3.1	2.6	2.5	2.5	2.5	2.5
Percent distribution of generation:							
Paper and paperboard	36.4	35.4	36.9	35.8	34.5	34.9	34.2
Glass	10.0	6.4	5.3	5.4	5.1	5.1	5.2
Metals	10.2	8.1	7.7	7.8	7.8	7.6	7.6
Plastics	4.5	8.3	10.7	11.2	11.5	11.8	11.8
Rubber and leather	2.8	2.8	2.7	2.8	2.8	2.7	2.7
Textiles	1.7	2.8	4.0	4.4	4.4	4.4	4.5
Wood	4.6	6.0	5.5	5.7	5.7	5.6	5.7
Food wastes	8.6	10.1	11.1	11.6	11.7	11.8	11.9
Yard wastes	18.1	17.1	12.8	12.0	13.1	12.8	13.1
Other wastes	3.2	3.0	3.3	3.3	3.3	3.3	3.4

Source: Franklin Associates, a Division of ERG, Prairie Village, KS, *Municipal Solid Waste in the United States: 2005 Facts and Figures*. Prepared for the U.S. Environmental Protection Agency. See also <http://www.epa.gov/epaoswer/non-hw/muncpl/msw99.htm>.

224 Geography and Environment

Table 364. Generation and Recovery of Selected Materials in Municipal Solid Waste: 1980 to 2005

[In millions of tons (151.6 represents 151,600,000), except as indicated. Covers postconsumer residential and commercial solid wastes which comprise the major portion of typical municipal collections. Excludes mining, agricultural and industrial processing, demolition and construction wastes, sewage sludge, and junked autos and obsolete equipment wastes. Based on material-flows estimating procedure and wet weight as generated]

Item and material	1980	1990	2000	2002	2003	2004	2005
Waste generated, total [1]	151.6	205.2	237.6	235.5	240.4	247.3	245.7
Paper and paperboard	55.2	72.7	87.7	84.2	83.0	86.4	84.0
Glass.	15.1	13.1	12.6	12.8	12.3	12.7	12.8
Metals: Ferrous	12.6	12.6	13.5	13.6	14.0	14.0	13.8
Aluminum	1.7	2.8	3.2	3.2	3.2	3.2	3.2
Other nonferrous	1.2	1.1	1.6	1.6	1.6	1.7	1.7
Plastics	6.8	17.1	25.3	26.3	27.6	29.2	28.9
Food, other	13.0	20.8	26.5	27.3	28.2	29.1	29.2
Yard trimmings.	27.5	35.0	30.5	28.3	31.5	31.8	32.1
Materials recovered, total [1]	14.5	33.2	69.1	70.5	74.8	77.7	79.0
Paper and paperboard	11.7	20.2	37.6	38.3	40.0	40.7	42.0
Glass.	0.8	2.6	2.9	2.5	2.7	2.7	2.8
Metals: Ferrous	0.4	2.2	4.6	4.9	5.1	5.1	4.9
Aluminum	0.3	1.0	0.9	0.8	0.7	0.7	0.7
Other nonferrous	0.5	0.7	1.1	1.1	1.1	1.2	1.3
Plastics	0.2	0.4	1.4	1.4	1.4	1.6	1.7
Food, other	(Z)	(Z)	0.7	0.7	0.8	0.7	0.7
Yard trimings	(Z)	4.2	15.8	16.0	18.3	19.8	19.9
Percent of generation recovered, total [1]	9.6	16.2	29.1	29.9	31.1	31.4	32.1
Paper and paperboard	21.3	27.8	42.8	45.5	48.2	47.1	50.0
Glass.	5.0	21.8	22.8	19.1	21.5	21.5	21.6
Metals: Ferrous	2.9	17.6	34.1	36.0	36.4	36.5	35.8
Aluminum	17.9	35.9	27.3	23.8	21.6	22.1	21.5
Other nonferrous	46.6	66.4	67.9	67.5	66.7	72.3	72.4
Plastics	3.0	2.2	5.3	5.2	5.1	5.5	5.7
Food, other	(Z)	(Z)	2.6	2.7	2.7	2.3	2.4
Yard trimings	(Z)	12.0	51.7	56.5	58.2	62.4	61.9

Z Less than 50,000 tons or .05 percent. [1] Includes products not shown separately.

Source: Franklin Associates, a Division of ERG, Prairie Village, KS, *Municipal Solid Waste in the United States: 2005 Facts and Figures*. Prepared for the U.S. Environmental Protection Agency. See also <http://www.epa.gov/epaoswer/non-hw/muncpl/msw99.htm>.

Table 365. Municipal Solid Waste—Generation, Recovery, and Discards by Selected Type of Product: 2005

[See headnote, Table 364]

Type of product	Generation (1,000 tons)	Recovery Products recovered (1,000 tons)	Recovery Percent of generation	Discards (1,000 tons)
Paper and paperboard products [1]	83,950	41,970	50.0	41,980
Nondurable goods.	44,910	19,030	42.4	25,880
Newspapers	9,790	8,730	89.2	1,060
Groundwood inserts	2,260	1,980	87.6	280
Magazines	2,520	970	38.5	1,550
Office papers	6,580	4,120	62.6	2,460
Standard mail	5,830	2,090	35.8	3,740
Other commercial printing	7,340	760	10.4	6,580
Containers and packaging	39,030	22,940	58.8	16,090
Corrugated boxes	30,930	22,100	71.5	8,830
Folding cartons	4,970	590	11.9	4,380
Glass products [1]	12,750	2,760	21.6	9,990
Containers and packaging	10,920	2,760	25.3	8,160
Beer and soft drink bottles	7,150	2,190	30.6	4,960
Wine and liquor bottles	1,640	250	15.2	1,390
Food and other bottles and jars	2,130	320	15.0	1,810
Metal products [1]	18,720	6,880	36.8	11,840
Ferrous	13,770	4,930	35.8	8,840
Aluminum.	3,210	690	21.5	2,520
Other nonferrous	1,740	1,260	72.4	480
Plastics [1]	28,910	1,650	5.7	27,260
Plastics in durable goods	8,710	370	4.2	8,340
Plastics in nondurable goods	6,550	(Z)	(Z)	6,550
Plastics in containers and packaging . . .	13,650	1,280	9.4	12,370
Rubber and leather [1]	6,700	960	14.3	5,740
Rubber in tires [1]	2,760	960	34.8	1,800

Z Less than 5,000 tons or .05 percent. [1] Includes products not shown separately.

Source: Franklin Associates, a Division of ERG, Prairie Village, KS, *Municipal Solid Waste in the United States: 2005 Facts and Figures*. Prepared for the U.S. Environmental Protection Agency. See also <http://www.epa.gov/epaoswer/non-hw/muncpl/msw99.htm>.

Geography and Environment 225

Table 366. Toxic Chemical Releases and Transfers by Media: 2000 to 2005

[In millions of pounds (6,187.9 represents 6,187,900,000), except as indicated. Based on reports filed as required by section 313 of the Emergency Planning and Community Right-to-Know Act (EPCRA, or Title III of the Superfund Amendments and Reauthorization Act of 1986), Public Law 99-499. Owners and operators of facilities that are classified within Standard Classification Code groups 10, 12, 20 through 39, 49, 5169, 5171, and 4953/7169; have 10 or more full-time employees, and that manufacture, process, or otherwise use any listed toxic chemical in quantities greater than the established threshold in the course of a calendar year are covered and required to report. Excludes all Persistent, Bioaccumulative, Toxic (PBT) chemicals and vanadium and vanadium compounds]

Media	2000	2001	2002	2003	2004	2005
Total facilities reporting............................	23,020	22,316	21,623	20,949	20,687	20,214
Total on- and off-site disposal or other releases........	6,187.9	5,046.8	4,268.3	3,906.2	3,716.2	3,805.7
On-site releases	5,742.9	4,597.9	3,828.9	3,463.4	3,243.4	3,314.7
Air emissions.............................	1,882.0	1,624.5	1,609.0	1,574.9	1,536.8	1,508.6
Surface water discharges	269.1	232.4	232.0	218.8	234.7	239.7
Underground injection class I................	239.9	192.5	205.1	205.8	208.7	209.2
Underground injection class II-V.............	29.7	16.0	13.6	14.7	19.2	14.4
RCRA subtitle C landfills [1]....................	231.9	149.3	136.9	150.3	130.4	140.2
Other landfills	275.6	274.0	229.9	216.6	218.2	219.8
Land treatment/application farming	15.8	15.9	22.5	17.0	19.1	20.3
Surface impoundments	963.1	800.9	631.6	666.3	587.3	631.2
Other land disposal	1,835.7	1,292.3	748.2	399.0	289.1	331.3
Off-site releases	445.0	448.9	439.4	442.8	472.7	491.0
Total transfers off-site for further waste management.....	3,811.3	3,683.9	3,548.8	3,399.3	3,616.1	3,536.1
Transfers to recycling	1,884.2	1,734.4	1,698.6	1,657.5	1,747.2	1,740.5
Transfers to energy recovery....................	745.8	774.6	737.7	649.0	649.9	607.1
Transfers to treatment	269.0	271.5	263.2	277.2	325.5	336.3
Transfers to POTWs [2]	341.2	343.2	303.9	269.6	258.2	263.6
Transfers to POTWs metal and metal compounds [2].....	2.9	2.2	1.9	1.8	1.6	1.7
Other off-site transfers	1.1	0.9	0.8	0.9	71.5	0.4
Transfers off-site for disposal or other releases [3]......	567.1	557.0	542.7	543.3	562.1	586.5
Total production-related waste managed..............	31,929.2	25,752.9	24,735.8	23,799.2	24,585.3	23,935.0
Recycled on-site	7,536.9	7,003.9	7,196.8	6,666.7	6,755.0	6,647.6
Recycled off-site	1,946.9	1,771.4	1,688.5	1,659.4	1,747.6	1,742.0
Energy recovery on-site	2,725.1	2,576.8	2,779.9	2,631.6	2,591.6	2,406.2
Energy recovery off-site	759.8	763.6	738.3	648.8	649.2	607.0
Treated on-site	12,272.3	7,858.8	7,373.4	7,638.0	8,457.7	8,042.0
Treated off-site	600.3	609.2	551.8	517.0	563.6	575.0
Quantity disposed or otherwise release of on- and off-site...	6,088.0	5,169.2	4,407.0	4,037.7	3,820.6	3,915.3
Non-production-related waste managed	240.0	34.3	15.4	22.2	16.2	19.0

[1] RCRA = Resource Conservation and Recovery Act.   [2] POTW (Publicly Owned Treatment Work) is a wastewater treatment facility that is owned by a state or municipality.   [3] Does not include off-site Disposal or Other Releases transferred to other TRI facilities that reported the amounts as on-site disposal or other releases.

Source: U.S. Environmental Protection Agency, Toxic Release Inventory (TRI) Program. *2005 TRI Public Data Release eReport.* See also <http://www.epa.gov/tri/tridata/tri05/index.htm> (released 22 March 2007).

Table 367. Toxic Chemical Releases by Industry: 2005

[In millions of pounds (4,339.5 represents 4,339,500,000), except as indicated. See headnote, Table 366]

Industry	1987 SIC[1] code	Total on- and off-site releases	On-site release — Total	On-site release — Point source air emissions	On-site release — Other surface impound-ments	Off-site releases/ transfers to disposal [2]
Total [3]	(X)	4,339.5	3,806.5	1,315.8	787.3	533.0
Metal mining	10	1,168.7	1,165.8	2.0	595.3	2.9
Coal mining.......................	12	14.5	14.5	0.1	1.7	0.0
Food and kindred products	20	165.2	157.8	33.5	0.2	7.4
Tobacco products..................	21	2.3	1.8	1.6	–	0.5
Textile mill products	22	4.3	3.6	2.8	0.2	0.7
Apparel and other textile products	23	0.4	0.2	0.2	–	0.2
Lumber and wood products	24	28.8	27.9	24.8	–	0.8
Furniture and fixtures	25	5.0	4.9	3.9	–	0.1
Paper and allied products	26	226.7	220.0	144.3	4.3	6.7
Printing and publishing	27	16.2	15.8	6.4	–	0.4
Chemical and allied products	28	531.5	478.8	145.0	16.6	52.7
Petroleum and coal products	29	67.8	63.7	30.4	–	4.1
Rubber and miscellaneous plastic products...	30	69.3	59.1	47.0	–	10.2
Leather and leather products	31	1.8	0.6	0.4	–	1.3
Stone, clay, glass products..........	32	53.6	46.1	38.6	0.2	7.5
Primary metal industries	33	479.2	195.4	36.1	36.4	283.8
Fabricated metals products	34	56.1	33.8	19.4	–	22.3
Industrial machinery and equipment...	35	11.7	6.0	3.5	–	5.7
Electronic, electric equipment	36	21.2	10.6	4.7	–	10.6
Transportation equipment	37	68.6	57.9	44.7	–	10.7
Instruments and related products	38	8.2	7.0	4.0	–	1.2
Miscellaneous	39	5.8	4.2	3.3	–	1.6
No codes [3]	(X)	21.9	21.1	2.5	1.3	0.8
Electric utilities....................	491/493	1,091.0	1,016.3	714.1	130.3	74.8
Chemical wholesalers...............	5169	1.6	1.5	0.6	–	0.2
Petroleum bulk terminals	5171	3.2	2.8	1.6	–	0.4
Hazardous Waste Management/Solvent Recovery	7389/4953	214.9	189.4	0.5	0.7	25.5

– Represents or rounds to zero.   X Not applicable.   [1] Standard Industrial Classification, see text, Section 12.   [2] Includes off-site disposal to underground injection for Class I wells, Class II to V wells, other surface impoundments, land releases, and other releases, not shown separately.   [3] Includes industries with no specific industry identified and several small industries in terms of releases, not shown separately.

Source: U.S. Environmental Protection Agency, Toxic Release Inventory (TRI) Program, *2005 TRI Public Data Release eReport.* See also <http://www.epa.gov/tri/tridata/tri05/index.htm> (released 22 March 2007).

226   Geography and Environment

Table 368.
Table 368. Toxic Chemical Releases by State and Outlying Area: 2005

[In millions of pounds (4,339.5 represents 4,339,500,000). Based on reports filed as required by section 313 of the Emergency Planning. See headnote, Table 366]

State and outlying area	Total on- and off-site re- leases	On-site release Total [1]	On-site release Point source air emis- sions	On-site release Other surface impound- ments	Off-site releases/ transfers to disposal	State and outlying area	Total on- and off-site re- leases	On-site release Total [1]	On-site release Point source air emis- sions	On-site release Other surface impound- ments	Off-site releases/ transfers to disposal
Total	4,339.5	3,806.5	1,315.8	787.3	533.0	NH	5.3	4.9	4.7	(Z)	0.4
U.S. total ..	4,330.8	3,798.4	1,308.9	787.3	532.4	NJ	23.9	20.4	12.1	(Z)	3.5
AL........	122.9	97.9	42.4	15.9	25.0	NM	15.1	13.1	0.6	0.3	2.0
AK........	548.7	548.4	2.0	230.3	0.3	NY	42.4	32.9	17.5	(Z)	9.6
AZ........	65.1	64.2	3.2	9.2	1.0	NC	139.5	126.4	97.6	5.7	13.1
AR........	49.5	41.9	14.5	1.8	7.5	ND	23.0	14.0	3.4	6.7	9.1
CA........	43.7	36.5	13.9	0.3	7.2	OH	276.9	220.2	117.7	12.6	56.7
CO........	25.7	19.1	2.1	3.3	6.6	OK	27.3	23.5	12.7	0.5	3.8
CT........	4.8	3.2	1.9	(Z)	1.5	OR	23.9	22.1	10.4	(Z)	1.8
DE........	12.8	8.4	6.2	(Z)	4.4	PA	156.7	106.9	80.8	1.3	49.7
DC	(Z)	(Z)	(Z)	(Z)	(Z)	RI	0.6	0.4	0.3	–	0.2
FL	129.9	125.8	61.7	8.2	4.1	SC	75.9	64.5	46.9	2.0	11.5
GA	130.4	126.9	86.1	17.1	3.5	SD	7.9	7.8	1.1	(Z)	0.1
HI	3.1	2.9	2.1	–	0.2	TN	143.8	128.3	71.5	21.5	15.5
ID	66.0	64.6	3.1	9.0	1.4	TX	261.9	235.8	51.7	5.0	26.1
IL	122.3	100.3	43.9	10.6	22.0	UT	172.6	170.8	7.5	88.9	1.8
IN	249.2	135.0	66.2	8.3	114.2	VT	0.4	0.2	–	–	0.2
IA	40.1	31.1	20.8	2.3	9.0	VA	73.9	65.5	43.0	1.5	8.5
KS	29.6	24.2	10.2	2.0	5.5	WA	35.9	33.6	8.5	18.4	2.2
KY	102.9	92.4	59.9	7.6	10.5	WV	97.1	87.4	67.4	2.9	9.6
LA	125.2	120.2	39.2	3.3	5.0	WI	45.6	30.0	18.4	(Z)	15.6
ME	11.5	9.9	4.2	(Z)	1.6	WY	15.6	14.6	1.7	1.1	1.1
MD	42.8	40.2	34.7	(Z)	2.6						
MA	7.7	5.5	4.7	0.1	2.2	American Samoa	(Z)	(Z)	(Z)	–	–
MI	101.9	68.9	48.7	5.9	33.0	Guam	0.2	0.2	0.1	(Z)	(Z)
MN	27.3	24.9	9.9	6.9	2.4	Northern Marianas...	(Z)	(Z)	(Z)	(Z)	(Z)
MS	58.6	56.9	20.2	10.3	1.7	Puerto Rico..	7.7	7.1	6.3	–	0.6
MO	121.3	109.7	18.9	62.2	11.6	U.S. Virgin Islands	0.8	0.8	0.5	(Z)	(Z)
MT	59.0	57.7	3.7	13.9	1.3						
NE........	37.5	33.8	7.8	(Z)	3.7						
NV........	326.1	324.9	1.2	190.4	1.2						

– Represents zero.   Z Less than 50,000.   [1] Includes other types of release not shown separately.
Source: U.S. Environmental Protection Agency, Toxic Release Inventory (TRI) Program, *2005 TRI Public Data Release eReport*. See also <http://www.epa.gov/tri/tridata/tri05/index.htm> (released 22 March 2007).

Table 369. Hazardous Waste Sites on the National Priority List by State and Outlying Area: 2006

[As of December 31. Includes both proposed and final sites listed on the National Priorities List for the Superfund program as authorized by the Comprehensive Environmental Response, Compensation, and Liability Act (CERCLA) of 1980 and the Superfund Amendments and Reauthorization Act (SARA) of 1986. For information on CERCLA and SARA, go to <http://www.epa.gov /superfund/action/law/cercla.htm/>]

State and outlying area	Total sites	Rank	Per- cent distri- bution	Fed- eral	Non- fed- eral	State and outlying area	Total sites	Rank	Per- cent distri- bution	Fed- eral	Non- fed- eral
Total	1,301	(X)	(X)	162	1,139	Montana	15	26	1.2	–	15
United States	1,286	(X)	(X)	161	1,125	Nebraska	13	31	1.0	1	12
Alabama........	15	24	1.2	3	12	Nevada	1	49	0.1	–	1
Alaska	5	44	0.4	5	–	New Hampshire	21	19	1.7	1	20
Arizona.........	8	41	0.6	2	6	New Jersey	118	1	9.5	8	110
Arkansas	10	40	0.8	–	10	New Mexico	13	32	1.0	1	12
California	95	2	7.6	24	71	New York	87	4	7.0	4	83
Colorado........	19	20	1.5	3	16	North Carolina	31	13	2.5	2	29
Connecticut......	15	25	1.2	1	14	North Dakota	–	50	0.0	–	–
Delaware	14	28	1.1	1	13	Ohio	37	11	3.0	5	32
District of Columbia .	1	(X)	0.1	1	–	Oklahoma.......	11	37	0.9	1	10
Florida	50	6	4.0	6	44	Oregon.........	11	38	0.9	2	9
Georgia	16	23	1.3	2	14	Pennsylvania	96	3	7.7	6	90
Hawaii	3	46	0.2	2	1	Rhode Island	12	36	1.0	2	10
Idaho	9	42	0.7	2	7	South Carolina	26	17	2.1	2	24
Illinois	48	8	3.8	5	43	South Dakota	2	47	0.2	1	1
Indiana.........	31	14	2.5	–	31	Tennessee	14	30	1.1	4	10
Iowa	12	33	1.0	1	11	Texas	45	9	3.6	4	41
Kansas.........	11	34	0.9	1	10	Utah	18	22	1.4	4	14
Kentucky	14	29	1.1	1	13	Vermont	11	39	0.9	–	11
Louisiana	14	27	1.1	1	13	Virginia	29	15	2.3	11	18
Maine..........	12	35	1.0	3	9	Washington	48	7	3.8	13	35
Maryland	18	21	1.4	9	9	West Virginia	9	43	0.7	2	7
Massachusetts.....	32	12	2.6	6	26	Wisconsin.......	38	10	3.0	–	38
Michigan........	68	5	5.5	1	67	Wyoming	2	48	0.2	1	1
Minnesota.......	25	18	2.0	2	23						
Mississippi	6	45	0.5	–	6	Guam	2	(X)	(X)	1	1
Missouri........	26	16	2.1	3	23	Puerto Rico.......	12	(X)	(X)	1	11
						Virgin Islands......	2	(X)	(X)	–	2

– Represents zero.   X Not applicable.
Source: U.S. Environmental Protection Agency, *Supplementary Materials: CERCLIS3/WasteLan Database*; (24 April 2007). See also <http://www.epa.gov/superfund/about.htm>.

Geography and Environment   227

Table 370. **Federal Funding for the Superfund, Brownfields, and Related Programs: 1995 to 2005**

[In millions of dollars (1,354 represents $1,354,000,000). For fiscal years ending in year shown; see text, Section 8. Represents either outlays or obligations; see footnotes below for further explanation. ATSDR = Agency for Toxic Substance and Disease Registry. NIEHS = National Institute for Environmental Health Sciences]

Program	1995	1996	1997	1998	1999	2000	2001	2002	2003	2004	2005
Current dollars											
Total	1,354	1,314	1,394	1,503	1,503	1,403	1,408	1,418	1,590	1,579	1,567
Superfund [1]	1,224	1,195	1,239	1,279	1,273	1,178	1,179	1,175	1,265	1,258	1,247
Brownfields [2]	2	8	37	89	91	92	91	95	167	170	164
ATSDR [3]	69	59	64	74	76	70	75	78	82	73	76
NIEHS [4]	59	52	54	61	63	63	63	70	76	78	80
Constant (2004) dollars [5]											
Total	1,589	1,514	1,578	1,682	1,660	1,519	1,489	1,473	1,622	1,579	1,537
Superfund [1]	1,437	1,377	1,403	1,431	1,406	1,275	1,247	1,220	1,290	1,258	1,223
Brownfields [2]	2	9	42	100	100	100	96	99	170	170	161
ATSDR [3]	81	68	72	83	84	76	79	81	84	73	75
NIEHS [4]	69	60	61	68	70	68	67	73	78	78	78

[1] Superfund program funding is the enacted appropriations excluding amounts designated for the Brownfields, Agency for Toxic Substances and Disease Registry (ATSDR), and National Institute for Environmental Health Sciences (NIEHS) programs. [2] Brownfields funding includes amounts received through the Superfund appropriations for fiscal years 1995 through 2002 and direct appropriations for fiscal years 2003 through 2005. [3] ATSDR and NIEHS funding includes amounts received through the Superfund appropriations for fiscal years 1995 through 2000 and direct appropriations for fiscal years 2001 through 2005. [4] The amount designated for the Brownfields program in fiscal year 1993 was 0.15 million in current year dollars and 0.18 in constant year 2004 dollars. [5] The current years' dollars adjusted for inflation using the Gross Domestic Product (Chained) Price Index, with 2004 as the reference year.

Source: U.S. Government Accountability Office, *Hazardous Waste Programs: Information on Appropriations and Expenditures for Superfund, Brownfields, and Related Programs*, series GAO-05-746R, June 30, 2005. See also <http://www.gao.gov/new.items /d05746r.pdf> (released 30 June 2005).

Table 371. **Hazardous Waste Generated, Shipped, and Received by State and Other Area: 2005**

[In thousands of tons (38,347.0 represents 38,347,000). Covers hazardous wastes regulated under the Resource Conservation and Recovery Act (RCRA)of 1976 as amended. The 2005 Report excludes the following data: Hazardous waste received from off site for storage/bulking and subsequently transferred off site for treatment or disposal is excluded from generation quantities. For further information on coverage, see report]

State and other areas	Generated	Shipped	Received	State and other areas	Generated	Shipped	Received
Total	38,347.0	7,686.3	8,545.9	Montana	7.2	6.0	–
				Nebraska	30.9	33.6	36.1
United States.	38,256.6	7,622.7	8,534.2	Nevada.	12.9	16.6	62.0
				New Hampshire	6.1	6.2	–
Alabama	874.7	210.0	120.9	New Jersey	993.1	322.4	166.2
Alaska	2.4	1.2	0.1	New Mexico.	944.6	5.9	9.0
Arizona..........	24.3	26.5	35.6	New York	1,124.2	195.5	286.5
Arkansas.........	443.7	284.5	273.3	North Carolina	384.1	106.5	91.1
California.........	747.2	710.8	1,770.3	North Dakota	549.7	1.6	0.6
Colorado.........	95.5	53.9	23.4	Ohio.............	2,145.4	946.7	853.2
Connecticut	44.0	55.4	22.7	Oklahoma	211.9	38.5	48.2
Delaware.........	14.4	14.1	0.4	Oregon	40.3	32.1	93.9
District of Columbia. . .	0.3	0.3	–	Pennsylvania	360.8	316.8	467.2
Florida	237.1	39.0	18.0	Rhode Island	6.3	10.3	38.6
Georgia	480.3	321.4	6.9	South Carolina	177.7	219.2	177.4
Hawaii	1.5	1.4	0.4	South Dakota.	1.0	1.2	0.1
Idaho	25.9	28.9	136.0	Tennessee	776.1	67.8	23.7
Illinois...........	1,164.1	407.7	437.5	Texas............	15,224.2	886.2	600.3
Indiana	1,017.4	426.6	642.5	Utah.............	78.1	77.8	154.4
Iowa............	52.7	52.5	0.5	Vermont	3.5	2.8	0.3
Kansas	229.2	132.2	193.9	Virginia	134.4	83.0	36.8
Kentucky.........	1,152.1	206.3	86.9	Washington	141.9	120.7	33.3
Louisiana	5,460.3	385.1	362.7	West Virginia	72.6	46.4	11.8
Maine...........	4.1	3.5	2.4	Wisconsin	108.3	111.5	53.8
Maryland.........	39.7	58.4	127.1	Wyoming..........	3.1	2.3	–
Massachusetts	372.7	70.1	28.0	Guam	0.1	0.1	0.1
Michigan	295.8	316.2	440.0	Navajo Nation......	0.1	0.1	–
Minnesota	249.5	62.1	303.6	Puerto Rico	87.5	61.2	11.6
Mississippi........	1,599.5	27.1	56.7	Trust Territories	0.0	0.0	–
Missouri	89.8	70.1	199.9	Virgin Islands	2.6	2.2	–

– Represents zero or rounds to zero.

Source: U.S. Environmental Protection Agency, *The National Biennial RCRA Harardous Waste Report (Based on 2005 Data)*, series EPA530-R-03-007. See also <http://www.epa.gov/epaoswer/hazwaste/data/br05/index.htm> (released December 2006).

228 Geography and Environment

Table 372. Environmental Industry—Revenues and Employment, by Industry Segment: 1990 to 2006

[150.7 represents $150,700,000,000. Covers approximately 59,000 private and public companies engaged in environmental activities]

Industry segment	Revenue (bil. dol.)				Employment			
	1990	1995	2000	2006	1990	1995	2000	2006
Industry total............	150.7	189.2	218.7	274.3	1,183,900	1,375,800	1,410,500	1,624,000
Analytical services [1].............	2.1	1.8	1.8	1.8	24,100	21,200	20,200	20,100
Wastewater treatment works [2]......	18.4	25.1	28.7	36.5	82,600	108,500	118,800	143,800
Solid waste management [3].........	26.1	32.5	39.4	49.2	205,500	243,400	221,400	261,600
Hazardous waste management [4].....	6.7	8.0	8.2	8.7	57,500	67,600	44,800	44,300
Remediation/industrial services......	9.9	9.9	10.1	10.9	118,900	112,000	100,200	94,200
Consulting and engineering........	12.5	15.5	17.4	23.5	147,100	180,200	184,000	230,500
Water equipment and chemicals.....	13.4	16.6	19.8	25.9	91,800	110,300	130,500	157,900
Instrument manufacturing	2.0	3.0	3.8	5.1	18,000	26,200	30,200	37,300
Air pollution control equipment [5]....	11.1	15.3	19.0	17.9	81,500	109,100	129,600	117,200
Waste management equipment [6]....	8.7	9.8	10.0	10.3	69,600	75,500	75,500	73,200
Process and prevention technology...	0.4	0.8	1.2	1.6	9,300	19,500	29,000	28,800
Water utilities [7]...............	19.8	25.3	29.9	36.2	98,500	118,200	130,000	148,500
Resource recovery [8].............	13.1	16.9	16.0	21.3	142,900	136,000	127,000	156,700
Clean energy systems and power [9]...	6.5	8.8	13.4	25.3	36,600	48,100	69,300	109,900

[1] Covers environmental laboratory testing and services. [2] Mostly revenues collected by municipal entities. [3] Covers such activities as collection, transportation, transfer stations, disposal, landfill ownership, and management for solid waste. [4] Transportation and disposal of hazardous, medical, and nuclear waste. [5] Includes stationary and mobile sources. [6] Includes vehicles, containers, liners, processing, and remediation equipment. [7] Revenues generated from the sale of water. [8] Revenues generated from the sale of recovered metals, paper, plastic, etc. [9] Revenues generated from the sale of equipment & systems and electricity.

Source: Environmental Business International, Inc., San Diego, CA, *Environmental Business Journal*, monthly (copyright). See also <http://www.ebiusa.com>.

Table 373. Threatened and Endangered Wildlife and Plant Species— Number: 2007

[As of April. Endangered species: One in danger of becoming extinct throughout all or a significant part of its natural range. Threatened species: One likely to become endangered in the foreseeable future]

Item	Mammals	Birds	Reptiles	Amphibians	Fishes	Snails	Clams	Crustaceans	Insects	Arachnids	Plants
Total listings.........	357	272	118	32	150	37	72	22	61	12	747
Endangered species, total...	325	251	78	21	85	26	64	19	51	12	599
United States..........	70	76	13	13	74	25	62	19	47	12	598
Foreign..............	255	175	65	8	11	1	2	–	4	–	1
Threatened species, total ...	32	21	40	11	65	11	8	3	10	–	148
United States..........	12	15	24	10	64	11	8	3	10	–	146
Foreign..............	20	6	16	1	1	–	–	–	–	–	2

– Represents zero.

Source: U.S. Fish and Wildlife Service, *Endangered Species Bulletin*, bimonthly; and <http://ecos.fws.gov/tess_public/Boxscore.do/> (accessed 05 May 2007).

Table 374. Tornadoes, Floods, Tropical Storms, and Lightning: 1995 to 2006

Weather type	1995	1998	1999	2000	2001	2002	2003	2004	2005	2006, prel.
Tornadoes: [1]										
Number [1]...........	1,235	1,424	1,343	1,071	1,216	941	1,376	1,819	1,264	1,032
Lives lost............	30	130	94	41	40	55	54	35	38	67
Injuries.............	650	1,868	1,842	882	743	968	1,087	396	537	989
Property loss (mil. dol.)..	410.8	1,714.2	1,989.9	423.6	630.1	801.3	1,263.2	537.1	421.8	752.1
Floods and flash floods:										
Lives lost............	80	136	68	38	48	49	85	82	43	76
Injuries.............	57	6,440	301	47	277	88	65	128	38	23
Property loss (mil. dol.)..	1,250.5	2,324.8	1,420.7	1,255.1	1,220.3	655.0	2,540.9	1,696.2	1,537.7	118,650.4
North Atlantic tropical storms and hurricanes [2]...	19	14	12	15	15	12	21	16	27	10
Direct deaths on U.S. mainland...........	17	9	19	–	24	51	14	34	1,016	–
Property loss in U.S. (bil.dol.)..........	5.9	3.5	4.2	8.1	5.2	1.1	1.9	18.9	93.0	2.4
Lightning:										
Deaths.............	85	44	46	51	44	51	44	32	38	47
Injuries.............	433	283	243	364	371	256	237	280	309	246

– Represents zero. [1] Source: U.S. National Weather Service, Internet site <http://www.spc.noaa.gov/climo/tom/monthlytornstats.html>. A violent, rotating column of air descending from a cumulonimbus cloud in the form of a tubular- or funnel-shaped cloud, usually characterized by movements along a narrow path and wind speeds from 100 to over 300 miles per hour. Also known as a "twister" or "waterspout." [2] Source: National Hurricane Center (NHC), Coral Gables, FL, unpublished data. For data on individual hurricanes, see the NHC Internet site at <http://www.nhc.noaa.gov/>.

Source: Except as noted, U.S. National Oceanic and Atmospheric Administration (NOAA), National Weather Service (NWS), *Office of Climate, Water, and Weather Services, Natural Hazard Statistics*, monthly. See also NOAA Web site at <http://www.nws.noaa.gov /om/hazstats.shtml>.

Geography and Environment 229

Table 375. Major U.S. Weather Disasters: 2000 to 2006

[10 represents $10,000,000,000. Covers only weather-related disasters costing $1 billion or more]

Event	Description	Time period	Estimated cost [1] (bil.dol.)	Deaths (²)
Widespread drought	Rather severe drought affected crops in states especially during the spring-summer, centered over the Great Plains region, with other areas affected across portions of the south and far west.	Spring-summer 2006	Over 6	(²)
Severe storms and tornadoes	Outbreak of tornadoes over portions of the midwest and south during a week-long period.	March 2006	Over 1	10+
Numerous wildfires	Wildfires mainly over the western half of the country, due to dry weather and high wind burning nearly 10 million acres (new record for period since 1960).	Entire year 2006	Over 1	28+
Hurricane Wilma	Category 3 hurricane makes landfall in southwest Florida, causing considerable damage from major flooding and strong winds in south-east Florida.	Oct. 2005	Over 10	35
Hurricane Rita	Category 3 hurricane makes landfall on the Texas-Lousiana border coastal region, causing surge/wind damage along the coast and flood damage in FL, MS, LA, AR, and TX.	Sept. 2005	Over 8	119
Hurricane Katrina	Category 3 hurricane makes landfall as a category 1 near Miami, FL, and on the LA, MS coast, causing massive damage in addition to flood and wind damage in Al, FL, TN, KY, OH, and GA.	Aug. 2005	Over 100	1,300+
Hurricane Dennis	Category 3 hurricane makes landfall in western Florida causing wind and surge damage, also causing wind and flood damage to GA, MS, and TN.	July 2005	Over 2	12+
Midwest drought	Midwest drought causing crop losses in AR, IL, IN, MO, OH, and WI.	Spring-summer 2005	Over 1.0	–
Hurricane Jeanne	Category 3 hurricane makes landfall in east-central Florida, causing considerable damage in Florida and some flood damage in GA, SC, NC, VA, MD, DE, NJ, PA, and NY.	Sept. 2004	Over 6.9	28
Hurricane Ivan	Category 3 hurricane makes landfall on Gulf coast of Alabama causing significant damage in AL and FL and wind/flood damage in GA, SC, NC, LA, MS, WV, MD, TN, KY, OH, DE, NJ, PA, and NY.	Sept. 2004	Over 14	57
Hurricane Frances	Category 2 hurricane makes landfall in east-central Florida causing significant damage in FL and considerable flood damage in GA, SC, NC, and NY.	Sept. 2004	Over 9	48
Hurricane Charley	Category 4 hurricane makes landfall in southwest FL resulting in major damage in FL and some damage in SC and NC.	Aug. 2004	15	34
Southern California wildfires	Dry weather, high winds, and resulting wildfire in southern CA burned 743,000 acres and destroyed 3700 homes.	Oct.- Nov. 2003	2.5	22
Hurricane Isabel	Category 2 hurricane makes landfall in eastern NC, causing damage along coasts of NC, VA, and MD with wind damage and flooding in NC, VA, MD, DE, WV, NJ, NY, and PA.	Sept. 2003	5	55
Midwest severe storms and tornadoes	Numerous tornadoes over the midwest, MS River valley, and OH/TN River valleys with record 400 tornadoes in one week.	May 2003	Over 3.4	51
Storms and hail	Severe storms and large hail over southern plains, lower MS River valley, and TX.	April 2003	Over 1.6	3
Widespread drought	Moderate to extreme drought over large portions of 30 states.	Spring to fall 2002	Over 10	–
Western fire season	Major fires over 11 western states from Rockies to west coast.	Spring to fall 2002	Over 2.0	21
Tropical Storm Allison	Tropical storm produced rainfall and severe flooding in coastal portions of TX and LA and damage in MS, FL, VA, and PA.	June 2001	5.0	43
Midwest and Ohio Valley hail and tornadoes	Storms, tornadoes, and hail in TX, OK, KS, NE, IA, MO, IL, IN, WI, MI, OH, KY, and PA.	April 2001	Over 1.9	3
Southern drought/heat wave	Severe drought and heat over south-central and south-eastern states caused significant losses in agriculture and related industries.	Spring-summer 2000	Over 4.0	140
Western fire season	Severe fire season in western states.	Spring-summer 2000	Over 2.0	–

– Represents zero. [1] Represents actual dollar costs at the time of event and is not adjusted for inflation. [2] Some deaths reported due to heat but not beyond typical annual averages.

Source: U.S. National Oceanic and Atmospheric Administration, National Climatic Data Center, "Billion Dollar U.S. Weather Disasters, 1980–2006"(released 17 January 2007). See also <http://www.ncdc.noaa.gov/oa/reports/billionz.html>.

Table 376. **Highest and Lowest Temperatures by State Through 2003**

State	Highest temperatures			Lowest temperatures		
	Station	Temperature (F)	Date	Station	Temperature (F)	Date
U.S. . . .	Greenland Ranch, CA. . .	134	Jul. 10, 1913	Prospect Creek, AK . . .	-80	Jan. 23, 1971
AL.	Centerville	112	Sep. 5, 1925	New Market	-27	Jan. 30, 1966
AK.	Fort Yukon	100	[1]Jun. 27, 1915	Prospect Creek Camp . .	-80	Jan. 23, 1971
AZ.	Lake Havasu City	128	Jun. 29, 1994	Hawley Lake	-40	Jan. 7, 1971
AR.	Ozark	120	Aug. 10, 1936	Pond.	-29	Feb. 13, 1905
CA.	Greenland Ranch	134	Jul. 10, 1913	Boca	-45	Jan. 20, 1937
CO	Bennett	118	Jul. 11, 1888	Maybell	-61	Feb. 1, 1985
CT.	Danbury	106	Jul. 15, 1995	Coventry	-32	[2]Jan. 22, 1961
DE.	Millsboro	110	Jul. 21, 1930	Millsboro	-17	Jan. 17, 1893
FL.	Monticello	109	Jun. 29, 1931	Tallahassee	-2	Feb. 13, 1899
GA	Greenville	112	Aug. 20, 1983	CCC Camp F-16.	-17	[1]Jan. 27, 1940
HI	Pahala	100	Apr. 27, 1931	Mauna Kea Obs. 111.2. .	12	May 17, 1979
ID	Orofino	118	Jul. 28, 1934	Island Park Dam	-60	Jan. 18, 1943
IL	East St. Louis.	117	Jul. 14, 1954	Congerville	-36	Jan. 5, 1999
IN	Collegeville	116	Jul. 14, 1936	New Whiteland	-36	Jan. 19, 1994
IA	Keokuk	118	Jul. 20, 1934	Elkader	-47	[2]Feb. 3, 1996
KS.	Alton (near)	121	[2]Jul. 24, 1936	Lebanon	-40	Feb. 13, 1905
KY.	Greensburg	114	Jul. 28, 1930	Shelbyville	-37	Jan. 19, 1994
LA.	Plain Dealing	114	Aug. 10, 1936	Minden	-16	Feb. 13, 1899
ME	North Bridgton	105	[2]Jul. 10, 1911	Van Buren	-48	Jan. 19, 1925
MD	Cumberland & Frederick. .	109	[2]Jul. 10, 1936	Oakland	-40	Jan. 13, 1912
MA	New Bedford & Chester . .	107	Aug. 2, 1975	Chester	-35	Jan. 12, 1981
MI	Mio.	112	Jul. 13, 1936	Vanderbilt	-51	Feb. 9, 1934
MN	Moorhead	114	[2]Jul. 6, 1936	Tower	-60	Feb. 2, 1996
MS	Holly Springs	115	Jul. 29, 1930	Corinth	-19	Jan. 30, 1966
MO	Warsaw & Union	118	[2]Jul. 14, 1954	Warsaw.	-40	Feb. 13, 1905
MT	Medicine Lake	117	Jul. 5, 1937	Rogers Pass	-70	Jan. 20, 1954
NE.	Minden	118	[2]Jul. 24, 1936	Oshkosh	-47	[2]Dec. 22, 1989
NV.	Laughlin	125	[2]Jun. 29, 1994	San Jacinto	-50	Jan. 8, 1937
NH	Nashua	106	Jul. 4, 1911	Mt. Washington.	-47	Jan. 29, 1934
NJ.	Runyon	110	Jul. 10, 1936	River Vale	-34	Jan. 5, 1904
NM	Waste Isolat Pilot Plt	122	Jun. 27, 1994	Gavilan	-50	Feb. 1, 1951
NY.	Troy	108	Jul. 22, 1926	Old Forge	-52	[2]Feb. 18, 1979
NC	Fayetteville.	110	Aug. 21, 1983	Mt. Mitchell	-34	Jan. 21, 1985
ND	Steele.	121	Jul. 6, 1936	Parshall.	-60	Feb. 15, 1936
OH	Gallipolis (near).	113	[2]Jul. 21, 1934	Milligan	-39	Feb. 10, 1899
OK	Tipton	120	[2]Jun. 27, 1994	Watts	-27	Jan. 18, 1930
OR	Pendleton	119	[2]Aug. 10, 1898	Seneca	-54	[2]Feb. 10, 1933
PA.	Phoenixville	111	[2]Jul. 10, 1936	Smethport	-42	[1]Jan. 5, 1904
RI.	Providence.	104	Aug. 2, 1975	Greene	-25	Feb. 5, 1996
SC.	Camden	111	[2]Jun. 28, 1954	Caesars Head	-19	Jan. 21, 1985
SD.	Gannvalley.	120	Jul. 5, 1936	McIntosh	-58	Feb. 17, 1936
TN.	Perryville	113	[2]Aug. 9, 1930	Mountain City	-32	Dec. 30, 1917
TX.	Monahans	120	[2]Jun. 28, 1994	Seminole	-23	[2]Feb. 8, 1933
UT.	Saint George	117	Jul. 5, 1985	Peter's Sink	-69	Feb. 1, 1985
VT.	Vernon	105	Jul. 4, 1911	Bloomfield	-50	Dec. 30, 1933
VA.	Balcony Falls	110	Jul. 15, 1954	Mtn. Lake Bio. Stn.	-30	Jan. 22, 1985
WA	Ice Harbor Dam	118	[2]Aug. 5, 1961	Mazama & Winthrop . . .	-48	Dec. 30, 1968
WV	Martinsburg	112	[2]Jul. 10, 1936	Lewisburg	-37	Dec. 30, 1917
WI	Wisconsin Dells	114	Jul. 13, 1936	Couderay.	-55	Feb. 4, 1996
WY	Basin	115	Aug. 8, 1983	Riverside R.S.	-66	Feb. 9, 1933

[1] Estimated.   [2] Also on earlier dates at the same or other places.

Source: U.S. National Oceanic and Atmospheric Administration, National Environmental Satellite, Data, and Information Services (NESDIS), National Climatic Data Center (NCDC), Temperature Extremes and Drought. <http://www.ncdc.noaa.gov/oa/climate/severeweather/temperatures.html>.

U.S. Census Bureau, Statistical Abstract of the United States: 2008

Table 377. Normal Daily Mean, Maximum, and Minimum Temperatures— Selected Cities

[In **Fahrenheit degrees.** Airport data except as noted. Based on standard 30-year period, 1971 through 2000]

State	Station	Daily mean temperature Jan.	July	Annual average	Daily maximum temperature Jan.	July	Annual average	Daily minimum temperature Jan.	July	Annual average
AL	Mobile	50.1	81.5	66.8	60.7	91.2	77.4	39.5	71.8	56.2
AK	Juneau	25.7	56.8	41.5	30.6	64.3	47.6	20.7	49.2	35.3
AZ	Phoenix	54.2	92.8	72.9	65.0	104.2	84.5	43.4	81.4	61.1
AR	Little Rock	40.1	82.4	62.1	49.5	92.8	72.7	30.8	72.0	51.5
CA	Los Angeles	57.1	69.3	63.3	65.6	75.3	70.6	48.6	63.3	56.1
	Sacramento	46.3	75.4	61.1	53.8	92.4	73.7	38.8	58.3	48.4
	San Diego	57.8	70.9	64.4	65.8	75.8	70.8	49.7	65.9	58.1
	San Francisco	49.4	62.8	57.3	55.9	71.1	65.1	42.9	54.5	49.6
CO	Denver	29.2	73.4	50.1	43.2	88.0	64.2	15.2	58.7	35.8
CT	Hartford	25.7	73.7	50.2	34.1	84.9	60.5	17.2	62.4	40.0
DE	Wilmington	31.5	76.6	54.4	39.3	86.0	63.6	23.7	67.3	45.1
DC	Washington	34.9	79.2	57.5	42.5	88.3	66.4	27.3	70.1	48.6
FL	Jacksonville	53.1	81.6	68.0	64.2	90.8	78.4	41.9	72.4	57.6
	Miami	68.1	83.7	76.7	76.5	90.9	84.2	59.6	76.5	69.1
GA	Atlanta	42.7	80.0	62.2	51.9	89.4	72.0	33.5	70.6	52.3
HI	Honolulu	73.0	80.8	77.5	80.4	87.8	84.7	65.7	73.8	70.2
ID	Boise	30.2	74.7	52.0	36.7	89.2	62.6	23.6	60.3	41.3
IL	Chicago	22.0	73.3	49.1	29.6	83.5	58.3	14.3	63.2	39.8
	Peoria	22.5	75.1	50.8	30.7	85.7	60.7	14.3	64.6	40.9
IN	Indianapolis	26.5	75.4	52.5	34.5	85.6	62.3	18.5	65.2	42.7
IA	Des Moines	20.4	76.1	50.0	29.1	86.0	59.8	11.7	66.1	40.2
KS	Wichita	30.2	81.0	56.4	40.1	92.9	67.4	20.3	69.1	45.2
KY	Louisville	33.0	78.4	57.0	41.0	87.0	66.0	24.9	69.8	47.9
LA	New Orleans	52.6	82.7	68.8	61.8	91.1	78.0	43.4	74.2	59.6
ME	Portland	21.7	68.7	45.8	30.9	78.8	55.2	12.5	58.6	36.3
MD	Baltimore	32.3	76.5	54.6	41.2	87.2	65.1	23.5	65.8	44.2
MA	Boston	29.3	73.9	51.6	36.5	82.2	59.3	22.1	65.5	43.9
MI	Detroit	24.5	73.5	49.8	31.1	83.4	58.4	17.8	63.6	41.0
	Sault Ste. Marie	13.2	63.9	40.1	21.5	75.7	49.6	4.9	52.0	30.5
MN	Duluth	8.4	65.5	39.1	17.9	76.3	48.7	-1.2	54.6	29.3
	Minneapolis-St. Paul	13.1	73.2	45.4	21.9	83.3	54.7	4.3	63.0	35.9
MS	Jackson	45.0	81.4	64.1	55.1	91.4	75.0	35.0	71.4	53.2
MO	Kansas City	26.9	78.5	54.2	36.0	88.8	64.3	17.8	68.2	44.0
	St. Louis	29.6	80.2	56.3	37.9	89.8	65.7	21.2	70.6	46.9
MT	Great Falls	21.7	66.2	43.8	32.1	82.0	56.4	11.3	50.4	31.1
NE	Omaha	21.7	76.7	50.7	31.7	87.4	61.5	11.6	65.9	39.8
NV	Reno	33.6	71.3	51.3	45.5	91.2	67.4	21.8	51.4	35.2
NH	Concord	20.1	70.0	45.9	30.6	82.9	57.7	9.7	57.1	34.1
NJ	Atlantic City	32.1	75.3	53.5	41.4	85.1	63.6	22.8	65.4	43.3
NM	Albuquerque	35.7	78.5	56.8	47.6	92.3	70.4	23.8	64.7	43.2
NY	Albany	22.2	71.1	47.6	31.1	82.2	57.6	13.3	60.0	37.5
	Buffalo	24.5	70.8	48.0	31.1	79.6	55.9	17.8	62.1	39.9
	New York	32.1	76.5	54.6	38.0	84.2	61.7	26.2	68.8	47.5
NC	Charlotte	41.7	80.3	61.4	51.3	90.1	71.7	32.1	70.6	51.0
	Raleigh	39.7	78.8	59.6	49.8	89.1	70.6	29.6	68.5	48.6
ND	Bismarck	10.2	70.4	42.3	21.1	84.5	54.5	-0.6	56.4	30.1
OH	Cincinnati	29.7	76.3	54.2	38.0	86.4	64.0	21.3	66.1	44.3
	Cleveland	25.7	71.9	49.7	32.6	81.4	58.1	18.8	62.3	41.2
	Columbus	28.3	75.1	52.9	36.2	85.3	62.6	20.3	64.9	43.2
OK	Oklahoma City	36.7	82.0	60.1	47.1	93.1	71.1	26.2	70.8	49.2
OR	Portland	39.9	68.1	53.5	45.6	79.3	62.1	34.2	56.9	44.8
PA	Philadelphia	32.3	77.6	55.3	39.0	85.5	63.2	25.5	69.7	47.4
	Pittsburgh	27.5	72.6	51.0	35.1	82.7	60.4	19.9	62.4	41.5
RI	Providence	28.7	73.3	51.1	37.1	82.6	60.2	20.3	64.1	42.0
SC	Columbia	44.6	82.0	63.6	55.1	92.1	74.8	34.0	71.8	52.5
SD	Sioux Falls	14.0	73.0	45.1	25.2	85.6	57.2	2.9	60.3	33.0
TN	Memphis	39.9	82.5	62.4	48.6	92.1	72.1	31.3	72.9	52.5
	Nashville	36.8	79.1	58.9	45.6	88.7	69.0	27.9	69.5	48.8
TX	Dallas-Fort Worth	44.1	85.0	65.5	54.1	95.4	75.8	34.0	74.6	55.1
	El Paso	45.1	83.3	64.7	57.2	94.5	77.1	32.9	72.0	52.1
	Houston	51.8	83.6	68.8	62.3	93.6	79.4	41.2	73.5	58.2
UT	Salt Lake City	29.2	77.0	52.0	37.0	90.6	62.9	21.3	63.4	41.2
VT	Burlington	18.0	70.6	45.2	26.7	81.4	54.5	9.3	59.8	35.8
VA	Norfolk	40.1	79.1	59.6	47.8	86.8	67.8	32.3	71.4	51.4
	Richmond	36.4	77.9	57.6	45.3	87.5	67.8	27.6	68.3	47.4
WA	Seattle-Tacoma	40.9	65.3	52.3	45.8	75.3	59.8	35.9	55.3	44.8
	Spokane	27.3	68.6	47.3	32.8	82.5	57.4	21.7	54.6	37.2
WV	Charleston	33.4	73.9	54.5	42.6	84.9	65.4	24.2	62.9	43.5
WI	Milwaukee	20.7	72.0	47.5	28.0	81.1	55.9	13.4	62.9	39.2
WY	Cheyenne	25.9	67.7	45.0	37.1	81.9	57.6	14.8	53.4	32.3
PR	San Juan	76.6	82.2	79.9	82.4	87.4	85.5	70.8	76.9	74.2

[1] City office data.

Source: U.S. National Oceanic and Atmospheric Administration. National Environmental Satellite, Data, and Information Services (NESDIS), National Climatic Data Center (NCDC). Temperature Extremes and Drought, Weather/Climate events. See also <http://www.ncdc.noaa.gov/oa/climate/online/ccd/nrmmax.txt>; <http://www.ncdc.noaa.gov/oa/climate/online/ccd/nrmmin.txt>; and <http://www.ncdc.noaa.gov/oa/climate/online/ccd/nrmavg.txt>.

232   Geography and Environment

Table 378. Highest Temperature of Record—Selected Cities

[In Fahrenheit degrees. Airport data, except as noted. For period of record through 2005]

State	Station	Length of record (years)	Jan.	Feb.	Mar.	Apr.	May	June	July	Aug.	Sept.	Oct.	Nov.	Dec.	Annual
AL	Mobile	64	84	82	90	94	100	102	104	105	99	93	87	81	105
AK	Juneau	61	57	57	61	74	82	86	90	84	73	61	56	54	90
AZ	Phoenix	68	88	92	100	105	113	122	121	116	118	107	95	88	122
AR	Little Rock	64	83	85	91	95	98	105	112	109	106	97	86	80	112
CA	Los Angeles	70	91	92	95	102	97	104	97	98	110	106	101	94	110
	Sacramento	55	70	76	88	92	95	105	115	114	110	108	104	87	115
	San Diego	65	88	90	93	98	96	101	95	98	111	107	97	88	111
	San Francisco	78	72	78	85	92	97	106	105	100	103	99	85	75	106
CO	Denver	63	73	76	84	90	96	104	105	101	97	89	79	75	105
CT	Hartford	51	66	73	89	96	99	100	102	102	99	91	81	76	102
DE	Wilmington	58	75	78	86	94	96	100	102	101	100	91	85	75	102
DC	Washington	64	79	82	89	95	99	101	104	105	101	94	86	79	105
FL	Jacksonville	64	85	88	91	95	100	103	105	102	100	96	88	84	105
	Miami	63	88	89	93	96	96	98	98	98	97	95	91	87	98
GA	Atlanta	57	79	80	89	93	95	101	105	102	98	95	84	79	105
HI	Honolulu	36	88	88	88	91	93	92	94	93	95	94	93	89	95
ID	Boise	66	63	71	81	92	99	109	111	110	102	94	78	65	111
IL	Chicago	47	65	72	88	91	93	104	104	101	99	91	78	71	104
	Peoria	66	70	72	86	92	93	105	104	103	100	90	81	71	105
IN	Indianapolis	66	71	76	85	89	93	102	104	102	100	90	81	74	104
IA	Des Moines	66	67	73	91	93	98	103	105	108	101	95	81	69	108
KS	Wichita	53	75	87	89	96	100	110	113	110	108	95	85	83	113
KY	Louisville	58	77	77	86	91	95	102	106	101	104	92	84	76	106
LA	New Orleans	59	83	85	89	92	96	100	101	102	101	94	87	84	102
ME	Portland	65	64	64	88	85	94	98	99	103	95	88	74	71	103
MD	Baltimore	55	75	79	89	94	98	101	104	105	100	92	83	77	105
MA	Boston	54	66	70	89	94	95	100	102	102	100	90	79	76	102
MI	Detroit	47	62	70	81	89	93	104	102	100	98	91	77	69	104
	Sault Ste. Marie	65	45	49	75	85	89	93	97	98	95	81	67	62	98
MN	Duluth	64	52	55	78	88	90	94	97	97	95	86	71	55	97
	Minneapolis-St. Paul	67	58	61	83	95	96	102	105	102	98	90	77	68	105
MS	Jackson	42	83	85	89	94	99	105	106	107	104	95	88	84	107
MO	Kansas City	33	71	77	86	93	95	105	107	109	106	92	82	74	109
	St. Louis	48	76	85	89	93	94	102	107	107	104	94	85	76	107
MT	Great Falls	68	67	70	78	89	93	101	105	106	98	91	76	69	106
NE	Omaha	69	69	78	89	97	99	105	114	110	104	96	83	72	114
NV	Reno	64	71	75	83	89	97	103	108	105	101	91	77	70	108
NH	Concord	64	68	67	89	95	97	98	102	101	98	90	80	73	102
NJ	Atlantic City	62	78	75	87	94	99	106	104	103	99	90	84	77	106
NM	Albuquerque	66	69	76	85	89	98	107	105	101	100	91	77	72	107
NY	Albany	59	65	68	89	92	94	99	100	99	100	89	82	71	100
	Buffalo	62	72	71	81	94	90	96	97	99	98	87	80	74	99
	New York [1]	137	72	75	86	96	99	101	106	104	102	94	84	75	106
NC	Charlotte	66	79	81	90	93	100	103	103	103	104	98	85	78	104
	Raleigh	61	80	84	92	95	97	104	105	105	104	98	88	80	105
ND	Bismarck	66	63	69	81	93	98	111	109	109	105	95	79	65	111
OH	Cincinnati	44	69	75	84	89	93	102	103	102	98	88	81	75	103
	Cleveland	64	73	74	83	88	92	104	103	102	101	90	82	77	104
	Columbus	66	74	75	85	89	94	102	100	101	100	90	80	76	102
OK	Oklahoma City	52	80	92	93	100	104	105	110	110	108	96	87	86	110
OR	Portland	65	66	71	80	90	100	100	107	107	105	92	73	65	107
PA	Philadelphia	64	74	74	87	95	97	100	104	101	100	96	81	73	104
	Pittsburgh	53	72	76	82	89	91	98	103	100	97	87	82	74	103
RI	Providence	52	69	72	85	98	95	97	102	104	100	86	78	77	104
SC	Columbia	58	84	84	91	94	101	107	107	107	101	101	90	83	107
SD	Sioux Falls	60	66	70	87	94	100	110	108	108	104	94	81	63	110
TN	Memphis	64	79	81	85	94	99	104	108	107	103	95	86	81	108
	Nashville	66	78	84	86	91	97	106	107	104	105	94	84	79	107
TX	Dallas-Fort Worth	52	88	95	96	96	103	110	109	111	102	89	89	89	113
	El Paso	66	80	83	89	98	105	114	112	108	104	96	87	80	114
	Houston	36	84	91	91	95	99	103	104	107	109	96	89	85	109
UT	Salt Lake City	77	63	69	78	86	99	104	107	106	100	89	75	69	107
VT	Burlington	62	66	62	84	91	93	100	100	101	98	85	75	67	101
VA	Norfolk	57	80	82	88	97	100	101	103	104	99	95	86	80	104
	Richmond	76	81	83	93	96	100	104	105	102	103	99	86	81	105
WA	Seattle-Tacoma	61	64	70	78	85	93	96	100	99	98	89	74	64	100
	Spokane	58	59	63	71	90	96	101	103	108	98	86	67	56	108
WV	Charleston	58	79	79	89	94	98	98	104	101	102	92	85	80	104
WI	Milwaukee	65	62	68	82	91	93	101	103	103	98	89	77	68	103
WY	Cheyenne	70	66	71	74	83	91	100	100	96	95	83	75	69	100
PR	San Juan	51	92	96	96	97	96	97	95	97	97	98	96	94	98

[1] City office data.

Source: U.S. National Oceanic and Atmospheric Administration, Comparative Climatic Data, annual. <http://www.ncdc.noaa.gov/oa/climate/online/ccd/hghtmp.txt>.

Table 379. **Lowest Temperature of Record—Selected Cities**

[In **Fahrenheit degrees.** Airport data, except as noted. For period of record through 2005]

State	Station	Length of record (years)	Jan.	Feb.	Mar.	Apr.	May	June	July	Aug.	Sept.	Oct.	Nov.	Dec.	Annual
AL	Mobile	64	3	11	21	32	43	49	60	59	42	30	22	8	3
AK	Juneau	61	-22	-22	-15	6	25	31	36	27	23	11	-5	-21	-22
AZ	Phoenix	68	17	22	25	32	40	50	61	60	47	34	25	22	17
AR	Little Rock	64	-4	-5	11	28	40	46	54	52	37	29	17	-1	-5
CA	Los Angeles	70	23	32	34	39	43	48	49	51	47	16	34	32	16
	Sacramento	55	23	23	26	31	36	41	48	49	43	36	26	18	18
	San Diego	65	29	36	39	41	48	51	55	57	51	43	38	34	29
	San Francisco	78	24	25	30	31	36	41	43	42	38	34	25	20	20
CO	Denver	63	-25	-30	-11	-2	22	30	43	41	17	3	-8	-25	-30
CT	Hartford	51	-26	-21	-6	9	28	35	44	36	30	17	1	-14	-26
DE	Wilmington	58	-14	-6	2	18	30	41	48	43	36	24	14	-7	-14
DC	Washington	64	-5	4	11	24	34	47	54	49	39	29	16	1	-5
FL	Jacksonville	64	7	19	23	34	45	47	61	59	48	36	21	11	7
	Miami	63	30	32	32	46	53	60	69	68	68	51	39	30	30
GA	Atlanta	57	-8	5	10	26	37	46	53	55	36	28	3	-	-8
HI	Honolulu	36	53	53	55	57	60	65	66	67	66	61	57	54	53
ID	Boise	66	-17	-15	6	19	22	31	35	34	23	11	-3	-25	-25
IL	Chicago	47	-27	-19	-8	7	24	36	40	41	28	17	1	-25	-27
	Peoria	66	-25	-19	-10	14	25	39	47	41	26	19	-2	-23	-25
IN	Indianapolis	66	-27	-21	-7	16	28	37	44	41	28	17	-2	-23	-27
IA	Des Moines	66	-24	-26	-22	9	30	38	47	40	26	14	-4	-22	-26
KS	Wichita	53	-12	-21	-2	15	31	43	51	48	31	18	1	-16	-21
KY	Louisville	58	-22	-19	-1	22	31	42	50	46	33	23	-1	-15	-22
LA	New Orleans	59	14	16	25	32	41	50	60	60	42	35	24	11	11
ME	Portland	65	-26	-39	-21	8	23	33	40	33	23	15	3	-21	-39
MD	Baltimore	55	-7	-3	6	20	32	40	50	45	35	25	13	-	-7
MA	Boston	54	-12	-4	6	16	34	45	50	47	38	28	15	-7	-12
MI	Detroit	47	-21	-15	-4	10	25	36	41	38	29	17	9	-10	-21
	Sault Ste. Marie	65	-36	-35	-24	-2	18	26	36	29	25	16	-10	-31	-36
MN	Duluth	64	-39	-39	-29	-5	17	27	35	32	22	8	-23	-34	-39
	Minneapolis-St. Paul	67	-34	-32	-32	2	18	34	43	39	26	13	-17	-29	-34
MS	Jackson	42	2	10	15	27	38	47	51	54	35	26	17	4	2
MO	Kansas City	33	-17	-19	-10	12	30	42	51	43	31	17	1	-23	-23
	St. Louis	48	-18	-12	-5	22	31	43	51	47	36	23	1	-16	-18
MT	Great Falls	68	-37	-35	-29	-6	15	31	36	30	16	-11	-25	-43	-43
NE	Omaha	69	-23	-21	-16	5	27	38	44	43	25	13	-9	-23	-23
NV	Reno	64	-16	-16	-2	13	18	21	33	24	20	8	1	-16	-16
NH	Concord	64	-33	-37	-16	8	21	30	35	29	21	10	-5	-22	-37
NJ	Atlantic City	62	-10	-11	5	12	25	37	42	40	32	20	10	-7	-11
NM	Albuquerque	66	-17	-5	8	19	16	40	52	50	37	21	-7	-7	-17
NY	Albany	59	-28	-21	-21	10	26	36	40	34	24	16	5	-22	-28
	Buffalo	62	-16	-20	-7	12	26	35	43	38	32	20	9	-10	-20
	New York [1]	137	-6	-15	3	12	32	44	52	50	39	28	5	-13	-15
NC	Charlotte	66	-5	5	4	24	32	45	53	50	39	24	11	2	5
	Raleigh	61	-9	-	11	23	31	38	48	46	37	19	11	4	-9
ND	Bismarck	66	-44	-43	-31	-12	15	30	35	33	11	-10	-30	-43	-44
OH	Cincinnati	44	-25	-11	-11	15	27	39	47	43	31	16	1	-20	-25
	Cleveland	64	-20	-15	-5	10	25	31	41	38	32	19	3	-15	-20
	Columbus	66	-22	-13	-6	14	25	35	43	39	31	20	5	-17	-22
OK	Oklahoma City	52	-4	-3	3	20	37	47	53	51	36	16	11	-8	-8
OR	Portland	65	-2	-3	19	29	29	39	43	44	34	26	13	6	-3
PA	Philadelphia	64	-7	-4	7	19	28	44	51	44	35	25	15	1	-7
	Pittsburgh	53	-22	-12	-1	14	26	34	42	39	31	16	-1	-12	-22
RI	Providence	52	-13	-7	1	14	29	41	48	40	33	20	6	-10	-13
SC	Columbia	58	-1	5	4	26	34	44	54	53	40	23	12	4	-1
SD	Sioux Falls	60	-36	-32	-23	5	17	33	38	34	22	9	-17	-28	-36
TN	Memphis	64	-4	-11	12	29	38	48	52	48	36	25	9	-13	-13
	Nashville	66	-17	-13	2	23	34	42	51	47	36	26	-1	-10	-17
TX	Dallas-Fort Worth	52	4	7	15	29	41	51	59	56	43	29	20	-1	-1
	El Paso	66	-8	8	14	23	31	46	57	56	41	25	1	5	-8
	Houston	36	12	3	22	31	44	52	62	60	48	29	19	7	3
UT	Salt Lake City	77	-22	-30	2	14	25	35	40	37	27	16	-14	-21	-30
VT	Burlington	62	-30	-30	-20	2	24	33	39	35	25	15	-2	-26	-30
VA	Norfolk	57	-3	8	18	28	36	45	54	49	45	27	20	7	-3
	Richmond	76	-12	-10	11	23	31	40	51	46	35	21	10	-1	-12
WA	Seattle-Tacoma	61	-	1	11	29	28	38	43	44	35	28	6	6	-
	Spokane	58	-22	-24	-7	17	24	33	37	35	22	7	-21	-25	-25
WV	Charleston	58	-16	-12	-	19	26	33	46	41	34	17	6	-12	-16
WI	Milwaukee	65	-26	-26	-10	12	21	33	40	44	28	18	-5	-20	-26
WY	Cheyenne	70	-29	-34	-21	-8	16	25	38	36	8	-1	-16	-28	-34
PR	San Juan	51	61	62	60	64	66	69	69	70	69	46	66	59	46

- Represents zero. [1] City office data.

Source: U.S. National Oceanic and Atmospheric Administration, *Comparative Climatic Data*, annual. See also <http://www.ncdc.noaa.gov/oa/climate/online/ccd/lowtmp.txt>.

U.S. Census Bureau, Statistical Abstract of the United States: 2008

Table 380. **Normal Monthly and Annual Precipitation—Selected Cities**

[**In inches.** Airport data, except as noted. The table data are the 30-year average values computed from the data recorded during the period 1971–2000]

State	Station	Jan.	Feb.	Mar.	Apr.	May	June	July	Aug.	Sept.	Oct.	Nov.	Dec.	Annual
AL	Mobile	5.75	5.10	7.20	5.06	6.10	5.01	6.54	6.20	6.01	3.25	5.41	4.66	66.29
AK	Juneau	4.81	4.02	3.51	2.96	3.48	3.36	4.14	5.37	7.54	8.30	5.43	5.41	58.33
AZ	Phoenix	0.83	0.77	1.07	0.25	0.16	0.09	0.99	0.94	0.75	0.79	0.73	0.92	8.29
AR	Little Rock	3.61	3.33	4.88	5.47	5.05	3.95	3.31	2.93	3.71	4.25	5.73	4.71	50.93
CA	Los Angeles	2.98	3.11	2.40	0.63	0.24	0.08	0.03	0.14	0.26	0.36	1.13	1.79	13.15
	Sacramento	3.84	3.54	2.80	1.02	0.53	0.20	0.05	0.06	0.36	0.89	2.19	2.45	17.93
	San Diego	2.28	2.04	2.26	0.75	0.20	0.09	0.03	0.09	0.21	0.44	1.07	1.31	10.77
	San Francisco	4.45	4.01	3.26	1.17	0.38	0.11	0.03	0.07	0.20	1.04	2.49	2.89	20.11
CO	Denver	0.51	0.49	1.28	1.93	2.32	1.56	2.16	1.82	1.14	0.99	0.98	0.63	15.81
CT	Hartford	3.84	2.96	3.88	3.86	4.39	3.85	3.67	3.98	4.13	3.94	4.06	3.60	46.16
DE	Wilmington	3.43	2.81	3.97	3.39	4.15	3.59	4.28	3.51	4.01	3.08	3.19	3.40	42.81
DC	Washington	3.21	2.63	3.60	2.77	3.82	3.13	3.66	3.44	3.79	3.22	3.03	3.05	39.35
FL	Jacksonville	3.69	3.15	3.93	3.14	3.48	5.37	5.97	6.87	7.90	3.86	2.34	2.64	52.34
	Miami	1.88	2.07	2.56	3.36	5.52	8.54	5.79	8.63	8.38	6.19	3.43	2.18	58.53
GA	Atlanta	5.02	4.68	5.38	3.62	3.95	3.63	5.12	3.67	4.09	3.11	4.10	3.82	50.20
HI	Honolulu	2.73	2.35	1.89	1.11	0.78	0.43	0.50	0.46	0.74	2.18	2.26	2.85	18.29
ID	Boise	1.39	1.14	1.41	1.27	1.27	0.74	0.39	0.30	0.76	0.76	1.38	1.38	12.19
IL	Chicago	1.75	1.63	2.65	3.68	3.38	3.63	3.51	4.62	3.27	2.71	3.01	2.43	36.27
	Peoria	1.50	1.67	2.83	3.56	4.17	3.84	4.02	3.16	3.12	2.76	2.99	2.40	36.03
IN	Indianapolis	2.48	2.41	3.44	3.61	4.35	4.13	4.42	3.82	2.88	2.76	3.61	3.03	40.95
IA	Des Moines	1.03	1.19	2.21	3.58	4.25	4.57	4.18	4.51	3.15	2.62	2.10	1.33	34.72
KS	Wichita	0.84	1.02	2.71	2.57	4.16	4.25	3.31	2.94	2.96	2.45	1.82	1.35	30.38
KY	Louisville	3.28	3.25	4.41	3.91	4.88	3.76	4.30	3.41	3.05	2.79	3.80	3.69	44.54
LA	New Orleans	5.87	5.47	5.24	5.02	4.62	6.83	6.20	6.15	5.55	3.05	5.09	5.07	64.16
ME	Portland	4.09	3.14	4.14	4.26	3.82	3.28	3.32	3.05	3.37	4.40	4.72	4.24	45.83
MD	Baltimore	3.47	3.02	3.93	3.00	3.89	3.43	3.85	3.74	3.98	3.16	3.12	3.35	41.94
MA	Boston	3.92	3.30	3.85	3.60	3.24	3.22	3.06	3.37	3.47	3.79	3.98	3.73	42.53
MI	Detroit	1.91	1.88	2.52	3.05	3.05	3.55	3.16	3.10	3.27	2.23	2.66	2.51	32.89
	Sault Ste. Marie	2.64	1.60	2.41	2.57	2.50	3.00	3.14	3.47	3.71	3.32	3.40	2.91	34.67
MN	Duluth	1.12	0.83	1.69	2.09	2.95	4.25	4.20	4.22	4.13	2.46	2.12	0.94	31.00
	Minneapolis-St. Paul. . .	1.04	0.79	1.86	2.31	3.24	4.34	4.04	4.05	2.69	2.11	1.94	1.00	29.41
MS	Jackson	5.67	4.50	5.74	5.98	4.86	3.82	4.69	3.66	3.23	3.42	5.04	5.34	55.95
MO	Kansas City	1.15	1.31	2.44	3.38	5.39	4.44	4.42	3.54	4.64	3.33	2.30	1.64	37.98
	St. Louis	2.14	2.28	3.60	3.69	4.11	3.76	3.90	2.98	2.96	2.76	3.71	2.86	38.75
MT	Great Falls	0.68	0.51	1.01	1.40	2.53	2.24	1.45	1.65	1.23	0.93	0.59	0.67	14.89
NE	Omaha	0.77	0.80	2.13	2.94	4.44	3.95	3.86	3.21	3.17	2.21	1.82	0.92	30.22
NV	Reno	1.06	1.06	0.86	0.35	0.62	0.47	0.24	0.27	0.45	0.42	0.80	0.88	7.48
NH	Concord	2.97	2.36	3.04	3.07	3.33	3.10	3.37	3.21	3.16	3.46	3.57	2.96	37.60
NJ	Atlantic City	3.60	2.85	4.06	3.45	3.38	2.66	3.86	4.32	3.14	2.86	3.26	3.15	40.59
NM	Albuquerque	0.49	0.44	0.61	0.50	0.60	0.65	1.27	1.73	1.07	1.00	0.62	0.49	9.47
NY	Albany	2.71	2.27	3.17	3.25	3.67	3.74	3.50	3.68	3.31	3.23	3.31	2.76	38.60
	Buffalo	3.16	2.42	2.99	3.04	3.35	3.82	3.14	3.87	3.84	3.19	3.92	3.80	40.54
	New York [1]	4.13	3.15	4.37	4.28	4.69	3.84	4.62	4.22	4.23	3.85	4.36	3.95	49.69
NC	Charlotte	4.00	3.55	4.39	2.95	3.66	3.42	3.79	3.72	3.83	3.66	3.36	3.18	43.51
	Raleigh	4.02	3.47	4.03	2.80	3.79	3.42	4.29	3.78	4.26	3.18	2.97	3.04	43.05
ND	Bismarck	0.45	0.51	0.85	1.46	2.22	2.59	2.58	2.15	1.61	1.28	0.70	0.44	16.84
OH	Cincinnati	2.92	2.75	3.90	3.96	4.59	4.42	3.75	3.79	2.82	2.96	3.46	3.28	42.60
	Cleveland	2.48	2.29	2.94	3.37	3.50	3.89	3.52	3.69	3.77	2.73	3.38	3.14	38.71
	Columbus	2.53	2.20	2.89	3.25	3.88	4.07	4.61	3.72	2.92	2.31	3.19	2.93	38.52
OK	Oklahoma City	1.28	1.56	2.90	3.00	5.44	4.63	2.94	2.48	3.98	3.64	2.11	1.89	35.85
OR	Portland	5.07	4.18	3.71	2.64	2.38	1.59	0.72	0.93	1.65	2.88	5.61	5.71	37.07
PA	Philadelphia	3.52	2.74	3.81	3.49	3.88	3.29	4.39	3.82	3.88	2.75	3.16	3.31	42.05
	Pittsburgh	2.70	2.37	3.17	3.01	3.80	4.12	3.96	3.38	3.21	2.25	3.02	2.86	37.85
RI	Providence	4.37	3.45	4.43	4.16	3.66	3.38	3.17	3.90	3.70	3.69	4.40	4.14	46.45
SC	Columbia	4.66	3.84	4.59	2.98	3.17	4.99	5.54	5.41	3.94	2.89	2.88	3.38	48.27
SD	Sioux Falls	0.51	0.51	1.81	2.65	3.39	3.49	2.93	3.01	2.58	1.93	1.36	0.52	24.69
TN	Memphis	4.24	4.31	5.58	5.79	5.15	4.30	4.22	3.00	3.31	3.31	5.76	5.68	54.65
	Nashville	3.97	3.69	4.87	3.93	5.07	4.08	3.77	3.28	3.59	2.87	4.45	4.54	48.11
TX	Dallas-Fort Worth	1.90	2.37	3.06	3.20	5.15	3.23	2.12	2.03	2.42	4.11	2.57	2.57	34.73
	El Paso	0.45	0.39	0.26	0.23	0.38	0.87	1.49	1.75	1.61	0.81	0.42	0.77	9.43
	Houston	3.68	2.98	3.36	3.60	5.15	5.35	3.18	3.83	4.33	4.50	4.19	3.69	47.84
UT	Salt Lake City	1.37	1.33	1.91	2.02	2.09	0.77	0.72	0.76	1.33	1.57	1.40	1.23	16.50
VT	Burlington	2.22	1.67	2.32	2.88	3.32	3.43	3.97	4.01	3.83	3.12	3.06	2.22	36.05
VA	Norfolk	3.93	3.34	4.08	3.38	3.74	3.77	5.17	4.79	4.06	3.47	2.98	3.03	45.74
	Richmond	3.55	2.98	4.09	3.18	3.95	3.54	4.67	4.18	3.98	3.60	3.06	3.12	43.91
WA	Seattle-Tacoma	5.13	4.18	3.75	2.59	1.77	1.49	0.79	1.02	1.63	3.19	5.90	5.62	37.07
	Spokane	1.82	1.51	1.53	1.28	1.60	1.18	0.76	0.68	0.76	1.06	2.24	2.25	16.67
WV	Charleston	3.25	3.19	3.90	3.25	4.30	4.09	4.86	4.11	3.45	2.67	3.66	3.32	44.05
WI	Milwaukee	1.85	1.65	2.59	3.78	3.06	3.56	3.58	4.03	3.30	2.49	2.70	2.22	34.81
WY	Cheyenne	0.45	0.44	1.05	1.55	2.48	2.12	2.26	1.82	1.43	0.75	0.64	0.46	15.45
PR	San Juan	3.02	2.30	2.14	3.71	5.29	3.52	4.16	5.22	5.60	5.06	6.17	4.57	50.76

[1] City office data.

Source: U.S. National Oceanic and Atmospheric Administration, *Comparative Climatic Data,* annual. See also <http://www.ncdc.noaa.gov/oa/climate/online/ccd/nrmpcp.txt>

Geography and Environment **235**

Table 381. Mean Number of Days With Precipitation of 0.01 Inch or More—Selected Cities

[0.01 is the smallest amount of precipitation numerically recorded, and includes the liquid water equivalent of frozen precipitation. Airport data, except as noted. For period of record through 2005]

State	Station	Length of record (years)	Jan.	Feb.	Mar.	Apr.	May	June	July	Aug.	Sept.	Oct.	Nov.	Dec.	Annual
AL	Mobile	64	11	9	10	7	8	12	16	14	10	6	8	10	121
AK	Juneau	61	19	17	18	17	17	15	17	18	21	24	20	21	223
AZ	Phoenix	66	4	4	4	2	1	1	4	5	3	3	2	4	36
AR	Little Rock	63	9	9	10	10	10	9	8	7	7	7	8	9	104
CA	Los Angeles	70	6	6	6	3	1	1	1	(Z)	1	2	3	5	35
	Sacramento	66	10	9	9	5	3	1	(Z)	(Z)	1	3	7	9	58
	San Diego	65	7	6	7	4	2	1	(Z)	--	1	2	4	6	42
	San Francisco	78	11	10	10	6	3	1	(Z)	(Z)	1	3	7	10	63
CO	Denver	63	6	6	9	9	11	9	9	9	6	5	6	5	89
CT	Hartford	51	11	10	12	11	12	11	10	10	9	9	11	12	128
DE	Wilmington	58	11	9	11	11	11	10	9	9	8	8	9	10	117
DC	Washington	64	10	9	11	10	11	10	10	9	8	7	8	9	113
FL	Jacksonville	64	8	8	8	6	8	13	14	15	13	9	6	8	116
	Miami	63	7	6	6	6	10	15	16	18	18	14	8	7	131
GA	Atlanta	71	11	10	11	9	9	10	12	9	8	6	8	10	115
HI	Honolulu	56	9	9	9	9	7	6	7	6	7	9	9	10	96
ID	Boise	66	12	10	10	8	8	6	2	3	4	6	10	11	89
IL	Chicago	47	11	9	12	12	11	10	10	9	9	9	11	11	124
	Peoria	66	9	8	11	12	12	10	9	8	8	8	9	10	113
IN	Indianapolis	66	12	10	13	12	12	10	10	9	8	8	10	12	126
IA	Des Moines	66	7	7	10	11	12	11	9	9	8	8	7	8	108
KS	Wichita	52	5	5	8	8	11	10	8	8	7	6	5	6	85
KY	Louisville	58	11	10	13	12	12	10	10	8	8	8	10	11	124
LA	New Orleans	57	10	9	9	7	8	11	14	13	10	6	8	10	114
ME	Portland	65	11	10	11	12	13	11	10	9	9	10	12	11	129
MD	Baltimore	55	10	9	11	11	11	10	9	9	8	8	9	9	115
MA	Boston	54	12	10	12	11	12	10	9	10	9	9	11	11	127
MI	Detroit	47	13	11	13	13	12	10	10	10	9	9	12	13	135
	Sault Ste. Marie	64	19	14	13	11	11	11	10	11	13	14	17	19	164
MN	Duluth	64	12	9	11	11	12	13	12	11	12	10	11	11	134
	Minneapolis-St. Paul	67	9	7	10	10	12	12	10	10	9	8	8	9	115
MS	Jackson	42	11	9	10	8	9	9	11	10	8	6	9	10	110
MO	Kansas City	33	7	7	10	11	12	10	8	9	8	8	8	7	104
	St. Louis	48	9	8	11	11	11	9	9	8	8	8	9	9	111
MT	Great Falls	68	8	8	9	9	11	12	7	8	7	6	7	7	100
NE	Omaha	69	6	7	8	10	12	11	10	9	8	6	6	6	99
NV	Reno	63	6	6	6	4	4	3	2	2	2	3	5	6	51
NH	Concord	64	11	9	11	12	12	11	10	10	9	9	11	11	127
NJ	Atlantic City	62	11	10	11	11	10	9	9	9	8	8	9	10	114
NM	Albuquerque	66	4	4	5	3	4	4	9	9	6	5	4	4	60
NY	Albany	59	13	10	12	12	13	11	10	11	10	9	12	12	136
	Buffalo	62	20	17	16	14	13	11	10	10	11	12	16	19	168
	New York [1]	136	11	10	11	11	11	10	10	10	8	8	9	10	121
NC	Charlotte	66	10	10	11	9	10	10	11	10	7	7	8	10	111
	Raleigh	61	10	10	10	8	9	10	10	8	7	8	8	9	113
ND	Bismarck	66	8	7	8	8	10	12	9	8	7	6	6	7	96
OH	Cincinnati	58	12	11	13	13	12	11	10	9	8	8	11	12	131
	Cleveland	64	17	14	15	14	13	11	10	10	10	11	14	16	156
	Columbus	66	14	12	13	13	13	11	11	9	8	9	11	13	138
OK	Oklahoma City	66	5	6	7	8	10	9	6	6	7	7	6	5	83
OR	Portland	65	18	16	17	15	12	9	4	5	7	13	18	19	153
PA	Philadelphia	65	11	9	11	11	11	10	9	9	8	8	9	10	118
	Pittsburgh	53	16	14	15	14	13	12	11	10	10	10	13	16	152
RI	Providence	52	11	10	12	11	12	11	9	10	9	9	11	12	124
SC	Columbia	58	10	9	10	8	9	10	12	11	8	6	7	9	109
SD	Sioux Falls	60	6	6	8	9	11	11	10	9	8	6	6	6	98
TN	Memphis	55	10	9	11	10	10	9	9	7	7	7	9	10	107
	Nashville	64	11	11	12	11	11	10	10	9	8	7	9	11	119
TX	Dallas-Fort Worth	52	7	7	7	8	9	7	5	5	6	6	6	6	79
	El Paso	66	4	3	2	2	2	3	8	8	5	4	3	4	49
	Houston	36	10	9	9	7	8	10	9	9	9	8	8	9	105
UT	Salt Lake City	77	10	9	10	10	8	5	4	5	5	6	8	9	91
VT	Burlington	62	14	11	13	12	14	13	12	12	12	12	14	15	154
VA	Norfolk	57	11	10	11	10	10	9	11	10	8	8	8	9	116
	Richmond	68	10	9	11	10	11	10	11	10	8	7	8	9	114
WA	Seattle-Tacoma	61	19	15	17	14	11	9	5	6	9	13	18	19	155
	Spokane	58	14	11	11	9	10	8	5	5	8	8	13	14	112
WV	Charleston	58	15	14	15	14	13	12	13	11	9	10	12	14	151
WI	Milwaukee	65	11	10	12	12	12	11	10	9	9	9	11	11	125
WY	Cheyenne	70	6	6	9	10	12	11	11	10	8	6	6	6	100
PR	San Juan	50	17	13	12	13	16	15	19	19	18	17	19	19	199

– Represents zero.   Z Less than 1/2 day.   [1] City office data.

Source: U.S. National Oceanic and Atmospheric Administration. *Comparative Climatic Data*, annual. See also <http://www.ncdc noaa.gov/oa/climate/online/ccd/prge01.txt>

Table 382. **Snow, Hail, Ice Pellets, and Sleet—Selected Cities**

[In inches. Airport data, except as noted. For period of record through 2005. T denotes trace. Stations may show snowfall (hail) during the warm months]

State	Station	Length of record (years)	Jan.	Feb.	Mar.	Apr.	May	June	July	Aug.	Sept.	Oct.	Nov.	Dec.	Annual
AL	Mobile.	63	0.1	0.1	0.1	T	T	–	T	–	–	–	T	0.1	0.4
AK	Juneau	61	25.8	18.6	14.6	3.3	T	T	–	–	T	1	11.7	21.2	96.2
AZ	Phoenix	62	T	–	T	T	T	–	–	–	–	T	–	T	T
AR	Little Rock	56	2.4	1.5	0.5	T	T	T	–	–	–	T	0.2	0.6	5.2
CA	Los Angeles	62	T	T	T	–	–	–	–	–	–	–	–	T	T
	Sacramento	50	T	T	T	–	T	–	–	–	–	–	–	T	T
	San Diego	60	T	–	T	T	–	–	–	–	–	–	T	T	T
	San Francisco	69	–	T	T	–	–	–	–	–	–	–	–	–	T
CO	Denver	61	8.1	7.5	12.5	8.9	1.6	–	T	T	1.6	3.7	9.1	7.3	60.3
CT	Hartford.	48	13.3	12.3	10.2	1.5	–	T	–	–	–	0.1	2.1	10.5	50.0
DE	Wilmington.	55	6.9	6.6	3.2	0.2	T	T	T	–	–	0.1	0.9	3.4	21.3
DC	Washington	62	5.5	5.5	2.3	T	T	T	T	T	–	–	0.8	3.0	17.1
FL	Jacksonville	60	T	–	–	T	–	T	T	–	–	–	–	–	T
	Miami	59	–	–	–	–	T	–	–	–	–	–	–	–	T
GA	Atlanta	66	1	0.5	0.4	T	–	–	T	–	–	T	T	0.2	2.1
HI	Honolulu	52	–	–	–	–	–	–	–	–	–	–	–	–	–
ID	Boise	66	6.5	3.6	1.7	0.6	0.1	T	T	T	T	0.1	2.3	5.7	20.6
IL	Chicago	46	11.5	7.7	6.7	1.6	0.1	T	T	T	T	0.4	2.1	8.1	38.2
	Peoria.	62	6.7	5.0	4.2	0.8	T	T	T	T	T	0.1	2.1	6.2	25.1
IN	Indianapolis	74	7	5.5	3.5	0.5	T	T	–	T	–	0.2	1.9	5.5	24.1
IA	Des Moines	62	8.3	7.3	6.1	1.9	T	T	T	T	T	0.3	3.1	6.6	33.6
KS	Wichita	52	4	4.2	2.7	0.2	T	T	T	T	T	–	1.3	3.5	15.9
KY	Louisville	58	5.3	4.2	3.1	0.1	T	T	T	T	–	0.1	1	2.5	16.3
LA	New Orleans	51	T	0.1	T	T	T	–	–	–	–	–	T	0.1	0.2
ME	Portland	65	19.3	16.5	13.5	2.9	0.2	–	T	–	T	0.2	3.3	14.7	70.6
MD	Baltimore.	55	6.3	7.1	3.6	0.1	T	T	T	–	–	T	1.0	3.3	21.4
MA	Boston	68	13.1	12.0	8.2	0.9	–	T	T	T	–	T	1.3	7.8	43.3
MI	Detroit.	47	11.1	9.1	6.9	1.9	T	–	–	–	T	0.2	2.5	10.2	41.9
	Sault Ste. Marie . .	58	29.2	18.2	14.6	5.8	0.5	T	T	T	0.1	2.4	15.6	31	117.4
MN	Duluth	62	18.3	12.1	13.8	6.7	0.7	T	T	T	0.1	1.6	12.8	15.4	81.5
	Minneapolis-St. Paul .	63	10.7	8.1	10.4	2.8	0.1	T	T	T	T	0.5	7.8	9.5	49.9
MS	Jackson.	38	0.5	0.2	0.2	T	–	–	T	–	–	–	T	0.1	1.0
MO	Kansas City	71	5.5	4.5	3.4	0.8	T	T	T	T	T	0.1	1.3	4.4	20.0
	St. Louis	69	5.4	4.5	3.7	0.5	T	T	T	–	–	T	1.4	4.0	19.5
MT	Great Falls.	68	9.4	8.4	10.8	7.0	1.9	0.3	T	0.1	1.5	3.4	7.5	8.1	58.4
NE	Omaha	70	7.5	7.0	6.3	1.1	0.1	T	T	T	T	0.3	2.6	5.7	30.6
NV	Reno	56	6.1	5.2	4.3	1.2	0.8	–	–	–	–	0.3	2.5	4.6	25.0
NH	Concord	64	18	14.2	11.6	2.7	0.1	T	–	–	T	0.1	3.8	14.0	64.5
NJ	Atlantic City	56	5	5.7	2.5	0.3	T	T	T	–	–	T	0.4	2.4	16.3
NM	Albuquerque.	66	2.5	2.1	1.8	0.6	T	T	T	T	T	0.1	1.2	2.7	11.0
NY	Albany	59	17.2	13.6	11.8	2.8	0.1	T	T	T	–	T	4.1	14.6	64.4
	Buffalo	62	24.7	17.8	12.6	3.3	0.2	T	T	T	T	0.3	11.2	24.2	94.1
	New York [1].	137	7.7	8.6	5.1	0.9	T	–	T	–	–	T	0.9	5.6	28.8
NC	Charlotte	66	2.2	1.8	1.2	T	T	T	–	–	–	T	0.1	0.5	5.8
	Raleigh	61	2.8	2.6	1.3	T	T	T	T	–	–	T	0.1	0.8	7.6
ND	Bismarck	66	7.9	6.8	8.5	3.9	0.9	T	T	T	0.2	1.9	6.9	6.9	43.9
OH	Cincinnati.	58	7.3	5.5	4.2	0.5	–	T	T	–	–	0.3	2.0	3.9	23.7
	Cleveland	64	14.4	12.2	11.0	2.7	0.1	T	T	–	–	0.6	5.2	12.8	59
	Columbus	58	8.9	6.2	4.5	1	T	T	T	T	–	0.1	2.2	5.5	28.4
OK	Oklahoma City	66	3.2	2.4	1.5	T	T	T	T	T	–	T	0.5	1.9	9.5
OR	Portland	55	3.2	1.1	0.4	T	–	T	–	T	–	–	0.4	1.4	6.5
PA	Philadelphia	63	6.3	7.0	3.4	0.3	T	T	–	–	–	T	0.7	3.4	21.1
	Pittsburgh	53	12	9.2	8.4	1.8	0.1	T	T	T	T	0.4	3.4	8.5	43.8
RI	Providence.	52	10	9.9	7.4	0.7	0.2	–	–	–	–	0.1	1.3	7.1	36.7
SC	Columbia	57	0.6	0.8	0.2	T	T	–	T	–	–	–	T	0.3	1.9
SD	Sioux Falls	60	7	8.0	9.3	3.0	T	T	T	T	T	0.9	6.2	7.0	41.4
TN	Memphis	49	2.2	1.4	0.8	T	T	T	–	–	–	T	0.1	0.6	5.1
	Nashville	59	3.8	3.0	1.5	–	–	T	T	–	–	–	0.4	1.4	10.1
TX	Dallas-Fort Worth . .	47	1.1	1.0	0.2	T	T	–	–	–	–	T	0.1	0.2	2.6
	El Paso	57	1.3	0.8	0.4	0.3	T	T	T	T	–	T	0.9	1.6	5.3
	Houston	71	0.2	0.2	T	T	T	T	–	–	–	–	T	T	0.4
UT	Salt Lake City.	77	13.5	9.9	9.0	4.9	0.6	T	T	T	0.1	1.3	6.9	11.9	58.1
VT	Burlington	62	19.4	16.5	13.8	4.1	0.2	–	T	T	T	0.2	6.6	18.4	79.2
VA	Norfolk	55	3	2.9	1.0	T	T	T	–	–	–	–	–	1.0	7.9
	Richmond	66	5	3.9	2.4	0.1	T	–	T	–	–	T	0.4	2.0	13.8
WA	Seattle-Tacoma. . . .	52	4.9	1.6	1.3	0.1	T	–	T	–	–	T	1.1	2.4	11.4
	Spokane	58	15.3	7.5	3.9	0.6	0.1	T	T	T	T	0.4	6.4	14.1	48.3
WV	Charleston	51	11	8.6	5.5	0.9	–	T	T	T	T	0.2	2.4	5.3	33.9
WI	Milwaukee	65	14	9.2	8.3	1.9	0.1	T	T	T	T	0.2	3.0	10.4	47.1
WY	Cheyenne	70	6.2	6.4	11.8	9.4	3.4	0.2	–	T	1.1	3.9	7.3	6.2	55.9
PR	San Juan.	50	–	–	–	–	–	–	–	–	–	T	–	–	T

– Represents zero. [1] City office data.

Source: U.S. National Oceanic and Atmospheric Administration, *Comparative Climatic Data*, annual. See also <http://www.ncdc.noaa.gov/oa/climate/online/ccd/avgsnf.txt>.

Geography and Environment 237

Table 383. Cloudiness, Average Wind Speed, Heating and Cooling Degree Days, and Average Relative Humidity—Selected Cities

[Airport data, except as noted. For period of record through 2005, except heating and cooling normals for period 1971–2000. M = morning. A = afternoon]

State	Station	Cloudiness-average percentage of days [1] Length of record (yr.)	An-nual	Average wind speed (m.p.h.) Length of record (yr.)	An-nual	Jan.	July	Heating degree days	Cooling degree days	Average relative humidity (percent) Length of record (yr.)	Annual M	A	Jan. M	A	July M	A
AL	Mobile	47	72.1	57	8.8	10.1	6.9	1,667	2,548	43	87	64	82	66	90	67
AK	Juneau	47	87.9	60	8.2	8.0	7.5	8,574	–	39	80	70	78	75	79	68
AZ	Phoenix	57	42.5	60	6.2	5.3	7.1	1,040	4,355	45	49	23	64	32	42	20
AR	Little Rock	35	67.7	63	7.8	8.4	6.7	3,084	2,086	41	82	62	80	66	86	61
CA	Los Angeles	60	60.0	57	7.5	6.7	7.9	1,286	682	46	79	66	72	62	86	69
	Sacramento	49	48.5	55	7.8	6.9	8.9	2,666	1,248	19	83	46	91	71	77	30
	San Diego	55	60.0	65	7.0	6.0	7.5	1,063	866	45	77	63	73	58	82	67
	San Francisco	68	56.2	78	10.6	7.2	13.6	2,862	142	46	84	63	87	69	87	60
CO	Denver	61	68.5	49	8.7	8.6	8.3	6,128	695	37	67	40	63	49	68	34
CT	Hartford	41	77.5	51	8.4	8.9	7.3	6,104	759	46	77	53	73	57	79	51
DE	Wilmington	47	73.4	57	9.0	9.8	7.8	4,887	1,125	58	79	55	75	60	80	55
DC	Washington	48	74.0	57	9.4	10.0	8.3	3,999	1,560	45	75	54	71	56	77	54
FL	Jacksonville	47	74.2	56	7.8	8.1	7.0	1,353	2,636	69	89	56	88	58	89	59
	Miami	46	79.5	56	9.2	9.5	7.9	155	4,383	41	83	61	85	60	83	63
GA	Atlanta	61	70.1	67	9.1	10.4	7.7	2,827	1,810	45	82	56	78	59	88	59
HI	Honolulu	47	75.3	56	11.3	9.4	13.1	–	4,561	36	72	56	81	62	68	52
ID	Boise	56	67.1	66	8.7	7.9	8.4	5,809	769	66	69	43	81	71	54	21
IL	Chicago	37	77.0	47	10.3	11.6	8.4	6,493	835	47	80	64	77	70	81	61
	Peoria	52	73.7	62	9.8	10.9	7.8	6,095	998	46	83	66	80	72	86	65
IN	Indianapolis	64	76.2	57	9.6	10.9	7.5	5,521	1,042	46	84	62	81	71	87	60
IA	Des Moines	46	71.5	56	10.7	11.4	8.9	6,432	1,052	44	80	65	77	70	83	63
KS	Wichita	39	64.9	52	12.2	11.9	11.3	4,765	1,658	52	80	60	79	66	79	55
KY	Louisville	47	74.8	58	8.3	9.5	6.8	4,352	1,443	45	81	59	78	65	85	58
LA	New Orleans	47	72.3	57	8.2	9.3	6.1	1,417	2,776	57	87	66	84	69	91	69
ME	Portland	54	72.3	65	8.7	9.0	7.6	7,325	347	65	79	59	76	60	80	60
MD	Baltimore	45	71.2	55	8.8	9.3	7.6	4,634	1,220	52	78	54	73	57	80	53
MA	Boston	60	73.2	48	12.4	13.7	11.0	5,630	777	41	73	58	68	58	74	57
MI	Detroit	37	79.5	47	10.2	11.8	8.5	6,449	727	47	81	60	80	70	82	54
	Sault Ste. Marie	54	81.9	64	9.2	9.6	7.8	9,230	145	64	85	66	81	74	88	62
MN	Duluth	47	79.2	56	11.0	11.6	9.4	9,742	189	44	81	67	78	73	85	65
	Minneapolis-St. Paul	57	74.0	67	10.5	10.5	9.4	7,882	699	46	78	64	75	70	80	60
MS	Jackson	30	69.6	42	6.9	8.2	5.2	2,368	2,290	42	90	64	86	69	93	66
MO	Kansas City	23	67.1	33	10.6	11.1	9.2	5,249	1,325	33	80	66	77	69	84	66
	St. Louis	47	72.6	56	9.6	10.6	8.0	4,757	1,561	45	81	63	80	69	83	61
MT	Great Falls	57	78.4	64	12.5	14.8	10.0	7,675	326	44	68	45	67	61	68	31
NE	Omaha	49	69.6	69	10.5	10.9	8.8	6,312	1,095	41	81	64	78	69	84	64
NV	Reno	53	56.7	63	6.6	5.6	7.2	5,601	493	42	68	31	80	51	59	19
NH	Concord	54	75.3	63	6.7	7.2	5.7	7,485	442	40	81	53	76	59	84	52
NJ	Atlantic City	37	74.2	47	9.8	10.7	8.3	5,113	935	41	82	57	78	59	83	57
NM	Albuquerque	56	54.2	66	8.9	8.0	8.9	4,281	1,290	45	58	29	68	39	59	27
NY	Albany	57	81.1	67	8.9	9.8	7.5	6,861	544	40	80	58	78	64	81	55
	Buffalo	52	85.2	66	11.8	13.9	10.2	6,693	548	45	80	63	79	73	79	56
	New York [2]	42	71.0	68	9.3	10.6	7.6	4,744	1,160	71	72	56	68	60	75	55
NC	Charlotte	49	70.4	56	7.4	7.8	6.6	3,208	1,644	45	82	54	78	55	87	57
	Raleigh	47	69.9	56	7.6	8.2	6.7	3,465	1,521	41	85	54	79	55	89	58
ND	Bismarck	56	74.5	66	10.2	10.0	9.2	8,809	471	46	80	62	76	71	84	55
OH	Cincinnati	44	77.8	58	9.0	10.4	7.2	5,200	1,053	43	82	60	80	69	86	58
	Cleveland	54	81.9	64	10.5	12.2	8.6	6,097	712	45	80	62	79	70	81	57
	Columbus	46	80.3	56	8.3	9.8	6.5	5,546	925	46	81	59	78	68	84	56
OK	Oklahoma City	44	61.9	57	12.2	12.5	10.9	3,663	1,907	40	79	61	78	64	80	57
OR	Portland	47	81.1	57	7.9	9.9	7.6	4,366	398	65	86	59	85	76	82	45
PA	Philadelphia	55	74.5	65	9.5	10.3	8.2	4,759	1,235	46	76	55	73	59	79	54
	Pittsburgh	43	83.8	53	9.0	10.4	7.3	5,829	726	45	80	58	77	66	83	55
RI	Providence	42	73.2	52	10.4	10.9	9.4	5,754	714	42	76	55	71	57	77	56
SC	Columbia	48	68.5	57	6.8	7.2	6.3	2,595	2,063	39	86	51	82	54	88	54
SD	Sioux Falls	50	71.2	57	11.0	10.9	9.8	7,746	757	42	82	66	78	72	84	61
TN	Memphis	43	67.7	57	8.8	10.0	7.5	3,033	2,190	66	80	60	78	65	84	61
	Nashville	54	71.8	64	8.0	9.1	6.5	3,658	1,656	40	83	63	79	67	87	63
TX	Dallas-Fort Worth	42	63.0	52	10.7	11.0	9.8	2,370	2,571	42	80	61	79	65	78	55
	El Paso	53	47.1	63	8.8	8.3	8.3	2,604	2,165	45	56	27	65	34	61	29
	Houston	26	75.3	36	7.6	8.1	6.6	1,525	2,893	36	89	67	85	70	91	65
UT	Salt Lake City	69	65.8	76	8.8	7.5	9.5	5,607	1,089	45	67	43	80	70	51	22
VT	Burlington	52	84.1	62	9.0	9.7	8.0	7,665	489	40	77	59	73	64	79	53
VA	Norfolk	47	71.2	57	10.5	11.4	8.9	3,342	1,630	57	79	58	75	59	82	59
	Richmond	50	72.9	57	7.7	8.1	6.9	3,878	1,466	71	83	53	80	57	85	56
WA	Seattle-Tacoma	51	84.4	57	8.8	9.5	8.1	4,797	173	46	84	62	82	75	82	49
	Spokane	48	76.4	58	8.9	8.7	8.6	6,820	394	46	78	52	86	80	64	27
WV	Charleston	47	82.2	58	5.8	6.9	4.8	4,589	1,064	58	84	57	78	63	91	60
WI	Milwaukee	55	75.3	65	11.5	12.6	9.7	7,096	616	45	79	67	76	70	81	65
WY	Cheyenne	60	71.2	48	12.9	15.1	10.4	7,289	280	46	65	45	58	50	69	37
PR	San Juan	40	80.0	50	8.3	8.3	9.6	–	5,426	50	79	65	82	65	79	67

– Represents zero.   [1] Percent of days that are either partly cloudy or cloudy.   [2] Airport data for sunshine.

Source: U.S. National Oceanic and Atmospheric Administration, *Comparative Climatic Data,* annual. See also <http://www.ncdc.noaa.gov/oa/climate/online/ccd/clpcdy.txt>;   <http://www.ncdc.noaa.gov/oa/climate/online/ccd/wndspd.txt>; <http://www.ncdc.noaa.gov/oa/climate/online/ccd/nrmhdd.txt>; <http://www.ncdc.noaa.gov/oa/climate/online/ccd/nrmcdd.txt>; and <http://www.ncdc.noaa.gov/oa/climate/online/ccd/relhum.txt>.

Elections

This section relates primarily to presidential, congressional, and gubernatorial elections. Also presented are summary tables on congressional legislation; state legislatures; Black, Hispanic, and female officeholders; population of voting age; voter participation; and campaign finances.

Official statistics on federal elections, collected by the Clerk of the House, are published biennially in *Statistics of the Presidential and Congressional Election* and *Statistics of the Congressional Election.* Federal and state elections data appear also in *America Votes,* a biennial volume published by CQ Press (a division of Congressional Quarterly, Inc.), Washington, DC. Federal elections data also appear in the U.S. Congress, *Congressional Directory,* and in official state documents. Data on reported registration and voting for social and economic groups are obtained by the U.S. Census Bureau as part of the Current Population Survey (CPS) and are published in Current Population Reports, Series P20 (see text, Section 1).

Almost all federal, state, and local governmental units in the United States conduct elections for political offices and other purposes. The conduct of elections is regulated by state laws or, in some cities and counties, by local charter. An exception is that the U.S. Constitution prescribes the basis of representation in Congress and the manner of electing the president and grants to Congress the right to regulate the times, places, and manner of electing federal officers. Amendments to the Constitution have prescribed national criteria for voting eligibility. The 15th Amendment, adopted in 1870, gave all citizens the right to vote regardless of race, color, or previous condition of servitude. The 19th Amendment, adopted in 1919, further extended the right to vote to all citizens regardless of sex. The payment of poll taxes as a prerequisite to voting in federal elections was banned by the 24th Amendment in

1964. In 1971, as a result of the 26th Amendment, eligibility to vote in national elections was extended to all citizens, 18 years old and over.

Presidential election—The Constitution specifies how the president and vice president are selected. Each state elects, by popular vote, a group of electors equal in number to its total of members of Congress. The 23d Amendment, adopted in 1961, grants the District of Columbia three presidential electors, a number equal to that of the least populous state. Subsequent to the election, the electors meet in their respective states to vote for president and vice president. Usually, each elector votes for the candidate receiving the most popular votes in his or her state. A majority vote of all electors is necessary to elect the president and vice president. If no candidate receives a majority, the House of Representatives, with each state having one vote, is empowered to elect the president and vice president, again, with a majority of votes required.

The 22nd Amendment to the Constitution, adopted in 1951, limits presidential tenure to two elective terms of 4 years each or to one elective term for any person who, upon succession to the presidency, has held the office or acted as President for more than 2 years.

Congressional election—The Constitution provides that representatives be apportioned among the states according to their population, that a census of population be taken every 10 years as a basis for apportionment, and that each state have at least one representative. At the time of each apportionment, Congress decides what the total number of representatives will be. Since 1912, the total has been 435, except during 1960 to 1962 when it increased to 437, adding one representative each for Alaska and Hawaii. The total reverted to 435 after

Elections 239

reapportionment following the 1960 census. Members are elected for 2-year terms, all terms covering the same period. The District of Columbia, American Samoa, Guam, and the Virgin Islands each elect one nonvoting delegate, and Puerto Rico elects a nonvoting resident commissioner.

The Senate is composed of 100 members, two from each state, who are elected to serve for a term of 6 years. One-third of the Senate is elected every 2 years. Senators were originally chosen by the state legislatures. The 17th Amendment to the Constitution, adopted in 1913, prescribed that senators be elected by popular vote.

Voter eligibility and participation— The Census Bureau publishes estimates of the population of voting age and the percent casting votes in each state for presidential and congressional election years. These voting-age estimates include a number of persons who meet the age requirement but are not eligible to vote, (e.g. aliens and some institutionalized persons). In addition, since 1964, voter participation and voter characteristics data have been collected during November of election years as part of the CPS. These survey data include noncitizens in the voting age population estimates, but exclude members of the Armed Forces and the institutional population.

Statistical reliability— For a discussion of statistical collection and estimation, sampling procedures, and measures of statistical reliability applicable to Census Bureau data, see Appendix III.

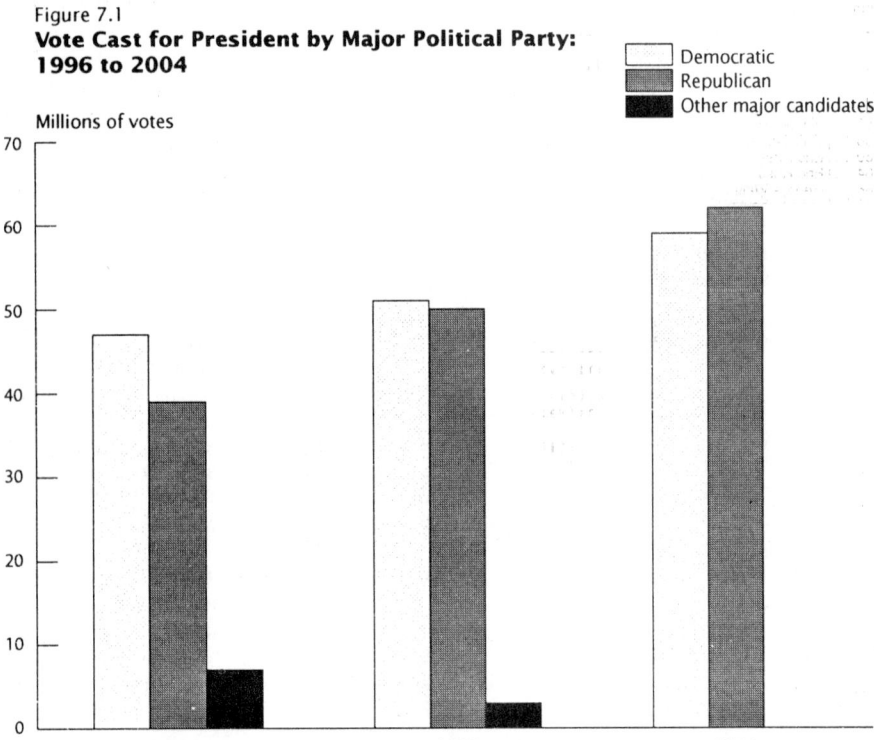

Figure 7.1
Vote Cast for President by Major Political Party: 1996 to 2004

Democratic
Republican
Other major candidates[1]

Millions of votes

[1]Candidates with 1 million or more votes: 1996—Reform, Ross Perot; 2000—Green, Ralph Nader.

Source: Chart prepared by U.S. Census Bureau. For data, see Tables 384 and 385.

240 Elections

Table 384. Vote Cast for President by Major Political Party: 1948 to 2004

[In thousands (48,834 represents 48,834,000). Prior to 1960, excludes Alaska and Hawaii; prior to 1964, excludes DC. Vote cast for major party candidates includes the votes of minor parties cast for those candidates]

Year	Candidates for President Democratic	Candidates for President Republican	Total popular vote [1] (1,000)	Democratic Popular vote Number (1,000)	Democratic Popular vote Per-cent	Democratic Electoral vote	Republican Popular vote Number (1,000)	Republican Popular vote Per-cent	Republican Electoral vote
1948. . . .	Truman	Dewey.	48,834	24,106	49.4	303	21,969	45.0	189
1952. , . .	Stevenson	Eisenhower . . .	61,552	27,315	44.4	89	33,779	54.9	442
1956. . . .	Stevenson	Eisenhower . . .	62,027	26,739	43.1	73	35,581	57.4	457
1960. . . .	Kennedy	Nixon	68,836	34,227	49.7	303	34,108	49.5	219
1964. . . .	Johnson	Goldwater	70,098	42,825	61.1	486	27,147	38.7	52
1968. . . .	Humphrey	Nixon	73,027	30,989	42.4	191	31,710	43.4	301
1972. . . .	McGovern	Nixon	77,625	28,902	37.2	17	46,740	60.2	520
1976. . . .	Carter.	Ford	81,603	40,826	50.0	297	39,148	48.0	240
1980. . . .	Carter.	Reagan.	86,497	35,481	41.0	49	43,643	50.5	489
1984. . . .	Mondale	Reagan	92,655	37,450	40.4	13	54,167	58.5	525
1988. . . .	Dukakis	Bush.	91,587	41,717	45.5	111	48,643	53.1	426
1992. . . .	Clinton	Bush.	104,600	44,858	42.9	370	38,799	37.1	168
1996. . . .	Clinton	Dole.	96,390	47,402	49.2	379	39,198	40.7	159
2000. . . .	Gore.	Bush.	105,594	50,996	48.3	266	50,465	47.8	271
2004. . . .	Kerry.	Bush.	122,349	58,895	48.1	251	61,873	50.6	286

[1] Include votes for minor party candidates, independents, unpledged electors, and scattered write-in votes.

Source: U.S. House of Representatives, Office of the Clerk, *Statistics of the Presidential and Congressional Election*, biennial. See <http://clerk.house.gov/member_info/election.html>.

Table 385. Vote Cast for Leading Minority Party Candidates for President: 1948 to 2004

[In thousands (1,169 represents 1,169,000). See headnote, Table 384. Data do not include write-ins, scatterings, or votes for candidates who ran on party tickets not shown]

Year	Candidate	Party	Popular vote (1,000)	Candidate	Party	Popular vote (1,000)
1948 . .	Strom Thurmond . . .	States' Rights.	1,169	Henry Wallace	Progressive	1,156
1952 ,	Vincent Hallinan. . . .	Progressive	135	Stuart Hamblen	Prohibition.	73
1956 [1]	T. Coleman Andrews.	States' Rights.	91	Eric Hass	Socialist Labor	41
1960 . .	Eric Hass	Socialist Labor	46	Rutherford Decker . .	Prohibition.	46
1964 . .	Eric Hass	Socialist Labor	43	Clifton DeBerry	Socialist Workers	22
1968 . .	George Wallace . . .	American Independent.	9,446	Henning Blomen	Socialist Labor	52
1972 [1]	John Schmitz.	American.	993	Benjamin Spock. . . .	People's	9
1976 . .	Eugene McCarthy . .	Independent	680	Roger McBride.	Libertarian	172
1980 . .	John Anderson	Independent	5,251	Ed Clark	Libertarian	920
1984 . .	David Bergland	Libertarian	227	Lyndon H. LaRouche.	Independent	79
1988 . .	Ron Paul	Libertarian	410	Lenora B. Fulani . . .	New Alliance	129
1992 . .	H. Ross Perot	Independent	19,722	Andre Marrou	Libertarian	281
1996 . .	H. Ross Perot	Reform	7,137	Ralph Nader	Green.	527
2000 . .	Ralph Nader	Green.	2,530	Pat Buchanan	Reform	324
2004 . .	Ralph Nader	Green.	116	Michael Badnarik . . .	Libertarian	369

[1] Data include write-ins, scatterings, and/or votes for candidates who ran on party tickets not shown.

Source: U.S. House of Representatives, Office of the Clerk, *Statistics of the Presidential and Congressional Election*, biennial. See <http://clerk.house.gov/member_info/election.html>.

Table 386. Democratic and Republican Percentages of Two-Party Presidential Vote by Selected Characteristics of Voters: 2000 and 2004

[In percent. Covers citizens of voting age living in private housing units in the contiguous United States. Percentages for Democratic Presidential vote are computed by subtracting the percentage Republican vote from 100 percent; third-party or independent votes are not included as valid data. Data are from the National Election Studies and are based on a sample and subject to sampling variability; for details, see source]

Characteristic	2000 Demo-cratic	2000 Repub-lican	2004 Demo-cratic	2004 Repub-lican	Characteristic	2000 Demo-cratic	2000 Repub-lican	2004 Demo-cratic	2004 Repub-lican
Total [1]	52	48	50	50	Race:				
					White	46	54	42	58
Year of birth:					Black	92	8	90	10
1975 or later.	63	37	66	34	Education:				
1959 to 1974	46	54	45	55	Less than high				
1943 to 1958	53	47	44	56	school	65	35	69	31
1927 to 1942	48	52	51	49	High school diploma/				
1911 to 1926	64	36	52	48	equivalent	53	47	46	54
1895 to 1910	−	100	−	−	Some college, no				
					degree	50	50	47	53
Sex:					College	50	50	50	50
Male	47	53	46	54	Union household	61	39	64	36
Female	56	44	53	47	Nonunion household . .	50	50	46	54

− Represents zero. [1] Includes other characteristics not shown separately.

Source: American National Election Studies. <http://www.electionstudies.org> (copyright).

Elections 241

Table 387. Electoral Vote Cast for President by Major Political Party—States: 1964 to 2004

[D = Democratic, R = Republican. For composition of regions, see map, inside front cover]

State	1964	1968 [1]	1972 [2]	1976 [3]	1980	1984	1988 [4]	1992	1996	2000 [5]	2004 [6]
Democratic . . .	486	191	17	297	49	13	111	370	379	266	251
Republican . . .	52	301	520	240	489	525	426	168	159	271	286
Northeast:											
Democratic	126	102	14	86	4	–	53	106	106	102	101
Republican	–	24	108	36	118	113	60	–	–	4	–
Midwest:											
Democratic	149	31	–	58	10	10	29	100	100	68	57
Republican	–	118	145	87	135	127	108	29	29	61	66
South:											
Democratic	121	45	3	149	31	3	8	68	80	15	16
Republican	47	77	165	20	138	174	168	116	104	168	173
West:											
Democratic	90	13	–	4	4	–	21	96	93	81	77
Republican	5	82	102	97	98	111	90	23	26	38	47
AL.	R-10	([1])	R-9	D-9	R-9	R-9	R-9	R-9	R-9	R-9	R-9
AK.	D-3	R-3	R-3	R-3	R-3	R-3	R-3	R-3	R-3	R-3	R-3
AZ.	R-5	R-5	R-6	R-6	R-6	R-7	R-7	R-8	D-8	R-8	R-10
AR.	D-6	([1])	R-6	D-6	R-6	R-6	R-6	D-6	D-6	R-6	R-6
CA.	D-40	R-40	R-45	R-45	R-45	R-47	R-47	D-54	D-54	D-54	D-55
CO.	D-6	R-6	R-7	R-7	R-7	R-8	R-8	D-8	R-8	R-8	R-9
CT.	D-8	D-8	R-8	R-8	R-8	R-8	R-8	D-8	D-8	D-8	D-7
DE.	D-3	R-3	R-3	D-3	R-3	R-3	R-3	D-3	D-3	D-3	D-3
DC.	D-3	D-3	D-3	D-3	D-3	D-3	D-3	D-3	D-3	[5]D-2	D-3
FL.	D-14	R-14	R-17	D-17	R-17	R-21	R-21	R-25	D-25	R-25	R-27
GA	R-12	([1])	R-12	D-12	D-12	R-12	R-12	D-13	R-13	R-13	R-15
HI	D-4	D-4	R-4	D-4	D-4	R-4	D-4	D-4	D-4	D-4	D-4
ID	D-4	R-4	R-4	R-4	R-4	R-4	R-4	R-4	R-4	R-4	R-4
IL	D-26	R-26	R-26	R-26	R-26	R-24	R-24	D-22	D-22	D-22	D-21
IN	D-13	R-13	R-13	R-13	R-13	R-12	R-12	R-12	R-12	R-12	R-11
IA	D-9	R-9	R-8	R-8	R-8	R-8	D-8	D-7	D-7	D-7	R-7
KS.	D-7	R-7	R-7	R-7	R-7	R-7	R-7	R-6	R-6	R-6	R-6
KY.	D-9	R-9	R-9	D-9	R-9	R-9	R-9	D-8	D-8	R-8	R-8
LA	R-10	([1])	R-10	D-10	R-10	R-10	R-10	D-9	D-9	R-9	R-9
ME	D-4	D-4	R-4	R-4	R-4	R-4	R-4	D-4	D-4	D-4	D-4
MD	D-10	D-10	R-10	D-10	D-10	R-10	R-10	D-10	D-10	D-10	D-10
MA	D-14	D-14	D-14	D-14	R-14	R-13	D-13	D-12	D-12	D-12	D-12
MI	D-21	D-21	R-21	R-21	R-21	R-20	R-20	D-18	D-18	D-18	D-17
MN	D-10	D-10	R-10	D-10	D-10	D-10	D-10	D-10	D-10	D-10	[6]D-9
MS	R-7	([1])	R-7	D-7	R-7	R-7	R-7	R-7	R-7	R-7	R-6
MO	D-12	R-12	R-12	D-12	R-12	R-11	R-11	D-11	D-11	R-11	R-11
MT	D-4	R-4	R-4	R-4	R-4	R-4	R-4	D-3	R-3	R-3	R-3
NE	D-5	R-5	R-5	R-5	R-5	R-5	R-5	R-5	R-5	R-5	R-5
NV	D-3	R-3	R-3	R-3	R-3	R-4	R-4	D-4	D-4	R-4	R-5
NH	D-4	R-4	R-4	R-4	R-4	R-4	R-4	D-4	D-4	R-4	D-4
NJ	D-17	R-17	R-17	R-17	R-17	R-16	R-16	D-15	D-15	D-15	D-15
NM	D-4	R-4	R-4	R-4	R-4	R-5	R-5	D-5	D-5	D-5	R-5
NY.	D-43	D-43	R-41	D-41	R-41	R-36	D-36	D-33	D-33	D-33	D-31
NC	D-13	[1]R-12	R-13	D-13	R-13	R-13	R-13	R-14	R-14	R-14	R-15
ND	D-4	R-4	R-3	R-3	R-3	R-3	R-3	R-3	R-3	R-3	R-3
OH	D-26	R-26	R-25	D-25	R-25	R-23	R-23	D-21	D-21	R-21	R-20
OK	D-8	R-8	R-8	R-8	R-8	R-8	R-8	R-8	R-8	R-8	R-7
OR	D-6	R-6	R-6	R-6	R-6	R-7	D-7	D-7	D-7	D-7	D-7
PA.	D-29	D-29	R-27	D-27	R-27	R-25	R-25	D-23	D-23	D-23	D-21
RI	D-4	D-4	R-4	D-4	D-4	R-4	D-4	D-4	D-4	D-4	D-4
SC.	R-8	R-8	R-8	D-8	R-8	R-8	R-8	R-8	R-8	R-8	R-8
SD.	D-4	R-4	R-4	R-4	R-4	R-3	R-3	R-3	R-3	R-3	R-3
TN.	D-11	R-11	R-10	D-10	R-10	R-11	R-11	D-11	D-11	R-11	R-11
TX.	D-25	R-25	R-26	D-26	R-26	R-29	R-29	R-32	R-32	R-32	R-34
UT.	D-4	R-4	R-4	R-4	R-4	R-5	R-5	R-5	R-5	R-5	R-5
VT.	D-3	R-3	R-3	R-3	R-3	R-3	R-3	D-3	D-3	D-3	D-3
VA.	D-12	R-12	[2]R-11	R-12	R-12	R-12	R-12	R-13	R-13	R-13	R-13
WA	D-9	D-9	R-9	[3]R-8	R-9	R-10	D-10	D-11	D-11	D-11	D-11
WV	D-7	D-7	R-6	D-6	D-6	R-6	[4]D-5	D-5	D-5	R-5	R-5
WI	D-12	R-12	R-11	D-11	R-11	R-11	D-11	D-11	D-11	D-11	D-10
WY	D-3	R-3	R-3	R-3	R-3	R-3	R-3	R-3	R-3	R-3	R-3

– Represents zero.   [1] Excludes 46 electoral votes cast for American Independent George C. Wallace as follows: AL 10, AR 6, GA 12, LA 10, MS 7, and NC 1.   [2] Excludes one electoral vote cast for Libertarian John Hospers in Virginia.   [3] Excludes one electoral vote cast for Ronald Reagan in Washington.   [4] Excludes one electoral vote cast for Lloyd Bentsen for President in West Virginia.   [5] Excludes one electoral vote left blank by a Democratic elector in the District of Columbia.   [6] Excludes one electoral vote cast for Democratic vice presidential nominee John Edwards in Minnesota.

Source: U.S. House of Representatives, Office of the Clerk, *Statistics of the Presidential and Congressional Election,* biennial. See also <http://clerk.house.gov/member_info/election.html>.

Table 388. **Popular Vote Cast for President by Political Party—States: 2000 and 2004**

[In thousands (105,594 represents 105,594,000), except percent]

State	2000			Percent of total vote		2004			Percent of total vote	
	Total [1]	Demo-cratic Party	Repub-lican Party	Demo-cratic Party	Repub-lican Party	Total [1]	Demo-cratic Party	Repub-lican Party	Demo-cratic Party	Repub-lican Party
United States. .	105,594	50,996	50,465	48.3	47.8	122,349	58,895	61,873	48.1	50.6
Alabama	1,666	693	941	41.6	56.5	1,883	694	1,176	36.8	62.5
Alaska	286	79	167	27.7	58.6	313	111	191	35.5	61.1
Arizona	1,532	685	782	44.7	51.0	2,013	894	1,104	44.4	54.9
Arkansas	922	423	473	45.9	51.3	1,055	470	573	44.5	54.3
California	10,966	5,861	4,567	53.4	41.7	12,421	6,745	5,510	54.3	44.4
Colorado.	1,741	738	884	42.4	50.8	2,130	1,002	1,101	47.0	51.7
Connecticut.	1,460	816	561	55.9	38.4	1,579	857	694	54.3	43.9
Delaware	328	180	137	55.0	41.9	375	200	172	53.3	45.8
District of Columbia .	202	172	18	85.2	9.0	228	203	21	89.2	9.3
Florida	5,963	2,912	2,913	48.8	48.8	7,610	3,584	3,965	47.1	52.1
Georgia	2,583	1,116	1,420	43.2	55.0	3,302	1,366	1,914	41.4	58.0
Hawaii	368	205	138	55.8	37.5	429	232	194	54.0	45.3
Idaho	502	139	337	27.6	67.2	598	181	409	30.3	68.4
Illinois	4,742	2,589	2,019	54.6	42.6	5,274	2,892	2,346	54.8	44.5
Indiana	2,199	902	1,246	41.0	56.6	2,468	969	1,479	39.3	59.9
Iowa	1,353	639	634	47.2	46.9	1,507	742	752	49.2	49.9
Kansas.	1,072	399	622	37.2	58.0	1,188	435	736	36.6	62.0
Kentucky	1,544	639	873	41.4	56.5	1,796	713	1,069	39.7	59.5
Louisiana	1,766	792	928	44.9	52.6	1,943	820	1,102	42.2	56.7
Maine.	652	320	287	49.1	44.0	741	397	330	53.6	44.6
Maryland	2,025	1,144	814	56.5	40.2	2,384	1,334	1,025	56.0	43.0
Massachusetts.	2,734	1,616	879	59.1	32.1	2,927	1,804	1,071	61.6	36.6
Michigan.	4,233	2,170	1,953	51.3	46.1	4,839	2,479	2,314	51.2	47.8
Minnesota.	2,439	1,168	1,110	47.9	45.5	2,828	1,445	1,347	51.1	47.6
Mississippi	994	405	573	40.7	57.6	1,140	458	673	40.2	59.0
Missouri	2,360	1,111	1,190	47.1	50.4	2,731	1,259	1,456	46.1	53.3
Montana	411	137	240	33.4	58.4	450	174	266	38.6	59.1
Nebraska	697	232	434	33.3	62.2	778	254	513	32.7	65.9
Nevada	609	280	302	45.9	49.5	830	397	419	47.9	50.5
New Hampshire	569	266	274	46.8	48.1	678	341	331	50.2	48.8
New Jersey	3,187	1,789	1,284	56.1	40.3	3,612	1,911	1,670	52.9	46.2
New Mexico	599	287	286	47.9	47.8	756	371	377	49.0	49.8
New York	6,960	4,108	2,403	59.0	34.5	7,448	4,181	2,807	56.1	37.7
North Carolina	2,915	1,258	1,631	43.1	56.0	3,501	1,526	1,961	43.6	56.0
North Dakota	288	95	175	33.1	60.7	313	111	197	35.5	62.9
Ohio	4,702	2,184	2,350	46.4	50.0	5,628	2,741	2,860	48.7	50.8
Oklahoma	1,234	474	744	38.4	60.3	1,464	504	960	34.4	65.6
Oregon.	1,534	720	714	47.0	46.5	1,837	943	867	51.3	47.2
Pennsylvania	4,912	2,486	2,281	50.6	46.4	5,770	2,938	2,794	50.9	48.4
Rhode Island	409	250	131	61.0	31.9	437	260	169	59.4	38.7
South Carolina	1,384	566	787	40.9	56.9	1,618	662	938	40.9	58.0
South Dakota	316	119	191	37.6	60.3	388	149	233	38.4	59.9
Tennessee	2,076	982	1,062	47.3	51.1	2,437	1,036	1,384	42.5	56.8
Texas	6,408	2,434	3,800	38.0	59.3	7,411	2,833	4,527	38.2	61.1
Utah	771	203	515	26.3	66.8	928	241	664	26.0	71.5
Vermont	294	149	120	50.6	40.7	312	184	121	58.9	38.8
Virginia.	2,739	1,217	1,437	44.4	52.5	3,195	1,455	1,717	45.5	53.7
Washington	2,487	1,248	1,109	50.2	44.6	2,859	1,510	1,305	52.8	45.6
West Virginia	648	295	336	45.6	51.9	756	327	424	43.2	56.1
Wisconsin	2,599	1,243	1,237	47.8	47.6	2,997	1,490	1,478	49.7	49.3
Wyoming	214	60	148	28.3	69.2	244	71	168	29.0	68.7

[1] Includes other parties.

Source: U.S. House of Representatives, Office of the Clerk, *Statistics of the Presidential and Congressional Election*, biannual. See also <http://clerk.house.gov/member_info/election.html>.

Elections 243

Table 389. **Vote Cast for United States Senators, 2004 and 2006, and Incumbent Senators, 2006—States**

[1,839 **represents** 1,839,000. D = Democrat, R = Republican, I = Independent]

State	2004 Total (1,000)[1]	2004 Percent for leading party	2006 Total (1,000)[1]	2006 Percent for leading party	Incumbent senators and year term expires — Name, party, and year	Name, party, and year
Alabama	1,839	R-67.5	(X)	(X)	Jeffrey Sessions (R) 2009	Richard Shelby (R) 2011
Alaska	308	R-48.6	(X)	(X)	Lisa Murkowski (R) 2011	Ted Stevens (R) 2009
Arizona	1,962	R-76.7	1,527	R-53.3	Jon Kyl (R) 2013	John McCain (R) 2011
Arkansas	1,039	D-55.9	(X)	(X)	Blanche Lincoln (D) 2011	Mark Pryor (D) 2009
California	12,053	D-57.7	8,541	D-59.4	Barbara Boxer (D) 2011	Dianne Feinstein (D) 2013
Colorado	2,107	D-51.3	(X)	(X)	Wayne Allard (R) 2009	Ken Salazar (D) 2011
Connecticut	1,425	D-66.4	1,135	D-39.7	Christopher Dodd (D) 2011	Joseph Lieberman (I) 2013
Delaware	(X)	(X)	243	D-70.2	Joseph Biden (D) 2009	Thomas Carper (D) 2013
Florida	7,430	R-49.4	4,794	D-60.3	Mel Martinez (R) 2011	Bill Nelson (D) 2013
Georgia	3,221	R-57.8	(X)	(X)	Saxby Chambliss (R) 2009	Johnny Isakson (R) 2011
Hawaii	415	D-75.5	343	D-61.3	Daniel Akaka (D) 2013	Daniel Inouye (D) 2011
Idaho	504	R-99.2	(X)	(X)	Larry Craig (R) 2009	Michael Crapo (R) 2011
Illinois	5,142	D-70.0	(X)	(X)	Richard Durbin (D) 2009	Barack Obama (D) 2011
Indiana	2,428	D-61.6	1,341	R-87.4	Evan Bayh (D) 2011	Richard Lugar (R) 2013
Iowa	1,479	D-70.2	(X)	(X)	Chuck Grassley (R) 2011	Tom Harkin (D) 2009
Kansas	1,129	R-69.2	(X)	(X)	Sam Brownback (R) 2011	Pat Roberts (R) 2009
Kentucky	1,724	R-50.7	(X)	(X)	Jim Bunning (R) 2011	Mitch McConnell (R) 2009
Louisiana[2]	1,848	R-51.0	(X)	(X)	Mary Landrieu (D) 2009	David Vitter (R) 2011
Maine	(X)	(X)	545	R-74.4	Susan Collins (R) 2009	Olympia Snowe (R) 2013
Maryland	2,322	D-64.8	62	R-68.0	Barbara Mikulski (D) 2011	Benjamin Cardin (D) 2013
Massachusetts	(X)	(X)	2,244	D-66.9	Edward Kennedy (D) 2013	John Kerry (D) 2009
Michigan	(X)	(X)	3,780	D-56.9	Carl Levin (D) 2009	Debbie Stabenow (D) 2013
Minnesota	(X)	(X)	2,203	D-58.1	Norm Coleman (R) 2009	Amy Klobuchar (D) 2013
Mississippi	(X)	(X)	611	R-63.6	Thad Cochran (R) 2009	Trent Lott (R) 2013
Missouri	2,706	R-56.1	2,128	D-49.6	Christopher Bond (R) 2011	Claire McCaskill (D) 2013
Montana	(X)	(X)	407	D-49.2	Max Baucus (D) 2009	John Tester (D) 2013
Nebraska	(X)	(X)	592	D-63.9	Chuck Hagel (R) 2009	Ben Nelson (D) 2013
Nevada	810	D-61.1	583	R-55.4	John Ensign (R) 2013	Harry Reid (D) 2011
New Hampshire	657	R-66.2	(X)	(X)	Judd Gregg (R) 2011	John Sununu (R) 2009
New Jersey	(X)	(X)	102	D-57.2	Robert Menendez (D) 2013	Frank Lautenberg (D) 2009
New Mexico	(X)	(X)	559	D-70.6	Jeff Bingaman (D) 2013	Pete Domenici (R) 2009
New York	7,448	D-58.9	4,701	D-57.4	Hillary Clinton (D) 2013	Charles Schumer (D) 2011
North Carolina	3,472	R-51.6	(X)	(X)	Richard Burr (R) 2011	Elizabeth Dole (R) 2009
North Dakota	311	D-68.3	218	D-68.8	Kent Conrad (D) 2013	Byron Dorgan (D) 2011
Ohio	5,426	R-63.8	2,258	D-100.0	Sherrod Brown (D) 2013	George Voinovich (R) 2011
Oklahoma	1,447	R-52.8	(X)	(X)	Tom Coburn (R) 2011	James Inhofe (R) 2009
Oregon	1,781	D-63.4	(X)	(X)	Gordon Smith (R) 2009	Ron Wyden (D) 2011
Pennsylvania	5,559	R-52.6	2,393	D-100.0	Robert Casey Jr. (D) 2013	Arlen Specter (R) 2011
Rhode Island	(X)	(X)	385	D-53.5	Sheldon Whitehouse (D) 2013	Jack Reed (D) 2009
South Carolina	1,597	R-53.7	(X)	(X)	Jim DeMint (R) 2011	Lindsey Graham (R) 2009
South Dakota	391	R-50.6	(X)	(X)	Tim Johnson (D) 2009	John Thune (R) 2011
Tennessee	(X)	(X)	1,834	R-50.7	Lamar Alexander (R) 2009	Bob Corker (R) 2013
Texas	(X)	(X)	4,315	R-61.7	John Cornyn (R) 2009	Kay Hutchison (R) 2013
Utah	912	R-68.7	571	R-62.4	Robert Bennett (R) 2011	Orrin Hatch (R) 2013
Vermont	307	D-70.6	262	R-32.4	Bernard Sanders (I) 2013	Patrick Leahy (D) 2011
Virginia	(X)	(X)	2,370	D-49.6	Jim Webb (D) 2013	John Warner (R) 2009
Washington	2,819	D-55.0	2,084	D-56.9	Maria Cantwell (D) 2013	Patty Murray (D) 2011
West Virginia	(X)	(X)	207	D-77.0	Robert Byrd (D) 2013	John Rockefeller (D) 2009
Wisconsin	2,950	D-55.4	2,138	D-67.3	Russell Feingold (D) 2011	Herb Kohl (D) 2013
Wyoming	(X)	(X)	196	R-68.9	Michael Enzi (R) 2009	Craig Thomas (R) 2013

X Not applicable.   [1] Includes vote cast for minor parties.   [2] Louisiana holds an open-primary election with candidates from all parties running on the same ballot. Any candidate who receives a majority is elected.

Source: U.S. House of Representatives, Office of the Clerk, *Statistics of the Presidential and Congressional Election*, biennial. See also <http://clerk.house.gov/member_info/electionInfo/index.html>.

Table 390. Vote Cast for United States Representatives by Major Political Party—States: 2002 to 2006

[In thousands (74,707 represents 74,707,000), except percent. R = Republican, D = Democrat, and I = Independent. In each state, totals represent the sum of votes cast in each Congressional District or votes cast for Representative-at-Large in states where only one member is elected. In all years there are numerous districts within the state where either the Republican or Democratic party had no candidate. In some states the Republican and Democratic vote includes votes cast for the party candidate by endorsing parties]

State	2002				2004				2006			
	Total[1]	Democratic	Republican	Percent for leading party	Total[1]	Democratic	Republican	Percent for leading party	Total[1]	Democratic	Republican	Percent for leading party
U.S. . . .	74,707	33,642	37,091	R-49.6	113,192	52,745	55,713	R-49.2	80,588	42,082	35,734	D-52.2
AL	1,269	507	695	R-54.7	1,793	708	1,080	R-60.2	1,199	502	686	R-57.2
AK	228	39	170	R-74.5	300	67	213	R-71.1	235	94	133	R-56.6
AZ	1,194	472	682	R-57.1	1,871	598	1,128	R-60.3	1,493	627	771	R-51.7
AR	688	392	284	D-57.0	791	426	358	D-53.9	763	457	306	D-59.8
CA	7,258	3,731	3,226	D-51.4	11,624	6,224	5,031	D-53.5	8,293	4,720	3,314	D-56.9
CO	1,397	589	753	R-53.9	2,039	995	992	D-48.8	1,539	833	624	D-54.1
CT	989	509	466	D-51.5	1,429	786	630	D-55.0	1,075	649	420	D-60.4
DE	228	61	165	R-72.1	356	106	246	R-69.1	252	98	144	R-57.2
FL [2]	3,767	1,537	2,161	R-57.4	5,627	2,212	3,319	R-59.0	3,852	1,600	2,183	R-56.7
GA	1,919	814	1,105	R-57.6	2,961	1,141	1,820	R-61.5	2,070	932	1,138	R-55.0
HI	360	232	117	D-64.5	417	262	148	D-62.9	338	220	118	D-65.0
ID	405	138	256	R-63.3	572	171	401	R-70.1	445	177	248	R-55.7
IL	3,429	1,741	1,657	D-50.8	4,989	2,675	2,272	D-53.6	3,453	1,986	1,423	D-57.5
IN	1,521	641	841	R-55.3	2,416	999	1,382	R-57.2	1,667	812	832	R-49.9
IA	1,013	454	546	R-54.0	1,458	625	823	R-56.4	1,033	493	522	R-50.6
KS	830	260	536	R-64.6	1,156	387	724	R-62.6	845	369	459	R-54.3
KY	1,094	351	694	R-63.4	1,635	602	1,017	R-62.2	1,254	602	612	R-48.8
LA	1,140	391	668	R-58.6	1,259	478	780	R-62.0	916	309	580	R-63.3
ME	495	290	206	D-58.5	710	418	283	D-58.9	536	351	163	D-65.4
MD	1,659	904	753	D-54.5	2,254	1,311	896	D-58.2	1,701	1,099	547	D-64.6
MA	2,220	1,529	290	D-68.8	2,927	2,060	435	D-70.4	2,244	1,632	199	D-72.7
MI	3,056	1,507	1,474	D-49.3	4,631	2,242	2,289	R-49.4	3,646	1,923	1,625	D-52.7
MN	2,202	1,098	1,030	D-49.9	2,722	1,400	1,236	D-51.4	2,179	1,153	925	D-52.9
MS	678	320	339	R-50.0	1,116	335	659	R-59.0	601	260	304	R-50.7
MO	1,854	829	986	R-53.2	2,667	1,193	1,430	R-53.6	2,097	992	1,049	R-50.0
MT	331	108	214	R-64.6	444	146	286	R-64.4	406	159	239	R-58.9
NE	474	47	387	R-81.6	765	231	515	R-67.3	596	262	334	R-56.1
NV	502	171	301	R-60.0	791	334	421	R-53.2	575	288	260	D-50.1
NH	443	176	255	R-57.5	652	244	396	R-60.8	403	209	190	D-52.0
NJ	2,006	1,030	934	D-51.4	3,285	1,721	1,515	D-52.4	2,137	1,208	903	D-56.5
NM	437	262	175	D-59.9	743	385	358	D-51.8	561	313	248	D-55.8
NY	4,701	1,778	1,526	D-37.8	7,448	3,457	2,209	D-46.4	4,687	2,538	1,160	D-54.1
NC	2,244	971	1,209	R-53.9	3,413	1,670	1,743	R-51.1	1,941	1,027	914	D-52.9
ND	231	121	110	D-52.4	311	185	126	D-59.6	218	143	75	D-65.7
OH	3,158	1,332	1,776	R-56.2	5,184	2,515	2,650	R-51.1	3,961	2,082	1,870	D-52.6
OK	1,002	392	547	R-54.6	1,375	389	875	R-63.7	905	373	518	R-57.2
OR	1,240	677	529	D-54.6	1,772	952	762	D-53.7	1,357	766	557	D-56.4
PA	3,310	1,349	1,859	R-56.2	5,151	2,478	2,565	R-49.8	4,011	2,229	1,732	D-55.6
RI	329	225	97	D-68.3	402	279	113	D-69.5	373	265	42	D-71.0
SC	984	345	569	R-57.8	1,439	486	913	R-63.5	1,086	473	600	R-55.2
SD	337	154	180	R-53.5	389	208	179	D-53.4	334	230	98	D-69.1
TN	1,529	708	771	R-50.4	2,219	1,032	1,161	R-52.3	1,715	861	800	D-50.2
TX	4,295	1,885	2,291	R-53.3	6,959	2,714	4,013	R-57.7	4,141	1,831	2,094	R-50.6
UT	557	221	322	R-57.8	909	362	520	R-57.6	570	244	292	R-51.3
VT	225	(X)	73	I-64.3	305	22	74	I-67.5	263	140	117	D-53.2
VA	1,516	440	956	R-63.0	3,004	1,023	1,817	R-60.5	2,297	947	1,223	R-53.2
WA	1,739	907	779	D-52.2	2,730	1,609	1,095	D-58.9	2,054	1,244	798	D-60.6
WV	400	264	136	D-66.0	722	415	303	D-57.6	455	264	191	D-58.0
WI	1,638	677	889	R-54.3	2,822	1,369	1,381	R-48.9	2,063	1,003	1,040	R-50.4
WY	182	66	110	R-60.5	239	100	132	R-55.2	196	92	93	R-47.6

X Not applicable.   [1] Includes votes cast for minor parties.   [2] State law does not require tabulation of votes for unopposed candidates.

Source: U.S. House of Representatives, Office of the Clerk, *Statistics of the Presidential and Congressional Election*, biennial. See also <http://clerk.house.gov/member_info/electionInfo/index.html>.

Table 391. Vote Cast for United States Representatives by Major Political Party—Congressional Districts: 2006

[In some states, the Democratic and Republican vote includes votes cast for the party candidate by endorsing parties]

State and district	Democratic candidate Name	Percent of total	Republican candidate Name	Percent of total	State and district	Democratic candidate Name	Percent of total	Republican candidate Name	Percent of total
AL	(X).......	(X)	(X).......	(X)	46th..	Brandt	36.69	Rohrabacher .	59.56
1st...	Beckerle....	31.82	Bonner.....	68.10	47th..	Sanchez....	62.33	Nguyen	37.67
2d ...	James	30.43	Everett.....	69.47	48th..	Young	37.23	Campbell ...	59.91
3d ...	Pierce	28.34	Rogers	70.11	49th..	Criscenzo ...	33.45	Issa........	63.30
4th...	Bobo	29.71	Aderholt	70.18	50th..	Busby	43.50	Bilbray	53.14
5th...	Cramer, Jr. ..	98.25	(¹).........	(¹)	51st..	Filner......	67.43	Miles	30.15
6th...	(¹).........	(¹)	Bachus.....	98.32	52d ..	Rinaldi	31.98	Hunter	64.64
7th...	Davis	99.04	(¹).........	(¹)	53d ..	Davis	67.56	Woodrum ...	30.00
AK	Benson	40.01	Young	56.57	CO	(X)........	(X)	(X)........	(X)
AZ	(X)........	(X)	(X)........	(X)	1st...	Degette	79.77	(¹).........	(¹)
1st...	Simon	43.45	Renzi	51.75	2d ...	Udall	68.24	Mancuso ...	28.31
2d ...	Thrasher....	38.89	Franks	58.62	3d ...	Salazar.....	61.59	Tipton	36.55
3d ...	Paine	38.23	Shadegg	59.27	4th...	Paccione ...	43.12	Musgrave ...	45.61
4th...	Pastor	72.52	Karg	23.92	5th...	Fawcett	40.35	Lamborn....	59.62
5th...	Mitchell.....	50.41	Hayworth ...	46.44	6th...	Winter	39.87	Tancredo ...	58.61
6th...	(¹).........	(¹)	Flake	74.80	7th...	Perlmutter ..	54.93	O'Donnell ...	42.06
7th...	Grijalva.....	61.09	Drake......	35.35	CT	(X)........	(X)	(X)........	(X)
8th...	Giffords	54.25	Graf.......	42.09	1st...	Larson	74.44	MacLean ...	25.54
AR	(X)........	(X)	(X)........	(X)	2d ...	Courtney ...	50.02	Simmons ...	49.98
1st...	Berry	69.26	Stumbaugh ..	30.74	3d ...	Delauro	76.01	Vollano.....	22.43
2d ...	Snyder.....	60.53	Mayberry ...	39.47	4th...	Farrell	47.58	Shays	50.96
3d ...	Anderson ...	37.77	Boozman ...	62.23	5th...	Murphy.....	56.46	Johnson.....	43.54
4th...	Ross	74.73	Ross	25.27	DE	Spivack	38.76	Castle	57.17
CA	(X)........	(X)	(X)........	(X)	FL	(X)........	(X)	(X)........	(X)
1st...	Thompson ..	66.23	Jones......	28.98	1st...	Roberts	31.46	Miller	68.54
2d ...	Sekhon	32.46	Herger	64.18	2d ...	Boyd	(²)	(¹).........	(¹)
3d ...	Durston	37.83	Lungren	59.48	3d ...	Brown	(²)	(¹).........	(¹)
4th...	Brown	45.87	Doolittle	49.05	4th...	Harms	30.32	Crenshaw...	69.67
5th...	Matsui	70.80	Yan	23.52	5th...	Russell.....	40.15	Brown-Waite .	59.85
6th...	Woolsey	70.22	Hooper.....	26.11	6th...	Bruderly	40.12	Stearns	59.88
7th...	Miller	83.99	(¹).........	(¹)	7th...	Chagnon ...	36.92	Mica	63.08
8th...	Pelosi......	80.39	Denunzio ...	10.72	8th...	Stuart......	45.73	Keller	52.79
9th...	Lee	86.35	Dendulk	10.73	9th...	Busansky ...	44.08	Bilirakis	55.91
10th..	Tauscher ...	66.43	Linn	33.54	10th..	Simpson	34.07	Young	65.93
11th..	McNerney ...	53.27	Pombo	46.73	11th..	Castor	69.65	Adams, Jr. ..	30.34
12th..	Lantos	76.05	Moloney	23.95	12th..	(¹).........	(¹)	Putnam	69.12
13th..	Stark	74.89	Bruno......	25.11	13th..	Jennings....	49.92	Buchanan ...	50.08
14th..	Eshoo	71.08	Smith......	24.22	14th..	Neeld......	35.63	Mack	64.37
15th..	Honda	72.33	Chukwu	27.67	15th..	Bowman	43.72	Weldon.....	56.28
16th..	Lofgren	72.71	Winston	27.29	16th..	Mahoney ...	49.55	Negron.....	47.66
17th..	Farr	77.07	De Maio	22.93	17th..	Meek	99.97	(¹).........	(¹)
18th..	Cardoza	65.48	Kanno	34.52	18th..	Patlak	37.85	Ros-Lehtinen.	62.15
19th..	Cox	39.42	Radanovich..	60.58	19th..	Wexler	(²)	(¹).........	(¹)
20th..	Costa......	100.00	(¹).........	(¹)	20th..	Schultz.....	(²)	(¹).........	(¹)
21st..	Haze	29.94	Nunes	66.74	21st..	Gonzalez ...	40.53	Diaz-Balart .	59.47
22d ..	Beery	29.30	McCarthy ...	70.70	22d ..	Klein	50.88	Shaw, Jr. ...	47.13
23d ..	Capps	65.17	Tognazzini ..	34.83	23d ..	Hastings....	(²)	(¹).........	(¹)
24th..	Martinez	37.97	Gallegly	62.02	24th..	Curtis......	42.06	Feeney.....	57.94
25th..	Rodriguez ...	35.66	McKeon	59.95	25th..	Calderin	41.53	Diaz-Balart .	58.47
26th..	Matthews ...	37.89	Dreier......	56.95	GA	(X)........	(X)	(X)........	(X)
27th..	Sherman ...	68.77	Hankwitz....	31.23	1st...	Nelson	31.50	Kingston	68.50
28th..	Berman	73.92	Kesselman ..	19.09	2d ...	Bishop, Jr. ..	67.87	Hughes	32.13
29th..	Schiff......	63.47	Bodell	27.42	3d ...	McGraw	32.35	Westmore-land	67.65
30th..	Waxman	71.45	Jones......	26.40	4th...	Johnson, Jr. .	75.36	Davis	24.64
31st..	Becerra	100.00	(¹).........	(¹)	5th...	Lewis	100.00	(¹).........	(¹)
32d ..	Solis	82.96	(¹).........	(¹)	6th...	Sinton	27.61	Price	72.39
33d ..	Watson	100.00	(¹).........	(¹)	7th...	Burns	29.09	Linder	70.91
34th..	Roybal-Allard .	76.80	Miller	23.20	8th...	Marshall	50.55	Collins	49.45
35th..	Waters	83.75	(¹).........	(¹)	9th...	Bradbury ...	23.37	Deal	76.63
36th..	Harman	63.39	Gibson	31.94	10th..	Holley	32.64	Norwood....	67.36
37th..	Millender-McDonald ..	82.40	(¹).........	(¹)	11th..	Pillion	28.94	Gingrey	71.06
38th..	Napolitano ..	75.33	Street.......	24.67	12th..	Barrow	50.30	Burns	49.70
39th..	Sanchez....	65.87	Andion	34.13	13th..	Scott	69.24	Honeycutt ...	30.76
40th..	Hoffman	30.68	Royce	66.76	HI	(X)........	(X)	(X)........	(X)
41st..	Contreras ...	33.07	Lewis	66.93	1st...	Abercrombie .	69.35	Hough	30.65
42d ..	(¹).........	(¹)	Miller	100.00	2d ...	Hirono	61.04	Hogue	38.96
43d ..	Baca	64.49	Folkens	35.51	ID	(X)........	(X)	(X)........	(X)
44th..	Vandenberg.	37.02	Calvert	59.98	1st...	Grant	44.80	Sali	49.94
45th..	Roth	39.34	Bono	60.66	2d ...	Hansen	34.43	Simpson	62.00

See footnotes at end of table.

246 Elections

Table 391. Vote Cast for United States Representatives by Major Political Party—Congressional Districts: 2006—Con.

[See headnote, p. 246]

State and district	Democratic candidate Name	Percent of total	Republican candidate Name	Percent of total
IL	(X)	(X)	(X)	(X)
1st . . .	Rush	84.06	Tabour	15.94
2d . .	Jackson, Jr. .	84.84	Belin	11.82
3d . . .	Lipinski	77.10	Wardingley . .	22.90
4th . . .	Gutierrez . . .	85.84	Melichar . . .	14.16
5th . . .	Emanuel . . .	77.99	White	22.00
6th . . .	Duckworth . .	48.65	Roskam . . .	51.35
7th . . .	Davis	86.70	Hutchinson . .	13.30
8th . . .	Bean	50.90	McSweeney .	44.01
9th . . .	Schakowsky .	74.59	Shannon . . .	25.41
10th . .	Seals	46.62	Kirk	53.38
11th . .	Pavich	44.90	Weller	55.10
12th . .	Costello	100.00	(1)	(1)
13th . .	Shannon . . .	41.66	Biggert	58.33
14th . .	Laesch	40.21	Hastert	59.79
15th . .	Gill	42.41	Johnson . . .	57.59
16th . .	Auman	32.13	Manzullo . . .	63.55
17th . .	Hare	57.17	Zinga	42.83
18th . .	Waterworth . .	32.72	LaHood	67.28
19th . .	Stover	39.29	Shimkus . . .	60.71
IN	(X)	(X)	(X)	(X)
1st . . .	Visclosky . .	69.65	Leyva	26.83
2d . . .	Donnelly	53.98	Chocola . . .	46.02
3d . . .	Hayhurst . . .	45.72	Souder	54.28
4th . . .	Sanders	37.62	Buyer	62.38
5th . . .	Carr	31.41	Burton	64.96
6th . . .	Welsh	39.99	Pence	60.01
7th . . .	Carson	53.76	Dickerson . .	46.24
8th . . .	Ellsworth . . .	61.02	Hostettler . . .	38.98
9th . . .	Hill	50.01	Sodrel	45.49
IA	(X)	(X)	(X)	(X)
1st . . .	Braley	55.10	Whalen	43.25
2d . . .	Loebsack . . .	51.43	Leach	48.57
3d . . .	Boswell . . .	51.90	Lamberti	46.50
4th . . .	Spencer	42.79	Latham	57.21
5th . . .	Schulte	35.58	King	58.53
KS	(X)	(X)	(X)	(X)
1st . . .	Doll	19.95	Moran	78.61
2d . . .	Boyda	50.60	Ryun	47.14
3d . . .	Moore	64.61	Ahner	33.68
4th . . .	McGinn	33.93	Tiahrt	63.53
KY	(X)	(X)	(X)	(X)
1st . . .	Barlow	40.42	Whitfield . . .	59.58
2d . . .	Weaver	44.59	Lewis	55.41
3d . . .	Yarmuth	50.62	Northup . . .	48.18
4th . . .	Lucas	43.38	Davis	51.69
5th . . .	Stepp	26.24	Rogers	73.76
6th . . .	Chandler . . .	85.46	(1)	(1)
LA 3 . . .	(X)	(X)	(X)	(X)
1st . . .	Gereighty . .	7.37	Jindal	88.10
2d . . .	Jefferson . . .	32.69	Lavigne	11.63
3d . . .	Melancon . .	55.03	Romero	40.31
4th . . .	Cash, Sr. . . .	16.95	McCrery . . .	57.40
5th . . .	Hearn	29.00	Alexander . .	68.26
6th . . .	(1)	(1)	Baker	82.81
7th . . .	Stagg	29.30	Boustany, Jr. .	70.70
ME	(X)	(X)	(X)	(X)
1st . . .	Allen	60.84	Curley	31.32
2d . . .	Michaud	70.52	D'Amboise . .	29.48
MD	(X)	(X)	(X)	(X)
1st . . .	Corwin	31.11	Gilchrest . . .	68.80
2d . . .	Ruppersberger . . .	69.21	Mathis	30.68
3d . . .	Sarbanes . .	64.03	White	33.76
4th . . .	Wynn	80.67	Starkman . .	18.64
5th . . .	Hoyer	82.68	(1)	(1)
6th . . .	Duck	38.43	Bartlett	58.97
7th . . .	Cummings . .	98.06	(1)	(1)
8th . . .	Hollen	76.52	Stein	21.90
MA	(X)	(X)	(X)	(X)
1st . . .	Olver	71.87	(1)	(1)
2d . . .	Neal	76.74	(1)	(1)
3d . . .	McGovern . .	77.63	(1)	(1)
4th . . .	Frank	77.79	(1)	(1)

State and district	Democratic candidate Name	Percent of total	Republican candidate Name	Percent of total
5th . . .	Meehan	73.38	(1)	(1)
6th . . .	Tierney	66.35	Barton	28.82
7th . . .	Markey	76.02	(1)	(1)
8th . . .	Capuano . . .	78.73	(1)	(1)
9th . . .	Lynch	72.25	Robinson . . .	20.09
10th . .	Delahunt . . .	62.08	Beatty	28.34
MI	(X)	(X)	(X)	(X)
1st . . .	Stupak	69.42	Hooper	27.99
2d . . .	Kotos	31.57	Hoekstra . . .	66.45
3d . . .	Rinck	34.58	Ehlers	63.10
4th . . .	Huckleberry . .	37.94	Camp	60.57
5th . . .	Kildee	72.89	Klammer . . .	25.23
6th . . .	Clark	37.93	Upton	60.59
7th . . .	Renier	45.98	Walberg . . .	49.93
8th . . .	Marcinkowski.	42.92	Rogers	55.27
9th . . .	Skinner	46.21	Knollenberg .	51.56
10th . .	Denison	31.32	Miller	66.22
11th . .	Trupiano . . .	42.99	McCotter . . .	54.05
12th . .	Levin	70.78	Shafer	26.34
13th . .	Kilpatrick . . .	99.99	(1)	(1)
14th . .	Conyers, Jr. .	85.30	Miles	14.70
15th . .	Dingell	87.95	(1)	(1)
MN	(X)	(X)	(X)	(X)
1st . . .	Walz	52.74	Gutknecht .	47.12
2d . . .	Rowley	40.04	Kline	56.20
3d . . .	Wilde	35.04	Ramstad . . .	64.85
4th . . .	McCollum . . .	69.54	Sium	30.23
5th . . .	Ellison	55.56	Fine	21.34
6th . . .	Wetterling . .	42.07	Bachmann . .	50.05
7th . . .	Peterson . . .	69.66	Barrett	28.99
8th . . .	Oberstar	63.61	Grams	34.39
MS	(X)	(X)	(X)	(X)
1st . . .	Hurt	34.08	Wicker	65.92
2d . . .	Thompson . .	64.27	Brown	35.73
3d . . .	(1)	(1)	Pickering . . .	77.67
4th . . .	Taylor	79.79	McDonnell . .	20.21
MO	(X)	(X)	(X)	(X)
1st . . .	Clay	72.89	Byrne	24.66
2d . . .	Weber	36.59	Akin	61.35
3d . . .	Carnahan . .	65.58	Bertelsen .	31.70
4th . . .	Skelton	67.64	Noland	29.40
5th . . .	Cleaver	64.25	Turk	32.30
6th . . .	Shettles . . .	35.73	Graves	61.64
7th . . .	Truman	30.11	Blunt	66.75
8th . . .	Hambacker. .	26.40	Emerson . . .	71.64
9th . . .	Burghard . . .	35.91	Hulshof	61.45
MT	Lindeen	39.13	Rehberg . . .	58.88
NE	(X)	(X)	(X)	(X)
1st . . .	Moul	41.64	Fortenberry .	58.36
2d . . .	Esch	45.34	Terry	54.66
3d . . .	Kleeb	45.01	Smith	54.99
NV	(X)	(X)	(X)	(X)
1st . . .	Berkley	64.84	Wegner	31.20
2d . . .	Derby	44.94	Heller	50.35
3d . . .	Hafen	46.57	Porter	48.46
NH	(X)	(X)	(X)	(X)
1st . . .	Shea-Porter .	51.27	Bradley	48.64
2d . . .	Hodes	52.71	Bass	45.61
NJ	(X)	(X)	(X)	(X)
1st . . .	Andrews	100.00	(1)	(1)
2d . . .	Thomas-Hughes . . .	35.60	LoBiondo . .	61.61
3d . . .	Sexton	41.04	Saxton	58.40
4th . . .	Gay	33.19	Smith	65.68
5th . . .	Aronsohn . . .	43.82	Garrett	54.91
6th . . .	Pallone, Jr. . .	68.59	Bellew	30.28
7th . . .	Stender	47.95	Ferguson . .	49.43
8th . . .	Pascrell, Jr. . .	70.89	Sandoval. . .	28.37
9th . . .	Rothman . . .	71.48	Micco	27.60
10th . .	Payne	100.00	(1)	(1)
11th . .	Wyka	36.64	Frelinghuysen .	62.09
12th . .	Holt	65.70	Sinagra	34.30
13th . .	Sires	77.52	Guarini	19.36

See footnotes at end of table.

U.S. Census Bureau, Statistical Abstract of the United States: 2008

Table 391. Vote Cast for United States Representatives by Major Political Party—Congressional Districts: 2006—Con.

[See headnote, p. 246]

State and district	Democratic candidate Name	Percent of total	Republican candidate Name	Percent of total
NM.....	(X).......	(X)	(X).......	(X)
1st	Madrid....	49.80	Wilson....	50.20
2d	Kissling	40.49	Pearce....	59.42
3d	Udall	74.64	Dolin	25.36
NY.....	(X).	(X)	(X).	(X)
1st	Bishop....	58.26	Zanzi....	35.36
2d	Israel....	64.35	Bugler	27.03
3d	Mejias....	41.39	King.	52.76
4th	McCarthy	59.69	Blessinger...	32.26
5th	Ackerman..	65.12	(¹)	(¹)
6th	Meeks	70.03	(¹)	(¹)
7th	Crowley	64.45	Brawley	12.31
8th	Nadler....	76.15	Friedman	12.22
9th	Weiner....	66.41	(¹)	(¹)
10th	Towns	70.05	Anderson	4.53
11th	Clarke	77.61	Finger	6.54
12th	Velazquez.	74.51	Romaguera..	8.51
13th	Harrison	38.89	Fossella	51.13
14th	Maloney	77.71	Maio	14.28
15th	Rangel	80.44	Daniels.	5.10
16th	Serrano	76.50	Mohamed	3.76
17th	Engel	65.95	Faulkner	20.32
18th	Lowey	62.35	Hoffman	25.82
19th	Hall	47.79	Kelly	45.52
20th	Gillibrand	50.01	Sweeney	44.17
21st	McNulty	72.27	Redlich.	20.16
22d	Hinchey	62.20	(¹)	(¹)
23d	Johnson	33.70	McHugh	57.74
24th	Arcuri	51.03	Meier	42.57
25th	Maffei.	47.12	Walsh	48.62
26th	Davis	45.06	Reynolds	48.78
27th	Higgins	79.27	McHale.	20.73
28th	Slaughter	66.87	Donnelly	24.52
29th	Massa	46.15	Kuhl, Jr.	48.93
NC.....	(X).	(X)	(X).	(X)
1st	Butterfield	100.00	(¹)	(¹)
2d	Etheridge	66.53	Mansell	33.47
3d	Weber	31.36	Jones	68.64
4th	Price	64.99	Acuff	35.01
5th	Sharpe	42.84	Foxx	57.16
6th	Blake	29.17	Coble	70.83
7th	McIntyre	72.80	Davis	27.20
8th	Kissell	49.86	Hayes	50.14
9th	Glass	33.47	Myrick	66.53
10th	Carsner	38.20	McHenry	61.80
11th	Shuler	53.79	Taylor.	46.21
12th	Watt	67.01	Fisher	32.99
13th	Miller	63.71	Robinson	36.29
ND.....	Pomeroy.	65.68	Mechtel	34.32
OH.....	(X).	(X)	(X).	(X)
1st	Cranley	47.75	Chabot.	52.25
2d	Wulsin	49.39	Schmidt	50.45
3d	Chema	41.46	Turner	58.54
4th	Siferd.	40.01	Jordan	59.99
5th	Weirauch	43.15	Gillmor	56.85
6th	Wilson	62.08	Blasdel.	37.92
7th	Conner.	39.38	Hobson	60.62
8th	Meier.	36.20	Boehner	63.80
9th	Kaptur	73.63	Leavitt	26.37
10th	Kucinich	66.41	Dovilla	33.59
11th	Jones.	83.44	String.	16.56
12th	Shamansky.	42.70	Tiberi	57.30
13th	Sutton	61.22	Foltin	38.78
14th	Katz	39.05	LaTourette	57.55
15th	Kilroy	49.72	Pryce.	50.20
16th	Shaw	41.66	Regula	58.34
17th	Ryan.	80.25	Manning II	19.75
18th	Space	62.06	Padgett	37.94
OK.....	(X).	(X)	(X).	(X)
1st	Gentges	30.87	Sullivan	63.64
2d	Boren.	72.74	Miller	27.26
3d	Barton	32.54	Lucas.	67.46
4th	Spake	35.39	Cole.	64.61
5th	Hunter	37.30	Fallin	60.38
OR.....	(X).	(X)	(X).	(X)
1st	Wu	62.83	Kitts.	33.71
2d	Voisin.	30.36	Walden.	66.81

State and district	Democratic candidate Name	Percent of total	Republican candidate Name	Percent of total
3d	Blumenauer .	73.49	Broussard...	23.47
4th	DeFazio	62.23	Feldkamp ...	37.59
5th	Hooley	53.99	Erickson	42.77
PA.....	(X).	(X)	(X).......	(¹)
1st	Brady.....	100.00	(¹)........	(¹)
2d	Fattah	88.56	Gessner	9.23
3d	Porter.	42.06	English.....	53.63
4th	Altmire	51.93	Hart.......	48.07
5th	Hilliard	39.91	Peterson	60.09
6th	Murphy.....	49.34	Gerlach	50.66
7th	Sestak	56.38	Weldon.....	43.62
8th	Murphy.....	50.30	Fitzpatrick ..	49.70
9th	Barr.......	39.67	Shuster.....	60.33
10th	Carney.....	52.95	Sherwood ...	47.05
11th	Kanjorski ...	72.47	Leonardi....	27.53
12th	Murtha	60.80	Irey	39.20
13th	Schwartz ...	66.13	Bhakta	33.87
14th	Doyle	90.09	(¹)........	(¹)
15th	Dertinger ...	43.50	Dent	53.57
16th	Herr.......	39.55	Pitts.......	56.57
17th	Holden	64.53	Wertz......	35.47
18th	Kluko	42.16	Murphy.....	57.84
19th	Avillo, Jr. ...	33.50	Platts......	63.97
RI.....	(X).	(X)	(X).......	(X)
1st	Kennedy	69.20	Scott	23.23
2d	Langevin ...	72.69	(¹)........	(¹)
SC.....	(X).	(X)	(X).......	(X)
1st	Maatta	37.86	Brown, Jr....	59.87
2d	Ellisor.....	37.29	Wilson	62.64
3d	Ballenger ...	37.10	Barrett	62.86
4th	Griffith.....	31.95	Inglis......	64.22
5th	Spratt, Jr. ...	56.90	Norman	43.06
6th	Clyburn	64.36	McLeod.....	34.15
SD.....	Herseth	69.09	Whalen.....	29.34
TN.....	(X).	(X)	(X).......	(X)
1st	Trent	36.97	Davis	61.11
2d	Greene.....	22.28	Duncan, Jr...	77.72
3d	Benedict....	34.31	Wamp	65.69
4th	Davis	66.45	Martin	33.55
5th	Cooper.....	69.00	Kovach	27.90
6th	Gordon.....	67.09	Davis	31.39
7th	Morrison....	31.82	Blackburn ...	66.05
8th	Tanner	73.18	Farmer.....	26.82
9th	Cohen	59.88	White......	17.96
TX.....	(X).	(X)	(X).......	(X)
1st	Owen......	30.25	Gohmert....	68.01
2d	Binderim	32.70	Poe	65.64
3d	Dodd	34.91	Johnson	62.51
4th	Melancon ...	33.45	Hall	64.44
5th	Thompson ...	35.59	Hensarling ..	61.76
6th	Harris......	37.08	Barton	60.46
7th	Henley	38.45	Culberson ...	59.19
8th	Wright	32.72	Brady......	67.28
9th	Green	100.00	(¹)........	(¹)
10th	Ankrum	40.40	McCaul.....	55.29
11th	(¹)........	(¹)	Conaway	100.00
12th	Morris......	31.09	Granger	66.95
13th	Waun	23.01	Thornberry ..	74.35
14th	Sklar	39.81	Paul.......	60.19
15th [4]	Hinojosa	61.78	Haring	23.72
16th	Reyes	78.67	(¹)........	(¹)
17th	Edwards	58.12	Taylor......	40.31
18th	Jackson-Lee .	76.62	Hassan	19.11
19th	Ricketts	29.77	Neugebauer .	67.70
20th	Gonzalez ...	87.35	(¹)........	(¹)
21st [4]	Courage	24.51	Smith......	60.11
22d [5,6]	Lampson	51.79	(¹)........	(¹)
23d [4,7]	Rodriguez ...	54.28	Bonilla	45.72
24th	Page	37.16	Marchant....	59.82
25th [4]	Doggett	67.26	Rostig......	26.30
26th	Barnwell	37.24	Burgess	60.21
27th	Ortiz......	56.77	Vaden	38.91
28th [4]	Cuellar	76.89	(¹)........	(¹)
29th	Green	73.54	Story	24.43
30th	Johnson	80.19	Aurbach	17.60
31st	Harrell	38.80	Carter	58.48
32d	Pryor	41.27	Sessions ...	56.42

See footnotes at end of table.

U.S. Census Bureau, Statistical Abstract of the United States: 2008

Table 391. Vote Cast for United States Representatives by Major Political Party—Congressional Districts: 2006—Con.

[See headnote, p. 246]

State and district	Democratic candidate Name	Percent of total	Republican candidate Name	Percent of total	State and district	Democratic candidate Name	Percent of total	Republican candidate Name	Percent of total
UT	(X).......	(X)	(X).......	(X)	4th...	Wright	40.07	Hastings....	59.93
1st...	Olsen. . .	32.45	Bishop	63.06	5th...	Goldmark . .	43.60	McMorris ...	56.40
2d ...	Matheson ...	59.00	Christensen. .	37.30	6th...	Dicks	70.60	Cloud......	29.40
3d ...	Burridge	32.24	Cannon	57.71	7th...	McDermott . .	79.41	Beren......	15.73
VT ...	Welch	53.22	Rainville	44.54	8th...	Burner	48.54	Reichert	51.46
VA	(X).......	(X)	(X).......	(X)	9th...	Smith......	65.72	Cofchin.....	34.28
1st...	O'Donnell ...	35.48	Davis	62.96	WV	(X)........	(X)	(X)........	(X)
2d ...	Kellam	48.45	Drake......	51.27	1st...	Mollohan. . .	64.29	Wakim	35.65
3d ...	Scott	96.08	(1)........	(1)	2d ...	Callaghan . .	42.82	Capito	57.18
4th. . .	(1)........	(1)	Forbes	76.12	3d ...	Rahall II	69.36	Wolfe......	30.64
5th...	Weed II	39.93	Goode, Jr....	59.11	WI.....	(X)........	(X)	(X)........	(X)
6th...	(1)........	(1)	Goodlatte	75.09	1st...	Thomas	37.17	Ryan	62.63
7th...	Nachman ...	34.40	Cantor	63.85	2d ...	Baldwin	62.82	Magnum....	37.09
8th...	Moran	66.40	O'Donoghue .	30.58	3d ...	Kind.......	64.79	Nelson	35.12
9th...	Boucher	67.76	Carrico.....	32.17	4th...	Moore	71.31	Rivera	28.42
10th. .	Feder......	40.96	Wolf.......	57.32	5th...	Kennedy....	35.68	Sensenbren-ner, Jr.	61.76
11th. .	Hurst......	43.57	Davis	55.45	6th...	(1)........	(1)	Petri.	98.92
WA....	(X)........	(X)	(X)........	(X)	7th...	Obey	62.17	Reid.......	34.97
1st...	Inslee......	67.72	Ishmael	32.28	8th...	Kagen	50.90	Gard	48.76
2d ...	Larsen	64.16	Roulstone ...	35.84	WY	Trauner	47.05	Cubin.	47.57
3d ...	Baird	63.12	Messmore...	36.88					

X Not applicable. [1] No candidate. [2] According to state law, it is not required to tabulate votes for unopposed candidates. [3] Louisiana holds an open-primary election with candidates from all parties running on the same ballot. Any candidate who receives a majority is elected; if no candidate receives 50 percent, there is a run-off election in November between the top two finishers. [4] On June 28, 2006, the U.S. Supreme Court declared that the Texas legislature's redistricting plan violated the Voting Rights Act. As a result, on August 4, 2006, replacement district boundaries were announced for the 2006 election for the 15th, 21st, 23rd, 25th, and 28th districts. On election day in November, these five redrawn districts held a special election, pursuant to section 204.021 of the Texas Election Code. If any candidate received over 50 percent, they were elected. Otherwise, a runoff election in December would decide the seat. [5] A special election was held to fill the unexpired term of Tom DeLay. Don Richardson (7,405 votes) and Shelley Sekula Gibbs (76,924 votes) ran as Republicans in the special election and as write-in candidates in the general election for the 22nd District. Sekula Gibbs won the special election and was sworn in on November 13, 2006, representing the district for the few remaining weeks of the 109th Congress. Lampson won the general election and was sworn in on January 4, 2007. [6] Reflects votes cast in the general election. [7] Reflects votes cast in the runoff election held on December 12, 2006.

Source: U.S. House of Representatives, Office of the Clerk, *Statistics of the Presidential and Congressional Election*, biennial. See also <http://clerk.house.gov/member_info/election.html>.

Table 392. Composition of Congress by Political Party: 1975 to 2007

[D = Democratic, R = Republican. As of beginning of first session of each Congress. Data reflect immediate result of elections. Vacancies and third party candidates are noted]

Year	Party and president	Congress	House Majority party	House Minority party	House Other	Senate Majority party	Senate Minority party	Senate Other
1975 [1]	R (Ford)	94th	D-291	R-144	–	D-61	R-37	2
1977 [2]	D (Carter)	95th	D-292	R-143	–	D-61	R-38	1
1979 [2]	D (Carter)	96th	D-277	R-158	–	D-58	R-41	1
1981 [2]	R (Reagan)	97th	D-242	R-192	1	R-53	D-46	–
1983	R (Reagan)	98th	D-269	R-166	–	R-54	D-46	–
1985	R (Reagan)	99th	D-253	R-182	–	R-53	D-47	–
1987	R (Reagan)	100th	D-258	R-177	–	D-55	R-45	–
1989	R (Bush)	101st	D-260	R-175	–	D-55	R-45	–
1991 [3]	R (Bush)	102d	D-267	R-167	1	D-56	R-44	–
1993 [3]	D (Clinton)	103d	D-258	R-176	1	D-57	R-43	–
1995 [3]	D (Clinton)	104th	R-230	D-204	1	R-52	D-48	–
1997 [4]	D (Clinton)	105th	R-226	D-207	2	R-55	D-45	–
1999 [4]	D (Clinton)	106th	R-223	D-211	1	R-55	D-45	–
2001 [4]	R (Bush)	107th	R-221	D-212	2	D-50	R-50	–
2003 [5, 6]	R (Bush)	108th	R-229	D-204	1	R-51	D-48	1
2005 [5]	R (Bush)	109th	R-232	D-202	1	R-55	D-44	1
2007 [7]	R (Bush)	110th	D-233	R-202	–	D-49	R-49	2

– Represents zero. [1] Senate had one Independent and one Conservative-Republican. [2] Senate had one Independent. [3] House had one Independent-Socialist. [4] House had one Independent-Socialist and one Independent. [5] House and Senate each had one Independent. [6] House had one vacancy. [7] Senate had two Independents.

Source: U.S. House of Representatives, Office of the Clerk, *Official List of Members*, annual. See also <http://clerk.house.gov /member_info/olm_110.pdf>.

Elections 249

Table 393. Composition of Congress by Political Party Affiliation—States: 2001 to 2007

[Figures are for the beginning of the first session (as of January 3). Dem. = Democratic; Rep. = Republican]

State	Representatives								Senators							
	107th Cong., [1, 2, 3] 2001		108th Cong., [1] 2003		109th Cong., [1, 4, 5] 2005		110th Cong., 2007		107th Cong., [6] 2001		108th Cong., [6] 2003		109th Cong., [4, 6] 2005		110th Cong., [7] 2007	
	Dem.	Rep.	Dem.	Rep.	Dem.	Rep.	Dem.	Rep.	Dem.	Rep.	Dem.	Rep.	Dem.	Rep.	Dem.	Rep.
U.S. ...	**211**	**221**	**205**	**229**	**202**	**231**	**233**	**202**	**50**	**50**	**48**	**51**	**44**	**55**	**49**	**49**
AL.......	2	5	2	5	2	5	2	5	–	2	–	2	–	2	–	2
AK.......	–	1	–	1	–	1	–	1	–	2	–	2	–	2	–	2
AZ.......	1	5	2	6	2	6	4	4	–	2	–	2	–	2	–	2
AR.......	3	1	3	1	3	1	3	1	1	1	2	–	2	–	2	–
CA.......	31	20	33	20	33	20	34	19	2	–	2	–	2	–	2	–
CO	2	4	2	5	3	4	4	3	–	2	–	2	1	1	1	1
CT.......	3	3	2	3	2	3	4	1	2	–	2	–	2	–	1	–
DE.......	–	1	–	1	–	1	–	1	2	–	2	–	2	–	2	–
FL.......	8	15	7	18	7	18	9	16	2	–	2	–	1	1	1	1
GA	3	8	5	8	6	7	6	7	2	–	1	1	–	2	–	2
HI	2	–	2	–	2	–	2	–	2	–	2	–	2	–	2	–
ID	–	2	–	2	–	2	–	2	–	2	–	2	–	2	–	2
IL	10	10	9	10	10	9	10	9	1	1	1	1	2	–	2	–
IN	4	6	3	6	2	7	5	4	1	1	1	1	1	1	1	1
IA	1	4	1	4	1	4	3	2	1	1	1	1	1	1	1	1
KS.......	1	3	1	3	1	3	2	2	–	2	–	2	–	2	–	2
KY.......	1	5	1	5	1	5	2	4	–	2	–	2	–	2	–	2
LA.......	2	5	3	4	2	5	2	5	2	–	2	–	1	1	1	1
ME	2	–	2	–	2	–	2	–	–	2	–	2	–	2	–	2
MD	4	4	6	2	6	2	6	2	2	–	2	–	2	–	2	–
MA	10	–	10	–	10	–	10	–	2	–	2	–	2	–	2	–
MI	9	7	6	9	6	9	6	9	2	–	2	–	2	–	2	–
MN	5	3	4	4	4	4	5	3	2	–	1	1	1	1	1	1
MS	3	2	2	2	2	2	2	2	–	2	–	2	–	2	–	2
MO	4	5	4	5	4	5	4	5	1	1	–	2	–	2	1	1
MT	–	1	–	1	–	1	–	1	1	1	1	1	1	1	2	–
NE.......	–	3	–	3	–	3	–	3	1	1	1	1	1	1	1	1
NV.......	1	1	1	2	1	2	1	2	1	1	1	1	1	1	1	1
NH.......	–	2	–	2	–	2	2	–	–	2	–	2	–	2	–	2
NJ.......	7	6	7	6	7	6	7	6	2	–	2	–	2	–	2	–
NM	1	2	1	2	1	2	1	2	1	1	1	1	1	1	1	1
NY.......	19	12	19	10	20	9	23	6	2	–	2	–	2	–	2	–
NC	5	7	6	7	6	7	7	6	1	1	1	1	–	2	–	2
ND	1	–	1	–	1	–	1	–	2	–	2	–	2	–	2	–
OH	8	11	6	12	6	11	7	11	–	2	–	2	–	2	1	1
OK	1	5	1	4	1	4	1	4	–	2	–	2	–	2	–	2
OR.......	4	1	4	1	4	1	4	1	1	1	1	1	1	1	1	1
PA.......	10	11	7	12	7	12	11	8	–	2	–	2	–	2	1	1
RI	2	–	2	–	2	–	2	–	1	1	1	1	1	1	2	–
SC.......	2	4	2	4	2	4	2	4	1	1	1	1	–	2	–	2
SD.......	–	1	–	1	1	–	1	–	2	–	2	–	1	1	1	1
TN.......	4	5	5	4	5	4	5	4	–	2	–	2	–	2	–	2
TX.......	17	13	17	15	11	21	13	19	–	2	–	2	–	2	–	2
UT.......	1	2	1	2	1	2	1	2	1	1	1	1	1	–	1	–
VT.......	–	–	–	–	–	1	–	1	1	1	1	–	1	–	1	–
VA.......	4	6	3	8	3	8	3	8	–	2	–	2	–	2	1	1
WA	6	3	6	3	6	3	6	3	2	–	2	–	2	–	2	–
WV	2	1	2	1	2	1	2	1	2	–	2	–	2	–	2	–
WI.......	5	4	4	4	4	4	5	3	2	–	2	–	2	–	2	–
WY.......	–	1	–	1	–	1	–	1	–	2	–	2	–	2	–	2

– Represents zero. [1] Vermont had one Independent–Socialist representative. [2] California had one vacancy. [3] Virginia had one Independent representative. [4] Vacancy due to the resignation of Rob Portman (OH) April 29, 2005. [5] As of June 28, 2005. [6] Vermont had one Independent senator. (Jeffords was reelected in Vermont in 2000 as a Republican, but subsequently switched to Independent status in June 2001.) [7] Vermont and Connecticut both had one Independent senator.

Source: U.S. Congress, Joint Committee on Printing, *Congressional Directory*, biennial through 2001; Starting in 2003, Office of the Clerk, *Official List of Members by State*, annual. See also <http://clerk.house.gov/member_info/olm_110.pdf>.

250 Elections

Table 394. Members of Congress—Selected Characteristics: 1991 to 2005

[As of beginning of first session of each Congress, (January 3). Figures for Representatives exclude vacancies]

Members of Congress and year	Male	Female	Black [1]	API [2]	His-panic [3]	Age [4] (in years) Under 40	40 to 49	50 to 59	60 to 69	70 and over	Seniority [5,6] Less than 2 yrs.	2 to 9 yrs.	10 to 19 yrs.	20 to 29 yrs.	30 yrs. or more
REPRESENTATIVES															
102d Cong., 1991 ...	407	28	[7]26	5	11	39	152	134	86	24	55	178	147	44	11
103d Cong., 1993 [8] ...	388	47	[7]38	7	17	47	151	128	89	15	118	141	132	32	12
104th Cong., 1995. ...	388	47	[9]40	7	17	53	155	135	79	13	92	188	110	36	9
106th Cong., 1999. ...	379	56	[9]39	6	19	23	116	173	87	35	41	236	104	46	7
107th Cong., 2001. ...	376	59	[9]39	7	19	14	97	167	117	35	44	155	158	63	14
108th Cong., 2003. ...	376	59	[9]39	5	22	19	86	174	121	32	54	178	140	48	13
109th Cong., 2005. ...	369	65	[9]42	4	23	22	96	175	113	28	37	173	158	48	18
SENATORS															
102d Cong., 1991 ...	98	2	–	2	–	–	23	46	24	7	5	34	47	10	4
103d Cong., 1993 [8] ...	93	7	1	2	–	1	16	48	22	12	15	30	39	11	5
104th Cong., 1995. ...	92	8	1	2	–	1	14	41	27	17	12	38	30	15	5
106th Cong., 1999. ...	91	9	–	2	–	–	14	38	35	13	8	39	33	14	6
107th Cong., 2001. ...	87	13	–	2	–	–	8	39	33	18	11	34	30	14	9
108th Cong., 2003. ...	86	14	–	2	–	1	12	29	34	24	9	42	29	13	7
109th Cong., 2005. ...	86	14	1	2	2	–	17	29	33	21	9	41	29	14	7

– Represents zero. [1] Source: Joint Center for Political and Economic Studies, Washington, DC, *Black Elected Officials: Statistical Summary*, annual (copyright). [2] Asian and Pacific Islanders. Source: Prior to 2005, Library of Congress, Congressional Research Service, "Asian Pacific Americans in the United States Congress," Report 94-767 GOV; starting 2005, U.S. House of Representatives, "House Press Gallery," <http://www.house.gov/daily/hpg.htm> (as of 4 January 2007) and U.S. Senate, "Minorities in the Senate," <http://www.senate.gov/artandhistory/history/common/briefing/minority_senators.htm>. [3] Source: National Association of Latino Elected and Appointed Officials, Washington, DC, *National Roster of Hispanic Elected Officials*, annual. [4] Some members do not provide date of birth. [5] Represents consecutive years of service. [6] Some members do not provide years of service. [7] Includes District of Columbia delegate but not Virgin Islands Delegate. [8] Includes members elected to fill vacant seats through June 14, 1993. [9] Includes District of Columbia and Virgin Islands delegate.

Source: Except as noted, compiled by U.S. Census Bureau from data published in *Congressional Directory*, biennial.

Table 395. U.S. Congress—Measures Introduced and Enacted and Time in Session: 1989 to 2006

[Excludes simple and concurrent resolutions]

Item	101st Cong., 1989–90	102d Cong., 1991–92	103d Cong., 1993–94	104th Cong., 1995–96	105th Cong., 1997–98	106th Cong., 1999–00	107th Cong., 2001–02	108th Cong., 2003–04	109th Cong., 2005–06
Measures introduced	6,664	6,775	8,544	6,808	7,732	9,158	9,130	8,625	10,703
Bills	5,977	6,212	7,883	6,545	7,532	8,968	8,953	8,468	10,560
Joint resolutions	687	563	661	263	200	190	177	157	143
Measures enacted	666	609	473	337	404	604	337	504	418
Public [1]	650	589	465	333	394	580	331	498	417
Private [2]	16	20	8	4	10	24	6	6	1
HOUSE OF REPRESENTATIVES									
Number of days	281	280	265	290	251	272	265	243	241
Number of hours	1,688	1,796	1,887	2,445	2,001	2,179	1,694	1,894	1,917
Number of hours per day...	6.0	6.4	7.1	8.4	8.0	8.0	6.4	7.8	8.0
SENATE									
Number of days	274	287	291	343	296	303	322	300	297
Number of hours	2,254	2,292	2,514	2,876	2,188	2,200	2,279	2,486	2,250
Number of hours per day...	8.2	8.0	8.6	8.4	7.4	7.3	7.1	8.3	7.6

[1] Laws on public matters that apply to all persons. [2] Laws designed to provide legal relief to specified persons or entities adversely affected by laws of general applicability.

Source: U.S. Congress, *Congressional Record* and *Daily Calendar*, selected issues. See also <http://www.senate.gov /pagelayout/reference/two_column_table/Resumes.htm>.

Table 396. Congressional Bills Vetoed: 1961 to 2007

Period	President	Total vetoes	Regular vetoes	Pocket vetoes	Vetoes sustained	Bills passed over veto
1961–63	John F. Kennedy	21	12	9	21	–
1963–69	Lyndon B. Johnson	30	16	14	30	–
1969–74	Richard M. Nixon	43	26	17	36	7
1974–77	Gerald R. Ford	66	48	18	54	12
1977–81	Jimmy Carter	31	13	18	29	2
1981–89	Ronald W. Reagan	78	39	39	69	9
1989–93	George Bush	44	29	15	43	1
1993–2001	William J. Clinton	37	36	1	34	2
2001–2007 [1]	George W. Bush	1	1	–	1	–

– Represents zero. [1] Through March 20, 2007.

Source: U.S. Congress, Senate Library, *Presidential Vetoes . . . 1789–1968*; U.S. Congress, *Calendars of the U.S. House of Representatives and History of Legislation*, annual. See also <http://clerk.house.gov/>.

U.S. Census Bureau, Statistical Abstract of the United States: 2008

Table 397. **Number of Governors by Political Party Affiliation: 1975 to 2007**

[Reflects figures after inaugurations for each year]

Year	Demo-cratic	Repub-lican	Indepen-dent/other	Year	Demo-cratic	Repub-lican	Indepen-dent/other	Year	Demo-cratic	Repub-lican	Indepen-dent/other
1975...	36	13	1	1996 [1]..	18	31	1	2002...	22	27	1
1980...	31	19	–	1997...	17	32	1	2003...	23	27	–
1985...	34	16	–	1998...	17	32	1	2004...	22	28	–
1990...	29	21	–	1999...	17	31	1	2005...	22	28	–
1994...	29	19	2	2000...	18	30	2	2006...	22	28	–
1995...	19	30	1	2001...	19	29	2	2007...	28	22	–

– Represents zero. [1] Arkansas's Democratic governor was succeeded midyear by a Republican.

Source: National Governors Association, Washington, DC, 1970–87 and 1991–2007, *Directory of Governors of the American States, Commonwealths & Territories*, annual; and 1988–90, *Directory of Governors*, annual (copyright).

Table 398. **Vote Cast for and Governor Elected by State: 2004 to 2006**

[In thousands (1,250 represents 1,250,000), except percent. D = Democratic, R = Republican]

State	2004 Total vote [1]	2004 Repub-lican	2004 Demo-crat	2004 Percent leading party	2006 Total vote [1]	2006 Repub-lican	2006 Demo-crat	2006 Percent leading party	Current governor [2]
AL....	(X)	(X)	(X)	(X)	1,250	718	520	R-57.4	Bob Riley
AK....	(X)	(X)	(X)	(X)	238	115	97	R-48.1	Sarah Palin
AZ....	(X)	(X)	(X)	(X)	1,534	544	960	D-62.6	Janet Napolitano
AR....	(X)	(X)	(X)	(X)	774	315	430	D-55.5	Mike Beebe
CA....	(X)	(X)	(X)	(X)	8,679	4,850	3,377	R-55.9	Arnold Schwarzenegger
CO ...	(X)	(X)	(X)	(X)	1,558	626	888	D-57.0	Bill Ritter
CT ...	(X)	(X)	(X)	(X)	1,123	710	398	R-63.2	M. Jodi Rell
DE....	365	167	186	D-50.9	(X)	(X)	(X)	(X)	Ruth Ann Minner
FL....	(X)	(X)	(X)	(X)	4,829	2,520	2,178	R-52.2	Charlie Crist
GA ...	(X)	(X)	(X)	(X)	2,122	1,230	811	R-57.9	Sonny Perdue
HI	(X)	(X)	(X)	(X)	349	215	122	R-61.7	Linda Lingle
ID	(X)	(X)	(X)	(X)	489	276	199	R-52.7	C. L. "Butch" Otter
IL	(X)	(X)	(X)	(X)	3,586	1,369	1,736	D-48.4	Rod Blagojevich
IN	2,448	1,303	1,114	R-53.2	(X)	(X)	(X)	(X)	Mitch Daniels
IA	(X)	(X)	(X)	(X)	1,059	467	569	D-53.7	Chet Culver
KS.[3]..	(X)	(X)	(X)	(X)	850	344	492	D-57.9	Kathleen Sebelius
KY [3] ..	1,083	596	487	R-55.0	(X)	(X)	(X)	(X)	Ernie Fletcher
LA [3] ..	1,416	369	872	D-52.0	(X)	(X)	(X)	(X)	Kathleen Blanco
ME ...	(X)	(X)	(X)	(X)	551	166	210	D-38.1	John Baldacci
MD ...	(X)	(X)	(X)	(X)	1,717	825	942	D-52.7	Martin O'Malley
MA ...	(X)	(X)	(X)	(X)	2,244	784	1,235	D-55.0	Deval Patrick
MI....	(X)	(X)	(X)	(X)	3,801	1,608	2,143	D 56.3	Jennifer M. Granholm
MN ...	(X)	(X)	(X)	(X)	2,218	1,029	1,007	R-46.4	Tim Pawlenty
MS [3] ..	894	470	410	R-52.6	(X)	(X)	(X)	(X)	Haley Barbour
MO ...	2,720	1,382	1,301	R-50.8	(X)	(X)	(X)	(X)	Matt Blunt
MT ...	456	205	225	D-50.4	(X)	(X)	(X)	(X)	Brian Schweitzer
NE....	(X)	(X)	(X)	(X)	593	436	145	R-73.3	Dave Heineman
NV....	(X)	(X)	(X)	(X)	582	279	256	R-47.9	Jim Gibbons
NH ...	684	326	340	D-51.0	404	105	298	D-74.0	John Lynch
NJ [4]..	2,290	985	1,225	D-53.5	(X)	(X)	(X)	(X)	Jon Corzine
NM ...	(X)	(X)	(X)	(X)	559	174	385	D-68.8	Bill Richardson
NY....	(X)	(X)	(X)	(X)	4,698	1,106	2,741	D-58.3	Eliot Spitzer
NC ...	3,487	1,495	1,939	D-55.6	(X)	(X)	(X)	(X)	Michael Easley
ND ...	310	221	85	R-71.3	(X)	(X)	(X)	(X)	John Hoeven
OH ...	(X)	(X)	(X)	(X)	4,184	1,471	2,428	D-58.0	Ted Strickland
OK ...	(X)	(X)	(X)	(X)	926	310	616	D-66.5	Brad Henry
OR ...	(X)	(X)	(X)	(X)	1,400	534	579	D-41.3	Ted Kulongoski
PA....	(X)	(X)	(X)	(X)	4,093	1,622	2,471	D-60.4	Edward Rendell
RI	(X)	(X)	(X)	(X)	387	197	190	R-51.0	Don Carcieri
SC....	(X)	(X)	(X)	(X)	1,092	602	489	R-55.1	Mark Sanford
SD....	(X)	(X)	(X)	(X)	356	207	121	R-61.7	Mike Rounds
TN....	(X)	(X)	(X)	(X)	1,819	541	1,247	D-68.6	Phil Bredesen
TX....	(X)	(X)	(X)	(X)	4,399	1,717	1,310	R-39.0	Rick Perry
UT....	907	525	374	R-57.8	(X)	(X)	(X)	(X)	Jon Huntsman
VT....	309	182	117	R-58.7	263	148	108	R-56.3	Jim Douglas
VA [4]..	1,984	912	1,026	D-52.0	(X)	(X)	(X)	(X)	Tim Kaine
WA ...	2,883	1,373	1,373	D-48.8	(X)	(X)	(X)	(X)	Chris Gregoire
WV....	744	253	473	D-63.5	(X)	(X)	(X)	(X)	Joe Manchin III
WI....	(X)	(X)	(X)	(X)	2,162	979	1,139	D-52.7	Jim Doyle
WY....	(X)	(X)	(X)	(X)	194	58	136	D-69.8	Dave Freudenthal

X Not applicable. [1] Includes minor party and scattered votes. [2] As of 13 August 2007. Source: National Governors Association, Washington, DC. See Internet site: <http://www.nga.org/portal/site/nga/menuitem.5dbb9333fc52447ae8ebb856a11010a0//>. [3] Voting year 2003. [4] Voting year 2005.
Source: Except as noted, the Council of State Governments, Lexington, KY, *The Book of States 2007*, annual (copyright).

U.S. Census Bureau, Statistical Abstract of the United States: 2008

Table 399. Composition of State Legislatures by Political Party Affiliation: 2006 and 2007

[Data reflect election results as of February in year shown, except as noted. Figures reflect immediate results of elections, including holdover members in state houses which do not have all of their members running for re-election. Dem. = Democrat, Rep. = Republican, Vac. = Vacancies. In general, Lower House refers to body consisting of state representatives; Upper House, of state senators]

State	Lower House								Upper House							
	2006				2007 [1]				2006				2007 [1]			
	Dem.	Rep.	Other	Vac.	Dem.	Rep.	Other	Vac.	Dem.	Rep.	Other	Vac.	Dem.	Rep.	Other	Vac.
U.S.	2,702	2,675	15	19	2,971	2,422	15	3	952	964	3	3	1,010	909	3	–
AL [2]	63	42	–	–	62	43	–	–	25	10	–	–	23	12	–	–
AK [3]	14	26	–	–	17	23	–	–	8	12	–	–	9	11	–	–
AZ [4]	21	39	–	–	27	33	–	–	12	18	–	–	13	17	–	–
AR [3]	72	28	–	–	75	25	–	–	27	8	–	–	27	8	–	–
CA [3]	48	32	–	–	48	32	–	–	25	15	–	–	25	15	–	–
CO [3]	35	30	–	–	39	26	–	–	18	17	–	–	20	15	–	–
CT [4]	99	52	–	–	107	44	–	–	24	12	–	–	24	12	–	–
DE [3]	15	25	1	–	18	23	–	–	13	8	–	–	13	8	–	–
FL [3]	36	84	–	–	41	79	–	–	14	26	–	–	14	26	–	–
GA [4]	80	99	1	–	74	106	–	–	22	34	–	–	22	34	–	–
HI [3]	41	10	–	–	43	8	–	–	20	5	–	–	20	5	–	–
ID [4]	13	57	–	–	19	51	–	–	7	28	–	–	7	28	–	–
IL [5]	65	53	–	–	66	52	–	–	31	27	1	–	37	22	–	–
IN [3]	48	52	–	–	51	49	–	–	17	33	–	–	17	33	–	–
IA [3]	49	51	–	–	54	46	–	–	25	25	–	–	30	20	–	–
KS [3]	42	83	–	–	47	78	–	–	10	30	–	–	10	30	–	–
KY [3]	57	43	–	–	61	39	–	–	15	22	1	–	16	21	1	–
LA [2]	67	37	1	–	59	43	1	2	24	15	–	–	24	15	–	–
ME [4]	76	73	2	–	89	60	2	–	19	16	–	–	18	17	–	–
MD [2]	98	43	–	–	104	37	–	–	33	14	–	–	33	14	–	–
MA [4]	137	20	–	3	141	19	–	–	34	6	–	–	35	5	–	–
MI [3]	50	58	–	2	58	52	–	–	16	22	–	–	17	21	–	–
MN [3]	66	68	–	–	85	49	–	–	35	31	1	–	44	23	–	–
MS [2]	74	47	–	1	74	47	–	1	28	24	–	–	25	27	–	–
MO [3]	64	96	–	3	71	92	–	–	11	22	–	1	13	21	–	–
MT [3]	50	50	–	–	49	50	1	–	27	23	–	–	26	24	–	–
NE [6]	(6)	(6)	(6)	(6)	(6)	(6)	(6)	(6)	(6)	(6)	(6)	(6)	(6)	(6)	(6)	(6)
NV [4]	26	15	–	1	27	15	–	–	9	12	–	–	10	11	–	–
NH [4]	149	247	–	4	239	161	–	–	8	16	–	–	14	10	–	–
NJ [3]	49	31	–	–	49	31	–	–	22	18	–	–	22	18	–	–
NM [3]	42	28	–	–	42	28	–	–	24	18	–	–	24	18	–	–
NY [4]	104	46	–	–	105	45	–	–	27	35	–	–	29	33	–	–
NC [4]	63	57	–	–	68	52	–	–	29	21	–	–	31	19	–	–
ND [2]	27	67	–	–	33	61	–	–	15	32	–	–	21	26	–	–
OH [3]	38	61	–	–	46	53	–	–	11	22	–	–	12	21	–	–
OK [3]	44	57	–	–	44	57	–	–	26	22	–	–	24	24	–	–
OR [3]	27	33	–	–	31	29	–	–	18	12	–	–	17	11	2	–
PA [3]	93	110	–	–	102	101	–	–	20	30	–	–	21	29	–	–
RI [4]	60	15	–	–	62	13	–	–	33	5	–	–	33	5	–	–
SC [3]	49	74	–	1	51	73	–	–	20	26	–	–	20	26	–	–
SD [4]	19	51	–	–	20	50	–	–	10	25	–	–	15	20	–	–
TN [3]	53	46	–	–	53	46	–	–	15	17	–	1	16	17	–	–
TX [3]	62	87	–	1	69	81	–	–	12	19	–	–	11	20	–	–
UT [3]	19	56	–	–	20	55	–	–	8	21	–	–	8	21	–	–
VT [4]	83	60	7	–	93	49	8	–	21	9	–	–	23	7	–	–
VA [3]	39	56	3	2	40	57	3	–	16	23	–	1	17	23	–	–
WA [3]	55	43	–	–	62	36	–	–	26	23	–	–	32	17	–	–
WV [3]	68	32	–	–	72	28	–	–	21	13	–	–	23	11	–	–
WI [3]	39	59	–	1	47	52	–	–	14	19	–	–	18	15	–	–
WY [3]	14	46	–	–	17	43	–	–	7	23	–	–	7	23	–	–

– Represents zero.   [1] As of 7 March 2007.   [2] Members of both houses serve 4-year terms.   [3] Upper House members serve 4-year terms and Lower House members serve 2-year terms.   [4] Members of both houses serve 2-year terms.   [5] Illinois—4- and 2-year term depending on district.   [6] Nebraska—4-year term and only state to have a nonpartisan legislature.

Source: The Council of State Governments, Lexington, KY, *The Book of States 2007*, annual (copyright).

U.S. Census Bureau, Statistical Abstract of the United States: 2008

Table 400. Political Party Control of State Legislatures by Party: 1983 to 2007

[As of beginning of year. Nebraska has a nonpartisan legislature]

Year	Legislatures under— Democratic control	Legislatures under— Split control or tie	Legislatures under— Republican control	Year	Legislatures under— Democratic control	Legislatures under— Split control or tie	Legislatures under— Republican control	Year	Legislatures under— Democratic control	Legislatures under— Split control or tie	Legislatures under— Republican control
1983 [1]	34	4	11	1994	24	17	8	2002	17	15	17
1985	27	11	11	1995	18	12	19	2003	16	12	21
1987 [2]	28	12	9	1996	16	15	18	2004	17	11	21
1989 [2]	28	13	8	1997	20	11	18	2005	19	10	20
1990	29	11	9	1999	20	12	17	2006	19	10	20
1992	29	14	6	2000	16	15	18	2007	22	12	15
1993	25	16	8	2001	16	15	18				

[1] Two 1984 midterm recall elections resulted in a change in control of the Michigan State Senate. At the time of the 1984 election, therefore, Democrats controlled 33 legislatures.　[2] A party change during the year by a Democratic representative broke the tie in the Indiana House of Representatives, giving the Republicans control of both chambers.

Source: National Conference of State Legislatures, Denver, CO, *State Legislatures*, periodic.

Table 401. Women Holding State Public Offices by Office and State: 2006

[As of January. For data on women in U.S. Congress, see Table 394]

State	Total	State-wide elective executive office [1]	State legislature Total	State legislature Percent [2]	State	Total	State-wide elective executive office [1]	State legislature Total	State legislature Percent [2]
U.S.	1,759	78	1,681	23	MO	45	3	42	21
					MT	38	1	37	25
AL	21	5	16	11	NE	14	2	12	([3])
AK	11	–	11	18	NV	22	1	21	33
AZ	33	3	30	33	NH	127	–	127	30
AR	23	–	23	17	NJ	23	–	23	19
CA	37	–	37	31	NM	38	3	35	31
CO	34	2	32	32	NY	48	1	47	22
CT	58	4	54	29	NC	43	4	39	23
DE	22	1	21	34	ND	25	–	23	16
FL	40	1	39	24	OH	26	2	24	18
GA	47	3	44	19	OK	27	5	22	15
HI	25	1	24	32	OR	26	1	25	28
ID	30	1	29	28	PA	35	1	34	13
IL	50	2	48	27	RI	19	–	19	17
IN	30	3	27	18	SC	16	1	15	9
IA	32	2	30	20	SD	17	–	17	16
KS	56	3	53	32	TN	22	–	22	17
KY	17	1	16	12	TX	39	3	36	20
LA	26	1	25	17	UT	22	–	22	21
ME	43	–	43	23	VT	61	1	60	33
MD	67	–	67	36	VA	24	–	24	17
MA	52	1	51	26	WA	51	2	49	33
MI	33	2	31	21	WV	22	1	21	16
MN	66	3	63	31	WI	37	3	34	26
MS	24	1	23	13	WY	15	1	14	16

– Represents zero.　[1] Excludes women elected to the judiciary, women appointed to state cabinet-level positions, women elected to executive posts by the legislature, and elected members of university Board of Trustees or Board of Education.　[2] Calculated by U.S. Census Bureau based on total state legislature (both upper and lower houses) data from Table 399.　[3] Nebraska—4-year term and only state to have a nonpartisan legislature.

Source: Center for the American Woman and Politics, Eagleton Institute of Politics, Rutgers University, New Brunswick, NJ, information releases, (copyright).

254　Elections

Table 402. Black Elected Officials by Office, 1970 to 2002, and State, 2002

[As of January 2002, no Black elected officials had been identified in Montana or South Dakota]

State	Total	U.S. and state legislatures[1]	City and county offices[2]	Law enforcement[3]	Education[4]	State	Total	U.S. and state legislatures[1]	City and county offices[2]	Law enforcement[3]	Education[4]
1970 (Feb.)..	1,469	179	715	213	362	MD	192	40	101	41	10
1980 (July)..	4,890	326	2,832	526	1,206	MA	79	6	60	2	11
1990 (Jan.)..	7,335	436	4,485	769	1,645	MI	353	24	153	62	114
1995 (Jan.)..	8,385	604	4,954	987	1,840	MN	20	2	4	10	4
1999 (Jan.)..	8,896	618	5,354	997	1,927	MS	950	46	646	121	137
2000 (Jan.)..	9,001	621	5,420	1,037	1,923	MO	206	19	145	17	25
2001 (Jan.)..	9,061	633	5,456	1,044	1,928	NE.	9	1	5	–	3
						NV.	13	5	4	2	2
2002 (Jan.)..	9,430	636	5,753	1,081	1,960	NH	5	5	–	–	–
AL.	757	36	569	56	96	NJ.	269	18	162	–	89
AK.	2	1	1	–	–	NM	4	1	–	2	1
AZ.	13	1	1	6	5	NY.	328	34	90	84	120
AR.	535	15	374	17	129	NC	523	28	369	31	95
CA.	234	10	78	76	70	ND	1	–	1	–	–
CO.	17	4	5	8	–	OH	305	21	197	35	52
CT.	69	14	46	3	6	OK	115	6	85	4	20
DE.	29	4	18	–	7	OR	5	3	1	1	–
DC	174	5[2]	169	–	3	PA.	215	19	85	75	36
FL.	275	25	180	43	27	RI.	8	7	1	–	–
GA.	640	53	413	48	126	SC.	547	32	345	12	158
HI.	1	1	–	–	–	TN.	195	18	118	28	31
ID.	1	–	1	–	–	TX.	466	19	306	47	94
IL.	619	28	327	59	205	UT.	5	1	3	1	–
IN.	94	13	54	13	14	VT.	1	1	–	–	–
IA.	12	1	8	1	2	VA.	248	16	132	16	84
KS.	16	7	4	3	2	WA	24	2	9	11	2
KY.	62	5	45	6	6	WV	19	2	13	3	1
LA.	739	32	408	132	167	WI.	33	8	15	5	5
ME.	2	–	1	–	1	WY	1	1	–	–	–

– Represents zero. [1] Includes elected state administrators. [2] County commissioners and councilmen, mayors, vice mayors, aldermen, regional officials, and other. [3] Judges, magistrates, constables, marshals, sheriffs, justices of the peace, and other. [4] Members of state education agencies, college boards, school boards, and other. [5] Includes one shadow senator, an elected official who lobbies Congress on DC issues, but is not sworn in at the federal level and has no voting privileges.

Source: Joint Center for Political and Economic Studies, Washington, DC, *Black Elected Officials: A Statistical Summary*, annual (copyright) and <http://www.jointcenter.org/publications_recent_publications/black_elected_officials>.

Table 403. Hispanic Public Elected Officials by Office, 1985 to 2006, and State, 2006

[As of January of year shown. For states not shown, no Hispanic public officials had been identified]

State	Total	State executives and legislators[1]	County and municipal officials	Judicial and law enforcement	Education and school boards	State	Total	State executives and legislators[1]	County and municipal officials	Judicial and law enforcement	Education and school boards
1985	3,147	129	1,316	517	1,185	MA	19	4	10	–	5
1990	4,004	144	1,819	583	1,458	MI	16	3	3	3	7
1994	5,459	199	2,197	651	2,412	MN	3	1	1	1	–
2000	5,019	217	1,852	447	2,503	MO	1	–	1	–	–
2001	5,205	223	1,846	454	2,682	MT	1	–	–	1	–
2002	4,303	227	1,960	532	1,603	NE.	3	1	1	–	1
2003	4,432	231	1,958	549	1,694	NV.	11	2	5	3	1
2004	4,651	253	2,059	638	1,723	NH.	3	2	1	–	–
2005	4,853	266	2,149	678	1,760	NJ.	109	5	61	–	43
						NM.	649	48	337	111	144
2006	4,932	244	2,151	693	1,835	NY.	63	16	30	15	2
AK.	1	–	1	–	–	NC.	3	2	1	–	–
AZ.	357	17	141	47	152	ND.	1	–	1	–	–
CA.	1,059	30	388	41	600	OH.	4	–	3	1	–
CO.	145	7	101	7	30	OK.	1	–	1	–	–
CT.	29	6	19	–	4	OR.	17	3	9	5	–
DE.	2	1	1	–	–	PA.	12	1	7	2	2
DC.	1	–	–	–	1	RI.	7	4	3	–	–
FL.	121	19	70	26	6	SC.	1	1	–	–	–
GA.	7	3	2	2	–	TN.	2	1	1	–	–
HI.	1	1	–	–	–	TX.	2,109	38	851	413	807
ID.	2	1	1	–	–	UT.	5	2	3	–	–
IL.	96	11	63	6	16	VA.	1	–	1	–	–
IN.	13	1	8	3	1	WA	13	3	4	–	6
KS.	11	4	6	–	1	WI.	13	1	5	4	3
LA.	3	–	1	2	–	WY	4	1	3	–	–
MD.	13	4	7	–	2						

– Represents zero. [1] Includes U.S. Senators and Representatives, not shown separately.

Source: National Association of Latino Elected and Appointed Officials (NALEO) Educational Fund, Washington, DC, *National Directory of Latino Elected Officials*, annual.

Elections 255

Table 404. Voting-Age Population, Percent Reporting Registered, and Voted: 1994 to 2006

[190.3 represents 190,300,000. As of November. Covers civilian noninstitutional population 18 years old and over. Includes aliens. Figures are based on Current Population Survey (see text, Section 1, Population, and Appendix III) and differ from those in Table 406 based on population estimates and official vote counts]

Characteristic	Voting-age population (mil.)							Percent reporting they registered							Percent reporting they voted						
								Presidential election years			Congressional election years				Presidential election years			Congressional election years			
	1994	1996	1998	2000	2002	2004	2006	1996	2000	2004	1994	1998	2002	2006	1996	2000	2004	1994	1998	2002	2006
Total [1]	190.3	193.7	198.2	202.6	210.4	215.7	220.6	65.9	63.9	65.9	62.0	62.1	60.9	61.6	54.2	54.7	58.3	44.6	41.9	42.3	43.6
18 to 20 years old	10.3	10.8	11.4	11.9	11.7	11.5	11.6	45.6	40.5	50.7	37.2	32.1	32.6	37.0	31.2	28.4	41.0	16.5	13.5	15.1	17.1
21 to 24 years old	14.9	13.9	14.1	14.9	15.6	16.4	16.2	51.2	49.3	52.1	45.5	35.0	42.5	44.9	33.4	35.4	42.5	22.3	19.2	18.7	21.9
25 to 34 years old	41.1	40.1	38.6	37.3	38.5	39.0	39.4	56.9	54.7	55.6	51.5	52.4	50.2	50.3	43.1	43.7	46.9	32.2	28.0	27.1	28.3
35 to 44 years old	41.9	43.3	44.4	44.5	43.7	43.1	42.6	66.5	63.8	64.2	63.3	62.4	60.0	59.3	54.9	55.0	56.9	46.0	40.7	40.2	40.1
45 to 64 years old	50.9	53.7	57.4	61.4	66.9	66.9	75.0	73.5	71.2	72.7	71.0	71.1	69.4	59.6	64.4	64.1	66.6	56.0	53.6	53.1	54.3
65 years old and over	31.1	31.9	32.3	32.8	33.9	34.7	35.8	77.0	76.1	76.9	75.6	75.4	75.8	75.4	67.0	67.6	68.9	60.7	59.5	61.0	60.5
Male	91.0	92.6	95.2	97.1	100.9	103.8	106.5	64.4	62.2	64.0	60.8	60.6	58.9	59.5	52.8	53.1	56.3	44.4	41.4	41.4	42.4
Female	99.3	101.0	103.0	105.5	109.5	111.9	114.1	67.3	65.6	67.6	63.2	63.5	62.8	63.5	55.5	56.2	60.1	44.9	42.4	43.0	44.7
White [2]	160.3	162.8	165.8	168.7	174.1	176.6	179.0	67.7	65.6	67.9	64.2	63.9	63.1	64.0	56.0	56.4	60.3	46.9	43.3	44.1	45.8
Black [2,3]	21.8	22.5	23.3	24.1	24.4	24.9	25.7	63.6	65.6	64.4	58.3	60.2	58.8	57.4	50.6	53.5	56.3	37.0	39.6	39.7	50.7
Asian	(NA)	(NA)	(NA)	8.0	9.6	9.3	9.9	(NA)	30.7	34.9	(NA)	(NA)	30.7	32.9	(NA)	25.4	29.8	(NA)	(NA)	19.4	21.8
Hispanic [4]	17.5	18.4	20.3	21.6	25.2	27.1	29.0	35.7	34.9	34.3	30.0	33.7	32.6	32.1	26.7	27.5	28.0	19.1	20.0	18.9	19.3
Region: [5]																					
Northeast	38.4	38.3	38.5	38.9	41.1	41.0	41.2	64.7	63.7	65.3	60.9	60.8	60.8	60.3	54.5	55.2	58.6	45.2	41.2	41.4	42.8
Midwest	44.5	45.2	45.9	46.4	48.8	48.4	49.1	71.6	70.2	72.8	68.7	68.2	66.5	68.3	59.3	60.9	65.0	48.8	47.3	47.1	50.7
South	66.4	68.1	70.1	71.8	74.2	77.2	80.0	65.9	64.5	65.5	60.7	62.7	61.6	62.0	52.2	53.5	56.4	40.5	38.6	41.6	40.3
West	41.0	42.1	43.7	45.5	46.3	49.1	50.4	60.8	56.9	60.1	58.1	56.0	54.0	55.4	51.8	49.9	54.4	46.4	42.3	39.0	42.4
School years completed:																					
8 years or less	14.7	14.1	13.3	12.9	12.3	12.6	12.1	40.7	36.1	32.5	40.1	40.2	32.4	29.5	28.1	26.8	23.6	23.2	24.6	19.4	17.1
High school:																					
Less than high school graduate	20.7	21.0	21.0	20.1	20.9	20.7	20.2	47.9	45.9	45.8	44.7	43.4	41.6	39.6	33.8	33.6	34.6	27.0	25.0	23.3	22.8
High school graduate or GED [6]	64.9	65.2	65.6	66.3	68.9	68.5	70.0	62.2	60.1	61.5	58.9	58.6	57.1	57.5	49.1	49.4	52.4	40.5	37.1	37.1	37.6
College:																					
Some college or associate's degree	50.4	50.9	52.9	55.3	57.3	58.9	60.2	72.9	70.0	73.7	68.4	68.3	66.7	68.3	60.5	60.3	66.1	49.1	46.2	45.8	47.3
Bachelor's or advanced degree	39.4	42.5	45.4	48.0	51.0	54.9	58.2	80.4	77.3	78.1	76.3	75.1	74.4	73.9	73.0	72.0	74.2	63.1	57.2	58.5	59.5
Employed	122.6	125.6	130.5	133.4	134.9	138.8	143.8	67.0	64.7	67.1	62.9	62.6	61.7	62.7	55.2	55.5	60.0	45.2	41.2	42.1	43.9
Unemployed	6.5	6.4	5.2	4.9	7.7	7.3	6.2	52.5	46.1	56.3	46.4	48.5	48.1	48.5	37.2	35.1	46.4	28.3	28.4	27.2	28.0
Not in labor force	61.2	61.6	62.5	64.2	67.8	69.6	70.5	65.1	63.8	64.4	61.9	62.1	60.9	60.7	54.1	54.5	56.2	45.3	44.5	44.2	44.3

NA Not available. [1] Includes other races not shown separately. [2] Beginning with the 2003 Current Population Survey (CPS), respondents could choose more than one race. 2004 data represent persons who selected this race group only and exclude persons reporting more than one race. The CPS in prior years only allowed respondents to report one race group. See also comments on race in the text for Section 1. [3] Prior to 2004, this category was Asian and Pacific Islanders; therefore rates are not comparable with prior years. [4] Hispanic persons may be any race. [5] For composition of regions, see map, inside cover. [6] The General Educational Development (GED) Test measures how well a non-high school graduate has mastered the skills and general knowledge that are acquired in a four-year high school education. Successfully passing the exam is a credential generally considered to be equivalent to a high school diploma.

Source: U.S. Census Bureau, Current Population Reports, P20-556, and earlier reports; "Voting and Registration in the Election of November 2004" (published 25 May 2005); <http://www.census.gov/population/www/socdemo/voting.html>; and unpublished data.

Table 405. Persons Reported Registered and Voted by State: 2006

[220,603 represents 220,603,000. As of November. See headnote, Table 404]

State	Voting-age population (1,000)	Percent of voting-age population Registered	Percent of voting-age population Voted	State	Voting-age population (1,000)	Percent of voting-age population Registered	Percent of voting-age population Voted
U.S......	220,603	61.6	43.6	MO	4,388	72.2	52.6
AL	3,447	72.0	48.4	MT	735	69.7	59.2
AK	469	70.9	52.9	NE	1,298	65.7	48.9
AZ	4,418	53.8	40.2	NV	1,839	49.2	37.3
AR	2,076	63.4	43.9	NH	1,015	67.7	47.0
CA	26,318	50.3	38.4	NJ	6,488	53.7	37.1
CO	3,464	65.7	49.9	NM	1,436	66.2	50.9
CT	2,640	62.5	46.2	NY	14,376	56.6	37.6
DE	647	63.0	42.6	NC	6,490	64.1	37.3
DC	419	65.8	44.6	ND	484	82.0	53.4
FL	13,929	56.4	38.4	OH	8,508	69.6	51.8
GA	6,630	59.6	40.3	OK	2,616	67.9	44.9
HI	967	50.9	40.1	OR	2,802	68.7	57.1
ID	1,064	62.0	49.1	PA	9,436	63.5	46.6
IL	9,392	61.5	42.2	RI	806	66.6	53.5
IN	4,629	63.6	44.3	SC	3,197	62.1	43.0
IA	2,252	73.9	52.4	SD	577	77.2	62.1
KS	2,035	62.6	44.3	TN	4,571	61.9	43.8
KY	3,142	71.3	48.0	TX	16,512	58.6	33.5
LA	3,071	71.0	39.1	UT	1,753	53.1	34.4
ME	1,034	78.5	57.5	VT	491	70.2	55.5
MD	4,175	65.1	51.4	VA	5,578	61.0	43.6
MA	4,864	65.4	50.0	WA	4,745	65.1	49.4
MI	7,458	70.5	54.8	WV	1,394	62.6	36.8
MN	3,855	74.2	61.6	WI	4,202	70.2	56.0
MS	2,083	69.0	42.2	WY	388	65.3	51.4

Source: U.S. Census Bureau, Current Population Reports, P20-556 and earlier reports; "Voting and Registration in the Election of November 2004" (published 25 May 2005); <http://www.census.gov/population/www/socdemo/voting.html>; and unpublished data.

Table 406. Participation in Elections for President and U.S. Representatives: 1932 to 2006

[75,768 represents 75,768,000. As of November, except as noted. Estimated resident population 21 years old and over, 1932–70, except as noted, and 18 years old and over thereafter; includes Armed Forces. Prior to 1958, excludes Alaska and prior to 1960, excludes Hawaii. District of Columbia is included in votes cast for President beginning 1964]

Year	Resident population (incl. aliens) of voting age (1,000)	Votes cast For President (1,000)	Per-cent of voting-age popu-lation	For U.S. Repre-senta-tives (1,000)	Per-cent of voting-age popu-lation	Year	Resident population (incl. aliens) of voting age (1,000)	Votes cast For President (1,000)	Per-cent of voting-age popu-lation	For U.S. Repre-senta-tives (1,000)	Per-cent of voting-age popu-lation
1932...	75,768	39,817	52.6	(NA)	(NA)	1970...	124,498	(X)	(X)	54,259	43.6
1934...	77,997	(X)	(X)	32,804	42.1	1972...	140,777	77,625	55.1	71,188	50.6
1936...	80,174	45,647	56.9	(NA)	(NA)	1974...	146,338	(X)	(X)	52,313	35.7
1938...	82,354	(X)	(X)	(NA)	(NA)	1976...	152,308	81,603	53.6	74,259	48.8
1940...	84,728	49,815	58.8	(NA)	(NA)	1978...	158,369	(X)	(X)	54,584	34.5
1942...	86,465	(X)	(X)	28,074	32.5	1980...	163,945	86,497	52.8	77,874	47.5
1944...	85,654	48,026	56.1	45,110	52.7	1982...	169,643	(X)	(X)	63,881	37.7
1946...	92,659	(X)	(X)	34,410	37.1	1984...	173,995	92,655	53.3	82,422	47.4
1948...	95,573	48,834	51.1	46,220	48.4	1986...	177,922	(X)	(X)	59,758	33.6
1950...	98,134	(X)	(X)	40,430	41.2	1988...	181,956	91,587	50.3	81,682	44.9
1952...	99,929	61,552	61.6	57,571	57.6	1990...	185,812	(X)	(X)	62,355	33.6
1954...	102,075	(X)	(X)	42,583	41.7	1992...	189,493	104,600	55.2	97,198	51.3
1956...	104,515	62,027	59.3	58,886	56.3	1994...	193,010	(X)	(X)	70,494	36.5
1958...	106,447	(X)	(X)	45,719	43.0	1996...	196,789	96,390	49.0	90,233	45.9
1960...	109,672	68,836	62.8	64,124	58.5	1998...	201,270	(X)	(X)	66,605	33.1
1962...	112,952	(X)	(X)	51,242	45.4	2000...	[2]209,851	105,594	50.3	98,800	47.1
1964...	114,090	70,098	61.4	65,879	57.7	2002...	[2]215,220	(X)	(X)	74,707	34.7
1966...	116,638	(X)	(X)	52,902	45.4	2004...	[2]220,344	122,349	55.5	113,192	51.4
1968...	120,285	73,027	60.7	66,109	55.0	2006...	[2]225,663	(X)	(X)	80,588	35.7

NA Not available. X Not applicable. [1] Population 18 and over in Georgia, 1944–70, and in Kentucky, 1956–70; 20 and over in Alaska and 20 and over in Hawaii, 1960–70. Source: Through 1992, U.S. Census Bureau, Current Population Reports, P25-1059 and earlier reports; also see <http://www.census.gov/population/www/socdemo/voting/past-voting.html#p25> (released July 31, 2000). For 1992–1998, "Projections of the Voting-Age Population for States: November 2000" (published 31 July 2000); also see <http://www.census.gov/population/socdemo/voting/proj00/tab03.txt>. Starting 2000, "Annual Estimates of the Population by Selected Age Groups and Sex for the United States: April 1, 2000 to July 1, 2006," (NC-EST2006-02); also see <http://www.census.gov/popest/national/asrh/NC-EST2006-sa.html/> (released 17 May 2007). [2] As of July 1.

Source: Except as noted, U.S. House of Representatives, Office of the Clerk, Statistics of the Presidential and Congressional Election, biennial. See also <http://clerk.house.gov/member_info/electionInfo/index.html>.

Elections 257

Table 407. **Resident Population of Voting Age and Percent Casting Votes—States: 2000 to 2006**

[209,851 represents 209,851,000. Estimated population, 18 years old and over. Includes Armed Forces stationed in each state, aliens, and institutional population]

State	Voting-age population (1,000) [1]			Percent casting votes for—				
				Presidential electors		U.S. Representatives		
	2000	2004	2006	2000	2004	2000	2004	2006
U.S.	209,851	220,344	225,663	50.3	55.5	47.1	51.4	35.7
AL	3,330	3,411	3,485	50.0	55.2	43.2	52.6	34.4
AK	437	472	489	65.3	66.2	62.8	63.5	48.0
AZ	3,792	4,224	4,538	40.4	47.7	38.7	44.3	32.9
AR	1,998	2,068	2,120	46.1	51.0	31.7	38.3	36.0
CA	24,739	26,325	26,925	44.3	47.2	42.2	44.2	30.8
CO	3,221	3,453	3,584	54.1	61.7	50.4	59.1	42.9
CT	2,571	2,655	2,687	56.8	59.5	51.1	53.8	40.0
DE	592	629	650	55.4	59.7	52.9	56.6	38.7
DC	457	463	467	44.2	49.1	(X)	(X)	(X)
FL	12,394	13,473	14,068	48.1	56.5	40.4	41.8	27.4
GA	6,053	6,581	6,909	42.7	50.2	39.9	45.0	30.0
HI	917	961	987	40.1	44.6	37.1	43.3	34.2
ID	930	1,015	1,072	54.0	58.9	53.0	56.4	41.5
IL	9,195	9,480	9,617	51.6	55.6	47.8	52.6	35.9
IN	4,518	4,654	4,736	48.7	53.0	47.7	51.9	35.2
IA	2,196	2,242	2,272	61.6	67.2	58.1	65.0	45.5
KS	1,980	2,038	2,068	54.2	58.3	52.3	56.7	40.9
KY	3,054	3,147	3,207	50.6	57.1	47.0	52.0	39.1
LA	3,252	3,321	3,198	54.3	58.5	37.0	37.9	28.6
ME	976	1,025	1,041	66.8	72.3	65.4	69.3	51.5
MD	3,954	4,179	4,255	51.2	57.1	48.7	53.9	40.0
MA	4,862	4,959	4,988	56.2	59.0	56.2	59.0	45.0
MI	7,361	7,560	7,617	57.5	64.0	55.3	61.3	47.9
MN	3,645	3,828	3,910	66.9	73.9	64.8	71.1	55.7
MS	2,074	2,131	2,151	47.9	53.5	47.6	52.4	27.9
MO	4,179	4,339	4,426	56.5	62.9	55.7	61.5	47.4
MT	674	707	727	61.0	63.7	60.9	62.9	55.9
NE	1,263	1,302	1,323	55.2	59.8	54.1	58.8	45.0
NV	1,502	1,739	1,861	40.6	47.7	39.0	45.5	30.9
NH	930	993	1,017	61.2	68.3	59.8	65.6	39.6
NJ	6,346	6,562	6,635	50.2	55.0	47.1	50.1	32.2
NM	1,314	1,396	1,446	45.6	54.2	44.7	53.2	38.8
NY	14,317	14,691	14,792	48.6	50.7	48.5	50.7	31.7
NC	6,110	6,452	6,701	47.7	54.3	45.5	52.9	29.0
ND	481	488	491	59.9	64.2	59.4	63.7	44.3
OH	8,479	8,651	8,708	55.5	65.1	54.1	59.9	45.5
OK	2,563	2,639	2,685	48.2	55.5	42.4	52.1	33.7
OR	2,584	2,742	2,844	59.4	67.0	55.7	64.6	47.7
PA	9,369	9,537	9,636	52.4	60.5	48.6	54.0	41.6
RI	803	833	830	51.0	52.5	47.9	48.3	44.9
SC	3,013	3,171	3,282	45.9	51.0	43.9	45.4	33.1
SD	553	575	587	57.2	67.5	56.9	67.8	56.8
TN	4,304	4,469	4,596	48.2	54.5	43.1	49.6	37.3
TX	15,047	16,272	17,014	42.6	45.5	39.8	42.8	24.3
UT	1,523	1,666	1,759	50.6	55.7	49.8	54.6	32.4
VT	462	483	491	63.6	64.7	61.3	63.2	53.6
VA	5,363	5,681	5,836	51.1	56.3	45.2	52.9	39.4
WA	4,396	4,689	4,870	56.6	61.0	54.2	58.2	42.2
WV	1,406	1,421	1,429	46.1	53.2	41.2	50.8	31.8
WI	4,005	4,168	4,244	64.9	71.9	62.6	67.7	48.6
WY	366	383	393	58.5	63.6	58.1	62.4	49.9

X Not applicable.   [1] As of July 1. Source: U.S. Census Bureau, "Annual Estimates of the Population by Selected Age Groups and Sex for the United States: April 1, 2000, to July 1, 2006." (NC-EST2006-02); see also <http://www.census.gov/popest/datasets.html>.

Source: Except as noted, U.S. House of Representatives, Office of the Clerk, *Statistics of the Presidential and Congressional Election*, biennial. See also <http://clerk.house.gov/member_info/electionInfo/index.html>.

258   Elections

Table 408. Political Action Committees—Number by Committee Type: 1980 to 2006

[As of December 31]

Committee type	1980	1990	1995	2000	2002	2003	2004	2005	2006
Total	2,551	4,172	4,016	3,706	4,027	4,023	4,867	4,343	4,183
Corporate	1,206	1,795	1,674	1,523	1,528	1,552	1,756	1,638	1,582
Labor	297	346	334	316	320	308	328	296	273
Trade/membership/health	576	774	815	812	975	877	986	912	937
Nonconnected	374	1,062	1,020	902	1,055	1,147	1,650	1,357	1,254
Cooperative	42	59	44	39	39	36	38	37	37
Corporation without stock	56	136	129	114	110	103	109	103	100

Source: U.S. Federal Election Commission, press release of January 2007.

Table 409. Political Action Committees—Financial Activity Summary by Committee Type: 2001 to 2006

[In millions of dollars (685.3 represents $685,300,000). Covers financial activity during 2-year calendar period indicated]

Committee type	Receipts			Disbursements [1]			Contributions to candidates		
	2001–02	2003–04	2005–06	2001–02	2003–04	2005–06	2001–02	2003–04	2005–06
Total............	685.3	915.7	477.4	656.5	842.9	394.1	282.0	310.5	141.1
Corporate	191.7	239.0	131.2	178.3	221.6	116.3	99.6	115.6	56.5
Labor...............	167.8	191.7	100.3	158.0	182.9	73.1	53.9	52.1	21.1
Trade/membership/health. . .	166.7	181.8	95.4	165.7	170.1	74.6	46.3	83.2	38.0
Nonconnected	145.8	289.4	141.6	141.3	255.2	122.6	75.1	52.5	22.0
Cooperative	3.7	4.2	2.7	3.6	3.9	1.9	2.7	2.9	1.4
Corporation without stock. . .	9.7	9.6	6.1	9.6	9.2	5.7	4.4	4.2	2.1

[1] Comprises contributions to candidates, independent expenditures, and other disbursements.

Source: U.S. Federal Election Commission, FEC Reports on Financial Activity, Final Report, Party and Non-party Political Committees, biennial.

Table 410. Presidential Campaign Finances—Federal Funds for General Election: 1992 to 2004

[In millions of dollars (110.4 represents $110,400,000). Based on FEC certifications, audit reports, and Dept. of Treasury reports]

1992		1996		2000		2004	
Candidate	Amount	Candidate	Amount	Candidate	Amount	Candidate	Amount
Total.....	110.4	Total	152.6	Total	147.7	Total	150.1
Bush	55.2	Clinton	61.8	Bush........	67.6	Bush........	74.6
Clinton	55.2	Dole	61.8	Gore	67.6	Kerry........	74.6
Perot	–	Perot	29.0	Buchanan ...	12.6	Nader	0.9

– Represents zero.

Source: U.S. Federal Election Commission, periodic press releases.

Table 411. Presidential Campaign Finances—Primary Campaign Receipts and Disbursements: 1995 to 2004

[In millions of dollars (243.9 represents $243,900,000). Covers campaign finance activity during 2-year calendar period indicated. Covers candidates who received Federal matching funds or who had significant financial activity]

Item	Total [1]			Democratic			Republican		
	1995–96	1999–00	2003–04	1995–96	1999–00	2003–04	1995–96	1999–00	2003–04
Receipts, total [2]	243.9	351.6	673.9	46.2	96.6	401.8	187.0	236.7	269.6
Individual contributions. . . .	126.4	238.2	611.4	31.3	66.7	351.0	93.1	159.1	258.9
Federal matching funds . . .	56.0	61.6	28.0	14.0	29.3	27.2	41.6	26.5	–
Disbursements	234.1	343.5	661.1	41.8	92.2	389.7	182.1	233.2	268.9

– Represents zero. [1] Includes other parties, not shown separately. [2] Includes other types of receipts, not shown separately.

Source: U.S. Federal Election Commission, FEC Reports on Financial Activity, Final Report, Presidential Pre-Nomination Campaigns, quadrennial.

Elections 259

Table 412. Congressional Campaign Finances—Receipts and Disbursements: 2001 to 2006

[643.3 represents $643,300,000. Covers all campaign finance activity during 2-year calendar period indicated for primary, general, run-off, and special elections. Data have been adjusted to eliminate transfers between all committees within a campaign. For further information on legal limits of contributions, see Federal Election Campaign Act of 1971, as amended]

Item	House of Representatives						Senate					
	Amount (mil. dol.)			Percent distribution			Amount (mil. dol.)			Percent distribution		
	2001–02	2003–04	2005–06	2001–02	2003–04	2005–06	2001–02	2003–04	2005–06	2001–02	2003–04	2005–06
Total receipts [1]	643.3	708.5	875.4	100	100	100	326.1	497.6	564.6	100	100	101
Individual contributions	322.5	396.7	478.9	50	56	55	214.3	324.1	383.2	66	65	68
Other committees	214.1	225.4	279.8	33	32	32	60.2	63.7	68.9	18	13	12
Candidate loans	72.0	47.4	56.1	11	7	6	28.1	39.8	47.0	9	8	8
Candidate contributions	9.2	7.8	14.7	1	1	2	0.8	38.2	37.5	(Z)	8	7
Democrats	314.2	307.4	417.5	49	43	48	162.9	250.6	291.8	50	50	52
Republicans	326.3	399.2	453.6	51	56	52	162.7	246.1	245.8	50	49	44
Others	2.8	1.9	4.2	(Z)	(Z)	(Z)	0.6	0.9	26.9	(Z)	(Z)	(Z)
Incumbents	369.8	452.6	532.6	57	64	61	145.0	171.7	278.4	44	35	49
Challengers [2]	107.0	118.2	188.7	17	17	22	109.7	79.5	186.6	34	16	33
Open seats [2]	166.5	137.8	154.1	26	19	18	71.4	246.4	99.6	22	50	18
Total disbursements	613.9	660.3	854.8	100	100	101	322.4	496.4	562.9	100	100	101
Democrats	301.1	288.5	395.5	49	44	46	162.9	254.6	288.6	51	51	51
Republicans	310.0	370.0	455.2	50	56	53	158.9	241.0	249.3	49	49	44
Others	2.9	1.8	4.1	(Z)	(Z)	(Z)	0.6	0.8	25.0	(Z)	(Z)	(Z)
Incumbents	343.9	410.1	519.2	56	62	61	145.6	171.7	274.3	45	35	49
Challengers [2]	103.9	116.6	185.6	17	18	22	108.4	76.6	187.1	34	15	33
Open seats [2]	166.1	133.6	150.0	27	20	18	68.5	248.1	101.5	21	50	18

Z Less than $50,000 or 0.5 percent.   [1] Includes other types of receipts, not shown separately.   [2] Elections in which an incumbent did not seek re-election.

Source: U.S. Federal Election Commission, *FEC Reports on Financial Activity, Final Report, U.S. Senate and House Campaigns*, biennial.

Table 413. Contributions to Congressional Campaigns by Political Action Committees (PAC) by Type of Committee: 1995 to 2006

[In millions of dollars (155.8 represents $155,800,000). Covers amounts given to candidates in primary, general, run-off, and special elections during the 2-year calendar period indicated. For number of political action committees, see Table 408]

Type of committee	Total [1]	Democrats	Republicans	Incumbents	Challengers	Open seats [2]
HOUSE OF REPRESENTATIVES						
1995–96	155.8	77.3	77.7	113.9	21.4	20.5
1997–98	158.7	77.6	80.9	124.0	14.9	19.8
1999–00	193.4	98.2	94.7	150.5	19.9	23.0
2001–02	206.9	102.6	104.2	161.0	13.8	32.1
2003–04	225.4	98.6	126.6	187.3	15.6	22.5
2005–06, total [3]	279.8	125.0	154.8	232.0	24.4	23.5
Corporate	96.1	31.7	64.4	90.4	1.5	4.2
Trade association [4]	79.6	30.3	49.3	70.7	3.2	5.7
Labor	47.6	42.1	5.5	32.8	9.8	5.0
Nonconnected [5]	50.3	18.2	32.1	32.4	9.7	8.2
SENATE						
1995–96	45.6	16.6	29.0	19.4	6.9	19.3
1997–98	48.1	20.7	27.3	34.3	6.6	7.2
1999–00	51.9	18.7	33.2	33.5	7.1	11.3
2001–02	59.2	25.4	33.8	37.0	14.2	8.1
2003–04	63.7	28.4	35.3	39.3	5.6	18.8
2005–06, total [3]	68.9	28.6	37.5	50.0	9.9	8.7
Corporate	27.3	9.1	17.1	23.1	1.7	2.6
Trade association [4]	16.4	6.0	9.8	12.6	1.8	2.1
Labor	6.7	5.8	0.5	3.4	2.1	1.2
Nonconnected [5]	17.1	7.1	9.5	9.9	4.3	2.8

[1] Includes other parties, not shown separately.   [2] Elections in which an incumbent did not seek reelection.   [3] Includes other types of political action committees not shown separately.   [4] Includes membership organizations and health organizations.   [5] Represents "ideological" groups as well as other issue groups not necessarily ideological in nature.

Source: U.S. Federal Election Commission, *FEC Reports on Financial Activity, Party and Non-Party Political Committees, Final Report*, biennial.

U.S. Census Bureau. Statistical Abstract of the United States: 2008

Section 8
State and Local Government Finances and Employment

This section presents data on revenues, expenditures, debt, and employment of state and local governments. Nationwide statistics relating to state and local governments, their numbers, finances, and employment are compiled primarily by the U.S. Census Bureau through a program of censuses and surveys. Every fifth year (for years ending in "2" and "7"), the Census Bureau conducts a census of governments involving collection of data for all governmental units in the United States. In addition, the Census Bureau conducts annual surveys which cover all the state governments and a sample of local governments.

Annually, the Census Bureau releases information on the Internet which presents financial data for the federal government, nationwide totals for state and local governments, and state-local data by states. Also released annually is a series on state, city, county, and school finances and on state and local public employment. There is also a series of quarterly data releases covering tax revenue and finances of major public employee retirement systems.

Basic information for Census Bureau statistics on governments is obtained by mail canvass from state and local officials; however, financial data for each of the state governments and for many of the large local governments are compiled from their official records and reports by Census Bureau personnel. In over two-thirds of the states, all or part of local government financial data are obtained through central collection arrangements with state governments. Financial data on the federal government are primarily based on the *Budget* published by the Office of Management and Budget (see text, Section 9, Federal Government Finances and Employment).

Governmental units—The governmental structure of the United States includes, in addition to the federal government and

the states, thousands of local governments—counties, municipalities, townships, school districts, and many "special districts." In 2002, 87,576 local governments were identified by the census of governments (see Tables 414–416). As defined by the census, governmental units include all agencies or bodies having an organized existence, governmental character, and substantial autonomy. While most of these governments can impose taxes, many of the special districts—such as independent public housing authorities and numerous local irrigation, power, and other types of districts—are financed from rentals, charges for services, benefit assessments, grants from other governments, and other nontax sources. The count of governments excludes semi-autonomous agencies through which states, cities, and counties sometimes provide for certain functions—for example, "dependent" school systems, state institutions of higher education, and certain other "authorities" and special agencies which are under the administrative or fiscal control of an established governmental unit.

Finances—The financial statistics relate to government fiscal years ending June 30 or at some date within the 12 previous months. The following governments are exceptions and are included as though they were part of the June 30 group; ending September 30, the state governments of Alabama and Michigan, the District of Columbia, and Alabama school districts; and ending August 31, the state governments of Nebraska, Texas, and Chicago school districts. New York State ends its fiscal year on March 31. The federal government ended the fiscal year June 30 until 1976 when its fiscal year, by an act of Congress, was revised to extend from Oct. 1 to Sept. 30. A 3-month quarter (July 1 to Sept. 30, 1976) bridged the transition.

Nationwide government finance statistics have been classified and presented in

U.S. Census Bureau, Statistical Abstract of the United States: 2008

terms of uniform concepts and categories, rather than according to the highly diverse terminology, organization, and fund structure utilized by individual governments.

Statistics on governmental finances distinguish among general government, utilities, liquor stores, and insurance trusts. *General government* comprises all activities except utilities, liquor stores, and insurance trusts. Utilities include government water supply, electric light and power, gas supply, and transit systems. Liquor stores are operated by 17 states and by local governments in 6 states. Insurance trusts relate to employee retirement, unemployment compensation, and other social insurance systems administered by the federal, state, and local governments.

Data for cities or counties relate only to municipal or county and their dependent agencies and do not include amounts for other local governments in the same geographic location. Therefore, expenditure figures for "education" do not include spending by the separate school districts which administer public schools within most municipal or county areas. Variations in the assignment of governmental responsibility for public assistance, health, hospitals, public housing, and other functions to a lesser degree also have an important effect upon reported amounts of city or county expenditure, revenue, and debt.

Employment and payrolls—These data are based mainly on mail canvassing of state and local governments. Payroll includes all salaries, wages, and individual fee payments for the month specified, and employment relates to all persons on governmental payrolls during a pay period of the month covered—including paid officials, temporary help, and (unless otherwise specified) part-time as well as full-time personnel. Effective with the 1997 Census of Governments, the reference period for measuring government employment was changed from October of the calendar year to March of the calendar year. As a result, there was no annual survey of government employment covering the October 1996 period. The prior reference month of October was used from 1958 to 1995. Figures shown for individual governments cover major dependent agencies such as institutions of higher education, as well as the basic central departments and agencies of the government.

Statistical reliability—For a discussion of statistical collection and estimation, sampling procedures, and measures of statistical reliability applicable to Census Bureau data, see Appendix III.

U.S. Census Bureau, Statistical Abstract of the United States: 2008

Table 414. **Number of Governmental Units by Type: 1952 to 2002**

Type of government	1952 [1]	1962	1967	1972	1977	1982	1987	1992	1997	2002
Total units	116,807	91,237	81,299	78,269	79,913	81,831	83,237	85,006	87,504	87,576
U.S. government	1	1	1	1	1	1	1	1	1	1
State government.	50	50	50	50	50	50	50	50	50	50
Local governments	116,756	91,186	81,248	78,218	79,862	81,780	83,186	84,955	87,453	87,525
County	3,052	3,043	3,049	3,044	3,042	3,041	3,042	3,043	3,043	3,034
Municipal.	16,807	18,000	18,048	18,517	18,862	19,076	19,200	19,279	19,372	19,429
Township and town . . .	17,202	17,142	17,105	16,991	16,822	16,734	16,691	16,656	16,629	16,504
School district.	67,355	34,678	21,782	15,781	15,174	14,851	14,721	14,422	13,726	13,506
Special district	12,340	18,323	21,264	23,885	25,962	28,078	29,532	31,555	34,683	35,052

[1] Adjusted to include units in Alaska and Hawaii which adopted statehood in 1959.

Source: U.S. Census Bureau, *Census of Governments, Volume 1, Number 1, Government Organization*, Series GC02(1)-1), quinquennial, <http://www.census.gov/govs/www/cog2002.html>.

Table 415. **Number of Local Governments by Type—States: 2002**

[Governments in existence in January. Limited to governments actually in existence. Excludes, therefore, a few counties and numerous townships and "incorporated places" existing as areas for which statistics can be presented as to population and other subjects, but lacking any separate organized county, township, or municipal government. See Appendix III]

State	All govern-mental units [1]	County	Municipal	Town-ship [1]	School district	Special district [2] Total [3]	Natural resources	Fire protection	Housing & community develop-ment
United States. . .	**87,525**	**3,034**	**19,429**	**16,504**	**13,506**	**35,052**	**6,979**	**5,725**	**3,399**
Alabama	1,171	67	451	–	128	525	68	12	152
Alaska	175	12	149	–	–	14	–	–	13
Arizona	638	15	87	–	231	305	83	151	–
Arkansas	1,588	75	499	–	310	704	258	80	122
California.	4,409	57	475	–	1,047	2,830	484	368	71
Colorado	1,928	62	270	–	182	1,414	178	250	91
Connecticut	580	–	30	149	17	384	1	64	93
Delaware.	339	3	57	–	19	260	239	–	3
District of Columbia.	2	–	1	–	–	1	–	–	–
Florida	1,191	66	404	–	95	626	124	57	105
Georgia	1,448	156	531	–	180	581	38	2	201
Hawaii	19	3	1	–	–	15	14	–	–
Idaho	1,158	44	200	–	116	798	176	142	10
Illinois.	6,903	102	1,291	1,431	934	3,145	979	823	112
Indiana	3,085	91	567	1,008	294	1,125	141	1	63
Iowa.	1,975	99	948	–	386	542	251	67	23
Kansas	3,887	104	627	1,299	324	1,533	261	–	199
Kentucky.	1,439	119	424	–	176	720	166	163	17
Louisiana	473	60	302	–	66	45	4	–	–
Maine	826	16	22	467	99	222	15	–	23
Maryland	265	23	157	–	–	85	44	–	21
Massachusetts	841	5	45	306	82	403	16	16	250
Michigan	2,804	83	533	1,242	580	366	80	4	–
Minnesota	3,482	87	854	1,793	345	403	114	–	167
Mississippi.	1,000	82	296	–	164	458	242	34	57
Missouri	3,422	114	946	312	536	1,514	183	317	136
Montana	1,127	54	129	–	352	592	125	155	12
Nebraska	2,791	93	531	446	575	1,146	80	421	125
Nevada	210	16	19	–	17	158	33	19	5
New Hampshire . . .	559	10	13	221	167	148	10	14	21
New Jersey	1,412	21	324	242	549	276	16	196	2
New Mexico.	858	33	101	–	96	628	583	–	6
New York	3,420	57	616	929	683	1,135	3	911	–
North Carolina	960	100	541	–	–	319	155	–	91
North Dakota	2,735	53	360	1,332	226	764	79	281	39
Ohio.	3,636	88	942	1,308	667	631	98	73	77
Oklahoma	1,798	77	590	–	571	560	97	26	105
Oregon	1,439	36	240	–	236	927	179	256	20
Pennsylvania	5,031	66	1,018	1,546	516	1,885	7	–	90
Rhode Island	118	–	8	31	4	75	2	34	25
South Carolina	701	46	269	–	85	301	48	86	46
South Dakota	1,866	66	308	940	176	376	102	72	40
Tennessee.	930	92	349	–	14	475	108	–	98
Texas	4,784	254	1,196	–	1,089	2,245	442	141	398
Utah.	605	29	236	–	40	300	81	19	16
Vermont	733	14	47	237	283	152	14	19	10
Virginia	521	95	229	–	1	196	47	–	–
Washington	1,787	39	279	–	296	1,173	170	387	41
West Virginia	686	55	234	–	55	342	15	–	39
Wisconsin	3,048	72	585	1,265	442	684	191	–	164
Wyoming	722	23	98	–	55	546	134	64	–

– Represents zero. [1] Includes "town" governments in the six New England States and in Minnesota, New York, and Wisconsin. [2] Single function districts. [3] Includes other special districts not shown separately.

Source: U.S. Census Bureau, *Census of Governments, Volume 1, Number 1, Government Organization*, Series GC02(1)-1), quinquennial, <http://www.census.gov/govs/www/cog2002.html>.

Table 416. County, Municipal, and Township Governments by Population Size: 2002

[Number of governments as of January 2002. Population enumerated as of April 1, 2000. (252,051 represents 252,051,000). Consolidated city-county governments are classified as municipal rather than county governments. Township governments include "towns" in the six New England states, Minnesota, New York, and Wisconsin. See Appendix III]

Population-size group	County governments			Municipal governments			Township governments		
	Number, 2002	Population, 2000		Number, 2002	Population, 2000		Number, 2002	Population, 2000	
		Number (1,000)	Percent		Number (1,000)	Percent		Number (1,000)	Percent
Total	3,034	252,051	100	19,429	174,882	100	16,504	57,365	100
300,000 or more.	161	131,575	52	58	47,768	27	3	1,527	3
200,000 to 299,999. . .	84	20,606	8	30	7,163	4	3	728	1
100,000 to 199,999. . .	228	31,576	13	153	21,076	12	30	3,974	7
50,000 to 99,999	383	27,160	11	364	24,960	14	97	6,588	11
25,000 to 49,999	638	22,913	9	643	22,576	13	273	9,275	16
10,000 to 24,999	869	14,488	6	1,436	22,589	13	773	12,067	21
5,000 to 9,999	385	2,911	1	1,637	11,644	7	1,085	7,560	13
2,500 to 4,999	173	643	(Z)	2,070	7,352	4	1,909	6,732	12
1,000 to 2,499	84	158	(Z)	3,677	5,951	3	3,679	5,905	10
Less than 1,000	29	21	(Z)	9,361	3,803	2	8,652	3,008	5

Z less than 0.5 percent.

Source: U.S. Census Bureau, Census of Governments, Volume 1, Number 1, Government Organization, Series GC02(1)-1), quinquennial, <http://www.census.gov/govs/www/cog2002.html>.

Table 417. State and Local Government Current Receipts and Expenditures in the National Income and Product Accounts: 1990 to 2006

[In billions of dollars (737.8 represents $737,800,000,000). For explanation of national income, see text, Section 13. Minus sign (−) indicates net loss]

Item	1990	1995	2000	2001	2002	2003	2004	2005	2006
Current receipts.	737.8	990.2	1,319.5	1,373.0	1,410.1	1,494.2	1,592.6	1,700.6	1,787.6
Current tax receipts	519.1	672.1	893.2	915.8	929.0	979.4	1,060.9	1,154.4	1,233.5
Personal current taxes	122.6	158.1	236.6	242.7	221.3	226.6	248.4	275.2	300.6
Income taxes	109.6	141.7	217.3	223.1	200.8	204.5	225.1	250.9	275.2
Other	13.0	16.4	19.4	19.6	20.5	22.2	23.4	24.4	25.4
Taxes on production and imports . . .	374.1	482.4	621.1	642.8	675.5	717.5	769.4	821.2	864.2
Sales taxes	184.3	242.7	316.6	321.1	330.2	347.7	370.3	394.1	413.9
Property taxes	161.5	202.6	254.6	269.3	290.1	307.9	329.8	350.4	369.3
Other	28.3	37.0	49.9	52.4	55.2	61.9	69.3	76.7	81.1
Taxes on corporate income.	22.5	31.7	35.5	30.2	32.2	35.3	43.1	58.0	68.7
Contributions for government social insurance	10.0	13.6	11.0	13.6	15.8	19.8	24.2	25.3	24.8
Income receipts on assets	68.4	68.4	92.2	88.8	78.2	72.9	73.3	75.3	77.6
Interest receipts	64.1	62.9	84.0	80.3	69.6	62.9	62.1	63.4	64.6
Dividends	0.2	1.0	1.9	2.0	2.0	2.2	2.4	2.4	2.6
Rents and royalties	4.2	4.5	6.3	6.5	6.6	7.9	8.7	9.5	10.4
Current transfer receipts	133.5	224.1	315.4	350.8	384.7	422.7	438.0	456.1	460.2
Federal grants-in-aid	111.4	184.1	247.3	276.1	304.6	338.5	349.0	361.1	358.0
From business (net)	7.1	13.5	28.8	31.4	32.6	33.5	34.7	36.7	39.5
From persons.	14.9	26.5	39.2	43.3	47.5	50.6	54.3	58.3	62.8
Current surplus of government enterprises	6.7	12.0	7.7	4.0	2.5	−0.6	−3.8	−10.5	−8.5
Current expenditures	730.5	978.2	1,269.5	1,368.2	1,444.3	1,514.5	1,605.5	1,703.9	1,785.0
Consumption expenditures.	544.6	696.1	917.8	969.8	1,025.3	1,073.8	1,130.3	1,207.2	1,288.3
Government social benefit payments to persons.	127.7	217.6	271.7	305.2	332.0	353.0	382.9	402.3	399.6
Interest payments.	57.9	64.2	79.5	85.5	86.0	87.7	91.8	94.2	96.7
Subsidies	0.4	0.3	0.5	7.7	0.9	0.1	0.4	0.4	0.4
Net state and local government saving.	7.2	12.0	50.0	4.8	−34.2	−20.4	−12.9	−3.3	2.5
Social insurance funds	2.0	4.0	2.0	2.6	1.7	3.8	7.5	7.3	5.7
Other.	5.3	8.0	47.9	2.2	−35.9	−24.1	−20.4	−10.6	−3.2

Source: U.S. Bureau of Economic Analysis, Survey of Current Business, April 2007. See also <http://www.bea.gov/national/nipaweb/SelectTable.asp?Selected=N>.

Table 418. Federal Grants-in-Aid to State and Local Governments: 1990 to 2007

[135,325 represents $135,325,000,000, except as indicated. For year ending Sept. 30. Minus sign (-) indicates decrease]

Year	Current dollars							Constant (2000) dollars	
	Total grants (mil. dol.)	Annual percent change [1]	Grants to individuals		Grants as percent of—			Total grants (bil. dol.)	Annual percent change [1]
			Total (mil. dol.)	Percent of total grants	State/local govt. expenditures [2]	Federal outlays	Gross domestic product		
1990	135,325	11.0	77,264	57.1	25.2	10.8	2.4	172.1	6.3
1993	193,612	8.7	124,155	64.1	29.6	13.7	3.0	223.9	5.9
1994	210,596	8.8	134,153	63.7	30.9	14.4	3.0	238.1	6.3
1995	224,991	6.8	144,427	64.2	31.5	14.8	3.1	247.9	4.1
1996	227,811	1.3	146,493	64.3	30.8	14.6	3.0	245.5	-1.0
1997	234,160	2.8	148,236	63.3	30.2	14.6	2.9	247.7	0.9
1998	246,128	5.1	160,305	65.1	30.3	14.9	2.9	257.3	3.9
1999	267,886	8.5	172,384	64.5	31.2	15.7	2.9	275.6	7.1
2000	285,874	6.6	182,592	64.1	27.4	16.0	2.9	285.9	3.7
2001	318,542	11.4	203,920	64.0	28.3	17.1	3.2	310.7	8.7
2002	352,895	10.8	227,373	64.4	29.4	17.5	3.4	338.4	8.9
2003	388,542	10.1	246,570	63.5	31.0	18.0	3.6	363.3	7.4
2004	407,512	4.9	262,177	64.3	31.1	17.8	3.5	370.4	2.0
2005	428,018	5.0	273,898	64.0	30.6	17.3	3.5	374.0	1.0
2006	434,099	1.4	272,858	62.9	28.9	16.3	3.3	362.9	-3.0
2007, est.	448,829	3.4	285,191	63.5	(NA)	16.1	3.3	366.0	0.9

NA Not available. [1] Average annual percent change from prior year shown. For explanation, see Guide to Tabular Presentation. For 1990, change from 1989. [2] Expenditures from own sources as defined in the national income and product accounts.

Source: U. S. Office of Management and Budget, *Budget of the United States Government, Historical Tables*, Annual; <http://www.whitehouse.gov/omb>.

Table 419. Total Outlays for Grants to State and Local Governments—Selected Agencies and Programs: 1990 to 2007

[In millions of dollars (135,325 represents $135,325,000,000). For year ending Sept 30. Includes trust funds]

Selected programs	1990	1995	2000	2003	2004	2005	2006	2007 est.
Total outlays for grants	135,325	224,991	285,874	388,542	407,512	428,018	434,099	448,829
Energy	461	492	433	589	608	636	651	654
Natural resources and environment [1]	3,745	3,985	4,595	5,593	6,009	5,858	6,062	5,881
Environmental Protection Agency [1]	2,874	2,912	3,490	3,917	4,018	3,734	3,966	3,712
Agriculture	1,285	780	724	800	995	933	749	778
Transportation	19,174	25,787	32,222	41,029	41,471	43,370	46,683	49,625
Grants for airports [1]	1,220	1,859	1,624	2,681	2,958	3,530	3,841	3,821
Federal-aid highways [2]	13,854	18,945	24,711	29,960	29,791	30,915	32,703	33,083
Urban mass transportation [1]	3,728	4,353	5,262	7,448	7,777	7,777	8,484	10,048
Community and regional development	4,965	7,230	8,665	15,082	12,604	20,167	21,285	18,891
Rural community advance program	139	333	479	800	797	814	773	726
Community development fund	2,818	4,333	4,955	5,569	5,388	4,985	5,012	7,828
Homeland Security	1,184	1,772	2,439	7,861	5,490	13,541	14,731	9,514
State and local programs	(NA)	(NA)	(NA)	550	1,535	2,116	2,601	1,956
Firefighter assistance grants	(NA)	(NA)	(NA)	31	508	1,185	228	565
Operations, planning, and support	11	79	192	(NA)	387	132	(NA)	(NA)
Mitigation grants	(NA)	(NA)	13	21	23	39	34	98
Disaster relief	1,173	1,693	2,234	7,259	3,037	10,069	11,868	6,895
Education, training, employment, social services	21,780	30,881	36,672	51,543	54,201	57,247	60,512	61,594
Education for the disadvantaged [3]	4,437	6,785	8,511	11,204	12,417	14,539	14,604	14,716
School improvement programs [3]	1,080	1,288	2,394	5,964	6,542	6,569	5,589	5,439
Special education	1,485	2,938	4,696	8,216	9,465	10,661	11,582	11,267
Social services—block grant	2,749	2,797	1,827	1,740	1,752	1,822	1,848	2,155
Children and family services programs	2,618	4,463	5,843	8,161	8,326	8,490	8,492	8,466
Training and employment services	3,042	3,620	2,957	4,291	3,883	3,372	4,566	4,489
Health	43,890	93,587	124,843	173,814	189,883	197,848	197,347	208,914
Substance abuse and mental health services [3]	1,241	2,444	1,931	2,171	2,241	3,203	3,183	2,308
Grants to states for Medicaid [3]	41,103	89,070	117,921	160,805	176,231	180,805	180,625	191,876
State children's health insurance fund [3]	(NA)	(NA)	1,220	4,355	4,607	5,129	5,451	5,647
Income security	36,768	58,366	68,653	86,476	85,983	90,885	89,816	91,807
Food stamp program [3]	2,130	2,740	3,508	4,162	4,204	4,385	4,608	4,638
Child nutrition programs [3]	4,871	7,387	9,060	10,664	11,035	11,726	12,263	13,482
Temporary assistance for needy families [3]	(NA)	(NA)	15,464	19,352	17,725	17,357	16,897	17,318
Veterans benefits and services [3]	134	253	434	428	493	552	625	608
Administration of justice	574	1,222	5,263	4,498	5,084	4,784	4,961	4,313

NA Not available. [1] Grants include trust funds. [2] Trust funds. [3] Includes grants for payments to individuals.

Source: U. S. Office of Management and Budget, *Budget of the United States Government, Historical Tables*, Annual; <http://www.whitehouse.gov/omb>.

State and Local Government Finances and Employment 265

Table 420. Federal Aid to State and Local Governments—Selected Programs by State: 2004

[In millions of dollars (408,143 represents $408,143,000,000). For fiscal year ending September 30]

State and island areas	Federal aid total [1]	Department of Agriculture — Food and nutrition service					Department of Education				
		Total	Child nutrition programs	Food stamp program [2]	Special supplemental food program (WIC)	Other	Total	Office of Elementary and Secondary Education — Special education programs	No child left behind act	Title 1 programs	Other
United States, total . . .	408,143	23,184	11,132	4,060	4,858	3,133	31,251	7,936	4,318	9,052	9,945
Alabama	6,057	382	217	32	78	56	522	141	82	167	132
Alaska	2,433	116	31	8	22	54	148	–	8	–	139
Arizona	7,815	457	245	41	114	57	740	143	86	183	327
Arkansas	4,124	263	130	26	54	52	351	107	64	103	78
California	47,283	2,887	1,407	410	848	222	4,411	1,026	513	1,330	1,543
Colorado	4,606	229	107	29	51	42	472	118	63	101	189
Connecticut	5,015	160	83	20	34	22	354	104	57	106	87
Delaware	1,113	62	29	9	10	14	119	27	26	30	36
District of Columbia	3,591	60	27	13	13	7	117	14	24	36	44
Florida	18,174	1,016	622	83	229	82	1,815	516	223	522	553
Georgia	9,540	729	445	59	150	75	97	2	12	–	83
Hawaii	1,805	128	49	10	29	40	233	44	24	34	131
Idaho	1,900	111	47	9	21	36	162	46	29	38	48
Illinois	14,949	771	431	91	167	81	1,529	450	203	472	404
Indiana	6,965	364	197	45	72	50	548	207	74	159	109
Iowa	3,612	209	95	21	39	54	355	102	50	71	132
Kansas	2,931	198	111	15	41	31	131	16	16	–	99
Kentucky	6,307	351	188	31	71	60	559	131	105	153	170
Louisiana	7,035	497	280	47	89	81	42	2	8	–	32
Maine	2,641	108	38	12	12	47	186	50	27	50	59
Maryland	6,646	275	148	35	61	32	583	197	74	124	187
Massachusetts	10,649	294	165	36	61	33	724	199	96	247	182
Michigan	12,210	612	295	94	127	97	1,186	328	200	427	231
Minnesota	6,331	357	172	49	67	70	108	7	11	–	89
Mississippi	5,297	359	194	33	58	75	418	93	80	146	99
Missouri	7,717	383	206	32	76	70	98	1	14	–	83
Montana	1,883	100	34	10	13	43	208	34	32	38	104
Nebraska	2,322	140	70	16	23	31	214	66	29	36	83
Nevada	2,093	114	53	12	27	21	203	60	29	50	65
New Hampshire	1,508	63	22	5	10	26	144	43	27	29	46
New Jersey	10,856	435	219	88	91	37	932	301	115	274	242
New Mexico	4,249	228	123	24	41	40	430	108	47	93	182
New York	42,576	1,425	748	236	338	104	2,722	612	376	1,050	684
North Carolina	11,354	659	366	65	133	96	939	269	123	248	298
North Dakota	1,316	81	27	8	10	36	143	22	27	29	65
Ohio	14,500	700	317	158	153	72	84	5	13	–	65
Oklahoma	4,937	356	183	43	65	65	538	117	77	129	216
Oregon	4,969	415	117	54	64	179	437	124	58	116	139
Pennsylvania	18,033	694	323	139	137	95	1,164	342	158	409	255
Rhode Island	1,981	65	33	8	15	10	17	–	1	–	16
South Carolina	5,544	324	197	22	62	43	104	7	21	–	76
South Dakota	1,407	92	34	10	14	33	71	1	2	–	68
Tennessee	9,129	448	240	37	100	70	662	199	86	190	188
Texas	25,674	1,963	1,212	159	448	144	2,876	714	442	970	749
Utah	2,639	171	85	21	33	33	259	77	40	37	105
Vermont	1,274	63	16	14	12	22	108	20	22	22	45
Virginia	6,598	65	6	3	5	51	765	208	78	172	307
Washington	7,855	427	169	46	103	109	624	181	101	152	190
West Virginia	3,384	163	79	15	31	37	229	49	55	75	51
Wisconsin	6,888	319	148	47	65	59	673	192	90	155	236
Wyoming	1,583	43	17	9	7	14	119	24	25	29	40
Island areas:											
American Samoa	137	22	10	5	6	–	25	5	1	–	19
Micronesia	65	1	–	–	–	–	6	3	1	–	2
Guam	275	18	6	3	5	4	44	16	1	–	28
Marshall Islands	49	–	–	–	–	–	4	1	1	–	2
Northern Marianas . . .	86	14	5	7	–	2	14	5	–	–	8
Palau	43	–	–	–	–	–	4	1	–	–	2
Puerto Rico	4,854	1,788	154	1,431	175	28	475	58	70	249	98
Virgin Islands	575	369	162	79	78	50	5	1	–	–	4
Undistributed amounts . .	760	39	–	–	–	39	–	–	–	–	–

See footnote at end of table.

Table 420. **Federal Aid to State and Local Governments—Selected Programs by State: 2004**—Con.

[In millions of dollars (2,508 represents $2,508,000,000). For fiscal year ending September 30]

State and island areas	FEMA total [4]	Department of Housing and Urban Development						Department of Labor			
			Public housing programs					State unemployment insurance and employment service			
		Total	Community development block grants	Low rent housing assistance	Housing certificate program	Capital program	Other	Total		Workforce investment	Other [3]
United States, total . . .	2,508	40,431	5,412	3,488	22,356	3,413	5,762	8,749	3,404	3,166	2,178
Alabama	44	534	70	109	213	75	66	138	43	71	24
Alaska	10	161	14	8	36	3	100	57	21	16	20
Arizona	7	480	82	17	165	10	206	138	42	57	39
Arkansas	43	295	37	25	180	27	26	72	27	28	17
California	585	4,677	581	115	3,184	121	677	1,193	490	532	171
Colorado	12	444	49	17	303	12	63	103	50	27	25
Connecticut	14	673	61	52	448	32	81	105	63	20	22
Delaware	8	113	9	9	65	8	22	22	11	5	6
District of Columbia	6	700	77	53	215	276	79	306	150	17	138
Florida	134	1,405	186	93	823	74	230	283	105	132	46
Georgia	26	919	118	109	495	88	108	174	69	67	38
Hawaii	3	167	28	10	93	16	20	48	19	11	17
Idaho	3	89	17	1	55	2	14	60	25	18	17
Illinois	13	2,188	225	254	1,246	202	262	384	162	138	84
Indiana	21	591	83	40	359	29	79	130	51	39	39
Iowa	10	247	48	5	157	7	30	69	33	16	19
Kansas	14	223	44	15	118	13	33	56	24	20	11
Kentucky	44	524	56	46	304	51	67	127	38	45	44
Louisiana	20	571	84	58	253	62	114	125	36	77	12
Maine	10	206	23	8	139	7	28	60	19	18	24
Maryland	42	840	81	69	475	60	155	190	66	41	82
Massachusetts	43	1,866	148	106	1,335	79	198	170	80	43	46
Michigan	19	960	154	50	542	44	170	341	147	124	71
Minnesota	18	634	70	36	386	44	98	125	47	35	43
Mississippi	18	315	54	27	164	26	44	87	35	36	16
Missouri	25	716	110	37	335	114	121	124	45	55	25
Montana	15	123	21	4	52	4	43	41	16	14	11
Nebraska	11	163	29	10	86	11	27	34	22	4	8
Nevada	6	178	22	15	107	5	29	61	32	20	8
New Hampshire	7	163	19	6	108	10	21	30	16	8	7
New Jersey	33	1,518	128	160	965	98	168	204	126	42	35
New Mexico	8	190	35	9	89	10	47	58	22	20	16
New York	156	5,420	958	874	2,515	563	511	531	205	229	97
North Carolina	115	829	93	96	456	66	117	273	78	76	119
North Dakota	16	111	14	2	64	5	27	25	13	6	5
Ohio	33	1,601	227	154	868	130	222	260	92	108	60
Oklahoma	28	469	58	25	190	22	174	79	30	30	20
Oregon	34	376	46	16	232	13	71	140	61	48	31
Pennsylvania	33	1,913	290	243	941	194	245	373	156	130	87
Rhode Island	2	266	21	20	173	18	35	30	17	6	7
South Carolina	15	380	51	30	219	28	52	109	41	43	25
South Dakota	5	125	20	3	55	2	46	34	13	8	14
Tennessee	50	609	62	89	291	70	97	163	54	55	53
Texas	126	1,939	297	113	1,143	148	239	546	174	229	143
Utah	15	166	30	4	99	3	31	56	32	13	10
Vermont	4	91	13	3	60	3	13	25	12	5	8
Virginia	194	743	76	62	449	50	105	247	53	44	150
Washington	48	702	89	35	373	43	161	263	92	108	63
West Virginia	39	216	48	16	114	11	28	54	22	20	11
Wisconsin	9	525	103	18	287	17	100	205	85	53	68
Wyoming	2	38	7	1	22	1	7	20	10	6	3
Island areas:											
American Samoa	3	2	1	–	–	–	–	1	–	–	1
Micronesia	4	–	–	–	–	–	1	1	–	1	–
Guam	31	42	3	3	32	3	1	8	1	6	2
Marshall Islands	–	–	–	–	–	–	–	1	–	1	–
Northern Marianas . . .	7	3	–	–	2	–	–	1	7	1	–
Palau	–	–	–	–	–	–	–	–	–	–	–
Puerto Rico	52	663	138	96	261	115	53	182	27	140	15
Virgin Islands	2	49	3	19	17	8	2	6	3	1	2
Undistributed amounts . .	216	278	–	–5	1	281	–	24	–	–	–

See footnote at end of table.

Table 420. Federal Aid to State and Local Governments—Selected Programs by State: 2004—Con.

[In millions of dollars (234,755 represents $234,755,000,000). For fiscal year ending September 30]

State and island areas	Department of Health and Human Services						Department of Transportation				Other federal aid [5]
	Administration for children			Centers for Medicare and Medicaid services						
	Total	Children & family services (Head Start)	Foster care and adoption assistance	Temporary assistance to needy families		Other	Total	Highway trust fund	Federal transit administration	Other	
United States, total . . .	234,755	8,263	6,331	17,468	180,115	22,576	40,080	28,881	6,818	4,393	27,187
Alaska	944	56	23	61	667	136	572	373	18	181	426
Arizona	4,745	158	82	244	3,851	410	680	450	165	66	567
Arkansas	2,416	90	48	41	2,045	192	459	375	17	67	224
California	27,395	1,041	1,550	3,765	18,448	2,591	3,801	2,365	1,080	357	2,333
Colorado	2,203	139	69	148	1,509	337	675	434	125	116	469
Connecticut	2,878	72	100	290	2,122	293	540	460	60	20	292
Delaware	569	15	9	29	441	75	102	91	4	7	118
District of Columbia	1,295	62	33	106	859	235	378	131	237	10	730
Florida	10,560	315	200	642	8,163	1,240	1,982	1,563	262	156	980
Georgia	5,957	220	89	380	4,705	562	1,021	788	127	105	617
Hawaii	890	35	27	76	655	97	162	97	38	27	174
Idaho	977	43	11	37	764	121	295	231	8	57	204
Illinois	8,245	343	358	688	5,928	928	1,067	611	341	115	750
Indiana	4,164	115	71	201	3,381	396	724	607	54	63	424
Iowa	2,056	71	52	135	1,587	211	397	339	23	35	269
Kansas	1,674	85	45	99	1,279	166	413	369	13	30	222
Kentucky	3,761	146	70	174	3,107	265	549	435	38	76	391
Louisiana	4,701	167	83	265	3,861	325	631	501	60	71	448
Maine	1,696	43	28	73	1,442	109	216	177	11	28	160
Maryland	3,611	108	128	265	2,677	432	624	426	74	124	481
Massachusetts	6,166	150	88	436	4,974	517	848	604	192	53	539
Michigan	7,372	297	226	803	5,256	791	1,019	799	88	133	700
Minnesota	3,981	119	93	247	3,120	401	671	453	139	78	437
Mississippi	3,313	189	8	99	2,774	243	465	362	12	90	322
Missouri	4,974	155	86	212	4,097	424	928	723	93	112	470
Montana	734	46	16	34	539	99	380	314	1	64	283
Nebraska	1,273	49	23	56	984	161	299	257	10	33	187
Nevada	895	35	21	42	659	137	319	199	53	67	318
New Hampshire	802	24	19	26	643	91	142	128	4	10	157
New Jersey	5,753	165	87	429	4,447	624	1,357	752	537	68	624
New Mexico	2,256	78	32	130	1,830	186	332	281	25	27	746
New York	28,156	528	726	2,480	22,518	1,903	2,610	1,470	1,011	129	1,555
North Carolina	6,819	202	93	332	5,551	641	1,110	977	73	59	610
North Dakota	524	37	15	25	368	80	245	181	3	61	171
Ohio	9,753	310	389	722	7,486	846	1,257	958	152	148	812
Oklahoma	2,581	129	35	171	1,959	287	559	487	19	52	325
Oregon	2,431	114	66	151	1,842	258	672	355	131	186	464
Pennsylvania	11,149	299	440	935	8,535	940	1,819	1,224	448	147	887
Rhode Island	1,282	32	21	96	1,038	95	185	157	12	16	133
South Carolina	3,507	106	30	101	2,969	300	737	670	24	43	367
South Dakota	577	41	8	25	414	89	228	182	2	43	275
Tennessee	5,855	149	50	214	5,017	425	749	622	57	69	592
Texas	13,597	593	221	523	10,814	1,446	3,302	2,827	255	219	1,325
Utah	1,377	57	29	98	1,027	166	327	245	50	32	268
Vermont	714	23	21	48	564	59	145	122	11	12	123
Virginia	3,190	187	102	176	2,262	463	831	588	162	81	564
Washington	4,253	167	102	412	3,106	466	903	486	264	154	634
West Virginia	1,988	64	33	128	1,585	177	430	331	8	91	266
Wisconsin	3,962	131	130	398	2,889	414	686	518	75	92	508
Wyoming	370	24	3	31	261	50	273	225	3	46	718
Island areas:											
American Samoa	17	6	–	–	5	7	13	7	–	6	54
Micronesia	1	–	–	–	–	–	–	–	–	–	53
Guam	30	6	–	–	9	14	12	9	–	3	90
Marshall Islands	–	–	–	–	–	–	–	–	–	–	44
Northern Marianas	10	3	–	–	3	4	9	1	–	8	29
Palau	–	–	–	–	–	–	–	–	–	–	39
Puerto Rico	898	265	14	54	273	291	188	47	127	14	609
Virgin Islands	44	12	–	3	8	20	4	–	1	3	97
Undistributed amounts	17	11	–	–	–	6	123	4	–	132	63

– Represents or rounds to zero   [1] Total includes programs not shown separately.   [2] For Puerto Rico, amount shown is for nutritional assistance grant program, all other amounts are grant payments for food stamp administration.   [3] Data have been revised.   [4] FEMA = Federal Emergency Management Agency. FEMA is part of Department of Homeland Security.   [5] Represents aid for other programs not shown.

Source: U.S. Census Bureau, Federal Aid to States For Fiscal Year 2004 (issued January 2006). See also <http://www.census.gov/prod/2006pubs/fas-04.pdf>.

Table 421. State and Local Governments—Summary of Finances: 1990 to 2004

[In millions of dollars (1,032,115 represents $1,032,115,000,000), except as indicated. For fiscal year ending in year shown; see text, this section. Local government amounts are estimates subject to sampling variation; see Appendix III and source]

Item	Total (millons of dollars)				Per capita [1] (dollars)			
	1990	2000	2003	2004	1990	2000	2003	2004
Revenue [2]	1,032,115	1,942,328	2,047,337	2,435,084	4,149	6,902	7,041	8,292
From federal government	136,802	291,950	389,264	425,683	550	1,037	1,339	1,450
Public welfare	59,961	148,549	199,789	217,176	241	528	687	740
Highways	14,368	24,414	30,052	30,692	58	87	103	105
Education	23,233	45,873	61,901	71,010	93	163	213	242
Health and hospitals	5,904	15,611	21,491	23,316	24	55	74	79
Housing and community development	9,655	17,690	24,713	26,560	39	63	85	90
Other and unallocable	23,683	39,812	51,317	56,929	95	141	176	194
From state and local sources	895,313	1,650,379	1,658,073	2,009,401	3,599	5,864	5,702	6,843
General, net intergovernmental	712,700	1,249,373	1,373,948	1,464,058	2,865	4,439	4,725	4,986
Taxes	501,619	872,351	938,972	1,010,277	2,016	3,100	3,229	3,440
Property	155,613	249,178	296,683	318,242	625	885	1,020	1,084
Sales and gross receipts	177,885	309,290	337,787	360,629	715	1,099	1,162	1,228
Individual income	105,640	211,661	199,407	215,215	425	752	686	733
Corporation net income	23,566	36,059	31,369	33,716	95	128	108	115
Other	38,915	66,164	73,726	82,475	156	235	254	281
Charges and miscellaneous	211,081	377,022	434,976	453,781	848	1,340	1,496	1,545
Utility and liquor stores	58,642	89,546	108,388	114,054	236	318	373	388
Water supply system	17,674	30,515	34,736	36,087	71	108	119	123
Electric power system	29,268	42,436	53,938	55,980	118	151	185	191
Gas supply system	5,216	8,049	8,985	9,783	21	29	31	33
Transit system	3,043	3,954	5,391	6,506	12	14	19	22
Liquor stores	3,441	4,592	5,338	5,698	14	16	18	19
Insurance trust revenue [3]	123,970	311,460	175,737	431,289	498	1,107	604	1,469
Employee retirement	94,268	273,881	120,157	365,265	379	973	413	1,244
Unemployment compensation	18,441	23,366	35,335	38,362	74	83	122	131
Direct expenditure	972,695	1,742,914	2,159,772	2,260,330	3,910	6,193	7,427	7,697
By function:								
Direct general expenditure [3]	831,573	1,502,768	1,817,513	1,903,194	3,342	5,340	6,250	6,481
Education [3]	288,148	521,612	621,335	655,361	1,158	1,853	2,137	2,232
Elementary and secondary	202,009	365,181	428,503	452,055	812	1,298	1,474	1,539
Higher education	73,418	134,352	164,187	173,086	295	477	565	589
Highways	61,057	101,336	117,696	118,179	245	360	405	402
Public welfare	107,287	233,350	306,463	335,257	431	829	1,054	1,142
Health	24,223	51,366	61,703	63,125	97	183	212	215
Hospitals	50,412	75,976	93,175	96,551	203	270	320	329
Police protection	30,577	56,798	67,361	69,707	123	202	232	237
Fire protection	13,186	23,102	27,854	28,330	53	82	96	96
Corrections	24,636	48,805	55,471	56,521	100	173	191	190
Natural resources	12,330	20,235	22,808	23,299	50	72	78	79
Sanitation and sewerage	28,453	45,261	51,723	55,908	114	161	178	190
Housing and community development	15,479	26,590	35,275	37,221	62	94	121	127
Parks and recreation	14,326	25,038	31,765	30,467	58	89	109	104
Financial administration	16,217	29,300	34,911	36,163	65	104	120	123
Interest on general debt [4]	49,739	69,814	77,277	81,723	200	248	266	278
Utility and liquor stores [4]	77,801	114,916	148,996	159,732	313	408	512	544
Water supply system	22,101	35,789	43,260	44,806	89	127	149	153
Electric power system	30,997	39,719	54,355	59,299	125	141	187	202
Gas supply system	2,989	3,724	5,300	6,717	12	13	18	23
Transit system	18,788	31,883	41,678	44,237	76	113	143	151
Liquor stores	2,926	3,801	4,402	4,673	12	14	15	16
Insurance trust expenditure [3]	63,321	125,230	193,263	197,405	255	445	665	672
Employee retirement	38,555	95,679	127,197	137,537	154	340	437	468
Unemployment compensation	16,499	18,648	51,547	43.278	66	66	177	147
By character and object:								
Current operation	700,131	1,288,746	1,579.290	1,662.510	2,814	4,579	5,431	5,661
Capital outlay	123,102	217.063	263,198	269,976	495	771	905	919
Construction	89,144	161,694	203,035	209,395	358	575	698	713
Equipment, land, and existing structures	33,958	55,369	60,162	60,581	136	197	207	206
Assistance and subsidies	27,227	31,375	35,080	36,922	109	111	121	126
Interest on debt (general and utility)	58,914	80,499	88,940	93,518	237	286	306	318
Insurance benefits and repayments	63,321	125,230	193,263	197,405	255	445	665	672
Expenditure for salaries and wages [5]	*340,654*	*548,796*	*647,211*	*666,041*	*1,369*	*1,950*	*2,226*	*2,268*
Debt outstanding, year end	858,006	1,451,815	1,812,667	1,951,661	3,449	5,159	6,234	6,646
Long-term	838,700	1,427.524	1,772.197	1,913.286	3,371	5.073	6,094	6,515
Short-term	19,306	24,291	40,470	38,374	78	86	139	131
Long-term debt:								
Issued	108,468	184,831	345,784	346.813	436	657	1,189	1,181
Retired	64,831	121.897	215,218	241.111	261	433	740	821

[1] 1990 and 2000 based on enumerated resident population as of April 1. Other years based on estimated resident population as of July 1. [2] Aggregates exclude duplicative transactions between state and local governments; see source [3] Includes amounts not shown separately. [4] Interest on utility debt included in "utility and liquor stores expenditure." For total interest on debt, see "Interest on debt (general and utility)." [5] Included in items above.

Source: U.S. Census Bureau; *Federal, State and Local Governments, State Government Finances,* series GF, No. 3 thereafter; <http://www.census.gov/govs/www/estimate04.html> (September 2006).

State and Local Government Finances and Employment 269

Table 422. **Table 422. State and Local Governments—Revenue and Expenditures by Function: 2004**

[In millions of dollars (2,435,084 represents $2,435,084,000,000), except as indicated. For fiscal year ending in year shown; see text, this section. Local government amounts are estimates subject to sampling variation; see Appendix III and source]

Item	Amount (mil. dol.) State and local	State	Local	Per capita (dol.)[1] State and local	State	Local
Revenue [2]	**2,435,084**	**1,586,665**	**1,247,463**	**8,292**	**5,413**	**4,248**
Intergovernmental revenue [2]	425,683	394,613	430,114	1,450	1,346	1,465
Total revenue from own sources [2]	2,009,401	1,192,052	817,349	6,843	4,067	2,783
General revenue from own sources	1,464,058	799,443	664,615	4,986	2,728	2,263
Taxes [3]	1,010,277	590,414	419,863	3,440	2,014	1,430
Property	318,242	10,714	307,528	1,084	37	1,047
Individual income	215,215	196,255	18,960	733	670	65
Corporation income	33,716	30,229	3,487	115	103	12
Sales and gross receipts	360,629	293,326	67,303	1,228	1,001	229
General sales	244,891	197,949	46,942	834	675	160
Selective sales [3]	115,738	95,377	20,361	394	325	69
Motor fuel	34,944	33,762	1,181	119	115	4
Alcoholic beverages	4,986	4,593	392	17	16	1
Tobacco products	12,626	12,303	323	43	42	1
Public utilities	21,427	10,709	10,717	73	37	36
Motor vehicle and operators' licenses	20,707	19,329	1,378	71	66	5
Death and gift	5,758	5,732	26	20	20	–
Charges and miscellaneous [3]	453,781	209,029	244,752	1,545	713	833
Current charges [3]	288,642	114,843	173,799	983	392	592
Education [3]	84,420	64,290	20,130	287	219	69
School lunch sales	6,326	21	6,305	22	–	21
Higher education	71,780	63,423	8,357	244	216	28
Natural resources	3,264	2,344	920	11	8	3
Hospitals	72,652	26,480	46,171	247	90	157
Sewerage	29,792	39	29,753	101	–	101
Solid waste management	12,083	422	11,661	41	1	40
Parks and recreation	7,982	1,328	6,653	27	5	23
Housing and community development	4,770	578	4,193	16	2	14
Airports	13,345	931	12,414	45	3	42
Sea and inland port facilities	3,107	879	2,227	11	3	8
Highways	8,991	5,533	3,458	31	19	12
Interest earnings	53,194	28,414	24,781	181	97	84
Special assessments	6,453	722	5,731	22	2	20
Sale of property	1,960	690	1,270	7	2	4
Utility and liquor store revenue	114,054	17,821	96,234	388	61	328
Insurance trust revenue	431,289	374,788	56,500	1,469	1,279	192
Expenditure [2]	**2,265,051**	**1,406,175**	**1,257,581**	**7,713**	**4,798**	**4,282**
Intergovernmental expenditure [2]	4,721	389,706	13,720	16	1,330	47
Direct expenditure [2]	2,260,330	1,016,469	1,243,861	7,697	3,468	4,236
General expenditure [3]	1,003,194	819,730	1,083,464	6,481	2,797	3,690
Education [3]	655,361	180,984	474,376	2,232	617	1,615
Elementary and secondary education	452,055	5,851	446,204	1,539	20	1,519
Higher education	173,086	144,913	28,173	589	494	96
Public welfare	335,257	291,968	43,289	1,142	996	147
Hospitals	96,551	40,011	56,541	329	137	193
Health	63,125	29,608	33,517	215	101	114
Highways	118,179	72,194	45,985	402	246	157
Police protection	69,707	9,471	60,236	237	32	205
Fire protection	28,330	–	28,330	96	–	96
Corrections	56,521	36,963	19,558	192	126	67
Natural resources	23,299	17,226	6,072	79	59	21
Sewerage	35,535	1,568	33,966	121	5	116
Solid waste management	20,373	2,952	17,421	69	10	59
Housing and community development	37,221	4,273	32,948	127	15	112
Governmental administration	100,741	43,453	57,289	343	148	195
Parks and recreation	30,467	4,571	25,896	104	16	88
Interest on general debt	81,723	32,953	48,770	278	112	166
Utility	155,059	21,676	133,382	528	74	454
Liquor store expenditure	4,673	3,924	749	16	13	3
Insurance trust expenditure	197,405	171,139	26,266	672	584	89
By character and object:						
Current operation	1,662,510	691,652	970,858	5,661	2,360	3,306
Capital outlay	269,976	90,950	179,026	919	310	610
Construction	209,395	73,372	136,022	713	250	463
Equipment, land, and existing structures	60,581	17,578	43,004	206	60	146
Assistance and subsidies	36,922	28,104	8,818	126	96	30
Interest on debt (general and utility)	93,518	34,624	58,894	318	118	201
Insurance benefits and repayments	197,405	171,139	26,266	672	584	89
Expenditure for salaries and wages [4]	*666,041*	*185,827*	*480,214*	*2,268*	*634*	*1,635*

– Represents or rounds to zero.   [1] Based on estimated resident population as of July 1. See Table 12.   [2] Aggregates exclude duplicative transactions between levels of government; see source.   [3] Includes amounts not shown separately.   [4] Included in items shown above.

Source: U.S. Census Bureau, Federal, State, and Local Governments, Finance, State and Local Government Finances, 2003–04. <http://www.census.gov/govs/www/estimate04.html> (September 2006).

Table 423. State and Local Governments—Capital Outlays: 1990 to 2004

[In millions of dollars (123,102 represents $123,102,000,000), except percent. For fiscal year ending in year shown; see text, this section. Local government amounts are subject to sampling variation; see Appendix III and source. Minus sign (−) indicates net loss.]

Level and function	1990	1995	1999	2000	2001	2002	2003	2004
State & local governments: Total . . .	**123,102**	**151,440**	**198,483**	**217,063**	**233,258**	**257,071**	**263,198**	**269,976**
Annual percent change [1]	9.0	10.1	9.1	9.4	7.5	10.2	2.4	2.6
By function:								
Education [2]	25,997	35,708	54,418	60,968	65,116	71,680	70,813	74,597
Elementary and secondary. . . .	18,057	24,808	40,768	45,150	48,404	53,294	51,118	52,977
Higher education	7,441	10,461	13,114	15,257	15,911	17,652	19,044	21,121
Highways	33,867	42,561	51,906	56,439	60,108	66,017	65,523	65,964
Health and hospitals	3,848	4,883	5,699	5,502	5,630	6,126	7,158	7,241
Natural resources	2,545	2,891	3,359	4,347	4,908	4,247	4,244	4,657
Housing [3]	3,997	4,527	5,615	6,184	5,888	6,939	7,660	7,578
Air transportation	3,434	3,802	6,666	6,717	8,420	8,551	9,066	9,731
Water transportation [4]	924	1,101	1,487	1,618	4,306	1,691	3,721	1,798
Sewerage	8,356	8,894	9,718	10,093	9,224	11,574	12,467	14,068
Parks and recreation	3,877	4,085	6,486	6,916	8,540	9,093	9,224	7,866
Utilities	16,601	19,028	21,861	24,847	24,553	30,241	34,538	37,432
Water	6,873	7,466	10,325	10,542	10,742	11,831	13,536	13,651
Electric	3,976	3,715	3,613	4,177	4,812	6,538	6,438	7,173
Gas	310	340	389	400	453	358	422	582
Transit	5,443	7,507	7,533	9,728	8,545	11,514	14,142	16,026
Other	19,657	23,961	31,268	33,431	36,566	40,912	38,784	39,044
State governments: Total.	**45,524**	**57,829**	**68,509**	**76,233**	**81,881**	**89,767**	**91,943**	**90,950**
Annual percent change [1]	5.6	9.3	6.3	11.3	7.4	9.6	2.4	−1.1
By function:								
Education [2]	7,253	10,042	12,294	14,077	14,936	16,589	17,727	19,632
Highways	24,850	31,687	37,986	41,651	44,761	49,119	48,719	48,566
Health and hospitals	1,531	2,402	2,276	2,228	2,390	2,241	2,930	2,763
Natural resources	1,593	1,956	2,349	2,758	3,105	2,766	2,788	2,957
Housing [3]	119	187	202	860	600	582	774	222
Air transportation	339	356	536	561	667	525	846	795
Water transportation [4]	202	223	270	310	362	346	410	388
Sewerage	333	853	627	403	393	405	405	881
Parks and recreation	601	650	1,023	1,044	1,185	1,483	1,098	945
Utilities	2,605	2,226	3,034	4,232	3,641	5,145	7,084	5,211
Other	6,098	7,246	7,912	8,108	9,840	10,567	9,163	8,589
Local governments: Total	**77,578**	**93,611**	**129,974**	**140,830**	**151,377**	**167,304**	**171,255**	**179,026**
Annual percent change [1]	4.5	10.6	10.7	8.4	7.5	10.5	2.4	4.5
By function:								
Education [2]	18,744	29,858	42,124	46,890	50,180	55,091	53,087	54,965
Elementary and secondary. . . .	17,669	28,402	40,160	44,629	47,808	52,804	50,475	52,261
Higher education	1,076	1,456	1,964	2,261	2,372	2,286	2,612	2,704
Highways	9,017	10,874	13,920	14,789	15,347	16,898	16,804	17,398
Health and hospitals	2,316	2,481	3,423	3,274	3,239	3,886	4,228	4,478
Natural resources	952	935	1,010	1,589	1,803	1,481	1,456	1,699
Housing [3]	3,878	4,340	5,413	5,324	5,288	6,358	6,886	7,356
Air transportation	3,095	3,446	6,129	6,156	7,753	8,026	8,221	8,936
Water transportation [4]	722	877	1,217	1,308	3,944	1,345	3,310	1,410
Sewerage	8,023	8,040	9,091	9,690	8,831	11,169	12,062	13,186
Parks and recreation	3,276	3,435	5,463	5,872	7,355	7,611	8,126	6,921
Utilities	13,996	16,801	18,827	20,615	20,912	25,096	27,455	32,221
Other	13,559	16,715	23,356	25,323	26,726	30,345	29,621	30,454

[1] Change from immediate/prior year except 1990, change from 1989. [2] Includes other education. [3] Includes community development. [4] Includes terminals.

Source: U.S. Census Bureau , *Federal, State, and Local Governments, Finance, State and Local Government Finances,* 2003–04, and unpublished data. See also <http://www.census.gov/govs/www/estimate04.html> (May 2007).

Table 424. State and Local Governments—Expenditure for Public Works: 1995 to 2004

[In millions of dollars (180,148 represents $180,148,000,000), except percent. Public works include expenditures for current operations and capital outlays on highways, airports, water transport terminals, and sewerage, solid waste management, water supply, and mass transit systems. Represents direct expenditures excluding intergovernmental grants]

Item	Total	Highways	Airport transpor-tation	Water transport and ter-minals	Sewer-age	Solid waste manage-ment	Water supply	Mass transit
1995, Total.	180,148	77,109	8,397	2,309	23,583	14,990	28,041	25,719
State	56,392	46,893	783	604	1,462	1,658	178	4,814
Local	123,756	30,216	7,614	1,706	22,121	13,331	27,863	20,904
Capital expenditures (percent) . .	40.7	55.2	45.3	47.7	37.7	13.2	26.6	29.2
2000, Total.	230,569	101,336	13,160	3,141	28,052	17,208	35,789	31,883
State	74,974	61,942	1,106	863	955	2,347	354	7,407
Local	155,595	39,394	12,054	2,277	27,098	14,861	35,435	24,476
Capital expenditures (percent) . .	41.9	55.7	51.0	51.5	36.0	8.9	29.5	30.5
2004, Total.	285,206	118,179	18,031	4,047	35,535	20,373	44,806	44,237
State	88,763	72,194	1,505	1,175	1,568	2,952	531	8,838
Local	196,443	45,985	16,525	2,872	33,966	17,421	44,275	35,399
Capital expenditures (percent) . .	43.1	55.8	54.0	44.4	39.6	8.8	30.5	36.2

Source: U.S. Census Bureau, *Federal, State, and Local Governments, Finance, State and Local Government Finances,* 2003–04, and unpublished data. See also <http://www.census.gov/govs/www/estimate04.html> (May 2007).

U.S. Census Bureau, Statistical Abstract of the United States: 2008

Table 425. State and Local Governments—Indebtedness: 1980 to 2004

[In billions of dollars (335.6 represents $335,600,000,000), except per capita. For fiscal year ending in year shown; see text, this section. Local government amounts are estimates subject to sampling variation; see Appendix III and source]

Item	Debt outstanding						Long term		
		Per capita [1] (dol.)	Long-term			Short-term	Net long-term [3]	Debt issued	Debt retired
	Total		Local schools [2]	Utilities	All other				
1980: Total	335.6	1,481	32.3	55.2	235.0	13.1	262.9	42.4	17.4
State	122.0	540	3.8	4.6	111.5	2.1	79.8	16.4	5.7
Local	213.6	943	28.5	50.6	123.5	11.0	183.1	25.9	11.7
1990: Total	858.0	3,449	60.4	134.8	643.5	19.3	474.4	108.5	64.8
State	318.3	1,282	4.4	12.3	298.7	2.8	125.5	43.5	22.9
Local	539.8	2,169	56.0	122.4	344.8	16.5	348.9	65.0	42.0
1992: Total	970.5	3,806	78.4	150.4	720.4	21.3	561.6	155.1	99.2
State	372.3	1,463	7.6	13.7	348.1	2.9	125.4	70.2	45.0
Local	598.1	2,345	70.9	136.7	373.1	18.4	409.1	85.0	54.3
1993: Total	1,017.7	3,943	89.8	157.6	747.5	22.7	617.1	195.6	147.0
State	389.7	1,515	9.4	14.8	361.7	3.9	176.9	77.1	60.7
Local	628.0	2,436	80.5	142.8	385.8	18.8	440.1	118.4	86.3
1994: Total	1,074.7	4,128	94.3	164.9	788.8	26.7	672.8	207.8	166.6
State	411.0	1,582	10.4	16.7	379.0	4.9	200.8	78.5	61.3
Local	663.7	2,549	83.9	148.2	409.7	21.8	472.0	129.3	105.3
1995: Total	1,115.4	4,244	118.2	163.9	806.2	27.0	697.3	129.3	95.1
State	427.2	1,629	11.3	17.0	392.8	6.1	205.3	52.6	37.5
Local	688.1	2,618	107.0	146.9	413.4	20.9	491.9	76.8	57.6
1996: Total	1,169.7	4,410	130.7	170.3	844.7	24.0	751.6	141.1	106.5
State	452.4	1,709	11.2	16.3	419.1	5.8	220.3	60.2	42.4
Local	717.3	2,705	119.5	154.0	425.6	18.2	531.3	80.9	64.1
1997: Total	1,224.5	4,573	139.0	179.1	889.8	16.6	797.7	151.3	109.3
State	456.7	1,709	11.7	16.0	426.8	2.1	222.7	54.4	41.1
Local	767.9	2,867	127.3	163.1	463.0	14.5	575.1	96.8	68.2
1998: Total	1,283.6	4,750	159.2	182.8	924.3	17.3	842.6	204.4	144.6
State	483.1	1,791	13.6	16.7	450.6	2.2	237.2	83.4	58.1
Local	800.4	2,962	145.5	166.1	473.8	15.1	605.4	120.9	86.5
1999: Total	1,369.3	5,021	180.7	194.9	975.7	17.8	907.3	229.4	153.1
State	510.5	1,876	15.4	16.7	475.8	2.7	249.4	83.2	55.6
Local	858.8	3,149	165.3	178.3	500.0	15.2	657.9	146.2	97.5
2000: Total	1,451.8	5,159	197.7	200.1	1,029.8	24.3	959.6	184.8	121.9
State	547.9	1,951	18.7	17.9	505.0	6.4	266.9	75.0	44.4
Local	903.9	3,212	179.0	182.2	524.8	17.9	692.7	109.8	77.5
2001: Total	1,554.0	5,447	225.3	210.4	1,096.2	22.1	1,038.6	199.6	130.6
State	576.5	2,025	21.5	18.7	532.6	3.7	287.4	81.3	50.7
Local	977.5	3,426	203.8	191.7	563.5	18.5	751.2	118.3	79.9
2002: Total	1,686.1	5,855	250.2	218.5	1,174.2	43.2	1,126.6	262.3	162.5
State	642.2	2,234	23.8	26.1	573.6	18.6	317.8	103.7	65.3
Local	1,043.9	3,625	226.4	192.4	600.5	24.6	808.8	158.6	97.2
2003: Total	1,812.7	6,234	272.7	238.4	1,261.1	40.5	1,242.7	345.8	215.2
State	697.9	2,405	24.0	36.1	621.7	16.1	366.2	148.8	85.9
Local	1,114.7	3,833	248.7	202.3	639.4	24.3	876.5	196.9	129.3
2004: Total	1,951.7	6,646	300.2	243.8	1,369.3	38.4	1,349.6	346.8	241.1
State	754.2	2,573	26.1	37.9	676.4	13.7	412.2	158.4	107.1
Local	1,197.5	4,078	274.1	205.9	692.9	24.6	937.4	188.5	134.0

[1] 1980, 1990, and 2000 based on enumerated resident population as of April 1; other years based on estimated resident population as of July 1. [2] Includes debt for education activities other than higher education. [3] Net long-term debt outstanding is the amount of long-term debt held by a government for which no funds have been set aside for its repayment.

Source: U.S. Census Bureau, 1990, *Government Finances*, Series GF, No. 5, annual; thereafter, *Federal, State, and Local Governments, Finance, State and Local Government Finances*, 2003–04, and unpublished data. See also <http://www.census.gov/govs/www/estimate04.html>.

Table 426. New Security Issues, State and Local Governments: 1990 to 2006

[In billions of dollars, (122.9 represents 122,900,000,000)]

Type of issue, issuer or use	1990	1995	1999	2000	2001	2002	2003	2004	2005	2006
All issues, new and refunding [1]	122.9	145.7	215.4	180.4	291.9	363.9	384.3	357.9	409.6	389.3
By type of issue:										
General obligation	39.5	57.0	73.3	64.5	118.6	145.3	144.1	130.5	145.8	115.0
Revenue	83.3	88.7	142.1	115.9	170.0	214.8	238.0	227.4	263.8	274.3
By type of issuer:										
State	15.0	14.7	16.4	19.9	30.1	33.9	49.8	47.4	31.6	28.3
Special district of statutory authority [2] . . .	75.9	93.5	152.4	121.2	197.5	259.1	253.5	234.2	298.6	293.2
Municipality, county, or township	32.0	37.5	46.6	39.3	61.0	67.1	79.0	76.3	79.4	67.8
Issues for new capital.	97.9	102.4	161.1	154.3	200.3	242.9	264.7	228.4	223.8	263.1
By use of proceeds:										
Education	17.1	24.0	36.6	38.7	50.1	57.9	70.4	65.4	71.0	70.3
Transportation	11.8	11.9	17.4	19.7	21.4	22.1	23.8	20.5	25.4	30.2
Utilities and conservation.	10.0	9.6	15.1	11.9	21.9	33.4	10.3	9.2	9.9	7.8
Industrial aid	6.6	6.6	9.1	7.1	6.6	7.2	22.3	19.1	18.6	35.0
Other purposes	31.7	30.8	47.9	47.3	55.7	73.0	97.7	80.4	60.6	72.7

[1] Par amounts of long-term issues based on date of sale. [2] Includes school districts.

Source: Board of Governors of the Federal Reserve System, *Statistical Supplement to the Federal Reserve Bulletin, monthly.* Based on data from Securities Data Company; <http://www.federalreserve.gov/pubs/supplement/2007/04/table145.htm>.

Table 427. State and Local Governments—Per Capita Summary of Finances by State: 2004

[In millions of dollars (2,435,084 represents $2,435,084,000,000), except as indicated. For fiscal year ending in year shown; see text, this section]

State	Revenue [1] All revenue Total	Per capita [2] (dol.)	General revenue Total	Per capita [2] (dol.)	Taxes Total	Per capita [2] (dol.)	Expenditures [1] Direct general expen- ditures	Per capita [2] (dol.)	Debt outstanding Total	Per capita [2] (dol.)
United States ..	2,435,084	8,292	1,889,741	6,435	1,010,277	3,440	1,903,194	6,481	1,951,661	6,646
Alabama........	32,065	7,086	25,535	5,643	10,535	2,328	27,089	5,987	21,629	4,780
Alaska.........	11,038	16,775	8,529	12,963	2,376	3,610	8,496	12,912	8,626	13,109
Arizona.........	38,388	6,688	30,195	5,260	16,481	2,871	30,075	5,240	29,844	5,199
Arkansas	18,027	6,555	14,745	5,362	6,973	2,536	14,577	5,301	10,409	3,785
California	358,673	10,007	251,889	7,028	133,894	3,736	260,960	7,281	269,935	7,531
Colorado........	38,744	8,419	28,128	6,112	14,582	3,169	28,424	6,176	33,841	7,354
Connecticut......	29,295	8,372	25,887	7,398	17,220	4,921	25,018	7,150	30,516	8,721
Delaware	7,102	8,557	6,249	7,529	2,994	3,608	6,191	7,459	6,053	7,292
District of Columbia	8,829	15,936	7,640	13,791	3,964	7,154	6,723	12,135	6,490	11,715
Florida	129,687	7,460	102,725	5,909	53,789	3,094	100,771	5,796	108,764	6,256
Georgia	57,902	6,493	47,336	5,308	25,655	2,877	50,211	5,630	34,848	3,908
Hawaii	9,983	7,910	8,221	6,514	4,812	3,813	8,673	6,872	9,027	7,153
Idaho..........	9,754	6,992	7,758	5,561	3,806	2,728	7,540	5,405	4,021	2,883
Illinois	100,247	7,886	76,266	6,000	45,191	3,555	79,495	6,254	102,304	8,048
Indiana.........	40,977	6,581	35,696	5,732	18,675	2,999	35,540	5,707	29,583	4,751
Iowa	22,545	7,634	18,396	6,230	9,019	3,054	18,396	6,230	11,335	3,839
Kansas.........	18,550	6,785	16,276	5,953	9,242	3,380	16,284	5,956	16,122	5,897
Kentucky	26,834	6,478	22,982	5,549	11,460	2,767	23,342	5,636	29,143	7,036
Louisiana	34,107	7,568	27,905	6,191	13,065	2,899	27,251	6,046	22,165	4,918
Maine..........	11,131	8,464	9,517	7,237	4,983	3,789	9,282	7,058	6,919	5,262
Maryland	44,288	7,964	36,777	6,613	22,331	4,016	34,111	6,134	27,795	4,998
Massachusetts....	60,795	9,489	47,172	7,363	27,015	4,217	48,446	7,561	72,898	11,378
Michigan........	80,185	7,936	65,501	6,483	33,478	3,313	67,643	6,695	57,609	5,702
Minnesota.......	42,956	8,428	35,230	6,912	19,424	3,811	36,637	7,188	33,670	6,606
Mississippi	20,670	7,125	16,914	5,831	7,089	2,444	17,282	5,957	10,189	3,512
Missouri	40,033	6,950	31,982	5,552	16,255	2,822	31,020	5,385	30,408	5,279
Montana........	7,088	7,646	5,796	6,252	2,431	2,623	5,547	5,983	4,297	4,635
Nebraska	15,479	8,855	11,669	6,676	6,308	3,609	10,776	6,165	8,829	5,051
Nevada	16,888	7,239	13,267	5,687	7,972	3,417	13,619	5,838	17,851	7,652
New Hampshire ...	8,703	6,700	7,440	5,728	4,070	3,133	7,549	5,811	8,135	6,262
New Jersey......	75,083	8,645	61,593	7,092	39,558	4,555	61,224	7,049	64,272	7,400
New Mexico	14,918	7,839	12,477	6,556	5,444	2,861	12,616	6,630	9,724	5,110
New York	224,429	11,640	179,380	9,303	101,426	5,260	175,803	9,118	219,358	11,377
North Carolina	63,458	7,431	48,768	5,711	25,012	2,929	48,490	5,678	37,973	4,447
North Dakota.....	6,524	10,259	4,348	6,836	1,901	2,989	4,157	6,537	3,143	4,941
Ohio	105,382	9,204	72,264	6,311	39,151	3,419	74,445	6,502	57,898	5,057
Oklahoma.......	23,954	6,797	19,215	5,453	9,435	2,677	18,148	5,150	13,265	3,764
Oregon.........	33,734	9,394	21,770	6,062	10,474	2,917	22,309	6,213	24,753	6,893
Pennsylvania.....	102,238	8,249	78,632	6,344	42,718	3,447	80,339	6,482	96,374	7,776
Rhode Island.....	9,665	8,949	7,761	7,186	4,202	3,891	7,643	7,077	8,237	7,627
South Carolina....	30,547	7,276	24,714	5,887	11,177	2,662	25,591	6,096	25,940	6,179
South Dakota	5,593	7,254	4,383	5,684	2,016	2,615	4,132	5,360	3,849	4,992
Tennessee	42,125	7,148	31,661	5,373	14,947	2,536	31,581	5,359	24,320	4,127
Texas..........	153,761	6,842	124,042	5,520	64,739	2,881	124,057	5,521	146,009	6,497
Utah	18,917	7,814	13,834	5,714	6,621	2,735	13,906	5,744	14,265	5,892
Vermont	5,266	8,480	4,569	7,357	2,286	3,681	4,398	7,082	3,327	5,358
Virginia.........	54,162	7,240	43,829	5,859	25,002	3,342	42,955	5,742	40,006	5,348
Washington......	54,738	8,819	39,758	6,405	21,425	3,452	42,579	6,860	50,370	8,115
West Virginia.....	14,117	7,787	·11,926	6,578	4,968	2,740	10,604	5,849	8,214	4,531
Wisconsin.......	48,698	8,848	35,528	6,455	20,441	3,714	36,714	6,670	35,272	6,409
Wyoming	6,816	13,471	5,663	11,193	2,245	4,437	4,535	8,961	1,835	3,627

[1] Includes items not shown separately. [2] Based on estimated resident population as of July 1, see Table 12.

Source: U.S. Census Bureau, *Federal, State, and Local Governments, Finance, State and Local Government Finances,* 2003-04; <http://www.census.gov/govs/www/estimate04.html> (accessed May 2007).

State and Local Government Finances and Employment **273**

Table 428. **State and Local Governments—Revenue by State: 2004**

[In millions of dollars (2,435,084 represents $2,435,084,000,000). For fiscal year ending in year shown, see text, this section]

State	Total revenue	General revenue Total	Intergovernmental from federal government	General revenue own sources	Taxes Total [1]	Property	Sales and gross receipts	Individual income [2]	Motor vehicle	Other taxes
United States ..	2,435,084	1,889,741	425,683	1,464,058	1,010,277	318,242	360,629	248,930	18,709	63,766
Alabama	32,065	25,535	6,819	18,716	10,535	1,662	5,217	2,636	198	822
Alaska.	11,038	8,529	2,421	6,109	2,376	859	358	340	58	760
Arizona	38,388	30,195	7,587	22,608	16,481	4,868	7,989	2,842	162	620
Arkansas	18,027	14,745	4,277	10,468	6,973	1,101	3,714	1,870	110	178
California	358,673	251,889	54,343	197,545	133,894	34,499	45,193	43,325	2,155	8,721
Colorado	38,744	28,128	5,203	22,925	14,582	4,722	5,390	3,653	226	590
Connecticut	29,295	25,887	4,503	21,384	17,220	6,802	4,900	4,699	197	621
Delaware	7,102	6,249	1,092	5,157	2,994	453	394	1,046	34	1,067
District of Columbia . .	8,829	7,640	2,706	4,934	3,964	1,028	1,153	1,218	24	541
Florida.	129,687	102,725	19,182	83,543	53,789	18,500	27,408	1,441	1,135	5,305
Georgia	57,902	47,336	9,903	37,433	25,655	7,845	9,423	7,325	280	782
Hawaii.	9,983	8,221	1,834	6,387	4,812	721	2,606	1,227	161	97
Idaho	9,754	7,758	1,875	5,883	3,806	1,084	1,427	1,012	112	171
Illinois	100,247	76,266	15,652	60,614	45,191	17,889	15,344	8,497	1,490	1,970
Indiana	40,977	35,696	7,337	28,360	18,675	6,074	6,992	4,877	178	555
Iowa	22,545	18,396	4,304	14,092	9,019	3,189	3,012	2,100	393	325
Kansas	18,550	16,276	3,137	13,140	9,242	3,247	3,427	2,082	165	321
Kentucky	26,834	22,982	6,242	16,741	11,460	2,136	4,313	4,011	208	792
Louisiana.	34,107	27,905	7,622	20,282	13,065	2,263	7,239	2,429	117	1,017
Maine	11,131	9,517	2,677	6,841	4,983	2,099	1,337	1,272	113	162
Maryland	44,288	36,777	7,262	29,515	22,331	6,019	5,456	8,856	319	1,682
Massachusetts	60,795	47,172	10,065	37,107	27,015	9,814	5,740	10,131	293	1,037
Michigan	80,185	65,501	15,110	50,391	33,478	11,979	11,066	8,203	1,067	1,164
Minnesota	42,956	35,230	7,161	28,069	19,424	4,920	6,564	6,347	521	1,071
Mississippi	20,670	16,914	5,643	11,272	7,089	1,860	3,459	1,306	118	347
Missouri.	40,033	31,982	8,018	23,964	16,255	4,304	6,695	4,258	266	733
Montana	7,088	5,796	1,880	3,915	2,431	959	440	673	148	211
Nebraska.	15,479	11,669	2,536	9,133	6,308	2,007	2,334	1,410	113	444
Nevada	16,888	13,267	1,920	11,348	7,972	2,147	4,568	–	139	1,117
New Hampshire	8,703	7,440	1,572	5,868	4,070	2,520	674	462	84	329
New Jersey	75,083	61,593	9,932	51,661	39,558	18,229	9,780	9,298	399	1,852
New Mexico	14,918	12,477	3,803	8,674	5,444	840	2,628	1,145	124	707
New York	224,429	179,380	45,695	133,686	101,426	32,334	27,397	36,108	834	4,753
North Carolina	63,458	48,768	11,910	36,858	25,012	6,093	8,951	8,348	467	1,153
North Dakota	6,524	4,348	1,314	3,034	1,901	585	742	264	55	256
Ohio	105,382	72,264	16,313	55,951	39,151	11,233	12,318	13,244	807	1,550
Oklahoma	23,954	19,215	4,819	14,396	9,435	1,637	3,639	2,452	554	1,153
Oregon	33,734	21,770	4,938	16,831	10,474	3,459	1,014	4,691	420	890
Pennsylvania	102,238	78,632	18,112	60,520	42,718	12,518	12,918	11,989	792	4,500
Rhode Island	9,665	7,761	2,124	5,637	4,202	1,759	1,311	969	57	106
South Carolina	30,547	24,714	6,211	18,503	11,177	3,704	4,012	2,635	151	674
South Dakota	5,593	4,383	1,360	3,023	2,016	705	1,071	47	66	127
Tennessee.	42,125	31,661	9,524	22,138	14,947	3,585	8,846	835	371	1,309
Texas	153,761	124,042	27,683	96,359	64,739	28,176	29,656	–	1,543	5,363
Utah	18,917	13,834	3,221	10,612	6,621	1,669	2,770	1,837	93	252
Vermont	5,266	4,569	1,369	3,200	2,286	950	693	492	63	88
Virginia	54,162	43,829	7,051	36,779	25,002	7,715	7,249	7,844	486	1,708
Washington	54,738	39,758	7,738	32,020	21,425	6,386	12,999	–	365	1,674
West Virginia	14,117	11,926	3,440	8,486	4,968	979	2,150	1,250	84	505
Wisconsin	48,698	35,528	7,262	28,266	20,441	7,429	5,915	5,933	331	833
Wyoming	6,816	5,663	1,982	3,682	2,245	684	734	–	64	764

See footnotes at end of table.

U.S. Census Bureau, Statistical Abstract of the United States: 2008

Table 428. State and Local Governments—Revenue by State: 2004—Con.

[See headnote page 274]

State	General revenue Current charges and miscellaneous revenue								Utility and liquor stores	Insurance trust revenue
		Current charges				Miscellaneous revenue				
	Total	Total [1]	Education	Hospitals	Sewerage	Total [1]	Interest earnings	Special assessments		
United States ..	453,781	288,642	84,420	72,652	29,792	165,139	53,194	6,453	114,054	431,289
Alabama	8,180	6,311	1,845	3,277	318	1,869	650	17	2,251	4,279
Alaska.	3,733	767	159	76	61	2,966	1,168	17	229	2,280
Arizona	6,126	3,628	1,389	417	433	2,499	728	83	3,099	5,094
Arkansas	3,495	2,476	855	782	188	1,019	402	12	688	2,594
California.	63,652	42,454	7,175	10,531	4,210	21,198	5,666	1,100	20,855	85,930
Colorado	8,344	5,286	1,839	1,091	520	3,058	970	350	1,761	8,855
Connecticut	4,164	2,264	801	419	246	1,900	654	29	538	2,870
Delaware.	2,163	1,018	392	29	120	1,145	269	316	236	617
District of Columbia . .	970	389	21	-	98	581	100	1	664	525
Florida.	29,754	17,680	3,266	4,287	1,762	12,073	3,713	1,207	6,311	20,652
Georgia	11,778	7,566	1,753	3,023	705	4,212	949	41	3,304	7,262
Hawaii.	1,575	1,183	255	208	151	392	160	15	208	1,554
Idaho	2,077	1,468	350	527	121	610	245	26	270	1,727
Illinois	15,423	9,043	3,457	1,086	914	6,380	2,356	259	2,842	21,139
Indiana	9,685	6,354	2,730	2,037	669	3,331	761	22	1,738	3,542
Iowa	5,073	3,709	1,332	1,471	269	1,364	396	38	820	3,328
Kansas	3,898	2,449	1,042	535	234	1,448	514	106	942	1,331
Kentucky	5,280	3,133	1,093	930	301	2,147	962	46	991	2,861
Louisiana	7,217	4,656	1,035	2,266	282	2,561	965	19	1,029	5,174
Maine	1,858	923	362	70	121	935	289	7	190	1,424
Maryland	7,184	4,537	2,076	95	690	2,647	653	94	790	6,721
Massachusetts	10,092	4,826	1,634	417	723	5,265	1,583	426	2,454	11,169
Michigan	16,913	11,207	4,305	2,423	1,284	5,706	1,717	241	2,511	12,173
Minnesota	8,645	5,620	1,972	1,110	509	3,025	997	318	1,641	6,085
Mississippi	4,183	3,314	846	1,767	158	869	321	5	794	2,961
Missouri.	7,709	4,875	1,881	1,464	451	2,834	1,063	115	1,276	6,775
Montana	1,484	884	391	43	60	600	234	49	135	1,157
Nebraska.	2,825	1,633	629	420	109	1,192	324	52	2,483	1,326
Nevada	3,376	2,416	464	509	345	960	285	116	946	2,675
New Hampshire	1,798	1,064	458	6	78	735	329	1	455	808
New Jersey	12,103	7,609	2,553	728	1,135	4,493	1,267	26	1,374	12,116
New Mexico	3,230	1,399	455	421	121	1,831	605	68	429	2,011
New York	32,259	19,868	3,580	5,248	1,564	12,391	3,312	101	10,576	34,473
North Carolina	11,846	8,862	2,461	3,405	1,080	2,984	1,161	24	3,216	11,474
North Dakota	1,133	746	318	4	35	387	127	47	96	2,080
Ohio	16,800	10,772	4,431	2,208	1,408	6,028	1,983	205	2,559	30,559
Oklahoma	4,961	3,437	1,501	845	232	1,524	436	7	1,125	3,614
Oregon	6,357	4,323	1,217	781	584	2,034	484	82	1,530	10,434
Pennsylvania	17,802	11,019	3,875	1,709	1,683	6,784	3,220	120	3,435	20,171
Rhode Island	1,435	669	312	4	70	766	291	3	163	1,741
South Carolina	7,327	5,292	1,562	2,415	280	2,035	594	57	2,470	3,362
South Dakota	1,007	518	232	33	50	488	216	16	200	1,010
Tennessee	7,191	5,482	1,456	2,125	444	1,709	504	53	6,423	4,040
Texas	31,620	18,895	6,117	5,483	2,103	12,725	4,900	118	7,948	21,771
Utah	3,991	2,881	1,189	537	209	1,110	384	27	1,617	3,466
Vermont	914	490	336	-	42	424	146	2	212	485
Virginia	11,776	7,557	2,441	1,754	839	4,219	1,332	125	1,755	8,578
Washington	10,595	7,616	1,983	1,970	1,041	2,979	1,005	107	4,955	10,025
West Virginia	3,518	1,954	562	301	134	1,564	486	11	224	1,967
Wisconsin	7,825	5,272	1,885	837	570	2,553	932	121	1,123	12,047
Wyoming	1,437	847	149	527	39	589	382	7	172	981

- Represents or rounds to zero. [1] Includes items not shown separately. [2] Includes individual and corporate income taxes.

Source: U.S. Census Bureau; *Federal, State and Local Governments, State Government Finances*; <http://www.census.gov/govs/www/estimate04.html> (accessed May 2007).

State and Local Government Finances and Employment **275**

[In millions of dollars (2,260,330 represents $2,260,330,000,000), except as indicated. For fiscal year ending in year shown; see text, this section]

State		General expenditure									
	Total expenditure [1]	Total		Direct general expenditure, total	Education and social services				Public safety		
		Amount	Per capita [2] (dol.)		Education	Public welfare	Health and hospitals	Highways	Police protection	Fire protection	Corrections
United States . .	2,260,330	1,907,915	6,497	1,903,194	655,361	335,257	159,676	118,179	69,707	28,330	56,521
Alabama	31,268	27,089	5,987	27,089	9,437	4,624	4,568	1,604	770	300	594
Alaska.	10,019	8,496	12,912	8,496	2,299	1,375	241	953	187	89	178
Arizona	36,072	30,075	5,240	30,075	10,074	4,969	2,010	2,076	1,417	555	1,175
Arkansas	16,323	14,577	5,301	14,577	5,429	3,012	1,075	1,279	441	159	458
California	324,606	264,383	7,376	260,960	84,395	40,209	24,281	11,053	11,163	4,232	9,481
Colorado	34,392	28,427	6,177	28,424	9,702	3,183	2,427	2,439	1,098	504	831
Connecticut	28,837	25,018	7,150	25,018	8,753	4,173	1,752	1,281	806	415	555
Delaware	6,921	6,192	7,460	6,191	2,191	1,020	348	498	202	22	203
District of Columbia . .	8,493	6,723	12,135	6,723	1,369	1,686	850	71	415	158	164
Florida.	115,547	100,771	5,796	100,771	29,396	16,117	8,779	7,060	5,015	2,169	3,550
Georgia	58,435	50,211	5,630	50,211	19,239	8,693	5,096	2,436	1,655	717	1,842
Hawaii.	9,869	8,673	6,873	8,673	2,488	1,367	674	352	264	112	158
Idaho	8,426	7,540	5,405	7,540	2,636	1,221	697	654	250	99	233
Illinois	95,419	79,497	6,254	79,495	28,621	11,534	5,399	4,969	3,459	1,505	1,829
Indiana	39,333	35,540	5,707	35,540	13,616	5,741	3,324	2,317	926	517	911
Iowa	20,586	18,444	6,246	18,396	7,020	3,081	2,131	1,583	493	156	316
Kansas	18,359	16,286	5,957	16,284	6,205	2,499	1,109	1,576	544	216	405
Kentucky	26,868	23,346	5,636	23,342	7,748	5,268	1,547	1,977	596	300	617
Louisiana	31,089	27,251	6,046	27,251	8,616	4,079	3,667	1,684	987	412	850
Maine	10,027	9,285	7,061	9,282	2,863	2,308	579	695	207	101	161
Maryland	38,540	34,111	6,134	34,111	12,519	5,610	1,736	1,940	1,429	588	1,311
Massachusetts . . .	58,027	48,626	7,590	48,446	14,654	10,305	1,927	3,490	1,480	863	1,019
Michigan	77,562	67,701	6,700	67,643	26,974	10,245	6,820	3,855	2,244	828	2,119
Minnesota	42,144	36,637	7,188	36,637	11,951	8,907	2,088	2,888	1,140	282	699
Mississippi	19,450	17,282	5,957	17,282	5,611	3,866	2,342	1,336	507	187	363
Missouri.	35,567	31,024	5,386	31,020	10,836	5,714	3,023	2,568	1,079	520	832
Montana	6,198	5,547	5,983	5,547	1,935	776	355	624	167	58	145
Nebraska.	14,057	10,794	6,175	10,776	4,041	1,943	728	1,034	283	122	299
Nevada	16,181	13,621	5,838	13,619	4,157	1,454	981	1,573	705	329	546
New Hampshire . .	8,346	7,549	5,811	7,549	2,753	1,515	178	525	239	144	130
New Jersey	72,568	61,316	7,060	61,224	24,712	8,147	2,810	3,260	2,687	728	1,814
New Mexico	14,068	12,616	6,630	12,616	4,657	2,556	859	820	445	164	423
New York	218,715	176,413	9,150	175,803	51,655	40,518	13,925	8,213	6,870	2,493	4,777
North Carolina . . .	56,543	48,490	5,678	48,490	17,240	8,570	5,951	3,468	1,623	624	1,326
North Dakota	4,486	4,157	6,637	4,157	1,525	779	115	501	85	29	59
Ohio	89,598	74,446	6,502	74,445	26,472	14,592	6,180	4,112	2,531	1,372	1,836
Oklahoma	20,838	18,189	5,162	18,148	6,921	3,527	1,305	1,280	582	315	582
Oregon	28,215	22,309	6,213	22,309	7,553	3,523	1,631	1,365	829	413	753
Pennsylvania	94,419	80,517	6,496	80,339	28,703	17,650	5,265	4,855	2,333	525	2,597
Rhode Island	8,910	7,670	7,101	7,643	2,441	1,939	321	369	284	223	162
South Carolina . . .	30,451	25,591	6,096	25,591	8,999	4,931	3,450	1,604	731	252	579
South Dakota	4,612	4,132	5,360	4,132	1,422	706	188	605	122	45	81
Tennessee	41,760	31,581	5,359	31,581	9,756	7,811	3,723	1,791	1,093	479	795
Texas	144,880	124,057	5,521	124,057	49,707	18,204	10,301	8,412	4,294	1,682	4,081
Utah	16,706	13,907	5,744	13,906	5,434	2,007	1,005	995	470	168	411
Vermont	4,812	4,398	7,082	4,398	1,761	1,016	111	333	115	39	93
Virginia	47,800	42,956	5,742	42,955	16,107	6,215	3,498	2,741	1,505	749	1,424
Washington	54,306	42,591	6,862	42,579	14,228	6,495	4,754	2,655	1,196	749	1,248
West Virginia	12,191	10,614	5,854	10,604	3,738	2,262	570	1,013	218	73	215
Wisconsin	42,410	36,714	6,670	36,714	13,366	6,858	2,280	2,875	1,388	509	1,157
Wyoming	5,080	4,535	8,961	4,535	1,437	506	700	520	138	42	132

See footnote at end of table.

U.S. Census Bureau, Statistical Abstract of the United States: 2008

Table 429. State and Local Governments—Expenditures and Debt by State: 2004—Con.

[See headnote page 276]

State	General expenditures							Utility and liquor store expenditures	Insurance trust expenditures	Debt outstanding
	Environment and housing				Govern-mental adminis-tration	Interest on general debt	Other general expen-ditures			
	Sewer-age	Solid waste man-age-ment	Parks and recre-ation	Hous-ing [3]						
United States..	**35,535**	**20,373**	**30,467**	**37,221**	**100,741**	**81,723**	**174,103**	**159,732**	**197,405**	**1,951,661**
Alabama	579	267	350	430	1,012	933	1,620	2,327	1,852	21,629
Alaska	72	65	85	194	593	400	1,764	337	1,186	8,626
Arizona	500	309	1,028	413	1,718	1,102	2,728	3,706	2,290	29,844
Arkansas	211	175	171	163	757	424	823	725	1,021	10,409
California	4,926	3,186	4,264	6,870	17,822	10,274	28,806	30,602	33,045	269,935
Colorado	605	82	951	505	1,624	1,461	3,011	2,676	3,293	33,841
Connecticut	346	342	377	553	1,437	1,578	2,648	859	2,960	30,516
Delaware	178	51	85	108	499	308	477	296	434	6,053
District of Columbia	296	34	110	327	445	279	518	1,646	124	6,490
Florida	2,032	1,942	2,308	1,373	5,859	4,879	10,292	8,250	6,526	108,764
Georgia	1,186	518	662	753	2,567	1,125	3,722	4,585	3,639	34,848
Hawaii	177	161	201	173	602	479	1,466	421	775	9,027
Idaho	160	97	97	42	491	208	644	272	614	4,021
Illinois	1,309	491	2,346	2,143	4,222	4,995	6,674	5,682	10,241	102,304
Indiana	814	219	411	700	1,756	1,231	3,057	1,894	1,899	29,583
Iowa	215	158	286	140	814	439	1,567	876	1,314	11,335
Kansas	259	108	200	100	978	708	1,378	933	1,142	16,122
Kentucky	304	186	253	307	978	1,517	1,744	1,062	2,463	29,143
Louisiana	444	287	471	482	1,573	1,295	2,404	1,209	2,629	22,165
Maine	119	112	66	199	434	366	1,073	156	589	6,919
Maryland	607	500	791	937	1,626	1,497	3,018	1,314	3,116	27,795
Massachusetts	1,275	406	324	1,588	2,218	3,133	5,762	4,007	5,574	72,898
Michigan	1,664	507	930	765	2,942	2,715	5,034	3,034	6,886	57,609
Minnesota	488	294	774	743	1,804	1,577	3,002	1,771	3,735	33,670
Mississippi	136	117	181	229	759	500	1,147	829	1,339	10,189
Missouri	539	143	473	546	1,500	1,231	2,016	1,613	2,934	30,408
Montana	53	58	56	97	345	190	688	123	528	4,297
Nebraska	142	68	273	148	479	256	960	2,816	465	8,829
Nevada	223	19	501	227	853	663	1,387	1,576	985	17,851
New Hampshire	80	91	88	214	396	402	793	404	393	8,135
New Jersey	1,163	1,070	871	1,012	2,851	2,409	7,689	3,202	8,142	64,272
New Mexico	106	193	247	111	720	350	964	441	1,011	9,724
New York	2,907	2,496	2,103	4,088	7,800	8,014	19,945	21,172	21,740	219,358
North Carolina	755	639	680	785	1,812	1,314	3,702	4,094	3,960	37,973
North Dakota	34	33	91	43	214	154	553	96	233	3,143
Ohio	1,762	490	1,019	1,785	4,688	2,904	4,702	3,035	12,118	57,898
Oklahoma	320	135	263	162	1,056	569	1,131	1,117	1,573	13,265
Oregon	623	131	378	494	1,688	925	2,002	1,755	4,151	24,753
Pennsylvania	1,501	639	707	1,692	4,170	4,563	5,140	4,860	9,221	96,374
Rhode Island	109	97	66	168	430	322	711	230	1,038	8,237
South Carolina	279	262	252	348	1,523	1,067	1,313	2,563	2,297	25,940
South Dakota	52	34	98	64	219	155	342	211	268	3,849
Tennessee	426	344	409	542	1,320	879	2,211	8,237	1,942	24,320
Texas	2,241	950	1,479	1,685	5,164	5,762	10,094	10,276	10,547	146,009
Utah	261	140	297	243	1,026	435	1,012	1,863	937	14,265
Vermont	52	33	29	111	203	169	333	209	205	3,327
Virginia	893	632	788	818	2,355	1,787	3,445	1,992	2,853	40,006
Washington	1,125	523	830	1,006	1,859	1,730	4,181	6,464	5,262	50,370
West Virginia	177	59	109	130	688	392	961	302	1,286	8,214
Wisconsin	759	432	544	445	1,571	1,562	2,969	1,427	4,269	35,272
Wyoming	51	44	95	15	277	94	482	182	364	1,835

[1] Includes items not shown separately. [2] Based on estimated resident population as of July 1; see Table 17. [3] Includes community development.

Source: U.S. Census Bureau; *Federal, State, and Local Governments, State and Local Government Finances* Census of Governments; <http://www.census.gov/govs/estimate/04.html>; (accessed May 2007).

State and Local Government Finances and Employment 277

Table 430. Bond Ratings for State Governments by State: 2006

[As of fourth quarter. Key to investment grade ratings are in declining order of quality. The ratings from AA to CCC may be modified by the addition of a (+) or (–) sign to show relative standing within the major rating categories. S&P: AAA, AA, A, BBB, BB, B, CCC, CC, C; Moody's: Aaa, Aa, A, Baa, Ba, B, Caa, Ca, C; Numerical modifiers 1, 2, and 3 are added to letter-rating. Fitch: AAA, AA, A, BBB, BB, B, CCC, CC, C]

State	Standard & Poor's	Moody's	Fitch	State	Standard & Poor's	Moody's	Fitch
Alabama	AA	Aa2	AA	Montana	AA–	Aa2	(NA)
Alaska	AA	Aa2	AA	Nebraska	AA+	([2])	(NA)
Arizona	AA	Aa3	(NA)	Nevada	AA+	Aa1	(NA)
Arkansas	AA	Aa2	(NA)	New Hampshire	AA	Aa2	AA
California	A+	A1	A+	New Jersey	AA	Aa3	AA–
Colorado	AA–	(NA)	(NA)	New Mexico	AA+	Aa1	(NA)
Connecticut	AA	Aa3	AA	New York	AA	Aa3	AA–
Delaware	AAA	Aaa	AAA	North Carolina	AAA	Aaa	AAA
Florida	AAA	Aa1	AA+	North Dakota	AA	Aa2	(NA)
Georgia	AAA	Aaa	AAA	Ohio	AA+	Aa1	AA+
Hawaii	AA	Aa2	AA	Oklahoma	AA	Aa3	AA
Idaho	AA–	[1]Aa2	(NA)	Oregon	AA–	Aa3	AA–
Illinois	AA	Aa3	AA–	Pennsylvania	AA	Aa2	AA
Indiana	AA+	[1]Aa1	(NA)	Rhode Island	AA	Aa3	AA
Iowa	AA+	[1]Aa1	(NA)	South Carolina	AA+	Aaa	AAA
Kansas	AA+	[1]Aa1	(NA)	South Dakota	AA	([2])	(NA)
Kentucky	AA–	[1]Aa2	(NA)	Tennessee	AA+	Aa2	AA
Louisiana	A	A2	A	Texas	AA	Aa1	AA+
Maine	AA–	Aa3	AA	Utah	AAA	Aaa	AAA
Maryland	AAA	Aaa	AAA	Vermont	AA+	Aaa	AA+
Massachusetts	AA	Aa2	(NA)	Virginia	AAA	Aaa	AAA
Michigan	AA	Aa2	AA–	Washington	AA	Aa1	AA
Minnesota	AAA	Aa1	AAA	West Virginia	AA–	Aa3	AA–
Mississippi	AA	Aa3	AA	Wisconsin	AA–	Aa3	AA–
Missouri	AAA	Aaa	AAA	Wyoming	AA	([2])	(NA)

NA Not available. [1] Issuer rating, no general obligation rating. [2] No General Obligation.

Source: Standard & Poor's, New York, NY (copyright), <http://www2.standardandpoors.com/portal/site/sp/en/us/page.home /home/0,0,0,0,0,0,0,0,0,0,0,0,0,0,0,0.html>; Moody's Investors Service, New York, NY (copyright), <http://www.moodys.com/cust/default_alt.asp>; Fitch Ratings, New York, NY (copyright), <http://www.fitchratings.com/>.

Table 431. Bond Ratings for City Governments by Largest Cities: 2006

[As of fourth quarter. See headnote in Table 430]

Cities ranked by 2000 population	Standard & Poor's	Moody's	Fitch	Cities ranked by 2000 population	Standard & Poor's	Moody's	Fitch
New York, NY	AA–	A1	A+	Oakland, CA	A+	A1	A+
Los Angeles, CA	AA–	Aa2	AA	Mesa, AZ	AA–	A1	(NA)
Chicago, IL	AA–	Aa3	AA	Tulsa, OK	AA	Aa2	(NA)
Houston, TX	AA–	Aa3	(NA)	Omaha, NE	AAA	Aaa	(NA)
Philadelphia, PA	BBB	Baa1	(NA)	Minneapolis, MN	AAA	Aa1	(NA)
Phoenix, AZ	AA+	Aa1	(NA)	Honolulu, HI	AA	Aa2	AA
San Diego, CA	([1])	A3	BBB+	Miami, FL	A+	A2	(NA)
Dallas, TX	AA+	Aa1	(NA)	Colorado Springs, CO	AA	Aa3	(NA)
San Antonio, TX	AA+	Aa2	(NA)	St. Louis, MO	A	A3	A–
Detroit, MI	BBB	Baa2	(NA)	Wichita, KS	AA	Aa2	(NA)
San Jose, CA	AA+	Aa1	(NA)	Santa Ana, CA	([1])	(NA)	(NA)
Indianapolis, IN	AAA	(NA)	(NA)	Pittsburgh, PA	BBB–	Baa2	BBB
San Francisco, CA	AA	Aa3	AA–	Arlington, TX	AA	Aa2	(NA)
Jacksonville, FL	([1])	Aa2	(NA)	Cincinnati, OH	AA+	Aa1	(NA)
Columbus, OH	AAA	Aaa	AAA	Anaheim, CA	AA	Aa2	(NA)
Austin, TX	AA+	Aa1	(NA)	Toledo, OH	A	A3	(NA)
Baltimore, MD	A+	A1	A+	Tampa, FL	([1])	[2]Aa2	(NA)
Memphis, TN	A+	A1	A+	Buffalo, NY	BBB	Baa2	(NA)
Milwaukee, WI	AA	Aa2	AA+	St. Paul, MN	AAA	Aa2	AA+
Boston, MA	AA+	Aa1	AA	Corpus Christi, TX	A+	A1	AA–
Washington, DC	A+	A2	(NA)	Aurora, CO	AA–	Aa2	(NA)
El Paso, TX	AA	Aa3	(NA)	Raleigh, NC	AAA	Aaa	AAA
Seattle, WA	AAA	Aa1	(NA)	Newark, NJ	AA	Baa2	(NA)
Denver, CO	AA+	Aa1	AA+	Lexington-Fayette, KY	AA+	(NA)	(NA)
Nashville-Davidson, TN	AA	Aa2	(NA)	Anchorage, AK	([1])	Aa3	(NA)
Charlotte, NC	AAA	Aaa	AAA	Louisville, KY	AA+	Aa2	(NA)
Fort Worth, TX	AA+	Aa1	(NA)	Riverside, CA	A+	(NA)	(NA)
Portland, OR	([1])	Aaa	(NA)	St Petersburg, FL	([1])	(NA)	(NA)
Oklahoma City, OK	AA+	Aa1	(NA)	Bakersfield, CA	([1])	([3])	(NA)
Tucson, AZ	AA	Aa3	(NA)	Stockton CA	A+	[2]A1	(NA)
New Orleans, LA	B	Ba1	(NA)	Birmingham, AL	AA	[2]Aa3	AA–
Las Vegas, NV	AA–	Aa3	(NA)	Jersey City, NJ	BBB	Baa3	(NA)
Cleveland, OH	A	A2	A+	Norfolk, VA	AA	A1	AA
Long Beach, CA	AA–	[2]Aa3	(NA)	Baton Rouge, LA	([1])	(NA)	(NA)
Albuquerque, NM	AA	Aa3	AA	Hialeah, FL	AA	Aa3	(NA)
Kansas City, MO	AA	Aa3	(NA)	Lincoln, NE	AAA	Aaa	(NA)
Fresno, CA	AA–	A1	(NA)	Greensboro, NC	AAA	Aaa	AAA
Virginia Beach, VA	AA+	Aa1	AA+	Plano, TX	AAA	Aaa	AAA
Atlanta, GA	AA–	Aa3	AA–	Rochester, NY	AA	A2	(NA)
Sacramento, CA	AA	Aa2	(NA)				

NA Not available. [1] Not reviewed. [2] Issuer Rating/No General Obligation. [3] General obligation withdrawn (WR) 12/15/06.

Source: Standard & Poor's, New York, NY (copyright), <http://www2.standardandpoors.com/portal/site/sp/en/us/page.home /home/0,0,0,0,0,0,0,0,0,0,0,0,0,0,0,0.html> Moody's Investors Service, New York, NY (copyright); <http://www.moodys.com/cust/default_alt.asp>; Fitch Ratings, New York, NY (copyright), <http://www.fitchratings.com/>.

278   State and Local Government Finances and Employment

Table 432. **State Resources, Expenditures, and Balances: 2005 and 2006**

[In millions of dollars (1,237,358 represents $1,237,358,000,000). For fiscal year ending in year shown; see text; this section. General funds exclude special funds earmarked for particular purposes, such as highway trust funds and federal funds; they support most on-going broad-based state services and are available for appropriation to support any governmental activity]

State	Expenditures by fund source				State general fund					
	Total, 2005	2006 [1]			Resources [3,4]		Expenditures [4]		Balance [5]	
		Total [2]	General fund	Federal fund	2005	2006 [1]	2005	2006 [1]	2005	2006 [1]
United States . .	1,237,358	1,338,139	584,648	377,662	598,404	658,751	553,900	602,251	38,488	50,802
Alabama	17,406	19,679	6,919	7,517	6,753	7,894	6,052	6,962	664	907
Alaska	8,689	9,912	2,997	3,119	3,055	3,247	3,055	3,247	9	–
Arizona	22,808	23,631	8,353	7,411	8,184	9,861	7,545	8,945	[6]639	[6]916
Arkansas	14,290	17,885	3,810	5,739	3,630	3,825	3,630	3,825	–	–
California	159,713	184,429	90,294	56,945	89,438	102,260	79,804	92,730	[6]9,634	[6]9,530
Colorado	14,218	15,295	6,292	3,560	6,448	7,786	6,113	7,097	[6]336	[6]689
Connecticut	21,169	22,337	14,681	1,952	14,063	14,999	13,699	14,552	364	446
Delaware	6,197	6,351	4,096	975	3,524	3,871	2,822	3,181	[6]701	691
Florida	58,332	65,436	26,475	20,411	28,010	30,712	24,440	27,140	3,571	3,572
Georgia	29,184	29,550	16,697	9,285	17,551	19,713	16,323	17,851	[6]1,228	1,863
Hawaii	8,753	9,594	4,666	1,762	4,671	5,411	4,185	4,679	486	732
Idaho	4,801	5,486	2,224	2,034	2,325	2,520	2,110	2,218	214	[6]302
Illinois	41,864	46,558	19,469	8,751	26,342	27,856	22,184	24,193	497	[6]590
Indiana	25,467	25,361	11,912	6,769	11,647	12,553	11,800	12,204	119	[6]411
Iowa	12,358	13,317	4,499	3,773	4,929	5,382	4,603	5,021	166	[6]149
Kansas	10,585	11,827	5,163	3,212	5,169	5,873	4,690	5,139	479	[6]734
Kentucky	19,333	22,162	8,357	7,451	8,238	9,294	7,698	8,436	469	[6]681
Louisiana	15,236	15,082	5,483	6,618	7,470	8,605	7,127	7,740	252	[6]827
Maine	6,754	7,151	2,874	2,660	2,818	2,984	2,784	2,872	34	[6]14
Maryland	24,708	27,238	12,356	6,420	12,438	13,703	11,264	12,342	1,174	[6]1,362
Massachusetts . . .	26,322	28,104	21,431	5,189	25,129	27,064	23,779	25,585	[6]2,487	[6]3,208
Michigan	40,571	41,877	8,982	12,933	8,865	9,141	8,644	9,032	221	[6]110
Minnesota	24,554	26,401	16,429	5,879	15,922	16,707	14,529	15,806	[6]1,393	[6]901
Mississippi	11,947	12,562	3,613	4,909	3,730	4,032	3,678	4,037	52	[6]–
Missouri	19,110	19,912	7,209	6,122	7,421	7,821	7,121	7,125	300	[6]695
Montana	3,954	4,664	1,588	1,772	1,662	1,994	1,365	1,583	297	406
Nebraska	7,472	9,121	3,072	2,936	3,124	3,482	2,720	2,916	403	[6]566
Nevada	7,055	8,407	2,691	2,037	3,262	3,210	3,101	2,916	161	294
New Hampshire. . .	4,420	4,531	1,355	1,420	1,407	1,411	1,325	1,334	82	[6]26
New Jersey	41,503	42,655	27,578	9,239	28,966	28,567	27,844	27,111	[6]778	[6]1,455
New Mexico	10,422	11,471	4,691	3,835	5,782	6,485	4,727	5,417	[6]688	781
New York	100,668	104,341	46,495	34,618	46,165	49,752	43,619	46,495	[6]2,546	[6]3,257
North Carolina. . . .	35,558	33,796	17,256	9,972	16,616	18,353	15,798	17,065	479	[6]749
North Dakota	3,182	3,742	979	1,320	1,073	1,163	904	966	69	197
Ohio	50,665	55,393	25,363	9,192	25,708	25,985	24,831	24,866	138	[6]632
Oklahoma	14,027	17,445	4,836	5,191	5,140	6,123	4,945	5,532	10	[6]133
Oregon	19,791	20,228	6,090	4,438	4,801	6,617	4,492	6,090	309	[6]527
Pennsylvania . . .	51,321	54,926	24,501	17,805	23,483	25,350	23,054	24,681	365	[6]514
Rhode Island . . .	6,038	6,807	3,124	2,049	2,979	3,124	2,927	3,100	39	[6]24
South Carolina . . .	17,992	17,966	5,617	6,889	5,712	6,759	5,073	5,640	[6]533	[6]988
South Dakota	3,403	3,313	1,090	1,364	991	1,057	989	1,056	–	[6]–
Tennessee	24,019	25,602	10,273	9,933	9,796	10,330	9,113	9,866	462	[6]311
Texas	64,964	70,126	32,646	24,699	34,398	40,962	29,711	32,283	3,739	[6]7,547
Utah	8,493	9,065	4,223	2,325	4,083	4,683	3,978	4,223	106	[6]460
Vermont	3,670	4,286	1,114	1,016	1,083	1,157	1,038	1,114	–	–
Virginia	31,712	31,923	13,590	5,961	14,436	16,609	13,879	15,232	557	1,377
Washington	27,498	32,459	13,621	6,391	13,089	14,323	12,220	13,621	870	[6]702
West Virginia	17,738	19,715	4,300	3,288	3,803	4,076	3,410	3,562	361	[6]469
Wisconsin.	31,868	33,482	12,385	7,166	11,773	12,814	11,860	12,385	[6]4	[6]49
Wyoming	5,556	5,538	1,789	1,410	1,304	1,252	1,299	1,242	5	[6]10

– Represents zero.   [1] Estimated.   [2] Includes bonds and other state funds not shown separately.   [3] Includes funds budgeted, adjustments, and balances from previous year.   [4] May or may not include budget stabilization fund transfers, depending on state accounting practices.   [5] Resources less expenditures.   [6] Ending balance includes the balance in a budget stabilization fund.

Source: National Association of State Budget Officers, Washington, DC, *2005 State Expenditure Report*, and *State General Fund from NASBO, Fiscal Survey of the States*, semiannual (copyright), <http://www.nasbo.org/publications.php>.

State and Local Government Finances and Employment **279**

Table 433. Estimated State and Local Taxes Paid by a Family of Four for Selected Largest City in Each State: 2005

[Data based on average family of four (two wage earners and two school-age children) owning their own home and living in a city where taxes apply. Comprises state and local sales, income, auto, and real estate taxes. For definition of median, see Guide to Tabular Presentation]

City	Total taxes paid by gross family income level (dollars)					Total taxes paid as percent of income				
	$25,000	$50,000	$75,000	$100,000	$150,000	$25,000	$50,000	$75,000	$100,000	$150,000
Albuquerque, NM	2,466	3,506	5,668	7,458	11,103	9.9	7.0	7.6	7.5	7.4
Atlanta, GA	3,238	4,465	7,244	9,558	14,328	13.0	8.9	9.7	9.6	9.6
Baltimore, MD	2,226	5,020	7,748	10,283	15,129	8.9	10.0	10.3	10.3	10.1
Boston, MA	3,131	5,878	7,976	9,701	13,143	12.5	11.8	10.6	9.7	8.8
Charlotte, NC	3,035	4,235	6,926	9,387	13,953	12.1	8.5	9.2	9.4	9.3
Chicago, IL	3,271	5,277	7,226	8,684	11,623	13.1	10.6	9.6	8.7	7.7
Columbus, OH	3,133	4,793	7,380	9,865	15,052	12.5	9.6	9.8	9.9	10.0
Denver, CO	2,885	3,455	5,475	7,113	10,379	11.5	6.9	7.3	7.1	6.9
Detroit, MI	3,445	5,571	8,049	10,215	14,714	13.8	11.1	10.7	10.2	9.8
Honolulu, HI	3,069	2,177	4,224	6,267	10,583	12.3	4.4	5.6	6.3	7.1
Houston, TX	2,470	3,277	4,724	5,573	7,222	9.9	6.6	6.3	5.6	4.8
Indianapolis, IN	3,087	6,113	8,321	10,385	14,517	12.3	12.2	11.1	10.4	9.7
Jacksonville, FL	2,444	2,344	3,455	4,203	5,749	9.8	4.7	4.6	4.2	3.8
Kansas City, MO	3,099	2,344	3,455	4,203	5,749	9.8	4.7	4.6	4.2	3.8
Las Vegas, NV	2,478	3,116	4,046	4,763	5,994	9.9	6.2	5.4	4.8	4.0
Los Angeles, CA	2,715	4,955	7,153	9,213	14,895	10.9	9.9	9.5	9.2	9.9
Memphis, TN	2,788	3,095	4,550	5,156	6,685	11.2	6.2	6.1	5.2	4.5
Milwaukee, WI	2,343	5,127	7,435	9,813	14,345	9.4	10.3	9.9	9.8	9.6
Minneapolis, MN	3,062	4,646	6,861	9,226	13,926	12.2	9.3	9.1	9.2	9.3
New Orleans, LA	2,778	3,511	5,943	7,833	11,482	11.1	7.0	7.9	7.8	7.7
New York City, NY	2,917	4,751	7,882	11,053	17,911	11.7	9.5	10.5	11.1	11.9
Oklahoma City, OK	3,033	3,561	6,314	8,397	12,428	12.1	7.1	8.4	8.4	8.3
Omaha, NE	2,639	4,385	7,039	9,451	14,484	10.6	8.8	9.4	9.5	9.7
Philadelphia, PA	4,130	6,838	9,444	11,841	16,645	16.5	13.7	12.6	11.8	11.1
Phoenix, AZ	2,887	3,690	5,443	6,910	9,953	11.5	7.4	7.3	6.9	6.6
Portland, OR	3,057	4,627	7,608	10,281	15,555	12.2	9.3	10.1	10.3	10.4
Seattle, WA	2,834	4,495	5,978	6,454	7,707	11.3	9.0	8.0	6.5	5.1
Virginia Beach, VA	3,005	3,843	6,090	7,960	11,788	12.0	7.7	8.1	8.0	7.9
Washington, DC	3,152	4,076	7,142	9,951	15,649	12.6	8.2	9.5	10.0	10.4
Wichita, KS	2,428	3,181	5,679	7,961	12,218	9.7	6.4	7.6	8.0	8.1
Average [1]	2,792	4,379	6,614	8,518	12,479	11.2	8.8	8.8	8.5	8.3
Median [1]	2,788	4,235	6,861	8,684	13,143	11.2	8.5	9.1	8.7	8.8

[1] Based on selected cities and District of Columbia. For complete list of cities, see Table 434.

Source: Government of the District of Columbia, Office of the Chief Financial Officer, *Tax Rates and Revenues, Tax Burden Comparisons, Nationwide Comparison*, annual, <http://www.cfo.dc.gov/cfo/site/>.

Table 434. Residential Property Tax Rates for Largest City in Each State: 2005

[The real property tax is a function of housing values, real estate tax rates, assessment levels, homeowner exemptions and credits. Effective rate is the amount each jurisdiction considers based upon assessment level used. Assessment level is ratio of assessed value to assumed market value. Nominal rates represent the "announced" rates levied by the jurisdiction.]

City	Effective tax rate per $100 Rank	Effective tax rate per $100 Rate	Assessment level (percent)	Nominal rate per $100	City	Effective tax rate per $100 Rank	Effective tax rate per $100 Rate	Assessment level (percent)	Nominal rate per $100
Indianapolis, IN	1	3.21	100.0	3.21	Columbus, OH	28	1.46	29.6	4.94
Houston, TX	2	3.01	100.0	3.01	Wilmington, DE	29	1.45	49.2	2.94
Providence, RI	3	3.00	100.0	3.00	Salt Lake City, UT	30	1.44	97.2	1.48
Bridgeport, CT	4	2.96	70.0	4.23	Phoenix, AZ	31	1.41	10.0	14.09
Manchester, NH	5	2.79	100.0	2.79	Little Rock, AR	32	1.38	20.0	6.90
Burlington, VT	6	2.72	100.0	2.72	Wichita, KS	33	1.30	11.5	11.35
Philadelphia, PA	7	2.64	32.0	8.26	Louisville, KY	34	1.26	100.0	1.26
Milwaukee, WI	8	2.36	96.0	2.46	Minneapolis, MN	36	1.24	90.7	1.36
Baltimore MD	9	2.31	100.0	2.31	Albuquerque, NM	35	1.24	33.3	3.73
Des Moines, IA	10	2.24	48.0	4.66	Portland, OR	38	1.23	64.2	1.91
Sioux Falls, SD	11	2.15	85.0	2.53	Boston, MA	37	1.23	100.0	1.23
Fargo, ND	12	2.09	4.4	48.08	Charlotte, NC	39	1.19	95.1	1.26
Newark, NJ	13	2.04	88.5	2.30	Oklahoma City, OK	40	1.18	11.0	10.70
Omaha, NE	14	2.01	96.0	2.10	Los Angeles, CA	41	1.10	100.0	1.10
Detroit, MI	15	1.94	28.6	6.77	Las Vegas, NV	42	1.09	35.0	3.11
Memphis, TN	16	1.87	25.0	7.47	Seattle, WA	43	1.03	95.3	1.08
Jacksonville, FL	17	1.86	100.0	1.86	Virginia Beach, VA	44	1.00	82.4	1.22
Boise, ID	18	1.75	98.9	1.76	Washington, DC	45	0.96	100.0	0.96
New Orleans, LA	19	1.72	10.0	17.17	Charleston, WV	46	0.87	60.0	1.45
Columbia, SC	21	1.71	4.0	42.76	Cheyenne, WY	47	0.72	9.5	7.60
Jackson, MS	20	1.71	10.0	17.11	Birmingham, AL	48	0.70	10.0	6.95
Atlanta, GA	22	1.68	40.0	4.20	New York City, NY	49	0.69	4.6	15.01
Portland, ME	23	1.63	81.0	2.01	Denver, CO	50	0.67	8.0	8.36
Anchorage, AK	24	1.63	100.0	1.63	Honolulu, HI	51	0.38	100.0	0.38
Billings, MT	25	1.57	80.0	1.96					
Kansas City, MO	26	1.50	19.0	7.91	Unweighted Average	(X)	1.64	59.9	6.31
Chicago, IL	27	1.49	20.4	7.30	Median	(X)	1.50	(X)	(X)

X Not applicable.

Source: Government of the District of Columbia, Office of the Chief Financial Officer, *Tax Rates and Revenues, Tax Burden Comparisons, Nationwide Comparison* annual. See also <http://www.cfo.dc.gov/cfo/site/>.

280   State and Local Government Finances and Employment

Table 435. Gross Revenue From Parimutuel and Amusement Taxes and Lotteries by State: 2002 to 2004

[In millions of dollars (43,653.3 represents $43,653,300,000). For fiscal years; see text, this section]

State	Gross revenue			2004					
						Lottery revenue			
							Apportionment of funds		
	2002	2003	2004	Amusement taxes [1]	Parimutuel taxes	Total [2]	Prizes	Administration	Proceeds available from ticket sales
United States..	43,653.3	46,673.7	50,758.5	4,990.7	301.9	45,465.9	27,654.7	2,790.2	15,021.1
Alabama........	3.7	3.5	3.3	0.1	3.2	(X)	(X)	(X)	(X)
Alaska.........	2.5	2.6	2.4		2.4	(X)	(X)	(X)	(X)
Arizona........	276.2	302.0	343.3	0.6	0.6	342.1	200.3	33.8	108.0
Arkansas.......	4.4	4.4	4.6	(X)	4.6	(X)	(X)	(X)	(X)
California.......	2,743.4	2,634.0	2,810.6	(X)	42.1	2,768.5	1,566.0	156.7	1,045.8
Colorado.......	478.2	464.6	510.8	99.1	4.5	407.2	242.5	51.0	113.7
Connecticut......	1,282.8	1,302.4	1,355.3	435.1	10.7	909.6	538.3	87.3	283.9
Delaware	397.1		379.6	(X)	0.2	379.4	53.2	42.3	283.9
Florida.........	2,232.9	2,743.5	2,928.5	(X)	26.7	2,901.7	1,724.5	134.9	1,042.3
Georgia........	2,162.8	2,284.1	2,376.3	(X)	(X)	2,376.3	1,480.3	112.4	783.6
Hawaii.........	(X)	(X)	(X)	(X)	(X)	(X)	(X)	(X)	(X)
Idaho..........	92.7	30.8	101.4	(X)	(X)	101.4	64.7	10.7	25.9
Illinois.........	2,064.4	2,152.2	2,370.4	785.9	12.0	1,572.5	973.8	56.5	542.1
Indiana........	1,094.8	1,281.2	1,439.4	765.7	4.8	668.9	436.5	31.6	200.8
Iowa..........	375.4	356.8	412.0	213.5	3.2	195.2	114.5	27.3	53.5
Kansas........	184.3	196.7	215.7	0.7	3.5	211.5	120.8	20.7	70.0
Kentucky.......	656.8	650.7	695.8	0.2	15.5	680.1	439.2	44.6	196.3
Louisiana.......	787.8	809.9	855.6	524.1	20.4	311.1	169.8	19.5	121.8
Maine..........	157.7	164.3	193.5	(X)	4.5	189.0	116.8	29.6	42.6
Maryland.......	1,314.5	1,336.9	1,408.9	10.1	3.0	1,395.4	789.8	139.4	466.2
Massachusetts.....	4,214.9	4,214.1	4,386.5	5.3	5.7	4,375.6	3,148.5	73.2	1,153.9
Michigan........	1,662.9	1,666.0	1,952.7	99.5	11.8	1,841.4	1,099.7	56.8	684.9
Minnesota.......	410.0	370.5	403.2	55.8	1.5	345.9	240.7	22.6	82.6
Mississippi......	184.2	184.6	167.3	167.3	(X)	(X)	(X)	(X)	(X)
Missouri........	769.2	952.6	1,049.5	307.1	(X)	742.5	484.8	38.4	219.3
Montana........	75.5	78.6	85.2	50.5	0.1	34.6	18.7	6.8	9.2
Nebraska.......	81.2	88.1	99.0	6.1	0.3	92.6	52.6	20.6	19.4
Nevada........	720.7	739.3	861.5	861.5	(X)	(X)	(X)	(X)	(X)
New Hampshire....	209.5	217.1	232.2	1.8	4.1	226.3	137.1	15.4	73.7
New Jersey......	2,306.0	2,307.6	2,533.7	468.1	(X)	2,065.7	1,196.8	73.1	795.9
New Mexico......	158.2	168.8	178.2	38.5	1.2	138.4	85.2	17.3	36.0
New York.......	4,506.6	5,109.8	5,528.5	0.6	36.1	5,491.8	3,306.3	226.3	1,959.2
North Carolina....	11.1	11.1	11.5	11.5	(X)	(X)	(X)	(X)	(X)
North Dakota.....	16.6	16.6	12.7	10.1	2.6	(X)	(X)	(X)	(X)
Ohio..........	2,000.5	2,093.8	2,170.6	(X)	15.9	2,154.7	1,276.0	277.8	600.9
Oklahoma........	10.1	9.4	8.2	5.4	2.8	(X)	(X)	(X)	(X)
Oregon........	1,421.8	1,526.5	1,612.5	0.1	2.9	1,609.5	1,148.9	264.7	195.9
Pennsylvania.......	1,805.7	1,987.6	2,1u9.5	0.6	26.6	2,162.4	1,305.9	19.2	837.3
Rhode Island.....	1,019.4	1,124.8	1,314.0	(X)	4.7	1,309.4	1,023.7	7.2	278.4
South Carolina.....	364.5	709.0	922.7	39.6	(X)	883.1	552.3	39.9	290.9
South Dakota	132.6	137.0	141.6	–	0.9	140.7	19.1	5.0	116.6
Tennessee.......	(X)	(X)	(X)	(X)	(X)	(X)	(X)	(X)	(X)
Texas..........	2,847.7	3,164.3	3,522.8	23.1	11.8	3,487.9	2,068.6	356.2	1,063.1
Utah..........	(X)	(X)	(X)	(X)	(X)	(X)	(X)	(X)	(X)
Vermont........	82.0	74.8	87.0	(X)	(X)	87.0	57.6	9.3	20.1
Virginia........	1,104.9	1,137.4	1,264.4	0.1	(X)	1,262.4	707.2	132.9	422.2
Washington.......	440.7	462.3	483.3	0.1	1.8	481.4	295.5	65.7	120.3
West Virginia......	461.5	566.8	683.3	(X)	9.5	673.8	123.3	30.1	520.5
Wisconsin.......	399.9	406.7	451.2	0.4	1.8	449.0	275.2	33.3	140.6
Wyoming........	0.2	0.2	0.2	(X)	0.2	(X)	(X)	(X)	(X)

– Rounds to zero. X Not applicable. [1] Represents nonlicense taxes. [2] Excludes commissions.

Source: U.S. Census Bureau, Federal, State and Local Governments, State Government Finances, Lottery, and unpublished data, <http://ftp2.census.gov/govs/state/04lottery.pdf>.

Table 436. Lottery Sales—Type of Game and Use of Proceeds: 1980 to 2006

[In millions of dollars (2,393 represents $2,393,000,000). For fiscal years]

Game	1980	1990	1995	2000	2003	2004	2005	2006
Total ticket sales.............	2,393	20,017	31,931	37,201	43,521	47,697	47,364	51,595
Instant [1]...................	527	5,204	11,511	15,459	20,387	23,011	25,946	28,342
Three-digit [2]................	1,554	4,572	5,737	5,341	5,394	5,389	5,428	5,456
Four-digit [2].................	55	1,302	1,941	2,711	3,059	3,195	3,300	3,400
Lotto [3].....................	52	8,563	10,594	9,160	9,655	10,472	9,707	11,015
Other [4].....................	206	376	2,148	4,530	5,026	5,630	2,983	3,382
State proceeds (net income) [5]....	978	7,703	11,100	11,404	13,991	15,094	15,779	17,220

[1] Player scratches a latex section on ticket which reveals instantly whether ticket is a winner. [2] Players choose and bet on three or four digits, depending on game, with various payoffs for different straight order or mixed combination bets. [3] Players typically select six digits out of a large field of numbers. Varying prizes are offered for matching three through six numbers drawn by lottery. [4] Includes break-open tickets, spiel, keno, video lottery, etc. [5] Sales minus prizes and expenses equal net government income.

Source: TLF Publications, Inc., Boyds, MD. 2007 World Lottery Almanac (copyright), <http://www.lafleurs.com/>.

U.S. Census Bureau, Statistical Abstract of the United States: 2008

Table 437. State Governments—Summary of Finances: 1990 to 2004

[(673,119 represents $673,119,000,000), For fiscal year ending in year shown; see text; this section]

Item	Total (million dollars)				Per capita (dollars) [1]			
	1990	2000	2003	2004	1990	2000	2003	2004
Borrowing and revenue	**673,119**	**1,336,798**	**1,430,303**	**1,727,347**	**2,712**	**4,760**	**4,928**	**5,893**
Borrowing...................	40,948	75,968	134,644	140,682	165	270	464	480
Total revenue	632,172	1,260,829	1,295,659	1,586,665	2,547	4,489	4,464	5,413
General revenue.............	517,429	984,783	1,112,349	1,194,056	2,085	3,506	3,833	4,074
Taxes	300,489	539,655	548,991	590,414	1,211	1,922	1,892	2,014
Sales and gross receipts	147,069	252,147	273,811	293,326	593	898	943	1,001
General...............	99,702	174,461	184,597	197,949	402	621	636	675
Motor fuels	19,379	29,968	32,269	33,762	78	107	111	115
Alcoholic beverages	3,191	4,104	4,399	4,593	13	15	15	16
Tobacco products	5,541	8,391	11,482	12,303	22	30	40	42
Other	19,256	35,222	41,065	44,718	78	125	141	153
Licenses.................	18,842	32,598	35,863	39,679	76	116	124	135
Motor vehicles	9,848	15,099	16,009	17,336	40	54	55	59
Corporations in general	3,099	6,460	6,129	6,339	12	23	21	22
Other	5,895	11,039	13,725	16,004	24	39	47	55
Individual income	96,076	194,573	181,933	196,255	387	693	627	670
Corporation net income	21,751	32,522	28,384	30,229	88	116	98	103
Property	5,848	10,996	10,471	10,714	24	39	36	37
Other..................	10,902	16,819	18,529	20,211	44	60	64	69
Charges and miscellaneous.....	90,612	170,747	201,741	209,029	365	608	695	713
Intergovernmental revenue	126,329	274,382	361,617	394,613	509	977	1,246	1,346
From federal government.....	118,353	259,114	343,308	374,694	477	923	1,183	1,278
Public welfare	59,397	147,150	196,954	214,528	239	524	679	732
Education	21,271	42,086	56,362	64,913	86	150	194	221
Highways	13,931	23,790	29,481	29,606	56	85	102	101
Health and hospitals	5,475	14,223	19,559	20,377	22	51	67	70
Other	18,279	31,865	40,951	45,270	74	113	141	154
From local governments	7,976	15,268	18,309	19,919	32	54	63	68
Utility revenue	3,305	4,513	12,518	12,955	13	16	43	44
Liquor store revenue	2,907	3,895	4,518	4,866	12	14	16	17
Insurance trust revenue [2]	108,530	267,639	166,274	374,788	437	953	573	1,279
Employee retirement	78,898	230,166	110,839	308,896	318	820	382	1,054
Unemployment compensation ...	18,370	23,260	35,191	38,230	74	83	121	130
**Expenditure and debt redemption.......... **	**592,213**	**1,125,828**	**1,426,715**	**1,497,114**	**2,386**	**4,009**	**4,916**	**5,108**
Total expenditure	572,318	1,084,097	1,359,048	1,406,175	2,306	3,860	4,683	4,798
General expenditure	508,284	964,723	1,163,968	1,209,436	2,048	3,435	4,010	4,126
Education.................	184,935	346,465	411,094	429,341	745	1,234	1,416	1,465
Public welfare	104,971	238,890	314,407	339,409	423	851	1,083	1,158
Health	20,029	42,066	50,221	49,559	81	150	173	169
Hospitals	22,637	32,578	38,395	40,426	91	116	132	138
Highways	44,249	74,415	85,726	86,166	178	265	295	294
Police protection	5,166	9,788	11,144	10,766	21	35	38	37
Corrections...............	17,266	35,129	39,188	39,314	70	125	135	134
Natural resources	9,909	15,967	18,517	18,652	40	57	64	64
Housing and community development	2,856	4,726	8,112	7,191	12	17	28	25
Other and unallocable	96,267	164,698	187,106	188,613	388	586	645	644
Utility expenditure	7,131	10,723	22,405	21,676	29	38	77	74
Liquor store expenditure. . . .	2,452	3,195	3,697	3,924	10	11	13	13
Insurance trust expenditure [2]	54,452	105,456	168,979	171,139	219	375	582	584
Employee retirement	29,562	75,971	103,049	111,376	119	271	355	380
Unemployment compensation ...	16,423	18,583	51,411	43,174	66	66	177	147
By character and object:								
Intergovernmental expenditure	175,028	327,070	382,197	389,706	705	1,165	1,317	1,330
Direct expenditure............	397,291	757,027	976,852	1,016,469	1,601	2,695	3,366	3,468
Current operation	258,046	523,114	656,989	691,652	1,040	1,863	2,264	2,360
Capital outlay	45,524	76,233	91,943	90,950	183	271	317	310
Construction	34,803	59,681	72,374	73,372	140	213	249	250
Land and existing structure ...	3,471	4,681	6,945	6,576	14	17	24	22
Equipment	7,250	11,871	12,623	11,002	29	42	43	38
Assistance and subsidies	16,902	22,136	25,901	28,104	68	79	89	96
Interest on debt	22,367	30,089	33,040	34,624	90	107	114	118
Insurance benefits [3].........	54,452	105,456	168,979	171,139	219	375	582	584
Debt redemption	19,895	41,730	67,666	90,939	80	149	233	310
**Debt outstanding, year end.... **	**318,254**	**547,876**	**697,929**	**754,150**	**1,282**	**1,951**	**2,405**	**2,573**
Long-term..................	315,490	541,497	681,796	740,414	1,271	1,928	2,349	2,526
Full-faith and credit	74,972	138,525	179,372	209,385	302	493	618	714
Nonguaranteed.............	240,518	402,972	502,424	531,030	969	1,435	1,731	1,812
Short-term.................	2,764	6,379	16,133	13,736	11	23	56	47
Net long-term [4]	125,524	266,870	366,207	412,194	506	950	1,262	1,406
Full-faith and credit only........	63,481	128,384	170,137	200,295	256	457	586	683

[1] 1990 and 2000 based on enumerated resident population as of April 1. Other years based on estimated resident population as of July 1.   [2] Includes other items not shown separately.   [3] Includes repayments.   [4] Less cash and investment assets specifically held for redemption of long-term debt.

Source: U.S. Census Bureau, *Federal, State, and Local Governments, Finance, Survey of State Government Finances*, 2004, and unpublished data. See also <http://www.census.gov/govs/www/state04.html>.

U.S. Census Bureau, *Statistical Abstract of the United States: 2008*

Table 438. State Governments—Revenue by State: 2004

[In millions of dollars (1,586,665 represents $1,586,665,000,000), except as noted. For fiscal year ending in year shown. See text this section. Includes local shares of state imposed taxes]

State	Total revenue [1,2]	General revenue Total	Per capita [3] Total (dol.)	Per capita [3] Rank	Intergovernmental Total	Intergovernmental From federal government	Taxes	Current charges and miscella-neous revenue	Utility and liquor store revenue	Insurance trust revenue
United States . .	1,586,665	1,194,056	4,074	(X)	394,613	374,694	590,414	209,029	17,821	374,788
Alabama	21,568	17,616	3,893	32	6,871	6,278	7,018	3,727	172	3,780
Alaska.	8,852	6,630	10,076	1	2,194	2,189	1,343	3,093	14	2,208
Arizona	23,784	18,980	3,307	45	6,987	6,582	9,637	2,355	25	4,779
Arkansas	14,225	11,680	4,247	20	4,042	4,019	5,581	2,057	–	2,545
California	229,289	154,485	4,310	19	49,556	45,553	85,721	19,207	4,367	70,437
Colorado	23,082	14,957	3,250	47	4,595	4,531	7,051	3,311	–	8,125
Connecticut	19,519	17,423	4,979	13	4,132	4,123	10,291	3,000	23	2,072
Delaware	5,698	5,144	6,198	3	1,054	1,022	2,375	1,715	10	544
Florida	75,331	56,673	3,260	46	16,737	16,609	30,534	9,402	19	18,640
Georgia	34,814	28,205	3,163	49	9,096	9,040	14,571	4,538	2	6,607
Hawaii.	8,229	6,675	5,290	7	1,640	1,633	3,849	1,186	–	1,554
Idaho	7,112	5,310	3,806	37	1,741	1,736	2,648	921	77	1,726
Illinois	59,474	44,738	3,519	44	14,173	12,650	23,710	6,856	–	14,736
Indiana	26,917	23,465	3,768	39	7,057	6,912	11,957	4,450	–	3,452
Iowa	15,363	11,917	4,035	28	4,038	3,912	5,215	2,664	136	3,310
Kansas	11,044	9,869	3,610	41	3,000	2,966	5,284	1,585	–	1,175
Kentucky	20,296	17,498	4,224	21	5,911	5,894	8,463	3,123	–	2,798
Louisiana.	23,441	18,867	4,186	24	6,996	6,900	7,741	4,130	5	4,569
Maine	8,283	6,769	5,147	11	2,574	2,560	2,870	1,325	91	1,424
Maryland	28,409	22,855	4,110	25	6,457	6,227	12,328	4,070	107	5,447
Massachusetts . . .	41,616	32,980	5,147	10	8,997	8,626	16,839	7,143	130	8,505
Michigan	56,048	45,366	4,490	16	13,750	13,483	22,647	8,969	676	10,006
Minnesota	29,708	24,217	4,751	14	6,380	6,207	14,735	3,102	–	5,491
Mississippi	15,351	12,196	4,204	22	5,425	5,229	5,125	1,647	194	2,961
Missouri.	26,320	20,287	3,522	43	7,412	7,237	9,120	3,756	–	6,033
Montana	5,452	4,245	4,580	15	1,705	1,694	1,626	915	50	1,157
Nebraska.	8,316	7,338	4,198	23	2,383	2,362	3,640	1,315	–	979
Nevada	10,114	7,296	3,127	50	1,625	1,569	4,717	954	143	2,675
New Hampshire . .	6,175	5,024	3,868	34	1,677	1,456	2,005	1,342	372	779
New Jersey	50,593	37,909	4,365	17	9,580	9,006	20,986	7,343	591	12,093
New Mexico	11,810	9,798	5,149	9	3,546	3,434	4,002	2,250	–	2,011
New York.	136,521	106,300	5,513	5	47,838	41,219	45,826	12,636	6,091	24,129
North Carolina . . .	44,371	32,951	3,853	35	11,609	11,045	16,836	4,506	–	11,420
North Dakota	5,228	3,172	4,987	12	1,221	1,191	1,229	723	–	2,056
Ohio	76,443	45,732	3,994	30	14,870	14,480	22,476	8,386	581	30,130
Oklahoma	17,520	13,700	3,888	33	4,566	4,483	6,427	2,708	353	3,467
Oregon	24,489	13,766	3,834	36	4,161	4,148	6,103	3,502	291	10,431
Pennsylvania	69,213	50,029	4,037	27	15,298	15,175	25,347	9,384	1,109	18,075
Rhode Island	7,266	5,619	5,203	8	2,096	1,987	2,409	1,114	22	1,625
South Carolina . . .	21,242	16,836	4,011	29	6,229	5,822	6,804	3,804	1,048	3,358
South Dakota	3,864	2,907	3,770	38	1,239	1,220	1,063	605	–	957
Tennessee	23,921	20,901	3,547	42	9,017	8,772	9,529	2,355	–	3,020
Texas	90,570	71,568	3,185	48	25,640	24,864	30,752	15,176	–	19,003
Utah	13,168	9,560	3,949	31	2,878	2,810	4,196	2,486	142	3,466
Vermont	4,303	3,795	6,111	4	1,315	1,314	1,767	713	35	472
Virginia	35,740	27,972	3,739	40	6,238	6,091	14,233	7,501	408	7,361
Washington	35,086	25,202	4,060	26	6,954	6,669	13,895	4,353	418	9,466
West Virginia	11,633	9,638	5,316	6	3,306	3,258	3,749	2,583	60	1,935
Wisconsin	34,753	23,934	4,348	18	6,832	6,596	12,638	4,464	–	10,819
Wyoming	5,098	4,061	8,026	2	1,977	1,912	1,505	580	56	981

–Represents or rounds to zero.   X Not applicable.   [1] Includes categories not shown separately.   [2] Duplicate intergovernmental transactions are excluded.   [3] Based on estimated resident population July 1.

Source: U.S. Census Bureau, *Federal, State, and Local Governments, Finance, Survey of State Government Finances,* 2004. See also <http://www.census.gov/govs/www/state04.html>.

State and Local Government Finances and Employment   283

Table 439. **State Government Tax Collections, by State: 2005**

[In millions of dollars (647,886 represents 647,886,000,000]

State	All taxes				Sales and gross receipts taxes						
		Per capita					Selective sales taxes				
	Total	Total (dol.)	Rank	Total property tax	General sales and gross receipts	Total	Total [1]	Alcoholic beverages and tobacco	Insurance and premiums	Motor fuels	Tobacco products
United States [2] . .	647,886	2,185	(X)	11,349	311,074	212,247	98,827	4,732	14,842	34,570	13,217
Alabama	7,800	1,715	44	231	3,989	2,033	1,955	144	273	560	153
Alaska	1,858	2,802	7	43	199	(X)	199	35	53	40	56
Arizona	11,008	1,849	40	374	6,699	5,208	1,491	59	397	706	291
Arkansas	6,552	2,361	16	557	3,458	2,574	884	43	125	437	148
California	98,435	2,723	9	2,164	37,673	29,967	7,706	314	2,233	3,366	1,096
Colorado	7,648	1,640	47	(X)	3,057	2,003	1,054	32	192	589	130
Connecticut	11,585	3,309	4	(X)	5,128	3,268	1,860	44	238	477	273
Delaware	2,725	3,237	5	(X)	397	(X)	397	14	69	114	80
Florida	33,895	1,908	37	300	25,486	19,056	6,430	623	765	2,094	466
Georgia	15,676	1,716	43	67	6,967	5,310	1,657	150	332	926	249
Hawaii	4,434	3,483	2	(X)	2,749	2,137	612	44	87	86	85
Idaho	2,934	2,053	30	(X)	1,501	1,128	373	7	87	220	52
Illinois	26,412	2,069	29	56	13,356	7,195	6,160	147	367	1,420	656
Indiana	12,854	2,051	31	9	7,195	5,001	2,194	39	187	807	343
Iowa	5,751	1,939	34	(X)	2,627	1,722	906	14	131	438	96
Kansas	5,599	2,037	32	61	2,779	1,991	788	90	122	426	124
Kentucky	9,091	2,179	23	475	4,252	2,595	1,657	82	358	496	38
Louisiana	8,639	1,917	36	45	4,586	2,861	1,724	54	363	603	106
Maine	3,071	2,330	18	44	1,362	935	427	13	81	228	92
Maryland	13,497	2,415	14	529	5,282	2,890	2,392	27	269	753	276
Massachusetts	18,015	2,800	8	-	5,782	3,891	1,891	69	402	686	424
Michigan	23,525	2,329	19	2,152	11,534	8,074	3,460	151	250	1,076	1,180
Minnesota	15,881	3,098	6	619	6,641	4,204	2,437	69	311	651	174
Mississippi	5,432	1,868	39	44	3,523	2,588	935	40	164	436	56
Missouri	9,544	1,646	46	23	4,599	3,036	1,563	28	288	742	110
Montana	1,876	2,006	33	185	455	(X)	455	22	61	192	61
Nebraska	3,797	2,159	24	2	1,973	1,517	456	24	39	305	71
Nevada	5,010	2,077	28	149	3,937	2,255	1,682	36	216	308	137
New Hampshire	2,022	1,547	48	392	705	(X)	705	12	80	132	102
New Jersey	22,934	2,635	10	3	10,172	6,552	3,620	99	454	525	800
New Mexico	4,471	2,322	20	41	2,171	1,557	614	35	95	223	48
New York	50,190	2,598	11	(X)	16,162	11,004	5,158	185	987	533	976
North Carolina	18,640	2,149	25	(X)	7,616	4,602	3,013	221	442	1,338	43
North Dakota	1,403	2,211	21	2	710	410	300	6	31	122	21
Ohio	24,007	2,093	27	37	11,146	8,194	2,952	90	440	1,672	579
Oklahoma	6,859	1,936	35	(X)	2,500	1,661	839	71	172	414	128
Oregon	6,523	1,792	41	24	699	-	699	14	55	373	244
Pennsylvania	27,263	2,198	22	58	13,227	8,065	5,162	237	677	1,908	1,031
Rhode Island	2,629	2,449	12	2	1,378	844	534	11	53	133	136
South Carolina	7,318	1,723	42	10	3,883	2,903	980	142	129	485	30
South Dakota	1,110	1,433	49	(X)	904	622	282	12	58	125	28
Tennessee	10,007	1,680	45	(X)	7,648	6,118	1,530	97	361	844	121
Texas	32,785	1,430	50	(X)	25,851	16,356	9,495	626	1,168	2,936	599
Utah	4,686	1,882	38	(X)	2,330	1,710	619	30	120	351	61
Vermont	2,243	3,604	1	745	778	311	467	18	52	86	48
Virginia	15,919	2,104	26	19	5,479	3,094	2,385	152	374	913	103
Washington	14,840	2,359	17	1,591	11,642	9,147	2,495	199	357	931	354
West Virginia	4,301	2,371	15	4	2,154	1,095	1,059	9	113	320	103
Wisconsin	13,452	2,434	13	112	6,091	4,039	2,051	49	145	957	610
Wyoming	1,740	3,419	3	181	642	522	119	1	20	68	27

See footnotes at end of table.

U.S. Census Bureau, Statistical Abstract of the United States: 2008

Table 439. State Government Tax Collections, by State: 2005—Con.

[See headnote, page 284]

State	License taxes Total¹	Selected license taxes Corporation	Motor vehicle operators	Occupancy and business n.e.c.³	Income taxes Total	Individual	Corporation net	Other taxes Total¹	Selected other taxes Death and gift	Severance
United States ² . .	42,703	7,145	18,221	12,068	258,946	220,255	38,691	23,815	5,342	8,131
Alabama.	438	81	191	123	2,934	2,537	397	207.919	14	145
Alaska	101	1	53	15	589	(X)	589	927.238	2	926
Arizona.	326	12	170	91	3,550	2,848	702	59.15	33	26
Arkansas	312	21	125	107	2,152	1,875	277	73.345	14	19
California	6,708	64	2,499	3,717	51,662	42,992	8,670	227.287	213	14
Colorado.	337	4	205	42	4,087	3,771	316	167.877	23	145
Connecticut.	377	17	206	94	5,608	5,033	575	471.009	265	(X)
Delaware	1,064	569	35	250	1,131	882	249	132.947	6	(X)
Florida	1,894	176	1,197	279	1,785	(X)	1,785	4429.268	295	59
Georgia	528	53	285	115	8,039	7,326	712	74.771	43	(X)
Hawaii	143	2	100	22	1,506	1,381	124	37.028	13	(X)
Idaho	238	2	114	50	1,181	1,041	141	13.928	9	2
Illinois	2,471	191	1,400	745	10,120	7,937	2,183	408.843	301	–
Indiana.	467	5	177	40	5,038	4,213	825	144.645	144	1
Iowa	589	38	382	82	2,441	2,254	186	93.409	77	(X)
Kansas.	291	51	165	23	2,299	2,051	248	169.15	52	117
Kentucky	554	199	195	107	3,515	3,036	479	295.267	63	229
Louisiana	520	289	111	75	2,745	2,393	352	742.167	30	712
Maine.	164	6	84	48	1,435	1,299	136	66.542	32	(X)
Maryland	734	65	479	133	6,469	5,661	807	483.614	183	(X)
Massachusetts.	686	26	317	145	11,023	9,690	1,333	522.768	255	(X)
Michigan.	1,340	20	903	144	8,016	6,109	1,907	483.076	101	68
Minnesota.	957	7	521	292	7,275	6,341	934	389.011	69	32
Mississippi	330	98	113	67	1,457	1,174	283	77.872	12	66
Missouri	642	119	264	133	4,233	4,015	218	47.243	39	–
Montana.	235	1	142	41	812	713	98	188.482	4	181
Nebraska	203	7	89	64	1,592	1,394	198	25.56	14	3
Nevada	704	59	155	363	(X)	(X)	(X)	220.405	21	40
New Hampshire	205	4	88	67	544	68	476	175.872	11	(X)
New Jersey.	1,289	247	423	491	10,449	8,224	2,225	1020.486	521	(X)
New Mexico	210	3	159	25	1,328	1,086	242	721.816	5	713
New York	1,277	69	739	157	30,885	28,100	2,785	1866.776	898	(X)
North Carolina	1,109	388	4C4	144	9,700	8,428	1,272	215.697	154	2
North Dakota.	110	(X)	51	40	318	242	76	264.39	2	262
Ohio	1,993	418	716	698	10,762	9,434	1,327	68.301	60	8
Oklahoma.	850	46	558	200	2,637	2,469	169	871.619	76	763
Oregon.	655	9	420	131	5,064	4,699	365	79.318	57	12
Pennsylvania.	2,725	845	824	847	9,979	8,276	1,703	1273.43	695	(X)
Rhode Island.	91	4	54	29	1,111	998	113	46.758	32	(X)
South Carolina.	403	68	131	124	2,938	2,691	247	84.588	19	(X)
South Dakota	150	3	44	64	49	(X)	49	7.441	4	3
Tennessee	1,090	517	262	229	961	155	806	309.101	86	1
Texas.	4,485	2,234	1,283	679	(X)	(X)	(X)	2449.186	102	2,348
Utah	165	2	97	29	2,116	1,927	189	76.396	3	73
Vermont	103	5	62	24	569	500	69	47.747	19	(X)
Virginia.	623	49	347	147	8,958	8,352	606	840.127	150	2
Washington.	726	21	355	203	(X)	(X)	(X)	880.198	(X)	43
West Virginia.	184	9	89	40	1,635	1,172	463	324.233	5	307
Wisconsin.	799	15	329	279	6,248	5,465	783	202.662	112	3
Wyoming	108	7	50	18	(X)	(X)	(X)	808.795	3	806

– Represents or rounds to zero.   X Not applicable.   ¹ Includes other items not shown separately.   ² Details will not add to the totals shown because of rounding.   ³ n.e.c means not elsewhere classified.

Source: U.S. Census Bureau, *Federal, State, and Local Governments, Tax collections, State government tax collections,* Annual. See also <http://www.census.gov/govs/www/statetax.html> (accessed May 2007).

State and Local Government Finances and Employment   285

Table 440. State Governments—Expenditures and Debt by State: 2004

[In millions of dollars (1,406,175 represents $1,406,175,000,000) except as indicated. For fiscal year ending in year shown; see text, this section]

State	Total expenditures[1]	General expenditure — Total — Amount	Per capita[2] (dol.)	Inter-govern-mental	Direct expenditures — Total[1]	Educa-tion	Public welfare	Health and hospitals	High-ways	Police protec-tion
United States..	1,406,175	1,209,436	4,126	389,706	819,730	180,984	291,968	69,619	72,194	9,471
Alabama	19,545	17,622	3,894	4,165	13,457	4,022	4,568	1,900	1,002	106
Alaska	8,089	6,835	10,387	1,050	5,785	983	1,370	116	817	57
Arizona.	21,749	19,541	3,404	7,544	11,997	2,686	4,336	1,137	1,271	181
Arkansas.	12,674	11,683	4,248	3,233	8,449	2,011	2,995	849	958	80
California.	203,815	171,079	4,773	80,132	90,946	18,377	26,258	7,294	5,603	1,183
Colorado.	18,061	15,035	3,267	4,861	10,174	3,059	2,617	1,057	1,099	99
Connecticut	19,523	16,669	4,764	3,397	13,273	2,166	4,059	1,629	859	171
Delaware.	5,388	4,915	5,921	923	3,992	873	1,020	329	387	76
Florida.	59,974	54,064	3,110	16,473	37,590	5,715	15,412	3,051	4,527	403
Georgia	34,197	30,869	3,461	9,335	21,534	5,731	8,547	1,297	1,394	223
Hawaii	7,856	7,081	5,611	134	6,947	2,488	1,346	638	214	11
Idaho	5,763	5,093	3,651	1,497	3,596	819	1,197	132	412	39
Illinois	53,429	45,809	3,604	13,304	32,505	7,072	11,045	3,502	2,407	365
Indiana	25,373	23,543	3,781	7,963	15,580	4,632	5,360	791	1,567	219
Iowa.	13,424	12,031	4,074	3,530	8,501	2,228	2,960	992	933	67
Kansas	11,207	10,103	3,695	2,879	7,224	1,982	2,463	362	1,059	70
Kentucky.	20,177	17,746	4,284	3,967	13,779	3,187	5,225	1,051	1,601	131
Louisiana	20,472	18,008	3,996	4,410	13,597	2,981	4,041	2,119	1,040	194
Maine	7,322	6,671	5,073	1,049	5,622	809	2,278	492	515	60
Maryland.	25,344	22,299	4,010	5,633	16,666	3,525	5,489	1,373	1,269	324
Massachusetts . . .	38,406	33,647	5,252	6,203	27,444	4,269	10,242	1,088	2,878	324
Michigan	52,685	46,507	4,603	19,035	27,472	7,636	9,483	2,955	1,697	286
Minnesota	28,832	25,384	4,980	9,638	15,746	3,692	7,387	567	1,143	187
Mississippi.	14,330	12,833	4,424	3,880	8,953	1,727	3,844	948	817	74
Missouri	22,039	19,487	3,383	5,260	14,227	2,579	5,567	1,696	1,579	135
Montana	4,691	4,120	4,444	955	3,165	688	743	249	516	31
Nebraska	6,980	6,646	3,802	1,696	4,950	1,231	1,881	330	595	54
Nevada.	8,686	7,556	3,239	2,948	4,607	1,099	1,260	345	831	62
New Hampshire . .	5,654	4,942	3,805	1,279	3,663	694	1,346	154	347	36
New Jersey	46,456	36,064	4,153	9,814	26,251	6,161	7,300	2,257	2,121	407
New Mexico.	11,025	10,013	5,262	3,031	6,982	1,589	2,493	726	620	99
New York	132,883	108,248	5,614	44,112	64,136	8,522	30,847	5,227	3,642	651
North Carolina . . .	37,051	33,009	3,865	10,327	22,682	6,052	7,328	1,868	3,007	351
North Dakota	3,198	2,975	4,677	614	2,361	635	682	85	325	14
Ohio	58,874	46,524	4,063	15,730	30,794	7,296	11,912	2,602	2,122	234
Oklahoma	14,915	13,078	3,711	3,715	9,363	2,605	3,489	502	773	103
Oregon	18,788	14,560	4,055	4,637	9,923	2,136	3,250	884	741	145
Pennsylvania	57,354	48,243	3,892	12,157	36,086	8,159	14,737	2,517	3,635	597
Rhode Island	6,387	5,371	4,973	869	4,502	711	1,932	314	256	49
South Carolina. . .	21,428	17,961	4,278	4,160	13,801	3,194	4,913	1,627	1,333	166
South Dakota. . . .	2,989	2,732	3,543	576	2,155	417	694	136	388	24
Tennessee.	22,165	20,594	3,495	5,302	15,292	3,078	7,644	1,305	1,168	136
Texas	77,338	67,661	3,011	17,032	50,629	12,606	17,885	3,711	5,707	459
Utah	10,794	9,753	4,028	2,113	7,640	2,438	1,972	775	690	112
Vermont	3,914	3,676	5,920	981	2,695	606	1,015	105	203	61
Virginia	30,370	27,618	3,692	8,819	18,799	4,943	4,993	2,442	2,184	239
Washington	32,510	27,010	4,352	6,912	20,098	5,576	6,399	2,541	1,485	171
West Virginia	9,879	8,555	4,719	1,942	6,613	1,329	2,258	307	948	59
Wisconsin	28,577	24,789	4,504	9,285	15,504	3,626	5,388	1,104	1,103	115
Wyoming.	3,596	3,186	6,295	1,204	1,981	344	496	138	408	31

See footnote at end of table.

286　State and Local Government Finances and Employment

Table 440. State Governments—Expenditures and Debt by State: 2004—Con.

[See headnote, page 286]

State	General expenditure—Con. Direct expenditures—Con. Correc-tions	Natural re-sources	Parks and recre-ation	Govern-mental admin-istration	Interest on general debt	Expenditures Utility	Liquor stores	Insur-ance trust	Debt outstanding Cash and security holdings	Debt out-standing, total	Per capita [2] (dollars)
United States. .	36,963	17,226	4,571	43,453	32,953	21,676	3,924	171,139	2,930,136	754,150	2,568
Alabama	392	235	23	434	236	–	178	1,745	29,992	6,364	1,409
Alaska	177	244	9	428	242	89	–	1,165	45,326	5,730	8,724
Arizona.	719	237	156	447	237	28	–	2,179	38,841	6,774	1,179
Arkansas.	351	197	81	476	123	–	–	992	18,988	3,749	1,365
California.	5,600	3,198	344	8,258	4,142	5,542	–	27,194	437,036	104,008	2,902
Colorado.	595	182	64	458	408	10	–	3,015	47,441	9,875	2,147
Connecticut	555	96	141	972	1,248	234	–	2,620	32,791	22,575	6,461
Delaware.	203	82	45	374	228	72	–	402	11,244	4,158	5,017
Florida	2,185	1,470	153	2,057	1,196	62	–	5,849	177,270	25,740	1,482
Georgia	1,257	518	139	738	461	2	–	3,325	64,062	8,664	970
Hawaii	158	110	58	440	356	–	–	775	13,195	5,746	4,563
Idaho	169	176	21	268	134	–	58	612	11,735	2,384	1,709
Illinois.	1,219	362	227	1,371	2,685	–	–	7,620	104,783	48,726	3,833
Indiana	646	266	58	601	447	39	–	1,791	36,948	13,080	2,102
Iowa.	216	207	17	460	161	1	93	1,299	27,063	4,858	1,645
Kansas	263	182	7	414	166	–	–	1,104	14,078	4,571	1,669
Kentucky	429	313	124	640	428	–	–	2,431	34,296	8,116	1,960
Louisiana	454	385	188	669	679	5	–	2,460	43,126	10,183	2,265
Maine	112	184	11	252	252	–	62	589	13,952	4,644	3,534
Maryland.	1,044	357	154	785	871	552	–	2,493	44,015	13,601	2,449
Massachusetts . . .	796	244	106	1,385	2,566	441	–	4,318	65,121	50,981	7,921
Michigan	1,576	425	115	813	1,097	–	550	5,627	70,892	20,960	2,077
Minnesota	347	412	129	642	378	101	–	3,347	50,533	6,666	1,308
Mississippi.	284	230	44	282	200	–	157	1,339	23,288	4,275	1,478
Missouri	609	294	46	584	639	–	–	2,552	59,431	16,218	2,819
Montana	121	276	13	214	123	–	43	528	11,724	3,049	3,291
Nebraska	187	136	30	178	96	–	–	334	10,273	1,950	1,116
Nevada.	232	100	19	201	140	145	–	985	21,351	3,607	1,547
New Hampshire . .	93	57	12	189	302	9	318	385	10,175	5,894	4,541
New Jersey	1,320	241	391	1,350	1,157	2,260	–	8,132	87,493	35,770	4,123
New Mexico.	255	173	58	391	164	–	–	1,011	33,923	5,411	2,847
New York	2,459	354	450	4,148	3,020	10,270	–	14,365	262,375	95,710	4,961
North Carolina . . .	1,039	491	140	729	441	102	–	3,939	73,703	14,103	1,653
North Dakota	44	118	13	122	77	–	–	223	7,302	1,662	2,614
Ohio.	1,403	362	84	1,865	1,193	–	366	11,985	166,739	22,183	1,935
Oklahoma	486	189	70	543	287	305	–	1,532	28,273	6,930	1,967
Oregon	394	344	63	941	376	9	144	4,074	59,095	10,496	2,924
Pennsylvania	1,433	580	153	1,939	1,123	48	1,018	8,044	104,532	25,996	2,100
Rhode Island	162	37	9	298	234	94	–	921	12,755	6,491	6,016
South Carolina . . .	416	196	65	742	453	1,174	–	2,293	30,436	11,163	2,661
South Dakota. . . .	51	89	27	108	99	–	–	258	9,468	2,613	3,393
Tennessee.	441	221	113	468	182	5	–	1,566	31,003	3,581	608
Texas	2,857	843	77	1,515	1,041	10	–	9,667	197,829	22,926	1,018
Utah.	276	168	41	566	186	–	104	937	19,473	4,962	2,049
Vermont	93	81	12	136	139	3	35	200	5,238	2,537	4,087
Virginia	955	176	75	824	722	19	350	2,383	57,643	15,314	2,049
Washington	796	528	62	606	754	25	351	5,124	66,904	15,774	2,542
West Virginia	183	182	57	439	190	15	51	1,258	12,389	4,745	2,620
Wisconsin	822	510	48	583	822	6	–	3,782	83,021	17,727	3,224
Wyoming.	90	164	26	110	48	–	47	364	11,570	910	1,799

– Represents or rounds to zero.   [1] Includes items not shown separately.   [2] Based on estimated resident population as of July 1.

Source: U.S. Census Bureau; Federal, State and Local Governments, State Government Finances. <http://www.census.gov/govs/www/state04.html> (accessed May 2007).

State and Local Government Finances and Employment   287

Table 441. Local Governments—Revenue by State: 2004

[In millions of dollars (1,247,463 represents $1,247,463,000,000), except as noted. For fiscal year ending in year shown; see text, this section]

State	Total revenue [1]	General revenue		Intergovernmental revenue			Taxes				
		Total	Per capita [2] (dol.)	Total	From federal government	From state governments	Total [1]	Property	Sales and gross receipts	Income [3]	Motor licenses
United States .	1,247,463	1,094,729	3,728	430,114	50,989	379,126	419,863	307,528	67,303	22,446	1,373
Alabama.......	15,475	12,897	2,850	4,926	542	4,385	3,517	1,440	1,541	101	25
Alaska........	3,051	2,764	4,201	1,092	232	860	1,032	812	185	–	15
Arizona.......	22,293	18,904	3,293	8,290	1,005	7,284	6,844	4,522	1,887	–	1
Arkansas	6,930	6,193	2,252	3,364	258	3,105	1,392	581	780	3	–
California.....	204,916	172,936	4,825	80,320	8,790	71,529	48,172	32,420	11,209	–	–
Colorado......	20,274	17,784	3,864	5,221	672	4,549	7,530	4,722	2,496	–	33
Connecticut.....	13,318	12,005	3,431	3,912	380	3,532	6,929	6,802	–	–	–
Delaware	2,412	2,112	2,545	1,045	70	975	619	453	11	47	–
District of Columbia	8,829	7,640	13,791	2,706	2,706	–	3,964	1,028	1,153	1,218	24
Florida.......	71,778	63,474	3,651	19,867	2,573	17,295	23,255	18,224	3,998	–	10
Georgia	32,101	28,145	3,156	9,820	863	8,957	11,084	7,780	2,954	–	–
Hawaii........	1,937	1,729	1,370	378	201	177	963	721	135	–	72
Idaho........	4,172	3,979	2,852	1,664	139	1,525	1,158	1,084	24	–	5
Illinois	56,388	47,143	3,709	17,095	3,003	14,092	21,481	17,832	2,880	–	120
Indiana........	21,266	19,438	3,122	7,486	425	7,061	6,718	6,065	86	424	19
Iowa.........	10,640	9,938	3,365	3,724	392	3,332	3,804	3,189	503	52	16
Kansas........	10,516	9,418	3,445	3,147	170	2,977	3,958	3,189	704	–	3
Kentucky	10,238	9,185	2,218	4,031	348	3,683	2,997	1,681	307	810	3
Louisiana	15,246	13,618	3,021	5,206	722	4,484	5,324	2,223	2,918	–	3
Maine........	3,979	3,881	2,951	1,235	116	1,119	2,112	2,054	3	–	31
Maryland	21,132	19,175	3,448	6,058	1,034	5,024	10,003	5,540	400	3,009	–
Massachusetts...	27,377	22,390	3,495	9,266	1,439	7,827	10,176	9,814	138	–	–
Michigan.......	42,170	38,168	3,778	19,393	1,627	17,766	10,831	9,887	221	489	2
Minnesota......	23,016	20,781	4,077	10,549	954	9,596	4,689	4,312	180	–	4
Mississippi	8,929	8,328	2,871	3,828	414	3,414	1,964	1,820	68	–	–
Missouri	18,776	16,758	2,909	5,669	781	4,888	7,136	4,282	2,226	313	11
Montana.......	2,525	2,439	2,631	1,064	187	877	806	775	–	–	3
Nebraska	8,781	5,950	3,404	1,772	174	1,597	2,668	2,005	346	–	24
Nevada	10,257	9,454	4,052	3,778	351	3,427	3,255	2,015	766	–	–
New Hampshire ..	4,062	3,950	3,041	1,429	116	1,313	2,064	2,026	–	–	–
New Jersey.....	35,658	34,853	4,013	11,520	926	10,594	18,572	18,226	40	–	–
New Mexico	6,280	5,851	3,074	3,429	369	3,060	1,442	787	589	–	2
New York	134,262	119,433	6,194	44,210	4,475	39,734	55,600	32,334	10,918	9,416	155
North Carolina...	29,694	26,424	3,094	10,908	865	10,043	8,176	6,093	1,682	–	27
North Dakota....	1,948	1,827	2,873	745	123	622	672	583	75	–	–
Ohio	44,859	42,452	3,708	17,363	1,833	15,530	16,676	11,192	1,535	3,478	93
Oklahoma......	9,775	8,856	2,513	3,595	337	3,258	3,008	1,637	1,299	–	1
Oregon........	13,968	12,727	3,544	5,500	791	4,710	4,371	3,444	265	100	1
Pennsylvania.....	48,267	43,845	3,538	18,055	2,936	15,119	17,371	12,450	388	2,988	–
Rhode Island....	3,498	3,242	3,001	1,128	137	991	1,793	1,758	6	–	–
South Carolina...	13,515	12,089	2,880	4,192	389	3,803	4,373	3,693	322	–	29
South Dakota ...	2,268	2,015	2,613	660	140	519	953	705	206	–	24
Tennessee	22,921	15,476	2,626	5,223	751	4,472	5,417	3,585	1,502	–	116
Texas........	82,942	72,226	3,214	21,795	2,820	18,976	33,987	28,176	5,035	–	311
Utah	8,014	6,538	2,701	2,608	411	2,197	2,425	1,669	628	–	–
Vermont	1,889	1,700	2,737	980	55	925	519	502	6	–	–
Virginia........	26,742	24,178	3,232	9,133	960	8,173	10,769	7,694	2,037	–	146
Washington.....	27,939	22,844	3,680	9,072	1,069	8,003	7,530	4,860	2,135	–	31
West Virginia....	4,259	4,064	2,241	1,910	182	1,728	1,218	976	57	–	–
Wisconsin.....	23,227	20,877	3,793	9,713	666	9,047	7,803	7,325	294	–	–
Wyoming	2,754	2,638	5,214	1,041	70	971	740	544	160	–	13

See footnotes at end of table.

U.S. Census Bureau, Statistical Abstract of the United States: 2008

Table 441. Local Governments—Revenue by State: 2004—Con.

[See headnote, page 288]

State	Current charges and miscellaneous general revenue	Current charges Total [1]	Education	Hospital	Sewerage	Miscellaneous general revenue Total [1]	Interest earnings	Special assessment	Utility revenue	Liquor store revenue	Insurance trust revenue
United States..	244,752	173,799	20,130	46,171	29,753	70,953	24,781	5,731	95,402	832	56,500
Alabama	4,454	3,643	303	2,407	318	811	356	17	2,078	–	499
Alaska	640	390	37	76	61	250	172	17	215	–	72
Arizona	3,771	2,458	424	417	433	1,313	517	83	3,073	–	315
Arkansas	1,437	932	148	209	188	505	266	12	688	–	49
California	44,444	31,067	2,078	6,820	4,210	13,377	3,363	1,100	16,487	–	15,492
Colorado	5,033	3,431	351	879	520	1,602	459	350	1,761	–	729
Connecticut	1,164	863	116	–	246	301	68	29	515	–	797
Delaware	448	303	15	–	120	146	50	20	226	–	73
District of Columbia	970	389	21	–	98	581	100	1	664	–	525
Florida	20,352	14,003	1,632	4,280	1,762	6,349	2,579	1,207	6,292	–	2,012
Georgia	7,240	5,177	276	2,650	705	2,063	724	41	3,301	–	655
Hawaii	388	301	–	–	151	88	28	11	208	–	–
Idaho	1,156	997	79	504	121	159	48	26	193	–	1
Illinois	8,568	5,831	1,089	725	914	2,737	760	259	2,842	–	6,403
Indiana	5,235	3,681	365	2,031	669	1,554	251	22	1,738	–	90
Iowa	2,409	1,933	395	814	269	476	143	38	684	–	18
Kansas	2,313	1,551	313	518	234	761	341	106	942	–	156
Kentucky	2,157	1,238	111	281	301	919	617	46	991	–	63
Louisiana	3,087	2,266	62	1,187	282	822	424	19	1,024	–	604
Maine	533	386	41	67	121	147	41	7	99	–	–
Maryland	3,114	2,232	596	–	690	882	253	94	500	183	1,274
Massachusetts	2,948	2,232	265	401	723	716	162	32	2,324	–	2,663
Michigan	7,944	5,822	953	711	1,284	2,122	515	241	1,835	–	2,167
Minnesota	5,543	3,717	438	963	509	1,826	707	318	1,422	219	594
Mississippi	2,536	2,103	272	1,359	158	434	185	5	601	–	–
Missouri	3,953	2,908	581	954	451	1,045	375	115	1,276	–	742
Montana	570	391	60	38	60	179	54	49	86	–	–
Nebraska	1,510	981	184	304	109	530	152	52	2,483	–	348
Nevada	2,422	1,811	109	496	345	611	120	115	803	–	–
New Hampshire ..	456	340	48	–	78	117	24	1	83	–	30
New Jersey	4,760	3,292	830	104	1,112	1,468	358	26	783	–	23
New Mexico	980	641	90	95	121	339	122	68	429	–	–
New York	19,624	13,331	1,187	2,762	1,560	6,293	1,408	101	4,485	–	10,344
North Carolina ...	7,340	6,068	579	2,800	1,080	1,272	450	24	2,803	413	54
North Dakota....	410	230	43	–	35	181	60	47	96	–	24
Ohio	8,413	5,669	985	984	1,405	2,745	1,270	205	1,977	–	429
Oklahoma	2,253	1,751	250	694	232	502	192	7	772	–	147
Oregon	2,855	2,179	412	182	584	676	182	82	1,239	–	2
Pennsylvania	8,418	5,312	717	34	1,683	3,107	1,962	120	2,326	–	2,097
Rhode Island	321	222	21	–	69	99	23	3	141	–	115
South Carolina ...	3,523	2,698	220	1,577	280	825	372	57	1,422	–	5
South Dakota....	402	309	59	33	50	93	33	16	183	17	53
Tennessee	4,836	3,945	377	2,061	444	891	349	53	6,423	–	1,021
Texas	16,444	11,867	1,848	3,468	2,098	4,576	2,510	118	7,948	–	2,768
Utah	1,505	1,028	65	26	209	477	129	26	1,475	–	–
Vermont	201	124	20	–	42	77	12	2	177	–	12
Virginia	4,276	3,085	256	175	839	1,191	475	125	1,347	–	1,217
Washington	6,242	4,729	285	1,260	1,041	1,514	541	107	4,537	–	558
West Virginia	935	611	32	240	131	325	175	11	164	–	32
Wisconsin	3,361	2,612	439	60	570	749	247	94	1,123	–	1,227
Wyoming	857	725	54	524	39	132	58	7	116	--	–

– Represents or rounds to zero. [1] Includes items not shown separately. [2] Based on estimated resident population as of July 1.

Source: U.S. Census Bureau; Federal, State and Local Governments, State Government Finances, <http://www.census .gov/govs/www/estimate04.html> (accessed May 2007).

State and Local Government Finances and Employment   289

Table 442. Local Governments—Expenditures and Debt by State: 2004

[In millions of dollars, (1,257,581 represents $1,257,581,000,000), except as indicated. For fiscal year ending in year shown; see text, this section]

State	Total expenditures [1]	General expenditures			Selected functions (direct expenditures)						
		Total amount	Per capita (dol.)	Direct general expenditures	Education	Public welfare	Health	Hospitals	Highways	Police protection	Fire protection
United States..	1,257,581	1,097,184	3,737	1,083,464	474,376	43,289	33,517	56,541	45,985	60,236	28,330
Alabama	15,901	13,644	3,020	13,632	5,416	55	271	2,397	602	664	300
Alaska	2,980	2,711	4,127	2,711	1,316	5	51	73	136	130	89
Arizona	22,418	18,629	3,242	18,078	7,388	633	272	601	806	1,236	555
Arkansas	6,884	6,129	2,231	6,128	3,417	17	29	197	321	361	159
California	201,350	170,440	4,755	170,013	66,017	13,951	8,406	8,581	5,450	9,980	4,232
Colorado	21,204	18,261	3,971	18,250	6,643	566	244	1,125	1,340	999	504
Connecticut	12,713	11,748	3,363	11,746	6,587	115	123	–	422	635	415
Delaware	2,473	2,216	2,674	2,199	1,318	–	20	–	111	126	22
District of Columbia	8,493	6,723	11,597	6,723	1,369	1,686	687	163	71	415	158
Florida	72,264	63,399	3,651	63,181	23,682	705	734	4,995	2,533	4,612	2,169
Georgia	33,637	28,741	3,217	28,677	13,508	147	984	2,816	1,042	1,433	717
Hawaii	2,153	1,732	1,375	1,727	–	21	36	–	138	253	112
Idaho	4,163	3,947	2,830	3,944	1,818	34	63	501	242	211	99
Illinois	55,321	47,018	3,698	46,990	21,548	489	588	1,309	2,562	3,095	1,505
Indiana	21,934	19,971	3,209	19,961	8,984	382	220	2,313	750	707	517
Iowa	10,771	9,975	3,377	9,895	4,791	120	279	860	650	425	156
Kansas	10,041	9,070	3,312	9,060	4,223	36	218	528	518	474	216
Kentucky	10,666	9,572	2,312	9,564	4,561	43	202	294	376	464	300
Louisiana	15,038	13,664	3,039	13,653	5,635	38	144	1,403	643	793	412
Maine	3,754	3,660	2,786	3,660	2,054	30	25	62	180	147	101
Maryland	19,047	17,662	3,180	17,444	8,994	120	363	–	670	1,105	588
Massachusetts . . .	26,487	21,664	3,366	21,002	10,385	63	118	721	612	1,155	863
Michigan	44,053	40,311	3,994	40,170	19,338	762	3,067	798	2,158	1,958	828
Minnesota	23,053	20,995	4,121	20,892	8,259	1,520	390	1,131	1,744	954	282
Mississippi	9,001	8,329	2,880	8,329	3,885	22	48	1,346	519	433	187
Missouri	18,798	16,803	2,921	16,793	8,257	147	318	1,009	989	944	520
Montana	2,466	2,385	2,575	2,382	1,247	33	62	43	108	137	58
Nebraska	8,777	5,830	3,337	5,826	2,810	62	57	342	439	228	122
Nevada	10,444	9,012	3,864	9,012	3,059	195	117	519	743	643	329
New Hampshire . .	4,049	3,963	3,054	3,885	2,059	169	23	–	178	203	144
New Jersey	36,221	35,268	4,065	34,973	18,552	847	417	137	1,139	2,281	728
New Mexico	6,102	5,661	2,978	5,634	3,067	63	45	88	200	347	164
New York	138,106	119,829	6,211	111,667	43,133	9,670	2,741	5,957	4,571	6,219	2,493
North Carolina . . .	30,237	26,226	3,074	25,808	11,188	1,242	1,482	2,601	461	1,272	624
North Dakota	1,911	1,805	2,839	1,796	891	37	30	–	177	71	29
Ohio	46,813	44,011	3,840	43,651	19,176	2,680	2,342	1,237	1,990	2,296	1,372
Oklahoma	9,640	8,786	2,494	8,785	4,315	38	116	687	508	479	315
Oregon	14,513	12,835	3,576	12,386	5,417	272	531	216	624	683	413
Pennsylvania	49,228	44,258	3,576	44,253	20,543	2,913	2,661	87	1,221	1,736	525
Rhode Island	3,393	3,141	2,911	3,141	1,730	7	7	1	112	235	223
South Carolina . . .	13,211	11,818	2,817	11,790	5,805	18	165	1,657	271	564	252
South Dakota	2,199	1,977	2,567	1,977	1,005	12	19	33	217	99	45
Tennessee	24,933	16,325	2,774	16,289	6,678	168	277	2,142	624	957	479
Texas	85,659	74,513	3,309	73,428	37,101	318	1,629	4,961	2,705	3,835	1,682
Utah	8,032	6,273	2,591	6,267	2,996	35	203	27	305	358	168
Vermont	1,880	1,703	2,743	1,703	1,155	1	7	–	130	53	39
Virginia	26,279	24,186	3,237	24,156	11,164	1,221	827	228	557	1,266	749
Washington	28,791	22,564	3,636	22,481	8,653	96	764	1,449	1,170	1,024	749
West Virginia	4,263	3,999	2,208	3,990	2,408	4	53	210	66	159	73
Wisconsin	23,155	21,247	3,864	21,210	9,741	1,471	995	181	1,771	1,273	509
Wyoming	2,688	2,554	5,051	2,553	1,093	10	48	514	112	107	42

See footnotes at end of table.

U.S. Census Bureau, Statistical Abstract of the United States: 2008

Table 442. **Local Governments—Expenditures and Debt by State: 2004**—Con.

[See headnote, page 290]

State	General expenditures—Con.								Utility expenditures	Insurance trust expenditures	Debt outstanding
	Selected functions (direct expenditures)—Con.										
	Corrections	Parks and recreation	Housing [3]	Sewerage	Solid waste	Governmental administration	Interest on general debt	Other			
United States ...	19,558	33,966	17,421	25,896	32,948	57,289	48,770	105,343	133,382	26,266	1,197,510
Alabama	202	579	262	327	426	579	697	856	2,150	107	15,265
Alaska	2	72	65	76	102	165	158	271	248	21	2,895
Arizona	456	500	267	872	357	1,271	865	1,999	3,678	111	23,070
Arkansas	107	198	160	90	159	281	301	331	725	29	6,660
California	3,881	4,786	2,200	3,920	6,651	9,564	6,132	16,263	25,060	5,850	165,927
Colorado	236	604	61	888	433	1,167	1,053	2,386	2,665	277	23,966
Connecticut	–	345	186	237	396	465	330	1,489	625	339	7,941
Delaware	–	178	13	41	57	126	81	107	225	32	1,895
District of Columbia	164	296	34	110	327	445	279	518	1,646	124	6,490
Florida	1,365	2,032	1,772	2,154	1,335	3,802	3,683	7,608	8,188	677	83,024
Georgia	585	1,186	495	523	716	1,830	664	2,034	4,583	313	26,184
Hawaii	–	176	161	143	87	162	123	315	421	–	3,280
Idaho	64	125	97	76	32	222	74	285	215	2	1,637
Illinois	610	1,260	443	2,119	2,106	2,851	2,310	4,196	5,682	2,621	53,578
Indiana	265	809	205	352	488	1,155	783	2,030	1,855	107	16,503
Iowa	100	210	155	269	129	354	277	1,120	782	15	6,478
Kansas	141	259	108	192	95	564	542	946	933	38	11,550
Kentucky	188	286	137	129	182	337	1,089	975	1,062	32	21,026
Louisiana	396	444	268	283	466	904	616	1,207	1,205	170	11,983
Maine	49	118	102	54	89	182	114	353	95	–	2,276
Maryland	267	508	475	637	725	842	626	1,523	604	623	14,194
Massachusetts	223	607	364	218	1,257	833	567	3,013	3,566	1,256	21,917
Michigan	543	1,664	458	815	380	2,130	1,618	3,654	2,484	1,258	36,649
Minnesota	352	488	257	645	691	1,162	1,199	1,817	1,437	388	27,005
Mississippi	79	136	117	137	225	477	300	418	672	–	5,914
Missouri	222	539	118	427	403	917	592	1,392	1,613	382	14,190
Montana	24	53	55	43	49	131	66	272	80	–	1,248
Nebraska	112	142	68	242	147	301	160	594	2,816	130	6,879
Nevada	314	223	14	482	214	653	523	986	1,431	–	14,244
New Hampshire	37	76	78	76	121	207	101	414	77	8	2,240
New Jersey	495	1,140	883	480	781	1,500	1,253	4,341	943	10	28,502
New Mexico	168	106	121	190	102	329	186	457	441	–	4,313
New York	2,319	2,847	2,259	1,653	3,876	3,652	4,993	15,284	10,902	7,375	123,648
North Carolina	286	754	578	540	648	1,083	874	2,175	3,648	21	23,871
North Dakota	15	34	33	78	36	93	78	195	96	10	1,480
Ohio	433	1,457	462	934	1,562	2,823	1,712	3,176	2,669	133	35,715
Oklahoma	96	320	131	193	149	514	283	642	813	41	6,335
Oregon	359	623	102	314	394	747	549	1,141	1,601	76	14,257
Pennsylvania	1,164	1,498	569	554	1,657	2,230	3,440	3,455	3,793	1,176	70,378
Rhode Island	–	80	44	57	153	132	88	272	136	116	1,746
South Carolina	164	279	258	188	238	781	614	536	1,389	3	14,777
South Dakota	30	52	34	71	51	110	56	143	197	10	1,236
Tennessee	354	426	324	295	514	853	697	1,501	8,233	376	20,739
Texas	1,224	2,241	788	1,402	1,659	3,649	4,721	5,514	10,266	879	123,084
Utah	135	255	126	257	187	460	249	505	1,758	–	9,303
Vermont	–	52	23	17	41	68	30	89	171	5	790
Virginia	469	829	592	713	708	1,530	1,065	2,236	1,623	470	24,692
Washington	452	1,125	478	767	810	1,253	977	2,715	6,089	138	34,596
West Virginia	32	139	51	52	111	249	201	181	236	28	3,469
Wisconsin	336	759	325	495	417	988	740	1,210	1,420	488	17,545
Wyoming	41	51	42	69	9	167	46	201	135	–	926

– Represents or rounds to zero. [1] Duplicate intergovernmental transactions are excluded. [2] Based on estimated population as of July 1. See Table 12. [3] Includes community development.

Source: U.S. Census Bureau, *Federal, State and Local Governments, State Governmental Finances;* <http://www.census.gov/govs/www/estimate04.html> (accessed May 2007).

State and Local Government Finances and Employment 291

Table 443. City Governments—Revenue for Largest Cities: 2004

[In millions of dollars (74,542 represents $74,542,000,000). For fiscal years ending in year shown; see text, this section. Cities ranked by estimated resident population as of July 1. Data reflect inclusion of fiscal activity of dependent school systems where applicable. Regarding intercity comparisons, see text, this section. See Appendix III]

Cities ranked by 2004 population	Total revenue [1]	General revenue Total	Intergovernmental Total	From federal govern-ment	From state/local govern-ment	From local govern-ment	General revenue from own sources Total [1]	Taxes Total [1]	Prop-erty	Sales and gross receipts Total	General sales	Public utilities	Current charges Total [1]	Parks and recre-ation	Sewer-age [2]	Miscellaneous Total [1]	Interest earn-ings	Utility revenue [3]	Employee retire-ment revenue
New York, NY [4]	74,542	60,966	23,939	3,154	20,689	96	37,027	28,680	11,831	5,351	4,042	422	5,423	63	1,075	2,924	534	3,232	10,344
Los Angeles, CA	13,471	6,741	978	300	540	138	5,763	2,774	991	1,061	381	572	2,300	107	494	689	292	2,918	3,812
Chicago, IL	7,752	5,065	1,253	433	820	—	3,812	2,166	729	1,192	187	513	958	—	142	687	175	318	2,369
Houston, TX	3,644	2,301	243	152	67	23	2,058	1,249	661	552	343	161	609	23	256	200	87	276	1,067
Philadelphia, PA [4]	6,563	5,054	2,203	743	1,153	306	2,851	2,135	381	198	108	76	594	13	215	122	51	919	590
Phoenix, AZ	2,862	2,388	868	416	405	47	1,520	821	224	540	411	24	540	27	191	159	112	247	227
San Antonio, TX	3,103	1,315	203	41	158	4	1,112	485	242	224	156	67	402	51	213	225	58	1,581	207
San Diego, CA	3,036	2,096	493	221	180	91	1,604	774	268	389	214	102	426	31	227	404	142	253	687
Dallas, TX	2,638	1,752	84	53	30	8	1,668	804	468	314	183	100	678	14	210	185	123	193	693
San Jose, CA	1,955	1,426	137	36	94	8	1,289	648	279	241	126	51	388	22	166	253	51	20	509
Detroit, MI	4,526	3,767	2,272	390	1,864	17	1,496	910	400	186	—	—	409	11	320	177	25	280	479
Indianapolis, IN [4]	3,150	1,797	561	58	491	11	1,236	764	611	43	—	101	357	12	23	115	42	607	45
Jacksonville, FL [4]	1,753	1,753	330	74	256	—	1,422	662	328	326	60	84	306	30	141	454	224	1,015	382
San Francisco, CA [4]	8,596	6,202	2,401	381	1,368	652	3,800	1,695	762	527	294	6	1,349	8	138	756	115	477	1,917
Columbus, OH	1,089	939	166	63	96	7	773	525	41	18	—	29	190	26	146	58	23	150	—
Austin, TX	2,395	976	115	52	41	23	861	417	233	170	110	14	340	7	152	104	52	1,052	367
Memphis, TN	3,380	1,618	1,088	172	425	491	530	358	301	43	—	27	106	10	65	66	33	1,290	473
Baltimore, MD [4]	3,037	2,561	1,350	257	1,056	36	1,211	864	532	69	71	—	232	4	134	116	34	153	373
Ft. Worth, TX	960	576	52	5	43	4	524	326	203	79	2	36	120	3	93	77	34	153	232
Charlotte, NC	1,126	1,019	252	53	63	135	767	349	261	31	69	—	209	4	124	209	54	60	47
El Paso, TX	597	486	79	58	19	2	407	245	131	107	—	—	122	3	69	40	15	60	52
Milwaukee, WI	1,929	930	442	75	312	56	488	233	222	31	—	36	188	4	104	67	20	65	934
Seattle, WA	2,512	1,320	135	38	92	4	1,185	713	268	278	71	114	346	40	266	127	22	860	332
Boston, MA	3,087	2,739	1,223	132	1,088	3	1,516	1,194	1,133	26	2	—	176	—	112	146	22	104	244
Denver, CO [4]	2,172	1,936	253	19	234	—	1,683	684	153	453	125	17	750	40	66	249	61	139	97
Louisville/Jefferson County, KY [4]	841	738	147	26	118	4	594	320	106	60	—	3	245	11	—	29	29	103	—
Washington, DC	8,087	7,535	2,751	2,474	139	139	4,922	3,964	1,028	1,153	726	224	389	12	99	570	93	66	355
Nashville-Davidson, TN [4]	2,914	1,745	653	8	405	240	1,092	701	602	55	306	7	242	11	80	149	90	872	296
Las Vegas, NV	881	800	142	43	43	56	658	377	229	175	175	41	237	22	175	44	17	80	1
Portland, OR	905	758	76	41	35	1	682	394	48	334	—	26	202	11	77	85	6	68	79
Oklahoma City, OK	757	757	297	11	218	68	460	201	100	49	132	43	173	8	75	37	3	118	—
Tucson, AZ	847	640	234	75	146	12	407	274	48	208	50	24	96	18	15	98	14	—	88
Albuquerque, NM	892	794	264	45	197	21	531	264	88	159	—	18	200	12	96	37	40	98	—
Long Beach, CA	1,340	1,175	196	103	92	—	250	124	100	124	—	60	632	19	80	98	—	161	4
Atlanta, GA	1,523	1,180	108	26	4	78	1,072	339	183	105	—	—	590	11	163	144	104	178	165

— Represents or rounds to zero.   [1] Includes revenue sources not shown separately.   [2] Includes solid waste management.   [3] Includes water, electric, and transit.   [4] Represents, in effect, city-county consolidated government.

Source: U.S. Census Bureau, Federal, State, and Local Governments, Government Finances, 2003–2004. See also <http://www.census.gov/govs/www/estimate04.html>.

U.S. Census Bureau, Statistical Abstract of the United States: 2008

Table 444. City Governments—Expenditures and Debt for Largest Cities: 2004

[In millions of dollars (74,821 represents $74,821,000,000). For fiscal year ending in year shown; see headnote, Table 443].

Cities ranked by 2004 population	Total expenditures [1]	Total direct expenditures	General expenditures: Total [1]	Education	Housing and community development	Public welfare	Health and hospitals	Police protection	Fire protection	Correction	Highways	Parks and recreation	Sewerage	Solid waste management	Governmental administration [2]	Interest on general debt	Utility expenditures [3]	Employee retirement expenditures	Debt outstanding
New York, NY [4]	74,821	69,075	58,666	15,098	3,456	9,428	5,889	3,626	1,268	1,257	1,470	649	1,823	1,118	1,044	2,698	8,780	7,375	75,703
Los Angeles, CA	10,896	10,895	6,401	–	207	–	50	1,209	433	–	341	326	565	227	332	396	3,154	1,340	14,670
Chicago, IL	7,064	6,878	5,648	1	231	160	192	1,177	362	–	622	80	121	185	133	654	371	1,044	14,985
Houston, TX	3,555	3,531	2,933	–	70	–	103	478	288	24	204	145	340	65	89	289	291	331	9,721
Philadelphia, PA [4]	6,275	6,250	4,649	23	193	536	1,066	531	171	342	83	99	155	96	358	112	964	662	5,219
Phoenix, AZ	2,874	2,863	2,307	20	112	–	–	343	178	11	67	292	129	87	108	188	488	79	4,792
San Antonio, TX	3,026	3,026	1,302	60	21	66	39	203	125	–	73	108	191	42	82	69	1,663	61	5,639
San Diego, CA	2,523	2,508	1,894	–	314	–	14	272	143	8	142	190	409	58	77	101	444	185	2,771
Dallas, TX	2,900	2,889	2,467	–	40	2	26	256	135	6	90	128	150	48	45	227	225	208	7,722
San Jose, CA	1,888	1,888	1,714	–	267	–	18	212	109	–	104	95	112	64	244	163	39	135	3,971
Detroit, MI	6,147	6,087	5,041	2,009	113	–	116	482	153	–	166	126	537	81	213	252	605	501	6,998
Indianapolis, IN	2,787	2,781	2,110	–	213	71	511	162	62	61	106	67	196	45	218	144	618	59	3,557
Jacksonville, FL [4]	3,615	3,528	2,015	–	68	41	103	178	77	53	213	71	322	72	147	229	1,448	152	9,795
San Francisco, CA [4]	7,222	7,217	5,596	104	184	415	1,311	351	201	138	147	115	209	87	188	610	1,129	496	8,153
Columbus, OH	1,064	1,053	922	–	21	–	32	183	124	13	80	66	146	36	66	96	142	–	1,387
Austin, TX	2,234	2,234	1,082	–	33	10	118	177	85	–	66	97	111	36	63	78	1,051	101	4,423
Memphis, TN	4,694	4,676	1,610	921	16	–	13	175	115	–	28	37	37	52	26	56	2,921	163	2,577
Baltimore, MD [4]	2,966	2,880	2,624	995	111	2	198	324	124	–	162	72	133	69	121	72	101	241	1,798
Ft. Worth, TX	881	881	625	–	12	2	7	101	83	4	47	40	106	39	32	32	181	75	1,196
Charlotte, NC	1,157	1,157	805	–	35	–	4	136	69	–	102	73	51	37	24	66	337	15	2,376
El Paso, TX	604	604	435	–	20	–	18	80	48	–	28	24	44	19	25	29	138	31	955
Milwaukee, WI	1,319	1,293	877	–	122	–	28	207	90	–	98	4	63	58	38	47	66	377	1,030
Seattle, WA	2,478	2,367	1,419	–	36	36	15	164	105	13	101	217	144	108	69	53	972	87	3,515
Boston, MA	2,986	2,743	2,561	856	134	92	178	247	138	102	38	37	150	56	59	59	104	320	1,598
Denver, CO [2]	2,554	2,497	2,229	–	64	106	55	153	74	66	82	160	69	–	135	250	239	86	5,428
Louisville/Jefferson County, KY [4]	870	863	812	–	12	22	52	118	58	42	35	35	–	20	40	171	58	–	2,560
Washington, DC	7,223	7,011	6,934	1,369	327	1,686	850	415	158	164	71	110	296	34	320	279	174	11	6,249
Nashville-Davidson, TN [4]	2,878	2,877	1,847	686	–	30	151	152	93	39	30	68	73	23	107	146	910	121	3,598
Las Vegas, NV	664	552	662	–	25	1	3	113	93	30	75	64	34	5	109	24	1	–	349
Portland, OR	1,059	1,059	890	–	47	–	–	127	73	–	109	76	245	3	50	84	94	75	2,250
Oklahoma City, OK	918	918	774	–	7	–	–	113	102	–	63	61	121	7	119	28	131	14	933
Tucson, AZ	807	807	588	–	56	–	–	111	46	–	48	60	–	28	58	43	188	32	1,057
Albuquerque, NM	789	789	697	–	35	9	17	101	49	44	42	89	33	42	29	31	91	–	954
Long Beach, CA	1,309	1,309	1,093	–	109	–	52	149	57	–	71	81	8	61	51	94	213	3	2,055

– Represents or rounds to zero. [1] Includes expenditure sources not shown separately. [2] Excludes public buildings. [3] Includes water, electric, and transit. [4] Represents, in effect, city–county consolidated government.

Source: U.S. Census Bureau, *Federal, State and Local Governments, Government Finances, 2003–2004*. See also <http://www.census.gov/govs/estimate.html>.

Table 445. County Governments—Revenue for Largest Counties: 2004

[In millions of dollars (17,547 represents $17,547,000,000). For fiscal year ending in year shown; see text, this section. See Appendix III]

Counties ranked by 2004 population	Total revenue [1]	General revenue: Total	Intergov.: Total [1]	Intergov.: Federal Total [1]	Intergov.: Federal Housing [2]	Intergov.: State Total [1]	Intergov.: State Public welfare	Intergov.: State Health and hospitals	Intergov.: From local government	Own sources: Total	Taxes: Total [1]	Taxes: Property	Taxes: Sales and gross receipts Total	Taxes: General sales	Current charges: Total [1]	Current charges: Parks and recreation	Current charges: Sewerage [3]	Current charges: Hospitals	Misc. general revenue: Total [1]	Misc. general revenue: Interest earnings
Los Angeles, CA	17,547	15,830	9,082	981	6	7,993	3,856	1,248	108	6,749	2,577	2,340	118	45	3,677	335	63	2,443	495	61
Cook, IL	3,573	2,537	542	49	43	489	259	-	4	1,995	1,383	806	554	332	532	44	-	298	79	28
Harris, TX	2,852	2,852	545	70	30	391	111	207	85	2,306	1,270	1,126	87	16	664	1	-	241	373	264
Maricopa, AZ	2,517	2,517	1,214	54	9	1,136	539	34	24	1,303	672	528	112	112	438	4	113	374	193	123
Orange, CA	3,819	2,971	1,707	105	8	1,516	614	130	86	1,264	462	376	46	44	528	54	17	-	275	113
San Diego, CA	4,139	3,535	2,530	137	103	2,316	916	519	78	1,005	583	489	28	21	192	20	-	-	230	46
Dade, FL	5,920	5,688	1,379	879	224	451	-	25	49	4,309	1,550	1,040	397	111	2,238	31	-	1,004	521	314
Dallas, TX	1,525	1,500	224	10	-	183	82	25	31	1,276	621	570	11	8	593	-	-	514	61	25
Riverside, CA	2,697	2,697	1,603	215	11	1,343	550	213	45	1,095	351	273	33	27	578	128	63	195	165	24
San Bernardino, CA	3,638	3,035	1,895	182	14	1,662	655	355	51	1,140	258	211	23	16	567	62	69	168	314	16
Wayne, MI	2,311	2,197	1,564	61	5	1,339	145	818	164	633	352	329	15	-	245	4	74	-	36	7
King, WA	2,055	1,952	505	110	21	274	-	174	121	1,447	902	411	463	376	452	4	318	-	93	35
Broward, FL	1,921	1,873	347	104	7	190	-	10	53	1,526	797	662	113	-	569	21	148	-	160	93
Clark, NV	3,654	3,262	706	43	12	561	495	18	103	2,555	1,315	550	543	192	995	45	125	452	246	50
Santa Clara, CA	3,148	3,148	1,603	126	22	1,441	-	389	36	1,545	639	591	7	4	717	50	-	544	189	17
Tarrant, TX	583	583	162	34	4	114	10	71	13	421	251	217	12	-	50	-	-	-	120	70
Bexar, TX	1,110	1,110	218	6	4	197	97	56	14	893	373	332	25	-	433	-	-	380	86	70
Suffolk, NY	2,594	2,457	602	38	6	555	308	73	9	1,856	1,556	529	997	994	170	8	22	-	129	33
Alameda, CA	2,903	1,990	1,073	59	3	983	459	324	31	917	385	342	24	13	413	17	-	185	119	17
Sacramento, CA	3,126	2,492	1,451	155	-	1,233	745	72	63	1,041	378	214	104	80	532	24	305	-	131	30
Nassau, NY	3,352	3,352	886	85	23	801	429	87	-	2,466	1,830	907	904	891	412	20	4	237	223	34
Cuyahoga, OH	1,843	1,843	811	20	20	786	422	205	5	1,031	491	279	172	157	340	9	84	305	200	149
Palm Beach, FL	1,426	1,354	193	58	10	133	5	-	4	1,162	708	542	151	-	239	8	-	-	215	65
Allegheny, PA	1,474	1,344	942	41	27	899	280	405	2	401	305	264	39	25	68	4	-	4	28	13
Oakland, MI	969	935	562	174	7	232	6	53	156	372	241	220	9	-	84	16	-	-	47	13
Hillsborough, FL	1,596	1,446	237	32	19	205	46	-	-	1,208	745	485	221	165	317	70	-	-	146	79
Hennepin, MN	1,696	1,696	672	182	7	479	279	91	10	1,025	470	464	-	-	476	73	3	291	79	31
Franklin, OH	1,032	1,030	396	7	2	364	123	143	25	634	416	311	98	81	84	6	52	-	134	119
Orange, FL	1,426	1,319	224	46	1	178	-	-	-	1,095	705	441	191	-	188	39	215	-	202	136
Contra Costa, CA	2,564	1,884	856	121	103	656	327	108	79	1,028	351	293	27	10	618	52	5	377	59	24
Fairfax, VA	4,538	3,716	925	99	49	774	138	78	52	2,791	2,241	1,775	262	159	375	14	11	-	176	96
St. Louis, MO	692	624	64	11	9	54	1	5	-	560	456	125	319	286	69	36	40	-	35	18
Salt Lake, UT	505	505	83	16	4	49	-	-	18	422	328	200	100	72	71	7	29	-	23	5
Fulton, GA	1,133	919	82	8	-	72	31	15	3	837	729	512	194	181	55	-	-	-	52	20
Westchester, NY	2,170	2,155	516	14	-	497	286	84	-	1,640	860	520	334	325	717	28	-	519	62	35

- Represents or rounds to zero. [1] Includes revenue sources not shown separately. [2] Includes community development. [3] Includes solid waste management.

Source: U.S. Census Bureau, Federal, State and Local Governments, Government Finances, 2003–2004. See also <http://www.census.gov/govs/estimate.html>.

Table 446. County Governments—Expenditures and Debt for Largest Counties: 2004

[In millions of dollars (16,647 represents $16,647,000,000). For fiscal year ending in year shown; see text, this section. See Appendix III]

Counties ranked by 2004 population	Total expenditures [1]	Total direct expenditures	General expenditures Total [1]	Education	Housing [2]	Public welfare	Health	Hospitals	Police protection	Correction	Highways	Parks and recreation	Natural resources	Sewerage and solid waste management	Governmental administration	Interest on general debt	Utility expenditures [3]	Employee retirement expenditures	Debt outstanding
Los Angeles, CA	16,647	16,128	15,199	880	4	5,074	1,695	2,494	1,062	913	256	189	212	53	1,506	129	–	1,448	3,543
Cook, IL	2,930	2,918	2,640	1	10	11	30	866	94	383	100	113	–	–	642	129	–	290	2,658
Harris, TX	3,358	3,358	3,358	–	128	31	214	792	341	70	423	48	213	–	405	338	–	–	8,021
Maricopa, AZ	2,396	2,086	2,086	36	12	788	85	357	53	327	96	8	77	101	338	100	–	6	2,005
Orange, CA	3,380	3,328	3,163	224	14	743	312	–	264	264	32	–	121	29	422	121	–	217	3,657
San Diego, CA	3,649	3,355	3,391	361	107	711	562	–	205	289	139	18	16	29	458	106	555	258	1,567
Dade, FL	6,305	6,277	5,749	–	269	128	62	1,378	378	208	57	253	37	407	221	629	–	–	9,514
Dallas, TX	1,474	1,474	1,463	331	28	6	56	947	26	127	25	14	–	–	151	27	4	11	464
Riverside, CA	2,669	2,527	2,665	320	38	626	192	323	208	152	119	16	66	56	269	32	–	–	1,246
San Bernardino, CA	3,153	3,021	2,920	–	7	882	268	402	199	163	60	60	51	65	236	47	46	188	2,024
Wayne, MI	2,299	2,231	2,194	1	5	193	899	53	25	234	175	72	18	76	321	65	–	105	661
King, WA	2,340	2,302	1,790	–	25	9	307	21	108	117	115	134	45	440	201	122	550	–	2,700
Clark, NV	1,981	1,793	1,923	–	19	136	113	468	258	180	71	209	21	141	153	151	187	–	3,084
Santa Clara, CA	3,558	3,558	3,005	225	9	549	63	676	361	151	433	31	85	71	177	241	553	–	5,708
Tarrant, TX	3,057	2,941	2,941	–	7	–	358	–	87	220	244	–	4	3	304	26	–	–	631
Bexar, TX	557	557	557	–	22	41	99	603	30	89	22	2	–	–	122	106	–	–	2,153
Suffolk, NY	1,066	1,042	1,066	272	6	520	46	–	34	70	29	28	9	69	98	70	166	174	954
Alameda, CA	2,473	2,188	2,307	34	3	655	159	355	407	116	39	1	20	–	244	59	35	146	1,458
Sacramento, CA	2,319	2,284	2,110	149	4	722	287	–	87	175	39	33	41	–	226	7	23	–	763
Nassau, NY	2,921	2,828	2,752	264	23	577	403	395	197	280	171	67	3	220	165	95	3	–	2,324
Cuyahoga, OH	3,191	2,793	3,189	–	18	444	199	516	552	195	60	–	–	86	242	186	–	–	3,468
Palm Beach, FL	1,961	1,944	1,961	–	25	43	312	–	24	90	55	70	35	12	109	168	150	–	2,755
Allegheny, PA	1,478	1,443	1,327	35	44	353	34	28	184	80	114	57	–	126	106	85	–	51	1,695
Oakland, MI	1,411	1,323	1,360	10	9	6	373	8	38	65	48	14	35	–	136	29	20	38	692
Hillsborough, FL	925	886	868	–	4	64	232	–	54	98	112	62	41	96	188	84	140	–	323
Hennepin, MN	1,594	1,569	1,453	–	13	454	118	393	145	109	94	–	61	67	167	23	6	–	2,281
Franklin, OH	1,643	1,638	1,638	–	7	285	153	–	67	87	68	21	–	53	140	110	154	–	574
Orange, FL	1,074	1,041	1,071	–	13	34	295	–	26	51	53	205	17	6	125	210	–	165	1,929
Contra Costa, CA	1,752	1,723	1,598	112	109	340	40	403	146	134	81	107	24	56	153	50	172	262	3,267
Fairfax, VA	2,056	2,009	1,891	1,903	89	204	186	–	79	102	168	72	3	20	105	165	2	22	1,226
St Louis, MO	4,111	4,044	3,677	–	1	24	160	–	176	33	24	13	8	248	75	165	154	–	3,413
Salt Lake, UT	721	510	696	–	13	86	53	–	38	55	17	59	1	11	85	23	–	165	292
Fulton, GA	501	501	501	–	1	86	70	77	62	56	89	13	–	94	213	15	134	262	340
Westchester, NY	1,156	934	973	87	10	454	106	613	26	154	36	59	1	166	94	64	42	49	531
Westchester, NY	2,373	2,074	2,331																1,381

– Represents or rounds to zero.
[1] Includes expenditure categories not shown separately. [2] Includes community development. [3] Includes water, electric, and transit.

Source: U.S. Census Bureau, Federal, State and Local Governments, Government Finances, 2003–2004. See also <http://www.census.gov/govs/estimate.html>.

Table 447. Governmental Employment and Payrolls: 1982 to 2005

[Employees in thousands (15,841 represents 15,841,000), payroll in millions of dollars (23,173 represents $23,173,000,000). Data are for the month of October through 1992. Beginning with the 1997 survey, data are for the month of March. There was no survey between October 1995 and March 1997. Covers both full-time and part-time employees. Local government data are estimates subject to sampling variation; see Appendix III and source]

Type of government	1982	1987	1992	1997	2000	2001	2002	2003	2004	2005
EMPLOYEES (1,000)										
Total	15,841	17,212	18,745	19,540	20,876	20,970	21,039	21,336	21,494	21,725
Federal (civilian)¹	2,848	3,091	3,047	2,807	2,899	2,698	2,690	2,717	2,733	2,720
State and local	12,993	14,121	15,698	16,733	17,976	18,272	18,349	18,649	18,759	19,004
Percent of total	82	82	84	86	86	87	87	87	87	87
State	3,744	4,116	4,595	4,733	4,877	4,985	5,072	5,042	5,041	5,078
Local	9,249	10,005	11,103	12,000	13,099	13,288	13,277	13,606	13,719	13,926
Counties	1,824	1,963	2,253	2,425	(NA)	(NA)	2,729	(NA)	(NA)	(NA)
Municipalities	2,397	2,493	2,665	2,755	(NA)	(NA)	2,972	(NA)	(NA)	(NA)
School districts	4,194	4,627	5,134	5,675	(NA)	(NA)	6,367	(NA)	(NA)	(NA)
Townships	356	393	424	455	(NA)	(NA)	488	(NA)	(NA)	(NA)
Special districts	478	529	627	691	(NA)	(NA)	721	(NA)	(NA)	(NA)
PAYROLLS (mil. dol.)										
Total	23,173	32,669	43,120	49,156	58,166	60,632	63,923	67,194	68,759	71,599
Federal (civilian)¹	5,959	7,924	9,937	9,744	11,485	11,370	11,599	12,672	12,844	13,475
State and local	17,214	24,745	33,183	39,412	46,681	49,262	52,323	54,522	55,914	58,123
Percent of total	74	76	77	80	80	81	82	81	81	81
State	5,022	7,263	9,828	11,413	13,279	14,136	14,838	15,116	15,477	16,062
Local	12,192	17,482	23,355	27,999	33,402	35,126	37,486	39,406	40,437	42,062
Counties	2,287	3,270	4,698	5,750	(NA)	(NA)	7,902	(NA)	(NA)	(NA)
Municipalities	3,428	4,770	6,207	7,146	(NA)	(NA)	9,714	(NA)	(NA)	(NA)
School districts	5,442	7,961	10,394	12,579	(NA)	(NA)	16,720	(NA)	(NA)	(NA)
Townships	370	522	685	869	(NA)	(NA)	1,124	(NA)	(NA)	(NA)
Special districts	665	959	1,370	1,654	(NA)	(NA)	2,026	(NA)	(NA)	(NA)

NA Not available. ¹ Includes employees outside the United States.

Source: U.S. Census Bureau, Federal, State, and Local Governments, Public Employment and Payroll Data; <http://www.census.gov/govs/www/apes.html>.

Table 448. All Governments—Employment and Payroll by Function: 2005

[Employees in thousands (21,725 represents 21,725,000); payroll in millions of dollars (71,599 represents $71,599,000,000). See headnote, Table 447]

Function	Employees (1,000)					Payrolls (mil. dol.)				
	Total	Federal (civilian)¹	State and local			Total	Federal (civilian)¹	State and local		
			Total	State	Local			Total	State	Local
Total	21,725	2,720	19,004	5,078	13,926	71,599	13,475	58,123	16,062	42,062
National defense²	696	696	(X)	(X)	(X)	2,639	2,639	(X)	(X)	(X)
Postal Service	778	778	(X)	(X)	(X)	3,502	3,502	(X)	(X)	(X)
Space research and technology	19	19	(X)	(X)	(X)	146	146	(X)	(X)	(X)
Elem. and secondary education	7,651	(X)	7,651	59	7,593	22,158	(X)	22,158	203	21,955
Higher education	2,861	(X)	2,861	2,303	558	7,396	(X)	7,396	6,133	1,263
Other education	108	11	97	97	(X)	396	63	333	333	–
Health	602	134	467	185	283	2,341	824	1,518	649	868
Hospitals	1,155	157	997	423	574	4,250	881	3,369	1,411	1,958
Public welfare	541	9	532	235	297	1,728	59	1,670	755	915
Social insurance administration	155	68	87	87	(X)	675	369	307	307	(X)
Police protection	1,131	157	973	104	869	4,847	861	3,986	461	3,526
Fire protection	450	(X)	450	(X)	450	1,571	(X)	1,571	(X)	1,571
Correction	755	35	720	469	251	2,662	171	2,491	1,612	879
Streets & highways	571	3	568	242	326	1,949	19	1,930	886	1,044
Air transportation	92	45	47	3	44	564	378	186	15	171
Water transport/terminals	18	5	13	5	8	69	13	56	21	35
Solid waste management	122	(X)	122	2	120	375	(X)	375	9	366
Sewerage	137	(X)	137	2	136	496	(X)	496	9	487
Parks & recreation	414	25	390	40	349	874	113	761	100	661
Natural resources	396	188	208	162	47	1,734	1,077	657	523	134
Housing & community development	139	16	122	–	122	528	101	427	–	427
Water supply	178	–	178	1	177	628	–	628	3	625
Electric power	80	–	80	4	75	403	–	403	23	380
Gas supply	13	–	13	–	13	45	–	45	–	45
Transit	235	(X)	235	34	202	1,019	(X)	1,019	165	854
Libraries	188	4	184	1	184	387	26	361	2	360
State liquor stores	9	(X)	9	9	(X)	20	(X)	20	20	(X)
Financial administration	541	110	431	173	258	2,052	623	1,429	625	804
Other government administration	494	24	470	61	409	1,220	148	1,072	217	855
Judicial and legal	503	61	441	169	272	2,077	363	1,714	736	979
Other & unallocable	694	175	518	207	311	2,845	1,099	1,746	846	900

– Represents or rounds to zero. X Not applicable. ¹ Includes employees outside the United States. ² Includes international relations.

Source: U.S. Census Bureau, Federal, State, and Local Governments, Public Employment and Payroll Data; <http://www.census.gov/govs/www/apes.html>.

Table 449. **State and Local Government—Employer Costs per Hour Worked: 2006**

[In dollars. As of March. Based on a sample; see source for details. Collection of severance pay and supplemental unemployment plans, which comprised "other benefits" and was published in all tables, was discontinued beginning with the March 2006 estimates. For additional data, see Table 632]

Occupation and industry	Total compensation	Wages and salaries	Benefit cost					
			Total	Paid leave	Supplemental pay	Insurance	Retirement and savings	Legally required benefits
Total workers	36.96	25.01	11.96	2.88	0.32	4.03	2.54	2.18
Occupational group:								
Management, professional, and related . . .	45.07	31.95	13.11	3.16	0.19	4.39	2.86	2.51
Professional and related	44.87	32.13	12.74	2.87	0.20	4.38	2.82	2.47
Teachers [1]	50.12	36.86	13.26	2.67	0.12	4.57	3.26	2.65
Primary, secondary, and special education school teachers	48.24	35.19	13.05	2.47	0.11	4.86	3.12	2.49
Sales and office	25.23	15.73	9.50	2.41	0.17	3.80	1.53	1.59
Office and administrative support	25.24	15.74	9.50	2.41	0.17	3.80	1.53	1.58
Service	28.21	17.19	11.02	2.58	0.62	3.35	2.71	1.76
Industry group:								
Education and health services	38.96	27.43	11.53	2.71	0.21	4.07	2.37	2.17
Educational services.	39.58	28.14	11.45	2.54	0.14	4.16	2.45	2.16
Elementary and secondary schools . .	38.62	27.47	11.15	2.21	0.12	4.37	2.38	2.08
Junior colleges, colleges, and universities	42.85	30.36	12.49	3.58	0.20	3.59	2.70	2.42
Health care and social assistance	34.98	22.96	12.02	3.78	0.68	3.49	1.85	2.22
Hospitals	31.39	20.46	10.93	3.24	0.75	3.19	1.66	2.09
Public administration.	33.88	21.19	12.69	3.19	0.49	3.96	2.95	2.10

[1] Includes postsecondary teachers; primary, secondary, and special education teachers; and other teachers and instructors.

Source: U.S. Bureau of Labor Statistics, *National Compensation Survey, Benefits, Archives, 2006 National Survey Compensation Publications List, Employer Costs for Employee Compensation News Release,* March 2006; <http://www.bls.gov/ncs/ncspubs.htm>; (accessed 1 June 2007).

Table 450. **State and Local Government—Full-Time Employment and Salary by Sex and Race/Ethnic Group: 1980 to 2003**

[As of June 30. (2,350 represents 2,350,000.) Excludes school systems and educational institutions. Based on reports from state governments (42 in 1980; 47 in 1983; 49 in 1981, and 1984 through 1987; and 50 in 1989 through 1991) and a sample of county, municipal, township, and special district jurisdictions employing 15 or more nonelected, nonappointed full-time employees. Beginning 1993, only for state and local governments with 100 or more employees. For definition of median, see Guide to Tabular Presentation]

Year and occupation	Employment (1,000)						Median annual salary ($1,000)					
	Male	Female	White [1]	Minority			Male	Female	White [1]	Minority		
				Total [2]	Black [1]	His-panic [3]				Total [2]	Black [1]	His-panic [3]
1980	2,350	1,637	3,146	842	619	163	15.2	11.4	13.8	11.8	11.5	12.3
1981	2,740	1,925	3,591	1,074	780	205	17.7	13.1	16.1	13.5	13.3	14.7
1983	2,674	1,818	3,423	1,069	768	219	20.1	15.3	18.5	15.9	15.6	17.3
1984	2,700	1,880	3,458	1,121	799	233	21.4	16.2	19.6	17.4	16.5	18.4
1985	2,789	1,952	3,563	1,179	835	248	22.3	17.3	20.6	18.4	17.5	19.2
1986	2,797	1,982	3,549	1,230	865	259	23.4	18.1	21.5	19.6	18.7	20.2
1987	2,818	2,031	3,600	1,249	872	268	24.2	18.9	22.4	20.9	19.3	21.1
1989	3,030	2,227	3,863	1,394	961	308	26.1	20.6	24.1	22.1	20.7	22.7
1990	3,071	2,302	3,918	1,456	994	327	27.3	21.8	25.2	23.3	22.0	23.8
1991	3,110	2,349	3,965	1,494	1,011	340	28.4	22.7	26.4	23.8	22.7	24.5
1993	2,820	2,204	3,588	1,436	948	341	30.6	24.3	28.5	25.9	24.2	26.8
1995	2,960	2,355	3,781	1,534	993	379	33.5	27.0	31.4	26.3	26.8	28.6
1997	2,898	2,307	3,676	1,529	973	392	34.6	27.9	32.2	30.2	27.4	29.5
1999	2,939	2,393	3,723	1,609	1,012	417	37.0	29.9	34.8	31.1	29.6	31.2
2001	3,080	2,554	3,888	1,746	1,077	471	39.8	32.1	37.5	34.0	31.5	33.8
2003, total	3,134	2,610	3,919	1,826	1,097	508	42.2	34.7	40.0	35.9	33.6	36.6
Officials/administrators . .	215	126	275	65	39	17	66.4	59.2	64.0	63.0	61.5	62.8
Professionals	654	819	1,064	409	228	96	52.2	44.9	48.6	46.6	43.1	45.6
Technicians	273	204	340	138	75	40	42.2	34.6	39.6	36.3	34.5	37.8
Protective service	923	209	795	337	205	107	43.0	35.5	42.2	40.1	37.3	44.0
Paraprofessionals	109	301	238	172	119	39	31.0	28.0	29.8	27.2	25.7	29.8
Admin. support	122	795	593	325	188	102	31.1	29.2	29.4	29.5	28.8	29.5
Skilled craft	401	23	308	116	67	37	38.6	32.9	38.4	38.0	36.2	38.2
Service/maintenance . . .	437	133	306	264	177	71	31.4	24.2	30.4	29.3	28.3	29.9

[1] Non-Hispanic. [2] Includes other minority groups not shown separately. [3] Persons of Hispanic origin may be of any race.

Source: U.S. Equal Employment Opportunity Commission, 1980–1991, *State and Local Government Information Report,* annual; beginning 1993, biennial.

State and Local Government Finances and Employment 297

Table 451. **State and Local Government Full-Time Equivalent Employment by Selected Function and State: 2005**

[In thousands (1,604.9 represents 1,604,900). For March. Local government amounts are estimates subject to sampling variation; see Appendix III and source]

State	Education Total[1]		Elem. & secondary		Higher education		Public welfare		Health		Hospitals	
	State	Local	State	Local	State	Local	State	Local	State	Local	State	Local
United States..	1,604.9	6,810.9	59.5	6,491.1	1,545.4	319.8	231.0	275.1	178.5	246.3	398.7	520.3
Alabama	36.7	99.9	–	99.9	36.7	–	4.3	1.3	5.3	4.6	11.4	24.2
Alaska.	8.9	17.2	4.0	17.1	4.9	0.1	1.7	0.2	0.7	0.4	0.2	0.6
Arizona	26.4	120.0	–	107.5	26.4	12.5	7.5	2.3	2.4	3.0	0.7	3.3
Arkansas	21.3	71.0	–	71.0	21.3	–	3.7	0.1	4.6	0.4	4.3	1.6
California	143.3	737.1	–	667.7	143.3	69.4	3.6	63.9	11.6	41.6	38.2	61.6
Colorado	37.0	98.4	–	97.2	37.0	1.3	1.9	6.0	1.2	3.4	3.5	9.0
Connecticut	15.8	87.8	–	87.8	15.8	–	4.4	1.8	1.9	1.6	10.4	–
Delaware	7.5	15.9	–	15.9	7.5	–	1.6	–	1.9	0.3	1.8	–
District of Columbia	(X)	12.7	(X)	11.9	(X)	0.8	(X)	1.5	(X)	1.8	(X)	1.7
Florida.	54.4	339.3	–	313.0	54.4	26.3	11.2	6.5	21.9	5.6	4.4	43.7
Georgia	48.0	228.4	–	228.0	48.0	0.4	8.6	1.4	4.5	11.9	8.0	22.8
Hawaii.	37.9	–	29.3	0.0	8.5	–	0.9	0.1	2.5	0.2	4.0	–
Idaho	8.5	32.1	–	30.4	8.5	1.7	1.8	0.1	1.0	1.0	0.8	5.5
Illinois	56.6	291.6	–	268.7	56.6	22.8	10.1	6.2	2.7	7.5	11.7	13.7
Indiana	54.6	135.4	–	135.4	54.6	–	5.6	1.2	1.8	3.7	3.8	23.3
Iowa	25.4	82.8	–	76.6	25.4	6.2	2.8	1.6	0.4	2.8	6.9	10.2
Kansas	19.3	84.7	–	77.1	19.3	7.6	2.8	0.7	1.0	3.1	2.4	7.5
Kentucky	31.3	106.5	–	106.5	31.3	–	6.8	0.7	2.2	5.6	5.8	4.1
Louisiana.	30.7	107.6	–	107.6	30.7	–	5.1	0.5	4.1	1.6	16.2	16.6
Maine	7.1	37.5	0.1	37.5	7.0	–	2.0	0.4	1.3	0.3	0.6	0.7
Maryland	26.4	118.5	–	109.0	26.4	9.5	6.8	3.4	6.8	4.2	5.0	–
Massachusetts . . .	24.9	149.0	0.1	148.9	24.8	0.1	7.6	2.5	7.3	2.8	6.9	–
Michigan	63.4	234.5	0.7	221.8	62.6	12.7	10.3	2.5	1.9	10.2	12.9	8.8
Minnesota	33.5	112.2	–	112.2	33.5	–	2.7	11.2	2.3	3.5	4.8	10.6
Mississippi	18.9	79.8	–	73.3	18.9	6.5	2.5	0.4	3.1	0.2	12.5	18.1
Missouri.	28.1	138.2	–	132.2	28.1	5.9	8.4	2.6	3.2	4.1	12.1	10.7
Montana	7.1	23.1	–	22.8	7.1	0.3	1.6	0.6	0.8	0.9	0.6	0.5
Nebraska.	12.2	43.8	–	40.9	12.2	3.0	2.5	0.8	0.6	0.6	4.3	4.3
Nevada	8.8	39.1	–	39.1	8.8	–	1.4	0.9	1.1	0.9	1.1	4.4
New Hampshire . .	6.7	34.3	–	34.3	6.7	–	1.5	2.5	0.8	0.2	0.8	–
New Jersey	55.5	213.6	24.5	203.0	31.0	10.6	7.5	10.6	4.6	4.4	18.5	1.9
New Mexico	17.5	50.7	–	47.1	17.5	3.6	1.6	0.8	2.3	0.4	10.4	0.9
New York.	51.0	490.8	–	468.1	51.0	22.7	6.3	48.4	9.2	17.8	41.1	48.1
North Carolina . . .	49.7	201.5	–	183.1	49.7	18.4	2.0	14.8	4.3	17.2	17.5	25.4
North Dakota	8.1	14.6	–	14.6	8.1	–	0.5	0.9	1.3	0.6	1.0	–
Ohio	66.7	262.6	–	256.7	66.7	5.9	3.0	24.2	3.7	18.5	11.2	12.0
Oklahoma	26.2	89.3	–	89.0	26.2	0.4	5.8	0.3	6.0	1.4	2.5	9.0
Oregon	18.6	71.5	–	63.3	18.6	8.2	5.7	0.8	2.7	4.5	4.8	2.1
Pennsylvania	57.8	256.1	–	246.3	57.8	9.8	12.5	21.0	1.6	5.4	12.5	–
Rhode Island	6.2	20.1	0.7	20.1	5.5	–	1.5	0.1	1.3	0.1	1.1	–
South Carolina . . .	28.7	97.4	–	97.4	28.7	–	4.4	0.3	6.7	2.3	7.9	18.6
South Dakota	5.0	20.0	–	19.6	5.0	0.4	1.1	0.3	0.6	0.2	0.9	0.5
Tennessee	34.0	130.0	–	130.0	34.0	–	6.3	1.5	3.6	3.9	7.9	22.3
Texas	100.8	668.7	–	629.2	100.8	39.4	19.1	3.3	12.8	21.5	30.7	47.7
Utah	23.6	48.3	–	48.3	23.6	–	3.2	0.5	2.0	1.3	5.7	0.5
Vermont	4.7	19.9	–	19.9	4.7	–	1.2	–	0.7	0.1	0.2	–
Virginia	50.1	187.3	–	185.9	50.1	1.3	2.3	8.2	5.1	6.2	12.9	3.2
Washington	51.1	98.3	–	98.3	51.1	–	9.9	1.9	5.6	4.2	9.7	12.4
West Virginia	11.0	40.5	–	40.5	11.0	–	3.3	–	0.9	1.4	1.7	2.2
Wisconsin	34.7	133.2	–	123.2	34.7	10.0	1.3	13.5	1.7	6.6	3.6	0.8
Wyoming	3.2	18.1	–	16.2	3.2	1.9	0.8	–	0.7	0.4	0.8	5.1

See footnote at end of table.

298   State and Local Government Finances and Employment

[In thousands (238.1 represents 238,100). For March. Local government amounts are estimates subject to sampling variation; see Appendix III and source]

State	Highways		Police protection		Fire protection		Corrections		Parks and recreation		Government administration	
	State	Local	State	Local	State	Local	State	Local	State	Local	State	Local
United States . .	**238.1**	**308.2**	**102.7**	**799.7**	**(X)**	**322.4**	**464.7**	**242.7**	**34.6**	**229.7**	**309.1**	**448.0**
Alabama	4.4	7.2	1.4	11.9	(X)	4.8	4.9	3.0	0.6	3.4	4.4	6.4
Alaska.	2.9	0.6	0.4	1.2	(X)	0.8	1.7	0.1	0.1	0.5	2.1	1.8
Arizona	2.9	5.7	2.0	17.7	(X)	7.0	10.3	5.0	0.4	6.5	4.8	12.1
Arkansas	3.6	3.7	1.1	7.0	(X)	2.8	4.5	1.8	0.8	1.1	3.6	4.5
California.	20.2	21.4	12.7	86.9	(X)	33.4	49.4	30.6	3.4	35.9	45.1	51.7
Colorado	3.1	6.2	1.2	11.9	(X)	5.2	6.5	3.7	0.3	6.0	3.6	9.1
Connecticut	2.9	3.5	2.0	8.9	(X)	4.8	7.7	–	0.2	2.3	4.3	4.7
Delaware.	1.6	0.6	0.9	1.6	(X)	0.2	2.7	–	0.3	0.3	1.3	1.3
District of Columbia	(X)	0.7	(X)	4.3	(X)	1.9	(X)	1.2	(X)	0.9	(X)	1.7
Florida.	7.6	15.3	4.4	59.4	(X)	26.2	28.0	15.6	1.4	19.4	11.8	29.0
Georgia.	5.8	8.4	2.0	24.2	(X)	10.7	19.5	8.3	2.9	6.2	7.5	12.2
Hawaii.	0.9	0.8	–	3.6	(X)	1.8	2.3	–	0.2	2.0	1.6	2.0
Idaho	1.8	1.6	0.5	3.2	(X)	1.2	1.8	1.1	0.2	0.7	2.5	2.6
Illinois	7.6	12.5	3.9	44.3	(X)	16.1	14.0	10.1	0.6	14.8	9.8	17.1
Indiana	4.3	6.6	2.0	15.6	(X)	7.0	9.0	5.6	0.2	3.4	4.8	10.3
Iowa	2.5	7.1	0.9	6.8	(X)	2.0	3.1	1.2	0.1	2.1	2.8	5.3
Kansas	3.6	5.7	1.1	8.1	(X)	3.3	3.6	2.6	0.6	2.5	2.8	6.0
Kentucky	5.1	3.3	2.3	8.6	(X)	4.0	3.9	4.1	1.5	1.6	4.8	4.8
Louisiana.	5.2	5.3	1.8	14.9	(X)	4.9	7.9	5.8	1.4	3.2	5.5	6.7
Maine	2.6	1.9	0.5	2.4	(X)	2.1	1.3	0.8	0.2	0.9	2.2	3.5
Maryland	4.7	4.6	2.5	14.1	(X)	6.0	12.0	3.2	0.5	6.2	6.0	5.3
Massachusetts . . .	3.9	6.8	5.7	17.8	(X)	13.0	6.6	2.8	0.8	2.1	7.6	9.7
Michigan	2.9	9.7	2.7	21.2	(X)	8.1	17.4	5.7	0.3	5.3	7.0	16.6
Minnesota	4.7	7.3	0.9	9.8	(X)	2.3	3.8	4.9	0.6	4.4	5.1	10.1
Mississippi	3.4	4.9	1.2	7.5	(X)	3.5	3.7	1.8	0.4	1.2	2.7	4.6
Missouri.	6.8	7.3	2.3	16.2	(X)	6.3	12.9	3.3	0.6	4.3	4.3	8.0
Montana	2.1	1.3	0.4	2.1	(X)	0.6	1.1	0.6	0.1	0.4	2.3	1.8
Nebraska.	2.2	3.6	0.7	4.3	(X)	1.3	2.5	1.2	0.3	1.0	1.2	3.9
Nevada	1.7	1.3	0.8	6.3	(X)	2.4	3.4	2.5	0.2	3.3	3.1	3.2
New Hampshire . .	1.8	1.7	0.4	3.3	(X)	1.7	1.4	0.6	0.2	0.4	1.6	1.7
New Jersey	7.4	11.5	4.5	31.8	(X)	8.3	10.3	6.6	2.1	5.4	10.1	14.5
New Mexico	2.3	1.8	0.6	5.4	(X)	2.1	4.2	1.8	0.8	2.0	2.8	4.0
New York.	12.4	28.4	6.5	78.9	(X)	23.8	33.5	24.8	2.5	11.5	25.7	27.2
North Carolina . . .	11.6	4.2	3.4	21.4	(X)	7.7	20.5	4.9	1.0	5.0	7.5	12.7
North Dakota	1.0	1.2	0.2	1.2	(X)	0.3	0.7	0.3	0.1	0.8	1.4	1.0
Ohio	7.1	14.9	2.7	30.5	(X)	18.0	16.4	8.8	0.7	9.7	11.4	17.9
Oklahoma	2.9	5.8	1.9	9.0	(X)	4.1	5.6	1.0	0.7	2.1	4.1	5.2
Oregon	3.4	4.0	1.2	7.7	(X)	3.7	5.0	3.6	0.4	3.2	7.6	6.0
Pennsylvania	13.6	10.8	6.0	25.2	(X)	6.3	17.2	12.3	1.4	3.2	14.6	15.8
Rhode Island	0.9	0.8	0.3	2.8	(X)	2.0	1.7	–	0.1	0.6	2.2	1.1
South Carolina . . .	4.9	2.6	1.9	10.9	(X)	4.7	7.4	2.8	0.6	3.1	5.2	5.3
South Dakota	1.0	1.6	0.3	1.6	(X)	0.4	0.8	0.5	0.1	0.4	1.0	1.6
Tennessee	4.4	6.9	2.0	15.6	(X)	6.7	7.1	6.7	1.1	3.4	5.5	8.1
Texas	14.8	21.8	4.1	57.4	(X)	23.9	45.5	22.9	1.1	16.0	16.8	27.5
Utah	1.7	1.7	0.8	4.9	(X)	1.8	3.4	1.8	0.3	2.5	2.7	3.8
Vermont	1.1	1.0	0.5	0.8	(X)	0.4	1.2	0.0	0.1	0.2	1.5	1.3
Virginia	9.5	3.7	2.7	17.9	(X)	8.5	14.2	6.9	0.9	7.7	6.5	13.1
Washington	7.0	7.3	2.2	12.0	(X)	8.0	9.1	4.6	0.7	6.1	6.8	11.1
West Virginia	5.2	1.0	1.0	3.0	(X)	1 0	3.3	0.2	0.6	0.7	3.6	2.9
Wisconsin	1.7	9.9	0.9	15.1	(X)	4.7	9.7	4.0	0.2	3.1	4.9	9.2
Wyoming	1.6	0.8	0.3	1.7	(X)	0.4	0.9	0.6	0.1	0.7	1.0	1.3

– Represents or rounds to zero.   X Not applicable.   [1] Includes other categories not shown separately.

Source: U.S. Census Bureau; "Public Employment and Payroll Data." See also <http://www.census.gov/govs/www/apes>. (accessed May 2007).

State and Local Government Finances and Employment   299

Table 452. State and Local Government Employment and Average Monthly Earnings by State: 1995 and 2005

[3,971 represents 3,971,000. 1995, as of October; 2005, as of March. Full-time equivalent employment is a derived statistic that provides an estimate of a government's total full-time employment by converting part-time employees to a full-time amount]

State	Full-time equivalent employment (1,000)				Full-time equivalent employment per 10,000 population [2]				Average monthly earnings [3] (dol.)			
	State		Local [1]		State		Local [1]		State		Local [1]	
	1995	2005	1995	2005	1995	2005	1995	2005	1995	2005	1995	2005
United States . . .	3,971	4,209	10,119	11,715	149	142	380	395	2,854	3,966	2,763	3,702
Alabama	81	85	165	188	188	188	384	414	2,421	3,572	2,017	2,728
Alaska	22	25	24	27	365	370	390	410	3,727	4,234	4,051	4,141
Arizona	58	69	161	213	131	116	362	357	2,570	3,541	2,689	3,684
Arkansas	48	54	90	106	188	195	357	382	2,353	3,335	1,823	2,570
California	338	387	1,141	1,384	107	107	360	383	3,664	5,319	3,523	4,927
Colorado	57	66	148	184	150	142	386	395	3,234	4,562	2,612	3,727
Connecticut	63	60	102	125	190	171	306	358	3,321	4,927	3,491	4,504
Delaware	22	25	19	23	302	292	264	268	2,743	3,869	2,755	3,815
District of Columbia . . .	(X)	(X)	47	46	(X)	(X)	806	790	(X)	(X)	3,425	4,775
Florida	175	186	534	657	120	105	367	370	2,488	3,407	2,485	3,476
Georgia	115	121	333	378	157	132	455	414	2,456	3,396	2,164	3,076
Hawaii	51	54	14	14	429	426	118	113	2,624	3,672	3,013	4,054
Idaho	21	23	46	54	177	160	393	380	2,476	3,454	2,165	2,954
Illinois	141	133	444	504	117	104	370	395	3,027	4,264	2,985	3,850
Indiana	89	93	217	240	151	148	371	383	2,583	3,512	2,375	3,209
Iowa	53	53	116	133	186	179	405	448	3,126	4,441	2,367	2,974
Kansas	48	44	118	137	184	161	454	500	2,325	3,622	2,315	2,950
Kentucky	73	79	133	159	189	190	341	381	2,488	3,421	2,523	2,786
Louisiana	93	91	171	192	212	202	390	427	2,359	3,455	1,860	2,638
Maine	21	21	45	55	172	160	363	416	2,618	3,608	2,349	2,931
Maryland	81	91	172	188	160	162	339	336	2,835	4,125	3,159	4,317
Massachusetts	82	89	220	234	133	138	358	363	3,068	4,420	2,961	4,097
Michigan	141	131	324	364	145	130	335	360	3,342	4,427	3,255	3,963
Minnesota	73	74	196	195	156	145	420	380	3,266	4,613	2,830	3,838
Mississippi	50	57	122	132	184	195	449	454	2,394	3,096	1,798	2,636
Missouri	79	92	192	227	147	158	357	391	2,232	3,087	2,297	2,971
Montana	18	20	38	36	206	209	436	384	2,534	3,309	2,347	2,821
Nebraska	30	32	76	79	179	185	460	450	2,290	3,263	2,413	3,368
Nevada	21	26	53	75	130	107	334	309	2,864	3,963	3,085	4,343
New Hampshire	17	19	38	50	146	149	332	380	2,669	3,630	2,641	3,199
New Jersey	125	154	312	348	155	177	386	399	3,563	4,855	3,553	4,640
New Mexico	42	50	68	78	247	261	397	404	2,390	3,160	2,119	2,785
New York	257	245	856	939	139	127	462	486	3,423	4,622	3,479	4,594
North Carolina	115	135	281	348	156	156	382	401	2,570	3,468	2,287	3,168
North Dakota	16	18	22	23	255	285	337	364	2,440	3,243	2,450	3,334
Ohio	143	136	425	484	127	119	379	422	3,083	3,909	2,696	3,532
Oklahoma	68	65	129	140	204	183	389	396	2,018	3,254	2,113	2,589
Oregon	52	58	114	124	164	159	358	342	2,848	3,725	2,896	3,748
Pennsylvania	152	160	369	417	125	129	303	336	3,025	3,923	2,911	3,791
Rhode Island	20	20	29	30	198	186	281	280	3,240	4,367	3,169	4,438
South Carolina	78	76	136	168	208	180	362	395	2,318	3,165	2,141	2,938
South Dakota	14	13	27	30	192	174	360	389	2,355	3,275	2,004	2,821
Tennessee	84	83	188	239	158	139	354	402	2,389	3,249	2,196	3,008
Texas	268	274	858	1,016	141	120	453	443	2,492	3,532	2,229	3,027
Utah	42	49	63	79	209	197	312	315	2,524	3,504	2,460	3,197
Vermont	13	14	21	25	214	231	361	403	2,471	3,896	2,455	2,976
Virginia	116	120	247	298	174	158	370	394	2,553	3,688	2,505	3,368
Washington	96	117	188	213	174	186	342	338	3,094	4,086	3,338	4,472
West Virginia	35	38	60	61	189	208	327	335	2,212	3,049	2,203	2,752
Wisconsin	64	70	201	224	124	127	388	404	3,153	4,321	2,900	3,771
Wyoming	11	12	27	32	224	231	558	629	2,203	3,389	2,309	3,182

X Not applicable. [1] Estimates subject to sampling variation; see Appendix III and source. [2] Based on estimated resident population as of July 1. See Table 12. [3] For full-time employees.

Source: U.S. Census Bureau; Governments Division; 2005 Annual Survey of Government Employment, May 2006. <http://www.census.gov/govs/www/apesstl.html> (accessed May 2007).

Table 453. City Government Employment and Payroll—Largest Cities: 1995 and 2005

[In thousands, (425.3 represents 425,300), except as noted. For 1995 as of October; 2005 as of March. See footnote 4, Table 443, for those areas representing city-county consolidated governments. See headnote, Table 452 for full-time equivalent employment definition]

Cities ranked by 2002 population [1]	Total employment (1,000)		Full-time equivalent employment				Payroll (mil. dol.)		Average monthly earnings for full-time employees (dol.)	
			Total (1,000)		Per 10,000 population					
	1995	2005	1995	2005	1995	2005	1995	2005	1995	2005
New York, NY [2,3]	425.3	443.4	388.1	410.8	529	508	1,306	1,958	3,454	4,919
Los Angeles, CA	47.9	53.5	46.9	51.7	136	136	191	304	4,133	5,894
Chicago, IL	41.5	42.6	41.5	42.1	152	146	156	171	3,757	4,100
Houston, TX	23.4	21.9	23.0	21.7	135	108	57	74	2,459	3,414
Philadelphia, PA	29.6	31.4	28.9	30.5	190	204	92	127	3,220	4,188
Phoenix, AZ	12.0	14.3	11.7	14.0	88	102	38	67	3,282	4,859
San Diego, CA	11.9	11.7	10.1	11.0	112	87	34	58	3,473	5,385
Dallas, TX	14.5	14.8	14.3	14.5	140	120	41	62	2,877	4,327
San Antonio, TX	15.7	17.3	14.8	16.4	148	138	37	62	2,539	3,826
Detroit, MI	17.8	37.4	17.2	33.5	173	363	50	143	2,909	4,294
San Jose, CA	6.5	9.4	6.0	8.6	105	95	27	52	4,700	6,319
Honolulu, HI	9.9	9.7	9.2	9.0	74	100	28	37	3,083	4,157
Indianapolis, IN	12.4	17.1	11.8	15.8	155	202	33	54	2,491	3,335
San Francisco, CA	26.5	29.2	26.5	29.2	361	383	98	191	3,711	6,541
Jacksonville, FL	9.8	11.4	9.3	11.3	132	148	28	46	3,064	4,201
Columbus, OH	8.3	8.4	8.0	8.1	391	112	26	35	3,325	4,369
Louisville, KY	5.3	8.4	4.4	7.7	125	111	9	26	2,224	3,390
Austin, TX	12.5	12.4	11.5	11.8	138	176	28	48	2,513	4,079
Memphis, TN [2]	21.8	28.9	20.6	26.3	336	406	54	90	2,679	3,522
Baltimore, MD [2]	28.0	27.2	27.5	25.7	102	402	81	103	3,011	4,093
Milwaukee, WI	8.8	8.0	8.5	7.9	679	134	23	32	2,794	4,031
Boston, MA [2]	22.0	22.4	21.5	20.8	393	353	49	97	2,279	4,696
Charlotte, NC	4.7	6.0	4.6	5.9	202	101	13	23	2,847	3,996
El Paso, TX	6.0	5.7	5.9	5.5	224	96	13	16	2,302	2,970
Washington, DC [2,3]	39.7	37.6	38.5	36.0	386	631	124	165	3,269	4,713
Seattle, WA	11.4	12.8	10.5	11.5	292	201	40	57	3,985	5,132
Ft. Worth, TX	5.8	6.4	5.3	6.1	178	107	12	24	2,403	4,089
Denver, CO	16.3	12.4	14.4	11.7	178	209	45	53	3,127	4,552
Nashville-Davidson, TN [2]	20.9	22.2	19.5	21.0	106	385	41	76	2,136	3,699
Portland, OR	5.8	6.2	5.1	5.4	117	100	19	27	3,950	5,210
Oklahoma City, OK	5.1	4.9	4.9	4.5	113	86	14	19	3,084	4,560
Las Vegas, NV	2.1	3.0	2.1	2.8	147	55	7	17	3,570	6,077
Tucson, AZ	5.8	6.8	5.3	6.0	106	118	14	24	2,882	4,300
New Orleans, LA	9.0	10.0	8.6	9.7	121	204	19	25	2,227	2,624
Long Beach, CA	5.7	6.0	5.4	5.6	125	119	21	28	3,947	5,194
Cleveland, OH	10.1	7.9	8.8	7.8	354	166	24	30	2,806	3,867
Albuquerque, NM	7.9	6.9	6.2	6.5	150	139	15	21	2,432	3,453
Fresno, CA	2.7	4.0	2.7	3.9	151	87	10	18	3,652	4,802
Kansas, MO	6.8	6.6	6.5	6.6	199	148	17	25	2,685	3,834
Sacramento, CA	4.4	5.1	4.0	4.4	70	100	14	23	3,713	5,796
Virginia Beach, VA [2]	16.9	21.8	15.2	18.8	111	433	35	55	2,386	3,124
Mesa, AZ	2.7	4.3	2.7	4.1	107	95	9	20	3,308	4,981
Atlanta, GA	8.1	8.0	7.9	7.8	92	184	20	29	2,542	3,748
Baton Rouge, LA	6.4	7.1	6.0	6.3	209	152	14	19	2,550	3,123
Oakland, CA	5.1	5.5	4.7	5.5	128	138	19	41	4,483	7,397
Omaha, NE	3.1	3.0	2.9	2.8	145	69	10	13	3,533	4,745
Tulsa, OK	4.3	4.3	4.2	4.2	206	106	11	15	2,735	3,598
Minneapolis, MN	6.9	5.9	6.3	5.5	179	146	23	24	3,922	4,482
Miami, FL	3.5	3.7	3.4	3.6	83	97	12	17	3,503	4,899
Colorado Springs, CO	6.4	7.7	5.9	7.2	63	195	19	31	3,243	4,370
Wichita, KS	3.5	4.0	3.2	3.3	95	93	8	11	2,617	3,541
Arlington, TX	2.5	2.7	2.1	2.4	187	69	6	10	2,992	4,178
Santa Ana, CA	2.2	2.5	2.0	2.1	87	60	8	13	4,813	7,069
St. Louis, MO	7.9	6.9	7.7	6.9	370	204	20	24	2,606	3,442
Anaheim, CA	3.7	3.5	2.3	2.4	102	73	10	16	4,635	6,693
Pittsburgh, PA	5.6	3.6	5.2	3.5	68	107	16	15	3,222	4,466
Cincinnati, OH	8.2	6.3	7.4	6.0	74	185	23	26	3,480	4,512
Tampa, FL	4.2	4.7	4.2	4.6	146	145	13	18	3,177	4,017
Toledo, OH	3.1	2.9	3.1	2.9	81	95	10	13	3,192	4,315
Raleigh, NC	2.9	3.8	2.6	3.3	118	108	7	12	2,705	3,715
Buffalo, NY [2]	12.4	11.9	11.6	10.8	163	375	40	48	3,733	4,661
Aurora, CO	2.1	2.7	2.1	2.6	151	92	6	12	2,972	4,579
St. Paul, MN	3.6	3.2	3.3	2.9	126	102	11	14	3,601	4,827
Corpus Christi, TX	3.4	3.1	3.3	3.0	206	108	8	10	2,384	3,338
Newark, NJ	5.5	6.9	5.3	5.9	343	212	18	31	3,545	5,352
Riverside, CA	2.3	2.4	2.3	2.1	84	77	9	11	4,122	5,699
Anchorage, AK	10.8	10.9	8.7	9.8	93	364	39	42	4,683	4,395
Lexington, KY	3.8	4.3	3.5	4.0	441	150	8	13	2,159	3,399
Stockton, CA	2.0	2.2	1.8	1.8	140	69	6	9	3,330	5,101
Bakersfield, CA	1.3	1.3	1.2	1.3	148	51	4	7	3,843	5,136
St. Petersburg, FL	3.9	3.9	3.3	3.4	109	137	9	13	2,836	3,990
Jersey City, NJ	3.7	3.8	3.6	3.5	398	144	13	17	3,755	5,274
Birmingham, AL	4.2	4.6	4.0	4.5	158	187	9	16	2,354	3,503
Norfolk, VA [2]	12.2	14.0	10.6	12.1	79	506	27	41	2,583	3,506
Plano, TX	1.6	2.4	1.4	2.2	137	93	5	9	3,430	4,244
Lincoln, NE	3.6	3.0	3.4	2.7	125	118	9	11	2,724	4,252

[1] 2002 based on estimated resident population as of July 1. [2] Includes city-operated elementary and secondary schools. [3] Includes city-operated university or college.

Source: U.S. Census Bureau, 2005 Annual Survey of Government Employment; see also <http://www.census.gov/govs/www/apesstl.html> (accessed May 2007).

Table 454. County Government Employment and Payroll—Largest Counties: 1995 and 2005

[In thousands, (93.2 represents 93,200), except as noted. For 1995 as of October; 2005 as of March. See text, this section. See headnote, Table 452, for full-time equivalent employment definition]

Counties ranked by 2002 population [1]	Total employment (1,000)		Full-time equivalent employment				Payroll (mil. dol.)		Average monthly earnings for full-time employees (dol.)	
			Total (1,000)		Per 10,000 population					
	1995	2005	1995	2005	1995	2005	1995	2005	1995	2005
Los Angeles, CA	93.2	99.5	87.7	95.3	96	97	339.8	475.0	3,858	5,033
Cook, IL	27.5	27.8	27.5	27.7	53	52	84.7	126.3	3,085	4,564
Harris, TX	20.0	21.7	19.8	20.8	65	59	50.2	77.4	2,550	3,746
Maricopa, AZ	17.0	16.4	16.3	16.2	69	49	35.6	54.9	2,197	3,397
Orange, CA	15.3	25.0	14.7	23.2	58	79	48.5	104.9	3,368	4,559
San Diego, CA	18.3	19.7	17.4	18.6	66	64	51.2	83.9	2,977	4,524
Dade, FL	36.1	43.8	34.8	42.5	172	182	113.8	190.8	3,359	4,615
Dallas, TX	11.8	15.2	11.2	14.3	58	62	26.5	54.5	2,290	3,823
Wayne, MI	6.0	5.8	5.8	5.8	28	28	18.6	25.1	3,276	4,344
San Bernardino, CA	15.0	19.9	13.9	18.5	90	102	41.9	84.0	3,052	4,593
King, WA	14.2	14.5	13.0	13.8	82	79	45.1	64.6	3,477	4,878
Broward, FL	10.7	12.9	10.3	12.6	75	74	29.7	48.4	2,922	3,897
Riverside, CA	13.2	20.1	12.6	18.8	93	111	42.3	90.6	3,437	4,812
Santa Clara, CA	17.6	18.0	15.3	17.1	98	102	57.4	100.4	3,840	5,942
Tarrant, TX	3.8	9.4	3.7	9.2	30	60	8.5	34.4	2,288	3,740
Clark, NV	12.5	19.1	11.4	17.3	121	114	39.0	88.4	3,536	5,225
Alameda, CA	11.2	11.3	10.2	10.8	77	73	37.7	60.9	3,649	5,687
Suffolk, NY	13.1	14.2	12.1	12.7	90	87	44.0	68.2	3,774	5,372
Bexar, TX	8.2	10.1	8.3	9.6	65	66	17.0	27.9	2,156	2,856
Cuyahoga, OH.	14.9	15.7	14.9	15.1	107	110	35.4	57.1	2,367	3,690
Nassau, NY.	19.0	16.8	17.3	15.1	133	112	64.6	76.6	3,939	5,156
Sacramento, CA.	12.1	14.9	11.7	14.1	107	108	37.0	71.0	3,195	5,046
Allegheny, PA	8.2	6.8	8.0	6.7	61	53	17.5	20.2	2,222	3,043
Oakland, MI	4.7	4.6	4.4	4.3	38	36	13.6	18.9	3,276	4,471
Palm Beach, FL.	8.3	10.5	8.1	10.0	84	84	25.4	40.4	3,196	4,100
Hennepin, MN	12.4	11.4	10.4	10.7	99	95	33.0	49.3	3,199	4,586
Franklin, OH	6.5	6.7	6.4	6.4	63	59	14.2	21.7	2,292	3,426
Hillsborough, FL.	13.3	13.9	12.6	11.4	144	108	31.6	39.1	2,565	3,690
St Louis, MO.	4.0	3.9	4.0	3.8	39	37	10.7	14.0	2,766	3,706
Fairfax, VA	32.3	44.7	31.2	38.1	354	382	95.6	165.4	3,152	4,389
Contra Costa, CA.	8.4	10.0	7.6	8.7	88	88	31.8	41.6	4,277	4,779
Orange, FL	9.2	10.5	8.3	9.7	113	103	21.7	35.7	2,631	3,735
Erie, NY	10.9	11.3	9.7	10.2	100	108	26.1	37.4	2,759	3,842
Westchester, NY	12.5	7.3	10.9	6.2	122	67	39.7	29.8	3,717	4,663
Milwaukee, WI.	9.5	9.3	9.6	9.0	102	96	23.9	35.7	2,523	3,981
Pinellas, FL.	5.7	6.6	5.6	6.4	65	69	14.0	25.7	2,500	3,998
Du Page, IL	3.2	3.6	3.0	3.4	35	37	8.1	14.1	2,801	4,155
Salt Lake, UT	4.9	5.9	3.9	4.3	49	46	10.1	13.9	2,920	3,576
Montgomery, MD	34.2	40.6	30.0	29.8	374	328	96.2	175.3	3,787	5,657
Shelby, TN	10.8	14.2	10.6	13.6	123	151	26.0	45.4	2,479	3,356
Bergen, NJ	7.5	5.7	7.0	4.9	83	54	20.6	23.7	3,207	4,959
Pima, AZ	7.4	7.2	6.7	6.7	92	76	16.7	22.5	2,585	5,505
Travis, TX	3.4	4.6	3.3	4.5	51	53	7.9	15.7	2,397	3,492
Fresno, CA	8.6	9.2	8.4	8.5	116	102	23.4	32.9	2,780	3,883
Hamilton, OH.	5.8	6.1	5.6	5.9	65	71	14.4	20.5	2,570	3,460
Prince Georges, MD	24.3	33.2	22.4	28.4	295	341	69.6	112.1	3,251	4,201
Fulton, GA	6.1	7.6	5.9	7.4	85	89	14.5	29.2	2,511	4,147
Macomb, MI	2.9	3.2	2.6	3.0	36	38	7.1	12.0	2,825	4,104
Essex, NJ	6.9	5.0	7.2	4.7	94	59	18.9	21.0	3,055	4,638
Ventura, CA	9.4	8.6	7.9	8.0	113	103	51.9	43.2	6,738	5,476
Middlesex, NJ	5.3	4.3	4.7	3.8	68	49	14.6	16.6	3,260	4,687
Baltimore, MD	25.6	27.5	21.5	22.8	302	296	61.3	92.9	3,051	4,252
Montgomery, PA.	3.3	4.1	3.2	3.7	46	48	6.5	12.4	2,108	3,266
Monroe, NY.	7.1	6.9	6.3	5.9	87	80	18.8	22.8	3,112	3,910
Mecklenburg, NC	19.2	27.1	16.8	23.5	299	318	40.4	82.1	2,473	3,494
Pierce, WA	3.2	3.6	3.0	3.4	48	46	10.2	16.6	3,531	4,966
San Mateo, CA	5.9	7.2	5.4	6.9	80	98	20.5	35.5	3,941	5,820
El Paso, TX.	3.5	4.7	3.4	4.4	51	64	7.5	15.3	2,277	3,484
Kern, CA	8.9	10.3	8.6	9.7	141	140	25.6	40.7	3,086	4,235
Multnomah, OR	4.5	5.0	4.0	4.5	65	67	10.0	16.6	2,559	3,659
Dekalb, GA	5.8	7.1	5.6	6.9	98	102	15.5	25.1	2,771	3,647
Wake, NC	14.7	21.0	13.2	18.8	267	278	30.8	65.3	2,352	3,436
Lake, IL	2.7	3.3	2.5	3.1	45	45	7.1	13.0	2,894	4,225
Oklahoma City, OK	1.8	2.3	1.7	2.2	27	32	3.1	5.7	1,928	2,687
Jefferson, AL.	4.9	4.5	4.8	4.4	73	67	12.3	16.9	2,555	3,839
Jackson, MO	2.0	1.9	2.0	1.9	32	29	4.0	5.8	1,998	3,030
Norfolk, MA.	0.9	0.5	0.9	0.5	14	7	2.3	2.0	2,540	4,227
Cobb, GA.	4.1	4.7	3.6	4.3	72	66	9.5	16.2	2,674	3,891
Gwinnett, GA.	3.4	4.5	3.2	4.3	74	66	8.1	16.7	2,599	3,966
Snohomish, WA	2.0	3.2	2.0	2.9	38	46	6.8	13.5	3,429	4,673
Monmouth, NJ	5.9	6.2	5.2	5.3	91	84	15.8	24.0	3,204	4,456
Hidalgo, TX.	1.5	2.2	1.5	2.2	32	35	2.5	5.6	1,711	2,584
San Joaquin, CA	7.0	7.7	6.6	6.9	127	113	19.3	30.4	3,067	4,385

[1] 2002 based on estimated resident population as of July 1. See Table 12.

Source: U.S. Census Bureau, *Governments Division; 2005 Annual Survey of Government Employment;* see also <http://www.census.gov/govs/www/apesstl.html> (accessed May 2007).

Section 9
Federal Government Finances and Employment

This section presents statistics relating to the financial structure and the civilian employment of the federal government. The fiscal data cover taxes, other receipts, outlays, and debt. The principal sources of fiscal data are the *Budget of the United States Government* and related documents, published annually by the Office of Management and Budget (OMB), and the U.S. Department of the Treasury's *United States Government Annual Report* and its *Appendix*. Detailed data on tax returns and collections are published annually by the Internal Revenue Service. The personnel data relate to staffing and payrolls. They are published by the Office of Personnel Management and the Bureau of Labor Statistics. Data on federally owned land and real property are collected by the General Services Administration and presented in its annual "Federal Real Property Report."

Budget concept—Under the unified budget concept, all federal monies are included in one comprehensive budget. These monies comprise both federal funds and trust funds. Federal funds are derived mainly from taxes and borrowing and are not restricted by law to any specific government purpose. Trust funds, such as the Unemployment Trust Fund, collect certain taxes and other receipts for use in carrying out specific purposes or programs in accordance with the terms of the trust agreement or statute. Fund balances include both cash balances with the Treasury and investments in U.S. securities. Part of the balance is obligated, part unobligated. Prior to 1985, the budget totals, under provisions of law, excluded some federal activities—including the Federal Financing Bank, the Postal Service, the Synthetic Fuels Corporation, and the lending activities of the Rural Electrification Administration. The Balanced Budget and Emergency Deficit Control Act of 1985 (P.L.99-177) repealed the off-budget status of these entities and placed social security (federal old-age and survivors

insurance and the federal disability insurance trust funds) off-budget. Though social security is now off-budget and, by law, excluded from coverage of the congressional budget resolutions, it continues to be a federal program.

Receipts arising from the government's sovereign powers are reported as governmental receipts; all other receipts; i.e., from business-type or market-oriented activities, are offset against outlays. Outlays are reported on a checks-issued (net) basis (i.e., outlays are recorded at the time the checks to pay bills are issued).

Debt concept—For most of U.S. history, the total debt consisted of debt borrowed by the Treasury (i.e., public debt). The present debt series includes both public debt and agency debt. The *gross federal debt* includes money borrowed by the Treasury and by various federal agencies; it is the broadest generally used measure of the federal debt. *Total public debt* is covered by a statutory debt limitation and includes only borrowing by the Treasury.

Treasury receipts and outlays—All receipts of the government, with a few exceptions, are deposited to the credit of the U.S. Treasury regardless of ultimate disposition. Under the Constitution, no money may be withdrawn from the Treasury unless appropriated by the Congress.

The day-to-day cash operations of the federal government clearing through the accounts of the U.S. Treasury are reported in the *Daily Treasury Statement*. Extensive detail on the public debt is published in the *Monthly Statement of the Public Debt of the United States*.

Budget receipts such as taxes, customs duties, and miscellaneous receipts, which are collected by government agencies, and outlays represented by checks issued and cash payments made by disbursing officers as well as government agencies

• U.S. Census Bureau, Statistical Abstract of the United States: 2008

are reported in the *Daily Treasury Statement of Receipts and Outlays of the United States Government* and in the Treasury's *United States Government Annual Report* and its *Appendix*. These deposits in and payments from accounts maintained by government agencies are on the same basis as the unified budget.

The quarterly *Treasury Bulletin* contains data on fiscal operations and related Treasury activities, including financial statements of government corporations and other business-type activities.

Income tax returns and tax collections—Tax data are compiled by the Internal Revenue Service of the Treasury Department. The annual *Internal Revenue Service Data Book* gives a detailed account of tax collections by kind of tax. The agency's annual *Statistics of Income* reports present detailed data from individual income tax returns and corporation income tax returns. The quarterly *Statistics of Income Bulletin* presents data on such diverse subjects as tax-exempt organizations, unincorporated businesses, fiduciary income tax and estate tax returns, sales of capital assets by individuals, international income and taxes reported by corporations and individuals, and estate tax wealth.

Employment and payrolls—The Office of Personnel Management collects employment and payroll data from all departments and agencies of the federal government, except the Central Intelligence Agency, the National Security Agency, and the Defense Intelligence Agency. Employment figures represent the number of persons who occupied civilian positions at the end of the report month shown and who are paid for personal services rendered for the federal government, regardless of the nature of appointment or method of payment. Federal payrolls include all payments for personal services rendered during the report month and payments for accumulated annual leave of employees who separate from the service. Since most federal employees are paid on a biweekly basis, the calendar month earnings are partially estimated on the basis of the number of work days in each month where payroll periods overlap.

Federal employment and payroll figures are published by the Office of Personnel Management in its *Federal Civilian Workforce Statistics—Employment and Trends*. It also publishes biennial employment data for minority groups, data on occupations of white- and blue-collar workers, and data on employment by geographic area; reports on salary and wage distribution of federal employees are published annually. General schedule is primarily white-collar; wage system primarily blue-collar. Data on federal employment are also issued by the Bureau of Labor Statistics in its *Monthly Labor Review* and in *Employment and Earnings* and by the U.S. Census Bureau in its annual publication *Public Employment*.

Figure 9.1
Federal Budget Summary: 1980 to 2007

Receipts, outlays, and surplus or deficit
Trillions of constant (2000) dollars

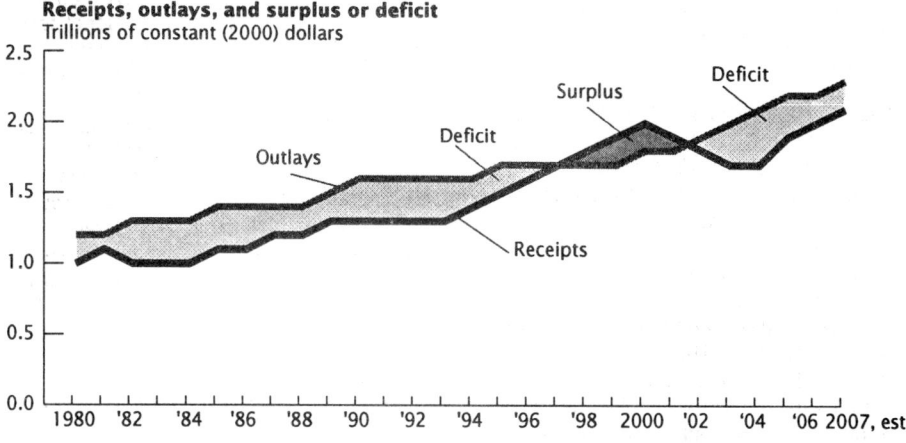

Outlays and federal debt as a percent of gross domestic product (GDP): 1980 to 2007
Percent

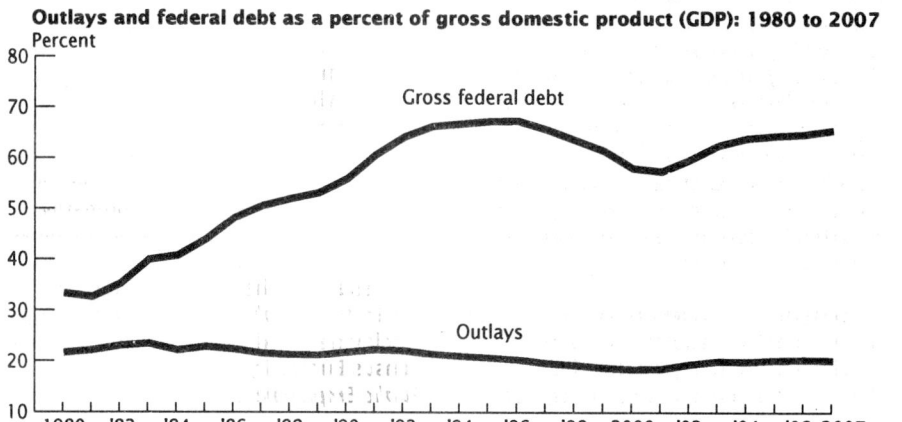

Gross federal debt: 1980 to 2007
Trillions of current dollars

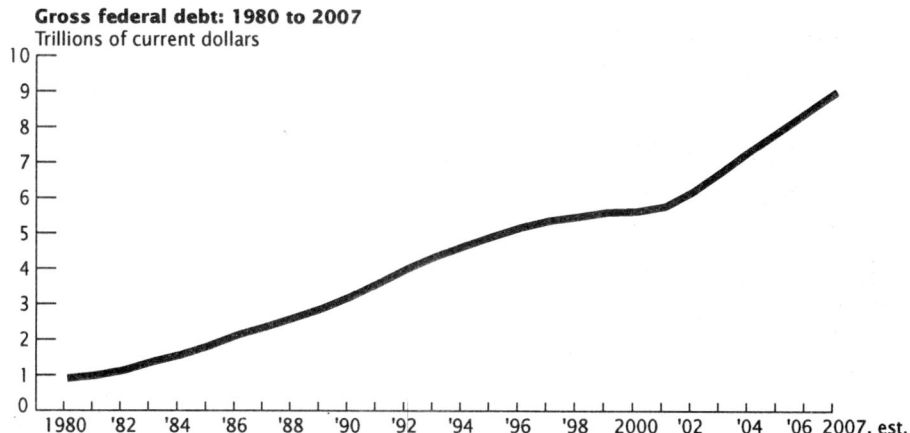

Source: Charts prepared by U.S. Census Bureau. For data, see Table 455 & 456.

Federal Government Finances and Employment   305

Table 455. Federal Budget—Receipts and Outlays: 1960 to 2007

[92.5 represents $92,500,000,000). For fiscal years ending in year shown; see text, Section 8. See also headnote, Table 457]

Fiscal year	In current dollars (bil. dol.)			In constant (2000) dollars (bil. dol.)			As percentage of GDP [1]		
	Receipts	Outlays	Surplus or deficit (−)	Receipts	Outlays	Surplus or deficit (−)	Receipts	Outlays	Surplus or deficit (−)
1960	92.5	92.2	0.3	528.5	526.8	1.7	17.9	17.8	0.1
1970	192.8	195.6	−2.8	815.9	828.0	−12.0	19.0	19.3	−0.3
1980	517.1	590.9	−73.8	1,028.3	1,175.1	−146.8	19.0	21.7	−2.7
1985	734.1	946.4	−212.3	1,082.6	1,395.7	−313.1	17.7	22.9	−5.1
1986	769.2	990.4	−221.2	1,107.3	1,425.7	−318.4	17.4	22.4	−5.0
1987	854.4	1,004.1	−149.7	1,196.1	1,405.7	−209.6	18.4	21.6	−3.2
1988	909.3	1,064.5	−155.2	1,235.6	1,446.5	−210.9	18.2	21.3	−3.1
1989	991.2	1,143.8	−152.6	1,298.9	1,498.9	−200.0	18.4	21.2	−2.8
1990	1,032.1	1,253.1	−221.0	1,309.4	1,589.9	−280.4	18.0	21.8	−3.9
1991	1,055.1	1,324.3	−269.2	1,282.6	1,609.9	−327.3	17.8	22.3	−4.5
1992	1,091.3	1,381.6	−290.3	1,282.7	1,623.9	−341.2	17.5	22.1	−4.7
1993	1,154.5	1,409.5	−255.1	1,323.2	1,615.5	−292.3	17.6	21.4	−3.9
1994	1,258.7	1,461.9	−203.2	1,414.0	1,642.2	−228.2	18.1	21.0	−2.9
1995	1,351.9	1,515.9	−164.0	1,482.4	1,662.2	−179.8	18.5	20.7	−2.2
1996	1,453.2	1,560.6	−107.4	1,557.9	1,673.0	−115.2	18.9	20.3	−1.4
1997	1,579.4	1,601.3	−21.9	1,661.2	1,684.2	−23.0	19.3	19.6	−0.3
1998	1,722.0	1,652.7	69.3	1,793.1	1,721.0	72.1	20.0	19.2	0.8
1999	1,827.6	1,702.0	125.6	1,874.9	1,746.0	128.9	20.0	18.7	1.4
2000	2,025.5	1,789.2	236.2	2,025.5	1,789.2	236.2	20.9	18.4	2.4
2001	1,991.4	1,863.2	128.2	1,945.9	1,820.6	125.3	19.8	18.5	1.3
2002	1,853.4	2,011.2	−157.8	1,777.8	1,929.2	−151.3	17.9	19.4	−1.5
2003	1,782.5	2,160.1	−377.6	1,665.5	2,018.2	−352.8	16.5	20.0	−3.5
2004	1,880.3	2,293.0	−412.7	1,707.3	2,082.1	−374.8	16.3	19.9	−3.6
2005	2,153.9	2,472.2	−318.3	1,888.2	2,167.3	−279.1	17.6	20.2	−2.6
2006	2,407.3	2,655.4	−248.2	2,037.1	2,247.1	−210.0	18.4	20.3	−1.9
2007 est.	2,540.1	2,784.3	−244.2	2,103.3	2,305.4	−202.2	18.5	20.2	−1.8

[1] Gross domestic product; see text, Section 13.

Source: U.S. Office of Management and Budget, *Budget of the United States Government, Historical Tables*, annual. See Internet site <http://www.whitehouse.gov/omb/budget/fy2008/>

Table 456. Federal Budget Debt: 1960 to 2007

[290.5 represents $290,500,000,000. As of the end of the fiscal year. See text, Section 8]

Fiscal year	Total (bil. dol.)					As percentage of GDP [1]				
	Gross federal debt	Federal govern- ment accounts	Held by the public			Gross federal debt	Federal govern- ment accounts	Held by the public		
			Total	Federal Reserve System	Other			Total	Federal Reserve System	Other
1960	290.5	53.7	236.8	26.5	210.3	56.1	10.4	45.7	5.1	40.6
1970	380.9	97.7	283.2	57.7	225.5	37.6	9.7	28.0	5.7	22.3
1980	909.0	197.1	711.9	120.8	591.1	33.3	7.2	26.1	4.4	21.7
1985	1,817.4	310.2	1,507.3	169.8	1,337.5	43.9	7.5	36.4	4.1	32.3
1986	2,120.5	379.9	1,740.6	190.9	1,549.8	48.1	8.6	39.4	4.3	35.1
1987	2,346.0	456.2	1,889.8	212.0	1,677.7	50.5	9.8	40.7	4.6	36.1
1988	2,601.1	549.5	2,051.6	229.2	1,822.4	51.9	11.0	41.0	4.6	36.4
1989	2,867.8	677.1	2,190.7	220.1	1,970.6	53.1	12.5	40.6	4.1	36.5
1990	3,206.3	794.7	2,411.6	234.4	2,177.1	55.9	13.9	42.0	4.1	38.0
1991	3,598.2	909.2	2,689.0	258.6	2,430.4	60.6	15.3	45.3	4.4	40.9
1992	4,001.8	1,002.1	2,999.7	296.4	2,703.3	64.1	16.1	48.1	4.8	43.3
1993	4,351.0	1,102.6	3,248.4	325.7	2,922.7	66.2	16.8	49.4	5.0	44.4
1994	4,643.3	1,210.2	3,433.1	355.2	3,077.9	66.7	17.4	49.3	5.1	44.2
1995	4,920.6	1,316.2	3,604.4	374.1	3,230.3	67.2	18.0	49.2	5.1	44.1
1996	5,181.5	1,447.4	3,734.1	390.9	3,343.1	67.3	18.8	48.5	5.1	43.5
1997	5,369.2	1,596.9	3,772.3	424.5	3,347.8	65.6	19.5	46.1	5.2	40.9
1998	5,478.2	1,757.1	3,721.1	458.2	3,262.9	63.5	20.4	43.1	5.3	37.8
1999	5,605.5	1,973.2	3,632.4	496.6	3,135.7	61.4	21.6	39.8	5.4	34.4
2000	5,628.7	2,218.9	3,409.8	511.4	2,898.4	58.0	22.9	35.1	5.3	29.9
2001	5,769.9	2,450.3	3,319.6	534.1	2,785.5	57.4	24.4	33.0	5.3	27.7
2002	6,198.4	2,658.0	3,540.4	604.2	2,936.2	59.7	25.6	34.1	5.8	28.3
2003	6,760.0	2,846.6	3,913.4	656.1	3,257.3	62.5	26.3	36.2	6.1	30.1
2004	7,354.7	3,059.1	4,295.5	700.3	3,595.2	63.9	26.6	37.3	6.1	31.2
2005	7,905.3	3,313.1	4,592.2	736.4	3,855.9	64.4	27.0	37.4	6.0	31.4
2006	8,451.4	3,622.4	4,829.0	768.9	4,060.0	64.7	27.7	37.0	5.9	31.1
2007, est.	9,007.8	3,924.5	5,083.3	(NA)	(NA)	65.5	28.5	36.9	(NA)	(NA)

NA Not available.   [1] Gross domestic product; see text, Section 13.

Source: U.S. Office of Management and Budget, *Budget of the United States Government, Historical Tables*, annual. See Internet site <http://www.whitehouse.gov/omb/budget/fy2008/>.

U.S. Census Bureau, Statistical Abstract of the United States: 2008

Table 457. Federal Budget Outlays by Type: 1990 to 2007

[1,253.1 represents $1,253,100,000,000. For years ending September 30. Given the inherent imprecision in deflating outlays, the data shown in constant dollars present a reasonable perspective—not precision. The deflators and the categories that are deflated are as comparable over time as feasible. Minus sign (–) indicates offset]

Type	Unit	1990	2000	2003	2004	2005	2006	2007, est.
Current dollar outlays	Bil. dol.. .	1,253.1	1,789.2	2,160.1	2,293.0	2,472.2	2,655.4	2,784.3
National defense [1]	Bil. dol. . .	299.3	294.4	404.8	455.8	495.3	521.8	571.9
Nondefense, total	Bil. dol. . .	953.8	1,494.8	1,755.3	1,837.2	1,976.9	2,133.6	2,212.4
Payments for individuals	Bil. dol. . .	585.7	1,054.5	1,331.7	1,397.4	1,490.0	1,591.8	1,681.3
Direct payments [2]	Bil. dol. . .	507.0	867.7	1,080.9	1,131.2	1,211.9	1,315.0	1,392.1
Grants to state and local governments .	Bil. dol. . .	78.7	186.8	250.8	266.2	278.1	276.8	289.2
All other grants	Bil. dol. . .	56.4	99.1	137.7	141.3	149.9	157.3	159.6
Net interest [2]	Bil. dol. . .	184.3	222.9	153.1	160.2	184.0	226.6	239.2
All other [2]	Bil. dol. . .	164.0	160.9	187.2	196.8	218.2	226.2	214.2
Undistributed offsetting receipts [2]	Bil. dol. . .	–36.6	–42.6	–54.4	–58.5	–65.2	–68.3	–81.8
Constant (2000) dollar outlays	Bil. dol.. .	1,589.9	1,789.2	2,018.2	2,082.1	2,167.3	2,247.1	2,305.4
National defense [1]	Bil. dol. . .	382.7	294.4	364.4	394.3	407.8	417.2	446.7
Nondefense, total	Bil. dol. . .	1,207.0	1,494.8	1,654.0	1,687.8	1,759.4	1,829.8	1,858.7
Payments for individuals	Bil. dol. . .	732.5	1,054.5	1,260.1	1,291.9	1,339.0	1,378.0	1,425.7
Direct payments [2]	Bil. dol. . .	634.0	867.7	1,022.8	1,045.8	1,089.3	1,138.6	1,180.6
Grants to state and local governments .	Bil. dol. . .	98.4	186.8	237.3	246.1	249.7	239.4	245.0
All other grants	Bil. dol. . .	73.3	99.1	126.2	124.5	124.5	123.8	121.4
Net interest [2]	Bil. dol. . .	226.9	222.9	143.8	146.8	163.5	195.4	201.1
All other [2]	Bil. dol. . .	228.0	160.9	172.6	174.4	185.1	186.2	173.2
Undistributed offsetting receipts [2]	Bil. dol. . .	–53.5	–42.6	–48.7	–49.7	–52.8	–53.5	–62.6
Outlays as percent of GDP [3]	Percent. .	21.8	18.4	20.0	19.9	20.2	20.3	20.2
National defense [1]	Percent . .	5.2	3.0	3.7	4.0	4.0	4.0	4.2
Nondefense, total	Percent . .	16.6	15.4	16.2	16.0	16.1	16.3	16.1
Payments for individuals	Percent . .	10.2	10.9	12.3	12.1	12.1	12.2	12.2
Direct payments [2]	Percent . .	8.8	8.9	10.0	9.8	9.9	10.1	10.1
Grants to state and local governments. . .	Percent . .	1.4	1.9	2.3	2.3	2.3	2.1	2.1
All other grants	Percent . .	1.0	1.0	1.3	1.2	1.2	1.2	1.2
Net interest [2]	Percent . .	3.2	2.3	1.4	1.4	1.5	1.7	1.7
All other [2]	Percent . .	2.9	1.7	1.7	1.7	1.8	1.7	1.6
Undistributed offsetting receipts [2]	Percent . .	–0.6	–0.4	–0.5	–0.5	–0.5	–0.5	–0.6

[1] Includes a small amount of grants to state and local governments and direct payments for individuals.   [2] Includes some off-budget amounts; most of the off-budget amounts are direct payments for individuals (social security benefits).   [3] GDP means Gross Domestic Product.

Source: U.S. Office of Management and Budget, *Budget of the United States Government, Historical Tables*, annual. See Internet site <http://www.whitehouse.gov/omb/budget/fy2008/>.

Table 458. Federal Budget Outlays by Agency: 1990 to 2007

[In billions of dollars (1,253.1 represents $1,253,100,000,000). For years ending September 30]

Department or other unit	1990	2000	2003	2004	2005	2006	2007, est.
Outlays, total [1]	1,253.1	1,789.2	2,160.1	2,293.0	2,472.2	2,655.4	2,784.3
Legislative Branch	2.2	2.9	3.4	3.9	4.0	4.1	4.3
The Judiciary Branch	1.6	4.1	5.1	5.4	5.5	5.8	5.8
Agriculture	45.9	75.1	72.8	71.6	85.3	93.5	88.8
Commerce	3.7	7.8	5.7	5.8	6.1	6.4	6.2
Defense-Military	289.7	281.1	388.7	437.0	474.4	499.4	548.9
Education	23.0	33.5	57.1	62.8	72.9	93.4	68.0
Energy	12.1	15.0	19.4	19.9	21.3	19.6	22.0
Health and Human Services	175.5	382.3	505.0	543.0	581.5	614.3	671.3
Homeland Security	7.2	13.2	32.0	26.6	38.7	69.1	50.4
Housing and Urban Development	20.2	30.8	37.4	45.0	42.5	42.4	42.8
Interior	5.8	8.0	9.2	8.6	9.3	9.1	10.9
Justice	5.9	16.8	20.8	29.6	22.4	23.3	23.0
Labor	26.1	31.9	69.6	56.7	46.9	43.1	47.4
State	4.8	6.7	9.3	10.9	12.7	13.0	16.3
Transportation	25.6	41.6	50.8	54.9	56.6	60.1	63.8
Treasury	253.9	390.5	368.3	375.8	410.2	464.7	490.5
Veterans Affairs	29.0	47.1	57.0	59.6	69.8	69.8	72.3
Corps of Engineers	3.3	4.2	4.7	4.7	4.7	6.9	7.6
Other Defense-Civil Programs	21.7	32.9	39.9	41.7	43.5	44.4	47.6
Environmental Protection Agency	5.1	7.2	8.0	8.3	7.9	8.3	8.0
Executive Office of the President	0.2	0.3	0.4	3.3	7.7	5.4	2.7
International Assistance Programs	10.1	12.1	13.5	13.7	15.0	13.9	17.1
National Aeronautics and Space Administration. . .	12.4	13.4	14.6	15.2	15.6	15.1	16.1
National Science Foundation	1.8	3.5	4.7	5.1	5.4	5.5	5.9
Office of Personnel Management	31.9	48.7	54.1	56.5	59.5	62.4	58.8
Social Security Administration (on-budget)	17.3	45.1	46.3	49.0	54.6	53.3	55.7
Social Security Administration (off-budget)	245.0	396.2	461.4	481.2	506.8	532.5	567.2
Undistributed offsetting receipts	–98.9	–173.0	–210.5	–212.5	–226.2	–237.5	–263.1

[1] Includes other agencies, not shown separately.

Source: U.S. Office of Management and Budget, *Budget of the United States Government, Historical Tables*, annual. See Internet site <http://www.whitehouse.gov/omb/budget/fy2008/>.

Federal Government Finances and Employment   307

Table 459. **Federal Outlays by Detailed Function: 1990 to 2007**

[In billions of dollars (1,253.1 represents $1,253,100,000,000). For years ending September 30]

Superfunction and function	1990	1995	2000	2003	2004	2005	2006	2007, est.
Total outlays.	**1,253.1**	**1,515.9**	**1,789.2**	**2,160.1**	**2,293.0**	**2,472.2**	**2,655.4**	**2,784.3**
National defense [1]	299.3	272.1	294.4	404.8	455.8	495.3	521.8	571.9
Department of Defense–Military.	289.7	259.4	281.1	387.2	436.5	474.1	499.3	548.9
Military personnel	75.6	70.8	76.0	106.7	113.6	127.5	127.5	128.8
Operation and maintenance.	88.3	91.0	105.8	151.4	174.0	188.1	203.8	224.8
Procurement.	81.0	55.0	51.7	67.9	76.2	82.3	89.8	104.3
Research, development, test, and evaluation . . .	37.5	34.6	37.6	53.1	60.8	65.7	68.6	71.1
Military construction	5.1	6.8	5.1	5.9	6.3	5.3	6.2	8.8
Atomic energy defense activities	9.0	11.8	12.1	16.0	16.6	18.0	17.5	17.9
International affairs [1]	13.8	16.4	17.2	21.2	26.9	34.6	29.5	35.1
International development and humanitarian assistance	5.5	7.6	6.5	10.3	13.8	17.7	16.7	15.8
International security assistance	8.7	5.3	6.4	8.6	8.4	7.9	7.8	9.3
Conduct of foreign affairs	3.1	4.2	4.7	6.7	7.9	9.1	8.6	11.2
General science, space, and technology.	14.4	16.7	18.6	20.9	23.1	23.6	23.6	24.9
General science and basic research.	2.8	4.1	6.2	8.0	8.4	8.9	9.1	9.4
Space flight, research, and supporting activities . . .	11.6	12.6	12.4	12.9	14.6	14.8	14.5	15.4
Energy.	3.3	4.9	–0.8	–0.7	–0.2	0.4	0.8	1.8
Energy supply	2.0	3.6	–1.8	–2.1	–1.6	–0.9	0.2	–
Natural resources and environment [1]	17.1	21.9	25.0	29.7	30.7	28.0	33.1	35.2
Water resources.	4.4	4.6	5.1	5.5	5.6	5.7	8.0	9.3
Conservation and land management	4.0	6.0	6.8	9.7	9.8	6.2	7.8	9.4
Recreational resources	1.4	2.0	2.6	2.9	3.0	3.0	3.1	3.0
Pollution control and abatement.	5.2	6.5	7.4	8.2	8.5	8.1	8.6	8.3
Agriculture	11.8	9.7	36.5	22.5	15.4	26.6	26.0	20.1
Farm income stabilization.	9.7	7.0	33.4	18.3	11.2	22.0	21.4	15.7
Agricultural research and services	2.1	2.6	3.0	4.2	4.3	4.5	4.6	4.5
Commerce and housing credit [1]	67.6	–17.8	3.2	0.7	5.3	7.6	6.2	0.2
Mortgage credit	3.8	–1.0	–3.3	–4.6	2.7	–0.9	–0.6	–3.7
Postal service.	2.1	–1.8	2.1	–5.2	–4.1	–1.2	–1.0	–5.6
Deposit insurance	57.9	–17.8	–3.1	–1.4	–2.0	–1.4	–1.1	–2.2
Transportation [1]	29.5	39.4	46.9	67.1	64.6	67.9	70.2	74.6
Ground transportation	19.0	25.3	31.7	37.5	40.7	42.3	45.2	48.3
Air transportation	7.2	10.0	10.6	23.3	16.7	18.8	18.0	18.3
Water transportation	3.2	3.7	4.4	5.9	6.9	6.4	6.7	7.6
Community and regional development [1]	8.5	10.7	10.6	18.9	15.8	26.3	54.5	32.6
Community development	3.5	4.7	5.5	6.3	6.2	5.9	5.8	8.7
Disaster relief and insurance.	2.1	3.3	2.6	10.1	7.3	17.7	46.1	21.3
Education, training, employment, and social services [1]	37.2	51.0	53.8	82.6	88.0	97.6	118.6	94.0
Elementary, secondary, and vocational education . .	9.9	14.7	20.6	31.5	34.4	38.3	39.7	40.0
Higher education	11.1	14.2	10.1	22.7	25.3	31.4	50.5	23.9
Research and general education aids	1.6	2.1	2.6	3.0	3.0	3.1	3.1	3.6
Training and employment	5.6	7.4	6.8	8.4	7.9	6.9	7.2	7.6
Social services	8.1	11.6	12.6	15.6	15.9	16.3	16.5	17.3
Health	57.7	115.4	154.5	219.6	240.1	250.6	252.8	268.5
Health care services	47.6	101.9	136.2	192.6	210.1	219.6	220.8	236.3
Health research and training	8.6	11.6	16.0	24.0	27.1	28.1	28.8	29.2
Consumer and occupational health and safety	1.5	1.9	2.3	2.9	2.9	2.9	3.1	3.0
Medicare	98.1	159.9	197.1	249.4	269.4	298.6	329.9	372.3
Income security [1]	148.7	223.8	253.7	334.6	333.1	345.8	352.5	365.4
General retirement and disability insurance (excluding social security).	5.1	5.1	5.2	7.0	6.6	7.0	4.6	7.9
Federal employee retirement and disability	52.0	65.9	77.2	85.2	88.7	93.4	98.3	104.8
Unemployment compensation	18.9	23.6	23.0	57.1	45.0	35.4	33.8	34.6
Housing assistance	15.9	27.6	28.9	35.5	36.8	37.9	38.3	39.0
Food and nutrition assistance	24.0	37.6	32.5	42.5	46.0	50.8	53.9	55.9
Social security	248.6	335.8	409.4	474.7	495.5	523.3	548.5	586.5
Veterans benefits and services [1]	29.1	37.9	47.1	57.0	59.8	70.2	69.8	72.4
Income security for veterans	15.3	19.0	24.9	29.1	30.8	35.8	35.8	37.0
Veterans education, training, and rehabilitation	0.2	1.1	1.3	2.1	2.6	2.8	2.6	3.0
Hospital and medical care for veterans	12.1	16.4	19.5	24.1	26.9	28.8	29.9	30.5
Veterans housing	0.5	0.3	0.4	0.5	–2.0	0.9	–1.2	–0.9
Administration of justice.	10.2	16.5	28.5	35.3	45.6	40.0	41.0	45.3
Federal law enforcement activities	4.8	6.6	12.1	15.7	19.1	19.9	20.0	24.8
Federal litigative and judicial activities.	3.6	6.1	7.8	9.1	9.7	9.6	10.1	10.5
Federal correctional activities	1.3	2.7	3.7	5.4	5.5	5.9	6.2	5.9
Criminal justice assistance	0.5	1.0	4.9	5.1	11.3	4.6	4.8	4.0
General government.	10.5	13.8	13.0	23.2	22.3	17.0	18.2	19.8
Net interest [1]	184.3	232.1	222.9	153.1	160.2	184.0	226.6	239.2
Interest on Treasury debt securities (gross)	264.7	332.4	361.9	318.1	321.7	352.3	405.9	433.0
Interest received by on-budget trust funds	–46.3	–59.9	–69.3	–72.5	–67.8	–69.2	–71.6	–75.1
Interest received by off-budget trust funds	–16.0	–33.3	–59.8	–83.5	–86.2	–91.8	–97.7	–106.2
Allowances	–	–	–	–	–	–	–	7.4
Undistributed offsetting receipts	–36.6	–44.5	–42.6	–54.4	–54.4	–58.5	–65.2	–81.8

– Represents or rounds to zero.   [1] Includes functions not shown separately.

Source: U.S. Office of Management and Budget, *Budget of the United States Government, Historical Tables,* annual. See Internet site <http://www.whitehouse.gov/omb/budget/fy2008/>.

U.S. Census Bureau, *Statistical Abstract of the United States: 2008*

Table 460. Outlays for Payments for Individuals by Category and Major Program: 1990 to 2007

[In billions of dollars (585.7 represents 585,700,000,000). For years ending September 30]

Category and Program	1990	1995	2000	2003	2004	2005	2006	2007, est.
Total, payments for individuals...	**585.7**	**877.5**	**1,054.5**	**1,332.2**	**1,397.8**	**1,490.7**	**1,592.7**	**1,682.2**
Social security and railroad retirement...	250.5	337.0	410.5	476.8	496.4	523.4	554.5	587.2
Social security:								
Old age and survivors insurance ...	221.9	292.7	351.4	400.2	414.8	434.0	457.7	482.2
Disability insurance	24.4	40.3	54.4	70.0	76.5	84.2	91.2	99.0
Railroad retirement (excl. social security)	4.1	4.0	4.6	6.6	5.2	5.3	5.6	6.0
Federal employees retirement and insurance	64.1	82.2	100.3	112.3	117.4	126.7	132.1	139.7
Military retirement.............	21.5	27.8	32.8	35.6	37.0	39.0	41.1	43.7
Civil service retirement	31.0	38.3	45.1	50.2	52.1	54.7	57.8	61.4
Veterans service-connected compensation	10.7	14.8	20.8	24.7	26.3	30.9	31.0	32.3
Other.....................	0.8	1.3	1.7	1.8	2.0	2.2	2.2	2.4
Unemployment assistance..........	17.4	21.9	21.1	55.0	43.1	33.1	31.9	32.6
Medical care...................	164.3	289.3	362.7	478.5	515.4	562.5	606.0	674.2
Medicare:								
Hospital insurance............	65.9	113.6	127.9	151.3	164.1	182.8	183.9	205.2
Supplementary medical insurance ..	41.5	63.5	87.2	121.8	131.8	151.0	191.7	225.1
State children's health insurance.....	–	–	1.2	4.4	4.6	5.1	5.5	5.6
Medicaid...................	41.1	89.1	117.9	160.7	176.2	181.7	180.6	191.9
Indian health	1.1	2.0	2.4	2.9	3.1	3.1	3.3	3.3
Hospital and medical care for veterans	12.0	16.2	19.3	24.5	21.6	23.1	24.4	26.1
Health resources and services	1.4	2.2	3.9	5.3	5.5	5.9	6.1	5.8
Substance abuse and mental health services	1.2	2.4	2.5	3.0	3.1	3.2	3.2	3.2
Health care tax credit	–	–	–	(Z)	0.1	0.1	0.1	0.1
Uniformed Services retiree health care fund	–	–	–	4.3	5.2	6.3	7.1	7.7
Other......................	(Z)	0.3	0.3	0.2	0.1	0.2	0.2	0.2
Assistance to students	11.2	14.8	10.9	22.8	25.7	32.1	51.7	30.0
Veterans education benefits	0.8	1.4	1.6	2.0	2.4	3.2	3.3	3.8
Student assistance, Department of Education and other	10.4	13.4	9.2	20.7	23.3	28.9	48.4	26.2
Housing assistance	15.9	25.6	24.1	29.7	30.8	31.8	32.1	32.5
Food and nutrition assistance	23.9	37.5	32.4	42.4	45.9	50.7	53.8	55.8
Food stamp program (including Puerto Rico)	15.9	25.6	18.3	25.3	28.6	32.6	34.6	35.6
Child nutrition and special milk programs	5.0	7.5	9.2	10.8	11.2	11.9	12.4	13.7
Supplemental feeding programs (WIC [1] and CSFP [2])	2.1	3.4	4.0	4.5	4.9	5.0	5.1	5.2
Commodity donations and other	0.8	1.0	0.9	1.7	1.2	1.2	1.7	1.4
Public assistance and related programs..	34.9	65.0	88.3	108.9	111.5	123.3	125.1	124.5
Supplemental security income program	11.5	23.6	29.5	30.4	31.2	35.3	34.3	33.4
Family support payments to states and TANF [3]	12.2	17.1	18.4	23.1	21.5	21.3	20.9	21.8
Low income home energy assistance..	1.3	1.4	1.5	2.0	1.9	2.1	2.6	2.6
Earned income tax credit..........	4.4	15.2	26.1	32.0	33.1	34.6	36.2	36.5
Legal services	0.3	0.4	0.3	0.3	0.3	0.3	0.3	0.3
Payments to states for daycare assistance	–	0.9	3.3	5.2	4.8	4.9	5.3	4.9
Veterans nonservice-connected pensions	3.6	3.0	3.0	3.2	3.3	3.7	3.5	3.4
Payments to states for foster care/adoption assistance	1.6	3.2	5.5	6.1	6.3	6.4	6.4	6.5
Payment where child credit exceeds tax liability................	–	–	0.8	6.4	8.9	14.6	15.5	14.9
Other public assistance	–	–	–	–	–	(Z)	0.1	0.1
All other payments for individuals	3.5	4.2	4.3	5.8	11.5	7.1	5.6	5.7
Coal miners and black lung benefits...	1.5	1.3	1.0	0.8	0.8	0.7	0.7	0.7
Veterans insurance and burial benefits.....................	1.4	1.4	1.4	1.3	1.4	1.4	1.4	1.4
D.C. employee retirement	–	–	0.4	0.5	0.5	2.2	0.5	0.5
Aging services programs	–	1.0	0.9	1.3	1.3	1.4	1.4	1.3
Energy employees compensation fund	–	–	–	0.3	0.3	0.6	0.9	0.9
September 11th victim compensation ..	–	–	–	0.7	6.3	(Z)	(Z)	–
Refugee assistance and other	0.6	0.6	0.6	0.9	0.9	0.8	0.8	0.8

– Represents zero.   Z Less than $50,000,000.   [1] WIC means Women, Infants, and Children.   [2] CSFP means Commodity Supplemental Food Program.   [3] TANF means Temporary Assistance for Needy Families.

Source: U.S. Office of Management and Budget, *Budget of the United States Government, Historical Tables,* annual. See Internet site <http://www.whitehouse.gov/omb/budget/fy2008/>.

Table 461. **Federal Budget Receipts by Source: 1990 to 2007**

[In billions of dollars (1,032.1 represents $1,032,100,000,000). For years ending September 30. Receipts reflect collections. Covers both federal funds and trust funds; see text, this section

Source	1990	1995	2000	2003	2004	2005	2006	2007, est.
Total federal receipts	1,032.1	1,351.9	2,025.5	1,782.5	1,880.3	2,153.9	2,407.3	2,540.1
Individual income taxes.	466.9	590.2	1,004.5	793.7	809.0	927.2	1,043.9	1,168.8
Corporation income taxes	93.5	157.0	207.3	131.8	189.4	278.3	353.9	342.1
Social insurance and retirement receipts . . .	380.0	484.5	652.9	713.0	733.4	794.1	837.8	873.4
Excise taxes	35.3	57.5	68.9	67.5	69.9	73.1	74.0	57.1
Other.	56.3	62.7	92.0	76.6	78.7	81.1	97.6	98.8
Social insurance and retirement receipts	380.0	484.5	652.9	713.0	733.4	794.1	837.8	873.4
Employment and general retirement	353.9	451.0	620.5	675.0	689.4	747.7	790.0	823.7
Old-age and survivors insurance (off-budget)	255.0	284.1	411.7	447.8	457.1	493.6	520.1	542.1
Disability insurance (off-budget)	26.6	67.0	68.9	76.0	77.6	83.8	88.3	92.0
Hospital insurance	68.6	96.0	135.5	147.2	150.6	166.1	177.4	185.2
Railroad retirement/pension fund	2.3	2.4	2.7	2.3	2.3	2.3	2.3	2.4
Unemployment insurance funds	21.6	28.9	27.6	33.4	39.5	42.0	43.4	45.0
Other retirement	4.5	4.6	4.8	4.6	4.6	4.5	4.4	4.7
Federal employees retirement— employee share	4.4	4.5	4.7	4.6	4.5	4.4	4.3	4.7
Excise taxes, total	35.3	57.5	68.9	67.5	69.9	73.1	74.0	57.1
Federal funds [1]	15.6	26.9	22.7	23.8	24.6	22.5	22.5	3.1
Alcohol	5.7	7.2	8.1	7.9	8.1	8.1	8.5	8.6
Tobacco	4.1	5.9	7.2	7.9	7.9	7.9	7.7	7.6
Telephone	3.0	3.8	5.7	5.8	6.0	6.0	4.9	−11.6
Ozone-depleting chemicals/products	0.4	0.6	0.1	−	−	−	−	−
Transportation fuels	−	8.5	0.8	0.9	1.4	−0.8	−2.4	−3.0
Trust funds [1]	19.8	30.5	46.2	43.7	45.3	50.5	51.5	53.9
Highway	13.9	22.6	35.0	33.7	34.7	37.9	38.4	39.7
Airport and airway	3.7	5.5	9.7	8.7	9.2	10.3	10.6	11.4
Black lung disability	0.7	0.6	0.5	0.5	0.6	0.6	0.6	0.6
Inland waterway	0.1	0.1	0.1	0.1	0.1	0.1	0.1	0.1
Oil spill liability.	0.1	0.2	0.2	−	−	−	0.1	0.2
Aquatic resources.	0.2	0.3	0.3	0.4	0.4	0.4	0.5	0.5
Tobacco assessments	−	−	−	−	−	0.9	0.9	1.0
Vaccine injury compensation.	0.2	0.1	0.1	0.1	0.1	0.1	0.2	0.2

− Represents zero.   [1] Includes other funds, not shown separately.

Source: U.S. Office of Management and Budget, *Budget of the United States Government, Historical Tables*, annual. See Internet site <http://www.whitehouse.gov/omb/budget/fy2008/>.

Table 462. **Federal Trust Fund Income, Outlays, and Balances: 2006 to 2008**

[In billions of dollars (11.2 represents $11,200,000,000). For years ending September 30. Receipts deposited. Outlays on a checks-issued basis less refunds collected. Balances: That which have not been spent. See text, this section, for discussion of the budget concept and trust funds]

Description	Income			Outlays			Balances [1]		
	2006	2007, est.	2008, est.	2006	2007, est.	2008, est.	2006	2007, est.	2008, est.
Airport and airway trust fund.	11.2	12.1	12.6	12.1	12.3	14.2	10.3	10.2	8.6
Federal civilian employees retirement funds	88.5	97.7	102.6	58.7	85.3	65.0	704.5	716.9	754.5
Federal employees health benefits fund . . .	33.5	34.8	37.1	31.3	33.2	36.4	14.8	16.4	17.1
Foreign military sales trust fund	14.2	15.1	13.1	13.0	15.1	13.1	7.9	7.9	7.9
Highway trust fund	38.5	39.9	41.0	36.0	39.1	44.4	15.1	15.8	12.2
Medicare:									
Hospital insurance (HI) trust fund	212.4	221.0	237.4	186.9	208.2	214.6	303.1	316.0	338.8
Supplemental medical insurance trust fund	211.3	236.8	252.2	194.9	228.2	245.9	33.3	41.9	48.2
Military retirement fund	52.4	51.9	53.2	41.1	43.7	45.7	206.0	214.2	221.7
Railroad retirement trust funds	12.2	12.5	11.8	10.6	11.4	11.8	27.3	28.3	28.4
Social security: Old-age, survivors and disability insurance trust funds	739.8	772.1	821.8	554.6	586.6	612.6	1,994.2	2,179.6	2,388.9
Unemployment trust funds	47.0	49.1	50.0	35.2	35.8	37.8	66.6	79.8	91.9
Veterans life insurance trust funds.	1.3	1.2	1.1	1.7	1.7	1.7	12.2	11.7	11.2
Other trust funds	23.2	23.6	27.2	20.2	21.5	24.2	42.4	44.4	47.4

[1] Balances available on a cash basis (rather than an authorization basis) at the end of the year. Balances are primarily invested in federal debt securities.

Source: U.S. Office of Management and Budget, *Budget of the United States Government, Analytical Perspectives*, annual. See Internet site <http://www.whitehouse.gov/omb/budget/fy2008/>.

Table 463. Tax Expenditures Estimates Relating to Individual and Corporate Income Taxes by Selected Function: 2006 to 2009

[In millions of dollars (3,100 represents $3,100,000,000). For years ending September 30. Tax expenditures are defined as revenue losses attributable to provisions of the federal tax laws which allow a special exclusion, exemption, or deduction from gross income or which provide a special credit, a preferential rate of tax, or a deferral of liability]

Function and provision	2006	2007	2008	2009
National defense:				
Exclusion of benefits and allowances to armed forces personnel	3,100	3,220	3,350	3,480
International affairs:				
Exclusion of income earned abroad by U.S. citizens	2,500	2,630	2,760	2,900
Extraterritorial income exclusion	4,400	1,630	–	–
Deferral of income from controlled foreign corporations (normal tax method)	11,160	11,940	12,770	13,650
Deferred taxes for financial firms on certain income earned overseas	2,260	2,370	2,490	1,060
General science, space, and technology:				
Expensing of research and experimentation expenditures (normal tax method) . . .	7,920	5,680	5,280	4,060
Credit for increasing research activities	2,180	10,320	4,960	2,100
Energy:				
Alternative fuel production credit.	2,980	2,370	780	10
Commerce and housing:				
Financial institutions and insurance:				
Exclusion of interest on life insurance savings	19,380	20,150	21,925	25,060
Housing:				
Deductibility of mortgage interest on owner-occupied homes	68,330	79,940	89,430	96,250
Deductibility of state and local property tax on owner-occupied homes.	21,260	15,540	12,620	12,590
Capital gains exclusion on home sales.	35,270	37,030	38,890	40,830
Exclusion of net imputed rental income	28,780	32,110	35,680	39,440
Exception from passive loss rules for $25,000 of rental loss.	6,590	7,150	7,520	7,790
Credit for low-income housing investments	4,420	4,660	4,940	5,250
Accelerated depreciation on rental housing (normal tax method)	10,340	11,240	12,300	13,480
Commerce:				
Capital gains (except agriculture, timber, iron ore, and coal).	48,610	51,770	51,960	52,230
Step-up basis of capital gains at death.	29,600	32,600	35,900	36,750
Accelerated depreciation of machinery and equipment (normal tax method) . . .	36,470	51,030	64,670	78,390
Expensing of certain small investments (normal tax method)	5,000	5,330	5,330	4,740
Graduated corporation income tax rate (normal tax method)	4,050	4,270	4,240	4,320
Deduction for U.S. production activities	9,950	10,700	13,810	14,500
Transportation:				
Exclusion of reimbursed employee parking expenses.	2,740	2,890	3,040	3,190
Education, training, employment, and social services:				
Education:				
HOPE tax credit.	3,900	3,330	3,350	3,600
Lifetime Learning tax credit	2,490	2,190	2,200	2,310
Exclusion of interest on bonds for private nonprofit educational facilities.	2,140	2,380	2,530	2,610
Parental personal exemption for students age 19 years or over	4,030	2,500	1,590	1,480
Deductibility of charitable contributions (education).	4,200	4,550	5,120	5,520
Training, employment, and social services:				
Child credit.	30,377	32,556	32,341	32,096
Credit for child and dependent care expenses.	3,190	2,810	1,740	1,650
Deductibility of charitable contributions, other than education and health	37,120	40,400	45,760	49,360
Health:				
Exclusion of employer contributions for medical insurance premiums [1]	125,000	141,270	160,190	179,580
Self-employed medical insurance premiums	3,970	4,370	3,730	4,180
Deductibility of medical expenses.	3,770	4,240	4,920	5,820
Exclusion of interest on hospital construction bonds.	3,420	3,770	4,010	4,130
Deductibility of charitable contributions (health).	4,190	4,560	5,160	5,570
Income security:				
Exclusion of workers' compensation benefits	5,660	5,740	5,830	5,920
Net exclusion of pension contributions and earnings:				
Employer plans	49,040	49,510	48,480	48,030
401(k) plans	40,760	42,410	43,970	45,980
Individual Retirement Accounts.	3,970	5,700	6,650	7,130
Keogh plans	10,130	10,860	11,890	13,010
Exclusion of other employee benefits:				
Premiums on group term life insurance	2,280	2,310	2,350	2,380
Earned income tax credit.	5,050	5,360	5,340	5,490
Social security:				
Exclusion of social security benefits:				
Social security benefits for retired workers	17,890	18,100	18,930	19,110
Social security benefits for disabled.	4,730	5,120	5,620	5,890
Social security benefits for dependents and survivors	3,360	3,340	3,400	3,330
Veterans' benefits and services:				
Exclusion of veterans' death benefits and disability compensation	3,580	3,770	3,890	4,030
General purpose fiscal assistance:				
Exclusion of interest on public purpose state and local bonds	22,980	25,430	27,150	27,960
Deductibility of nonbusiness state and local taxes other than on				
owner-occupied homes.	43,120	33,680	27,900	27,790
Addendum: Aid to state and local governments:				
Deductibility of:				
Property taxes on owner-occupied homes	21,260	15,540	12,620	12,590
Nonbusiness state and local taxes other than on owner-occupied homes	43,120	33,680	27,900	27,790
Exclusion of interest on state and local bonds for:				
Public purposes.	22,980	25,430	27,150	27,960
Private nonprofit educational facilities	2,140	2,380	2,530	2,610
Hospital construction	3,420	3,770	4,010	4,130

– Represents zero.   [1] Includes medical care.

Source: U.S. Office of Management and Budget, *Budget of the United States Government, Analytical Perspectives,* annual. See Internet site <http://www.whitehouse.gov/omb/budget/fy2008/>.

U.S. Census Bureau, Statistical Abstract of the United States: 2008

Table 464. U.S. Savings Bonds: 1990 to 2006

[In billions of dollars (122.5 represents $122,500,000,000), except percent. As of end of fiscal year, see text, Section 8]

Item	1990	1995	1998	1999	2000	2001	2002	2003	2004	2005	2006
Amounts outstanding, total [1]	122.5	181.5	180.7	166.5	177.7	179.5	185.5	192.6	194.1	189.9	189.2
Sales	7.8	7.2	4.8	6.5	5.6	8.0	12.5	13.2	10.3	6.5	8.5
Accrued discounts	8.0	9.5	9.1	8.4	6.9	8.4	7.7	7.3	6.9	6.7	7.5
Redemptions [2]	7.5	11.8	14.3	16.6	14.5	13.8	12.5	12.2	14.6	13.8	16.0
Percent of total outstanding...	6.1	6.5	7.9	10.0	8.2	7.7	6.7	6.3	7.5	7.3	8.5

[1] Interest-bearing debt only for amounts at end of year.   [2] Matured and unmatured bonds.

Source: U.S. Department of the Treasury, Bureau of Public Debt. See Internet site <http://www.treasurydirect.gov /govt/reports/pd/pd_sbntables_downloadable_files.htm> (accessed June 2007).

Table 465. Federal Funds—Summary Distribution by State: 2004

[In millions of dollars (2,161,948 represents $2,161,948,000,000), except as indicated. For year ending Sept. 30. Data for grants, salaries and wages, and direct payments to individuals are on an expenditures basis; procurement data are on an obligation basis]

State and island area	Federal funds		Agency		Object category			
	Total	Per capita [1] (dol.)	Defense	Non-defense	Direct payments	Procure-ment	Grants	Salaries and wages
United States [2]	2,161,948	7,222	347,689	1,814,259	1,136,514	339,681	460,152	225,601
Alabama...............	39,047	8,619	8,725	30,323	20,947	7,600	7,008	3,492
Alaska................	8,445	12,885	2,522	5,924	1,800	1,700	3,217	1,728
Arizona...............	41,979	7,309	11,135	30,844	20,211	9,797	8,364	3,608
Arkansas..............	19,489	7,080	1,596	17,893	12,449	848	4,683	1,509
California..............	232,387	6,474	42,723	189,664	115,570	40,254	54,534	22,029
Colorado..............	30,060	6,533	6,182	23,878	14,212	5,747	5,643	4,457
Connecticut............	30,304	8,649	9,735	20,569	13,637	9,509	5,556	1,602
Delaware..............	5,253	6,326	629	4,624	3,253	265	1,241	494
District of Columbia	37,630	67,982	5,264	32,366	4,552	13,347	4,205	15,526
Florida	121,934	7,009	17,419	104,514	80,482	11,447	19,610	10,395
Georgia	55,153	6,247	10,175	44,978	29,257	5,813	11,759	8,324
Hawaii	12,187	9,651	4,772	7,415	4,809	2,066	2,158	3,154
Idaho.................	8,968	6,437	744	8,225	4,702	1,373	1,995	898
Illinois................	76,828	6,043	5,918	70,910	46,708	6,583	16,531	7,007
Indiana...............	37,918	6,079	4,465	33,453	24,023	4,002	7,436	2,457
Iowa [2]	19,218	6,505	1,262	17,956	12,331	1,599	4,039	1,249
Kansas...............	19,131	6,993	2,948	16,183	11,213	2,242	3,469	2,208
Kentucky	31,714	7,649	5,132	26,582	17,102	4,637	6,743	3,231
Louisiana	32,954	7,298	4,433	28,521	18,931	3,418	7,787	2,818
Maine................	10,865	8,248	2,297	8,568	5,438	1,711	2,758	957
Maryland	64,726	11,645	13,796	50,930	24,562	20,804	8,837	10,523
Massachusetts.........	53,120	8,279	8,240	44,881	26,560	9,127	13,876	3,557
Michigan..............	60,488	5,981	3,783	56,706	39,532	4,119	13,227	3,610
Minnesota.............	28,791	5,644	2,112	26,679	16,950	2,329	7,209	2,302
Mississippi	22,338	7,695	3,624	18,713	12,493	2,372	5,379	2,094
Missouri..............	45,730	7,947	8,585	37,145	24,963	7,991	8,734	4,042
Montana..............	7,494	8,085	658	6,836	4,023	587	1,997	886
Nebraska.............	11,795	6,751	1,321	10,474	7,268	697	2,531	1,298
Nevada...............	12,769	5,469	1,612	11,158	7,501	1,600	2,322	1,347
New Hampshire.........	7,959	6,124	1,125	6,833	4,440	985	1,879	654
New Jersey............	55,264	6,353	5,843	49,421	33,471	6,132	11,333	4,328
New Mexico	19,864	10,437	2,471	17,393	7,157	5,973	4,663	2,072
New York	143,903	7,484	7,555	136,348	75,935	8,889	50,000	9,070
North Carolina.........	55,233	6,467	8,679	46,554	31,529	3,933	12,574	7,197
North Dakota..........	6,035	9,513	833	5,202	3,230	503	1,515	787
Ohio	73,195	6,388	7,539	65,656	44,170	6,936	16,514	5,576
Oklahoma.............	26,644	7,562	4,279	22,365	15,107	2,804	5,271	3,463
Oregon...............	21,871	6,084	1,311	20,560	13,500	1,283	5,185	1,903
Pennsylvania..........	94,900	7,649	9,037	85,864	59,064	9,311	19,916	6,609
Rhode Island..........	8,245	7,630	1,022	7,223	4,529	559	2,329	829
South Carolina.........	30,051	7,158	4,881	25,170	16,557	4,193	6,145	3,156
South Dakota	6,602	8,564	658	5,944	3,779	438	1,620	765
Tennessee............	45,441	7,701	3,770	41,670	23,983	8,118	9,863	3,476
Texas................	141,858	6,308	31,895	109,963	72,407	26,969	27,792	14,690
Utah	13,684	5,728	3,305	10,378	6,282	2,304	2,948	2,150
Vermont..............	4,633	7,456	623	4,010	2,264	541	1,423	405
Virginia...............	90,638	12,150	38,533	52,105	30,979	35,325	7,991	16,342
Washington...........	44,841	7,228	8,321	36,520	22,754	6,946	9,083	6,058
West Virginia..........	15,183	8,364	734	14,449	9,084	1,041	3,701	1,358
Wisconsin.............	31,554	5,728	2,414	29,140	19,534	2,641	7,484	1,895
Wyoming.............	4,393	8,673	412	3,981	1,834	403	1,636	521

[1] Based on U.S. Census Bureau estimated resident population as of July 1.   [2] Revised since originally published.

Source: U.S. Census Bureau, Consolidated Federal Federal Funds Report, 2004. See Internet site <http://www.census.gov /govs/www/cffr.html>.

Table 466. Internal Revenue Gross Collections by Type of Tax: 2002 to 2006

[2,017 represents $2,017,000,000,000. For years ending September 30. See text, this section, for information on taxes]

Type of tax	Gross collection (bil. dol.)					Percent of total				
	2002	2003	2004	2005	2006	2002	2003	2004	2005	2006
United States, total..........	2,017	1,953	2,019	2,269	2,519	100.0	100.0	100.0	100.0	100.0
Individual income taxes...........	1,038	987	990	1,108	1,236	51.5	50.5	49.1	48.8	49.1
Withheld by employers..........	751	735	747	787	849	37.2	37.6	37.0	34.7	33.7
Employment taxes..............	688	696	717	771	815	34.1	35.6	35.5	34.0	32.4
Old-age and disability insurance ...	677	685	706	760	803	33.6	35.1	35.0	33.5	31.9
Unemployment insurance........	7	7	7	7	8	0.3	0.3	0.3	0.3	0.3
Railroad retirement	5	4	4	5	5	0.2	0.2	0.2	0.2	0.2
Corporation income taxes	211	194	231	307	381	10.5	9.9	11.4	13.5	15.1
Estate and gift taxes.............	27	23	26	26	29	1.4	1.2	1.3	1.1	1.1
Excise taxes	52	53	55	57	58	2.6	2.7	2.7	2.5	2.3

Source: U.S. Internal Revenue Service, *IRS Data Book*, annual, (Publication 55B). See Internet site <http://www.irs.gov /taxstats/article/0,,id=102174,00.html>.

Table 467. Individual Income Tax Returns Filed—Examination Coverage: 1995 to 2006

[114,683 represents 114,683,000. See the annual *IRS Data Book* (Publication 55B) for a detailed explanation]

Year	Returns filed [1] (1,000)	Returns examined		Total recommended additional tax [3] ($1,000)	Average recommended additional tax per return [3] (dollars) [3]
		Total [2] (1,000)	Percent coverage		
1995	114,683	1,919	1.7	7,756,954	4,041
1996	116,060	1,942	1.7	7,600,191	3,915
1997	118,363	1,519	1.3	8,363,918	5,505
1998	120,342	1,193	1.0	6,095,698	5,110
1999	122,547	1,100	0.9	4,458,474	4,052
2000	124,887	618	0.5	3,388,905	5,486
2001	127,097	732	0.6	3,301,860	4,512
2002	129,445	744	0.6	3,636,486	4,889
2003	130,341	849	0.7	4,559,902	5,369
2004	130,134	997	0.8	6,201,693	6,220
2005	130,577	1,199	0.9	13,355,087	11,138
2006	132,276	1,284	1.0	13,045,221	10,160

[1] Returns filed in previous calendar year.   [2] Includes taxpayer examinations by correspondence.   [3] For 1995 to 1997, amount includes associated penalties.

Source: U.S. Internal Revenue Service. *IRS Data Book*, annual, Publication 55B. See Internet site <http://www.irs.gov /taxstats/article/0,,id=102174,00.html>.

Table 468. Federal Individual Income Tax Returns—Adjusted Gross Income, Taxable Income, and Total Income Tax: 2003 and 2004

[130,424 represents 130,424,000. For tax years. Based on a sample of returns, see source and Appendix III]

Item	2003		2004		Percent change in amount, 2003–04
	Number of returns (1,000)	Amount (mil. dol.)	Number of returns (1,000)	Amount (mil. dol.)	
Adjusted gross income (less deficit)......	130,424	6,207,109	132,226	6,788,805	9.4
Exemptions [1]....................	261,126	781,305	263,896	800,690	2.5
Taxable income	101,393	4,200,218	102,738	4,670,166	11.2
Total income tax...................	88,922	748,017	89,102	831,976	11.2
Alternative minimum tax...........	2,358	9,470	3,096	13,029	37.6

[1] The number of returns columns represent the number of exemptions.

Source: U.S. Internal Revenue Service, *Statistics of Income Bulletin*, Fall issues.

Federal Government Finances and Employment   313

Table 469. Federal Individual Income Tax Returns—Adjusted Gross Income (AGI) by Selected Source of Income and Income Class for Taxable Returns: 2004

[In millions of dollars (6,788,805 represents $6,788,805,000,000), except as indicated. For the tax year. Minus sign (–) indicates net loss was greater than net income. Based on sample; see Appendix III]

Item	Total [1]	Under $10,000	$10,000 to $19,999	$20,000 to $29,999	$30,000 to $39,999	$40,000 to $49,999	$50,000 to $99,999	$100,000 and over
Number of all returns (1,000)	132,226	25,661	22,937	18,217	13,915	10,571	28,167	12,757
Adjusted gross income [2]	6,788,805	35,654	342,224	451,385	482,760	473,381	1,982,014	3,021,387
Salaries and wages..........	4,921,806	114,528	253,887	369,232	403,103	389,371	1,604,977	1,786,709
Interest received..........	125,474	8,260	8,776	6,622	6,173	5,819	23,362	66,463
Dividends in AGI...........	146,839	5,791	5,013	4,661	4,563	4,790	22,588	99,433
Business; profession, net profit less loss [3]	247,217	5,498	23,258	16,901	13,724	13,360	54,353	120,122
Sales of property, net gain less loss	476,164	4,710	1,555	2,200	2,280	2,771	24,807	437,842
Pensions and annuities in AGI. . .	394,286	10,231	38,518	37,794	36,522	35,705	144,383	91,133
Rents and royalties, net income less loss [4]	24,334	–2,980	947	–164	–589	–330	41	27,408

[1] Includes a small number of taxable returns with no adjusted gross income. [2] Includes other sources, not shown separately. [3] Includes sales of capital assets and other property; net gain less loss. [4] Excludes rental passive losses disallowed in the computation of AGI; net income less loss.

Source: U.S. Internal Revenue Service, *Statistics of Income Bulletin*, Fall issues.

Table 470. Federal Individual Income Tax Returns—Total and Selected Sources of Adjusted Gross Income: 2003 and 2004

[130,424 represents 130,424,000. For tax years. Based on a sample of returns, see source and Appendix III. Minus sign (–) indicates decrease]

Item	2003 Number of returns (1,000)	2003 Amount (mil. dol.)	2004 Number of returns (1,000)	2004 Amount (mil. dol.)	Change in amount, 2003–04 Net change (mil. dol.)	Change in amount, 2003–04 Percent change
Adjusted gross income (less deficit) [1]	130,424	6,207,109	132,226	6,788,805	581,696	9.4
Salaries and wages....................	110,891	4,649,900	112,370	4,921,806	271,906	5.8
Taxable interest	59,459	127,160	57,606	125,474	–1,686	–1.3
Ordinary dividends	30,475	115,141	30,687	146,839	31,698	27.5
Qualified dividends	22,449	80,995	24,550	110,500	29,506	36.4
Business or profession net income (less loss) ..	19,416	229,655	20,252	247,217	17,562	7.6
Net capital gain	22,985	294,354	25,267	473,662	179,308	60.9
Capital gain distributions [2].............	7,265	4,695	10,733	15,336	10,641	226.6
Sales of property other than capital assets, net gain (less loss)	1,754	–330	1,750	2,503	2,833	(X)
Sales of property other than capital assets, net gain	799	8,139	858	10,473	2,335	28.7
Taxable social security benefits	10,975	97,768	11,692	110,462	12,694	13.0
Total rental and royalty net income (less net loss) [3]	9,564	29,227	9,751	27,384	–1,842	–6.3
Partnership and S corporation net income (less loss)	7,007	254,057	7,236	315,993	61,936	24.4
Estate and trust net income (less loss)	533	12,415	543	14,001	1,586	12.8
Farm net income (less loss)	1,997	–12,371	2,005	–13,239	–868	–7.0
Farm net income...................	592	7,473	589	7,371	–101	–1.4
Unemployment compensation	10,065	44,008	9,095	32,740	–11,268	–25.6
Taxable pensions and annuities............	22,823	372,931	23,123	394,286	21,354	5.7
Taxable Individual Retirement Account distributions	8,612	88,336	8,914	101,672	13,337	15.1
Other net income (less loss) [4].............	(NA)	21,289	5,892	23,198	1,908	9.0
Gambling earnings	1,540	19,150	1,709	23,313	4,164	21.7

NA Not available.   X Not applicable.   [1] Includes sources of income not shown separately.   [2] Includes both Schedule D and non-Schedule D capital gain distributions.   [3] Includes farm rental net income (less loss).   [4] Other net income (less loss) represents data reported on Form 1040, line 21, except net operating loss, the foreign-earned income exclusion, and gambling earnings.

Source: U.S. Internal Revenue Service, *Statistics of Income Bulletin*, Fall issues.

Table 471. **Federal Individual Income Tax Returns— Net Capital Gains and Capital Gain Distributions from Mutual Funds: 1988 to 2004**

[14,309 represents 14,309,000. For tax years. Based on a sample of returns, see source and Appendix III. Minus sign (–) indicates decrease]

Tax year	Net capital gain (less loss)				Capital gain distribution [2]			
	Number of returns (1,000)	Current dollars (mil. dol.)	Constant (1982–1984) dollars [1]		Number of returns (1,000)	Current dollars (mil. dol.)	Constant (1982–1984) dollars [1]	
			Amount (mil. dol.)	Percent change			Amount (mil. dol.)	Percent change
1988	14,309	153,768	129,981	(X)	4,274	3,879	3,279	(X)
1989	15,060	145,631	117,444	–9.6	5,191	5,483	4,422	34.9
1990	14,288	114,231	87,400	–25.6	5,069	3,905	2,988	–32.4
1991	15,009	102,776	75,460	–13.7	5,796	4,665	3,425	14.6
1992	16,491	118,230	84,269	11.7	5,917	7,426	5,293	54.5
1993	18,409	144,172	99,773	18.4	9,998	11,995	8,301	56.8
1994	18,823	142,288	96,011	–3.8	9,803	11,322	7,640	–8.0
1995	19,963	170,415	111,821	16.5	10,744	14,391	9,443	23.6
1996	22,065	251,817	160,495	43.5	12,778	24,722	15,757	66.9
1997	24,240	356,083	221,859	38.2	14,969	45,132	28,120	78.5
1998	25,690	446,084	273,671	23.4	16,070	46,147	28,311	0.7
1999	27,701	542,758	325,785	19.0	17,012	59,473	35,698	26.1
2000	29,521	630,542	366,169	12.4	17,546	79,079	45,923	28.6
2001	25,956	326,527	184,375	–49.6	12,216	13,609	7,685	–83.3
2002	24,189	238,789	132,734	–28.0	7,567	5,343	2,970	–61.4
2003	22,985	294,354	159,975	20.5	7,265	4,695	2,552	–14.1
2004	25,267	473,662	250,747	56.7	10,733	15,336	8,119	218.1

X Not applicable.   [1] Constant Dollars were calculated using the U.S. Bureau of Labor Statistics consumer price index for urban consumers (CPI-U, 1982–84 = 100). See Table 703.   [2] Capital gain distributions are included in net capital gain (less loss). For 1988–1996, and 1999–2004, capital gain distributions from mutual funds are the sum of the amounts reported on the Form 1040 and Schedule D. For 1997 and 1998, capital gain distributions were reported entirely on the Schedule D.

Source: U.S. Internal Revenue Service, *Statistics of Income Bulletin*, Fall issues.

Table 472. **Alternative Minimum Tax: 1986 to 2004**

[608.9 represents 608,900. For tax years. Based on a sample of returns, see source and Appendix III]

Tax year	Highest statutory alternative minimum tax rate	Alternative minimum tax		Tax year	Highest statutory alternative minimum tax rate	Alternative minimum tax	
		Number of returns (1,000)	Amount (mil. dol.)			Number of returns (1,000)	Amount (mil. dol.)
1986	20	608.9	6,713.1	1995	28	414.1	2,290.6
1987	21	139.8	1,674.9	1996	28	477.9	2,812.7
1988	21	113.6	1,027.9	1997	28	618.1	4,005.1
1989	21	117.5	831.0	1998	[1]28	853.4	5,014.5
				1999	[1]28	1,018.1	6,477.7
1990	21	132.1	830.3	2000	[1]28	1,304.2	9,600.8
1991	24	243.7	1,213.4	2001	[1]28	1,120.0	6,756.7
1992	24	287.2	1,357.1	2002	[1]28	1,910.8	6,853.9
1993	28	334.6	2,052.8	2003	[1]28	2,358.0	9,469.8
1994	28	369.0	2,212.1	2004	[1]28	3,096.3	13,029.2

[1] Top rate on most long-term capital gains was 20 percent. 15 percent for 2003 and 2004.

Source: Internal Revenue Service, *Statistics of Income Bulletin*, Winter 2006–2007, volume 26, no. 3. See also <http://www.irs.gov/taxstats/index.html>.

Federal Government Finances and Employment   315

Table 473. **Federal Individual Income Tax Returns—Sources of Net Losses Included in Adjusted Gross Income: 2003 and 2004**

[4,973 represents 4,973,000. For tax years. Based on a sample of returns, see source and Appendix III. Minus sign (–) indicates decrease]

Item	2003 Number of returns (1,000)	2003 Amount (mil. dol.)	2004 Number of returns (1,000)	2004 Amount (mil. dol.)	Percent change in amount, 2003–04
Total net losses	(NA)	279,243	(NA)	303,458	8.7
Business or profession net loss.	4,973	38,927	5,194	43,007	10.5
Net capital loss [1]	12,808	28,952	11,513	25,492	–12.0
Net loss, sales of property other than capital assets.	955	8,469	892	7,971	–5.9
Total rental and royalty net loss.	4,242	33,453	4,380	38,466	15.0
Partnership and S corporation net loss. . . .	2,553	78,972	2,498	82,697	4.7
Estate and trust net loss	33	1,084	36	1,436	32.4
Farm net loss	1,405	19,844	1,416	20,610	3.9
Net operating loss [2]	712	62,825	830	75,012	19.4
Other net loss [3]	290	6,718	359	8,768	30.5

NA Not available. [1] Includes only the portion of capital losses allowable in the calculation of adjusted gross income. Only $3,000 of net capital loss per return ($1,500 for married filing separately) are allowed to be included in negative total income. Any excess is carried forward to future years. [2] Net operating loss is a carryover of the loss from a business when taxable income from a prior year was less than zero. [3] Other net loss represents losses reported on Form 1040, line 21, except net operating loss and the foreign-earned income exclusion.

Source: U.S. Internal Revenue Service, *Statistics of Income Bulletin*, Fall issues.

Table 474. **Federal Individual Income Tax Returns—Number, Income Tax, and Average Tax by Size of Adjusted Gross Income: 2000 and 2004**

[129,374 represents 129,374,000. Based on sample of returns; see Appendix III]

Size of adjusted gross income	Number of returns (1,000) 2000	Number of returns (1,000) 2004	Adjusted gross income (AGI) (bil. dol.) 2000	Adjusted gross income (AGI) (bil. dol.) 2004	Income tax total [1] (bil. dol.) 2000	Income tax total [1] (bil. dol.) 2004	Tax as percent of AGI (for taxable returns only) 2000	Tax as percent of AGI (for taxable returns only) 2004	Average tax (for taxable returns only) (dol.) 2000	Average tax (for taxable returns only) (dol.) 2004
Total	129,374	132,226	6,365	6,789	981	832	16	13	10,129	9,337
Less than $1,000 [2]	2,966	3,622	–58	–85	–	–	2	(NA)	648	980
$1,000 to $2,999	5,385	4,812	11	10	–	1	7	1	134	61
$3,000 to $4,999	5,599	5,091	22	20	–	–	4	1	179	105
$5,000 to $6,999	5,183	4,790	31	29	1	–	5	1	297	120
$7,000 to $8,999	4,972	5,011	40	40	1	–	4	1	331	223
$9,000 to $10,999	5,089	4,814	51	48	1	1	5	1	470	247
$11,000 to $12,999.	4,859	4,620	58	55	2	1	6	2	704	406
$13,000 to $14,999	4,810	4,558	67	64	3	1	6	2	883	563
$15,000 to $16,999	4,785	4,598	76	74	3	2	7	2	1,052	740
$17,000 to $18,999	4,633	4,505	83	81	4	2	7	3	1,279	879
$19,000 to $21,999	6,502	6,160	133	126	7	4	8	3	1,565	1,113
$22,000 to $24,999	5,735	5,723	135	134	8	5	8	4	1,815	1,437
$25,000 to $29,999	8,369	8,512	229	234	16	11	8	5	2,248	1,825
$30,000 to $39,999	13,548	13,915	471	483	40	28	9	6	3,094	2,500
$40,000 to $49,999	10,412	10,571	466	473	46	34	10	7	4,462	3,582
$50,000 to $74,999	17,076	18,047	1,045	1,110	116	93	11	8	6,824	5,357
$75,000 to $99,999	8,597	10,120	738	872	100	86	14	10	11,631	8,538
$100,000 to $199,999 . . .	8,083	9,736	1,066	1,288	184	175	17	14	22,783	18,028
$200,000 to $499,999 . . .	2,136	2,348	614	677	146	139	24	21	68,628	59,350
$500,000 to $999,999 . . .	396	433	269	293	76	71	28	24	192,092	164,839
$1,000,000 or more	240	240	817	763	226	178	28	23	945,172	743,606

– Represents or rounds to zero. NA Not available. [1] Consists of income tax after credits (including alternative minimum tax). [2] In addition to low income taxpayers, this size class (and others) includes taxpayers with tax preferences, not reflected in adjusted gross income or taxable income which are subject to the "alternative minimum tax" (included in total income tax).

Source: U.S. Internal Revenue Service, *Statistics of Income Bulletin*, quarterly and Fall issues.

Table 475. **Federal Individual Income Tax Returns—Selected Itemized Deductions and the Standard Deduction: 2003 and 2004**

[43,950 represents 43,950,000. For tax years. Based on a sample of returns, see source and Appendix III. Minus sign (–) indicates decrease]

Item	2003 Number of returns [1] (1,000)	2003 Amount (mil. dol.)	2004 Number of returns [1] (1,000)	2004 Amount (mil. dol.)	Percent change, 2003–04 Number of returns [1]	Percent change, 2003–04 Amount
Total itemized deductions before limitation	43,950	930,812	46,335	1,035,000	5.4	11.2
Medical and dental expenses after 7.5-percent AGI limitation . [2]	8,678	56,007	9,531	61,503	9.8	9.8
Taxes paid [2]	43,062	310,897	46,009	362,609	6.8	16.6
State and local income taxes	(NA)	(NA)	33,516	202,306	(NA)	(NA)
State and local general sales taxes	(NA)	(NA)	11,249	17,527	(NA)	(NA)
Interest paid [3]	36,212	340,319	38,110	356,356	5.2	4.7
Home mortgage interest.	35,797	325,192	37,692	340,476	5.3	4.7
Charitable contributions.	38,627	145,702	40,623	165,564	5.2	13.6
Other than cash contributions	23,933	38,041	25,267	43,373	5.6	14.0
Casualty and theft losses.	90	1,605	185	3,510	106.3	118.8
Miscellaneous deductions after 2-percent AGI limitation. .	11,639	63,182	12,025	68,533	3.3	8.5
Total unlimited miscellaneous deductions	1,211	13,101	1,457	16,925	20.4	29.2
Itemized deductions in excess of limitation	5,221	28,947	5,724	36,762	9.6	27.0
Total itemized deductions after limitation	43,950	901,865	46,335	998,238	5.4	10.7
Total standard deduction	84,643	555,780	84,017	560,933	–0.7	0.9
Total deductions (after itemized deduction limitation)	128,593	1,457,645	130,352	1,559,171	1.4	7.0

NA Not available. [1] Returns with no adjusted gross income are excluded from the deduction counts. For this reason, the sum of the number of returns with total itemized deductions and the number of returns with total standard deduction is less than the total number of returns for all filers. [2] Includes real estate taxes, personal property taxes, and other taxes not shown separately. [3] Includes investment interest and deductible mortgage "points" not shown separately.

Source: U.S. Internal Revenue Service, *Statistics of Income Bulletin*, Fall issues.

Table 476. **Federal Individual Income Tax Returns—Statutory Adjustments: 2003 and 2004**

[30,382 represents 30,382,000. For tax years. Based on a sample of returns, see source and Appendix III. Minus sign (–) indicates decrease]

Item	2003 Number of returns [1] (1,000)	2003 Amount (mil. dol.)	2004 Number of returns [1] (1,000)	2004 Amount (mil. dol.)	Percent change in amount, 2003–04
Total statutory adjustments	30,382	87,576	32,154	98,047	12.0
Payments to an Individual Retirement Account	3,418	10,007	3,331	10,029	0.2
Educator expenses deduction.	3,241	806	3,402	858	6.5
Moving expenses adjustment	1,024	2,440	1,096	2,952	21.0
Student loan interest deduction.	6,953	4,410	7,527	4,399	–0.3
Tuition and fees deduction	3,571	6,684	4,710	10,589	58.4
Self-employment tax deduction.	15,373	19,791	15,920	21,109	6.7
Self-employment health insurance deduction.	3,802	16,454	3,884	18,457	12.2
Payments to a self-employed retirement (Keogh) plan. . .	1,209	17,796	1,201	19,296	8.4
Forfeited interest penalty	736	150	780	210	39.7
Alimony paid	587	7,520	574	8,470	12.6
Other adjustment [1]	(NA)	1,518	(NA)	1,677	10.5

NA Not available. [1] Includes foreign housing adjustment, Medical Savings Accounts deduction, certain business expenses of reservists, performing artists, etc., and other adjustments for 2003. For 2004, other adjustments include these plus the health savings account deduction (90,857 returns totaling $190.7 million).

Source: U.S. Internal Revenue Service, *Statistics of Income Bulletin*, Fall issues.

Federal Government Finances and Employment **317**

Table 477. Federal Individual Income Tax Returns—Itemized Deductions and Statutory Adjustments by Size of Adjusted Gross Income: 2004

[46,335 represents 46,335,000. Based on a sample of returns; see Appendix III]

Item	Unit	Total	Under $10,000	$10,000 to $19,999	$20,000 to $29,999	$30,000 to $39,999	$40,000 to $49,999	$50,000 to $99,999	$100,000 and over
Returns with itemized deductions:									
Number of returns [1,2]	1,000 ..	46,335	970	2,487	3,490	4,540	4,655	18,585	11,610
Amount [1,2]	Mil. dol..	998,238	13,525	32,521	46,079	61,388	67,717	334,536	442,473
Medical and dental expenses: [3]									
Returns	1,000 ..	9,531	625	1,459	1,507	1,402	1,138	2,812	587
Amount	Mil. dol..	94,670	5,742	11,556	11,774	11,079	10,096	31,101	13,321
Taxes paid:									
Returns [2]	1,000 ..	46,009	914	2,408	3,440	4,490	4,627	18,530	11,601
Amount, total	Mil. dol..	362,609	2,418	6,418	9,558	14,486	17,888	107,521	204,319
State and local taxes:									
Returns	1,000 ..	44,765	812	2,237	3,275	4,344	4,485	18,153	11,459
Amount	Mil. dol..	219,833	627	1,910	3,392	6,389	8,536	57,168	141,812
Real estate taxes:									
Returns	1,000 ..	40,458	701	1,871	2,601	3,600	3,957	16,771	10,957
Amount	Mil. dol..	132,252	1,682	4,160	5,629	7,314	8,522	46,224	58,722
Interest paid:									
Returns	1,000 ..	38,110	568	1,515	2,428	3,434	3,810	16,189	10,165
Amount	Mil. dol..	356,356	4,171	10,081	16,440	23,685	27,055	135,348	139,577
Home mortgage interest:									
Returns	1,000 ..	37,692	560	1,493	2,402	3,411	3,779	16,104	9,943
Amount	Mil. dol..	340,476	4,110	9,965	16,243	23,406	26,768	133,594	126,392
Charitable cash contributions:									
Returns	1,000 ..	38,567	574	1,724	2,591	3,465	3,671	15,855	10,687
Amount	Mil. dol..	122,875	899	2,741	4,567	6,243	7,163	36,253	65,009
Unreimbursed employee business expenses:									
Returns	1,000 ..	15,546	75	437	1,064	1,621	1,706	7,070	3,572
Amount	Mil. dol..	68,497	206	1,780	4,491	7,026	7,260	28,829	18,906
Returns with statutory adjustments:									
Number of returns [2]	1,000 ..	32,154	4,086	4,142	3,508	3,089	2,917	9,079	5,333
Amount of adjustments	Mil. dol..	98,047	5,740	5,751	6,387	6,151	6,401	24,559	43,057
Payments to IRAs: [4]									
Returns	1,000 ..	3,331	111	248	421	427	428	1,094	602
Amount	Mil. dol..	10,029	257	506	1,040	1,138	1,315	3,410	2,363
Student loan interest deduction	1,000 ..	7,527	368	755	1,030	1,075	972	2,784	544
Amount	Mil. dol..	4,399	182	317	515	628	596	1,913	248
Deduction for self-employment tax	1,000 ..	15,920	2,980	2,697	1,688	1,229	1,111	3,525	2,691
Amount	Mil. dol..	21,109	1,255	2,053	1,696	1,362	1,365	5,131	8,246
Payments to Keogh plans	1,000 ..	1,201	18	19	25	48	55	318	716
Amount	Mil. dol..	19,296	77	86	103	283	375	2,668	15,703

[1] After limitations. [2] Includes other deductions and adjustments, not shown separately. [3] Before limitation. [4] Individual Retirement Account.

Source: U.S. Internal Revenue Service, *Statistics of Income Bulletin*, Fall issues.

Table 478. Federal Individual Income Tax Returns—Selected Tax Credits: 2003 and 2004

[41,091 represents 41,091,000. For tax years. Based on a sample of returns, see source and Appendix III. Minus sign (–) indicates decrease]

Item	2003 Number of returns (1,000)	2003 Amount (mil. dol.)	2004 Number of returns (1,000)	2004 Amount (mil. dol.)	Percent change, 2003–04 Number of returns	Percent change, 2003–04 Amount
Total tax credits [1]	41,091	41,996	41,694	52,367	1.5	24.7
Child care credit	6,313	3,207	6,317	3,338	0.1	4.1
Earned income credit [2]	3,606	926	2,975	768	-17.5	-17.1
Foreign tax credit	4,145	5,806	4,700	6,758	13.4	16.4
General business credit	263	613	249	635	-5.4	3.7
Minimum tax credit	251	917	275	902	9.6	-1.6
Child tax credit [3]	25,672	22,788	25,989	32,300	1.2	41.7
Education credits	7,298	5,843	7,181	6,017	-1.6	3.0
Retirement savings contribution credit	5,297	1,034	5,289	1,012	-0.2	-2.2

[1] Includes credits not shown separately. [2] Represents portion of earned income credit used to offset income tax before credits. [3] Excludes refundable portion, which totaled $14.5 billion for 2004.

Source: U.S. Internal Revenue Service, *Statistics of Income Bulletin*, Fall issues.

U.S. Census Bureau, Statistical Abstract of the United States: 2008

Table 479. Federal Individual Income Tax Returns by State: 2004

[133,093 represents 133,093,000. For tax year. Data will not agree with data in other tables due to differing survey methodology used to derive state data]

State	Total number of returns (1,000)	Adjusted gross income (mil. dol)			Itemized deductions (mil. dol.)				Income tax (mil. dol.)
		Total [1]	Salary and wages	Net capital gain [2]	Total [1]	State and local income tax	Real estate tax	Interest paid	
U.S.. . . .	133,093	6,745,102	4,917,552	451,494	1,014,809	202,314	132,678	372,320	832,385
AL	1,910	80,885	60,102	3,723	10,259	1,699	446	3,476	8,607
AK	345	15,659	11,531	665	1,448	18	237	717	1,881
AZ	2,373	116,946	83,146	8,732	18,247	2,540	1,506	7,768	13,492
AR	1,136	44,374	32,902	2,116	5,259	1,200	243	1,490	4,505
CA	15,327	881,753	624,514	73,196	174,467	39,348	18,449	71,443	113,887
CO	2,110	114,780	82,079	9,486	18,702	3,130	1,534	9,589	14,003
CT	1,665	121,678	85,904	10,626	18,698	5,018	3,501	6,036	19,297
DE	396	21,274	15,102	1,355	2,817	661	219	1,144	2,610
DC	278	17,858	12,056	1,723	3,131	998	204	946	2,666
FL	8,173	415,063	262,773	47,235	54,906	1,796	8,027	21,854	55,276
GA	3,783	181,841	138,284	10,351	30,638	6,036	2,789	13,275	20,815
HI	606	28,114	20,084	1,992	4,277	980	196	1,960	3,109
ID	594	24,800	17,812	1,783	3,952	783	378	1,473	2,468
IL	5,763	312,952	228,116	21,421	43,252	5,847	8,257	16,575	40,695
IN	2,855	127,615	97,800	4,664	15,151	3,174	1,492	5,732	13,883
IA	1,334	58,022	43,144	2,286	7,318	1,738	819	2,168	5,929
KS	1,229	55,850	41,818	2,323	7,298	1,558	806	2,251	6,171
KY	1,758	72,675	54,957	2,897	9,686	2,697	728	3,118	7,506
LA	1,869	73,138	55,847	2,461	7,570	1,323	352	3,151	7,650
ME	619	26,305	19,062	1,521	3,552	920	527	1,120	2,698
MD	2,636	158,674	118,457	8,884	30,314	8,258	3,164	10,518	19,991
MA	3,061	192,413	137,406	15,652	29,050	7,331	4,534	10,368	27,013
MI	4,561	218,692	164,941	8,202	31,820	5,503	4,818	12,115	25,062
MN	2,408	128,345	95,761	6,596	20,479	5,187	2,149	7,817	15,424
MS	1,166	41,881	32,246	1,386	5,002	688	279	1,440	3,864
MO	2,586	114,809	85,445	5,063	15,267	3,140	1,515	5,126	12,640
MT	440	16,495	11,108	1,322	2,363	515	243	766	1,628
NE	809	35,717	26,551	1,917	4,785	994	651	1,386	3,823
NV	1,093	63,026	39,881	9,553	9,718	302	825	4,216	8,486
NH	643	35,041	26,127	2,514	4,457	360	1,118	1,807	4,377
NJ	4,107	264,918	199,029	14,730	45,119	9,800	10,347	13,916	37,548
NM	827	32,478	23,836	1,503	4,101	800	295	1,604	3,325
NY	8,625	509,011	359,826	45,111	87,796	28,546	13,533	21,255	72,289
NC	3,770	170,125	127,361	8,034	27,333	6,574	2,284	10,485	18,387
ND	305	12,162	8,774	562	969	130	147	276	1,252
OH	5,447	241,422	183,450	9,213	33,232	9,358	4,266	11,259	26,711
OK	1,476	60,731	43,736	3,181	7,931	1,835	552	2,260	6,479
OR	1,604	73,781	51,808	4,778	13,835	3,628	1,586	4,995	7,875
PA	5,811	278,531	207,054	13,125	35,607	7,590	5,978	11,986	33,211
RI	500	25,411	18,767	1,585	3,850	932	683	1,297	3,069
SC	1,844	76,865	56,796	3,966	11,683	2,461	856	5,009	7,793
SD	362	14,819	10,093	1,124	1,170	30	147	411	1,669
TN	2,607	114,815	87,191	6,677	12,184	309	1,088	4,741	13,253
TX	9,432	448,957	338,710	26,139	48,614	919	9,546	17,658	56,402
UT	996	44,972	33,823	2,533	8,487	1,535	591	3,004	4,388
VT	306	13,620	9,701	964	1,664	366	330	555	1,466
VA	3,491	197,533	146,928	11,204	30,787	6,734	3,486	12,498	24,698
WA	2,861	153,791	109,518	11,132	21,500	506	3,040	10,459	19,184
WV	748	28,133	21,411	749	2,286	593	126	751	2,733
WI	2,621	124,451	93,594	6,193	18,375	4,752	3,441	5,692	13,787
WY	244	12,319	7,831	1,597	1,115	44	78	398	1,565
Other [3]	1,580	49,583	53,353	5,747	3,289	1,130	272	966	5,843

[1] Includes other items, not shown separately.   [2] Less loss.   [3] Includes returns filed from Army Post Office and Fleet Post Office addresses by members of the armed forces stationed overseas; returns by other U.S. citizens abroad; and returns filed by residents of Puerto Rico with income from sources outside of Puerto Rico or with income earned as U.S. government employees.

Source: U.S. Internal Revenue Service, *Statistics of Income Bulletin*, Spring 2006, volume 25, no. 4.

Federal Government Finances and Employment   319

Table 480. Federal Individual Income Tax—Tax Liability and Effective and Marginal Tax Rates for Selected Income Groups: 2000 to 2006

[Refers to income after exclusions but before deductions for itemized or standard deductions and for personal exemptions. Tax liability is after reductions for tax credits. As a result of the tax credits, tax liability can be negative, which means that the taxpayer receives a payment from the government. The effective rate represents tax liability, which may be negative as a result of the tax credits, divided by stated income. The marginal tax rate is the percentage of the first additional dollar of income which would be paid in income tax. Tax credits which increase with income can result in negative marginal tax rates. Computations assume itemized deductions (in excess of floors) of 18 percent of adjusted gross income or the standard deduction, whichever is greater. All income is assumed to be from wages and salaries. Does not include social security and Medicare taxes imposed on most wages and salaries]

Adjusted gross income	2000	2002	2003	2004	2005	2006
TAX LIABILITY (dol.)						
Single person, no dependents						
$5,000	[1]-353	[1]-376	[1]-382	[1]-383	[1]-383	[1]-383
$10,000	[1]391	[1]149	[1]126	[1]91	[1]46	[1]-7
$20,000	1,920	1,545	1,480	1,450	1,405	1,355
$30,000	3,270	2,940	2,883	2,868	2,845	2,818
$40,000	4,988	4,392	4,248	4,163	4,075	4,048
$50,000	7,284	6,606	6,298	6,213	6,115	5,983
$75,000	13,024	12,141	11,423	11,338	11,240	11,108
$100,000	19,233	18,015	16,852	16,719	16,571	16,368
Married couple, two dependents, with one spouse working:						
$5,000	[1]-2,000	[1]-2,000	[1]-2,000	[1]-2,000	[1]-2,000	[1]-412
$10,000	[1]-3,888	[1]-4,000	[1]-4,000	[1]-4,000	[1]-4,000	[1]295
$20,000	[1,3]-2,349	[1,3,4]-3,951	[1,4]-4,044	[1,4]-4,643	[1,4]-4,986	[1,4]-1,867
$30,000	[1,3]475	[1,3,4]-1,065	[1,3,4]-2,158	[1,3,4]-2,359	[1,3,4]-2,810	[1,3,4]-3,447
$40,000	[3]2,218	[3]1,223	[3]45	[3,4]-30	[3,4]-150	[3,4]5,333
$50,000	[3]3,470	[3]2,550	[3]1,545	[3]1,470	[3]1,350	[3]7,733
$75,000	[3]7,384	[3]5,961	[3]4,695	[3]4,650	[3]4,575	[3]13,732
$100,000	[3]13,124	[3]11,496	[3]9,070	[3]8,875	[3]8,630	[3]20,287
EFFECTIVE RATE (percent)						
Single person, no dependents:						
$5,000	[1]-7.1	[1]-7.5	[1]-7.6	[1]-7.7	[1]-7.7	[1]-7.7
$10,000	[1]3.9	[1]1.5	[1]1.3	[1]0.9	[1]0.5	[1]-0.1
$20,000	9.6	7.7	7.4	7.3	7	6.8
$30,000	10.9	9.8	9.6	9.6	9.5	9.4
$40,000	12.5	11.0	10.6	10.4	10.2	10.1
$50,000	14.6	13.2	12.6	12.4	12.2	12.0
$75,000	17.4	16.2	15.2	15.1	15	14.8
$100,000	19.2	18.0	16.9	16.7	16.6	16.4
Married couple, two dependents, with one spouse working:						
$5,000	[1]-40.0	[1]-40.0	[1]-40.0	[1]-40.0	[1]-40.0	[1]-40.0
$10,000	[1]-38.9	[1]-40.0	[1]-40.0	[1]-40.0	[1]-40.0	[1]-39.3
$20,000	[1,3]-11.7	[1,3,4]-19.8	[1,4]-20.2	[1,4]-23.2	[1,4]-24.9	[1,4]-21.2
$30,000	[1,3]1.6	[1,3,4]-3.5	[1,3,4]-7.2	[1,3,4]-7.9	[1,3,4]-9.4	[1,3,4]-4.3
$40,000	[3]5.5	[3]3.1	[3]0.1	[3,4]-0.1	[3,4]-0.4	[3,4]1.6
$50,000	[3]6.9	[3]5.1	[3]3.1	[3]2.9	[3]2.7	[3]4.2
$75,000	[3]9.8	[3]7.9	[3]6.3	[3]6.2	[3]6.1	[3]6.9
$100,000	[3]13.1	[3]11.5	[3]9.1	[3]8.9	[3]8.6	[3]10.4
MARGINAL TAX RATE (percent)						
Single person, no dependents:						
$5,000	–	–	–	[1]-7.7	[1]-7.7	[1]-7.7
$10,000	[1]22.7	[1]17.7	[1]17.7	[1]17.7	[1]17.7	[1]17.7
$20,000	15.0	15.0	15.0	15.0	15.0	15.0
$30,000	15.0	15.0	15.0	15.0	15.0	15.0
$40,000	28.0	27.0	25.0	25.0	15.0	15.0
$50,000	28.0	27.0	25.0	25.0	25.0	25.0
$75,000	28.0	27.0	25.0	25.0	25.0	25.0
$100,000	31.0	30.0	28.0	28.0	28.0	28.0
Married couple, two dependents, with one spouse working:						
$5,000	[1]-40.0	[1]-40.0	[1]-40.0	[1]-40.0	[1]-40.0	[1]-40.0
$10,000	–	[1]-40.0	[1]-40.0	[1]-40.0	[1]-40.0	[1]-40.0
$20,000	[1,3]21.1	[1,3,4]11.1	[1,4]11.1	[1,4]6.1	[1,4]6.1	[1,4]6.1
$30,000	[1]36.1	[1,3,4]31.1	[1,3,4]31.1	[1,3,4]36.1	[1,3,4]36.1	[1,3,4]36.1
$40,000	15.0	15.0	15.0	[3,4]15.0	[3,4]15.0	[3,4]15.0
$50,000	15.0	15.0	15.0	15.0	15.0	15.0
$75,000	28.0	27.0	15.0	15.0	15.0	15.0
$100,000	28.0	27.0	15.0	25.0	25.0	25.0

– Represents zero. [1] Includes effect from the refundable earned income credit. [2] Includes effect from the rate reduction credit. [3] Includes effect from the child tax credit. [4] Includes effect from the additional (refundable) child tax credit.

Source: U.S. Department of the Treasury, Office of Tax Analysis, unpublished data.

Table 481. Federal Individual Income Tax—Current Income Equivalent to 2000 Constant Income for Selected Income Groups: 2000 to 2006

[Constant 2000 incomes calculated by using the U.S. Bureau of Labor Statistics Consumer Price Index for Urban Consumers (CPI-U); see Table 703, Section 14. See also headnote, Table 480]

Adjusted gross income Constant 2000 dollars	2000	2002	2003	2004	2005	2006
REAL INCOME EQUIVALENT (dol.)						
$5,000	5,000	5,220	5,340	5,480	5,670	5,850
$10,000	10,000	10,450	10,690	10,970	11,340	11,710
$20,000	20,000	20,890	21,370	21,940	22,680	23,410
$30,000	30,000	31,340	32,060	32,910	34,020	35,120
$40,000	40,000	41,790	42,740	43,880	45,370	46,830
$50,000	50,000	52,240	53,430	54,850	56,710	58,540
$75,000	75,000	78,350	80,140	82,270	85,060	87,800
$100,000	100,000	104,470	106,850	109,700	113,410	117,070
TAX LIABILITY (dol.)						
Single person, no dependents:						
$5,000	[1]-353	[1]-376	[1]-382	[1]-390	[1]-399	[1]-412
$10,000	[1]391	[1]228	[1]248	[1]262	[1]283	[1]295
$20,000	1,920	1,679	1,686	1,741	1,807	1,867
$30,000	3,270	3,105	3,136	3,225	3,339	3,447
$40,000	4,988	4,788	4,809	4,958	5,166	5,333
$50,000	7,284	7,102	7,001	7,207	7,491	7,733
$75,000	13,024	12,883	12,476	12,828	13,302	13,732
$100,000	19,233	19,115	18,425	18,946	19,649	20,287
Married couple, 2 dependents with one spouse working:						
$5,000	[1]-2,000	[1]-2,088	[1]-2,136	[1]-2,192	[1]-2,268	[1]-2,340
$10,000	[1]-3,888	[1,4]-4,150	[1,4]-4,223	[1,4]-4,333	[1,4]-4,451	[1,4]-4,598
$20,000	[1,3]-2,349	[1,3,4]-3,852	[1,4]-3,893	[1,4]-4,525	[1,4]-4,823	[1,4]-4,963
$30,000	[1,3]475	[1,3,4]-649	[1,3,4]-1,518	[1,3,4]-1,456	[1,3,4]-1,561	[1,3,4]-1,518
$40,000	[3]2,218	[3]1,491	[3]456	[3]552	[3]656	[3]745
$50,000	[3]3,470	[3]2,826	[3]2,042	[3]2,172	[3]2,325	[3]2,465
$75,000	[3]7,384	[3]6,703	[3]5,327	[3]5,544	[3]5,812	[3]6,064
$100,000	[3]13,124	[3]12,486	[3]10,474	[3]10,864	[3]11,579	[3]12,214
EFFECTIVE TAX RATE (percent)						
Single person, no dependents:						
$5,000	[1]-7.1	[1]-7.2	[1]-7.1	[1]-7.1	[1]-7.0	[1]-7.0
$10,000	[1]3.9	[1]2.2	[1]2.3	[1]2.4	[1]2.5	[1]2.5
$20,000	9.6	8.0	7.9	7.9	8.0	8.0
$30,000	10.9	9.9	9.8	9.8	9.8	9.8
$40,000	12.5	11.5	11.3	11.3	11.4	11.4
$50,000	14.6	13.6	13.1	13.1	13.2	13.2
$75,000	17.4	16.4	15.6	15.6	15.6	15.6
$100,000	19.2	18.3	17.2	17.3	17.3	17.3
Married couple, 2 dependents with one spouse working:						
$5,000	[1]-40.0	[1]-40.0	[1]-40.0	[1]-40.0	[1]-40.0	[1]-40.0
$10,000	[1]-38.9	[1,4]-39.7	[1,4]-39.5	[1,4]-39.5	[1,4]-39.3	[1,4]-39.3
$20,000	[1,3]-11.7	[1,3,4]-18.4	[1,4]-18.2	[1,4]-20.6	[1,4]-21.3	[1,4]-21.2
$30,000	[1,3]1.6	[1,3,4]-2.1	[1,3,4]-4.7	[1,3,4]-4.4	[1,3,4]-4.6	[1,3,4]-4.2
$40,000	[3]5.5	[3]3.6	[3]1.1	[3]1.3	[3]1.4	[3]1.6
$50,000	[3]6.9	[3]5.4	[3]3.8	[3]4.0	[3]4.1	[3]4.2
$75,000	[3]9.8	[3]8.6	[3]6.6	[3]6.7	[3]6.8	[3]6.9
$100,000	[3]13.1	[3]12.0	[3]9.8	[3]9.9	[3]10.2	[3]10.4
MARGINAL TAX RATE (percent)						
Single person, no dependents:						
$5,000	–	–	–	–	–	–
$10,000	[1]22.7	[1]17.7	[1]17.7	[1]17.7	[1]17.7	[1]1.7
$20,000	15.0	15.0	15.0	15.0	15.0	15.0
$30,000	15.0	15.0	15.0	15.0	15.0	15.0
$40,000	28.0	27.0	25.0	25.0	25.0	25.0
$50,000	28.0	27.0	25.0	25.0	25.0	25.0
$75,000	28.0	27.0	25.0	25.0	25.0	25.0
$100,000	31.0	30.0	28.0	28.0	28.0	28.0
Married couple, 2 dependents with one spouse working:						
$5,000	[1]-40.0	[4]-40.0	[4]-40.0	[4]-40.0	[1]-40.0	[4]-40.0
$10,000	–	[4]-10.0	[4]-10.0	[4]-15.0	[4]-15.0	[4]-15.0
$20,000	[1,3]21.1	[1,3,4]11.1	[1,4]11.1	[1,4]6.1	[1,4]6.1	[1,4]6.1
$30,000	[3]36.1	[1,3,4]31.1	[1,3,4]31.1	[1,3,4]36.1	[1,3,4]36.1	[1,3,4]36.1
$40,000	15.0	15.0	15.0	15.0	15.0	15.0
$50,000	15.0	15.0	15.0	15.0	15.0	15.0
$75,000	28.0	27.0	15.0	15.0	15.0	15.0
$100,000	28.0	27.0	25.0	25.0	[3]30.1	[3]30.1

– Represents zero. [1] Includes effect from the refundable earned income credit. [2] Includes effect from the rate reduction tax credit. [3] Includes effect from the child tax credit. [4] Includes effect from the additional (refundable) child tax credit.

Source: U.S. Department of the Treasury, Office of Tax Analysis, unpublished data.

Federal Government Finances and Employment 321

Table 482. **Federal Civilian Employment and Annual Payroll by Branch: 1970 to 2006**

[2,997 represents 2,997,000. For fiscal year ending in year shown. See text, Section 8. Includes employees in U.S. territories and foreign countries. Data represent employees in active-duty status, including intermittent employees. Annual employment figures are averages of monthly figures. Excludes Central Intelligence Agency, National Security Agency, and, as of November 1984, the Defense Intelligence Agency; and, as of October 1996, the National Imagery and Mapping Agency]

Year	Total (1,000)	Percent of U.S. employed [1]	Executive (1,000) Total	Executive (1,000) Defense	Legis-lative (1,000)	Judicial (1,000)	Payroll (mil. dol.) Total	Executive Total	Executive Defense	Legis-lative	Judicial
1970 . . .	[2]2,997	3.81	2,961	1,263	29	7	27,322	26,894	11,264	338	89
1975 . . .	2,877	3.35	2,830	1,044	37	10	39,126	38,423	13,418	549	154
1980 . . .	[2]2,987	3.01	2,933	971	40	14	58,012	56,841	18,795	883	288
1985 . . .	3,001	2.80	2,944	1,080	39	18	80,599	78,992	28,330	1,098	509
1990 . . .	[2]3,233	2.72	3,173	1,060	38	23	99,138	97,022	31,990	1,329	787
1995 . . .	2,943	2.36	2,880	852	34	28	118,304	115,328	31,753	1,598	1,379
2000 . . .	[2]2,879	2.10	2,816	681	31	32	130,832	127,472	29,607	1,619	1,741
2001 . . .	2,704	1.97	2,641	672	30	33	131,964	128,502	28,594	1,682	1,780
2002 . . .	2,699	1.98	2,635	671	31	34	136,611	132,893	28,845	1,781	1,938
2003 . . .	2,743	1.99	2,677	669	31	34	143,380	139,506	29,029	1,908	1,966
2004 . . .	2,714	1.95	2,649	668	30	34	148,037	144,134	29,128	1,977	1,927
2005 . . .	2,709	1.91	2,645	671	30	34	152,222	148,275	29,331	2,048	1,900
2006 . . .	2,700	1.87	2,636	676	30	34	160,570	156,543	29,580	2,109	1,918

[1] Civilian employed only. See Table 569, Section 12.   [2] Includes temporary census workers.

Source: U.S. Office of Personnel Management, *Federal Civilian Workforce Statistics—Employment and Trends*, bimonthly; and unpublished data. See Internet site <http://www.opm.gov/feddata>.

Table 483. Full-Time Federal Civilian Employment—Employees and Average Pay-by-Pay System: 1990 to 2006

[As of March 31 (2,036 represents 2,036,000). Excludes employees of Congress and federal courts, maritime seamen of Department of Commerce, and small number for whom rates were not reported. See text, this section, for explanation of general schedule and wage system]

Pay system	Employees (1,000) 1990	2000	2005	2006	Average annual pay (dol.) 1990	2000	2005	2006
Total, excluding postal . .	2,036	1,671	1,754	1,740	31,174	50,429	63,058	65,253
General Schedule	1,506	1,216	1,248	1,243	31,239	49,428	62,076	64,305
Wage System	369	205	186	185	26,565	37,082	43,907	45,522
Other	161	250	320	312	41,149	66,248	78,003	80,756
Postal pay system [1]	761	788	705	696	29,923	37,627	45,123	46,807

[1] Source: Career employees—U.S. Postal Service, *Annual Report of the Postmaster General*. See also <http://www.usps.com/financials/cspo/welcome.htm>; Average pay—U.S. Postal Service, *Comprehensive Statement of Postal Operations*, annual.

Source: Except as noted, U.S. Office of Personnel Management, "Pay Structure of the Federal Civil Service," annual (publication discontinued); and unpublished data. See Internet site <http://www.opm.gov/feddata/>.

Table 484. Paid Civilian Employment in the Federal Government by State: 2000 and 2004

[As of December 31. In thousands (2,766 represents 2,766,000). Excludes Central Intelligence Agency, Defense Intelligence Agency, seasonal and on-call employees, and National Security Agency]

State	2000	2004	State	2000	2004	State	2000	2004
U.S. [1] . . .	2,766	2,759	KY	30	31	OH	84	77
AL	48	49	LA	33	32	OK	43	43
AK	14	14	ME	13	14	OR	29	28
AZ	43	47	MD	130	130	PA	107	103
AR	20	20	MA	53	50	RI	10	10
CA	248	239	MI	58	55	SC	26	26
CO	51	51	MN	34	33	SD	9	10
CT	21	19	MS	24	23	TN	50	49
DE	5	5	MO	54	53	TX	162	168
DC	181	187	MT	11	12	UT	30	32
FL	113	123	NE	15	15	VT	6	6
GA	89	90	NV	13	15	VA	145	146
HI	23	25	NH	8	8	WA	62	64
ID	11	11	NJ	62	61	WV	18	19
IL	94	87	NM	25	26	WI	30	29
IN	37	35	NY	134	126	WY	6	6
IA	18	18	NC	57	57			
KS	25	25	ND	8	8			

[1] Includes employees outside the United States and in states not specified, not shown separately.

Source: U.S. Office of Personnel Management, "Employment by Geographic Area," biennial, (publication discontinued); and unpublished data. See Internet site: <http://www.opm.gov/feddata/>.

Table 485. **Federal Civilian Employment by Branch and Agency: 1990 to 2006**

[For years ending September 30. Annual averages of monthly figures. Excludes Central Intelligence Agency, National Security Agency; the Defense Intelligence Agency; and, as of October 1996, the National Imagery and Mapping Agency]

Agency	1990	1995	2000	2004	2005	2006
Total, all agencies	3,128,267	2,920,277	2,708,101	2,714,140	2,708,753	2,700,007
Legislative Branch	37,495	33,367	31,157	30,420	30,303	30,067
Judicial Branch	23,605	28,993	32,186	34,224	33,690	33,834
Executive Branch	3,067,167	2,857,917	2,644,758	2,649,496	2,644,764	2,636,106
Executive Office of the President	1,731	1,573	1,658	1,732	1,736	1,709
Executive departments	2,065,542	1,782,834	1,592,200	1,688,152	1,689,914	1,689,351
State	25,288	24,859	27,983	33,013	33,808	33,968
Treasury	158,655	155,951	143,508	117,344	114,194	112,000
Defense	1,034,152	832,352	676,268	668,009	670,790	676,452
Justice	83,932	103,262	125,970	103,536	105,102	106,159
Interior	77,679	76,439	73,818	74,500	73,599	71,593
Agriculture	122,594	113,321	104,466	106,186	104,989	101,887
Commerce [1]	69,920	36,803	47,652	37,641	38,927	40,335
Labor	17,727	16,204	16,040	16,095	15,599	15,434
Health & Human Services [2]	123,959	59,788	62,605	61,495	60,944	60,756
Housing & Urban Development	13,596	11,822	10,319	10,411	10,086	9,814
Transportation [3]	67,364	63,552	63,598	57,748	55,975	53,573
Energy	17,731	19,589	15,692	15,265	15,050	14,838
Education	4,771	4,988	4,734	4,482	4,429	4,257
Veterans Affairs	248,174	263,904	219,547	233,501	236,363	236,938
Homeland Security [3]	(X)	(X)	(X)	148,927	149,977	151,771
Independent agencies [4]	999,894	1,073,510	1,050,900	959,612	953,113	945,046
Board of Governors Federal Reserve System . .	1,525	1,704	2,372	1,820	1,851	1,869
Environmental Protection Agency	17,123	17,910	18,036	17,975	17,964	18,166
Equal Employment Opportunity Commission . . .	2,880	2,796	2,780	2,513	2,421	2,285
Federal Communications Commission	1,778	2,116	1,965	2,024	1,936	1,857
Federal Deposit Insurance Corporation	17,641	14,765	6,958	5,416	4,998	4,583
Federal Trade Commission	988	996	1,019	1,081	1,046	1,027
General Services Administration	20,277	16,500	14,334	12,764	12,685	12,460
National Archives & Records Administration . . .	3,120	2,833	2,702	3,029	3,048	3,051
National Aeronautics & Space Administration . .	24,872	21,635	18,819	19,105	19,105	18,448
National Labor Relations Board	2,263	2,050	2,054	1,934	1,822	1,832
National Science Foundation	1,318	1,292	1,247	1,327	1,325	1,325
Nuclear Regulatory Commission	3,353	3,212	2,858	3,124	3,230	3,297
Office of Personnel Management	6,636	4,354	3,780	3,409	4,333	4,954
Peace Corps	1,178	1,179	1,065	1,105	1,064	1,075
Railroad Retirement Board	1,772	1,544	1,176	1,110	1,010	1,004
Securities & Exchange Commission	2,302	2,852	2,955	3,632	3,933	3,760
Small Business Administration	5,128	5,085	4,150	3,520	4,288	6,148
Smithsonian Institution	5,092	5,444	5,065	5,034	4,981	4,953
Social Security Administration [2]	(X)	66,850	64,474	65,215	65,861	64,884
Tennessee Valley Authority	28,392	16,545	13,145	13,078	12,721	12,624
U.S. Information Agency	8,555	7,480	2,436	2,303	2,212	2,144
U.S. International Development Cooperation Agency	4,698	3,755	2,552	2,547	2,644	2,723
U.S. Postal Service	816,886	845,393	860,726	775,834	767,972	760,039

X Not applicable. [1] Includes enumerators for the 1990 and 2000 census. [2] Sizeable changes in 1995 due to the Social Security Administration which was separated from the Department of Health and Human Services to become an independent agency effective April 1995. [3] See text, Section 10, concerning the development of the Department of Homeland Security. [4] Includes agencies with fewer than 1,000 employees in 2005, not shown separately.

Source: U.S. Office of Personnel Management, *Federal Civilian Workforce Statistics—Employment and Trends*, bimonthly. See Internet site <http://www.opm.gov/feddata/>.

Table 486. **Federal Employees—Summary Characteristics: 1990 to 2005**

[As of September 30. In percent, except as indicated. For civilian employees, excluding U.S. Postal Service employees]

Characteristics	1990	1995	1999	2000	2001	2002	2003	2004	2005
Average age (years) [1]	42.3	44.3	45.9	46.3	46.5	46.5	46.7	46.8	46.9
Average length of service (years) [1]	13.4	15.5	16.9	17.1	17.1	16.8	16.8	16.6	16.4
Retirement eligible: [2]									
Civil Service Retirement System	8	10	15	17	19	23	27	30	33
Federal Employees Retirement System . . .	3	5	10	11	10	11	12	13	13
Bachelor's degree or higher	35	39	40	41	41	41	41	42	43
Sex: Male	57	56	55	55	55	55	55	56	56
Female	43	44	45	45	45	45	45	44	44
Race and national origin:									
Total minorities	27.4	28.9	30.0	30.4	30.6	30.8	31.1	31.4	31.7
Black	16.7	16.8	17.0	17.1	17.1	17.0	17.0	17.0	17.0
Hispanic	5.4	5.9	6.5	6.6	6.7	6.9	7.1	7.3	7.4
Asian/Pacific Islander	3.5	4.2	4.5	4.5	4.6	4.7	4.8	5.0	5.1
American Indian/Alaska Native	1.8	2.0	2.2	2.2	2.2	2.2	2.1	2.1	2.1
Disabled	7.0	7.0	7.0	7.0	7.0	7.0	7.0	7.0	7.0
Veterans preference	30.0	26.0	25.0	24.0	24.0	23.0	22.0	22.0	22.0
Vietnam era veterans	17.0	17.0	14.0	14.0	13.0	13.0	13.0	12.0	11.0
Retired military	4.9	4.2	3.9	3.9	4.2	4.4	4.6	4.9	5.4
Retired officers	0.5	0.5	0.5	0.5	0.6	0.7	0.8	0.9	1.0

[1] For full-time permanent employees. [2] Represents full-time permanent employees under the Civil Service Retirement System (excluding hires since January 1984), and the Federal Employees Retirement System (since January 1984).

Source: U.S. Office of Personnel Management, Office of Workforce Information, *The Fact Book, Federal Civilian Workforce Statistics*, annual. See Internet site <http://www.opm.gov/feddata/>.

Federal Government Finances and Employment 323

Table 487. Federal Executive Branch (Nonpostal) Employment by Race and National Origin: 1990 to 2006

[As of Sept. 30. Covers total employment for only Executive branch agencies participating in OPM's Central Personnel Data File (CPDF). For information on the CPDF, see <http://www.opm.gov/feddata/acpdf.pdf>]

Pay system	1990	1995	2000	2004	2005	2006
All personnel [1]	**2,150,359**	**1,960,577**	**1,755,689**	**1,851,349**	**1,856,966**	**1,848,339**
White, non-Hispanic	1,562,846	1,394,690	1,224,836	1,270,366	1,267,922	1,254,308
General schedule and related	1,218,188	1,101,108	961,261	972,737	973,767	948,740
Grades 1 to 4	132,028	79,195	55,067	48,798	46,671	43,450
Grades 5 to 8	337,453	288,755	239,128	231,765	227,387	219,168
Grades 9 to 12	510,261	465,908	404,649	405,825	408,111	399,400
Grades 13 to 15	238,446	267,250	262,417	286,349	291,598	286,722
Total executives/senior pay levels	9,337	13,307	14,332	16,337	16,409	16,118
Wage pay system	244,220	186,184	146,075	134,821	135,383	133,942
Other pay systems	91,101	94,091	103,168	146,471	142,363	155,508
Black	356,867	327,302	298,701	313,099	315,644	317,697
General schedule and related	272,657	258,586	241,135	244,736	24u,691	246,248
Grades 1 to 4	65,077	41,381	26,895	20,797	19,774	18,326
Grades 5 to 8	114,993	112,962	99,937	95,798	94,655	93,717
Grades 9 to 12	74,985	79,795	82,809	88,813	90,809	91,869
Grades 13 to 15	17,602	24,448	31,494	39,328	41,453	42,336
Total executives/senior pay levels	479	942	1,180	1,238	1,270	1,218
Wage pay system	72,755	55,637	42,590	37,798	37,666	37,378
Other pay systems	10,976	12,137	13,796	29,327	30,017	32,853
Hispanic	115,170	115,964	115,247	135,533	138,507	138,596
General schedule and related	83,218	86,762	89,911	102,612	104,927	105,236
Grades 1 to 4	15,738	11,081	8,526	7,969	7,768	6,854
Grades 5 to 8	28,727	31,152	31,703	34,380	33,653	33,834
Grades 9 to 12	31,615	34,056	36,813	43,868	46,268	46,951
Grades 13 to 15	7,138	10,473	12,869	16,395	17,238	17,597
Total executives/senior pay levels	154	382	547	656	682	699
Wage pay system	26,947	22,128	16,926	15,915	15,945	15,822
Other pay systems	4,851	6,692	7,863	16,350	16,953	16,839
American Indian, Alaska Native, Asian, and Pacific Islander	115,476	122,621	116,905	132,351	134,893	136,593
General schedule and related	81,499	86,768	86,074	96,014	97,866	97,870
Grades 1 to 4	15,286	11,854	9,340	8,528	8,357	7,877
Grades 5 to 8	24,960	26,580	25,691	27,601	27,417	26,986
Grades 9 to 12	31,346	33,810	33,167	37,172	38,276	38,492
Grades 13 to 15	9,907	14,524	17,876	22,713	23,816	24,515
Total executives/senior pay levels	148	331	504	760	804	873
Wage pay system	24,927	21,553	17,613	16,760	16,938	16,728
Other pay systems	8,902	13,969	12,714	18,817	19,285	21,122

[1] Beginning 2006, includes persons classified as multiracial, not shown separately.

Source: U.S. Office of Personnel Management, Central Personnel Data File.

Table 488. Area of Federally Owned Buildings in the United States by State: 2005

[3,200.1 represents 3,200,100,000. As of September 30. For executive branch agencies. For data on federal land by state, see Table 349]

State	Total building area [1] (mil. sq. ft)	Owned building area (mil. sq. ft)	Leased building area (mil. sq. ft.)	State	Total building area [1] (mil. sq. ft)	Owned building area (mil. sq. ft)	Leased building area (mil. sq. ft.)
U.S. [2] ...	**3,200.1**	**2,819.5**	**379.8**	MO	57.2	48.1	9.1
AL	59.4	53.5	5.9	MT	17.3	14.8	2.5
AK	55.9	50.8	5.1	NE	16.3	13.8	2.5
AZ	61.3	56.4	4.8	NV	34.4	31.7	2.7
AR	24.4	21.5	2.9	NH	4.6	3.3	1.3
CA	385.3	355.7	29.5	NJ	55.6	46.4	9.3
CO	62.9	54.5	8.4	NM	63.6	58.4	5.2
CT	18.9	17.0	1.8	NY	117.5	98.3	19.2
DE	8.3	7.8	0.5	NC	94.3	86.9	7.4
DC	91.1	68.4	22.7	ND	21.5	20.1	1.5
FL	132.5	115.6	16.7	OH	78.5	69.9	8.6
GA	125.9	112.7	13.2	OK	65.4	56.9	8.5
HI	61.3	60.0	1.3	OR	26.5	22.1	4.4
ID	20.7	17.8	3.0	PA	89.1	76.1	13.1
IL	89.7	81.0	8.7	RI	14.2	13.5	0.7
IN	36.3	31.7	4.5	SC	66.2	63.0	3.3
IA	16.3	12.5	3.8	SD	19.1	15.9	3.2
KS	45.5	41.1	4.3	TN	73.9	67.8	6.1
KY	55.8	51.5	4.3	TX	211.0	184.7	26.3
LA	47.8	41.4	6.4	UT	36.0	31.7	4.3
ME	13.4	11.9	1.6	VT	4.1	2.7	1.4
MD	135.3	112.8	22.5	VA	184.9	155.9	29.0
MA	41.0	34.9	6.0	WA	93.7	85.9	7.8
MI	35.7	28.7	6.9	WV	21.7	18.3	3.5
MN	22.8	19.4	3.4	WI	26.8	21.9	5.0
MS	38.5	35.0	3.5	WY	14.7	13.8	0.9

[1] Includes otherwised managed square feet, not shown separately.   [2] Includes location not reported, not shown separately.

Source: U.S. General Services Administration, Federal Real Property Council, *Federal Real Property Report*, June 2006 (revised since issued).

Section 10
National Security and Veterans Affairs

This section displays data for national security (national defense and homeland security) and benefits for veterans. Data are presented on national defense and its human and financial costs; active and reserve military personnel; and federally sponsored programs and benefits for veterans, and funding, budget and selected agencies for homeland security. The principal sources of these data are the annual *Selected Manpower Statistics* and the *Atlas/Data Abstract for the United States and Selected Areas* issued by the Office of the Secretary of Defense; *Annual Report of Secretary of Veterans Affairs*, U.S. Department of Veterans Affairs (VA), *Budget in Brief*, U.S. Department of Homeland Security; and *The Budget of the United States Government*, Office of Management and Budget. For more data on expenditures and personnel, see Section 30.

Department of Defense (DoD)—The U.S. Department of Defense is responsible for providing the military forces of the United States. It includes the Office of the Secretary of Defense, the Joint Chiefs of Staff, the Army, the Navy, the Air Force, and the defense agencies. The President serves as Commander-in-Chief of the Armed Forces; from him, the authority flows to the Secretary of Defense and through the Joint Chiefs of Staff to the commanders of unified and specified commands (e.g., U.S. Strategic Command).

Reserve components—The Reserve Components of the Armed Forces consist of the Army National Guard of the United States, Army Reserve, Naval Reserve, Marine Corps Reserve, Air National Guard, Air Force Reserve, and Coast Guard Reserve. They provide trained personnel and units available for active duty in the Armed Forces during times of war or national emergency, and at such other times as national security may require. The National Guard has dual federal/state responsibilities and uses jointly provided equipment, facilities, and budget support. The President is empowered to mobilize

the National Guard and to use such of the Armed Forces as he considers necessary to enforce federal authority in any state. There is in each Armed Force a ready reserve, a standby reserve, and a retired reserve. The Ready Reserve includes the Selected Reserve, which provides trained and ready units and individuals to augment the active forces during times of war or national emergency, or at other times when required; and the Individual Ready Reserve, which is a manpower pool that can be called to active duty during times of war or national emergency and would normally be used as individual fillers for active, guard, and reserve units, and as a source of combat replacements. Most of the Ready Reserve serves in an active status. See Table 502 for Standby Reserve and Retired Reserve detail.

Department of Veterans Affairs (VA)—A veteran is someone 18 years and older (there are a few 17-year-old veterans) who is not currently on active duty, but who once served on active duty in the United States Army, Navy, Air Force, Marine Corps, or Coast Guard, or who served in the Merchant Marine during World War II. There are many groups whose active service makes them veterans including: those who incurred a service-connected disability during active duty for training in the Reserves or National Guard, even though that service would not otherwise have counted for veteran status; members of a national guard or reserve component who have been ordered to active duty by order of the President or who have a full-time military job. The latter are called AGRs (Active Guard and Reserve). No one who has received a dishonorable discharge is a veteran.

The VA administers laws authorizing benefits for eligible former and present members of the Armed Forces and for the beneficiaries of deceased members. Veterans' benefits available under various acts of Congress include compensation for

U.S. Census Bureau, Statistical Abstract of the United States: 2008

service-connected disability or death; pensions for non-service-connected disability or death; vocational rehabilitation, education and training; home loan insurance; life insurance; health care; special housing and automobiles or other conveyances for certain disabled veterans; burial and plot allowances; and educational assistance to families of deceased or totally disabled veterans, servicemen missing in action, or prisoners of war. Since these benefits are legislated by Congress, the dates they were enacted and the dates they apply to veterans may be different from the actual dates the conflicts occurred. VA estimates of veterans cover all persons discharged from active U.S. military service under conditions other than dishonorable.

Homeland Security—In an effort to increase homeland security following the September 11, 2001, terrorist attacks on the United States, President George W. Bush issued the *National Strategy for Homeland Security* in July 2002 and signed legislation creating the Department of Homeland Security (DHS) in November 2002.

The *National Strategy* sets forth a plan to improve homeland security through 43 initiatives that fall within six critical mission areas. These mission areas are intelligence and warning, border and transportation security, domestic counterterrorism, protection of critical infrastructure, defense against catastrophic terrorism, and emergency preparedness and response.

The funding and activities of homeland security are not only carried out by DHS, but also by other federal agencies, state, and local entities. In addition to DHS, there are 32 other federal agencies that comprise federal homeland security funding. DHS, along with four other agencies—Department of Defense (DoD), Energy (DoE), Health and Human Services (HHS), and Justice (DoJ)—account for most of the federal spending for homeland security.

Department of Homeland Security (DHS)—The mission of DHS is to lead a unified effort to secure the United States. This effort is to prevent and deter terrorist attacks and to protect against and respond to threats and hazards to the nation. This effort is to ensure safe and secure borders, to welcome lawful immigrants and visitors, and to promote the free flow of commerce.

The creation of DHS, which began operations in March 2003, represents a fusion of 22 federal agencies (legacy agencies) to coordinate and centralize the leadership of many homeland security activities under a single department. Out of these agencies, the Secret Service and Coast Guard remain intact and report directly to the Secretary. Immigration and Naturalization Services (INS) adjudications and benefits programs report directly to the Deputy Secretary as the U.S. Citizenship and Immigration Services (USCIS).

The Customs and Border Protection (CBP) is responsible for managing, securing, and controlling U.S. borders. This includes carrying out traditional border-related responsibilities, such as stemming the tide of illegal drugs and illegal aliens; securing and facilitating legitimate global trade and travel; and protecting the food supply and agriculture industry from pests and disease. CBP is composed of the Border Patrol and Inspections (both moved from INS) along with Customs (absorbed from the U.S. Department of Treasury) and Animal and Plant Health Inspections Services (absorbed from the U.S. Department of Agriculture).

Immigration and Customs Enforcement (ICE) is the largest investigation arm of DHS. ICE is composed of four law enforcement divisions: Investigations, Intelligence, Federal Protective Service, and Apprehension, Detention, and Removal. ICE investigates a wide range of national security, financial and smuggling violations including drug smuggling, human trafficking, illegal arms exports, financial crimes, commercial fraud, human smuggling, document fraud, money laundering, child pornography/exploitation, and immigration fraud.

The Transportation Security Administration (TSA) was created as part of the Aviation and Transportation Security Act on November 19, 2001. TSA was originally part of the U.S. Department of Transportation, but was moved to DHS. TSA's mission is to provide security to our nation's transportation systems with a primary focus on aviation security.

U.S. Census Bureau, Statistical Abstract of the United States: 2008

Figure 10.1
Department of Defense Manpower: 2006
(In thousands)

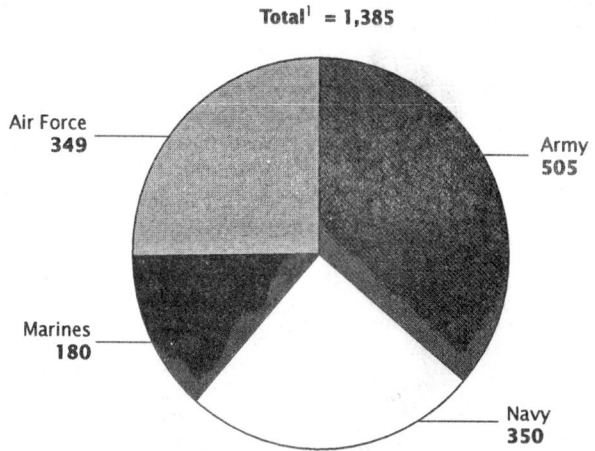

Total^1 = 1,385

Air Force 349

Army 505

Marines 180

Navy 350

^{1}Includes National Guard, Reserve, and retired regular personnel on extended or continuous active duty. Excludes Coast Guard.

Source: Chart prepared by U.S. Census Bureau. For data, see Table 498.

Figure 10.2
Living Veterans by Age: 2006
(In thousands)

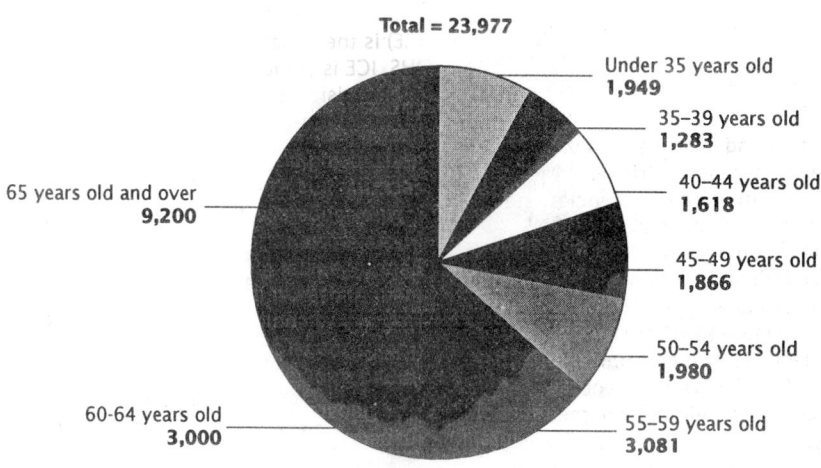

Total = 23,977

Under 35 years old 1,949

35–39 years old 1,283

40–44 years old 1,618

65 years old and over 9,200

45–49 years old 1,866

50–54 years old 1,980

60-64 years old 3,000

55–59 years old 3,081

Source: Chart prepared by U.S. Census Bureau. For data, see Table 506.

National Security and Veterans Affairs **327**

Table 489. National Defense Outlays and Veterans Benefits: 1960 to 2008

[In billions of dollars (53.5 represents $53,500,000,000) except percent. For fiscal year ending in year shown, see text, Section 8. Includes outlays of Department of Defense, Department of Veterans Affairs, and other agencies for activities primarily related to national defense and veterans programs. For explanation of average annual percent change, see Guide to Tabular Presentation. Minus sign (–) indicates decrease]

Year	National defense and veterans outlays (bil. dol.)				Annual percent change [1]			Defense outlays percent of—	
	Defense outlays								
	Total outlays	Current dollars	Constant (FY2000) dollars	Veterans outlays	Total outlays	Defense outlays	Veterans outlays	Federal outlays	Gross domestic product [2]
1960	53.5	48.1	300.2	5.4	2.5	2.4	3.1	52.2	9.3
1970	90.4	81.7	375.1	8.7	0.3	–1.0	13.6	41.8	8.1
1980	155.1	134.0	267.1	21.1	13.9	15.2	6.3	22.7	4.9
1990	328.4	299.3	382.7	29.1	–1.6	–1.4	–3.2	23.9	5.2
1995	310.0	272.1	305.9	37.9	–2.9	–3.4	0.8	17.9	3.7
1996	302.7	265.8	289.2	37.0	–2.3	–2.3	–2.4	17.0	3.5
1997	309.8	270.5	288.4	39.3	2.3	1.8	6.3	16.9	3.3
1998	310.0	268.2	282.4	41.8	0.1	–0.8	6.3	16.2	3.1
1999	320.2	274.8	286.6	43.2	3.3	2.5	3.4	16.1	3.0
2000	341.5	294.4	294.4	47.1	6.6	7.1	9.0	16.5	3.0
2001	349.8	304.8	297.2	45.0	2.4	3.5	–4.3	16.4	3.0
2002	399.5	348.5	329.3	51.0	14.2	14.3	13.2	17.3	3.4
2003	461.8	404.8	364.4	57.0	15.6	16.2	11.8	18.7	3.7
2004	515.6	455.8	394.3	59.8	11.7	12.6	4.8	19.9	4.0
2005	565.5	495.3	407.8	70.2	9.7	8.7	17.4	20.0	4.0
2006	591.7	521.8	417.2	69.8	4.6	5.4	–0.4	19.7	4.0
2007, est.	644.3	571.9	446.7	72.4	8.9	9.6	3.7	20.5	4.2
2008, est.	689.9	606.5	461.3	83.4	7.1	6.1	15.1	20.9	4.2

[1] Change from immediate prior year; for 1960, change from 1955. [2] Represents fiscal year GDP; for definition, see text, Section 13.

Source: U.S. Office of Management and Budget, *Budget of the United States Government, Historical Tables*, annual. See also <http://www.whitehouse.gov/omb>.

Table 490. National Defense Budget Authority and Outlays for Defense Functions: 1990 to 2007

[In billions of dollars (303.3 represents $303,300,000,000), except percent. For year ending September 30. Minus sign (–) indicates decrease]

Function	1990	1995	1999	2000	2001	2002	2003	2004	2005	2006	2007, est.
Total Budget Authority [1]	303.3	266.4	292.3	304.0	334.7	362.0	456.0	490.6	505.8	617.2	622.4
Department of Defense—Military	293.0	255.7	278.4	290.3	318.7	344.9	437.7	470.9	483.9	593.8	600.2
Military personnel	78.9	71.6	70.6	73.8	76.9	87.0	109.1	116.1	121.3	128.5	130.9
Operation and maintenance	88.4	93.7	104.9	108.7	125.2	133.2	178.3	189.8	179.2	213.5	240.7
Procurement	81.4	43.6	51.1	55.0	62.6	62.7	78.5	83.1	96.6	105.4	130.5
Research, development, test, and evaluation	36.5	34.5	38.3	38.7	41.6	48.7	58.1	64.6	68.8	72.9	77.1
Military construction	5.1	5.4	5.4	5.1	5.4	6.6	6.7	6.1	7.3	9.5	9.3
Family housing	3.1	3.4	3.6	3.5	3.7	4.0	4.2	3.8	4.1	4.4	3.8
Other	–0.4	3.4	4.5	5.5	3.3	2.6	2.9	7.4	6.6	59.6	7.9
Atomic energy defense activities	9.7	10.1	12.4	12.4	14.3	15.2	16.4	16.8	17.9	17.4	17.0
Defense-related activities	0.7	1.0	1.4	1.3	1.8	1.9	2.0	2.8	4.0	5.9	5.2
Total Outlays [1]	299.3	272.1	274.8	294.4	304.8	348.5	404.8	455.8	495.3	521.8	571.9
Department of Defense—Military	289.8	259.4	261.2	281.1	290.2	331.9	387.2	436.5	474.1	499.3	548.9
Military personnel	75.6	70.8	69.5	76.0	74.0	86.8	106.7	113.6	127.5	127.5	128.8
Operation and maintenance	88.3	91.0	96.3	105.8	112.0	130.0	151.4	174.0	188.1	203.8	224.8
Procurement	81.0	55.0	48.8	51.7	55.0	62.5	67.9	76.2	82.3	89.8	104.3
Research, development, test, and evaluation	37.5	34.6	37.4	37.6	40.5	44.4	53.1	60.8	65.7	68.6	71.1
Military construction	5.1	6.8	5.5	5.1	5.0	5.1	5.9	6.3	5.3	6.2	8.8
Family housing	3.5	3.6	3.7	3.4	3.5	3.7	3.8	3.9	3.7	3.7	4.3
Other	–1.2	–2.4	(Z)	1.5	0.3	–0.6	–1.6	1.6	1.5	–0.4	6.8
Atomic energy activities	9.0	11.8	12.2	12.1	12.9	14.8	16.0	16.6	18.0	17.5	17.9
Defense-related activities	0.6	0.9	1.4	1.2	1.6	1.8	1.6	2.8	3.2	5.1	5.1

Z Less than $50 million. [1] Includes defense budget authority, balances, and outlays by other departments.

Source: U.S. Office of Management and Budget, *Budget of the United States Government, Historical Tables, Budget Authority by Function and Subfunction, Outlay by Function and Subfunction*, annual. See also <http://www.whitehouse.gov/omb/budget>.

Table 491. U.S. Military Sales and Assistance to Foreign Governments: 1995 to 2005

[In millions of dollars (8,495 represents $8,495,000,000). Department of Defense (DoD) sales deliveries cover deliveries against sales orders authorized under Arms Export Control Act, as well as earlier and applicable legislation. For details regarding individual programs, see source. Table data has been updated throughout]

Item	1995	1998	1999	2000	2001	2002	2003	2004	2005
Military sales agreements	8,495	8,502	11,047	10,820	12,681	12,149	12,647	13,096	9,518
Military construction sales agreements	24	474	301	283	124	72	221	675	329
Military sales deliveries [1]	12,100	13,179	16,888	10,436	12,276	10,434	9,224	10,804	11,146
Military sales financing	3,712	3,420	3,370	4,333	3,535	4,032	5,955	4,584	4,956
Military assistance programs [2] . . .	117	95	268	86	41	46	257	135	293
Military assistance program delivery [3]	20	113	36	12	21	34	106	6	178
IMET program/deliveries [4]	26	50	49	50	54	70	79	89	85

[1] Includes military construction sales deliveries. [2] Also includes Military Assistance Service Funded (MASF) program data, Section 506(a) drawdown authority, and MAP Merger Funds. [3] Includes Military Assistance Service Funded (MASF) program data and Section 506(a) drawdown authority. [4] International Military Education & Training. Includes military assistance service funded and emergency draw downs.

Source: U.S. Department of Defense, Defense Security Cooperation Agency, DSCA Data and Statistics; see also <http://www.dsca.mil/programs/biz-ops/2005_facts/2005%20Facts%20Book%20Final.pdf>.

Table 492. U.S. Military Sales Deliveries by Selected Country: 1995 to 2005

[In millions of dollars (12,100 represents $12,100,000,000). For year ending September 30. Represents Department of Defense military sales. Table has been updated throughout]

Country	1995	1998	1999	2000	2001	2002	2003	2004	2005
Total [1]	12,100	13,179	16,888	10,436	12,276	10,434	9,224	10,804	11,146
Australia	303	207	269	330	308	232	213	185	391
Bahrain	40	62	48	54	335	82	96	78	62
Belgium	8	194	250	58	169	68	71	42	49
Canada	127	111	96	84	110	85	155	145	157
China: Taiwan	1,332	1,420	2,504	784	1,160	1,410	648	912	1,433
Denmark	54	159	157	46	112	23	14	22	41
Egypt	1,479	551	448	805	860	1,875	861	1,345	1,306
France	64	35	248	217	142	206	168	243	153
Germany	257	190	251	131	330	222	243	264	212
Greece	220	397	463	315	448	454	1,324	1,174	364
Israel	327	1,195	1,213	562	766	629	846	878	1,653
Italy	54	43	106	41	185	103	185	283	127
Japan	693	409	439	460	493	467	431	396	416
Jordan	47	47	49	52	80	57	69	106	142
Korea, South	442	836	585	1,400	735	526	554	593	610
Kuwait	471	323	316	321	502	131	143	212	259
Netherlands	153	344	321	161	412	242	224	271	179
Norway	25	119	64	199	192	88	123	80	106
Portugal	88	21	12	20	42	28	116	31	84
Saudi Arabia	3,567	3,800	4,686	2,000	1,891	1,308	1,013	1,224	1,009
Singapore	59	232	549	131	244	421	169	205	210
Spain	193	133	324	141	469	316	159	295	124
Thailand	356	144	133	113	118	168	132	179	92
Turkey	368	532	854	216	466	280	278	290	191
United Arab Emirates . . .	345	26	95	70	16	53	81	136	135
United Kingdom	419	430	365	347	525	386	350	453	390

[1] Includes countries not shown.

Source: U.S. Department of Defense, Defense Security Cooperation Agency, DSCA Data and Statistics; see also <http://www.dsca.mil/programs/biz-ops/2005_facts/2005%20Facts%20Book%20Final.pdf>.

National Security and Veterans Affairs 329

Table 493. Military and Civilian Personnel and Expenditures: 1990 to 2005

[Personnel in thousands (3,693 represents 3,693,000); expenditures in millions of dollars (209,904 represents 209,904,000,000). For year ending September 30. For definitions, see headnote, Tables 494 and 496]

Item	1990	1995	2000	2002	2003	2004	2005
Personnel, total [1] (1,000)....	3,693	3,391	2,791	2,811	2,806	2,764	2,848
Active duty military (including afloat)..	1,185	1,085	984	1,045	1,071	1,055	1,143
Civilian..............	931	768	634	628	631	634	639
Reserve and National Guard........	1,577	1,538	1,173	1,138	1,105	1,074	1,065
Expenditures, total........	209,904	209,695	229,072	276,281	316,648	345,891	381,290
Payroll outlays..............	88,650	98,396	103,447	114,950	122,270	139,490	141,018
Active duty military pay.........	33,705	35,188	36,872	40,945	46,614	50,489	50,482
Civilian pay...............	28,230	29,932	29,935	32,805	35,041	36,234	43,798
Reserve and National Guard pay...	5,556	5,681	4,646	7,523	7,306	10,303	11,087
Retired military pay .:........	21,159	27,595	31,994	33,677	33,309	42,465	35,651
Prime contract awards [2]	121,254	109,005	123,295	158,737	191,222	203,389	236,987
Grants..................	6,329	7,543	2,330	2,594	3,156	3,012	3,285

[1] Includes those based ashore and excludes those temporarily shore-based, in a transient status, or afloat. [2] Represents contract awards over $25,000.

Source: U.S. Department of Defense, *DoD Personnel and Procurement Statistics, Personnel, Publications, Atlas/Data Abstract for the United States and Selected Areas*, annual; <http://siadapp.dmdc.osd.mil>.

Table 494. Department of Defense Payroll and Contract Awards—States: 2005

[(In millions of dollars ($141,018 represents $141,018,000,000); For year ending September 30. *Payroll outlays* include the gross earnings of civilian and active duty military personnel for services rendered to the government and for cash allowances for benefits. Excludes employer's share of employee benefits, accrued military retirement benefits and most permanent change of station costs. *Contracts* refer to awards made in year specified; expenditures relating to awards may extend over several years. Military awards for supplies, services, and construction. Net value of contracts of over $25,000 for work in each state and DC. Figures reflect impact of prime contracting on state distribution of defense work. Often the state in which a prime contractor is located in is not the state where the subcontracted work is done. Undistributed civilians and military personnel, their payrolls, and prime contract awards for performance in classified locations are excluded]

State	Payroll Total	Retired military	Contract awards	Grants	State	Payroll Total	Retired military	Contract awards	Grants
U.S....	141,018	35,651	236,987	3,285	MO	2,196	563	6,981	35
AL......	3,432	928	7,069	70	MT......	402	127	233	47
AK......	1,402	143	1,924	44	NE......	928	238	479	23
AZ......	2,651	1,009	9,355	70	NV......	1,111	510	514	32
AR......	1,122	406	797	46	NH......	351	176	1,048	22
CA......	14,937	3,626	31,065	379	NJ......	1,991	330	6,101	68
CO......	3,144	990	3,690	47	NM......	1,446	401	1,154	24
CT......	765	179	8,753	56	NY......	2,548	500	5,962	156
DE......	407	128	174	24	NC......	6,859	1,406	2,949	76
DC......	1,957	58	3,486	40	ND......	511	62	270	24
FL......	8,819	3,826	10,318	98	OH......	3,049	689	5,460	89
GA......	6,809	1,497	5,741	51	OK......	3,074	539	1,994	31
HI......	3,554	301	1,991	39	OR......	767	358	589	59
ID......	517	200	155	28	PA......	3,030	759	7,483	194
IL......	3,132	566	3,572	105	RI......	608	107	418	18
IN......	1,363	337	4,428	32	SC......	3,288	937	2,001	61
IA......	481	155	867	37	SD......	402	100	368	27
KS......	1,506	356	1,881	27	TN......	1,513	787	2,804	38
KY......	2,602	398	4,300	20	TX......	10,925	3,412	20,697	132
LA......	1,791	445	3,029	57	UT......	1,681	237	2,181	28
ME......	801	190	1,744	23	VT......	137	54	403	11
MD......	5,196	992	10,864	224	VA......	16,386	3,516	26,810	76
MA......	1,096	308	8,333	145	WA......	5,283	1,281	4,453	59
MI......	1,273	383	3,962	104	WV......	414	149	394	18
MN......	695	237	1,703	66	WI......	638	255	2,563	39
MS......	1,726	422	3,294	52	WY......	302	76	184	14

Source: U.S. Department of Defense, *DoD Personnel and Procurement Statistics, Atlas/Data Abstract for the United States and Selected Areas*, annual; <http://siadapp.dmdc.osd.mil>.

Table 495. Expenditures and Personnel by Selected Major Locations: 2005

[In thousands of dollars (7,874,477 represents $7,874,477,000), except for personnel. For year ending September 30. See headnote, Table 494]

Major locations	Expenditures Total	Payroll outlays	Contracts/ grants	Major locations	Military and civilian personnel Total	Active duty military	Civilian
San Diego, CA........	7,874,477	3,537,765	4,336,712	San Diego, CA........	57,657	45,899	11,758
Fort Worth, TX........	6,762,558	257,140	6,505,418	Norfolk, VA........	55,210	46,757	8,453
Saint Louis, MO........	5,342,892	197,110	5,145,782	Fort Bragg, NC........	48,473	42,562	5,911
Washington, DC........	5,146,266	1,620,754	3,525,512	Fort Hood, TX........	47,948	43,150	4,798
Huntsville, AL........	4,892,281	283,842	4,608,439	Camp Pendleton, CA....	39,794	37,609	2,185
Arlington, VA........	4,693,320	2,330,309	2,363,011	Camp Lejeune, NC	34,231	31,532	2,699
Long Beach, CA......	4,364,908	57,625	4,307,283	Fort Campbell, KY....	31,957	29,432	2,525
Norfolk, VA........	4,350,652	2,957,657	1,392,995	Virginia Beach, VA.....	27,210	20,097	7,113
Sunnyvale, CA........	3,542,428	48,981	3,493,447	Fort Lewis, WA......	26,662	24,008	2,654
Tucson, AZ........	3,239,447	326,921	2,912,526	Fort Benning, GA	25,573	22,216	3,357

Source: U.S. Department of Defense, *DoD Personnel and Procurement Statistics, Personnel, Publications, Atlas/Data Abstract for the United States and Selected Areas*, annual; <http://siadapp.dmdc.osd.mil>.

330   National Security and Veterans Affairs

Table 496. Military and Civilian Personnel in Installations: 2005

[As of September 30. *Civilian personnel* includes United States citizens and foreign national direct-hire civilians subject to Office of Management and Budget (OMB) ceiling controls and civilian personnel involved in civil functions in the United States. Excludes indirect-hire civilians and those direct-hire civilians not subject to OMB ceiling controls. *Military personnel* include active duty personnel based ashore or afloat, excludes personnel temporarily shore-based in a transient status]

State	Active military personnel				Reserve and National Guard, total	Civilian personnel			
	Total [1]	Army	Navy/Marine Corps [2]	Air Force		Total [1]	Army	Navy/Marine Corps	Air Force
United States	1,143,303	404,788	446,191	292,324	1,065,227	639,253	229,874	171,480	155,929
Alabama	9,738	5,782	586	3,370	30,324	21,881	18,118	46	2,339
Alaska	18,169	9,020	130	9,019	5,959	4,605	2,512	18	1,731
Arizona	22,485	6,056	4,622	11,807	18,872	9,267	4,047	501	3,688
Arkansas	5,078	243	42	4,793	17,933	3,949	2,896	5	910
California	151,945	7,789	124,659	19,497	87,375	56,197	7,810	31,478	9,917
Colorado	32,483	17,893	929	13,661	17,105	10,623	2,907	37	5,406
Connecticut	7,133	30	7,073	30	8,067	2,417	506	1,014	258
Delaware	3,559	7	22	3,530	5,577	1,459	242	1	1,138
District of Columbia . .	13,633	4,821	4,753	4,059	8,621	15,081	4,165	9,296	913
Florida	58,850	2,475	30,976	25,399	49,222	26,549	3,294	11,436	9,210
Georgia	70,137	52,864	7,097	10,176	36,576	32,040	11,579	4,247	13,983
Hawaii	42,253	15,458	21,944	4,851	11,648	16,307	4,320	9,075	1,980
Idaho	4,230	37	105	4,088	6,804	1,596	756	47	736
Illinois	27,036	608	20,933	5,495	32,824	13,320	7,008	1,532	3,424
Indiana	994	509	365	120	22,906	8,996	1,928	3,109	1,043
Iowa	373	186	131	56	14,839	1,625	1,057	5	518
Kansas	14,865	11,873	171	2,821	15,267	6,391	4,902	1	1,099
Kentucky	38,596	38,176	225	195	15,956	9,027	7,593	198	225
Louisiana	15,953	8,190	1,702	6,061	24,399	6,857	3,642	1,109	1,729
Maine	1,949	220	1,709	20	6,010	6,311	330	5,259	272
Maryland	29,961	6,959	15,539	7,463	23,348	30,955	12,443	14,807	2,217
Massachusetts	2,243	261	507	1,475	19,079	6,556	2,396	228	2,917
Michigan	1,140	448	561	131	23,577	8,107	5,253	23	1,140
Minnesota	633	261	289	83	25,523	2,530	1,486	16	826
Mississippi	11,208	447	4,657	6,104	19,054	8,990	3,520	2,286	2,896
Missouri	16,189	10,960	1,618	3,611	25,598	9,458	6,385	255	1,236
Montana	3,700	27	27	3,646	5,843	1,311	530	–	734
Nebraska	7,070	147	596	6,327	8,617	3,828	1,384	17	2,079
Nevada	9,106	105	1,099	7,902	6,972	2,143	383	283	1,313
New Hampshire	613	8	556	49	4,852	1,056	526	46	324
New Jersey	6,552	928	866	4,758	20,761	13,822	9,571	1,937	1,542
New Mexico	10,965	259	204	10,502	6,583	6,968	3,057	41	3,398
New York	24,658	21,528	2,730	400	41,389	11,248	7,065	147	2,564
North Carolina	101,935	42,605	49,310	10,020	28,895	17,184	6,497	7,248	1,366
North Dakota	7,284	22	6	7,256	5,413	1,819	507	2	1,223
Ohio	7,014	457	596	5,961	36,482	21,483	1,401	73	12,300
Oklahoma	22,568	11,567	2,030	8,971	18,680	21,602	4,784	80	15,502
Oregon	647	215	378	54	13,625	3,333	2,420	19	868
Pennsylvania	2,790	1,037	1,500	253	44,121	25,494	9,152	7,029	1,591
Rhode Island	2,489	104	2,310	75	5,528	4,265	310	3,633	235
South Carolina	36,846	10,539	17,197	9,110	22,293	9,613	3,074	3,555	1,821
South Dakota	3,194	43	8	3,143	5,689	1,200	474	1	679
Tennessee	2,492	333	1,914	245	23,945	5,314	2,507	950	1,035
Texas	109,489	63,647	8,448	37,394	75,411	41,090	21,157	1,351	14,701
Utah	5,304	296	157	4,851	14,118	15,132	2,439	26	11,923
Vermont	73	20	28	25	4,253	593	294	1	263
Virginia	126,205	24,789	88,413	13,003	37,900	79,766	21,317	34,216	4,669
Washington	47,155	24,148	15,935	7,072	27,094	24,285	6,628	14,706	1,993
West Virginia	535	158	340	37	10,453	1,768	1,220	91	439
Wisconsin	513	229	198	86	20,231	2,827	1,846	13	863
Wyoming	3,273	4	–	3,269	3,616	1,015	236	–	739

– Represents zero. [1] Includes Other Defense Activities (ODA) not shown separately. [2] Beginning with the September 2005 report, Navy and Marine Corps personnel who are in afloat duty status at the time of the report are now included in the strength counts of their homeport locations.

Source: U.S. Department of Defense, DoD Personnel and Procurement Statistics, Personnel, Publications, *Atlas/Data Abstract for the United States and Selected Areas*, annual; <http://siadapp.dmdc.osd.mil/personnel/Pubs.htm>.

Table 497. Military Personnel on Active Duty by Location: 1980 to 2006

[In thousands (2,051 represents 2,051,000). As of September 30]

Location	1980	1985	1990	1995	2000	2002	2003	2004	2005	2006
Total	2,051	2,151	2,046	1,518	1,384	1,412	1,434	1,427	1,389	1,385
Shore-based [1]	1,840	1,920	1,794	1,351	1,237	1,262	1,287	1,291	1,262	1,263
Afloat [2]	211	231	252	167	147	150	148	136	127	121
United States [3]	1,562	1,636	1,437	1,280	1,127	1,181	1,182	1,139	1,098	1,100
Foreign countries	489	515	609	238	258	230	253	288	291	285

[1] Includes Navy personnel temporarily on shore. [2] Includes Marine Corps. [3] Includes Puerto Rico and Island areas.

Source: U.S. Department of Defense, DoD Personnel and Procurement Statistics, Personnel, Publications, *Atlas/Data Abstract for the United States and Selected Areas*, annual; <http://siadapp.dmdc.osd.mil/>.

National Security and Veterans Affairs 331

Table 498. Department of Defense Personnel: 1960 to 2006

[In thousands (2,475 represents 2,475,000). As of end of fiscal year; see text, Section 8. Includes National Guard, Reserve, and retired regular personnel on extended or continuous active duty. Excludes Coast Guard. Other officer candidates are included under enlisted personnel. Totals do not necessarily add due to rounding]

Year	Total [1,2]	Army Total [1]	Army Male Officers	Army Male Enlisted	Army Female Officers	Army Female Enlisted	Navy [2] Total [1]	Navy Male Officers	Navy Male Enlisted	Navy Female Officers	Navy Female Enlisted	Marine Corps Total [1]	Marine Corps Male Officers	Marine Corps Male Enlisted	Marine Corps Female Officers	Marine Corps Female Enlisted	Air Force Total [1]	Air Force Male Officers	Air Force Male Enlisted	Air Force Female Officers	Air Force Female Enlisted
1960	2,475	873	97	762	4.3	8.3	617	67	540	2.7	5.4	171	16	153	0.1	1.5	815	126	677	3.7	5.7
1965	2,654	969	108	846	3.8	8.5	670	75	583	2.6	5.3	190	17	172	0.1	1.4	825	128	685	4.1	4.7
1970	3,065	1,323	162	1,142	5.2	11.5	691	78	600	2.9	5.8	260	25	233	0.3	2.1	791	125	648	4.7	9.0
1975	2,128	784	98	640	4.6	37.7	535	62	449	3.7	17.5	196	19	174	0.3	2.8	613	100	478	5.0	25.2
1977	2,075	782	92	634	5.7	46.1	530	59	443	3.8	19.5	192	19	169	0.4	3.5	571	91	435	5.4	34.6
1978	2,062	772	92	619	6.3	50.5	530	59	442	4.0	21.3	191	18	167	0.4	4.7	570	89	429	6.0	41.1
1979	2,027	759	90	602	6.9	55.2	523	58	432	4.4	25.0	185	18	161	0.5	5.5	560	89	413	7.3	46.4
1980	2,051	777	91	612	7.6	61.7	527	58	430	4.9	30.1	189	18	164	0.5	6.2	558	90	404	8.5	51.9
1981	2,083	781	94	610	8.3	65.3	540	60	435	5.3	34.6	191	17	165	0.5	7.1	570	90	413	9.1	54.4
1982	2,109	780	94	609	9.0	64.1	553	61	444	5.7	37.3	192	18	165	0.6	7.9	583	92	421	9.9	54.5
1983	2,123	780	97	602	9.5	66.5	558	62	444	6.3	40.8	194	19	166	0.6	8.3	592	94	428	10.6	55.3
1984	2,138	780	98	601	10.2	67.1	565	62	448	6.6	42.6	196	19	167	0.6	8.6	597	95	430	11.2	55.9
1985	2,151	781	99	599	10.8	68.4	571	64	449	6.9	45.7	198	19	169	0.7	9.0	602	96	431	11.9	58.1
1986	2,169	761	99	597	11.3	69.7	581	65	457	7.3	47.2	200	19	170	0.6	9.2	608	97	434	12.4	61.2
1987	2,174	781	96	596	11.6	71.6	587	65	462	7.2	47.7	200	19	170	0.6	9.1	607	94	432	12.6	63.2
1988	2,138	772	95	588	11.8	72.0	593	65	466	7.3	49.7	197	19	168	0.7	9.0	576	92	405	12.9	61.5
1989	2,130	770	95	584	12.2	74.3	593	65	464	7.5	52.1	197	19	168	0.7	9.0	571	91	399	13.4	63.7
1990	2,044	732	92	553	12.4	71.2	579	64	451	7.8	52.1	197	19	168	0.7	8.7	535	87	370	13.3	60.8
1991	1,986	711	91	535	12.5	67.8	570	63	444	8.0	51.4	194	19	166	0.7	8.3	510	84	350	13.3	59.1
1992	1,807	610	83	449	11.7	61.7	542	61	417	8.3	51.0	185	18	157	0.6	7.9	470	77	320	12.7	54.5
1993	1,705	572	77	420	11.1	60.2	510	57	390	8.3	49.3	178	18	153	0.6	7.2	444	72	302	12.3	54.0
1994	1,610	541	74	394	10.9	59.0	469	54	355	8.0	47.9	174	17	149	0.6	7.0	426	69	287	12.3	
1995	1,518	509	72	365	10.8	57.3	435	51	324	7.9	47.9	175	17	150	0.7	7.4	400	66	266	12.1	52.1
1996	1,472	491	70	347	10.6	59.0	417	50	308	7.8	46.9	175	17	149	0.8	7.8	389	64	256	12.0	52.8
1997	1,439	492	69	346	10.4	62.4	396	48	290	7.8	44.8	174	17	148	0.8	8.5	377	62	246	12.0	53.8
1998	1,407	484	68	340	10.4	61.4	382	47	280	7.8	42.9	173	17	146	0.8	8.9	368	60	237	12.0	54.5
1999	1,386	479	67	337	10.5	61.5	373	46	271	7.7	43.9	173	17	145	0.9	9.3	361	58	232	11.8	54.6
2000	1,384	482	66	339	10.8	62.9	373	46	272	7.8	43.8	173	17	146	0.9	9.5	356	57	227	11.8	55.0
2001	1,385	481	66	337	11.0	63.4	378	46	273	8.0	46.6	173	17	145	1.0	9.6	354	57	224	12.0	55.6
2002	1,414	487	66	341	11.5	63.5	385	47	279	8.2	47.3	174	17	146	1.0	9.5	368	59	233	12.9	58.6
2003	1,434	499	68	352	12.0	63.5	382	47	276	8.2	47.3	178	18	149	1.0	9.6	375	61	237	13.5	60.0
2004	1,427	500	69	358	12.3	61.0	373	46	273	8.1	46.1	178	18	149	1.1	9.7	377	61	242	13.6	60.2
2005	1,389	493	69	353	12.4	57.9	363	45	266	7.8	44.5	180	18	151	1.1	9.8	354	60	225	13.4	60.2
2006	1,385	505	69	365	12.5	58.5	350	44	255	7.6	43.2	180	18	151	1.1	10	349	58	223	12.8	55.8

[1] Includes cadets, midshipmen, and other not shown separately. [2] Beginning 1980, excludes Navy Reserve personnel on active duty for Training and Administration of Reserves (TARS).

Source: U.S. Department of Defense, Selected Manpower Statistics, annual. See also <http://siadapp.dmdc.osd.mil.htm>.

Table 499. U.S. Military Personnel on Active Duty in Selected Foreign Countries: 1995 to 2006

[As of September 30]

Country	1995	2000	2001	2002	2003	2004	2005	2006
In foreign countries [1] . .	238,064	257,817	254,788	230,484	252,764	287,802	290,997	284,967
Ashore	208,836	212,858	211,947	208,479	226,570	265,594	268,214	262,586
Afloat	29,228	44,959	42,841	22,005	26,194	20,208	22,783	22,381
Argentina	26	26	22	28	28	29	28	26
Australia	314	175	803	171	574	196	196	347
Austria	35	18	24	20	24	21	23	25
Bahamas, The	36	24	64	22	25	41	41	36
Belgium	1,689	1,554	1,578	1,458	1,526	1,474	1,366	1,361
Bosnia and Herzegovina	1	5,708	3,116	3,082	3,041	951	263	232
Brazil	50	38	39	27	34	37	39	38
Canada.	214	156	163	148	141	156	150	133
Chile	28	26	337	28	25	23	29	29
China (includes Hong Kong) . . .	30	74	57	61	53	63	67	71
Colombia.	44	224	63	39	54	55	52	104
Cuba (Guantanamo)	5,129	688	557	549	697	682	950	953
Cyprus	24	41	30	28	34	20	43	37
Denmark. . . ₂	37	26	28	22	21	22	19	16
Diego Garcia [2]	897	625	590	548	528	816	683	157
Dominican Republic	13	12	14	55	14	14	11	13
Ecuador	86	20	22	35	33	32	32	35
Egypt	1,123	499	500	433	385	348	410	360
El Salvador	25	27	26	23	21	23	22	24
France	67	67	71	74	93	77	58	60
Germany.	73,280	69,203	70,998	68,701	74,796	76,058	66,418	64,319
Greece	489	678	506	593	583	473	428	395
Greenland	131	125	153	88	139	133	146	137
Haiti	1,616	21	13	15	13	26	14	11
Honduras	193	351	394	402	414	448	438	414
Hungary	16	375	29	19	15	18	16	19
Iceland	1,982	1,636	1,743	1,665	1,747	1,491	1,270	133
India.	27	20	18	19	26	30	31	33
Indonesia (includes Timor)	46	51	43	28	21	24	23	23
Israel	46	36	35	36	36	34	42	48
Italy	12,007	11,190	11,704	12,466	13,152	12,606	11,841	10,449
Japan.	39,134	40,159	40,217	41,848	40,519	36,365	35,571	33,453
Jordan	24	29	18	32	24	25	25	28
Kenya.	40	21	62	43	33	33	32	29
Korea, South	36,016	36,565	37,605	37,743	41,145	40,840	30,983	29,086
Kuwait	771	4,602	4,208	567	(³)	(³)	(³)	(³)
Mexico	36	29	27	31	30	32	30	29
Netherlands.	687	659	676	629	703	701	583	591
Norway	57	81	83	123	86	84	77	84
Oman	27	251	673	31	32	34	36	32
Pakistan	28	22	21	31	33	33	35	32
Peru	26	425	43	41	33	35	37	45
Philippines.	126	79	35	86	107	47	55	93
Portugal	1,066	1,005	1,005	992	1,094	1,006	970	922
Qatar	2	52	116	71	2,997	273	463	446
Russia	60	101	20	78	78	84	44	45
Saudi Arabia	1,077	7,053	4,805	776	953	235	258	282
Serbia (includes Kosovo)	13	5,427	5,679	2,804	319	1,814	1,801	1,721
Singapore	166	411	160	167	171	237	169	164
South Africa.	24	34	31	32	31	31	33	32
Spain	2,799	2,007	1,990	2,621	1,893	2,012	1,660	1,521
Switzerland	26	19	18	19	18	18	17	17
Thailand	99	526	113	125	132	122	114	108
Tunisia	20	12	15	17	15	15	14	14
Turkey	3,111	2,006	2,153	1,587	2,021	1,762	1,780	1,810
Ukraine	5	16	10	13	13	14	11	12
United Arab Emirates.	30	402	204	21	73	149	71	77
United Kingdom	12,131	11,207	11,318	10,258	11,616	11,469	10,752	10,331
Venezuela	35	28	31	27	21	28	21	21

[1] Includes areas not shown separately.   [2] British Indian Ocean Territory.   [3] Total (in/around Iraq as of September 30)— includes deployed Reserve/National Guard.

Source: U.S. Department of Defense, *DoD Personnel and Procurement Statistics, Selected Manpower Statistics, Table 2-4, Deployments.* See also <http://siadapp.dmdc.osd.mil/personnel/M01/fy05/m01fy05.pdf>.

National Security and Veterans Affairs   333

Table 500. U.S. Active Duty Military Deaths by Manner of Death: 1980 to 200⌣

[As of December 31. Table reflects addition of calendar year preliminary 2006 data and revised data for 2004 and 2005]

Manner of death	1980–2006	1980	1990	1995	1999	2000	2001	2002	2003	2004	2005	2006
Deaths, total.	42,108	2,392	1,507	1,040	796	758	891	999	1,228	1,874	1,942	1,858
Accident	22,773	1,556	880	538	436	398	437	547	440	604	632	465
Hostile action	2,677	–	–	–	–	–	3	18	344	739	739	753
Homicide	2,075	174	74	67	37	34	49	51	36	46	49	30
Illness	7,435	419	277	174	150	138	185	190	207	270	281	205
Pending.	375	–	–	–	13	–	1	6	16	19	72	238
Self-inflicted	5,690	231	232	250	145	151	140	160	167	188	150	155
Terrorist attack	426	1	1	7	–	17	55	–	–	–	–	–
Undetermined.	509	11	43	4	15	20	21	27	18	8	19	12
Deaths per 100,000 of personnel strength. . . .	**(X)**	**110.7**	**66.8**	**62.5**	**52.2**	**49.5**	**57.5**	**61.4**	**70.8**	**109.5**	**116.7**	**115.7**
Accident	(X)	72.0	39.0	32.4	28.6	26.0	28.2	33.6	25.4	35.3	38.0	27.9
Hostile action	(X)	–	–	–	–	–	0.2	1.1	19.9	43.2	44.4	45.3
Homicide	(X)	8.1	3.3	4.0	2.4	2.2	3.2	3.1	2.1	2.7	2.9	1.8
Illness	(X)	19.4	12.3	10.5	9.8	9.0	11.9	11.7	11.9	15.8	16.9	12.3
Pending.	(X)	–	–	–	0.9	–	0.1	0.4	0.9	1.1	4.3	14.3
Self-inflicted	(X)	10.7	10.3	15.0	9.5	9.9	9.0	9.8	9.6	11.0	9.0	9.3
Terrorist attack	(X)	–	–	0.4	–	1.1	3.5	–	–	–	–	–
Undetermined.	(X)	0.5	1.9	0.2	1.0	1.3	1.4	1.7	1.0	0.5	1.1	0.7

– Represents zero.   X Not applicable.

U.S. Department of Defense, DoD Personnel and Procurement Statistics, DoD Personnel and Military Casualty Statistics, Military Casualty Information <http://siadapp.dmdc.osd.mil/personnel/CASUALTY/castop.htm>.

Table 501. Military Personnel on Active Duty by Rank or Grade: 1990 to 2006

[In thousands (2,043.7 represents 2,043,700). As of Sept. 30]

Rank/grade	1990	1995	2000	2003	2004	2005	2006
Total	2,043.7	1,518.2	1,384.3	1,434.4	1,426.8	1,389.4	1,385.0
Total Officers	296.6	237.6	217.2	227.9	226.7	226.6	223.2
General-Admiral.	(Z)	(Z)	(Z)	(Z)	(Z)	(Z)	(Z)
Lieutenant General-Vice Admiral	0.1	0.1	0.1	0.1	0.1	0.1	0.1
Major General-Rear Admiral (U)	0.4	0.3	0.3	0.3	0.3	0.3	0.3
Brigadier General-Rear Admiral (L) . . .	0.5	0.4	0.4	0.4	0.4	0.4	0.5
Colonel-Captain	14.0	11.7	11.3	11.6	11.5	11.4	11.3
Lieutenant Colonel-Commander	32.3	28.7	27.5	28.5	28.4	28.1	27.5
Major-LT Commander	53.2	43.9	43.2	44.1	44.0	44.4	45.1
Captain-Lieutenant	106.6	84.3	68.1	68.1	69.5	72.5	71.9
1st Lieutenant-Lieutenant (JG)	37.9	26.1	24.7	29.9	31.1	27.5	24.9
2nd Lieutenant-Ensign	31.9	25.6	26.4	29.1	26.9	25.9	25.2
Chief Warrant Officer W-5	(Z)	(Z)	0.1	0.1	0.1	0.5	0.6
Chief Warrant Officer W-4	3.0	2.2	2.0	2.1	1.9	2.2	2.4
Chief Warrant Officer W-3	5.0	4.5	3.8	4.6	4.1	4.6	4.6
Chief Warrant Officer W-2	8.4	7.4	6.7	6.2	6.0	6.2	6.0
Warrant Officer W-1	3.2	2.0	2.1	2.4	3.1	2.5	2.9
Total Enlisted	1,733.8	1,268.5	1,154.6	1,193.9	1,172.0	1,149.9	1,148.6
E-9	15.3	11.1	10.2	10.8	10.7	10.5	10.4
E-8	38.0	28.8	26.0	27.7	27.1	27.1	26.7
E-7	134.1	109.3	97.7	101.4	99.6	97.8	99.3
E-6	239.1	180.5	164.9	172.4	173.1	172.4	170.3
E-5	361.5	261.4	229.5	250.7	251.1	248.5	248.8
E-4	427.8	317.2	251.0	264.5	264.1	261.7	261.4
E-3	280.1	197.1	196.3	222.1	220.1	201.7	185.4
E-2	140.3	99.7	99.0	85.1	84.3	70.8	83.5
E-1	97.6	63.4	80.0	59.2	55.8	59.5	62.8
Cadets and Midshipmen	13.3	12.1	12.5	12.6	12.6	12.9	13.2

Z Fewer than 50.

Source: U.S. Department of Defense, DoD Personnel and Procurement Statistics, Personnel, Military, Military Personnel Statistics, annual; <http://siadapp.dmdc.osd.mil>.

Table 502. Military Reserve Personnel: 1990 to 2006

[As of September 30. The Ready Reserve includes the Selected Reserve which is scheduled to augment active forces during times of war or national emergency, and the Individual Ready Reserve which, during times of war or national emergency, would be used to fill out Active, Guard, and Reserve units, and which would also be a source for casualty replacements; Ready Reservists serve in an active status (except the Inactive National Guard—a very small pool within the Army National Guard). The Standby Reserve cannot be called to active duty, other than for training, unless authorized by Congress under "full mobilization," and a determination is made that there are not enough qualified members in the Ready Reserve in the required categories who are readily available. The Retired Reserve represents a lower potential for involuntary mobilization]

Reserve status and branch of service	1990	1995	2000	2003	2004	2005	2006
Total reserves [1]	1,688,674	1,674,164	1,276,843	1,188,851	1,166,937	1,136,200	1,119,902
Ready reserve	1,658,707	1,648,388	1,251,452	1,167,101	1,145,035	1,113,427	1,101,565
Army [2]	1,049,579	999,462	725,771	682,522	663,209	636,355	631,856
Navy	240,228	267,356	184,080	152,855	148,643	140,821	131,802
Marine Corps........	81,355	103,668	99,855	98,868	101,443	99,820	100,522
Air Force [3]...........	270,313	263,011	229,009	219,895	219,159	223,551	224,637
Coast Guard	17,232	14,891	12,737	12,961	12,581	12,880	12,748
Standby reserve	29,967	25,776	25,391	21,750	21,902	22,773	18,337
Army	788	1,128	701	744	715	1,668	1,586
Navy	11,791	12,707	7,213	2,520	2,502	4,038	4,514
Marine Corps........	1,424	216	895	685	992	1,129	1,210
Air Force............	15,369	11,453	16,429	17,578	17,340	15,897	10,932
Coast Guard	595	272	153	223	353	41	95
Retired reserve......	462,371	505,905	573,305	601,611	614,904	627,424	637,262
Army	223,919	259,553	296,004	308,820	315,477	321,312	325,288
Navy	111,961	97,532	109,531	113,485	115,210	117,093	118,803
Marine Corps........	9,101	11,319	12,937	13,926	14,319	14,693	15,000
Air Force............	117,390	137,501	154,833	165,380	169,898	174,326	178,171

[1] Less retired reserves.   [2] Includes Army National Guard.   [3] Includes Air National.

Source: U.S. Department of Defense, DoD Personnel and Procurement Statistics, Personnel, Publications, *Atlas/Data Abstract for the United States and Selected Areas, Selected Manpower Statistics,* annual. See also <http://siadapp.dmdc.osd.mil>.

Table 503. Ready Reserve Personnel Profile—Race and Sex: 1990 to 2006

[In thousands (1,658.7 represents 1,658,700). As of September 30]

Year	Race						Sex			
	Total	White	Black	Asian	American Indian	Hispanic [1]	Officer Male	Officer Female	Enlisted Male	Enlisted Female
1990...	1,658.7	1,304.6	272.3	14.9	7.8	83.1	226.8	40.5	1,204.7	186.7
1994...	1,795.8	1,380.9	298.3	22.4	9.0	99.1	223.9	46.2	1,315.8	210.0
1995...	1,648.4	1,267.7	274.5	22.0	8.8	96.2	209.9	44.7	1,196.8	196.9
1996...	1,536.6	1,179.0	249.8	21.5	8.6	93.1	196.9	43.6	1,108.8	187.4
1997...	1,451.0	1,113.7	230.6	21.7	8.4	91.5	188.7	43.2	1,037.6	181.5
1998...	1,353.4	1,033.9	210.4	21.7	7.8	88.2	175.9	40.3	964.1	173.1
1999...	1,288.8	980.0	202.6	22.6	7.6	88.9	166.2	38.4	911.2	173.1
2000...	1,251.5	942.2	199.6	26.7	8.4	91.8	159.4	36.9	879.9	175.3
2001...	1,224.1	912.7	198.4	27.9	8.5	94.3	158.0	36.6	852.2	177.3
2002...	1,199.3	891.3	193.2	27.9	8.8	96.0	152.1	35.6	835.2	176.4
2003...	1,167.1	865.7	187.5	25.4	8.5	98.0	145.1	34.0	813.7	174.3
2004...	1,145.0	845.3	181.3	26.2	9.1	100.2	141.9	33.6	799.7	168.8
2005...	1,113.4	825.4	169.9	26.9	9.5	99.8	139.2	33.3	778.0	162.9
2006...	1,101.6	822.4	163.5	27.7	10.1	101.1	136.7	33.1	769.4	162.3

[1] Persons of Hispanic origin may be any race.

Source: U.S. Department of Defense, DoD Personnel and Procurement Statistics, Personnel, Publications, *Atlas/Data Abstract for the United States and Selected Areas, Selected Manpower Statistics,* annual. See also <http://siadapp.dmdc.osd.mil>.

Table 504. National Guard—Summary: 1980 to 2005

[In thousands (368 represents 368,000). As of September 30]

Item	Unit	1980	1990	1995	2000	2001	2002	2003	2004	2005
Army National Guard:										
Units	Number...	3,379	4,055	5,872	5,300	5,200	5,150	5,100	[1]5,100	[1]5,000
Personnel [2]........	1,000	368	444	375	353	352	352	351	343	334
Females	1,000	17	31	31	38	42	43	44	44	43
Funds obligated [3]....	Bil. dol. ...	1.8	5.2	6.0	6.9	7.7	8.0	10.0	[4]8.3	10.6
Value of equipment ...	Bil. dol. ...	7.6	29.0	33.0	35.0	35.0	35.0	36.0	[5]26.0	[5]25.0
Air National Guard:										
Units	Number...	1,054	1,339	1,604	1,550	1,500	1,500	1,500	[1]1,500	[1]1,400
Personnel [2]........	1,000	96	118	110	106	109	112	108	108	106
Funds obligated [3]....	Bil. dol. ...	1.7	3.2	4.2	5.6	5.8	6.8	6.4	7.6	7.9

[1] Includes units on active duty.   [2] Officers and enlisted personnel.   [3] Federal funds; includes personnel, operations, maintenance, and military construction.   [4] Dollar amounts allocated to the National Guard in the states and territories has declined due to large numbers of Army National Guard personnel on active federal service for the war in Iraq and Afghanistan.   [5] Decreased due to equipment left overseas by mobilized units.

Source: National Guard Bureau, *Annual Review of the Chief, National Guard Bureau;* and unpublished data. See also <http://www.ang.af.mil> and <http://www.arng.army.mil>.

Table 505. Veterans by Sex, Period of Service, and State: 2006

[In thousands (23,729 represents 23,729,000). As of September 30. VetPop 2004 Version 1.0 is the Department of Veterans Affairs (VA) latest official estimate and projection of the veteran population. It is based on published Census 2000 data supplemented by special extracts prepared for VA Office of the Actuary by the Census Bureau. This estimate and projection also uses administrative data and projections of service member separations from active duty provided by the Department of Defense (the Defense Manpower Data Center and the Office of the Actuary), as well as VA administrative data on veterans' benefits]

State	Total veterans [1,2]			Gulf War [3]	Vietnam era	Korean conflict	World War II	Peace-time
	Total	Male	Female					
United States [4]	23,729	22,015	1,714	4,604	7,879	3,045	3,122	6,075
Alabama	417	386	32	91	141	56	48	106
Alaska	66	59	7	19	26	4	3	16
Arizona.	550	507	43	106	177	81	81	135
Arkansas.	263	244	18	53	88	34	34	68
California.	2,204	2,039	165	404	746	295	306	557
Colorado.	420	384	36	100	151	45	40	106
Connecticut	252	237	15	32	82	36	42	66
Delaware.	79	73	6	15	26	10	10	21
District of Columbia.	35	32	3	6	11	5	5	9
Florida	1,747	1,614	133	316	529	271	305	432
Georgia	757	687	70	202	253	76	63	200
Hawaii	102	94	8	21	38	13	13	24
Idaho	132	122	10	32	43	15	15	31
Illinois.	852	799	53	152	273	110	120	218
Indiana	534	501	33	97	174	64	64	148
Iowa.	255	241	14	42	86	35	36	62
Kansas	238	221	16	48	82	29	31	57
Kentucky.	351	329	22	70	119	43	41	90
Louisiana	356	329	28	81	117	42	44	87
Maine	139	130	9	23	48	19	18	37
Maryland	471	427	44	107	153	53	52	127
Massachusetts	462	434	28	62	145	68	79	122
Michigan	804	756	48	133	267	98	105	217
Minnesota	410	387	23	63	143	52	51	110
Mississippi.	236	218	18	56	76	31	28	59
Missouri	538	503	35	98	179	70	69	141
Montana	100	93	7	19	36	12	12	25
Nebraska	154	143	11	32	52	21	19	36
Nevada.	244	225	20	48	87	33	28	64
New Hampshire	127	119	8	21	44	16	15	36
New Jersey	545	515	30	70	169	81	94	145
New Mexico.	176	161	15	36	63	23	21	43
New York	1,094	1,028	67	154	337	156	177	294
North Carolina	756	695	61	174	250	90	83	195
North Dakota	53	49	4	11	19	7	6	12
Ohio.	1,012	949	63	178	327	124	136	273
Oklahoma	347	323	24	74	124	44	42	81
Oregon	357	332	25	62	128	42	47	92
Pennsylvania	1,088	1,025	63	153	343	153	182	286
Rhode Island	86	81	5	12	28	13	15	22
South Carolina	410	377	33	97	141	49	43	105
South Dakota.	71	66	5	14	24	10	9	17
Tennessee	532	494	38	110	185	63	57	140
Texas	1,652	1,517	135	400	570	189	182	399
Utah	147	137	9	32	48	19	20	34
Vermont	56	52	4	8	19	7	7	16
Virginia	738	662	75	216	254	78	69	175
Washington	618	567	50	137	226	68	66	156
West Virginia	182	172	11	31	63	25	25	45
Wisconsin	457	430	28	75	150	58	59	125
Wyoming.	54	50	4	12	20	6	6	12

[1] Veterans serving in more than one period of service are counted only once in the total. [2] Current civilians discharged from active duty, other than for training only without service-connected disability. [3] Service from August 2, 1990, to the present. [4] Totals may not add due to rounding of numbers.

Source: Department of Veterans Affairs, Veteran Data and Information, Veteran Demographics. <http://www1.va.gov/vetdata/page.cfm?pg=2>.

Table 506. Veterans Living by Age and Period of Service: 2006

[In thousands (23,977 represents 23,977,000). As of September 30. Includes those living outside U.S. See headnote, Table 505]

Age	Total veterans	Wartime veterans					Peacetime veterans
		Total [1]	Gulf War [2]	Vietnam era	Korean conflict	World War II	
Total	23,977	17,835	4,647	7,956	3,086	3,151	6,142
Under 35 years old. . . .	1,949	1,937	1,937	–	–	–	12
35 to 39 years old	1,283	979	979	–	–	–	304
40 to 44 years old	1,618	633	633	–	–	–	985
45 to 49 years old	1,866	526	464	67	–	–	1,340
50 to 54 years old	1,980	1,393	321	1,188	–	–	588
55 to 59 years old	3,081	2,938	201	2,872	–	–	143
60 to 64 years old	3,000	2,616	80	2,600	–	–	384
65 years old and over . . .	9,200	6,813	32	1,229	3,086	3,151	2,387
Female, total	1,731	1,175	728	258	74	149	557

– Represents or rounds to zero. [1] Veterans who served in more than one wartime period are counted only once in the total. [2] Service from August 2, 1990 to the present.

Source: U.S. Department of Veterans Affairs, VetPop 2004, Ver 1.0, VA Office of the Actuary <http://www.va.gov/vetdata/demographics>.

Table 507. Veterans by Sex, Race, and Hispanic or Latino Origin: 2005

[In thousands (23,427.6 represents 23,427,600). Data are based on the American Community Survey (ACS). The survey universe is limited to the household population and excludes the population living in institutions, college dormitories, and other group quarters. Based on a sample and subject to sampling variability; see text of this section and Appendix III]

Characteristics	Total number	18 to 64 years	65 years and over
Total	23,427.6	14,401.6	9,026.0
Sex:			
Male	21,803.3	13,113.0	8,690.3
Female	1,624.3	1,288.6	335.7
White alone	19,919.3	11,656.8	8,262.5
Male	18,707.2	10,752.1	7,955.1
Female	1,212.1	904.7	307.4
Black or African American alone	2,361.0	1,859.2	501.8
Male	2,060.0	1,576.6	483.3
Female	301.1	282.6	18.5
American Indian/Alaska Native alone	170.4	132.0	38.4
Male	153.4	116.7	36.6
Female	17.0	15.2	1.8
Asian alone	293.3	197.6	95.8
Male	269.4	176.3	93.1
Female	23.9	21.2	2.7
Native Hawaiian and Other Pacific Islander alone	28.1	22.3	5.8
Male	24.6	19.3	5.3
Female	3.5	3.0	0.5
Some other race alone	373.1	314.2	58.9
Male	338.3	281.8	56.5
Female	34.8	32.4	2.4
Hispanic or Latino origin [1]	1,092.4	832.9	259.5
Male	997.7	746.9	250.8
Female	94.8	86.1	8.7

[1] Persons of Hispanic or Latino origin may be any race.

Source: U.S. Census Bureau, 2000 Census of Population and Housing, Summary File 3, using American FactFinder®, tables B21001, B21001A, B21001B, B21001C, B21001D, B21001E, B21001F, and B21001I (accessed 5 February 2007) <http://www.census.gov /prod/2003pubs/c2kbr-22.pdf> and <http://www.census.gov/acs/www/index.html>.

Table 508. Veterans Benefits—Expenditures by Program and Compensation for Service-Connected Disabilities: 1980 to 2006

[In millions of dollars (23,187 represents $23,187,000,000). For years ending September 30. Minus sign (-) indicates decrease]

Program	1980	1990	1995	2000	2003	2004	2005	2006
Total expenditures	23,187	28,998	37,775	47,086	56,892	59,555	69,564	72,447
Medical programs	6,042	11,582	16,255	19,637	25,188	28,158	29,191	31,308
Construction	300	661	641	466	411	318	480	497
General operating expenses	605	811	954	1,016	1,399	1,252	1,285	1,545
Compensation and pension	11,044	14,674	17,765	22,012	27,995	29,937	32,131	34,479
Vocational rehabilitation and education	2,350	452	1,317	1,610	2,565	2,827	3,033	3,198
All other [1]	2,846	818	844	2,345	-666	-2,937	3,445	1,421
Compensation for service-connected disabilities [2]	6,104	9,284	11,644	15,511	20,855	22,387	24,515	26,551

[1] Includes insurance, indemnities, and miscellaneous funds and expenditures. (Excludes expenditures from personal funds of patients.) [2] Represents veterans receiving compensation for service-connected disabilities.

Source: U.S. Department of Veterans Affairs, *Expenditures and Workload*, annual and unpublished data; <http://www1.va.gov /vetdata/page.cfm?pg=3>.

Table 509. Veterans Compensation and Pension Benefits—Number on Rolls by Period of Service and Status: 1980 to 2006

[In thousands (4,646 represents 4,646,000), except as indicated. As of September 30. Living refers to veterans receiving compensation for disability incurred or aggravated while on active duty and low-income war veterans receiving pension who have permanent and total mostly nonservice-connected disabilities or are age 65 or older. Deceased refers to deceased veterans whose dependents were receiving pensions and compensation benefits]

Period of service and veteran status	1980	1990	1995	2000	2003	2004	2005	2006
Total	4,646	3,584	3,330	3,236	3,369	3,432	3,503	3,582
Living veterans	3,195	2,746	2,669	2,672	2,832	2,899	2,973	3,056
Service-connected	2,273	2,184	2,236	2,308	2,485	2,556	2,637	2,726
Nonservice-connected	922	562	433	364	347	343	336	330
Deceased veterans	1,451	838	662	564	538	533	530	527
Service-connected	358	320	307	307	314	318	323	326
Nonservice-connected	1,093	518	355	257	224	215	207	201
Prior to World War I	14	4	2	1	1	(Z)	(Z)	(Z)
Living	(Z)	(Z)	(Z)	(Z)	(Z)	(Z)	(Z)	(Z)
World War I	692	198	89	34	19	16	13	11
Living	198	18	3	(Z)	(Z)	(Z)	(Z)	(Z)
World War II	2,520	1,723	1,307	968	813	766	718	674
Living	1,849	1,294	961	676	546	506	466	430
Korean conflict [1]	446	390	368	323	306	302	295	290
Living	317	305	290	255	241	237	231	226
Vietnam era [2]	662	774	868	969	1,120	1,172	1,218	1,260
Living	569	685	766	848	983	1,028	1,068	1,104
Gulf War [3]	(X)	(X)	138	334	490	552	630	716
Living	(X)	(X)	134	326	479	540	617	701
Peacetime	312	495	559	607	620	624	627	631
Living	262	444	514	567	583	587	591	596

X Not applicable.   Z Fewer than 500.   [1] Service during period June 27, 1950, to January 31, 1955.   [2] Service from August 5, 1964, to May 7, 1975.   [3] Service from August 2, 1990, to the present.

Source: U.S. Department of Veterans Affairs, 1980 to 1995, Annual Report of the Secretary of Veterans Affairs; beginning 2000, Annual Accountability Report and unpublished data; <http://www1.va.gov/vetdata/page.cfm?pg=2>.

National Security and Veterans Affairs   337

Table 510. Homeland Security Funding by Agency: 2005 to 2007

[In millions of dollars (52,657.2 represents $52,657,200,000). For year ending September 30. A total of 32 agencies comprise federal homeland security funding for 2007. Department of Homeland Security (DHS) is the designated department to coordinate and centralize the leadership of many homeland security activities under a single department. In addition to DHS, the Departments of Defense (DoD), Energy (DoE), Health and Human Services (HHS), and Justice (DoJ), account for most of the total government-wide homeland security funding]

Agency	2005 [1]	2006 [1]	2007
Total budget authority, excluding Bioshield [2, 3, 4, 5, 6]	52,657.2	54,639.4	56,403.0
Department of Agriculture	595.9	597.4	522.5
Department of Commerce	166.7	181.1	194.1
Department of Defense	16,107.7	16,479.3	16,538.3
Department of Education	23.9	24.7	24.0
Department of Energy	1,562.0	1,702.1	1,696.6
Department of Health and Human Services	4,229.4	4,351.8	4,313.2
Department of Homeland Security	23,979.9	25,154.9	26,872.2
Department of Housing and Urban Development	2.0	1.9	1.9
Department of the Interior	65.0	59.5	46.8
Department of Justice	2,690.8	2,995.4	3,089.3
Department of Labor	56.1	48.3	49.4
Department of State	824.1	1,107.9	1,239.6
Department of Transportation	219.3	181.0	178.6
Department of the Treasury	101.1	113.5	108.8
Department of Veterans Affairs	249.4	297.8	243.6
Corps of Engineers	89.0	72.0	43.0
Environmental Protection Agency	106.3	129.4	132.9
Executive Office of the President	29.5	20.8	20.8
General Services Administration	65.2	98.6	73.7
National Aeronautics and Space Administration	220.5	212.6	199.2
National Science Foundation	342.2	344.2	344.4
Office of Personnel Management	3.0	2.7	2.8
Social Security Administration	154.7	176.4	194.0
District of Columbia	15.0	13.5	8.0
Federal Communications Commission	1.8	2.3	2.3
Intelligence Community Management Account	72.4	56.0	56.0
National Archives and Records Administration	17.1	18.2	18.2
Nuclear Regulatory Commission	59.2	79.3	66.0
Postal Service	503.0	(X)	(X)
Securities and Exchange Commission	5.0	5.0	14.3
Smithsonian Institution	75.0	83.7	80.6
United States Holocaust Memorial Museum	8.0	7.8	7.8
Corporation for National and Community Service	17.0	20.4	20.4

X Not applicable. [1] FY 05 and 06 reflect the adjustments made for the Coast Guard (DHS) and reestimates for DoD. See "Source" for further details. [2] Actual budget for 2006. [3] Continuing resolution budget for 2007. [4] The federal spending estimates are for the Executive Branch's homeland security efforts. These estimates do not include the efforts of the Legislative or Judicial Branches. [5] The Department of Homeland Security Appropriations Act, 2004, provided $5.6 billion for Project BioShield, to remain available through 2013. Including this uneven funding stream can distort year-over-year comparisons. [6] The 2007 supplemental and emergency funding levels for the Departments of Homeland Security, Justice, and Treasury include both enacted and requested supplemental funding.

Source: U.S. Office of Management and Budget, Budget of the United States Government Fiscal Year 2008, The Budget Documents, *Analytical Perspectives, Budget of the United States Government Fiscal Year 2008, Crosscutting Programs, Homeland Security Funding Analysis*; <http://www.whitehouse.gov/omb/budget/fy2008/>.

Table 511. Homeland Security Funding by National Strategy Mission Area: 2005 to 2007

[In millions of dollars (52,657.2 represents $52,657,200,000). For Homeland Security funding analysis by OMB, agencies categorize their funding data based on the critical mission areas defined in the *National Strategy*]

Agency	2005 [1]	2006 [1]	2007
Total budget authority excluding Bioshield [2, 3, 4]	52,657.2	54,639.4	56,403.0
Intelligence and warning	349.8	443.0	500.3
Border and transportation security	16,652.3	18,042.3	19,528.1
Domestic counterterrorism	3,974.5	4,535.6	4,980.3
Protecting critical infrastructure and key assets	17,835.9	17,933.2	17,919.7
Defending against catastrophic threats	8,146.4	8,573.7	8,460.6
Emergency preparedness and response	5,645.5	4,992.3	4,935.9
Other	43.8	119.3	78.1

[1] FY 05 and 06 reflect the adjustments made for the Coast Guard and reestimates for DoD. See "Source" for further details. [2] Actual budget for 2006. [3] Continuing resolution budget for 2007. [4] See footnotes 5 and 6 in Table 510.

Source: U.S. Office of Management and Budget, Budget of the United States Government Fiscal Year 2008, The Budget Documents, *Analytical Perspectives, Budget of the United States Government Fiscal Year 2008, Crosscutting Programs, Homeland Security Funding Analysis*; <http://www.whitehouse.gov/omb/budget/fy2008/>.

Table 512. Department of Homeland Security Total Budget Authority and Personnel by Organization: 2006 and 2007

[Expenditures in thousands of dollars (40,568,610 represents $40,568,610,000). For the fiscal year ending September 30. Not all activities carried out by DHS constitute homeland security funding (e.g., Coast Guard search and rescue activities. For complete table footnotes see "Budget-in-Brief," "Overview," "Total Budget Authority by Organization," pages 19 and 20]

Organization	Expenditures		Full-time employees	
	2006 [1]	2007 [1]	2006 [1]	2007 [1]
Total Budget Authority [2]	40,568,610	43,117,414	183,274	185,569
Departmental Operations........................	559,230	626,123	846	846
Analysis and Operations	252,940	299,663	406	475
Office of the Inspector General.................	82,187	98,685	540	545
U.S. Customs & Border Protection..............	7,113,495	7,743,581	42,748	44,414
U.S. Immigration & Customs Enforcement	3,866,443	4,696,641	16,315	16,854
Transportation Security Administration	6,167,014	6,329,291	50,363	49,195
U.S. Coast Guard..............................	8,268,797	8,553,352	47,121	47,798
U.S. Secret Service	1,399,889	1,479,158	6,564	6,649
Counter-Terrorism Fund........................	1,980	(X)	(X)	(X)
Federal Emergency Management Agency (FEMA)	4,834,744	5,223,503	5,708	5,890
U.S. Citizenship & Immigration Services........	1,887,850	1,985,990	10,207	10,122
Federal Law Enforcement Training Center	279,534	253,279	1,001	1,047
Science & Technology Directorate (S&T)	1,487,075	973,109	387	383
Domestic Nuclear Detection Office	(X)	480,968	(X)	112
Legacy DHS Organizations [3]				
Preparedness Directorate......................	678,395	618,577	966	1,033
Preparedness: Office of Grants and Training ...	3,352,437	3,393,000	([4])	([4])
U.S. - VISIT	336,600	362,494	102	102

X Not applicable. [1] Revised enacted total. [2] Excludes BioShield funding, see footnote 4, Table 510. [3] Preparedness Directorate and U.S. VISIT are to become legacy organizations under the FY 2008 President's Budget. [4] Employee totals are included in the Preparedness Directorate totals.

Source: U.S. Department of Homeland Security, "Budget-in-Brief, Fiscal Year 2008;" <http://www.dhs.gov/xlibrary/assets /Budget_BIB-FY2008.pdf> (accessed 15 February 2007).

Table 513. Homeland Security Grants by State/Territories: 2005 and 2006

[In thousands of dollars (2,518,763 represents 2,518,763,000). For fiscal years ending September 30. Grants consist of the following programs: Citizen Corps Program (CCP), Law Enforcement Terrorism Prevention Program (LETPP), State Homeland Security Program (SHSP), Metropolitan Medical Response System (MMRS), and Urban Areas Security Initiative (UASI)]

State/Territory	2005	2006	State/Territory	2005	2006	State/Territory	2005	2006
Total ...	2,518,763	1,677,922	KY........	31,419	24,119	PA........	87,671	49,335
			LA........	42,670	30,437	RI	16,074	7,838
U.S.	2,475,564	1,650,306	ME........	16,609	7,785	SC........	26,284	14,679
			MD........	42,250	24,291	SD........	14,809	7,734
AL........	28,153	15,578	MA........	62,436	41,246	TN........	32,665	13,762
AK........	14,879	8,294	MI	64,075	46,899	TX........	138,570	89,880
AZ........	41,705	20,171	MN........	35,311	13,395	UT........	20,308	8,271
AR........	21,561	8,343	MS........	22,081	8,528	VT........	14,326	10,908
CA........	282,622	231,951	MO........	46,952	42,861	VA........	38,185	16,888
CO........	36,799	21,080	MT........	15,318	7,930	WA........	45,330	32,222
CT........	24,080	13,521	NE........	23,656	21,746	WV........	18,289	13,294
DE........	14,984	10,296	NV........	28,386	20,509	WI........	37,251	24,431
DC........	96,144	54,015	NH........	16,776	7,887	WY........	13,934	7,674
FL........	101,285	100,122	NJ........	60,811	51,983			
GA........	54,918	44,406	NM........	18,499	8,270	PR [1]	25,169	7,724
HI	23,130	12,935	NY........	298,351	183,674	VI........	4,612	2,742
ID	16,805	11,759	NC........	46,609	30,484	AS........	4,279	4,695
IL........	102,593	90,405	ND........	14,376	10,788	GU......	4,706	2,734
IN........	38,996	21,129	OH........	77,823	41,347	NM......	4,333	2,721
IA........	22,291	13,480	OK........	29,974	19,497	MH......	50	–
KS........	21,784	14,274	OR........	34,820	17,956	FM......	50	–

– Represents zero. [1] PR - Puerto Rico, VI - Virgin Islands, AS - America Samoa, GU - Guam, NM - Northern Mariana Islands, MH - Marshall Islands, and FM - Micronesia.

Source: U.S. Department of Homeland Security, Prevention and Protection, Grants, Homeland Security Grants. <http://www.dhs.gov/xgovt/grants/index.shtm>.

Table 514. Coast Guard Migrant Interdictions by Nationality of Alien: 2000 to 2006

[For the year ending September 30]

Year	Total	Haiti	Dominican Republic	China	Cuba	Mexico	Ecuador	Other
2000	4,210	1,113	499	261	1,000	49	1,244	44
2002	4,104	1,486	177	80	666	32	1,608	55
2003	6,068	2,013	1,748	15	1,555	–	703	34
2004	10,899	3,229	5,014	68	1,225	86	1,189	88
2005	9,455	1,850	3,612	32	2,712	55	1,149	45
2006	6,094	769	2,243	92	2,293	30	519	148

– Represents zero.

Source: U.S. Department of Homeland Security, United States Coast Guard, Fact File, Migrants Statistics, Statistics. <http://www.uscg.mil/hq/g-cp/comrel/factfile/index.htm> (accessed 22 January 2007).

National Security and Veterans Affairs 339

Table 515. Deportable Aliens Located by Border Patrol Sector: 2000 to 2005

[As of the end of September. Excludes Immigration and Customs Enforcement (ICE) Investigations' data. Data through 2004 comes from the Performance Analysis System (PAS). The 2005 data comes from the Enforcement Case Tracking System. Definitions for Immigration statistics <http://www.dhs.gov/ximgtn/statistics/stdfdef.shtm>]

Border Patrol Sector	2000	2002	2003	2004	2005
Total [1]	1,676,438	955,310	931,557	1,160,395	1,189,108
All southwest sectors	1,643,679	929,809	905,065	1,139,282	1,171,428
San Diego, CA............	151,681	100,681	111,515	138,608	126,909
El Centro, CA............	238,126	108,273	92,099	74,467	55,726
Yuma, AZ	108,747	42,654	56,638	98,060	138,438
Tucson, AZ	616,346	333,648	347,263	491,771	439,090
El Paso, TX.............	115,696	94,154	88,816	104,399	122,689
Marfa, TX	13,689	11,392	10,319	10,530	10,536
Del Rio, TX	157,178	66,985	50,145	53,794	68,510
Laredo, TX	108,973	82,095	70,521	74,706	75,342
Rio Grande Valley, TX	133,243	89,927	77,749	92,947	134,188
All other sectors.	32,759	25,501	26,492	21,113	17,680
Blaine, WA	2,581	1,732	1,380	1,354	1,001
Buffalo, NY	1,570	1,102	564	671	400
Detroit, MI	2,057	1,511	2,345	1,912	1,792
Grand Forks, ND	562	1,369	1,223	1,225	754
Havre, MT	1,568	1,463	1,406	986	949
Houlton, ME.	489	432	292	263	233
Livermore, CA [1]	6,205	4,371	3,565	1,850	117
Miami, FL	6,237	5,143	5,931	4,602	7,243
New Orleans, LA	6,478	4,665	5,151	2,889	1,358
Ramey, PR	1,731	835	1,688	1,813	1,619
Spokane, WA............	1,324	1,142	992	847	279
Swanton, VT	1,957	1,736	1,955	2,701	1,935

[1] Livermore sector closed July 30, 2004.

Source: U.S. Department of Homeland Security, Office of Immigration Statistics, *Yearbook of Immigration Statistics, 2005.* See also <http://www.dhs.gov/ximgtn/statistics/publications/yearbook.shtm>.

Table 516. Deportable Aliens Located: 1925 to 2005

[Includes all Border Patrol apprehensions and U.S. Immigration and Customs Enforcement (ICE) administrative apprehensions along with criminal arrests for fiscal years 1925 to 2003. Beginning in fiscal year 2004, excludes ICE criminal arrests. The number of aliens apprehended were first recorded in 1925. Prior to 1960, and after 1986, total deportable aliens located do not include nonwillful violator crewmen who violated the conditions of their stay in the United States because their vessel did not leave the United States within 29 days. For purposes of statistical reporting there is no difference between the terms "apprehension" and "deportable alien located"]

Year	Number	Year	Number	Year	Number	Year	Number
1925......	22,199	1946......	99,591	1967......	161,608	1988......	1,008,145
1926......	12,735	1947......	193,657	1968......	212,057	1989......	954,243
1927......	16,393	1948......	192,779	1969......	283,557	1990......	1,169,939
1928......	23,566	1949......	288,253	1970......	345,353	1991......	1,197,875
1929......	32,711	1950......	468,339	1971......	420,126	1992......	1,258,481
1930......	20,880	1951......	509,040	1972......	505,949	1993......	1,327,261
1931......	22,276	1952......	543,535	1973......	655,968	1994......	1,094,719
1932......	22,735	1953......	885,587	1974......	788,145	1995......	1,394,554
1933......	20,949	1954......	1,089,583	1975......	766,600	1996......	1,649,986
1934......	10,319	1955......	254,096	1976 [1].....	1,097,739	1997......	1,536,520
1935......	11,016	1956......	87,696	1977......	1,042,215	1998......	1,679,439
1936......	11,728	1957......	59,918	1978......	1,057,977	1999......	1,714,035
1937......	13,054	1958......	53,474	1979......	1,076,418	2000......	1,814,729
1938......	12,851	1959......	45,336	1980......	910,361	2001......	1,387,486
1939......	12,037	1960......	70,684	1981......	975,780	2002......	1,062,279
1940......	10,492	1961......	88,823	1982......	970,246	2003......	1,046,422
1941......	11,294	1962......	92,758	1983......	1,251,357	2004......	1,264,232
1942......	11,784	1963......	88,712	1984......	1,246,981	2005......	1,291,142
1943......	11,175	1964......	86,597	1985......	1,348,749		
1944......	31,174	1965......	110,371	1986......	1,767,400		
1945......	69,164	1966......	138,520	1987......	1,190,488		

[1] Includes the 15 months from July 1, 1975, to September 30, 1976, because the end date of fiscal years was changed from June 30 to September 30.

Source: U.S. Department of Homeland Security, Office of Immigration Statistics, *Yearbook of Immigration Statistics, 2005.* See also <http://www.dhs.gov/ximgtn/statistics/publications/yearbook.shtm>.

Table 517. **Principal Immigration-Related Activities of Immigration and Customs Enforcement (ICE) Investigations Activities: 2005**

[Data refer to criminal cases only; administrative cases are not included due to changes in reporting. Data in this table are not comparable with data reported in this table for previous years]

Activity	Criminal arrests	Criminal indict- ments	Criminal con- victions	Number seizures	Dollar value seizures
Total, all immigration-related categories....	9,874	6,406	6,763	3,819	95,718,829
Financial investigations [1]	72	34	42	273	16,935,323
Human smuggling and trafficking investigations [2]...	2,713	1,541	1,657	1,712	43,186,452
General and criminal alien investigations [3]....	5,412	3,571	3,741	348	30,363,657
Identity and benefit fraud (IBF) investigations [4]....	1,426	1,065	1,135	1,343	4,584,250
Compliance and worksite enforcement [5].........	251	195	188	143	649,146

[1] Financial investigations refer to cases developed to counteract organizations involved in money laundering and related financial crimes. [2] Human smuggling and trafficking investigations refer to cases targeted against persons or organizations that bring, transport, harbor, or smuggle illegal aliens into or within the United States. [3] General investigations refer to general investigative activities, including those targeting aliens who attempt illegal reentry, have absconded, or commit other crimes in the United States. Criminal alien investigations focus on large-scale organizations engaged in ongoing criminal activity. [4] Identity and benefit fraud investigations seek to penetrate fraud schemes that are used to violate immigration and related laws, or used to shield the true status of illegal aliens in order to obtain entitlement benefits from federal, state, or local agencies. [5] The compliance enforcement program focuses on preventing foreign nationals from exploiting the nations immigration system by developing cases for investigation from Department of Homeland Security systems containing information on the status of students and other nonimmigrants.

Source: U.S. Department of Homeland Security, Office of Immigration Statistics, *2005 Yearbook of Immigration Statistics*. See also <http://uscis.gov/graphics/shared/statistics/yearbook/index.htm> (accessed 8 June 2007).

Table 518. **Aliens Expelled and Aliens Removed by Administrative Reason for Removal: 2000 to 2005**

[As of the end of September. The administrative reason for formal removal is the legal basis for removal. Some aliens who are criminals may be removed under a different administrative reason (or charge) for the convenience of the government. See definitions of immigration enforcement terms, "Immigration Enforcement Actions 2005, Yearbook of Immigration Statistics"]

Violation	2000	2002	2003	2004	2005
Total Aliens Expelled:	1,862,218	1,084,907	1,076,971	1,239,767	1,174,059
Voluntary departures [1]...................	1,675,827	934,119	887,115	1,035,477	965,538
Formal removals [2]	186,391	150,788	189,856	204,290	208,521
Expedited removals.................	85,939	34,557	43,785	41,968	72,911
Administrative Reason for Forced Removal:					
Attempted entry without proper documents or through fraud or misrepresentation	89,935	41,392	52,728	50,727	75,532
Criminal violations	41,155	37,816	40,356	42,835	40,018
Failed to maintain status..............	748	1,257	1,334	1,125	1,042
Previously removed, ineligible for reentry	11,906	13,239	18,595	21,504	18,203
Present without authorization [3].........	40,501	55,733	75,329	86,313	72,229
Public charge	1,461	560	676	857	824
National security and related grounds	13	11	15	12	10
Smuggling or aiding illegal entry..........	494	582	624	729	540
Other	173	175	193	182	120
Unknown	5	23	6	6	3
Formal Removals by Leading Country of Nationality:					
Brazil.......................	1,097	2,585	3,877	5,877	5,938
Colombia	2,089	2,227	2,163	2,249	1,879
Dominican Republic.................	3,444	3,531	3,358	3,527	2,929
El Salvador	4,617	3,902	5,108	6,405	7,235
Guatemala	4,222	4,919	6,848	8,308	12,529
Honduras.....................	4,688	4,843	7,884	8,198	14,556
Jamaica......................	1,932	2,160	2,040	2,263	1,777
Mexico......................	150,656	109,703	139,750	149,289	144,840
Other	13,646	16,918	18,828	18,174	16,838

[1] Voluntary departures verified include aliens under docket control required to depart and voluntary departures not under docket control; first recorded in 1927. Beginning FY 2004, voluntary departures verified include both Deportable Alien Control System (DACS) cases under docket control and Performance Analysis System (PAS) Border Patrol voluntary departures verified-cases not under docket or aliens processed for removal under safeguard. The latter is used as a measure of border patrol voluntary departures verified-cases not under docket. In FY 2004, complete Detention and Removal Office district level figures for voluntary departures-cases not under docket are unavailable in PAS and as a result are excluded for that year. Prior to FY 2004, the reporting of voluntary departures verifed included all locations, Border Patrol Sectors and districts. [2] Formal removals include deportations, exclusions, and removals. [3] Includes those aliens charged under the statutes previous to April 1, 1997, as "entered without inspection" (EWI).

Source: U.S. Department of Homeland Security, Office of Immigration Statistics, *2005 Yearbook of Immigration Statistics*. See also <http://www.dhs.gov/ximgtn/statistics/publications/yearbook.shtm> (accessed 7 June 2007).

National Security and Veterans Affairs 341

Table 519. Customs and Border Protection (CBP)—Processed and Cleared Passengers, Planes, Vehicles, and Containers: 2000 to 2005

[In thousands (80,519.3 represents 80,519,300). For year ending September 30]

Characteristic	2000	2001	2002	2003	2004	2005
Air						
Passenger	80,519.3	79,675.8	71,607.9	72,959.3	80,866.4	86,123.4
Commercial plane [1]	829.3	839.2	768.9	789.8	823.8	866.3
Private plane	145.6	125.7	729.2	132.1	140.0	135.4
Land						
Passenger [2, 3]	397,312.2	381,477.3	333,651.7	329,998.2	326,692.7	317,765.2
Auto [2]	127,094.7	129,603.2	118,306.8	120,376.5	121,418.9	121,654.0
Rail containers.	2,156.5	2,257.1	2,430.1	2,471.9	2,587.6	2,655.4
Truck containers [4]	10,396.6	11,001.5	11,129.4	11,163.1	11,252.2	11,308.5
Sea						
Passenger [5]	10,990.1	11,290.9	12,224.4	15,127.5	22,234.2	26,228.2
Vessel [6]	211.2	215.4	211.6	203.6	142.2	113.2
Vessel containers [7]	5,813.2	5,944.0	7,247.6	9,092.3	9,796.3	11,340.8

[1] A commercial aircraft is any aircraft transporting passengers and/or cargo for some payment or other consideration, including money or services rendered. [2] See Table 1243 for more details. [3] Includes pedestrians. [4] Truck containers—number of trucks entering the U.S. [5] Does not include passengers on ferries. [6] Number of vessels. Includes every description of water craft or other contrivance used or capable of being used as a means of transportation on water, does not include aircraft. [7] Number of Vessel Containers.

Source: U.S. Department of Homeland Security, Customs and Border Protection, *About CBP, Statistics and Accomplishments, National Workload Statistics, 2000–2005.* See also <http://www.cbp.gov/xp/cgov/toolbox/about/accomplish/national _workload_stats.xml>.

Table 520. Prohibited Items Intercepted at U.S. Airport Screening Checkpoints: 2002 to 2006

[Passengers boarding aircraft in thousands (612,876 represents 612,876,000). For the calendar year. Transportation Security Administration (TSA) assumed responsibility for airport security on February 17, 2002, and by November 19, 2002, TSA assumed control over all passenger screenings from private contractors. TSA data are incomplete for 2002]

Year	2002	2003	2004	2005	2006
Passengers boarding aircraft total (1,000) [1]	612,876	646,275	702,921	738,692	744,454
Domestic.	560,107	592,412	640,698	670,418	671,606
International.	52,769	53,863	62,222	68,210	72,847
Total prohibited items	4,185,916	6,167,497	7,103,560	15,886,014	13,709,065
Knife [2]	1,147,843	1,969,003	2,055,306	1,822,846	1,607,014
Other cutting instrument [3]	2,063,729	3,029,318	3,409,724	3,276,936	163,419
Club [4]	13,134	25,578	28,998	20,531	12,295
Box cutter [5]	37,504	21,396	22,428	21,319	15,999
Firearm [6]	983	638	254	(NA)	(NA)
Incendiary [7]	83,086	485,792	697,242	371,711	94,096
Lighters [8]	(X)	(X)	(X)	9,420,653	11,616,217
Other [9]	839,637	635,772	889,608	952,018	200,025

NA Not Available. X Not applicable. [1] Data comes from the Air Transport Association. Dara are for U.S. passenger and cargo airlines only. [2] Knife includes any length and type except round-bladed, butter, and plastic cutlery. [3] Other cutting instruments refers to, e.g., scissors, screwdrivers, swords, sabers, and ice picks. [4] Club refers to baseball bats, night sticks, billy clubs, bludgeons; etc. [5] Box cutter. [6] Firearm refers to items like pistols, revolvers, rifles, automatic weapons, shotguns, parts of guns and firearms. [7] Incendiaries refer to categories of ammunition and gunpowder, flammables/irritants, and explosives. [8] As of April 14, 2005, passengers are prohibited from carrying all lighters on their person or in carry-on luggage or onboard an airplane. [9] Beginning December 22, scissors with a cutting edge of four inches or less and tools such as screwdrivers, wrenches, and pliers smaller than seven inches will be permitted on board. Scissors longer than four inches and tools such as crowbars, drills, hammers, and saws will continue to be prohibited from carry-on bags

Source: U.S. Department of Homeland Security, Transportation Security Administration, unpublished data; 13 April 2007 <http://www.tsa.gov>. Air Transport Association of America, Washington, DC. Annual Operations, Traffic, and Capacity. <http://www.airlines.org/home/default.aspx>.

Table 521. Seizure Statistics for Intellectual Property Rights (IPR): 2002 to 2006

[In thousands (98,990 represents 98,990,000). Customs and Border Protection (CBP) is dedicated to protecting against the importation of goods which infringe/violate Intellectual Property Rights (IPR) by devoting substantial resources toward identifying and seizing shipments of infringing articles]

Item	2002	2003	2004	2005	2006
Number of IPR Seizures	5,793	6,500	7,255	8,022	14,675
Total domestic value in U.S. dollars of IPR Seizures ($1,000) [1]	98,990	94,019	138,768	93,235	155,369
Selected IPR commodities seized by value ($1,000):					
Footwear.	(NA)	2,555	2,049	8,941	63,446
Wearing apparel	9,295	13,889	51,737	16,100	24,321
Handbags/wallets/backpacks	2,927	11,458	23,190	14,955	14,750
Cigarettes	37,580	41,720	24,161	9,649	(NA)
Consumer electronics [2]	5,307	3,780	8,880	8,794	7,057
Toys/electronic games	2,151	1,511	3,971	8,569	(NA)
Watches/parts.	3,919	3,384	2,543	3,071	(NA)
All others	6,154	5,697	13,184	13,550	13,060

NA Not available. [1] Domestic value is the cost of the seized goods, plus the costs of shipping and importing the goods into the U.S. and an amount for profit. [2] Consumer electronics includes cell phones and accessories, radios, and music on CD or tape.

Source: U.S. Department of Homeland Security, Customs and Border Protection, Import, Commercial Enforcement, Intellectual Property Rights, Seizure Statistics <www.cbp.gov/xp/cgov/import/commercial_enforcement/ipr/seizure/> (accessed 7 June 2007).

Section 11
Social Insurance and Human Services

This section presents data related to governmental expenditures for social insurance and human services; governmental programs for old-age, survivors, disability, and health insurance (OASDHI); governmental employee retirement; private pension plans; government unemployment and temporary disability insurance; federal supplemental security income payments and aid to the needy; child and other welfare services; and federal food programs. Also included here are selected data on workers' compensation and vocational rehabilitation, child support, child care, charity contributions, and philanthropic trusts and foundations.

The principal source for these data is the Social Security Administration's *Annual Statistical Supplement to the Social Security Bulletin* which presents current data on many of the programs.

Social insurance under the Social Security Act—Programs established by the Social Security Act provide protection against wage loss resulting from retirement, prolonged disability, death, or unemployment, and protection against the cost of medical care during old age and disability. The federal OASDI program provides monthly benefits to retired or disabled insured workers and their dependents and to survivors of insured workers. To be eligible, a worker must have had a specified period of employment in which OASDI taxes were paid. The age of eligibility for full retirement benefits had been 65 years old for many years. However, for persons born in 1938 or later that age gradually increases until it reaches age 67 for those born after 1959. Reduced benefits may be obtained as early as age 62. The worker's spouse is under the same limitations. Survivor benefits are payable to dependents of deceased insured workers. Disability benefits are payable to an insured worker under full retirement age with a prolonged disability and to the disabled worker's dependents on the same basis as

dependents of retired workers. Disability benefits are provided at age 50 to the disabled widow or widower of a deceased worker who was fully insured at the time of death. Disabled children, aged 18 or older, of retired, disabled, or deceased workers are also eligible for benefits. A lump-sum benefit is generally payable on the death of an insured worker to a spouse or minor children. For information on the Medicare program, see Section 3, Health and Nutrition.

Retirement, survivors, disability, and hospital insurance benefits are funded by a payroll tax on annual earnings (up to a maximum of earnings set by law) of workers, employers, and the self-employed. The maximum taxable earnings are adjusted annually to reflect increasing wage levels (see Table 527). Effective January 1994, there is no dollar limit on wages and self-employment income subject to the hospital insurance tax. Tax receipts and benefit payments are administered through federal trust funds. Special benefits for uninsured persons; hospital benefits for persons aged 65 and over with specified amounts of social security coverage less than that required for cash benefit eligibility; and that part of the cost of supplementary medical insurance not financed by contributions from participants are financed from federal general revenues.

Unemployment insurance is presently administered by the U.S. Employment and Training Administration and each state's employment security agency. By agreement with the U.S. Secretary of Labor, state agencies also administer unemployment compensation for eligible ex-military personnel and federal employees. Under state unemployment insurance laws, benefits related to the individual's past earnings are paid to unemployed eligible workers. State laws vary concerning the length of time benefits are paid and their amount. In most states, benefits are payable for 26 weeks and, during periods

U.S. Census Bureau, Statistical Abstract of the United States: 2008

of high unemployment, extended benefits are payable under a federal-state program to those who have exhausted their regular state benefits. Some states also supplement the basic benefit with allowances for dependents.

Unemployment insurance is funded by a federal unemployment tax levied on the taxable payrolls of most employers. Taxable payroll under the federal act and 12 state laws is the first $7,000 in wages paid each worker during a year. Forty-one states have taxable payrolls above $7,000. Employers are allowed a percentage credit of taxable payroll for contributions paid to states under state unemployment insurance laws. The remaining percent of the federal tax finances administrative costs, the federal share of extended benefits, and advances to states. About 97 percent of wage and salary workers are covered by unemployment insurance.

Retirement programs for government employees—The Civil Service Retirement System (CSRS) and the Federal Employees' Retirement System (FERS) are the two major programs providing age and service, disability, and survivor annuities for federal civilian employees. In general, employees hired after December 31, 1983, are covered under FERS and the social security program (OASDHI), and employees on staff prior to that date are members of CSRS and are covered under Medicare. CSRS employees were offered the option of transferring to FERS during 1987 and 1998. There are separate retirement systems for the uniformed services (supplementing OASDHI) and for certain special groups of federal employees. State and local government employees are covered for the most part by state and local retirement systems similar to the federal programs. In many jurisdictions these benefits supplement OASDHI coverage.

Workers' compensation—All states provide protection against work-connected injuries and deaths, although some states exclude certain workers (e.g., domestic workers). Federal laws cover federal employees, private employees in the District of Columbia, and longshoremen and harbor workers. In addition, the Department of Labor administers "black lung"

benefits programs for coal miners disabled by pneumoconiosis and for specified dependents and survivors. Specified occupational diseases are compensable to some extent. In most states, benefits are related to the worker's salary. The benefits may or may not be augmented by dependents' allowances or automatically adjusted to prevailing wage levels.

Income support—Income support programs are designed to provide benefits for persons with limited income and resources. The Supplemental Security Income (SSI) program and Temporary Assistance for Needy Families (TANF) program are the major programs providing monthly payments. In addition, a number of programs provide money payments or in-kind benefits for special needs or purposes. Several programs offer food and nutritional services. Also, various federal-state programs provide energy assistance, public housing, and subsidized housing to individuals and families with low incomes. General assistance may also be available at the state or local level.

The SSI program, administered by the Social Security Administration, provides income support to persons aged 65 or older and blind or disabled adults and children. Eligibility requirements and federal payment standards are nationally uniform. Most states supplement the basic SSI payment for all or selected categories of persons.

The Personal Responsibility and Work Opportunity Reconciliation Act of 1996 contained provisions that replaced the Aid to Families With Dependent Children (AFDC), Job Opportunities and Basic Skills (JOBS), and Emergency Assistance programs with the Temporary Assistance for Needy Families block grant program. This law contains strong work requirements, comprehensive child support enforcement, support for families moving from welfare to work, and other features. The TANF became effective as soon as each state submitted a complete plan implementing TANF, but no later than July 1, 1997. The AFDC program provided cash assistance based on need, income, resources, and family size.

Federal food stamp program—Under the food stamp program, single persons and those living in households meeting nationwide standards for income and assets may receive coupons redeemable for food at most retail food stores or provides benefits through electronic benefit transfer. The monthly amount of benefits or allotments a unit receives is determined by household size and income. Households without income receive the determined monthly cost of a nutritionally adequate diet for their household size. This amount is updated to account for food price increases. Households with income receive the difference between the amount of a nutritionally adequate diet and 30 percent of their income, after certain allowable deductions.

To qualify for the program, a household must have less than $2,000 in disposable assets ($3,000 if one member is aged 60 or older), gross income below 130 percent of the official poverty guidelines for the household size, and net income below 100 percent of the poverty guidelines. Households with a person aged 60 or older or a disabled person receiving SSI, social security, state general assistance, or veterans' disability benefits may have gross income exceeding 130 percent of the poverty guidelines. All households in which all members receive TANF or SSI are categorically eligible for food stamps without meeting these income or resource criteria. Households are certified for varying lengths of time, depending on their income sources and individual circumstances.

Health and welfare services— Programs providing health and welfare services are aided through federal grants to states for child welfare services, vocational rehabilitation, activities for the aged, maternal and child health services, maternity and infant care projects, comprehensive health services, and a variety of public health activities. For information about the Medicaid program, see Section 3, Health and Nutrition.

Noncash benefits—The U.S. Census Bureau annually collects data on the characteristics of recipients of noncash (in-kind) benefits to supplement the collection of annual money income data in the Current Population Survey (see text, Section 1, Population, and Section 14, Prices). Noncash benefits are those benefits received in a form other than money which serve to enhance or improve the economic well-being of the recipient. As for money income, the data for noncash benefits are for the calendar year prior to the date of the interview. The major categories of noncash benefits covered are public transfers (e.g., food stamps, school lunch, public housing, and Medicaid) and employer or union-provided benefits to employees.

Statistical reliability—For discussion of statistical collection, estimation, and sampling procedures and measures of statistical reliability applicable to HHS and Census Bureau data, see Appendix III.

U.S. Census Bureau, Statistical Abstract of the United States: 2008

Table 522. Government Transfer Payments to Individuals—Summary: 1980 to 2005

[In billions of dollars (263.4 represents $263,400,000,000)]

Year	Total	Retirement & disability insurance benefits	Medical payments	Income maintenance benefits	Unemployment insurance benefits	Veterans benefits	Federal education & training assistance payments [1]	Other [2]
1980	263.4	128.8	62.6	34.3	18.7	14.7	4.1	0.2
1990	561.5	264.2	188.8	63.5	18.2	17.7	7.3	1.8
1995	840.0	350.3	336.5	100.4	21.8	20.5	9.0	1.4
1996	883.1	364.9	361.7	102.6	22.4	21.4	8.6	1.6
1997	912.8	379.3	377.3	100.5	20.3	22.2	11.5	1.6
1998	932.6	391.8	383.7	101.1	19.9	23.2	11.2	1.8
1999	966.5	402.5	401.1	104.8	20.8	24.1	11.4	1.9
2000	1,018.1	424.8	427.7	106.6	20.7	24.9	11.0	2.4
2001	1,117.2	450.4	482.5	109.4	32.2	26.5	13.1	3.1
2002	1,220.0	474.9	525.4	119.7	53.7	29.3	14.5	2.4
2003	1,286.0	493.8	556.6	133.2	53.6	31.6	13.9	3.0
2004	1,365.5	516.8	611.9	143.2	37.1	33.8	15.0	7.6
2005	1,446.2	545.2	653.9	157.8	32.3	36.4	15.8	4.8

[1] See footnote 9, Table 523.   [2] See footnote 10, Table 523.

Source: U.S. Bureau of Economic Analysis, "Regional Accounts Data, Annual State Personal Income"; <http://www.bea.gov/bea/regional/spi/>; (accessed 14 December 2006).

Table 523. Government Transfer Payments to Individuals by Type: 1990 to 2005

[In millions of dollars (561,484 represents $561,484,000,000)]

Item	1990	1995	2000	2002	2003	2004	2005
Total	561,484	840,034	1,018,106	1,219,954	1,286,001	1,365,464	1,446,244
Retirement & disability insurance benefit payments	264,230	350,310	424,810	474,863	493,780	516,826	545,237
Old age, survivors', & disability insurance . . .	244,135	327,667	401,218	446,690	463,406	485,244	512,279
Railroad retirement and disability	7,221	8,028	8,265	8,700	8,855	9,009	9,191
Workers' compensation payments (federal & state)	8,618	10,530	10,845	13,318	14,547	15,145	15,767
Other government disability insurance & retirement [1]	4,256	4,085	4,482	6,155	6,972	7,428	8,000
Medical payments	188,808	336,506	427,689	525,387	556,843	611,871	653,880
Medicare	107,638	179,147	219,612	260,777	277,932	306,115	332,659
Public assistance medical çare [2]	78,176	155,007	205,021	258,560	273,916	299,952	314,984
Military medical insurance [3]	2,994	2,352	3,056	6,050	4,995	5,804	6,237
Income maintenance benefit payments	63,481	100,443	106,616	119,718	133,199	143,216	157,810
Supplemental Security Income (SSI).	16,670	27,726	31,675	34,664	35,703	37,299	38,780
Family assistance [4]	19,187	22,637	18,440	17,684	18,367	18,371	18,348
Food stamps	14,741	22,447	14,896	18,612	22,127	25,631	29,530
Other income maintenance [5]	12,883	27,633	41,605	48,758	57,002	61,915	71,152
Unemployment insurance benefit payments . . .	18,208	21,838	20,680	53,742	53,581	37,081	32,293
State unemployment insurance compensation	17,644	20,937	19,913	52,751	52,364	35,595	31,023
Unemployment compensation for federal civilian employees	215	339	226	331	333	281	224
Unemployment compensation for railroad employees	89	62	81	96	94	79	72
Unemployment compensation for veterans . .	144	320	182	281	365	431	446
Other unemployment compensation [6]	116	180	278	283	425	695	528
Veterans benefit payments.	17,687	20,546	24,935	29,333	31,610	33,823	36,385
Veterans pension and disability	15,550	17,565	21,895	25,933	27,955	29,968	32,376
Veterans readjustment [7]	257	1,086	1,323	1,666	1,936	2,161	2,399
Veterans life insurance benefits	1,868	1,884	1,707	1,723	1,707	1,682	1,596
Other assistance to veterans [8]	12	11	10	11	12	12	14
Federal education & training assistance payments [9]	7,300	9,007	10,985	14,523	13,946	15,045	15,798
Other payments to individuals [10]	1,770	1,384	2,391	2,388	3,042	7,602	4,841

[1] Consists largely of temporary disability payments, pension benefit guaranty payments, and black lung payments. [2] Consists of medicaid and other medical vendor payments. [3] Consists of payments made under the TriCare Management Program (formerly called CHAMPUS) for the medical care of dependents of active duty military personnel and of retired military personnel and their dependents at nonmilitary medical facilities. [4] Through 1995, consists of emergency assistance and aid to families with dependent children. Beginning with 1998, consists of benefits—generally known as temporary assistance for needy families—provided under the Personal Responsibility and Work Opportunity Reconciliation Act of 1996. [5] Consists largely of general assistance, expenditures for food under the supplemental program for women, infants, and children; refugee assistance; foster home care and adoption assistance; earned income tax credits; and energy assistance. [6] Consists of trade readjustment allowance payments, Redwood Park benefit payments, public service employment benefit payments, and transitional benefit payments. [7] Consists largely of veterans' readjustment benefit payments, educational assistance to spouses and children of disabled or deceased veterans, payments to paraplegics, and payments for auto and conveyances for disabled veterans. [8] Consists largely of state and local government payments to veterans. [9] Excludes veterans. Consists largely of federal fellowship payments (National Science Foundation fellowships and traineeships, subsistence payments to state maritime academy cadets, and other federal fellowships), interest subsidy on higher education loans, basic educational opportunity grants, and Job Corps payments. [10] Consists largely of Bureau of Indian Affairs payments, education exchange payments, Alaska Permanent Fund dividend payments, compensation of survivors of public safety officers, compensation of victims of crime, disaster relief payments, compensation for Japanese internment, and other special payments to individuals.

Source: U.S. Bureau of Economic Analysis, "Regional Accounts Data, Annual State Personal Income"; <http://www.bea.gov/bea/regional/spi/>; (accessed 13 December 2006).

Table 524. **Government Transfer Payments to Individuals by State: 2000 to 2005**

[In millions of dollars (1,018,106 represents $1,018,106,000,000)]

State	2000, total	2004, total	2005							
			Total	Retirement & disability insurance benefits	Medical payments	Income maintenance benefits	Unemployment insurance benefits	Veterans' benefits	Federal education & training assistance payments [1]	Other [2]
U.S. . . .	1,018,106	1,365,464	1,446,244	545,237	653,880	157,810	32,293	36,385	15,798	4,841
AL.	16,643	22,141	23,770	9,476	9,776	2,951	247	867	320	132
AK.	2,966	3,103	3,304	676	1,436	367	107	126	17	575
AZ.	15,959	24,223	26,484	10,562	11,674	2,480	295	861	470	142
AR.	10,006	13,691	14,661	5,753	6,196	1,667	271	571	183	20
CA.	114,559	156,257	162,896	56,062	73,724	23,401	4,535	3,125	1,914	135
CO	11,169	15,373	16,410	6,874	6,771	1,533	325	656	220	31
CT.	14,086	17,759	18,384	7,106	8,974	1,376	543	267	112	7
DE.	2,857	3,916	4,220	1,774	1,876	337	105	94	31	3
DC	2,709	3,374	3,647	717	2,176	512	61	110	61	11
FL.	64,208	88,061	93,896	38,439	41,744	8,852	912	2,924	893	133
GA	23,696	33,097	35,815	13,173	15,581	4,678	587	1,262	440	94
HI	3,844	5,004	5,362	2,196	2,190	639	93	197	45	2
ID	3,804	5,374	5,726	2,571	2,209	492	147	205	96	7
IL	41,726	53,715	58,409	22,350	26,557	6,163	1,821	829	645	43
IN	20,081	26,409	28,552	12,360	11,993	2,581	701	529	376	13
IA	10,046	12,811	13,544	6,151	5,553	1,026	312	287	205	10
KS.	8,908	11,594	12,290	5,244	5,057	1,227	274	317	162	9
KY.	15,778	20,645	21,714	8,579	9,158	2,643	428	616	281	8
LA.	16,582	23,056	26,648	7,539	11,203	4,581	690	682	304	1,649
ME	5,307	7,253	7,877	2,759	3,901	695	129	329	61	4
MD	16,981	22,936	24,668	9,251	11,998	2,122	463	595	221	17
MA	26,471	35,827	38,159	11,961	19,637	4,229	1,339	699	281	12
MI.	36,675	47,301	49,939	20,445	21,140	5,181	1,818	821	511	22
MN	15,748	21,653	22,387	8,920	10,258	1,719	656	576	242	17
MS	10,803	14,956	16,771	5,534	7,105	2,618	229	433	246	605
MO	20,904	27,972	29,804	11,736	13,771	2,770	471	725	309	22
MT	3,127	4,018	4,280	1,979	1,603	380	70	177	59	12
NE.	5,694	7,408	7,736	3,309	3,246	668	118	295	96	4
NV.	5,588	8,215	8,843	4,003	3,442	753	239	337	54	16
NH	3,918	5,327	5,476	2,502	2,326	338	84	181	44	2
NJ.	33,092	43,075	45,035	17,820	21,484	2,956	1,777	639	335	24
NM	6,014	8,578	9,105	3,167	4,064	1,131	127	454	131	92
NY.	95,735	128,208	127,043	37,326	69,856	14,674	2,431	1,460	1,250	46
NC	28,108	38,727	41,502	16,064	17,961	4,755	797	1,434	459	32
ND	2,322	2,747	2,902	1,282	1,189	225	45	93	46	23
OH	43,149	56,328	59,265	24,416	26,135	5,859	1,161	1,091	578	25
OK	11,999	15,981	17,112	6,748	7,124	1,911	177	887	242	23
OR	12,243	15,969	16,860	7,530	6,339	1,602	566	612	191	20
PA.	54,928	70,414	75,241	28,719	36,430	6,059	2,170	1,264	572	28
RI	4,748	6,349	6,614	2,382	3,245	574	203	138	69	3
SC.	14,340	19,853	21,105	8,386	8,790	2,587	370	720	235	18
SD.	2,490	3,222	3,424	1,445	1,418	290	28	140	54	48
TN.	21,864	29,325	31,055	11,658	14,076	3,638	483	864	299	37
TX.	59,911	83,272	91,088	31,925	40,380	12,307	1,432	3,233	1,251	561
UT.	4,962	6,756	7,237	3,222	2,808	671	130	191	194	21
VT.	2,245	2,987	3,231	1,198	1,533	300	80	89	30	2
VA.	19,916	27,251	29,303	12,575	11,512	3,292	382	1,213	310	18
WA	20,817	26,970	28,237	12,216	11,250	2,535	833	1,087	277	38
WV	8,894	11,417	12,031	5,323	4,871	1,126	172	412	121	5
WI.	17,902	23,410	24,847	10,759	10,254	2,171	819	599	227	20
WY	1,583	2,157	2,274	1,076	885	170	38	74	28	3

[1] Excludes veterans. Consists largely of federal fellowship payments (National Science Foundation, fellowships and traineeships, subsistence payments to state maritime academy cadets, and other federal fellowships), interest subsidy on higher education loans, basic educational opportunity grants, and Job Corps payments. [2] Consists largely of Bureau of Indian Affairs payments, education exchange payments, Alaska Permanent Fund dividend payments, compensation of survivors of public safety officers, compensation of victims of crime, disaster relief payments, compensation for Japanese internment, and other special payments to individuals.

Source: U.S. Bureau of Economic Analysis, "Regional Accounts Data, Annual State Personal Income"; <http://www.bea.gov/bea/regional/spi/>; (accessed 14 December 2006).

Social Insurance and Human Services **347**

Table 525. Number of Persons With Income by Specified Sources of Income: 2005

[In thousands (207,231 represents 207,231,000). Persons 15 years old and over as of March of the following year. Based on Current Population Survey; see text, Sections 1 and 13, and Appendix III]

Source of income	Total persons with income	Under 65 years old	65 years old and over	White [1]	Black [2]	Hispanic origin [3]
Total	**207,231**	**172,813**	**34,418**	**170,764**	**23,172**	**24,352**
Earnings	155,410	149,093	6,317	127,604	17,268	20,348
Wages and salary	145,904	140,599	5,305	119,302	16,728	19,363
Nonfarm self-employment	12,872	11,900	972	11,122	865	1,280
Farm self-employment	2,416	2,184	231	2,093	184	160
Unemployment compensation	5,816	5,657	160	4,546	937	663
State or local only	5,487	5,338	149	4,337	839	628
Combinations	329	318	11	209	98	35
Workers' compensation	2,013	1,839	174	1,646	259	239
State payments	786	746	39	657	85	116
Employment insurance	771	732	39	612	108	80
Own insurance	20	20	–	18	1	–
Other	469	372	97	389	67	47
Social security, railroad retirement	41,371	10,191	31,180	35,692	4,072	2,509
Supplemental Security Income (SSI)	5,215	4,039	1,176	3,529	1,290	749
Public assistance	2,177	2,114	63	1,253	746	428
TANF/Welfare (AFDC) only [4]	1,591	1,561	29	909	552	314
Other assistance only	537	504	34	328	167	107
Both	49	49	–	16	27	8
Veterans payments	2,527	1,461	1,066	2,166	264	113
Disability only	1,396	955	442	1,200	146	65
Survivors only	263	51	212	230	26	9
Pension only	551	256	295	459	61	21
Education only	67	65	2	57	7	3
Other only	113	65	49	99	13	3
Combinations	137	70	67	121	11	11
Means-tested	399	208	190	327	57	28
Nonmeans-tested	2,129	1,253	876	1,839	207	85
Survivors benefits	2,733	921	1,812	2,481	156	112
Company or union	1,233	264	969	1,139	59	56
Federal government	260	66	194	223	26	8
Military retirement	143	40	103	123	10	3
State or local government	255	75	180	229	20	13
Disability benefits	1,860	1,622	238	1,501	265	178
Workers' compensation	100	90	10	88	12	10
Company or union	492	425	67	394	69	31
Federal government	180	153	27	151	19	8
Military retirement	44	35	10	33	6	1
State or local government	298	257	40	238	47	42
Pensions	16,304	5,463	10,841	14,476	1,262	553
Company or union	11,352	3,459	7,893	10,192	798	405
Federal government	1,812	664	1,148	1,502	214	70
Military retirement	1,117	642	475	964	100	34
State or local government	4,257	1,789	2,469	3,746	359	173
Property income [5]	103,306	83,764	19,542	90,764	6,347	6,379
Interest	97,732	79,278	18,454	85,974	5,931	5,981
Dividends	35,784	28,577	7,207	32,461	1,385	1,176
Rents, royalties, estates or trusts	11,357	8,516	2,841	10,101	585	651
Education	8,278	8,237	41	6,358	1,245	771
Pell grant only	1,899	1,887	12	1,277	467	258
Other government only	1,220	1,214	6	934	204	117
Scholarships only	2,477	2,470	7	2,030	232	180
Child support	5,347	5,331	16	4,146	936	590
Alimony	414	357	57	385	20	29
Financial assistance from outside the household	2,023	1,862	162	1,530	289	224
Other income	1,012	831	181	775	156	63
Combinations of income types:						
Government transfer payments	59,374	26,898	32,476	49,134	7,461	4,684
Public assistance or SSI	7,133	5,915	1,218	4,621	1,956	1,148

– Represents or rounds to zero. [1] Beginning with the 2003 CPS, respondents could choose one or more races. For example, "White" refers to people who reported White and did not report any other race category. The use of this single-race population does not imply that it is the preferred method of presenting or analyzing data. Information on people who reported more than one race, such as "Asian and Black or African American," is available from Census 2000 through American FactFinder®. [2] "Black" refers to people who reported Black and did not report any other race category. [3] Persons of Hispanic origin may be of any race. [4] TANF—Temporary Assistance for Needy Families program; AFDC—Aid to Families with Dependent Children program. [5] Includes estates and trusts reported as survivor benefits.

Source: U.S. Census Bureau, "Table PINC-09. Source of Income in 2005—Number With Income and Mean Income of Specified Type in 2005 of People 15 Years Old and Over, by Race, Hispanic Origin and Sex." See also <http://pubdb3.census.gov/macro/032006/perinc/new09_000.htm>.

348 Social Insurance and Human Services

Table 526. **Persons Living in Households Receiving Selected Noncash Benefits: 2005**

[In thousands (293,135 represents 293,135,000), except percent. Persons, as of March 2006, who lived with someone (a nonrelative or a relative) who received aid. Not every person tallied here received the aid themselves. Persons living in households receiving more than one type of aid are counted only once. Excludes members of the Armed Forces except those living off post or with their families on post. Population controls for 2006 based on Census 2000 and an expanded sample of households. Based on Current Population Survey; see text of Section 1 and Appendix III]

Age, Sex, and Race	Total [1]	In household that received means-tested assistance [2]		In household that received means-tested cash assistance		In household that received food stamps		In household in which one or more persons were covered by Medicaid		Lived in public or authorized housing	
		Num-ber	Per-cent	Num-ber	Per-cent	Num-ber	Per-cent	Num-ber	Per-cent	Num-ber	Per-cent
Total	293,135	76,713	26.2	18,040	6.2	22,801	7.8	59,375	20.3	10,807	3.7
Under 18 years	73,285	28,383	38.7	5,555	7.6	9,733	13.3	21,927	29.9	4,005	5.5
18 to 24 years	27,965	7,873	28.2	1,791	6.4	2,338	8.4	6,242	22.3	1,155	4.1
25 to 34 years	39,480	10,904	27.6	2,104	5.3	3,297	8.4	8,630	21.9	1,391	3.5
35 to 44 years	43,121	10,369	24.0	2,180	5.1	2,707	6.3	7,746	18.0	1,045	2.4
45 to 54 years	42,797	7,840	18.3	2,410	5.6	1,957	4.6	6,143	14.4	1,006	2.4
55 to 59 years	17,827	2,914	16.3	1,133	6.4	755	4.2	2,307	12.9	352	2.0
60 to 64 years	13,153	2,138	16.3	847	6.4	584	4.4	1,666	12.7	346	2.6
65 years and over. . . .	35,505	6,292	17.7	2,021	5.7	1,430	4.0	4,714	13.3	1,506	4.2
65 to 74 years	18,554	3,286	17.7	1,037	5.6	809	4.4	2,544	13.7	679	3.7
75 years and over . .	16,951	3,007	17.7	984	5.8	620	3.7	2,170	12.8	827	4.9
Male.	143,803	35,654	24.8	8,212	5.7	9,696	6.7	27,677	19.2	4,250	3.0
Female	149,331	41,058	27.5	9,828	6.6	13,104	8.8	31,698	21.2	6,557	4.4
White alone	235,430	53,226	22.6	11,241	4.8	13,864	5.9	41,496	17.6	5,233	2.2
Black alone	36,802	17,230	46.8	5,157	14.0	7,297	19.8	12,929	35.1	4,630	12.6
Asian alone	12,580	2,883	22.9	707	5.6	408	3.2	2,293	18.2	413	3.3
Hispanic [3]	43,020	20,604	47.9	3,374	7.8	5,130	11.9	15,470	36.0	2,043	4.7
White alone, Non-Hispanic	195,553	34,203	17.5	8,251	4.2	9,256	4.7	27,295	14.0	3,450	1.8

[1] Number of persons living in households. [2] Means-tested assistance includes means-tested cash assistance, food stamps, Medicaid, and public or authorized housing. [3] People of Hispanic origin may be of any race.

Source: U.S. Census Bureau, *Current Population Reports*, P60-231. See also <http://pubdb3.census.gov/macro/032006 /pov/new26_001_03.htm>.

Table 527. **Social Security—Covered Employment, Earnings, and Contribution Rates: 1990 to 2006**

[164.0 represents 164,000,000. Includes Puerto Rico, Virgin Islands, American Samoa, and Guam. Represents all reported employment. Data are estimated. OASDHI = Old-age, survivors, disability, and health insurance; SMI = Supplementary medical insurance]

Item	Unit	1990	1995	1999	2000	2001	2002	2003	2004	2005	2006
Workers with insured status [1]	Million. . .	164.0	173.2	182.9	185.5	187.9	189.7	191.5	193.1	195.1	197.1
Male.	Million. . .	86.5	90.2	94.3	95.6	96.7	97.4	98.1	99.1	100.0	100.9
Female	Million. . .	77.5	83.0	88.6	89.8	91.2	92.2	93.3	94.0	95.1	96.2
Under 25 years	Million. . .	21.3	18.8	20.3	20.8	21.2	21.0	20.6	20.1	19.8	19.5
25 to 34 years	Million. . .	41.6	39.4	37.0	36.6	36.4	36.3	36.3	36.1	36.1	36.3
35 to 44 years	Million. . .	36.5	40.6	42.5	42.5	42.3	41.8	41.5	41.1	40.8	40.4
45 to 54 years	Million. . .	22.8	29.5	34.5	35.9	36.8	37.6	38.4	39.3	40.2	40.9
55 to 59 years	Million. . .	8.8	9.7	11.8	12.2	13.1	13.9	14.6	15.4	16.2	16.7
60 to 64 years	Million. . .	8.7	8.5	9.2	9.5	10.0	10.5	11.1	11.5	11.9	12.6
65 to 69 years	Million. . .	8.2	8.1	8.0	8.1	8.2	8.4	8.7	8.9	9.1	9.5
70 years and over.	Million. . .	16.3	18.5	19.6	19.9	20.0	20.2	20.4	20.7	20.9	21.1
Workers reported with—											
Taxable earnings [2]	Million. . .	134	141	152	155	156	155	155	157	159	162
Maximum earnings [2]	Million. . .	8	8	9	10	9	8	9	9	10	10
Earnings in covered employment [2]	Bil. dol. . .	2,704	3,406	4,479	4,839	4,940	4,955	5,089	5,403	5,698	6,077
Reported taxable [2]	Bil. dol. . .	2,359	2,920	3,749	4,008	4,170	4,250	4,357	4,564	4,768	5,057
Percent of total	Percent. .	87.2	85.7	83.7	82.8	84.4	85.8	85.6	84.5	83.7	83.2
Average per worker:											
Total earnings [2]	Dollars . .	20,244	24,082	29,383	31,162	31,758	31,990	32,844	34,436	35,819	37,545
Taxable earnings [2].	Dollars . .	17,662	20,641	24,592	25,812	26,810	27,439	28,115	29,088	29,971	31,247
Annual maximum taxable earnings [3]	Dollars . .	51,300	61,200	72,600	76,200	80,400	84,900	87,000	87,900	90,000	94,200
Contribution rates for OASDHI: [4]											
Each employer and employee . .	Percent. .	7.65	7.65	7.65	7.65	7.65	7.65	7.65	7.65	7.65	7.65
Self-employed [5]	Percent. .	15.30	15.30	15.30	15.30	15.30	15.30	15.30	15.30	15.30	15.30
SMI, monthly premium [6]	Dollars . .	28.60	46.10	45.50	45.50	50.00	54.00	58.70	66.60	78.20	88.50

[1] Estimated number fully insured for retirement and/or survivor benefits as of end of year. [2] Includes self-employment. Averages per worker computed with unrounded earnings and worker amounts, thus may not agree with rounded table amounts. [3] Beginning 1995, upper limit on earnings subject to HI taxes was repealed. [4] As of January 1, 2006, each employee and employer pays 7.65 percent and the self-employed pay 15.3 percent. [5] Self-employed pays 15.3 percent, and half of the tax is deductible for income tax purposes and for computing self-employment income subject to social security tax. [6] As of January 1.

Source: U.S. Social Security Administration, *Annual Statistical Supplement* to the *Social Security Bulletin;* and unpublished data. See also <http://www.ssa.gov/policy/docs/statcomps/supplement/2006/>.

Social Insurance and Human Services **349**

Table 528. Social Security (OASDI)—Benefits by Type of Beneficiary: 1990 to 2005

[39,832 represents 39,832,000. A person eligible to receive more than one type of benefit is generally classified or counted only once as a retired-worker beneficiary. OASDI = Old-age, survivors, and disability insurance. See also headnote, Table 527 and Appendix III]

Type of beneficiary	1990	1995	1998	1999	2000	2001	2002	2003	2004	2005
Number of benefits [1] (1,000) ..	39,832	43,387	44,246	44,596	45,415	45,878	46,444	47,038	47,688	48,434
Retired workers [2] (1,000)	24,838	26,673	27,511	27,775	28,499	28,837	29,190	29,532	29,953	30,461
Disabled workers [3] (1,000)	3,011	4,185	4,698	4,879	5,042	5,274	5,544	5,874	6,198	6,519
Wives and husbands [2,4] (1,000) . . .	3,367	3,290	3,054	2,987	2,963	2,899	2,833	2,773	2,722	2,680
Children (1,000)	3,187	3,734	3,769	3,795	3,803	3,839	3,910	3,961	3,986	4,025
Under age 18 . . . . . [5]	2,497	2,956	2,963	2,970	2,976	2,994	3,043	3,080	3,097	3,130
Disabled children [5]	600	686	713	721	729	737	745	753	759	769
Students [6]	89	92	93	104	98	109	123	128	130	127
Of retired workers	422	442	439	442	459	467	477	480	483	488
Of deceased workers	1,776	1,884	1,884	1,885	1,878	1,890	1,908	1,910	1,905	1,903
Of disabled workers	989	1,409	1,446	1,468	1,466	1,482	1,526	1,571	1,599	1,633
Widowed mothers [7] (1,000)	304	275	221	212	203	197	194	190	184	178
Widows and widowers [2,8] (1,000) . .	5,111	5,226	4,990	4,944	4,901	4,828	4,771	4,707	4,643	4,569
Parents [2] (1,000)	6	4	3	3	3	3	2	2	2	2
Special benefits [9] (1,000)	7	1	(Z)	(Z)	(Z)	(Z)	(Z)	(Z)	(Z)	(Z)
AVERAGE MONTHLY BENEFIT, CURRENT DOLLARS										
Retired workers [2]	603	720	780	804	844	874	895	922	955	1,002
Retired worker and wife [2]	1,027	1,221	1,318	1,357	1,420	1,466	1,494	1,535	1,586	1,660
Disabled workers [3]	587	682	733	754	786	814	834	862	894	938
Wives and husbands [2,4]	298	354	386	398	416	430	439	450	464	485
Children of retired workers	259	322	358	373	395	413	426	444	465	493
Children of deceased workers	406	469	510	526	550	571	585	603	625	656
Children of disabled workers	164	183	208	216	228	238	245	254	265	279
Widowed mothers [7]	409	478	545	566	595	621	640	664	689	725
Widows and widowers, nondisabled [2]	556	680	749	775	810	841	861	888	920	967
Parents [2]	482	591	651	674	704	729	753	779	810	851
Special benefits [9]	167	192	204	209	217	224	227	232	238	247
AVERAGE MONTHLY BENEFIT, CONSTANT (2005) DOLLARS [10]										
Retired workers [2]	887	923	936	940	955	974	974	985	988	1,002
Retired worker and wife [2]	1,511	1,565	1,583	1,587	1,606	1,632	1,625	1,639	1,640	1,660
Disabled workers [3]	863	874	880	882	889	907	907	920	925	938
Wives and husbands [2,4]	438	454	464	465	471	479	478	480	480	485
Children of deceased workers	597	601	612	615	622	636	636	644	647	656
Widowed mothers [7]	602	613	654	662	673	691	696	709	713	725
Widows and widowers, nondisabled [2]	818	872	899	906	916	936	937	948	952	967
Number of benefits awarded (1,000) . . . . [2]	3,717	3,882	3,800	3,917	4,290	4,162	4,336	4,322	4,459	4,672
Retired workers [2]	1,665	1,609	1,631	1,690	1,961	1,779	1,813	1,791	1,883	2,000
Disabled workers [3]	468	646	608	620	622	691	750	777	796	830
Wives and husbands [2,4]	379	322	311	322	385	358	363	353	367	379
Children . . . . . . [7]	695	809	763	773	777	796	846	852	859	908
Widowed mothers [7]	58	52	42	42	40	41	41	39	40	38
Widows and widowers [2,8]	452	445	444	470	505	496	523	508	514	517
Parents [2]	(Z)	(Z)	(Z)	(Z)	(Z)	(Z)	(Z)	(Z)	(Z)	(Z)
Special benefits [9]	(Z)	(Z)	(Z)	(Z)	(Z)	(Z)	(Z)	(Z)	(Z)	(Z)
BENEFIT PAYMENTS DURING YEAR (bil. dol.)										
Total [11]	247.8	332.6	375.0	385.8	407.6	431.9	453.8	470.8	493.3	520.8
Monthly benefits [12]	247.6	332.4	374.8	385.6	407.4	431.7	453.6	470.6	493.1	520.6
Retired workers [2]	156.8	205.3	232.3	238.5	253.5	269.0	281.6	291.5	304.5	321.7
Disabled workers [3]	22.1	36.6	43.5	46.5	49.8	54.2	59.9	64.8	71.7	78.4
Wives and husbands [2,4]	14.5	17.9	18.9	18.8	19.4	19.9	20.3	20.4	20.6	20.5
Children	12.0	16.1	18.1	18.6	19.3	20.4	21.5	22.3	23.3	24.5
Under age 18	9.0	11.9	13.3	13.6	14.1	14.8	15.7	16.2	17.0	17.9
Disabled children [5]	2.5	3.6	4.2	4.4	4.6	4.8	5.1	5.2	5.5	5.8
Students [6]	0.5	0.6	0.7	0.7	0.7	0.7	0.8	0.8	0.9	0.8
Of retired workers	1.3	1.7	1.9	2.0	2.1	2.3	2.5	2.6	2.7	2.9
Of deceased workers	8.6	10.7	11.9	12.1	12.5	13.1	13.7	14.1	14.5	15.1
Of disabled workers	2.2	3.7	4.2	4.4	4.7	4.9	5.3	5.7	6.1	6.5
Widowed mothers [7]	1.4	1.6	1.4	1.4	1.4	1.4	1.5	1.5	1.5	1.5
Widows and widowers [2,8]	40.7	54.8	60.5	61.8	63.9	66.8	68.8	70.1	71.7	73.4
Parents [2]	(Z)	(Z)	(Z)	(Z)	(Z)	(Z)	(Z)	(Z)	(Z)	(Z)
Special benefits [9]	(Z)	(Z)	(Z)	(Z)	(Z)	(Z)	(Z)	(Z)	(Z)	(Z)
Lump sum	0.2	0.2	0.2	0.2	0.2	0.2	0.2	0.2	0.2	0.2

Z Fewer than 500 or less than $50 million.   [1] Number of benefit payments in current-payment status, i.e., actually being made at a specified time with no deductions or with deductions amounting to less than a month's benefit.   [2] 62 years and over.   [3] Disabled workers under age 65.   [4] Includes wife beneficiaries with entitled children in their care and entitled divorced wives.   [5] 18 years old and over. Disability began before age 18.   [6] Full-time students aged 18 and 19.   [7] Includes surviving divorced mothers with entitled children in their care and widowed fathers with entitled children in their care.   [8] Includes widows aged 60–61, surviving divorced wives aged 60 and over, disabled widows and widowers aged 50 and over; and widowers aged 60–61.   [9] Benefits for persons aged 72 and over not insured under regular or transitional provisions of Social Security Act.   [10] Constant dollar figures are based on the consumer price index (CPI-U) for December as published by the U.S. Bureau of Labor Statistics.   [11] Represents total disbursements of benefit checks by the U.S. Department of the Treasury during the years specified.   [12] Distribution by type estimated.

Source: U.S. Social Security Administration, *Annual Statistical Supplement* to the *Social Security Bulletin*; and unpublished data.

Table 529. Social Security—Beneficiaries, Annual Payments, and Average Monthly Benefit, 1990 to 2005, and by State and Other Areas, 2005

[Number of beneficiaries in current-payment status (39,832 represents 39,832,000) and average monthly benefit as of December. Data based on 10 percent sample of administrative records. See also headnote, Table 528, and Appendix III]

Year, state, and other area	Number of beneficiaries (1,000)				Annual payments[2] (mil. dol.)				Average monthly benefit (dol.)		
	Retired workers and dependents Total	dependents[1]	Survivors	Disabled workers and dependents	Total	Retired workers and dependents[1]	Survivors	Disabled workers and dependents	Retired workers[3]	Disabled workers[4]	Widows and widowers[4]
1990	39,832	28,369	7,197	4,266	247,796	172,042	50,951	24,803	603	587	557
1995	43,380	30,139	7,379	5,862	332,581	224,381	67,302	40,898	720	682	680
2000	45,417	31,761	6,981	6,675	407,431	274,645	77,848	54,938	845	787	810
2003	46,448	32,360	6,870	7,220	470,546	314,024	85,621	70,899	922	862	888
2004	47,707	33,025	6,730	7,952	493,078	327,139	87,737	78,202	955	894	920
2005, total[5]	48,446	33,488	6,650	8,307	520,561	345,094	90,073	85,394	1,002	938	967
United States	47,255	32,727	6,431	8,097	512,221	340,499	88,098	83,623	(NA)	(NA)	(NA)
Alabama	904	546	140	218	9,259	5,370	1,741	2,149	960	907	897
Alaska	65	42	10	13	659	415	120	124	962	912	913
Arizona	919	654	110	155	10,030	6,887	1,505	1,638	1,023	970	1,002
Arkansas	558	346	80	132	5,564	3,332	961	1,271	935	887	868
California	4,460	3,193	571	697	48,106	32,751	7,946	7,409	1,003	955	995
Colorado	588	419	77	92	6,227	4,206	1,065	955	982	934	977
Connecticut	585	435	68	82	6,917	4,994	1,029	894	1,096	981	1,072
Delaware	152	108	19	26	1,725	1,173	268	284	1,054	984	1,040
District of Columbia	71	49	11	11	674	446	116	112	862	857	806
Florida	3,424	2,526	401	497	36,891	26,145	5,567	5,178	999	943	993
Georgia	1,231	799	182	250	12,846	8,048	2,261	2,537	978	924	913
Hawaii	203	157	23	23	2,162	1,607	302	253	990	964	945
Idaho	228	162	28	37	2,379	1,618	388	373	980	913	985
Illinois	1,898	1,347	271	281	21,364	14,497	3,899	2,967	1,040	966	1,031
Indiana	1,055	728	145	182	11,872	7,937	2,083	1,852	1,053	938	1,030
Iowa	548	397	76	75	5,946	4,102	1,087	757	1,000	896	992
Kansas	451	320	61	70	4,974	3,406	879	690	1,027	909	1,025
Kentucky	799	468	123	207	8,129	4,509	1,547	2,073	949	924	881
Louisiana	716	429	140	146	7,378	4,109	1,782	1,488	937	937	891
Maine	269	178	33	59	2,686	1,702	435	549	926	863	924
Maryland	772	549	110	113	8,512	5,766	1,516	1,231	1,012	967	986
Massachusetts	1,072	748	128	196	11,691	7,865	1,829	1,997	1,009	924	1,001
Michigan	1,743	1,189	247	306	20,106	13,193	3,599	3,315	1,080	994	1,043
Minnesota	786	575	100	112	8,525	5,959	1,425	1,140	1,004	922	988
Mississippi	552	322	88	142	5,395	3,052	998	1,344	920	880	838
Missouri	1,064	712	144	207	11,281	7,289	1,929	2,063	990	913	968
Montana	169	122	23	25	1,748	1,193	305	250	959	903	955
Nebraska	294	212	39	43	3,120	2,153	549	418	985	889	994
Nevada	348	254	38	55	3,830	2,666	538	626	1,008	1,008	1,012
New Hampshire	226	157	26	42	2,485	1,686	369	430	1,028	943	1,023
New Jersey	1,379	1,012	169	197	16,474	11,675	2,565	2,234	1,105	1,023	1,065
New Mexico	311	209	44	58	3,079	1,983	526	570	935	902	895
New York	3,064	2,170	378	516	34,797	23,800	5,427	5,570	1,059	989	1,020
North Carolina	1,511	1,006	192	313	15,856	10,269	2,400	3,187	984	921	907
North Dakota	115	82	19	14	1,174	780	257	137	935	873	927
Ohio	1,965	1,352	308	305	21,546	14,077	4,377	3,091	1,016	914	1,000
Oklahoma	635	427	94	114	6,606	4,226	1,227	1,152	962	924	939
Oregon	625	455	76	94	6,837	4,741	1,095	1,001	1,011	939	1,017
Pennsylvania	2,425	1,708	341	375	27,072	18,227	4,953	3,892	1,030	954	1,014
Rhode Island	192	134	21	36	2,089	1,418	302	368	1,006	913	1,013
South Carolina	774	505	104	164	8,100	5,139	1,283	1,677	982	932	904
South Dakota	142	103	21	19	1,415	966	269	180	920	877	916
Tennessee	1,098	708	159	231	11,406	7,109	2,010	2,288	978	904	923
Texas	2,955	1,990	475	490	30,684	19,643	6,178	4,864	975	924	940
Utah	272	198	36	39	2,913	2,037	495	380	1,009	928	1,033
Vermont	112	78	14	20	1,184	802	184	198	995	889	964
Virginia	1,139	772	155	212	12,115	7,883	2,045	2,187	989	945	930
Washington	937	674	113	150	10,474	7,218	1,646	1,611	1,042	952	1,032
West Virginia	413	239	70	104	4,417	2,377	932	1,108	988	981	927
Wisconsin	952	694	120	138	10,551	7,395	1,733	1,423	1,028	939	1,020
Wyoming	84	61	11	13	908	629	149	130	999	936	1,009
Puerto Rico	713	405	119	189	5,234	2,641	1,010	1,583	669	806	594
Guam	13	9	2	2	93	56	22	15	672	809	687
American Samoa	6	2	2	2	38	12	12	14	584	701	576
Virgin Islands	16	12	2	2	145	104	23	19	866	945	752
Northern Mariana Islands	2	1	1	(Z)	13	7	5	1	563	441	391
Abroad	442	332	94	16	2,817	1,775	903	139	565	819	627

NA Not available. Z Less than 500. [1] Includes special benefits for persons aged 72 and over not insured under regular or transitional provisions of Social Security Act. [2] Unnegotiated checks not deducted. 1990 and 1995 include lump-sum payments to survivors of deceased workers. [3] Excludes persons with special benefits. [4] Nondisabled only. [5] Includes those with state or area unknown.

Source: U.S. Social Security Administration, *Annual Statistical Supplement to the Social Security Bulletin*.

Social Insurance and Human Services 351

Table 530. **Social Security Trust Funds: 1990 to 2006**

[In billions of dollars (272.4 represents $272,400,000,000)]

Type of trust fund	1990	1995	2000	2001	2002	2003	2004	2005	2006
Old-age and survivors insurance (OASI):									
Net contribution income [1]	272.4	310.1	433.0	453.4	468.1	468.6	487.4	520.7	534.8
Interest received [2]	16.4	32.8	57.5	64.7	71.2	75.2	79.0	84.0	91.8
Benefit payments [3]	223.0	291.6	352.7	372.3	388.1	399.8	415.0	435.4	454.5
Assets, end of year	214.2	458.5	931.0	1,071.5	1,217.5	1,355.3	1,500.6	1,663.0	1,844.3
Disability insurance (DI):									
Net contribution income [1]	28.7	54.7	71.8	75.7	78.2	78.4	81.4	87.2	90.8
Interest received [2]	0.9	2.2	6.9	8.2	9.2	9.7	10.0	10.3	10.6
Benefit payments [3]	24.8	40.9	55.0	59.6	65.7	70.9	78.2	85.4	91.7
Assets, end of year	11.1	37.6	118.5	141.0	160.5	175.4	186.2	195.6	203.8

[1] Includes deposits by states and deductions for refund of estimated employee-tax overpayment. Includes government contributions on deemed wage credits for military service in 1957–2001. Includes taxation of benefits. [2] In 1990, includes interest on advance tax transfers. Includes interest on reimbursement for unnegotiated checks. [3] Includes payments for vocational rehabilitation services furnished to disabled persons receiving benefits because of their disabilities. Amounts reflect deductions for unnegotiated benefit checks.

Source: U.S. Social Security Administration, *Annual Report of Board of Trustees, OASI, DI, HI, and SMI Trust Funds*; <http://www.ssa.gov/OACT/TR/TR07>. Also published in *Social Security Bulletin*, quarterly.

Table 531. **Public Employee Retirement Systems—Participants and Finances: 1980 to 2005**

[4,629 represents 4,629,000. For fiscal year of retirement system, except data for the Thrift Savings Plan are for calendar year. For a definition of defined benefit, see headnote, Table 535]

Retirement plan	Unit	1980	1990	1995	2000	2001	2002	2003	2004	2005, proj.
TOTAL PARTICIPANTS [1]										
Federal retirement systems:										
Defined benefit:										
Civil Service Retirement System	1,000...	4,629	4,167	3,731	3,256	3,286	3,201	3,133	3,035	2,958
Federal Employees Retirement System [2]	1,000...	(X)	1,180	1,512	1,935	1,935	2,019	2,140	2,104	2,196
Military Service Retirement System [3]	1,000...	3,380	3,763	3,387	3,397	3,418	3,453	3,457	3,545	3,536
Thrift Savings Plan [4]	1,000...	(X)	1,625	2,195	2,500	2,600	3,000	3,200	3,400	3,600
State and local retirement systems [5,6]	1,000...	(NA)	16,858	14,734	16,834	17,021	17,264	17,650	17,890	17,932
ACTIVE PARTICIPANTS										
Federal retirement systems:										
Defined benefit:										
Civil Service Retirement System	1,000...	2,700	1,826	1,525	978	978	906	854	788	722
Federal Employees Retirement System [2]	1,000...	(X)	1,136	1,318	1,668	1,668	1,717	1,808	1,882	1,952
Military Service Retirement System [3]	1,000...	2,050	2,130	1,572	1,437	1,438	1,465	1,468	1,480	1,445
Thrift Savings Plan [4]	1,000...	(X)	1,419	1,930	1,900	1,900	2,300	2,400	2,500	2,800
State and local retirement systems [5,6]	1,000...	(NA)	11,345	12,524	13,917	13,977	14,123	14,249	14,181	14,116
ASSETS										
Total	Bil. dol..	258	1,047	1,655	2,950	2,976	3,016	3,092	3,472	3,697
Federal retirement systems	Bil. dol..	73	326	537	782	818	858	920	977	1,039
Defined benefit	Bil. dol..	73	318	502	684	717	756	791	825	866
Civil Service Retirement System	Bil. dol..	73	220	311	395	404	417	425	433	440
Federal Employees Retirement System [2]	Bil. dol..	(X)	18	60	126	144	162	183	204	228
Military Service Retirement System [3]	Bil. dol..	[7]	80	131	163	169	177	183	188	198
Thrift Savings Plan [4]	Bil. dol..	(X)	8	35	98	101	102	129	152	173
State and local retirement systems [5]	Bil. dol..	185	721	1,118	2,168	2,158	2,158	2,172	2,495	2,658
CONTRIBUTIONS										
Total	Bil. dol..	83	103	127	143	145	151	161	187	191
Federal retirement systems	Bil. dol..	19	61	67	78	80	85	86	95	100
Defined benefit	Bil. dol..	19	59	61	69	70	73	72	79	84
Civil Service Retirement System	Bil. dol..	19	28	31	33	33	34	29	34	33
Federal Employees Retirement System [2]	Bil. dol..	(X)	4	6	8	9	10	11	13	13
Military Service Retirement System [3]	Bil. dol..	[7]	27	24	28	28	30	32	32	38
Thrift Savings Plan [4]	Bil. dol..	(X)	2	6	9	10	12	14	16	16
State and local retirement systems [5]	Bil. dol..	64	42	60	65	65	66	75	92	91
BENEFITS										
Total	Bil. dol..	39	89	125	172	185	196	211	226	240
Federal retirement systems	Bil. dol..	27	53	66	81	84	86	89	93	99
Defined benefit	Bil. dol..	27	53	65	78	81	84	86	89	94
Civil Service Retirement System	Bil. dol..	15	31	37	44	46	47	48	50	52
Federal Employees Retirement System [2]	Bil. dol..	(X)	(Z)	1	1	1	2	2	2	3
Military Service Retirement System [3]	Bil. dol..	12	22	28	33	34	35	36	37	39
Thrift Savings Plan [4]	Bil. dol..	(X)	(Z)	1	3	3	2	3	4	5
State and local retirement systems [5]	Bil. dol..	12	36	59	91	101	110	122	133	141

NA Not available. X Not applicable. Z Less than $500 million. [1] Includes active, separated vested, retired employees, and survivors. [2] The Federal Employees Retirement System was established June 6, 1986. [3] Includes nondisability and disability retirees, surviving families, and all active personnel with the exception of active reserves. [4] The Thrift Savings Plan (a defined contribution plan) was established April 1, 1987. [5] Excludes state and local plans that are fully supported by employee contributions. [6] Not adjusted for double counting of individuals participating in more than one plan. [7] The Military Retirement System was unfunded until October 1, 1984.

Source: Employee Benefit Research Institute, Washington, DC, *EBRI Databook on Employee Benefits, Twelfth Edition*, and unpublished data (copyright). See also <http://www.ebri.org/>.

Table 532. Federal Civil Service Retirement: 1980 to 2005

[As of Sept. 30 or for year ending Sept. 30 (2,720 represents 2,720,000). Covers both Civil Service Retirement System and Federal Employees Retirement System]

Item	Unit	1980	1990	1995	2000	2001	2002	2003	2004	2005
Employees covered [1]	1,000	2,720	2,945	2,668	2,764	2,655	2,654	2,662	2,670	2,674
Annuitants, total	1,000	**1,675**	**2,143**	**2,311**	**2,376**	**2,383**	**2,383**	**2,389**	**2,404**	**2,433**
Age and service	1,000	905	1,288	1,441	1,501	1,509	1,513	1,523	1,544	1,568
Disability	1,000	343	297	263	242	239	236	234	231	229
Survivors	1,000	427	558	607	633	635	634	632	629	636
Receipts, total [2]	Mil. dol.	**24,389**	**52,689**	**65,684**	**75,967**	**77,949**	**80,069**	**78,366**	**82,412**	**83,691**
Employee contributions	Mil. dol.	3,686	4,501	4,498	4,637	4,593	4,475	4,522	4,483	4,353
Federal government contributions	Mil. dol.	15,562	27,368	33,130	37,722	38,442	39,692	36,583	42,240	43,093
Disbursements, total [3]	Mil. dol.	**14,977**	**31,416**	**38,435**	**45,194**	**47,356**	**48,970**	**50,368**	**52,277**	**54,790**
Age and service annuitants [4]	Mil. dol.	12,639	26,495	32,070	37,546	39,397	40,758	42,018	43,727	46,029
Survivors	Mil. dol.	1,912	4,366	5,864	7,210	7,533	7,790	7,951	8,127	8,338
Average monthly benefit:										
Age and service	Dollars	992	1,369	1,643	1,885	1,967	2,031	2,085	2,154	2,240
Disability	Dollars	723	1,008	1,164	1,240	1,269	1,286	1,291	1,305	1,327
Survivors	Dollars	392	653	819	952	992	1,024	1,044	1,073	1,106
Cash and security holdings	Bil. dol.	73.7	238.0	366.2	508.1	542.6	573.7	601.7	631.8	660.8

[1] Excludes employees in leave-without-pay status. [2] Includes interest on investments. [3] Includes refunds, death claims, and administration. [4] Includes disability annuitants.

Source: U.S. Office of Personnel Management, *Civil Service Retirement and Disability Trust Fund Annual Report.*

Table 533. State and Local Government Retirement Systems—Beneficiaries and Finances: 1990 to 2005

[In billions of dollars (111.3 represents 111,300,000,000), except as indicated. For fiscal years closed during the 12 months ending June 30]

Year and level of government	Num-ber of benefi-ciaries (1,000)	Receipts					Benefits and withdrawals			Cash and security holdings
		Total	Employee contribu-tions	Government contributions		Earn-ings on invest-ments	Total	Ben-efits	With-drawals	
				State	Local					
1990: All systems	4,026	111.3	13.9	14.0	18.6	64.9	38.4	36.0	2.4	721
State-administered	3,232	89.2	11.6	14.0	11.5	52.0	29.6	27.6	2.0	575
Locally administered	794	22.2	2.2	(Z)	7.0	12.9	8.8	8.4	0.4	145
1995: All systems	4,979	148.8	18.6	16.6	24.4	89.2	61.5	58.8	2.7	1,118
State-administered	4,025	123.3	15.7	16.2	15.4	76.0	48.0	45.8	2.2	914
Locally administered	954	25.5	2.9	0.4	9.0	13.3	13.5	13.0	0.5	204
2000: All systems	6,292	297.0	25.0	17.5	22.6	231.9	95.7	91.3	4.4	2,169
State-administered	4,786	247.4	20.7	17.2	16.7	192.8	76.0	72.2	3.8	1,798
Locally administered	1,506	49.7	4.3	0.4	5.9	39.1	19.8	19.1	0.7	371
2004: All systems	6,703	407.3	30.7	31.1	29.8	315.5	145.4	133.1	4.4	2,495
State-administered	5,631	339.6	26.3	30.7	18.5	264.1	117.6	107.7	3.6	2,078
Locally administered	1,072	67.7	4.4	(Z)	11.3	51.4	27.8	25.4	0.8	417
2005: All systems	6,903	351.5	31.3	24.1	35.1	260.9	155.3	141.3	3.8	2,658
State-administered	5,846	293.4	26.8	23.7	22.0	220.9	126.8	115.2	3.1	2,226
Locally administered	1,057	58.1	4.5	0.3	13.2	40.0	28.5	26.1	0.7	431

Z Less than $50 million.

Source: U.S. Census Bureau, through 1995, *Finances of Employee-Retirement Systems of State and Local Governments*, Series GF, No. 2, annual; beginning 2000, "Federal, State, and Local Governments, State and Local Government Public Employee Retirement Systems"; <http://www.census.gov/govs/www/retire.html>.

Table 534. Percent of Workers Participating In Retirement Benefits by Worker Characteristics: 2006

[Based on National Compensation Survey, a sample survey of 10,370 private industry establishments of all sizes, representing over 105 million workers; see Appendix III. Survey covers all 50 States and the District of Columbia. For a definition of defined benefit and defined contribution, see headnote, Table 535. See also Table 634]

Characteristic	Total [1]	Defined benefit	Defined contribu-tion	Characteristic	Total [1]	Defined benefit	Defined contribu-tion
Total	**51**	**20**	**43**	Full-time	60	23	51
White-collar occupations	60	22	53	Part-time	21	8	16
Blue-collar occupations	52	25	40	Union	80	68	44
Service occupations	24	7	20	Nonunion	47	14	43

[1] Total is less than the sum of the individual retirement items because many employees participated in both types of plans.

Source: U.S. Bureau of Labor Statistics, *Employee Benefits in Private Industry in the United States, March 2006*, Summary 06-05, August 2006. See also <http://www.bls.gov/ncs/ebs/sp/ebsm0004.pdf>.

Social Insurance and Human Services 353

Table 535. Private Pension Plans—Summary by Type of Plan: 1990 to 2004

[712.3 represents 712,300. "Pension plan" is defined by the Employee Retirement Income Security Act (ERISA) as "any plan, fund, or program which was heretofore or is hereafter established or maintained by an employer or an employee organization, or by both, to the extent that such plan (a) provides retirement income to employees, or (b) results in a deferral of income by employees for periods extending to the termination of covered employment or beyond, regardless of the method of calculating the contributions made to the plan, the method of calculating the benefits under the plan, or the method of distributing benefits from the plan." A defined benefit plan provides a definite benefit formula for calculating benefit amounts—such as a flat amount per year of service or a percentage of salary times years of service. A defined contribution plan is a pension plan in which the contributions are made to an individual account for each employee. The retirement benefit is dependent upon the account balance at retirement. The balance depends upon amounts contributed, investment experience, and, in the case of profit sharing plans, amounts which may be allocated to the account due to forfeitures by terminating employees. Employee Stock Ownership Plans (ESOP) and 401(k) plans are included among defined contribution plans. Data are based on Form 5500 series reports filed with the Department of Labor]

Item	Unit	Total				Defined contribution plan				Defined benefit plan			
		1990	1995	2000	2004	1990	1995	2000	2004	1990	1995	2000	2004
Number of plans [1]	1,000...	712.3	693.4	736.0	683.1	599.2	623.9	686.9	635.6	113.1	69.5	48.7	47.5
Total participants [2] ..	Million ..	76.9	87.5	103.3	106.3	38.1	47.7	61.7	64.6	38.8	39.7	41.6	41.7
Active participants [3] ..	Million ..	61.8	66.2	73.1	72.7	35.5	42.7	50.9	52.2	26.3	23.5	22.2	20.6
Assets [4]	Bil. dol..	1,674	2,724	4,203	4,693	712	1,322	2,216	2,587	962	1,402	1,986	2,106
Contributions [5]	Bil. dol..	98.8	158.8	231.9	323.0	75.8	117.4	198.5	228.6	23.0	41.4	33.4	94.4
Benefits [6]	Bil. dol..	129.4	183.0	341.0	333.3	63.0	97.9	213.5	192.9	66.4	85.1	127.5	140.4

[1] Excludes all plans covering only one participant. [2] Includes active, retired, and separated vested participants not yet in pay status. Also includes double counting of workers in more than one plan. [3] Includes any workers currently in employment covered by a plan and who are earning or retaining credited service under a plan. Also includes any nonvested former employees who have not yet incurred breaks in service. [4] Asset amounts shown exclude funds held by life insurance companies under allocated group insurance contracts for payment of retirement benefits. These excluded funds make up roughly 10 to 15 percent of total private fund assets. [5] Includes both employer and employee contributions. [6] Includes benefits paid directly from trust and premium payments made from plans to insurance carriers. Excludes benefits paid directly by insurance carriers.

Source: U.S. Department of Labor, Employee Benefits Security Administration, *Private Pension Plan Bulletin* (released March 2007). See also <http://www.dol.gov/ebsa/pdf/privatepensionplanbulletinhistoricaltables.pdf>.

Table. 536. Defined Benefit Retirement Plans—Selected Features: 2005

[In percent. Covers full-time employees in private industry. Based on National Compensation Survey, a sample survey of 3,227 private industry establishments of all sizes, representing over 102 million workers; see Appendix III. For a definition of defined benefit, see headnote, Table 535. See also Table 634]

Feature	All workers	White collar	Blue collar	Service	Goods producing	Service producing	1–99 workers	100 workers or more	Union	Non-union
Plan provisions:										
Benefits based on earnings	53	56	43	73	39	59	48	54	37	61
Early retirement benefits available ...	82	76	89	94	90	79	76	84	87	80
Availability of lump sum benefits at retirement	52	64	34	57	40	59	49	54	40	59
Benefit formula:										
Percent of terminal earnings	39	46	27	41	32	42	27	42	21	48
Percent of career earnings	14	10	16	32	7	17	21	12	15	13
Dollar amount formula	18	6	37	12	42	6	16	19	41	6
Percent of contribution formula	4	3	7	(Z)	7	3	9	3	10	1
Cash balance	23	33	12	14	10	30	25	23	12	29
Pension equity	2	2	2	1	2	2	1	2	(Z)	3
Requirements for normal retirement [1]:										
No age requirement	11	15	7	3	6	13	20	8	8	12
Less than 30 years of service	9	13	4	3	4	11	14	7	5	11
30 years of service	2	2	3	(S)	3	2	6	1	3	2
At age 55	1	1	2	(Z)	2	1	1	1	2	1
At age 60	9	8	10	16	7	10	8	10	14	7
At age 62	15	11	23	7	24	11	15	15	21	12
At age 65	59	63	48	74	55	60	47	62	43	67
Sum of age plus service [2]	1	1	1	(S)	2	(Z)	1	1	1	1

S Represents no employees in this category or data do not meet publication criteria.   Z Less than 0.5 percent.   [1] Normal retirement is defined as the point at which the participant could retire and immediately receive all accrued benefits by virtue of service and earnings, without reduction due to age. If a plan had alternative age and service requirements, the earliest age and associated service were tabulated; if one alternative did not specify an age, it was the requirement tabulated. Some age and service requirements are not shown separately.   [2] In some plans, participants must also satisfy a minimum age or service requirement.

Source: U.S. Bureau of Labor Statistics, *National Compensation Survey: Employee Benefits in Private Industry in the United States, 2005*, Bulletin 2589, May 2007. See also <http://www.bls.gov/ncs/ebs/sp/ebbl0022.pdf>.

Table 537. U.S. Households Owning IRAs: 2002 to 2005

[**43.2 represents** 43,200,000. Incidence of IRA ownership is based on an annual tracking survey of 3,000 randomly selected, representative U.S. households; see source for details]

Type of IRA	Number (mil.) [1]				Percent of U.S. households			
	2002	2003	2004	2005	2002	2003	2004	2005
Any type of IRA [2]	43.2	46.1	45.2	46.8	39.5	41.4	40.4	41.4
Traditional IRA	35.7	37.1	36.7	37.6	32.7	33.3	32.8	33.2
Roth IRA	13.2	16.2	14.3	16.1	12.1	14.6	12.8	14.2
SIMPLE IRA, SEP-IRA, or SAR-SEP IRA . . .	8.5	8.3	9.6	8.8	7.8	7.5	8.6	7.8

[1] The number of U.S. households owning IRAs in 2002 through 2005 is based on the following U.S. Census Bureau's total U.S. household estimates: 109.3 million in 2002, 111.3 million in 2003, 112.0 million in 2004, and 113.1 million in 2005 (U.S. Bureau of the Census, Current Population Reports, P60-226, August 2004).   [2] Excludes ownership of Coverdell Education Savings Accounts, which were referred to as Education IRAs before July 2001.

Source: Investment Company Institute, Washington, DC, *Fundamentals, Investment Company Institute Research in Brief*, "Appendix: Additional Data on IRA Ownership in 2005"; Vol. 15, No. 1A, January 2006 (copyright). See also <http://www.ici.org/statements /fundamentals/fm-v15n1appendix.pdf>.

Table 538. 401(k) Plans—Selected Features: 2005

[**In percent.** Covers full-time employees in private industry. Based on National Compensation Survey, a sample survey of 3,227 private industry establishments of all sizes, representing 102 million of workers; see Appendix III. See also Table 634]

Feature	All employees	White Collar	Blue Collar	Service
MAXIMUM PRETAX EMPLOYEE CONTRIBUTIONS [1]				
Percent of employee earnings	53	51	56	55
Specified dollar amount	(Z)	(Z)	(S)	(Z)
Up to the Internal Revenue code limit	46	47	44	39
Average maximum pretax contribution [2]	18.4	18.8	17.8	17.6
INVESTMENT CHOICES				
Employee permitted to choose investments	91	91	92	91
Employee not permitted to choose investments	1	1	(Z)	3

S Represents no employees in this category or data do not meet publication criteria.   Z Less than 0.5 percent.   [1] Includes contributions that are not matched by the employer. If maximum contributions vary, such as by length of service, the highest possible contribution was tabulated.   [2] The average is presented for all covered workers; averages exclude workers without the plan provision.

Source: U.S. Bureau of Labor Statistics, *National Compensation Survey: Employee Benefits in Private Industry in the United States, 2005*, Bulletin 2589, May 2007. See also <http://www.bls.gov/ncs/ebs/sp/ebbl0022.pdf>.

Table 539. State Unemployment Insurance—Summary: 1990 to 2006

[**2,522 represents** 2,522,000. Includes unemployment compensation for state and local government employees where covered by state law]

Item	Unit	1990	1995	2000	2001	2002	2003	2004	2005	2006
Insured unemployment, average weekly	1,000	2,522	2,572	2,110	2,974	3,585	3,531	2,950	2,661	2,476
Percent of covered employment [1]	Percent . . .	2.4	2.3	1.7	2.3	2.8	2.8	2.3	2.1	2.5
Percent of civilian unemployed	Percent . . .	35.8	34.7	37.6	44.2	43.2	40.7	36.8	35.7	36.0
Unemployment benefits, average weekly	Dollars . . .	161	187	221	238	257	262	263	267	277
Percent of weekly wage	Percent . . .	36.0	35.5	32.9	34.6	36.8	36.5	35.2	34.6	35.0
Weeks compensated.	Million	116.2	118.3	96.0	136.3	166.3	163.2	135.1	121.2	112.1
Beneficiaries, first payments	1,000	8,629	8,035	7,033	9,877	10,088	9,935	8,369	7,922	7,349
Average duration of benefits [2] . . .	Weeks. . . .	13.4	14.7	13.7	13.8	16.5	16.4	16.1	15.3	15.3
Claimants exhausting benefits . . .	1,000	2,323	2,662	2,144	2,827	4,416	4,417	3,532	2,856	2,666
Percent of first payment [3]	Percent . . .	29.4	34.3	31.8	34.1	42.5	43.4	39.0	35.9	35.1
Contributions collected [4]	Bil. dol. . . .	15.2	22.0	19.9	19.7	19.7	25.3	31.2	34.8	34.1
Benefits paid	Bil. dol. . . .	18.1	21.2	20.5	31.6	42.0	41.4	34.4	31.2	29.8
Funds available for benefits [5] . . .	Bil. dol. . . .	37.9	35.4	53.4	45.6	35.2	23.4	23.0	29.0	36.0
Average employer contribution rate [6]	Percent . . .	1.95	2.44	1.75	1.71	1.80	2.20	2.68	2.86	2.70

[1] Insured unemployment as percent of average covered employment in preceding year.   [2] Weeks compensated divided by first payment.   [3] Based on first payments for 12-month period ending June 30.   [4] Contributions from employers; also employees in states which tax workers.   [5] End of year. Sum of balances in state clearing accounts, benefit-payment accounts, and state accounts in federal unemployment trust funds.   [6] As percent of taxable wages.

Source: U.S. Department of Labor, Employment and Training Administration, *Unemployment Insurance Financial Data Handbook*. See also <http://www.ows.doleta.gov/unemploy/hb394.asp>.

Social Insurance and Human Services 355

Table 540. State Unemployment Insurance by State and Other Area: 2006

[7,349 represents 7,349,000. See headnote, Table 539. For state data on insured unemployment, see Table 611]

State or other area	Beneficiaries, first payments (1,000)	Benefits paid (mil. dol.)	Avg. weekly unemployment benefits (dol.)	State or other area	Beneficiaries, first payments (1,000)	Benefits paid (mil. dol.)	Avg. weekly unemployment benefits (dol.)
Total	7,349	29,807	277	MT	20	63	204
AL	105	206	184	NE	33	93	231
AK	41	110	198	NV	64	246	274
AZ	68	209	198	NH	25	78	256
AR	80	243	244	NJ	305	1,775	344
CA	948	4,485	289	NM	25	105	238
CO	69	288	312	NY	454	2,278	277
CT	119	559	304	NC	239	720	265
DE	23	97	251	ND	14	42	255
DC	16	93	283	OH	275	1,096	287
FL	240	719	231	OK	41	140	233
GA	198	537	256	OR	126	470	270
HI	21	97	365	PA	447	2,030	301
ID	40	101	241	RI	38	196	342
IL	335	1,649	292	SC	112	326	223
IN	187	731	286	SD	8	22	219
IA	93	310	282	TN	143	408	216
KS	54	210	287	TX	297	1,070	271
KY	111	382	271	UT	23	92	274
LA	60	294	191	VT	22	84	275
ME	31	106	246	VA	107	347	256
MD	96	391	274	WA	171	710	322
MA	210	1,255	366	WV	40	132	231
MI	476	1,960	294	WI	259	786	259
MN	141	663	333	WY	10	30	253
MS	53	161	186	PR	101	199	110
MO	135	411	212	VI	1	5	253

Source: U.S. Department of Labor, Employment and Training Administration, *Unemployment Insurance Financial Data Handbook.* See also <http://www.ows.doleta.gov/unemploy/hb394.asp>.

Table 541. Persons With Work Disability by Selected Characteristics: 2005

[In thousands, except percent (19,656 represents 19,656,000). As of March. Covers civilian noninstitutional population and members of Armed Forces living off post or with their families on post. Persons are classified as having a work disability if they (1) have a health problem or disability which prevents them from working or which limits the kind or amount of work they can do; (2) have a service-connected disability or ever retired or left a job for health reasons; (3) did not work in survey reference week or previous year because of long-term illness or disability; or (4) are under age 65, and are covered by medicare or receive supplemental security income. Based on Current Population Survey; see text, Section 1, and Appendix III]

Age and participation status in assistance programs	Total [1]	Male	Female	White [2]	Black [3]	Hispanic [4]
Persons with work disability	**19,656**	**9,668**	**9,989**	**14,828**	**3,620**	**2,204**
16 to 24 years old.	1,709	904	805	1,154	434	242
25 to 34 years old.	2,475	1,253	1,222	1,771	520	343
35 to 44 years old.	3,764	1,866	1,898	2,823	705	460
45 to 54 years old.	5,382	2,631	2,751	4,058	1,009	573
55 to 64 years old.	6,327	3,014	3,313	5,022	952	586
Percent work disabled of total population						
16 to 24 years old.	4.7	4.9	4.4	4.1	8.2	3.8
25 to 34 years old.	6.4	6.5	6.2	5.8	10.3	4.5
35 to 44 years old.	8.7	8.8	8.7	8.2	13.3	7.4
45 to 54 years old.	12.9	12.9	12.9	11.8	20.8	13.8
55 to 64 years old.	21.4	21.5	21.4	20.1	32.7	25.3
Percent of work disabled—						
Receiving social security income	34.1	33.9	34.2	35.5	31.4	25.6
Receiving food stamps	18.4	15.0	21.6	15.7	29.2	22.2
Covered by medicaid.	64.2	66.8	61.7	66.8	53.6	54.5
Residing in public housing	5.9	4.6	7.3	4.1	9.4	7.8
Residing in subsidized housing	3.9	3.0	4.6	3.3	6.9	4.5

[1] Includes other races not shown separately. [2] Beginning with the 2003 Current Population Survey, respondents were asked to choose one or more races. White alone refers to people who reported White and did not report any other race category. The use of this single-race population does not imply that it is the preferred method of presenting or analyzing data. The Census Bureau uses a variety of approaches. Information on people who reported more than one race, such as "White and American Indian and Alaska Native" or "Asian and Black or African American," is available from Census 2000 through American FactFinder®. About 2.6 percent of people reported more than one race in 2000. [3] Black alone refers to people who reported Black and did not report any other race category. [4] Hispanic persons may be of any race.

Source: U.S. Census Bureau, unpublished data.

Table 542. **Workers' Compensation Payments: 1990 to 2004**

[In billions of dollars, except as indicated (53.1 represents $53,100,000,000). See headnote, Table 543]

Item	1990	1995	1997	1998	1999	2000	2001	2002	2003	2004
Workers covered (mil.)	106	113	118	122	124	127	127	126	125	126
Premium amounts paid [1]	**53.1**	**57.1**	**53.5**	**53.4**	**55.4**	**58.5**	**64.7**	**73.8**	**81.7**	**87.4**
Private carriers [1]	35.1	31.6	29.9	30.4	32.6	35.7	37.9	41.6	45.4	48.7
State funds . . . . [2]	8.0	10.5	8.0	8.0	7.6	8.8	11.5	14.5	17.6	19.1
Federal programs [2]	2.2	2.6	3.4	3.5	3.5	3.6	3.8	3.9	4.0	4.1
Self-insurers	7.9	12.5	12.3	11.7	11.7	10.4	11.5	13.8	14.7	15.5
Annual benefits paid [1]	**38.2**	**43.5**	**42.4**	**43.9**	**45.6**	**46.9**	**49.5**	**53.2**	**54.7**	**56.0**
By private carriers [1]	22.2	21.4	21.6	23.0	25.7	26.9	28.0	28.8	28.5	28.3
From state funds [3]	8.8	10.9	7.3	7.2	6.9	7.4	8.0	9.3	10.5	11.0
Employers' self-insurance [4]	7.2	11.2	10.6	10.2	10.1	10.5	11.5	12.0	12.5	13.3
Type of benefit:										
Medical/hospitalization	15.1	16.6	17.2	17.9	19.1	20.9	22.8	24.5	25.5	26.1
Compensation payments	21.7	25.7	24.3	24.5	23.3	26.0	26.7	28.7	29.2	29.9
Percent of covered payroll: [1]										
Workers' compensation costs [5,6] . . .	2.18	1.82	1.49	1.38	1.33	1.30	1.40	1.60	1.73	1.76
Benefits [6]	1.57	1.38	1.18	1.11	1.10	1.06	1.10	1.16	1.16	1.13

[1] Premium and benefit amounts include estimated payments under insurance policy deductible provisions. Deductible benefits are allocated to private carriers and state funds. [2] Years 1990–1995 include federal employer compensation program and that portion of federal black lung benefits program financed from employer contributions. Years 1997–2002 include federal employer compensation program only due to changes in reporting methods. [3] Net cash and medical benefits paid by competitive and exclusive state funds and by federal workers' compensation programs. [4] Cash and medical benefits paid by self-insurers, plus value of medical benefits paid by employers carrying workers' compensation policies that exclude standard medical coverage. [5] Premiums written by private carriers and state funds, and benefits paid by self-insurers increased by 5–10 prior to 1995 and by 11 percent for 1995–2002 for administrative costs. Also includes benefits paid and administrative costs of federal system for government employees. [6] Excludes programs financed from general revenue—black lung benefits and supplemental pensions in some states.

Source: National Academy of Social Insurance, Washington, DC, *Workers' Compensation: Benefits, Coverage, and Costs*, annual. See also <http://www.nasi.org/>.

Table 543. **Workers' Compensation Payments by State: 2000 to 2004**

[In millions of dollars (47,695 represents $47,695,000,000). Calendar-year data. Payments represent compensation and medical benefits and include insurance losses paid by private insurance carriers (compiled from state workers' compensation agencies and A.M. Best Co.); disbursements of state funds (compiled from the A.M. Best Co. and state workers' compensation agencies); and self-insurance payments (compiled from state workers' compensation agencies and authors' estimates)]

State	2000	2001	2002	2003	2004	State	2000	2001	2002	2003	2004
Total	**47,695**	**50,533**	**53,309**	**54,715**	**55,968**	Montana	155	180	178	201	211
						Nebraska	230	248	283	290	283
Alabama	529	563	5ó5	580	576	Nevada	324	309	325	327	358
Alaska	139	163	180	184	194	New Hampshire	179	215	212	220	214
Arizona	498	436	505	531	585	New Jersey	1,183	1,256	1,329	1,379	1,398
Arkansas	214	218	221	225	226	New Mexico	144	159	176	189	196
California	9,449	10,083	11,582	12,404	12,460	New York	2,909	2,978	3,142	3,220	3,337
Colorado	810	566	761	757	835	North Carolina	873	905	988	1,067	1,159
Connecticut	638	641	676	675	685	North Dakota	70	71	74	78	83
Delaware	138	138	153	160	158	Ohio	2,099	2,248	2,388	2,442	2,442
District of Columbia .	86	91	94	89	98	Oklahoma	485	526	509	554	572
Florida	2,577	3,034	2,678	2,811	2,760	Oregon	425	473	475	471	507
Georgia	965	1,029	975	1,062	1,128	Pennsylvania	2,379	2,406	2,479	2,565	2,594
Hawaii	231	248	268	275	271	Rhode Island	127	136	141	131	142
Idaho	114	180	186	196	210	South Carolina	515	532	593	657	688
Illinois	1,948	2,080	2,124	2,104	2,213	South Dakota	63	71	73	74	76
Indiana	529	524	547	559	609	Tennessee	781	843	777	843	896
Iowa	343	390	400	424	446	Texas	2,160	2,212	2,307	1,857	1,574
Kansas	323	340	342	293	366	Utah	173	198	212	186	218
Kentucky	575	672	708	724	763	Vermont	102	98	119	120	128
Louisiana	547	588	563	585	589	Virginia	602	604	627	702	762
Maine	245	245	262	240	270	Washington	1,527	1,639	1,716	1,800	1,836
Maryland	641	682	664	701	768	West Virginia	693	713	833	829	741
Massachusetts	801	881	903	1,057	1,046	Wisconsin	768	924	897	840	1,043
Michigan	1,474	1,478	1,512	1,477	1,517	Wyoming	89	100	107	114	120
Minnesota	798	904	922	885	934	Federal total [1]	2,957	3,069	3,154	3,185	3,256
Mississippi	293	285	290	291	306	Federal employees . .	2,119	2,223	2,317	2,368	2,445
Missouri	780	959	1,116	1,081	1,120						

[1] Federal benefits include: those paid under the Federal Employees Compensation Act for civilian employees; the portion of the black lung benefit program that is financed by employers; and a portion of benefits under the Longshore and Harbor Workers Compensation Act that are not reflected in state data; namely, benefits paid by self-insured employers and by special funds under the LHWCA. See Appendix H of source for more information about federal programs.

Source: National Academy of Social Insurance, Washington, DC, *Workers' Compensation: Benefits, Coverage, and Costs*, annual. See also <http://www.nasi.org/>.

Social Insurance and Human Services 357

Table 544. Supplemental Security Income—Recipients and Payments: 1990 to 2005

[In thousands (4,817 represents 4,817,000), except as noted. Recipients and monthly payment as of December. Payments for calendar year. Persons with a federal SSI payment and/or federally administered state supplementation. See also Appendix III]

Program	Unit	1990	1995	2000	2001	2002	2003	2004	2005
Recipients, total	1,000.....	4,817	6,514	6,602	6,688	6,788	6,902	6,988	7,114
Aged	1,000.....	1,454	1,446	1,289	1,264	1,252	1,233	1,211	1,214
Blind	1,000.....	84	84	79	78	78	77	76	75
Disabled............	1,000.....	3,279	4,984	5,234	5,346	5,459	5,593	5,701	5,825
Payments, total [1]....	Mil. dol....	16,133	27,037	30,672	32,166	33,719	34,693	36,065	37,236
Aged	Mil. dol. ...	3,559	4,239	4,540	4,664	4,803	4,857	4,894	4,965
Blind	Mil. dol. ...	329	367	386	399	416	409	412	414
Disabled............	Mil. dol. ...	12,245	22,431	25,746	27,126	28,500	29,429	30,745	31,857
Average monthly payment, total	Dollars ...	276	335	379	394	407	417	428	439
Aged	Dollars....	208	250	300	314	330	342	351	360
Blind	Dollars....	319	355	413	428	445	455	463	475
Disabled...........	Dollars....	303	358	398	412	425	433	444	455

[1] Includes payments not distributed by reason for eligibility.

Source: U.S. Social Security Administration, *Social Security Bulletin*, quarterly and *Annual Statistical Supplement to the Social Security Bulletin*. See also <http://www.ssa.gov/policy/docs/statcomps/supplement/>.

Table 545. Supplemental Security Income (SSI)—Recipients and Payments by State and Other Area: 2000 to 2005

[Recipients as of December; payments for calendar year (6,602 represents 6,602,000). Data cover federal SSI payments and/or federally administered state supplementation. For explanation of methodology, see Appendix III]

State and other area	Recipients (1,000)		Payments for year (mil. dol.)			State and other area	Recipients (1,000)		Payments for year (mil. dol.)		
	2000	2005	2000	2004	2005		2000	2005	2000	2004	2005
Total ...	6,602	7,114	30,672	36,065	37,236	MO........	112	118	471	553	573
U.S......	6,601	7,113	30,669	36,061	37,232	MT........	14	15	57	66	70
AL........	159	164	659	761	776	NE........	21	22	85	101	103
AK........	9	11	37	51	53	NV........	25	33	108	154	163
AZ........	81	98	355	458	482	NH........	12	14	49	61	67
AR........	85	91	333	383	407	NJ	146	152	672	750	763
CA........	1,088	1,212	6,386	7,906	8,146	NM........	47	54	193	234	248
CO........	54	55	228	253	264	NY........	617	635	3,197	3,502	3,561
CT........	49	52	216	253	260	NC........	191	199	732	858	894
DE........	12	14	50	63	66	ND........	8	8	30	33	33
DC........	20	21	93	106	113	OH........	240	250	1,114	1,231	1,295
FL........	377	422	1,621	1,953	2,031	OK........	72	80	302	359	381
GA........	197	203	785	916	944	OR........	52	61	228	280	298
HI........	21	23	104	118	119	PA........	284	317	1,367	1,672	1,659
ID........	18	22	76	97	106	RI........	28	30	130	156	161
IL........	249	259	1,174	1,298	1,337	SC........	107	105	429	474	488
IN........	88	99	382	463	488	SD........	13	13	48	53	55
IA........	40	43	158	186	193	TN........	164	161	664	741	752
KS........	36	39	151	181	187	TX........	409	502	1,575	2,031	2,191
KY........	174	180	741	847	862	UT........	20	23	87	103	110
LA........	166	156	715	798	771	VT........	13	13	51	60	63
ME........	30	32	116	141	146	VA........	132	137	535	608	632
MD........	88	94	400	463	481	WA........	101	116	484	582	616
MA........	168	171	807	878	902	WV........	71	77	318	366	376
MI........	210	222	988	1,123	1,157	WI........	85	92	357	417	437
MN........	64	73	272	334	355	WY........	6	6	23	26	26
MS........	129	125	512	561	572	N. Mariana...	1	1	3	4	4

Source: U.S. Social Security Administration, *Annual Statistical Supplement* to the *Social Security Bulletin*. See also <http://www.ssa.gov/policy/docs/statcomps/supplement/>.

Table 546. Temporary Assistance for Needy Families (TANF)—Families and Recipients: 1980 to 2005

[In thousands (3,712 represents 3,712,000). Average monthly families and recipients for calendar year. Prior to TANF, the cash assistance program to families was called Aid to Families with Dependent Children (1980–1996). Under the new welfare law (Personal Responsibility and Work Opportunity Reconciliation Act of 1996), the program became TANF. See text, this section. Includes Puerto Rico, Guam, and Virgin Islands]

Year	Families	Recipients	Year	Families	Recipients	Year	Families	Recipients
1980	3,712	10,774	1990	4,057	11,695	1998	3,050	8,347
1983	3,686	10,761	1991	4,497	12,930	1999	2,554	6,824
1984	3,714	10,831	1992	4,829	13,773	2000	2,215	5,778
1985	3,701	10,855	1993	5,012	14,205	2001	2,104	5,359
1986	3,763	11,038	1994	5,033	14,161	2002	2,047	5,064
1987	3,776	11,027	1995	4,791	13,418	2003	2,024	4,929
1988	3,749	10,915	1996	4,434	12,321	2004	1,981	4,745
1989	3,799	10,993	1997	3,740	10,376	2005	1,909	4,492

Source: U.S. Department of Health and Human Services, Administration for Children and Families, unpublished data.

Table 547. Temporary Assistance for Needy Families (TANF)—Recipients by State and Other Areas: 2000 to 2005

[In thousands (2,215 represents 2,215,000). Average monthly families and recipients for calendar year. See headnote, Table 546]

State or other area	Families 2000	Families 2004	Families 2005	Recipients 2000	Recipients 2004	Recipients 2005	State or other area	Families 2000	Families 2004	Families 2005	Recipients 2000	Recipients 2004	Recipients 2005
Total ..	2,215	1,980	1,908	5,778	4,745	4,491	MT......	5	5	4	13	14	12
U.S.....	2,181	1,960	1,891	5,678	4,686	4,442	NE......	9	11	10	24	26	28
AL......	19	19	20	45	43	48	NV......	6	8	6	16	20	15
AK......	7	5	4	21	14	11	NH......	6	6	6	14	14	14
AZ......	33	48	43	84	111	96	NJ......	50	45	45	125	109	107
AR......	12	10	8	29	21	18	NM......	23	18	18	69	46	45
CA......	489	461	461	1,262	1,105	1,078	NY......	250	146	140	695	335	321
CO......	11	15	15	28	38	39	NC......	45	37	33	98	76	64
CT......	27	21	19	64	42	39	ND......	3	3	3	7	8	7
DE......	6	6	6	12	13	13	OH......	95	85	82	235	186	177
DC......	17	17	17	45	44	41	OK......	14	14	14	35	33	31
FL......	65	59	58	142	116	101	OR......	17	19	19	38	43	44
GA......	52	51	39	125	117	82	PA	88	91	97	241	239	254
HI	14	9	10	46	22	24	RI	16	12	10	44	31	26
ID	1	2	5	2	3	9	SC......	18	16	16	42	37	36
IL.......	78	37	38	234	91	96	SD......	3	3	3	7	6	6
IN	37	50	48	101	129	124	TN......	57	72	70	147	190	184
IA	20	18	17	53	45	42	TX......	129	100	82	347	237	189
KS......	13	17	18	32	45	46	UT......	8	9	9	21	23	22
KY......	38	36	34	87	78	74	VT......	6	5	5	16	12	11
LA......	27	18	16	71	42	36	VA......	31	10	10	69	28	28
ME......	11	10	9	28	27	25	WA	56	56	57	148	138	136
MD......	29	25	23	71	59	53	WV	13	14	12	33	33	26
MA......	43	50	48	100	107	102	WI	17	22	19	38	54	44
MI	72	80	81	198	213	215	WY	1	–	–	1	1	1
MN......	39	33	28	114	85	71	PR	30	17	15	88	47	41
MS......	15	18	15	34	41	33	GU	3	3	2	10	11	8
MO	47	41	40	125	99	96	VI.....	1	1	–	3	2	1

– Represents or rounds to zero.

Source: U.S. Department of Health and Human Services, Administration for Children and Families, unpublished data.

Table 548. Temporary Assistance for Needy Families (TANF)—Expenditures by State: 2000 to 2005

[In millions of dollars (24,781 represents $24,781,000,000). Represents federal and state funds expended in fiscal year]

State	2000, total	2004, total	2005 Total [1]	2005 Expenditures on assistance	State	2000, total	2004, total	2005 Total [1]	2005 Expenditures on assistance
U.S. ...	24.781	25,823	25,444	12,009	MO	321	300	299	125
AL......	96	114	123	51	MT......	44	45	44	23
AK......	93	76	74	48	NE......	79	89	78	54
AZ......	261	305	299	163	NV......	69	68	70	41
AR......	139	42	67	19	NH......	73	60	63	36
CA......	6,481	6,178	5,882	3,958	NJ......	321	889	858	309
CO......	205	212	214	78	NM.....	149	133	127	78
CT......	436	435	459	143	NY......	3,512	4,196	3,970	2,145
DE......	55	54	61	39	NC......	440	438	448	111
DC......	157	169	156	66	ND......	33	34	34	21
FL......	781	877	868	212	OH......	995	834	990	330
GA......	386	535	520	152	OK......	130	195	174	133
HI	162	128	128	82	OR.....	169	243	269	131
ID	43	41	40	7	PA	1,327	1,192	1,190	440
IL.......	879	981	998	127	RI	172	155	168	76
IN	342	314	307	115	SC.....	245	38	230	78
IA	163	163	162	78	SD.....	21	29	30	22
KS......	151	156	154	99	TN.....	293	236	233	138
KY......	203	196	216	123	TX.....	727	768	851	234
LA......	118	252	186	53	UT.....	100	114	108	51
ME......	108	102	127	102	VT.....	62	69	68	43
MD.....	336	350	349	124	VA.....	418	279	290	143
MA.....	690	681	689	352	WA.....	535	589	525	262
MI	1,264	1,281	1,175	446	WV	134	150	124	58
MN.....	381	402	392	137	WI	382	493	446	115
MS.....	62	103	79	27	WY	34	40	32	11

[1] Includes other items not shown separately.

Source: U.S. Department of Health and Human Services, Administration for Children and Families, *Temporary Assistance for Needy Families (TANF) Program, Annual Report to Congress.*

Social Insurance and Human Services 359

Table 549. **Child Support—Award and Recipiency Status of Custodial Parent: 2003**

[In thousands except as noted (13,951 represents 13,951,000). Custodial parents 15 years and older with own children under 21 years of age present from absent parents as of spring 2004. Covers civilian noninstitutional population. Based on Current Population Survey; see text, Section 1 and Appendix III. For definition of mean, see Guide to Tabular Presentation]

Award and recipiency status	All custodial parents				Custodial parents below the poverty level			
	Total				Total			
	Number	Percent distri- bution	Mothers	Fathers	Number	Percent distri- bution	Mothers	Fathers
Total	13,951	(X)	11,587	2,364	3,343	(X)	3,028	316
With child support agreement or award [1] . . .	8,376	(X)	7,436	940	1,964	(X)	1,819	145
Supposed to receive payments in 2003. . .	7,256	100.0	6,516	740	1,689	100.0	1,582	107
Actually received payments in 2003	5,548	76.5	5,018	530	1,159	68.6	1,103	56
Received full amount	3,290	45.3	2,948	342	594	35.2	562	32
Received partial payments.	2,258	31.1	2,070	188	565	33.5	542	24
Did not receive payments in 2003.	1,708	23.5	1,498	210	530	31.4	478	52
Child support not awarded	5,576	(X)	4,151	1,424	1,379	(X)	1,209	171
MEAN INCOME AND CHILD SUPPORT								
Received child support payments in 2003:								
Mean total money income (dol.).	28,612	(X)	26,715	46,570	7,458	(X)	7,494	6,748
Mean child support received (dol.)	4,577	(X)	4,647	3,906	3,713	(X)	3,712	3,733
Received the full amount due:								
Mean total money income (dol.)	32,259	(X)	30,174	50,246	8,242	(X)	8,173	9,461
Mean child support received (dol.). . .	6,242	(X)	6,380	5,052	5,970	(X)	5,985	5,692
Received partial payments:								
Mean total money income (dol.)	23,297	(X)	21,787	39,900	6,635	(X)	6,790	3,074
Mean child support received (dol.). . .	2,150	(X)	2,180	1,826	1,344	(X)	1,356	1,082
Received no payments in 2003:								
Mean total money income (dol.).	23,424	(X)	21,385	37,949	7,348	(X)	7,365	7,560
Without child support agreement or award:								
Mean total money income (dol.).	28,059	(X)	21,627	46,802	6,316	(X)	6,640	4,024

X Not applicable.   [1] As of April 2004.

Source: U.S. Census Bureau, unpublished data.

Table 550. **Child Support Enforcement Program—Caseload and Collections: 1990 to 2006**

[For years ending Sept. 30 (12,796 represents 12,796,000). Includes Puerto Rico, Guam, and the Virgin Islands. The child support enforcement program locates absent parents, establishes paternity of children born out of wedlock, and establishes and enforces support orders. By law, these services are available to all families that need them. The program is operated at the state and local government level, but 66 percent of administrative costs are paid by the federal government. Child support collected for families not receiving Temporary Assistance for Needy Families (TANF) goes to the family to help it remain self-sufficient. Most of the child support collected on behalf of TANF families goes to federal and state governments to offset TANF payments. Some states pass-through a portion of the CS collections to help families become self sufficient. Based on data reported by state agencies. Minus sign (–) indicates net outlay]

Item	Unit	1990	1995	2000	2002	2003	2004	2005	2006, prel.
Total cases [1]	1,000	12,796	19,162	17,334	16,066	15,923	15,854	15,861	15,844
Paternities established, total [2]. . .	1,000	393	659	867	697	663	692	690	675
Support orders established, total [3]. . . .	1,000	1,022	1,051	1,175	1,220	1,161	1,181	1,180	1,159
FINANCES									
Collections, total	Mil. dol. . .	6,010	10,827	17,854	20,137	21,176	21,861	23,006	23,933
TANF/FC collections [4].	Mil. dol. . . .	1,750	2,689	2,593	2,893	2,972	2,221	2,191	2,112
State share	Mil. dol. . . .	620	939	1,080	947	947	927	911	875
Estimated incentive payments to states	Mil. dol. . . .	264	400	353	338	356	361	365	402
Federal share [5]	Mil. dol. . . .	533	822	968	1,183	1,167	1,147	1,129	1,086
Current Assistance Medical Support Collections	Mil. dol. . . .	(NA)	(NA)	27	26	20	12	11	12
Current Assistance Payments to Families or Foster Care	Mil. dol. . . .	(NA)	(NA)	165	737	837	136	140	139
Non-TANF collections	Mil. dol. . . .	4,260	8,138	15,261	17,244	18,204	19,641	20,815	21,822
Administrative expenditures, total. . .	Mil. dol. . . .	1,606	3,012	4,526	5,183	5,216	5,322	5,353	5,561
State share	Mil. dol. . . .	545	918	1,519	1,752	1,765	1,803	1,813	1,884
Federal share	Mil. dol. . . .	1,061	2,095	3,006	3,432	3,450	3,519	3,540	3,677
Program savings, total	Mil. dol. . . .	–190	–852	–2,125	–3,053	–3,098	–3,249	–3,312	–3,600
State share	Mil. dol. . . .	338	421	–87	–466	–461	–515	–537	–607
Federal share	Mil. dol. . . .	–528	–1,273	–2,038	–2,587	–2,637	–2,734	–2,776	–2,993

NA Not Available.   [1] Passage of the Personal Responsibility and Work Opportunity Reconciliation Act of 1996 (PRWORA) mandated new categories in 1999 and cases were no longer double counted resulting in a 2 million case reduction.   [2] Does not include in-hospital paternities.   [3] Includes modifications to orders.   [4] Collections for current assistance cases where the children are: (1) recipients of TANF under title IV-A of the Social Security Act or (2) entitled to Foster Care (FC) maintenance under title IV-E of the Social Security Act plus collections distributed as assistance reimbursements. Includes assistance reimbursements, which are collections that will be divided between the state and federal governments to reimburse their respective shares of either Title IV-A assistance payments or Title IV-E Foster Care maintenance payments.   [5] Prior to fiscal year 2002, incentives were paid out of the federal share of collections and the net federal share was reported.

Source: U.S. Department of Health and Human Services, Office of Child Support Enforcement, *Annual Report to Congress.*

360   Social Insurance and Human Services

Table 551. Federal Food Programs: 1990 to 2006

[20.0 represents 20,000,000, except as noted. For years ending September 30. Program data include Puerto Rico, Virgin Islands, Guam, American Samoa, Northern Marianas, and the former Trust Territory when a federal food program was operated in these areas. Participation data are average monthly figures except as noted. Participants are not reported for the commodity distribution programs. Cost data are direct federal benefits to recipients; they exclude federal administrative payments and applicable state and local contributions. Federal costs for commodities and cash-in-lieu of commodities are shown separately from direct cash benefits for those programs receiving both]

Program	Unit	1990	1995	2000	2002	2003	2004	2005	2006
Food Stamp:									
Participants	Million	20.0	26.6	17.2	19.1	21.3	23.9	25.7	26.7
Federal cost	Mil. dol.	14,143	22,764	14,983	18,256	21,404	24,619	28,566	30,174
Monthly average coupon value per recipient	Dollars	58.78	71.27	72.62	79.67	83.90	85.99	92.72	94.05
Nutrition assistance program for Puerto Rico:									
Federal cost	Mil. dol.	937	1,131	1,268	1,351	1,395	1,413	1,495	1,518
National school lunch program (NSLP):									
Free lunches served	Million	1,662	2,090	2,205	2,277	2,335	2,397	2,477	2,496
Reduced-price lunches served	Million	273	308	409	441	453	462	479	488
Children participating [1]	Million	24.1	25.7	27.3	28.0	28.4	29.0	29.6	30.1
Federal cost	Mil. dol.	3,214	4,466	5,493	6,050	6,341	6,663	7,055	7,389
School breakfast (SB):									
Children participating [1]	Million	4.1	6.3	7.6	8.1	8.4	8.9	9.4	9.8
Federal cost	Mil. dol.	596	1,048	1,393	1,567	1,652	1,776	1,927	2,046
Special supplemental food program (WIC): [2]									
Participants	Million	4.5	6.9	7.2	7.5	7.6	7.9	8.0	8.1
Federal cost	Mil. dol.	1,637	2,512	2,853	3,130	3,230	3,562	3,603	3,599
Child and adult care (CAC): [3]									
Participants [4]	Million	1.5	2.3	2.7	2.8	2.9	3.0	3.1	3.1
Federal cost	Mil. dol.	719	1,296	1,500	1,657	1,726	1,812	1,905	1,945
Federal cost of commodities donated to— [5]									
Child nutrition (NSLP, CACFP, SFS, and SBP)	Mil. dol.	644	733	704	862	909	1,031	1,047	875
Emergency feeding [6]	Mil. dol.	282	100	182	380	396	363	322	250

[1] Average monthly participation (excluding summer months of June through August). Includes children in public and private elementary and secondary schools and in residential child care institutes. [2] WIC serves pregnant and postpartum women, infants, and children up to age five. [3] CACFP provides year-round subsidies to feed preschool children in child care centers and family day care homes. Certain care centers serving disabled or elderly adults also receive meal subsidies. [4] Average quarterly daily attendance at participating institutions. [5] Includes the federal cost of commodity entitlements, cash-in-lieu of commodities, and bonus foods. [6] Provides free commodities to needy persons for home consumption through food banks, hunger centers, soup kitchens, and similar nonprofit agencies. Includes the Emergency Food Assistance Program, the commodity purchases in soup kitchens/food banks program (FY 1989–96), and commodity disaster relief.

Source: U.S. Department of Agriculture, Food and Nutrition Service, "Food and Nutrition Service, Program Data"; <http://www.fns.usda.gov/pd/>; updated monthly.

Table 552. Federal Food Stamp Program by State: 2000 to 2006

[Participation data are average monthly numbers (17,194 represents 17,194,000). For years ending September 30. Food stamp costs are for benefits only and exclude administrative expenditures]

State	Persons (1,000) 2000	2005	2006	Benefits (mil. dol.) 2000	2005	2006	State	Persons (1,000) 2000	2005	2006	Benefits (mil. dol.) 2000	2005	2006
Total [1]	17,194	25,674	26,736	14,983	28,566	30,174	MS	276	391	511	226	463	507
U.S.	17,156	25,634	26,694	14,927	28,491	30,099	MO	423	766	796	358	736	740
AL	396	559	547	344	616	594	MT	59	81	82	51	89	90
AK	38	56	57	46	80	86	NE	82	117	120	61	120	124
AZ	259	550	541	240	634	626	NV	61	122	118	57	129	124
AR	247	374	385	206	401	414	NH	36	52	56	28	51	58
CA	1,831	1,992	2,000	1,639	2,313	2,363	NJ	345	392	406	304	437	456
CO	156	246	251	127	313	321	NM	169	241	245	140	251	253
CT	165	204	210	138	223	239	NY	1,439	1,755	1,786	1,361	2,136	2,240
DE	32	62	66	31	65	70	NC	488	800	854	403	856	921
DC	81	89	89	77	103	104	ND	32	42	43	25	45	46
FL	882	1,382	1,418	771	1,598	1,684	OH	610	1,007	1,064	520	1,155	1,266
							OK	253	424	436	208	440	467
GA	559	921	947	489	1,048	1,098	OR	234	429	434	198	456	463
HI	118	94	88	166	156	148	PA	777	1,043	1,092	656	1,105	1,182
ID	58	93	91	46	103	100	RI	74	76	73	59	79	81
IL	817	1,158	1,225	777	1,400	1,503							
IN	300	556	575	268	627	648	SC	295	521	534	249	566	589
IA	123	207	226	100	220	244	SD	43	56	58	37	61	66
KS	117	178	183	83	180	188	TN	496	850	870	415	942	976
KY	403	570	589	337	611	645	TX	1,333	2,442	2,623	1,215	2,659	2,939
LA	500	808	830	448	979	1,032	UT	82	133	132	68	141	140
ME	102	153	160	81	162	169	VT	41	45	47	32	45	50
							VA	336	488	507	263	500	526
MD	219	289	305	199	320	336	WA	295	508	536	241	539	595
MA	232	368	432	182	363	422	WV	227	262	268	185	258	266
MI	603	1,048	1,134	457	1,099	1,239	WI	193	346	368	129	317	347
MN	196	260	264	165	275	282	WY	22	25	24	19	27	26

[1] Includes Guam and the Virgin Islands. Several outlying areas receive nutrition assistance grants in lieu of food stamps (Puerto Rico, American Samoa, and the Northern Marianas).

Source: U.S. Department of Agriculture, Food and Nutrition Service. "Food and Nutrition Service, Program Data"; <http://www.fns.usda.gov/pd/>; updated monthly.

Social Insurance and Human Services **361**

Table 553. Selected Characteristics of Food Stamp Households and Participants: 1990 to 2005

[7,796 represents 7,796,000. For years ending September 30. Data for 1990 exclude Guam and the Virgin Islands. Based on a sample of households from the Food Stamp Quality Control System]

Year	Households				Participants		
	Total (1,000)	Percent of total			Total (1,000)	Percent of total	
		With children	With elderly [1]	With disabled [2]		Children	Elderly [1]
1990	7,796	60.3	18.1	8.9	20,049	49.6	7.7
1995	10,879	59.7	16.0	18.9	26,619	51.5	7.1
2000	7,325	53.9	21.0	27.5	17,139	51.3	10.0
2001	7,447	53.6	20.4	27.7	17,313	51.1	9.6
2002	8,193	54.1	18.7	27.0	19,098	51.0	8.9
2003	9,154	54.7	18.0	23.3	21,260	50.8	8.5
2004	10,279	54.3	17.3	22.9	23,858	50.2	8.2
2005	11,184	53.8	17.1	23.1	25,683	50.0	8.2

[1] Persons 60 years old and over. [2] The substantial increase in 1995 and decrease in 2003 are due in part to the changes in definition of a disabled household. Prior to 1995, disabled households were defined as households with SSI income but no members over age 59. In 1995, that definition changed to households with at least one member under 65 who received SSI, or at least one member age 18–61 who received social security, veterans' benefits, or other government benefits as a result of a disability. Because of changes to the QC data in 2003, the definition of a disabled household changed to households either SSI income or a medical expense deduction and without an elderly person, and households containing a nonelderly adult who does not appear to be working and who is receiving social security, veterans' benefits, or workers' compensation.

Source: U.S. Department of Agriculture, Food and Nutrition Service, Totals obtained from the National Data Bank. Percentages obtained from *Characteristics of Food Stamp Households: Fiscal Year 2005*, September 2006.

Table 554. Food Stamp Households and Participants—Summary: 2005

[10,854 represents 10,854,000. For year ending September 30. Based on a sample of 46,963 households from the Food Stamp Quality Control System. Figures are lower than official participation counts because they do not include ineligible participants or those receiving disaster food stamp assistance]

Household type and income source	Households		Age, sex, race, and Hispanic origin	Participants	
	Number (1,000)	Percent		Number (1,000)	Percent
Total	10,854	100.0	Total.................	24,881	100.0
With children	5,838	53.8	Children.................	12,429	50.0
Single-parent households	3,635	33.5	Under 5 years old...........	4,277	17.2
Married-couple households	1,037	9.6	5 to 17 years old	8,152	32.8
Other	1,166	11.6	Adults................	12,450	53.0
With elderly	1,856	17.1	18 to 35 years old	5,456	21.9
Living alone	1,456	13.4	36 to 59 years old	4,947	19.9
Not living alone...............	400	3.7	60 years old and over........	2,047	8.2
Disabled	2,505	23.1			
Living alone	1,386	12.8	Male	10,174	40.9
Not living alone...............	1,119	10.3	Female	14,701	59.1
Earned income..................	3,180	29.3	White, non-Hispanic...........	10,727	43.1
Wages and salaries	2,837	26.1	Black, non-Hispanic...........	8,299	33.4
Unearned income..................	7,393	68.1	Hispanic.................	4,786	19.2
TANF [1]	1,575	14.5	Asian..................	594	2.4
Supplemental security income	2,872	26.5	Native American	367	1.5
Social security	2,506	23.1	Other..................	108	0.4
No income	1,480	13.6			

[1] Temporary Assistance for Needy Families (TANF) program.

Source: U.S. Department of Agriculture, Food and Nutrition Service, *Characteristics of Food Stamp Households: Fiscal Year 2005*, September 2006. See also <http://www.fns.usda.gov/oane/menu/published/fsp/fspparthh.htm>.

Table 555. Head Start—Summary: 1980 to 2006

[For years ending September 30 (376 represents 376,000)]

Year	Enrollment (1,000)	Appropriation (mil. dol.)	Age and race	Enrollment, 2006 (percent)	Item	Number
1980 ...	376	735	Under 3 years old	10	Average cost per child:	
1990 ...	541	1,552	3 years old..........	35	1995	$4,534
1995 ...	751	3,534	4 years old.	51	2000	$5,951
1997 ...	794	3,981	5 years old and over ...	4	2006	$7,209
1998 ...	822	4,347				
1999 ...	826	4,658	White	40	Paid staff (1,000):	
2000 ...	858	5,267	Black	31	1995	147
2001 ...	905	6,200	Hispanic	34	2000	180
2002 ...	912	6,537	American Indian/		2006	218
2003 ...	910	6,668	Alaska Native	4	Volunteers (1,000):	
2004 ...	906	6,775	Asian	2	1995	1,235
2005 ...	907	6,843	Hawaiian/		2000	1,252
2006 ...	909	6,786	Pacific Islander	1	2006	1,365

Source: U.S. Department of Health and Human Services, Administration for Children and Families, "Head Start Statistical Fact Sheet"; <http://www.acf.hhs.gov/programs/hsb/about/index.html#factsheet>.

362   Social Insurance and Human Services

Table 556. Number of Emergency and Transitional Beds in Homeless Assistance Systems Nationwide: 2005

[The data are based on a nationally representative sample of 80 jurisdictions that collect data from emergency shelters and transitional providers. The data estimate homeless persons who used emergency shelters or transitional housing from February 2 through April 30, 2005. As a compliment to the survey, a "Continuum of Care" community was derived from each jurisdiction in order to estimate the number of unsheltered homeless persons and the number of emergency shelter and transitional housing beds available on a single night in January 2005. The data do not include homeless individuals living outside a sampled jurisdiction or homeless individuals not using an emergency shelter or a transitional housing program. For more information on data collection and methodology, see Appendix B of source]

| Homeless programs | Year-round units/beds [1] | | | | Other beds | |
	Family units	Family beds	Individual beds	Total year-round beds	Seasonal beds [2]	Overflow/voucher [3]
Emergency Shelters	30,593	100,730	117,217	217,947	24,923	48,622
Transitional Housing	33,580	115,225	105,140	220,365	(NA)	(NA)
Total Inventory	64,173	215,955	222,357	438,312	24,923	48,622
Permanent Supportive Housing.	32,159	84,051	124,602	208,653	(NA)	(NA)

NA Not available. [1] Year-round beds are available for use throughout the year and are considered part of the stable inventory of beds for homeless persons. [2] Seasonal beds are typically available during particularly high-demand seasons of the year (e.g. winter months in the North or summer months in the South) to accommodate increased need for emergency shelters to prevent illness or death due to the weather. [3] Overflow beds are typically used during unanticipated emergencies (e.g. precipititous temperature drops or a natural disaster displaces residents). Voucher beds are made available in a hotel or motel, and often function like overflow beds.

Source: U.S. Department of Housing and Urban Development, *Annual Homeless Assessment Report to Congress* (released February 2007). See also <http://huduser.org/publications/povsoc/annual_assess.html>.

Table 557. Social Assistance Services—Revenue for Employer Firms: 2000 to 2005

[In millions of dollars (77,032 represents $77,032,000,000). Based on the North American Industry Classification System, 1997, (NAICS), see text, Section 15. See Appendix III]

| Kind of business | NAICS code | 2000, total | 2004, total | 2005 | | |
				Total	Taxable firms	Tax-exempt firms
Social assistance.	624	77,032	103,745	109,261	23,956	85,305
Individual and family services	6241	37,311	50,177	51,737	6,894	44,843
Child and youth services	62411	7,517	9,755	10,103	861	9,242
Services for elderly and disabled persons . . .	62412	12,804	17,711	19,007	3,369	15,638
Other individual and family services	62419	16,990	22,711	22,627	2,664	19,963
Community, emergency and other relief services	6242	12,281	16,593	18,796	113	18,683
Community food services	62421	2,835	3,505	3,758	(S)	3,735
Community housing services	62422	4,888	6,397	6,548	67	6,481
Emergency and other relief services.	62423	4,558	6,691	8,490	(S)	8,467
Vocational rehabilitation services.	6243	9,458	13,025	13,546	2,424	11,122
Child day care services	6244	17,982	23,950	25,182	14,525	10,657

S Figure does not meet publication standards.

Source: U.S. Census Bureau, *Service Annual Survey*, 2005. See also <http://www.census.gov/svsd/www/services/sas/sas_data/sas62.htm>.

Table 558. Social Assistance—Nonemployer Establishments and Receipts: 1997 to 2004

[Receipts in millions of dollars (5,451 represents $5,451,000,000). Includes only firms subject to federal income tax. Nonemployers are businesses with no paid employees. Based on the North American Industry Classification System 2002 (NAICS), see text, Section 15]

| Kind of business | NAICS code | Establishments | | | Receipts | | |
		1997	2000	2004	1997	2000	2004
Social assistance, total	624	526,512	642,946	781,700	5,451	7,539	9,873
Individual & family services	6241	33,227	72,433	108,731	592	1,106	1,798
Community/emergency & other relief services. . .	6242	1,338	3,560	4,960	24	54	74
Vocational rehabilitation services	6243	3,213	7,314	10,676	82	151	233
Child day care services	6244	488,734	559,639	657,333	4,754	6,228	7,768

Source: U.S. Census Bureau, "Nonemployer Statistics"; <http://www.census.gov/epcd/nonemployer/index.html> (released July 2006).

Social Insurance and Human Services 363

Table 559. **Child Care Arrangements of Preschool Children by Type of Arrangement: 1991 to 2005**

[In percent, except as indicated (8,428 represents 8,428,000). Estimates are based on children 3 to 5 years old who have not entered kindergarten. Based on interviews from a sample survey of the civilian, noninstitutional population in households with telephones; see source for details. See also Appendix III]

Characteristic	Children		Type of nonparental arrangement [1]			
	Number (1,000)	Percent distribution	In relative care	In nonrelative care	In center-based program [2]	With parental care only
1991, total	8,428	100.0	16.9	14.8	52.8	31.0
1995, total	9,232	100.0	19.4	16.9	55.1	25.9
2005, total	**9,066**	**100.0**	**22.6**	**11.6**	**57.2**	**26.3**
Age:						
3 years old	4,070	44.9	24.0	14.4	42.5	33.4
4 years old	3,873	42.7	20.8	9.2	69.2	20.6
5 years old	1,123	12.4	23.8	9.9	68.7	20.4
Race-ethnicity:						
White, non-Hispanic	5,177	57.1	21.4	15.0	59.1	24.1
Black, non-Hispanic.	1,233	13.6	25.0	5.2	66.5	19.5
Hispanic	1,822	20.1	22.7	8.1	43.4	38.0
Other	834	9.2	26.4	8.1	61.5	24.7
Household income:						
Less than $10,001	795	8.8	25.1	8.6	53.4	33.4
$10,001 to $20,000	978	10.8	26.0	7.8	49.2	27.2
$20,001 to $30,000	1,183	13.1	25.4	6.3	43.9	38.5
$30,001 to $40,000	1,124	12.4	23.8	6.9	48.7	33.4
$40,001 to $50,000	808	8.9	21.8	11.6	50.0	35.4
$50,001 to $75,000	1,849	20.4	21.1	13.3	57.1	25.5
$75,001 or more	2,329	25.7	19.8	18.0	75.1	11.4

[1] Columns do not add to 100.0 because some children participated in more than one type of nonparental arrangement.
[2] Center-based programs include day care centers, Head Start programs, preschools, prekindergarten, and nursery schools.

Source: U.S. Department of Education, National Center for Education Statistics, Early Childhood Program Participation Survey of the National Household Education Surveys Program (NHES), 2005.

Table 560. **Licensed Child Care Centers and Family Child Care Providers by State and Other Areas: 2005**

[Centers as of February; family child care providers as of August. Licensed programs are required to have permission from the state to operate and must meet specified family child care or center standards. Some states may call their regulatory processes certification or registration. Family child care providers are programs that operate in the licensee's residence with at least one provider]

State	Licensed child care centers	Licensed family child care providers	State	Licensed child care centers	Licensed family child care providers	State	Licensed child care centers	Licensed family child care providers
US, total. .	**105,444**	**213,966**	KY [4]	2,256	1,029	OH	3,876	154
AL	1,372	1,722	LA [5]	1,993	[5]	OK	1,526	4,325
AK	107	324	ME	707	1,789	OR [6]	976	4,692
AZ [1]	2,182	371	MD	2,672	9,775	PA	3,989	5,197
AR [2]	1,762	987	MA	2,263	9,403	RI	460	1,314
CA	14,841	44,494	MI	4,588	13,715	SC [7]	1,339	303
CO	1,282	4,281	MN	1,577	13,085	SD [7]	298	92
CT	1,560	3,078	MS	1,588	126	TN	2,304	1,468
DE	409	1,614	MO	1,938	2,069	TX	8,889	10,154
DC	360	237	MT	271	1,141	UT [8]	268	2,342
FL.	4,248	2,409	NE	854	3,066	VT [8]	640	1,244
GA	3,019	6,736	NV	447	524	VA	2,700	1,678
HI	543	462	NH	798	359	WA	2,114	6,280
ID [3]	[3]	[3]	NJ [5]	4,262	[5]	WV	432	2,427
IL	2,898	10,643	NM	636	420	WI [9]	2,418	3,192
IN	617	3,111	NY	3,626	12,093	WY	207	546
IA	1,495	6,193	NC	4,400	4,671			
KS	1,270	7,316	ND	167	1,315			

[1] Voluntary licensing for family child care homes caring for four or fewer children. [2] Voluntary registration for family child care homes caring for five or fewer children. [3] Voluntary licensing for centers and family child care homes. [4] The state also has certified family child care homes. Information reported was only for licensed family child care homes. [5] Voluntary registration for family child care homes. [6] Voluntary licensing for public assistance reimbursement programs and programs caring for three or fewer children. [7] The state also has voluntarily registered family day care homes. [8] The state also has legally exempt child care. [9] The state also certifies small family care homes that wish to receive state subsidy reimbursement.

Source: National Association for Regulatory Administration, Conyers, GA, *Child Care Center Licensing Study*, 2005 (copyright). See also <http://www.nara.affiniscape.com/displaycommon.cfm?an=1&subarticlenbr=99>.

Table 561. **Foster Care and Adoption: 2004 and 2005**

[Data are preliminary and cover the period from October 1 of prior year through September 30 of year shown]

Characteristic	In foster care 2004	In foster care 2005	Entered foster care 2004	Entered foster care 2005	Exited foster care 2004	Exited foster care 2005	Waiting to be adopted 2004	Waiting to be adopted 2005	Adopted from foster care 2004	Adopted from foster care 2005
Total............	517,000	513,000	305,000	311,000	283,000	287,000	118,000	114,000	52,000	51,000
AGE										
Under 1 year.......	26,642	29,034	43,721	46,954	13,413	14,081	4,207	4,203	957	1,108
1 to 5 years	131,434	135,534	81,961	85,724	82,696	85,198	37,990	38,275	25,014	25,762
6 to 10 years	103,562	100,788	58,994	58,832	59,078	57,723	31,043	29,359	14,905	14,248
11 to 15 years., ...	150,621	142,935	86,442	84,612	66,146	64,587	34,302	33,282	9,178	8,327
16 to 20 years [1]	104,743	104,710	33,882	34,878	62,556	65,411	10,454	8,882	1,605	1,556
RACE										
White [2]	205,561	208,537	141,506	144,679	127,866	130,235	44,991	45,096	21,971	22,088
Black [2]...........	175,089	166,482	81,253	80,430	82,373	81,542	45,025	40,840	16,726	15,230
Asian [2]	3,099	2,973	2,468	2,454	2,400	2,328	484	448	258	337
Hispanic [3]	93,759	93,996	54,433	56,603	47,832	49,398	16,997	17,240	8,719	8,959
SEX										
Male	271,780	269,036	(NA)	(NA)	(NA)	(NA)	62,886	60,843	26,324	25,962
Female	245,220	243,964	(NA)	(NA)	(NA)	(NA)	55,114	53,157	25,676	25,038

NA Not available.   [1] For children waiting to be adopted, includes ages 16 to 17 only.   [2] Beginning with the 2000 Census, respondents could choose more than one race. Data represent persons who selected this race group only and exclude persons reporting more than one race. The census in prior years only allowed respondents to report one race group. See also comments on race in text, Section 1.   [3] Hispanic persons may be any race.

Source: U.S. Department of Health and Human Services, Administration for Children and Families, Adoption and Foster Care Analysis and Reporting System Reports, annual. See also <http://www.acf.hhs.gov/programs/cb/stats_research/index.htm#afcars>.

Table 562. **Private Philanthropy Funds by Source and Allocation: 1990 to 2005**

[In billions of dollars (101.4 represents $101,400,000,000). Estimates for sources of funds based on U.S. Internal Revenue Service reports of individual charitable deductions and household surveys of giving by Independent Sector and the Center on Philanthropy at Indiana University. For corporate giving, data are corporate charitable deductions from the U.S. Internal Revenue Service and the contributions made by corporate foundations as reported by the Foundation Center. Data about foundation donations are based upon surveys of foundations and data provided by the Foundation Center. Estimates of the allocation of funds were derived from surveys of nonprofits conducted by various sources]

Source and allocation	1990	1995	1996	1997	1998	1999	2000	2001	2002	2003	2004	2005
Total funds	101.4	124.0	138.6	159.4	177.4	201.0	227.7	229.0	234.1	236.7	245.2	260.3
Individuals.............	81.0	95.4	107.6	124.2	138.4	154.6	174.5	172.4	175.0	180.6	187.9	199.1
Foundations [1]	7.2	10.6	12.0	13.9	17.0	20.5	24.6	27.2	26.8	28.8	30.0
Corporations	5.5	7.4	7.5	8.6	8.5	10.2	10.7	11.7	12.9	11.2	12.0	13.8
Charitable bequests	7.6	10.7	11.5	12.6	13.6	15.6	17.9	17.7	19.2	18.1	19.8	17.4
Allocation:												
Religion................	49.8	58.1	61.9	64.7	68.3	71.3	77.0	79.9	82.8	84.6	88.0	93.2
Health................	9.9	12.6	13.9	14.0	16.9	18.0	18.8	19.3	18.9	20.9	22.0	22.5
Education	12.4	17.6	19.2	22.0	25.3	27.5	31.7	32.0	31.8	32.1	34.1	38.6
Human service	11.8	11.7	12.2	12.7	16.1	17.4	18.0	20.7	18.7	18.9	19.2	25.4
Arts, culture, and humanities ..	7.9	10.0	10.9	10.6	10.5	11.1	11.5	12.1	12.2	13.1	14.0	13.5
Public/societal benefit.......	4.9	7.1	7.6	8.4	10.9	11.0	11.6	11.8	11.6	12.1	13.0	14.0
Environment/wildlife	2.5	3.8	3.8	4.1	5.3	5.8	6.2	6.4	6.6	7.1	7.6	8.9
International	1.3	2.9	2.8	2.6	2.9	3.6	3.7	4.1	4.6	5.3	5.4	6.4
Gifts to foundations [1]	3.8	8.5	12.6	14.0	19.9	28.8	24.7	25.7	19.2	21.6	20.3	21.7
Unallocated [2]	-3.0	-8.2	-6.3	6.3	1.5	6.8	24.6	17.0	27.7	21.0	21.8	16.2

[1] Data are from the Foundation Center through 2001.   [2] Money deducted as a charitable contribution by donors but not allocated to sources. May include gifts to governmental entities, in-kind giving, gifts to new charities.

Source: Giving USA Foundation, Glenview, IL, researched and written by the Center on Philanthropy at Indiana University, Giving USA, annual (copyright).

Social Insurance and Human Services   365

Table 563. Foundations—Number and Finances: 1990 to 2005

[142.5 represents $142,500,000,000. Covers nongovernmental nonprofit organizations with funds and programs managed by their own trustees or directors, whose goals were to maintain or aid social, educational, religious, or other activities deemed to serve the common good. Excludes organizations that make general appeals to the public for funds, act as trade associations for industrial or other special groups, or do not currently award grants. Constant dollar figures based on Consumer Price Index, all urban consumers, supplied by U.S. Bureau of Labor Statistics. Minus sign (–) indicates decrease]

Year	Number of foundations	Assets Current dollars Amt. (bil. dol.)	Current dollars Percent change [1]	Constant (1975) dollars Amt. (bil. dol.)	Constant (1975) dollars Percent change [1]	Total giving [2] Current dollars Amt. (bil. dol.)	Current dollars Percent change [1]	Constant (1975) dollars Amt. (bil. dol.)	Constant (1975) dollars Percent change [1]	Gifts received Current dollars Amt. (bil. dol.)	Current dollars Percent change [1]	Constant (1978) dollars Amt. (bil. dol.)	Constant (1978) dollars Percent change [1]
1990 ..	32,401	142.5	3.6	58.7	-1.7	8.7	9.7	3.6	4.1	5.0	-10.0	2.5	-14.6
1995 ..	40,140	226.7	15.8	80.1	12.6	12.3	8.6	4.3	5.6	10.3	26.9	4.4	23.5
2000 ..	56,582	486.1	8.4	154.9	4.8	27.6	18.2	8.6	14.3	27.6	-13.9	10.5	-16.7
2005 ..	71,095	550.5	7.8	151.7	4.3	36.4	14.3	10.0	10.3	31.4	30.9	10.5	26.8

[1] Percent change from immediate preceding year. [2] Includes grants, scholarships, and employee matching gifts; exludes set-asides, loans, program-related investments (PRIs), and program expenses.

Source: The Foundation Center, New York, NY, FC Stats; <http://fdncenter.org/fc_stats/index.html>; (copyright).

Table 564. Foundations—Number and Finances by Asset Size: 2005

[Figures are for latest year reported by foundations (550,552 represents $550,552,000,000). See headnote, Table 563]

Asset size	Number	Assets (mil. dol.)	Gifts received (mil. dol.)	Expenditures (mil. dol.)	Total giving [1] (mil. dol.)	Percent distribution Number	Percent distribution Assets	Percent distribution Gifts received	Percent distribution Expenditures	Percent distribution Grants
Total	71,095	550,552	31,465	44,716	36,403	100.0	100.0	100.0	100.0	100.0
Under $50,000	12,360	187	2,495	2,784	2,682	17.4	(Z)	7.9	6.2	7.4
$50,000–$99,999	4,875	359	190	261	220	6.9	0.1	0.6	0.6	0.6
$100,000–$249,999	9,313	1,558	364	524	436	13.1	0.3	1.2	1.2	1.2
$250,000–$499,999	8,789	3,200	490	618	512	12.4	0.6	1.6	1.4	1.4
$500,000–$999,999	9,783	7,065	767	1,078	925	13.8	1.3	2.4	2.4	2.5
$1,000,000–$4,999,999	16,523	37,271	3,970	4,696	4,016	23.2	6.8	12.6	10.5	11.0
$5,000,000–$9,999,999	3,905	27,224	2,639	2,769	2,288	5.5	4.9	8.4	6.2	6.3
$10,000,000–$49,999,999. ...	4,198	88,849	7,068	8,133	6,770	5.9	16.1	22.5	18.2	18.6
$50,000,000–$99,999,999	678	46,920	3,588	3,848	2,980	1.0	8.5	11.4	8.6	8.2
$100,000,000–$249,999,999 ..	428	64,202	3,184	4,651	3,768	0.6	11.7	10.1	10.4	10.3
$250,000,000 or more	243	273,717	6,712	15,354	11,807	0.3	49.7	21.3	34.3	32.4

Z Less than 0.05 percent. [1] See footnote 2, Table 563.

Source: The Foundation Center, New York, NY, Foundation Yearbook, annual (copyright).

Table 565. Domestic Private Foundations—Information Returns: 1990 to 2003

[Money amounts in billions of dollars (122.4 represents $122,400,000,000). Minus sign (–) indicates loss]

Item	1990	1995	1996	1997	1998	1999	2000	2001	2002	2003
Number of returns..........	40,105	47,917	50,774	55,113	56,658	62,694	66,738	70,787	73,255	76,348
Nonoperating foundations ...	36,880	43,966	46,066	50,541	52,460	58,840	61,501	63,650	67,101	70,004
Operating foundations	3,226	3,951	4,708	4,572	4,198	3,854	5,238	7,137	6,154	6,344
Total assets, book value......	122.4	195.6	232.6	280.9	325.7	384.6	409.5	413.6	383.5	418.5
Total assets, fair market value..	151.0	242.9	288.6	342.7	397.1	466.9	471.6	455.4	413.0	475.0
Investments in securities....	115.0	190.7	225.1	272.4	317.9	363.4	361.4	329.4	294.4	344.3
Total revenue............	19.0	30.8	48.2	55.5	59.7	83.3	72.8	45.3	27.8	48.4
Total expenses...........	11.3	17.2	19.9	22.4	25.9	33.9	37.4	36.7	34.4	35.1
Contributions, gifts, and grants paid.........	8.6	12.3	14.5	16.4	19.4	22.8	27.6	27.4	26.3	26.7
Excess of revenue over expenses (net).......	7.7	13.6	28.4	33.0	33.8	49.4	35.3	8.6	-6.6	13.3
Net investment income [1]	11.9	20.4	26.2	34.8	39.3	57.1	48.8	25.7	17.6	25.2

[1] Represents income not considered related to a foundation's charitable purpose, e.g., interest, dividends, and capital gains. Foundations could be subject to an excise tax on such income.

Source: Internal Revenue Service, Statistics of Income, SOI Tax Stats—Charities & Other Tax-Exempt Organizations; <http://www.irs.gov/taxstats/charitablestats/article/0,,id=97176,00.html> (accessed 18 April 2007).

366 Social Insurance and Human Services

Table 566. Nonprofit Charitable Organizations—Information Returns: 1990 to 2003

[In billions of dollars (697.3 represents $697,300,000,000), except as indicated. Categories based on The National Taxonomy of Exempt Entities (NTEE), a classification system that uses 26 major field areas that are aggregated into 10 categories. Includes data reported by organizations described in Internal Revenue Code section 501(3), excluding private foundations and most religious organizations. Organizations with receipts under $25,000 were not required to file]

Year and category	Number of returns (1,000)	Total assets	Total fund balance or net worth	Revenue Total	Revenue Program service revenue [1]	Revenue Contributions, gifts, and grants	Total expenses	Excess of revenue over expenses (net)
1990.	141.8	697.3	375.3	435.6	306.9	85.3	409.4	26.1
2000.	230.2	1,562.5	1,023.2	866.2	579.1	199.1	796.4	69.8
2003, total	**263.4**	**1,899.9**	**1,164.3**	**1,072.2**	**754.6**	**230.0**	**1,009.7**	**62.5**
Arts, culture, and humanities .	27.3	76.1	62.0	24.9	6.4	14.0	21.1	3.7
Education.	47.1	619.9	440.7	201.6	110.2	59.9	175.5	26.1
Environment, animals	10.5	27.5	22.7	9.7	2.3	5.9	8.6	1.1
Health	35.1	741.8	386.5	611.1	537.7	44.3	591.9	19.3
Human services.	100.8	220.0	105.9	151.9	81.4	58.8	147.6	4.3
International, foreign affairs . .	3.1	12.7	9.2	14.3	0.8	13.1	14.3	(Z)
Mutual, membership benefit . .	0.5	12.5	9.6	2.5	1.6	0.2	1.9	0.6
Public, societal benefit.	23.3	171.1	113.1	48.8	13.0	28.7	42.4	6.4
Religion related	15.6	18.2	14.6	7.4	1.1	5.2	6.4	0.9

Z Less than 50 million. [1] Represents fees collected by organizations in support of their tax-exempt purposes, and income such as tuition and fees at educational institutions, hospital patient charges, and admission and activity fees collected by museums and other nonprofit organizations or institutions.

Source: Internal Revenue Service, Statistics of Income, SOI Tax Stats—Charities & Other Tax-Exempt Organizations Statistics. See also <http://www.irs.gov/taxstats/charitablestats/article/0,,id=97176,00.html> (accessed 18 April 2007).

Table 567. Individual Charitable Contributions by State: 2004

[In millions (40,426.9 represents 40,426,900,000)]

State	Charitable contribution Number	Charitable contribution Amount (mil. dol.)	State	Charitable contribution Number	Charitable contribution Amount (mil. dol.)
United States.	**40,426.9**	**162,198.7**	Missouri	687.9	2,595.7
Alabama	516.2	2,492.7	Montana	111.8	348.8
Alaska	69.7	260.4	Nebraska	218.6	848.8
Arizona.	789.3	2,726.7	Nevada.	346.7	1,500.6
Arkansas.	235.0	1,224.1	New Hampshire	196.9	547.5
California.	5,287.9	21,867.9	New Jersey	1,683.8	5,533.7
Colorado.	758.9	2,790.8	New Mexico.	182.6	597.8
Connecticut	666.9	2,690.0	New York	3,059.6	14,454.8
Delaware.	129.0	483.3	North Carolina	1,202.0	4,951.1
District of Columbia. . . .	104.3	663.5	North Dakota	47.5	177.3
Florida	2,182.1	9,481.9	Ohio.	1,549.0	4,899.6
Georgia	1,318.1	5,889.9	Oklahoma	384.8	1,848.9
Hawaii	178.4	560.9	Oregon	558.1	1,837.0
Idaho	175.0	707.0	Pennsylvania	1,640.8	5,687.3
Illinois.	1,840.4	7,054.5	Rhode Island	170.4	463.2
Indiana.	724.5	2,660.3	South Carolina	533.0	2,360.2
Iowa.	364.8	1,159.7	South Dakota	55.5	262.7
Kansas.	328.8	1,347.6	Tennessee.	563.7	3,027.3
Kentucky	461.1	1,642.6	Texas	1,991.6	9,927.6
Louisiana	347.9	1,476.7	Utah.	363.1	2,323.8
Maine	163.5	421.0	Vermont	74.2	212.7
Maryland.	1,177.5	4,887.2	Virginia	1,239.9	4,809.4
Massachusetts	1,134.3	3,930.4	Washington	886.7	3,435.4
Michigan	1,483.1	5,273.9	West Virginia	105.1	386.5
Minnesota	896.1	3,161.7	Wisconsin	861.0	2,397.3
Mississippi.	235.5	1,128.1	Wyoming.	41.4	322.2

Source: Internal Revenue Service, Statistics of Income Bulletin, Volume 25, Number 4, Spring 2006. See also <http://www.irs.gov /pub/irs-soi/spring06bul.pdf>.

Table 568. Volunteers by Selected Characteristics and Type of Main Organization: 2006

[In percent, except as noted. Data on volunteers relate to persons who performed unpaid volunteer activities for an organization at any point from September 1, 2005, through September 2006. Data represent the percent of the population involved in the activity]

Total and type of main organization [1]	Total both sexes	Sex — Men	Sex — Women	Age 16 to 24 years	Age 25 to 34 years	Age 35 to 44 years	Age 45 to 54 years	Age 55 to 64 years	Age 65 years and over	Race — White [2]	Race — Black [2]	Race — Asian [2]	Hispanic or Latino [3]	Educ. — Less than a high school diploma	Educ. — High school graduate, no college [5]	Educ. — Less than a bachelor's degree [6]	Educ. — College graduates	Civilian labor force — Total	Employed	Unemployed	Not in labor force
Total volunteers (1,000) . . .	61,199	25,546	35,653	8,044	9,096	13,308	13,415	8,819	8,518	52,850	5,211	1,881	4,212	2,615	11,537	15,196	23,808	43,579	41,861	1,718	17,621
Percent of population [7] . .	26.7	23.0	30.1	21.7	23.1	31.2	31.2	27.9	23.8	28.3	19.2	18.5	13.9	9.3	19.2	30.9	43.3	28.5	28.7	23.8	23.1
Median annual hours . .	52	52	50	40	36	48	52	63	104	52	52	30	42	50	52	52	55	48	48	48	70
Civic and political [8]	6.1	7.9	4.9	4.5	5.8	4.2	6.7	7.8	8.5	6.3	4.6	5.1	3.1	4.0	6.0	6.0	7.1	6.3	6.3	5.2	5.8
Educational or youth service	26.4	23.9	28.2	31.7	34.3	39.0	26.3	13.0	7.4	26.4	26.1	25.6	35.6	21.2	23.2	26.7	26.6	28.1	27.8	33.4	22.3
Environmental or animal care . . .	1.6	1.6	1.6	2.0	1.7	1.0	1.9	2.1	1.4	1.8	0.4	0.6	0.4	0.8	1.0	1.4	2.1	1.7	1.7	2.7	1.4
Hospital or other health . . .	8.1	6.1	9.6	8.0	8.8	6.1	7.5	10.4	9.4	8.4	5.2	9.8	5.5	6.0	8.2	8.6	8.1	8.2	8.2	7.7	8.0
Public safety	1.3	2.3	0.6	1.3	1.5	1.3	1.3	1.6	1.0	1.4	0.6	0.2	0.7	1.9	2.2	1.6	0.7	1.6	1.6	1.6	0.8
Religious	35.0	34.9	35.1	30.1	28.4	31.4	35.9	41.2	44.7	34.2	43.3	39.8	35.1	43.1	39.8	35.4	33.2	33.3	33.6	27.7	39.2
Social or community service	12.7	13.5	12.1	13.3	11.6	9.9	12.3	13.9	16.9	12.8	11.9	9.8	10.4	14.4	12.4	12.5	12.6	12.2	12.2	14.1	13.8
Sport and hobby [9]	3.7	4.6	3.1	3.2	3.1	3.1	3.7	4.7	4.5	3.9	1.8	3.1	3.9	3.1	3.0	3.6	4.3	3.8	3.8	3.0	3.5
Other	3.4	3.6	3.4	4.2	3.5	2.7	2.7	3.7	4.6	3.4	3.7	4.0	3.5	4.4	3.0	3.4	3.9	3.4	3.3	3.7	3.7
Not determined	1.5	1.7	1.4	1.8	1.4	1.2	1.7	1.5	1.6	1.4	2.5	1.9	1.9	1.2	1.2	1.0	1.9	1.5	1.5	0.9	1.5

[1] Main organization is defined as the organization for which the volunteer worked the most hours during the year. See headnote for more details. [2] Persons who selected this race group only; persons who selected more than one race group are not included. [3] Persons of Hispanic origin may be of any race. [4] Data refer to persons 25 years and over. [5] Includes high school diploma or equivalent. [6] Includes the categories, some college, no degree; and associate's degree. [7] For those reporting annual hours. [8] Includes professional and/or international. [9] Includes cultural and/or arts.

Source: U.S. Bureau of Labor Statistics, News, USDL 07-0019, January 10, 2007. See also <http://www.bls.gov/news.release/pdf/volun.pdf>.

Labor Force, Employment, and Earnings

This section presents statistics on the labor force; its distribution by occupation and industry affiliation; and the supply of, demand for, and conditions of labor. The chief source of these data is the Current Population Survey (CPS) conducted by the U.S. Census Bureau for the Bureau of Labor Statistics (BLS). Comprehensive historical and current data are available from the BLS Internet site <http://www.bls.gov/cps/>. These data are published on a current basis in the BLS monthly publication *Employment and Earnings*. Detailed data on the labor force are also available from the Census Bureau's decennial census of population.

Types of data—Most statistics in this section are obtained by two methods: household interviews or questionnaires and reports of establishment payroll records. Each method provides data that the other cannot suitably supply. Population characteristics, for example, are readily obtainable only from the household survey, while detailed industrial classifications can be readily derived only from establishment records.

Household data are obtained from a monthly sample survey of the population. The CPS is used to gather data for the calendar week including the 12th of the month and provides current comprehensive data on the labor force (see text, Section 1, Population). The CPS provides information on the work status of the population without duplication since each person is classified as employed, unemployed, or not in the labor force. Employed persons holding more than one job are counted only once, according to the job at which they worked the most hours during the survey week.

Monthly, quarterly, and annual data from the CPS are published by BLS in *Employment and Earnings*. Data presented include national totals of the number of persons in the civilian labor force by sex, race, Hispanic or Latino origin, and age; the number employed; hours of work; industry and occupational groups; and the number unemployed, reasons for, and duration of unemployment. Annual data shown in this section are averages of monthly figures for each calendar year, unless otherwise specified. Historical national CPS data are available on the Web site <http://www.bls.gov/cps/>.

The CPS also produces annual estimates of employment and unemployment for each state, 50 large metropolitan statistical areas, and selected cities. These estimates are published by BLS in its annual *Geographic Profile of Employment and Unemployment* available at <http://www.bls.gov/opub/gp/laugp.htm>. More detailed geographic data (e.g., for counties and cities) are provided by the decennial population censuses.

Data based on establishment records are compiled by BLS and cooperating state agencies as part of an ongoing Current Employment Statistics program. Survey data, gathered monthly from a sample of employers through electronic interviewing (including electronic data interchange, touchtone data entry, and computer-assisted telephone interviewing) or by mail, fax, on magnetic tape or computer diskette, are supplemented by data from other government agencies and adjusted at intervals to data from government social insurance program reports. The estimates exclude self-employed persons, private household workers, unpaid family workers, agricultural workers, and the Armed Forces. In March 2006, reporting establishments employed 3.9 million manufacturing workers (27 percent of the total manufacturing employment at the time), 20.8 million workers in private nonmanufacturing industries (21 percent of the total in private nonmanufacturing), and 15.5 million federal, state, and local government employees (70 percent of total government).

The establishment survey counts workers each time they appear on a payroll during the reference period (the payroll period that includes the 12th of the month). Thus, unlike the CPS, a person with two jobs is counted twice. The establishment survey is designed to provide detailed industry information for the nation, states, and metropolitan areas on non-farm wage and salary employment, average weekly hours, and average hourly and weekly earnings. Establishment survey data also are published in *Employment and Earnings*. Historical national data are available on the Web site <http://www.bls.gov/ces/>. Historical data for states and metropolitan areas are available on the Web site <http://www.bls.gov/sae/>.

In June 2003, BLS completed a comprehensive sample redesign of the establishment survey begun in June 2000, changing from a quota-based sample to a probability-based sample. Also in June 2003, all establishment survey employment, hours, and earnings series were converted from being classified by the 1987 Standard Industrial Classification (SIC) system to being classified by the 2002 North American Industry Classification System (NAICS). The NAICS conversion resulted in major definitional changes to many of the previously published SIC-based series. All establishment survey historical time series were reconstructed as part of the NAICS conversion process and all published series have a NAICS-based history extending back to at least 1990. For total nonfarm industries and other high-level aggregates, NAICS history was reconstructed back to the previously existing start date for the series, 1939 in most cases. More information on the sample redesign, the conversion to NAICS, and other changes to the establishment survey implemented in June 2003 appears in "Revisions to the Current Employment Statistics National Estimates Effective May 2003" in the June 2003 issue of *Employment and Earnings*, as well as the Establishment Data portion of the Explanatory Notes and Estimates of Error section of *Employment and Earnings*.

The completion of the sample redesign and the conversion to NAICS for state and metropolitan area establishment survey data were implemented in March 2003 with the release of January 2003 estimates. For a discussion of the changes to the state and area establishment survey data, see "Revisions to the Current Employment Statistics State and Area Estimates Effective January 2003" in the March 2003 issue of *Employment and Earnings*.

Labor force—According to the CPS definitions, the civilian labor force comprises all civilians in the noninstitutionalized population 16 years and over classified as "employed" or "unemployed" according to the following criteria: Employed civilians comprise (a) all civilians, who, during the reference week, did any work for pay or profit (minimum of an hour's work) or worked 15 hours or more as unpaid workers in a family enterprise and (b) all civilians who were not working but who had jobs or businesses from which they were temporarily absent for noneconomic reasons (illness, weather conditions, vacation, labor-management dispute, etc.) whether they were paid for the time off or were seeking other jobs. Unemployed persons comprise all civilians who had no employment during the reference week, who made specific efforts to find a job within the previous 4 weeks (such as applying directly to an employer or to a public employment service or checking with friends) and who were available for work during that week, except for temporary illness. Persons on layoff from a job and expecting recall also are classified as unemployed. All other civilian persons, 16 years old and over, are classified as "not in the labor force."

Various breaks in the CPS data series have occurred over time due to the introduction of population adjustments and other changes. For details on these breaks in series and the effect that they had on CPS data, see the section on noncomparability of labor force levels in the Household Data portion of the Explanatory Notes and Estimates of Error section of *Employment and Earnings* available on the site <http://www.bls.gov/cps/eetech_methods.pdf>.

Beginning in January 2006, the CPS data reflect the introduction of revised population controls. The effect of the revised

population controls on the monthly CPS estimates was to decrease the December 2005 employment level by 123,000 and the civilian noninstitutional population by 67,000. The updated controls had little or no effect on unemployment rates and other ratios. For additional information on the effects of the revised population controls on estimates from the CPS, see "Adjustments to Household Survey Population Estimates in January 2006" in the February 2006 issue of *Employment and Earnings*, available on the Internet at <http://www.bls.gov/cps/cps06adj.pdf>.

Hours and earnings—Average hourly earnings, based on establishment data, are gross earnings (i.e., earnings before payroll deductions) and include overtime premiums; they exclude irregular bonuses and value of payments in kind. Hours are those for which pay was received. Wages and salaries from the CPS consist of total monies received for work performed by an employee during the income year. It includes wages, salaries, commissions, tips, piece-rate payments, and cash bonuses earned before deductions were made for taxes, bonds, union dues, etc. Persons who worked 35 hours or more are classified as working full-time.

Industry and occupational groups—Industry data derived from the CPS for 1983–91 utilize the 1980 census industrial classification developed from the 1972 SIC. CPS data from 1971 to 1982 were based on the 1970 census classification system, which was developed from the 1967 SIC. Most of the industry categories were not affected by the change in classification.

The occupational classification system used in the 1980 census and in the CPS for 1983–91, evolved from the 1980 Standard Occupational Classification (SOC) system, first introduced in 1977. Occupational categories used in the 1980 census classification system are so radically different from the 1970 census system used in the CPS through 1982, that their implementation represented a break in historical data series. In cases where data have not yet been converted to the 1980 classifications and still reflect the 1970 classifications (e.g., Table 629), comparisons between the two systems should not be made.

Beginning in January 1992, the occupational and industrial classification systems used in the 1990 census were introduced into the CPS. (These systems were largely based on the 1980 SOC and the 1987 SIC systems, respectively.)

Beginning in 2003, the 2002 Census Bureau occupational and industrial classification systems were introduced into the CPS. These systems were derived from the 2000 SOC and the 2002 NAICS. The composition of detailed occupational and industrial classifications in the new classification systems was substantially changed from the previous systems in use, as was the structure for aggregating them into broad groups. Consequently, the use of the new classification systems created breaks in existing data series at all levels of aggregation. CPS data using the new classification systems are available beginning 2000. Additional information on the 2002 Census Bureau occupational and industrial classifications systems appears in "Revisions to the Current Population Survey Effective in January 2003" in the February 2003 issue of *Employment and Earnings*, available on the BLS Web site <http://www.bls.gov /cps/rvcps03.pdf>.

For details on the changes over time in the industrial and occupational classification systems used in the CPS, see the section on changes in the occupational and industrial classification systems in the Household Data portion of the Explanatory Notes and Estimates of Error section of *Employment and Earnings* available on the site <http://www.bls.gov/cps/eetech _methods.pdf>.

Establishments responding to the establishment survey are classified according to the 2002 NAICS. Previously they were classified according to the SIC manual. See text, Section 15, Business Enterprise, for information about the SIC manual and NAICS.

Productivity—BLS publishes data on productivity as measured by output per hour (labor productivity), output per combined unit of labor and capital input (multifactor productivity), and, for industry groups and industries, output per combined unit of capital, labor, energy, materials, and

purchased service inputs. Labor productivity and related indexes are published for the business sector as a whole and its major subsectors: nonfarm business, manufacturing, and nonfinancial corporations, and for over 200 detailed industries. Productivity indexes that take into account capital, labor, energy, materials, and service inputs are published for 18 major manufacturing industry groups, 86 detailed manufacturing industries, utility services, and air and railroad transportation. The major sector data are published in the BLS quarterly news release *Productivity and Costs* and in the annual *Multifactor Productivity Trends* release. Industry productivity measures are updated and published annually in the news releases *Productivity and Costs by Industry* and *Multifactor Productivity Trends by Industry*. The latest data are available at the Labor Productivity and Costs Web site <http://www.bls.gov/lpc/home.htm> and the Multifactor Productivity Web site <http://www.bls.gov/mfp.home.htm>. Detailed information on methods, limitations, and data sources appears in the BLS *Handbook of Methods*, BLS Bulletin 2490 (1997), Chapters 10 and 11.

Unions—As defined here, unions include traditional labor unions and employee associations similar to labor unions. Data on union membership status provided by BLS are for employed wage and salary workers and relate to their principal job. Earnings by union membership status are usual weekly earnings of full-time wage and salary workers. The information is collected through the Current Population Survey.

Work stoppages—Work stoppages include all strikes and lockouts known to BLS that last for at least 1 full day or shift and involve 1,000 or more workers. All stoppages, whether or not authorized by a union, legal or illegal, are counted. Excluded are work slowdowns and instances where employees report to work late or leave early to attend mass meetings or mass rallies.

Seasonal adjustment—Many economic statistics reflect a regularly recurring seasonal movement that can be estimated on the basis of past experience. By eliminating that part of the change which can be ascribed to usual seasonal variation (e.g., climate or school openings and closings), it is possible to observe the cyclical and other nonseasonal movements in the series. However, in evaluating deviations from the seasonal pattern—that is, changes in a seasonally adjusted series—it is important to note that seasonal adjustment is merely an approximation based on past experience. Seasonally adjusted estimates have a broader margin of possible error than the original data on which they are based, since they are subject not only to sampling and other errors, but also are affected by the uncertainties of the adjustment process itself.

Statistical reliability—For discussion of statistical collection, estimation, sampling procedures, and measures of statistical reliability applicable to Census Bureau and BLS data, see Appendix III.

Table 569. Civilian Population—Employment Status: 1970 to 2006

[In thousands (137,085 represents 137,085,000), except as indicated. Annual averages of monthly figures. Civilian noninstitutional population 16 years old and over. Based on Current Population Survey; see text, Section 1, and Appendix III]

Year	Civilian noninsti- tutional population	Civilian labor force						Not in labor force	
		Total	Percent of population	Employed	Employ- ment/ population ratio[1]	Unemployed			
						Number	Percent of labor force	Number	Percent of population
1970	137,085	82,771	60.4	78,678	57.4	4,093	4.9	54,315	39.6
1980	167,745	106,940	63.8	99,303	59.2	7,637	7.1	60,806	36.2
1985	178,206	115,461	64.8	107,150	60.1	8,312	7.2	62,744	35.2
1989	186,393	123,869	66.5	117,342	63.0	6,528	5.3	62,523	33.5
1990 [2]	189,164	125,840	66.5	118,793	62.8	7,047	5.6	63,324	33.5
1991	190,925	126,346	66.2	117,718	61.7	8,628	6.8	64,578	33.8
1992	192,805	128,105	66.4	118,492	61.5	9,613	7.5	64,700	33.6
1993 [2]	194,838	129,200	66.3	120,259	61.7	8,940	6.9	65,638	33.7
1994 [2]	196,814	131,056	66.6	123,060	62.5	7,996	6.1	65,758	33.4
1995	198,584	132,304	66.6	124,900	62.9	7,404	5.6	66,280	33.4
1996	200,591	133,943	66.8	126,708	63.2	7,236	5.4	66,647	33.2
1997 [2]	203,133	136,297	67.1	129,558	63.8	6,739	4.9	66,837	32.9
1998 [2]	205,220	137,673	67.1	131,463	64.1	6,210	4.5	67,547	32.9
1999 [2]	207,753	139,368	67.1	133,488	64.3	5,880	4.2	68,385	32.9
2000 [2]	212,577	142,583	67.1	136,891	64.4	5,692	4.0	69,994	32.9
2001	215,092	143,734	66.8	136,933	63.7	6,801	4.7	71,359	33.2
2002	217,570	144,863	66.6	136,485	62.7	8,378	5.8	72,707	33.4
2003 [2]	221,168	146,510	66.2	137,736	62.3	8,774	6.0	74,658	33.8
2004 [2]	223,357	147,401	66.0	139,252	62.3	8,149	5.5	75,956	34.0
2005 [2]	226,082	149,320	66.0	141,730	62.7	7,591	5.1	76,762	34.0
2006 [2]	228,815	151,428	66.2	144,427	63.1	7,001	4.6	77,387	33.8

[1] Civilian employed as a percent of the civilian noninstitutional population.   [2] Data not strictly comparable with data for earlier years. See text. this section, and February 1994, March 1996, February 1997–99, and February 2003–07 issues of *Employment and Earnings.*

Source: U.S. Bureau of Labor Statistics, Bulletin 2307; and *Employment and Earnings,* monthly, January 2007 issue. See Internet site <http://www.bls.gov/cps/home.htm>.

Table 570. Civilian Labor Force and Participation Rates With Projections: 1980 to 2014

[106.9 represents 106,900,000. Civilian noninstitutional population 16 years old and over. Annual averages of monthly figures. Rates are based on annual average civilian noninstitutional population of each specified group and represent proportion of each specified group in the civilian labor force. Based on Current Population Survey; see text, Section 1, and Appendix III]

Race, Hispanic origin, sex, and age	Civilian labor force (millions)						Participation rate (percent)					
	1980	1990 [1]	2000 [1]	2005 [1]	2006 [1]	2014, proj.	1980	1990 [1]	2000 [1]	2005 [1]	2006 [1]	2014, proj.
Total [2]	106.9	125.8	142.6	149.3	151.4	162.1	63.8	66.5	67.1	66.0	66.2	65.6
White [3]	93.6	107.4	118.5	122.3	123.8	129.9	64.1	66.9	67.3	66.3	66.5	65.9
Male	54.5	59.6	64.5	66.7	67.6	70.3	78.2	77.1	75.5	74.1	74.3	72.7
Female	39.1	47.8	54.1	55.6	56.2	59.6	51.2	57.4	59.5	58.9	59.0	59.3
Black [3]	10.9	13.7	16.4	17.0	17.3	19.4	61.0	64.0	65.8	64.2	64.1	63.4
Male	5.6	6.8	7.7	8.0	8.1	9.1	70.3	71.0	69.2	67.3	67.0	64.7
Female	5.3	6.9	8.7	9.0	9.2	10.4	53.1	58.3	63.1	61.6	61.7	62.3
Asian [3,4]	(NA)	(NA)	6.3	6.5	6.7	8.3	(NA)	(NA)	67.2	66.1	66.2	65.7
Male	(NA)	(NA)	3.4	3.5	3.6	4.4	(NA)	(NA)	76.1	74.8	75.0	74.4
Female	(NA)	(NA)	2.9	3.0	3.1	3.9	(NA)	(NA)	59.2	58.2	58.3	58.1
Hispanic [5]	6.1	10.7	16.7	19.8	20.7	25.8	64.0	67.4	69.7	68.0	68.7	69.2
Male	3.8	6.5	9.9	12.0	12.5	14.9	81.4	81.4	81.5	80.1	80.7	78.6
Female	2.3	4.2	6.8	7.8	8.2	10.8	47.4	53.1	57.5	55.3	56.1	59.3
Male..........	61.5	69.0	76.3	80.0	81.3	86.2	77.4	76.4	74.8	73.3	73.5	71.8
16 to 19 years	5.0	4.1	4.3	3.6	3.7	3.1	60.5	55.7	52.8	43.2	43.7	38.1
20 to 24 years	8.6	7.9	7.5	8.1	8.1	8.3	85.9	84.4	82.6	79.1	79.6	77.0
25 to 34 years	17.0	19.9	17.8	17.8	17.9	20.6	95.2	94.1	93.4	91.7	91.7	95.3
35 to 44 years	11.8	17.5	20.1	19.5	19.4	18.1	95.5	94.3	92.7	92.1	92.1	90.7
45 to 54 years	9.9	11.1	16.3	18.1	18.5	18.4	91.2	90.7	88.6	87.7	88.1	86.6
55 to 64 years	7.2	6.6	7.8	10.0	10.5	13.0	72.1	67.8	67.3	69.3	69.6	68.7
65 years and over ...	1.9	2.0	2.5	3.0	3.1	4.8	19.0	16.3	17.7	19.8	20.3	24.6
Female	45.5	56.8	66.3	69.3	70.2	75.9	51.5	57.5	59.9	59.3	59.4	59.7
16 to 19 years	4.4	3.7	4.0	3.6	3.6	3.2	52.9	51.6	51.2	44.2	43.7	40.4
20 to 24 years	7.3	6.8	6.7	7.1	7.0	7.6	68.9	71.3	73.1	70.1	69.5	70.6
25 to 34 years	12.3	16.1	14.9	14.5	14.6	16.2	65.5	73.5	76.1	73.9	74.4	75.4
35 to 44 years	8.6	14.7	17.5	16.5	16.4	15.3	65.5	76.4	77.2	75.8	75.9	75.4
45 to 54 years	7.0	9.1	14.8	16.3	16.7	17.2	59.9	71.2	76.8	76.0	76.0	78.1
55 to 64 years	4.7	4.9	6.6	8.9	9.5	12.6	41.3	45.2	51.9	57.0	58.2	61.9
65 years and over ...	1.2	1.5	1.8	2.3	2.4	3.9	8.1	8.6	9.4	11.5	11.7	15.9

NA Not available.   [1] See footnote 2, Table 569.   [2] Includes other races, not shown separately.   [3] The 2003 Current Population Survey (CPS) allowed respondents to choose more than one race. Beginning 2003, data represent persons who selected this race group only and exclude persons reporting more than one race. The CPS in prior years only allowed respondents to report one race group. See also comments on race in the text for Section 1.   [4] Prior to 2005, includes Pacific Islanders.   [5] Persons of Hispanic or Latino origin may be of any race.

Source: U.S. Bureau of Labor Statistics, *Employment and Earnings,* monthly, January 2007 issue; *Monthly Labor Review,* November 2005; and unpublished data. See Internet site <http://www.bls.gov/cps/home.htm>.

Labor Force, Employment, and Earnings   373

Table 571. Civilian Population—Employment Status by Sex, Race, and Ethnicity: 1970 to 2006

[In thousands (64,304 represents 64,304,000), except as indicated. Annual averages of monthly figures. See Table 569 for U.S. totals and coverage]

Year, sex, race, and Hispanic origin	Civilian noninstitutional population	Civilian labor force				Unemployed		Not in labor force	
		Total	Percent of population	Employed	Employment/ population ratio [1]	Number	Percent of labor force	Number	Percent of population
Male: 1970.....	64,304	51,228	79.7	48,990	76.2	2,238	4.4	13,076	20.3
1980	79,398	61,453	77.4	57,186	72.0	4,267	6.9	17,945	22.6
1990 [2]......	90,377	69,011	76.4	65,104	72.0	3,906	5.7	21,367	23.6
1995 [2]......	95,178	71,360	75.0	67,377	70.8	3,983	5.6	23,818	25.0
2000 [2]......	101,964	76,280	74.8	73,305	71.9	2,975	3.9	25,684	25.2
2004 [2]......	107,710	78,980	73.3	74,524	69.2	4,456	5.6	28,730	26.7
2005 [2]......	109,151	80,033	73.3	75,973	69.6	4,059	5.1	29,119	26.7
2006 [2]......	110,605	81,255	73.5	77,502	70.1	3,753	4.6	29,350	26.5
Female:									
1970	72,782	31,543	43.3	29,688	40.8	1,855	5.9	41,239	56.7
1980	88,348	45,487	51.5	42,117	47.7	3,370	7.4	42,861	48.5
1990 [2]......	98,787	56,829	57.5	53,689	54.3	3,140	5.5	41,957	42.5
1995 [2]......	103,406	60,944	58.9	57,523	55.6	3,421	5.6	42,462	41.1
2000 [2]......	110,613	66,303	59.9	63,586	57.5	2,717	4.1	44,310	40.1
2004 [2]......	115,647	68,421	59.2	64,728	56.0	3,694	5.4	47,225	40.8
2005 [2]......	116,931	69,288	59.3	65,757	56.2	3,531	5.1	47,643	40.7
2006 [2]......	118,210	70,173	59.4	66,925	56.6	3,247	4.6	48,037	40.6
White: [3]									
1970	122,174	73,556	60.2	70,217	57.5	3,339	4.5	48,618	39.8
1980 [2]	146,122	93,600	64.1	87,715	60.0	5,884	6.3	52,523	35.9
1990 [2]	160,625	107,447	66.9	102,261	63.7	5,186	4.8	53,178	33.1
1995 [2]	166,914	111,950	67.1	106,490	63.8	5,459	4.9	54,965	32.9
2000 [2]	176,220	118,545	67.3	114,424	64.9	4,121	3.5	57,675	32.7
2004 [2]	182,643	121,086	66.3	115,239	63.1	5,847	4.8	61,558	33.7
2005 [2]	184,446	122,299	66.3	116,949	63.4	5,350	4.4	62,148	33.7
2006 [2]	186,264	123,834	66.5	118,833	63.8	5,002	4.0	62,429	33.5
Black: [3]									
1973	14,917	8,976	60.2	8,128	54.5	846	9.4	5,941	39.8
1980	17,824	10,865	61.0	9,313	52.2	1,553	14.3	6,959	39.0
1985	19,664	12,364	62.9	10,501	53.4	1,864	15.1	7,299	37.1
1990 [2]	21,477	13,740	64.0	12,175	56.7	1,565	11.4	7,737	36.0
1995 [2]	23,246	14,817	63.7	13,279	57.1	1,538	10.4	8,429	36.3
2000 [2]	24,902	16,397	65.8	15,156	60.9	1,241	7.6	8,505	34.2
2004 [2]	26,065	16,638	63.8	14,909	57.2	1,729	10.4	9,428	36.2
2005 [2]	26,517	17,013	64.2	15,313	57.7	1,700	10.0	9,504	35.8
2006 [2]	27,007	17,314	64.1	15,765	58.4	1,549	8.9	9,693	35.9
Asian: [3, 4]									
2000 [2]	9,330	6,270	67.2	6,043	64.8	227	3.6	3,060	32.8
2004 [2]	9,519	6,271	65.9	5,994	63.0	277	4.4	3,248	34.1
2005 [2]	9,842	6,503	66.1	6,244	63.4	259	4.0	3,339	33.9
2006 [2]	10,155	6,727	66.2	6,522	64.2	205	3.0	3,427	33.7
Hispanic: [5]									
1980	9,598	6,146	64.0	5,527	57.6	620	10.1	3,451	36.0
1985	11,915	7,698	64.6	6,888	57.8	811	10.5	4,217	35.4
1990 [2]	15,904	10,720	67.4	9,845	61.9	876	8.2	5,184	32.6
1995 [2]	18,629	12,267	65.8	11,127	59.7	1,140	9.3	6,362	34.2
2000 [2]	23,938	16,689	69.7	15,735	65.7	954	5.7	7,249	30.3
2003 [2]	27,551	18,813	68.3	17,372	63.1	1,441	7.7	8,738	31.7
2004 [2]	28,109	19,272	68.6	17,930	63.8	1,342	7.0	8,837	31.4
2005 [2]	29,133	19,824	68.0	18,632	64.0	1,191	6.0	9,310	32.0
2006 [2]	30,103	20,694	68.7	19,613	65.2	1,081	5.2	9,409	31.3
Mexican:									
1986	7,377	4,941	67.0	4,387	59.5	555	11.2	2,436	33.0
1990 [2]	9,752	6,707	68.8	6,146	63.0	561	8.4	3,045	31.2
1995 [2]	11,609	7,765	66.9	7,016	60.4	750	9.7	3,844	33.1
2000 [2]	15,333	10,783	70.3	10,144	66.2	639	5.9	4,550	29.7
2004 [2]	17,900	12,340	68.9	11,449	64.0	892	7.2	5,559	31.1
2005 [2]	18,523	12,671	68.4	11,887	64.2	784	6.2	5,851	31.6
2006 [2]	19,036	13,158	69.1	12,477	65.5	681	5.2	5,877	30.9
Puerto Rican:									
1986	1,494	804	53.8	691	46.3	113	14.0	690	46.2
1990 [2]	1,718	960	55.9	870	50.6	91	9.5	758	44.1
1995 [2]	1,896	1,098	57.9	974	51.4	123	11.2	798	42.1
2000 [2]	2,193	1,411	64.3	1,318	60.1	92	6.6	783	35.7
2004 [2]	2,547	1,610	63.2	1,481	58.1	130	8.1	936	36.7
2005 [2]	2,654	1,619	61.0	1,492	56.2	126	7.8	1,035	39.0
2006 [2]	2,600	1,599	61.5	1,484	57.1	115	7.2	1,001	38.5
Cuban:									
1986	842	570	67.7	533	63.3	36	6.4	272	32.3
1990 [2]	918	603	65.7	559	60.9	44	7.2	315	34.3
1995 [2]	1,019	613	60.2	568	55.7	45	7.4	406	39.8
2000 [2]	1,174	740	63.1	707	60.3	33	4.5	434	37.0
2004 [2]	1,264	769	60.9	735	58.1	34	4.5	495	39.2
2005 [2]	1,259	755	60.0	730	58.0	25	3.3	503	40.0
2006 [2]	1,326	807	60.9	778	58.7	29	3.6	519	39.1

[1] Civilian employed as a percent of the civilian noninstitutional population. [2] See footnote 2, Table 569. [3] Beginning 2003, for persons in this race group only. See footnote 3, Table 570. [4] Prior to 2003, includes Pacific Islanders. [5] Persons of Hispanic or Latino ethnicity may be of any race. Includes persons of other Hispanic or Latino ethnicity, not shown separately.

Source: U.S. Bureau of Labor Statistics, Bulletin 2307; and *Employment and Earnings*, monthly. January 2007 issue. See Internet site <http://www.bls.gov/cps/home.htm>.

Table 572. Foreign-born and Native-born Populations—Employment Status by Selected Characteristics: 2006

[228,815 **represents** 228,815,000. Civilian noninstitutional population 16 years old and over, except as indicated. Annual averages of monthly figures. Based on Current Population Survey; see text, Section 1, and Appendix III]

Characteristic	Civilian noninstitutional population (1,000)	Civilian labor force			Unemployed (1,000)	
		Total (1,000)	Partici-pation rate [1]	Employed (1,000)	Number (1,000)	Unemploy-ment rate
Total	**228,815**	**151,428**	**66.2**	**144,427**	**7,001**	**4.6**
Male........................	110,605	81,255	73.5	77,502	3,753	4.6
Female......................	118,210	70,173	59.4	66,925	3,247	4.6
FOREIGN BORN						
Total [2]	**33,733**	**23,148**	**68.6**	**22,225**	**923**	**4.0**
Sex:						
Male	16,989	13,885	81.7	13,395	491	3.5
Female	16,743	9,263	55.3	8,831	432	4.7
Age:						
16 to 24 years old	4,156	2,501	60.2	2,318	183	7.3
25 to 34 years old	7,997	6,267	78.4	6,027	240	3.8
35 to 44 years old	8,022	6,552	81.7	6,325	227	3.5
45 to 54 years old	5,896	4,740	80.4	4,575	165	3.5
55 to 64 years old	3,707	2,428	65.5	2,340	87	3.6
Race and Hispanic ethnicity:						
White non-Hispanic	7,329	4,503	61.4	4,344	159	3.5
Black non-Hispanic	2,450	1,807	73.7	1,708	99	5.5
Asian non-Hispanic	7,481	5,060	67.6	4,917	142	2.8
Hispanic [3]	16,156	11,549	71.5	11,034	514	4.5
Educational attainment:						
Total 25 years old and over..........	29,576	20,647	69.8	19,908	739	3.6
Less than a high school diploma.......	9,361	5,865	62.7	5,566	299	5.1
High school graduates, no college [4] ...	7,358	5,032	68.4	4,855	177	3.5
Some college or associate's degree ...	4,511	3,346	74.2	3,232	114	3.4
Bachelor's degree and higher [5].......	8,347	6,405	76.7	6,255	149	2.3
NATIVE BORN						
Total [2]	**195,082**	**128,280**	**65.8**	**122,202**	**6,078**	**4.7**
Sex:						
Male	93,615	67,370	72.0	64,107	3,263	4.8
Female	101,467	60,910	60.0	58,095	2,815	4.6
Age:						
16 to 24 years old	32,787	19,893	60.7	17,723	2,170	10.9
25 to 34 years old	31,233	26,305	84.2	25,024	1,282	4.9
35 to 44 years old	34,731	29,296	84.3	28,244	1,051	3.6
45 to 54 years old	37,005	30,405	82.2	29,477	928	3.1
55 to 64 years old	27,668	17,557	63.5	17,049	508	2.9
65 years old and over	31,658	4,824	15.2	4,685	139	2.9
Race and Hispanic ethnicity:						
White non-Hispanic	150,979	100,126	66.3	96,262	3,864	3.9
Black non-Hispanic	23,668	14,905	63.0	13,500	1,405	9.4
Asian non-Hispanic	2,522	1,552	61.5	1,493	59	3.8
Hispanic [3]	13,947	9,145	65.6	8,578	567	6.2
Educational attainment:						
Total, 25 years old and over..........	162,295	108,387	66.8	104,479	3,908	3.6
Less than a high school diploma.......	18,181	6,893	37.9	6,326	567	8.2
High school graduates, no college [4] ...	53,390	33,322	62.4	31,847	1,475	4.4
Some college or associate's degree ...	44,500	32,064	72.1	30,911	1,152	3.6
Bachelor's degree and higher [4].......	46,224	36,108	78.1	35,394	714	2.0

[1] Civilian labor force as a percent of the civilian noninstitutional population. [2] Includes other races not shown separately. [3] Persons of Hispanic origin may be of any race. [4] Includes persons with a high school diploma or equivalent. [5] Includes persons with bachelor's, master's, professional, and doctoral degrees.

Source: U.S. Bureau of Labor Statistics, *Foreign-Born Workers: Labor Force Characteristics in 2006, News*, USDL 07-0603, April 25, 2007.

Labor Force, Employment, and Earnings **375**

Table 573. Civilian Labor Force—Percent Distribution by Sex and Age: 1980 to 2006

[106,940 represents 106,940,000. Civilian noninstitutional population 16 years old and over. Annual averages of monthly figures. Based on Current Population Survey; see text, Section 1, and Appendix III]

Year and sex	Civilian labor force (1,000)	Percent distribution						
		16 to 19 years	20 to 24 years	25 to 34 years	35 to 44 years	45 to 54 years	55 to 64 years	65 yrs. and over
Total: 1980	106,940	8.8	14.9	27.3	19.1	15.8	11.2	2.9
1990 [1]	125,840	6.2	11.7	28.6	25.5	16.1	9.2	2.7
2000 [1]	142,583	5.8	10.0	23.0	26.3	21.8	10.1	3.0
2005 [1]	149,320	4.8	10.1	21.7	24.1	23.0	12.7	3.5
2006 [1]	151,428	4.8	10.0	21.5	23.7	23.2	13.2	3.6
Male: 1980	61,453	8.1	14.0	27.6	19.3	16.1	11.8	3.1
1990 [1]	69,011	5.9	11.4	28.8	25.3	16.1	9.6	2.9
2000 [1]	76,280	5.6	9.9	23.4	26.3	21.3	10.2	3.3
2005 [1]	80,033	4.5	10.1	22.3	24.4	22.6	12.6	3.7
2006 [1]	81,255	4.5	10.0	22.1	23.9	22.8	12.9	3.8
Female: 1980	45,487	9.6	16.1	26.9	19.0	15.4	10.4	2.6
1990 [1]	56,829	6.5	12.0	28.3	25.8	16.1	8.7	2.6
2000 [1]	66,303	6.0	10.2	22.5	26.4	22.3	9.9	2.7
2005 [1]	69,288	5.2	10.2	20.9	23.9	23.6	12.9	3.3
2006 [1]	70,173	5.1	10.0	20.8	23.4	23.7	13.5	3.4

[1] See footnote 2, Table 569.

Source: U.S. Bureau of Labor Statistics, Bulletin 2307, and *Employment and Earnings*, monthly, January 2007 issue. See Internet site <http://www.bls.gov/cps/home.htm>.

Table 574. Civilian Labor Force and Participation Rates by Educational Attainment, Sex, Race, and Hispanic Origin: 1992 to 2006

[106,490 represents 106,490,000. Civilian noninstitutional population 25 years old and over. Annual averages of monthly figures. See Table 609 for unemployment data. Based on Current Population Survey; see text, Section 1, and Appendix III]

Year, sex, and race	Civilian labor force					Participation rate [1]				
	Total (1,000)	Percent distribution				Total	Less than high school diploma	High school gradu-ate, no degree	Less than a bach-elor's degree	College graduate
		Less than high school diploma	High school gradu-ate, no degree	Less than a bach-elor's degree	College graduate					
Total: [2]										
1992	106,490	12.6	35.6	25.4	26.4	66.5	41.2	66.4	75.3	81.3
1995	110,851	10.8	33.1	27.9	28.1	66.7	39.9	65.4	74.5	81.0
2000 [3]	120,061	10.4	31.4	27.7	30.5	67.3	43.5	64.4	73.9	79.4
2005 [3]	127,030	10.0	30.1	27.5	32.4	67.1	45.5	63.2	72.5	77.9
2006 [3]	129,034	9.9	29.7	27.4	32.9	67.2	46.3	63.1	72.2	77.9
Male:										
1992	58,439	14.1	34.0	24.0	27.9	77.0	54.7	78.3	83.9	86.9
1995	59,986	12.2	32.3	26.1	29.4	76.0	52.1	76.5	82.1	85.8
2000 [3] . . .	64,490	11.8	31.1	25.9	31.2	76.1	56.0	75.1	80.9	84.4
2005 [3] . . .	68,389	11.7	30.9	25.4	32.1	75.4	58.6	73.6	79.3	82.9
2006 [3] . . .	69,446	11.7	30.6	25.2	32.5	75.5	59.8	73.3	79.1	82.7
Female:										
1992	48,051	10.7	37.5	27.1	24.7	57.1	29.5	56.8	67.8	74.8
1995	50,865	9.2	34.2	30.0	26.6	58.3	29.2	56.4	68.1	75.4
2000 [3] . . .	55,572	8.8	31.8	29.7	29.7	59.4	32.3	55.5	68.0	74.0
2005 [3] . . .	58,641	8.0	29.2	30.0	32.8	59.4	32.9	53.8	66.8	72.9
2006 [3] . . .	59,588	7.8	28.7	30.0	33.5	59.6	33.2	53.8	66.6	73.1
White: [4]										
1992	90,627	11.8	35.5	25.5	27.2	66.3	41.1	65.4	74.6	81.0
1995	94,139	10.1	33.0	27.8	29.1	66.7	40.0	64.8	73.8	80.6
2000 [3] . . .	99,964	10.1	31.4	27.5	31.0	67.0	44.1	63.6	73.1	79.0
2005 [3] . . .	104,240	9.8	29.9	27.6	32.7	66.9	46.4	62.5	72.0	77.5
2006 [3] . . .	105,698	9.8	29.7	27.4	33.2	67.1	47.4	62.5	71.7	77.5
Black: [4]										
1992	11,583	18.2	39.5	26.4	15.9	66.7	40.6	72.9	80.9	86.2
1995	12,152	13.9	37.1	30.7	18.3	66.0	36.2	69.7	79.8	85.6
2000 [3] . . .	13,582	12.4	36.0	31.2	20.5	68.2	39.3	69.9	79.3	84.4
2005 [3] . . .	14,252	11.2	36.4	30.2	22.2	67.2	39.8	67.9	75.6	82.0
2006 [3] . . .	14,482	11.0	35.3	30.6	23.2	67.1	40.1	66.8	75.2	82.1
Asian: [5]										
2000 [3] . . .	5,402	9.1	20.7	20.2	50.1	70.9	46.0	65.6	76.4	79.1
2006 [3] . . .	6,065	7.5	17.8	17.2	57.5	69.9	44.4	62.8	72.6	77.5
Hispanic: [6]										
1992	8,728	38.9	29.6	20.0	11.5	68.3	56.3	75.5	82.2	83.2
1995	9,599	37.2	29.3	21.7	11.7	67.5	55.3	74.3	79.7	83.1
2000 [3] . . .	12,975	36.7	29.3	20.6	13.4	71.5	61.9	75.0	80.8	83.5
2005 [3] . . .	16,135	35.5	29.4	20.9	14.2	70.8	61.4	74.3	78.8	81.7
2006 [3] . . .	16,942	35.1	29.6	20.7	14.7	71.5	62.5	74.3	79.7	81.4

[1] See headnote, Table 570. [2] Includes other races, not shown separately. [3] See footnote 2, Table 569. [4] Beginning 2004, for persons in this race group only. See footnote 3, Table 570. [5] 2000 data include Pacific Islanders. [6] Persons of Hispanic or Latino origin may be of any race.

Source: U.S. Bureau of Labor Statistics, *Employment and Earnings*, monthly, January 2007 issue. See Internet site <http://www.bls.gov/cps/home.htm>.

Table 575. Characteristics of the Civilian Labor Force by State: 2005

[In thousands (149,320 represents 149,320,000), except ratio and rate. Civilian noninstitutional population, 16 years old and over. Annual averages of monthly figures. Because of separate processing and weighting procedures, the totals for the United States may differ from results obtained by aggregating totals for states]

State	Total		Employed		Employed popu- lation ratio [1]	Unemployed					Participation rate [3]	
						Total		Rate [2]				
	Number	Female	Total	Female		Number	Female	Total	Male	Female	Male	Female
United States. .	149,320	69,288	141,730	65,757	62.7	7,591	3,531	5.1	5.1	5.1	73.3	59.3
Alabama.	2,173	1,004	2,080	957	59.2	92	47	4.2	3.8	4.7	70.1	54.5
Alaska	343	159	320	151	67.3	23	9	6.7	7.6	5.6	77.2	66.9
Arizona.	2,806	1,242	2,673	1,181	60.8	133	62	4.8	4.6	5.0	72.4	55.6
Arkansas	1,367	636	1,297	603	61.0	70	33	5.1	5.1	5.2	71.6	57.6
California	17,823	7,911	16,872	7,481	62.1	951	431	5.3	5.2	5.4	74.4	57.1
Colorado.	2,525	1,140	2,401	1,080	68.2	124	60	4.9	4.6	5.3	79.4	64.2
Connecticut.	1,819	867	1,728	821	63.5	91	45	5.0	4.8	5.2	73.5	60.9
Delaware	440	212	421	202	64.3	19	10	4.3	4.0	4.7	72.9	62.0
District of Columbia .	296	152	278	142	63.4	18	10	6.2	5.7	6.7	71.8	64.1
Florida	8,715	4,046	8,401	3,888	60.5	314	158	3.6	3.3	3.9	70.1	56.0
Georgia	4,507	2,098	4,262	1,984	64.0	245	114	5.4	5.4	5.4	75.3	60.7
Hawaii	642	312	624	303	64.3	19	9	2.9	2.9	2.9	71.5	61.4
Idaho	743	340	713	325	67.2	30	15	4.0	3.6	4.5	76.8	63.2
Illinois	6,466	2,988	6,102	2,823	62.9	363	165	5.6	5.7	5.5	74.0	59.7
Indiana.	3,217	1,488	3,034	1,400	63.7	182	88	5.7	5.4	5.9	74.8	60.7
Iowa	1,659	793	1,585	759	68.4	74	34	4.5	4.7	4.3	76.6	66.9
Kansas.	1,476	683	1,401	649	67.3	75	34	5.1	5.1	5.0	78.2	64.0
Kentucky	2,007	959	1,883	898	58.5	123	61	6.1	5.9	6.4	67.7	57.4
Louisiana	2,095	1027	1,970	969	59.0	125	58	6.0	6.3	5.7	67.8	58.2
Maine.	714	344	678	328	63.7	35	16	5.0	5.3	4.6	72.1	62.2
Maryland	2,935	1,416	2,812	1,354	65.7	123	61	4.2	4.1	4.3	75.4	62.5
Massachusetts.	3,367	1,615	3,203	1,548	63.5	165	67	4.9	5.6	4.2	72.7	61.4
Michigan.	5,127	2,391	4,787	2,240	61.4	340	151	6.6	6.9	6.3	72.7	59.3
Minnesota.	2,928	1,386	2,814	1,340	70.6	114	46	3.9	4.4	3.3	78.7	68.5
Mississippi	1,330	636	1,238	589	56.8	92	47	6.9	6.4	7.4	67.7	55.1
Missouri	3,007	1,432	2,843	1,350	63.7	164	81	5.5	5.3	5.7	73.6	61.7
Montana.	497	232	475	222	64.2	22	10	4.4	4.6	4.2	72.8	61.9
Nebraska	984	461	945	442	70.5	39	18	4.0	4.0	4.0	79.9	67.2
Nevada	1,227	540	1174	517	63.9	53	23	4.3	4.4	4.3	74.4	59.1
New Hampshire	738	344	711	332	68.8	27	12	3.7	3.8	3.5	78.0	65.1
New Jersey.	4,468	2,042	4,271	1,946	63.5	197	96	4.4	4.2	4.7	75.3	58.2
New Mexico	949	439	898	418	61.3	50	20	5.3	5.9	4.7	72.3	57.7
New York	9,400	4,437	8,930	4,239	59.7	470	198	5.0	5.5	4.5	69.9	56.5
North Carolina	4,300	1,995	4,075	1,877	62.3	225	118	5.2	4.6	5.9	73.7	58.5
North Dakota.	359	169	347	164	69.6	12	5	3.4	4.0	2.7	77.6	66.6
Ohio	5,913	2,839	5,561	2,679	62.7	352	160	6.0	6.2	5.7	72.4	61.5
Oklahoma.	1,735	796	1,655	754	61.6	80	41	4.6	4.1	5.2	72.5	57.1
Oregon.	1,843	859	1,732	808	61.3	111	51	6.0	6.1	5.9	70.9	59.7
Pennsylvania.	6,286	2,971	5,976	2,821	61.3	310	149	4.9	4.8	5.0	71.2	58.3
Rhode Island.	575	279	545	266	64.2	30	14	5.2	5.4	4.9	73.3	62.6
South Carolina.	2,072	991	1,932	924	59.7	140	67	6.7	6.7	6.8	70.6	58.1
South Dakota	433	206	414	198	69.9	19	8	4.3	4.6	4.1	78.0	68.3
Tennessee	2,869	1,341	2,708	1,262	58.7	161	78	5.6	5.4	5.8	69.2	55.7
Texas.	11,238	5,029	10,630	4,755	63.5	608	274	5.4	5.4	5.5	76.1	58.6
Utah	1,234	545	1,183	520	68.5	51	25	4.1	3.8	4.5	80.9	62.3
Vermont	355	171	342	166	68.1	13	5	3.5	4.0	3.1	74.9	66.4
Virginia.	3,921	1,866	3,783	1,793	66.3	138	73	3.5	3.2	3.9	75.8	62.2
Washington	3,295	1,521	3,111	1,439	64.1	184	82	5.6	5.7	5.4	74.6	61.3
West Virginia.	800	380	758	363	52.1	42	17	5.3	6.0	4.5	59.8	50.6
Wisconsin.	3,024	1,433	2,882	1,367	66.7	142	66	4.7	4.8	4.6	75.2	65.0
Wyoming	283	128	273	123	68.2	10	5	3.6	3.6	3.6	78.2	63.4

[1] Civilian employment as a percent of civilian noninstitutional population.   [2] Percent unemployed of the civilian labor force.
[3] Percent of civilian noninstitutional population of each specified group in the civilian labor force.

Source: U.S. Bureau of Labor Statistics, Local Area Unemployment Statistics, *Geographic Profile of Employment and Unemployment, 2005 Annual Averages.* See Internet site <http://www.bls.gov/gps/>; (accessed 26 July 2007).

Labor Force, Employment, and Earnings   **377**

Table 576. Civilian Labor Force by Selected Metropolitan Area: 2006

[151,428 represents 151,428,000. Civilian noninstitutional population 16 years old and over. Annual averages of monthly figures. Data are derived from the Local Area Unemployment Statistics Program. For metro areas with a 2000 Census population of one million or more. For definition of metropolitan areas, see Appendix II. Metropolitan areas defined as of December 2005]

Metropolitan areas ranked by population, 2000	Civilian labor force (1,000)	Unem-ploy-ment rate [1]	Metropolitan areas ranked by population, 2000	Civilian labor force (1,000)	Unem-ploy-ment rate [1]
United States	151,428	4.6	Cleveland-Elyria-Mentor, OH.	1,093	5.4
New York-Northern New Jersey-Long Island, NY-NJ-PA.	9,290	4.5	Cincinnati-Middletown, OH-KY-IN.	1,110	5.2
Los Angeles-Long Beach-Santa Ana, CA	6,484	4.4	Portland-Vancouver-Beaverton, OR-WA	1,126	5.1
Chicago-Naperville-Joliet, IL-IN-WI	4,851	4.5	Kansas City, MO-KS	1,037	5.0
Philadelphia-Camden-Wilmington, PA-NJ-DE-MD	2,968	4.6	Sacramento–Arden-Arcade–Roseville, CA	1,040	4.7
Dallas-Fort Worth-Arlington, TX	3,106	4.8	San Jose-Sunnyvale-Santa Clara, CA. . .	859	4.5
Miami-Fort Lauderdale-Miami Beach, FL.	2,764	3.5	San Antonio, TX	929	4.6
Washington-Arlington-Alexandria, DC-VA-MD-WV.	2,964	3.1	Orlando-Kissimmee, FL	1,056	3.1
Houston-Sugar Land-Baytown, TX	2,707	4.9	Columbus, OH	939	4.7
Boston-Cambridge-Quincy, MA-NH NECTA.	2,471	4.6	Virginia Beach-Norfolk-Newport News, VA-NC	805	3.3
Detroit-Warren-Livonia, MI	2,170	7.2	Indianapolis-Carmel, IN	903	4.4
Atlanta-Sandy Springs-Marietta, GA	2,666	4.6	Milwaukee-Waukesha-West Allis, WI . . .	792	4.9
San Francisco-Oakland-Fremont, CA . . .	2,186	4.2	Las Vegas-Paradise, NV	925	4.1
Riverside-San Bernardino-Ontario, CA	1,771	4.9	Charlotte-Gastonia-Concord, NC-SC . . .	827	4.8
Phoenix-Mesa-Scottsdale, AZ	2,018	3.6	New Orleans-Metairie-Kenner, LA	492	4.8
Seattle-Tacoma-Bellevue, WA	1,775	4.5	Nashville-Davidson–Murfreesboro, TN . .	770	4.2
Minneapolis-St. Paul-Bloomington, MN-WI	1,845	3.7	Providence-Fall River-Warwick, RI-MA NECTA	713	5.4
San Diego-Carlsbad-San Marcos, CA. . .	1,518	4.0	Austin-Round Rock, TX	831	4.1
St. Louis, MO-IL	1,464	5.0	Memphis, TN-MS-AR.	610	5.7
Baltimore-Towson, MD.	1,408	4.1	Buffalo-Niagara Falls, NY	584	5.0
Pittsburgh, PA	1,204	4.9	Louisville-Jefferson County, KY-IN	628	5.5
Tampa-St. Petersburg-Clearwater, FL. . .	1,327	3.3	Jacksonville, FL	649	3.3
Denver-Aurora, CO	1,354	4.4	Richmond, VA	632	3.2
			Oklahoma City, OK	577	3.9
			Hartford-West Hartford-East Hartford, CT NECTA	578	4.4
			Birmingham-Hoover, AL	543	3.3
			Rochester, NY	535	4.4

[1] Percent unemployed of the civilian labor force.

Source: U.S. Bureau of Labor Statistics, Local Area Unemployment Statistics program. See Internet site <http://www.bls.gov/lau/>.

Table 577. School Enrollment and Labor Force Status: 1990 and 2005

[In thousands (31,421 represents 31,421,000), except percent. As of October. Civilian noninstitutional population 16 to 24 years old. Based on Current Population Survey; see text, Section 1, and Appendix III]

Characteristic	Population		Civilian labor force		Employed		Unemployed		
	1990	2005	1990	2005	1990	2005	1990, total	2005 Total	2005 Rate [1]
Total, 16 to 24 years old [2] . . .	31,421	36,761	20,679	22,338	18,317	20,032	2,363	2,306	10.3
Enrolled in school [2].	15,210	20,905	7,301	9,442	6,527	8,528	774	914	9.7
16 to 19 years old	10,118	13,582	4,244	4,937	3,645	4,267	599	670	13.6
20 to 24 years old	5,092	7,323	3,057	4,505	2,882	4,261	174	244	5.4
Sex:									
Male	7,704	10,269	3,635	4,344	3,215	3,912	420	432	9.9
Female	7,507	10,636	3,666	5,098	3,312	4,616	353	482	9.5
College level.	8,139	11,000	4,542	6,367	4,231	5,976	311	391	6.1
Full-time.	6,810	9,396	3,376	4,952	3,117	4,612	259	340	6.9
Race:									
White [3].	12,308	16,199	6,294	7,756	5,705	7,077	588	679	8.8
Below college	5,535	7,597	2,374	2,587	2,021	2,200	354	387	14.9
College level	6,772	8,603	3,919	5,169	3,685	4,877	234	292	5.7
Black [3].	2,129	2,893	718	948	576	777	142	171	18.1
Below college	1,207	1,565	306	292	212	190	94	102	35.0
College level	922	1,328	411	656	364	587	47	69	10.5
Asian [3].	(NA)	1,058	(NA)	400	(NA)	381	(NA)	19	4.8
Below college	(NA)	343	(NA)	74	(NA)	70	(NA)	4	([4])
College level	(NA)	715	(NA)	326	(NA)	311	(NA)	15	4.6
Not enrolled [2].	16,210	15,856	13,379	12,896	11,789	11,504	1,589	1,392	10.8
White [3]	13,317	12,412	11,276	10,285	10,193	9,323	1,083	962	9.4
Black [3]	2,441	2,448	1,752	1,843	1,298	1,506	454	338	18.3
Asian [3]	(NA)	419	(NA)	339	(NA)	314	(NA)	25	7.5

NA Not available. [1] Percent unemployed of civilian labor force in each category. [2] Includes other races, not shown separately. [3] 2005 data for persons in this race group only. See footnote 3, Table 570. [4] Data not shown where base is less than 75,000.

Source: U.S. Bureau of Labor Statistics, Bulletin 2307; College Enrollment and Work Activity of High School Graduates, News, USDL 06-514, March 24, 2006; and unpublished data. See Internet site <http://www.bls.gov/bls/newsrels.htm#OEUS>.

Table 578. **Labor Force Participation Rates by Marital Status, Sex, and Age: 1970 to 2005**

[For the civilian noninstitutional population 16 years old and over. Annual averages of monthly figures. See Table 575 for definition of participation rate. Based on Current Population Survey; see text, Section 1, and Appendix III]

Marital status and year	Male participation rate							Female participation rate						
	Total	16–19 years	20–24 years	25–34 years	35–44 years	45–64 years	65 and over	Total	16–19 years	20–24 years	25–34 years	35–44 years	45–64 years	65 and over
Single:														
1970	65.5	54.6	73.8	87.9	86.2	75.7	25.2	56.8	44.7	73.0	81.4	78.6	73.0	19.7
1980	72.6	59.9	81.3	89.2	82.2	66.9	16.8	64.4	53.6	75.2	83.3	76.9	65.6	13.9
1985 [1]	73.8	56.3	81.5	89.4	84.6	65.5	15.6	66.6	52.3	76.3	82.4	80.8	67.9	9.8
1990 [1]	74.8	55.1	81.6	89.9	84.5	67.3	15.7	66.7	51.7	74.5	80.9	80.8	66.2	12.1
1995	73.7	54.4	80.3	88.7	81.4	67.0	17.9	66.8	52.2	72.9	80.2	79.5	67.3	11.6
2000 [1]	73.6	52.5	80.5	89.4	82.9	69.7	17.3	68.9	51.1	76.1	83.9	80.9	69.9	10.8
2001	72.7	50.0	79.6	89.0	83.2	69.8	15.4	68.1	49.1	75.3	83.2	81.3	69.9	12.1
2002 [1]	71.7	47.2	78.7	88.7	83.1	69.6	16.9	67.4	47.3	74.5	83.3	79.9	69.6	14.3
2003 [1]	70.4	44.0	77.9	87.7	82.9	67.6	19.4	66.2	44.8	72.9	82.2	79.8	69.9	15.2
2004 [1]	70.2	43.6	77.7	87.9	82.7	67.8	20.3	65.9	43.8	73.1	81.8	80.5	70.9	14.7
2005 [1]	70.1	42.9	77.0	87.9	82.9	68.6	18.8	66.0	44.2	72.6	81.4	80.7	70.9	15.5
Married: [2]														
1970	86.1	92.3	94.7	98.0	98.1	91.2	29.9	40.5	37.8	47.9	38.8	46.8	44.0	7.3
1980	80.9	91.3	96.9	97.5	97.2	84.3	20.5	49.8	49.3	61.4	58.8	61.8	46.9	7.3
1985	78.7	91.0	95.6	96.8	96.8	81.7	16.8	53.8	49.6	65.3	65.8	68.1	49.4	6.6
1990 [1]	78.6	92.1	95.6	96.9	96.7	82.6	17.5	58.4	49.5	66.1	69.6	74.0	56.5	8.5
1995	77.5	89.2	94.9	96.3	95.4	82.4	18.0	61.0	51.6	64.7	72.0	75.7	62.7	9.1
2000 [1]	77.3	79.5	94.1	96.7	95.8	83.0	19.2	61.1	53.2	63.8	70.3	74.8	65.4	10.1
2001	77.4	77.7	94.2	95.9	95.6	83.7	19.1	61.2	45.1	63.9	69.9	74.5	66.1	10.3
2002 [1]	77.4	81.1	93.3	95.7	95.1	83.8	19.4	61.0	49.6	63.4	69.3	73.8	66.5	10.7
2003 [1]	77.3	76.6	93.2	95.3	95.1	83.5	19.9	61.0	46.7	62.6	68.5	73.3	67.4	11.3
2004 [1]	77.1	77.4	92.4	95.6	95.1	83.1	20.4	60.5	41.1	60.9	67.6	72.7	67.0	11.6
2005 [1]	77.2	71.4	93.4	95.3	95.2	83.6	21.4	60.7	44.1	61.1	68.4	73.0	67.0	12.5
Other: [3]														
1970	60.7	(B)	90.4	93.7	91.1	78.5	19.3	40.3	48.6	60.3	64.6	68.8	61.9	10.0
1980	67.5	(B)	92.6	94.1	91.9	73.3	13.7	43.6	50.0	68.4	76.5	77.1	60.2	8.2
1985	68.7	(B)	95.1	93.7	91.8	72.8	11.4	45.1	51.9	66.2	76.9	81.6	61.0	7.5
1990 [1]	68.9	(B)	93.1	93.0	90.7	74.9	12.0	47.2	53.9	65.4	77.0	82.1	65.0	8.4
1995	66.2	(B)	92.7	90.9	88.2	72.4	12.1	47.4	55.8	67.2	77.1	80.7	67.2	8.4
2000 [1]	66.8	60.5	88.1	93.2	89.9	73.9	12.9	49.0	46.0	74.0	83.1	82.9	69.8	8.7
2001	66.0	57.3	85.4	92.4	89.4	73.5	13.0	49.0	47.2	75.5	81.6	82.6	69.3	8.9
2002 [1]	65.5	57.5	87.4	91.2	89.6	74.1	13.2	49.2	46.2	74.7	80.7	82.7	69.7	8.9
2003 [1]	65.0	45.6	88.0	91.4	89.3	72.4	14.3	49.6	44.1	71.4	79.1	81.9	70.7	9.8
2004 [1]	64.9	53.1	87.2	90.6	88.6	72.8	14.3	49.6	48.7	70.0	79.4	81.7	69.8	10.4
2005 [1]	64.9	54.9	86.4	90.4	89.4	72.7	15.1	49.4	46.8	67.4	78.1	80.9	69.4	10.5

B Percentage not shown where base is less than 35,000. [1] See footnote 2, Table 569. [2] Spouse present. [3] Widowed, divorced, and married (spouse absent).

Source: U.S. Bureau of Labor Statistics, Bulletins 2217 and 2340; and unpublished data.

Table 579. **Marital Status of Women in the Civilian Labor Force: 1970 to 2005**

[31,543 represents 31,543,000. Civilian noninstitutional population 16 years and over. Annual averages of monthly figures. Based on the Current Population Survey; see text, Section 1, and Appendix III]

Year	Female civilian labor force (1,000)				Female participation rate [3]			
	Total	Single	Married [1]	Other [2]	Total	Single	Married [1]	Other [2]
1970	31,543	7,265	18,475	5,804	43.3	56.8	40.5	40.3
1975	37,475	9,125	21,484	6,866	46.3	59.8	44.3	40.1
1980	45,487	11,865	24,980	8,643	51.5	64.4	49.8	43.6
1985	51,050	13,163	27,894	9,993	54.5	66.6	53.8	45.1
1988	54,742	14,194	29,921	10,627	56.6	67.7	56.7	46.2
1989	56,030	14,377	30,548	11,104	57.4	68.0	57.8	47.0
1990 [4]	56,829	14,612	30,901	11,315	57.5	66.7	58.4	47.2
1991	57,178	14,681	31,112	11,385	57.4	66.2	58.5	46.8
1992	58,141	14,872	31,700	11,570	57.8	66.2	59.3	47.1
1993	58,795	15,031	31,980	11,784	57.9	66.2	59.4	47.2
1994 [4]	60,239	15,333	32,888	12,018	58.8	66.7	60.7	47.5
1995	60,944	15,467	33,359	12,118	58.9	66.8	61.0	47.4
1996	61,857	15,842	33,618	12,397	59.3	67.1	61.2	48.1
1997 [4]	63,036	16,492	33,802	12,742	59.8	67.9	61.6	48.6
1998 [4]	63,714	17,087	33,857	12,771	59.8	68.5	61.2	48.8
1999 [4]	64,855	17,575	34,372	12,909	60.0	68.7	61.2	49.1
2000 [4]	66,303	17,849	35,146	13,308	59.9	68.9	61.1	49.0
2001	66,848	18,021	35,236	13,592	59.8	68.1	61.2	49.0
2002	67,363	18,203	35,477	13,683	59.6	67.4	61.0	49.2
2003 [4]	68,272	18,397	36,046	13,828	59.5	66.2	61.0	49.6
2004 [4]	68,421	18,616	35,845	13,961	59.2	65.9	60.5	49.6
2005 [4]	69,288	19,183	35,941	14,163	59.3	66.0	60.7	49.4

[1] Husband present. [2] Widowed, divorced, or separated. [3] See footnote 3, Table 575 for definition of participation rate. [4] See footnote 2, Table 569.

Source: U.S. Bureau of Labor Statistics, Bulletin 2307; and unpublished data.

Labor Force, Employment, and Earnings 379

Table 580. Employment Status of Women by Marital Status and Presence and Age of Children: 1970 to 2005

[As of March (7.0 represents 7,000,000). Civilian noninstitutional population 16 years old and over. Based on the Current Population Survey; see text, Section 1, and Appendix III]

Item	Total Single	Total Mar-ried[1]	Total Other[2]	With any children – Total Single	Total Mar-ried[1]	Total Other[2]	Children 6 to 17 yrs. only Single	Children 6 to 17 yrs. only Mar-ried[1]	Children 6 to 17 yrs. only Other[2]	Children under 6 yrs. Single	Children under 6 yrs. Mar-ried[1]	Children under 6 yrs. Other[2]
IN LABOR FORCE (mil.)												
1970	7.0	18.4	5.9	(NA)	10.2	1.9	(NA)	6.3	1.3	(NA)	3.9	0.6
1980	11.2	24.9	8.8	0.6	13.7	3.6	0.2	8.4	2.6	0.3	5.2	1.0
1990	14.0	31.0	11.2	1.5	16.5	4.2	0.6	9.3	3.0	0.9	7.2	1.2
1995	15.0	33.6	12.0	2.1	18.0	4.6	0.8	10.2	3.3	1.3	7.8	1.3
2000	17.8	35.0	13.2	3.1	18.2	4.5	1.2	10.8	3.4	1.8	7.3	1.1
2003[3]	17.9	36.2	14.2	3.2	18.3	4.7	1.3	11.1	3.6	1.9	7.2	1.1
2004[3]	18.1	35.9	14.2	3.3	18.0	4.7	1.4	10.8	3.6	1.9	7.1	1.1
2005[3]	18.6	35.8	14.2	3.4	18.2	4.6	1.4	10.9	3.4	1.9	7.3	1.2
PARTICIPATION RATE[4]												
1970	53.0	40.8	39.1	(NA)	39.7	60.7	(NA)	49.2	66.9	(NA)	30.3	52.2
1980	61.5	50.1	44.0	52.0	54.1	69.4	67.6	61.7	74.6	44.1	45.1	60.3
1990	66.4	58.2	46.8	55.2	66.3	74.2	69.7	73.6	79.7	48.7	58.9	63.6
1995	65.5	61.1	47.3	57.5	70.2	75.3	67.0	76.2	79.5	53.0	63.5	66.3
2000	68.6	62.0	50.2	73.9	70.6	82.7	79.7	77.2	85.0	70.5	62.8	76.6
2003[3]	65.0	61.8	50.1	73.1	69.2	82.0	77.6	77.0	84.8	70.2	59.8	74.3
2004[3]	64.5	60.9	50.3	72.6	68.2	80.7	79.2	75.6	83.0	68.4	59.3	74.4
2005[3]	65.1	60.2	49.8	72.9	68.1	79.8	79.8	75.0	82.2	68.4	59.8	73.6
EMPLOYMENT (mil.)												
1970	6.5	17.5	5.6	(NA)	9.6	1.8	(NA)	6.0	1.2	(NA)	3.6	0.6
1980	10.1	23.6	8.2	0.4	12.8	3.3	0.2	8.1	2.4	0.2	4.8	0.9
1990	12.9	29.9	10.5	1.2	15.8	3.8	0.5	8.9	2.7	0.7	6.9	1.1
1995	13.7	32.3	11.3	1.8	17.2	4.2	0.7	9.8	3.1	1.1	7.3	1.2
2000	16.4	34.0	12.7	2.7	17.6	4.3	1.1	10.6	3.2	1.6	7.1	1.1
2003[3]	16.2	34.8	13.2	2.8	17.5	4.3	1.2	10.7	3.3	1.6	6.8	1.0
2004[3]	16.5	34.6	13.3	2.8	17.2	4.4	1.2	10.4	3.3	1.6	6.8	1.0
2005[3]	16.9	34.7	13.5	2.9	17.6	4.3	1.3	10.6	3.2	1.6	7.1	1.1
UNEMPLOYMENT RATE[5]												
1970	7.1	4.8	4.8	(NA)	6.0	7.2	(NA)	4.8	5.9	(NA)	7.9	9.8
1980	10.3	5.3	6.4	23.2	5.9	9.2	15.6	4.4	7.9	29.2	8.3	12.8
1990	8.2	3.5	5.7	18.4	4.2	8.5	14.5	3.8	7.7	20.8	4.8	10.2
1995	8.7	3.9	5.8	16.6	4.3	8.1	11.8	3.6	7.1	19.5	5.3	10.8
2000	7.3	2.7	4.3	11.0	2.9	5.1	8.7	2.6	4.8	12.6	3.5	5.9
2003[3]	9.4	3.8	6.5	13.4	4.1	8.9	11.6	3.6	7.7	14.7	4.9	13.0
2004[3]	0.0	3.7	6.1	13.1	4.1	7.2	10.6	3.7	6.3	14.8	4.7	9.9
2005[3]	8.9	3.0	5.3	15.0	3.1	6.9	10.7	2.9	5.9	14.8	3.4	9.9

NA Not available. [1] Husband present. [2] Widowed, divorced, or separated. [3] See footnote 2, Table 569. [4] Percent of women in each specific category in the labor force. [5] Unemployed as a percent of civilian labor force in specified group.

Source: U.S. Bureau of Labor Statistics, Bulletin 2307; and unpublished data.

Table 581. Labor Force Participation Rates for Wives, Husband Present by Age of Own Youngest Child: 1975 to 2005

[As of March. Civilian noninstitutional population, 16 years old and over. For definition of participation rate, see Table 584. Based on Current Population Survey; see text, Section 1, and Appendix III]

Presence and age of child	Total 1975	Total 1990	Total 2005	White[1] 1975	White[1] 1990	White[1] 2005	Black[1] 1975	Black[1] 1990	Black[1] 2005
Wives, total	44.4	58.2	60.2	43.6	57.6	59.8	54.1	64.7	66.3
No children under 18 years	43.8	51.1	53.8	43.6	50.8	53.5	47.6	52.9	57.0
With children under 18 years	44.9	66.3	68.1	43.6	65.6	67.8	58.4	75.6	76.4
Under 6 years, total	36.7	58.9	59.8	34.7	57.8	59.3	54.9	73.1	72.8
Under 3 years	32.7	55.5	57.0	30.7	54.9	56.7	50.1	67.5	68.7
1 year or under	30.8	53.9	55.8	29.2	53.3	55.5	50.0	64.4	65.5
2 years	37.1	60.9	61.0	35.1	60.3	61.0	56.4	75.4	72.6
3 to 5 years	42.2	64.1	64.2	40.1	62.5	63.2	61.2	80.4	77.7
3 years	41.2	63.1	62.7	39.0	62.3	62.1	62.7	74.5	80.3
4 years	41.2	65.1	64.8	38.7	63.2	64.5	64.9	80.6	74.8
5 years	44.4	64.5	67.4	43.8	62.0	65.4	56.3	86.2	84.4
6 to 13 years	51.8	73.0	73.0	50.7	72.6	72.8	65.7	77.6	78.7
14 to 17 years	53.5	75.1	79.6	53.4	74.9	80.1	52.3	78.8	80.4

[1] 2005 for persons in this race group only. See footnote 3, Table 570.

Source: U.S. Bureau of Labor Statistics, Bulletin 2340; and unpublished data.

Table 582. **Married Couple Households by Labor Force Status of Spouse: 1986 to 2006**

[50,933 represents 50,933,000. Data represent married couple households. Based on the Current Population Survey and subject to sampling error; for details see source and Appendix III]

Year	All married couples	Number (1,000)				Percent distribution			
		In labor force			Husband and wife not in labor force	In labor force			Husband and wife not in labor force
		Husband and wife	Husband only	Wife only		Husband and wife	Husband only	Wife only	
TOTAL									
1986	50,933	25,428	14,675	2,362	8,468	49.9	28.8	4.6	16.6
1990	52,317	28,056	13,013	2,453	8,794	53.6	24.9	4.7	16.8
1995	53,858	29,999	11,777	3,043	9,039	55.7	21.9	5.7	16.8
2000	55,311	31,095	11,815	3,301	9,098	56.2	21.4	6.0	16.4
2001	56,592	31,794	12,213	3,274	9,311	56.2	21.6	5.8	16.5
2002	56,747	31,637	12,327	3,388	9,395	55.8	21.7	6.0	16.6
2003	57,320	31,951	12,443	3,553	9,373	55.7	21.7	6.2	16.4
2004	57,719	31,536	12,980	3,684	9,519	54.6	22.5	6.4	16.5
2005	57,975	31,398	13,385	3,641	9,551	54.2	23.1	6.3	16.5
2006	58,179	31,783	12,990	3,754	9,652	54.6	22.3	6.5	16.6
WITH CHILDREN UNDER 18									
1986	24,630	14,606	8,916	518	590	59.3	36.2	2.1	2.4
1990	24,537	15,768	7,667	558	544	64.3	31.2	2.3	2.2
1995	25,241	17,024	6,863	756	598	67.4	27.2	3.0	2.4
2000	25,248	17,116	6,950	795	387	67.8	27.5	3.1	1.5
2001	25,980	17,563	7,210	784	422	67.6	27.8	3.0	1.6
2002	25,792	17,233	7,301	777	482	66.8	28.3	3.0	1.9
2003	25,914	17,065	7,499	893	457	65.9	28.9	3.4	1.8
2004	25,793	16,691	7,715	952	433	64.7	29.9	3.7	1.7
2005	25,919	16,789	7,806	925	400	64.8	30.1	3.6	1.5
2006	25,982	16,909	7,754	900	420	65.1	29.9	3.5	1.6
WITH CHILDREN UNDER 6									
1986	11,924	6,271	5,284	155	215	52.6	44.3	1.3	1.8
1990	12,051	6,932	4,692	192	235	57.5	38.9	1.6	2.0
1995	11,951	7,406	4,059	233	253	62.0	34.0	1.9	2.1
2000	11,393	6,984	4,077	211	121	61.3	35.8	1.9	1.1
2001	11,732	7,054	4,296	247	134	60.1	36.6	2.1	1.1
2002	11,531	6,796	4,311	250	175	58.9	37.4	2.2	1.5
2003	11,743	6,747	4,507	298	191	57.5	38.4	2.5	1.6
2004	11,711	6,657	4,579	317	158	56.8	39.1	2.7	1.3
2005	11,802	6,813	4,553	299	137	57.7	38.6	2.5	1.2
2006	11,984	6,939	4,572	324	149	57.9	38.2	2.7	1.2

Source: U.S. Bureau of the Census, Table MC-1, Married Couples by Labor Force Status of Spouses: 1986 to Present; released 22 March 2007. See Internet site <http://www.census.gov/population/www/socdemo/hh-fam.html>.

Table 583. **Employed Civilians and Weekly Hours: 1980 to 2006**

[In thousands (99,303 represents 99,303,000), except as indicated. Annual averages of monthly figures. For civilian noninstitutional population 16 years old and over. Based on Current Population Survey; see text, Section 1 and Appendix III]

Item	1980	1990 [1]	1995	2000 [1]	2004 [1]	2005 [1]	2006 [1]
Total employed	99,303	118,793	124,900	136,891	139,252	141,730	144,427
Age:							
16 to 19 years old	7,710	6,581	6,419	7,189	5,907	5,978	6,162
20 to 24 years old	14,087	13,401	12,443	13,229	13,723	13,792	13,878
25 to 34 years old	27,204	33,935	32,356	31,549	30,423	30,680	31,051
35 to 44 years old	19,523	30,817	34,202	36,433	34,580	34,630	34,569
45 to 54 years old	16,234	19,525	24,378	30,310	32,469	33,207	34,052
55 to 64 years old	11,586	11,189	11,435	14,002	17,331	18,349	19,389
65 years old and over	2,960	3,346	3,666	4,179	4,819	5,094	5,325
Class of worker:							
Nonagricultural industries [2]	95,938	115,570	121,460	134,427	137,020	139,532	142,221
Wage and salary worker [2]	88,525	106,598	112,448	125,114	127,463	129,931	132,449
Self-employed	7,000	8,719	8,902	9,205	9,467	9,509	9,685
Unpaid family workers	413	253	110	108	90	93	87
Agriculture and related industries	3,364	3,223	3,440	2,464	2,232	2,197	2,206
Wage and salary worker [2]	1,425	1,740	1,814	1,421	1,242	1,212	1,287
Self-employed	1,642	1,378	1,580	1,010	964	955	901
Unpaid family workers	297	105	45	33	27	30	18
Weekly hours:							
Nonagricultural industries:							
Wage and salary workers [2]	38.1	39.2	39.2	39.6	39.0	39.1	(NA)
Self-employed	41.2	40.8	39.4	39.7	38.4	38.4	(NA)
Unpaid family workers	34.7	34.0	33.5	32.5	31.3	32.2	(NA)
Agriculture and related industries:							
Wage and salary workers [2]	41.6	41.2	41.1	43.2	42.7	43.7	(NA)
Self-employed	49.3	46.8	43.5	45.3	44.4	43.6	(NA)
Unpaid family workers	38.6	38.5	42.0	38.3	37.3	44.0	(NA)

NA Not available. [1] See footnote 2, Table 569. [2] Includes the incorporated self-employed.

Source: U.S. Bureau of Labor Statistics, Employment and Earnings, monthly, January issues; and unpublished data. See Internet site <http://www.bls.gov/cps/home.htm>.

Labor Force, Employment, and Earnings 381

Table 584. Persons at Work by Hours Worked: 2006

[In thousands (138,681 represents 138,681,000), **except as indicated.** Annual averqages of monthly figures. Civilian noninstitutional population 16 years old and over. Based on Current Population Survey; see text, Section 1, and Appendix III. See headnote, Table 587 regarding industries]

Hours of work	Persons at work (1,000)			Percent distribution		
	Total	Agriculture and related industries	Non-agricultural industries	Total	Agriculture and related industries	Non-agricultural industries
Total	**138,681**	**2,110**	**136,571**	**100.0**	**100.0**	**100.0**
1 to 34 hours....................	32,421	560	31,861	23.4	26.6	23.3
1 to 4 hours..................	1,420	51	1,369	1.0	2.4	1.0
5 to 14 hours..................	4,922	140	4,781	3.5	6.6	3.5
15 to 29 hours................	15,941	250	15,691	11.5	11.8	11.5
30 to 34 hours................	10,139	119	10,020	7.3	5.7	7.3
35 hours and over	106,259	1,550	104,710	76.6	73.4	76.7
35 to 39 hours	9,391	97	9,294	6.8	4.6	6.8
40 hours	58,078	555	57,524	41.9	26.3	42.1
41 hours and over..............	38,790	898	37,892	28.0	42.5	27.7
41 to 48 hours	13,624	137	13,487	9.8	6.5	9.9
49 to 59 hours	14,642	271	14,371	10.6	12.8	10.5
60 hours and over	10,524	490	10,034	7.6	23.2	7.3
Average weekly hours: Persons at work . . .	39.2	43.1	39.2	(X)	(X)	(X)
Persons usually working full-time	42.9	49.3	42.8	(X)	(X)	(X)

X Not applicable.

Source: U.S. Bureau of Labor Statistics, *Employment and Earnings,* monthly, January 2007 issue. See Internet site <http://www.bls.gov/cps/home.htm>.

Table 585. Persons With a Job, But Not at Work: 1980 to 2005

[In thousands (5,881 represents 5,881,000), **except percent.** Civilian noninstitutional population 16 years old and over. Annual averages of monthly figures. Based on Current Population Survey; see text, Section 1 and Appendix III]

Reason for not working	1980	1990 [1]	1995	1998 [1]	1999 [1]	2000 [1]	2001	2002	2003 [1]	2004 [1]	2005 [1]
All industries, number	**5,881**	**6,160**	**5,582**	**5,586**	**5,407**	**5,681**	**5,631**	**5,394**	**5,469**	**5,482**	**5,511**
Percent of employed	5.9	5.2	4.5	4.2	4.1	4.2	4.1	4.0	4.0	3.9	3.9
Reason for not working:											
Vacation	3,320	3,529	2,982	3,033	2,899	3,109	3,039	2,929	2,922	2,923	2,892
Illness	1,426	1,341	1,084	1,095	1,096	1,156	1,095	1,072	1,090	1,058	1,088
Bad weather	155	90	122	130	104	89	100	97	123	133	145
Industrial dispute	105	24	21	10	7	14	9	7	18	10	6
All other	876	1,177	1,373	1,318	1,300	1,313	1,388	1,289	1,316	1,358	1,381

[1] See footnote 2, Table 569.

Source: U.S. Bureau of Labor Statistics, *Employment and Earnings,* monthly, January issues; and unpublished data. See Internet site <http://www.bls.gov/cps/home.htm>.

Table 586. Class of Worker by Sex and Selected Characteristic: 2005

[In percent, **except as indicated** (10,464 represents 10,464,000). Civilian noninstitutional population **16 years old and over.** Annual averages of monthly figures. Based on Current Population Survey; see text, Section 1 and Appendix III]

Characteristic	Unincorporated self-employed			Incorporated self-employed			Wage and salary workers [1]		
	Total	Male	Female	Total	Male	Female	Total	Male	Female
Total (1,000)	**10,464**	**6,632**	**3,832**	**5,254**	**3,828**	**1,425**	**125,889**	**65,467**	**60,423**
PERCENT DISTRIBUTION	100.0	100.0	100.0	100.0	100.0	100.0	100.0	100.0	100.0
Age: 16 to 19 years old	0.8	0.8	0.6	0.1	0.1	0.1	4.7	4.4	5.0
20 to 24 years old	3.0	3.3	2.4	1.1	1.0	1.4	10.7	10.7	10.6
25 to 34 years old	15.4	14.9	16.2	11.6	11.5	11.8	22.6	23.8	21.3
35 to 44 years old	24.4	23.7	25.7	26.6	26.3	27.3	24.4	24.7	23.9
45 to 54 years old	26.9	27.2	26.5	31.4	31.4	31.6	22.8	22.0	23.6
55 to 64 years old	19.8	19.5	20.3	20.9	21.2	20.1	12.0	11.6	12.5
65 years old and over	9.7	10.6	8.2	8.2	8.4	7.6	2.9	2.8	3.0
Race/ethnicity: White [2]...........	87.6	87.9	87.2	89.7	90.3	88.0	81.8	83.2	80.3
Black [2]	6.3	6.3	6.1	3.7	3.4	4.6	11.5	10.1	13.0
Asian [2]	4.1	3.8	4.6	5.3	5.0	6.0	4.4	4.4	4.3
Hispanic [3]	9.9	11.2	7.6	6.2	6.2	6.2	13.7	15.8	11.4
Country of birth: U.S.-born	86.6	85.5	88.3	86.6	86.8	86.2	85.0	82.8	87.4
Foreign-born................	13.7	14.7	12.0	13.4	13.2	13.9	15.0	17.2	12.6
U.S. citizen	6.2	6.2	6.1	8.7	8.7	8.8	5.9	5.8	5.9
Not a U.S. citizen...........	7.5	8.5	5.8	4.6	4.5	5.0	9.1	11.3	6.7

[1] Excludes the incorporated self-employed. [2] For persons in this race group only. See footnote 3, Table 570. [3] Persons of Hispanic or Latino origin may be of any race.

Source: U.S. Bureau of Labor Statistics, Current Population Survey, unpublished data.

382 Labor Force, Employment, and Earnings

Table 587. Self-Employed Workers by Industry and Occupation: 2000 to 2006

[In thousands (10,214 represents 10,214,000). Civilian noninstitutional population 16 years old and over. Annual averages of monthly figures. Data represent the unincorporated self-employed; the incorporated self-employed are considered wage and salary workers. Based on the occupational and industrial classification derived from those used in the 2000 census and are not comparable to those used in the 1990 census. See text, this section. Based on the Current Population Survey; see text, Section 1, and Appendix III]

Item	2000	2002	2003 [1]	2004 [1]	2005 [1]	2006 [1]
Total self-employed	10,214	9,926	10,295	10,431	10,464	10,586
Industry:						
Agriculture and related industries	1,010	1,003	951	964	955	901
Mining	12	13	9	13	11	10
Construction	1,728	1,598	1,717	1,848	1,830	1,910
Manufacturing	334	312	325	316	327	326
Wholesale and retail trade.	1,221	1,163	1,247	1,153	1,251	1,139
Transportation and utilities.	348	369	357	410	442	428
Information	139	145	152	146	126	120
Financial activities [2]	735	675	736	792	785	841
Professional and business services [2]	1,927	1,863	1,908	1,993	1,957	1,992
Education and health services [2]	1,107	1,119	1,138	1,105	1,071	1,158
Leisure and hospitality [2]	660	627	686	660	674	685
Other services [3]	993	1,041	1,071	1,031	1,036	1,076
Occupation:						
Management, professional, and related occupations. . .	4,169	4,064	4,176	4,179	4,085	(NA)
Service occupations	1,775	1,786	1,690	1,757	1,774	(NA)
Sales and office occupations	1,982	1,883	1,945	1,909	1,986	(NA)
Natural resources, construction, and maintenance occupations.	1,591	1,503	1,795	1,847	1,864	(NA)
Production, transportation, and material moving occupations.	698	690	689	739	756	(NA)

NA Not available. [1] See footnote 2, Table 569. [2] For composition of industries, see Table 607. [3] Includes private households.

Source: U.S. Bureau of Labor Statistics, *Employment and Earnings*, monthly, January issues. See Internet site <http://www.bls.gov /cps/home.htm>.

Table 588. Persons Doing Job-Related Work at Home: 2004

[136,602 represents 136,602,000. As of May. For persons at work 16 years and over in nonagricultural industries doing job-related work at home at least once a week as part of their primary job. Based on the Current Population Survey; see text, Section 1, and Appendix III. Industry and occupational classifications are those based on the 2000 census. See text, this section]

Characteristic	Total employed [1] (1,000)	Persons who usually worked at home [2]			Percent distribution by class of worker		
		Total (1,000)	Percent of employed	Total [3]	Wage and salary workers		Self employed [4]
					Paid work at home	Unpaid work at home	
Total [5]	136,602	20,673	15.1	100.0	16.2	49.3	33.7
SEX							
Male	72,417	10,780	14.9	100.0	14.7	47.3	37.6
Female	64,185	9,893	15.4	100.0	17.8	51.4	29.4
RACE AND HISPANIC ORIGIN							
White [6]	111,756	18,255	16.3	100.0	16.4	49.0	33.8
Black [6]	15,800	1,245	7.9	100.0	14.2	53.0	31.0
Asian [6]	5,630	718	12.7	100.0	14.2	52.1	33.7
Hispanic origin [7]	17,577	1,255	7.1	100.0	19.1	45.0	34.4
OCCUPATION							
Management, professional, and related occupations.	47,829	13,445	28.1	100.0	13.9	59.9	25.7
Management, business, and financial operations occupations.	19,205	5,602	29.2	100.0	16.2	46.6	36.9
Professional and related occupations . . .	28,623	7,842	27.4	100.0	12.2	69.5	17.7
Service occupations	22,752	1,414	6.2	100.0	20.6	20.9	54.8
Sales and office occupations	35,133	4,291	12.2	100.0	24.1	36.1	38.6
Sales and related occupations.	15,886	3,137	19.7	100.0	21.8	35.4	42.2
Office and administrative support occupations	19,247	1,154	6.0	100.0	30.5	38.0	28.9
Natural resources, construction, and maintenance occupations.	13,111	1,036	7.9	100.0	10.2	15.1	73.8
Farming, fishing, and forestry occupations	195	3	1.5	100.0	(B)	(B)	(B)
Construction and extraction occupations	7,927	705	8.9	100.0	6.1	13.3	80.6
Installation, maintenance, and repair occupations.	4,989	329	6.6	100.0	18.4	19.1	59.6
Production, transportation, and material moving occupations.	17,777	488	2.7	100.0	10.6	26.6	62.8
Production occupations	9,240	276	3.0	100.0	12.8	22.1	65.0
Transportation and material-moving occupations	8,538	212	2.5	100.0	7.7	32.5	59.8

B Data not shown where the base is less than 75,000. [1] Includes persons who did not report information on work at home. [2] Persons who worked at home at least once per week as part of their primary job. [3] Unpaid familiy workers and wage and salary workers who did not report pay status are included in the total but not shown separately. [4] Includes the incorporated and unincorporated self-employed. [5] Includes other races, not shown separately. [6] For persons in this race group only. See footnote 2, Table 570. [7] Persons of Hispanic origin may be of any race.

Source: U.S. Bureau of Labor Statistics, *Work at Home in 2004, News*, USDL 05-1768, September 22, 2005. See Internet site <http://www.bls.gov/bls/newsrels.htm#OEUS>.

Table 589. Persons on Flexible Schedules: 2004

[In thousands, **except percent**. **(99,778 represents 99,778,000) As of May.** For employed full-time wage and salary workers 16 years old and over. Excludes all self-employed persons, regardless of whether or not their businesses were incorporated. Data related to the primary job. Based on the Current Population Survey; see text, Section 1, and Appendix III]

Item	Total Total [1]	Total With flexible schedules Number	Total With flexible schedules Percent	Male Total [1]	Male With flexible schedules Number	Male With flexible schedules Percent	Female Total [1]	Female With flexible schedules Number	Female With flexible schedules Percent
Total	99,778	27,411	27.5	56,412	15,853	28.1	43,366	11,558	26.7
AGE									
16 to 19 years old.	1,427	336	23.6	903	185	20.5	524	151	28.9
20 years and over.	98,351	27,075	27.5	55,509	15,668	28.2	42,842	11,406	26.6
20 to 24 years old	9,004	2,058	22.9	5,147	1,065	20.7	3,856	993	25.8
25 to 34 years old	24,640	6,902	28.0	14,358	4,051	28.2	10,283	2,851	27.7
35 to 44 years old	26,766	7,807	29.2	15,424	4,605	29.9	11,342	3,202	28.2
45 to 54 years old	24,855	6,651	26.8	13,440	3,769	28.0	11,415	2,882	25.2
55 to 64 years old	11,745	3,181	27.1	6,383	1,865	29.2	5,361	1,316	24.5
65 years old and over	1,341	475	35.4	757	314	41.4	585	161	27.6
RACE AND HISPANIC ORIGIN									
White [2]	80,498	23,121	28.7	46,222	13,582	29.4	34,276	9,539	27.8
Black [2]	12,578	2,476	19.7	6,447	1,193	18.5	6,131	1,283	20.9
Asian [2]	4,136	1,132	27.4	2,300	720	31.3	1,836	412	22.4
Hispanic origin [3]	14,110	2,596	18.4	8,621	1,430	16.6	5,489	1,166	21.2
MARITAL STATUS									
Married, spouse present.	57,630	16,270	28.2	34,926	10,382	29.7	22,704	5,888	25.9
Not married	42,148	11,141	26.4	21,486	5,471	25.5	20,662	5,670	27.4
Never married.	25,144	6,693	26.6	14,469	3,605	24.9	10,676	3,088	28.9
Other marital status	17,004	4,448	26.2	7,018	1,866	26.6	9,986	2,582	25.9
PRESENCE AND AGE OF CHILDREN									
Without own children under 18	61,761	16,759	27.1	34,680	9,410	27.1	27,081	7,349	27.1
With own children under 18	38,018	10,652	28.0	21,733	6,443	29.6	16,285	4,209	25.8
With youngest child 6 to 17	21,739	5,960	27.4	11,477	3,341	29.1	10,262	2,619	25.5
With youngest child under 6	16,279	4,692	28.8	10,256	3,102	30.2	6,023	1,590	26.4

[1] Includes persons who did not provide information on flexible schedules.   [2] For persons in the race group only. See footnote 3, Table 570.   [3] Persons of Hispanic origin may be of any race.

Source: U.S. Bureau of Labor Statistics, *Workers on Flexible and Shift Schedules in May 2004, News*, USDL 05-1198, July 1, 2005. See Internet site <http://www.bls.gov/bls/newsrels.htm#OEUS>.

Table 590. Employed Workers With Alternative and Traditional Work Arrangements: 2005

[In thousands **(138,952 represents 138,952,000). As of February.** For employed workers 16 years old and over. Based on the Current Population Survey; see text, Section 1, Population, and Appendix III]

Characteristic	Total employed [1]	Workers with alternative arrangements Independent contractors	Workers with alternative arrangements On-call workers	Workers with alternative arrangements Temporary help agency workers	Workers with alternative arrangements Workers provided by contract firms	Workers with traditional arrangements
Total employed.	138,952	10,342	2,454	1,217	813	123,843
16 to 19 years old	5,510	89	133	33	7	5,194
20 to 24 years old	13,114	356	355	202	87	12,055
25 to 34 years old	30,103	1,520	535	362	205	27,427
35 to 44 years old	34,481	2,754	571	253	196	30,646
45 to 54 years old	32,947	2,799	417	200	186	29,324
55 to 64 years old	17,980	1,943	267	135	114	15,496
65 years old and over	4,817	881	175	33	18	3,701
Male.	73,946	6,696	1,241	574	561	64,673
16 to 19 years old	2,579	32	82	24	7	2,389
20 to 24 years old	6,928	194	200	107	61	6,331
25 to 34 years old	16,624	1,006	299	185	138	14,950
35 to 44 years old	18,523	1,824	252	120	140	16,130
45 to 54 years old	17,193	1,764	209	71	143	15,003
55 to 64 years old	9,485	1,287	108	52	70	7,954
65 years old and over	2,615	589	91	16	3	1,917
Female.	65,006	3,647	1,212	643	252	59,170
16 to 19 years old	2,931	57	52	9	–	2,805
20 to 24 years old	6,186	162	155	95	27	5,724
25 to 34 years old	13,480	514	236	177	67	12,477
35 to 44 years old	15,958	930	319	133	57	14,516
45 to 54 years old	15,754	1,035	208	129	43	14,322
55 to 64 years old	8,495	656	158	83	44	7,542
65 years old and over	2,202	292	84	17	15	1,785
Full-time workers	113,798	7,732	1,370	979	695	102,889
Part-time workers.	25,154	2,611	1,084	238	119	20,954

– Represents zero.   [1] Includes day laborers (an alternative arrangement) and a small number of workers who were both "on call" and "provided by contract firms," not shown separately.

Source: U.S. Bureau of Labor Statistics, *Contingent and Alternative Employment Arrangements, February 2005, News*, USDL 05-1443, July 27, 2005. See Internet site <http://www.bls.gov/bls/newsrels.htm#OEUS>.

384   Labor Force, Employment, and Earnings

Table 591. **Multiple Jobholders: 2006**

[Annual average of monthly figures (7,576 represents 7,576,000). Civilian noninstitutional population 16 years old and over. Multiple jobholders are employed persons who, either 1) had jobs as wage or salary workers with two employers or more; 2) were self-employed and also held a wage and salary job; or 3) were unpaid family workers on their primary jobs but also held a wage and salary job. Based on the Current Population Survey; see text, Section 1, Population, and Appendix III]

Characteristic	Total		Male		Female	
	Number (1,000)	Percent of employed	Number (1,000)	Percent of employed	Number (1,000)	Percent of employed
Total [1]	7,576	5.2	3,822	4.9	3,753	5.6
Age:						
16 to 19 years old	270	4.4	103	3.4	167	5.4
20 to 24 years old	774	5.6	341	4.6	432	6.7
25 to 54 years old	5,368	5.4	2,760	5.1	2,608	5.7
55 to 64 years old	988	5.1	517	5.1	471	5.1
65 years old and over	176	3.3	101	3.4	75	3.2
Race and Hispanic ethnicity:						
White [2]	6,321	5.3	3,199	4.9	3,122	5.8
Black [2]	818	5.2	404	5.5	415	4.9
Asian [2]	249	3.8	127	3.6	122	4.1
Hispanic [3]	598	3.0	337	2.8	261	3.4
Marital status:						
Married, spouse present	4,136	5.1	2,420	5.3	1,716	4.9
Widowed, divorced, or separated	1,308	5.6	440	4.4	868	6.3
Single, never married	2,131	5.3	962	4.4	1,169	6.5
Full- or part-time status:						
Primary job full-time, secondary job part-time ..	3,981	(X)	2,233	(X)	1,748	(X)
Both jobs part-time	1,676	(X)	508	(X)	1,168	(X)
Both jobs full-time	310	(X)	208	(X)	102	(X)
Hours vary on primary or secondary job	1,564	(X)	849	(X)	715	(X)

X Not applicable.   [1] Includes a small number of persons who work part-time on their primary job and full-time on their secondary job(s), not shown separately. Includes other races, not shown separately.   [2] For persons who selected this race group only. See footnote 3, Table 570.   [3] Persons of Hispanic or Latino ethnicity may be of any race.

Source: U.S. Bureau of Labor Statistics, *Employment and Earnings*, January 2007. See Internet site <http://www.bls.gov/cps /home.htm>.

Table 592. **Average Number of Jobs Held from Ages 18 to 40: 1978 to 2004**

[For persons 39 to 48 in 2004–05. A job is an uninterrupted period of work with a particular employer. Educational attainment as of 2004–05. Based on the National Longitudinal Survey of Youth 1979; see source for details]

Sex and educational attainment	Total [1]	Number of jobs held by age				
		18 to 21 years old	22 to 25 years old	26 to 30 years old	31 to 35 years old	36 to 40 years old
Total [2]	10.5	3.8	3.0	2.8	2.4	2.0
Less than a high school diploma	10.6	3.3	2.8	2.8	2.4	1.9
High school graduate, no college	10.2	3.6	2.8	2.7	2.4	2.1
Some college or associate's degree	10.9	3.9	3.0	2.9	2.4	2.2
Bachelor's degree or more	10.7	4.1	3.5	2.9	2.2	2.0
Male	10.7	3.9	3.2	3.0	2.5	2.1
Less than a high school diploma	12.0	3.9	3.3	3.3	2.7	2.1
High school graduate, no college	10.5	3.8	3.0	3.0	2.5	2.0
Some college or associate's degree	11.1	4.0	3.1	3.1	2.6	2.2
Bachelor's degree or more.	10.4	3.8	3.4	2.7	2.3	2.1
Female	10.3	3.6	2.9	2.7	2.2	2.0
Less than a high school diploma	8.6	2.4	2.0	2.1	2.0	1.8
High school graduate, no college	9.8	3.4	2.5	2.5	2.3	2.1
Some college or associate's degree	10.7	3.8	3.0	2.8	2.3	2.1
Bachelor's degree or more.	11.2	4.3	3.6	3.0	2.2	1.9
White, non-Hispanic	10.6	3.9	3.1	2.8	2.3	2.0
Less than a high school diploma	11.3	3.5	3.0	2.9	2.5	2.0
High school graduate, no college	10.1	3.8	2.8	2.7	2.4	2.0
Some college or associate's degree	11.1	4.1	3.1	3.0	2.4	2.1
Bachelor's degree or more.	10.7	4.1	3.5	2.8	2.2	1.9
Black, non-Hispanic	10.1	3.0	2.7	2.8	2.4	2.1
Less than a high school diploma	9.2	2.3	2.4	2.7	2.2	1.9
High school graduate, no college	10.3	3.0	2.6	2.8	2.5	2.1
Some college or associate's degree	10.0	3.2	2.7	2.8	2.5	2.2
Bachelor's degree or more.	10.5	3.6	3.4	3.1	2.6	2.2
Hispanic or Latino [3]	10.0	3.4	2.7	2.7	2.7	2.0
Less than a high school diploma	9.8	3.3	2.5	2.6	2.1	1.8
High school graduate, no college	10.0	3.1	2.6	2.7	2.4	2.1
Some college or associate's degree	10.1	3.6	2.9	2.8	2.1	2.2
Bachelor's degree or more.	10.4	3.6	3.1	2.9	2.6	2.1

[1] Jobs held in more than one age category were counted in each category, but only once in the total.   [2] Includes other races, not shown separately.   [3] Persons of Hispanic or Latino origin may be of any race.

Source: U.S. Bureau of Labor Statistics, *Number of Jobs Held, Labor Market Activity, and Earnings Growth Among Youngest Baby Boomers: Results from a Longitudinal Survey, News*, USDL 06-1496, August 25, 2006. See Internet site <http://www.bls.gov/nls /home.htm>.

Table 593. Distribution of Workers by Tenure With Current Employer: 2006

[125,668 represents 125,668,000. As of January. For employed wage and salary workers 16 years old and over. Data exclude the incorporated and unincorporated self-employed. Based on the Current Population Survey and subject to sampling error; see source and Appendix III]

Characteristic	Number employed (1,000)	Percent distribution by tenure with current employer								Median years [1]
		12 months or less	13 to 23 months	2 years	3 to 4 years	5 to 9 years	10 to 14 years	15 to 19 years	20 years or more	
Total [2]	125,668	24.4	7.0	5.2	16.9	20.9	9.5	6.7	9.4	4.0
AGE AND SEX										
16 to 19 years old	5,563	75.1	10.5	7.2	6.8	0.4	–	–	–	(NA)
20 to 24 years old	13,083	50.4	12.5	10.2	19.4	7.5	(Z)	–	–	1.3
25 to 34 years old	28,392	28.8	9.3	6.8	23.4	25.3	5.6	0.8	(Z)	2.9
35 to 44 years old	30,466	18.6	6.2	4.6	17.2	26.1	13.7	9.3	4.4	4.9
45 to 54 years old	28,845	13.5	4.6	3.2	14.0	21.7	12.7	11.1	19.2	7.3
55 to 64 years old	15,619	11.4	3.9	2.6	12.9	19.7	12.7	11.3	25.5	9.3
65 years old and over	3,699	10.4	3.1	2.8	12.6	22.6	12.8	10.3	25.4	8.8
Male	65,212	23.9	6.8	5.3	16.7	20.7	9.6	6.6	10.3	4.1
16 to 19 years old	2,696	74.1	9.9	8.3	7.2	0.4	–	–	–	(NA)
20 to 24 years old	6,840	49.7	12.0	10.2	20.8	7.3	0.1	–	–	1.4
25 to 34 years old	15,477	28.0	9.1	7.2	22.8	25.9	6.0	1.0	(Z)	2.9
35 to 44 years old	16,184	17.9	5.8	4.5	16.5	25.5	14.9	9.8	5.1	5.1
45 to 54 years old	14,392	13.0	4.3	3.1	13.0	20.6	12.5	11.3	22.2	8.1
55 to 64 years old	7,750	11.6	4.1	3.0	12.8	18.5	11.7	9.5	28.8	9.5
65 years old and over.	1,873	10.7	3.4	3.0	12.4	23.3	12.4	8.9	25.9	8.3
Female	60,456	24.9	7.2	5.0	17.2	21.2	9.3	6.8	8.4	3.9
16 to 19 years old	2,867	76.0	11.1	6.2	6.4	0.3	–	–	–	(NA)
20 to 24 years old	6,243	51.2	13.0	10.2	17.8	7.7	–	–	–	1.2
25 to 34 years old	12,915	29.8	9.5	6.5	24.0	24.6	5.2	0.5	–	2.8
35 to 44 years old	14,282	19.3	6.8	4.7	17.9	26.7	12.3	8.8	3.6	4.6
45 to 54 years old	14,453	14.0	4.9	3.4	14.9	22.8	13.0	10.8	16.2	6.7
55 to 64 years old	7,870	11.1	3.6	2.3	13.1	20.9	13.6	13.2	22.2	9.2
65 years old and over.	1,826	10.0	2.7	2.6	12.8	22.0	13.2	11.7	25.0	9.5
RACE AND HISPANIC ORIGIN										
White [3]	102,900	24.0	6.9	5.1	16.8	20.9	9.7	6.9	9.8	(NA)
Male	54,241	23.4	6.7	5.1	16.6	20.7	9.9	6.9	10.8	(NA)
Female	48,659	24.6	7.2	5.0	17.0	21.1	9.4	6.9	8.7	(NA)
Black [3]	14,265	26.2	6.6	5.7	17.2	21.1	8.4	6.5	8.2	(NA)
Male	6,501	26.4	6.7	6.4	17.8	19.8	8.6	5.5	8.9	(NA)
Female	7,764	26.1	6.6	5.1	16.7	22.2	8.2	7.5	7.7	(NA)
Asian [3]	5,463	23.7	8.3	5.8	19.0	22.5	9.9	4.3	6.4	(NA)
Male	2,941	23.1	9.0	6.2	17.5	24.9	9.3	3.5	6.5	(NA)
Female	2,522	24.5	7.4	5.3	20.7	19.8	10.7	5.2	6.4	(NA)
Hispanic origin [4]	17,741	30.1	6.5	7.3	20.2	20.3	7.2	4.6	3.7	(NA)
Male	10,550	29.7	6.0	7.7	20.5	20.5	7.4	4.7	3.5	(NA)
Female	7,191	30.6	7.4	6.8	19.7	20.1	7.0	4.4	4.1	(NA)

– Represents zero. NA Not available. Z Less that .05 percent. [1] For definition of median, see Guide to Tabular Presentation. [2] Includes other races, not shown separately. [3] For persons in this race group only. See footnote 3, Table 570. [4] Persons of Hispanic or Latino origin may be of any race.

Source: U. S. Bureau of Labor Statistics, News, *Employee Tenure in 2006, News, USDL* 06-1563, September 8, 2006. See Internet site <http://www.bls.gov/bls/newsrels.htm#OEUS>.

Table 594. Part-Time Workers by Reason: 2006

[In thousands (32,421 represents 32,421,000), **except hours.** For persons working 1 to 34 hours per week. For civilian noninstitutional population 16 years old and over. Annual average of monthly figures. Based on the Current Population Survey and subject to sampling error; see text, Section 1, and Appendix III]

Reason	All industries			Nonagriculture industries		
	Total	Usually work—		Total	Usually work—	
		Full-time	Part-time		Full-time	Part-time
Total working fewer than 35 hours	32,421	10,223	22,199	31,861	10,057	21,804
Economic reasons	4,162	1,554	2,608	4,071	1,504	2,567
Slack work or business conditions	2,658	1,294	1,363	2,596	1,259	1,337
Could find only part-time work	1,189	(S)	1,189	1,178	(S)	1,178
Seasonal work	175	119	56	158	106	52
Job started or ended during the week	141	141	(S)	139	139	(S)
Noneconomic reasons	28,259	8,669	19,591	27,790	8,553	19,237
Child-care problems	777	80	697	772	79	693
Other family or personal obligations	5,492	743	4,749	5,407	731	4,676
Health or medical limitations	799	(S)	799	778	(S)	778
In school or training	6,316	89	6,227	6,247	89	6,158
Retired or social security limit on earnings	2,096	(S)	2,096	1,988	(S)	1,988
Vacation or personal day	3,679	3,679	(S)	3,639	3,639	(S)
Holiday, legal or religious	1,156	1,156	(S)	1,147	1,147	(S)
Weather-related curtailment	388	388	(S)	365	365	(S)
Other	7,555	2,533	5,022	7,448	2,504	4,944
Average hours per week:						
Economic reasons	23.1	24.0	22.5	23.1	24.0	22.5
Noneconomic reasons	21.5	25.2	19.9	21.6	25.2	20.0

S No data or data do not meet publication standards.

Source: U.S. Bureau of Labor Statistics, *Employment and Earnings*, monthly, January 2007. See Internet site <http://www.bls.gov /cps/home.htm>.

Table 595. Displaced Workers by Selected Characteristics: 2006

[In percent, except total (3,815 represents 3,815,000). As of January. For persons 20 years old and over with tenure of 3 years or more who lost or left a job between January 2003 and December 2005 because of plant closings or moves, slack work, or the abolishment of their positions. Based on Current Population Survey and subject to sampling error; see source and Appendix III]

Characteristic	Total (1,000)	Employment status			Reason for job loss		
		Employed	Unemployed	Not in the labor force	Plant or company closed down or moved	Slack/ insufficient work	Position or shift abolished
Total [1]	3,815	69.9	13.4	16.7	49.0	22.2	28.8
20 to 24 years old	111	66.4	21.4	12.2	39.1	42.8	18.1
25 to 54 years old	2,841	74.5	13.4	12.0	48.5	22.6	28.9
55 to 64 years old	728	60.6	12.3	27.0	53.2	16.5	30.2
65 years old and over...	135	25.4	10.8	63.8	44.1	28.8	27.1
Males...........	2,076	73.5	13.6	12.9	48.8	24.8	26.5
20 to 24 years old	67	77.4	21.4	1.2	29.7	61.6	8.7
25 to 54 years old	1,552	78.6	12.8	8.5	48.2	24.5	27.3
55 to 64 years old	378	61.5	14.5	24.0	53.9	17.5	28.6
65 years old and over...	80	27.5	18.3	54.2	51.9	32.9	15.2
Females.........	1,739	65.6	13.1	21.3	49.2	19.2	31.6
20 to 24 years old	44	[2]	[2]	[2]	[2]	[2]	[2]
25 to 54 years old	1,289	69.6	14.2	16.2	48.9	20.3	30.8
55 to 64 years old	350	59.7	10.0	30.3	52.5	15.5	32.0
65 years old and over...	55	[2]	[2]	[2]	[2]	[2]	[2]
White [3]	3,169	70.0	13.2	16.8	49.5	22.1	28.4
Black [3]	452	71.2	13.4	15.4	42.5	19.7	37.8
Asian [3]	113	72.0	12.3	15.7	52.3	25.9	21.8
Hispanic origin [4]	416	60.2	22.9	16.9	59.6	26.1	14.3

[1] Includes other races, not shown separately. [2] Data not shown where base is less than 75,000. [3] For persons in this race group only. See footnote 3, Table 570. [4] Persons of Hispanic or Latino origin may be of any race.

Source: U.S. Bureau of Labor Statistics, News, *Worker Displacement, 2003–2005*, News, USDL 06-1454, August 17, 2006. See Internet site <http://www.bls.gov/bls/newsrels.htm#OEUS>.

Table 596. Labor Force Status of Persons With a Work Disability by Age: 2006

[In percent, except as indicated (24,461 represents 24,461,000). As of March. For civilians 16 to 74 who have a condition which prevents them from working or limits the amount of work they can do. Data from the Current Population Survey and subject to sampling error; see text, Section 1, and Appendix III]

Labor force status	Total	Age						
		16 to 24 years old	25 to 34 years old	35 to 44 years old	45 to 54 years old	55 to 64 years old	65 to 69 years old	70 to 74 years old
Number (1,000)	24,461	1,566	2,376	3,683	5,610	6,741	2,390	2,094
In labor force...........	22.6	31.0	37.5	29.6	26.4	18.0	9.8	6.5
Employed	19.7	23.2	30.6	26.5	23.2	16.5	9.2	5.8
Full-time...........	11.8	9.9	20.6	17.1	15.0	10.0	3.2	1.5
Not in labor force	77.4	69.0	62.5	70.4	73.6	82.0	90.2	93.5
Unemployment rate	12.8	25.1	18.3	10.4	12.0	8.3	6.5	11.8

Source: U.S. Census Bureau, "Disability Data from the March Current Population Survey"; <http://www.census.gov/hhes/www/disability /disabcps.html>; (accessed 22 February 2007).

Table 597. Persons Not in the Labor Force: 2006

[In thousands (77,387 represents 77,387,000). Annual average of monthly figures. Civilian noninstitutional population 16 years old and over. Based on the Current Population Survey; see text, Section 1, and Appendix III]

Status and reason	Total	Age			Sex	
		16 to 24 years old	25 to 54 years old	55 years old and over	Male	Female
Total not in the labor force	77,387	14,549	21,318	41,520	29,350	48,037
Do not want a job now [1]	72,602	12,867	19,221	40,514	27,248	45,354
Want a job now	4,786	1,682	2,097	1,006	2,102	2,684
In the previous year—						
Did not search for a job................	2,758	883	1,155	720	1,145	1,612
Did search for a job [2]	2,028	800	942	286	956	1,071
Not available for work now	580	282	252	46	226	354
Available for work now, not looking for work...	1,448	518	690	240	731	717
Reason for not currently looking for work:						
Discouraged over job prospects [3]	381	118	195	68	229	152
Family responsibilities..............	152	31	97	24	35	117
In school or training	207	177	28	2	111	96
Ill health or disability..............	130	18	76	36	63	68
Other [4]......................	578	174	294	110	292	285

[1] Includes some persons who are not asked if they want a job. [2] Persons who had a job in the prior 12 months must have searched since the end of that job. [3] Includes such things as believes no work available, could not find work, lacks necessary schooling or training, employer thinks too young or old, and other types of discrimination. [4] Includes such things as child care and transportation problems.

Source: U.S. Bureau of Labor Statistics, *Employment and Earnings*, monthly, January 2007 issue. See Internet site <http://www.bls.gov/cps/home.htm>.

Labor Force, Employment, and Earnings 387

Table 598. **Employed Civilians by Occupation, Sex, Race, and Hispanic Origin: 2006**

[144,427 represents 144,427,000. Civilian noninstitutional population 16 years old and over. Annual average of monthly figures. Based on Current Population Survey; see text, Section 1, and Appendix III. Occupational classifications are those used in the 2000 census and are not comparable to those used in the 1990 census]

Occupation	Total employed (1,000)	Percent of total			
		Female	Black [1]	Asian [1]	Hispanic [2]
Total, 16 years and over	144,427	46.3	10.9	4.5	13.6
Management, professional, and related occupations	**50,420**	**50.6**	**8.4**	**6.1**	**6.6**
Management, business, and financial operations occupations	21,233	41.9	7.3	4.8	7.0
Management occupations [3]	15,249	36.7	6.2	4.3	7.1
Chief executives	1,689	23.4	3.1	3.9	4.6
General and operations managers.....................	998	29.1	5.7	3.4	7.7
Advertising and promotions managers	75	52.5	5.4	1.7	5.1
Marketing and sales managers	888	40.2	4.8	3.8	5.3
Administrative services managers	87	24.4	7.3	5.2	8.3
Computer and information systems managers	401	27.2	6.4	9.1	4.7
Financial managers	1,083	55.0	7.0	5.5	7.7
Human resources managers	280	65.8	11.0	1.2	9.9
Industrial production managers.....................	298	16.4	3.0	3.2	8.0
Purchasing managers..........................	165	40.7	8.7	1.7	3.3
Transportation, storage, and distribution managers	249	14.6	9.8	2.9	14.9
Farm, ranch, and other agricultural managers	242	21.8	2.4	0.8	8.5
Farmers and ranchers..........................	784	25.0	0.8	1.0	2.0
Construction managers	1,010	7.8	3.7	2.3	8.3
Education administrators	796	63.9	14.2	2.2	7.2
Engineering managers...........................	103	7.3	2.9	10.9	3.4
Food service managers..........................	900	43.2	5.8	12.0	13.6
Lodging managers	174	51.0	6.5	13.3	8.5
Medical and health services managers.................	511	68.3	10.3	4.8	5.3
Property, real estate, and community association managers......	618	51.3	7.2	3.2	11.4
Social and community service managers	315	66.0	15.0	2.7	7.2
Business and financial operations occupations [3]	5,983	55.0	10.0	6.2	6.6
Wholesale and retail buyers, except farm products	222	55.8	3.2	3.5	8.9
Purchasing agents, except wholesale, retail, and farm products ...	290	51.1	7.9	3.2	7.0
Claims adjusters, appraisers, examiners, and investigators	283	58.2	14.1	3.4	6.7
Compliance officers, except agriculture, construction, health and safety, and transportation	149	54.0	17.4	5.8	8.3
Cost estimators	114	12.7	1.0	4.1	2.6
Human resources, training, and labor relations specialists	765	71.5	14.5	4.5	7.7
Management analysts............................	572	42.2	5.9	7.5	4.4
Accountants and auditors	1,779	60.2	10.2	9.4	6.0
Appraisers and assessors of real estate	134	35.7	1.5	2.2	4.6
Financial analysts..............................	103	38.4	4.0	12.3	3.9
Personal financial advisors........................	389	34.4	7.0	5.4	6.1
Insurance underwriters	92	69.2	16.2	2.5	5.2
Loan counselors and officers	468	52.7	11.1	5.6	10.8
Tax preparers	98	59.6	10.6	4.3	9.0
Professional and related occupations	29,187	56.9	9.3	7.1	6.4
Computer and mathematical occupations [3]	3,209	26.7	7.3	16.2	5.0
Computer scientists and systems analysts	715	31.9	9.5	12.7	5.0
Computer programmers..........................	562	25.3	3.9	18.1	5.3
Computer software engineers......................	846	21.8	5.8	26.9	3.4
Computer support specialists	314	28.9	10.5	7.4	7.2
Database administrators	90	37.0	8.9	14.8	3.0
Network and computer systems administrators	180	16.6	4.4	11.0	7.0
Network systems and data communications analysts	356	25.5	7.9	8.1	6.0
Operations research analysts	85	40.3	18.1	6.6	4.0
Architecture and engineering occupations [3]	2,830	14.5	5.6	9.7	5.9
Architects, except naval..........................	221	22.2	3.2	11.5	7.7
Aerospace engineers	110	13.1	5.6	12.9	5.1
Civil engineers................................	304	11.9	5.0	8.2	4.0
Computer hardware engineers	80	16.2	3.8	26.5	7.4
Electrical and electronics engineers..................	382	7.7	5.9	15.8	4.2
Industrial engineers, including health and safety	174	22.6	7.0	5.9	2.9
Mechanical engineers...........................	322	5.8	4.3	9.5	4.0
Drafters	181	21.8	3.0	6.8	10.3
Engineering technicians, except drafters................	396	20.6	9.3	5.3	11.2
Surveying and mapping technicians..... .[3]...........	96	9.9	3.0	0.3	8.5
Life, physical, and social science occupations [3].............	1,434	43.3	5.7	12.2	4.1
Biological scientists............................	116	46.6	3.5	11.9	3.8
Medical scientists.............................	164	45.4	5.3	35.6	2.4
Chemists and materials scientists	116	34.1	7.4	13.3	1.7
Environmental scientists and geoscientists..............	101	22.0	2.9	3.4	1.8
Market and survey researchers......................	129	61.3	9.0	8.7	3.4
Psychologists	189	67.7	2.6	2.2	3.5
Chemical technicians	76	35.9	11.4	4.4	8.8
Community and social services occupations [3].............	2,156	61.6	18.6	3.3	8.5
Counselors	614	66.8	17.9	2.3	8.2
Social workers................................	698	82.6	22.7	3.3	10.3
Miscellaneous community and social service specialists	293	70.5	23.9	3.2	11.8
Clergy	416	12.8	12.4	4.5	4.7

See footnotes at end of table.

U.S. Census Bureau, Statistical Abstract of the United States: 2008

[144,427 represents 144,427,000. Civilian noninstitutional population 16 years old and over. Annual average of monthly figures. Based on Current Population Survey; see text, Section 1, and Appendix III. Occupational classifications are those used in the 2000 census and are not comparable to those used in the 1990 census]

Occupation	Total employed (1,000)	Percent of total			
		Female	Black [1]	Asian [1]	Hispanic [2]
Professional and related occupations—Con.					
Legal occupations [3]	1,637	51.7	6.5	2.8	5.7
Lawyers	965	32.6	5.0	2.9	3.0
Paralegals and legal assistants	345	89.1	8.4	1.9	11.3
Miscellaneous legal support workers [3]	261	76.8	8.7	3.8	9.0
Education, training, and library occupations [3]	8,126	74.2	9.8	3.5	7.3
Postsecondary teachers	1,194	46.3	6.7	10.3	4.5
Preschool and kindergarten teachers	690	97.7	13.9	2.5	10.5
Elementary and middle school teachers	2,701	82.2	9.7	1.7	6.5
Secondary school teachers	1,098	56.0	7.3	1.9	6.5
Special education teachers	401	83.5	9.0	1.7	4.7
Other teachers and instructors	705	64.9	9.4	4.6	7.5
Librarians	229	84.2	8.8	1.1	2.9
Teacher assistants	942	92.3	14.9	2.3	14.1
Arts, design, entertainment, sports, and media occupations [3]	2,735	48.8	6.7	4.2	7.8
Artists and related workers	223	52.4	5.1	6.2	4.6
Designers	821	55.5	3.2	7.0	9.4
Producers and directors	134	40.0	6.4	3.3	6.9
Athletes, coaches, umpires, and related workers	270	36.9	9.5	2.2	5.8
Musicians, singers, and related workers	203	33.5	9.0	3.4	11.5
News analysts, reporters, and correspondents	78	53.4	4.0	2.5	4.2
Public relations specialists	141	64.6	8.8	1.3	3.7
Editors	157	53.7	5.1	1.3	5.6
Writers and authors	174	58.5	5.7	1.9	2.8
Broadcast and sound engineering technicians and radio operators	89	15.6	11.7	2.5	10.1
Photographers	127	43.3	7.1	1.7	6.7
Healthcare practitioner and technical occupations [3]	7,060	73.4	10.6	8.2	5.6
Dentists	196	22.6	3.1	11.4	4.3
Dietitians and nutritionists	96	91.0	21.2	7.6	4.6
Pharmacists	245	48.9	6.0	19.5	5.6
Physicians and surgeons	863	32.2	5.2	17.0	5.7
Physician assistants	85	71.7	10.9	6.2	6.7
Registered nurses	2,529	91.3	10.9	7.5	4.2
Occupational therapists	78	90.3	3.1	4.7	2.0
Physical therapists	198	62.7	5.8	13.7	5.0
Respiratory therapists	85	66.0	15.3	4.6	6.2
Speech-language pathologists	114	95.3	8.1	1.4	3.6
Clinical laboratory technologists and technicians	321	78.1	14.2	9.6	7.8
Dental hygienists	144	98.6	1.4	4.2	4.6
Diagnostic-related technologists and technicians	281	72.9	7.5	2.9	6.3
Emergency medical technicians and paramedics	156	31.9	11.9	2.2	7.4
Health diagnosing and treating practitioner support technicians	425	80.1	11.8	5.6	8.2
Licensed practical and licensed vocational nurses	556	94.2	23.2	3.1	7.0
Medical records and health information technicians	98	92.0	20.5	1.4	15.1
Service occupations	**23,811**	**57.3**	**15.9**	**4.3**	**19.5**
Healthcare support occupations [3]	3,132	89.4	24.7	4.1	13.1
Nursing, psychiatric, and home health aides	1,906	88.9	34.8	4.0	13.1
Massage therapists	124	84.1	5.4	5.0	8.0
Dental assistants	274	95.4	5.4	4.2	14.9
Protective service occupations [3]	2,939	22.3	19.7	1.7	10.2
First-line supervisors/managers of police and detectives	103	15.5	5.5	0.2	6.9
Firefighters	253	3.5	9.9	0.4	7.5
Bailiffs, correctional officers, and jailers	451	28.2	24.2	0.4	7.4
Detectives and criminal investigators	144	26.0	17.6	1.8	13.5
Police and sheriff's patrol officers	655	12.8	14.9	2.3	11.8
Private detectives and investigators	85	38.2	11.4	0.6	5.5
Security guards and gaming surveillance officers	835	23.0	29.8	3.1	12.2
Food preparation and serving-related occupations	7,606	56.6	11.7	5.3	21.1
Chefs and head cooks	313	23.9	14.1	15.8	19.1
First-line supervisors/managers of food preparation and serving workers	652	58.7	14.7	3.0	15.0
Cooks	1,868	43.4	17.4	6.2	31.6
Food-preparation workers	698	59.2	12.3	5.2	25.4
Bartenders	389	55.0	2.5	2.1	9.4
Combined food preparation and serving workers, including fast food	344	67.6	12.5	4.3	13.3
Counter attendants, cafeteria, food concession, and coffee shop	308	66.2	12.1	3.5	13.9
Waiters and waitresses	1,960	71.5	7.0	5.3	14.3
Food servers, nonrestaurant	155	65.3	23.7	5.1	13.2
Dining room and cafeteria attendants and bartender helpers	380	48.5	8.4	5.4	30.5
Dishwashers	279	23.9	10.0	3.1	36.7
Hosts and hostesses, restaurant, lounge, and coffee shop	257	86.4	6.3	4.3	14.7
Building and grounds cleaning and maintenance occupations	5,381	40.0	15.6	2.6	31.8
First-line supervisors/managers of housekeeping and janitorial workers	305	32.6	16.2	3.2	17.1
First-line supervisors/managers of landscaping, lawn service, and groundskeeping workers	235	8.0	5.8	1.0	17.2
Janitors and building cleaners	2,082	32.2	18.7	3.0	26.8
Maids and housekeeping cleaners	1,423	90.3	19.9	3.4	37.2
Pest control workers	78	2.2	7.7	2.2	21.8
Grounds maintenance workers	1,259	6.2	7.8	1.2	40.9

See footnotes at end of table.

Labor Force, Employment, and Earnings 389

Table 598. **Employed Civilians by Occupation, Sex, Race, and Hispanic Origin: 2006**—Con.

[144,427 represents 144,427,000. Civilian noninstitutional population 16 years old and over. Annual average of monthly figures. Based on Current Population Survey; see text, Section 1, and Appendix III. Occupational classifications are those used in the 2000 census and are not comparable to those used in the 1990 census]

Occupation	Total employed (1,000)	Percent of total			
		Female	Black [1]	Asian [1]	Hispanic [2]
Service occupations—Con.					
Personal care and service occupations [3]	4,754	78.7	15.0	6.4	13.0
First-line supervisors/managers of gaming workers	124	43.7	5.8	5.7	3.6
First-line supervisors/managers of personal service workers	176	66.7	11.2	10.9	6.0
Nonfarm animal caretakers	137	72.1	3.6	0.9	9.3
Gaming services workers	106	48.1	7.6	18.0	9.2
Barbers	100	17.7	36.7	1.9	10.0
Hairdressers, hairstylists, and cosmetologists	767	93.4	11.9	4.8	12.4
Miscellaneous personal appearance workers	230	83.0	6.5	45.5	8.0
Baggage porters, bellhops, and concierges	78	20.6	14.8	6.1	24.2
Transportation attendants	134	74.2	21.8	4.8	11.0
Child care workers	1,401	94.2	17.0	2.8	17.3
Personal and home care aides	703	87.3	22.4	5.8	14.9
Recreation and fitness workers	322	68.7	11.3	2.3	8.1
Sales and office occupations	**36,141**	**63.3**	**11.2**	**4.0**	**11.5**
Sales and related occupations [3]	16,641	49.1	9.0	4.6	11.1
First-line supervisors/managers of retail sales workers	3,435	41.8	7.4	4.5	9.6
First-line supervisors/managers of non retail sales workers	1,433	27.2	5.6	6.0	9.9
Cashiers	3,063	74.8	15.3	5.5	16.8
Counter and rental clerks	146	51.7	11.1	8.9	14.3
Parts salespersons	149	16.3	3.0	1.1	11.7
Retail salespersons	3,386	51.4	11.1	4.2	11.9
Advertising sales agents	220	53.9	6.7	4.2	7.2
Insurance sales agents	548	45.3	6.9	2.6	6.8
Securities, commodities, and financial services sales agents	398	29.3	9.3	7.9	5.5
Travel agents	82	77.3	7.1	8.8	6.6
Sales representatives, services, all other	563	32.8	5.9	2.9	8.0
Sales representatives, wholesale and manufacturing	1,422	27.2	2.9	2.5	7.3
Models, demonstrators, and product promoters	75	84.2	3.2	5.3	11.5
Real estate brokers and sales agents	1,046	59.9	5.8	5.9	9.1
Telemarketers	142	65.3	19.5	1.1	16.2
Door-to-door sales workers, news and street vendors, and related workers	261	62.4	6.5	3.0	14.6
Office and administrative support occupations [3]	19,500	75.4	13.1	3.6	11.9
First-line supervisors/managers of office and administrative support workers	1,543	72.2	9.0	2.7	9.9
Bill and account collectors	213	62.2	25.1	2.1	17.3
Billing and posting clerks and machine operators	422	88.1	13.3	3.5	10.7
Bookkeeping, accounting, and auditing clerks	1,511	90.3	7.8	3.7	8.4
Payroll and timekeeping clerks	158	92.4	11.0	2.3	11.9
Tellers	432	84.8	10.6	4.0	14.5
Court, municipal, and license clerks	114	80.7	12.4	1.4	13.9
Customer service representatives	1,916	70.4	18.3	3.6	13.8
File clerks	363	79.2	13.9	5.2	15.1
Hotel, motel, and resort desk clerks	117	63.7	18.1	3.7	18.3
Interviewers, except eligibility and loan	141	82.1	17.3	1.6	9.8
Library assistants, clerical	119	87.9	8.2	5.0	14.8
Loan interviewers and clerks	190	76.7	12.0	6.5	13.2
Order clerks	128	69.4	8.8	1.8	19.0
Receptionists and information clerks	1,403	92.7	10.8	3.8	12.6
Reservation and transportation ticket agents and travel clerks	156	64.8	19.3	5.0	13.1
Couriers and messengers	273	17.9	15.3	3.0	12.9
Dispatchers	303	53.4	11.7	1.0	13.5
Postal service clerks	153	49.5	22.7	12.4	7.8
Postal service mail carriers	329	35.7	15.7	5.0	8.7
Postal service mail sorters, processors, and processing machine operators	98	47.5	28.2	12.3	7.8
Production, planning, and expediting clerks	296	56.8	7.5	2.5	12.6
Shipping, receiving, and traffic clerks	543	30.1	14.0	2.6	20.1
Stock clerks and order fillers	1,462	39.1	17.8	3.4	16.4
Weighers, measurers, checkers, and samplers, recordkeeping	81	50.4	15.3	7.3	17.8
Secretaries and administrative assistants	3,455	96.9	9.8	2.2	8.6
Computer operators	185	49.6	15.2	7.7	10.3
Data entry keyers	475	81.6	15.2	6.1	11.8
Word processors and typists	256	91.2	18.1	1.9	9.5
Insurance claims and policy processing clerks	274	87.6	11.4	0.9	10.3
Mail clerks and mail machine operators, except postal service	123	54.2	25.8	7.5	8.4
Office clerks, general	1,035	81.9	12.4	5.8	14.5
Natural resources, construction, and maintenance occupations	**15,830**	**4.7**	**6.8**	**1.8**	**24.6**
Farming, fishing, and forestry occupations	961	22.0	4.9	1.6	39.7
Logging workers	78	0.2	7.5	0.0	3.0
Construction and extraction occupations [3]	9,507	3.1	6.6	1.2	29.3
First-line supervisors/managers of construction trades and extraction workers	976	2.6	4.6	1.3	12.0
Brickmasons, blockmasons, and stonemasons	244	1.6	7.1	0.1	40.3
Carpenters	1,843	2.4	4.5	1.6	26.6

See footnotes at end of table.

Table 598. **Employed Civilians by Occupation, Sex, Race, and Hispanic Origin: 2006**—Con.

[144,427 represents 144,427,000. Civilian noninstitutional population 16 years old and over. Annual average of monthly figures. Based on Current Population Survey; see text, Section 1, and Appendix III. Occupational classifications are those used in the 2000 census and are not comparable to those used in the 1990 census]

Occupation	Total employed (1,000)	Percent of total			
		Female	Black [1]	Asian [1]	Hispanic [2]
Construction and extraction occupations—Con.					
Carpet, floor, and tile installers and finishers	279	2.4	5.3	1.2	39.4
Cement masons, concrete finishers, and terrazzo workers	107	0.7	13.8	–	51.5
Construction laborers	1,693	3.7	7.5	1.4	44.7
Operating engineers and other construction equipment operators	451	1.7	8.3	0.3	9.7
Drywall installers, ceiling tile installers, and tapers	295	-2.9	3.8	0.1	51.8
Electricians	882	1.9	7.5	1.7	14.4
Painters, construction and maintenance	713	7.7	7.0	1.2	41.0
Pipelayers, plumbers, pipefitters, and steamfitters	662	1.8	8.5	0.4	20.9
Roofers	242	1.1	7.0	1.2	46.7
Sheet metal workers	125	3.1	2.2	2.8	13.7
Helpers, construction trades	132	6.2	9.9	0.4	43.2
Construction and building inspectors	102	8.8	10.1	1.3	12.3
Highway maintenance workers	103	3.8	10.5	0.6	23.1
Installation, maintenance, and repair occupations [3]	5,362	4.6	7.6	3.0	13.4
First-line supervisors/managers of mechanics, installers, and repairers	357	8.5	7.8	2.3	8.7
Computer, automated teller, and office machine repairers	371	9.7	8.4	6.8	10.2
Radio and telecommunications equipment installers and repairers	205	15.2	11.2	5.1	8.8
Aircraft mechanics and service technicians	141	5.3	6.6	3.7	7.6
Automotive body and related repairers	162	0.6	4.1	4.8	25.6
Automotive service technicians and mechanics	875	1.6	6.1	4.4	16.8
Bus and truck mechanics and diesel engine specialists	367	0.9	6.3	1.6	14.1
Heavy vehicle and mobile equipment service technicians and mechanics	237	1.4	2.6	0.3	13.5
Heating, air conditioning, and refrigeration mechanics and installers	405	2.7	4.8	1.1	13.7
Industrial and refractory machinery mechanics	436	3.8	9.1	2.5	11.7
Maintenance and repair workers, general	435	4.0	11.3	1.2	16.6
Electrical power-line installers and repairers	109	0.9	12.0	–	6.5
Telecommunications line installers and repairers	210	8.6	11.3	2.1	12.8
Production, transportation, and material occupations	**18,224**	**22.8**	**14.2**	**3.6**	**19.6**
Production occupations [3]	9,378	30.4	12.2	4.8	20.6
First-line supervisors/managers of production and operating workers	868	19.4	9.8	4.8	10.8
Electrical, electronics, and electromechanical assemblers	213	51.7	14.0	14.0	19.6
Bakers	186	57.9	9.4	4.6	28.5
Butchers and other meat, poultry, and fish processing workers	292	29.9	12.8	3.1	46.1
Food batchmakers	81	58.6	10.5	4.0	27.7
Cutting, punching, and press machine setters, operators, and tenders, metal and plastic	119	17.9	13.8	1.5	15.8
Machinists	415	6.7	5.2	4.1	12.1
Tool and die makers	105	0.9	3.0	–	5.4
Welding, soldering, and brazing workers	546	5.9	7.5	2.7	19.4
Printing machine operators	208	22.2	9.5	3.8	16.5
Laundry and dry-cleaning workers	190	62.4	18.3	5.2	32.1
Sewing machine operators	292	77.9	10.7	15.3	41.4
Tailors, dressmakers, and sewers	111	74.7	7.6	11.0	21.1
Cabinetmakers and bench carpenters	113	4.4	1.8	2.3	18.5
Stationary engineers and boiler operators	94	2.3	8.5	3.0	9.8
Water and liquid waste treatment plant and system operators	95	4.0	13.4	0.4	5.4
Crushing, grinding, polishing, mixing, and blending workers	105	11.2	19.3	5.1	24.6
Cutting workers	78	24.8	5.8	2.7	27.3
Inspectors, testers, sorters, samplers, and weighers	702	38.8	11.4	6.4	14.4
Medical, dental, and ophthalmic laboratory technicians	95	50.8	9.7	11.2	17.8
Packaging and filling machine operators and tenders	275	55.5	21.5	5.0	38.0
Painting workers	173	16.6	9.0	1.4	25.0
Transportation and material-moving occupations [3]	8,846	14.8	16.3	2.3	18.6
Supervisors, transportation and material-moving workers	228	16.7	13.0	2.2	12.1
Aircraft pilots and flight engineers	115	2.2	–	2.8	5.3
Bus drivers	565	49.6	29.4	1.3	12.2
Driver/sales workers and truck drivers	3,475	5.2	13.9	1.2	16.0
Taxi drivers and chauffeurs	282	16.0	23.8	12.6	15.0
Service station attendants	96	9.8	5.9	7.5	12.0
Industrial truck and tractor operators	574	7.2	20.1	0.8	25.8
Cleaners of vehicles and equipment	401	15.0	16.9	1.0	32.7
Laborers and freight, stock, and material movers, hand	1,899	16.9	16.2	2.7	19.4
Packers and packagers, hand	432	57.5	18.9	5.4	39.2
Refuse and recyclable material collectors	91	6.1	28.0	4.4	24.7

– Represents or rounds to zero. [1] The 2003 Current Population Survey (CPS) allowed respondents to choose more than one race. Data represent persons who selected this race group only and exclude persons reporting more than one race. The CPS in prior years only allowed respondents to report one race group. See comments on race in the text for Section 1. [2] Persons of Hispanic or Latino ethnicity may be of any race. [3] Includes other occupations, not shown separately.

Source: U.S. Bureau of Labor Statistics, *Employment and Earnings*, monthy, January 2007 issue. See Internet site <http://www.bls.gov/cps/home.htm>.

Labor Force, Employment, and Earnings 391

Table 599. Employed Civilians by Occupation—States: 2005

[In thousands (141,730 represents 141,730,000). Occupation classifications are those used in the 2000 Census and are not comparable to those in other tables using 1990 Census classifications. Based on the Current Population Survey and subject to sampling error; see text, Section 1, and Appendix III]

State	Total	Management, professional, and related occupations			Sales and office occupations		Natural resources, construction, and maintenance occupations			Production, transportation, and material moving occupations	
		Management, business, and financial operations	Professional and related occupations	Service occupations	Sales and related occupations	Office and administrative support occupations	Farming, fishing, and forestry occupations	Construction and extraction occupations	Installation, maintenance, and repair occupations	Production occupations	Transportation and material moving occupations
Total ...	141,730	20,450	28,795	23,133	16,433	19,529	976	9,145	5,226	9,378	8,664
AL.......	2,086	245	386	302	214	310	16	165	96	192	162
AK.......	318	43	70	51	32	48	4	25	13	9	22
AZ.......	2,697	411	499	488	341	377	8	218	114	128	113
AR.......	1,301	177	209	219	132	173	21	88	52	125	106
CA.......	16,724	2,632	3,450	2,670	2,080	2,183	204	1082	547	967	910
CO	2,406	404	500	379	306	316	10	181	79	104	126
CT	1,724	275	403	270	195	230	5	100	60	109	77
DE.......	421	60	86	69	48	60	2	31	17	23	24
DC	277	59	94	46	19	35	(Z)	8	4	3	9
FL.......	8,390	1,182	1,557	1,497	1,123	1,172	30	676	341	342	471
GA	4,334	643	813	659	506	601	27	302	184	322	278
HI	616	85	116	139	73	84	7	42	20	21	30
ID	721	104	128	108	83	106	21	57	33	35	46
IL	6,097	940	1,286	967	688	887	12	328	173	426	388
IN	3,032	389	535	438	339	380	17	172	146	364	252
IA	1,592	240	310	231	170	222	18	78	62	140	123
KS.......	1,406	216	287	231	147	185	12	84	56	102	87
KY.......	1,885	234	372	281	205	270	13	116	82	183	129
LA.......	1,973	241	348	347	238	274	17	138	80	135	156
ME	677	91	140	114	79	86	10	43	29	44	41
MD	2,800	480	709	439	284	389	10	173	87	100	128
MA	3,193	485	840	509	348	440	8	176	96	134	157
MI	4,773	613	992	792	550	594	20	267	186	458	299
MN	2,815	451	624	433	317	389	19	137	91	205	149
MS	1,241	132	239	203	130	160	23	82	55	135	83
MO	2,855	404	546	439	331	422	15	175	109	209	203
MT	476	75	87	86	62	53	11	44	17	18	24
NE......	948	140	190	142	110	135	13	53	35	69	60
NV......	1,167	147	155	291	145	170	(Z)	111	45	39	63
NH	708	113	167	102	86	92	2	47	24	45	31
NJ.......	4,244	700	981	645	497	594	8	204	130	211	273
NM......	897	144	183	143	98	117	9	75	30	39	60
NY.......	8,943	1,162	2,041	1,758	990	1,298	24	471	284	420	495
NC.......	4,092	564	764	629	470	534	37	300	174	360	261
ND	349	66	64	61	37	42	7	19	14	18	20
OH	5,558	738	1,046	916	628	799	22	275	204	537	394
OK	1,665	256	308	264	171	249	17	101	81	116	100
OR	1,745	261	371	259	212	241	26	99	55	110	109
PA.......	5,972	803	1,224	942	657	863	37	345	250	435	416
RI	541	74	115	94	63	78	2	27	16	44	29
SC.......	1,939	229	361	314	244	252	10	127	79	193	131
SD.......	414	70	73	70	44	59	8	24	13	30	24
TN.......	2,717	352	510	419	310	368	14	190	103	271	179
TX.......	10,629	1,476	2,010	1,745	1,272	1,484	85	846	434	625	651
UT.......	1,216	169	228	173	153	194	5	97	45	74	77
VT.......	342	49	86	55	33	41	4	24	11	23	16
VA.......	3,781	602	826	594	419	521	16	301	132	174	197
WA	3,114	487	721	486	343	409	38	173	100	166	190
WV	759	81	145	141	86	105	4	63	28	44	63
WI	2,881	407	550	433	300	406	22	158	97	292	215
WY	273	45	42	46	25	34	4	30	15	12	21

Z Less than 500.

Source: U.S. Bureau of Labor Statistics, Local Area Unemployment Statistics, *Geographic Profile of Employment and Unemployment, 2005.* See Internet site <http://www.bls.gov/gps/>.

U.S. Census Bureau, Statistical Abstract of the United States: 2008

Table 600. Employment Projections by Occupation: 2004 and 2014

[In thousands (624 represents 624,000), except percent and rank. Estimates based on the Current Employment Statistics Program; the Occupational Employment Statistics Survey; and the Current Population Survey. See source for methodological assumptions. Occupations based on the 2000 Standard Occupational Classification system]

Occupation	Employment (1,000)		Change 2002-2014		Quartile rank by 2004 median annual earnings [1]	Most significant source of postsecondary education or training
	2004	2014	Number (1,000)	Percent		
FASTEST GROWING						
Home health aides	624	974	350	56.0	VL	Short-term on-the-job training
Network systems and data communications analysts	231	357	126	54.6	VH	Bachelor's degree
Medical assistants	387	589	202	52.1	L	Moderate-term on-the-job training
Physician assistants	62	93	31	49.6	VH	Bachelor's degree
Computer software engineers, applications . .	460	682	222	48.4	VH	Bachelor's degree
Physical therapist assistants	59	85	26	44.2	H	Associate's degree
Dental hygienists	158	226	68	43.3	VH	Associate's degree
Computer software engineers, systems software	340	486	146	43.0	VH	Bachelor's degree
Dental assistants	267	382	114	42.7	L	Moderate-term on-the-job training
Personal and home care aides	701	988	287	41.0	VL	Short-term on-the-job training
Network and computer systems administrators	278	385	107	38.4	VH	Bachelor's degree
Database administrators	104	144	40	38.2	VH	Bachelor's degree
Physical therapists	155	211	57	36.7	VH	Master's degree
Forensic science technicians . . .	10	13	4	36.4	VH	Associate's degree
Veterinary technologists and technicians . . .	60	81	21	35.3	L	Associate's degree
Diagnostic medical sonographers	42	57	15	34.8	VH	Associate's degree
Physical therapist aides	43	57	15	34.4	L	Short-term on-the-job training
Occupational therapist assistants	21	29	7	34.1	H	Associate's degree
Medical scientists, except epidemiologists	72	97	25	34.1	VH	Doctoral degree
Occupational therapists	92	123	31	33.6	VH	Master's degree
Preschool teachers, except special education	431	573	143	33.1	L	Postsecondary vocational award
Cardiovascular technologists and technicians	45	60	15	32.6	H	Associate's degree
Postsecondary teachers	1,628	2,153	524	32.2	VH	Doctoral degree
Hydrologists	8	11	3	31.6	VH	Master's degree
Computer systems analysts	487	640	153	31.4	VH	Bachelor's degree
Hazardous materials removal workers	38	50	12	31.2	H	Moderate-term on-the-job training
LARGEST JOB GROWTH						
Retail salespersons	4,256	4,992	736	17.3	VL	Short-term on-the-job training
Registered nurses	2,394	3,096	703	29.4	VH	Associate's degree
Postsecondary teachers	1,628	2,153	524	32.2	VH	Doctoral degree
Customer service representatives	2,063	2,534	471	22.8	L	Moderate-term on-the-job training
Janitors and cleaners, except maids and housekeeping cleaners	2,374	2,813	440	18.5	VL	Short-term on-the-job training
Waiters and waitresses	2,252	2,627	376	16.7	VL	Short-term on-the-job training
Combined food preparation and serving workers, including fast food	2,150	2,516	367	17.1	VL	Short-term on-the-job training
Home health aides	624	974	350	56.0	VL	Short-term on-the-job training
Nursing aides, orderlies, and attendants . . .	1,455	1,781	325	22.3	L	Postsecondary vocational award
General and operations managers	1,807	2,115	308	17.0	VH	Bachelor's or higher degree, plus work experience
Personal and home care aides.	701	988	287	41.0	VL	Short-term on-the-job training
Elementary school teachers, except special education	1,457	1,722	265	18.2	H	Bachelor's degree
Accountants and auditors	1,176	1,440	264	22.4	VH	Bachelor's degree
Office clerks, general	3,138	3,401	263	8.4	L	Short-term on-the-job training
Laborers and freight, stock, and material movers, hand	2,430	2,678	248	10.2	VL	Short-term on-the-job training
Receptionists and information clerks	1,133	1,379	246	21.7	L	Short-term on-the-job training
Landscaping and groundskeeping workers . .	1,177	1,407	230	19.5	L	Short-term on-the-job training
Truck drivers, heavy and tractor-trailer	1,738	1,962	223	12.9	H	Moderate-term on-the-job training
Computer software engineers, applications. . .	460	682	222	48.4	VH	Bachelor's degree
Maintenance and repair workers, general . . .	1,332	1,533	202	15.2	H	Moderate-term on-the-job training
Medical assistants	387	589	202	52.1	L	Moderate-term on-the-job training
Executive secretaries and administrative assistants	1,547	1,739	192	12.4	H	Moderate-term on-the-job training
Sales representatives, wholesale and manufacturing, except technical and scientific products.	1,454	1,641	187	12.9	VH	Moderate-term on-the-job training
Carpenters	1,349	1,535	186	13.8	H	Long-term on-the-job training
Teacher assistants	1,296	1,478	183	14.1	VL	Short-term on-the-job training
Child care workers	1,280	1,456	176	13.8	VL	Short-term on-the-job training
Food preparation workers	889	1,064	175	19.7	VL	Short-term on-the-job training

[1] Quartile ranks based on the Occupational Employment Statistics annual earnings. VH = very high ($43,600 and over), H = high ($28,580 to $43,590), L = low ($20,190 to $28,570), and VL = very low (up to $20,180). The rankings were based on quartiles using one-fourth of total employment to define each quartile. Earnings are for wage and salary workers.

Source: U.S. Bureau of Labor Statistics "Occupational employment projections to 2014", *Monthly Labor Review*, November 2005. See Internet site <http://www.bls.gov/emp/home.htm>.

U.S. Census Bureau, Statistical Abstract of the United States: 2008

Table 601. **Occupations of the Employed by Selected Characteristic: 2005**

[In thousands (121,960 represents 121,960,000). Annual averages of monthly figures. Civilian noninstitutional population 25 years old and over. Based on Current Population Survey; see text, Section 1, and Appendix III. See headnote, Table 587, regarding occupations]

Sex, race, and educational attainment	Total employed	Managerial, profes- sional, and related	Service	Sales and office	Natural resources, construc- tion, and mainte nance	Production, transporta- tion, and material moving
Total [1]	121,960	46,303	17,448	29,322	13,173	15,714
Less than a high school diploma.	11,712	749	3,336	1,557	2,899	3,171
High school graduates, no college.	36,398	5,832	6,057	10,213	5,731	7,664
Less than a bachelor's degree	33,625	10,975	5,003	10,403	3,550	3,694
College graduates	40,225	28,748	2,151	7,150	992	1,184
White [2]	100,613	39,019	13,117	24,372	11,607	12,497
Less than a high school diploma	9,579	626	2,500	1,262	2,595	2,596
High school graduates, no college	29,911	5,038	5,067	8,649	5,076	6,081
Less than a bachelor's degree	27,771	9,321	3,868	8,574	3,099	2,909
College graduates.	33,352	24,034	1,682	5,887	838	911
Black [2]	13,177	3,730	3,036	3,159	983	2,268
Less than a high school diploma	1,369	65	578	183	185	358
High school graduates, no college	4,742	564	1,408	1,114	439	1,217
Less than a bachelor's degree	4,008	1,082	812	1,267	281	566
College graduates.	3,057	2,019	238	596	77	128
Asian [2]	5,601	2,753	818	1,198	249	583
Less than a high school diploma	440	36	165	70	40	130
High school graduates, no college	980	120	301	261	79	220
Less than a bachelor's degree	972	304	178	304	71	115
College graduates.	3,208	2,293	174	563	59	119
Hispanic [3]	15,362	2,880	3,553	3,008	2,953	2,968
Less than a high school diploma	5,367	180	1,623	536	1,600	1,427
High school graduates, no college	4,535	500	1,094	1,070	866	1,004
Less than a bachelor's degree	3,228	861	591	1,012	368	396
College graduates.	2,232	1,339	245	390	118	140

[1] Includes other races, not shown separately.   [2] For persons in this race group only. See footnote 3, Table 570.   [3] Persons of Hispanic or Latino ethnicity may be of any race.

Source: U.S. Bureau of Labor Statistics, unpublished data.

Table 602. **Employment by Industry: 2000 to 2006**

[In thousands (136,891 represents 136,891,000), except percent. See Table 584 regarding coverage and headnote Table 587 regarding industries]

Industry	2000	2004 [1]	2005 [1]	2006 [1]	2006, percent [1] Female	Black [2]	Asian [2]	His- panic [3]
Total employed	136,891	139,252	141,730	144,427	46.3	10.9	4.5	13.6
Agriculture and related industries.	2,464	2,232	2,197	2,206	24.6	2.7	1.2	19.4
Mining	475	539	624	687	13.0	4.9	0.7	13.6
Construction	9,931	10,768	11,197	11,749	9.6	5.5	1.4	25.1
Manufacturing	19,644	16,484	16,253	16,377	29.5	9.5	5.2	14.7
Durable goods	12,519	10,329	10,333	10,499	25.8	8.5	5.8	12.4
Nondurable goods	7,125	6,155	5,919	5,877	36.1	11.4	4.2	18.7
Wholesale trade	4,216	4,600	4,579	4,561	29.0	6.5	4.1	13.5
Retail trade	15,763	16,269	16,825	16,767	48.9	10.1	4.2	12.7
Transportation and utilities	7,380	7,013	7,360	7,455	24.2	16.5	3.6	12.7
Transportation and warehousing.	6,096	5,844	6,184	6,269	24.7	17.6	3.8	13.5
Utilities	1,284	1,168	1,176	1,186	21.9	10.9	2.5	8.2
Information	4,059	3,463	3,402	3,573	44.4	11.7	5.2	9.4
Financial activities.	9,374	9,969	10,203	10,490	55.5	10.2	5.1	10.0
Finance and insurance	6,641	6,940	7,035	7,254	58.2	10.5	5.6	8.5
Real estate and rental and leasing . . .	2,734	3,029	3,168	3,237	49.4	9.5	4.1	13.4
Professional and business services	13,649	14,108	14,294	14,868	42.5	9.8	5.7	13.0
Professional and technical services. . .	8,266	8,386	8,584	8,776	44.4	6.4	7.6	6.2
Management, administrative, and waste services	5,383	5,722	5,709	6,092	39.8	14.8	3.0	22.9
Education and health services.	26,188	28,719	29,174	29,938	74.9	14.2	4.7	9.1
Educational services	11,255	12,058	12,264	12,522	68.9	10.8	3.6	8.5
Health care and social assistance. . . .	14,933	16,661	16,910	17,416	79.1	16.7	5.4	9.5
Hospitals	5,202	5,700	5,719	5,712	76.6	16.4	7.0	7.6
Health services, except hospitals . .	7,009	8,118	8,332	8,639	78.6	15.3	5.3	9.5
Social assistance	2,722	2,844	2,860	3,065	85.4	21.2	2.9	12.9
Leisure and hospitality	11,186	11,820	12,071	12,145	51.3	10.5	5.9	19.4
Arts, entertainment, and recreation . . .	2,539	2,690	2,765	2,671	45.2	8.3	3.6	11.9
Accommodation and food services . . .	8,647	9,131	9,306	9,474	53.0	11.2	6.5	21.6
Other services	6,450	6,903	7,020	7,088	51.7	9.8	5.8	15.5
Other services, except private households.	5,731	6,124	6,208	6,285	46.5	9.6	6.2	13.3
Private households	718	779	812	803	92.5	11.1	2.5	32.8
Government workers	6,113	6,365	6,530	6,524	45.4	16.2	3.5	8.6

[1] See footnote 2, Table 569.   [2] Persons in this race group only. See footnote 3, Table 570.   [3] Persons of Hispanic or Latino origin may be of any race.
Source: U.S. Bureau of Labor Statistics, *Employment and Earnings,* monthly, January 2007 issue. See Internet site <http://www.bls.gov/cps/home.htm>.

Table 603. Employment Projections by Industry: 2004 to 2014

[15,034.5 represents 15,034,500. Estimates based on the Current Employment Statistics estimates. See source for methodological assumptions. Minus sign (–) indicates decline]

Industry	2002 NAICS code [1]	Employment (1,000)		Change, 2004–2014 (1,000)	Average annual rate of change 2004–2014
		2004	2014		
LARGEST GROWTH					
Retail trade	44,45	15,034.5	16,683.2	1,648.7	1.0
Employment services	5613	3,470.3	5,050.2	1,579.9	3.8
Food services and drinking places	722	8,850.0	10,300.8	1,450.8	1.5
Offices of health practitioners	6211,6212,6213	3,337.0	4,560.7	1,223.7	3.2
Construction	23	6,964.5	7,756.9	792.4	1.1
Local government educational services	(X)	7,762.5	8,545.5	783.0	1.0
Hospitals, private	622	4,293.6	4,981.9	688.3	1.5
Residential care facilities	6232,6233,6239	1,239.6	1,840.3	600.7	4.0
Home health care services	6216	773.2	1,310.3	537.1	5.4
Junior colleges, colleges, universities, and professsional schools	6112,6113	1,461.8	1,964.8	503.0	3.0
Local government enterprises except passenger transit	(X)	4,216.0	4,699.3	483.3	1.1
Wholesale trade	42	5,654.9	6,130.8	475.9	0.8
Management, scientific, and technical consulting services	5416	779.0	1,250.2	471.2	4.8
Computer systems design and related services	5415	1,147.4	1,600.3	452.9	3.4
Individual, family, community, and vocational rehabilitation services	6241,6242,6243	1,365.3	1,810.0	444.7	2.9
State government educational services	(X)	2,249.2	2,691.0	441.8	1.8
Amusement, gambling, and recreation industries	713	1,351.3	1,709.7	358.4	2.4
Services to buildings and dwellings	5617	1,694.1	2,049.7	355.6	1.9
Outpatient, laboratory, and other ambulatory care services	6214,6215,6219	836.1	1,160.4	324.3	3.3
Accommodation	721	1,795.9	2,100.1	304.2	1.6
MOST RAPID GROWTH					
Home health care services	6216	773.2	1,310.3	537.1	5.4
Software publishers	5112	238.7	400.0	161.3	5.3
Management, scientific, and technical consulting services	5416	779.0	1,250.2	471.2	4.8
Residential care facilities	6232,6233,6239	1,239.6	1,840.3	600.7	4.0
Facilities support services	5612	115.6	170.0	54.4	3.9
Employment services	5613	3,470.3	5,050.2	1,579.9	3.8
Independent artists, writers, and performers	7115	41.9	60.8	18.9	3.8
Office administrative services	5611	319.4	449.9	130.5	3.5
Computer systems design and related services	5415	1,147.4	1,600.3	452.9	3.4
Outpatient, laboratory, and other ambulatory care services	6214,6215,6219	836.1	1,160.4	324.3	3.3
Child day care services	6244	767.1	1,061.9	294.8	3.3
Other educational services	6114–17	475.3	649.9	174.6	3.2
Offices of health practitioners	6211,6212,6213	3,337.0	4,560.7	1,223.7	3.2
Accounting, tax prep..ration, bookkeeping, and payroll services	5412	816.0	1,099.9	283.9	3.0
Junior colleges, colleges, universities, and professional schools	6112,6113	1,461.8	1,964.8	503.0	3.0
Individual, family, community, and vocational rehabilitation services	6241,6242,6243	1,365.3	1,810.0	444.7	2.9
Scenic and sightseeing transportation	487	26.8	35.2	8.4	2.8
Waste treatment and disposal and waste management sevvices	5622,5629	206.3	267.9	61.6	2.6
Other professional, scientific, and technical services	5419	503.4	646.1	142.7	2.5
Specialized design services	5414	121.0	155.0	34.0	2.5
MOST RAPID DECLINE					
Cut-and-sew apparel manufacturing	3152	219.9	80.0	–139.9	–9.6
Fiber, yarn, and thread mills	3131	54.4	25.0	–29.4	–7.5
Apparel knitting mills	3151	42.0	20.0	–22.0	–7.2
Textile and fabric finishing and fabric coating mills	3133	68.5	35.0	–33.5	–6.5
Fabric mills	3132	115.7	60.0	–55.7	–6.4
Tobacco manufacturing	3122	29.4	16.6	–12.8	–5.6
Footwear manufacturing	3162	19.4	12.5	–6.9	–4.3
Apparel accessories and other apparel manufacturing	3159	23.0	15.0	–8.0	–4.2
Basic chemical manufacturing	3251	156.1	110.0	–46.1	–3.4
Metal ore mining	2122	27.3	19.3	–8.0	–3.4
Other textile product mills	3149	75.1	55.0	–20.1	–3.1
Household appliance manufacturing	3352	90.1	66.0	–24.1	–3.1
Commercial and service industry machinery manufacturing	3333	114.9	85.0	–29.9	–3.0
Federal enterprises, except the Postal Service and electrical utilities	(X)	70.5	53.0	–17.5	–2.8
Electrical equipment manufacturing	3353	153.1	117.0	–36.1	–2.7
Railroad rolling stock manufacturing	3365	24.7	18.9	–5.8	–2.6
Coal mining	2121	71.7	55.0	–16.7	–2.6
Rubber product manufacturing	3262	173.0	132.8	–40.2	–2.6

X Not applicable.   [1] Based on the North American Industry Classification System, 2002; see text, this section.

Source: U.S. Bureau of Labor Statistics, "Industry output and employment projections to 2014," *Monthly Labor Review*, November 2005. See Internet site <http://www.bls.gov/emp/home.htm>.

Labor Force, Employment, and Earnings   395

Table 604. Unemployed Workers—Summary: 1980 to 2006

[In thousands (7,637 represents 7,637,000), **except as indicated**. Civilian noninstitutional population 16 years old and over. Annual averages of monthly figures. Based on the Current Population Survey; see text Section 1, and Appendix III. For data on unemployment insurance, see Table 539]

Age, sex, race, Hispanic origin	1980	1990 [1]	1995	2000 [1]	2003 [1]	2004 [1]	2005 [1]	2006 [1]
UNEMPLOYED								
Total [2]	7,637	7,047	7,404	5,692	8,774	8,149	7,591	7,001
16 to 19 years old	1,669	1,212	1,346	1,081	1,251	1,208	1,186	1,119
20 to 24 years old	1,835	1,299	1,244	1,022	1,495	1,431	1,335	1,234
25 to 44 years old	2,964	3,323	3,390	2,340	3,775	3,362	3,061	2,800
45 to 64 years old	1,075	1,109	1,269	1,117	2,069	1,970	1,825	1,689
65 years and over	94	105	153	132	183	179	184	159
Male	4,267	3,906	3,983	2,975	4,906	4,456	4,059	3,753
16 to 19 years old.	913	667	744	599	697	664	667	622
20 to 24 years old.	1,076	715	673	547	841	811	775	705
25 to 44 years old.	1,619	1,803	1,776	1,159	2,085	1,819	1,559	1,452
45 to 64 years old.	600	662	697	587	1,176	1,057	955	887
65 years and over.	58	59	94	83	107	104	102	88
Female.	3,370	3,140	3,421	2,717	3,868	3,694	3,531	3,247
16 to 19 years old.	755	544	602	483	554	543	519	496
20 to 24 years old.	760	584	571	475	654	619	560	530
25 to 44 years old.	1,345	1,519	1,615	1,181	1,690	1,543	1,502	1,348
45 to 64 years old.	473	447	574	529	894	914	870	801
65 years and over.	36	46	60	50	76	75	82	71
White [3]	5,884	5,186	5,459	4,121	6,311	5,847	5,350	5,002
16 to 19 years old.	1,291	903	952	795	909	890	845	794
20 to 24 years old.	1,364	899	866	682	1,012	959	878	832
Black [3]	1,553	1,565	1,538	1,241	1,787	1,729	1,700	1,549
16 to 19 years old.	343	268	325	230	255	241	267	253
20 to 24 years old.	426	349	311	281	375	353	358	318
Asian [3, 4]	(NA)	(NA)	(NA)	227	366	277	259	205
16 to 19 years old.	(NA)	(NA)	(NA)	40	31	20	20	22
20 to 24 years old.	(NA)	(NA)	(NA)	41	47	46	35	28
Hispanic [5]	620	876	1,140	954	1,441	1,342	1,191	1,081
16 to 19 years old.	145	161	205	194	192	203	191	170
20 to 24 years old.	138	167	209	190	273	255	227	194
Full-time workers	6,269	5,677	5,909	4,538	7,361	6,762	6,175	5,675
Part-time workers	1,369	1,369	1,495	1,154	1,413	1,388	1,415	1,326
UNEMPLOYMENT RATE (percent) [6]								
Total [2]	7.1	5.6	5.6	4.0	6.0	5.5	5.1	4.6
16 to 19 years old	17.8	15.5	17.3	13.1	17.5	17.0	16.6	15.4
20 to 24 years old	11.5	8.8	9.1	7.2	10.0	9.4	8.8	8.2
25 to 44 years old	6.0	4.9	4.8	3.3	5.5	4.9	4.5	4.1
45 to 64 years old	3.7	3.5	3.4	2.5	4.1	3.8	3.4	3.1
65 years and over	3.1	3.0	4.0	3.1	3.8	3.6	3.5	2.9
Male	6.9	5.7	5.6	3.9	6.3	5.6	5.1	4.6
16 to 19 years old.	18.3	16.3	18.4	14.0	19.3	18.4	18.6	16.9
20 to 24 years old.	12.5	9.1	9.2	7.3	10.6	10.1	9.6	8.7
25 to 44 years old.	5.6	4.8	4.7	3.1	5.6	4.9	4.2	3.9
45 to 64 years old.	3.5	3.7	3.5	2.4	4.4	3.9	3.4	3.1
65 years and over.	3.1	3.0	4.3	3.3	4.0	3.7	3.4	2.8
Female.	7.4	5.5	5.6	4.1	5.7	5.4	5.1	4.6
16 to 19 years old.	17.2	14.7	16.1	12.1	15.6	15.5	14.5	13.8
20 to 24 years old.	10.4	8.5	9.0	7.1	9.3	8.7	7.9	7.6
25 to 44 years old.	6.4	4.9	5.0	3.6	5.4	5.0	4.8	4.3
45 to 64 years old.	4.0	3.2	3.3	2.5	3.7	3.7	3.4	3.1
65 years and over.	3.1	3.1	3.7	2.7	3.6	3.4	3.5	3.0
White [3]	6.3	4.8	4.9	3.5	5.2	4.8	4.4	4.0
16 to 19 years old.	15.5	13.5	14.5	11.4	15.2	15.0	14.2	13.2
20 to 24 years old.	9.9	7.3	7.7	5.9	8.4	7.9	7.2	6.9
Black [3]	14.3	11.4	10.4	7.6	10.8	10.4	10.0	8.9
16 to 19 years old.	38.5	30.9	35.7	24.5	33.0	31.7	33.3	29.1
20 to 24 years old.	23.6	19.9	17.7	15.0	19.8	18.4	18.3	16.2
Asian [3, 4]	(NA)	(NA)	(NA)	3.6	6.0	4.4	4.0	3.0
16 to 19 years old.	(NA)	(NA)	(NA)	14.2	17.5	11.5	12.4	14.0
20 to 24 years old.	(NA)	(NA)	(NA)	6.9	9.0	8.6	6.5	5.6
Hispanic [5]	10.1	8.2	9.3	5.7	7.7	7.0	6.0	5.2
16 to 19 years old.	22.5	19.5	24.1	16.6	20.0	20.4	18.4	15.9
20 to 24 years old.	12.1	9.1	11.5	7.5	10.2	9.3	8.6	7.2
Experienced workers [7]	6.9	5.3	5.4	3.8	5.8	5.3	4.8	(NA)
Women maintaining families	9.2	8.3	8.0	5.9	8.5	8.0	7.8	(NA)
Married men, wife present	4.2	3.4	3.3	2.0	3.8	3.1	2.8	2.4
Percent without work for—								
Fewer than 5 weeks	43.2	46.3	36.5	44.9	31.7	33.1	35.1	37.3
5 to 10 weeks	23.4	23.5	22.0	23.0	19.8	19.6	20.7	20.9
11 to 14 weeks	9.0	8.5	9.6	8.9	10.0	9.7	9.7	9.4
15 to 26 weeks.	13.8	11.7	14.6	11.8	16.4	15.9	14.9	14.7
27 weeks and over	10.7	10.0	17.3	11.4	22.1	21.8	19.6	17.6
Unemployment duration, average (weeks).	11.9	12.0	16.6	12.6	19.2	19.6	18.4	16.8

NA Not available. [1] See footnote 2, Table 569. [2] Includes other races, not shown separately. [3] Includes other ages, not shown separately. Also beginning 2003, for this race group only. See footnote 3, Table 570. [4] Prior to 2003, includes Pacific Islanders. [5] Persons of Hispanic or Latino origin may be of any race. Also includes ages not shown separately. [6] Unemployed as percent of civilian labor force in specified group. [7] Wage and salary workers.

Source: U.S. Bureau of Labor Statistics, *Employment and Earnings*, monthly, January 2007 issue; and unpublished data. See Internet site <http://www.bls.gov/cps/>.

Table 605. Unemployed Jobseekers Job Search Activities: 2006

[7,001 represents 7,001,000. For the civilian noninstitutional population 16 years old and over. Annual average of monthly data. Based on the Current Population Survey; see text, Section 1 and Appendix III]

Characteristic	Population (1,000)		Jobseekers job search methods (percent)							Average number of methods used
	Total unemployed	Total job-seekers [1]	Employer directly	Sent out a resume or filled out appli-cations	Placed or answer-ed ads	Friends or relatives	Public employ-ment agency	Private employ-ment agency		
Total, 16 years and over [2] ..	**7,001**	**6,080**	61.3	53.9	14.4	17.1	17.3	6.7		1.82
16 to 19 years old.	1,119	1,062	58.8	58.8	9.7	13.8	7.7	2.7		1.57
20 to 24 years old.	1,234	1,131	62.6	55.3	13.0	15.6	16.1	5.6		1.78
25 to 34 years old.	1,521	1,312	62.0	53.8	15.6	16.9	19.6	7.6		1.88
35 to 44 years old.	1,279	1,067	62.5	51.2	16.3	19.3	22.3	8.0		1.93
45 to 54 years old.	1,094	911	62.0	53.2	16.7	18.8	21.5	8.8		1.95
55 to 64 years old.	595	482	59.1	51.0	16.2	19.9	17.9	9.1		1.89
65 years old and over	159	114	56.8	37.8	13.1	18.2	12.5	5.2		1.58
Male.	3,753	3,181	63.0	51.4	14.4	18.5	17.0	7.0		1.83
16 to 19 years old	622	590	59.9	56.8	9.6	14.1	7.2	2.6		1.56
20 to 24 years old	705	635	63.3	52.7	13.3	17.5	16.2	5.8		1.78
25 to 34 years old	810	670	64.0	50.5	16.3	19.1	20.2	8.3		1.91
35 to 44 years old	642	512	64.5	47.8	16.0	21.1	21.5	8.4		1.94
45 to 54 years old	569	457	64.4	51.1	17.1	20.8	20.8	9.7		1.98
55 to 64 years old	318	255	62.4	49.6	15.9	20.4	18.6	9.7		1.94
65 years old and over . .	88	62	58.8	38.1	12.8	18.0	12.9	5.1		1.57
Female	3,247	2,899	59.4	56.5	14.3	15.5	17.7	6.4		1.81
16 to 19 years old	496	472	57.4	61.2	9.8	13.3	8.3	2.8		1.59
20 to 24 years old	530	496	61.7	58.5	12.6	13.0	16.0	5.4		1.78
25 to 34 years old	711	643	59.8	57.2	14.8	14.6	18.9	7.0		1.84
35 to 44 years old	637	555	60.6	54.4	16.6	17.6	23.0	7.6		1.92
45 to 54 years old	524	454	59.6	55.4	16.3	16.7	22.3	7.9		1.91
55 to 64 years old	277	227	55.4	52.6	16.5	19.4	17.0	8.5		1.83
65 years old and over . .	71	52	54.5	37.5	13.4	18.5	12.2	5.3		1.58
White [3]	5,002	4,238	61.5	54.1	14.9	17.8	16.2	6.9		1.84
Male	2,730	2,253	63.2	51.6	14.9	19.2	16.1	7.4		1.85
Female	2,271	1,985	59.6	56.9	14.9	16.2	16.3	6.3		1.82
Black [3]	1,549	1,434	61.0	53.2	13.0	14.8	21.1	6.5		1.78
Male	774	705	62.8	50.8	12.8	16.4	20.2	6.2		1.77
Female	775	730	59.4	55.6	13.1	13.2	21.9	6.7		1.79
Asian [3]	205	192	60.1	48.2	12.2	18.2	11.7	5.3		1.69
Male	110	103	64.1	47.2	12.4	20.6	12.6	5.4		1.75
Female	95	89	55.5	49.3	12.0	15.3	10.7	5.3		1.62
Hispanic [4]	1,081	922	61.1	46.1	11.1	24.3	16.8	6.3		1.75
Male	601	491	63.4	42.8	10.8	25.8	16.6	7.0		1.75
Female	480	431	58.5	49.9	11.6	22.5	17.1	5.4		1.74

[1] Excludes persons on temporary layoff.   [2] Includes other races, not shown separately.   [3] Data for this race group only. See footnote 3, Table 570.   [4] Persons of Hispanic or Latino origin may be of any race.

Source: U.S. Bureau of Labor Statistics, *Employment and Earnings*, monthly, January 2007 issue. See Internet site <http://www.bls.gov/cps/home.htm>.

Table 606. Unemployed Persons by Sex and Reason: 1980 to 2006

[In thousands (4,267 represents 4,267,000). Civilian noninstitutional population 16 years old and over. Annual averages of monthly figures. Based on Current Population Survey; see text, Section 1 and Appendix III]

Sex and reason	1980	1985	1990 [1]	1995	1999 [1]	2000 [1]	2001	2002	2003 [1]	2004 [1]	2005 [1]	2006 [1]
Male, total	4,267	4,521	3,906	3,983	3,066	2,975	3,690	4,597	4,906	4,456	4,059	3,753
Job losers [2]	2,649	2,749	2,257	2,190	1,563	1,516	2,119	2,820	3,024	2,603	2,188	2,021
Job leavers	438	409	528	407	389	387	422	434	422	437	445	406
Reentrants	776	876	806	1,113	895	854	925	1,068	1,141	1,070	1,067	1,015
New entrants.	405	487	315	273	219	217	223	274	320	346	359	312
Female, total	3,370	3,791	3,140	3,421	2,814	2,717	3,111	3,781	3,868	3,694	3,531	3,247
Job losers [2]	1,297	1,390	1,130	1,286	1,059	1,001	1,356	1,787	1,814	1,595	1,479	1,300
Job leavers	453	468	513	417	394	393	413	432	397	421	427	421
Reentrants	1,152	1,380	1,124	1,412	1,111	1,107	1,105	1,300	1,336	1,338	1,319	1,223
New entrants.	468	552	373	306	250	217	237	262	321	340	306	304

[1] See footnote 2, Table 569.   [2] Beginning 1995, persons who completed temporary jobs are identified separately and are included as job losers.

Source: U.S. Bureau of Labor Statistics, *Employment and Earnings*, monthly, January issues; Bulletin 2307; and unpublished data. See Internet site <http://www.bls.gov/cps/home.htm>.

Labor Force, Employment, and Earnings   397

Table 607. Unemployment Rates by Industry, 2000 to 2006, and by Sex, 2000 and 2006

[In percent. Civilian noninstitutional population 16 years old and over. Annual averages of monthly figures. Rate represents unemployment as a percent of labor force in each specified group. Based on Current Population Survey; see text, Section 1 and Appendix III. See headnote, Table 587, regarding industries]

Industry	2000	2004 [1]	2005 [1]	2006 [1]	Male 2000	Male 2006 [1]	Female 2000	Female 2006 [1]
All unemployed [2]	4.0	5.5	5.1	4.6	3.9	4.6	4.1	4.6
Industry: [3]								
Agriculture and related industries	9.0	9.9	8.3	7.2	8.3	6.6	11.5	8.9
Mining	4.4	3.9	3.1	3.2	4.6	3.1	2.8	4.0
Construction	6.2	8.4	7.4	6.7	6.4	6.8	5.1	5.7
Manufacturing	3.5	5.7	4.9	4.2	3.0	3.7	4.5	5.3
Wholesale trade	3.3	4.6	4.0	3.2	2.8	3.1	4.4	3.6
Retail trade	4.6	6.1	5.7	5.4	4.0	4.9	5.1	5.9
Transportation and utilities	3.4	4.4	4.1	4.0	3.2	3.8	4.2	4.6
Transportation and warehousing	3.8	4.9	4.5	4.3	1.9	4.2	4.6	5.0
Utilities	1.9	1.9	1.9	2.0	2.8	1.8	2.1	2.5
Information	3.2	5.7	5.0	3.7	2.7	3.5	3.7	4.1
Telecommunications	2.3	6.0	5.2	3.6	1.5	3.0	3.3	4.7
Financial activities	2.4	3.6	2.9	2.7	2.1	2.6	2.6	2.8
Finance and insurance	2.2	3.4	2.7	2.6	1.7	2.5	2.5	2.6
Real estate and rental and leasing	3.1	4.1	3.3	3.2	2.9	2.9	3.2	3.5
Professional and business services	4.8	6.8	6.2	5.6	4.4	5.4	5.2	6.0
Professional and technical services	2.5	4.1	3.5	3.0	2.2	2.6	2.9	3.4
Management, administrative, and waste services	8.1	10.6	10.2	9.3	7.6	8.9	8.8	9.9
Education and health services	2.5	3.4	3.4	3.0	2.2	2.8	2.5	3.1
Educational services	2.4	3.7	3.7	3.1	2.1	3.2	2.5	3.1
Health care and social assistance	2.5	3.4	3.3	3.0	2.3	2.6	2.5	3.1
Leisure and hospitality	6.6	8.3	7.8	7.3	6.2	7.0	7.0	7.6
Arts, entertainment, and recreation	5.9	7.2	6.9	7.2	6.1	7.2	5.7	7.2
Accommodation and food services	6.8	8.6	8.0	7.3	6.2	6.9	7.3	7.6
Other services [4]	3.9	5.3	4.8	4.7	3.7	4.6	4.0	4.8
Government workers	2.1	2.7	2.6	2.3	2.1	2.2	2.2	2.4

[1] See footnote 2, Table 569. [2] Includes the self-employed, unpaid family workers, and persons with no previous work experience, not shown separately. [3] Covers unemployed wage and salary workers. [4] Includes private household workers.

Source: U.S. Bureau of Labor Statistics, *Employment and Earnings*, monthly, January issues; and unpublished data. See Internet site <http://www.bls.gov/cps/home.htm>.

Table 608. Unemployment by Occupation, 2000 to 2006, and by Sex, 2006

[5,692 represents 5,692,000. Civilian noninstitutional population 16 years old and over. Annual averages of monthly data. Rate represents unemployment as a percent of the labor force for each specified group. Based on Current Population Survey; see text, Section 1 and Appendix III. See also headnote, Table 587, regarding occupations]

Occupation	Number (1,000) 2000	2005 [1]	2006 [1]	Unemployment rate 2000	2005 [1]	2006 [1]	2006 [1], by sex Male	Female
Total [2]	5,692	7,591	7,001	4.0	5.1	4.6	4.6	4.6
Management, professional, and related occupations	827	1,172	1,065	1.8	2.3	2.1	1.9	2.2
Management, business, and financial operations	320	464	427	1.6	2.2	2.0	1.8	2.2
Management	214	322	279	1.5	2.1	1.8	1.7	2.0
Business and financial operations	106	142	148	2.0	2.4	2.4	2.3	2.5
Professional and related occupations	507	708	638	1.9	2.4	2.1	2.1	2.2
Computer and mathematical	74	96	80	2.2	2.9	2.4	2.5	2.3
Architecture and engineering	51	60	49	1.7	2.1	1.7	1.6	2.6
Life, physical, and social science	18	39	27	1.4	2.7	1.8	1.7	2.0
Community and social services	40	52	50	2.0	2.4	2.3	2.4	2.2
Legal	18	27	22	1.2	1.6	1.3	0.9	1.8
Education, training, and library	136	210	196	1.8	2.5	2.4	2.4	2.4
Arts, design, entertainment, sports, and media	97	135	115	3.5	4.7	4.0	4.3	3.8
Healthcare practitioner and technical	73	90	98	1.2	1.3	1.4	0.7	1.6
Service occupations	1,132	1,587	1,485	5.2	6.4	5.9	6.0	5.8
Healthcare support	101	154	152	4.0	4.7	4.6	5.8	4.5
Protective service	70	121	105	2.7	4.0	3.4	2.9	5.3
Food preparation and serving related	469	615	590	6.6	7.7	7.2	7.5	6.9
Building and grounds cleaning and maintenance	301	429	402	5.8	7.6	7.0	6.9	7.0
Personal care and service	190	268	235	4.4	5.6	4.7	4.9	4.7
Sales and office occupations	1,446	1,820	1,667	3.8	4.8	4.4	3.9	4.7
Sales and related	673	874	812	4.1	5.0	4.7	3.4	5.9
Office and administrative support	773	946	856	3.6	4.6	4.2	4.9	4.0
Natural resources, construction, and maintenance	758	1,069	1,007	5.3	6.5	6.0	5.8	9.1
Farming, fishing, and forestry	133	103	101	10.2	9.6	9.5	8.4	13.2
Construction and extraction	507	751	699	6.2	7.6	6.8	6.7	9.9
Installation, maintenance, and repair	119	214	207	2.4	3.9	3.7	3.7	4.3
Production, transportation, and material moving	1,081	1,245	1,127	5.1	6.5	5.8	5.3	7.5
Production	575	677	544	4.8	6.7	5.5	4.7	7.2
Transportation and material moving	505	568	583	5.6	6.2	6.2	5.9	8.0

[1] See footnote 2, Table 569. [2] Includes persons with no previous work experience and those whose last job was in the Armed Forces.

Source: U.S. Bureau of Labor Statistics, *Employment and Earnings*, monthly, January issues; and unpublished data.

Table 609. Unemployed and Unemployment Rates by Educational Attainment, Sex, Race, and Hispanic Origin: 1992 to 2006

[6,543 represents 6,543,000. Annual averages of monthly figures. Civilian noninstitutional population 25 years old and over. See Table 574 for civilian labor force and participation rate data. Based on Current Population Survey; see text, Section 1 and Appendix III]

Year, sex, and race	Unemployed (1,000)					Unemployment rate [1]				
	Total	Less than high school diploma	High school gradu-ates, no degree	Less than a bach-elor's degree	BA degree or more	Total	Less than high school diploma	High school gradu-ates, no degree	Less than a bach-elor's degree	BA degree or more
Total: [2]										
1992 . . .	6,543	1,533	2,590	1,527	893	6.1	11.5	6.8	5.6	3.2
2000 [3] . . .	3,589	791	1,298	890	610	3.0	6.3	3.4	2.7	1.7
2006 [3] . . .	4,648	866	1,652	1,267	863	3.6	6.8	4.3	3.6	2.0
Male:										
1992 . . .	3,767	942	1,462	829	533	6.4	11.4	7.4	5.9	3.3
2000 [3] . . .	1,829	411	682	427	309	2.8	5.4	3.4	2.6	1.5
2006 [3] . . .	2,427	498	914	575	440	3.5	6.1	4.3	3.3	1.9
Female:										
1992 . . .	2,776	591	1,128	697	361	5.8	11.5	6.3	5.4	3.0
2000 [3] . . .	1,760	380	616	463	301	3.2	7.8	3.5	2.8	1.8
2006 [3] . . .	2,220	368	737	692	423	3.7	7.9	4.3	3.9	2.1
White: [4]										
1992 . . .	4,978	1,145	1,928	1,162	743	5.5	10.7	6.0	5.0	3.0
2000 [3] . . .	2,644	564	924	667	489	2.6	5.6	2.9	2.4	1.6
2006 [3] . . .	3,376	611	1,162	917	686	3.2	5.9	3.7	3.2	2.0
Black: [4]										
1992 . . .	1,269	322	565	301	81	11.0	15.3	12.3	9.8	4.4
2000 [3] . . .	731	179	315	169	68	5.4	10.7	6.4	4.0	2.5
2006 [3] . . .	979	204	408	274	93	6.8	12.8	8.0	6.2	2.8
Asian: [4, 5]										
2000 [3] . . .	146	28	34	35	49	2.7	5.7	3.0	3.2	1.8
2006 [3] . . .	154	17	33	32	72	2.5	3.8	3.1	3.1	2.1
Hispanic: [6]										
1992 . . .	853	434	235	134	50	9.8	12.8	9.1	7.7	5.0
2000 [3] . . .	569	297	150	85	38	4.4	6.2	3.9	3.2	2.2
2006 [3] . . .	716	328	207	125	56	4.2	5.5	4.1	3.6	2.2

[1] Percent unemployed of the civilian labor force. [2] Includes other races, not shown separately. [3] See footnote 2, Table 569. [4] 2006 data are for persons in this race group only. See footnote 3, Table 570. [5] 2000 data include Pacific Islanders. [6] Persons of Hispanic or Latino origin may be of any race.

Source: U.S. Bureau of Labor Statistics, *Employment and Earnings*, monthly, January issues. See Internet site <http://www.bls .gov/cps/home.htm>.

Table 610. Unemployed Persons by Reason of Unemployment: 2006

[7,001 represents 7,001,000. Annual averages of monthly data. Based on Current Population Survey; see text, Section 1 and Appendix III]

Age, sex, and reason	Total unem-ployed (1,000)	Percent distribution by duration				
		Less than 5 weeks	5 to 14 weeks	15 weeks and over		
				Total	15 to 26 weeks	27 weeks or longer
Total 16 years old and over	7,001	37.3	30.3	32.4	14.7	17.6
16 to 19 years old	1,119	46.9	33.2	19.9	10.7	9.2
Total 20 years old and over	5,882	35.5	29.7	34.7	15.5	19.2
Males	3,131	35.3	29.1	35.6	15.3	20.3
Job losers and persons who completed temporary jobs	1,927	37.3	29.6	33.2	15.6	17.6
On temporary layoff	540	53.5	31.9	14.6	10.1	4.5
Not on temporary layoff	1,387	30.9	28.7	40.4	17.7	22.6
Permanent job losers	948	28.4	29.2	42.4	19.1	23.3
Persons who completed temporary jobs	439	36.4	27.6	36.1	14.8	21.2
Job leavers	368	42.4	27.3	30.3	14.7	15.6
Reentrants	757	28.2	28.8	43.0	15.2	27.8
New entrants	78	21.8	29.5	48.7	12.6	36.1
Females	2,751	35.8	30.5	33.7	15.7	18.1
Job losers and persons who completed temporary jobs	1,249	37.2	29.7	33.0	17.1	15.9
On temporary layoff	324	57.3	29.7	13.0	8.1	5.0
Not on temporary layoff	925	30.2	29.7	40.0	20.3	19.7
Permanent job losers	685	27.0	29.0	44.0	22.1	22.0
Persons who completed temporary jobs	240	39.4	32.0	28.6	15.2	13.4
Job leavers	380	41.8	31.3	26.8	14.2	12.7
Reentrants	1,019	31.9	31.3	36.8	14.8	22.0
New entrants	103	34.5	28.4	37.1	11.4	25.7

Source: U.S. Bureau of Labor Statistics, *Employment and Earnings*, monthly, January 2007 issue. See Internet site <http://www.bls .gov/cps/home.htm>.

Table 611. Total Unemployed and Insured Unemployed by State: 1980 to 2005

[7,637 represents 7,637,000. Civilian noninstitutional population 16 years old and over. Annual averages of monthly figures. Total unemployment estimates based on the Current Population Survey; see text, Section 1 and Appendix III. U.S. totals derived by independent population controls; therefore state data may not add to U.S. totals]

State	Total unemployed Number (1,000) 1980	1990 [2]	2000 [2]	2005 [2]	Total unemployed Percent [1] 1980	1990 [2]	2000 [2]	2005 [2]	Insured unemployed [3] Number (1,000) 2000	2005	Insured unemployed Percent [4] 2000	2005
United States	7,637	7,047	5,692	7,591	7.1	5.6	4.0	5.1	[5]2,110.3	[5]2,661.4	[5]1.7	[5]2.1
Alabama	142	121	87	86	8.8	6.9	4.5	4.0	29.0	27.9	1.6	1.5
Alaska..........	18	19	20	23	9.7	7.0	6.7	6.8	12.3	12.4	4.9	4.5
Arizona	82	94	100	134	6.7	5.5	4.0	4.7	20.5	29.2	1.0	1.3
Arkansas	74	76	53	67	7.6	7.0	4.4	4.9	23.9	27.7	2.2	2.5
California	796	874	833	949	6.8	5.8	4.9	5.4	338.5	362.7	2.4	2.5
Colorado	88	91	65	129	5.9	5.0	2.8	5.0	15.0	25.2	0.7	1.2
Connecticut	93	90	39	89	5.9	5.2	2.2	4.9	28.3	39.6	1.7	2.5
Delaware	21	15	14	18	7.7	5.2	3.9	4.2	5.9	8.2	1.5	2.0
District of Columbia ..	23	20	18	19	7.3	6.6	5.7	6.5	5.7	4.5	1.3	1.0
Florida..........	262	405	300	325	5.9	6.0	3.6	3.8	70.8	88.7	1.1	1.2
Georgia	158	171	148	242	6.4	5.5	3.7	5.3	34.5	53.7	0.9	1.4
Hawaii..........	21	13	24	18	4.9	2.9	4.3	2.8	8.4	6.3	1.7	1.1
Idaho...........	30	27	31	28	7.9	5.9	4.9	3.8	12.1	13.1	2.3	2.3
Illinois	452	371	291	369	8.3	6.2	4.3	5.7	103.8	136.3	1.8	2.4
Indiana	253	142	92	174	9.6	5.3	3.2	5.4	31.8	54.1	1.1	1.9
Iowa	81	66	45	76	5.8	4.3	2.6	4.6	19.4	24.4	1.4	1.7
Kansas	54	55	53	75	4.5	4.5	3.7	5.1	15.6	20.0	1.2	1.6
Kentucky	134	107	83	121	8.0	5.9	4.1	6.1	25.4	30.3	1.5	1.8
Louisiana	123	110	101	148	6.7	6.3	5.4	7.1	24.0	65.7	1.3	3.6
Maine	38	33	22	34	7.8	5.2	3.5	4.8	8.9	10.7	1.6	1.8
Maryland	142	118	100	121	6.5	4.7	3.8	4.1	28.9	35.9	0.3	1.5
Massachusetts	164	204	92	162	5.6	6.0	2.6	4.8	60.1	82.1	1.9	2.7
Michigan	524	358	190	344	12.4	7.6	3.5	6.7	81.6	139.4	1.8	3.3
Minnesota	124	114	87	119	5.9	4.9	3.3	4.0	31.4	46.8	1.2	1.8
Mississippi	81	90	74	106	7.5	7.6	5.6	7.9	19.7	28.8	1.8	2.7
Missouri........	167	151	98	162	7.2	5.8	3.4	5.4	41.8	50.5	1.6	2.0
Montana	23	25	22	20	6.1	6.0	5.0	4.0	7.8	7.4	2.2	1.9
Nebraska	30	19	27	37	4.1	2.2	3.0	3.8	7.3	11.9	0.9	1.4
Nevada	28	33	48	49	6.2	4.9	4.0	4.1	19.5	18.5	2.0	1.6
New Hampshire.....	21	35	19	26	4.7	5.7	2.8	3.6	3.1	6.6	0.5	1.1
New Jersey	261	208	157	194	7.2	5.1	3.7	4.4	84.8	113.9	2.3	3.0
New Mexico	43	48	42	49	7.5	6.5	5.0	5.3	9.5	11.8	1.4	1.6
New York	601	469	416	472	7.5	5.3	4.6	5.0	146.2	190.7	1.8	2.3
North Carolina.....	182	145	155	227	6.6	4.2	3.6	5.2	54.3	76.9	1.5	2.1
North Dakota	15	13	10	12	5.0	4.0	3.0	3.4	3.9	3.5	1.3	1.1
Ohio	432	310	234	350	8.4	5.7	4.0	5.9	71.6	100.6	1.3	1.9
Oklahoma	61	86	52	76	4.8	5.7	3.1	4.4	12.2	16.9	0.9	1.2
Oregon	110	81	93	114	8.3	5.6	4.9	6.1	41.2	45.5	2.7	2.9
Pennsylvania	428	317	255	312	7.8	5.4	4.1	5.0	132.4	167.9	2.5	3.1
Rhode Island	33	32	23	29	7.2	6.8	4.1	5.0	12.2	12.4	2.7	2.7
South Carolina	93	84	71	142	6.9	4.8	3.8	6.8	27.1	38.5	1.5	2.2
South Dakota	16	13	11	17	4.9	3.9	2.3	3.9	2.0	2.6	0.6	0.7
Tennessee	151	132	115	162	7.3	5.3	3.9	5.6	42.2	43.7	1.6	1.7
Texas	350	552	452	596	5.2	6.3	4.2	5.3	107.9	127.9	1.2	1.4
Utah	41	36	38	54	6.3	4.3	3.3	4.3	10.5	10.6	1.1	1.0
Vermont.........	16	15	9	12	6.4	5.0	2.9	3.5	4.8	6.2	1.7	2.1
Virginia	133	143	82	136	5.0	4.3	2.2	3.5	22.2	31.3	0.7	0.9
Washington	157	131	151	182	7.9	4.9	5.2	5.5	70.6	58.8	2.7	2.2
West Virginia	75	65	44	40	9.4	8.4	5.5	5.0	14.1	14.0	2.1	2.1
Wisconsin........	172	113	101	144	7.2	4.4	3.6	4.7	53.1	72.7	2.0	2.7
Wyoming	9	13	10	10	4.0	5.5	3.9	3.6	2.9	2.8	1.3	1.2

[1] Total unemployment as percent of civilian labor force.   [2] See footnote 2, Table 569.   [3] Source: U.S. Employment and Training Administration, *Unemployment Insurance, Financial Handbook*, annual updates.   [4] Insured unemployment as percent of average covered employment in the previous year.   [5] Includes 49,800 in Puerto Rico and the Virgin Islands in 2000; and 43,600 in 2005.

Source: Except as noted, U.S. Bureau of Labor Statistics, *Geographic Profile of Employment and Unemployment*, annual. See Internet site <http://www.bls.gov/gps/>.

Table 612. Nonfarm Establishments—Employees, Hours, and Earnings by Industry: 1990 to 2006

[Annual averages of monthly data. (109,487 represents 109,487,000). Based on data from establishment reports. Includes all full- and part-time employees who worked during, or received pay for, any part of the pay period reported. Excludes proprietors, the self-employed, farm workers, unpaid family workers, private household workers, and Armed Forces. Establishment data shown here conform to industry definitions in the 2002 North American Industry Classification System (NAICS) and are adjusted to March 2006 employment benchmarks. Based on the Current Employment Statistics Program; see source and Appendix III]

Item and year	Total nonfarm	Total [1]	Con-struction	Manufac-turing	Whole-sale trade	Retail trade	Trans-portation and ware-housing	Utilities	Infor-mation	Finance and insur-ance	Real estate and rental and leasing	Profes-sional and tech-nical services	Adminis-trative and waste services	Educa-tional services	Health care and social assist-ance	Arts, entertain-ment, and recre-ation	Accom-moda-tions and food services	Govern-ment
EMPLOYEES (1,000)																		
1990	109,487	91,072	5,263	17,695	5,268	13,182	3,476	740	2,688	4,979	1,635	4,557	4,624	1,688	9,296	1,132	8,156	18,415
1995	117,298	97,866	5,274	17,241	5,433	13,897	3,838	666	2,843	5,072	1,755	5,101	6,057	2,010	11,278	1,459	9,042	19,432
2000	131,785	110,996	6,787	17,263	5,933	15,280	4,410	601	3,631	5,680	2,007	6,734	8,136	2,390	12,718	1,788	10,074	20,790
2003	129,999	108,416	6,735	14,510	5,608	14,917	4,185	577	3,188	5,923	2,054	6,630	7,670	2,695	13,893	1,813	10,360	21,583
2004	131,435	109,814	6,976	14,315	5,663	15,058	4,224	564	3,118	5,949	2,082	6,774	7,896	2,763	14,190	1,850	10,643	21,621
2005	133,703	111,899	7,336	14,226	5,764	15,280	4,361	554	3,061	6,023	2,130	7,053	8,142	2,836	14,536	1,892	10,923	21,804
2006	136,174	114,184	7,689	14,197	5,898	15,319	4,466	549	3,055	6,184	2,180	7,372	8,371	2,918	14,920	1,927	11,216	21,990
WEEKLY EARNINGS [2] (dol)																		
1990	(NA)	349.75	513.43	436.16	444.48	235.62	471.72	670.40	479.50	378.21	286.81	504.87	272.70	(NA)	319.80	219.02	147.89	(NA)
1995	(NA)	400.07	571.57	509.26	515.14	272.56	513.37	811.52	564.98	477.39	321.69	583.41	306.54	(NA)	379.66	240.57	165.47	(NA)
2000	(NA)	481.01	685.78	590.65	631.40	333.38	562.31	955.66	700.89	589.64	395.85	745.83	386.33	(NA)	449.27	273.79	207.44	(NA)
2003	(NA)	518.06	726.83	635.99	657.29	367.15	598.41	1,017.27	760.81	670.86	455.16	801.82	427.02	(NA)	516.03	305.85	217.51	(NA)
2004	(NA)	529.09	735.55	658.59	667.09	371.13	614.82	1,048.44	777.05	683.78	487.46	828.71	424.27	(NA)	537.87	313.01	221.68	(NA)
2005	(NA)	544.33	750.22	673.37	685.00	377.58	618.58	1,095.90	805.00	703.57	496.56	862.91	430.69	(NA)	560.43	330.19	226.48	(NA)
2006	(NA)	567.87	781.04	690.83	718.30	383.16	637.14	1,136.08	850.81	738.30		907.82	463.91	(NA)	581.64	332.29	236.65	(NA)
WEEKLY HOURS [2]																		
1990	(NA)	34.3	38.3	40.5	38.4	30.6	37.7	41.5	35.8	36.4	33.1	36.1	32.3	(NA)	31.8	26.1	25.9	(NA)
1995	(NA)	34.3	38.8	41.3	38.6	30.8	38.9	42.3	36.0	36.5	32.7	36.2	32.5	(NA)	31.9	26.3	25.8	(NA)
2000	(NA)	34.3	39.2	41.3	38.8	30.7	37.4	42.0	36.8	37.1	32.6	36.2	33.1	(NA)	32.1	25.6	26.2	(NA)
2003	(NA)	33.7	38.4	40.4	37.9	30.9	36.8	41.1	36.2	36.5	32.8	35.7	32.9	(NA)	32.5	25.5	25.6	(NA)
2004	(NA)	33.7	38.3	40.8	37.8	30.7	37.2	40.9	36.5	36.6	33.5	35.7	32.9	(NA)	32.7	25.7	25.6	(NA)
2005	(NA)	33.8	38.6	40.7	37.7	30.6	37.0	41.1	36.5	36.8	32.9	35.9	32.8	(NA)	32.9	25.1	25.7	(NA)
2006	(NA)	33.9	39.0	41.1	38.0	30.5	36.9	41.4	36.6	36.8			33.4	(NA)	32.8		25.8	(NA)
HOURLY EARNINGS [2] (dol)																		
1990	(NA)	10.20	13.42	10.78	11.58	7.71	12.50	16.14	13.40	10.40	8.66	13.99	8.45	(NA)	10.05	8.41	5.70	(NA)
1995	(NA)	11.65	14.73	12.34	13.34	8.85	13.18	19.19	15.68	13.07	9.85	16.32	9.43	(NA)	11.89	9.14	6.41	(NA)
2000	(NA)	14.02	17.48	14.32	16.28	10.86	15.05	22.75	19.07	15.90	12.14	20.61	11.66	(NA)	13.98	10.68	7.92	(NA)
2003	(NA)	15.37	18.95	15.74	17.36	11.90	16.25	24.77	21.01	18.37	13.32	22.54	13.00	(NA)	15.88	11.99	8.50	(NA)
2004	(NA)	15.69	19.23	16.15	17.65	12.08	16.52	25.61	21.40	18.70	13.88	23.24	12.90	(NA)	16.45	12.17	8.65	(NA)
2005	(NA)	16.13	19.46	16.56	18.16	12.36	16.70	26.68	22.06	19.09	14.55	24.15	13.13	(NA)	17.05	12.85	8.80	(NA)
2006	(NA)	16.76	20.02	16.80	18.91	12.58	17.28	27.42	23.23	20.05	15.07	25.26	13.91	(NA)	17.76	13.22	9.18	(NA)

NA Not available. [1] Includes other industries, not shown separately. [2] Average hours and earnings of production workers manufacturing, and construction; average hours and earnings of nonsupervisory workers for the service-providing industries.

Source: U.S. Bureau of Labor Statistics, the Current Employment Statistics program Internet site <http://www.bls.gov/ces/home.htm>.

Table 613. Employees in Nonfarm Establishments—States: 2006

[In thousands (136,174 represents 136,174,000). For coverage, see headnote, Table 612. National totals differ from the sum of the state figures because of differing benchmarks among states and differing industrial and geographic stratification. Based on North American Industry Classification System, 2002; see text, this section]

State	Total [1]	Construction	Manufacturing	Trade, transportation, and utilities	Information	Financial activities [2]	Professional and business services [3]	Education and health services [4]	Leisure and hospitality [5]	Other services [6]	Government
U.S. . . .	136,174	7,689	14,197	26,231	3,055	8,363	17,552	17,838	13,143	5,432	21,990
AL.	1,982	110	303	387	30	99	215	204	170	81	371
AK.	315	18	13	64	7	15	24	37	31	11	82
AZ.	2,644	246	187	511	45	183	395	291	267	101	410
AR.	1,200	57	199	249	20	53	115	151	97	44	208
CA.	15,073	939	1,505	2,874	473	941	2,225	1,618	1,519	507	2,447
CO.	2,279	168	149	419	76	161	332	231	265	91	368
CT.	1,680	67	194	311	38	144	204	280	132	64	246
DE.	436	[7]29	34	83	7	44	62	56	41	20	61
DC.	688	[7]13	2	28	22	30	153	94	54	60	233
FL.	8,007	637	403	1,597	167	546	1,341	971	905	337	1,098
GA.	4,086	[7]219	449	868	116	231	550	438	383	159	663
HI	617	[7]36	15	121	11	30	78	71	108	26	121
ID	640	52	66	128	11	32	82	70	60	19	116
IL.	5,935	276	683	1,198	117	406	853	763	525	260	846
IN	2,973	150	566	586	40	140	281	386	281	111	426
IA	1,503	75	231	309	33	101	117	199	133	57	247
KS	1,354	65	183	261	39	72	138	166	115	52	254
KY	1,845	83	261	379	30	91	178	238	168	76	318
LA	1,857	132	152	374	27	96	194	234	185	66	348
ME	615	31	60	126	11	34	52	114	60	20	105
MD.	2,588	[7]191	136	474	51	160	395	362	230	117	471
MA.	3,243	141	299	570	87	224	472	606	295	119	429
MI	4,341	180	648	795	67	216	588	584	407	178	670
MN.	2,760	130	347	531	58	181	323	406	246	118	414
MS.	1,142	58	176	227	14	46	94	123	119	37	240
MO	2,774	148	307	545	63	165	331	377	279	120	433
MT.	434	30	20	89	8	22	38	57	56	17	87
NE.	947	[7]48	102	201	20	66	102	131	81	36	162
NV.	1,282	144	51	226	15	66	158	87	337	36	150
NH.	639	30	77	142	13	40	61	100	64	21	91
NJ	4,075	174	325	876	99	281	602	569	339	161	649
NM.	833	59	38	142	16	35	103	108	87	29	198
NY.	8,612	337	568	1,506	270	726	1,109	1,570	678	357	1,487
NC.	4,021	244	553	755	73	206	473	487	371	176	675
ND.	353	19	26	76	8	19	29	50	32	15	76
OH.	5,441	231	797	1,046	89	307	657	778	501	223	801
OK.	1,552	70	149	284	30	84	175	188	137	75	318
OR.	1,702	100	207	336	35	106	193	205	165	59	287
PA	5,753	262	672	1,126	108	336	677	1,055	490	260	746
RI	493	23	53	80	11	35	57	97	50	23	65
SC.	1,903	124	252	368	27	102	217	193	207	76	330
SD.	399	22	42	80	7	30	26	59	43	16	75
TN.	2,783	131	400	608	50	144	320	339	270	101	415
TX.	10,053	604	926	2,044	223	626	1,226	1,218	943	347	1,712
UT.	1,203	95	123	235	33	71	155	134	108	35	204
VT	307	17	36	60	6	13	22	55	33	10	54
VA	3,726	249	289	663	92	196	627	405	338	182	674
WA	2,859	195	286	542	99	156	330	337	272	104	529
WV . . .	756	39	61	142	12	30	60	113	71	56	145
WI	2,861	127	505	544	49	161	269	392	258	136	416
WY	277	24	10	53	4	11	17	23	33	11	66

[1] Includes natural resources and mining, not shown separately. [2] Finance and insurance; real estate and rental and leasing. [3] Professional, scientific, and technical services; management of companies and enterprises; administrative and support and waste management and remediation services. [4] Education services; health care and social assistance. [5] Arts, entertainment, and recreation; accommodations and food services. [6] Includes repair and maintenance; personal and laundry services; and membership associations and organizations. [7] Natural resources and mining included with construction.

Source: U.S. Bureau of Labor Statistics, the Current Employment Statistics program Internet site <http://www.bls.gov/ces/home.htm> Compiled from data supplied by cooperating state agencies.

402   Labor Force, Employment and Earnings

Table 614. Nonfarm Industries—Employees and Earnings: 1990 to 2006

[Annual averages of monthly figures (109,487 represents 109,487,000). Covers all full- and part-time employees who worked during, or received pay for, any part of the pay period including the 12th of the month. See also headnote, Table 612]

Industry	2002 NAICS [1] code	All employees (1,000)					Average hourly earnings [2] (dol.)		
		1990	2000	2004	2005	2006	2000	2005	2006
Total nonfarm..............	(X)	109,487	131,785	131,435	133,703	136,174	(NA)	(NA)	(NA)
Goods-producing [3]..........	(X)	23,723	24,649	21,882	22,190	22,570	15.27	17.60	18.02
Service-providing [4].........	(X)	85,764	107,136	109,553	111,513	113,605	(NA)	(NA)	(NA)
Total private.................	(X)	91,072	110,996	109,814	111,899	114,184	14.02	16.13	16.76
Natural resources and mining..........	(X)	765	599	591	628	684	16.55	18.72	19.90
Mining........................	21	680	520	523	562	619	16.94	19.04	20.29
Oil and gas extraction...............	211	190	125	123	126	136	19.43	19.34	21.40
Mining, except oil and gas..........	212	302	225	205	213	221	18.07	20.18	20.59
Support activities for mining..........	213	188	171	195	224	262	14.55	17.89	19.65
Construction......................	23	5,263	6,787	6,976	7,336	7,689	17.48	19.46	20.02
Construction of buildings...........	236	1,413	1,633	1,630	1,712	1,806	16.74	19.05	19.73
Residential building..............	2361	673	823	896	960	1,018	15.18	17.72	18.39
Nonresidential building.............	2362	741	809	734	752	789	18.18	20.55	21.23
Heavy and civil engineering construction...	237	813	937	907	951	983	16.80	19.60	20.32
Highway, street, and bridge construction..	2373	289	340	347	351	349	18.17	20.12	20.67
Specialty trade contractors [5]........	238	3,037	4,217	4,439	4,673	4,900	17.91	19.55	20.05
Building foundation and exterior contractors.................	2381	703	919	1,010	1,083	1,132	16.93	18.44	18.95
Building equipment contractors........	2382	1,282	1,897	1,861	1,918	2,006	19.52	21.01	21.62
Building finishing contractors........	2383	665	857	932	992	1,036	16.44	18.82	19.18
Manufacturing......................	31–33	17,695	17,263	14,315	14,226	14,197	14.32	16.56	16.80
Durable goods..................	(X)	10,736	10,876	8,924	8,955	9,001	14.93	17.33	17.67
Wood products..................	321	541	613	550	559	560	11.63	13.16	13.40
Nonmetallic mineral products...........	327	528	554	506	505	508	14.53	16.61	16.59
Cement and concrete products.......	3273	195	234	235	240	248	14.64	16.68	16.80
Primary metals..................	331	689	622	467	466	462	16.64	18.94	19.35
Foundries...................	3315	214	217	165	164	162	14.72	17.50	17.90
Fabricated metal products [5]...........	332	1,610	1,753	1,497	1,522	1,554	13.77	15.80	16.17
Architectural and structural metals.....	3323	357	428	389	398	415	13.43	15.10	15.43
Machine shops and threaded products..	3327	309	365	327	345	352	14.53	16.43	16.98
Machinery [5].....................	333	1,408	1,455	1,143	1,163	1,191	15.22	17.03	17.20
Agricultural, construction, and mining machinery...................	3331	229	222	195	208	222	14.21	15.91	15.83
HVAC and commercial refrigeration equip.	3334	165	194	153	153	160	13.10	14.60	13.83
Metalworking machinery............	3335	267	274	202	202	203	16.66	17.86	18.63
Computer and electronic products [5].....	334	1,903	1,820	1,323	1,316	1,316	14.73	18.39	18.96
Computer and peripheral equipment....	3341	367	302	210	205	199	18.39	22.75	23.00
Communications equipment.........	3342	232	248	148	147	144	14.39	18.05	18.99
Semiconductors and electronic components..................	3344	574	676	454	452	463	13.46	17.03	17.30
Electronic instruments.............	3345	626	479	431	436	438	15.83	17.71	18.89
Electrical equipment and appliances......	335	633	591	445	434	436	13.23	15.24	15.53
Electrical equipment............	3353	244	210	154	152	156	13.28	15.31	15.88
Transportation equipment [5]...........	336	2,133	2,056	1,766	1,771	1,765	18.89	22.10	22.41
Motor vehicles.................	3361	271	291	256	248	236	24.45	29.01	29.05
Motor vehicle parts.............	3363	653	840	692	678	654	17.91	21.10	21.32
Aerospace products and parts........	3364	841	517	442	455	472	20.52	24.82	26.30
Furniture and related products...........	337	601	680	573	565	556	11.72	13.45	13.79
Household and institutional furniture....	3371	398	440	385	380	374	11.39	13.15	13.65
Miscellaneous manufacturing..........	339	690	733	656	652	652	11.93	14.08	14.36
Medical equipment and supplies.......	3391	288	310	301	305	309	12.70	14.71	14.99
Nondurable goods...............	(X)	6,959	6,388	5,391	5,272	5,197	13.31	15.27	15.32
Food manufacturing [5].............	311	1,507	1,553	1,494	1,478	1,484	11.77	13.04	13.13
Fruit and vegetable preserving and specialty food manufacturing........	3114	218	197	181	174	177	11.90	12.81	13.30
Animal slaughtering and processing....	3116	427	507	505	504	509	10.27	11.47	11.49
Bakeries and tortilla manufacturing.....	3118	292	306	285	280	281	11.45	12.57	12.63
Beverages and tobacco products........	312	218	207	195	192	195	17.40	18.76	18.19
Beverages...................	3121	173	175	166	167	171	17.19	18.28	17.44
Textile mills	313	492	378	237	218	196	11.23	12.38	12.55
Textile product mills...............	314	209	216	176	170	161	10.43	11.67	11.94
Apparel.......................	315	929	497	286	257	238	8.60	10.24	10.61
Cut and sew apparel	3152	776	394	221	200	186	8.40	10.05	10.29
Leather and allied products...........	316	133	69	42	40	37	10.35	11.50	11.44
Paper and paper products............	322	647	605	496	484	469	15.91	17.99	18.01
Pulp, paper, and paperboard mills......	3221	238	191	146	142	136	20.62	22.99	22.75
Converted paper products..........	3222	409	413	350	343	333	13.58	15.71	15.83
Printing and related support activities.....	323	809	807	663	646	636	14.09	15.74	15.80
Petroleum and coal products..........	324	153	123	112	112	114	22.80	24.47	24.08
Chemicals [5].................	325	1,036	980	887	872	869	17.09	19.67	19.60
Basic chemicals..............	3251	249	188	156	150	148	21.06	23.80	23.20
Pharmaceuticals and medicines	3254	207	274	290	288	292	17.27	21.31	21.34
Plastics and rubber products..........	326	826	952	806	803	797	12.69	14.80	14.96
Plastics products	3261	619	738	633	635	638	12.04	14.01	14.26
Rubber products	3262	207	214	172	168	159	14.82	17.58	17.70

See footnotes at end of table.

U.S. Census Bureau, Statistical Abstract of the United States: 2008

Table 614. Nonfarm Industries—Employees and Earnings: 1990 to 2006—Con.

[Annual averages of monthly figures (109,487 represents 109,487,000). Covers all full- and part-time employees who worked during, or received pay for, any part of the pay period including the 12th of the month. See also headnote, Table 612]

Industry	2002 NAICS [1] code	All employees (1,000)					Average hourly earnings [2] (dol.)		
		1990	2000	2004	2005	2006	2000	2005	2006
Trade, transportation, and utilities	(X)	22,666	26,225	25,533	25,959	26,231	13.31	14.92	15.40
Wholesale trade	42	5,268	5,933	5,663	5,764	5,898	16.28	18.16	18.91
Durable goods [5]	423	2,834	3,251	2,951	2,999	3,077	16.71	18.88	19.41
Motor vehicles and parts	4231	309	356	341	344	349	14.27	16.18	16.58
Lumber and construction supplies	4233	181	227	240	254	265	13.61	16.78	17.36
Commercial equipment	4234	597	722	640	639	654	20.29	23.67	24.14
Electric goods	4236	357	425	341	342	344	19.43	21.78	22.58
Hardware and plumbing	4237	216	247	236	245	255	15.07	16.47	17.12
Machinery and supplies	4238	690	725	650	659	676	16.47	18.71	19.05
Nondurable goods [5]	424	1,900	2,065	2,010	2,022	2,040	14.33	16.15	16.89
Paper and paper products	4241	162	177	151	152	153	15.65	17.23	17.50
Druggists' goods	4242	136	192	218	213	211	18.98	19.20	20.93
Grocery and related products	4244	623	689	691	699	709	13.57	15.38	15.96
Electronic markets and agents and brokers	425	535	618	702	743	781	20.79	20.71	22.32
Retail trade	44,45	13,182	15,280	15,058	15,280	15,319	10.86	12.36	12.58
Motor vehicle and parts dealers [5]	441	1,494	1,847	1,902	1,919	1,908	14.94	16.33	16.54
Automobile dealers	4411	983	1,217	1,257	1,261	1,247	16.95	17.85	17.93
Auto parts, accessories, and tire stores	4413	418	499	487	491	492	11.04	12.74	13.08
Furniture and home furnishings stores . . .	442	432	544	563	576	589	12.33	14.23	14.61
Furniture stores	4421	244	289	292	298	300	13.37	14.87	14.82
Home furnishings stores	4422	188	254	272	278	289	11.06	13.46	14.38
Electronics and appliance stores	443	382	564	516	536	538	13.67	17.73	18.26
Building material and garden supply stores	444	891	1,142	1,227	1,276	1,323	11.25	13.14	13.53
Building material and supplies dealers .	4441	753	982	1,083	1,134	1,176	11.30	13.24	13.64
Food and beverage stores	445	2,779	2,993	2,822	2,818	2,828	9.76	10.85	11.06
Grocery stores	4451	2,406	2,582	2,444	2,446	2,463	9.71	10.80	11.00
Specialty food stores	4452	232	270	242	236	229	9.97	11.04	11.37
Beer, wine, and liquor stores	4453	141	141	136	136	137	10.40	11.48	11.72
Health and personal care stores	446	792	928	941	954	956	11.68	14.03	14.31
Gasoline stations	447	910	936	876	871	861	8.05	8.92	9.00
Clothing & clothing accessories stores . . .	448	1,313	1,322	1,364	1,415	1,439	9.96	11.07	11.31
Clothing stores	4481	930	954	1,014	1,066	1,090	9.88	10.63	10.61
Shoe stores	4482	216	193	182	180	182	8.96	10.05	10.58
Jewelry, luggage, and leather goods stores	4483	167	175	169	169	167	11.48	14.10	15.35
Sporting goods, hobby, book, and music stores	451	532	686	641	647	647	9.33	10.35	10.69
Sporting goods and musical instrument stores	4511	352	437	432	447	457	9.55	10.68	10.97
Book, periodical, and music stores	4512	180	249	209	200	190	8.91	9.59	10.07
General merchandise stores	452	2,500	2,820	2,863	2,934	2,913	9.22	10.53	10.61
Department stores	4521	1,494	1,755	1,605	1,595	1,551	9.59	10.84	10.76
Miscellaneous store retailers [5]	453	738	1,007	914	900	885	10.20	11.22	11.22
Florists	4531	121	130	107	101	95	8.95	9.88	9.75
Office supplies, stationery, and gift stores	4532	358	471	402	391	379	10.46	11.65	11.71
Nonstore retailers	454	419	492	429	435	434	13.22	14.56	15.02
Electronic shopping and mail-order houses	4541	157	257	228	240	243	13.38	14.52	15.09
Transportation and warehousing	48,49	3,476	4,410	4,249	4,361	4,466	15.05	16.70	17.28
Air transportation	481	529	614	515	501	487	(NA)	(NA)	(NA)
Scheduled air transportation	4811	503	570	472	456	441	(NA)	(NA)	(NA)
Rail transportation	482	272	232	226	228	225	(NA)	(NA)	(NA)
Water transportation	483	57	56	56	61	64	(NA)	(NA)	(NA)
Truck transportation	484	1,122	1,406	1,352	1,398	1,437	15.86	16.74	17.24
General freight trucking	4841	807	1,013	950	981	1,004	16.37	17.20	17.54
Specialized freight trucking	4842	315	393	402	417	433	14.51	15.60	16.12
Transit and ground passenger transportation	485	274	372	385	389	394	11.88	13.00	13.23
Pipeline transportation	486	60	46	38	38	39	19.86	24.33	24.88
Scenic and sightseeing transportation . . .	487	16	28	27	29	27	14.57	13.75	15.57
Support activities for transportation	488	364	537	535	552	571	14.57	17.66	18.24
Freight transportation arrangement . . .	4885	111	178	171	177	180	13.46	16.94	17.23
Couriers and messengers	492	375	605	557	571	585	13.51	15.33	15.24
Couriers	4921	340	546	507	522	534	13.92	15.76	15.62
Warehousing and storage	493	407	514	558	595	636	14.46	15.06	15.04
Utilities	22	740	601	564	554	549	22.75	26.68	27.42
Power generation and supply	2211	550	434	409	401	397	23.13	27.63	28.36
Natural gas distribution	2212	155	121	109	107	106	23.41	26.86	27.66
Water, sewage and other systems	2213	35	46	46	45	46	16.93	17.70	18.39

See footnotes at end of table.

U.S. Census Bureau, Statistical Abstract of the United States: 2008

Table 614. Nonfarm Industries—Employees and Earnings: 1990 to 2006—Con.

[Annual averages of monthly figures (109,487 represents 109,487,000). Covers all full- and part-time employees who worked during, or received pay for, any part of the pay period including the 12th of the month. See also headnote, Table 612]

Industry	2002 NAICS[1] code	All employees (1,000)					Average hourly earnings[2] (dol.)		
		1990	2000	2004	2005	2006	2000	2005	2006
Information.	51	2,688	3,631	3,118	3,061	3,055	19.07	22.06	23.23
Publishing industries, except Internet	511	871	1,035	909	904	904	20.18	24.20	24.83
Newspaper, book, and directory publishers	5111	773	774	673	666	660	15.06	18.57	19.16
Software publishers	5112	98	261	236	238	243	28.48	38.11	38.42
Motion picture and sound recording industries	512	255	383	385	378	378	21.25	18.75	20.09
Motion picture and video industries	5121	232	352	363	357	357	21.33	18.88	20.33
Broadcasting, except Internet	515	284	344	325	328	331	16.74	21.22	23.07
Radio and television broadcasting.	5151	232	253	240	239	241	17.13	22.15	23.32
Cable and other subscription programming.	5152	52	91	86	89	90	(NA)	(NA)	(NA)
Internet publishing and broadcasting.	516	17	51	30	32	35	(NA)	(NA)	(NA)
Telecommunications[5]	517	980	1,263	1,035	992	973	17.81	22.09	23.52
Wired telecommunications carriers	5171	673	719	543	508	478	18.52	23.77	24.63
Wireless telecommunications carriers. . . .	5172	36	186	190	191	200	14.41	20.40	25.01
Telecommunications resellers	5173	180	214	147	135	129	19.99	22.28	22.64
Cable and other program distribution . . .	5175	70	123	130	134	144	14.67	17.23	17.80
ISPs, search portals, and data processing .	518	252	510	384	378	383	20.57	20.84	21.68
ISPs and Web search portals.	5181	41	194	117	115	122	25.60	22.79	24.50
Data processing and related services . .	5182	211	316	267	263	262	16.97	19.97	20.42
Other information services.	519	30	46	51	51	51	10.68	16.32	17.12
Financial activities	(X)	6,614	7,687	8,031	8,153	8,363	14.98	17.94	18.80
Finance and insurance[5].	52	4,979	5,680	5,949	6,023	6,184	15.90	19.09	20.05
Credit intermediation and related activities.	522	2,425	2,548	2,817	2,869	2,937	13.14	15.85	16.63
Depository credit intermediation.	5221	1,909	1,681	1,752	1,769	1,803	11.97	14.13	14.97
Commercial banking	52211	1,362	1,251	1,281	1,296	1,319	11.83	13.79	14.59
Nondepository credit intermediation . .	5222	398	644	757	770	784	15.30	19.24	19.76
Activities related to credit intermediation.	5223	119	222	309	330	350	15.39	16.48	17.52
Securities, commodity contracts, investments	523	458	805	766	786	816	20.20	26.59	28.44
Securities and commodity contracts, brokerage and exchanges	5232	338	566	493	498.9	509.7	20.07	27.68	29.15
Other financial investment activities . .	5239	120	239	274	287	307	20.48	24.69	27.25
Insurance carriers and related activities . .	524	2,016	2,221	2,259	2,259	2,316	17.37	20.66	21.40
Insurance carriers.	5241	1,338	1,433	1,399	1,386	1,428	17.92	21.67	22.39
Insurance agencies, brokerages, and related services	5242	678	788	860	874	888	16.28	18.88	19.64
Funds, trusts, and other financial vehicles	525	56	85	85	87.7	93.1	17.66	21.12	21.76
Real estate and rental and leasing[5] . .	53	1,635	2,007	2,082	2,130	2,180	12.14	14.55	15.07
Real estate	531	1,107	1,312	1,415	1,457	1,503	12.24	14.67	15.03
Lessors of real estate	5311	564	607	600	600	599	11.16	13.75	14.51
Offices of real estate agents and brokers	5312	217	281	331	356	381	12.57	14.90	15.06
Activities related to real estate	5313	327	424	484	502	523	13.60	15.64	15.61
Rental and leasing services[5]	532	514	667	641	646	647	11.69	14.05	14.77
Automotive equipment rental and leasing	5321	163	208	197	199	200	10.70	13.64	14.35
Consumer goods rental	5322	220	292	279	275	267	9.53	12.39	12.40
Professional and business services	(X)	10,848	16,666	16,395	16,954	17,552	15.52	18.08	19.12
Professional and technical services[5]	54	4,557	6,734	6,774	7,053	7,372	20.61	24.15	25.26
Legal services.	5411	944	1,066	1,163	1,168	1,173	21.38	23.96	25.19
Accounting and bookkeeping services . .	5412	664	866	806	849	889	14.42	17.45	17.98
Architectural and engineering services . .	5413	942	1,238	1,258	1,311	1,386	20.49	23.96	24.84
Computer systems design and related services	5415	410	1,254	1,149	1,195	1,278	27.13	31.64	33.02
Management and technical consulting services	5416	324	705	790	853	921	20.86	24.00	25.07
Scientific research and development services	5417	494	515	550	577	593	21.39	28.33	29.52
Advertising and related services	5418	382	497	429	446	458	16.99	19.49	20.88
Other professional and technical services.	5419	317	462	507	524	537	13.55	15.53	16.24
Management of companies and enterprises	55	1,667	1,796	1,724	1,759	1,809	15.28	18.08	19.71
Administrative and waste services	56	4,624	8,136	7,896	8,142	8,371	11.66	13.13	13.91
Administrative and support services[5] . . .	561	4,395	7,823	7,567	7,804	8,024	11.49	12.89	13.68
Office administrative services	5611	211	264	323	345	363	14.68	17.82	19.37
Employment services	5613	1,494	3,817	3,429	3,578	3,657	11.83	12.96	13.76
Temporary help services.	56132	1,156	2,636	2,387	2,549	2,631	11.79	12.00	12.73
Business support services	5614	505	787	758	766	791	11.08	13.14	13.52
Travel arrangement and reservation services	5615	250	299	226	224	227	12.72	14.55	15.31
Investigation and security services. . . .	5616	507	689	724	737	761	9.78	11.64	12.59
Services to buildings and dwellings . . .	5617	1,175	1.571	1,694	1,738	1,797	10.02	11.44	11.71
Waste management and remediation services	562	229	313	329	338	347	15.29	17.69	18.30

See footnotes at end of table.

Table 614. **Nonfarm Industries—Employees and Earnings: 1990 to 2006**—Con.

[Annual averages of monthly figures (109,487 represents 109,487,000). Covers all full- and part-time employees who worked during, or received pay for, any part of the pay period including the 12th of the month. See also headnote, Table 612]

Industry	2002 NAICS [1] code	All employees (1,000)					Average hourly earnings [2] (dol.)		
		1990	2000	2004	2005	2006	2000	2005	2006
Education and health services	(X)	10,984	15,109	16,953	17,372	17,838	13.95	16.71	17.38
Educational services	61	1,688	2,390	2,763	2,836	2,918	(NA)	(NA)	(NA)
Elementary and secondary schools	6111	461	716	824	837	847	(NA)	(NA)	(NA)
Junior colleges	6112	44	79	89	100	96	(NA)	(NA)	(NA)
Colleges and universities	6113	939	1,196	1,374	1,393	1,441	(NA)	(NA)	(NA)
Business, computer, and management training	6114	60	86	79	77	75	(NA)	(NA)	(NA)
Technical and trade schools	6115	72	91	99	102	104	(NA)	(NA)	(NA)
Other schools and instruction	6116	96	184	231	250	271	(NA)	(NA)	(NA)
Educational support services	6117	17	39	67	78	85	(NA)	(NA)	(NA)
Health care and social assistance	62	9,296	12,718	14,190	14,536	14,920	13.98	17.05	17.76
Ambulatory health care services [5]	621	2,842	4,320	4,952	5,114	5,283	14.99	17.86	18.63
Offices of physicians	6211	1,278	1,840	2,048	2,094	2,154	15.65	18.95	19.98
Offices of dentists	6212	513	688	760	774	784	15.96	19.40	20.51
Offices of other health practitioners	6213	276	438	527	549	571	14.24	16.70	17.27
Outpatient care centers	6214	261	386	451	473	489	15.29	18.96	19.33
Medical and diagnostic laboratories	6215	129	162	190	198	202	15.74	18.67	19.48
Home health care services	6216	288	633	777	821	867	12.86	14.42	14.78
Hospitals [5]	622	3,513	3,954	4,285	4,345	4,427	16.71	21.30	22.19
General medical and surgical hospitals	6221	3,305	3,745	4,042	4,096	4,167	16.75	21.40	22.30
Psychiatric and substance abuse hospitals	6222	113	86	92	93	98	14.97	17.79	18.64
Nursing and residential care facilities [5]	623	1,856	2,583	2,818	2,855	2,901	10.67	12.37	12.84
Nursing care facilities	6231	1,170	1,514	1,577	1,577	1,584	11.08	13.08	13.51
Residential mental health facilities	6232	269	437	490	497	512	9.96	11.30	11.85
Community care facilities for the elderly	6233	330	478	586	615	639	9.83	11.33	11.96
Social assistance	624	1,085	1,860	2,135	2,222	2,309	9.78	11.35	11.76
Individual and family services	6241	389	678	862	921	974	10.57	12.44	12.79
Emergency and other relief services	6242	67	117	131	129	129	10.95	13.48	14.22
Vocational rehabilitation services	6243	242	370	378	383	399	9.57	10.67	11.05
Child day care services	6244	388	696	765	790	807	8.88	10.14	10.53
Leisure and hospitality	(X)	9,288	11,862	12,493	12,816	13,143	8.32	9.38	9.75
Arts, entertainment, and recreation	71	1,132	1,788	1,850	1,892	1,927	10.68	12.85	13.22
Performing arts and spectator sports	711	273	382	368	376	399	13.11	18.67	18.53
Museums, historical sites, zoos, and parks	712	68	110	118	121	124	12.21	13.67	14.05
Amusements, gambling, and recreation	713	791	1,296	1,364	1,395	1,404	9.86	11.08	11.53
Accommodations and food services	72	8,156	10,074	10,643	10,923	11,216	7.92	8.80	9.18
Accommodations	721	1,616	1,884	1,790	1,819	1,833	9.48	10.75	11.24
Traveler and other longer-term accommodations	7211	1,582	1,837	1,737	1,765	1,780	9.49	10.78	11.28
RV parks and recreational camps	7212	34	47	52	53	54	9.03	9.78	9.76
Food services and drinking places	722	6,540	8,189	8,854	9,104	9,383	7.49	8.34	8.69
Full-service restaurants	7221	3,070	3,845	4,212	4,316	4,447	7.78	8.84	9.23
Limited-service eating places	7222	2,765	3,462	3,748	3,889	4,019	6.87	7.49	7.77
Special food services	7223	392	491	523	538	556	9.45	10.48	10.89
Drinking places, alcoholic beverages	7224	312	391	371	361	362	7.24	7.89	8.39
Other services	81	4,261	5,168	5,409	5,395	5,432	12.73	14.34	14.77
Repair and maintenance	811	1,009	1,242	1,229	1,236	1,249	13.28	14.82	15.07
Automotive repair and maintenance	8111	659	888	891	886	887	12.45	14.11	14.3
Personal and laundry services	812	1,120	1,243	1,273	1,277	1,284	10.18	11.81	12.02
Personal care services	8121	430	490	563	577	585	10.18	12.44	12.88
Death care services	8122	123	136	137	137	137	13.04	15.34	15.45
Dry-cleaning and laundry services	8123	371	388	352	347	344	9.17	10.18	10.22
Dry-cleaning and laundry services, except coin-operated	81232	215	211	185	180	178	8.14	9.14	9.18
Other personal services	8129	196	229	221	216	218	10.52	11.29	11.33
Pet care services, except veterinary	81291	23	41	44	49	(NA)	(NA)	(NA)	(NA)
Membership associations & organizations [5]	813	2,132	2,683	2,908	2,882	2,899	13.66	15.20	15.81
Grantmaking and giving services	8132	113	116	128	137	142	14.65	18.80	19.94
Social advocacy organizations	8133	126	143	175	174	178	12.08	13.89	14.52
Civic and social organizations	8134	377	404	409	409	413	9.85	11.16	11.38
Professional and similar organizations	8139	379	473	506	492	500	15.98	18.60	19.65
Government	92	18,415	20,790	21,621	21,804	21,990	(NA)	(NA)	(NA)
Federal	(X)	3,196	2,865	2,730	2,732	2,728	(NA)	(NA)	(NA)
State government	(X)	4,305	4,786	4,982	5,032	5,080	(NA)	(NA)	(NA)
Local government	(X)	10,914	13,139	13,909	14,041	14,182	(NA)	(NA)	(NA)

NA Not available.   X Not applicable.   [1] Based on the North American Industry Classification System, 2002. See text, this section.   [2] Production workers in the goods-producing industries and nonsupervisory workers in service-producing industries. See footnotes 3 and 4.   [3] Natural resources and mining, construction, and manufacturing.   [4] Trade, transportation and utilities, information, financial activities, professional and business services, education and health services, leisure and hospitality, other services, and government.   [5] Includes other industries not shown separately.

Source: U.S. Bureau of Labor Statistics, the Current Employment Statistics program; Internet site <http://www.bls.gov/ces /home.htm>.

Table 615. Private Sector Job Gains and Losses: 1998 to 2006

[In thousands (747 represents 747,000). For the three months ending in month shown. Data are for establishments and are seasonally adjusted. Based on the Quarterly Census of Employment and Wages; for details see source. Minus sign (–) indicates loss]

Year and month ending	Net change [1]	Gross job gains			Gross job losses		
		Total	Expanding establish-ments	Opening establish-ments	Total	Contracting establish-ments	Closing establish-ments
1998:							
March	747	8,788	6,633	2,155	8,041	6,107	1,934
June	666	8,722	6,569	2,153	8,056	6,218	1,838
September	659	8,539	6,574	1,965	7,880	6,161	1,719
December	759	8,576	6,778	1,798	7,817	6,060	1,757
1999:							
March	380	8,744	6,733	2,011	8,364	6,466	1,898
June	569	8,800	6,788	2,012	8,231	6,419	1,812
September	548	8,817	6,871	1,946	8,269	6,397	1,872
December	1,105	9,144	7,112	2,032	8,039	6,264	1,775
2000:							
March	818	8,906	6,988	1,918	8,088	6,361	1,727
June	541	8,764	6,975	1,789	8,223	6,509	1,714
September	146	8,724	6,834	1,890	8,578	6,719	1,859
December	336	8,690	6,862	1,828	8,354	6,582	1,772
2001:							
March	–101	8,555	6,768	1,787	8,656	6,756	1,900
June	–771	8,254	6,439	1,815	9,025	7,149	1,876
September	–1,380	7,749	5,990	1,759	9,129	7,174	1,955
December	–871	7,893	6,055	1,838	8,764	6,995	1,769
2002:							
March	–1	8,128	6,324	1,804	8,129	6,400	1,729
June	–80	8,050	6,246	1,804	8,130	6,411	1,719
September	–211	7,763	6,083	1,680	7,974	6,345	1,629
December	–175	7,702	6,059	1,643	7,877	6,267	1,610
2003:							
March	–404	7,472	5,932	1,540	7,876	6,321	1,555
June	–142	7,560	6,033	1,527	7,702	6,138	1,564
September	72	7,396	5,897	1,499	7,324	5,893	1,431
December	344	7,646	6,063	1,583	7,302	5,816	1,486
2004:							
March	435	7,745	6,231	1,514	7,310	5,871	1,439
June	594	7,857	6,292	1,565	7,263	5,726	1,537
September	191	7,789	6,123	1,666	7,598	5,953	1,645
December	869	8,081	6,365	1,716	7,212	5,727	1,485
2005:							
March	325	7,635	6,171	1,464	7,310	5,852	1,458
June	574	7,932	6,311	1,621	7,358	5,873	1,485
September	628	8,055	6,423	1,632	7,427	5,915	1,512
December	551	7,818	6,293	1,525	7,267	5,888	1,379
2006:							
March	784	7,556	6,205	1,351	6,772	5,536	1,236
June	466	7,761	6,286	1,475	7,295	5,937	1,358
September	19	7,364	5,985	1,379	7,345	6,010	1,335
December	516	7,734	6,255	1,479	7,218	5,885	1,333

[1] Difference between the total gross job gains and total gross job losses.

Source: U.S. Bureau of Labor Statistics, *Business Employment Dynamics: Fourth Quarter* 2006, USDL 07-1244, August 16, 2007. See Internet site <http://www.bls.gov/bdm/home.htm>.

Table 616. Average Percent Share of Private Sector Gross Job Gains and Losses by Firm Size: 1992 through 2006

[In percent. Covers third quarter 1992 through fourth quarter 2006. Data are for firms (legal businesses, either corporate or otherwise, which may consist of several establishments). Based on the Quarterly Census of Employment and Wages; for details see source]

Item	1 to 4 employ-ees	5 to 9 employ-ees	10 to 19 employ-ees	20 to 49 employ-ees	50 to 99 employ-ees	100 to 249 employ-ees	250 to 499 employ-ees	500 to 999 employ-ees	1,000 or more
Gross job gains	14.4	11.5	11.9	14.3	9.1	9.7	5.9	4.9	18.3
Expanding firms ...	7.0	10.6	12.0	15.2	10.0	11.1	6.8	5.7	21.6
Opening firms.....	52.3	16.0	11.6	9.7	4.2	3.0	1.3	0.8	1.1
Gross job losses	14.7	11.9	12.2	14.4	9.1	9.6	5.8	4.8	17.5
Contracting firms. ..	7.5	11.1	12.3	15.3	10.0	10.8	6.7	5.5	20.8
Closing firms	49.8	15.6	11.6	10.1	4.7	3.8	1.7	1.2	1.5
Net growth	9.5	6.3	8.0	12.3	9.4	11.7	7.4	6.2	29.2

Source: U.S. Bureau of the Census, *Business Employment Dynamics, Fourth Quarter 2006 News*, USDL 07-1244, August 16, 2007. See Internet site <http://www.bls.gov/bdm/home.htm>.

Table 617. **Hires and Separations Affecting Establishment Payrolls: 2003 to 2006**

[49,294 represents 49,294,000. Hires represent any additions to payrolls, including new and rehired employees, full- and part-time workers, short-term and seasonal workers, etc. Separations represent terminations of employment, including quits, layoffs, and discharges etc. Based on a monthly survey of private nonfarm establishments and governmental entities]

Industry	Annual hires (1,000)				Annual separations (1,000)			
	2003	2004	2005	2006	2003	2004	2005	2006
Total	49,294	54,721	57,491	59,400	48,294	51,779	54,609	55,422
Private industry	45,620	50,858	53,416	54,851	45,136	48,479	51,286	51,715
Natural resources and mining	216	229	257	257	218	216	206	227
Construction	4,580	4,677	5,150	4,513	4,555	4,638	4,847	4,653
Manufacturing	3,861	4,316	4,112	4,278	4,350	4,255	4,469	4,483
Durable goods	2,389	2,718	2,592	2,549	2,709	2,661	2,829	2,590
Nondurable goods	1,470	1,598	1,521	1,730	1,641	1,591	1,640	1,896
Trade, transporation, and utilities	10,389	11,988	12,289	12,640	10,682	11,704	11,983	11,995
Wholesale trade	1,481	1,702	1,720	1,629	1,647	1,720	1,602	1,716
Retail trade	7,423	8,392	8,530	8,909	7,378	8,177	8,424	8,517
Transportation, warehousing, and utilities..	1,489	1,893	2,039	2,100	1,657	1,810	1,955	1,760
Information	748	792	881	974	796	927	893	944
Financial activities.................	2,031	2,292	2,281	2,512	1,899	2,161	2,134	2,540
Finance and insurance	1,209	1,354	1,436	1,608	1,162	1,339	1,367	1,607
Real estate and rental and leasing	820	939	845	903	738	824	769	931
Professional and business services	7,842	9,416	10,554	11,328	7,362	8,568	9,816	10,061
Education and health services..........	5,164	5,253	5,619	5,905	4,500	4,710	4,969	5,099
Educational services	726	713	721	840	627	594	638	692
Health care and social assistance.......	4,439	4,541	4,898	5,066	3,874	4,118	4,331	4,410
Leisure and hospitality	8,628	9,670	9,893	10,336	8,589	9,012	9,674	9,734
Arts, entertainment, and recreation	1,349	1,495	1,503	1,509	1,334	1,493	1,409	1,328
Accommodation and food services	7,281	8,173	8,391	8,828	7,257	7,520	8,266	8,405
Other services	2,160	2,223	2,384	2,106	2,185	2,285	2,300	1,981
Government workers.................	3,674	3,863	4,075	4,549	3,158	3,298	3,325	3,706
Federal.......................	476	464	492	699	468	414	446	681
State and local	3,197	3,399	3,586	3,848	2,688	2,888	2,880	3,024

Source: U.S. Bureau of Labor Statistics, *Job Openings and Labor Turnover,* monthly, January 2007 release, *News,* USDL 07-0373, March 13, 2007. See Internet site <http://www.bls.gov/jlt/home.htm>.

Table 618. **Adults in Selected Work-Related Informal Learning Activities: 2002–03**

[(206,533 represents 206,533,000). Civilian noninstitutional population 16 years old and over not enrolled in elementary or secondary school. Based on the Adult Education for Work-Related Reasons Survey of the National Household Education Survey Program and subject to sampling error; see source and Appendix III for details]

Characteristic	Total adults (1,000)	Adults participating in work-related informal learning activities (percent)						
		Any activities	Self-paced study with books [1]	Attended confer-ences [2]	Informal presen-tations [3]	Self-paced study with soft-ware [4]	On the job pre-senta-tions [5]	Received super-vised train-ing [5, 6]
Total..................	206,533	58	31	23	21	21	56	43
Age:								
24 years old or younger	24,053	73	36	20	18	19	69	58
25 to 44 years old	82,223	70	37	28	26	26	57	45
45 to 64 years old	66,447	59	32	27	26	24	50	37
65 years old and over............	33,810	17	10	7	5	6	39	21
Sex:								
Male	98,793	62	33	27	23	23	55	42
Female	107,740	55	28	20	20	19	57	45
Race/ethnicity:								
White, non-Hispanic	149,135	59	30	24	23	21	57	45
Black, non-Hispanic	23,145	56	34	21	19	20	57	44
Asian or Pacific Islander, non-Hispanic.	6,330	67	44	34	32	39	51	40
Other, non-Hispanic	3,675	55	29	21	18	24	44	41
Hispanic [7]	24,248	57	33	20	14	17	46	35
Educational attainment:								
Less than high school............	32,357	31	17	8	5	7	43	25
High school diploma or equivalent....	61,194	50	26	15	13	14	53	40
Some college	58,055	65	35	24	23	24	58	48
BA degree or higher.............	32,122	75	38	35	34	34	61	51
Graduate degree or higher	22,804	78	43	51	46	37	59	47
Household income:								
$25,000 or less	53,796	40	22	12	9	10	50	35
$25,001 to 50,000	55,435	58	32	20	19	19	55	43
$50,001 to 75,000	43,189	64	32	24	24	24	56	46
$75,001 to 100,000	24,286	73	36	33	32	30	60	47
$100,001 or more	29,826	73	38	41	36	34	59	47

[1] Includes manuals and audio/video tapes. [2] Includes trade shows and conventions. [3] Such as "brown bag" events. [4] Includes from the Internet. [5] For adults employed in the past 12 months. [6] Or mentoring. [7] Persons of Hispanic origin may be of any race.

Source: U.S. National Center for Education Statistics, *Participation in Adult Education for Work-Related Reasons,* NCES 2006-040, November 2005.

408 Labor Force, Employment, and Earnings

Table 619. **Adults in Selected Work-Related Formal Learning Activities: 2004-2005**

[(211,607 represents 211,607,000). Civilian noninstitutional population 16 years old and over not enrolled in elementary or secondary school. Based on the Adult Education Survey of the National Household Education Survey Program and subject to sampling error; see source and Appendix III for details]

Characteristic	Total adults (1,000)	Adults participating in work-related formal learning activities (percent)				
		Any activities	College degree program	Vocational degree/ diploma program	Appren- ticeship	Work- related courses
Total	211,607	33	7	1	1	27
Age:						
24 years old or younger	25,104	46	28	3	3	21
25 to 44 years old	81,674	39	7	2	2	33
45 to 64 years old	70,908	34	2	1	–	33
65 years old and over	33,922	5	–	–	–	5
Sex:						
Male	101,596	31	6	2	1	24
Female	110,011	35	8	1	1	29
Race/ethnicity:						
White, non-Hispanic	146,614	34	7	1	1	29
Black, non-Hispanic	23,467	34	6	2	2	27
Asian or Pacific Islander, non-Hispanic	7,080	35	12	1	1	24
Other, non-Hispanic	8,346	34	11	2	2	23
Hispanic [1]	26,101	23	4	2	2	17
Educational attainment:						
Less than high school	38,538	8	1	1	2	6
High school diploma or equivalent	63,701	23	2	2	1	18
Some college	51,657	43	14	2	2	32
BA degree	37,244	49	9	1	–	44
Graduate degree or higher	20,466	55	8	1	1	51

– Represents or rounds to zero. [1] Persons of Hispanic origin may be of any race.

Source: U.S. National Center for Education Statistics, Adult Education Survey of the National Household Education Surveys Program 2005, unpublished data.

Table 620. **Average Hours Worked Per Day by Employed Persons: 2005**

[(150,748 represents 150,748,000). Civilian noninstitutional population 15 years old and over, except as indicated. Includes work at main and any other job(s). Excludes travel related to work. Based on the American Time Use Survey, a survey conducted continuously throughout the year, and subject to sampling error; see source for details]

Characteristic	Total employed (1,000)	Employed persons who worked on their diary day						
		Number (1,000)	Percent of employed	Hours of work	Worked at workplace		Worked at home [1]	
					Percent of employed [2]	Hours of work	Percent of employed [2]	Hours of work
Total	150,748	102,146	67.8	7.53	87.3	7.81	19.6	2.58
Work status:								
Full-time workers [3]	117,521	84,285	71.7	8.04	88.9	8.23	19.2	2.70
Part-time workers [3]	33,227	17,861	53.8	5.13	79.8	5.61	21.9	2.10
Male	79,988	56,302	70.4	7.90	87.8	8.13	20.9	2.57
Full-time workers [3]	68,598	50,167	73.1	8.27	89.2	8.42	20.5	2.60
Part-time workers [3]	11,390	6,135	53.9	4.85	75.9	5.31	24.0	2.38
Female	70,760	45,844	64.8	7.08	86.7	7.41	18.0	2.59
Full-time workers [3]	48,923	34,117	69.7	7.69	88.4	7.93	17.1	2.86
Part-time workers [3]	21,837	11,727	53.7	5.28	81.8	5.76	20.8	1.94
Jobholding status:								
Single jobholders	135,474	90,399	66.7	7.53	87.9	7.80	18.1	2.57
Multiple jobholders	15,274	11,746	76.9	7.57	82.3	7.90	31.3	2.62
Educational attainment: [4]								
Less than high school	10,635	7,244	68.1	7.90	93.9	7.95	(B)	(B)
High school diploma [5]	38,739	25,726	66.4	7.84	92.1	7.95	11.3	2.71
Some college	33,489	23,158	69.2	7.59	85.8	7.90	20.2	3.02
BA degree or higher	44,026	32,495	73.8	7.37	80.6	7.88	34.2	2.31

B Percent not shown where base is less than 800,000. [1] Represents doing activities that were "part of one's job." [2] Percent of employed who worked on their diary day. [3] Full-time workers usually worked 35 or more hours per week at all jobs combined; part-time workers fewer than 35 hours per week. [4] For those 25 years old and over. [5] Or equivalent.

Source: U.S. Bureau of Labor Statistics, *American Time Use Survey—2005 Results Announced by BLS, News,* USDL 06-1276, July 27, 2006. See Internet site <http://www.bls.gov/tus/home.htm>.

Labor Force, Employment, and Earnings 409

Table 621. **Annual Indexes of Output Per Hour for Selected NAICS Industries, 1987 to 2005**

[For a discussion of productivity measures, see text, this section. Minus sign (–) indicates decrease]

Industry	2002 NAICS code [1]	Indexes (1997 = 100)						Average annual percent change [2]
		1987	1990	1995	2000	2004	2005	
Mining	21	85.5	85.1	101.7	111.0	106.7	95.9	0.6
Oil and gas extraction	211	80.1	75.7	95.3	119.4	111.7	107.9	1.7
Mining, except oil and gas.	212	69.8	79.3	94.0	106.3	115.7	113.5	2.7
Utilities:								
Power generation and supply	2211	65.6	71.1	88.5	107.0	107.5	114.2	3.1
Natural gas distribution.	2212	67.8	71.4	89.0	113.2	118.3	123.5	3.4
Manufacturing:								
Fruit and vegetable preserving and specialty	3114	92.4	87.6	98.3	111.8	126.2	132.1	2.0
Dairy products	3115	82.7	91.1	97.6	95.9	107.4	109.5	1.6
Animal slaughtering and processing	3116	97.4	94.3	99.0	102.6	108.0	117.4	1.0
Bakeries and tortilla manufacturing	3118	100.9	94.5	100.7	108.3	113.8	115.4	0.7
Other food products	3119	97.5	92.5	104.1	112.6	119.3	115.4	0.9
Beverages	3121	77.1	87.6	103.2	90.8	114.1	119.4	2.5
Fabric mills.	3132	68.0	75.3	95.5	110.1	138.6	150.5	4.5
Cut and sew apparel	3152	69.8	70.1	85.2	119.8	108.4	113.1	2.7
Sawmills and wood preservation	3211	77.6	79.4	90.4	105.4	118.2	127.9	2.8
Plywood and engineered wood products	3212	99.7	102.8	101.4	98.8	102.9	110.3	0.6
Other wood products	3219	103.0	105.3	99.8	103.0	119.6	125.8	1.1
Pulp, paper, and paperboard mills	3221	81.7	84.0	98.4	116.3	148.0	148.9	3.4
Converted paper products.	3222	89.0	90.1	97.2	101.1	112.9	115.3	1.4
Printing and related support activities	3231	97.6	97.5	98.9	104.6	114.5	119.7	1.1
Petroleum and coal products	3241	71.1	75.4	89.9	113.5	123.4	123.8	3.1
Basic chemicals	3251	94.6	93.4	91.3	117.5	154.4	163.1	3.1
Resin, rubber, and artificial fibers	3252	77.4	76.4	95.4	109.8	121.9	127.8	2.8
Pharmaceuticals and medicines	3254	87.3	91.3	95.9	95.6	104.1	107.8	1.2
Soap, cleaning compounds, and toiletries	3256	84.4	84.8	96.1	102.8	135.3	152.6	3.3
Other chemical products and preparations	3259	75.4	77.8	93.5	119.7	121.3	123.5	2.8
Plastics products	3261	83.1	85.2	94.5	112.3	131.9	135.6	2.8
Rubber products	3262	75.5	83.5	92.9	101.7	114.4	119.3	2.6
Glass and glass products	3272	82.3	79.1	87.5	108.2	113.9	122.7	2.2
Cement and concrete products	3273	93.6	96.6	99.7	101.6	102.8	105.5	0.7
Foundries	3315	81.4	86.5	93.1	103.6	123.9	128.0	2.5
Forging and stamping	3321	85.4	89.0	93.9	121.1	142.0	146.7	3.0
Architectural and structural metals	3323	88.7	87.9	93.3	100.7	105.4	108.1	1.1
Machine shops and threaded products	3327	76.9	79.2	98.3	108.2	114.6	115.3	2.3
Coating, engraving, and heat treating metals	3328	75.5	81.3	102.2	105.5	125.3	136.0	3.3
Other fabricated metal products	3329	91.0	86.5	96.3	99.9	111.2	112.6	1.2
Agriculture, construction, and mining machinery . . .	3331	74.6	83.3	95.4	100.3	125.4	130.8	3.2
Industrial machinery.	3332	75.1	81.6	97.1	130.0	126.5	121.9	2.7
Commercial and service industry machinery	3333	86.9	95.6	103.6	100.9	106.4	113.4	1.5
HVAC and commercial refrigeration equipment . . .	3334	84.0	90.6	96.4	107.9	132.8	137.7	2.8
Metalworking machinery	3335	85.1	86.5	99.2	106.1	117.1	126.6	2.2
Other general purpose machinery.	3339	83.5	86.8	94.0	113.7	127.1	137.2	2.8
Computer and peripheral equipment	3341	11.0	14.7	49.9	234.9	416.6	576.5	24.6
Communications equipment	3342	39.8	48.4	74.4	164.1	148.4	144.4	7.4
Semiconductors and electronic components	3344	17.0	21.9	63.8	232.4	361.1	386.6	19.0
Electronic instruments	3345	70.2	78.5	97.9	116.7	145.4	139.8	3.9
Electrical equipment.	3353	68.7	73.6	98.0	99.4	110.8	116.7	3.0
Other electrical equipment and components	3359	78.8	76.1	92.0	119.7	115.6	121.7	2.4
Motor vehicles	3361	75.4	85.6	88.5	109.7	142.1	147.0	3.8
Motor vehicle bodies and trailers	3362	85.0	75.9	97.4	98.8	110.7	114.2	1.7
Motor vehicle parts	3363	78.7	76.0	92.3	112.3	138.0	144.4	3.4
Aerospace products and parts	3364	87.2	89.1	95.7	103.4	113.0	125.8	2.1
Ship and boat building	3366	95.5	99.6	93.1	121.9	138.7	133.2	1.9
Household and institutional furniture	3371	85.2	88.2	97.2	101.9	113.6	121.3	2.0
Office furniture and fixtures	3372	85.8	82.2	84.9	100.2	131.1	136.7	2.6
Medical equipment and supplies	3391	76.3	82.9	96.6	114.6	137.5	148.2	3.8
Other miscellaneous manufacturing	3399	85.4	90.5	95.9	113.6	128.6	139.0	2.7
Wholesale trade	42	73.2	79.8	94.0	116.2	134.7	135.5	3.5
Durable goods	423	62.3	67.5	90.1	124.6	159.8	164.8	5.5
Nondurable goods	424	91.0	98.9	98.5	105.1	113.5	114.2	1.3
Electronic markets and agents and brokers	425	64.3	74.3	95.4	119.3	107.4	98.1	2.4
Retail trade	44–45	79.1	81.4	94.0	116.1	138.0	142.7	3.3
Motor vehicle and parts dealers	441	78.3	82.7	95.5	114.3	127.4	128.0	2.8
Automobile dealers.	4411	79.2	84.1	95.8	113.7	124.7	123.4	2.5
Other motor vehicle dealers	4412	70.6	69.7	88.3	115.3	142.8	150.5	4.3
Auto parts, accessories, and tire stores	4413	71.8	79.0	95.2	108.4	110.3	118.6	2.8
Furniture and home furnishings stores.	442	75.1	79.0	93.7	115.9	147.0	149.4	3.9
Furniture stores	4421	77.3	84.8	93.6	112.0	139.4	138.4	3.3
Home furnishings stores	4422	71.3	71.0	93.3	121.0	157.1	163.8	4.7
Electronics and appliance stores	443	38.0	47.7	87.8	173.7	334.7	365.1	13.4
Building material and garden supply stores	444	75.8	79.5	91.9	113.3	134.6	135.1	3.3
Building material and supplies dealers	4441	77.6	81.6	93.4	115.1	134.0	134.6	3.1
Lawn and garden equipment and supplies stores.	4442	66.9	69.0	83.9	103.1	140.2	139.4	4.2
Food and beverage stores	445	110.9	107.5	102.3	101.1	113.1	119.1	0.4
Grocery stores.	4451	111.1	106.9	102.7	101.1	112.3	117.3	0.3
Specialty food stores	4452	138.5	127.2	102.9	98.5	121.1	137.4	(Z)
Beer, wine and liquor stores.	4453	94.7	98.7	95.4	107.0	129.9	147.6	2.5

See footnotes at end of table.

Table 621. **Annual Indexes of Output Per Hour for Selected NAICS Industries: 1987 to 2005**—Con.

[For a discussion of productivity measures, see text, this section. Minus sign (–) indicates decrease]

Industry	2002 NAICS code [1]	Indexes (1997 = 100)						Average annual percent change [2]
		1987	1990	1995	2000	2004	2005	
Retail trade—Con.								
Health and personal care stores	446	84.0	91.0	91.4	112.2	134.0	132.8	2.6
Gasoline stations	447	83.9	84.2	99.4	107.7	122.3	129.5	2.4
Clothing and clothing accessories stores	448	66.3	69.8	92.7	123.5	139.2	147.5	4.5
Clothing stores	4481	67.1	70.0	91.7	125.0	141.0	153.7	4.7
Shoe stores	4482	65.3	70.8	96.4	110.0	124.9	129.4	3.9
Jewelry, luggage, and leather goods stores	4483	64.5	68.1	94.1	130.5	144.5	137.2	4.3
Sporting goods, hobby, book, and music stores	451	74.4	82.1	95.0	121.1	151.1	164.2	4.5
Sporting goods and musical instrument stores	4511	70.5	79.5	94.7	127.8	160.1	172.8	5.1
Book, periodical, and music stores	4512	84.3	87.9	95.4	108.7	134.8	149.3	3.2
General merchandise stores	452	73.5	75.1	92.0	120.2	140.7	146.1	3.9
Department stores	4521	87.2	83.9	94.6	106.2	109.0	109.6	1.3
Other general merchandise stores	4529	54.8	61.2	87.2	147.3	192.9	203.5	7.6
Miscellaneous store retailers	453	65.1	69.5	88.8	114.1	131.2	142.0	4.4
Florists	4531	77.6	73.3	82.4	115.2	103.0	127.5	2.8
Office supplies, stationery, and gift stores	4532	61.4	66.4	91.7	127.3	173.0	182.6	6.2
Used merchandise stores	4533	64.5	70.4	85.9	116.5	155.7	168.1	5.5
Other miscellaneous store retailers	4539	68.3	75.0	88.9	104.4	97.2	104.3	2.4
Nonstore retailers	454	50.7	54.7	79.8	152.2	216.1	222.3	8.6
Electronic shopping and mail-order houses	4541	39.4	43.4	72.5	160.2	272.8	284.2	11.6
Vending machine operators	4542	95.5	95.1	86.4	91.1	110.4	112.7	0.9
Direct selling establishments	4543	70.8	74.1	93.2	122.5	131.8	128.7	3.4
Transportation and warehousing:								
Air transportation	481	81.1	77.5	95.3	98.1	126.0	135.7	2.9
Line-haul railroads	482111	58.9	69.8	92.0	114.3	146.4	138.5	4.9
General freight trucking, long-distance	48412	85.7	89.2	95.8	101.9	110.7	112.6	1.5
Used household and office goods moving	48421	106.7	112.6	101.4	94.8	88.7	88.5	–1.0
Postal service	491	90.9	94.2	97.7	105.5	110.0	111.2	1.1
Couriers and messengers	492	148.3	138.5	101.5	121.9	126.9	124.7	–1.0
Information:								
Newspaper, book, and directory publishers	5111	105.0	95.5	91.9	107.7	106.7	108.4	0.2
Software publishers	5112	10.2	28.5	73.4	119.2	160.7	171.0	17.0
Motion picture and video exhibition	51213	90.7	109.2	99.4	106.5	103.8	102.7	0.7
Broadcasting, except Internet	515	99.5	98.2	102.5	103.6	112.5	117.6	0.9
Radio and television broadcasting	5151	98.1	97.7	104.8	92.1	96.6	101.5	0.2
Cable and other subscription programming	5152	105.6	100.3	92.8	141.2	158.6	162.4	2.4
Wired telecommunications carriers	5171	56.9	66.0	87.6	122.7	133.9	140.2	5.1
Wireless telecommunications carriers	5172	75.6	70.4	90.0	152.8	292.0	392.4	9.6
Cable and other program distribution	5175	105.2	100.0	92.6	91.6	113.7	110.4	0.3
Finance and insurance:								
Commercial banking	52211	72.8	80.7	95.6	102.7	108.5	108.4	2.2
Real estate and rental and leasing:								
Passenger car rental	532111	92.7	90.8	100.7	112.3	118.3	110.5	1.0
Truck, trailer, and RV rental and leasing	53212	60.4	68.6	88.8	121.1	135.7	145.5	5.0
Video tape and disc rental	53223	77.0	97.1	119.5	134.9	154.5	155.6	4.0
Professional and technical services:								
Tax preparation services	541213	82.9	76.2	90.6	100.9	100.0	106.9	1.4
Architectural services	54131	90.0	93.8	106.5	107.6	118.3	123.9	1.8
Engineering services	54133	90.2	99.4	94.4	102.0	107.8	114.2	1.3
Advertising agencies	54181	95.9	107.9	102.5	107.5	133.0	131.2	1.8
Photography studios, portrait	541921	98.1	95.9	107.3	108.9	93.2	93.6	–0.3
Administrative and waste services:								
Employment placement agencies	56131	(NA)	(NA)	86.6	89.8	119.8	117.9	3.1
Travel agencies	56151	89.3	94.6	93.0	119.4	167.4	188.2	4.2
Janitorial services	56172	75.1	94.3	90.4	101.0	116.6	122.0	2.7
Health care and social assistance:								
Medical and diagnostic laboratories	6215	(NA)	(NA)	90.9	131.9	140.8	138.8	4.3
Medical laboratories	621511	(NA)	(NA)	91.3	127.4	130.7	127.1	3.4
Diagnostic imaging centers	621512	(NA)	(NA)	90.0	139.9	153.5	154.8	5.6
Arts, entertainment, and recreation:								
Amusement and theme parks	71311	112.0	112.5	96.3	106.0	101.4	110.0	–0.1
Bowling centers	71395	106.0	94.0	92.1	93.4	107.9	106.1	(Z)
Accommodation and food services:								
Traveler accommodations	7211	85.2	82.1	97.7	111.7	120.8	115.8	1.7
Food services and drinking places	722	96.0	102.4	100.3	103.5	107.1	108.8	0.7
Full-service restaurants	7221	92.1	99.4	96.2	103.0	104.9	107.5	0.9
Limited-service eating places	7222	96.5	103.6	104.1	102.0	106.9	106.8	0.6
Special food services	7223	89.9	99.8	100.8	115.0	118.8	122.8	1.8
Drinking places, alcoholic beverages	7224	136.7	123.3	104.6	100.6	112.6	119.7	–0.7
Other services:								
Automotive repair and maintenance	8111	85.9	89.9	103.2	109.4	112.0	112.5	1.5
Hair, nail, and skin care services	81211	83.5	82.1	93.4	108.2	125.0	130.4	2.5
Funeral homes and funeral services	81221	103.7	98.4	102.4	94.8	92.9	93.2	–0.6
Drycleaning and laundry services	8123	97.1	94.8	99.2	107.6	110.6	120.8	1.2
Photofinishing	81292	95.8	107.7	108.0	73.8	102.0	113.2	0.9

NA Not available.   Z Less than 0.05 percent.   [1] North American Industry Classification System, 2002 (NAICS); see text, this section.   [2] Average annual percent change, 1987 to 2005, based on compound rate formula. For NAICS industries 56131, 6215, 621511, and 621512 annual percent changes are for 1995–2005. The rates of change are calculated using index numbers to three decimal places.

Source: U.S. Bureau of Labor Statistics. Latest data available at: <http://www.bls.gov/lpc/home.htm> (accessed June 2007).

Table 622. **Annual Total Compensation and Wages and Salary Accruals Per Full-Time Equivalent Employee by Industry: 2000 to 2005**

[In dollars. Wage and salary accruals include executives' compensation, bonuses, tips, and payments-in-kind; total compensation includes in addition to wages and salaries, employer contributions for social insurance, employer contributions to private and welfare funds, director's fees, jury and witness fees, etc. Based on the 1997 North American Industry Classification System (NAICS); see text, this section]

Industry	Annual total compensation				Annual wages and salary			
	2000	2003	2004	2005	2000	2003	2004	2005
Domestic industries	46,407	51,341	53,498	55,465	38,762	41,628	43,265	44,702
Private industries	45,240	49,506	51,457	53,289	38,446	40,901	42,507	43,917
Agriculture, forestry, fishing, and hunting	29,332	26,452	29,972	32,709	25,847	23,152	26,573	29,093
Mining	70,413	79,488	83,744	90,429	58,291	63,237	67,681	72,983
Utilities	78,147	91,782	96,680	101,136	64,271	69,404	73,022	76,388
Construction	44,764	50,542	50,955	53,471	37,196	41,364	41,453	43,575
Manufacturing	54,219	62,113	63,890	66,414	44,216	46,753	48,732	50,180
Wholesale trade	56,264	63,247	66,294	68,832	48,017	52,964	55,287	57,238
Retail trade	30,225	32,295	33,400	34,096	26,307	27,393	28,197	28,670
Transportation and warehousing	48,336	50,964	53,118	53,990	39,463	40,854	42,455	42,911
Information	74,196	75,684	81,275	83,761	63,217	61,812	65,758	67,674
Finance and insurance	74,821	82,190	87,099	91,796	64,049	68,356	72,512	76,281
Real estate and rental and leasing	41,906	45,301	48,241	50,827	36,178	38,667	41,113	43,335
Professional, scientific, and technical services	68,436	74,761	78,356	81,448	58,886	63,669	66,437	69,045
Management of companies and enterprises [1]	89,496	90,151	96,163	102,468	75,984	76,010	80,718	86,413
Administrative and waste management services	28,540	33,880	33,999	35,819	25,181	29,232	29,097	30,678
Educational services	32,736	37,335	38,651	39,770	28,974	32,526	33,604	34,507
Health care and social assistance	40,897	45,631	47,441	48,898	35,127	38,752	40,210	41,373
Arts, entertainment, and recreation	35,898	39,893	40,881	40,853	31,259	34,234	34,923	34,693
Accommodation and food services	19,092	22,036	23,367	23,351	16,830	18,950	20,051	19,988
Other services, except government	28,630	31,888	33,071	34,127	25,495	28,069	29,023	29,791
Government	52,845	60,868	64,195	67,099	40,501	45,406	47,241	48,900
Federal	70,004	85,149	93,010	98,917	46,646	56,482	60,310	63,816
State and local	48,020	54,421	56,632	58,914	38,773	42,465	43,811	45,062

[1] Consists of offices of bank and other holding companies and of corporate, subsidiary, and regional managing offices.

Source: U.S. Bureau of Economic Analysis, Survey of Current Business, April 2007; and Internet site <http://www.bea.gov/bea/dn/nipaweb/SelectTable.asp?Selected=N> (accessed 15 May 2007).

Table 623. **Average Hourly Earnings by Private Industry Group: 1990 to 2006**

[In dollars. Average earnings include overtime. Data are for production workers in natural resources and mining, manufacturing, and construction, and nonsupervisory employees in other industries. See headnote, Table 612]

Private industry group	Current dollars					Constant (1982) dollars [1]				
	1990	2000	2004	2005	2006	1990	2000	2004	2005	2006
AVERAGE HOURLY EARNINGS										
Total private	10.20	14.02	15.69	16.13	16.76	7.66	8.04	8.24	8.18	8.24
Natural resources and mining	13.40	16.55	18.07	18.72	19.90	10.07	9.50	9.49	9.50	9.78
Construction	13.42	17.48	19.23	19.46	20.02	10.08	10.03	10.10	9.87	9.84
Manufacturing	10.78	14.32	16.15	16.56	16.80	8.10	8.22	8.48	8.40	8.26
Trade, transportation, and utilities	9.83	13.31	14.58	14.92	15.40	7.39	7.64	7.66	7.57	7.57
Information	13.40	19.07	21.40	22.06	23.23	10.07	10.94	11.24	11.19	11.42
Financial activities [2]	9.99	14.98	17.52	17.94	18.80	7.51	8.59	9.20	9.10	9.24
Professional and business services [2]	11.14	15.52	17.48	18.08	19.12	8.37	8.90	9.18	9.17	9.40
Education and health services [2]	10.00	13.95	16.15	16.71	17.38	7.51	8.00	8.48	8.48	8.54
Leisure and hospitality [2]	6.02	8.32	9.15	9.38	9.75	4.52	4.77	4.81	4.76	4.79
Other services	9.08	12.73	13.98	14.34	14.77	6.82	7.30	7.34	7.28	7.26
AVERAGE WEEKLY EARNINGS										
Total private	350	481	529	544	568	263	276	278	276	279
Natural resources and mining	603	735	804	854	908	453	422	422	433	446
Construction	513	686	736	750	781	386	393	386	381	384
Manufacturing	436	591	659	673	691	328	339	346	342	340
Trade, transportation, and utilities	332	450	488	498	515	249	258	257	253	253
Information	480	701	777	805	851	360	402	408	408	418
Financial activities [2]	355	537	623	645	672	266	308	327	327	331
Professional and business services [2]	381	535	598	619	662	286	307	314	314	326
Education and health services [2]	319	449	524	545	565	240	258	275	276	278
Leisure and hospitality [2]	156	217	235	241	250	117	125	123	122	123
Other services	298	413	433	443	457	224	237	227	225	224

[1] Earnings in current dollars divided by the Consumer Price Index (CPI-W) on a 1982 base; see text, Section 14, Prices.
[2] For composition of industries, see Table 607.

Source: U.S. Bureau of Labor Statistics, the Current Employment Statistics program Internet site <http://www.bls.gov/ces/home.htm>.

412 Labor Force, Employment, and Earnings

Table 624. **Mean Hourly Earnings and Weekly Hours by Selected Characteristics: 2005**

[Covers civilian workers in private industry establishments and state and local governments in the 50 states and DC. Excludes private households, federal government, and agriculture. Based on survey of 25,723 establishments representing over 84 million workers; see source and Appendix III for details about the National Compensation Survey]

Item	Mean hourly earnings (dol.) [1]			Mean weekly hours		
	Total	Private industry	State and local government	Total	Private industry	State and local government
Total	18.62	17.82	23.31	35.7	35.5	36.8
WORKER CHARACTERISTIC						
White-collar occupations	22.96	22.21	26.32	36.0	35.9	36.5
Professional specialty and technical	30.24	29.80	31.25	36.2	36.2	36.1
Executive, administrative, and managerial	33.69	34.21	31.04	39.8	40.0	38.6
Sales	15.32	15.33	13.75	32.4	32.4	33.3
Administrative support	14.53	14.44	14.98	36.5	36.5	36.6
Blue-collar occupations	15.87	15.75	17.96	38.1	38.1	37.7
Precision production, craft, and repair	19.95	19.93	20.24	39.6	39.6	39.7
Machine operators, assemblers, and inspectors	14.19	14.17	17.59	39.0	39.0	38.0
Transportation and material moving	15.28	15.10	17.01	37.7	38.1	34.5
Handlers, equipment cleaners, helpers, and laborers	11.63	11.43	14.90	35.3	35.1	38.6
Service occupations..................	10.89	9.38	17.55	31.7	30.6	37.0
Full-time [2].	19.70	18.95	23.73	39.6	39.7	38.8
Part-time [2].	10.52	10.15	15.80	20.5	20.6	19.1
Union [3]	22.65	20.67	25.49	36.7	36.6	36.8
Nonunion	17.77	17.43	21.22	35.5	35.4	36.8
Time [4]	18.33	17.43	23.31	35.5	35.3	36.8
Incentive [4].	24.12	24.11	(NA)	38.7	38.7	(NA)
ESTABLISHMENT CHARACTERISTIC						
Goods producing [5].	(X)	19.60	(X)	(X)	39.5	(X)
Service producing [5].	(X)	17.19	(X)	(X)	34.3	(X)
1 to 99 workers [6]	15.73	15.69	18.86	34.4	34.4	36.6
100 to 499 workers.	18.13	17.72	21.79	36.4	36.4	35.9
500 to 999 workers.	20.79	19.94	23.83	36.9	37.2	35.8
1,000 to 2,499 workers	21.65	21.07	23.37	36.9	37.0	36.4
2,500 workers or more.	25.44	27.05	24.06	37.3	37.1	37.5
GEOGRAPHIC REGION [7]						
New England.	20.81	19.97	26.72	34.3	34.1	35.5
Middle Atlantic	21.19	20.27	26.67	35.1	35.0	35.7
East North Central	18.91	18.11	24.27	35.3	35.2	36.1
West North Central	17.09	16.18	22.13	35.4	35.0	37.2
South Atlantic.	17.72	17.19	20.40	36.2	35.9	38.1
East South Central	14.66	14.06	19.16	37.0	37.0	37.3
West South Central.	16.36	15.73	19.64	36.6	36.3	38.3
Mountain.	17.30	16.31	23.27	35.8	35.5	37.1
Pacific	20.83	19.74	27.10	35.4	35.4	35.6

NA Not available.   X Not applicable.   [1] Earnings are straight time hourly wages or salary, including incentive pay, cost-of-living adjustments, and hazard pay. Excludes premium pay for overtime, vacations and holidays, nonproduction bonuses and tips.   [2] Based on definition used by each establishment.   [3] Workers whose wages are determined through collective bargaining.   [4] Time worker wages are based solely on an hourly rate or salary. Incentive workers wages are based at least in part on productivity payments such as piece rates or commissions.   [5] For private industry only. See footnotes 3 and 4, Table 614 for composition of goods and service producing industries.   [6] Private establishments employing 1 to 99 workers and state and local government establishments employing 50 to 99 workers.   [7] Composition of regions: NEW ENGLAND: Maine, New Hampshire, Vermont, Massachusetts, Rhode Island, Connecticut. MIDDLE ATLANTIC: New York, New Jersey, Pennsylvania. EAST NORTH CENTRAL: Ohio, Indiana, Illinois, Michigan, Wisconsin. WEST NORTH CENTRAL: Minnesota, Iowa, Missouri, North Dakota, South Dakota, Nebraska, Kansas. SOUTH ATLANTIC: Delaware, Maryland, District of Columbia, Virginia, West Virginia, North Carolina, South Carolina, Georgia, Florida. EAST SOUTH CENTRAL: Kentucky, Tennessee, Alabama, Mississippi. WEST SOUTH CENTRAL: Arkansas, Louisiana, Oklahoma, Texas. MOUNTAIN: Montana, Idaho, Wyoming, Colorado, New Mexico, Arizona, Utah, Nevada. PACIFIC: Washington, Oregon, California, Alaska, Hawaii.

Source: U.S. Bureau of Labor Statistics, *National Compensation Survey: Occupational Wages in the United States*, Bulletin 2581, August 2006. See Internet site <http://www.bls.gov/ncs/home.htm>.

Labor Force, Employment, and Earnings   413

Table 625. Employment and Wages: 1995 to 2005

[(115,488 represents 115,488,000). See headnote, Table 626]

Employment and wages	Unit	1995	2000	2001	2002	2003	2004	2005
Average annual employment:								
Total	1,000	115,488	129,877	129,636	128,234	127,796	129,278	131,572
Excluding federal	1,000	112,540	127,006	126,883	125,475	125,032	126,539	128,838
Private	1,000	96,895	110,015	109,305	107,577	107,066	108,490	110,611
State government	1,000	4,202	4,370	4,452	4,485	4,482	4,485	4,528
Local governments	1,000	11,442	12,620	13,126	13,413	13,484	13,564	13,699
Federal government	1,000	2,948	2,871	2,753	2,759	2,764	2,740	2,734
Annual wages:								
Total	Bil. dol.	3,216	4,588	4,695	4,714	4,826	5,088	5,352
Excluding federal	Bil. dol.	3,102	4,455	4,561	4,571	4,676	4,929	5,188
Private	Bil. dol.	2,659	3,888	3,952	3,931	4,016	4,246	4,480
State government	Bil. dol.	128	159	168	176	180	184	191
Local governments	Bil. dol.	315	409	440	464	481	499	517
Federal government	Bil. dol.	114	133	135	144	150	158	164
Average wage per employee:								
Total	Dol.	27,846	35,323	36,219	36,764	37,765	39,354	40,677
Excluding federal	Dol.	27,567	35,077	36,428	37,401	38,955	40,270
Private	Dol.	27,441	35,337	36,157	36,539	37,508	39,134	40,505
State government	Dol.	30,497	36,296	37,814	39,212	40,057	41,118	42,249
Local governments	Dol.	27,552	32,387	33,521	34,605	35,669	36,805	37,718
Federal government	Dol.	38,523	46,228	48,940	52,050	54,239	57,782	59,864
Average weekly wage per employee:								
Total	Dol.	536	679	697	707	726	757	782
Excluding federal	Dol.	530	675	691	701	719	749	774
Private	Dol.	528	680	695	703	721	753	779
State government	Dol.	586	698	727	754	770	791	812
Local governments	Dol.	530	623	645	665	686	708	725
Federal government	Dol.	741	889	941	1,001	1,043	1,111	1,151

Source: U.S. Bureau of Labor Statistics. "Employment and Wages, Annual Averages," 2004 and 2005. See Internet site <http://www.bls.gov/cew/home.htm>.

Table 626. Average Annual Wage by State: 2004 and 2005

[In dollars, except percent change. For workers covered by state unemployment insurance laws and for federal civilian workers covered by unemployment compensation for federal employees, approximately 97 percent of employees on nonfarm payrolls in 2005. Excludes most agricultural workers on small farms, all Armed Forces, elected officials in most states, railroad employees, most domestic workers, most student workers at school, employees of certain nonprofit organizations, and most self-employed individuals. Pay includes bonuses, stock options, cash value of meals and lodging, and tips and other gratuities]

State	Average annual pay 2004	Average annual pay 2005	Percent change, 2004–05	State	Average annual pay 2004	Average annual pay 2005	Percent change, 2004–05
United States	39,354	40,677	3.4	Missouri	34,845	35,951	3.2
Alabama	33,414	34,598	3.5	Montana	27,830	29,150	4.7
Alaska	39,062	40,216	3.0	Nebraska	31,507	32,422	2.9
Arizona	36,646	38,154	4.1	Nevada	37,106	38,763	4.5
Arkansas	30,245	31,266	3.4	New Hampshire	39,176	40,551	3.5
California	44,641	46,211	3.5	New Jersey	48,064	49,471	2.9
Colorado	40,276	41,601	3.3	New Mexico	31,411	32,605	3.8
Connecticut	51,007	52,954	3.8	New York	49,941	51,937	4.0
Delaware	42,487	44,622	5.0	North Carolina	34,791	35,912	3.2
District of Columbia	63,887	66,696	4.4	North Dakota	28,987	29,956	3.3
Florida	35,186	36,800	4.6	Ohio	36,441	37,333	2.4
Georgia	37,866	39,096	3.2	Oklahoma	30,743	31,721	3.2
Hawaii	35,198	36,353	3.3	Oregon	35,630	36,588	2.7
Idaho	29,871	30,777	3.0	Pennsylvania	38,555	39,661	2.9
Illinois	42,277	43,744	3.5	Rhode Island	37,651	38,751	2.9
Indiana	34,694	35,431	2.1	South Carolina	31,839	32,927	3.4
Iowa	32,097	33,070	3.0	South Dakota	28,281	29,149	3.1
Kansas	32,738	33,864	3.4	Tennessee	34,925	35,879	2.7
Kentucky	33,165	33,965	2.4	Texas	38,511	40,150	4.3
Louisiana	31,880	33,566	5.3	Utah	32,171	33,328	3.6
Maine	31,906	32,701	2.5	Vermont	33,274	34,197	2.8
Maryland	42,579	44,368	4.2	Virginia	40,534	42,287	4.3
Massachusetts	48,916	50,095	2.4	Washington	39,361	40,721	3.5
Michigan	40,373	41,214	2.1	West Virginia	30,382	31,347	3.2
Minnesota	40,398	40,800	1.0	Wisconsin	34,743	35,471	2.1
Mississippi	28,535	29,763	4.3	Wyoming	31,210	33,251	6.5

Source: U.S. Bureau of Labor Statistics. "Employment and Wages, Annual Averages," 2004 and 2005. See Internet site <http://www.bls.gov/cew/home.htm>.

Table 627. Full-Time Wage and Salary Workers—Number and Earnings: 2000 to 2006

[In current dollars of usual weekly earnings. Data represent annual averages (101,210 represents 101,210,000). Occupational classifications are those used in the 2000 census; see text this section. Based on the Current Population Survey; see text, Section 1, and Appendix III. For definition of median, see Guide to Tabular Presentation]

Characteristic	Number of workers (1,000)			Median weekly earnings (dol.)		
	2000	2005 [1]	2006 [1]	2000	2005 [1]	2006 [1]
All workers [2]	101,210	103,560	106,106	576	651	671
SEX						
Male	57,107	58,406	59,747	641	722	743
16 to 24 years old	6,770	6,396	6,559	375	409	418
25 years old and over	50,337	52,010	53,188	693	771	797
Female	44,103	45,154	46,358	493	585	600
16 to 24 years old	5,094	4,711	4,802	344	381	395
25 years old and over	39,009	40,443	41,556	516	612	627
RACE/ETHNICITY						
White [3]	83,228	84,110	86,055	590	672	690
Male	48,085	48,572	49,650	662	743	761
Female	35,143	35,538	36,405	502	596	609
Black [3]	12,410	12,388	12,745	474	520	554
Male	5,911	5,916	6,025	510	559	591
Female	6,500	6,472	6,720	429	499	519
Asian [3, 4]	4,598	4,651	4,840	615	753	784
Male	2,538	2,597	2,717	685	825	882
Female	2,060	2,054	2,123	547	665	699
Hispanic origin [5]	12,761	14,673	15,693	399	471	486
Male	8,077	9,433	10,007	417	489	505
Female	4,684	5,241	5,686	366	429	440
OCCUPATION						
Management, professional, and related occupations	34,831	36,908	37,824	810	937	967
Management, business, and financial operations	14,240	14,977	15,447	877	997	1,045
Management occupations	9,952	10,340	10,661	937	1,083	1,127
Business and financial operations occupations	4,288	4,637	4,786	760	871	930
Professional and related occupations	20,590	21,931	22,378	770	902	928
Computer and mathematical occupations	3,051	2,924	2,935	938	1,132	1,166
Architecture and engineering occupations	2,781	2,509	2,568	949	1,105	1,155
Life, physical, and social science occupations	989	1,164	1,220	811	965	984
Community and social services occupations	1,641	1,797	1,816	629	725	740
Legal occupations	1,039	1,162	1,156	919	1,052	1,144
Education, training, and library occupations	5,467	6,066	6,158	704	798	819
Arts, design, entertainment, sports, and media	1,488	1,488	1,476	724	819	841
Healthcare practitioner and technical occupations	4,134	4,821	5,048	727	878	905
Service occupations	12,595	14,123	14,749	365	413	422
Healthcare support occupations	1,731	2,085	2,231	358	410	423
Protective service occupations	2,281	2,549	2,633	591	678	693
Food preparation and serving-related occupations	3,483	4,007	4,212	317	356	371
Building and grounds cleaning and maintenance	3,354	3,425	3,594	351	394	406
Personal care and service occupations	1,746	2,057	2,079	351	409	407
Sales and office occupations	25,606	25,193	25,688	492	575	589
Sales and related occupations	9,650	10,031	10,336	525	622	628
Office and administrative support occupations	15,956	15,161	15,351	480	550	572
Natural resources, construction, and maintenance occupations	10,958	12,086	12,512	582	623	653
Farming, fishing, and forestry occupations	842	755	716	310	372	387
Construction and extraction occupations	5,852	6,826	7,166	580	604	619
Installation, maintenance, and repair occupations	4,263	4,504	4,630	628	705	742
Production, transportation, and material-moving occupations	17,221	15,251	15,332	475	540	557
Production occupations	10,378	8,403	8,391	471	538	559
Transportation and material-moving occupations	6,843	6,848	6,942	481	543	556

[1] See footnote 2, Table 569. [2] Includes other races, not shown separately. [3] Beginning 2005, for persons in this race group only. See footnote 3, table 570. [4] Prior to 2005, includes Pacific Islanders. [5] Persons of Hispanic or Latino origin may be of any race.

Source: U.S. Bureau of Labor Statistics, Bulletin 2307, and *Employment and Earnings*, monthly, January issues and unpublished data. See Internet site <http://www.bls.gov/cps/home.htm>.

Table. 628. Workers With Earnings by Occupation of Longest Held Job and Sex: 2005

[Covers persons 15 years old and over as of March 2006. (72,476, represents 72,476,000). Based on Current Population Survey; see text, Section 1, and Appendix III. For definition of median, see Guide to Tabular Presentation. Occupational classifications are those used in the 2000 census and are not comparable to those used in the 1990 census]

Major occupation of longest job held in 2005	All workers				Full-time, year-round			
	Women		Men		Women		Men	
	Number (1,000)	Median earnings (dol.)	Number (1,000)	Median earnings (dol.)	Number (1,000)	Median earnings (dol.)	Number (1,000)	Median earnings (dol.)
Total	72,476	23,074	82,934	34,349	43,351	31,858	61,500	41,386
Management, business, and financial occupations	9,126	41,484	12,422	61,030	7,142	46,795	10,736	65,767
Professional and related occupations . . .	17,234	35,520	12,959	52,774	10,800	42,012	10,112	61,025
Service occupations	15,374	12,658	11,520	19,139	7,066	20,733	7,021	26,706
Sales and office occupations.	25,154	21,665	14,141	31,093	14,967	29,286	10,139	40,106
Natural resources, construction, and maintenance	791	19,066	16,196	30,222	397	30,988	11,749	35,167
Production, transportation, and material moving occupations	4,704	18,206	15,020	29,434	2,905	22,893	11,152	34,597
Armed Forces	92	30,949	676	37,327	73	(B)	591	41,078

B Data not shown where base is less than 75,000.

Source: U.S. Census Bureau Internet site <http://pubdb3.census.gov/macro/032006/perinc/toc.htm>, Table PINC-06, "Occupation of Longest Job in 2005—People 15 years Old and Over, by Total Money Earnings in 2005, Work Experience in 2005 Race, Hispanic Origin, and Sex" (accessed 10 August 2007).

Table. 629. Employment Cost Index (ECI), Total Compensation by Occupation and Industry: 1985 to 2006

[As of December. The ECI is a measure of the rate of change in employee compensation (wages, salaries, and employer costs for employee benefits). Data are not seasonally adjusted: 1985 based on fixed employment counts from 1970 Census of Population; 1990 based on fixed employment counts from the 1980 Census of Population; 1995 to 2005, based primarily on 1990 Occupational Employment Statistics (OES) Survey; beginning in 2006, based primarily on 2002 OES Survey]

Item	Indexes (December 2005 = 100)						Percent change for 12 months ending Dec.—				
	1985	1990	1995	2000	2005	2006	1985	1990	1995	2000	2006
Civilian workers [1]	48.2	59.7	70.6	83.6	100.0	103.3	4.3	4.9	2.8	4.2	3.3
Workers, by occupational group:											
White-collar occupations	47.0	59.3	70.1	83.6	100.0	103.5	4.9	5.1	2.8	4.2	3.5
Blue-collar occupations	50.4	60.7	71.7	83.5	100.0	102.9	3.3	4.3	2.4	4.1	2.9
Service occupations	48.7	60.3	71.1	83.7	100.0	103.5	4.1	5.1	2.4	3.6	3.5
Workers, by industry division:											
Manufacturing	48.4	59.1	70.8	82.3	100.0	101.8	3.2	5.0	2.6	3.9	1.8
Nonmanufacturing:											
Service industries	46.5	61.0	71.6	84.3	100.0	103.5	4.7	6.3	2.3	3.9	3.5
Public administration [2]	46.6	59.4	70.1	81.0	100.0	103.8	4.7	5.3	3.4	2.7	3.8
State and local government. . . .	47.1	61.5	72.0	82.9	100.0	104.1	5.6	5.9	3.0	3.0	4.1
Workers, by occupational group:											
White-collar occupations	47.4	62.4	72.6	83.4	100.0	104.0	5.8	6.1	2.8	3.0	4.0
Blue-collar occupations	48.6	61.0	71.8	82.6	100.0	104.0	5.2	4.8	2.7	3.4	4.0
Workers, by industry division:											
Service industries	47.3	62.7	73.0	83.9	(NA)	(NA)	5.8	6.3	2.8	3.1	(NA)
Schools.	47.2	63.0	73.3	84.1	100.0	104.1	6.3	5.9	2.8	2.9	4.1
Elementary and secondary	47.5	63.7	73.9	84.1	100.0	104.2	6.3	6.3	2.8	2.7	4.2
Colleges and universities	(NA)	61.3	71.6	84.4	(NA)	(NA)	(NA)	5.3	2.6	3.6	(NA)
Services, excluding schools [3]	47.3	61.2	71.9	82.7	(NA)	(NA)	4.6	6.8	3.0	3.5	(NA)
Public administration [2]	46.6	59.4	70.1	81.0	100.0	103.8	4.7	5.3	3.4	2.7	3.8
Private industry workers [4]	48.4	59.3	70.2	83.6	100.0	103.2	3.9	4.6	2.5	4.2	3.2
Workers, by occupational group:											
White-collar occupations	47.0	58.4	69.4	83.6	100.0	103.3	4.9	4.8	2.8	4.6	3.3
Blue-collar occupations	50.5	60.7	71.7	83.6	100.0	102.8	3.1	4.3	2.4	4.2	2.8
Service occupations	50.9	61.8	72.1	85.3	100.0	103.1	3.0	4.7	1.8	3.9	3.1
Workers, by industry division:											
Manufacturing	48.4	59.1	70.8	82.3	100.0	101.8	3.2	5.0	2.6	3.9	1.8
Nonmanufacturing:											
Service industries	46.1	59.9	70.9	84.5	100.0	103.4	4.3	6.2	2.2	4.4	3.4
Business services	(NA)	59.2	69.7	87.4	100.0	103.5	(NA)	5.9	2.8	4.3	3.5
Health services	45.4	60.1	71.7	81.7	100.0	104.1	–	6.7	2.7	4.5	4.1
Hospitals	(NA)	58.0	68.9	79.2	100.0	103.9	(NA)	6.8	2.2	4.5	3.9
Workers, by bargaining status:											
Union.	49.8	58.6	70.5	81.1	100.0	103.0	2.7	4.3	2.8	4.0	3.0
Nonunion	47.9	59.5	70.2	84.1	100.0	103.2	4.6	4.8	2.6	4.3	3.2

– Represents or rounds to zero.   NA Not available.   [1] Includes private industry and state and local government workers and excludes farm, household, and federal government workers.   [2] Consists of executive, legislative, judicial, administrative, and regulatory activities.   [3] Includes library, social, and health services. Formerly called hospitals and other services.   [4] Excludes farm and household workers.

Source: U.S. Bureau of Labor Statistics, News, Employment Cost Index, quarterly; and Internet site <http://www.bls.gov/ncs/ect /home.htm>

Table 630. Federal Minimum Wage Rates: 1950 to 2009

Year	Current dollars	Year	Current dollars
1950	0.75	1980	3.10
1951	0.75	1981	3.35
1952	0.75	1982	3.35
1953	0.75	1983	3.35
1954	0.75	1984	3.35
1955	0.75	1985	3.35
1956	1.00	1986	3.35
1957	1.00	1987	3.35
1958	1.00	1988	3.35
1959	1.00	1989	3.35
1960	1.00	1990	3.80
1961	1.15	1991	4.25
1962	1.15	1992	4.25
1963	1.25	1993	4.25
1964	1.25	1994	4.25
1965	1.25	1995	4.25
1966	1.25	1996	4.75
1967	1.40	1997	5.15
1968	1.60	1998	5.15
1969	1.60	1999	5.15
1970	1.60	2000	5.15
1971	1.60	2001	5.15
1972	1.60	2002	5.15
1973	1.60	2003	5.15
1974	2.00	2004	5.15
1975	2.10	2005	5.15
1976	2.30	2006	5.15
1977	2.30	2007	5.85
1978	2.65	2008	6.55
1979	2.90	2009	7.25

Source: U.S. Employment Standards Administration, Internet site: <http://www.dol.gov/esa/whd/flsa/>.

Table 631. Workers Paid Hourly Rates by Selected Characteristics: 2006

[Data are annual averages (76,514 represents 76,514,000). For employed wage and salary workers, excluding the incorporated self-employed. Based on the Current Population Survey; see text, Section 1, and Appendix III]

Characteristic	Number of workers paid hourly rates (1,000)			Number of workers at or below $5.15	
	Total	Below $5.15	At $5.15	Number (1,000)	Percent of hourly paid workers
Total, 16 years and over [1]	76,514	1,283	409	1,692	2.2
16 to 24 years	16,649	619	247	866	5.2
25 years and over	59,865	664	162	826	1.4
Male, 16 years and over	38,193	422	146	569	1.5
16 to 24 years	8,583	198	98	296	3.4
25 years and over	29,609	224	49	273	0.9
Women, 16 years and over	38,321	861	263	1,124	2.9
16 to 24 years	8,065	421	149	570	7.1
25 years and over	30,256	440	114	553	1.8
White [2]	61,907	1,105	329	1,435	2.3
Black [2]	9,903	111	62	173	1.8
Asian [2]	2,654	30	8	38	1.4
Hispanic origin [3]	13,121	155	68	223	1.7
Full-time workers	58,452	554	99	653	1.1
Part-time workers [4]	17,930	724	310	1,034	5.8
Private sector industries	67,106	1,213	376	1,589	2.4
Public sector industries	9,407	70	34	104	1.1

[1] Includes races not shown separately. Also includes a small number of multiple jobholders whose full- or part-time status can not be determined for their principal job. [2] For persons in this race group only. See footnote 3, Table 570. [3] Persons of Hispanic or Latino origin may be of any race. [4] Working fewer than 35 hours per week.

Source: U.S. Bureau of Labor Statistics, Employment and Earnings, January 2007. See Internet site <http://www.bls.gov/cps/home.htm>.

Labor Force, Employment, and Earnings 417

Table 632. Employer Costs for Employee Compensation Per Hour Worked: 2006

[In dollars. As of December, for civilian workers. Based on a sample of establishments from the National Compensation Survey; see source for details. See also Appendix III]

Compensation component	Total civilian workers	State and local govern- ment workers	Private industry workers						
			Total	Goods produc- ing [1]	Service provid- ing [2]	Union workers	Non- union workers	Full- time workers	Part- time workers
Total compensation	27.54	38.26	25.67	30.02	24.55	35.60	24.52	29.18	14.08
Wages and salaries	19.24	25.74	18.11	19.92	17.64	21.91	17.66	20.26	10.99
Total benefits	8.30	12.52	7.57	10.10	6.92	13.69	6.85	8.92	3.09
Paid leave............	1.94	2.99	1.76	1.92	1.71	2.81	1.63	2.15	0.46
Vacation	0.91	1.03	0.89	1.01	0.86	1.41	0.83	(NA)	(NA)
Holiday	0.63	0.96	0.58	0.68	0.55	0.84	0.55	(NA)	(NA)
Sick	0.30	0.75	0.22	0.16	0.23	0.37	0.20	(NA)	(NA)
Other	0.10	0.24	0.08	0.07	0.08	0.18	0.06	(NA)	(NA)
Supplemental pay........	0.69	0.32	0.75	1.17	0.65	1.13	0.71	0.91	0.23
Insurance	2.26	4.22	1.92	2.66	1.73	4.04	1.67	2.30	0.66
Health insurance......	2.13	4.09	1.79	2.48	1.61	3.79	1.55	(NA)	(NA)
Retirement and savings....	1.21	2.75	0.94	1.54	0.79	2.57	0.75	1.16	0.21
Defined benefit........	0.76	2.46	0.47	0.99	0.34	1.94	0.30	(NA)	(NA)
Defined contributions....	0.44	0.30	0.47	0.54	0.45	0.63	0.45	(NA)	(NA)
Legally required	2.20	2.23	2.20	2.81	2.04	3.15	2.09	2.41	1.52
Social security and Medicare	1.54	1.71	1.62	1.70	1.47	1.93	1.47	(NA)	(NA)
Social security......	1.23	1.31	1.22	1.37	1.18	1.55	1.18	(NA)	(NA)
Medicare	0.31	0.39	0.30	0.33	0.29	0.37	0.29	(NA)	(NA)
Federal unemployment...	0.03	0.00	0.03	0.03	0.03	0.03	0.03	(NA)	(NA)
State unemployment	0.15	0.06	0.16	0.21	0.15	0.23	0.16	(NA)	(NA)
Workers compensation....	0.48	0.47	0.49	0.87	0.39	0.96	0.43	(NA)	(NA)

NA Not available. [1] Based on the North American Industry Classification System, 2002 (NAICS). See text, this section. Includes mining, construction, and manufacturing. The agriculture, forestry, farming, and hunting sector is excluded. [2] Based on the 2002 NAICS. Includes utilities; wholesale and retail trade; transportation and warehousing; information; finance and insurance; real estate and rental and leasing; professional and technical services; management of companies and enterprises, administrative and waste services; education services; health care and social assistance; arts, entertainment, and recreation; accommodations and food services; and other services, except public administration.

Source: U.S. Bureau of Labor Statistics, Employer Costs for Employee Compensation, News, USDL 07-0453, March 29, 2007. See Internet site <http://www.bls.gov/ncs/ect/home.htm>.

Table 633. Percent of Workers in Private Industry With Access to Retirement and Health Care Benefits by Selected Characteristics: 2006

[As of March. Based on National Compensation Survey, a sample survey of 10,376 private industry establishments of all sizes, representing over 105 million workers; see Appendix III. See also Tables 149 and 150]

Characteristic	Retirement benefits			Healthcare benefits			
	All plans [1]	Defined benefit	Defined contri- bution	Medical care	Dental care	Vision care	Outpatient prescrip- tion drug coverage
Total........................	60	21	54	71	46	29	67
WORKER CHARACTERISTICS							
White-collar occupations	69	23	65	77	53	32	72
Blue-collar occupations	62	25	53	77	46	31	73
Service occupations	34	8	30	45	27	19	43
Full-time [2].........................	69	24	63	85	55	34	81
Part-time [2]	29	9	25	22	15	11	21
Union [3]..........................	84	70	50	89	69	54	86
Nonunion [3]	57	15	55	68	43	26	64
Average wage less than $15 per hour	47	11	43	57	34	20	54
Average wage $15 per hour or more	77	34	69	88	62	40	84
ESTABLISHMENT SIZE							
1 to 99 workers	44	9	41	59	31	20	56
100 or more workers..................	78	35	70	84	64	40	80

[1] Employees may have access to both defined benefit and defined contribution plans. Total excludes duplication. [2] Employees are classified according to working either a full-time or part-time schedule based on the definition used by each establishment. [3] Union workers are those whose wages are determined through collective bargaining.

Source: U.S. Bureau of Labor Statistics, Employee Benefits in Private Industry in the United States, March 2006, Summary 06-05, August 2006. See Internet site <http://www.bls.gov/ncs/ebs/home.htm>.

Table 634. Percent of Workers in Private Industry With Access to Selected Employee Benefits: 2006

[As of March. Based on National Compensation Survey. The NCS benefits survey obtained data from 10,376 private industry establishments of all sizes, representing over 105 million workers; see Appendix III. See also Tables 149 and 150. For explanation of benefits, see source]

Characteristic	Paid holidays	Paid vacation	Paid military leave	Family leave Paid	Family leave Unpaid	Employer assistance for child care Total	Employer-provided funds	On-site and off-site child care	Child care resource and referral services	Adoption assistance	Long-term care insurance	Flexible work plans[1]	Subsidized commuting[2]
Total	**76**	**77**	**48**	**8**	**82**	**15**	**3**	**5**	**11**	**10**	**12**	**4**	**5**
WORKER CHARACTERISTICS													
White-collar occupations	84	83	57	11	86	20	4	7	15	15	17	7	7
Blue-collar occupations	80	79	43	4	78	8	1	2	7	7	7	1	3
Service occupations	50	59	32	5	75	10	2	5	5	2	4	1	2
Full-time [3]	88	90	53	9	85	16	4	6	12	12	13	5	6
Part-time [3]	37	36	29	3	70	10	2	4	6	5	6	2	2
Union [4]	83	83	55	6	89	19	3	6	17	14	15	3	6
Nonunion [4]	75	77	47	8	81	14	3	5	10	10	11	4	5
Average wage less than $15 per hour	67	69	39	5	77	9	2	3	5	5	7	2	2
Average wage $15 per hour or more	88	88	60	11	88	22	4	8	17	16	18	7	8
ESTABLISHMENT SIZE													
1 to 99 workers	68	70	35	6	73	5	1	2	3	4	5	3	2
100 or more workers	86	86	62	10	92	26	5	9	19	17	20	5	8
GEOGRAPHIC AREAS [5]													
New England division	81	77	56	10	85	17	4	8	13	13	12	5	7
Middle Atlantic division	78	79	54	6	84	16	4	6	11	13	13	6	7
East North Central division	76	76	50	8	79	17	3	7	12	12	12	3	3
West North Central division	76	73	44	6	81	15	2	7	8	10	10	3	4
South Atlantic division	77	79	49	9	82	13	3	4	10	11	12	3	3
East South Central division	76	78	41	6	88	9	3	4	5	5	9	3	3
West South Central division	77	78	44	8	77	15	4	6	10	8	11	4	7
Mountain division	72	74	47	6	79	14	3	2	12	9	12	4	3
Pacific division	74	77	42	10	83	15	2	4	12	8	12	4	8

[1] Arrangements permitting employees to work at home several days of the workweek.   [2] Employers subsidize employees' cost of commuting to and from work via public transportation, company-sponsored van pool, discounted subway fares, etc.   [3] Employees are classified as working either a full-time or part-time schedule based on the definition used by each establishment.   [4] Union workers are those whose wages are determined through collective bargaining.   [5] For composition of divisions, see map, inside front cover.

Source: U.S. Bureau of Labor Statistics, *Employee Benefits in Private Industry in the United States, March 2006*, Summary 06-05, August 2006. See Internet site <http://www.bls.gov/ncs/ebs/home.htm>.

Labor Force, Employment, and Earnings   419

Table 635. **Workers Killed or Disabled on the Job: 1970 to 2005**

[Data for 2005 are preliminary estimates (1.7 represents 1,700). Excludes homicides and suicides. Estimates based on data from the U.S. National Center for Health Statistics, state vital statistics departments, state industrial commissions, and beginning 1995, Bureau of Labor Statistics, Census of Occupational Fatalities. Numbers of workers based on data from the U.S. Bureau of Labor Statistics]

Year	Deaths Manufacturing Number (1,000)	Rate [1]	Non-manufacturing Number (1,000)	Rate [1]	Disabling injuries [2] (mil.)	Year and industry group	Deaths, 2005 Number	Rate [1]	Disabling injuries 2005 [2] (1,000)
1970 ...	1.7	9	12.1	21	2.2	Total, 2005 [3]	4,961	3.5	3,700
1975 ...	1.6	9	11.4	17	2.2	Agriculture [4]	696	31.6	80
1980 ...	1.7	8	11.5	15	2.2	Mining [5]	154	24.8	20
1985 ...	1.2	6	10.3	12	2.0	Construction.............	1,155	10.8	480
1990 ...	1.0	5	9.1	9	3.9	Manufacturing.............	358	2.2	450
1995 ...	0.6	3	4.4	4	3.6	Wholesale trade	192	4.2	130
1996 ...	0.7	3	4.4	4	3.9	Retail trade	197	1.2	470
1997 ...	0.7	3	4.5	4	3.8	Transportation and warehousing	827	16.6	270
1998 ...	0.6	3	4.5	4	3.8	Utilities	29	3.5	20
1999 ...	0.6	3	4.6	4	3.8	Information..............	57	1.8	40
2000 ...	0.6	3	4.4	4	3.9	Financial activities [6]	65	0.7	90
2001 ...	0.5	3	4.5	4	3.9	Professional & business services [6] ...	441	3.2	180
2002 ...	0.5	3	4.2	3	3.7	Educational & health services	119	0.6	530
2003 ...	0.4	2	4.3	4	3.4	Leisure & hospitality [6]	112	1.0	240
2004 ...	0.4	3	4.5	4	3.7	Other services [7]	148	2.1	140
2005 ...	0.4	2	4.6	4	3.7	Government	404	1.9	560

[1] Per 100,000 workers. [2] Disabling injury defined as one which results in death, some degree of physical impairment, or renders the person unable to perform regular activities for a full day beyond the day of the injury. Due to change in methodology, data beginning 1990 not comparable with prior years. [3] Includes deaths where industry is not known. [4] Includes forestry, fishing, and hunting. [5] Includes oil and gas extraction. [6] For composition of industry, see Table 613. [7] Excludes public service administration.

Source: National Safety Council, Itasca, IL, *Accident Facts*, annual through 1998 edition; thereafter, *Injury Facts*, annual (copyright).

Table 636. **Worker Deaths, Injuries, and Production Time Lost: 1995 to 2005**

[45.7 represents 45,700. Data may not agree with Table 638 because data here are not revised]

Item	Deaths 1,000) 1995	2000	2005	Disabling injuries [1] (mil.) 1995	2000	2005	Production time lost (mil. days) In the current year 1995	2000	2005	In future years [2] 1995	2000	2005
All accidents	45.7	47.0	54.3	9.9	10.5	11.9	225	240	275	455	460	535
On the job	5.3	5.2	5.0	3.6	3.9	3.7	75	80	80	65	60	65
Off the job	40.4	41.8	49.3	6.3	6.6	8.2	150	160	195	390	400	470
Motor vehicle.........	22.9	22.8	24.1	1.2	1.2	1.3	(NA)	(NA)	(NA)	(NA)	(NA)	(NA)
Public nonmotor vehicle..	7.5	8.3	10.0	2.3	2.8	3.3	(NA)	(NA)	(NA)	(NA)	(NA)	(NA)
Home...........	10.0	10.7	15.2	2.8	2.6	3.6	(NA)	(NA)	(NA)	(NA)	(NA)	(NA)

NA Not available. [1] See footnote 2, Table 635, for a definition of disabling injuries. [2] Based on an average of 5,850 days lost in future years per fatality and 565 days lost in future years per permanent injury.
Source: National Safety Council, Itasca, IL, *Accident Facts*, annual through 1998 edition; thereafter, *Injury Facts*, annual (copyright).

Table 637. **Industries With the Highest Total Case Incidence Rates for Nonfatal Injuries and Illnesses: 2005**

[Rates per 100 full-time employees. Rates refer to any Occupational Safety and Health Administration (OSHA)-recordable occupational injury or illness, whether or not it resulted in days away from work, job transfer or restriction. Incidence rates were calculated as: Number of injuries and illnesses divided by total hours worked by all employees during the year multiplied by 200,000 as base for 100 full-time equivalent workers (working 40 hours per week, 50 weeks per year)]

Industry	2002 NAICS [1] code	Rate	Industry	2002 NAICS [1] code	Rate
Private industry [2]	(X)	4.6	Animal (except poultry) slaughtering.....	311611	12.6
Beet sugar manufacturing	311313	18.3	Couriers	4921	12.4
Light truck and utility vehicle mfg.......	336112	17.8	Aluminum die-casting foundries........	331521	12.1
Iron foundries	331511	17.1	Boat building	336612	12.1
Truck trailer manufacturing	336212	16.8	Hog and pig farming [2]	1122	12.0
Prefabricated wood building mfg.......	321992	14.3	Cut stone and stone product mfg.	327991	11.8
Travel trailer and camper mfg...........	336214	14.1	Steel wire drawing	331222	11.5
Flat glass manufacturing	327211	13.6	Glass container manufacturing	327213	11.3
Framing contractors	23813	13.4	Amusement parks and arcades........	7131	11.3
Truss manufacturing	321214	13.3	Secondary smelting and alloying		
Aluminum foundries (except die-casting)..	331524	13.3	of aluminum..........................	331314	11.2
Iron and steel forging	332111	13.3	Ship building and repairing	336611	10.9
Heavy duty truck manufacturing	33612	13.1	Glass and glazing contractors	2381	10.7
Manufactured home (mobile home) mfg....	321991	12.9			

X Not applicable. [1] Based on the North American Industry Classification System, 2002 (NAICS). See text, this section. [2] Excludes farms with fewer than 11 employees.
Source: U.S. Bureau of Labor Statistics, *Workplace Injuries and Illnesses in 2005*. See Internet site <http://www.bls.gov/iif/>.

Table 638. Nonfatal Occupational Injury and Illness Incidence Rates: 2005

[Rates per 100 full-time employees. Except as noted, data refer to any Occupational Safety and Health Administration (OSHA) recordable occupational injury or illness, whether or not it resulted in days away from work, job transfer, or restriction. Incidence rates were calculated as: Number of injuries and illnesses divided by total hours worked by all employees during the year multiplied by 200,000 as base for 100 full-time equivalent workers (working 40 hours, per week, 50 weeks per year)]

Industry	2002 NAICS code [1]	Rate	Industry	2002 NAICS code [1]	Rate
Private industry [2]	(X)	4.6	Truck transportation	484	6.1
Agriculture, forestry, fishing, hunting [2]	11	6.1	Support activities for transportation	488	5.5
Crop production [2]	111	5.7	Couriers and messengers	492	11.6
Mining [3]	21	3.6	Warehousing and storage	493	8.2
Construction	23	6.3	Utilities	22	4.6
Construction of buildings	236	5.3	Information	51	2.1
Heavy and civil engineering construction .	237	5.6	Telecommunications	517	2.6
Specialty trade contractors	238	6.8	Finance and insurance [4]	52	1.0
Manufacturing [4]	31–33	6.3	Credit intermediation and related		
Food manufacturing	311	7.7	activities	522	1.0
Wood product manufacturing	321	9.4	Insurance carriers and related activities . .	524	1.2
Paper manufacturing	322	4.4	Real estate and rental and leasing	53	3.7
Printing and related support activities. . . .	323	4.1	Real estate	531	3.3
Chemical manufacturing	325	3.2	Rental and leasing services	532	4.6
Plastics and rubber products mfg.	326	7.1	Professional, scientific, and technical		
Nonmetallic mineral product mfg.	327	8.0	services	54	1.4
Primary metal manufacturing	331	9.1	Management of companies and		
Fabricated metal product mfg.	332	8.0	enterprises	55	2.4
Machinery manufacturing	333	6.5	Administrative and support and waste		
Computer and electronic product mfg. . . .	334	2.0	management and remediation services . . .	56	3.7
Electrical equipment, appliance, and			Administrative and support services.	561	3.4
component manufacturing	335	5.2	Waste management and remediation		
Transportation equipment manufacturing .	336	8.3	services	562	7.1
Furniture and related product mfg.	337	7.3	Educational services	61	2.4
Miscellaneous manufacturing	339	4.4	Health care and social assistance	62	5.9
Wholesale trade [4]	42	4.5	Ambulatory health care services	621	2.8
Merchant wholesalers, durable goods . . .	423	4.1	Hospitals	622	8.1
Merchant wholesalers, nondurable goods .	424	5.7	Nursing and residential care facilities	623	9.1
Retail trade [4]	44–45	5.0	Social assistance	624	4.3
Motor vehicle and parts dealers	441	4.8	Arts, entertainment, and recreation	71	6.1
Furniture and home furnishings stores . . .	442	5.0	Amusement, gambling, and recreation		
Building material and garden equipment			industries	713	5.6
and supplies dealers.	444	7.5	Accommodation and food services	72	4.5
Food and beverage stores.	445	6.0	Accommodation	721	6.1
Gasoline stations	447	3.5	Food services and drinking places	722	4.1
Clothing and clothing accessories stores .	448	2.7	Other services, except public admin.	81	3.2
General merchandise stores	452	6.7	Repair and maintenance	811	4.0
Miscellaneous store retailers	453	3.6	Personal and laundry services	812	2.7
Transportation and warehousing [4, 5]	48–49	7.0	Religious, grantmaking, civic,		
Air transportation	481	9.9	professional, and similar organizations . .	813	2.7

X Not applicable.   [1] North American Industry Classification System, 2002; see text, this section.   [2] Excludes farms with fewer than 11 employees.   [3] Data for mining operators in coal, metal, and nonmetal mining are provided to BLS by the Mine Safety and Health Administration (MHSA), U.S. Department of Labor. Independent mining contractors are excluded. Data provided by MSHA do not reflect 2002 OSHA recordkeeping requirements; therefore, estimates for these industries are not comparable with estimates for other industries.   [4] Includes other industries, not shown separately.   [5] Data for employers in railroad transportation are provided to BLS by the Federal Railroad Administration, U.S. Department of Transportation.

Source: U.S. Bureau of Labor Statistics, *Workplace Injuries and Illnesses in 2005*. See Internet site <http://www.bls.gov/iif/>.

Table 639. Fatal Work Injuries by Event or Exposure: 2005

[For the 50 states and DC. Based on the Census of Fatal Occupational Injuries. For details, see source. Due to methodological differences, data differ from National Safety Council data.]

Cause	Number of fatalities	Percent distri- bution	Cause	Number of fatalities	Percent distri- bution
Total	5,734	100	Contacts with objects and equipment [1] .	1,005	18
			Struck by object [1]	607	11
Transportation accidents [1]	2,493	43	Struck by falling objects	385	7
Highway accidents [1]	1,437	25	Struck by flying object	53	1
Collision between vehicles,			Caught in or compressed by—		
mobile equipment	718	13	equipment or objects	278	5
Noncollision accidents	318	6	Caught in or crushed in		
Nonhighway accident (farm,			collapsing materials	109	2
industrial premises).	340	6	Falls	770	13
Aircraft accidents	149	3	Exposure to harmful substances or		
Workers struck by a vehicle	391	7	environments [1]	501	9
Water vehicle accidents.	88	2	Contact with electric current	251	4
Railway accidents.	83	1	Exposure to caustic, noxious,		
			or allergenic substances	136	2
Assaults and violent acts [1]	792	14	Oxygen deficiency	59	1
Homicides [1]	567	10	Drowning, submersion	48	1
Shooting	441	8	Fires and explosions	159	3
Stabbing	60	1	Other events and exposures	14	(Z)
Self-inflicted injury	180	3			

Z Less than 0.5 percent.   [1] Includes other causes, not shown separately.

Source: U.S. Bureau of Labor Statistics, "Census of Fatal Occupational Injuries (CFOI)—Current and Revised Data." See Internet site <http://www.bls.gov/iif/oshcfoi1.htm>.

U.S. Census Bureau, Statistical Abstract of the United States: 2008

Table 640. **Workplace Violence Incidence and Security Measures: 2005**

[In percent. Covers period September 2004 to June 2006. Based on establishment survey and subject to sampling error; see source for details]

Incident or security measure	All establish- ments	Industry			Employment size class				
		Private industry [1]	State govern- ment	Local govern- ment	1 to 10 employ- ees	11 to 49 employ- ees	50 to 249 employ- ees	250 to 999 employ- ees	1,000 or more employ- ees
Any workplace violence incidents	5.3	4.8	32.2	14.7	2.4	9.1	16.0	28.8	49.9
Criminal	2.2	2.1	8.7	3.7	1.4	3.5	4.7	6.8	17.2
Customer or client.	2.2	1.9	15.4	10.3	1.0	3.9	6.4	12.2	28.3
Co-worker	2.3	2.1	17.7	4.3	0.6	4.6	8.1	16.8	34.1
Domestic violence.	0.9	0.8	5.5	2.1	0.1	2.0	2.9	9.0	24.1
No incident	92.1	92.5	65.3	85.1	95.6	87.8	77.8	63.9	43.8
Selected types of security provided:									
Intruder/burglar systems. . .	41.8	42.1	29.1	35.5	35.7	53.9	57.5	54.2	61.0
Surveillance cameras.	22.6	22.2	45.2	32.7	17.0	29.2	47.9	69.1	77.9
Motion detectors	26.9	27.1	14.8	21.3	24.0	32.9	33.7	28.3	36.4
Metal detectors.	0.9	0.7	16.0	4.3	0.5	1.1	2.5	7.2	15.7
Electronic badges [2]	6.3	6.0	35.6	9.0	3.9	7.2	20.8	45.1	60.1
Security guards	9.5	9.1	48.6	10.5	6.4	11.7	24.8	53.9	65.3
Limited access [3]	30.7	30.0	58.0	50.7	26.0	35.9	52.5	68.3	83.2
Physical barriers [4]	13.4	13.1	27.2	23.6	10.2	18.2	24.5	33.5	46.5
Lighting of work areas	39.1	38.7	55.8	48.5	32.2	50.0	62.1	71.9	80.4
Workplace violence training provided:									
Any training	20.8	20.2	58.0	32.3	14.6	29.1	45.7	64.2	67.8
No training.	78.4	78.9	42.0	67.6	84.3	70.5	54.0	35.6	32.0

[1] Excludes farms with fewer than 11 employees. [2] Or ID scanner at entry or exit. [3] Secured entry/locked doors. [4] Between work areas and the public.

Source: U.S. Bureau of the Census, *Survey of Workplace Violence and Prevention, 2005 News*, USDL 06-1860, October, 27, 2006. See Internet site, <http://www.bls.gov/iif/home.htm>.

Table 641. **Work Stoppages: 1960 to 2006**

[896 represents 896,000. Excludes work stoppages involving fewer than 1,000 workers and lasting less than 1 day. Information is based on reports of labor disputes appearing in daily newspapers, trade journals, and other public sources. The parties to the disputes are contacted by telephone, when necessary, to clarify details of the stoppages]

Year	Number of stop- pages [1]	Workers involved [2] (1,000)	Days idle		Year	Number of stop- pages [1]	Workers involved [2] (1,000)	Days idle	
			Number [3] (1,000)	Percent estimated working time [4]				Number [3] (1,000)	Percent estimated working time [4]
1960	222	896	13,260	0.09	1989	51	452	16,996	0.07
1965	268	999	15,140	0.10	1990	44	185	5,926	0.02
1970	381	2,468	52,761	0.29	1991	40	392	4,584	0.02
1974	424	1,796	31,809	0.16	1992	35	364	3,989	0.01
1975	235	965	17,563	0.09	1993	35	182	3,981	0.01
1976	231	1,519	23,962	0.12	1994	45	322	5,021	0.02
1977	298	1,212	21,258	0.10	1995	31	192	5,771	0.02
1978	219	1,006	23,774	0.11	1996	37	273	4,889	0.02
1979	235	1,021	20,409	0.09	1997	29	339	4,497	0.01
1980	187	795	20,844	0.09	1998	34	387	5,116	0.02
1981	145	729	16,908	0.07	1999	17	73	1,996	0.01
1982	96	656	9,061	0.04	2000	39	394	20,419	0.06
1983	81	909	17,461	0.08	2001	29	99	1,151	(Z)
1984	62	376	8,499	0.04	2002	19	46	660	(Z)
1985	54	324	7,079	0.03	2003	14	129	4,091	0.01
1986	69	533	11,861	0.05	2004	17	171	3,344	0.01
1987	46	174	5,4,481	0.02	2005	22	100	1,736	0.01
1988	40	118	5,4,381	0.02	2006	20	70	2,688	0.01

Z Less than 0.005 percent. [1] Beginning in year indicated. [2] Workers counted more than once if involved in more than one stoppage during the year. [3] Resulting from all stoppages in effect in a year, including those that began in an earlier year. [4] Agricultural and government employees are included in the total working time; private household and forestry and fishery employees are excluded. [5] Revised since originally published.

Source: U.S. Bureau of Labor Statistics, *Major Work Stoppages in 2006, News*, USDL 07-0304, February 27, 2007. See Internet site <http://www.bls.gov/cba/>.

classifications—federal general government and government enterprises and state and local general government and government enterprises.

The estimates by industry are available in current dollars and are derived from the estimates of gross domestic income, which consists of three components—the compensation of employees, gross operating surplus, and taxes on production and imports, less subsidies. Real, or inflation-adjusted, estimates are also prepared.

Regional Economic Accounts—These accounts consist of estimates of state and local area personal income and of gross domestic product by state and are consistent with estimates of personal income and gross domestic product in the Bureau's national economic accounts. BEA's estimates of state and local area personal income provide a framework for analyzing individual state and local economies, and they show how the economies compare with each other. The *personal income* of a state and/or local area is the income received by, or on behalf of, the residents of that state or area. Estimates of labor and proprietors' earnings by place of work indicate the economic activity of business and government within that area, and estimates of personal income by place of residence indicate the income within the area that is available for spending. BEA prepares estimates for states, counties, metropolitan areas, and BEA economic areas.

Gross domestic product by state estimates measure the value added to the nation's production by the labor and property in each state. GDP by state is often considered the state counterpart of the nation's GDP. The GDP by state estimates provide the basis for analyzing the regional impacts of national economic trends. GDP by state is measured as the sum of the distributions by industry and state of the components of gross domestic income; that is, the sum of the costs incurred and incomes earned in the production of GDP by state. The GDP estimates are presented in current dollars and in real (chained dollars) for 63 industries.

Consumer Expenditure Survey—The Consumer Expenditure Survey program was begun in 1980. The principal objective of the survey is to collect current consumer expenditure data, which provide a continuous flow of data on the buying habits of American consumers. The data are necessary for future revisions of the Consumer Price Index.

The survey conducted by the Census Bureau for the Bureau of Labor Statistics consists of two components: (1) an interview panel survey in which the expenditures of consumer units are obtained in five interviews conducted every 3 months, and (2) a diary or recordkeeping survey completed by participating households for two consecutive 1-week periods.

Each component of the survey queries an independent sample of consumer units representative of the U.S. total population. Over 52 weeks of the year, 7,500 consumer units are sampled for the diary survey. Each consumer unit keeps a diary for two 1-week periods yielding approximately 15,000 diaries a year. The interview sample is selected on a rotating panel basis, targeted at 7,500 consumer units per quarter. Data are collected in 102 areas of the country that are representative of the U.S. total population. The survey includes students in student housing. Data from the two surveys are combined; integration is necessary to permit analysis of total family expenditures because neither the diary nor quarterly interview survey was designed to collect a complete account of consumer spending.

Distribution of money income to families and individuals—Money income statistics are based on data collected in various field surveys of income conducted since 1936. Since 1947, the Census Bureau has collected the data on an annual basis and published them in *Current Population Reports*, P60 Series. In each of the surveys, field representatives interview samples of the population with respect to income received during the previous year. *Money income* as defined by the Census Bureau differs from the BEA concept of "personal income." Data on consumer income collected in the CPS by

Income, Expenditures, Poverty, and Wealth **427**

the Census Bureau cover money income received (exclusive of certain money receipts such as capital gains) before payments for personal income taxes, social security, union dues, medicare deductions, etc. Therefore, money income does not reflect the fact that some families receive part of their income in the form of noncash benefits (see Section 11) such as food stamps, health benefits, and subsidized housing; that some farm families receive noncash benefits in the form of rent-free housing and goods produced and consumed on the farm; or that noncash benefits are also received by some nonfarm residents which often take the form of the use of business transportation and facilities, full or partial payments by business for retirement programs, medical and educational expenses, etc. These elements should be considered when comparing income levels. None of the aggregate income concepts (GDP, national income, or personal income) is exactly comparable with money income, although personal income is the closest.

Poverty—Families and unrelated individuals are classified as being above or below poverty following the Office of Management and Budget's Statistical Policy Directive 14. The Census Bureau uses a set of thresholds that vary by family size and composition.

The poverty calculation is based solely on money income and does not reflect the fact that many low-income persons receive noncash benefits such as food stamps, medicaid, and public housing. The original thresholds were based on the U.S. Department of Agriculture's 1961 Economy Food Plan and reflected the different consumption requirements of families. The poverty thresholds are updated every year to reflect changes in the Consumer Price Index. The following technical changes to the thresholds were made in 1981: (1) distinctions based on sex of householder were eliminated, (2) separate thresholds for farm families were dropped, and (3) the matrix was expanded to families of nine or more persons from the old cutoff of seven or more persons. These changes were incorporated in the calculation of poverty data beginning with 1981. Besides the Census Bureau Web site at <http://www.census .gov/hhes/www/poverty/poverty.html>, information on poverty guidelines and research may be found at the U.S. Department of Human Services Web site at <http://aspe.hhs.gov/poverty/index .shtml>.

In the recent past, the Census Bureau has published a number of technical papers and reports that presented experimental poverty estimates based on income definitions that counted the value of selected government noncash benefits. The Census Bureau has also published reports on aftertax income.

Statistical reliability—For a discussion of statistical collection and estimation, sampling procedures, and measures of statistical reliability pertaining to Census Bureau data, see Appendix III.

Table 642. **Labor Union Membership by Sector: 1983 to 2006**

[See headnote, Table 644. (17,717.4 represents 17,717,400)]

Sector	1983	1985	1990	1995	2000	2003	2004	2005	2006
TOTAL (1,000)									
Wage and salary workers:									
Union members	17,717.4	16,996.1	16,739.8	16,359.6	16,258.2	15,776.0	15,471.6	15,685.4	15,359.1
Covered by unions	20,532.1	19,358.1	19,057.8	18,346.3	17,944.1	17,448.4	17,087.3	17,223.4	16,860.2
Public sector workers:									
Union members.	5,737.2	5,743.1	6,485.0	6,927.4	7,110.5	7,324.1	7,267.1	7,430.4	7,377.8
Covered by unions.	7,112.2	6,920.6	7,691.4	7,986.6	7,975.6	8,184.7	8,131.1	8,261.8	8,172.4
Private sector workers:									
Union members.	11,980.2	11,253.0	10,254.8	9,432.1	9,147.7	8,451.8	8,204.5	8,255.0	7,981.3
Covered by unions.	13,419.9	12,437.5	11,366.4	10,359.8	9,968.5	9,263.7	8,956.2	8,961.6	8,687.7
PERCENT									
Wage and salary workers:									
Union members	20.1	18.0	16.1	14.9	13.5	12.9	12.5	12.5	12.0
Covered by unions	23.3	20.5	18.3	16.7	14.9	14.3	13.8	13.7	13.1
Public sector workers:									
Union members.	36.7	35.7	36.5	37.7	37.5	37.2	36.4	36.5	36.2
Covered by unions.	45.5	43.1	43.3	43.5	42.0	41.5	40.7	40.5	40.1
Private sector workers:									
Union members.	16.5	14.3	11.9	10.3	9.0	8.2	7.9	7.8	7.4
Covered by unions	18.5	15.9	13.2	11.3	9.8	9.8	9.0	8.6	8.1

Source: The Bureau of National Affairs, Inc., Washington, DC, *Union Membership and Earnings Data Book: Compilations from the Current Population Survey (2007 edition)*, (copyright by BNA PLUS); authored by Barry Hirsch of Georgia State University and David Macpherson of Florida State University. Internet sites <http://plusdocs.bna.com/LaborReports.aspx> and <http://www.unionstats.com>.

Table 643. **Union Members by Selected Characteristics: 2006**

[Annual averages of monthly data (128,237 represents 128,237,000). Covers employed wage and salary workers 16 years old and over. Excludes self-employed workers whose businesses are incorporated although they technically qualify as wage and salary workers. Based on Current Population Survey, see text, Section 1, and Appendix III]

	Employed wage and salary workers			Median usual weekly earnings [3] (dol.)			
		Percent					
Characteristic	Total (1,000)	Union members [1]	Represented by unions [2]	Total	Union members [1]	Represented by unions [2]	Not represented by unions
Total [4]	128,237	12.0	13.1	671	833	827	642
16 to 24 years old	19,538	4.4	5.0	409	526	523	404
25 to 34 years old	28,805	10.1	11.1	621	773	766	606
35 to 44 years old	30,526	13.1	14.3	748	853	849	728
45 to 54 years old	29,401	16.0	17.5	773	888	884	750
55 to 64 years old	16,095	16.0	17.6	765	882	883	741
65 years and over	3,872	8.5	9.5	583	675	667	573
Men	66,811	13.0	14.0	743	887	885	717
Women	61,426	10.9	12.2	600	758	753	579
White [5]	104,668	11.7	12.8	690	859	854	659
Men	55,459	12.8	13.8	761	909	907	735
Women	49,209	10.5	11.7	609	777	772	588
Black [5]	14,878	14.5	16.1	554	707	694	520
Men	6,788	15.6	17.1	591	745	734	557
Women	8,090	13.7	15.2	519	665	656	502
Asian [5]	5,703	10.4	11.5	784	834	840	774
Men	3,015	9.5	10.5	882	838	852	888
Women	2,688	11.4	12.7	699	828	824	681
Hispanic [6]	18,121	9.8	10.7	486	686	681	469
Men	10,842	9.8	10.6	505	732	724	490
Women	7,279	9.7	10.9	440	607	614	420
Private sector industry	107,846	7.4	8.1	645	792	785	631
Agriculture and related industries.	1,059	2.3	2.6	422	(B)	(B)	420
Mining	632	7.5	8.8	912	(B)	1,044	899
Construction	8,444	13.0	13.6	642	969	956	610
Manufacturing	15,643	11.7	12.5	702	755	753	692
Wholesale and retail trade	19,245	5.0	5.3	578	637	632	575
Transportation and utilities	5,299	23.2	24.3	739	876	876	697
Information	3,105	12.0	13.0	871	998	990	841
Financial activities [7]	8,841	1.9	2.3	757	674	691	759
Professional and business services [7]	11,398	2.4	2.9	749	744	752	749
Education and health services [7]	17,853	8.3	9.5	648	751	745	635
Leisure and hospitality [7]	10,638	3.1	3.5	417	538	533	412
Other services	5,689	3.1	3.5	568	816	794	550
Public sector.	20,392	36.2	40.1	773	871	865	717

B Data not shown where base is less than 50,000. [1] Members of a labor union or an employee association similar to a labor union. [2] Members of a labor union or an employee association similar to a union as well as workers who report no union affiliation but whose jobs are covered by a union or an employee association contract. [3] For full-time employed wage and salary workers. [4] Includes races not shown separately. Also includes a small number of multiple jobholders whose full- and part-time status can not be determined for their principal job. [5] For persons in this race group only. See footnote 3, Table 570. [6] Persons of Hispanic or Latino ethnicity may be of any race. [7] For composition of industries, see Table 607.

Source: U.S. Bureau of Labor Statistics, *Employment and Earnings*, January 2007. See Internet site <http://www.bls.gov/cps/home.htm>.

Labor Force, Employment, and Earnings 423

Table 644. Labor Union Membership by State: 1983 and 2006

[Annual averages of monthly figures (17,717.4 represents 17,717,400). For wage and salary workers in agriculture and non-agriculture. Data represent union members by place of residence. Based on the Current Population Survey and subject to sampling error. For methodological details, see source]

State	Union members (1,000)		Workers covered by unions (1,000)		Percent of workers					
					Union members		Covered by unions		Private sector union members	
	1983	2006	1983	2006	1983	2006	1983	2006	1983	2006
United States.....	17,717.4	15,359.1	20,532.1	16,860.2	20.1	12.0	23.3	13.1	16.5	7.4
Alabama [1]..........	228.2	170.1	268.2	194.0	16.9	8.8	19.8	10.0	15.3	4.6
Alaska ., ...	41.7	62.1	49.2	66.6	24.9	22.2	29.3	23.8	17.3	12.3
Arizona [1]	125.0	196.9	156.4	249.8	11.4	7.6	14.3	9.7	8.6	4.4
Arkansas [1]	82.2	58.1	103.2	67.5	11.0	5.1	13.8	6.0	10.2	4.0
California	2,118.9	2,273.4	2,505.2	2,444.1	21.9	15.7	25.9	16.9	17.7	9.0
Colorado........	177.9	165.0	209.6	186.1	13.6	7.7	16.0	8.6	11.2	5.0
Connecticut.........	314.0	247.5	345.1	262.8	22.7	15.6	25.0	16.5	16.7	8.0
Delaware	49.2	42.6	54.1	45.1	20.1	10.8	22.1	11.4	15.9	5.8
District of Columbia	52.4	25.4	69.4	30.1	19.5	10.3	25.9	12.2	15.2	6.7
Florida [1]	393.7	397.0	532.9	497.4	10.2	5.2	13.8	6.5	7.1	2.3
Georgia [1]	267.0	175.8	345.1	229.7	11.9	4.4	15.3	5.8	11.1	3.4
Hawaii, ...	112.6	139.0	124.9	145.6	29.2	24.7	32.4	25.9	21.9	16.1
Idaho [1]	41.3	37.4	53.7	44.8	12.5	6.0	16.2	7.2	10.3	4.0
Illinois	1,063.8	931.2	1,205.1	979.3	24.2	16.4	27.4	17.2	21.5	11.1
Indiana...........	503.3	334.1	544.5	362.4	24.9	12.0	27.0	13.0	25.0	9.5
Iowa [1]	185.9	160.7	231.3	199.4	17.2	11.3	21.5	14.0	14.6	7.3
Kansas [1]	125.2	98.8	170.4	114.9	13.7	8.0	18.7	9.3	12.2	5.4
Kentucky , ...	223.7	172.1	259.8	196.3	17.9	9.8	20.8	11.2	18.2	8.5
Louisiana [1]	204.2	107.0	267.8	121.2	13.8	6.4	18.1	7.2	11.0	4.7
Maine...........	88.0	69.3	100.4	78.9	21.0	11.9	24.0	13.5	14.2	5.3
Maryland	346.5	342.4	423.1	386.5	18.5	13.1	22.6	14.8	14.4	7.5
Massachusetts.......	603.2	413.8	661.4	438.4	23.7	14.5	26.0	15.3	17.6	8.2
Michigan..........	1,005.4	841.8	1,084.6	878.6	30.4	19.6	32.8	20.4	25.3	13.7
Minnesota, ...	393.9	395.5	439.4	416.4	23.2	16.0	25.9	16.8	17.1	9.7
Mississippi [1]	79.4	60.0	99.7	77.6	9.9	5.6	12.5	7.3	9.0	4.1
Missouri	374.4	284.2	416.7	310.3	20.8	10.9	23.2	11.9	21.5	9.4
Montana.	49.5	48.3	55.5	52.2	18.3	12.2	20.5	13.1	14.8	5.5
Nebraska [1]	80.6	65.9	94.8	78.8	13.6	7.9	16.0	9.5	9.7	4.4
Nevada [1]	90.0	166.5	106.7	191.5	22.4	14.8	26.6	17.0	19.6	12.5
New Hampshire	48.5	62.9	60.8	70.1	11.5	10.1	14.4	11.3	7.5	4.4
New Jersey.........	822.1	770.3	918.2	825.3	26.9	20.1	30.0	21.6	21.1	11.2
New Mexico	52.6	62.2	70.6	91.6	11.8	7.8	15.8	11.5	10.1	4.9
New York , . , ...	2,155.6	1,981.3	2,385.9	2,060.2	32.5	24.4	36.0	25.4	24.0	14.7
North Carolina [1]	178.7	125.6	238.1	155.1	7.6	3.3	10.2	4.1	5.4	1.8
North Dakota [1].......	28.4	20.3	35.1	24.0	13.2	6.8	16.3	8.0	9.5	3.7
Ohio	1,011.0	733.7	1,125.0	801.3	25.1	14.2	27.9	15.5	22.5	9.3
Oklahoma [2]........	131.5	92.8	168.2	112.4	11.5	6.4	14.7	7.7	9.1	3.5
Oregon...........	222.9	210.7	261.9	224.6	22.3	13.8	26.2	14.7	16.4	7.5
Pennsylvania........	1,195.7	744.5	1,350.0	802.3	27.5	13.6	31.1	14.7	23.2	8.0
Rhode Island........	85.8	76.3	93.7	79.5	21.5	15.3	23.5	16.0	13.7	7.8
South Carolina [1]	69.6	58.7	100.6	74.3	5.9	3.3	8.6	4.2	3.9	2.2
South Dakota [1]	26.8	20.8	34.8	25.1	11.5	5.9	14.9	7.2	8.0	2.8
Tennessee [1]	252.4	153.0	300.9	174.0	15.1	6.0	18.0	6.8	12.4	3.1
Texas [1]	583.7	476.2	712.8	575.8	9.7	4.9	11.9	5.9	8.1	2.8
Utah [1]	81.6	60.7	100.9	68.5	15.2	5.4	18.9	6.1	11.3	2.7
Vermont, ...	25.9	33.7	31.5	39.3	12.6	11.0	15.3	12.9	6.7	5.0
Virginia [1]	268.3	139.5	346.1	179.3	11.7	4.0	15.1	5.2	10.2	3.1
Washington.........	419.9	548.5	499.7	582.6	27.1	19.8	32.3	21.0	22.0	12.5
West Virginia........	142.7	100.7	160.6	110.1	25.3	14.2	28.5	15.5	26.1	10.3
Wisconsin, ...	465.5	385.5	526.7	415.2	23.8	14.9	26.9	16.1	19.8	9.0
Wyoming [1]	27.1	19.4	31.8	23.5	13.9	8.3	16.2	10.0	10.4	6.1

[1] Right to work state. [2] Passed right to work law in 2001.

Source: The Bureau of National Affairs (BNA), Inc., Washington, DC, *Union Membership and Earnings Data Book: Compilations from the Current Population Survey (2007 edition),* (copyright by BNA PLUS); authored by Barry Hirsch of Georgia State University and David Macpherson of Florida State University. Internet sites <http://bnaplus.bna.com/LaborReports.aspx> and <http://www.unionstats.com>.

Section 13
Income, Expenditures, Poverty, and Wealth

This section presents data on gross domestic product (GDP), gross national product (GNP), national and personal income, saving and investment, money income, poverty, and national and personal wealth. The data on income and expenditures measure two aspects of the U.S. economy. One aspect relates to the National Income and Product Accounts (NIPA), a summation reflecting the entire complex of the nation's economic income and output and the interaction of its major components; the other relates to the distribution of money income to families and individuals or consumer income.

The primary source for data on GDP, GNP, national and personal income, gross saving and investment, and fixed assets and consumer durables is the *Survey of Current Business*, published monthly by the Bureau of Economic Analysis (BEA). A comprehensive revision to the NIPA was released beginning in December 2003. Discussions of the revision appeared in the January, June, August, September, and December 2003 issues of the *Survey of Current Business*. Summary historical estimates appeared in the February 2004 issue of the *Survey of Current Business*. Detailed historical data can be found on BEA's Web site at <http://www.bea.gov/>.

Sources of income distribution data are the decennial censuses of population, the Current Population Survey (CPS), and the American Community Survey, all products of the U.S. Census Bureau (see text, Section 1 and Section 4). Annual data on income of families, individuals, and households are presented in *Current Population Reports, Consumer Income*, P60 Series, in print. Many data series are also found on the Census Web site at <http://www.census.gov/hhes/www/income.html>. Data on the household sector's saving and assets are published by the Board of Governors of the Federal Reserve System in the quarterly statistical release *Flow of Funds Accounts*. The Federal Reserve Board also periodically conducts the *Survey of Consumer Finances*, which presents financial information on family assets and net worth. Detailed information on personal wealth is published periodically by the Internal Revenue Service (IRS) in *SOI Bulletin*.

National income and product—Gross domestic product is the total output of goods and services produced by labor and property located in the United States, valued at market prices. GDP can be viewed in terms of the expenditure categories that comprise its major components: purchases of goods and services by consumers and government, gross private domestic investment, and net exports of goods and services. The goods and services included are largely those bought for final use (excluding illegal transactions) in the market economy. A number of inclusions, however, represent imputed values, the most important of which is the rental value of owner-occupied housing. GDP, in this broad context, measures the output attributable to the factors of production located in the United States. Gross domestic product by state is the gross market value of the goods and services attributable to labor and property located in a state. It is the state counterpart of the nation's gross domestic product.

The featured measure of real GDP is an index based on chain-type annual weights. Changes in this measure of real output and prices are calculated as the average of changes based on weights for the current and preceding years. (Components of real output are weighted by price, and components of prices are weighted by output.) These annual changes are "chained" (multiplied) together to form a time series that allows for the effects of changes in relative prices and changes in the composition of output over time. Quarterly and monthly changes are based on quarterly and

U.S. Census Bureau, Statistical Abstract of the United States: 2008

monthly weights, respectively. The new output indexes are expressed as 2000 = 100, and for recent years, in 2000 dollars; the price indexes are also based to 2000 = 100. For more information on chained-dollar indexes, see the article on this subject in the November 2003 issue of the *Survey of Current Business.*

Chained (2000) dollar estimates of most components of GDP are not published for periods prior to 1990, because during periods far from the base period, the levels of the components may provide misleading information about their contributions to an aggregate. Values are published in index form (2000 = 100) for 1929 to the present to allow users to calculate the percent changes for all components, which are accurate for all periods. In addition, BEA publishes estimates of contributions of major components to the percent change in GDP for all periods.

Gross national product measures the output attributable to all labor and property supplied by United States residents. GNP differs from "national income" mainly in that GNP includes allowances for depreciation—that is, consumption of fixed capital.

National Income includes all net incomes net of consumption of fixed capital (CFC), earned in production. National income is the sum of compensation of employees, proprietors' income with inventory valuation adjustment (IVA) and capital consumption adjustment (CCAdj), rental income of persons with CCAdj, corporate profits with IVA and CCAdj, net interest and miscellaneous payments, taxes on production and imports, business current transfer payments (net), current surplus of government enterprises, less subsidies.

Capital consumption adjustment for corporations and for nonfarm sole proprietorships and partnerships is the difference between capital consumption based on income tax returns and capital consumption measured using empirical evidence on prices of used equipment and structures in resale markets, which have shown that depreciation for most types of assets approximates a geometric pattern. The tax return data are valued at historical costs and reflect changes over time in

service lives and depreciation patterns as permitted by tax regulations. *Inventory valuation adjustment* represents the difference between the book value of inventories used up in production and the cost of replacing them.

Personal income is the current income received by persons from all sources minus their personal contributions for government social insurance. Classified as "persons" are individuals (including owners of unincorporated firms), nonprofit institutions that primarily serve individuals, private trust funds, and private noninsured welfare funds. Personal income includes personal current transfer receipts (payments not resulting from current production) from government and business such as social security benefits, public assistance, etc., but excludes transfers among persons. Also included are certain nonmonetary types of income chiefly, estimated net rental value to owner-occupants of their homes and the value of services furnished without payment by financial intermediaries. Capital gains (and losses) are excluded.

Disposable personal income is personal income less personal current taxes. It is the income available to persons for spending or saving. Personal current taxes are tax payments (net of refunds) by persons (except personal contributions for government social insurance) that are not chargeable to business expense. Personal taxes include income taxes, personal property taxes, motor vehicle licenses, and other miscellaneous taxes.

Gross domestic product by industry—The BEA also prepares estimates of value added by industry. *Value added* is a measure of the contribution of each private industry and of government to the nation's GDP. It is defined as an industry's gross output (which consists of sales or receipts and other operating income, commodity taxes, and inventory change) minus its intermediate inputs (which consists of energy, raw materials, semi-finished goods, and services that are purchased from domestic industries or from foreign sources). These estimates of value added are produced for 61 private industries and for 4 government

426 Income, Expenditures, Poverty, and Wealth

the Census Bureau cover money income received (exclusive of certain money receipts such as capital gains) before payments for personal income taxes, social security, union dues, medicare deductions, etc. Therefore, money income does not reflect the fact that some families receive part of their income in the form of noncash benefits (see Section 11) such as food stamps, health benefits, and subsidized housing; that some farm families receive noncash benefits in the form of rent-free housing and goods produced and consumed on the farm; or that noncash benefits are also received by some nonfarm residents which often take the form of the use of business transportation and facilities, full or partial payments by business for retirement programs, medical and educational expenses, etc. These elements should be considered when comparing income levels. None of the aggregate income concepts (GDP, national income, or personal income) is exactly comparable with money income, although personal income is the closest.

Poverty—Families and unrelated individuals are classified as being above or below poverty following the Office of Management and Budget's Statistical Policy Directive 14. The Census Bureau uses a set of thresholds that vary by family size and composition.

The poverty calculation is based solely on money income and does not reflect the fact that many low-income persons receive noncash benefits such as food stamps, medicaid, and public housing. The original thresholds were based on the U.S. Department of Agriculture's 1961 Economy Food Plan and reflected the different consumption requirements of families. The poverty thresholds are updated every year to reflect changes in the Consumer Price Index. The following technical changes to the thresholds were made in 1981: (1) distinctions based on sex of householder were eliminated, (2) separate thresholds for farm families were dropped, and (3) the matrix was expanded to families of nine or more persons from the old cutoff of seven or more persons. These changes were incorporated in the calculation of poverty data beginning with 1981. Besides the Census Bureau Web site at <http://www.census.gov/hhes/www/poverty/poverty.html>, information on poverty guidelines and research may be found at the U.S. Department of Human Services Web site at <http://aspe.hhs.gov/poverty/index.shtml>.

In the recent past, the Census Bureau has published a number of technical papers and reports that presented experimental poverty estimates based on income definitions that counted the value of selected government noncash benefits. The Census Bureau has also published reports on aftertax income.

Statistical reliability—For a discussion of statistical collection and estimation, sampling procedures, and measures of statistical reliability pertaining to Census Bureau data, see Appendix III.

classifications—federal general government and government enterprises and state and local general government and government enterprises.

The estimates by industry are available in current dollars and are derived from the estimates of gross domestic income, which consists of three components—the compensation of employees, gross operating surplus, and taxes on production and imports, less subsidies. Real, or inflation-adjusted, estimates are also prepared.

Regional Economic Accounts—These accounts consist of estimates of state and local area personal income and of gross domestic product by state and are consistent with estimates of personal income and gross domestic product in the Bureau's national economic accounts. BEA's estimates of state and local area personal income provide a framework for analyzing individual state and local economies, and they show how the economies compare with each other. The *personal income* of a state and/or local area is the income received by, or on behalf of, the residents of that state or area. Estimates of labor and proprietors' earnings by place of work indicate the economic activity of business and government within that area, and estimates of personal income by place of residence indicate the income within the area that is available for spending. BEA prepares estimates for states, counties, metropolitan areas, and BEA economic areas.

Gross domestic product by state estimates measure the value added to the nation's production by the labor and property in each state. GDP by state is often considered the state counterpart of the nation's GDP. The GDP by state estimates provide the basis for analyzing the regional impacts of national economic trends. GDP by state is measured as the sum of the distributions by industry and state of the components of gross domestic income; that is, the sum of the costs incurred and incomes earned in the production of GDP by state. The GDP estimates are presented in current dollars and in real (chained dollars) for 63 industries.

Consumer Expenditure Survey—The Consumer Expenditure Survey program was begun in 1980. The principal objective of the survey is to collect current consumer expenditure data, which provide a continuous flow of data on the buying habits of American consumers. The data are necessary for future revisions of the Consumer Price Index.

The survey conducted by the Census Bureau for the Bureau of Labor Statistics consists of two components: (1) an interview panel survey in which the expenditures of consumer units are obtained in five interviews conducted every 3 months, and (2) a diary or recordkeeping survey completed by participating households for two consecutive 1-week periods.

Each component of the survey queries an independent sample of consumer units representative of the U.S. total population. Over 52 weeks of the year, 7,500 consumer units are sampled for the diary survey. Each consumer unit keeps a diary for two 1-week periods yielding approximately 15,000 diaries a year. The interview sample is selected on a rotating panel basis, targeted at 7,500 consumer units per quarter. Data are collected in 102 areas of the country that are representative of the U.S. total population. The survey includes students in student housing. Data from the two surveys are combined; integration is necessary to permit analysis of total family expenditures because neither the diary nor quarterly interview survey was designed to collect a complete account of consumer spending.

Distribution of money income to families and individuals—Money income statistics are based on data collected in various field surveys of income conducted since 1936. Since 1947, the Census Bureau has collected the data on an annual basis and published them in *Current Population Reports*, P60 Series. In each of the surveys, field representatives interview samples of the population with respect to income received during the previous year. *Money income* as defined by the Census Bureau differs from the BEA concept of "personal income." Data on consumer income collected in the CPS by

Income, Expenditures, Poverty, and Wealth 427

[In billions of dollars (526 represents $526,000,000,000). For explanation of gross domestic product and chained dollars, see text, this section. Minus sign (–) indicates net imports]

Item	1960	1970	1980	1990	1994	1995	1996	1997	1998	1999	2000	2001	2002	2003	2004	2005	2006
CURRENT DOLLARS																	
Gross domestic product.....	526	1,039	2,790	5,803	7,072	7,398	7,817	8,304	8,747	9,268	9,817	10,128	10,470	10,961	11,713	12,456	13,247
Personal consumption expenditures	332	649	1,757	3,840	4,743	4,976	5,257	5,547	5,880	6,283	6,739	7,055	7,351	7,704	8,212	8,742	9,269
Durable goods	43	85	214	474	582	612	653	693	750	818	863	884	924	943	986	1,033	1,070
Nondurable goods	153	272	696	1,250	1,437	1,485	1,556	1,619	1,684	1,805	1,947	2,017	2,080	2,190	2,345	2,539	2,715
Services	136	292	847	2,116	2,724	2,879	3,049	3,236	3,446	3,660	3,929	4,154	4,347	4,571	4,880	5,170	5,484
Gross private domestic investment	79	152	479	861	1,097	1,144	1,240	1,390	1,509	1,626	1,736	1,614	1,582	1,664	1,888	2,057	2,213
Fixed investment	76	150	486	846	1,033	1,113	1,210	1,318	1,438	1,559	1,679	1,646	1,570	1,650	1,831	2,036	2,163
Change in private inventories	3	2	-6	15	64	31	31	72	71	67	57	-32	12	14	57	21	50
Net exports of goods and services	4	4	-13	-78	-94	-91	-96	-102	-160	-261	-380	-367	-424	-499	-613	-717	-763
Exports	27	60	281	552	721	812	869	955	956	991	1,096	1,033	1,006	1,041	1,178	1,303	1,466
Imports	23	56	294	630	815	904	965	1,057	1,116	1,252	1,476	1,400	1,430	1,540	1,791	2,020	2,229
Government consumption expenditures and gross investment	112	234	566	1,180	1,326	1,369	1,416	1,469	1,518	1,621	1,722	1,826	1,961	2,093	2,226	2,373	2,528
Federal	64	114	244	508	519	519	527	531	530	556	579	613	680	756	826	878	927
National defense	53	88	168	374	354	349	355	350	346	361	370	393	437	497	551	589	621
Nondefense	11	26	76	134	166	171	173	181	185	195	209	220	243	259	275	289	306
State and local	48	120	322	672	806	850	889	938	988	1,065	1,143	1,213	1,282	1,336	1,400	1,494	1,601
CHAINED (2000) DOLLARS																	
Gross domestic product.....	2,502	3,772	5,162	7,113	7,836	8,032	8,329	8,704	9,067	9,470	9,817	9,891	10,049	10,301	10,704	11,049	11,415
Personal consumption expenditures	1,597	2,452	3,374	4,770	5,291	5,434	5,619	5,832	6,126	6,439	6,739	6,910	7,099	7,295	7,577	7,841	8,091
Durable goods	(NA)	(NA)	(NA)	454	529	553	596	647	720	805	863	901	965	1,021	1,086	1,145	1,203
Nondurable goods	(NA)	(NA)	(NA)	1,484	1,604	1,639	1,680	1,725	1,794	1,877	1,947	1,987	2,037	2,103	2,179	2,277	2,362
Services	(NA)	(NA)	(NA)	2,852	3,177	3,260	3,356	3,468	3,615	3,758	3,929	4,023	4,100	4,179	4,324	4,437	4,550
Gross private domestic investment	267	427	645	895	1,100	1,134	1,234	1,388	1,524	1,643	1,736	1,598	1,557	1,613	1,771	1,866	1,946
Fixed investment	(NA)	(NA)	(NA)	887	1,042	1,110	1,209	1,321	1,455	1,576	1,679	1,629	1,545	1,597	1,714	1,842	1,895
Change in private inventories	(NA)	(NA)	(NA)	15	64	30	29	71	73	69	57	-13	12	14	53	20	43
Net exports of goods and services	91	161	324	-55	-79	-71	-80	-105	-204	-296	-380	-399	-471	-519	-591	-619	-618
Exports	103	213	311	553	707	778	843	944	967	1,008	1,096	1,037	1,013	1,026	1,120	1,196	1,303
Imports	(NA)	(NA)	(NA)	607	786	849	923	1,048	1,170	1,304	1,476	1,436	1,485	1,545	1,711	1,815	1,921
Government consumption expenditures and gross investment	715	1,013	1,115	1,530	1,541	1,550	1,565	1,594	1,624	1,687	1,722	1,780	1,859	1,905	1,941	1,958	1,998
Federal	(NA)	(NA)	(NA)	659	596	580	574	568	561	574	579	601	643	687	717	728	742
National defense	(NA)	(NA)	(NA)	479	405	389	384	373	365	372	370	385	413	449	475	484	493
Nondefense	(NA)	(NA)	(NA)	179	192	191	190	195	196	202	209	217	230	238	241	244	249
State and local	(NA)	(NA)	(NA)	868	943	968	991	1,026	1,063	1,113	1,143	1,179	1,215	1,218	1,224	1,230	1,256
Residual	-65	-68	14	-91	-64	-51	-39	-24	-15	-6	–	2	3	3	–	-11	-26

– Represents or rounds to zero. NA Not available.

Source: U.S. Bureau of Economic Analysis, Survey of Current Business, April 2007. See also <http://www.bea.gov/national/nipaweb/SelectTable.asp?Selected=N>.

Income, Expenditures, Poverty, and Wealth   429

U.S. Census Bureau. Statistical Abstract of the United States: 2008

Table 646. GDP Components in Real (2000) Dollars—Annual Percent Change: 1990 to 2006

[Change from immediate previous year; for example, 1990, change from 1989. Minus sign (–) indicates decrease]

Component	1990	1995	1999	2000	2001	2002	2003	2004	2005	2006
Gross domestic product (GDP)...	1.9	2.5	4.5	3.7	0.8	1.6	2.5	3.9	3.2	3.3
Personal consumption expenditures	2.0	2.7	5.1	4.7	2.5	2.7	2.8	3.9	3.5	3.2
Durable goods.................	-0.3	4.4	11.7	7.3	4.3	7.1	5.8	6.4	5.5	5.0
Nondurable goods	1.6	2.2	4.6	3.8	2.0	2.5	3.2	3.6	4.5	3.7
Services....................	2.9	2.6	4.0	4.5	2.4	1.9	1.9	3.5	2.6	2.6
Gross private domestic investment	-3.4	3.1	7.8	5.7	-7.9	-2.6	3.6	9.8	5.4	4.3
Fixed investment	-2.1	6.5	8.3	6.5	-3.0	-5.2	3.4	7.3	7.5	2.9
Nonresidential	0.5	10.5	9.2	8.7	-4.2	-9.2	1.0	5.9	6.8	7.2
Structures	1.5	6.4	-0.4	6.8	-2.3	-17.1	-4.1	2.2	1.1	9.0
Equipment and software.......	–	12.0	12.7	9.4	-4.9	-6.2	2.8	7.3	8.9	6.5
Residential	-8.6	-3.2	6.0	0.8	0.4	4.8	8.4	9.9	8.6	-4.2
Exports	9.0	10.1	4.3	8.7	-5.4	-2.3	1.3	9.2	6.8	8.9
Goods.....................	8.4	11.7	3.8	11.2	-6.1	-4.0	1.8	9.0	7.5	10.5
Services...................	10.5	6.3	5.6	2.9	-3.7	1.9	–	9.7	5.1	5.4
Imports	3.6	8.0	11.5	13.1	-2.7	3.4	4.1	10.8	6.1	5.8
Goods.....................	3.0	9.0	12.4	13.5	-3.2	3.7	4.9	10.9	6.7	5.9
Services...................	6.5	3.3	6.9	11.1	-0.3	2.1	–	10.0	2.8	5.3
Government consumption expenditures and gross investment..............	3.2	0.5	3.9	2.1	3.4	4.4	2.5	1.9	0.9	2.1
Federal	2.0	-2.7	2.2	0.9	3.9	7.0	6.8	4.3	1.5	2.0
National defense	–	-3.8	1.9	-0.5	3.9	7.4	8.7	5.9	1.7	1.9
Nondefense.................	8.3	-0.4	2.8	3.5	3.9	6.3	3.4	1.2	1.1	2.1
State and local	4.1	2.6	4.7	2.7	3.2	3.1	0.2	0.5	0.5	2.1

– Represents or rounds to zero.

Source: U.S. Bureau of Economic Analysis, *Survey of Current Business*, April 2007. See also <http://www.bea.gov/national/nipaweb/SelectTable.asp?Selected=N>.

Table 647. Gross Domestic Product in Current and Real (2000) Dollars by Type of Product and Sector: 1990 to 2006

[In billions of dollars (5,803 represents $5,803,000,000,000). For explanation of chained dollars, see text, this section]

Type of product and sector	1990	1995	2000	2001	2002	2003	2004	2005	2006
CURRENT DOLLARS									
Gross domestic product	5,803	7,398	9,817	10,128	10,470	10,961	11,713	12,456	13,247
PRODUCT									
Goods	2,156	2,661	3,449	3,413	3,442	3,524	3,714	3,887	4,143
Durable goods	958	1,236	1,689	1,589	1,585	1,585	1,651	1,743	1,834
Nondurable goods	1,198	1,425	1,760	1,824	1,867	1,939	2,063	2,144	2,309
Services [1]	3,114	4,098	5,426	5,726	6,031	6,367	6,798	7,220	7,662
Structures	534	638	942	990	996	1,069	1,201	1,349	1,442
SECTOR									
Business...................	4,463	5,701	7,667	7,841	8,041	8,412	9,008	9,613	10,237
Nonfarm	4,386	5,632	7,595	7,768	7,970	8,323	8,893	9,518	10,143
Farm.....................	77	69	72	73	71	88	115	96	94
Households and institutions	619	816	1,081	1,160	1,227	1,269	1,357	1,420	1,519
General government	722	882	1,070	1,126	1,202	1,280	1,348	1,423	1,491
Federal	259	285	315	326	353	384	412	437	452
State and local	463	597	754	801	849	896	937	986	1,039
CHAINED (2000) DOLLARS									
Gross domestic product	7,113	8,032	9,817	9,891	10,049	10,301	10,704	11,049	11,415
PRODUCT									
Goods	2,253	2,639	3,449	3,391	3,433	3,538	3,712	3,881	4,121
Durable goods	877	1,125	1,689	1,613	1,627	1,682	1,782	1,890	2,006
Nondurable goods	1,407	1,532	1,760	1,777	1,805	1,856	1,931	1,996	2,120
Services	4,170	4,655	5,426	5,553	5,693	5,811	5,994	6,129	6,273
Structures	718	754	942	946	922	952	1,001	1,048	1,053
SECTOR									
Business...................	5,287	6,077	7,667	7,691	7,807	8,050	8,402	8,718	9,048
Nonfarm	5,238	6,030	7,595	7,626	7,737	7,974	8,320	8,635	8,962
Farm.....................	49	50	72	66	70	76	82	82	86
Households and institutions	841	945	1,081	1,110	1,131	1,129	1,176	1,201	1,234
General government	1,004	1,021	1,070	1,089	1,110	1,124	1,131	1,141	1,149
Federal	372	334	315	317	323	332	335	337	336
State and local	634	687	754	772	787	792	796	804	813

[1] Includes government consumption expenditures, which are for services (such as education and national defense) produced by government. In current dollars, these services are valued at their cost of production.

Source: U.S. Bureau of Economic Analysis, *Survey of Current Business*, April 2007. See also <http://www.bea.gov/national/nipaweb/SelectTable.asp?Selected=N>.

430   Income, Expenditures, Poverty, and Wealth

Table 648. Gross Domestic Product in Current and Real (2000) Dollars by Industry: 2000 to 2006

[In billions of dollars (9,817 represents $9,817,000,000,000). Data are based on the 1997 North American Industry Classification System (NAICS); see text, section 15. Data include nonfactor charges (capital consumption allowances, indirect business taxes, etc.) as well as factor charges against gross product; corporate profits and capital consumption allowances have been shifted from a company to an establishment basis]

Industry	Current dollars				Chained (2000) dollars			
	2000	2004	2005	2006	2000	2004	2005	2006
Gross domestic product	9,817	11,713	12,456	13,247	9,817	10,704	11,049	11,415
Private industries	8,614	10,222	10,892	11,610	8,614	9,435	9,749	10,111
Agriculture, forestry, and fishing	98	142	123	122	98	111	111	116
Farms	72	115	96	(NA)	72	82	82	(NA)
Agricultural services	27	27	27	(NA)	27	28	28	(NA)
Mining	121	172	233	256	121	108	105	104
Oil and gas extraction	81	116	160	(NA)	81	77	74	(NA)
Mining, except oil and gas	27	29	32	(NA)	27	24	23	(NA)
Mining support activities	13	27	42	(NA)	13	9	10	(NA)
Utilities	189	235	248	263	189	206	208	211
Construction	436	541	611	648	436	426	442	448
Manufacturing	1,426	1,435	1,513	1,601	1,426	1,491	1,523	1,574
Durable goods	865	820	854	916	865	914	959	1,023
Wood products	31	38	39	(NA)	31	31	32	(NA)
Nonmetallic mineral products	46	50	53	(NA)	46	49	48	(NA)
Primary metals	48	54	61	(NA)	48	49	48	(NA)
Fabricated metal products	122	118	131	(NA)	122	114	119	(NA)
Machinery	109	104	111	(NA)	109	105	109	(NA)
Computer and electronic products	186	130	135	(NA)	186	259	310	(NA)
Electrical equipment, appliances, and components	51	46	48	(NA)	51	47	48	(NA)
Motor vehicles, bodies & trailers, & parts	118	110	95	(NA)	118	129	125	(NA)
Other transportation equipment	64	66	71	(NA)	64	57	59	(NA)
Furniture and related products	33	37	37	(NA)	33	36	35	(NA)
Miscellaneous manufacturing	58	67	73	(NA)	58	65	70	(NA)
Nondurable goods	561	615	658	686	561	578	571	566
Food & beverage & tobacco	155	156	176	(NA)	155	146	153	(NA)
Textile mills and textile product mills	27	23	24	(NA)	27	24	24	(NA)
Apparel and leather and allied products	25	17	17	(NA)	25	18	18	(NA)
Paper products	56	53	55	(NA)	56	56	58	(NA)
Printing and related support activities	49	46	47	(NA)	49	45	46	(NA)
Petroleum and coal products	26	54	64	(NA)	26	38	30	(NA)
Chemical products	157	198	209	(NA)	157	184	181	(NA)
Plastics and rubber products	67	67	68	(NA)	67	68	67	(NA)
Wholesale trade	592	688	743	789	592	661	670	682
Retail trade	662	781	824	863	662	771	810	844
Transportation and warehousing	302	330	345	364	302	322	335	341
Air transportation	58	45	41	(NA)	58	71	76	(NA)
Rail transportation	26	30	32	(NA)	26	27	26	(NA)
Water transportation	7	9	9	(NA)	7	6	7	(NA)
Truck transportation	93	108	114	(NA)	93	96	100	(NA)
Transit & ground passenger transport	15	17	17	(NA)	15	14	14	(NA)
Pipeline transportation	9	10	9	(NA)	9	9	11	(NA)
Other transportation & support	70	82	89	(NA)	70	72	73	(NA)
Warehousing and storage	25	30	33	(NA)	25	29	32	(NA)
Information	458	529	555	579	458	559	609	653
Publishing industries (includes software)	117	134	150	(NA)	117	139	157	(NA)
Motion picture and sound recording	33	40	41	(NA)	33	37	37	(NA)
Broadcasting and telecommunications	271	301	304	(NA)	271	329	353	(NA)
Information and data processing services	38	54	60	(NA)	38	53	61	(NA)
Finance and insurance	741	917	958	1,028	741	835	854	891
Real estate and rental and leasing	1,191	1,491	1,578	1,731	1,191	1,325	1,370	1,452
Professional, scientific, and technical services	675	795	864	930	675	750	801	843
Legal services	136	169	181	(NA)	136	140	141	(NA)
Computer systems design, related services	126	131	141	(NA)	126	138	148	(NA)
Miscellaneous services	413	495	543	(NA)	413	473	514	(NA)
Management of companies & enterprises	183	211	226	239	183	196	199	200
Admin/support waste management/ remediation services	282	341	369	396	282	298	314	329
Educational services	79	108	116	123	79	86	88	89
Health care and social assistance	599	806	860	912	599	701	727	751
Ambulatory health care services	308	409	442	(NA)	308	373	395	(NA)
Hospitals, nursing, residential care	239	326	342	(NA)	239	262	263	(NA)
Social assistance	53	71	75	(NA)	53	67	71	(NA)
Arts, entertainment, and recreation	89	111	114	122	89	97	97	100
Performing arts, spectator sports, museums, and related activities	40	52	54	(NA)	40	45	44	(NA)
Amusements, gambling, & recreation	49	59	60	(NA)	49	53	53	(NA)
Accommodation and food services	261	313	331	350	261	279	284	292
Accommodation	91	99	105	(NA)	91	90	91	(NA)
Food services and drinking places	171	214	226	(NA)	171	188	193	(NA)
Other services, except public administration	229	274	283	296	229	229	228	230
Government	1,203	1,491	1,564	1,636	1,203	1,254	1,263	1,270
Federal	379	478	499	515	379	393	392	389
State and local	824	1,013	1,065	1,121	824	861	871	881

NA Not available.

Source: U.S. Bureau of Economic Analysis, Survey of Current Business, May 2007. See also <http://www.bea.gov/newsreleases /industry/gdpindustry/gdpindnewsrelease.htm> (released 24 April 2007).

Income, Expenditures, Poverty, and Wealth   431

Table 649. Gross Domestic Product by State in Current and Real (2000) Dollars by State: 2000 to 2006

[In billions of dollars (9,749.1 represents $9,749,100,000,000). For definition of gross domestic product or chained dollars, see text, this section]

State	Current dollars					Chained (2000) dollars				
	2000	2003	2004	2005	2006, prel.	2000	2003	2004	2005	2006, prel.
United States [1]	9,749.1	10,886.2	11,633.6	12,372.9	13,149.0	9,749.1	10,225.7	10,608.9	10,924.0	11,291.4
Alabama..............	114.6	130.2	141.7	151.3	160.6	114.6	121.6	128.0	132.5	136.6
Alaska	27.0	31.2	34.7	39.4	41.1	27.0	27.4	28.6	29.1	29.3
Arizona.............	158.5	182.0	194.1	212.3	232.5	158.5	174.2	181.1	193.1	206.2
Arkansas	66.8	75.7	81.8	87.0	91.8	66.8	70.8	73.9	76.4	78.4
California	1,287.1	1,406.5	1,515.5	1,616.4	1,727.4	1,287.1	1,337.8	1,403.4	1,457.1	1,518.9
Colorado.............	171.9	187.4	198.4	214.3	230.5	171.9	176.5	181.6	189.5	198.7
Connecticut...........	160.4	169.9	183.9	193.5	204.1	160.4	159.5	167.8	171.9	176.4
Delaware	41.5	48.6	52.5	56.7	60.4	41.5	44.9	46.9	49.0	50.6
District of Columbia	58.7	71.7	77.8	82.6	87.7	58.7	64.7	67.5	69.5	72.3
Florida	471.3	559.0	607.2	666.6	713.5	471.3	520.4	548.1	585.1	610.0
Georgia	290.9	317.9	337.6	358.4	379.6	290.9	299.7	310.0	320.4	331.1
Hawaii	40.2	46.4	50.8	54.8	58.3	40.2	42.6	45.0	46.9	49.0
Idaho...............	35.0	38.1	42.7	45.9	49.9	35.0	36.5	39.7	42.2	45.3
Illinois	464.2	510.3	534.4	555.6	589.6	464.2	479.3	488.0	492.3	507.0
Indiana.............	194.4	215.4	229.6	236.4	248.9	194.4	203.5	210.9	210.9	215.0
Iowa	90.2	102.2	111.6	117.6	124.0	90.2	95.3	100.7	103.6	106.3
Kansas..............	82.8	93.6	99.1	105.2	111.7	82.8	86.7	88.9	91.5	94.6
Kentucky	111.9	124.9	131.8	138.6	146.0	111.9	117.2	120.1	122.8	125.5
Louisiana	131.5	146.7	162.6	180.3	193.1	131.5	131.9	138.6	138.8	141.2
Maine...............	35.5	40.2	43.1	44.9	47.0	35.5	37.3	38.9	39.3	40.1
Maryland	180.4	213.3	229.2	244.4	257.8	180.4	198.0	206.3	213.8	219.9
Massachusetts..........	274.9	293.8	309.5	320.1	337.6	274.9	280.9	289.3	292.2	300.8
Michigan.............	337.2	359.0	363.4	372.1	381.0	337.2	341.1	338.3	339.5	337.9
Minnesota............	185.1	208.2	222.6	231.4	244.5	185.1	196.7	204.8	207.4	213.4
Mississippi	64.3	72.3	76.5	79.8	84.2	64.3	66.6	68.0	68.3	70.0
Missouri	176.7	195.5	204.7	215.1	225.9	176.7	183.2	186.6	190.5	194.5
Montana.............	21.4	25.5	27.8	29.9	32.3	21.4	23.3	24.3	25.2	26.4
Nebraska	55.5	64.6	68.0	72.2	75.7	55.5	59.9	60.6	63.0	64.4
Nevada	73.7	87.8	99.3	110.2	118.4	73.7	81.6	89.1	95.4	99.4
New Hampshire.........	43.5	48.2	51.7	54.1	56.3	43.5	45.9	47.9	48.9	49.5
New Jersey...........	344.8	389.1	409.2	427.7	453.2	344.8	366.6	375.1	380.5	391.6
New Mexico	50.7	57.5	63.9	69.7	75.9	50.7	53.0	57.2	58.9	62.5
New York	777.2	850.2	908.3	961.4	1,021.9	777.2	808.4	841.7	870.0	900.0
North Carolina..........	273.7	306.0	324.6	350.7	374.5	273.7	286.4	296.1	310.2	323.2
North Dakota..........	17.8	21.7	22.7	24.9	26.4	17.8	19.9	19.9	21.3	21.9
Ohio	372.0	402.4	424.6	442.2	461.3	372.0	378.7	388.6	392.9	397.2
Oklahoma............	89.8	103.5	111.4	121.6	134.7	89.8	94.3	97.1	99.1	105.7
Oregon..............	112.4	121.6	135.0	141.8	151.3	112.4	117.9	128.0	132.7	139.3
Pennsylvania..........	389.6	440.7	464.5	486.1	510.3	389.6	411.6	420.8	426.0	433.3
Rhode Island..........	33.6	39.4	42.2	43.6	45.7	33.6	36.5	38.0	38.1	38.7
South Carolina.........	112.5	127.9	132.3	140.1	149.2	112.5	119.6	120.3	123.7	128.1
South Dakota	23.1	27.4	29.5	30.5	32.3	23.1	25.7	26.5	27.0	28.0
Tennessee	174.9	200.3	214.4	225.0	238.0	174.9	188.5	196.8	201.1	207.3
Texas...............	727.2	828.8	904.4	989.3	1,065.9	727.2	771.0	808.1	831.8	867.9
Utah	67.6	75.4	81.1	88.4	97.7	67.6	70.2	73.1	77.0	82.5
Vermont	17.8	20.6	22.0	23.1	24.2	17.8	19.6	20.4	20.9	21.5
Virginia..............	260.7	302.5	325.5	350.7	369.3	260.7	281.5	295.0	308.8	318.7
Washington...........	222.0	240.8	252.4	271.4	293.5	222.0	225.0	229.2	240.0	253.4
West Virginia..........	41.5	46.5	49.9	53.1	55.7	41.5	42.6	44.0	44.7	45.0
Wisconsin............	175.7	195.9	208.3	217.0	227.2	175.7	184.1	190.4	193.2	196.6
Wyoming	17.3	21.7	23.9	27.2	29.6	17.3	18.8	19.4	19.7	20.2

[1] For chained (2000) dollar estimates, states will not add to U.S. total.

Source: U.S. Bureau of Economic Analysis, *Survey of Current Business*, July 2007; and "Gross Domestic Product by State"; published 7 June 2007; <http://www.bea.gov/bea/regional/gsp/default.cfm?series=NAICS>.

Table 650. Gross Domestic Product by Selected Industries and State: 2006

[In billions of dollars (13,149.0 represents $13,149,000,000,000). Preliminary data. For definition of gross state product, see text, this section. Industries based on 1997 North American Industry Classification System; see text, Section 15]

State	Total [1]	Con-struc-tion	Manu-facturing	Whole-sale trade	Retail trade	Finance and insur-ance	Real estate, rental, and leasing	Profes-sional and tech-nical serv-ices	Health care and social assis-tance	Govern-ment [2]
United States . . .	13,149.0	647.9	1,601.2	788.7	863.2	1,027.5	1,731.1	929.6	911.7	1,538.6
Alabama	160.6	8.1	30.0	9.2	12.7	8.3	15.4	9.2	11.2	24.2
Alaska	41.1	1.9	0.9	0.8	1.9	1.2	3.3	1.4	2.3	7.3
Arizona	232.5	18.1	18.8	13.6	19.9	19.6	33.6	13.5	16.3	28.1
Arkansas	91.8	4.1	18.0	6.3	6.8	3.6	8.0	3.4	6.9	12.5
California	1,727.4	82.7	169.0	101.8	119.7	115.1	292.8	147.9	103.7	189.9
Colorado	230.5	14.3	15.0	12.5	13.8	13.7	30.4	20.6	13.2	26.5
Connecticut	204.1	6.7	23.5	11.4	11.7	33.6	28.5	15.4	15.3	18.3
Delaware	60.4	(D)	4.6	2.3	2.5	19.8	7.1	3.5	3.1	5.2
District of Columbia . . .	87.7	(D)	0.2	0.8	1.2	4.0	9.6	18.0	3.7	28.9
Florida	713.5	55.8	35.9	47.0	56.6	48.4	122.2	45.4	51.3	78.9
Georgia	379.6	19.8	49.0	30.2	25.4	22.3	45.6	24.7	22.2	48.9
Hawaii	58.3	3.5	1.0	2.0	4.3	2.6	10.5	2.7	3.9	12.8
Idaho	49.9	3.4	7.2	2.7	4.3	2.3	5.8	3.4	3.3	6.3
Illinois	589.6	28.0	77.6	42.3	33.9	55.0	77.9	49.6	38.4	56.8
Indiana	248.9	10.8	70.0	14.1	15.8	14.1	24.4	9.4	18.0	24.4
Iowa	124.0	5.2	26.1	7.2	7.5	15.1	11.3	3.8	8.2	14.3
Kansas	111.7	4.5	15.3	7.1	7.6	6.6	10.8	5.7	7.8	16.6
Kentucky	146.0	6.1	27.3	9.1	10.1	7.1	13.6	5.9	11.8	21.4
Louisiana	193.1	8.9	40.5	8.8	12.8	6.3	15.3	7.3	10.4	19.9
Maine	47.0	2.5	5.4	2.5	4.2	3.2	6.5	2.2	5.1	6.6
Maryland	257.8	15.9	14.1	13.2	16.2	16.5	43.8	26.3	19.0	42.4
Massachusetts	337.6	14.7	33.3	20.7	17.8	33.3	50.2	36.9	30.2	29.6
Michigan	381.0	16.0	68.4	23.4	25.9	23.3	47.1	29.6	29.6	41.1
Minnesota	244.5	11.3	33.9	17.7	14.7	22.9	32.0	14.6	20.3	25.5
Mississippi	84.2	4.3	12.9	4.6	7.5	3.6	7.6	3.0	6.1	14.2
Missouri	225.9	10.8	34.3	14.7	15.5	13.5	24.1	13.4	16.9	26.1
Montana	32.3	2.2	1.5	1.7	2.3	1.6	3.8	1.5	2.9	5.2
Nebraska	75.7	3.3	8.9	4.5	4.8	7.5	7.1	3.5	5.5	10.4
Nevada	118.4	11.9	5.8	5.0	9.1	8.1	17.6	6.0	5.7	11.8
New Hampshire	56.3	2.7	6.6	3.6	4.7	4.6	8.3	3.7	4.8	5.2
New Jersey	453.2	19.1	41.6	36.5	28.4	37.3	78.2	38.5	32.1	45.0
New Mexico	75.9	3.6	7.3	2.6	4.7	2.3	7.1	5.3	4.7	13.0
New York	1,021.9	32.2	64.1	51.7	54.4	158.6	156.9	88.1	77.1	102.0
North Carolina	374.5	18.7	74.0	20.8	24.0	41.7	36.7	17.8	23.1	46.8
North Dakota	26.4	1.3	2.5	2.1	1.9	1.6	2.5	0.9	2.2	4.0
Ohio	461.3	18.2	89.3	28.6	31.0	38.3	49.1	25.4	37.0	49.5
Oklahoma	134.7	5.2	14.0	6.4	9.0	5.8	12.5	5.5	8.5	20.6
Oregon	151.3	7.3	26.5	10.2	8.7	8.5	20.4	7.2	11.3	20.5
Pennsylvania	510.3	24.0	75.4	30.9	32.5	37.2	60.4	37.4	48.0	49.8
Rhode Island	45.7	2.3	4.5	2.3	2.8	5.3	6.9	2.6	4.2	5.5
South Carolina	149.2	9.1	26.3	9.1	12.0	7.4	16.9	6.6	8.7	23.4
South Dakota	32.3	1.4	3.4	1.8	2.3	5.5	2.8	0.8	2.8	4.2
Tennessee	238.0	10.5	42.4	16.2	19.9	12.9	24.8	12.3	20.8	25.1
Texas	1,065.9	57.8	139.7	70.8	67.3	58.7	101.3	68.0	61.5	112.9
Utah	97.7	6.2	11.0	4.9	7.2	8.5	10.7	6.4	5.7	13.2
Vermont	24.2	1.3	2.9	1.3	2.0	1.5	2.9	1.4	2.4	3.3
Virginia	369.3	19.6	34.2	16.2	22.4	22.8	49.7	43.3	19.8	63.1
Washington	293.5	14.7	32.9	18.2	21.4	16.6	42.0	17.7	19.3	39.5
West Virginia	55.7	2.5	6.1	2.9	4.4	2.2	5.2	2.2	5.3	9.5
Wisconsin	227.2	10.3	47.2	13.4	14.3	16.9	27.8	9.6	18.6	24.7
Wyoming	29.6	1.8	1.0	1.1	1.6	0.7	2.5	0.9	1.2	3.8

D Data withheld to avoid disclosure.   [1] Includes industries not shown separately.   [2] Includes federal civilian and military and state and local government.

Source: U.S. Bureau of Economic Analysis, *Survey of Current Business*, July 2007; and "Gross Domestic Product by State"; published 7 June 2007; <http://www.bea.gov/bea/regional/gsp/default.cfm?series=NAICS>.

Income, Expenditures, Poverty, and Wealth   433

Table 651. **Relation of GDP, GNP, Net National Product, National Income, Personal Income, Disposable Personal Income, and Personal Saving: 1990 to 2006**

[In billions of dollars (5,803 represents $5,803,000,000,000). For definitions, see text, this section]

Item	1990	1995	2000	2002	2003	2004	2005	2006
Gross domestic product (GDP)	5,803	7,398	9,817	10,470	10,961	11,713	12,456	13,247
Plus: Income receipts from the rest of the world	189	234	383	306	337	410	513	666
Less: Income payments to the rest of the world	154	198	344	275	280	364	482	636
Equals: Gross national product (GNP).	5,838	7,433	9,856	10,500	11,018	11,759	12,488	13,277
Less: Consumption of fixed capital	683	878	1,188	1,292	1,337	1,436	1,605	1,577
Equals: Net national product	5,155	6,555	8,668	9,208	9,681	10,323	10,883	11,700
Less: Statistical discrepancy	66	101	-127	-21	49	67	71	-3
Equals: National income.	5,089	6,454	8,795	9,229	9,632	10,256	10,812	11,702
Less: Corporate profits [1]	438	697	818	886	993	1,183	1,331	1,616
Taxes on production and imports less subsidies	399	524	665	724	759	819	865	913
Contributions for government social insurance	410	533	703	750	779	826	881	945
Net interest and miscellaneous payments on assets	442	367	559	521	525	485	483	509
Business current transfer payments (net)	39	47	87	84	84	86	74	93
Current surplus of government enterprises	2	11	5	1	2	-5	-15	-10
Wage accruals less disbursements . . .	–	16	–	–	15	-15	–	13
Plus: Personal income receipts on assets	924	1,016	1,387	1,333	1,337	1,428	1,519	1,656
Personal current transfer receipts	595	877	1,084	1,286	1,351	1,427	1,527	1,602
Equals: Personal income	4,879	6,152	8,430	8,882	9,164	9,731	10,239	10,883
Less: Personal current taxes	593	744	1,236	1,052	1,001	1,050	1,203	1,361
Equals: Disposable personal income. .	4,286	5,408	7,194	7,830	8,163	8,682	9,036	9,523
Less: Personal outlays	3,986	5,157	7,026	7,645	7,988	8,507	9,071	9,626
Equals: Personal saving	299	251	169	185	175	174	-35	-103

– Represents or rounds to zero. [1] Corporate profits with inventory valuation and capital consumption adjustments.

Source: U.S. Bureau of Economic Analysis, *Survey of Current Business*, April 2007. See also <http://www.bea.gov /national/nipaweb/SelectTable.asp?Selected=N>.

Table 652. **Gross Saving and Investment: 1990 to 2006**

[In billions of dollars (940 represents $940,000,000,000)]

Item	1990	1995	2000	2002	2003	2004	2005	2006
Gross saving	940	1,185	1,771	1,489	1,459	1,544	1,612	1,834
Net saving	258	306	583	197	123	108	7	257
Net private saving	423	491	343	479	515	502	320	408
Personal saving	299	251	169	185	175	174	-35	-103
Undistributed corporate profits with IVA and CCA [1]	123	224	175	295	325	343	355	499
Wage accruals less disbursements	–	16	–	–	15	-15	–	13
Net government saving	-165	-185	239	-282	-393	-395	-313	-151
Federal	-172	-197	190	-248	-372	-382	-309	-154
State and local	7	12	50	-34	-20	-13	-3	3
Consumption of fixed capital.	683	878	1,188	1,292	1,337	1,436	1,605	1,577
Private	552	713	991	1,080	1,118	1,205	1,353	1,311
Domestic business.	466	600	836	894	917	970	1,059	1,051
Households and institutions.	85	113	155	187	202	236	294	260
Government.	131	165	197	212	218	231	252	266
Federal	68	82	87	89	90	94	99	104
State and local	63	83	110	123	128	137	153	161
Gross domestic investment, capital acct. transactions, and net lending	1,007	1,286	1,643	1,468	1,508	1,610	1,683	1,832
Gross domestic investment	1,077	1,377	2,040	1,926	2,020	2,259	2,455	2,644
Gross private domestic investment.	861	1,144	1,736	1,582	1,664	1,888	2,057	2,213
Gross government investment	216	233	305	344	356	371	397	431
Capital account transactions (net)	7	1	1	3	3	2	4	4
Net lending or net borrowing	-77	-92	-397	-460	-516	-651	-776	-816
Statistical discrepancy	66	101	-127	-21	49	67	71	-3
Addenda:								
Gross private saving	974	1,205	1,334	1,560	1,633	1,708	1,672	1,720
Gross government saving.	-34	-20	436	-71	-174	-164	-60	115
Federal	-104	-115	277	-159	-282	-288	-210	-49
State and local	70	95	160	89	107	124	150	164
Net domestic investment	394	498	852	634	684	823	850	1,067
Gross saving as a percentage of gross national income	16.3	16.2	17.7	14.2	13.3	13.2	13.0	13.8
Net saving as a percentage of gross national income	4.5	4.2	5.8	1.9	1.1	0.9	0.1	1.9

– Represents or rounds to zero. [1] IVA and CCA = Inventory valuation adjustment and capital consumption adjustment.

Source: U.S. Bureau of Economic Analysis, *Survey of Current Business*, April 2007. See also <http://www.bea.gov /national/nipaweb/SelectTable.asp?Selected=N>.

Table 653. Flow of Funds Accounts—Composition of Individuals' Savings: 1990 to 2006

[In billions of dollars (518.0 represents $518,000,000,000). Combined statement for households, farm business, and nonfarm noncorporate business. Minus sign (−) indicates decrease]

Composition of savings	1990	1995	2000	2002	2003	2004	2005	2006
Increase in financial assets	518.0	521.2	366.4	632.0	992.3	1,234.9	971.5	743.2
Foreign deposits	1.4	4.6	7.6	1.3	2.2	5.4	5.2	7.3
Checkable deposits and currency	−9.5	−43.3	−78.6	0.4	−54.0	61.2	5.0	−4.5
Time and savings deposits	33.8	143.4	352.6	338.5	379.0	387.0	453.9	533.9
Money market fund shares	31.4	102.0	152.4	−40.9	−118.3	−47.9	63.0	159.4
Securities	210.3	12.7	−653.9	23.3	352.4	198.2	21.0	−407.6
Open market paper	5.8	2.0	12.4	13.1	−4.5	30.2	28.1	23.4
U.S. savings bonds	8.5	5.1	−1.7	4.5	8.9	0.6	0.7	−2.7
Other Treasury securities	89.3	−17.6	−209.0	−110.1	22.5	71.9	−92.0	−68.8
Agency and GSE-backed securities [1]	36.3	28.2	32.8	−156.7	143.7	87.9	223.1	−14.8
Municipal securities	34.7	−59.9	4.6	97.4	28.4	36.9	74.7	44.1
Corporate and foreign bonds	52.5	78.0	81.1	194.9	−84.3	−19.2	−15.6	14.7
Corporate equities [2]	−48.4	−82.3	−632.0	−145.4	−2.8	−259.2	−463.9	−740.4
Mutual fund shares	31.5	59.3	57.9	125.6	240.5	249.0	266.0	336.8
Life insurance reserves	26.5	45.8	50.2	60.1	66.8	33.1	16.1	14.2
Pension fund reserves	191.0	176.8	271.6	186.5	200.3	241.4	152.6	154.1
Miscellaneous and other assets	33.0	79.2	264.6	62.8	164.0	356.5	254.6	286.4
Gross investment in tangible assets	808.0	1,012.4	1,487.2	1,571.8	1,680.6	1,829.7	1,978.5	2,048.6
Minus: Consumption of fixed capital	558.8	712.1	940.9	1,007.9	1,057.5	1,141.8	1,274.7	1,232.1
Equals: Net investment in tangible assets	249.2	300.3	546.3	563.9	623.0	687.9	703.8	816.5
Net increase in liabilities	230.5	410.6	944.5	985.1	1,117.5	1,541.7	1,602.5	1,437.5
Mortgage debt on nonfarm homes	205.5	168.1	416.7	731.0	796.1	1,049.9	1,121.7	817.2
Other mortgage debt [3]	−2.4	5.8	119.0	105.0	153.8	166.0	241.4	243.1
Consumer credit	15.1	147.9	181.0	112.6	103.9	116.1	94.3	111.1
Policy loans	4.1	10.5	2.8	1.0	−0.7	1.6	0.8	3.9
Security credit	−3.7	3.5	7.2	−48.2	34.3	81.5	−31.6	59.7
Other liabilities [3]	11.9	74.9	217.8	83.8	30.2	126.4	175.8	202.5
Personal saving with consumer durables [4]	551.8	431.6	4.6	241.1	512.6	396.8	89.1	139.9
Personal saving without consumer durables [4]	475.8	335.9	−201.3	35.9	306.8	188.6	−121.2	−91.7
Personal saving (NIPA, excludes consumer durables) [5]	299.4	250.9	168.5	184.7	174.9	174.3	−34.8	−102.1

[1] GSE = government-sponsored enterprises. [2] Only directly held and those in closed-end and exchange-traded funds. Other equities are included in mutual funds, life insurance, and pension reserves. [3] Includes corporate farms. [4] Flow of Funds measure. [5] National Income and Product Accounts measure.

Source: Board of Governors of the Federal Reserve System, "Federal Reserve Statistical Release, Z.1, Flow of Funds Accounts of the United States"; published: 8 March 2007; <http://www.federalreserve.gov/releases/z1/20070308/>.

Table 654. Government Consumption Expenditures and Gross Investment in Current and Real (2000) Dollars by Level of Government and Type: 2000 to 2006

[In billions of dollars (1,721.6 represents $1,721,600,000,000). Government consumption expenditures are services (such as education and national defense) produced by government that are valued at their cost of production. Excludes government sales to other sectors and government own-account investment (construction and software). Gross government investment consists of general government and government enterprise expenditures for fixed assets; inventory investment is included in government consumption expenditures. For explanation of national income and chained dollars, see text, Section 13]

Item	Current dollars				Chained (2000) dollars			
	2000	2004	2005	2006	2000	2004	2005	2006
Government consumption expenditures and gross investment, total	1,721.6	2,226.2	2,372.8	2,527.7	1,721.6	1,940.6	1,958.0	1,998.4
Consumption expenditures	1,417.1	1,854.8	1,975.7	2,096.3	1,417.1	1,595.6	1,609.3	1,635.9
Gross investment	304.5	371.4	397.1	431.3	304.5	344.7	348.5	362.9
Structures	189.3	233.1	248.9	273.6	189.3	202.4	198.4	204.2
Equipment and software	115.2	138.3	148.1	157.8	115.2	144.1	153.4	162.8
Federal	578.8	825.9	878.3	926.6	578.8	716.6	727.5	741.9
Consumption expenditures	499.3	724.5	768.6	808.0	499.3	615.6	620.8	629.4
Gross investment	79.5	101.4	109.8	118.6	79.5	101.4	107.9	114.5
Structures	13.3	14.7	15.4	16.4	13.3	12.9	12.6	12.6
Equipment and software	66.2	86.7	94.4	102.2	66.2	89.0	95.8	102.9
National defense	370.3	551.2	589.3	621.0	370.3	475.4	483.6	492.8
Consumption expenditures	321.5	483.7	516.9	542.0	321.5	408.3	413.3	418.1
Gross investment	48.8	67.5	72.4	79.0	48.8	67.5	71.2	76.4
Structures	5.0	5.1	5.2	5.8	5.0	4.4	4.2	4.4
Equipment and software	43.8	62.4	67.2	73.3	43.8	63.3	67.3	72.3
Nondefense	208.5	274.7	289.0	305.6	208.5	241.0	243.7	248.9
Consumption expenditures	177.8	240.7	251.7	266.1	177.8	207.0	207.3	211.2
Gross investment	30.7	33.9	37.4	39.5	30.7	33.9	36.7	38.2
Structures	8.3	9.6	10.2	10.6	8.3	8.5	8.4	8.2
Equipment and software	22.3	24.3	27.1	28.9	22.3	25.6	28.6	30.5
State and local	1,142.8	1,400.3	1,494.4	1,601.1	1,142.8	1,223.9	1,230.4	1,256.4
Consumption expenditures	917.8	1,130.3	1,207.2	1,288.3	917.8	979.6	988.0	1,006.0
Gross investment	225.0	270.0	287.3	312.8	225.0	244.1	242.1	250.2
Structures	176.0	218.4	233.5	257.2	176.0	189.5	185.7	191.7
Equipment and software	49.0	51.6	53.8	55.6	49.0	55.0	57.3	59.6

Source: U.S. Bureau of Economic Analysis, Survey of Current Business, April 2007. See also <http://www.bea.gov/national/nipaweb/SelectTable.asp?Selected=N>.

Table 655. Personal Consumption Expenditures in Current and Real (2000) Dollars by Type: 2000 to 2005

[In billions of dollars (6,739.4 represents $6,739,400,000,000). For definition of "chained" dollars, see text, this section]

Expenditure	Current dollars 2000	2003	2004	2005	Chained (2000) dollars 2000	2003	2004	2005
Total expenditures [1]	6,739.4	7,703.6	8,211.5	8,742.4	6,739.4	7,295.3	7,577.1	7,841.2
Food and tobacco [1]	1,003.7	1,134.0	1,202.3	1,291.4	1,003.7	1,051.1	1,082.2	1,134.7
Food purchased for off-premise consumption	566.7	636.0	677.9	734.0	566.7	598.7	619.0	659.2
Purchased meals and beverages [2]	348.8	399.0	425.5	455.1	348.8	368.7	381.6	395.8
Tobacco products	78.5	88.0	87.5	90.0	78.5	74.1	72.3	70.7
Clothing, accessories, and jewelry [1]	397.0	418.8	442.1	464.8	397.0	440.4	463.9	489.5
Shoes	47.0	50.3	51.9	54.2	47.0	52.1	53.9	54.8
Clothing	250.4	260.0	272.9	287.2	250.4	281.6	296.7	317.9
Jewelry and watches	50.6	52.8	56.5	58.9	50.6	56.3	59.8	63.3
Personal care [1]	93.4	100.4	106.6	112.2	93.4	97.1	102.0	105.7
Toilet articles and preparations	55.0	56.0	58.2	61.7	55.0	56.1	58.3	61.6
Barbershops, beauty parlors, and health clubs	38.4	44.4	48.4	50.5	38.4	41.0	43.6	44.1
Housing [1]	1,006.5	1,161.8	1,236.1	1,304.1	1,006.5	1,051.9	1,091.6	1,122.6
Owner-occupied nonfarm dwellings-space rent	712.2	846.4	910.1	963.3	712.2	764.9	804.2	831.9
Tenant-occupied nonfarm dwellings-space rent	227.5	245.3	248.9	257.0	227.5	220.4	218.1	218.6
Household operation [1]	719.3	781.1	824.4	881.7	719.3	765.9	801.9	829.8
Furniture [3]	67.6	70.2	75.5	79.0	67.6	73.9	79.7	84.4
Semidurable house furnishings [4]	36.5	39.0	41.2	43.5	36.5	44.5	49.1	53.2
Cleaning and polishing preparations	61.6	69.0	72.9	77.7	61.6	67.1	70.6	73.8
Household utilities [1]	209.9	242.0	255.6	285.8	209.9	215.4	216.5	219.6
Electricity	102.3	115.6	121.1	134.2	102.3	105.7	108.7	113.5
Gas	41.0	51.7	55.5	65.5	41.0	41.8	41.3	40.9
Water and other sanitary services	50.8	57.8	60.7	64.2	50.8	52.5	52.0	52.2
Telephone and telegraph	125.1	129.7	132.9	136.0	125.1	133.5	139.6	144.1
Medical care [1]	1,218.3	1,556.5	1,670.4	1,784.1	1,218.3	1,411.0	1,457.7	1,508.3
Drug preparations and sundries [5]	169.4	233.6	251.3	265.7	169.4	208.6	218.3	224.2
Physicians	236.8	300.6	322.2	342.4	236.8	288.1	302.6	315.9
Dentists	61.8	74.6	80.2	85.5	61.8	65.9	67.5	68.2
Hospitals and nursing homes [6]	482.6	610.8	645.8	691.3	482.6	541.5	549.2	565.1
Health insurance	84.0	112.8	130.4	142.2	84.0	98.8	102.9	108.2
Medical care [7]	68.4	95.0	111.2	121.6	68.4	79.2	82.8	87.6
Personal business [1]	539.1	559.7	612.4	647.9	539.1	528.4	560.6	579.7
Brokerage charges and investment counseling	100.6	77.4	86.6	90.5	100.6	85.9	94.3	97.1
Bank service charges, trust services, and safe deposit box rental	64.2	81.8	89.3	99.9	64.2	76.5	80.3	87.2
Expense of handling life insurance [8]	96.1	85.9	98.7	106.9	96.1	77.8	84.7	89.0
Legal services	63.9	78.1	82.0	85.6	63.9	67.1	67.2	67.4
Transportation [1]	853.4	921.7	976.2	1,048.9	853.4	905.3	919.7	922.3
User-operated transportation [1]	793.8	866.0	917.3	988.2	793.8	845.9	857.4	859.9
New autos	103.6	97.2	97.7	103.7	103.6	100.6	101.7	107.0
Net purchases of used autos	60.7	54.8	54.9	58.5	60.7	56.3	56.0	57.2
Other motor vehicles	173.2	227.6	231.0	227.3	173.2	236.1	241.5	234.5
Tires, tubes, accessories, etc.	49.0	52.0	54.4	58.7	49.0	49.5	51.4	54.3
Repair, greasing, washing, parking, storage, rental, and leasing	183.5	186.8	189.5	195.6	183.5	173.0	173.0	173.3
Gasoline and oil	175.7	192.7	230.4	280.2	175.7	183.2	186.0	185.9
Insurance	43.0	49.2	53.7	58.1	43.0	43.8	44.5	44.6
Purchased intercity transportation	47.4	42.7	45.0	46.0	47.4	48.1	51.3	51.2
Recreation [1, 9]	585.7	659.9	708.4	756.3	585.7	689.0	744.4	802.7
Magazines, newspapers, and sheet music	35.0	36.3	39.6	43.8	35.0	34.3	36.3	39.1
Nondurable toys and sport supplies	56.6	60.6	63.5	67.2	56.6	70.7	77.0	86.0
Wheel goods, sports and photographic equipment, boats, and pleasure aircraft	57.6	65.6	71.4	81.5	57.6	68.3	75.1	86.1
Video and audio goods, including musical instruments	72.8	76.5	81.8	85.8	72.8	91.5	104.6	117.9
Computers, peripherals, and software	43.8	46.6	51.6	55.4	(NA)	(NA)	(NA)	(NA)
Commercial participant amusements	75.8	91.2	100.7	107.3	75.8	84.4	90.8	93.9
Education and research	163.8	203.1	213.6	226.5	163.8	176.0	174.8	176.1
Higher education	86.4	112.6	119.6	126.8	86.4	96.2	95.9	96.4
Religious and welfare activities	172.3	207.1	219.0	224.5	172.3	189.5	194.4	193.2
Foreign travel and other, net [1]	-13.0	-0.5	0.1	-	-13.0	-6.5	-7.2	-7.5
Foreign travel by U.S. residents	84.4	80.5	91.8	99.9	84.4	72.1	78.4	81.7
Less: Expenditures in the United States by nonresidents	100.7	85.8	96.7	104.9	100.7	82.1	88.8	92.1

- Represents or rounds to zero. NA Not available. [1] Includes other expenditures not shown separately. [2] Consists of purchases (including tips) of meals and beverages from retail, service, and amusement establishments; hotels; dining and buffet cars; schools; school fraternities; institutions; clubs; and industrial lunch rooms. Includes meals and beverages consumed both on- and off-premise. [3] Includes mattresses and bedsprings. [4] Consists largely of textile house furnishings including piece goods allocated to house furnishing use. Also includes lamp shades, brooms, and brushes. [5] Excludes drug preparations and related products dispensed by physicians, hospitals, and other medical services. [6] Consists of (1) current expenditures (including consumption of fixed capital) of nonprofit hospitals and nursing homes and (2) payments by patients to proprietary and government hospitals and nursing homes. [7] Consists of (1) premiums, less benefits and dividends, for health hospitalization and accidental death and dismemberment insurance provided by commercial insurance carriers and (2) administrative expenses (including consumption of fixed capital) of Blue Cross and Blue Shield plans and of other independent prepaid and self-insured health plans. [8] Consists of (1) operating expenses of life insurance carriers and private noninsured pension plans and (2) premiums less benefits and dividends of fraternal benefit societies. Excludes expenses allocated by commercial carriers to accident and health insurance. [9] For additional details, see Table 1212.

Source: U.S. Bureau of Economic Analysis, *Survey of Current Business*, April 2007. See also <http://www.bea.gov/national/nipaweb/SelectTable.asp?Selected=N>.

Table 656. **Personal Income and Its Disposition: 1990 to 2006**

[In billions of dollars (4,879 represents $4,879,000,000,000), except as indicated. For definition of personal income and chained dollars, see text, this section]

Item	1990	1995	2000	2002	2003	2004	2005	2006
Personal income.	**4,879**	**6,152**	**8,430**	**8,882**	**9,164**	**9,731**	**10,239**	**10,883**
Compensation of employees, received . .	3,338	4,177	5,783	6,091	6,310	6,665	7,030	7,477
Wage and salary disbursements.	2,754	3,419	4,829	4,981	5,113	5,392	5,665	6,023
Supplements to wages and salaries . .	584	758	953	1,110	1,198	1,273	1,366	1,454
Proprietors' income [1]	381	492	728	768	811	911	971	1,015
Farm.	32	23	23	11	29	36	30	23
Nonfarm	349	470	706	758	782	875	940	993
Rental income of persons [1]	51	122	150	153	133	127	73	77
Personal income receipts on assets	924	1,016	1,387	1,333	1,337	1,428	1,519	1,656
Personal interest income.	755	763	1,011	936	914	891	945	1,017
Personal dividend income	169	253	376	397	423	537	574	640
Personal current transfer receipts.	595	877	1,084	1,286	1,351	1,427	1,527	1,602
Government social benefits to persons	573	858	1,042	1,249	1,317	1,398	1,481	1,567
Old-age, survivors, disability, and health insurance benefits	352	507	621	708	741	791	845	931
Other current transfer receipts, from business (net)	22	19	42	37	34	28	46	35
Less: Contributions for government social insurance	410	533	703	750	779	826	881	945
Less: Personal current taxes	593	744	1,236	1,052	1,001	1,050	1,203	1,361
Equals: Disposable personal income . . .	**4,286**	**5,408**	**7,194**	**7,830**	**8,163**	**8,682**	**9,036**	**9,523**
Less: Personal outlays	*3,986*	*5,157*	*7,026*	*7,645*	*7,988*	*8,507*	*9,071*	*9,626*
Personal consumption expenditures	3,840	4,976	6,739	7,351	7,704	8,212	8,742	9,269
Personal interest payments.	116	133	205	196	183	186	209	230
Personal current transfer payments	30	49	82	98	102	110	119	126
Equals: Personal saving	**299**	**251**	**169**	**185**	**175**	**174**	**-35**	**-103**
Personal saving as a percentage of disposable personal income	7.0	4.6	2.3	2.4	2.1	2.0	-0.4	-1.1
Addenda:								
Disposable personal income:								
Total, billions of chained (2000) dollars . .	5,324	5,906	7,194	7,562	7,730	8,011	8,105	8,313
Per capita:								
Current dollars	17,131	20,287	25,479	27,157	28,031	29,531	30,440	31,773
Chained (2000) dollars	21,281	22,153	25,479	26,228	26,545	27,250	27,302	27,737

[1] With inventory valuation adjustments and capital consumption adjustment.

Source: U.S. Bureau of Economic Analysis, *Survey of Current Business*, April 2007. See also <http://www.bea.gov /national/nipaweb/SelectTable.asp?Selected=N>.

Table 657. **Selected Per Capita Income and Product Measures in Current and Real (2000) Dollars: 1960 to 2006**

[In dollars. Based on U.S. Census Bureau estimated population including Armed Forces abroad; based on quarterly averages. For explanation of chained dollars, see text, this section]

Year	Current dollars					Chained (2000) dollars			
	Gross domestic product	Gross national product	Personal income	Disposable personal income	Personal consumption expenditures	Gross domestic product	Gross national product	Disposable personal income	Personal consumption expenditures
1960	2,912	2,929	2,277	2,022	1,835	13,840	13,938	9,735	8,837
1965	3,700	3,727	2,860	2,563	2,283	16,420	16,554	11,594	10,331
1970	5,064	5,095	4,090	3,587	3,162	18,391	18,520	13,563	11,955
1975	7,586	7,646	6,181	5,498	4,789	19,961	20,133	15,291	13,320
1980	12,249	12,400	10,134	8,822	7,716	22,666	22,956	16,940	14,816
1985	17,695	17,806	14,787	13,037	11,406	25,382	25,548	19,476	17,040
1990	23,195	23,335	19,500	17,131	15,349	28,429	28,600	21,281	19,067
1991	23,650	23,770	19,923	17,609	15,722	28,007	28,150	21,109	18,848
1992	24,668	24,783	20,870	18,494	16,485	28,556	28,693	21,548	19,208
1993	25,578	25,700	21,356	18,872	17,204	28,940	29,079	21,493	19,593
1994	26,844	26,944	22,176	19,555	18,004	29,741	29,850	21,812	20,082
1995	27,749	27,884	23,078	20,287	18,665	30,128	30,271	22,153	20,382
1996	28,982	29,112	24,176	21,091	19,490	30,881	31,015	22,546	20,835
1997	30,424	30,544	25,334	21,940	20,323	31,886	32,010	23,065	21,365
1998	31,674	31,752	26,880	23,161	21,291	32,833	32,912	24,131	22,183
1999	33,181	33,302	27,933	23,968	22,491	33,904	34,027	24,564	23,050
2000	34,769	34,907	29,855	25,479	23,869	34,769	34,907	25,479	23,869
2001	35,491	35,644	30,572	26,236	24,723	34,660	34,810	25,698	24,216
2002	36,311	36,417	30,805	27,157	25,494	34,852	34,957	26,228	24,622
2003	37,641	37,836	31,469	28,031	26,455	35,375	35,562	26,545	25,053
2004	39,841	39,999	33,102	29,531	27,932	36,409	36,556	27,250	25,774
2005	41,960	42,067	34,493	30,440	29,450	37,219	37,318	27,302	26,415
2006	44,197	44,297	36,313	31,773	30,926	38,087	38,175	27,737	26,997

Source: U.S. Bureau of Economic Analysis, *Survey of Current Business*, April 2007. See also <http://www.bea.gov /national/nipaweb/SelectTable.asp?Selected=N>.

Income, Expenditures, Poverty, and Wealth   **437**

Table 658. Personal Income in Current and Constant (2000) Dollars by State:200

[In billions of dollars (8,422.1 represents $8,422,100,000,000). Represents a measure of income received from all sources during the calendar year by residents of each state. Data exclude federal employees overseas and U.S. residents employed by private U.S. firms on temporary foreign assignment. Totals may differ from those in Tables 651, 656, and 657]

State	Current dollars					Constant (2000) dollars [1]				
	2000	2003	2004	2005	2006, prel.	2000	2003	2004	2005	2006, prel.
United States	8,422.1	9,150.3	9,716.4	10,220.9	10,860.9	8,422.1	8,665.3	8,965.7	9,167.3	9,480.9
Alabama..........	105.8	118.4	126.7	134.7	143.9	105.8	112.1	116.9	120.8	125.6
Alaska...........	18.7	21.2	22.3	23.6	25.0	18.7	20.1	20.5	21.2	21.8
Arizona..........	132.6	150.6	164.1	178.7	194.0	132.6	142.6	151.4	160.3	169.3
Arkansas	58.7	66.5	70.9	74.1	78.5	58.7	63.0	65.4	66.4	68.5
California	1,103.8	1,187.0	1,268.0	1,335.4	1,420.2	1,103.8	1,124.1	1,170.1	1,197.7	1,239.8
Colorado.	144.4	154.8	164.7	174.9	186.3	144.4	146.6	152.0	156.9	162.6
Connecticut.......	141.6	148.8	158.6	165.9	174.7	141.6	140.9	146.3	148.8	152.5
Delaware	24.3	27.4	29.3	31.2	33.3	24.3	25.9	27.0	28.0	29.1
District of Columbia ...	23.1	26.9	29.1	30.7	32.4	23.1	25.5	26.9	27.6	28.3
Florida	457.5	514.4	565.0	604.1	647.6	457.5	487.1	521.3	541.9	565.3
Georgia	230.4	250.8	264.7	282.3	298.6	230.4	237.5	244.3	253.2	260.7
Hawaii	34.5	37.8	41.1	43.9	46.7	34.5	35.8	38.0	39.4	40.7
Idaho............	31.3	34.8	38.2	40.7	43.9	31.3	33.0	35.3	36.5	38.3
Illinois	400.4	426.9	442.3	462.9	490.4	400.4	404.3	408.2	415.2	428.1
Indiana..........	165.3	178.7	187.5	195.3	205.4	165.3	169.2	173.0	175.2	179.3
Iowa	77.8	83.9	91.2	93.9	99.1	77.8	79.5	84.2	84.2	86.5
Kansas...........	74.6	81.1	85.5	90.3	96.0	74.6	76.8	78.9	81.0	83.8
Kentucky	98.8	106.3	111.9	118.0	123.5	98.8	100.7	103.2	105.8	107.8
Louisiana	103.2	115.7	121.8	111.2	132.7	103.2	109.6	112.4	99.7	115.9
Maine...........	33.2	37.5	39.2	40.6	42.7	33.2	35.5	36.2	36.4	37.3
Maryland	182.0	205.7	220.6	234.6	247.5	182.0	194.8	203.6	210.4	216.1
Massachusetts.......	240.2	254.0	268.0	279.9	295.3	240.2	240.5	247.3	251.0	257.8
Michigan..........	294.2	313.5	320.3	331.3	341.7	294.2	296.9	295.5	297.2	298.3
Minnesota.........	158.0	173.5	184.2	191.2	200.0	158.0	164.3	170.0	171.5	174.6
Mississippi	59.8	66.3	69.4	72.9	77.2	59.8	62.8	64.1	65.4	67.4
Missouri	152.7	166.1	173.1	181.1	191.1	152.7	157.3	159.7	162.4	166.8
Montana..........	20.7	24.2	25.8	27.1	29.0	20.7	22.9	23.8	24.3	25.3
Nebraska.........	47.3	53.4	55.8	57.9	60.8	47.3	50.6	51.5	51.9	53.1
Nevada	61.4	71.2	79.4	86.2	92.6	61.4	67.4	73.2	77.3	80.8
New Hampshire......	41.4	44.3	47.2	49.4	51.7	41.4	42.0	43.6	44.3	45.1
New Jersey........	323.6	342.9	363.2	381.5	404.3	323.6	324.7	335.1	342.1	353.0
New Mexico........	40.3	46.7	50.7	53.7	58.0	40.3	44.2	46.8	48.2	50.6
New York	663.0	693.5	742.2	772.0	818.4	663.0	656.8	684.9	692.4	714.4
North Carolina......	218.7	235.0	252.3	269.2	285.5	218.7	222.5	232.8	241.5	249.2
North Dakota.......	16.1	18.2	18.5	19.9	20.7	16.1	17.2	17.1	17.8	18.1
Ohio	320.5	341.1	352.6	365.5	382.7	320.5	323.1	325.3	327.8	334.0
Oklahoma..........	84.3	92.6	100.0	106.1	115.3	84.3	87.7	92.3	95.2	100.6
Oregon.	96.4	105.2	111.3	117.5	124.6	96.4	99.6	102.7	105.4	108.8
Pennsylvania.......	364.8	393.9	413.6	433.4	456.3	364.8	373.0	381.6	388.7	398.3
Rhode Island.......	30.7	35.1	36.7	37.9	39.9	30.7	33.2	33.8	34.0	34.8
South Carolina......	98.3	107.2	113.6	120.1	127.5	98.3	101.5	104.9	107.7	111.3
South Dakota	19.4	22.4	24.1	25.2	26.5	19.4	21.2	22.2	22.6	23.2
Tennessee	148.8	165.4	174.5	184.4	195.1	148.8	156.6	161.0	165.4	170.3
Texas............	593.1	649.4	690.5	744.3	805.3	593.1	615.0	637.1	667.5	703.0
Utah	53.6	59.4	63.5	68.0	74.2	53.6	56.3	58.6	61.0	64.8
Vermont	16.9	18.7	19.5	20.4	21.4	16.9	17.7	18.0	18.3	18.7
Virginia.	220.8	250.6	266.8	283.7	299.4	220.8	237.3	246.1	254.4	261.4
Washington	187.9	202.9	216.9	223.2	239.3	187.9	192.2	200.2	200.2	208.9
West Virginia	39.6	43.8	45.8	47.9	50.7	39.6	41.5	42.3	43.0	44.3
Wisconsin	153.5	168.1	176.5	183.9	192.8	153.5	159.2	162.8	165.0	168.3
Wyoming	14.1	16.4	17.7	19.0	20.9	14.1	15.5	16.4	17.0	18.3

[1] Constant dollar estimates are computed by the U.S. Census Bureau using the national implicit price deflator for personal consumption expenditures from the Bureau of Economic Analysis. Any regional differences in the rate of inflation are not reflected in these constant dollar estimates.

Source: Except as noted, U.S. Bureau of Economic Analysis, Survey of Current Business, April 2007. See also <http://www.bea.gov/bea/regional/spi.htm>.

Table 659. Personal Income Per Capita in Current and Constant (2000) Dollars by State: 2000 to 2006

[In dollars, except as indicated. 2006 preliminary. See headnote, Table 658]

State	Current dollars				Constant (2000) dollars [1]				Income rank	
	2000	2004	2005	2006	2000	2004	2005	2006	2000	2006
United States	**29,843**	**33,090**	**34,471**	**36,276**	**29,843**	**30,533**	**30,918**	**31,667**	(X)	(X)
Alabama	23,764	28,037	29,623	31,295	23,764	25,871	26,569	27,319	44	40
Alaska	29,865	33,889	35,564	37,271	29,865	31,271	31,898	32,535	15	16
Arizona	25,656	28,564	30,019	31,458	25,656	26,357	26,925	27,461	37	39
Arkansas	21,924	25,794	26,681	27,935	21,924	23,801	23,931	24,385	48	48
California	32,458	35,380	36,936	38,956	32,458	32,647	33,129	34,006	8	11
Colorado	33,367	35,810	37,510	39,186	33,367	33,043	33,643	34,207	7	8
Connecticut	41,485	45,384	47,388	49,852	41,485	41,878	42,503	43,518	1	1
Delaware	30,867	35,354	37,088	39,022	30,867	32,623	33,265	34,064	13	10
District of Columbia	40,456	50,240	52,811	55,755	40,456	46,358	47,367	48,671	(X)	(X)
Florida	28,507	32,534	34,001	35,798	28,507	30,020	30,496	31,249	20	20
Georgia	27,988	29,628	30,914	31,891	27,988	27,339	27,727	27,839	26	38
Hawaii	28,422	32,660	34,489	36,299	28,422	30,137	30,934	31,687	22	19
Idaho	24,073	27,414	28,478	29,952	24,073	25,296	25,542	26,146	42	43
Illinois	32,182	34,794	36,264	38,215	32,182	32,106	32,526	33,359	9	13
Indiana	27,130	30,134	31,173	32,526	27,130	27,806	27,960	28,393	31	33
Iowa	26,552	30,887	31,670	33,236	26,552	28,501	28,405	29,013	33	30
Kansas	27,691	31,230	32,866	34,743	27,691	28,817	29,478	30,328	27	21
Kentucky	24,411	27,020	28,272	29,352	24,411	24,932	25,358	25,622	40	46
Louisiana	23,079	27,088	24,664	30,952	23,079	24,995	22,122	27,019	45	41
Maine	25,968	29,861	30,808	32,348	25,968	27,554	27,632	28,238	35	34
Maryland	34,256	39,725	41,972	44,077	34,256	36,656	37,645	38,476	5	4
Massachusetts	37,753	41,636	43,501	45,877	37,753	38,419	39,017	40,048	3	3
Michigan	29,551	31,730	32,804	33,847	29,551	29,279	29,422	29,546	17	27
Minnesota	32,014	36,163	37,290	38,712	32,014	33,369	33,446	33,793	10	12
Mississippi	21,005	24,009	25,051	26,535	21,005	22,154	22,469	23,163	50	50
Missouri	27,240	30,081	31,231	32,705	27,240	27,757	28,012	28,549	30	31
Montana	22,928	27,841	29,015	30,688	22,928	25,690	26,024	26,789	46	42
Nebraska	27,622	31,957	32,923	34,397	27,622	29,488	29,529	30,026	29	23
Nevada	30,433	34,021	35,744	37,089	30,433	31,393	32,059	32,376	14	17
New Hampshire	33,393	36,402	37,768	39,311	33,393	33,590	33,875	34,316	6	7
New Jersey	38,362	41,858	43,831	46,344	38,362	38,624	39,313	40,455	2	2
New Mexico	22,133	26,679	27,889	29,673	22,133	24,618	25,014	25,903	47	44
New York	34,895	38,473	39,967	42,392	34,895	35,501	35,847	37,005	4	5
North Carolina	27,067	29,569	31,041	32,234	27,067	27,284	27,841	28,138	32	36
North Dakota	25,104	29,109	31,357	32,552	25,104	26,860	28,125	28,416	38	32
Ohio	28,205	30,763	31,860	33,338	28,205	28,386	28,576	29,102	24	29
Oklahoma	24,406	28,394	29,948	32,210	24,406	26,200	26,861	28,117	41	37
Oregon	28,093	31,017	32,289	33,666	28,093	28,621	28,961	29,388	25	28
Pennsylvania	29,693	33,415	34,937	36,680	29,693	30,833	31,336	32,019	16	18
Rhode Island	29,212	33,996	35,324	37,388	29,212	31,369	31,683	32,637	18	15
South Carolina	24,424	27,090	28,285	29,515	24,424	24,997	25,369	25,765	39	45
South Dakota	25,718	31,231	32,523	33,929	25,718	28,818	29,170	29,618	36	26
Tennessee	26,096	29,641	30,969	32,304	26,096	27,351	27,777	28,199	34	35
Texas	28,310	30,664	32,460	34,257	28,310	28,295	29,114	29,904	23	25
Utah	23,874	26,214	27,321	29,108	23,874	24,189	24,505	25,409	43	47
Vermont	27,678	31,442	32,717	34,264	27,678	29,013	29,344	29,910	28	24
Virginia	31,085	35,608	37,503	39,173	31,085	32,940	33,637	34,196	12	9
Washington	31,775	34,956	35,479	37,423	31,775	32,255	31,822	32,668	11	14
West Virginia	21,898	25,302	26,419	27,897	21,898	23,347	23,696	24,352	49	49
Wisconsin	28,568	32,095	33,278	34,701	28,568	29,615	29,848	30,292	19	22
Wyoming	28,458	35,058	37,305	40,676	28,458	32,349	33,459	35,508	21	6

X Not applicable.   [1] Constant dollar estimates are computed by the U.S. Census Bureau using the national implicit price deflator for personal consumption expenditures from the Bureau of Economic Analysis. Any regional differences in the rate of inflation are not reflected in these constant dollar estimates.

Source: Except as noted, U.S. Bureau of Economic Analysis, *Survey of Current Business*, April 2007. See also <http://www.bea.gov/bea/regional/spi>.

U.S. Census Bureau, *Statistical Abstract of the United States: 2008*

Table 660. **Disposable Personal Income Per Capita in Current and Constant (2000) Dollars by State: 2000 to 2006**

[In dollars, except percent. 2006 preliminary. Disposable personal income is the income available to persons for spending or saving; it is calculated as personal income less personal tax and nontax payments]

State	Current dollars				Constant (2000) dollars [1]				Percent of U.S. average	
	2000	2004	2005	2006	2000	2004	2005	2006	2000	2006
United States	**25,468**	**29,518**	**30,418**	**31,735**	**25,468**	**27,237**	**27,282**	**27,703**	**100.0**	**100.0**
Alabama	21,046	25,610	26,845	28,185	21,046	23,631	24,078	24,604	82.6	88.8
Alaska	26,424	31,022	32,280	33,595	26,424	28,625	28,952	29,326	103.8	105.9
Arizona	22,323	25,759	26,769	27,763	22,323	23,769	24,010	24,235	87.7	87.5
Arkansas	19,374	23,517	24,108	25,112	19,374	21,700	21,623	21,921	76.1	79.1
California	26,712	31,152	32,059	33,373	26,712	28,745	28,754	29,132	104.9	105.2
Colorado	28,233	31,986	33,173	34,332	28,233	29,515	29,753	29,970	110.9	108.2
Connecticut	33,380	38,612	39,574	40,973	33,380	35,629	35,495	35,767	131.1	129.1
Delaware	26,276	31,192	32,350	33,683	26,276	28,782	29,015	29,403	103.2	106.1
District of Columbia . . .	33,408	43,799	45,343	47,515	33,408	40,415	40,669	41,478	131.2	149.7
Florida	24,808	29,366	30,314	31,635	24,808	27,097	27,189	27,615	97.4	99.7
Georgia	24,052	26,518	27,450	28,109	24,052	24,469	24,620	24,537	94.4	88.6
Hawaii	24,842	29,217	30,502	31,856	24,842	26,960	27,358	27,808	97.5	100.4
Idaho	20,957	24,919	25,667	26,754	20,957	22,994	23,021	23,355	82.3	84.3
Illinois	27,409	31,016	31,973	33,419	27,409	28,620	28,677	29,173	107.6	105.3
Indiana	23,646	27,201	27,916	28,979	23,646	25,099	25,038	25,297	92.8	91.3
Iowa	23,388	28,134	28,596	29,808	23,388	25,960	25,648	26,020	91.8	93.9
Kansas	24,045	28,249	29,481	30,935	24,045	26,066	26,442	27,004	94.4	97.5
Kentucky	21,343	24,312	25,257	26,104	21,343	22,434	22,653	22,787	83.8	82.3
Louisiana	20,574	24,921	22,603	28,553	20,574	22,996	20,273	24,925	80.8	90.0
Maine	22,488	26,860	27,459	28,777	22,488	24,785	24,628	25,120	88.3	90.7
Maryland	28,799	34,553	36,144	37,574	28,799	31,883	32,418	32,800	113.1	118.4
Massachusetts	30,308	36,050	37,229	38,794	30,308	33,265	33,391	33,865	119.0	122.2
Michigan	25,434	28,586	29,338	30,117	25,434	26,377	26,314	26,290	99.9	94.9
Minnesota	27,184	31,925	32,599	33,494	27,184	29,458	29,239	29,238	106.7	105.5
Mississippi	18,935	22,304	23,102	24,360	18,935	20,581	20,721	21,265	74.3	76.8
Missouri	23,675	27,156	27,932	29,066	23,675	25,058	25,053	25,373	93.0	91.6
Montana	20,233	25,324	26,092	27,419	20,233	23,367	23,402	23,935	79.4	86.4
Nebraska	24,087	28,987	29,568	30,676	24,087	26,747	26,520	26,778	94.6	96.7
Nevada	26,319	30,326	31,427	32,290	26,319	27,983	28,187	28,187	103.3	101.7
New Hampshire	28,564	32,976	33,852	34,964	28,564	30,428	30,362	30,521	112.2	110.2
New Jersey	32,007	36,771	38,017	39,840	32,007	33,930	34,098	34,778	125.7	125.5
New Mexico	19,576	24,401	25,354	26,839	19,576	22,516	22,740	23,429	76.9	84.6
New York	28,879	33,054	33,791	35,407	28,879	30,500	30,308	30,908	113.4	111.6
North Carolina	23,395	26,505	27,555	28,553	23,395	24,457	24,715	24,738	91.9	89.3
North Dakota	22,594	26,776	28,661	29,515	22,594	24,707	25,707	25,765	88.7	93.0
Ohio	24,262	27,334	28,052	29,223	24,262	25,222	25,160	25,510	95.3	92.1
Oklahoma	21,516	25,806	27,014	28,895	21,516	23,812	24,229	25,223	84.5	91.1
Oregon	23,902	27,557	28,369	29,310	23,902	25,428	25,445	25,586	93.9	92.4
Pennsylvania	25,572	29,865	30,932	32,222	25,572	27,558	27,743	28,128	100.4	101.5
Rhode Island	25,056	30,260	31,135	32,734	25,056	27,922	27,926	28,575	98.4	103.1
South Carolina	21,501	24,590	25,481	26,406	21,501	22,690	22,854	23,051	84.4	83.2
South Dakota	23,161	29,043	30,026	31,116	23,161	26,799	26,931	27,162	90.9	98.0
Tennessee	23,408	27,394	28,423	29,456	23,408	25,278	25,493	25,713	91.9	92.8
Texas	24,961	28,190	29,603	31,012	24,961	26,012	26,551	27,071	98.0	97.7
Utah	20,798	23,678	24,420	25,792	20,798	21,849	21,903	22,515	81.7	81.3
Vermont	24,008	28,341	29,188	30,317	24,008	26,151	26,179	26,465	94.3	95.5
Virginia	26,213	31,359	32,527	33,628	26,213	28,936	29,174	29,355	102.9	106.0
Washington	27,305	31,813	31,885	33,334	27,305	29,355	28,598	29,098	107.2	105.0
West Virginia	19,534	23,188	24,006	25,204	19,534	21,396	21,531	22,001	76.7	79.4
Wisconsin	24,497	28,612	29,395	30,439	24,497	26,401	26,365	26,571	96.2	95.9
Wyoming	24,495	31,868	33,526	36,176	24,495	29,406	30,070	31,579	96.2	114.0

[1] Constant dollar estimates are computed by the Census Bureau using the national implicit price deflator for personal consumption expenditures from the Bureau of Economic Analysis. Any regional differences in the rate of inflation are not reflected in these constant dollar estimates.

Source: Except as noted, U.S. Bureau of Economic Analysis, *Survey of Current Business*, April 2007. See also <http://www.bea.gov/bea/regional/spi>.

Table 661. Personal Income by Selected Large Metropolitan Area: 2000 to 2005

[8,422,074 represents $8,422,074,000,000. Metropolitan areas as defined December 2006. MSA = Metropolitan Statistical Area. See Appendix II. Minus sign (–) indicates decrease]

Metropolitan area ranked by 2005 population	Personal income 2000 (mil. dol.)	Personal income 2004 (mil. dol.)	Personal income 2005 (mil. dol.)	Annual percent change, 2004–2005	Per capita personal income 2000 (dol.)	Per capita personal income 2004 (dol.)	Per capita personal income 2005 (dol.)	Percent of national average, 2005
United States	8,422,074	9,716,351	10,220,942	5.2	29,843	33,090	34,471	100.0
New York-Northern New Jersey-Long Island, NY-NJ-PA MSA	732,799	816,254	851,660	4.3	39,912	43,496	45,268	131.3
Los Angeles-Long Beach-Santa Ana, CA MSA	385,053	453,033	475,263	4.9	31,039	35,115	36,746	106.6
Chicago-Naperville-Joliet, IL-IN-WI MSA	318,439	350,111	367,957	5.1	34,914	37,268	38,951	113.0
Dallas-Fort Worth-Arlington, TX MSA	176,530	202,282	216,667	7.1	33,966	35,521	37,209	107.9
Philadelphia-Camden-Wilmington, PA-NJ-DE-MD MSA	193,919	224,974	236,467	5.1	34,058	38,869	40,727	118.1
Miami-Fort Lauderdale-Pompano Beach, FL MSA	157,015	190,430	203,465	6.8	31,220	35,589	37,507	108.8
Houston-Sugar Land-Baytown, TX MSA	161,398	191,918	209,818	9.3	34,035	36,676	39,199	113.7
Washington-Arlington-Alexandria, DC-VA-MD-WV MSA	196,093	239,826	255,740	6.6	40,667	46,311	48,697	141.3
Atlanta-Sandy Springs-Marietta, GA MSA	141,817	161,795	173,159	7.0	33,120	33,553	34,825	101.0
Detroit-Warren-Livonia, MI MSA	151,793	161,831	168,038	3.8	34,045	36,094	37,515	108.8
Boston-Cambridge-Quincy, MA-NH MSA	182,380	201,089	209,847	4.4	41,433	45,195	47,168	136.8
San Francisco-Oakland-Fremont, CA MSA	199,989	207,385	218,475	5.3	48,333	49,989	52,543	152.4
Riverside-San Bernardino-Ontario, CA MSA	74,787	97,251	104,074	7.0	22,806	25,705	26,618	77.2
Phoenix-Mesa-Scottsdale, AZ MSA	92,975	114,926	125,718	9.4	28,359	30,892	32,414	94.0
Seattle-Tacoma-Bellevue, WA MSA	115,203	131,813	133,475	1.3	37,740	41,593	41,608	120.7
Minneapolis-St. Paul-Bloomington, MN-WI MSA	109,818	127,315	132,210	3.8	36,833	40,915	42,091	122.1
San Diego-Carlsbad-San Marcos, CA MSA	92,654	113,062	119,136	5.4	32,799	38,536	40,569	117.7
St. Louis, MO-IL MSA	84,222	94,075	98,979	5.2	31,171	34,011	35,573	103.2
Baltimore-Towson, MD MSA	85,144	103,138	109,543	6.2	33,293	39,032	41,320	119.9
Tampa-St. Petersburg-Clearwater, FL MSA	68,891	82,692	87,999	6.4	28,652	32,000	33,250	96.5
Pittsburgh, PA MSA	74,361	83,356	87,003	4.4	30,609	34,810	36,530	106.0
Denver-Aurora, CO MSA	82,196	94,402	100,066	6.0	37,843	40,583	42,369	122.9
Cleveland-Elyria-Mentor, OH MSA	67,935	72,723	75,278	3.5	31,623	34,078	35,423	102.8
Portland-Vancouver-Beaverton, OR-WA MSA	62,190	70,144	74,282	5.9	32,117	34,018	35,430	102.8
Cincinnati-Middletown, OH-KY-IN MSA	61,393	70,041	73,103	4.4	30,474	33,758	34,961	101.4
Sacramento-Arden-Arcade-Roseville, CA MSA	54,236	68,308	72,404	6.0	29,985	33,919	35,463	102.9
Kansas City, MO-KS MSA	58,247	66,426	69,560	4.7	31,605	34,498	35,769	103.8
Orlando-Kissimmee, FL MSA	44,751	55,966	60,951	8.9	27,015	30,068	31,557	91.5
San Antonio, TX MSA	45,997	53,643	57,384	7.0	26,751	28,981	30,393	88.2
San Jose-Sunnyvale-Santa Clara, CA MSA	92,947	83,986	88,883	5.8	53,395	48,226	50,468	146.4
Las Vegas-Paradise, NV MSA	41,239	54,475	59,793	9.8	29,597	33,049	34,980	101.5
Columbus, OH MSA	49,770	56,971	59,674	4.7	30,740	33,725	34,960	101.4
Virginia Beach-Norfolk-Newport News, VA-NC MSA	41,659	51,739	54,438	5.2	26,364	31,587	33,163	96.2
Indianapolis-Carmel, IN MSA	48,862	56,900	59,683	4.9	31,913	35,180	36,391	105.6
Providence-New Bedford-Fall River, RI-MA MSA	45,976	54,685	56,721	3.7	28,970	33,639	35,025	101.6
Charlotte-Gastonia-Concord, NC-SC MSA	43,120	51,652	55,931	8.3	32,179	35,075	36,761	106.6
Milwaukee-Waukesha-West Allis, WI MSA	49,151	55,370	57,604	4.0	32,716	36,644	38,164	110.7
Austin-Round Rock, TX MSA	41,157	46,192	50,102	8.5	32,542	32,726	34,441	99.9
Nashville-Davidson-Murfreesboro-Franklin, TN MSA	40,309	48,620	52,092	7.1	30,599	34,888	36,655	106.3
New Orleans-Metairie-Kenner, LA MSA	34,606	40,230	26,552	-34.0	26,302	30,611	20,210	58.6
Memphis, TN-MS-AR MSA	34,459	40,258	42,133	4.7	28,519	32,342	33,529	97.3
Jacksonville, FL MSA	33,151	40,348	42,785	6.0	29,435	33,014	34,288	99.5
Louisville-Jefferson County, KY-IN MSA	34,250	39,044	40,842	4.6	29,394	32,522	33,749	97.9
Hartford-West Hartford-East Hartford, CT MSA	42,568	47,840	50,237	5.0	36,980	40,504	42,369	122.9
Richmond, VA MSA	33,603	40,189	42,873	6.7	30,545	34,808	36,537	106.0
Oklahoma City, OK MSA	29,092	35,735	37,970	6.3	26,499	31,325	32,875	95.4
Buffalo-Niagara Falls, NY MSA	31,806	35,617	36,715	3.1	27,208	30,912	32,071	93.0
Birmingham-Hoover, AL MSA	29,898	36,526	38,809	6.3	28,383	33,816	35,663	103.5
Salt Lake City, UT MSA	27,081	31,341	33,634	7.3	27,847	30,731	32,133	93.2
Rochester, NY MSA	30,455	33,821	35,106	3.8	29,326	32,531	33,857	98.2
Raleigh-Cary, NC MSA	27,062	31,680	33,907	7.0	33,650	34,615	35,624	103.3
Tucson, AZ MSA	20,514	24,881	26,704	7.3	24,173	27,467	28,869	83.7
Honolulu, HI MSA	26,605	31,278	33,316	6.5	30,391	34,832	36,828	106.8
Bridgeport-Stamford-Norwalk, CT MSA	52,190	57,845	60,615	4.8	58,977	64,224	67,269	195.1
Tulsa, OK MSA	24,984	28,763	30,723	6.8	29,002	32,692	34,685	100.6
Fresno, CA MSA	17,628	21,859	22,796	4.3	21,972	25,257	25,961	75.3
Albany-Schenectady-Troy, NY MSA	25,168	29,084	30,159	3.7	30,442	34,452	35,590	103.2
New Haven-Milford, CT MSA	28,379	31,856	33,182	4.2	34,395	37,803	39,292	114.0
Dayton, OH MSA	24,210	25,935	26,744	3.1	28,548	30,746	31,792	92.2
Omaha-Council Bluffs, NE-IA MSA	24,230	29,025	30,435	4.9	31,503	36,191	37,444	108.6
Albuquerque, NM MSA	18,910	23,280	24,631	5.8	25,846	29,836	30,884	89.6
Oxnard-Thousand Oaks-Ventura, CA MSA	25,364	30,534	32,139	5.3	33,517	38,367	40,358	117.1
Allentown-Bethlehem-Easton, PA-NJ MSA	22,220	25,282	26,698	5.6	29,944	32,447	33,808	98.1
Worcester, MA MSA	24,539	27,565	28,806	4.5	32,598	35,433	36,851	106.9
Grand Rapids-Wyoming, MI MSA	20,818	23,610	24,519	3.9	28,022	30,832	31,836	92.4
Bakersfield, CA MSA	13,891	17,660	18,924	7.2	20,925	24,067	24,999	72.5
Baton Rouge, LA MSA	17,206	20,162	21,687	7.6	24,323	27,782	29,654	86.0
El Paso, TX MSA	12,650	15,727	16,771	6.6	18,560	22,074	23,256	67.5
Akron, OH MSA	20,593	22,573	23,425	3.8	29,588	32,181	33,396	96.9
Columbia, SC MSA	17,429	20,139	21,288	5.7	26,851	29,419	30,810	89.4

Source: U.S. Bureau of Economic Analysis, *Survey of Current Business*, May 2007. See also <http://www.bea.gov/regional/reis>.

Income, Expenditures, Poverty, and Wealth   441

Table 662. **Average Annual Expenditures of All Consumer Units by Selected Major Types of Expenditure: 1990 to 2005**

[In dollars, except as indicated (96,968 represents 96,968,000). Based on Consumer Expenditure Survey. Data are averages for the noninstitutional population. Expenditures reported here are out-of-pocket]

Type	1990	1995	2000	2001	2002	2003	2004	2005
Number of consumer units (1,000)	96,968	103,123	109,367	110,339	112,108	115,356	116,282	117,356
Expenditures, total [1]	$28,381	$32,264	$38,045	$39,518	$40,677	$40,817	$43,395	$46,409
Food	4,296	4,505	5,158	5,321	5,375	5,340	5,781	5,931
Food at home [1]	2,485	2,803	3,021	3,086	3,099	3,129	3,347	3,297
Meats, poultry, fish, and eggs	668	752	795	828	798	825	880	764
Dairy products	295	297	325	332	328	328	371	378
Fruits and vegetables	408	457	521	522	552	535	561	552
Other food at home	746	856	927	952	970	999	1,075	1,158
Food away from home	1,811	1,702	2,137	2,235	2,276	2,211	2,434	2,634
Alcoholic beverages	293	277	372	349	376	391	459	426
Housing [1]	8,703	10,458	12,319	13,011	13,283	13,432	13,918	15,167
Shelter	4,836	5,928	7,114	7,602	7,829	7,887	7,998	8,805
Utilities, fuels, public services	1,890	2,191	2,489	2,767	2,684	2,811	2,927	3,183
Apparel and services	1,618	1,704	1,856	1,743	1,749	1,640	1,816	1,886
Transportation [1]	5,120	6,014	7,417	7,633	7,759	7,781	7,801	8,344
Vehicle purchases	2,129	2,638	3,418	3,579	3,665	3,732	3,397	3,544
Gasoline and motor oil	1,047	1,006	1,291	1,279	1,235	1,333	1,598	2,013
Other vehicle expenses	1,642	2,015	2,281	2,375	2,471	2,331	2,365	2,339
Health care	1,480	1,732	2,066	2,182	2,350	2,416	2,574	2,664
Entertainment	1,422	1,612	1,863	1,953	2,079	2,060	2,218	2,388
Reading	153	162	146	141	139	127	130	126
Tobacco products, smoking supplies . . .	274	269	319	308	320	290	288	319
Personal insurance and pensions	2,592	2,964	3,365	3,737	3,899	4,055	4,823	5,204
Life and other personal insurance . . .	345	373	399	410	406	397	390	381
Pensions and Social Security	2,248	2,591	2,966	3,326	3,493	3,658	4,433	4,823

[1] Includes expenditures not shown separately.

Source: U.S. Bureau of Labor Statistics, *Consumer Expenditures in 2005*; <http://stats.bls.gov/cex/home.htm>.

Table 663. **Average Annual Expenditures of All Consumer Units by Metropolitan Area: 2004–2005**

[In dollars. Covers 2-year period, 2004–2005. Metropolitan areas defined June 30, 1983, CMSA = Consolidated Metropolitan Statistical Area; MSA = Metropolitan Statistical Area; PMSA = Primary Metropolitan Statistical Area. See text, Section 1, and Appendix II. See headnote, Table 662]

Metropolitan area	Total expendi- tures	Food	Housing			Transportation			Health care
			Total [1]	Shel- ter	Utility fuels [2]	Total [1]	Vehicle pur- chases	Gaso- line and motor oil	
Anchorage, AK MSA	59,427	6,412	18,764	11,391	3,228	12,596	6,082	2,157	3,397
Atlanta, GA MSA	39,992	5,496	14,346	8,497	3,430	6,044	2,359	1,695	1,837
Baltimore, MD MSA	39,217	4,324	14,714	9,487	2,944	5,799	2,052	1,541	2,215
Boston-Lawrence-Salem, MA-NH CMSA	51,679	7,223	17,805	11,364	3,169	8,586	3,759	1,747	2,624
Chicago-Gary-Lake County, IL-IN-WI CMSA	54,935	6,456	18,962	11,440	3,541	8,875	4,013	1,754	2,933
Cleveland-Akron-Lorain, OH CMSA . . .	38,476	4,526	13,349	7,560	3,412	6,095	2,056	1,449	2,600
Dallas-Fort Worth, TX CMSA . . .	50,637	6,426	16,706	9,453	3,833	8,838	3,587	1,982	3,027
Denver-Boulder-Greeley, CO CMSA . .	49,996	6,251	15,772	10,078	3,013	8,646	3,529	1,755	2,724
Detroit-Ann Arbor, MI CMSA	51,219	6,780	16,490	9,656	3,511	9,246	2,914	2,129	2,261
Honolulu, HI MSA	54,937	8,089	17,400	10,887	2,813	9,921	4,768	1,658	2,600
Houston-Galveston-Brazoria, TX CMSA	52,998	5,862	16,609	9,245	3,877	10,326	4,584	2,249	2,942
Los Angeles-Long Beach, CA PMSA . .	55,760	7,062	19,911	13,030	2,908	10,972	4,996	2,312	2,275
Miami-Fort Lauderdale, FL CMSA . . .	37,673	5,522	14,807	9,465	3,140	6,282	2,013	1,633	2,003
Minneapolis-St. Paul, MN-WI MSA . . .	58,900	6,850	19,341	11,245	3,070	8,550	3,140	1,853	3,100
New York-Northern New Jersey- Long Island, NY-NJ-CT CMSA	54,121	7,283	20,065	13,271	3,528	7,581	2,316	1,495	2,412
Philadelphia-Wilmington-Trenton, PA-NJ-DE-MD CMSA	47,289	6,481	15,915	9,289	3,600	8,084	3,802	1,477	2,254
Phoenix-Mesa, AZ MSA	49,009	6,434	14,719	8,414	3,057	10,549	5,490	1,769	2,890
Pittsburgh-Beaver Valley, PA CMSA . .	39,891	5,205	12,031	6,429	3,103	7,456	3,307	1,538	2,528
Portland-Vancouver, OR-WA CMSA. . .	50,313	6,377	16,039	9,862	2,878	8,845	3,964	1,742	2,693
San Diego, CA MSA.	59,805	6,437	21,484	14,511	2,767	11,301	5,681	2,094	3,038
San Francisco-Oakland-San Jose, CA CMSA	60,992	7,581	22,885	15,947	2,711	9,518	3,347	1,922	2,773
Seattle-Tacoma, WA CMSA	54,027	6,904	17,483	10,741	2,769	9,491	3,897	1,914	2,910
St. Louis-East St. Louis-Alton, MO-IL CMSA.	48,365	6,266	14,409	7,620	3,251	8,649	4,095	1,853	2,980
Washington, DC-MD-VA MSA.	55,977	5,831	21,523	13,997	3,618	7,876	2,758	1,726	2,510

[1] Includes expenditures not shown separately. [2] Includes public services.

Source: U.S. Bureau of Labor Statistics, *Consumer Expenditures in 2005*; <http://stats.bls.gov/cex/home.htm>.

442 Income, Expenditures, Poverty, and Wealth

Table 664. Average Annual Expenditures of All Consumer Units by Race, Hispanic Origin, and Age of Householder: 2005

[In **dollars.** Based on Consumer Expenditure Survey. Data are averages for the noninstitutional population. Expenditures reported here are out-of-pocket]

Type	All consumer units [1]	White and all other races	Asian	Black or African American	Hispanic or Latino	Age of householder Under 25 years	Age of householder 65 years and over
Expenditures, total	46,409	48,077	52,054	32,849	40,123	27,776	32,866
Food	5,931	6,127	6,632	4,319	5,551	3,933	4,163
Food at home	3,297	3,373	3,580	2,663	3,344	1,917	2,605
Cereals and bakery products	445	455	492	363	400	273	366
Cereals and cereal products	143	142	216	132	147	106	106
Bakery products	302	313	276	231	253	167	261
Meats, poultry, fish, and eggs	764	757	892	787	876	449	569
Beef	228	234	196	193	285	149	150
Pork	153	151	164	170	160	79	126
Other meats	103	106	82	90	99	59	79
Poultry	134	128	147	177	177	83	85
Fish and seafood	113	107	259	121	109	59	102
Eggs	33	32	45	35	46	21	28
Dairy products	378	399	303	245	364	214	308
Fresh milk and cream	146	153	137	98	162	90	119
Other dairy products	232	246	166	147	202	124	189
Fruits and vegetables	552	559	814	428	640	298	490
Fresh fruits	182	186	284	122	219	87	170
Fresh vegetables	175	177	312	122	210	90	147
Processed fruits	106	106	125	99	119	69	101
Processed vegetables	89	90	93	85	92	51	72
Other food at home	1,158	1,204	1,078	840	1,064	684	871
Nonalcoholic beverages	303	314	279	230	321	186	203
Food away from home	2,634	2,754	3,052	1,657	2,207	2,015	1,558
Alcoholic beverages	426	465	319	173	286	401	248
Housing	15,167	15,496	19,017	11,650	14,338	8,940	11,058
Shelter	8,805	8,961	12,659	6,524	8,937	5,538	5,836
Owned dwellings [2]	5,958	6,236	8,623	3,188	4,886	1,263	3,903
Mortgage interest and charges	3,317	3,416	5,354	1,998	3,166	835	1,060
Property taxes	1,541	1,626	2,203	734	1,058	287	1,524
Rented dwellings	2,345	2,182	3,479	3,148	3,876	4,085	1,492
Other lodging	502	544	556	189	175	190	440
Utilities, fuels, and public services	3,183	3,181	3,018	3,253	2,986	1,755	2,813
Natural gas	473	464	454	549	378	191	489
Electricity	1,155	1,157	942	1,205	1,071	645	1,029
Fuel oil and other fuels	142	159	58	45	43	36	195
Telephone	1,048	1,032	1,166	1,124	1,130	744	733
Water and other public services	366	369	398	330	365	140	367
Household operations	801	833	948	530	605	387	650
Personal services	322	321	449	289	336	237	113
Other household expenses	479	512	499	241	268	151	538
Housekeeping supplies	611	653	439	352	508	242	534
Household furnishings and equipment [2] . .	1,767	1,868	1,954	991	1,303	1,018	1,225
Household textiles	132	136	172	93	95	58	91
Furniture	467	491	478	298	487	297	306
Floor coverings	56	60	97	16	20	17	28
Major appliances	223	229	377	143	171	95	204
Miscellaneous household equipment . . .	782	838	737	393	445	483	503
Apparel and services	1,886	1,868	2,035	1,981	2,195	1,577	957
Men and boys	440	441	467	420	529	316	191
Women and girls	754	748	877	765	787	678	448
Children under 2 years old	82	82	97	77	149	97	22
Footwear	320	297	303	493	442	297	159
Other apparel products and services	290	299	291	226	288	189	137
Transportation	8,344	8,674	8,899	5,850	7,900	5,987	5,171
Vehicle purchases (net outlay) [2]	3,544	3,715	3,516	2,350	3,280	2,721	2,007
Cars and trucks, new	1,931	2,037	2,568	988	1,710	720	1,370
Cars and trucks, used	1,531	1,590	898	1,307	1,551	1,907	630
Gasoline and motor oil	2,013	2,080	2,011	1,546	2,171	1,538	1,208
Other vehicle expenses [2]	2,339	2,426	2,395	1,710	2,068	1,536	1,594
Vehicle finance charges	297	310	218	229	269	199	110
Maintenance and repair	671	707	619	433	586	444	542
Vehicle insurance	913	937	914	747	837	626	658
Public transportation	448	454	978	245	380	191	362
Health care [3]	2,664	2,853	2,262	1,448	1,520	704	4,193
Entertainment [4]	2,388	2,573	1,804	1,242	1,494	1,393	1,593
Personal care products and services	541	551	519	472	501	337	462
Reading	126	137	117	52	55	49	143
Education	940	967	1,759	500	558	1,359	211
Tobacco products and smoking supplies . . .	319	342	124	216	158	308	165
Miscellaneous	808	864	794	416	665	263	839
Cash contributions	1,663	1,749	1,188	1,204	927	393	1,889
Personal insurance and pensions	5,204	5,411	6,584	3,325	3,974	2,133	1,775
Life and other personal insurance	381	390	465	292	140	45	403
Pensions and social security	4,823	5,021	6,119	3,033	3,834	2,088	1,372
Personal taxes	**2,408**	**2,683**	**1,966**	**603**	**982**	**373**	**929**

[1] Includes other householders not shown separately.   [2] Includes other types not shown separately.   [3] For additional health care expenditures, see Table 133.   [4] For additional recreation expenditures, see Section 26.

Source: U.S. Bureau of Labor Statistics, *Consumer Expenditures in 2005*. See also <http://www.bls.gov/cex/2005/Standard/race.pdf> and <http://www.bls.gov/cex/2005/Standard/hispanic.pdf> and <http://www.bls.gov/cex/2005/Standard/age.pdf> (released February 2007).

Table 665. Average Annual Expenditures of All Consumer Units by Region and Size of Unit: 2005

[**In dollars.** For composition of regions, see map, inside front cover. See headnote, Table 662]

Type	Region				Size of consumer unit				
	North-east	Mid-west	South	West	One person	Two per-sons	Three per-sons	Four per-sons	Five or more
Expenditures, total	47,921	45,027	42,504	52,891	26,773	48,492	55,096	62,215	62,618
Food	6,495	5,754	5,491	6,339	3,073	5,851	7,088	8,622	9,078
Food at home..................	3,645	3,232	3,011	3,527	1,638	3,142	3,925	4,846	5,583
Cereals and bakery products	508	454	400	456	227	411	513	666	793
Cereals and cereal products.....	162	143	129	148	69	124	165	223	277
Bakery products	346	311	270	307	158	286	347	442	516
Meats, poultry, fish, and eggs......	885	712	732	767	332	738	941	1,140	1,332
Beef......................	243	220	227	222	90	212	304	344	408
Pork......................	163	150	157	143	67	156	182	228	253
Other meats	125	109	89	101	45	102	115	155	188
Poultry	159	121	129	135	61	119	170	204	253
Fish and seafood	158	85	100	125	52	117	133	164	178
Eggs	37	26	30	40	18	32	38	46	53
Dairy products................	424	391	332	401	193	350	448	556	668
Fresh milk and cream	151	150	137	152	74	126	182	216	270
Other dairy products	273	240	195	249	118	223	265	340	398
Fruits and vegetables	652	517	475	624	290	543	645	780	889
Fresh fruits	214	175	148	214	100	178	209	254	290
Fresh vegetables	217	150	149	206	91	177	210	245	261
Processed fruits	127	106	89	117	58	102	118	155	176
Processed vegetables	95	87	89	87	42	86	108	126	161
Other food at home	1,176	1,158	1,072	1,279	597	1,100	1,378	1,704	1,901
Nonalcoholic beverages........	306	300	291	324	161	282	366	459	477
Food away from home	2,850	2,522	2,480	2,813	1,435	2,709	3,163	3,776	3,495
Alcoholic beverages	441	460	350	503	327	507	485	412	377
Housing	16,421	14,151	13,402	18,016	9,835	15,273	17,466	20,076	20,342
Shelter	10,071	7,886	7,167	11,337	6,179	8,704	10,006	11,333	11,626
Owned dwellings [1]	6,681	5,688	4,900	7,337	3,055	6,052	7,086	8,702	8,795
Mortgage interest and charges ...	3,049	3,001	2,815	4,693	1,429	2,994	4,146	5,535	5,673
Property taxes	2,344	1,671	1,085	1,452	907	1,741	1,699	2,003	1,899
Rented dwellings	2,765	1,664	1,911	3,398	2,889	1,966	2,341	2,066	2,344
Other lodging	624	534	355	601	235	686	579	566	487
Utilities, fuels, and public services	3,409	3,158	3,240	2,923	2,024	3,270	3,725	4,059	4,313
Natural gas.................	621	725	294	375	312	482	514	628	654
Electricity.................	1,102	994	1,401	969	719	1,196	1,360	1,473	1,565
Fuel oil and other fuels	391	106	75	73	99	161	160	151	163
Telephone..................	1,035	1,000	1,085	1,047	664	1,054	1,275	1,340	1,412
Water and other public services	261	333	385	459	230	377	417	467	520
Household operations	765	759	777	913	383	675	1,064	1,434	1,169
Personal services.............	307	346	313	323	42	107	553	901	697
Other household expenses	458	413	464	590	341	568	511	533	473
Housekeeping supplies...........	654	618	573	629	321	673	682	843	824
Household furnishings and equipment [1].	1,522	1,730	1,646	2,214	928	1,951	1,988	2,406	2,410
Household textiles	132	144	128	128	65	145	167	189	153
Furniture....................	385	395	463	621	218	519	566	593	717
Floor coverings	58	56	56	55	25	65	62	61	105
Major appliances	210	210	214	264	104	260	222	315	333
Miscellaneous household equipment .	638	817	697	1,009	454	843	840	1,132	967
Apparel and services	2,036	1,750	1,836	1,975	980	1,657	2,441	2,850	3,123
Men and boys.................	467	388	421	499	223	389	572	649	756
Women and girls..............	848	728	738	724	386	656	998	1,183	1,178
Children under 2 years old	87	77	76	93	16	43	158	149	202
Footwear....................	354	280	322	330	172	240	401	542	587
Other apparel products and services...	281	278	279	329	183	328	311	327	401
Transportation.................	7,732	7,537	7,990	10,068	4,030	9,124	10,438	11,553	10,963
Vehicle purchases (net outlay) [1]	2,911	3,085	3,543	4,572	1,395	4,043	4,639	5,044	4,536
Cars and trucks, new	1,760	1,700	1,777	2,571	673	2,452	2,372	2,697	2,238
Cars and trucks, used..........	1,114	1,298	1,689	1,874	669	1,514	2,163	2,209	2,226
Gasoline and motor oil . , ...	1,761	1,975	2,069	2,180	1,032	2,043	2,524	2,802	2,964
Other vehicle expenses [1]	2,424	2,313	2,085	2,708	1,336	2,489	2,796	3,160	2,992
Vehicle finance charges	241	274	336	304	121	301	405	459	413
Maintenance and repair..........	641	648	587	860	437	728	769	841	799
Vehicle insurance.............	967	845	879	993	521	944	1,118	1,261	1,186
Public transportation	637	380	293	608	267	549	479	548	471
Health care [2] . , ...	2,581	2,841	2,606	2,647	1,750	3,359	2,815	2,786	2,718
Entertainment [3]	2,263	2,384	2,112	2,950	1,335	2,622	2,615	3,152	3,364
Personal care products and services	540	514	508	623	328	583	626	732	631
Reading	148	132	94	155	103	149	123	136	117
Education	1,387	998	674	926	500	766	1,265	1,491	1,559
Tobacco products and smoking supplies ..	330	374	318	254	227	338	391	361	361
Miscellaneous	822	837	654	1,016	563	947	852	887	908
Cash contributions	1,370	1,868	1,710	1,627	1,313	1,900	1,683	1,648	1,932
Personal insurance and pensions	5,353	5,212	4,760	5,789	2,409	5,418	6,809	7,510	7,145
Life and other personal insurance.....	374	380	419	326	162	407	452	515	657
Pensions and social security	4,980	4,832	4,341	5,462	2,247	5,010	6,358	6,995	6,488
Personal taxes..............	**2,160**	**2,326**	**2,265**	**2,938**	**1,425**	**2,868**	**3,001**	**2,855**	**2,270**

[1] Includes other types not shown separately. [2] For additional health care expenditures, see Table 133. [3] For additional recreation expenditures, see Section 26.

Source: U.S. Bureau of Labor Statistics, *Consumer Expenditures in 2005.* See also <http://www.bls.gov/cex/2005/Standard/cusize.pdf> and <http://www.bls.gov/cex/2005/Standard/region.pdf> (released February 2007).

Table 666. Average Annual Expenditures of All Consumer Units by Income Level: 2005

[In dollars. Based on Consumer Expenditure Survey. Data are averages for the noninstitutional population. Expenditures reported here are out-of-pocket]

Income level	Total expenditures [1]	Food	Housing Total [1]	Shelter	Utility fuels [2]	Transportation Total [1]	Vehicle purchases	Gasoline and motor oil	Health care
All consumer units	46,409	5,931	15,167	8,805	3,183	8,344	3,544	2,013	2,664
Consumer units with complete reporting:									
Less than $70,000	32,444	4,535	11,172	6,448	2,697	5,973	2,422	1,610	2,220
$70,000 to $79,999.	57,697	7,421	17,849	10,394	3,682	10,761	4,517	2,603	3,278
$80,000 to $99,999.	65,280	8,060	20,505	11,750	4,094	12,137	5,093	2,935	3,533
$100,000 and over	99,128	10,702	30,563	18,040	4,856	16,859	7,777	3,242	4,104
$100,000 to $119,999.	78,351	9,349	23,641	13,462	4,400	15,108	7,388	3,168	3,782
$120,000 to $149,999	88,974	10,171	27,393	16,192	4,636	15,685	6,940	3,214	3,908
$150,000 and over	125,934	12,324	39,358	23,685	5,443	19,357	8,753	3,332	4,549

[1] Includes expenditures not shown separately. [2] Includes public service.

Source: U.S. Bureau of Labor Statistics, *Consumer Expenditures in 2005*. See also <http://www.bls.gov/cex/2005/share/higherincome.pdf> (released February 2007).

Table 667. Annual Expenditure Per Child by Husband-Wife Families by Family Income and Expenditure Type: 2006

[In dollars. Data are for a child in a two-child family. Excludes expenses for college. Expenditures based on data from the 1990–92 Consumer Expenditure Survey updated to 2006 dollars using the Consumer Price Index. For more on the methodology, see report cited below and Notes sheet]

Family income and age of child	Total	Housing	Food	Transportation	Clothing	Health care	Child care and education	Miscellaneous [1]
INCOME: LESS THAN $44,500								
Less than 2 years old	7,580	2,880	1,030	910	350	570	1,150	690
3 to 5 years old.	7,750	2,840	1,140	880	340	540	1,300	710
6 to 8 years old.	7,780	2,750	1,470	1,030	380	630	770	750
9 to 11 years old.	7,710	2,480	1,760	1,120	420	680	470	780
12 to 14 years old.	8,570	2,760	1,850	1,260	700	690	330	980
15 to 17 years old.	8,540	2,230	2,000	1,690	620	730	550	720
INCOME: $44,500 TO $74,900								
Less than 2 years old	10,600	3,890	1,230	1,360	410	750	1,890	1,070
3 to 5 years old.	10,910	3,860	1,420	1,330	400	720	2,090	1,090
6 to 8 years old.	10,780	3,760	1,810	1,480	440	820	1,340	1,130
9 to 11 years old.	10,610	3,490	2,130	1,570	490	890	880	1,160
12 to 14 years old.	11,340	3,780	2,140	1,710	820	890	640	1,360
15 to 17 years old.	11,660	3,240	2,380	2,160	730	940	1,110	1,100
INCOME: MORE THAN $74,900								
Less than 2 years old	15,760	6,180	1,630	1,910	540	860	2,850	1,790
3 to 5 years old.	16,140	6,150	1,840	1,870	530	830	3,110	1,810
6 to 8 years old.	15,790	6,050	2,220	2,020	570	940	2,140	1,850
9 to 11 years old.	15,490	5,790	2,580	2,110	620	1,020	1,490	1,880
12 to 14 years old.	16,310	6,070	2,710	2,250	1,040	1,020	1,140	2,080
15 to 17 years old.	16,970	5,540	2,850	2,730	940	1,080	2,010	1,820

[1] Expenses include personal care items, entertainment, and reading materials.

Source: U.S. Department of Agriculture, Center for Nutrition Policy and Promotion, *Expenditures on Children by Families, 2006 Annual Report*. See also <http:www.cnpp.usda.gov/Publications/CRC/crc2006.pdf> (released April 2007).

Income, Expenditures, Poverty, and Wealth   445

Table 668. Money Income of Households—Percent Distribution by Income Level, Race, and Hispanic Origin, in Constant (2005) Dollars: 1980 to 2005

[Constant dollars based on CPI-U-RS deflator. Households as of March of following year. (82,368 represents 82,368,000). Based on Current Population Survey, Annual Social and Economic Supplement (ASEC); see text, Sections 1 and 13, and Appendix III. For data collection changes over time, see <http://www.census.gov/hhes/www/income/histinc/hstchg.html>. For definition of median, see Guide to Tabular Presentation]

Year	Number of house- holds (1,000)	Percent distribution							Median income (dollars)
		Under $15,000	$15,000– $24,999	$25,000– $34,999	$35,000– $49,999	$50,000– $74,999	$75,000– $99,999	$100,000 and over	
ALL HOUSEHOLDS [1]									
1980	82,368	17.5	14.0	13.0	17.6	20.6	9.7	7.7	39,739
1990 [2]	94,312	15.9	12.8	12.2	16.4	19.7	10.9	12.0	43,366
2000 [2]	108,209	13.7	12.0	11.6	14.9	18.7	11.9	17.2	47,599
2004 [3]	113,343	14.9	12.7	11.6	14.6	18.3	11.2	16.7	45,817
2005	114,384	14.7	12.4	11.4	14.9	18.4	11.1	17.2	46,326
WHITE									
1980	71,872	15.5	13.5	13.0	17.8	21.6	10.2	8.3	41,925
1990 [2]	80,968	13.8	12.5	12.2	16.8	20.3	11.6	12.8	45,232
2000 [2]	90,030	12.5	11.6	11.4	14.9	19.1	12.4	18.2	49,782
2004 [3, 4, 5]	92,880	13.3	12.3	11.4	14.6	18.7	11.7	17.8	48,218
2005 [4, 5]	93,588	12.8	12.0	11.4	14.9	18.9	11.6	18.3	48,554
BLACK									
1980	8,847	33.6	18.6	13.0	15.3	12.6	4.7	2.3	24,153
1990 [2]	10,671	32.2	15.3	12.9	14.0	14.9	5.6	5.1	27,048
2000 [2]	13,174	23.1	15.8	13.3	15.5	16.2	7.8	8.2	33,630
2004 [3, 4, 6]	13,809	26.2	15.9	13.8	14.7	14.8	7.4	7.2	31,101
2005 [4, 6]	14,002	26.0	16.1	12.6	15.1	15.1	7.3	7.8	30,858
ASIAN AND PACIFIC ISLANDER									
1990 [2]	1,958	12.0	9.8	8.3	13.6	23.1	13.1	20.0	55,687
2000 [2]	3,963	10.5	8.0	9.1	13.2	18.0	14.6	26.6	63,205
2004 [3, 4, 7]	4,123	11.4	8.9	8.5	12.7	19.5	12.6	26.4	59,427
2005 [4, 7]	4,273	12.4	8.5	7.1	12.2	19.2	13.1	27.5	61,094
HISPANIC [8]									
1980	3,906	22.4	18.8	15.6	17.4	16.7	5.7	3.3	30,631
1990 [2]	6,220	22.5	16.9	14.6	17.3	16.4	6.7	5.6	32,340
2000 [2]	10,034	16.5	16.2	14.1	17.6	18.1	9.2	8.3	37,598
2004 [3]	12,178	18.1	17.1	14.4	17.0	16.7	8.0	8.8	35,417
2005	12,519	17.4	16.2	15.0	17.1	17.2	8.2	8.8	35,967

[1] Includes other races not shown separately. [2] Data reflect implementation of Census 2000-based population controls and a 28,000 household sample expansion to 78,000 households. [3] Data have been revised to reflect a correction to the weights in the 2005 ASEC. [4] Beginning with the 2003 Current Population Survey (CPS), the questionnaire allowed respondents to choose more than one race. For 2002 and later, data represent persons who selected this race group only and excludes persons reporting more than one race. The CPS in prior years allowed respondents to report only one race group. See also comments on race in the text for Section 1. [5] Data represent White alone, which refers to people who reported White and did not report any other race category. [6] Data represent Black alone, which refers to people who reported Black and did not report any other race category. [7] Data represent Asian alone, which refers to people who reported Asian and did not report any other race category. [8] People of Hispanic origin may be of any race.

Source: U.S. Census Bureau, *Current Population Reports*, P60-231; and Internet sites <http://www.census.gov/prod/2006pubs/p60-231.pdf> (released August 2006) and <http://www.census.gov/hhes/www/income/histinc/h17.htm>.

Table 669. Money Income of Households—Median Income by Race and Hispanic Origin, in Current and Constant (2005) Dollars: 1980 to 2005

[In dollars. See headnote, Table 668]

Year	Median income in current dollars					Median income in constant (2005) dollars				
	All house- holds [1]	White [2]	Black [3]	Asian, Pacific Islander [4]	His- panic [5]	All house- holds [1]	White [2]	Black [3]	Asian, Pacific Islander [4]	His- panic [5]
1980	17,710	18,684	10,764	(NA)	13,651	39,739	41,925	24,153	(NA)	30,631
1990	29,943	31,231	18,676	38,450	22,330	43,366	45,232	27,048	55,687	32,340
1995 [6]	34,076	35,766	22,393	40,614	22,860	43,346	45,496	28,485	51,662	29,079
1997	37,005	38,972	25,050	45,249	26,628	44,883	47,269	30,383	54,882	32,297
1998 [7]	38,885	40,912	25,351	46,637	28,330	46,508	48,933	30,321	55,780	33,884
1999 [7]	40,696	42,325	27,910	50,960	30,746	47,671	49,580	32,694	59,695	36,016
2000 [8]	41,990	43,916	29,667	55,757	33,168	47,599	49,782	33,630	63,205	37,598
2001	42,228	44,517	29,470	53,635	33,565	46,569	49,093	32,499	59,148	37,015
2002 [9]	42,409	45,086	29,026	52,626	33,103	46,036	48,942	31,509	57,127	35,934
2003 [10]	43,318	45,631	29,645	55,699	32,997	45,970	48,424	31,460	59,109	35,017
2004 [10]	44,334	46,668	30,095	57,504	34,271	45,817	48,218	31,101	59,427	35,417
2005	46,326	48,554	30,858	61,094	35,967	46,326	48,554	30,858	61,094	35,967

NA Not available. [1] Includes other races not shown separately. [2] Beginning with 2002, data represent White alone, which refers to people who reported White and did not report any other race category. [3] Beginning with 2002, data represent Black alone, which refers to people who reported Black and did not report any other race category. [4] Beginning with 2002, data represent Asian alone, which refers to people who reported Asian and did not report any other race category. [5] People of Hispanic origin may be of any race. [6] Data reflect full implementation of 1990 census-based sample design and metropolitan definitions. [7] 7,000 household sample reduction, and revised race edits. [8] Implementation of Census 2000-based population controls. [9] Implementation of a 28,000 household sample expansion. [10] Data have been revised to reflect a correction to the weights in the 2005 ASEC.

Source: U.S. Census Bureau, *Current Population Reports*, P60-231; and Internet sites <http://www.census.gov/prod/2006pubs/p60-231.pdf> (released August 2006) and <http://www.census.gov/hhes/www/income/histinc/h05.html>.

Table 670. Money Income of Households—Distribution by Income Level and Selected Characteristics: 2005

[114,384 represents 114,384,000. Households as of **March of the following year**. Based on Current Population Survey; see text, Sections 1 and 13, and Appendix III. For definition of median, see Guide to Tabular Presentation]

Characteristic	Number of households (1,000)								Median income (dollars)
	Total	Under $15,000	$15,000–$24,999	$25,000–$34,999	$35,000–$49,999	$50,000–$74,999	$75,000–$99,999	$100,000 and over	
Total	114,384	16,733	14,139	13,030	17,004	21,031	12,734	19,716	46,326
Age of householder:									
15 to 24 years	6,795	1,697	1,226	1,073	1,103	991	378	330	28,770
25 to 34 years	19,120	2,190	2,175	2,377	3,325	4,307	2,303	2,445	47,379
35 to 44 years	23,016	2,043	1,999	2,216	3,425	4,867	3,327	5,139	58,084
45 to 54 years	23,731	2,273	1,826	2,023	3,277	4,676	3,478	6,181	62,424
55 to 64 years	18,264	2,329	1,873	1,838	2,671	3,482	2,092	3,980	52,260
65 years and over.	23,459	6,203	5,044	3,501	3,202	2,710	1,159	1,641	26,036
Region: [1]									
Northeast	21,054	3,034	2,340	2,174	2,790	3,847	2,423	4,442	50,882
Midwest	26,351	3,721	3,295	2,977	4,137	5,083	3,126	4,011	45,950
South	41,805	6,716	5,691	5,106	6,338	7,358	4,304	6,293	42,138
West.	25,174	3,260	2,813	2,773	3,741	4,740	2,878	4,969	50,002
Size of household:									
One person	30,453	9,797	6,016	4,126	4,499	3,461	1,190	1,361	23,736
Two people	37,775	3,659	4,544	4,877	6,051	7,676	4,378	6,589	49,294
Three people	18,924	1,597	1,652	1,745	2,810	4,131	2,762	4,230	58,917
Four people	15,998	951	1,062	1,282	2,057	3,332	2,671	4,641	69,605
Five people	7,306	466	559	628	965	1,528	1,204	1,956	66,487
Six people	2,562	169	176	229	408	596	337	645	61,342
Seven or more people	1,366	90	133	144	216	301	189	293	56,796
Type of household:									
Family household	77,402	6,365	7,489	8,142	11,439	16,071	10,679	17,219	57,278
Married-couple	58,179	2,524	4,329	5,462	8,174	12,863	9,204	15,622	66,067
Male householder, wife absent	5,130	524	590	681	945	1,116	559	715	46,756
Female householder, husband absent.	14,093	3,317	2,571	1,999	2,319	2,093	911	883	30,650
Nonfamily household	36,982	10,369	6,649	4,889	5,564	4,959	2,056	2,496	27,326
Male householder	16,753	3,518	2,713	2,300	2,886	2,603	1,236	1,497	34,048
Female householder	20,230	6,850	3,936	2,590	2,679	2,356	819	999	22,688
Educational attainment of householder: [2]									
Total	107,589	15,037	12,915	11,956	15,901	20,040	12,355	19,386	47,716
Less than 9th grade	6,088	2,268	1,314	892	728	556	198	131	20,224
9th to 12th grade (no diploma)	9,130	2,741	1,872	1,378	1,312	1,086	425	312	24,675
High school graduate	32,345	5,364	5,114	4,293	5,416	6,111	3,038	3,011	38,191
Some college, no degree.	19,311	2,192	2,161	2,356	3,272	3,926	2,434	2,965	48,284
Associate's degree	9,563	858	893	1,028	1,567	2,152	1,385	1,679	54,709
Bachelor's degree or more. . . .	31,153	1,610	1,560	2,011	3,603	6,207	4,874	11,288	77,179
Bachelor's degree	19,843	1,185	1,138	1,434	2,458	4,051	3,199	6,377	72,424
Master's degree	7,943	307	334	428	892	1,647	1,232	3,101	81,023
Professional degree	1,789	54	52	85	128	247	209	1,011	100,000
Doctorate degree	1,578	62	35	64	123	259	235	799	100,000
Number of earners:									
No earners	24,224	10,875	5,441	3,120	2,393	1,417	477	501	16,893
One earner	42,066	5,184	7,023	6,838	8,177	7,562	3,029	4,253	37,541
Two earners and more.	48,095	672	1,675	3,071	6,433	12,053	9,227	14,961	75,293
Two earners	38,327	634	1,567	2,787	5,579	10,044	7,032	10,688	70,952
Three earners.	7,337	33	100	246	752	1,627	1,705	2,874	87,905
Four earners or more.	2,430	6	8	39	103	382	493	1,399	100,000
Work experience of householder:									
Total	114,384	16,733	14,139	13,030	17,004	21,031	12,734	19,716	46,326
Worked.	79,087	5,101	7,394	8,273	12,527	17,236	11,075	17,481	57,802
Worked at full-time jobs . . .	67,123	3,026	5,586	6,835	10,794	15,263	9,932	15,685	60,909
50 weeks or more . . .	57,418	1,521	4,188	5,707	9,232	13,464	8,888	14,422	63,610
27 to 49 weeks	6,231	628	890	716	1,088	1,215	760	934	46,873
26 weeks or less	3,473	881	506	415	473	585	282	329	32,985
Worked at part-time jobs. . .	11,964	2,072	1,807	1,438	1,734	1,974	1,143	1,796	40,171
50 weeks or more	6,521	864	972	819	931	1,122	665	1,149	44,044
27 to 49 weeks	2,582	451	388	273	424	414	261	371	40,834
26 weeks or less	2,862	758	447	347	379	436	215	277	30,832
Did not work	35,297	11,631	6,746	4,758	4,476	3,794	1,659	2,234	23,801
Tenure:									
Owner-occupied	78,330	7,348	7,659	7,835	11,281	15,867	10,644	17,696	56,992
Renter-occupied	34,581	8,868	6,183	5,000	5,544	5,006	2,040	1,938	29,031
Occupier paid no cash rent. .	1,474	515	299	195	178	158	46	82	22,149

[1] For composition of regions, see map, inside front cover. [2] People 25 years old and over.

Source: U.S. Census Bureau, *Current Population Reports*, P60-231; and Internet site <http://pubdb3.census.gov/macro/032006/hhinc /toc.htm> (released 29 August 2006).

U.S. Census Bureau, Statistical Abstract of the United States: 2008

Table 671. Money Income of Households—Number and Distribution by Race and Hispanic Origin: 2005

[Households as of **March of the following year. (114,384 represents 114,384,000).** Based on Current Population Survey (CPS); see text, Sections 1 and 13, and Appendix III. The 2006 CPS allowed respondents to choose more than one race. Data represent persons who selected this race group only and excludes persons reporting more than one race. See also comments on race in the text for Section 1]

Income interval	Number (1,000)					Percent distribution				
	All races	White alone	Black alone	Asian alone	Hispanic [1]	All races	White alone	Black alone	Asian alone	Hispanic [1]
All households ...	**114,384**	**93,588**	**14,002**	**4,273**	**12,519**	**100.0**	**100.0**	**100.0**	**100.0**	**100.0**
Under $10,000........	9,401	6,355	2,405	335	1,258	8.2	6.8	17.2	7.8	10.0
$10,000 to $14,999	7,332	5,705	1,241	195	928	6.4	6.1	8.9	4.6	7.4
$15,000 to $19,999	7,115	5,589	1,195	175	1,017	6.2	6.0	8.5	4.1	8.1
$20,000 to $24,999	7,024	5,607	1,058	188	1,014	6.1	6.0	7.6	4.4	8.1
$25,000 to $29,999	6,618	5,378	913	163	893	5.8	5.7	6.5	3.8	7.1
$30,000 to $34,999	6,412	5,286	845	140	981	5.6	5.6	6.0	3.3	7.8
$35,000 to $39,999	5,976	4,893	775	175	773	5.2	5.2	5.5	4.1	6.2
$40,000 to $44,999	5,770	4,767	714	164	718	5.0	5.1	5.1	3.8	5.7
$45,000 to $49,999	5,258	4,324	624	184	650	4.6	4.6	4.5	4.3	5.2
$50,000 to $59,999	9,352	7,765	1,025	362	1,031	8.2	8.3	7.3	8.5	8.2
$60,000 to $74,999	11,679	9,898	1,095	458	1,128	10.2	10.6	7.8	10.7	9.0
$75,000 to $84,999	6,101	5,268	492	232	497	5.3	5.6	3.5	5.4	4.0
$85,000 to $99,999	6,633	5,609	530	327	532	5.8	6.0	3.8	7.7	4.2
$100,000 to $149,999	12,132	10,520	760	635	744	10.6	11.2	5.4	14.9	5.9
$150,000 to $199,999	4,031	3,488	207	289	213	3.5	3.7	1.5	6.8	1.7
$200,000 to $249,999	1,529	1,347	46	116	75	1.3	1.4	0.3	2.7	0.6
$250,000 and above....	2,023	1,786	74	135	66	1.8	1.9	0.5	3.2	0.5

[1] Persons of Hispanic origin may be of any race.

Source: U.S. Census Bureau, *Current Population Reports*, P60-231; and Internet site <http://pubdb3.census.gov/macro/032006/hhinc/new06_000.htm> (released 29 August 2006).

Table 672. Money Income of Families—Number and Distribution by Race and Hispanic Origin: 2005

[Households as of **March of the following year. (77,418 represents 77,418,000).** Based on Current Population Survey (CPS); see text, Sections 1 and 13, and Appendix III. The 2006 CPS allowed respondents to choose more than one race. Data represent persons who selected this race group only and excludes persons reporting more than one race. See also comments on race in the text for Section 1]

Income interval	Number (1,000)					Percent distribution				
	All races	White alone	Black alone	Asian alone	Hispanic [1]	All races	White alone	Black alone	Asian alone	Hispanic [1]
All families [1]	**77,418**	**63,414**	**9,051**	**3,208**	**9,868**	**100.0**	**100.0**	**100.0**	**100.0**	**100.0**
Under $10,000........	4,055	2,552	1,202	147	812	5.2	4.0	13.3	4.6	8.2
$10,000 to $14,999......	2,890	2,024	652	105	636	3.7	3.2	7.2	3.3	6.4
$15,000 to $19,999......	3,709	2,726	751	138	805	4.8	4.3	8.3	4.3	8.2
$20,000 to $24,999......	4,056	3,154	666	110	807	5.2	5.0	7.4	3.4	8.2
$25,000 to $29,999......	4,113	3,242	621	126	712	5.3	5.1	6.9	3.9	7.2
$30,000 to $34,999......	4,183	3,417	579	100	790	5.4	5.4	6.4	3.1	8.0
$35,000 to $39,999......	3,813	3,114	486	121	612	4.9	4.9	5.4	3.8	6.2
$40,000 to $44,999......	3,844	3,197	451	108	580	5.0	5.0	5.0	3.4	5.9
$45,000 to $49,999......	3,644	3,018	394	147	521	4.7	4.8	4.4	4.6	5.3
$50,000 to $59,999......	6,693	5,572	711	269	864	8.6	8.8	7.9	8.4	8.8
$60,000 to $74,999......	9,061	7,744	777	363	938	11.7	12.2	8.6	11.3	9.5
$75,000 to $84,999......	4,861	4,180	398	184	409	6.3	6.6	4.4	5.7	4.1
$85,000 to $99,999......	5,610	4,770	437	276	464	7.2	7.5	4.8	8.6	4.7
$100,000 to $149,999	10,327	8,983	646	532	626	13.3	14.2	7.1	16.6	6.3
$150,000 to $199,999	3,457	2,987	178	255	178	4.5	4.7	2.0	7.9	1.8
$200,000 to $249,999	1,355	1,190	39	110	68	1.8	1.9	0.4	3.4	0.7
$250,000 and above	1,747	1,546	65	116	46	2.3	2.4	0.7	3.6	0.5

[1] Persons of Hispanic origin may be of any race.

Source: U.S. Census Bureau, *Current Population Report*, P60-231; and Internet site at <http://pubdb3.census.gov/macro/032006/faminc/new07_000.htm> (released 29 August 2006).

448 Income, Expenditures, Poverty, and Wealth

Table 673. Money Income of Families—Percent Distribution by Income Level in Constant (2005) Dollars: 1980 to 2005

[Constant dollars based on CPI-U-RS deflator. Families as of March of the following year (60,309 represents 60,309,000). Based on Current Population Survey, Annual Social and Economic Supplement (ASEC); see text, Sections 1 and 13, and Appendix III. For data collection changes over time, see <http://www.census.gov/hhes/www/income/histinc/hstchg.html>. For definition of median, see Guide to Tabular Presentation]

Year	Number of families (1,000)	Percent distribution Under $15,000	$15,000– $24,999	$25,000– $34,999	$35,000– $49,999	$50,000– $74,999	$75,000– $99,999	$100,000 and over	Median income (dollars)
ALL FAMILIES [1]									
1980	60,309	10.3	12.1	12.6	18.9	24.5	12.0	9.6	47,173
1990 [2]	66,322	10.2	10.6	11.3	16.8	22.6	13.4	15.2	51,202
2000 [2]	73,778	8.1	9.7	10.7	15.0	20.7	14.3	21.5	57,508
2004 [3]	76,866	9.2	10.3	10.6	14.5	20.4	13.6	21.4	55,869
2005	77,418	8.9	10.0	10.7	14.6	20.3	13.5	21.8	56,194
WHITE									
1980	52,710	8.4	11.3	12.5	19.2	25.6	12.7	10.3	49,150
1990 [2]	56,803	7.8	10.0	11.2	17.2	23.4	14.2	16.2	53,464
2000 [2,4,5]	61,330	6.7	9.0	10.3	15.0	21.2	14.9	22.8	60,112
2004 [3,4,5]	63,084	7.6	9.7	10.3	14.3	20.9	14.3	22.9	58,620
2005 [4,5]	63,414	7.2	9.3	10.5	14.7	21.0	14.1	23.2	59,317
BLACK									
1980	6,317	26.1	19.0	13.6	16.7	15.5	6.1	3.0	28,439
1990 [2]	7,471	27.0	15.1	13.1	14.4	16.9	7.0	6.4	31,027
2000 [2]	8,731	17.6	15.4	13.6	15.9	18.0	9.4	10.1	38,174
2004 [3,4,6]	8,906	20.8	14.9	13.1	15.4	17.1	9.3	9.4	36,323
2005 [4,6]	9,051	20.5	15.6	13.3	14.7	16.4	9.2	10.2	35,464
ASIAN AND PACIFIC ISLANDER									
1990 [2]	1,536	8.7	9.0	8.0	12.8	23.4	15.2	22.7	61,185
2000 [2]	2,982	6.9	6.9	8.1	12.6	18.9	16.0	30.6	70,981
2004 [3,4,7]	3,142	6.2	7.5	8.3	13.1	20.4	13.7	30.8	67,608
2005 [4,7]	3,208	7.8	7.7	7.0	11.8	19.7	14.4	31.6	68,957
HISPANIC ORIGIN [8]									
1980	3,235	18.5	18.9	16.1	18.6	18.3	6.2	3.6	33,021
1990 [2]	4,981	19.9	17.0	14.8	17.3	17.4	7.3	6.2	33,935
2000 [2]	8,017	14.5	16.1	14.3	17.8	18.8	9.5	8.9	39,043
2004 [3]	9,521	15.4	17.6	15.0	16.7	17.5	8.3	9.5	36,625
2005	9,868	14.7	16.3	15.2	17.4	18.2	8.9	9.3	37,867

[1] Includes other races not shown separately.   [2] Data reflect implementation of Census 2000-based population controls and a 28,000 household sample expansion to 78,000 households.   [3] Data have been revised to reflect a correction to the weights in the 2005 ASEC.   [4] Beginning with the 2003 Current Population Survey (CPS), the questionnaire allowed respondents to choose more than one race. For 2002 and later, data represent persons who selected this race group only and excludes persons reporting more than one race. The CPS in prior years allowed respondents to report only one race group. See also comments on race in the text for Section 1.   [5] Data represent White alone, which refers to people who reported White and did not report any other race category.   [6] Data represent Black alone, which refers to people who reported Black and did not report any other race category.   [7] Data represent Asian alone, which refers to people who reported Asian and did not report any other race category.   [8] People of Hispanic origin may be of any race.

Source: U.S. Census Bureau, Current Population Reports, P60-231; and Internet sites <http://www.census.gov/prod/2006pubs/p60-231.pdf> (released August 2006) and <http://www.census.gov/hhes/www/income/histinc/f23.html>.

Table 674. Money Income of Families—Median Income by Race and Hispanic Origin in Current and Constant (2005) Dollars: 1980 to 2005

[See headnote, Table 673]

Year	Median income in current dollars All families [1]	White [2]	Black [3]	Asian, Pacific Islander [4]	Hispanic [5]	Median income in constant (2005) dollars All families [1]	White [2]	Black [3]	Asian, Pacific Islander [4]	Hispanic [5]
1980	21,023	21,904	12,674	(NA)	14,716	47,173	49,150	28,439	(NA)	33,021
1990	35,353	36,915	21,423	42,246	23,431	51,202	53,464	31,027	61,185	33,935
1995 [6]	40,611	42,646	25,970	46,356	24,570	51,659	54,247	33,035	58,966	31,254
1997	44,568	46,754	28,602	51,850	28,142	54,056	56,707	34,691	62,888	34,133
1998	46,737	49,023	29,404	52,826	29,608	55,900	58,634	35,169	63,182	35,413
1999 [7]	48,831	51,079	31,850	56,127	31,523	57,201	59,834	37,309	65,747	36,926
2000 [8]	50,732	53,029	33,676	62,617	34,442	57,508	60,112	38,174	70,981	39,043
2001	51,407	54,067	33,598	60,158	34,490	56,691	59,625	37,052	66,342	38,035
2002 [9]	51,680	54,633	33,525	60,984	34,185	56,100	59,306	36,392	66,200	37,109
2003	52,680	55,768	34,369	63,251	34,272	55,905	59,182	36,473	67,123	36,370
2004 [10]	54,061	56,723	35,148	65,420	35,440	55,869	58,620	36,323	67,608	36,625
2005	56,194	59,317	35,464	68,957	37,867	56,194	59,317	35,464	68,957	37,867

NA Not available.   [1] Includes other races not shown separately.   [2] Beginning with 2002, data represent White alone, which refers to people who reported White and did not report any other race category.   [3] Beginning with 2002, data represent Black alone, which refers to people who reported Black and did not report any other race category.   [4] Beginning with 2002, data represent Asian alone, which refers to people who reported Asian and did not report any other race category.   [5] People of Hispanic origin may be of any race.   [6] Data reflect full implementation of the 1990 census-based sample design and metropolitan definitions.   [7] 7,000 household sample reduction, and revised race edits.   [7] Implementation of Census 2000-based population controls.   [8] Implementation of a 28,000 household sample expansion.   [9] See footnote 4, Table 673. See also comments on race in the text for Section 1.   [10] Data have been revised to reflect a correction to the weights in the 2005 ASEC.

Source: U.S. Census Bureau, Current Population Reports, P60-231; and Internet sites <http://www.census.gov/prod/2006pubs/p60-231.pdf> (released August 2006) and <http://www.census.gov/hhes/www/income/histinc/f05.html>.

Income, Expenditures, Poverty, and Wealth   449

Table 675. Share of Aggregate Income Received by Each Fifth and Top 5 Percent of Households: 1980 to 2005

[Families as of March of the following year (82,368 represents 82,368,000). Income in constant 2005 CPI-U-RS adjusted dollars. Based on the Current Population Survey; see text, Sections 1 and 13, and Appendix III. For data collection changes over time, see <http://www.census.gov/hhes/www/income/histinc/hstchg.html>]

Year	Number of households (1,000)	Income at selected positions (dollars)					Percent distribution of aggregate income					
		Upper limit of each fifth				Top 5 percent	Lowest 5th	Second 5th	Third 5th	Fourth 5th	Highest 5th	Top 5 percent
		Lowest	Second	Third	Fourth							
1980 . . .	82,368	16,780	31,468	48,243	70,637	113,677	4.2	10.2	16.8	24.7	44.1	16.5
1990 . . .	94,312	18,104	34,270	52,428	79,953	137,223	3.8	9.6	15.9	24.0	46.6	18.5
1995 [1] . .	99,627	18,317	34,236	53,428	82,840	143,740	3.7	9.1	15.2	23.3	48.7	21.0
1997 . . .	102,528	18,678	35,416	55,793	86,721	153,490	3.6	8.9	15.0	23.2	49.4	21.7
1998 . . .	103,874	19,275	36,369	57,813	89,703	158,116	3.6	9.0	15.0	23.2	49.2	21.4
1999 [2] . .	106,434	20,073	37,391	59,020	92,813	166,340	3.6	8.9	14.9	23.2	49.4	21.5
2000 [3] . .	108,209	20,314	37,408	59,143	92,688	164,617	3.6	8.9	14.8	23.0	49.8	22.1
2001 . . .	109,297	19,817	36,738	58,448	92,083	165,969	3.5	8.7	14.6	23.0	50.1	22.4
2002 . . .	111,278	19,448	36,232	57,709	91,202	162,831	3.5	8.8	14.8	23.3	49.7	21.7
2003 . . .	112,000	19,085	36,081	57,786	92,185	163,555	3.4	8.7	14.8	23.4	49.8	21.4
2004 [4] . .	113,343	19,104	35,835	57,077	90,945	162,408	3.4	8.7	14.7	23.2	50.1	21.8
2005 . . .	114,384	19,178	36,000	57,660	91,705	166,000	3.4	8.6	14.6	23.0	50.4	22.2

[1] Data reflect full implementation of the 1990 census-based sample design and metropolitan definitions, 7,000 household sample reduction, and revised race edits. [2] Implementation of Census 2000-based population controls. [3] Implementation of a 28,000 household sample expansion. [4] Data have been revised to reflect a correction to the weights in the 2005 ASEC.

Source: U.S. Census Bureau, Current Population Reports, P60-231; and Internet sites <http://www.census.gov/prod/2006pubs/p60-231.pdf> (released August 2006), <http://www.census.gov/hhes/www/income/histinc/h01ar.html>, and <http://www.census.gov/hhes/www/income/histinc/h02ar.html>.

Table 676. Money Income of Families—Distribution by Family Characteristics and Income Level: 2005

[(77,418 represents 77,418,000). See headnote, Table 673. For composition of regions, see map inside front cover]

Characteristic	Number of families (1,000)								Median income (dollars)
	Total	Under $15,000	$15,000 to $24,999	$25,000 to $34,999	$35,000 to $49,999	$50,000 to $74,999	$75,000 to $99,999	$100,000 and over	
All families	77,418	6,945	7,765	8,296	11,301	15,754	10,471	16,886	56,194
Age of householder:									
15 to 24 years old	3,696	984	622	543	566	542	226	211	28,691
25 to 34 years old	13,497	1,672	1,556	1,594	2,124	2,983	1,709	1,860	48,405
35 to 44 years old	18,069	1,422	1,415	1,632	2,411	3,829	2,855	4,505	62,944
45 to 54 years old	17,468	990	1,036	1,198	2,157	3,618	2,991	5,475	72,881
55 to 64 years old	12,447	754	939	1,010	1,771	2,687	1,771	3,514	65,834
65 years old and over	12,241	1,123	2,195	2,321	2,270	2,095	916	1,321	37,765
Region:									
Northeast	14,153	1,154	1,270	1,429	1,766	2,762	2,000	3,773	62,133
Midwest	17,567	1,398	1,603	1,765	2,688	3,870	2,650	3,595	57,453
South	28,444	2,939	3,288	3,287	4,287	5,636	3,571	5,436	51,352
West	17,254	1,453	1,603	1,817	2,561	3,487	2,252	4,082	57,985
Type of family:									
Married-couple families	58,189	2,546	4,353	5,481	8,182	12,885	9,182	15,560	65,906
Male householder, no spouse present	5,134	626	698	764	949	1,003	511	581	41,111
Female householder, no spouse present	14,095	3,772	2,714	2,050	2,172	1,863	778	745	27,244
Unrelated subfamilies	504	182	104	92	64	34	19	5	21,982
Education attainment of householder:									
Persons 25 years old and over, total	73,722	5,961	7,143	7,753	10,736	15,212	10,245	16,675	57,804
Less than 9th grade	3,870	818	940	728	615	480	186	107	26,973
9th to 12th grade (no diploma) . .	6,085	1,252	1,197	1,072	1,044	909	353	260	30,275
High school graduate (includes equivalency)	22,097	2,121	2,796	2,874	3,976	5,027	2,637	2,668	47,045
Some college, no degree	13,370	930	1,118	1,500	2,166	2,998	2,063	2,596	56,841
Associate's degree	6,694	342	417	610	982	1,680	1,187	1,478	64,294
Bachelor's degree or more	21,605	500	677	969	1,953	4,122	3,819	9,567	91,010
Bachelor's degree	13,788	368	517	704	1,390	2,848	2,581	5,379	84,337
Master's degree	5,427	93	119	186	420	958	950	2,703	99,675
Professional degree	1,319	13	27	43	74	165	161	838	100,000
Doctoral degree	1,071	25	13	70	70	151	130	647	100,000

Source: U.S. Census Bureau, Current Population Reports, P60-231; and Internet site <http://pubdb3.census.gov/macro/032006/faminc/new01_000.htm> (released 29 August 2006).

450   Income, Expenditures, Poverty, and Wealth

Table 677. **Median Income of Families by Type of Family in Current and Constant (2005) Dollars: 1980 to 2005**

[In dollars. See headnote, Table 673. For definition of median, see Guide to Tabular Presentation]

	Current dollars						Constant (2005) dollars					
	Married-couple families				Male house-holder, no spouse present	Female house-holder, no spouse present	Married-couple families				Male house-holder, no spouse present	Female house-holder, no spouse present
Year	Total	Wife Total	Wife in paid labor force	Wife not in paid labor force			Total	Wife Total	Wife in paid labor force	Wife not in paid labor force		
1980...	21,023	23,141	26,879	18,972	17,519	10,408	47,173	51,926	60,313	42,571	39,311	23,354
1990...	35,353	39,895	46,777	30,265	29,046	16,932	51,202	57,780	67,747	43,833	42,067	24,523
1995 [1]...	40,611	47,062	55,823	32,375	30,358	19,691	51,659	59,865	71,009	41,182	38,616	25,048
1997...	44,568	51,591	60,669	36,027	32,960	21,023	54,056	62,574	73,584	43,697	39,977	25,498
1998...	46,737	54,180	63,751	37,161	35,681	22,163	55,900	64,802	76,249	44,446	42,676	26,508
1999 [2]...	48,831	56,501	66,478	38,480	37,339	23,762	57,201	66,186	77,873	45,076	43,739	27,835
2000 [3]...	50,732	59,099	69,235	39,982	37,727	25,716	57,508	66,993	78,483	45,322	42,766	29,151
2001...	51,407	60,335	70,834	40,782	36,590	25,745	56,691	66,537	78,115	44,974	40,351	28,391
2002...	51,680	61,130	72,806	40,102	37,739	26,423	56,100	66,358	79,033	43,532	40,967	28,683
2003...	52,680	62,281	75,170	41,122	38,032	26,550	55,905	66,094	79,772	43,639	40,360	28,175
2004 [4]...	54,061	63,626	76,854	42,215	40,361	26,969	55,869	65,754	79,424	43,627	41,711	27,871
2005...	56,194	65,906	78,755	44,457	41,111	27,244	56,194	65,906	78,755	44,457	41,111	27,244

[1] Data reflect full implementation of the 1990 census-based sample design and metropolitan definitions, 7,000 household sample reduction, and revised race edits. [2] Implementation of Census 2000-based population controls. [3] Implementation of a 28,000 household sample expansion. [4] Data have been revised to reflect a correction to the weights in the 2005 ASEC.

Source: U.S. Census Bureau, *Current Population Reports*, P60-231; and Internet sites <http://www.census.gov/prod/2006pubs/p60-231.pdf> (released August 2006) and <http://www.census.gov/hhes/www/income/histinc/f07ar.html>.

Table 678. **Married-Couple Families—Number and Median Income by Work Experience of Husbands and Wives and Presence of Children: 2005**

[(58,189 represents 58,189,000). See headnote, Table 673. For definition of median, see Guide to Tabular Presentaton]

	Number (1,000)					Median income (dollars)				
Work experience of husband or wife	All married-couple families	No related children	One or more related children under 18 years old			All married-couple families	No related children	One or more related children under 18 years old		
			Total	One child	Two or more			Total	One child	Two or more
All married-couple families.	58,189	31,042	27,147	10,574	16,573	65,906	61,507	70,853	72,323	69,918
Husband worked.............	45,794	20,193	25,601	9,784	15,817	75,370	78,046	72,792	75,500	71,465
Wife worked..............	33,430	15,198	18,233	7,478	10,754	81,891	85,010	79,954	81,379	78,300
Wife did not work..........	12,364	4,995	7,369	2,306	5,063	55,429	59,206	52,469	53,181	52,199
Husband year-round, full-time worker...................	38,254	15,850	22,403	8,548	13,855	79,136	83,896	75,868	78,359	74,553
Wife worked..............	28,265	12,365	15,899	6,534	9,365	85,565	89,793	82,390	83,790	81,506
Wife did not work..........	9,989	3,485	6,504	2,014	4,490	59,643	62,382	56,204	55,980	56,319
Husband did not work.......	12,394	10,849	1,545	790	756	33,758	33,774	33,621	37,206	30,710
Wife worked..............	3,671	2,735	936	487	449	46,759	49,116	40,390	41,712	38,562
Wife did not work..........	8,723	8,114	609	302	307	29,639	29,946	22,703	27,150	18,186

Source: U.S. Census Bureau, *Current Population Reports*, P60-231; and Internet site <http://pubdb3.census.gov/macro/032006/faminc/new04_000.htm> (released 29 August 2006).

Table 679. **Median Income of People With Income in Constant (2005) Dollars by Sex, Race, and Hispanic Origin: 1990 to 2005**

[In dollars. People as of March of following year. People 15 years old and over. Constant dollars based on CPI-U-RS deflator. Based on the Current Population Survey; see text, Sections 1 and 13, and Appendix III. For data collection changes over time, see <http://www.census.gov/hhes/www/income/histinc/hstchg.html>]

	Male					Female				
Race and Hispanic origin	1990	2000 [1]	2003 [2]	2004 [3]	2005	1990	2000 [1]	2003 [2]	2004 [3]	2005
All races [4].........	29,390	32,129	31,763	31,537	31,275	14,584	18,209	18,316	18,258	18,576
White [5].............	30,660	33,777	32,613	32,393	32,179	14,942	18,227	18,489	18,291	18,669
Black [6].............	18,637	24,194	23,332	23,449	22,653	12,061	18,002	17,596	17,940	17,631
Asian [7].............	(NA)	(NA)	34,268	34,123	34,215	(NA)	(NA)	18,761	21,208	21,641
Hispanic [8]...........	19,509	22,102	22,342	22,277	22,089	10,909	13,884	14,477	14,935	15,036
White non-Hispanic.......	31,802	35,717	34,310	34,804	35,345	15,324	18,891	19,421	19,052	19,451

NA Not available. [1] Implementation of Census 2000-based population controls and sample expanded by 28,000 households. [2] Beginning with the 2003 Current Population Survey (CPS), the questionnaire allowed respondents to choose more than one race. For 2002 and later, data represent persons who selected this race group only and excludes persons reporting more than one race. The CPS in prior years allowed respondents to report only one race group. See also comments on race in the text for Section 1. [3] Data have been revised to reflect a correction to the weights in the 2005 ASEC. [4] Includes other races not shown separately. [5] Beginning with 2002, data represent White alone, which refers to people who reported White and did not report any other race category. [6] Beginning with 2002, data represent Black alone, which refers to people who reported Black and did not report any other race category. [7] Beginning with 2002, data represent Asian alone, which refers to people who reported Asian and did not report any other race category. [8] People of Hispanic origin may be of any race.

Source: U.S. Census Bureau, *Current Population Reports*, P60-231; and Internet sites <http://www.census.gov/prod/2006pubs/p60-231.pdf> (released August 2006) and <http://www.census.gov/hhes/www/income/histinc/p02.html>.

Income, Expenditures, Poverty, and Wealth   451

Table 680. Money Income of People—Selected Characteristics by Income Level: 2005

[People as of March 2006 (113,163 represents 113,163,000). Covers people 15 years old and over. Median income in constant dollars based on CPI-U-RS deflator. For definition of median, see Guide to Tabular Presentation. For composition of regions, see map, inside front cover. Based on the Current Population Survey (CPS), see Appendix III]

Characteristic	All persons (1,000)	Persons with income									Median income (dollars)
		Number (1,000)									
		Total (1,000)	Under $5,000 [1]	$5,000 to $9,999	$10,000 to $14,999	$15,000 to $24,999	$25,000 to $34,999	$35,000 to $49,999	$50,000 to $74,999	$75,000 and over	
MALE											
Total	113,163	102,986	7,659	7,375	9,182	17,425	14,566	16,711	15,304	14,764	31,275
15 to 24 years old.	20,930	14,182	4,425	2,451	1,922	2,826	1,392	717	318	129	10,469
25 to 34 years old.	19,827	18,897	827	1,070	1,456	3,681	3,625	3,775	2,844	1,619	31,161
35 to 44 years old.	21,372	20,566	657	770	1,092	2,767	3,046	4,137	4,037	4,058	40,964
45 to 54 years old.	20,973	20,152	707	835	1,023	2,435	2,562	3,751	4,201	4,636	43,627
55 to 64 years old.	14,876	14,369	633	736	993	1,883	1,873	2,559	2,653	3,038	40,654
65 yrs. old and over . . .	15,185	14,820	409	1,515	2,695	3,832	2,066	1,770	1,250	1,285	21,784
Region:											
Northeast.	21,080	19,237	1,517	1,313	1,495	3,080	2,583	3,050	3,052	3,147	32,623
Midwest.	25,169	23,379	1,907	1,544	1,992	3,717	3,337	4,214	3,696	2,972	31,988
South	40,493	36,520	2,526	2,841	3,540	6,652	5,323	5,782	5,014	4,845	29,984
West	26,420	23,850	1,709	1,677	2,155	3,976	3,324	3,664	3,544	3,802	31,586
Education attainment of householder: [2]											
Total	92,233	88,804	3,232	4,925	7,260	14,599	13,173	15,992	14,985	14,637	35,758
Less than 9th grade . . .	5,868	5,475	297	968	1,214	1,578	762	439	157	61	16,321
9th to 12th grade [3] . . .	7,940	7,276	458	871	996	2,056	1,340	927	438	190	20,934
High school graduate [4] .	29,380	28,077	1,122	1,730	2,738	5,802	5,118	5,675	4,060	1,831	30,134
Some college, no degree	15,001	14,505	475	586	1,014	2,171	2,407	3,199	2,853	1,798	36,930
Associate's degree	7,135	7,000	220	226	332	871	1,037	1,602	1,715	996	41,903
Bachelor's degree or more.	26,910	26,470	660	544	964	2,120	2,509	4,150	5,761	9,761	58,114
Bachelor's degree	17,082	16,764	484	411	686	1,509	1,872	2,918	3,704	5,180	51,700
Master's degree	6,205	6,137	126	88	181	426	418	891	1,406	2,600	64,468
Professional degree . .	1,937	1,912	31	20	47	106	111	171	315	1,114	90,878
Doctorate degree . . .	1,686	1,656	20	25	51	80	107	168	338	868	76,937
Tenure:											
Owner-occupied	81,901	75,234	5,654	4,377	5,797	10,860	9,950	12,737	12,686	13,174	35,805
Renter-occupied	29,902	26,564	1,893	2,855	3,201	6,257	4,449	3,858	2,518	1,534	22,742
Occupier paid no cash rent	1,360	1,187	111	143	184	307	167	114	102	59	20,039
FEMALE											
Total	120,031	104,245	14,956	15,758	13,328	19,809	13,816	12,632	8,771	5,174	18,576
15 to 24 years old. . . .	20,379	13,484	4,858	2,716	1,908	2,383	1,017	427	137	42	8,220
25 to 34 years old. . . .	19,653	17,058	2,227	1,653	1,720	3,621	3,005	2,660	1,572	599	22,815
35 to 44 years old. . . .	21,750	19,552	2,597	1,790	1,775	3,446	3,015	3,104	2,343	1,483	25,435
45 to 54 years old. . . .	21,824	19,919	2,054	1,859	1,797	3,671	2,976	3,317	2,632	1,615	26,476
55 to 64 years old. . . .	16,104	14,635	1,910	1,799	1,568	2,608	2,199	2,035	1,513	1,005	22,122
65 yrs. old and over . . .	20,320	19,598	1,311	5,943	4,560	4,080	1,605	1,092	575	433	12,495
Region:											
Northeast.	22,692	20,025	2,866	2,958	2,505	3,597	2,498	2,392	1,935	1,273	19,467
Midwest.	26,730	24,022	3,493	3,426	3,041	4,784	3,435	3,063	1,904	875	18,857
South	43,675	37,378	5,283	6,056	4,772	7,262	5,055	4,453	2,885	1,611	18,011
West	26,933	22,820	3,313	3,318	3,010	4,167	2,828	2,724	2,049	1,412	18,569
Education attainment of householder: [2]											
Total	99,651	90,762	10,098	13,043	11,420	17,427	12,801	12,208	8,635	5,130	20,806
Less than 9th grade . . .	5,874	4,579	711	1,748	1,002	786	191	81	38	23	9,496
9th to 12th grade [3] . . .	8,215	6,812	949	2,066	1,432	1,457	538	250	82	36	11,136
High school graduate [4] .	31,518	28,409	3,251	4,960	4,552	7,008	4,205	2,742	1,206	483	16,695
Some college, no degree	17,610	16,402	1,916	1,960	1,922	3,494	2,824	2,436	1,273	578	21,545
Associate's degree	9,625	9,070	817	806	950	1,742	1,681	1,598	1,108	365	26,074
Bachelor's degree or more.	26,810	25,490	2,455	1,504	1,562	2,937	3,360	5,100	4,930	3,644	37,055
Bachelor's degree	18,071	17,090	1,844	1,135	1,172	2,224	2,580	3,364	2,917	1,853	32,668
Master's degree	6,848	6,560	501	295	287	596	654	1,487	1,616	1,121	44,385
Professional degree . .	1,113	1,090	77	57	54	61	79	132	197	433	59,934
Doctorate degree . . .	778	749	33	16	49	55	48	115	198	234	56,820
Tenure:											
Owner-occupied	86,485	76,379	11,028	10,700	9,051	13,612	10,133	9,915	7,391	4,549	20,215
Renter-occupied	32,221	26,735	3,711	4,814	4,055	5,971	3,585	2,654	1,341	606	16,007
Occupier paid no cash rent	1,324	1,131	217	245	223	227	100	63	40	18	12,339

[1] Includes persons with income deficit. [2] Persons 25 years and over. [3] No diploma attained. [4] Includes high school equivalency.

Source: U.S. Census Bureau, *Current Population Reports*, series P60-231; and Internet site <http://pubdb3.census.gov /macro/032005/perinc/new01_000.htm> (released 29 August 2006).

Table 681. Average Earnings of Year-Round, Full-Time Workers by Educational Attainment: 2005

[In dollars. For people 18 years old and over as of March 2006. See headnote, Table 679]

Sex and Age	All workers	Less than 9th grade	High school — 9th to 12th grade (no diploma)	High school graduate[1]	College — Some college, no degree	Associate's degree	Bachelor's degree or more
Male, total	56,187	25,557	30,202	40,112	48,369	51,894	87,777
18 to 24 years old	24,715	17,556	21,507	24,053	24,708	26,984	34,775
25 to 34 years old	42,913	22,052	27,002	33,866	42,196	42,666	61,027
35 to 44 years old	59,495	26,968	30,871	42,133	52,402	54,914	90,836
45 to 54 years old	66,973	28,087	33,926	46,622	54,949	57,295	103,658
55 to 64 years old	66,616	30,680	39,800	47,151	59,459	60,556	91,656
65 years old and over . . .	71,889	27,147	32,929	43,431	51,258	70,542	117,611
Female, total	39,046	18,072	21,656	28,657	34,291	37,556	55,222
18 to 24 years old	22,443	(B)	15,458	19,412	21,468	25,407	31,409
25 to 34 years old	35,270	17,409	22,337	25,783	30,924	32,498	45,755
35 to 44 years old	41,911	16,802	22,026	29,301	36,401	37,979	59,781
45 to 54 years old	43,069	19,189	24,353	31,246	38,239	40,924	62,064
55 to 64 years old	41,451	19,206	21,882	31,757	38,262	42,812	58,248
65 years old and over . . .	34,616	(B)	18,227	26,712	37,443	37,693	55,128

B Base figure too small to meet statistical standards for reliability of derived figure. [1] Includes equivalency.
Source: U.S. Census Bureau, *Current Population Reports*, series P60-231; and Internet site <http://pubdb3.census.gov/macro/032006/perinc/new04_000.htm> (released 29 August 2006).

Table 682. Per Capita Money Income in Current and Constant (2005) Dollars by Race and Hispanic Origin: 1990 to 2005

[In dollars. Constant dollars based on CPI-U-RS deflator. People as of March of following year. Based on the Current Population Survey, Annual Social and Economic Supplement (ASEC); see text, Sections 1 and 13, and Appendix III. For data collection changes over time see <http://www.census.gov/hhes/www/income/histinc/hstchg.html>]

Year	Current dollars — All races[1]	White[2]	Black[3]	Asian, Pacific Islander[4]	Hispanic[5]	Constant (2005) dollars — All races[1]	White[2]	Black[3]	Asian, Pacific Islander[4]	Hispanic[5]
1990	14,387	15,265	9,017	(NA)	8,424	20,837	22,108	13,059	(NA)	12,200
1995 [6] . . .	17,227	18,304	10,982	16,567	9,300	21,913	23,283	13,969	21,074	11,830
1999 [7] . . .	21,239	22,451	14,362	21,454	11,566	24,879	26,299	16,824	25,131	13,548
2000 [8] . . .	22,346	23,582	14,796	23,350	12,651	25,331	26,732	16,772	26,469	14,341
2001	22,851	24,127	14,953	24,277	13,003	25,200	26,607	16,490	26,773	14,340
2002 [9] . . .	22,794	24,142	15,441	24,131	13,487	24,744	26,207	16,762	26,195	14,641
2003	23,276	24,626	15,775	24,604	13,492	24,701	26,134	16,741	26,110	14,318
2004 [10] . . .	23,857	25,223	16,025	26,165	14,105	24,655	26,067	16,561	27,040	14,577
2005	25,036	26,496	16,874	27,331	14,483	25,036	26,496	16,874	27,331	14,483

NA Not available. [1] Includes other races not shown separately. [2] Beginning with 2002, data represent White alone, which refers to people who reported White and did not report any other race category. [3] Beginning with 2002, data represent Black alone, which refers to people who reported Black and did not report any other race category. [4] Beginning with 2002, data represent Asian alone, which refers to people who reported Asian and did not report any other race category. [5] Beginning with 2002, data represent Asian alone, which refers to people who reported Asian and did not report any other race category. [5] Persons of Hispanic origin may be of any race. [6] Data reflect full implementation of the 1990 census-based sample design and metropolitan definitions. [7] 7,000 household sample reduction, and revised race edits. [8] Implementation of Census 2000-based population controls. [8] Implementation of a 28,000 household sample expansion. [9] See footnote 4, Table 673. See also comments on race in the text for Section 1. [10] Data have been revised to reflect a correction to the weights in the 2005 ASEC.
Source: U.S. Census Bureau, *Current Population Reports*, P60-231; and Internet sites <http://www.census.gov/prod/2006pubs/p60-231.pdf> (released August 2006) and <http://www.census.gov/hhes/www/income/histinc/p01ar.html> (released August 2006).

Table 683. Money Income of People—Number by Income Level and by Sex, Race, and Hispanic Origin: 2005

[In thousands (113,163 represents 113,163,000). People as of March of the following year. Based on Current Population Survey (CPS); see text, Sections 1 and 13, and Appendix III]

Income interval	Male — All races[1]	White[2]	Black[3]	Asian[4]	Hispanic[5]	Female — All races[1]	White[2]	Black[3]	Asian[4]	Hispanic[5]
All households [1] . . .	113,163	92,958	12,538	4,851	15,779	120,031	96,663	15,173	5,331	14,861
Under $10,000 [6]	25,211	18,423	4,588	1,296	4,242	46,499	36,740	6,208	2,251	7,914
$10,000 to $19,999	17,944	14,718	2,150	602	3,631	23,917	19,460	3,062	814	2,946
$20,000 to $29,999	15,922	13,113	1,835	579	3,076	16,467	13,310	2,195	602	1,683
$30,000 to $39,999	13,670	11,579	1,318	464	1,871	11,681	9,504	1,447	480	1,030
$40,000 to $49,999	10,348	8,835	931	352	1,041	7,520	6,186	864	321	516
$50,000 to $59,999	7,535	6,483	582	323	653	4,620	3,782	549	203	258
$60,000 to $74,999	7,769	6,726	525	366	502	4,151	3,406	403	276	246
$75,000 to $84,999	3,454	3,029	192	178	193	1,490	1,224	138	114	87
$85,000 to $99,999	2,877	2,551	124	158	168	1,222	988	129	82	62
$100,000 to $149,999 . . .	4,997	4,380	204	342	272	1,710	1,420	137	131	81
$150,000 to $199,999 . . .	1,648	1,502	32	98	60	434	365	25	41	23
$200,000 to $249,999 . . .	636	581	16	36	23	136	124	6	3	9
$250,000 and above	1,152	1,036	41	56	49	182	155	12	14	4

[1] Includes races not shown separately. [2] White alone refers to people who reported Black and did not report any other race category. [3] Black alone refers to people who reported Black and did not report any other race category. [4] Asian alone refers to people who reported Asian and did not report any other race category. [5] Persons of Hispanic origin may be of any race. [6] Includes persons without income.
Source: U.S. Census Bureau, *Current Population Reports*, P60-231; and Internet site <http://pubdb3.census.gov/macro/032006/perinc/new11_000.htm> (released 29 August 2006).

Income, Expenditures, Poverty, and Wealth **453**

Table 684. Household Income—Distribution by Income Level and State: 2005

[In thousands (111,091 represents 111,091,000), except as indicated. The American Community Survey universe is limited to the household population and excludes the population living in institutions, college dormitories, and other group quarters. Based on a sample and subject to sampling variability; see Appendix III. For definition of median, see Guide to Tabular Presentation]

State	Number of households (1,000)								Median income (dollars)
	Total	Under $25,000	$25,000–$49,999	$50,000–$74,999	$75,000–$99,999	$100,000–$149,999	$150,000–$199,999	$200,000 and over	
United States..	111,091	29,785	29,497	21,001	12,648	11,258	3,544	3,358	46,242
Alabama.........	1,789	630	497	304	163	131	33	30	36,879
Alaska.........	233	47	54	49	33	34	10	6	56,234
Arizona.........	2,204	582	642	422	241	200	63	55	44,282
Arkansas	1,088	392	325	186	93	62	16	13	34,999
California	12,098	2,764	2,863	2,230	1,496	1,583	580	581	53,629
Colorado........	1,819	426	471	358	230	211	65	58	50,652
Connecticut.......	1,324	260	284	247	188	192	71	82	60,941
Delaware	318	67	82	65	44	39	12	9	52,499
District of Columbia .	248	70	59	40	25	24	12	17	47,221
Florida	7,049	1,965	2,085	1,308	720	595	183	193	42,433
Georgia	3,320	897	898	634	378	315	102	96	45,604
Hawaii..........	430	81	104	88	59	63	21	14	58,112
Idaho...........	532	154	164	109	56	34	8	8	41,443
Illinois	4,691	1,145	1,187	919	578	535	170	157	50,260
Indiana..........	2,443	657	712	499	281	203	51	41	43,993
Iowa	1,201	325	354	256	135	88	22	20	43,609
Kansas..........	1,072	296	313	208	117	93	24	21	42,920
Kentucky........	1,654	571	471	297	154	110	28	23	37,369
Louisiana	1,677	605	444	280	160	127	30	31	36,729
Maine...........	542	155	156	113	56	41	11	10	42,801
Maryland	2,086	377	468	394	297	332	116	102	61,592
Massachusetts.....	2,448	558	512	456	332	352	124	115	57,184
Michigan.........	3,888	1,039	1,041	757	460	388	113	90	46,039
Minnesota........	2,020	438	527	425	269	236	67	58	52,024
Mississippi	1,084	419	313	175	87	61	16	13	32,938
Missouri	2,285	664	663	444	239	182	49	43	41,974
Montana.........	368	116	112	75	33	22	5	5	39,301
Nebraska........	696	187	203	149	77	55	13	11	43,849
Nevada	907	210	250	186	118	98	23	22	49,169
New Hampshire....	497	93	122	111	73	63	20	15	56,768
New Jersey.......	3,142	621	659	571	424	493	185	190	61,672
New Mexico	728	244	210	128	66	51	15	14	37,492
New York	7,114	1,903	1,684	1,281	817	835	283	312	49,480
North Carolina....	3,410	1,043	986	632	336	264	78	71	40,729
North Dakota......	270	79	83	56	26	18	4	4	41,030
Ohio	4,508	1,274	1,265	884	502	402	98	82	43,493
Oklahoma........	1,381	467	413	249	122	85	24	21	37,063
Oregon..........	1,425	406	405	278	156	118	35	28	42,944
Pennsylvania......	4,860	1,363	1,316	937	549	444	133	118	44,537
Rhode Island......	406	102	96	79	52	50	17	11	51,458
South Carolina.....	1,636	530	464	307	157	120	30	28	39,316
South Dakota	310	95	94	64	30	19	4	5	40,310
Tennessee	2,366	768	680	432	226	165	47	48	38,874
Texas...........	7,978	2,369	2,198	1,412	832	725	226	216	42,139
Utah	792	173	240	173	97	75	19	16	47,934
Vermont	249	64	70	51	27	26	6	5	45,686
Virginia..........	2,890	626	706	553	368	374	135	127	54,240
Washington.......	2,450	593	648	483	299	274	88	66	49,262
West Virginia......	741	283	216	127	58	39	9	9	33,452
Wisconsin........	2,220	542	626	477	286	196	47	44	47,105
Wyoming	205	51	59	44	27	17	4	4	46,202

Source: U.S. Census Bureau, *Income, Earnings, and Poverty From the 2005 American Community Survey*, series ACS-01; and 2005 American Community Survey; B19001. Household Income in the Past 12 Months; B19013. Median Household Income in the Past 12 Months (In 2005 Inflation-Adjusted Dollars); using American FactFinder®; <http://factfinder.census.gov/>; (accessed 9 January 2007).

Table 685. Family Income—Distribution by Income Level and State: 2005

[In thousands (74,341 represents 74,341,000), except as indicated. The American Community Survey universe is limited to the household population and excludes the population living in institutions, college dormitories, and other group quarters. Based on a sample and subject to sampling variability; see Appendix III. For definition of median, see Guide to Tabular Presentation]

State	Number of families (1,000)								Median income (dol.)
	Total	Under $25,000	$25,000–$49,999	$50,000–$74,999	$75,000–$99,999	$100,000–$149,999	$150,000–$199,999	$200,000 and over	
United States..	74,341	14,015	18,992	15,590	10,255	9,541	3,048	2,901	55,832
Alabama.........	1,224	312	346	246	143	118	30	28	46,086
Alaska	157	23	33	33	26	28	8	5	67,084
Arizona.........	1,459	293	411	305	185	166	53	46	51,458
Arkansas........	742	194	231	154	80	55	15	12	43,134
California	8,281	1,465	1,899	1,559	1,137	1,267	472	483	61,476
Colorado........	1,164	180	272	247	180	177	57	52	62,470
Connecticut......	893	102	168	173	150	163	62	74	75,541
Delaware	216	29	52	49	36	33	10	8	63,863
District of Columbia .	108	28	26	14	10	12	8	11	51,411
Florida	4,595	933	1,340	939	571	496	155	162	50,465
Georgia	2,285	462	595	473	311	269	90	85	53,744
Hawaii	306	40	70	64	49	54	18	11	66,472
Idaho	372	76	115	88	49	30	7	7	48,775
Illinois	3,126	505	737	667	472	460	148	136	61,174
Indiana.........	1,640	284	461	394	238	180	45	37	54,077
Iowa	790	129	221	204	118	80	20	17	54,971
Kansas.........	716	124	201	169	100	82	22	19	53,998
Kentucky	1,119	282	324	235	136	98	25	20	46,214
Louisiana	1,137	306	306	222	138	111	26	27	45,730
Maine..........	355	66	101	88	48	34	10	9	52,338
Maryland	1,398	159	275	266	231	275	102	90	74,879
Massachusetts.....	1,570	221	295	310	253	286	105	101	71,655
Michigan........	2,594	458	656	571	382	343	103	82	57,277
Minnesota.......	1,329	171	307	314	225	202	59	52	63,998
Mississippi	760	225	226	148	77	56	15	12	40,917
Missouri	1,521	303	430	345	202	159	44	38	51,477
Montana........	237	49	74	59	28	18	4	4	47,959
Nebraska	455	75	125	117	67	49	12	10	55,073
Nevada	589	95	158	132	88	80	18	18	57,079
New Hampshire....	338	37	75	80	59	56	17	14	67,354
New Jersey......	2,172	275	406	401	330	427	164	169	75,311
New Mexico	483	125	143	96	52	43	13	11	44,097
New York	4,616	878	1,053	905	624	671	229	256	59,686
North Carolina	2,290	508	652	487	282	231	69	61	49,339
North Dakota.....	166	26	50	43	23	16	3	4	53,103
Ohio	2,987	553	808	681	426	358	88	74	54,086
Oklahoma.......	934	224	283	201	107	79	21	19	45,990
Oregon.........	909	174	250	206	125	100	30	24	52,698
Pennsylvania.....	3,200	561	845	716	462	394	117	105	55,904
Rhode Island.....	259	41	54	57	41	41	15	10	64,657
South Carolina....	1,103	267	305	240	135	105	28	24	48,100
South Dakota	204	39	61	51	26	18	4	4	50,461
Tennessee	1,604	376	457	345	194	146	42	43	47,950
Texas..........	5,598	1,329	1,481	1,077	691	629	201	190	49,769
Utah	593	91	177	141	85	68	17	14	54,595
Vermont	157	25	40	39	23	21	5	4	57,170
Virginia.........	1,939	280	439	395	289	307	116	111	65,174
Washington......	1,574	252	391	342	233	226	73	57	60,077
West Virginia.....	500	134	157	108	52	35	8	7	42,852
Wisconsin.......	1,441	213	370	360	243	173	41	39	58,647
Wyoming	134	20	38	33	21	15	3	3	55,343

Source: U.S. Census Bureau, *Income, Earnings, and Poverty From the 2005 American Community Survey*, series ACS-01; and 2005 American Community Survey; B19101. Family Income in the Past 12 Months; B19113. Median Family Income in the Past 12 Months (In 2005 Inflation-Adjusted Dollars); using American FactFinder®; <http://factfinder.census.gov/>; (accessed 9 January 2007).

Income, Expenditures, Poverty, and Wealth 455

Table 686. Household Income, Family Income, and Per Capita Income and Individual and Family Below Poverty Level by City: 2005

[For number and percent below poverty, see headnote, Table 687. The American Community Survey universe is limited to the household population and excludes the population living in institutions, college dormitories, and other group quarters. Based on a sample and subject to sampling variability; see Appendix III. For definition of median, see Guide to Tabular Presentation]

City	Median household income (dol.)	Median family income (dol.)	Per capita income (dol.)	Number below poverty level Individuals	Number below poverty level Families	Percent below poverty level Individuals	Percent below poverty level Families
Albuquerque, NM	41,820	54,570	24,576	66,345	12,198	13.7	9.9
Anaheim, CA	52,158	56,478	20,794	38,309	6,862	11.7	9.6
Anchorage municipality, AK	61,217	72,931	29,581	25,040	4,541	9.5	6.7
Arlington, TX	48,992	56,186	22,693	46,180	9,028	13.3	10.5
Atlanta, GA	39,752	42,010	33,590	105,928	20,349	26.9	25.5
Aurora, CO	48,309	56,029	23,060	38,228	7,588	13.1	10.7
Austin, TX	43,731	60,592	27,760	122,141	20,689	18.1	13.8
Bakersfield, CA	45,174	51,601	20,937	51,617	9,599	18.1	14.6
Baltimore, MD	32,456	41,542	20,749	136,256	23,836	22.6	18.9
Boston, MA	42,562	49,320	30,167	116,110	20,086	22.3	17.8
Buffalo, NY	27,311	33,027	17,348	68,607	14,479	26.9	23.6
Charlotte, NC	47,131	56,960	28,875	78,124	15,575	13.0	10.2
Chicago, IL	41,015	46,888	23,449	573,486	107,418	21.3	18.0
Cincinnati, OH	29,554	38,763	20,593	71,767	13,456	25.0	19.7
Cleveland, OH	24,105	28,990	14,825	133,886	27,977	32.4	28.6
Colorado Springs, CO	47,854	59,886	26,001	43,780	9,297	11.7	9.7
Columbus, OH	40,405	47,229	22,134	128,163	24,089	18.5	14.1
Corpus Christi, TX	39,698	44,773	20,039	51,866	10,198	18.6	14.5
Dallas, TX	36,403	38,717	24,477	251,987	48,157	22.1	18.8
Denver, CO	42,370	52,139	27,715	83,044	14,367	15.3	12.0
Detroit, MI	28,069	33,640	15,042	261,497	51,145	31.4	27.0
El Paso, TX	32,205	35,562	15,248	158,216	34,695	27.2	23.8
Fort Worth, TX	40,663	47,064	21,249	112,971	23,414	18.8	15.7
Fresno, CA	37,800	42,793	17,586	115,278	21,604	24.3	20.1
Honolulu, HI [1]	50,793	64,892	27,661	43,468	8,583	12.0	9.4
Houston, TX	36,894	40,172	22,534	443,757	91,562	22.9	20.0
Indianapolis, IN [2]	41,578	50,584	22,566	114,963	22,343	15.1	11.5
Jacksonville, FL	44,173	52,138	23,076	93,377	19,179	12.2	9.6
Kansas City, MO	41,069	50,540	24,567	72,226	13,758	16.5	12.9
Las Vegas, NV	47,863	57,471	24,887	62,678	12,810	11.7	9.7
Lexington-Fayette, KY	42,442	60,067	26,343	37,821	6,450	14.9	9.8
Long Beach, CA	43,746	46,477	23,266	88,868	16,125	19.2	16.4
Los Angeles, CA	42,667	47,434	24,587	747,613	131,329	20.1	16.7
Memphis, TN	33,244	40,111	20,279	150,704	32,860	23.6	21.1
Mesa, AZ	44,861	53,730	22,325	52,067	9,767	11.9	8.9
Miami, FL	25,211	28,784	17,531	101,883	20,881	28.3	24.6
Milwaukee, WI	32,666	35,675	17,696	137,760	27,268	24.9	21.3
Minneapolis, MN	41,829	57,316	26,886	72,681	10,643	20.8	14.6
Nashville-Davidson, TN [2]	40,214	49,748	25,005	75,968	15,891	14.6	11.8
New Orleans, LA	30,711	39,428	21,998	106,666	19,748	24.5	21.8
New York, NY	43,434	49,374	27,233	1,512,112	307,345	19.1	16.7
Newark, NJ	30,665	34,816	15,346	62,866	12,967	24.8	22.9
Oakland, CA	44,124	47,283	25,739	68,148	14,053	18.3	16.9
Oklahoma City, OK	37,375	49,769	22,190	95,947	19,943	18.7	14.9
Omaha, NE	40,484	51,637	23,500	57,020	11,588	15.3	13.1
Philadelphia, PA	32,573	40,534	19,140	343,547	64,162	24.5	19.9
Phoenix, AZ	42,353	47,559	22,471	225,117	42,456	16.4	13.5
Pittsburgh, PA	30,278	41,633	22,018	65,726	11,799	23.2	17.1
Portland, OR	42,287	55,321	26,677	90,689	14,020	17.8	11.8
Raleigh, NC	48,131	65,033	29,464	48,612	7,209	15.5	9.6
Riverside, CA	50,416	57,913	20,924	41,164	6,964	14.1	10.5
Sacramento, CA	44,867	50,653	22,841	85,181	15,056	19.2	14.7
San Antonio, TX	40,186	47,150	20,407	224,014	44,091	18.7	15.5
San Diego, CA	55,637	67,925	29,497	161,978	26,935	13.5	9.7
San Francisco, CA	57,496	73,180	39,554	87,823	12,626	12.2	8.9
San Jose, CA	70,921	79,413	30,769	88,182	15,760	10.0	7.5
Santa Ana, CA	47,438	46,154	14,110	51,134	8,969	17.3	15.8
Seattle, WA	49,297	69,795	36,392	66,068	7,468	12.3	6.6
St. Louis, MO	30,874	36,282	19,153	84,435	15,199	25.4	21.9
St. Paul, MN	44,103	55,606	23,541	48,468	8,467	18.6	14.2
St. Petersburg, FL	37,947	50,108	26,446	33,456	6,726	14.4	11.4
Stockton, CA	41,118	47,101	18,976	55,740	10,093	20.1	16.1
Tampa, FL	38,568	47,329	26,265	57,252	10,763	18.3	14.2
Toledo, OH	33,044	42,179	17,953	66,606	12,738	23.4	18.4
Tucson, AZ	34,241	41,529	18,813	101,034	19,754	20.0	16.3
Tulsa, OK	35,966	43,802	23,762	65,140	14,492	17.6	15.1
Virginia Beach, VA	58,545	66,102	28,064	31,631	7,125	7.4	6.3
Washington, DC	47,221	51,411	37,569	97,617	18,159	19.0	16.7
Wichita, KS	40,115	48,696	22,379	52,433	10,968	14.8	12.2

[1] Data shown for census designated place (CDP).   [2] Represents the portion of a consolidated city that is not within one or more separately incorporated places.

Source: U.S. Census Bureau, *Income, Earnings, and Poverty From the 2005 American Community Survey*, series ACS-01; and 2005 American Community Survey; using American FactFinder®; <http://factfinder.census.gov/>; (accessed 9 January 2007).

Table 687. Individuals and Families Below Poverty Level—Number and Rate by State: 2000 and 2005

[In thousands (33,311 represents 33,311,000), except as indicated. Represents number and percent below poverty in the past 12 months. The American Community Survey universe is limited to the household population and excludes the population living in institutions, college dormitories, and other group quarters. Based on a sample and subject to sampling variability; see Appendix III]

State	Number below poverty level (1,000)				Percent below poverty level			
	Individuals		Families		Individuals		Families	
	2000	2005	2000	2005	2000	2005	2000	2005
United States.........	33,311	38,231	6,615	7,605	12.2	13.3	9.3	10.2
Alabama...............	672	754	146	168	15.6	17.0	12.4	13.7
Alaska................	55	71	11	13	9.1	11.2	6.8	8.3
Arizona...............	780	824	150	159	15.6	14.2	11.6	10.9
Arkansas..............	439	462	96	100	17.0	17.2	13.0	13.4
California.............	4,520	4,673	832	850	13.7	13.3	10.7	10.3
Colorado..............	363	504	64	97	8.7	11.1	5.7	8.3
Connecticut...........	254	281	51	55	7.7	8.3	5.8	6.2
Delaware	70	85	14	17	9.3	10.4	6.7	7.6
District of Columbia	94	98	17	18	17.5	19.0	15.4	16.7
Florida	1,987	2,214	387	445	12.8	12.8	9.3	9.7
Georgia	999	1,266	206	264	12.6	14.4	10.0	11.6
Hawaii	103	121	19	23	8.8	9.8	6.8	7.7
Idaho.................	144	192	26	38	11.4	13.9	7.7	10.3
Illinois	1,335	1,484	262	287	11.1	12.0	8.6	9.2
Indiana...............	592	740	113	148	10.1	12.2	7.1	9.0
Iowa	281	310	53	59	10.0	10.9	7.0	7.5
Kansas................	247	310	43	60	9.5	11.7	6.2	8.4
Kentucky	640	680	148	150	16.4	16.8	13.5	13.4
Louisiana.............	862	864	182	183	20.0	19.8	16.0	16.1
Maine.................	124	161	22	32	10.1	12.6	6.6	9.0
Maryland	477	448	89	84	9.3	8.2	6.6	6.0
Massachusetts..........	586	637	110	119	9.6	10.3	7.1	7.6
Michigan..............	975	1,300	196	257	10.1	13.2	7.7	9.9
Minnesota.............	328	457	66	81	6.9	9.2	5.1	6.1
Mississippi............	498	600	104	127	18.2	21.3	14.2	16.8
Missouri	606	748	118	152	11.2	13.3	7.7	10.0
Montana..............	117	130	23	25	13.4	14.4	9.5	10.5
Nebraska	158	186	28	37	9.6	10.9	6.5	8.2
Nevada	194	262	34	52	9.9	11.1	6.9	8.9
New Hampshire.........	63	95	11	18	5.3	7.5	3.5	5.3
New Jersey............	651	739	126	147	7.9	8.7	6.0	6.8
New Mexico	320	348	64	69	18.0	18.5	14.2	14.3
New York	2,391	2,566	491	513	13.1	13.8	10.7	11.1
North Carolina.........	1,018	1,263	203	269	13.1	15.1	9.6	11.7
North Dakota..........	71	68	14	12	11.6	11.2	8.1	7.5
Ohio	1,216	1,451	246	297	11.1	13.0	8.4	9.9
Oklahoma.............	459	565	100	122	13.8	16.5	11.0	13.1
Oregon................	439	499	84	91	13.2	14.1	9.5	10.1
Pennsylvania...........	1,240	1,420	247	274	10.5	11.9	7.8	8.6
Rhode Island...........	108	126	23	25	10.7	12.3	8.5	9.5
South Carolina.........	557	639	123	138	14.4	15.6	11.7	12.5
South Dakota	83	101	16	20	11.5	13.6	8.4	9.7
Tennessee	745	900	158	200	13.5	15.5	10.5	12.5
Texas.................	3,056	3,905	639	796	15.1	17.6	12.3	14.2
Utah	192	246	40	47	8.8	10.2	7.2	8.0
Vermont	63	69	12	12	10.7	11.5	7.5	7.7
Virginia...............	630	729	124	143	9.2	10.0	6.8	7.4
Washington............	667	729	127	133	11.6	11.9	8.6	8.4
West Virginia..........	327	317	72	70	18.6	18.0	14.7	14.0
Wisconsin.............	461	546	75	100	8.9	10.2	5.6	7.0
Wyoming	55	47	10	8	11.4	9.5	7.9	6.3

Source: U.S. Census Bureau, 2005 American Community Survey; B17001. Poverty Status in the Past 12 Months by Sex and Age, and B17010. Poverty Status in the Past 12 Months of Familes by Family Type by Presence of Related Children under 18 Years by Age of Related Children; using American FactFinder®; <http://factfinder.census.gov/>; (accessed 10 January 2007).

Income, Expenditures, Poverty, and Wealth   457

Table 688. Weighted Average Poverty Thresholds by Size of Unit: 1980 to 2005

[In dollars. For information on the official poverty thresholds; see text, this section. For data collection changes over time, see <http://www.census.gov/hhes/www/income/histinc/hstch.html>]

Size of family unit	1980	1990	1995	2000 [1]	2001	2002	2003	2004 [2]	2005
One person (unrelated individual)	4,190	6,652	7,763	8,791	9,039	9,183	9,393	9,646	9,973
Under 65 years old	4,290	6,800	7,929	8,959	9,214	9,359	9,573	9,827	10,160
65 years old and over	3,949	6,268	7,309	8,259	8,494	8,628	8,825	9,060	9,367
Two persons	5,363	8,509	9,933	11,235	11,569	11,756	12,015	12,335	12,755
Householder under 65 years old	5,537	8,794	10,259	11,589	11,920	12,110	12,384	12,714	13,145
Householder 65 years old and over . .	4,983	7,905	9,219	10,418	10,715	10,885	11,133	11,430	11,815
Three persons	6,565	10,419	12,158	13,740	14,128	14,348	14,680	15,066	15,577
Four persons	8,414	13,359	15,569	17,604	18,104	18,392	18,810	19,307	19,971
Five persons	9,966	15,792	18,408	20,815	21,405	21,744	22,245	22,830	23,613
Six persons	11,269	17,839	20,804	23,533	24,195	24,576	25,122	25,787	26,683
Seven persons	12,761	20,241	23,552	26,750	27,517	28,001	28,544	29,233	30,249
Eight persons	14,199	22,582	26,237	29,701	30,627	30,907	31,589	32,641	33,610
Nine or more persons	16,896	26,848	31,280	35,150	36,286	37,062	37,656	39,062	40,288

[1] Implementation of Census-2000-based population controls and sample expanded by 28,000 households.   [2] The 2004 data have been revised to reflect a correction to the weights in the 2005 ASEC.

Source: U.S. Census Bureau, *Current Population Reports*, P60-231; and Internet site <http://www.census.gov/prod/2006pubs/p60-231.pdf>.

Table 689. People Below Poverty Level and Below 125 Percent of Poverty Level by Race and Hispanic Origin: 1980 to 2005

[29,272 represents 29,272,000. People as of March of the following year. Based on Current Population Survey, Annual Social and Economic Supplement (ASEC); See text, Section 1, and Appendix III. For data collection changes over time, see <http://www.census.gov/hhes/www/income/histinc/hstchg.html>]

Year	Number below poverty level (1,000)					Percent below poverty level					Below 125 percent of poverty level	
	All races [1]	White [2]	Black [3]	Asian and Pacific Islander [4]	His- panic [5]	All races [1]	White [2]	Black [3]	Asian and Pacific Islander [4]	His- panic [5]	Num- ber (1,000)	Percent of total popu- lation
1980	29,272	19,699	8,579	(NA)	3,491	13.0	10.2	32.5	(NA)	25.7	40,658	18.1
1985	33,064	22,860	8,926	(NA)	5,236	14.0	11.4	31.3	(NA)	29.0	44,166	18.7
1986	32,370	22,183	8,983	(NA)	5,117	13.6	11.0	31.1	(NA)	27.3	43,486	18.2
1987 [6] . .	32,221	21,195	9,520	1,021	5,422	13.4	10.4	32.4	16.1	28.0	43,032	17.9
1988	31,745	20,715	9,356	1,117	5,357	13.0	10.1	31.3	17.3	26.7	42,551	17.5
1989	31,528	20,785	9,302	939	5,430	12.8	10.0	30.7	14.1	26.2	42,653	17.3
1990	33,585	22,326	9,837	858	6,006	13.5	10.7	31.9	12.2	28.1	44,837	18.0
1991 [7] . .	35,708	23,747	10,242	996	6,339	14.2	11.3	32.7	13.8	28.7	47,527	18.9
1992 [7] . .	38,014	25,259	10,827	985	7,592	14.8	11.9	33.4	12.7	29.6	50,592	19.7
1993 [8] . .	39,265	26,226	10,877	1,134	8,126	15.1	12.2	33.1	15.3	30.6	51,801	20.0
1994	38,059	25,379	10,196	974	8,416	14.5	11.7	30.6	14.6	30.7	50,401	19.3
1995	36,425	24,423	9,872	1,411	8,574	13.8	11.2	29.3	14.6	30.3	48,761	18.5
1996	36,529	24,650	9,694	1,454	8,697	13.7	11.2	28.4	14.5	29.4	49,310	18.5
1997	35,574	24,396	9,116	1,468	8,308	13.3	11.0	26.5	14.0	27.1	47,853	17.8
1998	34,476	23,454	9,091	1,360	8,070	12.7	10.5	26.1	12.5	25.6	46,036	17.0
1999 [9] . .	32,791	22,169	8,441	1,285	7,876	11.9	9.8	23.6	10.7	22.7	45,030	16.3
2000 [10] . .	31,581	21,645	7,982	1,258	7,747	11.3	9.5	22.5	9.9	21.5	43,612	15.6
2001	32,907	22,739	8,136	1,275	7,997	11.7	9.9	22.7	10.2	21.4	45,320	16.1
2002 [11] . .	34,570	23,466	8,602	1,161	8,555	12.1	10.2	24.1	10.1	21.8	47,084	16.5
2003 [12] . .	35,861	24,272	8,781	1,401	9,051	12.5	10.5	24.4	11.8	22.5	48,687	16.9
2004 [12] . .	37,040	25,327	9,014	1,201	9,122	12.7	10.8	24.7	9.8	21.9	49,693	17.1
2005	36,950	24,872	9,168	1,402	9,368	12.6	10.6	24.9	11.1	21.8	49,327	16.8

NA Not available.   [1] Includes other races not shown separately.   [2] Beginning 2002, data represent White alone, which refers to people who reported White and did not report any other race category.   [3] Beginning 2002, data represent Black alone, which refers to people who reported Black and did not report any other race category.   [4] Beginning 2002, data represent Asian alone, which refers to people who reported Asian and did not report any other race category.   [5] People of Hispanic origin may be of any race.   [6] Implementation of a new March CPS processing system.   [7] Implementation of 1990 census population controls.   [8] The March 1994 income supplement was revised to allow for the coding of different income amounts on selected questionnaire items. Limits either increased or decreased in the following categories: earnings increased to $999,999; social security increased to $49,999; supplemental security income and public assistance increased to $24,999; veterans' benefits increased to $99,999; child support and alimony decreased to $49,999.   [9] Implementation of Census-2000-based population controls.   [10] Implementation of 28,000 household sample expansion.   [11] Beginning with the 2003 Current Population Survey (CPS), the questionnaire allowed respondents to choose more than one race. For 2002 and later, data represent persons who selected this race group only and excludes persons reporting more than one race. The CPS in prior years allowed respondents to report only one race group. See also comments on race in the text for Section 1, Population.   [12] Data have been revised to reflect a correction to the weights in the 2005 ASEC.

Source: U.S. Census Bureau, *Current Population Reports*, P60-231; and Internet sites <http://www.census.gov/prod/2006pubs/p60-231.pdf> (released August 2006) and <http://www.census.gov/hhes/www/poverty/histpov/perindex.html>.

Table 690. Children Below Poverty Level by Race and Hispanic Origin: 1980 to 2005

[11,114 represents 11,114,000. Persons as of March of the following year. Covers only related children in families under 18 years old. Based on Current Population Survey, Annual Social and Economic Supplement (ASEC); see text, this section and Section 1, and Appendix III. For data collection changes over time, see <http://www.census.gov/hhes/www/income/histinc/hstchg.html>]

Year	Number below poverty level (1,000)					Percent below poverty level				
	All races [1]	White [2]	Black [3]	Asian and Pacific Islander [4]	His-panic [5]	All races [1]	White [2]	Black [3]	Asian and Pacific Islander [4]	His-panic [5]
1980	11,114	6,817	3,906	(NA)	1,718	17.9	13.4	42.1	(NA)	33.0
1985	12,483	7,838	4,057	(NA)	2,512	20.1	15.6	43.1	(NA)	39.6
1986	12,257	7,714	4,037	(NA)	2,413	19.8	15.3	42.7	(NA)	37.1
1987 [6]	12,275	7,398	4,234	432	2,606	19.7	14.7	44.4	22.7	38.9
1988	11,935	7,095	4,148	458	2,576	19.0	14.0	42.8	23.5	37.3
1989	12,001	7,164	4,257	368	2,496	19.0	14.1	43.2	18.9	35.5
1990	12,715	7,696	4,412	356	2,750	19.9	15.1	44.2	17.0	37.7
1991	13,658	8,316	4,637	348	2,977	21.1	16.1	45.6	17.1	39.8
1992 [7]	14,521	8,752	5,015	352	3,440	21.6	16.5	46.3	16.0	39.0
1993 [8]	14,961	9,123	5,030	358	3,666	22.0	17.0	45.9	17.6	39.9
1994	14,610	8,826	4,787	308	3,956	21.2	16.3	43.3	17.9	41.1
1995	13,999	8,474	4,644	532	3,938	20.2	15.5	41.5	18.6	39.3
1996	13,764	8,488	4,411	553	4,090	19.8	15.5	39.5	19.1	39.9
1997	13,422	8,441	4,116	608	3,865	19.2	15.4	36.8	19.9	36.4
1998	12,845	7,935	4,073	542	3,670	18.3	14.4	36.4	17.5	33.6
1999 [9]	11,678	7,194	3,698	367	3,561	16.6	13.1	32.8	11.5	29.9
2000 [10]	11,005	6,834	3,495	407	3,342	15.6	12.4	30.9	12.5	27.6
2001	11,175	7,086	3,423	353	3,433	15.8	12.8	30.0	11.1	27.4
2002 [11]	11,646	7,203	3,570	302	3,653	16.3	13.1	32.1	11.4	28.2
2003	12,340	7,624	3,750	331	3,982	17.2	13.9	33.6	12.1	29.5
2004 [12]	12,473	7,876	3,702	269	3,985	17.3	14.3	33.4	9.4	28.6
2005	12,335	7,652	3,743	312	3,977	17.1	13.9	34.2	11.0	27.7

NA Not available.   [1] Includes other races not shown separately.   [2] Beginning 2002, data represent White alone, which refers to people who reported White and did not report any other race category.   [3] Beginning 2002, data represent Black alone, which refers to people who reported Black and did not report any other race category.   [4] Beginning 2002, data represent Asian alone, which refers to people who reported Asian and did not report any other race category.   [5] People of Hispanic origin may be of any race.   [6] Implementation of a new March CPS processing system.   [7] Implementation of 1990 census population controls.   [8] The March 1994 income supplement was revised to allow for the coding of different income amounts on selected questionnaire items. Limits either increased or decreased in the following categories: earnings increased to $999,999; social security increased to $49,999; supplemental security income and public assistance increased to $24,999; veterans' benefits increased to $99,999; child support and alimony decreased to $49,999.   [9] Implementation of Census-2000-based population controls.   [10] Implementation of 28,000 household sample expansion.   [11] Beginning with the 2003 Current Population Survey (CPS), the questionnaire allowed respondents to choose more than one race. For 2002 and later, data represent persons who selected this race group only and exclude persons reporting more than one race. The CPS in prior years allowed respondents to report only one race group. See also comments on race in the text for Section 1.   [12] Data have been revised to reflect a correction to the weights in the 2005 ASEC.

Source: U.S. Census Bureau, *Current Population Reports,* P60-231; and Internet sites <http://www.census.gov/prod/2006pubs/p60-231.pdf> (released August 2006) and <http://www.census.gov/hhes/www/poverty/histpov/hstpov3.html>.

Table 691. Persons Below Poverty Level by Selected Characteristics: 2005

[36,950 represents 36,950,000. People as of March 2006. Based on Current Population Survey (CPS); see text, this section and Section 1, and Appendix III. The 2006 CPS allowed respondents to choose more than one race. For 2005, data represent persons who selected this race group only and exclude persons reporting more than one race. The CPS in prior years allowed respondents to report only one race group. See also comments on race in the text for Section 1. For composition of regions, see map, inside front cover]

Characteristic	Number below poverty level (1,000)					Percent below poverty level				
	All races [1]	White alone	Black alone	Asian alone	His-panic [2]	All races [1]	White alone	Black alone	Asian alone	His-panic [2]
Total	36,950	24,872	9,168	1,402	9,368	12.6	10.6	24.9	11.1	21.8
Male	15,950	10,750	3,840	666	4,360	11.1	9.2	22.4	11.0	19.7
Female	21,000	14,122	5,328	736	5,008	14.1	11.9	27.1	11.3	23.9
Under 18 years old	12,896	8,085	3,841	317	4,143	17.6	14.4	34.5	11.1	28.3
18 to 24 years old	5,094	3,509	1,142	241	1,128	18.2	16.1	28.1	20.8	23.2
25 to 34 years old	4,965	3,342	1,157	269	1,504	12.6	10.8	22.4	12.0	19.2
35 to 44 years old	4,186	2,950	889	172	1,185	9.7	8.6	16.6	7.8	18.3
45 to 54 years old	3,504	2,361	834	172	563	8.2	6.7	16.7	9.7	12.8
55 to 59 years old	1,441	1,036	316	43	210	8.1	6.9	17.7	6.0	14.5
60 to 64 years old	1,260	888	289	44	175	9.6	8.0	22.2	9.3	17.0
65 years old and over	3,603	2,700	701	143	460	10.1	8.7	23.3	12.8	19.9
65 to 74 years old	1,648	1,159	369	86	241	8.9	7.3	21.7	13.1	17.7
75 years old and over	1,955	1,541	332	57	219	11.5	10.3	25.4	12.4	23.1
Northeast	6,103	4,026	1,548	386	1,378	11.3	9.2	23.4	13.8	22.7
Midwest	7,419	5,027	1,945	163	736	11.4	9.0	29.8	11.2	21.3
South	14,854	9,222	4,941	253	3,392	14.0	11.4	24.3	11.1	22.0
West	8,573	5,696	735	600	3,863	12.6	12.0	21.9	9.9	21.4
Native	31,080	20,593	8,672	478	5,581	12.1	9.7	25.7	10.4	21.6
Foreign born	5,870	4,278	496	924	3,787	16.5	18.0	16.4	11.6	22.0
Naturalized citizen	1,441	949	139	326	645	10.4	11.6	10.7	7.9	15.0
Not a citizen	4,429	3,329	357	598	3,142	20.4	21.4	20.7	15.4	24.4

[1] Includes other races not shown separately.   [2] Persons of Hispanic origin may be any race.

Source: U.S. Census Bureau, *Current Population Reports,* P60-231; and Internet stie <http://pubdb3.census.gov/macro/032006/pov/toc.htm> (released 29 August 2006).

Income, Expenditures, Poverty, and Wealth   459

Table 692. **Work Experience During 2005 by Poverty Status, Sex, and Age: 20**___

[104,876 **represents** 104,876,000. Covers only persons 16 years old and over. Based on Current Population Survey; see text, this section, Section 1, and Appendix III]

Sex and age	Worked full-time year-round			Did not work full-time year-round			Did not work		
		Below poverty level			Below poverty level			Below poverty level	
	Number (1,000)	Number (1,000)	Percent	Number (1,000)	Number (1,000)	Percent	Number (1,000)	Number (1,000)	Percent
BOTH SEXES									
Total	104,876	2,894	2.8	50,251	6,446	12.8	73,735	16,041	21.8
16 to 17 years old	90	7	8.1	2,714	204	7.5	6,208	1,117	18.0
18 to 64 years old	102,126	2,861	2.8	43,859	6,139	14.0	38,360	11,450	29.8
18 to 24 years old. . . .	8,048	454	5.6	12,273	2,109	17.2	7,645	2,531	33.1
25 to 34 years old. . . .	23,745	896	3.8	9,306	1,682	18.1	6,429	2,387	37.1
35 to 54 years old. . . .	55,430	1,299	2.3	16,272	1,908	11.7	14,217	4,484	31.5
55 to 64 years old. . . .	14,903	213	1.4	6,008	440	7.3	10,069	2,048	20.3
65 years old and over . . .	2,660	25	1.0	3,678	103	2.8	29,167	3,475	11.9
MALE									
Total	61,510	1,609	2.6	21,225	2,607	12.3	28,225	5,890	20.9
16 to 17 years old	67	6	(B)	1,366	95	6.9	3,181	562	17.7
18 to 64 years old	59,810	1,581	2.6	17,929	2,469	13.8	13,421	4,279	31.9
18 to 24 years old. . . .	4,726	210	4.4	5,915	840	14.2	3,471	1,018	29.3
25 to 34 years old. . . .	14,294	550	3.8	3,800	628	16.5	1,733	734	42.4
35 to 54 years old. . . .	32,325	720	2.2	5,749	824	14.3	4,270	1,732	40.6
55 to 64 years old. . . .	8,465	101	1.2	2,465	177	7.2	3,947	795	20.1
65 years old and over . . .	1,632	22	1.3	1,930	43	2.2	11,623	1,049	9.0
FEMALE									
Total	43,366	1,285	3.0	29,026	3,839	13.2	45,510	10,151	22.3
16 to 17 years old	23	1	(B)	1,348	109	8.1	3,028	555	18.3
18 to 64 years old	42,316	1,280	3.0	25,929	3,669	14.2	24,939	7,170	28.8
18 to 24 years old. . . .	3,322	244	7.3	6,357	1,269	20.0	4,173	1,513	36.3
25 to 34 years old. . . .	9,451	346	3.7	5,506	1,054	19.1	4,696	1,653	35.2
35 to 54 years old. . . .	23,105	579	2.5	10,522	1,083	10.3	9,947	2,752	27.7
55 to 64 years old. . . .	6,438	112	1.7	3,543	263	7.4	6,123	1,253	20.5
65 years old and over . . .	1,027	4	0.3	1,749	61	3.5	17,544	2,426	13.8

B Base figure too small to meet statistical standards for reliability of a derived figure.

Source: U.S. Census Bureau, *Current Population Reports*, series P60-231; and Internet site <http://pubdb3.census.gov /macro/032006/pov/new22_100_01.htm> (released 29 August 2006).

Table 693. **Families Below Poverty Level and Below 125 Percent of Poverty by Race and Hispanic Origin: 1980 to 2005**

[6,217 **represents** 6,217,000. **Families as of March of the following year** . Based on Current Population Survey. See text, this section, Section 1, and Appendix III. For data collection changes over time, see <http://www.census.gov/hhes/www/income/histinc /hstchg.htm>]

Year	Number below poverty level (1,000)					Percent below poverty level					Below 125 percent of poverty level	
	All races [1]	White [2]	Black [3]	Asian and Pacific Islander [4]	His- panic [5]	All races [1]	White [2]	Black [3]	Asian and Pacific Islander [4]	His- panic [5]	Num- ber (1,000)	Percent
1980 . . .	6,217	4,195	1,826	(NA)	751	10.3	8.0	28.9	(NA)	23.2	8,764	14.5
1985 . . .	7,223	4,983	1,983	(NA)	1,074	11.4	9.1	28.7	(NA)	25.5	9,753	15.3
1990 . . .	7,098	4,622	2,193	169	1,244	10.7	8.1	29.3	11.0	25.0	9,564	14.4
1995 . . .	7,532	4,994	2,127	264	1,695	10.8	8.5	26.4	12.4	27.0	10,223	14.7
1996 . . .	7,708	5,059	2,206	284	1,748	11.0	8.6	26.1	12.7	26.4	10,476	14.9
1997 . . .	7,324	4,990	1,985	244	1,721	10.3	8.4	23.6	10.2	24.7	10,032	14.2
1998 . . .	7,186	4,829	1,981	270	1,648	10.0	8.0	23.4	11.0	22.7	9,714	13.6
1999 [6] . .	6,792	4,447	1,887	258	1,593	9.3	7.3	21.8	10.3	20.5	9,320	12.9
2000 [7] . .	6,400	4,333	1,686	233	1,540	8.7	7.1	19.3	7.8	19.2	9,032	12.2
2001 . . .	6,813	4,579	1,829	234	1,649	9.2	7.4	20.7	7.8	19.4	9,525	12.8
2002 [8] . .	7,229	4,862	1,923	210	1,792	9.6	7.8	21.5	7.4	19.7	9,998	13.2
2003 . . .	7,607	5,058	1,986	311	1,925	10.0	8.1	22.3	10.2	20.8	10,360	13.6
2004 [9] . .	7,835	5,293	2,035	232	1,953	10.2	8.4	22.8	7.4	20.5	10,499	13.7
2005 . . .	7,657	5,068	1,997	289	1,948	9.9	8.0	22.1	9.0	19.7	10,442	13.5

NA Not available. [1] Includes other races not shown separately. [2] Beginning 2002, data represent White alone, which refers to people who reported White and did not report any other race category. [3] Beginning 2002, data represent Black alone, which refers to people who reported Black and did not report any other race category. [4] Beginning 2002, data represent Asian alone, which refers to people who reported Asian and did not report any other race category. [5] People of Hispanic origin may be of any race. [6] Implementation of Census 2000-based population controls. [7] Implementation of Census 2000-based population controls and sample expanded by by 28,000 households. [8] Beginning with the 2003 Current Population Survey (CPS), the questionnaire allowed respondents to choose more than one race. For 2002 and later, data represent persons who selected this race group only and exclude persons reporting more than one race. The CPS in prior years allowed respondents to report only one race group. See also comments on race in the text for Section 1, Population. [9] Data have been revised to reflect a correction to the rights in the 2005 ASEC.

Source: U.S. Census Bureau, *Current Population Reports*, P60-231; and Internet sites <http://www.census.gov /prod/2006pubs/p60-231.pdf> (released August 2006) and <http://www.census.gov/hhes/www/poverty/histpov/hstpov4.html>.

460   Income, Expenditures, Poverty, and Wealth

Table 694. Families Below Poverty Level by Selected Characteristics: 2005

[7,657 represents 7,657,000. Families as of March 2006. Based on Current Population Survey (CPS); see text, this section, Section 1, and Appendix III. The 2006 CPS allowed respondents to choose more than one race. For 2005, data represent persons who selected this race group only and exclude persons reporting more than one race. See also comments on race in the text for Section 1. For composition of regions, see map, inside front cover]

Characteristic	Number below poverty level (1,000)					Percent below poverty level				
	All races [1]	White alone	Black alone	Asian alone	His- panic [2]	All races [1]	White alone	Black alone	Asian alone	His- panic [2]
Total families	7,657	5,068	1,997	289	1,948	9.9	8.0	22.1	9.0	19.7
Age of householder:										
15 to 24 years old.	1,029	664	288	14	255	29.5	25.5	45.7	12.9	30.6
25 to 34 years old.	2,137	1,385	606	65	643	15.8	13.2	31.4	10.6	23.5
35 to 44 years old.	1,879	1,263	470	75	568	10.4	8.7	20.7	8.1	20.9
45 to 54 years old.	1,133	743	283	62	240	6.5	5.1	14.3	8.9	13.0
55 to 64 years old.	719	491	165	35	111	5.8	4.7	13.8	7.0	12.5
65 years old and over	723	498	174	37	110	5.9	4.7	17.3	10.7	14.4
Region:										
Northeast	1,264	813	347	76	313	8.9	7.0	21.3	10.9	21.5
Midwest	1,510	1,012	415	24	144	8.6	6.6	26.2	6.8	18.5
South	3,158	1,947	1,067	55	704	11.1	8.8	21.3	9.1	19.4
West.	1,725	1,297	167	133	786	10.0	9.2	20.5	8.6	19.6
Type of family:										
Married couple	2,944	2,317	341	193	917	5.1	4.6	8.3	7.5	13.8
Male householder, no spouse present.	669	439	170	20	155	13.0	11.2	21.1	8.3	15.9
Female householder, no spouse present.	4,044	2,312	1,486	76	876	28.7	25.3	36.1	19.7	38.9

[1] Includes other races not shown separately.   [2] Hispanic persons may be of any race.

Source: U.S. Census Bureau, *Current Population Reports*, P60-231; and Internet site <http://pubdb3.census.gov/macro/032006/pov/toc.htm> (released 29 August 2006).

Table 695. People and Families With Alternative Definitions of Income Below Poverty: 2004

[290,605 represents 290,605,000. People and families as of March 2005]

Race and Hispanic origin	Number (1,000)	Alternative definitions of income, percent below poverty			
		Money income [1]	Market income [2]	Post-social insurance income [3]	Disposable income [4]
PEOPLE					
Total [5]	290,605	12.6	19.4	12.9	10.4
White alone or in combination.	238,453	10.8	17.6	11.0	9.0
White alone [6].	233,702	10.7	17.5	10.9	8.9
White alone, not Hispanic.	195,054	8.6	15.7	8.5	7.2
Black alone or in combination.	38,016	24.6	32.1	25.6	19.6
Black alone [7]	36,423	24.6	32.2	25.5	19.7
Asian alone or in combination.	13,356	9.9	13.9	10.8	9.1
Asian alone [8]	12,301	10.0	14.0	10.9	9.3
Hispanic [9].	41,688	21.8	26.9	23.0	17.9
FAMILIES					
Total [5]	77,019	10.5	17.4	10.8	8.5
White alone or in combination.	64,128	8.8	15.7	8.9	7.1
White alone [6].	63,227	8.7	15.6	8.8	7.0
White alone, not Hispanic.	54,388	6.7	13.9	6.7	5.4
Black alone or in combination.	9,113	23.4	30.6	24.1	18.7
Black alone [7]	8,908	23.4	30.6	24.1	18.7
Asian alone or in combination.	3,295	7.8	12.1	8.4	7.1
Asian alone [8]	3,155	7.8	12.0	8.4	7.0
Hispanic [9].	9,537	21.1	26.9	22.2	17.1

[1] Money income concept includes all money income received by individuals who are 15 years or older. It consists of income before deductions for taxes and other expenses and does not include lump-sum payments or capital gains. It also does not include the value of noncash benefits such as food stamps. This income concept is the basis for the official U.S. poverty measure.   [2] Market income concept includes money income except government cash transfers; includes imputed realized capital gains and losses; includes imputed rate of return on home equity; and subtracts imputed work expenses.   [3] Post-Social insurance income concept includes money income except government means-tested cash transfers; includes imputed realized capital gains and losses; includes imputed rate of return on home equity; and subtracts imputed work expenses.   [4] Disposable income concept includes money income; includes the value of noncash transfers (food stamps, public or subsidized housing, and free or reduced-price school lunches); includes imputed realized capital gains and losses; includes imputed rate of return on home equity; and subtracts imputed work expenses, federal payroll taxes, federal and state income taxes, and property taxes on owner-occupied homes.   [5] Data for American Indians and Alaska Natives, Asian, and Native Hawaiian and Other Pacific Islanders are not shown separately.   [6] White alone refers to people who reported White and did not report any other race category.   [7] Black alone refers to people who reported Black and did not report any other race category.   [8] Asian alone refers to people who reported Asian and did not report any other race category.   [9] Persons of Hispanic origin may be of any race.

Source: U.S. Census Bureau, *The Effects of Government Taxes and Transfers on Income and Poverty: 2004*. See also <http://www.census.gov/hhes/www/poverty/effect2004/effectofgovtandt2004.pdf> (released 14 February 2006).

Income, Expenditures, Poverty, and Wealth   461

Table 696. Top Wealth Holders With Gross Assets of $675,000 or More by Type of Property, Sex, and Size of Net Worth: 2001

[7,357 represents 7,357,000. Net worth is defined as assets minus liabilities. Based on a sample of federal estate tax returns (Form 706). Based on the estate multiplier technique; for more information on this methodology, see source]

Sex and net worth	Number of top wealth holders (1,000)	Assets (mil. dol.)				
		Total [1]	Personal residences	Other real estate	Closely held stock	Publicly traded stock
Both sexes, total	**7,357**	**15,181,904**	**1,790,586**	**1,483,808**	**1,228,657**	**3,492,512**
Size of net worth:						
Negative net worth [2]	32	34,900	6,897	4,116	2,209	8,058
$1 under $600,000	1,508	980,726	282,507	140,049	29,826	68,119
$600,000 under $1,000,000	2,307	2,080,347	411,849	221,197	49,671	333,887
$1,000,000 under $2,500,000	2,569	4,127,949	585,453	451,974	203,716	814,725
$2,500,000 under $5,000,000	573	2,106,827	211,564	259,276	165,506	487,587
$5,000,000 under $10,000,000	243	1,771,701	143,179	175,206	173,792	450,143
$10,000,000 under $20,000,000	77	1,128,102	74,680	96,322	154,327	300,377
$20,000,000 or more..............	46	2,951,351	74,457	135,669	449,612	1,029,617
Males, total	**3,953**	**8,890,276**	**887,979**	**848,748**	**883,579**	**1,946,329**
Size of net worth:						
Negative net worth [2]	26	32,272	5,907	3,400	2,209	8,026
$1 under $600,000	919	562,062	158,339	74,712	23,875	38,808
$600,000 under $1,000,000	1,083	984,350	162,180	114,128	35,262	141,310
$1,000,000 under $2,500,000	1,363	2,243,244	284,976	247,600	145,384	385,646
$2,500,000 under $5,000,000	333	1,222,038	110,947	143,503	121,794	253,438
$5,000,000 under $10,000,000	155	1,148,462	83,846	115,265	150,390	269,144
$10,000,000 under $20,000,000	42	624,240	30,216	50,809	77,985	159,053
$20,000,000 or more..............	31	2,073,608	51,568	99,331	326,681	690,904
Females, total	**3,404**	**6,291,628**	**902,607**	**635,060**	**345,078**	**1,546,183**
Size of net worth:						
Negative net worth [2]	6	2,628	990	716	(Z)	32
$1 under $600,000	589	418,664	124,168	65,337	5,951	29,311
$600,000 under $1,000,000	1,224	1,095,997	249,669	107,069	14,409	192,577
$1,000,000 under $2,500,000	1,206	1,884,705	300,477	204,374	58,332	429,079
$2,500,000 under $5,000,000	240	884,789	100,617	115,773	43,712	234,149
$5,000,000 under $10,000,000	88	623,239	59,333	59,941	23,402	180,999
$10,000,000 under $20,000,000	35	503,862	44,464	45,513	76,342	141,324
$20,000,000 or more..............	15	877,743	22,889	36,338	122,931	338,713

Z Less than $500,000.   [1] Includes other types of assets not shown separately.   [2] Includes individuals with zero net worth.

Source: U.S. Internal Revenue Service, *Statistics of Income Bulletin*, Winter 2005–2006, Volume 25, No. 3. See also <http://www.irs.gov/taxstats/indtaxstats/article/0,,id=96426,00.html>.

Table 697. Top Wealth Holders With Net Worth of $1 Million or More—Number and Net Worth by State: 2001

[3,510 represents 3,510,000. Millionaire is defined as those adults with net worth (assets minus liabilities) of $1 million or more. Based on a sample of federal estate tax returns (Form 706). Estimates of wealth by state can be subject to significant year-to-year fluctuations and this is especially true for individuals at the extreme tail of the net worth distribution and for states with relatively small decedent populations. Based on the estate mulitipler technique; for more information on this methodology, see source]

State	Number of millionaires (1,000)	Net worth (mil. dol.)	State	Number of millionaires (1,000)	Net worth (mil. dol.)
Total	**3,510**	**11,275,755**	Montana	11	29,836
Alabama	35	88,579	Nebraska	14	66,470
Alaska	6	15,689	Nevada............	26	97,954
Arizona	45	152,533	New Hampshire	17	42,208
Arkansas...........	22	58,856	New Jersey	178	579,085
California...........	572	1,940,734	New Mexico.........	18	47,827
Colorado...........	59	267,715	New York..........	317	1,315,450
Connecticut	83	322,668	North Carolina	83	266,524
Delaware...........	11	30,846	North Dakota	5	8,831
District of Columbia....	11	38,063	Ohio..............	114	328,870
Florida	249	837,498	Oklahoma	22	106,653
Georgia	86	220,277	Oregon	41	111,321
Hawaii	13	29,387	Pennsylvania	135	372,109
Idaho	13	34,559	Rhode Island	13	28,121
Illinois.............	185	522,196	South Carolina	40	110,356
Indiana	53	128,883	South Dakota	10	20,185
Iowa..............	32	60,127	Tennessee.........	49	141,637
Kansas............	28	62,142	Texas	182	577,967
Kentucky...........	26	65,622	Utah.............	14	38,342
Louisiana	34	89,790	Vermont	3	9,355
Maine	12	26,130	Virginia	94	229,300
Maryland...........	69	186,861	Washington	73	257,268
Massachusetts.......	105	455,761	West Virginia	10	29,580
Michigan...........	88	237,762	Wisconsin	54	165,763
Minnesota..........	60	180,335	Wyoming..........	7	24,221
Mississippi..........	11	32,457			
Missouri	58	155,805	Other areas [1]	9	29,251

[1] Includes U.S. territories and possessions.

Source: U.S. Internal Revenue Service, *Statistics of Income Bulletin*, Winter 2005–2006, Volume 25, No. 3. See also <http://www.irs.gov/taxstats/indtaxstats/article/0,,id=96426,00.html>.

462   Income, Expenditures, Poverty, and Wealth

Table 698. Nonfinancial Assets Held by Families by Type of Asset: 2004

[172.9 represents $172,900. Families include one-person units and, as used in this table, are comparable to the U.S. Census Bureau household concept. For definition of family, see text, Section 1. Based on Survey of Consumer Finance; see Appendix III. For data on financial assets, see Table 1140. For definition of median, see Guide to Tabular Presentation]

Family characteristic	Total [1]	Vehicles	Primary residence	Other residential property	Equity in nonresidential property	Business equity	Other	Any nonfinancial asset
PERCENT OF FAMILIES HOLDING ASSET								
All families, total	97.9	86.3	69.1	12.5	8.3	11.5	7.8	92.5
Age of family head:								
Under 35 years old	96.5	82.9	41.6	5.1	3.3	6.9	5.5	88.6
35 to 44 years old	97.7	89.4	68.3	9.4	6.4	13.9	6.0	93.0
45 to 54 years old	98.3	88.8	77.3	16.3	11.4	15.7	9.7	94.7
55 to 64 years old	97.5	88.6	79.1	19.5	12.8	15.8	9.2	92.6
65 to 74 years old	99.5	89.1	81.3	19.9	10.6	8.0	9.0	95.6
75 years old and over	99.6	76.9	85.2	9.7	7.7	5.3	8.5	92.5
Race or ethnicity of respondent:								
White non-Hispanic	99.3	90.3	76.1	14.0	9.2	13.6	9.3	95.8
Non-White or Hispanic	94.4	76.1	50.8	8.9	5.8	5.9	3.8	84.0
Tenure:								
Owner-occupied	100.0	92.3	100.0	15.7	11.0	14.7	9.2	100.0
Renter-occupied or other	93.3	73.0	(X)	5.4	2.4	4.3	4.6	75.9
MEDIAN VALUE [2] ($1,000)								
All families, total	172.9	14.2	160.0	100.0	60.0	100.0	15.0	147.8
Age of family head:								
Under 35 years old	39.2	11.3	135.0	82.5	55.0	50.0	5.0	32.3
35 to 44 years old	173.4	15.6	160.0	80.0	42.2	100.0	10.0	151.3
45 to 54 years old	234.9	18.8	170.0	90.0	43.0	144.0	20.0	184.5
55 to 64 years old	351.2	18.6	200.0	135.0	75.0	190.9	25.0	226.3
65 to 74 years old	233.2	12.4	150.0	80.0	78.0	100.0	30.0	161.1
75 years old and over	185.2	8.4	125.0	150.0	85.8	80.3	11.0	137.1
Race or ethnicity of respondent:								
White non-Hispanic	224.5	15.7	165.0	105.0	66.0	135.0	16.5	164.8
Non-White or Hispanic	59.6	9.8	130.0	80.0	30.0	66.7	10.0	64.1
Tenure:								
Owner-occupied	289.9	17.5	160.0	100.0	62.0	122.8	17.5	201.6
Renter-occupied or other	12.2	7.2	(X)	80.0	56.0	50.0	8.0	8.4

X Not applicable.   [1] Any financial or nonfinancial asset.   [2] Median value of asset for families holding such assets.

Source: Board of Governors of the Federal Reserve System, "2004 Survey of Consumer Finances"; published 28 February 2006; <http://www.federalreserve.gov/pubs/oss/oss2/2004/scf2004home.html>.

Table 699. Family Net Worth—Mean and Median Net Worth in Constant (2004) Dollars by Selected Family Characteristics: 1995 to 2004

[Net worth in thousands of constant (2004) dollars (260.8 represents $260,800). Constant dollar figures are based on consumer price index for all urban consumers published by U.S. Bureau of Labor Statistics. Families include one-person units and as used in this table are comparable to the U.S. Census Bureau household concept. Based on Survey of Consumer Finance; see Appendix III. For definition of mean and median, see Guide to Tabular Presentation]

Family characteristic	1995 Mean	1995 Median	1998 Mean	1998 Median	2001 Mean	2001 Median	2004 Mean	2004 Median
All families	260.8	70.8	327.5	83.1	422.9	92.2	448.2	93.1
Age of family head:								
Under 35 years old	53.2	14.8	74.0	10.6	96.6	12.5	73.5	14.2
35 to 44 years old	176.8	64.2	227.6	73.5	276.6	82.6	299.2	69.4
45 to 54 years old	364.8	116.8	420.2	122.3	517.6	141.6	542.7	144.7
55 to 64 years old	471.1	141.9	617.0	148.2	779.5	197.4	843.8	248.7
65 to 74 years old	429.3	136.6	541.1	169.8	722.6	189.4	690.9	190.1
75 years old and over	317.9	114.5	360.3	145.6	499.6	165.4	528.1	163.1
Race or ethnicity of respondent:								
White non-Hispanic	308.7	94.3	391.4	111.0	520.2	130.2	561.8	140.7
Non-White or Hispanic	94.9	19.5	116.5	19.3	125.1	19.1	153.1	24.8
Tenure:								
Owner-occupied	373.7	128.1	468.7	153.2	596.9	183.8	624.9	184.4
Renter-occupied or other	53.8	6.0	50.4	4.9	58.6	5.1	54.1	4.0

Source: Board of Governors of the Federal Reserve System, "2004 Survey of Consumer Finances"; published 28 February 2006; <http://www.federalreserve.gov/pubs/oss/oss2/2004/scf2004home.html>.

U.S. Census Bureau, Statistical Abstract of the United States: 2008

Table 700. Household and Nonprofit Organization Sector Balance Sheet: 1990 to 2006

[In billions of dollars (23,916 represents $23,916,000,000,000). As of December 31. For details of financial assets and liabilities, see Tables 1139 and 1141]

Item	1990	1995	2000	2001	2002	2003	2004	2005	2006
Assets	23,916	32,612	48,767	48,378	47,577	53,767	58,992	64,014	68,920
Tangible assets [1]	9,353	11,226	15,803	17,013	18,516	20,219	22,499	25,129	26,804
Real estate	7,380	8,750	12,644	13,714	15,074	16,655	18,734	21,178	22,642
Consumer durable goods	1,899	2,371	3,015	3,144	3,273	3,380	3,567	3,738	3,923
Financial assets [1]	14,563	21,386	32,964	31,365	29,062	33,548	36,494	38,885	42,115
Deposits [1]	3,304	3,332	4,350	4,842	5,122	5,288	5,619	6,049	6,670
Time and savings deposits	2,485	2,306	3,062	3,332	3,656	3,991	4,399	4,805	5,302
Money market fund shares	392	477	960	1,113	1,070	960	903	957	1,110
Credit market instruments [1]	1,750	2,182	2,238	2,118	2,192	2,524	2,746	3,030	3,029
Agency and GSE-backed securities [2]	119	200	510	403	245	389	440	646	631
Municipal securities	648	533	531	581	679	708	743	817	861
Corporate and foreign bonds	238	427	397	466	737	739	712	682	698
Corporate equities	1,960	4,369	8,036	6,377	4,536	5,612	5,714	5,483	5,483
Mutual fund shares	512	1,314	2,856	2,734	2,421	3,085	3,611	4,121	4,963
Security credit	62	128	412	454	413	475	578	575	656
Life insurance reserves	392	566	819	880	921	1,013	1,060	1,083	1,119
Pension fund reserves	3,308	5,715	9,166	8,766	8,068	9,673	10,637	11,177	12,192
Equity in noncorporate business	3,032	3,465	4,716	4,804	4,967	5,403	6,004	6,797	7,386
Liabilities [1]	3,711	5,052	7,389	7,998	8,780	9,810	11,010	12,220	13,293
Credit market instruments [1]	3,589	4,855	7,000	7,649	8,460	9,450	10,565	11,804	12,816
Home mortgages	2,497	3,325	4,802	5,286	5,968	6,824	7,808	8,883	9,676
Consumer credit	824	1,169	1,749	1,900	2,012	2,116	2,232	2,327	2,438
Net worth	20,205	27,560	41,378	40,380	38,797	43,956	47,982	51,795	55,626
Replacement cost value of structures:									
Residential	4,624	6,105	8,468	9,142	9,766	10,657	11,876	12,857	13,616
Households	4,367	5,817	8,106	8,761	9,369	10,239	11,427	12,387	13,132
Farm households	149	171	223	235	245	260	279	292	300
Nonprofit organizations	108	117	140	146	151	158	170	178	184
Nonresidential (nonprofits)	472	591	813	867	907	958	1,060	1,166	1,242
Owners' equity in household real estate	4,082	4,644	6,607	7,188	7,796	8,417	9,357	10,520	10,945
Owners' equity as percentage of household real estate	62.0	58.3	57.9	57.6	56.6	55.2	54.5	54.2	53.1

[1] Includes types of assets and/or liabilities not shown separately.   [2] GSE = Government-sponsored enterprises.

Source: Board of Governors of the Federal Reserve System, "Federal Reserve Statistical Release, Z.1, Flow of Funds Accounts of the United States"; published: 8 March 2007; <http://www.federalreserve.gov/releases/z1/20070308/>.

Table 701. Net Stock of Fixed Reproducible Tangible Wealth in Current and Real (2000) Dollars: 1990 to 2005

[In billions of dollars (18,111 represents $18,111,000,000,000). As of December 31. For explanation of chained dollars, see text, this section]

Item	1990	1995	1999	2000	2001	2002	2003	2004	2005
CURRENT DOLLARS									
Net stock, total	18,111	22,670	28,081	29,917	31,609	33,061	34,805	37,988	40,989
Fixed assets	16,212	20,299	25,246	26,902	28,465	29,788	31,424	34,421	37,251
Private	12,611	15,794	19,847	21,190	22,485	23,523	24,917	27,193	29,344
Nonresidential	6,500	7,954	9,860	10,514	11,020	11,330	11,692	12,533	13,544
Equipment and software	2,469	3,067	3,822	4,077	4,203	4,271	4,381	4,554	4,743
Information processing equipment and software	622	811	1,109	1,238	1,294	1,319	1,350	1,394	1,448
Structures	4,031	4,887	6,038	6,437	6,817	7,059	7,311	7,979	8,801
Residential	6,111	7,840	9,987	10,676	11,465	12,193	13,225	14,660	15,800
Housing units	4,955	6,354	8,106	8,663	9,320	9,922	10,771	11,942	12,831
Government	3,601	4,505	5,399	5,713	5,980	6,266	6,508	7,228	7,907
Nonresidential	3,452	4,317	5,179	5,481	5,733	6,002	6,228	6,925	7,585
Equipment and software	551	675	698	703	711	723	738	787	815
Structures	2,900	3,642	4,481	4,778	5,022	5,279	5,490	6,138	6,770
Residential	149	188	220	232	247	264	280	304	322
Federal	1,079	1,291	1,399	1,425	1,447	1,470	1,499	1,593	1,681
Defense	735	865	891	896	904	914	928	985	1,033
State and local	2,522	3,213	4,000	4,288	4,533	4,796	5,009	5,635	6,226
Consumer durable goods	1,899	2,371	2,835	3,015	3,144	3,273	3,380	3,567	3,738
Motor vehicles and parts	670	842	1,021	1,092	1,156	1,214	1,256	1,327	1,376
Furniture and household equipment	814	1,011	1,196	1,260	1,292	1,335	1,366	1,439	1,507
Other	415	518	618	662	696	725	759	801	856
CHAINED (2000) DOLLARS									
Net stock, total	22,580	25,156	28,524	29,528	30,393	31,189	32,004	32,872	33,747
Fixed assets	20,726	22,939	25,700	26,498	27,170	27,759	28,368	29,031	29,704
Private	16,029	17,804	20,190	20,880	21,438	21,901	22,384	22,922	23,484
Nonresidential	7,809	8,638	9,986	10,392	10,669	10,841	10,986	11,155	11,345
Equipment and software	2,532	2,972	3,823	4,091	4,249	4,343	4,422	4,529	4,671
Structures	5,347	5,702	6,163	6,302	6,422	6,499	6,568	6,634	6,694
Residential	8,223	9,174	10,203	10,488	10,769	11,068	11,401	11,763	12,126
Government	4,700	5,137	5,510	5,618	5,731	5,857	5,984	6,108	6,219
Nonresidential	4,507	4,926	5,285	5,390	5,501	5,623	5,747	5,867	5,976
Equipment and software	631	686	699	706	714	727	739	758	780
Structures	3,872	4,237	4,587	4,684	4,786	4,896	5,007	5,109	5,196
Residential	201	220	225	227	231	234	238	241	244
Consumer durable goods	1,903	2,242	2,824	3,030	3,228	3,441	3,662	3,888	4,118

Source: U.S. Bureau of Economic Analysis, *Survey of Current Business*, September 2006, and <http://www.bea.gov/bea/dn/FA2004/SelectTable.asp> (released 15 August 2006).

Prices

This section presents indexes of producer and consumer prices, actual prices for selected commodities, and energy prices. The primary sources of these data are monthly publications of the U.S. Department of Labor, Bureau of Labor Statistics (BLS), which include *Monthly Labor Review, Consumer Price Index, Detailed Report, Producer Price Indexes,* and *U.S. Import and Export Price Indexes.* The U.S. Department of Commerce, Bureau of Economic Analysis is the source for gross domestic product measures. Cost of living data for many urban and metropolitan areas are provided by the ACCRA, a private organization in Alexandria, VA. Table 707 on housing price indexes appears in this edition from the Office of Federal Housing Enterprise Oversight, *Housing Price Index.* Other commodity, housing, and energy prices may be found in the Energy and Utilities, Natural Resources, and Construction and Housing sections.

Consumer price indexes (CPI)—The CPI is a measure of the average change in prices over time in a "market basket" of goods and services purchased either by urban wage earners and clerical workers or by all urban consumers. In 1919, BLS began to publish complete indexes at semiannual intervals, using a weighting structure based on data collected in the expenditure survey of wage-earner and clerical-worker families in 1917–19 (BLS Bulletin 357, 1924). The first major revision of the CPI occurred in 1940, with subsequent revisions in 1953, 1964, 1978, 1987, and 1998.

Beginning with the release of data for January 1988 in February 1988, most consumer price indexes shifted to a new reference base year. All indexes previously expressed on a base of 1967 = 100, or any other base through December 1981, have been rebased to 1982–84 = 100. The expenditure weights are based upon data tabulated from the Consumer Expenditure Surveys.

BLS publishes CPIs for two population groups: (1) a CPI for all urban consumers (CPI-U), which covers approximately 80 percent of the total population; and (2) a CPI for urban wage earners and clerical workers (CPI-W), which covers 32 percent of the total population. The CPI-U includes, in addition to wage earners and clerical workers, groups which historically have been excluded from CPI coverage, such as professional, managerial, and technical workers; the self-employed; short-term workers; the unemployed; and retirees and others not in the labor force.

The current CPI is based on prices of food, clothing, shelter, fuels, transportation fares, charges for doctors' and dentists' services, drugs, etc. purchased for day-to-day living. Prices are collected in 87 areas across the country from over 50,000 housing units and 23,000 establishments. Area selection was based on the 1990 census. All taxes directly associated with the purchase and use of items are included in the index. Prices of food, fuels, and a few other items are obtained every month in all 87 locations. Prices of most other commodities and services are collected monthly in the three largest geographic areas and every other month in other areas.

In calculating the index, each item is assigned a weight to account for its relative importance in consumers' budgets. Price changes for the various items in each location are then averaged. Local data are then combined to obtain a U.S. city average. Separate indexes are also published for regions, area size-classes, cross-classifications of regions and size-classes, and for 26 local areas, usually consisting of the Metropolitan Statistical Area (MSA); see Appendix II. Area definitions are those established by the Office of Management and Budget in 1983. Definitions do not include revisions made since 1992. Area indexes do not measure differences in the level of prices among cities; they only measure the average

change in prices for each area since the base period. For further detail regarding the CPI, see the BLS *Handbook of Methods,* Bulletin 2490, Chapter 17; the *Consumer Price Index,* and the CPI home page: <http://www.bls.gov/cpi/>. In January 1983, the method of measuring home-ownership costs in the CPI-U was changed to a rental equivalence approach. This treatment calculates homeowner costs of shelter based on the implicit rent owners would pay to rent the homes they own. The rental equivalence approach was introduced into the CPI-W in 1985. The CPI-U was used to prepare the consumer price tables in this section.

Producer price index (PPI)—This index, dating from 1890, is the oldest continuous statistical series published by BLS. It is designed to measure average changes in prices received by domestic producers of all commodities, at various stages of processing.

The index has undergone several revisions (see *Monthly Labor Review,* February 1962, April 1978, and August 1988). It is now based on approximately 10,000 individual products and groups of products along with about 100,000 quotations per month. Indexes for the net output of manufacturing and mining industries have been added in recent years. Prices used in constructing the index are collected from sellers and generally apply to the first significant large-volume commercial transaction for each commodity—i.e., the manufacturer's or other producer's selling price or the selling price on an organized exchange or at a central market.

The weights used in the index represent the total net selling value of commodities produced or processed in this country. Values are f.o.b. (free on board) production point and are exclusive of excise taxes. Effective with the release of data for January 1988, many important producer price indexes were changed to a new reference base year, 1982 = 100, from 1967 = 100. The reference year of the PPI shipment weights has been taken primarily from the 2002 Census of Manufactures. For further detail regarding

the PPI, see the BLS *Handbook of Methods,* Bulletin 2490 (April 1997), Chapter 14. The PPI Web page is <http://www.bls.gov/ppi/>.

BEA price indexes—Chain-weighted price indexes, produced by the Bureau of Economic Analysis (BEA), are weighted averages of the detailed price indexes used in the deflation of the goods and services that make up the gross domestic product (GDP) and its major components. Growth rates are constructed for years and quarters using quantity weights for the current and preceding year or quarter; these growth rates are used to move the index for the preceding period forward a year or quarter at a time. All chain-weighted price indexes are expressed in terms of the reference year value 2000 = 100.

Personal consumption expenditures (PCE) price and quantity indexes are based on market transactions for which there are corresponding price measures. The price index provides a measure of the prices paid by persons for domestic purchases of goods and services, which may be a useful measure of consumer prices for some analytical purposes. PCEs are defined as market value of spending by individuals and not-for-profit institutions on all goods and services. Personal consumption expenditures also Include the value of certain imputed goods and services—such as the rental value of owner-occupied homes and compensation paid in kind—such as employer-paid health and life insurance premiums. More information on this index may be found at <http://www.bea.gov/bea/mp _National.htm>.

Measures of inflation—Inflation is defined as a time of generally rising prices for goods and factors of production. The BLS samples prices of items in a representative market basket and publishes the result as the CPI. The media invariably announce the inflation rate as the percent change in the CPI from month to month. A much more meaningful indicator of inflation is the percent change from the same month of the prior year. The PPI measures prices at the producer level only. The PPI shows the same general pattern of inflation as does the CPI but is more volatile. The PPI can be

roughly viewed as a leading indicator. It often tends to foreshadow trends that later occur in the CPI.

Other measures of inflation include the gross domestic purchases chain-weighted price index, the index of industrial materials prices; the Futures Price and Spot Market prices from the Commodity Research Bureau; the Employment Cost Index, the Hourly Compensation Index, or the Unit Labor Cost Index found in Section 12 on Labor Force, Employment, and Earnings, as a measure of the change in cost of the labor factor of production; and changes in long-term interest rates that are often used to measure changes in the cost of the capital factor of production.

International price indexes—The BLS International Price Program produces export and import price indexes for non-military goods traded between the United States and the rest of the world.

The export price index provides a measure of price change for all products sold by U.S. residents to foreign buyers. The import price index provides a measure of price change for goods purchased from other countries by U.S. residents. The reference period for the indexes is 2000 = 100, unless otherwise indicated. The product universe for both the import and export indexes includes raw materials, agricultural products, semifinished manufactures, and finished manufactures, including both capital and consumer goods. Price data for these items are collected primarily by mail questionnaire. In nearly all cases, the data are collected directly from the exporter or importer, although in a few cases, prices are obtained from other sources.

To the extent possible, the data gathered refer to prices at the U.S. border for exports and at either the foreign border or the U.S. border for imports. For nearly all products, the prices refer to transactions completed during the first week of the month. Survey respondents are asked to indicate all discounts, allowances, and rebates applicable to the reported prices, so that the price used in the calculation of the indexes is the actual price for which the product was bought or sold.

Table 702. **Purchasing Power of the Dollar: 1950 to 2006**

[Indexes: PPI, 1982 = $1.00; CPI, 1982-84 = $1.00. Producer prices prior to 1961, and consumer prices prior to 1964, exclude Alaska and Hawaii. Producer prices based on finished goods index. Obtained by dividing the average price index for the 1982 = 100, PPI; 1982–84 = 100, CPI base periods (100.0) by the price index for a given period and expressing the result in dollars and cents. Annual figures are based on average of monthly data]

Year	Annual average as measured by—		Year	Annual average as measured by—	
	Producer prices	Consumer prices		Producer prices	Consumer prices
1950	3.546	4.151	1979	1.289	1.380
1951	3.247	3.846	1980	1.136	1.215
1952	3.268	3.765	1981	1.041	1.098
1953	3.300	3.735	1982	1.000	1.035
1954	3.289	3.717	1983	0.984	1.003
1955	3.279	3.732	1984	0.964	0.961
1956	3.195	3.678	1985	0.955	0.928
1957	3.077	3.549	1986	0.969	0.913
1958	3.012	3.457	1987	0.949	0.880
1959	3.021	3.427	1988	0.926	0.846
1960	2.994	3.373	1989	0.880	0.807
1961	2.994	3.340	1990	0.839	0.766
1962	2.985	3.304	1991	0.822	0.734
1963	2.994	3.265	1992	0.812	0.713
1964	2.985	3.220	1993	0.802	0.692
1965	2.933	3.166	1994	0.797	0.675
1966	2.841	3.080	1995	0.782	0.656
1967	2.809	2.993	1996	0.762	0.638
1968	2.732	2.873	1997	0.759	0.623
1969	2.632	2.726	1998	0.765	0.613
1970	2.545	2.574	1999	0.752	0.600
1971	2.469	2.466	2000	0.725	0.581
1972	2.392	2.391	2001	0.711	0.565
1973	2.193	2.251	2002	0.720	0.556
1974	1.901	2.029	2003	0.698	0.543
1975	1.718	1.859	2004	0.673	0.529
1976	1.645	1.757	2005	0.642	0.512
1977	1.546	1.649	2006 [1]	0.624	0.496
1978	1.433	1.532			

[1] PPI data are preliminary.

Source: U.S. Bureau of Labor Statistics. *CPI Detailed Report*, monthly, and at <http://www.bls.gov/cpi/cpi_dr.htm>. See also *Monthly Labor Review* at <http://www.bls.gov/opub/mlr/welcome.htm> and *Producer Price Indexes*, monthly and annual.

Figure 14.1
Annual Percent Change in Consumer Price Indexes: 1990 to 2006

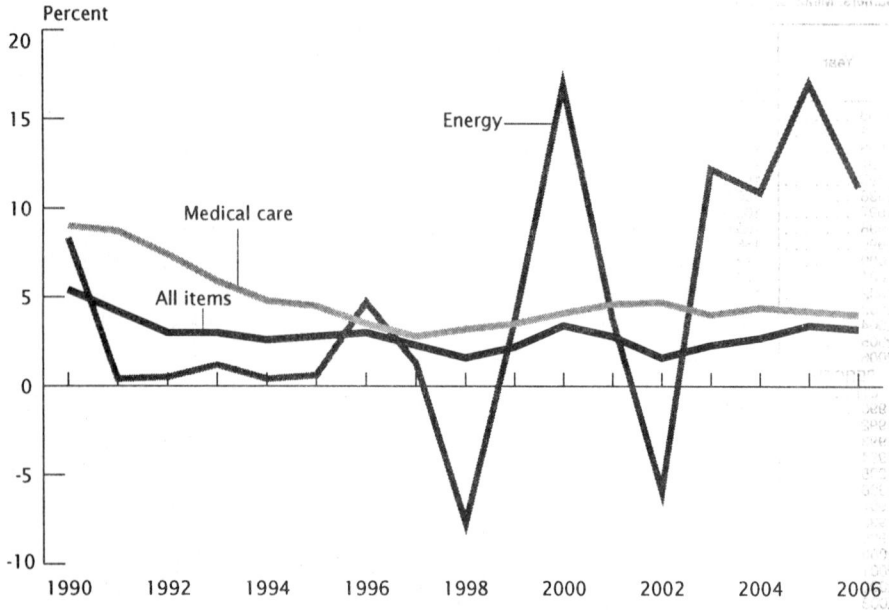

Source: Chart prepared by U.S. Census Bureau. For data, see Table 703.

Figure 14.2
Percent Change in Single-Family Housing Price Indexes: 2005 to 2006

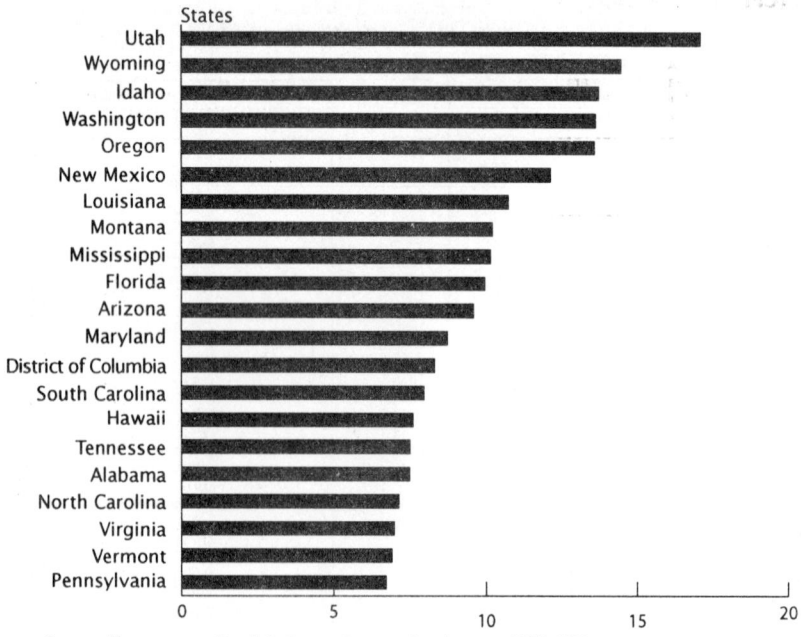

Source: Chart prepared by U.S. Census Bureau. For data, see Table 707.

468   Prices

U.S. Census Bureau, Statistical Abstract of the United States: 2008

Table 703. **Consumer Price Indexes (CPI-U) by Major Groups: 1990 to 2006**

[1982–84 = 100, except as indicated. Represents annual averages of monthly figures. Reflects buying patterns of all urban consumers. Minus sign (–) indicates decrease. See text, this section]

Year	All items	Com- mod- ities	Ser- vices	Food	Energy	All items less food and energy	Food and bever- ages	Shel- ter	Trans- por- tation	Med- ical care	Apparel	Education and commun- ication [1]
1990	130.7	122.8	139.2	132.4	102.1	135.5	132.1	140.0	120.5	162.8	124.1	(NA)
1992	140.3	129.1	152.0	137.9	103.0	147.3	138.7	151.2	126.5	190.1	131.9	(NA)
1993	144.5	131.5	157.9	140.9	104.2	152.2	141.6	155.7	130.4	201.4	133.7	85.5
1994	148.2	133.8	163.1	144.3	104.6	156.5	144.9	160.5	134.3	211.0	133.4	88.8
1995	152.4	136.4	168.7	148.4	105.2	161.2	148.9	165.7	139.1	220.5	132.0	92.2
1996	156.9	139.9	174.1	153.3	110.1	165.6	153.7	171.0	143.0	228.2	131.7	95.3
1997	160.5	141.8	179.4	157.3	111.5	169.5	157.7	176.3	144.3	234.6	132.9	98.4
1998	163.0	141.9	184.2	160.7	102.9	173.4	161.1	182.1	141.6	242.1	133.0	100.3
1999	166.6	144.4	188.8	164.1	106.6	177.0	164.6	187.3	144.4	250.6	131.3	101.2
2000	172.2	149.2	195.3	167.8	124.6	181.3	168.4	193.4	153.3	260.8	129.6	102.5
2001	177.1	150.7	203.4	173.1	129.3	186.1	173.6	200.6	154.3	272.8	127.3	105.2
2002	179.9	149.7	209.8	176.2	121.7	190.5	176.8	208.1	152.9	285.6	124.0	107.9
2003	184.0	151.2	216.5	180.0	136.5	193.2	180.5	213.1	157.6	297.1	120.9	109.8
2004	188.9	154.7	222.8	186.2	151.4	196.6	186.6	218.8	163.1	310.1	120.4	111.6
2005	195.3	160.2	230.1	190.7	177.1	200.9	191.2	224.4	173.9	323.2	119.5	113.7
2006	201.6	164.0	238.9	195.2	196.9	205.9	195.7	232.1	180.9	336.2	119.5	116.8
PERCENT CHANGE [2]												
1990	5.4	5.2	5.5	5.8	8.3	5.0	5.8	5.4	5.6	9.0	4.6	(NA)
1992	3.0	2.0	3.9	1.2	0.5	3.7	1.4	3.3	2.2	7.4	2.5	(NA)
1993	3.0	1.9	3.9	2.2	1.2	3.3	2.1	3.0	3.1	5.9	1.4	(NA)
1994	2.6	1.7	3.3	2.4	0.4	2.8	2.3	3.1	3.0	4.8	-0.2	3.9
1995	2.8	1.9	3.4	2.8	0.6	3.0	2.8	3.2	3.6	4.5	-1.0	3.8
1996	3.0	2.6	3.2	3.3	4.7	2.7	3.2	3.2	2.8	3.5	-0.2	3.4
1997	2.3	1.4	3.0	2.6	1.3	2.4	2.6	3.1	0.9	2.8	0.9	3.3
1998	1.6	0.1	2.7	2.2	-7.7	2.3	2.2	3.3	-1.9	3.2	0.1	1.9
1999	2.2	1.8	2.5	2.1	3.6	2.1	2.2	2.9	2.0	3.5	-1.3	0.9
2000	3.4	3.3	3.4	2.3	16.9	2.4	2.3	3.3	6.2	4.1	-1.3	1.3
2001	2.8	1.0	4.1	3.2	3.8	2.6	3.1	3.7	0.7	4.6	-1.8	2.6
2002	1.6	-0.7	3.1	1.8	-5.9	2.4	1.8	3.7	-0.9	4.7	-2.6	2.6
2003	2.3	1.0	3.2	2.2	12.2	1.4	2.1	2.4	3.1	4.0	-2.5	1.8
2004	2.7	2.3	2.9	3.4	10.9	1.8	3.4	2.7	3.5	4.4	-0.4	1.6
2005	3.4	3.6	3.3	2.4	17.0	2.2	2.5	2.6	6.6	4.2	-0.7	1.9
2006	3.2	2.4	3.8	2.4	11.2	2.5	2.4	3.4	4.0	4.0	–	2.7

– Represents zero.   NA Not available.   [1] Dec. 1997 = 100.   [2] Change from immediate prior year. 1990 change from 1989.
Source: U.S. Bureau of Labor Statistics, *CPI Detailed Report*, monthly, and at <http://www.bls.gov/cpi/cpi_dr.htm>. See also *Monthly Labor Review* at <http://www.bls.gov/opub/mlr/welcome.htm>.

Table 704. **Annual Percent Changes From Prior Year in Consumer Price Indexes (CPI-U)—Selected Areas: 2006**

[Represents percent changes of annual averages of monthly figures. Local area CPI indexes are by-products of the national CPI program. Each local index has a smaller sample size than the national index and is therefore subject to substantially more sampling and other measurement error. As a result, local area indexes show greater volatility than the national index, although their long-term trends are similar. Area definitions are those established by the Office of Management and Budget in 1983. For further detail, see the U.S. Bureau of Labor Statistics Handbook of Methods, Bulletin 2285, Chapter 19, the Consumer Price Index, and Report 736, the CPI: 1987 Revision. Minus sign (–) indicates decrease. See also text, this section and Appendix III]

Area	All items	Food and bever- ages	Food	Hous- ing	Apparel	Trans- porta- tion	Medi- cal care	Fuel and other utilities
U.S. city average.	3.2	2.4	2.4	3.8	–	4.0	4.0	8.8
Anchorage, AK MSA.	3.2	1.8	1.8	4.0	4.6	4.0	3.5	11.9
Atlanta, GA MSA	2.6	2.1	2.4	2.7	0.8	3.9	-1.2	3.0
Boston, MA MSA	3.1	2.9	2.9	3.5	1.4	1.7	4.5	15.8
Chicago-Gary, IL-IN MSA	2.1	2.0	2.1	1.7	-0.6	3.7	4.4	-4.1
Cincinnati-Hamilton, OH-KY-IN CMSA	3.9	1.9	1.8	4.1	0.8	4.9	8.1	14.8
Cleveland-Akron-Lorain, OH CMSA	1.7	2.5	2.5	1.3	-8.3	3.2	4.6	3.0
Dallas-Fort Worth, TX CMSA	2.9	3.9	3.6	2.4	6.1	4.0	4.1	11.0
Denver-Boulder-Greely, CO CMSA	3.6	1.3	1.0	2.3	19.3	5.1	7.4	-2.5
Detroit-Ann Arbor-Flint, MI CMSA	3.0	1.6	1.6	3.8	-6.3	4.8	4.0	10.7
Honolulu, HI MSA.	5.9	4.5	4.6	8.4	1.9	5.5	(NA)	13.1
Houston-Galveston-Brazoria, TX CMSA	2.8	1.7	1.6	3.7	-1.8	3.8	4.5	19.9
Kansas City, MO-KS CMSA	2.6	2.5	2.3	1.7	0.1	4.0	7.8	2.9
Los Angeles-Anaheim-Riverside, CA CMSA	4.3	2.0	2.2	6.0	0.5	3.9	4.0	14.3
Miami-Fort Lauderdale, FL CMSA	4.9	1.7	1.7	7.4	6.1	3.1	4.5	18.4
Milwaukee, WI PMSA	2.5	3.5	3.6	2.0	-0.4	3.7	2.5	6.1
Minneapolis-St. Paul, MN-WI MSA	1.6	1.9	1.7	-0.2	1.2	3.8	5.5	1.9
New York-Northern New Jersey-Long Island, NY-NJ-CT CMSA	3.8	3.0	3.1	5.1	-1.5	3.8	4.0	7.6
Philadelphia-Wilmington-Trenton, PA-NJ-DE-MD CMSA. .	3.9	1.9	1.8	5.8	-2.5	2.8	4.2	13.2
Pittsburgh, PA MSA	3.1	2.4	2.4	4.5	-3.2	2.6	5.6	6.6
Portland, OR MSA	2.6	2.5	2.5	1.9	5.3	4.9	5.1	5.1
San Diego, CA MSA	3.4	2.3	2.3	4.1	3.3	2.6	(NA)	9.9
San Francisco-Oakland-San Jose, CA CMSA	3.2	1.8	1.8	3.0	1.6	3.5	10.0	12.9
Seattle-Tacoma, WA CMSA	3.7	2.9	2.9	4.8	3.1	4.1	3.2	6.3
St. Louis-East St. Louis, MO-IL CMSA	1.8	2.6	2.5	0.9	-6.5	4.0	5.0	10.3
Tampa-St. Petersburg-Clearwater, FL MSA	4.0	2.7	2.7	5.2	2.9	5.0	5.3	10.1
Washington-Baltimore, DC-MD-VA-WV CMSA	3.6	2.7	2.8	4.4	0.9	3.9	2.3	7.7

– Represents zero.   NA Not available.
Source: U.S. Bureau of Labor Statistics, *CPI Detailed Report*, monthly, and at <http://www.bls.gov/cpi/cpi_dr.htm>. See also *Monthly Labor Review* at <http://www.bls.gov/opub/mlr/welcome.htm>.

U.S. Census Bureau, Statistical Abstract of the United States: 2008

Table 705. **Consumer Price Indexes for All Urban Consumers (CPI-U) for Selected Items and Groups: 2000 to 2006**

[1982–84 = 100, except as noted. Annual averages of monthly figures. See headnote, Table 703]

Item	2000	2001	2002	2003	2004	2005	2006	Annual percentage change, 2005–2006
All items	172.2	177.1	179.9	184.0	188.9	195.3	201.6	3.2
Food and beverages.	168.4	173.6	176.8	180.5	186.6	191.2	195.7	2.4
Food	167.8	173.1	176.2	180.0	186.2	190.7	195.2	2.4
Food at home	167.9	173.4	175.6	179.4	186.2	189.8	193.1	1.7
Cereals and bakery products	188.3	193.8	198.0	202.8	206.0	209.0	212.8	1.8
Cereals and cereal products	175.9	178.7	181.8	185.2	186.2	186.7	187.3	0.3
Bakery products	194.1	201.3	206.1	211.7	216.2	220.5	226.4	2.7
Bread [1]	107.4	112.5	115.4	118.5	121.1	126.2	130.4	3.3
Cakes, cupcakes, and cookies. . . .	187.9	192.0	196.7	202.8	206.4	209.8	214.2	2.1
Other bakery products	191.5	199.1	203.0	207.3	211.8	211.4	215.5	1.9
Meats, poultry, fish, and eggs	154.5	161.3	162.1	169.3	183.7	184.7	186.6	1.0
Meats, poultry, and fish	155.5	162.4	163.2	169.7	182.3	186.7	188.2	0.8
Meats	150.7	159.3	160.3	169.0	183.2	187.5	188.8	0.7
Beef and veal	148.1	160.5	160.6	175.1	195.3	200.4	202.1	0.8
Uncooked ground beef.	125.2	135.5	138.1	149.2	166.3	175.1	176.3	0.7
Uncooked beef steaks [1]	109.1	118.1	116.6	127.6	144.7	145.1	146.1	0.7
Pork	156.5	162.4	161.8	164.9	174.2	177.7	177.3	-0.2
Other meats	152.0	156.4	161.9	166.0	173.4	177.5	180.7	1.8
Poultry.	159.8	164.9	167.0	169.1	181.7	185.3	182.0	-1.8
Chicken [1]	102.5	105.5	107.6	108.9	118.2	120.6	117.6	-2.5
Fish and seafood.	190.4	191.1	188.1	190.0	194.3	200.1	209.5	4.7
Dairy products	160.7	167.1	168.1	167.9	180.2	182.4	181.4	-0.5
Milk [1]	107.8	112.7	110.6	111.5	125.0	127.0	125.5	-1.2
Cheese and related products	162.8	167.6	170.0	169.4	180.8	183.3	180.8	-1.4
Fruits and vegetables	204.6	212.2	220.9	225.9	232.7	241.4	252.9	4.8
Fresh fruits and vegetables.	238.8	247.9	258.4	265.3	274.7	285.3	300.4	5.3
Fresh fruits.	258.3	265.1	270.2	279.1	286.8	297.4	315.2	6.0
Fresh vegetables.	219.4	230.6	245.4	250.5	262.1	271.7	284.3	4.6
Processed fruits and vegetables [1] . . .	105.6	109.0	113.1	114.1	115.5	119.3	122.8	2.9
Nonalcoholic beverages and beverage materials	137.8	139.2	139.2	139.8	140.4	144.4	147.4	2.1
Juices and nonalcoholic drinks [1]	105.6	107.5	107.8	108.0	108.5	110.6	113.2	2.4
Carbonated drinks	123.4	125.4	125.6	125.6	127.9	131.9	134.2	1.7
Nonfrozen noncarbonated juices and drinks [1]	104.2	106.0	106.4	106.5	105.7	106.5	109.5	2.8
Beverage materials including coffee and tea [1]	97.9	97.0	96.3	97.4	97.6	102.4	104.1	1.7
Other food at home	155.6	159.6	160.8	162.6	164.9	167.0	169.6	1.6
Sugar and sweets.	154.0	155.7	159.0	162.0	163.2	165.2	171.5	3.8
Candy and chewing gum [1]	103.8	104.3	106.2	107.8	108.4	109.5	112.2	2.5
Fats and oils	147.4	155.7	155.4	157.4	167.8	167.7	168.0	0.2
Other food.	172.2	176.0	177.1	178.8	179.7	182.5	185.0	1.4
Frozen and freeze dried prepared food	148.5	152.4	152.6	150.6	152.5	153.2	153.7	0.3
Snacks	166.3	169.0	168.7	173.1	173.7	173.7	178.5	1.5
Spices, seasonings, condiments, sauces.	175.6	181.4	184.6	185.5	185.3	188.0	190.3	1.2
Other miscellaneous food [1]	107.5	108.9	109.2	110.3	110.4	111.3	113.9	2.3
Food away from home . . . . [1] . .	169.0	173.9	178.3	182.1	187.5	193.4	199.4	3.1
Full service meals and snacks [1]	106.8	110.3	113.0	115.3	118.4	121.9	125.7	3.1
Limited service meals and snacks [1] . . .	106.3	109.6	112.7	114.9	118.6	122.4	126.0	2.9
Food at employee sites and schools [1] . .	104.4	105.5	108.2	112.4	115.5	118.6	122.6	3.4
Other food away from home [1]	109.0	113.4	117.7	121.3	125.3	131.3	136.6	4.0
Alcoholic beverages	174.7	179.3	183.6	187.2	192.1	195.9	200.7	2.5
Alcoholic beverages at home	158.1	161.1	164.0	166.5	170.2	172.3	174.9	1.5
Beer, ale, and other malt beverages at home [1]	156.8	160.7	164.7	168.5	174.6	176.4	178.1	1.0
Wine at home	151.6	151.5	152.3	153.1	153.8	156.2	159.8	2.3
Alcoholic beverages away from home	207.1	215.2	222.5	228.6	236.6	244.5	254.6	4.1
Housing	169.6	176.4	180.3	184.8	189.5	195.7	203.2	3.8
Shelter	193.4	200.6	208.1	213.1	218.8	224.4	232.1	3.4
Rent of primary residence	183.9	192.1	199.7	205.5	211.0	217.3	225.1	3.6
Lodging away from home [1]	117.5	118.6	118.3	119.3	125.9	130.3	136.0	4.4
Other lodging away from home including hotels and motels	252.4	254.0	251.4	252.2	265.3	274.2	285.6	4.2
Owners' equivalent rent of primary residence [2]	198.7	206.3	214.7	219.9	224.9	230.2	238.2	3.5
Tenants' and household insurance [1]	103.7	106.2	108.7	114.8	116.2	117.6	116.5	-0.9
Fuels and utilities	137.9	150.2	143.6	154.5	161.9	179.0	194.7	8.8
Household energy	122.8	135.4	127.2	138.2	144.4	161.6	177.1	9.6
Fuel oil and other fuels	129.7	129.3	115.5	139.5	160.5	208.6	234.9	12.6
Fuel oil	130.3	125.8	111.5	136.6	160.0	216.4	244.6	13.0
Propane, kerosene, and firewood [3] . .	155.5	168.7	154.8	181.9	202.1	240.6	268.8	11.7

See footnotes at end of table.

U.S. Census Bureau, Statistical Abstract of the United States: 2008

[1982–84 = 100, except as noted. Annual averages of monthly figures. See headnote, Table 703]

Item	2000	2001	2002	2003	2004	2005	2006	Annual percentage change, 2005–2006
Gas (piped) and electricity	128.0	142.4	134.4	145.0	150.6	166.5	182.1	9.4
Electricity	128.5	137.8	136.2	139.5	142.1	150.8	169.2	12.2
Utility (piped) gas service	132.0	158.3	135.3	166.3	180.1	215.4	220.8	2.5
Water and sewer and trash collection services [1]	106.5	109.6	113.0	117.2	124.0	130.3	136.8	5.0
Water and sewerage maintenance.	227.5	234.6	242.5	251.7	268.1	283.4	297.2	4.9
Garbage and trash collection [4]	269.8	275.5	283.0	291.9	303.3	314.0	330.1	5.1
Household furnishings and operations	128.2	129.1	128.3	126.1	125.5	126.1	127.0	0.7
Window and floor coverings and other linens [1]	100.9	98.4	96.2	91.5	88.8	87.4	84.2	-3.7
Furniture and bedding	134.4	132.2	129.4	127.7	127.3	125.9	127.0	0.9
Bedroom furniture	138.4	136.6	135.3	133.9	137.3	142.7	145.4	1.9
Living room, kitchen, and dining room furniture [1]	102.4	101.5	98.6	97.2	95.9	92.7	92.8	0.1
Appliances [1]	96.3	94.7	92.7	89.5	85.9	86.9	88.1	1.4
Other household equipment and furnishings [1]	98.0	96.7	93.8	89.3	87.4	85.5	80.4	-6.0
Clocks, lamps, and decorator items	111.7	107.5	103.3	96.2	91.4	88.0	79.6	-9.5
Tools, hardware, outdoor equipment, and supplies [1]	97.0	96.7	95.7	94.0	93.5	94.4	94.6	0.2
Tools, hardware, and supplies [1]	97.3	96.7	95.5	93.3	94.8	98.1	99.4	1.3
Outdoor equipment and supplies [1]	96.8	96.5	95.7	94.2	92.6	92.4	92.1	-0.3
Housekeeping supplies.	153.4	158.4	159.8	157.5	157.4	159.9	166.6	4.2
Household cleaning products [1]	105.1	109.1	109.9	108.2	107.0	107.9	111.6	3.4
Household paper products [1]	113.8	118.7	119.2	117.2	120.8	125.4	132.0	5.3
Miscellaneous household products [1] . . .	104.3	105.9	107.4	106.1	105.3	106.4	111.0	4.3
Household operations [1]	110.5	115.6	119.0	121.8	125.0	130.3	136.6	4.8
Domestic services [1]	109.7	113.9	118.3	121.3	123.8	128.3	133.1	3.7
Gardening and lawncare services [1] . . .	111.4	116.6	118.3	120.2	122.9	127.9	(NA)	(NA)
Apparel	129.6	127.3	124.0	120.9	120.4	119.5	119.5	–
Men's and boy's apparel	129.7	125.7	121.7	118.0	117.5	116.1	114.1	-1.7
Men's apparel	133.1	128.9	125.7	122.1	121.4	121.4	119.8	-1.3
Men's shirts and sweaters [1]	98.3	93.9	88.8	85.2	85.3	84.2	84.7	0.6
Women's and girl's apparel	121.5	119.3	115.8	113.1	113.0	110.8	110.7	-0.1
Women's apparel.	121.9	119.9	116.1	113.1	113.3	111.8	112.5	0.6
Women's suits and separates [1]	98.2	95.8	91.4	88.1	89.8	87.3	88.2	1.0
Women's underwear, nightwear, sportswear, and accessories [1]	101.8	101.5	97.1	95.9	94.2	95.4	94.4	-1.0
Footwear.	123.8	123.0	121.4	119.6	119.3	122.6	123.5	0.7
Men's footwear	129.5	125.6	125.9	120.7	119.7	121.3	123.5	1.8
Women's footwear	119.6	120.9	119.0	118.4	118.4	121.9	122.8	0.7
Jewelry and watches [3]	137.0	136.9	133.2	128.7	129.5	127.6	130.7	2.4
Jewelry [3]	141.2	141.7	138.1	133.2	133.6	131.3	134.8	2.7
Transportation	153.3	154.3	152.9	157.6	163.1	173.9	180.9	4.0
Private transportation.	149.1	150.0	148.8	153.6	159.4	170.2	177.0	4.0
New and used motor vehicles [1]	100.8	101.3	99.2	96.5	94.2	95.6	95.6	–
New vehicles.	142.8	142.1	140.0	137.9	137.1	137.9	137.6	-0.2
Used cars and trucks	155.8	158.7	152.0	142.9	133.3	139.4	140.0	0.4
Leased cars and trucks [5]	(NA)	(NA)	99.0	96.8	93.6	92.7	93.1	0.4
Motor fuel	129.3	124.7	116.6	135.8	160.4	195.7	221.0	12.9
Gasoline (all types).	128.6	124.0	116.0	135.1	159.7	194.7	219.9	12.9
Motor vehicle parts and equipment	101.5	104.8	106.9	107.8	108.7	111.9	117.3	4.8
Motor vehicle maintenance and repair	177.3	183.5	190.2	195.6	200.2	206.9	215.6	4.2
Motor vehicle maintenance and servicing	162.7	168.8	175.0	179.5	182.8	189.2	195.7	3.4
Motor vehicle repair [1]	108.2	111.8	116.0	119.6	122.7	126.7	132.7	4.7
Motor vehicle insurance	256.7	268.1	291.6	314.4	323.2	329.9	331.8	0.6
Motor vehicle fees [1]	107.3	109.3	112.5	116.5	131.0	134.7	138.8	3.0
State and local registration and license [1]	105.1	105.6	108.5	112.7	131.3	133.2	137.3	3.1
Public transportation	209.6	210.6	207.4	209.3	209.1	217.3	226.6	4.3
Airline fare	239.4	239.4	231.6	231.3	227.2	236.6	247.3	4.5
Medical care	260.8	272.8	285.6	297.1	310.1	323.2	336.2	4.0
Medical care commodities	238.1	247.6	256.4	262.8	269.3	276.0	285.9	3.6
Prescription drugs	285.4	300.9	316.5	326.3	337.1	349.0	363.9	4.3
Nonprescription drugs and medical supplies [3]	149.5	150.6	150.4	152.0	152.3	151.7	154.6	1.9
Internal and respiratory over-the-counter drugs	176.9	178.9	178.8	181.2	180.9	179.7	183.4	2.1
Medical care services	266.0	278.8	292.9	306.0	321.3	336.7	350.6	4.1
Professional medical services	237.7	246.5	253.9	261.2	271.5	281.7	289.3	2.7
Physicians' services	244.7	253.6	260.6	267.7	278.3	287.5	291.9	1.5
Dental services	258.5	269.0	281.0	292.5	306.9	324.0	340.9	5.2
Services by other medical professionals [3]	161.9	167.3	171.8	177.1	181.9	186.8	192.2	2.9
Hospital and related services.	317.3	338.3	367.8	394.8	417.9	439.9	468.1	6.4
Hospital services [6]	115.9	123.6	134.7	144.7	153.4	161.6	172.1	6.5

See footnotes at end of table.

U.S. Census Bureau, Statistical Abstract of the United States: 2008

Table 705. **Consumer Price Indexes for All Urban Consumers (CPI-U) for Selected Items and Groups: 2000 to 2006**—Con.

[1982–84 = 100, except as noted. Annual averages of monthly figures. See headnote, Table 703]

Item	2000	2001	2002	2003	2004	2005	2006	Annual percent-age change, 2005–2006
Recreation [1]	103.3	104.9	106.2	107.5	108.6	109.4	110.9	1.4
Video and audio [1]	101.0	101.5	102.8	103.6	104.2	104.2	104.6	0.4
Cable and satellite television and radio service [4]	266.8	278.4	295.0	309.5	322.4	331.9	344.9	3.9
Pets, pet products, and services [1]	106.1	109.7	113.2	115.7	120.1	123.6	128.4	3.9
Pets and pet products	144.3	146.7	149.7	150.3	154.5	155.8	161.7	3.8
Pet services including veterinary [1]	114.6	121.8	128.2	134.9	142.3	150.3	156.5	4.1
Sporting goods	119.0	118.5	116.4	115.3	115.0	115.5	117.1	1.4
Sports vehicles, including bicycles	130.9	132.8	131.8	130.3	130.8	133.2	138.0	3.6
Other recreational goods [1]	87.8	84.6	80.5	76.1	73.3	69.5	67.2	-3.3
Recreation services [1]	111.7	116.1	119.6	124.5	127.5	130.5	135.1	3.5
Club membership dues and fees for participant sports [1]	108.9	111.7	112.9	116.1	116.7	117.4	121.9	3.8
Admissions	230.5	242.4	251.4	263.2	272.9	282.3	291.9	3.4
Education and communication [1]	102.5	105.2	107.9	109.8	111.6	113.7	116.8	2.7
Education [1]	112.5	118.5	126.0	134.4	143.7	152.7	162.1	6.2
Tuition/child care fees and other school fees	324.0	341.1	362.1	386.7	414.3	440.9	468.1	6.2
College tuition and fees	331.9	348.8	372.6	403.9	442.1	475.1	507.0	6.7
Elementary and high school tuition and fees	349.9	372.6	398.4	424.9	453.5	483.2	511.2	5.8
Child care and nursery school [7]	156.3	164.1	172.5	180.3	187.1	195.4	206.0	5.4
Communication [1]	93.6	93.3	92.3	89.7	86.7	84.7	84.1	-0.7
Information and information processing [1]	92.8	92.3	90.8	87.8	84.6	82.6	81.7	-1.1
Telephone services [1]	98.5	99.3	99.7	98.3	95.8	94.9	95.8	0.9
Land-line telephone services, local charges	175.6	184.8	193.2	201.1	204.1	209.6	213.9	2.1
Land-line telephone services, long distance charges [1]	91.8	88.8	84.9	77.8	70.9	67.5	68.3	1.2
Wireless telephone services [1]	76.0	68.1	67.4	66.8	66.2	65.0	64.6	-0.6
Information technology, hardware, and services [8]	25.9	21.3	18.3	16.1	14.8	13.6	12.5	-8.1
Other goods and services	271.1	282.6	293.2	298.7	304.7	313.4	321.7	2.6
Tobacco and smoking products	394.9	425.2	461.5	469.0	478.0	502.8	519.9	3.4
Cigarettes [1]	159.9	172.5	187.7	190.4	193.5	203.5	210.4	3.4
Personal care	165.6	170.5	174.7	178.0	181.7	185.6	190.2	2.5
Personal care products	153.7	155.1	154.7	153.5	153.9	154.4	155.8	0.9
Hair, dental, shaving, and miscellaneous personal care products [1]	103.3	104.4	104.4	102.5	102.1	101.8	102.6	0.8
Cosmetics, perfume, bath, nail preparations, and implements	166.8	168.1	167.2	168.0	169.5	171.3	173.1	1.1
Personal care services	178.1	184.3	188.4	193.2	197.6	203.9	209.7	2.8
Haircuts and other personal care services [1]	108.7	112.5	114.9	117.9	120.6	124.4	127.9	2.8
Miscellaneous personal services	252.3	263.1	274.4	283.5	293.9	303.0	313.6	3.5
Legal services [3]	189.3	199.5	211.1	221.7	232.3	241.8	250.0	3.4
Funeral expenses [3]	187.8	194.6	204.1	212.1	221.3	228.8	240.6	5.2
SPECIAL AGGREGATE INDEXES								
Commodities	149.2	150.7	149.7	151.2	154.7	160.2	164.0	2.4
Commodities less food and beverages	137.7	137.2	134.2	134.5	136.7	142.5	145.9	2.4
Nondurables less food and beverages	147.4	147.1	145.1	149.7	157.2	168.4	176.7	4.9
Nondurables less food, beverages, and apparel	162.5	163.4	162.2	171.5	183.9	202.6	216.3	6.8
Durables	125.4	124.6	121.4	117.5	114.8	115.3	114.5	-0.7
Services	195.3	203.4	209.8	216.5	222.8	230.1	238.9	3.8
Rent of shelter [2]	201.3	208.9	216.7	221.9	227.9	233.7	241.9	3.5
Transportation services	196.1	201.9	209.1	216.3	220.6	225.7	230.8	2.3
Other services	229.9	238.0	246.4	254.4	261.3	268.4	277.5	3.4
All items less food	173.0	177.8	180.5	184.7	189.4	196.0	202.7	3.4
All items less shelter	165.7	169.7	170.8	174.6	179.3	186.1	191.9	3.1
All items less medical care	167.3	171.9	174.3	178.1	182.7	188.7	194.7	3.2
Commodities less food	139.2	138.9	136.0	136.5	138.8	144.5	148.0	2.4
Nondurables less food	149.1	149.1	147.4	151.9	159.3	170.1	178.2	4.8
Nondurables less food and apparel	162.9	164.1	163.3	172.1	183.8	201.2	213.9	6.3
Nondurables	158.2	160.6	161.1	165.3	172.2	180.2	186.7	3.6
Apparel less footwear	126.2	123.6	120.1	116.8	116.3	114.4	114.1	-0.3
Services less rent of shelter [2]	202.9	212.3	217.5	226.4	233.5	243.2	253.3	4.2
Services less medical care services	188.9	196.6	202.5	208.7	214.5	221.2	229.6	3.8
Energy	124.6	129.3	121.7	136.5	151.4	177.1	196.9	11.2
All items less energy	178.6	183.5	187.7	190.6	194.4	198.7	203.7	2.5
All items less food and energy	181.3	186.1	190.5	193.2	196.6	200.9	205.9	2.5
Commodities less food and energy commodities	144.9	145.3	143.7	140.9	139.6	140.3	140.6	0.2
Energy commodities	129.5	125.2	117.1	136.7	161.2	197.4	223.0	13.0
Services less energy services	202.1	209.6	217.5	223.8	230.2	236.6	244.7	3.4
Domestically produced farm food	170.1	176.5	179.2	183.7	191.7	195.0	198.1	1.6
Utilities and public transportation	152.6	161.0	158.4	164.3	167.5	176.6	186.7	5.7

– Represents zero. NA Not available. [1] December 1997 = 100. [2] December 1982 = 100. [3] December 1986 = 100. [4] December 1983 = 100. [5] December 2001 = 100. [6] December 1996 = 100. [7] December 1990 = 100. [8] December 1988 = 100.
Source: Bureau of Labor Statistics, *CPI Detailed Report*, monthly, and at <http://www.bls.gov/cpi/cpi_dr.htm> See also *Monthly Labor Review* at <http://www.bls.gov/opub/mlr/welcome.htm>.

Table 706. Cost of Living Index—Selected Urban Areas: Fourth Quarter 2006

[Data are for a selected urban area within the larger metropolitan area shown. Measures relative price levels for consumer goods and services in participating areas for a mid-management standard of living. The nationwide average equals 100, and each index is read as a percent of the national average. The index does not measure inflation, but compares prices at a single point in time. Excludes taxes. Metropolitan areas as defined by the Office of Management and Budget. For definitions, urban areas, and components of metropolitan areas, see source]

Metropolitan areas and metropolitan divisions	Composite index (100%)	Grocery items (13%)	Housing (29%)	Utilities (10%)	Transportation (10%)	Health care (4%)	Misc. goods and services (35%)
Birmingham-Hoover, AL	94.2	97.7	80.9	99.2	96.9	98.9	100.7
Huntsville, AL	91.6	93.8	77.7	84.4	98.8	95.4	101.4
Mobile, AL	93.1	98.2	77.8	99.5	92.1	82.3	103.0
Montgomery, AL	94.9	97.2	91.5	98.5	97.9	88.9	95.6
Anchorage, AK	126.6	122.7	141.3	103.7	122.0	139.4	122.8
Phoenix-Mesa-Scottsdale, AZ	102.5	98.4	107.2	94.3	103.6	100.5	102.5
Tucson, AZ	99.8	102.2	99.2	97.0	101.8	101.2	99.5
Fayetteville-Springdale-Rogers, AR-MO	89.9	91.8	76.8	108.8	93.2	92.6	92.9
Fort Smith, AR-OK	87.0	91.1	71.3	97.4	85.7	100.9	93.8
Little Rock-North Little Rock, AR	97.9	105.6	80.6	109.4	99.8	95.1	105.3
Fresno, CA	119.5	116.1	152.2	102.6	116.5	107.4	101.6
Los Angeles-Long Beach-Glendale, CA metro. div.	147.0	117.5	256.5	84.8	112.6	100.3	103.2
Oakland-Fremont-Hayward, CA metro. div.	146.5	143.9	207.4	89.4	115.7	119.2	127.0
Riverside-San Bernardino-Ontario, CA:							
Palm Springs, CA	125.2	108.0	163.6	102.8	117.9	105.3	111.7
Riverside City, CA	116.3	110.3	151.0	81.6	116.0	100.2	102.8
San Francisco-San Mateo-Redwood City, CA metro. div.	172.9	144.1	274.3	89.1	122.4	126.9	146.3
San Jose-Sunnyvale-Santa Clara, CA	151.0	140.4	244.1	102.8	109.4	119.9	109.7
Colorado Springs, CO	95.4	99.0	92.3	87.0	109.1	104.7	93.9
Denver-Aurora, CO	103.4	103.5	107.9	102.3	99.2	107.5	100.7
Fort Collins-Loveland, CO	103.3	104.7	97.2	98.9	107.3	100.5	108.1
Greeley, CO	95.0	97.1	92.0	100.2	101.6	103.9	92.3
Dover, DE	103.2	97.2	97.7	137.5	100.1	101.5	101.0
Wilmington, DE-MD-NJ metro. div.	105.3	107.1	104.5	115.8	97.5	112.4	103.6
Washington-Arlington-Alexandria, DC-VA-MD-WV metro. div.	138.8	111.2	211.8	121.8	109.9	113.1	106.6
Cape Coral-Fort Myers, FL	103.1	94.6	106.2	95.2	110.2	104.6	103.8
Fort Lauderdale-Pompano Beach-Deerfield Beach, FL metro. div.	119.2	101.7	165.2	96.3	108.1	103.7	100.4
Jacksonville, FL	97.7	98.0	95.8	90.2	100.1	99.5	100.3
Miami-Miami Beach-Kendall, FL metro. div.	113.8	104.8	135.4	102.2	115.0	108.7	103.5
Orlando-Kissimmee, FL	101.8	95.2	102.5	111.1	105.1	98.3	100.4
Sarasota-Bradenton-Venice, FL:							
Bradenton, FL	99.8	97.2	108.0	95.7	100.7	104.4	94.5
Sarasota, FL	105.0	103.7	113.8	105.6	103.9	110.3	98.0
Tampa-St. Petersburg-Clearwater, FL:							
St. Petersburg-Clearwater, FL	99.1	106.5	98.6	109.5	98.8	93.7	94.4
Tampa, FL	98.2	98.1	98.3	96.4	102.6	93.1	98.1
Atlanta-Sandy Springs-Marietta, GA:							
Atlanta, GA	95.6	99.1	92.0	85.9	100.4	105.2	97.4
Marietta, GA	98.8	91.0	99.7	103.3	95.9	100.2	100.4
Honolulu, HI	163.5	157.7	252.7	116.5	127.6	110.8	124.0
Boise City-Nampa, ID	97.7	91.2	88.8	99.4	111.2	103.1	102.2
Champaign-Urbana, IL	96.4	91.2	90.9	114.0	97.1	98.9	97.3
Chicago-Naperville-Joliet, IL metro. div.:							
Chicago, IL	109.8	103.5	124.0	109.8	110.5	108.8	100.7
Joliet-Will County, IL	97.2	102.0	96.2	90.0	101.9	102.4	96.4
Peoria, IL	98.6	105.7	93.5	102.9	104.4	100.7	96.8
Springfield, IL	92.7	95.7	87.2	83.7	97.4	110.3	95.2
Fort Wayne, IN	90.1	92.0	84.0	95.7	96.4	91.2	90.9
Indianapolis, IN	97.6	101.4	99.9	97.8	99.2	95.1	94.1
South Bend-Mishawaka, IN-MI	91.3	97.6	86.7	89.4	97.6	97.3	90.6
Cedar Rapids, IA	92.8	88.0	80.2	94.3	102.0	108.4	99.9
Davenport-Moline-Rock Island, IA-IL	94.9	96.2	89.3	95.8	101.7	90.9	97.2
Des Moines, IA	89.4	86.8	86.5	88.7	88.2	91.3	93.1
Lawrence, KS	91.7	89.1	90.4	95.2	89.6	92.5	93.1
Cincinnati-Middletown, OH-KY-IN	93.6	96.9	82.6	94.1	98.8	92.3	99.6
Louisville, KY-IN	99.1	95.8	90.7	89.8	116.5	100.1	104.6
Baton Rouge, LA	91.7	94.1	85.6	90.8	98.2	98.8	93.4
Lafayette, LA	96.7	90.8	99.9	84.1	98.2	96.6	99.4
New Orleans-Metairie-Kenner, LA	101.3	110.5	103.8	87.3	102.3	93.2	100.5
Shreveport-Bossier City, LA	92.8	91.5	87.9	94.5	91.6	93.2	97.1

See footnotes at end of table.

U.S. Census Bureau, Statistical Abstract of the United States: 2008

[Data are for a selected urban area within the larger metropolitan area shown. Measures relative price levels for consumer goods and services in participating areas for a mid-management standard of living. The nationwide average equals 100, and each index is read as a percent of the national average. The index does not measure inflation, but compares prices at a single point in time. Excludes taxes. Metropolitan areas as defined by the Office of Management and Budget. For definitions, urban areas, and components of metropolitan areas, see source]

Metropolitan areas and metropolitan divisions	Composite index (100%)	Grocery items (13%)	Housing (29%)	Utilities (10%)	Transportation (10%)	Health care (4%)	Misc. goods and services (35%)
Baltimore-Towson, MD	120.4	107.2	157.4	118.5	107.5	107.1	101.5
Bethesda-Gaithersburg-Frederick, MD metro. div.	133.2	109.6	189.3	129.2	118.2	112.8	104.8
Boston-Quincy, MA metro. div.	134.5	121.8	169.3	117.7	103.2	132.0	125.4
Cambridge-Newton-Framingham, MA metro. div.	123.8	115.7	146.0	126.7	108.2	113.3	113.8
Grand Rapids-Wyoming, MI	108.1	112.3	107.0	124.1	96.0	96.8	107.6
Kalamazoo-Portage, MI.............	97.4	107.0	92.1	95.5	101.5	106.5	96.3
Rochester, MN.	96.0	89.0	90.5	93.9	96.5	103.0	102.5
St. Cloud, MN	99.0	95.6	90.7	99.7	103.0	100.7	105.2
Jackson, MS	92.4	90.5	81.6	104.3	92.7	104.1	96.9
Kansas City, MO-KS..............	95.6	90.6	89.5	104.3	95.9	96.9	99.6
St. Louis, MO-IL.................	98.0	112.7	93.1	101.9	94.1	96.1	96.8
Springfield, MO	89.4	91.8	75.8	95.6	93.0	94.0	96.0
Missoula, MT...................	102.7	116.6	97.0	101.9	102.7	100.6	102.4
Omaha-Council Bluffs, NE-IA	88.8	88.9	80.9	87.8	97.1	95.3	92.2
Las Vegas-Paradise, NV	109.4	99.6	126.5	111.6	114.0	105.9	97.8
Reno-Sparks, NV	105.4	108.0	111.3	84.9	112.9	115.9	102.4
Edison, NJ metro. div..............	127.0	101.5	171.1	108.9	104.1	108.9	114.8
Newark-Union, NJ-PA metro. div..	130.7	111.9	175.8	109.5	101.6	107.0	118.6
New York-White Plains-Wayne NY-NJ metro. div.	131.8	112.2	179.4	109.1	105.9	107.2	117.8
Albuquerque, NM................	98.9	98.5	105.0	86.7	99.1	101.6	97.2
Nassau-Suffolk, NY metro. div.	154.3	121.4	230.0	145.5	114.8	117.5	123.9
New York-White Plains-Wayne, NY-NJ metro. div.:							
New York (Manhattan), NY	214.7	152.5	394.0	151.2	128.2	131.0	146.7
New York (Queens), NY	146.0	130.5	209.0	132.6	115.1	111.0	118.2
Syracuse, NY	99.3	103.1	80.9	118.5	106.9	99.2	104.9
Asheville, NC..................	101.2	97.1	107.4	84.5	103.2	100.9	102.1
Charlotte-Gastonia-Concord, NC-SC:							
Charlotte, NC..................	92.7	99.8	79.9	82.4	98.0	115.1	99.2
Gastonia, NC..................	87.7	99.5	71.1	86.7	93.2	96.9	94.2
Durham, NC	90.4	96.7	86.3	89.2	92.7	93.2	90.8
Greenville, NC..................	97.1	110.8	78.8	107.1	90.6	106.1	104.7
Hickory-Lenoir-Morganton, NC	92.2	95.7	92.5	84.2	89.3	99.7	93.0
Raleigh-Cary, NC	99.1	100.6	92.9	97.7	98.3	103.5	103.7
Wilmington, NC.................	103.8	101.2	109.3	94.6	105.0	100.0	103.1
Winston-Salem, NC	91.2	100.8	80.3	82.9	89.6	101.8	98.0
Bismarck, ND	90.3	89.3	81.7	85.8	99.5	94.3	95.7
Fargo, ND-MN..................	94.9	93.8	83.3	125.9	95.9	95.7	95.4
Akron, OH.	95.7	107.1	84.9	115.3	106.3	93.9	91.7
Cincinnati-Middletown, OH-KY-IN	91.9	89.8	83.0	95.2	91.9	94.7	98.4
Cleveland-Elyria-Mentor, OH	97.8	107.6	88.1	110.9	97.3	101.0	98.1
Columbus, OH.	100.1	98.3	96.5	116.6	101.2	105.1	98.1
Dayton, OH....................	96.0	98.7	85.6	99.9	100.1	92.6	101.5
Oklahoma City, OK.	92.3	86.7	84.5	87.4	100.1	101.0	98.8
Tulsa, OK	92.0	93.6	77.6	91.7	99.8	102.4	99.6
Portland-Vancouver-Beaverton, OR-WA ...	121.1	113.4	135.0	106.0	120.4	109.9	118.6
Erie, PA	99.1	102.4	88.9	131.9	97.3	99.3	97.3
Lancaster, PA	109.3	100.1	120.1	110.4	99.9	96.5	107.8
Philadelphia, PA metro. div.	125.6	124.9	152.0	118.0	108.3	107.0	113.9
Pittsburgh, PA	98.7	102.8	100.8	111.0	99.4	87.3	93.1
York-Hanover, PA.	101.1	93.7	109.2	98.3	97.6	90.6	100.4
Providence-New Bedford-Fall River, RI-MA.	124.7	115.3	143.3	121.6	105.5	114.0	120.9
Charleston-North Charleston, SC	98.1	100.0	92.0	99.8	99.2	109.6	100.0
Columbia, SC:							
Camden, SC	93.1	97.7	81.3	88.5	84.8	92.0	104.5
Columbia, SC..................	91.8	96.8	83.6	96.9	90.5	104.5	94.1
Myrtle Beach-Conway-North Myrtle Beach, SC	93.5	102.4	78.9	91.5	98.8	92.2	101.0
Spartanburg, SC	90.4	93.2	82.2	81.1	91.1	93.6	97.9
Kingsport-Bristol-Bristol, TN-VA........	89.6	108.0	77.4	82.7	89.4	92.3	94.2
Knoxville, TN.	89.3	90.0	81.2	89.3	87.7	92.1	95.7
Memphis, TN-MS-AR	92.8	93.5	82.4	83.1	90.7	100.6	103.4
Nashville-Davidson-Murfreesboro, TN	95.3	100.1	83.3	99.3	105.7	100.0	98.6
Amarillo, TX	88.3	88.9	81.6	95.5	93.5	92.6	89.4
Austin-Round Rock, TX:							
Austin, TX	97.8	94.2	87.0	95.5	100.9	100.1	107.3
Round Rock , TX	92.8	84.5	76.8	107.1	98.2	106.3	101.5
Brownsville-Harlingen, TX:							
Brownsville, TX.................	88.4	86.4	72.6	105.6	101.1	94.1	92.7
Harlingen, TX..................	87.1	92.2	70.2	95.2	104.5	94.4	90.6
Corpus Christi, TX	89.0	93.4	77.9	92.8	91.2	87.8	94.8

See footnotes at end of table.

U.S. Census Bureau, Statistical Abstract of the United States: 2008

Table 706. Cost of Living Index—Selected Urban Areas: Fourth Quarter 2006—Con.

[Data are for a selected urban area within the larger metropolitan area shown. Measures relative price levels for consumer goods and services in participating areas for a mid-management standard of living. The nationwide average equals 100, and each index is read as a percent of the national average. The index does not measure inflation, but compares prices at a single point in time. Excludes taxes. Metropolitan areas as defined by the Office of Management and Budget. For definitions, urban areas, and components of metropolitan areas, see source]

Metropolitan areas and metropolitan divisions	Com-posite index (100%)	Grocery items (13%)	Housing (29%)	Utilities (10%)	Transpor tation (10%)	Health care (4%)	Misc. goods and services (35%)
Dallas-Plano-Irving, TX metro. div.:							
Dallas, TX	91.8	96.1	74.7	100.4	101.7	98.8	97.8
Plano, TX	98.0	103.8	82.4	103.3	99.3	100.5	106.2
El Paso, TX	93.7	115.9	77.6	91.6	98.2	104.4	96.3
Fort Worth-Arlington, TX metro. div.:							
Arlington, TX	89.1	88.3	77.5	100.9	94.2	101.0	92.5
Fort Worth, TX	86.9	92.1	73.9	98.3	93.0	94.5	89.6
Houston-Sugar Land-Baytown, TX	90.0	84.3	72.5	111.6	95.0	103.3	96.9
Killeen-Temple-Fort Hood, TX	88.0	82.0	73.6	98.8	103.5	97.2	93.2
Lubbock, TX	86.4	89.9	71.6	85.4	93.7	97.4	93.9
McAllen-Edinburg-Mission, TX	84.4	83.4	69.3	79.3	95.1	97.5	93.8
San Antonio, TX	94.1	84.8	81.8	89.5	97.5	103.9	106.5
Waco, TX	90.5	84.3	79.5	103.2	99.4	94.2	95.0
Salt Lake City, UT	102.2	104.1	99.0	87.5	110.8	95.6	106.4
Burlington-South Burlington, VT	118.4	105.6	132.3	123.5	109.4	108.3	114.4
Richmond, VA	108.3	98.2	115.6	105.2	105.4	110.7	107.8
Roanoke, VA	90.7	91.3	86.9	90.5	91.6	97.3	92.6
Virginia Beach-Norfolk-Newport News, VA-NC	105.7	98.9	114.5	116.7	91.6	98.8	102.7
Washington-Arlington-Alexandria, DC-VA-MD-WV metro. div.	124.2	99.4	167.2	118.4	97.8	107.5	110.0
Richland-Kennewick-Pasco, WA	97.5	100.9	85.3	91.9	115.2	118.7	100.0
Olympia, WA	105.0	109.7	98.3	94.4	113.0	119.7	107.8
Spokane, WA	97.9	100.3	88.1	85.5	113.6	108.8	102.7
Tacoma, WA metro. div.	112.5	121.8	123.0	100.2	103.9	119.6	105.9
Charleston, WV	91.5	88.7	84.8	103.6	95.9	93.7	93.1
Appleton, WI	93.3	90.9	78.1	89.8	110.6	103.6	101.3
Green Bay, WI	93.8	93.5	85.3	110.7	101.7	95.5	93.5
Cheyenne, WY	99.6	104.4	95.4	112.8	103.0	96.9	96.7

Source: C2ER, P.O. Box 100127, Arlington, VA 22210, *ACCRA Cost of Living Index,* Fourth Quarter 2006 (copyright).

Table 707. Single-Family Housing Price Indexes by State: 1990 to 2006

[**Index 1980, 1st quarter = 100.** The index reflects average price changes in repeat sales or refinancings on the same properties. Since the data are for the fourth quarter, the index represents the annual percentage change in home values in the fourth quarter of the year shown relative to the fourth quarter of the previous year. The information is obtained by reviewing repeat mortgage transactions on single-family properties whose mortages have been purchased or securitized by either Fannie Mae or Freddie Mac; for more information on methodology, see Appendix III]

State	1990	2000	2005	2006	Percent change 2005– 2006	State	1990	2000	2005	2006	Percent change 2005– 2006
U.S.	170	244	386	408	5.59						
AL	140	204	265	284	7.47	MT	124	220	339	374	10.20
AK	115	170	258	275	6.24	NE	127	205	251	257	2.22
AZ	132	207	395	433	9.58	NV	146	194	398	414	4.00
AR	129	186	244	258	5.63	NH	216	296	497	510	2.60
CA	228	284	618	647	4.58	NJ	230	295	552	585	6.07
CO	130	280	359	369	2.90	NM	137	204	295	331	12.12
CT	241	279	465	482	3.67	NY	278	362	635	662	4.33
DE	226	277	477	508	6.50	NC	164	242	310	332	7.11
DC	194	266	610	660	8.29	ND	114	167	233	244	4.85
FL	152	213	445	489	9.95	OH	145	223	271	273	0.62
GA	162	248	323	340	5.34	OK	102	151	193	201	4.20
HI	251	238	499	537	7.58	OR	135	255	401	455	13.59
ID	128	204	306	348	13.73	PA	198	246	383	409	6.70
IL	170	251	360	380	5.53	RI	254	299	596	614	2.99
IN	140	211	254	259	1.70	SC	150	223	294	317	7.94
IA	120	193	245	251	2.58	SD	123	203	270	286	5.71
KS	120	186	235	243	3.66	TN	147	221	281	302	7.48
KY	142	220	278	288	3.77	TX	117	166	205	219	6.63
LA	104	164	221	244	10.72	UT	119	241	307	360	17.08
ME	236	297	498	522	4.84	VT	214	261	432	462	6.89
MD	201	247	494	537	8.72	VA	184	239	439	469	6.96
MA	291	441	732	732	0.03	WA	178	279	430	489	13.63
MI	147	262	323	322	-0.38	WV	111	162	224	235	4.74
MN	139	240	367	373	1.55	WI	137	233	323	333	2.94
MS	122	182	229	252	10.14	WY	91	156	235	269	14.46
MO	145	215	291	303	4.27						

Source: Office of Federal Housing Enterprise Oversight, *Housing Price Index,* 4th quarter 2006, at <http://www.ofheo.gov/media /pdf/4q06hpi.pdf> (released 01 March 2007). For most recent release, see <http://www.ofheo.gov/HPIHistData.asp>.

Prices   475

Table 708. Weekly Food Cost of a Nutritious Diet by Type of Family: 2000 and 2006

[In dollars. Assumes that food for all meals and snacks is purchased at the store and prepared at home. See source for details on estimation procedures]

Family type	December 2000				December 2006			
	Thrifty plan	Low-cost plan	Moderate-cost plan	Liberal plan	Thrifty plan	Low-cost plan	Moderate-cost plan	Liberal plan
FAMILIES								
Family of two:								
20 to 50 years old	60.60	78.20	96.40	120.00	72.40	91.30	112.70	141.40
51 years old and over	57.60	75.20	93.10	111.50	68.40	87.80	108.60	131.00
Family of four:								
Couple, 20 to 50 years old and children—								
1 to 2 and 3 to 5 years old	88.40	112.60	137.60	169.40	104.50	130.90	160.60	198.90
6 to 8 and 9 to 11 years old	101.90	132.60	165.30	199.20	121.50	155.30	193.30	234.70
INDIVIDUALS [1]								
Child:								
1 year old	16.10	19.80	23.20	28.20	18.30	23.20	26.90	32.80
2 years old	16.00	19.80	23.20	28.20	18.30	22.80	27.20	32.80
3 to 5 years old	17.30	21.70	26.80	32.10	20.30	25.00	30.90	37.50
6 to 8 years old	21.50	28.80	35.90	41.70	25.70	34.00	42.00	49.10
9 to 11 years old	25.30	32.70	41.80	48.40	30.00	38.20	48.80	57.10
Male:								
12 to 14 years old	26.20	36.90	45.70	53.80	31.20	43.20	53.20	63.30
15 to 19 years old	27.00	38.00	47.40	54.70	32.50	44.70	55.30	64.70
20 to 50 years old	28.90	37.90	47.20	57.20	34.60	44.40	55.30	67.60
51 years old and over	26.40	36.10	44.50	53.40	31.50	42.20	52.00	62.80
Female:								
12 to 19 years old	26.30	31.80	38.60	46.70	31.00	37.40	45.10	54.90
20 to 50 years old	26.20	33.20	40.40	51.90	31.20	38.70	47.20	60.90
51 years old and over	26.00	32.30	40.10	48.00	30.70	37.50	46.70	56.20

[1] The costs given are for individuals in 4-person families. For individuals in other size families, the following adjustments are suggested: 1-person, add 20 percent; 2-person, add 10 percent; 3-person, add 5 percent; 5- or 6-person, subtract 5 percent; 7- (or more) person, subtract 10 percent.

Source: U.S. Department of Agriculture, *Official USDA Food Plans: Cost of Food at Home at Four Levels*, monthly. See also <http://www.cnpp.usda.gov/Publications/FoodPlans/2006/CostofFoodDec06.pdf> (released January 2007).

Table 709. Food—Retail Prices of Selected Items: 2000 to 2006

[In dollars per pound, except as indicated. As of December. See Appendix III]

Food	2000	2005	2006	Food	2000	2005	2006
Cereals and bakery products:				Fresh fruits and vegetables:			
Flour, white, all purpose	0.28	0.30	0.32	Apples, red Delicious	0.82	0.97	1.03
Rice, white, lg. grain, raw	(NA)	0.52	0.56	Bananas	0.49	0.48	0.50
Spaghetti and macaroni	0.88	0.87	0.89	Oranges, navel	0.62	0.89	0.96
Bread, white, pan	0.99	1.05	1.14	Grapefruit	0.58	1.10	0.97
Bread, whole wheat	1.36	1.29	1.62	Grapes, Thompson seedless	2.36	2.76	2.89
Beef:				Lemons	1.11	1.51	1.66
Ground beef, 100% beef.	1.63	2.30	2.26	Pears, Anjou	(NA)	1.00	1.24
Ground chuck, 100% beef.	1.98	2.61	2.61	Potatoes, white	0.35	0.50	0.52
Ground beef, lean and extra lean	2.33	2.91	2.95	Lettuce, iceberg	0.85	0.85	0.90
Round steak, USDA Choice.	3.28	4.12	3.99	Tomatoes, field grown	1.57	1.85	1.64
Sirloin steak, boneless	4.81	5.93	5.79	Processed fruits and vegetables:			
Pork:				Orange juice, frozen concentrate,			
Bacon, sliced	3.03	3.33	3.46	12 oz. can, per 16 oz.	1.88	1.78	2.23
Chops, center cut, bone-in	3.46	3.28	3.15	Potatoes, frozen, french-fried.	1.09	(NA)	(NA)
Ham, boneless, excluding canned	2.75	3.09	3.09	Sugar and sweets:			
Poultry, fish, and eggs:				Sugar, white, all sizes.	0.41	0.45	0.51
Chicken, fresh, whole.	1.08	1.06	1.06	Sugar, white, 33–80 oz. pkg.	0.40	0.43	0.48
Chicken legs, bone-in.	1.26	1.33	1.23	Fats and oils:			
Turkey, frozen, whole	0.99	1.07	0.99	Margarine, stick.	(NA)	0.84	0.88
Tuna, light, chunk, canned	1.92	(NA)	(NA)	Margarine, tubs, soft	0.84	0.91	1.14
Eggs, Grade A, large, (dozen)	0.96	1.35	1.54	Shortening, vegetable oil blends.	1.07	(NA)	(NA)
Dairy products:				Peanut butter, creamy, all sizes	1.96	1.70	1.72
Milk, fresh, whole, fortified (per gal.) . .	2.79	3.24	3.00	Nonalcoholic beverages:			
Butter, salted, grade AA, stick	2.80	2.98	2.89	Coffee, 100% ground roast, all sizes. . .	3.21	3.24	3.11
American processed cheese	3.69	3.92	3.61	Other prepared foods:			
Cheddar cheese, natural.	3.76	4.43	4.02	Potato chips, per 16 oz.	3.44	3.46	3.41
Ice cream, prepack., bulk, reg.(1/2 gal.).	3.66	3.69	3.90				

NA Not available.

Source: Bureau of Labor Statistics, *CPI Detailed Report*, monthly, and at <http://www.bls.gov/cpi/cpi_dr.htm>. See also *Monthly Labor Review* at <http://www.bls.gov/opub/mlr/welcome.htm>.

Table 710. Average Prices of Selected Fuels and Electricity: 1990 to 2006

[In dollars per unit, except electricity, in cents per kWh. Represents price to end-users, except as noted]

Type	Unit [1]	1990	1995	1999	2000	2001	2002	2003	2004	2005	2006
Crude oil, composite [2]	Barrel	22.22	17.23	17.51	28.26	22.95	24.10	28.53	36.98	50.24	60.23
Motor gasoline: [3]											
Unleaded regular	Gallon	1.16	1.15	1.17	1.51	1.46	1.36	1.59	1.88	2.30	2.59
Unleaded premium	Gallon	1.35	1.34	1.36	1.69	1.66	1.56	1.78	2.07	2.49	2.81
No. 2 heating oil.	Gallon	0.73	0.56	0.56	0.93	0.83	0.74	0.93	1.17	1.71	1.97
No. 2 diesel fuel. .	Gallon	0.73	0.56	0.58	0.94	0.84	0.76	0.94	1.24	1.79	2.08
Propane, consumer grade . .	Gallon	0.75	0.49	0.46	0.60	0.51	0.42	0.58	0.84	1.09	1.36
Residual fuel oil	Gallon.	0.44	0.39	0.37	0.60	0.53	0.57	0.70	0.74	1.05	1.22
Natural gas, residential	1,000 cu/ft. .	5.80	6.06	6.69	7.76	9.63	7.89	9.63	10.75	12.84	13.76
Electricity, residential.	kWh.	7.83	8.40	8.16	8.24	8.58	8.44	8.72	8.95	9.45	10.40

[1] See headnote.   [2] Refiner acquisition cost.   [3] Average, all service.

Source: U.S. Energy Information Administration, *Monthly Energy Review*. For most current issue, see <http://www.eia.doe.gov/emeu/mer/contents.html>.

Table 711. Retail Gasoline Prices—Selected Areas: 2004 to 2006

[In cents per gallon. Prices are annual averages]

Area	Regular			Midgrade			Premium		
	2004	2005	2006	2004	2005	2006	2004	2005	2006
Boston, MA	185.8	225.7	256.3	195.8	236.3	268.2	205.6	246.4	278.7
Chicago, IL	190.0	231.8	266.3	200.1	241.9	276.6	209.9	251.9	286.8
Cleveland, OH	180.2	222.0	249.4	190.2	232.2	259.7	200.4	243.0	270.6
Denver,CO	180.4	223.9	253.1	191.9	235.4	264.7	201.8	245.4	274.5
Houston, TX	171.2	216.8	246.6	181.0	226.8	256.7	190.7	236.5	266.6
Los Angeles, CA	214.7	249.0	283.3	224.8	258.6	293.4	234.6	268.1	303.3
Miami, FL	191.3	238.9	267.1	202.0	249.3	277.9	210.5	258.5	286.9
New York, NY	190.4	230.0	263.1	201.0	241.5	275.8	209.2	251.3	286.4
San Francisco, CA	214.8	248.1	279.1	225.9	259.4	291.0	235.7	269.4	301.1
Seattle, WA	194.9	236.3	268.3	205.9	247.3	278.9	216.0	257.6	289.1

Source: U.S. Energy Information Administration, *Weekly U.S. Retail Gasoline Prices*, Gasoline Historical Data. See also <http://www.eia.doe.gov/oil_gas/petroleum/data_publications/wrgp/mogas_history.html>.

Table 712. Producer Price Indexes by Stage of Processing: 1990 to 2006

[1982 = 100, except as indicated. See Appendix III]

Year	Crude materials				Inter-mediate materials, supplies, and components	Finished goods			Finished consumer foods	
	Total	Food-stuffs and feed-stuffs	Fuel	Crude nonfood materials except fuel		Con-sumer goods	Capital equip-ment	Crude	Pro-cessed	Finished consumer goods excl. food
1990	108.9	113.1	84.8	107.3	114.5	118.2	122.9	123.0	124.4	115.3
1992	100.4	105.1	84.0	94.2	114.7	121.7	129.1	107.6	124.4	120.8
1993	102.4	108.4	87.1	94.1	116.2	123.0	131.4	114.4	126.5	121.7
1994	101.8	106.5	82.4	97.0	118.5	123.3	134.1	111.3	127.9	121.6
1995	102.7	105.8	72.1	105.8	124.9	125.6	136.7	118.8	129.8	124.0
1996	113.8	121.5	92.6	105.7	125.7	129.5	138.3	129.2	133.8	127.6
1997	111.1	112.2	101.3	103.5	125.6	130.2	138.2	126.6	135.1	128.2
1998	96.8	103.9	86.7	84.5	123.0	128.9	137.6	127.2	134.8	126.4
1999	98.2	98.7	91.2	91.1	123.2	132.0	137.6	125.5	135.9	130.5
2000	120.6	100.2	136.9	118.0	129.2	138.2	138.8	123.5	138.3	138.4
2001	121.0	106.1	151.4	101.5	129.7	141.5	139.7	127.7	142.4	141.4
2002	108.1	99.5	117.3	101.0	127.8	139.4	139.1	128.5	141.0	138.8
2003	135.3	113.5	185.7	116.9	133.7	145.3	139.5	130.0	147.2	144.7
2004	159.0	127.0	211.4	149.2	142.6	151.7	141.4	138.2	153.9	150.9
2005 [1]	182.2	122.7	279.7	176.7	154.0	160.4	144.6	140.2	156.9	161.9
2006 [1]	185.4	119.3	244.5	210.0	164.0	165.9	146.8	151.1	157.1	169.1
PERCENT [2] CHANGE										
1990	5.6	1.7	−0.6	12.0	2.2	5.4	3.5	2.8	4.9	5.9
1992	−0.8	−0.4	1.3	−3.4	0.3	1.0	1.9	−9.8	–	1.8
1993	2.0	3.1	3.7	−0.1	1.3	1.1	1.8	6.3	1.7	0.7
1994	−0.6	−1.8	−5.4	3.1	2.0	0.2	2.1	−2.7	1.1	−0.1
1995	0.9	−0.7	−12.5	9.1	5.4	1.9	1.9	6.7	1.5	2.0
1996	10.8	14.8	28.4	−0.1	0.6	3.1	1.2	8.8	3.1	2.9
1997	−2.4	−7.7	9.4	−2.1	−0.1	0.5	−0.1	−2.0	1.0	0.5
1998	−12.9	−7.4	−14.4	−18.4	−2.1	−1.0	−0.4	0.5	−0.2	−1.4
1999	1.4	−5.0	5.2	7.8	0.2	2.4	0.0	−1.3	0.8	3.2
2000	22.8	1.5	50.1	29.5	4.9	4.7	0.9	−1.6	1.8	6.1
2001	0.3	5.9	10.6	−14.0	0.4	2.4	0.6	3.4	3.0	2.2
2002	−10.7	−6.2	−22.5	−0.5	−1.5	−1.5	−0.4	0.6	−1.0	−1.8
2003	25.2	14.1	58.3	15.7	4.6	4.2	0.3	1.2	4.4	4.3
2004	17.5	11.9	13.8	27.6	6.7	4.4	1.4	6.3	4.6	4.3
2005	14.6	−3.4	32.3	18.4	8.0	5.7	2.3	1.4	1.9	7.3
2006 [1]	1.8	−2.8	−12.6	18.8	6.5	3.4	1.5	7.8	0.1	4.4

– Represents or rounds to zero.   [1] Preliminary.   [2] Change from immediate prior year. 1990, change from 1989.

Source: U.S. Bureau of Labor Statistics, *Producer Price Indexes*, monthly and annual. See also *Monthly Labor Review* at <http://www.bls.gov/opub/mlr/welcome.htm>.

Table 713. Producer Price Indexes by Stage of Processing: 1990 to 2006

[1982 = 100, except as indicated. See Appendix III]

Stage of processing	1990	1995	2000	2002	2003	2004	2005	2006 [1]
Finished goods	**119.2**	**127.9**	**138.0**	**138.9**	**143.3**	**148.5**	**155.7**	**160.3**
Finished consumer goods	**118.2**	**125.6**	**138.2**	**139.4**	**145.3**	**151.7**	**160.4**	**165.9**
Finished consumer foods	**124.4**	**129.0**	**137.2**	**140.1**	**145.9**	**152.7**	**155.7**	**156.7**
Fresh fruits and melons	118.1	85.8	91.4	91.5	84.1	104.9	102.8	110.7
Fresh and dry vegetables	118.1	144.4	126.7	136.5	135.7	129.4	142.6	153.3
Eggs for fresh use (Dec. 1991 = 100)	(NA)	86.3	84.9	82.9	106.6	100.0	79.6	90.0
Bakery products	141.0	164.3	182.3	189.9	195.0	196.3	201.1	207.8
Milled rice	102.5	113.1	101.2	80.3	102.5	135.5	120.1	135.7
Pasta products (June 1985 = 100)	114.1	125.0	121.6	121.7	126.4	127.3	127.9	128.1
Beef and veal	116.0	100.9	113.7	114.7	137.9	141.2	147.4	142.1
Pork	119.8	101.5	113.4	109.0	115.7	132.7	131.9	128.4
Processed young chickens	111.0	113.5	110.4	109.7	119.7	138.9	136.2	117.4
Processed turkeys	107.6	104.9	98.7	95.3	92.5	107.8	105.1	104.2
Finfish and shellfish	147.2	170.8	198.1	191.2	195.3	206.3	222.6	237.1
Dairy products	117.2	119.7	133.7	136.2	139.4	155.9	154.5	147.4
Processed fruits and vegetables	124.7	122.4	128.6	132.6	133.8	135.2	140.4	148.8
Soft drinks	122.3	133.1	144.1	151.3	153.0	156.5	159.1	163.1
Roasted coffee	113.0	146.5	133.5	121.5	127.3	130.1	151.1	153.8
Shortening and cooking oils	123.2	142.5	132.4	140.8	160.8	193.7	176.7	184.0
Finished consumer goods excluding foods	**115.3**	**124.0**	**138.4**	**138.8**	**144.7**	**150.9**	**161.9**	**169.1**
Alcoholic beverages	117.2	128.5	140.6	147.0	148.9	152.8	158.5	160.0
Apparel	117.5	124.2	127.4	125.5	125.7	125.6	125.6	125.8
Women's/girls/infants' cut & sew apparel (December 2003 = 100	(NA)	(NA)	(NA)	(NA)	(NA)	100.2	100.3	100.2
Men's and boy's cut and sew apparel (December 2003 = 100)	(NA)	(NA)	(NA)	(NA)	(NA)	99.9	98.7	97.9
Textile house furnishings	109.5	119.5	122.0	122.3	122.4	123.4	122.9	123.1
Footwear	125.6	139.2	144.9	146.0	147.1	146.2	148.1	149.3
Residential electric power (Dec. 1990 = 100)	(NA)	111.8	110.8	115.4	118.8	121.4	126.4	134.7
Residential gas (Dec. 1990 = 100)	(NA)	104.4	135.5	131.9	167.6	183.2	216.8	226.9
Gasoline	78.7	63.7	94.6	83.3	102.7	128.1	168.6	197.2
Fuel oil No. 2	73.3	56.6	93.5	75.0	95.3	120.7	178.4	208.0
Soaps and synthetic detergents	117.7	122.9	128.2	130.0	130.9	132.9	134.6	142.7
Cosmetics and other toilet preparations	121.6	129.0	137.4	139.4	140.4	140.6	143.0	145.1
Tires, tubes, and tread	96.8	100.2	93.0	95.2	97.9	102.5	108.1	114.7
Sanitary papers and health products	135.3	144.4	146.7	149.3	150.5	148.5	154.6	160.1
Book publishing	153.4	185.0	218.2	234.8	243.1	253.1	264.0	275.2
Household furniture	125.1	141.8	152.7	157.1	158.2	160.5	166.5	172.3
Floor coverings	119.0	123.7	129.6	130.5	133.6	136.7	146.4	154.0
Household appliances	110.8	112.4	107.3	104.6	102.4	101.5	103.3	103.9
Home electronic equipment	82.7	78.9	71.8	69.0	67.7	65.2	62.6	60.3
Household glassware	132.5	153.2	166.0	169.9	168.9	171.4	174.7	172.0
Household flatware	122.1	138.3	142.6	144.7	145.2	145.4	147.7	150.8
Lawn and garden equipment, except tractors	123.0	130.4	132.0	133.9	133.5	134.5	134.5	135.2
Passenger cars	118.3	134.1	132.8	129.5	129.5	131.7	131.8	127.9
Toys, games, and children's vehicles	118.1	124.3	121.9	124.8	124.9	125.1	127.0	128.5
Sporting and athletic goods	112.6	122.0	126.1	125.5	124.0	123.4	124.6	126.7
Tobacco products	221.4	231.3	397.2	459.4	431.6	434.0	457.8	460.1
Mobile homes	117.5	145.6	161.3	166.6	169.6	186.6	200.8	208.9
Jewelry, platinum, and karat gold	122.8	127.8	127.2	130.0	132.4	135.3	138.6	149.3
Costume jewelry and novelties	125.3	135.1	141.6	144.2	144.9	147.9	153.5	153.9
Capital Equipment	**122.9**	**136.7**	**138.8**	**139.1**	**139.5**	**141.4**	**144.6**	**146.8**
Agricultural machinery and equipment	121.7	142.9	153.7	158.5	160.9	165.9	174.7	178.8
Construction machinery and equipment	121.6	136.7	148.6	151.1	153.2	158.5	168.3	175.4
Metal cutting machine tools	129.8	148.0	161.9	152.4	150.6	151.4	155.1	163.4
Metal forming machine tools	128.7	145.7	161.8	166.8	167.6	171.6	178.9	183.3
Pumps, compressors, and equipment	119.2	139.4	154.1	161.0	162.9	167.5	178.5	186.2
Electronic computers (Dec. 1990 = 100)	(NA)	850.1	261.6	153.5	122.3	107.3	85.5	66.4
Textile machinery	128.8	146.7	156.2	157.0	157.6	158.1	160.5	161.7
Paper industries machinery (June 1982 = 100)	134.8	151.0	164.7	168.9	170.3	173.7	178.1	180.6
Printing trades machinery	124.9	133.6	142.1	143.7	143.1	143.4	144.3	146.5
Transformers and power regulators	120.9	128.9	135.8	131.7	131.9	135.7	150.3	172.6
Communication/related equip.(Dec. 1985 = 100)	106.1	112.1	110.6	107.6	105.5	105.3	102.5	102.5
X-ray and electromedical equipment	109.8	111.8	101.5	100.9	100.5	97.5	95.7	95.1
Mining machinery and equipment	121.0	135.6	146.1	151.8	155.2	163.4	175.9	183.8
Office and store machines and equipment	109.5	111.5	112.7	112.5	112.3	113.2	115.1	114.6
Commercial furniture	133.4	148.2	158.4	160.9	162.3	165.6	172.7	177.0
Light motor trucks	130.0	159.0	157.6	150.5	150.2	151.3	148.4	143.0
Heavy motor trucks	120.3	144.1	148.0	152.2	154.2	155.7	162.4	168.7
Truck trailers	110.8	131.7	139.4	138.1	139.4	139.4	148.1	164.5
Civilian aircraft (Dec. 1985 = 100)	115.3	141.8	159.6	171.3	179.9	190.5	202.2	212.2
Ships (Dec. 1985 = 100)	110.1	132.8	146.9	150.6	159.4	171.4	176.6	183.3
Railroad equipment	118.6	134.8	135.7	134.9	136.3	143.9	160.4	169.4
Intermediate materials, supplies, and components	**114.5**	**124.9**	**129.2**	**127.8**	**133.7**	**142.6**	**154.0**	**164.0**
Intermediate foods and feeds	**113.3**	**114.8**	**111.7**	**115.5**	**125.9**	**137.1**	**133.8**	**135.4**
Flour	103.6	123.0	103.8	116.2	123.6	129.0	133.6	145.9
Refined sugar	122.7	119.3	110.6	117.7	121.8	120.7	124.9	150.2
Soft drink beverage bases (December 1985 = 100)	126.2	148.3	167.1	172.6	174.3	176.2	180.4	188.4
Prepared animal feeds	107.4	109.1	102.9	105.7	112.8	124.8	115.6	119.1

See footnotes at end.

U.S. Census Bureau, Statistical Abstract of the United States: 2008

Table 713. Producer Price Indexes by Stage of Processing: 1990 to 2006—Con.

[1982 = 100, except as indicated. See Appendix III]

Stage of processing	1990	1995	2000	2002	2003	2004	2005	2006 [1]
Intermediate materials less foods and feeds.	114.5	125.5	130.1	128.5	134.2	143.0	155.1	165.4
Synthetic fibers	106.7	109.4	107.2	106.2	106.4	106.6	112.3	115.1
Processed yarns and threads	112.6	112.8	107.9	102.6	103.6	108.7	111.7	114.0
Leather	177.5	191.4	182.2	202.5	214.0	220.6	219.6	223.7
Liquefied petroleum gas	77.4	65.1	127.1	104.5	150.9	193.3	244.7	266.4
Commercial electric power	115.3	131.7	131.5	137.5	140.0	142.0	149.8	161.3
Industrial electric power	119.6	130.8	131.5	139.9	145.8	147.2	156.2	172.8
Commercial natural gas (Dec. 1990 = 100)	(NA)	96.5	134.7	135.0	173.6	194.9	232.5	240.0
Industrial natural gas (Dec. 1990 = 100)	(NA)	90.9	139.0	136.5	180.5	201.7	249.4	245.2
Natural gas to electric utilities (Dec. 1990 = 100)	(NA)	87.7	120.7	103.9	158.2	171.6	204.0	191.2
Jet fuels	76.0	55.0	88.5	71.6	86.3	112.6	169.6	199.1
No. 2 diesel fuel	74.1	57.0	93.3	77.9	100.5	128.2	189.1	216.9
Residual fuel	57.7	52.6	84.7	75.4	101.2	100.2	148.9	161.1
Industrial chemicals	113.2	128.4	129.1	127.3	141.7	162.8	188.5	213.2
Prepared paint	124.8	142.1	160.8	166.9	170.8	175.7	187.9	201.5
Fats and oils, inedible	88.1	126.9	70.1	90.3	123.4	153.6	146.9	151.6
Mixed fertilizers	103.3	111.1	112.4	113.9	119.1	127.8	138.9	144.6
Plastic resins and materials	124.1	143.5	141.6	130.7	146.1	163.1	193.0	199.0
Synthetic rubber	111.9	126.3	119.1	119.3	125.7	132.4	151.3	161.6
Plastic construction products	117.2	133.8	135.8	136.1	138.6	144.6	158.8	182.1
Unsupported plastic film, sheet, and shapes	119.0	135.6	133.2	136.5	142.8	149.1	164.8	175.2
Plastic parts and components for manufacturing	112.9	115.9	117.3	116.2	116.3	116.5	119.8	130.1
Softwood lumber	123.8	178.5	178.6	170.8	170.8	209.8	203.6	189.1
Hardwood lumber	131.0	167.0	185.9	178.3	188.8	199.3	196.6	195.1
Plywood	114.2	165.3	157.6	151.7	167.0	198.5	186.8	172.8
Paper	128.8	159.0	149.8	144.7	146.1	149.4	159.6	167.4
Paperboard	135.7	183.1	176.7	164.3	162.7	170.2	175.5	191.9
Paper boxes and containers	129.9	163.8	172.6	172.8	172.9	177.6	183.7	192.6
Building paper and board	112.2	144.9	138.8	129.3	159.9	192.4	184.9	172.8
Commercial printing (June 1982 = 100)	128.0	144.5	155.2	157.0	158.3	159.4	161.6	165.0
Foundry and forge shop products	117.2	129.3	136.5	136.8	137.4	144.0	156.2	162.8
Primary nonferrous metals	133.4	146.8	113.6	100.8	104.8	133.6	158.2	237.7
Nonferrous wire and cable	142.6	151.5	143.7	134.3	134.5	152.5	169.4	227.8
Metal containers	114.0	117.2	106.8	107.8	109.2	116.2	123.9	126.7
Hardware	125.9	141.1	151.2	156.0	156.5	161.6	168.0	173.9
Plumbing fixtures and brass fittings	144.3	166.0	180.4	181.9	183.4	188.3	197.6	207.1
Heating equipment	131.6	147.5	155.6	157.9	163.2	169.5	179.9	185.7
Fabricated ferrous wire products (June 1982 = 100)	114.6	125.7	130.0	129.7	131.3	149.3	157.1	162.7
Mechanical power transmission equipment	125.3	146.9	163.9	169.5	171.7	179.3	189.5	196.7
Air conditioning and refrigeration equipment	122.1	130.2	135.3	136.9	137.2	139.4	146.2	150.4
Ball and roller bearings	130.6	152.0	168.8	170.0	171.3	177.1	187.1	193.1
Wiring devices	132.2	147.2	152.9	153.8	152.9	169.0	176.6	188.1
Motors, generators, motor generator sets	132.9	143.9	146.2	146.8	147.4	149.8	157.8	165.1
Switchgear and switchboard equipment	124.4	140.3	153.0	158.4	159.9	163.8	170.2	179.0
Electronic components and accessories	118.4	113.6	97.1	92.4	90.8	88.8	87.0	88.6
Internal combustion engines	120.2	135.6	143.8	144.4	144.6	145.8	147.7	152.5
Flat glass	107.5	113.2	109.7	111.2	111.0	108.6	111.0	113.5
Cement	103.7	128.1	150.1	152.6	152.0	156.8	176.4	199.1
Concrete products	113.5	129.4	147.8	152.7	153.6	161.2	177.2	195.1
Asphalt felts and coatings	97.1	100.0	104.1	110.9	116.4	117.7	130.8	144.3
Gypsum products	105.2	154.5	201.4	168.9	171.5	198.8	229.6	275.1
Glass containers	120.4	130.5	127.4	135.6	140.2	144.4	146.4	152.9
Motor vehicle parts	111.2	116.0	113.6	112.9	111.8	112.0	113.1	116.3
Aircraft engines and engine parts (Dec. 1985 = 100)	113.5	132.8	141.0	145.7	153.8	163.0	165.9	172.2
Photographic supplies	127.6	126.8	125.2	121.6	117.5	115.1	120.1	121.6
Medical/surgical/personal aid devices	127.3	141.3	146.0	150.9	154.7	157.8	159.2	161.3
Crude materials for further processing	108.9	102.7	120.6	108.1	135.3	159.0	182.2	185.4
Crude foodstuffs and feedstuffs	113.1	105.8	100.2	99.5	113.5	127.0	122.7	119.3
Wheat	87.6	118.6	80.3	97.9	98.5	106.0	102.7	116.9
Corn	100.9	109.0	76.4	89.4	93.8	97.5	75.9	95.7
Slaughter cattle	122.5	99.5	104.1	100.8	124.3	126.2	131.5	126.2
Slaughter hogs	94.1	70.2	72.7	55.4	66.1	87.8	82.7	77.2
Slaughter broilers/fryers	119.5	129.1	127.6	125.9	149.3	188.5	181.0	156.1
Slaughter turkeys	116.9	120.3	120.7	104.3	102.8	122.0	131.1	140.5
Fluid milk	100.8	93.6	92.0	90.8	93.8	120.1	113.5	96.3
Soybeans	100.8	102.2	83.4	87.7	108.8	130.0	102.6	96.8
Crude nonfood materials	101.5	96.8	130.4	111.4	148.2	179.2	223.4	231.7
Raw cotton	118.2	156.2	95.2	61.5	92.9	85.6	78.9	79.2
Coal	97.5	95.0	87.9	99.8	99.9	109.2	116.8	126.5
Natural gas	80.4	66.6	155.5	122.5	214.5	245.9	335.4	284.4
Crude petroleum	71.0	51.1	85.2	67.9	83.0	108.2	150.1	176.1
Logs and timber	142.8	220.4	196.4	180.1	181.8	193.3	197.4	200.8
Wastepaper	138.9	371.1	282.5	173.1	197.3	231.4	230.9	234.8
Iron ore	83.3	91.8	94.8	95.2	95.9	98.2	116.9	133.4
Iron and steel scrap	166.0	202.7	142.1	141.4	182.6	323.7	289.8	335.1
Nonferrous metal ores (Dec. 1983 = 100)	98.3	101.6	68.0	68.1	78.5	113.7	150.0	216.5
Copper base scrap	181.3	193.5	123.7	111.4	128.4	186.5	258.6	432.8
Aluminum base scrap	172.6	209.4	177.0	158.0	168.7	194.1	210.1	275.8
Construction sand, gravel, and crushed stone	125.4	142.3	163.1	173.0	177.1	183.3	195.8	214.1
Industrial sand	117.6	132.5	146.0	155.1	160.4	165.3	174.4	183.2

NA Not available.   [1] Preliminary data.

Source: U.S. Bureau of Labor Statistics, *Producer Price Indexes*, monthly and annual. See also *Monthly Labor Review* at <http://www.bls.gov/opub/mlr/welcome.htm>.

U.S. Census Bureau, Statistical Abstract of the United States: 2008

Table 714. Producer Price Indexes for the Net Output of Selected Industries: 2002 to 2006

[Indexes are based on selling prices reported by establishments of all sizes by probability sampling. Manufacturing industries selected by shipment value. N.e.c.= not elsewhere classified. See text, Section 22. See Appendix III]

Industry	NAICS code [1]	Index base [2]	2002	2003	2004	2005	2006 [3]
Logging	113310	12/81	165.1	168.8	175.3	179.2	176.6
Total mining industries	**21**	12/84	**96.6**	**131.3**	**153.4**	**201.0**	**209.6**
Crude petroleum & natural gas extraction	211111	06/02	(NA)	152.3	183.4	253.5	254.2
Natural gas liquid extraction	211112	06/02	(NA)	181.2	216.5	285.4	259.4
Bituminous coal & lignite surface mining	212111	12/01	101.9	101.5	107.1	111.9	117.3
Anthracite mining	212113	12/79	163.0	168.4	180.9	205.4	234.7
Iron ore mining	212210	12/84	94.2	95.0	97.2	115.7	132.1
Gold ore mining	212221	06/85	92.4	107.6	121.6	131.7	177.2
Silver ore mining	212222	12/83	(NA)	(NA)	(NA)	(NA)	(NA)
Copper ore & nickel ore mining	212234	06/88	80.1	90.1	150.1	200.8	362.2
Dimension stone mining and quarrying	212311	06/85	164.0	169.9	173.4	182.0	185.6
Crushed and broken limestone mining and quarrying	212312	12/83	154.7	159.2	165.4	174.3	189.6
Crushed and broken granite mining and quarrying	212313	12/83	193.2	197.5	203.7	217.3	243.6
Other crushed and broken stone mining and quarrying	212319	12/83	160.8	164.0	170.3	187.1	201.5
Construction sand and gravel mining	212321	06/82	185.8	188.9	195.0	209.9	229.2
Industrial sand mining	212322	06/82	157.1	162.1	167.1	176.1	186.2
Kaolin and ball clay mining	212324	06/84	118.8	121.0	122.7	126.2	134.4
Clay and ceramic and refractory minerals mining	212325	06/84	140.9	142.5	144.4	148.3	156.9
Potash, soda, and borate mineral mining	212391	12/84	107.7	106.1	110.8	130.7	153.2
Drilling oil and gas wells	213111	12/85	153.5	153.5	168.0	258.8	376.6
Oil and gas operations support activities	213112	12/85	137.4	135.6	141.8	161.3	187.4
Nonmetallic minerals support activity (except fuels)	213115	06/85	110.5	114.6	119.6	127.5	137.1
Total manufacturing industries	**31-33**	12/84	**133.7**	**137.1**	**142.9**	**150.8**	**156.9**
Dog and cat food mfg.	311111	12/85	135.7	136.2	144.0	145.8	147.7
Flour milling	311211	06/83	107.6	113.7	117.4	117.5	127.5
Rice milling	311212	06/84	72.2	87.6	113.1	102.1	114.2
Soybean processing	311222	12/79	72.1	87.1	102.3	91.5	94.7
Fats and oils refining and blending	311225	12/81	138.1	158.1	186.8	171.7	177.6
Chocolate and confectionery mfg. from cacao beans	311320	06/83	148.1	156.2	155.0	157.5	161.1
Confectionery mfg. (purchased chocolate)	311330	12/03	(NA)	(NA)	100.1	102.2	103.8
Frozen fruit, juice, and vegetable mfg.	311411	06/81	144.1	147.8	149.3	156.0	170.7
Frozen specialty food mfg.	311412	12/82	139.0	139.2	142.1	143.6	144.3
Fruit and vegetable canning	311421	06/81	143.7	144.8	146.5	151.4	155.8
Specialty canning	311422	12/82	174.6	176.1	177.5	184.0	188.5
Fluid milk	311511	12/82	146.4	147.7	162.5	165.2	163.2
Ice cream and frozen dessert mfg.	311520	06/83	158.8	160.4	166.0	168.2	171.5
Animal (except poultry) slaughtering	311611	12/80	113.1	130.1	137.8	141.0	136.4
Meat processed from carcasses	311612	12/82	121.1	129.7	132.9	136.6	137.2
Poultry processing	311615	12/81	115.9	121.9	137.5	135.3	123.7
Seafood canning	311711	12/84	110.3	110.2	114.5	114.0	118.4
Fresh and frozen seafood processing	311712	12/82	157.2	161.5	164.1	171.1	171.8
Frozen cakes, pies, and other pastries mfg.	311813	06/91	120.9	124.8	127.5	129.2	135.2
Cookie and cracker manufacturing	311821	06/85	175.0	181.6	183.4	184.4	187.8
Flour mixes and dough mfg. from purchased flour	311822	06/85	126.4	131.9	134.0	135.9	139.4
Dry pasta manufacturing	311823	06/85	122.0	126.3	127.1	127.8	127.6
Coffee and tea manufacturing	311920	06/81	133.8	139.4	142.2	161.0	164.3
Mayonnaise, dressing, and other sauces mfg.	311941	12/03	(NA)	(NA)	101.6	102.9	104.9
Spice and extracts manufacturing	311942	12/03	(NA)	(NA)	100.3	99.1	99.7
Soft drinks manufacturing	312111	06/81	159.5	161.5	165.3	168.6	173.3
Bottled water manufacturing	312112	12/03	(NA)	(NA)	100.7	101.5	101.7
Breweries	312120	06/82	142.7	145.8	151.9	158.4	158.2
Wineries	312130	12/83	141.7	140.8	140.0	144.8	152.7
Distilleries	312140	06/83	164.9	165.1	164.7	165.5	167.6
Tobacco stemming and redrying	312210	06/84	114.7	117.5	119.4	119.9	109.8
Cigarettes	312221	12/82	442.8	411.7	412.6	437.0	440.1
Other tobacco product mfg.	312229	12/03	(NA)	(NA)	99.6	103.0	106.8
Broadwoven fabric finishing mills	313311	12/03	(NA)	(NA)	99.9	103.2	106.9
Textile/fabric finishing (exc. broadwoven) mills	313312	12/03	(NA)	(NA)	99.6	100.8	101.5
Underwear and nightwear knitting mills	315192	06/82	130.1	129.1	128.6	128.6	127.3
Men's/boys' cut & sew trouser/slack/jean mfg.	315224	12/81	132.2	128.4	126.6	123.2	121.0
Women's/girls' cut & sew dress mfg.	315233	12/80	122.1	122.8	124.9	123.7	123.2
Women's/girls' cut & sew other outerwear mfg.	315239	06/83	111.5	112.9	112.8	113.3	112.2
Sawmills	321113	12/80	139.1	141.1	163.4	162.0	158.1
Wood preservation	321114	06/85	151.6	154.0	167.7	175.7	169.5
Hardwood veneer and plywood manufacturing	321211	06/85	142.3	138.6	143.6	146.2	149.8
Softwood veneer or plywood, mfg.	321212	12/80	131.8	154.4	189.0	172.7	151.1
Engineered wood member (exc. truss) mfg.	321213	12/03	(NA)	(NA)	110.1	121.0	118.0
Truss mfg.	321214	12/03	(NA)	(NA)	112.5	119.6	119.0
Reconstituted wood product mfg.	321219	06/91	112.3	139.1	168.2	162.2	152.5
Wood window and door mfg.	321911	12/03	(NA)	(NA)	101.9	103.1	106.8
Manufactured homes (mobile homes) mfg.	321991	06/81	172.6	175.8	190.0	204.4	212.5
Pulp mills	322110	12/82	116.5	120.9	131.3	137.4	144.8
Paper (except newsprint) mills	322121	12/03	(NA)	(NA)	102.4	108.4	112.5
Newsprint mills	322122	12/03	(NA)	(NA)	104.0	115.7	124.7
Paperboard mills	322130	12/82	179.7	180.4	190.1	196.2	212.9
Digital printing	323115	12/03	(NA)	(NA)	99.3	98.4	97.7
Book printing	323117	12/83	150.7	150.2	151.5	154.9	158.3
Petroleum refineries	324110	06/85	96.3	121.2	151.5	205.3	240.9
Petroleum lubricating oils and greases	324191	12/80	185.5	191.5	199.4	231.2	284.8
Industrial gas manufacturing	325120	12/03	(NA)	(NA)	108.3	118.3	122.4

See footnotes at end of table.

480 Prices

[See headnote, page 480]

Industry	NAICS code [1]	Index base [2]	2002	2003	2004	2005	2006 [3]
Plastics material and resins manufacturing.	325211	12/80	148.9	167.8	192.0	228.5	236.1
Synthetic rubber manufacturing	325212	06/81	119.1	125.2	131.6	150.6	161.6
Nitrogenous fertilizer manufacturing	325311	12/79	131.6	177.0	203.9	236.9	245.9
Phosphatic fertilizer manufacturing	325312	12/79	132.8	145.4	161.3	173.3	183.8
Fertilizer (mixing only) manufacturing	325314	12/79	143.3	149.2	156.7	169.0	174.1
Pesticide and other agricultural chemical manufacturing . .	325320	06/82	138.2	138.1	138.6	140.7	143.6
Pharmaceutical preparation mfg.	325412	06/81	326.7	343.3	360.1	378.7	398.0
Photo film, paper, plate and chemical mfg.	325992	12/03	(NA)	(NA)	99.1	102.6	103.6
Plastics pipe and pipe fitting manufacturing	326122	06/93	114.6	124.7	140.8	171.9	214.0
Cement manufacturing	327310	06/82	151.1	150.5	155.4	175.2	197.6
Lime	327410	12/85	126.1	128.1	133.1	144.6	156.7
Cut stone and stone products	327991	12/84	149.3	149.7	149.5	151.6	153.9
Steel investment foundries	331512	06/81	205.6	199.8	197.7	204.8	216.7
Steel foundries (except investment)	331513	06/81	135.3	137.5	146.2	160.1	170.1
Aluminum die-casting foundries	331521	06/91	109.6	111.5	114.1	116.4	125.1
Iron and steel forging	332111	12/83	112.9	112.8	117.5	128.1	133.4
Hand and edge tools, except machine tools and handsaws	332212	06/83	164.7	165.1	168.8	177.0	183.7
Saw blade and handsaw mfg.	332213	06/83	142.0	142.9	142.9	146.0	150.2
Metal window and door manufacturing	332321	06/83	159.2	161.0	166.5	175.2	183.6
Sheetmetal work mfg.	332322	12/82	142.9	144.4	159.4	165.6	171.4
Heating equipment (except warm air furnaces) mfg.	333414	06/80	196.3	199.8	206.2	215.4	222.0
Electronic computer mfg.	334111	12/98	61.1	49.1	107.4	92.4	82.7
Computer storage device mfg.	334112	12/98	64.2	55.4	105.7	98.6	91.4
Computer terminal mfg.	334113	12/93	88.5	86.4	85.3	85.9	86.6
Telephone apparatus mfg.	334210	12/85	104.6	100.9	95.8	93.7	91.9
Radio/TV broadcast & wireless comm. equip. mfg.	334220	12/91	98.2	95.1	93.3	92.6	92.1
Audio and video equipment mfg. . . .	334310	03/80	74.0	72.8	71.1	69.2	67.8
Laboratory apparatus and furniture	339111	12/91	132.7	137.3	141.2	148.1	152.5
Surgical and medical instrument mfg.	339112	06/82	130.8	133.1	134.6	135.2	133.9
Services Industries							
Material recyclers	429930	12/86	129.3	151.6	220.7	219.8	269.7
New car dealers	441110	12/99	108.7	111.5	113.5	116.3	122.2
Recreational vehicle dealers	441210	06/01	112.2	109.7	121.4	133.6	132.7
Boat dealers.	441222	06/01	107.9	113.8	116.4	121.9	125.4
Automotive parts and accessories stores	441310	12/03	(NA)	(NA)	106.8	110.9	119.4
Household appliance stores	443111	06/03	(NA)	(NA)	93.3	100.5	104.4
Radio, TV, and other electronics stores	443112	06/03	(NA)	(NA)	100.4	99.5	98.4
Computer and software stores	443120	06/03	(NA)	(NA)	92.7	90.0	89.5
Hardware stores	444130	06/03	(NA)	(NA)	103.5	108.6	112.9
Nursery, garden, and farm supply stores	444220	12/02	(NA)	102.1	112.4	117.2	118.4
Grocery (except convenience) stores	445110	12/99	113.6	117.9	123.6	132.1	135.6
Specialty food stores	445200	12/03	(NA)	(NA)	107.1	110.2	115.2
Beer, wine, and liquor stores	445310	06/00	103.5	106.9	110.7	111.0	111.4
Food (health) supplement stores	446191	12/99	130.6	139.1	144.9	149.2	165.1
Gasoline stations with convenience stores	447110	12/03	(NA)	(NA)	102.5	104.3	109.9
Men's clothing stores	448110	06/02	(NA)	102.2	103.8	105.8	102.6
Women's clothing stores	448120	06/03	(NA)	(NA)	105.1	105.6	111.0
Family clothing stores	448140	06/03	(NA)	(NA)	103.7	108.3	110.6
Luggage and leather goods stores	448320	06/00	93.6	94.7	98.5	103.4	107.4
Sporting goods stores	451110	06/00	107.2	104.4	99.1	100.3	103.5
Book stores	451211	06/00	106.9	113.7	118.2	114.5	116.6
Department stores, except discount	452111	12/03	(NA)	(NA)	104.5	103.1	103.3
Discount department stores.	452112	12/03	(NA)	(NA)	106.1	106.7	107.4
Office supplies and stationery stores.	453210	06/00	114.8	124.3	127.1	130.2	134.5
Manufactured (mobile) home dealers	453930	12/02	(NA)	103.6	113.8	123.3	130.4
Scheduled passenger air transportation	481111	12/89	200.4	205.7	205.8	217.1	227.7
Scheduled freight air transportation	481112	12/03	(NA)	(NA)	100.2	104.9	108.5
General freight trucking, local	484110	12/03	(NA)	(NA)	105.2	111.5	115.2
General freight trucking, long-distance.	484121	12/03	(NA)	(NA)	102.7	108.6	112.0
Marine cargo handling	488320	12/91	110.9	111.5	113.2	115.1	117.9
Navigational services to shipping	488330	12/92	127.4	129.3	133.1	138.6	149.3
Freight transportation arrangement	488510	12/94	99.5	99.9	100.9	101.1	101.0
United States Postal Service	491110	06/89	150.2	155.0	155.0	155.0	164.7
Couriers	492110	12/03	(NA)	(NA)	105.6	115.0	123.2
Newspaper publishers	511110	12/79	381.8	395.6	409.7	426.2	439.2
Periodical publishers	511120	12/79	320.4	332.3	339.1	347.6	354.8
Software publishers	511210	12/97	98.0	96.9	94.3	94.3	94.6
Cellular and other wireless carriers.	517212	06/99	91.6	92.3	90.9	79.6	74.5
Commercial banking	522110	12/03	(NA)	(NA)	102.8	106.1	113.0
Savings institutions	522120	12/03	(NA)	(NA)	100.9	98.8	101.1
Direct life insurance carriers	524113	12/98	101.6	103.4	105.2	106.4	106.9
Direct health and medical insurance carriers	524114	12/02	(NA)	106.2	111.8	116.8	121.4
Direct property and casualty insurance carriers	524126	06/98	108.8	115.1	118.8	121.1	121.8
Insurance agencies and brokerages	524210	12/02	(NA)	102.3	104.4	105.4	105.3
Nursing care facilities.	623110	12/94	144.6	149.4	155.6	161.4	166.1
Hotels (except casino hotels) and motels.	721110	12/03	(NA)	(NA)	103.5	110.0	113.9
Casino hotels	721120	12/03	(NA)	(NA)	105.0	107.5	111.2

NA Not available.   [1] North American Industry Classification System, 1997.   [2] Index base year equals 100.   [3] Preliminary data.

Source: U.S. Bureau of Labor Statistics, *Producer Price Indexes*, monthly and annual. See also *Monthly Labor Review* at <http://www.bls.gov/opub/mlr/welcome.htm>.

Prices   481

Table 715. Commodity Research Bureau Futures Price Index: 1990 to 2006

[1967 = 100. Index computed daily. Represents unweighted geometric average of commodity futures prices (through 6 months forward) of 17 major commodity futures markets. Represents end of year index]

Item	1990	1995	1997	1998	1999	2000	2001	2002	2003	2004	2005	2006
All commodities	222.6	243.2	229.1	191.2	205.1	227.8	190.6	234.5	255.3	283.9	347.9	394.9
Softs [1]	276.0	354.4	408.7	344.8	280.9	254.4	252.8	303.7	250.5	343.5	420.5	475.9
Industrials	245.5	272.5	210.9	185.3	192.9	211.0	141.8	176.6	256.6	232.1	302.5	368.8
Grains and oilseeds [2]	171.2	218.6	210.7	172.8	156.6	174.9	159.0	188.2	225.8	177.0	193.8	279.1
Energy	246.0	180.0	180.4	135.0	221.0	355.8	204.9	320.7	358.7	457.3	705.3	591.6
Oilseeds [3]	223.6	277.5	(3)	(3)	(3)	(3)	(3)	(3)	(3)	(3)	(3)	(3)
Livestock and meats	226.2	192.4	238.1	186.7	239.6	253.6	247.4	251.0	237.8	303.6	300.3	294.6
Metals (precious)	257.8	276.0	249.3	234.3	253.4	265.7	246.8	289.1	364.1	396.6	478.1	611.9

[1] Prior to 1997, reported as imported. Softs include commodities that are grown and not mined such as coffee, cocoa, lumber, cotton, and sugar. [2] Prior to 1997, reported as grains. [3] Incorporated into grains and oilseeds beginning 1997.

Source: Commodity Research Bureau (CRB), Chicago, IL, *CRB Commodity Index Report*, weekly (copyright).

Table 716. Indexes of Spot Primary Market Prices: 1990 to 2006

[1967 = 100. Computed weekly for 1980; daily thereafter. Represents unweighted geometric average of price quotations of 23 commodities; much more sensitive to changes in market conditions than is a monthly producer price index]

Items and number of commodities	1990	1995	1997	1998	1999	2000	2001	2002	2003	2004	2005	2006
All commodities (23)	258.1	289.1	271.8	235.2	227.3	224.0	212.1	244.3	283.6	293.0	303.3	368.2
Foodstuffs (10).	206.4	236.4	227.3	197.5	178.1	184.7	201.6	238.1	250.2	256.0	241.7	276.0
Raw industrials (13)	301.2	332.2	307.5	265.3	268.9	255.8	217.3	248.6	309.1	321.5	354.7	449.3
Livestock and products (5)	292.7	307.4	306.1	232.3	265.7	265.5	257.2	317.8	365.9	365.0	326.6	378.6
Metals (5)	283.2	300.6	269.8	218.5	261.6	214.0	172.5	184.5	276.7	357.7	440.9	744.7
Textiles and fibers (4)	257.6	274.3	261.5	237.5	223.8	245.7	217.4	230.2	255.2	237.9	252.5	254.4
Fats and oils (4).	188.7	226.7	257.1	236.0	174.8	163.6	175.8	234.0	297.2	262.6	223.4	273.9

Source: Commodity Research Bureau, Chicago, IL, *CRB Commodity Index Report*, weekly (copyright).

Table 717. Chain-Type Price Indexes for Gross Domestic Product: 1990 to 2006

[2000 = 100. For explanation of "chain-type," see text, Section 13]

Component	1990	1995	2000	2002	2003	2004	2005	2006
Gross domestic product	81.6	92.1	100.0	104.2	106.4	109.4	112.7	116.1
Personal consumption expenditures. . . .	80.5	91.6	100.0	103.5	105.6	108.4	111.5	114.6
Durable goods	104.6	110.7	100.0	95.8	92.4	90.8	90.2	89.0
Nondurable goods.	84.2	90.6	100.0	102.1	104.1	107.6	111.5	115.0
Services	74.2	88.3	100.0	106.0	109.4	112.9	116.5	120.5
Gross private domestic investment	96.4	100.9	100.0	101.6	103.2	106.6	110.3	113.8
Fixed investment	95.5	100.3	100.0	101.7	103.3	106.8	110.5	114.2
Nonresidential.	104.7	106.2	100.0	99.5	99.6	100.8	103.4	106.4
Structures.	74.0	83.9	100.0	110.0	113.9	121.0	134.6	150.0
Equipment and software	118.2	115.2	100.0	96.0	94.9	94.5	94.1	93.9
Residential.	74.9	85.8	100.0	107.2	112.4	120.6	126.7	131.8
Net exports of goods and services:								
Exports	100.0	104.4	100.0	99.3	101.4	105.2	108.9	112.5
Goods	108.0	109.2	100.0	98.7	100.6	104.4	107.6	111.2
Services	82.5	93.1	100.0	100.8	103.3	107.0	112.1	115.8
Imports	103.8	106.4	100.0	96.3	99.7	104.7	111.3	116.0
Goods	108.2	108.6	100.0	95.3	98.1	103.0	109.6	114.5
Services	85.7	96.1	100.0	101.9	108.3	113.8	119.9	124.0
Government consumption expenditures and gross investment	77.1	88.4	100.0	105.5	109.8	114.7	121.2	126.5
Federal	77.1	89.5	100.0	105.6	110.1	115.2	120.7	124.9
National defense	78.0	89.6	100.0	105.8	110.8	116.0	121.9	126.0
Nondefense	75.3	89.4	100.0	105.3	108.9	114.0	118.6	122.8
State and local	77.4	87.8	100.0	105.4	109.7	114.4	121.5	127.4

Source: U.S. Bureau of Economic Analysis, *Survey of Current Business*, April 2007. See also <http://www.bea.gov /bea/dn/nipaweb/SelectTable.asp?Selected=N> (released February 2007).

Table 718. **Price Indexes For Personal Consumption Expenditures by Type of Expenditure: 1990 to 2005**

[2000 = 100. See also Table 655]

Type of expenditure	1990	1995	2000	2002	2003	2004	2005
Total expenditures [1]	80.5	91.6	100.0	103.5	105.6	108.4	111.5
Food and tobacco [1]	78.2	86.8	100.0	105.9	107.9	111.1	113.8
Food purchased for off-premise consumption. . . . . [2]	82.7	90.4	100.0	104.4	106.2	109.5	111.3
Purchased meals and beverages [2].	78.6	88.2	100.0	105.9	108.2	111.5	115.0
Tobacco products	46.7	57.6	100.0	116.8	118.8	121.0	127.3
Clothing, accessories, and jewelry [1].	105.6	105.7	100.0	97.0	95.1	95.3	95.0
Shoes.	103.7	106.2	100.0	98.0	96.6	96.3	99.0
Clothing.	109.4	106.3	100.0	94.9	92.3	92.0	90.4
Jewelry and watches	114.4	117.9	100.0	97.3	93.9	94.5	93.1
Personal care	83.1	91.8	100.0	102.9	103.4	104.6	106.1
Housing [1]	74.5	86.1	100.0	107.8	110.4	113.2	116.2
Owner-occupied nonfarm dwellings— space rent	74.8	86.2	100.0	108.0	110.7	113.2	115.8
Tenant-occupied nonfarm dwellings—space rent	75.4	86.2	100.0	108.3	111.3	114.1	117.6
Household operation [1].	89.3	96.6	100.0	100.9	102.0	102.8	106.3
Furniture [3].	91.9	99.6	100.0	96.3	95.0	94.7	93.7
Semidurable house furnishings [4]	112.0	111.0	100.0	94.8	87.7	83.9	81.7
Cleaning and polishing preparations	84.2	89.5	100.0	104.4	102.8	103.2	105.3
Household utilities.	80.9	90.3	100.0	104.5	112.3	118.1	130.1
Electricity	91.5	100.9	100.0	106.8	109.3	111.4	118.3
Gas.	73.2	77.3	100.0	101.2	123.8	134.3	160.3
Water and other sanitary services	66.1	87.1	100.0	106.2	110.2	116.7	122.9
Fuel oil and coal	76.9	69.9	100.0	91.7	109.7	125.4	159.5
Telephone and telegraph	103.8	107.0	100.0	98.1	97.2	95.2	94.4
Medical care [1]	70.1	88.0	100.0	106.5	110.3	114.6	118.3
Drug preparations and sundries [5].	72.7	87.2	100.0	109.0	112.0	115.1	118.5
Physicians.	71.2	92.3	100.0	102.8	104.3	106.5	108.4
Dentists.	60.6	80.1	100.0	108.7	113.2	118.7	125.3
Hospitals and nursing homes [6]	70.1	87.7	100.0	108.1	112.8	117.6	122.3
Health insurance.	62.0	82.4	100.0	103.5	114.2	126.8	131.4
Medical care [7].	60.3	84.2	100.0	107.1	120.0	134.4	138.9
Personal business [1]	76.0	90.3	100.0	103.9	105.9	109.2	111.8
Expense of handling life insurance [8]. . . .	61.7	75.2	100.0	106.7	110.4	116.6	120.2
Legal services	65.7	80.5	100.0	111.5	116.5	122.0	127.0
Funeral and burial expenses	63.7	82.1	100.0	108.6	113.0	117.8	121.8
Transportation	79.9	90.8	100.0	99.0	101.8	106.1	113.7
User-operated transportation [1].	79.5	90.8	100.0	99.6	102.4	107.0	114.9
New autos	87.5	99.9	100.0	98.4	96.6	96.0	96.9
Net purchases of used autos	69.1	95.6	100.0	103.9	97.4	98.0	102.3
Tires, tubes, accessories, etc.	102.2	101.8	100.0	104.3	105.2	105.7	108.2
Repair, greasing, washing, parking, storage, rental, and leasing	77.6	90.4	100.0	106.1	108.0	109.6	112.9
Gasoline and oil	78.4	77.8	100.0	90.4	105.2	123.9	150.8
Purchased local transportation.	77.0	90.2	100.0	105.3	112.8	119.5	125.0
Mass transit systems	77.9	90.9	100.0	105.3	112.8	119.5	125.0
Taxicab	75.0	88.7	100.0	105.3	112.8	119.5	125.0
Purchased intercity transportation [1]	87.9	91.4	100.0	87.1	88.9	87.8	89.8
Railway (commutation)	76.2	85.7	100.0	108.7	107.6	98.4	99.2
Bus.	86.8	86.6	100.0	106.6	110.5	114.8	118.9
Airline	91.5	93.0	100.0	82.9	84.8	83.3	84.8
Recreation [1]	104.9	109.0	100.0	97.2	95.8	95.2	94.2
Magazines, newspapers, and sheet music.	73.9	89.4	100.0	103.8	105.9	109.0	111.8
Nondurable toys and sport supplies	115.9	118.4	100.0	90.6	85.8	82.4	78.2
Video and audio products, including musical instruments and computer goods	284.8	205.9	100.0	77.1	68.7	62.9	56.8
Computers, peripherals, and software . . .	1,516.2	516.5	100.0	60.2	49.2	43.6	37.6
Education and research.	66.6	82.6	100.0	109.6	115.4	122.2	128.6
Higher education.	62.9	82.8	100.0	110.7	117.0	124.7	131.5
Religious and welfare activities	73.1	84.5	100.0	105.9	109.3	112.6	116.2
Foreign travel and other, net:							
Foreign travel by U.S. residents.	80.1	95.1	100.0	105.0	111.6	117.1	122.3
Expenditures abroad by U.S. residents . . .	102.0	124.1	100.0	105.9	124.3	137.8	145.9
Less: Expenditures in the United States by nonresidents.	76.9	87.3	100.0	101.4	104.5	109.0	113.9

[1] Includes other expenditures not shown separately.   [2] Consists of purchases (including tips) of meals and beverages from retail, service, and amusement establishments; hotels; dining and buffet cars; schools; school fraternities; institutions; clubs; and industrial lunch rooms. Includes meals and beverages consumed both on- and off-premise.   [3] Includes mattresses and bedsprings.   [4] Consists largely of textile house furnishings including piece goods allocated to house furnishing use. Also includes lamp shades, brooms, and brushes.   [5] Excludes drug preparations and related products dispensed by physicians, hospitals, and other medical services.   [6] Consists of (1) current expenditures (including consumption of fixed capital) of nonprofit hospitals and nursing homes and (2) payments by patients to proprietary and government hospitals and nursing homes.   [7] Consists of (1) premiums, less benefits and dividends, for health hospitalization and accidental death and dismemberment insurance provided by commercial insurance carriers and (2) administrative expenses (including consumption of fixed capital) of Blue Cross and Blue Shield plans and of other independent prepaid and self-insured health plans.   [8] Consists of (1) operating expenses of life insurance carriers and private noninsured pension plans and (2) premiums less benefits and dividends of fraternal benefit societies. Excludes expenses allocated by commercial carriers to accident and health insurance.

Source: U.S. Bureau of Economic Analysis, *Survey of Current Business*, September 2006. See also <http://www.bea.doc.gov /bea/dn/nipaweb/SelectTable.asp?Selected=N> (released as August 2006).

Table 719. Export Price Indexes—Selected Commodities: 1990 to 2006

[2000 = 100. As of June. Indexes are weighted by 2000 export values according to the Schedule B classification system of the U.S. Census Bureau. Prices used in these indexes were collected from a sample of U.S. manufacturers of exports and are factory transaction prices, except as noted. N.e.s. = not elsewhere specified]

Commodities	1990	1995	2000 [1]	2002	2003	2004	2005	2006
All commodities.	**95.1**	**104.5**	**100.1**	**98.0**	**99.5**	**103.4**	**106.7**	**111.2**
Food and live animals	102.4	112.1	100.6	99.8	107.5	123.9	124.3	126.8
Meat	81.4	95.7	104.8	90.0	102.9	127.3	140.2	130.8
Fish	86.8	107.1	100.6	97.9	108.2	108.6	110.1	115.8
Cereals and cereal preparations	126.5	133.2	100.0	106.5	118.5	141.2	118.7	136.0
Fruits and vegetables	93.2	107.2	97.9	99.0	99.6	111.1	133.6	125.9
Feeding stuff for animals	99.5	104.9	100.4	101.2	108.8	131.9	118.1	127.0
Miscellaneous food products	94.0	94.8	100.0	100.7	101.5	101.6	108.1	107.1
Beverages and tobacco	84.9	98.2	100.0	98.2	98.2	101.6	103.3	101.5
Tobacco and tobacco manufactures	85.0	98.1	99.9	97.6	96.6	100.0	101.6	99.9
Crude materials	96.7	125.4	101.6	95.3	103.9	125.7	130.3	151.8
Oil seeds and oleaginous fruits	116.1	115.6	103.3	102.9	122.7	168.5	136.5	119.5
Cork and wood	76.5	117.5	99.8	87.1	90.4	98.3	97.6	100.0
Pulp and waste paper	70.9	122.2	106.9	89.3	90.1	100.8	101.5	101.3
Textile fibers	118.2	154.3	100.5	88.6	103.2	108.7	103.1	110.4
Metalliferous ores and metal scrap	105.9	132.2	99.2	99.8	109.0	167.5	212.9	346.1
Mineral fuels and related materials	67.2	68.5	97.4	93.9	107.6	131.8	181.0	232.3
Coal, coke, and briquettes	109.5	106.4	99.5	110.9	(NA)	(NA)	(NA)	(NA)
Crude petroleum and petroleum products	57.5	59.6	96.8	87.9	102.7	129.7	188.7	251.7
Chemicals and related products	90.4	108.4	100.9	95.8	100.8	105.8	115.7	123.4
Chemical materials and products, n.e.s.	86.4	100.7	99.7	97.5	101.6	104.9	106.1	110.7
Intermediate manufactured products	86.8	100.6	100.2	98.1	100.0	107.0	113.9	124.2
Rubber manufactures	81.4	95.7	100.1	102.7	110.1	111.2	115.5	121.1
Paper and paperboard products	90.8	115.6	100.5	94.8	98.3	99.2	103.9	109.5
Textiles	91.2	102.8	100.2	100.0	100.7	105.4	111.7	109.5
Nonmetallic mineral manufactures	85.8	94.3	100.4	102.2	100.4	99.9	103.5	105.7
Nonferrous metals	87.1	98.2	98.5	85.3	80.3	95.4	106.1	156.5
Manufactures of metals, n.e.s.	81.2	92.3	100.9	102.5	104.8	108.4	118.3	127.5
Machinery and transport equipment [2]	97.9	102.8	100.0	98.9	97.8	98.2	98.7	98.7
Power generating machinery [3]	77.0	88.5	99.7	104.5	107.2	108.7	111.3	114.2
Machinery specialized for particular industries	82.7	94.0	100.2	101.8	102.6	105.4	110.7	116.7
Metalworking machinery	82.1	92.3	99.3	99.9	101.0	100.0	103.7	104.7
General industrial machines, parts, n.e.s.	82.5	92.0	100.1	102.3	102.4	104.9	109.3	111.8
Computer equipment and office machines	193.2	147.5	99.9	90.4	88.1	87.2	80.9	77.0
Computer equipment	234.5	160.7	99.7	92.1	88.1	83.9	77.5	71.3
Telecommunications [4]	97.3	103.8	100.3	97.7	93.8	91.8	89.7	87.8
Electrical machinery and equipment	112.7	117.2	99.8	93.9	89.7	88.2	87.4	84.0
Road vehicles	88.7	96.1	100.0	100.3	101.1	102.4	103.0	104.4
Miscellaneous manufactured articles	90.5	98.6	99.7	100.4	101.2	100.9	102.1	103.7

[2] NA Not available. [1] June 2000 may not equal 100 because indexes were reweighted to an "average" trade value in 2000. [2] Excludes military and commercial aircraft. [3] Includes equipment. [4] Includes sound recording and reproducing equipment.

Source: U.S. Bureau of Labor Statistics, *U.S. Import and Export Price Indexes*, monthly.

Table 720. Import Price Indexes—Selected Commodities: 1990 to 2006

[2000 = 100. As of June. Indexes are weighted by the 2000 Tariff Schedule of the United States Annotated, a scheme for describing and reporting product composition and value of U.S. imports. Import prices are based on U.S. dollar prices paid by importer]

Commodity	1990	1995	2000 [1]	2002	2003	2004	2005	2006
All commodities.	**90.8**	**101.4**	**100.2**	**94.1**	**96.2**	**101.7**	**109.2**	**117.1**
Food and live animals	92.1	108.6	99.0	94.5	99.4	106.9	113.9	117.3
Meat	118.4	100.8	100.8	104.0	102.9	128.9	138.5	137.8
Fish	70.9	92.5	99.3	79.8	81.3	84.1	87.8	94.9
Beverages and tobacco	76.5	88.6	100.4	103.0	103.9	105.3	108.5	109.7
Crude materials	90.4	109.5	99.4	96.4	99.5	125.8	130.5	137.6
Mineral fuels and related products	54.7	61.9	101.3	86.1	101.7	131.5	179.0	228.8
Crude petroleum and petroleum products	54.8	63.0	102.2	85.9	97.6	130.0	182.4	241.1
Natural gas	54.9	49.3	95.2	83.6	130.1	140.0	148.5	151.5
Chemicals and related products	93.7	106.8	99.8	97.0	100.1	103.8	112.4	116.6
Intermediate manufactured products	91.3	102.7	100.4	92.8	94.4	106.1	112.8	126.5
Machinery and transport equipment	100.8	112.4	100.1	97.1	95.8	95.1	95.0	94.2
Computer equipment and office machines	198.5	167.2	99.9	87.8	81.8	75.5	70.5	65.2
Computer equipment	284.6	198.4	100.4	80.3	71.9	64.9	58.2	53.3
Telecommunications [2]	120.9	119.1	100.2	94.4	89.3	84.7	82.1	78.7
Electrical machinery and equipment	111.3	122.9	100.7	97.1	95.4	94.7	94.4	95.3
Road vehicles	82.0	97.3	100.1	100.2	100.7	102.4	103.8	104.2
Miscellaneous manufactured articles	94.7	103.2	99.7	98.6	99.7	99.9	101.0	102.0
Plumbing, heating, and lighting fixtures	102.0	107.4	99.2	98.5	94.8	93.5	96.4	97.2
Furniture and parts	96.0	103.1	99.6	98.8	100.2	102.3	106.4	105.9
Articles of apparel and clothing	96.5	99.0	99.6	99.7	100.6	100.7	100.6	100.5
Footwear	96.5	99.3	99.6	99.2	100.0	100.4	100.5	100.9

[1] June 2000 may not equal 100 because indexes were reweighted to an "average" trade value in 2000. [2] Includes sound recording and reproducing equipment.

Source: U.S. Bureau of Labor Statistics, *U.S. Import and Export Price Indexes*, monthly.

Business Enterprise

This section relates to the place and behavior of the business firm and to business initiative in the American economy. It includes data on the number, type, and size of businesses; financial data of domestic and multinational U.S. corporations; business investments, expenditures, and profits; and sales and inventories.

The principal sources of these data are the *Survey of Current Business*, published by the Bureau of Economic Analysis (BEA), the *Statistical Supplement to the Federal Reserve Bulletin*, issued by the Board of Governors of the Federal Reserve System, the annual *Statistics of Income (SOI)* reports of the Internal Revenue Service (IRS), and the Census Bureau's Economic Census, *County Business Patterns, Quarterly Financial Report for Manufacturing, Mining, and Trade Corporations (QFR), Survey of Business Owners*, and *Annual Capital Expenditures Survey*.

Business firms—A firm is generally defined as a business organization under a single management and may include one or more establishments. The terms firm, business, company, and enterprise are used interchangeably throughout this section. A firm doing business in more than one industry is classified by industry according to the major activity of the firm as a whole.

The IRS concept of a business firm relates primarily to the legal entity used for tax reporting purposes. A sole proprietorship is an unincorporated business owned by one person and may include large enterprises with many employees and hired managers and part-time operators. A partnership is an unincorporated business owned by two or more persons, each of whom has a financial interest in the business. A corporation is a business that is legally incorporated under state laws. While many corporations file consolidated tax returns, most corporate tax returns represent individual corporations, some

of which are affiliated through common ownership or control with other corporations filing separate returns.

Economic census—The economic census is the major source of facts about the structure and functioning of the nation's economy. It provides essential information for government, business, industry, and the general public. It furnishes an important part of the framework for such composite measures as the gross domestic product estimates, input/output measures, production and price indexes, and other statistical series that measure short-term changes in economic conditions. The Census Bureau takes the economic census every 5 years, covering years ending in "2" and "7."

The economic census is collected on an establishment basis. A company operating at more than one location is required to file a separate report for each store, factory, shop, or other location. Each establishment is assigned a separate industry classification based on its primary activity and not that of its parent company. Establishments responding to the establishment survey are classified into industries on the basis of their principal product or activity (determined by annual sales volume). The statistics issued by industry in the 2002 Economic Census are classified primarily on the 2002 North American Industry Classification System (NAICS) and, to a lesser extent, on the 1997 NAICS used in the previous census (see below).

More detailed information about the scope, coverage, methodology, classification system, data items, and publications for each of the economic censuses and related surveys is published in the *Guide to the 2002 Economic Census* at <http://www.census.gov/econ/census02/guide/>.

Data from the 2002 Economic Census were released through the Census Bureau's American FactFinder® service, on

Business Enterprise   485

DVD-ROM, in Adobe Acrobat PDF reports and in hypertext "drill-down" tables available on the Census Bureau Web site. For more information on these various media of release, see the following page on the Census Bureau Web site <http://www .census.gov/econ/census02/>.

Survey of Business Owners—The Survey of Business Owners (SBO), formerly known as the Surveys of Minority- and Women-Owned Business Enterprises (SMOBE/SWOBE), provides statistics that describe the composition of U.S. businesses by gender, Hispanic or Latino origin, and race. Data from SBO are published in a series of reports: *American Indian- and Alaska Native-Owned Firms, Asian-Owned Firms, Black-Owned Firms, Hispanic-Owned Firms, Native Hawaiian- and Other Pacific Islander-Owned Firms, Women-Owned Firms*, and *Company Summary*. Data are presented by industry classifications and/or geographic area and size of firm (employment and receipts). The reports include totals for all U.S. businesses based on the 2002 Economic Census and estimates of business ownership by gender, Hispanic or Latino origin, and race based on the 2002 SBO. Each owner had the option of selecting more than one race and therefore is included in each race selected. For information on confidentiality protection and survey methodology, see Appendix III and the SBO Web site <http://www.census .gov/csd/sbo/>.

North American Industry Classification System (NAICS)—NAICS has replaced the previous Standard Industrial Classification (SIC) system.

NAICS 2002 is the same as NAICS 1997 for 14 of the 20 sectors. Construction and wholesale trade are substantially changed, but the revisions also modify a number of retail classifications and the organization of the information sector. Very minor boundary adjustments affect administrative and support services and mining. A key feature of NAICS is the revision for the Information sector. A few of the new and important industries created in this section include: Internet service providers and Web search portals, and Internet publishing and broadcasting. Included in the Retail Trade sector is electronic shopping and electronic auctions.

Quarterly Financial Report—The Quarterly Financial Report (QFR) program publishes quarterly aggregate statistics on the financial conditions of U.S. corporations. The QFR requests companies to report estimates from their statements of income and retained earnings, and balance sheets. The statistical data are classified and aggregated by type of industry and asset size. The QFR sample includes manufacturing companies with assets of $250 thousand and above, and mining, wholesale, and retail companies with assets of $50 million and above. The data are available quarterly in the *Quarterly Financial Report for Manufacturing, Mining, and Trade Corporations* on the Internet at <http://www.census.gov/csd /qfr/>.

Multinational Companies—BEA collects financial and operating data on U.S. multinational companies. These data provide a picture of the overall activities of foreign affiliates and U.S. parent companies, using a variety of indicators of their financial structure and operations. The data on foreign affiliates cover the entire operations of the affiliate, irrespective of the percentage of U.S. ownership. These data cover items that are needed in analyzing the characteristics, performance, and economic impact of multinational companies, such as sales, value added, employment and compensation of employees, capital expenditures, exports and imports, and research and development expenditures. Separate tabulations are available for all affiliates and for affiliates that are majority-owned by their U.S. parent(s).

Statistical reliability—For a discussion of statistical collection, estimation, and sampling procedures and measures of reliability applicable to data from the Census Bureau and the Internal Revenue Service, see Appendix III.

Table 721. **Number of Returns, Receipts, and Net Income by Type of Business: 1990 to 2004**

[14,783 represents 14,783,000. Covers active enterprises only. Figures are estimates based on sample of unaudited tax returns; see Appendix III]

Item	Number of returns (1,000)			Business receipts [1] (bil. dol.)			Net income (less loss) [2] (bil. dol.)		
	Nonfarm propri- etor- ships	Partner- ships	Corpora- tions	Nonfarm propri- etor- ships	Partner- ships	Corpora tions	Nonfarm propri- etor- ships	Partner- ships	Corpora- tions
1990	14,783	1,554	3,717	731	541	10,914	141	17	371
1991	15,181	1,515	3,803	713	539	10,963	142	21	345
1992	15,495	1,485	3,869	737	571	11,272	154	43	402
1993	15,848	1,468	3,965	757	627	11,814	156	67	498
1994	16,154	1,494	4,342	791	732	12,858	167	82	577
1995	16,424	1,581	4,474	807	854	13,969	169	107	714
1996	16,955	1,654	4,631	843	1,042	14,890	177	145	806
1997	17,176	1,759	4,710	870	1,297	15,890	187	168	915
1998	17,409	1,855	4,849	918	1,534	16,543	202	187	838
1999	17,576	1,937	4,936	969	1,829	18,009	208	228	929
2000	17,905	2,058	5,045	1,021	2,316	19,593	215	269	928
2001	18,338	2,132	5,136	1,017	2,569	19,308	217	276	604
2002	18,926	2,242	5,267	1,030	2,669	18,849	221	271	564
2003	19,710	2,375	5,401	1,050	2,818	19,755	230	301	780
2004	20,591	2,547	5,558	1,140	3,142	21,717	248	385	1,112

[1] Excludes investment income except for partnerships and corporations in finance, insurance, and real estate before 1998. Beginning 1998, finance and insurance, real estate, and management of companies included investment income for partnerships and corporations. Excludes investment income for S corporations. [2] Net income (less loss) is defined differently by form of organization, basically as follows: (a) Proprietorships: Total taxable receipts less total business deductions, including cost of sales and operations, depletion, and certain capital expensing, excluding charitable contributions and owners' salaries; (b) Partnerships: Total taxable receipts (including investment income except capital gains) less deductions, including cost of sales and operations and certain payments to partners, excluding charitable contributions, oil and gas depletion, and certain capital expensing; (c) Corporations: Total taxable receipts (including investment income, capital gains, and income from foreign subsidiaries deemed received for tax purposes, except for S corporations) less business deductions, including cost of sales and operations, depletion, certain capital expensing, and officers' compensation excluding S corporation charitable contributions and investment expenses; net income is before income tax.

Source: U.S. Internal Revenue Service, *Statistics of Income*, various publications.

Table 722. **Number of Returns and Business Receipts by Size of Receipts: 2000 to 2004**

[5,045 represents 5,045,000. Covers active enterprises only. Figures are estimates based on sample of unaudited tax returns; see Appendix III]

Size-class of receipts	Returns (1,000)					Business receipts [1] (bil. dol.)				
	2000	2001	2002	2003	2004	2000	2001	2002	2003	2004
Corporations	5,045	5,136	5,267	5,401	5,558	19,593	19,308	18,849	19,755	21,717
Under $25,000 [2]	1,220	1,248	1,283	1,280	1,317	4	3	4	3	4
$25,000 to $49,999	302	296	314	346	334	10	11	12	13	12
$50,000 to $99,999	477	485	514	522	545	35	36	38	39	40
$100,000 to $499,999	1,515	1,550	1,583	1,649	1,703	397	388	395	412	424
$500,000 to $999,999	582	601	611	623	635	407	428	434	441	448
$1,000,000 or more	946	956	962	981	1,023	18,738	18,442	17,967	18,848	20,788
Partnerships	2,058	2,132	2,242	2,375	2,547	2,316	2,569	2,669	2,818	3,142
Under $25,000 [2]	1,105	1,130	1,204	1,284	1,373	5	5	5	5	5
$25,000 to $49,999	183	183	185	192	193	7	7	7	7	7
$50,000 to $99,999	187	192	195	206	226	13	14	14	15	16
$100,000 to $499,999	353	373	394	410	436	82	88	92	95	102
$500,000 to $999,999	92	103	105	111	121	66	73	74	78	86
$1,000,000 or more	137	151	159	172	198	2,143	2,383	2,478	2,619	2,925
Nonfarm proprietorship	17,905	18,338	18,926	19,710	20,591	1,021	1,017	1,030	1,050	1,140
Under $25,000 [2]	11,997	12,345	12,716	13,308	13,916	82	86	87	93	97
$25,000 to $49,999	2,247	2,239	2,358	2,450	2,536	80	79	83	87	90
$50,000 to $99,999	1,645	1,704	1,752	1,805	1,792	117	121	124	128	128
$100,000 to $499,999	1,733	1,759	1,803	1,851	2,020	355	353	362	373	405
$500,000 to $999,999	190	197	203	200	218	126	133	138	135	147
$1,000,000 or more	92	93	93	96	109	261	245	234	235	273

[1] Finance and insurance, real estate, and management of companies included investment income for partnerships and corporations. [2] Includes firms with no receipts.

Source: U.S. Internal Revenue Service, *Statistics of Income Bulletin*; and unpublished data.

Business Enterprise 487

Table 723. Number of Returns, Receipts, and Net Income by Type of Business and Industry: 2004

[20,591 represents 20,591,000. Covers active enterprises only. Figures are estimates based on sample of unaudited tax returns; see Appendix III. Based on the North American Industry Classification System (NAICS), 2002; see text, this section. Minus sign (–) indicates net loss]

Industry	2002 NAICS code	Number of returns (1,000)			Business receipts [1] (bil. dol.)			Net income (less loss) (bil. dol.)		
		Non-farm propri-etor-ships	Partner-ships	Corpo-rations	Non-farm propri-etor-ships	Partner-ships	Corpo-rations	Non-farm propri-etor-ships	Partner-ships	Corpo-rations
Total	(X)	20,591	2,547	5,558	1,140	3,142	21,717	248	385	1,112
Agriculture, forestry, fishing, and hunting [2]	11	282	120	142	16	21	125	1	(Z)	3
Mining	21	126	26	31	9	77	213	1	27	19
Utilities	22	12	4	7	(Z)	136	526	(Z)	1	4
Construction	23	2,587	155	722	198	226	1,240	31	19	47
Special trade contractors	238	2,084	58	430	135	39	493	25	2	14
Manufacturing	31–33	351	43	281	26	616	5,893	3	38	291
Wholesale and retail trade [3]	(X)	2,750	179	1,001	228	639	6,167	13	12	162
Wholesale trade	42	351	43	376	41	357	2,973	5	10	80
Retail trade [4]	44–45	2,399	136	621	187	282	3,193	8	2	82
Motor vehicle and parts dealers	441	159	17	93	37	96	827	1	1	8
Food and beverage stores	445	85	14	96	26	50	486	1	(Z)	6
Gasoline stations........	447	21	6	37	23	40	194	(Z)	(Z)	1
Transportation and warehousing	48–49	983	34	183	65	71	599	9	5	6
Information [4]	51	295	35	124	8	178	864	2	6	23
Broadcasting (except Internet)	515	[5]44	3	7	[5]2	32	88	[5](Z)	(Z)	1
Telecommunications	517	(5)	5	19	(5)	102	375	(5)	(Z)	-12
Finance and insurance	52	673	269	239	73	339	2,873	18	136	363
Real estate and rental and leasing	53	1,179	1,180	604	71	231	223	28	54	10
Professional, scientific, and technical services [4]	54	2,951	164	780	138	232	722	57	56	18
Legal services	5411	353	28	99	35	105	72	16	38	6
Accounting, tax preparation, bookkeeping, and payroll services	5412	408	18	65	11	38	27	4	8	2
Management, scientific, and technical consulting services	5416	735	39	227	31	28	152	16	6	7
Management of companies and enterprises	55	(NA)	24	50	(NA)	34	729	(NA)	10	116
Administrative and support and waste management and remediation services	56	1,995	52	246	50	53	398	14	4	11
Educational services	61	474	8	44	7	3	32	2	(Z)	2
Health care and social assistance	62	1,778	57	370	104	119	492	42	16	20
Arts, entertainment, and recreation	71	1,132	45	119	26	35	75	6	-1	3
Accommodation and food services	72	384	91	281	40	114	376	1	1	12
Accommodation	721	49	29	37	5	52	88	(Z)	-1	3
Food services and drinking places	722	335	61	244	35	63	289	1	1	9
Other services [4]	81	2,355	58	333	77	17	169	18	1	9
Auto repair and maintenance	8111	345	15	107	24	6	61	3	(Z)	1
Personal and laundry services.............	812	1,339	33	134	34	8	69	11	(Z)	3
Religious, grantmaking, civic, professional, and similar organizations	813	266	(Z)	39	4	(Z)	10	2	(Z)	–
Unclassified..............	(X)	284	3	3	4	(Z)	–	1	(Z)	–

– Represents zero.   NA Not available.   X Not applicable.   Z Less than 500 or $500 million.   [1] Includes investment income for partnerships and corporations in finance and insurance, real estate, and management of companies' industries. Excludes investment income for S corporations.   [2] For corporations, represents agricultural services only.   [3] For corporations, includes trade business not identified as wholesale or retail.   [4] Includes other industries not shown separately.   [5] Broadcasting includes telecommunications.

Source: U.S. Internal Revenue Service, *Statistics of Income*, various publications.

Table 724. **Nonfarm Sole Proprietorships—Selected Income and Deduction Items: 1990 to 2004**

[In billions of dollars (731 represents $731,000,000,000) except as indicated. All figures are estimates based on samples. Tax law changes have affected the comparability of the data over time; see *Statistics of Income* reports for a description. See Appendix III]

Item	1990	1995	1998	1999	2000	2001	2002	2003	2004
Number of returns (1,000)	14,783	16,424	17,409	17,576	17,905	18,338	18,926	19,710	20,591
Returns with net income (1,000).	11,222	12,213	13,080	13,159	13,308	13,604	13,751	14,448	15,053
Business receipts	731	807	918	969	1,021	1,017	1,030	1,050	1,140
Income from sales and operations . . .	719	797	905	955	1,008	1,002	1,015	1,034	1,122
Business deductions [1].	589	638	716	761	806	800	809	820	892
Cost of goods sold/operations [1]. . . .	291	307	341	370	387	363	352	338	371
Purchases	210	219	231	256	269	247	227	218	239
Labor costs.	23	24	27	29	29	28	30	28	32
Materials and supplies	30	34	42	42	43	44	46	47	53
Advertising.	(NA)	(NA)	9	9	10	11	11	12	13
Car and truck expenses	22	33	40	41	46	47	50	53	59
Commissions	9	10	11	11	12	12	14	14	13
Depreciation.	24	27	29	31	32	33	37	42	43
Insurance.	13	13	13	13	14	14	16	17	19
Interest paid.	13	10	11	11	12	13	11	11	11
Office expenses	(NA)	(NA)	10	10	10	11	11	12	12
Rent paid.	23	28	30	31	33	34	35	36	37
Repairs	9	10	11	12	12	12	13	13	15
Salaries and wages (net)	47	54	59	61	63	64	66	68	71
Supplies	(NA)	(NA)	20	22	22	23	25	26	27
Taxes paid	10	13	14	14	14	14	15	15	16
Utilities	14	17	18	18	19	20	21	22	21
Net income (less loss) [2].	141	169	202	208	215	217	221	230	248
Net income [2]	162	192	226	233	245	250	257	269	291
Constant (2000) Dollars [3]									
Business receipts	896	877	952	991	1,021	993	991	991	1,045
Business deductions	722	693	742	778	806	781	778	774	818
Net income (less loss)	173	184	210	213	215	212	213	217	227
Net income.	198	208	235	239	245	244	248	254	266

NA Not available. [1] Includes other amounts not shown separately. [2] After adjustment for the passive loss carryover from prior years. Therefore, "business receipts" minus "total deductions" do not equal "net income." [3] Based on the overall implicit price deflator for gross domestic product.

Source: U.S. Internal Revenue Service, *Statistics of Income Bulletin.*

Table 725. **Partnerships—Selected Income and Balance Sheet Items: 1990 to 2004**

[In billions of dollars (1,735 represents $1,735,000,000,000), except as indicated. Covers active partnerships only. All figures are estimates based on samples. See Appendix III]

Item	1990	1995	1998	1999	2000	2001	2002	2003	2004
Number of returns (1,000)	1,554	1,581	1,855	1,937	2,058	2,132	2,242	2,375	2,547
Returns with net income (1,000).	854	955	1,171	1,226	1,261	1,301	1,325	1,357	1,441
Number of partners (1,000).	17,095	15,606	15,663	15,924	13,660	14,232	14,328	14,108	15,557
Assets [1, 2].	1,735	2,719	5,127	5,999	6,694	8,428	8,867	9,675	11,608
Depreciable assets (net)	681	767	1,153	1,314	1,487	1,646	1,792	1,846	1,988
Inventories, end of year	57	88	176	174	150	208	203	214	276
Land.	215	221	291	326	359	392	423	455	509
Liabilities [1, 2].	1,415	1,886	3,151	3,453	3,696	4,835	4,972	5,303	6,248
Accounts payable	67	91	191	244	230	362	346	276	336
Short-term debt [3].	88	124	230	232	252	289	283	274	296
Long-term debt [4].	498	544	884	989	1,132	1,286	1,375	1,389	1,546
Nonrecourse loans	470	466	523	582	639	700	770	800	854
Partners' capital accounts [2]	320	832	1,976	2,546	2,999	3,593	3,895	4,372	5,360
Receipts [1]	566	890	1,603	1,907	2,405	2,665	2,773	2,923	3,260
Business receipts [5]	483	854	1,534	1,829	2,316	2,569	2,669	2,818	3,142
Interest received	21	31	51	62	82	85	70	71	88
Deductions [1]	550	784	1,416	1,679	2,136	2,389	2,502	2,621	2,876
Cost of goods sold/operations	243	395	737	902	1,226	1,338	1,430	1,523	1,666
Salaries and wages	56	80	143	170	201	231	238	245	269
Taxes paid	9	13	24	27	31	35	36	39	42
Interest paid.	30	43	73	74	93	97	68	65	64
Depreciation.	60	23	43	52	59	72	83	84	90
Net income (less loss)	17	107	187	228	269	276	271	301	385
Net income.	116	179	298	348	410	446	440	469	566

[1] Includes items not shown separately. [2] Assets, liabilities, and partners' capital accounts are understated because not all partnerships file complete balance sheets. [3] Mortgages, notes, and bonds payable in less than 1 year. [4] Mortgages, notes, and bonds payable in 1 year or more. [5] Excludes investment income except for partnerships in finance, insurance, and real estate in 1995. Beginning 1998, finance and insurance, real estate, and management of companies included investment income for partnerships.

Source: U.S. Internal Revenue Service, *Statistics of Income,* various issues.

Business Enterprise **489**

Table 726. Partnerships—Selected Items by Industry: 2004

[In billions of dollars (11,608 represents $11,608,000,000,000), except as indicated. Covers active partnerships only. Figures are estimates based on samples. Based on the North American Industry Classification System (NAICS), 2002; see text, this section. See Appendix III. Minus sign (–) indicates net loss]

Industry	2002 NAICS code	Number of partnerships (1,000) Total	With net income	With net loss	Total assets [1]	Business receipts [2]	Total deductions	Net income less loss	Net income	Net loss
Total [3]	(X)	2,547	1,441	1,106	11,608	3,142	2,876	384.7	566.2	181.5
Agriculture, forestry, fishing, and hunting	11	120	64	55	95	21	28	(Z)	5.2	5.2
Mining	21	26	18	8	173	77	58	27.2	31.8	4.6
Utilities	22	4	2	2	149	136	137	1.3	6.3	5.0
Construction	23	155	87	68	200	226	214	19.0	24.5	5.5
Manufacturing	31–33	43	19	24	427	616	595	37.7	49.4	11.7
Wholesale trade	42	43	21	22	104	357	352	10.0	13.2	3.2
Retail trade	44–45	136	62	74	100	282	287	2.1	6.9	4.7
Transportation and warehousing	48–49	34	17	18	108	71	71	4.9	8.5	3.6
Information	51	35	14	21	516	178	187	6.1	24.8	18.7
Finance and insurance	52	269	192	77	6,321	339	203	136.0	155.6	19.7
Real estate and rental and leasing	53	1,180	661	519	2,638	231	186	54.4	120.8	66.4
Professional, scientific, and technical services	54	164	100	64	107	232	190	56.0	62.5	6.5
Management of companies and enterprises	55	24	14	11	338	34	24	9.9	17.5	7.6
Admin/support waste mgt/ remediation services	56	52	30	22	30	53	51	3.8	5.2	1.4
Educational services	61	8	5	4	2	3	3	0.2	0.4	0.3
Health care and social assistance	62	57	36	20	70	119	111	16.0	19.9	3.9
Arts, entertainment, and recreation	71	45	19	27	59	35	41	–1.2	4.3	5.5
Accommodation and food services	72	91	46	45	155	114	120	0.6	7.6	7.1
Other services	81	58	35	24	13	17	17	0.7	1.8	1.1

X Not applicable. Z Less than $50 million dollars. [1] Total assets are understated because not all partnerships file complete balance sheets. [2] Finance and insurance, real estate, and management of companies includes investment income for partnerships. [3] Includes businesses not allocable to individual industries.

Source: U.S. Internal Revenue Service, *Statistics of Income*, various issues.

Table 727. Nonfarm Noncorporate Business-Sector Balance Sheet: 1990 to 2006

[In billions of dollars (3,712 represents $3,712,000,000,000), except as noted. Represents year-end outstandings]

Item	1990	1995	2000	2001	2002	2003	2004	2005	2006
Assets	3,712	4,092	6,434	6,712	7,020	7,473	8,242	9,221	10,056
Tangible assets	3,356	3,544	5,011	5,133	5,363	5,731	6,200	6,879	7,481
Real estate [1]	3,045	3,193	4,573	4,689	4,904	5,255	5,698	6,349	6,916
Residential	2,126	2,349	3,386	3,523	3,711	4,018	4,386	4,895	5,271
Nonresidential	919	845	1,187	1,166	1,193	1,237	1,312	1,454	1,645
Equipment and software [2]	263	294	367	377	390	405	424	447	478
Residential [3]	32	36	39	40	40	40	42	45	49
Nonresidential	232	259	329	338	350	365	382	402	428
Inventories [2]	47	56	70	67	69	71	78	83	87
Financial assets	356	548	1,423	1,579	1,657	1,742	2,042	2,343	2,575
Checkable deposits and currency	71	105	164	165	167	173	259	298	328
Time and savings deposits	51	71	248	255	269	314	318	366	402
Money market fund shares	7	17	49	59	61	53	62	71	78
Treasury securities	13	24	40	43	43	45	50	58	64
Municipal securities	–	2	2	4	3	3	4	5	6
Mortgages	31	22	23	27	26	26	31	35	39
Trade receivables	98	140	342	344	363	338	364	419	461
Miscellaneous assets	86	167	554	684	724	791	954	1,091	1,197
Insurance receivables	39	44	46	48	52	57	60	65	68
Equity investment in GSEs [4]	1	1	2	2	2	2	2	2	2
Other	47	122	506	634	670	732	891	1,024	1,128
Liabilities	1,349	1,396	2,674	2,890	3,084	3,173	3,517	3,897	4,233
Credit market instruments	1,093	1,062	1,796	1,959	2,107	2,199	2,443	2,748	3,036
Bank loans n.e.c. [5]	136	165	361	405	430	442	466	516	571
Other loans and advances	94	92	128	125	127	132	133	134	149
Mortgages	863	805	1,308	1,429	1,550	1,625	1,844	2,097	2,317
Trade payables	60	86	260	255	281	255	277	308	332
Taxes payable	32	33	65	69	70	70	78	85	90
Miscellaneous liabilities	164	215	553	607	626	649	718	756	775
Net worth	2,363	2,695	3,760	3,822	3,936	4,300	4,726	5,324	5,823
Debt/net worth (percent)	46.3	39.4	47.8	51.2	53.5	51.1	51.7	51.6	52.1

– Represents or rounds to zero. [1] At market value. [2] At replacement (current) cost. [3] Durable goods in rental properties. [4] GSEs = government-sponsored enterprises. Equity in the Farm Credit System. [5] Not elsewhere classified.

Source: Board of Governors of the Federal Reserve System, "Federal Reserve Statistical Release, Z.1, Flow of Funds Accounts of the United States"; published: 8 March 2007; <http://www.federalreserve.gov/releases/z1/20070308/>.

490 Business Enterprise

Table 728. Nonfinancial Corporate Business-Sector Balance Sheet: 1990 to 2006

[In billions of dollars (9,683 represents $9,683,000,000,000). Represents year-end outstandings]

Item	1990	1995	2000	2001	2002	2003	2004	2005	2006
Assets	9,683	11,460	19,016	19,125	19,474	20,065	21,668	23,056	24,621
Tangible assets	6,108	6,501	9,244	9,226	9,532	9,956	10,737	11,690	12,890
Real estate [1]	3,388	3,145	4,844	4,793	5,035	5,360	5,903	6,637	7,552
Equipment and software [2]	1,819	2,287	3,067	3,167	3,193	3,250	3,357	3,484	3,687
Inventories [2]	901	1,070	1,334	1,266	1,303	1,345	1,477	1,569	1,652
Financial assets [3]	3,575	4,959	9,772	9,899	9,942	10,109	10,932	11,366	11,731
Foreign deposits	15	17	24	16	21	38	54	71	72
Time and savings deposits	75	100	272	201	291	363	420	454	427
Money market fund shares	20	60	191	302	330	291	319	355	444
Commercial paper	14	20	58	60	65	76	95	111	123
Mortgages	53	58	44	47	50	52	67	81	96
Consumer credit	67	85	81	73	75	58	59	59	57
Trade receivables	967	1,185	1,939	1,818	1,720	1,702	1,831	1,989	2,077
Mutual fund shares [1]	10	46	122	113	95	125	140	156	182
Liabilities [3]	4,729	6,010	9,611	9,809	9,923	9,867	10,349	10,505	10,493
Credit market instruments	2,536	2,911	4,531	4,729	4,742	4,853	5,018	5,263	5,697
Commercial paper	117	157	278	178	120	85	102	94	117
Municipal securities [4]	115	135	154	158	161	164	169	177	182
Corporate bonds [5]	1,008	1,344	2,230	2,578	2,710	2,869	2,946	3,006	3,227
Bank loans n.e.c. [6]	545	602	853	744	636	561	563	624	690
Other loans and advances	473	454	649	653	665	667	684	723	742
Mortgages	277	220	366	419	450	507	554	639	740
Trade payables	626	878	1,541	1,438	1,457	1,403	1,500	1,643	1,702
Taxes payable	38	40	78	81	93	81	88	93	91
Net worth (market value)	4,954	5,450	9,405	9,316	9,551	10,197	11,319	12,551	14,128
Debt/net worth (percent)	51.2	53.4	48.2	50.8	49.6	47.6	44.3	41.9	40.3

[1] At market value. [2] At replacement (current) cost. [3] Includes items not shown separately. [4] Industrial revenue bonds. Issued by state and local governments to finance private investment and secured in interest and principal by the industrial user of the funds. [5] Through 1992, corporate bonds include net issues by Netherlands Antillean financial subsidiaries. [6] Not elsewhere classified.

Source: Board of Governors of the Federal Reserve System, "Federal Reserve Statistical Release, Z.1, Flow of Funds Accounts of the United States"; published: 8 March 2007; <http://www.federalreserve.gov/releases/z1/20070308/>.

Table 729. Corporate Funds—Sources and Uses: 1990 to 2006

[In billions of dollars (238 represents $238,000,000,000). Covers nonfarm nonfinancial corporate business]

Item	1990	1995	2000	2001	2002	2003	2004	2005	2006
Profits before tax (book)	238	419	422	310	336	424	623	931	1,089
– Taxes on corporate income	98	141	170	111	97	135	185	251	288
– Net dividends	117	177	250	243	253	291	365	226	396
+ Capital consumption allowance [1]	365	463	629	678	734	733	750	599	604
= U.S. internal funds, book	388	564	632	633	721	732	823	1,053	1,009
+ Foreign earnings retained abroad	45	53	100	111	93	113	108	-34	124
+ Inventory valuation adjustment (IVA)	-13	-18	-14	11	-2	-14	-40	-33	-45
= Internal funds + IVA	420	598	718	755	811	831	892	986	1,088
Gross investment	369	653	900	885	782	819	996	976	1,130
Capital expenditures	429	618	929	803	737	750	822	882	1,010
Fixed investment [2]	422	577	882	841	734	748	787	873	967
Inventory change + IVA	12	40	55	-30	14	13	47	20	43
Nonproduced nonfinancial assets	-5	1	-9	-9	-11	-11	-11	-11	1
Net financial investment	-59	36	-28	82	45	69	174	94	119
Net acquisition of financial assets [3]	124	426	1,209	178	130	83	783	415	302
Checkable deposits and currency	6	4	15	-65	-35	52	-35	-23	-120
Time and savings deposits	-6	3	35	9	10	71	58	34	-27
Money market fund shares	9	23	37	111	28	-39	28	36	89
Commercial paper	(-Z)	1	10	2	5	11	19	16	12
Municipal securities	-8	-20	7	-3	3	3	-4	-1	4
Trade receivables	29	78	282	-121	-98	-17	129	157	89
Mutual fund shares [3]	-1	5	4	4	1	11	2	7	7
Miscellaneous assets [3]	114	320	819	253	192	-10	555	143	238
U.S. direct investment abroad [4]	36	90	128	119	130	123	220	-8	187
Insurance receivables	13	8	(-Z)	10	17	18	19	21	11
Net increase in liabilities [3]	184	391	1,237	95	85	13	609	320	183
Net funds raised in markets	73	169	224	167	-29	47	39	-118	-165
Net new equity issues	-63	-58	-118	-48	-42	-42	-127	-363	-602
Credit market instruments [3]	136	227	342	215	13	89	165	245	437
Commercial paper	10	18	48	-83	-58	-35	17	-8	23
Municipal securities [5]	(-Z)	3	1	3	3	3	5	7	5
Corporate bonds [4]	47	91	163	348	132	158	78	60	220
Bank loans n.e.c. [6]	3	75	44	-110	-108	-86	2	61	66
Other loans and advances [3]	56	32	64	4	12	2	17	39	22
Finance companies	16	24	55	-14	3	-2	9	25	17
Mortgages	22	8	22	53	32	46	47	86	100
Trade payables	28	81	313	-104	20	25	97	143	56
Miscellaneous liabilities [3]	82	141	694	29	82	33	466	291	295
Foreign direct investment in U.S.	59	54	192	85	28	24	29	43	108

Z Less than $500 million. [1] Consumption of fixed capital plus capital consumption adjustment. [2] Nonresidential fixed investment plus residential fixed investment. [3] Includes other items not shown separately. [4] 1990, corporate bonds include net issues by Netherlands Antillean financial subsidiaries, and U.S. direct investment abroad excludes net inflows from these bond issues. [5] Industrial revenue bonds. Issued by state and local governments to finance private investment and secured in interest and principal by industrial user of the funds. [6] Not elsewhere classified.

Source: Board of Governors of the Federal Reserve System, "Federal Reserve Statistical Release, Z.1, Flow of Funds Accounts of the United States"; published: 8 March 2007; <http://www.federalreserve.gov/releases/z1/20070308/>.

Business Enterprise 491

Table 730. Corporations—Selected Financial Items: 1990 to 2004

[In billions of dollars (18,190 represents $18,190,000,000,000), except as noted. Covers active corporations only. All corporations are required to file returns except those specifically exempt. See source for changes in law affecting comparability of historical data. Based on samples; see Appendix III]

Item	1990	1995	1998	1999	2000	2001	2002	2003	2004
Number of returns (1,000)	3,717	4,474	4,849	4,936	5,045	5,136	5,267	5,401	5,558
Number with net income (1,000)	1,911	2,455	2,761	2,812	2,819	2,822	2,801	2,932	3,116
S Corporation returns [1] (1,000)	1,575	2,153	2,588	2,726	2,860	2,986	3,154	3,342	3,518
Assets [2]	18,190	26,014	37,347	41,464	47,027	49,154	50,414	53,645	60,118
Cash	771	962	1,336	1,597	1,820	1,926	1,923	2,120	2,730
Notes and accounts receivable	4,198	5,307	7,062	7,745	8,754	8,756	8,886	8,995	10,691
Inventories	894	1,045	1,139	1,198	1,272	1,208	1,221	1,267	1,386
Investments in government obligations	921	1,363	1,366	1,340	1,236	1,392	1,527	1,656	1,571
Mortgage and real estate	1,538	1,713	2,414	2,555	2,822	3,229	3,687	4,073	4,627
Other investments	4,137	7,429	13,201	15,799	17,874	18,344	18,728	20,536	22,657
Depreciable assets	4,318	5,571	6,541	6,936	7,292	7,614	7,678	7,805	7,974
Depletable assets	129	154	193	184	191	199	226	237	270
Land	210	242	271	286	303	320	326	342	363
Liabilities [2]	18,190	26,014	37,347	41,464	47,027	49,154	50,414	53,645	60,118
Accounts payable	1,094	1,750	2,501	2,792	3,758	3,927	4,074	4,338	5,645
Short-term debt [3]	1,803	2,034	3,216	3,658	4,020	4,132	3,814	4,002	4,399
Long-term debt [4]	2,665	3,335	4,813	5,448	6,184	6,782	7,185	7,384	8,154
Net worth	4,739	8,132	13,108	15,363	17,349	17,615	17,545	18,819	20,814
Capital stock	1,585	2,194	3,244	3,522	3,966	4,253	4,000	3,151	2,308
Paid-in or capital surplus	2,814	5,446	8,610	10,186	12,265	13,920	15,287	15,258	16,160
Retained earnings [5]	1,410	2,191	3,373	3,373	3,627	2,132	1,111	2,282	3,278
Receipts [2,6]	11,410	14,539	17,324	18,892	20,606	20,273	19,749	20,690	22,712
Business receipts [6,7]	9,860	12,786	15,010	16,314	17,637	17,504	17,297	18,264	19,976
Interest [8]	977	1,039	1,277	1,354	1,628	1,549	1,282	1,182	1,368
Rents and royalties	133	145	200	223	254	251	252	270	274
Deductions [2,6]	11,033	13,821	16,489	17,967	19,692	19,683	19,199	19,941	21,636
Cost of sales and operations [7]	6,611	8,206	9,362	10,284	11,135	11,042	10,607	11,319	12,498
Compensation of officers	205	304	357	374	401	383	381	389	417
Rent paid on business property	185	232	308	347	380	398	411	407	420
Taxes paid	251	326	355	371	390	392	397	417	447
Interest paid	825	744	967	1,019	1,272	1,203	913	818	939
Depreciation	333	437	542	584	614	650	711	692	691
Advertising	126	163	198	216	234	220	218	225	239
Net income (less loss) [6,9]	371	714	838	929	928	604	564	780	1,112
Net income	553	881	1,091	1,229	1,337	1,112	1,053	1,176	1,456
Deficit	182	166	253	300	409	509	489	396	344
Income subject to tax	366	565	663	694	760	635	601	699	857
Income tax before credits [10]	119	194	231	242	266	221	210	244	300
Tax credits	32	42	50	49	62	54	56	66	75
Foreign tax credit	25	30	37	38	49	41	42	50	57
Income tax after credits [11]	96	156	182	193	204	167	154	178	224

[1] Represents certain small corporations with up to 75 shareholders (35 for 1990 and 1995), mostly individuals, electing to be taxed at the shareholder level. [2] Includes items not shown separately. [3] Payable in less than 1 year. [4] Payable in 1 year or more. [5] Appropriated and unappropriated and "adjustments to shareholders' equity." [6] Receipts, deductions and net income of S corporations are limited to those from trade or business. Those from investments are excluded. [7] Includes gross sales and cost of sales of securities, commodities, and real estate by exchanges, brokers, or dealers selling on their own accounts. Excludes investment income. [8] Includes tax-exempt interest in state and local government obligations. [9] Excludes regulated investment companies. [10] Consists of regular (and alternative tax) only. [11] Includes minimum tax, alternative minimum tax, adjustments for prior year credits, and other income-related taxes.

Source: U.S. Internal Revenue Service, Statistics of Income, Corporation Income Tax Returns, annual.

Table 731. **Corporations by Receipt-Size Class and Industry: 2004**

[Number of returns in thousands (5,558 represents 5,558,000); receipts and net income in billions of dollars (21,717 represents $21,717,000,000,000). Covers active enterprises only. Figures are estimates based on a sample of unaudited tax returns; see Appendix III. Numbers in parentheses represent North American Industry Classification System 2002 codes, see text, this section]

Industry	Total	Under $1 mil.[1]	$1 mil.–$4.9 mil.	$5 mil.–$9.9 mil.	$10 mil.–$49.9 mil.	$50 mil. or more
Total: [2]						
Number of returns [3]	5,558	4,535	762	121	111	30
Business receipts [3]	21,717	929	1,618	941	2,271	16,057
Net income (less loss)	1,112	11	48	26	93	934
Agriculture, forestry, fishing, and hunting (11):						
Number	142	126	13	2	1	–
Business receipts [3]	125	21	27	13	19	45
Mining (21):						
Number	31	25	4	1	1	–
Business receipts [3]	213	4	10	5	16	177
Utilities (22):						
Number	7	6	1	–	–	–
Business receipts [3]	526	1	1	1	3	521
Construction (23):						
Number	722	558	126	20	16	2
Business receipts [3]	1,240	137	269	140	297	397
Manufacturing (31–33):						
Number	281	173	68	16	17	6
Business receipts [3]	5,893	46	156	115	361	5,216
Wholesale and retail trade (42,44–45):						
Number	1,001	687	218	40	44	12
Business receipts [3]	6,167	182	491	283	943	4,269
Transportation and warehousing (48–49):						
Number	183	147	26	5	4	1
Business receipts [3]	599	27	56	32	79	405
Information (51):						
Number	124	106	12	2	3	1
Business receipts [3]	864	16	27	15	53	754
Finance and insurance (52):						
Number	239	196	28	5	6	3
Business receipts [3]	2,873	36	62	38	137	2,599
Real estate and rental and leasing (53):						
Number	604	577	22	2	2	–
Business receipts [3]	223	55	47	15	32	74
Professional, scientific, and technical services (54):						
Number	780	691	72	9	6	1
Business receipts [3]	722	116	138	62	114	291
Management of companies & enterprises (55):						
Number	50	43	3	1	2	–
Business receipts [3]	729	1	7	10	36	675
Administrative and support and waste management and remediation services (56):						
Number	246	206	33	4	2	1
Business receipts [3]	398	43	68	27	45	215
Educational services (61):						
Number	44	41	3	–	–	–
Business receipts [3]	32	6	6	1	5	14
Health care and social assistance (62):						
Number	370	302	57	5	5	1
Business receipts [3]	492	92	113	37	79	171
Arts, entertainment, and recreation (71):						
Number	119	108	9	1	1	1
Business receipts [3]	75	16	20	5	9	25
Accommodation and food services (72):						
Number	281	233	42	4	1	–
Business receipts [3]	376	67	77	26	27	179
Other services (81):						
Number	333	304	25	2	1	–
Business receipts [3]	169	63	43	16	19	29

– Represents or rounds to zero.   [1] Includes businesses without receipts.   [2] Includes businesses not allocable to individual industries.   [3] Includes investment income for corporations in finance and insurance and management of companies' industries. Excludes investment income for S corporations (certain small corporations with up to 75 shareholders, mostly individuals, electing to be taxed at the shareholder level).

Source: U.S. Internal Revenue Service, *Statistics of Income, Corporation Income Tax Returns,* annual.

Business Enterprise   **493**

Table 732. **Corporations by Asset-Size Class and Industry: 2004**

[In **billions of dollars** (137 represents $137,000,000,000), **except number of returns.** Covers active corporations only. Excludes corporations not allocable by industry. Numbers in parentheses represent North American Industry Classification System 2002 codes. See text, this section]

Industry	Total	Under $10 mil. [1]	$10– $24.9 mil.	$25– $49.9 mil.	$50– $99.9 mil.	$100– $249.9 mil.	$250 mil. and over
Agriculture, forestry, fishing, and hunting (11):							
Returns.	141,553	140,581	623	184	86	53	25
Total receipts	137	79	12	9	7	10	20
Mining (21):							
Returns.	30,909	29,687	555	251	136	106	174
Total receipts	233	28	7	6	7	10	174
Utilities (22):							
Returns.	7,096	6,702	104	59	30	48	152
Total receipts	569	7	3	2	4	6	549
Construction (23):							
Returns.	721,803	715,171	4,612	1,155	499	219	148
Total receipts	1,263	756	132	70	57	47	201
Manufacturing (31–33):							
Returns.	281,448	266,865	7,190	2,865	1,681	1,267	1,579
Total receipts	6,357	517	200	160	171	258	5,050
Wholesale and retail trade (42, 44–45):							
Returns.	1,001,211	983,364	11,635	3,246	1,380	771	816
Total receipts	6,309	1,882	582	337	257	279	2,972
Transportation and warehousing (48–49):							
Returns.	182,614	180,903	960	313	160	135	143
Total receipts	623	182	30	18	16	27	349
Information (51):							
Returns.	123,862	121,100	1,246	539	309	263	406
Total receipts	993	95	21	17	17	29	815
Finance and insurance (52):							
Returns.	239,011	219,963	3,515	2,531	2,717	3,580	6,704
Total receipts	2,873	188	27	26	29	66	2,536
Real estate and rental and leasing (53):							
Returns.	603,789	597,993	3,891	1,068	439	235	162
Total receipts	254	140	17	11	8	9	68
Professional, scientific, and technical services (54):							
Returns.	779,510	775,853	1,897	885	366	282	227
Total receipts	754	438	47	30	26	41	170
Management of companies and enterprises (55):							
Returns.	49,800	43,154	1,129	1,011	1,315	1,630	1,560
Total receipts	729	30	2	2	6	15	674
Administrative and support and waste management and remediation services (56):							
Returns.	245,725	244,656	551	213	110	93	101
Total receipts	416	198	25	15	17	19	142
Educational services (61):							
Returns.	43,956	43,801	72	28	21	19	14
Total receipts	33	17	2	1	1	3	9
Health care and social assistance (62):							
Returns.	370,384	369,332	552	210	109	98	82
Total receipts	506	336	18	14	12	17	109
Arts, entertainment, and recreation (71):							
Returns.	118,854	118,175	401	143	49	52	34
Total receipts	83	48	5	3	3	6	17
Accommodation and food services (72):							
Returns.	280,517	279,223	740	236	101	92	124
Total receipts	405	188	15	11	10	20	161
Other services (81):							
Returns.	332,662	332,187	307	72	40	30	26
Total receipts	174	138	7	3	4	5	17

[1] Includes returns with zero assets.

Source: U.S. Internal Revenue Service, *Statistics of Income, Corporation Income Tax Returns*, annual.

494 Business Enterprise

Table 733. **Economic Census Summary (NAICS 1997 Basis): 1997 and 2002**

[25 represents 25,000. Covers establishments with payroll. Data are based on the 1997 and 2002 economic censuses which are subject to nonsampling error. Data for the construction sector are also subject to sampling errors. For details on survey methodology and nonsampling and sampling errors, see Appendix III]

Kind of business	NAICS code [1]	Establishments (1,000)		Sales, receipts or shipments (bil. dol.)		Annual payroll (bil. dol.)		Paid employees [2] (1,000)	
		1997	2002	1997	2002	1997	2002	1997	2002
Mining	21	25	24	174	184	20.8	21.6	509	488
Oil & gas extraction	211	8	8	103	113	5.5	5.3	111	99
Mining (except oil & gas)	212	7	7	51	47	9.4	8.9	229	195
Mining support activities	213	9	9	20	24	5.9	7.3	169	194
Utilities	22	16	17	412	399	36.6	42.4	703	663
Construction	23	656	709	859	1,207	174.2	253.6	5,665	7,174
Manufacturing	31–33	363	351	3,835	3,915	569.8	575.2	16,805	14,664
Wholesale trade	42	453	439	4,060	4,637	214.9	260.2	5,797	5,903
Wholesale trade, durable goods	421	291	286	2,180	2,460	133.2	164.1	3,398	3,530
Wholesale trade, nondurable goods	422	163	153	1,880	2,178	81.7	96.1	2,398	2,373
Retail trade	44–45	1,118	1,111	2,461	3,054	237.2	301.5	13,991	14,623
Motor vehicle & parts dealers	441	123	121	645	799	50.2	64.0	1,719	1,821
Furniture & home furnishings stores	442	65	65	72	92	10.0	12.8	483	535
Electronics & appliance stores	443	43	47	69	82	7.1	9.3	345	391
Bldg. material & garden equipment & supplies dealers	444	(NA)	88	(NA)	247	(NA)	30.1	(NA)	1,160
Food & beverage stores	445	149	149	402	457	40.6	48.7	2,893	2,839
Health & personal care stores	446	83	82	118	178	15.2	20.3	904	1,024
Gasoline stations	447	127	121	198	249	11.5	13.7	922	927
Clothing & clothing accessories stores	448	157	150	136	168	16.6	21.4	1,280	1,427
Sporting goods, hobby, book, & music stores	451	69	62	62	73	7.1	8.7	561	611
General merchandise stores	452	36	41	330	445	30.9	42.6	2,508	2,525
Miscellaneous store retailers	453	130	129	78	91	10.2	12.8	753	792
Nonstore retailers	454	44	55	113	173	12.3	17.1	506	571
Transportation & warehousing [3]	48–49	178	200	318	382	82.3	116.0	2,921	3,651
Information [3]	51	114	138	623	898	129.5	195.4	3,066	3,749
Publishing industries	511	34	33	179	247	43.4	67.2	1,006	1,114
Motion picture & sound recording industries	512	22	22	56	78	9.4	12.7	276	304
Broadcasting & telecommunications	513	43	59	346	490	63.5	86.9	1,434	1,737
Information & data processing services	514	15	23	42	83	13.3	28.6	350	594
Finance & insurance [4]	52	395	440	2,198	2,804	264.6	377.8	5,835	6,579
Real estate & rental & leasing [4]	53	288	323	241	336	41.6	60.2	1,702	1,949
Professional, scientific, & technical services [3]	54	621	740	595	868	231.4	369.6	5,361	6,978
Management of companies & enterprises	55	47	49	92	108	154.2	179.2	2,618	2,608
Admin/support waste management/remediation services [3]	56	276	273	296	397	137.3	194.9	7,347	8,261
Administrative & support services [3]	561	260	255	257	346	128.4	182.6	7,067	7,929
Waste management & remediation services [3]	562	16	19	39	51	8.9	12.2	281	332
Educational services [3]	61	41	49	20	31	6.4	10.2	321	430
Health care and social assistance	62	646	709	885	1,211	378.2	497.4	13,562	15,144
Ambulatory health care services	621	455	489	355	489	155.9	203.4	4,414	4,925
Hospitals	622	7	6	379	500	155.8	197.2	4,933	5,174
Nursing & residential care facilities	623	57	69	93	127	42.2	59.0	2,471	2,831
Social assistance	624	126	144	57	95	24.4	37.9	1,744	2,213
Arts, entertainment, & recreation	71	99	110	105	142	32.8	45.2	1,588	1,849
Performance arts, spectator sports, & related industries	711	31	38	38	58	14.5	21.2	327	423
Museums, historical sites, & like institutions	712	6	7	7	9	1.8	2.9	92	123
Amusement, gambling, & recreation industries	713	63	66	58	75	20.8	21.0	1,146	1,303
Accommodation & food services	72	545	566	350	449	97.0	127.6	9,451	10,121
Accommodation	721	58	61	98	128	26.7	35.0	1,697	1,813
Food services & drinking places	722	487	505	252	321	70.3	92.6	7,755	8,308
Other services (except public administration) [3]	81	520	525	266	302	65.5	81.0	3,256	3,352
Repair & maintenance [3]	811	235	231	105	118	29.9	35.1	1,276	1,286
Personal and laundry services [3]	812	185	193	58	71	18.6	22.4	1,217	1,263
Religious/grantmaking/prof/like organizations	813	99	101	103	113	17.1	23.4	763	803

NA Not available. [1] Based on North American Industry Classification System, 1997; see text this section. [2] For pay period including March 12. [3] Enterprise support establishments are included in the 2002 data but not in the 1997 data affecting comparability for this industry. [4] For detailed industries, see Table 1133.

Source: U.S. Census Bureau, "2002 Economic Census, Comparative Statistics for United States, Summary Statistics by 1997 NAICS"; published 31 July 2006; <http://www.census.gov/econ/census02/data/comparative/USCS.HTM>.

Table 734. **Nonemployer Establishments and Receipts by Industry: 2000 to 2004**

[Establishments: 16,530 represents 16,530,000. Includes only firms subject to federal income tax. Nonemployers are businesses with no paid employees. Data originate chiefly from administrative records of the Internal Revenue Service; see Appendix III. Data for 2000 based on the North American Industry Classification System (NAICS), 1997; beginning 2003 based on NAICS 2002, see text, this section]

Kind of business	NAICS code	Establishments (1,000)			Receipts (mil. dol.)		
		2000	2003	2004	2000	2003	2004
All industries	(X)	16,530	18,649	19,524	709,379	829,819	887,002
Forestry, fishing & hunting, & ag support services	113–115	223	226	231	9,196	9,558	10,180
Mining	21	86	88	91	5,227	6,278	7,025
Utilities	22	14	14	16	504	600	653
Construction	23	2,014	2,239	2,392	107,538	126,479	140,052
Manufacturing	31–33	285	300	303	13,022	14,105	14,748
Wholesale trade.	42	388	376	384	31,684	31,400	33,227
Retail trade	44–45	1,743	1,880	1,893	73,810	80,548	82,916
Transportation & warehousing.	48–49	747	859	916	37,824	44,953	51,537
Information	51	238	260	283	7,620	8,518	9,470
Finance & insurance	52	692	695	718	49,058	47,345	44,032
Real estate & rental & leasing.	53	1,696	2,046	2,218	133,398	176,079	189,905
Professional, scientific, & technical services .	54	2,420	2,648	2,725	90,272	102,911	110,596
Admin/support waste mgt/ remediation services	56	1,032	1,294	1,337	23,754	28,885	30,932
Educational services	61	283	374	410	3,736	5,002	5,588
Health care & social assistance.	62	1,317	1,543	1,609	36,550	45,500	47,883
Arts, entertainment, & recreation	71	782	888	923	11,201	21,010	22,448
Accommodation & food services	72	218	260	275	13,418	15,271	15,510
Other services (except public administration).	81	2,350	2,660	2,800	55,056	65,377	70,299

X Not applicable.

Source: U.S. Census Bureau, "Nonemployer Statistics"; <http://www.census.gov/epcd/nonemployer/>.

Table 735. **Establishments, Employees, and Payroll by Employment-Size Class: 1990 to 2004**

[6,176 represents 6,176,000. Excludes most government employees, railroad employees, self-employed persons. Employees are for the week including March 12. Covers establishments with payroll. An *establishment* is a single physical location where business is conducted or where services or industrial operations are performed. For statement on methodology, see Appendix III]

Employment-size class	Unit	1990	1995	1999	2000	2001	2002	2003	2004
Establishments, total	1,000 . .	6,176	6,613	7,008	7,070	7,095	7,201	7,255	7,388
Under 20 employees.	1,000 . .	5,354	5,733	6,036	6,069	6,083	6,199	6,240	6,359
20 to 99 employees	1,000 . .	684	730	802	826	836	835	845	856
100 to 499 employees	1,000 . .	122	135	152	157	157	149	151	154
500 to 999 employees.	1,000 . .	10	10	12	12	12	11	11	12
1,000 or more employees	1,000 . .	6	6	7	7	7	7	7	7
Employees, total	1,000 . .	93,476	100,335	110,706	114,065	115,061	112,401	113,398	115,075
Under 20 employees.	1,000 . .	24,373	25,785	27,289	27,569	27,681	28,116	28,313	28,701
20 to 99 employees	1,000 . .	27,414	29,202	32,193	33,147	33,555	33,335	33,760	34,288
100 to 499 employees	1,000 . .	22,926	25,364	28,707	29,736	29,692	28,101	28,549	28,976
500 to 999 employees.	1,000 . .	6,551	7,021	7,923	8,291	8,357	7,743	7,638	7,815
1,000 or more employees	1,000 . .	12,212	12,962	14,594	15,322	15,776	15,105	15,138	15,295
Annual payroll, total	Bil. dol..	2,104	2,666	3,555	3,879	3,989	3,943	4,041	4,254
Under 20 employees.	Bil. dol. .	485	608	773	818	839	866	885	926
20 to 99 employees	Bil. dol. .	547	696	925	1,006	1,037	1,041	1,068	1,124
100 to 499 employees	Bil. dol. .	518	675	931	1,031	1,052	1,021	1,054	1,106
500 to 999 employees.	Bil. dol. .	174	219	298	336	342	329	334	355
1,000 or more employees	Bil. dol. .	381	467	628	690	719	685	700	743

Source: U.S. Census Bureau, "County Business Patterns"; see <http://www.census.gov/epcd/cbp/view/cbpview.html>.

Table 736. **Establishments, Employees, and Payroll by Employment-Size Class and Industry: 2000 to 2004**

[Establishments and employees in thousands (7,070.0 represents 7,070,000); payroll in billions of dollars. See headnote, Table 735. Data for 2000 based on the North American Industry Classification System (NAICS), 1997; beginning 2003, data based on NAICS 2002. See text, this section]

Industry	NAICS code	2000, total	2003, total	2004 Total	Under 20 employ- ees	20 to 99 employ- ees	100 to 499 employ- ees	500 to 999 employ- ees	1,000 or more employ- ees
Establishments, total [1].......	(X)	**7,070.0**	**7,254.7**	**7,387.7**	**6,359.5**	**856.3**	**153.6**	**11.5**	**6.8**
Agriculture, forestry, fishing & hunting...	11	26.1	25.9	25.5	23.8	1.6	0.2	(Z)	(Z)
Mining	21	23.7	23.6	23.8	19.4	3.6	0.7	0.1	(Z)
Utilities....................	22	17.3	18.4	17.7	12.5	3.8	1.2	0.1	(Z)
Construction	23	709.6	732.2	760.4	693.0	59.7	7.2	0.4	0.1
Manufacturing	31–33	354.5	341.8	339.1	233.1	76.8	25.6	2.5	1.1
Wholesale trade	42	446.2	432.5	429.5	367.6	53.8	7.4	0.5	0.2
Retail trade	44–45	1,113.6	1,115.9	1,119 8	964.0	129.9	25.2	0.6	0.1
Transportation and warehousing	48–49	190.0	202.7	206.9	172.2	27.9	5.9	0.6	0.3
Information	51	133.6	140.0	139.7	112.2	21.2	5.3	0.6	0.3
Finance and insurance	52	423.7	460.6	470.6	423.1	39.2	6.9	0.9	0.6
Real estate and rental and leasing.....	53	300.2	333.6	348.7	333.0	13.9	1.6	0.1	(Z)
Professional, scientific, and technical services.....................	54	722.7	780.9	804.6	743.3	52.1	8.2	0.7	0.3
Management of companies and enterprises.....................	55	47.4	47.4	46.3	30.3	10.9	4.1	0.7	0.4
Admin/support waste mgt/remediation services.....................	56	351.5	348.7	358.9	298.8	44.0	14.2	1.1	0 7
Educational services	61	68.0	76.4	78.8	59.9	15.0	3.1	0.4	0.4
Health care and social assistance	62	658.6	716.4	731.9	621.1	86.9	20.4	1.7	1.9
Arts, entertainment, and recreation	71	103.8	114.0	118.8	99.8	16.0	2.8	0.2	0.1
Accommodation and food services.....	72	542.4	575.3	591.0	425.9	154.7	9.8	0.4	0.2
Other services [2]	81	723.3	732.0	734.5	685.4	45.1	3.8	0.1	0.1
Unclassified establishments	99	99.0	36.5	41.2	41.0	0.2	(Z)	–	–
Employees, total [1].........	**(X)**	**114,065**	**113,398**	**115,075**	**28,701**	**34,288**	**28,976**	**7,815**	**15,295**
Agriculture, forestry, fishing & hunting...	11	184	181	182	86	(NA)	(NA)	6	(NA)
Mining	21	456	455	470	91	(NA)	138	39	(NA)
Utilities....................	22	655	676	635	66	170	232	87	78
Construction	23	6,573	6,381	6,648	2,597	2,288	1,294	237	232
Manufacturing	31–33	16,474	14,132	13,822	1,350	3,361	5,148	1,682	2,281
Wholesale trade	42	6,112	5,864	5,907	1,773	2,093	1,384	309	347
Retail trade	44–45	14,841	14,868	15,351	5,117	5,269	4,541	343	82
Transportation and warehousing	48–49	3,790	4,068	4,099	712	1,157	1,125	382	722
Information	51	3,546	3,600	3,472	510	899	1,053	418	59^
Finance and insurance	52	5,963	6,464	6,481	1,876	1,513	1,378	646	1,06
Real estate and rental and leasing.....	53	1,942	2,045	2,086	1,125	523	(NA)	78	(NA)
Professional, scientific, and technical services.....................	54	6,816	7,340	7,570	2,560	2,010	1,570	440	991
Management of companies and enterprises.....................	55	2,874	2,879	2,825	169	485	889	449	831
Admin/support waste mgt/remediation services.....................	56	9,138	8,511	8,708	1,165	1,934	2,806	751	2,051
Educational services	61	2,532	2,777	2,893	288	629	603	278	1,095
Health care and social assistance	62	14,109	15,472	15,815	3,288	3,472	3,776	1,209	4,070
Arts, entertainment, and recreation	71	1,741	1,833	1,889	376	672	511	105	225
Accommodation and food services.....	72	9,881	10,440	10,750	2,589	5,960	1,543	266	392
Other services [2]	81	5,293	5,367	5,416	2,912	1,646	654	89	115
Unclassified establishments	99	144	46	55	50	(NA)	(NA)	–	–
Annual payroll, total [1].......	**(X)**	**3,879**	**4,041**	**4,254**	**926**	**1,124**	**1,106**	**355**	**743**
Agriculture, forestry, fishing & hunting...	11	5	5	5	2	(D)	(D)	(Z)	(D)
Mining	21	22	25	27	4	(D)	8	3	(D)
Utilities....................	22	41	45	45	4	11	17	7	7
Construction	23	240	253	268	91	96	60	11	10
Manufacturing	31–33	644	576	593	46	127	212	77	131
Wholesale trade	42	270	272	291	78	98	71	19	24
Retail trade	44–45	303	319	334	105	117	100	8	3
Transportation and warehousing	48–49	126	143	148	24	40	40	14	31
Information	51	209	204	200	26	47	63	24	40
Finance and insurance	52	347	393	422	94	100	98	45	86
Real estate and rental and leasing.....	53	59	69	74	36	20	(D)	3	(D)
Professional, scientific, and technical services.....................	54	362	398	427	120	120	103	29	55
Management of companies and enterprises.....................	55	211	212	222	15	36	69	35	68
Admin/support waste mgt/remediation services.....................	56	210	219	236	38	56	68	19	54
Educational services	61	62	75	80	6	15	17	6	36
Health care and social assistance	62	431	526	560	125	111	107	44	172
Arts, entertainment, and recreation	71	43	48	51	13	12	17	3	5
Accommodation and food services.....	72	126	139	147	35	71	24	6	11
Other services [2]	81	110	118	123	61	37	18	3	4
Unclassified establishments	99	4	1	1	1	(D)	(D)	–	–

– Represents zero.   D Data withheld to avoid disclosure.   NA Not available.   X Not applicable.   Z Less than 50 establishments or 500 million dollars.   [1] Totals for 2000 include auxiliaries. Beginning 2003, cases previously classified under NAICS code 95 (auxiliaries) are coded in the operating NAICS sector of the establishment.   [2] Except public administration.

Source: U.S. Census Bureau, "County Business Patterns"; see <http://www.census.gov/epcd/cbp/view/cbpview.html>.

Table 737. **Employer Firms, Establishments, Employment, and Annual Payroll by Enterprise Size: 1990 to 2004**

[In thousands except as noted (5,074 represents 5,074,000). Firms are an aggregation of all establishments owned by a parent company with some annual payroll. Establishments are locations with active payroll in any quarter. This table illustrates the changing importance of enterprise sizes over time, not job growth, as enterprises can grow or decline and change enterprise size cells over time]

Item		All industries—employment size of enterprise						
	Total	0 to 4 [1]	5 to 9	10 to 19	20 to 99	100 to 499	Less than 500	500 or more
Firms:								
1990	5,074	3,021	952	563	454	70	5,060	14
1995	5,369	3,250	981	577	470	76	5,354	15
1999	5,608	3,389	1,013	606	502	81	5,591	17
2000	5,653	3,397	1,021	617	516	84	5,635	17
2001	5,658	3,402	1,019	616	518	85	5,640	17
2002	5,698	3,466	1,011	614	508	82	5,681	17
2003	5,767	3,504	1,025	620	515	85	5,750	17
2004	5,886	3,580	1,043	633	526	87	5,869	17
Establishments:								
1990	6,176	3,032	971	600	590	255	5,448	728
1995	6,613	3,260	998	618	639	284	5,799	814
1999	7,008	3,398	1,027	643	671	309	6,048	960
2000	7,070	3,406	1,035	652	674	312	6,080	990
2001	7,095	3,410	1,034	650	670	316	6,080	1,015
2002	7,201	3,471	1,024	653	693	333	6,173	1,028
2003	7,255	3,510	1,038	655	687	331	6,222	1,033
2004	7,388	3,586	1,056	667	693	330	6,331	1,056
Employment:								
1990	93,469	5,117	6,252	7,543	17,710	13,545	50,167	43,302
1995	100,315	5,395	6,440	7,734	18,422	14,660	52,653	47,662
1999	110,706	5,606	6,652	8,130	19,703	15,638	55,729	54,977
2000	114,065	5,593	6,709	8,286	20,277	16,260	57,124	56,941
2001	115,061	5,630	6,698	8,275	20,370	16,410	57,383	57,678
2002	112,401	5,698	6,640	8,246	19,874	15,909	56,366	56,034
2003	113,398	5,768	6,732	8,330	20,187	16,430	57,448	55,950
2004	115,075	5,845	6,853	8,500	20,643	16,758	58,597	56,477
Annual payroll (bil. dol.):								
1990	2,104	117	114	144	352	279	1,007	1,097
1995	2,666	142	137	175	437	361	1,252	1,414
1999	3,555	177	167	218	565	475	1,601	1,954
2000	3,879	186	174	231	608	528	1,727	2,152
2001	3,989	188	179	237	624	539	1,768	2,222
2002	3,943	194	182	241	624	536	1,777	2,166
2003	4,041	197	187	247	635	552	1,818	2,222
2004	4,254	206	196	258	670	588	1,917	2,337

[1] Employment is measured in March, thus some firms (start-ups after March, closures before March, and seasonal firms) will have zero employment and some annual payroll.

Source: U.S. Small Business Administration, Office of Advocacy, "Statistics of U.S. Businesses"; <http://www.sba.gov/advo/research/data.html>; accessed 20 March 2007.

Table 738. **Firm Births and Deaths by Employment Size of Enterprise: 1990 to 2004**

[In thousands (541.1 represents 541,100). Data represent activity from March of the beginning year to March of the ending year. Establishments with no employment in the first quarter of the beginning year were excluded. This table provides the number of births and deaths of initial establishments (based on Census ID) as an approximation of firm births and deaths]

Item	Births (initial locations)				Deaths (initial locations)			
	Total	Less than 20 employees	Less than 500 employees	500 employees or more	Total	Less than 20 employees	Less than 500 employees	500 employees or more
Firms:								
1990 to 1991	541.1	515.9	540.9	0.3	546.5	517.0	546.1	0.4
1995 to 1996	597.8	572.4	597.5	0.3	512.4	485.5	512.0	0.4
1998 to 1999	579.6	554.3	579.3	0.3	544.5	514.3	544.0	0.4
1999 to 2000	574.3	548.0	574.0	0.3	542.8	514.2	542.4	0.5
2000 to 2001	585.1	558.0	584.8	0.3	553.3	524.0	552.8	0.5
2001 to 2002 [1]	569.8	541.5	568.3	1.5	586.9	557.1	586.5	0.4
2002 to 2003	612.3	585.6	612.0	0.3	540.7	514.6	540.3	0.3
2003 to 2004	628.9	601.9	628.7	0.3	541.0	515.0	540.7	0.3
Employment:								
1990 to 1991	3,105	1,713	2,907	198	3,208	1,723	3,044	164
1995 to 1996	3,256	1,845	3,056	200	3,100	1,560	2,808	291
1998 to 1999	3,225	1,670	2,991	235	3,180	1,645	2,969	210
1999 to 2000	3,229	1,793	3,031	198	3,177	1,654	2,946	230
2000 to 2001	3,418	1,821	3,109	310	3,262	1,701	3,050	212
2001 to 2002	3,370	1,748	3,034	336	3,660	1,755	3,257	403
2002 to 2003	3,667	1,856	3,174	493	3,324	1,608	2,880	445
2003 to 2004	3,575	1,889	3,241	334	3,221	1,615	2,868	353

[1] A change in methodology ("based on Census ID" rather than "plant number") has affected the allocation of firms by employment size.

Source: U.S. Small Business Administration, Office of Advocacy, "Firm Size Data, Statistics of U.S. Businesses and Nonemployer Statistics"; <http://www.sba.gov/advo/research/data.html>; accessed 6 April 2007.

Table 739. **Employer Firms, Employment, and Annual Payroll by Enterprise Size and Industry: 2004**

[5,886 represents 5,886,000. A firm is an aggregation of all establishments owned by a parent company (within a geographic location and/or industry) with some annual payroll. A firm may be a single location or it can include multiple locations. Employment is measured in March and payroll is annual leading to some firms with zero employment. Numbers in parentheses represent North American Industry Classification System codes, 2002; see text, this section]

Industry and data type	Unit		All industries—employment size of enterprise							
		Total	0	1 to 4	5 to 9	10 to 19	20 to 99	100 to 499	Less than 500	500 or more
Total [1]:										
Firms	1,000. . .	5,886	802	2,778	1,043	633	526	87	5,869	17
Employment	1,000. . .	115,075	–	5,845	6,853	8,500	20,643	16,758	58,597	56,477
Annual payroll	Bil. dol. .	4,254	40	166	196	258	670	588	1,917	2,337
Construction (23):										
Firms	1,000. . .	751	128	361	125	73	56	6	750	1
Employment	1,000. . .	6,648	–	755	820	980	2,097	1,094	5,746	902
Annual payroll	Bil. dol. .	268	5	22	26	35	85	49	223	46
Manufacturing (31–33):										
Firms	1,000. . .	293	21	95	54	46	58	14	289	4
Employment	1,000. . .	13,822	–	215	364	634	2,369	2,499	6,080	7,741
Annual payroll	Bil. dol. .	593	2	6	11	21	86	97	223	370
Wholesale trade (42):										
Firms	1,000. . .	338	35	155	59	40	38	8	335	3
Employment	1,000. . .	5,907	–	324	389	540	1,391	994	3,637	2,270
Annual payroll	Bil. dol. .	291	2	12	15	23	61	46	159	132
Retail trade (44–45):										
Firms	1,000. . .	735	85	342	151	85	61	9	733	2
Employment	1,000. . .	15,351	–	768	989	1,124	2,264	1,327	6,472	8,880
Annual payroll	Bil. dol. .	334	3	14	19	24	62	39	161	173
Transportation & warehousing (48–49):										
Firms	1,000. . .	165	25	80	23	16	15	3	163	2
Employment	1,000. . .	4,099	–	154	153	215	570	479	1,571	2,528
Annual payroll	Bil. dol. .	148	1	4	4	6	18	16	49	99
Information (51):										
Firms	1,000. . .	75	12	32	11	8	8	2	74	1
Employment	1,000. . .	3,472	–	65	75	111	328	329	909	2,564
Annual payroll	Bil. dol. .	200	1	3	3	5	16	18	46	155
Finance & insurance (52):										
Firms	1,000. . .	252	31	145	37	17	16	4	250	2
Employment	1,000. . .	6,481	–	297	235	229	643	705	2,108	4,374
Annual payroll	Bil. dol. .	422	2	11	11	13	37	43	116	306
Professional, scientific & technical services (54):										
Firms	1,000. . .	735	119	409	103	56	39	7	732	3
Employment	1,000. . .	7,570	–	787	670	744	1,428	1,030	4,661	2,909
Annual payroll	Bil. dol. .	427	6	30	28	36	82	63	246	181
Management of companies & enterprises (55):										
Firms	1,000. . .	27	1	3	1	1	6	8	20	7
Employment	1,000. . .	2,825	–	5	4	7	71	255	343	2,482
Annual payroll	Bil. dol. .	222	(Z)	(Z)	(Z)	(Z)	4	15	20	202
Admin/support waste mgt/ remediation services (56):										
Firms	1,000. . .	310	57	138	47	29	28	8	307	3
Employment	1,000. . .	8,708	–	287	308	388	1,109	1,490	3,583	5,125
Annual payroll	Bil. dol. .	236	3	8	8	11	31	36	96	139
Educational services (61):										
Firms	1,000. . .	71	9	25	11	9	13	3	70	1
Employment	1,000. . .	2,893	–	53	72	122	534	548	1,330	1,564
Annual payroll	Bil. dol. .	80	(Z)	1	1	2	12	15	33	47
Health care and social assistance (62):										
Firms	1,000. . .	588	52	245	137	78	57	15	584	4
Employment	1,000. . .	15,815	–	551	904	1,038	2,255	2,918	7,666	8,149
Annual payroll	Bil. dol. .	560	4	22	33	39	78	82	257	303
Accommodation & food services (72):										
Firms	1,000. . .	453	67	131	88	77	80	9	452	2
Employment	1,000. . .	10,750	–	311	590	1,051	3,027	1,589	6,568	4,182
Annual payroll	Bil. dol. .	147	3	4	6	11	36	20	81	66
Other services (except public administration) (81):										
Firms	1,000. . .	671	58	363	136	67	41	4	670	1
Employment	1,000. . .	5,416	–	787	883	884	1,480	637	4,673	744
Annual payroll	Bil. dol. .	123	1	15	17	19	32	17	101	21

– Represents zero.   Z Less than $500 million.   [1] Includes other industries not shown separately.

Source: U.S. Small Business Administration, Office of Advocacy, "Statistics of U.S. Businesses"; <http://www.sba.gov/advo/research/data.html>; accessed 20 March 2007.

Business Enterprise   499

Table 740. **Employer Firms, Employment, and Payroll by Employment Size of Enterprise and State: 2000 and 2004**

[5,652.5 represents 5,652,500. A firm is an aggregation of all establishments owned by a parent company (within a state) with some annual payroll. A firm may be a single location or it can include multiple locations. Employment is measured in March and payroll is annual leading to some firms with zero employment]

State	Employer firms (1,000)					Employment, 2004 (mil.)			Annual payroll, 2004 (bil. dol.)		
	2000		2004								
	Total	Less than 20 employees	Total	Less than 20 employees	Less than 500 employees	Total	Less than 20 employees	Less than 500 employees	Total	Less than 20 employees	Less than 500 employees
U.S....	5,652.5	5,035.0	5,885.8	5,255.8	5,868.7	115.1	21.2	58.6	4,254.0	659.3	1,917.4
AL	79.9	68.2	79.4	67.6	77.3	1.6	0.3	0.8	49.8	7.7	22.6
AK	15.9	14.0	16.5	14.5	16.0	0.2	0.1	0.1	9.1	2.1	4.9
AZ	93.0	79.3	101.2	86.4	98.4	2.0	0.3	1.0	69.2	10.7	30.6
AR	52.4	45.4	53.2	45.9	51.7	1.0	0.2	0.5	28.7	4.5	12.2
CA	664.6	581.1	696.3	612.2	690.9	13.3	2.4	7.0	554.7	88.2	257.5
CO	116.2	101.5	124.3	109.6	121.5	1.9	0.4	1.0	71.6	12.6	33.1
CT	78.5	67.2	78.0	66.8	76.0	1.5	0.3	0.8	72.8	10.8	31.5
DE	20.2	16.6	21.0	17.0	19.6	0.4	0.1	0.2	16.1	2.1	6.1
DC	16.3	12.4	15.9	11.8	14.7	0.4	0.1	0.2	24.3	2.9	10.8
FL......	354.0	319.3	404.1	366.3	399.9	6.9	1.3	3.1	219.8	38.6	96.4
GA	160.4	138.3	172.4	149.2	168.7	3.5	0.6	1.6	121.3	17.8	50.6
HI	24.3	20.8	25.8	21.9	25.0	0.5	0.1	0.3	15.1	2.8	7.9
ID	32.2	28.0	35.6	31.2	34.6	0.5	0.1	0.3	14.2	3.1	7.4
IL	254.1	218.1	259.7	224.3	255.6	5.2	0.9	2.6	207.9	30.8	94.1
IN	116.3	98.1	117.7	99.7	114.9	2.6	0.4	1.3	85.1	11.6	37.4
IA	65.6	56.2	65.8	56.5	64.2	1.2	0.2	0.7	37.6	5.7	17.7
KS	61.6	52.4	61.8	52.8	60.0	1.1	0.2	0.6	35.7	5.6	16.9
KY	72.3	61.0	72.9	61.7	70.8	1.5	0.3	0.8	46.2	6.8	20.6
LA	81.7	69.5	83.1	70.3	81.1	1.6	0.3	0.9	49.0	8.0	23.7
ME	34.1	30.1	35.4	31.2	34.5	0.5	0.1	0.3	15.4	3.3	8.7
MD	106.0	90.4	112.3	96.0	109.7	2.2	0.4	1.1	84.3	13.5	40.9
MA	148.2	127.8	146.3	126.3	143.5	3.0	0.5	1.5	135.2	19.6	60.2
MI.	193.9	167.2	193.7	167.6	190.7	3.9	0.7	2.0	147.7	21.9	65.7
MN	116.2	99.4	123.2	106.2	120.8	2.4	0.4	1.2	92.4	12.9	40.8
MS	48.3	41.5	48.4	41.3	46.9	0.9	0.2	0.5	24.8	4.0	11.3
MO	118.1	101.1	125.5	108.2	122.8	2.4	0.4	1.2	79.2	11.6	35.3
MT	28.0	25.0	30.5	27.3	29.9	0.3	0.1	0.2	8.3	2.3	5.4
NE	41.4	35.5	42.2	36.2	40.9	0.8	0.1	0.4	23.7	3.6	10.8
NV	40.3	33.4	46.5	38.7	44.5	1.0	0.1	0.5	34.8	5.4	15.3
NH	32.1	27.3	33.1	28.2	32.0	0.6	0.1	0.3	20.0	4.0	10.9
NJ.	202.2	178.4	207.4	183.4	204.3	3.6	0.7	1.8	160.2	26.2	71.7
NM	35.5	30.1	36.6	30.9	35.2	0.6	0.1	0.3	16.8	3.3	8.9
NY	424.8	379.2	441.2	395.7	437.1	7.4	1.5	3.9	353.3	53.2	154.7
NC	163.6	142.0	170.0	147.2	166.8	3.4	0.6	1.6	109.6	16.7	47.0
ND	17.2	14.7	17.6	15.0	17.0	0.3	0.1	0.2	7.3	1.4	4.2
OH	212.5	180.5	211.4	180.3	207.8	4.8	0.8	2.4	162.6	22.7	71.7
OK	70.2	61.0	71.5	62.1	69.7	1.2	0.3	0.7	35.6	6.4	17.5
OR	85.1	74.2	88.5	77.5	86.5	1.4	0.3	0.8	46.3	8.4	23.1
PA	237.5	204.6	241.2	208.2	237.4	5.1	0.9	2.6	181.8	26.2	81.4
RI......	25.2	21.5	26.5	22.6	25.6	0.4	0.1	0.3	15.0	2.8	8.0
SC	78.4	67.2	81.1	69.6	78.9	1.6	0.3	0.8	46.7	7.6	20.8
SD	20.6	17.7	21.3	18.4	20.7	0.3	0.1	0.2	8.4	1.7	5.0
TN	102.4	86.7	102.0	86.1	99.1	2.3	0.4	1.1	76.9	10.5	32.8
TX	369.0	321.3	381.6	332.2	376.8	8.1	1.4	3.9	293.6	43.1	122.2
UT	46.2	39.3	53.2	45.9	51.5	0.9	0.2	0.5	28.6	4.7	13.5
VT	19.1	16.7	19.5	17.0	18.9	0.3	0.1	0.2	8.0	1.9	4.7
VA	139.7	120.3	150.4	129.7	147.3	3.1	0.5	1.5	114.9	16.9	50.6
WA	138.2	120.9	143.7	126.5	141.2	2.3	0.5	1.3	90.2	14.9	42.3
WV	33.5	28.8	32.9	28.2	31.8	0.6	0.1	0.3	15.6	2.7	7.5
WI.	115.6	98.2	117.6	100.0	115.3	2.4	0.4	1.3	82.8	12.2	38.9
WY	15.9	13.9	17.0	14.8	16.4	0.2	0.1	0.1	5.7	1.5	3.5

Source: U.S. Small Business Administration, Office of Advocacy, "Statistics of U.S. Businesses"; <http://www.sba.gov/advo /research/data.html>; accessed 20 March 2007.

Table 741. Employer Firm Births and Deaths and Business Bankruptcies by State: 2004 to 2006

[Births represent an employing unit which is determined, for the first time, as meeting the definition of "employer" in the state unemployment compensation law or a previously terminated employing unit which again is determined as meeting the definition of employer]

State	Births			Deaths			Business bankruptcies		
	2004	2005	2006	2004	2005	2006	2004	2005	2006
United States [1]....	904,784	938,942	933,657	934,045	935,743	971,894	34,317	39,201	19,695
Alabama	9,413	10,575	10,096	10,104	10,168	11,128	325	331	219
Alaska.	1,848	1,982	1,904	2,650	2,294	2,239	64	83	45
Arizona	12,421	21,339	21,555	17,553	18,249	2 62,075	480	525	261
Arkansas	7,052	7,591	9,551	6,481	7,021	7,289	376	426	276
California.	117,016	121,482	115,684	143,115	151,944	149,212	3,748	4,236	2,098
Colorado	23,694	26,610	22,708	9,734	14,035	24,158	786	1,120	435
Connecticut	9,064	9,220	9,516	11,018	11,131	11,214	132	156	219
Delaware	3,270	3,299	3,153	3,362	3,355	3,295	276	218	244
District of Columbia . . .	4,393	4,316	4,232	3,440	3,952	3,111	41	46	27
Florida.	77,754	84,890	79,870	54,498	58,737	64,423	1,183	1,622	991
Georgia	29,547	29,804	31,677	27,835	29,315	29,787	2,090	2,232	1,148
Hawaii	3,698	3,763	3,813	3,754	3,794	3,789	47	81	25
Idaho	7,814	9,312	9,159	5,716	6,334	6,713	160	141	56
Illinois	28,453	30,445	30,230	33,472	32,846	33,426	912	1,042	669
Indiana	13,906	14,545	14,653	15,282	16,504	13,851	524	758	376
Iowa	5,954	6,004	5,877	7,391	6,802	7,248	360	455	208
Kansas	6,742	7,095	6,973	7,250	7,330	7,000	268	410	158
Kentucky	8,807	9,617	8,973	8,597	8,515	10,230	319	409	200
Louisiana.	9,875	9,393	11,034	9,668	9,123	8,972	622	718	476
Maine	4,300	4,251	4,497	4,987	4,711	4,769	138	144	85
Maryland	21,751	22,083	21,535	20,636	21,769	20,745	417	760	333
Massachusetts	18,822	19,723	17,800	20,270	18,878	22,376	315	406	253
Michigan	24,625	24,642	23,508	24,584	26,971	21,268	681	1,071	753
Minnesota	15,167	12,555	13,739	15,209	15,302	14,403	1,374	1,721	381
Mississippi	6,141	6,071	6,862	7,380	8,423	7,898	170	200	187
Missouri.	16,155	17,239	15,805	17,924	20,109	18,124	354	438	284
Montana	4,588	4,768	4,727	4,896	4,394	4,469	109	129	39
Nebraska.	4,849	5,127	4,820	5,051	4,982	5,117	207	296	182
Nevada	10,483	11,299	10,743	9,012	8,485	8,423	257	333	178
New Hampshire	4,865	4,758	4,703	5,401	5,406	5,481	158	586	218
New Jersey	35,895	33,022	36,258	50,034	32,751	32,959	684	765	493
New Mexico	5,683	5,272	5,536	5,592	5,670	5,274	727	828	95
New York	62,854	62,045	61,718	64,013	62,667	61,190	4,070	2,112	1,201
North Carolina	23,387	25,906	26,729	22,055	22,867	23,165	486	612	403
North Dakota	1,747	1,893	1,821	2,621	2,512	2,181	85	95	32
Ohio	22,725	22,542	22,213	21,328	23,429	25,412	1,432	2,099	957
Oklahoma	9,263	8,609	9,962	8,018	7,231	7,829	659	944	236
Oregon	13,481	14,445	15,085	14,407	14,804	14,039	852	1,160	301
Pennsylvania	33,188	36,609	34,928	34,507	36,989	35,805	1,138	1,356	742
Rhode Island	3,932	3,677	3,739	4,250	4,164	4,572	74	136	48
South Carolina	11,745	12,341	12,273	10,975	10,681	11,661	175	176	82
South Dakota	1,691	2,102	2,003	2,251	2,354	2,449	108	196	47
Tennessee	17,415	17,484	17,207	16,520	17,135	16,395	548	574	397
Texas	54,098	55,858	58,943	55,792	55,839	54,479	3,094	3,590	2,081
Utah	11,357	11,536	13,379	11,597	11,871	11,190	440	449	148
Vermont	2,322	1,911	1,957	2,578	2,346	2,365	85	78	36
Virginia	24,134	25,061	23,686	19,919	21,359	20,972	750	476	283
Washington	31,955	30,353	32,726	47,141	40,944	36,331	665	786	401
West Virginia	3,937	3,493	3,823	5,136	4,869	4,854	247	282	114
Wisconsin	13,093	13,656	13,371	12,711	13,397	13,060	742	820	307
Wyoming	2,519	2,632	2,570	2,737	2,689	2,773	65	84	40

[1] Includes Puerto Rico and Virgin Islands, not shown separately. Bankruptcy data also includes Guam and Northern Mariana Islands. [2] Data not comparable with prior years.

Source: U.S. Employment and Training Administration, unpublished data, and Administrative Office of the U.S. Courts, "Bankruptcy Statistics"; <http://www.uscourts.gov/bnkrpctystats/statistics.htm>.

Table 742. Small Business Administration Loans to Minority-Owned Small Businesses: 2000 to 2006

[3,634 represents $3,634,000,000. For year ending September 30. A small business must be independently owned and operated, must not be dominant in its particular industry, and must meet standards set by the Small Business Administration as to its annual receipts or number of employees]

Minority group	Number of loans					Amount (mil. dol.)				
	2000	2003	2004	2005	2006	2000	2003	2004	2005	2006
Total minority loans.	11,999	20,184	25,413	29,722	33,772	3,634	4,215	5,144	6,132	6,606
Percent of all loans	24.8	27.2	28.4	28.3	31.5	29.4	29.2	29.3	30.2	32.6
African American	2,120	3,769	4,827	6,635	7,231	388	399	481	627	693
Asian American	5,838	9,507	12,100	13,456	14,446	2,383	2,756	3,400	4,056	4,239
Hispanic American	3,500	6,112	7,686	8,796	11,214	761	942	1,151	1,325	1,561
Native American	541	796	800	835	881	101	118	113	123	114

Source: U.S. Small Business Administration, Management Information Summary, unpublished data.

Census Bureau, Statistical Abstract of the United States: 2008

Table 743. U.S. Firms—Ownership by Women, Race, and Hispanic or Latino Origin Groups: 2002

[22,975 represents 22,975,000. A Hispanic firm may be of any race and, therefore may be included in more than one race group. See text, this section and Appendix III]

Group	All firms [1]			Firms with paid employees			
	Firms (1,000)	Sales and receipts (bil. dol.)		Firms (1,000)	Sales and receipts (bil. dol.)	Employees (1,000)	Annual payroll (bil. dol.)
All firms [2]	22,975	22,604		5,525	21,836	110,767	3,812
Female-owned	6,489	940		917	803	7,141	174
Male-owned	13,184	7,061		3,525	6,564	42,429	1,320
Equally male-/female-owned.	2,693	732		718	627	5,665	130
Publicly held and other firms [3]	494	13,820		353	13,797	55,398	2,186
Hispanic or Latino origin	1,573	222		200	180	1,537	37
Mexican, Mexican American, Chicano.	701	97		89	77	720	16
Puerto Rican	109	12		12	10	77	2
Cuban	152	35		28	31	206	6
Other Spanish/Hispanic/Latino.	596	74		67	59	504	12
Black	1,198	89		95	66	754	18
American Indian and Alaska Native . . .	201	27		24	22	191	5
Asian	1,104	327		319	291	2,214	56
Asian Indian.	223	88		82	80	610	18
Chinese	286	105		89	96	649	15
Filipino	125	14		20	11	132	4
Japanese	87	31		22	28	205	6
Korean	158	47		57	41	321	7
Vietnamese	147	16		26	12	126	3
Other Asian	89	24		25	22	161	4
Native Hawaiian and Other Pacific Islander	29	4		4	4	29	1
Native Hawaiian	17	3		2	2	20	1
Samoan	2	(Z)		(Z)	(Z)	2	(Z)
Guamanian or Chamorro	4	1		(S)	(S)	(S)	(S)
Other Pacific Islander	6	(Z)		(Z)	(Z)	4	(Z)

S Does not meet publication standards.   Z Less than 500 or $500 million.   [1] Both firms with paid employees and firms with no paid employees.   [2] U.S. totals are based on the 2002 Economic Census, whereas the gender, Hispanic or Latino origin, and race estimates are based on the 2002 Survey of Business Owners.   [3] Publicly held and other firms not classifiable by gender, Hispanic or Latino origin, and race.

Source: U.S. Census Bureau, 2002 Economic Census, Survey of Business Owners, Women-Owned Firms: 2002 (SB02-00CS-WMN)(RV); Hispanic-Owned Firms: 2002 (SB02-00CS-HISP)(RV); Black-Owned Firms: 2002 (SB02-00CS-BLK)(RV); American Indian- and Alaska Native-Owned Firms: 2002 (SB02-00CS-AIAN)(RV); Asian-Owned Firms: 2002 (SB02-00CS-ASIAN)(RV); and Native Hawaiian- and Other Pacific Islander-Owned Firms: 2002 (SB02-00CS-NHPI)(RV).

Table 744. Women-Owned Firms by Kind of Business and Receipts Size: 2002

[6,489 represents 6,489,000. Based on the 2002 Survey of Business Owners; see text, this section and Appendix III]

Kind of business and receipts size	2002 NAICS code [1]	All firms [2]		Firms with paid employees			
		Firms (1,000)	Sales and receipts (mil. dol.)	Firms (1,000)	Sales and receipts (mil. dol.)	Employees (1,000)	Annual payroll (mil. dol.)
Total [3]	(X)	6,489	939,538	917	802,851	7,141	173,529
Construction	23	202	68,423	52	62,366	456	15,977
Manufacturing	31-33	110	93,168	40	91,286	636	20,386
Wholesale trade.	42	121	210,405	42	206,290	378	12,812
Retail trade.	44-45	945	148,947	146	131,483	851	15,293
Real estate and rental and leasing . . .	53	504	48,318	50	24,247	170	4,797
Professional, scientific, and technical services.	54	935	79,133	133	57,176	573	21,288
Admin/support waste mgt/ remediation services	56	569	48,062	61	40,567	1,004	19,589
Health care and social assistance	62	1,036	68,383	116	51,519	961	21,819
Accommodation and food services . . .	72	167	38,688	87	35,980	909	10,276
Other services (except public administration) [4]	81	1,016	36,216	86	19,622	386	6,559
Less than $5,000	(X)	1,831	4,372	13	32	31	1,112
$5,000 to $9,999	(X)	1,168	7,876	16	112	6	63
$10,000 to $24,999	(X)	1,405	21,642	51	876	34	281
$25,000 to $49,999	(X)	731	25,408	80	2,953	86	869
$50,000 to $99,999	(X)	496	34,580	141	10,330	238	2,898
$100,000 to $249,999	(X)	423	66,287	240	39,208	710	10,775
$250,000 to $499,999	(X)	197	68,982	154	54,463	838	15,125
$500,000 to $999,999	(X)	122	84,729	106	73,701	986	20,913
$1,000,000 or more	(X)	117	625,662	114	621,175	4,213	121,492

X Not applicable.   [1] Based on the 2002 North American Industry Classification System (NAICS); see text, this section.   [2] Both firms with paid employees and firms with no paid employees.   [3] Firms with more than one establishment are counted in each industry in which they operate, but only once in the total. Includes other kinds of businesses not shown separately.   [4] Excludes religious, grantmaking, civic, professional, and similar organizations (NAICS 813) and private households (NAICS 814).

Source: U.S. Census Bureau, 2002 Economic Census, Survey of Business Owners, Women-Owned Firms: 2002 (SB02-00CS-WMN)(RV).

U.S. Census Bureau, Statistical Abstract of the United States: 2008

Table 745. **Hispanic- or Latino-Owned Firms by Kind of Business and Receipts Size: 2002**

[1,573 represents 1,573,000. Based on the 2002 Survey of Business Owners; see text, this section and Appendix III]

Kind of business and receipts size	2002 NAICS code [1]	All firms [2]			Firms with paid employees			
		Firms (1,000)	Sales and receipts (mil. dol.)	Firms (1,000)	Sales and receipts (mil. dol.)	Employees (1,000)	Annual payroll (mil. dol.)
Total [3]	(X)	1,573	221,927	200	179,508	1,537	36,712
Construction	23	210	31,446	25	22,662	190	5,280
Manufacturing	31–33	31	17,965	10	17,245	125	3,739
Wholesale trade	42	34	39,323	12	37,503	86	2,831
Retail trade	44–45	151	40,424	26	35,511	156	3,271
Transportation and warehousing [4]	48–49	126	10,671	9	5,622	54	1,341
Professional, scientific, and technical services	54	138	15,017	19	11,529	98	4,167
Admin/support waste mgt/ remediation services	56	208	12,206	16	9,087	243	4,099
Health care and social assistance	62	182	13,758	20	11,208	140	4,237
Accommodation and food services	72	48	11,265	22	10,384	237	2,812
Other services (except public administration) [5]	81	249	10,082	19	5,329	74	1,486
Less than $5,000	(X)	328	814	2	5	2	79
$5,000 to $9,999	(X)	301	2,065	3	21	2	28
$10,000 to $24,999	(X)	391	5,865	9	156	6	57
$25,000 to $49,999	(X)	190	6,550	15	571	16	160
$50,000 to $99,999	(X)	138	9,726	29	2,109	40	534
$100,000 to $249,999	(X)	112	17,481	51	8,341	129	2,072
$250,000 to $499,999	(X)	51	17,894	36	12,892	176	3,323
$500,000 to $999,999	(X)	33	22,825	26	18,461	229	4,901
$1,000,000 or more	(X)	29	138,708	28	136,953	938	25,559

X Not applicable.   [1] Based on the 2002 North American Industry Classification System (NAICS); see text, this section.   [2] Both firms with paid employees and firms with no paid employees.   [3] Firms with more than one establishment are counted in each industry in which they operate, but only once in the total. Includes other kinds of businesses not shown separately.   [4] Excludes large certificated passenger carriers that report to the Office of Airline Information, U.S. Department of Transportation. Also excludes railroad transportation and U.S. Postal Service.   [5] Excludes religious, grantmaking, civic, professional, and similar organizations (NAICS 813) and private households (NAICS 814).

Source: U.S. Census Bureau, *2002 Economic Census, Survey of Business Owners, Hispanic-Owned Firms: 2002* (SB02-00CS-HISP)(RV).

Table 746. **Women-Owned and Minority-Owned Firms With Paid Employees by Employment Size: 2002**

[917 represents 917,000. Employment reflects number of paid employees during the March 12 pay period. Based on the 2002 Survey of Business Owners; see text, this section and Appendix III]

Item	Unit		Number of employees						
		Total	None [1]	1 to 4	5 to 9	10 to 19	20 to 49	50 to 99	100 to 499	500 or more
WOMEN-OWNED										
Firms	1,000	917	161	462	149	83	43	11	7	1
Sales and receipts	Mil. dol.	802,851	23,539	113,447	96,282	103,160	117,875	74,053	114,484	160,012
Employees	1,000	7,141	–	939	971	1,105	1,269	750	1,194	913
Annual payroll	Mil. dol.	173,529	3,953	20,483	21,360	25,946	31,578	19,316	30,015	20,877
HISPANIC-OWNED										
Firms	1,000	200	37	100	31	18	9	3	1	(Z)
Sales and receipts	Mil. dol.	179,508	6,703	28,292	26,627	26,945	29,496	19,447	27,206	14,792
Employees	1,000	1,537	–	202	205	248	267	185	244	186
Annual payroll	Mil. dol.	36,712	1,153	4,568	4,958	5,705	6,393	4,817	5,900	3,217
BLACK-OWNED										
Firms	1,000	95	19	47	14	7	4	1	1	(Z)
Sales and receipts	Mil. dol.	65,799	2,986	10,679	7,773	7,769	10,912	9,697	11,193	4,790
Employees	1,000	754	–	96	92	100	133	87	162	82
Annual payroll	Mil. dol.	17,550	541	2,251	2,133	2,279	3,034	2,154	3,623	1,535
AMERICAN INDIAN- AND ALASKA NATIVE-OWNED										
Firms	1,000	24	5	12	4	2	1	(Z)	(Z)	(Z)
Sales and receipts	Mil. dol.	21,987	1,021	3,378	2,411	2,996	3,814	3,092	2,842	2,433
Employees	1,000	191	–	26	23	28	36	23	26	29
Annual payroll	Mil. dol.	5,135	137	578	528	706	945	675	773	793
ASIAN-OWNED										
Firms	1,000	319	54	161	55	30	15	3	2	(Z)
Sales and receipts	Mil. dol.	291,163	10,287	56,967	46,155	44,109	50,950	30,759	32,955	18,980
Employees	1,000	2,214	–	347	353	393	437	226	302	155
Annual payroll	Mil. dol.	56,045	1,616	7,946	7,992	9,130	10,947	6,048	8,211	4,154
NATIVE HAWAIIAN- AND OTHER PACIFIC ISLANDER-OWNED										
Firms	1,000	4	1	2	1	(Z)	(Z)	(Z)	(Z)	–
Sales and receipts	Mil. dol.	3,502	73	520	413	574	805	420	698	–
Employees	1,000	29	–	4	4	5	7	4	5	–
Annual payroll	Mil. dol.	826	12	133	99	123	228	100	132	–

– Represents zero.   Z Less than 500.   [1] Firms reported annual payroll, but did not report any employees on their payroll during specified period in 2002.

Source: U.S. Census Bureau, *2002 Economic Census, Survey of Business Owners, Women-Owned Firms: 2002* (SB02-00CS-WMN)(RV); *Hispanic-Owned Firms: 2002* (SB02-00CS-HISP)(RV); *Black-Owned Firms: 2002* (SB02-00CS-BLK)(RV); *American Indian- and Alaska Native-Owned Firms: 2002* (SB02-00CS-AIAN)(RV); *Asian-Owned Firms: 2002* (SB02-00CS-ASIAN)(RV); and *Native Hawaiian- and Other Pacific Islander-Owned Firms: 2002* (SB02-00CS-NHPI)(RV).

Business Enterprise   503

Table 747. Black-Owned Firms by Kind of Business and Receipts Size: 2002

[1,198 represents 1,198,000. Based on the 2002 Survey of Business Owners; see text, this section and Appendix III]

Kind of business and receipts size	2002 NAICS code [1]	All firms [2]		Firms with paid employees			
		Firms (1,000)	Sales and receipts (mil. dol.)	Firms (1,000)	Sales and receipts (mil. dol.)	Employees (1,000)	Annual payroll (mil. dol.)
Total [3]	(X)	1,198	88,642	95	65,799	754	17,550
Construction	23	75	9,632	9	7,504	55	1,718
Manufacturing	31-33	10	4,647	2	4,456	31	1,022
Wholesale trade	42	12	5,604	2	5,136	11	392
Retail trade	44-45	102	13,587	9	11,550	45	982
Transportation and warehousing [4]	48-49	99	5,445	5	2,160	26	555
Professional, scientific, and technical services	54	116	9,395	11	7,097	71	2,879
Admin/support waste mgt/ remediation services	56	121	6,416	10	4,908	134	2,316
Health care and social assistance	62	246	11,828	20	8,415	164	3,495
Accommodation and food services . . .	72	25	5,033	7	4,416	115	1,171
Other services (except public administration) [5]	81	210	5,178	9	2,092	32	571
Less than $5,000	(X)	360	863	1	4	3	163
$5,000 to $9,999	(X)	249	1,688	2	14	1	6
$10,000 to $24,999	(X)	295	4,453	6	101	5	45
$25,000 to $49,999	(X)	125	4,286	9	342	10	103
$50,000 to $99,999	(X)	74	5,159	15	1,122	26	325
$100,000 to $249,999	(X)	52	7,912	25	4,094	77	1,158
$250,000 to $499,999	(X)	21	7,233	15	5,359	86	1,580
$500,000 to $999,999	(X)	12	8,295	10	6,927	99	2,218
$1,000,000 or more	(X)	11	48,753	10	47,835	447	11,951

X Not applicable. [1] Based on the 2002 North American Industry Classification System (NAICS); see text, this section. [2] Both firms with paid employees and firms with no paid employees. [3] Firms with more than one establishment are counted in each industry in which they operate, but only once in the total. Includes other kinds of businesses not shown separately. [4] Excludes large certificated passenger carriers that report to the Office of Airline Information, U.S. Department of Transportation. Also excludes railroad transportation and U.S. Postal Service. [5] Excludes religious, grantmaking, civic, professional, and similar organizations (NAICS 813) and private households (NAICS 814).

Source: U.S. Census Bureau, 2002 Economic Census, Survey of Business Owners, Black-Owned Firms: 2002 (SB02-00CS-BLK)(RV).

Table 748. American Indian- and Alaska Native-Owned Firms by Kind of Business and Receipts Size: 2002

[201.4 represents 201,400. Based on the 2002 Survey of Business Owners; see text, this section and Appendix III]

Kind of business and receipts size	2002 NAICS code [1]	All firms [2]		Firms with paid employees			
		Firms (1,000)	Sales and receipts (mil. dol.)	Firms (1,000)	Sales and receipts (mil. dol.)	Employees (1,000)	Annual payroll (mil. dol.)
Total [3]	(X)	201.4	26,873	24.5	21,987	191.3	5,135
Construction	23	32.3	6,055	4.8	4,866	31.3	1,072
Manufacturing	31-33	6.0	3,125	1.4	3,016	20.0	657
Wholesale trade	42	4.3	2,162	0.8	2,048	5.7	191
Retail trade	44-45	20.5	4,967	3.0	4,382	21.1	437
Transportation and warehousing [4] . . .	48-49	10.0	942	0.9	501	4.8	129
Real estate and rental and leasing . . .	53	9.3	715	0.6	342	2.3	69
Professional, scientific, and technical services	54	22.5	2,091	3.3	1,570	15.3	641
Admin/support waste mgt/ remediation services	56	15.7	1,699	1.8	1,505	31.2	638
Health care and social assistance	62	24.4	1,234	2.1	920	17.5	369
Other services (except public administration) [5]	81	26.7	935	1.7	447	6.3	116
Less than $5,000	(X)	54.2	130	0.4	1	0.3	4
$5,000 to $9,999	(X)	36.4	245	0.5	3	0.2	5
$10,000 to $24,999	(X)	43.3	662	1.1	17	0.9	7
$25,000 to $49,999	(X)	24.2	841	1.9	71	2.0	18
$50,000 to $99,999	(X)	16.9	1,188	3.4	252	4.2	63
$100,000 to $249,999	(X)	13.3	2,086	6.4	1,064	17.4	277
$250,000 to $499,999	(X)	6.1	2,141	4.4	1,534	19.8	391
$500,000 to $999,999	(X)	3.5	2,338	2.9	1,975	22.9	530
$1,000,000 or more	(X)	3.6	17,242	3.5	17,069	123.5	3,840

X Not applicable. [1] Based on the 2002 North American Industry Classification System (NAICS); see text, this section. [2] Both firms with paid employees and firms with no paid employees. [3] Firms with more than one establishment are counted in each industry in which they operate, but only once in the total. Includes other kinds of businesses not shown separately. [4] Excludes large certificated passenger carriers that report to the Office of Airline Information, U.S. Department of Transportation. Also excludes railroad transportation and U.S. Postal Service. [5] Excludes religious, grantmaking, civic, professional, and similar organizations (NAICS 813) and private households (NAICS 814).

Source: U.S. Census Bureau, 2002 Economic Census, Survey of Business Owners, American Indian- and Alaska Native-Owned Firms: 2002 (SB02-00CS-AIAN).

Table 749. Asian-Owned Firms by Kind of Business and Receipts Size: 2002

[1,104 represents 1,104,000. Based on the 2002 Survey of Business Owners; see text, this section and Appendix III]

Kind of business and receipts size	2002 NAICS code [1]	All firms [2]		Firms with paid employees			
		Firms (1,000)	Sales and receipts (mil. dol.)	Firms (1,000)	Sales and receipts (mil. dol.)	Employees (1,000)	Annual payroll (mil. dol.)
Total [3]	(X)	1,104	326,663	319	291,163	2,214	56,045
Construction	23	39	9,715	7	8,129	47	1,665
Manufacturing	31-33	24	26,434	12	25,924	170	5,115
Wholesale trade	42	47	87,083	25	83,924	155	5,590
Retail trade	44-45	152	65,143	62	58,564	292	5,004
Finance and insurance [4]	52	30	6,970	5	5,169	26	1,357
Real estate and rental and leasing	53	75	9,759	9	4,778	35	1,032
Professional, scientific, and technical services	54	154	27,234	30	23,360	196	9,963
Health care and social assistance	62	123	29,951	45	26,689	280	10,315
Accommodation and food services	72	105	32,830	75	31,094	671	7,697
Other services (except public administration) [5]	81	189	11,266	31	7,184	113	2,004
Less than $5,000	(X)	175	437	2	6	17	638
$5,000 to $9,999	(X)	143	960	4	28	1	14
$10,000 to $24,999	(X)	200	3,129	12	201	7	65
$25,000 to $49,999	(X)	140	4,923	20	738	19	204
$50,000 to $99,999	(X)	122	8,651	38	2,785	56	716
$100,000 to $249,999	(X)	141	22,424	84	13,874	228	3,305
$250,000 to $499,999	(X)	82	28,992	65	23,266	303	5,561
$500,000 to $999,999	(X)	52	36,158	46	31,787	369	7,753
$1,000,000 or more	(X)	50	220,991	49	218,477	1,214	37,790

X Not applicable. [1] Based on the 2002 North American Industry Classification System (NAICS); see text, this section. [2] Both firms with paid employees and firms with no paid employees. [3] Firms with more than one establishment are counted in each industry in which they operate, but only once in the total. Includes other kinds of businesses not shown separately. [4] Excludes funds, trusts, and other financial vehicles (NAICS 525), except real estate investment trusts (NAICS 525930). [5] Excludes religious, grantmaking, civic, professional, and similar organizations (NAICS 813) and private households (NAICS 814).

Source: U.S. Census Bureau, 2002 Economic Census, Survey of Business Owners, Asian-Owned Firms: 2002 (SB02-00CS-ASIAN)(RV).

Table 750. Native Hawaiian- and Other Pacific Islander-Owned Firms by Kind of Business and Receipts Size: 2002

[4,279.6 represents $4,279,600,000. Based on the 2002 Survey of Business Owners; see text, this section and Appendix III]

Kind of business and receipts size	2002 NAICS code [1]	All firms [2]		Firms with paid employees			
		Firms	Sales and receipts (mil. dol.)	Firms	Sales and receipts (mil. dol.)	Employees	Annual payroll (mil. dol.)
Total [3]	(X)	28,948	4,279.6	3,693	3,502.2	29,319	826.2
Construction	23	2,853	906.3	(S)	(S)	(S)	(S)
Manufacturing	31-33	324	184.1	84	177.0	1,478	45.4
Wholesale trade	42	377	482.2	146	469.1	1,078	35.9
Retail trade	44-45	3,601	645.5	459	552.7	2,492	56.6
Transportation and warehousing [4]	48-49	1,412	190.3	243	140.4	2,758	46.6
Information	51	311	144.6	58	135.3	427	27.1
Real estate and rental and leasing	53	1,851	153.2	266	80.5	732	21.7
Professional, scientific, and technical services	54	3,239	267.3	321	172.7	1,351	53.4
Admin/support waste mgt/ remediation services	56	3,362	451.6	(S)	(S)	(S)	(S)
Accommodation and food services	72	511	137.7	193	130.0	2,645	33.2
Less than $5,000	(X)	7,316	17.5	(S)	(S)	(S)	(S)
$5,000 to $9,999	(X)	6,164	42.3	(S)	(S)	(S)	(S)
$10,000 to $24,999	(X)	5,951	89.0	221	3.5	131	1.1
$25,000 to $49,999	(X)	2,933	101.9	166	5.9	161	1.5
$50,000 to $99,999	(X)	2,173	150.5	343	24.6	495	4.9
$100,000 to $249,999	(X)	2,241	338.3	857	139.5	2,094	44.1
$250,000 to $499,999	(X)	962	347.6	804	295.7	3,847	80.3
$500,000 to $999,999	(X)	480	335.2	452	315.3	4,444	99.7
$1,000,000 or more	(X)	727	2,857.3	(S)	(S)	(S)	(S)

S Data do not meet publication standards. X Not applicable. [1] Based on the 2002 North American Industry Classification System (NAICS); see text, this section. [2] Both firms with paid employees and firms with no paid employees. [3] Firms with more than one establishment are counted in each industry in which they operate, but only once in the total. Includes other kinds of businesses not shown separately. [4] Excludes large certificated passenger carriers that report to the Office of Airline Information, U.S. Department of Transportation. Also excludes railroad transportation and U.S. Postal Service.

Source: U.S. Census Bureau, 2002 Economic Census, Survey of Business Owners, Native Hawaiian- and Other Pacific Islander-Owned Firms: 2002 (SB02-00CS-NHPI)(RV).

Table 751. **Bankruptcy Petitions Filed and Pending by Type and Chapter: 1990 to 2006**

[For years ending June 30. Covers only bankruptcy cases filed under the Bankruptcy Reform Act of 1978. *Bankruptcy:* legal recognition that a company or individual is insolvent and must restructure or liquidate. Petitions "filed" means the commencement of a proceeding through the presentation of a petition to the clerk of the court; "pending" is a proceeding in which the administration has not been completed]

Item	1990	1995	2000	2001	2002	2003	2004	2005	2006
Total filed.	725,484	858,104	1,276,922	1,386,606	1,505,306	1,650,279	1,635,725	1,637,254	1,484,570
Business [1].	64,688	51,288	36,910	37,135	39,201	37,182	35,739	32,406	31,562
Nonbusiness.[2]	660,796	806,816	1,240,012	1,349,471	1,466,105	1,613,097	1,599,986	1,604,848	1,453,008
Chapter 7 [3]	468,171	552,244	864,183	950,724	1,030,372	1,144,658	1,146,761	1,174,681	1,142,958
Chapter 11 [4].	2,116	1,755	722	745	894	966	935	847	749
Chapter 13 [5].	190,509	252,817	375,107	397,996	434,835	467,466	452,286	429,315	309,298
Voluntary.	723,886	856,991	1,276,146	1,385,840	1,504,500	1,649,543	1,635,099	1,636,678	1,484,085
Involuntary	1,598	1,113	776	766	806	736	626	576	485
Chapter 7 [3].	505,337	581,390	885,447	972,659	1,053,230	1,165,993	1,167,101	1,196,212	1,164,815
Chapter 9 [6].	7	12	8	10	8	7	7	6	10
Chapter 11 [4].	19,591	13,221	9,947	10,272	11,401	10,602	11,048	6,703	6,224
Chapter 12 [7]	1,351	904	732	206	367	775	302	290	360
Chapter 13 [5].	199,186	262,551	380,770	403,418	440,231	472,811	457,171	433,945	313,085
Section 304 [8].	12	26	18	41	69	91	96	98	36
Chapter 15 [9]	(X)	(X)	(X)	(X)	(X)	(X)	(X)	(X)	40
Total pending. . .	961,919	1,090,446	1,400,416	1,535,903	1,613,742	1,729,139	1,697,267	1,750,562	1,411,212

X Not applicable.   [1] Business bankruptcies include those filed under chapters 7, 9, 11, or 12.   [2] Includes Section 304 petitions not shown separately.   [3] Chapter 7, liquidation of nonexempt assets of businesses or individuals.   [4] Chapter 11, individual or business reorganization.   [5] Chapter 13, adjustment of debts of an individual with regular income.   [6] Chapter 9, adjustment of debts of a municipality.   [7] Chapter 12, adjustment of debts of a family farmer with regular income, effective November 26, 1986.   [8] Chapter 11, U.S.C., Section 304, cases ancillary to foreign proceedings.   [9] Chapter 15 was added and Section 304 was terminated by changes in the Bankruptcy Laws effective October 17, 2005.

Source: Administrative Office of the U.S. Courts, *Statistical Tables for the Federal Judiciary* and "Bankruptcy Statistics"; <http://www.uscourts.gov/bnkrpctystats/statistics.htm>.

Table 752. **Bankruptcy Cases Filed by State: 2000 to 2006**

[In thousands (1,276.9 represents 1,276,900). For years ending June 30. Covers only bankruptcy cases filed under the Bankruptcy Reform Act of 1978. *Bankruptcy:* legal recognition that a company or individual is insolvent and must restructure or liquidate. Petitions "filed" means the commencement of a proceeding through the presentation of a petition to the clerk of the court]

State	2000	2004	2005	2006	State	2000	2004	2005	2006
Total [1].	1,276.9	1,635.7	1,637.3	1,484.6	Missouri	26.3	38.0	39.2	38.6
					Montana	3.3	4.4	4.4	4.3
Alabama	31.4	42.4	42.6	34.8	Nebraska	5.6	8.8	9.6	8.7
Alaska	1.4	1.5	1.6	1.7	Nevada.	14.3	19.4	16.3	17.2
Arizona	21.7	31.8	32.4	26.7	New Hampshire	3.9	4.5	4.9	4.2
Arkansas	16.3	24.2	25.5	21.5					
California.	160.6	132.5	122.6	117.6	New Jersey	38.7	42.5	40.7	34.2
					New Mexico.	7.1	9.4	10.1	8.2
Colorado	15.6	27.4	30.2	31.1	New York	61.7	80.2	81.7	77.4
Connecticut	11.4	11.8	11.8	11.5	North Carolina	25.8	37.7	37.5	31.6
Delaware.	4.9	3.8	3.6	3.3	North Dakota	2.0	2.3	2.5	2.5
District of Columbia. .	2.6	2.1	1.9	1.7					
Florida	74.0	92.2	85.8	73.5	Ohio.	53.6	90.9	95.8	98.8
					Oklahoma	19.3	27.2	28.2	27.7
Georgia	57.9	79.8	77.3	61.3	Oregon	18.1	24.9	25.3	22.9
Hawaii	5.0	3.5	3.2	3.2	Pennsylvania	43.8	59.1	62.3	56.4
Idaho	7.3	9.7	9.7	8.2	Rhode Island	4.8	4.3	4.4	4.0
Illinois.	62.3	81.3	83.6	76.6					
Indiana	37.5	55.7	55.9	60.0	South Carolina	11.7	15.9	15.2	10.9
					South Dakota.	2.1	2.9	2.9	3.0
Iowa.	8.2	13.0	14.3	12.8	Tennessee.	47.1	62.9	60.8	49.2
Kansas.	11.4	16.3	17.3	16.3	Texas	62.9	92.2	97.5	86.8
Kentucky.	20.8	29.3	29.2	30.0	Utah.	14.4	21.3	20.5	14.0
Louisiana	23.1	30.2	31.1	25.3					
Maine	4.1	4.6	4.7	4.6	Vermont	1.6	1.8	1.7	2.0
					Virginia	37.1	42.1	38.8	30.9
Maryland.	31.1	32.0	28.5	24.6	Washington	31.2	40.1	37.7	32.3
Massachusetts	16.7	18.2	19.6	19.6	West Virginia	8.2	11.4	12.6	12.1
Michigan	36.4	63.0	68.5	67.2	Wisconsin	18.0	27.7	29.0	27.2
Minnesota	15.4	19.1	19.4	18.5	Wyoming.	2.0	2.4	2.5	2.2
Mississippi	17.9	21.2	21.8	16.2					

[1] Includes island areas not shown separately.

Source: Administrative Office of the U.S. Courts, *Statistical Tables for the Federal Judiciary* and "Bankruptcy Statistics"; <http://www.uscourts.gov/bnkrpctystats/statistics.htm>.

Table 753. Patents and Trademarks: 1990 to 2006

[In thousands (99.2 represents 99,200). Calendar year data. Covers U.S. patents issued to citizens of the United States and residents of foreign countries. For data on foreign countries, see Table 1355]

Type	1990	1995	2000	2001	2002	2003	2004	2005	2006
Patents issued	99.2	113.8	176.0	184.0	184.4	187.0	181.3	157.7	196.4
Inventions	90.4	101.4	157.5	166.0	167.3	169.0	164.3	143.8	173.8
Individuals	17.3	17.4	22.4	21.7	20.5	19.6	17.6	14.7	16.6
Corporations:									
United States	36.1	44.0	70.9	74.3	74.2	75.3	73.0	65.2	78.9
Foreign [1]	36.0	39.1	63.3	69.0	71.8	73.2	72.9	63.2	77.4
U.S. government	1.0	1.0	0.9	1.0	0.9	0.9	0.8	0.7	0.8
Designs	8.0	11.7	17.4	16.9	15.5	16.6	15.7	13.0	21.0
Botanical plants	0.3	0.4	0.5	0.6	1.1	1.0	1.0	0.7	1.1
Reissues	0.4	0.3	0.5	0.5	0.5	0.4	0.3	0.2	0.5
U.S. residents	52.8	64.4	96.9	98.6	97.1	98.6	94.1	82.6	102.2
Foreign country residents	46.2	49.4	79.1	85.4	87.3	88.5	87.2	75.2	94.2
Percent of total	46.7	43.4	44.9	46.4	47.3	47.3	48.1	47.6	48.0
Trademarks:									
Applications filed	127.3	181.0	361.8	277.3	264.1	271.7	304.5	334.7	362.3
Issued	60.8	92.5	115.2	142.9	176.0	166.6	146.0	154.8	193.7
Trademarks	53.6	85.6	106.4	109.6	146.9	130.9	113.7	121.6	153.3
Trademark renewals	7.2	6.9	8.8	33.3	29.2	35.6	32.3	33.3	40.4

[1] Includes patents to foreign governments.

Source: U.S. Patent and Trademark Office, "Statistical Reports Available For Viewing, Calendar Year Patent Statistics"; <http://www.uspto.gov/web/offices/ac/ido/oeip/taf/reports.htm> and unpublished data.

Table 754. Patents by State and Island Areas: 2006

[Includes only U.S. patents granted to residents of the United States and territories]

State	Total	Inventions	Designs	Botanical plants	Re-issues	State	Total	Inventions	Designs	Botanical plants	Re-issues
Total	102,239	89,823	11,691	430	295	Missouri	863	721	135	5	2
Alabama.	429	357	70	1	1	Montana	136	121	15	–	–
Alaska	45	36	9	–	–	Nebraska	239	186	51	2	–
Arizona.	1,893	1,705	183	–	5	Nevada	472	386	84	–	2
Arkansas	185	138	43	3	1	New Hampshire . .	657	602	53	–	2
California	25,039	22,275	2,531	165	68	New Jersey	3,627	3,172	434	6	15
Colorado.	2,349	2,118	223	–	8	New Mexico	354	344	10	–	–
Connecticut	1,857	1,652	196	5	4	New York	6,406	5,627	753	8	18
Delaware	396	357	38	–	1	North Carolina . . .	2,232	1,974	247	8	3
District of Columbia	69	63	6	–	–	North Dakota. . . .	77	66	8	3	–
Florida	3,261	2,600	582	64	15	Ohio	3,291	2,630	652	3	6
Georgia	1,719	1,487	202	26	4	Oklahoma	584	544	34	2	–
Hawaii	101	84	14	2	1	Oregon.	2,536	2,060	421	50	5
Idaho	1,717	1,663	48	–	6	Pennsylvania. . . .	3,186	2,842	330	4	10
Illinois	4,053	3,294	737	12	10	Rhode Island. . . .	354	269	84	1	–
Indiana.	1,499	1,165	319	7	8	South Carolina. . .	691	577	113	–	1
Iowa	732	666	65	–	1	South Dakota . . .	79	74	4	1	–
Kansas.	581	492	86	–	3	Tennessee	817	669	144	1	3
Kentucky	471	413	57	–	1	Texas.	6,716	6,308	385	2	21
Louisiana	365	321	37	6	1	Utah	800	684	110	–	6
Maine.	156	142	13	1	–	Vermont	486	437	49	–	–
Maryland	1,556	1,410	136	1	9	Virginia.	1,231	1,094	128	–	9
Massachusetts. . .	4,368	4,011	336	8	13	Washington.	3,620	3,286	322	3	9
Michigan.	4,178	3,758	404	9	7	West Virginia. . . .	111	103	8	–	–
Minnesota.	3,268	2,957	290	16	5	Wisconsin	2,150	1,688	452	3	7
Mississippi	152	119	31	–	2	Wyoming	56	48	8	–	–
						Island areas	29	28	1	–	–

- Represents zero.

Source: U.S. Patent and Trademark Office, unpublished data.

Table 755. Copyright Registration by Subject Matter: 1990 to 2006

[In thousands (590.7 represents 590,700). For years ending September 30. Comprises claims to copyrights registered for both U.S. and foreign works. Semiconductor chips and renewals are not considered copyright registration claims]

Subject matter	1990	2000	2005	2006	Subject matter	1990	2000	2005	2006
Total copyright claims . .	590.7	497.6	515.2	509.7	Works of the visual arts [3] . . .	76.7	85.8	82.5	90.7
Monographs [1]	179.7	169.7	191.4	182.7					
Serials	111.5	69.0	57.7	61.1	Semiconductor chip				
Sound recordings	37.5	34.2	49.9	50.8	products.	1.0	0.7	0.5	0.3
Musical works [2]	185.3	138.9	133.7	124.4	Renewals.	51.8	16.8	15.8	10.7

[1] Includes computer software and machine readable works. [2] Includes dramatic works, accompanying music, choreography, pantomimes, motion pictures, and filmstrips. [3] Two-dimensional works of fine and graphic art, including prints and art reproductions; sculptural works; technical drawings and models; photographs; commercial prints and labels; works of applied arts, cartographic works, and multimedia works.

Source: The Library of Congress, Copyright Office, Annual Report.

Table 756. Net Stock of Private Fixed Assets by Industry: 2000 to 2005

[In billions of dollars (21,190 represents $21,190,000,000,000). Estimates as of Dec. 31. Net stock estimates are presented in terms of current cost and cover equipment, software, and structures]

Industry	NAICS code [1]	2000	2003	2004	2005
Private fixed assets	(X)	21,190	24,917	27,193	29,344
Agriculture, forestry, fishing, and hunting.	11	406	452	485	517
Farms [2]	111, 112	379	424	454	484
Forestry, fishing, and related activities.	113-115	27	29	31	33
Mining	21	580	683	758	1,007
Oil and gas extraction	211	442	539	603	833
Mining, except oil and gas	212	92	95	104	114
Mining support activites	213	46	49	51	60
Utilities.	22	1,039	1,170	1,254	1,322
Construction	23	173	191	205	222
Manufacturing	31-33	1,759	1,809	1,876	1,953
Durable goods	(X)	996	1,029	1,063	1,107
Wood products	321	31	31	33	34
Nonmetallic mineral products.	327	55	58	61	64
Primary metals	331	124	120	123	126
Fabricated metal products.	332	112	115	119	125
Machinery	333	140	150	156	164
Computer and electronic products	334	245	252	257	263
Electrical equipment, appliances, and components	335	45	46	48	50
Motor vehicles, bodies and trailers, and parts	3361-3363	105	110	114	119
Other transportation equipment	3364, 3365, 3369	79	84	88	92
Furniture and related products	337	16	17	18	19
Miscellaneous manufacturing.	339	43	45	48	51
Nondurable goods.	(X)	763	780	813	846
Food and beverage and tobacco products	311, 312	182	187	195	204
Textile mills and textile product mills	313, 314	44	41	42	42
Apparel and leather and allied products.	315, 316	17	16	17	17
Paper products	322	100	97	98	100
Printing and related support activities	323	41	43	45	47
Petroleum and coal products	324	92	98	104	109
Chemical products.	325	220	229	240	252
Plastics and rubber products	326	67	70	72	75
Wholesale trade.	42	348	375	397	420
Retail trade.	44-45	641	730	803	877
Transportation and warehousing	48-49	805	866	903	938
Air transportation	481	196	230	238	246
Railroad transportation	482	267	280	284	292
Water transportation	483	39	45	49	54
Truck transportation.	484	68	66	69	73
Transit and ground passenger transportation	485	34	36	37	38
Pipeline transportation	486	74	83	94	101
Other transportation and support activites [3]	487, 488, 492	105	103	104	106
Warehousing and storage.	493	22	25	27	29
Information	51	817	875	907	945
Publishing industries (includes software)	511	50	51	53	55
Motion picture and sound recording industries	512	32	32	33	35
Broadcasting and telecommunications	513	716	767	793	824
Information and data processing services	514	19	26	28	31
Finance and insurance	52	822	905	982	1,059
Federal Reserve banks	521	11	13	14	16
Credit intermediation and related activities.	522	465	511	549	586
Securities, commodity contracts, and investments.	523	86	93	101	108
Insurance carriers and related activities.	524	165	178	190	202
Funds, trusts, and other financial vehicles	525	95	110	128	147
Real estate and rental and leasing	53	11,476	14,121	15,627	16,839
Real estate	531	11,233	13,832	15,323	16,518
Rental and leasing services and lessors of intangible assets [4]	532, 533	243	289	305	321
Professional, scientific, and technical services	54	205	253	275	298
Legal services	5411	20	22	23	25
Computer systems design and related services	5415	50	58	64	71
Miscellaneous professional, scientific, and technical services [5]	(5)	135	173	188	202
Management of companies and enterprises [6]	551111, 551112	269	308	340	372
Admin/support waste management/remediation services	56	153	176	189	196
Administrative and support services	561	84	104	114	123
Waste management and remediation services	562	68	72	75	73
Educational services	61	213	269	300	333
Health care and social assistance	62	693	831	912	994
Ambulatory health care services	621	190	223	242	261
Hospitals.	622	449	546	601	658
Nursing and residential care facilities	623	29	35	39	43
Social assistance	624	24	28	30	33
Arts, entertainment, and recreation	71	128	157	173	189
Performing arts, spectator sports, museums, and related activities	711, 712	48	60	67	74
Amusements, gambling, and recreation industries.	713	80	97	106	115
Accommodation and food services	72	336	374	403	429
Accommodation	721	177	190	202	213
Food services and drinking places.	722	160	185	200	215
Other services, except public administration	81	329	373	404	436

X Not applicable. [1] Based on North American Industry Classification System, 1997; see text this section. [2] NAICS crop and animal production. [3] Consists of scenic and sightseeing transportation; transportation support activities; and couriers and messengers. [4] Intangible assets include patents, trademarks, and franchise agreements, but not copyrights. [5] Consists of accounting, tax preparation, bookkeeping, and payroll services (NAICS code 5412); architectural, engineering, and related services (5413); specialized design services (5414); management, scientific, and technical consulting services (5416); scientific research and development services (5417); advertising and related services (5418); and other professional, scientific, and technical services (5419). [6] Consists of bank and other holding companies.

Source: U.S. Bureau of Economic Analysis, "Table 3.1ES. Current-Cost Net Stock of Private Fixed Assets by Industry"; published 15 August 2006; <http://www.bea.gov/bea/dn/FA2004/SelectTable.asp#S3>.

508 Business Enterprise

Table 757. **Gross Private Domestic Investment in Current and Real (2000) Dollars: 1990 to 2005**

[In billions of dollars (861 represents $861,000,000,000). Covers equipment, software, and structures. For explanation of chained dollars, see text, Section 13]

Item	1990	1995	2000	2001	2002	2003	2004	2005
CURRENT DOLLARS								
Gross private domestic investment. . .	861	1,144	1,736	1,614	1,582	1,664	1,888	2,057
Less: Consumption of fixed capital	552	713	991	1,076	1,080	1,118	1,205	1,353
Equals: Net private domestic investment , . .	309	431	745	539	502	546	683	705
Fixed investment	846	1,113	1,679	1,646	1,570	1,650	1,831	2,036
Less: Consumption of fixed capital . . .	552	713	991	1,076	1,080	1,118	1,205	1,353
Equals: Net fixed investment	295	400	688	571	490	532	625	684
Nonresidential	622	810	1,232	1,177	1,066	1,077	1,155	1,266
Residential	224	303	447	469	504	572	675	770
Change in private inventories	15	31	57	-32	12	14	57	21
CHAINED (2000) DOLLARS								
Gross private domestic investment. . .	895	1,134	1,736	1,598	1,557	1,613	1,771	1,866
Less: Consumption of fixed capital	572	707	991	1,072	1,080	1,108	1,167	1,270
Equals: Net private domestic investment	323	427	745	527	477	505	603	596
Fixed investment	887	1,110	1,679	1,629	1,545	1,597	1,714	1,842
Nonresidential	595	763	1,232	1,181	1,072	1,082	1,146	1,224
Residential	299	353	447	449	470	509	560	608
Change in private inventories	15	30	57	-32	13	14	53	20

Source: U.S. Bureau of Economic Analysis, "Table 5.2.5. Gross and Net Domestic Investment by Major Type" and "Table 5.2.6. Real Gross and Net Domestic Investment by Major Type, Chained Dollars"; published 2 August 2006; <http://www.bea.gov/national/nipaweb/SelectTable.asp?Selected=N>.

Table 758. **Information and Communications Technology (ICT) Equipment and Computer Software Expenditures: 2004 and 2005**

[In millions of dollars (90,655 represents $90,655,000,000). Covers only companies with employees. The Information and Communication Technology Survey collects noncapitalized and capitalized data on information and communication technology equipment, including computer software. This survey is sent to a sample of approximately 46,000 private nonfarm employer businesses operating in the United States]

Type of expenditure and industry	2002 NAICS code[1]	Noncapitalized expenditures[2]		Capitalized expenditures[3]	
		2004	2005	2004	2005
Total expenditures for ICT equipment and computer software.	(X)	90,655	91,809	137,344	141,602
Total equipment expenditures	(X)	38,447	37,558	(NA)	(NA)
Purchases.	(X)	17,376	18,186	86,792	91,832
Computer and peripheral equipment	(X)	11,801	12,162	51,424	53,833
Information and communication technology equipment	(X)	5,323	5,740	31,015	32,918
Electromedical and electrotherapeutic apparatus	(X)	252	285	4,354	5,082
Operating leases and rental payments	(X)	21,070	19,372	(NA)	(NA)
Computer and peripheral equipment	(X)	14,026	12,938	(NA)	(NA)
Information and communication technology equipment	(X)	5,555	5,439	(NA)	(NA)
Electromedical and electrotherapeutic apparatus	(X)	1,489	996	(NA)	(NA)
Total computer software expenditures	(X)	52,208	54,249	(NA)	(NA)
Purchases and payroll for developing software.	(X)	30,671	31,450	50,552	49,769
Software licensing and service/maintenance agreements	(X)	21,537	22,799	(NA)	(NA)
Forestry, fishing, and agricultural services.	113-115	73	70	71	85
Mining.	21	562	693	703	896
Utilities.	22	1,436	1,323	2,349	2,541
Construction.	23	1,095	863	1,571	1,587
Manufacturing	31-33	16,969	16,591	16,828	15,932
Durable goods industries	321,327,33	11,560	11,282	10,103	9,501
Nondurable goods industries.	31,322–326	5,409	5,309	6,725	6,431
Wholesale trade.	42	3,648	2,970	5,368	4,867
Retail trade	44-45	4,304	4,406	10,712	10,495
Transportation and warehousing	48-49	1,639	1,631	3,092	3,315
Information	51	14,926	15,310	35,612	37,117
Finance and insurance	52	19,091	19,910	23,878	24,333
Real estate and rental and leasing	53	900	1,028	2,340	2,083
Professional, scientific, and technical services.	54	12,781	13,922	11,210	13,050
Management of companies and enterprises	55	546	395	811	707
Admin/support and waste management/remediation services	56	2,490	2,245	3,200	3,354
Educational services.	61	1,506	1,633	2,094	2,027
Health care and social assistance	62	5,862	5,891	12,885	14,049
Arts, entertainment, and recreation	71	391	527	1,109	858
Accommodation and food services	72	674	794	1,327	1,979
Other services (except public administration).	81	1,298	1,210	2,206	1,912
Equipment expenditures serving multiple industry codes	(X)	465	397	518	414

NA Not available. X Not applicable. [1] Based on North American Industry Classification System, 2002; see text, this section. [2] Expenses for ICT equipment including computer software not charged to asset accounts for which depreciation or amortization accounts are ordinarily maintained. [3] Expenses for ICT equipment including computer software chargeable to asset accounts for which depreciation or amortization accounts are ordinarily maintained.

Source: U.S. Census Bureau, *Information and Communication Technology: 2005*, ICT/05, April 2007. See also <http://www.census.gov/csd/ict/>.

Table 759. Capital Expenditures: 2000 to 2005

[In billions of dollars (1,161 represents $1,161,000,000,000). Based on a sample survey and subject to sampling error; see source for details]

Item	All companies				Companies with employees				Companies without employees			
	2000	2003	2004	2005	2000	2003	2004	2005	2000	2003	2004	2005
Capital expenditures, total.............	1,161	975	1,042	1,146	1,090	887	953	1,064	71	88	89	82
Structures...............	364	345	369	402	338	314	335	369	26	31	33	33
New.................	329	305	325	366	309	282	300	341	20	23	24	25
Used................	35	39	44	36	29	32	35	28	6	7	9	8
Equipment and software.....	797	630	673	744	752	573	618	695	45	58	56	49
New.................	751	579	628	702	718	541	588	666	32	39	41	36
Used................	46	51	45	42	34	32	30	29	12	19	15	13
Capital leases	20	16	18	18	19	15	18	18	(Z)	(Z)	(Z)	(Z)

Z Less than $500 million.

Source: U.S. Census Bureau, *Annual Capital Expenditures: 2005*, ACE/05, February 2007. See also <http://www.census.gov/csd/ace/>.

Table 760. Capital Expenditures by Industry: 2000 and 2005

[In billions of dollars (1,090 represents $1,090,000,000,000). Covers only companies with employees. Based on the North American Industry Classification System (NAICS), 2002; see text, this section. Based on a sample survey and subject to sampling error; see source for details]

Industry	2002 NAICS code	2000	2005	Industry	2002 NAICS code	2000	2005
Total expenditures.....	(X)	1,090	1,064	Professional, scientific, and technical services.........	54	34	33
Forestry, fishing, and agricultural services	113-115	1	3	Management of companies and enterprises	55	5	3
Mining.................	21	43	67	Admin/support waste mgt/ remediation services.......	56	18	18
Utilities................	22	61	58	Educational services........	61	18	18
Construction.............	23	25	30	Health care and social assistance	62	52	74
Manufacturing............	31-33	215	165	Arts, entertainment, and recreation.............	71	19	14
Durable goods..........	321, 327, 33	134	92	Accommodation and food services	72	26	31
Nondurable goods	31, 322–326	81	73	Other services (except public administration)...........	81	21	20
Wholesale trade	42	34	40				
Retail trade.............	44-45	70	74	Structure and equipment expenditures serving multiple industry categories ..	(X)	2	2
Transportation and warehousing	48-49	60	57				
Information	51	160	91				
Finance and insurance	52	134	162				
Real estate and rental and leasing................	53	92	103				

X Not applicable.

Source: U.S. Census Bureau, *Annual Capital Expenditures: 2005*, ACE/05, February 2007. See also <http://www.census.gov/csd/ace/>.

Table 761. Business Cycle Expansions and Contractions—Months of Duration: 1945 to 2001

[A trough is the low point of a business cycle; a peak is the high point. Contraction, or recession, is the period from peak to subsequent trough; expansion is the period from trough to subsequent peak. Business cycle reference dates are determined by the National Bureau of Economic Research, Inc.]

Business cycle reference date				Contraction (peak to trough)	Expansion (previous trough to this peak)	Length of cycle	
Peak		Trough				Trough from previous trough	Peak from previous peak
Month	Year	Month	Year				
February.............	1945	October	1945	8	[1]80	[1]88	[2]93
November............	1948	October	1949	11	37	48	45
July	1953	May..........	1954	10	45	55	56
August	1957	April	1958	8	39	47	49
April	1960	February	1961	10	24	34	32
December	1969	November	1970	11	106	117	116
November	1973	March	1975	16	36	52	47
January	1980	July..........	1980	6	58	64	74
July	1981	November	1982	16	12	28	18
July	1990	March	1991	8	92	100	108
March...............	2001	November	2001	8	120	128	128
Average, all cycles: 1945 to 2001 (10 cycles).				10	57	67	67
Average, peacetime cycles: 1945 to 2001 (8 cycles) .				10	52	63	63

[1] Previous trough: June 1938.   [2] Previous peak: May 1937.

Source: National Bureau of Economic Research, Inc., Cambridge, MA, "Business Cycle Expansions and Contractions"; <http://www.nber.org/cycles.html>; (accessed: 30 May 2007).

U.S. Census Bureau, Statistical Abstract of the United States: 2008

Table 762. **Composite Indexes of Leading, Coincident, and Lagging Economic Indicators: 2000 to 2006**

[299.3 represents 299,300]

Item	Unit	2000	2002	2003	2004	2005	2006
Leading index, composite	1996 = 100	115.0	118.4	124.3	132.8	136.2	137.8
Average weekly hours, manufacturing	Hours	41.2	40.5	40.4	40.8	40.6	41.1
Average weekly initial claims for unemployment insurance	1,000	299.3	403.9	401.8	343.0	331.8	313.1
Manufacturers' new orders, consumer goods and materials (1982 dol.)	Mil. dol.	152,031	143,867	143,459	144,002	143,535	141,738
Vendor performance, slower deliveries diffusion index [1]	Percent	53.3	53.3	53.0	62.6	54.1	54.3
Manufacturers' new orders, nondefense capital goods (1982 dol.)	Mil. dol.	49,780	37,792	39,282	39,024	46,312	50,061
Building permits, new private housing units	1,000	1,598	1,749	1,888	2,058	2,159	1,835
Stock prices, 500 common stocks [1]	1941–43 = 10	1,426.8	995.6	963.7	1,130.6	1,207.1	1,310.0
Money supply, M2 (chain 2000 dol.)	Bil. dol.	4,798	5,423	5,691	5,780	5,860	5,971
Interest rate spread, 10-year Treasury bonds less federal funds	Percent	-0.20	2.90	2.90	2.93	1.08	-0.17
Index of consumer expectations [1]	1966:1 = 100	102.7	84.6	81.4	88.5	77.4	75.9
Coincident index, composite	1996 = 100	115.4	114.1	114.5	116.7	119.2	122.2
Employees on nonagricultural payrolls	1,000	131,792	130,342	129,993	131,423	133,696	136,173
Personal income less transfer payments (chain 2000 dol.)	Bil. dol.	7,345	7,336	7,415	7,649	7,814	8,113
Industrial production	2002 = 100	103.5	100.0	100.6	103.6	106.9	111.3
Manufacturing and trade sales (chain 2000 dol.)	Mil. dol.	844,794	844,978	861,783	889,019	917,952	954,416
Lagging index, composite	1996 = 100	116.7	116.4	116.4	117.3	121.4	125.0
Average duration of unemployment	Weeks	12.7	16.7	19.2	19.6	18.4	16.8
Inventories to sales ratio, manufacturing and trade (chain 2000 dol.)	Ratio	1.40	1.40	1.40	1.35	1.33	1.32
Change in labor cost per unit of output, manufacturing	Percent	2.3	0.6	2.7	-1.1	-0.7	-0.1
Average prime rate	Percent	9.2	4.7	4.1	4.3	6.2	8.0
Commercial and industrial loans outstanding (chain 2000 dol.)	Mil. dol.	953,143	686,318	588,372	540,405	571,318	602,118
Consumer installment credit to personal income ratio	Percent	19.2	21.2	21.5	22.1	22.1	21.6
Change in consumer price index for services	Percent	3.8	3.2	3.0	3.0	3.5	3.7

[1] Data are from private sources and provided through the courtesy of the compilers and are subject to their copyrights: stock prices, Standard & Poor's Corporation; index of consumer expectations, University of Michigan's Survey Research Center; vendor performance, Institute for Supply Management.

Source: The Conference Board, New York, NY 10022-6601, *Business Cycle Indicators*, monthly, <http://www.conference-board.org/economics/bci/> (copyright).

Table 763. **Manufacturing and Trade—Sales and Inventories: 1992 to 2006**

[In billions of dollars (541 represents $541,000,000,000), except ratios. Based on North American Industry Classification System (NAICS) 2002; see text, this section]

Year	Sales, average monthly [1]				Inventories [2]				Inventory-sales ratios [3]			
	Total	Manu-facturing	Retail trade	Mer-chant whole-salers	Total	Manu-facturing	Retail trade	Mer-chant whole-salers	Total	Manu-facturing	Retail trade	Mer-chant whole-salers
1992	541	242	151	147	837	379	261	197	1.53	1.57	1.67	1.31
1993	568	252	162	154	864	380	280	205	1.50	1.50	1.68	1.30
1994	610	270	176	165	927	400	305	222	1.46	1.44	1.66	1.29
1995	655	290	185	180	986	425	323	238	1.48	1.44	1.72	1.29
1996	687	300	197	190	1,006	431	334	241	1.46	1.43	1.67	1.27
1997	724	320	206	198	1,047	444	345	259	1.42	1.37	1.64	1.27
1998	743	325	216	202	1,079	449	357	272	1.43	1.38	1.62	1.31
1999	787	336	234	217	1,138	464	385	290	1.40	1.35	1.59	1.29
2000	834	351	249	235	1,197	482	407	308	1.41	1.35	1.59	1.28
2001	819	331	256	232	1,119	428	395	296	1.42	1.38	1.58	1.31
2002	824	326	261	236	1,139	423	417	299	1.36	1.29	1.56	1.25
2003	854	335	272	247	1,145	408	433	303	1.34	1.24	1.56	1.22
2004	923	359	290	275	1,235	440	463	333	1.30	1.18	1.56	1.22
2005	1,001	395	308	299	1,312	479	476	358	1.27	1.17	1.51	1.16
2006	1,066	412	325	329	1,389	510	491	388	1.28	1.21	1.49	1.14

[1] Averages of monthly not-seasonally-adjusted figures.   [2] Seasonally adjusted end-of-year data.   [3] Averages of seasonally adjusted monthly ratios.

Source: U.S. Council of Economic Advisors, *Economic Indicators*, May 2007.

Table 764. Industrial Production Indexes by Industry and Major Market Groups: 1990 to 2006

[2002 = 100. Except as noted, based on the North American Industry Classification System (NAICS); 2002; see text, this section]

Industry and market group	2002 NAICS code	1990	1995	2000	2001	2003	2004	2005	2006
Total index	(X)	68.7	79.8	103.6	100.0	101.1	103.6	106.9	111.1
INDUSTRY GROUP									
Manufacturing (SIC) [1]	(X)	65.9	77.8	104.3	100.0	101.1	104.0	108.0	113.0
Manufacturing (NAICS)	31–33	64.5	77.1	104.0	99.8	101.3	104.4	108.6	113.9
Durable goods	(X)	51.4	66.0	105.4	100.4	102.3	106.3	112.1	120.4
Wood products	321	84.4	91.3	104.2	97.5	100.9	104.5	111.1	107.5
Nonmetallic mineral products	327	83.8	89.5	104.2	100.3	100.9	104.1	108.2	112.5
Primary metals	331	96.2	105.4	110.3	99.8	98.9	109.3	107.1	112.0
Fabricated metal products	332	80.7	95.0	111.2	103.1	98.9	99.1	103.3	108.9
Machinery	333	86.8	102.3	117.7	104.1	99.6	103.7	110.0	117.1
Computers and electronic products	334	11.9	24.9	101.8	103.5	111.5	126.2	141.0	169.1
Electrical equipment, appliances, and components	335	88.4	103.7	122.9	110.4	97.4	99.1	100.7	105.8
Motor vehicles and parts	3361–3	55.5	79.0	99.5	90.6	103.5	103.8	103.7	101.9
Aerospace and other misc. transportation equipment	3364–9	123.0	87.4	99.5	105.8	96.0	94.5	104.2	122.4
Furniture and related products	337	74.6	81.5	102.3	95.8	98.2	101.0	104.6	104.7
Miscellaneous products	339	66.8	78.5	96.5	95.3	103.1	103.2	111.8	116.9
Nondurable goods	(X)	87.7	95.8	102.3	99.0	100.1	102.0	104.5	106.7
Food, beverage, and tobacco products	311,2	90.0	97.3	101.2	100.9	102.0	102.6	106.3	109.8
Textile and product mills	313,4	99.7	112.5	112.7	101.1	96.1	94.6	96.1	92.7
Apparel and leather	315,6	172.8	180.5	151.2	128.5	93.1	81.8	80.0	80.7
Paper	322	97.2	106.8	105.0	99.0	97.3	98.0	98.6	98.5
Printing and related support	323	102.1	107.3	113.1	106.3	96.3	97.0	98.9	103.3
Petroleum and coal products	324	86.9	89.8	96.9	96.4	98.1	106.2	110.0	110.3
Chemical	325	78.3	83.5	95.0	93.3	101.4	105.7	108.0	110.3
Plastics and rubber products	326	67.7	85.6	103.5	97.4	100.1	101.3	102.3	105.7
Other manufacturing (non-NAICS) [2]	1133, 5111	96.7	90.9	109.6	103.2	97.0	97.8	99.6	98.0
Mining	21	106.9	104.4	103.5	104.5	99.9	99.2	97.6	100.2
Utilities	2211,2	77.9	87.2	97.4	97.0	101.9	103.3	105.5	105.3
Electric power generation, transmission and distribution	2211	76.7	85.7	97.2	96.9	102.1	104.2	107.2	108.1
Natural gas distribution	2212	85.6	96.9	98.6	97.2	100.9	99.0	97.2	91.8
MAJOR MARKETS									
Final products and nonindustrial supplies	(X)	72.7	82.6	103.3	100.6	101.2	103.3	107.5	111.2
Consumer goods	(X)	75.9	87.1	99.3	98.1	101.3	102.8	105.7	106.9
Durable	(X)	56.7	75.6	99.2	94.9	103.4	104.8	105.9	105.6
Automotive products	(X)	50.9	71.0	93.9	90.8	105.6	105.2	102.6	99.4
Home electronics	(X)	6.7	31.0	98.6	100.0	110.5	126.9	145.1	169.9
Appliances, furniture, carpeting	(X)	77.8	86.3	103.1	98.7	99.8	103.1	106.2	104.4
Miscellaneous goods	(X)	82.3	93.0	106.9	99.3	100.1	101.7	105.8	108.1
Nondurable	(X)	84.9	92.3	99.3	99.4	100.5	102.0	105.5	107.2
Nonenergy	(X)	86.3	93.5	100.3	100.1	100.5	101.7	105.2	107.7
Foods and tobacco	(X)	91.3	98.5	101.8	101.7	101.4	102.9	106.5	109.5
Clothing	(X)	171.5	180.2	150.1	128.1	93.1	81.0	78.8	79.5
Chemical products	(X)	63.1	71.1	86.9	91.5	101.6	104.7	108.4	110.6
Paper products	(X)	84.6	87.7	103.7	100.9	96.6	97.4	100.8	101.6
Energy	(X)	78.5	86.6	95.1	96.2	100.6	103.0	106.9	106.1
Business equipment	(X)	57.3	70.8	114.6	107.6	100.2	104.5	112.8	125.9
Transit	(X)	109.7	90.4	116.9	111.3	94.8	99.4	111.5	138.9
Information processing	(X)	24.5	41.6	117.1	115.2	104.5	111.8	122.1	137.4
Industrial and other	(X)	82.6	96.3	112.7	101.7	99.6	102.2	108.2	115.4
Defense and space equipment	(X)	141.4	105.8	92.1	100.6	103.8	104.0	109.7	112.0
Construction supplies	(X)	76.6	86.7	105.1	100.5	99.8	101.8	106.7	110.4
Business supplies	(X)	71.3	80.8	104.2	100.0	101.5	103.7	107.1	110.3
Materials	(X)	63.8	76.1	104.0	99.1	100.9	104.0	106.2	111.0
Nonenergy	(X)	56.9	71.3	105.0	98.8	101.3	105.6	109.4	115.7
Durable	(X)	43.5	60.1	105.2	99.3	102.5	108.3	113.8	123.4
Consumer parts	(X)	58.6	85.1	107.4	95.0	98.9	99.0	100.3	100.7
Equipment parts	(X)	20.2	32.8	101.8	100.4	108.3	120.0	133.1	159.9
Other	(X)	81.2	94.6	107.9	100.3	99.5	103.8	106.1	109.6
Nondurable	(X)	92.1	98.1	104.6	98.0	99.3	101.2	102.4	104.0
Textile	(X)	103.5	118.8	112.1	99.2	94.6	90.1	89.5	86.3
Paper	(X)	102.2	109.0	108.5	102.0	96.7	98.0	99.1	100.5
Chemical	(X)	85.8	90.5	101.6	94.6	101.0	106.6	107.6	109.4
Energy	(X)	95.6	98.0	101.0	100.0	99.9	99.7	98.4	99.8

X Not applicable. [1] Standard Industrial Classification (SIC); see text, this section. [2] Those industries—logging and newspaper, periodical, book, and directory publishing—that have traditionally been considered to be manufacturing.

Source: Board of Governors of the Federal Reserve System, *Statistical Supplement to the Federal Reserve Bulletin*, monthly; and *Industrial Production and Capacity Utilization*, Statistical Release G.17, monthly. See also <http://www.federalreserve.gov/releases/g17/>.

Table 765. Index of Industrial Capacity: 1990 to 2006

[2002 output = 100. Annual figures are averages of monthly data. Capacity represents estimated quantity of output relative to output in 2002 which the current stock of plant and equipment was capable of producing]

Year	Index of capacity		Relation of output to capacity (percent)				
				Stage of process			
	Total industry	Manufacturing	Total industry	Crude [1]	Primary and semifinished [2]	Finished [3]	Manufacturing
1990	83.4	80.7	82.4	89.2	82.7	80.3	81.6
1995	95.0	93.6	84.0	88.6	86.8	79.5	83.1
1997	106.3	106.4	83.9	90.2	85.9	80.1	83.0
1998	114.3	115.5	82.8	87.3	84.0	80.5	81.7
1999	120.9	123.1	81.9	86.6	84.1	78.5	80.8
2000	126.9	130.3	81.7	88.2	84.3	77.0	80.1
2001	131.4	135.4	76.1	85.3	77.6	72.4	73.9
2002	133.6	137.1	74.8	82.9	77.2	70.6	73.0
2003	132.8	136.2	76.1	84.6	78.3	71.7	74.2
2004	132.5	135.7	78.1	86.5	80.7	73.1	76.6
2005	133.3	137.1	80.2	86.4	82.6	75.5	78.8
2006	136.1	140.6	81.8	88.7	83.4	77.6	80.4

[1] Crude processing, covers a relatively small portion of total industrial capacity and consists of logging (NAICS 1133), much of mining (excluding stone, sand, and gravel mining, and oil and gas drilling, which are NAICS 21231, 21221-2, and 213111) and some basic manufacturing industries, including basic chemicals (NAICS 3251); fertilizers, pesticides, and other agricultural chemicals (NAICS 32531,2); pulp, paper, and paperboard mills (NAICS 3221); and alumina, aluminum, and other nonferrous production and processing mills (NAICS 3313,4).   [2] Primary and semifinished processing loosely corresponds to the previously published aggregate, primary processing. Includes utilities and portions of several 2-digit SIC industries included in the former advanced processing group. These include printing and related support activities (NAICS 3231); paints and adhesives (NAICS 3255); and newspaper, periodical, book, and directory publishers (NAICS 5111).   [3] Finished processing generally corresponds to the previously published aggregate, advanced processing. Includes oil and gas well drilling and carpet and rug mills.

Source: Board of Governors of the Federal Reserve System, *Industrial Production and Capacity Utilization*, Statistical Release G.17, monthly. (Based on data from Federal Reserve Board, U.S. Dept. of Commerce, U.S. Bureau of Labor Statistics, and McGraw-Hill Information Systems Company, New York, NY; and other sources.)

Table 766. Productivity and Related Measures: 1990 to 2006

[See text, Section 12. Minus sign (–) indicates decrease]

Item	1990	1995	2000	2001	2002	2003	2004	2005	2006
INDEXES (1992 = 100)									
Output per hour, business sector...........	94.4	101.5	116.1	119.1	123.9	128.7	132.6	135.4	137.7
Nonfarm business...............	94.5	102.0	115.7	118.6	123.5	128.0	131.8	134.6	136.7
Manufacturing.................	93.8	110.7	139.4	141.5	151.5	160.9	163.8	171.6	178.4
Output, [1] business sector................	96.9	114.4	140.5	141.0	143.1	147.5	154.0	159.8	165.8
Nonfarm business...............	97.1	111.8	140.8	141.3	143.4	147.8	154.2	160.0	166.1
Manufacturing.................	98.5	115.8	144.1	136.8	136.0	137.3	139.1	144.2	151.4
Hours, [2] business sector	102.7	109.7	121.0	118.4	115.4	114.6	116.1	118.0	120.4
Nonfarm business...............	102.7	109.6	121.7	119.2	116.1	115.4	117.0	118.9	121.5
Manufacturing.................	105.0	104.6	103.4	96.6	89.8	85.4	85.0	84.0	84.9
Compensation per hour, [3] business sector	90.6	105.8	134.7	140.4	145.3	151.2	156.9	163.5	171.6
Nonfarm business...............	90.4	105.3	134.2	139.5	144.6	150.4	155.9	162.3	170.4
Manufacturing.................	90.5	107.3	134.7	137.9	147.9	158.3	161.4	168.9	175.7
Real hourly compensation, [3] business sector...	96.2	98.7	112.0	113.5	115.7	117.7	119.0	119.9	121.9
Nonfarm business...............	96.0	98.8	111.6	112.8	115.1	117.1	118.2	119.1	121.0
Manufacturing.................	96.1	100.1	112.0	111.5	117.7	123.2	122.3	123.9	124.8
Unit labor costs, [4] business sector...........	96.0	104.2	116.0	117.9	117.3	117.5	118.3	120.7	124.6
Nonfarm business...............	95.7	103.8	116.0	117.7	117.1	117.5	118.3	120.6	124.6
Manufacturing.................	96.4	96.9	96.7	97.4	97.6	98.4	98.5	98.4	98.5
ANNUAL PERCENT CHANGE [5]									
Output per hour, business sector...........	2.1	0.1	2.9	2.6	4.1	3.8	3.1	2.1	1.7
Nonfarm business...............	1.9	0.5	2.8	2.5	4.1	3.7	2.9	2.1	1.6
Manufacturing.................	2.2	4.4	4.4	1.5	7.0	6.2	1.8	4.8	4.0
Output, [1] business sector................	1.5	2.9	3.9	0.3	1.5	3.1	4.4	3.7	3.8
Nonfarm business...............	1.5	3.2	3.8	0.4	1.5	3.1	4.3	3.8	3.8
Manufacturing.................	–0.4	5.2	2.7	–5.1	–0.6	1.0	1.3	3.6	5.0
Hours, [2] business sector	–0.6	2.8	1.0	–2.2	–2.5	–0.7	1.3	1.6	2.1
Nonfarm business...............	–0.4	2.7	1.0	–2.0	–2.6	–0.6	1.4	1.6	2.1
Manufacturing.................	–2.5	0.8	–1.6	–6.5	–7.1	–4.9	–0.5	–1.1	1.0
Compensation per hour, [3] business sector	6.3	2.1	7.1	4.2	3.5	4.1	3.8	4.2	5.0
Nonfarm business...............	6.1	2.1	7.2	4.0	3.6	4.0	3.6	4.1	5.0
Manufacturing.................	4.4	1.9	9.2	2.3	7.3	7.0	2.0	4.7	4.1
Real hourly compensation, [3] business sector...	1.3	–0.3	3.7	1.4	1.9	1.7	1.1	0.8	1.6
Nonfarm business...............	1.0	–0.3	3.7	1.2	2.0	1.7	0.9	0.8	1.6
Manufacturing.................	–0.5	–0.5	5.7	–0.5	5.6	4.7	–0.7	1.3	0.7
Unit labor costs, [4] business sector...........	4.1	1.9	4.1	1.6	–0.5	0.2	0.7	2.0	3.2
Nonfarm business...............	4.1	1.6	4.2	1.5	–0.5	0.3	0.7	2.0	3.3
Manufacturing.................	2.2	–2.4	4.5	0.8	0.2	0.8	0.2	–0.1	0.1

[1] Refers to gross sectoral product, annual weighted.   [2] Hours at work of all persons engaged in the business and nonfarm business sectors (employees, proprietors, and unpaid family workers); employees' and proprietors' hours in manufacturing. [3] Wages and salaries of employees plus employers' contributions for social insurance and private benefit plans. Also includes an estimate of same for self-employed. Real compensation deflated by the consumer price index for all urban consumers, see text, Section 14.   [4] Hourly compensation divided by output per hour.   [5] All changes are from the immediate prior year.

Source: U.S. Bureau of Labor Statistics, *Productivity and Costs*, News USDL 07-0821, June 6, 2007; and Internet site <http://www.bls.gov/lpc/home.htm>.

Business Enterprise   513

Table 767. **Corporate Profits, Taxes, and Dividends: 1990 to 2006**

[In billions of dollars (438 represents $438,000,000,000). Covers corporations organized for profit and other entities treated as corporations. Represents profits to U.S. residents, without deduction of depletion charges and exclusive of capital gains and losses; intercorporate dividends from profits of domestic corporations are eliminated; net receipts of dividends, reinvested earnings of incorporated foreign affiliates, and earnings of unincorporated foreign affiliates are added. CCA = capital consumption adjustment]

Item	1990	2000	2002	2003	2004	2005	2006
Corporate profits with IVA and CCA	438	818	886	993	1,183	1,331	1,616
Taxes on corporate income	145	265	193	243	300	399	475
Profits after tax with IVA and CCA	292	553	694	750	883	931	1,141
Net dividends	169	378	399	425	540	577	642
Undistributed profits with IVA and CCA	123	175	295	325	343	355	499
Cash flow:							
Net cash flow with IVA and CCA	491	865	1,037	1,085	1,139	1,211	1,365
Undistributed profits with IVA and CCA	123	175	295	325	343	355	499
Consumption of fixed capital	368	690	742	760	796	857	866
Less: Inventory valuation adjustment (IVA)	-13	-14	-2	-14	-40	-33	-34
Equals: Net cash flow	504	879	1,039	1,099	1,179	1,244	1,399

Source: U.S. Bureau of Economic Analysis, *Survey of Current Business*, monthly. See also <http://www.bea.gov/national /nipaweb/Index.asp>.

Table 768. **Corporate Profits With Inventory Valuation and Capital Consumption Adjustments—Financial and Nonfinancial Industries: 2000 to 2006**

[In billions of dollars (818 represents $818,000,000,000). Based on the North American Industry Classification System 1997; see text, this section. Minus sign (–) indicates loss. See headnote, Table 767]

Item	2000	2002	2003	2004	2005	2006
Corporate profits with IVA/CCA [1]	818	886	993	1,183	1,331	1,616
Domestic industries	672	731	828	1,006	1,134	1,373
Rest of the world	146	156	166	176	197	243
Corporate profits with IVA [1]	759	766	895	1,105	1,486	1,777
Domestic industries	614	610	729	928	1,289	1,533
Financial [2]	200	276	317	344	389	499
Nonfinancial	413	334	412	584	900	1,035
Utilities	24	11	12	16	30	49
Manufacturing	144	48	76	150	255	312
Wholesale trade	60	49	55	70	98	106
Retail trade	60	79	87	89	114	130
Transportation and warehousing	15	-1	7	12	21	35
Information	-18	-9	3	38	78	88
Other nonfinancial [3]	128	156	172	209	305	316
Rest of the world	146	156	166	176	197	243

[1] Inventory valuation adjustment and capital consumption adjustment. [2] Consists of finance and insurance and bank and other holding companies. [3] Consists of agriculture, forestry, fishing, and hunting; mining; construction; real estate and rental and leasing; professional, scientific, and technical services; administrative and waste management services; educational services; health care and social assistance; arts, entertainment, and recreation; accommodation and food services; and other services, except government.

Source: U.S. Bureau of Economic Analysis, *Survey of Current Business*, May 2007. See also <http://www.bea.gov/national /nipaweb/Index.asp>.

Table 769. **Corporate Profits Before Taxes by Industry: 2000 to 2005**

[In billions of dollars (773 represents $773,000,000,000). Profits are without inventory valuation and capital consumption adjustments. Minus sign (–) indicates loss. See headnote, Table 767]

Industry	1997 NAICS code [1]	2000	2002	2003	2004	2005
Corporate profits before tax	(X)	773	768	908	1,144	1,519
Domestic industries	(X)	628	613	743	968	1,322
Agriculture, forestry, fishing, and hunting	11	2	(Z)	2	3	5
Mining	21	15	5	16	22	39
Utilities	221	25	11	12	17	31
Construction	23	42	47	39	55	83
Manufacturing	31–33	153	48	83	172	271
Wholesale trade	42	62	52	60	79	104
Retail trade	44–45	61	79	88	95	120
Transportation and warehousing	48–49	15	-1	7	12	22
Information	51	-18	-9	3	37	77
Finance and insurance	52	113	158	196	204	222
Real estate and rental and leasing	53	9	10	10	12	24
Professional, scientific, and technical services	54	1	20	26	31	42
Management of companies and enterprises [2]	551111,551112	87	119	121	141	167
Admin/support waste mgt/remediation services	56	9	10	14	16	21
Educational services	61	2	3	3	4	5
Health care and social assistance	62	25	37	40	40	52
Arts, entertainment, and recreation	71	2	4	3	4	6
Accommodation and food services	72	14	13	12	16	22
Other services, except public administration	81	8	7	8	8	10
Rest of the world [3]	(X)	146	156	165	176	197

X Not applicable. Z Less than $500 million. [1] Based on North American Industry Classification System, 1997; see text, this section. [2] Consists of bank and other holding companies. [3] Consists of receipts by all U.S. residents, including both corporations and persons, of dividends from foreign corporations and, for U.S. corporations, their share of reinvested earnings of their incorporated foreign affiliates, and earnings of unincorporated foreign affiliates, net of corresponding payments.

Source: U.S. Bureau of Economic Analysis, *Survey of Current Business*, August 2006. See also <http://www.bea.gov/national /nipaweb/Index.asp>.

514 Business Enterprise

Table 770. Manufacturing, Mining, and Trade Corporations—Profits and Stockholders' Equity by Industry: 2005 and 2006

[Averages of quarterly figures at annual rates. Manufacturing data exclude estimates for corporations with less than $250,000 in assets at time of sample selection. Based on sample; see source for discussion of methodology. Based on North American Industry Classification System (NAICS), 2002; see text, this section. Minus sign (−) indicates loss]

Industry	2002 NAICS code	Ratio of profits after taxes to stockholders' equity (percent)		Profits after taxes per dollar of sales (cents)		Ratio of stockholders' equity to debt	
		2005	2006	2005	2006	2005	2006
Manufacturing.	31–33	**16.6**	**18.0**	**7.4**	**8.3**	**1.9**	**2.0**
Nondurable manufacturing	(X)	21.7	21.9	9.0	9.8	1.6	1.8
Food.	311	17.5	19.0	4.8	5.3	1.1	1.1
Beverage and tobacco products.	312	25.8	24.6	16.3	17.1	1.2	1.5
Textile mills and textile product mills.	313, 314	9.9	8.0	3.1	3.0	1.5	1.8
Apparel and leather products.	315, 316	20.7	20.3	7.1	7.7	2.1	2.4
Paper.	322	7.2	11.4	2.9	4.3	0.9	1.0
Printing and related support activities	323	12.4	18.6	2.6	4.0	0.8	0.7
Petroleum and coal products.	324	30.4	28.3	10.1	10.6	3.0	3.1
Chemicals.	325	18.8	19.4	12.6	13.9	1.7	1.9
Plastics and rubber products.	326	16.1	15.5	3.6	3.6	0.7	0.8
Durable manufacturing.	(X)	12.4	14.4	5.9	6.8	2.2	2.3
Wood products.	321	17.8	17.7	4.5	4.8	1.3	1.3
Nonmetallic mineral products.	327	0.2	23.3	−0.5	7.7	1.1	1.1
Primary metals.	331	17.9	23.8	6.7	8.7	1.8	2.0
Fabricated metal products.	332	20.4	24.6	6.1	7.5	1.4	1.6
Machinery.	333	13.6	17.7	5.8	7.7	1.8	2.1
Computer and electronic products	334	11.7	13.4	10.4	12.0	4.4	4.3
Electrical equipment, appliances, & components.	335	14.9	18.1	12.0	14.1	3.9	3.8
Transportation equipment.	336	6.3	2.0	1.6	0.5	1.3	1.2
Furniture and related products.	337	17.2	17.7	5.1	5.2	1.5	1.2
Miscellaneous manufacturing.	339	15.7	11.1	10.4	8.1	2.2	2.7
All mining.	21	**20.6**	**20.4**	**25.2**	**27.0**	**2.3**	**2.4**
All wholesale trade.	42	**16.0**	**14.8**	**2.4**	**2.1**	**1.8**	**1.7**
Durable goods.	421	12.8	13.5	2.5	2.6	1.9	1.8
Nondurable goods.	422	21.3	17.6	2.3	1.6	1.6	1.4
All retail trade.	44–45	**16.8**	**16.2**	**3.2**	**3.2**	**1.8**	**1.8**
Food and beverage stores.	445	12.6	13.8	1.5	1.7	1.0	1.2
Clothing and general merchandise stores.	448, 452	17.0	15.3	4.1	3.9	2.0	2.2
All other retail trade.	(X)	17.7	18.0	3.3	3.3	1.9	1.7

X Not applicable.

Source: U.S. Census Bureau, *Quarterly Financial Report for Manufacturing, Mining, and Trade Corporations.*

Table 771. Value Added, Employment, and Capital Expenditures of Nonbank U.S. Multinational Companies: 1994 to 2004

[Value added and capital expenditures in billions of dollars (1,717 represents $1,717,000,000,000); employees in thousands. See headnote, Table 772. MNC = Multinational company. MOFA = Majority-owned foreign affiliate. Minus sign (−) indicates decrease]

Item	1994 [1]	1999	2000	2001	2002	2003	2004	Percent change at annual rates	
								1994– 1999	1999– 2004
VALUE ADDED									
MNCs worldwide:									
Parents and all affiliates.	(NA)	(NA)	(NA)	(NA)	(NA)	(NA)	(NA)	(NA)	(NA)
Parents and MOFAs.	1,717	2,481	2,748	2,478	2,460	2,656	3,040	7.6	4.2
Parents.	1,314	1,914	2,141	1,892	1,859	1,958	2,216	7.8	3.0
Affiliates, total.	(NA)	(NA)	(NA)	(NA)	(NA)	(NA)	(NA)	(NA)	(NA)
MOFAs.	404	566	607	586	602	698	824	7.0	7.8
Other.	(NA)	(NA)	(NA)	(NA)	(NA)	(NA)	(NA)	(NA)	(NA)
EMPLOYEES									
MNCs worldwide:									
Parents and all affiliates.	25,670	32,227	33,598	32,539	31,894	30,762	31,406	4.7	−0.5
Parents and MOFAs.	24,273	30,773	32,057	30,929	30,373	29,347	29,995	4.9	−0.5
Parents.	18,565	23,007	23,885	22,735	22,118	21,105	21,378	4.4	−1.5
Affiliates, total.	7,105	9,220	9,713	9,804	9,776	9,658	10,028	5.4	1.7
MOFAs.	5,707	7,766	8,171	8,194	8,256	8,242	8,617	6.4	2.1
Other.	1,398	1,454	1,542	1,610	1,520	1,415	1,411	0.8	−0.6
CAPITAL EXPENDITURES									
MNCs worldwide:									
Parents and all affiliates.	328	514	(NA)	(NA)	(NA)	(NA)	(NA)	(NA)	(NA)
Parents and MOFAs.	303	483	507	524	443	425	432	9.4	−3.2
Parents.	232	370	396	413	333	315	309	9.8	−4.9
Affiliates, total.	96	144	(NA)	(NA)	(NA)	(NA)	(NA)	(NA)	(NA)
MOFAs.	71	113	111	111	110	110	123	7.9	2.2
Other.	25	31	(NA)	(NA)	(NA)	(NA)	(NA)	(NA)	(NA)

NA Not available. [1] Data for 1994 are not strictly comparable with data beginning 1999; see source.

Source: U.S. Bureau of Economic Analysis, *Survey of Current Business,* November 2006.

Business Enterprise 515

Table 772. U.S. Multinational Companies—Selected Characteristics: 2004

[Preliminary. In billions of dollars (15,778 represents $15,778,000,000,000), except as indicated. Consists of nonbank U.S. parent companies and their nonbank foreign affiliates. U.S. parent comprises the domestic operations of a multinational and is a U.S. person that owns or controls directly or indirectly, 10 percent or more of the voting securities of an incorporated foreign business enterprise, or an equivalent interest in an unincorporated foreign business enterprise. A U.S. person can be an incorporated business enterprise. A majority-owned foreign affiliate (MOFA) is a foreign business enterprise in which a U.S. parent company owns or controls more than 50 percent of the voting securities]

| Industry [1] | 2002 NAICS code | U.S. parents | | | | MOFAs | | |
		Total assets	Capital expen-ditures	Value added	Employ-ment (1,000)	Capital expen-ditures	Value added	Employ-ment (1,000)
All industries................	(X)	15,778	308.7	2,216	21,378	123.1	824	8,617
Mining	21	227	15.4	40	183	29.0	95	164
Utilities	22	685	29.4	93	310	3.1	10	60
Manufacturing [2]	31–33	4,848	119.1	1,011	7,864	51.1	391	4,309
Petroleum and coal products.	324	427	16.0	120	212	3.4	61	39
Chemicals	325	770	19.4	176	924	9.9	76	562
Computers and electronic products	334	508	13.5	111	944	7.1	39	645
Transportation equipment	336	1,678	34.2	202	1,858	11.9	55	946
Wholesale trade	42	432	18.9	104	795	7.0	122	734
Information [2]	51	1,407	47.2	259	1,787	4.2	37	318
Broadcasting (except Internet) and telecommunications	515,517	931	39.5	165	1,054	2.7	11	83
Finance (except depository institutions) and insurance	52 exc. 521, 522	6,805	17.9	177	1,217	7.6	39	243
Professional, scientific, and technical services	54	264	7.9	115	959	3.1	46	475
Other industries [2].	(X)	1,110	52.9	416	8,262	17.9	87	2,315
Retail trade	44–45	344	22.8	175	3,919	3.7	32	724

X Not applicable.   [1] Represents North American Industry Classification System 2002-based industry of U.S. parent or industry of foreign affiliate.   [2] Includes other industries not shown separately.

Source: U.S. Bureau of Economic Analysis, *Survey of Current Business*, November 2006 and unpublished data.

Table 773. U.S. Multinational Companies—Value Added: 2000 and 2004

[In billions of dollars (2,748 represents $2,748,000,000,000). See headnote, Table 772. Data are by industry of U.S. parent. Based on the North American Industry Classification System, 2002 (NAICS); see text this section]

| Industry | 2002 NAICS code | U.S. multinationals | | U.S. parents | | Majority-owned foreign affiliates | |
		2000	2004	2000	2004	2000	2004
All industries	(X)	2,748	3,040	2,141	2,216	607	824
Mining	21	39	64	28	40	11	24
Utilities	22	86	101	81	93	5	8
Manufacturing [1]	31–33	1,410	1,574	995	1,011	415	563
Petroleum and coal products	324	232	282	112	120	120	162
Chemicals	325	212	275	141	176	71	99
Computers and electronic products	334	188	164	142	111	46	54
Transportation equipment	336	271	281	209	202	62	79
Wholesale trade	42	133	134	99	104	34	30
Information [1]	51	325	295	302	259	22	36
Broadcasting (except Internet) and telecommunications	515,517	226	175	218	165	8	10
Finance (except depository institutions) and insurance	52 exc. 521,522	181	217	157	177	24	40
Professional, scientific, and technical services . . .	54	141	166	101	115	41	51
Other industries [1]	(X)	433	488	379	416	54	72
Retail trade	44–45	166	196	149	175	18	21

X Not applicable.   [1] Includes other industries not shown separately.

Source: U.S. Bureau of Economic Analysis, *Survey of Current Business*, November 2003 and November 2006.

Table 774. U.S. Majority-Owned Foreign Affiliates—Value Added by Industry of Affiliate and Country: 2004

[In millions of dollars (824,336 represents $824,336,000,000. See headnote, Table 772. Numbers in parentheses represent North American Industry Classification System 2002 codes; see text, this section]

| Country | All industries [1] | Mining (21) | Manufacturing (31–33) | | | | Wholesale trade (42) | Professional, scientific, and technical services (54) |
			Total [1]	Chemicals (325)	Transporta-tion equip-ment (336)		
All countries [2].	824,336	94,662	390,714	76,457	55,476	121,597	45,804
United Kingdom	132,527	11,081	53,473	8,648	5,222	13,890	12,260
Canada	94,205	15,259	47,554	5,442	11,680	7,366	2,027
Germany	74,184	1,478	41,825	5,286	11,162	18,165	3,725
France	47,717	105	26,194	6,278	3,851	7,792	2,371
Japan	46,491	4	20,244	4,664	490	7,525	6,006
Australia	29,853	4,393	11,227	1,882	1,853	4,870	2,720
Italy	29,292	18	20,230	3,914	1,396	4,221	1,529
Netherlands	28,220	1,025	14,900	3,933	1,896	4,442	2,323
Ireland	27,022	17	19,187	8,696	63	3,027	569
Mexico	22,383	1,228	14,703	3,158	4,646	1,116	415

[1] Includes other industries not shown separately.   [2] Includes other countries not shown separately.

Source: U.S. Bureau of Economic Analysis, *Survey of Current Business*, November 2006.

516   Business Enterprise

Science and Technology

This section presents statistics on scientific, engineering, and technological resources, with emphasis on patterns of research and development (R&D) funding and on scientific, engineering, and technical personnel; education; and employment. Also included are statistics on space program outlays. Principal sources of these data are the National Science Foundation (NSF) and the National Aeronautics and Space Administration (NASA).

NSF gathers data chiefly through recurring surveys. Current NSF publications containing data on funds for research and development and on scientific and engineering personnel include detailed statistical tables; issue briefs; and annual, biennial, triennial, and special reports. Titles or the areas of coverage of these reports include the following: *Science and Engineering Indicators; National Patterns of R&D Resources; Women, Minorities, and Persons with Disabilities in Science and Engineering*—science and technology data presented in chart and tabular form in a pocket-sized publication—*Federal Funds for Research and Development*; Federal R&D Funding by Budget Function; Federal Support to Universities, Colleges, and Selected Nonprofit Institutions; *Research and Development in Industry*; R&D expenditures and graduate enrollment and support in academic science and engineering; and characteristics of doctoral scientists and engineers and of recent graduates in the United States. Statistical surveys in these areas pose problems of concept and definition and the data should therefore be regarded as broad estimates rather than precise, quantitative statements. See sources for methodological and technical details.

The National Science Board's biennial *Science and Engineering Indicators* contains data and analysis of international and domestic science and technology, including measures of inputs and outputs.

The *Budget of the United States Government*, published by the U.S. Office of Management and Budget, contains summary financial data on federal R&D programs.

Research and development outlays— NSF defines research as "systematic study directed toward fuller scientific knowledge of the subject studied" and development as "the systematic use of scientific knowledge directed toward the production of useful materials, devices, systems, or methods, including design and development of prototypes and processes."

National coverage of R&D expenditures is developed primarily from periodic surveys in four principal economic sectors: (1) *Government,* made up primarily of federal executive agencies; (2) *industry,* consisting of manufacturing and nonmanufacturing firms and the federally funded research and development centers (FFRDCs) they administer; (3) *universities and colleges,* composed of universities, colleges, and their affiliated institutions, agricultural experiment stations, and associated schools of agriculture and of medicine, and FFRDCs administered by educational institutions; and (4) *other nonprofit institutions,* consisting of such organizations as private philanthropic foundations, nonprofit research institutes, voluntary health agencies, and FFRDCs administered by nonprofit organizations.

The R&D funds reported consist of current operating costs, including planning and administration costs, except as otherwise noted. They exclude funds for routine testing, mapping and surveying, collection of general-purpose data, dissemination of scientific information, and training of scientific personnel.

Scientists, engineers, and technicians—Scientists and engineers are defined as persons engaged in scientific and engineering work at a level requiring a knowledge of sciences equivalent at least to that acquired through completion

of a 4-year college course. Technicians are defined as persons engaged in technical work at a level requiring knowledge acquired through a technical institute, junior college, or other type of training less extensive than 4-year college training. Craftsmen and skilled workers are excluded.

Table 775. Research and Development (R&D) Expenditures by Source and Objective: 1970 to 2006

[In millions of dollars (26,271 represents $26,271,000,000), except as indicated. For calendar years]

Year	Sources of funds						Objective (percent of total)			Character of work		
	Total	Federal government	Industry	Universities/colleges	Non-profit	Non-federal government[1]	Defense related[2]	Space related[3]	Other	Basic research	Applied research	Development
1970 ...	26,271	14,984	10,449	259	343	237	33	10	56	3,594	5,752	16,925
1971 ...	26,952	15,210	10,824	290	366	262	33	10	58	3,720	5,833	17,399
1972 ...	28,740	16,039	11,715	312	393	282	33	8	59	3,850	6,147	18,743
1973 ...	30,952	16,587	13,299	343	422	302	32	7	61	4,099	6,655	20,197
1974 ...	33,359	17,287	14,885	393	474	320	29	7	64	4,511	7,344	21,504
1975 ...	35,671	18,533	15,824	432	534	348	28	8	65	4,875	8,091	22,706
1976 ...	39,435	20,292	17,702	480	592	369	27	8	65	5,373	8,976	25,085
1977 ...	43,338	22,071	19,642	569	662	394	27	7	66	6,008	9,662	27,667
1978 ...	48,719	24,414	22,457	679	727	443	26	6	68	6,959	10,704	31,056
1979 ...	55,379	27,225	26,097	785	791	482	25	6	70	7,836	12,097	35,445
1980 ...	63,224	29,986	30,929	920	871	519	24	5	70	8,745	13,714	40,765
1981 ...	72,292	33,739	35,948	1,058	967	581	24	5	70	9,658	16,329	46,305
1982 ...	80,748	37,133	40,692	1,207	1,095	621	26	5	69	10,651	18,218	51,879
1983 ...	89,950	41,451	45,264	1,357	1,220	658	28	4	68	11,880	20,298	57,771
1984 ...	102,244	46,470	52,187	1,514	1,351	721	29	3	68	13,332	22,451	66,461
1985 ...	114,671	52,641	57,962	1,743	1,491	834	30	3	67	14,748	25,401	74,522
1986 ...	120,249	54,622	60,991	2,019	1,647	969	31	3	66	17,154	27,240	75,855
1987 ...	126,360	58,609	62,576	2,262	1,849	1,065	32	3	65	18,481	27,951	79,929
1988 ...	133,880	60,130	67,977	2,527	2,081	1,165	30	4	66	19,786	29,528	84,566
1989 ...	141,889	60,464	74,966	2,852	2,333	1,274	28	4	69	21,889	32,277	87,723
1990 ...	151,990	61,607	83,208	3,187	2,589	1,399	25	4	71	23,028	34,896	94,067
1991 ...	160,872	60,780	92,300	3,457	2,852	1,483	22	5	73	27,139	38,629	95,104
1992 ...	165,347	60,912	96,229	3,568	3,113	1,525	22	4	74	27,604	37,933	99,810
1993 ...	165,726	60,524	96,549	3,709	3,388	1,557	21	4	74	28,742	37,280	99,704
1994 ...	169,201	60,773	99,203	3,938	3,665	1,622	20	5	76	29,649	36,615	102,937
1995 ...	183,618	62,964	110,870	4,110	3,924	1,751	19	5	77	29,609	40,932	113,077
1996 ...	197,338	63,388	123,416	4,435	4,239	1,860	18	4	78	32,797	43,165	121,375
1997 ...	212,142	64,567	136,227	4,837	4,590	1,921	17	4	79	36,915	46,551	128,676
1998 ...	226,455	66,375	147,845	5,162	5,101	1,971	16	4	80	35,331	46,388	144,736
1999 ...	245,036	67,045	164,660	5,618	5,616	2,098	15	3	82	38,872	52,096	154,068
2000 ...	267,557	66,403	186,135	6,230	6,542	2,246	13	2	84	42,763	56,932	167,862
2001 ...	277,736	72,820	188,439	6,824	7,256	2,396	14	2	84	47,785	64,706	165,245
2002 ...	276,591	77,691	180,711	7,341	8,291	2,556	15	2	82	51,400	51,033	174,157
2003 ...	289,025	83,596	186,174	7,648	8,868	2,740	16	2	82	55,109	61,448	172,468
2004 ...	300,060	88,908	191,376	7,932	8,962	2,882	17	2	81	56,670	70,093	173,297
2005[4] ..	323,546	94,635	207,556	8,413	9,949	2,993	17	2	81	60,157	75,252	188,138
2006[4] ..	342,886	96,847	223,042	8,909	10,924	3,164	12	2	86	63,648	79,291	199,947

[1] Nonfederal R&D expenditures to university and college performers.   [2] R&D spending by the Department of Defense, including space activities and a portion of the Department of Energy funds.   [3] For the National Aeronautics and Space Administration only.   [4] Preliminary.

Source: U.S. National Science Foundation, *National Patterns of R&D Resources*, annual. See also <http://www.nsf.gov/statistics/>.

Table 776. Performance Sector of Research and Development (R&D) Expenditures: 1995 to 2006

[In millions of dollars (183,618 represents $183,618,000,000). For calendar year. FFRDCs are federally funded research and development centers. For most academic institutions and the federal government before 1997, began on July 1 instead of October 1]

Year	Total	Federal government	Industry — Total	Industry — Funded by Federal government	Industry — Funded by Industry[1]	Industry FFRDCs	Universities and colleges — Total	U&C — Federal government	U&C — Nonfederal government[2]	U&C — Industry	U&C — Universities & colleges	U&C — Non-profits	University & college FFRDCs[3]	Other nonprofit institutions — Total	ONP — Federal government	ONP — Industry	ONP — Non-profits
RESEARCH AND DEVELOPMENT TOTAL																	
1995	183,618	16,904	129,830	21,178	108,652	2,273	22,610	13,587	1,751	1,547	4,110	1,616	5,367	5,527	2,847	671	2,308
2000	267,557	17,917	199,961	17,117	182,844	2,001	30,688	17,714	2,246	2,174	6,230	2,325	5,742	9,782	4,847	1,118	4,217
2003	289,025	22,752	200,724	17,798	182,926	2,458	40,457	25,106	2,740	2,129	7,648	2,833	7,301	12,839	5,686	1,118	6,035
2004	300,060	23,044	208,301	20,266	188,035	2,485	43,090	27,140	2,882	2,190	7,932	2,946	7,658	12,838	5,671	1,151	6,016
2005, prel.	323,546	24,744	225,983	21,990	203,994	2,565	45,831	28,944	2,993	2,311	8,413	3,170	7,786	13,822	5,791	1,251	6,779
2006, prel.	342,886	24,408	241,809	22,516	219,293	2,426	49,090	31,223	3,164	2,400	8,909	3,395	7,720	14,539	5,721	1,349	7,530
BASIC RESEARCH																	
1995	29,609	2,689	5,569	190	5,379	530	15,145	9,634	1,069	945	2,510	987	2,702	2,899	1,170	390	1,338
2000	42,763	3,765	7,040	925	6,115	547	22,860	13,912	1,549	1,499	4,296	1,603	2,874	5,061	2,099	621	2,341
2003	55,109	4,664	8,330	1,386	6,944	299	30,354	19,823	1,880	1,461	5,246	1,943	3,747	6,656	2,714	621	3,351
2004	55,670	4,734	7,835	1,072	6,763	175	32,397	21,380	1,991	1,513	5,479	2,035	3,729	6,728	2,749	639	3,340
2005, prel.	60,157	4,921	8,500	1,163	7,337	135	34,437	22,734	2,074	1,602	5,830	2,197	3,780	7,245	2,756	695	3,764
2006, prel.	63,648	4,938	9,078	1,191	7,887	128	36,887	24,524	2,189	1,661	6,164	2,349	3,746	7,657	2,768	749	4,181
APPLIED RESEARCH																	
1995	40,932	4,952	26,919	3,164	23,755	535	5,655	2,775	559	494	1,311	516	1,050	1,692	934	170	589
2000	56,932	6,105	39,176	2,682	36,494	269	6,652	3,350	572	553	1,586	592	1,329	3,183	1,831	283	1,069
2003	61,448	7,672	37,334	4,473	32,861	1,434	8,589	4,637	705	548	1,969	729	1,756	4,300	2,487	283	1,529
2004	70,093	7,532	45,432	4,775	40,657	1,521	8,997	4,951	731	556	2,012	747	1,935	4,312	2,496	292	1,525
2005, prel.	75,252	7,870	49,289	5,181	44,108	1,532	9,625	5,374	753	582	2,118	798	1,918	4,611	2,576	317	1,718
2006, prel.	79,291	7,750	52,721	5,305	47,416	1,482	10,325	5,812	799	606	2,250	857	1,805	4,809	2,559	342	1,908
DEVELOPMENT																	
1995	113,077	9,262	97,342	17,824	79,518	1,208	1,810	1,178	123	108	288	113	1,616	1,236	744	111	381
2000	167,862	8,047	153,745	13,510	140,235	1,185	1,177	452	125	121	348	130	1,539	1,537	517	214	807
2003	172,468	10,416	155,060	11,939	143,121	725	1,514	646	155	120	432	160	1,798	1,853	485	214	1,155
2004	173,297	10,778	155,034	14,419	140,615	789	1,696	808	161	122	442	164	1,993	1,798	426	220	1,151
2005, prel.	188,138	11,952	168,195	15,645	152,549	899	1,769	836	165	128	465	175	2,088	1,996	460	239	1,297
2006, prel.	199,947	11,720	180,010	16,020	163,990	816	1,877	887	175	133	494	188	2,168	2,094	395	258	1,441

[1] Includes all nonfederal sources of industry R&D expenditures. [2] Includes all nonfederal sources. [3] Includes all R&D expenditures of FFRDCs administered by academic institutions and funded by the federal government.

Source: National Science Foundation. Data derived from: *Research and Development in Industry*, annual; *Academic Research and Development Expenditures*, annual; and *Federal Funds For Research and Development*, annual. See also <http://www.nsf.gov/statistics/>.

Science and Technology 519

Table 777. **National Research and Development (R&D) Expenditures as a Percent of Gross Domestic Product by Country: 1985 to 2005**

Year	Total R&D						Nondefense R&D[1]		
	United States	Japan[2]	Unified Germany[3]	France	United Kingdom	Italy	Canada	Russia	Total OECD[4]
1985	2.72	2.58	2.60	2.15	2.24	1.10	1.42	(NA)	2.22
1990	2.62	2.81	2.61	2.33	2.15	1.25	1.51	2.03	2.26
1995	2.48	2.71	2.19	2.29	1.95	0.97	1.70	0.85	2.07
2000	2.73	3.05	2.45	2.15	1.86	1.05	1.92	1.05	2.23
2002	2.64	3.18	2.49	2.23	1.83	1.13	2.04	1.25	2.24
2003	2.63	3.20	2.52	2.17	1.79	1.11	2.01	1.28	2.25
2004	2.56	3.18	2.50	2.14	1.73	1.10	2.01	1.16	2.25
2005	2.59	(NA)	2.51	2.13	(NA)	(NA)	1.98	1.07	(NA)

NA Not available.   [1] Estimated.   [2] Data on Japanese research and development in 2000 and later years may not be consistent with data in earlier years because of changes in methodology.   [3] Data for 1985–90 are for West Germany only.   [4] Organization for Economic Cooperation and Development.

Source: National Science Foundation, *National Patterns of R&D Resources*, annual; and Organization for Economic Cooperation and Development.

Table 778. **Federal Obligations for Research in Current and Constant (2000) Dollars by Field of Science: 1980 to 2006**

[In millions of dollars (11,597 represents $11,597,000,000). For fiscal years ending in year shown; see text, Section 8. Excludes R&D plant]

Field of science	1980	1990	1995	2000	2002	2003	2004	2005, prel.	2006, prel.
CURRENT DOLLARS									
Research, total	11,597	21,622	28,434	38,471	48,007	51,072	53,358	55,546	54,979
Basic....................	4,674	11,286	13,877	19,570	23,668	24,751	26,121	26,919	26,938
Applied	6,923	10,337	14,557	18,901	24,338	26,320	27,237	28,627	28,041
Life sciences..............	4,192	8,830	11,811	17,965	25,477	27,772	27,729	28,543	28,207
Psychology...............	199	449	623	1,627	906	1,104	1,855	1,916	1,934
Physical sciences	2,001	3,809	4,278	4,788	4,983	5,022	5,211	5,473	5,394
Environmental sciences	1,261	2,174	2,854	3,329	3,418	3,741	3,742	3,876	3,754
Mathematics and computer sciences ...	241	841	1,579	2,206	2,631	2,672	2,949	3,115	3,081
Engineering	2,830	4,227	5,708	6,346	8,275	8,405	8,866	9,481	9,397
Social sciences	524	630	679	1,050	983	1,026	1,090	1,132	1,178
Other sciences, n.e.c.[1]	350	664	902	1,160	1,334	1,329	1,916	2,010	2,034
CONSTANT (2000) DOLLARS[2]									
Research, total	21,848	26,622	30,850	38,471	46,014	48,018	48,988	49,644	47,916
Basic....................	8,806	13,896	15,056	19,570	22,686	23,271	23,982	24,059	23,478
Applied	13,043	12,727	15,794	18,901	23,328	24,747	25,007	25,585	24,439
Life sciences..............	7,898	10,872	12,814	17,965	24,419	26,112	25,458	25,510	24,584
Psychology...............	375	553	676	1,627	868	1,038	1,703	1,712	1,686
Physical sciences	3,770	4,690	4,641	4,788	4,776	4,721	4,784	4,892	4,701
Environmental sciences	2,376	2,677	3,096	3,329	3,276	3,517	3,435	3,464	3,272
Mathematics and computer sciences ...	454	1,035	1,713	2,206	2,521	2,513	2,708	2,784	2,685
Engineering	5,332	5,204	6,193	6,346	7,931	7,903	8,140	8,473	8,190
Social sciences .... .¹.....	987	776	737	1,050	942	964	1,000	1,011	1,026
Other sciences, n.e.c.[1]	659	818	979	1,160	1,279	1,250	1,759	1,797	1,773

[1] Not elsewhere classified.   [2] Based on gross domestic product implicit price deflator.

Source: U.S. National Science Foundation, *Federal Funds for Research and Development*, annual. See also <http://www.nsf.gov/statistics/>.

Table 779. **Federal Budget Authority for Research and Development (R&D) in Current and Constant (2000) Dollars by Selected Budget Functions: 2004 to 2007**

[In millions of dollars (121,867 represents $121,867,000,000). For year ending September 30. Excludes R&D plant. Represents budget authority. Functions shown are those for which $1 billion or more was authorized since 1995]

Function	Current dollars				Constant (2000) dollars[1]			
	2004	2005	2006	2007, prel.	2004	2005	2006	2007, prel.
Total[2]	121,867	126,601	130,087	132,578	112,309	113,158	112,795	112,117
National defense	69,593	74,047	76,154	77,781	64,135	66,184	66,031	65,777
Health	28,251	28,824	28,949	28,902	26,035	25,763	25,101	24,441
Space research and technology	7,612	7,300	8,256	9,268	7,015	6,525	7,159	7,838
Energy	1,343	1,296	1,370	1,346	1,238	1,158	1,188	1,138
General science.............	6,466	6,570	6,672	7,294	5,959	5,872	5,785	6,168
Natural resources and environment ...	2,168	2,168	2,136	2,004	1,998	1,938	1,852	1,695
Transportation	1,863	1,847	1,723	1,488	1,717	1,651	1,494	1,258
Agriculture	1,750	1,820	1,866	1,610	1,613	1,627	1,618	1,362

[1] Based on gross domestic product implicit price deflator.   [2] Includes other functions, not shown separately.

Source: U.S. National Science Foundation, *Federal R&D Funding by Budget Function*, annual. See also <http://www.nsf.gov/statistics/> (released December 2006).

520   Science and Technology

Table 780. Research and Development (R&D) Expenditures in Science and Engineering at Universities and Colleges in Current and Constant (2000) Dollars: 1990 to 2005

[In millions of dollars (16,286 represents $16,286,000,000). Totals may not add due to rounding]

Characteristic	Current dollars				Constant (2000) dollars [1]			
	1990	1995	2000	2005	1990	1995	2000	2005
Total................	16,286	22,172	30,070	45,750	20,051	24,056	30,070	40,893
Basic research [2]	10,643	14,810	22,454	34,384	13,103	16,068	22,454	30,733
Applied R&D [2]	5,643	7,362	7,616	11,367	6,948	7,987	7,616	10,160
Source of funds:								
All governments ...	0,008	13,333	17,536	29,167	11,866	14,466	17,536	26,070
Institutions' own funds ...	1,324	1,690	2,200	2,940	1,630	1,834	2,200	2,628
Industry.............	3,006	4,048	5,924	8,258	3,701	4,392	5,924	7,381
Other..............	1,127	1,489	2,156	2,292	1,388	1,616	2,156	2,049
Fields:								
Physical sciences	1,807	2,256	2,712	3,704	2,225	2,448	2,712	3,311
Environmental sciences ...	1,069	1,434	1,765	2,546	1,316	1,556	1,765	2,276
Mathematical sciences....	222	279	342	495	273	303	342	442
Computer sciences	515	682	876	1,406	634	740	876	1,257
Life sciences	8,726	12,189	17,469	27,603	10,743	13,224	17,469	24,672
Psychology	253	371	517	826	311	402	517	738
Social sciences.........	703	1,019	1,299	1,675	866	1,106	1,299	1,498
Other sciences........	336	427	535	767	414	463	535	686
Engineering	2,656	3,516	4,555	6,728	3,270	3,814	4,555	6,013

[1] Based on gross domestic product implicit price deflator.   [2] Basic research and applied R&D statistics were reestimated for FY 2001 and forward. These data are not directly comparable to those from earlier years.
Source: U.S. National Science Foundation, *Survey of Research and Development Expenditures at Universities and Colleges,* annual.

Table 781. Federal Research and Development (R&D) Obligations to Selected Universities and Colleges: 2003 and 2004

[In millions of dollars (22,804.3 represents $22,804,300,000). For years ending September 30. For the top 40 institutions receiving federal R&D funds in 2004. Awards to the administrative offices of university systems are excluded from totals for individual institutions because that allocation of funds is unknown, but those awards are included in "total all institutions"]

Major institution ranked by total 2004 federal R&D obligations	2003	2004	Major institution ranked by total 2004 federal R&D obligations	2003	2004
Total, all institutions [1]...........	22,804.3	23,810.8	University of North Carolina at Chapel Hill	313.2	305.7
Johns Hopkins University	961.9	1,034.9	University Southern California	269.3	288.3
University of Washington	565.5	589.6	Vanderbilt University	235.0	259.5
University of Pennsylvania	454.8	494.2	Baylor College of Medicine	251.8	252.6
University of Michigan	470.5	477.3	University of California—Berkeley......	212.3	246.9
Stanford University	436.6	472.3	Case Western Reserve University......	195.0	241.5
University of California—Los Angeles ...	448.6	471.0	University of Rochester	215.0	236.3
University of California—San Diego ...	414.1	420.3	The Scripps Research Institute	209.9	229.1
University of California—San Francisco .	368.5	395.5	Emory University...............	204.6	214.0
Duke University.................	377.1	392.6	University of Alabama—Birmingham	211.6	211.6
Washington University............	398.1	386.4	University of Chicago	192.6	209.1
Harvard University...............	346.2	379.1	Boston University	197.2	208.7
University of Pittsburgh............	362.4	371.9	Northwestern University	194.6	208.5
Columbia University—City of NY	363.7	369.5	University of Arizona	190.0	206.9
University of Wisconsin—Madison	346.6	364.0	University of California—Davis.......	192.1	205.1
Yale University.................	321.6	343.0	Ohio State University............	185.4	202.9
Massachusetts Institute of Technology. ..	273.6	340.2	University of Illinois—Urbana Champaign.	205.9	198.2
University of Colorado	313.6	336.7	University of Virginia	172.8	188.8
University of Minnesota	311.8	328.7	University of Florida..............	175.1	179.0
Cornell University	294.3	328.6	University of Iowa	169.8	178.1
Pennsylvania State University	299.1	316.2			

[1] Includes other institutions, not shown separately.
Source: U.S. National Science Foundation, *Federal S&E Support to Universities and Colleges and Nonprofit Institutions,* annual.

Table 782. Graduate Science/Engineering Students in Doctorate-Granting Colleges by Characteristic and Field: 1990 to 2005

[In thousands (397.8 represents 397,800). As of fall. Includes outlying areas]

Field of science or engineering	Characteristic										
	Total			Female			Foreign		Part-time		
	1990	2000	2005	1990	2000	2005	2000	2005	1990	2000	2005
Total, all surveyed fields .	397.8	433.3	524.5	149.7	195.3	253.5	122.3	141.3	123.2	118.2	146.6
Science/engineering	350.6	366.7	433.3	113.4	145.6	183.6	116.9	134.2	100.7	94.7	113.3
Engineering, total	99.9	98.4	114.3	13.6	19.6	25.2	46.1	52.2	35.9	27.8	32.1
Sciences, total	250.7	268.3	319.0	99.8	126.0	158.4	70.8	81.9	64.8	66.9	81.1
Physical sciences.......	32.5	29.3	35.4	7.6	8.7	11.3	11.5	14.4	3.6	3.2	3.5
Environmental.........	12.9	12.7	10.7	3.8	5.2	6.4	2.6	2.7	3.0	2.6	3.0
Mathematical sciences ...	17.3	13.8	18.5	5.3	4.9	6.6	5.7	7.3	4.0	2.7	3.9
Computer sciences......	27.7	39.5	44.3	6.4	11.4	10.8	19.3	18.7	12.9	16.3	16.7
Agricultural sciences.....	10.9	11.2	12.2	3.2	4.7	5.7	2.4	2.6	2.0	2.3	3.1
Biological sciences......	46.0	52.3	64.4	21.0	27.4	36.0	11.5	16.2	6.8	7.2	8.7
Psychology	35.8	37.7	46.7	23.6	27.0	35.0	2.1	2.8	10.3	9.5	13.8
Social sciences.......	67.7	71.8	87.8	29.0	36.8	46.6	15.7	17.3	22.1	23.0	28.5
Health fields, total........	47.2	66.6	91.2	36.3	49.6	69.9	5.4	7.1	22.5	23.5	33.3

Source: U.S. National Science Foundation, *Survey of Graduate Science Engineering Students and Postdoctorates,* annual.

Science and Technology **521**

[For a description of science and engineering degree categories, see Appendix B of source <http://www.nsf.gov/statistics/nsf07307/content.cfm?pub_id=3634&id=4>]

Academic year ending	Bachelor's degrees awarded				Master's degrees awarded				Doctoral degrees awarded			
	Total S&E	Men	Women	Percent women	Total S&E	Men	Women	Percent women	Total S&E	Men	Women	Percent women
1980	304,695	191,215	113,480	37.2	64,089	46,004	18,085	28.2	17,775	13,814	3,961	22.3
1985	332,273	203,402	128,871	38.8	70,578	48,247	22,331	31.6	18,934	14,043	4,891	25.8
1990	329,094	189,082	140,012	42.5	77,788	51,230	26,558	34.1	22,869	16,498	6,371	27.9
1995	378,148	202,217	175,931	46.5	94,309	58,518	35,791	38.0	26,536	18,117	8,287	31.4
2000	398,622	197,669	200,953	50.4	95,683	54,213	41,470	43.3	25,966	16,521	9,393	36.2
2001	400,206	197,623	202,583	50.6	98,986	55,593	43,393	43.8	25,548	16,174	9,331	36.6
2002	415,611	204,408	211,203	50.8	99,173	55,701	43,472	43.8	24,588	15,374	9,159	37.3
2003	439,434	218,057	221,377	50.4	107,739	61,140	46,599	43.3	25,289	15,728	9,477	37.6
2004	454,978	225,566	229,412	50.4	118,379	66,764	51,615	43.6	26,275	16,405	9,819	37.4

Source: U.S. National Science Foundation, *Science and Engineering Degrees: 1966–2004* (published January 2007). See also <http://www.nsf.gov/statistics/nsf07307/>.

Table 784. College Graduates by Education and Occupation: 1993 and 2003

[In percent, except as noted. S&E stands for science and engineering. College graduates includes individuals with degrees at the bachelor level or higher]

Field and occupation	1993	2003	Field and occupation	1993	2003
All college graduates (1,000)	29,021	40,621	S&E-related or non-S&E occupations . .	78	77
S&E occupations	11	12	Not employed	16	17
S&E-related or non-S&E occupations	71	69	Non-S&E degrees only (1,000)	15,723	21,395
Not employed.	18	20	S&E occupations	3	3
			S&E-related or non-S&E occupations . .	78	75
S&E degrees only (1,000)	7,153	10,118	Not employed	19	21
S&E occupations	30	31	Degrees in more than one broad		
S&E-related or non-S&E occupations . .	52	50	field [1] (1,000)	3,676	5,568
Not employed	18	19	S&E occupations	11	12
S&E-related degrees only (1,000)	2,469	3,540	S&E-related or non-S&E occupations . .	76	72
S&E occupations	6	6	Not employed	13	16

[1] S&E, S&E-related, and non-S&E.

Source: U.S. National Science Foundation, National Survey of College Graduates: 1993 and 2003.

Table 785. Profile of Employed College Graduates by Employment Sector and Occupation Group: 2003

[In thousands (32,575 represents $32,575,000,000), except as noted. S&E stands for science and engineering. Includes individuals with degrees at the bachelor's level or higher]

Characteristic	All employed graduates (1,000)	Occupation (percent)			Median annual salary (dollars)			
		S&E	S&E-related	Non-S&E	All employed graduates	S&E	S&E-related	Non-S&E
HIGHEST LEVEL OF DEGREE ATTAINMENT								
All degree levels	32,575	14	15	70	50,000	69,000	55,000	47,000
Bachelor's	20,359	12	14	74	47,000	67,000	48,000	43,000
Master's	8,675	17	14	70	54,000	70,000	55,000	50,000
Doctorate	1,271	50	7	43	70,000	71,000	77,000	65,000
Professional	2,270	4	44	52	95,000	80,000	112,000	80,000
EMPLOYMENT SECTOR								
Educational institutions	7,156	11	17	71	42,000	49,000	44,000	40,000
4-year colleges, medical schools, university-affiliated research institutes . .	2,003	32	22	46	47,000	50,000	50,000	44,000
2-year colleges.	295	31	2	67	40,000	40,000	40,000	40,000
Precollege and other institutions	4,857	1	16	82	41,000	50,000	42,000	40,000
Government	3,527	16	13	71	53,000	64,000	56,000	50,000
Federal	1,232	23	13	65	66,000	75,000	65,000	62,000
State	1,044	16	13	71	43,000	50,000	45,000	42,000
Local	1,251	10	13	77	45,000	54,000	44,000	44,000
Business/industry	21,893	15	15	70	56,000	73,000	60,000	50,000
For-profit	13,771	19	13	68	61,000	75,000	67,000	55,000
Self-employed, incorporated	3,403	11	18	71	60,000	72,000	85,000	50,000
Self-employed, not incorporated	2,583	7	14	78	40,000	50,000	65,000	35,000
Nonprofit	2,534	7	28	65	42,000	53,000	50,000	35,000

Source: U.S. National Science Foundation, National Survey of College Graduates: 2003.

Table 786. Doctorates Conferred by Characteristics of Recipients: 2000 and 2005

[In percent, except as indicated. Based on the Survey of Earned Doctorate Awards; for description of methodology, see source]

Characteristic	2000, total [1]	2005									
		All fields [1]	Engineering	Physical sciences [2]	Earth sciences	Mathematics	Computer sciences	Biological sci [3]	Agricultural	Social sciences [4]	Psychology
Total conferred											
(number)......	41,361	43,354	6,404	3,647	713	1,203	1,136	6,368	1,038	4,138	3,327
Male..........	56.0	54.7	81.4	73.3	65.9	72.7	80.0	51.1	63.5	55.2	31.9
Female........	43.8	45.1	18.3	26.7	34.1	27.1	19.8	48.8	36.2	44.7	68.0
CITIZENSHIP [5]											
Total conferred											
(number)......	39,596	40,736	6,038	3,450	675	1,143	1,072	6,073	972	3,904	3,101
U.S. citizen......	70.7	64.6	33.1	51.2	62.4	42.0	37.8	68.2	54.2	60.5	90.6
Foreign citizen.....	29.3	35.4	66.9	48.8	37.6	58.0	62.2	31.8	45.8	39.5	9.4
RACE/ETHNICITY [6]											
Total conferred											
(number)......	29,936	27,912	2,284	1,900	442	541	473	4,396	557	2,540	2,891
White [7].........	79.2	76.9	70.2	79.0	86.9	76.3	69.1	75.9	87.3	76.2	79.1
Black [7]........	5.8	6.4	4.4	2.9	1.4	4.1	3.2	3.6	2.9	6.7	5.7
Asian/Pacific [7]...	7.6	7.8	17.7	10.3	4.1	12.2	19.5	12.2	3.9	6.6	4.5
Indian/Alaskan [7]...	0.6	0.5	0.4	0.2	0.9	0.0	0.2	0.3	0.5	0.7	0.5
Hispanic........	4.4	5.1	3.9	3.9	4.1	4.4	2.5	5.2	3.2	5.9	6.5
Other/unknown [8]...	2.4	3.2	3.4	3.7	2.7	3.0	5.5	2.9	2.2	4.0	3.7

[1] Includes other fields, not shown separately. [2] Astronomy, physics, and chemistry. [3] Biochemistry, botany, microbiology, physiology, zoology, and related fields. [4] Anthropology, sociology, political science, economics, international relations and related fields. [5] For those with known citizenship, includes those with temporary visas. [6] Excludes those with temporary visas. [7] Non-Hispanic. [8] For the year 2004, includes Native Hawaiians and Other Pacific Islanders, respondents choosing multiple races (excluding those selecting an Hispanic ethnicity), and respondents with unknown race/ethnicity.

Source: U.S. National Science Foundation, *Science and Engineering Doctorate Awards*, annual. See also <http://www.nsf.gov/statistics /nsf07305/> (released December 2006).

Table 787. Doctorates Awarded by Field of Study and Year of Doctorate: 1999 to 2005

Field of study	1999	2000	2001	2002	2003	2004	2005
Grand total, all fields...........	41,092	41,361	40,651	39,953	40,740	42,117	43,354
Science and engineering, total..........	25,931	25,966	25,496	24,582	25,274	26,272	27,974
Engineering, total................	5,330	5,323	5,508	5,077	5,279	5,775	6,404
Aeronautical/astronautical............	206	214	203	209	200	201	219
Chemical......................	674	726	730	705	648	725	875
Civil.........................	584	556	595	627	673	673	757
Electrical.....................	1,478	1,543	1,577	1,393	1,465	1,650	1,852
Industrial/manufacturing............	211	176	206	230	214	217	222
Materials/metallurgical.............	469	451	497	396	474	511	540
Mechanical....................	855	864	953	827	814	852	978
Other.......................	853	793	747	690	791	946	961
Science, total...................	20,601	20,643	19,988	19,505	19,995	20,497	21,570
Biological/agricultural sciences.......	6,646	6,890	6,668	6,699	6,753	6,984	7,406
Agricultural sciences............	1,065	1,037	975	1,009	1,060	1,045	1,038
Biological sciences.............	5,581	5,853	5,693	5,690	5,693	5,939	6,368
Earth, atmospheric, and ocean sciences, total................	723	694	660	689	683	686	713
Atmospheric..................	124	143	116	117	139	126	144
Earth.......................	452	387	393	426	374	420	420
Ocean sciences...............	147	164	151	146	170	140	149
Mathematical/computer sciences, total....	1,939	1,910	1,832	1,726	1,859	2,024	2,339
Computer sciences..............	856	860	825	807	866	948	1,136
Mathematics..................	1,083	1,050	1,007	919	993	1,076	1,203
Physical sciences, total.............	3,562	3,378	3,364	3,185	3,289	3,338	3,647
Astronomy...................	159	185	186	141	167	165	186
Chemistry....................	2,132	1,989	1,981	1,921	2,041	1,987	2,127
Physics.....................	1,271	1,204	1,197	1,123	1,081	1,186	1,334
Psychology....................	3,668	3,616	3,385	3,197	3,273	3,327	3,327
Social sciences, total..............	4,063	4,155	4,079	4,009	4,138	4,138	4,138
Economics...................	1,075	1,086	1,081	1,026	1,050	1,069	1,184
Political science...............	1,016	986	984	938	1,024	946	990
Sociology....................	572	637	577	566	612	599	555
Other social sciences...........	1,400	1,446	1,437	1,479	1,452	1,524	1,409
Nonscience and engineering, total........	15,161	15,395	15,155	15,371	15,466	15,845	15,380
Education....................	6,546	6,432	6,332	6,491	6,638	6,633	6,229
Health......................	1,407	1,591	1,541	1,653	1,633	1,719	1,777
Humanities...................	5,035	5,213	5,160	5,029	5,018	5,013	4,947
Professional/other/unknown...........	2,173	2,159	2,122	2,198	2,177	2,480	2,427

Source: U.S. National Science Foundation, *Science and Engineering Doctorate Awards*, annual. See also <http://www.nsf.gov /statistics/nsf07305/> (released December 2006).

Table 788. **Non-U.S. Citizens Awarded Doctorates in Science and Engineering by Visa Type and Country of Citizenship: 1996 to 2005**

[For description of science and engineering fields, see Table 787]

Visa and country/economy	1996	1997	1998	1999	2000	2001	2002	2003	2004	2005
All non-U.S. citizens	10,911	9,788	9,734	8,892	9,067	9,213	8,861	9,480	10,154	11,516
Canada.	278	263	286	289	294	306	315	323	380	365
Mexico	162	148	176	172	208	206	182	217	181	206
Brazil	209	151	164	164	131	142	126	108	136	156
United Kingdom	118	92	124	142	100	138	134	109	109	107
Germany.	171	181	210	183	229	220	197	191	185	180
China	3,033	2,395	2,502	2,233	2,378	2,404	2,401	2,495	2,877	3,448
Japan	169	155	155	158	201	149	157	201	186	211
Korea	991	901	822	760	753	865	856	956	1,056	1,170
Taiwan	1,166	1,093	909	746	676	539	469	440	394	442
Thailand	119	97	122	134	153	236	264	312	272	251
India.	1,287	1,281	1,134	915	834	817	681	769	863	1,103
Iran	152	113	93	92	80	100	58	68	60	136
Turkey	153	170	172	192	275	307	343	373	344	340
Science	7,356	6,640	6,677	6,297	6,266	6,127	5,940	6,304	6,604	7,477
Engineering	3,555	3,148	3,057	2,595	2,801	3,086	2,921	3,176	3,550	4,039
Permanent visa	3,009	2,281	1,991	1,654	1,409	1,270	1,170	1,098	1,003	1,112
Temporary visa.	7,902	7,507	7,743	7,238	7,658	7,943	7,691	8,382	9,151	10,404

Source: U.S. National Science Foundation, *Science and Engineering Doctorate Awards*, annual. See also <http://www.nsf.gov/statistics/nsf07305/> (released December 2006).

Table 789. **Civilian Employment of Scientists, Engineers, and Technicians by Occupation and Industry: 2004**

[In thousands (6,834.8 represents 6,834,800). Based on sample and subject to sampling error. For details, see source]

Occupation	Total [1]	Mining [2]	Wage and salary workers							Self employed [3]
			Construction	Manufacturing	Information	Professional, scientific and technical services	Government	Other service-providing industries		
Scientists, engineers, and technicians, total	6,834.8	45.6	76.4	1,251.2	516.7	1,874.7	1,118.8	1,603.4		336.2
Scientists	1,080.8	7.8	2.5	104.6	31.1	225.8	331.3	252.4		118.4
Physical scientists.	250.4	7.4	0.5	43.8	0.8	82.8	84.2	22.9		6.5
Life scientists	231.7	(NA)	(NA)	28.8	0.1	44.8	96.2	41.4		16.2
Mathematical science occupations . .	107.0	0.1	0.1	7.2	8.3	23.2	20.5	45.9		1.7
Social scientists and related occupations	491.7	0.3	2.0	24.9	21.9	75.0	130.3	142.3		94.0
Computer specialists	3,045.8	6.0	9.0	272.5	411.0	868.8	332.2	996.3		150.1
Engineers [4].	1,448.9	19.1	36.6	554.7	49.7	378.1	194.2	174.9		40.9
Civil engineers	237.3	0.4	19.6	3.3	1.2	115.1	75.6	9.5		12.7
Electrical/electronics engineers	298.8	0.5	4.5	103.4	33.6	69.5	31.5	45.1		10.6
Mechanical engineers	225.9	0.7	4.1	122.1	0.4	55.8	13.5	23.5		5.7
Drafters, engineering, and mapping technicians [5]	850.9	3.9	24.2	260.9	24.2	281.2	122.1	113.8		19.8
Electrical/electronics engineering technicians.	181.6	1.1	2.3	64.8	17.3	26.8	24.8	43.5		0.6
Other engineering technicians	350.3	1.7	4.2	128.2	4.0	91.3	78.5	41.0		1.1
Drafters.	254.0	0.5	16.9	67.6	2.5	119.3	7.2	25.1		14.9
Surveying and mapping technicians	65.0	0.7	0.9	0.3	0.4	43.8	11.6	4.2		3.1
Life, physical, and social science technicians	341.9	8.2	0.3	58.3	0.5	73.2	129.4	64.0		4.3
Surveyors, cartographers, and photogrammetrists	66.5	0.5	3.7	0.1	0.2	47.7	9.6	1.9		2.7

NA Not available. [1] Includes agriculture, forestry, and fishing not shown separately. [2] Includes oil and gas extraction. [3] Includes secondary jobs. [4] Includes kinds of engineers and technicians not shown separately. [5] Includes other drafters, technicians, and mapping technicians, not shown separately.

Source: U.S. Bureau of Labor Statistics, *National Industry-Occupation Employment Matrix*, February 2006 (data collected biennially).

524 Science and Technology

Table 790. Individuals in Science and Engineering (S&E) Occupations as Share of Workforce by State and Other Areas: 2006

[In thousands (3,661.3 represents 3,661,300), except as noted. As of May 2006. The Occupational Employment Statistics Survey (OES) collects data in six semiannual panels over a 3-year period on occupational employment and wages of wage and salary workers in nonfarm establishments in the United States, Guam, Puerto Rico, and the Virgin Islands. The OES survey uses the Standard Occupational Classification (SOC) system to categorize workers in 1 of 801 detailed occupations. For a list of occupations see <http://www.bls.gov/oes/current/oes_stru.htm>. For more information about methodology, see <http://www.bls.gov/oes/current/oes_tec.htm>]

State	2006			State	2006		
	S&E occupations [1]	Employed workforce	Workforce in S&E occupations [1] (percent)		S&E occupations [1]	Employed workforce	Workforce in S&E occupations [1] (percent)
United States.	3,661.3	132,605.0	2.8	Nebraska	19.3	901.1	2.1
				Nevada.	25.0	1,257.9	2.0
Alabama	50.5	1,912.2	2.6	New Hampshire	16.6	627.6	2.6
Alaska	12.2	303.9	4.0	New Jersey	99.5	3,957.5	2.5
Arizona.	75.5	2,574.2	2.9	New Mexico.	30.6	789.4	3.9
Arkansas.	20.8	1,166.8	1.8	New York	194.2	8,387.8	2.3
California.	481.4	15,065.8	3.2	North Carolina	91.7	3,892.7	2.4
Colorado.	83.3	2,207.1	3.8	North Dakota	7.7	335.7	2.3
Connecticut	51.1	1,659.0	3.1	Ohio.	125.5	5,354.2	2.3
Delaware.	7.3	424.3	1.7	Oklahoma	35.9	1,503.4	2.4
District of Columbia. . .	35.2	609.4	5.8	Oregon	53.2	1,648.7	3.2
Florida	177.5	7,869.2	2.3	Pennsylvania	148.2	5,631.5	2.6
Georgia	76.0	4,001.6	1.9	Rhode Island	11.9	482.6	2.5
Hawaii	14.9	599.1	2.5	South Carolina	46.0	1,840.2	2.5
Idaho	24.9	624.3	4.0	South Dakota	7.9	381.2	2.1
Illinois.	130.8	5,826.7	2.2	Tennessee.	48.5	2,718.4	1.8
Indiana	63.6	2,913.2	2.2	Texas	294.1	9,761.0	3.0
Iowa.	28.3	1,470.2	1.9	Utah.	35.6	1,151.0	3.1
Kansas	35.4	1,321.2	2.7	Vermont	9.4	299.6	3.1
Kentucky.	32.5	1,779.8	1.8	Virginia	119.0	3,608.4	3.3
Louisiana	40.8	1,777.0	2.3	Washington	116.1	2,736.9	4.2
Maine	13.8	596.9	2.3	West Virginia	15.9	710.6	2.2
Maryland	92.9	2,531.2	3.7	Wisconsin	75.7	2,744.2	2.8
Massachusetts	120.9	3,170.5	3.8	Wyoming.	8.6	262.3	3.3
Michigan	167.6	4,294.3	3.9				
Minnesota	81.6	2,682.9	3.0	Guam	1.1	54.7	2.1
Mississippi.	6.7	1,113.0	0.6	Puerto Rico	23.7	1,031.7	2.3
Missouri	58.8	2,700.5	2.2	Virgin Islands	0.4	44.3	0.9
Montana	14.5	427.1	3.4				

[1] Science and Engineering includes those occupations listed under SOC 17-0000 and SOC 19-0000.

Source: U.S. Department of Labor, Bureau of Labor Statistics, Occupational Employment and Wage Estimates; and Local Area Unemployment Statistics. See also <http://www.bls.gov/oes/home.htm>.

Table 791. Research and Development (R&D) Scientists and Engineers— Employment and Cost by Industry: 2002 to 2004

[1,073.3 represents 1,073,300]

Industry	NAICS [1] code	Employed scientists and engineers [2] (1,000)			Cost per scientist or engineer, Constant (2000) dollars [3,4] ($1,000)		
		2002	2003	2004	2002	2003	2004
All industries [5]	(X)	1,073.3	1,115.8	1,133.7	181.5	180.8	181.3
Chemicals.	325	84.2	89.1	105.0	239.2	245.1	302.3
Machinery.	333	56.2	55.9	59.0	115.4	111.5	109.8
Electrical equipment, appliances, and components. . .	335	23.8	15.2	17.9	149.8	(D)	(D)
Motor vehicles, trailers, and parts	3361–3363	69.6	41.6	(NA)	(D)	(D)	(D)
Aerospace products and parts	3364	25.8	36.6	39.3	(D)	405.9	320.3
Transportation and warehousing services	48, 49	0.4	–	–	(D)	(D)	(D)
Software publishing	5112	81.0	93.6	100.1	163.0	155.3	168.7
Architectural, engineering, and related services	5413	28.0	35.3	39.9	152.7	141.9	111.6
Computer systems design and related services	5415	76.8	77.8	69.7	133.2	152.7	163.8
Scientific R&D services	5417	55.0	48.5	45.8	260.2	258.1	293.1
Management of companies and enterprises	55	1.5	1.0	(NA)	167.6	162.2	(NA)

– Represents or rounds to zero. D Withheld to avoid disclosure. NA Not available. X Not applicable. [1] North American Industry Classification System 1997 (NAICS); see text, Section 15. [2] The mean number of full-time equivalent R&D scientists and engineers employed in January of the year shown and the following January. [3] Based on gross domestic product implicit price deflator. [4] Represents the arithmetic mean of the numbers of R&D scientists and engineers reported in each industry for January in 2 consecutive years divided into total R&D expenditures in each industry. [5] Includes other industries not shown separately.

Source: U.S. National Science Foundation, *Research and Development in Industry*, annual (released February 2007). See also <http://www.nsf.gov/statistics/showpub.cfm?TopID=5&SubID=36>.

Science and Technology 525

Industry	NAICS [1] code	Total R&D funds as a percent of net sales			Company R&D funds as a percent of net sales		
		2002	2003	2004	2002	2003	2004
All industries, total.................	(X)	3.9	3.5	3.7	3.6	3.2	3.4
All manufacturing industries, total........	(X)	3.7	3.5	3.8	3.3	3.1	3.4
Food....................................	311	(D)	(D)	0.6	0.6	0.6	0.6
Paper, printing, and support activities..........	322, 326	(D)	(D)	(D)	1.3	1.1	1.5
Petroleum and coal products	324	(D)	(D)	0.4	0.4	0.3	0.4
Chemicals................................	325	6.0	5.7	(D)	5.9	5.6	6.6
Plastic and rubber products	326	(D)	2.1	(D)	1.8	2.1	1.6
Nonmetallic mineral products	327	(D)	1.0	1.8	1.2	1.0	1.8
Primary metals...........................	331	0.7	0.7	0.7	0.7	0.7	0.7
Fabricated metal products	332	1.5	1.6	1.5	1.4	1.5	1.4
Machinery...............................	333	4.4	4.2	3.7	4.3	4.2	3.6
Navigational, measuring, electromedical, and control instruments	3345	8.7	12.9	13.8	5.4	7.2	7.1
Electrical equipment, appliances, and components...	335	2.8	2.2	2.8	2.7	2.2	2.7
Motor vehicles, trailers, and parts	3361-3363	(D)	(D)	2.4	3.1	2.4	2.4
Aerospace products and parts	3364	4.1	6.8	5.7	2.3	3.5	4.0
All nonmanufacturing industries, total	(X)	4.4	3.6	3.5	4.1	3.3	3.2
Transportation and warehousing services	48, 49	(D)	0.4	(D)	0.5	0.4	0.5
Software publishing	5112	21.5	(D)	(D)	21.4	23.4	23.3
Architectural, engineering, and related services	5413	7.8	12.3	12.2	5.3	7.8	6.6
Computer systems design and related services	5415	16.5	11.1	12.1	14.3	9.8	11.7
Scientific R&D services	5417	21.3	19.4	35.8	17.6	16.5	29.6
Management of companies and enterprises	55	7.6	4.1	(NA)	7.6	4.1	(NA)

D Figure withheld to avoid disclosure of information pertaining to a specific organization or individual.   NA Not available.
X Not applicable. [1] North American Industry Classification System 1997 (NAICS); see text, Section 15.

Source: U.S. National Science Foundation, *Research and Development in Industry*, annual. See also <http://www.nsf.gov /statistics/pubseri.cfm?TopID=2&SubID=5&SeriID=26>.

Table 793. **Funds for Performance of Industrial Research and Development (R&D) by Selected Industries: 2001 to 2004**

[In millions of dollars (202,017 represents $202,017,000,000). For calendar years. Covers basic research, applied research, and development. Based on the Survey of Industry Research and Development]

Industry	NAICS [1] code	2001	2002	2003	2004
CURRENT DOLLARS					
Total funds [2].................................	(X)	202,017	193,868	200,724	208,301
Company and other funds	(X)	185,118	177,467	182,926	188,035
Federal funds................................	(X)	16,899	16,401	20,699	20,266
Petroleum and coal products....................	324	(D)	(D)	(D)	1,603
Chemicals and allied products...................	325	17,892	20,641	23,001	(D)
Pharmaceuticals and medicines	3254	10,371	(D)	(D)	31,477
Machinery	333	6,404	6,429	6,304	6,579
Computer and electronic products	334	47,079	38,881	39,001	48,296
Navigational, measuring, electromedical, and control instruments...	3345	12,947	13,729	14,014	15,214
Electrical equipment, appliances, and components	335	4,980	2,039	2,073	2,664
Motor vehicles, trailers, and parts...................	3361-3363	(D)	(D)	(D)	15,677
Aerospace products and parts...................	3364	7,868	9,654	13,205	13,086
Information.................................	51	(D)	17,880	(D)	22,593
Professional, scientific, and technical services	54	27,704	30,358	27,967	28,709
Computer systems design and related services.........	5415	9,154	11,983	9,032	11,575
Scientific R&D services	5417	14,244	13,034	12,460	11,355
All other [2]	(X)	(D)	(D)	(D)	(D)
CONSTANT (2000) DOLLARS [3]					
Total funds [2].................................	(X)	197,282	186,072	188,828	190,927
Company and other funds	(X)	180,779	170,330	172,085	172,351
Federal funds	(X)	16,503	15,741	19,472	18,576
Petroleum and coal products....................	324	(D)	(D)	(D)	1,469
Chemicals	325	17,473	19,811	21,638	(D)
Pharmaceuticals and medicines	3254	10,128	(D)	(D)	28,852
Machinery	333	6,254	6,170	5,930	6,030
Computer and electronic products	334	45,976	37,317	36,690	44,268
Navigational, measuring, electromedical, and control instruments...	3345	12,644	13,177	13,183	13,945
Electrical equipment, appliances, and components	335	4,863	1,957	1,950	2,442
Motor vehicles, trailers, and parts...................	3361-3363	(D)	(D)	(D)	14,369
Aerospace products and parts...................	3364	7,684	9,266	12,422	11,995
Information.................................	51	(D)	17,151	(D)	20,709
Professional, scientific, and technical services	54	27,055	29,137	26,310	26,314
Computer systems design and related services.........	5415	8,939	11,501	8,497	10,610
Scientific R&D services	5417	13,910	12,510	11,722	10,408
All other [2]	(X)	(D)	(D)	(D)	(D)

D Figure withheld to avoid disclosure of information pertaining to a specific organization or individual.   X Not applicable.
[1] North American Industry Classification System, 1997; see text, Section 15.   [2] Includes other industries not shown separately.
[3] Based on gross domestic product implicit price deflator.

Source: U.S. National Science Foundation, *Research and Development in Industry*, annual. See also <http://www.nsf.gov /statistics/pubseri.cfm?TopID=2&SubID=5&SeriID=26>.

Table 794. Space Vehicle Systems—Net Sales and Backlog Orders: 1970 to 2005

[In millions of dollars (1,956 represents $1,956,000,000). Backlog orders as of Dec. 31. Based on data from major companies engaged in manufacture of aerospace products. Includes parts but excludes engines and propulsion units, except where noted]

Year	Net sales			Backlog orders			Year	Net sales			Backlog orders		
	Total	Military	Non-military	Total	Military	Non-military		Total	Military	Non-military	Total	Military	Non-military
1970...	1,956	1,025	931	1,184	786	398	2000...	8,164	3,723	4,441	21,395	8,942	12,453
1975...	2,119	1,096	1,023	1,304	1,019	285	2001 [1]..	9,032	(D)	(D)	24,425	(D)	(D)
1980...	3,183	1,461	2,022	1,014	951	863	2002 [1]..	7,946	(D)	(D)	21,968	(D)	(D)
1985...	6,300	4,241	2,059	6,707	4,941	1,766	2003 [1]..	7,325	(D)	(D)	14,037	(D)	(D)
1990...	9,691	6,556	3,135	12,462	8,130	4,332	2004 [1]..	7,320	(D)	(D)	19,413	(D)	(D)
1995...	11,314	4,782	6,532	15,650	5,872	9,778	2005 [1]..	3,258	(D)	(D)	19,337	(D)	(D)

D Withheld to avoid disclosing data for individual companies. [1] Includes engines and/or propulsion units for space vehicles, including parts.

Source: U.S. Census Bureau, Current Industrial Reports, M336G, Civil Aircraft and Aircraft Engines; and Aerospace Industry, annual. See also <http://www.census.gov/industry/1/m336g0513.pdf>.

Table 795. Federal Outlays for General Science, Space, and Other Technology, 1970 to 2006, and Projections, 2007 and 2008

[In billions of dollars (4.5 represents $4,500,000,000). For fiscal years ending in year shown; see text, Section 8]

Year	Current dollars			Constant (2000) dollars		
	Total	General science/basic research	Space and other technologies	Total	General science/basic research	Space and other technologies
1970	4.5	0.9	3.6	19.3	4.0	15.2
1980	5.8	1.4	4.5	12.0	2.8	9.1
1985	8.6	2.0	6.6	13.7	3.2	10.5
1990	14.4	2.8	11.6	20.0	3.9	16.1
1995 [1]	16.7	4.1	12.6	18.7	4.6	14.1
2000	18.6	6.2	12.4	18.6	6.2	12.4
2001	19.7	6.5	13.2	19.3	6.4	12.9
2002	20.7	7.2	13.5	19.7	6.9	12.8
2003	20.8	7.9	12.9	19.2	7.3	11.9
2004	23.0	8.3	14.6	20.4	7.4	13.0
2005	23.6	8.8	14.8	20.0	7.5	12.5
2006	23.5	9.0	14.5	19.3	7.4	11.9
2007, proj.	24.7	9.3	15.4	20.0	7.5	12.5
2008, proj.	26.5	9.9	16.6	21.0	7.8	13.1

[1] Due to the effects of the Credit Reform Act of 1990 on the measurement and classification of federal credit activities, the discretionary outlays for years prior to 1995 are not strictly comparable to those for 1995 and after. However, the discretionary outlays shown after 1995 are no more than $1 billion higher than they would have been if measured on the same (pre-credit reform) basis as the 1990 outlays.

Source: U.S. Office of Management and Budget, Budget of the United States, Historical Tables, Fiscal Year 2008, annual. See also <http://www.gpoaccess.gov/usbudget/fy08/hist.html>.

Table 796. U.S. and Worldwide Commercial Space Industry Revenue by Type: 2002 to 2005

[In billions of dollars (19.3 represents $19,300,000,000). For calendar years]

Industry	U.S.				World			
	2002	2003	2004	2005	2002	2003	2004	2005
Revenue, total	19.3	24.6	26.5	30.8	71.3	74.3	82.7	88.8
Satellite manufacturing [1]	4.4	4.6	3.9	3.2	11.0	9.8	10.2	7.8
Launch industry	1.0	2.1	1.5	1.5	3.7	3.2	2.8	3.0
Satellite services [2]	13.9	17.9	21.1	26.1	35.6	39.8	46.9	52.8
Ground equipment manufacturing [3]	(NA)	(NA)	(NA)	(NA)	21.0	21.5	22.8	25.2

NA Not available. [1] Includes revenues from the construction and sale of satellites to both commercial and government. [2] Includes revenues derived from transponder leasing and subscription/retail services such as direct-to-home television, satellite radio, remote sensing, and satellite mobile and data communications. [3] Includes revenues from the manufacture of gateways and satellite control stations, satellite news-gathering trucks, very small aperture terminals, direct-to-home television equipment and mobile satellite phones.

Source: Satellite Industry Association/Futron Corporation, Bethesda, MD, 2005–2006 Satellite Industry Indicators Survey (copyright). See also <http://www.sia.org/>.

Science and Technology 527

Table 797. **National Aeronautics and Space Administration—Budget Appropriations, 2007, and Projections, 2008 to 2012**

[In millions of dollars (16,792.3 represents $16,792,300,000). Figures may not add due to rounding]

Item	2007	2008	2009	2010	2011	2012
Appropriations, total...............	16,792.3	17,309.4	17,614.2	18,026.3	18,460.4	18,905.0
Science, exploration, & aeronautics...........	10,650.6	10,483.1	10,868.4	11,364.2	15,386.5	15,888.6
Science....................	5,466.8	5,516.1	5,555.3	5,600.6	5,656.9	5,802.7
Earth science....................	1,464.5	1,497.3	1,545.8	1,520.1	1,411.2	1,353.2
Heliophysics.....................	1,028.1	1,057.2	1,028.4	1,091.3	1,241.2	1,307.5
Planetary science..................	1,411.2	1,395.8	1,676.9	1,720.3	1,738.3	1,748.2
Astrophysics.....................	1,563.0	1,565.8	1,304.2	1,268.9	1,266.2	1,393.8
Exploration systems..................	4,152.5	3,923.8	4,312.8	4,757.8	8,725.2	9,076.8
Constellation systems.............	3,232.5	3,068.0	3,451.2	3,784.9	7,666.0	7,993.0
Advanced capabilities...............	920.0	855.8	861.6	973.0	1,059.1	1,083.9
Aeronautics research & technology.........	529.3	554.0	546.7	545.3	549.8	554.7
Cross-agency support programs...........	502.0	489.2	453.5	460.4	454.7	454.4
Education........................	167.4	153.7	152.8	152.7	149.8	149.6
Advanced business systems...........	97.4	103.1	69.4	71.6	67.6	67.5
Innovative partnerships program..........	215.1	198.1	197.2	199.8	200.0	200.0
Shared capability assets program.........	22.1	34.3	34.2	36.2	37.3	37.2
Exploration capabilities..................	6,108.3	6,791.7	6,710.3	6,625.7	3,036.6	2,978.0
Space operations..................	6,108.3	6,791.7	6,710.3	6,625.7	3,036.6	2,978.0
International space station..............	1,762.6	2,238.6	2,515.1	2,609.2	2,547.5	2,600.8
Space shuttle.....................	4,017.6	4,007.5	3,650.9	3,634.4	116.2	–
Space & flight support...............	328.1	545.7	544.3	382.0	372.9	377.2
Inspector General.....................	33.5	34.6	35.5	36.4	37.3	38.3

– Represents or rounds to zero.

Source: U.S. National Aeronautics and Space Administration, *Fiscal Year 2008 Budget* <http://www.nasa.gov/about/budget/index.html> (accessed 11 May 2007).

Table 798. **Nobel Prize Laureates in Selected Sciences: 1901 to 2004**

[Presented by location of award-winning research and by date of award]

Country	1901–2004				1901–1930	1931–1945	1946–1960	1961–1975	1976–1990	1991–2003	2004
	Total	Physics	Chemistry	Physiology/ Medicine							
Total.........	502	174	146	182	93	49	74	92	98	82	8
United States.......	225	80	54	91	6	14	38	41	63	59	6
United Kingdom.....	76	21	27	28	15	11	14	20	9	6	–
Germany [1].........	63	19	29	15	27	11	4	8	7	4	–
France...........	25	11	7	7	13	2	–	5	2	3	–
Soviet Union Russia..	12	9	1	2	2	–	4	3	1	2	–
Japan............	8	4	4	–	–	–	1	2	1	4	–
Other countries......	93	30	24	39	30	11	13	13	15	4	2

– Represents zero.   [1] Between 1946 and 1991, data are for the former West Germany only.

Source: U.S. National Science Foundation, unpublished data.

528   Science and Technology

Agriculture

This section presents statistics on farms and farm operators; land use; farm income, expenditures, and debt; farm output, productivity, and marketings; foreign trade in agricultural products; specific crops; and livestock, poultry, and their products.

The principal sources are the reports issued by the National Agricultural Statistics Service (NASS) and the Economic Research Service (ERS) of the U.S. Department of Agriculture (USDA). The information from the 2002 Census of Agriculture is available in printed form in the Volume 1, Geographic Area Series; in electronic format on CD-ROM; and on the Internet site <http://www.agcensus.usda.gov /Publications/2002/index.asp>. The Department of Agriculture publishes annually *Agricultural Statistics,* a general reference book on agricultural production, supplies, consumption, facilities, costs, and returns. The ERS publishes data on farm assets, debt, and income on the Internet site <http://www.ers.usda .gov/briefing/farmincome/>. Sources of current data on agricultural exports and imports include *Outlook for U.S. Agricultural Trade,* published by the ERS; the ERS Internet site <http://www.ers.usda.gov /briefing/AgTrade/>; and the foreign trade section of the U.S. Census Bureau Web site <http://www.census.gov /foreign-trade/statistics/index.html>.

The field offices of the NASS collect data on crops, livestock and products, agricultural prices, farm employment, and other related subjects mainly through sample surveys. Information is obtained on crops and livestock items as well as scores of items pertaining to agricultural production and marketing. State estimates and supporting information are sent to the Agricultural Statistics Board of NASS, which reviews the estimates and issues reports containing state and national data. Among these reports are annual summaries such as *Crop Production, Crop Values, Agricultural Prices,* and *Livestock*

Production, Disposition and Income. For more information about concepts and methods underlying USDA's statistical series, see *Major Statistical Series of the U.S. Department of Agriculture* (Agricultural Handbook No. 671), a 12-volume set of publications.

Farms and farmland—The definitions of a farm have varied through time. Since 1850, when minimum criteria defining a farm for census purposes first were established, the farm definition has changed nine times. The current definition, first used for the 1974 census, is any place from which $1,000 or more of agricultural products were produced and sold, or normally would have been sold, during the census year.

Acreage designated as "land in farms" consists primarily of agricultural land used for crops, pasture, or grazing. It also includes woodland and wasteland not actually under cultivation or used for pasture or grazing, provided it was part of the farm operator's total operation. Land in farms includes acres set aside under annual commodity acreage programs as well as acres in the Conservation Reserve and Wetlands Reserve Programs for places meeting the farm definition. Land in farms is an operating unit concept and includes land owned and operated as well as land rented from others. All grazing land, except land used under government permits on a per-head basis, was included as "land in farms" provided it was part of a farm or ranch.

An evaluation of coverage has been conducted for each census of agriculture since 1945 to provide estimates of the completeness of census farm counts. The 2002 coverage evaluation shows the census covered 96 percent of the farms with $50,000 or more in sales, but only 78 percent of farms with less than $50,000 in sales. The overall coverage of all farms was 82 percent. The census covered nearly 98 percent of all land in farms and

97 percent of the market value of agricultural products sold. In 2002, census farm counts and totals were statistically adjusted for coverage and reported at the county level. The size of the adjustments varies considerably by state. In general, farms not on the census mail list tended to be small in acreage, production, and sales of farm products. For more explanation about census mail list compilation, collection methods, coverage measurement, and adjustments, see Appendixes A and C, 2002 Census of Agriculture, Volume 1 reports.

Farm income—The final agricultural sector output comprises cash receipts from farm marketings of crops and livestock, federal government payments made directly to farmers for farm-related activities, rental value of farm homes, value of farm products consumed in farm homes, and other farm-related income such as machine hire and custom work. Farm marketings represent quantities of agricultural products sold by farmers multiplied by prices received per unit of production at the local market. Information on prices received for farm products is generally obtained by the NASS Agricultural Statistics Board from surveys of firms (such as grain elevators, packers, and processors) purchasing agricultural commodities directly from producers. In some cases, the price information is obtained directly from the producers.

Crops—Estimates of crop acreage and production by the NASS are based on current sample survey data obtained from individual producers and objective yield counts, reports of carlot shipments, market records, personal field observations by field statisticians, and reports from other sources. Prices received by farmers are marketing year averages. These averages are based on U.S. monthly prices weighted by monthly marketings during specific periods. U.S. monthly prices are state average prices weighted by marketings during the month. Marketing year average prices do not include allowances for outstanding loans, government purchases, deficiency payments or disaster payments.

All state prices are based on individual state marketing years, while U.S. marketing year averages are based on standard marketing years for each crop. For a listing of the crop marketing years and the participating states in the monthly program, see *Crop Values*. Value of production is computed by multiplying state prices by each state's production. The U.S. value of production is the sum of state values for all states. Value of production figures shown in Tables 824–827, 831, and 832 should not be confused with cash receipts from farm marketings which relate to sales during a calendar year, irrespective of the year of production.

Livestock—Annual inventory numbers of livestock and estimates of livestock, dairy, and poultry production prepared by the Department of Agriculture are based on information from farmers and ranchers obtained by probability survey sampling methods.

Statistical reliability—For a discussion of statistical collection and estimation, sampling procedures, and measures of statistical reliability pertaining to Department of Agriculture data, see Appendix III.

Table 799. Farms by Size and Type of Organization: 1974 to 2002

[2,314 represents 2,314,000. For comments on adjustment, see text, this section]

Size and type of organization	Unit	Not adjusted for coverage						1997 [1]	2002 [1]
		1974	1978	1982	1987	1992	1997		
Farms.................	1,000	2,314	2,258	2,241	2,088	1,925	1,912	2,216	2,129
Land in farms.............	Mil. acres...	1,017	1,015	987	964	946	932	955	938
Average size of farm........	Acres	440	449	440	462	491	487	431	441
Farms by size:									
Under 10 acres..........	1,000	128	151	188	183	166	154	205	179
10 to 49 acres..........	1,000	380	392	449	412	388	411	531	564
50 to 179 acres..........	1,000	828	759	712	645	584	593	694	659
180 to 499 acres.........	1,000	616	582	527	478	428	403	428	389
500 to 999 acres.........	1,000	207	213	204	200	186	176	179	162
1,000 to 1,999 acres	1,000	93	98	97	102	102	101	103	99
2,000 acres or more	1,000	62	63	65	67	71	75	74	78
Farms by type of organization:									
Family or individual	1,000	(NA)	1,966	1,946	1,809	1,653	1,643	1,923	1,910
Partnership	1,000	(NA)	233	223	200	187	169	186	130
Corporation	1,000	(NA)	50	60	67	73	84	90	74
Other [2]	1,000	(NA)	9	12	12	12	15	17	16

NA Not available.   [1] Data have been adjusted for coverage; see text, this section.   [2] Cooperative, estate or trust, institutional, etc.

Source: U.S. Department of Agriculture, National Agricultural Statistics Service, *2002 Census of Agriculture*, Vol. 1.

Table 800. Farms—Number and Acreage by Size of Farm: 1997 and 2002

[2,216 represents 2,216,000. Data have been adjusted for coverage; see text, this section]

Size of farm	Number of farms (1,000)		Land in farms (mil. acres)		Cropland harvested (mil. acres)		Percent distribution 2002		
	1997	2002	1997	2002	1997	2002	Number of farms	All land in farms	Cropland harvested
Total	2,216	2,129	954.8	938.3	318.9	302.7	100.0	100.0	100.0
Under 10 acres	205	179	0.9	0.8	0.3	0.2	8.4	0.1	0.1
10 to 49 acres	531	564	14.0	14.7	4.3	4.1	26.5	1.6	1.4
50 to 69 acres	154	152	9.0	8.8	2.7	2.5	7.1	0.9	0.8
70 to 99 acres	200	191	16.5	15.7	5.2	4.7	9.0	1.7	1.5
100 to 139 acres	187	175	21.7	20.2	7.0	6.1	8.2	2.2	2.0
140 to 179 acres	153	142	24.1	22.3	8.4	7.3	6.7	2.4	2.4
180 to 219 acres	100	91	19.8	18.0	7.2	6.2	4.3	1.9	2.1
220 to 259 acres	79	72	18.8	17.1	7.5	6.5	3.4	1.8	2.1
260 to 499 acres	249	226	89.2	80.6	40.1	34.1	10.6	8.6	11.3
500 to 999 acres	179	162	124.6	112.4	66.5	56.7	7.6	12.0	18.7
1,000 to 1,999 acres...	103	99	140.7	135.7	75.9	72.8	4.7	14.5	24.0
2,000 acres or more ...	74	78	475.6	491.9	94.1	101.6	3.7	52.4	33.6

Source: U.S. Department of Agriculture, National Agricultural Statistics Service, *2002 Census of Agriculture*, Vol. 1.

Table 801. Farms—Number, Acreage, and Value by Tenure of Principal Operator and Type of Organization: 1997 and 2002

[2,216 represents 2,216,000. Full owners own all the land they operate. Part owners own a part and rent from others the rest of the land they operate. A principal operator is the person primarily responsible for the on-site, day-to-day operation of the farm or ranch business. Data have been adjusted for coverage; see text, this section]

Item and year	Unit	Total [1]	Tenure of operator			Type of organization		
			Full owner	Part owner	Tenant	Family or indi- vidual	Partner- ship	Corpora- tion
NUMBER OF FARMS								
1997......................	1,000	2,216	1,385	616	215	1,923	186	90
2002, total.................	1,000	2,129	1,428	551	150	1,910	130	74
Under 50 acres	1,000	743	639	64	41	697	24	18
50 to 179 acres	1,000	659	487	131	41	611	31	12
180 to 499 acres	1,000	389	203	153	33	344	29	12
500 to 999 acres	1,000	162	54	91	17	133	17	10
1,000 acres or more..........	1,000	177	46	112	18	125	29	21
LAND IN FARMS								
1997......................	Mil. acres...	955	332	512	111	605	151	133
2002......................	Mil acres...	938	357	495	87	622	146	108
Value of land and buildings, 2002 [2] ...	Bil. dol.	1,145	495	551	99	836	158	129
Value of farm products sold, 2002	Bil. dol.	201	88	91	22	104	37	57

[1] Includes other types, not shown separately.   [2] Based on a sample of farms.

Source: U.S. Department of Agriculture, National Agricultural Statistics Service, *2002 Census of Agriculture*, Vol. 1.

Agriculture   531

Table 802. Farms—Number and Acreage: 1990 to 2006

[As of June 1 (2,146 represents 2,146,000). Based on 1974 census definition; for definition of farms and farmland, see text of this section. Activities included as agriculture have undergone changes in recent years. Data for period 1995 to 2006 are not directly comparable with data for 1990. Data for 2002 have been adjusted for underenumeration. Minus sign (-) indicates decrease]

Year	Unit	1990	1995	2000	2001	2002	2003	2004	2005	2006
Number of farms	1,000.	2,146	2,196	2,167	2,149	2,135	2,127	2,113	2,099	2,090
Annual change [1] . . .	1,000.	-29	-1	-21	-18	-13	-9	-14	-14	-9
Land in farms	Mil. acres . . .	987	963	945	942	940	939	936	933	932
Average per farm. . .	Acres.	460	438	436	438	440	441	443	445	446

[1] Annual change from immediate preceding year.

Source: U.S. Dept. of Agriculture, National Agricultural Statistics Service, *Farms and Land in Farms, Final Estimates, 1988–1992; Farms and Land in Farms, Final Estimates, 1993–1997; Farm Numbers and Land in Farms, Final Estimates, 1998–2002;* and *Farms, Land in Farms, and Livestock Operations,* annual.

Table 803. Farms—Number and Acreage by State: 2000 and 2006

[2,167 represents 2,167,000. See headnote, Table 802]

State	Farms (1,000) 2000	2006	Acreage (mil.) 2000	2006	Acreage per farm 2000	2006	State	Farms (1,000) 2000	2006	Acreage (mil.) 2000	2006	Acreage per farm 2000	2006
U.S	2,167	2,090	945	932	436	446	Montana	28	28	59	60	2,133	2,139
Alabama.	47	43	9	9	191	200	Nebraska	52	48	46	46	887	960
Alaska	1	1	1	1	1,569	1,406	Nevada	3	3	6	6	2,065	2,100
Arizona.	11	10	27	26	2,514	2,610	New Hampshire.	3	3	(Z)	(Z)	133	132
Arkansas	48	47	15	14	304	308	New Jersey.	10	10	1	1	86	81
California	83	76	28	26	337	346	New Mexico	18	18	45	45	2,494	2,543
Colorado.	30	31	32	31	1,053	1,000	New York	38	35	8	8	205	214
Connecticut. . . .	4	4	(Z)	(Z)	86	86	North Carolina . . .	56	48	9	9	166	183
Delaware	3	2	1	1	215	224	North Dakota. . . .	31	30	39	39	1,279	1,300
Florida	44	41	10	10	236	244	Ohio	79	76	15	14	187	188
Georgia	49	49	11	11	222	220	Oklahoma	85	83	34	34	400	406
Hawaii	6	6	1	1	251	236	Oregon.	40	39	17	17	433	435
Idaho	25	25	12	12	486	472	Pennsylvania. . . .	59	58	8	8	130	131
Illinois	77	72	28	27	357	377	Rhode Island. . . .	1	1	(Z)	(Z)	75	71
Indiana.	63	59	15	15	240	254	South Carolina. . .	24	25	5	5	203	197
Iowa	94	89	33	32	346	356	South Dakota. . . .	32	31	44	44	1,358	1,396
Kansas.	65	64	48	47	736	738	Tennessee	88	82	12	11	134	139
Kentucky	90	84	14	14	152	163	Texas.	228	230	131	130	573	564
Louisiana	29	27	8	8	277	291	Utah	16	15	12	12	748	768
Maine.	7	7	1	1	190	192	Vermont	7	6	1	1	192	197
Maryland	12	12	2	2	172	170	Virginia.	49	47	9	9	180	182
Massachusetts. . .	6	6	1	1	89	85	Washington.	37	34	16	15	420	444
Michigan.	53	53	10	10	192	191	West Virginia. . . .	21	21	4	4	173	170
Minnesota.	81	79	28	27	344	346	Wisconsin	78	76	16	15	206	201
Mississippi	42	42	11	11	266	262	Wyoming	9	9	35	34	3,750	3,780
Missouri	109	105	30	30	277	287							

Z Less than 500,000 acres.

Source: U.S. Department of Agriculture, National Agricultural Statistics Service, *Farm Numbers and Land in Farms, Final Estimates, 1998–2002* and *Farms, Land in Farms, and Livestock Operations,* annual.

Table 804. Certified Organic Farmland Acreage and Livestock: 2000 to 2005

["Certified organic" means that agricultural products have been grown and processed according to USDA's national organic standards and certified by USDA-accredited state and private certification organizations]

Item	Unit	2000	2004	2005	Crop	Certified organic acreage (1,000) 2000	2005
Certified growers	Number. . .	6,592	8,021	8,493	Corn	78	131
					Wheat	181	277
Certified organic acreage,					Oats	30	46
total	1,000	1,776	3,045	4,054	Barley	42	39
Pastureland and rangeland. . .	1,000	557	1,593	2,331	Rice	27	26
Cropland	1,000	1,219	1,452	1,723	Millet.	15	14
					Soybeans	136	122
Certified animals:					Dry beans	14	11
Beef cows	1,000	13.8	36.7	36.1	Dry peas and lentils.	10	18
Milk cows	1,000	38.2	74.8	87.1	Flax	25	31
Other cows	1,000	(NA)	36.6	58.8	Lettuce	11	12
Hogs and pigs	1,000	1.7	4.9	10.0	Tree nuts	4	16
Sheep and lambs	1,000	2.3	4.3	4.5	Apples	9	13
Layer hens	1,000	1,114	1,788	2,415	Grapes	13	23
Broilers	1,000	1,925	4,769	10,406	Peanuts.	2	12
Turkeys.	1,000	9	164	144	Trees for maple syrup . . .	12	12

NA Not available.

Source: U.S. Department of Agriculture, Economic Research Service, "Organic Production"; <http://www.ers.usda.gov /data/organic>.

532 Agriculture

Table 805. Balance Sheet of the Farming Sector: 1990 to 2005

[In billions of dollars, except as indicated (841 represents $841,000,000,000). As of December 31]

Item	1990	1995	1997	1998	1999	2000	2001	2002	2003	2004	2005
Assets	841	966	1,051	1,083	1,139	1,203	1,256	1,304	1,379	1,585	1,805
Real estate	619	740	808	840	887	946	996	1,046	1,112	1,308	1,521
Livestock and poultry [1]	71	58	67	63	73	77	79	76	79	79	81
Machinery, motor vehicles [2]	86	88	89	90	90	90	93	94	96	102	105
Crops [3]	23	27	33	30	28	28	25	23	24	24	24
Purchased inputs	3	3	5	5	4	5	4	6	6	6	6
Financial assets	38	49	50	55	57	57	59	60	62	66	67
Claims	841	966	1,051	1,083	1,139	1,203	1,256	1,304	1,379	1,585	1,805
Debt [4]	131	143	157	165	168	178	186	193	198	202	215
Real estate debt	68	72	79	83	87	91	96	103	108	107	116
Nonreal estate debt	63	71	78	82	80	87	90	90	90	94	100
Equity	709	823	894	919	971	1,026	1,070	1,111	1,181	1,383	1,590
FINANCIAL RATIOS (percent)											
Farm debt/equity ratio	18.5	17.4	17.5	17.9	17.3	17.3	17.4	17.4	16.8	14.6	13.6
Farm debt/asset ratio	15.6	14.8	14.9	15.2	14.7	14.8	14.8	14.8	14.4	12.7	11.9
Rate of return on assets from:											
Total	3.5	4.3	5.7	5.1	5.3	5.1	4.6	3.2	6.6	11.4	(NA)
Current income [5]	4.1	2.2	3.0	2.4	1.8	2.0	2.0	0.7	2.2	3.4	(NA)
Real capital gains [6]	-0.7	2.1	2.7	2.7	3.4	3.1	2.6	2.5	4.4	8.0	(NA)
Rate of return on equity from:											
Total	3.0	3.9	5.5	4.8	5.1	5.0	4.4	2.8	6.8	13.4	(NA)
Current income [7]	3.0	1.1	2.0	1.4	0.7	0.9	1.1	-0.4	1.5	3.1	(NA)
Real capital gains [8]	0.1	2.8	3.5	3.4	4.3	4.1	3.4	3.2	5.2	10.4	(NA)

NA Not available.   [1] Excludes horses, mules, and broilers.   [2] Includes only farm share value for trucks and autos.   [3] All non-CCC crops held on farms plus the value above loan rate for crops held under Commodity Credit Corporation.   [4] Excludes debt for nonfarm purposes.   [5] Returns to farm assets from current income/farm business assets. Measures how efficiently the farm business uses its assets; the per dollar return on farm assets from current income only.   [6] Real capital gains on farm business assets/farm business assets. The per dollar return on farm assets from real capital gains.   [7] Returns to farm assets from current income minus interest/farm business equity. Measures the returns to equity capital employed in farm business from current income less interest.   [8] Real capital gains on farm business assets/farm business equity. The per dollar return on farm equity from real capital gains.

Source: U.S. Department of Agriculture, Economic Research Service, "Farm Balance Sheet"; published 31 August 2006; <http://www.ers.usda.gov/Data/FarmBalanceSheet/FBSDMU.HTM>.

Table 806. Farm Sector Output and Value Added: 1990 to 2005

[In billions of dollars (180.1 represents $180,100,000,000). For definition of value added, see text, Section 13. Minus sign (–) indicates decrease]

Item	1990	1995	1997	1998	1999	2000	2001	2002	2003	2004	2005
CURRENT DOLLARS											
Farm output, total	180.1	192.0	222.0	208.9	198.5	203.6	210.8	202.1	227.7	260.8	253.2
Cash receipts from farm marketings	172.1	194.3	211.2	199.0	190.2	196.6	200.1	194.6	214.8	238.4	238.0
Farm products consumed on farms	0.7	0.5	0.5	0.5	0.5	0.6	0.5	0.5	0.5	0.5	0.5
Other farm income	4.9	6.3	7.4	8.5	9.4	8.4	9.5	10.6	11.8	13.3	14.1
Change in farm finished goods inventories	2.4	-9.2	2.8	0.8	-1.6	-2.0	0.6	-3.7	0.7	8.5	0.6
Less: Intermediate goods and services consumed [1]	103.5	123.5	133.9	130.0	129.8	132.1	137.7	131.2	139.5	146.2	157.3
Equals: Gross farm value added	76.6	68.5	88.1	78.9	68.8	71.5	73.1	70.8	88.3	114.6	95.9
Less: Consumption of fixed capital	18.6	19.6	20.3	20.9	21.2	21.3	27.4	27.0	27.7	29.5	31.5
Equals: Net farm value added	58.0	48.9	67.8	58.0	47.6	50.2	45.7	43.9	60.6	85.1	64.4
Compensation of employees	13.4	15.4	17.1	18.2	18.9	19.7	20.9	20.8	20.0	22.5	24.3
Taxes on production and imports	3.8	4.2	4.4	4.3	4.9	4.7	4.8	5.0	4.9	5.1	6.1
Less: Subsidies to operators	7.6	6.1	6.4	10.5	18.6	19.6	18.3	9.6	14.9	11.5	21.1
Net operating surplus	48.5	35.4	52.6	46.0	42.4	45.4	38.3	27.7	50.6	69.0	55.1
CHAINED (2000) DOLLARS [2]											
Farm output, total	164.5	179.6	198.4	198.4	200.5	203.6	200.7	201.4	207.9	211.9	215.1
Cash receipts from farm marketings	159.0	183.5	189.2	189.2	192.0	196.6	190.1	194.1	195.5	192.3	200.4
Farm products consumed on farms	0.7	0.5	0.5	0.6	0.6	0.6	0.5	0.5	0.4	0.4	0.4
Other farm income	4.8	5.8	6.5	7.9	9.5	8.4	9.4	10.1	10.7	11.5	12.7
Change in farm finished goods inventories	2.1	-8.8	2.5	0.9	-1.8	-2.0	0.6	-3.6	0.6	6.2	0.4
Less: Intermediate goods and services consumed [1]	117.5	134.4	133.7	137.5	138.1	132.1	135.3	131.3	131.7	129.4	131.7
Equals: Gross farm value added	49.3	49.6	64.4	61.6	62.9	71.5	65.6	70.1	76.0	81.6	82.4
Less: Consumption of fixed capital	23.0	21.3	21.3	21.6	21.6	21.3	27.0	26.2	26.5	27.3	27.9
Equals: Net farm value added	29.4	30.4	42.9	40.2	41.5	50.2	39.0	44.2	49.7	54.3	54.6

[1] Includes rent paid to nonoperator landlords.   [2] See text, Section 13.

Source: U.S. Bureau of Economic Analysis, Survey of Current Business, August 2006. See also <http://www.bea.gov/national/nipaweb/SelectTable.asp?Selected=N>.

Agriculture   533

Table 807. **Value Added to Economy by Agricultural Sector: 1990 to 2005**

[In billions of dollars (188.5 represents $188,500,000,000). Data are consistent with the net farm income accounts and include income and expenses related to the farm operator dwellings. The concept presented is consistent with that employed by the Organization for Economic Co-operation and Development]

Item	1990	1995	1997	1998	1999	2000	2001	2002	2003	2004	2005
Value of agricultural sector production	**188.5**	**203.6**	**230.5**	**220.2**	**213.4**	**221.2**	**230.3**	**221.2**	**244.3**	**283.2**	**275.4**
Value of crop production	83.2	95.9	112.5	102.1	92.8	94.8	95.0	98.4	108.4	125.3	112.7
Food grains	7.5	10.4	10.4	8.8	6.9	6.5	6.4	6.8	8.0	8.9	8.4
Feed crops	18.7	24.5	27.1	22.6	19.5	20.5	21.5	24.0	24.7	27.4	25.3
Cotton	5.5	6.9	6.3	6.1	4.6	2.9	3.6	3.4	6.4	4.8	5.8
Oil crops	12.3	15.5	19.8	17.4	13.4	13.5	13.3	15.0	18.0	17.9	18.3
Tobacco	2.7	2.5	2.9	2.8	2.3	2.3	1.9	1.7	1.6	1.6	1.1
Fruits and tree nuts	9.4	11.0	13.0	12.0	12.0	12.4	12.0	12.6	13.5	15.8	16.8
Vegetables	11.3	15.0	14.7	15.0	15.0	15.5	15.4	17.2	16.9	16.8	16.9
All other crops	12.9	15.2	17.2	17.6	18.4	18.6	19.2	20.2	20.7	21.0	21.3
Home consumption	0.1	0.2	0.2	0.2	0.2	0.2	0.2	0.2	0.1	0.1	0.1
Value of inventory adjustment	2.8	-5.3	1.0	-0.3	0.5	2.2	1.5	-2.9	-1.6	11.0	-1.3
Value of livestock production	90.0	87.8	96.3	94.2	95.2	99.1	106.4	93.5	105.0	124.4	126.9
Meat animals	51.1	44.9	49.7	43.4	45.7	53.0	53.3	48.1	56.2	62.4	64.8
Dairy products	20.2	19.9	20.9	24.1	23.2	20.6	24.7	20.6	21.2	27.4	26.7
Poultry and eggs	15.3	19.1	22.3	23.0	22.9	21.9	24.6	21.1	24.0	29.5	28.9
Miscellaneous livestock	2.5	3.4	3.6	3.8	3.9	4.2	4.1	4.1	4.2	4.3	4.5
Home consumption	0.5	0.3	0.2	0.2	0.1	0.1	0.1	0.1	0.1	0.2	0.3
Value of inventory adjustment	0.4	0.2	-0.4	-0.3	-0.7	-0.6	-0.4	-0.6	-0.8	0.6	1.7
Services and forestry	15.3	19.9	21.7	23.9	25.4	27.3	28.9	29.3	30.9	33.5	35.8
Machine hire and customwork	1.8	1.9	2.4	2.2	2.0	2.2	2.1	2.2	3.0	3.4	2.8
Forest products sold	1.8	2.8	2.8	3.0	2.7	2.8	2.6	2.5	2.2	2.4	2.5
Other farm income	4.5	5.8	6.9	8.7	10.1	8.7	10.1	10.2	10.5	11.2	12.4
Gross imputed rental value of farm dwellings	7.2	9.4	9.6	10.0	10.6	13.5	14.1	14.5	15.2	16.5	18.2
Less: Purchased inputs	92.2	108.8	120.0	117.7	118.7	121.8	125.7	123.1	130.0	136.6	146.7
Farm origin	39.5	41.8	46.9	44.8	45.5	47.9	48.2	48.3	53.7	57.5	57.9
Feed purchased	20.4	23.8	26.3	25.0	24.5	24.5	24.8	25.0	27.5	29.7	28.2
Livestock and poultry purchased	14.6	12.5	13.8	12.6	13.8	15.9	15.2	14.4	16.8	18.1	19.2
Seed purchased	4.5	5.5	6.7	7.2	7.2	7.5	8.2	8.9	9.4	9.6	10.4
Manufactured inputs	22.0	26.1	29.2	28.1	27.1	28.7	29.4	28.5	28.5	31.7	35.5
Fertilizers and lime	8.2	10.0	10.9	10.6	9.9	10.0	10.3	9.6	10.0	11.4	12.9
Pesticides	5.4	7.7	9.0	9.0	8.6	8.5	8.6	8.3	8.4	8.6	8.9
Petroleum fuel and oils	5.8	5.4	6.2	5.6	5.6	7.2	6.9	6.6	6.8	8.2	10.3
Electricity	2.6	3.0	3.0	2.9	3.0	3.0	3.6	3.9	3.3	3.4	3.4
Other purchased inputs	30.7	40.9	43.9	44.8	46.1	45.2	48.1	46.4	47.8	47.5	53.3
Repair and maintenance of capital items	8.6	9.6	10.6	10.5	10.7	10.9	11.2	10.4	10.3	12.0	11.9
Machine hire and custom work	3.0	3.9	4.0	4.6	4.4	4.1	4.0	4.0	3.5	3.6	3.5
Marketing, storage, and transportation expenses	4.2	7.2	7.1	6.9	7.3	7.5	7.8	7.5	7.3	7.2	8.8
Contract labor	1.6	2.0	2.5	2.4	2.5	2.7	3.1	2.7	3.2	3.0	3.0
Miscellaneous expenses	13.4	18.2	19.7	20.4	21.3	19.9	21.9	21.7	23.6	21.7	26.1
Plus: Net government transactions [1]	3.1	0.4	0.4	5.3	14.3	15.8	15.0	5.2	9.2	5.4	15.8
Direct Government payments	9.3	7.3	7.5	12.4	21.5	23.2	22.4	12.4	16.5	13.0	24.3
Motor vehicle registration and licensing fees	0.4	0.4	0.5	0.5	0.4	0.5	0.5	0.4	0.5	0.5	0.6
Property taxes	5.8	6.4	6.7	6.6	6.8	6.9	6.9	6.8	6.8	7.0	8.0
Equals: Gross value added	**99.3**	**95.1**	**110.9**	**107.8**	**109.0**	**115.2**	**119.7**	**103.2**	**123.5**	**152.0**	**144.6**
Less: Capital consumption	18.1	18.9	19.3	19.6	19.8	20.1	20.6	21.0	21.5	23.1	24.1
Equals: Net value added	**81.2**	**76.2**	**91.7**	**88.2**	**89.2**	**95.1**	**99.1**	**82.2**	**102.0**	**128.9**	**120.4**
Less: Employee compensation	12.4	14.3	15.9	16.8	17.4	17.9	18.8	19.1	1.8	20.5	21.0
Less: Net rent received by nonoperator landlords	9.0	9.6	11.2	10.9	10.4	11.2	11.1	9.8	10.1	9.9	10.5
Less: Real estate and nonreal estate interest	13.5	12.6	13.2	13.5	13.8	14.7	13.6	13.1	12.7	13.1	15.1
Equals: Net farm income	**46.3**	**39.8**	**51.3**	**47.1**	**47.7**	**51.3**	**55.6**	**40.2**	**60.4**	**85.4**	**73.8**

[1] Direct government payments minus motor vehicle registration and licensing fees and property taxes.

Source: U.S. Dept. of Agriculture, Economic Research Service, "United States and State Farm Income Data"; <http://www.ers.usda.gov/Data/farmincome/finfidmu.htm>; accessed 12 December 2006.

Table 808. **Cash Receipts for Selected Commodities—Leading States: 2005**

[In millions of dollars (49,209 represents $49,209,000,000). See headnote, Table 809]

State	Value	State	Value	State	Value	State	Value
Cattle and calves	49,209	Dairy products	26,738	Broilers	20,902	Corn	19,125
Texas	7,580	California	5,223	Georgia	2,897	Iowa	3,636
Nebraska	6,458	Wisconsin	3,528	Arkansas	2,652	Illinois	3,564
Kansas	6,089	New York	1,914	Alabama	2,410	Nebraska	2,086
Colorado	3,138	Pennsylvania	1,774	North Carolina	2,232	Minnesota	1,635
Oklahoma	2,697	Idaho	1,418	Mississippi	2,055	Indiana	1,511

Source: U.S. Department of Agriculture, Economic Research Service, "Farm Income"; published 14 August 2006; <http://www.ers.usda.gov/Data/farmincome/firkdmu.htm>.

534 Agriculture

Table 809. Farm Income—Cash Receipts From Farm Marketings: 2000 to 2005

[In millions of dollars (192,028 represents $192,028,000,000). Represents gross receipts from commercial market sales as well as net Commodity Credit Corporation loans. The source estimates and publishes individual cash receipt values only for major commodities and major producing states. The U.S. receipts for individual commodities, computed as the sum of the reported states, may understate the value of sales for some commodities. The degree of underestimation in some of the minor commodities can be substantial]

Commodity	2000	2003	2004	2005	Commodity	2000	2003	2004	2005
Total.........	192,028	215,503	237,878	238,941	Lettuce [1].........	1,863	2,288	2,021	1,986
Livestock and products [1]......	99,635	105,638	123,627	124,980	Head	1,202	1,233	1,116	988
Cattle and calves......	40,783	45,092	47,507	49,209	Romaine	299	627	440	458
Hogs...........	11,758	10,618	14,333	15,037	Leaf	356	426	459	537
Sheep and lambs	470	502	512	562	Onions	713	1,003	998	1,037
Dairy products........	20,587	21,239	27,387	26,738	Peppers, green	531	473	538	465
Broilers	13,989	15,215	20,446	20,902	Tomatoes........	1,845	1,910	2,160	2,277
Chicken eggs	4,289	5,273	5,239	4,000	Fresh	1,195	1,333	1,440	1,654
Turkeys	2,771	2,632	2,996	3,158	Processing.......	650	577	720	622
Horses/mules [2]......	1,239	1,018	1,161	1,228	Watermelons.......	240	343	313	410
Aquaculture [1,2]......	798	776	848	852					
Catfish	501	425	480	482	Fruits/nuts	12,435	13,478	15,822	16,840
					Grapefruit.........	377	270	348	748
Crops [1]........	92,394	109,865	114,250	113,962	Oranges	1,775	1,441	1,714	1,605
Rice	837	1,225	1,768	1,574	Apples	1,466	1,688	1,767	1,591
Wheat	5,672	6,745	7,124	6,810	Cherries..........	327	422	507	549
Barley	556	668	601	548	Grapes [1]........	3,100	2,610	3,011	3,461
Corn	15,162	18,939	21,199	19,125	Wine	1,909	1,543	1,605	2,215
Hay..............	3,855	4,214	4,691	4,742	Raisins	487	374	624	568
Sorghum grain	864	800	818	714	Peaches..........	470	454	462	510
Cotton	2,950	6,420	4,784	5,796	Strawberries	1,045	1,375	1,460	1,383
Tobacco	2,316	1,612	1,578	1,096	Almonds	666	1,600	2,189	2,337
Peanuts..........	897	799	814	846	Pecans...........	239	278	327	407
Soybeans.........	12,047	16,602	16,441	16,793	Walnuts	296	378	452	540
Vegetables [1]......	15,540	16,887	16,817	16,880	Pistachios	245	145	465	577
Beans, dry	436	475	439	491	Sugar beets	1,113	1,270	1,107	1,107
Potatoes..........	2,375	2,669	2,386	2,377	Cane for sugar ...	881	1,004	926	821
Broccoli	622	616	638	564	Greenhouse/nursery [1]..	13,710	15,435	15,863	16,202
Carrots...........	390	549	573	587	Floriculture	4,576	5,082	5,284	5,363
Corn, sweet.......	709	780	794	819	Christmas trees	502	506	499	485
					Mushrooms.........	867	943	886	879

[1] Includes other commodities not shown separately. [2] See also Table 862.

Source: U.S. Department of Agriculture, Economic Research Service, "United States and State Farm Income Data"; <http://www.ers.usda.gov/Data/farmincome/finfidmu.htm>. accessed: 11 December 2006.

Table 810. Farm Output, Income, and Government Payments by State: 2004 and 2005

[In millions of dollars (283,192 represents $283,192,000,000). Farm income data are after inventory adjustment and include income and expenses related to the farm operator's dwelling]

State	Final agricultural sector output 2004	2005	Net farm income 2004	2005	Government payments, 2005	State	Final agricultural sector output 2004	2005	Net farm income 2004	2005	Government payments, 2005
U.S.	283,192	275,446	85,400	73,834	24,349	MT......	2,647	2,887	818	703	382
AL.....	4,907	4,905	2,059	1,924	251	NE......	13,400	12,968	3,568	2,700	1,414
AK.....	61	58	13	8	5	NV......	528	560	160	122	12
AZ.....	3,473	3,537	1,474	1,123	126	NH......	220	213	54	58	8
AR.....	7,566	6,891	3,131	1,903	588	NJ......	1,041	1,019	238	278	26
CA.....	34,641	33,789	11,191	9,118	703	NM......	2,757	2,865	953	760	117
CO.....	6,279	6,346	1,517	1,216	382	NY......	4,043	4,046	921	1,111	143
CT.....	619	618	156	189	11	NC......	10,206	9,984	2,986	3,616	1,193
DE.....	1,065	1,236	360	490	29	ND......	4,250	4,602	854	1,280	831
FL.....	7,555	8,215	2,752	3,217	435	OH......	6,903	6,506	1,579	1,452	614
GA.....	7,070	7,171	2,729	2,536	665	OK......	5,988	6,156	1,408	1,439	312
HI.....	625	636	123	103	5	OR......	4,473	4,725	1,380	1,053	129
ID......	4,971	5,009	1,752	1,125	191	PA......	5,771	5,527	1,703	1,730	140
IL......	11,551	9,014	3,866	1,065	1,773	RI......	83	83	27	31	5
IN......	7,493	6,369	2,550	1,390	914	SC......	2,303	2,116	814	732	261
IA......	17,316	16,104	5,569	3,446	2,284	SD......	5,885	5,614	2,091	1,926	807
KS.....	11,020	11,379	2,018	2,526	1,080	TN......	3,493	3,413	596	894	509
KY.....	5,246	5,232	1,334	2,082	828	TX......	20,435	19,918	7,028	6,296	2,094
LA.....	2,592	2,454	756	663	338	UT......	1,507	1,553	452	329	55
ME.....	669	617	185	179	22	VT......	639	650	169	213	21
MD.....	2,182	2,101	726	745	85	VA......	3,560	3,574	750	1,005	235
MA.....	559	551	114	131	13	WA	6,726	6,590	1,773	1,048	240
MI.....	5,210	5,164	1,219	1,337	386	WV......	600	621	65	55	17
MN.....	11,222	11,016	2,758	3,059	1,388	WI......	8,148	8,258	1,824	1,742	584
MS.....	4,899	4,731	1,853	1,837	857	WY.....	1,222	1,283	264	300	131
MO.....	7,572	6,572	2,725	1,548	711						

Source: U.S. Department of Agriculture, Economic Research Service, "Farm Income Summary Totals for 50 States"; <http://www.ers.usda.gov/Data/FarmIncome/50State/50stmenu.htm>; accessed 13 December 2006.

Agriculture 535

Table 811. **Farm Income—Farm Marketings, 2004 and 2005, and Principal Commodities, 2005, by State**

[In millions of dollars (237,878 represents $237,878,000,000). Cattle include calves; sheep include lambs, and greenhouse includes nursery]

State	2004 Total	2004 Crops	2004 Live-stock	2005 Total	2005 Crops	2005 Live-stock	State rank for total farm marketings and four principal commodities in order of marketing receipts
U.S....	237,878	114,250	123,627	238,941	113,962	124,980	Cattle, dairy products, broilers, corn
AL	4,074	695	3,379	4,097	722	3,375	24-Broilers, cattle, chicken eggs, greenhouse
AK	51	24	27	49	25	24	50-Greenhouse, hay, dairy products, potatoes
AZ	3,007	1,606	1,401	3,106	1,693	1,412	29-Cattle, dairy products, lettuce, cotton
AR	6,465	2,289	4,176	6,320	2,105	4,215	11-Broilers, rice, soybeans, cattle
CA	31,675	23,126	8,550	31,707	23,253	8,454	1-Dairy products, greenhouse, grapes, almonds
CO	5,511	1,337	4,174	5,386	1,396	3,990	16-Cattle, dairy products, greenhouse, corn
CT	513	339	174	511	351	160	44-Greenhouse, dairy products, chicken eggs, aquaculture
DE	935	193	743	1,068	175	893	38-Broilers, corn, greenhouse, soybeans
FL......	7,113	5,620	1,493	7,760	6,306	1,453	9-Greenhouse, oranges, tomatoes, grapefruit
GA	6,102	2,030	4,072	6,130	2,131	3,999	12-Broilers, cotton, greenhouse, peanuts
HI	549	456	92	556	468	88	42-Greenhouse, pineapples, sugar cane, macadamia nuts
ID	4,387	1,849	2,538	4,484	1,901	2,584	21-Dairy products, cattle, potatoes, wheat
IL	8,931	6,993	1,938	8,847	6,859	1,988	7-Corn, soybeans, hogs, cattle
IN	6,096	4,028	2,069	5,580	3,537	2,043	15-Corn, soybeans, hogs, dairy products
IA	14,032	6,749	7,284	14,621	6,674	7,947	3-Hogs, corn, soybeans, cattle
KS	9,255	2,835	6,420	9,975	3,107	6,868	5-Cattle, wheat, corn, soybeans
KY	4,125	1,387	2,739	3,971	1,270	2,701	25-Horses/mules, broilers, cattle, tobacco
LA	2,174	1,296	878	2,125	1,205	920	34-Sugar cane, cattle, cotton, rice
ME	562	222	340	535	240	295	43-Dairy products, potatoes, chicken eggs, greenhouse
MD	1,746	736	1,010	1,617	686	931	36-Broilers, greenhouse, dairy products, corn
MA	415	321	94	404	313	91	47-Greenhouse, cranberries, dairy products, sweet corn
MI	4,259	2,490	1,769	4,160	2,432	1,727	22-Dairy products, greenhouse, soybeans, corn
MN	9,558	4,628	4,930	9,301	4,338	4,963	6-Hogs, corn, soybeans, dairy products
MS	3,993	1,281	2,712	4,135	1,234	2,901	23-Broilers, cotton, soybeans, aquaculture
MO	5,726	2,651	3,075	5,615	2,514	3,101	14-Cattle, soybeans, corn, hogs
MT	2,225	946	1,278	2,324	1,038	1,286	33-Cattle, wheat, barley, hay
NE	11,236	3,898	7,337	11,470	3,925	7,545	4-Cattle, corn, soybeans, hogs
NV	467	160	306	479	172	307	45-Cattle, hay, dairy products, onions
NH	169	96	73	163	93	70	48-Greenhouse, dairy products, cattle, apples
NJ	865	679	187	858	677	181	40-Greenhouse, horses/mules, blueberries, peaches
NM	2,581	577	2,004	2,611	621	1,990	31-Dairy products, cattle, hay, pecans
NY	3,621	1,319	2,303	3,630	1,326	2,305	28-Dairy products, greenhouse, apples, cattle
NC	8,315	2,962	5,353	8,264	2,662	5,602	8-Broilers, hogs, greenhouse, turkeys
ND	3,843	2,904	939	3,921	2,925	997	26-Wheat, cattle, soybeans, corn
OH	5,219	3,147	2,072	5,182	3,138	2,044	18-Soybeans, corn, dairy products, greenhouse
OK	5,014	1,109	3,904	5,247	1,032	4,215	17-Cattle, hogs, broilers, wheat
OR	3,693	2,650	1,043	3,747	2,716	1,031	27-Greenhouse, cattle, dairy products, hay
PA	4,983	1,661	3,322	4,782	1,548	3,234	20-Dairy products, cattle, greenhouse, mushrooms
RI	65	55	10	64	54	10	49-Greenhouse, dairy products, sweet corn, cattle
SC	1,918	822	1,096	1,819	728	1,091	35-Broilers, greenhouse, cattle, turkeys
SD	4,579	2,147	2,432	4,863	2,262	2,601	19-Cattle, corn, soybeans, wheat
TN	2,560	1,261	1,298	2,525	1,258	1,267	32-Cattle, broilers, greenhouse, soybeans
TX	16,545	5,340	11,205	16,355	5,694	10,662	2-Cattle, cotton, broilers, greenhouse
UT	1,263	279	983	1,326	289	1,037	37-Cattle, dairy products, hogs, hay
VT	580	82	499	563	80	483	41-Dairy products, cattle, greenhouse, hay
VA	2,692	910	1,782	2,702	830	1,872	30-Broilers, cattle, dairy products, turkeys
WA	5,823	4,088	1,736	5,810	3,987	1,823	13-Apples, dairy products, cattle, wheat
WV	426	77	349	452	76	376	46-Broilers, cattle, chicken eggs, dairy products
WI	6,845	1,752	5,094	6,759	1,745	5,014	10-Dairy products, cattle, corn, greenhouse
WY	1,097	147	951	966	151	815	39-Cattle, hay, sugar beets, sheep

Source: U.S. Department of Agriculture, Economic Research Service, "United States and State Farm Income Data"; <http://www.ers.usda.gov/Data/farmincome/finfidmu.htm>; accessed 7 December 2006.

Table 812. **Indexes of Prices Received and Paid by Farmers: 2000 to 2006**

[1990–1992 = 100, except as noted]

Item	2000	2004	2005	2006	Item	2000	2004	2005	2006
Prices received, all products	96	119	116	116	Prices paid, total [2]..........	118	132	141	148
					Production	116	131	139	146
					Feed	102	121	117	127
Crops	96	117	112	120	Livestock & poultry.......	110	128	138	133
Food grains	85	120	111	134	Seed	124	158	168	182
Feed grains and hay......	86	110	95	109	Fertilizer.............	110	140	164	174
Cotton	82	90	70	79	Agricultural chemicals.....	120	121	123	128
Tobacco	107	94	94	91	Fuels	134	165	216	239
Oil-bearing crops	85	134	105	100	Supplies & repairs	124	134	140	145
Fruits and nuts	98	127	130	155	Autos and trucks	119	114	114	112
Commercial vegetables [1]...	121	129	139	138	Farm machinery.........	139	162	173	181
Potatoes & dry beans	93	102	109	128	Building materials........	121	134	142	152
All other crops........	110	115	117	119	Farm services	119	128	132	138
					Rent	110	115	123	121
Livestock and products......	97	122	120	113	Interest	113	96	119	138
Meat animals	94	116	120	116	Taxes	123	128	154	162
Dairy products	94	123	116	99	Wage rates	140	160	165	171
Poultry and eggs	106	132	124	117	Parity ratio (1910–14 = 100) [3]...	38	43	39	37

[1] Excludes potatoes and dry beans. [2] Includes production items, interest, taxes, wage rates, and a family living component. The family living component is the Consumer Price Index for all urban consumers from the Bureau of Labor Statistics. See text, Section 14, and Table 703. [3] Ratio of prices received by farmers to prices paid.

Source: U.S. Department of Agriculture, National Agricultural Statistics Service, *Agricultural Prices: Annual Summary.*

536 Agriculture

Table 813. Civilian Consumer Expenditures for Farm Foods: 1990 to 2005

[In billions of dollars, except percent (449.8 represents $449,800,000,000). Excludes imported and nonfarm foods, such as coffee and seafood, as well as food consumed by the military, or exported]

Item	1990	1995	1997	1998	1999	2000	2001	2002	2003	2004	2005
Consumer expenditures, total. . .	449.8	529.5	566.5	585.0	625.3	661.1	687.5	709.4	744.2	788.9	830.7
Farm value, total . ., ...	106.2	113.8	121.9	119.6	122.2	123.3	130.0	132.5	140.2	155.5	157.8
Marketing bill, total [1]	343.6	415.7	444.6	465.4	503.1	537.8	557.5	576.9	604.0	633.4	672.9
Percent of total consumer expenditures	76.4	78.5	78.5	79.6	80.5	81.3	81.1	81.3	81.2	80.3	81.0
At-home expenditures [2]	276.2	316.9	339.2	346.8	370.7	390.2	403.9	416.8	437.2	463.5	488.1
Farm value . ., ...	80.2	76.1	79.0	77.0	78.7	79.6	83.9	85.7	91.4	101.3	102.8
Marketing bill [1]	196.0	240.8	260.2	269.8	292.0	310.6	320.0	331.1	345.8	362.2	385.3
Away-from-home expenditures	173.6	212.6	227.3	238.2	254.6	270.9	283.6	292.6	307.0	325.4	342.6
Farm value	26.0	37.7	42.9	42.6	43.5	43.7	46.1	46.8	48.8	54.2	55.0
Marketing bill [1]	147.6	174.9	184.4	195.6	211.1	227.2	237.5	245.8	258.2	271.2	287.6
Marketing bill cost components:											
Labor cost	154.0	196.6	216.9	229.9	241.5	252.9	263.8	273.1	285.9	303.7	319.8
Packaging materials	36.5	48.2	48.7	50.4	50.9	53.5	55.0	56.8	59.5	63.1	66.5
Rail and truck transport	19.8	22.3	23.6	24.4	25.2	26.4	27.5	28.4	29.7	31.6	33.2
Corporate profits before taxes	13.2	19.5	22.3	25.5	29.2	31.1	32.0	33.0	34.6	35.5	37.4
Fuels and electricity.	15.2	18.6	20.2	20.7	22.0	23.1	24.1	24.9	26.1	27.6	31.6
Advertising	17.1	19.8	22.1	23.4	24.8	26.1	27.5	28.1	29.4	30.8	32.7
Depreciation	16.3	18.9	21.0	21.6	23.0	24.2	24.5	25.3	26.5	27.8	29.5
Net interest	13.5	11.6	12.5	12.9	14.4	16.9	18.6	19.2	20.1	21.1	22.4
Net rent	13.9	19.8	21.8	23.7	25.3	26.7	29.4	30.3	31.7	33.2	35.3
Repairs	6.2	7.9	8.8	9.0	9.6	10.1	10.6	10.9	11.4	12.0	12.7
Taxes	15.7	19.1	19.8	20.9	22.2	23.5	24.1	24.9	26.1	27.4	29.1
Other	22.2	13.4	6.9	3.0	15.0	23.3	20.4	22.0	23.0	19.6	22.7

[1] The difference between expenditures for domestic farm-originated food products and the farm value or payment farmers received for equivalent farm products. [2] Food primarily purchased from retail food stores for use at home.

Source: U.S. Department of Agriculture, Economic Research Service, *Food Cost Review, 1950–97*, ERS Agricultural Economic Report No. AER780, June 1999; and "ERS/USDA Briefing Room—Food marketing and price spreads: USDA marketing bill"; <http://www.ers.usda.gov/Briefing/FoodPriceSpreads/bill/>.

Table 814. Agricultural Exports and Imports—Volume by Principal Commodities: 1990 to 2006

[In thousands of metric tons, except fruit juices, wine, and malt beverages in thousands of hectoliters (7,703 represents 7,703,000). Includes Puerto Rico, U.S. territories, and shipments under foreign aid programs. Excludes fish, forest products, distilled liquors, manufactured tobacco, and products made from cotton; but includes raw tobacco, raw cotton, rubber, beer and wine, and processed agricultural products]

Commodity	1990	1995	2000	2003	2004	2005	2006
EXPORTS							
Fruit juices and wine . . . ., . .	7,703	10,688	14,356	13,714	15,383	13,982	14,436
Beef, pork, lamb, and poultry meats [1]. . .	1,451	3,723	4,935	5,127	4,033	4,620	4,953
Wheat, unmilled	27,384	32,317	27,568	25,117	31,044	27,040	23,316
Wheat products	863	1,142	844	420	381	313	282
Rice, paddy, milled	2,534	3,275	3,241	4,469	3,518	4,388	3,845
Feed grains	61,066	66,795	54,946	48,428	53,324	50,865	62,784
Feed grain products	1,430	2,018	2,062	4,241	4,393	5,436	6,041
Feeds and fodders [2]	10,974	13,338	13,065	11,839	11,393	11,422	11,367
Fresh fruits and nuts	2,648	3,323	3,450	3,490	3,450	3,607	3,518
Fruit products	390	462	471	504	531	483	504
Vegetables, fresh	1,297	1,708	2,029	2,048	2,034	2,077	1,981
Vegetables, frozen and canned	529	892	1,112	1,008	1,046	1,086	1,156
Oilcake and meal	5,079	6,404	6,462	5,951	5,526	6,905	7,967
Oilseeds	15,820	23,596	28,017	31,789	26,091	26,462	29,266
Vegetable oils	1,226	2,532	2,043	2,251	1,939	1,937	2,220
Tobacco, unmanufactured	223	209	180	156	164	154	180
Cotton, excluding linters.	1,696	2,039	1,485	2,674	2,885	3,405	3,506
IMPORTS							
Fruit juices.	33,116	21,922	31,154	35,531	33,670	43,077	38,980
Wine	2,510	2,781	4,584	6,215	6,549	7,262	7,944
Malt beverages	10,382	13,251	23,464	27,618	27,946	29,947	34,356
Coffee, including products	1,214	989	1,370	1,302	1,323	1,307	1,359
Rubber and allied gums, crude . . . ., . .	840	1,044	1,232	1,120	1,158	1,169	1,012
Beef, pork, lamb, and poultry meats [1]. . .	1,169	1,050	1,579	1,665	1,876	1,804	1,631
Grains [3]	2,071	4,553	4,622	3,484	3,701	3,726	4,729
Biscuits, pasta, and noodles	300	489	711	904	934	1,001	1,033
Feeds and fodders [2]	959	1,247	1,224	1,157	1,063	963	1,023
Fruits, nuts, and preparations [4]	5,401	6,530	8,354	9,054	9,122	9,570	9,899
Vegetables, fresh or frozen.	1,898	2,777	3,763	4,813	5,061	5,183	5,404
Tobacco, unmanufactured	173	190	216	288	254	233	256
Oilseeds and oilnuts	509	713	1,056	531	800	818	1,091
Vegetable oils and waxes.	1,204	1,509	1,846	1,841	2,274	2,386	2,908
Oilcake and meal	316	805	1,254	1,314	1,779	1,541	1,663

[1] Includes variety meats. [2] Excluding oil meal. [3] Includes wheat, corn, oats, barley, and rice. [4] Includes bananas and plantains.

Source: U.S. Department of Agriculture, Economic Research Service, "Foreign Agricultural Trade of the United States (FATUS)"; <http://www.ers.usda.gov/data/fatus/> and "U.S. Trade Internet System"; <http://www.fas.usda.gov/ustrade>.

Agriculture **537**

Table 815. Agricultural Exports and Imports—Value: 1990 to 2006

[In billions of dollars, except percent (16.6 represents $16,600,000,000). Includes Puerto Rico, U.S. territories, and shipments under foreign aid programs. Excludes fish, forest products, distilled liquors, manufactured tobacco, and products made from cotton; but includes raw tobacco, raw cotton, rubber, beer and wine, and processed agricultural products]

Year	Trade balance	Exports, domestic products	Percent of all exports	Imports for consumption	Percent of all imports	Year	Trade balance	Exports, domestic products	Percent of all exports	Imports for consumption	Percent of all imports
1990...	16.6	39.5	11	22.9	5	2000...	12.3	51.3	7	39.0	3
1994...	19.2	46.2	10	27.0	4	2001...	14.3	53.7	8	39.4	3
1995...	26.0	56.2	10	30.3	4	2002...	11.2	53.1	8	41.9	4
1996...	26.8	60.4	10	33.5	4	2003...	12.0	59.4	9	47.4	4
1997...	21.0	57.1	9	36.1	4	2004...	7.4	61.4	8	54.0	4
1998...	14.9	51.8	8	36.9	4	2005...	3.9	63.2	8	59.3	4
1999...	10.7	48.4	8	37.7	4	2006...	5.7	71.0	8	65.3	4

Source: U.S. Department of Agriculture, Economic Research Service, "Foreign Agricultural Trade of the United States (FATUS)"; <http://www.ers.usda.gov/data/fatus/> and U.S. Department of Agriculture, Foreign Agricultural Service, "U.S. Trade Internet System"; <http://www.fas.usda.gov/ustrade>.

Table 816. Agricultural Imports—Value by Selected Commodity: 1990 to 2006

[22,918 represents $22,918,000,000. See headnote, Table 815]

Commodity	Value (mil. dol.)							Percent distribution		
	1990	2000	2002	2003	2004	2005	2006	1990	2000	2006
Total [1].............	22,918	38,974	41,909	47,376	53,977	59,317	65,333	100.0	100.0	100.0
Cattle, live.........	978	1,152	1,446	867	543	1,039	1,546	4.3	3.0	2.4
Beef and veal	1,872	2,399	2,741	2,623	3,626	3,651	3,220	8.2	6.2	4.9
Pork...............	938	997	1,001	1,190	1,367	1,281	1,197	4.1	2.6	1.8
Dairy products	891	1,671	1,783	1,978	2,424	2,686	2,711	3.9	4.3	4.1
Grains and feeds	1,188	3,076	3,666	3,910	4,292	4,527	5,324	5.2	7.9	8.1
Fruits and preparations ...	2,167	3,846	4,356	4,722	5,079	5,842	6,516	9.5	9.9	10.0
Vegetables and preparations..........	1,979	3,958	4,659	5,349	6,077	6,410	7,008	8.6	10.2	10.7
Sugar and related products	1,213	1,555	1,854	2,129	2,107	2,494	3,045	5.3	4.0	4.7
Wine	917	2,207	2,671	3,268	3,416	3,762	4,151	4.0	5.7	6.4
Malt beverages	923	2,179	2,581	2,681	2,767	3,096	3,583	4.0	5.6	5.5
Oilseeds and products....	952	1,847	1,730	2,013	2,944	2,998	3,510	4.2	4.7	5.4
Coffee and products	1,915	2,700	1,693	1,958	2,263	2,976	3,312	8.4	6.9	5.1
Cocoa and products	1,072	1,404	1,761	2,439	2,484	2,751	2,659	4.7	3.6	4.1
Rubber, crude natural	707	842	751	1,047	1,466	1,552	2,029	3.1	2.2	3.1

[1] Includes other commodities not shown separately.

Source: U.S. Department of Agriculture, Economic Research Service, "Foreign Agricultural Trade of the United States (FATUS)"; <http://www.ers.usda.gov/data/fatus/> and U.S. Department of Agriculture, Foreign Agricultural Service, "U.S. Trade Internet System"; <http://www.fas.usda.gov/ustrade>.

Table 817. Agricultural Imports—Value by Selected Countries of Origin: 1990 to 2006

[22,918 represents $22,918,000,000. See headnote, Table 815]

Country	Value (mil. dol.)							Percent distribution		
	1990	2000	2002	2003	2004	2005	2006	1990	2000	2006
Total [1].............	22,918	38,974	41,909	47,376	53,977	59,317	65,333	100.0	100.0	100.0
European Union [2]......	4,991	8,276	8,911	10,956	12,331	13,333	14,381	21.8	21.2	22.0
Canada..............	3,171	8,661	10,350	10,286	11,453	12,270	13,433	13.8	22.2	20.6
Mexico	3,614	5,077	5,518	6,301	7,262	8,331	9,390	15.8	13.0	14.4
Australia	1,174	1,592	1,894	2,120	2,486	2,421	2,487	5.1	4.1	3.8
China [3].............	273	812	1,002	1,288	1,615	1,872	2,262	1.2	2.1	3.5
Brazil	1,563	1,144	1,154	1,550	1,662	1,975	2,237	6.8	2.9	3.4
Indonesia	638	998	931	1,227	1,490	1,702	2,023	2.8	2.6	3.1
Chile	481	1,026	1,154	1,216	1,342	1,521	1,774	2.1	2.6	2.7
New Zealand	855	1,132	1,199	1,317	1,597	1,712	1,669	3.7	2.9	2.6
Colombia............	790	1,123	929	1,031	1,162	1,437	1,480	3.4	2.9	2.3
Thailand	470	779	733	926	1,083	1,094	1,334	2.0	2.0	2.0
Costa Rica	400	812	803	869	899	916	1,163	1.7	2.1	1.8
India...............	285	826	671	687	858	923	1,043	1.2	2.1	1.6
Argentina	389	672	602	572	616	831	990	1.7	1.7	1.5
Guatemala	497	710	685	764	784	920	924	2.2	1.8	1.4

[1] Includes other countries not shown separately. [2] For consistency, data for all years are shown on the basis of 25 countries in the European Union; see footnote 3, Table 1339. [3] See footnote 2, Table 1298.

Source: U.S. Department of Agriculture, Foreign Agricultural Service, "U.S. Trade Internet System"; <http://www.fas.usda.gov/ustrade>; (accessed: 25 April 2007).

Table 818. Selected Farm Products—United States and World Production and Exports: 2000 to 2006

[In metric tons, except as indicated (61 represents 61,000,000). Metric ton = 1.102 short tons or .984 long tons]

Commodity	Unit	Amount United States			Amount World			United States as percent of world		
		2000	2005	2006	2000	2005	2006	2000	2005	2006
PRODUCTION [1]										
Wheat	Million	61	57	49	581	621	593	10.4	9.2	8.3
Corn for grain	Million	252	282	268	590	695	693	42.7	40.6	38.6
Soybeans	Million	75	83	87	176	220	229	42.6	37.9	37.8
Rice, milled	Million	5.9	7.1	6.2	398	418	415	1.5	1.7	1.5
Cotton [2]	Million bales [3] . . .	17.0	23.3	23.9	87.7	120.1	113.9	19.3	19.4	21.0
EXPORTS [4]										
Wheat [5]	Million	28.0	27.4	24.5	104.0	113.6	110.7	26.9	24.2	22.1
Corn	Million	48.3	56.2	56.0	76.4	83.1	85.0	63.3	67.6	65.9
Soybeans	Million	27.1	25.8	29.9	53.9	64.1	69.5	50.3	40.2	43.1
Rice, milled basis	Million	2.8	3.9	3.4	22.8	29.0	28.4	12.5	13.3	11.9
Cotton [2]	Million bales [3] . . .	6.8	14.4	18.0	27.1	35.0	44.7	24.9	41.3	40.4

[1] Production years vary by commodity. In most cases, includes harvests from July 1 of the year shown through June 30 of the following year. [2] For production and trade years ending in year shown. [3] Bales of 480 lb. net weight. [4] Trade years may vary by commodity. Wheat, corn, and soybean data are for trade year beginning in year shown. Rice data are for calendar year. [5] Includes wheat flour on a grain equivalent.

Source: U.S. Department of Agriculture, Foreign Agricultural Service, *Foreign Agricultural Commodity Circular Series*, periodic; <http://www.fas.usda.gov/commodities.asp>.

Table 819. Percent of U.S. Agricultural Commodity Output Exported: 1990 to 2005

[All export shares are estimated from export and production weights]

Commodity group	1990–94, average	1995–99, average	2000–04, average	2000	2002	2003	2004	2005
Total agriculture	21.9	22.1	21.3	21.6	20.8	21.1	20.9	20.1
Livestock [1]	4.1	4.6	4.4	4.6	4.4	4.5	3.8	3.6
Red meat	4.1	7.1	8.0	8.1	8.5	9.1	5.8	7.3
Poultry meat	7.4	15.5	14.7	15.5	13.9	14.2	13.4	14.2
Dairy products	3.4	1.4	1.0	1.0	1.0	1.2	1.0	1.1
Crops [2]	25.1	25.4	24.6	24.9	24.2	24.5	24.1	23.6
Wheat and rice [3]	50.8	47.5	47.9	45.9	46.7	50.6	49.4	48.9
Coarse grains [4]	24.7	24.9	22.5	24.1	21.1	22.7	20.9	21.2
Oilseeds/meal/oil [5]	22.2	23.4	22.7	23.1	23.6	20.4	22.4	19.9
Fruits and nuts [6]	18.1	19.2	20.5	18.6	21.2	20.4	21.6	21.9
Vegetables [7]	9.9	12.1	12.7	13.0	12.3	13.1	12.0	12.7
Cotton and tobacco	40.7	38.1	58.8	43.7	60.3	66.6	66.6	72.5

[1] Includes live animals, eggs, fats and oils, wool, and fresh bovine hides. [2] Includes sugar, honey, maple syrup. Excludes beer and confections. [3] Includes wheat flour and other wheat products. [4] Includes corn, barley, sorghum, oats, rye, and their products. [5] The oilseed equivalent weights of oilmeals and vegetable oils are used. [6] Includes fruit juices and wine, whose volume measures are converted to farm weight. [7] Includes pulses (legumes) and hops. Frozen and canned exports are in farm-weight equivalent.

Source: U.S. Department of Agriculture, Economic Research Service, USDA's commodity yearbooks, "Foreign Agricultural Trade of the U.S."; <http://www.ers.usda.gov/data/fatus/>, and "Production, Supply, and Distribution database"; <http://www.fas.usda.gov/psd/>.

Table 820. Top 10 U.S. Export Markets for Selected Commodities: 2006

[In thousands of metric tons (57,686 represents 57,686,000)]

Corn Country	Amount	Wheat [1] Country	Amount	Soybeans Country	Amount	Cotton [2] Country	Amount
World, total	57,686	World, total. . .	23,316	World, total. . .	28,102	World, total. . .	3,506
Japan	16,245	Japan	2,997	China [3]	10,328	China [3]	1,631
Mexico	7,835	Nigeria	2,453	Mexico	3,743	Turkey	419
Korea, South	6,044	Mexico	2,219	Japan	3,308	Mexico	327
Taiwan [3]	4,289	Philippines	1,782	Netherlands	2,032	Indonesia	205
Egypt	3,936	Iraq	1,608	Taiwan [3]	1,856	Taiwan [3]	129
Colombia	3,004	Egypt	1,522	Indonesia	1,183	Thailand	111
Canada	1,865	Korea, South	1,132	Turkey	608	Pakistan	78
Syria	1,256	Venezuela	928	Thailand	475	Korea, South	74
Dominican Republic. .	1,211	Taiwan [3]	795	Korea, South	440	Colombia	56
Algeria	1,191	Yemen	680	Egypt	396	Hong Kong	55
Rest of world	10,809	Rest of world. . . .	7,200	Rest of world. . . .	3,735	Rest of world. . . .	421

[1] Unmilled. [2] Excluding linters. [3] See footnote 2, Table 1298.

Source: U.S. Department of Agriculture, Foreign Agricultural Service, "FAS Online, U.S. Trade Exports - FATUS Commodity Aggregations"; <http://www.fas.usda.gov/ustrade/USTExFatus.asp>; (accessed: 25 April 2007).

Table 821. **Agricultural Exports—Value by Principal Commodities: 1990 to 2006**

[(39,495 represents $39,495,000,000). See headnote, Table 815]

Commodity	Value (mil. dol.)							Percent distribution		
	1990	2000	2002	2003	2004	2005	2006	1990	2000	2006
Total agricultural exports	39,495	51,265	53,143	59,392	61,426	63,182	70,993	100.0	100.0	100.0
Animals and animal products [1]	6,648	11,600	11,087	12,161	10,369	12,226	13,527	16.8	22.6	19.1
Meat and meat products	2,558	5,276	5,042	5,741	3,240	4,299	5,196	6.5	10.3	7.3
Poultry and poultry products	910	2,235	2,064	2,287	2,577	3,138	2,952	2.3	4.4	4.2
Grains and feeds [1]	14,386	13,620	14,395	15,054	17,692	16,439	19,285	36.4	26.6	27.2
Wheat and products	4,035	3,578	3,845	4,099	5,273	4,520	4,379	10.2	7.0	6.2
Corn	6,026	4,469	4,845	4,724	5,875	4,789	7,034	15.3	8.7	9.9
Fruits and preparations	2,007	2,743	2,781	2,973	3,162	3,468	3,759	5.1	5.4	5.3
Fresh fruits	1,486	2,080	2,134	2,273	2,394	2,697	2,870	3.8	4.1	4.0
Nuts and preparations	976	1,319	1,525	1,762	2,220	2,917	3,072	2.5	2.6	4.3
Vegetables and preparations	1,836	3,112	3,030	3,056	3,258	3,571	3,906	4.6	6.1	5.5
Oilseeds and products	5,725	8,584	9,627	11,652	10,439	10,229	11,276	14.5	16.7	15.9
Soybeans	3,548	5,258	5,677	7,960	6,668	6,274	6,909	9.0	10.3	9.7
Tobacco, unmanufactured	1,441	1,204	1,050	1,038	1,044	990	1,141	3.6	2.3	1.6
Cotton, excluding linters	2,783	1,873	2,015	3,361	4,226	3,921	4,501	7.0	3.7	6.3
Other	3,693	7,210	7,634	8,336	9,016	9,421	10,527	9.4	14.1	14.8

[1] Includes commodities not shown separately.

Source: U.S. Department of Agriculture, Economic Research Service, "Foreign Agricultural Trade of the United States (FATUS)"; <http://www.ers.usda.gov/data/fatus/> and U.S. Department of Agriculture, Foreign Agricultural Service, "U.S. Trade Internet System"; <http://www.fas.usda.gov/ustrade>.

Table 822. **Agricultural Exports—Value by Selected Countries of Destination: 1990 to 2006**

[(39,495 represents $39,495,000,000). See headnote, Table 815]

Country	Value (mil. dol.)							Percent distribution		
	1990	2000	2002	2003	2004	2005	2006	1990	2000	2006
Total agricultural exports [1]	39,495	51,265	53,143	59,392	61,426	63,182	70,993	100.0	100.0	100.0
Canada	4,214	7,643	8,662	9,315	9,742	10,618	11,930	10.7	14.9	16.8
Mexico	2,560	6,410	7,238	7,891	8,510	9,429	10,896	6.5	12.5	15.3
Caribbean	1,015	1,408	1,518	1,590	1,850	1,913	2,118	2.6	2.7	3.0
Central America	483	1,121	1,252	1,338	1,429	1,589	1,843	1.2	2.2	2.6
South America	1,063	1,704	1,790	1,912	1,955	1,943	2,368	2.7	3.3	3.3
Asia, excluding Middle East [2]	15,857	19,877	19,729	23,688	23,009	22,544	25,796	40.1	38.8	36.3
Japan	8,142	9,292	8,384	8,906	8,147	7,931	8,422	20.6	18.1	11.9
Korea, South	2,650	2,546	2,673	2,886	2,489	2,234	2,851	6.7	5.0	4.0
Taiwan [3]	1,663	1,996	1,966	2,025	2,065	2,301	2,479	4.2	3.9	3.5
China [3, 4]	818	1,716	2,068	5,017	5,542	5,233	6,724	2.1	3.3	9.5
Indonesia [2]	275	668	810	996	925	958	1,102	0.7	1.3	1.6
Europe/Eurasia [2]	10,162	7,676	7,696	7,815	8,319	8,568	8,765	25.7	15.0	12.3
European Union [5]	7,249	6,489	6,342	6,663	6,789	6,855	7,290	18.4	12.7	10.3
Russia	(X)	580	552	579	802	972	836	(X)	1.1	1.2
Middle East [2]	1,728	2,323	2,260	2,549	2,833	2,844	3,336	4.4	4.5	4.7
Turkey	226	658	675	921	944	1,062	1,030	0.6	1.3	1.5
Africa	1,848	2,308	2,297	2,489	2,953	2,773	3,056	4.7	4.5	4.3
Oceania	343	490	512	621	601	742	760	0.9	1.0	1.1

X Not applicable.   [1] Totals include transshipments through Canada, but transshipments are not distributed by country after 1998.   [2] Includes areas not shown separately.   [3] See footnote 2, Table 1298.   [4] China includes Macao. However Hong Kong remains separate economically until 2050 and is not included.   [5] For consistency, data for all years are shown on the basis of 25 countries in the European Union; see footnote 3, Table 1339.

Source: U.S. Department of Agriculture, Economic Research Service, "Foreign Agricultural Trade of the United States (FATUS)"; <http://www.ers.usda.gov/data/fatus/> and U.S. Department of Agriculture, Foreign Agricultural Service, "U.S. Trade Internet System"; <http://www.fas.usda.gov/ustrade>.

Table 823. **Cropland Used for Crops and Acreages of Crops Harvested: 1990 to 2006**

[In millions of acres, except as indicated (341 represents 341,000,000)]

Item	1990	1995	1999	2000	2001	2002	2003	2004	2005	2006
Cropland used for crops	341	332	344	345	340	340	342	336	337	330
Index (1977 = 100)	90	88	91	91	90	90	90	89	89	87
Cropland harvested [1]	310	302	316	314	311	307	316	312	314	304
Crop failure	6	8	8	11	10	17	10	9	6	11
Cultivated summer fallow	25	22	20	20	19	16	16	15	16	15
Cropland idled by all federal programs	62	55	30	31	34	34	34	35	35	37
Acres of crops harvested [2]	322	314	327	325	321	316	324	321	321	312

[1] Land supporting one or more harvested crops.   [2] Area in principal crops harvested as reported by Crop Reporting Board plus acreages in fruits, vegetables for sale, tree nuts, and other minor crops.

Source: U.S. Department of Agriculture, Economic Research Service, *Major Uses of Land in the United States, 2002,* 2006; Also in *Agricultural Statistics,* annual. Beginning 1995 *Agricultural Resources and Environmental Indicators,* periodic, and *AREI Updates: Cropland Use.* See also ERS Briefing Room at <http://www.ers.usda.gov/Briefing/LandUse/majorlandusechapter.htm#trends>.

[67.0 represents 67,000,000. Marketing year beginning January 1 for potatoes, May 1 for hay, June 1 for wheat, August 1 for cotton, September 1 for soybeans and corn. Acreage, production, and yield of all crops periodically revised on basis of census data]

Item	Unit	1990	2000	2002	2003	2004	2005	2006
CORN FOR GRAIN								
Acreage harvested	Million	67.0	72.4	69.3	70.9	73.6	75.1	70.6
Yield per acre	Bushel.	119	137	129	142	160	148	149
Production , ...	Mil. bu.	7,934	9,915	8,967	10,089	11,807	11,114	10,535
Farm price [1]	Dol./bu.	2.28	1.85	2.32	2.42	2.06	2.00	3.20
Farm value	Mil. dol.	18,192	18,499	20,882	24,477	24,381	22,198	33,837
Total supply [2] . . . . [3] . . .	Mil. bu.	9,282	11,639	10,578	11,190	12,776	13,237	12,512
Total disappearance [3] . . .	Mil. bu.	7,761	9,740	9,491	10,232	10,662	11,270	11,760
Ethanol	Mil. bu.	(NA)	(NA)	996	1,168	1,323	1,603	2,150
Exports	Mil. bu.	1,725	1,941	1,588	1,900	1,818	2,147	2,250
Ending stocks	Mil. bu.	1,521	1,899	1,087	958	2,114	1,967	752
SOYBEANS								
Acreage harvested	Million	56.5	72.4	72.5	72.5	74.0	71.3	74.6
Yield per acre	Bushel.	34.1	38.1	38.0	33.9	42.2	43.0	42.7
Production , ...	Mil. bu.	1,926	2,758	2,756	2,454	3,124	3,063	3,188
Farm price [1]	Dol./bu.	5.74	4.54	5.53	7.34	5.74	5.66	6.20
Farm value	Mil. dol.	11,042	12,467	15,253	18,014	17,895	17,269	19,694
Total supply [2] . . . . [3] . . .	Mil. bu.	2,169	3,052	2,969	2,638	3,242	3,322	3,642
Total disappearance [3] . . .	Mil. bu.	1,840	2,804	2,791	2,525	2,986	2,873	3,046
Exports	Mil. bu.	557	996	1,044	887	1,097	947	1,100
Ending stocks	Mil. bu.	329	248	178	112	256	449	595
HAY								
Acreage harvested	Million	61.0	59.9	63.9	63.4	62.0	61.7	60.8
Yield per acre	Sh. tons.	2.40	2.54	2.34	2.49	2.55	2.45	2.33
Production , . [5]	Mil. sh. tons . . .	146	152	149	158	158	151	142
Farm price [4], [5]	Dol./ton	80.60	84.60	92.40	85.50	92.00	98.20	109.00
Farm value	Mil. dol.	10,462	11,417	12,338	12,007	12,212	12,585	13,506
WHEAT								
Acreage harvested	Million	69.1	53.1	45.8	53.1	50.0	50.1	46.8
Yield per acre	Bushel.	39.5	42.0	35.0	44.2	43.2	42.0	38.7
Production , ...	Mil. bu.	2,730	2,228	1,606	2,345	2,158	2,105	1,812
Farm price [1]	Dol./bu.	2.61	2.62	3.56	3.40	3.40	3.42	4.25
Farm value	Mil. dol.	7,184	5,782	5,637	7,929	7,283	7,171	7,721
Total supply [2] . . . . [3] . . .	Mil. bu.	3,303	3,268	2,460	2,899	2,775	2,727	2,498
Total disappearance [3] . . .	Mil. bu.	2,435	2,392	1,969	2,353	2,235	2,155	2,026
Exports	Mil. bu.	1,069	1,062	850	1,158	1,066	1,009	875
Ending stocks	Mil. bu.	868	876	491	546	540	571	472
COTTON								
Acreage harvested	Million	11.7	13.1	12.4	12.0	13.1	13.8	12.7
Yield per acre	Pounds	634	632	665	730	855	831	819
Production [6]	Mil. bales [7]. . . .	15.5	17.2	17.2	18.3	23.3	23.9	21.7
Farm price [1]	Cents/lb.	68.2	51.6	45.7	63.0	43.5	49.7	49.6
Farm value	Mil. dol.	5,076	4,260	3,777	5,517	4,854	5,695	5,176
Total supply [2] . . . . [3] . . .	Mil. bales [7]. . . .	18.5	21.1	24.7	23.7	26.7	29.4	27.8
Total disappearance [3] . . .	Mil. bales [7]. . . .	16.5	15.6	19.2	20.0	21.1	23.9	19.5
Exports	Mil. bales [7]. . . .	7.8	6.7	11.9	13.8	14.4	18.0	14.5
Ending stocks [8]	Mil. bales [7]. . . .	2.3	6.0	5.4	3.5	5.5	6.1	8.3
POTATOES								
Acreage harvested	Million	1.4	1.3	1.3	1.2	1.2	1.1	1.1
Yield per acre	Cwt. [9]	293	381	362	367	391	390	390
Production , ...	Mil. cwt. [9]. . . .	402	514	458	458	456	424	435
Farm price [1]	Dol./cwt. [9]	6.08	5.08	6.67	5.89	5.66	7.06	7.42
Farm value	Mil. dol.	2,431	2,591	3,045	2,686	2,575	2,991	3,226

NA Not available.　[1] Marketing year average price. U.S. prices are computed by weighting U.S. monthly prices by estimated monthly marketings and do not include an allowance for outstanding loans and government purchases and payments. [2] Comprises production, imports, and beginning stocks.　[3] Includes feed, residual, and other domestic uses not shown separately.　[4] Prices are for hay sold baled.　[5] Season average prices received by farmers. U.S. prices are computed by weighting state prices by estimated sales.　[6] State production figures, which conform with annual ginning enumeration with allowance for cross-state ginnings, rounded to thousands and added for U.S. totals.　[7] Bales of 480 pounds, net weight.　[8] Stock estimates based on Census Bureau data which results in an unaccounted difference between supply and use estimates and changes in ending stocks.　[9] Cwt = hundred weight (100 pounds).

Source: Production—U.S. Department of Agriculture, National Agricultural Statistics Service, *Crop Production*, annual; and *Crop Values*, annual. Supply and disappearance—U.S. Department of Agriculture, Economic Research Service, *Feed Situation*, quarterly; *Fats and Oils Situation*, quarterly; *Wheat Situation*, quarterly; *Cotton and Wool Outlook Statistics*, periodic; and *Agricultural Supply and Demand Estimates*, periodic. Data are also in *Agricultural Statistics*, annual; and "Agricultural Outlook: Statistical Indicators"; <http://www.ers.usda.gov/publications/agoutlook/aotables/>.

Agriculture　541

Table 825. Corn—Acreage, Production, and Value by Leading States: 2004 to 2006

[73,631 represents 73,631,000. One bushel of corn = 56 pounds]

State	Acreage harvested (1,000 acres) 2004	2005	2006	Yield per acre (bu.) 2004	2005	2006	Production (mil. bu.) 2004	2005	2006	Price ($/bu.) 2004	2005	2006	Farm value (mil. dol.) 2004	2005	2006
U.S.[1]	73,631	75,117	70,648	160	148	149	11,807	11,114	10,535	2.06	2.00	3.20	24,381	22,198	33,837
IA	12,400	12,500	12,350	181	173	166	2,244	2,163	2,050	1.99	1.94	3.15	4,466	4,195	6,458
IL	11,600	11,950	11,150	180	143	163	2,088	1,709	1,817	2.14	2.08	3.35	4,468	3,554	6,088
NE	7,950	8,250	7,750	166	154	152	1,320	1,271	1,178	2.02	1.92	3.15	2,666	2,439	3,711
MN	7,050	6,850	6,850	159	174	161	1,121	1,192	1,103	1.94	1.86	3.15	2,175	2,217	3,474
IN	5,530	5,770	5,380	168	154	157	929	889	845	1.99	2.00	3.35	1,849	1,777	2,830
OH	3,110	3,250	2,960	158	143	159	491	465	471	2.04	1.98	3.30	1,002	920	1,553
WI	2,600	2,900	2,800	136	148	143	354	429	400	2.15	1.94	3.30	760	833	1,321
MO	2,880	2,970	2,630	162	111	138	467	330	363	2.03	2.03	3.10	947	669	1,125
KS	2,880	3,450	3,000	150	135	115	432	466	345	2.12	2.07	3.20	916	964	1,104
SD	4,150	3,950	3,220	130	119	97	540	470	312	1.82	1.79	2.95	982	841	921
MI	1,920	2,010	1,960	134	143	147	257	287	288	1.97	1.88	3.20	507	540	922
TX	1,680	1,850	1,450	139	114	121	234	211	175	2.60	2.47	3.20	607	521	561
ND	1,150	1,200	1,400	105	129	111	121	155	155	1.88	1.80	3.00	227	279	466
KY	1,140	1,180	1,040	152	132	146	173	156	152	2.24	2.21	3.30	388	344	501
CO	1,040	950	860	135	148	156	140	141	134	2.23	2.23	3.25	313	314	436
PA	980	960	960	140	122	122	137	117	117	2.25	2.30	3.55	309	269	416
NC	740	700	740	117	120	132	87	84	98	2.44	2.33	2.95	211	196	288
TN	615	595	500	140	130	125	86	77	63	2.17	2.07	2.85	187	160	178
NY	500	460	480	122	124	129	61	57	62	2.37	2.29	3.30	145	131	204
MD	425	400	425	153	135	142	65	54	60	2.17	2.19	3.35	141	118	202
VA	360	360	345	145	118	120	52	42	41	2.17	2.14	3.00	113	91	124

[1] Includes other states, not shown separately.

Source: U.S. Department of Agriculture, National Agricultural Statistics Service, Crop Production, annual; and Crop Values, annual.

Table 826. Soybeans—Acreage, Production, and Value by Leading States: 2004 to 2006

[73,958 represents 73,958,000. One bushel of soybeans = 60 pounds]

State	Acreage harvested (1,000 acres) 2004	2005	2006	Yield per acre (bu.) 2004	2005	2006	Production (mil. bu.) 2004	2005	2006	Price ($/bu.) 2004	2005	2006	Farm value (mil. dol.) 2004	2005	2006
U.S.[1]	73,958	71,251	74,602	42	43	43	3,124	3,063	3,188	5.74	5.66	6.20	17,895	17,269	19,694
IA	10,150	10,000	10,100	49	53	51	497	525	510	5.76	5.54	6.25	2,865	2,909	3,188
IL	9,900	9,450	10,050	50	47	48	495	439	482	5.84	5.76	6.40	2,891	2,531	3,087
MN	7,050	6,800	7,250	33	45	44	233	306	319	5.90	5.53	5.95	1,373	1,692	1,898
IN	5,520	5,380	5,680	52	49	50	284	264	284	5.66	5.78	6.30	1,609	1,524	1,789
NE	4,750	4,660	5,010	46	51	50	219	235	251	5.54	5.55	5.90	1,210	1,306	1,478
OH	4,420	4,480	4,620	47	45	47	208	202	217	5.74	5.74	6.25	1,192	1,157	1,357
MO	4,960	4,910	5,110	45	37	38	223	182	194	5.62	5.67	6.30	1,254	1,030	1,223
SD	4,120	3,850	3,850	34	35	34	140	135	131	5.58	5.39	5.70	782	726	746
ND	3,570	2,900	3,870	23	36	31	82	104	120	5.75	5.37	5.85	472	561	702
AR	3,150	3,000	3,070	39	34	35	123	102	107	5.88	5.92	6.50	722	604	698
KS	2,710	2,850	3,080	41	37	32	111	105	99	5.39	5.45	6.10	599	575	601
MI	1,980	1,990	1,990	38	39	45	75	77	90	5.72	5.73	6.10	430	439	546
WI	1,550	1,580	1,640	35	44	44	53	70	72	5.70	5.64	5.90	305	392	426
KY	1,300	1,240	1,370	44	43	44	57	53	60	5.87	5.86	6.75	336	312	407

[1] Includes other states, not shown separately.

Source: U.S. Department of Agriculture, National Agricultural Statistics Service, Crop Production, annual; and Crop Values, annual.

Table 827. Wheat—Acreage, Production, and Value by Leading States: 2004 to 2006

[49,999 represents 49,999,000. One bushel of wheat = 60 pounds]

State	Acreage harvested (1,000 acres) 2004	2005	2006	Yield per acre (bu.) 2004	2005	2006	Production (mil. bu.) 2004	2005	2006	Price ($/bu.) 2004	2005	2006	Farm value (mil. dol.) 2004	2005	2006
U.S.[1]	49,999	50,119	46,810	43.2	42.0	38.7	2,158	2,105	1,812	3.40	3.42	4.25	7,283	7,171	7,721
KS	8,500	9,500	9,100	37.0	40.0	32.0	315	380	291	3.25	3.31	4.60	1,022	1,258	1,340
ND	7,775	8,835	8,290	39.4	34.4	30.4	307	304	252	3.40	3.55	4.50	1,043	1,077	1,129
MT	5,025	5,235	5,215	34.5	36.8	29.4	173	192	153	3.61	3.63	4.60	623	698	703
WA	2,275	2,225	2,225	63.1	62.6	62.9	144	139	140	3.68	3.32	4.40	524	456	616
ID	1,190	1,200	1,195	85.5	83.8	75.6	102	101	90	3.61	3.31	4.05	365	330	365
SD	2,798	3,193	2,576	46.0	41.8	32.6	129	133	84	3.35	3.65	4.50	432	485	378
OK	4,700	4,000	3,400	35.0	32.0	24.0	165	128	82	3.32	3.39	4.85	546	434	396
MN	1,636	1,745	1,695	54.8	41.0	47.4	90	71	80	3.32	3.66	4.55	298	261	369

[1] Includes other states, not shown separately.

Source: U.S. Department of Agriculture, National Agricultural Statistics Service, Crop Production, annual; and Crop Values, annual.

Table 828. Greenhouse and Nursery Crops—Value of Production, Trade, and Consumption: 1990 to 2005

[In millions of dollars, except as noted (8,764 represents $8,764,000,000). Includes all floriculture and nursery crops except cut Christmas trees, seeds, and food crops grown under cover. Domestic production based on grower wholesale receipts. Domestic consumption equals supply minus exports. Supply equals domestic production plus imports]

Year	Production and trade				Consumption			
	Domestic production	Imports	Supply	Exports	Domestic consumption	Per household [1] (dol.)	Per capita [1] (dol.)	Import share (percent)
1990	8,764	536	9,300	195	9,105	99	36	5.9
2000	13,796	1,159	14,955	265	14,691	139	52	7.9
2001	14,396	1,150	15,546	253	15,292	143	54	7.5
2002	15,181	1,132	16,313	243	16,070	149	56	7.0
2003	15,632	1,249	16,881	261	16,620	152	57	7.5
2004	14,877	1,378	16,254	283	15,971	145	54	8.6
2005, total	15,218	1,383	16,601	302	16,299	147	55	8.5
Nursery and other greenhouse crops	9,855	513	10,368	242	10,127	91	34	5.1
Floriculture crops	5,363	870	6,233	60	6,172	56	21	14.1
Flowering plants and other floriculture crops [2]	4,966	160	5,127	35	5,092	46	17	3.2
Cut flowers	397	709	1,106	25	1,081	10	4	65.6

[1] Based on Census Bureau estimates of households and population. [2] Includes potted flowering plants, foliage plants for indoor or patio use, bedding and garden plants, cut cultivated greens, and propagative material.

Source: U.S. Department of Agriculture, Economic Research Service, *Floriculture and Nursery Crops Yearbook*.

Table 829. Fresh Fruits and Vegetables—Supply and Use: 2000 to 2006

[In millions of pounds, except per capita in pounds (8,355 represents 8,355,000,000)]

Year	Utilized production [1]	Imports [2]	Supply, total [1]	Exports [2]	Consumption Total	Per capita [3]
FRUITS						
Citrus:						
2000	8,355	720	9,075	2,445	6,630	23.5
2002	8,256	707	8,962	2,245	6,718	23.4
2003	8,442	969	9,411	2,456	6,955	23.9
2004	8,156	993	9,149	2,495	6,654	22.7
2005	7,320	1,123	8,443	2,035	6,408	21.6
2006	7,053	1,235	8,288	2,034	6,254	20.9
Noncitrus: [4]						
2000	13,850	11,225	25,074	3,389	21,685	76.6
2002	12,833	11,552	24,385	2,902	21,483	74.4
2003	13,386	12,164	25,550	2,835	22,716	77.9
2004	14,335	12,325	26,660	3,079	23,581	80.1
2005	14,389	12,459	26,848	3,478	23,370	78.7
VEGETABLES AND MELONS						
2000	46,922	6,719	54,986	4,200	48,563	172.0
2002	46,724	7,697	55,762	4,265	49,388	171.4
2003	46,901	8,076	56,227	4,251	49,944	171.6
2004	48,247	8,193	57,693	4,363	50,700	172.7
2005	47,553	8,708	57,753	4,363	51,452	173.6
2006	46,945	9,261	57,486	3,956	51,703	173.0
POTATOES						
2000	13,185	806	13,990	677	13,313	47.1
2002	12,567	883	13,450	693	12,757	44.3
2003	13,349	872	14,221	590	13,631	46.8
2004	13,181	755	13,936	479	13,457	45.8
2005	12,428	788	13,216	639	12,577	42.4
2006	12,377	817	13,195	626	12,569	42.1

[1] Crop-year basis for fruits. Supply data for vegetables include ending stocks of previous year. [2] Fiscal year for fruits; calendar year for vegetables and potatoes. [3] Based on Census Bureau estimated total population. [4] Includes bananas.

Source: U.S. Department of Agriculture, Economic Research Service, *Fruit and Tree Nuts Situation and Outlook Yearbook*, and *Vegetables and Melons Situation and Outlook Yearbook*.

Table 830. Nuts—Supply and Use: 2000 to 2005

[In millions of pounds (shelled) (331 represents 331,000,000)]

Year	Beginning stocks	Marketable production [1]	Imports	Supply, total	Consumption	Exports	Ending stocks
2000	331	1,117	293	1,741	723	781	237
2002	252	1,562	363	2,177	926	928	323
2003	323	1,504	431	2,258	998	963	297
2004	297	1,533	504	2,334	985	1,039	309
2005	309	1,484	433	2,226	813	1,121	293

[1] Utilized production minus inedibles and noncommercial usage.

Source: U.S. Department of Agriculture, Economic Research Service, *Fruit and Tree Nuts Situation and Outlook Yearbook*.

Agriculture   543

Table 831. Commercial Vegetable and Other Specified Crops—Area, Production, and Value, 2004 to 2006, and Leading Producing States, 2006

[294 represents 294,000. Except as noted, relates to commercial production for fresh market and processing combined. Includes market garden areas but excludes minor producing acreage in minor producing states. Excludes production for home use in farm and nonfarm gardens. Value is for season or crop year and should not be confused with calendar-year income]

Crop	Area [1] (1,000 acres)			Production [2] (1,000 short tons)			Value [3] (mil. dol.)			Leading states in order of production, 2006
	2004	2005	2006	2004	2005	2006	2004	2005	2006	
Beans, snap	294	303	300	1,124	1,096	1,104	393	415	448	WI, OR, NY [4]
Beans, dry edible	1,219	1,534	1,538	889	1,339	1,212	453	516	518	ND, MI, NE
Broccoli [5]	134	135	139	992	997	1,010	638	570	653	CA, AZ
Cabbage [5]	76	74	74	1,249	1,214	1,284	322	326	355	CA, NY, TX
Cantaloupes [5]	87	90	90	1,094	1,056	989	322	336	341	CA, AZ, GA [5]
Carrots	98	99	98	1,764	1,805	1,746	573	597	577	CA, MI, TX [5]
Cauliflower	38	42	43	321	364	380	196	222	254	CA, AZ
Celery	28	27	26	974	934	896	289	259	332	CA, MI, NC
Corn, sweet	649	642	616	4,362	4,526	4,423	751	814	825	(NA)
Fresh market	243	238	232	1,394	1,351	1,337	537	597	619	FL, CA, GA
Processed	406	404	385	2,968	3,175	3,086	214	217	206	MN, WA, WI
Cucumbers [5]	170	166	158	1,096	1,025	1,001	363	362	400	MI, FL [4]
Lettuce, head [5]	181	177	175	3,311	3,287	2,935	1,119	1,019	977	CA, AZ
Lettuce, leaf [5]	62	65	71	740	794	858	455	531	599	CA, AZ
Lettuce, Romaine [5]	53	60	61	918	997	990	350	386	428	CA, AZ
Mushrooms [6]	31	29	28	421	419	415	878	862	841	PA, CA
Onions	169	165	163	4,153	3,675	3,582	672	849	868	CA, WA, ID
Peppers, bell	53	57	61	820	802	862	517	535	586	CA, FL, GA
Potatoes	1,167	1,087	1,116	22,802	21,196	21,734	2,575	2,991	3,226	ID, WA, WI
Spinach	52	55	55	444	477	380	153	183	191	CA, AZ [5]
Squash	53	55	58	388	417	474	223	214	229	GA, MI, CA
Sweet potatoes	93	88	87	806	787	822	282	283	298	NC, CA, MS
Tomatoes	430	408	422	14,170	12,107	12,454	2,149	2,220	2,274	(NA)
Fresh market	130	126	123	1,903	1,913	1,842	1,430	1,599	1,596	FL, CA, VA
Processed	301	282	299	12,266	10,193	10,612	719	621	677	CA, IN
Watermelons	142	138	143	1,844	1,920	2,104	313	446	435	FL, TX, GA

NA Not available. [1] Area of crops for harvest for fresh market, including any partially harvested or not harvested because of low prices or other factors, plus area harvested for processing. [2] Excludes some quantities not marketed. [3] Fresh market vegetables valued at f.o.b. shipping point. Processing vegetables are equivalent returns at packinghouse door. [4] Processed only. [5] Fresh market only. [6] Area is shown in million square feet. All data are for marketing year ending June 30.

Source: U.S. Department of Agriculture, National Agricultural Statistics Service, *Vegetables, 2006 Summary*, January 2007. Also in *Agricultural Statistics*, annual.

Table 832. Fruits and Nuts—Utilized Production and Value, 2004 to 2006, and Leading Producing States, 2006

[5,220 represents 5,220,000]

Fruit or nut	Unit	Utilized production [1]			Farm value (mil. dol.)			Leading states in order of production, 2006
		2004	2005	2006	2004	2005	2006	
Apples [2]	1,000 tons	5,220	4,860	5,036	1,403	1,681	2,099	WA, NY
Apricots	1,000 tons	93	77	45	35	40	30	CA, WA
Avocados	1,000 tons	179	312	(NA)	291	351	(NA)	CA, FL
Blackberries, cultivated (OR)	1,000 tons	24	24	21	34	37	35	OR
Blueberries	1,000 tons	137	149	175	297	381	558	MI, NJ, OR
Cherries, sweet	1,000 tons	279	244	287	437	484	487	WA, OR, CA
Cherries, tart	1,000 tons	107	134	125	70	64	53	MI, UT, WA
Cranberries	1,000 tons	308	312	338	203	215	251	WI, MA, NJ
Grapefruit	1,000 tons	2,165	1,018	1,232	307	383	368	FL, CA
Grapes (13 states)	1,000 tons	6,230	7,811	6,335	3,010	3,489	3,162	CA, WA, NY
Lemons	1,000 tons	798	870	942	276	306	392	CA, AZ
Nectarines	1,000 tons	252	251	238	86	127	124	CA
Oranges	1,000 tons	12,872	9,252	8,898	1,774	1,475	1,766	FL, CA
Peaches	1,000 tons	1,230	1,145	987	462	512	513	CA, SC, GA
Pears	1,000 tons	873	822	830	293	294	325	WA, CA, OR
Pineapples	1,000 tons	220	212	188	83	79	76	HI
Plums (CA)	1,000 tons	144	171	158	74	92	110	CA
Prunes (dried basis) (CA)	1,000 tons	49	94	162	72	138	241	CA
Raspberries	1,000 tons	79	91	92	245	256	285	CA
Strawberries	1,000 tons	1,107	1,161	1,202	1,295	1,396	1,515	CA, FL
Tangerines	1,000 tons	417	335	417	112	127	138	FL, CA
Almonds (shelled basis) (CA)	Mil. lb.	1,005	915	1,095	2,189	2,526	2,198	CA
Hazelnuts (in the shell)	1,000 tons	38	28	41	54	62	45	OR
Macadamia nuts	1,000 tons	28	27	28	41	44	39	HI
Pecans (in the shell) (11 states)	1,000 tons	93	140	94	327	407	301	NM, GA, TX
Pistachios	1,000 tons	174	142	119	465	580	457	CA
Walnuts, English (in the shell)	1,000 tons	325	355	350	452	557	(NA)	CA

NA Not available. [1] Excludes quantities not harvested or not marketed. [2] Production in commercial orchards with 100 or more bearing age trees.

Source: U.S. Department of Agriculture, National Agricultural Statistics Service, *Noncitrus Fruits and Nuts, 2006 Preliminary Summary*, January 2007; and *Citrus Fruits, 2006 Summary*, September 2006.

Table 833. Meat Supply and Use: 1990 to 2006

[In millions of pounds (carcass weight equivalent) (62,255 represents 62,255,000,000). Carcass weight equivalent is the weight of the animal minus entrails, head, hide, and internal organs; includes fat and bone. Covers federal and state inspected, and farm slaughter]

Year and type of meat	Production	Imports	Supply [1]	Exports	Consumption [2]	Ending stocks
RED MEAT AND POULTRY						
1990	62,255	3,295	66,673	2,472	62,937	1,263
2000	82,372	4,136	88,480	9,344	77,068	2,069
2003	85,187	4,376	91,902	9,740	80,138	2,025
2004	85,140	4,992	92,157	8,090	81,875	2,192
2005	86,781	4,846	93,819	9,274	82,333	2,212
2006	89,005	4,331	95,547	10,125	83,275	2,147
ALL RED MEATS						
1990	38,787	3,295	42,742	1,250	40,784	707
2000	46,299	4,127	51,340	3,760	46,559	1,021
2003	46,710	4,359	52,307	4,242	47,006	1,059
2004	45,555	4,959	51,573	2,650	47,735	1,187
2005	45,846	4,804	51,837	3,372	47,385	1,080
2006	47,544	4,271	52,895	4,159	47,570	1,166
Beef:						
1990	22,743	2,356	25,434	1,006	24,031	397
2000	26,888	3,032	30,332	2,468	27,338	525
2003	26,339	3,006	30,036	2,518	27,000	518
2004	24,650	3,679	28,847	460	27,750	637
2005	24,784	3,599	29,020	698	27,751	571
2006	26,172	3,073	29,816	1,150	28,035	631
Pork:						
1990	15,354	898	16,565	238	16,031	296
2000	18,952	965	20,406	1,287	18,642	478
2003	19,966	1,185	21,684	1,717	19,436	532
2004	20,529	1,099	22,160	2,181	19,437	543
2005	20,706	1,025	22,274	2,665	19,115	494
2006	21,017	1,005	22,516	2,991	19,012	513
Veal:						
1990	327	(NA)	331	(NA)	325	6
2000	225	(NA)	230	(NA)	225	5
2003	202	(NA)	209	(NA)	204	5
2004	176	(NA)	181	(NA)	177	4
2005	165	(NA)	169	(NA)	164	5
2006	166	(NA)	171	(NA)	165	6
Lamb and mutton:						
1990	363	41	412	6	397	8
2000	234	130	372	5	354	13
2003	203	168	378	7	367	4
2004	200	180	384	9	372	3
2005	191	180	374	9	355	10
2006	189	193	392	18	358	16
POULTRY, TOTAL						
1990	23,468	–	23,931	1,222	22,153	556
2000	36,073	9	37,140	5,584	30,508	1,048
2003	38,477	17	39,595	5,498	33,131	966
2004	39,585	33	40,584	5,440	34,139	1,005
2005	40,935	42	41,981	5,902	34,947	1,132
2006	41,461	60	42,653	5,966	35,705	981
Broilers:						
1990	18,430	–	18,651	1,143	17,266	242
2000	30,209	6	31,011	4,918	25,295	798
2003	32,399	12	33,173	4,920	27,645	608
2004	33,699	27	34,334	4,784	28,837	713
2005	34,986	34	35,733	5,203	29,607	924
2006	35,347	45	36,316	5,260	30,300	756
Mature chicken:						
1990	523	–	530	25	496	9
2000	531	2	540	220	311	9
2003	502	3	510	95	413	3
2004	504	2	509	214	292	3
2005	516	1	520	130	388	2
2006	503	3	508	160	343	4
Turkeys:						
1990	4,514	–	4,750	54	4,390	306
2000	5,333	1	5,589	445	4,902	241
2003	5,576	2	5,911	484	5,074	354
2004	5,383	5	5,741	442	5,010	288
2005	5,432	8	5,728	570	4,952	206
2006	5,611	12	5,830	546	5,062	221

– Represents zero. NA Not available. [1] Total supply equals production plus imports plus ending stocks of previous year.
[2] Includes shipments to territories.

Source: U.S. Department of Agriculture, Economic Research Service, *Food Consumption, Prices, and Expenditures, 1970–1997*; and "Agricultural Outlook: Statistical Indicators"; <http://www.ers.usda.gov/publications/agoutlook/aotables/>.

U.S. Census Bureau, Statistical Abstract of the United States: 2008

Table 834. Livestock Inventory and Production: 1990 to 2007

[95.8 represents 95,800,000. Production in live weight; includes animals-for-slaughter market, younger animals shipped to other states for feeding or breeding purposes, farm slaughter and custom slaughter consumed on farms where produced, minus livestock shipped into states for feeding or breeding with an adjustment for changes in inventory]

Type of livestock	Unit	1990	1995	2000	2001	2002	2003	2004	2005	2006	2007
ALL CATTLE [1]											
Inventory: [2] Number on farms	Mil.	95.8	102.8	98.2	97.3	96.7	96.1	94.9	95.4	96.7	97.0
Total value	Bil. dol. . .	59.0	63.2	67.1	70.5	72.3	69.9	77.6	87.4	97.6	89.5
Value per head	Dol.	616	615	683	725	747	728	818	916	1,009	922
Production: Quantity	Bil. lb. . .	39.2	42.5	43.0	42.6	42.4	42.2	41.5	41.4	42.1	(NA)
Beef, price per 100 lb.	Dol.	74.60	61.80	68.60	71.30	66.50	79.70	85.80	89.70	87.20	(NA)
Calves, price per 100 lb.	Dol. . . .	95.60	73.10	104.00	106.00	96.40	102.00	119.00	135.00	133.00	(NA)
Value of production	Bil. dol. . .	29.3	24.7	28.5	29.4	27.1	32.1	34.8	36.6	35.7	(NA)
HOGS AND PIGS											
Inventory: [3] Number on farms	Mil.	53.8	59.7	59.3	59.1	59.7	59.6	60.4	61.0	61.4	62.1
Total value	Bil. dol. . .	4.3	3.2	4.3	4.5	4.6	4.2	4.0	6.3	5.8	5.6
Value per head	Dol.	79	53	72	77	77	71	67	103	95	90
Production: Quantity	Bil. lb. . .	21.3	24.4	25.7	25.9	26.3	26.3	26.7	27.4	28.1	(NA)
Price per 100 lb.	Dol. . . .	53.70	40.50	42.30	44.40	33.40	37.20	49.30	50.20	46.00	(NA)
Value of production	Bil. dol. . .	11.3	9.8	10.8	11.4	8.7	9.7	13.1	13.6	12.7	(NA)
SHEEP AND LAMBS											
Inventory: [2] Number on farms	Mil.	11.4	9.0	7.0	6.9	6.6	6.3	6.1	6.1	6.2	6.2
Total value	Mil.. dol..	901	663	670	690	614	657	724	799	875	826
Value per head	Dol.	79	75	95	100	92	104	119	130	141	134
Production: Quantity	Mil.. lb.. .	781	602	512	501	485	470	464	473		(NA)
Sheep, price per 100 lb.	Dol.	23.20	28.00	34.30	34.60	28.20	34.90	38.80	45.10	35.20	(NA)
Lambs, price per 100 lb.	Dol.	55.50	78.20	79.80	66.90	74.10	94.40	101.00	110.00	95.50	(NA)
Value of production	Mil.. dol..	374	414	365	303	314	349	392	411	453	368	(NA)

NA Not available.   [1] Includes milk cows.   [2] As of January 1.   [3] As of December 1 of preceding year.

Source: U.S. Department of Agriculture, National Agricultural Statistics Service, *Meat Animals—Production, Disposition, and Income Final Estimates 1998–2002,* May 2004; *Meat Animals Production, Disposition, and Income,* annual; and annual livestock summaries. Also in *Agricultural Statistics,* annual.

Table 835. Livestock Operations by Size of Herd: 2000 to 2006

[In thousands (1,076 represents 1,076,000). An operation is any place having one or more head on hand at any time during the year]

Size of herd	2000	2005	2006	Size of herd	2000	2005	2006
CATTLE [1]				**MILK COWS [2]**			
Total operations	1,076	983	971	Total operations	105	78	75
1 to 49 head	671	612	605	1 to 49 head	53	37	35
50 to 99 head	186	164	161	50 to 99 head	31	23	22
100 to 499 head	192	178	176	100 head or more	21	18	18
500 to 999 head	19	19	19	**HOGS AND PIGS**			
1,000 head or more	10	10	10	Total operations	87	67	66
BEEF COWS [2]				1 to 99 head	50	41	40
Total operations	831	770	763	100 to 499 head	17	10	9
1 to 49 head	655	597	591	500 to 999 head	6	5	4
50 to 99 head	100	95	94	1,000 to 1,999 head	6	4	4
100 to 499 head	71	73	73	2,000 to 4,999 head	5	5	5
500 head or more	6	5	6	5,000 head or more	2	2	2

[1] Includes calves.   [2] Included in operations with cattle.

Source: U.S. Department of Agriculture, National Agricultural Statistics Service, *Livestock Operations Final Estimates 1998–2002,* April 2004; *Farms, Land in Farms, and Livestock Operations 2006 Summary,* February 2007; and *Agricultural Statistics,* annual.

Table 836. Hogs and Pigs—Number, Production, and Value by State: 2004 to 2006

[60,975 represents 60,975,000. See headnote, Table 834]

State	Number on farms [1] (1,000)			Quantity produced (mil. lb.)			Value of production (mil. dol.)			Commercial slaughter [2] (mil. lb.)	
	2004	2005	2006	2004	2005	2006	2004	2005	2006	2005	2006
U.S. [3]	60,975	61,449	62,149	26,689	27,416	28,140	13,072	13,607	12,704	27,828	28,143
IA	16,300	16,600	17,200	7,196	7,788	8,212	3,265	3,636	3,495	8,079	8,023
NC	9,900	9,800	9,500	3,852	3,840	3,779	2,067	2,089	1,890	2,847	2,891
MN	6,500	6,600	6,800	3,110	3,238	3,338	1,511	1,570	1,507	2,443	2,452
IN	3,200	3,250	3,300	1,426	1,487	1,494	679	704	648	1,873	1,947
IL	4,100	4,000	4,200	1,733	1,614	1,454	938	902	749	2,611	2,648
NE	2,850	2,850	3,000	1,374	1,368	1,411	717	730	699	1,934	1,943
MO	2,900	2,700	2,750	1,142	1,115	1,294	552	537	528	(4)	(4)

[1] As of December 1.   [2] Includes slaughter in federally inspected and other slaughter plants; excludes animals slaughtered on farms.   [3] Includes other states not shown separately.   [4] Included in U.S. total. Not printed to avoid disclosing individual operation.

Source: U.S. Department of Agriculture, National Agricultural Statistics Service, *Meat Animals—Production, Disposition and Income,* annual; and *Livestock Slaughter,* annual.

Table 837. Cattle and Calves—Number, Production, and Value by State: 2004 to 2007

[95,438 represents 95,438,000. Includes milk cows. See headnote, Table 834]

State	Number on farms [1] (1,000)			Quantity produced (mil. lb.)			Value of production (mil. dol.)			Commercial slaughter [2] (mil. lb.)	
	2005	2006	2007	2004	2005	2006	2004	2005	2006	2005	2006
U.S. [3]	95,438	96,702	97,003	41,497	41,448	42,102	34,831	36,629	35,741	40,689	42,820
TX........	13,700	14,100	14,000	7,402	7,304	6,804	6,187	6,437	5,010	7,483	7,817
NE........	6,350	6,500	6,650	4,392	4,499	4,811	3,605	3,831	4,055	9,078	9,288
KS........	6,600	6,650	6,400	3,862	3,993	4,132	2,796	2,973	2,971	9,097	9,509
OK........	5,350	5,450	5,250	1,968	2,064	2,134	1,942	2,187	2,111	28	31
CA........	5,400	5,450	5,500	1,983	1,929	1,997	1,267	1,214	1,177	1,813	2,016
CO........	2,500	2,650	2,700	1,915	1,797	1,940	1,849	1,813	1,934	2,655	2,753
IA........	3,600	3,800	3,950	1,611	1,730	1,820	1,329	1,410	1,468	(4)	(4)
SD........	3,700	3,750	3,700	1,546	1,501	1,541	1,446	1,528	1,499	(4)	(4)
WI........	3,350	3,400	3,400	1,055	1,075	1,167	801	858	872	1,948	2,117
MO........	4,400	4,500	4,450	1,170	1,215	1,127	1,191	1,316	1,188	(4)	104
ID........	2,060	2,110	2,180	1,056	1,032	1,065	847	868	858	483	(4)

[1] As of January 1. [2] Data cover cattle only. Includes slaughter in federally inspected and other slaughter plants; excludes animals slaughtered on farms. [3] Includes other states not shown separately. [4] Included in U.S. total. Not printed to avoid disclosing individual operation.

Source: U.S. Department of Agriculture, National Agricultural Statistics Service, Meat Animals—Production, Disposition and Income, annual; and Livestock Slaughter, annual.

Table 838. Milk Cows—Number, Production, and Value by State: 2004 to 2006

[9,012 represents 9,012,000]

State	Number on farms [1] (1,000)			Milk produced on farms (mil. lb.)			Value of production [2] (mil. dol.)		
	2004	2005	2006	2004	2005	2006	2004	2005	2006
United States [3] ...	9,012	9,043	9,112	170,934	176,929	181,798	27,568	26,874	23,574
California........	1,725	1,755	1,780	36,465	37,564	38,830	5,371	5,229	4,497
Wisconsin........	1,241	1,236	1,243	22,085	22,866	23,398	3,732	3,567	3,112
New York........	655	648	638	11,650	12,078	12,045	1,957	1,920	1,614
Idaho	424	455	488	9,093	10,161	10,895	1,364	1,423	1,286
Pennsylvania	562	561	554	10,062	10,503	10,742	1,771	1,775	1,568
Minnesota	463	453	450	8,102	8,195	8,364	1,353	1,262	1,087
New Mexico	326	328	355	6,737	6,951	7,638	1,017	994	924
Texas	319	320	335	6,009	6,442	7,145	979	986	950
Michigan	303	312	320	6,330	6,750	7,100	1,032	1,040	944

[1] Average number during year. Represents cows and heifers that have calved, kept for milk; excluding heifers not yet fresh. [2] Valued at average returns per 100 pounds of milk in combined marketings of milk and cream. Includes value of milk fed to calves. [3] Includes other states not shown separately.

Source: U.S. Department of Agriculture, National Agricultural Statistics Service, Dairy Products, annual; and Milk: Production, Disposition, and Income, annual.

Table 839. Milk Production and Manufactured Dairy Products: 1990 to 2006

[193 represents 193,000]

Item	Unit	1990	1995	2000	2001	2002	2003	2004	2005	2006
Number of farms with milk cows	1,000	193	140	105	97	91	86	82	78	75
Cows and heifers that have calved, kept for milk.	Mil. head...	10.0	9.5	9.2	9.1	9.1	9.1	9.0	9.0	9.1
Milk produced on farms.	Bil. lb.....	148	155	167	165	170	170	171	177	182
Production per cow	1,000 lb....	14.8	16.4	18.2	18.2	18.6	18.8	19.0	19.6	20.0
Milk marketed by producers [1]	Bil. lb.....	146	154	166	164	169	169	170	176	181
Value of milk produced	Bil. dol....	20.4	20.1	20.8	24.9	20.7	21.4	27.6	26.9	23.6
Cash receipts from marketing of milk and cream [1]	Bil. dol....	20.1	19.9	20.6	24.7	20.6	21.2	27.4	26.7	23.4
Number of dairy manufacturing plants	Number....	1,723	1,495	1,164	1,179	1,149	1,119	1,093	1,088	1,080
Manufactured dairy products:										
Butter (incl. whey butter)	Mil. lb.....	1,302	1,264	1,256	1,232	1,355	1,242	1,247	1,347	1,448
Cheese, total [2]	Mil. lb.....	6,059	6,917	8,258	8,261	8,547	8,557	8,873	9,149	9,534
American (excl. full-skim American)...	Mil. lb.....	2,894	3,131	3,642	3,544	3,691	3,622	3,739	3,808	3,913
Cream and Neufchatel	Mil. lb.....	431	544	687	645	686	677	699	715	752
All Italian varieties	Mil. lb.....	2,207	2,674	3,289	3,426	3,470	3,524	3,662	3,803	3,989
Cottage cheese: Creamed [3]	Mil. lb.....	832	711	735	742	748	769	788	784	775
Condensed bulk milk.	Mil. lb.....	1,426	1,372	1,202	1,110	1,191	1,047	1,021	1,182	1,333
Evaporated and condensed canned milk .	Mil. lb.....	615	503	465	468	593	595	549	548	517
Nonfat dry milk [4]	Mil. lb.....	902	1,243	1,457	1,419	1,596	1,589	1,412	1,210	1,224
Dry whey [5]	Mil. lb.....	1,143	1,147	1,188	1,046	1,115	1,085	1,085	1,100	1,100
Yogurt, plain and fruit-flavored	Mil. lb.....	(NA)	1,646	1,837	2,003	2,311	2,507	2,707	3,058	3,295
Ice cream, regular	Mil. gal....	824	862	980	970	1,005	993	920	960	966
Ice cream, lowfat [6]	Mil. gal....	352	357	373	380	339	398	387	360	372

NA Not available. [1] Comprises sales to plants and dealers, and retail sales by farmers direct to consumers. [2] Includes varieties not shown separately. [3] Includes partially creamed (low fat). [4] Includes dry skim milk for animal feed through 2001. [5] Includes animal but excludes modified whey production. [6] Includes freezer-made milkshake in most states.

Source: U.S. Department of Agriculture, National Agricultural Statistics Service, Dairy Products, annual; and Milk: Production, Disposition, and Income, annual.

Table 840. Milk Production and Commercial Use: 1990 to 2006

[In billions of pounds milkfat basis (147.7 represents 147,700,000,000) except as noted]

Year	Production	Farm use	Commercial Farm marketings	Beginning stock	Imports	Commercial supply, total	CCC net removals [1]	Commercial Ending stock	Disappearance	Milk price per 100 lb. [2] (dol.)
1990	147.7	2.0	145.7	4.1	2.7	152.5	8.5	5.1	138.8	13.68
1995	155.3	1.6	153.7	4.3	2.9	160.9	2.1	4.1	154.7	12.78
2000	167.4	1.3	166.1	6.1	4.4	176.7	0.8	6.8	169.0	12.40
2002	170.1	1.1	168.9	7.0	5.1	181.1	0.3	9.9	170.9	12.19
2003	170.4	1.1	169.3	9.9	5.0	184.2	1.2	8.3	174.7	12.52
2004	170.9	1.1	169.8	8.3	5.3	183.4	-0.1	7.2	176.4	16.05
2005	176.9	1.1	175.9	7.2	5.0	188.0	–	8.0	180.0	15.14
2006	181.8	1.1	180.7	8.0	5.0	193.7	–	9.5	184.2	12.90

– Represents zero. [1] Removals from commercial supply by Commodity Credit Corporation (CCC). [2] Wholesale price received by farmers for all milk delivered to plants and dealers.

Source: U.S. Department of Agriculture, Economic Research Service, "Agricultural Outlook: Statistical Indicators"; <http://www.ers.usda.gov/publications/agoutlook/aotables/>.

Table 841. Broiler, Turkey, and Egg Production: 1990 to 2006

[For year ending November 30 (353 represents 353,000,000)]

Item	Unit	1990	1995	1999	2000	2001	2002	2003	2004	2005	2006
Chickens:[1]											
Number [2]	Million	353	388	437	437	444	444	450	454	453	453
Value per head [2]	Dollars	2.29	2.41	2.64	2.44	2.41	2.38	2.48	2.48	2.52	2.60
Value, total [2]	Mil. dol	808	935	1,156	1,064	1,069	1,055	1,116	1,123	1,141	1,176
Number sold	Million	208	180	214	218	202	200	190	192	193	172
Price per lb.	Cents	9.6	6.5	7.1	5.7	4.5	4.8	4.9	5.8	6.5	5.8
Value of sales	Mil. dol	94	60	75	64	47	50	48	58	65	53
PRODUCTION											
Broilers: [3]											
Number	Million	5,864	7,326	8,146	8,284	8,390	8,591	8,493	8,741	8,872	8,882
Weight	Bil. lb.	25.6	34.2	40.8	41.6	42.5	44.1	44.0	45.8	47.9	48.8
Price per lb.	Cents	32.6	34.4	37.1	33.6	39.3	30.5	34.6	44.6	43.6	38.6
Production value	Mil. dol	8,366	11,762	15,129	13,989	16,696	13,437	15,215	20,446	20,878	18,851
Turkeys:											
Number	Million	282	292	270	270	273	275	274	264	252	262
Weight	Bil. lb.	6.0	6.8	6.9	7.0	7.2	7.5	7.5	7.3	7.1	7.4
Price per lb.	Cents	39.6	41.0	40.6	40.6	39.0	36.5	36.1	42.0	44.9	47.9
Production value	Mil. dol	2,393	2,769	2,807	2,828	2,797	2,732	2,700	3,065	3,183	3,551
Eggs:											
Number	Billion	68.1	74.8	82.9	84.7	86.1	87.3	87.5	89.1	90.0	90.9
Price per dozen	Cents	70.8	62.5	62.0	61.6	62.0	58.9	73.2	71.4	54.0	57.9
Production value	Mil. dol	4,021	3,893	4,287	4,346	4,446	4,281	5,333	5,299	4,049	4,388

[1] Excludes commercial broilers. [2] As of December 1. [3] Young chickens of the heavy breeds and other meat-type birds, to be marketed at 2–5 lbs. live weight and from which no pullets are kept for egg production.

Source: U.S. Department of Agriculture, National Agricultural Statistics Service, Poultry Production and Value Final Estimates 1998–2002, April 2004; Turkeys Final Estimates 1998–2002, April 2004; Chickens and Eggs Final Estimates 1998–2002, April 2004; Poultry—Production and Value, annual; Turkeys, annual; and Chickens and Eggs, annual.

Table 842. Broiler and Turkey Production by State: 2004 to 2006

[In millions of pounds, live weight production (45,796 represents 45,796,000,000)]

State	Broilers 2004	Broilers 2005	Broilers 2006	Turkeys 2004	Turkeys 2005	Turkeys 2006	State	Broilers 2004	Broilers 2005	Broilers 2006	Turkeys 2004	Turkeys 2005	Turkeys 2006
U.S. [1]	45,796	47,856	48,795	7,305	7,096	7,418	MS	4,387	4,775	4,662	(NA)	(NA)	(NA)
AL	5,470	5,604	5,688	(NA)	(NA)	(NA)	MO	(NA)	(NA)	(NA)	667	628	634
AR	6,208	6,314	6,283	527	566	585	NC	4,537	4,852	5,093	1,069	1,054	1,125
CA	(NA)	(NA)	(NA)	414	396	428	ND	(NA)	(NA)	(NA)	26	30	35
DE	1,492	1,612	1,803	(NA)	(NA)	(NA)	OH	225	228	242	220	224	191
FL	463	458	443	(NA)	(NA)	(NA)	OK	1,243	1,325	1,347	(NA)	(NA)	(NA)
GA	6,495	6,752	7,187	(NA)	(NA)	(NA)	PA	708	800	783	234	207	195
IL	(NA)	(NA)	(NA)	89	93	90	SC	1,186	1,280	1,408	463	310	386
IN	(NA)	(NA)	(NA)	410	429	462	SD	(NA)	(NA)	(NA)	151	138	158
IA	(NA)	(NA)	(NA)	324	306	274	TN	999	1,003	1,089	(NA)	(NA)	(NA)
KY	1,570	1,638	1,590	(NA)	(NA)	(NA)	TX	3,166	3,265	3,330	(NA)	(NA)	(NA)
MD	1,366	1,390	1,305	13	15	26	VA	1,341	1,328	1,332	435	502	555
MI	(NA)	(NA)	(NA)	188	169	175	WV	354	363	359	71	68	93
MN	232	230	260	1,228	1,202	1,211	WI	152	160	169	(NA)	(NA)	(NA)

NA Not available. [1] Includes other states not shown separately.

Source: U.S. Department of Agriculture, National Agricultural Statistics Service, Poultry—Production and Value, annual.

Section 18
Natural Resources

This section presents data on the area, ownership, production, trade, reserves, and disposition of natural resources. Natural resources is defined here as including forestry, fisheries, and mining and mineral products.

Forestry—Presents data on the area, ownership, and timber resource of commercial timberland; forestry statistics covering the National Forests and Forest Service cooperative programs; product data for lumber, pulpwood, woodpulp, paper and paperboard, and similar data.

The principal sources of data relating to forests and forest products are *Forest Resources of the United States, 2002; Timber Demand and Technology Assessment; U.S. Timber Production, Trade, Consumption, and Price Statistics, 1965– 2002; Land Areas of the National Forest System,* issued annually by the Forest Service of the U.S. Department of Agriculture; *Agricultural Statistics* issued by the Department of Agriculture; and reports of the annual survey of manufactures, and the annual *Current Industrial Reports,* issued by the U.S. Census Bureau on the Internet and in print in the annual *Manufacturing Profiles.* Additional information is published in the monthly *Survey of Current Business* of the Bureau of Economic Analysis, and the annual *Wood Pulp* and *Fiber Statistics* and *The Statistics of Paper, Paperboard, and Wood Pulp* of the American Forest and Paper Association, Washington, DC.

The completeness and reliability of statistics on forests and forest products vary considerably. The data for forest land area and stand volumes are much more reliable for areas that have been recently surveyed than for those for which only estimates are available. In general, more data are available for lumber and other manufactured products such as particle board and softwood panels, etc., than for the primary forest products such as poles and piling and fuelwood.

Fisheries—The principal source of data relating to fisheries is *Fisheries of the United States,* issued annually by the National Marine Fisheries Service (NMFS), National Oceanic and Atmospheric Administration (NOAA). The NMFS collects and disseminates data on commercial landings of fish and shellfish. Annual reports include quantity and value of commercial landings of fish and shellfish disposition of landings and number and kinds of fishing vessels and fishing gear. Reports for the fish-processing industry include annual output for the wholesaling and fish processing establishments, annual and seasonal employment. The principal source for these data is the annual *Fisheries of the United States.*

Mining and mineral products— Presents data relating to mineral industries and their products, general summary measures of production and employment, and more detailed data on production, prices, imports and exports, consumption, and distribution for specific industries and products. Data on mining and mineral products may also be found in Sections 19, 21, and 28 of this *Abstract;* data on mining employment may be found in Section 12.

Mining comprises the extraction of minerals occurring naturally (coal, ores, crude petroleum, natural gas) and quarrying, well operation, milling, refining and processing, and other preparation customarily done at the mine or well site or as a part of extraction activity. (Mineral preparation plants are usually operated together with mines or quarries.) Exploration for minerals is included as is the development of mineral properties.

The principal governmental sources of these data are the *Minerals Yearbook* and *Mineral Commodity Summaries,* published by the U.S. Geological Survey, U.S. Department of the Interior, and various monthly and annual publications of the Energy

Information Administration, U.S. Department of Energy. See text, Section 19, for a list of Department of Energy publications. In addition, the Census Bureau conducts a census of mineral industries every 5 years.

Nongovernment sources include the *Annual Statistical Report* of the American Iron and Steel Institute, Washington, DC; *Metals Week* and the monthly *Engineering and Mining Journal*, issued by the McGraw-Hill Publishing Co., New York, NY; *The Iron Age*, issued weekly by the Chilton Co., Philadelphia, PA; and the *Joint Association Survey of the U.S. Oil and Gas Industry*, conducted jointly by the American Petroleum Institute, Independent Petroleum Association of America, and Mid-Continent Oil and Gas Association.

Mineral statistics, with principal emphasis on commodity detail, have been collected by the U.S. Geological Survey and the former Bureau of Mines since 1880. Current data in U.S. Geological Survey publications include quantity and value of nonfuel minerals produced, sold, or used by producers, or shipped; quantity of minerals stocked; crude materials treated and prepared minerals recovered; and consumption of mineral raw materials.

Censuses of mineral industries have been conducted by the Census Bureau at various intervals since 1840. Beginning with the 1967 census, legislation provides for a census to be conducted every 5 years for years ending in "2" and "7." The most recent results, published for 2002, are based on the North American Industry Classification System (NAICS). The censuses provide, for the various types of mineral establishments, information on operating costs, capital expenditures, labor, equipment, and energy requirements in relation to their value of shipments and other receipts. Commodity statistics on many manufactured mineral products are also collected by the Census Bureau at monthly, quarterly, or annual intervals and issued in its *Current Industrial Reports* series.

In general, figures shown in the individual commodity tables include data for outlying areas and may therefore not agree with summary tables. Except for crude petroleum and refined products, the export and import figures include foreign trade passing through the customs districts of United States and Puerto Rico but exclude shipments between U.S. territories and the customs districts.

Table 843. **Gross Domestic Product of Natural Resource-Related Industries in Current and Real (2000) Dollars by Industry: 2000 to 2006**

[In billions of dollars (9,817.0 represents $9,817,000,000,000). Data are based on the 2002 North American Industry Classification System (NAICS); see text, Section 15. Data include nonfactor charges (capital consumption allowances, indirect business taxes, etc.) as well as factor charges against gross product; corporate profits and capital consumption allowances have been shifted from a company to an establishment basis]

Industry	Current dollars				Chained (2000) dollars			
	2000	2004	2005	2006	2000	2004	2005	2006
All industries, total [1]	9,817.0	11,712.5	12,455.8	13,246.6	9,817.0	10,703.5	11,048.6	11,415.3
Industries covered	306.3	405.2	450.0	(NA)	306.3	305.8	305.3	(NA)
Percent of all industries	3.1	3.5	3.6	(NA)	3.1	2.9	2.8	(NA)
Agriculture, forestry, fishing, and hunting. .	98.0	142.0	123.1	122.4	98.0	110.5	110.6	116.1
Farms	71.5	114.6	95.9	(NA)	71.5	81.6	82.4	(NA)
Forestry, fishing and related activities . .	26.5	27.4	27.2	(NA)	26.5	28.4	27.5	(NA)
Mining	121.3	172.1	233.3	256.0	121.3	107.6	104.8	104.1
Oil and gas extraction	81.0	116.4	159.6	(NA)	81.0	77.2	73.6	(NA)
Mining, except oil and gas	27.0	29.3	31.5	(NA)	27.0	23.5	22.7	(NA)
Support activities for mining	13.4	26.5	42.2	(NA)	13.4	9.1	9.7	(NA)
Timber-related manufacturing	87.0	91.1	93.6	(NA)	87.0	87.7	89.9	(NA)
Wood products	31.4	38.3	39.0	(NA)	31.4	31.4	32.4	(NA)
Paper products	55.6	52.8	54.6	(NA)	55.6	56.3	57.5	(NA)

NA Not available.   [1] Includes industries, not shown separately.

Source: U.S. Bureau of Economic Analysis, *Survey of Current Business*, May 2007. See also <http://www.bea.gov /industry/gdpbyind_data.htm> (released 24 April 2007).

Table 844. Natural Resource-Related Industries—Establishments, Sales, Payroll, and Employees by Industry: 1997 and 2002

[174 represents $174,000,000,000. Includes only establishments of firms with payroll. Data are based on the 1997 and 2002 economic censuses, which are subject to nonsampling error. For details on methodology and nonsampling and sampling errors, see Appendix III]

Industry	1997 NAICS code [1]	Establishments (number)		Value of shipments (bil. dol.)		Annual payroll (bil. dol.)		Paid employees [2] (1,000)	
		1997	2002	1997	2002	1997	2002	1997	2002
Mining	21	25,000	24,284	174	184	21	22	509	488
Oil & gas extraction	211	8,312	7,722	103	113	6	5	111	99
Mining (except oil & gas) ...	212	7,348	7,196	51	47	9	9	229	195
Mining support activities	213	9,340	9,366	20	24	6	7	169	194
Manufacturing [3]	31–33	362,829	350,728	3,835	3,915	570	575	16,805	14,664
Wood product mfg	321	17,367	17,255	88	89	14	16	570	543
Paper mfg	322	5,868	5,495	150	153	22	21	574	489
Petroleum & coal products manufacturing	324	2,146	2,268	177	216	6	6	108	104

[1] North American Industry Classification System, 1997.   [2] For pay period including March 12.   [3] Includes other industries not shown separately.

Source: U.S. Census Bureau, 2002 Economic Census, *Comparative Statistics*, Series EC02-00C-Comp, issued July 2006; <http://www.census.gov/econ/census02>.

Table 845. Natural Resource-Related Industries—Establishments, Employees, and Annual Payroll by Industry: 2000 and 2004

[1,791.3 represents 1,791,300. Excludes government employees, railroad employees, self-employed persons, etc. See "General Explanation" in source for definitions and statement on reliability of data. An establishment is a single physical location where business is conducted or where services or industrial operations are performed]

Industry	2002 NAICS code [1]	Establishments (number)		Number of employees [2] (1,000)		Annual payroll (bil. dol.)	
		2000	2004	2000	2004	2000	2004
Natural resource-related industries, total . .	(X)	72,932	71,575	1,791.3	1,652.1	66.58	70.76
Forestry, fishing, hunting, and agriculture support	11	26,076	25,528	183.6	182.1	4.68	5.22
Forestry and logging..................	113	13,347	11,707	83.1	76.0	2.26	2.31
Timber tract operations	1131	469	521	3.3	5.0	0.13	0.21
Forest nurseries & gathering forest products	1132	258	260	1.7	1.9	0.07	0.06
Logging........................	1133	12,620	10,926	78.1	69.0	2.06	2.04
Fishing, hunting & trapping.............	114	2,671	2,493	10.0	8.7	0.34	0.34
Fishing	1141	2,308	2,098	7.5	6.0	0.27	0.25
Hunting & trapping	1142	363	395	2.5	2.7	0.08	0.08
Agriculture & forestry support activities	115	10,058	11,328	90.4	97.5	2.08	2.58
Crop production support activities	1151	5,061	5,243	57.6	61.1	1.35	1.68
Animal production support activities	1152	3,450	4,299	18.2	21.2	0.38	0.50
Forestry support activities...........	1153	1,547	1,786	14.7	15.2	0.35	0.40
Mining	21	23,738	23,842	456.1	470.3	22.09	26.75
Oil & gas extraction	211	7,740	7,372	83.0	82.9	5.39	6.56
Mining (except oil & gas)	212	7,231	6,991	204.3	189.7	9.34	9.92
Coal mining....................	2121	1,253	1,100	70.7	69.9	3.54	3.99
Metal ore mining.................	2122	522	300	34.8	25.6	1.72	1.57
Nonmetallic mineral mining & quarrying.....	2123	5,456	5,591	98.8	94.3	4.08	4.36
Mining support activities.............	213	8,767	9,479	168.8	197.7	7.35	10.27
Timber-related manufacturing..............	(X)	23,118	22,205	1,151.6	999.7	39.80	38.78
Wood product manufacturing	321	17,328	16,783	597.7	534.8	16.51	17.19
Sawmills & wood preservation..........	3211	4,695	4,244	131.4	113.1	3.78	3.77
Veneer, plywood & engineered wood product manufacturing..............	3212	1,904	1,915	120.6	112.9	3.75	4.05
Other wood product manufacturing........	3219	10,729	10,624	345.8	308.8	8.95	9.37
Paper manufacturing..................	322	5,790	5,422	553.9	464.9	23.29	21.59
Pulp, paper, & paperboard mills..........	3221	597	649	177.1	150.3	9.48	8.77
Converted paper product manufacturing	3222	5,193	4,773	376.8	314.6	13.82	12.82

X Not applicable.   [1] North American Industry Classification System, 2002.   [2] Covers full- and part-time employees who are on the payroll in the pay period including March 12.

Source: U.S. Census Bureau, County Business Patterns; annual. See also <http://www.census.gov/epcd/cbp/view/cbpview.html>.

Natural Resources 551

[89,085,026 represents $89,085,026,000. Includes only establishments or firms with payroll. Data based on the 2002 Economic Census. See Appendix III]

Industry	2002 NAICS code [1]	Establishments	Value of shipments ($1,000)	Annual payroll ($1,000)	Paid employees
Wood product manufacturing	321	17,202	89,085,026	16,054,554	540,565
Sawmills and wood preservation	3211	4,318	25,922,616	3,496,055	108,045
Saw mills	321113	3,805	21,388,581	3,123,879	95,724
Wood preservation	321114	513	4,534,035	372,176	12,321
Veneer, plywood, and engineered wood product manufacturing	3212	1,925	20,201,016	3,681,187	114,300
Other wood product manufacturing	3219	10,959	42,961,394	8,877,312	318,220
Millwork	32191	4,725	22,557,817	4,415,940	151,245
Wood container and pallet manufacturing	32192	2,948	5,055,879	1,154,283	51,003
All other wood product manufacturing	32199	3,286	15,347,698	3,307,089	115,972
Paper manufacturing	322	5,520	153,766,022	21,497,243	491,436
Pulp, paper, and paperboard mills	3221	561	70,031,347	8,854,439	158,619
Pulp mills	32211	31	3,650,916	487,324	8,043
Paper mills	32212	327	45,163,754	5,700,302	102,571
Paperboard mills	32213	203	21,216,677	2,666,813	48,005
Converted paper product manufacturing	3222	4,959	83,734,675	12,642,804	332,817
Paperboard container manufacturing	32221	2,669	43,494,303	7,091,160	184,884
Paper bag and coated and treated paper manufacturing	32222	929	18,242,228	2,640,583	66,296
Stationery product manufacturing	32223	636	7,977,966	1,300,452	38,595
Other converted paper product manufacturing	32229	725	14,020,178	1,610,609	43,042

[1] North American Industry Classification System, 2002.

Source: U.S. Census Bureau, 2002 Economic Census, Manufacturing, General Summary, issued October 2005. See also <http://www.census.gov/econ/census02>.

Table 847. Timber-Based Manufacturing Industries—Employees, Payroll, and Shipments: 2005

[In thousands (13,169 represents 13,169,000). Based on the Annual Survey of Manufactures; see Appendix III]

Selected industry	2002 NAICS code [1]	All employees Number (1,000)	Payroll Total (mil. dol.)	Payroll Per employee (dol.)	Production workers, total (1,000)	Value added by manufactures Total (mil. dol.)	Value added by manufactures Per production worker (dol.)	Value of shipments (mil. dol.)
Manufacturing, all industries [2]	31–33	13,169	579,891	44,035	9,230	2,204,095	238,793	4,735,384
Timber-based manufacturing, total	321–322	969	38,533	39,779	765	120,651	157,791	274,866
Percent of total manufacturing	(X)	7	6.64	(X)	8.28	5.47	(X)	5.80
Wood product manufacturing	321	539	17,832	33,078	431	44,763	103,830	112,018
Sawmills & wood preservation	3211	105	3,876	36,800	87	10,946	125,701	32,786
Veneer, plywood, & engineered wood product	3212	115	4,112	35,612	93	11,078	119,160	26,609
Other wood product	3219	318	9,844	30,927	251	22,738	90,568	52,623
Millwork	32191	158	5,151	32,512	125	11,382	91,340	28,611
Wood container & pallet	32192	50	1,258	25,077	41	2,717	65,809	5,955
All other wood products	32199	110	3,436	31,312	85	8,640	101,441	18,056
Paper manufacturing	322	430	20,701	48,189	334	75,889	227,544	162,848
Pulp, paper, & paperboard mills	3221	136	8,227	60,675	108	38,619	358,927	75,428
Pulp mills	32211	7	467	65,337	6	1,678	297,475	4,044
Paper mills	32212	91	5,504	60,430	73	26,952	371,313	50,530
Paperboard mills	32213	37	2,256	60,379	29	9,989	340,110	20,854
Converted paper product	3222	294	12,474	42,430	226	37,270	164,973	87,420
Paperboard container	32221	163	6,975	42,842	125	17,628	141,288	46,127
Paper bag & coated & treated paper	32222	62	2,719	43,971	46	8,970	193,401	19,943
Stationery product	32223	33	1,256	37,641	26	3,261	125,035	8,002
Other converted paper products	32229	36	1,524	42,356	29	7,411	258,323	13,347

X Not applicable.   [1] North American Industry Classification System, 2002; see text, Section 15.   [2] Includes other industries not shown separately.

Source: U.S. Census Bureau, Annual Survey of Manufactures, 2005, Series M05(AS)-1. See also <http://www.census.gov /prod/2006pubs/am0531gs1.pdf> (issued November 2006).

Table 848. **Forest Land and Timberland by Type of Owner and Region: 2002**

[In thousands of acres (748,923 represents 748,923,000). As of January 1. Forest land is land at least 10 percent stocked by forest trees of any size, including land that formerly had such tree cover and that will be naturally or artificially regenerated. The minimum area for classification of forest land is 1 acre or strips of timber with a crown width of at least 120 feet wide. Timberland is forest land that is producing or is capable of producing crops of industrial wood and that is not withdrawn from timber utilization by statute or administrative regulation]

Region	Forest land, total	Total	Federal Total	Federal National forest	Federal Other	State, county, and municipal	Private Total	Private National forest	Private Farmer and other private [1]
Total	748,923	541,098	147,278	96,644	50,634	37,559	356,261	65,595	290,666
North	169,684	179,998	32,547	9,840	22,707	21,285	126,166	14,648	111,518
Northeast	85,031	85,834	10,085	2,164	7,921	7,464	68,285	10,855	57,430
North Central	84,653	94,164	22,462	7,676	14,786	13,821	57,881	3,793	54,088
South	214,605	208,051	21,227	11,246	9,981	5,378	181,446	35,915	145,531
Southeast	88,561	87,429	9,609	4,710	4,899	2,655	75,165	14,180	60,985
South Central	126,044	120,622	11,618	6,536	5,082	2,723	106,281	21,735	84,546
Rocky Mountains	144,343	73,467	50,268	43,959	6,309	2,839	20,360	2,926	17,434
Great Plains.	4,783	4,521	1,277	1,020	257	180	3,064	–	3,064
Intermountain	139,560	68,946	48,991	42,939	6,052	2,659	17,296	2,926	14,370
Pacific Coast	220,291	79,582	43,236	31,599	11,637	8,057	28,289	12,106	16,183
Alaska	126,869	16,209	9,094	3,772	5,322	4,344	2,771	–	2,771
Pacific Northwest [2] . .	51,441	44,386	23,505	17,911	5,594	3,207	17,674	9,174	8,500
Pacific Southwest [2] . . .	41,981	18,987	10,637	9,916	721	506	7,844	2,932	4,912

– Represents or rounds to zero. [1] Includes Indian lands. [2] Includes Hawaii.

Source: U.S. Department of Agriculture, National Agricultural Statistics Service, *Agricultural Statistics, 2006.* See also <http://www.nass.usda.gov/Publications/Ag_Statistics/index.asp>.

Table 849. **Timber Volume, Growth, and Removal on Timberland by Species, Group, and Region: 2002**

[856,061 represents 856,061,000,000]

Region	Net volume [1] — Growing stock [2] (mil. cu. ft.) All species	Soft-woods	Hard-woods	Sawtimber [3] (bil. board ft.) All species	Soft-woods	Hard-woods	Timber growth [4] (mil. cu. ft.) All species	Soft-woods	Hard-woods	Timber removals [5] (mil. cu. ft.) All species	Soft-woods	Hard-woods
Total	856,061	491,803	364,258	3,317	2,270	1,047	23,689	13,651	9,971	16,012	10,064	5,948
North	217,624	49,878	167,746	598	149	449	5,418	1,167	4,184	2,865	680	2,185
Northeast	123,667	31,476	92,191	334	94	239	2,833	658	2,175	1,275	414	861
North Central	93,957	18,402	75,555	264	55	209	2,585	525	2,061	1,590	266	1,324
South	267,965	108,018	159,947	895	400	495	11,522	6,467	5,055	10,126	6,506	3,620
Southeast	124,002	52,758	71,244	396	177	219	5,157	3,097	2,059	4,363	2,881	1,482
South Central	143,963	55,260	88,703	499	223	276	6,365	3,370	2,995	5,763	3,625	2,138
Rocky Mountains	131,659	120,837	10,822	516	492	24	2,062	1,858	204	532	502	30
Great Plains	4,260	1,880	2,380	15	7	8	87	42	45	37	21	16
Intermountain	127,399	118,957	8,442	501	485	16	1,975	1,816	159	495	481	14
Pacific Coast	238,813	213,070	25,743	1,308	1,229	79	4,687	4,159	528	2,489	2,376	113
Alaska	31,997	29,124	2,873	146	142	5	207	122	85	140	137	3
Pacific Northwest . .	148,635	135,591	13,044	843	795	47	3,154	2,841	313	1,721	1,621	99
Pacific Southwest [6] .	58,181	48,355	9,826	319	292	28	1,326	1,196	131	628	618	10

[1] As of January 1. [2] Live trees of commercial species meeting specified standards of quality or vigor. Cull trees are excluded. Includes only trees 5.0-inches in diameter or larger at 4 1/2 feet above ground. [3] Live trees of commercial species containing at least one 12-foot sawlog or two noncontiguous 8-foot logs, and meeting regional specifications for freedom from defect. Softwood trees must be at least 9.0 inches in diameter and hardwood trees must be at least 11.0-inches in diameter at 4 1/2 feet above ground. [4] The net increase in the volume of trees during a specified year. Components include the increment in net volume of trees at the beginning of the specific year surviving to its end, plus the net volume of trees reaching the minimum size class during the year, minus the volume of trees that died during the year, and minus the net volume of trees that became cull trees during the year. [5] The net volume of trees removed from the inventory during a specified year by harvesting, cultural operations such as timber stand improvement, or land clearing. [6] Includes Hawaii.

Source: U.S. Department of Agriculture, National Agricultural Statistics Service, *Agricultural Statistics, 2006.* See also <http://www.nass.usda.gov/Publications/Ag_Statistics/index.asp>.

Natural Resources 553

Timber Removals—Roundwood Product Output by Source and Species Group: 2002

[In million cubic feet (16,001 represents 16,001,000,000)]

Source and species group	Total	Sawlogs	Pulpwood	Veneer logs	Other products [1]	Fuelwood [2]
Total................	16,001	7,237	4,977	1,353	814	1,621
Softwoods................	10,107	5,218	2,865	1,183	444	397
Hardwoods...............	5,894	2,019	2,112	170	370	1,224
Growing stock [3]............	13,750	6,793	4,352	1,285	728	592
Softwoods.............	9,167	4,962	2,528	1,124	396	156
Hardwoods	4,583	1,831	1,824	160	331	436
Other sources [4]............	2,251	444	625	68	86	1,029
Softwoods..............	941	256	337	58	48	241
Hardwoods	1,310	187	288	9	38	788

[1] Includes such items as cooperage, pilings, poles, posts, shakes, shingles, board mills, charcoal, and export logs. [2] Downed and dead wood volume left on the ground after trees have been cut on timberland. [3] Includes live trees of commercial species meeting specified standards of quality or vigor. Cull trees are excluded. Includes only trees 5.0-inches in diameter or larger at 4 1/2 feet above the ground. [4] Includes salvable dead trees, rough and rotten trees, trees of noncommercial species, trees less than 5.0-inches in diameter at 4 1/2 feet above the ground, tops, and roundwood harvested from nonforest land (for example, fence rows).
Source: U.S. Department of Agriculture, National Agricultural Statistics Service, *Agricultural Statistics, 2006.* See also <http://www.nass.usda.gov/Publications/Ag_Statistics/index.asp>.

Table 851. **Total Wildland Fires and Acres: 1970 to 2006**

[Includes only nonstructure fires that occur in the wildland. Data do not include prescribed fires, which are ignited by management action under certain predetermined conditions to meet specific objectives related to hazardous fuels or habitat improvement]

Year	Fires	Acres (1,000)	Year	Fires	Acres (1,000)	Year	Fires	Acres (1,000)	Year	Fires	Acres (1,000)
1970 ..	121,736	3,279	1992 ..	87,394	2,070	1998 ..	81,043	2,330	2004 [1]	65,461	8,098
1975 ..	134,872	1,791	1993 ..	58,810	1,798	1999 ..	92,487	5,626	2005 ..	66,753	8,689
1980 ..	234,892	5,261	1994 ..	79,107	4,074	2000 ..	92,250	7,393	2006 ..	96,385	9,874
1985 ..	133,840	4,435	1995 ..	82,234	1,841	2001 ..	84,079	3,571			
1990 ..	122,763	5,453	1996 ..	96,363	6,066	2002 ..	73,457	7,185			
1991 ..	75,754	2,954	1997 ..	66,196	2,857	2003 ..	63,629	3,961			

[1] 2004 fires and acres do not include state lands for North Carolina.
Source: National Interagency Coordination Center, *Wildland Fires and Acres* (1960–2006); <http://www.nifc.gov/stats/fires_acres.html> (accessed 18 April 2007).

Table 852. **Timber Products—Production, Foreign Trade, and Consumption by Type of Product: 1990 to 2006**

[In millions of cubic feet, roundwood equivalent (15,577 represents 15,577,000,000)]

Type of product	1990	1995	1998	1999	2000	2001	2002	2003	2004	2005	2006
Industrial roundwood:											
Domestic production	15,577	15,537	15,620	15,632	15,436	14,634	14,902	14,571	15,139	15,465	(NA)
Softwoods	10,968	10,191	10,097	10,381	10,201	9,859	10,124	10,290	10,710	11,002	(NA)
Hardwoods	4,609	5,347	5,523	5,251	5,235	4,775	4,778	4,282	4,428	4,463	(NA)
Imports	3,091	3,907	4,157	4,370	4,529	4,605	4,505	5,096	5,805	5,802	(NA)
Exports	2,307	2,282	1,951	1,964	1,996	1,759	1,769	1,535	1,604	1,646	(NA)
Consumption	16,361	17,161	17,827	18,038	17,969	17,481	17,637	18,132	19,339	19,622	(NA)
Softwoods	11,779	11,961	12,339	12,754	12,659	12,552	12,790	13,398	14,357	14,652	(NA)
Hardwoods	4,582	5,200	5,488	5,284	5,310	4,929	4,847	4,734	4,983	4,970	(NA)
Lumber:											
Domestic production ...	7,317	6,815	7,093	7,379	7,199	6,820	7,060	7,131	7,510	7,889	(NA)
Imports	1,909	2,522	2,721	2,807	2,845	2,903	3,036	3,193	3,704	3,737	4,328
Exports	589	460	350	404	428	354	353	347	348	389	437
Consumption........	8,637	8,877	9,463	9,782	9,616	9,369	9,744	9,977	10,866	11,237	(NA)
Plywood and veneer:											
Domestic production ...	1,423	1,303	1,201	1,208	1,187	1,067	1,074	1,054	1,086	1,068	(NA)
Imports	97	107	131	160	155	173	205	240	354	373	(NA)
Exports	109	89	55	45	42	32	31	35	43	37	(NA)
Consumption........	1,410	1,321	1,277	1,323	1,300	1,208	1,249	1,259	1,397	1,403	(NA)
Pulp products:											
Domestic production ...	5,313	6,079	6,114	5,813	5,881	5,691	5,708	5,557	5,692	5,679	(NA)
Imports	1,038	1,248	1,269	1,355	1,459	1,458	1,180	1,579	1,669	1,570	(NA)
Exports	646	905	818	768	842	801	810	643	680	708	(NA)
Consumption........	5,704	6,422	6,565	6,400	6,498	6,348	6,078	6,493	6,680	6,541	(NA)
Logs:											
Imports	4	13	30	47	68	70	81	80	73	114	97
Exports	674	451	316	326	331	307	309	356	366	345	356
Pulpwood chips, exports ...	288	377	412	422	353	265	265	155	168	166	192
Fuelwood consumption	3,019	2,937	2,523	2,542	2,561	2,571	2,581	1,515	1,540	1,550	(NA)

NA Not available.
Source: U.S. Forest Service, *U.S. Timber Production, Trade, Consumption, and Price Statistics, 1965–1999*, Research Paper FPL-RP-595; and unpublished data. See also <http://www.fpl.fs.fed.us/documnts/fplrp/fplrp595.pdf>.

554 Natural Resources

Table 853. Selected Timber Products—Imports and Exports: 1990 to 2006

[In million board feet (13,063 represents 13,063,000,000) except as indicated]

Product	Unit	1990	1995	2000	2001	2002	2003	2004	2005	2006
IMPORTS [1]										
Lumber, total [2]	Mil. bd. ft. . .	13,063	17,524	19,906	20,443	21,434	21,981	25,493	25,738	23,648
From Canada	Percent. . .	91	97	92	93	90	90	83	85	85
Logs, total	Mil. bd. ft. [3]	23	80	435	452	525	497	454	710	528
From Canada . .	Percent. . . .	84	70	96	97	97	98	97	85	97
Paper and board [4] . . .	1,000 tons . .	12,195	14,292	17,555	18,513	19,433	20,034	21,140	20,438	18,194
Woodpulp	1,000 tons₂	4,893	5,969	7,227	7,348	7,247	6,691	6,726	6,762	6,939
Plywood	Mil. sq. ft. [5]	1,687	1,951	2,917	3,246	3,868	4,489	5,896	6,325	9,799
EXPORTS										
Lumber, total [2]	Mil. bd. ft. . .	4,623	2,958	2,700	2,190	2,186	2,193	3,842	2,682	2,386
To: Canada	Percent. . . .	14	22	26	26	27	29	12	28	11
Japan	Percent. . . .	28	33	12	10	7	7	11	3	4
Europe.	Percent. . . .	15	17	19	18	16	16	9	15	16
Logs, total	Mil. bd. ft. [3]	4,213	2,820	2,068	1,918	1,934	2,224	2,287	2,157	1,944
To: Canada	Percent. . . .	9	25	41	46	50	54	49	54	48
Japan	Percent. . . .	62	61	45	39	34	29	28	27	29
China.	Percent. . . .	9	1	–	1	2	2	3	4	5
Paper and board [4] . . .	1,000 tons . .	5,163	7,621	10,003	11,504	11,564	11,868	12,566	13,434	12,805
Woodpulp	1,000 tons₄	5,905	8,261	6,409	6,167	6,254	5,847	6,225	6,413	5,168
Plywood	Mil. sq. ft. [5]	1,766	1,517	754	580	563	640	783	568	675

– Represents zero. [1] Customs value of imports; see text, Section 28. [2] Includes railroad ties. [3] Log scale. [4] Includes paper and board products. Excludes hardboard. [5] 3/8 inch basis.

Source: U.S. Forest Service, *U.S. Timber Production, Trade, Consumption, and Price Statistics, 1965–1999*, Research Paper FPL-RP-595; and unpublished data. See also <http://www.fpl.fs.fed.us/documnts/fplrp/fplrp595.pdf>.

Table 854. Lumber Consumption by Species Group and End Use: 1996 to 2006

[In billion board feet (62.2 represents 62,200,000,000), except per capita in board feet. Per capita consumption based on estimated resident population as of July 1]

Item	1996	1997	1998	1999	2000	2001	2002	2003	2004	2005	2006
Consumption, total	62.2	63.0	65.1	68.3	66.1	64.6	67.5	67.0	73.1	75.6	71.3
Per capita	234	235	241	250	240	227	235	230	249	255	238
SPECIES GROUP											
Softwoods.	50.2	50.9	52.1	54.5	54.0	53.7	56.4	56.5	62.0	64.4	60.7
Hardwoods	12.0	12.1	13.0	13.8	12.2	11.0	11.1	10.5	11.1	11.2	10.6
END USE											
New housing.	19.0	19.2	20.6	22.1	20.6	20.1	23.4	24.0	26.1	28.6	(NA)
Residential upkeep and improvements	17.7	15.1	14.7	15.1	16.4	17.0	17.8	18.3	20.0	20.6	(NA)
New nonresidential construction [1].	4.6	7.5	7.8	7.6	5.1	5.6	4.5	4.4	4.4	4.3	(NA)
Manufacturing	7.6	8.4	8.4	(NA)	(NA)	(NA)	(NA)	8.1	7.9	7.7	(NA)
Shipping.	6.3	6.9	7.2	7.4	7.7	8.1	8.0	7.5	7.8	7.6	(NA)
Other [2].	(NA)	(NA)	(NA)	16.1	16.3	13.8	13.8	4.7	6.9	7.0	(NA)

NA Not available. [1] In addition to new construction, includes railroad ties laid as replacements in existing track and lumber used by railroads for railcar repair. [2] Includes upkeep and improvement of nonresidential buildings and structures; made-at-home projects, such as furniture, boats, and picnic tables; made-on-the-job items such as advertising and display structures; and miscellaneous products and uses.

Source: U.S. Forest Service, *U.S. Timber Production, Trade, Consumption, and Price Statistics, 1965–1999*, Research Paper FPL-RP-595; and unpublished data. See also <http://www.fpl.fs.fed.us/documnts/fplrp/fplrp595.pdf>.

Table 855. Selected Species—Stumpage Prices in Current and Constant (1996) Dollars: 2000 to 2005

[In dollars per 1,000 board feet. Stumpage prices are based on sales of sawtimber from national forests]

Species	Current dollars				Constant (1996) dollars [1]			
	2000	2003	2004	2005	2000	2003	2004	2005
Softwoods:								
Douglas fir [2].	433	193	93	321	397	140	64	260
Southern pine [3]	258	164	183	193	237	119	125	157
Sugar pine [4]	187	95	94	114	172	69	64	93
Ponderosa pine [4][5]	155	111	65	103	142	81	44	84
Western hemlock [6]	46	86	63	70	42	62	43	57
Hardwoods:								
All eastern hardwoods [7].	341	284	427	415	313	206	292	337
Oak, white, red, and black [7]	258	304	291	329	237	221	199	267
Maple, sugar [8]	314	560	618	648	288	406	422	526

[1] Deflated by the producer price index, all commodities. [2] Western Washington and western Oregon. [3] Southern region. [4] Pacific Southwest region (formerly California region). [5] Includes Jeffrey pine. [6] Pacific Northwest region. [7] Eastern and Southern regions. [8] Eastern region.

Source: U.S. Forest Service, *Timber Demand and Technology Assessment*, RWU-4851. Also in *Agricultural Statistics*, annual.

[1982 = 100. For information about producer prices, see text, Section 14]

Product	1990	1995	2000	2001	2002	2003	2004	2005	2006
Lumber and wood products [1]	129.7	178.1	178.2	174.4	173.3	177.4	195.6	196.5	194.2
Lumber	124.6	173.4	178.8	171.6	170.6	174.3	203.6	198.6	188.3
Softwood lumber	123.8	178.5	178.6	170.1	170.8	170.8	209.8	203.6	189.1
Hardwood lumber	131.0	167.0	185.9	181.3	178.3	188.8	199.3	196.6	195.1
Millwork [1]	130.4	163.8	176.4	179.2	179.8	181.8	191.9	197.2	201.7
General millwork	132.0	165.4	178.0	181.8	183.3	185.4	193.1	196.1	201.3
Prefabricated structural members	122.3	163.5	175.1	173.5	168.5	171.0	193.7	206.9	206.5
Plywood	114.2	165.3	157.6	154.3	151.7	167.0	198.5	186.8	172.8
Softwood plywood	119.6	188.1	173.3	167.8	164.1	195.9	250.9	223.5	190.6
Hardwood plywood and related products	102.7	122.2	130.2	130.4	131.5	129.0	134.4	138.1	(NA)
Other wood products [1]	114.7	143.7	130.5	130.5	127.2	129.9	134.3	139.2	143.0
Boxes	119.1	145.0	155.2	154.5	154.3	157.6	163.1	164.9	167.3
Pulp, paper, and allied products [1]	141.2	172.2	183.7	184.8	185.9	190.0	195.7	202.6	209.8
Pulp, paper, and prod., excl. bldg. paper [1]	132.9	163.4	161.4	157.7	155.3	157.1	162.1	169.8	178.4
Woodpulp	151.3	183.2	145.3	125.8	116.2	121.4	132.2	138.0	144.1
Wastepaper	138.9	371.1	282.5	148.6	173.1	197.3	231.4	230.9	234.8
Paper [1]	128.8	159.0	149.8	150.6	144.7	146.1	149.4	159.6	167.4
Writing and printing papers	129.1	158.4	146.6	146.4	143.8	144.7	146.0	156.1	162.7
Newsprint	119.6	161.8	127.5	138.6	105.7	112.1	124.5	138.5	152.3
Paperboard	135.7	183.1	176.7	172.1	164.3	162.7	170.2	175.5	191.9
Converted paper and paperboard products [1]	135.2	157.0	162.7	164.5	163.8	165.3	168.3	176.1	184.1
Office supplies and accessories	121.4	134.9	133.8	136.9	135.7	137.4	137.6	143.1	145.9
Building paper & building board mill prods	112.2	144.9	138.8	129.3	129.3	159.9	192.4	184.9	172.8

NA Not available.   [1] Includes other products not shown separately.

Source: U.S. Bureau of Labor Statistics, *Producer Price Indexes*, monthly.

Table 857. Pulpwood Consumption, Woodpulp Production, and Paper and Board Production and Consumption: 1995 to 2005

Item	Unit	1995	1998	1999	2000	2001	2002	2003	2004	2005
Pulpwood consumption [1]	1,000 cords [2]	97,052	96,305	94,265	95,904	92,181	90,500	85,436	87,110	88,595
Woodpulp production [3]	1,000 tons	67,103	65,163	62,914	62,758	58,198	58,069	53,197	54,301	60,267
Paper and board [4]:										
Production	1,000 tons	89,509	94,510	97,020	94,491	88,913	89,636	80,712	83,612	91,031
Consumption or new supply	1,000 tons	96,126	100,978	104,873	103,147	97,303	97,227	94,422	95,068	101,864
Per capita	Pounds	731	747	768	731	683	676	629	627	687

[1] Revised to match data from American Forest and Paper Association and American Pulpwood Association.   [2] One cord equals 128 cubic feet.   [3] Includes changes in stocks.   [4] Excludes defibrated and exploded woodpulp used for hard pressed board.

Source: U.S. Department of Agriculture, National Agricultural Statistics Service, *Agricultural Statistics, 2006*. See also <http://www.nass.usda.gov/Publications/Ag_Statistics/index.asp>.

Table 858. Paper and Paperboard—Production and New Supply: 1990 to 2005

[In millions of short tons (80.45 represents 80,450,000). 1 short ton = 2,000 lbs]

Item	1990	1995	1999	2000	2001	2002	2003	2004	2005
Production, total	80.45	91.33	98.65	96.05	90.38	91.11	89.81	93.41	92.64
Paper, total	39.36	42.87	45.98	45.52	42.10	41.56	40.37	41.82	41.43
Paperboard, total	39.32	46.64	51.04	48.97	46.81	48.13	48.02	50.09	49.71
Unbleached kraft	20.36	22.70	23.11	21.80	20.44	21.09	21.73	22.67	22.58
Semichemical	5.64	5.66	6.01	5.95	5.58	5.84	6.10	6.53	6.41
Bleached kraft	4.40	5.30	5.71	5.44	5.30	5.30	5.36	5.65	5.66
Recycled	8.92	12.98	16.21	15.79	15.50	15.91	14.83	15.24	15.06
Wet machine board	0.15	0.15	0.06	0.06	0.05	0.05	0.05	0.05	0.05
Building paper	0.81	0.81	0.66	0.64	0.58	0.55	0.55	0.58	0.57
Insulating board	0.86	0.86	0.91	0.86	0.85	0.83	0.83	0.88	0.88
New supply, all grades, excluding products	87.68	98.16	106.90	105.02	83.58	100.57	99.76	103.74	101.59
Paper, total	49.49	52.77	57.30	57.13	37.69	53.66	53.22	54.88	53.47
Newsprint	13.41	12.76	13.09	12.92	–	11.18	11.05	10.84	9.87
Printing/writing papers	25.46	29.55	32.53	32.99	30.62	31.09	31.03	32.68	31.99
Packaging and ind. conv. papers	4.72	4.24	4.71	4.27	–	4.20	3.96	4.14	4.05
Tissue	5.90	6.22	6.98	6.95	7.07	7.20	7.18	7.22	7.56
Paperboard, total	36.30	43.45	47.59	46.02	44.09	45.29	44.95	47.20	46.51
Construction and other	1.90	1.95	2.00	1.88	1.80	1.62	1.59	1.66	1.61

-- Represents or rounds to zero.

Source: American Forest and Paper Association, Washington, DC, *Monthly Statistical Summary of Paper, Paperboard and Woodpulp*.

Table 859. Fishery Products—Domestic Catch, Imports, and Disposition: 1990 to 2005

[Live weight, in millions of pounds (16,349 represents 16,349,000,000). For data on commercial catch for selected countries, see Table 1337, Section 30]

Item	1990	1995	1999	2000	2001	2002	2003	2004	2005
Total	16,349	16,484	17,378	17,338	18,115	19,028	19,850	20,413	20,529
For human food	12,662	13,584	14,462	14,738	15,303	16,007	17,187	17,648	18,147
For industrial use	3,687	2,900	2,916	2,599	2,812	3,021	2,663	2,765	2,382
Domestic catch.	9,404	9,788	9,339	9,069	9,489	9,397	9,507	9,683	9,624
For human food	7,041	7,667	6,832	6,912	7,311	7,205	7,521	7,794	7,989
For industrial use.	2,363	2,121	2,507	2,157	2,178	2,192	1,986	1,889	1,635
Imports [1]	6,945	6,696	8,039	8,269	8,626	9,631	10,343	10,730	10,905
For human food	5,621	5,917	7,630	7,827	7,992	8,802	9,666	9,854	10,158
For industrial use [2]	1,324	779	409	442	634	829	677	876	747
Exports [1]	4,627	5,166	5,208	5,757	7,107	6,979	6,756	8,203	8,420
For human food	3,832	4,175	4,130	4,586	5,774	5,587	5,392	6,462	6,385
For industrial use [2]	795	991	1,078	1,171	1,333	1,392	1,364	1,741	2,035
Disposition of domestic catch. . .	9,404	9,788	9,339	9,069	9,489	9,397	9,507	9,683	9,624
Fresh and frozen	6,501	7,099	6,416	6,657	7,082	6,826	7,266	7,488	7,763
Canned.	751	769	712	530	536	652	498	552	563
Cured.	126	90	133	119	123	117	119	137	160
Reduced to meal, oil, etc.	2,026	1,830	2,078	1,763	1,748	1,802	1,624	1,506	1,138

[1] Excludes imports of edible fishery products consumed in Puerto Rico; includes landings of tuna caught by foreign vessels in American Samoa. [2] Fish meal and sea herring.

Source: U.S. National Oceanic and Atmospheric Administration, National Marine Fisheries Service, *Fisheries of the United States*, annual. See also <http://www.st.nmfs.gov/st1/fus/fus05/index.html> (released February 2007).

Table 860. Fisheries—Quantity and Value of Domestic Catch: 1980 to 2005

Im millions of pounds (6,482 represents 6,482,000,000), except as noted]

Year	Quantity (mil. lb. [1])			Value (mil. dol.)	Average price per lb. (cents)	Year	Quantity (mil. lb. [1])			Value (mil. dol.)	Average price per lb. (cents)
	Total	For human food	For indus- trial prod- ucts [2]				Total	For human food	For indus- trial prod- ucts [2]		
1980 . . .	6,482	3,654	2,828	2,237	34.5	1998 . . .	9,194	7,174	2,020	3,128	34.0
1985 . . .	6,258	3,294	2,964	2,326	37.2	1999 . . .	9,339	6,832	2,507	3,464	37.1
1990 . . .	9,404	7,041	2,363	3,522	37.5	2000 . . .	9,069	6,912	2,157	3,549	39.1
1993 . . .	[3]10,467	8,214	2,253	3,471	33.2	2001 . . .	9,489	7,311	2,178	3,218	34.0
1994 . . .	10,461	7,936	2,525	3,807	36.8	2002 . . .	9,397	7,205	2,192	3,092	32.9
1995 . . .	9,788	7,667	2,121	3,770	38.5	2003 . . .	9,507	7,521	1,986	3,347	35.2
1996 . . .	9,565	7,474	2,091	3,487	36.5	2004 . . .	9,683	7,794	1,889	3,756	38.8
1997 . . .	9,846	7,248	2,597	3,447	35.0	2005 . . .	9,624	7,989	1,635	3,933	40.9

[1] Live weight. [2] Meal, oil, fish solubles, homogenized condensed fish, shell products, bait, and animal food. [3] Represents record catch.

Source: U.S. National Oceanic and Atmospheric Administration, National Marine Fisheries Service, *Fisheries of the United States*, annual. See also <http://www.st.nmfs.gov/st1/fus/fus05/index.html> (released February 2007).

Table 861. Domestic Fish and Shellfish Catch and Value by Major Species Caught: 1990 to 2005

[In thousands (9,403,571 represents 9,403,571,000)]

Species	Quantity (1,000 lb.)				Value ($1,000)			
	1990	2000	2004	2005	1990	2000	2004	2005
Total	9,403,571	9,068,985	9,682,981	9,624,172	3,521,995	3,549,481	3,755,778	3,932,532
Fish, total [1]	8,091,068	7,689,661	8,415,959	8,452,569	1,900,097	1,594,815	1,748,308	1,831,900
Cod: Atlantic	95,881	25,060	16,069	13,910	61,329	26,384	21,691	20,816
Pacific	526,396	530,505	590,650	548,746	91,384	142,330	148,982	150,738
Flounder	254,519	412,723	359,781	419,410	112,921	109,910	123,956	135,097
Halibut	70,454	75,190	80,056	76,955	96,700	143,826	176,405	177,157
Herring, sea; Atlantic	113,095	160,269	189,281	215,565	5,746	9,972	15,084	20,467
Herring, sea; Pacific	108,120	74,835	75,330	87,295	32,178	12,043	15,246	13,801
Menhaden	1,962,160	1,760,498	1,497,617	1,243,698	93,896	112,403	72,447	62,455
Pollock, Alaska.	3,108,031	2,606,802	3,353,874	3,410,539	268,344	160,525	271,630	306,929
Salmon	733,146	628,638	738,726	899,445	612,367	270,213	302,641	330,670
Tuna	62,393	50,779	56,541	44,394	105,040	95,176	91,138	85,707
Whiting (Atlantic, silver) . .	44,500	26,855	18,965	16,561	11,281	11,370	9,918	8,284
Whiting (Pacific, hake)	21,232	452,718	474,528	566,926	1,229	18,809	21,823	29,047
Shellfish, total [1]	1,312,503	1,379,324	1,267,022	1,171,603	1,621,898	1,954,666	2,007,470	2,100,632
Clams.	139,198	118,482	119,411	105,624	130,194	153,973	166,407	173,540
Crabs.	499,416	299,006	315,643	297,747	483,837	405,006	449,821	413,035
Lobsters: American	61,017	83,180	88,386	87,550	154,677	301,300	366,006	414,188
Oysters.	29,193	41,146	38,654	33,957	93,718	90,667	112,122	110,611
Scallops, sea	39,917	32,747	64,580	56,704	153,696	164,609	321,377	433,522
Shrimp	346,494	332,486	309,295	261,122	491,433	690,453	427,619	406,506
Squid, Pacific	36,082	259,508	89,580	125,711	2,636	27,077	19,831	31,670

[1] Includes other types of fish and shellfish, not shown separately.

Source: U.S. National Oceanic and Atmospheric Administration, National Marine Fisheries Service, *Fisheries of the United States*, annual. See also <http://www.st.nmfs.gov/st1/fus/fus05/index.html> (released February 2007).

Natural Resources 557

Table 662. **U.S. Private Aquaculture—Trout and Catfish Production and Value:. 1990 to 2006**

[67.8 represents 67,800,000. Data are for calendar year and foodsize fish (those over 12 inches long)]

Item	Unit	1990	1995	2000	2002	2003	2004	2005	2006
TROUT FOODSIZE									
Number sold	Mil.	67.8	60.2	58.4	50.2	46.1	49.6	55.5	49.2
Total weight	Mil. lb.	56.8	55.6	59.0	54.4	50.8	57.6	59.7	61.5
Total value of sales	Mil. dol. . . .	64.6	60.8	63.3	58.5	52.9	59.4	62.7	67.7
Average price received by									
processors	Dol./lb.	1.14	1.09	1.07	1.08	1.04	1.03	1.05	1.10
Percent sold to processors	Percent . . .	58	68	70	69	68	73	66	71
CATFISH FOODSIZE									
Number sold	Mil.	272.9	321.8	420.1	407.0	381.7	389.3	405.4	368.7
Total weight	Mil. lb.	392.4	481.5	633.8	675.8	699.3	682.2	638.9	583.6
Total value of sales	Mil. dol. . . .	305.1	378.1	468.8	380.0	397.1	450.9	450.2	452.1
Average price received by									
processors	Dol./lb.	0.78	0.79	0.74	0.56	0.57	0.66	0.70	0.77
Fish sold to processors	Mil. lb.	360.4	446.9	593.6	630.6	661.5	630.5	600.7	566.1
Avg. price paid by processors	Cents/lb. . . .	75.8	78.6	75.1	56.8	58.1	69.7	72.5	79.5
Processor sales.	Mil. lb.	183.1	227.0	297.2	317.6	319.3	306.8	300.0	284.0
Avg. price received by processors. . .	Dol./lb.	2.24	2.40	2.36	2.07	2.05	2.23	2.29	2.46
Inventory (Jan. 1)	Mil. lb.	9.4	10.9	13.6	12.3	13.6	15.2	13.7	18.2

Source: U.S. Department of Agriculture, National Agricultural Statistics Service, *Trout Production*, released February; *Catfish Production*, released January; and *Catfish Processing*, released May. Also in *Agricultural Statistics*, annual.

Table 863. **Supply of Selected Fishery Items: 1990 to 2005**

[In millions of pounds (734 represents 734,000,000). Totals available for U.S. consumption are supply minus exports plus imports. Round weight is the complete or full weight as caught]

Species	Unit	1990	1995	1999	2000	2001	2002	2003	2004	2005
Shrimp	Heads-off weight . . .	734	832	1,084	1,172	1,312	1,430	1,608	1,670	1,559
Tuna, canned	Canned weight	856	875	1,020	980	796	922	982	874	895
Snow crab	Round weight	37	42	216	122	171	172	198	168	171
Clams	Meat weight	152	144	125	133	139	144	143	132	120
Salmon, canned.	Canned weight	148	147	123	95	81	135	111	98	123
American lobster	Round weight	95	94	122	124	125	135	128	138	144
Spiny lobster	Round weight	89	89	91	99	79	87	93	93	83
Scallops	Meat weight	74	62	64	78	76	91	94	94	86
Sardines, canned	Canned weight	61	44	57	(NA)	(NA)	(NA)	(NA)	(NA)	(NA)
Oysters	Meat weight	56	63	55	71	58	62	69	53	47
King crab	Round weight	19	21	52	41	38	47	47	52	78
Crab meat, canned.	Canned weight	9	12	26	29	35	44	47	56	59

NA Not available.

Source: U.S. National Oceanic and Atmospheric Administration, National Marine Fisheries Service, *Fisheries of the United States*, annual. See also <http://www.st.nmfs.gov/st1/fus/fus05/index.html> (released February 2007).

Table 864. **Canned, Fresh, and Frozen Fishery Products—Production and Value: 1990 to 2005**

[In millions of pounds (1,178 represents 1,178,000,000). Fresh fishery products exclude Alaska and Hawaii. Canned fishery products data are for natural pack only]

Product	Production (mil. lb.)					Value (mil. dol.)				
	1990	1995	2000	2004	2005	1990	1995	2000	2004	2005
Canned, total [1]	1,178	1,927	1,747	1,106	1,082	1,562	1,887	1,626	1,100	1,210
Tuna	581	667	671	434	446	902	939	856	569	628
Salmon	196	244	171	199	219	366	419	288	251	301
Clam products	110	129	127	108	123	76	110	120	113	126
Sardines, Maine	13	14	(Z)	(NA)	(NA)	17	24	(Z)	(NA)	(NA)
Shrimp	1	1	2	1	1	3	7	11	5	3
Crabs	1	(Z)	(Z)	(Z)	(Z)	4	(Z)	(Z)	(Z)	(Z)
Oysters [2]	1	(Z)	(Z)	(Z)	(Z)	1	(Z)	1	1	(Z)
Fish fillets and steaks [3] .	441	385	368	567	612	843	841	823	933	1,119
Cod	65	65	56	15	46	132	152	167	54	114
Flounder	54	35	27	20	20	154	86	71	66	65
Haddock	7	3	6	10	24	24	11	24	42	88
Ocean perch, Atlantic	1	(Z)	(Z)	1	1	1	1	1	4	4
Rockfish	33	25	11	4	3	53	38	25	9	7
Pollock, Atlantic	12	4	2	3	2	21	10	4	6	4
Pollock, Alaska.	164	135	160	384	383	174	184	178	366	404
Other	105	118	106	129	133	284	359	353	387	433

NA Not available. Z Less than 500,000 pounds or $500,000. [1] Includes other products, not shown separately. [2] Includes oyster specialties. [3] Fresh and frozen.

Source: U.S. National Oceanic and Atmospheric Administration, National Marine Fisheries Service, *Fisheries of the United States*, annual. See also <http://www.st.nmfs.gov/st1/fus/fus05/index.html> (released February 2007).

Table 865. **Mineral Industries—Employment, Hours, and Earnings: 1990 to 2006**

[In thousands (680 represents 680,000), except as noted. Based on the Current Employment Statistics Program, see Appendix III]

Industry and item	Unit	1990	1995	2000	2002	2003	2004	2005	2006
All mining:									
All employees	1,000	680	558	520	512	503	523	562	619
Production workers	1,000	469	391	383	378	364	384	419	465
Avg. weekly hours	Number	46.1	46.8	45.5	43.9	44.4	45 4	46.4	46.3
Avg. weekly earnings	Dollars	630	711	771	769	796	837	884	939
Coal mining:									
All employees	1,000	136	97	72	74	70	71	74	79
Production workers	1,000	110	78	59	63	59	59	61	68
Avg. weekly hours	Number	44.7	45.7	45.6	45.4	46.2	47.7	48.5	49.5
Avg. weekly earnings	Dollars	822	929	945	934	963	1,029	1,071	1,093
Oil and gas extraction:									
All employees	1,000	190	152	125	122	120	123	126	136
Production workers	1,000	84	73	67	68	67	70	72	79
Avg. weekly hours	Number	44.4	43.6	41.3	39.5	41.1	43.5	44.3	43.0
Avg. weekly earnings	Dollars	591	677	802	761	778	808	856	921
Metal ore mining:									
All employees	1,000	53	48	38	29	27	28	29	33
Production workers	1,000	43	39	29	22	20	20	22	26
Avg. weekly hours	Number	42.5	43.4	43.4	42.8	43.7	45.2	44.2	43.5
Avg. weekly earnings	Dollars	646	788	871	878	957	1,035	1001	974
Nonmetallic minerals mining, and quarrying:									
All employees	1,000	113	108	115	107	106	107	110	110
Production workers	1,000	85	81	87	80	78	81	84	82
Avg. weekly hours	Number	45.0	46.3	46.1	45.2	45.1	44.6	45.9	46.1
Avg. weekly earnings	Dollars	532	632	722	749	773	791	830	863

Source: U.S. Bureau of Labor Statistics, the Current Employment Statistics program Internet site <http://www.bls.gov /ces/home.htm>.

Table 866. **Mine Safety: 1995 to 2005**

[Reported injury rates per 200,000 employee hours]

Item	All mines			Coal			Metal and nonmetal		
	1995	2000	2005	1995	2000	2005	1995	2000	2005
Number of mines	13,859	14,413	14,666	2,946	2,124	2,063	10,913	12,289	12,603
Number of miners	361,647	348,548	344,837	132,111	108,098	116,436	229,536	240,450	228,401
Fatalities	100	85	57	47	38	22	53	47	35
Fatal injury rate	0.03	0.03	0.02	0.04	0.04	0.02	0.03	0.02	0.02
All injury rate	6.30	5.13	3.92	8.22	6.64	4.62	5.24	4.45	3.54
Coal production (mil. tons)	1,030	1,078	1,133	1,030	1,078	1,133	(X)	(X)	(X)
Total mining area inspection hours/mine	56	57	50	153	178	176	25	28	23
Citations and orders	123,147	120,269	128,225	82,121	58,394	69,124	41,026	61,875	59,101
S&S [1] citations and orders (percent)	42	36	32	49	42	39	28	31	23
Amount assessed [2] (mil. dol.)	25.1	24.7	23.9	18.4	12.0	14.4	6.7	12.7	9.5

X Not applicable. [1] A violation that "significantly and substantially" contributes to the cause and effect of a coal or other mine safety or health hazard. [2] Government penalties or fines.

Source: U.S. Mine Safety and Health Administration, Office of Program Education and Outreach Services, "Mine Safety and Health At a Glance" (accessed 22 December 2006); <http://www.msha.gov/MSHAINFO/FactSheets/MSHAFCT10.HTM>.

Table 867. **Mining and Primary Metal Production Indexes: 1990 to 2006**

[Index 2002 = 100]

Industry group	NAICS code [1]	1990	1995	2000	2001	2002	2003	2004	2005	2006
Mining [2]	21	106.9	104.4	103.5	104.5	100.0	99.9	99.2	97.6	100.2
Oil and gas extraction [2]	211	107.3	104.0	101.0	102.0	100.0	99.0	96.4	92.6	94.2
Crude oil and natural gas	211111	109.2	104.8	100.9	102.2	100.0	99.7	96.4	92.7	94.3
Coal mining	2121	98.3	96.8	99.2	103.9	100.0	97.5	100.8	102.1	106.9
Metal ore mining	2122	112.1	122.6	120.2	109.2	100.0	94.3	94.0	101.8	103.1
Iron ore	21221	109.8	121.8	122.2	90.1	100.0	90.3	102.1	102.0	99.0
Gold ore and silver ore	21222	99.6	106.6	118.8	112.7	100.0	92.8	82.9	87.1	82.6
Copper, nickel, lead, and zinc	21223	120.2	137.7	121.8	114.6	100.0	97.8	100.9	101.7	105.7
Oil and gas drilling	213111	102.3	89.5	114.4	138.6	100.0	116.2	126.9	142.5	164.4
Primary metal manufacturing [2]	331	96.2	105.4	110.3	99.8	100.0	98.9	109.3	107.1	112.0
Iron and steel	3311	95.1	105.6	110.9	100.3	100.0	100.8	116.4	109.9	117.0
Aluminum	3313	102.4	98.0	103.4	92.3	100.0	95.7	96.3	102.3	98.9
Nonferrous metals [2]	3314	109.2	120.7	109.0	99.2	100.0	100.6	104.3	103.4	106.6
Copper	33142	142.5	263.1	133.9	112.1	100.0	86.9	91.0	77.0	76.8

[1] Based on the 2002 North American Industry Classification System (NAICS). [2] Includes other industries not shown separately.

Source: Board of Governors of the Federal Reserve System, *The Statistical Supplement to the Federal Reserve Bulletin*, monthly; and *Industrial Production and Capacity Utilization*, Statistical Release G.17, monthly.

Natural Resources   559

Table 868. Mineral Production: 1990 to 2006

[In millions of short tons (1,029.1 represents 1,029,100,000). Data represent production as measured by mine shipments, mine sales, or marketable production; see Appendix IV]

Minerals and Metals	Unit	1990	1995	2000	2005	2006, est.
FUEL MINERALS						
Coal, total	Mil. sh. tons	1,029.1	1,033.0	1,073.6	1,131.5	1,161.4
Bituminous	Mil. sh. tons	693.2	613.8	574.3	571.2	(NA)
Subbituminous	Mil. sh. tons	244.3	328.0	409.2	474.7	(NA)
Lignite	Mil. sh. tons	88.1	86.5	85.6	83.9	(NA)
Anthracite	Mil. sh. tons	3.5	4.7	4.6	1.7	(NA)
Natural gas (marketed production)	Tril. cu. ft.	18.59	19.51	20.20	18.95	19.36
Petroleum (crude)	Mil. bbl. [1]	2,685	2,394	2,131	1,890	(NA)
Uranium (recoverable content)	Mil. lb	8.9	6.0	4.0	2.7	(NA)
NONFUEL MINERALS						
Asbestos (sales)	1,000 metric tons . .	(D)	9	5	–	–
Barite, primary, sold/used by producers . .	1,000 metric tons . .	430	543	392	489	540
Boron minerals, sold or used by producers	1,000 metric tons . .	1,090	1,190	1,070	1,150	1,150
Bromine, sold or used by producers	1,000 metric tons . .	177	218	228	226	226
Cement:						
Portland [2]	Mil. metric tons	67	73	84	94	94
Masonry [3]	Mil. metric tons	3	4	4	5	5
Clays	1,000 metric tons . .	42,900	43,000	40,800	41,600	41,300
Diatomite	1,000 metric tons . .	631	722	677	653	800
Feldspar [4]	1,000 metric tons . .	630	880	790	750	760
Fluorspar, finished shipments	1,000 metric tons . .	64	51	–	–	–
Garnet (industrial)	1,000 metric tons . .	47	46	60	40	35
Gypsum, crude	Mil. metric tons	15	17	20	21	21
Helium [5]	Mil. cu. meters	85	101	98	76	76
Lime, sold or used by producers	Mil. metric tons	16	19	20	20	21
Mica, scrap & flake, sold/used by producers	1,000 metric tons . .	109	108	101	78	93
Peat, sales by producers	1,000 metric tons . .	721	660	847	751	721
Perlite, processed, sold or used	1,000 metric tons . .	576	700	672	508	457
Phosphate rock (marketable)	Mil. metric tons	46	44	39	36	31
Potash (K₂O equivalent) sales	1,000 metric tons . .	1,710	1,480	1,300	1,200	1,200
Pumice & pumicite, producer sales	1,000 metric tons . .	443	529	1,050	1,270	1,580
Salt, common, sold/used by producers . .	Mil. metric tons	37	41	46	45	46
Sand & gravel, sold/used by producer . .	Mil. metric tons	855	935	1,148	1,301	1,312
Construction	Mil. metric tons	829	907	1,120	1,270	1,280
Industrial	Mil. metric tons	26	28	28	31	32
Sodium carbonate (natural) (soda ash) . .	1,000 metric tons . .	9,100	10,100	10,200	11,000	10,900
Sodium sulfate (natural)	1,000 metric tons . .	349	327	(NA)	467	480
Stone [6]	Mil. metric tons	1,110	2,420	2,810	3,200	3,200
Crushed and broken	Mil. metric tons	1,110	1,260	1,560	1,690	1,670
Dimension [7]	1,000 metric tons . .	1,120	1,160	1,250	1,510	1,530
Sulfur: Total shipments	1,000 metric tons . .	11,500	12,100	10,700	9,430	9,200
Sulfur: Frasch mines (shipments)	1,000 metric tons . .	3,680	3,150	900	–	–
Talc and pyrophyllite, crude	1,000 metric tons . .	1,270	1,060	851	856	880
Vermiculite concentrate	1,000 metric tons . .	209	171	150	100	100
METALS						
Antimony ore and concentrate	Metric tons	(D)	262	(D)	–	–
Aluminum	1,000 metric tons . .	4,048	3,375	3,668	2,481	2,280
Bauxite (dried)	1,000 metric tons . .	(D)	(D)	(NA)	(NA)	(NA)
Copper (recoverable content)	1,000 metric tons . .	1,590	1,850	1,450	1,140	1,200
Gold (recoverable content)	Metric tons	294	317	353	256	260
Iron ore (gross weight) [8]	Mil. metric tons	57	61	61	53	53
Lead (recoverable content)	1,000 metric tons . .	426	386	449	426	430
Magnesium metal	1,000 metric tons . .	139	142	(D)	(D)	(D)
Manganiferous ore (gross weight) [9] . . .	1,000 metric ton . . .	(D)	(D)	–	(NA)	(NA)
Mercury [10]	Metric tons	(NA)	(D)	(NA)	(NA)	(NA)
Molybdenum (concentrate)	1,000 metric tons . .	62	61	41	58	61
Nickel ore (recovered Ni content)	1,000 metric tons . .	330	1,560	–	–	–
Palladium metal	Kilograms	5,930	5,260	10,300	13,300	13,600
Platinum metal	Kilograms	1,810	1,590	4,390	3,920	4,000
Silicon (Si content)	1,000 metric tons . .	418	396	367	270	143
Silver (recoverable content)	Metric tons	2,120	1,560	1,860	1,230	1,140
Titanium concentrate (TiO₂ content)	1,000 metric tons . .	(D)	(D)	300	300	300
Tungsten ore and concentrate [11]	Metric tons	(D)	–	–	–	–
Zinc (recoverable content)	1,000 metric tons . .	515	603	805	748	725

– Represents zero. D Withheld to avoid disclosing individual company data. NA Not available. [1] 42 gal. bbl.
[2] Includes Puerto Rico until 1995. [3] Excludes Puerto Rico for 2000–2006. [4] Beginning 1995, includes aplite. [5] Refined.
[6] Excludes abrasive stone, bituminous limestone and sandstone, and ground soapstone, all included elsewhere in table; Includes calcareous marl and slate. [7] Includes Puerto Rico, 1990 to 1995. [8] Represents shipments; includes by-product ores.
[9] 5- to 35-percent manganiferous ore. [10] Covers mercury recovered as a by-product of gold ores only. [11] Content of ore and concentrate.

Source: Nonfuels, through 1995, U.S. Bureau of Mines, thereafter, U.S. Geological Survey, *Minerals Yearbook* and *Mineral Commodities Summaries*, annual; fuels, U.S. Energy Information Administration, *Annual Energy Review*, 2005; most recent year from *Monthly Energy Review* and *Annual Coal Report*. See also <http://www.eia.doe.gov>.

560 Natural Resources

Table 869. Nonfuel Mineral Commodities—Summary: 2006

[In thousands of metric tons (2,300 represents 2,300,000), except as indicated. Preliminary estimates. Average price in dollars per metric tons, except as noted; see Appendix IV]

Mineral	Unit	Production	Exports	Net import reliance [1] (percent)	Consumption, apparent	Average price per unit (dollars)	Employment (number)
Aluminum	1,000 metric tons	2,300 [3]	2,800	44	6,100	[2]1.20	59,000
Antimony (contained)	Metric tons	—	2,900	88	27,600	[2]2.25	10
Asbestos	1,000 metric tons	—	3	100	3	(NA)	—
Barite	1,000 metric tons	540	78	83	3,200	[4]39.00	330
Bauxite and alumina (metal equivalent)	1,000 metric tons	(NA)	760	100	2,500	[4]28.00	(NA)
Beryllium (contained)	Metric tons	100	160	[5]	90	(NA)	(NA)
Bismuth (contained)	Metric tons	—	150	96	(NA)	[2]4.40	(NA)
Boron (B_2O_3 content)	1,000 metric tons	612	200	[5]	400	[4,6]400–425	1,300
Bromine (contained)	1,000 metric tons	226	11	[5]	225	[7,8]74.20	1,200
Cadmium (contained)	Metric tons	[3]892	597	29	1,250	[2,9]1.27	(NA)
Cement	1,000 metric tons	99,800	800	24	131,000	[4]98.00	16,300
Chromium	1,000 metric tons	[10]125	60	75	510	(NA)	(NA)
Clays	1,000 metric tons	41,300	5,890	[5]	35,700	(NA)	1,270
Cobalt (contained)	Metric tons	[10]2,200	2,900	81	11,300	[2]15.90	(NA)
Columbium (contained)	Metric tons	—	560	100	10,300	(NA)	(NA)
Copper (mine, recoverable)	1,000 metric tons	1,200	950	40	2,300	[3]15.00	7.2
Diamond (industrial)	Million carats	293	83	51	601	[11]0.28	(NA)
Diatomite	1,000 metric tons	655	145	[5]	510	[4]274.00	1,000
Feldspar	1,000 metric tons	760	10	[5]	755	[4]57.00	400
Fluorspar	1,000 metric tons	—	15	100	684	(NA)	—
Garnet (industrial)	Metric tons	35,300	13,200	53	74,300	[4]50–2,000	160
Gemstones	Million dollars	61	9,930	99	8,430	(NA)	1,200
Germanium (contained)	Kilograms	4,600	7100	(NA)	(NA)	[7]880.00	65
Gold (contained)	Metric tons	260	340	[5]	(NA)	[12]610.00	7,900
Graphite (crude)	1,000 metric tons	—	22	100	33	[4,13]528.00	(NA)
Gypsum (crude)	1,000 metric tons	21,200	150	27	41,600	[4]7.50	5,900
Iodine	Metric tons	1,220	2,700	71	4,190	[7,14]18.69	30
Iron ore (usable)	Million metric tons	54.00	8	5	57	[4]52.00	4,450
Iron and steel scrap (metal)	Million metric tons	76	11	[5]	55	[4,15]235.00	30,000
Iron and steel slag (metal)	1,000 metric tons	21,500	(NA)	7	21,500	[4]17.50	2,500
Lead (contained)	1,000 metric tons	430	275	2	1,590	[2]77.00	2,690
Lime	1,000 metric tons	21,200	116	1	21,500	80.50	5,300
Magnesium compounds	1,000 metric tons	305	30	53	645	(NA)	370
Magnesium metal	1,000 metric tons	(D)	13	54	120	[2]1.15	400
Manganese (gross weight)	1,000 metric tons	—	2	100	870	[16]3.61	(NA)
Mercury	Metric tons	[10](NA)	350	[5]	(NA)	[17]650.00	(NA)
Mica, scrap and flake	1,000 metric tons	93	7	30	133	[4]250.00	(NA)
Molybdenum (contained)	Metric tons	60,500	33,500	[5]	44,500	[7]53.10	910
Nickel (contained)	Metric tons	—	[18]63,900	60	147,000	[19]24,244.00	—
Nitrogen (fixed)-ammonia	1,000 metric tons	7,900	240	42	13,600	[20]300.00	1,150
Peat	1,000 metric tons	618	35	59	1,510	[4]30.31	700
Perlite	1,000 metric tons	457	32	35	700	[4]42.72	114
Phosphate rock	1,000 metric tons	30,700	—	6	(NA)	[4]27.78	2,500
Platinum-group metals	Kilograms	17,600	78,000	93	(NA)	[13,21]1,200.00	1,600
Potash (K_2O equivalent)	1,000 metric tons	1,200	400	80	5,200	[4,22]290.00	1,130
Pumice and pumicite	1,000 metric tons	1,580	22	12	1,800	[4]32.00	110
Salt	1,000 metric tons	46,000	1,000	16	55,700	[4,23]45.00	4,100
Silicon (contained)	1,000 metric tons	[24]143	32	[25]	[26]356	[27]62.00	(NA)
Silver (contained)	Metric tons	1,140	1,600	65	6,110	[13]11.57	800
Sodium carbonate (soda ash)	1,000 metric tons	10,900	4,800	[5]	6,000	[28]170.00	2,500
Sodium sulfate	1,000 metric tons	480	140	[5]	405	[29]134.00	225
Stone (crushed)	Million metric tons	1,670	1	(Z)	1,690	[4]7.75	79,700
Sulfur (all forms)	1,000 metric tons	9,240	800	26	12,400	[4,30]28.00	2,700
Talc	1,000 metric tons	880	185	11	985	[4]85.00	435
Thallium (contained)	Kilograms	—	1,290	100	(NA)	[7]5,170.00	(NA)
Tin (contained)	Metric tons	[10]3,000	5,500	79	58,100	[2]5.20	—
Titanium dioxide	1,000 metric tons	1,360	524	[5]	1,140	[2,31]1.17	4,300
Tungsten (contained)	Metric tons	[10]4,500	7,290	66	13,200	[32]205.00	(NA)
Vermiculite	1,000 metric tons	100	5	31	145	[4]143.00	100
Zinc (contained)	1,000 metric tons	725	761	76	1,120	[4,33]1.49	900
Zirconium (ZrO_2)	Metric tons	(D)	56,200	[5]	(D)	[4,24]710.00	(NA)

– Represents or rounds to zero. D Withheld to avoid disclosure. NA Not available. Z Less than half the unit of measure. [1] Calculated as a percent of apparent consumption. [2] Dollars per pound. [3] Refinery production. [4] Dollars per metric ton. [5] Net exporter. [6] Granulated pentahydrate borax in bulk, f.o.b mine. [7] Dollars per kilogram. [8] Bulk, purified bromine. [9] 1- to 5-short ton lots. [10] Secondary production. [11] Value of imports, dollars per carat. [12] Dollars per troy ounce. [13] Price of flake imports. [14] C.i.f. value, crude, per kilogram. [15] Delivered, No. 1 Heavy Melting composite price. [16] 46–48 percent Mn metallurgical ore, per unit contained Mn, c.i.f. U.S. ports. [17] Dollars per 76-pound flask. [18] Exports include both primary and secondary materials. [19] London Metal Exchange cash price. [20] F.o.b. gulf coast. [21] Dealer price of platinum. [22] Dealer price of K_2O, muriate. [23] Vacuum and open pan, bulk, pellets and packaged, f.o.b. mine and plant. [24] Price for imported zircon, f.o.b. U.S. East Coast. [25] Value less than or equal to 50,000 metric tons. Includes silicon metal only. [26] Ferrosilicon only. [27] Ferrosilicon, 50 percent Si. [28] Quoted year-end price, dense, bulk, f.o.b. Green River, WY, dollars per short ton. [29] Quoted price, bulk, f.o.b. works, East, dollars per short ton. [30] Elemental sulfur, f.o.b. mine and/or plant. [31] Rutile, list, year-end. [32] Dollars per metric ton unit WO_3 (7.93 kilograms of contained tungsten per metric ton unit). [33] London Metal Exchange cash price for Special High Grade zinc.
Source: U.S. Geological Survey, Mineral Commodity Summaries, annual. See also <http://minerals.er.usgs.gov/minerals/pubs/mcs/2007/mcs2007.pdf> (released 12 January 2007).

Table 870. Selected Mineral Products—Average Prices: 1990 to 2006

[Excludes Alaska and Hawaii, except as noted]

Year	Nonfuels								Fuels		
	Copper, cathode [1] (cents per lb.)	Platinum [2] (dol./ troy oz.)	Gold (dol./ troy oz.[3])	Silver (dol./ troy oz.[3])	Lead [4] (cents per lb.)	Tin (New York) [5] (cents per lb.)	Zinc [6] (cents per lb.)	Sulfur, crude [7] (dol./ metric ton)	Bituminous coal [8] (dol./ short ton)	Crude petroleum [8] (dol./ bbl.)	Natural gas [8] (dol./ 1,000 cu. ft.)
1990	123	467	385	4.82	46	386	75	80.14	27.43	20.03	1.71
1993	92	370	361	4.30	32	350	46	31.86	26.15	14.25	2.04
1994	111	411	385	5.29	37	369	49	30.08	25.68	13.19	1.85
1995	138	425	386	5.15	42	416	56	44.46	25.56	14.62	1.55
1996	109	398	389	5.19	49	412	51	34.11	25.17	18.46	2.17
1997	107	397	332	4.89	47	381	65	36.06	24.64	17.23	2.32
1998	79	375	295	5.54	45	373	51	29.14	24.87	10.87	1.96
1999	76	379	280	5.25	44	366	53	37.81	23.92	15.56	2.19
2000	88	549	280	5.00	44	370	56	24.73	24.15	26.72	3.68
2001	77	533	272	4.39	44	315	44	10.01	25.36	21.84	4.00
2002	76	543	311	4.62	44	292	39	11.84	26.57	22.51	2.95
2003	85	694	365	4.91	44	340	41	28.71	26.73	27.56	4.88
2004	134	849	411	6.69	51	547	53	32.50	30.56	36.77	5.46
2005	173	900	446	7.34	61	483	67	30.92	37.51	50.28	7.33
2006	315	1,200	610	11.6	77	520	145	28.00	(NA)	59.69	6.42

NA Not available. [1] U.S. producer price. [2] Average annual dealer prices. [3] 99.95 percent purity. [4] Nationwide delivered basis. [5] Composite price. [6] Platt's Metals Week price for North American Special High Grade zinc. Average prices for 1990 are for U.S. High Grade Zinc. [7] F.o.b. (Free on Board) works. [8] Average value at the point of production or domestic first purchase price.

Source: Nonfuels, through 1994, U.S. Bureau of Mines, thereafter, U.S. Geological Survey, *Minerals Yearbook* and *Mineral Commodities Summaries*, annual; fuels, U.S. Energy Information Administration, *Annual Energy Review* and most recent year from *Monthly Energy Review.*

Table 871. Value of Domestic Nonfuel Mineral Production by State: 2000 to 2006

[In millions of dollars (39,400 represents $39,400,000,000). For similar data on fuels, see Table 876]

State	2000	2005	2006 [1]	State	2000	2005	2006 [1]
United States . .	[2]39,400	55,200	64,400				
Alabama	930	1,120	1,200	Montana	[3]96	847	1,040
Alaska	1,140	1,470	2,850	Nebraska	[3]84	110	112
Arizona	2,510	4,350	6,710	Nevada	2,980	3,880	5,240
Arkansas	484	591	617	New Hampshire	[3]57	88	100
California	3,270	4,240	4,500	New Jersey	[3]291	344	369
Colorado	592	1,750	1,670	New Mexico	786	1,150	1,460
Connecticut	[3]112	157	169	New York	1,020	1,290	1,330
Delaware	[3]14	20	22	North Carolina	744	792	872
Florida	1,820	2,890	2,790	North Dakota	35	46	56
Georgia	1,620	1,810	1,970	Ohio	999	1,210	1,260
Hawaii	[3]92	100	107	Oklahoma	473	606	622
Idaho	358	906	810	Oregon	299	432	428
Illinois	913	1,210	1,280	Pennsylvania	[3]1,250	1,550	1,670
Indiana	695	883	963	Rhode Island	[3]20	35	38
Iowa	503	641	704	South Carolina	[3]551	659	730
Kansas	629	870	913	South Dakota	233	215	204
Kentucky	501	765	918	Tennessee	737	770	807
Louisiana	325	393	362	Texas	1,950	2,720	2,910
Maine	96	141	155	Utah	1,430	2,790	3,990
Maryland	[3]358	577	596	Vermont	[3]67	97	101
Massachusetts	[3]200	250	262	Virginia	710	1,160	1,230
Michigan	1,640	1,750	2,010	Washington	607	633	720
Minnesota	1,460	2,190	2,740	West Virginia	172	200	211
Mississippi	149	215	212	Wisconsin	[3]372	562	591
Missouri	1,370	1,940	2,130	Wyoming	978	1,300	1,250

[1] Preliminary. [2] Includes undistributed not shown separately. [3] Partial data only; excludes values withheld to avoid disclosing individual company data.

Source: U.S. Geological Survey, *Minerals Yearbook*, annual, and *Mineral Commodities Summaries*, annual. See also <http://minerals.er.usgs.gov/minerals/pubs/mcs/2007/mcs2007.pdf> (released 12 January 2007).

Table 872. **Principal Fuels, Nonmetals, and Metals—World Production and the U.S. Share: 1990 to 2006**

[In millions of short tons (5,348 represents 5,348,000,000), except as indicated; see Appendix IV]

Mineral	Unit	World production				Percent U.S. of world			
		1990	1995	2000	2006	1990	1995	2000	2006
Fuels: [1]									
Coal.	Mil. sh. tons	5,348	5,096	4,935	(NA)	19	20	22	(NA)
Petroleum (crude).	Bil. bbl.	22.1	22.8	25.0	(NA)	12	11	9	(NA)
Natural gas (dry, marketable)	Tril. cu. ft.	73.6	78.0	88.3	(NA)	24	24	22	(NA)
Natural gas plant liquids	Bil. bbl.	1.7	2.1	2.4	(NA)	34	31	29	(NA)
Nonmetals:									
Asbestos	1,000 metric tons . .	4,010	2,180	2,110	2,300	(D)	(Z)	(Z)	–
Barite.	1,000 metric tons . .	5,770	4,870	6,470	8,080	7	11	6	7
Feldspar.	1,000 metric tons . .	5,990	7,910	9,580	13,300	11	11	8	6
Fluorspar	1,000 metric tons . .	5,120	4,170	4,470	5,350	1	1	(NA)	–
Gypsum	Mil. metric tons . . .	104	98	106	119	15	17	19	18
Mica (incl. scrap)	1,000 metric tons . .	217	328	328	280	51	43	31	33
Nitrogen (N content)	Mil. metric tons . . .	98	100	108	122	13	13	11	6
Phosphate rock (gross wt.).	Mil. metric tons . . .	162	130	132	145	29	33	30	21
Potash (K₂O equivalent)	Mil. metric tons . . .	28	25	27	30	6	6	4	4
Sulfur, elemental basis	Mil. metric tons . . .	58	54	58	66	20	22	19	14
Metals, mine basis:									
Bauxite.	Mil. metric tons . . .	113	112	136	177	(D)	(D)	(NA)	(NA)
Columbian concentrates (Nb content). .	1,000 metric tons . .	12	18	33	60	–	–	–	–
Copper. . . . .'.	1,000 metric tons . .	8,950	10,100	13,200	15,000	18	18	11	8
Gold	Metric tons	2,180	2,230	2,590	2,500	14	14	14	10
Iron ore (gross wt.)	Mil. metric tons . . .	983	1,030	1,070	1,690	6	6	6	3
Lead [2]	1,000 metric tons . .	3,370	2,830	3,184	3,360	15	14	15	13
Mercury [2]	Metric tons	4,523	3,160	1,350	1,400	12	(D)	(NA)	(D)
Molybdenum	1,000 metric tons . .	111	126	133	179	55	48	31	34
Nickel [2]	1,000 metric tons . .	974	1,040	1,270	1,550	(Z)	(Z)	(Z)	–
Silver	1,000 metric tons . .	16	15	18	20	13	10	11	6
Tantalum concentrates (Ta content) . . .	Metric tons	344	356	1,040	1,290	–	–	–	–
Titanium concentrates:									
Ilmenite (gross wt.)	1,000 metric tons . .	4,070	4,010	5,010	[3]4,080	(D)	(D)	7	[3, 4]6
Rutile (gross wt.)	1,000 metric tons . .	481	416	387	[5]462	(D)	(D)	(D)	(D)
Tungsten [2]	1,000 metric tons . .	52	39	44	73	(D)	–	(NA)	–
Vanadium [2]	1,000 metric tons . .	33	34	56	62	6	6	–	–
Zinc [2]	1,000 metric tons . .	7,180	7,280	8,788	10,000	7	8	10	7
Metals, smelter basis:									
Aluminum	1,000 metric tons . .	19,300	19,700	24,400	33,100	21	17	15	7
Cadmium	1,000 metric tons . .	20	20	20	21	8	7	10	4
Copper.	1,000 metric tons . .	9,472	10,400	11,000	13,900	15	15	9	4
Iron, pig	Mil. metric tons . . .	539	525	573	858	9	10	8	5
Lead [6]	1,000 metric tons . .	5,950	5,590	6,580	4,840	22	25	22	26
Magnesium [4]	1,000 metric tons . .	354	395	428	650	39	36	(D)	(D)
Raw Steel	Mil. metric tons . . .	777	752	845	1,200	12	13	12	8
Tin [7]	1,000 metric tons . .	220	189	271	273	–	–	2	–
Zinc.	1,000 metric tons . .	7,180	7,370	9,137	10,800	5	5	4	3

– Represents or rounds to zero.   D Withheld to avoid disclosing company data.   NA Not available.   Z Less than half the unit of measure.   [1] Source: Energy Information Administration, *International Energy Annual*.   [2] Content of ore and concentrate.   [3] Includes U.S. production of rutile.   [4] Primary production; no smelter processing necessary.   [5] Excludes U.S. production.   [6] Refinery production.   [7] Production from primary sources only.

Source: Nonfuels, through 1990, U.S. Bureau of Mines; thereafter, U.S. Geological Survey, *Minerals Yearbook*, annual, and *Mineral Commodities Summaries*, annual; fuels, U.S. Energy Information Administration, *International Energy Annual*. See also <http://minerals.er.usgs.gov/minerals/pubs/mcs/2007/mcs2007.pdf> (published 12 January 2007).

Table 873. **Net U.S. Imports of Selected Minerals and Metals as Percent of Apparent Consumption: 1980 to 2006**

[In percent. Based on net imports which equal the difference between imports and exports plus or minus government stockpile and industry stock changes]

Minerals and metals	1980	1990	1995	2000	2002	2003	2004	2005	2006 [1]
Bauxite [2]	94	98	99	100	100	100	100	100	100
Columbium	100	100	100	100	100	100	100	100	100
Fluorspar.	87	91	92	100	100	100	100	100	100
Manganese	98	100	100	100	100	100	100	100	100
Mica (sheet).	100	100	100	100	100	100	100	100	100
Strontium	100	100	100	100	100	100	100	100	100
Vanadium	35	(D)	84	100	100	100	100	100	100
Platinum	87	78	(NA)	78	91	91	92	93	95
Tantalum.	90	86	80	80	83	79	89	90	87
Barite	44	71	65	84	78	77	78	84	83
Cobalt.	93	84	79	78	72	79	77	83	81
Potash	65	68	75	80	80	80	80	80	80
Tin	79	71	84	88	88	89	92	78	79
Zinc	60	64	71	72	75	72	73	69	76
Chromium	67	80	75	77	64	66	70	76	75
Titanium	(NA)	(NA)	70	79	74	68	58	71	71
Tungsten.	53	81	90	66	69	63	73	68	66
Silver	7	(NA)	(NA)	43	60	65	53	61	65
Nickel	76	64	60	55	52	50	55	55	60
Iron and steel.	13	13	21	18	15	10	14	15	21
Iron ore.	25	21	14	10	10	12	6	4	5

D Withheld to avoid disclosure.   NA Not available.   [1] Preliminary.   [2] Includes alumina.

Source: Through 1990, U.S. Bureau of Mines; thereafter, U.S. Geological Survey, *Mineral Commodity Summaries and Minerals Yearbook*, annual and *Historical Statistics for Mineral and Material Commodities in the United States*; import and export data from U.S. Census Bureau.

Natural Resources   **563**

Table 874. Petroleum Industry—Summary: 1980 to 2005

[548 represents 548,000. Includes all costs incurred for drilling and equipping wells to point of completion as productive wells or abandonment after drilling becomes unproductive. Based on sample of operators of different size drilling establishments]

Item	Unit	1980	1990	1995	2000	2001	2002	2003	2004	2005 [1]
Crude oil producing wells (Dec. 31)..	1,000 ...	548	602	574	534	530	529	513	510	506
Daily output per well [2]........	Bbl.....	15.7	12.2	11.4	10.9	10.9	10.9	11.1	10.7	10.1
Completed wells drilled, total......	1,000 ..	58.25	26.92	18.19	25.64	31.00	24.34	28.24	30.16	37.75
Crude oil...................	1,000 ..	31.18	11.78	7.28	7.32	7.86	5.99	7.14	7.36	8.19
Gas.....................	1,000 ..	15.36	10.43	7.87	15.63	20.43	16.03	18.67	20.43	26.30
Dry.....................	1,000 ..	11.70	4.70	3.04	2.70	2.72	2.33	2.42	2.37	3.27
Average depth per well.........	Feet....	4,166	4,653	5,523	4,723	4,893	5,125	5,408	5,733	5,706
Average cost per well..........	$1,000 ..	368	384	513	755	943	1,054	1,200	1,673	(NA)
Average cost per foot..........	Dollars ..	77.02	76.07	87.22	142.16	181.94	195.31	216.27	292.57	(NA)
Crude oil production, total.......	Mil. bbl..	3,146	2,685	2,394	2,131	2,118	2,097	2,073	1,983	1,869
Value at wells [3]...........	Bil. dol..	67.93	53.77	35.00	56.93	46.25	47.21	57.14	72.93	93.94
Average price per barrel.......	Dollars ..	21.59	20.03	14.62	26.72	21.84	22.51	27.56	36.77	50.26
Lower 48 states [4]...........	Mil. bbl..	2,555	2,037	1,853	1,776	1,766	1,738	1,718	1,651	1,554
Alaska..................	Mil. bbl..	592	647	542	355	351	359	356	332	315
Onshore.................	Mil. bbl..	2,768	2,290	1,838	1,482	1,416	1,366	1,339	1,294	1,235
Offshore................	Mil. bbl..	379	395	557	649	702	731	735	689	634
Imports: Crude oil [5]...........	Mil. bbl..	1,926	2,151	2,639	3,320	3,405	3,336	3,528	3,692	3,670
Refined petroleum products.....	Mil. bbl..	603	775	586	874	928	872	949	1,119	1,267
Exports: Crude oil...........	Mil. bbl..	104.9	39.7	34.5	18.4	7.4	3.3	4.5	9.8	15.1
Proved reserves.............	Bil. bbl..	29.8	26.3	22.4	22.0	22.4	22.7	21.9	21.4	(NA)
Operable refineries...........	Number..	319	205	175	158	155	153	149	149	148
Capacity (Jan. 1)...........	Mil. bbl..	6,566	5,684	5,633	6,027	6,057	6,127	6,116	6,166	6,251
Refinery input, total..........	Mil. bbl..	5,133	5,325	5,555	5,964	5,979	5,955	6,027	6,135	6,106
Crude oil.............	Mil. bbl..	4,934	4,894	5,100	5,514	5,522	5,456	5,586	5,664	5,550
Natural gas plant liquids......	Mil. bbl..	169	171	172	139	156	156	153	154	158
Other liquids............	Mil. bbl..	30	260	283	311	301	344	289	317	398
Refinery output, total [6].........	Mil. bbl..	5,352	5,574	5,838	6,311	6,309	6,305	6,383	6,520	6,464
Motor gasoline...........	Mil. bbl..	2,376	2,540	2,722	2,910	2,928	2,987	2,991	3,025	3,014
Jet fuel..............	Mil. bbl..	366	543	517	588	558	553	543	566	561
Distillate fuel oil.........	Mil. bbl..	974	1,067	1,152	1,310	1,349	1,311	1,353	1,396	1,441
Residual fuel oil.........	Mil. bbl..	578	347	288	255	263	219	241	240	228
Liquefied petroleum gases....	Mil. bbl..	121	182	239	258	243	245	240	236	210
Utilization rate............	Percent..	75.4	87.1	92.0	92.6	92.6	90.7	92.6	93.0	90.4

NA Not available. [1] Preliminary. [2] Based on number of wells producing at end of year. [3] Includes lease condensate. Values based on domestic first purchase price. [4] Excluding Alaska and Hawaii. [5] Includes imports for the Strategic Petroleum Reserve. [6] Includes other products not shown separately.

Source: U.S. Energy Information Administration, *Annual Energy Review 2005*. See also <http://www.eia.doe.gov/emeu/aer/contents.html>.

Table 875. U.S. Petroleum Balance: 1980 to 2005

[In millions of barrels (6,242 represents 6,242,000,000). Minus sign (–) indicates decrease]

Item	1980	1990	1995	2000	2001	2002	2003	2004	2005
Petroleum products supplied for domestic use	**6,242**	**6,201**	**7,087**	**7,211**	**7,172**	**7,213**	**7,312**	**7,588**	**7,593**
Production of products...............	5,765	5,934	6,940	6,903	6,942	6,925	6,979	7,198	(NA)
Crude input to refineries.........	4,934	4,894	5,718	5,514	5,522	5,456	5,586	5,664	5,555
Oil, field production [1].........	3,138	2,685	2,406	2,125	2,118	2,097	2,073	1,983	1,890
Alaska..................	592	647	542	354	351	359	356	332	315
Lower 48 states	2,555	2,037	1,853	1,771	1,766	1,738	1,718	1,651	1,575
Net imports	1,821	2,112	2,604	3,301	3,398	3,333	3,523	3,682	3,684
Imports (gross excluding SPR) [2] ..	1,910	2,142	2,639	3,317	3,401	3,330	3,528	3,692	3,677
SPR [2] imports	16	10	–	3	4	6	–	–	–
Exports	-105	40	35	18	7	7	5	10	12
Other sources	33	98	102	82	7	26	-11	2	(NA)
Natural gas liquids (NGL), supply	577	574	708	799	801	798	756	844	783
Other liquids	253	465	514	589	619	671	637	691	(NA)
Net imports of refined products	484	326	101	305	303	249	312	392	389
Imports	578	598	407	648	636	581	660	742	757
Exports	94	272	307	343	333	332	348	350	369
Stock withdrawal, refined products	-7	-59	46	2	-73	39	21	-2	-1
TYPE OF PRODUCT SUPPLIED									
Total products supplied for domestic use	**6,242**	**6,201**	**6,469**	**7,211**	**7,172**	**7,213**	**7,312**	**7,588**	**7,593**
Finished motor gasoline	2,407	2,641	2,843	3,101	3,143	3,229	3,261	3,333	3,343
Distillate fuel oil................	1,049	1,103	1,170	1,362	1,404	1,378	1,433	1,485	1,503
Residual fuel oil	918	449	311	333	296	255	282	316	336
Liquefied petroleum gases [3]	414	568	693	816	746	789	757	780	741
Other	1,454	1,440	1,452	1,598	1,583	1,561	1,579	1,673	(NA)
ENDING STOCKS									
Ending stocks, all oils............	**1,392**	**1,621**	**1,563**	**1,468**	**1,586**	**1,548**	**1,568**	**1,645**	**1,698**
Crude oil and lease condensate........	358	323	303	286	312	278	269	286	(NA)
Strategic Petroleum Reserve (SPR)	108	586	592	541	550	599	638	676	685
Other	926	712	668	641	724	671	661	683	(NA)

– Represents zero. [1] See footnote 2, Table 876. [2] SPR = Strategic petroleum reserve. [3] Includes ethane.

Source: U.S. Energy Information Administration, *Petroleum Supply Annual*, volume 1. See also <http://www.eia.doe.gov/pub/oil_gas/petroleum/data_publications/petroleum_supply_annual/psa_volume1/current/pdf/volume1_all.pdf> (released 23 October 2006).

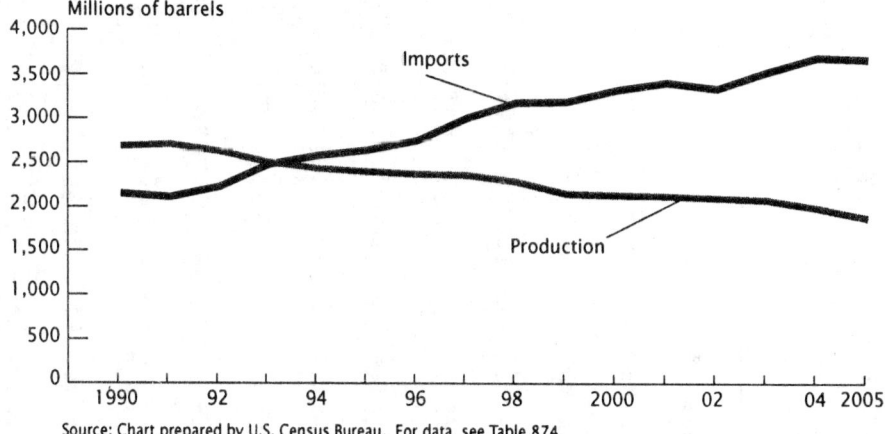

Figure 18.1
Crude Oil Production and Imports: 1990 to 2005

Millions of barrels

Imports

Production

Source: Chart prepared by U.S. Census Bureau. For data, see Table 874.

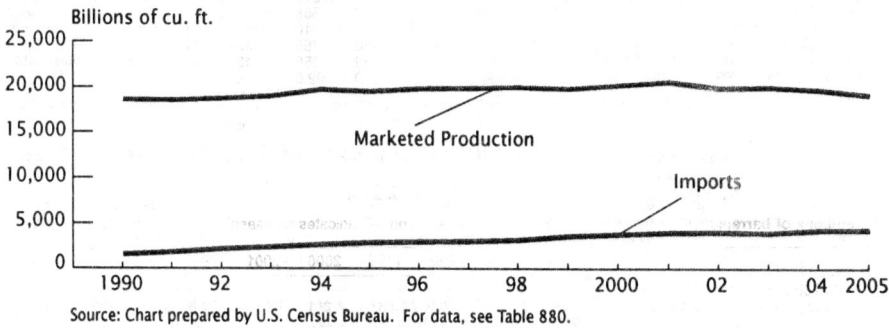

Figure 18.2
Natural Gas Marketed Production and Imports: 1990 to 2005

Billions of cu. ft.

Marketed Production

Imports

Source: Chart prepared by U.S. Census Bureau. For data, see Table 880.

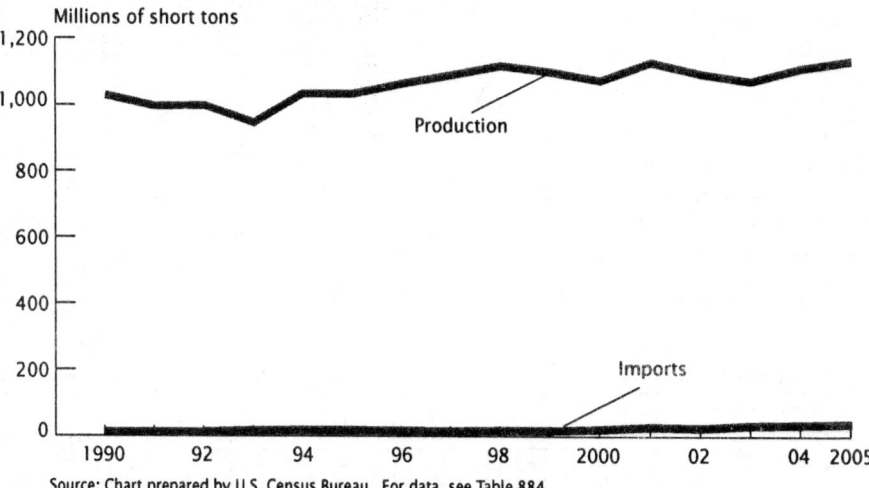

Figure 18.3
Coal Production and Imports: 1990 to 2005

Millions of short tons

Production

Imports

Source: Chart prepared by U.S. Census Bureau. For data, see Table 884.

Natural Resources 565

Table 876. Crude Petroleum and Natural Gas—Production and Value by Major Producing States: 2003 to 2005

[2,073 represents 2,073,000,000 barrels]

State	Crude petroleum Quantity (mil. bbl.)			Value (mil. dol.)			Natural gas marketed production [1] Quantity (bil. cu. ft.)			Value (mil. dol.)		
	2003	2004	2005	2003	2004	2005	2003	2004	2005	2003	2004	2005
Total [2]	2,073	1,983	1,890	57,144	72,926	95,035	19,974	19,517	18,951	97,555	106,522	138,988
AL	8	7	8	228	289	419	346	316	297	2,051	2,103	2,751
AK	356	332	315	18,583	23,868	31,933	490	472	487	1,179	1,612	2,313
AR	7	7	6	192	247	323	170	187	191	877	1,063	1,383
CA	250	240	230	6,608	8,280	10,842	337	320	318	1,698	1,808	2,365
CO	21	22	23	648	892	1,263	1,011	1,079	1,133	4,591	5,622	8,418
FL	3	3	3	(NA)	(NA)	(NA)	3	3	3	(NA)	(NA)	(NA)
IL	12	11	10	340	426	523	(Z)	(Z)	(Z)	(Z)	(NA)	(NA)
IN	2	2	2	53	67	88	1	3	3	8	21	29
KS	34	34	34	974	1,327	1,806	419	397	377	1,815	1,961	2,456
KY	3	3	3	69	94	125	88	94	93	398	495	634
LA	90	83	75	2,750	3,376	4,080	1,350	1,353	1,296	7,614	8,071	11,305
MI	7	6	6	190	251	298	237	260	261	950	1,000	1,383
MS	17	17	18	456	635	877	134	63	53	688	369	437
MT	19	25	33	554	953	1,730	86	97	108	321	437	709
NE	3	3	2	79	96	126	1	1	1	5	5	5
NM	66	64	61	1,952	2,521	3,205	1,604	1,633	1,645	7,307	8,119	11,369
NY	(Z)	(Z)	(Z)	(NA)	(NA)	(NA)	36	46	55	209	321	429
ND	29	31	36	861	1,224	1,868	56	55	53	197	315	441
OH	6	6	6	159	221	302	94	90	84	552	602	728
OK	65	63	62	1,942	2,497	3,384	1,558	1,656	1,670	7,737	9,146	12,044
PA	2	3	4	72	100	215	160	197	169	(NA)	(NA)	(NA)
TX	406	393	388	11,821	15,239	20,396	5,244	5,067	5,255	27,171	29,561	39,651
UT	13	15	17	378	576	899	268	278	301	1,103	1,458	2,157
WV	1	1	2	37	51	84	188	197	217	(NA)	(NA)	(NA)
WY	52	52	52	1,396	1,812	2,356	1,539	1,592	1,639	6,362	7,893	11,245
Federal offshore	135	130	131	32,434	40,652	80,118	(NA)	(NA)	(NA)	(NA)	(NA)	(NA)
Lower 48 states	1,718	1,651	1,575	38,562	49,058	63,101	19,485	19,046	18,463	(NA)	(NA)	(NA)

NA Not available.   Z Less than 500,000 barrels or 500 million cubic feet.   [1] Excludes nonhydrocarbon gases.   [2] Includes other states not shown separately. State production does not include state offshore production. U.S. level totals shown in Tables 874 and 880 may contain revisions not carried to state level.

Source: U.S. Energy Information Administration, *Petroleum Supply Annual*, Vol. 2, and *Petroleum Marketing Annual*; and *Natural Gas Annual*, and *Natural Gas Monthly*.

Table 877. Crude Oil, Natural Gas, and Natural Gas Liquids—Reserves by State: 2003 to 2005

[21,891 mil. bbl. represents 21,891,000,000 bbl. As of December 31. Proved reserves are estimated quantities of the mineral, which geological and engineering data demonstrate with reasonable certainty, to be recoverable in future years from known reservoirs under existing economic and operating conditions. Based on a sample of operators of oil and gas wells]

Area	2003 Crude oil proved reserves (mil. bbl.)	Natural gas (bil. cu. ft.)	Natural gas liquids (mil. bbl.)	2004 Crude oil proved reserves (mil. bbl.)	Natural gas (bil. cu. ft.)	Natural gas liquids (mil. bbl.)	2005 Crude oil proved reserves (mil. bbl.)	Natural gas (bil. cu. ft.)	Natural gas liquids (mil. bbl.)
United States [1]	21,891	189,044	7,459	21,371	192,513	7,928	21,757	204,385	8,165
Alabama	52	4,301	60	53	4,120	50	55	3,965	61
Alaska	4,446	8,285	387	4,327	8,407	369	4,171	8,171	352
Arkansas	50	1,663	3	51	1,835	3	40	1,964	3
California	3,452	2,450	101	3,376	2,634	122	3,435	3,228	137
Colorado	217	15,436	395	225	14,743	465	250	16,596	484
Florida	68	79	17	65	78	12	59	77	7
Illinois	125	(NA)	(NA)	92	(NA)	(NA)	95	(NA)	(NA)
Indiana	19	(NA)	(NA)	11	(NA)	(NA)	16	(NA)	(NA)
Kansas	243	4,819	248	245	4,652	271	281	4,314	224
Kentucky	25	1,889	66	27	1,880	72	23	2,151	70
Louisiana	452	9,325	295	427	9,588	263	432	10,447	292
Michigan	75	3,428	48	53	3,091	48	62	2,910	39
Mississippi	169	746	7	178	691	6	189	755	7
Montana	315	1,059	8	364	995	6	427	986	9
Nebraska	16	(NA)	(NA)	15	(NA)	(NA)	16	(NA)	(NA)
New Mexico	677	17,020	875	669	18,512	864	690	18,201	840
New York	(NA)	365	(NA)	(NA)	324	(NA)	(NA)	349	(NA)
North Dakota	353	448	45	389	417	43	418	453	49
Ohio	66	1,126	(NA)	49	974	(NA)	46	898	(NA)
Oklahoma	588	15,401	686	570	16,238	790	630	17,123	839
Pennsylvania	13	2,487	(NA)	13	2,361	(NA)	14	2,782	(NA)
Texas	4,583	45,730	2,517	4,613	49,955	2,801	4,919	56,507	3,080
Utah	221	3,516	([2])	215	3,866	([2])	256	4,295	([2])
Virginia	(NA)	1,717	(NA)	(NA)	1,742	(NA)	(NA)	2,018	(NA)
West Virginia	13	3,306	[3]68	11	3,397	85	21	4,459	[3]85
Wyoming	517	21,744	[3]898	628	22,632	[3]927	704	23,774	[3]879
Federal offshore	5,120	22,570	725	4,691	19,271	721	4,483	17,831	696
Lower 48 states	17,445	180,759	7,072	17,044	184,106	7,559	17,586	196,214	7,813

NA Not available.   [1] Includes states not shown separately.   [2] Included with Wyoming.   [3] Includes Utah.
Source: Energy Information Administration, *U.S. Crude Oil, Natural Gas, and Natural Gas Liquids Reserves, 2005 Annual Report*, 5 December 2006. See also <http://www.eia.doe.gov/oil_gas/natural_gas/data_publications/crude_oil_natural_gas_reserves /cr.html>.

Table 878. **Federal Offshore Leasing, Exploration, Production, and Revenue: 1990 to 2006**

[In millions (56.79 represents 56,790,000), except as indicated. See source for explanation of terms and for reliability statement]

Item	Unit	1990	1995	2000	2002	2003	2004	2005	2006
Tracts offered..............	Number..	10,459	10,995	7,992	8,548	12,147	9,123	11,447	7,905
Tracts leased..............	Number..	825	835	553	804	957	888	989	763
Acres offered..............	Millions..	56.79	59.70	42.89	45.69	64.77	48.35	61.08	42.24
Acres leased..............	Millions..	4.30	4.34	2.92	4.20	5.03	4.69	5.24	4.12
Bonus paid for leased tracts.....	Bil. dol...	0.6	0.4	0.3	0.1	0.4	0.6	0.7	0.9
New wells being drilled:									
Active	Number..	120	124	224	119	135	156	242	209
Suspended..............	Number..	266	247	146	72	48	56	67	61
Cumulative wells (since 1953):									
Wells completed	Number..	13,167	13,475	13,718	13,282	18,424	18,260	18,001	17,801
Wells plugged and abandoned..	Number..	14,677	18,008	22,814	25,232	32,251	33,746	34,878	36,407
Revenue, total [1]............	Bil. dol...	3.4	2.7	5.2	4.1	5.9	5.3	6.3	7.6
Bonuses	Bil. dol...	0.8	0.4	0.4	0.1	1.1	0.5	0.6	0.9
Oil and gas royalties [1]	Bil. dol...	2.6	2.1	4.1	3.8	4.5	4.6	5.5	6.5
Rentals	Bil. dol...	0.09	0.09	0.21	0.20	0.25	0.21	0.22	0.22
Sales value [2]..............	Bil. dol...	17.0	13.8	27.4	25.2	29.0	30.6	37.2	45.6
Oil	Bil. dol...	7.0	6.3	11.5	11.4	8.3	8.4	15.4	24.2
Natural gas	Bil. dol...	9.5	7.5	15.9	13.8	20.7	22.2	21.8	21.4
Sales volume: [3]									
Oil	Mil. bbls..	324	409	566	530	310	248	332	391
Natural gas	Bil. cu. ft..	5,093	4,692	4,723	4,343	3,501	3,941	3,504	2,581

[1] Includes condensate royalties. [2] Production value is value at time of production, not current value. [3] Excludes sales volumes for gas lost, gas plant products, or sulfur.

Source: U.S. Dept. of the Interior, Minerals Management Service, *Federal Offshore Statistics*, annual; for revenue, sales value, and sales volume data after 2000, Minerals Revenue Management, Annual Reported Royalty Revenue Statistical Information; <http://www.mrm.mms.gov/MRMWebStats/Home.aspx>.

Table 879. **Oil and Gas Extraction Industry—Establishments, Employees, and Payroll by State: 2004**

[5,564,509 represents 5,564,509,000. Excludes government employees, railroad employees, self-employed persons, etc. See "General Explanation" in source for definitions and statement on reliability of data. An establishment is a single physical location where business is conducted or where services or industrial operations are performed. See Appendix III]

State	Crude petroleum and natural gas extraction (211111) [1]			State	Natural gas liquid extraction (211112) [1]		
	Establish- ments	Number of employees [2]	Annual payroll ($1,000)		Establish- ments	Number of employees [2]	Annual payroll ($1,000)
United States ..	6,883	69,723	5,564,509	United States ..	489	13,156	1,000,175
Alabama	29	408	24,054	Alabama	9	113	11,227
Colorado	345	3,247	349,706	Colorado	25	611	58,118
Florida...........	25	108	4,775	Florida...........	11	62	4,172
Kansas	355	2,851	129,234	Kansas	17	249	15,284
Louisiana	356	7,333	666,193	Louisiana	52	1,478	104,442
Mississippi	66	353	22,248	Mississippi	6	158	12,611
New Mexico	147	1,625	105,011	New Mexico	30	813	55,932
Ohio	199	1,332	57,444	Oklahoma	34	495	28,175
Oklahoma	1,014	8,555	612,094	Texas	135	5,386	437,626
Texas	2,791	27,186	2,417,808	Utah	8	86	6,196
Utah	53	719	56,374	Wyoming	32	716	48,188
Wyoming	185	1,939	111,537				

[1] Based on North American Industry Classification System, 2002. [2] Covers full- and part-time employees who are on the payroll in the pay period including March 12.

Source: U.S. Census Bureau, County Business Patterns; annual. See also <http://www.census.gov/epcd/cbp/view/cbpview.html>.

Table 880. **Natural Gas—Supply, Consumption, Reserves, and Marketed Production: 1980 to 2005**

[182 represents 182,000)]

Item	Unit	1980	1990	1995	2000	2001	2002	2003	2004	2005
Producing wells (year-end)	1,000	182	269	299	342	373	388	393	405	395
Production value at wells	Bil. of dol.	32.1	31.8	30.2	74.3	82.3	58.7	97.5	107.5	140.1
Avg. per 1,000 cu. ft.	Dollars	1.59	1.71	1.55	3.68	4.00	2.95	4.88	5.46	7.33
Proved reserves [1]	Tril. cu. ft.	199	169	165	177	183	187	189	193	204
Marketed production [2]	Bil. cu. ft.	20,180	18,594	19,506	20,198	20,570	19,885	19,974	19,684	19,115
Minus: Extraction losses [3]	Bil. cu. ft.	777	784	908	1,016	954	957	876	927	900
Equals: Dry production	Bil. cu. ft.	19,403	17,810	18,599	19,182	19,616	18,928	19,099	18,757	18,215
Plus: Supplemental gas supplies	Bil. cu. ft.	155	123	110	90	86	68	68	68	70
Equals: Dry production with supplemental gas	Bil. cu. ft.	19,558	17,932	18,709	19,272	19,703	18,996	19,166	18,825	18,285
Plus: Withdrawals from storage	Bil. cu. ft.	1,972	1,986	3,025	3,550	2,344	3,180	3,161	3,088	3,048
Plus: Imports	Bil. cu. ft.	985	1,532	2,841	3,782	3,977	4,015	3,944	4,259	4,285
Plus: Balancing item [4]	Bil. cu. ft.	-640	307	396	-306	99	45	44	315	148
Equals: Total supply	Bil. cu. ft.	21,875	21,758	24,971	26,298	26,122	26,237	26,314	26,486	25,766
Minus: Exports	Bil. cu. ft.	49	86	154	244	373	516	680	854	787
Minus: Additions to storage [5]	Bil. cu. ft.	1,949	2,499	2,610	2,721	3,510	2,713	3,358	3,202	2,998
Equals: Consumption, total	Bil. cu. ft.	19,877	19,174	22,207	23,333	22,239	23,007	22,277	22,430	21,981
Lease and plant fuel	Bil. cu. ft.	1,026	1,236	1,220	1,151	1,119	1,113	1,122	1,098	1,066
Pipeline fuel	Bil. cu. ft.	635	660	700	642	625	667	591	572	560
Residential	Bil. cu. ft.	4,752	4,391	4,850	4,996	4,771	4,889	4,885	5,079	4,837
Commercial [6]	Bil. cu. ft.	2,611	2,623	3,031	3,182	3,023	3,144	3,179	3,142	3,054
Industrial	Bil. cu. ft.	8,198	8,255	9,384	9,293	8,463	8,620	8,273	8,349	7,710
Vehicle fuel	Bil. cu. ft.	(NA)	(Z)	5	13	15	15	18	21	22
Electric power sector	Bil. cu. ft.	3,682	3,245	4,237	5,206	5,342	5,672	5,135	5,463	5,797
World production (dry)	Tril. cu. ft.	53.4	73.6	78.0	88.3	90.5	92.2	95.4	98.6	(NA)
U.S. production (dry)	Tril. cu. ft.	19.4	17.8	18.6	19.2	19.6	18.9	19.1	18.8	(NA)
Percent U.S. of world	Percent	36.4	24.2	23.9	21.7	21.7	20.5	20.0	19.0	(NA)

Z Less than 500 million cubic feet. NA Not available. [1] Estimated, end of year. Source: U.S. Energy Information Administration, *U.S. Crude Oil, Natural Gas, and Natural Gas Liquids Reserves*, annual. [2] Marketed production includes gross withdrawals from reservoirs less quantities used for reservoir repressuring and quantities vented or flared. Excludes nonhydrocarbon gases subsequently removed. [3] Volumetric reduction in natural gas resulting from the removal of natural gas plant liquids, which are transferred to petroleum supply. [4] Quantities lost and imbalances in data due to differences among data sources. Since 1980, excludes intransit shipments that cross U.S.-Canada border (i.e., natural gas delivered to its destination via the other country). [5] Underground storage. Through 2004, includes liquefied natural gas (LNG) storage in above-ground tanks. [6] Includes deliveries to municipalities and public authorities for institutional heating and other purposes.

Source: Except as noted, U.S. Energy Information Administration, *Annual Energy Review; International Energy Annual; U.S. Crude Oil, Natural Gas, and Natural Gas Liquids Reserves;* and *Natural Gas Annual.* See also <http://www.eia.doe.gov>.

Table 881. **Liquefied Petroleum Gases—Summary: 1980 to 2006**

[In millions of 42-gallon barrels (561 barrels represents 561,000,000 barrels). Includes ethane, propane, normal butane, and isobutane]

Item	1980	1990	1995	2000	2002	2003	2004	2005	2006
Production	561	638	760	843	822	767	795	737	757
At natural gas plants	441	456	521	587	577	527	559	530	538
At refineries	121	182	234	258	245	240	235	209	220
Imports	79	68	53	79	67	82	96	120	117
Refinery input	85	107	105	87	90	83	87	92	104
Exports	9	14	21	27	24	20	16	19	20
Stocks, Dec. 31	116	98	93	83	106	94	104	109	113

Source: U.S. Energy Information Administration, *Monthly Energy Review*, May 2007 issue. See also <http://www.eia.doe.gov/emeu/mer/petro.html>.

Table 882. **Natural Gas Plant Liquids—Production and Value: 1980 to 2005**

[Barrels of 42 gallons (567 represents 567,000,000)]

Item	Unit	1980	1990	1995	2000	2001	2002	2003	2004	2005
Field production [1]	Mil. bbl.	567	566	643	699	682	686	686	662	627
Pentanes plus	Mil. bbl.	126	112	122	112	112	109	109	101	97
Liquefied petroleum gases	Mil. bbl.	441	454	521	587	570	577	577	561	529
Natural gas processed	Tril. cu. ft.	15	15	17	17	17	16	15	15	15

[1] Includes other finished petroleum products, not shown separately.

Source: U.S. Energy Information Administration, *Petroleum Supply Annual* and *Natural Gas Annual.* See also <http://www.eia.doe.gov>.

568 Natural Resources

Table 883. Coal Supply, Disposition, and Prices: 2000 to 2006

[In millions of short tons (1,073.6 represents 1,073,600,000). 1 short ton equals 2,000 lbs]

Item	2000	2001	2002	2003	2004	2005	2006
United States, total supply	1,073.6	1,127.7	1,094.3	1,071.8	1,112.1	1,131.5	1,161.4
Consumption by sector:							
Total	1,084.1	1,060.1	1,066.4	1,094.9	1,107.3	1,125.5	1,114.2
Electric power	985.8	964.4	977.5	1,005.1	1,016.3	1,037.5	1,026.5
Coke plants	28.9	26.1	23.7	24.2	23.7	23.4	23.0
Other industrial plants	65.2	65.3	60.7	61.3	62.2	60.3	23.0
Combined heat and power (CHP). . . .	(NA)	25.8	26.2	24.0	26.6	25.9	60.5
Noncombined heat and power	(NA)	39.5	34.5	36.4	35.6	34.5	25.8
Residential/commercial users	4.1	4.4	4.4	4.2	5.1	4.2	34.8
							4.2
Year-end coal stocks:							
Total	140.0	181.9	192.1	165.5	154.0	144.3	184.2
Electric power	102.0	138.5	141.7	121.6	106.7	101.1	139.7
Coke plants	1.5	1.5	1.4	0.9	1.3	2.6	2.9
Other industrial plants	4.6	6.0	5.8	4.7	4.8	5.6	6.5
Producers/distributors	31.9	35.9	43.3	38.3	41.2	35.0	35.1
U.S. coal trade:							
Net exports	46.0	28.9	22.7	18.0	20.7	19.5	13.4
Exports	58.5	48.7	39.6	43.0	48.0	49.9	49.6
Steam coal.	25.7	23.3	18.1	20.9	21.2	21.3	22.1
Metallurgical coal.	32.8	25.4	21.5	22.1	26.8	28.7	27.5
Imports	12.5	19.8	16.9	25.0	27.3	30.5	36.2
Average delivered price (dollars per							
short ton):							
Electric utilities [1]	24.28	24.68	24.74	25.82	27.30	30.91	34.31
Independent power producers [1]	(NA)	(NA)	27.96	26.2	27.27	30.26	32.44
Coke plants	44.38	46.42	50.67	50.63	61.50	83.79	92.87
Other industrial plants	31.46	32.26	35.49	34.70	39.30	47.63	51.67
Average free alongside ship (f.a.s.):							
Exports	34.90	36.97	40.44	35.98	54.11	67.10	70.93
Steam coal.	29.67	31.88	34.51	26.94	42.03	47.64	46.25
Metallurgical coal.	38.99	41.63	45.41	44.55	63.63	81.56	90.81
Imports	30.10	34.00	35.51	31.45	37.52	46.71	49.10

NA Not available.   [1] Average delivered price is through November 2006.

Source: U.S. Energy Information Administration, *U.S. Coal Supply and Demand: 2006 Review*, annual. See also <http://www.eia.doe.gov/cneaf/coal/page/special/feature.html>.

Table 884. Coal and Coke—Summary: 1980 to 2005

[In millions of short tons (830 represents 830,000,000), except as indicated. Includes coal consumed at mines. Recoverability varies between 40 and 90 percent for individual deposits; 50 percent or more of overall U.S. coal reserve base is believed to be recoverable]

Item	Unit	1980	1990	1995	2000	2002	2003	2004	2005
COAL									
Coal production, total [1, 2]	Mil. sh. tons . . .	830	1,029	1,033	1,074	1,094	1,072	1,112	1,133
Value [3]	Bil. dol.	20.45	22.39	19.45	18.02	19.68	19.13	22.16	27.33
Anthracite production [2]	Mil. sh. tons . . .	6.1	3.5	4.7	4.6	1.4	1.3	1.7	1.7
Bituminous coal and lignite [4]	Mil. sh. tons . . .	824	1,026	1,028	1,069	1,093	1,070	1,110	1,132
Underground	Mil. sh. tons . . .	338	425	396	374	357	353	368	369
Surface [2]	Mil. sh. tons . . .	492	605	637	700	737	719	745	765
Exports	Mil. sh. tons . . .	92	106	89	58	40	43	48	50
Imports.	Mil. sh. tons . . .	1	3	9	13	17	25	27	30
Consumption [5]	Mil. sh. tons . . .	703	904	962	1,084	1,066	1,095	1,107	1,128
Electric power sector.	Mil. sh. tons . . .	569	783	850	986	978	1,005	1,016	1,039
Industrial.	Mil. sh. tons . . .	127	115	106	94	84	86	86	84
Number of mines	Number	5,598	3,243	2,104	1,453	1,426	1,316	1,379	1,415
Daily employment.	1,000	225	131	90	72	75	71	74	79
Production, by state:									
Alabama	Mil. sh. tons . . .	26	29	25	19	19	20	22	21
Illinois	Mil. sh. tons . . .	63	60	48	33	33	32	32	32
Indiana	Mil. sh. tons . . .	31	36	26	28	35	35	35	34
Kentucky	Mil. sh. tons . . .	150	173	154	131	124	113	114	120
Montana	Mil. sh. tons . . .	30	38	39	38	37	37	40	40
Ohio	Mil. sh. tons . . .	39	35	26	22	21	22	23	25
Pennsylvania	Mil. sh. tons . . .	93	71	62	75	68	64	66	67
Virginia	Mil. sh. tons . . .	41	47	34	33	30	32	31	28
West Virginia	Mil. sh. tons . . .	122	169	163	158	150	140	148	154
Wyoming	Mil. sh. tons . . .	95	184	264	339	373	376	396	404
Other states	Mil. sh. tons . . .	140	187	192	197	202	202	204	207
World production	Mil. sh. tons . . .	4,182	5,348	5,096	4,935	5,265	5,648	6,079	(NA)
Percent U.S. of world.	Percent	19.8	19.2	20.3	21.8	20.8	19.0	18.3	(NA)
COKE									
Production	Mil. sh. tons . . .	46.1	27.6	23.7	20.8	16.8	17.2	16.9	16.7
Imports.	Mil. sh. tons . . .	0.7	0.8	3.8	3.8	3.2	2.8	6.9	3.5
Exports	Mil. sh. tons . . .	2.1	0.6	1.4	1.1	0.8	0.7	1.3	1.7
Consumption [6]	Mil. sh. tons . . .	41.3	27.8	25.8	23.2	19.6	19.4	22.5	18.2

NA Not available.   [1] Includes bituminous coal, subbituminous coal, lignite, and anthracite.   [2] Beginning 2002, includes a small amount of refuse recovery.   [3] Coal values are based on free-on-board rail/barge prices, which are the free-on-board prices of coal at the point of first sale, excluding freight or shipping and insurance costs.   [4] Includes subbituminous.   [5] Includes some categories not shown separately.   [6] Consumption is calculated as the sum of production and imports minus exports and stock change.

Source: U.S. Energy Information Administration, *Annual Energy Review*, *International Energy Annual*, and *Annual Coal Report*.

Table 885. Demonstrated Coal Reserves by Major Producing State: 2004 and 2005

[In millions of short tons (494,450 represents 494,450,000,000). As of January 1. The demonstrated reserve base represents the sum of coal in both measured and indicated resource categories of reliability. Measured resources of coal are estimates that have a high degree of geologic assurance from sample analyses and measurements from closely spaced and geological well known sample sites. Indicated resources are estimates based partly from sample and analyses and measurements and partly from reasonable geologic projections]

State	2004 Total reserves	2004 Under-ground	2004 Surface	2005 Total reserves	2005 Under-ground	2005 Surface
United States [1]	494,450	335,468	158,982	492,935	334,876	158,059
Alabama...................	4,242	1,034	3,208	4,205	1,007	3,198
Alaska	6,112	5,423	689	6,110	5,423	687
Colorado..................	16,293	11,529	4,764	16,223	11,461	4,762
Illinois	104,529	87,972	16,557	104,469	87,919	16,550
Indiana...................	9,534	8,764	771	9,483	8,741	742
Iowa	2,189	1,732	457	2,189	1,732	457
Kentucky	30,225	17,202	13,023	30,020	17,055	12,965
Kentucky, Eastern............	10,671	1,282	9,389	10,516	1,178	9,337
Kentucky, Western	19,554	15,920	3,634	19,504	15,877	3,628
Missouri	5,990	1,479	4,511	5,989	1,479	4,510
Montana..................	119,280	70,958	48,322	119,230	70,958	48,272
New Mexico	12,172	6,171	6,001	12,131	6,156	5,975
North Dakota...............	9,090	–	9,090	9,053	–	9,053
Ohio	23,342	17,577	5,765	23,300	17,546	5,754
Oklahoma.................	1,557	1,232	325	1,554	1,231	323
Pennsylvania..............	27,597	23,330	4,267	27,472	23,221	4,251
Anthracite	7,200	3,844	3,356	7,198	3,844	3,355
Bituminous	20,397	19,486	911	20,274	19,377	896
Texas....................	12,442	–	12,442	12,385	–	12,385
Utah	5,445	5,177	268	5,396	5,128	268
Virginia...................	1,740	1,163	576	1,693	1,130	562
Washington................	1,341	1,332	8	1,340	1,332	8
West Virginia...............	33,220	29,366	3,854	32,960	29,184	3,775
Wyoming	64,325	42,501	21,824	63,819	42,500	21,319

– Represents or rounds to zero.   NA Not available.   [1] Includes other states not shown separately.

Source: U.S. Energy Information Administration, *Annual Coal Report*, 2005. See also <http://www.eia.doe.gov/cneaf/coal/page/acr /acr_sum.html>.

Table 886. Uranium Concentrate (U$_3$O$_8$) Industry—Summary: 1990 to 2006

[In millions of feet (1.7 represents 1,700,000), except as indicated. See also Table 908 in Section 19]

Item	Unit	1990	1995	2000	2001	2002	2003	2004	2005	2006 [1]
Exploration and development, surface drilling............	Mil. ft........	1.7	1.3	1.0	0.7	(D)	(D)	1.2	1.7	2.7
Expenditures	Mil. dol.......	(NA)	2.6	5.6	2.7	(D)	(D)	10.6	18.1	40.1
Number of mines operated.....	Number......	39	12	10	7	6	4	6	10	11
Underground	Number......	27	–	1	–	–	1	2	4	5
Openpit	Number......	2	–	–	–	–	–	–	–	–
In situ leaching	Number......	7	5	4	3	3	2	3	4	5
Other sources...........	Number......	3	7	5	4	3	1	1	2	1
Mine production	1,000 pounds ..	5,876	3,528	3,123	2,647	2,405	2,200	2,452	3,045	4,692
Underground	1,000 pounds ..	(D)	–	(D)	(D)	(D)	(D)	(D)	(D)	(D)
Openpit	1,000 pounds ..	1,881	–	–	–	–	–	–	–	–
In situ leaching	1,000 pounds ..	(D)	3,372	2,995	(D)	(D)	(D)	(D)	2,681	4,259
Other sources...........	1,000 pounds ..	3,995	156	128	(D)	(D)	(D)	(D)	(D)	(D)
Uranium concentrate production .	1,000 pounds ..	8,886	6,043	3,958	2,639	2,344	2,000	2,282	2,689	4,106
Concentrate shipments from mills and plants...........	1,000 pounds ..	12,957	5,500	3,187	2,203	3,810	1,600	2,280	2,702	3,838
Employment..............	Person-years ..	1,335	1,107	627	423	426	321	420	648	755

– Represents zero.   D Data withheld to avoid disclosing figures for individual companies.   NA Not available.   [1] Preliminary.

Source: U.S. Department of Energy, through 2002, *Uranium Industry*, annual. Thereafter, *Domestic Uranium Production Report*, annual. See also <http://www.eia.doe.gov/cneaf/nuclear/dupr/dupr.html>.

Section 19
Energy and Utilities

This section presents statistics on fuel resources, energy production and consumption, electric energy, hydroelectric power, nuclear power, solar energy, wood energy, and the electric and gas utility industries. The principal sources are the U.S. Department of Energy's Energy Information Administration (EIA), the Edison Electric Institute, Washington, DC, and the American Gas Association, Arlington, VA. The Department of Energy was created in October 1977 and assumed and centralized the responsibilities of all or part of several agencies including the Federal Power Commission (FPC), the U.S. Bureau of Mines, the Federal Energy Administration, and the U.S. Energy Research and Development Administration. For additional data on transportation, see Section 23; on fuels, see Section 18; and on energy-related housing characteristics, see Section 20.

The EIA, in its *Annual Energy Review,* provides statistics and trend data on energy supply, demand, and prices. Information is included on petroleum and natural gas, coal, electricity, hydroelectric power, nuclear power, solar, wood, and geothermal energy. Among its annual reports are *Annual Energy Review, Electric Power Annual, Natural Gas Annual, Petroleum Supply Annual, State Energy Data Report, State Energy Price and Expenditure Report, Performance Profiles of Major Energy Producers, Annual Energy Outlook,* and *International Energy Annual.* These various publications contain state, national, and international data on production of electricity, net summer capability of generating plants, fuels used in energy production, energy sales and consumption, and hydroelectric power. The EIA also issues the *Monthly Energy Review,* which presents current supply, disposition, and price data and monthly publications on petroleum, coal, natural gas, and electric power. Data on residential energy consumption, expenditures, and conservation activities are available from EIA's Residential Energy Consumption Survey and are published every 4 years.

The Edison Electric Institute's monthly bulletin and annual *Statistical Year Book of the Electric Utility Industry for the Year* contain data on the distribution of electric energy by public utilities; information on the electric power supply, expansion of electric generating facilities, and the manufacture of heavy electric power equipment is presented in the annual *Year-End Summary of the Electric Power Situation in the United States.* The American Gas Association, in its monthly and quarterly bulletins and its yearbook, *Gas Facts,* presents data on gas utilities and financial and operating statistics.

Btu conversion factors—Various energy sources are converted from original units to the thermal equivalent using British thermal units (Btu). A Btu is the amount of energy required to raise the temperature of 1 pound of water 1 degree Fahrenheit (F) at or near 39.2 degrees F. Factors are calculated annually from the latest final annual data available; some are revised as a result. The following list provides conversion factors used in 2006 for production and consumption, in that order, for various fuels: Petroleum, 5.800 and 5.352 mil. Btu per barrel; total coal, 20.333 and 20.204 mil. Btu per short ton; and natural gas (dry), 1,029 Btu per cubic foot for both. The factors for the production of nuclear power and geothermal power were 10,427 and 21,017 Btu per kilowatt-hour, respectively. The fossil fuel steam-electric power plant generation factor of 10,022 Btu per kilowatt-hour was used for hydroelectric power generation and for wood and waste, wind, photovoltaic, and solar thermal energy consumed at electric utilities.

In the past few years, EIA has restructured the industry categories it once used to gather and report electricity statistics. The electric power industry, previously divided into electric utilities and non-utilities, now consists of the Electric Power Sector, the Commercial Sector, and the Industrial Sector.

The Electric Power Sector is composed of electricity-only and combined-heat-and-power plants (CHPs) whose primary business is to sell electricity, or electricity and heat, to the public.

Electricity-only plants are composed of traditional electric utilities, and nontraditional participants, including energy service providers, power marketers, independent power producers (IPPs), and the portion of CHPs that produce only electricity.

A utility is defined as a corporation, person, agency, authority, or other legal entity or instrumentality aligned with distribution facilities for delivery of electric energy for use primarily by the public. Electric utilities include investor-owned electric utilities, municipal and state utilities, federal electric utilities, and rural electric cooperatives. In total, there are more than 3,100 electric utilities in the United States.

An independent power producer is an entity defined as a corporation, person, agency, authority, or other legal entity or instrumentality that owns or operates facilities whose primary business is to produce electricity for use by the public. They are not generally aligned with distribution facilities and are not considered electric utilities.

Combined-heat-and-power producers are plants designed to produce both heat and electricity from a single heat source. These types of electricity producers can be independent power producers or industrial or commercial establishments. As some independent power producers are CHPs, their information is included in the data for the combined-heat-and-power sector. There are approximately 2,800 unregulated independent power producers and CHPs in the United States.

The Commercial Sector consists of commercial CHPs and commercial electricity-only plants. Industrial CHPs and industrial electricity-only plants make up the Industrial Sector. For more information, please refer to the *Electric Power Annual 2005* Web site located at <http://www.eia.doe.gov/cneaf/electricity/epa/epa_sum.html>.

U.S. Census Bureau, Statistical Abstract of the United States: 2008

Table 887. Utilities—Establishments, Revenue, Payroll, and Employees by Kind of Business: 2002

[398,907 represents $398,907,000,000. Includes only establishments or firms with payroll. Data based on the 2002 Economic Census. See headnote, Table 733 and Appendix III]

Kind of business	2002 NAICS code [1]	Establish- ments (number)	Revenue Total (mil. dol.)	Revenue Per paid employee (dol.)	Annual payroll Total (mil. dol.)	Annual payroll Per paid employee (dol.)	Paid employees for pay period including March 12 (number)
Utilities.	22	17,103	398,907	601,630	42,418	63,974	663,044
Electric power generation, transmission, & distribution	2211	9,394	325,028	606,764	35,560	66,383	535,675
Electric power generation	22111	1,997	79,432	646,917	9,062	73,801	122,785
Hydroelectric power generation	221111	371	2,729	429,013	369	58,008	6,360
Fossil fuel electric power generation. . .	221112	1,245	56,048	776,734	5,233	72,524	72,159
Nuclear electric power generation	221113	73	12,032	383,845	2,493	79,513	31,347
Other electric power generation.	221119	308	8,622	667,421	967	74,853	12,919
Electric power transmission, control & distribution	22112	7,397	245,597	594,824	26,498	64,178	412,890
Electric bulk power transmission & control	221121	72	1,588	552,587	195	67,710	2,874
Electric power distribution.	221122	7,325	244,009	595,120	26,304	64,153	410,016
Natural gas distribution.	2212	2,376	66,515	778,438	5,370	62,844	85,447
Water, sewage, & other systems	2213	5,333	7,363	175,647	1,488	35,496	41,922
Water supply & irrigation systems	22131	4,603	5,886	169,722	1,220	35,184	34,682
Sewage treatment facilities	22132	667	832	147,425	181	32,099	5,643
Steam & air-conditioning supply	22133	63	645	404,050	87	54,272	1,597

[1] North American Industry Classification System, 2002; see text, Section 15.

Source: U.S. Census Bureau, *2002 Economic Census*, Series EC02-22A-1US, issued August 2005. See also <http://www.census.gov/econ/census02/>.

Table 888. Private Utilities—Employees, Annual Payroll, and Establishments by Industry: 2004

[44,766 represents 44,766,000,000. Excludes government employees, railroad employees, self-employed persons, etc. An establishment is a single physical location where business is conducted or where services or industrial operations are performed. See Appendix III]

Year and industry	2002 NAICS code [1]	Number of employ- ees [2]	Annual payroll (mil. dol.)	Aver- age payroll per em- ployee (dol.)	Establishment by employment size-class Total	Establishment by employment size-class Under 20 em- ployees	Establishment by employment size-class 20 to 99 em- ployees	Establishment by employment size-class 100 to 499 em- ployees	Establishment by employment size-class 500 and over employ- ees
Utilities, total	22	634,734	44,766	70,527	17,675	12,511	3,803	1,187	174
Electric power generation, transmission and distribution	2211	510,598	37,648	73,732	9,743	5,688	2,933	962	160
Electric power generation.	22111	124,256	9,717	78,201	2,249	1,385	591	230	43
Hydroelectric power generation. . . .	221111	6,130	449	73,209	396	325	59	12	–
Fossil fuel electric power generation.	221112	77,673	5,830	75,061	1,424	794	423	197	10
Nuclear electric power generation . .	221113	30,223	2,690	89,013	71	21	13	7	30
Other electric power generation . . .	221119	10,230	748	73,094	358	245	96	14	3
Electric power transmission, control & distribution.	22112	386,342	27,931	72,295	7,494	4,303	2,342	732	117
Electric bulk power transmission & control.	221121	5,501	419	76,210	101	60	24	15	2
Electric power distribution	221122	380,841	27,511	72,239	7,393	4,243	2,318	717	115
Natural gas distribution	2212	81,466	5,430	66,649	2,513	1,757	566	178	12
Water, sewage, & other systems	2213	42,670	1,689	39,574	5,419	5,066	304	47	2
Water supply & irrigation systems. . . .	22131	35,271	1,395	39,562	4,600	4,334	220	45	1
Sewage treatment facilities	22132	5,934	212	35,663	731	667	61	2	1
Steam & air-conditioning supply	22133	1,465	82	55,688	88	65	23	–	–

– Represents zero. [1] North American Industry Classification System, 2002, see text, Section 15. [2] Covers full- and part-time employees who are on the payroll in the pay period including March 12.

Source: U.S. Census Bureau, "County Business Patterns"; <http://www.census.gov/epcd/cbp/view/cbpview.html> (released June 2006).

Energy and Utilities **573**

Table 889. Energy Supply and Disposition by Type of Fuel: 1960 to 2005

[In quadrillion British thermal units (Btu) (42.80 represents 42,800,000,000,000,000). For definition of Btu, see source and text, this section]

Year	Production Total[1]	Crude oil[2]	Natural gas	Coal	Nuclear power	Renewable Total[1]	Hydro-electric power[3]	biofuel[4]	Solar energy	Net imports total[5]	Consumption Total[1]	Petro-leum[6,7]	Natural gas[8]	Coal	Nuclear power	Renewable energy[3] total
1960	42.80	14.93	12.66	10.82	0.01	2.93	1.61	1.32	(NA)	2.71	45.09	19.92	12.39	9.84	0.01	2.93
1970	63.50	20.40	21.67	14.61	0.24	4.08	2.63	1.43	(NA)	5.71	67.84	29.52	21.79	12.26	0.24	4.08
1975	61.36	17.73	19.64	14.99	1.90	4.72	3.15	1.50	(NA)	11.71	72.00	32.73	19.95	12.66	1.90	4.72
1976	61.60	17.26	19.48	15.65	2.11	4.77	2.98	1.71	(NA)	14.59	76.01	35.17	20.35	13.58	2.11	4.77
1977	62.05	17.45	19.57	15.75	2.70	4.25	2.33	1.84	(NA)	17.90	78.00	37.12	19.93	13.92	2.70	4.25
1978	63.14	18.43	19.49	14.91	3.02	5.04	2.94	2.04	(NA)	17.19	79.99	37.97	20.00	13.77	3.02	5.04
1979	65.95	18.10	20.08	17.54	2.78	5.17	2.93	2.15	(NA)	16.60	80.90	37.12	20.67	15.04	2.78	5.17
1980	67.23	18.25	19.91	18.60	2.74	5.49	2.90	2.48	(NA)	12.10	78.28	34.20	20.39	15.42	2.74	5.49
1981	67.01	18.15	19.70	18.38	3.01	5.47	2.76	2.59	(NA)	9.41	76.34	31.93	19.93	15.91	3.01	5.47
1982	66.61	18.31	18.32	18.64	3.13	6.02	3.27	2.65	(NA)	7.25	73.29	30.23	18.51	15.32	3.13	6.02
1983	64.15	18.39	16.59	17.25	3.20	6.53	3.53	2.88	(NA)	8.06	73.15	30.05	17.36	15.89	3.20	6.53
1984	68.89	18.85	18.01	19.72	3.55	6.49	3.39	2.94	(Z)	8.68	76.79	31.05	18.51	17.07	3.55	6.49
1985	67.76	18.99	16.98	19.33	4.08	6.14	2.97	2.98	(Z)	7.58	76.58	30.92	17.83	17.48	4.08	6.14
1986	67.13	18.38	16.54	19.51	4.38	6.18	3.07	2.88	(Z)	10.13	76.83	32.20	16.71	17.26	4.38	6.18
1987	67.61	17.67	17.14	20.14	4.75	5.68	2.63	2.82	(Z)	11.59	79.22	32.87	17.74	18.01	4.75	5.68
1988	68.98	17.28	17.60	20.74	5.59	5.51	2.33	2.96	(Z)	12.93	82.87	34.22	18.55	18.85	5.59	5.51
1989 [9]	69.41	16.12	17.85	21.35	5.60	6.34	2.84	3.10	0.06	14.11	85.00	34.21	19.71	19.07	5.60	6.34
1990	70.79	15.57	18.33	22.46	6.10	6.16	3.05	2.69	0.06	14.06	84.73	33.55	19.73	19.17	6.10	6.16
1991	70.43	15.70	18.23	21.59	6.42	6.18	3.02	2.73	0.06	13.19	84.67	32.85	20.15	18.99	6.42	6.18
1992	70.00	15.22	18.38	21.63	6.48	5.93	2.62	2.87	0.06	14.44	86.01	33.53	20.84	19.12	6.48	5.93
1993	68.33	14.49	18.58	20.25	6.41	6.19	2.89	2.84	0.07	17.01	87.65	33.84	21.35	19.84	6.41	6.19
1994	70.72	14.10	19.35	22.11	6.69	6.07	2.68	2.95	0.07	18.33	89.29	34.67	21.84	19.91	6.69	6.07
1995	71.13	13.89	19.08	22.03	7.08	6.62	3.21	3.02	0.07	17.75	91.20	34.55	22.78	20.09	7.08	6.62
1996	72.47	13.72	19.34	22.68	7.09	7.11	3.59	3.10	0.07	19.07	94.23	35.76	23.20	21.00	7.09	7.11
1997	72.46	13.66	19.39	23.21	6.60	7.11	3.64	3.04	0.07	20.70	94.80	36.27	23.33	21.45	6.60	7.11
1998	72.84	13.24	19.61	23.94	7.07	6.57	3.30	2.84	0.07	22.28	95.20	36.93	22.94	21.66	7.07	6.57
1999	71.71	12.45	19.34	23.19	7.61	6.60	3.27	2.89	0.07	23.54	96.84	37.96	23.01	21.62	7.61	6.60
2000	71.29	12.36	19.66	22.62	7.86	6.17	2.81	2.92	0.07	24.97	98.98	38.40	23.92	22.58	7.86	6.17
2001	71.91	12.28	20.20	23.49	8.03	5.35	2.24	2.67	0.07	26.39	96.50	38.33	22.91	21.91	8.03	5.35
2002	70.86	12.16	19.44	22.62	8.14	5.93	2.69	2.75	0.06	25.74	97.97	38.40	23.63	21.90	8.14	5.93
2003	70.14	12.03	19.69	21.97	7.96	6.14	2.82	2.81	0.06	27.01	98.27	39.05	22.97	22.32	7.96	6.14
2004	70.39	11.50	19.26	22.71	8.22	6.22	2.69	2.98	0.06	29.11	100.41	40.59	23.04	22.47	8.22	6.22
2005 [10]	69.17	10.84	18.76	23.05	8.13	6.06	2.71	2.78	0.06	29.62	99.89	40.44	22.64	22.83	8.13	6.06

NA Not available. Z Less than 5 trillion. [1] Includes types of fuel not shown separately. [2] Includes lease condensate. [3] Electricity net generation from conventional hydroelectric power, geothermal, solar, and wind; consumption of wood, waste, and alcohol fuels; geothermal heat pump and direct use energy; and solar thermal direct use energy. [4] Wood, waste, and alcohol (ethanol blended into motor gasoline). [5] Imports minus exports. [6] Beginning in 1993, ethanol blended into motor gasoline is included in petroleum. [7] Petroleum products supplied, including natural gas plant liquids and crude oil burned as fuel. [8] Includes supplemental gaseous fuels. [9] There is a discontinuity in this time series between 1989 and 1990. [10] Preliminary.

Source: U.S. Energy Information Administration, Annual Energy Review, 2005. See also <http://www.eia.doe.gov/emeu/aer/overview.html> (released 27 July 2006).

Table 890. Energy Supply and Disposition by Type of Fuel— Estimates, 2004 and 2005, and Projections, 2006 to 2020

[Quadrillion Btu (70.98 represents 70,980,000,000,000,000) per year. Btu = British thermal unit. For definition of Btu, see source and text, this section. Mcf = 1,000 cubic feet. Projections are "reference" or mid-level forecasts. See report for methodology and assumptions used in generating projections]

Type of fuel	2004	2005	Projections			
			2006	2010	2015	2020
Production, total	70.98	69.80	71.09	76.13	79.12	82.09
Crude oil and lease condensate	11.58	10.96	10.79	11.99	12.52	12.48
Natural gas plant liquids	2.46	2.33	2.36	2.43	2.45	2.38
Natural gas, dry	19.32	18.77	19.13	19.93	20.19	21.41
Coal	22.85	23.20	23.77	24.47	25.74	26.61
Nuclear power	8.22	8.13	8.20	8.23	8.47	9.23
Renewable energy [1]	6.26	6.18	6.80	8.42	8.78	9.10
Other [2]	0.29	0.22	0.04	0.67	0.98	0.89
Imports, total	33.30	34.52	34.39	34.18	36.97	39.66
Crude oil [3]	22.02	22.09	22.01	21.88	22.96	24.72
Petroleum products [4]	6.11	7.16	7.35	6.02	6.56	7.05
Natural gas	4.36	4.42	4.12	5.36	6.43	6.17
Other imports [5]	0.82	0.85	0.90	0.92	1.02	1.73
Exports, total	4.19	4.33	4.61	4.52	4.39	4.33
Petroleum [6]	2.07	2.31	2.73	2.71	2.77	2.84
Natural gas	0.87	0.75	0.74	0.69	0.66	0.69
Coal	1.25	1.27	1.14	1.12	0.96	0.80
Consumption, total	100.67	100.19	100.75	106.50	112.28	118.16
Petroleum products [7]	40.79	40.61	40.57	41.76	44.26	46.52
Natural gas	23.05	22.63	22.37	24.73	26.07	27.04
Coal	22.60	22.87	23.14	24.24	25.64	27.29
Nuclear power	8.22	8.13	8.20	8.23	8.47	9.23
Renewable energy [1], other [8]	6.02	5.93	6.47	7.54	7.84	8.09
Net imports of petroleum	26.06	26.94	26.63	25.19	26.75	28.92
Prices (2004 dollars per unit):						
Imported crude oil price [9]	37.09	49.19	61.75	51.20	44.61	46.47
Gas wellhead price (dol. per mcf) [10]	5.80	7.51	6.67	5.76	4.99	5.22
Coal minemouth price (dol. per ton)	20.68	23.34	24.02	24.20	22.41	21.58
Average electric price (cents per kWh)	7.85	8.10	8.32	8.07	7.69	7.90

[1] Includes grid-connected electricity from conventional hydroelectric; wood and wood waste; landfill gas; municipal solid waste; other biomass; wind; photovoltaic and solar thermal sources; nonelectric energy from renewable sources, such as active and passive solar systems, and wood. Excludes electricity imports using renewable sources and nonmarketed renewable energy. [2] Includes liquid hydrogen, methanol, and some domestic inputs to refineries. [3] Includes imports of crude oil for the Strategic Petroleum Reserve. [4] Includes imports of finished petroleum products, imports of unfinished oils, alcohols, ethers, blending components, and renewable fuels such as ethanol. [5] Includes coal, coal coke (net), and electricity (net). [6] Includes crude oil and petroleum products. [7] Includes petroleum-derived fuels and non-petroleum-derived fuels, such as ethanol and biodiesel. Petroleum coke, which is a solid, is included. Also included are natural gas plant liquids, crude oil consumed as a fuel, and liquid hydrogen. [8] Includes net electricity imports and natural gas losses. [9] Weighted average price delivered to U.S. refiners. [10] Represents lower 48 onshore and offshore supplies.

Source: U.S. Energy Information Administration, *Annual Energy Outlook 2007*. See also <http://www.eia.doe.gov/oiaf/aeo/excel /aeotab_1.xls> (released February 2007).

Table 891. Energy Consumption by End-Use Sector: 1970 to 2005

[67.84 represents 67,840,000,000,000,000 Btu. Btu = British thermal units. For definition of Btu, see source and text, this section. See Appendix III]

Year	Total (quad. Btu)	Residential and commercial [1] (quad. Btu)	Industrial [2] (quad. Btu)	Transportation (quad. Btu)	Percent of total		
					Residential and commercial [1]	Industrial [2]	Transportation
1970	67.84	22.11	29.64	16.10	32.6	43.7	23.7
1975	72.00	24.31	29.45	18.24	33.8	40.9	25.3
1980	78.28	26.43	32.15	19.70	33.8	41.1	25.2
1985	76.58	27.60	28.89	20.09	36.0	37.7	26.2
1990	84.73	30.41	31.90	22.42	35.9	37.7	26.5
1995	91.20	33.34	34.01	23.85	36.6	37.3	26.1
1997	94.80	34.79	35.26	24.75	36.7	37.2	26.1
1998	95.20	35.05	34.89	25.26	36.8	36.6	26.5
1999	96.84	36.07	34.81	25.95	37.2	35.9	26.8
2000	98.98	37.72	34.70	26.55	38.1	35.1	26.8
2001	96.50	37.51	32.71	26.27	38.9	33.9	27.2
2002	97.97	38.40	32.72	26.85	39.2	33.4	27.4
2003	98.27	38.64	32.61	27.02	39.3	33.2	27.5
2004	100.41	39.02	33.44	27.95	38.9	33.3	27.8
2005 [3]	99.89	39.84	31.98	28.06	39.9	32.0	28.1

[1] Commercial sector fuel use, including that at commercial combined-heat-and-power (CHP) and industrial electricity-only plants. [2] Industrial sector fuel use, including that at industrial combined-heat-and-power (CHP) and industrial electricity-only plants. [3] Preliminary.

Source: U.S. Energy Information Administration, *Annual Energy Review 2005*. See also <http://www.eia.doe.gov/emeu/aer/pdf/pages /sec2_4.pdf> (released 27 July 2006).

Table 892. Energy Consumption—End-Use Sector and Selected Source, by State: 2003

[In trillions of Btu (98,605 represents 98,605,000,000,000,000), except as indicated. For definition of Btu, see source and text, this section. Data are preliminary]

State	Total [1]	Per capita [2] (mil. Btu)	End-use sector [3] Resi-dential	End-use sector [3] Com-mercial	End-use sector [3] Indus-trial [1]	End-use sector [3] Trans-por-tation	Source Petro-leum	Source Natural gas (dry) [4]	Source Coal	Source Hydro electric power [5]	Source Nuclear electric power
United States..	98,605	339	21,251	17,475	32,795	27,084	39,051	23,293	22,324	2,825	7,959
Alabama.........	2,014	447	385	259	915	455	580	351	874	130	330
Alaska	762	1,175	53	58	432	219	284	446	13	16	–
Arizona.........	1,371	246	354	317	203	498	537	275	407	73	298
Arkansas	1,133	416	221	156	473	283	377	259	254	27	153
California	8,130	229	1,469	1,484	1,903	3,275	3,837	2,267	70	373	371
Colorado........	1,352	297	317	290	368	376	463	438	394	13	–
Connecticut......	889	255	295	220	125	248	436	155	42	6	168
Delaware	313	383	69	56	121	67	148	48	47	–	–
District of Columbia	184	329	38	116	5	25	30	34	(Z)	–	–
Florida	4,288	252	1,306	1,017	570	1,394	1,940	720	724	3	323
Georgia	3,004	343	689	508	924	883	1,058	396	819	42	347
Hawaii	310	248	36	42	68	164	270	3	19	1	–
Idaho..........	467	341	103	76	171	116	139	71	10	86	–
Illinois	3,918	310	985	778	1,207	948	1,313	1,000	1,021	1	987
Indiana.........	2,913	470	538	368	1,341	666	901	542	1,571	4	–
Iowa	1,176	400	240	195	461	280	393	232	445	8	42
Kansas.........	1,118	410	226	198	410	285	434	293	390	(Z)	93
Kentucky	1,877	456	354	249	830	445	664	230	943	40	–
Louisiana	3,693	822	371	283	2,271	768	1,610	1,360	248	9	168
Maine..........	479	366	116	79	154	130	262	75	8	33	–
Maryland	1,551	281	428	280	428	415	561	203	330	27	143
Massachusetts.....	1,589	248	486	407	249	447	734	471	109	11	52
Michigan........	3,158	313	839	604	925	790	1,010	923	753	14	291
Minnesota.......	1,796	355	410	345	529	512	694	375	391	8	140
Mississippi	1,184	411	232	166	413	372	484	266	179	–	114
Missouri	1,842	322	498	388	366	590	737	267	796	7	101
Montana........	376	410	74	66	134	102	161	68	189	89	–
Nebraska	646	372	150	127	198	171	231	119	227	10	83
Nevada	654	292	153	117	170	214	242	190	183	18	–
New Hampshire....	328	254	97	72	53	106	198	55	42	14	97
New Jersey......	2,578	298	634	595	484	867	1,233	639	107	(Z)	310
New Mexico.....	663	353	102	120	212	229	250	234	306	2	–
New York	4,221	220	1,235	1,353	544	1,088	1,776	1,179	304	249	424
North Carolina....	2,644	314	676	535	721	711	947	228	772	74	426
North Dakota.....	395	624	63	58	186	88	121	59	421	18	–
Ohio	3,986	349	960	701	1,339	987	1,340	872	1,428	5	88
Oklahoma........	1,491	425	302	228	520	441	545	558	394	18	–
Oregon.........	1,049	295	259	205	279	307	370	220	45	341	–
Pennsylvania......	3,973	321	998	701	1,286	988	1,466	730	1,444	34	775
Rhode Island.....	228	212	79	59	26	64	102	81	(Z)	(Z)	–
South Carolina.....	1,614	389	337	243	642	392	517	147	420	38	525
South Dakota	264	345	64	54	62	85	113	45	43	44	–
Tennessee	2,269	388	508	374	762	626	782	268	621	123	252
Texas...........	12,370	560	1,624	1,345	6,706	2,694	5,628	4,553	1,604	9	349
Utah	705	296	142	138	203	223	276	163	379	4	–
Vermont	156	252	47	31	26	52	86	9	(Z)	12	46
Virginia.........	2,429	329	598	557	561	712	965	272	460	18	259
Washington.......	1,935	316	464	371	517	583	793	255	118	735	79
West Virginia......	784	433	159	109	347	169	255	134	983	14	–
Wisconsin........	1,833	335	429	329	656	418	597	398	488	19	127
Wyoming	461	919	41	51	250	119	162	121	494	6	–

– Represents zero. Z Less than .5 trillion Btu. [1] U.S. total energy and U.S. industrial sector include 50.5 trillion Btu of net imports of coal coke that is not allocated to the states. [2] Based on estimated resident population as of July 1. [3] End-use sector data include electricity sales and associated electrical system energy losses. [4] Includes supplemental gaseous fuels. [5] Conventional hydroelectric power. Does not include pumped-storage hydroelectricity. A negative number in this column results from pumped storage for which, overall, more electricity is expended than created to provide electricity during peak demand periods.

Source: U.S. Energy Information Administration, State Energy Data, 2003. See also <http://www.eia.doe.gov/emeu/states /_seds.html> (released 24 October 2006).

Table 893. **Commercial Buildings—Energy Consumption and Expenditures: 2003**

[4,645 represents 4,645,000. Covers buildings using one or more major fuel. Excludes industrial buildings, predominantly residential buildings, and buildings of less than 1,000 sq. ft. Based on a sample survey of building representatives and energy suppliers; therefore, subject to sampling variability. For characteristics of commercial buildings, see Table 968 in Section 20. For composition of regions, see inside front cover]

Building characteristic	All buildings using any major fuel		Consumption (tril. Btu)			Expenditures (mil. dol.)		
	Number (1,000)	Square feet (mil.)	Major fuel, total [1]	Electricity	Natural gas	Major fuel, total [1]	Electricity	Natural gas
All buildings	**4,645**	**64,783**	**5,820**	**3,037**	**1,928**	**92,577**	**69,032**	**14,525**
Region:								
Northeast	726	12,905	1,271	503	428	21,344	14,262	3,553
Midwest	1,266	17,080	1,690	737	705	21,521	14,172	4,844
South	1,775	23,489	1,948	1,278	474	31,595	25,540	3,866
West......................	878	11,310	911	519	320	18,118	15,057	2,261
Year constructed:								
1919 or before	330	3,769	302	90	143	4,131	2,319	1,134
1920 to 1945	527	6,871	620	208	229	8,670	5,123	1,708
1946 to 1959	562	7,045	565	231	216	8,540	5,729	1,610
1960 to 1969	579	8,101	737	327	255	11,378	7,714	1,872
1970 to 1979	731	10,772	1,023	572	351	16,129	12,637	2,466
1980 to 1989	707	10,332	1,034	627	291	17,346	13,902	2,270
1990 to 1999	876	12,360	1,098	690	314	18,761	15,236	2,452
Principal activity within building:								
Education	386	9,874	820	371	268	12,008	8,111	1,889
Food sales	226	1,255	251	208	39	4,990	4,627	332
Food service	297	1,654	427	217	203	6,865	5,176	1,615
Health care	129	3,163	594	248	243	7,440	4,882	1,538
Inpatient	8	1,905	475	178	204	5,329	3,198	1,241
Outpatient	121	1,258	119	69	38	2,111	1,684	297
Lodging..................	142	5,096	510	235	215	7,445	5,288	1,581
Retail (other than mall).........	443	4,317	319	211	91	5,980	5,132	719
Office	824	12,208	1,134	719	269	20,841	17,050	2,201
Public assembly	277	3,939	370	167	102	5,790	3,943	775
Public order and safety	71	1,090	126	57	29	1,917	1,216	234
Religious worship	370	3,754	163	62	82	2,457	1,628	664
Service	622	4,050	312	149	139	4,779	3,485	1,096
Warehouse and storage........	597	10,078	456	244	132	6,894	5,034	976
Other	79	1,738	286	133	87	4,420	3,049	684
Vacant	182	2,567	54	15	28	751	412	220
Square footage:								
1,001 to 5,000	2,552	6,789	672	386	250	12,812	10,348	2,155
5,001 to 10,000	889	6,585	516	262	209	9,398	7,296	1,689
10,001 to 25,000	738	11,535	776	407	309	13,140	10,001	2,524
25,001 to 50,000	241	8,668	673	350	258	10,392	7,871	1,865
50,001 to 100,000..........	129	9,057	759	405	244	11,897	8,717	1,868
100,001 to 200,000............	65	9,064	934	483	249	13,391	9,500	1,737
200,001 to 500,000...........	25	7,176	725	361	205	10,347	7,323	1,343
500,001 and over	7	5,908	766	383	204	11,201	7,977	1,344

[1] Includes fuel oil, propane, and purchased steam not shown separately.

Source: U.S. Energy Information Administration, *Commercial Buildings Energy Survey: Consumption and Expenditures, 2003.* See also <http://www.eia.doe.gov/emeu/cbecs/cbecs2003/detailed_tables_2003/detailed_tables_2003.html> (released December 2006).

Table 894. **Fossil Fuel Prices by Type of Fuel: 1990 to 2005**

[In dollars per million British thermal units (Btu), except as indicated. For definition of Btu and mineral fuel conversions, see source and text, this section. All fuel prices taken as close to the point of production as possible]

Fuel	Current dollars					Constant (2000) dollars				
	1990	1995	2000	2004	2005 [1]	1990	1995	2000	2004	2005 [1]
Composite [2]...	1.84	1.47	2.60	3.62	4.81	2.26	1.60	2.60	3.32	4.29
Crude oil [3] . ,....	3.45	2.52	4.61	6.34	8.67	4.23	2.74	4.61	5.81	7.73
Natural gas [4]	1.55	1.40	3.32	4.95	6.80	1.90	1.52	3.32	4.53	6.06
Coal [5]	1.00	0.88	0.80	0.98	1.19	1.22	0.96	0.80	0.89	1.06

[1] Preliminary. [2] Derived by multiplying the price per Btu of each fossil fuel by the total Btu content of the production of each fossil fuel and dividing this accumulated value of total fossil fuel production by the accumulated Btu content of total fossil fuel production. [3] Domestic first purchase prices. [4] Wellhead prices. [5] Free-on-board (f.o.b.) rail/barge prices, which are the f.o.b. prices of coal at the point of first sale, excluding freight or shipping and insurance costs. Includes bituminous coal, subbituminous coal, and lignite.

Source: U.S. Energy Information Administration, *Annual Energy Review 2005.* See also <http://www.eia.doe.gov/emeu/aer/pdf/pages /sec3_3.pdf> (released 27 July 2006).

Table 895. Energy Expenditures—End-Use Sector and Selected Source, by State: 2003

[In millions of dollars (753,412 represents $753,412,000,000). Data are preliminary. End-use sector and electric utilities exclude expenditures on energy sources such as hydroelectric, photovoltaic, solar thermal, wind, and geothermal. Also excludes expenditures for reported amounts of energy consumed by the energy industry for production, transportation, and processing operations]

State	Total [1]	End-use sector				Source			
		Residential	Commercial	Industrial	Transportation	Petroleum products	Natural gas	Coal	Electricity sales
U.S.	753,412	178,797	129,234	150,110	295,271	379,145	144,434	29,224	257,081
AL.	12,680	2,894	1,723	3,266	4,796	5,817	2,220	1,254	4,825
AK.	2,843	413	383	245	1,802	2,108	261	25	580
AZ.	11,842	2,804	2,093	1,096	5,850	6,329	1,639	525	4,706
AR.	7,591	1,623	878	1,974	3,116	3,846	1,561	312	2,347
CA.	79,565	14,716	15,488	11,355	38,007	40,765	14,986	119	27,481
CO	9,861	2,316	1,724	1,509	4,312	5,062	1,994	383	3,118
CT.	9,212	3,158	2,046	928	3,080	4,875	1,429	79	3,235
DE.	2,267	606	391	495	774	1,179	359	75	871
DC	1,600	363	889	33	316	376	420	(Z)	810
FL.	34,672	10,213	6,813	2,823	14,823	17,914	4,467	1,270	16,774
GA	21,445	5,492	3,277	3,725	8,951	10,338	3,260	1,416	7,778
HI	3,393	560	579	492	1,763	2,288	54	30	1,479
ID	3,162	640	408	716	1,398	1,640	417	18	1,107
IL	30,513	7,965	5,500	6,004	11,045	13,365	7,896	1,228	9,298
IN	18,979	3,991	2,262	5,451	7,275	8,795	4,341	2,103	5,344
IA	8,553	1,975	1,212	2,231	3,135	4,269	1,683	419	2,519
KS.	8,053	1,709	1,257	2,116	2,972	4,319	1,516	395	2,320
KY.	11,513	2,186	1,356	3,182	4,788	6,153	1,554	1,201	3,727
LA	20,173	2,793	2,002	8,752	6,627	10,479	5,743	333	5,270
ME	4,044	1,229	671	543	1,601	2,738	480	16	1,172
MD	12,575	3,526	1,897	2,046	5,106	6,314	1,855	535	4,594
MA	16,400	5,268	3,787	1,891	5,454	7,941	3,860	221	5,862
MI	24,279	6,596	4,155	4,388	9,141	11,481	5,630	1,078	7,409
MN	13,322	3,177	2,171	2,294	5,680	7,012	2,582	429	3,766
MS	8,152	1,749	1,133	1,701	3,569	4,336	1,494	280	2,888
MO	14,463	3,602	2,270	2,065	6,526	7,836	2,224	739	4,472
MT	2,575	542	432	444	1,158	1,449	336	119	779
NE.	4,699	1,022	725	1,044	1,909	2,478	773	141	1,458
NV.	5,758	1,268	912	1,069	2,510	2,736	1,171	255	2,453
NH	3,443	1,054	662	430	1,296	2,061	437	71	1,188
NJ.	22,523	5,867	4,928	2,845	8,884	11,326	4,847	191	7,219
NM	4,419	868	826	568	2,159	2,596	672	437	1,331
NY.	43,407	14,236	13,653	3,327	12,191	17,854	9,902	500	17,920
NC	20,337	5,583	3,458	3,266	8,029	10,112	1,824	1,375	8,329
ND	2,245	429	319	629	868	1,218	243	463	569
OH	31,263	7,840	4,995	7,145	11,283	14,106	6,944	1,745	10,175
OK	10,096	2,211	1,424	2,189	4,272	4,986	2,974	385	3,185
OR	7,960	1,766	1,235	1,290	3,669	4,137	1,306	57	2,796
PA	32,128	9,395	5,525	6,197	11,011	14,818	6,059	1,922	11,184
RI	2,388	843	539	211	795	1,173	676	(Z)	816
SC.	11,102	2,619	1,580	2,631	4,272	5,195	1,153	656	4,684
SD.	2,029	478	317	345	889	1,191	262	59	577
TN.	15,350	3,361	2,424	3,010	6,556	7,665	1,896	800	5,651
TX.	80,710	13,664	9,450	31,819	25,777	44,648	20,163	2,023	23,787
UT.	4,781	933	720	646	2,482	2,781	758	371	1,276
VT.	1,667	528	301	185	653	1,012	66	(Z)	588
VA.	18,173	4,830	3,187	2,283	7,874	9,864	2,229	775	6,342
WA	13,352	2,882	2,138	1,727	6,606	7,378	1,550	171	4,534
WV	4,942	1,047	622	1,423	1,851	2,605	789	1,258	1,439
WI	14,246	3,685	2,234	3,107	5,220	6,711	3,096	589	4,436
WY	2,503	286	267	797	1,154	1,468	387	382	616

Z Less than $500,000.   [1] Includes sources not shown separately, such as electricity imports and exports and coal coke net imports ($169.1 million in 2003, which are not allocated to the states). Total expenditures are the sum of purchases for each source (including electricity sales) less electric utility purchases of fuel.

Source: U.S. Energy Information Administration, *State Energy Data, 2003.* See also <http://www.eia.doe.gov/emeu/states/_seds.html> (released 24 October 2006).

Table 896. **Energy Expenditures and Average Fuel Prices by Source and Sector: 1970 to 2004**

[In millions of dollars (82,911 represents $82,911,000,000), except as indicated. For definition of Btu, see text, this section. End-use sector and electric utilities exclude expenditures and prices on energy sources such as hydropower, solar, wind, and geothermal. Also excludes expenditures for reported amounts of energy consumed by the energy industry for production, transportation, and processing operations]

Source and sector	1970	1980	1985	1990	1995	2000	2001	2002	2003	2004
EXPENDITURES (mil. dol.)										
Total [1]	82,911	374,346	438,184	[5]472,539	514,049	689,199	694,066	661,772	753,397	869,319
Natural gas	10,891	51,061	72,938	65,278	75,020	119,092	139,296	111,415	144,453	163,024
Petroleum products	47,955	237,676	223,928	235,368	236,905	360,751	336,377	320,002	379,145	468,290
Motor gasoline	31,596	124,408	118,048	126,558	136,647	193,947	185,892	179,511	209,597	253,233
Coal	4,630	22,607	29,678	28,602	27,431	28,080	28,202	28,612	29,402	31,764
Electricity sales	23,345	98,095	149,233	176,691	205,876	231,577	245,449	248,357	257,082	268,465
Residential sector [2]	20,213	69,418	99,772	111,097	128,388	156,089	168,504	161,478	178,832	190,734
Commercial sector [3]	10,628	46,932	70,396	79,284	91,788	112,870	125,910	119,916	128,951	137,749
Industrial sector [4]	16,691	94,316	106,518	[5]102,402	107,060	141,536	138,331	128,736	150,342	176,497
Transportation sector	35,379	163,680	161,498	179,757	186,813	278,703	261,322	251,641	295,271	364,337
Motor gasoline	30,525	121,809	115,205	123,845	134,641	191,620	182,122	175,729	204,883	247,139
Electric utilities [2]	4,344	37,838	43,503	40,467	38,755	57,775	62,204	53,496	63,542	70,498
AVERAGE FUEL PRICES (dol. per mil. Btu)										
All sectors	1.65	6.89	8.37	[5]8.25	8.28	10.33	10.73	10.07	11.41	12.91
Residential sector [2]	2.10	7.46	10.91	11.88	12.63	14.27	15.72	14.74	15.82	17.16
Commercial sector [3]	1.98	7.85	11.65	11.89	12.64	13.93	15.62	14.70	15.56	16.55
Industrial sector [4]	0.84	4.71	6.03	[5]5.23	4.97	6.49	6.80	6.28	7.47	8.54
Transportation sector	2.31	8.61	8.27	8.28	8.09	10.78	10.21	9.63	11.21	13.37
Electric utilities [2]	0.32	1.77	1.88	1.48	1.28	1.64	1.78	1.51	1.80	1.96

[1] Includes other sources not shown separately.   [2] There are no direct fuel costs for geothermal, photovoltaic, or solar thermal energy.   [3] There are no direct fuel costs for hydroelectric, geothermal, photovoltaic, or solar thermal energy.   [4] There are no direct fuel costs for hydroelectric, geothermal, wind, photovoltaic, or solar thermal energy.   [5] There is a discontinuity in the total time series and the industrial time series between 1985 and 1990 due to the expanded coverage of nonelectric utility use of wood and waste beginning in 1989.
Source: U.S. Energy Information Administration, *State Energy Data: Prices and Expenditures*, annual. See also <http://www.eia.doe.gov/emeu/states/state.html?q_state_a=us&q_state=UNITED%20STATES> (published 1 June 2007).

Table 897. **Renewable Energy Consumption Estimates by Source: 1995 to 2005**

[In quadrillion Btu (6.62 represents 6,620,000,000,000,000). For definition of Btu, see source and text, this section. Renewable energy is obtained from sources that are essentially inexhaustible unlike fossil fuels of which there is a finite supply]

Source and sector	1995	2000	2001	2002	2003	2004	2005 [1]
Consumption, total	6.62	6.17	5.35	5.93	6.14	6.22	6.06
Conventional hydroelectric power [2]	3.21	2.81	2.24	2.69	2.82	2.69	2.71
Geothermal energy [3]	0.29	0.32	0.31	0.33	0.33	0.34	0.35
Biomass [4]	3.02	2.92	2.67	2.75	2.81	2.98	2.78
Solar energy [5]	0.07	0.07	0.07	0.06	0.06	0.06	0.06
Wind energy [6]	0.03	0.06	0.07	0.11	0.11	0.14	0.15
Residential [7]	0.59	0.50	0.44	0.45	0.47	0.48	0.49
Biomass [4]	0.52	0.43	0.37	0.38	0.40	0.41	0.42
Geothermal [3]	0.01	0.01	0.01	0.01	0.01	0.01	0.02
Solar [5, 8]	0.06	0.06	0.06	0.06	0.06	0.06	0.06
Commercial [9]	0.12	0.13	0.11	0.12	0.13	0.14	0.13
Biomass [4]	0.11	0.12	0.11	0.11	0.12	0.13	0.12
Geothermal [3]	(Z)	0.01	0.01	0.01	0.01	0.01	0.01
Hydroelectric [2]	(Z)	(Z)	(Z)	(Z)	(Z)	(Z)	(Z)
Industrial [10]	1.90	1.83	1.63	1.61	1.58	1.67	1.41
Biomass [4]	1.85	1.78	1.59	1.56	1.53	1.64	1.37
Geothermal [3]	(Z)	(Z)	(Z)	(Z)	(Z)	(Z)	(Z)
Hydroelectric [2]	0.05	0.04	0.03	0.04	0.04	0.03	0.03
Transportation:							
Alcohol fuels [11]	0.12	0.14	0.15	0.17	0.24	0.30	0.34
Electric power [12]	3.89	3.58	3.02	3.58	3.73	3.62	3.69
Biomass [4]	0.42	0.45	0.45	0.52	0.52	0.51	0.53
Geothermal [3]	0.28	0.30	0.29	0.30	0.30	0.31	0.32
Hydroelectric [2]	3.15	2.77	2.21	2.65	2.78	2.66	2.68
Solar [5]	0.01	0.01	0.01	0.01	0.01	0.01	0.01
Wind [6]	0.03	0.06	0.07	0.11	0.11	0.14	0.15

Z Less than 5 trillion Btu.   [1] Preliminary.   [2] Power produced from natural streamflow as regulated by available storage.   [3] As used at electric power plants, hot water or steam extracted from geothermal reservoirs in the Earth's crust that is supplied to steam turbines at electric power plants that drive generators to produce electricity.   [4] Organic nonfossil material of biological origin constituting a renewable energy source.   [5] Includes small amounts of distributed solar thermal and photovoltaic energy.   [6] Energy present in wind motion that can be converted to mechanical energy for driving pumps, mills, and electric power generators. Wind pushes against sails, vanes, or blades radiating from a central rotating shaft.   [7] Consists of living quarters for private households, but excludes institutional living quarters.   [8] The radiant energy of the sun, which can be converted into other forms of energy, such as heat or electricity.   [9] Consists of service-providing facilities and equipment of businesses, governments, and other private and public organizations. Includes institutional living quarters and sewage treatment facilities.   [10] Consists of all facilities and equipment used for producing, processing, or assembling goods.   [11] Ethanol primarily derived from corn.   [12] Consists of electricity only and combined heat and power plants who sell electricity and heat to the public.
Source: U.S. Energy Information Administration, *Annual Energy Review*, 2005. See also <http://www.eia.doe.gov/emeu/aer/renew.html> (released 27 July 2006).

Table 898. **Renewable Energy, Consumption by Sector and Source: 2004 to 2030**

[In quadrillions of Btu per year. For definition of Btu, see source and text, this section. Data represent actual heat rates used to determine fuel consumption for all renewable fuels except hydropower, solar, and wind. Consumption at hydroelectric, solar, and wind facilities determined by using the fossil fuel equivalent of 10,280 Btu per kilowatthour]

Sector and source	2004	2005	2010	2015	2020	2025	2030
MARKETED RENEWABLE ENERGY [1]							
Total marketed renewable energy	**6.27**	**6.19**	**8.45**	**8.82**	**9.15**	**9.56**	**9.86**
Residential (wood)	0.40	0.41	0.43	0.41	0.40	0.40	0.39
Commercial (biomass)	0.12	0.12	0.12	0.12	0.12	0.12	0.12
Industrial [2]	1.91	1.69	2.28	2.45	2.59	2.76	2.93
Conventional hydroelectric	0.05	0.03	0.03	0.03	0.03	0.03	0.03
Municipal waste [3]	0.01	0.01	0.01	0.01	0.01	0.01	0.01
Biomass	1.64	1.40	1.55	1.67	1.77	1.88	2.01
Biofuels heat and coproducts	0.21	0.24	0.69	0.74	0.78	0.83	0.88
Transportation	0.30	0.34	0.95	1.01	1.10	1.19	1.27
Ethanol used in E85 [4]	–	–	–	–	–	0.01	0.02
Ethanol used in gasoline blending . . .	0.29	0.33	0.91	0.98	1.05	1.14	1.20
Biodiesel used in distillate blending. . .	–	–	0.04	0.03	0.04	0.05	0.05
Electric power [5]	3.55	3.64	4.67	4.83	4.93	5.09	5.15
Conventional hydroelectric	2.66	2.68	2.99	3.04	3.05	3.06	3.06
Geothermal	0.31	0.32	0.36	0.37	0.44	0.48	0.53
Municipal waste [3]	0.27	0.28	0.29	0.33	0.33	0.33	0.34
Biomass	0.16	0.21	0.51	0.55	0.56	0.68	0.67
Dedicated plants	0.14	0.09	0.11	0.11	0.12	0.17	0.26
Cofiring	0.02	0.11	0.40	0.44	0.44	0.50	0.41
Solar thermal	0.01	0.01	0.01	0.02	0.02	0.02	0.02
Solar photovoltaic	–	–	–	–	–	–	–
Wind	0.14	0.15	0.50	0.52	0.53	0.53	0.53
Ethanol, total	**0.29**	**0.33**	**0.91**	**0.98**	**1.06**	**1.15**	**1.22**
Sources:							
Corn	0.28	0.33	0.87	0.93	0.99	1.07	1.13
Cellulose	–	–	0.01	0.02	0.02	0.02	0.02
Imports	0.01	0.01	0.02	0.03	0.05	0.06	0.07
NONMARKETED RENEWABLE ENERGY [6]							
Selected consumption:							
Residential.	0.03	0.03	0.04	0.05	0.06	0.07	0.08
Solar hot water heating.	0.03	0.03	0.03	0.04	0.05	0.06	0.06
Geothermal heat pumps	–	–	0.01	0.01	0.01	0.01	0.02
Solar photovoltaic	–	–	–	–	–	–	–
Commercial	0.02	0.03	0.03	0.03	0.03	0.03	0.04
Solar thermal	0.02	0.02	0.03	0.03	0.03	0.03	0.03
Solar photovoltaic	–	–	–	–	–	0.01	0.01

– Represents or rounds to zero. [1] Includes nonelectric renewable energy groups for which the energy source is bought and sold in the marketplace, although all transactions may not necessarily be marketed, and marketed renewable energy inputs for electricity entering the marketplace on the electric power grid. Excludes electricity imports. [2] Includes all electricity production by industrial and other combined heat and power for the grid and for own use. [3] Includes municipal solid waste, landfill gas, and municipal sewage sludge. All municipal solid waste is included, although a portion of the municipal solid waste stream contains petroleum-derived plastics and other nonrenewable sources. For municipal waste used to produce electric power, incremental growth is assumed to be for landfill gas facilities. [4] Excludes motor gasoline component of E85. [5] Includes consumption of energy by electricity-only and combined heat and power plants whose primary business is to sell electricity, or electricity and heat, to the public. Includes small power producers and exempt wholesale generators. [6] Includes selected renewable energy consumption data for which the energy is not bought or sold, either directly or indirectly as an input to marketed energy.

Source: U.S. Energy Information Administration, Annual Energy Outlook 2007. See also <http://www.eia.doe.gov/oiaf/aeo/aeoref_tab.html> (released February 2007).

Table 899. Energy Imports and Exports by Type of Fuel: 1980 to 2005

[In quadrillion of Btu. (12.10 represents 12,100,000,000,000,000 Btu). For definition of Btu, see text, this section]

Type of fuel	1980	1985	1990	1995	1999	2000	2001	2002	2003	2004	2005 [1]
Net imports, total [2] . . .	12.10	7.58	14.06	17.75	23.54	24.97	26.39	25.74	27.01	29.11	29.62
Coal.	-2.39	-2.39	-2.70	-2.08	-1.30	-1.21	-0.77	-0.61	-0.49	-0.57	-0.51
Natural gas (dry) . . .	0.96	0.90	1.46	2.74	3.50	3.62	3.69	3.58	3.36	3.50	3.59
Petroleum [3]	13.50	8.95	15.29	16.89	21.18	22.38	23.36	22.63	24.07	26.00	26.41
Other [4]	0.04	0.13	0.01	0.19	0.16	0.18	0.10	0.13	0.07	0.18	0.13
Imports, total.	15.80	11.78	18.82	22.26	27.25	28.97	30.16	29.41	31.06	33.54	34.26
Coal.	0.03	0.05	0.07	0.24	0.23	0.31	0.49	0.42	0.63	0.68	0.76
Natural gas (dry) . . .	1.01	0.95	1.55	2.90	3.66	3.87	4.07	4.10	4.04	4.37	4.39
Petroleum [3]	14.66	10.61	17.12	18.88	23.13	24.53	25.40	24.68	26.22	28.21	28.87
Other [4]	0.10	0.17	0.08	0.24	0.23	0.26	0.19	0.21	0.17	0.29	0.24
Exports, total	3.69	4.20	4.75	4.51	3.71	4.01	3.77	3.67	4.05	4.43	4.64
Coal.	2.42	2.44	2.77	2.32	1.53	1.53	1.27	1.03	1.12	1.25	1.27
Natural gas (dry) . . .	0.05	0.06	0.09	0.16	0.16	0.25	0.38	0.52	0.69	0.86	0.79
Petroleum	1.16	1.66	1.82	1.99	1.95	2.15	2.04	2.04	2.15	2.21	2.46
Other [4]	0.07	0.04	0.07	0.05	0.07	0.08	0.09	0.07	0.10	0.11	0.11

[1] Preliminary.   [2] Net imports equals imports minus exports. Minus sign (−) denotes an excess of exports over imports.
[3] Includes imports into the Strategic Petroleum Reserve.   [4] Coal coke and small amounts of electricity transmitted across U.S. borders with Canada and Mexico.

Source: U.S. Energy Information Administration, *Annual Energy Review, 2005*. See also <http://www.eia.doe.gov/emeu/aer/pdf/pages/sec1_11.pdf> (released 27 July 2006).

Table 900. U.S. Foreign Trade in Selected Mineral Fuels: 1980 to 2005

[985 represents 985,000,000,000 cu. ft. Minus sign (−) indicates an excess of imports over exports]

Mineral fuel	Unit	1980	1985	1990	1995	2000	2002	2003	2004	2005 [1]
Natural gas:										
Imports	Bil. cu. ft.	985	950	1,532	2,841	3,782	4,015	3,944	4,259	4,285
Exports	Bil. cu. ft.	49	55	86	154	244	516	680	854	787
Net trade	Bil. cu. ft.	−936	−894	−1,447	−2,687	−3,538	−3,499	−3,264	−3,404	−3,498
Crude oil:										
Imports [2]	Mil. bbl.	1,926	1,168	2,151	2,639	3,320	3,336	3,528	3,692	3,670
Exports	Mil. bbl.	105	75	40	35	18	3	5	10	15
Net trade	Mil. bbl.	−1,821	−1,094	−2,112	−2,604	−3,301	−3,333	−3,523	−3,682	−3,655
Petroleum products:										
Imports	Mil. bbl.	603	681	775	586	874	872	949	1,119	1,267
Exports	Mil. bbl.	94	211	273	312	362	356	370	374	414
Net trade	Mil. bbl.	−508	−471	−502	−274	−512	−517	−579	−745	−853
Coal:										
Imports	Mil. sh. tons . . .	1.2	2.0	2.7	9.5	12.5	16.9	25.0	27.3	30.5
Exports	Mil. sh. tons . . .	91.7	92.7	105.8	88.5	58.5	39.6	43.0	48.0	49.9
Net trade	Mil. sh. tons . . .	90.5	90.7	103.1	79.1	46.0	22.7	18.0	20.7	19.5

[1] Preliminary.   [2] Includes strategic petroleum reserve imports.
Source: U.S. Energy Information Administration, *Annual Energy Review 2005*. See also <http://www.eia.doe.gov/emeu/aer/contents.html> (released 27 July 2006).

Table 901. Crude Oil Imports Into the U.S. by Country of Origin: 1980 to 2006

[In millions of barrels (1,921 represents 1,921,000,000). Barrels contain 42 gallons. Crude oil imports are reported by the PAD District in which they are to be processed. Includes crude oil imported for storage in the Strategic Petroleum Reserve (SPR). Total OPEC excludes, and non-OPEC includes, petroleum imported into the United States indirectly from members of OPEC, primarily from Carribean and West European areas, as petroleum products that were refined from crude oil produced by OPEC]

Country of origin	1980	1985	1990	1995	2000	2001	2002	2003	2004	2005	2006
Total imports . . .	1,921	1,168	2,151	2,639	3,311	3,405	3,336	3,521	3,674	3,670	3,685
OPEC, [1, 2, 3] total	1,410	479	1,283	1,219	1,659	1,770	1,490	1,671	1,836	1,738	1,745
Algeria	166	31	23	10	(Z)	4	11	41	79	83	130
Iraq	10	17	188	−	226	290	168	171	238	190	202
Kuwait [4]	10	1	29	78	96	87	79	75	88	79	65
Libya	200	−	−	−	−	−	−	−	7	16	24
Saudi Arabia [4]	456	48	436	460	556	588	554	629	547	525	519
Indonesia	115	107	36	23	13	15	18	10	12	7	6
Nigeria	307	102	286	227	319	307	215	306	389	387	381
Venezuela	57	112	243	420	446	471	438	436	473	449	416
Non-OPEC, total [5]	511	689	869	1,419	1,652	1,635	1,846	1,850	1,838	1,932	1,940
Angola	(NA)	(NA)	86	131	108	117	117	132	112	164	187
Brazil	(NA)	(NA)	−	−	2	5	21	17	19	34	49
Canada.	73	171	235	380	492	495	527	565	590	600	651
Colombia.	(NA)	(NA)	51	76	116	95	86	59	51	57	52
Ecuador [2]	6	20	(NA)	35	46	41	37	50	83	101	99
Mexico	185	261	251	375	479	509	548	580	584	566	575
Norway	53	11	35	94	110	103	127	60	54	43	36
Russia	(NA)	(NA)	(Z)	5	3	−	31	60	54	55	39
United Kingdom	63	101	57	124	106	89	148	127	86	70	47

− Represents zero.   NA Not available.   Z Represents less than 500,000 barrels.   [1] OPEC (Organization of Petroleum Exporting Countries) includes the Persian Gulf nations shown below, except Bahrain, which is not a member of OPEC, and also includes Iran, Qatar, and United Arab Emirates.   [2] Ecuador withdrew from OPEC on Dec. 31, 1992; therefore, it is included under OPEC for the period 1973 to 1992.   [3] Gabon withdrew from OPEC on Dec. 31, 1994; therefore, it is included under OPEC for the period 1973 to 1994.   [4] Imports from the Neutral Zone between Kuwait and Saudi Arabia are included in Saudi Arabia.   [5] Non-OPEC total includes nations not shown.

Source: U.S. Energy Information Administration, *Petroleum Supply Monthly*, February 2007. See also <http://www.eia.doe.gov/pub/oil_gas/petroleum/data_publications/petroleum_supply_monthly/current/pdf/table38.pdf>.

Table 902. **Crude Oil and Refined Products—Summary: 1980 to 2006**

[13,481 represents 13,481,000 bbl. Barrels (bbl.) of 42 gallons. Data are averages]

Year	Crude oil (1,000 bbl. per day)					Refined oil products (1,000 bbl. per day)			Total oil imports [3] (1,000 bbl. per day)	Crude oil stocks [4] (mil. bbl.)	
	Input to refineries	Domestic production	Imports			Domestic demand	Imports	Exports		Total	Strategic reserve [5]
			Total [1]	Strategic reserve [2]	Exports						
1980......	13,481	8,597	5,263	44	287	17,056	1,646	258	6,909	[6]466	108
1985......	12,002	8,971	3,201	118	204	15,726	1,866	577	5,067	814	493
1990......	13,409	7,355	5,894	27	109	16,988	2,123	748	8,018	908	586
1995......	13,973	6,560	7,230	–	95	17,725	1,605	855	8,835	895	592
1997......	14,662	6,452	8,225	–	108	18,620	1,936	896	10,162	868	563
1998......	14,889	6,252	8,706	–	110	18,917	2,002	835	10,708	895	571
1999......	14,804	5,881	8,731	8	118	19,519	2,122	822	10,852	852	567
2000......	15,067	5,822	9,071	8	50	19,701	2,389	990	11,459	826	541
2001......	15,128	5,801	9,328	11	20	19,649	2,543	951	11,871	862	550
2002......	14,947	5,746	9,140	16	9	19,761	2,390	975	11,530	877	599
2003......	15,304	5,681	9,665	–	12	20,034	2,599	1,014	12,264	907	638
2004......	15,475	5,419	10,088	77	27	20,731	3,057	1,021	13,145	961	676
2005......	15,220	5,178	10,126	52	32	20,802	3,588	1,133	13,714	1,008	685
2006......	15,240	5,136	10,095	6	25	20,588	3,517	1,309	13,612	998	689

– Represents zero. [1] Includes Strategic Petroleum Reserve. [2] SPR is the Strategic Petroleum Reserve. Through 2003, includes imports by SPR only; beginning in 2004, includes imports by SPR, and imports into SPR by others. [3] Crude oil (including Strategic Petroleum Reserve imports) plus refined products. [4] Crude oil at end of period. Includes commercial and Strategic Petroleum Reserve stocks. [5] Crude oil stocks in the Strategic Petroleum Reserve include non-U.S. stocks held under foreign or commercial storage agreements. [6] Stocks of Alaskan crude oil in transit are included from January 1985 forward.

Source: U.S. Energy Information Administration, *Monthly Energy Review*, April 2007 issue.

Table 903. **Petroleum and Coal Products Corporations—Sales, Net Profit, and Profit Per Dollar of Sales: 1990 to 2006**

[318.5 represents $318,500,000,000. Represents SIC group 29 (NAICS group 324). Through 2000, based on Standard Industrial Classification code; beginning 2001, based on North American Industry Classification System, 1997 (NAICS). Profit rates are averages of quarterly figures at annual rates. Beginning 1990, excludes estimates for corporations with less than $250,000 in assets]

Item	Unit	1990	1995	1998	1999	2000	2001	2002	2003	2004	2005	2006
Sales..........	Bil. dol...	318.5	283.1	250.4	277.0	455.2	472.5	474.9	597.8	767.7	956.0	1,048.5
Net profit:												
Before income taxes....	Bil. dol...	23.1	16.5	9.7	20.3	55.5	47.2	22.4	52.8	89.7	120.2	140.5
After income taxes.....	Bil. dol...	17.8	13.9	8.3	17.2	42.6	35.8	19.5	43.6	71.8	96.3	111.5
Depreciation[1]	Bil. dol...	18.7	16.7	14.7	13.5	15.5	17.2	17.8	19.4	18.5	18.6	20.6
Profits per dollar of sales:												
Before income taxes....	Cents ...	7.3	5.8	3.5	7.1	12.2	9.7	4.6	10.4	15.5	17.9	17.6
After income taxes.....	Cents ...	5.6	4.9	3.1	6.0	9.4	7.4	4.2	8.6	12.4	14.3	13.9
Profits on stockholders' equity:												
Before income taxes....	Percent..	16.4	12.6	6.0	13.0	29.4	21.8	9.7	20.8	32.9	38.0	35.7
After income taxes.....	Percent..	12.7	10.6	5.2	11.0	22.6	16.5	8.4	17.1	26.3	30.4	28.3

[1] Includes depletion and accelerated amortization of emergency facilities.
Source: U.S. Census Bureau, *Quarterly Financial Report for Manufacturing, Mining and Trade Corporations.*

Table 904. **Major Petroleum Companies—Financial Summary: 1980 to 2006**

[32.9 represents $32,900,000,000. Data represent a composite of approximately 42 major worldwide petroleum companies aggregated on a consolidated total company basis]

Item	1980	1990	1995	2000	2001	2002	2003	2004	2005	2006
FINANCIAL DATA (bil. dol.)										
Net income................	32.9	26.8	24.3	76.4	62.0	44.3	85.5	120.5	170.6	187.6
Depreciation, depletion, etc.............	32.5	38.7	43.1	53.3	63.4	61.2	68.0	76.9	76.5	85.8
Cash flow [1]	65.4	65.5	67.4	129.7	140.0	118.0	157.7	205.1	239.9	261.2
Dividends paid.............	9.3	15.9	17.6	23.0	29.7	27.3	27.5	33.5	37.5	39.2
Net internal funds available for investment or debt repayment [2]	56.1	49.6	49.8	106.7	110.4	90.7	130.3	171.5	202.4	221.7
Capital and exploratory expenditures	62.1	59.6	59.8	72.8	99.9	88.7	90.7	112.4	140.4	193.1
Long-term capitalization.............	211.4	300.0	304.3	516.9	543.8	548.1	606.1	700.1	800.4	910.6
Long-term debt.................	49.8	90.4	85.4	112.8	143.2	153.5	142.1	161.0	165.2	177.4
Preferred stock...................	2.0	5.2	5.7	5.4	6.7	2.5	2.2	1.3	3.5	3.4
Common stock and retained earnings [3]..	159.6	204.4	213.2	398.7	393.9	392.1	461.8	537.8	631.7	729.8
Excess of expenditures over cash income [4]	6.0	10.0	10.0	–33.9	–10.5	–2.0	–39.5	–59.2	–62.0	–28.9
RATIOS [5] (percent)										
Long-term debt to long-term capitalization..	23.6	30.1	28.1	21.8	26.7	28.3	26.5	24.1	23.5	19.9
Net income to total average capital	17.0	9.1	8.1	15.7	12.3	8.7	15.2	18.9	23.0	22.3
Net income to average common equity....	22.5	13.5	11.6	20.5	16.3	11.5	20.1	24.2	29.3	27.8

[1] Generally represents internally generated funds from operations. Sum of net income and noncash charges such as depreciation, depletion, and amortization. [2] Cash flow minus dividends paid. [3] Includes common stock, capital surplus, and earned surplus accounts after adjustments. [4] Capital and exploratory expenditures plus dividends paid minus cash flow. [5] Represents approximate year-to-year comparisons because of changes in the makeup of the group due to mergers and other corporate changes.

Source: Carl H. Pforzheimer & Co., New York, NY, *Comparative Oil Company Statements*, annual.

582   Energy and Utilities

Table 905. **Nuclear Power Plants—Number, Capacity, and Generation: 1980 to 2006**

[51.8 represents 51,800,000 kW]

Item	1980	1985	1990	1995	1999	2000	2001	2002	2003	2004	2005	2006
Operable generating units [1,2] ...	71	96	112	109	104	104	104	104	104	104	104	104
Net summer capacity [2,3] (mil. kW)	51.8	79.4	99.6	99.5	97.4	97.9	98.2	98.7	99.2	99.6	100.0	100.0
Net generation (bil. kWh)......	251.1	383.7	576.9	673.4	728.3	753.9	768.8	780.1	763.7	788.5	782.0	787.2
Percent of total electricity net generation .,.........	11.0	15.5	19.0	20.1	19.7	19.8	20.6	20.2	19.7	19.9	19.3	19.4
Capacity factor [4] (percent)	56.3	58.0	66.0	77.4	85.3	88.1	89.4	90.3	87.9	90.1	89.3	89.9

[1] Total of nuclear generating units holding full-power licenses, or equivalent permission to operate, at the end of the year. Although Browns Ferry 1 was shut down in 1985, the unit has remained fully licensed and thus has continued to be counted as operable during the shutdown. [2] As of year-end. [3] Net summer capacity is the peak steady hourly output that generating equipment is expected to supply to system load, exclusive of auxiliary and other power plant, as demonstrated by test at the time of summer peak demand. [4] Weighted average of monthly capacity factors. Monthly factors are derived by dividing actual monthly generation by the maximum possible generation for the month (number of hours in the month multiplied by the net summer capacity at the end of the month).

Source: U.S. Energy Information Administration, *Monthly Energy Review*, April 2007. See also <http://www.eia.doe.gov/emeu/mer /nuclear.html> (accessed 23 May 2007).

Table 906. **Nuclear Power Plants—Number of Units, Net Generation, and Net Summer Capacity by State: 2005**

[781,986 represents 781,986,000,000 kWh]

State	Number of units	Net generation Total (mil. kWh)	Net generation Percent of total [1]	Net summer capacity Total (mil. kW)	Net summer capacity Percent of total [1]	State	Number of units	Net generation Total (mil. kWh)	Net generation Percent of total [1]	Net summer capacity Total (mil. kW)	Net summer capacity Percent of total [1]
U.S.	104	781,986	19.3	99.99	10.2	MS	1	10,078	22.4	1.27	7.5
AL	5	31,694	23.0	5.01	16.3	MO	1	8,031	8.8	1.19	5.8
AZ	3	25,807	25.4	3.88	15.6	NE	2	8,802	28.0	1.24	17.6
AR	2	13,690	28.6	1.83	13.0	NH	1	9,456	39.8	1.22	28.2
CA	4	36,155	18.1	4.32	7.0	NJ	1	31,392	51.8	3.98	22.7
CT	2	15,562	46.4	2.04	25.6	NY	6	42,443	28.9	5.15	13.2
FL.......	5	28,759	13.1	3.90	7.3	NC	5	39,982	30.8	4.94	18.2
GA	4	31,534	23.1	4.06	11.1	OH	3	14,803	9.4	2.11	6.2
IL.......	11	93,263	48.0	11.39	26.8	PA	9	76,289	35.0	9.20	20.5
IA.......	1	4,538	10.3	0.58	5.2	SC	7	53,138	51.8	6.47	28.7
KS	1	8,821	19.2	1.17	10.6	TN	3	27,803	28.6	3.40	16.4
LA	2	15,676	16.9	2.12	7.9	TX	4	38,232	9.6	4.86	4.8
MD	2	14,703	27.9	1.74	13.9	VT	1	4,072	71.2	0.51	50.5
MA	1	5,475	11.5	0.69	4.9	VA	4	27,918	35.4	3.43	15.2
MI.......	3	32,872	27.0	3.98	13.1	WA	1	8,242	8.1	1.13	4.1
MN	3	12,835	24.2	1.62	13.4	WI	3	9,921	16.0	1.58	9.8

[1] For total generation and capacity, see Table 912.

Source: U.S. Energy Information Administration, *Electric Power Annual 2005*. See also <http://www.eia.doe.gov/cneaf/electricity /epa/epa_sprdshts.html> (released 6 November 2006).

Table 907. **Solar Collector Shipments by Type, End Use, and Market Sector: 1980 to 2005**

[Shipments in thousands of square feet (19,398 represents 19,398,000). Solar collector is a device for intercepting sunlight, converting the light to heat, and carrying the heat to where it will be either used or stored. 1985 data are not available. Based on the Annual Solar Thermal Collector Manufacturers Survey]

Year	Number of manufacturers	Total shipments [1,2]	Collector type Low temperature [1,2]	Collector type Medium temperature, special, other [2]	End use Pool heating	End use Hot water	End use Space heating	Market sector Residential	Market sector Commercial	Market sector Industrial
1980 , ...	233	19,398	12,233	7,165	12,029	4,790	1,688	16,077	2,417	488
1986 [4]	98	9,360	3,751	1,111	3,494	1,181	127	4,131	703	13
1990 [4]	51	11,409	3,645	2,527	5,016	1,091	2	5,835	294	22
1995	36	7,666	6,813	840	6,763	755	132	6,966	604	82
2000	26	8,354	7,948	400	7,863	367	99	7,473	810	57
2003	26	11,444	10,877	560	10,800	511	76	10,506	864	71
2004 , ...	24	14,114	13,608	506	13,634	452	13	12,864	1,178	70
2005 [5]	25	16,041	15,224	702	15,041	640	228	14,681	1,160	31

[1] Includes shipments of high temperature collectors to the government, including some military, but excluding space applications. Also includes end uses such as process heating, utility, and other market sectors not shown separately. [2] Includes imputation of shipment data to account for nonrespondents. [3] Total shipments include all domestic and export shipments and may include imported collectors that subsequently were shipped to domestic or foreign customers. [4] Declines between 1986 and 1990 are primarily due to the expiration of the federal energy tax credit and industry consolidation. [5] Preliminary.

Source: U.S. Energy Information Administration, 1980–1990, *Solar Collector Manufacturing Activity*, annual reports; 1995–2002, *Renewable Energy Annual*; thereafter, *Solar Thermal and Photovoltaic Collector Manufacturing Activities 2005*. See also <http://www.eia.doe.gov/cneaf/solar.renewables/page/solarreport/solar.html> (released August 2006).

Table 908. **Uranium Concentrate—Supply, Inventories, and Average Prices: 1980 to 2005**

[43.70 represents 43,700,000 pounds (lbs.). Years ending Dec. 31. For additional data on uranium, see Section 18]

Item	Unit	1980	1990	1995	2000	2001	2002	2003	2004	2005
Production [1].....................	Mil. lb....	43.70	8.89	6.04	3.96	2.64	2.34	2.00	2.28	2.69
Exports [2].....................	Mil. lb....	5.8	2.0	9.8	13.6	11.7	15.4	13.2	13.2	20.5
Imports [2].....................	Mil. lb....	3.6	23.7	41.3	44.9	46.7	52.7	53.0	66.1	65.5
Electric plant purchases from domestic suppliers..............	Mil. lb....	(NA)	20.5	22.3	24.3	27.5	22.7	21.7	28.2	27.3
Loaded into U.S. nuclear reactors [3]...	Mil. lb....	(NA)	(NA)	51.1	51.5	52.7	57.2	62.3	50.1	58.3
Inventories, total...............	Mil. lb....	(NA)	129.1	72.5	111.3	103.8	102.1	85.5	95.2	93.8
At domestic suppliers...........	Mil. lb....	(NA)	26.4	13.7	56.5	48.1	48.7	39.9	37.5	29.0
At electric plants	Mil. lb....	(NA)	102.7	58.7	54.8	55.6	53.5	45.6	57.7	64.8
Average price per pound: Purchased imports.............	Dollars...	(NA)	12.55	10.20	9.84	9.51	10.05	10.59	12.25	14.83
Domestic purchases...........	Dollars...	(NA)	15.70	11.11	11.45	10.45	10.35	10.84	11.91	13.98

NA Not available. [1] Data are for uranium concentrate, a yellow or brown powder obtained by the milling of uranium ore, processing of in situ leach mining solutions, or as a byproduct of phosphoric acid production. [2] Trade data prior to 1990 were for transactions conducted by uranium suppliers only. For 1990 forward, transactions by uranium buyers (consumers) have been included. Buyer imports and exports prior to 1990 are believed to be small. [3] Does not include any fuel rods removed from reactors and later reloaded into the reactor.

Source: U.S. Energy Information Administration, *Annual Energy Review 2005*. Also see <http://www.eia.doe.gov/emeu/aer/pdf /pages/sec9_7.pdf> (released 27 July 2006).

Table 909. **Electricity Net Generation by Sector and Fuel Type: 1990 to 2005**

[3,038.0 represents 3,038,000,000,000 kWh. Data are for fuels consumed to produce electricity. Also includes fuels consumed to produce useful thermal output at a small number of electric utility combined-heat-and-power (CHP) plants]

Source and sector	Unit	1990	1995	2000	2002	2003	2004	2005 [1]
Net generation, total.............	Bil. kWh. ...	3,038.0	3,353.5	3,802.1	3,858.5	3,883.2	3,970.6	4,038.0
Electric power sector, total	Bil. kWh.....	2,901.3	3,194.2	3,637.5	3,698.5	3,721.2	3,808.4	3,883.4
Electricity-only plants [2].........	Bil. kWh.....	2,840.0	3,052.8	3,472.9	3,504.8	3,525.5	3,624.1	3,705.5
Combined-heat-and-power plants [3]..	Bil. kWh.....	61.3	141.5	164.6	193.7	195.7	184.3	177.9
Commercial sector [4]...........	Bil. kWh.....	5.8	8.2	7.9	7.4	7.5	8.3	8.2
Industrial sector [5]............	Bil. kWh.....	130.8	151.0	156.7	152.6	154.5	153.9	146.3
Net generation by source, all sectors:								
Fossil fuels, total	Bil. kWh.....	2,103.8	2,293.9	2,692.5	2,730.2	2,758.6	2,825.0	2,903.3
Coal [6]......................	Bil. kWh.....	1,594.0	1,709.4	1,966.3	1,933.1	1,973.7	1,978.6	2,014.2
Petroleum [7]	Bil. kWh.....	126.6	74.6	111.2	94.6	119.4	120.6	121.9
Natural gas [8]	Bil. kWh.....	372.8	496.1	601.0	691.0	649.9	709.0	751.5
Other gases [9]................	Bil. kWh.....	10.4	13.9	14.0	11.5	15.6	16.8	15.6
Nuclear electric power............	Bil. kWh.....	576.9	673.4	753.9	780.1	763.7	788.5	780.5
Hydroelectric pumped storage [10]...	Bil. kWh.....	-3.5	-2.7	-5.5	-8.7	-8.5	-8.5	-6.6
Renewable energy, total	Bil. kWh.....	357.2	384.8	356.5	351.3	363.2	358.8	357.2
Conventional hydroelectric power..	Bil. kWh.....	292.9	310.8	275.6	264.3	275.8	268.4	265.1
Biomass, total	Bil. kWh.....	45.8	56.9	60.7	61.5	61.3	60.9	61.8
Wood [11]	Bil. kWh.....	32.5	36.5	37.6	38.7	37.5	37.6	37.8
Waste [12]	Bil. kWh.....	13.3	20.4	23.1	22.9	23.7	23.3	24.0
Geothermal	Bil. kWh.....	15.4	13.4	14.1	14.5	14.4	14.8	15.1
Solar [13]...................	Bil. kWh.....	0.4	0.5	0.5	0.6	0.5	0.6	0.5
Wind.	Bil. kWh.....	2.8	3.2	5.6	10.4	11.2	14.1	14.6
Other [14]	Bil. kWh.....	3.6	4.1	4.8	5.7	6.1	6.7	3.7
Consumption of fuels for electricity generation:								
Coal [6]	Mil. sh. tons..	792.5	860.6	994.9	987.6	1,014.1	1,026.0	1,051.2
Petroleum, total	Mil. bbl.....	219.0	132.6	195.2	168.6	206.7	209.5	215.0
Distilate fuel oil [15]	Mil. bbl.....	18.1	19.6	31.7	23.3	29.7	20.7	21.9
Residual fuel oil [16]	Mil. bbl.....	190.8	95.5	143.4	109.2	142.5	145.2	146.8
Other liquids [17]	Mil. bbl.....	0.4	0.7	1.4	1.9	2.9	4.0	3.7
Petroleum coke	Mil. sh. tons..	1.9	3.4	3.7	6.8	6.3	7.9	8.5
Natural gas [8]	Bil. cu. ft....	3,691.6	4,737.9	5,691.5	6,126.1	5,616.1	6,111.3	6,466.0
Other gases [9]	Tril. Btu.....	111.8	132.5	126.0	131.2	156.3	187.0	188.6
Biomass [5]	Tril. Btu.....	653.5	795.6	825.9	1,004.1	902.4	924.5	1,039.6
Wood [11]	Tril. Btu.....	442.3	479.9	495.8	605.1	519.3	533.5	624.7
Waste [12]	Tril. Btu.....	211.2	315.7	330.1	399.1	383.1	390.9	414.8
Other [14]	Tril. Btu.....	36.0	42.0	46.2	49.0	58.7	51.3	32.9

[1] Preliminary. [2] Electricity-only plants within the NAICS 22 category whose primary business is to sell electricity to the public. Data also include a small number of electric utility combined-heat-and-power plants (CHP). [3] Combined-heat-and-power plants within the NAICS 22 category whose primary business is to sell electricity and heat to the public. Data do not include electric utility CHP plants—these are included under electricity-only plants. [4] Commercial combined-heat-and-power (CHP) and commercial electricity-only plants. [5] Industrial combined-heat-and-power (HCP) and industrial electricity-only plants. Through 1988, data are for industrial hydroelectric power only. [6] Anthracite, bituminous coal, subbituminous coal, lignite, waste coal, and coal synfuel. [7] Distillate fuel oil, residual fuel oil, petroleum coke, jet fuel, kerosene, other petroleum, and waste oil. [8] Includes a small amount of supplemental gaseous fuels that cannot be identified separately. [9] Blast furnace gas, propane gas, and other manufactured and waste gases derived from fossil fuels. [10] Pumped storage facility production minus energy used for pumping. [11] Wood, black liquor, and other wood waste. [12] Municipal solid waste, landfill gas, sludge waste, tires, agricultural byproducts, and other biomass. [13] Solar thermal and photovoltaic energy. [14] Batteries, chemicals, hydrogen, pitch, purchased steam, sulfur, and miscellaneous technologies. [15] Fuel oil numbers 1, 2, and 4. Prior to 2001, electric utility data also include small amounts of kerosene and jet fuel. [16] Fuel oil numbers 5 and 6. Prior to 2001, electric utility data also include a small amount of fuel oil number 4. [17] Jet fuel, kerosene, other petroleum liquids, and waste oil.

Source: U.S. Energy Information Administration, *Annual Energy Review 2005*. See also <http://www.eia.doe.gov/emeu/aer /contents.html> (released 27 July 2006).

Table 910. **Total Electric Net Summer Capacity, All Sectors: 1990 to 2005**

[In million kilowatts (734.1 represents 734,100,000). Data are at end of year. For plants that use multiple sources of energy, capacity is assigned to the predominant energy source]

Source	1990	1995	1999	2000	2001	2002	2003	2004	2005 [1]
Net summer capacity, total	734.1	769.5	785.9	811.7	848.3	905.3	948.4	962.9	978.5
Fossil fuels, total	527.8	554.2	572.6	598.9	634.9	689.5	731.2	745.4	758.8
Coal [2]	307.4	311.4	315.5	315.1	314.2	315.4	313.0	313.0	313.5
Petroleum [3]	49.0	43.7	35.6	35.9	39.7	38.2	36.4	33.7	33.8
Natural gas [4]	56.2	75.4	70.0	06.7	125.8	171.7	208.4	224.3	234.5
Dual fired [5]	113.6	122.0	146.0	149.8	153.5	162.3	171.3	172.2	174.7
Other gases [6]	1.6	1.7	1.9	2.3	1.7	2.0	2.0	2.3	2.4
Nuclear electric power	99.6	99.5	97.4	97.9	98.2	98.7	99.2	99.6	99.8
Hydroelectric pumped storage	19.5	21.4	19.6	19.5	19.7	20.4	20.5	20.8	20.9
Renewable energy, total	86.8	93.9	95.3	94.9	95.1	96.1	96.9	96.4	98.2
Conventional hydroelectric power . . .	73.9	78.6	79.4	79.4	78.9	79.4	78.7	77.6	77.7
Biomass, total	8.1	10.3	10.5	10.0	9.7	9.7	9.7	9.8	9.8
Wood [7]	5.5	6.7	6.8	6.1	5.9	5.8	5.9	6.2	6.2
Waste [8]	2.5	3.5	3.7	3.9	3.8	3.8	3.8	3.6	3.6
Geothermal	2.7	3.0	2.8	2.8	2.2	2.3	2.1	2.2	2.2
Solar [9]	0.3	0.3	0.4	0.4	0.4	0.4	0.4	0.4	0.4
Wind	1.8	1.7	2.3	2.4	3.9	4.4	6.0	6.5	8.2
Other [10]	0.5	0.5	1.0	0.5	0.4	0.6	0.6	0.7	0.9

[1] Preliminary. [2] Anthracite, bituminous coal, subbituminous coal, lignite, waste coal, and coal synfuel. [3] Distillate fuel oil, residual fuel oil, petroleum coke, jet fuel, kerosene, other petroleum, and waste oil. [4] Includes a small amount of supplemental gaseous fuels that cannot be identified separately. [5] Petroleum and natural gas. [6] Blast furnace gas, propane gas, and other manufactured and waste gases derived from fossil fuels. [7] Wood, black liquor, and other wood waste. [8] Municipal solid waste, landfill gas, sludge waste, tires, agricultural byproducts, and other biomass. [9] Solar thermal and photovoltaic energy. [10] Batteries, chemicals, hydrogen, pitch, purchased steam, sulfur, and miscellaneous technologies.

Source: U.S. Energy Information Administration, *Annual Energy Review 2005*. See also <http://www.eia.doe.gov/emeu/aer /elect.html> (released 27 July 2006).

Table 911. **Electricity—End Use and Average Retail Prices: 1980 to 2005**

[Beginning 2003, the category "other" has been replaced by "transportation," and the categories "commercial" and "industrial" have been redefined. Data represent revenue from electricity retail sales divided by the amount of retail electricity sold (in kilowatt-hours). Prices include state and local taxes, energy or demand charges, customer service charges, environmental surcharges, franchise fees, fuel adjustments, and other miscellaneous charges applied to end-use customers during normal billing operations. Prices do not include deferred charges, credits, or other adjustments, such as fuel or revenue from purchased power, from previous reporting periods. Data are for a census of electric utilities. Beginning in 1999, data also include energy service providers selling to retail customers]

Item	1990	1995	1999	2000	2001	2002	2003	2004	2005 [1]
END USE (Billion kilowatt-hours)									
Total end use [2]	2,837.1	3,164.0	3,483.7	3,592.4	3,544.7	3,632.3	3,657.5	3,716.7	3,813.4
Direct use [3]	124.5	150.7	171.6	170.9	162.6	166.2	168.3	168.5	160.5
Retail sales [4]									
Residential	924.0	1,042.5	1,144.9	1,192.4	1,201.1	1,265.4	1,273.6	1,293.6	1,361.1
Commercial [5]	838.3	953.1	1,103.8	1,159.3	1,191.2	1,205.1	1,197.2	1,229.0	1,266.7
Industrial [6]	945.5	1,012.7	1,058.2	1,064.2	984.5	990.1	1,011.6	1,018.5	1,016.7
Transportation [7]	4.8	5.0	5.1	5.4	5.2	5.5	6.8	7.1	8.3
AVERAGE RETAIL PRICES (Cents per kilowatt-hour)									
Total									
Nominal	6.57	6.89	6.64	6.81	7.31	7.22	7.42	7.62	8.09
Real	8.05	7.48	6.78	6.81	7.14	6.93	6.98	6.98	7.21
Residential									
Nominal	7.83	8.40	8.16	8.24	8.63	8.46	8.70	8.97	9.42
Real	9.60	9.12	8.34	8.24	8.43	8.12	8.18	8.22	8.40
Commercial [8]									
Nominal	7.34	7.69	7.26	7.43	7.95	7.90	8.00	8.16	8.68
Real	9.00	8.35	7.42	7.43	7.76	7.58	7.53	7.48	7.74
Industrial [6]									
Nominal	4.74	4.66	4.43	4.64	4.98	4.91	5.12	5.27	5.57
Real	5.81	5.06	4.53	4.64	4.86	4.71	4.82	4.83	4.97
Transportation [7]									
Nominal	(NA)	(NA)	(NA)	(NA)	(NA)	(NA)	7.55	7.13	7.44
Real	(NA)	(NA)	(NA)	(NA)	(NA)	(NA)	7.10	6.54	6.63
Other [9]									
Nominal	6.40	6.88	6.35	6.56	7.44	6.75	(X)	(X)	(X)
Real	7.84	7.47	6.49	6.56	7.27	6.48	(X)	(X)	(X)

NA Not available. X Not applicable. [1] Preliminary. [2] The sum of "total retail sales" and "direct use." [3] Use of electricity that is 1) self-generated, 2) produced by either the same entity that consumes the power or an affiliate, and 3) used in direct support of a service or industrial process located within the same facility or group of facilities that house the generating equipment. Direct use is exclusive of station use. [4] Electricity retail sales to ultimate customers reported by electric utilities and, beginning in 1996, other energy service providers. [5] Includes public street and highway lighting, interdepartmental sales, and other sales to public authorities. [6] Beginning 2003, includes agriculture and irrigation. [7] Includes sales to railroads and railways. [8] Beginning 2003, includes public street and highway lighting, interdepartmental sales, and other sales to public authorities. [9] Public street and highway lighting, interdepartmental sales, other sales to public authorities, agriculture and irrigation, and transportation including railroads and railways.

Source: U.S. Energy Information Administration, *Annual Energy Review 2005*. See also <http://www.eia.doe.gov/emeu/aer /elect.html> (released 27 July 2006).

Energy and Utilities **585**

Table 912. Electric Power Industry—Net Generation and Net Summer Capacity by State: 2000 to 2005

[Capacity as of December 31. (3,802.1 represents 3,802,100,000,000). Covers utilities for public use]

State	Net generation (bil. kWh)			2005		Net summer capacity (mil. kW)			
	2000	2003	2004	Total	Percent from coal	2000	2003	2004	2005
United States	3,802.1	3,883.2	3,970.6	4,054.7	49.7	811.7	948.4	962.9	978.0
Alabama	124.4	137.5	137.4	137.9	56.6	23.5	30.2	30.6	30.7
Alaska.	6.2	6.3	6.5	6.6	9.5	2.1	1.9	1.9	1.9
Arizona	88.9	94.4	104.6	101.5	39.6	15.3	23.5	24.3	24.9
Arkansas	43.9	50.4	51.9	47.8	48.2	9.7	13.5	13.5	14.1
California	208.1	192.8	194.8	200.3	1.1	51.9	57.9	58.3	61.7
Colorado	44.2	46.6	47.9	49.6	71.7	8.4	10.4	11.1	11.1
Connecticut	33.0	29.5	32.6	33.5	11.9	6.4	7.6	7.9	8.0
Delaware	6.0	7.4	7.9	8.1	59.4	2.1	3.4	3.4	3.4
District of Columbia	0.1	0.1	(Z)	0.2	–	0.8	0.8	0.8	0.8
Florida.	191.8	212.6	218.1	220.3	28.4	41.5	49.4	50.7	53.2
Georgia	123.9	124.1	126.8	136.7	63.8	27.8	34.8	35.3	36.5
Hawaii.	10.6	11.0	11.4	11.5	14.2	2.4	2.3	2.3	2.4
Idaho	11.9	10.4	10.9	10.8	0.9	3.0	3.0	3.0	3.2
Illinois	178.5	189.1	192.0	194.1	47.5	36.3	45.5	42.0	42.5
Indiana	127.8	124.9	127.8	130.4	94.2	23.3	25.6	26.7	27.0
Iowa	41.5	42.1	43.2	44.2	77.6	9.1	10.1	10.9	11.1
Kansas	44.8	46.6	46.8	45.9	75.2	10.1	10.9	10.9	11.0
Kentucky	93.0	91.7	94.5	97.8	91.1	16.8	19.1	19.6	20.0
Louisiana	92.9	94.9	98.2	92.6	24.9	21.0	25.7	26.5	26.8
Maine	14.0	19.0	19.1	18.8	1.7	4.2	4.3	4.2	4.2
Maryland	51.1	52.2	52.1	52.7	55.7	10.4	12.5	12.5	12.5
Massachusetts	38.7	48.4	47.5	47.5	25.3	12.4	13.9	14.0	14.0
Michigan	104.2	111.3	118.5	121.6	57.8	25.8	30.4	30.4	30.4
Minnesota	51.4	55.1	52.4	53.0	62.1	10.3	11.5	11.6	12.1
Mississippi	37.6	40.1	43.7	45.1	36.9	9.0	17.3	17.0	16.9
Missouri.	76.6	87.2	87.6	90.8	85.3	17.3	20.0	20.2	20.5
Montana	26.5	26.3	26.8	27.9	63.8	5.2	5.2	5.1	5.3
Nebraska.	29.1	30.5	32.0	31.5	66.2	6.0	6.7	6.7	7.0
Nevada	35.5	33.2	37.7	40.2	45.7	6.7	7.5	8.7	8.7
New Hampshire	15.0	21.6	23.9	23.7	17.2	2.9	4.2	4.3	4.3
New Jersey	58.1	57.4	55.9	60.5	19.2	16.5	18.6	18.2	17.5
New Mexico	34.0	32.7	32.9	35.1	85.2	5.6	6.3	6.3	6.5
New York.	138.1	137.6	138.0	146.9	14.0	35.6	36.7	37.8	39.1
North Carolina	122.3	127.6	126.3	129.7	60.5	24.5	27.3	27.1	27.1
North Dakota	31.3	31.3	29.9	31.9	94.8	4.7	4.7	4.8	4.8
Ohio	149.1	146.6	148.3	157.0	87.2	28.4	34.1	34.1	33.9
Oklahoma	55.6	60.6	60.7	68.6	53.0	14.1	18.2	19.4	19.8
Oregon	51.8	49.0	51.4	49.3	7.0	11.3	12.9	12.1	12.2
Pennsylvania	201.7	206.3	214.7	218.1	55.5	36.7	42.4	45.1	44.9
Rhode Island	6.0	5.6	4.9	6.1	–	1.2	1.7	1.7	1.7
South Carolina	93.3	93.8	97.9	102.5	38.7	18.7	20.7	22.2	22.6
South Dakota	9.7	7.9	7.5	6.5	46.0	2.8	2.7	2.7	2.8
Tennessee	95.8	92.2	97.6	97.1	61.0	19.5	20.9	20.9	20.7
Texas	377.7	379.2	390.3	396.7	37.4	81.7	99.6	101.1	101.0
Utah	36.6	38.0	38.2	38.2	94.2	5.2	5.8	6.2	6.5
Vermont	6.3	6.0	5.5	5.7	–	1.0	1.0	1.0	1.0
Virginia	77.2	75.3	78.9	78.9	44.9	19.4	21.3	22.5	22.6
Washington	108.2	100.1	102.2	102.0	10.3	26.1	27.7	27.6	27.8
West Virginia	92.9	94.7	89.7	93.6	97.6	15.0	16.1	16.4	16.5
Wisconsin	59.6	60.1	60.4	61.8	67.4	13.6	14.3	14.7	16.2
Wyoming	45.5	43.6	44.8	45.6	95.1	6.2	6.6	6.6	6.7

– Represents zero.   Z Represents less than 50 million kWh or 50,000 kW.

Source: U.S. Energy Information Administration, *Electric Power Annual 2005*. See also <http://www.eia.doe.gov/cneaf /electricity/epa/epa_sprdshts.html> (released 9 November 2006).

Table 913. Electric Power Industry—Capability, Peak Load, and Capacity Margin: 1980 to 2006

[558,237 represents 558,237,000 kW. Excludes Alaska and Hawaii. Capability represents the maximum kilowatt output with all power sources available and with hydraulic equipment under actual water conditions, allowing for maintenance, emergency outages, and system operating requirements. Capacity margin is the difference between capability and peak load]

Year	Capability at the time of— Summer peak load (1,000 kW) Amount	Change from prior year	Winter peak load (1,000 kW) Amount	Change from prior year	Noncoincident peak load Summer (1,000 kW)	Winter (1,000 kW)	Capacity margin Summer Amount (1,000 kW)	Percent of capability	Winter Amount (1,000 kW)	Percent of capability
1980	558,237	13,731	572,195	17,670	427,058	384,567	131,179	23.5	187,628	32.8
1985	621,597	17,357	636,475	14,350	460,503	423,660	161,094	25.9	212,815	33.4
1987	648,118	14,827	662,977	16,256	496,185	448,277	151,933	23.4	214,700	32.4
1988	661,580	13,462	676,940	13,963	529,460	466,533	132,120	20.0	210,407	31.1
1989	673,316	11,736	685,249	8,309	524,110	496,378	149,206	22.2	188,871	27.6
1990	685,091	11,775	696,757	11,508	546,331	484,231	138,760	20.3	212,526	30.5
1991	690,915	5,824	703,212	6,455	551,418	485,761	139,497	20.2	217,451	30.9
1992	695,436	4,521	707,752	4,540	548,707	492,983	146,729	21.1	214,769	30.3
1993	694,250	-1,186	711,957	4,205	575,356	521,733	118,894	17.1	190,224	26.7
1994	702,985	8,735	715,090	3,133	585,320	518,253	117,665	16.7	196,837	27.5
1995	714,222	11,237	727,679	12,589	620,249	544,684	93,973	13.2	182,995	25.1
1996	724,728	10,506	737,637	9,958	616,790	554,081	107,938	14.9	183,556	24.9
1997	725,829	1,101	736,666	-971	637,677	529,874	88,152	12.1	206,792	28.1
1998	724,193	-1,636	735,090	-1,576	660,293	567,558	63,900	8.8	167,532	22.8
1999	733,481	9,288	748,271	13,181	682,122	570,915	51,359	7.0	177,356	23.7
2000	750,771	17,290	767,505	19,234	678,413	588,426	72,358	9.6	179,079	23.3
2001	783,737	32,966	806,598	39,093	687,812	576,312	95,925	12.2	230,286	28.6
2002	825,145	41,408	850,984	44,386	714,565	604,986	110,580	13.4	245,998	28.9
2003	853,649	28,504	882,120	31,136	709,375	593,874	144,274	16.9	288,246	32.7
2004	851,766	-1,883	864,849	-17,271	704,459	618,701	147,307	17.3	246,148	28.5
2005	860,137	8,371	878,110	13,261	758,876	626,365	101,261	11.8	251,745	28.7
2006 [1]	870,480	10,343	888,698	10,588	762,228	635,597	108,252	12.4	253,101	28.5

[1] Preliminary.

Source: Edison Electric Institute, Washington, DC, *Statistical Yearbook of the Electric Power Industry*, annual.

Table 914. Electric Energy Retail Sales by Class of Service and State: 2005

[In billions of kilowatt-hours (3,661.0 represents 3,661,000,000,000)]

State	Total [1]	Residential	Commercial	Industrial	State	Total [1]	Residential	Commercial	Industrial
United States...	3,661.0	1,359.2	1,275.1	1,019.2					
Alabama	89.2	31.3	21.6	36.3	Missouri	80.9	34.4	29.6	16.9
Alaska	5.9	2.1	2.7	1.2	Montana	13.5	4.2	4.5	4.8
Arizona	69.4	30.5	27.5	11.4	Nebraska	27.0	9.3	8.8	8.8
Arkansas	46.2	17.1	11.4	17.7	Nevada	32.5	11.1	8.5	12.9
California	254.2	85.6	117.6	50.2	New Hampshire	11.2	4.5	4.6	2.2
Colorado	48.4	16.4	19.8	12.1	New Jersey	81.9	30.0	39.8	11.9
Connecticut	33.1	13.8	13.9	5.2	New Mexico	20.6	5.9	8.4	6.4
Delaware	12.1	4.6	4.2	3.3	New York	150.1	50.5	76.8	19.9
District of Columbia	11.8	1.9	9.3	0.3	North Carolina	128.3	54.1	44.2	30.1
Florida	225.0	115.8	89.4	19.7	North Dakota	10.8	3.8	4.0	3.1
Georgia	132.3	52.8	44.7	34.6	Ohio	160.2	53.9	46.9	59.4
Hawaii	10.5	3.2	3.5	3.9	Oklahoma	53.7	21.3	17.5	14.9
Idaho	21.9	7.6	5.6	8.6	Oregon	46.4	18.3	15.4	12.7
Illinois	145.0	48.6	50.0	45.9	Pennsylvania	148.3	53.7	45.8	48.0
Indiana	106.5	33.6	24.0	48.9	Rhode Island	8.0	3.2	3.6	1.2
Iowa	42.8	13.6	11.3	17.9	South Carolina	81.3	28.7	20.5	32.1
Kansas	39.0	13.4	14.5	11.2	South Dakota	9.8	4.0	4.0	1.8
Kentucky	89.4	26.9	19.1	43.3	Tennessee	103.9	41.1	29.1	33.6
Louisiana	77.4	28.7	21.7	27.0	Texas	334.3	126.6	110.8	96.8
Maine	12.4	4.5	4.2	3.7	Utah	25.0	7.6	9.4	8.0
Maryland	68.4	28.4	17.9	21.5	Vermont	5.9	2.2	2.1	1.6
Massachusetts	57.2	20.5	26.4	9.9	Virginia	108.8	44.7	44.7	19.4
Michigan	110.4	36.1	39.6	34.7	Washington	83.4	33.2	28.1	22.1
Minnesota	66.0	21.7	22.0	22.3	West Virginia	30.2	11.4	7.5	11.3
Mississippi	45.9	18.0	12.7	15.3	Wisconsin	70.3	22.5	22.5	25.4
					Wyoming	14.1	2.4	3.8	8.0

[1] Includes transportation, not shown separately.

Source: U.S. Energy Information Administration, *Electric Sales and Revenue 2005*. See also <http://www.eia.doe.gov/cneaf /electricity/esr/table2.xls> (released November 2006).

Table 915. Electric Energy Price by Class of Service and State: 2005

[Revenue (in cents) per kilowatt hour (kWh). Data include both bundled and unbundled consumers]

State	Total[1]	Resi-dential	Com-mercial	Indus-trial	State	Total[1]	Resi-dential	Com-mercial	Indus-trial
United States	8.14	9.45	8.67	5.73	Missouri	6.13	7.08	5.92	4.54
Alabama	6.46	8.00	7.50	4.52	Montana	6.72	8.10	7.43	4.83
Alaska	11.72	13.30	11.56	9.29	Nebraska	5.87	7.14	5.98	4.43
Arizona	7.79	8.86	7.40	5.85	Nevada	9.02	10.20	9.48	7.71
Arkansas	6.30	8.00	6.18	4.74	New Hampshire	12.53	13.51	12.06	11.48
California	11.63	12.51	11.92	9.55					
					New Jersey	10.89	11.74	10.61	9.76
Colorado	7.64	9.06	7.62	5.74	New Mexico	7.51	9.13	7.81	5.61
Connecticut	12.06	13.64	11.53	9.40	New York	13.95	15.72	14.36	8.23
Delaware	7.76	9.01	7.60	6.21	North Carolina	7.19	8.65	6.86	5.04
District of Columbia	9.18	9.10	9.13	14.13	North Dakota	5.92	6.99	6.11	4.32
Florida	8.76	9.62	8.16	6.46					
					Ohio	7.08	8.51	7.93	5.10
Georgia	7.43	8.64	7.67	5.28	Oklahoma	6.85	7.95	7.00	5.11
Hawaii	18.33	20.70	19.04	15.79	Oregon	6.34	7.25	6.51	4.83
Idaho	5.12	6.29	5.42	3.91	Pennsylvania	8.27	9.86	8.50	6.29
Illinois	6.95	8.34	7.75	4.61	Rhode Island	11.97	13.04	11.71	10.01
Indiana	5.88	7.50	6.57	4.42					
					South Carolina	6.72	8.67	7.39	4.55
Iowa	6.69	9.27	6.95	4.56	South Dakota	6.60	7.77	6.20	4.95
Kansas	6.55	7.90	6.60	4.85	Tennessee	6.31	6.98	7.17	4.73
Kentucky	5.01	6.57	6.01	3.60	Texas	9.14	10.93	8.85	7.14
Louisiana	8.03	8.87	8.56	6.71	Utah	5.92	7.52	6.07	4.24
Maine	10.57	13.23	10.63	7.28					
					Vermont	10.95	12.96	11.33	7.77
Maryland	8.13	8.46	8.97	7.01	Virginia	6.64	8.16	6.05	4.46
Massachusetts	12.18	13.44	12.42	9.22	Washington	5.87	6.54	6.33	4.27
Michigan	7.23	8.40	7.84	5.32	West Virginia	5.15	6.21	5.53	3.85
Minnesota	6.61	8.28	6.59	5.02	Wisconsin	7.48	9.66	7.67	5.39
Mississippi	7.54	8.71	8.48	5.37	Wyoming	5.16	7.48	6.17	3.99

[1] Includes transportation, not shown separately.

Source: U.S. Energy Information Administration, *Electric Sales and Revenue 2005*. See also <http://www.eia.doe.gov/cneaf /electricity/esr/esr_sum.html> (released November 2006).

Table 916. Total Electric Power Industry—Generation, Sales, Revenue, and Customers: 1990 to 2006

[2,808 represents 2,808,000,000,000 kWh. Sales and revenue are to and from ultimate customers. Commercial and Industrial are not wholly comparable on a year-to-year basis due to changes from one classification to another. For the 2003 period forward, the Energy Information Administration replaced the "Other" sector with the Transportation sector. The Transportation sector consists entirely of electrified rail and urban transit systems. Data previously reported in "Other" have been relocated to the Commercial sector, except for Agriculture (i.e., irrigation load), which have been relocated to the Industrial sector]

Class	Unit	1990	1995	2000	2001	2002	2003	2004	2005	2006[1]
Generation[2]	Bil kWh..	2,808	3,353	3,802	3,737	3,858	3,883	3,971	4,055	4,053
Sales[3]	Bil. kWh..	2,713	3,013	3,421	3,382	3,466	3,489	3,548	3,661	3,665
Residential or domestic ..	Bil. kWh ..	924	1,043	1,192	1,201	1,265	1,274	1,294	1,359	1,354
Percent of total	Percent ..	34.1	34.6	34.9	35.5	36.5	36.5	36.5	37.1	37.0
Commercial[4]	Bil. kWh ..	751	863	1,055	1,088	1,105	1,197	1,229	1,275	1,301
Industrial[5]	Bil. kWh..	946	1,013	1,064	985	990	1,012	1,019	1,019	1,002
Revenue[3]	Bil. dol..	178.2	207.7	233.2	247.3	250.2	258.9	270.5	298.0	324.3
Residential or domestic ..	Bil. dol. ..	72.4	87.6	98.2	103.7	107.1	110.8	116.0	128.4	140.8
Percent of total	Percent ..	40.6	42.2	42.1	41.9	42.8	42.8	42.9	43.1	43.4
Commercial[4]	Bil. dol. ..	55.1	66.4	78.4	86.5	87.3	95.8	100.3	110.5	121.7
Industrial[5]	Bil. dol. ..	44.9	47.2	49.4	49.1	48.6	51.8	53.7	58.4	61.0
Ultimate customers, Dec. 31[3]	Million...	110.6	118.3	127.6	131.4	133.6	134.5	136.1	138.4	139.9
Residential or domestic ..	Million ..	97.1	103.9	111.7	114.9	116.6	117.3	118.8	120.8	122.1
Commercial[4]	Million ...	12.1	12.9	14.3	14.9	15.3	16.5	16.6	16.9	17.1
Industrial[5]	Million ...	0.5	0.6	0.5	0.6	0.6	0.7	0.7	0.7	0.7
Avg. kWh used per customer	1,000....	24.5	25.5	26.8	25.7	25.9	25.9	26.1	26.5	26.2
Residential	1,000..	9.5	10.0	10.7	10.5	10.9	10.9	10.9	11.3	11.1
Commercial[4]	1,000....	62.2	66.6	73.5	73.2	72.0	72.3	74.0	75.6	76.1
Avg. annual bill per customer	Dollar ...	1,612	1,756	1,828	1,883	1,872	1,924	1,987	2,154	2,318
Residential	Dollar ..	745	843	879	902	918	945	977	1,063	1,154
Commercial[4]	Dollar ..	4,562	5,124	5,464	5,821	5,693	5,786	6,037	6,551	7,122
Avg. revenue per kWh sold	Cents ...	6.57	6.89	6.81	7.31	7.22	7.42	7.62	8.14	8.85
Residential	Cents ...	7.83	8.40	8.24	8.63	8.46	8.70	8.97	9.45	10.4
Commercial[4]	Cents ...	7.34	7.69	7.43	7.95	7.90	8.00	8.16	8.67	9.36
Industrial[5]	Cents ...	4.74	4.66	4.64	4.98	4.91	5.12	5.27	5.73	6.09

[1] Preliminary. [2] "Generation" includes batteries, chemicals, hydrogen, pitch, sulfur, purchased steam, and miscellaneous technologies, which are not separately displayed. [3] Includes other types not shown separately. Data for 1990 are as of December 31st. Data for following years are average yearly customers. [4] Small light and power. [5] Large light and power.

Source: Edison Electric Institute, Washington, DC, *Statistical Yearbook of the Electric Power Industry*, annual.

588 Energy and Utilities

U.S. Census Bureau. Statistical Abstract of the United States: 2008

Table 917. Revenue and Expense Statistics for Major U.S. Investor-Owned Electric Utilities: 1995 to 2005

[In millions of nominal dollars (199,967 represents $199,967,000,000). Covers approximately 180 investor-owned electric utilities that during each of the last 3 years met any one or more of the following conditions—1 mil. megawatt-hours of total sales; 100 megawatt-hours of sales for resale, 500 megawatt-hours of gross interchange out, and 500 megawatt-hours of wheeling for other]

Item	1995	2000	2001	2002	2003	2004	2005
Utility operating revenues	199,967	235,336	267,525	219,389	226,227	240,318	267,534
Electric utility	183,655	214,707	244,219	200,135	202,369	213,539	235,570
Other utility	16,312	20,630	23,306	19,254	23,858	26,779	31,964
Utility operating expenses	165,321	210,324	235,198	188,745	197,459	207,161	238,590
Electric utility	150,599	191,329	213,733	171,291	175,473	182,337	208,461
Operation	91,881	132,662	159,929	116,374	122,723	131,962	151,150
Production	68,983	107,352	136,089	90,649	96,181	104,287	121,058
Cost of fuel	29,122	32,555	29,490	24,132	26,476	28,678	36,161
Purchased power	29,981	61,969	98,231	58,828	62,173	67,354	78,279
Other	9,880	12,828	8,368	7,688	7,532	8,256	6,638
Transmission	1,425	2,699	2,365	3,494	3,585	4,519	5,687
Distribution	2,561	3,115	3,217	3,113	3,185	3,301	3,517
Customer accounts	3,613	4,246	4,434	4,165	4,180	4,087	4,243
Customer service	1,922	1,839	1,856	1,821	1,893	2,012	2,289
Sales	348	403	282	261	234	238	219
Administrative and general	13,028	13,009	11,686	12,872	13,466	13,519	14,113
Maintenance	11,767	12,185	11,167	10,843	11,141	11,774	12,058
Depreciation	19,885	22,761	20,845	17,319	16,962	16,373	17,177
Taxes and other	27,065	23,721	21,792	26,755	24,648	22,228	26,848
Other utility	14,722	18,995	21,465	17,454	21,986	24,823	30,129
Net utility operating income	34,646	25,012	32,327	30,644	28,768	33,158	28,944

Source: U.S. Energy Information Administration, *Electric Power Annual 2005.* See also <http://www.eia.doe.gov/cneaf/electricity /epa/epat8p1.html> (released 4 October 2006).

Table 918. Total Renewable Energy Net Generation of Electricity by Source and State: 2002

[In millions of kilowatt hours (351,251 represents 351,251,000,000). MSW = municipal solid waste]

State	Total [1]	Hydro-electric	MSW/landfill gas	Other bio-mass [2]	Wood/wood waste	State	Total [1]	Hydro-electric	MSW/landfill gas	Other bio-mass [2]	Wood/wood waste
U.S.	351,251	264,329	20,185	2,672	38,665	MO	1,423	1,357	(NA)	66	(Z)
AL	12,575	8,825	(NA)	23	3,727	MT	9,630	9,567	(NA)	(NA)	63
AK	1,452	1,439	(NA)	11	1	NE	1,119	1,097	(NA)	13	(NA)
AZ	7,569	7,427	50	91	(NA)	NV	3,395	2,268	(NA)	(NA)	(NA)
AR	5,021	3,436	(NA)	5	1,581	NH	2,066	1,141	225	(NA)	700
CA	54,821	31,141	1,858	434	3,958	NJ	1,342	12	1,315	16	(NA)
CO	1,378	1,209	(NA)	30	(NA)	NM	284	265	(NA)	19	(NA)
CT	1,961	335	1,437	188	(NA)	NY	27,671	25,048	2,129	(NA)	412
DE	(NA)	(NA)	(NA)	(NA)	(NA)	NC	5,310	3,492	106	30	1,683
DC	(NA)	(NA)	(NA)	(NA)	(NA)	ND	1,593	1,593	(NA)	(Z)	(NA)
FL	5,328	184	3,309	282	1,553	OH	640	488	23	2	126
GA	9,131	2,716	28	168	6,219	OK	2,227	1,988	(NA)	(NA)	239
HI	609	95	301	139	(NA)	OR	35,500	34,413	87	(NA)	624
ID	9,278	8,769	(NA)	(NA)	508	PA	4,968	2,211	1,925	9	766
IL	974	129	592	254	(NA)	RI	101	4	98	(NA)	(NA)
IN	543	411	124	7	(NA)	SC	2,634	1,390	16	(NA)	1,229
IA	1,964	946	78	21	(Z)	SD	4,360	4,354	(NA)	(NA)	4,360
KS	479	13	(NA)	(NA)	(NA)	TN	8,776	7,974	38	10	751
KY	4,390	4,025	(NA)	(NA)	365	TX	5,117	1,123	53	211	1,073
LA	3,754	891	(NA)	114	2,749	UT	687	458	11	(NA)	(NA)
ME	7,198	2,768	408	298	3,724	VT	1,481	1,115	(NA)	(NA)	356
MD	2,438	1,661	594	(Z)	183	VA	3,386	868	1,106	4	1,408
MA	2,914	863	1,918	27	107	WA	79,955	78,167	225	21	1,126
MI	4,171	1,669	945	81	1,475	WV	1,097	1,066	(NA)	22	(Z)
MN	2,886	809	791	3	377	WI	3,676	2,515	396	74	645
MS	949	12	(NA)	(Z)	937	WY	1,031	584	(NA)	(NA)	(NA)

NA Not available. Z Less than 500,000 million kilowatt hours. [1] Includes types not shown separately. [2] Agriculture byproducts/crops, sludge waste, tires, and other biomass solids, liquids, and gases.

Source: Energy Information Administration, *Renewable Energy Trends 2004.* See also <http://www.eia.doe.gov/cneaf/solar .renewables/page/trends/table17.pdf> (released August 2005).

Energy and Utilities 589

Table 919. **Carbon Dioxide Emissions by Sector and Source—1980 to 2005, and Projections, 2010 to 2020**

[In million metric tons (4,728.5 represents 4,728,500,000), except as noted]

Sector	1980	1990	1995	2000	2004	2005 [1]	2010	2015	2020
Total [2]	4,728.5	4,984.8	5,265.8	5,810.2	5,923.2	5,945.3	6,213.9	6,588.9	6,944.5
Petroleum [3]	2,039.0	2,068.6	2,132.0	2,352.1	2,499.9	2,513.6	2,559.6	2,724.6	2,872.7
Natural gas.	865.4	850.4	955.2	956.2	902.1	859.2	854.0	893.8	947.8
Coal	298.3	262.3	236.2	216.6	199.0	193.3	196.7	203.7	209.5
Electricity [4]	1,529.0	1,803.1	1,936.8	2,279.3	2,309.4	2,375.0	2,505.1	2,676.6	2,831.6
Residential	909.0	953.7	1,030.7	1,171.9	1,213.9	1,253.8	1,320.0	1,391.8	1,456.4
Petroleum	123.1	98.0	95.9	107.2	105.9	105.3	105.3	106.8	104.8
Natural gas	256.3	238.6	263.1	269.2	264.8	261.7	175.0	192.1	204.0
Coal.	5.7	2.9	1.6	1.0	1.3	0.9	1.0	1.0	1.0
Electricity [4]	523.9	614.2	670.0	794.4	841.9	885.7	940.0	1,001.8	1,063.8
Commercial	652.5	780.7	841.1	1,006.4	1,034.1	1,050.6	1,124.4	1,233.2	1,329.9
Petroleum	95.6	69.4	53.0	54.1	54.3	55.4	54.1	57.1	57.3
Natural gas	140.7	142.4	164.5	171.8	170.3	166.3	175.0	192.1	204.0
Coal.	8.3	11.6	11.0	8.1	9.5	7.8	9.2	9.2	9.2
Electricity [4]	407.9	557.2	612.6	772.4	799.9	821.1	886.1	974.7	1,059.4
Industrial [5]	1,780.8	1,683.6	1,728.6	1,778.0	1,736.0	1,682.3	1,732.1	1,775.2	1,817.3
Petroleum . [3].	470.7	373.5	359.1	375.7	437.3	431.2	406.0	418.9	422.6
Natural gas [3]	434.1	433.5	489.4	479.7	434.9	399.7	466.0	468.5	493.1
Coal.	284.3	247.7	223.6	207.5	188.1	184.5	186.5	193.5	199.3
Electricity [4]	594.9	628.5	650.9	708.9	662.9	662.8	673.7	694.3	702.2
Transportation	1,386.2	1,566.8	1,665.3	1,854.0	1,939.2	1,958.6	2,037.4	2,188.7	2,340.9
Petroleum [6] [7]	1,349.6	1,527.7	1,624.0	1,815.0	1,902.5	1,921.7	1,994.2	2,141.8	2,288.0
Natural gas [7]	34.3	35.9	38.2	35.5	32.1	31.5	38.0	41.1	46.7
Electricity [4] . . . . [8] . . .	2.3	3.2	3.2	3.6	4.6	5.4	5.3	5.8	6.2
Electric power sector [8] . . .	1,529.0	1,803.1	1,936.8	2,279.3	2,309.4	2,375.0	2,505.1	2,676.6	2,831.7
Petroleum	202.8	100.9	60.1	90.9	98.0	100.3	69.2	74.6	74.1
Natural gas	200.8	176.9	229.4	281.4	296.2	318.9	345.7	385.2	389.9
Coal.	1,125.3	1,519.1	1,636.8	1,896.6	1,903.7	1,944.2	2,078.0	2,203.0	2,354.0

[1] Preliminary. [2] Includes other items not shown separately. [3] Includes lease and plant fuel. [4] Emissions from the electric power sector are distributed to the end-use sectors. [5] Includes emissions from geothermal power and nonbiogenic emissions from municipal solid waste. [6] Fuel consumption includes energy for combined-heat-and-power plants (CHP), except those plants whose primary business is to sell electricity, or electricity and heat, to the public. [7] This includes carbon dioxide from international bunker fuels, both civilian and military, which are excluded from the accounting of carbon dioxide emissions under the United Nations convention. [8] Includes pipeline fuel natural gas and compressed natural gas used as vehicle fuel.

Source: U.S. Energy Information Administration, 1980, *State Energy Data Report;* 1990 to 2005, *Emissions of Greenhouse Gases in the U.S. 2005;* and projections, *Annual Energy Outlook 2007.* See also, <http://www.eia.doe.gov>.

Table 920. **Privately Owned Gas Utility Industry—Balance Sheet and Income Account: 1990 to 2005**

[In millions of dollars (121,686 represents $121,686,000,000). The gas utility industry consists of pipeline and distribution companies. Excludes operations of companies distributing gas in bottles or tanks]

Item	1990	1995	1999	2000	2001	2002	2003	2004	2005
COMPOSITE BALANCE SHEET									
Assets, total	121,686	141,965	155,413	165,709	171,681	185,064	174,756	168,306	196,215
Total utility plant	112,863	143,636	166,134	162,206	175,530	197,717	188,807	180,884	207,976
Depreciation and amortization. . . .	49,483	62,723	73,823	69,366	73,753	85,038	76,642	79,889	91,794
Utility plant (net).	63,380	80,912	92,311	92,839	101,777	112,679	112,165	100,996	116,183
Investment and fund accounts . . .	23,872	26,489	17,344	10,846	10,237	13,000	13,430	12,716	16,331
Current and accrued assets	23,268	18,564	22,443	35,691	29,345	25,786	22,905	22,107	32,325
Deferred debits [1]	9,576	13,923	20,922	24,279	28,553	31,928	24,663	31,033	29,574
Liabilities, total	121,686	141,965	155,413	165,709	171,681	185,064	174,756	168,306	196,215
Capitalization, total	74,958	90,581	95,244	96,079	107,310	117,362	112,089	105,799	120,949
Capital stock	43,810	54,402	48,569	47,051	56,870	58,067	57,605	54,252	62,470
Long-term debts	31,148	35,548	46,906	48,267	49,739	58,962	54,179	51,327	58,264
Current and accrued liabilities. . . .	29,550	28,272	32,683	42,312	34,962	30,856	28,599	25,515	34,936
Deferred income taxes [2]	11,360	14,393	17,120	17,157	20,445	24,612	23,888	23,944	24,937
Other liabilities and credits	5,818	8,715	10,365	10,161	8,964	12,235	10,179	13,048	15,393
COMPOSITE INCOME ACCOUNT									
Operating revenues, total . .	66,027	58,390	59,142	72,042	79,276	68,352	75,527	80,194	102,018
Minus: Operating expenses [3] . . .	60,137	50,760	38,752	64,988	71,209	60,041	66,677	71,719	89,385
Operation and maintenance . . .	51,627	37,966	41,415	54,602	58,873	48,521	55,036	59,920	77,673
Federal, state, and local taxes. .	4,957	6,182	5,605	6,163	7,394	6,249	6,581	6,472	7,513
Equals: Operating income	5,890	7,630	20,390	7,053	8,068	8,310	8,852	8,475	12,632
Utility operating income	6,077	7,848	16,614	7,166	8,192	8,564	9,198	8,619	12,812
Income before interest charges. . .	8,081	9,484	17,531	7,589	8,266	9,305	10,053	9,609	13,972
Net income	4,410	5,139	10,420	4,245	4,038	4,792	6,198	5,942	9,777
Dividends	3,191	4,037	5,595	3,239	3,560	3,887	3,765	2,111	2,419

[1] Includes capital stock discount and expense and reacquired securities. [2] Includes reserves for deferred income taxes. [3] Includes expenses not shown separately.

Source: American Gas Association, Arlington, VA, *Gas Facts,* annual (copyright).

Table 921. Gas Utility Industry—Summary: 1990 to 2005

[54,261 represents 54,261,000. Covers natural, manufactured, mixed, and liquid petroleum gas. Based on a questionnaire mailed to all privately and municipally owned gas utilities in the United States, except those with annual revenues less than $25,000]

Item	Unit	1990	1995	2000	2001	2002	2003	2004	2005
End users [1]	1,000	54,261	58,728	61,262	61,385	62,034	62,610	63,297	64,395
Residential	1,000	49,802	53,955	56,494	56,680	57,293	57,802	58,501	59,569
Commercial	1,000	4,246	4,530	4,610	4,546	4,590	4,661	4,641	4,678
Industrial and other	1,000	166	181	157	156	149	145	152	145
Sales [2]	Tril. Btu [3]	9,842	9,221	9,232	8,667	8,864	8,927	8,766	8,848
Residential	Tril. Btu	4,468	4,803	4,741	4,525	4,589	4,722	4,566	4,516
Percent of total	Percent	45	52	51	52	52	53	52	51
Commercial	Tril. Btu	2,192	2,281	2,077	2,053	2,055	2,125	2,075	2,056
Industrial	Tril. Btu	3,010	1,919	1,698	1,461	1,748	1,672	1,763	1,654
Other	Tril. Btu	171	218	715	627	472	408	363	622
Revenues [2]	Mil. dol.	45,153	46,436	59,243	69,150	57,112	72,606	79,929	96,909
Residential	Mil. dol.	25,000	28,742	35,828	42,454	35,062	43,664	47,275	55,680
Percent of total	Percent	55	62	60	61	61	60	59	57
Commercial	Mil. dol.	10,604	11,573	13,339	16,848	13,512	17,349	18,689	22,653
Industrial	Mil. dol.	8,996	5,571	7,432	7,513	6,841	9,478	11,230	13,751
Other	Mil. dol.	553	549	2,645	2,335	1,698	2,115	2,735	4,825
Prices per mil. Btu [3]	Dollars	4.59	5.05	6.42	7.98	6.44	8.13	9.13	10.95
Residential	Dollars	5.60	6.00	7.56	9.38	7.64	9.25	10.37	12.33
Commercial	Dollars	4.84	5.07	6.42	8.20	6.57	8.17	9.01	11.02
Industrial	Dollars	2.99	2.98	4.38	5.14	3.84	5.67	6.37	8.31
Gas mains mileage	1,000	1,189	1,278	1,369	1,374	1,411	1,424	1,462	1,438
Field and gathering	1,000	32	31	27	20	22	22	24	23
Transmission	1,000	292	297	297	287	310	304	299	297
Distribution	1,000	865	950	1,046	1,066	1,080	1,098	1,140	1,118
Construction expenditures [4]	Mil. dol.	7,899	10,760	8,624	9,516	11,552	13,034	16,567	10,089
Transmission	Mil. dol.	2,886	3,380	1,590	3,212	5,184	7,317	3,205	3,368
Distribution	Mil. dol.	3,714	5,394	5,437	4,546	4,890	3,870	11,636	5,129
Production and storage	Mil. dol.	309	367	138	113	73	258	181	179
General	Mil. dol.	770	1,441	1,273	1,457	1,156	1,350	1,271	1,070
Underground storage	Mil. dol.	219	177	185	187	249	239	274	343

[1] Annual average. [2] Excludes sales for resale. [3] For definition of Btu, see text, this section. [4] Includes general.

Source: American Gas Association, Arlington, VA, *Gas Facts*, annual (copyright).

Table 922. Gas Utility Industry—Customers, Sales, and Revenues by State: 2004

[64,395 represents 64,395,000. See headnote, Table 921. For definition of Btu, see text, this section]

State	Customers [1] (1,000)		Sales [2] (tril. Btu)		Revenues [2] (mil. dol.)		State	Customers [1] (1,000)		Sales [2] (tril. Btu)		Revenues [2] (mil. dol.)	
	Total	Resi-dential	Total	Resi-dential	Total	Resi-dential		Total	Resi-dential	Total	Resi-dential	Total	Resi-dential
U.S.	64,395	59,569	8,848	4,516	96,909	55,680							
							MO	1,493	1,349	169	110	2,006	1,354
AL	866	799	103	43	1,294	660	MT	272	241	31	20	325	212
AK	121	108	96	19	348	103	NE	468	428	61	33	586	346
AZ	1,100	1,043	84	37	915	484	NV	725	688	84	37	872	454
AR	626	556	63	35	741	459	NH	110	94	16	8	228	117
CA	10,559	10,092	715	496	7,922	5,709	NJ	2,721	2,508	386	229	4,795	2,989
CO	1,663	1,525	197	128	1,887	1,278	NM	577	530	54	34	544	370
CT	526	475	85	45	1,182	714	NY	4,253	3,929	556	349	7,304	5,027
DE	149	137	20	11	262	151	NC	1,104	993	133	66	1,782	982
DC	134	127	15	11	247	186	ND	131	114	24	11	247	122
FL	685	644	43	16	665	318	OH	2,328	2,160	284	208	3,605	2,699
GA	356	323	56	19	656	256	OK	959	880	94	61	1,023	692
HI	29	26	3	1	70	16	OR	701	627	93	41	975	513
ID	335	301	34	22	345	229	PA	2,636	2,422	338	232	4,572	3,214
IL	3,843	3,623	507	397	5,620	4,465	RI	247	224	29	20	402	282
IN	1,801	1,651	233	147	2,635	1,731	SC	600	542	112	29	1,302	424
IA	948	850	116	69	1,299	827	SD	179	157	24	13	253	143
KS	936	853	94	67	1,059	780	TN	1,176	1,049	161	68	1,923	894
KY	826	743	105	55	1,246	697	TX	4,308	3,979	1,495	190	12,466	2,309
LA	956	897	316	42	3,010	540	UT	799	744	96	60	847	564
ME	26	19	4	1	63	19	VT	38	33	8	3	80	38
MD	956	897	98	72	1,385	1,045	VA	1,091	1,007	135	79	1,855	1,175
MA	1,417	1,297	181	122	2,637	1,827	WA	1,062	966	134	76	1,451	869
MI	3,322	3,073	494	353	4,947	3,613	WV	410	374	52	31	625	387
MN	1,492	1,364	273	132	2,734	1,442	WI	1,754	1,593	246	135	2,639	1,565
MS	495	440	85	25	912	322	WY	85	76	13	7	122	67

[1] Averages for the year. [2] Excludes sales for resale.

Source: American Gas Association, Arlington, VA, *Gas Facts*, annual (copyright).

Census Bureau, Statistical Abstract of the United States: 2008

Table 923. **Public Drinking Water Systems by Size of Community Served and Source of Water: 2005**

[As of September. Covers systems that provide water for human consumption through pipes and other constructed conveyances to a least 15 service connections or serve an average of at least 25 persons for at least 60 days a year. Based on reported data in the Safe Drinking Water Information System maintained by the Environmental Protection Agency]

Type of system	Total	Size of community served					Water source	
		500 or fewer persons	501 to 3,300 persons	3,301 to 10,000 persons	10,001 to 100,000	100,001 persons or more	Ground water	Surface water
Total systems	157,908	129,330	19,541	4,961	3,686	390	143,565	14,343
COMMUNITY WATER SYSTEMS [1]								
Number of systems	52,554	29,654	14,120	4,748	3,646	386	40,686	11,868
Percent of systems	100	56	27	9	7	1	77	23
Population served (1,000).	281,504	4,924	20,048	27,515	102,712	126,305	88,797	192,707
Percent of population	100	2	7	10	36	45	32	68
NONTRANSIENT NONCOMMUNITY WATER SYSTEM [2]								
Number of systems	19,169	16,345	2,705	102	17	–	18,561	608
Percent of systems	100	85	14	1	–	–	97	3
Population served (1,000).	6,052	2,282	2,707	558	505	–	5,442	610
Percent of population	100	38	45	9	8	–	90	10
TRANSIENT NONCOMMUNITY WATER SYSTEM [3]								
Number of systems	86,185	83,331	2,716	111	23	4	84,318	1,867
Percent of systems	100	97	3	–	–	–	98	2
Population served (1,000).	14,151	7,297	2,657	599	604	2,994	11,348	2,803
Percent of population	100	52	19	4	4	21	80	20

– Represents zero. [1] A public water system that supplies water to the same population year-round. [2] A public water system that regularly supplies water to at least 25 of the same people at least 6 months per year, but not year-round. Some examples are schools, factories, and office buildings which have their own water systems. [3] A public water system that provides water in a place such as a gas station or campground where people do not remain for long periods of time.

Source: U.S. Environmental Protection Agency, *Factoids: Drinking Water and Ground Water Statistics for 2005*, annual reports. See also <http://www.epa.gov/safewater/data/getdata.html> (published December 2006).

Table 924. **Sewage Treatment Facilities: 2004**

[Based on the North American Industry Classification System (NAICS), 2002; see text, Section 15]

State	Sewage treatment facilities (NAICS 22132)		State	Sewage treatment facilities (NAICS 22132)	
	Number of establishments	Paid employees		Number of establishments	Paid employees
U.S.	731	5,934	MO	24	(1)
AL.	6	(1)	MT.	10	(1)
AK.	4	(3)	NE.	3	(3)
AZ	11	39	NV	2	(3)
AR	6	32	NH	2	(3)
CA	21	(2)	NJ	12	(2)
CO	13	40	NM	8	43
CT	7	139	NY	31	(2)
DE	1	(3)	NC	25	69
DC.	(NA)	(NA)	ND	(NA)	(NA)
FL	68	803	OH	13	76
GA	8	(1)	OK	6	(1)
HI	14	79	OR	3	(3)
ID	7	(1)	PA	88	536
IL.	40	(4)	RI	3	(1)
IN	41	192	SC	13	70
IA	5	(1)	SD	4	(3)
KS	3	(1)	TN	10	(1)
KY	10	104	TX	63	(5)
LA	26	241	UT	3	(3)
ME.	3	(3)	VT	3	(3)
MD.	2	(3)	VA	11	(2)
MA	12	(2)	WA	7	(1)
MI	19	(1)	WV	17	109
MN.	8	(1)	WI	11	(1)
MS.	20	(2)	WY	3	(1)

NA Not available. [1] 20–99 employees. [2] 100–249 employees. [3] 0–19 employees. [4] 250–499 employees. [5] 1,000–2,499 employees.

Source: U.S. Census Bureau, "County Business Patterns"; annual. See also <http://www.census.gov/epcd/cbp/view/cbpview.html>.

Section 20
Construction and Housing

This section presents data on the construction industry and on various indicators of its activity and costs; on housing units and their characteristics and occupants; and on the characteristics and vacancy rates for commercial buildings. This edition contains data from the 2005 American Housing Survey.

The principal source of these data is the U.S. Census Bureau, which issues a variety of current publications, as well as data from the decennial census. Current construction statistics compiled by the Census Bureau appear in its *New Residential Construction* and *New Residential Sales* press releases and Web site <http://www.census.gov/const/www/>. Statistics on expenditures by owners of residential properties are issued quarterly and annually in *Expenditures for Residential Improvements and Repairs. Value of New Construction Put in Place* presents data on all types of construction. Reports of the censuses of construction industries (see below) are also issued on various topics.

Other Census Bureau publications include the *Current Housing Reports* series, which comprise the quarterly *Housing Vacancies*, the quarterly *Market Absorption of Apartments*, the biennial *American Housing Survey* (formerly *Annual Housing Survey)*, and reports of the censuses of housing and of construction industries.

Other sources include the monthly *Dodge Construction Potentials* of McGraw-Hill Construction, New York, NY, which present national and state data on construction contracts; the National Association of Home Builders with state-level data on housing starts; the NATIONAL ASSOCIATION OF REALTORS®, which presents data on existing home sales; the Bureau of Economic Analysis, which presents data on residential capital and gross housing product; and the U.S. Energy Information Administration, which provides data on commercial buildings through its periodic sample surveys.

Censuses and surveys—Censuses of the construction industry were first conducted by the Census Bureau for 1929, 1935, and 1939; beginning in 1967, a census has been taken every 5 years (through 2002, for years ending in "2" and "7"). The latest reports are part of the 2002 Economic Census. See text, Section 15, Business Enterprise.

The construction sector of the economic census, covers all employer establishments primarily engaged in (1) building construction by general contractors or operative builders; (2) heavy (nonbuilding) construction by general contractors; and (3) construction by special trade contractors. This sector includes construction management and land subdividers and developers. The 2002 census was conducted in accordance with the 2002 North American Industrial Classification System (NAICS). See text, Section 15, Business Enterprise.

From 1850 through 1930, the Census Bureau collected some housing data as part of its censuses of population and agriculture. Beginning in 1940, separate censuses of housing have been taken at 10-year intervals. For the 1970 and 1980 censuses, data on year-round housing units were collected and issued on occupancy and structural characteristics, plumbing facilities, value, and rent; for 1990 such characteristics were presented for all housing units.

The American Housing Survey (*Current Housing Reports* Series H-150 and H-170), which began in 1973, provided an annual and ongoing series of data on selected housing and demographic characteristics until 1983. In 1984, the name of the survey was changed from the Annual Housing Survey. Currently, national data are collected every other year, and data for

selected metropolitan areas are collected on a rotating basis. All samples represent a cross section of the housing stock in their respective areas. Estimates are subject to both sampling and nonsampling errors; caution should therefore be used in making comparisons between years.

Data on residential mortgages were collected continuously from 1890 to 1970, except 1930, as part of the decennial census by the Census Bureau. Since 1973, mortgage status data, limited to single family homes on less than 10 acres with no business on the property, have been presented in the American Housing Survey. Data on mortgage activity are covered in Section 25, Banking and Finance.

Housing units—In general, a housing unit is a house, an apartment, a group of rooms or a single room occupied or intended for occupancy as separate living quarters; that is, the occupants live separately from any other individual in the building, and there is direct access from the outside or through a common hall. Transient accommodations, barracks for workers, and institutional-type quarters are not counted as housing units.

Statistical reliability—For a discussion of statistical collection and estimation, sampling procedures, and measures of statistical reliability applicable to Census Bureau data, see Appendix III.

U.S. Census Bureau, Statistical Abstract of the United States: 2008

Table 925. **Construction—Establishments, Employees, and Payroll by Kind of Business (NAICS Basis): 2003 and 2004**

[6,381 represents 6,381,000. Covers establishments with payroll. Excludes most government employees, railroad employees, and self-employed persons. Kind-of-business classification based on North American Industry Classification System (NAICS) 2002. For statement on methodology, see Appendix III]

Industry	2002 NAICS code [1]	Establishments		Paid employees [2] (1,000)		Annual payroll (mil. dol.)	
		2003	2004	2003	2004	2003	2004
Construction	23	732,175	760,372	6,381	6,648	252,940	268,268
Construction of buildings	236	219,899	233,617	1,492	1,579	62,827	68,877
Residential building construction	2361	176,600	190,924	789	873	30,252	35,236
New single-family housing construction (except operative builders).............	236115	105,329	113,948	400	444	13,346	15,883
New multifamily housing construction (except operative builders).............	236116	4,878	4,955	46	47	1,958	2,116
New housing operative builders	236117	10,959	10,774	140	158	8,428	9,944
Residential remodelers	236118	55,434	61,247	204	224	6,521	7,293
Nonresidential building construction	2362	43,299	42,693	702	706	32,575	33,641
Industrial building construction	23621	1,773	1,884	71	73	2,900	3,192
Commercial and institutional building construction ....'.................	23622	41,526	40,809	631	633	29,674	30,448
Heavy and civil engineering construction	237	50,905	50,146	911	908	42,678	43,423
Utility system construction	2371	21,166	20,843	462	452	20,138	19,938
Water and sewer line and related structures . . .	23711	14,105	13,810	185	192	7,917	8,409
Oil and gas pipeline and related structures....	23712	1,751	1,702	85	84	3,959	3,741
Power and communication line and related structures...................	23713	5,310	5,331	192	176	8,262	7,789
Land subdivision......................	2372	11,986	11,915	61	64	2,717	3,203
Highway, street, and bridge construction	2373	12,446	12,030	309	313	16,109	16,496
Other heavy and civil engineering construction...	2379	5,307	5,358	80	80	3,715	3,786
Specialty trade contractors..............	238	461,371	476,609	3,979	4,161	147,434	155,968
Foundation, structure, and building exterior contractors	2381	112,299	113,498	984	1,044	32,913	35,089
Poured concrete foundation and structures contractors	23811	27,517	26,534	265	277	9,463	9,933
Structural steel and precast concrete contractors	23812	3,547	3,500	63	64	2,556	2,596
Framing contractors..................	23813	18,456	18,127	149	162	4,266	4,804
Masonry contractors..................	23814	24,723	26,470	208	225	6,679	7,200
Glass and glazing contractors	23815	5,163	5,292	46	48	1,702	1,779
Roofing contractors	23816	18,999	19,170	172	181	5,644	5,935
Siding contractors	23817	10,082	10,091	50	51	1,428	1,531
Other foundation, structure, and building exterior contractors	23819	3,812	4,314	31	36	1,176	1,311
Building equipment contractors	2382	165,428	171,809	1,746	1,785	70,976	73,626
Electrical contractors	23821	68,211	72,817	725	744	29,929	30,917
Plumbing, heating, and air-conditioning contractors	23822	91,111	92,898	912	933	35,907	37,416
Other building equipment contractors	23829	6,106	6,094	109	108	5,140	5,293
Building finishing contractors..............	2383	115,155	123,276	802	863	26,294	28,764
Drywall and insulation contractors..........	23831	18,773	20,406	273	294	9,590	10,333
Painting and wall covering contractors.......	23832	39,174	39,495	208	217	6,052	6,512
Flooring contractors	23833	14,088	15,707	75	82	2,606	2,907
Tile and terrazzo contractors	23834	8,737	10,226	55	63	1,805	2,076
Finish carpentry contractors.............	23835	28,639	31,501	135	150	4,284	4,871
Other building finishing contractors	23839	5,744	5,941	56	58	1,958	2,065
Other specialty trade contractors	2389	68,489	68,026	447	469	17,251	18,488
Site preparation contractors..............	23891	36,198	35,622	257	269	10,352	11,017
All other specialty trade contractors.........	23899	32,291	32,404	190	200	6,899	7,471

[1] North American Industry Classification System code, 2002; see text, Section 15. [2] Employees on the payroll for the pay period including March 12.

Source: U.S. Census Bureau, "County Business Patterns"; annual. See <http://www.census.gov/epcd/cbp/view/cbpview.html>.

Construction and Housing **595**

Table 926. Construction—Establishments, Employees, Payroll, Value of Construction, Costs, and Capital Expenditures by Kind of Business (NAICS Basis): 2002

[For establishments with payroll. (254,292 represents $254,292,000,000). Based on the 2002 Economic Censuses; See Appendix III]

Kind of business	2002 NAICS code[1]	Number of establishments	Number of employees	Average number of construction workers	Total payroll (mil. dol.)	Total payroll construction workers (mil. dol.)	Value of construction work (mil. dol.)	Net value of construction work (mil. dol.)	Value added (mil. dol.)	Cost of materials, components, and supplies (mil. dol.)	Capital expenditures excluding land (mil. dol.)
Construction	**23**	**710,307**	**7,193,069**	**5,317,758**	**254,292**	**173,250**	**1,196,556**	**874,853**	**560,885**	**326,144**	**20,578**
New single-family general contractors	236115	58,488	273,202	179,473	8,268	4,484	61,876	38,629	19,708	19,311	622
New multifamily general contractors	236116	4,370	43,726	27,398	1,717	931	16,724	7,505	4,163	3,642	191
New housing operative builders	236117	26,046	241,069	120,071	10,504	4,116	139,221	87,271	51,444	36,833	907
Residential remodelers	236118	82,750	320,208	207,637	8,704	4,929	45,034	30,628	18,286	12,542	528
Industrial building construction	236210	2,799	95,130	71,429	3,960	2,626	17,515	9,899	6,436	3,614	222
Commercial building construction	236220	37,391	696,056	461,787	29,260	16,569	241,480	108,486	72,170	38,096	1,426
Water and sewer system construction	237110	12,395	198,622	156,692	7,361	5,296	32,482	26,818	16,022	10,984	1,205
Oil and gas pipeline construction	237120	1,418	94,323	79,237	4,033	3,208	11,580	10,333	7,751	2,717	315
Power and communication system construction	237130	5,995	246,669	189,336	10,422	7,703	34,078	30,025	22,532	8,129	782
Land subdivision	237210	8,444	52,607	18,736	2,004	619	13,927	10,836	9,146	2,187	249
Highway, street, and bridge construction	237310	11,348	410,822	319,768	15,654	11,282	81,412	62,095	35,976	28,062	2,902
Other heavy construction	237990	10,227	140,202	106,800	4,849	3,422	20,739	17,270	11,477	6,125	1,048
Poured concrete structure contractors	238110	27,149	301,737	254,375	9,181	7,170	33,772	30,512	18,119	12,508	814
Steel and precast concrete contractors	238120	4,329	76,861	62,510	2,906	2,218	8,724	7,986	5,822	2,210	199
Framing contractors	238130	14,438	153,636	130,863	4,415	3,520	14,429	12,650	8,588	4,214	195
Masonry contractors	238140	25,763	256,634	217,735	7,166	5,794	20,270	19,210	13,173	6,088	419
Glass and glazing contractors	238150	5,294	49,840	33,114	1,758	1,088	6,270	6,003	3,502	2,629	74
Roofing contractors	238160	23,222	219,329	169,958	6,026	4,097	23,012	21,120	12,812	8,399	450
Siding contractors	238170	2,839	43,000	30,241	1,192	801	4,288	3,842	2,273	1,615	67
Other building exterior contractors	238190	2,850	32,850	24,125	1,193	803	3,676	3,389	2,136	1,287	56
Electrical contractors	238210	62,862	763,949	597,200	29,573	22,336	82,663	78,140	52,085	26,770	1,196
Plumbing and HVAC contractors	238220	87,936	954,095	696,890	36,019	25,681	118,447	105,962	67,464	39,440	1,849
Other building equipment contractors	238290	6,090	118,606	85,344	4,930	3,578	14,476	13,654	10,076	3,813	285
Drywall and insulation contractors	238310	19,644	295,730	247,522	9,772	7,595	30,825	27,061	18,068	9,075	349
Painting and wall covering contractors	238320	39,025	232,489	182,454	6,014	4,452	16,869	15,330	11,524	3,895	327
Flooring contractors	238330	12,886	76,601	49,089	2,397	1,433	9,388	8,279	4,789	3,622	128
Tile and terrazzo contractors	238340	8,927	58,774	43,723	1,834	1,260	5,853	5,634	3,748	1,942	96
Finish carpentry contractors	238350	35,094	171,836	122,460	4,708	3,236	18,134	15,621	9,737	6,189	321
Other building finishing contractors	238390	3,776	50,837	37,545	1,728	1,175	4,877	4,574	3,415	1,202	75
Site preparation contractors	238910	30,589	284,528	222,469	9,770	7,153	37,755	32,534	23,287	9,783	2,332
All other specialty trade contractors	238990	32,098	239,098	171,778	6,974	4,677	26,760	23,558	15,157	9,220	946

[1] North American Industry Classification System, 2002; see text, this section and Section 15.

Source: U.S. Census Bureau, "2002 Economic Census, Construction, Subject Series Reports." See Internet site <http://www.census.gov/econ/census02/guide/SUBSUMM.HTM>.

Table 927. Construction Materials—Producer Price Indexes: 1990 to 2006

[1982 = 100, except as noted. Data for 2006 are preliminary. For discussion of producer price indexes, see text, Section 14. This index, more formally known as the special commodity grouping index for construction materials, covers materials incorporated as integral parts of a building or normally installed during construction and not readily removable. Excludes consumer durables such as kitchen ranges, refrigerators, etc. This index is not the same as the stage-of-processing index of intermediate materials and components for construction]

Commodity	1990	1995	2000	2001	2002	2003	2004	2005	2006
Construction materials	119.6	138.8	144.1	142.8	144.0	147.1	161.5	169.6	180.2
Interior solvent-based paint	133.0	164.5	191.1	190.2	190.5	198.0	(NA)	(NA)	(NA)
Architectural coatings	132.7	152.3	168.7	174.3	175.2	180.6	187.4	203.3	220.0
Construction products from plastics	117.2	133.8	135.8	132.9	136.1	138.6	144.6	158.8	182.1
Douglas fir, dressed	138.4	198.8	185.2	178.1	178.5	176.7	(NA)	(NA)	(NA)
Southern pine, dressed	111.2	166.9	161.0	152.5	145.2	145.4	(NA)	(NA)	(NA)
Softwood lumber	123.8	178.5	178.6	170.1	170.8	170.8	209.8	203.6	189.1
Millwork	130.4	163.8	176.4	179.2	179.8	181.8	191.9	197.2	201.7
Softwood plywood	119.6	188.1	173.3	167.8	164.1	195.9	250.9	223.5	190.6
Hardwood plywood and related products	102.7	122.2	130.2	130.4	131.5	129.0	134.4	138.1	(NA)
Hardwood veneer and plywood [1]	(NA)	(NA)	(NA)	(NA)	(NA)	(NA)	(NA)	(NA)	101.5
Softwood plywood veneer, excluding reinforced/backed	142.3	203.5	182.2	175.5	172.8	184.1	209.5	206.2	(NA)
Building paper and building board mill products	112.2	144.9	138.8	129.3	129.3	159.9	192.4	184.9	172.8
Steel pipe and tubes [2]	102.6	104.4	106.6	104.0	106.7	113.3	166.3	193.3	201.6
Builders' hardware	133.0	153.2	163.8	166.4	169.3	170.3	172.9	179.2	187.5
Plumbing fixtures and brass fittings	144.3	166.0	180.4	180.8	181.9	183.4	188.3	197.6	207.1
Heating equipment	131.6	147.5	155.6	157.1	157.9	163.2	169.5	179.9	185.7
Metal doors, sash, and trim	131.4	156.5	165.1	167.1	168.0	169.9	175.8	184.9	193.1
Siding, aluminum [3]	(NA)	132.4	142.2	141.5	141.0	152.6	(NA)	(NA)	(NA)
Sheet metal products	129.2	138.9	144.0	143.7	145.2	146.6	162.6	169.4	176.2
Outdoor lighting equipment, including parts [4]	113.0	120.8	124.7	125.7	126.2	126.9	129.4	131.8	137.8
Commercial fluorescent fixtures [5]	113.0	121.0	117.7	113.6	114.0	115.2	113.6	(NA)	(NA)
Commercial and industrial lighting fixtures	127.5	138.9	140.3	140.2	139.5	141.9	142.3	147.0	151.9
Architectural and ornamental metalwork [6]	118.7	128.0	139.8	141.7	144.2	147.2	172.5	185.4	191.2
Fabricated ferrous wire products [2]	114.6	125.7	130.0	129.8	129.7	131.3	149.3	157.1	162.7
Elevators, escalators, and other lifts.	110.1	113.0	118.7	119.4	120.0	118.7	120.5	123.5	126.0
Stamped metal switch and receptacle box	158.0	183.5	183.0	195.4	195.4	196.1	205.2	(NA)	(NA)
Electrical conduit and conduit fittings [7]	(NA)	(NA)	(NA)	(NA)	(NA)	(NA)	(NA)	106.6	116.3
Other noncurrent-carrying wiring devices [7]	(NA)	(NA)	(NA)	(NA)	(NA)	(NA)	(NA)	102.3	107.9
Concrete ingredients and related products	115.3	134.7	155.6	159.1	162.6	164.8	170.4	185.3	205.0
Concrete products	113.5	129.4	147.8	151.7	152.7	153.6	161.2	177.2	195.1
Clay construction products excluding refractories . . .	129.9	144.3	152.8	155.7	152.8	154.2	156.6	165.4	176.7
Prep asphalt and tar roofing and siding products . . .	95.8	97.8	100.0	103.3	106.6	110.6	111.9	125.0	136.9
Gypsum product	105.2	154.5	201.4	156.4	168.9	171.5	198.8	229.6	275.1
Insulation materials	108.4	118.8	128.6	127.6	128.3	128.8	137.2	142.2	150.2
Paving mixtures and blocks	101.2	105.8	130.4	134.6	136.2	142.6	144.9	156.9	199.8

NA Not available.   [1] December 2005 = 100.   [2] June 1982 = 100.   [3] December 1982 = 100.   [4] June 1985 = 100.   [5] Recessed nonair.   [6] December 1983 = 100.   [7] December 2004 = 100.

Source: U.S. Bureau of Labor Statistics, Producer Price Indexes, monthly and annual. See Internet site <http://www.bls.gov/ppi/home.htm>.

Table 928. Value of New Construction Put in Place: 1980 to 2006

[In millions of dollars (273,936 represents $273,936,000,000). Represents value of construction put in place during year; differs from building permit and construction contract data in timing and coverage. Includes installed cost of normal building service equipment and selected types of industrial production equipment (largely site fabricated). Excludes cost of shipbuilding, land, and most types of machinery and equipment. For methodology, see Appendix III. For details, see Tables 929 and 930]

Year		Private			Public		
	Total	Total	Residential buildings	Non-residential	Total	Federal	State and local
1980	273,936	210,290	100,381	109,909	63,646	9,642	54,004
1985	403,416	325,601	160,520	165,081	77,815	12,004	65,811
1990	476,778	369,300	191,103	178,197	107,478	12,099	95,379
1991	432,592	322,483	166,251	156,232	110,109	12,845	97,264
1992	463,661	347,814	199,393	148,421	115,847	14,376	101,471
1993	502,435	375,073	225,067	150,006	127,362	14,424	112,938
1994	549,420	418,999	258,561	160,438	130,421	14,440	115,981
1995	567,896	427,885	247,351	180,534	140,011	15,751	124,260
1996	623,313	476,638	281,115	195,523	146,675	15,325	131,350
1997	656,171	502,734	289,014	213,720	153,437	14,087	139,350
1998	706,779	552,001	314,607	237,394	154,778	14,318	140,460
1999	768,811	599,729	350,562	249,167	169,082	14,025	155,057
2000	831,075	649,750	374,457	275,293	181,325	14,166	167,157
2001	864,159	662,247	388,324	273,922	201,912	15,081	186,830
2002	873,090	659,651	421,912	237,739	213,438	16,578	196,860
2003	921,403	705,276	475,941	229,335	216,127	17,913	198,214
2004	1,023,487	803,305	564,827	238,478	220,183	18,342	201,841
2005	1,132,149	897,989	641,345	256,644	234,160	17,300	216,860
2006	1,192,238	937,047	641,332	295,715	255,191	17,603	237,588

Source: U.S. Census Bureau, "Construction Spending," Internet site <http://www.census.gov/const/www/c30index.html>.

Construction and Housing   597

Census Bureau, Statistical Abstract of the United States: 2008

Table 929. **Value of Private Construction Put in Place: 1995 to 2006**

[In millions of dollars (427,885 represents $427,885,000,000). Represents value of construction put in place during year; differs from building permit and construction contract data in timing and coverage. See Appendix III and Tables 928 and 930]

Type of construction	1995	1999	2000	2001	2002	2003	2004	2005	2006
Total construction [1]	427,885	599,729	649,750	662,247	659,651	705,276	803,305	897,989	937,047
Residential	247,351	350,562	374,457	388,324	421,912	475,941	564,827	641,345	641,332
New single family	153,515	223,837	236,788	249,086	265,889	310,575	377,557	433,510	415,997
New multifamily	17,889	27,434	28,259	30,305	32,952	35,116	39,944	47,297	53,020
Improvements	75,947	99,290	109,410	108,933	123,071	130,250	147,326	160,538	172,315
Nonresidential	180,534	249,167	275,293	273,922	237,739	229,335	238,478	256,644	295,715
Lodging	7,131	15,955	16,304	14,519	10,467	9,930	11,982	12,666	17,687
Office	22,996	45,052	52,407	49,745	35,296	30,579	32,879	37,276	46,194
General	20,569	41,745	49,637	47,136	32,356	27,380	28,679	32,962	41,390
Financial	2,339	3,125	2,689	2,586	2,857	3,174	4,186	4,285	4,742
Commercial [1]	44,096	59,376	64,055	63,606	59,000	57,505	63,195	66,584	72,148
Automotive [1]	4,191	5,904	5,967	5,650	5,807	5,039	5,235	5,614	5,463
Sales	883	1,573	1,629	2,014	2,235	2,099	2,443	2,834	2,306
Service/parts	2,448	3,270	3,009	2,394	2,308	1,866	1,978	1,805	2,089
Parking	860	1,062	1,330	1,242	1,265	1,074	814	975	1,068
Food/beverage [1]	7,169	8,277	8,786	8,765	7,914	8,369	8,232	7,795	7,417
Food	3,062	4,610	4,792	4,300	4,207	4,234	3,590	3,128	2,773
Dining/drinking	3,408	2,874	2,935	3,441	2,916	3,321	3,937	4,078	3,735
Fast food	699	793	1,058	1,024	792	813	705	590	908
Multiretail [1]	11,976	15,234	14,911	16,373	15,581	15,400	18,828	22,750	29,126
General merchandise	5,339	4,668	5,100	5,066	6,009	5,341	6,416	6,740	5,849
Shopping center	4,086	7,187	6,803	7,769	6,605	6,867	9,256	12,462	18,446
Shopping mall	2,175	2,873	2,523	2,701	2,108	2,231	2,138	2,631	3,320
Other commercial [1]	8,432	11,179	13,537	11,945	12,083	11,249	13,341	11,744	10,574
Drug store	536	1,645	1,682	1,185	1,644	1,790	1,427	1,315	1,301
Building supply store	1,372	1,588	2,592	3,016	2,471	2,268	2,521	2,416	2,628
Other stores	5,653	6,849	8,136	6,995	7,145	6,214	8,229	7,075	5,707
Warehouse	9,299	13,702	14,822	15,691	11,908	12,345	12,074	12,827	14,292
General commercial	8,944	12,756	13,511	14,440	10,934	11,004	10,830	11,468	13,298
Farm	3,014	5,059	5,988	5,135	5,611	5,103	5,485	5,854	5,277
Health care	15,259	18,388	19,455	19,506	22,438	24,217	26,272	28,495	33,183
Hospital	8,807	9,491	10,183	11,313	13,925	15,234	16,147	18,250	22,860
Medical building	4,064	4,910	5,066	4,638	4,924	6,068	7,615	8,031	7,292
Special care	2,388	3,987	4,206	3,555	3,538	2,915	2,510	2,213	3,032
Educational [1]	5,699	9,756	11,683	12,846	13,109	13,424	12,701	12,788	13,745
Preschool	326	663	770	874	593	711	674	516	489
Primary/secondary	1,245	2,420	2,948	3,536	3,605	3,204	3,2C2	2,718	3,205
Higher education [1]	3,055	5,204	6,333	6,597	6,875	7,259	6,496	6,946	7,561
Instructional	1,712	2,258	3,058	3,210	3,619	3,701	3,200	3,556	3,454
Dormitory	483	1,274	1,356	1,555	1,528	1,761	1,669	1,537	2,085
Sports/recreation	192	515	645	755	772	677	739	821	854
Other educational	817	1,232	1,318	1,421	1,651	1,785	1,998	2,294	2,067
Gallery/museum	571	778	920	990	1,312	1,371	1,335	1,745	1,675
Religious	4,348	7,371	8,030	8,393	8,335	8,559	8,153	7,715	7,690
House of worship	2,951	5,057	5,656	6,040	6,021	6,238	6,015	5,992	6,231
Other religious	1,389	2,314	2,347	2,330	2,312	2,322	2,138	1,723	1,459
Auxiliary building	619	1,252	1,280	1,247	1,358	1,296	1,258	1,251	1,190
Public safety	185	465	423	274	217	185	289	408	448
Amusement and recreation [1]	5,886	9,550	8,768	7,828	7,478	7,781	8,432	7,507	9,041
Theme/amusement park	563	919	747	462	230	270	198	200	386
Sports	910	1,495	1,068	1,067	1,427	1,306	900	807	839
Fitness	637	1,137	1,152	1,294	1,286	1,262	1,141	1,425	1,999
Performance/meeting center	365	546	732	977	900	844	1,054	1,072	783
Social center	1,558	2,006	2,368	2,337	2,285	1,996	2,594	1,626	1,478
Movie theater/studio	848	2,376	1,461	792	568	855	1,218	1,248	1,214
Transportation [1]	4,759	6,525	6,879	7,058	6,773	6,568	6,841	7,124	7,937
Air	666	1,106	1,804	1,993	1,281	1,012	869	748	715
Land	4,008	5,164	4,907	4,883	5,325	5,462	5,800	6,214	7,049
Railroad	3,509	4,670	4,263	4,456	4,584	4,851	5,392	5,816	6,589
Communication	11,112	18,405	18,799	19,596	18,384	14,456	15,468	18,846	21,621
Power [1]	22,006	22,040	29,344	31,499	32,608	33,619	27,360	26,314	30,481
Electricity	14,274	15,489	23,374	25,270	24,998	25,592	20,431	19,192	21,660
Gas	6,279	4,918	4,891	5,078	6,080	6,358	5,096	5,239	5,741
Oil	929	1,489	1,003	943	1,193	1,068	1,579	1,293	1,876
Sewage and waste disposal	576	516	508	402	246	278	331	240	284
Water supply	670	413	714	563	397	393	405	326	445
Manufacturing [1]	35,364	35,126	37,583	37,815	22,744	21,434	23,667	29,886	34,278
Food/beverage/tobacco	4,525	3,654	3,985	4,088	2,817	2,695	3,157	4,677	4,892
Textile/apparel/leather & allied	824	490	413	307	284	218	188	415	146
Wood	616	460	483	343	477	376	485	982	1,505
Paper	1,448	896	479	1,265	584	818	548	467	562
Print/publishing	1,197	924	848	1,232	666	630	654	777	748
Petroleum/coal	4,741	1,004	1,255	1,171	887	717	1,204	771	1,666
Chemical	5,531	6,632	3,798	4,896	5,625	5,368	5,507	6,588	9,239
Plastic/rubber	1,475	2,388	1,645	1,379	776	659	936	877	839
Nonmetallic mineral	856	1,282	1,898	2,216	536	865	896	1,163	1,961
Primary metal	2,533	2,137	1,976	773	241	436	312	836	1,489
Fabricated metal	808	2,046	2,148	1,447	833	662	595	699	568
Machinery	1,275	1,040	864	863	797	707	645	917	924
Computer/electronic/electrical	6,332	4,748	6,392	6,029	1,918	1,444	2,835	4,247	4,324
Transportation equipment	2,382	3,683	6,318	6,901	3,832	3,314	2,610	3,702	2,557
Furniture	213	232	148	232	148	278	217	96	131

[1] Includes other types of construction, not shown separately

Source: U.S. Census Bureau, "Construction Spending," Internet <http://www.census.gov/const/www/c30index.html>.

Table 930. Value of State and Local Government Construction Put in Place: 1995 to 2006

[In millions of dollars (124,260 represents $124,260,000,000). See headnote, Table 928 and also Table 929]

Type of construction	1995	1999	2000	2001	2002	2003	2004	2005	2006
Total construction [1]	124,260	155,057	167,157	186,830	196,860	198,214	201,841	216,860	237,588
Residential	4,483	3,206	2,962	3,493	3,754	3,724	4,110	4,047	4,340
Multifamily	4,410	3,193	2,945	3,440	3,671	3,593	3,956	3,740	4,027
Nonresidential	119,778	151,851	164,196	183,337	193,106	194,490	197,731	212,813	233,248
Office	3,275	3,576	4,494	5,557	6,274	6,116	6,024	5,211	5,478
Commercial [1]	1,117	1,004	1,020	2,402	2,422	2,207	1,979	1,882	1,580
Automotive	808	1,515	1,233	1,927	1,714	1,599	1,501	1,490	1,199
Parking	664	1,347	1,143	1,913	1,693	1,562	1,356	1,357	1,054
Warehouse	199	271	330	301	293	318	276	218	189
Health care	2,648	2,503	2,829	2,942	3,490	4,005	5,025	5,059	5,514
Hospital	1,644	1,754	1,949	2,124	2,539	2,685	3,324	3,429	4,014
Medical building	673	390	490	487	509	876	1,211	1,168	904
Special care	331	359	390	390	442	444	490	463	597
Educational [1]	27,458	39,767	46,818	52,813	59,463	59,340	59,741	65,750	70,931
Primary/secondary [1]	18,708	29,489	33,764	36,670	41,972	40,316	40,990	44,184	48,691
Elementary	5,598	9,973	12,272	14,105	15,154	13,430	14,308	14,251	14,194
Middle/junior high	3,999	5,794	5,820	6,923	8,410	7,921	8,132	9,069	10,948
High	5,144	10,694	13,326	14,072	17,142	18,561	17,950	19,892	22,952
Higher education [1]	7,354	8,624	10,749	13,365	14,280	15,451	15,864	18,033	19,102
Instructional	4,566	5,098	6,317	7,874	7,982	9,042	8,699	9,275	9,496
Parking	169	355	514	561	432	508	765	1,013	913
Administration	136	260	294	199	456	236	303	387	654
Dormitory	348	778	1,078	1,429	1,620	2,074	2,673	2,918	3,414
Library	321	316	308	374	440	544	524	588	492
Student union/cafeteria	254	288	322	618	1,031	702	632	880	996
Sports/recreation	667	743	966	1,287	1,546	1,329	1,370	1,769	1,783
Infrastructure	844	679	835	835	545	613	867	1,138	1,249
Other educational	1,185	1,328	1,645	2,164	2,629	2,687	2,357	2,735	2,335
Library/archive	752	915	976	1,675	2,118	1,815	1,501	2,098	1,870
Public safety [1]	4,956	6,209	5,854	6,056	5,960	5,844	5,477	6,013	6,618
Correctional	4,056	5,193	4,754	4,894	4,554	4,204	3,771	3,958	4,609
Detention	3,383	4,215	3,907	3,838	3,418	3,148	2,787	2,936	3,302
Police/sheriff	673	978	848	1,057	1,135	1,056	985	1,022	1,307
Other public safety	858	1,016	1,100	1,161	1,406	1,640	1,705	2,055	2,009
Fire/rescue	546	867	994	991	1,227	1,359	1,441	1,675	1,626
Amusement and recreation [1]	5,140	7,239	7,583	9,143	9,215	8,354	7,794	7,340	8,943
Sports	1,369	2,684	2,289	2,709	2,569	2,065	1,746	1,587	1,864
Performance/meeting center	1,466	1,244	2,075	2,915	2,915	2,260	2,061	1,921	2,043
Convention center	1,025	868	1,397	2,268	2,130	1,545	1,350	1,350	1,409
Social center	648	1,107	1,152	1,432	1,446	1,606	1,476	1,006	1,251
Neighborhood center	487	836	886	1,065	934	1,221	1,312	866	1,060
Park/camp	1,418	2,042	1,930	1,846	1,928	1,999	2,303	2,728	3,657
Transportation	9,559	11,402	13,000	15,868	17,312	16,483	16,440	16,256	17,447
Air [1]	4,104	6,021	6,700	7,849	8,123	8,146	8,715	8,993	9,651
Passenger terminal	1,289	2,235	2,930	2,770	3,040	3,778	3,972	3,310	3,728
Runway	2,313	3,138	3,196	4,354	4,305	3,793	4,049	4,861	4,915
Land [1]	4,278	4,312	5,165	6,253	7,291	7,207	6,415	5,936	6,518
Passenger terminal	1,224	1,259	1,253	1,557	1,860	2,099	1,368	907	981
Mass transit	1,851	1,357	1,484	2,492	3,375	3,160	3,067	3,208	3,152
Railroad	492	1,044	1,471	1,095	674	449	349	552	307
Water [1]	1,177	1,069	1,136	1,766	1,899	1,130	1,309	1,327	1,278
Dock/marina	737	663	863	1,258	1,203	894	1,028	930	916
Dry dock/marine terminal	217	406	236	483	695	235	281	397	362
Power	5,686	2,851	5,501	5,267	3,771	6,785	7,044	8,320	7,804
Electrical	4,087	2,245	5,257	4,963	3,244	6,041	5,851	7,091	7,143
Distribution	1,323	1,319	2,087	1,397	1,158	2,144	1,856	1,786	2,213
Highway and street [1]	38,553	51,003	51,574	56,428	56,660	56,251	57,351	63,157	70,946
Pavement	29,883	37,822	37,929	41,125	40,962	39,294	40,274	45,177	46,018
Lighting	676	944	856	1,228	888	1,156	1,146	1,232	1,059
Retaining wall	192	846	1,099	624	742	565	552	675	1,542
Tunnel	354	959	894	1,069	657	619	521	373	199
Bridge	6,788	8,793	9,302	10,910	11,741	12,980	13,150	14,244	19,905
Toll/weigh	156	289	325	104	217	180	233	320	660
Maintenance building	54	367	293	407	297	244	170	96	213
Rest facility/streetscape	172	974	878	961	1,155	1,213	1,306	1,042	1,351
Sewage and waste disposal [1]	12,976	14,491	14,000	14,157	15,334	15,625	17,084	18,336	21,292
Sewage/dry waste [1]	7,452	9,753	9,338	9,038	9,956	9,812	10,836	11,717	13,244
Plant	2,527	2,998	2,765	2,404	2,680	2,735	3,095	3,369	3,355
Line/pump station	4,581	6,352	6,326	6,375	7,082	6,934	7,574	8,243	9,718
Waste water	5,413	4,730	4,663	5,120	5,378	5,813	6,248	6,620	8,048
Plant	3,777	3,600	3,229	3,818	4,227	4,403	4,658	5,231	6,019
Line/drain	1,636	1,130	1,434	1,302	1,151	1,410	1,591	1,389	2,029
Water supply [1]	7,270	9,590	9,528	11,447	11,674	11,711	11,977	13,483	14,227
Plant	1,846	2,963	3,067	4,070	3,824	4,309	4,418	4,943	5,010
Well	331	320	378	394	555	365	318	360	622
Line	3,889	4,252	4,644	5,300	5,195	4,944	5,307	6,234	5,840
Pump station	444	786	625	684	852	767	705	776	1,293
Reservoir	320	563	266	410	463	450	503	502	695
Tank/tower	376	678	548	588	785	876	727	668	767
Conservation and development [1]	1,068	1,061	933	1,077	1,012	1,020	1,466	1,752	2,021
Dam/levee	275	414	303	242	279	231	297	405	603
Breakwater/jetty	300	300	270	490	397	514	654	726	811

[1] Includes other types of construction, not shown separately.

Source: U.S. Census Bureau, "Construction Spending," Internet site <http://www.census.gov/const/www/c30index.html>.

Construction and Housing 599

Table 931. **Construction Contracts—Value of Construction and Floor Space of Buildings by Class of Construction: 1980 to 2006**

[151.8 reresents $151,800,000,000. Building construction includes new structures and additions; nonbuilding construction includes major alterations to existing structures which affect only valuation, since no additional floor area is created by "alteration"]

Year		Resi- dential build- ings	Nonresidential buildings									Non- build- ing con- struc- tion
	Total		Total	Com- mer- cial [1]	Manu- fac- turing	Educa- tional [2]	Health	Public build- ings	Reli- gious	Social and recrea- tional	Mis- cella- neous	
VALUE (bil. dol.)												
1980	151.8	60.4	56.9	27.7	9.2	7.4	5.4	1.6	1.2	2.7	1.7	34.5
1985	235.6	102.1	92.1	54.6	8.1	10.0	7.8	3.1	2.0	4.0	2.5	41.4
1990	246.0	100.9	95.4	44.8	8.4	16.6	9.2	5.7	2.2	5.3	3.1	49.7
1995	306.5	127.9	114.2	46.6	13.8	22.9	10.8	6.3	2.8	7.1	3.8	64.4
1998	405.6	179.8	154.5	74.0	12.1	30.1	12.9	6.6	4.3	10.8	3.6	71.3
1999	447.2	195.0	168.7	77.2	11.3	37.1	13.6	8.2	4.5	11.6	5.1	83.5
2000	472.9	208.3	173.3	80.9	8.9	40.9	12.4	7.5	4.6	13.8	4.4	91.3
2001	496.5	219.7	169.1	70.2	8.0	47.0	14.4	7.8	4.8	12.0	4.8	107.7
2002	504.0	248.7	155.1	59.6	5.5	45.3	16.1	7.3	5.1	11.5	4.7	100.2
2003	531.8	283.4	156.1	58.9	6.9	47.8	15.7	7.1	4.5	11.0	4.3	92.4
2004	592.4	333.0	164.3	67.2	8.0	43.9	17.5	7.2	4.5	11.6	4.4	95.0
2005	667.4	383.3	180.8	71.6	9.9	48.8	21.9	7.9	4.1	11.6	4.9	103.3
2006	676.9	340.9	212.5	89.8	13.0	53.3	24.1	8.3	4.0	14.0	5.8	123.5
FLOOR SPACE (mil. sq. ft.)												
1980	3,102	1,839	1,263	738	220	103	55	18	28	49	52	(X)
1985	3,853	2,324	1,529	1,039	165	111	73	28	32	44	38	(X)
1990	3,020	1,817	1,203	694	128	152	69	47	29	51	32	(X)
1995	3,454	2,172	1,281	700	163	186	70	40	33	56	33	(X)
1998	4,812	3,015	1,797	1,107	166	219	96	42	47	85	34	(X)
1999	5,091	3,253	1,838	1,115	141	261	98	49	48	87	39	(X)
2000	4,982	3,113	1,869	1,180	111	273	88	44	49	94	29	(X)
2001	4,828	3,159	1,669	988	93	295	92	44	50	81	27	(X)
2002	4,792	3,356	1,436	810	68	277	97	37	52	71	26	(X)
2003	5,093	3,689	1,405	795	75	270	92	35	45	67	26	(X)
2004	5,517	4,060	1,457	875	86	231	94	34	43	68	27	(X)
2005	5,854	4,338	1,517	921	77	245	107	33	37	67	29	(X)
2006	5,240	3,642	1,597	982	82	253	110	34	34	71	32	(X)

X Not applicable.   [1] Includes nonindustrial warehouses.   [2] Includes science.

Source: McGraw-Hill Construction, a Division of the McGraw-Hill Companies, New York, NY (copyright).

Table 932. **Construction Contracts—Value by State: 2000 to 2006**

[In millions of dollars (472,930 represents $472,930,000,000). Represents value of construction in states in which work was actually done. See headnote, Table 932]

State			2006			State			2006		
	2000	2005	Total [1]	Resi- den- tial	Non- resi- den- tial		2000	2005	Total [1]	Resi- den- tial	Non- resi- den- tial
U.S.	472,930	667,440	676,931	340,940	212,453	MO	7,498	12,000	11,349	5,480	3,913
AL	7,225	9,664	9,886	5,703	2,507	MT	1,004	1,563	1,591	730	424
AK	1,327	1,813	2,124	558	793	NE	2,646	4,433	3,827	1,216	1,561
AZ	13,966	24,150	20,058	12,223	5,724	NV	6,978	12,614	15,708	5,942	6,864
AR	3,739	4,838	4,847	2,505	1,417	NH	2,514	2,699	2,233	1,107	749
CA	52,858	72,250	66,833	33,376	21,399	NJ	10,940	14,361	13,679	5,531	5,093
CO	12,491	16,461	16,585	8,740	4,401	NM	3,140	4,198	6,084	2,368	2,837
CT	5,181	5,833	7,221	2,363	3,905	NY	20,756	26,680	31,469	10,565	13,935
DE	1,350	1,986	1,722	955	436	NC	17,258	24,550	25,107	17,187	6,002
DC	1,763	1,446	1,855	354	1,030	ND	854	1,142	1,556	482	564
FL	35,079	71,341	64,029	41,767	14,396	OH	16,270	19,373	17,403	6,592	6,956
GA	20,419	27,038	28,551	16,290	7,316	OK	5,330	6,314	7,345	3,355	2,617
HI	1,409	3,164	4,230	2,703	929	OR	6,020	10,074	9,047	5,201	2,063
ID	2,521	4,934	4,988	3,498	1,065	PA	14,861	17,263	19,988	6,958	7,730
IL	17,167	24,645	25,068	12,461	8,135	RI	1,063	1,830	1,418	586	701
IN	11,011	14,205	13,549	5,808	5,207	SC	7,759	12,829	12,477	8,609	2,805
IA	3,776	6,460	6,292	2,394	2,491	SD	1,221	1,637	1,833	700	687
KS	4,463	5,055	5,643	2,258	1,815	TN	10,108	13,651	14,449	8,417	4,078
KY	6,625	7,427	8,488	3,342	2,661	TX	41,124	56,873	67,211	35,053	18,579
LA	5,528	7,331	9,183	4,300	2,075	UT	4,420	8,269	8,579	5,272	2,135
ME	1,710	2,474	2,352	1,152	719	VT	602	1,271	1,020	493	232
MD	7,836	10,226	11,624	5,010	4,819	VA	13,634	18,598	16,028	8,644	5,334
MA	11,983	11,189	8,953	4,119	3,442	WA	10,332	17,046	18,779	9,620	5,265
MI	14,735	14,224	12,713	4,902	5,500	WV	1,856	2,851	3,177	1,226	1,033
MN	8,838	10,064	9,596	4,755	2,905	WI	8,044	11,085	12,152	4,588	3,323
MS	2,917	4,291	5,112	2,676	1,496	WY	778	1,752	1,919	805	390

[1] Includes nonbuilding construction, not shown separately.

Source: McGraw-Hill Construction, a Division of the McGraw-Hill Companies, New York, NY, (copyright).

Table 933. **New Privately Owned Housing Units Authorized by State: 2000 and 2006**

[1,592.3 represents 1,592,300. Based on about 19,000 places in United States having building permit systems in 2000 and 20,000 in 2006]

State	Housing units (1,000) 2000	2006 Total	2006 1 unit	Valuation (mil. dol.) 2000	2006 Total	2006 1 unit	State	Housing units (1,000) 2000	2006 Total	2006 1 unit	Valuation (mil. dol.) 2000	2006 Total	2006 1 unit
U.S. ..	1,592.3	1,838.9	1,378.2	185,744	291,314	245,687	MO ...	24.3	29.2	19.9	2,569	4,087	3,427
AL ...	17.4	32.0	24.1	1,718	4,402	3,431	MT ...	2.6	4.5	3.4	235	723	598
AK ...	2.1	2.7	1.6	333	511	364	NE ...	9.1	8.2	6.6	830	1,065	968
AZ ...	61.5	65.4	55.6	7,158	11,203	10,176	NV ...	32.3	39.4	26.7	3,312	5,383	3,689
AR ...	9.2	13.9	10.8	859	1,794	1,586	NH ...	6.7	5.7	4.8	937	1,037	956
CA ...	145.6	160.5	107.7	23,344	29,614	23,454	NJ ...	34.6	34.3	17.1	3,376	4,383	3,067
CO ...	54.6	38.3	30.4	6,822	7,770	6,797	NM ...	8.9	13.6	12.3	1,073	2,316	2,211
CT ...	9.4	9.2	7.1	1,425	1,874	1,723	NY ...	44.1	54.4	20.0	4,992	7,078	4,137
DE ...	4.6	6.5	5.0	414	785	663	NC ...	78.4	100.0	82.7	8,643	16,074	14,692
DC ...	0.8	2.1	0.1	54	300	20	ND ...	2.1	3.5	2.3	190	462	353
FL ...	155.3	203.2	146.2	17,462	35,716	27,902	OH ...	49.7	34.4	27.5	6,154	5,920	5,378
GA ...	91.8	104.2	86.1	8,722	14,455	12,952	OK ...	11.1	15.8	14.1	1,204	2,322	2,232
HI ...	4.9	7.5	5.6	823	1,761	1,476	OR ...	19.9	26.6	19.9	2,533	4,942	4,254
ID ...	10.9	17.1	14.8	1,359	2,987	2,729	PA ...	41.1	39.1	33.1	4,616	6,354	5,829
IL ...	51.9	58.8	37.9	6,528	9,470	7,691	RI ...	2.6	2.4	1.8	296	384	312
IN ...	37.9	29.1	24.4	4,414	4,688	4,344	SC ...	32.8	50.8	41.7	3,533	7,592	6,636
IA ...	12.5	13.4	10.3	1,333	2,006	1,700	SD ...	4.2	5.3	4.0	369	659	572
KS ...	12.5	14.6	11.1	1,397	1,995	1,768	TN ...	32.2	46.0	39.2	3,378	6,782	6,224
KY ...	18.5	16.6	13.5	1,767	2,261	2,054	TX ...	141.2	216.6	162.8	15,418	29,206	25,240
LA ...	14.7	28.7	23.8	1,553	3,818	3,428	UT ...	17.6	25.9	22.6	2,138	4,847	4,476
ME ...	6.2	7.3	6.5	723	1,125	1,053	VT ...	2.5	2.6	2.1	319	422	374
MD ...	30.4	23.3	17.9	3,232	3,890	3,242	VA ...	48.4	47.7	39.0	5,052	7,707	6,845
MA ...	18.0	19.6	10.9	2,741	3,249	2,387	WA ...	39.0	50.0	35.6	4,426	8,540	6,961
MI ...	52.5	29.2	24.8	6,256	4,493	4,100	WV ...	3.8	5.6	5.2	360	944	914
MN ...	32.8	26.4	20.9	4,204	4,843	4,145	WI ...	34.2	27.3	19.6	3,917	4,424	3,716
MS ...	11.3	16.6	14.1	918	2,011	1,837	WY ...	1.6	3.5	3.1	314	639	601

Source: U.S. Census Bureau, Construction Reports, "New Residential Construction." See Internet site <http://www.census.gov/const/www/newresconstindex.html>.

Table 934. **New Privately Owned Housing Units Started—Selected Characteristics: 1970 to 2006**

[In thousands (1,434 represents 1,434,000). For composition of regions, see map inside front cover]

Year	Total units	Structures with— 1 unit	2 to 4 units	5 or more units	Region North-east	Mid-west	South	West	Units for sale Total	Single-family	Multi-family
1970	1,434	813	85	536	218	294	612	311	(NA)	(NA)	(NA)
1975	1,160	892	64	204	149	294	442	275	576	531	45
1980	1,292	852	110	331	125	218	643	306	689	526	163
1981	1,084	705	91	288	117	165	562	240	584	426	158
1982	1,062	663	80	320	117	149	591	205	549	409	140
1983	1,703	1,068	113	522	168	218	935	382	923	713	210
1984	1,750	1,084	121	544	204	243	866	436	934	728	206
1985	1,742	1,072	93	576	252	240	782	468	867	713	154
1986	1,805	1,179	84	542	294	296	733	483	925	782	143
1987	1,621	1,146	65	409	269	298	634	420	862	732	130
1988	1,488	1,081	59	348	235	274	575	404	808	709	99
1989	1,376	1,003	55	318	179	266	536	396	735	648	87
1990	1,193	895	38	260	131	253	479	329	585	529	56
1991	1,014	840	36	138	113	233	414	254	531	490	41
1992	1,200	1,030	31	139	127	288	497	288	659	618	41
1993	1,288	1,126	29	133	127	298	562	302	760	716	44
1994	1,457	1,198	35	224	138	329	639	351	815	763	52
1995	1,354	1,076	34	244	118	290	615	331	763	712	51
1996	1,477	1,161	45	271	132	322	662	361	833	774	59
1997	1,474	1,134	45	296	137	304	670	363	843	784	59
1998	1,617	1,271	43	303	149	331	743	395	941	882	59
1999	1,641	1,302	32	307	156	347	746	392	981	912	69
2000	1,569	1,231	39	299	155	318	714	383	946	871	75
2001	1,603	1,273	37	293	149	330	732	391	990	919	71
2002	1,705	1,359	39	308	158	350	782	416	1,070	999	71
2003	1,848	1,499	34	315	163	374	839	472	1,207	1,120	87
2004	1,956	1,611	42	303	175	356	909	516	1,360	1,240	120
2005	2,068	1,716	41	311	190	357	996	525	1,508	1,358	150
2006	1,801	1,465	43	293	167	280	910	444	1,272	1,121	151

NA Not available.

Source: U.S. Census Bureau, Construction Reports, "New Residential Construction." See Internet site <http://www.census.gov/const/www/newresconstindex.html>.

Construction and Housing **601**

Table 935. New Privately Owned Housing Units Started by State: 2000 to 2006

[In thousands of units (1,573 represents 1,573,000)]

State	2000	2004, est.	2005, est.	2006, est. Total units	2006, est. Single-family units	State	2000	2004, est.	2005, est.	2006, est. Total units	2006, est. Single-family units
U.S.	1,573	1,724	1,658	1,614	1,319	MO	27.4	27.7	27.5	27.5	24.3
AL......	21.2	20.8	20.9	21.1	18.2	MT	2.4	2.9	2.9	2.8	2.0
AK......	2.0	2.3	2.3	2.3	1.6	NE......	9.2	10.5	10.0	9.7	8.5
AZ......	59.4	64.4	61.9	60.1	53.2	NV......	31.0	37.8	36.1	35.0	27.9
AR......	12.5	13.8	13.6	13.6	10.4	NH......	6.4	7.4	7.0	6.6	5.6
CA......	137.1	177.7	165.0	154.2	120.3	NJ......	31.4	27.2	26.5	26.1	20.7
CO......	52.5	35.9	36.8	37.7	31.7	NM......	7.3	10.6	10.3	10.1	8.9
CT......	8.9	8.6	8.5	8.5	7.7	NY......	41.1	41.0	38.8	37.5	22.0
DE......	4.4	6.2	5.9	5.7	5.4	NC......	76.1	72.8	71.1	70.2	59.3
DC......	0.4	0.4	0.4	0.4	0.1	ND......	2.4	3.6	3.4	3.3	2.3
FL......	147.9	185.7	173.6	165.4	123.7	OH......	47.8	51.2	49.7	48.8	41.7
GA......	90.4	89.3	86.1	84.1	71.0	OK......	14.1	14.6	14.3	14.2	12.6
HI	4.7	6.8	6.5	6.2	5.1	OR......	18.8	19.2	19.6	20.0	15.6
ID	11.3	13.5	13.1	12.8	11.1	PA......	39.2	40.4	39.4	39.0	34.6
IL......	51.3	61.5	58.5	56.6	45.2	RI	2.6	2.4	2.4	2.4	2.0
IN	38.2	40.4	39.4	38.8	33.5	SC	31.6	35.1	33.4	32.3	27.2
IA	12.8	15.3	14.6	14.1	11.5	SD	4.4	5.2	4.9	4.8	4.0
KS.....	13.4	14.0	13.8	13.8	11.7	TN	34.6	34.3	34.2	34.3	30.4
KY.....	21.8	20.4	20.4	20.5	17.9	TX	145.0	163.3	154.9	149.1	117.8
LA	15.5	18.7	18.0	17.7	15.2	UT......	18.1	20.2	19.9	19.8	16.7
ME.....	6.3	7.3	6.8	6.5	6.0	VT.....	2.6	2.8	2.7	2.6	2.4
MD.....	28.7	27.4	27.1	27.0	22.5	VA	47.5	53.4	51.8	50.6	43.2
MA.....	17.1	16.2	16.0	16.0	12.8	WA	36.9	38.8	38.3	38.2	29.9
MI......	50.4	53.4	51.7	50.7	45.2	WV	5.3	5.4	5.4	5.4	5.1
MN.....	32.9	41.7	39.0	37.1	31.9	WI.....	32.6	38.1	36.7	35.8	27.9
MS.....	14.1	12.8	12.8	12.9	11.1	WY	1.9	2.2	2.2	2.3	2.1

Source: National Association of Home Builders, Economics Division, Washington, DC. Data provided by the Econometric Forecasting Service.

Table 936. Characteristics of New Privately Owned One-Family Houses Completed: 1990 to 2006

[Percent distribution, except total houses. (966 represents 966,000). Data are percent distribution of characteristics for all houses completed (includes new houses completed, houses built for sale completed, contractor-built and owner-built houses completed, and houses completed for rent). Percents exclude houses for which characteristics specified were not reported]

Characteristic	1990	2000	2005	2006	Characteristic	1990	2000	2005	2006
Total houses (1,000)	966	1,242	1,636	1,654	Bedrooms............	100	100	100	100
					2 or less............	15	11	12	12
Construction type	100	100	100	100	3.................	57	54	49	49
Site built.............	(NA)	94	96	95	4 or more	29	35	39	39
Modular	(NA)	3	3	2					
Other...............	(NA)	3	2	2	Bathrooms	100	100	100	100
					1 1/2 or less	13	7	4	5
Exterior wall material	100	100	100	100	2.................	42	39	36	36
Brick	18	20	20	21	2 1/2 or more	45	54	59	59
Wood................	39	14	7	8					
Stucco	18	17	22	22	Heating fuel..........	100	100	100	100
Vinyl siding [1]	(NA)	39	34	30	Gas	59	70	66	62
Aluminum siding	5	1	1	(Z)	Electricity	33	27	31	35
Other [1]	20	7	16	18	Oil.................	5	3	2	1
					Other...............	3	1	1	1
Floor area	100	100	100	100					
Under 1,200 sq. ft ...	11	6	4	4	Heating system	100	100	100	100
1,200 to 1,599 sq. ft.....	22	18	16	14	Warm air furnace	65	71	67	63
1,600 to 1,999 sq. ft.....	22	23	20	20	Electric heat pump	23	23	29	33
2,000 to 2,399 sq. ft	17	18	18	17	Other	12	6	4	5
2,400 sq. ft. and over	29	35	42	44					
Average (sq. ft.)........	2,080	2,266	2,434	2,469	Central air-conditioning ...	100	100	100	100
Median (sq. ft.)	1,905	2,057	2,227	2,248	With................	76	85	89	89
					Without	24	15	11	11
Number of stories	100	100	100	100					
1..................	46	47	44	43	Fireplaces............	100	100	100	100
2 or more	49	52	55	57	No fireplace	34	40	45	47
Split level	4	1	(Z)	(Z)	1 or more	66	60	55	53
Foundation	100	100	100	100	Parking facilities	100	100	100	100
Full or partial basement...	38	37	31	29	Garage..............	82	89	91	91
Slab................	40	46	53	56	Carport..............	2	1	1	1
Crawl space	21	17	16	15	No garage or carport	16	11	8	9

NA Not available.   Z Less than 0.5 percent.   [1] Prior to 1995, "other" includes vinyl siding.

Source: U.S. Census Bureau, "Characteristics of New Housing." See Internet site <http://www.census.gov/const/www/charindex.html>.

U.S. Census Bureau, Statistical Abstract of the United States: 2008

Table 937. **Housing Starts and Average Length of Time from Start to Completion of New Privately Owned One-Unit Residential Buildings: 1980 to 2006**

[(852 represents 852,000.) For buildings started in permit issuing places]

Year	Total [1]	Purpose of construction			Region [2]			
		Built for sale	Contractor built	Owner built	Northeast	Midwest	South	West
STARTS (1,000)								
1980	852	526	149	164	87	142	428	196
1985	1,072	713	177	157	182	148	504	239
1990	895	529	196	147	104	193	371	226
1995	1,076	712	199	133	102	234	485	256
1997	1,134	784	189	131	111	238	507	278
1998	1,271	882	209	144	122	273	574	303
1999	1,302	912	208	142	126	289	580	308
2000	1,231	871	195	128	118	260	556	297
2001	1,273	919	186	129	111	269	590	303
2002	1,359	999	198	125	118	277	628	336
2003	1,499	1,120	205	127	116	309	686	388
2004	1,611	1,240	198	130	128	306	743	433
2005	1,716	1,358	197	129	138	306	831	441
2006	1,465	1,121	189	119	118	235	757	356
COMPLETION (months)								
1980	6.9	6.2	5.5	10.1	7.7	8.0	6.1	7.4
1985	6.2	5.4	4.9	10.6	7.2	6.0	5.7	6.7
1990	6.4	5.9	5.3	10.3	9.3	5.6	5.7	6.9
1995	5.9	5.2	5.8	9.5	7.4	6.0	5.4	6.0
1997	6.0	5.2	5.9	9.8	7.3	6.2	5.6	5.8
1998	6.0	5.4	6.0	9.5	7.1	6.2	5.5	6.1
1999	6.1	5.5	6.4	9.2	7.0	6.4	5.7	6.3
2000	6.2	5.6	6.5	9.2	7.5	6.4	5.9	6.0
2001	6.2	5.6	7.0	9.2	7.6	6.5	5.8	6.3
2002	6.1	5.5	6.6	9.6	7.3	6.4	5.6	6.2
2003	6.2	5.5	6.8	9.9	7.5	6.7	5.7	6.2
2004	6.2	5.7	7.0	9.1	7.3	6.7	5.8	6.3
2005	6.4	5.9	7.6	9.8	7.7	6.6	6.0	6.8
2006	6.9	6.3	7.8	10.7	8.3	7.1	6.3	7.4

[1] Includes units built for rent, not shown separately.   [2] For composition of regions, see map inside front cover.

Source: U.S. Census Bureau, "New Residential Construction." See Internet site <http://www.census.gov/const/www/newresconstindex .html>.

Table 938. **Price Indexes of New One-Family Houses Sold, by Region: 1980 to 2006**

[1996 = 100. Based on kinds of homes sold in 1996. Includes value of the lot. For composition of regions, see map, inside front cover]

Year	Total	Northeast	Midwest	South	West
1980	59.5	48.0	56.8	63.2	58.4
1982	65.7	54.0	63.9	70.9	62.8
1983	67.1	57.3	63.7	72.8	64.0
1984	69.8	62.2	67.5	75.2	66.3
1985	70.7	68.5	66.4	76.7	66.7
1986	73.4	78.6	70.2	79.0	68.4
1987	77.4	89.2	74.9	81.9	72.0
1988	80.3	91.5	78.2	83.7	75.9
1989	83.5	94.1	80.0	86.1	80.7
1990	85.1	92.2	80.7	86.3	84.6
1991	86.2	89.2	82.8	87.9	85.1
1992	87.3	96.1	84.3	88.8	85.6
1993	91.1	93.3	90.0	93.0	88.7
1994	95.5	94.5	94.4	96.4	94.9
1995	98.2	96.7	98.1	99.4	96.5
1996	100.0	100.0	100.0	100.0	100.0
1997	102.9	102.8	103.3	102.8	102.9
1998	105.5	104.5	105.3	106.0	105.1
1999	110.7	108.8	110.3	110.5	111.7
2000	115.4	114.6	114.4	114.7	117.3
2001	119.5	122.6	115.8	117.8	123.9
2002	124.8	127.5	120.7	121.2	132.5
2003	131.9	137.5	124.7	126.5	144.3
2004	141.9	149.1	132.6	133.0	161.5
2005	153.1	152.9	139.2	140.8	185.5
2006	159.2	152.9	141.9	147.4	195.3

Source: U.S. Census Bureau, "Construction Price Indexes." See Internet site <http://www.census.gov/const/www/constpriceindex .html>.

Construction and Housing   603

Table 939. New Privately Owned One-Family Houses Sold by Region and Type of Financing, 1980 to 2006, and by Sales-Price Group, 2006

[In thousands (545 represents 545,000). Based on a national probability sample of monthly interviews with builders or owners of one-family houses for which building permits have been issued or, for nonpermit areas, on which construction has started. For details, see source and Appendix III. For composition of regions, see map inside front cover]

Year and sales-price group	Total sales	Region				Financing type			
		North-east	Midwest	South	West	Conven-tional [1]	FHA and VA	Rural Housing Service [2]	Cash
1980	545	50	81	267	145	302	196	14	32
1985	688	112	82	323	170	403	208	11	64
1990	534	71	89	225	149	337	138	10	50
1995	667	55	125	300	187	490	129	9	39
1999	880	76	168	395	242	689	143	6	41
2000	877	71	155	406	244	695	138	4	40
2001	908	66	164	439	239	726	141	2	39
2002	973	65	185	450	273	788	140	4	42
2003	1,086	79	189	511	307	911	130	4	41
2004	1,203	83	210	562	348	1,047	105	6	46
2005	1,283	81	205	638	358	1,150	79	1	52
2006	1,051	63	161	559	267	948	63	1	38
Under $200,000	369	9	73	263	25	305	51	–	13
$200,000 to $299,999	300	15	49	158	79	274	11	–	15
$300,000 to $499,999	258	24	29	100	104	248	1	–	8
$500,000 and over	123	14	10	38	60	119	–	–	3

– Represents or rounds to zero.   [1] Includes houses reporting other types of financing.   [2] Prior to 1999, the Farmers Home Administration.

Source: U.S. Census Bureau and U.S. Dept. of Housing and Urban Development, Current Construction Reports, Series C25, *Characteristics of New Housing*, annual; and *New One-Family Houses Sold*, monthly; publications discontinued in 2001. See New Residential Sales at <http://www.census.gov/const/www/newressalesindex.html>.

Table 940. Median Sales Price of New Privately Owned One-Family Houses Sold by Region: 1980 to 2006

[In dollars. For definition of median, see Guide to Tabular Presentation. For composition of regions, see map inside front cover. See Appendix III. See also headnote, Table 939]

Year	U.S.	North-east	Mid-west	South	West	Year	U.S.	North-east	Mid-west	South	West
1980	64,600	69,500	63,400	59,600	72,300	2001	175,200	246,400	172,600	155,400	213,600
1985	84,300	103,300	80,300	75,000	92,600	2002	187,600	264,300	178,000	163,400	238,500
1990	122,900	159,000	107,900	99,000	147,500	2003	195,000	264,500	184,300	168,100	260,900
1995	133,900	180,000	134,000	124,500	141,400	2004	221,000	315,800	205,000	181,100	283,100
1999	161,000	210,500	164,000	145,900	173,700	2005	240,900	343,800	216,900	197,300	332,600
2000	169,000	227,400	169,700	148,000	196,400	2006	246,500	346,000	213,500	208,200	337,700

Source: U.S. Census Bureau and U.S. Department of Housing and Urban Development, Current Construction Reports, Series C25, *Characteristics of New Housing*, annual; and *New One-Family Houses Sold*, monthly; publications discontinued in 2001. See New Residential Sales at <http://www.census.gov/const/www/newressalesindex.html>.

Table 941. New Manufactured (Mobile) Homes Placed for Residential Use and Average Sales Price by Region: 1980 to 2006

[233.7 represents 233,700. A mobile home is a moveable dwelling, 8 feet or more wide and 40 feet or more long, designed to be towed on its own chassis, with transportation gear integral to the unit when it leaves the factory, and without need of permanent foundation. Excluded are travel trailers, motor homes, and modular housing. Data are based on a probability sample and subject to sampling variability; see source. For composition of regions, see map inside front cover]

Year	Units placed (1,000)					Average sales price (dol.)				
	Total	North-east	Mid-west	South	West	U.S.	North-east	Mid-west	South	West
1980	233.7	12.3	32.3	140.3	48.7	19,800	18,500	18,600	18,200	25,400
1985	283.4	20.2	38.6	187.6	36.9	21,800	22,700	21,500	20,400	28,700
1990	195.4	18.8	37.7	108.4	30.6	27,800	30,000	27,000	24,500	39,300
1995	319.4	15.0	57.5	203.2	43.7	35,300	35,800	35,700	33,300	44,100
1996	337.7	16.2	58.8	218.2	44.4	37,200	37,300	38,000	35,500	45,000
1997	336.3	14.3	55.3	219.4	47.3	39,800	41,300	40,300	38,000	47,300
1998	373.7	14.7	58.3	250.3	50.4	41,600	42,200	42,400	40,100	48,400
1999	338.3	14.1	53.6	227.2	43.5	43,300	44,000	44,400	41,900	49,600
2000	280.9	14.9	48.7	178.7	38.6	46,400	47,000	47,900	44,300	54,100
2002	174.3	11.8	34.2	101.0	27.2	51,300	53,200	51,700	48,000	62,600
2003	139.8	11.2	25.2	77.2	26.1	54,900	57,300	55,100	50,500	67,700
2004	124.4	11.0	20.6	67.4	25.5	58,200	60,200	58,800	52,300	73,200
2005	122.9	9.2	17.1	68.1	28.5	62,600	67,000	60,600	55,700	79,900
2006	111.3	7.6	14.5	65.2	24.0	64,200	66,100	59,000	58,500	83,400

Source: U.S. Census Bureau, "Manufactured Housing." See Internet site <http://www.census.gov/const/www/mhsindex.html>.

604   Construction and Housing

Table 942. Existing One-Family Homes Sold and Price by Region: 1990 to 2006

[2,914 represents 2,914,000. Includes existing detached single-family homes and townhomes; excludes condos and co-ops. Based on data (adjusted and aggregated to regional and national totals) reported by participating real estate multiple listing services. For definition of median, see Guide to Tabular Presentation. See Table 945 for data on condos and co-ops. For composition of regions, see map inside front cover]

Year	Homes sold (1,000)					Median sales price (dol.)				
	Total	North-east	Mid-west	South	West	Total	North-east	Mid-west	South	West
1990	2,914	510	806	1,010	587	97,300	140,200	76,700	86,300	141,200
1991	2,885	515	808	992	569	102,700	149,300	81,000	89,800	147,400
1992	3,150	578	906	1,049	618	105,500	149,000	84,600	92,900	143,300
1993	3,427	611	961	1,173	681	109,100	149,300	87,600	95,800	144,400
1994	3,544	615	963	1,220	746	113,500	149,300	90,900	97,200	151,900
1995	3,519	609	944	1,219	747	117,000	146,500	96,500	99,200	153,600
1996	3,797	652	988	1,289	868	122,600	147,800	102,800	105,000	160,200
1997	3,964	678	1,009	1,363	914	129,000	152,400	108,900	111,300	169,000
1998	4,495	741	1,136	1,598	1,020	136,000	157,100	116,300	118,000	179,500
1999	4,649	728	1,144	1,705	1,072	141,200	160,700	121,600	122,100	189,400
2000	4,603	714	1,116	1,706	1,066	147,300	161,200	125,600	130,300	199,200
2001	4,734	709	1,155	1,793	1,076	156,600	169,400	132,300	139,600	211,700
2002	4,975	731	1,217	1,871	1,155	167,600	190,100	138,300	149,700	234,300
2003	5,443	769	1,322	2,072	1,280	180,200	220,300	143,700	159,700	254,700
2004	5,958	821	1,389	2,310	1,438	195,200	254,400	151,500	171,800	289,100
2005	6,180	838	1,411	2,457	1,474	219,000	281,600	168,300	181,100	340,300
2006	5,677	787	1,314	2,352	1,224	221,900	280,300	164,800	183,700	350,500

Source: NATIONAL ASSOCIATION OF REALTORS, Washington, DC, *Real Estate Outlook; Market Trends & Insights*, monthly, (copyright). See Internet site <http://www.realtor.org/research>.

Table 943. Median Sales Price of Existing One-Family Homes by Selected Metropolitan Area: 2005 and 2006

[In thousands of dollars (219.0 represents $219,000). Includes existing detached single-family homes and townhouses. Areas are metropolitan statistical areas defined by Office of Management and Budget as of 2004, except as noted]

Metropolitan area	2005	2006	Metropolitan area	2005	2006
United States, total	219.0	221.9	New York-Northern New Jersey-		
			Long Island, NY-NJ-PA.	445.2	469.5
Allentown-Bethlehem-Easton, PA-NJ	243.4	248.1	New York-Wayne-White Plains, NY-NJ. .	495.2	537.8
Anaheim-Santa Ana-Irvine, CA [1]	691.9	709.0	NY: Edison, NJ	375.5	387.7
Atlantic City, NJ	256.1	254.8	NY: Nassau-Suffolk, NY	465.2	474.7
Baltimore-Towson, MD.	265.3	279.9	NY: Newark-Union, NJ-PA.	416.8	436.5
Barnstable Town, MA.	398.3	389.5	Norwich-New London, CT.	255.9	264.4
Boston-Cambridge-Quincy, MA-NH [2]	413.2	402.2	Orlando, FL	243.6	270.4
Boulder, CO.	348.4	366.4	Palm Bay-Melbourne-Titusville, FL.	209.7	212.0
Bridgeport-Stamford-Norwalk, CT.	482.4	473.7	Philadelphia-Camden-		
			Wilmington, PA-NJ-DE-MD	215.3	230.2
Cape Coral-Fort Myers, FL.	269.2	268.2	Phoenix-Mesa-Scottsdale, AZ	247.4	268.2
Charleston-North Charleston, SC.	197.0	212.4	Pittsfield, MA	207.3	212.9
Chicago-Naperville-Joliet, IL	264.2	273.5	Portland-South Portland-Biddeford, ME. . .	246.6	243.8
Colordo Springs, CO	205.9	218.2	Portland-Vancouver-Beaverton, OR-WA . .	244.9	280.8
Deltona-Daytona Beach-			Providence-New Bedford-		
Ormond Beach, FL	192.5	205.8	Fall River, RI-MA.	293.4	289.6
Denver-Aurora, CO	247.1	249.5	Raleigh-Cary, NC	194.9	213.7
Dover, DE.	180.4	206.9	Reno-Sparks, NV	349.9	347.2
Eugene-Springfield, OR	197.6	230.6	Richmond, VA	201.9	225.5
Gainesville, FL	184.0	213.2	Riverside-San Bernardino-Ontario, CA [1] . .	374.2	400.1
Hagerstown-Martinsburg, MD-WV	208.7	223.1	Sacramento-Arden-Arcade-		
Hartford-West Hartford-			Roseville, CA [1]	375.9	374.8
East Hartford, CT	253.3	258.1	Salem, OR	177.7	212.9
Honolulu, HI.	590.0	630.0	San Diego-Carlsbad-San Marcos, CA [1] . .	604.3	601.8
Kingston, NY	251.0	252.7	San Francisco-Oakland-Fremont, CA [1] . .	715.7	736.8
Las Vegas-Paradise, NV	304.7	317.4	San Jose-Sunnyvale-Santa Clara, CA [1] . .	744.5	775.0
Los Angeles-Long Beach-			Sarasota-Bradenton-Venice, FL.	354.2	334.3
Santa Ana, CA [1]	[1]529.0	584.8	Seattle-Tacoma-Bellevue, WA	316.8	361.2
Madison, WI	218.3	223.2	Springfield, MA.	201.8	209.6
Miami-Fort Lauderdale-			Tampa-St.Petersburg-Clearwater, FL	205.3	228.9
Miami Beach, FL.	370.1	371.2	Trenton-Ewing, NJ	261.1	289.6
Milwaukee-Waukesha-West Allis, WI	215.7	220.9	Tucson, AZ	231.6	244.9
Minneapolis-St. Paul-			Virginia Beach-Norfolk-		
Bloomington, MN-WI	234.8	232.3	Newport News, VA-NC.	197.2	235.5
New Haven-Milford, CT	279.1	287.7	Washington-Arlington-		
			Alexandria, DC-VA-MD-WV	425.8	431.0
			Worcester, MA	290.7	281.7

[1] California data supplied by the California Association of REALTORS.   [2] Excludes areas in New Hampshire.

Source: NATIONAL ASSOCIATION OF REALTORS, Washington, DC, *Real Estate Outlook: Market Trends & Insights*, monthly, (copyright). See Internet site <http://www.realtor.org/research>.

Construction and Housing   605

Existing Home Sales by State: 2000 to 2006

[In thousands (5,174 represents 5,174,000). Includes condos and co-ops as well as single-family homes. Data shown here reflect revisions from prior estimates]

State	2000	2004	2005	2006	State	2000	2004	2005	2006
United States ..	5,174	6,779	7,075	6,480	Missouri.........	110.2	141.8	143.2	135.3
Alabama	67.0	112.0	128.0	125.8	Montana	17.4	24.2	25.7	26.8
Alaska..........	14.3	23.0	25.6	30.8	Nebraska........	32.3	39.8	41.2	38.7
Arizona	104.8	186.8	199.0	142.9	Nevada	44.6	99.8	98.0	69.7
Arkansas	45.0	60.9	75.3	82.6	New Hampshire....	26.7	(NA)	(NA)	(NA)
California	573.5	610.1	599.6	458.4	New Jersey	161.1	188.6	184.4	154.1
Colorado	111.5	126.0	130.4	123.7	New Mexico	29.9	50.6	57.5	58.2
Connecticut	61.5	75.1	80.4	70.8	New York	273.3	307.5	319.8	303.4
Delaware	12.9	18.9	19.3	17.8	North Carolina.....	134.2	192.6	215.7	234.8
District of Columbia ..	10.6	13.4	12.1	10.1	North Dakota	10.8	14.5	15.8	14.1
Florida	393.6	526.5	546.1	395.3	Ohio	216.4	275.7	286.9	275.4
Georgia	143.6	215.8	242.1	248.8	Oklahoma	67.3	93.6	104.6	106.0
Hawaii	22.1	35.5	36.8	31.5	Oregon	62.6	90.7	100.5	85.8
Idaho...........	24.1	32.0	(NA)	37.0	Pennsylvania	195.9	248.2	255.2	234.5
Illinois	246.8	307.5	315.3	289.0	Rhode Island	17.0	19.2	19.8	17.4
Indiana	111.0	130.5	138.3	147.4	South Carolina	64.3	99.3	114.6	115.2
Iowa	53.3	71.1	75.0	74.6	South Dakota	12.6	17.3	18.3	18.3
Kansas	52.6	73.4	77.9	76.1	Tennessee	100.4	156.1	170.9	173.6
Kentucky	66.0	89.3	96.2	96.9	Texas	381.8	485.5	531.6	578.6
Louisiana	66.8	79.6	87.2	92.2	Utah	35.5	43.6	51.7	51.7
Maine	27.6	33.6	33.3	30.7	Vermont..........	12.1	14.2	15.0	15.0
Maryland	100.5	140.6	135.5	113.2	Virginia	130.0	186.0	181.8	140.1
Massachusetts	112.3	141.7	148.6	128.1	Washington	112.4	147.6	167.7	154.2
Michigan	185.0	213.4	208.1	182.4	West Virginia	22.9	36.0	38.4	32.6
Minnesota	96.3	137.4	134.9	115.4	Wisconsin........	91.6	116.8	123.0	117.5
Mississippi	38.7	58.1	61.4	63.8	Wyoming	9.6	13.2	14.3	13.6

NA Not available.

Source: NATIONAL ASSOCIATION OF REALTORS, Washington, DC, *Real Estate Outlook: Market Trends & Insights*, monthly (copyright). See Internet site <http://www.realtor.org/research>.

Table 945. **Existing Apartment Condos and Co-ops—Units Sold and Median Sales Price by Region: 1990 to 2006**

[272 represents 272,000. Data shown here reflect revisions from prior estimates. For definition of median, see Guide to Tabular Presentation. For composition of regions, see map inside front cover]

Year	Units sold (1,000)					Median sales price (dol.)				
	U.S.	North-east	Mid-west	South	West	U.S.	North-east	Mid-west	South	West
1990	272	73	55	80	64	86,900	107,500	70,200	64,200	114,600
1995	333	108	66	96	63	89,000	92,500	90,700	67,800	114,800
1998	471	157	92	126	95	102,500	100,900	106,400	76,800	137,700
1999	534	182	102	145	105	110,100	109,800	114,600	80,700	143,900
2000	571	197	106	160	108	114,000	108,500	121,700	84,200	149,100
2001	601	203	116	174	108	125,600	121,200	134,800	93,200	160,400
2002	657	221	129	193	114	144,900	143,500	148,600	109,900	187,000
2003	732	250	146	211	125	168,500	178,100	162,600	126,900	222,400
2004	820	292	161	230	137	197,100	214,100	181,000	156,600	258,000
2005	896	331	177	245	143	223,900	245,100	189,100	187,300	283,800
2006	801	299	169	211	122	221,900	249,700	190,900	184,000	264,700

Source: NATIONAL ASSOCIATION OF REALTORS, Washington, DC, *Real Estate Outlook: Market Trends & Insights*, monthly (copyright). See Internet site <http://www.realtor.org/research>.

Table 946. **New Unfurnished Apartments Completed and Rented in 3 Months by Region: 2000 to 2006**

[226.2 represents 226,200. Structures with five units or more, privately-financed, nonsubsidized, unfurnished rental apartments. Based on sample and subject to sampling variability; see source for details. For composition of regions, see map, inside front cover]

Year and rent	Number (1,000)					Percent rented in 3 months				
	U.S.	North-east	Mid-west	South	West	U.S.	North-east	Mid-west	South	West
2000	226.2	14.8	39.5	125.9	45.9	72	85	76	67	77
2004	153.8	13.1	31.7	72.7	36.3	62	75	59	60	65
2005	113.0	4.7	20.5	57.8	30.0	64	75	64	62	64
2006, prel..........	117.2	6.0	12.6	69.9	28.6	55	41	58	60	56
Less than $750	20.0	0.7	6.3	12.1	0.9	73	93	75	76	61
$750 to $849............	13.5	(Z)	1.3	10.2	1.9	62	7	66	66	72
$850 to $949............	14.7	0.1	1.1	10.6	2.9	52	78	33	60	61
$950 to $1,049	11.6	0.2	0.8	8.8	1.8	50	83	37	51	58
$1,050 to $1,149	10.6	0.2	0.5	6.6	3.4	49	99	30	56	53
$1,150 or more	46.7	4.7	2.7	21.7	17.6	48	29	36	53	53
Median monthly asking rent (dollars) ..	$1,039	([1])	$752	$973	([1])	(X)	(X)	(X)	(X)	(X)

X Not applicable.   Z Fewer than 50 units or less than one-half of 1 percent.   [1] Over $1,150.

Source: U.S. Census Bureau, *Current Housing Reports*, Series H130, *Market Absorption of Apartments*, and unpublished data. See Internet site: <http://www.census.gov/prod/www/abs/apart.html>.

Table 947. **Total Housing Inventory for the United States: 1980 to 2006**

[In thousands (87,739 represents 87,739,000), except percent. Based on the Current Population Survey and the Housing Vacancy Survey and subject to sampling error; see source and Appendix III for details]

Item	1980	1985	1990	1995	2000	2002 [1]	2003	2004	2005	2006
All housing units	87,739	97,333	106,283	112,655	119,628	119,297	120,834	122,187	123,925	126,012
Vacant	8,101	9,446	12,059	12,669	13,908	14,332	15,274	15,599	15,694	16,437
Year-round vacant.	5,996	7,400	9,128	9,570	10,439	10,771	11,631	11,884	11,916	12,459
For rent	1,575	2,221	2,662	2,946	3,024	3,347	3,676	3,802	3,721	3,737
For sale only.	734	1,006	1,064	1,022	1,148	1,220	1,308	1,307	1,451	1,836
Rented or sold	623	664	660	810	850	842	976	991	1,060	1,108
Held off market	3,064	3,510	4,742	4,793	5,411	5,362	5,671	5,784	5,684	5,778
Occasional use	814	977	1,485	1,667	1,892	1,819	1,989	1,967	1,884	1,858
Usual residence elsewhere	568	659	1,068	801	1,037	995	994	1,068	1,128	1,198
Other	1,683	1,875	2,189	2,325	2,482	2,548	2,688	2,749	2,672	2,722
Seasonal [2].	2,106	2,046	2,931	3,099	3,469	3,561	3,643	3,715	3,778	3,978
Total occupied	79,638	87,887	94,224	99,985	105,720	104,965	105,560	106,588	108,231	109,575
Owner	52,223	56,152	60,248	64,739	71,250	71,278	72,054	73,575	74,553	75,380
Renter	27,415	31,736	33,976	35,246	34,470	33,687	33,506	33,013	33,678	34,195
PERCENT DISTRIBUTION										
All housing units	100.0	100.0	100.0	100.0	100.0	100.0	100.0	100.0	100.0	100.0
Vacant	9.2	9.7	11.3	11.2	11.6	12.0	12.6	12.8	12.7	13.0
Total occupied	90.8	90.3	88.7	88.8	88.4	88.0	87.4	87.2	87.3	87.0
Owner	59.5	57.7	56.7	57.5	59.6	59.7	59.6	60.2	60.2	60.3
Renter	31.2	32.6	32.0	31.3	28.8	28.2	27.7	27.0	27.2	27.5

[1] Revised. Based on 2000 census controls.   [2] Beginning 1990, includes vacant seasonal mobile homes. For years shown, seasonal vacant housing units were underreported prior to 1990.

Source: U.S. Census Bureau, "Housing Vacancies and Home Ownership" <http://www.census.gov/hhes/www/housing/hvs/hvs.html>.

Table 948. **Occupied Housing Inventory by Age of Householder: 1985 to 2006**

[In thousands (87,887 represents 87,887,000). Based on the Current Population Survey/Housing Vacancy Survey; see source for details]

Age of householder	1985	1990	1995	2000	2001	2002 [1]	2003	2004	2005	2006
Total [2]	87,887	94,224	99,986	105,719	107,009	104,965	105,560	106,588	108,231	109,576
Under 25 years old	5,483	5,143	5,502	6,221	6,460	6,372	6,441	6,538	6,536	6,578
25 to 29 years old	9,543	9,508	8,662	8,482	8,358	8,231	8,213	8,491	8,790	8,975
30 to 34 years old	10,288	11,213	11,206	10,219	10,301	10,176	10,084	9,865	9,583	9,423
35 to 39 years old	9,615	10,914	11,993	11,834	11,587	10,924	10,777	10,438	10,526	10,520
40 to 44 years old	7,919	9,893	11,151	12,377	12,504	11,839	11,748	11,768	11,722	11,484
45 to 49 years old	6,517	8,038	10,080	11,164	11,529	11,204	11,341	11,583	11,780	11,988
50 to 54 years old	6,157	6,532	7,882	9,834	10,288	10,123	10,194	10,316	10,595	10,896
55 to 59 years old	6,558	6,182	6,355	7,602	7,827	8,261	8,550	8,928	9,504	9,919
60 to 64 years old	6,567	6,446	5,860	6,215	6,345	6,422	6,776	7,112	7,336	7,604
65 to 69 years old	5,976	6,407	6,088	5,816	5,749	5,644	5,570	5,656	5,900	6,074
70 to 74 years old	5,003	5,397	5,693	5,567	5,496	5,137	5,163	5,065	5,016	5,057
75 years old and over. . . .	7,517	8,546	9,514	10,388	10,565	10,632	10,703	10,827	10,943	11,058

[1] Revised. Based on 2000 census controls.   [2] 1985 total includes ages not reported. Thereafter cases allocated by age.

Source: U.S. Census Bureau, "Housing Vacancies and Home Ownership" <http://www.census.gov/hhes/www/housing/hvs/hvs.html>.

Table 949. **Vacancy Rates for Housing Units—Characteristics: 2000 to 2006**

[In percent. Rate is relationship between vacant housing for rent or for sale and the total rental and homeowner supply, which comprises occupied units, units rented or sold and awaiting occupancy, and vacant units available for rent or sale. Based on the Current Population/Housing Vacancy Survey; see source for details. For composition of regions, see map, inside front cover]

Characteristic	Rental units				Homeowner units			
	2000	2004 [1]	2005	2006	2000	2004 [1]	2005	2006
Total units	8.0	10.2	9.8	9.7	1.6	1.7	1.9	2.4
Northeast	5.6	7.3	6.5	7.1	1.2	1.1	1.5	1.7
Midwest	8.8	12.2	12.6	12.4	1.3	2.0	2.2	2.6
South	10.5	12.6	11.8	11.6	1.9	2.0	2.1	2.7
West	5.8	7.5	7.3	6.8	1.5	1.4	1.4	2.1
Units in structure:								
1 unit	7.0	9.3	9.9	9.8	1.5	1.6	1.7	2.1
2 units or more	8.7	10.9	10.0	9.9	4.7	5.2	6.2	8.3
5 units or more	9.2	11.5	10.4	10.2	5.8	4.8	6.6	9.0
Units with—								
3 rooms or less	10.3	12.4	12.1	11.8	10.4	9.5	12.0	13.2
4 rooms	8.2	10.4	9.6	9.7	2.9	3.3	3.3	4.4
5 rooms	6.9	9.3	9.3	9.0	2.0	2.0	2.2	2.6
6 rooms or more	5.2	8.2	8.1	8.2	1.1	1.2	1.4	1.7

[1] Revised.

Source: U.S. Census Bureau, "Housing Vacancies and Home Ownership" <http://www.census.gov/hhes/www/housing/hvs/hvs.html>.

Construction and Housing **607**

Table 950. **Housing Units and Tenure—States: 2005**

[124,522 represents 124,522,000. The American Community Survey universe is limited to the household population and excludes the population living in institutions, college dormitories, and other group quarters. Based on a sample and subject to sampling variability; see Appendix III]

State	Housing units						Housing tenure			
			Vacant (1,000)		Vacancy rate		Owner-occupied units		Renter-occupied units	
	Total (1,000)	Occu-pied (1,000)	Total	For sea-sonal use [1]	Home-owner [2]	Renter [3]	Total (1,000)	Average house-hold size	Total (1,000)	Average house-hold size
United States...	124,522	111,091	13,431	3,884	1.7	7.9	74,319	2.70	36,772	2.39
Alabama.........	2,082	1,789	293	51	2.0	9.4	1,261	2.55	527	2.32
Alaska..........	274	233	41	21	1.6	7.0	147	2.93	86	2.45
Arizona.........	2,545	2,204	341	139	1.5	8.7	1,502	2.70	702	2.52
Arkansas........	1,249	1,088	162	37	1.9	9.7	737	2.53	351	2.39
California.......	12,989	12,098	891	247	1.2	4.7	7,070	3.01	5,028	2.78
Colorado........	2,053	1,819	234	84	2.6	9.5	1,234	2.64	585	2.22
Connecticut......	1,423	1,324	100	21	1.0	6.7	920	2.72	404	2.20
Delaware........	375	318	57	31	1.5	9.3	230	2.62	88	2.46
District of Columbia..	278	248	30	1	2.2	5.7	106	2.20	143	1.98
Florida.........	8,257	7,049	1,208	596	1.7	7.9	4,904	2.50	2,145	2.40
Georgia.........	3,771	3,320	451	65	2.7	11.7	2,218	2.73	1,102	2.51
Hawaii..........	491	430	61	32	0.9	4.7	257	3.04	173	2.64
Idaho..........	596	532	63	30	1.4	4.9	380	2.71	152	2.41
Illinois.........	5,145	4,691	454	44	1.7	9.6	3,278	2.79	1,413	2.34
Indiana.........	2,724	2,443	281	34	2.5	10.9	1,759	2.60	684	2.22
Iowa...........	1,307	1,201	106	18	1.8	7.3	878	2.50	323	2.07
Kansas.........	1,196	1,072	124	11	2.1	10.2	745	2.62	327	2.18
Kentucky........	1,866	1,654	212	34	2.0	8.1	1,168	2.54	486	2.24
Louisiana........	1,940	1,677	264	41	1.7	8.0	1,137	2.72	540	2.40
Maine..........	684	542	142	101	1.5	7.5	389	2.48	153	2.08
Maryland........	2,274	2,086	188	42	1.2	6.2	1,439	2.75	647	2.33
Massachusetts.....	2,688	2,448	240	94	1.1	5.6	1,568	2.74	880	2.14
Michigan........	4,479	3,888	591	240	2.4	10.3	2,903	2.65	985	2.21
Minnesota.......	2,252	2,020	232	106	1.3	8.4	1,531	2.61	489	2.04
Mississippi......	1,235	1,084	151	25	1.8	8.7	757	2.66	327	2.49
Missouri........	2,593	2,285	308	70	2.3	9.4	1,614	2.57	671	2.20
Montana........	428	368	60	28	1.5	6.6	254	2.56	114	2.27
Nebraska.......	767	696	71	14	1.7	8.3	475	2.61	221	2.13
Nevada........	1,019	907	113	29	3.1	7.4	550	2.72	357	2.49
New Hampshire.....	583	497	86	58	1.1	6.9	363	2.71	134	2.16
New Jersey.......	3,444	3,142	302	114	1.2	6.5	2,114	2.85	1,028	2.42
New Mexico......	839	728	111	34	1.5	7.6	504	2.66	223	2.43
New York.......	7,853	7,114	739	239	1.4	4.9	3,936	2.82	3,178	2.38
North Carolina.....	3,941	3,410	531	153	2.1	10.1	2,325	2.54	1,085	2.31
North Dakota......	304	270	34	12	0.9	7.2	182	2.43	88	1.90
Ohio...........	5,007	4,508	499	46	2.2	10.5	3,153	2.60	1,355	2.18
Oklahoma........	1,589	1,381	208	28	2.5	10.1	937	2.57	444	2.32
Oregon.........	1,558	1,425	133	39	1.4	6.5	909	2.61	516	2.30
Pennsylvania......	5,422	4,860	562	149	1.5	8.1	3,474	2.60	1,386	2.12
Rhode Island......	448	406	42	14	1.3	6.9	255	2.72	151	2.25
South Carolina......	1,928	1,636	292	78	2.3	11.7	1,147	2.57	489	2.40
South Dakota......	348	310	38	13	1.4	6.3	214	2.50	96	2.19
Tennessee.......	2,637	2,366	271	44	2.0	8.9	1,639	2.54	727	2.27
Texas..........	9,026	7,978	1,048	182	2.2	10.8	5,163	2.92	2,815	2.56
Utah...........	873	792	81	33	1.0	7.0	559	3.23	233	2.66
Vermont........	307	249	59	45	0.8	6.2	177	2.57	72	2.05
Virginia.........	3,175	2,890	285	62	1.1	7.4	2,012	2.63	877	2.33
Washington......	2,652	2,450	201	59	1.2	5.8	1,585	2.65	866	2.25
West Virginia......	872	741	132	38	1.9	7.7	558	2.46	182	2.19
Wisconsin........	2,499	2,220	279	146	1.2	6.6	1,556	2.57	663	2.07
Wyoming........	236	205	31	14	1.4	3.9	147	2.51	58	2.19

[1] For seasonal, recreational, or occasional use.   [2] Proportion of the homeowner housing inventory which is vacant for sale.
[3] Proportion of the rental inventory which is vacant for rent.

Source: U.S. Census Bureau, 2005 American Community Survey Tables B25002. Occupancy Status; B25003. Tenure; B25004. Vacancy Status; and B25010. Average Household Size of Units by Tenure; using American FactFinder®. See Internet site <http://factfinder.census.gov/>; (accessed 15 December 2006).

Table 951. Housing Units—Characteristics by Tenure and Region: 2005

[In thousands of units (124,377 represents 124,377,000), except as indicated. As of fall. Based on the American Housing Survey; see Appendix III. For composition of regions, see map, inside front cover]

Characteristic	Total housing units	Sea-sonal	Total	Owner	Renter	North-east	Mid-west	South	West	Vacant
			Total	Occupied						
Total units.	124,377	3,845	108,871	74,931	33,040	20,337	24,955	39,722	23,858	11,660
Percent distribution.	100.0	3.1	87.5	68.8	31.2	18.7	22.9	36.5	21.9	9.4
Units in structure:										
Single family detached.	77,703	2,287	69,996	61,699	8,297	11,044	17,707	26,254	14,992	5,420
Single family attached	7,046	197	6,158	3,976	2,182	1,825	1,042	2,035	1,256	691
2 to 4 units	10,071	188	8,379	1,550	6,829	2,604	1,863	2,073	1,840	1,504
5 to 9 units	6,073	125	5,109	502	4,607	917	1,004	1,824	1,364	840
10 to 19 units.	5,696	94	4,739	563	4,175	817	902	1,830	1,190	863
20 to 49 units.	4,402	125	3,639	436	3,203	1,041	601	964	1,033	638
50 or more units . . . . ¹.	4,757	186	3,912	689	3,222	1,589	682	809	831	659
Manufactured/mobile home ¹.	8,630	644	6,940	5,516	1,424	500	1,155	3,932	1,352	1,047
Single-wide.	5,584	457	4,257	3,093	1,164	371	843	2,443	600	869
Double-wide.	2,897	174	2,558	2,302	255	126	312	1,435	685	165
Triple-wide or larger	118	7	107	103	4	–	–	44	64	4
Stories in structure: ²										
1 story	39,963	1,553	34,814	26,278	8,537	1,139	4,031	19,192	10,453	3,596
2 stories	41,189	984	36,283	24,026	12,257	6,187	10,111	11,154	8,832	3,922
3 stories	26,287	393	23,714	16,375	7,340	8,482	8,342	4,353	2,537	2,180
4 to 6 stories	5,819	137	5,128	2,248	2,880	2,932	999	719	478	554
7 or more stories	2,488	135	1,992	488	1,504	1,097	317	372	206	362
Foundation: ³										
Full basement	26,882	350	24,984	22,612	2,372	8,586	10,745	3,793	1,860	1,547
Partial building	9,431	153	8,735	7,840	894	2,378	3,626	1,590	1,140	544
Crawlspace	22,292	1,151	19,038	15,646	3,392	732	2,575	10,037	5,694	2,103
Concrete slab.	25,514	660	23,012	19,317	3,695	1,129	1,720	12,675	7,488	1,843
Other	629	169	384	259	125	44	82	192	66	75
Equipment:										
Lacking complete facilities	5,345	462	1,695	257	1,438	298	345	536	515	3,188
With complete facilities.	119,032	3,384	107,177	74,674	32,502	20,038	24,610	39,186	23,343	8,472
Kitchen sink.	123,262	3,644	108,656	74,889	33,767	20,296	24,923	39,663	23,775	10,962
Refrigerator	121,035	3,466	108,673	74,856	33,818	20,311	24,909	39,640	23,814	8,895
Cooking stove or range	121,208	3,475	108,140	74,718	33,422	20,179	24,812	39,506	23,642	9,593
Burners only, no stove or range. . . .	189	32	131	60	71	31	19	37	43	26
Microwave oven only.	481	23	397	106	291	104	68	98	126	61
Dishwasher	75,239	1,677	68,508	54,060	14,448	11,132	14,491	26,271	16,614	5,055
Washing machine	95,272	1,979	89,287	71,997	17,290	15,039	20,969	34,138	19,141	4,006
Clothes dryer.	92,179	1,949	86,169	70,348	15,821	13,976	20,765	32,893	18,534	4,062
Disposal in kitchen sink	58,906	1,217	53,299	38,595	14,704	5,107	12,423	18,584	17,185	4,390
Trash compactor.	4,513	125	4,077	3,343	734	601	659	1,638	1,179	311
Main heating equipment:										
Warm-air furnace	76,665	1,727	68,275	50,459	17,817	8,546	20,331	23,735	15,664	6,662
Steam or hot water system.	14,074	176	12,880	7,719	5,161	9,496	1,996	588	800	1,018
Electric heat pump	14,551	605	12,484	9,074	3,411	344	664	9,993	1,483	1,462
Built-in electric units	5,607	310	4,699	2,116	2,583	1,065	1,116	918	1,600	598
Floor, wall, or pipeless furnace	5,916	149	5,102	2,172	2,930	443	399	1,300	2,961	664
Room heaters with flue	1,615	111	1,294	752	542	165	172	646	310	211
Room heaters without flue	1,627	76	1,327	881	447	18	42	1,222	45	224
Portable electric heaters.	1,127	73	907	441	467	29	20	642	216	146
Stoves	1,171	183	896	742	155	150	143	304	299	93
Fireplaces ⁴	251	47	190	166	24	24	22	69	74	15
Other	505	65	298	167	131	18	31	159	90	142
Cooking stoves.	148	–	120	50	70	34	–	50	36	28
None	1,120	324	399	194	205	4	20	96	279	397
Air conditioning: Central.	80,511	1,662	72,629	55,849	16,780	6,535	17,401	36,249	12,443	6,220
One or more room units	27,124	579	24,863	14,326	10,537	10,132	5,707	5,697	3,326	1,681
Source of water:										
Public system or private company . .	108,210	2,638	95,313	62,991	32,322	17,168	20,874	34,871	22,401	10,260
Well serving 1 to 5 units.	15,372	1,014	13,132	11,607	1,525	3,079	4,008	4,648	1,396	1,227
Other	795	194	427	334	93	90	73	203	61	174
Means of sewage disposal:										
Public sewer	98,013	1,976	86,850	55,496	31,355	16,107	20,053	29,617	21,073	9,187
Septic tank, cesspool, chemical toilet.	25,976	1,685	21,967	19,403	2,564	4,229	4,888	10,067	2,783	2,323
Other	388	184	54	32	22	–	13	38	2	151

– Represents or rounds to zero.   ¹ Includes trailers. Includes width not reported, not shown separately.   ² Excludes mobile homes; includes basements and finished attics.   ³ Limited to single-family units.   ⁴ With and without inserts.

Source: U.S. Census Bureau, Current Housing Reports, Series H150/05, *American Housing Survey for the United States*. See Internet site <http://www.census.gov/hhes/www/housing/ahs/nationaldata.html>.

Construction and Housing   609

Table 952. Housing Units by Units in Structure and State: 2005

[In percent, except as indicated (124,522 represents 124,522,000). The American Community Survey universe is limited to the household population and excludes the population living in institutions, college dormitories, and other group quarters. Based on a sample and subject to sampling variability; see Appendix III]

State	Total housing units (1,000)	\multicolumn{9}{c}{Percent of units by units in structure—}
		1-unit detached	1-unit attached	2 units	3 or 4 units	5 to 9 units	10 to 19 units	20 or more units	Mobile homes	Boat, RV, van, etc.
U.S. . . .	**124,522**	**61.1**	**5.7**	**4.0**	**4.6**	**5.0**	**4.5**	**8.0**	**7.0**	**0.1**
AL.	2,082	67.3	1.9	2.3	3.1	4.8	2.7	3.2	14.6	0.1
AK.	274	59.4	8.0	5.2	7.5	6.1	2.8	5.3	5.6	0.1
AZ.	2,545	60.1	5.3	1.4	3.7	4.7	5.2	7.0	12.1	0.5
AR.	1,249	70.1	1.6	3.1	3.3	3.4	3.1	2.1	13.3	(Z)
CA.	12,989	57.8	7.1	2.6	5.7	6.2	5.1	11.3	4.1	0.1
CO.	2,053	62.0	7.0	2.0	3.7	5.2	5.8	9.4	4.8	0.1
CT.	1,423	59.4	5.1	8.2	8.7	5.4	3.8	8.6	0.9	(Z)
DE.	375	56.3	14.0	1.7	2.4	4.3	5.4	4.6	11.2	0.1
DC.	278	12.7	25.2	3.6	7.8	6.9	12.0	31.5	(Z)	0.1
FL.	8,257	53.4	5.9	2.5	4.2	5.3	5.8	12.3	10.5	0.1
GA	3,771	65.4	3.3	2.5	3.5	5.4	4.8	4.4	10.5	(Z)
HI	491	53.5	6.0	2.8	4.8	7.0	5.4	20.1	0.2	0.1
ID	596	70.9	3.2	2.7	4.3	3.0	2.4	2.7	10.8	0.1
IL	5,145	58.6	5.6	6.3	6.6	6.3	4.2	9.2	3.1	(Z)
IN	2,724	71.9	3.6	3.0	3.7	4.7	3.6	3.7	5.9	(Z)
IA	1,307	74.1	3.0	2.9	3.8	3.6	3.7	4.5	4.4	(Z)
KS.	1,196	72.2	4.2	2.8	3.7	4.0	3.5	3.9	5.7	(Z)
KY.	1,866	68.0	2.2	2.9	3.9	4.5	2.9	2.8	12.7	(Z)
LA.	1,940	65.2	3.9	3.7	4.3	3.8	2.7	3.8	12.5	(Z)
ME	684	67.2	2.4	5.8	6.1	4.5	1.8	2.6	9.6	(Z)
MD	2,274	51.7	20.6	2.0	2.5	5.7	8.2	7.6	1.8	(Z)
MA	2,688	52.4	4.6	11.0	11.1	6.2	4.4	9.5	0.9	(Z)
MI.	4,479	70.8	4.6	2.8	2.8	4.3	3.8	4.8	6.2	(Z)
MN	2,252	68.1	6.8	2.6	2.1	2.1	3.8	10.4	4.0	(Z)
MS	1,235	68.6	1.7	2.4	3.4	4.6	1.8	1.8	15.7	(Z)
MO	2,593	70.1	3.3	3.4	5.0	3.5	3.4	3.8	7.5	(Z)
MT	428	68.4	2.7	3.3	5.1	3.1	1.6	2.9	12.9	0.1
NE.	767	72.3	3.9	2.1	2.9	3.8	4.6	5.7	4.5	(Z)
NV.	1,019	56.4	5.4	1.5	6.3	9.7	6.4	6.5	7.4	0.3
NH	583	62.8	5.7	5.9	6.0	4.4	3.1	5.7	6.5	(Z)
NJ.	3,444	54.0	9.0	9.8	6.2	4.8	5.2	10.0	1.0	(Z)
NM	839	62.6	3.6	2.1	3.9	3.0	2.5	4.3	17.8	0.2
NY.	7,853	42.1	5.0	10.8	7.0	5.2	4.3	22.9	2.6	(Z)
NC	3,941	64.6	3.1	2.5	3.0	4.6	3.8	2.9	15.5	(Z)
ND	304	62.0	4.1	2.5	4.0	4.4	5.7	8.3	9.0	0.2
OH	5,007	67.8	4.4	5.0	4.6	4.7	4.1	5.1	4.3	(Z)
OK	1,589	72.6	2.2	1.7	3.2	3.9	3.3	3.3	9.7	0.1
OR	1,558	62.7	3.9	3.0	4.3	4.4	4.3	7.5	9.6	0.3
PA.	5,422	56.6	18.1	5.1	4.3	3.4	2.6	5.3	4.5	(Z)
RI	448	54.7	2.9	11.3	13.6	5.2	3.9	7.0	1.4	–
SC.	1,928	61.7	2.5	2.4	3.2	5.3	3.0	3.2	18.5	0.1
SD.	348	68.5	2.8	2.1	3.4	3.3	3.8	5.5	10.6	(Z)
TN.	2,637	67.8	3.0	3.3	3.5	5.1	3.6	3.2	10.5	0.1
TX.	9,026	64.6	2.7	2.1	3.4	5.4	6.6	7.2	7.9	0.1
UT.	873	67.8	4.8	3.9	5.0	3.6	4.3	6.1	4.3	(Z)
VT.	307	65.2	3.8	6.3	6.9	5.6	1.8	2.8	7.6	(Z)
VA.	3,175	62.6	10.0	1.8	3.0	4.9	6.1	5.8	5.9	(Z)
WA	2,652	62.3	3.3	2.8	4.0	4.8	5.9	8.8	7.8	0.2
WV	872	71.2	1.5	2.4	2.8	2.6	1.7	2.3	15.4	0.1
WI.	2,499	66.2	3.8	7.7	3.7	4.9	3.2	6.4	4.1	(Z)
WY	236	66.3	3.8	2.9	4.5	3.4	2.0	2.2	14.8	(Z)

– Represents zero. Z Less than .05 percent.

Source: U.S. Census Bureau, 2005 American Community Survey Table B25024. Units in Structure; using American FactFinder®. See Internet site <http://factfinder.census.gov/>; (accessed 15 December 2006).

Table 953. **Housing Units—Size of Units and Lot: 2005**

[In thousands (124,377 represents 124,377,000), except as indicated. As of fall. Based on the American Housing Survey; see Appendix III. For composition of regions, see map inside front cover]

Item	Total housing units	Sea-sonal	Year-round units Occupied — Total	Owner	Renter	North-east	Mid-west	South	West	Vacant
Total units	124,377	3,845	108,871	74,931	33,940	20,337	24,955	39,722	23,858	11,660
Rooms:										
1 room	637	80	379	9	370	128	50	40	160	177
2 rooms	1,399	106	989	46	943	338	141	185	325	303
3 rooms	10,941	622	8,692	1,043	7,649	2,173	1,815	2,489	2,215	1,627
4 rooms	22,774	1,175	18,141	6,829	11,312	3,316	3,964	6,571	4,290	3,458
5 rooms	28,619	932	24,763	16,949	7,814	3,713	5,831	10,007	5,211	2,924
6 rooms	25,325	516	23,096	19,493	3,603	4,343	5,103	8,822	4,828	1,714
7 rooms	15,284	226	14,332	13,086	1,247	2,677	3,468	5,268	2,920	725
8 rooms or more	19,399	187	18,480	17,477	1,003	3,649	4,582	6,340	3,908	732
Complete bathrooms:										
No bathrooms	2,115	497	554	224	330	157	89	198	110	1,063
1 bathroom	47,221	1,591	39,920	16,983	22,937	9,754	9,992	12,253	7,922	5,710
1 and one-half bathrooms	17,205	346	15,876	12,362	3,514	3,871	5,129	4,256	2,621	982
2 or more bathrooms	57,837	1,412	52,520	45,361	7,159	6,555	9,745	23,015	13,205	3,905
Square footage of unit:										
Single detached and mobile homes	86,333	2,931	76,936	67,215	9,720	11,544	18,862	30,186	16,344	6,467
Less than 500	1,037	215	622	395	227	104	112	248	158	200
500 to 749	2,652	454	1,775	1,092	683	235	373	822	345	423
750 to 999	6,211	463	4,959	3,597	1,362	579	1,358	2,020	1,002	789
1,000 to 1,499	20,301	610	18,135	15,144	2,991	2,035	4,284	7,588	4,228	1,556
1,500 to 1,999	19,546	375	18,035	16,161	1,875	2,415	4,190	7,056	4,374	1,135
2,000 to 2,499	13,465	240	12,559	11,732	827	2,096	3,234	4,624	2,605	666
2,500 to 2,999	6,964	95	6,565	6,255	310	1,187	1,600	2,496	1,281	304
3,000 to 3,999	6,446	112	5,932	5,745	187	1,119	1,631	2,024	1,157	403
4,000 or more	3,952	58	3,662	3,468	193	817	901	1,313	631	232
Other [1]	5,759	308	4,691	3,626	1,066	957	1,179	1,992	563	759
Median square footage	1,758	1,146	1,795	1,858	1,344	1,985	1,824	1,742	1,747	1,463
Lot size:										
Single detached and attached units and mobile homes	90,932	2,913	81,115	69,484	11,631	12,959	19,456	31,669	17,032	6,903
Less than one-eighth acre	12,409	555	10,402	8,139	2,263	2,005	2,429	2,849	3,119	1,451
One-eighth to one-quarter acre . .	25,467	747	22,916	18,910	4,005	2,916	5,686	7,473	6,840	1,804
One-quarter to one-half acre . . .	17,808	432	16,203	14,359	1,844	2,464	3,929	6,461	3,349	1,172
One-half up to one acre	11,757	307	10,650	9,492	1,159	1,983	2,183	5,164	1,319	800
1 up to 5 acres	16,318	481	14,809	13,037	1,772	2,662	3,216	7,299	1,631	1,029
5 up to 10 acres	2,628	94	2,367	2,204	163	326	685	982	374	167
10 acres or more	4,545	297	3,767	3,343	424	602	1,328	1,440	398	480
Median acreage	0.36	0.34	0.36	0.38	0.24	0.41	0.35	0.46	0.22	0.29

[1] Represents units not reported or size unknown.

Source: U.S. Census Bureau, Current Housing Reports, Series H150/05, *American Housing Survey for the United States*. See Internet site <http://www.census.gov/hhes/www/housing/ahs/nationaldata.html>.

Table 954. **Occupied Housing Units—Tenure by Race of Householder: 1991 to 2005**

[In thousands (93,147 represents 93,147,000), except percent. As of fall. Based on the American Housing Survey; see Appendix III]

Race of householder and tenure	1991	1993	1995	1997	1999	2001	2003 [1]	2005
ALL RACES [2]								
Occupied units, total	93,147	94,724	97,693	99,487	102,803	106,261	105,842	108,871
Owner-occupied	59,796	61,252	63,544	65,487	68,796	72,265	72,238	74,931
Percent of occupied	64.2	64.7	65.0	65.8	66.9	68.0	68.3	68.8
Renter-occupied.	33,351	33,472	34,150	34,000	34,007	33,996	33,604	33,940
WHITE [3]								
Occupied units, total	79,140	80,029	81,611	82,154	83,624	85,292	87,483	89,449
Owner-occupied	53,749	54,878	56,507	57,781	60,041	62,465	63,126	65,023
Percent of occupied	67.9	68.6	69.2	70.3	71.8	73.2	72.2	72.7
Renter-occupied.	25,391	25,151	25,104	24,372	23,583	22,826	24,357	24,426
BLACK [3]								
Occupied units, total	10,832	11,128	11,773	12,085	12,936	13,292	13,004	13,447
Owner-occupied	4,635	4,788	5,137	5,457	6,013	6,318	6,193	6,471
Percent of occupied	42.8	43.0	43.6	45.2	46.5	47.5	47.6	48.1
Renter-occupied.	6,197	6,340	6,637	6,628	6,923	6,974	6,811	6,975
HISPANIC ORIGIN [4]								
Occupied units, total	6,239	6,614	7,757	8,513	9,041	9,814	11,038	11,651
Owner-occupied	2,423	2,788	3,245	3,646	4,087	4,731	5,106	5,752
Percent of occupied	38.8	42.2	41.8	42.8	45.2	48.2	46.3	49.4
Renter-occupied.	3,816	3,826	4,512	4,867	4,955	5,083	5,931	5,899

[1] Based on 2000 census controls. [2] Includes other races, not shown separately. [3] The 2003 American Housing Survey (AHS) allowed respondents to choose more than one race. Beginning in 2003, data represent householders who selected this race group only and exclude householders reporting more than one race. The AHS in prior years only allowed respondents to report one race group. See also comments on race in the text. [4] Persons of Hispanic origin may be of any race.

Source: U.S. Census Bureau, Current Housing Reports, Series H150/91, H150/93, H150/95RV, H150/97, H150/99, H150/01, H150/03, and H150/05, *American Housing Survey for the United States*. See Internet site <http://www.census.gov/hhes/www/housing/ahs/nationaldata.html>.

Table 955. Homeownership Rates by Age of Householder and Household Type: 1985 to 2006

[In percent. Represents the proportion of owner households to the total number of occupied households. Based on the Current Population Survey/Housing Vacancy Survey; see source and Appendix III for details]

Age of householder and household type	1985	1990	1995	2000	2001	2002	2003	2004	2005	2006
United States.......	63.9	63.9	64.7	67.4	67.8	67.9	68.3	69.0	68.9	68.8
AGE OF HOUSEHOLDER										
Less than 25 years old	17.2	15.7	15.9	21.7	22.5	22.9	22.8	25.2	25.7	24.8
25 to 29 years old	37.7	35.2	34.4	38.1	38.9	38.8	39.8	40.2	40.9	41.8
30 to 34 years old	54.0	51.8	53.1	54.6	54.8	54.9	56.5	57.4	56.8	55.9
35 to 39 years old	65.4	63.0	62.1	65.0	65.5	65.2	65.1	66.2	66.6	66.4
40 to 44 years old	71.4	69.8	68.6	70.6	70.8	71.7	71.3	71.9	71.7	71.2
45 to 49 years old	74.3	73.9	73.7	74.7	75.4	74.8	75.4	76.3	75.0	74.9
50 to 54 years old	77.5	76.8	77.0	78.5	78.2	77.9	77.9	78.2	78.3	77.7
55 to 59 years old	79.2	78.8	78.8	80.4	81.0	80.8	80.9	81.2	80.6	80.4
60 to 64 years old	79.9	79.8	80.3	80.3	81.8	81.6	81.9	82.4	81.9	81.5
65 to 69 years old	79.5	80.0	81.0	83.0	82.4	82.9	82.5	83.2	82.8	82.4
70 to 74 years old	76.8	78.4	80.9	82.6	82.5	82.5	82.0	84.4	82.9	83.0
75 years old and over......	69.8	72.3	74.6	77.7	78.1	78.4	78.7	78.8	78.4	79.1
Less than 35 years old	39.9	38.5	38.6	40.8	41.2	41.3	42.2	43.1	43.0	42.6
35 to 44 years old	68.1	66.3	65.2	67.9	68.2	68.6	68.3	69.2	69.3	68.9
45 to 54 years old	75.9	75.2	75.2	76.5	76.7	76.3	76.6	77.2	76.6	76.2
55 to 64 years old	79.5	79.3	79.5	80.3	81.3	81.1	81.4	81.9	81.2	80.9
65 years and over	74.8	76.3	78.1	80.4	80.3	80.6	80.5	81.1	80.6	80.9
TYPE OF HOUSEHOLD										
Family households:										
Married-couple families ...	78.2	78.1	79.6	82.4	82.9	82.9	83.3	84.0	84.2	84.1
Male householder, no spouse present......	57.8	55.2	55.3	57.5	57.9	57.3	57.9	59.6	59.1	58.9
Female householder, no spouse present......	45.8	44.0	45.1	49.1	49.9	49.2	49.6	50.9	51.0	51.3
Nonfamily households:										
One-person	45.8	49.0	50.5	53.6	54.4	54.9	55.2	55.8	55.6	55.7
Male householder	38.8	42.4	43.8	47.4	48.2	48.6	50.0	50.5	50.3	50.5
Female householder ...	51.3	53.6	55.4	58.1	59.0	59.6	59.1	59.9	59.6	59.8
Other:										
Male householder	30.1	31.7	34.2	38.0	38.6	38.7	40.0	41.7	41.7	40.8
Female householder ...	30.6	32.5	33.0	40.6	41.0	41.9	43.1	43.5	44.8	45.5

Source: U.S. Census Bureau, "Housing Vacancies and Home Ownership." See Internet site <http://www.census.gov/hhes/www/hvs.html>.

Table 956. Homeownership Rates by State: 1985 to 2006

[In percent. See headnote, Table 955]

State	1985	1990	1995	2000	2005	2006	State	1985	1990	1995	2000	2005	2006
United States .	63.9	63.9	64.7	67.4	68.9	68.8	Missouri	69.2	64.0	69.4	74.2	72.3	71.9
Alabama........	70.4	68.4	70.1	73.2	76.6	74.2	Montana	66.5	69.1	68.7	70.2	70.4	69.5
Alaska	61.2	58.4	60.9	66.4	66.0	67.2	Nebraska	68.5	67.3	67.1	70.2	70.2	67.6
Arizona........	64.7	64.5	62.9	68.0	71.1	71.6	Nevada.........	57.0	55.8	58.6	64.0	63.4	65.7
Arkansas........	66.6	67.8	67.2	68.9	69.2	70.8	New Hampshire ...	65.5	65.0	66.0	69.2	74.0	74.2
California.......	54.2	53.8	55.4	57.1	59.7	60.2	New Jersey	62.3	65.0	64.9	66.2	70.1	69.0
Colorado.......	63.6	59.0	64.6	68.3	71.0	70.1	New Mexico......	68.2	68.6	67.0	73.7	71.4	72.0
Connecticut.....	69.0	67.9	68.2	70.0	70.5	71.1	New York	50.3	53.3	52.7	53.4	55.9	55.7
Delaware.......	70.3	67.7	71.7	72.0	75.8	76.8	North Carolina ...	68.0	69.0	70.1	71.1	70.9	70.2
Dist. of Columbia ..	37.4	36.4	39.2	41.9	45.8	45.9	North Dakota	69.9	67.2	67.3	70.7	68.5	68.3
Florida	67.2	65.1	66.6	68.4	72.4	72.4	Ohio............	67.9	68.7	67.9	71.3	73.3	72.1
Georgia	62.7	64.3	66.6	69.8	67.9	68.5	Oklahoma	70.5	70.3	69.8	72.7	72.9	71.6
Hawaii	51.0	55.5	50.2	55.2	59.8	59.9	Oregon.........	61.5	64.4	63.2	65.3	68.2	68.1
Idaho	71.0	69.4	72.0	70.5	74.2	75.1	Pennsylvania	71.6	73.8	71.5	74.7	73.3	73.2
Illinois..........	60.6	63.0	66.4	67.9	70.9	70.4	Rhode Island	61.4	58.5	57.9	61.5	63.1	64.6
Indiana........	67.6	67.0	71.0	74.9	75.0	74.2	South Carolina ...	72.0	71.4	71.3	76.5	73.9	74.2
Iowa..........	69.9	70.7	71.4	75.2	73.9	74.0	South Dakota	67.6	66.2	67.5	71.2	68.4	70.6
Kansas........	68.3	69.0	67.5	69.3	69.5	70.0	Tennessee.......	67.6	68.3	67.0	70.9	72.4	71.3
Kentucky.......	68.5	65.8	71.2	73.4	71.6	71.7	Texas	60.5	59.7	61.4	63.8	65.9	66.0
Louisiana	70.2	67.8	65.3	68.1	72.5	71.3	Utah...........	71.5	70.1	71.5	72.7	73.9	73.5
Maine.........	73.7	74.2	76.7	76.5	73.9	75.3	Vermont........	69.5	72.6	70.4	68.7	74.2	74.0
Maryland........	65.6	64.9	65.8	69.9	71.2	72.6	Virginia	68.5	69.8	68.1	73.9	71.2	71.1
Massachusetts....	60.5	58.6	60.2	59.9	63.4	65.2	Washington	66.8	61.8	61.6	63.6	67.6	66.7
Michigan........	70.7	72.3	72.2	77.2	76.4	77.4	West Virginia	75.9	72.0	73.1	75.9	81.3	78.4
Minnesota......	70.0	68.0	73.3	76.1	76.5	75.6	Wisconsin.......	63.8	68.3	67.5	71.8	71.1	70.2
Mississippi......	69.6	69.4	71.1	75.2	78.8	76.2	Wyoming........	73.2	68.9	69.0	71.0	72.8	73.7

Source: U.S. Census Bureau, "Housing Vacancies and Home Ownership." See Internet site <http://www.census.gov/hhes/www/hvs.html>.

Table 957. Occupied Housing Units—Costs by Region: 2005

[74,931 represents 74,931,000. As of fall. See headnote, Table 958, for an explanation of housing costs. Based on the American Housing Survey; see Appendix III. For composition of regions, see map inside front cover]

Category	Number (1,000)					Percent distribution				
	Total units	North-east	Mid-west	South	West	Total units	North-east	Mid-west	South	West
OWNER-OCCUPIED UNITS										
Total	74,931	13,217	18,360	28,003	15,350	100.0	100.0	100.0	100.0	100.0
Monthly housing costs:										
Less than $300	12,426	1,027	2,652	6,942	1,804	16.6	7.8	14.4	24.8	11.8
$300 to $399	6,763	997	2,008	2,538	1,220	9.0	7.5	10.9	9.1	7.9
$400 to $499	5,096	977	1,456	1,844	819	6.8	7.4	7.9	6.6	5.3
$500 to $599	4,704	1,059	1,235	1,756	654	6.3	8.0	6.7	6.3	4.3
$600 to $699	4,192	847	1,118	1,636	591	5.6	6.4	6.1	5.8	3.9
$700 to $799	3,933	763	1,105	1,436	629	5.2	5.8	6.0	5.1	4.1
$800 to $999	7,632	1,336	2,089	2,885	1,322	10.2	10.1	11.4	10.3	8.6
$1,000 to $1,249	8,031	1,249	2,272	2,821	1,689	10.7	9.4	12.4	10.1	11.0
$1,250 to $1,499	6,184	1,213	1,595	1,884	1,492	8.3	9.2	8.7	6.7	9.7
$1,500 or more	15,971	3,749	2,830	4,261	5,130	21.3	28.4	15.4	15.2	33.4
Median (dol.) [1]	809	941	764	656	1,094	(X)	(X)	(X)	(X)	(X)
RENTER-OCCUPIED UNITS										
Total	33,940	7,120	6,595	11,719	8,507	100.0	100.0	100.0	100.0	100.0
Monthly housing costs:										
Less than $300	2,922	736	637	1,036	514	8.6	10.3	9.7	8.8	6.0
$300 to $399	1,859	316	493	765	285	5.5	4.4	7.5	6.5	3.4
$400 to $499	3,353	515	890	1,380	568	9.9	7.2	13.5	11.8	6.7
$500 to $599	3,897	625	927	1,648	698	11.5	8.8	14.1	14.1	8.2
$600 to $699	4,099	723	952	1,488	936	12.1	10.2	14.4	12.7	11.0
$700 to $799	3,694	703	721	1,317	953	10.9	9.9	10.9	11.2	11.2
$800 to $999	5,273	1,274	817	1,643	1,540	15.5	17.9	12.4	14.0	18.1
$1,000 to $1,249	3,178	816	360	847	1,154	9.4	11.5	5.5	7.2	13.6
$1,250 to $1,499	1,644	421	146	343	733	4.8	5.9	2.2	2.9	8.6
$1,500 or more	1,886	576	201	350	760	5.6	8.1	3.0	3.0	8.9
No cash rent.	2,134	415	449	904	366	6.3	5.8	6.8	7.7	4.3
Median (dol.) [1]	694	762	613	639	915	(X)	(X)	(X)	(X)	(X)

X Not applicable.   [1] For explanation of median, see Guide to Tabular Presentation.

Source: U.S. Census Bureau, Current Housing Reports, Series H150/05, *American Housing Survey for the United States.* See Internet site <http://www.census.gov/hhes/www/housing/ahs/nationaldata.html>.

Table 958. Occupied Housing Units—Financial Summary by Selected Characteristics of the Householder: 2005

[In thousands of units (108,871 represents 108,871,000), except as indicated. As of fall. Housing costs include real estate taxes, property insurance, utilities, fuel, water, garbage collection, homeowner association fees, mobile home fees, and mortgage. Based on the American Housing Survey; see Appendix III]

Characteristic	Total occu-pied units	Tenure		Black [1]		Hispanic origin [2]		Elderly [3]		Households below poverty level	
		Owner	Renter	Owner	Renter	Owner	Renter	Owner	Renter	Owner	Renter
Total units [4]	108,871	74,931	33,940	6,471	6,975	5,752	5,899	17,818	4,379	6,450	8,674
Monthly housing costs:											
Less than $300	15,348	12,426	2,922	1,272	879	861	343	5,695	818	2,412	1,844
$300 to $399	8,622	6,763	1,859	613	426	399	225	3,008	366	850	736
$400 to $499	8,449	5,096	3,353	466	760	292	509	1,963	427	614	1,037
$500 to $599	8,601	4,704	3,897	474	880	284	735	1,562	386	480	1,052
$600 to $699	8,291	4,192	4,099	402	768	306	797	1,069	400	367	864
$700 to $799	7,627	3,933	3,694	404	899	309	687	735	340	282	708
$800 to $999	12,905	7,632	5,273	733	1,067	674	1,115	1,125	498	414	802
$1,000 or more.	36,893	30,186	6,708	2,107	916	2,627	1,271	2,661	666	1,032	828
Median amount (dol.) [5]	753	809	694	702	646	926	734	409	588	395	530
Monthly housing costs as percent of income: [6]											
Less than 5 percent	4,304	4,051	253	300	42	217	35	732	10	20	12
5 to 9 percent	11,687	10,761	925	790	178	626	87	2,858	57	69	48
10 to 14 percent	13,771	11,412	2,359	873	373	625	338	2,989	140	172	68
15 to 19 percent	14,960	11,499	3,462	898	620	716	507	2,294	172	243	140
20 to 24 percent	12,605	8,947	3,658	746	725	627	565	1,693	297	269	215
25 to 29 percent	10,394	6,788	3,607	586	678	570	692	1,265	459	267	453
30 to 34 percent	7,652	4,658	2,994	367	613	484	659	922	355	238	449
35 to 39 percent	5,561	3,344	2,217	334	495	376	368	773	266	355	312
40 percent or more	23,967	12,628	11,339	1,469	2,617	1,463	2,288	4,182	2,062	4,041	5,278
Median amount (percent) [5] . .	23	20	32	22	35	25	34	20	44	75	77

[1] For persons who selected this race group only. See footnote 3, Table 954.   [2] Persons of Hispanic origin may be of any race.   [3] Householders 65 years old and over.   [4] Includes units with no cash rent not shown separately.   [5] For explanation of median, see Guide to Tabular Presentation.   [6] Money income before taxes.

Source: U.S. Census Bureau, Current Housing Reports, Series H150/05, *American Housing Survey for the United States.* See Internet site <http://www.census.gov/hhes/www/housing/ahs/nationaldata.html>.

U.S. Census Bureau, Statistical Abstract of the United States: 2008

Table 959. Owner-Occupied Housing Units—Value and Costs by State: 2005

[In percent, except as indicated (74,319 represents 74,319,000). The American Community Survey universe is limited to the household population and excludes the population living in institutions, college dormitories, and other group quarters. Based on a sample and subject to sampling variability; see Appendix III. For definition of median, see Guide to Tabular Presentation]

State	Total (1,000)	Percent of units with value of— $99,999 or less	$100,000 to $199,999	$200,000 or more	Median value (dol.)	Median selected monthly owner costs [1] (dol.)	Selected monthly owner costs as a percent of household income in the past 12 months [1] Less than 15 percent	15.0 to 24.9 percent	25.0 to 29.9 percent	30 percent or more
U.S. ...	74,319	27.2	31.0	41.8	167,500	961	18.1	34.6	12.5	34.5
AL......	1,261	51.4	32.5	16.1	97,500	624	25.7	36.7	10.2	26.9
AK......	147	16.0	35.1	48.9	197,100	1,182	20.1	37.7	11.2	30.7
AZ......	1,502	19.4	35.0	45.5	185,400	952	18.7	34.7	12.5	33.7
AR......	737	58.1	29.5	12.4	87,400	580	26.8	37.3	9.9	25.6
CA......	7,070	6.0	6.6	87.4	477,700	1,564	12.1	26.8	12.9	47.7
CO	1,234	9.9	30.9	59.2	223,300	1,220	15.4	33.4	14.0	36.9
CT......	920	4.2	25.1	70.8	271,500	1,415	16.8	34.2	14.0	34.8
DE......	230	16.7	32.1	51.2	203,800	993	23.0	37.0	11.1	28.6
DC......	106	2.8	15.5	81.7	384,400	1,351	21.0	33.8	11.1	33.3
FL......	4,904	21.1	32.0	46.9	189,500	925	15.5	31.2	12.2	40.6
GA......	2,218	28.8	40.8	30.4	147,500	974	20.1	36.0	11.7	31.8
HI......	257	2.7	9.2	88.1	453,600	1,278	14.6	31.8	13.4	39.7
ID......	380	29.9	44.8	25.3	134,900	805	19.0	35.8	12.8	32.0
IL......	3,278	23.2	31.3	45.5	183,900	1,107	16.4	33.5	12.6	37.2
IN......	1,759	41.3	42.7	16.0	114,400	822	22.4	39.2	12.3	25.9
IA......	878	46.1	39.0	14.9	106,600	724	22.4	41.2	11.9	24.3
KS......	745	46.7	36.1	17.3	107,800	776	21.4	40.8	12.1	25.4
KY......	1,168	48.0	36.3	15.6	104,900	655	24.1	37.3	11.0	27.1
LA......	1,137	49.2	35.7	15.1	101,700	629	25.6	35.3	10.1	28.5
ME	389	28.8	36.2	35.0	155,300	781	22.3	35.0	12.6	29.8
MD	1,439	10.4	21.5	68.1	280,200	1,307	19.6	35.9	12.8	31.3
MA	1,568	2.6	12.2	85.2	361,500	1,426	15.1	33.2	14.0	37.3
MI	2,903	26.7	43.2	30.2	149,300	941	18.5	36.3	12.5	32.4
MN	1,531	16.1	34.4	49.5	198,800	1,066	17.4	36.7	14.3	31.4
MS	757	61.2	28.1	10.7	82,700	580	21.7	35.5	10.4	31.6
MO	1,614	38.3	40.2	21.4	123,100	765	22.9	39.1	11.4	26.3
MT	254	35.1	37.9	27.0	131,600	700	19.9	34.5	10.7	34.4
NE......	475	42.0	41.8	16.2	113,200	804	20.7	39.8	12.8	26.4
NV......	550	9.5	19.7	70.8	283,400	1,247	12.9	30.6	13.3	42.4
NH	363	10.3	24.7	65.0	240,100	1,253	14.3	33.0	14.7	37.8
NJ......	2,114	5.7	17.0	77.4	333,900	1,545	14.6	31.0	13.3	40.7
NM	504	37.7	37.8	24.4	125,500	669	21.6	36.1	11.2	30.6
NY......	3,936	22.8	19.8	57.4	258,900	1,163	17.6	31.5	11.7	38.9
NC......	2,325	35.6	40.5	23.9	127,600	831	20.1	36.6	12.0	30.9
ND......	182	58.0	33.2	8.8	88,600	599	24.3	40.3	13.8	21.5
OH......	3,153	32.7	46.3	21.0	129,600	896	19.5	37.7	12.7	29.9
OK......	937	57.5	31.8	10.7	89,100	631	24.9	37.7	11.1	25.9
OR......	909	12.9	36.7	50.4	201,200	1,030	14.9	35.1	13.8	35.8
PA......	3,474	36.3	35.7	28.1	131,900	840	19.1	36.9	12.7	31.0
RI	255	2.6	17.3	80.1	281,300	1,315	16.4	32.3	13.3	37.8
SC......	1,147	44.0	34.9	21.1	113,100	720	20.8	36.9	11.3	30.6
SD......	214	49.1	36.4	14.5	101,700	658	21.6	41.1	11.7	25.5
TN......	1,639	42.7	38.3	19.0	114,000	717	21.6	36.8	11.6	29.5
TX......	5,163	47.0	35.9	17.1	106,000	878	18.2	36.7	12.1	32.4
UT......	559	12.2	53.8	34.1	167,200	1,024	17.0	35.9	14.1	32.8
VT......	177	19.4	40.0	40.6	173,400	987	15.0	37.6	13.8	33.3
VA......	2,012	19.6	27.8	52.5	212,300	1,095	19.5	36.4	13.0	30.8
WA	1,585	11.5	29.8	58.7	227,700	1,169	14.8	34.7	14.2	36.0
WV	558	60.8	28.2	11.1	84,400	447	28.7	36.1	9.1	25.5
WI	1,556	23.1	46.4	30.5	152,600	974	15.0	38.1	14.3	32.4
WY	147	32.1	43.8	24.2	135,000	698	24.6	38.4	11.3	25.5

[1] For homes with a mortgage. Includes all forms of debt where the property is pledged as security for repayment of the debt, including deeds of trust, land contracts, home equity loans, etc. Also includes cost of property insurance, utilities, real estate taxes, etc.

Source: U.S. Census Bureau, 2005 American Community Survey Tables B25075. Value for Owner-Occupied Housing Units; B25077. Median Value for Owner-Occupied Housing Units; B25088. Median Selected Monthly Owner Costs by Mortgage Status; B25091. Mortgage Status by Selected Monthly Owner Cost as a Percentage of Household Income; using American FactFinder®. See Internet site <http://factfinder.census.gov/> (accessed 16 May 2007).

Table 960. Renter-Occupied Housing Units—Gross Rent by State: 2005

[In percent, except as indicated (36,772 represents 36,772,000. The American Community Survey universe is limited to the household population and excludes the population living in institutions, college dormitories, and other group quarters. Based on a sample and subject to sampling variability; see Appendix III]

State	Total [1] (1,000)	Percent of units with gross rent of—					Median gross rent (dol.)	Gross rent as a percent of household income in the past 12 months			
		$299 or less	$300 to $499	$500 to $749	$750 to $999	$1,000 or more		Less than 15 percent	15.0 to 24.9 percent	25.0 to 29.9 percent	30 percent or more
U.S...	36,772	6.9	13.6	29.1	22.0	22.4	728	12.0	23.8	10.9	45.7
AL	527	11.7	26.4	31.9	12.9	4.9	535	13.7	22.7	10.4	38.8
AK	86	2.9	6.2	25.2	25.5	27.2	832	14.2	23.4	10.6	38.7
AZ	702	3.8	12.0	36.1	22.7	19.2	717	12.0	24.2	11.3	44.6
AR	351	10.4	25.7	36.4	12.0	4.0	549	13.0	24.0	10.3	40.0
CA	5,028	3.5	5.4	16.9	25.0	45.5	973	9.5	22.5	11.2	51.7
CO	585	5.0	10.9	31.0	23.4	24.9	757	9.9	24.6	12.6	46.5
CT	404	8.7	7.5	21.0	26.9	30.8	839	12.1	24.4	11.9	44.8
DE	88	6.3	7.7	26.5	30.4	22.6	793	12.4	26.9	10.8	42.5
DC	143	9.3	7.9	23.9	23.1	34.2	832	12.2	25.0	12.1	46.3
FL	2,145	4.3	8.0	27.0	30.3	25.4	809	8.6	22.5	11.0	50.9
GA	1,102	6.7	13.8	31.5	25.6	15.5	709	11.9	25.0	10.1	44.2
HI	173	3.7	6.9	13.0	21.6	44.4	995	9.9	23.5	10.4	43.9
ID	152	9.2	21.2	37.5	16.2	7.9	594	13.0	25.5	9.6	42.2
IL	1,413	7.4	12.4	29.9	25.5	19.9	734	12.6	23.7	10.5	46.1
IN	684	7.6	19.9	40.1	18.6	7.6	615	13.6	25.2	10.1	43.4
IA	323	9.7	25.0	37.9	13.5	5.8	559	15.5	26.1	9.8	39.7
KS	327	7.8	23.3	35.7	16.5	8.7	588	13.7	25.6	11.4	40.2
KY	486	12.6	27.4	33.9	11.7	3.9	527	14.0	24.6	9.2	40.0
LA	540	10.7	22.0	36.3	13.5	6.2	569	13.4	20.5	9.3	42.9
ME	153	12.3	18.1	32.6	18.0	11.2	623	13.2	24.2	10.7	43.4
MD	647	5.9	6.5	19.6	26.7	36.2	891	10.8	26.5	11.2	45.3
MA	880	10.5	8.9	16.0	21.1	39.5	902	11.3	23.9	12.2	46.4
MI	985	7.7	16.7	36.6	21.0	12.6	655	11.6	22.6	10.4	47.6
MN	489	9.7	12.7	33.6	21.9	16.7	692	11.3	25.5	11.6	44.8
MS	327	13.1	24.6	30.9	14.0	3.9	538	11.7	21.7	9.7	41.3
MO	671	9.0	22.5	36.1	17.1	7.8	593	13.9	24.5	11.5	41.4
MT	114	11.0	25.6	33.8	12.6	6.9	552	16.4	21.9	10.4	40.3
NE	221	9.2	25.0	34.3	14.9	8.4	569	15.5	27.9	11.6	35.6
NV	357	2.5	6.9	23.1	31.9	31.8	861	11.4	23.8	12.8	46.9
NH	134	7.4	6.6	20.9	29.7	30.9	854	10.2	28.3	12.7	42.6
NJ	1,028	6.4	4.9	15.6	28.8	40.4	935	11.2	24.5	11.3	47.6
NM	223	8.8	24.0	32.7	17.0	8.6	587	14.5	22.0	9.1	44.3
NY	3,178	7.9	10.0	22.1	22.1	34.3	841	13.5	22.4	10.4	48.3
NC	1,085	7.0	17.7	37.8	19.3	9.1	635	13.2	23.3	10.5	42.3
ND	88	13.9	36.0	28.2	10.0	2.5	479	20.5	28.1	8.5	32.8
OH	1,355	8.4	19.5	38.6	18.7	8.7	613	12.9	24.4	10.6	44.1
OK	444	8.1	27.6	35.2	13.5	5.6	547	14.2	24.3	8.9	40.9
OR	516	4.9	13.1	38.2	23.4	15.2	689	10.6	23.7	10.8	48.1
PA	1,386	8.5	18.4	32.9	20.2	13.6	647	13.7	24.3	11.1	42.9
RI	151	12.6	8.7	23.7	30.8	20.8	775	12.0	24.2	13.4	45.3
SC	489	7.7	19.8	35.4	17.7	8.2	611	13.0	22.6	9.1	41.9
SD	96	16.8	28.0	31.1	9.8	3.7	500	16.9	25.7	11.0	34.7
TN	727	9.7	21.5	37.5	15.4	6.9	583	13.2	23.8	10.8	41.3
TX	2,815	5.5	14.3	38.2	22.0	13.6	671	11.6	24.6	10.4	45.3
UT	233	4.3	14.5	41.3	20.3	13.8	665	13.2	25.0	13.4	41.6
VT	72	10.0	11.1	36.0	21.0	14.9	683	10.7	22.2	13.7	45.7
VA	877	6.3	11.0	23.6	21.8	30.8	812	12.5	25.6	12.0	42.2
WA	866	5.4	11.0	32.4	25.0	21.3	741	11.2	25.6	11.3	46.0
WV	182	14.5	30.3	27.6	8.6	2.8	483	12.6	20.8	10.0	38.6
WI	663	7.2	17.0	39.8	21.2	10.0	643	13.9	27.1	11.7	41.6
WY	58	9.1	26.9	34.9	10.6	7.8	537	22.6	26.3	9.3	30.6

[1] Includes units with no cash rent.

Source: U.S. Census Bureau, 2004 American Community Survey Tables B25063. Gross Rent; B25064. Median Gross Rent; B25070. Gross Rent as a Percentage of Household Income; using American FactFinder. See Internet site <http://factfinder.census.gov/> (accessed 17 May 2007).

Construction and Housing   615

[In thousands (74,931 represents 74,931). As of fall Based on the American Housing Survey, see Appendix III]

Mortgage characteristic	Total owner-occu-pied units	New con-struc-tion[1]	Mobile homes	Black[2]	His-panic[3]	Elderly[4]	Moved in past year	Below poverty level
		Housing unit characteristics		Household characteristics				
ALL OWNERS								
Total	74,931	4,919	5,516	6,471	5,752	17,818	6,591	6,450
Mortgages currently on property:								
None, owned free and clear.	24,776	839	3,066	2,078	1,539	12,139	1,258	3,690
Regular and home equity mortgages....	48,394	3,987	2,352	4,190	4,098	5,224	5,192	2,512
Regular mortgage...............	44,652	3,843	2,233	3,971	3,964	4,115	5,064	2,338
Home equity lump sum mortage	4,385	269	87	264	253	527	269	164
Home equity line of credit.	10,044	712	132	438	476	1,320	652	297
Not reported	1,694	87	96	201	115	391	139	243
Number of regular and home equity mortgages:[5]								
1 mortgage.................	33,409	2,815	2,053	3,208	3,085	3,878	3,634	1,824
2 mortgages.................	10,877	921	108	558	719	688	1,149	259
3 mortgages or more	1,164	100	5	56	90	77	146	40
Type of mortgage:								
Regular and home equity lump sum[5] ...	2,958	224	15	157	183	162	208	96
With home equity line of credit	587	38	–	23	44	45	54	27
No home equity line of credit	2,348	183	15	131	137	115	151	69
Regular no home equity lump sum[5] ...	41,694	3,619	2,218	3,814	3,781	3,953	4,855	2,242
With home equity line of credit	6,835	572	70	290	366	455	509	144
No home equity line of credit	31,992	2,899	1,962	3,162	3,223	2,936	4,089	1,714
Home equity lump sum no regular[5]	1,427	45	73	107	70	365	61	68
With home equity line of credit	307	3	15	14	3	76	22	19
No home equity line of credit	1,099	42	57	91	66	280	40	46
No regular or home equity lump sum[5].....	28,851	1,031	3,210	2,393	1,718	13,338	1,466	4,045
With home equity line of credit	2,315	99	46	112	64	744	67	107
No home equity line of credit	24,842	845	3,068	2,081	1,539	12,203	1,260	3,695
OWNERS WITH ONE OR MORE REGULAR OR LUMP SUM HOME EQUITY MORTGAGES								
Total[5]	46,079	3,888	2,306	4,078	4,034	4,480	5,125	2,405
Type of primary mortgage:								
FHA	4,689	450	111	820	615	298	551	238
VA........................	1,809	160	37	231	115	150	203	66
RHS/RD[6]...................	364	41	13	44	31	23	50	29
Other types.................	35,908	3,087	1,894	2,561	3,049	3,332	4,059	1,621
Mortgage origination:								
Placed new mortgage(s)	45,798	3,879	2,264	4,032	3,977	4,448	5,077	2,371
Primary obtained when property acquired	27,592	3,401	1,872	2,844	2,771	2,304	4,940	1,718
Obtained later	18,206	478	392	1,188	1,206	2,144	138	653
Assumed	231	3	40	41	47	27	43	32
Wrap-around.................	11	6	2	–	3	3	5	–
Combination of the above	40	–	–	5	8	2	–	2
Payment plan of primary mortgage:								
Fixed payment, self amortizing	37,392	3,187	1,853	3,227	3,284	3,297	3,955	1,677
Adjustable rate mortgage	2,441	235	92	194	253	178	404	98
Adjustable term mortgage	160	–	15	13	7	43	7	14
Graduated payment mortgage	517	71	19	49	47	36	133	26
Balloon	518	76	45	22	51	37	102	32
Combination of the above	474	67	5	26	28	59	91	14
Payment plan of secondary mortgage:[5]								
Units with two or more mortgages[5].....	5,286	494	27	339	478	260	834	143
Fixed payment, self amortizing	3,897	334	25	287	344	171	571	108
Adjustable rate mortgage	460	67	–	11	37	21	110	3
Adjustable term mortgage	156	13	–	3	27	29	13	5
Graduated payment mortgage.......	70	13	–	5	16	–	35	2
Balloon	106	11	3	5	11	3	15	5
Other......................	5	–	–	–	–	–	–	–
Combination of the above	174	31	–	2	5	4	29	4
Reason primary refinanced:								
Units with a refinanced primary mortgage[7]	17,685	535	302	1,102	1,192	1,502	133	513
To get a lower interest rate.........	15,322	453	195	851	978	1,186	80	369
To increase payment period	568	10	13	31	57	45	10	12
To reduce payment period	2,007	29	13	68	126	111	2	128
To renew or extend a loan that has fallen due	178	–	3	20	12	17	–	12
To receive cash	2,375	60	36	169	230	261	25	70
Other reason	1,646	42	95	137	116	185	23	67
Cash received in primary mortgage refinance:								
Units receiving refinance cash	2,375	60	36	169	230	261	25	70
Median amount received (dol.)	28,084	(NA)	(NA)	19,608	31,701	33,553	(NA)	21,390

– Represents or rounds to zero. NA Not available. [1] Constructed in the past 4 years. [2] For persons who selected this race group only. See footnote 3, Table 954. [3] Persons of Hispanic origin may be of any race. [4] 65 years old and over. [5] Includes "don't know" and "not reported." [6] Rural Housing Service/Rural Development Mortgage, formerly Farmers Home Administration. [7] Persons reporting more than one reason are counted once in the total.

Source: U.S. Census Bureau, Current Housing Reports, Series H150/05, *American Housing Survey for the United States*. See Internet site <http://www.census.gov/hhes/www/housing/ahs/nationaldata.html>.

Table 962. **Occupied Housing Units—Neighborhood Indicators by Selected Characteristics of the Householder: 2005**

[In thousands (108,871 represents 108,871,000). As of fall. Based on the American Housing Survey; see Appendix III]

Characteristic	Total occupied units	Tenure		Black [1]		Hispanic origin [2]		Elderly [3]		Households below poverty level	
		Owner	Renter	Owner	Renter	Owner	Renter	Owner	Renter	Owner	Renter
Total units	108,871	74,931	33,940	6,471	6,975	5,752	5,899	17,818	4,379	6,450	8,674
Street noise or traffic present [4] . .	28,436	16,918	11,519	1,797	2,565	1,363	1,757	4,188	1,221	1,609	2,978
Condition not bothersome	16,866	9,988	6,878	1,078	1,510	731	973	2,869	880	942	1,720
Condition bothersome	11,522	6,906	4,616	719	1,048	633	782	1,314	340	664	1,252
So bothersome they want to move	4,370	2,314	2,056	274	596	230	365	311	126	241	658
Neighborhood crime present [4] . . .	16,419	9,203	7,215	1,340	1,968	885	1,351	1,825	566	920	2,115
Condition not bothersome	6,944	4,025	2,920	587	777	339	439	936	312	359	808
Condition bothersome	9,447	5,166	4,280	748	1,179	546	912	881	255	558	1,302
So bothersome they want to move	4,003	1,646	2,357	288	724	253	562	216	80	191	806
Odors present [4]	5,991	3,445	2,546	362	685	330	495	644	207	366	797
Condition not bothersome	2,279	1,397	882	160	211	113	119	293	76	131	246
Condition bothersome	3,708	2,048	1,660	202	474	217	374	351	129	235	550
So bothersome they want to move	1,415	617	799	87	283	72	196	95	49	69	312
Other problems:											
Noise	2,552	1,458	1,094	155	260	137	224	314	91	144	318
Litter or housing deterioration . .	1,918	1,226	691	168	237	130	138	289	37	80	209
Poor city or county services. . .	844	513	330	102	128	84	59	106	18	41	85
People	4,057	2,530	1,527	283	381	249	272	456	67	247	505
With public transportation [4]	58,623	35,092	23,531	3,888	5,455	3,584	4,542	8,315	3,063	2,768	6,000
Household uses it at least weekly	11,219	4,148	7,071	902	2,218	616	1,838	771	859	454	2,285
Household uses it less than weekly	8,641	5,095	3,545	592	803	430	642	1,007	483	321	999
Household does not use	37,978	25,425	12,553	2,329	2,362	2,498	2,019	6,440	1,679	1,958	2,627
No public transportation	46,499	37,361	9,138	2,392	1,268	1,958	1,196	8,956	1,188	3,422	2,393
Not reported	3,750	2,478	1,271	192	251	210	161	548	128	261	280
Police protection:											
Satisfactory	96,834	66,895	29,939	5,543	5,923	4,948	5,149	16,024	4,000	5,449	7,390
Unsatisfactory	8,391	5,714	2,676	693	781	633	572	1,195	183	726	923
Secured communities [5]:											
Community access secured with walls or fences	6,925	3,150	3,775	223	846	357	893	974	543	221	844
Community access not secured	101,136	71,201	29,935	6,163	6,069	5,353	4,977	16,690	3,803	6,137	7,754
Secured multiunits: [5]											
Multiunit access secured.	5,841	1,061	4,781	81	1,029	99	694	389	1,306	154	1,308
Multiunit access not secured . .	19,792	2,645	17,147	269	3,824	277	3,339	774	1,926	252	4,416
Senior citizen communities:											
Households with persons 55 years old and over	42,934	34,557	8,377	2,865	1,533	1,945	1,086	17,818	4,379	3,902	2,537
Community age restricted [6]	2,834	1,435	1,399	47	198	45	106	1,118	1,228	222	536
Access to structure:											
Enter building from outside [4, 7]	25,778	3,740	22,038	349	4,882	380	4,053	1,179	3,248	411	5,757
Use of steps not required . .	10,049	1,498	8,550	97	1,738	165	1,634	556	1,777	165	2,517
Use of steps required	15,692	2,229	13,463	252	3,139	214	2,412	621	1,460	241	3,238
Enter home from outside [4, 8] . .	83,093	71,191	11,903	6,122	2,093	5,372	1,845	16,639	1,131	6,039	2,916
Use of steps not required . .	39,953	34,712	5,241	2,869	903	3,197	945	8,271	527	2,689	1,228
Use of steps required	43,043	36,393	6,650	3,247	1,187	2,167	900	8,340	604	3,341	1,688
Community quality:											
Some or all activities present. .	38,786	25,667	13,119	2,219	2,632	1,783	1,836	6,522	2,210	1,815	3,281
Community center or clubhouse	23,287	14,379	8,908	1,243	1,782	961	1,172	4,111	1,696	982	2,094
Golf in the community	6,236	4,678	1,558	306	200	233	184	1,159	209	255	338
Trails in the community	18,641	13,581	5,061	1,012	733	801	630	2,955	767	738	1,091
Shuttle bus	9,565	5,831	3,734	429	542	411	500	2,084	1,142	474	1,145
Daycare	14,531	9,883	4,648	1,111	1,209	691	722	2,212	533	736	1,319
Private or restricted beach, park, or shoreline	6,556	4,937	1,620	244	278	267	194	1,190	193	316	368
Trash, litter, or junk on street: [9]											
None.	96,984	68,345	28,639	5,503	5,451	5,077	4,824	16,494	4,011	5,601	6,969
Minor accumulation	6,578	3,273	3,305	479	889	373	637	617	225	406	1,036
Major accumulation	2,757	1,450	1,308	216	414	148	322	336	70	198	467

[1] For persons who selected this race group only. See footnote 3, Table 954.   [2] Persons of Hispanic origin may be of any race.   [3] Householders 65 years old and over.   [4] Includes those not reporting.   [5] Public access is restricted (walls, gates, private security). Includes high rise apartments, retirement communities, resorts, etc.   [6] At least one family member must be aged 55 years old or older.   [7] Restricted to multi-units.   [8] Restricted to single units.   [9] Or on any properties within 300 feet.

Source: U.S. Census Bureau, Current Housing Reports, Series H150/05, *American Housing Survey for the United States*. See Internet site <http://www.census.gov/hhes/www/housing/ahs/nationaldata.html>.

Construction and Housing **617**

[97,693 represents 97,693,000. As of fall. Based on American Housing Survey. See Appendix III]

Type of equipment or fuel	Number (1,000)					Percent distribution	
	1995	1999	2001	2003 [1]	2005	1995	2005
Occupied units, total.	97,693	102,803	106,261	105,842	108,871	100.0	100.0
Heating equipment:							
Warm air furnace.	53,165	62,018	65,262	65,380	68,275	54.4	62.7
Steam or hot water	13,669	13,153	13,441	13,257	12,880	14.0	11.8
Heat pumps	9,406	10,992	11,080	11,347	12,484	9.6	11.5
Built-in electric units.	7,035	4,939	5,063	4,760	4,699	7.2	4.3
Floor, wall, or pipeless furnace. . .	4,963	5,310	5,343	5,322	5,102	5.1	4.7
Room heaters with flue.	1,620	1,624	1,542	1,432	1,294	1.7	1.2
Room heaters without flue.	1,642	1,790	1,558	1,509	1,327	1.7	1.2
Fireplaces, stoves, portable							
heaters or other.	5,150	2,434	2,571	2,396	2,411	5.3	2.2
None.	1,044	544	401	439	399	1.1	0.4
House main heating fuel:							
Electricity.	26,771	31,142	32,590	32,341	34,263	27.4	31.5
Utility gas.	49,203	52,366	54,689	54,928	56,317	50.4	51.7
Bottled, tank, or LP gas	4,251	5,905	6,079	6,134	6,228	4.4	5.7
Fuel oil, kerosene, etc..	12,029	10,750	10,473	10,136	9,929	12.3	9.1
Coal or coke.	210	168	128	126	95	0.2	0.1
Wood and other fuel	4,186	1,927	1,902	1,735	1,640	4.3	1.5
None.	1,042	545	400	441	398	1.1	0.4
Cooking fuel:							
Electricity.	57,621	61,315	63,685	62,859	65,297	59.0	60.0
Gas [2]	39,218	41,051	42,161	42,612	43,316	40.1	39.8
Other fuel	566	69	66	62	51	0.6	(Z)
None.	287	368	349	309	206	0.3	0.2

Z Less than .05 percent   [1] Based on 2000 census controls.   [2] Includes utility, bottled, tank, and LP gas.

Source: U.S. Census Bureau, Current Housing Reports, Series H150/95RV, H150/99, H150/01, H150/03, and H150/05, *American Housing Survey for the United States.* See Internet site <http://www.census.gov/hhes/www/housing/ahs/nationaldata.html>.

Table 964. **Occupied Housing Units—Housing Indicators by Selected Characteristics of the Householder: 2005**

[In thousands of units (108,871 represents 108,871,000). As of fall. Based on the American Housing Survey; see Appendix III]

Characteristic	Total occupied units	Tenure		Black [1]		Hispanic origin [2]		Elderly [3]		Households below poverty level	
		Owner	Renter	Owner	Renter	Owner	Renter	Owner	Renter	Owner	Renter
Total units	108,871	74,931	33,940	6,471	6,975	5,752	5,899	17,818	4,379	6,450	8,674
Amenities:											
Porch, deck, balcony, or patio	92,659	68,940	23,719	5,633	4,651	5,118	3,932	16,276	2,605	5,661	5,586
Telephone available	105,741	73,152	32,589	6,265	6,671	5,599	5,672	17,486	4,209	6,218	8,232
Usable fireplace	37,804	33,757	4,047	2,123	559	1,900	567	6,879	304	1,736	571
Separate dining room . . .	52,782	43,119	9,663	3,833	2,197	3,074	1,574	9,842	929	3,176	2,122
With 2 or more living rooms or rec. rooms . . .	32,544	30,183	2,360	2,128	327	1,572	203	6,431	204	1,468	371
Garage or carport with home	68,238	57,322	10,917	3,785	1,364	4,266	1,969	13,917	1,238	3,895	1,873
Cars and trucks available:											
No cars, trucks, or vans. .	9,227	2,462	6,765	526	2,186	158	1,224	1,528	1,938	794	3,232
Other households without cars.	13,794	9,614	4,180	625	556	881	864	1,760	269	904	921
1 car with or without trucks or vans	51,687	34,948	16,740	3,090	3,328	2,449	2,687	10,216	1,945	3,379	3,774
2 cars	26,066	20,773	5,294	1,685	791	1,653	944	3,695	199	1,082	645
3 or more cars.	8,097	7,134	962	544	113	612	180	621	28	290	102
Selected deficiencies:											
Signs of rats in last 3 months.	880	464	416	48	131	102	156	57	25	50	154
Signs of mice in last 3 months.	6,140	3,917	2,223	366	669	233	520	737	180	420	669
Holes in floors	981	489	492	46	139	47	115	77	20	119	184
Open cracks or holes . . .	5,241	2,797	2,445	279	620	259	415	448	143	404	737
Broken plaster or peeling paint (interior of unit)	2,218	1,059	1,159	147	320	118	216	215	87	174	359
No electrical wiring	50	40	10	–	–	3	–	10	2	15	2
Exposed wiring	700	459	240	55	46	32	29	100	30	71	90
Rooms without electric outlet	1,543	898	645	113	160	88	119	196	60	161	180
Water leakage from inside structure [4]	9,049	5,210	3,840	494	876	422	665	825	286	422	1,003
Water leakage from outside structure [4].	11,701	8,391	3,310	784	719	498	493	1,562	244	668	853

– Represents or rounds to zero.   [1] For persons who selected this race group only. See footnote 3, Table 954.   [2] Persons of Hispanic origin may be of any race.   [3] Householders 65 years old and over.   [4] During the 12 months prior to the survey.

Source: U.S. Census Bureau, Current Housing Reports, Series H150/05, *American Housing Survey for the United States.* See Internet site <http://www.census.gov/hhes/www/housing/ahs/nationaldata.html>.

Table 965. Net Stock of Residential Fixed Assets: 1990 to 2005

[In billions of dollars (6,260.2 represents $6,260,200,000,000). End of year estimates]

Item	1990	1995	1999	2000	2001	2002	2003	2004	2005
Total residential fixed assets...	6,260.2	8,028.0	10,206.7	10,907.4	11,711.5	12,456.7	13,504.3	14,963.6	16,121.7
By type of owner and legal form of organization:									
Private	6,111.0	7,839.8	9,986.7	10,675.7	11,464.8	12,193.1	13,224.7	14,659.8	15,800.1
Corporate	65.7	76.6	94.5	99.5	105.0	110.1	116.1	126.1	135.3
Noncorporate	6,045.3	7,763.3	9,892.2	10,576.1	11,359.8	12,083.0	13,108.7	14,533.7	15,664.7
Government	149.2	188.2	219.9	231.7	246.7	263.6	279.5	303.7	321.7
Federal	51.8	61.6	72.2	75.4	79.2	82.9	87.9	93.9	99.4
State and local	97.3	126.6	147.7	156.4	167.5	180.7	191.6	209.8	222.2
By industry:									
Private	6,111.0	7,839.8	9,986.7	10,675.7	11,464.8	12,193.1	13,224.7	14,659.8	15,800.1
Farm	48.7	51.3	67.0	72.2	77.2	80.6	85.9	90.7	95.6
Nonfarm	6,062.4	7,788.6	9,919.8	10,603.4	11,387.6	12,112.5	13,138.8	14,569.1	15,704.5
By tenure group: [1]									
Owner-occupied	4,515.6	5,987.9	7,752.3	8,328.7	8,996.0	9,614.3	10,499.0	11,706.3	12,678.5
Farm	48.7	51.3	67.0	72.2	77.2	80.6	85.9	90.7	95.6
Nonfarm	4,467.0	5,936.7	7,685.3	8,256.4	8,918.8	9,533.7	10,413.1	11,615.5	12,582.9
Tenant-occupied	1,718.8	2,011.3	2,420.6	2,543.0	2,677.2	2,802.0	2,961.8	3,209.9	3,393.5

[1] Excludes stocks of other nonfarm residential assets, which consists primarily of dormitories, and of fraternity and sorority houses.

Source: U.S. Bureau of Economic Analysis, Internet site <http://www.bea.gov/bea/dn/FA2004/SelectTable.asp> (accessed May 2007).

Table 966. Home Remodeling—Work Done and Amount Spent: 2006

[In thousands, except percent (3,762 represents 3,762,000). As of fall 2006. For work done in the prior 12 months. Based on household survey and subject to sampling error; see source]

Remodeling project	Households with work done [1]			Amount spent (dol.)		
	Number	Percent of house-holds	Done by outside contractor	Under $1,000	$1,000 to $2,999	Over $3,000
Conversion of garage/attic/basement into living space	3,762	1.7	651	525	967	1,259
Remodel bathroom	14,453	6.6	3,332	6,355	2,501	2,280
Remodel kitchen	9,619	4.4	2,836	2,881	1,464	3,202
Remodel bedroom	8,032	3.7	1,021	4,316	1,077	635
Remodel/convert room to home office	3,467	1.6	172	1,713	528	205
Remodel other rooms	7,039	3.2	1,046	3,170	1,022	942
Add bathroom	1,926	0.9	542	266	283	710
Add/extend garage	1,080	0.5	227	87	109	527
Add other rooms—exterior addition	2,040	0.9	665	288	331	844
Add deck/porch/patio	7,047	3.2	2,128	1,979	1,493	1,998
Roofing	9,279	4.3	5,501	1,829	1,950	3,670
Siding—vinyl/metal	2,940	1.4	1,558	432	505	1,229
Aluminum windows	1,683	0.8	657	394	388	244
Clad-wood/Wood windows	1,131	0.5	428	245	236	414
Vinyl windows	4,819	2.2	2,635	1,143	1,242	1,548
Ceramic tile floors	6,963	3.2	2,426	3,246	1,175	808
Hardwood floors	5,049	2.3	2,460	1,151	1,259	1,234
Laminate flooring	5,616	2.6	1,418	3,039	1,203	572
Vinyl flooring	4,164	1.9	1,216	2,350	495	89
Carpeting	10,576	4.8	6,164	3,590	3,465	1,148
Kitchen cabinets	4,658	2.1	1,590	1,206	723	1,364
Kitchen counter tops	4,798	2.2	2,298	1,761	900	1,103
Skylights	807	0.4	395	457	91	110
Exterior doors	6,720	3.1	2,907	4,040	959	568
Interior doors	4,653	2.1	1,095	2,962	330	175
Garage doors	3,139	1.4	2,098	1,238	1,028	132
Concrete or masonry work	5,055	2.3	2,621	1,896	1,157	1,062
Swimming pool—inground	756	0.4	359	38	101	426
Wall paneling	1,450	0.7	155	750	81	45
Ceramic wall tile	2,735	1.3	698	1,410	572	134

[1] Includes no response and amount unknown.

Source: Mediamark Research Inc., New York, NY, Top-Line Reports, (copyright) Internet site <http://www.mediamark.com/>.

U.S. Census Bureau, Statistical Abstract of the United States: 2008

[In millions of dollars (124,971 represents $124,971,000,000). Based on personal interviews and mail surveys; see source for details]

		Owner-occupied one-unit properties						
	All			Materials purchased by owners			Year structure built		
Type of expenditure	residential properties	Total [1]	Payments to contractors	Total	For jobs done by owners	For jobs done under contract	Before 1960	1960 to 1979	1980 to 2003
Total:									
1995.	124,971	79,003	63,017	15,987	12,305	3,682	30,080	28,157	14,718
2000.	152,975	100,161	84,778	15,382	11,682	3,700	30,451	27,872	32,717
2003.	176,899	115,876	101,207	14,669	11,750	2,920	40,497	29,498	45,881
2004.	198,556	136,080	114,197	21,883	17,213	4,670	39,452	36,035	60,594
2005.	215,030	159,458	133,684	25,774	20,365	5,409	40,821	45,505	73,132
2006.	228,208	167,154	141,439	25,715	21,615	4,100	43,582	39,196	84,376
Maintenance and repairs:									
1995	47,032	25,460	19,487	5,973	5,498	476	9,979	8,388	5,511
2000	42,236	22,411	18,260	4,151	3,384	767	8,074	5,226	6,788
2003	44,094	18,381	15,714	2,667	2,387	279	5,583	4,545	8,253
2004	50,611	26,575	20,655	5,920	5,356	564	8,197	6,401	11,977
2005	53,293	32,888	24,574	8,314	7,869	444	9,315	8,022	15,551
2006	53,389	31,078	23,299	7,778	7,133	645	8,633	8,405	14,040
Improvements:									
1995	77,940	53,543	43,530	10,013	6,807	3,206	20,101	19,768	9,208
2000	110,739	77,750	66,517	11,232	8,298	2,934	22,377	22,646	25,929
2003	132,805	97,495	85,494	12,003	9,362	2,640	34,914	24,953	37,628
2004	147,945	109,506	93,542	15,962	11,857	4,106	31,254	29,634	48,617
2005	161,737	126,570	109,110	17,460	12,496	4,964	31,507	37,483	57,581
2006	174,819	136,076	118,140	17,936	14,481	3,455	34,950	30,790	70,336

[1] Includes year built not reported, not shown separately.
Source: U.S. Census Bureau, "Residential Improvement and Repair Statistics." See Internet site <http://www.census.gov/const/www/c50index.html>.

Table 968. **Commercial Buildings—Summary: 2003**

[4,645 represents 4,645,000. Excludes mall buildings. Building type based on predominant activity in which the occupants were engaged. Based on a sample survey of building representatives conducted in 2003, therefore subject to sampling variability. For commercial building energy consumption and expenditures, see Table 893, Section 19]

Characteristic	All buildings (1,000)	Total floorspace (mil. sq. ft.)	Total workers in all buildings (1,000)	Mean square foor per building [1] (1,000)	Mean square foot per worker [1]	Mean operating hours per week [1]
All buildings	**4,645**	**64,783**	**72,807**	**13.9**	**890**	**61**
Building floorspace (sq. ft.):						
1,001 to 5,000	2,552	6,789	9,936	2.7	683	57
5,001 to 10,000	889	6,585	7,512	7.4	877	61
10,001 to 25,000	738	11,535	10,787	15.6	1,069	67
25,001 to 50,000	241	8,668	8,881	35.9	976	72
50,001 to 100,000.	129	9,057	8,432	70.4	1,074	80
100,001 to 200,000	65	9,064	11,662	138.8	779	89
200,001 to 500,000	25	7,176	6,883	289.0	1,043	100
Over 500,000	7	5,908	8,744	896.1	676	115
Principal activity within building:						
Education	386	9,874	12,489	25.6	791	50
Food sales	226	1,255	1,430	5.6	877	107
Food service	297	1,654	3,129	5.6	528	86
Health care	129	3,163	6,317	24.6	501	59
Inpatient	8	1,905	3,716	241.4	513	168
Outpatient	121	1,258	2,600	10.4	484	52
Lodging.	142	5,096	2,457	35.8	2,074	167
Retail (other than mall).	443	4,317	3,463	9.7	1,246	59
Office	824	12,208	28,154	14.8	434	55
Public assembly	277	3,939	2,395	14.2	1,645	50
Public order and safety	71	1,090	1,347	15.5	809	103
Religious worship	370	3,754	1,706	10.1	2,200	32
Service	622	4,050	3,667	6.5	1,105	55
Warehouse and storage	597	10,078	4,369	16.9	2,306	66
Other	79	1,738	1,819	21.9	956	63
Vacant	182	2,567	(NA)	14.1	(NA)	(NA)
Energy sources: [2]						
Electricity.	4,404	63,307	72,708	14.4	871	62
Natural gas	2,391	43,468	51,956	18.2	837	65
Fuel oil	451	15,157	19,625	33.6	772	68
District heat	67	5,443	10,190	81.4	534	79
District chilled water	33	2,853	7,189	86.7	397	79
Propane	502	7,076	5,858	14.1	1,208	60
Wood	62	289	262	4.6	1,105	46

NA Not available. [1] For explanation of mean, see Guide to Tabular Presentation. [2] More than one type may apply.
Source: U.S. Energy Information Administration, "2003 Commercial Buildings Energy Consumption Buildings (CBECS) Detailed Tables"; Table B1. See Internet site <http://www.eia.doe.gov/emeu/cbecs/cbecs2003/detailed_tables_2003/detailed_tables_2003.html> (accessed 11 July 2007).

Section 21

Manufactures

This section presents summary data for manufacturing as a whole and more detailed information for major industry groups and selected products. The types of measures shown at the different levels include data for establishments, employment and payroll, value and quantity of production and shipments, value added by manufacture, inventories, and various indicators of financial status.

The principal sources of these data are U.S. Census Bureau reports of the censuses of manufactures conducted every 5 years, the *Annual Survey of Manufactures*, and *Current Industrial Reports*. Reports on current activities of industries or current movements of individual commodities are compiled by such government agencies as the Bureau of Labor Statistics; the Economic Research Service of the U.S. Department of Agriculture; the International Trade Administration; and by private research or trade associations.

Data on financial aspects of manufacturing industries are collected by the Census Bureau (see especially Tables 983–985) as part of the Quarterly Financial Report. Industry aggregates in the form of balance sheets, profit and loss statements, analyses of sales and expenses, lists of subsidiaries, and types and amounts of security issues are published for leading manufacturing corporations registered with the Securities and Exchange Commission. The BEA issues data on capital in manufacturing industries and capacity utilization rates in manufacturing. See also Section 15, Business Enterprise.

Several private trade associations provide industry coverage for certain sections of the economy. They include the Aluminum Association (Table 992), American Iron and Steel Institute (Tables 993 and 994), Consumer Electronics Association (Table 1000), and the Aerospace Industries Association (Tables 1005 and 1007). Machine tool consumption data (Table 996) is produced jointly by the Association for Manufacturing Technology and American Machine Tool Distributors Association.

Censuses and annual surveys—The first census of manufactures covered the year 1809. Between 1809 and 1963, a census was conducted at periodic intervals. Since 1967, it has been taken every 5 years (for years ending in "2" and "7"). Results from the 2002 census are presented in this section utilizing the North American Industry Classification System (NAICS). For additional information see text, Section 15, Business Enterprise, and the Census Bureau Web site at <http://www.census.gov/econ/census02/>. Census data, either directly reported or estimated from administrative records, are obtained for every manufacturing plant with one or more paid employees.

The *Annual Survey of Manufactures* (ASM), conducted for the first time in 1949, collects data for the years between censuses for the more general measure of manufacturing activity covered in detail by the censuses. The annual survey data are estimates derived from a scientifically selected sample of establishments. The 2004 annual survey is based on a sample of about 50,000 from a universe of 346,000 establishments. These establishments represent all manufacturing establishments of multiunit companies and all single-establishment manufacturing companies mailed schedules in the 2002 Census of Manufactures. For the current panel of the ASM sample, all establishments of companies with 2002 shipments in manufacturing in excess of $500 million were included in the survey with certainty. For the remaining portion of the mail survey, the establishment was defined as the sampling unit. For this portion, all establishments with 500 employees or more and establishments with a very large value of shipments also were included. Therefore, of the 50,000 establishments included in the ASM panel, approximately 24,000 are selected with certainty. Smaller establishments in the remaining portion of the mail survey were selected by sample.

U.S. Census Bureau, Statistical Abstract of the United States: 2008

Establishments and classification—
Each of the establishments covered in the
2002 Economic Census—Manufacturing
was classified in 1 of 480 industries (473
manufacturing industries and 7 former
manufacturing industries) in accordance
with the industry definitions in the 2002
NAICS manual. In the NAICS system, an
industry is generally defined as a group
of establishments that have similar production processes. To the extent practical, the system uses supply-based or
production-oriented concepts in defining
industries. The resulting group of establishments must be significant in terms of
number, value added by manufacture,
value of shipments, and number of
employees.

Establishments frequently make products
classified both in their industry (primary
products) and other industries (secondary
products). Industry statistics (employment, payroll, value added by manufacture, value of shipments, etc.) reflect the
activities of the establishments, which
may make both primary and secondary
products. Product statistics, however, represent the output of all establishments
without regard for the classification of the
producing establishment. For this reason,
when relating the industry statistics,
especially the value of shipments, to the
product statistics, the composition of the
industry's output should be considered.

Establishment—Establishment signifies
a single physical plant site or factory. It is
not necessarily identical to the business
unit or company, which may consist of
one or more establishments. A company
operating establishments at more than
one location is required to submit a separate report for each location and include
establishments with payroll at any time
during the year. An establishment
engaged in distinctly different lines of
activity and maintaining separate payroll
and inventory records is also required to
submit separate reports.

Durable goods—Items with a normal
life expectancy of 3 years or more.
Automobiles, furniture, household appliances, and mobile homes are common
examples.

Nondurable goods—Items which
generally last for only a short time
(3 years or less). Food, beverages, clothing, shoes, and gasoline are common
examples.

Statistical reliability—For a discussion
of statistical collection and estimation,
sampling procedures, and measures of
statistical reliability applicable to Census
Bureau data, see Appendix III.

U.S. Census Bureau, Statistical Abstract of the United States: 2008

Table 969. Gross Domestic Product in Current and Real (2000) Dollars by Industry: 2000 to 2006

[In billions of dollars (9,817.0 represents $9,817,000,000,000). Data include nonfactor charges (capital consumption allowances, indirect business taxes, etc.) as well as factor charges against gross product; corporate profits and capital consumption allowances have been shifted from a company to an establishment basis]

Industry	2002 NAICS code [1]	2000	2002	2003	2004	2005	2006
CURRENT DOLLARS							
Gross domestic product, total [2]	(X)	**9,817.0**	**10,469.6**	**10,960.8**	**11,712.5**	**12,455.8**	**13,246.6**
Private industries	(X)	8,614.3	9,131.2	9,542.3	10,221.5	10,892.2	11,610.4
Manufacturing	31–33	1,426.2	1,352.6	1,359.3	1,434.8	1,512.5	1,601.2
Durable goods	(X)	865.3	774.8	771.8	819.6	854.3	915.7
Wood products	321	31.4	30.4	32.1	38.3	39.0	(NA)
Nonmetallic mineral products	327	45.7	45.9	45.1	49.5	53.3	(NA)
Primary metals	331	48.2	41.9	38.4	54.3	61.1	(NA)
Fabricated metal products	332	121.7	107.4	106.3	118.4	130.5	(NA)
Machinery	333	109.3	96.5	94.3	104.4	111.1	(NA)
Computer and electronic products	334	185.6	124.2	124.0	129.5	135.3	(NA)
Electrical equipment, appliances, and components	335	50.6	48.8	48.8	45.7	47.8	(NA)
Motor vehicles, bodies and trailers, and parts	3361–63	118.1	118.9	124.1	109.8	95.4	(NA)
Other transportation equipment	3364, 66, 69	64.4	69.6	62.4	65.7	71.1	(NA)
Furniture and related products	337	32.7	31.1	33.4	36.7	37.1	(NA)
Miscellaneous manufacturing	339	57.5	60.0	62.9	67.4	72.6	(NA)
Nondurable goods	(X)	561.0	577.9	587.5	615.2	658.2	685.5
Food and beverage and tobacco products	311, 312	154.8	172.9	167.9	156.2	175.7	(NA)
Textile mills and textile product mills	313, 314	26.5	21.9	23.1	23.4	23.8	(NA)
Apparel and leather and allied products	315, 316	25.1	20.9	18.3	17.1	16.8	(NA)
Paper products	322	55.6	50.3	50.3	52.8	54.6	(NA)
Printing and related support activities	323	49.0	45.7	45.2	46.4	46.9	(NA)
Petroleum and coal products	324	26.2	26.2	39.1	53.8	63.5	(NA)
Chemical products	325	157.1	174.4	179.5	198.4	209.2	(NA)
Plastics and rubber products	326	66.7	65.5	64.0	67.1	67.7	(NA)
CHAINED (2000) DOLLARS							
Gross domestic product, total [2]	(X)	**9,817.0**	**10,048.8**	**10,301.0**	**10,703.5**	**11,048.6**	**11,415.3**
Private industries	(X)	8,614.3	8,817.1	9,050.9	9,434.5	9,748.8	10,110.8
Manufacturing	31-33	1,426.2	1,384.4	1,400.1	1,490.7	1,523.1	1,573.8
Durable goods	(X)	865.3	827.7	849.4	914.4	959.0	1,023.1
Wood products	321	31.4	30.3	30.4	31.4	32.4	(NA)
Nonmetallic mineral products	327	45.7	45.5	45.2	48.6	48.4	(NA)
Primary metals	331	48.2	44.1	42.3	48.7	48.3	(NA)
Fabricated metal products	332	121.7	104.4	104.6	113.6	119.1	(NA)
Machinery	333	109.3	93.3	91.6	104.7	109.0	(NA)
Computer and electronic products	334	185.6	185.8	214.6	258.5	309.9	(NA)
Electrical equipment, appliances, and components	335	50.6	48.8	50.1	46.7	47.5	(NA)
Motor vehicles, bodies and trailers, and parts	3361–63	118.1	127.5	137.0	128.8	125.1	(NA)
Other transportation equipment	3364, 66, 69	64.4	64.2	55.5	57.0	59.2	(NA)
Furniture and related products	337	32.7	29.2	31.4	35.6	34.8	(NA)
Miscellaneous manufacturing	339	57.5	56.4	59.1	64.7	70.1	(NA)
Nondurable goods	(X)	561.0	555.7	551.2	578.4	571.1	565.8
Food and beverage and tobacco products	311, 312	154.8	153.7	151.4	145.9	152.9	(NA)
Textile mills and textile product mills	313, 314	26.5	21.4	23.6	23.5	24.0	(NA)
Apparel and leather and allied products	315, 316	25.1	21.1	18.5	17.7	17.7	(NA)
Paper products	322	55.6	50.8	52.1	56.3	57.5	(NA)
Printing and related support activities	323	49.0	43.5	43.5	45.3	45.9	(NA)
Petroleum and coal products	324	26.2	32.5	30.7	38.1	30.0	(NA)
Chemical products	325	157.1	170.5	169.6	183.6	180.5	(NA)
Plastics and rubber products	326	66.7	62.9	63.0	68.1	67.1	(NA)

NA Not available.   X Not applicable.   [1] North American Industry Classification System, 2002; see text Section 15.
[2] Includes industries, not shown separately. For additional industries, see Table 648.

Source: U.S. Bureau of Economic Analysis, *Survey of Current Business*, May 2007. See also <http://www.bea.gov /newsreleases/industry/gdpindustry/gdpindnewsrelease.htm>(released 24 April 2007).

Manufactures   623

Table 970. **Manufacturing—Establishments, Employees, and Annual Payroll by Industry: 2003 and 2004**

[(113,398 represents 113,398,000). Excludes government employees, railroad employees, self-employed persons, etc. An *establishment* is a single physical location where business is conducted or where services or industrial operations are performed. See "General Explanation" in source for definitions and statement on reliability of data. See Appendix III]

Industry	2002 NAICS [1] code	2003 Establishments, number	2003 Employees [2] (1,000)	2003 Annual payroll (mil. dol.)	2004 Establishments, number	2004 Employees [2] (1,000)	2004 Annual payroll (mil. dol.)
All industries, total	(X)	7,254,745	113,398	4,040,889	7,387,724	115,075	4,253,996
Manufacturing, total	31–33	341,849	14,132	576,058	339,083	13,822	592,830
Percent of all industries	(X)	4.7	12.5	14.3	4.6	12.0	13.9
Food manufacturing	311	27,274	1,496	46,593	26,767	1,482	47,540
Beverage & tobacco products	312	3,212	155	7,111	3,359	155	7,211
Textile mills	313	3,840	255	7,366	3,638	224	6,875
Textile product mills	314	7,289	188	4,997	7,117	171	4,905
Apparel manufacturing	315	13,376	304	7,065	12,314	280	6,804
Leather & allied products	316	1,519	44	1,265	1,475	43	1,307
Wood products	321	16,808	524	15,891	16,783	535	17,194
Paper	322	5,456	482	21,668	5,422	465	21,590
Printing & related support activities	323	36,024	700	25,033	35,321	673	24,997
Petroleum & coal products	324	2,299	98	6,487	2,457	104	7,776
Chemical	325	13,247	841	48,532	13,364	823	48,816
Plastics & rubber products	326	15,019	921	32,126	14,886	908	33,160
Nonmetallic mineral products	327	16,446	468	18,087	16,714	472	18,963
Primary metal	331	5,725	480	20,863	5,426	451	21,486
Fabricated metal products	332	59,407	1,518	55,778	59,373	1,515	58,581
Machinery	333	27,459	1,129	48,994	27,037	1,088	50,459
Computer & electronic products	334	15,426	1,189	66,583	15,097	1,108	66,318
Electrical equip, appliance & component. . .	335	6,383	460	17,617	6,294	439	17,797
Transportation equipment	336	12,503	1,607	79,967	12,705	1,626	85,128
Furniture & related products	337	21,716	564	16,796	21,735	555	17,221
Miscellaneous	339	31,421	708	27,239	31,799	703	28,702

X Not applicable. [1] North American Industry Classification System, 2002; see text, Section 15. [2] Covers full- and part-time employees who are on the payroll in the pay period including March 12.

Source: U.S. Census Bureau, "County Business Patterns." See <http://www.census.gov/epcd/cbp/view/cbpview.html>.

Table 971. **Manufacturing Establishments, Employees, and Annual Payroll by State: 2004**

[(13,822 represents 13,822,000). Data are for North American Industry Classification System (NAICS) 2002 codes 31–33. Excludes government employees, railroad employees, self-employed persons, etc. An *establishment* is a single physical location where business is conducted or where services or industrial operations are performed. See "General Explanation" in source for definitions and statement on reliability of data. See Appendix III]

State	Establishments	Employees [1] (1,000)	Annual payroll (mil. dol.)	State	Establishments	Employees [1] (1,000)	Annual payroll (mil. dol.)
United States	339,083	13,822	592,830	Missouri	7,019	303	11,703
				Montana	1,267	18	688
Alabama	4,964	274	10,068	Nebraska	1,998	104	3,633
Alaska	501	10	396	Nevada.	1,844	43	1,789
Arizona	4,818	167	7,493	New Hampshire	2,191	76	3,529
Arkansas.	3,144	201	6,551	New Jersey	9,962	326	17,001
California.	46,110	1,476	70,372	New Mexico	1,549	33	1,297
Colorado	5,235	138	6,275	New York	19,994	599	25,307
Connecticut	5,174	188	9,579	North Carolina	10,327	571	20,691
Delaware.	696	36	1,645	North Dakota	741	24	780
District of Columbia. . . .	147	2	74	Ohio	16,887	815	35,719
Florida	14,433	372	14,635	Oklahoma	3,941	141	5,371
Georgia	8,709	433	15,894	Oregon	5,541	177	7,532
Hawaii	928	15	479	Pennsylvania	15,915	668	27,931
Idaho	1,805	60	2,415	Rhode Island	2,024	58	2,261
Illinois	16,363	685	29,467	South Carolina	4,270	275	10,796
Indiana	9,068	544	23,739	South Dakota	923	40	1,274
Iowa	3,811	219	8,644	Tennessee	6,804	392	15,268
Kansas	3,179	173	6,986	Texas	20,780	829	36,255
Kentucky	4,174	258	10,716	Utah	3,113	111	4,321
Louisiana	3,416	149	6,980	Vermont	1,152	39	1,638
Maine	1,845	63	2,526	Virginia	5,817	295	12,026
Maryland	3,813	141	6,747	Washington	7,401	254	12,232
Massachusetts	8,263	294	15,590	West Virginia	1,453	67	2,598
Michigan	14,447	662	32,391	Wisconsin	9,804	489	20,479
Minnesota	8,067	333	15,026	Wyoming	546	10	432
Mississippi	2,710	174	5,594				

[1] Covers full- and part-time employees who are on the payroll in the pay period including March 12.

Source: U.S. Census Bureau, "County Business Patterns." See <http://www.census.gov/epcd/cbp/view/cbpview.html>.

Table 972. **Manufactures—Summary by Selected Industry: 2005**

[13,168.8 represents 13,168,800. Based on the Annual Survey of Manufactures; see Appendix III]

Industry based on shipments	2002 NAICS code [1]	All employees [2]			Production workers (1,000)	Value added by manufactures [3] (mil.dol.)	Value of shipments [4] (mil. dol.)
		Number (1,000)	Payroll Total (mil. dol.)	Per employee (dol.)			
Manufacturing, total	31-33	13,168.8	579,891	44,035	9,230.2	2,204,095	4,735,384
Food [5]	311	1,438.8	47,797	33,219	1,094.7	235,673	534,878
Grain and oilseed milling	3112	52.9	2,625	49,599	39.7	22,190	59,480
Sugar and confectionery products	3113	68.4	2,699	39,464	53.0	15,946	28,641
Fruit and vegetable preserving and specialty foods	3114	167.0	5,614	33,627	137.6	27,126	54,951
Dairy products	3115	127.8	5,316	41,603	88.9	25,376	76,926
Meat products	3116	486.0	13,286	27,339	416.9	53,632	150,437
Bakeries and tortillas	3118	278.6	8,810	31,624	174.7	35,139	53,666
Beverage and tobacco products	312	144.6	7,049	48,762	82.6	80,716	123,636
Beverage	3121	123.7	5,771	46,664	67.0	43,436	80,922
Tobacco	3122	20.9	1,278	61,181	15.6	37,280	42,714
Textile mills	313	195.1	6,252	32,043	163.5	17,560	41,149
Textile product mills	314	156.6	4,587	29,285	122.0	14,835	36,706
Apparel	315	223.7	5,429	24,272	171.2	16,319	31,650
Cut and sew apparel	3152	171.9	4,111	23,924	130.7	12,627	24,375
Leather and allied products [5]	316	37.4	1,101	29,445	29.0	2,865	6,013
Wood products [5]	321	539.1	17,832	33,078	431.1	44,763	112,018
Sawmills and wood preservation	3211	105.3	3,876	36,800	87.1	10,946	32,786
Veneer, plywood, and engineered wood products	3212	115.5	4,112	35,612	93.0	11,078	26,609
Paper	322	429.6	20,701	48,189	333.5	75,889	162,848
Pulp, paper, and paperboard mills	3221	135.6	8,227	60,675	107.6	38,619	75,428
Converted paper products	3222	294.0	12,474	42,430	225.9	37,270	87,420
Printing and related support activities	323	642.3	24,893	38,753	456.7	58,930	97,095
Petroleum and coal products	324	102.9	7,927	77,027	65.2	117,541	476,075
Chemical [5]	325	761.2	45,798	60,169	433.3	328,440	604,501
Basic chemical	3251	156.4	10,593	67,729	92.2	75,396	169,863
Resin, syn rubber, and artificial and syn. fibers and filaments	3252	85.5	5,198	60,816	58.9	32,909	89,987
Pharmaceutical and medicine	3254	236.0	15,684	66,445	113.4	124,586	165,969
Plastics and rubber products	326	885.4	33,156	37,445	688.0	96,348	200,489
Plastics products	3261	727.7	26,398	36,275	563.6	78,946	163,927
Nonmetallic mineral products	327	464.9	19,147	41,181	359.7	64,545	114,321
Cement and concrete products	3273	222.0	9,175	41,319	169.1	30,407	56,257
Primary metal [5]	331	428.0	21,311	49,794	338.6	77,179	201,835
Iron and steel mills and ferroalloy	3311	102.4	6,635	64,780	82.6	32,933	82,370
Foundries	3315	161.2	6,842	42,433	132.0	16,429	30,522
Fabricated metal products [5]	332	1,460.3	59,342	40,638	1,079.2	154,928	288,068
Architectural and structural metals	3323	355.2	13,825	38,920	252.9	36,072	73,557
Machine shops, turned product and screw, nut, and bolt	3327	362.6	14,870	41,005	274.0	31,623	50,562
Coating, engraving, heat treating, and allied activities	3328	126.6	4,788	37,820	97.3	12,943	22,661
Machinery [5]	333	1,062.7	50,233	47,269	682.6	142,488	302,204
Agriculture, construction, and mining machinery	3331	174.2	7,592	43,588	118.5	29,172	70,237
Metalworking machinery	3335	166.4	8,289	49,827	116.0	16,574	26,349
Computer and electronic products [5]	334	1,003.7	59,834	59,614	464.9	226,319	373,932
Computer and peripheral equipment	3341	101.0	6,301	62,388	35.0	36,407	68,469
Communications equipment	3342	128.0	8,041	62,843	50.4	32,413	59,060
Semiconductor and other electronic components	3344	348.2	18,302	52,569	198.4	81,946	120,106
Navigational, measuring, medical, control instruments	3345	375.3	24,958	66,496	147.8	68,730	108,223
Electrical equipment, appliance, and component	335	420.6	17,523	41,657	293.8	54,318	112,008
Electrical equipment	3353	142.5	6,179	43,358	92.7	16,983	33,708
Transportation equipment [5]	336	1,554.8	83,947	53,993	1,103.8	254,665	687,288
Motor vehicles	3361	202.2	14,100	69,746	175.1	66,480	259,467
Motor vehicle bodies and trailers	3362	149.2	5,272	35,337	118.3	12,292	33,515
Motor vehicle parts	3363	613.2	30,033	48,976	478.7	81,600	206,342
Aerospace products and parts	3364	382.7	25,989	67,918	182.2	71,221	137,105
Ship and boat building	3366	140.6	5,617	39,946	102.1	13,587	25,516
Furniture and related products [5]	337	535.8	17,491	32,642	414.3	46,801	84,291
Household and institutional furniture and kitchen cabinets	3371	354.6	10,694	30,158	281.2	26,710	48,549
Miscellaneous manufacturing	339	681.3	28,541	41,895	422.5	92,974	144,382
Medical equipment and supplies	3391	308.2	14,629	47,460	179.2	53,187	75,207

[1] North American Industry Classification System, 2002; see text, Section 15. [2] Includes employment and payroll at administrative offices and auxiliary units. All employees represent the average of production workers plus all other employees for the payroll period ended nearest the 12th of March. Production workers represent the average of the employment for the payroll periods ended nearest the 12th of March, May, August, and November. [3] Adjusted value added; takes into account (a) value added by merchandising operations (that is, difference between the sales value and cost of merchandise sold without further manufacture, processing, or assembly), plus (b) net change in finished goods and work-in-process inventories between beginning and end of year. [4] Includes extensive and unmeasurable duplication from shipments between establishments in the same industry classification. [5] Includes industries not shown separately.

Source: U.S. Census Bureau, *Annual Survey of Manufactures, Statistics for Industry Groups and Industries: 2005 Series* M05(AS-1) (issued November 2006). See Internet site <http://www.census.gov/mcd/asm-as1.html>.

Table 973. Manufactures—Summary by State: 2005

[13,168.8 represents 13,168,800. Data are for North American Industry Classification System (NAICS) 2002 codes 31–33. Sum of state totals may not add to U.S. total because U.S. and state figures were independently derived. See Appendix III]

State	All employees [1]			Production workers [1]		Value added by manufactures [2]		
		Payroll					Per	Value of
	Number (1,000)	Total (mil. dol.)	Per employee (dol.)	Total (1,000)	Wages (mil. dol.)	Total (mil. dol.)	production worker (dol.)	ship-ments [3] (mil. dol.)
United States.....	13,168.8	579,891	44,035	9,230.2	337,490	2,204,095	238,793	4,735,384
Alabama	264.2	10,016	37,917	205.5	6,879	38,373	186,733	87,841
Alaska...........	10.8	384	35,481	9.1	285	1,805	198,857	6,571
Arizona	159.0	7,604	47,826	99.6	3,742	23,736	238,291	43,234
Arkansas	185.7	6,325	34,069	149.3	4,504	26,982	180,762	58,188
California........	1,397.9	65,923	47,159	881.6	30,787	217,546	246,764	434,238
Colorado	128.5	6,032	46,950	85.8	3,193	19,463	226,804	37,420
Connecticut	180.9	9,294	51,378	108.6	4,502	28,973	266,900	46,549
Delaware.........	35.6	1,712	48,071	25.5	1,046	14,313	560,904	23,362
District of Columbia ...	1.8	72	40,369	1.0	36	160	164,190	261
Florida..........	347.5	14,209	40,892	229.8	7,344	47,290	205,820	91,573
Georgia..........	414.2	15,758	38,042	316.9	10,344	63,015	198,821	143,960
Hawaii...........	13.3	481	36,092	8.5	283	1,809	212,380	6,407
Idaho	55.5	2,181	39,293	37.6	1,205	10,512	279,874	18,232
Illinois..........	655.0	29,231	44,627	455.5	17,089	105,325	231,215	231,332
Indiana	534.6	23,898	44,706	403.3	16,128	90,120	223,445	199,872
Iowa	220.2	8,779	39,861	162.3	5,591	39,080	240,776	86,427
Kansas	173.0	7,145	41,291	120.3	4,286	22,827	189,730	62,064
Kentucky	243.6	10,417	42,764	186.1	7,041	38,686	207,886	106,365
Louisiana.........	139.2	6,870	49,347	102.0	4,462	69,911	685,431	163,163
Maine	56.3	2,343	41,651	40.9	1,522	7,857	191,947	14,918
Maryland	135.7	6,689	49,297	84.7	3,271	21,353	252,122	39,774
Massachusetts	295.0	15,129	51,280	174.9	6,654	46,044	263,199	80,702
Michigan	611.7	30,915	50,535	449.5	20,521	92,336	205,418	222,075
Minnesota	329.5	14,902	45,232	222.0	8,042	48,304	217,563	97,999
Mississippi........	166.1	5,579	33,593	132.0	3,830	17,208	130,315	49,661
Missouri..........	286.7	12,449	43,417	214.1	8,255	47,340	221,096	107,661
Montana	16.7	708	42,399	11.9	446	2,645	221,581	7,949
Nebraska.........	101.4	3,680	36,304	78.1	2,506	14,650	187,701	38,258
Nevada..........	44.3	1,936	43,723	28.7	996	7,290	254,028	12,281
New Hampshire	75.7	3,661	48,388	46.4	1,675	9,188	197,845	16,872
New Jersey	301.7	15,200	50,375	195.1	7,592	51,299	262,975	103,236
New Mexico........	31.4	1,333	42,380	22.3	760	20,401	913,919	26,748
New York.........	547.2	24,208	44,241	355.0	12,736	87,756	247,218	154,682
North Carolina	539.6	20,098	37,244	402.3	12,696	101,268	251,721	186,665
North Dakota	22.4	827	36,970	17.0	565	3,556	209,129	8,978
Ohio	768.3	34,830	45,332	561.6	22,647	124,986	222,573	278,577
Oklahoma	129.9	5,364	41,284	96.5	3,451	20,451	212,028	55,096
Oregon	178.7	7,805	43,683	126.7	4,648	34,808	274,809	61,770
Pennsylvania	652.7	28,194	43,198	458.6	16,677	104,858	228,661	214,876
Rhode Island	52.9	2,220	41,997	33.3	1,092	6,541	196,473	11,548
South Carolina	253.0	10,517	41,577	191.9	6,775	37,668	196,330	87,499
South Dakota	37.0	1,273	34,359	28.1	844	4,989	177,775	10,361
Tennessee........	381.6	15,311	40,123	284.9	9,807	62,828	220,495	137,388
Texas	779.2	35,615	45,705	529.8	19,627	172,960	326,461	463,953
Utah	110.2	4,560	41,390	73.8	2,479	15,703	212,900	33,572
Vermont	38.8	1,763	45,440	24.4	918	5,419	222,136	10,686
Virginia	275.4	11,346	41,197	204.6	7,288	49,167	240,328	88,966
Washington	248.4	11,920	47,989	160.1	6,092	46,164	288,347	93,099
West Virginia	58.0	2,411	41,580	43.3	1,573	9,186	212,196	21,573
Wisconsin	473.0	20,328	42,975	342.1	12,456	66,965	195,728	144,244
Wyoming..........	9.9	444	45,012	7.4	301	2,979	403,340	6,660

[1] Includes employment and payroll at administrative offices and auxiliary units. All employees represent the average of production workers plus all other employees for the payroll period ended nearest the 12th of March. Production workers represent the average of the employment for the payroll periods ended nearest the 12th of March, May, August, and November. [2] Adjusted value added; takes into account (a) value added by merchandising operations (that is, difference between the sales value and cost of merchandise sold without further manufacture, processing, or assembly), plus (b) net change in finished goods and work-in-process inventories between beginning and end of year. [3] Includes extensive and unmeasurable duplication from shipments between establishments in the same industry classification.

Source: U.S. Census Bureau, *Annual Survey of Manufactures, Geographic Area Statistics: 2005 Series M05(AS-3)* (issued November 2006). See Internet site <http://www.census.gov/mcd/asm-as3.html>.

626 Manufactures

Table 974. **Manufacturers' E-Commerce Shipments by Industry: 2004 and 2005**

[(**4,308,971** represents $4,308,971,000,000). Based on the Annual Survey of Manufactures; subject to sampling variability. For businesses with paid employees. E-commerce is the value of goods and services sold over computer-mediated networks (open or proprietary)]

Industry	2002 NAICS code [1]	2004				2005			
		Ship-ments, total (mil. dol).	E-commerce			Ship-ments, total (mil.dol).	E-commerce		
			Ship-ments, total (mil.dol.)	Percent of total ship ments	Percent distri-bution		Ship-ments, total (mil.dol.)	Percent of total ship-ments	Percont distri-bution
Manufacturing, total . . .	31–33	4,308,971	996,174	23.1	100.0	4,735,387	1,265,987	26.7	100.0
Food products	311	512,340	64,121	12.5	6.4	534,878	94,553	17.7	7.5
Beverage and tobacco	312	113,737	52,783	46.4	5.3	123,636	60,653	49.1	4.8
Textile mills	313	40,898	4,416	10.8	0.4	41,149	6,709	16.3	0.5
Textile product mills	314	33,636	8,472	25.2	0.9	36,706	9,875	26.9	0.8
Apparel	315	32,873	8,694	26.4	0.9	31,650	8,628	27.3	0.7
Leather and allied products. . .	316	5,812	611	10.5	0.1	6,013	716	11.9	0.1
Wood products	321	104,135	7,974	7.7	0.8	112,018	12,153	10.8	1.0
Paper	322	155,381	19,631	12.6	2.0	162,848	29,885	18.4	2.4
Printing and related support activities	323	93,595	8,259	8.8	0.8	97,095	15,690	16.2	1.2
Petroleum and coal products. .	324	330,439	77,527	23.5	7.8	476,075	120,334	25.3	9.5
Chemicals	325	540,883	102,967	19.0	10.3	604,501	158,327	26.2	12.5
Plastics and rubber products . .	326	184,711	33,220	18.0	3.3	200,489	42,288	21.1	3.3
Nonmetallic mineral products. .	327	102,880	10,850	10.5	1.1	114,321	15,892	13.9	1.3
Primary metals . . . . : .	331	181,602	33,410	18.4	3.4	201,835	43,346	21.5	3.4
Fabricated metal products. . . .	332	261,101	33,992	13.0	3.4	288,068	48,921	17.0	3.9
Machinery	333	272,123	52,292	19.2	5.2	302,204	71,711	23.7	5.7
Computer and electronic products.	334	365,545	76,197	20.8	7.6	373,932	85,572	22.9	6.8
Electrical equipment, appli-ances, and components . . .	335	105,084	25,177	24.0	2.5	112,008	29,327	26.2	2.3
Transportation equipment	336	662,001	346,473	52.3	34.8	687,288	370,309	53.9	29.3
Furniture and related products	337	78,279	11,264	14.4	1.1	84,291	16,013	19.0	1.3
Miscellaneous.	339	131,916	17,844	13.5	1.8	144,382	25,084	17.4	2.0

[1] North American Industry Classification System, 2002; see text, Section 15.

Source: U.S. Census Bureau, "E-Stats" (released 25 May 2007). See Internet site <http://www.census.gov/eos/www/ebusiness614.htm>.

Table 975. **Manufacturing Employer Costs for Employee Compensation Per Hour Worked: 1990 to 2007**

[As of March, for private industry workers. Based on a sample of establishments in the National Compensation Survey; see Appendix III and source for details. See also Table 632, Section 12]

Compensation component	Cost (dol.)					Percent distribution				
	1990	2000	2005	2006	2007	1990	2000	2005	2006	2007
Total compensation	17.33	23.41	28.48	29.40	30.37	100.0	100.0	100.0	100.0	100.0
Wages and salaries.	11.86	16.01	18.26	19.18	20.00	68.4	68.4	64.1	65.2	65.8
Total benefits	5.47	7.40	10.21	10.22	10.38	31.6	31.6	35.9	34.8	34.2
Paid leave	1.31	1.74	2.07	2.26	2.37	7.6	7.4	7.3	7.7	7.8
Vacation.	0.67	0.86	1.04	1.16	1.23	3.9	3.7	3.7	3.9	4.0
Holiday	0.48	0.65	0.76	0.81	0.85	2.8	2.8	2.7	2.8	2.8
Sick.	0.12	0.13	0.16	0.20	0.21	0.7	0.6	0.6	0.7	0.7
Other.	0.05	0.10	0.10	0.09	0.09	0.3	0.4	0.3	0.3	0.3
Supplemental pay	0.65	1.04	1.25	1.15	1.23	3.8	4.4	4.4	3.9	4.1
Premium pay.	0.34	0.58	0.61	0.54	0.52	2.0	2.5	2.1	1.8	1.7
Nonproduction bonuses. . .	0.22	0.36	0.53	0.47	0.57	1.3	1.5	1.8	1.6	1.9
Shift pay.	0.09	0.10	0.12	0.13	0.14	0.5	0.4	0.4	0.5	0.5
Insurance.	1.37	1.85	2.68	2.87	2.97	7.9	7.9	9.4	9.8	9.8
Health insurance	(NA)	1.69	2.48	2.67	2.76	(NA)	7.2	8.7	9.1	9.1
Retirement and savings	0.56	0.75	1.64	1.44	1.24	3.2	3.2	5.8	4.9	4.1
Defined benefit	(NA)	0.34	1.13	0.90	0.67	(NA)	1.5	4.0	3.1	2.2
Defined contributions	(NA)	0.41	0.51	0.53	0.57	(NA)	1.8	1.8	1.8	1.9
Legally required	1.54	1.92	2.45	2.51	2.56	8.9	8.2	8.6	8.5	8.4
Social security.	1.02	1.38	1.60	1.67	1.74	5.9	5.9	5.6	5.7	5.7
Federal unemployment . . .	0.03	0.03	0.03	0.03	0.03	0.2	0.1	0.1	0.1	0.1
State unemployment.	0.12	0.11	0.19	0.20	0.19	0.7	0.5	0.7	0.7	0.6
Workers compensation . . .	0.36	0.40	0.64	0.61	0.60	2.1	1.7	2.2	2.1	2.0
Other benefits [1].	0.04	0.09	0.12	(NA)	(NA)	0.2	0.4	0.4	(NA)	(NA)

NA Not available. [1] Includes severance pay, and supplemental unemployment benefits.

Source: U.S. Bureau of Labor Statistics, *Employer Costs for Employee Compensation, News*, USDL 07-0877, June 21, 2007. See Intenet site <http://www.bls.gov/ncs/ect/home.htm>.

Manufactures 627

Table 976. **Manufacturing Industries—Employment by Industry: 1990 to 2006**

[Annual averages of monthly figures (109,487 represents 109,487,000). Covers all full- and part-time employees who worked during, or received pay for, any part of the pay period including the 12th of the month. Minus sign (−) indicates decrease. See also headnote, Table 614]

Industry	2002 NAICS code[1]	All employees (1,000)						Percent change	
		1990	2000	2003	2004	2005	2006	1990–2000	2000–2006
All industries	(X)	109,487	131,785	129,999	131,435	133,703	136,174	20.4	3.3
Manufacturing	31–33	17,695	17,263	14,510	14,315	14,226	14,197	−2.4	−17.8
Percent of all industries	(X)	16.2	13.1	11.2	10.9	10.6	10.4	(X)	(X)
Durable goods	(X)	10,736	10,876	8,963	8,924	8,955	9,001	1.3	−17.2
Wood products	321	541	613	538	550	559	560	13.4	−8.6
Sawmills & wood preservation	3211	148	134	117	119	119	119	−9.6	−11.5
Plywood & engineered wood products . .	3212	96	122	114	118	123	120	28.2	−1.7
Other wood products	3219	297	357	306	313	317	322	20.1	−9.9
Nonmetallic mineral products	327	528	554	494	506	505	508	4.9	−8.4
Clay products & refractories.	3271	84	82	66	65	62	61	−1.9	−26.0
Glass & glass products.	3272	152	141	115	113	108	103	−7.6	−26.8
Cement & concrete products	3273	195	234	224	235	240	248	20.1	6.1
Lime, gypsum, & other nonmetallic mineral products	3279	98	97	89	94	96	96	−0.3	−1.6
Primary metals	331	689	622	477	467	466	462	−9.7	−25.7
Iron & steel mills & ferroalloy production	3311	187	135	102	95	96	94	−27.7	−30.1
Steel products from purchased steel . . .	3312	70	73	61	61	61	60	4.0	−18.2
Alumina & aluminum production	3313	108	101	75	74	73	73	−7.3	−27.7
Other nonferrous metal production	3314	109	96	74	71	72	73	−11.7	−24.2
Foundries.	3315	214	217	166	165	164	162	1.4	−25.2
Fabricated metal products	332	1,610	1,753	1,479	1,497	1,522	1,554	8.9	−11.3
Forging & stamping	3321	128	138	109	110	111	113	7.9	−18.0
Cutlery & hand tools	3322	79	79	61	59	56	54	0.3	−31.5
Architectural & structural metals	3323	357	428	380	389	398	415	20.0	−3.2
Boilers, tanks, & shipping containers . .	3324	117	107	91	92	91	92	−9.1	−13.9
Hardware	3325	57	50	40	38	36	34	−12.8	−31.9
Spring & wire products	3326	78	81	64	62	59	58	4.3	−28.0
Machine shops & threaded products . . .	3327	309	365	311	327	345	352	18.4	−3.7
Coating, engraving, & heat treating metals	3328	143	175	143	143	145	149	22.7	−14.8
Other fabricated metal products	3329	344	330	281	278	282	287	−4.0	−13.0
Machinery	333	1,408	1,455	1,149	1,143	1,163	1,191	3.3	−18.1
Agricultural, construction, & mining machinery	3331	229	222	188	195	208	222	−2.8	−0.4
Industrial machinery	3332	152	163	123	121	124	123	7.5	−24.7
Commercial & service industry machinery	3333	147	147	118	115	111	111	0.3	−24.5
HVAC & commercial refrigeration equipment	3334	165	194	157	153	153	160	17.8	−17.7
Metalworking machinery	3335	267	274	205	202	202	203	2.5	−25.9
Turbine & power transmission equipment	3336	114	111	94	93	98	100	−2.4	−9.9
Other general purpose machinery.	3339	335	343	265	265	268	273	2.4	−20.3
Computer & electronic products.	334	1,903	1,820	1,355	1,323	1,316	1,316	−4.3	−27.7
Computer & peripheral equipment	3341	367	302	224	210	205	199	−17.8	−34.2
Communications equipment.	3342	232	248	155	148	147	144	7.0	−41.7
Audio & video equipment	3343	60	52	37	33	32	32	−13.3	−39.2
Semiconductors & electronic components	3344	574	676	461	454	452	463	17.8	−31.6
Electronic instruments	3345	626	479	430	431	436	438	−23.6	−8.6
Magnetic media manufacturing & reproduction	3346	43	63	48	46	45	41	46.4	−35.2
Electrical equipment & appliances	335	633	591	460	445	434	436	−6.7	−26.3
Electric lighting equipment.	3351	81	85	67	65	61	59	5.0	−30.5
Household appliances	3352	114	106	93	90	85	82	−7.0	−22.1
Electrical equipment.	3353	244	210	160	154	152	156	−13.9	−25.8
Other electrical equipment & components	3359	195	191	140	137	136	139	−2.3	−27.2
Transportation equipment [2]	336	2,133	2,056	1,774	1,766	1,771	1,765	−3.6	−14.1
Motor vehicles	3361	271	291	265	256	248	236	7.4	−19.0
Motor vehicle bodies & trailers	3362	130	183	153	165	171	180	40.8	−1.4
Motor vehicle parts	3363	653	840	708	692	678	654	28.6	−22.1
Aerospace products & parts	3364	841	517	442	442	455	472	−38.5	−8.7
Ship & boat building	3366	173	153	146	148	153	156	−11.4	1.7
Other transportation equipment	3369	35	40	38	38	39	40	14.0	−0.8

See footnotes at end of table.

U.S. Census Bureau, Statistical Abstract of the United States: 2008

[Annual averages of monthly figures (109,487 represents 109,487,000). Covers all full- and part-time employees who worked during, or received pay for, any part of the pay period including the 12th of the month. Minus sign (-) indicates decrease. See also headnote, Table 614]

Industry	2002 NAICS code[1]	All employees (1,000)						Percent change	
		1990	2000	2003	2004	2005	2006	1990–2000	2000–2006
Furniture & related products	337	601	680	573	573	565	556	13.0	-18.2
Household & institutional furniture.	3371	398	440	382	385	380	374	10.6	-15.2
Office furniture & fixtures.	3372	156	181	139	135	133	132	16.0	-27.0
Other furniture-related products	3379	47	58	52	53	52	51	23.1	-13.1
Miscellaneous manufacturing	339	690	733	663	656	652	652	6.2	-11.1
Medical equipment & supplies	3391	288	310	304	301	305	309	7.7	-0.4
Other miscellaneous manufacturing . . .	3399	403	423	359	354	347	343	5.1	-19.0
Nondurable goods	**(X)**	**6,959**	**6,388**	**5,547**	**5,391**	**5,272**	**5,197**	**-8.2**	**-18.6**
Food manufacturing	311	1,507	1,553	1,518	1,494	1,478	1,484	3.0	-4.4
Animal food	3111	57	55	50	50	49	50	-4.2	-7.9
Grain & oilseed milling	3112	71	65	62	60	61	61	-9.1	-6.6
Sugar & confectionery products	3113	99	92	85	83	79	75	-7.3	-18.7
Fruit & vegetable preserving & specialty.	3114	218	197	185	181	174	177	-9.5	-10.1
Dairy products	3115	145	136	135	131	132	132	-5.9	-3.2
Animal slaughtering & processing.	3116	427	507	516	505	504	509	18.6	0.4
Seafood product preparation & packaging.	3117	54	45	42	42	41	40	-17.2	-10.9
Bakeries & tortilla manufacturing	3118	292	306	292	285	280	281	4.9	-8.5
Other food products	3119	143	150	152	156	159	160	5.0	6.5
Beverages & tobacco products	312	218	207	200	195	192	195	-4.9	-5.9
Beverages	3121	173	175	169	166	167	171	1.2	-2.0
Textile mills	313	492	378	261	237	218	196	-23.1	-48.3
Fiber, yarn, & thread mills	3131	102	81	57	54	50	48	-20.5	-40.4
Fabric mills.	3132	270	192	130	115	104	90	-29.0	-53.2
Textile & fabric finishing mills	3133	120	105	74	68	63	58	-12.1	-45.4
Textile product mills.	314	209	216	179	176	170	161	3.3	-25.5
Textile furnishings mills.	3141	127	129	105	101	96	90	1.3	-29.9
Other textile product mills	3149	82	88	74	75	74	71	6.4	-19.0
Apparel.	315	929	497	312	286	257	238	-46.5	-52.0
Apparel knitting mills	3151	112	69	45	42	37	34	-38.4	-50.7
Cut & sew apparel.	3152	776	394	243	221	200	186	-49.3	-52.9
Accessories & other apparel	3159	41	34	24	23	21	19	-16.9	-45.1
Leather & allied products	316	133	69	45	42	40	37	-48.3	-45.6
Footwear	3162	83	31	20	19	18	17	-62.8	-43.3
Leather & hide tanning & finishing & other leather products.	3169	51	38	25	23	22	20	-25.0	-47.4
Paper & paper products	322	647	605	516	496	484	469	-6.6	-22.4
Pulp, paper, & paperboard mills	3221	238	191	151	146	142	136	-19.7	-28.9
Converted paper products	3222	409	413	365	350	343	333	1.1	-19.3
Printing & related support activities.	323	809	807	681	663	646	636	-0.2	-21.2
Petroleum & coal products	324	153	123	114	112	112	114	-19.4	-7.2
Chemicals	325	1,036	980	906	887	872	869	-5.3	-11.4
Basic chemicals	3251	249	188	162	156	150	148	-24.4	-21.7
Resin, rubber, & artificial fibers.	3252	158	136	112	110	108	105	-14.2	-22.5
Agricultural chemicals.	3253	52	48	42	42	40	39	-8.8	-19.0
Pharmaceuticals & medicines	3254	207	274	292	290	288	292	32.4	6.6
Paints, coatings, & adhesives	3255	85	79	69	68	68	67	-6.6	-14.6
Soaps, cleaning compounds, and toiletries	3256	132	129	119	115	114	113	-2.4	-12.4
Other chemical products and preparations	3259	153	127	111	107	104	105	-17.1	-17.2
Plastics & rubber products	326	826	952	815	806	803	797	15.3	-16.3
Plastics products	3261	619	738	639	633	635	638	19.3	-13.6
Rubber products	3262	207	214	177	172	168	159	3.5	-25.7

X Not applicable.   [1] Based on the North American Industry Classification System (NAICS), 2002; see text, this section and Section 15.   [2] Includes railroad rolling stock manufacturing not shown separately.

Source: U.S. Bureau of Labor Statistics, the Current Employment Statistics program Internet site <http://www.bls.gov/ces /home.htm>.

Table 977. **Average Hourly Earnings of Production Workers in Manufacturing Industries by State: 2003 to 2006**

[In dollars. Data are based on the North American Industry Classification System (NAICS) 2002. Based on the Current Employment Statistics Program; see headnote Table 618 and Appendix III]

State	2003	2004	2005	2006	State	2003	2004	2005	2006
United States	**15.74**	**16.15**	**16.56**	**16.80**	Missouri	18.22	17.92	17.42	17.16
Alabama	13.56	14.33	14.93	15.56	Montana	14.02	14.87	15.62	15.90
Alaska	12.18	12.01	14.22	14.30	Nebraska	14.86	15.19	15.44	15.04
Arizona.	14.38	14.20	14.55	14.88	Nevada.	14.63	14.60	14.98	15.47
Arkansas.	13.55	13.49	13.71	13.35	New Hampshire	14.85	15.48	15.87	16.56
California.	15.04	15.36	15.70	15.95	New Jersey	15.45	15.89	16.33	16.55
Colorado.	16.89	16.46	15.91	16.58	New Mexico.	13.19	13.13	13.66	14.06
Connecticut	17.74	18.35	18.96	19.78	New York	16.78	17.29	17.77	18.29
Delaware.	16.91	17.66	17.74	18.13	North Carolina	13.66	14.25	14.38	14.57
District of Columbia [1] . . .	15.76	16.73	16.80	17.30	North Dakota	14.04	14.35	15.29	14.97
Florida	14.09	13.84	13.89	14.75	Ohio.	17.99	18.47	19.07	19.16
Georgia	14.08	14.54	14.56	14.74	Oklahoma	14.13	14.24	14.56	14.77
Hawaii	12.90	13.50	14.34	15.89	Oregon	15.20	15.34	15.49	15.57
Idaho	13.72	14.15	14.96	16.89	Pennsylvania	14.99	15.16	15.26	15.37
Illinois.	15.20	15.61	15.84	16.03	Rhode Island	12.88	13.03	13.12	13.42
Indiana	17.84	17.92	18.14	18.57	South Carolina	14.19	14.73	15.23	15.03
Iowa.	15.70	16.17	16.25	16.40	South Dakota	13.13	13.37	13.47	13.75
Kansas	15.83	16.57	17.14	17.68	Tennessee.	13.56	13.84	14.02	14.04
Kentucky	16.01	16.50	16.65	16.92	Texas	13.94	13.98	14.03	14.01
Louisiana	16.86	16.40	17.30	17.94	Utah.	14.90	15.38	14.73	15.25
Maine	16.28	16.97	17.28	18.57	Vermont	14.54	14.60	15.06	15.79
Maryland	15.74	16.47	16.98	17.87	Virginia	15.90	16.11	16.40	16.75
Massachusetts	16.53	16.89	17.66	18.26	Washington	18.02	18.28	18.83	19.90
Michigan	21.20	21.51	21.50	21.83	West Virginia	16.05	16.57	17.14	17.89
Minnesota	15.43	16.04	16.63	17.23	Wisconsin	16.12	16.19	16.29	16.54
Mississippi	12.89	13.12	13.53	13.78	Wyoming.	16.75	16.58	17.08	17.44

[1] Represents the Washington-Arlington-Alexandria Metropolitan Area.

Source: U.S. Bureau of Labor Statistics, the Current Employment Statistics program, see Internet site <http://www.bls.gov/ces/home.htm>.

Table 978. **Manufacturing Full-Time Equivalent Employees and Wages by Industry: 2000 to 2005**

[124,707 represents 124,707,000. Full-time equivalent employees equals the number of employees on full-time schedules plus the number of employees for part-time schedules converted to full-time basis]

Industry	2002 NAICS code [1]	Full-time equivalent (FTE) employees (1,000)				Wage and salary accruals per FTE worker (dol.)			
		2000	2003	2004	2005	2000	2003	2004	2005
All domestic industries, total .	(X)	124,707	123,314	124,422	126,865	38,762	41,628	43,265	44,702
Manufacturing	31-33	16,947	14,306	14,117	14,044	44,216	46,753	48,732	50,180
Percent of all industries.	(X)	13.6	11.6	11.3	11.1	114.1	112.3	112.6	112.3
Durable goods.	(X)	10,713	8,856	8,809	8,864	47,007	49,046	51,111	52,408
Wood products.	321	606	544	556	564	30,360	32,124	33,715	35,077
Nonmetallic mineral products	327	545	492	495	496	38,879	41,657	42,967	44,876
Primary metals.	331	611	467	458	459	45,745	48,499	51,693	52,694
Fabricated metal products	332	1,738	1,457	1,469	1,504	37,688	40,335	41,957	43,013
Machinery	333	1,420	1,136	1,125	1,148	46,882	48,976	51,591	53,036
Computer and electronic products	334	1,813	1,336	1,300	1,296	71,372	70,695	74,597	77,965
Electrical equipment, appliances, and components.	335	568	455	440	429	42,732	43,983	46,736	48,155
Motor vehicles, bodies and trailers, and parts	3361-3363 3364-	1,283	1,106	1,106	1,093	49,727	54,204	54,719	54,241
Other transportation equipment . . .	3365	736	642	648	669	52,612	59,859	62,513	64,176
Furniture and related products . . .	337	664	559	561	556	29,660	32,088	33,081	33,990
Miscellaneous manufacturing	339	728	662	650	651	38,504	43,153	45,673	46,062
Nondurable goods	(X)	6,235	5,451	5,308	5,180	39,420	43,028	44,784	46,368
Food and beverage and tobacco products	311-312	1,719	1,670	1,648	1,627	34,110	36,788	37,658	38,682
Textile mills and textile product mills	313-314	584	436	405	376	29,018	31,219	32,839	33,633
Apparel and leather and allied products	315	538	359	332	301	24,769	27,883	29,678	31,222
Paper products	322	596	502	485	469	45,578	50,192	51,422	52,949
Printing and related support activities	323	767	675	663	644	38,966	39,353	40,610	41,944
Petroleum and coal products	324	120	114	109	109	62,310	68,709	75,830	82,380
Chemical products	325	968	891	872	862	60,928	66,223	69,574	72,298

X Not applicable   [1] North American Industry Classification System, 2002; see text, this section.

Source: U.S. Bureau of Economic Analysis, *Survey of Current Business*, monthly. See also <http://www.bea.gov/bea/dn/nipaweb/SelectTable.asp?Selected=N> (released 04 August 2006).

630 Manufactures

[In billions of dollars (2,904 represents $2,904,000,000,000), except ratio. Based on a sample survey; for methodology, see source]

Year	Shipments	Inventories (Dec. 31)[1]	Ratio of inventories to shipments[2]	New orders	Unfilled orders (Dec. 31)
1992	2,904	370	1.57	(NA)	448
1993	3,020	371	1.51	2,960	422
1994	3,238	391	1.48	3,200	431
1995	3,480	415	1.47	3,427	443
1996	3,597	421	1.44	3,567	485
1997	3,835	433	1.39	3,780	508
1998	3,900	439	1.38	3,808	492
1999	4,032	453	1.38	3,957	501
2000	4,209	470	1.37	4,161	545
2001	3,970	417	1.29	3,872	510
2002	3,915	412	1.30	3,802	458
2003	4,015	398	1.22	3,964	474
2004	4,309	428	1.22	4,255	492
2005	4,735	466	1.21	4,735	567
2006	4,940	496	1.24	4,975	682

NA Not available.   [1] Inventories are stated at current cost.   [2] Ratio based on December seasonally adjusted data.

Source: U.S. Census Bureau, Current Industrial Reports, Benchmark Report for Manufacturers' Shipments, Inventories, and Orders: January 2001 through December 2006, Series M3-3 (06) (released May 2007); see <http://www.census.gov/indicator/www/m3>. See also <http://www.census.gov/indicator/www/m3/PastPressReleases/Prel/2006/dec06prel.pdf>(released 02 February 2007).

[Based on a sample survey; for methodology, see source]

Industry	2002 NAICS code[1]	2000	2001	2002	2003	2004	2005	2006
INVENTORIES-TO-SHIPMENTS RATIO								
All manufacturing industries	(X)	1.37	1.29	1.30	1.22	1.22	1.21	1.24
Durable goods	(X)	1.55	1.48	1.47	1.38	1.41	1.42	1.46
Wood products	321	1.32	1.28	1.29	1.26	1.26	1.28	1.26
Nonmetallic mineral products	327	1.23	1.17	1.15	1.17	1.16	1.09	1.19
Primary metals	331	1.69	1.70	1.68	1.61	1.62	1.57	1.62
Fabricated metals	332	1.56	1.50	1.53	1.46	1.56	1.55	1.63
Machinery	333	2.08	1.95	1.98	1.81	1.82	1.81	1.81
Computers and electronic products	334	1.54	1.43	1.55	1.40	1.41	1.29	1.35
Electrical equipment, appliances, and components	335	1.44	1.38	1.47	1.42	1.41	1.38	1.42
Transportation equipment	336	1.35	1.28	1.20	1.14	1.14	1.26	1.29
Furniture and related products	337	1.35	1.26	1.25	1.19	1.25	1.22	1.22
Miscellaneous products	339	1.90	1.88	1.72	1.68	1.72	1.74	1.75
Nondurable goods	(X)	1.14	1.07	1.09	1.03	1.02	1.00	1.00
Food products	311	0.88	0.80	0.82	0.77	0.74	0.75	0.79
Beverages and tobacco products	312	1.51	1.47	1.67	1.61	1.60	1.41	1.35
Textile mills	313	1.49	1.40	1.30	1.24	1.25	1.25	1.30
Textile product mills	314	1.75	1.70	1.32	1.28	1.20	1.20	1.18
Apparel	315	1.89	1.31	1.63	1.45	1.65	1.61	1.41
Leather and allied products	316	2.10	1.32	1.74	1.65	1.65	1.77	1.66
Paper products	322	1.11	1.09	1.13	1.08	1.11	1.10	1.10
Printing	323	0.79	0.74	0.78	0.76	0.79	0.81	0.80
Petroleum and coal products	324	0.71	0.75	0.86	0.83	0.77	0.76	0.78
Basic chemicals	325	1.40	1.33	1.28	1.21	1.20	1.19	1.19
Plastics and rubber products	326	1.21	1.11	1.10	1.08	1.15	1.17	1.17
UNFILLED ORDERS-TO-SHIPMENTS RATIO								
All manufacturing industries	(X)	1.57	1.55	1.41	1.43	1.38	1.44	1.66
Durable goods	(X)	2.78	2.84	2.61	2.67	2.63	2.83	3.23
Primary metals	331	1.45	1.51	1.36	1.58	1.48	1.59	1.39
Fabricated metals	332	2.02	1.92	1.74	1.80	1.92	2.07	2.16
Machinery	333	2.51	2.61	2.21	2.40	2.35	2.52	2.86
Computers and electronic products	334	3.08	3.33	3.20	3.30	3.31	3.14	3.38
Electrical equipment, appliances, and components	335	1.77	1.60	1.72	1.70	1.79	1.95	2.19
Transportation equipment	336	4.91	5.04	4.56	4.52	4.50	5.27	6.57
Furniture and related products	337	1.14	1.11	1.01	1.06	1.12	1.08	0.98
Miscellaneous products	339	0.62	0.41	0.45	0.54	0.54	0.41	0.43

X Not applicable.   [1] Based on the North American Industry Classification System, 2002; see text, this section and Section 15.

Source: U.S. Census Bureau, Current Industrial Reports, Benchmark Report for Manufacturers' Shipments, Inventories, and Orders: January 2001 through December 2006, Series M3-3 (06) (released May 2007); see <http://www/census/gov/indicator/www/m3/>. See also <http://www.census.gov.indicator/www/m3/PastPressReleases/Prel/2006/dec06prel.pdf>(released 02 February 2007).

Manufactures   631

Table 981. Value of Manufacturers' Shipments, Inventories, and New Orders by Industry: 2000 to 2006

[In millions of dollars (4,208,584 represents $4,208,584,000,000). Based on a sample survey; for methodology, see source]

Industry	2002 NAICS code [1]	2000	2002	2003	2004	2005	2006
SHIPMENTS							
All manufacturing industries	(X)	4,208,584	3,914,723	4,015,388	4,308,970	4,735,385	4,939,953
Durable goods	(X)	2,373,688	2,123,621	2,142,589	2,264,667	2,420,344	2,537,908
Wood products	321	93,669	89,020	92,069	104,135	112,017	104,970
Nonmetallic mineral products.	327	97,329	95,064	96,945	102,880	114,321	120,851
Primary metals	331	156,598	139,436	138,270	181,602	201,835	232,809
Fabricated metals	332	268,213	246,847	245,340	261,101	288,068	305,268
Machinery	333	291,548	255,321	257,429	272,123	302,202	327,886
Computers and electronic products. . .	334	510,639	357,324	352,273	365,545	373,932	393,953
Electrical equipment, appliances, and components	335	125,443	102,845	99,906	105,084	112,007	122,693
Transportation equipment	336	639,861	636,711	655,871	662,000	687,289	690,493
Furniture and related products	337	75,107	75,841	75,275	78,280	84,291	87,208
Miscellaneous products	339	115,281	125,212	129,211	131,917	144,382	151,777
Nondurable goods	(X)	1,834,896	1,791,102	1,872,799	2,044,303	2,315,041	2,402,045
Food products	311	435,229	458,206	488,518	512,339	534,879	537,879
Beverages and tobacco products	312	111,692	105,456	109,080	113,737	123,636	128,639
Textile mills	313	52,112	45,497	42,653	40,898	41,149	37,295
Textile product mills	314	33,654	32,082	31,256	33,636	36,706	36,614
Apparel	315	60,339	41,901	38,645	32,873	31,650	32,712
Leather and allied products	316	9,647	5,906	5,807	5,812	6,013	6,366
Paper products	322	165,298	153,755	151,098	155,380	162,848	168,602
Printing	323	104,396	95,612	92,553	93,595	97,095	101,015
Petroleum and coal products	324	235,134	215,513	247,119	330,439	476,075	514,901
Basic chemicals	325	449,159	462,499	487,742	540,884	604,501	630,363
Plastics and rubber products	326	178,236	174,675	178,328	184,710	200,489	207,659
INVENTORIES (Dec. 31)							
All manufacturing industries	(X)	470,084	412,328	397,631	428,321	466,171	496,115
Durable goods	(X)	298,232	253,198	239,946	258,736	278,602	300,664
Wood products	321	10,329	9,502	9,605	10,836	11,829	10,872
Nonmetallic mineral products.	327	9,799	9,488	9,171	9,726	10,373	11,737
Primary metals	331	22,199	19,620	18,566	24,563	26,437	31,412
Fabricated metals	332	34,085	30,650	29,189	33,090	36,358	40,464
Machinery	333	49,151	40,955	37,653	40,071	44,065	47,940
Computers and electronic products. . .	334	63,024	44,608	39,779	41,597	38,819	42,882
Electrical equipment, appliances, and components	335	14,505	12,100	11,359	11,897	12,413	14,044
Transportation equipment	336	69,199	61,198	59,783	60,745	69,721	71,303
Furniture and related products	337	8,261	7,703	7,298	7,912	8,321	8,612
Miscellaneous products	339	17,680	17,374	17,543	18,299	20,266	21,398
Nondurable goods	(X)	171,852	159,130	157,685	169,585	187,569	195,451
Food products	311	31,882	31,334	31,465	31,776	33,494	35,711
Beverages and tobacco products	312	14,331	14,882	14,717	15,234	14,598	14,520
Textile mills	313	6,243	4,759	4,261	4,139	4,190	3,939
Textile product mills	314	4,698	3,397	3,229	3,256	3,557	3,494
Apparel	315	9,170	5,462	4,474	4,333	4,079	3,715
Leather and allied products	316	1,634	829	773	777	864	861
Paper products	322	15,205	14,286	13,444	14,237	14,781	15,239
Printing	323	6,445	5,775	5,500	5,781	6,128	6,250
Petroleum and coal products	324	12,840	14,258	15,786	19,431	27,783	30,844
Basic chemicals	325	51,623	48,328	48,295	53,210	58,935	61,071
Plastics and rubber products	326	17,781	15,820	15,741	17,411	19,160	19,807
NEW ORDERS							
All manufacturing industries	(X)	4,161,472	3,801,734	3,964,423	4,255,188	4,734,955	4,974,738
Durable goods	(X)	2,326,576	2,010,632	2,091,624	2,210,885	2,419,914	2,572,693
Wood products	321	93,669	89,020	92,069	104,135	112,017	104,970
Nonmetallic mineral products.	327	97,329	95,064	96,945	102,880	114,321	120,851
Primary metals	331	153,625	138,014	140,637	185,893	206,072	233,261
Fabricated metals	332	270,021	242,338	246,219	265,864	295,699	310,265
Machinery	333	294,608	244,326	261,968	273,909	312,139	342,503
Computers and electronic products. . .	334	436,415	272,217	287,319	297,237	295,399	327,403
Electrical equipment, appliances, and components	335	126,196	102,411	99,345	106,517	114,507	126,790
Transportation equipment	336	663,396	625,786	661,287	663,460	741,909	767,538
Furniture and related products	337	74,532	75,563	75,525	78,879	84,569	86,796
Miscellaneous products	339	116,855	125,893	130,315	132,111	143,282	152,316
Nondurable goods	(X)	1,834,896	1,791,102	1,872,799	2,044,303	2,315,041	2,402,045

X Not applicable. [1] Based on the North American Industry Classification System, 2002; see text, this section and Section 15.

Source: U.S. Census Bureau, *Current Industrial Reports, Benchmark Report for Manufacturers' Shipments, Inventories, and Orders: January 2001 through December 2006,* Series M3-3 (06) (released May 2007); see <http://www.census.gov/indicator/www/m3/>. See also <http://www.census.gov/indicator/www/m3/PastPressReleases/Prel/2006/dec06prel.pdf>(released 02 February 2007).

Table 982. **Value of Manufacturers' Shipments, Inventories, and New Orders by Market Grouping: 2000 to 2006**

[In millions of dollars (4,028,584 represents $4,028,584,000,000). Based on a sample survey; for methodology, see source]

Market grouping	2000	2001	2002	2003	2004	2005	2006
SHIPMENTS							
All manufacturing industries	4,208,584	3,970,499	3,914,723	4,015,388	4,308,970	4,735,385	4,939,953
Consumer goods	1,500,532	1,480,495	1,494,575	1,584,329	1,700,835	1,896,690	1,946,415
Consumer durable goods	391,463	367,522	395,953	418,821	419,182	422,386	415,425
Consumer nondurable goods.	1,109,069	1,112,973	1,098,622	1,165,508	1,281,653	1,474,304	1,530,990
Aircraft and parts	111,658	118,226	108,639	102,931	105,850	113,985	130,105
Defense aircraft and parts.	24,560	27,777	34,136	39,096	41,515	37,930	40,053
Nondefense aircraft and parts	87,098	90,449	74,503	63,835	64,335	76,055	90,052
Construction materials and supplies . . .	444,812	424,517	424,008	429,183	463,148	509,674	529,032
Motor vehicles and parts	471,180	427,175	469,561	491,713	494,567	499,325	485,954
Computers and related products	110,242	89,529	73,807	69,073	63,270	68,469	66,547
Information technology industries.	399,751	353,237	284,799	274,829	287,837	295,446	311,629
Nondefense capital goods	808,345	728,466	652,500	633,878	661,217	728,878	787,596
Excluding aircraft.	757,617	678,229	609,654	600,699	629,207	685,318	730,560
Defense capital goods	67,051	73,533	76,085	85,724	91,688	91,552	95,225
Durables excluding capital goods.	1,498,292	1,372,407	1,395,036	1,422,987	1,511,762	1,599,914	1,655,087
INVENTORIES (Dec. 31)							
All manufacturing industries	470,084	417,487	412,328	397,631	428,321	466,171	496,115
Consumer goods	128,148	118,835	121,561	121,435	128,535	142,222	150,576
Consumer durable goods	26,108	24,275	24,513	23,831	25,215	27,290	28,026
Consumer nondurable goods.	102,040	94,560	97,048	97,604	103,320	114,932	122,550
Aircraft and parts	36,091	35,332	33,282	31,792	31,107	34,545	38,240
Defense aircraft and parts.	9,423	9,007	8,970	10,233	10,840	12,134	12,109
Nondefense aircraft and parts	26,668	26,325	24,312	21,559	20,267	22,411	26,131
Construction materials and supplies . . .	49,389	45,205	45,347	44,073	49,202	53,745	57,179
Motor vehicles and parts	22,283	19,868	20,890	20,795	21,991	23,325	24,219
Computers and related products	8,350	5,291	5,275	4,112	3,955	4,105	4,257
Information technology industries.	50,795	41,443	37,700	34,097	35,853	32,837	34,904
Nondefense capital goods	127,162	111,042	104,643	96,430	99,245	104,657	115,041
Excluding aircraft.	106,669	90,403	85,830	79,592	84,158	86,799	94,214
Defense capital goods	17,153	13,543	14,025	15,150	15,361	19,327	16,238
Durables excluding capital goods.	153,917	135,686	134,530	128,366	144,130	154,618	169,385
NEW ORDERS							
All manufacturing industries	4,161,472	3,872,490	3,801,734	3,964,423	4,255,188	4,734,955	4,974,738
Consumer goods	1,501,810	1,478,656	1,494,722	1,585,292	1,701,298	1,895,570	1,946,282
Consumer durable goods	392,741	365,683	396,100	419,784	419,645	421,266	415,292
Consumer nondurable goods.	1,109,069	1,112,973	1,098,622	1,165,508	1,281,653	1,474,304	1,530,990
Aircraft and parts	130,575	110,560	102,930	99,843	104,962	150,109	194,309
Defense aircraft and parts.	31,326	36,299	39,161	44,552	31,758	30,031	42,108
Nondefense aircraft and parts	99,249	74,261	63,769	55,291	73,204	120,078	152,201
Construction materials and supplies . . .	446,792	419,920	422,093	429,281	466,301	517,392	531,638
Motor vehicles and parts	468,470	425,554	470,049	493,589	495,286	502,107	488,996
Computers and related products	107,656	89,208	74,089	68,048	61,678	67,351	66,344
Information technology industries.	409,500	344,402	265,375	276,841	293,619	295,010	325,779
Nondefense capital goods	831,335	698,447	621,802	634,697	672,945	787,502	869,149
Excluding aircraft.	767,754	664,855	582,751	609,117	630,331	698,076	756,423
Defense capital goods	79,598	83,789	70,927	96,858	92,191	91,910	106,475
Durables excluding capital goods.	1,415,643	1,294,161	1,317,903	1,360,069	1,445,749	1,540,502	1,597,069

Source: U.S. Census Bureau, *Current Industrial Reports, Benchmark Report for Manufacturers' Shipments, Inventories, and Orders: January 2001 through December 2006*, Series M3-3 (06) (released May 2007); see <http://www.census.gov/indicator/www/m3/>. See also <http://www.census.gov/indicator/www/m3/PastPressReleases/Prel/2006/dec06prel.pdf> (released 02 February 2007).

Table 983. **Finances and Profits of Manufacturing Corporations: 1990 to 2006**

[In billions of dollars (2,811 represents $2,811,000,000,000). Data exclude estimates for corporations with less than $250,000 in assets at time of sample selection. See Table 770 for individual industry data]

Item	1990 [1]	1995 [1]	2000 [1]	2001 [1]	2001 [2]	2002 [2]	2003 [2]	2004 [2]	2005 [2]	2006 [2]
Net sales.	2,811	3,528	4,548	4,308	4,295	4,217	4,397	4,934	5,411	5,800
Net operating profit	173	268	348	185	186	225	237	320	359	411
Net profit:										
Before taxes	160	274	381	82	83	196	306	447	524	617
After taxes	112	198	275	36	36	135	237	348	401	481
Cash dividends.	62	81	132	102	103	106	115	143	179	167
Net income retained in business . .	49	117	143	-67	-66	28	122	205	222	314

[1] Based on Standard Industrial Classification system. [2] Based on the North American Industry Classification System, 2002; see Text, Section 15.

Source: U.S. Census Bureau, *Quarterly Financial Report for Manufacturing, Mining, and Trade Corporations*. See also 2006 4th quarter press release issued April 2007 <http://www.census.gov/csd/qfr/>.

Manufactures **633**

Table 984. Manufacturing Corporations—Assets and Profits by Asset Size: 1990 to 2006

[In millions of dollars (2,629,458 represents $2,629,458,000,000). Corporations and assets as of end of 4th quarter; profits for entire the year. Through 2000, based on Standard Industrial Classification code; beginning 2001, based on North American Industry Classification System; see text, Section 15. For corporations above a certain asset value based on complete canvass. The asset value for complete canvass was raised in 1988 to $50 million and in 1995 to $250 million. Asset sizes less than these values are sampled, except as noted. For details regarding methodology, see source for first quarter, 1988. Minus sign (–) indicates loss]

Year	Total [1]	Under $10 mil. [1]	$10– $25 mil.	$25– $50 mil.	$50– $100 mil.	$100– $250 mil.	$250– $1 bil.	$1 bil. and over
Assets:								
1990	2,629,458	142,498	74,477	55,914	72,554	123,967	287,512	1,872,536
1991	2,688,422	140,056	70,567	58,549	72,694	127,748	295,743	1,923,066
1992	2,798,625	143,766	70,446	65,718	75,967	132,742	302,287	2,007,698
1993	2,904,869	149,763	72,854	61,243	81,389	134,388	317,774	2,087,457
1994	3,080,231	148,751	81,505	66,405	82,116	138,950	358,100	2,204,404
1995	3,345,229	155,618	87,011	68,538	87,262	159,133	370,263	2,417,403
1996	3,574,407	163,928	87,096	69,722	93,205	156,702	398,651	2,605,102
1997	3,746,797	167,921	87,398	76,034	85,186	157,130	397,559	2,775,570
1998	3,967,309	170,068	87,937	69,627	86,816	148,060	419,153	2,985,647
1999	4,382,814	170,058	85,200	67,352	97,810	138,143	398,881	3,425,370
2000	4,852,106	171,666	85,482	72,122	90,866	149,714	389,537	3,892,720
2001 [2]	4,747,789	169,701	84,664	67,493	88,088	131,617	393,752	3,812,474
2002	4,823,219	166,191	82,369	62,654	81,667	134,821	407,423	3,888,095
2003	5,162,852	161,462	80,681	62,592	77,205	126,826	392,192	4,261,894
2004	5,538,113	163,072	80,085	71,674	81,741	126,950	414,144	4,600,447
2005	5,828,716	165,195	85,785	68,731	87,818	142,900	423,917	4,854,370
2006	6,305,267	170,904	94,846	77,892	94,028	155,200	419,731	5,292,666
Net profit: [3]								
1990	110,128	8,527	5,160	2,769	2,661	3,525	7,110	80,377
1991	66,407	6,820	4,271	2,564	1,704	1,707	5,027	44,316
1992	22,085	9,567	4,748	3,245	3,034	4,553	5,919	–8,979
1993	83,156	11,195	5,415	3,439	3,218	3,584	4,555	51,750
1994	174,874	14,131	7,057	4,072	4,996	6,745	14,626	123,250
1995	198,151	13,224	5,668	3,767	5,771	7,000	16,549	146,172
1996	224,869	15,802	6,872	4,266	5,664	7,935	16,059	168,271
1997	244,505	17,948	8,383	4,153	4,675	7,074	18,433	183,836
1998	234,386	18,350	6,421	3,790	4,681	5,610	14,364	181,170
1999	257,805	17,398	7,618	3,504	4,798	4,795	12,756	206,934
2000	275,313	16,578	6,820	3,403	2,742	3,510	15,121	227,136
2001 [2]	36,168	8,387	3,366	–408	403	–543	–6,782	31,746
2002	134,686	10,003	2,784	807	1,699	3,356	–1,227	117,262
2003	237,041	9,821	3,374	2,005	2,256	2,973	4,115	212,497
2004	348,151	14,970	5,745	3,858	3,080	5,140	12,787	302,571
2005	401,344	17,357	6,057	4,066	3,781	7,678	15,967	346,438
2006	481,002	22.409	8,667	5,214	5,749	9,140	22,308	407,515

[1] Excludes estimates for corporations with less than $250,000 in assets at time of sample selection. [2] Beginning 2001, data reported on a NAICS basis. [3] After taxes.
Source: U.S. Census Bureau, *Quarterly Financial Report for Manufacturing, Mining, and Trade Corporations.* See also 2006 4th quarter press release issued April 2007; <http://www.census.gov/csd/qfr>.

Table 985. Manufacturing Corporations—Selected Finances: 1990 to 2006

[In billions of dollars (2,811 represents $2,811,000,000,000). Data are not necessarily comparable from year to year due to changes in accounting procedures, industry classifications, sampling procedures, etc.; for detail, see source. Through 2000, based on Standard Industrial Classification code; beginning 2001, based on North American Industry Classification System; see text, Section 15]

Year	All manufacturing corps. Sales	Profits [1] Before taxes	Profits [1] After taxes	Durable goods industries Sales	Profits [1] Before taxes	Profits [1] After taxes	Nondurable goods industries Sales	Profits [1] Before taxes	Profits [1] After taxes
1990	2,811	158	110	1,357	57	41	1,454	101	69
1991	2,761	99	66	1,304	14	7	1,457	85	59
1992 [2]	2,890	31	22	1,390	–34	–24	1,500	65	46
1993	3,015	118	83	1,490	39	27	1,525	79	56
1994	3,256	244	175	1,658	121	87	1,598	123	88
1995	3,528	275	198	1,808	131	94	1,721	144	104
1996	3,758	307	225	1,942	147	106	1,816	160	119
1997	3,922	331	244	2,076	167	121	1,847	164	123
1998	3,949	315	234	2,169	175	128	1,781	140	107
1999	4,149	355	258	2,314	199	140	1,835	157	117
2000	4,548	381	275	2,457	191	132	2,091	190	144
2001 [3]	4,295	83	36	2,321	–69	–76	1,974	152	112
2002	4,217	196	135	2,261	45	21	1,955	149	113
2003	4,397	306	237	2,283	118	88	2,114	188	149
2004	4,934	447	348	2,537	200	157	2,397	248	192
2005	5,411	524	401	2,731	211	161	2,681	313	240
2006	5,800	617	481	2,919	256	199	2,881	361	282

[1] Beginning 1998, profits before and after income taxes reflect inclusion of minority stockholders' interest in net income before and after income taxes. [2] Data for 1992 (most significantly 1992: first qtr.) reflect the early adoption of Financial Accounting Standards Board Statement 106 (Employer's Accounting for Post-Retirement Benefits Other Than Pensions) by a large number of companies during the fourth quarter of 1992. Data for 1993: first qtr. also reflect adoption of Statement 106. Corporations must show the cumulative effect of a change in accounting principle in the first quarter of the year in which the change is adopted. [3] Beginning 2001, data reported on a NAICS basis.
Source: U.S. Census Bureau, *Quarterly Financial Report for Manufacturing, Mining, and Trade Corporations.* See also 2006 4th quarter press release issued April 2007 <http://www.census.gov/csd/qfr/>.

U.S. Census Bureau, Statistical Abstract of the United States: 2008

Table 986. Tobacco Products—Summary: 1990 to 2006

[710 represents 710,000,000,000]. Production data are for calendar years. Excludes cigars produced in customs bonded manufacturing warehouses. 2006 data are preliminary]

Item	Unit	1990	1995	2000	2001	2002	2003	2004	2005	2006
PRODUCTION										
Cigarettes, total	Billions	710	747	565	562	532	499	494	489	484
Nonfilter tip	Billions	23	15	7	6	5	6	5	4	(NA)
Filter tip	Billions	687	732	558	556	527	494	488	486	(NA)
Cigars	Billions	1.9	2.1	2.8	3.7	3.8	4.0	4.4	3.7	4.1
Tobacco [1]	Mil. lb.	142	131	133	130	133	137	135	143	141
Smoking	Mil. lb.	16	12	14	13	16	18	16	17	17
Chewing tobacco	Mil. lb.	73	63	49	47	45	43	39	39	38
Snuff	Mil. lb.	53	60	70	70	73	76	79	87	86
EXPORTS										
Cigarettes	Bil. cigarettes	164.3	231.1	147.9	133.9	127.4	121.5	118.7	113.3	109.9
Cigars	Bil. cigars	72.0	94.0	113.0	124.0	122.7	130.2	171.0	301.0	180.0
Smoking tobacco	Bil. lb	0.8	0.3	0.5	11.0	7.9	0.7	0.2	0.2	0.4
IMPORTS										
Cigarettes	Bil. cigarettes	1.4	3.0	11.3	14.7	20.8	23.1	22.7	18.1	16.2
Cigars	Bil. cigars	111.0	195.0	497.0	543.4	413.5	508.0	616.0	445.0	340.0
Smoking tobacco	Bil. lb	2.9	4.2	4.2	1.9	2.1	2.1	1.5	3.0	3.1
CONSUMPTION										
Tobacco products per person [2]	Lb. [3]	5.6	4.8	4.1	4.3	4.2	4.0	3.3	3.7	3.5
Cigarettes per person [2]	1,000	2.8	2.5	2.1	2.1	2.0	1.9	1.8	1.7	1.7
EXPENDITURES										
Consumer expenditures, total	Bil. dol.	43.8	48.7	77.5	82.9	88.2	86.8	86.3	88.7	(NA)
Cigarettes	Bil. dol.	41.6	45.8	72.9	77.8	82.8	81.1	79.9	82.0	(NA)
Cigars	Bil. dol.	0.7	1.0	1.8	2.1	2.2	2.5	2.9	3.1	(NA)
Other	Bil. dol.	1.5	2.5	2.7	3.0	3.1	3.2	3.4	3.7	(NA)

NA Not available. [1] Smoking and chewing tobacco and snuff output. [2] Based on estimated population, 18 years old and over, as of July 1, including Armed Forces abroad. [3] Unstemmed processing weight equivalent.

Source: U.S. Dept. of Agriculture, Economic Research Service, *Tobacco Situation and Outlook*, quarterly. See also <http://usda.mannlib.cornell.edu/usda/ers/TBS-2000s/2007/TBS-04-24-2007.pdf> (released 24 April 2007).

Table 987. Cotton, Wool, and Manmade Fibers—Consumption by End-Use: 2001 to 2005

[16,077 represents 16,077,000,000. Represents products manufactured by U.S. mills. Excludes glass fiber]

Year	Total (mil. lb.)	Cotton Total (mil. lb.)	Cotton Percent of end-use	Wool Total (mil. lb.)	Wool Percent of end-use	Manufactured fibers Total (mil. lb.)	Manufactured fibers Percent of end-use	Artificial Total (mil. lb.)	Artificial Percent of end-use	Synthetic Total (mil. lb.)	Synthetic Percent of end-use
Total:											
2001	16,077	4,484	27.9	120	0.7	11,472	71.4	276	1.7	11,196	69.6
2002	15,715	4,044	25.7	102	0.6	11,568	73.6	250	1.6	11,314	72.0
2003	14,754	3,465	23.5	98	0.7	11,191	75.9	227	1.5	10,964	74.3
2004	14,131	2,911	20.6	91	0.6	11,129	78.8	218	1.5	10,911	77.2
2005	13,840	2,850	20.6	82	0.6	10,908	78.8	210	1.5	10,697	77.3
Apparel:											
2001	5,338	2,651	49.7	73	1.4	2,613	49.0	135	2.5	2,479	46.4
2002	4,798	2,298	47.9	64	1.3	2,437	50.8	113	2.4	2,325	48.4
2003	4,155	1,904	45.8	65	1.6	2,187	52.6	93	2.2	2,094	50.4
2004	3,627	1,602	44.2	60	1.7	1,965	54.2	76	2.1	1,889	52.1
2005	3,450	1,600	46.4	51	1.5	1,799	52.1	62	1.8	1,736	50.3
Home textiles:											
2001	2,537	1,450	57.2	13	0.5	1,074	42.3	52	2.0	1,022	40.3
2002	2,385	1,365	57.4	10	0.4	1,004	42.1	48	2.0	951	39.9
2003	2,069	1,180	57.0	12	0.6	877	42.4	43	2.1	834	40.3
2004	1,745	940	53.9	10	0.6	794	45.5	40	2.3	753	43.2
2005	1,559	854	54.8	9	0.6	695	44.6	36	2.3	659	42.3
Floor coverings:											
2001	4,089	30	0.7	25	0.6	4,034	98.7	–	–	4,034	98.7
2002	4,373	30	0.7	20	0.5	4,323	98.9	–	–	4,323	98.9
2003	4,414	32	0.7	14	0.3	4,369	99.0	–	–	4,369	99.0
2004	4,490	32	0.7	14	0.3	4,444	99.0	–	–	4,444	99.0
2005	4,524	29	0.6	16	0.4	4,479	99.0	–	–	4,479	99.0
Industrial: [1]											
2001	4,114	353	8.6	10	0.2	3,751	91.2	90	2.2	3,661	89.0
2002	4,159	346	8.3	8	0.2	3,804	91.5	88	2.1	3,716	89.3
2003	4,116	349	8.5	8	0.2	3,759	91.3	91	2.2	3,668	89.1
2004	4,270	337	7.9	6	0.1	3,926	91.9	102	2.4	3,824	89.6
2005	4,307	367	8.5	5	0.1	3,934	91.3	112	2.6	3,822	88.7

– Represents or rounds to zero. [1] Includes consumer-type products.

Source: Fiber Economics Bureau, Inc., Arlington, VA, *Fiber Organon*, monthly (copyright).

Manufactures 635

Table 988. Textiles—Production and Foreign Trade: 2005

[2,072,405 represents 2,072,405,000. Fabric blends as shown in the report are reported based on the chief weight of the fiber; whereas, fabrics blends as shown for imports are based on the chief value of the fiber]

Product description	Manufacturers' production (quantity) (1,000)	Imports for consumption Quantity	Value ($1,000)[1]	Percent imports to manufacturers' production	Exports of domestic merchandise Quantity	Value ($1,000)	Percent exports to manufacturers' production
YARN (quantity 1,000 kilograms)							
Spun yarn	2,072,405	226,342	768,559	10.9	(S)	786,289	(S)
Textured, crimped, twisted, or bulked filament yarn	1,539,478	146,210	481,165	9.5	78,141	242,268	5.1
BROADWOVEN FABRICS [2] (quantity 1,000 square meters)							
Spun yarn fabrics	3,232,752	1,521,034	1,885,922	47.1	376,762	754,252	11.7
85 percent or more filament yarn fabrics, manmade	4,313,207	980,109	721,380	22.7	(NA)	(NA)	(NA)
Spun/filament combinations (except blue denim and other yarn dyed)	421,048	199,647	272,155	47.4	61,093	119,206	14.5
Silk fabrics	(D)	41,268	311,252	(D)	3,894	21,962	(D)
KNIT FABRICS (quantity 1,000 kilograms)							
Pile fabrics	56,790	175,305	239,270	308.7	36,810	178,458	64.8
Elastic fabric	27,649	28,642	293,657	103.6	(S)	399,404	(S)
Other warp knit fabrics	49,225	27,214	178,498	55.3	10,123	100,386	20.6
Other weft knit fabrics	341,254	97,205	448,273	28.5	224,662	1,074,864	65.8
Other narrow knit fabrics	4,032	1,102	14,882	27.3	(S)	25,185	(S)
SHEETS, PILLOWCASES, AND TOWELS (quantity 1,000 dozens)							
Sheets and pillowcases	16,023	36,679	1,814,441	228.9	946	68,918	5.9
Finished towels	29,971	133,621	1,542,183	445.8	2,209	49,388	7.4

D Withheld to avoid disclosing data for individual companies.   NA Not available.   S Does not meet publication standards. [1] Dollar value represents the c.i.f. (cost, insurance, and freight) at the first port of entry in the United States plus calculated import duty.   [2] Represents production of gray broadwoven fabrics; import and export data represent gray as well as finished broadwoven fabrics.

Source: U.S. Census Bureau, *Current Industrial Reports, Textiles*, Series MQ313A. <http://www.census.gov/cir/www/index.html>.

Table 989. Footwear—Consumption, Production, and Imports: 1990 to 2004

[In millions of pairs of shoes (1,305.2 represents 1,305,200,000), except as indicated]

Item	1990	2000	2003	2004	Item	1990	2000	2003	2004
CONSUMPTION					Other	(NA)	2.0	0.2	0.2
Consumption, total	1,305.2	1,851.5	2,007.9	2,159.0	Rubber or fabric	(NA)	20.6	11.3	8.5
Production	184.6	86.6	39.8	35.2	Plastic or protective	(NA)	7.2	6.2	6.8
Imports	1,120.7	1,764.9	1,968.1	2,123.8	IMPORTS				
Percent of consumption	85.9	95.3	98.0	98.4	Men's	102.1	200.5	213.3	220.5
					Men's work	13.2	24.1	26.5	27.8
PRODUCTION					Women's	415.2	587.2	730.5	814.4
Men's	(NA)	24.0	12.7	12.1	Juveniles'	132.8	228.3	251.5	259.8
Men's work	(NA)	9.2	8.1	8.9	Athletic	212.3	288.1	345.2	361.8
Women's	(NA)	9.8	5.2	4.7	Slippers	17.9	76.3	84.5	124.9
Juveniles'	(NA)	1.4	0.3	0.2	Other	3.9	9.9	9.4	9.6
Athletic	(NA)	0.3	0.1	0.1	Rubber or fabric	199.2	317.3	225.7	188.4
Slippers	(NA)	31.2	3.9	2.7	Plastic or protective	23.9	10.4	18.3	19.2

NA Not available.

Source: American Apparel and Footwear Association, Arlington, VA, *Shoe Stats*, annual. See also <http://www.apparelandfootwear.org/>.

Table 990. Pharmaceutical Preparations—Value of Shipments: 2000 to 2005

[In millions of dollars (79,262 represents 79,262,000,000]

Product description	Product code	2000	2001	2002	2003	2004	2005
Pharmaceutical preparations, except biologicals	(X)	79,262	90,182	100,741	107,561	109,852	116,301
Affecting neoplasms, endocrine systems, and metabolic disease	3254121100	9,784	14,819	17,499	20,065	20,789	23,341
Acting on the central nervous system and sense organs	3254124100	18,508	18,975	24,345	24,759	25,001	25,044
Acting on the cardiovascular system	3254127100	8,993	9,798	10,339	9,671	10,224	10,246
Acting on the respiratory system	325412A100	10,179	11,692	12,504	13,758	15,148	16,216
Acting on the digestive system	325412D100	10,046	12,616	13,373	15,052	15,252	16,776
Acting on the skin	325412G100	2,941	2,708	2,844	3,083	3,283	3,245
Vitamin, nutrient, and hematinic preps	325412L100	5,676	5,884	6,029	6,877	6,683	6,827
Affecting parasitic and infective disease	325412P100	11,037	11,193	11,337	11,848	10,819	11,244
Pharmaceutical preps for veterinary use	325412T100	2,096	2,497	2,471	2,449	2,653	3,362

X Not applicable.

Source: U.S. Census Bureau, *Current Industrial Reports, Pharmaceutical Preparations, Except Biologicals* Series MA325G. See <http://www.census.gov/mcd/index.html>.

Table 991. **Inorganic Chemicals and Fertilizers—Production: 2000 to 2005**

[15,809 represents 15,809,000]

Product description	Product code	Unit	2000	2003	2004	2005
INORGANIC FERTILIZERS						
Ammonia, synthetic anhydrous	3253111120 ...	1,000 short tons ...	15,809	11,130	12,058	11,181
Ammonium nitrate, original solution	3253111201 ...	1,000 short tons ...	7,979	6,328	7,229	7,212
Ammonium sulfate	3253111240 ...	1,000 short tons ...	2,808	2,871	3,005	2,906
Urea (100%)......................	3253114100 ...	1,000 short tons ...	7,682	6,375	6,344	5,807
Nitric acid (100%)	3253111111. ...	1,000 short tons ...	8,708	7,189	7,129	7,398
Phosphoric acid (100% P2O5).........	3253121100 ...	1,000 short tons ...	12,492	12,537	12,693	12,609
Sulfuric acid, gross (100%)...........	3251881100 ...	1,000 short tons ...	43,643	41,144	41,934	40,956
Superphosphates and other fertilizer materials (100% P2O5)..............	3253124100 ...	1,000 short tons ...	8,899	8,837	8,737	8,141
INORGANIC CHEMICALS						
Chlorine gas....................	3251811111 ...	1,000 metric tons...	14,000	10,361	12,329	10,277
Sodium hydroxide, total liquid	3251814111 ...	1,000 metric tons...	11,523	8,796	9,620	8,520
Potassium hydroxide liquid	3251817111 ...	1,000 metric tons...	539	471	525	527
Finished sodium bicarbonate.........	3251817131 ...	1,000 metric tons...	536	540	579	581
Hydrochloric acid..............	3251884131 ...	1,000 metric tons...	4,717	(S)	5,302	4,619
Aluminum oxide	3313110100 ...	1,000 metric tons...	(D)	(D)	(D)	(D)
Aluminum sulfate (commercial)	3251887151 ...	1,000 metric tons...	1,076	965	972	967
Sodium chlorate	325188A141 ...	1,000 metric tons...	940	669	556	523
Sodium phosphate tripoly	325188A174 ...	1,000 metric tons...	(D)	(D)	(D)	(D)
Sodium silicates [1]	325188A181 ...	1,000 metric tons...	1,136	1,074	1,112	1,031
Sodium metasilicates............	325188A187 ...	1,000 metric tons...	72	61	58	59
Sodium sulfate [2].............	325188A1A7...	1,000 metric tons...	509	89	86	93
Carbon activated [2]............	325998H1E7...	1,000 metric tons...	166	112	(D)	(D)
Hydrogen peroxide	325188G181...	1,000 metric tons...	1,083	340	357	365
Phosphorous, oxychloride, and trichlorde...	325188G1F1...	1,000 metric tons...	(D)	(D)	(D)	(D)

D Withheld to avoid disclosing data for individual companies.   S Does not meet publication standards.   [1] Other than metasilicates.   [2] Granular and pulverized.

Source: U.S. Census Bureau, *Current Industrial Reports, Inorganic Chemicals*, Series MQ325A and *Fertilizers and Related Chemicals*, Series MQ325B. See <http://www.census.gov/cir/www/index.html>.

Table 992. **Aluminum—Supply, Shipments, and Foreign Trade: 1990 to 2006**

[In millions of pounds (17,334 represents 17,334,000,000)]

Item	1990	1995	2000	2002	2003	2004	2005	2006, prel.
SUPPLY								
Aluminum supply, total.	**17,334**	**20,425**	**23,586**	**21,117**	**21,145**	**22,281**	**23,571**	**22,836**
Primary production	8,925	7,441	8,087	5,964	5,962	5,549	5,468	5,029
Recovery from scrap.............	5,276	7,030	7,606	6,453	6,215	6,669	6,592	6,658
Imports of ingot and mill products	3,133	5,956	7,893	8,701	8,968	10,063	11,510	11,149
Aluminum net shipments, total	**17,188**	**21,019**	**24,496**	**23,607**	**23,392**	**24,950**	**25,541**	**25,982**
PRODUCT [1]								
Mill products, total	13,013	15,716	17,676	15,701	15,693	17,122	17,734	17,936
Sheet, plate, and foil	9,297	11,168	12,116	10,570	10,562	11,463	11,810	11,794
Rod, bar, and wire.............	370	534	690	591	576	631	660	698
Electrical conductor.............	542	566	681	708	694	763	794	850
Extruded shapes and tube	2,546	3,102	3,792	3,457	3,468	3,821	4,018	4,137
Powder and paste...........	106	108	142	142	146	155	144	140
Forgings and impacts	152	238	255	233	247	289	308	317
Ingot for castings and other [2]........	4,175	5,303	6,820	7,906	7,699	7,828	7,807	8,046
MARKET [1]								
Domestic, total.	14,637	18,152	21,680	21,211	21,403	22,901	23,060	23,151
Building and construction	2,663	2,679	3,204	3,437	3,432	3,692	3,683	3,624
Transportation	3,205	5,749	7,947	7,523	7,804	8,509	8,683	8,666
Consumer durables	1,122	1,369	1,692	1,504	1,498	1,585	1,561	1,644
Electrical	1,309	1,395	1,704	1,491	1,433	1,580	1,644	1,701
Machinery and equipment	992	1,257	1,496	1,427	1,452	1,610	1,634	1,676
Containers and packaging	4,772	5,088	4,992	4,979	4,941	5,098	5,115	5,113
Other	574	615	645	850	843	827	740	727
Exports	2,551	2,867	2,816	2,396	1,988	2,049	2,481	2,834
FOREIGN TRADE [3]								
Exports	3,753	3,846	4,100	3,746	3,662	4,416	5,629	6,592
Imports.....................	3,718	6,899	9,358	9,679	9,884	11,221	12,607	12,322

[1] Statistics on shipments and markets for 1990 to 2000 represent total U.S. producer's shipments plus imports by consumers. Beginning 2002, figures include Canada.   [2] Net ingot for foundry castings, export, and destructive uses.   [3] U.S. imports and exports of aluminum ingot, mill products, and scrap.

Source: The Aluminum Association, Inc., Washington, DC, *Aluminum Statistical Review*, annual.

Manufactures   637

Table 993. Iron and Steel Industry—Summary: 1990 to 2005

[95.5 represents 95,500,000 tons. For financial data, the universe in 1992 consists of the companies that produced 68 percent of the total reported raw steel production. The financial data represent the operations of the steel segment of the companies. Minus sign (−) indicates net loss]

Item	Unit	1990	1995	2000	2001	2002	2003	2004	2005
Steel mill products, apparent supply . . .	Mil. tons [1]	95.5	109.6	131.9	116.4	117.8	116.1	131.8	120.8
Net shipments	Mil. tons [1]	85.0	97.5	109.1	98.9	100.0	106.0	111.4	105.0
Exports	Mil. tons [1]	4.3	7.1	6.5	6.1	6.0	8.2	7.9	9.4
Imports	Mil. tons [1]	17.2	24.4	29.4	30.1	32.6	23.1	35.8	32.1
Scrap consumed	Mil. tons [1]	50.1	62.0	65.0	63.0	62.0	61.8	57.3	55.3
Scrap inventory	Mil. tons [1]	3.6	4.1	5.3	4.9	4.2	4.5	4.8	(NA)
Iron and steel products: Exports	Mil. tons [1]	5.3	8.2	7.7	7.2	7.0	9.3	9.6	11.3
Imports	Mil. tons [1]	21.9	27.3	42.6	34.4	37.3	27.9	41.2	37.8
Capacity by steelmaking process.	Mil. net tons . . .	116.7	112.4	130.3	125.5	113.7	121.6	116.1	119.5
Revenue	Bil. dol.	30.9	35.1	38.8	31.0	31.6	34.3	38.6	41.3
Net income	Bil. dol.	0.1	1.5	−1.1	−3.9	−1.3	−6.9	3.2	2.9
Stockholders' equity	Bil. dol.	4.3	8.6	9.9	5.5	1.4	−5.0	10.5	11.2
Total assets	Bil. dol.	28.3	35.1	43.9	38.1	34.1	29.8	29.1	29.7
Capital expenditures	Bil. dol.	2.6	2.5	2.1	1.1	1.1	2.1	1.3	1.6
Working capital ratio [2]	Ratio.	1.6	1.5	1.7	1.6	1.3	0.9	2.3	2.4
Inventories	Bil. dol.	4.7	5.1	6.8	5.7	5.5	4.9	4.6	4.8
Average employment.	1,000	169.0	122.6	99.5	88.0	74.4	42.5	39.7	37.5
Hours worked.	Million	350.0	269.2	219.7	186.4	157.1	90.6	87.8	80.5

NA Not available.   [1] In millions of short tons.   [2] Current assets to current liabilities.

Source: American Iron and Steel Institute, Washington, DC, *Annual Statistical Report* (copyright).

Table 994. Steel Products—Net Shipments by Market Classes: 1990 to 2005

[In thousands of short tons (84,981 represents 84,981,000). Comprises carbon, alloy, and stainless steel]

Market class	1990	1995	2000	2001	2002	2003	2004	2005
Net shipments, total.	**84,981**	**97,494**	**109,050**	**99,448**	**99,191**	**105,974**	**111,385**	**104,971**
Automotive.	11,100	14,622	16,063	14,059	12,562	15,883	13,858	14,477
Steel service centers, distributors	21,111	23,751	30,108	27,012	22,828	28,551	34,667	30,558
Construction, incl. maintenance [1]	9,245	14,892	20,290	21,543	15,729	23,787	23,810	23,967
Containers, packaging, shipping.	4,474	4,139	3,708	3,232	3,251	3,028	2,592	3,022
Machinery, industrial equipment, tools . .	2,388	2,310	1,784	1,456	1,137	1,178	1,853	1,653
Steel for converting and processing	9,441	10,440	12,708	10,311	7,201	9,448	8,151	5,562
Rail transportation	1,080	1,373	1,307	981	751	938	1,185	1,258
Contractors' products	2,870	([1])	([1])	([1])	([1])	([1])	([1])	([1])
Oil and gas industries	1,892	2,643	2,885	2,953	1,658	2,112	2,487	3,062
Electrical equipment.	2,453	2,397	2,055	1,684	1,336	1,099	2,026	1,183
Appliances, utensils, and cutlery	1,540	1,589	1,907	1,820	1,734	2,018	919	1,925
Other	17,387	19,338	16,235	14,337	31,004	17,932	19,837	18,304

[1] Beginning 1995, contractors' products included with construction.

Source: American Iron and Steel Institute, Washington, DC, *Annual Statistical Report* (copyright).

Table 995. Metalworking Machinery—Value of Shipments: 2005

[In thousands of dollars (2,800,272 represents $2,800,272,000)]

Product description	Product code	2005
Metalworking machinery	(X)	2,800,272
Metal cutting type [1, 2, 3]	(X)	2,079,874
Boring and drilling machines	333512A1	110,971
Gear cutting machines [1]	33351211	(D)
Grinding and polishing machines	33351221	265,035
Lathes [2, 3, 4, 5]	33351231	248,240
Milling machines [2, 6]	33351241	53,582
Machining centers.	33351271	619,563
Station type machines	33351281	104,481
Other metal cutting machine tools	33351291	431,962
Remanufactured metal cutting machine tools	3335126111	93,404
Metal forming type [7, 8]	(X)	720,398
Punching and shearing machines	33351311 pt.	125,808
Bending and forming machines	33351311 pt.	218,465
Presses, except forging [7]	33351331	139,924
Other metal forming type machines [7, 8]	33351351 pt.	206,547
Remanufactured metal forming machine tools [8]	3335137121	(D)

D Withheld to avoid disclosing data for individual companies.   X Not applicable.   [1] Data for "Gear cutting machines" are included in total "Metal cutting type."   [2] Data for "All lathes (turning machines) valued under $3,025 each" and "All Milling machines valued under $3,025 each" are included in total "Metal cutting type."   [3] Data for product code 3335123126, "Vertical NC turning machines," are included in total "Metal cutting type."   [4] Product class 33351231, "Lathes," excludes the values for product code 3335123131, "All lathes (turning machines) valued under $3,025 each."   [5] Product class 33351231, "Lathes," excludes the values for product code 3335123126, "Vertical NC turning machines."   [6] Product class 33351241, "Milling machines," excludes the value for product code 3335124101, "All milling machines valued under $3,025 each."   [7] Data for product code 3335133101, "All presses valued under $3,025 each" and 33351351101, "All other metal forming type machine tools valued under $3,025 each," are included in total "Metal forming Type."   [8] Product code 3335137121 was included in product class 33351351 to avoid disclosing data for individual companies.

Source: U.S. Census Bureau, *Current Industrial Reports, Metalworking Machinery*, Series MQ333W. See <http://www.census.gov /cir/www/index.html>.

Table 996. U.S. Machine Tool Consumption—Gross New Orders and Exports: 2005 and 2006

[Value in millions of dollars (3,581 represents $3,581,000,000)]

Item	2005				2006			
	Total	Metal cutting machines	Metal forming machines	Other manufacturing technology	Total	Metal cutting machines	Metal forming machines	Other manufacturing technology
New order units, total	23,058	19,540	979	2,539	27,288	23,670	1,183	2,435
Northeast [1]	3,633	3,107	169	357	4,561	3,989	185	387
South [2]	3,941	3,255	204	482	4,189	3,441	253	495
Midwest [3]	6,935	5,581	319	1,035	7,412	6,241	294	877
Central [4]	4,931	4,316	169	446	6,571	5,836	307	428
West [5]	3,618	3,281	118	219	4,555	4,163	144	248
New order value, total	3,581	2,871	178	532	4,380	3,708	182	490
Northeast [1]	475	400	25	51	641	558	24	58
South [2]	586	440	46	99	587	459	37	91
Midwest [3]	1,266	998	67	201	1,380	1,158	53	169
Central [4]	782	629	25	128	1,115	956	47	111
West [5]	472	403	16	53	657	577	20	60
Export order units [6]	1,915	1,443	202	270	1,918	1,435	176	307
Export order value [6]	533	394	46	92	577	429	36	112

[1] Covers Maine, New Hampshire, Vermont, New York, Massachusetts, Connecticut, Rhode Island, New Jersey, and Pennsylvania. [2] Covers Delaware, Maryland, Virginia, West Virginia, Kentucky, North Carolina, South Carolina, Tennessee, Mississippi, Alabama, Georgia, and Florida. [3] Covers Wisconsin, Michigan, Ohio, Illinois, and Indiana. [4] Covers Minnesota, North Dakota, South Dakota, Montana, Wyoming, Idaho, Iowa, Nebraska, Kansas, Missouri, Oklahoma, Arkansas, Louisiana, Texas, New Mexico, Colorado, and Utah. [5] Covers Washington, Oregon, California, Nevada, and Arizona. [6] Represents orders placed with U.S. builders.

Source: The Association for Manufacturing Technology, McLean, VA, (copyright); and American Machine Tool Distributors Association, Rockville, MD, *U.S. Machine Tool Consumption Report*, monthly.

Table 997. Semiconductors, Electronic Components, and Semiconductor Manufacturing Equipment—Value of Shipments: 2000 to 2005

[In millions of dollars (703 represents $703,000,000)]

Product description	Product code	2000	2001	2002	2003	2004	2005
Semiconductor machinery	3332950	(NA)	(NA)	(NA)	(NA)	(NA)	7,969
Transmittal, industrial, and special-purpose electron tubes (except x-ray)	3344111	703	700	584	629	641	652
Receiving type electron tubes and cathode ray picture tubes	3344114	3,458	2,847	2,486	1,508	1,049	621
Electron tube parts	3344117	144	125	91	63	78	84
Bare printed circuit boards	3344120	11,892	8,911	5,764	4,871	4,709	4,794
Integrated microcircuits (semiconductor networks)	3344131	73,664	46,337	49,726	54,830	60,097	62,984
Transistors	3344134	1,569	913	818	608	656	598
Diodes and rectifiers	3344137	621	403	370	391	305	323
Other semiconductor devices	334413A	9,757	7,632	6,632	6,519	7,247	8,390
Capacitors for electronic circuitry	3344141	2,786	1,734	1,338	1,192	1,184	1,031
Resistors for electronic circuitry	3344150	982	776	653	636	744	650
Electronic coil, transformer, and other indicator manufacturing	3344160	1,719	1,362	1,154	957	1,116	1,202
Coaxial connectors	3344171	805	506	464	402	403	376
Cylindrical connectors	3344174	725	688	528	563	631	506
Rack and panel connectors	3344177	532	359	264	268	291	304
Printed circuit connectors	334417A	1,811	1,147	776	834	1,013	939
Other connectors including parts	334417D	2,059	2,052	1,436	1,418	1,079	1,145
Printed circuit assemblies, loaded boards, and modules	334418B	37,273	31,214	23,171	19,715	19,566	19,151
Crystals, filters (except microwave) and piezoelectric devices	3344191	1,168	984	726	601	654	771
All other miscellaneous transducers	3344194	1,519	1,331	1,203	1,219	1,495	1,519
Switches, mechanical types for electronic circuitry	3344197	903	828	836	739	716	742
Microwave components and devices	334419A	2,435	1,848	1,511	1,415	1,326	1,158
All other electronic components	334419E	8,332	6,173	4,366	4,060	4,158	4,183

NA Not available.

Source: U.S. Census Bureau, *Current Industrial Reports, Semiconductors, Electronic Components, and Semiconductor Manufacturing Equipment*, Series MA334Q. See <http://www.census.gov/cir/www/index.html>.

Manufactures 639

Table 998. Computers Perpherial Equipment—Value of Shipments: 2000 to 2005

[In millions of dollars (62,857 represents $62,857,000,000)]

Product	Product code	2000	2001	2002	2003	2004	2005
Electronic computers [1]	334111	62,857	48,543	40,448	38,271	37,895	38,386
Host computers (multiusers)	3341111	22,877	16,469	13,053	12,237	10,993	11,759
Single-user computers	3341117	38,981	31,492	26,586	25,164	26,309	25,906
Other computers	334111D	998	581	809	870	593	721
Computer storage devices (except parts, attachments, and accessories)	3341121	8,995	7,319	5,027	5,101	5,034	6,100
Parts, attachments, and accessories for computer storage devices	3341124	1,692	1,699	1,578	1,130	1,039	1,441
Computer terminals [1]	3341131	415	361	266	258	274	245
Parts, attachments, and accessories for computer terminals [1]	3341134	(D)	(D)	(D)	1	2	(D)
All other miscellaneous computer peripheral equipment	3341191	(S)	(S)	(S)	(S)	4,705	4,425
Parts, subassemblies, and accessories for computer peripheral equipment	3341194	2,766	2,360	1,905	1,849	2,257	2,743
Point-of-sale terminals and funds-transfer devices	3341197	852	977	632	732	513	497
Parts and attachments for point-of-sale terminals and funds-transfer devices	334119D	(NA)	(NA)	(NA)	(NA)	(D)	(D)
Magnetic and optical recording media	3346130	3,206	2,228	2,207	2,271	1,586	1,303

D Withheld to avoid disclosing data for individual companies.   NA Not available.   S Does not meet publication standards.
[1] Excludes point-of-sale and funds transfer devices.

Source: U.S. Census Bureau, *Current Industrial Reports, Computers and Peripheral Equipment*, Series MA334R (beginning with 2006, MQ334R). See <http://www.census.gov/cir/www/index.html>.

Table 999. Computers and Peripheral Equipment—Shipments: 2004 and 2005

[27,335 represents 27,335,000]

Product	Product code	Number of companies, 2005	Quantity (1,000) 2004	Quantity (1,000) 2005	Value (mil. dol.) 2004	Value (mil. dol.) 2005
Electronic computers [1]	334111	93	27,335	24,947	37,895	38,385
Host computers, multiusers	3341111	40	(D)	(D)	10,993	11,759
Single-user computers, microprocessor-based, capable of supporting attached peripherals [1]	3341117	56	23,256	22,878	26,309	25,906
Personal computers	3341117107	24	16,252	(D)	15,690	(D)
Workstations	3341117109	32	1,045	(D)	1,848	(D)
Other computers (array, analog, hybrid, and special-use computers)	334111D	29	(D)	(D)	593	721
Computer storage devices (except parts, attachments, and accessories)	3341121	42	(X)	(X)	5,034	6,100
Disk subsystem and disk arrays for multiuser computer systems	3341121109	15	116	225	1,362	2,008
Disk drives (all sizes)	3341121112	13	(X)	(X)	69	11
Storage Area Networks(SANs)	3341121123	3	(D)	391	(D)	10
Tape drives (all sizes)	3341121138	10	(X)	(X)	278	289
USB Flash memory (thumb drives)	3341121141	–	(NA)	–	(NA)	–
Other computer storage devices	3341121145	22	(D)	1,162	(D)	3,781
Parts, attachments, and accessories for computer storage devices	3341124	13	(X)	(X)	1,039	1,441
Computer terminals (except point-of-sale and funds-transfer devices, parts, attachments, and accessories)	3341131	19	(X)	(X)	274	245
Parts, attachments, and accessories for computer terminals (except point-of-sale and funds-transfer devices)	3341134	6	(X)	(X)	2	(D)
All other miscellaneous computer peripheral (input/output) equipment (except parts, attachments and accessories)	3341191	128	(X)	(X)	4,705	4,425
Parts, subassemblies, and accessories for computer peripheral equipment	3341194	34	(X)	(X)	2,256	2,743
Point-of-sale terminals and funds-transfer devices	3341197	17	427	292	513	497
Magnetic and optical recording media	3346130	19	(X)	(X)	1,586	1,303

– Represents zero.   D Withheld to avoid disclosing data for individual companies.   NA Not available.   X Not applicable.
[1] Includes other products, not shown separately.

Source: U.S. Census Bureau, *Current Industrial Reports, Computers and Peripheral Equipment*, Series MA334R (beginning with 2006, MQ334R). See <http://www.census.gov/cir/www/index.html>.

640   Manufactures

Table 1000. **U.S. Consumer Electronics Sales and Forecasts by Product Category: 2003 to 2007**

[In millions of dollars (106,318 representes $106,318,000,000). Factory sales include imports]

Product category	2003	2004	2005	2006	2007, proj.
Total	106,318	117,033	128,895	145,744	155,202
In-the-home technologies total	58,806	64,022	67,135	73,297	75,719
TV sets and displays	14,528	16,783	19,022	25,085	26,574
Digital TV sets and displays [1]	8,692	12,300	15,563	23,661	26,301
Digital direct-view TV receivers	673	728	821	1,583	1,286
Digital projection TV	3,678	5,543	4,441	4,266	3,156
Direct-view LCD	664	1,579	3,258	8,480	12,224
Plasma	1,590	2,347	3,609	5,705	6,044
Front projection	2,087	2,103	2,914	2,943	2,993
Analog displays . [1]	5,836	4,483	3,459	1,424	273
Video components [1]	4,862	4,668	4,491	4,498	4,431
Component DVD players/recorders	2,698	2,183	2,053	2,254	2,100
Set-top boxes	1,757	2,355	2,359	2,196	2,315
Personal video recorders (PVRs) . . . . [1] . .	178	459	701	1,104	1,366
Home information technologies and security [1]	33,428	36,315	38,187	38,947	40,202
Personal computers	15,584	18,233	19,400	19,666	20,264
Aftermarket computer monitors	1,856	2,214	2,315	2,218	2,175
Computer printers	4,734	4,053	3,995	3,953	3,675
Modems/fax modems	1,419	1,465	1,525	1,455	1,360
Other computer peripherals	2,707	3,032	3,375	3,656	4,045
Personal computer software	5,060	5,162	5,250	5,325	5,475
Home security systems	2,055	2,150	2,322	2,670	3,204
Audio separates/systems	3,000	3,390	2,862	2,634	2,590
Audio separates components	981	1,325	1,318	1,330	1,390
Communications [1]	2,988	2,866	2,573	2,133	1,922
Telephone answering devices	1,210	1,274	1,279	1,085	1,025
Fax machines	242	186	151	127	111
In-the-vehicle technologies total	6,388	7,062	7,860	8,809	9,708
Entertainment devices [1]	5,842	6,426	7,140	7,556	8,169
Aftermarket autosound equipment	2,180	2,336	2,270	2,056	2,036
Domestic factory-installed autosound	3,245	3,569	4,318	4,821	5,344
Information and security	546	636	720	1,253	1,539
Portable and transportable navigation	163	261	349	887	1,177
Anywhere technologies total	29,600	32,037	39,026	47,899	51,356
Digital imaging	5,923	6,390	7,315	9,492	8,536
Digital cameras	3,921	4,739	5,611	7,805	6,945
All camcorders	2,002	1,651	1,704	1,687	1,591
Portable entertainment	1,779	2,281	5,003	6,105	6,356
MP3 players	424	1,289	4,229	5,535	5,863
Electronic gaming	10,253	10,512	11,070	13,022	16,077
Electronic gaming hardware	3,188	3,162	3,029	4,016	5,990
Electronic gaming software	7,065	7,350	8,041	9,006	10,087
Portable communication	11,645	12,854	15,638	19,280	20,387
Wireless telephones	9,922	11,258	14,265	17,934	19,099
Consumer electronic enhancements	11,524	13,911	14,874	15,740	18,420
Accessories	7,774	8,453	9,170	10,007	11,124
Electronic accessories	2,368	2,723	3,268	3,987	4,984
Primary batteries	5,406	5,730	5,902	6,020	6,140
Blank media [1]	3,750	5,458	5,704	5,733	7,296
Blank computer media	1,800	1,841	2,189	1,966	2,249
Flash media	1,346	3,102	3,087	3,385	4,694

[1] Includes categories, not shown separately.

Source: Consumer Electronics Association, Washington, DC, *U.S. Consumer Electronics Sales and Forecasts, 2002–2007* (copyright).

Table 1001. **Telecommunication Equipment—Value of Shipments: 2000 to 2005**

[In millions of dollars (15,174 represents $15,174,000,000]

Product description	Product code	2000	2001	2002	2003	2004	2005
Telephone switching and switchboard equipment	3342101	15,174	12,188	7,437	4,900	3,294	1,576
Carrier line equipment and noncomsumer modems . . .	3342104	13,112	10,943	4,488	3,045	3,598	2,824
Wireline voice and data network equipment	3342107	28,971	22,841	13,886	12,272	12,052	12,289
Communication systems and equipment [1]	3342201	36,357	36,501	25,104	25,805	31,230	30,272
Broadcast, studio, and related electronic equipment . .	3342202	4,029	3,491	3,304	2,932	2,763	3,289
Alarm systems	3342901	2,755	2,374	2,440	2,258	2,014	1,910
Vehicular and pedestrian traffic control equipment [2] . .	3342902	838	806	928	945	898	1,020
Intercommunications systems [3]	3342903	447	451	385	428	455	416
External modems, consumer	3344184	95	179	112	75	100	98
Laser sources	3359997	(S)	1,051	929	833	928	1,041

S Does not meet publication standards. [1] Includes microwave and space satellites. [2] Includes electrical railway signals and attachments. [3] Includes inductive paging systems (selective calling).

Source: U.S. Census Bureau, *Current Industrial Reports, Telecommunications*, Series MA334P. See <http://www.census.gov/cir/www/index.html>.

U.S. Census Bureau, Statistical Abstract of the United States: 2008

Table 1002. **Motor Vehicle Manufactures—Summary by Selected Industry: 2005**

[49,404 represents $49,404,000,000. Based on the Annual Survey of Manufactures; see Appendix III]

Industry	2002 NAICS code[1]	All employees[2]			Produc-tion workers[2]	Value of ship-ments[3] (mil. dol.)
		Number	Payroll			
			Total (mil. dol.)	Per employee (dol.)		
Motor vehicle manufacturing, total	3361–3363	964,597	49,404	51,217	772,130	499,323
Motor vehicle, total	3361	202,157	14,100	69,746	175,108	259,467
Automobile & light duty motor vehicle	33611	169,139	12,654	74,814	148,305	234,394
Automobile	336111	69,571	5,222	75,055	59,581	86,761
Light truck & utility vehicle	336112	99,568	7,432	74,646	88,724	147,634
Heavy duty truck	33612	33,018	1,446	43,785	26,803	25,073
Motor vehicle body & trailer.	3362	149,222	5,272	35,327	118,349	33,515
Motor vehicle body.	336211	48,342	1,806	37,350	36,307	10,797
Truck trailer	336212	29,965	1,012	33,783	24,829	7,133
Motor home	336213	21,924	774	35,293	17,841	6,241
Travel trailer & camper	336214	48,991	1,680	34,291	39,373	9,344
Motor vehicle parts	3363	613,218	30,033	48,976	478,673	206,342
Motor vehicle gasoline engine & engine parts	33631	74,159	4,273	57,618	57,537	35,400
Motor vehicle electrical and electronic equipment. .	33632	81,104	3,578	44,112	58,501	22,714
Motor vehicle steering and suspension	33633	37,576	1,866	49,650	29,728	10,853
Motor vehicle brake system	33634	38,185	1,559	40,823	29,635	14,077
Motor vehicle transmission & power train parts . . .	33635	80,070	5,105	63,754	65,597	34,615
Motor vehicle seating & interior trim.	33636	47,258	1,993	42,166	34,315	18,249
Motor vehicle metal stamping	33637	99,345	5,459	54,954	80,996	26,707
Other motor vehicle parts	33639	155,523	6,201	39,874	122,364	43,726

[1] North American Industry Classification System, 2002; see text, Section 15. [2] Production workers represent average number of production workers for March 12, June 12, September 12, and December 12 pay periods. All employees include production workers and other employees for the pay period that includes the 12th of March. [3] Includes extensive and unmeasurable duplication from shipments between establishments in the same industry classification.

Source: U.S. Census Bureau, *Annual Survey of Manufactures, Statistics for Industry Groups and Industries: 2005*, Series M05(AS-1) (issued November 2006). See Internet site <http://www.census.gov/mcd/asm-as1.html>.

Table 1003. **Motor Vehicle Manufactures—Employees, Payroll, and Shipments by Major State: 2005**

[14,100 represents $14,100,000,000. Industry based on the North American Industry Classification System (NAICS), 2002. See text, Section 15. See footnote 3, Table 1002, for information regarding shipments. Based on the Annual Survey of Manufactures; see Apppendix III]

Major state based on employment	Motor vehicle manufacturing (NAICS 3361)			Motor vehicle parts manufacturing (NAICS 3363)		
	Employees	Payroll (mil. dol.)	Shipments (mil. dol.)	Employees	Payroll (mil. dol.)	Shipments (mil. dol.)
United States[1]	202,157	14,100	259,467	613,218	30,033	206,342
Alabama.	6,895	488	6,795	14,222	603	4,687
Arkansas	(²)	(D)	(D)	5,777	182	1,084
California	6,550	490	7,626	24,971	990	6,068
Florida	–	–	–	4,500	164	1,079
Georgia	5,713	384	6,764	9,366	344	2,458
Illinois	6,390	457	7,991	24,593	1,089	6,888
Indiana.	13,129	914	19,839	74,992	3,957	23,024
Iowa	–	–	–	6,739	258	1,698
Kentucky	17,286	1,333	25,527	29,120	1,192	9,722
Michigan.	37,251	2,923	55,587	133,650	7,985	50,419
Mississippi	(³)	(D)	(D)	5,888	215	2,025
Missouri	14,535	1,082	20,282	13,627	555	3,885
New Jersey	1,163	77	320	–	–	–
New York	–	–	–	179,791	1,052	6,729
North Carolina	(⁴)	(D)	(D)	18,200	721	7,165
Ohio	25,186	1,852	38,504	86,342	4,678	31,115
Oklahoma.	(³)	(D)	(D)	4,470	185	1,268
Oregon.	3,469	142	1,243	1,794	82	360
Pennsylvania.	(²)	(D)	(D)	11,849	461	2,874
South Carolina	(⁴)	(D)	(D)	15,760	744	6,417
Tennessee	13,100	907	11,109	36,778	1,519	15,985
Texas.	4,841	350	8,309	12,373	475	3,565
Utah	–	–	–	4,785	167	1,843
Virginia.	(³)	(D)	(D)	6,782	283	2,085
Washington.	(²)	(D)	(D)	2,128	86	443

– Represents zero. D Withheld to avoid disclosing data on individual companies. [1] Includes states not shown separately. [2] Employee class size of 1,000 to 2,499. [3] Employee class size of 2,500 to 4,999. [4] Employee class size of 5,000 to 9,999.

Source: U.S. Census Bureau, *Annual Survey of Manufactures, Geographic Area Statistics: 2005 Series M05(AS-3)* (issued November 2006). See Internet site <http://www.census.gov/mcd/asm-as3.html>.

642 Manufactures

Table 1004. Aerospace—Sales, New Orders, and Backlog: 2000 to 2005

[In billions of dollars (109.3 represents $109,300.000,000), except as indicated. Reported by establishments in which the principal business is the development and/or production of aerospace products]

Item	2000	2001	2002	2003	2004	2005
Net sales	109.3	117.1	115.2	116.4	124.3	122.1
Percent U.S. government	37.5	38.6	46.1	52.9	51.7	54.0
Complete aircraft and parts [1]	57.2	58.7	53.9	49.6	49.6	51.7
Aircraft engines and parts	12.5	15.9	14.8	13.8	16.1	16.3
Missiles and space vehicles, parts	15.6	15.5	15.6	15.6	14.2	9.7
Other products, services	24.0	26.9	30.9	07.4	44.4	44.3
Net, new orders	140.1	122.3	114.8	117.7	131.7	181.5
Backlog, Dec. 31	215.0	220.1	222.5	226.9	234.3	293.6

[1] Except engines sold separately.

Source: U.S. Census Bureau, Current Industrial Reports, Civil Aircraft and Aircraft Engines; and Aerospace Industry, Series MA336G. See <http://www.census.gov/cir/www/index.html>.

Table 1005. Net Orders for U.S. Civil Jet Transport Aircraft: 1990 to 2006

[1990 data are net new firm orders; beginning 1995, net announced orders. Minus sign (–) indicates net cancellations. In 1997, Boeing acquired McDonnell Douglas]

Type of aircraft and customer	1990	1995	2000	2002	2003	2004	2005	2006
Total number [1]	670	421	585	174	237	267	1,004	1,058
U.S. customers	259	138	412	89	84	23	220	321
Foreign customers	411	283	193	172	185	204	811	737
Boeing 737, total	189	189	378	117	204	142	571	739
U.S. customers	38	85	302	64	74	16	152	242
Foreign customers	151	104	86	127	145	92	439	497
Boeing 747, total	153	35	24	17	4	10	43	72
U.S. customers	24	2	1	–	–	1	13	18
Foreign customers	129	33	18	13	9	10	30	54
Boeing 757, total	66	-7	43	–	-1	–	–	–
U.S. customers	33	-6	38	2	-7	–	–	–
Foreign customers	33	-1	14	–	6	–	–	–
Boeing 767, total	60	26	6	-2	10	9	15	10
U.S. customers	23	4	-2	1	–	–	–	–
Foreign customers	37	22	14	12	15	1	20	10
Boeing 777, total	34	83	113	26	12	42	154	76
U.S. customers	34	–	60	-1	11	–	10	35
Foreign customers	–	83	53	27	8	43	146	41
Boeing 787, total	–	–	–	–	–	56	235	161
U.S. customers	–	–	–	–	–	–	45	26
Foreign customers	–	–	–	–	–	56	190	135
McDonnell Douglas MD-11, total	52	-6	–	–	–	–	–	–
U.S. customers	16	3	–	–	–	–	–	–
Foreign customers	36	-9	–	–	–	–	–	–
McDonnell Douglas MD-80/90, total	116	51	–	–	–	–	–	–
U.S. customers	91	–	–	–	–	–	–	–
Foreign customers	25	51	–	–	–	–	–	–
McDonnell Douglas MD-95, total	–	50	21	16	8	8	-14	–
U.S. customers	–	50	13	23	6	6	–	–
Foreign customers	–	–	8	-7	2	2	-14	–

– Represents zero.   [1] Beginning 2000, includes unidentified customers.

Source: Aerospace Industries Association of America, Washington, DC, Research Center, Statistical Series 23, Internet site at <http://www.aia-aerospace.org/stats/aero_stats/aero_stats.cfm>.

Table 1006. U.S. Aircraft Shipments, 1990 to 2005, and Projections, 2006

[Value in millions of dollars (64,567 represents $64,567,000,000)]

Year	Total Units	Total Value	Large transports Units	Large transports Value	General aviation [1] Units	General aviation [1] Value	Helicopters Units	Helicopters Value	Military Units	Military Value
1990	3,321	64,567	521	22,215	1,144	2,007	603	254	1,053	40,091
1992	2,585	64,740	567	28,750	941	1,840	324	142	753	34,008
1993	2,585	59,103	408	24,133	964	2,144	258	113	955	32,713
1994	2,309	52,718	309	18,124	928	2,357	308	185	764	32,052
1995	2,436	49,381	256	15,263	1,077	2,842	292	194	811	31,082
1996	2,220	55,583	269	18,915	1,115	3,048	278	193	558	33,427
1997	2,757	65,129	374	26,929	1,549	4,593	346	231	488	33,376
1998	3,533	75,724	559	35,663	2,193	5,534	363	252	418	34,275
1999	3,799	80,974	620	38,171	2,475	6,803	345	200	359	35,800
2000	4,113	72,669	485	30,327	2,802	8,040	493	270	333	34,032
2001	3,902	77,608	526	34,155	2,616	7,991	415	247	345	35,215
2002	3,251	73,112	379	27,547	2,196	7,261	318	157	358	38,147
2003	3,221	68,006	281	21,033	2,080	6,205	517	366	343	40,402
2004	3,804	74,526	283	20,484	2,296	6,918	805	515	343	46,609
2005	4,649	81,515	290	22,116	2,853	8,632	947	815	420	49,952
2006, proj.	4,909	91,930	398	28,030	3,146	10,361	880	758	575	52,781

[1] Excludes off-the-shelf military aircraft.

Source: U.S. Department of Commerce, International Trade Administration, Internet site at <http://www.ita.doc.gov/td/aerospace/aerospace_statistics.htm>.

Table 1007. **Aerospace Industry Sales by Product Group and Customer: 1990 to 2007**

[In billions of dollars (134.4 represents $134,400,000,000). Due to reporting practices and tabulating methods, figures may differ from those in Table 1004]

Group	1990	1995	2000	2002	2003	2004	2005	2006[1]	2007[2]
CURRENT DOLLARS									
Total sales	134.4	107.8	144.7	152.3	146.6	155.7	170.1	184.4	195.4
Product group:									
Aircraft, total................	71.4	55.0	81.6	79.5	72.8	79.1	89.1	100.3	108.1
Civil[4]...................	31.3	24.0	47.6	41.3	32.4	32.5	39.2	47.5	54.6
Military...................	40.1	31.1	34.0	38.1	40.4	46.6	50.0	52.8	53.5
Missiles...................	14.2	7.4	9.3	12.8	13.5	14.7	15.3	14.9	15.8
Space...................	26.4	27.4	29.7	34.6	35.9	35.9	37.3	38.6	39.4
Related products and services[5]...	22.4	18.0	24.1	25.4	24.4	26.0	28.3	30.7	32.2
Customer group:									
Aerospace, total	112.0	89.8	120.6	127.0	122.2	129.8	141.7	153.7	163.2
DOD[6]...................	60.5	42.4	47.5	57.7	64.0	70.1	74.3	77.0	78.8
NASA[7] and other agencies	11.1	11.4	13.4	16.4	15.5	16.0	17.4	17.9	18.3
Other customers[8].........	40.4	36.0	59.7	52.9	42.7	43.8	50.1	58.8	66.2
Related products and services[5]...	22.4	18.0	24.1	25.4	24.4	26.0	28.3	30.7	32.2
CONSTANT (1987)DOLLARS[3]									
Total sales	123.5	86.1	108.2	109.4	102.3	105.1	110.4	115.1	117.7
Product group:									
Aircraft, total................	65.6	44.0	61.0	57.1	50.8	53.4	57.8	62.5	65.1
Civil[4]...................	28.7	19.1	35.6	29.7	22.6	22.0	25.4	29.6	32.9
Military...................	36.8	24.8	25.4	27.4	28.2	31.5	32.4	32.9	32.2
Missiles...................	13.0	5.9	6.9	9.2	9.4	9.9	9.9	9.3	9.5
Space...................	24.3	21.9	22.2	24.9	25.0	24.3	24.2	24.1	23.7
Related products and services[5]...	20.6	14.3	18.0	18.2	17.1	17.5	18.4	19.2	19.4
Customer group:									
Aerospace, total	102.9	71.7	90.1	91.2	85.3	87.6	92.0	95.9	98.3
DOD[6]...................	55.6	33.9	35.5	41.5	44.7	47.3	48.2	48.0	47.4
NASA[7] and other agencies	10.2	9.1	10.0	11.8	10.8	10.8	11.3	11.2	11.0
Other customers[8].........	37.1	28.8	44.6	38.0	29.8	29.5	32.5	36.7	39.8
Related products and services[5]...	20.6	14.3	18.0	18.2	17.1	17.5	18.4	19.2	19.4

[1] Preliminary. [2] Estimate. [3] Based on AIA's aerospace composite price deflator. [4] All civil sales of aircraft (domestic and export sales of jet transports, commuters, business, and personal aircraft and helicopters). [5] Electronics, software, and ground support equipment, plus sales of nonaerospace products which are produced by aerospace-manufacturing use technology, processes, and materials derived from aerospace products. [6] Department of Defense. [7] National Aeronautics and Space Administration. [8] Includes civil aircraft sales (see footnote 4), commercial space sales, all exports of military aircraft and missiles, and related propulsion and parts.

Source: Aerospace Industries Association of America, Inc., Washington, DC, *2006 Year-end Review and Forecast*; and Internet site <http://www.aia-aerospace.org>.

Table 1008. **Major Household Appliances—Value of Shipments: 2000 to 2005**

[In millions of dollars (2,170 represents $2,170,000,000)]

Product description	Product code	2000	2001	2002	2003	2004	2005
Electric household ranges, ovens and surface cooking units, equipment, and parts...	3352211	2,170	2,004	1,824	2,176	2,285	2,555
Gas household ranges, ovens, and surface cooking units, equipment, and parts......	3352213	779	902	929	1,018	1,120	1,390
Other household ranges, cooking equipment, and outdoor cooking equipment[1].......	3352215	1,251	1,027	1,051	967	914	964
Household refrigerators, including combination refrigerator-freezers........	3352221	5,396	5,227	5,080	4,993	5,002	5,405
Household laundry machines and parts	3352240	4,047	4,162	4,447	4,770	5,130	5,236
Water heaters, electric...............	3352281	573	556	576	570	545	638
Water heaters, except electric............	3352283	844	799	842	986	884	974
Household appliances, n.e.c.[2].........	3352285	2,066	2,033	2,009	2,056	2,297	2,481

[1] Includes parts and accessories. [2] N.e.c. means not elsewhere classified.

Source: U.S. Census Bureau, *Current Industrial Reports, Major Household Appliances MA335F.* See also <http://www.census.gov/cir/www/index.html>.

Section 22
Wholesale and Retail Trade

This section presents statistics relating to the distributive trades, specifically wholesale trade and retail trade. Data shown for the trades are classified by kind of business and cover sales, establishments, employees, payrolls, and other items. The principal sources of these data are from the Census Bureau and include the *2002 Economic Census*, annual and monthly surveys, and the *County Business Patterns* program. These data are supplemented by several tables from trade associations, such as the National Automobile Dealers Association (Table 1025). Several notable research groups are also represented, such as Claritas (Table 1023), National Research Bureau (Tables 1030 and 1031), Jupiter Research, Inc. (Table 1022), and Forrester Research, Inc. (Table 1021).

Data on wholesale and retail trade also appear in several other sections. For instance, labor force employment and earnings data appear in Section 12, Labor Force, Employment, and Earnings; gross domestic product of the industry (Table 646) appears in Section 13, Income, Expenditures, Poverty, and Wealth; financial data (several tables) from the quarterly *Statistics of Income Bulletin*, published by the Internal Revenue Service, appear in Section 15, Business Enterprise.

Censuses—Censuses of wholesale trade and retail trade have been taken at various intervals since 1929. Beginning with the 1967 census, legislation provides for a census of each area to be conducted every 5 years (for years ending in "2" and "7"). For more information on the most recent census, see the *Guide to the 2002 Economic Census* found at <http://www.census.gov/econ/census02/guide/>. The industries covered in the censuses and surveys of business are defined in the *North American Industry Classification System*, (NAICS). *Retail trade* refers to places of business primarily engaged in retailing merchandise to the general public; and *wholesale trade*, to establishments primarily engaged in selling goods to other businesses and normally operating from a warehouse or office that have little or no display of merchandise. Most Census Bureau tables in this section are utilizing the 2002 NAICS codes, which replaced the Standard Industrial Classification (SIC) system. NAICS made substantial structural improvements and identifies over 350 new industries. At the same time, it causes breaks in time series far more profound than any prior revision of the previously used SIC system. For information on this system and how it affects the comparability of wholesale and retail statistics historically, see text, Section 15, Business Enterprise, and especially the Census Bureau Web site at <http://www.census.gov/epcd/www/naics.html>. In general, the 2002 Economic Census has three series of publications for these two sectors: 1) subject series with reports such as product lines and establishment and firm sizes, 2) geographic reports with individual reports for each state, and 3) industry series with individual reports for industry groups. For information on these series, see the Census Bureau Web site at <http://www.census.gov/econ/census02/>.

Current surveys—Current sample surveys conducted by the Census Bureau cover various aspects of wholesale and retail trade. Its *Monthly Retail Trade and Food Services* release <http://www.census.gov/mrts/www/mrts.html> contains monthly estimates of sales, inventories, and inventory/sales ratios for the United States, by kind of business. Annual figures on retail sales, year-end inventories, purchases, accounts receivable, and gross margins by kind of business are located on the Census Bureau Web site at <http://www.census.gov/svsd/www/artstbl.html>. Additionally, annual data for accommodation and food services are located at the same site.

Statistics from the Bureau's monthly wholesale trade survey include national estimates of sales, inventories, and inventory/sales ratios for merchant

wholesalers excluding manufacturers' sales branches and offices. Data are presented by major summary groups "durable and nondurable," and 4-digit NAICS industry groups. Merchant wholesalers excluding manufacturers' sales branches and offices are those wholesalers who take title to the goods they sell (e.g., jobbers, exporters, importers, industrial distributors). These data, based on reports submitted by a sample of firms, appear in the *Monthly Wholesale Trade Report* <http://www.census.gov /mwts/www/mwts/html>. This report, along with monthly sales, inventories, and inventories/sales ratios, also provides data on annual sales, inventories, and year-end inventories/sales ratios. The Annual Wholesale Trade Survey provides data on merchant wholesalers excluding manufacturer sales branches and offices as well as summary data for all merchant wholesalers. This report also provides separate data for manufacturer sales branches and offices, and electronic markets, agents, brokers, and commission merchants. This report provides data on annual sales, year-end inventories, inventories/sales ratios, operating expenses, purchases, and gross margins. Data are presented by major summary groups "durable and nondurable" and 4-digit NAICS industry groups for sales, end-of-year inventories, and operating expenses. The reports are available as documents on the Census Bureau Web site

at <http://www.census .gov/econ/www /retmenu.html>.

E-commerce—Electronic commerce (or e-commerce) is sales of goods and services over the Internet and extranet, electronic data interchange (EDI), or other online systems. Payment may or may not be made online. This edition has several tables on e-commerce sales, such as Tables 1019 to 1023 in this section, 974 in Section 21, Manufactures, and 1250 in Section 27, Accommodation, Food Services, and Other Services. Also, there are several private sources for similar data such as Forrester Research Inc., Cambridge MA; and Jupiter Research, Inc., New York, NY. These sources show estimated and projected online retail sales by key categories from business to consumers or to other businesses. Their methods of collecting the data vary widely between the sources and consequently these estimates of this activity vary also. Users of these estimates may want to contact the sources for descriptions of their methodology. Methodology for Census Bureau estimates can be found at <www.census.gov/eos/www /ebusiness614.htm>.

Statistical reliability—For a discussion of statistical collection and estimation, sampling procedures, and measures of statistical reliability applicable to Census Bureau data, see Appendix III.

Table 1009. **Wholesale and Retail Trade—Establishments, Sales, Payroll, and Employees: 2002**

[4,635 represents $4,635,000,000,000. Covers establishments with payroll. For statement on methodology, see Appendix III]

Kind of business	2002 NAICS code [1]	Establishments	Sales (bil. dol.)	Annual payroll (bil. dol.)	Paid employees (1,000)
Wholesale trade	42	435,521	4,635	260	5,878
Durable goods wholesalers (except agents, brokers, and electronic markets)	423	260,445	2,171	157	3,357
Nondurable goods wholesalers (except agents, brokers, and electronic markets)	424	142,661	1,980	93	2,273
Wholesale electronic markets and agents and brokers	425	32,415	483	10	249
Retail trade	44–45	1,114,637	3,056	302	14,648
Motor vehicle and parts dealers	441	125,139	802	65	1,845
Furniture and home furnishings stores	442	65,204	92	13	535
Electronics and appliance stores	443	46,779	82	9	391
Building material and garden equipment and supplies dealers	444	88,314	247	30	1,160
Food and beverage stores	445	148,804	457	49	2,839
Health and personal care stores	446	81,797	178	20	1,024
Gasoline stations	447	121,446	249	14	927
Clothing and clothing accessories stores	448	149,810	168	21	1,427
Sporting goods, hobby, book, and music stores	451	62,236	73	9	611
General merchandise stores	452	40,723	445	43	2,525
Miscellaneous store retailers	453	129,464	91	13	792
Nonstore retailers	454	54,921	173	17	571

[1] North American Industry Classification System; see text, Section 15.
Source: U.S. Census Bureau, 2002 Economic Census, *Wholesale Trade, Geographic Area Series, United States: 2002* (EC02-42A-1US) and *Retail Trade, Geographic Area Series, United States: 2002* (EC02-44A-1US).

Table 1010. Wholesale Trade—Establishments, Employees, and Payroll: 2003 and 2004

[432.5 represents 432,500. Covers establishments with payroll. Employees are for the week including March 12. Excludes most government employees, railroad employees, and self-employed persons. Kind-of-business classification based on North American Industry Classification System (NAICS), 2002; see text, Section 15, Business Enterprise. For statement on methodology, see Appendix III]

Kind of business	2002 NAICS code	Establishments (1,000)		Employees (1,000)		Payroll (bil. dol.)	
		2003	2004	2003	2004	2003	2004
Wholesale trade	42	432.5	429.5	5,864	5,907	272.2	290.6
Merchant wholesalers, durable goods	423	254.0	248.5	3,313	3,319	162.0	173.4
Motor vehicles and motor vehicle parts & supplies ...	4231	26.0	25.1	364	358	14.1	14.6
Furniture & home furnishings	4232	13.8	13.2	162	157	6.6	6.7
Lumber & other construction materials	4233	18.0	18.1	236	248	10.0	11.1
Professional & commercial equipment & supplies	4234	36.4	37.4	703	718	42.6	45.8
Metal & mineral (except petroleum)	4235	10.7	10.5	147	146	6.7	7.6
Electrical goods	4236	31.4	30.0	469	461	29.1	31.6
Hardware, & plumbing & heating equipment & supplies................................	4237	19.0	19.0	212	217	9.3	9.9
Machinery, equipment, & supplies	4238	62.2	60.4	688	688	30.8	32.7
Miscellaneous durable goods	4239	36.6	34.8	330	326	12.8	13.4
Merchant wholesalers, nondurable goods	424	138.9	134.6	2,288	2,294	99.3	104.8
Paper & paper products.....................	4241	12.9	12.5	215	201	8.8	9.5
Drugs & druggists' sundries	4242	7.7	7.7	252	268	16.6	18.1
Apparel, piece goods & notions	4243	17.3	16.4	197	190	9.1	9.3
Grocery & related products...................	4244	35.2	34.3	757	764	29.3	31.0
Farm product raw materials	4245	7.3	7.0	65	64	2.2	2.3
Chemical & allied products	4246	13.1	12.7	146	141	7.6	7.6
Petroleum & petroleum products	4247	7.7	7.4	105	105	4.7	5.0
Beer, wine, and distilled alcoholic beverages	4248	4.3	4.2	169	170	7.7	8.1
Miscellaneous nondurable goods	4249	33.4	32.3	383	389	13.4	14.0
Wholesale electronic markets and agents and brokers ..	425	39.7	46.5	264	294	10.8	12.4

Source: U.S. Census Bureau, "County Business Patterns"; <http://www.census.gov/epcd/cbp/view/cbpview.html>.

Table 1011. Merchant Wholesale Trade Sales—Total and E-Commerce: 2005

[3,585,038 represents $3,585,038,000,000. Covers only businesses with paid employees. Excludes manufacturers' sales branches and offices. Based on the Annual Trade Survey, see Appendix III]

Kind of business	2002 NAICS code [1]	Value of sales (mil. dol.)		E-commerce as percent of total sales	Percent distribution of e-commerce sales
		Total	E-commerce		
Merchant wholesalers, total	42	3,585,038	474,801	13.2	100.0
Durable goods	423	1,778,412	199,539	11.2	42.0
Motor vehicles and motor vehicle parts and supplies ..	4231	294,376	77,174	26.2	16.3
Furniture and home furnishings	4232	60,978	5,160	8.5	1.1
Lumber and other construction materials	4233	140,905	4,267	3.0	0.9
Professional & commercial equipment & supplies	4234	311,454	46,316	14.9	9.8
Computer, peripheral equipment, and software	42343	164,348	24,667	15.0	5.2
Metal and mineral, (except petroleum)	4235	136,831	1,582	1.2	(S)
Electrical goods	4236	266,112	30,101	11.3	6.3
Hardware, and plumbing and heating equipment and supplies	4237	84,550	9,041	10.7	1.9
Machinery, equipment and supplies	4238	291,514	10,415	3.6	2.2
Miscellaneous durable goods	4239	191,692	15,483	8.1	3.3
Nondurable goods	424	1,806,626	275,262	15.2	58.0
Paper and paper products	4241	87,829	11,481	13.1	2.4
Drugs and druggists' sundries	4242	330,917	169,123	51.1	35.6
Apparel, piece goods and notions	4243	112,719	22,328	19.8	4.7
Grocery and related products	4244	429,290	35,866	8.4	7.6
Farm product raw materials	4245	115,288	4,217	3.7	0.9
Chemical and allied products	4246	87,295	(D)	(D)	(D)
Petroleum and petroleum products	4247	353,387	(D)	(D)	(D)
Beer, wine, and distilled alcoholic beverages	4248	91,316	4,223	4.6	0.9
Miscellaneous nondurable goods	4249	198,585	16,331	8.2	3.4

D Data withheld to avoid disclosing data of individual companies.   S Figure does not meet publication standards.   [1] North American Industry Classification System, 2002; see text, Section 15.

Source: U.S. Census Bureau, "E-Stats, 2005 E-commerce Multi-sector Report"; published 25 May 2007; <http://www.census.gov /eos/www/ebusiness614.htm>.

Table 1012. **Merchant Wholesalers—Summary: 1995 to 2006**

[In billions of dollars (2,159.0 represents $2,159,000,000,000), except ratios. Inventories and inventories/sales ratios, as of December, seasonally adjusted. Excludes manufacturers' sales branches and offices. Data reflect latest revision. Based on data from the Annual Wholesale Trade Survey and the Monthly Wholesale Trade Survey; see Appendix III]

Kind of business	2002 NAICS code [1]	1995	2000	2002	2003	2004	2005	2006
SALES								
Merchant wholesalers	42	2,159.0	2,814.6	2,835.5	2,962.3	3,296.5	3,585.0	3,952.0
Durable goods	423	1,141.7	1,486.7	1,421.5	1,448.9	1,654.6	1,778.4	1,942.8
Motor vehicles, parts, and supplies	4231	169.7	222.2	251.9	257.3	277.8	294.4	324.0
Furniture and home furnishings	4232	36.6	52.7	53.5	54.8	58.3	61.0	67.9
Lumber and construction materials	4233	66.3	87.2	95.1	105.7	128.6	140.9	146.9
Professional and commercial equipment	4234	197.9	282.2	272.5	272.6	296.3	311.5	332.2
Computer, peripheral equipment and software	42343	(NA)	174.8	150.6	144.3	157.5	164.3	173.3
Metals and minerals (except petroleum)	4235	87.0	93.8	81.7	81.4	121.2	136.8	156.3
Electrical and electronic goods	4236	186.6	260.0	223.0	227.1	253.8	266.1	293.0
Hardware, plumbing and heating equipment	4237	56.4	72.1	70.4	71.2	77.5	84.6	92.3
Machinery, equipment and supplies	4238	191.3	256.1	227.8	230.8	260.2	291.5	320.7
Miscellaneous durable goods	4239	149.9	160.3	145.6	148.0	181.0	191.7	209.5
Nondurable goods	424	1,017.3	1,327.9	1,414.0	1,513.3	1,641.9	1,806.6	2,009.3
Paper and paper products	4241	66.1	77.8	72.6	73.9	81.6	87.8	93.9
Drugs and druggists' sundries	4242	83.7	176.0	245.6	273.5	296.6	330.9	374.0
Apparel, piece goods, and notions	4243	67.6	96.5	105.8	104.4	108.4	112.7	122.9
Grocery and related products	4244	309.0	374.7	385.9	405.3	409.7	429.3	454.2
Farm-product raw materials	4245	125.5	102.7	103.4	115.1	123.0	115.3	131.9
Chemical and allied products	4246	50.3	62.3	67.7	69.7	76.4	87.3	93.7
Petroleum and petroleum products	4247	126.5	195.8	192.7	225.7	274.9	353.4	430.2
Beer, wine, and distilled beverages	4248	52.5	71.3	79.2	82.2	85.6	91.3	96.1
Miscellaneous nondurable goods	4249	136.0	170.9	161.1	163.4	185.7	198.6	212.3
INVENTORIES								
Merchant wholesalers	42	238.4	308.0	298.8	303.3	332.8	357.5	388.2
Durable goods	423	154.1	201.9	185.3	187.7	212.9	228.8	248.4
Motor vehicles, parts, and supplies	4231	23.0	29.1	30.3	31.8	33.7	36.8	38.2
Furniture and home furnishings	4232	4.9	6.4	6.3	6.5	6.8	7.1	7.7
Lumber and construction materials	4233	6.7	8.7	9.0	10.5	13.4	14.5	15.1
Professional and commercial equipment	4234	23.6	28.1	25.2	25.3	27.4	28.1	31.1
Computer, peripheral equipment and software	42343	(NA)	12.3	9.5	10.1	10.9	10.8	11.4
Metals and minerals (except petroleum)	4235	11.0	13.3	12.1	12.2	19.1	19.1	24.9
Electrical and electronic goods	4236	23.9	31.7	25.8	25.1	27.5	29.2	32.4
Hardware, plumbing and heating equipment	4237	8.7	11.8	11.3	11.4	12.7	13.8	14.6
Machinery, equipment and supplies	4238	36.1	52.1	47.2	45.4	50.7	57.0	62.3
Miscellaneous durable goods	4239	16.2	20.7	18.2	19.5	21.7	23.2	22.1
Nondurable goods	424	84.3	106.0	113.5	115.6	119.9	128.8	139.8
Paper and paper products	4241	5.3	6.5	5.2	5.2	5.9	6.3	6.4
Drugs and druggists' sundries	4242	10.4	23.0	30.4	30.5	30.1	29.2	31.3
Apparel, piece goods, and notions	4243	11.6	13.9	14.4	13.7	14.0	14.7	15.1
Grocery and related products	4244	18.1	20.2	20.1	20.1	20.6	22.8	25.0
Farm-product raw materials	4245	10.6	9.1	9.1	11.1	8.4	9.9	14.8
Chemical and allied products	4246	4.9	6.1	6.9	6.9	7.6	8.3	8.7
Petroleum and petroleum products	4247	4.3	5.0	5.7	6.2	9.0	11.6	12.2
Beer, wine, and distilled beverages	4248	5.1	7.1	7.6	7.8	8.3	8.9	9.6
Miscellaneous nondurable goods	4249	13.9	15.2	14.1	14.1	16.1	17.0	16.8
INVENTORIES/SALES RATIO								
Merchant wholesalers	42	1.28	1.28	1.24	1.18	1.16	1.14	1.14
Durable goods	423	1.55	1.65	1.59	1.49	1.46	1.47	1.49
Motor vehicles, parts, and supplies	4231	1.60	1.55	1.43	1.40	1.44	1.43	1.30
Furniture and home furnishings	4232	1.60	1.45	1.47	1.41	1.37	1.33	1.28
Lumber and construction materials	4233	1.21	1.19	1.16	1.14	1.20	1.13	1.33
Professional and commercial equipment	4234	1.33	1.26	1.12	1.09	1.07	1.04	1.08
Computer, peripheral equipment and software	42343	(NA)	0.93	0.77	0.82	0.79	0.79	0.73
Metals and minerals (except petroleum)	4235	1.53	1.71	1.86	1.63	1.67	1.53	1.88
Electrical and electronic goods	4236	1.47	1.44	1.40	1.29	1.26	1.29	1.23
Hardware, plumbing and heating equipment	4237	1.73	1.95	2.00	1.90	1.90	1.81	1.88
Machinery, equipment and supplies	4238	2.06	2.49	2.54	2.31	2.13	2.19	2.29
Miscellaneous durable goods	4239	1.27	1.57	1.53	1.47	1.29	1.39	1.29
Nondurable goods	424	0.96	0.90	0.92	0.89	0.85	0.81	0.81
Paper and paper products	4241	0.96	0.98	0.86	0.82	0.83	0.82	0.81
Drugs and druggists' sundries	4242	1.40	1.45	1.43	1.29	1.18	1.00	0.98
Apparel, piece goods, and notions	4243	1.98	1.66	1.71	1.53	1.49	1.48	1.45
Grocery and related products	4244	0.68	0.63	0.61	0.61	0.59	0.62	0.63
Farm-product raw materials	4245	1.02	1.02	0.91	1.02	0.85	1.03	1.29
Chemical and allied products	4246	1.12	1.12	1.24	1.17	1.11	1.09	1.06
Petroleum and petroleum products	4247	0.40	0.26	0.30	0.31	0.37	0.35	0.33
Beer, wine, and distilled beverages	4248	1.14	1.17	1.09	1.11	1.13	1.19	1.15
Miscellaneous nondurable goods	4249	1.16	1.04	1.05	1.08	1.00	0.99	0.95

NA Not available. [1] North American Industry Classification System, 2002; see text, Section 15.

Source: U.S. Census Bureau, "Annual Revision of Monthly Wholesale Distributors: Sales and Inventories: January 1992 Through January 2007" published 29 March 2007; <http://www.census.gov/mwts/www/mwtshist.html>.

Table 1013. **Wholesale and Retail Trade—Establishments, Employees, and Payroll by State: 2000 and 2004**

[6,112 **represents** 6,112,000. Covers establishments with payroll. Employees are for the week including March 12. Excludes most government employees, railroad employees, and self-employed persons. Kind-of-business classification for 2000 based on North American Industry Classification System (NAICS) 1997; data for 2004 based on NAICS 2002. See text, Section 15. For statement on methodology, see Appendix III]

State	Wholesale trade (NAICS 42)						Retail trade (NAICS 44, 45)					
	Number of establishments		Number of employees (1,000)		Annual payroll (mil. dol.)		Number of establishments		Number of employees (1,000)		Annual payroll (mil. dol.)	
	2000	2004	2000	2004	2000	2004	2000	2004	2000	2004	2000	2004
U.S. . . .	446,237	429,489	6,112	5,907	270,122	290,576	1,113,573	1,119,849	14,841	15,351	302,553	334,018
AL.	6,132	5,534	82	76	2,892	2,993	19,723	19,424	230	238	4,074	4,548
AK.	752	738	7	8	281	366	2,733	2,692	33	34	790	883
AZ.	6,731	6,548	86	92	3,627	4,102	16,911	17,730	255	296	5,694	6,827
AR.	3,505	3,426	45	46	1,402	1,693	12,211	11,940	135	142	2,268	2,627
CA.	58,326	58,553	808	802	40,011	44,720	107,987	110,875	1,491	1,662	36,073	41,732
CO	7,452	7,304	97	97	4,906	5,062	18,748	19,055	252	249	5,883	6,073
CT.	5,076	4,702	77	79	4,481	4,783	14,111	13,958	191	197	4,540	5,025
DE.	1,009	971	19	20	1,117	1,318	3,742	3,843	52	55	1,048	1,250
DC	372	412	5	7	282	353	1,945	1,774	19	19	431	450
FL.	30,671	31,398	315	308	12,536	13,028	67,396	71,456	903	960	18,044	21,259
GA	13,892	13,816	199	199	9,064	9,776	33,788	34,425	464	474	9,365	9,778
HI	1,809	1,881	19	20	627	747	4,924	4,887	63	67	1,313	1,563
ID	2,012	1,981	24	23	845	839	5,871	5,951	70	73	1,347	1,545
IL	21,509	20,032	344	323	16,683	17,306	43,800	43,154	637	626	12,992	13,721
IN	8,642	8,204	120	115	4,607	4,926	24,261	23,775	354	352	6,332	6,783
IA	5,155	4,822	65	61	2,173	2,376	14,382	13,809	184	178	3,169	3,401
KS.	4,876	4,553	62	62	2,333	2,663	12,261	11,748	153	150	2,747	2,848
KY.	4,939	4,595	74	69	2,536	2,739	16,988	16,670	221	223	3,804	4,227
LA	6,192	5,713	79	74	2,723	2,857	17,755	17,708	232	232	4,032	4,423
ME	1,740	1,672	22	19	744	771	7,015	7,003	77	82	1,436	1,780
MD	6,098	6,013	95	95	4,526	4,848	19,539	19,529	285	299	6,062	6,887
MA	9,735	8,881	156	143	9,114	8,665	25,813	25,905	353	370	7,729	8,705
MI	13,576	12,260	191	173	8,887	8,920	38,862	38,533	545	523	10,667	10,530
MN	9,294	8,789	137	136	6,399	7,674	20,862	20,967	304	312	5,980	6,840
MS	3,116	2,918	40	35	1,222	1,259	12,794	12,498	141	142	2,384	2,587
MO	9,072	8,319	146	131	5,458	5,050	23,911	23,769	318	321	6,258	6,527
MT	1,537	1,476	15	14	433	471	5,101	5,124	52	56	920	1,110
NE.	3,061	2,899	41	37	1,346	1,450	8,248	8,090	110	107	1,895	2,089
NV.	2,556	2,724	31	35	1,238	1,586	6,940	7,770	108	128	2,533	3,179
NH	2,105	1,994	25	25	1,184	1,399	6,545	6,641	93	97	1,930	2,254
NJ.	17,157	16,555	279	273	14,724	16,274	34,841	35,133	439	470	9,897	11,169
NM	2,162	1,975	22	20	753	772	7,249	7,242	91	96	1,745	2,039
NY.	36,606	35,701	422	407	20,941	21,866	75,500	77,750	844	888	18,116	20,220
NC	12,364	11,760	173	165	7,153	7,262	35,785	35,878	450	458	8,739	9,290
ND	1,543	1,478	18	17	532	624	3,435	3,443	42	43	719	810
OH	16,646	15,559	261	235	10,437	10,706	42,708	41,560	644	619	11,903	12,433
OK	5,005	4,646	62	54	2,126	2,111	14,147	13,751	168	171	2,913	3,273
OR	5,836	5,661	79	73	3,266	3,359	14,256	14,368	193	195	4,126	4,411
PA	16,796	15,818	243	245	10,287	11,988	48,518	47,430	668	678	12,556	13,898
RI	1,530	1,440	21	19	768	822	4,342	4,216	53	55	1,149	1,272
SC.	5,091	4,828	65	64	2,353	2,561	18,619	18,557	224	223	4,083	4,326
SD.	1,390	1,272	16	15	472	526	4,181	4,258	50	50	879	971
TN.	8,006	7,391	127	118	4,848	5,260	24,624	23,814	311	320	5,908	6,590
TX.	32,631	31,081	458	438	20,176	21,680	74,758	76,032	1,021	1,061	21,846	22,698
UT.	3,294	3,377	44	45	1,583	1,855	7,952	8,400	124	128	2,455	2,674
VT.	889	862	11	10	401	461	3,974	3,910	38	40	750	916
VA.	7,893	7,707	110	113	4,651	5,282	28,794	29,202	399	433	7,949	9,154
WA	9,869	9,522	125	125	5,412	5,995	22,700	22,602	313	319	7,181	7,642
WV	1,869	1,674	22	21	698	795	7,788	7,349	92	90	1,493	1,615
WI.	7,928	7,288	119	120	4,636	5,368	21,354	21,312	322	321	5,891	6,533
WY	790	766	7	7	229	271	2,881	2,939	28	30	515	631

Source: U.S. Census Bureau, "County Business Patterns"; <http://www.census.gov/epcd/cbp/view/cbpview.html>.

Wholesale and Retail Trade **649**

Table 1014. **Retail Trade—Establishments, Employees, and Payroll: 2000 and 2004**

[1,113.6 represents 1,113,600. Covers establishments with payroll. Employees are for the week including March 12. Most government employees are excluded. For statement on methodology, see Appendix III]

Kind of business	NAICS code [1]	Establishments (1,000)		Employees (1,000)		Payroll (bil. dol.)	
		2000	2004	2000	2004	2000	2004
Retail trade, total	**44-45**	**1,113.6**	**1,119.8**	**14,841**	**15,351**	**302.6**	**334.0**
Motor vehicle & parts dealers	441	124.5	127.8	1,866	1,959	63.9	70.9
Automobile dealers	4411	50.9	52.3	1,222	1,301	47.8	53.2
New car dealers	44111	26.2	26.5	1,112	1,179	44.8	49.7
Used car dealers	44112	24.7	25.8	110	121	3.1	3.6
Other motor vehicle dealers	4412	14.5	16.5	127	161	3.8	5.3
Motorcycle and boat and other motor vehicle dealers	44122	11.4	13.4	91	119	2.7	3.8
Automotive parts, accessories, & tire stores	4413	59.1	59.1	517	498	12.2	12.3
Furniture & home furnishings stores	442	64.8	65.7	549	577	13.4	14.5
Furniture stores	4421	29.7	28.8	284	274	7.5	7.8
Home furnishings stores	4422	35.1	37.0	265	303	5.9	6.7
Floor covering stores	44221	15.8	15.0	103	100	3.2	3.3
Electronics & appliance stores [2]	443	45.6	49.0	407	458	11.2	11.0
Appliance, TV, & other electronics stores	44311	29.6	35.5	279	357	6.6	8.3
Household appliance stores	443111	9.8	10.1	62	76	1.5	2.0
Radio, television, and other electronics stores	443112	19.8	25.3	217	280	5.1	6.3
Computer & software stores	44312	12.9	11.1	106	84	4.2	2.3
Bldg material & garden equip & supp dealers	444	91.9	86.7	1,235	1,223	32.5	33.8
Building material & supplies dealers [2]	4441	70.9	66.1	1,055	1,047	28.4	29.6
Home centers	44411	4.4	5.9	351	456	7.6	10.7
Hardware stores	44413	15.0	14.4	146	143	2.5	2.8
Lawn & garden equip & supplies stores	4442	21.0	20.7	180	176	4.0	4.2
Nursery and garden centers	44422	16.5	16.4	152	150	3.4	3.5
Food & beverage stores	445	154.5	152.5	3,004	2,957	48.4	51.7
Grocery stores	4451	98.3	96.1	2,717	2,661	44.0	46.8
Supermarkets & other grocery (except convenience) stores	44511	68.8	67.2	2,544	2,511	41.8	44.8
Convenience stores	44512	29.5	28.9	173	149	2.2	2.1
Specialty food stores	4452	27.8	27.0	154	154	2.4	2.5
Beer, wine & liquor stores [3]	4453	28.5	29.4	134	142	2.1	2.3
Health & personal care stores [2]	446	81.2	84.1	914	1,049	19.3	24.3
Pharmacies & drug stores	44611	40.6	40.1	680	771	14.5	18.4
Cosmetics, beauty supplies, & perfume stores	44612	9.6	12.5	61	97	0.8	1.3
Optical goods stores	44613	14.3	12.6	74	73	1.7	1.7
Gasoline stations	447	119.6	118.1	937	935	13.3	14.3
Gasoline stations with convenience stores	44711	80.5	92.6	653	734	8.9	10.6
Other gasoline stations	44719	39.1	25.5	284	201	4.4	3.7
Clothing & clothing accessories stores	448	150.9	149.8	1,369	1,555	20.2	23.7
Clothing stores [2]	4481	90.0	92.4	1,015	1,196	13.7	16.6
Men's clothing stores	44811	10.7	8.8	85	65	1.6	1.4
Women's clothing stores	44812	35.6	33.8	302	326	3.9	4.5
Children's & infants' clothing stores	44813	5.6	6.5	59	74	0.7	0.9
Family clothing stores	44814	20.6	24.1	453	589	5.9	7.9
Shoe stores	4482	29.7	27.3	185	194	2.6	3.0
Jewelry, luggage, & leather goods stores	4483	31.3	30.2	168	165	3.9	4.1
Jewelry stores	44831	29.3	28.8	156	157	3.6	3.9
Sporting goods, hobby, book, & music stores	451	65.0	62.2	616	621	8.8	9.5
Sporting goods/hobby/musical instrument stores [2]	4511	43.6	43.4	389	414	6.0	6.8
Sporting goods stores	45111	22.6	22.9	185	202	2.9	3.5
Hobby, toy, and game stores	45112	10.9	10.3	131	130	1.8	1.9
Book, periodical, & music stores [2]	4512	21.4	18.8	228	208	2.8	2.7
Book stores	451211	11.7	11.2	142	142	1.7	1.9
Prerecorded tape, CD, & record stores	45122	7.7	5.9	76	57	0.9	0.7
General merchandise stores	452	39.6	44.1	2,526	2,657	39.8	47.4
Department stores	4521	10.4	9.4	1,766	1,442	27.2	24.9
Other general merchandise stores	4529	29.2	34.8	760	1,214	12.6	22.5
Warehouse clubs & superstores	45291	2.0	3.0	478	923	8.7	18.5
All other general merchandise stores	45299	27.2	31.8	283	292	3.8	4.1
Miscellaneous store retailers [2]	453	131.0	128.9	850	824	13.8	14.2
Florists	4531	24.2	21.7	122	110	1.6	1.5
Office supplies, stationery, and gift stores	4532	43.0	43.2	350	325	5.2	5.2
Office supplies and stationery stores	45321	8.6	9.2	135	120	2.7	2.6
Gift, novelty, and souvenir stores	45322	34.4	34.0	215	205	2.5	2.6
Used merchandise stores	4533	17.5	18.1	114	128	1.6	2.0
Other miscellaneous store retailers	4539	46.4	46.0	264	260	5.4	5.6
Pet and pet supplies stores	45391	8.1	8.1	68	83	0.9	1.3
Nonstore retailers [2]	454	44.8	50.8	567	536	18.1	18.7
Electronic shopping & mail-order houses	4541	11.8	15.6	277	262	10.4	10.3
Direct selling establishments	4543	26.8	29.6	223	219	6.1	6.9
Fuel dealers	45431	11.8	10.5	106	98	3.1	3.3

[1] Data for 2000 based on North American Industry Classification System 1997; 2004 data based on NAICS 2002. See text, Section 15. [2] Includes other kinds of business not shown separately. [3] Includes government employees.

Source: U.S. Census Bureau, County Business Patterns; <http://www.census.gov/epcd/cbp/view/cbpview.html>.

Table 1015. **Retail Trade and Food Services—Sales by Kind of Business: 1995 to 2006**

[In billions of dollars (2,456.1 represents $2,456,100,000,000)]

Kind of business	2002 NAICS code [1]	1995	2000	2001	2002	2003	2004	2005	2006
Retail & food services sales, total . .	44, 45, 722	2,456.1	3,294.2	3,385.6	3,466.1	3,615.2	3,846.3	4,088.0	4,330.5
Retail sales, total	44, 45	2,222.5	2,988.8	3,067.7	3,134.3	3,265.5	3,474.3	3,693.4	3,904.3
GAFO, total [2]		651.1	863.9	883.9	913.9	948.2	1,007.2	1,065.5	1,120.4
Motor vehicle and parts dealers	441	580.8	797.6	816.0	820.3	841.2	864.5	888.3	901.1
Automobile and other motor vehicle dealers	4411, 4412	528.7	733.9	755.6	757.4	776.6	797.3	816.9	827.4
Automobile dealers	4411	502.5	688.7	708.6	707.7	721.0	734.7	750.0	761.5
New car dealers.	44111	464.6	630.1	649.4	645.8	656.9	665.9	675.7	683.1
Used car dealers	44112	37.8	58.6	59.2	61.9	64.1	68.8	74.3	78.5
Automotive parts, accessories, and tire stores	4413	52.1	63.7	61.3	62.9	64.6	67.2	71.4	73.7
Furniture, home furnishings, electronics and appliance stores	442, 443	128.5	173.7	172.0	178.5	184.5	200.1	214.6	230.2
Furniture and home furnishings stores . .	442	63.6	91.3	91.6	94.6	97.5	105.3	112.4	121.2
Furniture stores.	4421	37.0	50.7	50.6	51.3	52.1	56.5	60.3	63.9
Home furnishings stores	4422	26.6	40.6	41.0	43.3	45.5	48.8	52.1	57.3
Electronics and appliance stores [3]	443	64.9	82.4	80.4	83.9	87.0	94.8	102.2	109.0
Appliance, television, and other electronics stores.	44311	42.1	58.3	60.2	63.3	66.1	72.2	77.5	84.0
Household appliance stores	443111	10.0	12.6	13.5	14.2	14.5	15.7	17.0	18.1
Radio, television, and other electronics stores	443112	32.2	45.6	46.8	49.1	51.6	56.5	60.5	65.9
Computer and software stores	44312	20.5	20.7	16.9	17.3	17.5	19.1	21.1	21.3
Building materials, garden equipment, & supply stores	444	164.8	229.3	239.7	248.9	265.1	298.8	327.4	358.6
Building materials & supply dealers	4441	141.2	197.9	207.3	217.4	232.0	263.6	290.3	317.2
Hardware stores	44413	13.8	16.2	16.6	17.0	17.6	18.1	18.8	19.5
Food and beverage stores [3]	445	391.3	445.7	463.3	465.8	477.1	495.0	516.9	541.7
Grocery stores	4451	356.9	403.0	418.6	420.3	430.0	444.6	463.6	482.8
Beer, wine, and liquor stores.	4453	22.1	28.7	29.8	30.1	30.7	32.4	34.4	37.7
Health and personal care stores	446	101.7	155.4	166.7	180.1	192.2	198.9	208.7	224.2
Pharmacies and drug stores	44611	85.9	130.9	141.8	153.9	164.6	167.2	175.4	189.3
Gasoline stations	447	181.3	250.0	251.5	250.8	273.6	320.4	373.3	404.5
Clothing and clothing accessories stores [3] .	448	131.6	168.0	167.6	172.6	178.8	190.1	201.9	214.7
Clothing stores [3].	4481	90.8	118.2	119.3	123.0	128.3	137.1	146.3	155.4
Women's clothing stores	44812	28.7	31.5	31.5	31.3	32.5	34.7	36.9	39.4
Family clothing stores.	44814	40.0	58.9	60.2	64.3	67.3	72.0	77.5	82.7
Shoe stores	4482	20.4	22.9	22.9	23.2	23.2	23.7	25.5	27.2
Jewelry stores	44831	19.2	25.0	23.7	24.8	25.5	27.5	28.2	30.1
Sporting goods, hobby, book, & music stores [3].	451	60.9	76.1	77.1	77.0	77.3	80.1	82.5	87.2
Sporting goods stores	45111	20.0	25.4	26.3	26.3	27.2	28.9	31.2	35.2
Book stores	451211	11.2	14.9	15.1	15.5	16.2	16.8	17.0	16.6
General merchandise stores	452	300.6	404.3	427.6	446.6	468.7	497.2	525.0	552.2
Department stores (excl. L.D.) [4].	4521	205.9	232.5	228.4	220.7	214.4	215.7	214.2	212.2
Department stores (incl. L.D.) [4]	4521	210.9	239.9	235.6	227.8	221.0	222.0	220.5	218.0
Other general merchandise stores	4529	94.7	171.9	199.2	225.9	254.3	281.5	310.7	340.0
Warehouse clubs and superstores . . .	45291	65.1	139.6	164.7	191.3	216.3	242.4	270.2	297.9
Miscellaneous store retailers	453	77.2	108.1	104.4	104.2	103.1	105.3	110.6	119.5
Nonstore retailers [3]	454	103.7	180.7	180.8	189.5	203.9	224.0	243.3	270.5
Electronic shopping & mail order houses.	4541	52.7	113.9	114.8	122.3	131.2	147.2	161.6	182.4
Fuel dealers.	45431	19.8	26.7	26.1	24.0	29.0	31.9	37.2	38.3
Food services and drinking places [5] . .	**722**	**233.6**	**305.5**	**317.9**	**331.8**	**349.7**	**372.0**	**394.6**	**426.2**

[1] North American Industry Classification System, 2002; see text, Section 15.   [2] GAFO (General Merchandise, Apparel, Furniture, and Office Supplies) represents stores classified in the following NAICS codes: 442, 443, 448, 451, 452, and 4532.   [3] Includes other kinds of business not shown separately.   [4] L.D. represents leased departments.   [5] See also Table 1253.

Source: U.S. Census Bureau, *Current Business Reports, Annual Revision of Monthly Retail and Food Services: Sales and Inventories—January 1992 Through February 2007*, Series BR/06-A.

Table 1016. **Retail Trade Corporations—Sales, Net Profit, and Profit Per Dollar of Sales: 2005 and 2006**

[Represents North American Industry Classification System, 1997 (NAICS) groups 44 and 45. Profit rates are averages of quarterly figures at annual rates. Covers corporations with assets of $50,000,000 or more]

Item	Unit	Total retail trade		Food and beverage stores (NAICS 445)		Clothing and general merchandise stores (NAICS 448 and 452)		All other retail stores	
		2005	2006	2005	2006	2005	2006	2005	2006
Sales	Bil. dol . .	1,812	1,929	375	375	663	703	774	851
Net profit:									
Before income taxes	Bil. dol .	87.2	92.2	8.6	9.4	40.9	41.8	37.7	41.0
After income taxes	Bil. dol .	58.6	62.0	5.5	6.4	27.8	27.5	25.4	28.1
Profits per dollar of sales:									
Before income taxes	Cents. . .	4.8	4.8	2.3	2.5	6.1	5.9	4.9	4.8
After income taxes	Cents. . .	3.2	3.2	1.5	1.7	4.1	3.9	3.3	3.3
Profits on stockholders' equity:									
Before income taxes	Percent .	25.0	24.1	19.9	20.3	25.1	23.3	26.3	26.2
After income taxes	Percent .	16.8	16.2	12.6	13.8	17.0	15.3	17.7	18.0

Source: U.S. Census Bureau, *Quarterly Financial Report for Manufacturing, Mining and Trade Corporations*, annual; <http://www.census.gov/csd/qfr/>.

Wholesale and Retail Trade   651

Table 1017. **Retail Trade and Food Services—Estimated Per Capita Sales by Selected Kinds of Business: 1995 to 2006**

[In dollars. As of Dec. 31. Based on estimated resident population estimates as of July. For statement on methodology, see Appendix III]

Kind of business	2002 NAICS code [1]	1995	2000	2001	2002	2003	2004	2005	2006
Retail and food service sales	44–45, 722	9,224	11,673	11,870	12,030	12,432	13,099	13,787	14,464
Retail sales, total	44–45	8,347	10,590	10,755	10,878	11,229	11,832	12,456	13,040
Total (excluding motor vehicle and parts dealers).............	44–45 ex 441	6,165	7,764	7,891	8,031	8,337	8,888	9,461	10,031
Motor vehicle and parts dealers	441	2,181	2,826	2,864	2,847	2,893	2,944	2,996	3,010
Furniture and home furnishings stores	442	239	324	321	328	335	359	379	405
Electronics and appliance stores........	443	244	292	282	291	299	323	345	364
Building material and garden equipment and supplies dealers..............	444	619	813	840	864	911	1,018	1,104	1,198
Food and beverage stores............	445	1,470	1,579	1,624	1,617	1,641	1,686	1,743	1,809
Health and personal care stores	446	382	551	584	625	661	677	704	749
Gasoline stations	447	681	886	882	870	941	1,091	1,259	1,351
Clothing and clothing accessories stores ..	448	494	595	588	599	615	647	681	717
Sporting goods, hobby, book, and music stores....................	451	229	270	270	267	266	273	278	291
General merchandise stores...........	452	1,129	1,433	1,499	1,550	1,612	1,693	1,770	1,844
Miscellaneous store retailers	453	290	383	366	362	354	358	373	399
Nonstore retailers................	454	389	640	634	658	701	763	824	903
Food services and drinking places ...	722	877	1,082	1,114	1,152	1,203	1,267	1,331	1,423

[1] North American Industry Classification System, 2002; see text, Section 15.

Source: U.S. Census Bureau, unpublished data.

Table 1018. **Retail Trade—Merchandise Inventories and Inventory/Sales Ratio by Kind of Business: 2000 to 2006**

[Inventories in billions of dollars (407.0 represents $407,000,000,000). As of Dec. 31. Estimates exclude food services. Includes warehouses. Adjusted for seasonal variations. Sales data also adjusted for holiday and trading-day differences. Based on data from the Monthly Retail Trade Survey, Annual Retail Trade Survey, and administrative records; see Appendix III. Data have been adjusted using results of the 2002 Economic Census]

Kind of business	2002 NAICS code [1]	Inventories				Inventory/sales ratio			
		2000	2004	2005	2006	2000	2004	2005	2006
Total [2]...................	44–45	407.0	462.6	475.5	490.9	1.62	1.55	1.52	1.49
Excluding motor vehicle and parts dealers................	44–45 ex 441	278.5	307.3	321.2	335.8	1.49	1.37	1.34	1.33
Motor vehicle and parts dealers	441	128.5	155.3	154.3	155.2	2.01	2.07	2.10	2.01
Furniture, home furnishings, electronics, and appliance stores......	442,443	25.7	30.6	31.5	32.1	1.86	1.79	1.73	1.64
Building material and garden equipment and supplies dealers	444	34.5	42.6	46.4	46.8	1.76	1.64	1.63	1.60
Food and beverage stores............	445	32.1	33.3	33.9	34.6	0.84	0.79	0.77	0.75
Clothing and clothing accessories stores....................	448	36.9	41.9	44.2	49.7	2.62	2.60	2.57	2.72
General merchandise stores...........	452	64.9	70.9	73.1	75.3	1.87	1.67	1.64	1.60
Department stores	4521	42.7	37.4	37.2	36.9	2.17	2.06	2.10	2.09

[1] North American Industry Classification System, 2002; see text, Section 15.   [2] Includes kind of business not shown separately.

Source: U.S. Census Bureau, *Current Business Reports, Annual Revision of Monthly Retail and Food Services: Sales and Inventories—January 1992 Through February 2007*, Series BR/06-A.

Table 1019. **Retail Trade Sales—Total and E-Commerce by Kind of Business: 2005**

[3,693,430 represents $3,693,430,000,000. Covers retailers with and without payroll. Based on the Annual Retail Trade Survey; see Appendix III]

Kind of business	2002 NAICS code [1]	Value of sales (mil. dol.)		E-commerce as percent of total sales	Percent distribution of E-commerce sales
		Total	E-commerce		
Retail trade, total [2].................	44–45	3,693,430	93,280	2.5	100.0
Motor vehicle and parts dealers	441	888,307	16,729	1.9	17.9
Furniture and home furnishings stores	442	112,403	544	0.5	0.6
Electronics and appliance stores.............	443	102,176	1,303	1.3	1.4
Food and beverage stores.................	445	516,851	530	0.1	0.6
Clothing and clothing accessories stores	448	201,896	1,786	0.9	1.9
Sporting goods, hobby, book, and music stores...	451	82,456	1,116	1.4	1.2
Miscellaneous store retailers	453	110,593	1,771	1.6	1.9
Nonstore retailers	454	244,333	68,054	27.9	73.0
Electronic shopping and mail-order houses	454110	161,598	65,387	40.5	70.1

[1] North American Industry Classification System, 2002; see text, Section 15.   [2] Includes other kinds of business not shown separately.

Source: U.S. Census Bureau, "E-Stats, 2005 E-commerce Multi-sector Report"; published 25 May 2007; <http://www.census .gov/eos/www/ebusiness614.htm>.

Table 1020. Electronic Shopping and Mail-Order Houses—Total and E-Commerce Sales by Merchandise Line: 2004 and 2005

[147,199 represents $147,199,000,000 in sales. Represents NAICS code 454110, which comprises establishments primarily engaged in retailing all types of merchandise using nonstore means, such as catalogs, toll-free telephone numbers, or electronic media, such as interactive television or computer. Covers businesses with and without paid employees. Based on the Annual Retail Survey; see Appendix III]

Merchandise line	Value of sales, total, 2004 (mil. dol.)	2005 Value of sales (mill. dol.) Total	2005 Value of sales (mill. dol.) E-commerce	2005 E-commerce as percent of total sales	2005 Percent distribution Total	2005 Percent distribution E-commerce
Total	147,199	161,598	65,387	40.5	100.0	100.0
Books and magazines.	5,699	5,966	3,225	54.1	3.7	4.9
Clothing and clothing accessories (includes footwear)	13,984	15,893	7,921	49.8	9.8	12.1
Computer hardware	19,422	19,895	9,079	45.6	12.3	13.9
Computer software	3,224	3,680	1,850	50.3	2.3	2.8
Drugs, health aids, beauty aids.	40,067	43,150	6,450	14.9	26.7	9.9
Electronics and appliances.	7,464	8,996	5,997	66.7	5.6	9.2
Food, beer and wine. . . . ͘.	2,354	3,062	1,369	44.7	1.9	2.1
Furniture and home furnishings.	8,279	9,707	5,075	52.3	6.0	7.8
Music and videos.	4,154	3,645	2,164	59.4	2.3	3.3
Office equipment and supplies	6,533	7,068	4,288	60.7	4.4	6.6
Sporting goods	2,618	3,290	1,568	47.7	2.0	2.4
Toys, hobby goods, and games	3,338	3,609	1,809	50.1	2.2	2.8
Other merchandise [1] . . . . ͘.	22,127	25,345	9,930	39.2	15.7	15.2
Nonmerchandise receipts [2]	7,936	8,292	4,662	56.2	5.1	7.1

[1] Includes other merchandise such as jewelry, collectibles, souvenirs, auto parts and accessories, hardware, and lawn and garden equipment and supplies. [2] Includes nonmerchandise receipts such as auction commissions, shipping and handling, customer training, customer support, and advertising.

Source: U.S. Census Bureau, "E-Stats, 2005 E-commerce Multi-sector Report"; published 25 May 2007; <http://www.census.gov/eos/www/ebusiness614.htm>.

Table 1021. Projected Online Retail Sales: 2006 to 2011

[In billions of dollars (132.1 represents $132,100,000,000)]

Online product or service	2006	2007	2008	2009	2010	2011
Retail trade, total [1]	132.1	157.4	184.4	212.6	241.6	271.1
Apparel/accessories/footwear	13.8	16.4	19.3	22.2	25.2	28.2
Appliances/tools	5.9	7.0	8.3	9.6	11.0	12.5
Auto/auto parts.	15.9	19.0	22.2	25.5	28.6	31.4
Computer hardware/software	16.8	19.0	21.2	23.2	25.5	27.8
Consumer electronics	9.8	11.9	14.4	17.1	20.1	23.4
Food/beverages/groceries	6.2	7.2	8.4	9.7	11.1	12.7
Home furnishings	10.2	12.5	15.0	17.7	20.3	23.0
Music/videos	8.2	9.9	11.8	13.7	15.6	17.6

[1] Excludes travel. Includes other products/services not shown separately.

Source: Forrester Research, Inc., Cambridge, MA, US eCommerce: Five-Year Forecast And Data Overview, October 12, 2006 (copyright).

Table 1022. Online Retail Spending, 2001 to 2006, and Projections, 2007

[31.0 represents $31,000,000,000]

Category	Online retail spending (bil.dol.) 2001	2004	2005	2006	2007, proj.	Percentage of total retail spending by category 2001	2004	2005	2006	2007, proj.
Total.	31.0	67.3	83.7	100.1	115.6	(NA)	(NA)	(NA)	(NA)	(NA)
Computer hardware and software. .	11.0	16.1	18.1	20.0	21.9	26.4	34.1	36.1	38.3	40.5
Consumer electronics	1.5	3.4	4.7	6.0	7.2	20.2	24.2	26.0	27.4	28.0
Books, music, and videos.	3.8	6.2	7.5	8.4	9.3	7.7	11.7	13.4	14.6	15.7
Tickets	1.8	3.9	4.6	5.3	5.8	6.9	13.6	15.4	17.0	17.9
Consumer health.	0.4	1.8	2.6	3.2	4.0	0.5	1.8	2.5	3.0	3.5
Apparel, accessories, footwear, and jewelry.	4.7	10.7	14.0	16.8	19.7	1.6	3.4	4.2	4.7	5.3
Grocery and pet food.	0.8	3.0	4.1	5.4	6.7	0.1	0.5	0.6	0.8	1.0
Toys and video games	1.0	2.5	2.9	3.6	4.2	3.2	7.3	8.5	10.0	11.0
Sporting goods	0.7	1.6	2.0	2.3	2.5	2.9	6.7	7.9	8.7	9.2
Flowers and specialty gifts	1.2	2.6	3.1	3.6	4.0	2.3	4.8	5.6	6.4	7.0
Home	1.8	7.4	10.0	13.6	17.1	0.5	1.6	2.0	2.6	3.2
Office products	0.6	2.6	3.2	3.8	4.2	2.0	7.3	9.0	10.2	10.9
Other	1.8	5.4	6.7	8.0	9.0	(NA)	(NA)	(NA)	(NA)	(NA)

NA Not available.

Source: Jupiter Research, Inc., New York, NY, unpublished data (copyright).

Wholesale and Retail Trade 653

Table 1023. **Retail Trade and Food Services—Sales by Type of Store and State: 2006**

[In millions of dollars (4,806,715 represents $4,806,715,000,000). Kind-of-business classification based on North American Industry Classification System (NAICS), 1997; see text, Section 15. Data are estimates]

State	Total retail sales plus food services and drinking places (NAICS 44-45, 722)	All retail stores [1] (NAICS 44-45)	Motor vehicle and parts dealers (NAICS 441)	Furniture and home furnishings (NAICS 442)	Electronics and appliances (NAICS 443)	Building material & garden equip. & supplies dealers (NAICS 444)	Food and beverage stores (NAICS 445)	Health and personal care (NAICS 446)
U.S....	4,806,715	4,346,489	914,102	130,664	116,233	538,107	567,719	240,772
AL	78,929	73,212	16,037	2,026	1,216	9,765	7,550	4,503
AK	13,365	12,047	2,330	274	278	1,291	1,875	210
AZ	117,291	107,923	23,978	4,056	3,600	11,609	12,964	4,596
AR	47,330	44,117	10,004	986	682	6,465	3,918	2,084
CA	621,462	562,962	126,271	18,853	21,626	67,234	80,510	27,758
CO	89,113	80,894	17,492	2,826	2,567	10,462	12,812	2,553
CT	65,224	59,884	11,815	1,945	1,343	7,841	8,572	3,732
DE	19,518	18,018	3,861	857	535	2,706	2,400	960
DC	7,401	4,808	98	238	130	328	1,328	857
FL......	378,048	344,556	83,908	13,089	8,911	40,699	42,532	20,092
GA	158,054	142,873	31,490	4,719	3,445	18,427	17,466	7,596
HI......	25,969	22,251	4,120	595	487	2,089	3,363	1,395
ID......	26,917	25,155	6,097	841	497	4,139	2,806	754
IL......	211,648	190,752	36,511	5,441	5,012	23,202	23,758	9,653
IN......	104,965	95,994	20,319	2,298	2,466	12,208	9,732	5,238
IA......	48,722	45,271	9,070	1,123	870	6,613	5,410	2,060
KS	41,866	38,428	7,934	919	983	4,670	4,846	1,771
KY	66,364	60,633	11,355	1,581	1,117	8,085	7,227	3,878
LA	69,739	63,630	14,139	1,665	1,533	7,898	6,638	3,771
ME	26,741	24,906	4,390	483	338	3,273	3,521	941
MD	57,025	47,973	10,689	1,633	1,330	6,424	7,378	2,171
MA	122,242	110,159	21,878	3,790	3,106	14,704	18,322	8,110
MI......	88,197	75,420	16,359	1,909	1,995	10,713	8,452	4,937
MN	94,668	86,902	16,236	2,218	2,568	12,074	11,353	3,896
MS	47,933	44,548	8,714	942	779	5,841	3,965	2,781
MO	103,409	94,615	19,329	2,320	2,329	11,515	8,918	5,070
MT	18,974	17,400	3,329	579	422	2,795	1,909	471
NE	32,270	29,830	5,688	851	641	4,139	2,730	1,211
NV	59,461	53,582	11,433	1,762	1,679	5,167	5,826	1,990
NH	35,253	33,135	6,465	760	1,116	4,891	5,041	1,153
NJ......	162,627	149,285	30,668	5,172	3,816	17,651	28,873	9,844
NM	32,770	29,947	6,341	702	635	3,302	2,646	1,161
NY	308,752	278,935	46,771	8,333	8,931	31,564	43,591	26,232
NC	151,718	138,825	31,326	4,873	2,476	19,621	15,405	8,824
ND	13,343	12,541	2,610	277	303	1,958	1,282	581
OH	177,644	160,927	33,227	3,955	3,739	18,796	23,330	8,813
OK	52,831	48,422	11,314	1,097	848	6,066	4,053	2,360
OR	66,291	60,095	13,258	1,818	1,689	7,185	8,646	2,078
PA	213,638	197,034	39,773	4,745	4,060	22,095	26,242	13,165
RI......	17,758	15,796	3,239	445	359	1,980	2,396	1,671
SC	71,641	65,051	12,747	1,891	1,287	9,191	8,075	4,175
SD	16,901	15,855	2,963	336	342	2,382	1,390	533
TN	60,958	51,632	10,810	1,366	1,047	6,981	5,347	3,989
TX	213,144	178,241	41,095	4,867	4,817	18,714	21,662	6,702
UT	23,695	20,728	4,621	743	462	2,599	2,314	484
VT	13,336	12,483	2,370	304	209	1,946	1,838	656
VA	78,948	66,244	13,757	2,242	1,900	8,977	8,333	2,947
WA	118,549	108,923	21,317	3,043	2,915	12,618	15,487	4,002
WV	28,307	26,133	5,011	500	454	3,324	2,777	1,931
WI......	94,746	87,340	17,337	2,189	2,185	12,713	9,913	4,230
WY	11,018	10,172	2,207	186	155	1,177	997	202

See footnotes at end of table.

U.S. Census Bureau, Statistical Abstract of the United States: 2008

Table 1023. **Retail Trade and Food Services—Sales by Type of Store and State: 2006**—Con.

[See headnote, page 654]

State	Gasoline stations (NAICS 447)	Clothing and clothing accessories (NAICS 448)	Sporting goods, hobby, book & music stores (NAICS 451)	General merchandise (NAICS 452)	Miscellaneous stores (NAICS 453)	Nonstore retailers (NAICS 454)	Food services & drinking places (NAICS 722)
U.S...	509,115	228,384	92,217	580,846	129,109	299,220	460,226
AL	10,349	3,194	1,096	12,409	1,838	3,229	5,717
AK	1,330	486	365	2,574	480	554	1,318
AZ	12,549	4,357	2,159	16,317	3,049	8,689	9,369
AR	6,649	1,481	664	8,640	1,370	1,176	3,212
CA	52,736	33,526	13,274	71,475	16,112	33,587	58,500
CO	7,713	3,732	2,665	11,937	2,636	3,499	8,219
CT	5,511	3,784	1,485	6,002	1,518	6,336	5,340
DE	1,561	897	432	2,192	918	699	1,500
DC	349	612	251	293	134	191	2,593
FL......	33,261	19,487	5,706	44,450	9,760	22,660	33,492
GA	21,793	7,694	2,321	19,555	3,651	4,716	15,182
HI......	1,816	2,846	549	3,642	992	357	3,718
ID......	3,307	637	613	3,702	883	879	1,762
IL......	19,266	10,761	4,280	26,092	4,784	21,992	20,897
IN......	14,568	3,899	1,748	14,735	3,007	5,777	8,970
IA......	7,467	1,435	854	6,787	946	2,637	3,450
KS	5,652	1,464	766	6,488	1,069	1,866	3,438
KY	9,573	2,162	1,039	10,565	2,260	1,792	5,731
LA	9,257	2,899	1,144	11,111	2,169	1,407	6,108
ME	3,544	1,040	417	2,893	725	3,340	1,835
MD	4,396	3,024	1,159	5,753	1,151	2,866	9,051
MA	9,516	7,254	2,882	8,975	3,018	8,606	12,083
MI......	8,499	3,479	1,620	11,194	2,713	3,550	12,777
MN	10,686	3,612	2,195	12,821	2,181	7,063	7,766
MS	8,045	1,821	642	8,923	1,333	762	3,385
MO	15,025	3,743	1,621	14,144	2,584	8,016	8,795
MT	3,344	467	495	2,524	640	424	1,574
NE	4,272	950	634	3,898	606	4,210	2,440
NV	5,775	4,304	869	6,930	1,828	6,020	5,879
NH	3,178	1,484	748	3,773	973	3,552	2,117
NJ......	11,633	9,476	3,357	12,244	3,674	12,877	13,342
NM	5,131	1,187	553	5,158	1,185	1,944	2,823
NY	21,526	25,673	7,315	26,303	11,742	20,952	29,817
NC	19,274	6,004	2,223	18,420	3,952	6,427	12,894
ND	2,397	345	221	1,493	309	765	802
OH	21,086	6,657	3,211	19,733	4,299	14,080	16,718
OK	8,247	1,754	952	9,040	1,832	858	4,409
OR	5,745	2,685	1,617	9,778	2,112	3,483	6,196
PA	22,849	8,928	4,172	22,881	5,876	22,248	16,604
RI......	1,745	860	289	1,222	451	1,139	1,963
SC	10,417	3,578	1,158	9,291	1,936	1,303	6,590
SD	2,563	337	293	2,020	349	2,346	1,046
TN	7,023	2,482	940	7,543	1,521	2,583	9,326
TX	24,639	8,430	3,846	26,768	4,854	11,847	34,903
UT	2,530	732	558	3,097	516	2,072	2,967
VT	1,852	447	338	653	474	1,396	853
VA	9,110	3,542	1,482	9,441	1,739	2,775	12,704
WA	10,357	4,866	2,579	16,975	3,696	11,068	9,627
WV	4,626	753	349	4,444	761	1,202	2,173
WI......	12,889	2,898	1,875	12,112	2,136	6,864	7,406
WY	2,493	221	196	1,434	365	539	846

[1] Includes other types of stores, not shown separately.

Source: Market Statistics, a division of Claritas Inc., Arlington, VA, The Survey of Buying Power Data Service, annual (copyright).

Wholesale and Retail Trade **655**

Table 1024. **Retail Trade—Nonemployer Establishments and Receipts by Kind of Business: 2000 to 2004**

[1,743 represents 1,743,000. Includes only firms subject to federal income tax. Nonemployers are businesses with no paid employees. Data for 2000 based on the North American Industry Classification System (NAICS), 1997; beginning 2003, based on NAICS 2002, see text, Section 15]

Kind of business	NAICS code	Establishments (1,000)			Receipts (mil. dol.)		
		2000	2003	2004	2000	2003	2004
Retail trade, total [1]	44–45	1,743	1,880	1,893	73,810	80,548	82,916
Motor vehicle & parts dealers [1]	441	122	143	145	17,355	19,432	20,097
Used car dealers	44112	74	84	85	13,255	14,429	14,739
Motorcycle & boat & other MV dealers	44122	21	26	28	1,969	2,440	2,644
Automotive parts, accessories, & tire stores	4413	25	29	29	1,872	2,280	2,353
Furniture & home furnishings stores	442	37	42	43	2,574	2,962	3,049
Bldg material & garden equip & supp dealers	444	28	31	32	2,182	2,427	2,603
Building material & supplies dealers	4441	20	23	24	1,677	1,883	2,044
Food & beverage stores [1]	445	82	90	89	8,493	8,983	8,951
Grocery stores	4451	39	41	40	4,609	4,644	4,567
Specialty food stores	4452	33	38	39	2,135	2,474	2,522
Health & personal care stores	446	92	115	118	1,915	2,349	2,487
Clothing & clothing accessories stores	448	89	102	106	4,464	4,808	5,023
Clothing stores	4481	60	67	70	2,718	2,930	3,067
Sporting goods, hobby, book, & music stores	451	96	96	95	3,761	3,815	3,873
Miscellaneous store retailers	453	339	334	325	12,963	13,467	13,719
Gift, novelty, & souvenir stores	45322	73	75	72	2,104	2,166	2,172
Nonstore retailers [1]	454	792	857	867	15,401	17,425	18,218
Electronic shopping & mail-order houses	4541	49	58	67	1,391	1,941	2,310
Direct selling establishments	4543	708	767	769	13,047	14,562	15,002

[1] Includes other kinds of business not shown separately.

Source: U.S. Census Bureau, "Nonemployer Statistics"; <http://www.census.gov/epcd/nonemployer/>.

Table 1025. **Franchised New Car Dealerships—Summary: 1990 to 2006**

[316 represents $316,000,000,000]

Item	Unit	1990	1995	1999	2000	2001	2002	2003	2004	2005	2006
Dealerships [1]	Number	24,825	22,800	22,400	22,250	21,800	21,725	21,650	21,640	21,495	21,200
Sales	Bil. dol	316	456	607	650	690	680	699	714	699	675
New cars sold [2]	Millions	9.3	8.6	8.7	8.8	8.4	8.1	7.6	7.5	7.7	7.8
Used vehicles sold	Millions	14.2	18.5	20.1	20.5	21.4	19.4	19.5	19.7	19.7	19.2
Employment	1,000	924	996	1,081	1,114	1,130	1,130	1,130	1,130	1,138	1,120
Dealer pretax profits as a percentage of sales	Percent	1.0	1.4	1.8	1.6	2.0	1.9	1.7	1.7	1.6	1.5
Inventory: [3]											
Domestic: [4]											
Total	1,000	2,537	2,974	2,901	3,183	2,824	2,727	3,085	3,267	2,991	2,943
Days' supply	Days	73	71	62	68	63	63	63	75	70	71
Imported: [4]											
Total	1,000	707	445	378	468	508	521	618	646	566	605
Days' supply	Days	72	72	47	50	51	49	49	59	52	51

[1] At beginning of year. [2] Data provided by "Ward's Automotive Reports." [3] Annual average. Includes light trucks. [4] Classification based on where automobiles are produced (i.e., automobiles manufactured by foreign companies but produced in the U.S. are classified as domestic).

Source: National Automobile Dealers Association, McLean, VA, NADA Data, annual.

Table 1026. **Retail Sales and Leases of New and Used Vehicles: 1990 to 2005**

[In thousands, except as noted (51,390 represents 51,390,000)]

Item	1990	1995	1999	2000	2001	2002	2003	2004	2005
Vehicle sales and leases, total	51,390	56,476	57,618	58,964	59,742	59,835	60,215	59,410	61,086
New vehicle sales and leases	13,860	14,718	16,879	17,344	17,118	16,810	16,643	16,865	16,948
New vehicle sales [1]	13,285	12,070	12,468	13,181	13,510	13,639	13,594	13,608	13,551
Passenger cars	8,766	6,841	6,396	6,580	6,407	6,370	5,932	5,737	5,806
Light trucks	4,519	5,228	6,073	6,601	7,103	7,269	7,663	7,871	7,745
New vehicle leases [2]	575	2,648	4,411	4,163	3,608	3,171	3,049	3,257	3,397
Passenger cars	534	1,795	2,301	2,272	2,015	1,732	1,683	1,768	1,861
Light trucks	41	853	2,110	1,891	1,593	1,439	1,366	1,489	1,536
Used vehicle sales [3]	37,530	41,758	40,739	41,620	42,624	43,025	43,572	42,545	44,138
New and used vehicle sales, total value (bil. dol.) [4]	446	611	698	737	737	721	738	759	780
New vehicle sales (bil. dol.)	227	292	348	380	369	371	382	392	413
Used vehicle sales (bil. dol.)	219	319	350	357	367	350	356	367	367

[1] New vehicle sales data is calculated by subtracting CNW Marketing's vehicle leasing data from Bureau of Economic Analysis' data which combines sales and leases. [2] Consumer leases only. [3] Used car sales include sales from franchised dealers, independent dealers, and casual sales. [4] Includes leased vehicles.

Source: U.S. Bureau of Transportation Statistics, National Transportation Statistics, annual. See Internet site <http://www.bts.gov/publications/national_transportation_statistics/>. Data supplied by following sources: New vehicle sales and leases—U.S. Department of Commerce, Bureau of Economic Analysis; New vehicle leases—CNW Marketing/Research, personal communication, Mar. 2, 2005; Used vehicle sales and value: Manheim, Used Car Market Report, Atlanta, GA.

Table 1027. **New Motor Vehicle Sales and Car Production: 1990 to 2006**

[In thousands (14,137 represents 14,137,000). Includes leases]

Type of vehicle	1990	1995	2000	2002	2003	2004	2005	2006
New motor vehicle sales	14,137	15,106	17,806	17,137	16,971	17,297	17,445	17,048
New-car sales and leases.	9,300	8,636	8,852	8,102	7,615	7,505	7,667	7,781
Domestic	6,897	7,129	6,833	5,871	5,527	5,350	5,480	5,436
Import	2,403	1,507	2,019	2,231	2,087	2,155	2,187	2,345
New-truck sales and leases.	4,838	6,469	8,954	9,035	9,356	9,792	9,777	9,268
Light	4,560	6,081	8,492	8,713	9,028	9,361	9,281	8,723
Domestic	3,957	5,691	7,651	7,647	7,801	8,115	8,065	7,377
Import	603	391	841	1,066	1,227	1,246	1,216	1,347
Other.	278	388	462	322	328	432	497	544
Domestic-car production	6,231	6,340	5,542	5,019	4,510	4,230	4,321	4,367

Source: U.S. Bureau of Economic Analysis, "Auto and Truck Seasonal Adjustment"; <http://www.bea.gov/national/xls/gaphist.xls>, accessed April 2007. Data are mainly from "Ward's Automotive Reports" published by Ward's Communications, Southfield, MI.

Table 1028. **Retail Foodstores—Number and Sales by Type: 2000 to 2005**

{119.6 represents 119,600. Based on North American Industry Classification System (NAICS), 2002; see text, Section 15]

Type of foodstore	Number [1] (1,000)				Sales [2] (bil. dol.)				Percent distribution			
									Number		Sales	
	2000	2003	2004	2005	2000	2003	2004	2005	2000	2004	2000	2005
Total	119.6	120.2	120.5	(NA)	417.3	446.4	463.1	484.3	100.0	100.0	100.0	100.0
Grocery stores.	95.9	95.3	95.1	(NA)	403.1	430.0	445.1	463.9	80.2	78.9	96.6	95.8
Supermarkets [3]	21.9	21.1	21.0	20.2	310.3	327.2	318.0	349.8	18.3	17.4	74.4	72.2
Conventional	7.2	4.1	3.6	3.0	58.3	66.8	70.5	72.8	6.0	3.0	14.0	15.0
Superstore [4]	7.9	8.1	8.2	8.0	131.0	132.4	126.0	142.3	6.6	6.8	31.4	29.4
Warehouse [5].	2.4	3.2	3.2	2.7	20.2	13.0	10.4	13.4	2.0	2.6	4.8	2.8
Combination food and drug [6]. . . .	3.7	5.0	5.2	5.6	75.3	92.2	88.3	96.9	3.1	4.3	18.0	20.0
Super warehouse [7]	0.5	0.5	0.5	0.5	16.0	11.5	10.9	12.6	0.4	0.4	3.8	2.6
Hypermarket [8].	0.2	0.2	0.3	0.3	9.5	11.2	11.9	11.9	0.2	0.2	2.3	2.5
Convenience stores [9]	28.2	29.4	30.4	26.1	19.2	21.0	22.6	19.9	23.6	25.2	4.6	4.1
Superette [10]	45.8	44.8	43.8	(NA)	73.6	81.8	104.5	94.2	38.3	36.3	17.6	19.5
Specialized food stores [11]	23.7	24.9	25.4	(NA)	14.2	16.4	18.0	20.4	19.8	21.1	3.4	4.2

NA Not available. [1] Estimated. [2] Includes nonfood items. [3] A grocery store, primarily self-service in operation, providing a full range of departments, and having at least $2.5 million in annual sales in 1985 dollars. [4] Contains greater variety of products than conventional supermarkets, including specialty and service departments, and considerable nonfood (general merchandise) products. [5] Contains limited product variety and fewer services provided, incorporating case lot stocking and shelving practices. [6] Contains a pharmacy, a nonprescription drug department, and a greater variety of health and beauty aids than that carried by conventional supermarkets. [7] A larger warehouse store that offers expanded product variety and often service meat, deli, or seafood departments. [8] A very large store offering a greater variety of general merchandise—like clothes, hardware, and seasonal goods—and personal care products than other grocery stores. [9] A small grocery store selling a limited variety of food and nonfood products, typically open extended hours. [10] A grocery store, primarily self-service in operation, selling a wide variety of food and nonfood products with annual sales below $2.5 million (1985 dollars). [11] Primarily engaged in the retail sale of a single food category such as meat and seafood stores and retail bakeries.

Source: U.S. Department of Agriculture, Economic Research Service, The U.S. Food Marketing System, 2002, Agricultural Economic Report 811, August 2002; and unpublished data.

Table 1029. **Food and Alcoholic Beverage Sales by Sales Outlet: 1990 to 2005**

[In billions of dollars (554.0 represents $554,000,000,000)]

Sales outlet	1990	1995	1999	2000	2001	2002	2003	2004	2005
Food sales, total [1]	554.0	652.8	777.4	813.1	847.3	876.8	916.0	964.3	1,023.2
Food at home	305.3	349.8	412.7	423.4	445.0	457.8	476.1	496.9	527.0
Food stores [2].	256.4	275.3	299.6	303.5	313.1	312.0	323.9	335.6	351.3
Other stores [3].	32.3	54.7	83.0	89.4	103.0	116.6	122.2	129.9	143.4
Home-delivered, mail order.	5.3	8.6	18.8	19.2	18.0	17.9	18.2	19.0	20.5
Farmers, manufacturers, wholesalers . . .	3.5	4.1	4.6	4.6	4.6	4.6	4.8	4.9	5.1
Home production and donations	7.7	7.0	6.7	6.6	6.4	6.7	7.0	7.4	6.7
Food away from home [4]	248.8	303.0	364.7	389.7	402.3	419.0	439.9	467.4	496.2
Alcoholic beverage sales, total	72.6	80.3	99.9	104.9	110.1	115.4	119.1	124.3	132.3
Packaged alcoholic beverages	38.0	41.5	51.5	52.5	54.8	56.7	57.1	59.5	63.9
Liquor stores	18.6	19.0	22.9	24.5	25.3	25.5	26.0	27.8	29.9
Food stores	10.8	12.3	15.2	15.9	16.9	17.4	17.8	18.6	19.4
All other	8.6	10.3	13.5	12.1	12.6	13.9	13.3	13.2	14.7
Alcoholic drinks	34.5	38.8	48.4	52.4	55.4	58.7	62.0	64.8	68.3
Eating and drinking places [5]	26.5	30.3	38.1	41.5	44.1	47.1	50.1	52.4	55.5
Hotels and motels	3.8	3.9	4.5	4.9	5.2	5.3	5.4	5.5	5.6
All other	4.2	4.6	5.8	6.1	6.1	6.3	6.5	6.8	7.2

[1] Includes taxes and tips. [2] Excludes sales to restaurants and institutions. [3] Includes eating and drinking establishments, trailer parks, commissary stores, and military exchanges. [4] Includes food furnished and donations. [5] Includes tips.

Source: U.S. Department of Agriculture, Economic Research Service, "Food CPI, Prices, and Expenditures: Food Expenditure Tables"; published 8 June 2006; <http://www.ers.usda.gov/briefing/CPIFoodAndExpenditures/Data/>.

[4,390 represents 4,390,000,000. As of December 31. A shopping center is a group of architecturally unified commercial establishments built on a site that is planned, developed, owned, and managed as an operating unit related in its location, size, and type of shops to the trade area that the unit serves. The unit provides on-site parking in definite relationship to the types and total size of the stores. The data base attempts to include all centers with three or more stores. Estimates are based on a sample of data available on shopping center properties; for details, contact source]

Year	Total	Gross leasable area (square feet)					
		Less than 100,001	100,001– 200,000	200,001– 400,000	400,001– 800,000	800,001– 1,000,000	More than 1 million
NUMBER							
1990	36,515	23,231	8,756	2,781	1,102	288	357
1995	41,235	26,001	9,974	3,345	1,234	301	380
2000	45,115	28,062	10,958	3,935	1,424	326	410
2003	47,104	29,234	11,336	4,233	1,540	334	427
2004	47,835	29,710	11,471	4,315	1,573	335	430
2005	48,695	30,270	11,617	4,405	1,628	338	437
Percent distribution	100.0	62.2	23.9	9.0	3.3	0.7	0.9
Percent change, 2004–2005	1.8	1.9	1.3	2.1	3.5	0.9	1.6
GROSS LEASABLE AREA							
1990 (mil. sq. ft.)	4,390	1,125	1,197	734	618	259	457
1995 (mil. sq. ft.)	4,967	1,267	1,368	886	689	271	486
2000 (mil. sq. ft.)	5,566	1,383	1,514	1,059	790	294	526
2003 (mil. sq. ft.)	5,865	1,446	1,569	1,147	854	301	548
2004 (mil. sq. ft.)	5,953	1,469	1,588	1,171	872	302	552
2005 (mil. sq. ft.)	6,060	1,486	1,608	1,196	903	305	561
Percent distribution	100.0	24.5	26.5	19.7	14.9	5.0	9.3
Percent change, 2004–2005	1.8	1.2	1.3	2.2	3.6	0.9	1.6
RETAIL SALES							
1990 (bil. dol.)	706.4	205.1	179.5	108.0	91.7	45.1	77.0
1995 (bil. dol.)	893.8	259.6	227.1	136.4	115.8	57.0	97.8
2000 (bil. dol.)	1,181.1	342.8	300.0	180.5	152.8	75.2	129.8
2003 (bil. dol.)	1,339.2	388.5	340.1	204.8	173.1	85.2	147.5
2004 (bil. dol.)	1,432.6	415.5	363.8	219.2	185.1	91.1	158.0
2005 (bil. dol.)	1,530.4	443.8	388.6	234.2	197.6	97.3	168.9
Percent distribution	100.0	29.0	25.4	15.3	12.9	6.4	11.0
Percent change, 2004–2005	6.8	6.8	6.8	6.9	6.8	6.8	6.9

Source: National Research Bureau (a subsidiary of CoStar Group), Chicago, IL, (copyright) "2006 NRB Shopping Centers Census"; <http://www.icsc.org/srch/rsrch/census/>.

Table 1031. Shopping Centers—Gross Leasable Area and Retail Sales, by State: 2005

[6,060 represents 6,060,000,000. See headnote, Table 1030]

State	Gross leasable area, (mil. sq. ft.)	Retail sales (bil. dol.)	Retail sales per sq. ft. (dol.)	Percent change, 2004–2005		State	Gross leasable area, (mil. sq. ft.)	Retail sales (bil. dol.)	Retail sales per sq. ft. (dol.)	Percent change, 2004–2005	
				Gross leasable area	Retail sales					Gross leasable area	Retail sales
U.S.	6,060	1,530.4	253	1.8	6.8	MO	129	33.0	255	1.9	6.5
AL	84	21.7	258	0.8	5.8	MT	10	3.0	293	–	6.8
AK	8	3.3	429	–	8.5	NE	40	8.3	207	1.7	6.3
AZ	150	36.8	245	3.2	7.0	NV	64	10.2	158	3.3	7.4
AR	41	10.2	252	5.7	5.4	NH	27	7.6	283	0.1	9.9
CA	755	182.8	242	1.6	6.7	NJ	191	43.9	230	1.8	7.7
CO	125	35.3	282	4.9	7.6	NM	32	9.1	281	–	6.0
CT	102	29.8	293	0.7	8.3	NY	266	65.2	245	0.3	6.6
DE	25	6.9	280	4.0	8.2	NC	207	42.1	203	3.6	6.5
DC	11	2.5	237	–	6.7	ND	10	3.2	313	–	9.4
FL	488	144.5	296	2.3	7.6	OH	270	59.9	222	1.1	6.3
GA	205	45.5	222	1.9	6.4	OK	63	17.8	284	1.3	5.1
HI	21	7.4	346	2.0	10.1	OR	63	14.3	227	1.5	7.4
ID	20	4.6	228	0.1	5.7	PA	270	59.8	221	1.3	6.9
IL	282	63.4	225	1.3	7.2	RI	24	5.6	237	2.8	6.9
IN	132	30.7	232	1.2	6.2	SC	95	22.3	235	2.8	6.2
IA	52	10.9	208	2.9	6.4	SD	8	1.9	244	9.0	6.3
KS	62	16.7	268	1.1	6.3	TN	142	33.5	237	1.3	6.6
KY	71	19.8	279	1.0	6.1	TX	410	127.0	310	2.8	6.5
LA	92	26.9	291	2.4	6.3	UT	41	9.0	219	1.5	5.7
ME	19	6.8	351	–	8.6	VT	9	2.8	318	–	8.2
MD	136	36.8	271	1.1	6.8	VA	187	47.9	256	1.4	7.2
MA	123	35.7	291	1.8	7.4	WA	107	26.7	249	0.8	7.1
MI	155	37.0	238	0.9	6.6	WV	23	5.1	216	–	5.2
MN	76	20.7	272	1.7	6.8	WI	82	21.7	264	0.7	6.9
MS	48	11.0	230	4.5	4.9	WY	6	1.9	308	–	5.8

– Represents zero.

Source: National Research Bureau (a subsidiary of CoStar Group), Chicago, IL, (copyright) "2006 NRB Shopping Centers Census"; <http://www.icsc.org/srch/rsrch/census/>.

Section 23
Transportation

This section presents data on civil air transportation, both passenger and cargo, and on water transportation, including inland waterways, oceanborne commerce, the merchant marine, cargo, and vessel tonnages.

This section also presents statistics on revenues, passenger and freight traffic volume, and employment in various revenue-producing modes of the transportation industry, including motor vehicles, trains, and pipelines. Data are also presented on highway mileage and finances, motor vehicle travel, accidents, and registrations; and characteristics of public transit, railroads, and pipelines.

Principal sources of air and water transportation data are the annual *National Transportation Statistics,* issued by the U.S. Bureau of Transportation Statistics; the *Annual Report* issued by the Air Transport Association of America, Washington, DC; and the annual *Waterborne Commerce of the United States* issued by the Corps of Engineers of the Department of the Army. In addition, the U.S. Census Bureau in its commodity flow survey (part of the census of transportation, taken every 5 years through 2002, for years ending in "2" and "7") provides data on the type, weight, and value of commodities shipped by manufacturing establishments in the United States, by means of transportation, origin, and destination. The latest reports for 2002 are part of the 2002 Economic Census. This census was conducted in accordance with the 2002 North American Industry Classification System (NAICS). See text, Section 15, Business Enterprise, for a discussion of the 2002 Economic Census and NAICS.

The principal compiler of data on public roads and on operation of motor vehicles is the U.S. Department of Transportation's (DOT) Federal Highway Administration (FHWA). These data appear in FHWA's annual *Highway Statistics* and other publications.

The U.S. National Highway Traffic Safety Administration issues data on traffic accident deaths and death rates in two annual reports: the *Fact Book* and the *Fatal Accident Reporting System Annual Report.* DOT's Federal Railroad Administration presents data on accidents involving railroads in its annual *Accident/Incident Bulletin,* and the *Rail-Highway Crossing Accident/Incident and Inventory Bulletin.*

Data are also presented in many nongovernment publications. Among them are the weekly and annual *Cars of Revenue Freight Loaded* and the annual *Yearbook of Railroad Facts,* both published by the Association of American Railroads, Washington, DC; *Transit Fact Book,* containing electric railway and motorbus statistics, published annually by the American Public Transit Association, Washington, DC; and *Injury Facts,* issued by the National Safety Council, Chicago, IL.

Civil aviation—Federal promotion and regulation of civil aviation have been carried out by the Federal Aviation Administration (FAA) and the Civil Aeronautics Board (CAB). The CAB promoted and regulated the civil air transportation industry within the United States and between the United States and foreign countries. The Board granted licenses to provide air transportation service, approved or disapproved proposed rates and fares, and approved or disapproved proposed agreements and corporate relationships involving air carriers. In December 1984, the CAB ceased to exist as an agency. Some of its functions were transferred to the DOT, as outlined below. The responsibility for investigation of aviation accidents resides with the National Transportation Safety Board.

The Office of the Secretary, DOT aviation activities include: negotiation of international air transportation rights, selection of U.S. air carriers to serve capacity-controlled international markets, oversight of international rates and fares,

U.S. Census Bureau, Statistical Abstract of the United States: 2008

maintenance of essential air service to small communities, and consumer affairs. DOT's Bureau of Transportation Statistics (BTS) handles aviation information functions formerly assigned to CAB. Prior to BTS, the Research and Special Programs Administration handled these functions.

The principal activities of the FAA include: the promotion of air safety; controlling the use of navigable airspace; prescribing regulations dealing with the competency of airmen, airworthiness of aircraft and air traffic control; operation of air route traffic control centers, airport traffic control towers, and flight service stations; the design, construction, maintenance, and inspection of navigation, traffic control, and communications equipment; and the development of general aviation.

The CAB published monthly and quarterly financial and traffic statistical data for the certificated route air carriers. BTS continues these publications, including both certificated and noncertificated (commuter) air carriers. The FAA annually publishes data on the use of airway facilities; data related to the location of airmen, aircraft, and airports; the volume of activity in the field of nonair carrier (general aviation) flying; and aircraft production and registration.

General aviation comprises all civil flying (including such commercial operations as small demand air taxis, agriculture application, powerline patrol, etc.) but excludes certificated route air carriers, supplemental operators, large-aircraft commercial operators, and commuter airlines.

Air carriers and service—The CAB previously issued "certificates of public convenience and necessity" under Section 401 of the Federal Aviation Act of 1958 for scheduled and nonscheduled (charter) passenger services and cargo services. It also issued certificates under Section 418 of the Act to cargo air carriers for domestic all-cargo service only. The DOT Office of the Secretary now issues the certificates under a "fit, willing, and able" test of air carrier operations. Carriers operating only a 60-seat-or-less aircraft are given exemption authority to carry passengers, cargo, and mail in scheduled and

nonscheduled service under Part 298 of the DOT (formerly CAB) regulations. Exemption authority carriers who offer scheduled passenger service to an essential air service point must meet the "fit, willing, and able" test.

Vessel shipments, entrances, and clearances—Shipments by dry cargo vessels comprise shipments on all types of watercraft, except tanker vessels; shipments by tanker vessels comprise all types of cargo, liquid and dry, carried by tanker vessels.

A vessel is reported as entered only at the first port which it enters in the United States, whether or not cargo is unloaded at that port. A vessel is reported as cleared only at the last port at which clearance is made to a foreign port, whether or not it takes on cargo. Army and Navy vessels entering or clearing without commercial cargo are not included in the figures.

Units of measurement—Cargo (or freight) tonnage and shipping weight both represent the gross weight of the cargo including the weight of containers, wrappings, crates, etc. However, shipping weight excludes lift and cargo vans and similar substantial outer containers. Other tonnage figures generally refer to stowing capacity of vessels, 100 cubic feet being called 1 ton. Gross tonnage comprises the space within the frames and the ceiling of the hull, together with those closed-in spaces above deck available for cargo, stores, passengers, or crew, with certain minor exceptions. Net or registered tonnage is the gross tonnage less the spaces occupied by the propelling machinery, fuel, crew quarters, master's cabin, and navigation spaces. Substantially, it represents space available for cargo and passengers. The net tonnage capacity of a ship may bear little relation to weight of cargo. Deadweight tonnage is the weight in long tons required to depress a vessel from light water line (that is, with only the machinery and equipment on board) to load line. It is, therefore, the weight of the cargo, fuel, etc., which a vessel is designed to carry with safety.

Federal-aid highway systems—The Intermodal Surface Transportation Efficiency Act (ISTEA) of 1991 eliminated the

historical Federal-Aid Highway Systems and created the National Highway System (NHS) and other federal-aid highway categories. The final NHS was approved by Congress in December of 1995 under the National Highway System Designation Act.

Functional systems—Roads and streets are assigned to groups according to the character of service intended. The functional systems are (1) arterial highways that generally handle the long trips, (2) collector facilities that collect and disperse traffic between the arterials and the lower systems, and (3) local roads and streets that primarily serve direct access to residential areas, farms, and other local areas.

Regulatory bodies—The Interstate Commerce Commission (ICC), created by the U.S. Congress to regulate transportation in interstate commerce, has jurisdiction over railroads, trucking companies, bus lines, freight forwarders, water carriers, coal slurry pipelines, and transportation brokers. The Federal Energy Regulatory Commission is responsible for setting rates and charges for transportation and sale of natural gas and for establishing rates or charges for transportation.

Motor carriers—For 1960–73, Class I for-hire motor carriers of freight were classified by the ICC as those with $1 million or more of gross annual operating revenue; 1974–79, the class minimum was $3 million. Effective January 1, 1980, Class I carriers are those with $5 million or more in revenue. For 1960–68, Class I motor carriers of passengers were classified by the ICC as those with $200,000 or more of gross annual operating revenue; for 1969–76, as those with revenues of $1 million or more; and since 1977, as those with $3 million or more. Effective January 1, 1988, Class I motor carriers of passengers are those with $5 million or more in operating revenues; Class II less than $5 million in operating revenues.

Railroads—Railroad companies reporting to the ICC are divided into specific groups as follows: (1) regular line-haul (interstate) railroads (and their nonoperating subsidiaries), (2) switching and terminal railroads, (3) private railroads prior to 1964 (identified by ICC as "circular" because they reported on brief circulars), and (4) unofficial railroads, so designated when their reports are received too late for tabulation. For the most part, the last three groups are not included in the statistics shown here.

For years prior to 1978, Class I railroads were those with annual revenues of $1 million or more for 1950–55; $3 million or more for 1956–64; $5 million or more for 1965–75; and $10 million or more for 1976–77. In 1978, the classification became Class I, those having more than $50 million gross annual operating revenue; Class II, from $10 million to $50 million; and Class III, less than $10 million. Effective January 1, 1982, the ICC adopted a procedure to adjust the threshold for inflation by restating current revenues in constant 1978 dollars. In 1988, the criteria for Class I and Class II railroads were $92.0 million and $18.4 million, respectively. Also effective January 1, 1982, the ICC adopted a Carrier Classification Index Survey Form for carriers not filing annual report Form R-1 with the commission. Class II and Class III railroads are currently exempted from filing any financial report with the Commission. The form is used for reclassifying carriers.

The Surface Transportation Board (STB) was established pursuant to the ICC Termination Act of 1995, Pub. L. No. 104-88, 109 Stat. 803 (1995) (ICCTA), to assume certain of the regulatory functions that had been administered by the ICC. The Board has broad economic regulatory oversight of railroads, addressing such matters as rate reasonableness, car service and interchange, mergers and line acquisitions, line construction, and line abandonments (49 U.S.C. 10101-11908). Other ICC regulatory functions were either eliminated or transferred to the Federal Highway Administration or the Bureau of Transportation Statistics within DOT.

Class I Railroads are regulated by the STB and subject to the Uniform System of Accounts and required to file annual and periodic reports. Railroads are classified based on their annual operating revenues. The class to which a carrier belongs is determined by comparing its adjusted

U.S. Census Bureau, Statistical Abstract of the United States: 2008

operating revenues for 3 consecutive years to the following scale: Class I, $250 million or more; Class II, $20 million to $250 million; and Class III, $0 to $20 million.

Postal Service—The U.S. Postal Service provides mail processing and delivery services within the United States. The Postal Reorganization Act of 1970 created the Postal Service, effective July 1971, as an independent establishment of the Federal Executive Branch.

Revenue and cost analysis describes the Postal Service's system of attributing revenues and costs to classes of mail and service. This system draws primarily upon probability sampling techniques to develop estimates of revenues, volumes, and weights, as well as costs by class of mail and special service. The costs attributed to classes of mail and special services are primarily incremental costs which vary in response to changes in volume; they account for roughly 60 percent of the total costs of the Postal Service. The balance represents "institutional costs." Statistics on revenues, volume of mail, and distribution of expenditures are presented in the Postal Service's annual report, *Cost and Revenue Analysis,* and its *Annual Report of the Postmaster General* and its annual *Comprehensive Statement on Postal Operations.*

Statistical reliability—For a discussion of statistical collection and estimation, sampling procedures, and measures of statistical reliability applicable to Census Bureau data, see Appendix III.

Table 1032. **Transportation-Related Components of U.S. Gross Domestic Product: 2000 to 2005**

[In billions of dollars (1,089.5 represents $1,089,500,000,000), except percent]

Item	2000	2001	2002	2003	2004	2005
CURRENT DOLLARS						
Total transportation-related final demand [1]	1,089.5	1,103.9	1,106.4	1,138.0	1,212.5	1,323.7
Total gross domestic product (GDP)	9,817.0	10,128.0	10,649.6	10,960.8	11,712.5	12,455.8
Transportation as a percent of GDP	11.1	10.9	10.4	10.4	10.4	10.6
Personal consumption of transportation	853.5	872.3	882.2	921.7	976.1	1,048.8
Motor vehicles and parts	386.5	407.9	429.3	431.7	437.9	448.2
Gasoline and oil	175.7	171.6	164.5	192.7	230.4	280.2
Transportation services	291.3	292.8	288.4	297.3	307.8	320.4
Gross private domestic investment	167.4	148.6	132.8	124.4	148.1	165.1
Transportation structures	6.6	6.9	6.5	6.1	6.5	6.8
Transportation equipment	160.8	141.7	126.3	118.3	141.6	158.3
Net exports of transportation-related goods and service [2]	−109.0	−108.2	−112.1	−125.4	−134.9	−131.0
Exports (+)	179.0	174.3	175.5	174.5	195.5	222.5
Civilian aircraft, engines,and parts	48.1	52.6	50.4	46.7	50.0	60.8
Automotive vehicles, engines, and parts	80.4	75.4	78.9	80.6	89.2	98.6
Passenger fares	20.7	17.9	17.0	15.7	18.9	20.9
Other transportation	29.8	28.4	29.2	31.5	37.4	42.2
Imports (−)	288.0	282.5	287.6	299.9	330.4	353.5
Civilian aircraft, engines,and parts	26.4	31.4	25.5	24.1	24.3	25.8
Automotive vehicles, engines, and parts	195.9	189.8	203.7	210.1	228.2	239.5
Passenger fares	24.3	22.6	20.0	21.0	23.7	26.1
Other transportation	41.4	38.7	38.4	44.7	54.2	62.1
Government transportation-related purchases	177.6	191.2	203.5	217.3	223.2	240.8
Federal purchases [3]	19.2	21.1	26.4	29.6	29.0	30.3
State and local purchases [3]	149.4	160.3	166.6	171.5	177.5	192.4
Defense-related purchases [4]	9.0	9.8	10.5	16.2	16.7	18.1
CHAINED (2000) DOLLARS						
Total transportation-related final demand [1]	1,089.5	1,098.7	1,100.7	1,098.8	1,118.3	1,139.0
Total gross domestic product (GDP)	9,817.0	9,890.7	10,048.8	10,301.0	10,703.5	11,048.6
Transportation as a percent of GDP	11.1	11.1	11.0	10.7	10.4	10.3
Personal consumption of transportation	853.5	872.1	891.1	905.9	920.5	923.2
Motor vehicles and parts	386.5	405.8	429.0	442.1	450.5	452.9
Gasoline and oil	175.7	178.3	181.9	183.2	186.0	185.9
Transportation services	291.3	288.0	280.2	280.6	284.0	284.4
Gross private domestic investment	167.4	149.4	132.1	119.4	134.6	151.3
Transportation structures	6.6	6.6	6.1	5.6	5.8	5.9
Transportation equipment	160.8	142.8	126.0	113.8	128.8	145.4
Net exports of transportation-related goods and service [2]	−109.0	−108.5	−114.5	−126.1	−132.6	−129.9
Exports (+)	179.0	171.6	170.7	164.6	178.9	194.1
Civilian aircraft, engines,and parts	48.1	49.9	46.5	41.5	42.7	49.8
Automotive vehicles, engines, and parts	80.4	75.2	78.3	79.4	87.2	95.2
Passenger fares	20.7	17.8	16.5	13.6	14.8	15.2
Other transportation	29.8	28.7	29.4	30.1	34.2	33.9
Imports (−)	288.0	280.1	285.2	290.7	311.5	324.0
Civilian aircraft, engines,and parts	26.4	30.2	24.2	22.8	22.2	22.7
Automotive vehicles, engines, and parts	195.9	189.9	203.3	208.5	222.7	231.2
Passenger fares	24.3	20.7	17.4	17.9	20.6	21.7
Other transportation	41.4	39.3	40.3	41.5	46.0	48.4
Government transportation-related purchases	177.6	185.7	192.0	199.6	195.8	194.4
Federal purchases [3]	19.2	20.6	25.0	27.1	25.4	25.5
State and local purchases [3]	149.4	155.8	157.3	158.5	156.3	154.2
Defense-related purchases [4]	9.0	9.3	9.7	14.0	14.1	14.7

[1] Sum of total personal consumption of transportation, total gross private domestic investment, net exports of transportation-related goods and services, and total government transportation-related purchases. [2] Sum of exports and imports. [3] Federal purchases and state and local purchases are the sum of consumption expenditures and gross investment. [4] Defense-related purchases are the sum of transportation of material and travel.
Source: U.S. Bureau of Transportation Statistics, *National Transportation Statistics,* annual. See Internet site <http://www.bts.gov/publications/national_transportation_statistics/>.

Table 1033. **Employment in Transportation and Warehousing: 1990 to 2006**

[In thousands (3,476 represents 3,476,000). Annual average of monthly figures. Based on Current Employment Statistics program; see Appendix III]

Industry	2002 NAICS code [1]	1990	1995	2000	2003	2004	2005	2006
Transportation and warehousing	48,49	3,476	3,838	4,410	4,185	4,249	4,361	4,466
Air transportation	481	529	511	614	528	515	501	487
Rail transportation	482	272	233	232	218	226	228	225
Water transportation	483	57	51	56	55	56	61	64
Truck transportation	484	1,122	1,249	1,406	1,326	1,352	1,398	1,437
Transit and ground	485	274	328	372	382	385	389	394
Pipeline transportation	486	60	54	46	40	38	38	39
Scenic and sightseeing	487	16	22	28	27	27	29	27
Support activities	488	364	430	537	520	535	552	571
Couriers and messengers	492	375	517	605	562	557	571	585
Warehousing and storage	493	407	444	514	528	558	595	636

[1] North American Industry Classification System 2002, see text, Sections 12 and 15.
Source: U.S. Bureau of Labor Statistics, the Current Employment Statistics program Internet site <http://www.bls.gov/ces/home.htm>.

U.S. Census Bureau, *Statistical Abstract of the United States: 2008*

Table 1034. **Transportation System Mileage Within the U.S.: 1980 to 2005**

[3,860 represents 3,860,000]

System	1980	1985	1990	1995	2000	2002	2003	2004	2005
Highway (1,000).......	3,860	3,864	3,867	3,912	3,936	3,966	3,974	3,982	3,996
Class 1 rail.........	164,822	145,764	119,758	108,264	99,250	100,125	99,126	97,662	95,830
Amtrak............	24,000	24,000	24,000	24,000	23,000	23,000	22,675	22,256	22,007
Transit:									
Commuter rail [1].....	(NA)	3,574	4,132	4,160	5,209	6,831	6,809	6,875	7,118
Heavy rail [2].......	(NA)	1,293	1,351	1,458	1,558	1,572	1,597	1,596	1,622
Light rail [3]........	(NA)	384	483	568	834	960	996	1,187	1,188
Navigable channels	26,000	26,000	26,000	26,000	26,000	26,000	26,000	26,000	26,000
Oil pipeline [4]........	218,393	213,605	208,752	181,912	176,996	160,990	159,889	159,889	159,512
Gas pipeline [5] (1,000)...	1,052	1,119	1,189	1,278	1,369	1,411	1,424	1,462	1,438

NA Not available. [1] Also called metropolitan rail or regional rail. [2] Also called metro, subway, rapid transit, or rapid rail. [3] Also called streetcar, tramway, or trolley. [4] Includes trunk and gathering lines for crude-oil pipeline. [5] Excludes service pipelines.

Source: U.S. Bureau of Transportation Statistics, *National Transportation Statistics*, annual. See Internet site <http://www.bts.gov/publications/national_transportation_statistics>.

Table 1035. **U.S. Aircraft, Vehicles, and Other Conveyances: 1980 to 2005**

[121,601 represents 121,601,000]

System	1980	1990	1995	2000	2001	2002	2003	2004	2005
Air:									
Air carrier [1].............	3,808	6,083	7,411	8,055	8,497	8,194	8,176	8,186	8,225
General aviation [2] (active fleet).....	211,045	198,000	188,089	217,533	211,446	211,244	209,708	219,426	224,352
Highway, registered vehicles (1,000):									
Passenger car...............	121,601	133,700	128,387	133,621	137,633	135,921	135,670	136,431	136,568
Motorcycle	5,694	4,259	3,897	4,346	4,903	5,004	5,370	5,768	6,227
Van, pick-up, SUV	27,876	48,275	65,738	79,085	84,188	85,011	87,187	91,845	95,337
Truck...................	5,791	6,196	6,719	8,023	7,858	7,927	7,757	8,171	8,482
Bus....................	529	627	686	746	750	761	777	795	807
Transit: [3]									
Motor bus....	59,411	58,714	67,107	75,013	76,075	76,190	77,328	81,033	82,027
Light rail cars [4]............	1,013	913	999	1,577	1,366	1,445	1,482	1,622	1,645
Heavy rail cars [5]	9,641	10,419	10,157	10,591	10,718	10,718	10,754	10,858	11,110
Trolley bus	823	832	885	951	600	600	672	597	615
Commuter rail cars and locomotives..............	4,500	4,415	4,565	5,073	5,124	5,300	5,959	6,228	6,392
Demand response	(X)	16,471	29,352	33,080	34,661	34,699	35,954	37,078	41,958
Other [6]	(NA)	1,197	2,809	5,208	5,727	6,330	6,272	6,566	7,251
Rail:									
Class I, freight cars 1,000)........	1,168	659	583	560	500	478	467	474	475
Class I, locomotive............	28,094	18,835	18,812	20,028	19,745	20,506	20,774	22,015	22,779
Nonclass I freight cars	102,161	103,527	84,724	132,448	125,470	130,590	124,580	120,169	120,195
Car companies' and shippers' freight cars	440,552	449,832	550,717	688,194	688,806	691,329	687,337	693,978	717,211
Amtrak, passenger train car.......	2,128	1,863	1,722	1,894	2,084	2,896	1,623	1,211	1,186
Amtrak, locomotive............	419	318	313	378	401	372	442	276	258
Water:									
Non-self-propelled vessels [7].......	31,662	31,209	31,360	33,152	33,042	32,381	31,335	31,296	32,052
Self-propelled vessels [8].........	7,126	8,236	8,281	8,202	8,546	8,621	8,648	8,994	8,976
Ocean-going steam and motor ships (1,000 gross tons and over)	849	635	512	461	454	443	416	412	357
Recreational boats (1,000)........	8,578	10,997	11,735	12,782	12,876	12,854	12,795	12,781	12,942

NA Not available. X Not applicable. [1] Air carrier aircraft are those carrying passengers or cargo for hire under 14 CFR 121 and 14 CFR 135. [2] Includes air taxi aircraft. [3] 2005 data are preliminary. [4] Fixed rail streetcar or trolley, for example. [5] Metro, subway, or rapid transit, for example. [6] Includes aerial tramway, automated guideway transit, cablecar, ferry boat, inclined plane, monorail, and vanpool. [7] Includes dry-cargo barges, tank barges, and railroad-car floats. [8] Includes dry-cargo and/or passenger, offshore supply vessels, railroad-car ferries, tankers, and towboats.

Source: U.S. Bureau of Transportation Statistics, *National Transportation Statistics*, annual. See Internet site <http://www.bts.gov/publications/national_transportation_statistics/>.

U.S. Census Bureau, Statistical Abstract of the United States: 2008

Table 1036. U.S. Freight Gateways—Value of Shipments: 2005

[In billions of dollars, except as indicated (2,421.7 represents $2,421,700,000,000). For the top 50 gateways ranked by value of shipments. Excludes imports of less than $1,250, exports less than $2,500, and intransit shipments]

Port	Mode	Rank	Total trade	Exports	Imports	Exports as a percent of total
Total U.S. merchandise trade	(X)	(X)	2,421.7	821.8	1,599.9	33.9
Top 50 gateways.	(X)	(X)	2,031.7	712.1	1,319.6	35.1
As a percent of total.	(X)	(X)	83.9	86.7	82.5	(X)
JFK International Airport, NY	Air	1	134.9	59.3	75.6	43.9
Port of Los Angeles, CA	Water	2	134.3	18.4	116.0	13.7
Port of Detroit, MI.	Land	3	130.5	68.8	61.7	52.7
Port of New York, NY and NJ	Water	4	130.4	26.2	104.2	20.1
Port of Long Beach, CA	Water	5	124.6	21.2	103.4	17.0
Port of Laredo, TX	Land	6	93.7	40.9	52.8	43.7
Port of Houston, TX	Water	7	86.1	33.8	52.3	39.3
Chicago, IL.	Air	8	73.4	29.1	44.3	39.7
Los Angeles International Airport, CA.	Air	9	72.9	36.5	36.4	50.1
Port of Buffalo-Niagara Falls, NY.	Land	10	70.5	32.5	38.0	46.2
Port of Huron, MI.	Land	11	68.2	23.6	44.6	34.6
San Francisco International Airport, CA	Air	12	57.2	25.2	32.0	44.0
Port of Charleston, SC	Water	13	52.4	15.9	36.5	30.4
Port of El Paso, TX.	Land	14	43.0	18.9	24.1	43.9
Port of Norfolk Harbor, VA	Water	15	39.6	15.0	24.5	37.9
Port of Baltimore, MD	Water	16	35.6	8.6	27.0	24.0
Dallas-Fort Worth, TX	Air	17	35.1	15.4	19.7	44.0
Port of Seattle, WA.	Water	18	35.0	7.7	27.3	22.0
Anchorage, AK	Air	19	34.7	8.7	26.0	25.1
Port of Tacoma, WA	Water	20	33.8	5.0	28.7	14.9
Port of Savannah, GA.	Water	21	33.4	11.3	22.1	33.7
Port of Oakland, CA	Water	22	32.6	8.9	23.7	27.3
Atlanta, GA.	Air	23	29.9	11.6	18.3	38.7
New Orleans, LA	Air	24	29.7	11.8	17.9	39.9
Miami International Airport, FL	Air	25	27.4	17.8	9.7	64.8
Port of Otay Mesa Station, CA	Land	26	24.4	9.3	15.1	38.0
Cleveland, OH.	Air	27	23.6	15.1	8.6	63.7
Port of Morgan City, LA	Water	28	21.0	0.1	20.9	0.4
Port of New Orleans, LA	Water	29	20.5	8.9	11.6	43.4
Port of Miami, FL	Water	30	19.8	8.4	11.4	42.6
Port of Philadelphia, PA.	Water	31	19.2	1.5	17.7	8.0
Port of Champlain-Rouses Pt., NY.	Land	32	18.3	6.7	11.6	36.7
Port of Hidalgo, TX.	Land	33	18.3	7.6	10.7	41.6
Port of Beaumont, TX	Water	34	17.0	1.2	15.8	7.1
Port of Jacksonville, FL.	Water	35	16.2	6.1	10.1	37.8
Port of Blaine, WA	Land	36	15.6	7.3	8.4	46.4
Newark, NJ	Air	37	15.5	3.4	12.1	21.8
Port of Corpus Christi, TX	Water	38	15.5	2.2	13.3	14.2
Port of South Louisiana, LA	Water	39	15.3	5.5	9.9	35.7
Port of Port Everglades, FL	Water	40	15.3	6.0	9.3	39.2
Port of Nogales, AZ	Land	41	14.1	5.0	9.1	35.6
Boston Logan Airport, MA	Air	42	13.6	8.0	5.6	59.0
Port of Pembina, ND.	Land	43	12.7	7.2	5.5	56.4
Port of Alexandria Bay, NY.	Land	44	11.8	4.6	7.3	38.6
Port of Portland, OR	Water	45	11.5	2.2	9.3	18.9
Port of Brownsville-Cameron, TX.	Land	46	11.4	6.3	5.1	55.1
Port of Texas City, TX	Water	47	10.8	1.6	9.2	14.9
Port of Calexico-East, CA	Land	48	10.8	4.7	6.0	43.7
San Juan International Airport, PR.	Air	49	10.4	6.1	4.3	58.9
Port of Sweetgrass, MT.	Land	50	10.1	5.0	5.1	49.7

X Not applicable.

Source: U.S. Bureau of Transportation Statistics, *National Transportation Statistics*, annual. See Internet site <http://www.bts.gov/publications/national_transportation_statistics/>.

Transportation 665

Table 1037. **Transportation and Warehousing—Establishments, Revenue, Payroll, and Employees by Industry: 2002**

[382,152 represents $382,152,000,000. For establishments with payroll. Based on the 2002 Economic Censuses; See Appendix III]

Kind of business	2002 NAICS code [1]	Number of establishments	Revenue (mil. dol.)	Annual payroll (mil. dol.)	Paid employees (1,000)
Transportation and warehousing	48–49	199,618	382,152	115,989	3,650.9
Air transportation [2]	481	3,847	19,735	3,805	99.1
Scheduled air transportation [2]	4811	1,665	12,157	2,281	67.1
Nonscheduled air transportation	4812	2,182	7,578	1,524	32.0
Water transportation	483	1,890	23,331	3,194	66.2
Deep sea, coastal, and Great Lakes water transportation	4831	1,314	19,788	2,329	47.9
Truck transportation	484	112,642	164,219	47,750	1,435.2
General freight trucking	4841	59,011	110,239	34,121	989.2
Specialized freight trucking	4842	53,631	53,980	13,630	446.0
Transit and ground passenger transportation [3]	485	17,260	18,850	7,675	398.4
Urban transit systems	4851	1,025	2,808	1,694	53.6
Taxi and limousine service	4853	6,988	4,248	1,185	66.1
School and employee bus transportation	4854	4,515	5,928	2,610	174.7
Charter bus industry	4855	1,249	1,762	565	29.3
Pipeline transportation [3]	486	2,188	22,031	2,477	36.8
Pipeline transportation of crude oil	4861	252	3,402	485	6.5
Pipeline transportation of natural gas	4862	1,431	14,797	1,575	23.7
Scenic and sightseeing transportation	487	2,523	1,859	526	22.5
Support activities for transportation [3]	488	33,942	57,414	16,202	465.6
Support activities for air transportation	4881	4,976	12,181	3,746	129.6
Support activities for water transportation	4883	2,366	8,812	2,604	64.0
Support activities for road transportation	4884	7,927	4,003	1,356	56.0
Freight transportation arrangement	4885	16,504	27,656	6,868	168.6
Couriers and messengers	492	12,655	58,165	17,175	561.5
Couriers	4921	7,382	54,821	16,180	514.9
Local messengers and local delivery	4922	5,273	3,344	995	46.6
Warehousing and storage	493	12,671	16,548	17,183	565.5

[1] North American Industry Classification System, 2002; see text, Section 15. [2] Excludes large certificated passenger carriers that do not report to the Office of Airline Information, U.S. Department of Transportation. [3] Includes other industries, not shown separately.

Source: U.S. Census Bureau, "2002 Economic Census, Geographic Area Series Reports, Transportation and Warehousing," Series EC02-48A-US, issued August 2005. See Internet site <http://www.census.gov/econ/census02/guide/geosumm.htm>.

Table 1038. **U. S. Scheduled Airline Industry—Summary: 1995 to 2006**

[For calendar years or Dec. 31 (547.8 represents 547,800,000). For domestic and international operations. Covers carriers certificated under Section 401 of the Federal Aviation Act. Minus sign (-) indicates loss]

Item	Unit	1995	2000	2001 [1]	2002 [1]	2003 [2]	2004	2005	2006
SCHEDULED SERVICE									
Revenue passengers enplaned	Mil.	547.8	666.2	622.1	612.9	646.3	702.9	738.6	744.6
Revenue passenger miles	Bil.	540.7	692.8	651.7	641.1	656.9	733.6	779.0	797.4
Available seat miles	Bil.	807.1	957.0	930.5	892.6	893.8	971.4	1,003.3	1,006.4
Revenue passenger load factor	Percent	67.0	72.4	70.0	71.8	73.5	75.5	77.6	79.2
Mean passenger trip length [3]	Miles	987	1,040	1,048	1,046	1,016	1,044	1,055	1,071
Cargo ton miles	Mil.	16,921	23,888	22,003	24,591	26,735	27,978	28,036	29,283
Aircraft departures	1,000	8,062	9,035	8,788	9,187	10,839	11,398	11,562	11,268
FINANCES [4]									
Total operating revenue [5]	Mil. dol.	95,117	130,839	115,526	106,985	117,920	134,300	151,255	163,824
Passenger revenue	Mil. dol.	69,835	93,622	80,947	73,577	77,379	85,669	93,500	101,208
Cargo revenue	Mil. dol.	9,882	14,456	14,129	13,525	15,003	17,146	20,704	22,544
Charter revenue	Mil. dol.	3,742	4,913	4,449	4,225	5,589	5,503	6,074	5,562
Total operating expense	Mil. dol.	89,266	123,840	125,852	115,552	120,028	135,782	150,828	156,279
Operating profit (or loss)	Mil. dol.	5,852	6,999	-10,326	-8,566	-2,108	-1,491	427	7,545
Interest income (or expense)	Mil. dol.	-2,426	-2,193	-2,506	-3,263	-3,442	-3,715	-4,209	-4,147
Net profit (or loss)	Mil. dol.	2,283	2,486	-8,275	-11,008	-2,371	-7,643	-5,782	3,045
Revenue per passenger mile	Cents	12.9	13.5	12.4	11.5	11.8	11.7	12.0	12.7
Operating profit margin	Percent	6.2	5.3	-8.9	-8.0	-1.8	-1.1	0.3	4.6
Net profit margin	Percent	2.4	1.9	-7.2	-10.3	-2.0	-5.7	-3.8	1.9
EMPLOYEES [6]									
Total	1,000	547.0	680.0	672.0	601.4	569.8	569.5	562.5	544.5
Pilots and copilots	1,000	55.4	72.4	73.8	68.8	67.8	82.0	74.5	69.2

[1] Includes cash compensation remitted to carriers under the Air Transportation Safety and System Stabilization Act (P.L. 107–42). [2] Includes security costs reimbursements remitted to carriers under the Emergency Wartime Supplemental Appropriations Act (P.L. 108–11). [3] For definition of mean, see Guide to Tabular Presentation. [4] 2006 data are preliminary. [5] Includes other types of revenues, not shown separately. [6] Average full-time equivalents.

Source: Air Transport Association of America, Washington, DC, Air Transport Annual Report.

Table 1039. **Transportation and Warehousing—Establishments, Employees, and Payroll by Kind of Business (NAICS Basis): 2000 and 2004**

[3,790.0 represents 3,790,000. Covers establishments with payroll. Employees are for the week including March 12. Excludes most government employees, railroad employees, and self-employed persons. For statement on methodology, see Appendix III. County Business Patterns excludes rail transportation (NAICS 482) and the National Postal Service (NAICS 491)]

Industry	2002 NAICS code [1]	Establishments		Paid employees [2] (1,000)		Annual payroll (mil. dol.)	
		2000	2004	2000	2004	2000	2004
Transportation & warehousing	48–49	190,044	206,878	3,790.8	4,098.9	125,592.4	148,244.6
Air transportation	481	5,429	5,722	615.6	489.1	26,569.3	24,867.7
Scheduled air transportation	4811	3,324	3,309	570.9	450.0	24,484.5	22,891.8
Scheduled passenger air transportation . .	481111	2,740	2,794	536.2	428.0	23,470.7	22,138.7
Scheduled freight air transportation	481112	584	515	34.7	22.1	1,013.8	753.2
Nonscheduled air transportation	4812	2,105	2,413	44.7	39.0	2,084.8	1,975.8
Water transportation	483	1,900	1,854	67.6	66.8	3,003.2	3,565.0
Deep sea, coastal, & Great Lakes water transportation	4831	1,254	1,231	47.8	47.2	2,214.2	2,659.9
Inland water transportation	4832	646	623	19.7	19.6	789.0	905.1
Inland water freight transportation	483211	402	360	16.3	13.6	673.9	673.1
Inland water passenger transportation . . .	483212	244	263	3.5	6.1	115.1	232.0
Truck transportation	484	110,416	113,926	1,415.8	1,428.5	46,451.5	50,792.6
General freight trucking	4841	55,874	62,335	922.7	982.1	31,614.0	35,847.7
General freight trucking, local.	48411	20,329	24,760	153.3	187.6	4,529.8	6,226.5
General freight trucking, long distance. . . .	48412	35,545	37,575	769.5	794.5	27,084.2	29,621.2
Specialized freight trucking	4842	54,542	51,591	493.1	446.3	14,837.5	14,944.9
Used household & office goods moving . . .	48421	9,147	8,516	128.9	108.7	3,661.4	3,325.0
Specialized freight (except used goods) trucking, local	48422	32,493	31,485	200.4	194.2	5,692.4	6,373.4
Specialized freight (except used goods) trucking, long-distance	48423	12,902	11,590	163.7	143.4	5,483.7	5,246.5
Transit & ground passenger transportation	485	16,383	17,132	386.9	401.0	7,214.7	8,044.6
Urban transit systems	4851	705	919	43.1	46.2	1,295.8	1,424.3
Mixed mode systems	485111	152	53	6.2	1.7	146.9	43.3
Commuter rail.	485112	15	18	(D)	0.4	(D)	12.1
Bus and other motor vehicle mode systems	485113	505	809	31.4	43.1	925.1	1,335.9
Other	485119	33	39	(D)	1.1	(D)	33.0
Interurban & rural bus transportation	4852	444	491	26.8	18.3	709.7	495.0
Taxi & limousine service.	4853	6,806	6,960	67.8	65.6	1,244.3	1,327.0
Taxi service	48531	3,116	3,025	30.4	29.3	485.2	547.4
Limousine service	48532	3,690	3,935	37.5	36.4	759.1	779.6
School & employee bus transportation . . .	4854	4,217	4,353	162.9	183.5	2,322.6	2,961.0
Charter bus industry	4855	1,451	1,265	34.1	29.9	668.7	658.5
Other transit & ground passenger transportation	4859	2,760	3,144	52.2	57.6	973.6	1,178.8
Special needs transportation	485991	1,914	2,102	34.8	43.4	648.9	904.4
Pipeline transportation.	486	2,802	2,597	53.0	39.6	3,828.6	2,996.9
Pipeline transportation of crude oil	4861	307	307	6.7	7.1	425.6	643.2
Pipeline transportation of natural gas	4862	1,938	1,595	39.2	24.8	2,961.1	1,800.2
Other pipeline transportation	4869	557	695	7.0	7.7	441.9	553.4
Scenic & sightseeing transportation	487	2,254	2,651	23.6	22.1	583.5	623.5
Scenic & sightseeing transportation, land . .	4871	454	639	8.7	8.7	192.8	215.2
Scenic & sightseeing transportation, water. .	4872	1,642	1,841	13.0	11.3	331.2	335.3
Scenic & sightseeing transportation, other . . .	4879	158	171	2.0	2.0	59.5	73.1
Support activities for transportation	488	31,440	35,486	472.4	526.9	16,507.0	20,631.0
Support activities for air transportation	4881	4,368	5,116	126.7	145.4	3,634.0	4,949.8
Airport operations	48811	1,834	1,597	67.9	65.9	1,569.5	1,571.5
Air traffic control.	488111	137	165	0.8	1.8	29.9	84.8
Other support activities for air transportation	48819	2,534	3,519	58.8	79.5	2,064.6	3,378.3
Support activities for rail transportation	4882	821	908	21.4	26.0	714.4	964.5
Support activities for water transportation	4883	2,543	2,389	81.6	89.9	3,250.7	4,341.9
Port and harbor operations	48831	196	234	7.4	6.9	265.8	300.7
Marine cargo handling	48832	607	551	53.5	58.6	2,194.7	2,899.7
Navigational services to shipping	48833	863	804	11.8	11.9	478.7	591.5
Other	48839	877	800	8.9	12.5	311.5	550.0
Support activities for road transportation	4884	7,010	8,922	56.2	67.1	1,308.8	1,760.8
Motor vehicle towing	48841	6,078	7,390	41.8	50.0	961.7	1,313.0
Freight transportation arrangement.	4885	15,177	16,597	161.7	174.9	6,620.3	7,779.1
Other support activities for transportation . . .	4889	1,521	1,554	24.7	23.6	978.6	834.8
Couriers & messengers.	492	12,297	14,195	619.3	549.8	17,399.4	17,113.9
Couriers	4921	6,667	9,000	548.9	501.6	15,890.5	16,013.9
Local messengers & local delivery	4922	5,630	5,195	70.5	48.2	1,508.9	1,100.1
Warehousing & storage	493	7,123	13,315	135.9	575.2	4,035.3	19,609.4

D Figure withheld to avoid disclosure pertaining to individual companies.   [1] Based on the North American Industry Classification System (NAICS), 2002; see text, Section 15.   [2] For employees on the payroll for the pay period including March 12.

Source: U.S. Census Bureau, "County Business Patterns." See <http://www.census.gov/epcd/cbp/view/cbpview.html>.

U.S. Census Bureau, Statistical Abstract of the United States: 2008

Table 1040. Transportation Accidents, Deaths, and Injuries: 1980 to 2005

[6,216 represents 6,216,000]

Mode	Accidents 1980	1990	1995	2000	2005	Deaths 1980	1990	1995	2000	2005	Injuries 1980	1990	1995	2000	2005
Transit type:															
Land:															
Highway crashes(1,000) [1]	6,216	6,471	6,699	6,394	6,159	51.1	44.6	41.8	41.9	43.4	2,848	3,231	3,465	3,189	2,699
Passenger car occupants	(NA)	5,561	5,594	4,926	(NA)	27.4	24.1	22.4	20.7	18.4	(NA)	2,376	2,469	2,052	1,573
Motorcyclists	(NA)	103	66	69	(NA)	5.1	3.2	2.2	2.9	4.6	(NA)	84	57	58	87
Light truck occupants	(NA)	2,152	2,750	3,208	(NA)	7.5	8.6	9.6	11.5	13.0	(NA)	505	722	887	872
Large truck occupants	(NA)	372	363	438	(NA)	1.3	0.7	0.6	0.8	0.8	(NA)	42	30	31	27
Bus occupants	(NA)	60	59	56	(NA)	(Z)	(Z)	(Z)	(Z)	0.1	(NA)	33	19	18	11
Pedestrians	(NA)	(NA)	(NA)	(NA)	(NA)	8.1	6.5	5.6	4.8	4.9	(NA)	105	86	78	64
Pedacyclists	(NA)	(NA)	(NA)	(NA)	(NA)	1.0	0.9	0.8	0.7	0.8	(NA)	75	67	51	45
Other	(NA)	(NA)	(NA)	(NA)	(NA)	0.7	0.6	0.5	0.6	0.9	(NA)	11	14	15	18
Railroad [2]	18,817	8,594	7,092	6,485	6,294	1,417	1,297	1,146	937	885	62,246	25,143	14,440	11,643	9,231
Highway-rail grade crossing	10,612	5,715	4,633	3,502	3,052	833	698	579	425	357	3,550	2,407	1,894	1,219	1,012
Railroad [2]	8,205	2,879	2,459	2,983	3,242	584	599	567	512	528	58,696	22,736	12,546	10,424	8,219
Rapid rail transit [3]	6,789	12,178	14,327	12,782	(NA)	83	117	79	80	(NA)	6,801	10,036	11,238	10,848	(NA)
Air:															
Air carrier [4]	19	24	36	56	40	1	39	168	92	22	19	29	25	29	13
Commuter [5]	38	15	12	12	6	37	6	9	5	-	14	11	17	7	'
On-demand [6]	171	107	75	80	66	105	51	52	71	18	43	36	14	12	23
General aviation	3,590	2,242	2,056	1,837	1,669	1,239	770	735	596	563	681	409	396	309	270
Water:															
Recreational [7]	5,513	6,411	8,019	7,740	4,969	1,360	865	829	701	697	2,650	3,822	4,141	4,355	3,451
Waterborne (vessel related) [8]	4,624	3,613	5,349	5,403	(NA)	206	85	53	53	(NA)	180	175	154	150	(NA)
Pipeline: [9]															
Gas	1,524	198	161	234	(NA)	15	6	18	37	14	177	69	53	77	45
Hazard liquid	246	180	188	146	(NA)	4	3	3	1	2	15	7	11	4	2
Other transit [10]	(NA)	77,985	48,144	47,116	(NA)	(NA)	222	195	215	(NA)	(NA)	44,520	45,958	45,849	(NA)
Hazardous materials [11]	15,719	8,879	14,853	17,557	(NA)	19	8	7	16	(NA)	626	423	400	251	(NA)

NA Not available. Z Less than 50. [1] Data on deaths are from U.S. National Highway Traffic Safety Administration and are based on deaths within 30 days of the accident. Includes only police reported crashes. For more details, see Table 1079. [2] Accidents which result in damages to railroad property. Grade crossing accidents are also included when classified as a train accident. Deaths exclude fatalities in railroad-highway grade crossing accidents. [3] Reporting criteria and source of data changed between 1989 and 1990; these data from 1990 to present are not comparable to earlier years. [4] See footnote 1, Table 1045. Injuries classified as serious. [5] See footnote 2, Table 1045. Injuries classified as serious. [6] See footnote 3, Table 1045. Injuries classified as serious. [7] Accidents resulting in death, injury, or requiring medical treatment beyond first aid; damages exceeding $500; or a person's disappearance. [8] Covers accidents involving commercial vessels which must be reported to U.S. Coast Guard if there is property damage exceeding $25,000; material damage affecting the seaworthiness or efficiency of a vessel; stranding or grounding; loss of life; or injury causing a person's incapacity for more than 3 days. [9] Beginning 1985, pipeline accidents/incidents are credited to year of occurrence; prior data are credited to the year filed. [10] Other transit includes bus, light rail, commuter rail, demand response, van pool, and automated guideway. Excludes cable car, inclined plane, jitney, and ferry boat. [11] Incidents, deaths, and injuries involving hazardous materials cover all types of transport; excludes pipelines and bulk, nonpackaged water incidents.

Source: U.S. Bureau of Transportation Statistics, *National Transportation Statistics*, annual. See Internet site <http://www.bts.gov/publications/national_transportation_statistics/>.

Table 1041. Airline Cost Indexes: 1980 to 2006

[2000 = 100. Covers U.S. major and national passenger carriers. Major carriers have operating revenues of $1 billion or more; nationals have operating revenues from $100 million to $1 billion]

Index	1980	1985	1990	1995	2000	2001	2002	2003	2004	2005	2006
Composite index [1]	81.5	91.5	103.3	99.5	100.0	106.5	106.8	112.0	125.2	150.6	176.1
Labor costs	84.7	109.6	119.9	150.0	100.0	110.0	118.2	121.0	119.6	113.0	114.2
Fuel	123.4	122.0	101.9	71.1	100.0	91.9	93.9	113.7	151.1	215.0	262.9
Aircraft ownership [2]	25.8	39.0	58.2	72.0	100.0	94.7	90.6	77.8	88.9	85.4	80.9
Nonaircraft ownership	37.8	52.8	88.8	104.0	100.0	140.0	112.0	112.9	105.0	102.3	102.4
Professional services	28.8	46.7	68.3	86.9	100.0	103.2	96.4	96.5	97.1	105.4	110.1
Food and beverage	91.4	97.3	125.9	107.6	100.0	92.2	86.8	72.7	67.3	62.6	59.1
Landing fees	55.6	60.9	83.2	97.7	100.0	111.7	117.1	108.7	118.6	126.1	134.7
Maintenance material	65.1	76.6	115.3	91.2	100.0	94.7	72.8	57.5	57.6	54.3	58.7
Aircraft insurance	221.8	357.6	117.1	264.7	100.0	117.0	218.3	151.2	149.0	125.0	127.7
Nonaircraft insurance	71.1	124.5	70.4	229.4	100.0	169.8	540.0	423.9	352.2	307.4	245.2
Passenger commissions	121.8	171.5	226.7	184.8	100.0	86.6	57.9	42.7	38.0	33.1	30.5
Communication	53.3	74.6	86.9	88.2	100.0	110.9	101.4	85.1	77.3	74.4	70.7
Advertising and promotion	117.4	160.0	165.8	108.5	100.0	85.4	74.3	68.2	77.1	75.5	81.8
Utilities and office supplies	65.8	84.0	94.2	84.6	100.0	108.0	90.1	78.8	78.4	81.8	88.7
Transportation-related expenses	(NA)	(NA)	45.4	47.8	100.0	111.5	107.0	202.2	285.4	379.5	411.3
Other operating expenses	85.5	86.2	101.9	93.9	100.0	99.9	112.9	91.6	96.1	111.6	99.7
Interest [3]	153.1	171.5	170.6	165.3	100.0	96.8	87.9	91.6	91.5	124.8	121.6

NA Not available. [1] Weighted average of all components, including interest. [2] Includes lease, aircraft and engine rentals, depreciation, and amortization. [3] Interest on long-term debt and capital and other interest expense

Source: Air Transport Association of America, Washington, DC, *Airline Cost Index, Major and National Carriers, First Quarter 2007.* See Internet site <http://www.airlines.org/economics/> (accessed 17 July 2007).

Table 1042. Top 40 Airports in 2005—Passengers Enplaned: 1995 and 2005

[In thousands (558,593 represents 558,593,000), except rank. For calendar year. Airports ranked by total passengers enplaned by large certificated air carriers on scheduled and nonscheduled operations, 2005]

Airport	1995 Total	Rank	2005 Total	Rank	Airport	1995 Total	Rank	2005 Total	Rank
All airports	558,593	(X)	701,509	(X)	Greater Cincinnati, OH	5,943	30	11,238	22
Total, top 40.	399,293	(X)	533,901	(X)	Salt Lake City Intl, UT.....	8,223	23	10,592	23
Atlanta, GA (Hartsfield Intl)..	27,509	2	41,596	1	Fort Lauderdale-Hollywood Intl, FL....	4,059	12	10,242	24
Chicago, IL (O'Hare Intl)	29,689	1	34,529	2	Baltimore, MD (BWI Intl) ...	5,649	28	9,592	25
Dallas-Ft. Worth Intl, TX	25,636	3	27,741	3	Tampa Intl, FL.........	4,942	27	9,137	26
Los Angeles, Intl, CA	20,965	4	22,939	4	San Diego, CA (Lindbergh Field)	6,317	22	8,568	27
Las Vegas, NV (McCarran Intl)	11,322	17	20,697	5	Washington, DC (Ronald Reagan Washington National)..	6,884	25	8,522	28
Denver, Intl, CO........	14,210	6	20,485	6	Chicago, IL (Midway)	4,148	33	8,381	29
Phoenix Sky Harbor Intl, AZ.	13,517	7	20,110	7	Honolulu Intl, HI.........	8,518	35	8,302	30
Houston, Intercontinental, TX	10,904	10	18,409	8	Metropolitan Oakland Intl, CA..............	4,738	26	6,935	31
Minneapolis-St. Paul Intl, MN	11,397	32	17,906	9	St. Louis, MO (Lambert-St. Louis Intl)	12,634	31	6,825	32
Detroit, MI (Wayne County) .	12,883	19	17,389	10	Portland Intl, OR	5,441	21	6,670	33
Orlando Intl, FL	8,863	13	15,629	11	Memphis Intl, TN	3,750	39	5,630	34
Philadelphia Intl, PA	7,940	9	15,005	12	Cleveland, OH (Cleveland-Hopkins Intl)	4,960	36	5,513	35
Newark Intl, NJ	11,614	5	14,880	13	San Juan, PR (Luis Munoz Marin Intl)	4,412	37	5,234	36
New York, NY (JFK Intl)....	9,239	8	14,495	14	San Jose Intl, CA........	4,265	29	5,234	37
Charlotte-Douglas Intl, NC .	9,579	16	13,936	15	Pittsburgh Intl, PA.......	9,132	24	5,183	38
Seattle-Tacoma Intl, WA ...	10,691	20	13,924	16	Kansas City Intl, MO......	4,500	46	5,052	39
San Francisco Intl, CA	14,916	18	13,829	17	Sacramento Intl, CA	3,195	45	5,049	40
New York, NY (La Guardia) .	9,665	15	12,512	18					
Miami Intl, FL	12,023	14	12,334	19					
Boston, MA (Logan Intl)	10,462	38	11,901	20					
Washington, DC (Dulles Intl)	4,560	11	11,756	21					

X Not applicable.

Source: U.S. Bureau of Transportation Statisics, Office of Airline Information, BTS Form 41, Schedule T-3, unpublished data.

Table 1043. Domestic Airline Markets: 2006

[In thousands (3,783 represents 3,783,000). For calendar year. Data are for the 25 top markets and include all commercial airports in each metro area. Data represent origin and final destination of travel]

Market	Passengers	Market	Passengers
Fort Lauderdale to—from New York........	3,783	Chicago to—from Las Vegas	1,617
New York to—from Orlando	3,576	New York to—from San Juan	1,589
Chicago to—from New York	3,292	Dallas/Fort Worth to—from Houston	1,580
Atlanta to—from New York	2,654	Chicago to—from Los Angeles	1,565
Los Angeles to—from New York	2,642	Dallas/Fort Worth to—from New York	1,459
New York to—from West Palm Beach	1,980	Chicago to—from Orlando	1,438
Boston to—from New York............	1,867	Chicago to—from Phoenix	1,386
Las Vegas to—from New York	1,786	Chicago to—from Washington	1,345
New York to—from Tampa	1,776	Las Vegas to—from Los Angeles	1,330
New York to—from San Francisco	1,767	Atlanta to—from Washington	1,289
Miami to—from New York	1,735	Orlando to—from Philadelphia	1,262
Honolulu to—from Kahului...........	1,677	Chicago to—from Dallas/Fort Worth	1,261
New York to—from Washington	1,672		

Source: Air Transport Association of America, Washington, DC, *Annual Report.*

Table 1044. **Worldwide Airline Fatalities: 1987 to 2006**

[For scheduled air transport operations. Excludes accidents due to acts of unlawful interference]

Year	Fatal accidents	Passenger deaths	Death rate [1]	Year	Fatal accidents	Passenger deaths	Death rate [1]
1987	25	900	0.06	1997	25	921	0.04
1988	29	742	0.04	1998	20	904	0.03
1989	29	879	0.05	1999	21	499	0.02
1990	27	544	0.03	2000	18	757	0.03
1991	29	638	0.03	2001	13	577	0.02
1992	28	1,070	0.06	2002	14	791	0.03
1993	33	864	0.04	2003	7	466	0.02
1994	27	1,170	0.05	2004	9	203	0.01
1995	25	711	0.03	2005	17	712	0.02
1996	24	1,146	0.05	2006	23	755	0.02

[1] Rate per 100 million passenger kilometers flown.

Source: International Civil Aviation Organization, Montreal, Canada, *Civil Aviation Statistics of the World*, annual.

Table 1045. **Aircraft Accidents: 1990 to 2006**

[For years ending December 31]

Item	Unit	1990	1995	2000	2003	2004	2005	2006, prel.
Air carrier accidents, all services [1]	Number...	24	36	56	54	30	40	31
Fatal accidents.................	Number...	6	3	3	2	2	3	2
Fatalities	Number...	39	168	92	22	14	22	50
Aboard...................	Number...	12	162	92	21	14	20	49
Rates per 100,000 flight hours:								
Accidents..................	Rate.....	0.198	0.267	0.306	0.309	0.159	0.206	0.158
Fatal accidents	Rate.....	0.049	0.022	0.016	0.011	0.011	0.015	0.010
Commuter air carrier accidents [2]	Number...	15	12	12	2	4	6	3
Fatal accidents.................	Number...	3	2	1	1	–	–	1
Fatalities	Number...	6	9	5	2	–	–	2
Aboard...................	Number...	4	9	5	2	–	–	2
Rates per 100,000 flight hours:								
Accidents..................	Rate.....	0.641	0.457	3.247	0.627	1.324	2.034	1.071
Fatal accidents	Rate.....	0.128	0.076	0.271	0.313	–	–	0.357
On-demand air taxi accidents [3]	Number...	107	75	80	73	66	66	54
Fatal accidents.................	Number...	29	24	22	18	23	11	10
Fatalities	Number...	51	52	71	42	64	18	16
Aboard...................	Number...	49	52	68	40	63	16	16
Rates per 100,000 flight hours:								
Accidents..................	Rate.....	4.76	3.02	2.04	2.49	2.04	1.73	1.50
Fatal accidents	Rate.....	1.29	0.97	0.56	0.61	0.71	0.29	0.28
General aviation accidents [4]	Number...	2,242	2,056	1,837	1,740	1,619	1,669	1,515
Fatal accidents.................	Number...	444	413	345	352	314	321	303
Fatalities	Number...	770	735	596	633	559	563	698
Aboard...................	Number...	765	728	585	630	559	558	538
Rates per 100,000 flight hours:								
Accidents..................	Rate.....	7.85	8.21	6.57	6.68	6.49	7.20	6.64
Fatal accidents	Rate.....	1.55	1.63	1.21	1.34	1.26	1.38	1.32

– Represents zero.   [1] U.S. air carriers operating under 14 CFR 121. Beginning 2000, includes aircraft with 10 or more seats, previously operating under 14 CFR 135.   [2] All scheduled service of U.S. air carriers operating under 14 CFR 135. Beginning 2000, only aircraft with fewer than 10 seats.   [3] All nonscheduled service of U.S. air carriers operating under 14 CFR 135.   [4] U.S. civil registered aircraft not operated under 14 CFR 121 or 135. Data from 2006 include 154 deaths aboard a foreign registed aircraft when it collided with a business general aviation aircraft over the Brazilian Amazon jungle. There were no fatalities in the general aviation aircraft.

Source: U.S. National Transportation Safety Board, "Aviation Accident Statistics," Internet site <http://www.ntsb.gov/aviation /stats.htm> (accessed 11 July 2007).

Table 1046. **U.S. Carrier Delays, Cancellations, and Diversions: 1995 to 2005**

[In thousands (5,327.4 represents 5,327,400). For calendar year. See headnote, table 1047]

Item	1995	1997	1998	1999	2000	2001	2002	2003	2004	2005
Total operations...	5,327.4	5,411.8	5,384.7	5,527.9	5,683.0	5,967.8	5,271.4	6,488.5	7,129.3	7,140.6
Delays:										
Late departures [1]	827.9	846.9	870.4	937.3	1,131.7	953.8	717.4	834.4	1,187.6	1,279.4
Late arrivals [2]	1,039.3	1,083.8	1,070.1	1,152.7	1,356.0	1,104.4	868.2	1,057.8	1,421.4	1,466.1
Cancellations [3]	91.9	97.8	144.5	154.3	187.5	231.2	65.1	101.5	127.8	133.7
Diversions [4]	10.5	12.1	13.2	13.6	14.3	12.9	8.4	11.4	13.8	14.0

[1] Late departures comprise flights departing 15 minutes or more after the scheduled departure time.   [2] Late arrivals comprise flights arriving 15 minutes or more after the scheduled arrival time.   [3] A cancelled flight is one that was not operated, but was listed in a carrier's computer reservation system within seven days of the scheduled departure.   [4] A diverted flight is one that left from the scheduled departure airport but flew to a destination point other than the scheduled destination point.

Source: U.S. Bureau of Transportation Statistics, *National Transportation Statistics*, annual. See also Internet site <http://www.bts.gov/programs/airline_information/annual_airline_on_time_performance>.

670 Transportation

[In percent. Quarterly, based on gate arrival and departure times for domestic scheduled operations of U.S. major airlines. All U.S. airlines with 1 percent or more of total U.S. domestic scheduled airline passenger revenues are required to report on-time data. A flight is considered on time if it operated less than 15 minutes after the scheduled time shown in the carrier's computerized reservation system. See source for data on individual airlines]

Airport	On-time arrivals				On-time departures			
	1st qtr.	2d qtr.	3d qtr.	4th qtr.	1st qtr.	2d qtr.	3d qtr.	4th qtr.
Total major airports	77.0	76.7	75.6	73.7	79.0	78.5	77.7	76.8
Atlanta, Hartsfield...	73.9	75.5	68.0	70.4	76.0	74.3	66.2	70.2
Boston, Logan International	75.6	66.8	71.9	72.8	80.5	74.8	76.5	77.9
Baltimore/Washington International	82.6	77.7	79.0	80.8	80.3	75.9	78.2	80.3
Charlotte, Douglas	81.2	76.1	74.3	73.0	81.8	75.8	76.5	75.7
Cincinnati, Greater Cincinnati	86.4	84.7	82.0	78.9	87.6	87.0	84.2	78.4
Washington, Reagan National..........	80.6	76.4	74.9	73.4	84.9	81.7	81.0	80.2
Denver International................	77.5	81.7	80.4	75.0	75.3	80.3	79.7	76.6
Dallas-Fort Worth International	79.6	78.8	79.8	76.8	77.5	74.2	76.7	75.1
Detroit, Metro Wayne County	80.6	79.6	76.1	69.4	79.6	79.6	78.2	73.4
Newark International.................	63.5	63.0	64.5	59.3	74.6	71.8	70.1	71.1
Fort Lauderdale-Hollywood International. . .	80.2	79.3	75.8	74.7	80.4	81.3	81.7	79.0
Washington/Dulles	78.7	75.7	73.6	74.6	77.9	74.3	71.9	75.2
Houston, George Bush	77.4	76.0	80.8	76.5	80.5	77.0	81.9	79.7
New York, JFK International	72.7	73.7	67.3	65.2	77.6	81.1	71.9	71.2
Las Vegas, McCarran International	75.2	77.6	77.3	75.7	74.1	75.5	76.1	75.3
Los Angeles International.............	76.4	78.7	76.3	75.3	79.7	81.9	81.0	79.2
New York, La Guardia................	66.2	64.5	64.9	61.0	76.5	74.4	74.6	73.5
Orlando International	81.7	79.9	78.6	79.4	81.9	80.9	79.8	81.5
Chicago, Midway	81.1	75.3	77.3	78.3	74.7	68.5	72.0	73.6
Miami International..................	79.2	77.2	71.8	76.7	80.0	79.2	73.8	79.9
Minneapolis-St. Paul International	80.0	83.3	79.9	75.6	81.5	84.6	80.9	78.0
Oakland International	75.3	79.1	80.9	77.9	76.6	79.1	81.0	76.3
Chicago, O'Hare	70.7	70.4	68.5	63.3	70.2	70.7	68.6	66.0
Portland International	75.3	79.7	79.6	74.3	83.3	86.3	86.1	82.1
Philadelphia International.............	75.0	70.6	68.1	68.0	75.9	71.3	69.5	72.0
Phoenix, Sky Harbor International	80.5	81.3	80.3	78.9	79.4	79.2	79.2	79.2
San Diego, Lindbergh Field	76.4	79.0	78.8	77.5	80.9	83.1	83.8	81.8
Seattle-Tacoma International	72.6	77.9	74.6	70.1	78.5	81.8	78.2	75.3
San Francisco International	66.2	71.6	74.3	69.2	72.5	77.0	79.1	74.3
Salt Lake City International	78.9	86.3	85.4	80.4	83.3	88.3	87.2	83.7
St. Louis, Lambert	82.5	77.2	77.8	76.8	83.1	78.1	80.3	78.7
Tampa, Tampa International	79.9	78.9	76.6	79.2	82.5	82.2	81.1	83.7

Source: U.S. Department of Transportation, Aviation Consumer Protection Division, *Air Travel Consumer Report*, monthly. See Internet site <http://airconsumer.ost.dot.gov>.

Table 1048. Consumer Complaints Against U.S. Airlines: 1990 to 2006

[Calendar year data. Represents complaints filed by consumers to the U.S. Department of Transportation, Aviation Consumer Protection Division, regarding service problems with air carrier personnel. See source for data on individual airlines]

Complaint category	1990	1995	2000	2001	2002	2003	2004	2005	2006
Total	7,703	4,629	20,564	14,076	7,697	4,601	5,839	6,900	6,448
Flight problems [1]	3,034	1,133	8,698	5,048	1,808	1,049	1,462	1,942	1,845
Customer service [2].........	758	667	4,074	2,531	1,478	584	742	800	870
Baggage..........	1,329	628	2,753	1,965	,082	802	1,085	1,586	1,400
Ticketing/boarding [3]	624	666	1,405	1,310	898	643	637	679	708
Refunds	701	576	803	942	737	428	376	530	485
Fares [4]	312	185	708	568	436	243	180	219	172
Disability [5]	(NA)	(NA)	612	457	420	325	467	430	365
Oversales [6]	399	263	759	539	364	223	263	284	275
Discrimination [7]	(NA)	(NA)	(NA)	164	176	71	96	100	90
Advertising	96	66	42	42	43	13	41	45	30
Tours	29	18	25	11	(8)	(8)	(8)	(8)	(8)
Animals	(NA)	(NA)	1	6	–	–	–	–	–
Smoking.............	74	15	(9)	(9)	(9)	(9)	(9)	(9)	(9)
Credit.............	5	4	(9)	(9)	(9)	(9)	(9)	(9)	(9)
Other.............	342	408	684	493	255	218	487	282	205

– Represents zero.   NA Not available.   [1] Cancellations, delays, etc. from schedule.   [2] Unhelpful employees, inadequate meals or cabin service, treatment of delayed passengers.   [3] Errors in reservations and ticketing; problems in making reservations and obtaining tickets.   [4] Incorrect or incomplete information about fares, discount fare conditions, and availability, etc.   [5] Prior to 2000, included in ticketing/boarding.   [6] All bumping problems, whether or not airline complied with DOT regulations.   [7] Allegations of discrimination by airlines due to factors other than disability, such as race, religion, national origin, or sex.   [8] Included in "Other" beginning 2002.   [9] Included in "Other" beginning 2000.

Source: U.S. Department of Transportation, Aviation Consumer Protection Division, *Air Travel Consumer Report*, monthly. See Internet site <http://airconsumer.ost.dot.gov>.

Transportation   671

Table 1049. **Commuter/Regional Airline Operations Summary: 2003 to 2006**

[Calendar year data (112.6 represents 112,600,000). Commuter/regional airlines operate primarily aircraft of predominately 75 passengers or less and 18,000 pounds of payload capacity serving short haul and small community markets. Represents operations within all North America by U.S. Regional Carriers. Averages are means. For definition of mean, see Guide to Tabular Presentation]

Item	Unit	2003	2004	2005	2006
Passenger carriers operating	Number	73	75	75	71
Passengers enplaned	Millions.	112.6	134.1	154.2	155.7
Average passengers enplaned per carrier.	1,000	1,542.5	1,787.7	2,055.6	2,193.5
Revenue passenger miles (RPM)	Billions	47.7	62.6	73.8	74.4
Average RPMs per carrier	Millions.	652.8	835.1	983.7	1,047.2
Available seat miles	Billions	72.2	91.6	104.8	100.9
Average load factor	Percent	66.0	68.4	70.4	73.7
Departures completed.	Millions.	4.6	5.0	5.3	5.1
Airports served	Number	823	846	846	896
Average trip length	Miles	423.2	467.1	478.5	477.4
Average seating capacity (seats).	Number	48.9	54.4	54.4	53.6
Fleet flying hours	1,000	5,940.3	6,595.5	7,333.0	7,132.7

Source: Compiled by the Regional Airline Association and BACK Aviation from DOT Form 41 data, *Annual Report of the Regional Airline Industry* (copyright).

Table 1050. **Airports, Aircraft, and Airmen: 1980 to 2005**

[As of December 31 or for years ending December 31]

Item	1980	1985	1990	1995	2000	2003	2004	2005
Airports, total [1]	15,161	16,319	17,490	18,224	19,281	19,581	19,820	19,854
Public	4,814	5,858	5,589	5,415	5,317	5,286	5,288	5,270
Percent—with lighted runways	66.2	68.1	71.4	74.3	75.9	76.2	76.3	76.8
With paved runways	72.3	66.7	70.7	73.3	74.3	74.5	74.5	74.8
Private	10,347	10,461	11,901	12,809	13,964	14,295	14,532	14,584
Percent—with lighted runways	15.2	9.1	7.0	6.4	7.2	8.6	9.0	9.2
With paved runways	13.3	17.4	31.5	33.0	32.0	32.7	32.8	33.2
Certificated [2]	730	700	680	667	651	628	599	575
Civil	(X)	(X)	(X)	572	563	555	542	(NA)
Civil military	(X)	(X)	(X)	95	88	73	57	(NA)
General aviation	14,431	15,619	16,810	17,557	18,630	18,953	19,221	19,279
Active air carrier fleet [3]	3,805	4,678	6,083	7,411	8,055	8,176	8,186	8,225
Fixed wing	3,803	4,673	6,072	7,293	8,016	8,144	8,150	8,182
Helicopter.	2	5	11	118	39	32	36	43
General aviation fleet [4]	211,043	196,500	198,000	188,089	217,533	209,708	219,426	224,352
Fixed-wing	200,094	184,700	184,500	162,342	183,276	176,624	182,867	185,373
Turbojet	2,992	4,100	4,100	4,559	7,001	7,997	9,298	9,823
Turboprop	4,089	5,000	5,300	4,995	5,762	7,689	8,379	7,942
Piston.	193,013	175,600	175,200	152,788	170,513	160,938	165,189	167,608
Rotorcraft	6,001	6,000	6,900	5,830	7,150	6,525	7,821	8,728
Other.	4,945	5,800	6,600	4,741	6,700	6,008	5,939	6,454
Gliders	(X)	(X)	(X)	2,182	2,041	2,002	2,116	2,074
Lighter than air.	(X)	(X)	(X)	2,559	4,660	4,006	3,823	4,380
Experimental	(X)	(X)	(X)	15,176	20,407	20,550	22,800	23,627
Airman certificates held: [5]								
Pilot, total	827,071	709,540	702,659	639,184	625,581	625,011	618,633	609,737
Women.	52,902	43,082	40,515	38,032	36,757	36,757	37,694	36,584
Student.	199,833	146,652	128,663	101,279	93,064	87,296	87,910	87,213
Recreational	(X)	(X)	87	232	340	310	291	278
Airplane:								
Private	357,479	311,086	299,111	261,399	251,561	241,045	235,994	228,619
Commercial	183,442	151,862	149,666	133,980	121,858	123,990	122,592	120,614
Air transport	69,569	82,740	107,732	123,877	141,596	143,504	142,160	141,992
Rotorcraft only [6]	6,030	8,123	9,567	7,183	7,775	7,916	8,586	9,518
Glider only.	7,039	8,168	7,833	11,234	9,387	20,950	21,100	21,369
Flight instructor certificates	60,440	58,940	63,775	77,613	80,931	87,816	89,596	90,555
Instrument ratings	260,462	258,559	297,073	298,798	311,944	315,413	313,546	311,828
Nonpilot [7]	368,356	395,139	492,237	651,341	547,453	509,835	515,293	644,016
Mechanic	250,157	274,100	344,282	405,294	344,434	313,032	317,111	320,293
Repairman	(X)	(X)	(X)	61,233	38,208	37,248	39,231	40,030
Parachute rigger.	9,547	9,395	10,094	11,824	10,477	7,883	8,011	8,150
Ground instructor	61,550	58,214	66,882	96,165	72,326	72,692	73,735	74,378
Dispatcher.	6,799	8,511	11,002	15,642	16,340	16,955	17,493	18,079
Flight navigator	1,936	1,542	1,290	916	570	382	336	298
Flight engineer.	38,367	43,377	58,687	60,267	65,098	61,643	59,376	57,756

NA Not available.   X Not applicable.   [1] Existing airports, heliports, seaplane bases, etc. recorded with FAA. Includes military airports with joint civil and military use. Includes U.S. outlying areas. Airport-type definitions: Public—publicly owned and under control of a public agency; private—owned by a private individual or corporation. May or may not be open for public use. [2] Certificated airports serve air-carriers with aircraft seating more than 30 passengers.   [3] Air-carrier aircraft are aircraft carrying passengers or cargo for hire under 14 CFR 121 (large aircraft—more than 30 seats) and 14 CFR 135 (small aircraft—30 seats or fewer).   [4] Beginning 1995, excludes commuters.   [5] Source: U.S. Federal Aviation Administration. See Internet site <http://www .faa.gov/data_statistics/>. Prior years in the *Statistical Handbook of Aviation*, annual.   [6] Data for 1980 and 1985 are for helicopters only.   [7] All certificates on record. No medical examination required.

Source: Except as noted, U.S. Bureau of Transportation Statistics, *National Transportation Statistics*, annual. See Internet site <http://www.bts.gov/publications/national_transportation_statistics/>.

Table 1051. **Freight Carried on Major U.S. Waterways: 1980 to 2005**

[In millions of tons (4.0 represents 4,000,000)]

Item	1980	1985	1990	1995	2000	2002	2003	2004	2005
Atlantic intracoastal waterway	4.0	3.1	4.2	3.5	3.1	1.9	1.9	2.3	2.7
Great Lakes.................	183.5	148.1	167.1	177.8	187.5	167.2	156.5	178.4	169.4
Gulf intracoastal waterway	94.5	102.5	115.4	118.0	113.8	107.7	117.8	123.3	116.1
Mississippi River system [1]	584.2	527.8	659.1	707.2	715.5	712.8	676.8	699.8	678.0
Mississippi River mainstem	441.5	384.0	475.3	520.3	515.6	501.7	478.0	496.9	464.6
Ohio River system [2]	179.3	203.9	260.0	267.6	274.4	280.9	261.3	271.5	280.1
Columbia River...............	49.2	42.4	51.4	57.1	55.2	45.0	47.2	53.5	51.5
Snake River................	5.1	3.5	4.0	6.8	6.7	4.3	5.3	5.7	5.3

[1] Main channels and all tributaries of the Mississippi, Illinois, Missouri, and Ohio Rivers.   [2] Main channels and all navigable tributaries and embayments of the Ohio, Tennessee, and Cumberland Rivers.

Source: U.S. Army Corps of Engineers, *Waterborne Commerce of the United States*, annual. See Internet site <http://www.iwr.usace.army.mil/ndc/wcsc/wcsc.htm>.

Table 1052. **Waterborne Commerce by Type of Commodity: 1995 to 2005**

[In millions of short tons (2,240.4 represents 2,240,400,000). One short ton equals 2,000 lbs. Domestic trade includes all commercial movements between United States ports and on inland rivers, Great Lakes, canals, and connecting channels of the United States, Puerto Rico, and Virgin Islands]

Commodity	1995	2000	2004	2005 Total	2005 Domestic	2005 Foreign imports	2005 Foreign exports
Total	2,240.4	2,424.6	2,551.9	2,527.6	1,028.9	1,096.9	401.8
Coal.........	324.5	297.0	306.1	316.6	235.3	31.2	50.2
Petroleum and petroleum products	907.1	1,044.0	1,127.1	1,111.4	362.7	685.3	63.4
Crude petroleum ...	504.6	571.4	616.2	602.7	79.4	522.8	0.5
Petroleum products [1]	402.5	472.4	510.9	508.8	283.3	162.5	63.0
Gasoline	114.4	125.2	149.1	156.1	83.5	63.0	9.6
Distillate fuel oil	76.7	91.7	139.1	141.1	72.8	52.7	15.6
Residual fuel oil........	111.9	131.6	92.9	96.1	78.8	13.8	3.5
Chemicals and related products	153.7	172.4	180.3	174.9	72.7	45.5	56.7
Fertilizers................	35.7	35.1	34.3	34.5	12.6	8.9	13.0
Other chemicals and related products	118.0	137.3	146.0	140.4	60.0	36.6	43.7
Crude material, inedible............	381.7	380.3	390.3	386.0	213.4	117.2	55.4
Forest products, wood and chips	47.2	33.1	27.8	29.4	9.3	11.0	9.1
Pulp and waste paper	14.9	13.6	17.5	18.7	0.1	2.1	16.5
Soil, sand, gravel, rock, and stone [1]	152.5	165.0	179.8	177.9	128.8	44.9	4.2
Limestone	54.0	67.4	73.2	73.5	52.4	17.9	3.1
Phosphate rock...............	10.7	3.4	6.4	6.0	3.3	2.7	–
Sand & gravel...............	77.0	79.0	83.6	80.2	69.1	10.4	0.8
Iron ore and scrap..............	104.9	97.9	94.8	85.7	55.0	14.8	15.9
Marine shells	0.5	0.3	–	–	–	–	–
Nonferrous ores and scrap	27.9	29.2	25.4	29.2	6.2	18.9	4.1
Sulphur, clay, and salt	23.4	11.3	8.3	8.7	1.2	2.8	4.7
Slag..................	1.9	4.0	6.2	6.0	2.5	3.5	–
Other nonmetal minerals	8.4	25.9	30.5	30.4	10.4	19.1	1.0
Primary manufactured goods	106.3	153.0	159.6	166.4	44.9	102.4	19.1
Papers products	13.1	12.1	13.1	13.7	0.3	6.7	6.8
Lime, cement, and glass..........	33.9	55.9	55.3	62.4	20.5	40.3	1.6
Primary iron and steel products	44.1	57.1	54.0	52.1	16.2	33.7	2.1
Primary nonferrous metal products......	12.3	25.5	32.6	33.5	7.8	17.3	8.3
Primary wood products..............	2.9	2.5	4.6	4.8	0.1	4.4	0.3
Food and farm products...............	303.2	283.3	271.3	251.3	77.7	35.9	137.7
Fish	3.6	2.4	2.9	3.0	0.1	1.7	1.1
Grain [1]	167.9	145.2	141.8	124.0	44.6	1.4	78.0
Wheat	48.5	43.4	44.8	36.4	8.9	0.2	27.2
Corn	105.0	88.2	86.4	75.2	31.9	0.1	43.2
Oilseeds	46.1	57.6	48.4	47.2	19.0	0.3	27.9
Soybeans..................	42.0	47.3	42.7	40.8	16.4	0.1	24.2
Vegetables products	9.0	8.9	9.1	8.3	1.0	4.0	3.3
Processed grain and animal feed.......	33.0	23.1	19.3	18.4	6.5	0.7	11.3
Other agricultural products	43.5	46.1	49.7	50.5	6.6	27.8	16.1
All manufactured equip, machinery and products .... [2]	57.0	83.6	102.7	110.3	20.2	73.5	16.6
Waste and scrap, n.e.c. [2]...........	5.4	4.3	3.0	2.0	2.0	–	–
Unknown or not elsewhere classified	1.6	6.8	11.6	8.7	0.1	5.9	2.7

– Represents or rounds to zero.   [1] Includes commodities not shown separately.   [2] N.e.c. means not elsewhere classified.

Source: U.S. Army Corps of Engineers, *Waterborne Commerce of the United States*, annual. See Internet site <http://www.iwr.usace.army.mil/ndc/wcsc/wcsc.htm>.

Transportation 673

Table 1053. **Selected U.S. Ports by Tons of Traffic: 2005**

[In thousands of short tons (44,113 represents 44,113,000), except rank. One short ton equals 2,000 lbs. For calendar year for the top 30 ports. Represents tons of cargo shipped from or received by the specified port. Excludes cargo carried on general ferries; coal and petroleum products loaded from shore facilities directly onto bunkers of vessels for fuel; and amounts of less than 100 tons of government owned equipment in support of Corps of Engineers projects]

Port name	Rank	Total	Foreign Total	Foreign Inbound	Foreign Outbound	Domestic
Baltimore, MD	18	44,113	28,235	21,507	6,727	15,878
Baton Rouge, LA	9	59,294	22,405	17,585	4,820	36,889
Beaumont, TX	6	78,887	60,102	55,505	4,597	18,784
Corpus Christi, TX	7	77,647	53,808	45,418	8,390	23,839
Duluth-Superior, MN and WI	16	44,722	14,513	561	13,952	30,209
Freeport, TX	22	33,602	28,445	25,416	3,030	5,156
Houston, TX	2	211,666	145,051	103,190	41,861	66,615
Huntington - Tristate	4	83,889	–	–	–	83,889
Lake Charles, LA	13	52,725	32,106	27,083	5,023	20,619
Long Beach, California	5	79,858	63,301	44,493	18,808	16,557
Los Angeles, CA	12	54,894	46,926	33,994	12,932	7,968
Mobile, AL	11	57,665	31,376	21,224	10,152	26,289
New Orleans, LA	8	65,876	33,079	21,252	11,827	32,797
New York, NY and NJ	3	152,132	87,799	76,567	11,232	64,333
Norfolk Harbor, VA	21	35,281	26,444	8,568	17,876	8,837
Pascagoula, MS	26	29,324	19,894	16,542	3,352	9,429
Paulsboro, NJ	23	32,072	18,383	18,134	249	13,689
Philadelphia, PA	20	39,365	26,237	25,915	323	13,127
Pittsburgh, PA	19	43,624	–	–	–	43,624
Plaquemines, LA, Port of	15	47,872	15,953	8,039	7,914	31,918
Portland, ME	27	29,286	28,193	28,039	154	1,093
Portland, OR	29	28,127	16,356	4,411	11,945	11,771
Savannah, GA	25	30,114	28,300	18,216	10,084	1,814
Seattle, WA	30	28,081	20,983	10,476	10,507	7,098
South Louisiana, LA, Port of	1	212,245	94,574	43,490	51,084	117,672
St. Louis, MO and IL	24	30,347	–	–	–	30,347
Tacoma, WA	28	28,289	20,674	7,659	13,015	7,615
Tampa, FL	14	49,174	20,109	11,838	8,271	29,065
Texas City, TX	10	57,839	43,467	38,005	5,462	14,372
Valdez, AK	17	44,448	–	–	–	44,448

– Represents zero.

Source: U.S. Army Corps of Engineers, *"Waterborne Commerce of the United States, 2005."* See Internet site <http://www.iwr.usace.army.mil/ndc/wcsc/wcsc.htm> (accessed 27 June 2007).

Table 1054. **Selected U.S. Ports/Waterways by Container Traffic: 2005**

[In thousands of twenty-foot equivalent units (TEUS). 30,058.9 represents 30,058,900. For calendar year. For the 30 leading ports/waterways in total TEUS. A TEUS is a measure of containerized cargo capacity equal to 1 standard 20-foot length by 8-foot width by 8-foot 6-inch height container]

Port/waterway name	Rank	Total loaded	Domestic Total[1]	Domestic Inbound loaded	Domestic Outbound loaded	Foreign loaded Total	Foreign loaded Inbound
Total[2]	(X)	30,058.9	5,244.1	2,088.2	2,088.2	25,882.6	17,329.4
Anchorage, AK	17	293.3	317.2	231.3	59.9	2.2	0.3
Baltimore, MD	16	486.8	128.4	55.1	50.8	380.9	244.0
Boston, MA	20	160.2	30.0	16.7	13.4	130.2	73.9
Camden-Gloucester, NJ.	29	65.9	39.8	6.1	21.9	37.9	31.3
Charleston, SC	6	1,513.6	13.1	1.3	3.3	1,509.0	897.0
Chester, PA	26	100.0	–	–	–	100.0	56.1
Gulfport, MS	21	150.8	–	–	–	150.8	93.6
Honolulu, HI	11	855.8	1,146.3	545.0	271.0	39.7	22.9
Houston, TX	10	1,289.8	68.2	23.1	33.3	1,233.4	624.8
Jacksonville, FL	15	581.8	432.1	75.5	329.3	177.0	52.2
Kahului, Maui, HI	28	82.2	110.0	62.9	19.2	–	–
Kawaihae Harbor, HI	30	60.3	84.3	46.9	13.4	–	–
Long Beach, CA	1	5,200.1	437.3	48.0	272.0	4,880.1	3,733.8
Los Angeles, CA	2	4,375.4	10.2	1.9	7.9	4,365.6	3,465.5
Miami, FL	12	777.5	8.9	2.3	0.8	774.4	445.7
New Orleans, LA	18	176.5	15.1	6.5	3.2	166.8	69.1
New York, NY and NJ	3	3,580.6	193.4	72.6	105.3	3,402.6	2,428.3
Newport News, VA	25	103.2	–	–	–	103.2	61.3
Norfolk Harbor, VA	9	1,436.2	140.9	60.8	57.5	1,317.9	778.7
Oakland, CA	4	1,560.6	285.8	46.2	168.0	1,346.3	759.1
Palm Beach, FL	22	138.7	–	–	–	138.7	35.5
Philadelphia, PA	24	131.1	1.3	0.2	1.1	129.8	109.0
Port Everglades, FL	14	591.4	16.4	–	15.9	575.5	276.4
Portland, OR	23	131.6	19.2	9.1	0.3	122.3	60.8
San Juan, PR	13	725.8	561.4	424.6	97.2	204.0	162.5
Savannah, GA	7	1,485.8	11.3	1.4	0.7	1,483.8	801.5
Seattle, WA	8	1,443.0	302.5	44.9	150.5	1,247.5	818.4
Tacoma, WA	5	1,545.2	335.6	62.6	251.0	1,231.6	838.1
Wilmington, DE	19	161.6	–	–	–	161.6	120.4
Wilmington, NC	27	91.6	–	–	–	91.6	61.6

– Represents zero. [1] Includes empty TEUS. [2] Includes other ports/waterways not shown separately.

Source: U.S. Army Corps of Engineers, "U.S. Waterborne Container Traffic for U.S. Port/Waterway in 2005." See Internet site <http://www.iwr.usace.army.mil/ndc/wcsc/wcsc.htm> (accessed 27 June 2007).

U.S. Census Bureau, Statistical Abstract of the United States: 2008

Table 1055. Highway Mileage—Urban and Rural by Ownership: 1980 to 2005

[In thousands (3,955 represents 3,955,000). As of Dec. 31. Includes Puerto Rico beginning 2000]

Type and control	1980	1985	1990	1995	2000	2002	2003	2004	2005
Total mileage [1]	[2]3,955	3,862	3,880	3,912	3,951	3,982	3,991	3,997	4,012
Urban mileage [3]	624	691	757	819	859	902	954	994	1,023
Under state control	79	111	96	112	112	112	127	130	144
Under local control	543	578	661	706	746	787	828	862	874
Rural mileage	[2]3,331	3,171	3,123	3,093	3,092	3,080	3,036	3,003	2,989
Under state control	702	773	703	691	664	685	653	650	637
Under local control	2,270	2,173	2,242	2,231	2,311	2,297	2,263	2,236	2,228
Under federal control	262	225	178	170	117	118	120	118	123

[1] Beginning 1985, includes only public road mileage, as defined in 23 USC 402. [2] Includes 98,000 miles of nonpublic road mileage previously contained in other rural categories. [3] Includes a small amount of road owned by the federal government, such as roads in federal parks that are not part of a state or local highway system.

Source: U.S. Federal Highway Administration, Highway Statistics, annual. See Internet site <http://www.fhwa.dot.gov/policy/ohpi/hss /hsspubs.htm>.

Table 1056. Hazardous Shipments—Value, Tons, and Ton-Miles: 2002

[660,181 represents $660,181,000,000. For business establishments in mining, manufacturing, wholesale trade, and selected retail industries. 2002 classified by the 1997 North American Industry Classification System (NAICS). Selected auxiliary establishments are also included. Based on the 2002 Economic Census; see Appendix III]

Mode of transportation	Value (mil. dol.)		Tons (1,000)		Ton-miles (mil.)		Average miles per shipment
	Total	Percent	Total	Percent	Total	Percent	
All modes	660,181	100.0	2,191,519	100.0	326,727	100.0	136
Single modes	644,489	97.6	2,158,533	98.5	311,897	95.5	105
Truck [1]	419,630	63.6	1,159,514	52.9	110,163	33.7	86
For-hire truck	189,803	28.8	449,503	20.5	65,112	19.9	285
Private truck	226,660	34.3	702,186	32.0	44,087	13.5	38
Rail	31,339	4.7	109,369	5.0	72,087	22.1	695
Water	46,856	7.1	228,197	10.4	70,649	21.6	(S)
Air (includes truck and air)	1,643	0.2	64	–	85	–	2,080
Pipeline [2]	145,021	22.0	661,390	30.2	(S)	(S)	(S)
Multiple modes	9,631	1.5	18,745	0.9	12,488	3.8	849
Parcel, U.S. Postal Service or courier .	4,268	0.6	245	–	119	–	837
Other multiple modes	5,363	0.8	18,500	0.8	12,369	3.8	1,371
Other and unknown modes	6,061	0.9	14,241	0.6	2,342	0.7	57
Class of material	660,181	100.0	2,191,519	100.0	326,727	100.0	136
Class 1, explosives	7,901	1.2	5,000	0.2	1,568	0.5	651
Class 2, gasses	73,932	11.2	213,358	9.7	37,262	11.4	95
Class 3, flammable liquids	490,238	74.3	1,788,986	81.6	218,574	66.9	106
Class 4, flammable solids	6,566	1.0	11,300	0.5	4,391	1.3	158
Class 5, oxidizers and organic peroxides	5,471	0.8	12,670	0.6	4,221	1.3	407
Class 6, toxic (poison)	8,275	1.3	8,459	0.4	4,254	1.3	626
Class 7, radioactive materials	5,850	0.9	57	–	44	–	(S)
Class 8, corrosive materials	38,324	5.8	90,671	4.1	36,260	11.1	301
Class 9, miscellaneous dangerous goods	23,625	3.6	61,018	2.8	20,153	6.2	368

– Rounds to zero.   S Data do not meet publication standards due to high sampling variability or other reasons.   [1] Truck as a single mode includes shipments that went by private truck only, for-hire truck only, or a combination of private truck and for-hire truck.   [2] Commodity Flow Survey data exclude shipments of crude oil.

Source: U.S. Bureau of Transportation Statistics and U.S. Census Bureau, 2002 Economic Census, Transportation, "2002 Commodity Flow Survey, Hazardous Shipments" Series EC02TCF-US(HM), issued December 2004. See Internet site <http://www.census.gov/svsd/www/cfsmain.html>.

Table 1057. Highway Mileage by State—Functional Systems and Urban/Rural: 2005

[As of Dec. 31. Excludes Puerto Rico. For definition of fuctional systems see text, this section]

State	Total	Functional systems					Urban	Rural
		Interstate	Other free-ways and express-ways	Arterial	Collector	Local		
U.S.	3,995,635	46,608	10,560	394,040	790,495	2,753,932	1,009,839	2,985,796
AL.	96,046	909	29	9,123	20,284	65,701	21,627	74,419
AK.	14,367	1,081	–	1,515	2,837	8,934	2,255	12,112
AZ.	59,789	1,169	156	5,720	8,163	44,581	22,722	37,067
AR.	98,661	656	99	6,876	20,327	70,703	10,935	87,726
CA.	169,906	2,460	1,494	26,982	31,869	107,101	85,433	84,473
CO	87,597	956	314	8,922	16,250	61,155	18,819	68,778
CT.	21,193	346	237	2,759	3,198	14,653	15,040	6,153
DE.	6,093	41	14	664	1,040	4,334	2,885	3,208
DC	1,500	13	22	264	152	1,049	1,500	–
FL.	120,557	1,471	550	12,845	14,268	91,423	81,090	39,467
GA	117,644	1,243	121	14,061	22,856	79,363	36,986	80,658
HI	4,322	55	34	753	832	2,648	2,287	2,035
ID	47,129	612	–	4,011	10,373	32,133	4,740	42,389
IL	138,833	2,169	92	14,454	21,707	100,411	38,476	100,357
IN	95,575	1,169	135	7,963	22,682	63,626	21,230	74,345
IA	113,971	781	–	9,697	31,522	71,971	11,115	102,856
KS.	135,462	874	191	9,507	33,510	91,380	11,767	123,695
KY.	78,020	762	65	5,865	16,076	55,252	12,320	65,700
LA	60,949	903	53	5,570	10,032	44,391	15,517	45,432
ME	22,806	367	20	2,174	5,986	14,259	2,970	19,836
MD	30,961	481	289	3,781	5,002	21,408	16,997	13,964
MA	35,900	573	312	6,175	4,825	24,015	27,947	7,953
MI	121,456	1,243	328	14,462	24,562	80,861	35,423	86,033
MN	132,048	915	154	12,933	29,607	88,439	16,407	115,641
MS	74,181	682	72	7,345	15,445	50,637	10,630	63,551
MO	125,823	1,182	348	10,146	24,815	89,332	19,350	106,473
MT	69,339	1,192	–	6,038	16,367	45,742	2,754	66,585
NE.	93,311	482	21	8,048	20,747	64,013	6,061	87,250
NV.	34,624	562	57	3,007	5,007	25,991	6,929	27,695
NH	15,567	225	52	1,534	2,742	11,014	4,721	10,846
NJ.	38,552	431	404	5,760	4,151	27,806	31,233	7,319
NM	63,759	1,000	5	5,083	8,483	49,186	7,974	55,785
NY.	113,341	1,674	798	13,502	20,557	76,810	41,224	72,117
NC	103,128	1,083	385	9,518	17,457	74,685	32,112	71,016
ND	86,793	571	–	5,880	11,769	68,573	1,845	84,948
OH	124,840	1,574	483	10,912	22,560	89,311	44,470	80,370
OK	112,938	933	188	8,197	25,314	78,306	15,315	97,623
OR	64,544	728	55	7,020	17,681	39,060	12,795	51,749
PA	120,668	1,758	546	13,222	19,837	85,305	44,482	76,186
RI	6,491	71	85	831	882	4,622	5,226	1,265
SC.	66,238	843	92	7,180	15,044	43,079	16,452	49,786
SD.	83,909	678	12	6,376	19,099	57,744	2,624	81,285
TN.	90,451	1,104	137	9,014	17,860	62,336	21,418	69,033
TX.	304,171	3,233	1,183	28,598	63,511	207,646	83,449	220,722
UT.	43,573	940	14	3,455	7,745	31,419	10,578	32,995
VT.	14,397	320	20	1,303	3,130	9,624	1,396	13,001
VA.	71,964	1,118	240	8,306	14,074	48,226	21,489	50,475
WA	83,381	764	373	7,404	16,848	57,992	20,148	63,233
WV	37,028	554	10	3,246	8,774	24,444	4,183	32,845
WI	114,141	743	268	12,398	21,608	79,124	21,932	92,209
WY	27,698	914	3	3,641	11,026	12,114	2,561	25,137

– Represents zero.

Source: U.S. Federal Highway Administration, *Highway Statistics*, annual. See Internet site <http://www.fhwa.dot.gov/policy/ohpi/hss/hsspubs.htm>.

Table 1058. Bridge Inventory—Total and Deficient, 1996 to 2006, and by State, 2006

[Based on the National Bridge Inventory program; for details, see source]

State and year	Number of bridges	Total number	Percent	Deficient and obsolete Structurally deficient [1] Number	Percent	Functionally obsolete [2] Number	Percent
1996, total	581,862	182,726	31.4	101,518	17.4	81,208	14.0
1997, total	582,751	175,885	30.2	98,475	16.9	77,410	13.3
1998, total	502,984	172,582	29.6	93,076	16.0	79,506	13.6
1999, total	585,542	170,050	29.0	88,150	15.1	81,900	14.0
2000, total	587,755	167,993	28.6	87,106	14.8	80,887	13.8
2001, total	590,066	165,099	28.0	83,630	14.2	81,469	13.8
2002, total	591,220	163,010	27.6	81,437	13.8	81,573	13.8
2003, total	592,246	160,819	27.2	79,811	13.5	81,008	13.7
2004, total	593,885	158,318	26.7	77,758	13.1	80,560	13.6
2005, total	594,616	156,177	26.3	75,871	12.8	80,306	13.5
U.S. total, 2006	**596,842**	**153,990**	**25.8**	**73,764**	**12.4**	**80,226**	**13.4**
Alabama	15,879	4,307	27.1	2,102	13.2	2,205	13.9
Alaska	1,210	318	26.3	151	12.5	167	13.8
Arizona	7,248	737	10.2	161	2.2	576	7.9
Arkansas	12,502	2,974	23.8	1,068	8.5	1,906	15.2
California	23,625	6,708	28.4	2,994	12.7	3,714	15.7
Colorado	8,311	1,397	16.8	575	6.9	822	9.9
Connecticut	4,166	1,401	33.6	351	8.4	1,050	25.2
Delaware	849	132	15.5	35	4.1	97	11.4
District of Columbia	245	156	63.7	22	9.0	134	54.7
Florida	11,553	2,036	17.6	305	2.6	1,731	15.0
Georgia	14,523	2,911	20.0	1,113	7.7	1,798	12.4
Hawaii	1,110	513	46.2	156	14.1	357	32.2
Idaho	4,062	771	19.0	334	8.2	437	10.8
Illinois	25,943	4,284	16.5	2,447	9.4	1,837	7.1
Indiana	18,364	4,053	22.1	2,066	11.3	1,987	10.8
Iowa	24,825	6,661	26.8	5,152	20.8	1,509	6.1
Kansas	25,440	5,431	21.3	3,038	11.9	2,393	9.4
Kentucky	13,637	4,289	31.5	1,362	10.0	2,927	21.5
Louisiana	13,347	4,063	30.4	1,869	14.0	2,194	16.4
Maine	2,380	820	34.5	343	14.4	477	20.0
Maryland	5,059	1,380	27.3	410	8.1	970	19.2
Massachusetts	4,947	2,560	51.7	586	11.8	1,974	39.9
Michigan	10,887	3,055	28.1	1,746	16.0	1,309	12.0
Minnesota	13,008	1,586	12.2	1,135	8.7	451	3.5
Mississippi	16,952	4,460	26.3	3,170	18.7	1,290	7.6
Missouri	24,024	7,736	32.2	4,595	19.1	3,141	13.1
Montana	5,002	1,040	20.8	500	10.0	540	10.8
Nebraska	15,452	3,741	24.2	2,413	15.6	1,328	8.6
Nevada	1,630	196	12.0	50	3.1	146	9.0
New Hampshire	2,359	748	31.7	317	13.4	431	18.3
New Jersey	6,420	2,292	35.7	760	11.8	1,532	23.9
New Mexico	3,848	692	18.0	401	10.4	291	7.6
New York	17,335	6,611	38.1	2,110	12.2	4,501	26.0
North Carolina	17,666	5,072	28.7	2,256	12.8	2,816	15.9
North Dakota	4,482	1,030	23.0	776	17.3	254	5.7
Ohio	27,946	6,933	24.8	2,884	10.3	4,049	14.5
Oklahoma	23,460	7,858	33.5	6,299	26.8	1,559	6.6
Oregon	7,234	1,784	24.7	645	8.9	1,139	15.7
Pennsylvania	22,327	9,571	42.9	5,582	25.0	3,989	17.9
Rhode Island	753	425	56.4	191	25.4	234	31.1
South Carolina	9,238	2,090	22.6	1,275	13.8	815	8.8
South Dakota	5,945	1,520	25.6	1,186	19.9	334	5.6
Tennessee	19,803	4,242	21.4	1,324	6.7	2,918	14.7
Texas	49,518	10,162	20.5	2,219	4.5	7,943	16.0
Utah	2,827	497	17.6	239	8.5	258	9.1
Vermont	2,710	938	34.6	436	16.1	502	18.5
Virginia	13,357	3,418	25.6	1,197	9.0	2,221	16.6
Washington	7,548	2,015	26.7	381	5.0	1,634	21.6
West Virginia	6,956	2,593	37.3	1,075	15.5	1,518	21.8
Wisconsin	13,770	2,127	15.4	1,335	9.7	792	5.8
Wyoming	3,027	611	20.2	381	12.6	230	7.6
Puerto Rico	2,133	1,045	49.0	246	11.5	799	37.5

[1] Bridges are structurally deficient if they have been restricted to light vehicles, require immediate rehabilitation to remain open, or are closed. [2] Bridges are functionally obsolete if they have deck geometry, load carrying capacity, clearance or approach roadway alignment that no longer meet the criteria for the system of which the bridge is carrying a part.

Source: U.S. Federal Highway Administration, Office of Bridge Technology; <http://www.fhwa.dot.gov/bridge/nbi.htm>.

Transportation 677

Table 1059. **Funding for Highways and Disposition of Highway-User Revenue: 1990 to 2005**

[In millions of dollars (75,444 represents $75,444,000,0000). Data compiled from reports of state and local authorities]

Type	1990	1995	1999	2000	2001	2002	2003	2004	2005
Total receipts	75,444	96,269	121,650	131,115	132,324	138,878	139,246	145,315	154,690
Current income	69,880	87,620	110,376	119,815	119,659	123,802	124,593	129,521	137,668
Highway-user revenues	44,346	59,331	74,222	81,335	77,719	79,487	79,280	83,006	90,343
Other taxes and fees...........	19,827	21,732	29,380	31,137	34,190	36,168	37,783	38,956	39,214
Investment income, other receipts ..	5,707	6,557	6,774	7,342	7,749	8,147	7,530	7,560	8,111
Bond issue proceeds [1]	5,564	8,649	11,274	11,301	12,665	15,076	14,654	15,794	17,022
Funds from (+) or to (–) reserves	–36	–2,791	–5,639	–8,418	–2,423	–239	4,359	2,174	–1,990
Total funds available	75,408	93,478	116,011	122,697	129,900	138,639	143,605	147,489	152,700
Total disbursements	75,408	93,478	116,011	122,697	129,900	138,639	143,605	147,489	152,700
Current disbursements	72,457	88,994	111,097	117,592	124,815	131,694	136,213	139,478	144,629
Capital outlay...............	35,151	44,228	57,227	61,323	65,968	68,794	70,004	70,274	75,162
Maintenance and traffic services	20,365	24,319	29,997	30,636	31,677	33,893	35,011	36,327	37,882
Administration and research	6,501	8,419	9,130	10,020	10,423	10,934	11,986	12,737	11,126
Law enforcement and safety......	7,235	8,218	10,393	11,031	11,977	12,548	13,501	14,322	14,066
Interest on debt	3,205	3,810	4,350	4,583	4,770	5,526	5,711	5,819	6,392
Bond retirement [1]..............	2,951	4,484	4,914	5,105	5,086	6,945	7,393	8,011	8,071

[1] Excludes issue and redemption of short-term notes or refunding bonds.
Source: U.S. Federal Highway Administration, *Highway Statistics*, annual. See Internet site <http://www.fhwa.dot.gov/policy/ohpi /hss/hsspubs.htm>.

Table 1060. **Federal Aid to State and Local Governments for Highway Trust Fund and Federal Transit Administration (FTA) by State: 2004**

[Year ending Sept. 30. (28,881 represents $28,881,000,000)]

State	Highway trust fund Total (mil. dol.)	Per capita (dol.)[1]	FTA Total (mil. dol.)	Per capita (dol.)[1]	State	Highway trust fund Total (mil. dol.)	Per capita (dol.)[1]	FTA Total (mil. dol.)	Per capita (dol.)[1]	State	Highway trust fund Total (mil. dol.)	Per capita (dol.)[1]	FTA Total (mil. dol.)	Per capita (dol.)[1]
U.S. [2] .	28,881	97	6,818	23	KS....	369	135	13	5	ND.....	181	285	3	5
U.S. [3] .	28,813	98	6,689	23	KY.....	435	105	38	9	OH.....	958	84	152	13
AL	491	108	19	4	LA.....	501	111	60	13	OK.....	487	138	19	6
AK	373	569	18	27	ME....	177	134	11	8	OR.....	355	99	131	37
AZ.....	450	78	165	29	MD....	426	77	74	13	PA.....	1,224	99	448	36
AR.....	375	136	17	6	MA....	604	94	192	30					
CA.....	2,365	66	1,080	30	MI	799	79	88	9	RI	157	145	12	11
CO.....	434	94	125	27	MN....	453	89	139	27	SC.....	670	160	24	6
CT.....	460	131	60	17	MS....	362	125	12	4	SD.....	182	236	2	3
DE.....	91	110	4	5	MO....	723	126	93	16	TN.....	622	105	57	10
DC.....	131	237	237	428	MT....	314	339	1	2	TX.....	2,827	126	255.	11
FL.....	1,563	90	262	15	NE....	257	147	10	6	UT.....	245	103	50	21
GA.....	788	89	127	14	NV....	199	85	53	23	VT.....	122	197	11	18
HI	97	77	38	30	NH....	128	99	4	3	VA.....	588	79	162	22
ID	231	166	8	6	NJ.....	752	87	537	62	WA	486	78	264	43
IL	611	48	341	27	NM....	281	147	25	13	WV	331	182	8	4
IN	607	97	54	9	NY.....	1,470	76	1,011	53	WI	518	94	75	14
IA	339	115	23	8	NC....	977	114	73	9	WY ...	225	444	3	5

[1] Based on estimated population as of July 1. [2] Includes outlying areas and undistributed funds, not shown separately.
[3] For the 50 states and D.C.
Source: U.S. Census Bureau, *Federal Aid to States for Fiscal Year, 2004*. See Inernet site <http://www.census.gov/prod/www /abs/fas.html>.

Table 1061. **State Motor Fuel Tax Receipts, 2004 and 2005, and Gasoline Tax Rates, 2005**

[603 represents $603,000,000]

State	Net receipts (mil. dol.) 2004	2005	Tax rate,[1] 2005	State	Net receipts (mil. dol.) 2004	2005	Tax rate,[1] 2005	State	Net receipts (mil. dol.) 2004	2005	Tax rate,[1] 2005
AL	603	617	18.00	KY ...	461	470	18.50	ND	107	107	23.00
AK	30	33	8.00	LA	558	576	20.00	OH	1,656	1,788	28.00
AZ	652	685	18.00	ME	217	222	26.00	OK	415	435	17.00
AR	447	444	21.70	MD	743	758	23.50	OR	406	401	24.00
CA	3,350	3,404	18.00	MA	684	687	21.00	PA	1,788	1,911	30.00
CO	553	519	22.00	MI.....	1,074	1,067	19.00	RI	148	148	30.00
CT	454	473	25.00	MN....	648	652	20.00	SC	478	509	16.00
DE	112	113	23.00	MS	414	402	18.40	SD	131	131	22.00
DC	29	26	20.00	MO	700	710	17.00	TN	762	765	21.40
FL.....	1,982	2,041	14.50	MT	190	184	27.75	TX	2,928	2,941	20.00
GA	502	503	7.50	NE	317	303	25.30	UT	336	345	24.50
HI.....	80	80	16.00	NV	424	443	24.80	VT	88	86	20.00
ID.....	219	218	25.00	NH	154	157	19.50	VA	871	890	17.50
IL.....	1,346	1,349	19.00	NJ.....	617	564	10.50	WA	900	923	31.00
IN.....	862	886	18.00	NM	243	250	18.88	WV	395	287	27.00
IA.....	418	427	20.70	NY	1,587	1,567	23.25	WI.	935	956	29.90
KS	422	433	24.00	NC	1,275	1,356	27.10	WY	93	99	14.00

[1] State gasoline tax rates in cents per gallon. In effect December 31.
Source: U.S. Federal Highway Administration, *Highway Statistics*, annual. See Internet site <http://www.fhwa.dot.gov/policy/ohpi /hss/hsspubs.htm>.

Table 1062. **Public Highway Debt—State and Local Governments: 1980 to 2005**

[In millions of dollars (2,381 represents $2,381,000,000). Long-term obligations. Data are for varying calendar and fiscal years. Excludes duplicated and interunit obligations]

Item	1980	1985	1990	1995	2000	2002	2003	2004	2005
Total debt issued	2,381	8,194	5,708	11,305	14,513	19,089	22,127	19,694	(NA)
State	1,160	5,397	3,147	4,718	9,067	13,250	16,618	13,344	19,784
Local [1]	1,221	2,797	2,561	6,587	5,446	5,839	5,509	6,350	(NA)
Total debt redeemed.	1,987	5,294	3,120	5,634	8,623	13,537	16,171	12,252	(NA)
State	1,114	3,835	1,648	2,930	3,897	9,988	11,550	8,292	14,072
Local [1]	873	1,459	1,472	2,695	4,726	3,549	3,621	3,960	(NA)
Total debt outstanding [2] . . .	27,616	32,690	46,586	68,733	96,383	111,226	119,571	129,933	(NA)
State	20,210	21,277	28,362	39,228	61,434	70,826	77,592	85,565	88,187
Local [1]	7,406	11,413	18,224	29,505	34,949	40,400	41,979	44,368	(NA)

NA Not available. [1] Local data estimated. [2] End-of-year.

Source: U.S. Federal Highway Administration, *Highway Statistics*, annual. See Internet site <http://www.fhwa.dot.gov/policy/ohpi/hss /hsspubs.htm>.

Table 1063. **State Disbursements for Highways by State: 1995 to 2005**

[In millions of dollars (67,615 represents $67,615,000,000). Comprises disbursements from current revenues or loans for construction, maintenance, interest and principal payments on highway bonds, transfers to local units, and miscellaneous. Includes transactions by state toll authorities. Excludes amounts allocated for collection expenses and nonhighway purposes, and mass transit]

State	1995	1999	2000	2001	2002	2003	2004	2005
United States.	67,615	83,675	89,832	94,513	104,977	109,403	104,677	116,517
Alabama.	1,002	1,085	1,246	1,433	1,575	1,572	1,562	1,519
Alaska	438	416	501	482	541	618	623	643
Arizona.	1,199	1,860	2,040	2,149	2,445	2,453	2,569	2,458
Arkansas	666	736	817	976	1,161	1,176	1,219	1,078
California	5,966	6,876	6,750	6,795	8,570	9,349	7,967	8,308
Colorado.	922	1,260	1,392	1,616	2,195	1,788	1,870	1,652
Connecticut.	1,153	1,094	1,304	1,236	1,848	1,743	1,677	1,434
Delaware	441	507	595	647	738	929	798	1,104
District of Columbia	140	242	244	406	336	368	369	327
Florida	3,421	3,992	4,208	4,348	4,985	6,664	5,804	7,369
Georgia	1,437	1,763	1,567	1,748	1,945	1,756	1,935	2,070
Hawaii	360	355	272	263	275	375	314	506
Idaho	350	445	492	480	508	547	568	608
Illinois	3,006	2,957	3,447	3,788	4,286	4,595	4,289	4,201
Indiana	1,433	1,522	1,932	3,202	1,975	2,445	2,578	2,235
Iowa	1,078	1,253	1,494	1,388	1,405	1,419	1,401	1,392
Kansas.	1,019	1,155	1,206	1,271	1,951	1,891	1,387	1,394
Kentucky	1,397	1,578	1,651	1,612	1,776	2,152	1,907	1,723
Louisiana	1,198	1,237	1,301	1,154	1,287	1,498	1,576	1,387
Maine.	379	458	488	505	744	579	702	616
Maryland	1,289	1,554	1,599	1,673	1,803	1,885	1,831	2,049
Massachusetts.	2,501	4,407	3,524	3,965	3,783	3,547	3,612	3,196
Michigan	1,974	2,629	2,748	2,920	2,859	2,799	2,930	3,561
Minnesota.	1,210	1,534	1,692	1,683	1,866	1,969	1,995	2,131
Mississippi	662	968	1,039	911	1,040	1,014	1,087	1,081
Missouri	1,313	1,600	1,818	2,044	2,110	2,120	2,135	2,069
Montana.	388	434	474	469	535	578	657	664
Nebraska	578	681	745	661	867	839	859	876
Nevada	484	557	651	668	631	807	1,045	865
New Hampshire	328	416	387	445	522	453	389	389
New Jersey	2,102	2,905	4,503	4,276	4,863	6,364	3,849	7,119
New Mexico	535	753	1,162	1,119	983	862	1,164	911
New York	4,584	5,347	5,307	5,301	7,161	6,592	6,094	9,638
North Carolina	1,871	2,441	2,621	2,868	3,001	3,013	3,557	3,698
North Dakota.	270	413	385	358	385	379	388	456
Ohio	2,637	3,158	3,351	3,493	3,580	3,660	3,657	4,040
Oklahoma.	828	1,322	1,417	1,443	1,839	1,379	1,175	1,163
Oregon.	888	1,009	1,010	984	1,029	1,183	1,000	1,628
Pennsylvania.	3,153	4,143	4,517	4,875	5,365	5,258	4,283	4,567
Rhode Island.	290	316	256	380	380	299	373	407
South Carolina.	668	885	970	1,104	1,201	1,191	1,254	1,360
South Dakota	286	371	466	463	437	441	455	466
Tennessee	1,230	1,398	1,440	1,563	1,622	1,661	1,549	1,718
Texas.	3,593	4,840	5,665	5,716	6,019	6,758	7,134	8,918
Utah	431	1,072	1,072	941	956	879	1,871	986
Vermont	194	252	287	297	265	312	297	310
Virginia.	2,107	2,771	2,678	2,909	3,185	3,419	3,002	3,384
Washington	1,909	1,780	1,871	2,042	2,276	2,288	2,469	2,625
West Virginia.	781	930	1,170	1,289	1,210	1,169	1,056	1,425
Wisconsin.	1,252	1,614	1,663	1,793	2,204	1,904	1,942	2,363
Wyoming	272	386	396	360	460	468	458	429

Source: U.S. Federal Highway Administration, *Highway Statistics*, annual. See Internet site <http://www.fhwa.dot.gov/policy/ohpi /hss/hsspubs.htm>.

Table 1064. **State Motor Vehicle Registrations: 1980 to 2005**

[In thousands (155,796 represents 155,796,000). Compiled principally from information obtained from state authorities, but it was necessary to draw on other sources and to make numerous estimates in order to complete series. Excludes motorcycles; see Table 1066]

Item	1980	1990	1995	2000	2003	2004	2005
All motor vehicles	155,796	188,798	201,530	221,475	231,390	237,243	241,194
Private and commercial	153,265	185,541	197,941	217,567	227,476	233,266	237,140
Publicly owned..............	2,531	3,257	3,589	3,908	3,914	3,977	4,054
Automobiles [1]	121,601	133,700	128,387	133,621	135,670	136,431	136,568
Private and commercial	120,743	132,164	126,900	132,247	134,337	135,077	135,192
Publicly owned..............	857	1,536	1,487	1,374	1,333	1,354	1,376
Buses	529	627	686	746	777	795	807
Private and commercial	254	275	288	314	325	330	331
Publicly owned..............	275	351	398	432	452	465	476
Trucks [1]	33,667	54,470	72,458	87,108	94,943	100,017	103,819
Private and commercial	32,268	53,101	70,754	85,005	92,814	97,860	101,616
Publicly owned..............	1,399	1,369	1,704	2,103	2,129	2,157	2,203

[1] Trucks include pickups, panels, and delivery vans. Beginning 1990, personal passenger vans, passenger minivans, and utility-type vehicles are no longer included in automobiles but are included in trucks.

Source: U.S. Federal Highway Administration, *Highway Statistics*, annual. See Internet site <http://www.fhwa.dot.gov/policy/ohpi /hss/hsspubs.htm>.

Table 1065. **Alternative Fueled Vehicles in Use by Fuel Type: 1995 to 2004**

[2004 data are projections. 276,643 represents 276,643,000]

Vehicles and fuel consumption	Total [1]	Liquified petroleum gases (LPG)	Compressed natural gas (CNG)	Liquified natural gas (LNG)	Methanol, 85 percent (M85) [2]	Ethanol, 85 percent (E85) [2]	Electricity [3]
ALTERNATIVE FUELED VEHICLES							
1995	246,855	172,806	50,218	603	18,319	1,527	2,860
1996	265,006	175,585	60,144	663	20,265	4,536	3,280
1997	280,205	175,679	68,571	813	21,040	9,130	4,453
1998	295,030	177,183	78,782	1,172	19,648	12,788	5,243
1999	322,302	178,610	91,267	1,681	18,964	24,604	6,964
2000	394,664	181,994	100,750	2,090	10,426	87,570	11,830
2001	425,457	185,053	111,851	2,576	7,827	100,303	17,847
2002	471,098	187,680	120,839	2,708	5,873	120,951	33,047
2003	510,805	190,438	132,988	3,030	4,917	133,776	45,656
2004	547,904	194,389	143,742	3,134	4,592	146,195	55,852
FUEL CONSUMPTION (1,000 gasoline-equivalent gallons)							
1995	276,643	232,701	35,162	2,759	2,023	190	663
1996	295,616	239,158	46,923	3,247	1,775	694	773
1997	312,589	238,356	65,192	3,714	1,554	1,280	1,010
1998	323,790	241,386	72,412	5,343	1,212	1,727	1,202
1999	302,287	209,817	79,620	5,828	1,073	3,916	1,524
2000	322,307	212,576	86,745	7,259	585	12,071	3,058
2001	348,421	215,876	104,496	8,921	439	14,623	4,066
2002	378,589	223,143	120,670	9,382	337	17,783	7,274
2003	412,725	230,486	141,726	10,514	274	20,092	9,633
2004	447,198	242,368	159,464	10,868	257	22,405	11,836

[1] Inlcudes methanol, neat (M100) and ethanol, 95 percent (E95) through 2000, not shown separately. [2] The remaining portion is gasoline. [3] Excludes gasoline-electric hybrids.

Source: U.S. Energy Information Administration, *Renewable and Alternative Fuels*. See Internet site <http://www.eia.doe.gov /fuelrenewable.html>.

Table 1066. **State Motor Vehicle Registrations, 1980 to 2005, and Licensed Drivers and Motorcycle Registrations by State: 2005**

[In thousands (155,796 represents 155,796,000). Motor vehicle registrations cover publicly, privately, and commercially owned vehicles. For uniformity, data have been adjusted to a calendar-year basis as registration years in states differ; figures represent net numbers where possible, excluding reregistrations and nonresident registrations. See also Table 1064]

State	Motor vehicle registrations [1]						2005		Motor-cycle registra-tion [2] 2005	Licensed drivers, 2005
	1980	1985	1990	1995	2000	2004	Total	Auto-mobiles (incl. taxis)		
U.S.	155,796	171,689	188,798	201,530	221,475	237,243	241,194	136,568	6,184	200,549
AL......	2,938	3,383	3,744	3,553	3,960	4,508	4,545	1,762	93	3,637
AK......	262	353	477	542	594	660	673	250	22	487
AZ......	1,917	2,235	2,825	2,873	3,795	3,776	3,972	2,121	98	3,943
AR......	1,574	1,384	1,448	1,613	1,840	1,918	1,940	951	50	2,024
CA......	16,873	18,899	21,926	22,432	27,698	31,400	32,487	19,639	659	22,896
CO	2,342	2,759	3,155	2,812	3,626	2,023	1,808	859	117	3,341
CT......	2,147	2,465	2,623	2,622	2,853	3,042	3,059	2,028	65	2,740
DE......	397	465	526	592	630	711	737	428	19	610
DC	268	306	262	243	242	239	237	185	1	330
FL......	7,614	9,865	10,950	10,369	11,781	15,057	15,691	8,312	510	13,374
GA	3,818	4,580	5,489	6,120	7,155	7,882	8,063	4,209	141	5,940
HI......	570	651	771	802	738	947	948	518	24	856
ID......	834	854	1,054	1,043	1,178	1,344	1,374	583	56	978
IL......	7,477	7,527	7,873	8,973	8,973	9,232	9,458	5,705	291	7,871
IN......	3,826	3,824	4,366	5,072	5,571	5,525	4,955	2,695	147	4,246
IA......	2,329	2,696	2,632	2,814	3,106	3,369	3,398	1,842	146	2,033
KS......	2,007	2,148	2,012	2,085	2,296	2,347	2,368	865	66	1,974
KY......	2,593	2,615	2,909	2,631	2,826	3,319	3,428	1,914	56	2,861
LA......	2,779	3,012	2,995	3,286	3,557	3,767	3,819	1,960	55	3,084
ME	724	840	977	967	1,024	1,068	1,075	589	40	1,004
MD	2,803	3,276	3,607	3,654	3,848	4,120	4,322	2,597	76	3,710
MA	3,749	3,738	3,726	4,502	5,265	5,456	5,420	3,368	140	4,613
MI......	6,488	6,727	7,209	7,674	8,436	8,399	8,247	4,753	263	7,105
MN	3,091	3,385	3,508	3,882	4,630	4,593	4,647	2,506	201	3,084
MS	1,577	1,746	1,875	2,144	2,289	1,964	1,978	1,119	27	1,965
MO	3,271	3,558	3,905	4,255	4,580	4,812	4,589	2,539	81	4,135
MT	680	652	783	968	1,026	1,009	1,009	433	48	716
NE......	1,254	1,258	1,384	1,467	1,619	1,689	1,703	836	31	1,321
NV......	655	709	853	1,047	1,220	1,281	1,349	673	50	1,596
NH......	704	974	946	1,122	1,052	1,178	1,174	652	69	998
NJ......	4,761	5,164	5,652	5,906	6,390	6,224	6,262	3,957	158	5,871
NM	1,068	1,226	1,301	1,484	1,529	1,543	1,548	686	37	1,305
NY......	8,002	9,042	10,196	10,274	10,235	11,099	11,863	8,973	190	11,072
NC	4,532	4,501	5,162	5,682	6,223	6,198	6,148	3,584	105	6,228
ND	627	655	630	695	694	701	695	341	23	467
OH	7,771	8,102	8,410	9,810	10,467	10,636	10,634	6,362	308	7,708
OK.....	2,583	2,911	2,649	2,856	3,014	3,151	3,725	1,933	82	2,234
OR.....	2,081	2,204	2,445	2,785	3,022	3,003	2,897	1,393	72	2,693
PA.....	6,926	7,209	7,971	8,481	9,260	9,821	9,864	5,888	305	8,461
RI.....	623	610	672	699	760	808	812	517	29	746
SC.....	1,996	2,222	2,521	2,833	3,095	3,257	3,339	1,933	63	2,988
SD.....	601	657	704	709	793	841	854	385	46	566
TN.....	3,271	3,754	4,444	5,400	4,820	5,035	4,980	2,833	122	4,352
TX.....	10,475	12,444	12,800	13,682	14,070	16,907	17,470	8,912	328	14,659
UT.....	992	1,099	1,206	1,447	1,628	2,084	2,210	1,090	48	1,600
VT.....	347	398	462	492	515	523	508	269	22	563
VA.....	3,626	4,253	4,938	5,613	6,046	6,497	6,591	4,067	77	5,178
WA	3,225	3,526	4,257	4,503	5,116	5,535	5,598	3,061	171	4,682
WV	1,320	1,143	1,225	1,425	1,442	1,396	1,352	700	17	1,328
WI.....	2,941	3,187	3,815	3,993	4,366	4,705	4,725	2,562	303	3,993
WY	467	500	528	601	586	641	646	232	33	383

[1] Automobiles, trucks, and buses (excludes motorcycles). Excludes vehicles owned by military services. [2] Private and commercial.

Source: U.S. Federal Highway Administration, *Highway Statistics*, annual. See Internet site <http://www.fhwa.dot.gov/policy/ohpi /hss/hsspubs.htm>.

Transportation 681

Table 1067. Roadway Congestion: 2003

[15,919 represents 15,919,000. Various federal, state, and local information sources were used to develop the data base with the primary source being the Federal Highway Administration's Highway Performance Monitoring System. Areas shown are rated the top 73 in annual per-person hours of delay]

Urbanized area	Freeway daily vehicle miles of travel		Annual person hours of delay		Annual congestion cost		
	Total miles (1,000)	Per lane-mile of freeway	Total hours (1,000)	Per person	Per person (dol.)	Delay and fuel cost (mil. dol.)	Fuel wasted (gal. per person)
Total, average	15,919	16,206	43,802	25	422	742	15
Akron, OH	5,435	12,494	3,672	6	105	62	4
Albany-Schenectady, NY	5,820	10,582	3,784	7	122	64	4
Albuquerque, NM	4,285	12,985	9,258	16	269	156	9
Allentown-Bethlehem, PA-NJ	4,600	11,646	5,618	9	151	95	6
Atlanta, GA	43,590	19,077	103,618	34	584	1,754	24
Austin, TX	9,200	15,726	23,201	27	457	391	16
Baltimore, MD.	26,050	17,026	62,436	27	458	1,057	17
Beaumont, TX	1,685	12,481	1,101	8	127	18	4
Birmingham, AL	9,020	13,363	9,705	14	242	165	10
Boston, MA-NH-RI.	37,300	15,738	100,237	25	424	1,692	15
Bridgeport-Stamford, CT-NY	10,000	16,667	14,550	17	291	250	13
Buffalo, NY	6,720	10,500	6,981	6	104	118	3
Cape Coral, FL.	435	9,667	2,712	8	141	46	5
Charleston-North, Charleston, SC. . .	3,130	12,275	6,364	14	228	107	8
Charlotte, NC-SC	7,755	15,990	16,692	23	389	282	15
Chicago, IL-IN	52,010	19,516	252,822	31	526	4,274	19
Cincinnati, OH-KY-IN	17,635	15,203	27,288	17	287	461	10
Cleveland, OH	17,390	12,647	10,709	6	97	182	4
Colorado Springs, CO	3,435	11,845	6,953	14	243	117	8
Columbus, OH	14,665	15,356	18,550	16	264	314	10
Dallas-Fort Worth-Arlington, TX	51,870	16,705	151,840	35	592	2,545	19
Dayton, OH	6,870	12,491	4,438	6	102	75	4
Denver-Aurora, CO	17,960	15,754	64,506	31	530	1,087	18
Detroit, MI	33,465	17,521	119,581	30	499	2,019	18
El Paso, TX-NM	4,030	14,393	6,491	10	164	110	6
Fresno, CA	3,280	12,377	4,180	7	120	72	5
Grand Rapids, MI	4,515	12,203	5,852	10	169	99	6
Hartford, CT.	10,425	13,196	7,434	8	144	127	6
Honolulu, HI.	5,930	14,289	7,476	11	184	129	6
Houston, TX.	46,665	18,970	135,652	36	609	2,283	22
Indianapolis, IN.	11,290	15,466	21,358	21	350	362	14
Jacksonville, FL	10,275	13,980	16,850	18	308	285	11
Kansas City, MO-KS	20,185	11,404	13,874	9	156	235	6
Las Vegas, NV	8,275	17,062	22,245	16	279	380	11
Los Angeles-Long Beach-Santa Ana, CA	136,000	23,248	623,796	50	855	10,686	33
Louisville, KY-IN	11,500	15,972	19,916	22	377	336	14
Memphis, TN-MS-AR	7,815	14,081	17,465	18	295	294	10
Miami, FL	36,685	19,057	147,294	29	487	2,486	17
Milwaukee, WI	10,465	14,950	18,249	13	214	310	8
Minneapolis-St. Paul, MN	27,580	17,346	57,537	23	394	975	15
Nashville-Davidson, TN	13,085	13,702	18,890	20	331	318	11
New Haven, CT	7,450	14,327	5,848	11	181	100	7
New Orleans, LA.	5,960	14,024	10,853	10	167	183	6
New York-Newark, NY-NJ-CT	112,555	15,698	404,480	23	383	6,780	11
Oklahoma City, OK	9,500	12,102	7,218	7	112	122	4
Omaha, NE-IA	3,600	12,000	7,984	13	211	134	7
Orlando, FL	10,570	13,551	38,157	30	510	643	18
Oxnard-Ventura, CA	6,700	18,873	10,249	18	307	176	12
Pensacola, FL-AL	1,200	10,909	2,977	10	162	50	5
Philadelphia, PA-NJ-DE-MD	33,875	14,728	112,309	21	357	1,884	11
Phoenix, AZ	23,610	17,819	76,662	26	431	1,294	15
Pittsburgh, PA.	12,210	9,768	14,530	8	135	243	4
Portland, OR-WA	12,945	18,105	33,387	20	341	569	13
Providence, RI-MA	11,095	12,328	21,668	18	295	363	9
Raleigh-Durham, NC	8,145	13,352	11,481	15	248	194	10
Richmond, VA.	10,830	10,995	8,305	9	153	140	5
Riverside-San Bernardino, CA. . . .	19,500	21,429	50,155	30	517	863	21
Sacramento, CA	13,705	19,303	35,929	22	374	619	15
Salem, OR.	1,245	12,450	1,714	5	135	29	5
Salt Lake City, UT	8,300	15,660	15,094	16	279	257	11
San Antonio, TX	16,100	14,977	23,788	18	301	401	11
San Diego, CA	36,195	19,460	81,756	28	492	1,411	21
San Francisco-Oakland, CA	48,985	20,242	152,352	37	631	2,605	23
San Jose, CA	16,565	18,508	48,134	29	492	823	18
Sarasota-Bradenton, FL	825	12,692	5,772	10	170	97	6
Seattle, WA	30,700	17,593	72,461	25	427	1,237	17
St. Louis, MO-IL	26,145	14,647	39,936	19	326	675	13
Tampa-St. Petersburg, FL.	9,855	14,600	51,360	25	422	865	14
Toledo, OH-MI	4,115	12,470	3,391	7	110	57	4
Tucson, AZ	3,285	13,408	13,767	19	324	233	12
Tulsa, OK	7,025	10,036	5,419	7	113	91	4
Virginia Beach, VA.	12,875	13,697	21,746	14	239	367	9
Washington, DC-VA-MD	37,815	18,537	145,484	34	577	2,465	21

Source: Texas Transportation Institute, College Station, Texas; 2005 Urban Mobility Study (issued May 2005). (Copyright). See <http://mobility.tamu.edu/ums/>.

682 Transportation

Table 1068. **Commuting to Work by State: 2005**

[In percent, except as indicated (133,091 represents 133,091,000). **For workers 16 years old and over.** The American Community Survey universe is limited to the household population and excludes the population living in institutions, college dormitories, and other group quarters. Based on a sample and subject to sampling variability; see Appendix III]

State	Total workers (1,000)	Commuted by car, truck, or van — Drove alone	Commuted by car, truck, or van — Car-pooled	Used public transportation [1]	Walked	Used other means [2]	Worked at home	Mean travel time to work (min.)
U.S.	133,091	77.0	10.7	4.7	2.5	1.6	3.6	25.1
AL.........	1,941	84.0	10.9	0.4	1.2	1.3	2.2	23.4
AK.........	295	68.2	15.1	1.2	6.6	4.8	4.1	18.3
AZ.........	2,575	75.5	14.2	1.9	2.1	2.2	4.0	24.8
AR.........	1,201	81.7	12.3	0.3	1.6	1.4	2.6	21.0
CA.........	15,547	74.0	12.5	4.7	2.5	2.0	4.3	27.0
CO.........	2,280	76.4	10.0	2.7	2.9	1.9	6.0	23.5
CT.........	1,657	81.1	8.2	4.2	2.0	1.2	3.3	24.8
DE.........	397	80.3	10.6	2.2	1.8	1.5	3.7	23.7
DC.........	250	37.5	7.7	37.7	10.0	2.6	4.4	29.3
FL.........	7,701	80.0	11.1	1.8	1.6	2.0	3.6	26.0
GA	4,099	80.0	11.3	2.2	1.3	1.6	3.6	27.2
HI	584	68.4	15.6	5.7	3.3	2.4	4.6	25.7
ID	656	76.2	12.2	0.9	3.3	2.4	4.9	19.8
IL	5,794	75.0	9.4	8.2	2.6	1.4	3.4	28.1
IN	2,835	83.1	9.4	0.9	1.9	1.5	3.1	22.5
IA	1,471	80.1	10.1	0.8	3.2	1.6	4.3	18.4
KS.........	1,330	82.6	9.1	0.4	2.5	1.5	4.0	18.4
KY.........	1,766	82.8	10.9	0.9	1.7	1.0	2.8	22.5
LA	1,858	81.0	11.0	1.9	1.7	2.0	2.3	24.9
ME	641	79.8	10.1	0.7	3.6	1.2	4.6	23.3
MD	2,706	73.6	10.9	8.5	2.1	1.3	3.7	30.8
MA	3,031	75.0	8.5	8.1	3.8	1.2	3.4	27.0
MI	4,399	84.3	8.7	1.1	1.8	1.0	3.1	23.5
MN	2,596	79.0	9.5	2.8	2.7	1.3	4.7	22.2
MS	1,182	82.4	12.4	0.4	1.3	1.6	1.9	23.5
MO	2,683	81.6	10.5	1.3	1.8	1.2	3.6	23.0
MT	455	75.2	11.0	0.6	4.6	2.6	6.0	17.3
NE	884	81.0	10.0	0.6	2.7	1.2	4.5	17.9
NV.........	1,138	78.1	11.7	3.0	2.3	1.9	3.0	23.3
NH	668	82.4	8.8	0.7	2.8	1.1	4.2	25.0
NJ.........	3,985	72.8	9.3	10.3	3.1	1.5	3.0	29.5
NM	832	76.6	13.6	0.9	2.5	1.6	4.8	21.2
NY.........	8,423	55.4	7.8	25.8	5.6	1.9	3.5	31.2
NC	3,908	81.2	11.9	0.9	1.4	1.5	3.2	23.3
ND	329	78.2	10.8	0.4	4.1	1.3	5.2	16.3
OH	5,173	84.0	8.4	1.7	1.9	1.0	3.0	22.4
OK	1,567	81.8	11.0	0.6	1.8	1.7	3.2	20.1
OR	1,670	73.4	11.5	4.1	3.2	2.6	5.1	21.9
PA.........	5,539	77.3	9.7	5.1	3.6	1.1	3.1	25.1
RI	501	81.6	8.9	2.7	2.5	1.5	2.8	22.7
SC.........	1,853	82.4	11.5	0.7	1.5	1.6	2.4	23.6
SD.........	382	77.5	11.0	0.3	4.0	1.1	6.1	16.6
TN.........	2,657	83.6	10.4	0.7	1.4	1.2	2.8	23.6
TX.........	9,969	79.3	12.5	1.7	1.5	1.8	3.3	24.6
UT.........	1,152	76.5	12.8	2.3	2.1	1.6	4.7	20.5
VT.........	316	75.8	11.0	0.9	5.2	1.5	5.5	21.2
VA.........	3,603	78.4	11.4	3.7	1.7	1.3	3.5	27.0
WA	2,913	74.3	11.9	4.7	2.9	1.7	4.6	24.7
WV	724	81.9	10.9	0.7	2.5	1.2	2.9	24.9
WI	2,715	81.1	9.0	1.5	2.9	1.6	3.8	20.8
WY	258	74.3	12.5	1.6	4.4	1.6	5.7	17.3

[1] Excluding taxicabs. [2] Includes taxicabs, motorcycles, bicycles, and other means.

Source: U.S. Census Bureau; 2005 American Community Survey; B08006. Sex of Worker by Means of Transportation to Work; and R0801. Mean Travel Time to Work of Workers 16 Years Old and Over Who Did Not Work At Home (minutes); using American FactFinder; <http://factfinder.census.gov/>; (accessed (8 January 2007).

Transportation 683

Table 1069. **Motor Vehicle Distance Traveled by Type of Vehicle: 1970 to 2005**

[1,110 represents 1,110,000,000,000. Travel estimates based on automatic vehicle classification data]

Year	Vehicle-miles of travel (bil.)					Average miles per vehicle (1,000)				
	Total [1]	Cars [1]	Buses [2]	Vans, pickups, SUVs	Trucks [3]	Total [1]	Cars [1]	Buses [2]	Vans, pickups, SUVs	Trucks [3]
1970 . . .	1,110	920	4.5	123	62	10.0	10.0	12.0	8.7	13.6
1980 . . .	1,527	1,122	6.1	291	108	9.5	8.8	11.5	10.4	18.7
1984 . . .	1,720	1,236	4.6	358	122	10.0	9.2	8.0	11.2	22.6
1985 . . .	1,775	1,256	4.5	391	124	10.0	9.4	7.5	10.5	20.6
1986 . . .	1,835	1,280	4.7	424	127	10.1	9.5	7.9	10.8	22.1
1987 . . .	1,921	1,325	5.3	457	134	10.5	9.7	8.9	11.1	23.3
1988 . . .	2,026	1,380	5.5	502	138	10.7	10.0	8.9	11.5	22.5
1989 . . .	2,096	1,412	5.7	536	143	10.9	10.2	9.1	11.7 ⸳	22.9
1990 . . .	2,144	1,418	5.7	575	146	11.1	10.3	9.1	11.9	23.6
1991 . . .	2,172	1,367	5.8	649	150	11.3	10.3	9.1	12.2	24.2
1992 . . .	2,247	1,381	5.8	707	153	11.6	10.6	9.0	12.4	25.4
1993 . . .	2,296	1,385	6.1	746	160	11.6	10.5	9.4	12.4	26.3
1994 . . .	2,358	1,416	6.4	765	170	11.7	10.8	9.6	12.2	25.8
1995 . . .	2,423	1,438	6.4	790	178	11.8	11.2	9.4	12.0	26.5
1996 . . .	2,486	1,470	6.6	817	183	11.8	11.3	9.4	11.8	26.1
1997 . . .	2,562	1,503	6.8	851	191	12.1	11.6	9.8	12.1	27.0
1998 . . .	2,632	1,550	7.0	868	196	12.2	11.8	9.8	12.2	25.4
1999 . . .	2,691	1,569	7.7	901	203	12.2	11.9	10.5	12.0	26.0
2000 . . .	2,747	1,600	7.6	923	206	12.2	11.9	10.2	11.7	25.7
2001 . . .	2,797	1,628	7.1	943	209	11.9	11.8	9.4	11.2	26.6
2002 . . .	2,856	1,658	6.8	966	215	12.2	12.2	9.0	11.4	27.1
2003 . . .	2,890	1,672	6.8	984	218	12.2	12.3	8.7	11.3	28.1
2004 . . .	2,965	1,700	6.8	1,027	221	12.2	12.5	8.5	11.2	27.0
2005 . . .	2,989	1,690	6.6	1,059	223	12.1	12.4	8.2	11.1	26.3

[1] Motorcycles included with cars through 1994; thereafter in total, not shown separately. [2] Includes school buses. [3] Includes combinations.

Source: U.S. Federal Highway Administration, *Highway Statistics*, annual. See Internet site <http://www.fhwa.dot.gov/policy/ohpi/hss/hsspubs.htm>.

Table 1070. **Domestic Motor Fuel Consumption by Type of Vehicle: 1970 to 2005**

[92.3 represents 92,300,000,000. Comprises all fuel types used for propulsion of vehicles under state motor fuels laws. Excludes federal purchases for military use. Minus sign (−) indicates decrease]

Year	Annual fuel consumption (bil. gal.)					Average miles per gallon				
	All vehicles [1]	Avg. annual percent change [2]	Cars [1]	Buses [3]	Vans, pickups, SUVs	Trucks [4]	All vehicles [1]	Cars [1]	Buses [3]	Vans, pickups, SUVs	Trucks [4]
1970 . . .	92.3	4.8	67.8	0.8	12.3	11.3	12.0	13.5	5.5	10.0	5.5
1980 . . .	115.0	−5.9	70.2	1.0	23.8	20.0	13.3	16.0	6.0	12.2	5.4
1984 . . .	118.7	2.2	70.8	0.8	25.6	21.4	14.5	17.4	5.7	14.0	5.7
1985 . . .	121.3	2.2	71.7	0.8	27.4	21.4	14.6	17.5	5.4	14.3	5.8
1986 . . .	125.2	3.2	73.4	0.9	29.1	21.9	14.7	17.4	5.3	14.6	5.8
1987 . . .	127.5	1.8	73.5	0.9	30.6	22.5	15.1	18.0	5.8	14.9	5.9
1988 . . .	130.1	2.0	73.5	0.9	32.7	22.9	15.6	18.8	5.8	15.4	6.0
1989 . . .	131.9	1.4	74.1	0.9	33.3	23.5	15.9	18.0	6.0	16.1	6.1
1990 . . .	130.8	−0.8	69.8	0.9	35.6	24.5	16.4	20.3	6.4	16.1	6.0
1991 . . .	128.6	−1.7	64.5	0.9	38.2	25.0	16.9	21.2	6.7	17.0	6.0
1992 . . .	132.9	3.3	65.6	0.9	40.9	25.5	16.9	21.0	6.6	17.3	6.0
1993 . . .	137.3	3.3	67.2	0.9	42.9	26.2	16.7	20.6	6.6	17.4	6.1
1994 . . .	140.8	2.5	68.1	1.0	44.1	27.7	16.7	20.8	6.6	17.3	6.1
1995 . . .	143.8	2.1	68.1	1.0	45.6	29.0	16.8	21.1	6.6	17.3	6.1
1996 . . .	147.4	2.5	69.2	1.0	47.4	29.6	16.9	21.2	6.6	17.2	6.2
1997 . . .	150.4	2.0	69.9	1.0	49.4	29.9	17.0	21.5	6.7	17.2	6.4
1998 . . .	155.4	3.3	71.7	1.1	50.5	32.0	16.9	21.6	6.7	17.2	6.1
1999 . . .	161.4	3.9	73.2	1.1	52.8	33.9	16.7	21.4	6.7	17.0	6.0
2000 . . .	162.5	0.7	73.1	1.1	52.9	35.2	16.9	21.9	6.8	17.4	5.8
2001 . . .	163.5	0.6	73.6	1.0	53.5	35.2	17.1	22.1	6.9	17.6	5.9
2002 . . .	168.7	3.2	75.5	1.0	55.2	36.8	16.9	22.0	6.8	17.5	5.8
2003 . . .	170.0	0.8	75.5	1.0	60.7	32.7	17.0	22.2	7.0	16.2	6.7
2004 . . .	173.5	2.1	75.4	1.3	63.4	33.1	17.1	22.5	5.0	16.2	6.7
2005 . . .	174.3	0.5	73.9	1.3	65.4	33.4	17.2	22.9	5.0	16.2	6.7

[1] Motorcycles included with cars through 1994; thereafter in total, not shown separately. [2] Change from immediate prior year. [3] Includes school buses. [4] Includes combinations.

Source: U.S. Federal Highway Administration, *Highway Statistics*, annual. See Internet site <http://www.fhwa.dot.gov/policy/ohpi/hss/hsspubs.htm>.

684 Transportation

Table 1071. Motor Vehicle Accidents—Number and Deaths: 1980 to 2005

[17.9 represents 17,900,000]

Item	Unit	1980	1985	1990	1995	2000	2002	2003	2004	2005
ACCIDENTS										
Motor vehicle accidents [1]	Million ...	17.9	19.3	11.5	10.7	13.4	18.3	11.8	10.9	10.7
Vehicles involved:										
Cars	Million ...	22.8	25.6	14.3	12.3	15.9	18.1	11.5	10.8	(NA)
Trucks	Million ...	5.5	6.1	4.4	4.5	8.8	12.2	8.2	8.1	(NA)
Motorcycles	1,000 ...	560	480	180	152	130	190	150	150	(NA)
DEATHS										
Motor vehicle deaths within 1 yr. [2] ...	1,000 ...	53.2	45.9	46.8	43.4	43.4	45.4	44.1	46.2	45.8
Noncollision accidents	1,000 ...	(NA)	(NA)	4.9	4.4	4.8	5.3	5.1	5.2	5.3
Collision accidents:										
With other motor vehicles	1,000 ...	23.0	19.9	19.9	19.0	19.1	19.2	19.8	20.6	19.2
With pedestrians	1,000 ...	9.7	8.5	7.3	6.4	5.9	6.1	5.7	5.9	6.2
With fixed objects..........	1,000 ...	(NA)	(NA)	13.1	12.1	12.3	13.6	12.4	13.3	13.7
Deaths within 30 days [3]	1,000 ...	51.1	43.8	44.6	41.8	41.9	43.0	42.9	42.8	43.4
Occupants.................	1,000 ...	36.8	31.5	33.9	33.1	33.5	34.1	33.6	33.3	33.0
Passenger cars	1,000 ...	27.4	23.2	24.1	22.4	20.7	20.6	19.7	19.2	18.4
Light trucks [4]	1,000 ...	7.5	6.7	8.6	9.6	11.5	12.3	12.5	12.7	13.0
Large trucks [4]	1,000 ...	1.3	1.0	0.7	0.6	0.8	0.7	0.7	0.8	0.8
Buses	1,000 ...	(Z)	0.1	(Z)	(Z)	(Z)	(Z)	(Z)	0.0	0.1
Other/unknown............	1,000 ...	0.5	0.5	0.5	0.4	0.5	0.5	0.6	0.6	0.8
Motorcycle riders [5].........	1,000 ...	5.1	4.6	3.2	2.2	2.9	3.3	3.7	4.0	4.6
Nonoccupants.............	1,000 ...	9.2	7.8	7.5	6.5	5.6	5.6	5.5	5.5	5.8
Pedestrians	1,000 ...	8.1	6.8	6.5	5.6	4.8	4.9	4.8	4.7	4.9
Pedalcyclist.............	1,000 ...	1.0	0.9	0.9	0.8	0.7	0.7	0.6	0.7	0.8
Other/unknown	1,000 ...	0.1	0.1	0.1	0.1	0.1	0.1	0.1	0.1	0.2
Traffic death rates: [3, 6]										
Per 100 million vehicle miles	Rate	3.3	2.5	2.1	1.7	1.5	1.5	1.5	1.4	1.5
Per 100,000 licensed drivers	Rate	35.2	27.9	26.7	23.7	22.0	22.1	21.9	21.5	21.7
Per 100,000 registered vehicles ...	Rate	34.8	26.4	24.2	21.2	19.3	19.1	18.6	18.0	17.7
Per 100,000 resident population...	Rate	22.5	18.4	17.9	15.9	14.9	14.9	14.8	14.6	14.7

NA Not available.   Z Fewer than 50.   [1] Covers only accidents occurring on the road. Data are estimated. Year-to-year comparisons should be made with caution.   [2] Deaths that occur within 1 year of accident. Includes collision categories not shown separately.   [3] Within 30 days of accident. Source: U.S. National Highway Traffic Safety Administration, Traffic Safety Facts, annual; and unpublished data. See Internet site <http://www.nhtsa.dot.gov/people/Crash/Index.html>.   [4] See footnotes 2 and 3 in Table 1075.   [5] Includes motorized cycles.   [6] Based on 30-day definition of traffic deaths.

Source: Except as noted, National Safety Council, Itasca, IL, Injury Facts, annual (copyright). See Internet site <http://www.nsc.org/>.

Table 1072. Traffic Fatalities by State: 1980 to 2005

[For deaths within 30 days of the accident]

State	1980	1990	2000	2005	Fatality rate [1] 1980	Fatality rate [1] 2005	State	1980	1990	2000	2005	Fatality rate [1] 1980	Fatality rate [1] 2005
U.S. ...	51,091	44,599	41,945	43,443	3.3	1.5	MO	1,175	1,097	1,157	1,257	3.4	1.8
							MT......	325	212	237	251	4.9	2.3
AL	940	1,121	996	1,131	3.2	1.9	NE......	396	262	276	276	3.5	1.4
AK	88	98	106	72	3.3	1.4	NV......	346	343	323	427	5.7	2.1
AZ	947	869	1,036	1,177	5.3	2.0	NH......	194	158	126	166	3.0	1.2
AR	588	604	652	648	3.6	2.0	NJ	1,120	886	731	748	2.2	1.0
CA	5,496	5,192	3,753	4,329	3.5	1.3	NM.....	606	499	432	488	5.4	2.0
CO	709	544	681	606	3.2	1.3	NY......	2,610	2,217	1,460	1,429	3.4	1.0
CT	575	385	341	274	3.0	0.9	NC......	1,503	1,385	1,557	1,534	3.6	1.5
DE	153	138	123	134	3.6	1.4	ND......	151	112	86	123	2.9	1.6
DC	41	48	48	48	1.2	1.3	OH......	2,033	1,638	1,366	1,323	2.8	1.2
FL	2,825	2,891	2,999	3,543	3.6	1.8	OK......	959	641	650	802	3.5	1.7
GA	1,508	1,562	1,541	1,729	3.5	1.5	OR......	646	579	451	488	3.4	1.4
HI	186	177	132	140	3.3	1.4	PA	2,089	1,646	1,520	1,616	2.9	1.5
ID	331	244	276	275	4.8	1.9	RI	129	84	80	87	2.4	1.1
IL	1,975	1,589	1,418	1,361	3.0	1.3	SC	852	979	1,065	1,093	3.8	2.2
IN	1,166	1,049	886	938	3.0	1.3	SD	228	153	173	186	3.7	2.2
IA	626	465	445	450	3.3	1.5	TN	1,153	1,177	1,307	1,270	3.4	1.8
KS	595	444	461	428	3.4	1.4	TX	4,366	3,250	3,779	3,504	3.8	1.5
KY......	820	849	820	985	3.2	2.1	UT	334	272	373	282	3.1	1.1
LA	1,219	959	938	955	5.0	2.1	VT	137	90	76	73	3.7	1.0
ME......	265	213	169	169	3.5	1.1	VA	1,045	1,079	929	947	2.7	1.2
MD......	756	707	588	614	2.6	1.1	WA	971	825	631	647	3.4	1.2
MA......	881	605	433	442	2.5	0.8	WV	523	481	411	374	4.9	1.8
MI	1,750	1,571	1,382	1,129	2.8	1.1	WI	972	769	799	815	3.1	1.4
MN......	848	566	625	559	3.0	1.0	WY	245	125	152	170	4.9	1.9
MS......	695	750	949	931	4.2	2.2							

[1] Deaths per 100 million vehicle miles traveled.

Source: U.S. National Highway Safety Traffic Administration, Traffic Safety Facts, annual. See Internet site <http://www.nhtsa.dot.gov/people/Crash/Index.html>.

Transportation   685

Table 1073. **Fatal Motor Vehicle Accidents—National Summary: 1990 to 2005**

[Based on data from the Fatality Analysis Reporting System (FARS). FARS gathers data on accidents that result in loss of human life. FARS is operated and maintained by National Highway Traffic Safety Administration's (NHTSA) National Center for Statistics and Analysis (NCSA). FARS data are gathered on motor vehicle accidents that occurred on a roadway customarily open to the public, resulting in the death of a person within 30 days of the accident. Collection of these data depend on the use of police, hospital, medical examiner/coroner, and Emergency Medical Services reports; State vehicle registration, driver licensing, and highway department files; and vital statistics documents and death certificates. See source for further detail]

Item	1990	1995	2000	2001	2002	2003	2004	2005
Fatal crashes, total	**39,836**	**37,241**	**37,526**	**37,862**	**38,491**	**38,477**	**38,444**	**39,189**
One vehicle involved	23,445	21,250	21,117	21,510	22,164	21,775	21,836	22,653
Two or more vehicles involved.	16,391	15,991	16,409	16,352	16,327	16,702	16,608	16,536
Persons killed in fatal crashes [1]	**44,599**	**41,817**	**41,945**	**42,196**	**43,005**	**42,884**	**42,836**	**43,443**
Occupants	37,134	35,291	36,348	36,440	37,375	37,341	37,304	37,594
Drivers.	25,750	24,390	25,567	25,869	26,659	26,779	26,871	27,472
Passengers	11,276	10,782	10,695	10,469	10,604	10,458	10,355	10,036
Other	108	119	86	102	112	104	78	86
Nonoccupants	7,465	6,526	5,597	5,756	5,630	5,543	5,532	5,849
Pedestrians	6,482	5,584	4,763	4,901	4,851	4,774	4,675	4,881
Pedalcyclists.	859	833	693	732	665	629	727	784
Other	124	109	141	123	114	140	130	184
Occupants killed by vehicle type:								
Passenger cars	24,092	22,423	20,699	20,320	20,569	19,725	19,192	18,440
Mini-compact (95 inches)	3,556	2,207	1,113	887	813	636	599	452
Subcompact (95 to 99 inches)	4,753	4,584	3,660	3,571	3,435	3,081	2,718	2,527
Compact (100 to 104 inches).	5,310	6,899	7,022	6,731	7,061	6,769	6,650	6,245
Intermediate (105 to 109) inches	4,849	4,666	5,204	5,402	5,514	5,583	5,667	5,548
Full-size (110 to 114) inches	2,386	2,116	2,287	2,344	2,434	2,451	2,354	2,483
Largest (115 inches and over)	2,249	1,297	897	864	828	782	807	793
Unknown	989	654	516	521	484	423	397	392
Motorcycles	3,129	2,114	2,783	3,077	3,150	3,583	3,827	4,398
Other motorized cycles	115	113	114	120	120	131	201	155
Light trucks [2]	8,601	9,568	11,526	11,723	12,274	12,546	12,674	12,975
Pickup.	5,979	5,938	6,003	6,139	6,100	5,957	5,838	6,038
Utility.	1,214	1,935	3,358	3,530	4,031	4,483	4,760	4,807
Van.	1,154	1,639	2,129	2,019	2,109	2,080	2,046	2,105
Other . . . . [3] . . .	254	56	36	35	34	26	30	25
Large trucks [3]	705	648	754	702	689	726	766	803
Medium trucks	134	96	106	82	87	82	99	117
Heavy trucks	571	552	648	620	602	644	667	686
Buses.	32	33	22	34	45	41	42	58
Other vehicles	296	307	401	401	424	477	512	487
Unknown.	164	85	49	63	104	112	90	278
Persons involved in fatal crashes.	**107,777**	**102,102**	**100,716**	**101,175**	**101,784**	**101,862**	**100,760**	**101,034**
Occupants	99,297	94,621	94,325	94,706	95,403	95,470	94,579	94,405
Drivers.	58,893	56,164	57,280	57,586	58,113	58,517	58,395	59,104
Passengers	40,229	38,252	36,889	36,892	37,080	36,743	35,992	35,138
Other	175	205	156	228	210	210	192	163
Nonoccupants	8,480	7,481	6,391	6,469	6,381	6,392	6,181	6,629
Vehicle miles traveled (VMT) (bil.)	2,144	2,423	2,747	2,797	2,856	2,890	2,965	2,990
Licensed drivers (1,000)	167,015	176,628	190,625	191,276	194,602	196,166	198,889	200,665
Registered vehicles (1,000)	184,275	197,065	217,028	221,230	225,685	230,788	237,949	245,642
Percent distribution of fatal accidents by the highest blood alcohol concentration (BAC) in accident:								
0.00 percent	49.5	57.7	58.7	58.9	59.2	60.2	60.5	61.1
0.01 to 0.07 percent	6.5	5.7	5.9	5.9	5.6	5.6	5.4	5.3
0.08 percent and over	44.0	36.7	35.4	35.2	35.3	34.3	34.2	33.6
Fatalities per 100,000 resident population:								
Under 5 years old	4.9	4.3	3.7	3.4	3.1	3.1	3.2	2.9
5 to 15 years old	6.4	6.0	4.7	4.3	4.3	4.4	4.4	3.9
16 to 24 years old.	35.2	30.7	28.5	28.6	29.3	28.1	27.7	27.4
25 to 44 years old	19.7	17.2	16.1	16.2	16.2	16.0	15.8	16.3
45 to 64 years old	14.9	13.6	13.8	13.5	13.8	14.0	13.9	14.2
65 to 79 years old.	18.8	18.5	17.1	17.1	17.0	16.3	16.3	16.2
80 years old and over	26.8	28.0	25.0	24.5	23.3	24.5	22.4	21.3
Fatalities per 100 million VMT [4]	2.1	1.7	1.5	1.5	1.5	1.5	1.4	1.5
Fatalities per 100,000 licensed drivers	26.7	23.7	22.0	22.1	22.1	21.9	21.5	21.7
Licensed driver per person.	0.7	0.7	0.7	0.7	0.7	0.7	0.7	0.7
VMT [3] per registered vehicle	11,637	12,294	12,657	12,644	12,653	12,522	12,461	12,172
Fatalities per 100,000 registered vehicles . .	24.2	21.2	19.3	19.1	19.1	18.6	18.0	17.7
Fatal crashes per 100 million VMT [3]	1.9	1.5	1.4	1.4	1.3	1.3	1.3	1.3
Involved vehicles per fatal crash	1.5	1.5	1.5	1.5	1.5	1.5	1.4	1.4
Fatalities per fatal crash	1.1	1.1	1.1	1.1	1.1	1.1	1.1	1.1
Fatalities per 100,000 resident population	17.9	15.9	14.9	14.8	14.9	14.8	14.6	14.7

[1] Deaths within 30 days of the accident.   [2] Trucks with a gross vehicle weight rating of 10,000 pounds or less, including pickups, vans, truck-based station wagons, and utility vehicles.   [3] Trucks with a gross vehicle weight rating of over 10,000 pounds.   [4] VMT = vehicle miles of travel.

Source: U.S. National Highway Traffic Safety Administration, *Fatality Analysis Reporting System,* annual. See Internet site <http://www.nhtsa.dot.gov/people/Crash/Index.html>.

Table 1074. **Motor Vehicle Occupants and Nonoccupants Killed and Injured: 1980 to 2005**

[For deaths within 30 days of the accident. (3,416 represents 3,416,000)]

Year	Total	Occupants						Motor-cycle riders[2]	Nonoccupants			
		Total	Passenger cars	Light trucks[1]	Large trucks[1]	Buses	Other/unknown[3]		Total	Pedestrian	Pedal-cyclist	Other/unknown[3]
KILLED												
1980	51,091	36,783	27,449	7,486	1,262	46	540	5,144	9,164	8,070	965	129
1985	43,825	31,479	23,212	6,689	977	57	544	4,564	7,782	6,808	890	84
1990	44,599	33,890	24,092	8,601	705	32	460	3,244	7,465	6,482	859	124
1994	40,716	31,998	21,997	8,904	670	18	409	2,320	6,398	5,489	802	107
1995	41,817	33,064	22,423	9,568	648	33	392	2,227	6,526	5,584	833	109
1996 [4]	42,065	33,534	22,505	9,932	621	21	455	2,161	6,368	5,449	765	154
1997	42,013	33,609	22,199	10,249	723	18	420	2,116	6,288	5,321	814	153
1998	41,501	33,088	21,194	10,705	742	38	409	2,294	6,119	5,228	760	131
1999	41,717	33,392	20,862	11,265	759	59	447	2,483	5,842	4,939	754	149
2000	41,945	33,451	20,699	11,526	754	22	450	2,897	5,597	4,763	693	141
2001	42,196	33,243	20,320	11,723	708	34	458	3,197	5,756	4,901	732	123
2002	43,005	34,105	20,569	12,274	689	45	528	3,270	5,630	4,851	665	114
2003	42,884	33,627	19,725	12,546	726	41	589	3,714	5,543	4,774	629	140
2004	42,836	33,276	19,192	12,674	766	42	602	4,028	5,532	4,675	727	130
2005	43,443	33,041	18,440	12,975	803	58	765	4,553	5,849	4,881	784	184
INJURED (1,000)												
1988	3,416	3,119	2,585	478	37	15	4	105	192	110	75	8
1990	3,231	2,960	2,376	505	42	33	4	84	187	105	75	7
1994	3,266	3,045	2,364	631	30	16	4	57	164	92	62	9
1995	3,465	3,246	2,469	722	30	19	4	57	162	86	67	10
1996	3,483	3,277	2,458	761	33	20	4	55	151	82	58	11
1997	3,348	3,149	2,341	755	31	17	6	53	146	77	58	11
1998	3,192	3,012	2,201	763	29	16	4	49	131	69	53	8
1999	3,236	3,047	2,138	847	33	22	7	50	140	85	51	3
2000	3,189	2,997	2,052	887	31	18	10	58	134	78	51	5
2001	3,033	2,841	1,927	861	29	15	9	60	131	78	45	8
2002	2,926	2,735	1,805	879	26	19	6	65	126	71	48	7
2003	2,889	2,697	1,756	889	27	18	7	67	124	70	46	8
2004	2,788	2,594	1,643	900	27	16	7	76	118	68	41	9
2005	2,699	2,494	1,573	872	27	11	10	87	118	64	45	8

[1] See footnotes 2 and 3 in Table 1075. [2] Includes motorized cycles. [3] Includes combination trucks. [4] Total includes two fatalities of unknown person type, not specified in distribution.

Source: U.S. National Highway Traffic Safety Administration, *Traffic Safety Facts*, annual; and unpublished data. See Internet site <http://www.nhtsa.dot.gov/people/Crash/Index.html>.

Table 1075. **Vehicles Involved in Crashes by Vehicle Type, Rollover Occurrence, and Crash Severity: 2005**

[10,775.1 represents 10,775,100. Excludes motorcycles]

Vehicle type	Total		Rollover occurrence			
			Yes		No	
	Number (1,000)	Percent	Number (1,000)	Percent	Number (1,000)	Percent
Vehicles involved in all crashes [1]	10,755.1	100.0	279.9	2.6	10,475.2	97.4
Passenger cars	6,087.2	100.0	108.7	1.8	5,978.6	98.2
Light trucks: [2]						
Pickup	1,652.6	100.0	60.7	3.7	1,592.0	96.3
Utility	1,583.4	100.0	75.9	4.8	1,507.5	95.2
Van	795.3	100.0	15.4	1.9	779.9	98.1
Other	119.8	100.0	2.1	1.8	117.7	98.2
Large truck [3]	441.5	100.0	14.2	3.2	427.4	96.8
Bus	51.4	100.0	0.4	0.8	50.9	99.2
Other/unknown	23.7	100.0	2.5	10.7	21.2	89.3
Fatal crashes	54.7	100.0	11.5	21.1	43.2	78.9
Passenger cars	25.0	100.0	4.1	16.4	20.9	83.6
Light trucks: [2]						
Pickup	10.9	100.0	2.9	26.7	8.0	73.3
Utility	8.1	100.0	2.9	35.4	5.3	64.6
Van	3.7	100.0	0.7	18.8	3.0	81.2
Other	0.1	100.0	(Z)	21.3	0.1	78.8
Large truck [3]	4.9	100.0	0.7	13.6	4.3	86.4
Bus	0.3	100.0	(Z)	2.5	0.3	97.5
Other/unknown	1.6	100.0	0.2	14.2	1.4	85.8

Z Less than 50. [1] Includes injury and property-only crashes, not shown separately. [2] Trucks of 10,000 pounds gross vehicle weight rating or less, including pickups, vans, truck-based station wagons and utility vehicles. [3] Trucks over 10,000 pounds gross vehicle weight rating.

Source: U.S. National Highway Safety Traffic Administration, *Traffic Safety Facts*, annual. See Internet site <http://www.nhtsa.dot.gov/people/Crash/Index.html>.

Table 1076. **Speeding-Related Traffic Fatalities by State and Road Type and Speed Limit: 2005**

[Speeding consists of exceeding the posted speed limit or driving too fast for the road conditions or any speed-related violation charged (racing, driving above speed limit, speed greater than reasonable, exceeding special speed limit)]

State	Traffic fatalities, total	Speeding-related fatalities by road type and speed limit								
		Interstate			Noninterstate					
		Total [1]	Over 55 mph	At or under 55 mph	55 mph	50 mph	45 mph	40 mph	35 mph	Under 35 mph
United States	43,443	13,113	1,384	342	3,462	510	1,719	886	1,453	1,341
Alabama	1,131	493	53	7	118	15	175	31	39	25
Alaska.	72	27	7	3	4	–	2	1	5	3
Arizona	1,177	460	109	15	36	23	71	73	32	35
Arkansas	648	104	5	–	52	3	11	7	17	5
California.	4,329	1,471	203	30	344	60	145	131	181	156
Colorado	606	204	16	11	25	10	30	24	22	30
Connecticut	274	92	3	7	1	–	9	9	9	49
Delaware.	134	52	1	5	4	26	–	5	6	2
District of Columbia . . .	48	17	–	5	–	–	–	–	2	10
Florida.	3,543	239	14	7	30	11	52	20	33	33
Georgia	1,729	340	22	5	105	6	51	5	43	18'
Hawaii.	140	69	–	6	6	1	6	1	25	20
Idaho	275	95	14	–	11	11	7	5	8	8
Illinois	1,361	525	68	22	199	16	48	46	62	61
Indiana	938	258	19	17	59	10	42	34	27	46
Iowa	450	44	5	–	19	2	5	–	7	4
Kansas	428	119	16	–	37	2	6	4	4	19
Kentucky	985	187	12	6	117	–	22	2	17	10
Louisiana.	955	180	14	3	70	4	34	7	27	13
Maine	169	86	11	3	9	9	21	11	9	10
Maryland	614	214	14	15	19	34	22	29	30	46
Massachusetts	442	146	11	3	4	3	11	21	28	57
Michigan	1,129	243	26	11	120	4	24	2	14	25
Minnesota	559	152	13	4	85	7	6	4	2	20
Mississippi	931	254	36	–	91	20	45	9	21	8
Missouri.	1,257	529	59	9	197	6	31	28	66	51
Montana	251	97	17	–	2	2	4	–	9	10
Nebraska.	276	51	10	–	5	11	2	3	8	5
Nevada	427	160	24	–	10	8	23	1	23	9
New Hampshire	166	56	4	1	4	5	1	6	14	16
New Jersey	748	79	–	3	10	21	12	3	9	13
New Mexico.	488	165	33	2	28	1	12	7	10	11
New York.	1,429	456	13	13	173	15	27	37	21	77
North Carolina	1,534	560	40	7	287	4	121	1	72	14
North Dakota	123	28	2	1	8	2	–	1	–	3
Ohio	1,323	277	23	6	123	4	28	7	51	21
Oklahoma	802	292	27	2	64	8	71	13	18	15
Oregon	488	161	10	2	76	3	11	7	19	14
Pennsylvania	1,616	757	44	18	195	18	167	91	144	54
Rhode Island	87	40	6	3	1	3	2	2	6	17
South Carolina	1,093	480	59	2	158	9	93	22	55	24
South Dakota	186	62	7	–	26	–	1	3	4	4
Tennessee	1,270	266	12	10	9	–	9	4	4	4
Texas	3,504	1,426	162	49	174	35	147	117	121	143
Utah	282	75	38	–	3	3	2	6	7	6
Vermont	73	33	2	–	–	13	3	3	5	3
Virginia	947	313	42	19	128	3	52	8	35	19
Washington	647	247	14	4	18	54	12	19	57	41
West Virginia	374	82	10	–	33	3	13	8	6	6
Wisconsin	815	294	16	6	157	2	27	7	18	42
Wyoming	170	56	18	–	8	–	3	1	1	6

– Represents zero.   [1] Includes fatalities that occurred on roads for which the speed limit was unknown.

Source: U.S. National Highway Traffic Safety Administration, *Traffic Safety Facts, Speeding,* annual. See Internet site <http://www.nhtsa.dot.gov/people/Crash/Index.html>.

U.S. Census Bureau, Statistical Abstract of the United States: 2008

Table 1077. **Fatalities by Highest Blood Alcohol Concentration in the Crash: 1985 to 2005**

[BAC means blood alcohol concentration; g/dl means grams per deciliter]

Item	1985	1990	1995	2000	2002	2003	2004	2005
Total fatalities · · · · · · · · · · · · ·	43,825	44,599	41,817	41,945	43,005	42,884	42,836	43,443
Fatalities in alcohol-related crashes . . .	23,167	22,587	17,732	17,380	17,524	17,105	16,919	16,885
Percent	52.9	50.6	42.4	41.4	40.7	40.0	39.5	38.9
BAC = 0.01-0.07 g/dl:								
Number	3,081	2,980	2,490	2,511	2,432	2,427	2,325	2,346
Percent	7.0	6.7	6.0	6.0	5.7	6.0	5.4	5.4
BAC = 0.08 g/dl or more:								
Number	20,086	19,607	15,242	14,870	15,093	14,678	14,593	14,539
Percent	45.8	44.0	36.5	35.5	35.1	34.0	34.1	33.5
Fatalities with BAC = 0.00 g/dl:								
Number.	20,659	22,012	24,085	24,565	25,481	25,779	25,918	26,558
Percent.	47.1	49.4	57.6	58.6	59.3	60.0	60.5	61.1

Source: U.S. National Highway Traffic Safety Administration, *Traffic Safety Facts*, annual; and unpublished data. See Internet site <http://www.nhtsa.dot.gov/people/Crash/Index.html>.

Table 1078. **Traffic Fatalities by State and Highest Blood Alcohol Concentration (BAC) in the Crash: 2005**

[BAC means blood alcohol concentration; g/dl means grams per deciliter]

State	Traffic fatalities, total	No alcohol (BAC = 0.00 g/dl)		Any alcohol (BAC = 0.01 g/dl or more)					
						Low alcohol (BAC = 0.01-0.07 g/dl)		High alcohol (BAC = 0.08 g/dl or more)	
		Number	Percent	Number	Percent	Number	Percent	Number	Percent
United States . . .	43,443	26,558	61.1	16,885	38.9	2,346	5.4	14,539	33.5
Alabama	1,131	708	62.6	423	37.4	42	3.7	382	33.7
Alaska	72	37	51.7	35	48.3	4	5.7	31	42.6
Arizona	1,177	685	58.2	492	41.8	58	4.9	434	36.9
Arkansas	648	415	64.1	233	35.9	25	3.9	208	32.0
California	4,329	2,610	60.3	1,719	39.7	254	5.9	1,466	33.9
Colorado	606	362	59.7	244	40.3	31	5.2	213	35.1
Connecticut	274	154	56.3	120	43.7	19	7.0	101	36.8
Delaware	134	68	51.0	66	49.0	6	4.8	59	44.2
District of Columbia . . .	48	22	45.4	26	54.6	5	10.8	21	43.8
Florida	3,543	2,072	58.5	1,471	41.5	201	5.7	1,271	35.9
Georgia	1,729	1,184	68.5	545	31.5	82	4.7	463	26.8
Hawaii	140	69	49.2	71	50.8	13	9.1	58	41.7
Idaho	275	186	67.6	89	32.4	5	1.6	85	30.7
Illinois	1,361	781	57.4	580	42.6	103	7.6	477	35.1
Indiana	938	618	65.9	320	34.1	47	5.0	273	29.1
Iowa	450	332	73.8	118	26.2	16	3.6	102	22.6
Kansas	428	277	64.7	151	35.3	30	6.9	122	28.4
Kentucky	985	672	68.2	313	31.8	47	4.7	267	27.1
Louisiana	955	561	58.7	394	41.3	47	5.0	347	36.3
Maine	169	110	65.3	59	34.7	8	5.0	50	29.8
Maryland	614	379	61.7	235	38.3	44	7.1	191	31.2
Massachusetts	442	271	61.3	171	38.7	21	4.7	150	34.0
Michigan	1,129	708	62.7	421	37.3	58	5.1	363	32.1
Minnesota	559	358	64.0	201	36.0	26	4.6	176	31.4
Mississippi	931	560	60.2	371	39.8	40	4.3	331	35.5
Missouri.	1,257	742	59.0	515	41.0	81	6.4	434	34.5
Montana	251	127	50.6	124	49.4	12	4.9	112	44.5
Nebraska	276	185	67.1	91	32.9	13	4.6	78	28.3
Nevada	427	268	62.8	159	37.2	16	3.8	143	33.4
New Hampshire	166	106	64.0	60	36.0	5	3.0	55	33.0
New Jersey	748	485	64.9	263	35.1	46	6.2	217	29.0
New Mexico	488	299	61.2	189	38.8	17	3.5	172	35.3
New York	1,429	905	63.3	524	36.7	91	6.3	434	30.3
North Carolina	1,534	985	64.2	549	35.8	65	4.2	484	31.6
North Dakota	123	65	52.7	58	47.3	13	10.2	46	37.2
Ohio	1,323	818	61.9	505	38.1	96	7.3	409	30.9
Oklahoma	802	519	64.8	283	35.2	34	4.2	249	31.0
Oregon	488	311	63.8	177	36.2	38	7.7	139	28.5
Pennsylvania	1,616	980	60.7	636	39.3	77	4.8	559	34.6
Rhode Island	87	44	50.5	43	49.5	10	11.0	34	38.5
South Carolina	1,093	629	57.5	464	42.5	68	6.2	396	36.2
South Dakota	186	106	57.0	80	43.0	4	1.9	76	41.1
Tennessee	1,270	806	63.5	464	36.5	67	5.3	397	31.2
Texas	3,504	1,935	55.2	1,569	44.8	198	5.6	1,371	39.1
Utah	282	245	86.9	37	13.1	2	0.7	35	12.3
Vermont	73	44	60.0	29	40.0	1	1.5	28	38.5
Virginia	947	600	63.4	347	36.6	63	6.6	284	30.0
Washington	647	353	54.6	294	45.4	41	6.4	253	39.1
West Virginia	374	248	66.3	126	33.7	11	2.8	116	30.9
Wisconsin	815	446	54.7	369	45.3	41	5.0	328	40.2
Wyoming	170	105	61.9	65	38.1	9	5.1	56	33.0

Source: U.S. National Highway Traffic Safety Administration, *Traffic Safety Facts*, annual. See Internet site <http://www.nhtsa.dot.gov/people/Crash/Index.html>.

Transportation 689

Table 1079. **Crashes by Crash Severity: 1990 to 2005**

[6,471 represents 6,471,000. A crash is a police-reported event that produces injury and/or property damage, involves a vehicle in transport and occurs on a trafficway or while the vehicle is in motion after running off the trafficway]

Item	1990	1995	1999	2000	2001	2002	2003	2004	2005
Crashes (1,000).............	6,471	6,699	6,279	6,394	6,323	6,316	6,328	6,181	6,159
Fatal	39.8	37.2	37.1	37.5	37.9	38.5	38.5	38.4	39.2
Nonfatal injury..............	2,122	2,217	2,054	2,070	2,003	1,929	1,925	1,862	1,816
Property damage only	4,309	4,446	4,188	4,286	4,282	4,348	4,365	4,281	4,304
Percent of total crashes:									
Fatal	0.6	0.6	0.6	0.6	0.6	0.6	0.6	0.6	0.6
Nonfatal injury..............	32.8	33.1	32.7	32.4	31.7	30.5	30.4	30.1	29.5
Property damage only	66.6	66.4	66.7	67.0	67.7	68.8	69.0	69.3	69.9

Source: U.S. National Highway Safety Traffic Administration. *Traffic Safety Facts.* annual. See Internet site <http://www.nhtsa.dot.gov/people/Crash/Index.html>.

Table 1080. **Alcohol Involvement for Drivers in Fatal Crashes: 1995 and 2005**

[BAC = blood alcohol concentration]

Age, sex, and vehicle type	1995		2005	
	Number of drivers	Percentage with BAC of .08% or greater	Number of drivers	Percentage with BAC of .08% or greater
Total drivers involved in fatal crashes [1]	56,164	22.0	59,104	20.2
Drivers by age group:				
Under 16 years old....................	410	9.3	304	8.9
16 to 20 years old....................	7,725	15.6	7,293	16.4
21 to 24 years old....................	6,263	31.8	6,548	31.9
25 to 34 years old....................	13,048	30.3	11,378	27.8
35 to 44 years old....................	10,677	26.1	10,733	23.2
45 to 54 years old....................	6,815	17.7	9,403	18.6
55 to 64 years old....................	4,079	13.6	6,041	11.8
65 to 74 years old....................	3,251	7.6	3,212	6.5
75 years old and over	2,989	4.0	3,003	3.9
Drivers by sex:				
Male.....................	41,235	25.0	43,060	23.0
Female...................	14,184	12.9	14,974	12.5
Drivers by vehicle type:				
Passenger cars	30,773	22.6	24,908	22.0
Light trucks [2]	17,483	24.6	22,757	21.3
Large trucks [2]	4,410	2.3	4,881	1.3
Motorcycles.....................	2,262	33.0	4,652	26.8
Buses.....................	269	0.8	276	1.2

[1] Includes age and sex unknown, and other and unknown types of vehicles. [2] See footnotes 2 and 3 in Table 1075.

Source: U.S. National Highway Safety Traffic Administration, *Traffic Safety Facts*, annual. See Internet site <http://www.nhtsa.dot.gov/people/Crash/Index.html>.

Table 1081. **Licensed Drivers and Number in Accidents by Age: 2005**

[201,500 represents 201,500,000]

Age group	Licensed drivers		Drivers in accidents				Accident rates per number of drivers	
			Fatal		All			
	Number (1,000)	Percent	Number	Percent	Number (1,000)	Percent	Fatal [1]	All [2]
Total..............	201,500	100.0	62,300	100.0	18,400	100.0	31	9
19 years old and under	9,396	4.7	6,300	10.1	2,490	13.5	67	27
Under 16 years old	52	(Z)	400	0.6	250	1.4	(³)	(³)
16 years old...........	1,271	0.6	900	1.4	410	2.2	71	32
17 years old...........	2,197	1.1	1,300	2.1	570	3.1	59	26
18 years old...........	2,758	1.4	1,800	2.9	650	3.5	65	24
19 years old...........	3,118	1.5	1,900	3.0	610	3.3	61	20
20 to 24 years old	16,886	8.4	8,900	14.3	2,640	14.3	53	16
20 years old...........	3,217	1.6	1,800	2.9	610	3.3	56	19
21 years old...........	3,245	1.6	1,900	3.0	540	2.9	59	17
22 years old...........	3,394	1.7	1,900	3.0	500	2.7	56	15
23 years old...........	3,460	1.7	1,700	2.7	500	2.7	49	14
24 years old...........	3,570	1.8	1,600	2.6	490	2.7	45	14
25 to 34 years old	36,003	17.9	11,300	18.1	3,820	20.8	31	11
35 to 44 years old	40,394	20.0	10,400	16.7	3,420	18.6	26	8
45 to 54 years old	39,851	19.8	9,600	15.4	3,060	16.6	24	8
55 to 64 years old	29,685	14.7	6,600	10.6	1,610	8.8	22	5
65 to 74 years old	16,492	8.2	4,200	6.7	800	4.3	25	5
75 years old and over	12,793	6.3	5,000	8.0	560	3.0	39	4

Z Less than 0.05. [1] Per 100,000 licensed drivers. [2] Per 100 licensed drivers. [3] Rates for drivers under age 16 are substantially overstated due to the high proportion of unlicensed drivers involved.

Source: National Safety Council, Itasca, IL, *Injury Facts, 2006,* (copyright). See Internet site <http://www.nsc.org/>.

Table 1082. Passenger Transit Industry—Summary: 1980 to 2005

[6,510 represents $6,510,000,000. Includes Puerto Rico. Includes aggregate information for all transit systems in the United States. Excludes nontransit services such as taxicab, school bus, unregulated jitney, sightseeing bus, intercity bus, and special application mass transportation systems (e.g., amusement parks, airports, island, and urban park ferries). Includes active vehicles only]

Item	Unit	1980	1985	1990	1995	2000	2004	2005
Operating systems	Number. .	1,044	4,972	5,078	5,973	6,000	6,429	6,429
Motor bus systems	Number. .	1,040	2,681	2,688	2,250	2,262	1,500	1,500
Revenue vehicles, active	Number. .	75,388	94,368	93,553	116,473	131,918	143,822	150,827
Motor bus	Number. .	59,411	64,258	58,714	67,107	75,013	81,033	82,027
Commuter rail.	Number. .	4,500	4,035	5,007	5,164	5,498	6,228	6,392
Demand response.	Number. .	(NA)	14,490	16,471	29,352	33,080	37,078	41,958
Heavy rail	Number. .	9,641	9,326	10,419	10,157	10,591	10,858	11,110
Light rail	Number. .	1,013	717	913	999	1,577	1,622	1,645
Trolley bus.	Number. .	823	676	832	885	951	597	615
Other	Number. .	(NA)	867	1,197	2,809	5,208	6,406	7,080
Operating funding, total	Mil. dol. . .	6,510	12,195	16,053	18,241	24,243	29,718	31,708
Passenger funding. . . . [1]	Mil. dol. . .	2,557	4,575	5,891	6,801	8,746	9,775	10,269
Other operating funding [1]	Mil. dol. . .	248	702	895	2,812	4,217	4,960	4,983
Operating assistance	Mil. dol. . .	3,705	6,918	9,267	8,628	11,280	14,983	16,456
Federal	Mil. dol. . .	1,094	940	970	817	994	2,086	2,303
Local [2]	Mil. dol. . .	2,611	5,979	5,327	3,981	5,319	6,184	6,658
State [2]	Mil. dol. . .	(NA)	(NA)	2,970	3,830	4,967	6,713	7,495
Operating expense	Mil. dol. . .	6,247	12,381	15,742	17,849	22,646	28,506	30,295
Vehicle operations	Mil. dol. . .	3,248	5,655	6,654	8,282	10,111	12,866	13,793
Maintenance.	Mil. dol. . .	1,774	3,672	4,631	5,047	6,445	7,833	8,259
General administration	Mil. dol. . .	1,224	2,505	3,450	2,590	3,329	3,974	4,075
Purchased transportation	Mil. dol. . .	(NA)	549	1,008	1,930	2,761	3,833	4,168
Capital and planning grants, federal [3] . . .	Mil. dol. . .	2,787	2,559	2,428	5,534	7,366	7,913	(NA)
Capital expenditures	Mil. dol. . .	(NA)	(NA)	(NA)	7,230	9,587	13,246	12,383
Vehicle-miles operated.	Million . . .	2,287	2,791	3,242	3,550	4,081	4,471	4,601
Motor bus	Million . . .	1,677	1,863	2,130	2,184	2,315	2,471	2,485
Trolley bus.	Million . . .	13	16	14	14	14	13	13
Heavy rail	Million . . .	385	451	537	537	595	642	646
Light rail	Million . . .	18	17	24	35	53	67	69
Commuter rail.	Million . . .	179	183	213	238	271	295	303
Demand response.	Million . . .	(NA)	247	306	507	759	890	978
Other	Million . . .	15	15	18	37	74	92	107
Trips taken	Million . . .	8,567	8,636	8,799	7,763	9,363	9,575	9,815
Motor bus	Million . . .	5,837	5,675	5,677	4,848	5,678	5,731	5,855
Trolley bus.	Million . . .	142	142	126	119	122	106	107
Heavy rail	Million . . .	2,108	2,290	2,346	2,033	2,632	2,748	2,808
Light rail	Million . . .	133	132	175	251	320	350	381
Commuter rail.	Million . . .	280	275	328	344	413	414	423
Demand response.	Million . . .	(NA)	59	68	88	105	114	125
Other	Million . . .	67	63	79	80	93	112	117
Avg. fare per trip . . . . [4]	Cents . . .	30	53	67	88	93	102	102
Employees, number (avg.) [4]	1,000 . . .	187	270	273	311	360	359	367
Payroll, employee	Mil. dol. . .	3,281	5,843	7,226	8,213	10,400	12,487	12,177
Fringe benefits, employee	Mil. dol. . .	1,353	2,868	3,986	4,484	5,413	8,172	8,093

NA Not available. [1] Beginning 1995, includes taxes levied directly by transit agency and other dedicated funds, formerly included in Local. [2] Includes other operating revenue, nonoperating revenue, and auxiliary income. Data for 1985 are state and local combined. [3] 1980, capital grants only. [4] Through 1990, represents employee equivalents of 2,080 hours = one employee; beginning 1995, equals actual employees.

Source: American Public Transportation Association, Washington, DC, *Public Transportation Fact Book*, annual. See Internet site <http://www.apta.com/>.

Table 1083. Transit Buses Equipped for Disabilities: 1995 to 2005

[Represents ADA (Americans with Disabilities Act of 1992) lift- or ramp-equipped buses. Includes buses of transit agencies receiving federal funding for bus purchases and buses of agencies not receiving federal funds that voluntarily report data to the Federal Transit Administration]

Item	1995	1999	2000	2001	2002	2003	2004	2005
Transit buses, total	**57,322**	**63,618**	**65,324**	**67,379**	**68,418**	**68,596**	**68,789**	**69,504**
Percent ADA equipped	61.7	80.5	83.6	87.2	94.1	95.3	98.1	96.5
Small buses, total [1]	5,372	8,265	8,850	9,622	9,822	10,084	10,248	11,118
Percent ADA equipped	84.5	93.4	94.5	95.4	99.2	99.2	98.5	97.6
Medium buses, total [1]	3,879	6,613	7,455	7,830	8,693	9,346	10,031	10,681
Percent ADA equipped	66.0	90.1	92.9	93.7	98.4	97.7	100.0	98.8
Large buses, total [1]	46,355	46,891	47,017	47,925	47,764	46,608	45,919	45,524
Percent ADA equipped	59.2	76.8	79.9	84.5	92.2	93.9	97.4	95.5
Articulated buses, total [1]	1,716	1,849	2,002	2,002	2,139	2,558	2,591	2,231
Percent ADA equipped	50.2	81.3	85.5	88.5	97.2	96.4	99.8	99.7

[1] Small buses have fewer than 25 seats; medium buses have 25 to 35 seats; large ones have more than 35 seats; articulated buses are extra long and measure between 54 and 60 feet.

Source: U.S. Bureau of Transportation Statistics, *National Transportation Statistics*, annual. See Internet site <http://www.bts.gov/>.

Transportation 691

Table 1084. **Characteristics of Rail Transit by Transit Authority: 2004**

Mode and transit agency	Primary city served	States served	Directional route-miles [1]	Number of highway-rail crossings	Number of stations	Number of ADA-accessible stations [2]
Total [3]	34	28	9,762.1	6,533	2,912	1,696
Heavy rail	11	12	1,596.1	27	1,023	428
Metropolitan Atlanta Rapid Transit Authority	Atlanta	GA	96.1	–	38	38
Maryland Transit Administration.	Baltimore	MD	29.4	–	14	14
Massachusetts Bay Transportation Authority	Boston	MA	76.3	–	53	42
Chicago Transit Authority	Chicago	IL	206.3	25	144	72
Greater Cleveland Regional Transit Authority	Cleveland	OH	38.1	–	18	10
L.A. County Metropolitan Transportation Authority	Los Angeles	CA	31.9	–	16	16
Miami-Dade Transit Agency	Miami	FL	45.0	–	22	22
MTA New York City Transit.	New York	NY	493.8	–	468	54
MTA Staten Island Railway.	New York	NY	28.6	–	23	4
Port Authority Trans-Hudson Corporation .	New York	NY, NJ	28.6	2	13	7
Port Authority Transit Corporation	Philadelphia	PA, NJ	31.5	–	13	5
Southeastern Pennsylvania Transportation Authority	Philadelphia	PA	74.9	–	75	18
San Francisco Bay Area Rapid Transit District	San Francisco	CA	209.0	–	43	43
Washington Metropolitan Area Transit Authority	Washington	DC, MD, VA	206.6	–	83	83
Commuter rail [4]	16	18	6,971.2	2,754	1,166	679
Alaska Railroad Corporation.	Anchorage	AK	92.4	27	10	10
Maryland Transit Administration.	Baltimore	MD, DC, WV	400.4	40	42	22
Massachusetts Bay Transportation Authority	Boston	MA, RI	702.1	233	126	82
NE Illinois Regional Commuter Rail Corporation	Chicago	IL, WI	940.4	512	230	139
Northern Indiana Commuter Transportation District	Chicago	IL, IN	179.8	117	20	12
Dallas Area Rapid Transit	Dallas	TX	29.0	15	4	4
Fort Worth Transportation Authority	Dallas	TX	40.5	19	5	5
Connecticut Department of Transportation	New Haven	CT	101.2	3	8	8
Southern California Regional Rail Authority	Los Angeles	CA	778.0	442	53	53
South Florida Regional Transportation Authority	Miami	FL	142.2	72	18	18
MTA Metro-North Railroad	New York	NY, NJ, CT	545.7	160	109	32
MTA Long Island Rail Road	New York	NY	638.2	395	124	99
New Jersey Transit Corporation	New York	NY, NJ, PA	1,070.2	329	167	68
Pennsylvania Department of Transportation	Philadelphia	PA	144.4	7	12	4
Southeastern Pennsylvania Transportation Authority	Philadelphia	PA	446.9	116	156	51
North San Diego County Transit Development Board	San Diego	CA	82.2	34	8	8
Peninsula Corridor Joint Powers Board.	San Francisco	CA	153.7	49	34	24
Central Puget Sound Regional Transit Authority	Seattle	WA	146.9	34	9	9
Altamont Commuter Express Authority . . .	San Jose	CA	172.0	127	10	10
OnTrack	Syracuse	NY	3.5	(NA)	3	3
Virginia Railway Express	Washington	DC, VA	161.5	23	18	18

– Represents zero.   NA Not available.   [1] The mileage in each direction over which public transportation vehicles travel while in revenue service. The mileage is computed without regard to the number of traffic lanes or rail tracks existing in the right-of-way.   [2] Number of stations that comply with the Americans with Disabilities Act of 1992 (ADA). Additional stations may be wheelchair accessible but not comply with other provisions of the ADA.   [3] Includes light rail, not shown separately.   [4] Excludes commuter-type services operated independently by AMTRAK.

Source: U.S. Bureau of Transportation Statistics, *State Transportation Statistics, 2005* See Internet site <http://www.bts.gov/>.

692   Transportation

Table 1085. Transit Ridership in Selected Urbanized Areas: 2004

[Areas ranked by 2000 population size]

Urbanized area	2000 Population [1] Total (1,000)	Rank	Annual unlinked passenger trips [2] (mil.)	Motor bus	Heavy rail [3]	Light rail [4]	Commuter rail [5]	Other [6]
U.S. urbanized areas [7] . . .	193,768	(X)	8,852	57.2	31.0	4.0	4.7	3.2
Atlanta, GA.	3,500	11	363.3	45.5	19.0	12.4	–	23.0
Austin,TX	902	40	35.7	98.2	–	–	–	1.8
Baltimore, MD	2,076	18	114.3	77.4	10.9	5.3	5.9	0.6
Boston, MA-NH-RI	4,032	7	396.1	30.6	39.8	17.8	10.1	1.7
Buffalo, NY	977	38	23.1	76.0	–	23.7	–	0.3
Charlotte, NC-SC.	759	47	18.9	97.6	–	–	–	2.4
Chicago, IL-IN.	8,308	3	582.8	56.2	30.7	–	12.2	0.9
Cincinnati, OH-KY-IN	1,503	26	27.1	98.4	–	–	–	1.6
Cleveland, OH.	1,787	21	58.9	82.0	12.4	4.3	–	1.3
Columbus, OH	1,133	36	14.7	98.9	–	–	–	1.1
Dallas-Fort Worth-Arlington, TX . . .	4,146	6	85.8	76.1	–	19.1	2.5	2.3
Denver-Aurora, CO	1,985	20	82.4	86.6	–	12.2	–	1.2
Detroit, MI	3,903	9	45.4	95.8	–	–	–	4.2
Hartford, CT	852	45	15.9	87.5	–	–	2.5	10.0
Houston, TX	3,823	10	95.9	91.7	–	5.6	–	2.7
Indianapolis, IN	1,219	33	9.3	96.4	–	–	–	3.6
Jacksonville, FL.	882	43	10.2	87.6	–	–	–	12.4
Kansas City, MO-KS.	1,362	29	13.8	95.9	–	–	–	4.1
Las Vegas, NV	1,314	31	51.3	98.6	–	–	–	1.4
Los Angeles-Long Beach-Santa Ana, CA	11,789	2	606.8	86.8	5.1	5.4	1.6	1.1
Louisville, KY-IN	864	44	15.5	97.7	–	–	–	2.3
Memphis, TN-MS-AR	972	39	12.7	90.3	–	7.7	–	1.9
Miami, FL.	4,919	5	151.2	80.1	10.3	–	1.9	7.7
Milwaukee, WI.	1,309	32	56.4	97.9	–	–	–	2.1
Minneapolis-St. Paul, MN	2,389	16	67.4	92.6	–	4.4	–	3.1
Nashville-Davidson, TN.	750	48	6.4	97.8	–	0.0	–	2.2
New Orleans, LA	1,009	37	54.9	77.2	–	16.2	–	6.6
New York-Newark, NY-NJ-CT.	17,800	1	3,383.9	37.8	54.1	0.3	7.0	0.8
Oklahoma City, OK	747	49	4.0	96.1	–	–	–	3.9
Orlando, FL	1,157	35	23.4	96.8	–	–	–	3.2
Philadelphia, PA-NJ-DE-MD.	5,149	4	350.5	55.7	27.7	7.2	8.7	0.7
Phoenix-Mesa, AZ	2,907	13	55.3	97.0	–	–	–	3.0
Pittsburgh, PA	1,753	22	69.1	85.5	–	9.6	–	4.8
Portland, OR-WA.	1,583	23	105.7	69.0	–	29.8	–	1.1
Providence, RI-MA.	1,175	34	17.2	95.7	–	–	–	4.3
Richmond, VA	819	46	12.1	97.2	–	–	–	2.8
Riverside-San Bernardino, CA	1,507	25	24.2	96.0	–	–	–	4.0
Sacramento, CA	1,393	28	32.4	64.9	–	34.1	–	1.1
Salt Lake City, UT	888	42	26.6	57.3	–	37.6	–	5.0
San Antonio, TX	1,328	30	43.2	97.7	–	–	–	2.3
San Diego, CA	2,674	15	88.6	66.2	–	30.0	1.6	2.3
San Francisco-Oakland, CA.	3,229	12	199.4	45.4	48.9	–	3.3	2.3
San Jose, CA	1,538	24	39.8	83.9	–	13.8	–	2.3
Seattle, WA	2,712	14	156.3	64.3	–	0.8	0.6	34.3
St. Louis, MO-IL	2,078	17	47.9	67.1	–	30.3	–	2.6
Tampa-St. Petersburg, FL	2,062	19	21.0	95.4	–	2.5	–	2.1
Tucson, AZ.	720	50	16.9	98.0	–	–	–	2.0
Virginia Beach, VA	1,394	27	20.5	96.2	–	–	–	3.8
Washington, DC-VA-MD	3,934	8	442.9	42.2	56.6	–	0.8	0.4

– Represents zero. X Not applicable. [1] As of April 1. Based on the 2000 decennial census. [2] The number of times passengers board public transportation vehicles. [3] Also called metro, subway, rapid transit, or rapid rail. [4] Also called streetcar, tramway, or trolley. [5] Also called metropolitan rail or regional rail. [6] Includes such modes as trolley, bus, ferry, cable car, vanpool, and demand response. [7] Includes Puerto Rico and other areas, not shown separately.

Source: U.S. Bureau of Transportation Statistics, *State Transportation Statistics, 2006.* See Internet site <http://www.bts.gov/publications/state_transportation_profiles/>.

Transportation **693**

Table 1086. Truck Transportation, Couriers and Messengers, and Warehousing and Storage—Estimated Revenue: 2000 to 2005

[In millions of dollars (237,812 represents $237,812,000,000). For taxable and tax-exempt employer firms. Estimates have been adjusted to the results of the 2002 Economic Census. Based on the North American Industry Classification System, 2002; see text, Section 15]

Kind of business	2002 NAICS code [1]	2000	2004	2005
Selected transportation and warehousing industries	48, 49	237,812	265,942	292,330
Truck transportation	484	165,421	185,945	206,466
General freight trucking	4841	108,051	124,970	138,908
General freight trucking, local.	48411	17,254	20,112	22,311
General freight trucking, long-distance.	48412	90,797	104,858	116,597
General freight trucking, long-distance, truckload	484121	61,562	75,854	84,604
General freight trucking, long-distance, less than truckload	484122	29,235	29,004	31,993
Specialized freight trucking	4842	57,370	60,975	67,558
Used household and office goods moving	48421	14,484	13,891	15,101
Specialized freight (except used goods) trucking, local	48422	21,912	25,263	28,254
Specialized freight (except used goods) trucking, long-distance	48423	20,974	21,821	24,203
Couriers and messengers	492	57,776	62,246	66,445
Couriers	4921	54,114	58,797	63,106
Local messengers and local delivery	4922	3,662	3,449	3,339
Warehousing and storage	493	14,615	17,751	19,419
General warehousing and storage	49311	8,967	10,930	11,668
Refrigerated warehousing and storage	49312	2,859	3,167	3,276
Farm product warehousing and storage	49313	776	691	773
Other warehousing and storage.	49319	2,013	2,963	3,702

[1] Based on the 2002 North American Industry Classification System; see text Section 15.

Source: U.S. Census Bureau, "2005 Service Annual Survey, Truck Transportation, Messenger Services and Warehousing." See <http://www.census.gov/econ/www/servmenu.html> (released February 2007).

Table 1087. Truck Transportation—Summary: 2000 to 2005

[In millions of dollars (165,421 represents $165,421,000,000). For taxable and tax-exempt employer firms. Covers NAICS 484. Estimates have been adjusted to the results of the 2002 Economic Census. Based on the North American Industry Classification System, 2002; see text, Section 15]

Item	2000	2003	2004	2005
Total operating revenue	165,421	168,486	185,945	206,466
Total motor carrier revenue	152,810	156,633	173,227	191,893
Local trucking [1]	48,837	52,409	56,657	63,214
Long-distance trucking [1].	103,973	104,224	116,570	128,679
Size of shipments:				
Less-than-truckload	36,453	37,472	40,264	42,025
Truckload	116,357	119,161	132,963	149,868
Commodities handled:				
Agricultural and fish products.	13,666	14,803	15,574	17,232
Grains, alcohol, and tobacco products.	4,912	6,047	6,253	7,005
Stone, nonmetallic minerals, and metallic ores	8,703	10,256	11,025	12,479
Coal and petroleum products.	5,812	5,924	6,692	7,662
Pharmaceutical and chemical products	9,929	8,615	9,370	10,034
Wood products, textiles, and leathers	14,281	14,141	16,429	17,229
Base metal and machinery	12,239	12,883	14,852	15,804
Electronic, motorized vehicles, and precision instruments	11,939	13,118	14,451	15,547
Used household and office goods.	11,078	9,309	10,807	12,045
New furniture and miscellaneous manufactured products . .	17,244	17,927	19,626	22,008
Other goods	43,007	43,610	48,148	54,848
Origin and destination of shipments:				
U.S. to U.S.	145,985	150,472	167,162	184,593
U.S. to Canada	1,390	1,315	1,383	1,550
U.S. to Mexico	1,434	1,477	(S)	(S)
Canada to U.S.	1,184	1,032	1,134	1,350
Mexico to U.S.	1,283	1,134	(S)	(S)
All other destinations	1,534	1,203	1,255	1,514
Inventory of revenue generating equipment (1,000):				
Trucks	201	208	212	216
Owned	168	183	188	192
Leased	33	26	24	25
Truck-tractors.	916	872	836	865
Owned	772	731	707	728
Leased	144	141	129	136
Trailers	1,893	1,863	1,858	1,930
Owned	1,572	1,584	1,513	1,568
Leased	321	278	346	363
Highway miles traveled (mil.):				
Total.	84,910	85,279	85,599	90,001
By loaded or partially loaded vehicles	67,558	68,506	69,693	72,856

S Data do not meet publication standards. [1] Local trucking is the carrying of goods within a single metro area and its adjacent nonurban areas; long-distance trucking is the carrying of goods between metro areas.

Source: U.S. Census Bureau, "2005 Service Annual Survey, Truck Transportation, Messenger Services, and Warehousing." See <http://www.census.gov/econ/www/servmenu.html> (released February 2007).

694 Transportation

Table 1088. Railroads, Class I—Summary: 1990 to 2005

[As of Dec. 31, or calendar year data, except as noted (216 represents 216,000). Compiled from annual reports of class I railroads only, except where noted. Minus sign (–) indicates deficit]

Item	Unit	1990	1995	2000	2001	2002	2003	2004	2005
Class I line-hauling companies [1]	Number..	14	11	8	8	7	7	7	7
Employees [2]	1,000 ...	216	188	168	162	157	155	158	162
Compensation	Mil. dol...	8,654	9,070	9,623	9,430	9,387	9,576	10,337	10,879
Average per hour	Dollars ..	15.8	19.0	21.5	22.1	22.7	23.4	24.2	25.7
Average per year	Dollars ..	39,987	48,188	57,157	58,153	59,650	61,920	65,550	66,975
Mileage:									
Railroad line owned [3]	1,000 ...	146	137	121	119	118	117	123	121
Railroad track owned [4]	1,000 ...	244	228	205	204	200	200	211	208
Equipment:									
Locomotives in service	Number..	18,835	18,812	20,028	19,745	20,506	20,774	22,015	22,779
Average horsepower	1,000 lb..	2,665	2,927	3,261	3,275	3,378	3,415	3,458	3,467
Cars in service:									
Freight train [5]	1,000 ...	1,212	1,219	1,381	1,314	1,300	1,279	1,288	1,312
Freight cars [6]	1,000 ...	659	583	560	500	478	467	474	475
Average capacity	Tons	87.5	88.6	92.3	92.7	93.1	93.7	94.3	95.1
Income and expenses:									
Operating revenues	Mil. dol...	28,370	32,279	34,102	34,576	35,327	36,639	40,517	46,118
Operating expenses	Mil. dol...	24,652	27,897	29,040	29,164	29,592	31,440	35,107	37,843
Net revenue from operations	Mil. dol...	3,718	4,383	5,062	5,412	5,735	5,199	5,410	8,275
Income before fixed charges	Mil. dol...	4,627	5,016	5,361	5,517	6,179	5,220	5,523	8,361
Provision for taxes [7]	Mil. dol...	1,088	1,556	1,430	1,614	1,823	1,494	1,543	2,224
Ordinary income	Mil. dol...	1,961	2,439	2,501	2,740	3,201	2,683	2,867	4,917
Net income	Mil. dol...	1,977	2,324	2,500	2,740	3,201	2,687	2,867	4,917
Net railway operating income	Mil. dol...	2,648	2,858	3,924	4,111	4,248	4,078	4,147	6,075
Total taxes [8]	Mil. dol...	3,780	4,075	4,379	4,673	4,724	4,316	4,480	5,176
Indus. return on net investment	Percent..	8.1	7.0	6.5	6.9	7.0	6.3	6.1	8.5
Gross capital expenditures	Mil. dol...	3,591	5,720	5,290	5,113	5,605	5,989	6,345	7,068
Equipment	Mil. dol...	996	2,343	1,508	1,013	1,021	1,300	1,301	1,026
Roadway and structures	Mil. dol...	2,644	3,651	4,549	4,421	4,645	4,561	4,941	5,364
Other	Mil. dol...	–49	–275	–767	–321	–61	128	102	678
Balance sheet:									
Total property investment	Mil. dol...	70,348	86,186	106,136	108,588	117,770	122,902	135,941	141,400
Accrued depreciation and amortization	Mil. dol...	22,222	23,439	23,989	24,635	26,649	29,215	29,771	32,508
Net investment	Mil. dol...	48,126	62,746	82,147	83,953	91,121	93,686	106,170	108,892
Shareholder's equity	Mil. dol...	23,662	31,419	32,401	34,822	39,675	41,151	51,955	55,828
Net working capital	Mil. dol...	–3,505	–2,634	–5,783	–6,282	–6,037	–6,750	–5,171	–4,729
Cash dividends	Mil. dol...	2,074	1,518	819	2,120	870	1,406	1,888	1,267
AMTRAK passenger traffic:									
Passenger revenue	Mil. dol...	941.9	734.1	1,201.6	1,299.9	1,304.3	1,421.1	1,432.6	1,461.7
Revenue passengers carried	1,000 ...	22,382	20,349	22,985	23,444	23,269	24,595	25,215	25,076
Revenue passenger miles	Million ...	6,125	5,401	5,574	5,571	5,314	5,680	5,511	5,381
Averages:									
Revenue per passenger	Dollars ...	42.1	36.1	52.3	55.4	56.1	57.8	56.8	58.3
Revenue per passenger mile	Cents ...	15.4	13.6	21.6	23.3	24.5	25.0	26.0	27.2
Freight service:									
Freight revenue	Mil. dol...	24,471	31,356	33,083	33,533	34,110	35,413	39,131	44,457
Per ton-mile	Cents ...	2.7	2.4	2.3	2.2	2.3	2.3	2.4	2.6
Per ton originated	Dollar ...	19.3	20.2	19.0	19.3	19.3	19.7	21.2	23.4
Revenue-tons originated	Million ...	1,425	1,550	1,738	1,742	1,767	1,799	1,844	1,899
Revenue-tons carried	Million ...	2,024	2,322	2,179	2,187	2,207	2,240	2,398	2,448
Tons carried one mile	Billion ...	1,034	1,306	1,466	1,495	1,507	1,551	1,663	1,696
Average miles of road operated	1,000 ...	133	125	121	121	123	122	121	121
Revenue ton-miles per mile of road	1,000 ...	7,763	10,439	12,156	12,358	12,245	12,686	13,695	14,071
Revenue per ton-mile	Cents ...	3	2	2	2	2	2	2	3
Train miles	Million ...	380	458	504	500	500	516	535	548
Net ton-miles per train-mile [9]	Number..	2,755	2,870	2,923	3,005	3,030	3,024	3,126	3,115
Net ton-miles per loaded car-mile [9]	Number..	69.1	73.6	73.1	72.4	71.5	71.4	78.5	79.0
Train-miles per train-hour	Miles....	24	22	21	21	21	20	19	19
Haul per ton, U.S. as a system	Miles....	726	843	843	858	853	862	902	893
Accidents/incidents: [10]									
Casualties—all railroads:									
Persons killed	Number..	1,297	1,146	937	971	951	868	895	886
Persons injured	Number..	25,143	14,440	11,643	10,985	11,103	9,254	9,141	9,332
Class I railroads:									
Persons killed	Number..	1,166	994	778	805	796	749	784	738
Persons injured	Number..	19,284	9,571	7,655	7,232	7,722	6,161	6,170	6,159

[1] See text, this section, for definition of Class I. [2] Average midmonth count. [3] Represents the aggregate length of roadway of all line-haul railroads. Excludes yard tracks, sidings, and parallel lines. (Includes estimate for Class II and III railroads). [4] Includes multiple main tracks, yard tracks, and sidings owned by both line-haul and switching and terminal. (Includes estimate for Class II and III railroads). [5] Includes cars owned by all railroads, private car companies, and shippers. [6] Class I railroads only. [7] Includes state income taxes. [8] Includes payroll, income, and other taxes. [9] Revenue and nonrevenue freight. [10] Source: Federal Railroad Admin., Railroad Safety Statistics, annual. Includes highway grade crossing casualties. See Internet site <http://www.fra.dot.gov/>.

Source: Except as noted, Association of American Railroads, Washington, DC, Railroad Facts, Statistics of Railroads of Class I, annual, and Analysis of Class I Railroads, annual. See Internet site <http://www.aar.org/AboutTheIndustry/AboutTheIndustry.asp>.

Transportation 695

Table 1089. **Railroads, Class-I Cars of Revenue Freight Loaded, 1970 to 2006, and by Commodity Group, 2005 and 2006**

[In thousands (27,160 represents 27,160,000). Figures are 52-week totals]

Year	Car-loads [1]	Commodity group	Carloads 2005 [2]	2006 [2]	Commodity group	Carloads 2005 [2]	2006 [2]
1970....	27,160	Coal...................	6,907	7,233	Metals and products..........	630	671
1980....	22,598	Metallic ores............	250	253	Stone, clay, and glass products...	524	497
1990....	16,177	Chemicals, allied products	1,493	1,482	Crushed stone, gravel, sand.....	1,006	1,027
2000 [2]...	16,354	Grain	1,126	1,177	Nonmetallic minerals..........	371	316
2001 [2]...	16,286	Motor vehicles and equipment....	1,154	1,087	Waste and scrap materials......	498	500
2002 [2]...	16,101	Pulp, paper, allied products.....	443	425	Lumber, wood products........	308	280
2003 [2]...	16,159	Primary forest products	162	139	Coke...................	295	287
2004 [2]...	16,600	Food and kindred products.....	432	451	Petroleum products	308	319
2005 [2]...	16,691	Grain mill products	485	479	All other carloads...........	300	314
2006 [2]...	16,937						

[1] Beginning 1990 excludes intermodal.   [2] Excludes 3 Class I railroads. 2006 data preliminary.

Source: Association of American Railroads, Washington, DC, *Weekly Railroad Traffic*, annual. See Internet site <http://www.aar.org/AboutTheIndustry/AboutTheIndustry.asp>.

Table 1090. **Railroads, Class-I Line-Haul-Revenue Freight Originated by Commodity Group: 1990 to 2006**

[21,401 represents 21,401,000]

Commodity group	1990	1995	2000	2001	2002	2003	2004	2005	2006
Carloads (1,000) [1]........	21,401	23,726	27,763	27,205	27,901	28,870	30,095	31,142	32,114
Farm products..............	1,689	1,692	1,437	1,461	1,471	1,519	1,519	1,510	1,590
Metallic ores	508	463	322	251	328	331	339	662	674
Coal......................	5,912	6,095	6,954	7,295	7,088	7,037	7,102	7,202	7,574
Nonmetallic minerals...........	1,202	1,159	1,309	1,280	1,310	1,370	1,430	1,488	1,470
Food and kindred products.......	1,307	1,377	1,377	1,446	1,472	1,478	1,461	1,448	1,487
Lumber and wood products	780	719	648	603	619	612	616	611	548
Pulp, paper, allied products	611	628	633	601	646	667	669	679	671
Chemicals, allied products	1,531	1,642	1,820	1,777	1,866	1,913	1,981	1,937	1,943
Petroleum and coal products	573	596	565	547	533	606	651	689	689
Stone, clay, and glass products....	539	516	541	528	559	581	594	603	570
Primary metal products	477	575	723	642	656	648	701	680	728
Fabricated metal products	31	32	30	51	38	36	39	36	50
Machinery, exc. electrical	39	41	35	46	38	38	45	42	43
Transportation equipment.......	1,091	1,473	1,984	1,777	1,831	1,811	1,849	1,923	1,871
Waste and scrap materials.......	439	623	619	591	617	651	725	706	701
Tons (mil.) [1]..............	1,425	1,550	1,738	1,742	1,767	1,799	1,844	1,899	1,957
Farm products..............	147	154	136	137	138	141	142	140	149
Metallic ores	47	44	32	25	31	33	33	60	61
Coal......................	579	627	758	801	785	784	792	804	852
Nonmetallic minerals...........	109	110	126	123	126	133	140	146	141
Food and kindred products.......	81	91	94	98	102	102	100	102	105
Lumber and wood products	53	51	49	46	48	47	47	48	43
Pulp, paper, allied products	33	36	36	34	37	39	38	38	37
Chemicals, allied products	126	138	155	157	162	167	165	167
Petroleum and coal products	40	43	42	42	42	49	54	57	57
Stone, clay, and glass products....	44	43	48	46	49	51	53	55	52
Primary metal products	38	47	60	53	55	54	59	57	61
Fabricated metal products	1	1	1	1	1	1	1	1	1
Machinery, exc. electrical	1	1	1	1	1	1	1	1	1
Transportation equipment.......	23	30	42	37	38	36	37	38	36
Waste and scrap materials.......	28	38	40	37	39	41	46	47	48
Gross revenue (mil. dol.) [1]...	29,775	33,782	36,331	36,063	36,742	38,434	41,622	46,743	52,639
Farm products..............	2,422	3,020	2,673	2,741	2,711	2,870	3,176	3,628	4,205
Metallic ores	408	394	338	288	285	289	317	485	529
Coal......................	6,954	7,356	7,794	8,181	7,797	7,890	8,418	9,393	10,821
Nonmetallic minerals...........	885	875	969	945	967	1,041	1,131	1,293	1,462
Food and kindred products.......	2,188	2,464	2,424	2,579	2,657	2,760	2,892	3,253	3,730
Lumber and wood products	1,390	1,385	1,524	1,519	1,628	1,745	1,924	2,278	2,335
Pulp, paper, allied products	1,486	1,543	1,526	1,457	1,567	1,646	1,730	1,953	2,124
Chemicals, allied products	3,933	4,553	4,636	4,504	4,658	4,779	5,100	5,432	6,049
Petroleum and coal products	918	997	1,010	1,014	1,026	1,123	1,268	1,500	1,722
Stone, clay, and glass products....	931	1,044	1,113	1,090	1,149	1,211	1,323	1,505	1,664
Primary metal products	979	1,199	1,371	1,292	1,288	1,349	1,518	1,734	2,157
Fabricated metal products	42	44	48	65	61	47	50	55	79
Machinery, exc. electrical	67	69	61	73	61	60	72	91	109
Transportation equipment.......	3,100	3,269	3,843	3,590	3,731	3,707	3,746	3,960	4,228
Waste and scrap materials......	504	685	706	685	717	799	956	1,070	1,190

[1] Includes commodity groups and small packaged freight shipments, not shown separately.

Source: Association of American Railroads, Washington, DC, *Freight Commodity Statistics*, annual. See Internet site <http://www.aar.org/AboutTheIndustry/AboutTheIndustry.asp>.

696   Transportation

Table 1091. **Line Haul Railroads—Producer Price Indexes: 2000 to 2006**

[Index base date = 100]

Commodity	Index base date	2000	2001	2002	2003	2004	2005	2006, prel.
Line-haul railroads	Dec. 1984	114.5	116.6	118.9	121.4	126.5	139.6	151.8
Railroad transportation, freight (carload)	Dec. 1996	101.9	104.1	106.3	109.0	114.7	128.1	139.3
Coal............................	Dec. 1984	108.7	110.6	110.1	111.4	114.6	(NA)	(NA)
Farm products	Dec. 1984	123.1	124.5	125.5	132.1	146.4	(NA)	(NA)
Food products	Dec. 1984	100.4	102.8	102.7	101.7	107.5	(NA)	(NA)
Metallic ores	Dec. 1984	105.9	107.0	107.0	105.9	110.0	(NA)	(NA)
Chemicals and allied products..........	Dec. 1984	121.3	122.3	126.2	131.7	140.7	(NA)	(NA)
Nonmetallic minerals	Dec. 1984	122.1	123.0	124.3	125.7	131.1	(NA)	(NA)
Lumber and wood products	Dec. 1984	109.0	112.2	120.5	123.3	131.5	(NA)	(NA)
Transportation equipment	Dec. 1984	112.6	118.7	130.5	136.6	141.8	(NA)	(NA)
Pulp, paper, and allied products.........	Dec. 1984	119.0	122.4	122.4	124.4	134.4	(NA)	(NA)
Primary metal products	Dec. 1984	124.1	128.8	132.5	136.1	141.1	(NA)	(NA)
Stone, clay, glass, and concrete products ..	Dec. 1984	128.7	129.0	124.3	127.1	132.8	(NA)	(NA)
Petroleum and coal products...........	Dec. 1984	124.6	126.8	127.5	129.6	132.2	(NA)	(NA)
Railroad transportation, freight (intermodal)...	Dec. 1996	102.9	103.2	103.8	106.4	107.6	113.2	123.4
Railroad transportation, passenger	Dec. 1996	116.3	119.1	124.6	115.3	111.1	115.1	123.4

NA Not available.

Source: U.S. Bureau of Labor Statistics, *Producer Price Indexes*, monthly and annual. See Internet site <http://www.bls.gov/ppi/>.

Table 1092. **Petroleum Pipeline Companies—Characteristics: 1980 to 2005**

[173 represents 173,000. Covers pipeline companies operating in interstate commerce and subject to jurisdiction of the Federal Energy Regulatory Commission]

Item	Unit	1980	1985	1990	1995	2000	2002	2003	2004	2005
Miles of pipeline, total ..	1,000	173	171	168	177	152	150	140	142	131
Gathering lines......	1,000	36	35	32	35	18	16	14	15	14
Trunk lines.........	1,000	136	136	136	142	134	133	126	127	118
Total deliveries.......	Mil. Bbl.......	10,600	10,745	11,378	12,862	14,450	13,343	13,236	13,394	12,732
Crude oil...........	Mil. Bbl.......	6,405	6,239	6,563	6,952	6,923	7,019	6,941	6,612	6,675
Products	Mil. Bbl.......	4,195	4,506	4,816	5,910	7,527	6,324	6,295	6,782	6,057
Total trunk line traffic...	Bil. Bbl.-miles ..	3,405	3,342	3,500	3,619	3,508	3,563	3,591	3,652	3,485
Crude oil...........	Bil. Bbl.-miles ..	1,948	1,842	1,891	1,899	1,602	1,620	1,609	1,604	1,571
Products	Bil. Bbl.-miles ..	1,458	1,500	1,609	1,720	1,906	1,943	1,982	2,049	1,914
Carrier property value ..	Mil. dol........	19,752	21,605	25,828	27,460	29,648	32,605	32,018	29,552	29,536
Operating revenues ..	Mil. dol........	6,356	7,461	7,149	7,711	7,483	7,812	7,704	8,020	7,917
Net income	Mil. dol........	1,912	2,431	2,340	2,670	2,705	3,409	3,470	3,323	3,076

Source: PennWell Publishing Co., Houston, Texas, *Oil & Gas Journal*, annual (copyright).

Table 1093. **U.S. Postal Service Rates for Letters and Postcards: 1991 to 2007**

[In dollars. Rates exclude Canada and Mexico]

Domestic mail date of rate change	Letters First ounce	Letters Each added ounce	Postcards	Express mail—first 1/2 pound	International air mail date of rate change	Letters—first ounce [1]	Post-cards	Aero grammes
1991 (Feb. 3)	0.29	0.23	0.19	9.95	2001 (Jan. 7)	0.80	0.70	0.70
1995 (Jan. 1)......	0.32	0.23	0.20	10.75	2006 (Jan. 8) [2]	0.84	0.75	0.75
1999 (Jan. 10).....	0.33	0.22	0.20	11.75	2007 (May 14) [2]	0.90	0.90	([3])
2001 (Jan. 7)......	0.34	0.21	0.20	12.25				
2001 (July 1).....	0.34	0.23	0.21	12.45				
2002 (June 30)....	0.37	0.23	0.23	13.65				
2006 (Jan. 8).....	0.39	0.24	0.24	14.40				
2007 (May 14).....	0.41	0.17	0.26	16.25				

[1] The rates after the first ounce may differ depending on whether a country is primarily European; is in a rate group comprising Australia, New Zealand, and Japan; or is categorized "rest of the world." [2] On January 8, 2006, the process of converting the rates for Micronesia and the Marshall Islands from the domestic schedule to the international schedule was initiated. During the transition period, the rates to these two countries have increased and will continue to increase incrementally until they equal the international rate to the rest of the world. [3] Discontinued.

Source: U.S. Postal Service, "United States Domestic Postage Rate: Recent History" and unpublished data. See Internet site <http://www.usps.com/rates/welcome.htm>.

Table 1094. U.S. Postal Service—Summary: 1980 to 2006

[106,311 represents 106,311,000,000. For years ending September 30. Includes Puerto Rico and all outlying areas. See text, this section]

Item	1980	1990	1995	2000	2004	2005	2006
Offices, stations, and branches	**39,486**	**40,067**	**39,149**	**38,060**	**37,159**	**37,142**	**36,826**
Number of post offices	30,326	28,959	28,392	27,876	27,505	27,385	27,318
Number of stations and branches	9,160	11,108	10,757	10,184	9,654	9,757	9,508
Delivery points (mil.)	(NA)	(NA)	(NA)	135.9	142.3	144.3	146.2
Residential	(NA)	(NA)	(NA)	123.9	129.6	131.3	133.0
City	(NA)	(NA)	(NA)	76.1	78.0	78.5	78.9
P.O. Box	(NA)	(NA)	(NA)	15.9	15.6	15.6	15.6
Rural/highway contract	(NA)	(NA)	(NA)	31.9	36.0	37.2	38.4
Business	(NA)	(NA)	(NA)	12.1	12.7	13.0	13.2
Pieces of mail handled (mil.)	**106,311**	**166,301**	**180,734**	**207,882**	**206,106**	**211,743**	**213,138**
Domestic [1]	105,348	165,503	179,933	206,782	205,262	210,891	212,345
First class mail [2]	60,276	89,270	96,296	103,526	97,926	98,071	97,618
Express Mail	17	59	57	71	54	56	56
Priority Mail	248	518	869	1,223	849	888	924
Periodicals (formerly 2d class)	10,220	10,680	10,194	10,365	9,135	9,070	9,023
Standard Mail (formerly Standard A)	30,381	63,725	71,112	90,057	95,564	100,942	102,460
Package Services (formerly Standard B)	633	663	936	1,128	1,132	1,166	1,175
Mailgram	39	14	5	4	2	2	–
U.S. Postal Service	2,992	538	412	363	529	621	1,016
Free for the blind	28	35	52	47	71	76	75
International economy mail (surface)	450	166	106	79	26	23	19
International airmail	513	632	696	1,021	818	829	774
Employees, total (1,000)	**667**	**843**	**875**	**901**	**808**	**803**	**796**
Career	643	761	753	788	707	705	696
Headquarters	3	2	2	2	3	3	3
Headquarters support	(NA)	6	4	6	3	4	4
Inspection Service	5	4	4	4	4	3	3
Inspector General	(X)	(X)	(X)	1	1	1	1
Field Career	634	749	743	775	697	693	685
Postmasters	29	27	27	26	26	25	25
Supervisors/managers	36	43	35	39	34	33	33
Professional, administrative, and technical	5	10	11	10	9	9	9
Clerks	263	290	274	282	226	222	214
Mail handlers	37	51	57	61	55	56	57
City carriers	187	236	240	241	228	228	224
Motor vehicle operators	6	7	8	9	9	9	9
Rural carriers	33	42	46	57	63	64	66
Special delivery messengers	2	2	2	(X)	(X)	(X)	(X)
Building and equipment maintenance	27	33	38	42	40	40	40
Vehicle maintenance	5	5	5	6	6	5	6
Other [3]	4	1	2	2	2	2	2
Noncareer	25	83	122	114	100	98	100
Casuals	5	27	26	30	21	19	23
Transitional	(X)	(X)	32	13	10	8	5
Rural substitutes	20	43	50	58	56	57	59
Relief/Leave replacements	(X)	12	13	12	12	12	12
Nonbargaining temporary	(X)	(Z)	1	1	1	1	1
Compensation and employee benefits (mil. dol.)	16,541	34,214	41,931	49,532	52,134	53,932	56,281
Avg. salary per employee (dol.) [4]	24,799	37,570	45,001	50,103	60,261	62,635	62,348
Pieces of mail per employee, (1,000)	159	197		231	255	264	268
Total revenue (mil. dol.) [5]	**19,253**	**40,074**	**54,509**	**64,540**	**69,029**	**69,993**	**72,817**
Operating postal revenue	17,143	39,201	54,176	64,476	68,960	69,798	72,551
Mail revenue [6]	16,377	37,892	52,490	62,284	65,869	66,649	69,144
First class mail	10,146	24,023	31,955	35,516	36,377	36,062	37,039
Priority Mail [7]	612	1,555	3,075	4,837	4,421	4,634	5,043
Express Mail [8]	184	630	711	996	853	872	918
Mailgram	15	8	2	2	1	1	(X)
Periodicals (formerly 2d class)	863	1,509	1,972	2,171	2,192	2,161	2,215
Standard Mail (formerly Standard A)	2,412	8,082	11,792	15,193	18,123	18,954	19,877
Package Services (formerly Standard B)	805	919	1,525	1,912	2,207	2,201	2,259
International economy mail (surface)	154	222	205	180	145	134	128
International airmail	442	941	1,254	1,477	1,551	1,631	1,666
Service revenue	765	1,310	1,687	2,191	3,091	3,150	3,407
Registry [9]	157	174	118	98	75	77	73
Certified [9]	120	310	560	385	630	601	632
Insurance [9]	55	47	52	109	128	132	137
Collect-on-delivery	21	26	21	22	11	9	10
Money orders	95	155	196	235	231	208	193
Other [9]	244	592	737	1,342	2,017	2,122	2,363
Operating expenses (mil. dol.) [10]	19,413	40,490	50,730	62,992	65,851	68,283	71,684

– Represents or rounds to zero.   NA Not available.   X Not applicable.   Z Fewer than 500.   [1] Data for 1980 includes penalty and franked mail, not shown separately.   [2] Items mailed at 1st class rates and weighing 11 ounces or less.   [3] Includes discontinued operations, area offices, and nurses.   [4] For career bargaining unit employees. Includes fringe benefits.   [5] Net revenues after refunds of postage. Includes operating reimbursements, stamped envelope purchases, indemnity claims, and miscellaneous revenue and expenditure offsets. Shown in year which gave rise to the earnings.   [6] For 1980, includes penalty and franked mail, not shown separately. Later years have that mail distributed into the appropriate class.   [7] Provides 2 to 3 day delivery service.   [8] Overnight delivery of packages weighing up to 70 pounds.   [9] Beginning 2000, return receipt revenue broken out from reqistry, certified, and insurance and included in "other."   [10] Shown in year in which obligation was incurred.

Source: U.S. Postal Service, *Annual Report of the Postmaster General* and *Comprehensive Statement on Postal Operations*, annual; and unpublished data.

Section 24
Information and Communications

This section presents statistics on the various information and communications media: publishing, including newspapers, periodicals, books, and software; motion pictures, sound recordings, broadcasting, and telecommunications; and information services, such as libraries. Statistics on computer use and Internet access are also included. Data on the usage, finances, and operations of the U.S. Postal Service previously shown in this section are now presented in Section 23, Transportation.

Information industry—The U.S. Census Bureau's *Service Annual Survey, Information Services Sector*, provides estimates of operating revenue of taxable firms and revenues and expenses of firms exempt from federal taxes for industries in the information sector of the economy. Similar estimates were previously issued in the *Annual Survey of Communications Services*. Data are based on the North American Industry Classification System (NAICS), and the information sector is a newly created economic sector. It comprises establishments engaged in the following processes: (a) producing and distributing information and cultural products, (b) providing the means to transmit or distribute these products as well as data or communications, and (c) processing data. It includes establishments previously classified in the Standard Industrial Classification (SIC) in manufacturing (publishing); transportation, communications, and utilities (telecommunications and broadcasting); and services (software publishing, motion picture production, data processing, online information services, and libraries).

This new sector is comprised of industries which existed previously, were revised from previous industry definitions, or are completely new industries. Among those which existed previously are newspaper publishers, motion picture and video production, and online information services.

Revised industries include book publishers and libraries and archives. Newly created industries include database and directory publishers, record production, music publishers, sound recording studios, cable networks, wired telecommunications carriers, paging, and satellite telecommunications.

Data from 1998 to 2003 are based on the 1997 NAICS; beginning 2004, data are based on the 2002 NAICS. Major revisions in many communications industries affect the comparability of these data. The following URL contains detailed information about NAICS <http://www.census.gov /epcd/www/naics.html>. See also the text in Section 15, Business Enterprise.

Beginning 2001, the Service Annual Survey estimates reflect the introduction of the provisional North American Product Classification System (NAPCS) for the information sector. Data for prior years are not comparable. See <http://www.census.gov/eos/www /napcs/napcs.htm>.

The 1997 Economic Census was the first economic census to cover the new information sector of the economy. The census, conducted every 5 years, for the years ending "2" and "7," provides information on the number of establishments, receipts, payroll, and paid employees for the United States and various geographic levels. The most recent reports are from the 2002 Economic Census. This census was conducted in accordance with the 2002 NAICS.

The Federal Communications Commission (FCC), established in 1934, regulates wire and radio communications. Only the largest carriers and holding companies file annual financial reports which are publically available. The FCC has jurisdiction over interstate and foreign communication services but not over intrastate or local services. The gross operating revenues of the telephone carriers reporting

U.S. Census Bureau, Statistical Abstract of the United States: 2008

publically available data annually to the FCC, however, are estimated to cover about 90 percent of the revenues of all U.S. telephone companies. Data are not comparable with Census Bureau *Annual Survey* because of coverage and different accounting practices for those telephone companies which report to the FCC.

Reports filed by the broadcasting industry cover all radio and television stations operating in the United States. The private radio services represent the largest and most diverse group of licensees regulated by the FCC. These services provide voice, data communications, point-to-point, and point-to-multipoint radio communications for fixed and mobile communicators. Major users of these services are small businesses, the aviation industry, the maritime trades, the land transportation industry, the manufacturing industry, state and local public safety and governmental authorities, emergency medical service providers, amateur radio operators, and personal radio operations (CB and the General Mobile Radio Service). The FCC also licenses entities as private and common carriers. Private and common carriers provide fixed and land mobile communications service on a for-profit basis. Principal sources of wire,

radio, and television data are the FCC's *Annual Report* and its annual *Statistics of Communications Common Carriers.*

Statistics on publishing are available from the Census Bureau, as well as from various private agencies. Editor & Publisher Co., New York, NY, presents annual data on the number and circulation of daily and Sunday newspapers in its *International Year Book.* The Book Industry Study Group, New York, NY, collects data on books sold and domestic consumer expenditures. Data on academic and public libraries are collected by the U.S. National Center for Education Statistics. Data on Internet use by adults are collected by the Pew Internet and American Life Project, Washington, DC, and Mediamark Research, New York, NY.

Advertising—Data on advertising previously shown in this section are now presented in Section 27, Accommodation, Food Services, and Other Services.

Statistical reliability—For a discussion of statistical collection and estimation, sampling procedures, and measures of statistical reliability applicable to Census Bureau data, see Appendix III.

U.S. Census Bureau, Statistical Abstract of the United States: 2008

[For establishments with payroll (3,599.9 represents 3,599,900). Excludes most government employees, railroad employees, and self-employed persons. For statement on methodology, see Appendix III]

Industry	2002 NAICS code[1]	Establishments (number) 2003	2004	Paid employees[2] (1,000) 2003	2004	Annual payroll (mil. dol.) 2003	2004
Information industries	51	140,027	139,681	3,599.9	3,472.4	204,024	200,447
Publishing industries	511	31,336	31,528	1,049.6	1,033.5	66,312	66,887
Newspaper, periodical, book, and database publishers	5111	22,179	22,443	705.4	704.9	30,842	32,020
Newspaper publishers	51111	8,376	8,435	384.7	383.1	13,735	14,009
Periodical publishers	51112	7,176	7,602	155.8	154.4	8,933	9,418
Book publishers	51113	3,377	3,377	83.6	85.0	4,357	4,622
Database and directory publishers	51114	1,808	1,740	52.0	56.3	2,610	2,871
Other publishers	51119	1,442	1,289	29.3	26.1	1,207	1,099
Greeting card publishers	511191	114	120	14.3	13.1	617	583
All other publishers	511199	1,328	1,169	15.0	13.0	590	517
Software publishers	5112	9,157	9,085	344.2	328.6	35,470	34,866
Motion picture and sound recording industries	512	22,207	22,753	283.8	307.8	13,046	13,286
Motion picture and video industries	5121	18,914	19,348	257.5	282.7	10,999	11,321
Motion picture and video production	51211	11,255	11,751	93.0	122.2	7,723	8,264
Motion picture and video distribution	51212	449	452	3.5	3.4	198	214
Motion picture and video exhibition	51213	5,110	5,029	136.0	134.9	1,514	1,327
Motion picture theaters (except drive-ins) . . .	512131	4,834	4,756	134.6	133.5	1,494	1,301
Drive-in motion picture theaters	512132	276	273	1.4	1.4	20	26
Postproduction and other motion picture ar;d video industries	51219	2,100	2,116	25.0	22.1	1,564	1,516
Teleproduction and other postproduction services	512191	1,786	1,784	21.0	17.4	1,302	1,194
Other motion picture and video industries . . .	512199	314	332	4.0	4.7	262	323
Sound recording industries	5122	3,293	3,405	26.3	25.1	2,047	1,965
Record production	51221	328	353	1.4	1.4	72	74
Integrated record production/distribution.	51222	402	415	11.0	9.7	1,297	1,196
Music publishers	51223	612	606	4.5	4.7	305	329
Sound recording studios	51224	1,482	1,513	5.4	5.4	213	205
Other sound recording industries	51229	469	518	4.0	3.8	160	162
Broadcasting (except Internet)	515	10,372	10,099	286.4	288.0	16,004	16,198
Radio and television broadcasting	5151	9,688	9,466	254.6	247.7	13,029	12,521
Radio broadcasting	51511	7,711	7,492	131.4	127.0	5,493	5,514
Radio networks	515111	669	729	10.4	11.9	611	728
Radio stations	515112	7,042	6,763	121.0	115.1	4,882	4,786
Television broadcasting.	51512	1,977	1,974	123.2	120.6	7,535	7,006
Cable and other subscription programming	5152	684	633	31.8	40.4	2,976	3,677
Internet publishing and broadcasting	516	2,038	2,133	35.6	37.0	2,324	2,546
Telecommunications	517	50,142	49,786	1,415.2	1,327.4	77,957	72,683
Wired telecommunications carriers	5171	27,607	27,596	855.2	781.4	51,445	45,280
Wireless telecommunications carriers (except satellite).	5172	13,020	13,183	266.3	262.1	13,500	13,971
Paging.	517211	1,508	1,224	17.2	11.5	684	503
Cellular and other wireless telecommunications	517212	11,512	11,959	249.0	250.6	12,816	13,468
Telecommunications resellers	5173	2,726	2,886	36.6	46.6	1,660	2,211
Satellite telecommunications	5174	698	649	14.6	18.4	890	1,201
Cable and other program distribution	5175	5,383	4,844	234.1	210.7	9,961	9,437
Other telecommunications	5179	708	628	8.3	8.3	500	583
Internet service providers, Web search portals, and data processing service	518	19,643	19,489	473.9	426.4	26,516	27,002
Internet service providers and Web search portals.	5181	5,365	5,422	70.9	60.4	4,803	5,234
Internet service providers	518111	4,790	4,851	60.9	49.2	3,539	3,083
Web search portals	518112	575	571	10.0	11.2	1,264	2,151
Data processing, hosting, and related services. . .	5182	14,278	14,067	403.0	365.9	21,713	21,767
Other information services	519	4,289	3,893	55.4	52.2	1,865	1,846
News syndicates.	51911	623	559	11.5	11.2	693	677
Libraries and archives	51912	2,951	2,677	32.3	31.7	717	735
All other information services	51919	715	657	11.6	9.3	455	434

[1] North American Industry Classification System, 2002; see text, this section and Section 15.   [2] For employees on the payroll for the pay period including March 12.

Source: U.S. Census Bureau, "County Business Patterns"; <http://www.census.gov/epcd/cbp/view/cbpview.html>.

Table 1096. **Information Sector Services—Estimated Revenue and Expenses: 2004 and 2005**

[In millions of dollars (955,083 represents $955,083,000,000), except percent. For taxable and tax-exempt employer firms. Estimates have been adjusted to the results of the 2002 Economic Census. Based on the Service Annual Survey; see Appendix III. Minus sign (−) indicates decrease]

Industry	2002 NAICS code [1]	Operating revenue			Operating expenses		
		2004	2005	Percent change, 2004–05	2004	2005	Percent change, 2004–05
Information industries	51	955,083	1,005,252	5.3	784,704	809,923	3.2
Publishing industries (except Internet)	511	256,301	268,838	4.9	193,091	195,815	1.4
Newspaper, periodical, book, and directory publishers	5111	144,040	149,215	3.6	104,811	109,119	4.1
Newspaper publishers	51111	48,366	49,717	2.8	39,920	40,978	2.7
Periodical publishers	51112	42,290	45,365	7.3	34,583	36,294	4.9
Book publishers	51113	27,904	27,729	−0.6	16,415	17,375	5.8
Directory and mailing list publishers	51114	18,040	19,371	7.4	10,722	11,295	5.3
Other publishers	51119	7,440	7,033	−5.5	3,171	3,177	0.2
Greeting card publishers	511191	5,075	4,552	−10.3	1,857	1,774	−4.5
All other publishers	511199	2,365	2,481	4.9	1,314	1,403	6.8
Software publishers.	5112	112,261	119,623	6.6	88,280	86,696	−1.8
Motion picture and sound recording industries . .	512	88,269	92,129	4.4	72,820	76,241	4.7
Motion picture and video industries	5121	71,774	73,369	2.2	60,288	61,406	1.9
Motion picture and video production and distribution	51211,12	56,605	58,346	3.1	47,959	49,279	2.8
Motion picture and video exhibition	51213	11,180	10,789	−3.5	8,631	8,500	−1.5
Motion picture theaters (except drive-ins)	512131	11,069	10,669	−3.6	8,557	8,421	−1.6
Drive-in motion picture theaters.	512132	111	120	8.1	(S)	(S)	(S)
Postproduction services and other motion picture and video industries	51219	3,989	4,234	6.1	3,698	3,627	−1.9
Teleproduction and other postproduction services	512191	3,193	3,373	5.6	3,002	2,857	−4.8
Other motion picture and video industries	512199	796	861	8.2	696	770	10.6
Sound recording industries	5122	16,495	18,760	13.7	12,532	14,835	18.4
Record production	51221	352	341	−3.1	275	262	−4.7
Integrated record production/distribution. . .	51222	11,021	12,866	16.7	8,918	11,112	24.6
Music publishers	51223	3,885	4,204	8.2	2,164	2,184	0.9
Sound recording studios	51224	724	767	5.9	635	672	5.8
Other sound recording industries	51229	513	582	13.5	540	605	12.0
Broadcasting (except Internet)	515	83,466	88,752	6.3	63,709	68,010	6.8
Radio and television broadcasting	5151	52,093	53,520	2.7	42,268	44,376	5.0
Radio broadcasting	51511	16,494	17,223	4.4	14,303	15,600	9.1
Radio networks	515111	2,677	3,510	31.1	4,389	5,450	24.2
Radio stations	515112	13,817	13,713	−0.8	9,914	10,150	2.4
Television broadcasting.	51512	35,599	36,297	2.0	27,965	28,776	2.9
Cable and other subscription programming . .	5152	31,373	35,232	12.3	21,441	23,634	10.2
Internet publishing and broadcasting	516	8,695	10,339	18.9	7,583	8,918	17.6
Telecommunications	517	429,430	449,344	4.6	372,243	382,374	2.7
Wired telecommunications carriers	5171	211,176	206,781	−2.1	187,746	176,600	−5.9
Wireless telecommunications carriers (except satellite)	5172	127,602	143,308	12.3	106,688	123,817	16.1
Paging.	517211	1,909	2,002	4.9	1,550	1,736	12.0
Cellular and other wireless telecommunications	517212	125,693	141,306	12.4	105,138	122,081	16.1
Telecommunications resellers	5173	9,849	11,230	14.0	5,981	6,759	13.0
Satellite telecommunications	5174	6,030	5,521	−8.4	5,826	4,841	−16.9
Cable and other program distribution	5175	73,317	80,493	9.8	64,957	69,031	6.3
Other telecommunications	5179	(S)	(S)	(S)	1,045	1,326	26.9
Internet service providers, Web search portals, and data processing services	518	82,491	88,730	7.6	70,226	73,102	4.1
Internet service providers and Web search portals.	5181	25,161	25,966	3.2	18,790	17,544	−6.6
Internet service providers	518111	20,201	18,914	−6.4	16,301	14,283	−12.4
Web search portals	518112	4,960	7,052	42.2	2,489	3,261	31.0
Data processing, hosting, and related services.	5182	57,330	62,764	9.5	51,436	55,558	8.0
Other information services	519	6,431	7,120	10.7	5,032	5,463	8.6
News syndicates	51911	1,972	2,162	9.6	1,724	1,863	8.1
Libraries and archives	51912	1,879	2,032	8.1	1,582	1,676	5.9
Other information services.	51919	2,580	2,926	13.4	1,726	1,924	11.5

S Data do not meet publication standards.   [1] North American Industry Classification System (NAICS), 2002; see text this section.

Source: U.S. Census Bureau, "2005 Service Annual Survey, Information Sector Services." See <http://www.census.gov/econ/www/servmenu.html> (released February 2007).

Table 1097. **Information Industries—Establishments, Revenue, Payroll and Employees by Kind of Business: 2002**

[For establishments with payroll. (891,846 represents $891,846,000,000). Based on the 2002 Economic Census; see Appendix III]

Kind of business	2002 NAICS code [1]	Number of establish-ments	Receipts (mil. dol.)	Annual payroll (mil. dol.)	Paid employees (1,000)
Information industries...............	51	137,678	891,846	194,670	3,736.1
Publishing industries (except Internet)...........	511	32,287	242,216	65,681	1,089.6
Motion picture & sound recording industries.......	512	22,458	78,250	12,599	303.1
Motion picture & video industries..............	5121	19,074	62,927	10,353	271.2
Sound recording industries..................	5122	3,384	15,324	2,246	31.9
Broadcasting (except Internet)................	515	9,540	73,962	14,439	291.4
Radio & television broadcasting..............	5151	8,851	48,589	11,591	252.2
Cable & other subscription programming........	5152	689	25,373	2,848	39.1
Internet publishing & broadcasting..............	516	2,057	6,363	2,346	40.0
Telecommunications......................	517	49,275	411,645	72,182	1,440.1
Wired telecommunications carriers.............	5171	27,955	237,697	47,496	842.4
Wireless telecommunications carriers (except satellite).............................	5172	11,155	99,193	13,207	281.4
Telecommunications resellers.................	5173	2,525	9,717	1,397	34.5
Satellite telecommunications.................	5174	646	5,748	915	14.4
Cable & other program distribution.............	5175	6,288	57,709	8,553	256.0
Other telecommunications...................	5179	706	1,581	614	11.4
Internet service providers, Web search portals, & data processing......................	518	18,589	74,508	25,719	514.0
Internet service providers & Web search portals....	5181	4,820	21,419	4,451	79.8
Data processing, hosting, & related services......	5182	13,769	53,089	21,267	434.3
Other information services..................	519	3,472	4,901	1,705	57.8

[1] North American Industry Classification System, 2002; see text, this section and Section 15, Business Enterprise.

Source: U.S. Census Bureau, "2002 Economic Census, Geographic Area Series Reports, Information." See Internet site: <http://www.census.gov/econ/census02/guide/geosumm.htm>; (accessed January 2007).

Table 1098. **Media Usage and Consumer Spending: 2000 to 2010**

[Estimates for time spent were derived using rating data for broadcast television and cable and satellite television, survey research for radio, mobile, out-of-home media and yellow pages, and consumer purchase data (units, admissions, access) for books, home video, Internet, newspapers, consumer books, consumer magazines, recorded music, videogames, and box office. Adults 18 and older were the basis for estimates for newspapers, consumer books, consumer magazines, out-of-home media, yellow pages and home video. Persons 12 and older were the basis for the estimates for broadcast television, cable & satellite television, radio, recorded music, box office, videogames, Internet and mobile content]

Item	2000	2003	2004	2005	2006, proj.	2007, proj.	2008, proj.	2009, proj.	2010, proj.
HOURS PER PERSON PER YEAR [1]									
Total [2].................	3,340	3,508	3,530	3,543	3,553	3,567	3,592	3,601	3,620
Television...............	1,502	1,615	1,620	1,659	1,673	1,686	1,704	1,713	1,733
Broadcast television [3]........	812	729	711	679	684	672	666	657	650
Network stations	717	629	612	576	579	567	558	546	538
Independent stations [4]......	95	100	100	101	105	105	108	110	112
Cable & satellite television [3].....	690	886	909	980	989	1,014	1,038	1,057	1,083
Basic cable and satellite television..............	568	728	753	807	823	840	862	880	902
Premium cable and satellite television [4]............	122	157	156	173	166	174	176	176	181
Broadcast and satellite radio [3]......	784	834	821	805	794	786	785	778	776
Recorded music [3]...........	259	189	195	189	191	191	188	187	180
Newspapers [3].............	201	194	191	184	181	177	173	169	165
Pure-play Internet services [3]......	100	155	165	172	177	180	181	182	183
Out-of-home media..........	118	123	126	130	134	137	141	145	150
Consumer magazines [3]........	135	122	125	124	122	121	122	120	119
Consumer books [3]...........	107	109	108	108	107	107	107	108	108
Videogames [3]..............	65	76	78	73	75	78	80	84	86
Home video [5].............	43	60	67	63	63	64	65	66	67
CONSUMER SPENDING PER PERSON PER YEAR (dol.)									
Total [2].................	610.35	739.65	772.58	787.44	817.06	850.61	880.87	909.37	933.52
Television	173.58	236.82	258.73	283.47	306.70	329.39	350.03	368.55	384.55
Cable and satellite television [3]....	173.58	236.79	258.63	283.08	305.70	327.55	347.26	364.79	379.92
Broadcast television [3]..........	(Z)	0.03	0.09	0.40	1.00	1.84	2.77	3.75	4.63
Home video [5].............	81.41	122.28	125.45	115.24	114.24	115.54	116.78	118.33	119.36
Consumer books [3]...........	87.45	91.84	92.49	95.62	97.04	100.32	101.85	104.05	106.38
Pure-play Internet services [3]......	45.43	59.72	59.60	57.11	55.84	56.29	57.26	58.67	59.77
Recorded music [3]...........	61.20	49.46	52.03	51.18	52.00	52.25	52.23	51.87	51.08
Newspapers [3].............	51.92	53.62	51.97	50.56	49.65	48.65	47.53	46.29	44.94
Consumer magazines [3]........	47.58	46.56	47.38	47.64	47.30	47.28	47.93	47.35	47.73
Box office [3]..............	32.72	39.10	38.88	36.38	37.15	36.30	35.67	35.39	35.29
Videogames [3].............	28.01	32.98	33.59	32.23	33.59	35.55	37.38	39.98	41.52

Z Less than $.005   [1] Can include concurrent use of media, such as watching television and reading e-mail simultaneously. Does not include media use at work.   [2] Includes other media, not shown separately.   [3] Online and mobile use and spending on traditional media platforms, such as downloaded music, newspaper Web sites, e-books, cable modems, online video of television programs and Internet radio were included in the traditional media segment, not in pure-play Internet services or pure-play mobile content. Pure-play Internet services and pure-play mobile content included telecommunications access, such as DSL, Internet-only Web sites such as Yahoo!, GameSpy, eHarmoney, and mobile-only services, such as MobiTV or text messaging services from telecommunication providers.   [4] Telemundo and Univson affiliates included in independent and public stations. Pay-per-view, interactive channels, home shopping and audio-only feeds included in premium cable & satellite services.   [5] Playback of prerecorded VHS cassettes and DVDs only.

Source: Veronis Suhler Stevenson, New York, NY, *Communications Industry Forecast & Report,* annual (copyright).

Information and Communications   703

Table 1099. Utilization of Selected Media: 1980 to 2005

[78.6 represents 78,600,000]

Item	Unit	1980	1990	1995	1999	2000	2001	2002	2003	2004	2005
Households with—											
Telephone service [1]	Percent ...	93.0	93.3	93.9	94.0	94.6	94.6	95.5	95.5	94.2	92.4
Radio [2]	Millions ...	78.6	94.4	98.0	(NA)	100.5	101.9	105.1	106.7	108.3	109.9
Percent of total households...	Percent ...	99.0	99.0	99.0	99.0	99.0	99.0	99.0	99.0	99.0	99.0
Average number of sets	Number ...	5.5	5.6	5.6	5.6	5.6	5.6	5.6	8.0	8.0	8.0
Television [3]	Millions ...	76	92	96	101	101	102	106	107	109	110
Percent of total households...	Percent ...	97.9	98.2	98.3	98.2	98.2	98.2	98.2	98.2	98.2	98.2
Television sets in homes	Millions ...	128	193	217	240	245	248	254	260	268	287
Average number of sets per home	Number ...	1.7	2.0	2.3	2.4	2.4	2.4	2.4	2.4	2.5	2.6
Color set households	Millions ...	63	90	94	99	101	102	105	107	108	109
Wired cable television [4]	Millions ...	15.2	51.9	60.5	67.1	68.6	69.5	73.2	74.4	73.8	73.9
Percent of TV households...	Percent ...	19.9	56.4	63.4	67.5	68.0	68.0	69.4	69.8	68.1	67.5
Alternative delivery system (ADS) households [4]	Millions ...	(NA)	(NA)	4.0	9.4	11.7	14.7	17.4	19.7	21.2	23.3
Percent of TV households...	Percent ...	(NA)	(NA)	4.2	9.3	11.4	14.1	16.3	18.2	19.3	20.8
VCRs [4]	Millions ...	1	63	77	84	86	88	96	98	98	99
Percent of TV households...	Percent ...	1.1	68.6	81.0	84.6	85.1	86.2	91.2	91.5	90.8	90.2
Computers [5]	Percent ...	(NA)	(NA)	(NA)	(NA)	51.0	56.2	(NA)	61.8	(NA)	(NA)
Internet connections [5]	Percent ...	(NA)	(NA)	(NA)	(NA)	41.5	50.3	(NA)	54.6	(NA)	(NA)
Broadband Internet [5]	Percent ...	(NA)	(NA)	(NA)	(NA)	4.4	9.1	(NA)	19.9	(NA)	(NA)
Commercial radio stations: [2]											
AM	Number ...	4,589	4,987	4,909	4,783	4,685	4,727	4,804	4,802	4,770	4,758
FM	Number ...	3,282	4,392	5,296	5,766	5,892	6,051	6,161	6,207	6,217	6,215
Television stations: [6] Total	Number ...	1,011	1,442	1,532	1,615	1,663	1,686	1,714	1,730	1,748	1,749
Commercial	Number ...	734	1,092	1,161	1,243	1,288	1,309	1,333	1,349	1,366	1,370
VHF	Number ...	516	542	562	561	567	572	581	587	589	589
UHF	Number ...	218	545	599	682	721	737	752	762	777	781
Cable television systems [7]	Number ...	4,225	9,575	11,218	10,700	10,400	10,300	9,900	9,400	8,875	(NA)
Daily newspaper circulation [8]	Millions ...	62.2	62.3	58.2	56.0	55.8	55.6	55.2	55.2	54.6	53.3

NA Not available. [1] For occupied housing units. 1980 as of April 1; all other years as of March. Source: U.S. Census Bureau, *1980 Census of Housing*, vol. 1; thereafter, Federal Communications Commission, *Trends in Telephone Service*, annual. [2] 1980–1995 as of December 31. Source: M Street Corp. as reported by Radio Advertising Bureau New York, NY; through 1990, *Radio Facts*, annual (copyright); beginning 1995, *Radio Marketing Guide and Fact Book for Advertisers*, annual (copyright). Number of stations on the air compiled from Federal Communications Commission reports. Beginning 1999, Federal Communications Commission, unpublished data as of Sept. 30. See Internet site <http://www.fcc.gov/mb/audio/totals>. [3] As of January of year shown. Excludes Alaska and Hawaii. Source: Television Bureau of Advertising, Inc., *Trends in Television*, annual (copyright). [4] Wired cable and VCR as of February; ADS for fourth quarter. Excludes Alaska and Hawaii. Source: See footnote 3. [5] As of August 2000, September 2001, and October 2003. Source: U.S. Department of Commerce, National Telecommunications and Information Administration, *A Nation Online: Entering the Broadband Age*, September 2004. See Internet site <http://www.ntia.doc.gov/reports/anol/index.html>. [6] Source: Beginning 1999, Federal Communications Commission, unpublished data. See Internet site <http://www.fcc.gov/mb/audio/totals>. Beginning 1999, as of September. For prior years data, see footnote 3. [7] As of January 1. Source: Warren Communications News, Washington DC, *Television and Cable Factbook* (copyright). [8] As of September 30. Source: Editor & Publisher, Co., New York, NY, *Editor & Publisher International Year Book*, annual (copyright).

Source: Compiled from sources mentioned in footnotes.

Table 1100. Multimedia Audiences—Summary: 2006

[In percent, except total (218,289 represents 218,289,000). As of fall. For persons 18 years old and over. Represents the percent of persons participating during the prior week, except as indicated. Based on sample and subject to sampling error; see source for details]

Item	Total population (1,000)	Television viewing	Television prime time viewing	Cable viewing [1]	Radio listening	Newspaper reading	Accessed Internet [2]
Total	218,289	94.1	84.2	79.4	81.7	75.7	65.6
18 to 24 years old	28,098	90.1	74.2	74.5	85.3	69.0	78.3
25 to 34 years old	39,485	91.9	82.2	77.4	86.3	71.5	75.6
35 to 44 years old	43,532	93.8	84.6	80.2	88.0	75.1	75.0
45 to 54 years old	42,127	94.3	85.2	81.4	86.9	78.5	72.2
55 to 64 years old	29,660	96.4	88.5	83.3	80.5	79.7	61.8
65 years old and over	35,387	97.7	89.1	78.6	60.9	79.6	27.9
Male	105,176	94.2	84.3	79.5	83.3	76.1	64.6
Female	113,113	93.9	84.1	79.2	80.3	75.3	66.5
Not high school graduate	34,355	93.7	83.4	64.5	71.4	57.0	22.1
High school graduate	69,653	95.4	86.2	80.9	80.4	74.0	53.5
Attended college	59,432	94.4	84.0	82.8	85.6	80.2	80.4
College graduate	54,849	92.2	82.5	83.0	85.6	84.7	92.0
Household income:							
Less than $10,000	13,121	93.2	83.1	60.9	71.3	64.6	31.7
$10,000 to $19,999	21,735	94.4	84.9	65.0	68.5	67.4	33.1
$20,000 to $29,999	24,022	94.2	84.7	70.3	75.8	72.4	40.5
$30,000 to $34,999	11,935	93.8	85.2	77.2	78.2	69.4	53.2
$35,000 to $39,999	11,090	96.1	85.2	76.0	80.6	73.1	58.2
$40,000 to $49,999	20,898	94.0	82.7	79.4	83.2	75.6	62.3
$50,000 to $74,999	43,599	94.1	84.1	83.1	85.5	77.0	74.9
$75,000 to $99,999	28,599	94.5	85.6	87.5	87.6	79.3	84.9
$100,000 or more	43,289	93.4	83.3	89.4	87.6	83.7	90.7

[1] In the past 7 days. [2] In the last 30 days.

Source: Mediamark Research Inc., New York, NY, *Multimedia Audiences*, fall 2006 (copyright).

704   Information and Communications

Table 1101. Newspaper Publishers—Estimated Revenue, Expenses, and Inventories: 2004 and 2005

[In millions of dollars (48,366 represents $48,366,000,000). For taxable and tax-exempt employer firms. Covers NAICS 51111. Estimates have been adjusted to the results of the 2002 Economic Census. Based on the North American Industry Classification System (NAICS), 2002. See text, this section, and Section 15. See also Appendix III. Minus sign (–) indicates decrease]

Item	2004	2005	Percent change 2004–05
Operating revenue [1]...............................	48,366	49,717	2.8
Breakdown of revenue by media type:			
Print	41,104	42,468	3.3
Online	1,808	2,092	15.7
Other media	749	451	–39.8
Operating expenses.............................	39,920	40,978	2.7
Personnel costs......	19,407	19,807	2.1
Gross annual payroll......	15,355	15,680	2.1
Employer's cost for fringe benefits.....	3,771	3,882	2.9
Temporary staff and leased employee expense	282	245	–13.1
Expensed materials, parts and supplies (not for resale)............	4,379	4,369	–0.2
Expensed equipment......	97	98	1.0
Expensed purchase of other materials, parts and supplies	4,282	4,270	–0.3
Expensed purchased services	3,054	3,223	5.5
Expensed software	80	89	11.3
Expensed electricity and fuels (except motor fuel).....	292	335	14.7
Lease and rental payments	537	560	4.3
Purchased repair and maintenance	383	380	–0.8
Purchased advertising and promotional services......	617	660	7.0
Purchased printing services	1,145	1,200	4.8
Other operating expenses	13,080	13,579	3.8
Depreciation and amortization charges......	2,031	2,048	0.8
Government taxes and license fees......	377	382	1.3
All other operating expenses......	10,672	11,149	4.5
Inventories at end of year.......................	688	713	3.6
Finished good	(S)	33	(S)
Work-in-process......	15	17	13.3
Materials, fuels, supplies etc.	644	663	3.0

S Data do not meet publication standards.   [1] Includes other types of revenue (e.g., printing services) not shown separately.

Source: U.S. Census Bureau, "2005 Service Annual Survey, Information Sector Services." See <http://www.census.gov/econ/www/servmenu.html> (released February 2007).

Table 1102. Daily and Sunday Newspapers—Number and Circulation: 1970 to 2006

[Number of newspapers as of February 1 the following year. Circulation figures as of September 30 of year shown (62.1 represents 62,100,000). For English language newspapers only]

Type	1970	1975	1980	1985	1990	1995	2000	2002	2003	2004	2005	2006
NUMBER												
Daily: Total [1]...............	1,748	1,756	1,745	1,676	1,611	1,533	1,480	1,457	1,456	1,457	1,452	1,437
Morning	334	339	387	482	559	656	766	777	787	814	817	833
Evening	1,429	1,436	1,388	1,220	1,084	891	727	692	680	653	645	614
Sunday	586	639	736	798	863	888	917	913	917	915	914	907
NET PAID CIRCULATION (mil.)												
Daily: Total [1]...............	62.1	60.7	62.2	62.8	62.3	58.2	55.8	55.2	55.2	54.6	53.3	52.3
Morning	25.9	25.5	29.4	36.4	41.3	44.3	46.8	46.6	46.9	46.9	46.1	45.4
Evening	36.2	35.2	32.8	26.4	21.0	13.9	9.0	8.6	8.3	7.7	7.2	6.9
Sunday	49.2	51.1	54.7	58.8	62.6	61.5	59.4	58.8	58.5	57.8	55.3	53.2
PER CAPITA CIRCULATION [2]												
Daily: Total [1]...............	0.30	0.28	0.27	0.26	0.25	0.22	0.20	0.19	0.19	0.19	0.18	0.17
Morning	0.13	0.12	0.13	0.15	0.17	0.17	0.17	0.16	0.16	0.16	0.16	0.15
Evening	0.18	0.16	0.14	0.11	0.08	0.05	0.03	0.03	0.03	0.03	0.02	0.02
Sunday	0.24	0.24	0.24	0.25	0.25	0.23	0.21	0.20	0.20	0.20	0.19	0.18

[1] All-day newspapers are counted in both morning and evening columns but only once in total. Circulation is divided equally between morning and evening.   [2] Based on U.S. Census Bureau estimated resident population as of July 1.

Source: Editor & Publisher Co., New York, NY, *Editor & Publisher International Year Book*, annual (copyright).

Information and Communications 705

Table 1103. **Daily Newspapers—Number and Circulation by Size of City: 1980 to 2006**

[Number of newspapers as of February 1 the following year. Circulation as of September 30 (29,413 represents 29,413,000). For English language newspapers only. See Table 32 for number of cities by population size. All-day newspapers are counted in both morning and evening columns; circulation is divided equally between morning and evening]

Type of daily and population-size class	Number					Net paid circulation (1,000)				
	1980	1990	1995	2000	2006	1980	1990	1995	2000	2006
Morning dailies, total...	387	559	656	766	833	29,413	41,311	44,310	46,772	45,441
In cities of—										
1,000,001 or more	20	18	25	26	30	8,795	6,508	10,173	10,820	10,416
500,001 to 1,000,000	27	22	22	25	35	5,705	4,804	5,587	5,412	6,539
100,001 to 500,000	99	138	153	163	161	8,996	20,051	17,214	17,469	15,976
50,001 to 100,000	75	100	138	162	164	2,973	4,373	5,602	5,887	5,474
25,001 to 50,000	64	102	115	141	162	1,701	3,209	3,150	3,899	3,690
Less than 25,000........	102	179	203	249	281	1,243	2,365	2,584	3,285	3,346
Evening dailies, total...	1,388	1,084	891	727	614	32,788	21,017	13,883	9,000	6,888
In cities of—										
1,000,001 or more	11	7	3	1	1	2,984	1,423	390	1	1
500,001 to 1,000,000	23	12	7	3	5	4,101	1,350	1,017	519	404
100,001 to 500,000	123	71	45	32	22	8,178	4,687	2,529	1,603	1,141
50,001 to 100,000	156	94	72	54	40	4,896	2,941	2,029	1,332	977
25,001 to 50,000	246	204	158	124	101	5,106	4,278	2,819	1,898	1,421
Less than 25,000........	829	696	606	513	445	7,523	6,338	5,099	3,648	2,945

Source: Editor & Publisher Co., New York, NY, *Editor & Publisher International Year Book,* annual (copyright).

Table 1104. **Daily and Sunday Newspapers—Number and Circulation, 1991 to 2005 and by State, 2006**

[Number of newspapers as of February 1 the following year. Circulation as of September 30 (60,687 represents 60,687,000). For English language newspapers only. California, New York, Massachusetts, and Virginia Sunday newspapers include national circulation]

State	Daily			Sunday		State	Daily			Sunday	
		Circulation [1]			Net paid circulation (1,000)			Circulation [1]			Net paid circulation (1,000)
	Num-ber	Net paid (1,000)	Per capita [2]	Num-ber			Num-ber	Net paid (1,000)	Per capita [2]	Num-ber	
Total, 1991 ..	1,586	60,687	0.24	875	62,068	LA	24	682	0.16	18	748
Total, 1992 ..	1,570	60,164	0.23	891	62,160	ME	7	218	0.16	4	182
Total, 1993 ..	1,556	59,812	0.23	884	62,566	MD	11	465	0.08	8	607
Total, 1994 ..	1,548	59,305	0.23	886	62,294	MA	32	1,350	0.21	16	1,291
Total, 1995 ..	1,533	58,193	0.22	888	61,529	MI	48	1,563	0.15	27	1,769
Total, 1996 ..	1,520	56,983	0.21	890	60,798	MN	25	825	0.16	15	1,058
Total, 1997 ..	1,509	56,728	0.21	903	60,484	MS	23	350	0.12	19	351
Total, 1998 ..	1,489	56,182	0.20	898	60,066	MO	42	888	0.15	21	1,074
Total, 1999 ..	1,483	55,979	0.20	905	59,894	MT	11	184	0.19	7	185
Total, 2000 ..	1,480	55,773	0.20	917	59,421	NE	16	388	0.22	6	372
Total, 2001 ..	1,468	55,578	0.19	913	59,090	NV	8	292	0.12	4	316
Total, 2002 ..	1,457	55,186	0.19	913	58,780	NH	11	205	0.16	4	206
Total, 2003 ..	1,456	55,185	0.19	917	58,495	NJ	18	1,186	0.14	15	1,458
Total, 2004 ..	1,457	54,626	0.19	915	57,753	NM	17	266	0.14	12	275
Total, 2005 ..	1,452	53,345	0.18	914	55,270	NY	60	6,832	0.35	38	5,026
						NC	47	1,232	0.14	39	1,362
Total, 2006 ..	**1,437**	**52,329**	**0.17**	**907**	**53,175**	ND	10	150	0.24	7	157
AL	25	604	0.13	21	673	OH	84	2,155	0.19	41	2,379
AK..........	7	103	0.15	5	114	OK	39	571	0.16	31	701
AZ..........	16	721	0.12	11	822	OR	19	630	0.17	12	658
AR..........	28	453	0.16	16	523	PA	80	2,526	0.20	43	2,953
CA..........	86	5,177	0.14	57	5,297	RI	6	196	0.18	3	238
CO	30	950	0.20	16	1,089	SC..........	16	586	0.14	14	678
CT..........	17	630	0.18	13	708	SD..........	11	150	0.19	4	130
DE..........	2	128	0.15	2	156	TN..........	26	819	0.14	19	966
DC	3	1,017	1.75	2	972	TX..........	82	2,644	0.11	77	3,339
FL..........	40	3,020	0.17	37	3,637	UT..........	6	332	0.13	6	367
GA	35	966	0.10	30	1,214	VT..........	8	107	0.17	3	81
HI	6	266	0.21	6	294	VA..........	23	3,146	0.41	17	929
ID	12	210	0.14	8	227	WA	22	952	0.15	16	1,084
IL	66	2,125	0.17	32	2,337	WV	20	373	0.21	14	385
IN	67	1,235	0.20	25	1,180	WI	34	827	0.15	17	1,001
IA	37	576	0.19	13	613	WY	9	88	0.17	5	73
KS..........	41	384	0.14	13	336						
KY..........	24	583	0.14	14	586						

[1] Circulation figures based on the principal community served by a newspaper which is not necessarily the same location as the publisher's office. [2] Per capita based on estimated resident population as of July 1, except 2000, enumerated resident population as of April 1.

Source: Editor & Publisher Co., New York, NY, *Editor & Publisher International Year Book,* annual (copyright).

706 Information and Communications

Table 1105. **Periodical Publishers—Estimated Revenue, Expenses, and Inventories: 2004 and 2005**

[In millions of dollars (42,290 represents $42,290,000,000). For taxable and tax-exempt employer firms. Covers NAICS 51112. Estimates have been adjusted to the results of the 2002 Economic Census. Based on the North American Industry Classification System (NAICS), 2002. See text, this section, and Section 15. See also Appendix III. Minus sign (–) indicates decrease]

Item	2004	2005	Percent change, 2004–05
Operating revenue [1]	42,290	45,365	7.3
Breakdown of revenue by media type:			
Print	29,375	30,991	5.5
Online	1,461	1,713	17.2
Other media	391	428	9.5
Operating expenses	34,583	36,294	4.9
Personnel	12,847	13,644	6.2
Gross annual payroll	10,370	10,925	5.4
Employer's cost for fringe benefits	2,064	2,290	10.9
Temporary staff and leased employee expense	413	429	3.9
Expensed materials, parts and supplies (not for resale)	1,531	1,521	–0.7
Expensed equipment	246	201	–18.3
Expensed purchase of other materials, parts and supplies	1,284	1,319	2.7
Expensed purchased services	7,375	7,701	4.4
Expensed software	475	(S)	(S)
Expensed electricity and fuels (except motor fuel)	116	136	17.2
Lease and rental payments	1,130	1,248	10.4
Purchased repair and maintenance	247	297	20.2
Purchased advertising and promotional services	2,358	2,519	6.8
Purchased printing services	3,049	3,183	4.4
Other operating expenses	12,830	13,429	4.7
Depreciation and amortization charges	1,714	1,674	–2.3
Government taxes and license fees	174	190	9.2
All other	10,942	11,565	5.7
Inventories at end of year	1,635	1,834	12.2
Finished good	1,118	1,245	11.4
Work-in-process	110	129	17.3
Materials, fuels, supplies etc.	406	460	13.3

S Data do not meet publication standards.   [1] Includes other types of revenue (e.g., printing services) not shown separately.

Source: U.S. Census Bureau, "2005 Service Annual Survey, Information Sector Services." See <http://www.census.gov/econ/www/servmenu.html> (released February 2007).

Table 1106. **Quantity of Books Sold and Value of Consumer Domestic Expenditures: 2006 to 2010**

[(3,096 represents 3,096,000,000). Represents net publishers' shipments after returns. Includes all titles released by publishers in the United States and imports which appear under the imprints of American publishers. Multivolume sets, such as encyclopedias, are counted as one unit. Due to changes in methodology and scope, these data are not comparable to those previously published]

Type of publication	Net publishers' shipments (mil.)					Domestic U.S. consumer expenditures (mil. dol.)				
	2006	2007, proj.	2008, proj.	2009, proj.	2010 proj.	2006	2007, proj.	2008, proj.	2009, proj.	2010 proj.
Total	3,096	3,141	3,173	3,199	3,216	53,616	55,696	57,455	59,333	61,054
Trade	2,273	2,302	2,316	2,323	2,329	25,372	26,307	26,930	27,618	28,342
Adult	824	828	831	834	837	16,134	16,618	17,023	17,443	17,899
Hardback	406	407	408	408	409	9,615	9,877	10,122	10,351	10,603
Paperback	418	421	423	425	427	6,519	6,740	6,901	7,093	7,296
Juvenile	873	891	895	895	894	5,996	6,319	6,427	6,589	6,759
Hardback	273	291	284	288	291	2,796	3,048	3,036	3,145	3,243
Paperback	600	600	610	606	603	3,200	3,271	3,391	3,443	3,516
Mass market paperbacks— rack-sized	575	583	590	595	598	3,242	3,371	3,480	3,586	3,685
Religious	263	270	278	285	292	4,685	4,919	5,169	5,416	5,674
Hardback	94	96	99	102	105	2,796	2,929	3,082	3,234	3,387
Paperback	169	174	178	183	188	1,889	1,990	2,087	2,183	2,287
Professional	281	282	283	284	285	11,020	11,340	11,631	11,925	12,209
Hardback	100	100	101	101	102	6,920	7,125	7,314	7,503	7,684
Paperback	181	182	183	183	184	2,993	3,080	3,160	3,241	3,321
Subscription reference	(X)	(X)	(X)	(X)	(X)	1,107	1,135	1,157	1,182	1,205
University press	25	24	24	24	24	642	656	670	683	696
Hardback	9	9	9	9	9	224	230	234	239	243
Paperback	15	15	15	15	15	418	426	435	444	453
Elementary/high school text	177	186	194	204	207	5,375	5,766	6,161	6,607	6,851
Hardback	60	65	69	72	73	2,570	2,882	3,089	3,315	3,431
Paperback	118	120	126	132	134	2,805	2,884	3,073	3,292	3,420
College text	77	77	78	78	79	6,522	6,710	6,895	7,084	7,282
Hardback	34	34	34	35	35	4,346	4,477	4,609	4,743	4,865
Paperback	43	43	43	43	44	2,176	2,232	2,285	2,341	2,417

X Not applicable.

Source: Book Industry Study Group, Inc., New York, NY, *Book Industry Trends, 2007,* annual (copyright).

Information and Communications 707

Table 1107. Book Publishers—Estimated Revenue and Inventories: 2004 and 2005

[In millions of dollars (27,904 represents $27,904,000,000), except percent. For taxable and tax-exempt employer firms. Covers NAICS 51113. Estimates have been adjusted to the results of the 2002 Economic Census. Based on the North American Industry Classification System (NAICS), 2002. See text, this section, and Section 15. See also Appendix III. Minus sign (−) indicates decrease]

Item	2004	2005	Percent change, 2004–05
Operating revenue, total............................	27,904	27,729	−0.6
Sources of revenue:			
Books, print..	24,735	24,423	−1.3
Textbooks...	9,198	9,410	2.3
Children's books.................................	2,029	2,099	3.4
General reference books........................	1,964	(S)	(S)
Professional, technical, and scholarly books.	3,446	3,413	−1.0
Adult trade......................................	8,099	(S)	(S)
All other operating revenue.....................	3,169	3,306	4.3
Breakdown of revenue by media type:			
Print books......................................	(S)	26,111	(S)
Online books....................................	(S)	(S)	(S)
Other media books..............................	(S)	813	(S)
Inventories at end of year........................	4,421	4,508	2.0
Finished goods..................................	3,702	3,748	1.2
Work-in-process.................................	553	599	8.3
Materials, supplies, fuel, etc....................	167	161	−3.6

S Data do not meet publication standards.

Source: U.S. Census Bureau, "2005 Service Annual Survey, Information Sector Services." See <http://www.census.gov/econ/www/servmenu.html> (released February 2007).

Table 1108. Directory and Mailing List Publishers—Estimated Revenue, Expenses, and Inventories: 2004 and 2005

[In millions of dollars (18,040 represents $18,040,000,000). For taxable and tax-exempt employer firms. Covers NAICS 51114. Estimates have been adjusted to the results of the 2002 Economic Census. Based on the North American Industry Classification System (NAICS), 2002. See text, this section, and Section 15. See also Appendix III. Minus sign (−) indicates decrease]

Item	2004	2005	Percent change, 2004–05
Operating revenue [1].............................	18,040	19,371	7.4
Breakdown of revenue by media type:			
Print...	12,896	13,318	3.3
Online..	3,111	3,986	28.1
Other media....................................	491	311	−36.7
Operating expenses.............................	10,722	11,295	5.3
Personnel..	4,165	4,612	10.7
Gross annual payroll............................	3,094	3,464	12.0
Employer's cost for fringe benefits..............	(S)	996	(S)
Temporary staff and leased employee expense	201	152	−24.4
Expensed materials, parts and supplies (not for resale)....	840	845	0.6
Expensed equipment............................	23	29	26.1
Expensed purchase of other materials, parts and supplies	817	817	(Z)
Expensed purchased services	(S)	(S)	(S)
Expensed software	41	43	4.9
Expensed electricity and fuels (except motor fuel)..............	(S)	19	(S)
Lease and rental payments	269	278	3.3
Purchased repair and maintenance	(S)	71	(S)
Purchased advertising and promotional services.	(S)	375	(S)
Purchased printing services	756	(S)	(S)
Other operating expenses	4,201	4,178	−0.5
Depreciation and amortization charges..........	698	735	5.3
Government taxes and license fees..............	(S)	(S)	(S)
All other..	(S)	3,364	(S)
Inventories at end of year.......................	442	459	3.8
Finished good...................................	182	206	13.2
Work-in-process.................................	32	32	(Z)
Materials, fuels, supplies etc....................	228	221	−3.1

S Data do not meet publication standards.   Z Less than 0.05.   [1] Includes other types of revenue (e.g., sales of mailing lists), not shown separately.

Source: U.S. Census Bureau, "2005 Service Annual Survey, Information Sector Services." See <http://www.census.gov/econ/www/servmenu.html> (released February 2007).

Table 1109. **Software Publishers—Estimated Revenue, Expenses, and Inventories: 2004 and 2005**

[In millions of dollars (112,261 represents $112,261,000,000), except percent. For taxable and tax-exempt employer firms. Covers NAICS 5112. Estimates have been adjusted to the results of the 2002 Economic Census. Based on the North American Industry Classification System (NAICS), 2002. See text, this section, and Section 15. Minus sign (−) indicates decrease]

Item	2004	2005	Percent change, 2004–05
Operating revenue.............................	112,261	119,623	6.6
Source of revenue:			
System software publishing [1]...................	43,696	46,965	7.5
Operating system software......................	17,836	18,250	2.3
Network software.............................	10,952	12,708	16.0
Database management software..................	6,304	6,651	5.5
Development tools and programming languages software........	3,579	3,538	−1.1
Application software publishing [1].................	40,680	42,690	4.9
General business productivity and home use applications.........	18,391	19,162	4.2
Cross-industry application software..............	12,150	12,658	4.2
Vertical market application software.............	6,726	7,153	6.3
Utilities software.............................	925	1,000	8.1
Other services [1].............................	27,885	29,969	7.5
Customization and integration of packaged software............	4,454	5,219	17.2
Information technology technical consulting services............	4,000	4,412	10.3
Resale of computer hardware and software.........	2,648	2,303	−13.0
Information technology-related training services...........	1,497	1,567	4.7
Operating expenses...........................	88,280	86,696	−1.8
Personnel costs..............................	49,950	49,516	−0.9
Gross annual payroll..........................	41,817	40,339	−3.5
Employer's cost for fringe benefits...............	6,116	6,709	9.7
Temporary staff and leased employee expense...........	2,017	2,468	22.4
Expensed materials, parts and supplies (not for resale)..........	(S)	2,306	(S)
Expensed equipment..........................	663	770	16.1
Expensed purchase of other materials, parts and supplies........	(S)	1,536	(S)
Expensed purchased services [1]..................	9,378	9,276	−1.1
Purchased electricity and fuels (except motor fuel)............	253	292	15.4
Lease and rental payments.....................	2,509	2,326	−7.3
Purchased repair and maintenance...............	377	427	13.3
Purchased advertising and promotional services............	4,989	5,162	3.5
Other operating expenses......................	25,702	25,598	−0.4
Inventories at end of year......................	1,549	1,686	8.8
Finished goods..............................	965	1,227	27.2
Works-in-process.............................	56	53	−5.4
Materials, supplies, fuel, etc....................	528	406	−23.1

S Data do not meet publication standards. [1] Includes other sources of revenue and other expenses, not shown separately.

Source: U.S. Census Bureau, "2005 Service Annual Survey, Information Sector Services." See <http://www.census.gov/econ/www/servmenu.html> (released February 2007).

Table 1110. **Motion Picture and Video Exhibition—Estimated Revenue and Expenses: 2004 and 2005**

[In millions of dollars (11,180 represents $11,180,000,000), except percent. For taxable and tax-exempt employer firms. For NAICS 51213. Estimates have been adjusted to the results of the 2002 Economic Census. Based on the North American Industry Classification System (NAICS), 2002. See text, this section, and Section 15. See also Appendix III. Minus sign (−) indicates decrease]

Item	2004	2005	Percent change, 2004–05
Operating revenue, total......................	11,180	10,789	−3.5
Sources of revenue:			
Feature film exhibition revenue.................	7,522	7,178	−4.6
Admission to domestic films....................	7,358	6,996	−4.9
Admission to foreign films.....................	165	182	10.3
Other revenue [1].............................	3,657	3,611	−1.3
Food and beverage sales......................	3,124	3,049	−2.4
Advertising services..........................	222	217	−2.3
Coin-operated games and rides.................	43	41	−4.7
Operating expenses...........................	8,631	8,500	−1.5
Personnel costs..............................	1,697	1,663	−2.0
Gross annual payroll..........................	1,495	1,461	−2.3
Employer's cost for fringe benefits...............	162	163	0.6
Temporary staff and leased employee expense...........	40	39	−2.5
Expensed materials, parts and supplies (not for resale)........	191	177	−7.3
Expensed purchased services [1]..................	1,970	2,056	4.4
Purchased electricity and fuels (except motor fuel)............	299	314	5.0
Lease and rental payments.....................	1,248	1,310	5.0
Purchased repair and maintenance..............	223	228	2.2
Purchased advertising and promotional services..........	197	201	2.0
Other operating expenses......................	4,773	4,603	−3.6

[1] Includes other sources of revenue and other expenses, not shown separately.

Source: U.S. Census Bureau, "2005 Service Annual Survey, Information Sector Services." See <http://www.census.gov/econ/www/servmenu.html> (released February 2007).

Information and Communications 709

Table 1111. Recording Media—Manufacturers' Shipments and Value: 1999 to 2006

[1,160.6 represents 1,160,600,000. Based on reports of RIAA member companies who distributed about 84 percent of the pre-recorded music in 2006. These data are supplemented by other sources]

Medium	1999	2000	2001	2002	2003	2004	2005	2006
UNITS SHIPPED (mil.)								
Total [1]	1,160.6	1,079.2	968.5	859.7	798.4	958.0	1,301.8	1,583.2
Physical:								
Compact disks [2]	938.9	942.5	881.9	803.3	746.0	767.0	705.4	614.9
Music video [3]	19.8	18.2	17.7	14.7	19.9	32.8	33.8	23.1
Other albums [4]	126.5	78.2	47.6	33.3	20.5	7.7	4.4	1.7
Other singles [5]	75.4	40.3	21.3	8.4	12.1	6.6	5.0	2.9
Digital:								
Download single	(X)	(X)	(X)	(X)	(X)	139.4	366.9	586.4
Download album	(X)	(X)	(X)	(X)	(X)	4.6	13.6	27.6
Kiosk [6]	(X)	(X)	(X)	(X)	(X)	(X)	0.7	1.4
Music video	(X)	(X)	(X)	(X)	(X)	(X)	1.9	9.9
Mobile [7]	(X)	(X)	(X)	(X)	(X)	(X)	170.0	315.3
Subscription [8]	(X)	(X)	(X)	(X)	(X)	(X)	1.3	1.7
VALUE (mil. dol.)								
Total [1]	14,584.7	14,323.7	13,740.9	12,614.2	11,854.4	12,338.1	12,269.5	11,510.2
Physical:								
Compact disks [2]	12,816.3	13,214.5	12,909.4	12,044.1	11,232.9	11,446.5	10,520.2	9,162.9
Music video [3]	376.7	281.9	329.2	288.4	399.9	607.2	602.2	451.0
Other albums [4]	1,093.4	653.7	396.8	238.8	164.2	66.1	48.5	22.1
Other singles [5]	298.3	173.6	105.5	42.9	57.4	34.9	24.2	15.4
Digital:								
Download single	(X)	(X)	(X)	(X)	(X)	138.0	363.3	580.6
Download album	(X)	(X)	(X)	(X)	(X)	45.5	135.7	275.9
Kiosk [6]	(X)	(X)	(X)	(X)	(X)	(X)	1.0	1.9
Music video	(X)	(X)	(X)	(X)	(X)	(X)	3.7	19.7
Mobile [7]	(X)	(X)	(X)	(X)	(X)	(X)	421.6	774.5
Subscription [8]	(X)	(X)	(X)	(X)	(X)	(X)	149.2	206.2

X Not applicable. [1] Net, after returns. [2] Includes DualDisc. [3] Includes DVD video. [4] Includes cassette, LP/EP, DVD audio, and SACD. [5] Includes CD single, cassette single, and vinyl single. [6] Includes singles and albums. [7] Includes Master Ringtunes, Ringbacks, full-length downloads, and other mobile. [8] Weighted annual average. Number of units not included in total.

Source: Recording Industry Association of America, Washington, DC, *2006 Year-end Statistics* and earlier issues (copyright). See Internet site <http://www.riaa.com> (accessed 15 May 2007).

Table 1112. Profile of Consumer Expenditures for Sound Recordings—Percent Distribution: 1990 to 2006

[In percent. Based on monthly telephone surveys of the population 10 years old and over]

Item	1990	1995	2000	2002	2003	2004	2005	2006
Total [1]	100.0	100.0	100.0	100.0	100.0	100.0	100.0	100.0
Age: 10 to 14 years	7.6	8.0	8.9	8.9	8.6	9.4	8.6	7.6
15 to 19 years	18.3	17.1	12.9	13.3	11.4	11.9	11.9	12.8
20 to 24 years	16.5	15.3	12.5	11.5	10.0	9.2	12.7	9.8
25 to 29 years	14.6	12.3	10.6	9.4	10.9	10.0	12.1	12.7
30 to 34 years	13.2	12.1	9.8	10.8	10.1	10.4	11.3	10.2
35 to 39 years	10.2	10.8	10.6	9.8	11.2	10.7	8.8	10.6
40 to 44 years	7.8	7.5	9.6	9.9	10.0	10.9	9.2	9.0
45 years and over	11.1	16.1	23.8	25.5	26.6	26.4	25.5	26.1
Sex: Male	54.4	53.0	50.6	49.4	49.1	49.5	51.8	50.4
Female	45.6	47.0	49.4	50.6	50.9	50.5	48.2	49.6
Sales outlet:								
Record store	69.8	52.0	42.4	36.8	33.2	32.5	39.4	35.4
Other store.	18.5	28.2	40.8	50.7	52.8	53.8	32.0	32.7
Tape/record club	8.9	14.3	7.6	4.0	4.1	4.4	8.5	10.5
Ad or 800 number	2.5	4.0	2.4	2.0	1.5	1.7	2.4	2.4
Internet [2]	(NA)	(NA)	3.2	3.4	5.0	5.9	8.2	9.1
Digital download	(NA)	(NA)	(NA)	(NA)	(NA)	(NA)	6.0	6.8
Music type: [3]								
Rock.	36.1	33.5	24.8	24.7	25.2	23.9	31.5	34.0
Country	9.6	16.7	10.7	10.7	10.4	13.0	12.5	13.0
Rap/Hip Hop.	8.5	6.7	12.9	13.8	13.3	12.1	13.3	11.4
R&B/Urban.	11.6	11.3	9.7	11.2	10.6	11.3	10.2	11.0
Pop	13.7	10.1	11.0	9.0	8.9	10.0	8.1	7.1
Religious	2.5	3.1	4.8	6.7	5.8	6.0	5.3	5.5
Jazz	4.8	3.0	2.9	3.2	2.9	2.7	1.8	2.0
Children's.	0.5	0.5	0.6	0.4	0.6	2.8	2.3	2.9

NA Not available. [1] Percent distributions exclude nonresponses and responses of "Don't know." Some types of music and sales outlets are not shown separately. [2] Excludes record club purchases over the Internet or digital downloads. [3] As classified by respondent.

Source: Recording Industry Association of America, Washington, DC, *2006 Consumer Profile* and earlier issues (copyright). See Internet site <http://www.riaa.com> (accessed 15 May 2007).

710   Information and Communications

Table 1113. Radio and Television Broadcasting—Estimated Revenue and Expenses: 2004 and 2005

[In millions of dollars (2,677 represents $2,677,000,000). For taxable and tax-exempt employer firms. Estimates have been adjusted to the results of the 2002 Economic Census. Based on the North American Industry Classification System (NAICS), 2002. See text, this section, and Section 15]

Item	Radio networks (NAICS 515111)		Radio stations (NAICS 515112)		TV broadcasting (NAICS 51512)	
	2004	2005	2004	2005	2004	2005
Operating revenue	2,677	3,510	13,817	13,713	35,599	36,297
Air time	925	1,471	12,268	12,086	25,972	26,052
National/regional air time	723	1,242	2,799	2,723	16,284	16,261
Local advertising revenue.............	202	229	9,469	9,363	9,689	9,790
Other operating revenue	1,752	2,039	1,548	1,626	9,627	10,245
Network compensation.................	269	286	224	223	5,783	6,341
Public and noncommercial programming services	484	730	(S)	(S)	(S)	(S)
All other operating revenue.............	999	1,022	803	835	2,536	2,630
Operating expenses	4,389	5,450	9,914	10,150	27,965	28,776
Personnel costs......................	1,069	1,223	4,998	5,117	7,161	7,554
Gross annual payroll...................	893	1,036	4,203	4254	6,093	6,423
Employer's cost for fringe benefits	119	133	550	612	958	1,012
Temporary staff and leased employee expense	57	53	246	251	110	120
Expensed materials, parts and supplies (not for resale)..	187	232	111	123	221	223
Expensed equipment.....................	96	106	35	41	61	57
Expensed purchase of other materials, parts and supplies........................	91	126	76	82	161	165
Expensed purchased services	1,126	1,433	979	1,045	1,897	1,997
Expensed purchases of software	14	16	(S)	(S)	33	33
Purchased electricity and fuels (except motor fuel) . . .	15	17	131	144	(S)	(S)
Lease and rental payments................	113	131	304	342	412	427
Purchased repair and maintenance	(S)	(S)	82	85	(S)	(S)
Purchased advertising and promotional services.....	975	1,259	416	429	879	944
Other operating expenses	2,007	2,563	3,825	3,866	18,686	19,001
Broadcast rights and music license fees	256	338	567	586	11,700	12,023
Network compensation fees	161	173	(S)	(S)	660	697
Depreciation and amortization fees	473	475	566	491	1,413	1,385
Government taxes and license fees	13	16	477	489	177	150
All other operating expenses.................	1,104	1,561	2,132	2,218	4,736	4,746

S Data do not meet publication standards.

Source: U.S. Census Bureau, "2005 Service Annual Survey, Information Sector Services." See <http://www.census.gov/econ/www /servmenu.html> (released February 2007).

Table 1114. Cable and Pay TV—Summary: 1975 to 2006

[9,800 represents 9,800,000. Cable TV for calendar year. Pay TV as of December 31 of year shown]

Year	Cable TV				Pay TV					
	Avg. basic sub-scribers (1,000)	Avg. monthly basic rate (dol.)	Revenue [1] (mil. dol.)		Units [2] (1,000)			Monthly rate (dol.)		
			Total	Basic	Total pay [3]	Pay cable	Non-cable delivered premium	All pay weighted average [3]	Pay cable	Non-cable delivered premium
1975	9,800	6.50	804	764	194	194	(NA)	(NA)	7.85	(NA)
1980	17,500	7.69	2,609	1,615	8,581	7,336	(NA)	8.91	8.62	(NA)
1985	35,440	9.73	8,831	4,138	29,885	29,418	(NA)	10.29	10.25	(NA)
1990	50,520	16.78	17,582	10,174	39,902	39,751	(NA)	10.35	10.30	(NA)
1994	58,373	21.62	21,531	15,144	47,478	42,528	4,950	8.19	8.33	6.99
1995	60,550	23.07	24,137	16,763	55,723	46,798	8,925	8.29	8.54	6.99
1996	62,300	24.41	26,195	18,249	63,705	49,728	13,977	7.98	8.12	7.50
1997	63,600	26.48	28,931	20,213	72,785	51,933	20,852	8.31	8.43	8.00
1998	64,650	27.81	31,191	21,574	80,605	55,280	25,325	8.58	8.74	8.22
1999	65,500	28.92	34,095	22,732	88,455	59,005	29,450	8.73	8.85	8.50
2000	66,250	30.37	36,756	24,142	102,590	65,918	36,672	8.69	8.81	8.48
2001	66,732	32.87	42,238	26,324	115,325	75,433	39,892	8.95	9.10	8.66
2002	66,472	34.71	48,623	27,690	125,662	81,128	44,534	9.19	9.29	9.00
2003	66,050	36.59	53,991	29,000	127,377	83,421	43,956	9.37	9.45	9.23
2004	65,727	38.14	59,559	30,080	140,060	90,843	49,217	10.03	10.11	9.88
2005	65,337	39.63	65,684	31,075	149,067	96,910	52,157	10.08	10.16	9.93
2006	65,319	41.17	72,993	32,274	157,936	101,331	56,605	10.13	10.21	9.98

NA Not available. [1] Includes installation revenue, subscriber revenue, and nonsubscriber revenue; excludes telephony and high-speed access. [2] Individual program services sold to subscribers. [3] Includes multipoint distribution service (MDS), satellite TV (STV), multipoint multichannel distribution service (MMDS), satellite master antenna TV (SMATV), C-band satellite, and DBS satellite. Includes average pay unit price based on data for major premium pay movie services.

Source: SNL Kagan, a division of SNL Financial LC. From the Broadband Cable Financial Databook 2004, 2005, 2006, 2007 (copyright); the Cable Cable Program Investor and Cable TV Investor: Deals & Finance newsletters (monthly); and various other SNL Kagan publications.

Information and Communications   711

Table 1115. **Cable and Other Subscription Programming—Estimated Revenue and Expenses: 2004 and 2005**

[In millions of dollars (31,373 represents $31,373,000,000), except percent. For taxable and tax-exempt employer firms. Covers NAICS 51521. Estimates have been adjusted to the results of the 2002 Economic Census. Based on the North American Industry Classification System (NAICS), 2002. See text, this section, and Section 15]

Item	2004	2005	Percent change, 2004-05
Operating revenue	31,373	35,232	12.3
Source of revenue:			
Licensing of rights to broadcast specialty programming [1]	16,483	18,627	13.0
Air time	12,879	14,193	10.2
All other operating services revenue	2,011	2,411	19.9
Operating expenses	21,441	23,634	10.2
Personnel costs	3,986	4,650	16.7
Gross annual payroll	3,151	3,695	17.3
Employer's cost for fringe benefits	553	630	13.9
Temporary staff and leased employee expense	283	325	14.8
Expensed materials, parts and supplies (not for resale)	267	309	15.7
Expensed equipment	60	63	5.0
Expensed purchase of other materials, parts and supplies	207	246	18.8
Expensed purchased services	1,978	2,122	7.3
Expensed purchases of software	39	44	12.8
Purchased electricity and fuels (except motor fuel)	(S)	42	(S)
Lease and rental payments	448	512	14.3
Purchased repair and maintenance	(S)	95	(S)
Purchased advertising and promotional services	1,329	1,429	7.5
Other operating expenses	15,210	16,553	8.8
Network compensation fees	11,626	12,568	8.1
Depreciation and amortization charges	1,368	1,453	6.2
Government taxes and license fees	124	126	1.6
All other operating expenses	2,092	2,406	15.0

S Data do not meet publication standards. [1] Protected by copyright.

Source: U.S. Census Bureau, "2005 Service Annual Survey, Information Sector Services." See <http://www.census.gov/econ/www/servmenu.html> (released February 2007).

Table 1116. **Internet Publishing and Broadcasting—Estimated Revenue and Expenses: 2004 and 2005**

[In millions of dollars (8,695 represents $8,695,000,000). For taxable and tax-exempt employer firms. Covers NAICS 516. Estimates have been adjusted to the results of the 2002 Economic Census. Based on the North American Industry Classification System (NAICS), 2002. See text, this section, and Section 15. Minus sign (–) indicates decrease]

Item	2004	2005	Percent change, 2004-05
Operating revenue	8,695	10,339	18.9
Source of revenue:			
Publishing and broadcasting of content on the Internet	4,482	4,763	6.3
Online advertising space	1,525	1,969	29.1
Licensing of rights to use intellectual property	384	479	24.7
All other operating revenue	2,303	3,128	35.8
Breakdown of revenue by type of customer:			
Government	(S)	(S)	(S)
Business firms and not-for-profit organizations	6,330	7,405	17.0
Household consumers and individual users	2,022	2,416	19.5
Operating expenses	7,583	8,918	17.6
Personnel	3,358	3,838	14.3
Gross annual payroll	2,747	3,260	18.7
Employer's cost for fringe benefits	360	419	16.4
Temporary staff and leased employee expense	251	160	–36.3
Expensed materials, parts and supplies (not for resale)	268	224	–16.4
Expensed equipment	102	78	–23.5
Expensed purchase of other materials, parts and supplies	166	(S)	(S)
Expensed purchased services	1,227	1,401	14.2
Expensed purchases of software	61	66	8.2
Purchased electricity and fuels (except motor fuel)	20	17	–15.0
Lease and rental payments	303	290	–4.3
Purchased repair and maintenance	36	77	113.9
Purchased advertising and promotional services	807	951	17.8
Other operating expenses	2,730	3,455	26.6
Depreciation and amortization charges	360	614	70.6
Government taxes and license fees	27	85	214.8
All other operating expenses	2,343	2,755	17.6

S Data do not meet publication standards.

Source: U.S. Census Bureau, "2005 Service Annual Survey, Information Sector Services." See <http://www.census.gov/econ/www/servmenu.html> (released February 2007).

Table 1117. **Telecommunications Industry—Carriers and Revenue: 1995 to 2004**

[Revenue in millions of dollars (190,076 represents $190,076,000,000). Data based on carrier filings to the FCC. Because of reporting changes, data beginning 2000 are not strictly comparable with previous years; see source for details]

Category	Carriers					Telecommunications revenue				
	1995	2000	2002 [1]	2003	2004	1995	2000	2002	2003	2004
Total [2]	3,058	4,879	4,390	4,636	5,031	190,076	292,762	292,341	291,123	291,734
Local service providers......	1,675	2,641	2,531	2,681	2,864	103,792	128,075	130,941	126,860	123,067
Incumbent local exchange carriers (ILECs)........	1,347	1,335	1,310	1,303	1,304	102,820	116,158	114,990	109,480	105,496
Pay telephone providers ...	271	699	606	605	642	349	972	641	523	445
Competitors of ILECs.....	57	607	615	773	918	623	10,945	15,310	16,857	17,126
CAPs and CLECs [3].....	57	479	451	601	690	623	9,814	13,043	15,509	15,112
Local resellers........	([4])	105	100	100	136	([4])	879	1,538	721	1,215
Other local exchange carriers............	([4])	23	64	72	92	([4])	11	406	338	245
Private carriers........	([4])	([4])	([4])	([4])	([4])	([4])	39	281	267	532
Shared tenant service providers..........	([4])	([4])	([4])	([4])	([4])	([4])	202	42	22	22
Wireless service providers [5]..	930	1,430	927	939	963	18,627	63,280	80,467	89,342	99,465
Telephony [6]............	792	783	422	413	396	17,208	59,823	78,568	88,168	98,329
Paging service providers...	138	425	346	347	360	([4])	3,102	1,473	1,007	872
Toll service providers.......	453	808	932	1,026	1,204	76,447	101,407	80,934	74,920	69,204
Interexchange carriers	130	212	229	232	257	70,938	87,311	68,146	61,246	51,589
Operator service providers..	25	20	18	17	19	500	635	554	567	523
Prepaid service providers ..	8	23	27	50	67	16	727	460	812	1,635
Satellite service carriers ...	([4])	25	33	40	40	([4])	336	406	663	721
Toll resellers..........	260	493	574	642	751	4,220	10,641	9,279	9,294	12,192
Other toll carriers........	30	35	51	45	70	773	1,758	2,089	2,339	2,543

[1] Counts dropped in 2002 because many affiliated filers were allowed to file consolidated reports. [2] Revenue data include adjustments, not shown separately. For 1995, revenue data include some nontelecommunications revenue, formerly reported as local exchange wireless revenue. [3] Competitive access providers (CAPs) and competitive local exchange carriers (CLECs). [4] Data not available separately. [5] Beginning 2000, includes specialized mobile radio services and other services, not shown separately. [6] Cellular service, personal communications service, and specialized mobile radio.

Source: U.S. Federal Communications Commission, *Trends in Telephone Service*, annual.

Table 1118. **Wired Telecommunications—Estimated Revenue and Expenses: 2004 and 2005**

[In millions of dollars (211,176 represents $211,176,000,000). For taxable and tax-exempt employer firms. Covers NAICS 5171. Estimates have been adjusted to the results of the 2002 Economic Census. Based on the North American Industry Classification System (NAICS), 2002. See text, this section, and Section 15. Minus sign (–) indicates decrease]

Item	2004	2005	Percent change, 2004–05
Operating revenue.............................	211,176	206,781	-2.1
Fixed total [1]	105,511	99,814	-5.4
Fixed local...........................	70,355	66,551	-5.4
Fixed long-distance....................	33,210	29,529	-11.1
Fixed all distance	1,945	3,734	92.0
Other communication services [1]	89,204	90,939	1.9
Carrier services	37,221	36,641	-1.6
Private network services	25,530	26,204	2.6
Subscriber line charges	8,616	8,291	-3.8
Internet access services.............	10,240	12,034	17.5
Reselling services for telecommunications equipment, retail	4,096	3,984	-2.7
All other	16,462	16,028	-2.6
Operating expenses............................	187,746	176,600	-5.9
Personnel costs................................	63,309	60,408	-4.6
Gross annual payroll......................	40,867	40,116	-1.8
Employer's cost for fringe benefits	18,258	16,733	-8.4
Temporary staff and leased employee expense	4,184	3,559	-14.9
Expensed materials, parts and supplies (not for resale)............	4,650	4,413	-5.1
Expensed equipment......................	439	393	-10.5
Expensed purchase of other materials, parts, and supplies........	4,211	4,019	-4.6
Expensed purchased services	11,058	10,325	-6.6
Expensed purchases of software	1,575	1,532	-2.7
Purchased electricity and fuels (except motor fuel)	1,648	1,671	1.4
Lease and rental payments	3,574	3,398	-4.9
Purchased repair and maintenance	2,116	2,005	-5.2
Purchased advertising and promotional services............	2,145	1,719	-19.9
Other operating expenses............................	108,730	101,454	-6.7
Access charges	30,647	29,221	-4.7
Universal service contributions (USC) and other similar charges	2,827	3,673	29.9
Depreciation and amortization charges.................	39,454	35,502	-10.0
Government taxes and license fees	4,004	3,755	-6.2
All other operating expenses.....................	31,798	29,304	-7.8

[1] Includes and other sources of revenue, not shown separately.

Source: U.S. Census Bureau, "2005 Service Annual Survey, Information Sector Services." See <http://www.census.gov/econ /www/servmenu.html> (released February 2007).

Information and Communications 713

Table 1119. **Telephone Systems—Summary: 1985 to 2004**

[**112 represents 112,000,000.** Covers principal carriers filing annual reports with Federal Communications Commission]

Item	Unit	1985	1990	1995	1999	2000	2001[1]	2002[1]	2003[1]	2004[1]
LOCAL EXCHANGE CARRIERS[2]										
Carriers[3]	Number...	55	51	53	52	52	30	29	28	28
Access lines	Millions	112	130	166	228	245	253	262	268	270
Business access lines	Millions	31	36	46	57	58	54	54	49	46
Residential access lines	Millions	79	89	101	115	115	112	ₒ103	99	100
Other access lines (public, mobile, special)	Millions	2	6	19	55	72	87	105	120	124
Number of local calls (originating)	Billions	365	402	484	554	537	515	459	425	420
Number of toll calls (originating)	Billions	(NA)	63	94	102	106	98	90	81	92
Gross book cost of plant	Bil. dol.	191	240	284	342	362	360	367	368	(NA)
Depreciation and amortization reserves	Bil. dol.	49	89	127	176	190	194	210	222	(NA)
Net plant	Bil. dol.	142	151	157	166	172	166	157	146	(NA)
Total assets	Bil. dol.	162	180	197	204	214	208	195	182	(NA)
Total stockholders equity	Bil. dol.	63	74	72	67	72	66	58	47	(NA)
Operating revenues	Bil. dol.	73	84	96	113	117	109	103	108	(NA)
Local revenues	Bil. dol.	32	37	46	58	60	55	51	51	50
Operating expenses[4]	Bil. dol.	48	62	72	79	81	77	79	83	(NA)
Net operating income[5]	Bil. dol.	13	14	14	20	20	19	23	9	(NA)
Net income	Bil. dol.	9	11	11	13	15	11	8	4	(NA)
Employees	(1,000)	(NA)	569	447	436	434	386	333	303	(NA)
Compensation of employees	Bil. dol.	(NA)	23	21	24	24	23	23	23	23
Average monthly residential local telephone rate[6]	Dollars	(NA)	19.24	20.01	19.93	20.78	22.62	23.38	24.31	24.52
Average monthly single-line business telephone rate[6]	Dollars	(NA)	41.21	41.80	41.21	41.80	42.43	43.59	43.75	43.49
LONG DISTANCE CARRIERS										
Number of carriers with prescribed lines	Number	(NA)	325	583	(NA)	(NA)	(NA)	(NA)	(NA)	(NA)
Number of presubscribed lines	Millions	(NA)	132	153	(NA)	(NA)	(NA)	(NA)	(NA)	(NA)
Total toll service revenues[7]	Bil. dol.	55	67	90	108	110	99	84	77	71
Interstate switched access minutes	Bil. min.	167	307	432	553	567	538	486	444	423
INTERNATIONAL TELEPHONE SERVICE[8]										
Number of U.S. billed calls	Millions	425	984	2,830	5,305	5,742	6,265	5,926	7,350	10,890
Number of U.S. billed minutes	Millions	3,446	8,030	15,889	28,515	30,135	33,287	35,063	42,664	63,553
U.S. billed revenues	Mil. dol.	3,487	8,059	14,335	14,980	14,909	11,380	9,773	8,944	9,178
U.S. carrier revenue net of settlements with foreign carriers	Mil. dol.	2,332	5,188	9,397	10,379	10,982	8,034	6,931	5,964	5,546
Revenue from private-line service	Mil. dol.	172	201	514	1,216	1,480	1,467	988	620	458
Revenue from resale service	Mil. dol.	(NA)	167	1,756	4,528	7,600	5,341	4,871	5,420	5,248

NA Not available. [1] Beginning 2001, detailed financial data only filed by regional Bell-operating companies. Access lines and calls reported by 50 reporting companies. [2] Gross operating revenues, gross plant, and total assets of reporting carriers estimated at more than 90 percent of total industry. New accounting rules became effective in 1990; prior years may not be directly comparable on an one-to-one basis. Includes Virgin Islands, and prior to 1995, Puerto Rico. [3] The reporting threshold for carriers is $100 million in annual operating revenue. [4] Excludes taxes. [5] After tax deductions. [6] Based on surveys conducted by FCC. [7] Series revised to include all toll revenues: toll, wireless, ILECs, carriers (ILECs) and competitive local exchange carriers (CLECs). [8] Beginning 1995, data are for all U.S. points, and include calls to and from Alaska, Hawaii, Puerto Rico, Guam, the U.S. Virgin Islands, and offshore U.S. points. Beginning 1995, carriers first started reporting traffic to and from Canada and Mexico. Data for Canada and Mexico in prior years are staff estimates.

Source: U.S. Federal Communications Commission, *Statistics of Communications Common Carriers*, annual; *Trends in Telephone Service*, annual; and *Trends in the International Telecommunications Industry*, annual.

Table 1120. **Cellular Telecommunications Industry: 1990 to 2006**

[**Calendar year data, except as noted (5,283 represents 5,283,000).** Based on a survey sent to all facilities-based cellular, personal communications services, and enhanced special mobile radio (ESMR) systems. The number of operational systems beginning 2000 differs from that reported for previous periods as a result of the consolidated operation of ESMR systems in a broader service area instead of by a city-to-city basis]

Item	Unit	1990	1995	2000	2002	2003	2004	2005	2006
Systems	Number...	751	1,627	2,440	2,846	3,123	(NA)	(NA)	(NA)
Subscribers	1,000	5,283	33,786	109,478	140,766	158,722	182,140	207,896	233,041
Cell sites[1]	Number	5,616	22,663	104,288	139,338	162,986	175,725	183,689	195,613
Employees	Number...	21,382	68,165	184,449	192,410	205,629	226,016	233,067	253,793
Service revenue	Mil. dol.	4,548	19,081	52,466	76,508	87,624	102,121	113,538	125,457
Roamer revenue[2]	Mil. dol.	456	2,542	3,883	3,896	3,766	4,210	3,786	3,494
Capital investment[3]	Mil. dol.	6,282	24,080	89,624	126,922	145,867	173,794	199,025	223,449
Average monthly bill[4]	Dollars	80.90	51.00	45.27	48.40	49.91	50.64	49.98	50.56
Average length of call[4]	Minutes	2.20	2.15	2.56	2.73	2.87	3.05	3.00	3.03

NA Not available. [1] The basic geographic unit of a wireless PCS or cellular system. A city or county is divided into smaller "cells," each of which is equipped with a low-powered radio transmitter/receiver. The cells can vary in size depending upon terrain, capacity demands, etc. By controlling the transmission power, the radio frequencies assigned to one cell can be limited to the boundaries of that cell. When a wireless PCS or cellular phone moves from one cell toward another, a computer at the switching office monitors the movement and at the proper time, transfers or hands off the phone call to the new cell and another radio frequency. [2] Service revenue generated by subscribers' calls outside of their system areas. [3] Beginning 2005, cumulative capital investment figure reached by summing the incremental capital investment in year shown with cumulative capital investment of prior year. [4] As of December 31.

Source: CTIA-The Wireless Association®, Washington, DC, *Semi-annual Wireless Survey* (copyright).

Table 1121. **Cellular and Other Wireless (except Paging) Telecommunications— Estimated Revenue and Expenses: 2004 and 2005**

[In millions of dollars (125,693 represents $125,693,000,000). For taxable and tax-exempt employer firms. Covers NAICS 517212. Estimates have been adjusted to the results of the 2002 Economic Census. Based on the North American Industry Classification System (NAICS), 2002. See text, this section, and Section 15. Minus sign (–) indicates decrease]

Item	2004	2005	Percent change 2004–05
Operating revenue...............................	125,693	141,306	12.4
Mobile services......................................	101,192	113,591	12.3
Mobile telephony..................................	54,871	58,981	7.5
Mobile long distance.............................	3,314	3,672	10.8
Mobile all-distance...............................	36,308	43,000	18.4
Other mobile services..........	6,699	7,939	18.5
Other telecommunications services [1]...................	6,744	6,867	1.8
Internet access services........................	668	1,140	70.7
Reselling services for telecommunications equipment, retail......	5,447	4,971	-8.7
All other operating revenue..........................	17,756	20,848	17.4
Operating expenses............................	105,138	122,081	16.1
Personnel costs......................................	19,910	21,344	7.2
Gross annual payroll.............................	14,408	14,958	3.8
Employer's cost for fringe benefits.................	3,686	3,505	-4.9
Temporary staff and leased employee expense.......	1,816	2,881	58.6
Expensed materials, parts and supplies (not for resale)...........	10,010	10,441	4.3
Expensed equipment..............................	931	1,007	8.2
Expensed purchase of other materials, parts and supplies.......	9,079	9,434	3.9
Expensed purchased services	15,780	16,572	5.0
Expensed purchases of software...............	930	1,027	10.4
Purchased electricity and fuels (except motor fuel).............	718	853	18.8
Lease and rental payments	4,839	5,584	15.4
Purchased repair and maintenance................	(S)	1,151	(S)
Purchased advertising and promotional services............	7,901	7,957	0.7
Other operating expenses	59,438	73,724	24.0
Access charges....................................	5,603	5,792	3.4
Universal service contributions (USC) and other similar charges....	1,869	2,554	36.7
Depreciation and amortization charges....................	17,143	22,506	31.3
Government taxes and license fees..................	1,215	1,362	12.1
All other operating expenses........................	33,606	41,510	23.5

S Data do not meet publication standards.   [1] Includes other sources of revenue, not shown separately.

Source: U.S. Census Bureau, "2005 Service Annual Survey, Information Sector Services." See <http://www.census.gov/econ /www/servmenu.html> (released February 2007).

Table 1122. **Cable and Other Programming Distribution—Estimated Revenue and Expenses: 2004 and 2005**

[In millions of dollars (73,317 represents $73,317,000,000). For taxable and tax-exempt employer firms. Covers NAICS 5175. Estimates have been adjusted to the results of the 2002 Economic Census. Based on the North American Industry Classification System (NAICS), 2002. See text, this section, and Section 15. Minus sign (–) indicates decrease]

Item	2004	2005	Percent change, 2004–05
Operating revenue...............................	73,317	80,493	9.8
Source of revenue:			
Multichannel programming distribution services...............	49,256	53,090	7.8
Basic programming package...................	37,563	40,734	8.4
Premium programming package	8,654	8,993	3.9
Pay-per-view......................................	3,039	3,363	10.7
Other revenue [1]...................................	24,061	27,402	13.9
Air time..	3,383	3,572	5.6
Rental and reselling services for program distribution equipment....	2,308	2,509	8.7
Internet access services........................	9,435	11,139	18.1
Operating expenses............................	64,957	69,031	6.3
Personnel costs......................................	11,871	13,385	12.8
Gross annual payroll.............................	8,782	10,229	16.5
Employer's cost for fringe benefits.................	2,354	2,409	2.3
Temporary staff and leased employee expense........	734	747	1.8
Expensed materials, parts and supplies (not for resale)...........	1,313	1,571	19.6
Expensed equipment.............................	856	1,030	20.3
Expensed purchase of other materials, parts and supplies.......	457	541	18.4
Expensed purchased services	4,261	4,183	-1.8
Expensed purchases of software...............	231	264	14.3
Purchased electricity and fuels (except motor fuel).............	(S)	503	(S)
Lease and rental payments	846	794	-6.1
Purchased repair and maintenance................	(S)	693	(S)
Purchased advertising and promotional services............	1,644	1,930	17.4
Other operating expenses	47,513	49,892	5.0
Program and production costs....................	20,363	22,162	8.8
Depreciation and amortization charges................	13,977	14,379	2.9
Government taxes and license fees.................	1,969	1,819	-7.6
All other operating expenses........................	11,204	11,532	2.9

S Data do not meet publication standards.   [1] Includes other sources of revenue, not shown separately.

Source: U.S. Census Bureau, "2005 Service Annual Survey, Information Sector Services." See <http://www.census.gov/econ /www/servmenu.html> (released February 2007).

Information and Communications   **715**

Table 1123. **Internet Service Providers and Data Processing, Hosting, and Related Services—Estimated Revenue and Expenses: 2004 and 2005**

[In millions of dollars (20,201 represents $20,201,000,000). For taxable and tax-exempt employer firms. Estimates have been adjusted to the results of the 2002 Economic Census. Based on the North American Industry Classification System (NAICS), 2002. See text, this section, and Section 15]

Item	Internet service provider (NAICS 518111)		Data processing, hosting, and related services (NAICS 5182)	
	2004	2005	2004	2005
Operating revenue, (NAICS 518111) [1]	20,201	18,914	(X)	(X)
Internet access service	14,081	12,240	(X)	(X)
Online advertising space	2,830	3,332	(X)	(X)
Internet backbone services	1,013	1,094	(X)	(X)
Internet telephony	68	140	(X)	(X)
Operating revenue, (NAICS 5182)	(X)	(X)	57,330	62,764
Data processing IT infrastructure provising, and hosting services [1]	(X)	(X)	26,978	29,772
Business processing management services	(X)	(X)	16,956	18,557
Data management services	(X)	(X)	5,095	5,426
Application service provising	(X)	(X)	3,132	3,693
Other operating revenue [1]	(X)	(X)	(S)	(S)
IT technical consulting services	(X)	(X)	990	976
Information and document transformation services	(X)	(X)	2,508	2,690
Software publishing	(X)	(X)	1,164	1,567
Reselling services for computer hardware and software, retail	(X)	(X)	1,116	1,115
Operating expenses	16,301	14,283	51,436	55,558
Personnel costs	(S)	5,199	24,932	27,659
Gross annual payroll	3,924	3,981	19,695	21,048
Employer's cost for fringe benefits	(S)	708	3,371	3,913
Temporary staff and leased employee expense	(S)	510	1,866	2,698
Expensed materials, parts and supplies (not for resale)	(S)	(S)	1,814	1,975
Expensed equipment	(S)	95	736	761
Expensed purchase of other materials, parts and supplies	(S)	(S)	1,077	1,214
Expensed purchased services	(S)	3,155	7,319	7,971
Expensed purchases of software	86	107	1,304	1,430
Purchased electricity and fuels (except motor fuels)	127	128	264	306
Lease and rental payments	518	485	2,988	3,237
Purchased repair and maintenance	127	115	1,681	1,782
Purchased advertising and promotional services	(S)	2,320	1,081	1,217
Other operating expenses	(S)	5,744	17,372	17,953
Depreciation and amortization charges	(S)	1,750	4,690	4,238
Government taxes abd license fees	121	110	340	369
All other operating expenses	(S)	3,884	12,342	13,347

S Data do not meet publication standards. X Not applicable. [1] Includes other sources of revenue, not shown separately.

Source: U.S. Census Bureau, "2005 Service Annual Survey, Information Sector Services." See <http://www.census.gov/econ/www/servmenu.html> (released February 2007).

Table 1124. **Academic Libraries—Summary: 2004**

[For fiscal year 200,204 represents 200,204,000. For 2- and 4-year degree-granting institutions. Based on the Academic Libraries Survey; see source for details]

Item	Number of libraries	Circulation [1] (1,000)	Gate count [2] (1,000)	Volumes held [3] (1,000)	Staff [4]		Expenditures			Electronic services (percent)	
					Total	Librarians (percent)	Total (mil. dol.)	Salary [5] (percent)	Reference service by e-mail or Web	Technology for persons with disabilities
Total	3,653	200,204	19,369	982,590	94,085	27.6	5,751	50.7	69.0	49.0
Control: Public	1,581	132,836	13,125	590,977	57,071	26.6	3,437	52.2	79.6	73.7
Private	2,072	67,368	6,243	391,613	37,013	29.1	2,314	48.3	61.0	30.2
Level:										
4-year degree and above [7]	2,217	174,158	15,181	924,214	80,412	27.1	5,166	48.4	74.4	47.1
Doctorate	597	124,956	9,453	668,301	54,963	26.2	3,887	46.6	85.4	68.0
Master's	918	34,455	4,094	184,926	18,352	28.5	925	54.2	76.5	47.7
Bachelor's	668	13,009	1,500	67,062	6,567	29.9	308	54.7	61.7	27.8
Less than 4-year	1,436	26,046	4,188	58,375	13,673	30.3	585	70.9	60.7	51.9
Enrollment: [4]										
Less than 1,500	1,802	18,293	2,572	99,624	11,554	31.2	516	55.4	53.9	26.1
1,500 to 4,999	1,175	38,791	4,934	186,100	21,461	29.4	1,121	54.0	80.3	61.9
5,000 or more	676	143,120	11,863	696,865	61,070	26.2	4,114	49.1	89.5	87.6

[1] Includes reserves. [2] In a typical week. [3] At end of year. [4] Full-time equivalent. [5] Salary and wages. [6] Level of highest degree offered. [7] Includes 34 institutions granting "other" degrees, not shown separately.

Source: U.S. National Center for Education Statistics, "Academic Libraries: 2004," NCES 2007-301, November 2006.

716   Information and Communications

Table 1125. **Public Libraries by Selected Characteristics: 2004**

[9,130 **represents** $9,130,000,000. Based on survey of public libraries. Data are for public libraries in the 50 states and the District of Columbia. The response rates for these items are between 98 and 100 percent]

Population of service area	Number of—			Operating income—			Paid staff [3]		Public use Internet terminals, average per stationary outlet
					Source (percent)				
	Public libraries	Stationary outlets [1]	Total (mil. dol.) [2]	State govern- ment	Local govern- ment	Total	Librar- ians with ALA- MLS [4]		
Total	9,207	16,549	9,130	10.0	81.5	136,014	30,560		10.3
1,000,000 or more . . .	25	1,036	1,383	6.6	80.9	16,350	4,571		19.5
500,000 to 999,000. . .	55	1,136	1,378	11.1	81.9	18,807	4,728		17.7
250,000 to 499,999. . .	96	1,084	1,079	12.2	81.2	15,260	3,804		14.9
100,000 to 249,999. . .	332	2,017	1,491	9.8	83.0	22,667	4,912		13.3
50,000 to 99,999	538	1,617	1,156	11.8	81.3	17,884	3,983		12.8
25,000 to 49,999	930	1,708	1,118	10.2	82.4	17,332	4,012		11.2
10,000 to 24,999	1,771	2,268	943	8.9	81.8	15,670	3,223		9.3
5,000 to 9,999	1,476	1,639	339	11.2	77.7	6,484	940		6.8
2,500 to 4,999	1,341	1,383	141	7.4	76.8	2,999	267		4.9
1,000 to 2,499	1,619	1,633	81	5.2	74.4	1,943	102		3.6
Fewer than 1,000	1,024	1,028	21	6.7	72.4	619	20		2.6

[1] The sum of central and branches' libraries. The total number of central libraries was 9,047 the total of branch libraries was 7,502. [2] Includes income from the federal government (0.5%) and other sources (8.0%), not shown separately. [3] Full-time equivalents. [4] Librarians with master's degrees from a graduate library education program accredited by the American Library Association (ALA). Total librarians, including those without ALA-MLS, were 45,037.

Source: U.S. National Center for Education Statistics, *Public Libraries in the United States: 2004*, NCES 2006-349, August 2006.

Table 1126. **Public Library Use of the Internet: 2007**

[In percent, except number of outlets. As of spring. Based on sample survey; see source for details]

Item		Metropolitan status [1]			Poverty status [2]		
	Total	Urban	Sub- urban	Rural	Less than 20 percent	20 to 40 percent	More than 40 percent
All libraries' outlets [3]	16,192	2,868	5,270	8,054	13,579	2,432	181
Connected to the Internet	99.7	100.0	99.8	99.5	99.8	99.3	97.6
Connected with public access.	99.1	99.4	99.3	98.9	99.2	99.0	95.3
Average number of workstations	10.7	18.3	12.7	7.1	10	14.3	25.4
Speed of access:							
128kbps or less.	7.5	1.6	4.5	11.4	7.2	9.1	4.9
129kbps to 768kbps.	15.6	4.2	10.5	22.7	16.4	11.5	5.0
769kbps to 1.5mbps.	32.9	40.5	38.4	26.8	31.9	38.1	40.1
1.6mbps to 5mbps.	13.6	21.7	15.2	9.9	13.8	12.5	14.2
Greater than 5mbps	15.6	26.2	16.6	11.4	14.9	18.6	33.2
Don't know	14.8	5.8	14.8	17.8	15.8	10.2	2.6
Public library availability of wireless Internet access:							
Currently available	54.2	66.8	60.7	45.8	55.6	47.0	50.1
Plan to make available within the next year	17.4	18.8	17.3	17.0	17.0	19.3	25.8

[1] Urban = inside central city; Suburban = In metro area, outside of a central city; Rural = outside a metro area. [2] Determined by the 2000 poverty status of the service area of the outlet. [3] Central libraries and branches; excludes bookmobiles.

Source: Information Use Management and Policy Institute, College of Information, Florida State University, Tallahassee, FL, *Public Libraries and the Internet 2007: Survey Results and Findings*, by John Carlo Bertot, et al., Florida State University, Tallahassee, FL. Study funded by the American Library Association.

Table 1127. Internet Access and Usage and Online Service Usage: 2006

[For persons 18 years old and over (218,289 represents 218,289,000). As of fall. Based on sample and subject to sampling error; see source for details]

Item	Total adults	Have Internet access			Used the Internet in the last 30 days		
		Home or work or other	Home	Work	Home or work or other	Home	Work
Total adults [1] (1,000)...........	218,289	176,641	142,072	80,577	143,111	123,090	69,118
PERCENT DISTRIBUTION							
Total......................	100.0	100.0	100.0	100.0	100.0	100.0	100.0
Age:							
18 to 34 years old...............	31.0	33.3	31.4	33.2	36.2	33.8	33.2
35 to 54 years old...............	39.2	42.3	44.9	52.1	44.1	45.4	52.6
55 years old and over	29.8	24.4	23.7	14.7	19.7	20.8	14.2
Sex:							
Male.......................	48.2	48.2	48.9	49.5	47.5	48.1	49.4
Female.....................	51.8	51.8	51.1	50.5	52.5	51.9	50.6
Census region: [2]							
Northeast	19.0	20.0	21.3	19.5	20.3	21.1	19.5
Midwest	22.5	23.4	22.3	22.6	22.9	22.3	22.3
South	36.2	33.8	33.0	33.9	33.2	32.6	33.4
West.......................	22.3	22.8	23.4	24.1	23.5	24.0	24.8
Household size:							
1 to 2 persons	46.9	43.4	40.7	41.2	42.0	41.3	41.9
3 to 4 persons	37.6	40.9	43.2	44.4	42.5	43.4	44.4
5 or more persons.............	15.4	15.7	16.1	14.4	15.5	15.4	13.7
Any child in household...........	40.6	43.7	44.8	47.2	45.0	44.9	46.9
Marital status:							
Single......................	24.8	25.8	23.2	23.5	27.1	24.6	23.7
Married.....................	56.4	58.8	63.6	63.6	59.5	63.0	64.0
Other	18.8	15.5	13.2	12.9	13.4	12.4	12.3
Educational attainment:							
Graduated college plus	25.1	30.0	34.6	46.1	35.3	37.8	49.7
Attended college.............	27.2	30.8	31.9	31.3	33.4	33.3	30.8
Did not attend college	47.6	39.3	33.5	22.6	31.3	28.8	19.5
Employed full-time	53.3	58.5	60.4	87.0	63.0	62.6	87.8
Employed part-time...............	11.2	12.2	12.5	12.6	12.8	12.8	11.9
Occupation of the employed:							
Professional..................	13.4	16.3	18.6	29.9	19.3	20.6	31.3
Management/business/financial	9.6	11.5	12.9	20.6	13.2	13.7	22.4
Sales/office	16.0	18.6	18.8	29.5	20.9	19.6	30.1
Natural resources/construction/ maintenance	7.0	6.5	6.4	5.4	6.1	6.0	4.7
Other.....................	18.5	17.8	16.4	14.2	16.3	15.5	11.1
Type of firm of the employed:							
Business.....................	35.0	37.6	38.3	52.0	40.0	39.4	51.8
Government..................	10.2	12.1	12.9	20.8	13.7	13.7	21.4
Other	19.3	21.1	21.7	26.8	22.1	22.3	26.5
Household income:							
Less than $50,000	47.1	38.7	31.0	22.1	32.8	28.9	19.8
$50,000 to $74,999..............	20.0	22.1	23.4	22.1	22.8	23.0	21.9
$75,000 to $149,999	24.7	29.2	33.6	40.0	32.9	35.2	41.2
$150,000 or more	8.3	10.0	11.9	15.7	11.5	12.9	17.1

[1] Includes other labor force status, not shown separately.   [2] For composition of regions, see map inside front cover.

Source: Mediamark Research Inc., New York, NY, *CyberStats*, fall 2006 (copyright). See Internet site <http://www.mriplus.com /pocketpiece.html>.

U.S. Census Bureau, Statistical Abstract of the United States: 2008

Table 1128. **Adult Computer and Adult Internet Users, by Selected Characteristics: 1995 to 2006**

[Percent of persons 18 years old and over. Represents persons who use a computer or the Internet at a workplace, school, home, or anywhere else, on at least an occasional basis. Based on telephone surveys of persons with land-line telephones. In 2006, 2,373 persons were interviewed and the response rate was 27 percent. For 1995, Internet users include those who ever use a home, work, or school computer and modem to connect to information services, bulletin boards, or other computers over the Internet. For 2000, Internet users include persons who ever go online to access the Internet or World Wide Web or to send and receive e-mail. For 2005 and 2006, Internet users include those who at least occasionally use the Internet or send and receive e-mail]

Characteristic	Adult computer users				Adult Internet users				All adults, by type of home connection, 2006	
	1995	2000	2005	2006	1995	2000	2005	2006	Broad-band	Dial-up
Total adults.	54	65	71	73	14	53	69	70	44	16
Age:										
18 to 29 years old	70	82	83	84	21	72	82	83	58	13
30 to 49 years old	66	76	81	84	18	62	80	82	55	17
50 to 64 years old	46	61	72	74	9	48	68	70	40	20
65 years old and over	12	21	31	35	2	15	28	33	16	12
Sex:										
Male	58	66	72	73	18	56	70	71	47	16
Female. . , ...	51	64	70	73	10	51	67	69	42	16
Race/ethnicity:										
White, non-Hispanic	54	66	72	74	14	55	70	72	45	17
Black, non-Hispanic	50	59	60	63	11	42	54	58	37	11
English-speaking Hispanic . . .	64	64	75	74	21	48	73	69	45	12
Educational attainment:										
Less than high school	17	28	36	38	2	19	35	36	16	10
High school graduate [1]	46	56	63	63	8	41	59	59	32	17
Some college	72	80	81	87	20	69	80	84	53	17
College graduate or higher. . .	82	88	90	92	29	79	88	91	68	16
Annual household income:										
Less than $30,000	37	48	52	52	8	35	50	49	24	13
$30,000 to $49,999.	61	74	76	78	15	61	74	75	46	20
$50,000 to $74,999.	(NA)	85	88	90	23	74	86	90	61	22
$75,000 or more	(NA)	90	92	94	32	81	91	93	73	14

NA Not available.   [1] Includes those with a GED certificate.

Source: 1995 data based on the Times Mirror Center for the People & the Press survey from May and June of 1995; thereafter, Pew Internet & American Life Project Surveys from September–December 2000; September and December of 2005; and November and December of 2006. See Internet site <http://www.pewinternet.org/index.asp>.

Table 1129. **Internet Activities of Adults, by Type of Home Internet Connection: 2006**

[For Internet users 18 years old and over (128 represents 128,000,000). For persons who have ever performed the activity. Based on telephone surveys of persons with land-line telephones. In December 2006, 2,373 persons were interviewed and the response rate was 27 percent]

Activity	Survey date (month,year)	Adult Internet users (mil)	Percent of users performing activity	Percent of home dial-up users performing activity	Percent of home broadband users performing activity
Send or read e-mail	Dec, 06	128	91	93	95
Use a search engine to find information	Dec, 06	128	91	87	95
Search for a map or driving directions	Dec, 06	121	86	83	90
Buy a product online.	Aug, 06	100	71	61	81
Get news online.	Dec, 06	95	67	53	76
Visit a local, state or federal government Web site	Aug, 06	93	66	66	72
Buy or make a reservation for travel	Aug, 06	89	63	55	70
Look for news or information about politics	Aug, 06	76	54	48	59
Take a virtual tour of a location online	Aug, 06	72	51	41	62
Look online for info about a job.	Aug, 06	65	46	39	48
Get sports scores and info online	Aug, 06	63	45	34	52
Read someone else's blog.	Jan, 06	57	39	31	47
Look online for info about a place to live.	Aug, 06	55	39	30	45
Send instant messages.	Aug, 06	55	39	39	43
Play online games	Aug, 06	49	35	29	37
Rate a product, service, or person.	Aug, 06	45	32	23	38
Log onto the Internet using a wireless device . .	Feb–Apr, 06	44	30	13	43
Download music.	Feb–Apr, 06	40	27	19	34
Participate in an online auction	Aug, 06	38	27	22	33
Download video files to your computer.	Feb–Apr, 06	28	19	12	26

Source: Pew Internet & American Life Project Surveys. See Internet site <http://www.pewinternet.org/index.asp>.

U.S. Census Bureau, Statistical Abstract of the United States: 2008

Table 1130. **Daily Typical Internet Activities of Adult Internet Users: 2006**

[Percent of Internet users 18 years old and over. Represents persons who report doing the activity "yesterday." Based on telephone surveys of persons with land-line telephones. In December 2006, 2,373 persons were interviewed and the response rate was 27 percent]

Activity	Survey date (month-year)	Total	Age				Sex	
			18 to 29 years old	30 to 49 years old	50 to 64 years old	65 years old and over	Male	Female
Send or read e-mail	Dec, 06	54	48	58	54	49	56	52
Use a search engine to find information	Dec, 06	41	44	47	33	20	45	37
Search for a map or driving directions	Dec, 06	10	11	11	9	4	12	9
Buy a product online	Aug, 06	6	10	5	4	2	7	5
Get news online	Dec, 06	31	31	36	25	27	37	25
Visit a local, state, or federal government Web site	Aug, 06	14	11	18	11	7	16	12
Buy or make a reservation for travel	Aug, 06	3	1	4	3	2	3	3
Look for news or information about politics	Aug, 06	19	21	21	14	12	24	14
Take a virtual tour of a location online	Aug, 06	4	4	3	4	2	3	4
Look online for info about a job.	Aug, 06	5	6	8	3	1	7	4
Get sports scores and info online . . .	Aug, 06	15	18	15	16	11	24	7
Look online for info about a place to live.	Aug, 06	5	9	5	3	1	7	4
Send instant messages	Aug, 06	10	20	9	5	1	10	10
Play online games	Aug, 06	9	13	8	9	8	10	8
Rate a product, service, or person. . .	Dec, 06	3	2	3	3	3	3	3
Log onto the Internet using a wireless device.	Feb–Apr, 06	15	20	16	12	5	19	11
Download music.	Feb–Apr, 06	4	9	4	1	(Z)	6	2
Participate in an online auction	Aug, 06	3	3	3	2	2	4	1
Download video files to your computer	Feb–Apr, 06	4	7	3	2	1	6	2
Pay to access or download digital content online	Aug, 06	4	3	5	3	3	6	2
Use an online social or professional networking site	Aug, 06	9	31	4	2	(Z)	11	8
Sell something online	Aug, 06	1	1	(Z)	2	3	2	(Z)
Download a podcast so you can listen to it or view it later	Aug, 06	1	2	1	(Z)	2	2	(Z)

Z Less than .05 percent.

Source: Pew Internet & American Life Project Surveys. See Internet site <http://www.pewinternet.org/index.asp>.

Table 1131. **Primary News Sources of Adults: 2005**

[Percent of persons 18 years old and over. Represents where people said they got their news "yesterday." Based on December 2005 telephone survey of 3,011 persons with land-line telephones. The response rate was 29 percent]

News source	All adults	All Internet users	All non-Internet users	Home dial-up users	Home broadband users
TV.	59	60	57	66	57
National TV.	47	49	43	50	49
Radio.	44	49	34	52	49
Local paper.	38	38	37	41	38
National paper.	12	14	9	12	17
Internet, total.	(X)	35	(X)	26	43
National TV news site	(X)	14	(X)	9	17
Portal	(X)	16	(X)	13	21
Local daily paper site.	(X)	9	(X)	6	11
Local TV news site	(X)	8	(X)	6	10
National daily paper site.	(X)	6	(X)	4	8
International news site	(X)	3	(X)	3	5
News blogs	(X)	3	(X)	2	5
Radio news organization	(X)	2	(X)	2	3
Alternative news organization	(X)	2	(X)	1	2
Online listervs	(X)	2	(X)	2	2

X Not applicable.

Source: Pew Internet & American Life Project December 2005 Survey. See Internet site <http://www.pewinternet.org/index.asp>.

U.S. Census Bureau, Statistical Abstract of the United States: 2008

Section 25
Banking, Finance, and Insurance

This section presents data on the nation's finances, various types of financial institutions, money and credit, securities, insurance, and real estate. The primary sources of these data are publications of several departments of the federal government, especially the U.S. Treasury Department, and independent agencies such as the Federal Deposit Insurance Corporation, the Board of Governors of the Federal Reserve System, and the Securities and Exchange Commission. National data on insurance are available primarily from private organizations, such as the American Council of Life Insurers and the Insurance Information Institute.

Flow of funds—The flow of funds accounts of the Federal Reserve Board bring together statistics on all of the major forms of financial instruments to present an economy-wide view of asset and liability relationships. In flow form, the accounts relate borrowing and lending to one another and to the nonfinancial activities that generate income and production. Each claim outstanding is included simultaneously as an asset of the lender and as a liability of the debtor. The accounts also indicate the balance between asset totals and liability totals over the economy as a whole. Several publications of the Federal Reserve Board contain information on the flow of funds accounts: Summary data on flows and outstandings, in the *Statistical Supplement to the Federal Reserve Bulletin, Flow of Funds Accounts of the United States* (quarterly); and concepts and organization of the accounts in *Guide to the Flow of Funds Accounts* (2000). Data are also available on the Federal Reserve Board's Web site <http://www .federalreserve .gov/>.

Survey of Consumer Finances (SCF)—The Federal Reserve Board, in cooperation with the Treasury Department, sponsors this survey, which is conducted every 3 years to provide detailed information on the finances of U.S. families. Among the topics covered are the balance sheet, pension, income, and other demographic characteristics of U.S. families. The survey also gathers information on the use of financial institutions. Since 1992, data for the SCF have been collected by the National Organization for Social Science and Survey Research at the University of Chicago. Data and information on the survey are available on the Web site of the Federal Reserve Board: <http://www .federalreserve.gov/pubs /oss/oss2/scfindex.html>.

Banking system—Banks in this country are organized under the laws of both the states and the federal government and are regulated by several bank supervisory agencies. National banks are supervised by the Comptroller of the Currency. *Reports of Condition* have been collected from national banks since 1863. Summaries of these reports are published in the Comptroller's *Annual Report,* which also presents data on the structure of the national banking system.

The Federal Reserve System was established in 1913 to exercise central banking functions, some of which are shared with the U.S. Treasury. It includes national banks and such state banks that voluntarily join the system. Statements of state bank members are consolidated by the Federal Reserve Board with data for national banks collected by the Comptroller of the Currency into totals for all member banks of the system. Balance sheet data for member banks and other commercial banks are published quarterly in the *Statistical Supplement to the Federal Reserve Bulletin* (also available on the Web at <http://www.federalreserve.gov>.

The Federal Deposit Insurance Corporation (FDIC), established in 1933, insures each depositor up to $100,000. Major item balance sheet and income data for all insured financial institutions are published in the *FDIC Quarterly Banking Profile.* This publication is also available on the Internet at the following address: <http://www.fdic.gov>. Quarterly financial information for individual institutions

Banking, Finance, and Insurance   721

is available through the FDIC and Federal Financial Institutions Examination Council Web sites at <http://www.fdic.gov> and <http://www.ffiec.gov>.

Credit unions—Federally chartered credit unions are under the supervision of the National Credit Union Administration. State-chartered credit unions are supervised by the respective state supervisory authorities. The administration publishes comprehensive program and statistical information on all federal and federally insured state credit unions in the *Annual Report of the National Credit Union Administration*.

Other credit agencies—Insurance companies, finance companies dealing primarily in installment sales financing, and personal loan companies represent important sources of funds for the credit market. Statistics on loans, investments, cash, etc., of life insurance companies are published principally by the American Council of Life Insurers in its *Life Insurers Fact Book*. Consumer credit data are published currently in the *Statistical Supplement to the Federal Reserve Bulletin*.

Government corporations and credit agencies make available credit of specified types or to specified groups of private borrowers, either by lending directly or by insuring or guaranteeing loans made by private lending institutions. Data on operations of government credit agencies, along with other government corporations, are available in reports of individual agencies; data on their debt outstanding are published in the *Statistical Supplement to the Federal Reserve Bulletin*.

Securities—The Securities and Exchange Commission (SEC) was established in 1934 to protect the interests of the public and investors against malpractices in the securities and financial markets and to provide the fullest possible disclosure of information regarding securities to the investing public.

Data on the securities industry and securities transactions are also available from a number of private sources. The Securities Industry Association, New York, NY, <http://www.sia.com/>, publishes the *Securities Industry Fact Book, Securities*

Industry Yearbook, and the periodic *Securities Industry Trends*. The Investment Company Institute, Washington, DC, <http://www.ici.org/>, publishes a reference book, research newsletters, and a variety of research reports that examine the industry, its shareholders, or industry issues. The annual *Mutual Fund Fact Book* is a guide to trends and statistics observed in the investment company industry. *Fundamentals* is a newsletter summarizing the findings of major Institute research projects. Institute research reports provide a detailed examination of shareholder demographics and other aspects of fund ownership.

Among the many sources of data on stock and bond prices and sales are the New York Stock Exchange, New York, NY, <http://www.nyse.com/>; NASDAQ, Washington, DC, <http://www.nasdaq.com/>; Global Financial Data, Los Angeles, CA, <http://www.globalfindata.com/>; Dow-Jones & Company, Inc., New York, NY, <http://www.djindexes.com/mdsidx/>; and the Bond Market Association, New York, NY, <http://www.bondmarkets.com/>.

Insurance—Insuring companies, which are regulated by the various states or the District of Columbia, are classified as either life or property. Both life and property insurance companies may underwrite health insurance. Insuring companies, other than those classified as life, are permitted to underwrite one or more property lines provided they are so licensed and have the necessary capital or surplus.

There are a number of published sources for statistics on the various classes of insurance—life, health, fire, marine, and casualty. Organizations representing certain classes of insurers publish reports for these classes. The American Council of Life Insurers publishes statistics on life insurance purchases, ownership, benefit payments, and assets in its *Life Insurers Fact Book*.

Statistical reliability—For a discussion of statistical collection, estimation, and sampling procedures and measures of reliability applicable to data from the Census Bureau and the Federal Reserve Board's Survey of Consumer Finances, see Appendix III.

Figure 25.1
Interest Rates and Bond Yields: 1990 to 2006
(Annual averages)

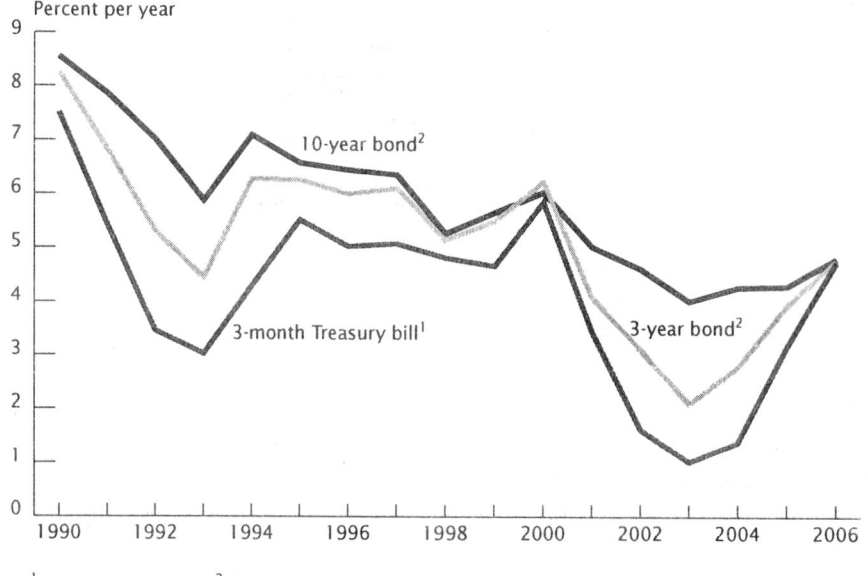

Percent per year

¹New issues.   ² U.S. Treasury, constant maturities.

Source: Chart prepared by U.S. Census Bureau. For data, see Tables 1166 and 1167.

Figure 25.2
Foreign Holdings of U.S. Treasury Securities by Country: 2006
(In billion dollars)

Total = 2,115

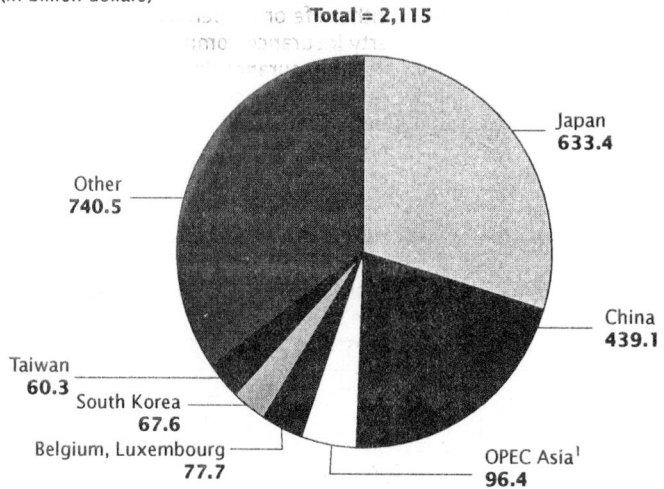

Japan
633.4

Other
740.5

China
439.1

Taiwan
60.3

South Korea
67.6

Belgium, Luxembourg
77.7

OPEC Asia¹
96.4

¹Comprises Indonesia, Iran, Iraq, Kuwait, Qatar, Saudi Arabia, and the United Arab Emirates.

Source: Chart prepared by U.S. Census Bureau. For data, see Table 1175.

Banking, Finance, and Insurance   723

Table 1132. **Gross Domestic Product in Finance, Insurance, Real Estate, Rental, and Leasing in Current and Real (2000) Dollars: 2000 to 2006**

[In billions of dollars, except percent (741 represents $741,000,000,000). Represents value added by industry. For definition of gross domestic product and explanation of chained dollars, see text, Section 13]

Industry	1997 NAICS code [1]	Current dollars				Chained (2000) dollars			
		2000	2004	2005	2006	2000	2004	2005	2006
Finance & insurance, total	52	741	917	958	1,028	741	835	854	891
Percent of gross domestic product . . .		7.5	7.8	8.1	8.1	7.5	7.8	7.7	7.8
Monetary authorities—central bank, credit intermediation & related activities.	521,522	319	445	475	(NA)	319	385	397	(NA)
Security, commodity contracts, & like activity	523	168	157	167	(NA)	168	189	205	(NA)
Insurance carriers & related activities.	524	238	296	296	(NA)	238	243	237	(NA)
Funds, trusts, & other financial vehicles (part)	525	16	20	20	(NA)	16	16	17	(NA)
Real estate & rental & leasing, total . .	53	1,191	1,491	1,578	1,731	1,191	1,325	1,370	1,452
Percent of gross domestic product . . .		12.1	12.7	12.7	13.1	12.1	12.4	12.4	12.7
Real estate	531	1,082	1,386	1,473	(NA)	1,082	1,226	1,274	(NA)
Rental & leasing services [2]	532,533	108	105	106	(NA)	108	99	95	(NA)

NA Not available. [1] See footnote 1, Table 1133. [2] Includes lessors of other nonfinancial intangible assets.

Source: U.S. Bureau of Economic Analysis, *Survey of Current Business*, May 2007. See also <http://www.bea.gov/newsreleases /industry/gdpindustry/gdpindnewsrelease.htm>.

Table 1133. **Finance and Insurance/Real Estate and Rental and Leasing— Establishments, Revenue, Payroll, and Employees by Kind of Business (1997 NAICS Basis): 1997 and 2002**

[2,198 represents $2,198,000,000,000. For establishments with payroll. Based on the 1997 and 2002 Economic Censuses; see Appendix III]

Kind of business	1997 NAICS code [1]	Number of establishments		Revenue (bil. dol.)		Annual payroll (bil. dol.)		Paid employees (1,000)	
		1997	2002	1997	2002	1997	2002	1997	2002
Finance & insurance	52	395,203	440,268	2,198	2,804	264.6	377.8	5,835	6,579
Monetary authorities—central bank	521	42	47	25	29	0.9	1.2	22	22
Credit intermediation & related activities	522	166,882	196,451	809	1,056	98.7	151.2	2,745	3,300
Security, commodity contracts, & like activity	523	54,491	72,338	275	316	71.3	103.4	706	832
Insurance carriers & related activities. . .	524	172,299	169,520	1,073	1,380	92.2	120.6	2,327	2,406
Funds, trusts, and other financial vehicles (part)	525	1,489	1,912	17	23	1.4	1.3	35	19
Real estate & rental & leasing.	53	288,273	322,805	241	336	41.6	60.2	1,702	1,949
Real estate	531	221,650	256,086	153	224	27.9	41.7	1,117	1,305
Rental & leasing services.	532	64,472	64,334	76	95	12.6	16.9	559	617
Lessors of other nonfinancial intangible assets	533	2,151	2,385	11	17	1.1	1.7	26	27

[1] 1997 North American Industry Classification System; see text, Section 15.

Source: U.S. Census Bureau, "2002 Economic Census; Comparative Statistics for United States Summary Statistics by 1997 NAICS"; published 31 July 2006; <http://www.census.gov/econ/census02/data/comparative/USCS.HTM>.

Table 1134. **Finance and Insurance—Nonemployer Establishments and Receipts by Kind of Business: 2000 to 2004**

[691.8 represents 691,800. Includes only firms subject to federal income tax. Nonemployers are businesses with no paid employees. Data originate chiefly from administrative records of the Internal Revenue Service; see Appendix III. Data for 2000 based on the 1997 North American Industry Classification System (NAICS); beginning 2003 based on 2002 NAICS, see text, Section 15]

Kind of business	NAICS code	Establishments (1,000)			Receipts (mil. dol.)		
		2000	2003	2004	2000	2003	2004
Finance and insurance	52	691.8	695.0	717.5	49,058	47,345	44,032
Credit intermediation & related activities.	522	165.3	77.2	81.4	4,848	4,605	4,652
Depository credit intermediation	5221	6.5	7.0	7.7	197	248	248
Nondepository credit intermediation	5222	134.1	26.4	28.3	3,624	2,138	2,295
Activities related to credit intermediation	5223	24.7	43.8	45.4	1,028	2,219	2,108
Security, commodity contracts, & like activity.	523	181.5	251.8	259.5	29,379	25,737	21,316
Scrty & comdty contracts interm & brokerage . . .	5231	29.6	32.8	33.2	6,395	5,327	4,657
Investment banking and securities dealing. . .	52311	5.6	7.7	7.8	2,043	1,861	1,324
Securities brokerage	52312	19.5	20.3	20.6	3,712	2,736	2,621
Commodity contracts dealing	52313	1.0	1.2	1.2	238	143	236
Commodity contracts brokerage.	52314	3.6	3.7	3.7	402	588	476
Securities & commodity exchanges	5232	1.6	2.0	1.9	1,495	1,082	867
Other financial investment activities	5239	150.2	217.1	224.4	21,488	19,328	15,793
Insurance carriers & related activities	524	345.0	366.0	376.6	14,831	17,003	18,064
Insurance carriers.	5241	1.0	0.6	0.6	98	50	42
Agencies & other insurance-related activities. . .	5242	344.0	365.4	376.0	14,733	16,953	18,022
Insurance agencies & brokerages	52421	245.5	250.8	255.2	11,570	12,880	13,560
Other insurance related activities	52429	98.5	114.6	120.8	3,163	4,073	4,462

Source: U.S. Census Bureau, "Nonemployer Statistics"; <http://www.census.gov/epcd/nonemployer/>.

Table 1135. **Finance and Insurance—Establishments, Employees, and Payroll: 2000 and 2004**

[423.7 represents 423,700. Covers establishments with payroll. Kind-of-business classification for 2000 based on North American Industry Classification System (NAICS) 1997; data for 2004 based on NAICS 2002. See text, Section 15. Employees are for the week including March 12. Most government employees are excluded. For statement on methodology, see Appendix III]

Kind of business	NAICS code	Establishments (1,000) 2000	2004	Employees (1,000) 2000	2004	Payroll (bil. dol.) 2000	2004
Finance & insurance, total	52	423.7	470.6	5,963	6,481	346.8	422.4
Monetary authorities—central bank	521	0.1	0.1	22	21	1.1	1.2
Credit intermediation & related activities	522	176.3	208.6	2,753	3,190	116.1	162.4
Depository credit intermediation [1]	5221	105.6	115.7	1,935	2,115	78.5	100.8
Commercial banking	52211	73.9	83.0	1,493	1,631	63.6	80.7
Savings institutions	52212	15.9	16.4	244	249	9.2	12.0
Credit unions	52213	15.6	16.0	192	229	5.4	7.7
Nondepository credit intermediation [1]	5222	49.3	54.0	621	733	29.6	45.5
Real estate credit	522292	19.8	24.9	238	361	10.8	24.5
Activities related to credit intermediation	5223	21.4	38.9	198	343	7.9	16.1
Security, commodity contracts & like activity	523	72.9	85.0	866	863	119.5	121.4
Security & commodity contracts intermediate & brokerage [1]	5231	38.1	42.5	539	517	80.2	76.5
Investment banking & securities dealing	52311	6.3	6.0	138	137	31.2	31.1
Securities brokerage	52312	29.5	33.9	378	356	47.0	42.8
Securities & commodity exchanges	5232	(Z)	0.1	7	7	0.5	0.8
Other financial investment activities [1]	5239	34.8	42.3	320	339	38.8	44.2
Portfolio management	52392	11.6	13.2	156	159	24.9	27.9
Insurance carriers & related activities	524	172.2	173.7	2,290	2,376	108.1	134.8
Insurance carriers [1]	5241	37.4	33.6	1,489	1,494	74.7	91.6
Direct life/health/medical insurance carriers . . .	52411	13.9	12.8	813	799	40.0	49.8
Direct life insurance carriers	524113	10.7	8.9	491	373	25.7	24.1
Direct health & medical insurance carriers . .	524114	3.1	3.9	322	426	14.3	25.7
Other direct insurance carriers [1]	52412	23.0	20.1	660	673	33.5	39.5
Direct property & casualty insurance carriers	524126	19.8	13.4	609	586	31.1	34.3
Agencies & other insurance-related activities [1] . .	5242	134.8	140.1	801	881	33.3	43.2
Insurance agencies & brokerages	52421	121.5	127.7	596	689	24.7	33.7
Funds, trusts, & other financial vehicles (part)	525	2.3	3.3	32	32	2.1	2.6

Z Less than 50.   [1] Includes industries not shown separately.

Source: U.S. Census Bureau, "County Business Patterns"; <http://www.census.gov/epcd/cbp/view/cbpview.html>.

Table 1136. **Flow of Funds Accounts—Financial Assets of Financial and Nonfinancial Institutions by Holder Sector: 1990 to 2006**

[In billions of dollars (35,902 represents $35,902,000,000,000). As of Dec. 31]

Sector	1990	1995	1999	2000	2001	2002	2003	2004	2005	2006
All sectors	35,902	53,461	86,373	89,531	90,741	89,587	100,211	109,892	117,956	128,917
Households [1]	14,563	21,386	34,349	32,964	31,365	29,062	33,548	36,494	38,885	42,115
Nonfinancial business	3,979	5,568	9,335	11,260	11,545	11,671	11,928	13,057	13,797	14,398
Farm business	47	61	65	65	67	72	77	83	88	92
Nonfarm noncorporate	356	548	1,176	1,423	1,579	1,657	1,742	2,042	2,343	2,575
Nonfinancial corporations	3,575	4,959	8,094	9,772	9,899	9,942	10,109	10,932	11,366	11,731
State and local government	1,020	1,122	1,601	1,662	1,748	1,800	1,908	2,015	2,168	2,286
U.S. government	442	442	561	514	615	611	653	615	605	611
Monetary authorities	342	472	697	636	683	754	797	841	879	908
Commercial banking	3,337	4,494	5,986	6,469	6,829	7,329	7,843	8,564	9,324	10,204
U.S.-chartered commercial banks	2,644	3,322	4,434	4,774	5,015	5,427	5,840	6,398	6,904	7,613
Foreign banking offices in U.S.	367	666	751	789	792	801	766	637	787	790
Bank-holding companies	298	467	741	842	942	1,026	1,153	1,429	1,524	1,695
Banks in U.S.-affiliated areas	28	39	59	63	80	75	84	100	109	106
Savings institutions	1,323	1,013	1,150	1,218	1,291	1,349	1,465	1,649	1,789	1,715
Credit unions	217	311	415	441	506	564	617	655	686	719
Life insurance companies	1,351	2,064	3,068	3,136	3,225	3,335	3,773	4,130	4,351	4,709
Property-casualty insurance companies .	533	740	873	862	860	940	1,060	1,161	1,250	1,365
Private pension funds	1,629	2,899	4,594	4,468	4,048	3,547	4,476	4,925	5,120	5,558
Defined benefit plans	900	1,466	2,075	1,979	1,810	1,584	1,980	2,128	2,149	2,280
Defined contribution plans	729	1,433	2,519	2,489	2,238	1,963	2,496	2,797	2,971	3,278
State and local government employee retirement funds	730	1,327	2,326	2,293	2,207	1,930	2,344	2,572	2,701	2,979
Federal government retirement funds . . .	340	541	774	797	860	894	958	1,023	1,074	1,142
Money market mutual funds	493	741	1,580	1,812	2,241	2,224	2,016	1,880	2,007	2,313
Mutual funds	608	1,853	4,538	4,433	4,135	3,638	4,654	5,436	6,049	7,093
Closed-end funds	53	136	152	142	140	151	206	246	271	294
Exchange-traded funds	–	1	34	66	83	102	151	226	296	423
Government-sponsored enterprises (GSE)	478	897	1,723	1,965	2,309	2,549	2,786	2,870	2,805	2,841
Agency- and GSE-backed mortgage pools	1,020	1,571	2,294	2,493	2,832	3,159	3,489	3,542	3,677	3,965
Asset-backed securities issuers	268	663	1,313	1,476	1,690	1,873	2,070	2,402	3,067	3,599
Finance companies	596	705	1,017	1,213	1,304	1,446	1,680	1,858	1,857	1,889
Real estate investment trusts	28	33	69	66	76	102	136	253	330	396
Security brokers and dealers	262	568	1,001	1,221	1,466	1,335	1,613	1,845	2,127	2,742
Funding corporations	251	383	1,065	1,179	1,375	1,374	1,451	1,522	1,815	2,101
Rest of the world	2,036	3,531	5,861	6,746	7,309	7,848	8,589	10,112	11,025	12,552

– Represents zero.   [1] Includes nonprofit organizations.

Source: Board of Governors of the Federal Reserve System, "Federal Reserve Statistical Release, Z.1, Flow of Funds Accounts of the United States"; published 8 March 2007; <http://www.federalreserve.gov/releases/z1/20070308/>.

Banking, Finance, and Insurance **725**

Table 1137. **Flow of Funds Accounts—Credit Market Debt Outstanding: 1990 to 2006**

[In billions of dollars (13,771 represents $13,771,000,000,000). As of December 31]

Item	1990	1995	1999	2000	2001	2002	2003	2004	2005	2006
Credit market debt	13,771	18,458	25,321	27,030	29,258	31,722	34,607	37,695	41,000	44,549
Domestic nonfinancial	10,839	13,657	17,230	18,091	19,212	20,593	22,310	24,323	26,602	28,699
Households [1]	3,589	4,855	6,408	7,000	7,649	8,460	9,450	10,565	11,804	12,816
Corporations...............	2,536	2,911	4,189	4,531	4,729	4,742	4,853	5,018	5,263	5,697
Nonfarm noncorporate business...	1,093	1,062	1,600	1,796	1,959	2,107	2,199	2,443	2,748	3,036
Farm business	135	145	170	182	192	200	208	219	232	259
State and local government......	987	1,047	1,182	1,198	1,303	1,447	1,568	1,683	1,854	2,006
U.S. government	2,498	3,637	3,681	3,385	3,379	3,637	4,033	4,395	4,702	4,885
Rest of the world	318	568	748	815	863	1,072	1,244	1,425	1,466	1,720
Financial sectors.............	2,614	4,233	7,342	8,124	9,183	10,057	11,052	11,947	12,932	14,129
Commercial banking	198	251	449	509	562	612	661	739	824	998
Savings institutions	140	115	260	288	286	262	268	333	349	287
Credit unions	–	–	3	3	5	7	9	11	15	19
Life insurance companies	–	1	3	2	3	5	8	11	11	14
Government-sponsored enterprises (GSE)	399	807	1,594	1,826	2,131	2,350	2,594	2,659	2,575	2,634
Agency- and GSE-backed mortgage pools	1,020	1,571	2,294	2,493	2,832	3,159	3,489	3,542	3,677	3,965
Asset-backed securities issuers ...	269	666	1,323	1,483	1,696	1,878	2,075	2,407	3,071	3,603
Finance companies	398	500	721	807	818	884	995	1,130	1,109	1,145
Real estate investment trusts.....	28	45	165	168	171	198	230	343	402	452
Security brokers and dealers	15	29	25	41	42	41	47	62	62	69
Funding corporations	147	249	504	503	637	660	675	709	838	942

– Represents or rounds to zero.   [1] Includes nonprofit organizations.

Source: Board of Governors of the Federal Reserve System, "Federal Reserve Statistical Release, Z.1, Flow of Funds Accounts of the United States"; published 8 March 2007; <http://www.federalreserve.gov/releases/z1/20070308/>.

Table 1138. **Flow of Funds Accounts—Financial Assets and Liabilities of Foreign Sector: 1990 to 2006**

[In billions of dollars (2,036 represents $2,036,000,000,000). As of December 31]

Type of instrument	1990	1995	1999	2000	2001	2002	2003	2004	2005	2006
Total financial assets [1]	2,036	3,531	5,861	6,746	7,309	7,848	8,589	10,112	11,025	12,552
Net interbank assets	53	229	140	161	116	120	110	118	106	96
U.S. checkable deposits and currency..	108	194	279	287	306	327	356	398	443	491
U.S. time deposits.............	49	50	126	109	121	152	143	216	258	319
Security RPs [2]	20	68	80	91	151	190	460	665	713	780
Credit market instruments	926	1,593	2,420	2,776	3,213	3,737	4,169	4,981	5,640	6,465
Open market paper............	11	43	105	114	108	127	136	181	189	227
Treasury securities	438	817	1,058	1,021	1,095	1,285	1,514	1,804	1,994	2,135
Official	286	490	618	640	720	812	986	1,241	1,289	1,410
Private	152	327	441	382	375	474	527	562	705	725
Agency- and GSE-backed securities [3]	50	146	300	441	535	648	653	778	953	1,173
Official	5	18	76	116	127	158	200	258	361	481
Private	45	129	224	325	408	490	453	520	593	692
Municipal securities...........	2	4	8	8	8	12	20	26	30	34
U.S. corporate bonds [4]	253	461	829	1,074	1,351	1,539	1,722	2,061	2,314	2,738
Loans to U.S. corporate business ...	172	122	120	117	116	126	125	131	160	159
U.S. corporate equities	244	550	1,612	1,643	1,573	1,336	1,840	2,123	2,303	2,831
Trade receivables	42	45	45	45	42	44	46	45	52	64
Miscellaneous assets...........	594	803	1,158	1,634	1,789	1,943	1,465	1,566	1,510	1,505
Foreign direct investment in U.S. [5]..	505	680	1,102	1,421	1,518	1,500	1,577	1,727	1,874	2,074
Other.....................	89	123	57	213	270	443	-112	-162	-365	-569
Total liabilities	1,419	2,126	3,226	3,562	3,747	4,283	4,515	5,436	5,541	5,584
U.S. official foreign exchange and net IMF position..............	61	64	50	46	47	56	62	62	46	46
U.S. private deposits	298	419	676	803	810	831	868	958	1,044	1,174
Credit market instruments [1]	318	568	748	815	863	1,072	1,244	1,425	1,466	1,720
Commercial paper	75	56	89	121	196	254	267	330	368	461
Bonds .... [6]	145	413	548	573	557	705	874	993	988	1,140
Bank loans n.e.c. [6]	19	35	59	71	63	69	61	63	76	91
U.S. government loans	63	55	48	47	46	44	42	38	34	28
Trade payables	31	53	54	46	44	41	48	51	57	66
Miscellaneous liabilities [1].........	710	1,026	1,698	1,844	1,981	2,282	2,293	2,941	2,928	2,577
U.S. direct investment abroad [4,5]...	630	886	1,414	1,532	1,693	1,867	2,060	2,399	2,454	2,682

[1] Includes other items not shown separately.   [2] Repurchase agreements.   [3] GSE = Government-sponsored enterprises.
[4] Through 1992, corporate bonds include net issues by Netherlands Antillean financial subsidiaries; U.S. direct investment abroad excludes net inflows from those bond issues.   [5] Direct investment is valued on a current-cost basis.   [6] Not elsewhere classified.

Source: Board of Governors of the Federal Reserve System, "Federal Reserve Statistical Release, Z.1, Flow of Funds Accounts of the United States"; published 8 March 2007; <http://www.federalreserve.gov/releases/z1/20070308/>.

Table 1139. **Flow of Funds Accounts—Assets of Households: 1990 to 2006**

[As of December 31 (14,563 represents $14,563,000,000,000). Includes nonprofit organizations. See also Table 700]

Type of instrument	Total (bil. dol.)							Percent distribution		
	1990	2000	2002	2003	2004	2005	2006	1990	2000	2006
Total financial assets	14,563	32,964	29,062	33,548	36,494	38,885	42,115	100.0	100.0	100.0
Deposits	3,304	4,350	5,122	5,288	5,619	6,049	6,670	22.7	13.2	15.8
Foreign deposits	13	48	50	52	58	63	70	0.1	0.1	0.2
Checkable deposits and currency...	413	279	346	285	259	224	188	2.8	0.8	0.4
Time and savings deposits	2,485	3,062	3,656	3,991	4,399	4,805	5,302	17.1	9.3	12.6
Money market fund shares	392	960	1,070	960	903	957	1,110	2.7	2.9	2.6
Credit market instruments.........	1,750	2,238	2,192	2,524	2,746	3,030	3,029	12.0	6.8	7.2
Open-market paper	94	97	110	106	136	164	188	0.6	0.3	0.4
Treasury securities	509	585	288	441	565	563	486	3.5	1.8	1.2
Agency and GSE-backed securities [1]...............	119	510	245	389	440	646	631	0.8	1.5	1.5
Municipal securities	648	531	679	708	743	817	861	4.4	1.6	2.0
Corporate and foreign bonds	238	397	737	739	712	682	698	1.6	1.2	1.7
Mortgages	143	117	133	141	149	157	166	1.0	0.4	0.4
Corporate equities [2]	1,960	8,036	4,536	5,612	5,714	5,483	5,483	13.5	24.4	13.0
Mutual fund shares	512	2,856	2,421	3,085	3,611	4,121	4,963	3.5	8.7	11.8
Security credit	62	412	413	475	578	575	656	0.4	1.3	1.6
Life insurance reserves...........	392	819	921	1,013	1,060	1,083	1,119	2.7	2.5	2.7
Pension fund reserves [3].........	3,308	9,166	8,068	9,673	10,637	11,177	12,192	22.7	27.8	28.9
Equity in noncorporate business	3,032	4,716	4,967	5,403	6,004	6,797	7,386	20.8	14.3	17.5
Miscellaneous assets.............	243	371	423	474	524	570	619	1.7	1.1	1.5

[1] GSE = government-sponsored enterprises.   [2] Only those directly held and those in closed-end and exchange-traded funds. Other equities are included in mutual funds and life insurance and pension reserves.   [3] See also Table 1190.

Source: Board of Governors of the Federal Reserve System, "Federal Reserve Statistical Release, Z.1, Flow of Funds Accounts of the United States"; published 8 March 2007; <http://www.federalreserve.gov/releases/z1/20070308/>.

Table 1140. **Financial Assets Held by Families by Type of Asset: 2001 and 2004**

[Median value in thousands of constant 2004 dollars (29.8 represents $29,800). All dollar figures are adjusted to 2004 dollars using the "current methods" version of the consumer price index for all urban consumers published by U.S. Bureau of Labor Statistics. Families include one-person units; for definition of family, see text, Section 1. Based on Survey of Consumer Finances; see Appendix III]

Age of family head and family income	Any financial asset [1]	Transaction accounts [2]	Certificates of deposit	Savings bonds	Stocks [3]	Pooled investment funds [4]	Retirement accounts [5]	Life insurance [6]	Other managed [7]
PERCENT OF FAMILIES OWNING ASSET									
2001, total..........	93.4	91.4	15.7	16.7	21.3	17.7	52.2	28.0	6.6
2004, total	93.8	91.3	12.7	17.6	20.7	15.0	49.7	24.2	7.3
Under 35 years old........	90.1	86.4	5.6	15.3	13.3	8.3	40.2	11.0	2.9
35 to 44 years old	93.6	90.8	6.7	23.3	18.5	12.3	55.9	20.1	3.7
45 to 54 years old	93.6	91.8	11.9	21.0	23.2	18.2	57.7	26.0	6.2
55 to 64 years old	95.2	93.2	18.1	15.2	29.1	20.6	62.9	32.1	9.4
65 to 74 years old	96.5	93.9	19.9	14.9	25.4	18.6	43.2	34.8	12.8
75 years old and over......	97.6	96.4	25.7	11.0	18.4	16.6	29.2	34.0	16.7
Percentiles of income: [8]									
Less than 20	80.1	75.5	5.0	6.2	5.1	3.6	10.1	14.0	3.1
20 to 39.9	91.5	87.3	12.7	8.8	8.2	7.6	30.0	19.2	4.9
40 to 59.9	98.5	95.9	11.8	15.4	16.3	12.7	53.4	24.2	7.9
60 to 79.9	99.1	98.4	14.9	26.6	28.2	18.6	69.7	29.8	7.8
80 to 89.9	99.8	99.1	16.3	32.3	35.8	26.2	81.9	29.5	12.1
90 to 100	100.0	100.0	21.5	29.9	55.0	39.1	88.5	38.1	13.0
MEDIAN VALUE [9]									
2001, total............	29.8	4.2	16.0	1.1	21.3	37.3	30.9	10.7	74.6
2004, total............	23.0	3.8	15.0	1.0	15.0	40.4	35.2	6.0	45.0
Under 35 years old........	5.2	1.8	4.0	0.5	4.4	8.0	11.0	3.0	5.0
35 to 44 years old	19.0	3.0	10.0	0.5	10.0	15.9	27.9	5.0	18.3
45 to 54 years old	38.6	4.8	11.0	1.0	14.5	50.0	55.5	8.0	43.0
55 to 64 years old	78.0	6.7	29.0	2.5	25.0	75.0	83.0	10.0	65.0
65 to 74 years old	36.1	5.5	20.0	3.0	42.0	60.0	80.0	8.0	60.0
75 years old and over	38.8	6.5	22.0	5.0	50.0	60.0	30.0	5.0	50.0

[1] Includes other types of financial assets, not shown separately, money market mutual funds, and call accounts at brokerages.   [2] Checking, savings, and money market deposit accounts.   [3] Covers only those stocks that are directly held by families outside mutual funds, retirement accounts, and other managed assets.   [4] Excludes money market mutual funds and indirectly held mutual funds and includes all other types of directly held pooled investment funds, such as traditional open-ended and closed-end mutual funds, real estate investment trusts, and hedge funds.   [5] The tax-deferred retirement accounts consist of IRAs, Keogh accounts, and certain employer-sponsored accounts. Employer-sponsored accounts include 401(k), 403(b), and thrift saving accounts from current or past jobs; other current job plans from which loans or withdrawals can be made; and accounts from past jobs from which the family expects to receive the account balance in the future.   [6] The value of such policies according to their current cash value, not their death benefit.   [7] Includes personal annuities and trusts with an equity interest and managed investment accounts.   [8] Percentiles of income distribution in 2004 dollars: 20th: $18,900; 40th: $33,900; 60th: $53,600; 80th: $89,300; 90th: $129,400. Percentile: A value on a scale of zero to 100 that indicates the percent of a distribution that is equal to or below it. For example, a family with income in the 80th percentile has income equal to or better than 80 percent of all other families.   [9] Median value of financial asset for families holding such assets.

Source: Board of Governors of the Federal Reserve System, "2004 Survey of Consumer Finances"; published 28 February 2006; <http://www.federalreserve.gov/pubs/oss/oss2/2004/scf2004home.html>.

Banking, Finance, and Insurance   727

Table 1141. Flow of Funds Accounts—Liabilities of Households: 1990 to 2006

[As of December 31 (3,711 represents $3,711,000,000,000). Includes nonprofit organizations. n.e.c. = Not elsewhere classified. See also Table 700]

Type of instrument	Total (bil. dol.)							Percent distribution		
	1990	2000	2002	2003	2004	2005	2006	1990	2000	2006
Total liabilities	3,711	7,389	8,780	9,810	11,010	12,220	13,293	100.0	100.0	100.0
Credit market instruments	3,589	7,000	8,460	9,450	10,565	11,804	12,816	96.7	94.7	96.4
Home mortgages [1]	2,497	4,802	5,968	6,824	7,808	8,883	9,676	67.3	65.0	72.8
Consumer credit	824	1,749	2,012	2,116	2,232	2,327	2,438	22.2	23.7	18.3
Municipal securities	86	138	164	178	189	205	227	2.3	1.9	1.7
Bank loans, n.e.c.	18	65	21	39	23	47	96	0.5	0.9	0.7
Other loans	82	120	121	119	119	119	124	2.2	1.6	0.9
Commercial mortgages	83	127	174	174	193	223	255	2.2	1.7	1.9
Security credit	39	235	148	183	264	232	292	1.0	3.2	2.2
Trade payables	67	135	152	157	159	161	163	1.8	1.8	1.2
Unpaid life insurance premiums [2] . . .	16	20	20	21	22	22	23	0.4	0.3	0.2

[1] Includes loans made under home equity lines of credit and home equity loans secured by junior liens.   [2] Includes deferred premiums.

Source: Board of Governors of the Federal Reserve System, "Federal Reserve Statistical Release, Z.1, Flow of Funds Accounts of the United States"; published 8 March 2007; <http://www.federalreserve.gov/releases/z1/20070308/>.

Table 1142. Financial Debt Held by Families by Type of Debt: 2001 and 2004

[Median debt in thousands of constant 2004 dollars (41.3 represents $41,300). See headnote, Table 1140]

Age of family head and family income	Any debt	Secured by residential property		Lines of credit not secured by residential property	Installment loans	Credit card balances [2]	Other [3]
		Primary residence [1]	Other				
PERCENT OF FAMILIES HOLDING DEBT							
2001, total	75.1	44.6	4.6	1.5	45.2	44.4	7.2
2004, total	76.4	47.9	4.0	1.6	46.0	46.2	7.6
Under 35 years old	79.8	37.7	2.1	2.2	59.4	47.5	6.2
35 to 44 years old	88.6	62.8	4.0	1.5	55.7	58.8	11.3
45 to 54 years old	88.4	64.6	6.3	2.9	50.2	54.0	9.4
55 to 64 years old	76.3	51.0	5.9	0.7	42.8	42.1	8.4
65 to 74 years old	58.8	32.1	3.2	0.4	27.5	31.9	4.0
75 years old and over	40.3	18.7	1.5	(B)	13.9	23.6	2.5
Percentiles of income: [4]							
Less than 20	52.6	15.9	(B)	(B)	26.9	28.8	4.6
20 to 39.9	69.8	29.5	1.5	1.5	39.9	42.9	5.8
40 to 59.9	84.0	51.7	2.6	1.8	52.4	55.1	8.0
60 to 79.9	86.6	65.8	4.1	1.8	57.8	56.0	8.3
80 to 89.9	92.0	76.8	7.5	2.6	60.0	57.6	12.3
90 to 100	86.3	76.2	15.4	2.5	45.7	38.5	10.6
MEDIAN DEBT [5]							
2001, total	41.3	74.6	42.6	4.2	10.3	2.0	3.2
2004, total	55.3	95.0	87.0	3.0	11.5	2.2	4.0
Under 35 years old	33.6	107.0	62.5	1.0	11.9	1.5	3.0
35 to 44 years old	87.2	110.0	75.0	1.9	12.0	2.5	4.0
45 to 54 years old	83.2	97.0	87.0	7.0	12.0	2.9	4.0
55 to 64 years old	48.0	83.0	108.8	14.0	12.9	2.2	5.5
65 to 74 years old	25.0	51.0	100.0	4.0	8.3	2.2	5.0
75 years old and over	15.4	31.0	39.0	(B)	6.7	1.0	2.0

B Base figure too small.   [1] First and second mortgages and home equity loans and lines of credit secured by the primary residence.   [2] Families that had an outstanding balance on any of their credit cards after paying their most recent bills.   [3] Includes loans on insurance policies, loans against pension accounts, borrowing on margin accounts and unclassified loans.   [4] See footnote 8, Table 1140.   [5] Median amount of financial debt for families holding such debts.

Source: Board of Governors of the Federal Reserve System, "2004 Survey of Consumer Finances"; published 28 February 2006; <http://www.federalreserve.gov/pubs/oss/oss2/2004/scf2004home.html>.

Table 1143. Amount of Debt Held by Families—Percent Distribution: 2001 and 2004

[See headnote, Table 1140]

Type of debt	2001	2004	Purpose of debt	2001	2004	Type of lending institution	2001	2004
Total	100.0	100.0	Total.	100.0	100.0	Total	100.0	100.0
Secured by residential property:			Primary residence:			Commercial bank	34.1	35.1
Primary residence . .	75.2	75.2	Purchase	70.9	70.2	Thrift institution	6.1	7.3
Other	6.2	8.5	Improvement	2.0	1.9	Credit union	5.5	3.6
Lines of credit not			Other residential			Finance or loan company.	4.3	4.1
secured by			property	6.5	9.5	Brokerage	2.3	2.5
residential property . .	0.5	0.7	Investments, excluding			Real estate lender [1] . . .	38.0	39.4
Installment loans	12.3	11.0	real estate	2.8	2.2	Individual lender	2.0	1.7
Credit card balances . .	3.4	3.0	Vehicles	7.8	6.7	Other nonfinancial	1.4	2.0
Other	2.3	1.6	Goods and services . .	5.8	6.0	Government	1.1	0.7
			Education.	3.1	3.0	Credit card issuer	3.7	3.0
			Other loans	1.1	0.6	Other loans	0.8	0.5

[1] Includes mortgage lender.

Source: Board of Governors of the Federal Reserve System, "2004 Survey of Consumer Finances"; published 28 February 2006; <http://www.federalreserve.gov/pubs/oss/oss2/2004/scf2004home.html>.

Table 1144. **Ratios of Debt Payments to Family Income: 1995 to 2004**

[In percent. All dollar figures are adjusted to 2004 dollars using the "current methods" version of the consumer price index for all urban consumers published by U.S. Bureau of Labor Statistics. Families include one-person units; for definition of family, see text, Section 1. Based on Survey of Consumer Finance; see Appendix III. For definition of median, see Guide to Tabular Presentation]

Age of family head and family income (constant (2004) dollars)	Ratio of debt payments to family income						Percent of debtors with—					
	Aggregate			Median			Ratios above 40 percent			Any payment 60 days or more past due		
	1995	2001	2004	1995	2001	2004	1995	2001	2004	1995	2001	2004
All families	14.1	12.9	14.4	16.2	16.7	18.0	11.7	11.8	12.2	7.1	7.0	8.9
Under 35 years old.	17.8	17.2	17.8	16.8	17.7	18.0	12.1	12.0	12.8	8.7	11.9	13.7
35 to 44 years old	17.2	15.1	18.2	18.3	17.8	20.6	9.9	10.1	12.6	7.7	5.9	11.7
45 to 54 years old	15.1	12.8	15.3	16.6	17.4	18.4	12.3	11.6	13.1	7.4	6.2	7.6
55 to 64 years old	11.8	10.9	11.5	14.2	14.3	15.8	15.1	12.3	10.2	3.2	7.1	4.2
65 to 74 years old	7.2	9.2	8.7	12.3	16.0	15.6	11.3	14.7	11.6	5.3	1.5	3.4
75 years old and over	2.5	3.9	7.1	2.9	8.0	12.8	7.4	14.6	10.7	5.4	0.8	3.9
Percentiles of income: [1]												
Less than 20	19.1	16.1	18.2	13.3	19.2	19.7	27.5	29.3	27.0	10.2	13.4	15.9
20 to 39.9	17.0	15.8	16.7	17.5	16.7	17.4	18.0	16.6	18.6	10.1	11.7	13.8
40 to 59.9	15.6	17.1	19.4	15.7	17.6	19.5	9.9	12.3	13.7	8.7	7.9	10.4
60 to 79.9	17.9	16.8	18.5	18.9	18.1	20.6	7.7	6.5	7.1	6.6	4.0	7.1
80 to 89.9	16.6	17.0	17.3	16.8	17.3	18.1	4.7	3.5	2.4	2.8	2.6	2.3
90 to 100	9.5	8.1	9.3	12.6	11.2	12.7	2.3	2.0	1.8	1.0	1.3	0.3

[1] See footnote 8, Table 1140.

Source: Board of Governors of the Federal Reserve System, "2004 Survey of Consumer Finances"; published 28 February 2006; <http://www.federalreserve.gov/pubs/oss/oss2/2004/scf2004home.html>.

Table 1145. **Household Debt-Service Payments and Financial Obligations as a Percentage of Disposable Personal Income: 1980 to 2006**

[As of end of year, seasonally adjusted. Household debt service ratio is an estimate of the ratio of debt payments to disposable personal income. Debt payments consist of the estimated required payments on outstanding mortgage and consumer debt. The financial obligations ratio adds automobile lease payments, rental payments on tenant-occupied property, homeowners' insurance, and property tax payments to the debt service ratio]

Year	Household debt service ratio	Financial obligations ratio			Year	Household debt service ratio	Financial obligations ratio		
		Total	Home-owner	Renter			Total	Home-owner	Renter
1980 . . .	10.58	15.37	13.33	23.62	2002 . . .	13.56	18.83	16.73	29.10
1990 . . .	11.97	17.35	15.48	24.71	2003 . . .	13.50	18.53	16.85	26.79
1995 . . .	11.84	17.45	15.17	26.89	2004 . . .	13.56	18.42	16.98	25.84
2000 . . .	12.88	18.24	15.76	30.55	2005 . . .	14.29	19.15	17.90	25.46
2001 . . .	13.38	18.85	16.32	31.32	2006 . . .	14.53	19.40	18.20	25.56

Source: Board of Governors of the Federal Reserve System, "Household Debt Service and Financial Obligations Ratios;" <http://www.federalreserve.gov/releases/housedebt/default.htm>.

Table 1146. **Selected Financial Institutions—Number and Assets by Asset Size: 2006**

[As of December. 10,090.8 represents $10,090,800,000,000. FDIC = Federal Deposit Insurance Corporation]

Asset size	Number of institutions			Assets (bil. dol.)		
	F.D.I.C.-insured		Credit unions [1]	F.D.I.C.-insured		Credit unions [1]
	Commercial banks	Savings institutions		Commercial banks [2]	Savings institutions	
Total	7,402	1,279	8,362	10,090.8	1,769.7	709.9
Less than $25.0 million	545	75	5,384	9.3	1.1	39.9
$25.0 million to $49.9 million	1,034	119	1,032	38.7	4.4	36.6
$50.0 million to $99.9 million	1,666	193	746	122.3	14.0	52.1
$100.0 million to $499.9 million. . .	3,161	576	913	697.0	135.4	196.7
$500.0 million to $999.9 million. . .	502	161	172	342.8	115.1	116.9
$1.0 billion to $2.9 billion	289	88	96	468.5	140.3	148.3
$3.0 billion or more.	205	67	19	8,412.2	1,359.4	119.4
	Percent distribution					
Total	100.0	100.0	100.0	100.0	100.0	100.0
Less than $25.0 million	7.4	5.9	64.4	0.1	0.1	5.6
$25.0 million to $49.9 million	14.0	9.3	12.3	0.4	0.2	5.2
$50.0 million to $99.9 million	22.5	15.1	8.9	1.2	0.8	7.3
$100.0 million to $499.9 million. . .	42.7	45.0	10.9	6.9	7.7	27.7
$500.0 million to $999.9 million. . .	6.8	12.6	2.1	3.4	6.5	16.5
$1.0 billion to $2.9 billion	3.9	6.9	1.1	4.6	7.9	20.9
$3.0 billion or more.	2.8	5.2	0.2	83.4	76.8	16.8

[1] Source: National Credit Union Administration, *National Credit Union Administration Year-end Statistics 2006.* Excludes nonfederally insured state chartered credit unions and federally insured corporate credit unions. [2] Includes foreign branches of U.S. banks.

Source: Except as noted, U.S. Federal Deposit Insurance Corporation, *Statistics on Banking, 2006.*

Banking, Finance, and Insurance **729**

Table 1147. FDIC-Insured Financial Institutions—Number, Assets, and Liabilities: 1990 to 2006

[In billions of dollars, except as indicated (4,649 represents $4,649,000,000,000). As of Dec. 31. 2006 data preliminary. Includes island areas. Except as noted, includes foreign branches of U.S. banks]

Item	1990	1995	2000	2001	2002	2003	2004	2005	2006
All banking offices	84,240	81,179	86,165	86,749	87,594	88,687	91,024	92,877	94,669
Commercial bank offices, total[1]	62,630	65,717	72,045	72,587	73,648	74,799	77,264	79,657	82,067
Number of main offices	12,376	9,972	8,331	8,096	7,903	7,783	7,643	7,538	7,404
Number of branches	50,254	55,745	63,714	64,491	65,745	67,016	69,621	72,119	74,663
Savings institutions offices, total	21,610	15,462	14,120	14,162	13,946	13,888	13,760	13,220	12,602
Number of main offices	2,815	2,030	1,589	1,534	1,466	1,411	1,345	1,307	1,279
Number of branches	18,795	13,432	12,531	12,628	12,480	12,477	12,415	11,913	11,323
Number of financial institutions reporting	15,158	11,970	9,905	9,613	9,354	9,181	8,976	8,833	8,681
Assets, total[2]	4,649	5,338	7,462	7,868	8,436	9,075	10,106	10,877	11,860
Net loans and leases	2,867	3,198	4,576	4,687	4,968	5,349	6,037	6,639	7,156
Real estate loans	1,586	1,690	2,396	2,561	2,850	3,144	3,680	4,141	4,508
1-4 family residential mortgages	859	1,006	1,340	1,380	1,513	1,611	1,833	2,042	2,176
Commercial real estate	328	349	525	570	628	682	752	826	904
Construction and development	171	90	197	232	245	272	338	450	565
Home equity loans[3]	86	98	151	184	256	346	491	534	559
Commercial and industrial loans	646	674	1,086	1,020	953	922	968	1,086	1,214
Loans to individuals	451	576	672	701	772	848	930	948	955
Credit cards and related plans	142	224	266	250	292	339	399	395	385
Farm loans	33	40	49	48	47	47	49	52	54
Other loans and leases	245	294	448	440	435	478	496	494	504
Less: Reserve for losses	65	60	71	80	85	86	82	77	78
Less: Unearned income	29	15	3	3	4	3	3	3	2
Securities	890	1,099	1,361	1,465	1,633	1,771	1,860	1,893	1,980
Domestic office assets	4,259	4,753	6,702	7,119	7,684	8,251	9,160	9,824	10,557
Foreign office assets	390	585	760	749	752	824	945	1,053	1,303
Liabilities and capital, total	4,649	5,338	7,462	7,868	8,436	9,075	10,106	10,877	11,860
Noninterest-bearing deposits	511	641	802	927	1,002	1,028	1,173	1,267	1,270
Interest-bearing deposits	3,127	3,129	4,113	4,262	4,566	4,926	5,412	5,875	6,555
Other borrowed funds	569	849	1,467	1,496	1,571	1,735	1,905	2,063	2,121
Subordinated debt	28	46	90	99	99	107	119	131	161
Other liabilities	128	238	356	377	422	450	459	423	505
Equity capital	286	436	634	707	776	831	1,039	1,119	1,248
Domestic office deposits	3,344	3,315	4,208	4,560	4,911	5,213	5,719	6,221	6,631
Foreign office deposits	293	454	707	630	658	741	866	921	1,194
Estimated insured deposits[4]	2,629	2,662	3,054	3,210	3,382	3,452	3,621	3,890	4,146

[1] Includes insured branches of foreign banks that file a Call Report. [2] Includes other items not shown separately. [3] For one- to four-family residential properties. [4] Excludes foreign office deposits which are uninsured.

Source: U.S. Federal Deposit Insurance Corporation, The FDIC Quarterly Banking Profile, Annual Report, Statistics on Banking, annual; and FDIC Quarterly Banking Profile Graph Book.

Table 1148. FDIC-Insured Financial Institutions—Income and Selected Measures of Financial Condition: 1990 to 2006

[In billions of dollars, except as indicated (437.7 represents $437,700,000,000). 2006 data preliminary. Includes island areas. Includes foreign branches of U.S. banks]

Item	1990	1995	2000	2001	2002	2003	2004	2005	2006
Interest income	437.7	373.4	512.2	486.8	429.5	404.6	418.4	523.4	643.5
Interest expense	295.9	190.7	276.5	251.8	152.9	122.6	123.3	205.0	313.3
Net interest income	141.8	182.7	235.7	235.1	276.6	281.9	295.2	318.4	330.1
Provisions for loan losses	41.4	14.7	32.0	46.3	51.5	37.3	29.0	29.7	29.3
Noninterest income	62.2	89.5	164.8	168.8	183.5	202.7	202.6	222.0	240.7
Percent of net operating revenue[1]	30.5	32.9	41.1	40.1	39.9	41.8	40.7	41.1	42.2
Noninterest expense	144.2	171.6	241.6	251.1	263.7	279.7	295.5	317.3	332.3
Income taxes	9.1	30.3	43.7	44.0	51.9	58.9	58.6	64.6	68.3
Net income	11.3	56.4	81.7	87.2	105.0	120.5	122.3	133.9	145.7
PERFORMANCE RATIOS									
Return on assets[2] (percent)	0.24	1.10	1.14	1.14	1.30	1.38	1.28	1.30	1.28
Return on equity[3] (percent)	3.95	13.63	13.55	12.99	14.12	15.04	13.20	12.73	12.34
Net interest margin[4] (percent)	3.47	4.05	3.78	3.78	3.96	3.73	3.54	3.52	3.31
Net charge-offs[5]	34.8	14.4	26.3	38.9	47.0	40.8	32.0	31.6	26.7
Net charge-offs to loans and leases, total (percent)	1.19	0.46	0.59	0.83	0.97	0.78	0.56	0.50	0.38
Net charge-off rate, credit card loans (percent)	3.39	3.39	4.37	5.15	5.47	5.75	4.99	4.76	3.44
CONDITION RATIOS									
Equity capital to assets (percent)	6.16	8.16	8.49	8.99	9.20	9.15	10.28	10.29	10.52
Noncurrent assets plus other real estate owned to assets[6] (percent)	3.16	0.92	0.71	0.88	0.90	0.75	0.53	0.50	0.53
Percentage of banks losing money	16.5	3.1	7.5	8.2	6.7	6.0	6.0	6.2	7.6
Number of problem institutions	1,492	193	94	114	136	116	80	52	50
Assets of problem institutions	640	31	24	40	39	30	28	7	8
Number of failed/assisted institutions	169	6	7	4	11	3	4	–	–

– Represents zero. [1] Net operating revenue equals net interest income plus noninterest income. [2] Net income (including securities transactions and nonrecurring items) as a percentage of average total assets. [3] Net income as a percentage of average total equity capital. [4] Interest income less interest expense as a percentage of average earning assets (i.e. the profit margin a bank earns on its loans and investments). [5] Total loans and leases charged off (removed from balance sheet because of uncollectibility), less amounts recovered on loans and leases previously charged off. [6] Noncurrent assets: the sum of loans, leases, debt securities, and other assets that are 90 days or more past due, or in nonaccrual status. Other real estate owned: primarily foreclosed property.

Source: U.S. Federal Deposit Insurance Corporation, Annual Report; Statistics on Banking, annual; and FDIC Quarterly Banking Profile.

Table 1149. FDIC-Insured Financial Institutions by Asset Size: 2006

[(10,091 represents $10,091,000,000,000). Preliminary. See headnote, Table 1148]

Item	Unit	Total	Less than $100 million	$100 million to $1 billion	$1 billion to $10 billion	Greater than $10 billion
COMMERCIAL BANKS						
Institutions reporting	Number...	7,402	3,246	3,662	406	88
Assets, total	Bil. dol. ...	10,091	170	1,040	1,076	7,804
Deposits	Bil. dol. ...	6,731	141	847	768	4,975
Net income	Bil. dol	120	2	12	14	101
Return on assets	Percent...	1.33	0.95	1.24	1.35	1.35
Return on equity	Percent...	13.06	7.38	12.20	12.65	13.40
Equity capital to assets	Percent...	10.21	12.74	10.21	10.99	10.05
Noncurrent assets plus other real estate owned to assets	Percent...	0.51	0.72	0.60	0.51	0.50
Net charge-offs to loans and leases	Percent...	0.40	0.18	0.18	0.24	0.47
SAVINGS INSTITUTIONS						
Institutions reporting	Number...	1,279	387	737	124	31
Assets, total	Bil. dol. ...	1,770	20	250	321	1,178
Deposits	Bil. dol. ...	1,094	15	188	225	666
Net income	Bil. dol. ...	17	(Z)	2	3	12
Return on assets	Percent...	1.00	0.78	0.88	0.83	1.07
Return on equity	Percent...	8.70	5.06	8.08	7.69	9.17
Equity capital to assets	Percent...	12.31	15.58	11.15	10.97	12.86
Noncurrent assets plus other real estate owned to assets	Percent...	0.63	0.79	0.57	0.55	0.66
Net charge-offs to loans and leases	Percent...	0.29	0.11	0.07	0.09	0.40

Z Less than $500 million.

Source: U.S. Federal Deposit Insurance Corporation, *Annual Report; Statistics on Banking*, annual; and *FDIC Quarterly Banking Profile*. See also <http://www.fdic.gov/bank/index.html>.

Table 1150. FDIC-Insured Financial Institutions—Number and Assets by State and Island Areas: 2006

[In billions of dollars, except as indicated (11,860.2 represents $11,860,200,000,000). As of Dec. 31. Information is obtained primarily from the Federal Financial Institutions Examination Council (FFIEC) Call Reports and the Office of Thrift Supervision's Thrift Financial Reports. Data are based on the location of each reporting institution's main office. Reported data may include assets located outside of the reporting institution's home state]

State or island area	Number of institutions	Assets by asset size of bank				State or island area	Number of institutions	Assets by asset size of bank			
		Total	Less than $1 bil.	$1 bil. to $10 bil.	Greater than $10 bil.			Total	Less than $1 bil.	$1 bil. to $10 bil.	Greater than $10 bil.
Total...	8,681	11,860.2	1,479.9	1,397.7	8,982.6	NV	38	1,416.0	4.8	23.8	1,387.5
						NH	26	19.7	7.9	1.6	10.2
AL	159	233.3	28.6	9.1	195.6	NJ	132	139.7	32.4	59.4	47.9
AK	7	4.3	2.0	2.3	–	NM	54	17.7	8.7	9.1	–
AZ	55	18.9	8.2	10.8	–	NY	200	523.5	42.5	109.1	371.9
AR	156	48.4	28.9	19.5	–	NC	110	1,913.6	26.5	19.3	1,867.8
CA	304	573.8	59.6	156.2	358.0	ND	96	18.4	11.1	7.3	–
CO	164	47.2	26.3	20.8	–	OH	276	1,874.7	43.5	32.2	1,799.1
CT	57	63.3	15.1	20.6	27.5	OK	264	67.3	33.4	8.4	25.5
DE	34	559.6	4.0	20.8	534.8	OR	40	35.4	7.2	14.1	14.2
DC	7	1.2	1.2	–	–	PA	251	415.2	57.5	76.3	281.5
FL	306	165.8	65.3	86.7	13.8	RI	13	29.6	1.8	14.0	13.9
GA	352	284.8	69.3	32.8	182.6	SC	94	45.4	19.4	26.0	–
HI	9	37.5	1.3	13.6	22.6	SD	89	499.0	12.8	7.8	478.4
ID	19	6.9	6.9	–	–	TN	201	88.6	39.8	11.2	37.6
IL	685	381.0	108.7	80.7	191.6	TX	650	255.9	93.1	82.3	80.5
IN	172	71.8	33.8	38.0	–	UT	69	292.4	12.7	17.0	262.6
IA	401	56.6	48.7	7.8	–	VT	19	8.6	4.1	4.5	–
KS	362	59.2	38.2	21.0	–	VA	126	247.3	31.9	21.8	193.6
KY	220	45.7	33.7	12.0	–	WA	99	65.5	24.5	41.0	–
LA	166	76.4	29.8	5.6	41.0	WV	70	21.3	10.9	10.4	–
ME	36	56.3	11.9	4.8	39.6	WI	302	141.6	52.4	20.7	68.5
MD	112	54.2	24.8	29.4	–	WY	45	7.1	7.1	–	–
MA	194	244.7	55.7	35.7	153.4						
MI	171	231.5	33.6	25.6	172.2						
MN	448	80.1	51.0	14.3	14.7	AS	1	0.1	0.1	–	–
MS	98	50.6	17.5	21.0	12.0	GU	3	1.0	1.0	–	–
MO	368	106.9	55.2	27.8	24.0	FM	1	0.1	0.1	–	–
MT	83	17.1	10.8	6.2	–	PR	10	98.8	–	40.2	58.6
NE	254	39.6	22.5	17.2	–	VI	3	0.2	0.2	–	–

– Represents zero.

Source: U.S. Federal Deposit Insurance Corporation, *Statistics on Banking*, annual.

Banking, Finance, and Insurance 731

Table 1151. **FDIC-Insured Financial Institutions—Number of Offices and Deposits by State: 2006**

[As of June 30 (6,449.9 represents $6,449,900,000,000). Includes insured U.S. branches of foreign banks. The term "offices" includes both main offices and branches. "Banking office" is defined to include all offices and facilities that actually hold deposits, and does not include loan production offices, computer centers, and other nondeposit installations, such as automated teller machines (ATMs). Several institutions have designated home offices that do not accept deposits; these have been included to provide a more complete listing of all offices. The figures for each geographical area only include deposits of offices located within that area. Based on the Summary of Deposits survey]

State	Number of offices	Total deposits (bil. dol.)	State	Number of offices	Total deposits (bil. dol.)	State	Number of offices	Total deposits (bil. dol.)
Total [1] ..	94,752	6,449.9	IA	1,598	54.0	NC	2,606	195.2
U.S.	94,102	6,386.4	KS	1,518	50.7	ND	434	12.9
AL	1,470	71.4	KY	1,781	60.6	OH	4,034	208.6
AK	133	6.7	LA	1,578	71.9	OK	1,311	53.3
AZ	1,219	78.9	ME	510	19.6	OR	1,071	45.3
AR	1,445	44.2	MD	1,749	92.8	PA	4,700	250.2
CA	6,894	725.9	MA	2,158	175.7	RI	243	23.8
CO	1,539	76.3	MI	3,111	152.6	SC	1,331	59.2
CT	1,232	79.2	MN	1,808	97.1	SD	468	75.2
DE	262	153.9	MS	1,163	40.2	TN	2,168	102.0
DC	220	24.3	MO	2,309	98.1	TX	6,259	402.5
FL	5,310	363.4	MT	371	13.7	UT	604	143.3
GA	2,741	169.5	NE	1,045	33.8	VT	276	9.9
HI	289	25.7	NV	532	126.2	VA	2,512	172.8
ID	496	16.9	NH	428	20.6	WA	1,871	99.6
IL	4,831	329.7	NJ	3,279	213.3	WV	645	24.8
IN	2,373	87.2	NM	498	20.9	WI	2,336	103.5
			NY	5,126	800.1	WY	217	9.5

[1] Includes Puerto Rico and other areas, not shown separately.

Source: U.S. Federal Deposit Insurance Corporation, *Bank and Thrift Branch Office Data Book*, annual.

Table 1152. **U.S. Banking Offices of Foreign Banks—Summary: 1990 to 2006**

[In billions of dollars, except as indicated (791 represents $791,000,000,000). As of December. Data cover foreign-bank branches and agencies in the 50 states and the District of Columbia, New York investment companies (through September 1996); U.S. commercial banks of which more than 25 percent is owned by foreign banks, and International Banking Facilities. Foreign banks are those owned by institutions located outside of the United States and its affiliated insular areas. Beginning 2000 data include U.S. chartered entities that are completely or partially owned by foreign companies that are not banks themselves]

Item	1990	1995	2000	2002	2003	2004	2005	2006	Share [1] 1990	Share [1] 2000	Share [1] 2005	Share [1] 2006
Assets	791	984	1,303	1,392	1,431	1,712	2,025	2,404	21.4	20.1	21.7	23.1
Loans, total	398	461	535	500	478	603	746	852	18.0	13.8	14.0	14.4
Business	193	249	300	246	203	217	260	324	30.8	26.7	24.7	27.2
Deposits	384	523	708	705	724	919	1,049	1,244	14.5	17.7	18.2	19.8

[1] Percent of "domestically owned" commercial banks plus U.S. offices of foreign banks.

Source: Board of Governors of the Federal Reserve System, "Share Data for U.S. Offices of Foreign Banks"; published March 2007; <http://www.federalreserve.gov/releases/lba/Share/SHRTBL1.html>.

Table 1153. **Federal and State-Chartered Credit Unions—Summary: 1990 to 2006**

[Except as noted, as of December 31 (36,241 represents 36,241,000). Federal data include District of Columbia, Puerto Rico, Guam, and Virgin Islands. Excludes state-insured, privately insured, and noninsured state-chartered credit unions and corporate central credit unions which have mainly other credit unions as members]

Year	Operating credit unions Federal	Operating credit unions State	Number of failed institu- tions [1]	Members (1,000) Federal	Members (1,000) State	Assets (mil. dol.) Federal	Assets (mil. dol.) State	Loans outstanding (mil. dol.) Federal	Loans outstanding (mil. dol.) State	Savings (mil. dol.) Federal	Savings (mil. dol.) State
1990...	8,511	4,349	164	36,241	19,454	130,073	68,133	83,029	44,102	117,892	62,082
1995...	7,329	4,358	26	42,163	24,927	193,781	112,860	120,514	71,606	170,300	99,838
1999...	6,566	4,062	23	44,076	31,308	239,316	172,086	155,578	116,366	207,614	149,305
2000...	6,336	3,980	29	43,883	33,705	242,881	195,363	163,851	137,485	210,188	169,053
2001...	6,118	3,866	22	43,817	35,560	270,123	231,432	170,326	152,112	235,201	201,923
2002...	5,953	3,735	15	44,600	36,300	301,238	255,837	181,768	160,881	261,819	222,372
2003...	5,776	3,593	13	46,153	36,287	336,611	273,572	202,898	173,236	291,484	236,856
2004...	5,572	3,442	21	46,858	36,710	358,701	288,294	223,878	190,376	308,317	247,804
2005...	5,393	3,302	27	47,612	36,895	377,804	300,868	249,515	208,728	321,820	255,804
2006...	5,189	3,173	22	48,262	37,487	394,125	315,817	270,420	223,917	333,914	267,275

[1] 1990 for year ending September 30; 1995 reflects 15-month period from October 1994 through December 1995; beginning 1999, reflects calendar year. A failed institution is defined as a credit union which has ceased operation because it was involuntarily liquidated or merged with assistance from the National Credit Union Share Insurance Fund.

Source: National Credit Union Administration, *Annual Report of the National Credit Union Administration*, and unpublished data.

U.S. Census Bureau, Statistical Abstract of the United States: 2008

Table 1154. **Percentage of Households Using Selected Electronic Banking Technologies: 1995 to 2004**

[Covers only those households that access services (other than by check or credit card) at a bank, thrift institution, or credit union. Based on sample surveys. For details on the Survey of Consumer Finances, see Appendix III and the Web site of the Federal Reserve Board: <www.federalreserve.gov/boarddocs/surveys>. The Reuters/University of Michigan Survey of Consumers is based on data from approximately 1,000 respondents. For details, see the Web site of the University of Michigan: <www.umich.edu>]

Technology	Survey of Consumer Finances				Reuters/ University of Michigan Survey of Consumers	
	1995	1998	2001	2004	1999	2003
ELECTRONIC						
Direct deposit of any type.	53	67	71	75	65	70
ATM card	35	55	57	65	59	65
Debit card [1]	20	37	50	62	(NA)	54
Preauthorized debts	25	40	43	50	31	46
Automated phone system.	(NA)	26	22	20	40	44
Computer banking	4	7	19	34	10	32
Smart card [2]	1	2	3	(NA)	(NA)	6
Prepaid card [2]	(NA)	(NA)	(NA)	(NA)	(NA)	73
NONELECTRONIC						
In person	87	81	78	78	(NA)	(NA)
Mail	59	55	51	51	(NA)	(NA)
Phone (talk in person)	(NA)	43	42	42	(NA)	(NA)

NA Not available. [1] A debit card is a card that automatically deducts the amount of a purchase from the money in an account. [2] A smart card is a type of payment card containing a computer chip which is set to hold a sum of money. As the card is used, purchases are subtracted from that sum. Prepaid cards are cards that contain a stored value, or a value that has been paid up-front, allowing you to use the card much like cash. As you use the card, the prepaid value is drawn down. Examples are phone cards and gift cards. Smart cards are different from prepaid cards in that you can add money to the card at special machines designed for smart cards or sometimes at ATMs.

Source: Board of Governors of the Federal Reserve System, *Federal Reserve Bulletin*, winter 2004 and unpublished data.

Table 1155. **Percent of U.S. Households That Use Selected Payment Instruments: 1995 to 2004**

[In percent. Based on Survey of Consumer Finances conducted by the Board of Governors of the Federal Reserve System; see Appendix III]

Age and education of head of household	Any of these instruments		ATM [1]		Debit card		Direct deposit		Automatic bill paying		Software [2]	
	1995	2004	1995	2004	1995	2004	1995	2004	1995	2004	2001	2004
All households	77.7	90.4	62.5	74.4	17.6	59.3	46.7	71.2	21.8	47.4	18.0	19.3
Under 30 years old	76.3	87.3	72.3	83.0	24.4	74.4	31.0	54.0	17.7	36.5	17.0	20.4
30 to 60 years old.	78.7	90.3	68.6	82.3	19.7	67.6	42.8	68.2	24.4	50.3	22.0	21.9
61 years old and over	76.1	91.9	44.2	51.6	9.6	32.5	63.3	87.0	18.2	46.5	9.0	12.8
No college degree	71.4	86.2	54.7	67.4	14.3	54.9	40.3	64.3	18.1	39.5	10.9	12.4
College degree	91.8	97.5	80.4	86.4	25.2	67.0	61.0	83.2	30.1	61.1	31.8	31.3

[1] The question on ATMs asked whether any member of the household had an ATM card, not whether the member used it. The other questions asked about usage of other instruments. [2] The question on software asked whether the respondent or spouse/partner uses any type of computer software to help in managing their money.

Source: Mester, Loretta J., "Changes in the Use of Electronic Means of Payment: 1995–2004," *Business Review*, Second Quarter 2006, published by Federal Reserve Bank of Philadelphia. See also <http://www.philadelphiafed.org/files/br/brq2-2006-4changes-electronic-means.pdf>.

Table 1156. **Debit Cards—Holders, Number, Transactions, and Volume, 2000 and 2005, and Projections, 2010**

[174 represents 174,000,000]

Type of debit card	Cardholders (mil.)		Number of cards (mil.)			Number of transactions (mil.)			Volume (bil. dol.)		
	2005	2010, proj.	2000	2005	2010, proj.	2000	2005	2010, proj.	2000	2005	2010, proj.
Total [1]	174	185	235	280	361	9,797	25,265	42,529	448	1,180	2,179
Bank [2]	223	282	137	270	351	6,797	16,681	26,223	327	829	1,422
EFT systems [3]	173	184	223	269	281	2,979	8,564	16,256	119	350	755
Other [4]	11	13	11	11	13	22	19	50	1	1	2

[1] Cardholders may hold more than one type of card. Bank cards and EFT cards are the same pieces of plastic that carry multiple brands. The total card figure shown does not include any duplication. [2] Visa and MasterCard debit cards. [3] Cards issued by financial institution members of regional and national switches such as Star, Interlink, Pulse, Nyce, etc. EFT = Electronic funds transfer. [4] Retail cards such as those issued by supermarkets.

Source: The Nilson Report, Carpinteria, CA, Twice-monthly newsletter. (Copyright used by permission.)

Banking, Finance, and Insurance 733

Table 1157. Credit Cards—Holders, Number, Spending, and Debt, 2000 and 2005, and Projections, 2010

[159 represents 159,000,000]

Type of credit card	Cardholders (mil.)			Number of cards (mil.)			Credit card spending volume (bil. dol.)			Credit card debt outstanding (bil. dol.)		
	2000	2005	2010, proj.	2000	2005	2010, proj.	2000	2005	2010, proj.	2000	2005	2010, proj.
Total [1]	159	164	176	1,425	1,395	1,466	1,458	2,052	3,378	680	832	1,091
Bank [2]	(NA)	(NA)	(NA)	455	546	623	938	1,373	2,157	480	612	775
Store	114	114	114	597	500	491	120	134	197	92	87	102
Oil company	76	60	55	98	79	76	50	67	126	5	9	13
Other [3]	132	125	113	275	270	276	350	477	898	103	124	201

NA Not available. [1] Cardholders may hold more than one type of card. [2] Visa and MasterCard credit cards. [3] Includes Universal Air Travel Plan (UATP), phone cards, automobile rental, and miscellaneous cards. Except for data on cardholders, also includes Discover and American Express.

Source: The Nilson Report, Carpinteria, CA, Twice-monthly newsletter. (Copyright used by permission.)

Table 1158. Usage of General Purpose Credit Cards by Families: 1995 to 2004

[General purpose credit cards include Mastercard, Visa, Optima, and Discover cards. Excludes cards used only for business purposes. All dollar figures are given in constant 2004 dollars based on consumer price index data as published by U.S. Bureau of Labor Statistics. Families include one-person units; for definition of family, see text, Section 1. Based on Survey of Consumer Finances; see Appendix III. For definition of median, see Guide to Tabular Presentation]

Age of family head and family income	Percent having a general purpose credit card	Median number of cards	Median new charges on last month's bills (dol.)	Percent having a balance after last month's bills	Median balance (dol.) [1]	Percent of cardholding families who—		
						Almost always pay off the balance	Some-times pay off the balance	Hardly ever pay off the balance
1995, total	66.5	2	200	56.0	1,800	52.4	20.1	27.5
1998, total	67.5	2	200	54.7	2,200	53.8	19.3	26.9
2001, total	72.7	2	200	53.7	1,900	55.3	19.1	25.6
2004, total	71.5	2	300	56.2	2,100	55.7	20.3	24.0
Under 35 years old	60.6	2	200	66.1	1,500	49.0	20.4	30.6
35 to 44 years old	73.3	2	300	70.8	2,400	41.6	26.2	32.2
45 to 54 years old	77.5	2	300	61.2	3,000	49.3	23.9	26.8
55 to 64 years old	78.2	2	400	46.1	2,500	66.8	16.8	16.5
65 to 74 years old	75.5	2	300	37.7	2,300	70.7	13.4	15.9
75 years old and over	65.4	2	200	32.2	1,100	77.5	12.9	9.7
Less than $10,000	31.5	1	100	59.4	1,200	50.9	17.3	31.9
$10,000 to $24,999	48.6	1	100	59.7	1,200	49.9	17.0	33.1
$25,000 to $49,999	71.2	2	200	64.3	2,000	46.9	20.3	32.8
$50,000 to $99,999	88.2	2	300	56.1	2,800	56.1	22.0	21.8
$100,000 and more	96.6	2	1,200	42.8	3,400	71.1	20.2	8.7

[1] Among families having a balance.

Source: Board of Governors of the Federal Reserve System, unpublished data.

Table 1159. Consumer Credit Outstanding and Finance Rates: 1990 to 2006

[In billions of dollars, except percent (808 represents $808,000,000,000). Covers most short- and intermediate-term credit extended to individuals, excluding loans secured by real estate. Estimated amounts of seasonally adjusted credit outstanding as of end of year; finance rates, annual averages]

Type of credit	1990	1995	1999	2000	2001	2002	2003	2004	2005	2006
Total....................	808	1,141	1,533	1,722	1,872	1,984	2,088	2,202	2,296	2,405
Revolving	239	444	609	683	716	749	771	801	827	879
Nonrevolving [1]	570	698	923	1,039	1,155	1,235	1,317	1,401	1,469	1,526
FINANCE RATES (percent)										
Commercial banks:										
New automobiles (48 months)	11.78	9.57	8.44	9.34	8.50	7.62	6.93	6.60	7.08	7.72
Other consumer goods (24 months)	15.46	13.94	13.39	13.90	13.22	12.54	11.95	11.89	12.05	12.41
Credit-card plans.............	18.17	15.99	15.19	15.78	14.87	13.40	12.30	12.71	12.51	13.21
Finance companies:										
New automobiles.............	12.54	11.19	6.66	6.61	5.65	4.29	3.40	4.36	5.46	4.96
Used automobiles	15.99	14.48	12.60	13.55	12.18	10.74	9.72	8.96	9.03	9.67

[1] Comprises automobile loans and all other loans not included in revolving credit, such as loans for mobile homes, education, boats, trailers, or vacations. These loans may be secured or unsecured.

Source: Board of Governors of the Federal Reserve System, Statistical Supplement to the Federal Reserve Bulletin, monthly.

Table 1160. **Consumer Credit by Type of Holder: 1990 to 2006**

[In billions of dollars (824 represents $824,000,000,000). As of December 31. Not seasonally adjusted]

Type of holder	1990	1995	1999	2000	2001	2002	2003	2004	2005	2006
Total	824	1,169	1,557	1,749	1,900	2,012	2,116	2,232	2,327	2,438
Nonfinancial corporations	67	85	76	81	73	75	58	59	59	57
U.S. government	–	10	51	67	80	93	94	98	102	103
Commercial banking	382	502	508	551	568	603	669	704	707	741
Savings institutions	50	40	62	65	71	69	78	91	109	96
Credit unions	92	132	168	184	190	196	206	215	229	236
Government-sponsored enterprises	19	34	34	37	39	37	21	–	–	–
Asset-backed securities issuers	77	213	457	528	598	633	597	572	605	671
Finance companies	138	152	202	234	280	308	393	492	517	534

– Represents or rounds to zero.

Source: Board of Governors of the Federal Reserve System, "Federal Reserve Statistical Release, Z.1, Flow of Funds Accounts of the United States"; published 8 March 2007; <http://www.federalreserve.gov/releases/z1/20070308/>.

Table 1161. **Mortgage Debt Outstanding by Type of Property and Holder: 1990 to 2006**

[In billions of dollars (3,803 represents $3,803,000,000,000). As of December 31]

Type of property and holder	1990	1995	1999	2000	2001	2002	2003	2004	2005	2006
Total mortgages [1]	3,803	4,550	6,233	6,796	7,486	8,364	9,369	10,672	12,134	13,306
Home [2]	2,615	3,451	4,691	5,110	5,639	6,371	7,169	8,238	9,366	10,190
Multifamily residential	288	276	375	404	446	485	556	609	680	731
Commercial	821	739	1,064	1,171	1,282	1,383	1,511	1,683	1,940	2,221
Farm	79	85	103	110	118	125	134	142	148	163
Commercial banking	849	1,090	1,495	1,660	1,790	2,058	2,256	2,595	2,957	3,403
Savings institutions	802	597	668	723	758	781	870	1,057	1,153	1,074
Credit unions	50	66	111	125	141	159	183	213	246	279
Life insurance companies	268	213	231	236	243	250	261	273	285	304
Government-sponsored enterprises (GSE)	156	250	242	264	297	357	463	478	477	480
Agency- and GSE-backed mortgage pools	1,020	1,571	2,294	2,493	2,832	3,159	3,489	3,542	3,677	3,965
Asset-backed securities issuers	68	248	552	610	711	796	968	1,424	2,109	2,464
Finance companies	114	105	195	238	258	331	370	476	541	598
Real estate investment trusts	8	14	24	19	18	30	50	119	159	172
HOME MORTGAGES [2]										
Total [1]	2,615	3,451	4,691	5,110	5,639	6,371	7,169	8,238	9,366	10,190
Commercial banking	430	647	880	966	1,024	1,222	1,347	1,568	1,773	2,053
Savings institutions	600	482	548	594	620	631	703	875	955	870
Credit unions	50	66	111	125	141	159	183	213	246	279
Government-sponsored enterprises (GSE)	115	205	189	205	226	271	363	363	348	343
Agency- and GSE-backed mortgage pools	991	1,543	2,235	2,426	2,749	3,064	3,367	3,417	3,546	3,822
Asset-backed securities issuers	55	194	354	377	434	489	611	1,014	1,587	1,835
Finance companies	80	66	147	187	210	286	320	422	490	539

[1] Includes other holders not shown separately. [2] Mortgages on one- to four-family properties.

Source: Board of Governors of the Federal Reserve System, "Federal Reserve Statistical Release, Z.1, Flow of Funds Accounts of the United States"; published 8 March 2007; <http://www.federalreserve.gov/releases/z1/20070308/>.

Table 1162. **Characteristics of Conventional First Mortgage Loans for Purchase of Single-Family Homes: 1990 to 2006**

[In percent, except as indicated (154.1 represents $154,100). Annual averages. Covers fully amortized conventional mortgage loans used to purchase single-family nonfarm homes. Excludes refinancing loans, nonamortized and balloon loans, loans insured by the Federal Housing Administration, and loans guaranteed by the Veterans Administration. Based on a sample of mortgage lenders, including savings and loans associations, savings banks, commercial banks, and mortgage companies]

Loan characteristics	New homes						Previously occupied homes					
	1990	2000	2003	2004	2005	2006	1990	2000	2003	2004	2005	2006
Contract interest rate, [1]												
all loans	9.7	7.4	5.7	5.7	5.9	6.5	9.8	7.9	5.7	5.7	5.8	6.5
Fixed-rate loans	10.1	8.0	5.9	6.0	6.1	6.6	10.1	8.2	5.8	6.0	6.0	6.6
Adjustable-rate loans [2]	8.9	6.5	5.1	5.4	5.3	6.2	8.9	7.2	5.0	5.1	5.6	6.4
Initial fees, charges [3]	1.98	0.69	0.63	0.50	0.54	0.67	1.74	0.66	0.32	0.37	0.33	0.33
Effective interest rate, [4]												
all loans	10.1	7.5	5.8	5.8	5.9	6.6	10.1	8.1	5.7	5.7	5.9	6.6
Fixed-rate loans	10.4	8.2	6.0	6.0	6.2	6.7	10.4	8.3	5.9	6.0	6.0	6.6
Adjustable-rate loans [2]	9.2	6.5	5.2	5.4	5.3	6.2	9.2	7.2	5.0	5.2	5.6	6.4
Term to maturity (years)	27.3	29.2	28.7	28.8	29.2	29.5	27.0	28.6	26.5	27.7	28.3	28.9
Purchase price ($1,000)	154.1	234.9	275.3	293.6	328.5	346.4	140.3	191.8	237.0	253.2	291.3	295.9
Loan-to-price ratio	74.9	77.4	77.9	76.0	75.2	75.4	74.9	77.9	72.6	74.6	74.6	76.9
Percent of number of loans with adjustable rates	31	40	21	42	29	21	27	21	17	33	30	22

[1] Initial interest rate paid by the borrower as specified in the loan contract. [2] Loans with a contractual provision for periodic adjustments in the contract interest rate. [3] Includes all fees, commissions, discounts, and "points" paid by the borrower, or seller, in order to obtain the loan. Excludes those charges for mortgage, credit, life, or property insurance; for property transfer; and for title search and insurance. [4] Contract interest rate plus fees and charges amortized over a 10-year period.

Source: U.S. Federal Housing Finance Board, *Rates & Terms on Conventional Home Mortgages, Annual Summary.*

Banking, Finance, and Insurance **735**

Table 1163. Mortgage Originations and Delinquency and Foreclosure Rates: 1990 to 2006

[In percent, except as indicated (459 represents $459,000,000,000). Covers one- to four-family residential nonfarm mortgage loans. Mortgage origination is the making of a new mortgage]

Item	1990	1995	2000	2001	2002	2003	2004	2005	2006
MORTGAGE ORIGINATIONS									
Total (bil. dol.)	459	640	1,139	2,243	2,854	3,812	2,773	2,908	2,815
Purchase (bil. dol.)	389	494	905	960	1,097	1,280	1,309	1,512	1,459
Refinance (bil. dol.)	70	145	234	1,283	1,757	2,532	1,463	1,397	1,357
DELINQUENCY RATES [1]									
Total	4.7	4.2	4.4	5.1	5.1	4.7	4.5	4.5	4.6
Prime conventional loans	(NA)	(NA)	2.3	2.7	2.6	2.5	2.3	2.3	2.4
Subprime conventional loans	(NA)	(NA)	11.9	14.0	14.3	12.2	10.8	10.8	12.3
Federal Housing Administration loans .	6.7	7.6	9.1	10.8	11.5	12.2	12.2	12.5	12.7
Veterans Administration loans	6.3	6.4	6.8	7.7	7.9	8.0	7.3	7.0	6.7
FORECLOSURE RATES [2]									
Total	0.9	0.9	1.2	1.5	1.5	1.3	1.2	1.0	1.2
Prime conventional loans	(NA)	(NA)	0.4	0.5	0.5	0.6	0.5	0.4	0.5
Subprime conventional loans	(NA)	(NA)	9.4	9.4	8.0	5.6	3.8	3.3	4.5
Federal Housing Administration loans .	1.3	1.3	1.7	2.2	2.8	2.9	2.7	2.3	1.9
Veterans Administration loans	1.2	1.3	1.2	1.3	1.6	1.6	1.5	1.1	1.0

NA Not available.   [1] Number of loans delinquent 30 days or more as percentage of mortgage loans serviced in survey. Annual average of quarterly figures.   [2] Percentage of loans in the foreclosure process at year-end, not seasonally adjusted.

Source: Mortgage Bankers Association of America, Washington, DC, "1-4 Family Mortgage Originations 1990–2005"; <http://www.mbaa.org/ResearchandForecasts/MarketEnvironment/1-4FamilyMortgageOriginations1990-2005.htm>; accessed 16 June 2006; and *National Delinquency Survey*, quarterly, and unpublished data.

Table 1164. Delinquency Rates on Loans at Insured Commercial Banks: 1990 to 2006

[In percent. Annual averages of quarterly figures, not seasonally adjusted. Delinquent loans are those past due 30 days or more and still accruing interest as well as those in nonaccrual status. They are measured as a percentage of end-of-period loans]

Type of loan	1990	1995	2000	2001	2002	2003	2004	2005	2006
Total loans	5.33	2.48	2.18	2.61	2.69	2.33	1.80	1.57	1.57
Real estate	6.10	2.94	1.89	2.13	1.99	1.76	1.44	1.38	1.48
Residential [1]	(NA)	2.20	2.11	2.29	2.11	1.83	1.55	1.55	1.73
Commercial [2]	(NA)	3.94	1.49	1.79	1.71	1.54	1.20	1.07	1.11
Consumer	3.83	3.09	3.55	3.67	3.51	3.28	3.08	2.81	2.90
Credit cards	(NA)	3.74	4.50	4.86	4.87	4.47	4.11	3.70	4.01
Other	(NA)	2.67	2.98	3.03	2.79	2.67	2.46	2.23	2.21
Leases	1.97	0.79	1.59	2.11	2.24	1.91	1.33	1.28	1.26
Commercial and industrial	5.34	1.95	2.22	3.08	3.84	3.34	2.19	1.51	1.28
Agricultural	3.84	2.50	2.54	2.63	2.51	2.50	1.68	1.30	1.31

NA Not available.   [1] Residential real estate loans include loans secured by one- to four-family properties, including home equity lines of credit.   [2] Commercial real estate loans include construction and land development loans, loans secured by multifamily residences, and loans secured by nonfarm, nonresidential real estate.

Source: Federal Financial Institutions Examination Council (FFIEC), *Consolidated Reports of Condition and Income* (1990–2000: FFIEC 031 through 034; beginning 2001. FFIEC 031 & 041).

Table 1165. Money Stock: 1990 to 2006

[In billions of dollars (825 represents $825,000,000,000). As of December. Seasonally adjusted averages of daily figures]

Item	1990	1995	1999	2000	2001	2002	2003	2004	2005	2006
M1, total	825	1,127	1,123	1,088	1,182	1,219	1,306	1,375	1,373	1,366
Currency [1]	246	372	518	531	581	626	663	698	724	750
Travelers' checks [2]	8	9	9	8	8	8	8	8	7	7
Demand deposits [3]	277	389	353	310	336	306	325	342	324	306
Other checkable deposits [4]	294	357	243	238	257	279	310	327	317	303
M2, total	3,279	3,641	4,649	4,931	5,451	5,801	6,062	6,412	6,669	7,021
M1	825	1,127	1,123	1,088	1,182	1,219	1,306	1,375	1,373	1,366
Non-M1 components of M2	2,454	2,514	3,526	3,844	4,269	4,582	4,756	5,036	5,296	5,655
Retail money funds	358	448	831	921	982	910	777	701	703	803
Savings deposits (including MMDAs [5])	923	1,134	1,740	1,878	2,313	2,779	3,169	3,518	3,619	3,688
Commercial banks	581	775	1,289	1,424	1,739	2,061	2,337	2,631	2,770	2,895
Thrift institutions	342	360	452	454	573	718	831	887	849	792
Small time deposits [6]	1,173	931	955	1,045	975	892	810	818	975	1,164
Commercial banks	611	575	635	700	635	590	537	546	635	765
Thrift institutions	563	357	320	345	340	302	274	272	340	399

[1] Currency outside U.S. Treasury, Federal Reserve Banks and the vaults of depository institutions.   [2] Outstanding amount of U.S. dollar-denominated travelers' checks of nonbank issuers. Travelers' checks issued by depository institutions are included in demand deposits.   [3] Demand deposits at domestically chartered commercial banks, U.S. branches and agencies of foreign banks, and Edge Act corporations (excluding those amounts held by depository institutions, the U.S. government, and foreign banks and official institutions) less cash items in the process of collection and Federal Reserve float.   [4] Negotiable order of withdrawal (NOW) and automatic transfer service (ATS) balances at domestically chartered commercial banks, U.S. branches, and agencies of foreign banks, Edge Act corporations, and thrift institutions, credit union share draft balances, and demand deposits at thrift institutions.   [5] Money market deposit accounts (MMDAs).   [6] Small-denomination time deposits are those issued in amounts of less than $100,000. All Individual Retirement Account (IRA) and Keogh account balances at commercial banks and thrift institutions are subtracted from small time deposits.

Source: Board of Governors of the Federal Reserve System, *Statistical Supplement to the Federal Reserve Bulletin*, monthly, and *Money Stock Measures, Federal Reserve Statistical Release H.6*, weekly.

Table 1166. Money Market Interest Rates and Mortgage Rates: 1980 to 2006

[Percent per year. Annual averages of monthly data, except as indicated]

Type	1980	1985	1990	1994	1995	1996	1997	1998	1999	2000	2001	2002	2003	2004	2005	2006
Federal funds, effective rate	13.35	8.10	8.10	4.21	5.83	5.30	5.46	5.35	4.97	6.24	3.88	1.67	1.13	1.35	3.22	4.97
Prime rate charged by banks[1]	15.26	9.93	10.01	7.15	8.83	8.27	8.44	8.35	8.00	9.23	6.91	4.67	4.12	4.34	6.19	7.96
Discount rate[1]	11.77	7.69	6.98	3.60	5.21	5.02	5.00	4.92	4.62	5.73	3.40	1.17	2.12	2.34	4.19	5.96
Eurodollar deposits, 3-month	14.00	8.27	8.16	4.63	5.93	5.38	5.61	5.45	5.31	6.45	3.70	1.73	1.14	1.55	3.51	5.19
Large negotiable CDs:																
3-month, secondary market	13.02	8.04	8.15	4.63	5.92	5.39	5.62	5.47	5.33	6.46	3.71	1.73	1.15	1.57	3.51	5.16
6-month, secondary market[2]	12.94	8.24	8.17	4.96	5.98	5.47	5.73	5.44	5.46	6.59	3.66	1.81	1.17	1.74	3.73	5.24
Taxable money market funds[2]	12.68	7.71	7.82	3.75	5.48	4.95	5.10	5.04	4.64	5.89	3.67	1.29	0.64	0.82	2.66	4.51
Tax-exempt money market funds[2]	(NA)	4.90	5.45	2.38	3.39	2.99	3.14	2.94	2.72	3.54	2.24	0.94	0.53	0.66	1.87	2.90
Certificates of deposit (CDs):[3]																
6-month	(NA)	8.05	7.79	3.42	4.92	4.68	4.86	4.58	4.27	5.09	3.43	1.67	1.02	1.14	2.37	3.29
1-year	(NA)	8.53	7.92	4.01	5.39	4.95	5.15	4.81	4.55	5.46	3.60	1.98	1.20	1.45	2.77	3.64
2½-year	(NA)	9.32	7.96	4.58	5.69	5.14	5.40	4.93	4.73	5.64	3.97	2.74	1.77	2.21	3.18	3.75
5-year	(NA)	9.99	8.06	5.42	6.00	6.46	5.66	5.08	4.93	5.97	4.58	3.96	2.93	3.34	3.75	4.02
U.S. government securities:																
Secondary market:[4]																
3-month Treasury bill	11.39	7.47	7.50	4.25	5.49	5.01	5.06	4.78	4.64	5.82	3.40	1.61	1.01	1.37	3.15	4.73
6-month Treasury bill	11.32	7.65	7.46	4.64	5.56	5.08	5.18	4.83	4.75	5.90	3.34	1.68	1.05	1.58	3.39	4.81
Auction average:[5]																
3-month Treasury bill	11.51	7.48	7.51	4.29	5.51	5.02	5.07	4.81	4.66	5.85	3.45	1.62	1.02	1.38	3.16	4.73
Home mortgages:																
New-home mortgage yields[6]	12.66	11.55	10.05	7.49	7.87	7.80	7.71	7.07	7.04	7.52	7.00	6.43	5.80	5.77	5.94	6.60
Conventional, 15 yr. fixed[3]	(NA)	11.48	9.73	7.77	7.39	7.28	7.16	6.58	7.09	7.76	6.53	6.02	5.25	5.23	5.50	6.13
Conventional, 30 yr. fixed[3]	(NA)	11.85	9.97	8.28	7.86	7.76	7.57	6.91	7.46	8.08	7.01	6.56	5.89	5.86	5.93	6.47

NA Not available. [1] Rate for the Federal Reserve Bank of New York. Beginning 2003, the rate charged for discounts made and advances extended under the Federal Reserve's primary credit discount window program, which became effective January 9, 2003. The rate replaced that for adjustment credit, which was discontinued after January 8, 2003. [2] 12-month return for period ending December 31. Source: iMoneyNet, Inc., Westborough, MA, Money Market Insight, monthly, <http://www.imoneynet.com> (copyright). [3] Annual averages. Source: Bankrate, Inc., North Palm Beach, FL, Bank Rate Monitor, weekly (copyright). <http://www.bankrate.com>. [4] Averages based on daily closing bid yields in secondary market, bank discount basis. [5] Averages computed on an issue-date basis; bank discount basis. Source: U.S. Council of Economic Advisors, Economic Indicators, monthly. [6] Effective rate (in the primary market) on conventional mortgages, reflecting fees and charges as well as contract rate and assumed, on the average, repayment at end of ten years. Source: U.S. Federal Housing Finance Board, Rates & Terms on Conventional Home Mortgages, Annual Summary.

Source: Except as noted, Board of Governors of the Federal Reserve System, Statistical Supplement to the Federal Reserve Bulletin, monthly.

Banking, Finance, and Insurance   737

Table 1167. Bond Yields: 1980 to 2006

[Percent per year. Annual averages of daily figures, except as indicated]

Type	1980	1985	1990	1995	2000	2001	2002	2003	2004	2005	2006
U.S. Treasury, constant maturities: [1,2]											
1-year	12.00	8.42	7.89	5.94	6.11	3.49	2.00	1.24	1.89	3.62	4.94
2-year	11.73	9.27	8.16	6.15	6.26	3.83	2.64	1.65	2.38	3.85	4.82
3-year	11.51	9.64	8.26	6.25	6.22	4.09	3.10	2.10	2.78	3.93	4.77
5-year	11.45	10.12	8.37	6.38	6.16	4.56	3.82	2.97	3.43	4.05	4.75
7-year	11.40	10.50	8.52	6.50	6.20	4.88	4.30	3.52	3.87	4.15	4.76
10-year	11.43	10.62	8.55	6.57	6.03	5.02	4.61	4.01	4.27	4.29	4.80
20-year	(NA)	(NA)	(NA)	6.95	6.23	5.63	5.43	4.96	5.04	4.64	5.00
State and local govt. bonds, Aaa rating [3]	7.84	8.60	6.96	5.79	5.58	5.01	4.87	4.52	4.50	4.28	4.15
State and local govt. bonds, Baa rating [3]	8.99	9.59	7.30	6.05	6.19	5.75	5.64	5.20	5.09	4.86	4.71
Municipal (Bond Buyer, 20 bonds)	8.55	9.11	7.27	5.95	5.71	5.15	5.04	4.75	4.68	4.40	4.40
High-grade municipal bonds (Standard & Poor's) [4]	8.51	9.18	7.25	5.95	5.77	5.19	5.05	4.73	4.63	4.29	4.42
Corporate Aaa rating/seasoned [3,5]	11.94	11.37	9.32	7.59	7.62	7.08	6.49	5.66	5.63	5.23	5.59
Corporate Baa rating/seasoned [3]	13.67	12.72	10.36	8.20	8.37	7.95	7.80	6.76	6.39	6.06	6.48
Corporate seasoned, all industries [3]	12.75	12.05	9.77	7.83	7.98	7.49	7.10	6.24	6.00	5.57	5.98

NA Not available. [1] Yields on actively traded non-inflation-indexed issues adjusted to constant maturities. Data from U.S. Treasury. [2] Through 1995, yields are based on closing bid prices quoted by at least five dealers. Beginning 2000, yields are based on closing indicative prices quoted by secondary market participants. [3] Data from Moody's Investors Service, New York, NY. [4] Source: U.S. Council of Economic Advisors, *Economic Indicators*, monthly [5] Moody's Aaa rates through December 6, 2001, are average of Aaa utility and Aaa industrial bond rates. As of December 7, 2001, these rates are averages of Aaa industrial bonds only.

Source: Board of Governors of the Federal Reserve System, *Statistical Supplement to the Federal Reserve Bulletin*, monthly.

Table 1168. Volume of Debt Markets by Type of Security: 1990 to 2006

[In billions of dollars (1,081 represents $1,081,000,000,000). Covers debt markets as represented by the source]

Type of security	1990	1995	2000	2003	2004	2005	2006
NEW ISSUE VOLUME [1]							
Total	1,081	1,640	2,592	6,843	5,525	5,715	6,236
U.S. Treasury securities [2]	398	511	312	745	853	746	789
Federal agency debt [3]	55	228	447	1,268	882	669	747
Municipal	128	160	201	383	360	408	387
Mortgage-backed securities [4]	380	348	708	3,071	1,779	1,966	2,003
Asset-backed securities [5]	44	113	337	600	870	1,172	1,252
Corporate debt [6]	77	280	587	776	781	753	1,059
DAILY TRADING VOLUME							
Total	111.2	246.3	357.6	754.5	821.2	923.0	898.9
U.S. Treasury securities [2,7]	111.2	193.2	206.6	433.5	499.0	554.5	524.7
Federal agency debt [7]	(NA)	23.7	72.8	81.7	78.8	78.8	74.4
Municipal [8]	(NA)	(NA)	8.8	12.6	14.8	16.9	22.5
Mortgage-backed securities [4,7]	(NA)	29.4	69.5	206.0	207.4	251.8	254.6
Corporate [6]	(NA)	(NA)	(NA)	20.7	21.2	21.0	22.7
VOLUME OF SECURITIES OUTSTANDING							
Total	7,745	11,229	16,961	22,030	23,692	25,256	27,391
U.S. Treasury securities [2]	2,196	3,307	2,967	3,575	3,944	4,166	4,323
Federal agency debt [9]	435	845	1,855	2,637	2,745	2,614	2,660
Municipal	1,184	1,294	1,481	1,901	2,031	2,226	2,404
Mortgage-backed securities [4]	1,333	2,352	3,566	5,239	5,456	5,916	6,492
Asset-backed securities [5,6]	90	316	1,072	1,694	1,828	1,955	2,130
Money market instruments [10]	1,157	1,177	2,663	2,526	2,904	3,420	4,008
Corporate debt [6,9]	1,350	1,938	3,358	4,459	4,785	4,960	5,374

NA Not available. [1] Covers only long-term issuance. [2] Marketable public debt. [3] Includes overnight discount notes. [4] Includes only Government National Mortgage Association (GNMA), Federal National Mortgage Association (FNMA), Federal Home Loan Mortgage Corporation (FHLMC) mortgage-backed securities (MBS) and collateralized mortgage obligations (CMOs) and private-label MBS/CMOs. [5] Excludes mortgage-backed assets. [6] Includes nonconvertible corporate debt, Yankee bonds, and MTNs (Medium-Term Notes), but excludes all issues with maturities of one year or less, agency debt, and all certificates of deposit. [7] Primary dealer transactions. [8] Includes customer-to-dealer and dealer-to-dealer transactions. [9] The Securities Industry and Financial Markets Association estimates. [10] Commercial paper, bankers acceptances, and large time deposits.

Source: The Securities Industry and Financial Markets Association, New York, NY. Copyright. Based on data supplied by Board of Governors of the Federal Reserve System, U.S. Dept. of Treasury, Thompson Financial Securities Data Company, Inside MBS & ABS, FHLMC, FNMA, GNMA, Federal Home Loan Banks, Student Loan Marketing Association, Federal Farm Credit Banks, Tennessee Valley Authority, Bloomberg, and Municipal Securities Rulemaking Board.

Table 1169. **Total Returns of Stocks, Bonds, and Treasury Bills: 1980 to 2006**

[In percent. Average annual percent change. Stock return data are based on the Standard & Poor's 500 index. Minus sign (–) indicates loss]

Period	Stocks				Treasury bills, total return	Bonds (10-year), total return
	Total return	Capital gains	Dividends and reinvestment	Total return after inflation		
1980 to 1989	17.55	12.59	4.40	11.85	0.10	13.01
1990 to 1999	18.21	15.31	2.51	14.85	4.95	8.02
2000 to 2006	1.13	–0.49	1.63	–1.10	3.07	6.76
2001	–11.89	–13.04	1.32	–13.68	3.32	5.51
2002	–22.10	–23.37	1.65	–23.91	1.61	15.15
2003	28.68	26.38	1.82	26.31	1.03	0.54
2004	10.88	8.99	1.73	7.38	1.43	4.59
2005	4.91	3.00	1.85	1.45	3.30	3.16
2006	15.80	13.62	1.91	11.97	4.97	2.36

Source: Global Financial Data, Los Angeles, CA, "GFD Guide to Total Returns"; <http://www.globalfindata.com/articles/total_return_worksheet.xls>; and unpublished data (copyright).

Table 1170. **Equities, Corporate Bonds, and Treasury Securities—Holdings and Net Purchases by Type of Investor: 2000 to 2006**

[In billions of dollars (17,627 represents $17,627,000,000,000). Holdings as of Dec. 31. Minus sign (–) indicates net sales]

Type of investor	Holdings					Net purchases				
	2000	2003	2004	2005	2006	2000	2003	2004	2005	2006
EQUITIES [1]										
Total [2]	17,627	15,618	17,389	18,278	20,603	5.3	138.6	66.4	–152.6	–409.5
Household sector [3]	8,036	5,612	5,714	5,483	5,483	–632.0	–2.8	–259.2	–463.9	–740.4
Rest of the world [4]	1,643	1,840	2,123	2,303	2,831	193.6	34.0	61.8	86.6	108.8
Property-casualty insurance companies	194	183	202	205	233	0.7	–2.7	–3.5	–5.8	2.2
Life insurance companies	892	919	1,054	1,162	1,405	111.3	45.5	51.5	65.9	73.4
Private pension funds	1,971	2,082	2,329	2,417	2,668	62.8	–101.0	–11.0	–53.0	–41.4
State and local retirement funds	1,299	1,422	1,607	1,729	1,958	11.6	–0.6	–22.6	–3.0	–11.0
Mutual funds	3,227	3,051	3,694	4,176	5,018	193.1	136.8	158.5	129.6	131.4
Exchange-traded funds	66	146	218	281	402	42.4	15.1	51.2	47.1	68.3
CORPORATE & FOREIGN BONDS										
Total [2]	4,768	6,889	7,673	8,360	9,298	343.5	642.3	712.4	784.4	937.4
Household sector [3]	397	739	712	682	698	81.1	–84.3	–19.2	–15.6	14.7
Rest of the world [4]	1,074	1,722	2,061	2,314	2,738	168.2	220.8	259.5	330.4	423.8
Commercial banking	266	482	560	686	781	56.0	44.6	77.3	126.5	94.4
Property-casualty insurance companies	188	219	245	263	279	6.4	20.0	26.4	17.5	15.9
Life insurance companies	1,222	1,620	1,768	1,841	1,882	49.0	171.0	147.8	78.9	41.1
Private pension funds	266	275	267	267	285	–76.3	20.9	–7.7	8.9	8.7
Money market mutual funds	180	259	261	263	368	27.3	30.5	2.3	2.2	105.1
Mutual funds	362	548	623	699	814	–6.2	77.4	74.5	76.4	114.5
Government-sponsored enterprises	131	226	337	385	406	19.1	36.6	110.8	48.0	21.4
Brokers and dealers	113	228	252	338	397	19.3	36.4	23.9	85.4	59.5
TREASURY SECURITIES										
Total [2]	3,358	4,008	4,371	4,678	4,862	–294.9	398.4	362.5	307.3	183.7
Household sector [3]	585	441	565	563	486	–213.6	29.4	67.2	–98.8	–77.3
State and local governments	310	364	387	456	484	5.5	9.5	23.2	68.8	28.0
Rest of the world [4]	1,021	1,514	1,804	1,994	2,135	–70.5	276.0	346.8	287.1	141.1
Monetary authority	512	667	718	744	779	33.7	37.3	51.2	26.4	34.7

[1] Excludes mutual fund shares. For mutual fund shares, see Table 1187. [2] Includes other types not shown separately. [3] Includes nonprofit organizations. [4] Holdings and net purchases of U.S. issues by foreign residents.

Source: Board of Governors of the Federal Reserve System, "Federal Reserve Statistical Release, Z.1, Flow of Funds Accounts of the United States"; published 8 March 2007; <http://www.federalreserve.gov/releases/z1/20070308/>.

Table 1171. **New Security Issues of Corporations by Type of Offering: 2000 to 2006**

[In billions of dollars (1,082.2 represents $1,082,200,000,000). Represents gross proceed of issues maturing in more than one year. Figures are the principal amount or the number of units multiplied by the offering price. Excludes secondary offerings, employee stock plans, investment companies other than closed-end, intracorporate transactions, and Yankee bonds. Stock data include ownership securities issued by limited partnerships]

Type of offering	2000	2005	2006	Type of offering	2000	2005	2006
Total [1]	1,082.2	2,439.0	2,710.0				
Bonds, total	947.3	2,323.7	2,590.9				
Sold in the United States	824.5	2,141.5	2,318.4	Stocks, total	311.9	200.5	240.5
Sold abroad	122.8	182.2	272.5	Public	134.9	115.3	119.2
				Nonfinancial	118.4	54.7	56.0
Nonfinancial	259.2	216.1	344.0	Financial	16.5	60.5	63.1
Financial	688.1	2,107.7	2,246.9	Private placement	177.0	85.2	121.4

[1] Excludes private placements of stocks.

Source: Board of Governors of the Federal Reserve System, *Statistical Supplement to the Federal Reserve Bulletin*, monthly.

Table 1172. **Purchases and Sales by U.S. Investors of Foreign Bonds and Stocks, 1990 to 2006, and by Selected Country, 2006**

[In billions of dollars (31.2 represents $31,200,000,000). Covers transactions in all types of long-term foreign securities as reported by banks, brokers, and other entities in the United States. Data cover new issues of securities, transactions in outstanding issues, and redemptions of securities. Includes transactions executed in the United States for the account of foreigners, and transactions executed abroad for the account of reporting institutions and their domestic customers. Data by country show the country of location of the foreign buyers and sellers who deal directly with reporting institutions in the United States. The data do not necessarily indicate the country of beneficial owner or issuer. The term "foreigner" covers all institutions and individuals domiciled outside the United States, including U.S. citizens domiciled abroad, and the foreign branches, subsidiaries, and other affiliates abroad of U.S. banks and businesses; the central governments, central banks, and other official institutions of foreign countries; and international and regional organizations. "Foreigner" also includes persons in the United States to the extent that they are known by reporting institutions to be acting on behalf of foreigners. Minus sign (–) indicates net sales by U.S. investors or a net inflow of capital into the United States]

Year and country	Net purchases			Total transactions [1]			Bonds		Stocks	
	Total	Bonds	Stocks	Total	Bonds	Stocks	Pur- chases	Sales	Pur- chases	Sales
1990	31.2	21.9	9.2	907	652	255	337	315	132	123
1995	98.7	48.4	50.3	2,569	1,827	741	938	890	396	346
1996	110.6	51.4	59.3	3,239	2,279	960	1,165	1,114	510	450
1997	89.1	48.1	40.9	4,505	2,952	1,553	1,500	1,452	797	756
1998	11.1	17.3	-6.2	4,527	2,674	1,853	1,346	1,328	923	930
1999	-10.0	5.7	-15.6	3,941	1,602	2,339	804	798	1,162	1,177
2000	17.1	4.1	13.1	5,539	1,922	3,617	963	959	1,815	1,802
2001	19.6	-30.5	50.1	5,135	2,290	2,845	1,130	1,160	1,448	1,398
2002	-27.0	-28.5	1.5	5,253	2,716	2,537	1,344	1,372	1,269	1,268
2003	56.5	-32.0	88.6	5,580	2,883	2,698	1,425	1,457	1,393	1,305
2004	152.8	67.9	85.0	6,399	2,986	3,413	1,527	1,459	1,749	1,664
2005	172.4	45.1	127.3	7,572	2,965	4,608	1,505	1,460	2,367	2,240
2006, total [2]	246.0	139.7	106.3	11,383	3,878	7,505	2,009	1,869	3,806	3,699
United Kingdom	158.0	97.0	61.0	3,939	1,475	2,463	786	689	1,262	1,201
Cayman Islands	-27.7	-4.1	-23.7	1,640	447	1,193	221	225	585	609
Japan	-2.2	-4.3	2.1	924	140	784	68	72	393	391
Canada	18.8	11.1	7.6	748	426	323	218	207	165	158
Ireland	14.5	14.7	-0.2	548	507	41	261	246	20	20
Hong Kong	19.4	-1.9	21.2	453	30	423	14	16	222	201
Bermuda	7.9	6.2	1.7	403	58	345	32	26	173	172
France	3.9	-1.1	5.1	211	44	167	22	23	86	81
Bahamas, The	-1.7	-1.5	-0.3	209	101	108	50	51	54	54
Australia	8.8	2.8	6.1	202	48	155	25	22	80	74
Germany	-8.3	-11.6	3.2	138	60	78	24	36	41	38
Sweden	-1.2	-1.5	0.2	124	13	111	6	7	56	55
Netherlands	-7.3	-4.3	-3.0	117	27	90	12	16	43	46
Singapore	0.8	-4.8	5.6	113	21	92	8	13	49	43

[1] Total purchases plus total sales.   [2] Includes other countries, not shown separately.
Source: U.S. Dept. of Treasury, *Treasury Bulletin*, quarterly.

Table 1173. **U.S. Holdings of Foreign Stocks and Bonds by Country: 2004 to 2006**

[In billions of dollars (2,560.4 represents $2,560,400,000,000). See also Table 1261]

Country	Stocks			Country	Bonds		
	2004	2005	2006, prel.		2004	2005	2006, prel.
Total holdings	2,560.4	3,317.7	4,251.5	Total holdings	993.0	1,028.2	1,180.8
Europe [1]	1,356.2	1,614.0	2,069.4	Europe [1]	478.2	482.0	631.3
United Kingdom	461.8	544.5	734.2	United Kingdom	178.6	193.9	296.6
France	164.6	205.1	268.0	Belgium & Luxembourg	31.8	33.5	66.9
Switzerland	138.2	191.9	236.9	Netherlands	55.1	51.8	49.0
Germany	123.7	158.0	196.1	France	41.8	47.8	46.7
Netherlands	136.5	132.8	158.8	Germany	13.8	16.9	31.7
Spain	63.0	63.5	77.7	Ireland	5.1	5.7	21.3
Italy	57.5	63.9	77.1	Spain	151.9	157.5	169.0
Finland	33.9	44.4	55.4	Canada	129.3	137.1	142.8
Sweden	38.3	40.5	49.7	Caribbean financial centers [1] . .	114.4	118.4	117.7
Canada	180.4	247.8	310.9	Cayman Islands			
Caribbean financial centers [1] . .	257.5	330.1	380.8	Latin America, excluding			
Bermuda	153.5	173.8	214.2	Caribbean financial centers [1]	83.8	87.0	95.0
Cayman Islands	69.7	102.6	107.3	Mexico	28.6	28.2	25.3
Latin America, excluding				Brazil	19.9	21.7	23.7
Caribbean financial centers [1] . .	105.8	154.3	212.6	Asia [1]	78.9	84.9	60.9
Brazil	43.1	68.6	98.1	Japan	36.4	35.1	31.0
Mexico	37.5	57.9	76.3	Africa [1]	6.3	6.4	5.9
Asia [1]	565.8	849.9	1,114.9	South Africa	3.0	2.6	2.3
Japan	330.4	493.3	603.9	Other countries [1]	64.6	73.3	75.9
Korea, South	66.6	110.3	146.1	Australia	40.4	48.6	50.8
Taiwan [2]	34.6	57.1	80.2				
Hong Kong	35.4	44.5	76.7				
Africa [1]	28.9	39.9	56.0				
South Africa	21.6	31.6	44.5				
Other countries [1]	65.8	81.7	106.8				
Australia	57.1	71.1	93.4				

[1] Includes other countries not shown separately.   [2] See footnote 3, Table 1175.
Source: U.S. Bureau of Economic Analysis, *Survey of Current Business*, July 2007.

740 Banking, Finance, and Insurance

Table 1174. Foreign Purchases and Sales of U.S. Securities by Type of Security, 1990 to 2006, and by Selected Country, 2006

[In billions of dollars (18.7 represents $18,700,000,000). Covers transactions in all types of long-term domestic securities by foreigners as reported by banks, brokers, and other entities in the United States (except nonmarketable U.S. Treasury notes, foreign series; and nonmarketable U.S. Treasury bonds and notes, foreign currency series). See headnote, Table 1172. Minus sign (-) indicates net sales by foreigners or a net outflow of capital from the United States]

Year and country	Net purchases					Total transactions [4]				
	Total	Treasury bonds and notes [1]	U.S. govt. corpora tions [2] bonds	Corporate bonds [3]	Corporate stocks	Total	Treasury bonds and notes [1]	U.S govt. corpora tions [2] bonds	Corporate bonds [3]	Corporate stocks
1990	18.7	17.9	6.3	9.7	-15.1	4,204	3,620	104	117	362
1995	231.9	134.1	28.7	57.9	11.2	7,243	5,828	222	278	915
1996	370.2	232.2	41.7	83.7	12.5	8,965	7,134	241	422	1,169
1997	388.0	184.2	49.9	84.4	69.6	12,759	9,546	469	617	2,126
1998	277.8	49.0	56.8	121.9	50.0	14,989	10,259	992	641	3,097
1999	350.2	-10.0	92.2	160.4	107.5	14,617	8,586	880	577	4,574
2000	457.8	-54.0	152.8	184.1	174.9	16,910	7,795	1,305	775	7,036
2001	520.8	18.5	164.0	222.0	116.4	20,003	10,517	2,239	1,260	5,986
2002	547.6	119.9	195.1	182.3	50.2	25,498	14,409	3,261	1,459	6,369
2003	719.9	263.6	155.8	265.7	34.7	26,332	15,739	2,725	1,694	6,174
2004	916.5	352.1	226.4	309.5	28.5	29,441	17,520	2,192	2,033	7,696
2005	1,011.5	338.1	219.3	372.2	82.0	33,303	19,764	1,976	2,182	9,382
2006, total [5]	1,142.1	198.6	290.8	503.0	149.8	41,060	21,714	2,854	2,834	13,657
United Kingdom	462.3	92.6	53.6	240.7	75.5	14,201	9,909	642	1,229	2,421
Cayman Islands	113.6	-18.7	31.8	73.0	27.4	10,169	3,679	823	641	5,026
France	41.5	-1.6	-0.3	21.6	21.7	2,982	1,686	29	54	1,215
Bermuda	22.0	2.7	2.6	10.6	6.1	2,605	948	86	95	1,477
Canada	49.6	18.0	11.7	8.2	11.8	1,344	907	100	72	265
Japan	59.1	2.0	45.1	12.7	-0.7	1,206	821	240	56	88
Ireland	15.0	-1.3	4.2	13.9	-1.8	1,071	885	44	64	77
Bahamas, The	-7.6	-8.1	0.4	2.1	-2.0	689	344	18	50	276
China [6]	105.0	37.7	35.6	31.3	0.5	468	241	169	45	14
Norway	19.1	5.1	8.8	5.7	-0.6	458	284	117	15	41
Germany	-14.1	1.5	4.5	-11.9	-8.2	435	165	20	50	199
Hong Kong	62.7	16.2	32.1	14.8	-0.5	403	264	75	26	38
Netherlands	-2.0	0.7	-0.6	3.4	-5.4	285	135	24	17	109
Switzerland	8.1	-2.9	-0.2	10.0	1.2	259	51	14	38	156

[1] Marketable bonds and notes.   [2] Includes federally sponsored agencies.   [3] Includes transactions in directly placed issues abroad by U.S. corporations and issues of states and municipalities.   [4] Total purchases plus total sales.   [5] Includes other countries, not shown separately.   [6] See footnote 3, Table 1175.

Source: U.S. Dept. of Treasury, Treasury Bulletin, quarterly.

Table 1175. Foreign Holdings of U.S. Securities by Country: 2004 to 2006

[In billions of dollars (1,813.6 represents $1,813,600,000,000). Covers only private holdings of U.S. securities, except as noted. See also Table 1261]

Type of security and country	2004	2005	2006	Type of security and country	2004	2005	2006
U.S. Treasury securities [1,2]	1,813.6	1,984.4	2,115.0	Japan	213.7	241.2	243.5
Japan [3]	684.3	659.1	633.4	China [3]	33.6	48.9	67.2
China [3]	245.2	327.1	439.1	Africa	2.1	2.8	3.0
OPEC Asia [4]	48.1	69.5	96.4	Other countries	18.2	23.3	29.1
Belgium and Luxembourg	56.1	62.8	77.7				
Korea, South	56.7	67.2	67.6	Corporate stocks	1,960.4	2,109.9	2,538.7
Taiwan [3]	66.3	66.4	60.3	Europe [2]	1,098.7	1,162.4	1,401.0
Hong Kong	43.3	40.5	54.6	United Kingdom	292.4	291.4	390.3
Brazil	15.8	28.9	52.5	Belgium and Luxembourg	162.6	191.9	241.3
Germany	41.7	44.2	43.7	Netherlands	156.5	163.1	173.7
United Kingdom	51.7	74.7	36.5	Switzerland	134.4	139.8	159.2
				France	67.4	82.9	118.8
Corporate and agency bonds	2,035.1	2,243.1	2,689.8	Germany	81.9	80.2	77.3
Europe [2]	1,295.8	1,396.1	1,660.1	Ireland	56.6	63.4	74.3
United Kingdom	463.7	482.8	634.8	Sweden	49.9	47.7	50.3
Belgium and Luxembourg	517.3	542.7	571.5	Denmark	23.1	26.4	32.7
Netherlands	60.8	83.1	98.2	Italy	34.2	30.2	30.5
Ireland	56.2	69.8	93.7	Canada	220.2	253.6	311.0
Switzerland	60.2	63.8	79.0	Caribbean financial centers [2]	281.7	317.2	388.8
Germany	62.5	70.6	66.3	Cayman Islands	139.5	164.8	217.0
France	25.1	31.5	54.0	Bermuda	56.7	59.9	68.8
Canada	52.0	63.8	83.2	Netherlands Antilles	23.3	25.8	29.2
Caribbean financial centers [2]	329.8	356.4	476.9	Latin America, excluding Caribbean financial centers	31.8	33.9	40.0
Cayman Islands	197.6	228.9	326.9	Asia [2]	256.1	268.4	310.1
Bermuda	96.0	96.5	106.6	Japan	179.4	187.6	214.8
Latin America, excluding Caribbean financial centers	28.3	30.0	38.5	Africa	4.9	4.7	5.1
Asia [2]	308.9	370.7	399.0	Other countries [2]	67.0	69.7	82.7
				Australia	59.3	61.2	72.3

[1] Includes foreign official holdings.   [2] Includes other countries not shown separately.   [3] With the establishment of diplomatic relations with China on January 1, 1979, the U.S. government recognized the People's Republic of China as the sole legal government of China and acknowledged the Chinese position that there is only one China and that Taiwan is part of China.   [4] Comprises Indonesia, Iran, Iraq, Kuwait, Qatar, Saudi Arabia, and the United Arab Emirates.

Source: U.S. Bureau of Economic Analysis, Survey of Current Business, July 2007.

Banking, Finance, and Insurance   741

Table 1176. **Stock Prices and Yields: 2000 to 2006**

[Closing values as of end of December, except as noted]

Index	2000	2001	2002	2003	2004	2005	2006
STOCK PRICES							
Standard & Poor's indices: [1]							
S&P 500 composite (1941–43 = 10)	1,320	1,148	880	1,112	1,212	1,248	1,418
S&P 400 MidCap Index (1982 = 100)	517	508	430	576	663	738	804
S&P 600 Small Cap Index (Dec. 31, 1993 = 100)	220	232	197	270	329	351	400
S&P 500/Barra Value Index (Dec. 31, 1974 = 35)	636	552	428	552	626	648	764
S&P 500/Barra Growth Index (Dec. 31, 1974 = 35)	688	595	449	556	582	597	653
Russell indices: [2]							
Russell 1000 (Dec. 31, 1986 = 130)	700	605	466	595	651	679	770
Russell 2000 (Dec. 31, 1986 = 135)	484	489	383	557	652	673	788
Russell 3000 (Dec. 31, 1986 = 140)	726	634	490	630	694	723	822
N.Y. Stock Exchange Common Stock Index:							
Composite (Dec. 31, 2002 = 5000)	6,946	6,236	5,000	6,440	7,250	7,754	9,139
Yearly high	7,165	7,048	6,445	6,470	7,373	7,868	9,188
Yearly low	6,095	5,331	4,452	4,419	6,211	6,903	7,708
American Stock Exchange Composite Index (Dec. 29, 1995 = 550)	898	848	824	1,174	1,434	1,759	2,056
NASDAQ Composite Index (Feb. 5, 1971 = 100)	2,471	1,950	1,336	2,003	2,175	2,205	2,415
NASDAQ-100 (Jan. 31, 1985 = 125)	2,342	1,577	984	1,468	1,621	1,645	1,757
Industrial (Feb. 5, 1971 = 100)	1,483	1,389	1,030	1,604	1,858	1,860	2,090
Banks (Feb. 5, 1971 = 100)	1,939	2,135	2,231	2,899	3,218	3,078	3,417
Computers (Oct. 29, 1993 = 200)	1,295	981	623	935	965	992	1,053
Transportation (Feb. 5, 1971 = 100)	1,160	1,285	1,298	1,754	2,229	2,438	2,582
Telecommunications (Oct. 29, 1993 = 200)	463	237	109	184	198	184	235
Biotech (Oct. 29, 1993 = 200)	1,085	909	497	724	769	790	798
Dow-Jones and Co., Inc.:							
Composite (65 stocks)	3,317	2,892	2,375	3,001	3,396	3,638	4,121
Industrial (30 stocks)	10,787	10,022	8,342	10,454	10,783	10,718	12,463
Transportation (20 stocks)	2,947	2,640	2,310	3,007	3,797	4,196	4,560
Utility (15 stocks)	412	294	215	267	335	405	457
Dow Jones Wilshire 5000 Composite Index [3] (Dec. 31, 1980 = 1404.596)	12,176	10,708	8,343	10,799	11,971	12,518	14,258
COMMON STOCK YIELDS (percent)							
Standard & Poor's Composite Index (500 stocks): [4]							
Dividend-price ratio [5]	1.15	1.32	1.61	1.77	1.72	1.83	1.87
Earnings-price ratio [6]	3.63	2.95	2.92	3.84	4.89	5.36	5.78

[1] Standard & Poor's Indices are market-value weighted and are chosen for market size, liquidity, and industry group representation. The S&P 500 index represents 500 large publicly-traded companies. The S&P MidCap Index tracks mid-cap companies. The S&P Small Cap Index consists of 600 domestic small-cap stocks. [2] The Russell 1000 and 3000 indices show respectively the 1000 and 3000 largest capitalization stocks in the United States. The Russell 2000 index shows the 2000 largest capitalization stocks in the United States after the first 1000. [3] The Dow Jones Wilshire 5000 Composite Index measures the performance of all U.S. headquartered equity securities with readily available prices. Source: Dow Jones & Company, Inc., New York, NY, Dow Jones Indexes, (copyright). [4] Source: U.S. Council of Economic Advisors, Economic Indicators, monthly. [5] Aggregate cash dividends (based on latest known annual rate) divided by aggregate market value based on Wednesday closing prices. Averages of monthly figures. [6] Averages of quarterly ratios which are ratio of earnings (after taxes) for 4 quarters ending with particular quarter-to-price index for last day of that quarter.

Source: Except as noted, Global Financial Data, Los Angeles, CA, <http://www.globalfindata.com/> (copyright).

Table 1177. **Dow Jones U.S. Total Market Index by Industry: 2000 to 2006**

[As of end of year]

Industry	2000	2001	2002	2003	2004	2005	2006
U.S. Total Market Index, total	306.88	266.71	204.51	262.68	289.38	302.37	343.25
Basic materials	154.49	153.22	136.97	181.10	200.33	205.79	236.22
Consumer goods	219.82	212.88	198.48	240.91	266.44	265.88	298.60
Consumer services	279.11	284.94	212.34	280.07	306.85	298.62	338.32
Oil and gas	272.96	236.74	200.29	246.08	319.76	422.12	510.72
Financial	440.91	404.50	346.36	445.96	492.54	510.02	592.98
Health care	360.18	310.76	242.87	286.04	295.22	315.50	332.38
Industrials	276.11	245.14	179.78	235.69	272.24	280.72	314.41
Technology	749.01	535.89	327.84	493.02	499.78	513.48	561.85
Telecommunications	210.38	180.62	115.04	119.12	136.84	126.90	168.11
Utilities	177.80	127.04	95.75	114.54	136.79	152.41	178.78

Source: Dow Jones & Company, Inc., New York, NY, Dow Jones Indexes (copyright).

742 Banking, Finance, and Insurance

Table 1178. **Transaction Activity in Equities, Options, and Security Futures, 1990 to 2006, and by Exchange, 2006**

[In billions of dollars (2,229 represents $2,229,000,000,000). Market value of all sales of equities and options listed on an exchange or subject to last-sale reporting. Also reported are the value of such options that were exercised and the value of single-stock futures that were delivered. Excludes options and futures on indexes]

Year and exchange	Total	Equity trading	Option trading	Option exercises and futures deliveries
1990	2,229	2,154	27	48
1995	6,321	6,208	51	63
1997	11,693	11,488	105	100
1998	15,164	14,903	140	121
1999	23,219	22,813	260	145
2000	36,275	35,557	485	233
2001	26,138	25,636	278	224
2002	23,028	22,658	161	209
2003	22,737	22,292	164	282
2004	27,876	27,158	223	495
2005	34,567	33,222	350	995
2006, total [1]	**43,939**	**41,796**	**531**	**1,611**
American Stock Exchange	721	542	45	134
Chicago Board Options Exchange	531	18	130	383
Chicago Stock Exchange	449	449	–	–
International Securities Exchange	525	–	132	393
NASD	15,436	15,436	–	–
Nasdaq Stock Market	2,390	2,390	–	–
National Stock Exchange	468	468	–	–
New York Stock Exchange	16,311	16,311	–	–
The Pacific Exchange	6,512	6,047	112	352
Philadelphia Stock Exchange	373	31	88	255

– Represents zero.   [1] Includes other exchanges not shown separately.

Source: U.S. Securities and Exchange Commission, "Select SEC and Market Data"; <http://www.sec.gov/about.shtml>.

Table 1179. **Volume of Trading on New York Stock Exchange: 1990 to 2006**

[39,946 represents 39,946,000,000. *Round lot:* A unit of trading or a multiple thereof. On the NYSE the unit of trading is generally 100 shares in stocks. For some inactive stocks, the unit of trading is 10 shares. *Odd lot:* An amount of stock less than the established 100-share unit or 10-share unit of trading]

Item	Unit	1990	1995	2000	2001	2002	2003	2004	2005	2006
Shares traded	Million	39,946	87,873	265,499	311,290	369,069	356,767	372,718	523,811	597,724
Round lots [1]	Million	39,665	87,218	262,478	307,509	363,136	352,398	367,099	516,743	588,127
Average daily shares	Million	157	346	1,042	1,240	1,441	1,398	1,457	2,051	2,343
High day	Million	292	653	1,561	2,368	2,813	1,886	2,690	3,628	3,853
Low day	Million	57	118	403	414	462	360	509	694	797
Odd lots	Million	282	656	3,021	3,781	5,933	4,370	5,619	7,068	9,597
Value of shares traded	Bil. dol	1,336	3,110	11,205	10,645	10,491	9,847	11,841	18,174	22,247
Round lots [1]	Bil. dol.	1,325	3,083	11,060	10,489	10,278	9,692	11,618	17,858	21,790
Odd lots	Bil. dol.	11	27	145	155	213	154	223	316	458
Bond volume [2]	Mil. dol.	10,893	6,979	2,328	2,668	3,646	2,502	1,291	951	419
Daily average	Mil. dol	43.1	27.7	9.2	10.8	14.5	10.0	5.1	3.8	1.7

[1] Beginning 2005 reflects trades of NYSE Group.   [2] Par value.

Source: New York Stock Exchange, Inc., New York, NY, "Facts & Figures"; <http://www.nysedata.com/factbook> (copyright).

Table 1180. **Securities Listed on New York Stock Exchange: 1990 to 2006**

[As of December 31 (1,689 represents $1,689,000,000,000)]

Item	Unit	1990	1995	1998	1999	2000	2001	2002	2003	2004	2005	2006
BONDS												
Number of issuers	Number	743	564	474	416	392	369	343	312	228	211	205
Number of issues	Number	2,912	2,097	1,858	1,736	1,627	1,447	1,323	1,273	1,059	971	850
Face value	Bil. dol	1,689	2,773	2,554	2,402	2,125	1,654	1,378	1,355	1,080	968	919
STOCKS [1]												
Shares listed	Billions	90.7	154.7	239.3	280.9	313.9	341.5	349.9	359.7	382.7	403.2	411.4
Market value	Bil. dol	2,820	6,013	10,864	12,296	12,372	11,714	9,603	12,158	13,562	14,910	16,934
Average price [2]	Dollars	31.08	38.86	45.40	43.77	42.14	34.11	28.39	33.80	35.43	36.97	41.17

[1] Beginning 2004, data are for NYSE Group.   [2] This average cannot be used as an index of price trend due to changes in shares listed caused by new listings, suspensions, stock splits, and stock dividends.

Source: New York Stock Exchange, Inc., New York, NY, "Facts & Figures"; <http://www.nysedata.com/factbook> (copyright).

Banking, Finance, and Insurance   743

Table 1181. Stock Ownership by Age of Head of Family and Family Income: 1995 to 2004

[Median value in thousands of constant 2004 dollars (18.0 represents $18,000). Constant dollar figures are based on consumer price index data published by U.S. Bureau of Labor Statistics. Families include one-person units; for definition of family, see text, Section 1. Based on Survey of Consumer Finance; see Appendix III. For definition of median, see Guide to Tabular Presentation]

Age of family head and family income (constant (2004) dollars)	Families having direct or indirect stock holdings [1] (percent)			Median value among families with holdings			Stock holdings' share of total financial assets (percent)		
	1995	2001	2004	1995	2001	2004	1995	2001	2004
All families	40.4	52.2	50.2	18.0	36.7	32.5	40.1	56.1	51.3
Under 35 years old	36.6	49.0	40.8	6.3	7.5	8.0	27.2	52.5	40.3
35 to 44 years old.	46.4	59.5	54.5	12.3	29.3	20.0	39.5	57.2	53.5
45 to 54 years old.	48.9	59.3	56.5	31.9	53.3	50.0	43.1	59.1	53.8
55 to 64 years old.	40.0	57.4	62.8	38.2	85.7	71.1	44.5	56.2	55.0
65 to 74 years old	34.4	40.0	46.9	41.9	160.1	70.0	35.8	55.4	51.5
75 years old and over	27.9	35.7	34.8	24.6	117.2	85.9	39.8	51.8	39.3
Percentiles of income: [2]									
Less than 20	6.5	12.9	11.7	4.6	8.0	7.5	14.2	37.4	32.0
20 to 39.9	24.7	34.1	29.8	7.8	8.3	10.0	26.7	35.6	30.9
40 to 59.9	41.5	52.5	51.6	7.7	16.0	15.0	28.5	46.8	43.4
60 to 79.9	54.3	75.7	69.9	15.6	30.5	26.2	35.6	52.0	41.8
80 to 89.9	69.7	82.0	83.7	30.8	68.8	55.5	41.3	57.3	48.9
90 to 100	80.0	89.7	92.7	73.9	263.8	204.9	45.7	60.5	57.5

[1] Indirect holdings are those in retirement accounts and other managed assets.   [2] See footnote 8, Table 1140.

Source: Board of Governors of the Federal Reserve System, "2004 Survey of Consumer Finances"; published 28 February 2006; <http://www.federalreserve.gov/pubs/oss/oss2/2004/scf2004home.html> and unpublished data.

Table 1182. Household Ownership of Equities: 2005

[56.9 represents 56,900,000. Based on a national probability sample of 4,927 household financial decision-makers. Further questions about equity ownership were asked of those 2,476 decision-makers who indicated they owned equities]

Type of holding	Households owning equities		Number of individual investors (mil.)
	Number (mil.)	Percent of all households	
Any type of equity (net) [1].	56.9	50.3	91.1
Any equity inside employer-sponsored retirement plans	37.6	33.2	48.8
Any equity outside employer-sponsored retirement plans	39.3	34.7	58.9
Individual stock (net) [1]	28.4	25.1	42.6
Individual stock inside employer-sponsored retirement plans.	7.6	6.7	9.9
Individual stock outside employer-sponsored retirement plans.	23.3	20.6	35.0
Stock mutual funds (net) [1]	51.8	45.8	77.7
Stock mutual funds inside employer-sponsored retirement plans	36.0	31.8	46.8
Stock mutual funds outside employer-sponsored retirement plans . . .	31.1	27.5	46.7

[1] Net figure adjusted for multiple responses.

Source: Investment Company Institute, Washington, DC, and Securities Industry Association, New York, NY, *Equity Ownership in America, Fall 2005* (copyright).

Table 1183. Characteristics of Equity Owners: 2005

[In percent, except as indicated. See headnote, Table 1182. For definition of median, see Guide to Tabular Presentation]

Item	Total	Age					Household income		
		18 to 34 years old	35 to 44 years old	45 to 54 years old	55 to 64 years old	65 years old and over	Less than $50,000	$50,000 to $99,999	$100,000 and over
Median age of owner (years).	51	30	40	50	59	72	52	46	49
Median household income (dol.). . . .	65,000	62,000	70,000	70,000	65,000	45,000	30,000	70,000	133,300
Median household financial assets [1] (dol.).	125,000	40,000	80,000	152,700	275,700	350,000	46,500	116,800	367,900
Equity investments owned:									
Individual stock (net) [2]	49	38	46	45	53	63	38	44	61
Inside retirement plans [3]	12	9	14	17	12	8	5	13	20
Outside retirement plans [3] . . .	43	32	41	39	47	57	32	36	55
Stock mutual funds (net) [2]	90	94	92	93	92	81	88	93	92
Inside retirement plans [3] . . .	66	77	77	77	61	32	55	75	79
Outside retirement plans [3] . . .	55	47	52	51	64	60	50	50	60
Have retirement plan coverage [3] . . .	78	84	85	84	77	58	68	86	87
Have Individual Retirement Account (IRA).	67	61	64	65	74	70	57	66	76

[1] Includes assets in employer-sponsored retirement plans but excludes value of primary residence.   [2] Net figure adjusted for multiple responses.   [3] Employer-sponsored.

Source: Investment Company Institute, Washington, DC, and Securities Industry Association, New York, NY, *Equity Ownership in America, Fall 2005* (copyright).

Table 1184. **Households Owning Mutual Funds by Age and Income: 2000 and 2006**

[In percent. Ownership includes money market, stock, bond, and hybrid mutual funds, variable annuities, and mutual funds owned through Individual Retirement Accounts (IRAs), Keoghs, and employer-sponsored retirement plans. In 2006 an estimated 54,900,000 households owned mutual funds. Based on an annual survey of 3,000 households; for details, see source. For definition of mutual fund, see headnote, Table 1186]

Age of household head and household income	Percent distribution, 2006	As percent of all households		Age of household head and household income	Percent distribution, 2006	As percent of all households	
		2000	2006			2000	2006
Total	100	49	48	Less than $25,000......	8	17	16
Less than 35 years old...	17	43	35	$25,000 to $34,999.....	7	37	29
35 to 44 years old......	24	58	55	$35,000 to $49,999.....	13	49	40
45 to 54 years old......	27	59	60	$50,000 to $74,999.....	25	66	58
55 to 64 years old......	17	54	53	$75,000 to $99,999.....	17	77	71
65 years old and over ...	15	32	38	$100,000 and over	30	79	83

Source: Investment Company Institute, Washington, DC, *Fundamentals, Investment Company Institute Research in Brief,* Vol. 9, No. 4, August 2000; and Vol. 15, No. 6, October 2006 (copyright).

Table 1185. **Characteristics of Mutual Fund Owners: 2004**

[In percent, except as indicated. Mutual fund ownership includes holdings of money market, stock, bond, and hybrid mutual funds; and funds owned through variable annuities, Individual Retirement Accounts (IRAs), Keoghs, and employer-sponsored retirement plans. Based on a national probability sample of 3,613 primary financial decision-makers in households with mutual fund investments. For definition of mutual fund, see headnote, Table 1186. For definition of median, see Guide to Tabular Presentation]

Characteristic	Total	Age			Household income		
		Under 40 years old	40 to 64 years old	65 years old and over	Less than $50,000	$50,000 to $99,999	$100,000 or more
Median age (years)................	48	33	51	71	48	46	46
Median household income (dol.)..........	68,700	65,000	75,000	45,000	32,500	70,000	130,000
Median household financial assets [1] (dol.)	125,000	50,000	200,000	207,100	50,000	110,000	350,000
Own an IRA	69	63	72	64	58	65	77
Household has a defined contribution retirement plan(s), net [2]................	84	86	87	67	74	89	88
401(k) plan	67	78	71	28	56	72	76
403(b) plan	14	12	15	6	9	13	19
State, local, or federal government plan	35	27	37	46	32	38	31
Median mutual fund assets (dol.)...........	48,000	20,000	70,000	60,000	17,600	43,800	95,000
Median number of mutual funds owned	4	4	5	3	3	4	6
Own: [2]							
Equity funds....................	80	79	83	74	70	80	91
Bond funds	44	41	46	39	35	41	50
Own mutual funds bought: [2]							
Outside employer-sponsored retirement plan(s)	68	59	69	84	63	60	74
Inside employer-sponsored retirement plan(s)	63	69	67	30	55	68	68

[1] Includes assets in employer-sponsored retirement plans but excludes value of primary residence.   [2] Net figure adjusted for multiple responses. For definition of defined contribution plan, see headnote, Table 535.

Source: Investment Company Institute, Washington, DC, *Profile of Mutual Fund Shareholders, 2004* (copyright).

Table 1186. **Mutual Funds—Summary: 1990 to 2006**

[Number of funds and assets as of December 31 (1,065 represents $1,065,000,000,000). A mutual fund is an open-end investment company that continuously issues and redeems shares that represent an interest in a pool of financial assets. Excludes data for funds that invest in other mutual funds. Minus sign (–) indicates net redemptions]

Type of fund	Unit	1990	1995	2000	2001	2002	2003	2004	2005	2006
Number of funds, total	Number..	3,079	5,725	8,155	8,305	8,244	8,126	8,041	7,975	8,120
Equity funds	Number..	1,099	2,139	4,385	4,716	4,747	4,599	4,547	4,586	4,770
Hybrid funds	Number..	193	412	523	483	473	508	510	505	508
Bond funds	Number..	1,046	2,177	2,208	2,091	2,035	2,045	2,041	2,013	1,993
Money market funds, taxable [1] ...	Number..	506	674	703	689	679	662	639	595	576
Money market funds, tax-exempt [2]..	Number..	235	323	336	326	310	312	304	276	273
Assets, total	Bil. dol.	1,065	2,811	6,965	6,975	6,390	7,414	8,107	8,905	10,414
Equity funds	Bil. dol. ..	239	1,249	3,962	3,418	2,662	3,684	4,384	4,940	5,912
Hybrid funds	Bil. dol. ..	36	210	346	346	325	430	519	567	653
Bond funds	Bil. dol. ..	291	599	811	925	1,130	1,248	1,290	1,357	1,494
Money market funds, taxable [1]	Bil. dol. ..	415	630	1,607	2,013	1,997	1,764	1,603	1,707	1,988
Money market funds, tax-exempt [2]..	Bil. dol. ..	84	123	238	272	275	288	310	334	366
Equity, hybrid, and bond funds:										
Sales	Bil. dol. ..	149	475	1,630	1,383	1,434	1,430	1,471	1,589	1,852
Redemptions	Bil. dol. ..	98	313	1,330	1,177	1,228	1,148	1,178	1,286	1,483
Net sales	Bil. dol. ..	51	163	300	206	206	282	293	303	369
Money market funds, taxable: [1]										
Sales	Bil. dol. ..	1,219	2,729	8,691	10,701	11,012	10,150	9,717	11,064	14,089
Redemptions	Bil. dol. ..	1,183	2,617	8,499	10,314	11,075	10,402	9,874	10,998	13,831
Net sales	Bil. dol. ..	36	112	192	386	–63	–252	–157	67	258
Money market funds, tax-exempt: [2]										
Sales	Bil. dol. ..	197	396	788	783	750	873	1,082	1,389	1,594
Redemptions	Bil. dol. ..	190	385	757	751	736	866	1,066	1,365	1,561
Net sales	Bil. dol. ..	7	11	31	31	14	7	16	24	33

[1] Funds invest in short-term, high-grade securities sold in the money market.   [2] Funds invest in municipal securities with relatively short maturities.

Source: Investment Company Institute, Washington, DC, *Mutual Fund Fact Book,* annual (copyright).

Table 1187. Mutual Fund Shares—Holdings and Net Purchases by Type of Investor: 2000 to 2006

[In billions of dollars (4,433 represents $4,433,000,000,000). Holdings as of Dec. 31. For definition of mutual fund, see headnote, Table 1186. Excludes money market mutual funds. Minus sign (–) indicates net sales]

Type of investor	Holdings					Net purchases				
	2000	2003	2004	2005	2006	2000	2003	2004	2005	2006
Total	4,433	4,654	5,436	6,049	7,093	237.6	288.6	298.2	260.2	333.2
Households, nonprofit organizations	2,856	3,085	3,611	4.121	4,963	57.9	240.5	249.0	266.0	336.8
Nonfinancial corporate business. . .	122	125	140	156	182	3.5	11.3	2.0	7.4	7.4
State and local governments	31	26	27	28	30	1.2	–5.2	–1.5	–0.2	–2.5
Commercial banking	15	17	18	17	24	2.5	–6.2	–0.9	–1.8	3.9
Credit unions	2	4	3	2	2	–0.3	0.5	–0.9	–1.0	–0.1
Life insurance companies	97	92	114	109	120	5.6	0.5	12.8	–9.9	2.0
Private pension funds	1,132	1,097	1,292	1,376	1,507	117.3	39.9	36.2	–0.1	–12.1
State and local government retirement funds	178	208	231	238	266	49.9	7.3	1.6	–0.2	–2.1

Source: Board of Governors of the Federal Reserve System, "Federal Reserve Statistical Release, Z.1, Flow of Funds Accounts of the United States"; published 8 March 2007; <http://www.federalreserve.gov/releases/z1/20070308/>.

Table 1188. Mutual Fund Retirement Assets: 1990 to 2005

[In billions of dollars, except percent (205 represents $205,000,000,000). Based on data from the Institute's Annual Questionnaire for Retirement Statistics. The 2005 survey gathered data from 16,089 mutual fund share classes representing approximately 84 percent of mutual fund industry assets. Assets were estimated for all nonreporting funds. Estimates of retirement assets in street name and omnibus accounts were derived from data reported on the Annual Questionnaire for Retirement Statistics and the Annual Institutional Survey. For definition of mutual fund, see headnote, Table 1186]

Type of account	1990	1995	2000	2001	2002	2003	2004	2005
Mutual fund retirement assets	205	913	2,492	2,360	2,105	2,682	3,084	3,444
Percent of total retirement assets . . .	5	13	21	21	20	22	23	24
Individual retirement accounts (IRAs)	139	468	1,236	1,173	1,052	1,319	1,497	1,668
Employer-sponsored defined contribution retirement plans	67	445	1,256	1,188	1,053	1,363	1,588	1,776
401(k) plans [1]	35	266	819	798	712	927	1,096	1,238
Percent of total 401(k) assets.	9	31	47	47	45	47	48	51
403(b) plans [2]	15	120	265	237	198	262	295	321
457 plans [3]	2	9	45	43	36	44	51	59
Other defined contribution plans [4]	15	50	127	110	106	130	146	158
Percent of all mutual funds:								
Mutual fund retirement assets	19	32	36	34	33	36	38	39
Individual retirement accounts (IRAs)	13	16	18	17	16	18	18	19
Employer-sponsored retirement plans.	6	16	18	17	17	18	20	20

[1] A 401(k) plan is a qualified retirement plan that allows participants to have a portion of their compensation (otherwise payable in cash) contributed pretax to a retirement account on their behalf. Predominantly 401(k) assets, but may also include some profit-sharing plan assets that do not have a 401(k) feature.   [2] Section 403(b) of the Internal Revenue Code permits employees of certain charitable organizations, nonprofit hospitals, universities, and public schools to establish tax-sheltered retirement programs. These plans may invest in either annuity contracts or mutual fund shares.   [3] These plans are deferred compensation arrangements for government employees and employees of certain tax-exempt organizations.   [4] Includes Keoghs and defined contribution plans (profit-sharing, thrift-savings, stock bonus, and money purchase) without 401(k) features.

Source: Investment Company Institute, Washington, DC, Fundamentals, Investment Company Institute Research in Brief, "The U.S. Retirement Market, 2005"; Vol. 15, No. 5, July 2006; and "Appendix: Additional Data on the U.S. Retirement Market"; Vol. 15, No. 5A, July 2006; <http://www.ici.org> (copyright).

Table 1189. Individual Retirement Accounts (IRA) Plans—Value by Institution: 1990 to 2005

[As of December 31 (637 represents $637,000,000,000). Estimated]

Institution	Amount (bil. dol.)								Percent distribution		
	1990	1995	2000	2001	2002	2003	2004	2005	1990	2000	2005
Total IRA assets	637	1,288	2,629	2,619	2,533	2,991	3,336	3,667	100	100	100
Bank and thrift deposits [1]	266	261	252	254	263	268	270	273	42	10	7
Life insurance companies [2]	40	81	203	211	268	285	311	333	6	8	9
Mutual funds	139	468	1,236	1,173	1,052	1,319	1,497	1,668	22	47	45
Securities held in brokerage accounts [3]	192	479	939	982	949	1,118	1,259	1,393	30	36	38

[1] Includes Keogh deposits.   [2] Annuities held by IRAs, excluding variable annuity mutual fund IRA assets.   [3] Excludes mutual fund assets held through brokerage accounts, which are included in mutual funds.

Source: Investment Company Institute, Washington, DC, Fundamentals, Investment Company Institute Research in Brief, "The U.S. Retirement Market, 2005"; Vol. 15, No. 5, July 2006; and "Appendix: Additional Data on the U.S. Retirement Market"; Vol. 15, No. 5A, July 2006; <http://www.ici.org> (copyright).

Table 1190. Assets of Private and Public Pension Funds by Type of Fund: 1990 to 2006

[In billions of dollars (3,269 represents $3,269,000,000,000). As of end of year. Except for corporate equities, represents book value. Excludes social security trust funds; see Table 530]

Type of pension fund	1990	1995	2000	2001	2002	2003	2004	2005	2006
Total, all types	3,269	5,658	9,084	8,673	7,976	9,581	10,548	11,094	12,117
Private funds	2,199	3,789	5,994	5,607	5,152	6,279	6,953	7,318	7,996
Insured [1]	570	891	1,526	1,559	1,605	1,803	2,028	2,197	2,438
Noninsured [2,3]	1,629	2,899	4,468	4,048	3,547	4,476	4,925	5,120	5,558
Credit market instruments [3]	464	608	622	586	577	646	646	659	694
Agency- and GSE-backed securities [4] .	133	213	197	203	183	221	233	231	252
Corporate and foreign bonds	158	241	266	243	254	275	267	276	285
Corporate equities	606	1,257	1,971	1,909	1,559	2,082	2,329	2,417	2,668
Mutual fund shares	40	357	1,132	963	832	1,097	1,292	1,376	1,507
Unallocated insurance contracts [5]	215	322	308	276	250	317	328	338	369
State and local govt. employee retirement funds [3]	730	1,327	2,293	2,207	1,930	2,344	2,572	2,701	2,979
Credit market instruments [3]	402	510	743	689	639	650	677	674	694
Agency- and GSE-backed securities [4]. . .	63	63	179	181	193	248	293	291	297
Corporate equities	285	704	1,299	1,260	1,057	1,422	1,607	1,729	1,958
Mutual fund shares.	8	63	178	184	167	208	231	238	266
Federal government retirement funds [6]	340	541	797	860	894	958	1,023	1,074	1,142

[1] Annuity reserves held by life insurance companies, excluding unallocated contracts held by private pension funds.
[2] Private defined benefit plans and defined contribution plans (including 401(k) type plans). [3] Includes other types of assets not shown separately. [4] GSE = Government-sponsored enterprises. [5] Assets held at life insurance companies (e.g., guaranteed investment contracts (GICs), variable annuities). [6] Includes the Federal Employees Thrift Savings Plan, the National Railroad Retirement Investment Trust, and nonmarketable government securities held by federal government retirement funds.

Source: Board of Governors of the Federal Reserve System, "Federal Reserve Statistical Release, Z.1, Flow of Funds Accounts of the United States"; published 8 March 2007; <http://www.federalreserve.gov/releases/z1/20070308/>.

Table 1191. Annual Revenues of Selected Securities Industries: 2000 to 2005

[In millions of dollars (384,992 represents $384,992,000,000). Covers taxable and tax-exempt employer firms only. Based on the North American Industry Classification System (NAICS), 2002; see text, Section 15. Based on Service Annual Survey. Estimates have been adjusted to the results of the 2002 Economic Census. See Appendix III]

Kind of business	2002 NAICS code	2000	2002	2003	2004	2005
Total	523x	384,992	292,647	311,525	349,166	411,331
Securities and commodity contracts intermediation and brokerage	5231	296,045	212,237	225,299	250,080	298,016
Investment banking & securities dealing	52311	145,416	98,930	108,306	127,257	158,868
Securities brokerage	52312	144,631	107,199	110,689	115,626	131,101
Commodity contracts dealing	52313	2,945	3,044	3,329	3,858	4,142
Commodity contracts brokerage	52314	3,053	3,053	2,975	3,339	3,905
Other financial investment activities [1]	5239x	88,947	80,410	86,226	99,086	113,315
Portfolio management	52392	75,349	67,370	71,535	80,872	91,120
Investment advice	52393	13,598	13,040	14,691	18,214	22,195

[1] Excludes NAICS 52391 (miscellaneous intermediation) and NAICS 52399 (all other financial investment activities).

Source: U.S. Census Bureau, *Service Annual Survey: 2005.*

Table 1192. Securities Industry—Financial Summary: 1990 to 2005

[In billions of dollars, except as indicated. (71.4 represents $71,400,000,000)]

Type	1990	1995	1999	2000	2001	2002	2003	2004	2005
Number of firms	8,437	7,722	7,461	7,258	7,002	6,768	6,565	6,284	6,016
Revenues, total.	71.4	143.4	266.8	349.5	280.1	221.8	219.0	242.9	332.5
Commissions	12.0	23.2	45.9	54.1	44.8	45.0	45.5	47.6	46.8
Trading/investment gains	15.7	29.0	55.5	70.8	39.0	24.2	38.8	30.7	30.7
Underwriting profits	3.7	8.9	17.8	18.7	16.9	14.7	17.2	19.1	19.9
Margin interest	3.2	6.5	15.2	24.5	13.9	6.4	5.3	7.0	13.3
Mutual fund sales	3.2	7.4	16.7	19.4	16.4	15.7	16.2	18.5	20.7
Other	33.4	68.5	115.7	161.9	149.1	115.8	96.0	120.1	201.2
Expenses, total.	70.6	132.1	237.7	310.4	260.7	206.5	193.3	219.7	311.3
Interest expense	28.1	56.9	87.5	131.9	98.9	56.4	44.4	59.7	140.2
Compensation	22.9	41.5	81.7	95.2	83.5	74.9	77.4	83.5	88.8
Commissions/clearance paid	3.0	5.7	13.5	15.5	14.0	15.0	16.3	17.4	18.6
Other	16.6	28.0	55.0	67.8	64.2	60.3	55.1	59.2	63.6
Net income, pretax	0.8	11.3	29.1	39.1	19.4	15.3	25.7	23.2	21.2
Pretax profit margin (percent)	1.1	7.9	10.9	11.2	6.9	6.9	11.7	9.5	6.4
Pretax return on equity (percent) . .	2.2	20.1	27.8	31.1	13.8	10.7	17.6	15.0	13.1
Assets.	657	1,494	2,537	2,866	3,371	3,261	3,980	4,831	5,215
Liabilities	623	1,435	2,423	2,728	3,227	3,119	3,831	4,671	5,051
Ownership equity	34	59	114	138	144	142	149	160	164

Source: U.S. Securities and Exchange Commission, "Select SEC and Market Data Fiscal 2006"; <http://www.sec.gov /about/secstats2006.pdf>.

Table 1193. **Life Insurance in Force and Purchases in the United States—Summary: 1990 to 2005**

[As of December 31 or calendar year, as applicable (389 represents 389,000,000). Covers life insurance with life insurance companies only. Represents all life insurance in force on lives of U.S. residents whether issued by U.S. or foreign companies]

Year	Number of policies, total (mil.)	Life insurance in force			Life insurance purchases [2]					
		Value (bil. dol.)			Number (1,000)			Amount (bil. dol.)		
		Total [1]	Individual	Group	Total	Individual	Group	Total	Individual	Group
1990	389	9,393	5,391	3,754	28,791	14,199	14,592	1,529	1,070	459
1995	370	11,696	6,890	4,605	31,999	12,595	19,404	1,577	1,039	538
1998	358	14,471	8,523	5,735	31,891	11,559	20,332	2,064	1,325	740
1999	367	15,496	9,172	6,110	38,584	11,673	26,912	2,367	1,400	967
2000	369	15,953	9,376	6,376	34,882	13,345	21,537	2,515	1,594	921
2001	377	16,290	9,346	6,765	40,095	14,059	26,036	2,773	1,600	1,172
2002	375	16,346	9,312	6,876	38,713	14,692	24,020	2,767	1,753	1,014
2003	379	17,044	9,655	7,236	35,767	13,821	21,946	2,823	1,773	1,050
2004	373	17,508	9,717	7,631	38,453	12,581	25,872	2,948	1,846	1,102
2005	373	18,399	9,970	8,263	34,519	11,407	23,112	2,836	1,796	1,040

[1] Includes other types of policies not shown separately. [2] Excludes revivals, increases, dividend additions, and reinsurance acquired. Includes long-term credit insurance (life insurance on loans of more than 10 years' duration).

Source: American Council of Life Insurers, Washington, DC, *Life Insurers Fact Book*, annual (copyright).

Table 1194. **U.S. Life Insurance Companies—Summary: 1990 to 2005**

[As of December 31 or calendar year, as applicable (402.2 represents $402,200,000,000). Covers domestic and foreign business of U.S. companies. Beginning 1995 includes annual statement data for companies that primarily are health insurance companies]

Item	Unit	1990	1995	1998	1999	2000	2001	2002	2003	2004	2005
U.S. companies [1]	Number .	2,195	1,650	1,444	1,347	1,269	1,341	1,284	1,227	1,179	1,119
Income	**Bil. dol.** .	402.2	528.1	663.4	726.9	811.5	724.4	734.0	727.0	756.8	779.0
Life insurance premiums . .	Bil. dol..	76.7	102.8	119.9	120.3	130.6	125.3	134.5	127.3	139.7	142.3
Annuity considerations [2]	Bil. dol..	129.1	158.4	229.5	270.2	306.7	251.3	269.3	268.6	276.7	277.1
Health insurance premiums. . . .	Bil. dol..	58.3	90.0	94.9	100.0	105.6	103.4	108.7	115.8	125.8	118.3
Investment and other.	Bil. dol..	138.2	176.9	219.1	236.4	268.5	244.5	221.5	215.3	214.7	241.4
Payments under life insurance and annuity contracts	Bil. dol. .	88.4	227.6	301.8	355.3	375.2	304.9	301.3	307.1	331.7	365.7
Payments to life insurance beneficiaries.	Bil. dol..	24.6	34.5	40.1	41.4	44.1	46.5	48.2	51.7	51.6	53.0
Surrender values under life insurance [3]	Bil. dol..	18.0	19.5	26.8	32.8	27.2	30.7	32.9	35.9	35.5	39.2
Surrender values under annuity contracts [3, 4]	Bil. dol..	(NA)	105.4	154.5	198.3	214.0	151.3	142.9	140.3	162.9	190.3
Policyholder dividends	Bil. dol..	12.0	17.8	18.9	19.1	20.0	20.0	21.0	20.8	19.0	17.9
Annuity payments [4]	Bil. dol..	32.6	48.5	60.4	62.5	68.7	55.2	55.0	57.1	61.2	63.9
Matured endowments	Bil. dol..	0.7	1.0	0.6	0.5	0.6	0.5	0.6	0.6	0.6	0.6
Other payments	Bil. dol..	0.6	0.9	0.6	0.6	0.6	0.6	0.6	0.7	0.9	0.7
Health insurance benefit payments	Bil. dol. .	40.0	64.7	70.0	74.5	78.8	76.3	78.7	81.9	88.5	79.6
BALANCE SHEET											
Assets	**Bil. dol.** .	1,408	2,144	2,827	3,071	3,182	3,269	3,380	3,887	4,253	4,482
Government bonds	Bil. dol..	211	409	379	362	364	377	481	538	563	590
Corporate securities	Bil. dol..	711	1,241	1,898	2,180	2,238	2,263	2,266	2,666	2,965	3,136
Percent of total assets . . .	Percent .	50	58	67	71	70	69	67	69	70	70
Bonds	Bil. dol..	583	869	1,140	1,190	1,241	1,354	1,475	1,644	1,785	1,850
Stocks	Bil. dol..	128	372	758	990	997	909	791	1,022	1,180	1,285
Mortgages.	Bil. dol..	270	212	216	230	237	244	251	269	283	295
Real estate	Bil. dol..	43	52	41	38	36	32	33	31	31	33
Policy loans	Bil. dol..	63	96	105	99	102	104	105	107	109	110
Other	Bil. dol..	110	133	187	163	204	248	244	276	303	319
Interest earned on assets [5]	Percent .	8.89	7.41	6.95	6.71	7.05	6.31	5.38	5.03	4.80	4.90
Obligations and surplus funds [6] . .	Bil. dol..	1,408	2,144	2,826	3,071	3,182	3,269	3,380	3,888	4,253	4,482
Policy reserves	**Bil. dol.**	1,197	1,812	2,377	2,610	2,719	2,446	2,507	2,895	3,160	3,360
Annuities [7]	Bil. dol..	798	1,213	1,608	1,781	1,841	1,516	1,550	1,835	2,024	2,174
Group	Bil. dol..	516	619	845	907	960	571	570	662	712	758
Individual	Bil. dol..	282	594	763	874	881	945	980	1,173	1,312	1,415
Supplementary contracts [8] . .	Bil. dol..	17	25	31	32	34	13	14	15	16	16
Life insurance	Bil. dol..	349	511	656	705	742	816	833	921	988	1,029
Health insurance	Bil. dol..	33	63	82	92	96	101	111	123	134	141
Liabilities for deposit-type contracts [9]	Bil. dol..	18	20	21	21	21	338	364	405	445	456
Capital and surplus	Bil. dol..	91	151	173	181	188	191	202	231	250	256

NA Not available. [1] Beginning 1995, includes life insurance companies that sell accident and health insurance. [2] Beginning 2001, excludes certain deposit-type funds from income due to codification. [3] Beginning with 1995, "surrender values" include annuity withdrawals of funds, which were not included in prior years. [4] Beginning 2001, excludes payments under deposit-type contracts. [5] Net rate. [6] Includes other obligations not shown separately. [7] Beginning 2001, excludes reserves for guaranteed interest contracts (GICs). [8] Through 2000, includes reserves for contracts with and without life contingencies; beginning 2001, includes only reserves for contracts with life contingencies. [9] Policyholder dividend accumulations for all years. Beginning 2001, also includes liabilities for guaranteed interest contracts, supplementary contracts without life contingencies, and premium and other deposits.

Source: American Council of Life Insurers, Washington, DC, *Life Insurers Fact Book*, annual (copyright).

748 Banking, Finance, and Insurance

Table 1195. Property and Casualty Insurance—Summary: 2000 to 2005

[In billions of dollars (305.1 represents $305,100,000,000). Minus sign (−) indicates loss]

Item	2000	2001	2002	2003	2004	2005
Premiums, net written [1]	305.1	327.8	373.1	407.5	425.7	427.4
Automobile, private [2]	120.0	128.1	139.6	151.3	157.6	159.7
Automobile, commercial [2]	19.8	21.8	24.6	25.5	26.7	26.8
Fire	(NA)	5.1	7.4	8.4	8.1	7.9
Homeowners' multiple peril	32.7	35.4	40.2	46.0	50.0	53.0
Commercial multiple peril	(NA)	22.5	25.4	27.4	20.1	29.7
Marine, inland and ocean	8.0	8.7	9.4	10.4	10.8	11.2
Accident and health	14.5	15.6	15.6	11.9	9.8	9.6
Workers' compensation	26.2	27.1	30.6	32.9	36.7	39.7
Medical malpractice	(NA)	6.3	7.4	8.8	9.1	9.7
Other liability [3]	(NA)	20.0	29.3	36.1	39.8	39.1
Reinsurance	(NA)	11.8	15.1	15.5	13.7	6.6
Losses and expenses	321.3	361.8	377.4	389.4	407.7	421.7
Underwriting gain/loss	−27.3	−52.6	−30.8	−4.9	4.3	−5.9
Net investment income	41.5	38.6	39.5	39.8	40.3	50.3
Operating earnings after taxes	4.4	−13.6	4.3	23.5	29.4	33.3
Assets	914.0	949.1	1,061.3	1,193.2	1,300.5	1,398.2
Policyholders' surplus	320.5	294.9	296.9	359.5	404.6	437.9

NA Not available. [1] Excludes state funds. [2] Includes premiums for automobile liability and physical damage. [3] Coverages protecting against legal liability resulting from negligence, carelessness, or failure to act.
Source: Insurance Information Institute, New York, NY, The III Insurance Fact Book, annual (copyright). See also <http://www.iii.org>.

Table 1196. Automobile Insurance—Average Expenditures Per Insured Vehicle by State: 2000 to 2004

[In dollars. Average expenditure equals total premiums written divided by liability car-years. A car-year is equal to 365 days of insured coverage for a single vehicle. The average expenditures for automobile insurance in a state are affected by a number of factors, including the underlying rate structure, the coverages purchased, the deductibles and limits selected, the types of vehicles insured, and the distribution of driver characteristics. The NAIC does not rank state average expenditures and does not endorse any conclusions drawn from this data]

State	2000	2003	2004	State	2000	2003	2004	State	2000	2003	2004
U.S.	690	823	838	KS	540	611	603	ND	477	537	562
				KY	616	739	758	OH	579	672	680
AL	594	657	677	LA	806	1,015	1,062	OK	603	689	690
AK	770	938	974	ME	528	633	650	OR	625	736	753
AZ	792	921	931	MD	757	893	947	PA	699	813	843
AR	606	698	708	MA	946	1,052	1,113	RI	825	997	1,034
CA	672	828	833	MI	702	950	980	SC	620	745	763
CO	755	923	850	MN	696	837	829	SD	482	564	587
CT	871	988	991	MS	654	710	749	TN	592	650	666
DE	849	977	1,022	MO	612	702	702	TX	678	837	847
DC	996	1,135	1,185	MT	530	675	683	UT	620	733	722
FL	781	1,018	1,062	NE	533	624	637	VT	568	683	693
GA	674	759	779	NV	829	914	939	VA	576	658	702
HI	702	776	817	NH	665	779	798	WA	722	825	839
ID	505	586	590	NJ	977	1,193	1,221	WV	680	844	875
IL	652	762	760	NM	674	732	728	WI	545	621	636
IN	570	671	671	NY	939	1,168	1,172	WY	496	618	629
IA	479	581	580	NC	564	605	597				

Source: National Association of Insurance Commissioners (NAIC), Kansas City, MO, Auto Insurance Database Report, annual (copyright). Reprinted with permission of the NAIC. Further reprint or distribution strictly prohibited without prior written permission of the NAIC.

Table 1197. Renters and Homeowners Insurance—Average Premiums by State: 2004

[In dollars. Average premium equals premiums divided by exposure per house-years. A house-year is equal to 365 days of insured coverage for a single dwelling and is the standard measurement for homeowners insurance]

State	Renters [1]	Homeowners [2]	State	Renters [1]	Homeowners [2]	State	Renters [1]	Homeowners [2]
U.S.	195	729	KS	180	833	ND	130	704
			KY	165	615	OH	169	523
AL	226	793	LA	253	1,074	OK	257	991
AK	191	810	ME	145	513	OR	174	492
AZ	227	642	MD	160	652	PA	150	593
AR	229	768	MA	215	759	RI	194	769
CA	265	835	MI	184	726	SC	190	768
CO	181	811	MN	156	767	SD	127	601
CT	201	777	MS	262	907	TN	212	681
DE	163	488	MO	182	689	TX [3]	277	1,362
DC	189	894	MT	163	661	UT	151	473
FL	199	929	NE	153	730	VT	157	608
GA	215	635	NV	217	632	VA	153	616
HI	209	726	NH	162	599	WA	177	590
ID	159	448	NJ	181	641	WV	175	616
IL	186	659	NM	203	585	WI	128	483
IN	181	636	NY	220	785	WY	164	650
IA	144	575	NC	155	623			

[1] Based on the HO-4 renters insurance policy for tenants. Includes broad named-peril coverage for the personal property of tenants. [2] Based on the HO-3 homeowner package policy for owner-occupied dwellings, 1–4 family units. Provides "all risks" coverage (except those specifically excluded in the policy) on buildings, broad named-peril coverage on personal property, and is the most common package policy. [3] The Texas Insurance Commissioner promulgates residential policy forms which are similar but not identical to the standard forms.
Source: National Association of Insurance Commissioners (NAIC), Kansas City, MO, Dwelling Fire, Homeowners Owner-Occupied, and Homeowners Tenant and Condominium/Cooperative Unit Owners Insurance (copyright). Reprinted with permission of the NAIC. Further reprint or distribution strictly prohibited without prior written permission of the NAIC.

U.S. Census Bureau, Statistical Abstract of the United States: 2008

Table 1198. **Real Estate and Rental and Leasing—Nonemployer Establishments and Receipts by Kind of Business: 2000 to 2004**

[1,696 represents 1,696,000. Includes only firms subject to federal income tax. Nonemployers are businesses with no paid employees. Data originate chiefly from administrative records of the Internal Revenue Service; see Appendix III. Data for 2000 based on the North American Industry Classification System (NAICS), 1997; beginning 2003 based on NAICS 2002, see text, Section 15]

Kind of business	NAICS code	Establishments (1,000)			Receipts (mil. dol.)		
		2000	2003	2004	2000	2003	2004
Real estate & rental & leasing, total . . .	53	1,696	2,046	2,218	133,398	176,079	189,905
Real estate	531	1,616	1,964	2,135	127,862	170,133	183,662
Lessors of real estate.	5311	714	789	820	86,934	106,472	110,672
Offices of real estate agents & brokers	5312	522	629	703	22,623	29,442	34,288
Activities related to real estate	5313	380	546	612	18,305	34,220	38,701
Rental & leasing services.	532	79	80	82	5,440	5,807	6,102
Automotive equipment rental & leasing	5321	19	20	20	995	950	974
Consumer goods rental	5322	17	17	18	766	764	811
General rental centers	5323	3	3	4	252	316	338
Commercial/industrial equipment rental & leasing.	5324	41	40	40	3,426	3,778	3,979
Lessors of other nonfinancial intangible assets.	533	1	1	1	96	138	141

Source: U.S. Census Bureau, "Nonemployer Statistics"; <http://www.census.gov/epcd/nonemployer/>.

Table 1199. **Real Estate and Rental and Leasing—Establishments, Employees, and Payroll: 2000 and 2004**

[300.2 represents 300,200. Covers establishments with payroll. Kind-of-business classification for 2000 based on North American Industry Classification System (NAICS) 1997; data for 2004 based on NAICS 2002. See text, Section 15, Business Enterprise. Employees are for the week including March 12. Most government employees are excluded. For statement on methodology, see Appendix III]

Kind of business	NAICS code	Establishments (1,000)		Employees (1,000)		Payroll (bil. dol.)	
		2000	2004	2000	2004	2000	2004
Real estate & rental & leasing, total . . .	53	300.2	348.7	1,942	2,086	59.2	74.1
Real estate	531	234.9	282.1	1,280	1,432	40.4	53.5
Lessors of real estate.	5311	108.2	114.1	501	527	12.5	15.5
Offices of real estate agents & brokers	5312	65.1	93.9	271	323	10.6	15.2
Activities related to real estate	5313	61.6	74.2	507	582	17.3	22.8
Rental & leasing services.	532	63.2	64.3	636	625	17.2	18.5
Automotive equipment rental & leasing	5321	11.1	11.4	182	172	5.1	5.7
Passenger car rental & leasing.	53211	5.2	5.4	129	121	3.4	3.7
Truck, utility trailer, & RV rental & leasing.	53212	5.8	6.0	53	52	1.7	2.0
Consumer goods rental [1]	5322	33.1	34.2	255	264	4.2	5.1
Video tape & disk rental	53223	19.6	19.1	152	154	1.6	1.8
General rental centers	5323	6.4	5.2	42	33	1.2	1.0
Commercial/industrial equipment rental & leasing	5324	12.6	13.5	157	155	6.7	6.8
Lessors of other nonfinancial intangible assets.	533	2.1	2.3	26	29	1.6	2.1

[1] Includes other kinds of business not shown separately.

Source: U.S. Census Bureau, "County Business Patterns"; <http://www.census.gov/epcd/cbp/view/cbpview.html>.

Table 1200. **Rental and Leasing Services—Revenue by Kind of Business: 2000 to 2005**

[In millions of dollars (98,504 represents $98,504,000,000). Based on the North American Industry Classification System (NAICS) 2002; see text, Section 15. Covers taxable and tax-exempt employer firms. Estimates have been adjusted using the results of the 2002 Economic Census. Based on Service Annual Survey; see Appendix III]

Kind of business	2002 NAICS code	2000	2001	2002	2003	2004	2005
Rental & leasing services	532	98,504	96,932	95,108	96,387	102,863	109,959
Automotive equipment rental & leasing.	5321	37,231	36,035	35,779	37,007	41,126	43,785
Passenger car rental & leasing	53211	22,949	22,485	22,683	23,007	24,793	25,957
Truck, utility trailer, & RV rental & leasing . . .	53212	14,282	13,550	13,096	14,000	16,333	17,828
Consumer goods rental [1]	5322	20,159	20,760	20,701	21,923	23,412	23,641
Video tape & disk rental	53223	9,569	9,584	9,364	10,053	10,604	10,243
General rental centers.	5323	3,636	3,337	3,387	3,611	3,710	3,791
Commercial/industrial equip rental & leasing . . .	5324	37,478	36,800	35,241	33,846	34,615	38,742

[1] Includes other kinds of business not shown separately.

Source: U.S. Census Bureau, "Service Annual Survey: 2005"; published February 2007; <http://www.census.gov/econ/www/servmenu.html>.

Arts, Recreation, and Travel

This section presents data on the arts, entertainment, and recreation economic sector of the economy, and personal recreational activities, the arts and humanities, and domestic and foreign travel.

Arts, Entertainment, and Recreation Industry—The U.S. Census Bureau's *Service Annual Survey, Arts, Entertainment, and Recreation Sector,* provides estimates of operation revenue of taxable firms and revenues and expenses of firms exempt from federal taxes for industries in this sector of the economy. Data beginning 1998 are based on the North American Industry Classification System (NAICS). Most establishments were previously classified in the Standard Industrial Classification (SIC) in services, some in retail trade.

This new sector is comprised of industries which existed previously, were revised from previous industry definitions, or are completely new industries. Among those which existed previously are amusement and theme parks. Revised industries include museums. New industries include theater companies and dinner theaters. The following URL contains detailed information about NAICS and provides a comparison of the SIC and NAICS <http://www.census.gov/epcd/www/naics.html>. See also the text in Section 15, Business Enterprise.

The Economic Census, conducted every 5 years, for the years ending "2" and "7," provides information on the number of establishments, receipts, payroll, and paid employees for the U.S. and various geographic levels.

Recreation and leisure activities— Data on the participation in various recreation and leisure time activities are based on several sample surveys. Data on participation in fishing, hunting, and other forms of wildlife-associated recreation are published periodically by the U.S. Department of Interior, Fish and Wildlife Service. The most recent data are from the 2001 survey. Data on participation in various sports recreation activities are published by the National Sporting Goods Association. Mediamark, Inc. also conducts periodic surveys on sports and leisure activities, as well as other topics.

Parks and recreation—The Department of the Interior has responsibility for administering the national parks. The National Park Service publishes information on visits to national park areas in its annual report, *National Park Statistical Abstract.* The National Parks: Index (year) is an annual report which contains brief descriptions, with acreages, of each area administered by the service, plus certain "related" areas. This information can be found at: <http://www2.nature.nps.gov/stats>. Statistics for state parks are compiled by the National Association of State Park Directors.

Travel—Statistics on arrivals and departures to the United States are reported by the International Trade Administration (ITA), Office of Travel & Tourism Industries (OTTI). Data on domestic travel, business receipts and employment of the travel industry, and travel expenditures are published by the research department of the Travel Industry Association (TIA). Other data on household transportation characteristics are in Section 23, Transportation.

Statistical reliability—For a discussion of statistical collection and estimation, sampling procedures, and measures of statistical reliability applicable to Census Bureau data, see Appendix III.

Table 1201. Arts, Entertainment, and Recreation Services—Estimated Revenue: 2000 to 2005

[In millions of dollars (127,394 represents $127,394,000,000), except percent. For taxable and tax-exempt employer firms. Except where indicated, estimates adjusted using the results of the 2002 Economic Census. Minus sign (–) indicates decrease. Based on the Service Annual Survey, see Appendix III]

Industry	2002 NAICS code [1]	2000 [2]	2002 [2]	2003 [2]	2004 [2]	2005	Percent change, 2004–2005
Arts, entertainment, and recreation	71	127,394	141,902	149,360	158,557	165,540	4.4
Performing arts, spectator sports.	711	51,149	58,285	60,367	62,796	64,891	3.3
Performing arts companies	7111	10,746	10,864	11,070	11,554	11,987	3.7
Spectator sports	7112	19,339	22,313	22,445	23,659	24,489	3.5
Sports teams and clubs	711211	10,739	13,025	13,257	14,115	14,010	-0.7
Racetracks.	711212	6,349	6,702	6,582	7,022	7,570	7.8
Other spectator sports	711219	2,251	2,586	2,606	2,522	2,909	15.3
Promoters of performing arts, sports, and similar events	7113	10,098	12,168	12,872	13,571	14,135	4.2
Agents and managers for artists, athletes, entertainers, and other public figures	7114	3,184	3,602	3,604	3,819	3,672	-3.8
Independent artists, writers, and performers.	7115	7,782	9,338	10,376	10,193	10,608	4.1
Museums, historical sites, and similar institutions . . .	712	9,350	8,607	9,082	9,688	10,088	4.1
Amusement, gambling, and recreation industries . . .	713	66,895	75,010	79,911	86,073	90,561	5.2
Amusement parks and arcades	7131	9,441	9,443	9,930	10,561	11,113	5.2
Amusement and theme parks	71311	8,245	8,174	8,737	9,344	9,886	5.8
Amusement arcades	71312	1,196	1,269	1,193	1,217	1,227	0.8
Gambling industries.	7132	14,621	18,893	22,370	25,698	28,000	9.0
Casinos (except casino hotels).	71321	9,592	12,387	14,601	16,664	18,074	8.5
Other gambling industries	71329	5,029	6,506	7,769	9,034	9,926	9.9
Other amusement and recreation industries.	7139	42,833	46,674	47,611	49,814	51,448	3.3
Golf courses and country clubs	71391	16,692	17,533	16,987	17,880	18,529	3.6
Skiing facilities	71392	1,551	1,801	1,839	1,980	(S)	(S)
Marinas.	71393	3,379	3,352	3,382	3,393	3,670	8.2
Fitness and recreational sports centers	71394	12,543	14,987	16,130	16,839	17,487	3.8
Bowling centers.	71395	2,762	3,075	3,293	3,505	3,415	-2.6
All other amusement and recreation	71399	5,906	5,926	5,980	6,217	6,298	1.3

S Data do not meet publication standards.   [1] Based on the North American Industry Classification System (NAICS) 2002; see text, this section and Section 15.   [2] Data has been revised.

Source: U.S. Census Bureau, "2005 Service Annual Survey, Arts, Entertainment, and Recreation Services." See <http://www.census.gov/econ/www/servmenu.html>; issued February 2007 .

Table 1202. Arts, Entertainment, and Recreation—Establishments, Revenue, Payroll, and Employees by Kind of Business (1997 NAICS Basis): 1997 and 2002

[(104,715 represents $104,715,000,000) For establishments with payroll. Data are based on the 1997 and 2002 economic censuses which are subject to nonsampling error. For details on survey methodology, sampling and nonsampling errors, see Appendix III. Based on the North American Industry Classification System (NAICS), 1997, see text, Section 15]

Kind of business	1997 NAICS code	Number of establishments		Revenue (mil. dol.)		Annual payroll (mil. dol.)		Paid employees (1,000)	
		1997	2002	1997	2002	1997	2002	1997	2002
Arts, entertainment and recreation, total	71	99,099	110,324	104,715	141,923	32,787	45,175	1,588	1,849
Performing arts, spectator sports, and related industries [1]	711	30,566	37,737	37,619	58,286	14,456	21,232	327	423
Performing arts companies	7111	9,199	9,303	8,570	10,864	2,725	3,267	122	138
Spectator sports	7112	3,881	4,072	13,656	22,313	6,151	10,206	92	108
Promoters of performing arts, sports and similar events	7113	3,941	4,521	6,622	11,698	1,401	2,020	72	99
Agents and managers for artists, athletes, entertainers and others . . .	7114	2,532	3,977	2,410	4,073	911	1,415	13	21
Museums, historical sites, and similar institutions [1]	712	5,580	6,664	6,764	8,609	1,837	2,936	92	123
Amusement, gambling, and recreation industries [1]	713	62,914	65,923	58,463	75,028	20,792	21,007	1,146	1,303
Amusement parks and arcades	7131	3,344	3,015	8,418	9,443	1,962	2,069	139	122
Gambling industries	7132	2,060	2,075	13,673	18,902	2,728	3,599	146	158
Other amusement and recreation services	7139	57,510	60,833	36,372	46,682	11,310	15,339	862	1,023

[1] Includes other industries not shown separately.

Source: U.S. Census Bureau, "2002 Economic Census, Comparative Statistics for United States; Arts, Entertainment, and Recreation; <http://www.census.gov/econ/census02/data/comparative/USCS_71.HTM> (accessed 14 June 2007).

Table 1203. **Arts, Entertainment, and Recreation—Nonemployer Establishments and Receipts by Kind of Business (NAICS Basis): 2000 to 2004**

[(781.7 represents 781,700). Includes only firms subject to federal income tax. Nonemployers are businesses with no paid employees]

Kind of business	2002 NAICS code [1]	Establishments (1,000)			Receipts (mil. dol.)		
		2000	2003	2004	2000	2003	2004
Arts, entertainment, and recreation	71	781.7	888.1	923.1	17,713	21,010	22,448
Performing arts, spectator sports, and related industries	711	645.4	751.8	781.8	13,008	15,536	16,637
Performing arts companies	7111	19.3	27.4	29.3	576	700	766
Spectator sports	7112	67.3	91.5	91.0	1,481	1,820	1,894
Promoters of performing arts, sports, and similar events	7113	23.1	31.8	33.9	851	1,203	1,292
Agents/managers for artists, athletes, and other public figures	7114	27.1	30.5	31.8	857	1,051	1,111
Independent artists, writers and performers.......................	7115	508.6	570.6	595.8	9,244	10,763	11,573
Museums, historical sites, and similar institutions.......................	712	3.6	4.7	5.5	52	68	80
Amusement, gambling, and recreation industries	713	132.7	131.7	135.8	4,653	5,406	5,732
Amusement parks and arcades	7131	5.4	5.3	5.7	291	339	372
Gambling industries................	7132	5.9	7.2	7.8	532	927	1,049
Other amusement and recreation services...	7139	121.3	119.1	122.4	3,830	4,140	4,311

[1] Based on the 2002 North American Industry Classification System (NAICS); see text, Section 15.
Source: U.S. Census Bureau, "Nonemployer Statistics;" published July 2006; <http://www.census.gov/epcd/nonemployer/index.html>.

Table 1204. **Arts, Entertainment, and Recreation—Establishments, Payroll, and Employees by Kind of Business (NAICS Basis): 2000 and 2004**

[(1,741.5 represents 1,741,500). For establishments with payroll. See Appendix III]

Kind of business	2002 NAICS [1] code	Establishments		Paid employees [2] (1,000)		Annual payroll (mil. dol.)	
		2000	2004	2000	2004	2000	2004
Arts, entertainment, & recreation	71	103,816	118,827	1,741.5	1,889.0	43,204	50,710
Performing arts, spectator sports	711	33,859	40,464	351.9	398.1	19,090	23,193
Performing arts companies	7111	9,253	9,284	126.4	125.9	3,251	3,417
Theater companies & dinner theaters......	71111	3,367	3,607	63.4	67.0	1,469	1,668
Dance companies..................	71112	584	566	10.7	9.3	216	204
Musical groups & artists..............	71113	4,497	4,561	44.0	42.6	1,341	1,336
Other performing arts companies.	71119	805	550	8.3	7.0	226	208
Spectator sports	7112	4,461	4,350	100.2	112.5	9,215	11,155
Sports teams & clubs	711211	684	770	36.3	44.7	7,587	9,240
Racetracks	711212	899	747	45.8	49.7	994	1,165
Other spectator sports...............	711219	2,878	2,833	18.1	18.1	633	750
Promoters of performing arts, sports, and similar events	7113	4,394	5,542	71.8	98.7	1,917	2,295
Promoters of performing arts, sports, & similar events with facilities.	71131	1,107	1,995	44.3	74.6	787	1,416
Promoters of performing arts, sports, & similar events without facilities........	71132	3,287	3,547	27.6	24.1	1,130	879
Agents/managers for artists, athletes, and other public figures..................	7114	3,048	3,410	16.0	16.4	1,117	1,462
Independent artists, writers, & performers.....	7115	12,703	17,878	37.5	44.6	3,589	4,863
Museums, historical sites, & similar institutions ...	712	5,777	6,934	110.4	118.9	2,549	3,062
Museums	71211	3,988	4,714	75.4	78.7	1,765	2,050
Historical sites....................	71212	892	995	8.3	9.7	143	205
Zoos & botanical gardens	71213	414	611	20.5	25.4	509	675
Nature parks & other similar institutions	71219	483	614	6.2	5.1	133	133
Amusement, gambling, & recreation industries ...	713	64,180	71,429	1,279.2	1,372.1	21,564	24,455
Amusement parks & arcades	7131	2,879	2,964	124.0	138.8	2,277	2,644
Amusement & theme parks	71311	716	563	102.8	111.8	2,011	2,295
Amusement arcades	71312	2,163	2,401	21.3	27.1	266	349
Gambling industries	7132	2,191	2,305	202.6	179.0	4,757	4,785
Casinos (except casino hotels)	71321	537	459	150.2	124.6	3,592	3,383
Other gambling industries	71329	1,654	1,846	52.4	54.5	1,165	1,401
Other amusement & recreation services......	7139	59,110	66,160	952.6	1,054.2	14,531	17,026
Golf courses & country clubs	71391	11,885	12,070	297.9	303.7	6,243	7,244
Skiing facilities....................	71392	389	383	56.9	73.1	452	566
Marinas	71393	4,126	4,092	24.8	28.1	640	815
Fitness & recreational sports centers	71394	23,003	30,624	382.8	479.2	4,499	5,838
Bowling centers	71395	5,234	4,747	87.9	85.3	888	945
All other amusement & recreation industries	71399	14,473	14,244	102.4	84.8	1,808	1,617

[1] North American Industry Classification System code (NAICS); see text, this section and Section 15. [2] For employees on the payroll for the period including March 12.
Source: U.S. Census Bureau, "County Business Patterns;" annual. See <http://www.census.gov/epcd/cbp/view/cbpview.html>.

Arts, Recreation, and Travel 753

Table 1205. **Expenditures Per Consumer Unit for Entertainment and Reading: 1985 to 2005**

[Data are annual averages. In dollars, except as indicated. Based on Consumer Expenditure Survey (CE); see text in Section 13 for description of survey. See also headnote, Table 664. Consumer Expenditures Survey has implemented multiple imputation of income data, starting with the publication of the 2004 tables. Because of income imputation, data for 2004 are not strictly comparable to data from previous years, especially for income tables. Thus, income data are available for all consumer units and data are no longer shown for complete income reporters. For more information, go to <http://www.bls.gov/cex/csxann04.pdf>, page 4. For composition of regions, see map, inside front cover]

| Year and characteristic | Entertainment and reading | | Entertainment | | | | |
	Total	Percent of total expenditures	Total	Fees and admissions	Audio and visual equipment, and services	Other entertainment supplies, equipment, and services [1]	Reading
1985	1,311	5.6	1,170	320	371	479	141
1989	1,581	5.7	1,424	377	429	618	157
1990	1,575	5.6	1,422	371	454	597	153
1991	1,635	5.5	1,472	378	468	627	163
1992	1,662	5.6	1,500	379	492	629	162
1993	1,792	5.8	1,626	414	590	621	166
1994	1,732	5.5	1,567	439	533	595	165
1995	1,775	5.5	1,612	433	542	637	163
1996	1,993	5.9	1,834	459	561	814	159
1997	1,977	5.7	1,813	471	577	766	164
1998	1,907	5.4	1,746	449	535	762	161
1999	2,050	5.5	1,891	459	608	824	159
2000	2,009	5.3	1,863	515	622	727	146
2001	2,094	5.3	1,953	526	660	767	141
2002	2,218	5.5	2,079	542	692	845	139
2003	2,187	5.4	2,060	494	730	835	127
2004	2,348	5.4	2,218	528	788	903	130
2005, total	**2,514**	**5.4**	**2,388**	**588**	**888**	**912**	**126**
Age of reference person:							
Under 25 years old	1,442	5.2	1,393	249	631	512	49
25 to 34 years old	2,544	5.6	2,455	489	943	1,023	89
35 to 44 years old	2,886	5.2	2,765	753	1,029	984	121
45 to 54 years old	3,177	5.7	3,034	753	1,046	1,236	143
55 to 64 years old	2,596	5.2	2,429	633	862	934	167
65 to 74 years old	2,297	6.0	2,143	548	797	798	154
75 years old and over	1,164	4.3	1,032	282	484	266	132
Hispanic or Latino origin of reference person:							
Hispanic	1,549	3.9	1,494	337	716	441	55
Non-Hispanic	2,629	5.6	2,494	618	908	968	135
Race of reference person:							
White, Asian, and other races	2,680	5.6	2,543	641	900	1,002	137
Black	1,294	3.9	1,242	201	797	245	52
Region of residence:							
Northeast	2,411	5.0	2,263	615	903	746	148
Midwest	2,516	5.6	2,384	614	839	931	132
South	2,206	5.2	2,112	451	868	793	94
West	3,105	5.9	2,950	760	959	1,232	155
Size of consumer unit:							
One person	1,438	5.4	1,335	336	591	408	103
Two or more persons	2,958	5.4	2,822	692	1,011	1,118	136
Two persons	2,771	5.7	2,622	605	897	1,120	149
Three persons	2,738	5.0	2,615	634	1,051	930	123
Four persons	3,288	5.3	3,152	876	1,110	1,166	136
Five persons or more	3,481	5.6	3,364	821	1,182	1,361	117
Income before taxes:							
Quintiles of income:							
Lowest 20 percent	943	4.9	891	145	459	287	52
Second 20 percent	1,421	4.9	1,336	243	623	471	85
Third 20 percent	1,918	4.9	1,813	349	799	665	105
Fourth 20 percent	3,028	5.6	2,885	633	1,036	1,216	143
Highest 20 percent	5,256	5.8	5,009	1,568	1,521	1,920	247
Education:							
Less than a high school graduate	1,194	4.4	1,152	123	553	476	42
High school graduate	1,964	5.1	1,877	331	777	769	87
High school graduate with some college	2,563	5.8	2,450	489	909	1,052	113
Associate's degree	2,828	5.7	2,709	564	993	1,153	119
Bachelor's degree	3,358	5.5	3,174	1,049	1,089	1,036	184
Master's, professional, doctoral degree	4,092	5.6	3,797	1,403	1,194	1,200	295

[1] Other equipment and services include pets, toys, and playground equipment; sports, exercise, and photographic equipment; and recreational vehicles.

Source: U.S. Bureau of Labor Statistics, *Consumer Expenditure Survey*, annual and Current Standard Tables. See also <http://www.bls.gov/cex/home/htm>.

Table 1206. **Personal Consumption Expenditures for Recreation: 1990 to 2005**

[In billions of dollars (290.2 represents $290,200,000,000), except percent. Represents market value of purchases of goods and services by individuals and nonprofit institutions]

Type of product or service	1990	1995	2000	2002	2003	2004	2005
Total recreation expenditures	290.2	418.1	585.7	629.9	659.9	708.4	756.3
Percent of total personal consumption [1]	7.6	8.4	8.7	8.6	8.6	8.6	8.7
Books and maps	16.2	23.2	33.7	37.1	38.7	40.6	42.2
Magazines, newspapers, and sheet music	21.6	27.5	35.0	35.1	36.3	30.6	43.8
Nondurable toys and sport supplies	32.8	44.4	56.6	59.2	60.6	63.5	67.2
Wheel goods, sports, and photographic equipment [2]	29.7	39.7	57.6	61.4	65.6	71.4	81.5
Video and audio products, computer equipment, and musical instruments	53.0	81.5	116.6	120.0	123.1	133.4	141.2
Video and audio goods, including musical instruments	44.1	57.2	72.8	75.4	76.5	81.8	85.8
Computers, peripherals, and software	8.9	24.3	43.8	44.6	46.6	51.6	55.4
Radio and television repair.	3.2	3.6	4.2	4.1	4.1	4.6	4.8
Flowers, seeds, and potted plants	10.9	14.0	18.0	18.0	17.9	18.3	19.7
Admissions to specified spectator amusements	15.1	21.1	30.4	34.8	36.0	37.4	38.3
Motion picture theaters	5.1	5.6	8.6	9.6	9.9	9.9	9.7
Legitimate theaters and opera, and entertainments of nonprofit institutions [3]	5.2	8.1	10.3	11.7	11.9	12.4	12.7
Spectator sports [4]	4.8	7.4	11.5	13.5	14.3	15.1	15.9
Clubs and fraternal organizations except insurance [5]	13.5	17.4	19.0	21.1	22.2	22.3	23.5
Commercial participant amusements [6]	25.2	48.8	75.8	83.7	91.2	100.7	107.3
Parimutuel net receipts	3.5	3.7	5.0	5.3	5.2	5.6	6.2
Other [7]	65.4	93.4	133.9	150.0	158.9	170.9	180.0

[1] See Table 655. [2] Includes boats and pleasure aircraft. [3] Except athletic. [4] Consists of admissions to professional and amateur athletic events and to racetracks, including horse, dog, and auto. [5] Consists of current expenditures (including consumption of fixed capital) of nonprofit clubs and fraternal organizations and dues and fees paid to proprietary clubs. [6] Consists of billiard parlors; bowling alleys; dancing, riding, shooting, skating, and swimming places; amusement devices and parks; golf courses; sightseeing buses and guides; private flying operations; casino gambling; and other commercial participant amusements. [7] Consists of net receipts of lotteries and expenditures for purchases of pets and pet care services, cable TV, film processing, photographic studios, sporting and recreation camps, video cassette rentals, and recreational services, not elsewhere classified.

Source: Bureau of Economic Analysis, *Survey of Current Business*, April 2007. See also <http://www.bea.gov/bea/dn/nipaweb/index.asp>.

Table 1207. **Performing Arts—Selected Data: 1990 to 2005**

[Sales, receipts, and expenditures in millions of dollars (282 represents $282,000,000). For season ending in year shown, except as indicated]

Item	1990	1995	1998	1999	2000	2001	2002	2003	2004	2005
Legitimate theater: [1]										
Broadway shows:										
New productions	40	33	33	39	37	28	37	36	39	39
Attendance (mil.)	8.0	9.0	11.5	11.7	11.4	11.9	11.0	11.4	11.6	11.5
Playing weeks [2, 3]	1,070	1,120	1,442	1,441	1,464	1,484	1,434	1,544	1,451	1,494
Gross ticket sales	282	406	558	588	603	666	643	721	771	769
Broadway road tours: [4]										
Attendance (mil.)	11.1	15.6	15.2	14.6	11.7	11.0	11.7	12.4	12.9	18.2
Playing weeks.	944	1,242	1,127	1,082	888	823	863	877	1,060	1,389
Gross ticket sales	367	701	721	707	572	541	593	642	714	934
Nonprofit professional theatres: [5]										
Companies reporting [6]	185	215	189	313	262	363	1,146	1,274	1,477	1,490
Gross income.	307.6	444.4	570.0	740.0	791.0	961.1	1,436.0	1,481.0	1,570.8	1,646.6
Earned income	188.4	281.2	342.0	442.0	466.0	554.5	761.0	787.0	856.2	845.0
Contributed income	119.2	163.1	228.0	298.0	325.0	406.6	675.0	694.0	714.6	801.6
Gross expenses	306.3	444.9	518.5	701.0	708.0	923.6	1,405.0	1,476.0	1,464.4	1,529.8
Productions	2,265	2,646	2,135	3,921	3,241	4,787	10,000	13,000	11,000	12,000
Performances.	46,131	56,608	46,628	64,556	66,123	81,828	157,000	170,000	169,000	169,000
Total attendance (mil.)	15.2	18.6	14.6	18.0	22.0	21.1	32.2	34.3	32.1	32.5
OPERA America professional member companies: [7]										
Number of companies reporting [8] . . .	98	88	89	95	98	96	86	89	95	93
Expenses [8]	321.2	435.0	556.3	591.1	636.7	685.1	684.4	691.6	677.9	754.5
Performances [9]	2,336	2,251	2,222	2,200	2,153	2,031	1,868.0	1,730	1,946	2,097
Total attendance (mil.) [9, 10]	7.5	6.5	6.6	6.6	6.7	6.5	4.9	5.9	5.1	5.1
Main season attendance (mil.) [9, 11] . .	4.1	3.9	3.7	4.0	4.3	4.2	3.2	3.1	3.4	3.3
Symphony orchestras: [12]										
Concerts	18,931	29,328	31,766	31,549	33,154	36,437	37,118	38,182	37,263	(NA)
Attendance (mil.).	24.7	30.9	32.2	30.8	31.7	31.5	30.3	27.8	27.7	(NA)
Gross revenue	377.5	536.2	627.6	671.8	734.0	774.7	763.6	781.2	826.8	(NA)
Operating expenses	621.7	858.8	1,012.0	1,088.0	1,126.3	1,285.9	1,311.9	1,314.8	1,482.6	(NA)
Support	257.8	351.0	459.7	486.0	521.0	556.9	580.0	575.7	639.4	(NA)

NA Not available. [1] Source: The League of American Theaters and Producers, Inc, New York, NY. For season ending in year shown. [2] All shows (new productions and holdovers from previous seasons). [3] Eight performances constitute one playing week. [4] North American Tours include U.S. and Canadian companies. [5] Source: Theatre Communications Group, New York, NY. For years ending on or prior to Aug. 31. [6] Beginning in 2002, nonprofit theatre data is based on survey responses and extrapolated data from IRS Form 990. [7] Source: OPERA America, New York, NY. For years ending on or prior to Aug 31. [8] U.S. companies. [9] Prior to 1993, and for 1999, U.S. and Canadian companies; 1993 to 1998 and 2000 to 2004, U.S. companies only. [10] Includes educational performances, outreach, etc. [11] For paid performances. [12] Source: American Symphony Orchestra League, Inc., New York, NY. For years ending Aug. 31. Prior to 1995, represents 254 U.S. orchestras; beginning 1995, represents all U.S. orchestras, excluding college/university and youth orchestras. Also, beginning 1995, data based on 1,200 orchestras.

Source: Compiled from sources listed in footnotes. See also <http://www.livebroadway.com>; <http://www.tcg.org>; <http://www.operaamerica.org/>; <http://www.symphony.org>.

Arts, Recreation, and Travel 755

Table 1208. Arts and Humanities—Selected Federal Aid Programs: 1990 to 2005

[In millions of dollars (170.8 represents $170,800,000), except as indicated. For fiscal year ending September 30]

Type of fund and program	1990	1995	1999	2000	2001	2002	2003	2004	2005
National Endowment for the Arts:									
Funds available [1]	170.8	152.1	85.0	85.2	94.0	98.6	101.0	105.5	108.8
Program appropriation	124.3	109.0	66.0	66.0	86.7	95.8	95.1	99.3	99.5
Grants awarded (number)	4,475	3,685	1,675	1,882	2,093	2,138	1,925	2,150	2,161
Funds obligated [2,3]	157.6	147.9	82.6	83.5	92.5	96.2	99.3	102.6	104.4
National Endowment for the Humanities:									
Funds available [1]	140.6	152.3	95.5	102.6	106.8	110.1	111.6	127.1	119.8
Program appropriation	114.2	125.7	80.0	82.7	86.4	89.9	89.3	98.7	99.9
Matching funds [4]	26.3	25.7	13.9	15.1	15.6	16.1	16.0	15.9	15.9
Grants awarded (number)	2,195	1,871	874	1,230	1,290	1,252	963	1,246	1,174
Funds obligated [2]	141.0	151.8	92.1	100.0	105.7	106.1	100.1	125.1	117.8
Education programs	16.3	19.2	10.3	13.0	12.1	12.1	11.3	17.4	14.6
State programs	29.6	32.0	29.3	30.6	32.1	32.8	33.0	36.3	36.9
Research grants	22.5	22.2	6.6	6.9	7.0	7.0	7.9	8.4	7.1
Fellowship program	15.3	16.5	5.6	6.1	7.0	7.7	6.9	8.1	8.9
Challenge [5]	14.6	13.8	9.9	10.8	11.9	13.4	8.3	12.6	12.7
Public programs	25.4	25.8	12.2	11.8	16.3	13.2	12.7	18.3	14.4
Preservation and access	17.5	22.2	18.2	20.7	19.2	19.8	20.7	23.7	22.4

[1] Includes other funds, not shown separately. Excludes administrative funds. [2] Includes obligations for new grants, supplemental awards on previous years' grants, and program contracts. [3] Beginning with 1997 data, the grantmaking structure changed from discipline-based categories to thematic ones. [4] Represents federal funds obligated only upon receipt or certification by endowment of matching nonfederal gifts. [5] Program designed to stimulate new sources and higher levels of giving to institutions for the purpose of guaranteeing long-term stability and financial independence. Program usually requires a match of at least 3 private dollars to each federal dollar. Funds for challenge grants are not allocated by program area because they are awarded on a grant-by-grant basis.

Source: U.S. National Endowment for the Arts, *Annual Report;* and U.S. National Endowment for the Humanities, *Annual Report.* See also <http://arts.endow.gov/>and <http://www.neh.gov/>.

Table 1209. Budgets for Selected U.S. Federal and Quasi-Governmental Organizations Funding Arts and Culture: 2004 and 2006

[In millions (489 represents 489,000,000). Independent of the Arts Endowment and its state and regional partners, other public agencies also support arts and culture. Some have the ability to offer direct funding to artists and arts-related or cultural organizations, but many others specialize in producing, archiving, or exhibiting artworks or performances for the public's benefit]

Organization	2004	2006	Organization	2004	2006
Smithsonian Institution [1]	489	517	Department of Education (Arts in Education Model Development Program)	10	13
Corporation for Public Broadcasting	377	460	Commission of Fine Arts	8	2
Institute of Museum and Library Services	262	247	National Capital Planning Commission	8	8
National Endowment for the Humanities	135	142	General Services Administration (Art-in-architecture Program)	5	7
National Endowment for the Arts	121	124	Advisory Council on Historic Preservation	4	5
National Gallery of Art	88	95	Department of State (Bureau of Education and Cultural Affairs' cultural exchanges, presentations, and diplomacy)	(NA)	5
Department of Interior (Save America's Treasures)	30	28			
Kennedy Center for the Performing Arts	17	18			

NA Not available. [1] Exclusive of buildings and facilities capital.

Source: National Endowment for the Arts, How the United States Funds the Arts. See also <http://www.nea.gov/pub/how.pdf>.

Table 1210. Participation in Various Arts Activities: 2002

[In percent. For persons 18 years old and over. Covers activities engaged in at least once in the prior 12 months. See headnote in Table 1211]

Item	Classical music	Other dance [1]	Painting	Pottery [2]	Sewing	Photo-graphy [3]	Writing	Purchased art recently	Choir/chorale
Total	1.8	4.2	8.6	6.9	16.0	11.5	7.0	29.5	4.8
Sex:									
Male	1.5	3.3	6.4	4.9	2.4	10.8	5.8	29.7	3.8
Female	2.1	4.9	10.6	8.7	28.5	12.1	8.2	29.3	5.7
Race and ethnicity:									
White alone	2.1	4.1	9.4	7.6	17.6	12.8	7.6	28.9	4.5
African American alone	0.4	3.5	5.6	4.1	9.4	7.6	7.4	35.9	9.1
Other alone	2.3	5.8	7.4	6.5	14.9	11.9	5.3	26.3	3.5
Hispanic	0.7	4.2	6.8	5.1	12.5	6.7	4.0	37.5	2.9
Age:									
18 to 24 years old	2.5	6.0	15.4	9.3	10.4	12.9	12.7	41.0	4.9
25 to 34 years old	1.4	4.5	10.2	7.8	13.0	12.3	7.9	39.1	3.9
35 to 44 years old	1.8	3.9	8.1	7.4	15.3	14.1	6.7	31.2	4.8
45 to 54 years old	2.5	4.2	8.2	7.5	18.6	12.1	6.8	27.9	5.1
55 to 64 years old	1.5	3.4	6.7	5.6	19.1	10.5	5.0	26.1	5.6
65 to 74 years old	1.4	3.7	4.8	4.6	20.5	8.1	4.1	23.7	5.3
75 years old and older	0.7	2.5	3.1	2.4	18.0	3.8	3.7	11.4	3.7

[1] Other dance refers to dance other than ballet, including modern, folk and tap. [2] Includes ceramics, jewelry, leatherwork, and metalwork. [3] Includes making movies or video as an artistic activity.

Source: U.S. National Endowment for the Arts, *Research Division Report #45, 2002 Survey of Public Participation in the Arts;* <http://www.nea.gov/pub/ResearchReports_chrono.html>.

756   Arts, Recreation, and Travel

Table 1211. Attendance Rates for Various Arts Activities: 2002

[In percent. For persons 18 years and over. Represents attendance at least once in the prior 12 months. Excludes elementary and high school performances. Based on the 2002 household survey Public Participation in the Arts. See also Tables 1210 and 1212]

Item	Jazz	Classical music	Musicals	Non-musical plays	Ballet	Art museums/ galleries	Art/craft fairs and festivals	Historic sites[1]	Literature[2]
Total	10.8	11.6	17.1	12.3	3.9	26.5	33.4	31.6	46.7
Sex: Male	10.7	10.3	14.0	10.3	2.5	24.6	27.0	30.5	37.6
Female	10.8	12.7	20.0	14.2	5.1	28.2	39.2	32.5	55.1
Race and Ethnicity:									
White alone	11.4	13.7	20.1	14.2	4.7	29.5	38.0	36.0	51.4
African American alone	12.7	4.5	10.3	7.1	1.5	14.8	9.7	17.8	37.1
Other alone	7.3	10.3	11.9	10.0	2.3	32.7	25.8	30.4	43.7
Hispanic	6.2	5.5	6.9	6.2	1.6	16.1	20.3	17.2	26.5
Age:									
18 to 24 years old	10.5	7.8	14.8	11.4	2.6	23.7	29.2	28.3	42.8
25 to 34 years old	10.8	9.0	15.4	10.7	3.5	26.7	33.5	33.3	47.7
35 to 44 years old	13.0	10.7	19.1	13.0	4.9	27.4	37.2	35.8	46.6
45 to 54 years old	13.9	15.2	19.3	15.2	5.1	32.9	38.8	38.0	51.6
55 to 64 years old	8.8	15.6	19.7	13.8	3.3	27.8	35.1	31.6	48.9
65 to 74 years old	7.6	12.5	16.6	13.0	3.3	23.4	31.1	24.2	45.3
75 years old and older	3.9	9.5	10.1	5.4	2.2	13.4	15.7	12.8	36.7
Education:									
Grade school	0.9	1.5	1.6	1.1	–	4.5	8.4	6.3	14.0
Some high school	2.7	1.9	4.1	3.7	0.8	7.7	14.0	11.4	23.4
High school graduate	5.3	4.5	9.1	5.7	1.2	14.2	25.7	20.2	37.7
Some college	12.2	11.5	19.4	12.7	3.9	29.0	38.2	36.5	52.9
College graduate	19.4	21.9	30.2	22.5	7.2	46.6	49.3	51.2	63.1
Graduate school	24.0	34.1	37.6	31.8	12.9	58.6	51.9	56.8	74.3
Income:									
Less than $10,000	5.1	6.7	7.6	5.3	1.5	12.4	19.7	14.1	32.1
$10,000 to $19,999	5.4	5.2	8.2	5.4	1.9	14.0	21.4	14.9	37.5
$20,000 to $29,999	6.3	6.3	8.6	6.0	2.4	16.2	24.5	20.8	37.5
$30,000 to $39,999	10.9	10.3	13.6	10.0	2.8	23.3	33.2	28.6	44.1
$40,000 to $49,999	10.3	12.9	16.1	12.2	3.6	25.3	34.6	32.7	47.9
$50,000 to $74,999	11.2	12.4	21.5	14.0	4.3	30.4	40.3	39.1	52.3
$75,000 or More	18.2	19.9	29.3	21.8	7.2	44.6	46.5	50.9	60.8

– Represents or rounds to zero.   [1] Parks, historic buildings, neighborhoods.   [2] Read a book (literature) during the previous twelve months. Includes novels, short stories, poetry, and/or plays.

Source: U.S. National Endowment for the Arts, *Research Division Report #45, 2002 Survey of Public Participation in the Arts.* See also <http://www.arts.endow.gov/pub/ResearchReports_chrono.html>.

Table 1212. Participation in Various Leisure Activities: 2002

[In percent, except as indicated (205.9 represents 205,900,000). For persons 18 years old and over. Covers activities engaged in at least once in the prior 12 months. See headnote, Table 1211]

Item	Adult population (mil.)	Attendance at— Movies	Sports events	Amusement park	Participation in— Exercise program	Playing sports	Charity work	Home improvement/ repair	Gardening
Total	205.9	60.0	35.0	41.7	55.1	30.4	29.0	42.4	47.3
Sex:									
Male	98.7	59.5	41.4	40.4	55.0	38.8	25.6	46.3	37.1
Female	107.2	60.5	29.2	42.9	55.1	22.7	32.1	38.9	56.7
Race and Ethnicity:									
White alone	150.1	63.0	38.4	42.8	59.1	33.0	32.5	47.7	52.3
African American alone	23.7	49.2	27.0	36.6	46.1	23.1	22.7	26.3	30.3
Other alone	9.5	58.1	22.3	43.9	50.4	26.9	22.5	33.8	41.3
Hispanic	22.7	52.5	26.4	38.9	40.1	22.3	15.3	28.0	34.8
Age:									
18 to 24 years old	26.8	82.8	46.0	57.6	61.3	49.4	25.3	21.1	20.7
25 to 34 years old	36.9	73.3	41.8	56.2	60.2	39.6	26.0	41.1	41.4
35 to 44 years old	44.2	68.0	42.2	53.3	59.5	36.6	33.2	53.0	51.8
45 to 54 years old	39.0	60.4	35.8	37.1	58.6	28.6	33.4	54.9	55.4
55 to 64 years old	25.9	46.6	25.5	27.1	48.4	16.0	28.1	44.8	56.6
65 to 74 years old	17.6	32.2	19.7	18.4	47.0	13.7	28.8	38.4	57.2
75 years old and over	15.5	19.5	11.1	9.6	31.3	6.0	21.3	22.1	47.9
Education:									
Grade school	11.6	19.5	9.4	17.2	21.0	6.9	8.2	19.5	32.5
Some high school	20.1	39.4	17.4	30.6	32.7	17.2	12.5	24.9	31.2
High school graduate	63.8	51.7	28.3	37.9	45.6	22.6	20.2	35.6	43.8
Some college	56.9	68.7	39.9	48.9	62.3	35.2	33.1	46.5	49.6
College graduate	36.1	77.1	51.0	50.1	73.2	45.2	42.6	56.0	56.1
Graduate school	17.4	77.5	48.3	44.0	77.3	43.6	53.1	61.6	63.3
Income:									
Less than $10,000	14.4	38.7	16.5	30.4	36.5	15.0	16.2	19.7	32.2
$10,000 to $19,999	22.7	41.8	20.1	30.7	42.0	18.5	18.8	23.5	38.8
$20,000 to $29,999	25.0	48.3	23.0	34.7	45.2	21.4	20.7	28.4	40.9
$30,000 to $39,999	24.2	57.5	30.0	39.3	53.3	26.6	27.4	42.0	46.6
$40,000 to $49,999	17.6	63.1	34.8	42.6	55.0	29.3	29.1	46.0	49.1
$50,000 to $74,999	34.7	69.3	44.8	50.2	63.0	36.0	35.3	53.6	54.4
$75,000 or more	45.8	79.4	53.3	54.0	72.5	48.0	41.5	61.2	56.3
Not reported	21.5	51.0	28.4	31.4	45.1	22.6	23.2	33.6	42.9

Source: U.S. National Endowment for the Arts, Research Division Report #45, 2002 Survey of Public Participation in the Arts. <http://www.nea.gov/pub/ResearchReports_chrono.html>.

Arts, Recreation, and Travel   757

Table 1213. Adult Participation in Selected Leisure Activities by Frequency: 2006

[In thousands (14,504 represents 14,504,000), except percent. For fall 2006. Based on sample and subject to sampling error; see source]

Activity	Participated in the last 12 months [1] Number	Participated in the last 12 months [1] Percent	Two or more times a week Number	Two or more times a week Percent	Once a week Number	Once a week Percent	Two to three times a month Number	Two to three times a month Percent	Once a month Number	Once a month Percent
Adult education courses	14,504	6.6	3,247	1.5	2,044	0.9	634	0.3	1,225	0.6
Attend auto shows	16,906	7.7	196	0.1	216	0.1	338	0.2	879	0.4
Attend classical music/opera performances	10,567	4.8	88	(Z)	80	(Z)	531	0.2	1,081	0.5
Attend country music performances	10,901	5.0	54	(Z)	237	0.1	257	0.1	501	0.2
Attend dance performances	7,567	3.5	178	0.1	154	0.1	78	(Z)	458	0.2
Attend horse races	5,382	2.5	145	0.1	104	0.1	265	0.1	386	0.2
Attend other music performances [2]	23,794	10.9	306	0.1	367	0.2	877	0.4	2,043	0.9
Attend rock music performances	20,285	9.3	302	0.1	183	0.1	659	0.3	1,131	0.5
Backgammon	3,556	1.6	431	0.2	181	0.1	443	0.2	423	0.2
Baking	41,264	18.9	7,988	3.7	6,321	2.9	8,828	4.0	6,363	2.9
Barbecuing	74,050	33.9	11,323	5.2	12,115	5.6	16,245	7.4	10,760	4.9
Billiards/pool	19,698	9.0	1,433	0.7	1,349	0.6	2,663	1.2	2,377	1.1
Bird watching	12,123	5.6	5,747	2.6	917	0.4	1,219	0.6	738	0.3
Board games	39,275	18.0	3,117	1.4	3,552	1.6	6,725	3.1	7,072	3.2
Book clubs	6,071	2.8	244	0.1	312	0.1	626	0.3	2,125	1.0
Ceramics/pottery	2,221	1.0	186	0.1	167	0.1	241	0.1	365	0.2
Chess	6,948	3.2	763	0.4	511	0.2	784	0.4	1,382	0.6
Concerts on radio	7,319	3.4	1,464	0.7	744	0.3	834	0.4	732	0.3
Cooking for fun	40,142	18.4	13,998	6.4	6,705	3.1	5,624	2.6	4,131	1.9
Crossword puzzles	30,538	14.0	12,913	5.9	3,748	1.7	3,443	1.6	2,286	1.1
Dance/go dancing	20,179	9.2	1,730	0.8	1,909	0.9	2,682	1.2	2,682	1.2
Dining out	106,180	48.6	21,214	9.7	26,009	11.9	23,636	10.8	12,809	5.9
Electronic games (not TV)	17,974	8.2	5,605	2.6	2,835	1.3	2,203	1.0	1,727	0.8
Entertain friends or relatives at home	87,801	40.2	8,048	3.7	10,685	4.9	18,406	8.4	17,714	8.1
Fantasy Sports League	6,008	2.8	2,129	1.0	1,214	0.6	137	0.1	343	0.2
Fly kites	5,732	2.6	103	0.1	133	0.1	109	0.1	389	0.2
Furniture refinishing	6,922	3.2	433	0.2	131	0.1	471	0.2	515	0.2
Go to bars/night clubs	39,944	18.3	3,323	1.5	4,341	2.0	6,788	3.1	6,109	2.8
Go to beach	49,871	22.9	2,975	1.4	2,105	1.0	4,589	2.1	4,514	2.1
Go to live theater	27,283	12.5	155	0.1	558	0.3	1,205	0.6	3,104	1.4
Go to museums	25,387	11.6	309	0.1	210	0.1	563	0.3	2,458	1.1
Home decoration and furnishing	27,019	12.4	1,050	0.5	1,592	0.7	2,932	1.3	4,851	2.2
Karaoke	8,409	3.9	393	0.2	592	0.3	661	0.3	1,121	0.5
Model making	3,182	1.5	171	0.1	102	0.1	344	0.2	318	0.2
Painting, drawing	12,356	5.7	2,710	1.2	1,432	0.7	1,391	0.6	1,335	0.6
PC/computer games	42,736	19.6	20,285	9.3	5,086	2.3	4,362	2.0	3,316	1.5
Photo album/scrap book	18,042	8.3	1,400	0.6	1,267	0.6	2,741	1.3	2,577	1.2
Photography	28,504	13.1	4,431	2.0	3,144	1.4	6,119	2.8	4,825	2.2
Picnic	21,819	10.0	564	0.3	581	0.3	1,562	0.7	2,809	1.3
Play bingo	9,301	4.3	713	0.3	723	0.3	878	0.4	1,124	0.5
Play cards	47,591	21.8	5,316	2.4	5,432	2.5	6,865	3.1	8,053	3.7
Play musical instrument	16,852	7.7	6,838	3.1	1,713	0.8	1,684	0.8	1,639	0.8
Reading books	84,444	38.7	45,929	21.0	7,982	3.7	7,230	3.3	4,987	2.3
Reading comic books	4,233	1.9	1,100	0.5	412	0.2	528	0.2	506	0.2
Trivia games	12,409	5.7	1,914	0.9	1,286	0.6	1,671	0.8	1,534	0.7
Video games	22,727	10.4	8,072	3.7	2,741	1.3	2,677	1.2	1,901	0.9
Woodworking	9,703	4.5	1,757	0.8	988	0.5	1,352	0.6	1,278	0.6
Word games	18,787	8.6	6,583	3.0	2,274	1.0	2,155	1.0	1,964	0.9
Zoo attendance	25,954	11.9	245	0.1	87	(Z)	405	0.2	1,426	0.7

Z represents less than 0.05. [1] Includes those participating less than once a month not shown separately. [2] Excluding country and rock.

Source: Mediamark Research, Inc., New York, NY, Top-line Reports (copyright). See also <http://www.mediamark.com/mri/docs/TopLineReports.html>.

Table 1214. Household Pet Ownership: 2001

[Based on a sample survey of 80,000 households in 2001; for details, see source]

Item	Unit	Dogs	Cats	Birds	Horses
Percent of households owning companion pets [1]	Percent	36.1	31.6	4.6	1.7
Average number owned	Number	1.6	2.1	2.1	2.9
Households obtaining veterinary care [2]	Percent	83.6	65.3	11.7	54.6
Average visits per household per year	Number	2.7	1.8	0.3	2.1
PERCENT OF HOUSEHOLDS OWNING PETS					
Annual household income:					
Under $20,000	Percent	29.7	28.1	5.1	1.0
$20,000 to $34,999	Percent	33.9	30.9	4.5	1.3
$35,000 to $54,999	Percent	37.9	32.2	4.8	2.0
$55,000 to $84,999	Percent	40.5	34.3	4.4	2.1
$85,000 and over	Percent	39.7	33.7	4.2	2.1
Household size: [1]					
One person	Percent	20.8	23.5	2.8	0.7
Two persons	Percent	34.3	31.3	4.0	1.6
Three persons	Percent	46.2	37.4	5.9	2.2
Four persons	Percent	50.6	38.2	6.3	2.3
Five or more persons	Percent	53.0	39.7	8.3	3.2

[1] As of December 31, 2001. [2] During 2001.

Source: American Veterinary Medical Association, Schaumburg, IL, U.S. Pet Ownership and Demographics Sourcebook, 2002 (copyright). See also <http://www.avma.org/>.

Table 1215. Retail Sales and Household Participation in Lawn and Garden Activities: 2002 to 2006

[(39,635 represents $39,635,000,000). For calendar year. Subject to sampling variability; see source]

Activity	Retail sales (mil. dol.)					Percent households engaged in activity				
	2002	2003	2004	2005	2006	2002	2003	2004	2005	2006
Total	39,635	38,371	36,778	35,208	34,077	79	78	75	83	74
Lawn care..............	11,963	10,413	8,887	9,657	8,558	55	54	48	54	48
Indoor houseplants.......	2,128	1,571	1,495	1,464	1,156	44	41	39	42	35
Flower gardening........	3,131	3,025	2,735	3,003	2,572	41	38	36	41	33
Insect control...........	2,281	2,053	1,823	1,869	1,746	32	30	28	30	26
Shrub care	1,072	1,042	1,027	1,109	840	27	27	26	31	25
Vegetable gardening......	1,270	1,408	1,058	1,154	1,164	25	24	22	25	22
Tree care	2,790	2,359	3,067	2,820	2,322	26	25	24	26	21
Landscaping	8,854	10,507	11,346	9,078	10,893	34	33	33	31	30
Flower bulbs	1,191	1,036	892	945	786	29	26	26	29	22
Fruit trees	695	635	589	507	640	12	12	11	13	11
Container gardening......	1,362	1,219	1,196	1,295	948	23	24	21	26	18
Raising transplants[1]......	262	230	258	237	257	12	10	9	11	9
Herb gardening.........	444	345	367	371	296	15	14	14	17	12
Growing berries	171	345	141	151	121	7	6	6	8	6
Ornamental gardening.....	580	831	769	678	493	8	9	9	12	7
Water gardening	1,441	1,565	1,128	870	1,285	14	15	13	11	14

[1] Starting plants in advance of planting in ground.

Source: The National Gardening Association, Burlington, VT, *National Gardening Survey*, annual (copyright). See also <http://www.garden.org/home>.

Table 1216. Selected Recreational Activities: 1990 to 2006

[41 represents 41,000,000]

Activity	Unit	1990	1995	2000	2002	2003	2004	2005	2006
Softball, amateur:[1]									
Total participants[2]	Million	41	42	31	31	30	28	27	25
Youth participants	1,000	1,100	1,350	1,370	1,365	1,351	1,356	1,447	1,459
Adult teams[3]	1,000	188	187	155	143	119	132	128	127
Youth teams[3]	1,000	46	74	81	80	79	80	85	86
Golf facilities[4]	Number...	12,846	14,074	15,489	15,827	15,899	16,057	16,052	15,990
Tennis players[5]	1,000	21,000	17,820	22,900	23,200	24,100	24,000	24,720	24,720
Tenpin bowling[6]									
Establishments........	Number...	7,611	7,049	6,247	5,973	5,811	5,761	5,818	5,566
Membership, total[7]......	1,000	6,588	4,925	3,756	3,382	3,246	3,112	2,896	2,728
Skiing: [8]									
Skier visits[9]..........	Million	50.0	52.7	52.2	54.4	57.6	57.1	56.9	58.9
Operating resorts	Number...	591	520	503	493	490	494	492	478
Motion picture screens[10]....	1,000	24	28	37	35	36	37	39	39
Receipts, box office......	Mil. dol....	5,022	5,494	7,468	9,272	9,165	9,215	8,832	9,137
Attendance	Million	1,189	1,263	1,385	1,596	1,520	1,484	1,378	1,395
Boating: [11]									
People participating in recreational boating[12,13]	Million	67.5	70.3	64.4	67.1	65.0	65.4	67.5	72.6
Retail expenditures on boating[14]	Mil. dol....	13,731	17,226	27,065	31,563	30,283	32,953	37,317	39,493
Recreational boats in use by boat type[15]..........	Million	16.0	15.4	16.8	17.2	17.2	17.4	17.7	17.7
Outboard..............	Million	(NA)	(NA)	8.3	8.3	8.4	8.4	8.5	8.5
Inboard...............	Million	(NA)	(NA)	1.0	1.1	1.1	1.1	1.1	1.1
Sterndrive.............	Million	(NA)	(NA)	1.6	1.5	1.6	1.7	1.7	1.7
Personal watercraft	Million	(NA)	(NA)	1.2	1.2	1.2	1.3	1.2	1.2
Sailboats.............	Million	(NA)	(NA)	1.6	1.6	1.6	1.6	1.6	1.6
Other	Million	(NA)	(NA)	3.1	3.4	3.4	3.4	3.6	3.6

NA Not available. [1] Source: Amateur Softball Association, Oklahoma City, OK. [2] Amateur Softball Association teams and other amateur softball teams. [3] Amateur Softball Association teams only. [4] Source: National Golf Foundation, Jupiter, FL. [5] Source: Tennis Industry Association, Hilton Head, SC. Players for persons 12 years old and over who played at least once. [6] Source: United States Bowling Congress, Greendale, WI. [7] Membership totals are for U.S., Canada, and for U.S. military personnel worldwide. [8] Source: National Ski Areas Association, Kottke National End of Season Survey 2005/06—final report (copyright). [9] Represents one person visiting a ski area for all or any part of a day or night, and includes full-end half-day, night, complimentary, adult, child, season, and other types of tickets. Data are estimated and are for the season ending in the year shown. [10] Source: Motion Picture Association of America, Inc., Encino, CA. [11] Source: National Marine Manufacturers Association, Chicago, IL. (copyright). [12] People participating is now measured as adults 18 years and older. [13] Data for 1990-2005 have been revised, see report. [14] Represents estimated expenditures for new and used boats, motors and engines, accessories, safety equipment, fuel, insurance, docking, maintenance, launching, storage, repairs, and other expenses. [15] 2006 data are estimated.

Source: Compiled from sources listed in footnotes.

U.S. Census Bureau, Statistical Abstract of the United States: 2008

Table 1217. College and Professional Football Summary: 1990 to 2006

[35,330 represents 35,330,000. For definition of median, see Guide to Tabular Presentation]

Sport	Unit	1990	1995	2000	2002	2003	2004	2005	2006
Football:									
NCAA college:[1]									
Teams	Number.	533	565	606	617	617	612	615	615
Attendance	1,000 ..	35,330	35,638	39,059	44,556	46,145	43,106	43,487	47,909
National Football League:[2]									
Teams	Number.	28	30	31	32	32	32	32	32
Attendance, total	1,000 ..	17,666	19,203	20,954	21,505	21,639	21,709	21,792	22,200
Regular season	1,000 ..	13,960	15,044	16,387	16,833	16,914	17,001	17,012	17,341
Average per game....	Number.	62,321	62,682	66,078	65,755	66,328	66,409	66,455	67,738
Postseason games[3]...	1,000 ..	848	(NA)	809	782	806	789	802	776
Players' salaries:[4]									
Average	$1,000 .	354	584	787	1,180	1,259	1,331	1,400	1,700
Median base salary....	$1,000 .	275	301	441	525	534	537	569	722

NA Not available. [1] Source: National Collegiate Athletic Assn., Indianapolis, IN; <www.ncaasports.com> (copyright). [2] Source: National Football League, New York, NY; <http://www.nfl.com/>. [3] Includes Pro Bowl (a nonchampionship game) and Super Bowl. [4] Source: National Football League Players Association, Washington, DC.; <http://www.nflpa.org/>.

Table 1218. Selected Spectator Sports: 1990 to 2006

[55,512 represents 55,512,000]

Sport	Unit	1990	1995	2000	2002	2003	2004	2005	2006
Baseball, major leagues:[1]									
Attendance.............	1,000 ..	55,512	51,288	74,339	69,428	69,501	74,822	76,286	77,524
Regular season	1,000 ..	54,824	50,469	72,748	67,859	67,568	73,023	74,926	76,043
Playoffs[2]	1,000 ..	479	533	1,314	1,262	1,568	1,625	1,191	1,218
World Series	1,000 ..	209	286	277	306	365	174	168	225
Players' salaries:[3]									
Average	$1,000 .	598	1,111	1,896	2,296	2,372	2,313	2,476	2,699
Basketball:[4, 5]									
NCAA—Men's college:									
Teams	Number.	767	868	932	936	967	981	983	984
Attendance	1,000 ..	28,741	28,548	29,025	29,395	30,124	30,761	30,569	30,940
NCAA—Women's college:									
Teams	Number.	782	864	956	975	1,009	1,008	1,036	1,018
Attendance[6]........	1,000 ..	2,777	4,962	8,698	9,533	10,164	10,016	9,940	9,903
National Hockey League:[7]									
Regular season attendance..	1,000 ..	12,580	9,234	18,800	20,615	20,409	20,356	([8])	20,854
Playoffs attendance	1,000 ..	1,356	1,329	1,525	1,691	1,636	1,709	([8])	1,530
Professional rodeo:[9]									
Rodeos	Number.	754	739	688	666	657	671	662	649
Performances	Number.	2,159	2,217	2,081	2,207	1,949	1,982	1,940	1,884
Members	Number.	5,693	6,894	6,255	6,209	6,158	6,247	6,127	5,892
Permit-holders (rookies)	Number.	3,290	3,835	3,249	2,543	3,121	2,990	2,701	2,468
Total prize money	Mil. dol.	18.2	24.5	32.3	33.3	34.3	35.5	36.6	36.2

[1] Source: Major League Baseball (previously, The National League of Professional Baseball Clubs), New York, NY, National League Green Book; and The American League of Professional Baseball Clubs, New York, NY, American League Red Book. [2] Beginning 1997, two rounds of playoffs were played. Prior years had one round. [3] Source: Major League Baseball Players Association, New York, NY. [4] Season ending in year shown. [5] Source: National Collegiate Athletic Association, Indianapolis, IN (copyright). [6] For women's attendance total, excludes double-headers with men's teams. [7] For season ending in year shown. Source: National Hockey League, Montreal, Quebec. [8] In September 2004, franchise owners locked out their players upon the expiration of the collective bargaining agreement. The entire season was cancelled in February 2005. [9] Source: Professional Rodeo Cowboys Association, Colorado Springs, CO, Official Professional Rodeo Media Guide, annual (copyright). Source: Compiled from sources listed in footnotes.

Table 1219. Adult Attendance at Sports Events by Frequency: 2006

[In thousands (1,867 represents 1,867,000), except percent. For fall 2006. Based on survey and subject to sampling error; see source]

Event	Attend one or more times a month Num-ber	Attend one or more times a month Per-cent	Attend less than once a month Num-ber	Attend less than once a month Per-cent	Event	Attend one or more times a month Num-ber	Attend one or more times a month Per-cent	Attend less than once a month Num-ber	Attend less than once a month Per-cent
Auto racing—NASCAR ..	1,867	0.9	9,566	4.4	Weekend				
Auto racing—other	1,974	0.9	7,111	3.3	professional games ..	3,875	1.8	11,501	5.3
Baseball	8,154	3.7	18,630	8.5	Golf	1,401	0.6	6,229	2.9
Basketball:					High school sports	11,093	5.1	9,141	4.2
College games	3,597	1.7	9,303	4.3	Horse racing:				
Professional games...	2,826	1.3	10,763	4.9	Flats, runners.......	1,156	0.5	5,000	2.3
Bowling	1,440	0.7	5,015	2.3	Trotters/harness	594	0.3	4,372	2.0
Boxing	967	0.4	4,624	2.1	Ice hockey	2,065	1.0	7,923	3.6
Equestrian events	702	0.3	4,834	2.2	Motorcycle racing.....	371	0.2	4,995	2.3
Figure skating	527	0.2	4,804	2.2	Pro beach volleyball	109	0.1	4,259	2.0
Fishing tournaments	693	0.3	4,910	2.3	Rodeo/bull riding	980	0.5	5,455	2.5
Football:					Soccer	3,538	1.6	5,819	2.7
College games	5,959	2.7	11,605	5.3	Tennis	792	0.4	5,242	2.4
Monday night					Truck and tractor pull/				
professional games ..	1,990	0.9	6,301	2.9	mud racing	924	0.4	5,523	2.5
					Wrestling—professional ..	878	0.4	4,979	2.3

Source: Mediamark Research, Inc., New York, NY, Top-line Reports (copyright). See also <http://www.mediamark.com/mri/docs/TopLineReports.html>.

U.S. Census Bureau, Statistical Abstract of the United States: 2008

Table 1220. **Participation in NCAA Sports: 2005 to 2006**

Sport	Males			Females		
	Teams	Athletes	Average squad	Teams	Athletes	Average squad
Total [1]	8,137	224,926	(X)	9,150	168,583	(X)
Baseball	890	28,767	32.3	(X)	(X)	(X)
Basketball	1,013	16,571	16.4	1,000	15,090	14.5
Bowling [2]	2	33	16.5	44	383	8.7
Cross country	879	11,893	13.5	958	13,228	13.8
Equestrian [2,3]	8	95	11.9	45	1,286	28.6
Fencing [3]	35	632	18.1	44	658	15.0
Field hockey	(X)	(X)	(X)	258	5,468	21.2
Football [3]	618	61,252	99.1	(X)	(X)	(X)
Golf [3]	777	8,250	10.6	504	3,981	7.9
Gymnastics	19	321	16.9	86	1,414	16.4
Ice hockey	133	3,973	29.9	75	1,727	23.0
Lacrosse	222	7,871	35.5	271	5,999	22.1
Rifle [3]	36	207	5.8	37	217	5.9
Rowing [2]	60	2,139	35.7	142	6,902	48.6
Rugby [2]	2	84	42.0	4	149	37.3
Sailing [2]	24	417	17.4	(X)	(X)	(X)
Skiing [3]	36	525	14.6	40	503	12.6
Soccer	752	19,793	26.3	930	21,709	23.3
Softball	(X)	(X)	(X)	932	16,609	17.8
Squash [2]	25	395	15.8	26	360	13.8
Swimming/diving [3]	381	7,771	20.4	497	11,011	22.2
Synchronized swimming [2]	(X)	(X)	(X)	8	97	12.1
Tennis	754	7,599	10.1	888	8,534	9.6
Track, indoor [3]	567	19,135	33.7	630	19,090	30.3
Track, outdoor [3]	670	22,075	32.9	722	20,871	28.9
Volleyball	82	1,210	14.8	992	14,010	14.1
Water polo	45	942	20.9	61	1,173	19.2
Wrestling	228	6,139	26.9	(X)	(X)	(X)

X Not applicable. [1] Includes other sports, not shown separately. [2] Sport recognized by the NCAA but does not have an NCAA championship. [3] Co-ed championship sport.

Source: The National Collegiate Athletic Association (NCAA), Indianapolis, IN, *2005–06 Participation Study* (copyright); <http://www.ncaa.org/wps/portal>.

Table 1221. **Participation in High School Athletic Programs by Sex: 1975 to 2006**

[Data based on number of state associations reporting and may underrepresent the number of schools with and participants in athletic programs]

Year	Participants [1]		Sex and sport	Most popular sports, 2005–2006 [2]	
	Males	Females		Schools	Participants
1975–76	4,109,021	1,645,039	MALE		
1977–78	4,367,442	2,083,040			
1978–79	3,709,512	1,854,400	Football (11-player)	13,727	1,071,775
1979–80	3,517,829	1,750,264	Basketball	17,535	546,335
1980–81	3,503,124	1,853,789	Track & field (outdoor)	15,497	533,985
1981–82	3,409,081	1,810,671	Baseball	15,290	470,671
1982–83	3,355,558	1,779,972	Soccer	10,580	358,935
1983–84	3,303,599	1,747,346	Wrestling	9,744	251,534
1984–85	3,354,284	1,757,884	Cross country	13,110	208,303
1985–86	3,344,275	1,807,121	Golf	13,267	161,284
1986–87	3,364,082	1,836,356	Tennis	9,706	153,006
1987–88	3,425,777	1,849,684	Swimming & diving	6,224	107,468
1988–89	3,416,844	1,839,352			
1989–90	3,398,192	1,858,659	FEMALE		
1990–91	3,406,355	1,892,316	Basketball	17,275	452,929
1991–92	3,429,853	1,940,801	Track & field (outdoor)	15,417	439,200
1992–93	3,416,389	1,997,489	Volleyball	14,578	390,034
1993–94	3,472,967	2,130,315	Softball (fast pitch)	14,710	369,094
1994–95	3,536,359	2,240,461	Soccer	9,970	321,555
1995–96	3,634,052	2,367,936	Cross country	12,989	175,954
1996–97	3,706,225	2,474,043	Tennis	9,816	173,753
1997–98	3,763,120	2,570,333	Swimming & diving	6,559	147,413
1998–99	3,832,352	2,652,726	Competitive spirit squads	3,914	98,570
1999–00	3,861,749	2,675,874	Golf	8,816	64,195
2000–01	3,921,069	2,784,154			
2001–02	3,960,517	2,806,998			
2002–03	3,988,738	2,856,358			
2003–04	4,038,253	2,865,299			
2004–05	4,110,319	2,908,390			
2005–06	4,206,549	2,953,355			

[1] A participant is counted in the number of sports participated in. [2] Ten most popular sports for each sex in terms of number of participants.

Source: National Federation of State High School Associations, Indianapolis, IN, *The 2005–2006 High School Athletics Participation Survey* (copyright); <http://www.nfhs.org/>.

Table 1222. Participation in Selected Sports Activities: 2005

[In thousands (260,861 represents 260,861,000), except rank. For persons 7 years of age or older. Except as indicated, a participant plays a sport more than once in the year]

Activity	All persons		Sex		Age								Household income (dol.)					
	Number	Rank	Male	Female	7-11 years	12-17 years	18-24 years	25-34 years	35-44 years	45-54 years	55-64 years	65 years and over	Under 15,000	15,000-24,999	25,000-34,999	35,000-49,999	50,000-74,999	75,000 and over
SERIES I SPORTS [1]																		
Total	260,861	(X)	128,001	132,860	19,675	23,337	28,729	37,232	43,062	42,229	29,931	36,666	30,442	28,281	29,466	40,495	53,699	78,477
Number participated in—																		
Aerobic exercising [2]	33,692	11	9,960	23,732	903	1,708	5,089	8,412	7,579	4,584	2,796	2,620	2,031	2,546	2,437	5,641	7,815	13,223
Backpacking [3]	13,253	20	8,486	4,767	1,032	1,887	2,501	3,332	2,517	1,472	346	165	1,871	1,072	1,012	2,654	2,545	4,100
Baseball	14,627	17	11,358	3,269	4,700	3,536	1,588	1,689	1,594	912	314	293	1,155	862	1,395	2,763	3,654	4,798
Basketball	29,881	12	20,460	9,420	6,071	7,705	6,087	3,912	3,250	1,719	791	348	3,398	2,706	2,630	4,394	6,970	9,781
Bicycle riding [2]	43,138	6	24,196	18,942	9,816	7,373	3,724	5,540	6,787	5,561	2,272	2,063	4,181	3,814	4,019	7,718	8,351	15,054
Billiards	37,259	9	23,558	13,701	1,500	3,565	8,861	8,601	7,279	5,009	1,666	778	3,206	4,235	3,787	6,704	7,232	12,096
Bowling	45,383	5	23,928	21,455	5,553	6,618	8,090	8,503	7,967	5,224	1,831	1,597	3,706	3,700	4,539	7,059	10,617	15,762
Camping [4]	45,997	4	25,350	20,648	4,946	6,102	5,566	8,561	9,791	6,163	3,068	1,801	3,353	4,015	5,307	8,047	10,700	14,575
Exercise walking [2]	85,991	1	34,148	51,843	3,181	4,066	8,739	13,924	16,633	16,147	11,491	11,809	9,231	7,533	9,145	13,147	18,325	28,610
Exercising with equipment [2]	54,248	3	25,532	28,715	721	4,450	8,733	10,238	10,668	8,515	5,606	5,317	3,467	3,912	4,600	7,950	12,487	21,832
Fishing (net) [2]	41,643	7	28,594	13,049	3,963	4,848	5,330	6,278	7,741	6,713	3,935	2,836	5,020	4,332	5,325	6,539	8,826	11,601
Fishing—fresh water	37,487	8	25,933	11,554	3,791	4,648	4,695	5,483	6,888	6,113	3,377	2,493	4,295	3,923	4,935	5,995	8,153	10,187
Fishing—salt water	9,969	23	6,930	3,039	487	674	1,254	1,660	2,056	1,765	1,345	729	1,493	728	1,117	1,500	1,832	3,299
Football—tackle	9,933	24	8,702	1,232	1,672	3,453	2,416	1,005	742	325	195	123	1,364	956	910	1,517	2,266	2,920
Golf	24,671	15	19,489	5,181	747	2,169	2,909	4,400	5,178	4,157	2,874	2,237	1,165	933	1,790	3,015	5,644	12,123
Hiking	29,768	13	16,388	13,380	2,383	2,932	3,898	5,788	6,259	4,467	2,639	1,402	2,579	2,622	2,819	5,364	6,134	10,250
Hunting with firearms	19,428	16	17,052	2,376	686	2,625	2,335	3,663	3,803	3,271	1,891	1,153	1,272	1,766	2,440	3,798	4,020	6,132
Running/jogging [2]	29,246	14	16,368	12,878	2,266	4,833	6,937	6,310	4,584	2,306	1,254	756	2,619	2,077	2,044	5,214	6,307	10,985
Soccer	14,142	18	8,382	5,760	5,136	3,780	2,013	1,472	1,028	462	193	58	1,543	1,300	807	2,142	3,069	5,279
Softball	14,092	19	6,959	7,133	2,039	2,553	2,419	2,570	2,479	1,213	593	226	864	1,193	1,363	2,020	3,638	5,013
Swimming [2]	57,592	2	28,522	29,400	8,774	9,157	7,475	8,610	10,215	7,144	3,629	2,968	4,603	4,528	5,728	10,269	12,308	20,536
Tennis	11,121	22	5,777	5,344	1,053	2,216	1,945	1,858	1,853	1,285	568	343	908	1,157	802	1,470	2,329	4,456
Volleyball [2]	13,205	21	6,333	6,872	1,195	3,381	3,097	2,364	1,663	1,014	250	241	1,615	1,039	1,374	2,109	3,030	4,038
Weightlifting	35,534	10	22,785	12,749	323	4,974	7,139	7,594	7,156	4,609	2,313	1,427	2,429	2,175	2,295	5,523	7,994	15,119

See footnotes at end of table.

U.S. Census Bureau, Statistical Abstract of the United States: 2008

Table 1222. Participation in Selected Sports Activities: 2005—Con.

[See headnote, page 762]

Activity	All persons Number	All persons Rank	Sex Male	Sex Female	Age 7–11 years	Age 12–17 years	Age 18–24 years	Age 25–34 years	Age 35–44 years	Age 45–54 years	Age 55–64 years	Age 65 years and over	Household income (dol.) Under 15,000	15,000–24,999	25,000–34,999	35,000–49,999	50,000–74,999	75,000 and over
Total	260,860	(X)	128,001	132,859	19,676	23,339	28,729	37,232	43,062	42,228	29,931	36,664	31,631	26,015	31,074	40,751	52,198	79,191
Number participating in—																		
Archery (target)	6,764	10	5,360	1,404	1,076	1,454	1,159	905	1,151	513	395	110	475	613	1,158	1,267	1,185	2,066
Boating—motor/power	27,539	2	15,994	11,545	2,194	3,134	3,194	4,998	5,024	4,883	2,875	1,237	1,738	1,313	2,799	4,270	6,077	11,342
Cheerleading	3,299	16	198	3,101	1,192	1,068	648	130	114	81	15	51	211	173	205	673	979	1,058
Hockey (ice)	2,432	17	2,006	426	410	781	261	130	274	159	50	101	193	100	304	243	482	1,110
Hunting with bow and arrow	6,623	13	5,837	786	100	695	1,349	1,002	1,928	601	548	401	574	651	1,010	1,450	1,368	1,570
In-line roller skating	13,115	4	6,955	6,160	4,252	3,811	1,587	1,365	1,281	356	214	249	895	1,273	1,295	2,082	3,433	4,137
Mountain biking—off road	9,210	7	5,707	3,503	1,173	1,334	1,238	1,816	1,968	1,260	256	164	819	403	1,278	1,545	1,816	3,350
Muzzleloading	4,099	15	3,774	326	22	212	641	470	1,188	655	659	253	287	289	441	770	1,117	1,196
Paintball games	8,022	8	7,037	985	670	3,223	1,803	996	708	405	201	16	813	444	830	1,317	1,634	2,984
Scooter riding	10,415	6	6,404	4,011	5,295	2,976	498	353	625	217	253	199	880	612	844	1,539	2,215	4,325
Skateboarding	12,042	5	8,996	3,046	4,786	4,691	996	401	688	82	108	291	800	1,103	916	1,832	2,840	4,551
Skiing—alpine	6,900	9	3,491	3,408	1,062	1,153	990	795	1,356	1,064	299	179	174	136	193	375	1,864	4,157
Skiing—cross country	1,873	18	950	923	98	246	137	124	433	470	277	88	71	115	211	159	281	1,036
Snowboarding	5,987	14	4,444	1,543	781	2,310	1,281	711	526	226	65	87	559	394	476	799	1,218	2,540
Target shoot	21,867	3	16,831	5,036	938	2,901	3,752	3,828	4,219	3,208	2,142	879	1,316	2,046	3,389	3,786	5,601	5,729
Target shoot—air gun	6,656	12	5,790	866	1,465	1,979	1,023	328	733	494	396	238	381	765	940	1,075	1,246	2,251
Water skiing	6,725	11	3,893	2,832	552	1,342	876	1,514	900	824	507	209	305	189	423	666	2,099	3,042
Work-out at club	34,725	1	14,617	20,108	447	2,368	5,495	7,297	6,829	5,904	3,410	2,976	2,254	1,414	3,090	3,941	8,340	15,686

SERIES II SPORTS 5

X Not applicable. 1 Based on a sampling of 15,000 households. 2 Participant engaged in activity at least six times in the year. 3 Includes wilderness camping. 4 Vacation/overnight. 5 Based on a sampling of 20,000 households.

Source: National Sporting Goods Association, Mt. Prospect, IL, Sports Participation in 2005: Series 1 and Series II (copyright) <http://www.nsga.org/public/pages/index.cfm?pageid=864>.

U.S. Census Bureau, Statistical Abstract of the United States: 2008

Table 1223. Sporting Goods Sales by Product Category: 1990 to 2006

[In millions of dollars (50,725 represents $50,725,000,000), except percent. Based on a sample survey of consumer purchases of 80,000 households, (100,000 beginning 1995), except recreational transport, which was provided by industry associations. Excludes Alaska and Hawaii. Minus sign (–) indicates decrease]

Selected product category	1990	1995	2000	2001	2002	2003	2004	2005	2006, proj.
Sales, all products	50,725	59,794	74,442	74,337	77,726	79,779	85,811	89,836	89,866
Annual percent change [1]	(NA)	6.5	4.6	–0.1	4.6	2.6	7.6	4.7	–
Percent of retail sales	(NA)	2.5	2.5	2.4	2.5	2.4	2.5	2.4	2.3
Athletic and sport clothing [2]	10,130	10,311	11,030	10,217	9,801	10,543	11,201	11,650	12,292
Athletic and sport footwear [2]	11,654	11,415	13,026	13,814	14,144	14,446	14,752	15,711	16,268
Aerobic shoes	611	372	292	281	239	222	237	261	259
Basketball shoes	918	999	786	761	789	890	877	878	887
Cross training shoes	679	1,191	1,528	1,476	1,421	1,407	1,327	1,437	1,466
Golf shoes	226	225	226	223	243	222	230	259	251
Gym shoes, sneakers	2,536	1,741	1,871	2,004	2,042	2,059	2,221	2,314	2,499
Jogging and running shoes	1,110	1,043	1,638	1,670	1,733	1,802	1,989	2,157	2,221
Tennis shoes	740	480	533	505	503	544	508	528	538
Walking shoes	2,950	2,841	3,317	3,280	3,415	3,468	3,496	3,673	3,746
Athletic and sport equipment [2]	14,439	18,809	21,608	21,594	21,699	22,394	23,328	23,981	24,450
Archery	265	287	259	276	279	320	332	362	37?
Baseball and softball	217	251	319	316	334	340	352	372	38?
Billiards and indoor games	192	304	516	528	574	625	622	572	56?
Camping	1,072	1,205	1,354	1,371	1,442	1,487	1,531	1,442	1,456
Exercise	1,824	2,960	3,610	3,889	4,378	4,957	5,074	5,207	5,363
Fishing tackle	1,910	2,010	2,030	2,058	2,024	1,981	2,026	2,139	2,182
Golf	2,514	3,194	3,805	3,871	3,258	3,046	3,198	3,474	3,509
Hunting and firearms	2,202	3,003	2,274	2,206	2,449	2,654	3,175	3,351	3,418
Optics	438	655	729	783	826	847	859	887	922
Skin diving and scuba	294	328	355	348	348	338	351	358	365
Skiing, downhill	475	562	495	515	527	462	452	442	457
Tennis	333	297	383	371	358	343	362	397	405
Recreational transport [2]	14,502	19,259	28,779	28,712	32,083	32,397	36,531	38,493	36,856
Bicycles and supplies	2,423	3,390	5,131	4,725	4,961	4,736	4,898	5,343	4,940
Pleasure boats, motors, & accessories	7,644	9,064	13,224	14,558	15,382	14,705	16,054	17,017	17,358
Recreational vehicles	4,113	5,895	9,529	8,598	10,960	12,058	14,753	15,394	13,789
Snowmobiles	322	910	894	831	779	898	826	739	769

– Rounds to zero. NA Not available. [1] Represents change from immediate prior year. [2] Includes other products not shown separately.

Source: National Sporting Goods Association, Mt. Prospect, IL, *The Sporting Goods Market in 2006*; and prior issues (copyright); <http://www.nsga.org/public/pages/index.cfm?pageid=869>.

Table 1224. Consumer Purchases of Sporting Goods by Consumer Characteristics: 2005

[In percent. Based on sample survey of consumer purchases of 100,000 households. Excludes Alaska and Hawaii]

Characteristic	Total households	Footwear					Equipment				
		Aerobic shoes	Gym shoes/ sneakers	Jog- ging/ run- ning shoes	Skate- board- ing shoes	Walk- ing shoes	Multi pur- pose home gyms	Rod/ reel combi- nation	Golf club set	Rifles	Soccer balls
Total	100	100	100	100	100	100	100	100	100	100	100
Age of user:											
Under 14 years old	19.2	6.4	47.0	9.0	42.0	5.6	–	8.6	4.4	3.0	63.1
14 to 17 years old	5.7	3.2	10.9	6.8	28.1	2.2	–	0.8	6.8	0.4	11.3
18 to 24 years old	10.0	5.7	6.2	10.1	13.4	5.4	6.9	2.8	1.1	6.3	5.1
25 to 34 years old	13.6	28.5	10.0	26.1	10.9	10.5	37.1	13.4	18.6	23.3	8.4
35 to 44 years old	15.0	19.5	10.8	20.5	4.7	15.7	31.1	30.7	21.1	22.2	2.0
45 to 64 years old	24.1	30.7	11.7	23.1	0.7	40.9	17.3	31.1	34.4	38.4	3.4
65 years old and over	12.4	6.0	3.4	4.4	0.2	19.7	7.6	10.4	13.6	6.4	0.0
Multiple ages	–	–	–	–	–	–	–	2.2	–	–	6.7
Sex of user:											
Male	49.2	15.4	53.3	50.8	74.8	38.0	57.0	75.7	77.9	86.6	62.4
Female	50.8	84.6	46.7	49.2	25.2	62.0	32.8	16.1	22.1	9.5	34.2
Household use	–	–	–	–	–	–	10.2	8.2	–	3.9	3.4
Annual household income:											
Under $15,000	14.2	8.8	9.4	3.8	5.6	9.0	6.2	5.7	4.8	7.0	4.0
$15,000 to $24,999	14.1	6.1	10.7	6.7	8.5	12.0	1.2	10.7	6.1	16.6	8.0
$25,000 to $34,999	11.6	14.7	11.3	7.9	14.3	10.9	8.0	15.1	6.9	9.7	8.6
$35,000 to $49,999	15.2	14.7	15.5	16.0	19.7	14.7	22.4	19.8	7.5	24.8	14.8
$50,000 to $74,999	17.8	21.0	20.8	20.4	20.8	19.5	26.5	18.1	20.9	17.0	24.9
$75,000 to $99,999	12.3	13.3	15.4	18.5	16.0	16.3	12.2	17.5	20.3	10.8	13.9
$100,000 and over	14.8	21.4	16.9	26.7	15.1	17.6	23.5	13.1	33.5	14.1	25.8

– Represents or rounds to zero.

Source: National Sporting Goods Association, Mt. Prospect, IL, *The Sporting Goods Market in 2006* (copyright). <http://www.nsga.org.public/pages/index.cfm?pageid=869>.

U.S. Census Bureau, Statistical Abstract of the United States: 2008

Table 1225. **National Park System—Summary: 1990 to 2006**

[For year ending September 30, except as noted. (986 represents $986,000,000). Includes data for five areas in Puerto Rico and Virgin Islands, one area in American Samoa, and one area in Guam]

Item	1990	1995	2000	2002	2003	2004	2005	2006
Finances (mil. dol.): [1]								
Expenditures reported	986	1,445	1,833	2,161	2,315	2,371	2,451	2,463
Salaries and wages	459	633	799	876	934	956	984	998
Improvements, maintenance	160	234	299	311	344	332	361	389
Construction	109	192	215	296	293	354	381	300
Other	259	386	520	678	744	729	725	776
Funds available	1,506	2,225	3,316	3,940	4,099	4,087	4,218	4,242
Appropriations	1,053	1,325	1,881	2,257	3,298	2,388	2,425	2,450
Other [2]	453	900	1,435	1,683	1,801	1,699	1,793	1,792
Revenue from operations	79	106	234	245	274	264	286	308
Recreation visits (millions): [3]								
All areas	258.7	269.6	285.9	277.3	266.1	276.9	273.5	272.6
National parks [4]	57.7	64.8	66.1	64.5	63.4	63.8	63.5	60.4
National monuments	23.9	23.5	23.8	20.3	20.0	19.8	20.9	19.6
National historical, commemorative, archaeological [5]	57.5	56.9	72.2	70.2	66.6	77.0	74.9	73.6
National parkways	29.1	31.3	34.0	35.7	31.1	31.7	31.7	32.6
National recreation areas [4]	47.2	53.7	50.0	48.2	47.7	46.6	46.8	47.8
National seashores and lakeshores. . .	23.3	22.5	22.5	23.3	22.6	21.3	21.7	19.6
National Capital Parks	7.5	5.5	5.4	3.8	3.5	4.7	4.3	6.2
Recreation overnight stays (millions). . . .	17.6	16.8	15.4	14.7	14.2	13.7	13.5	13.2
In commercial lodgings.	3.9	3.8	3.7	3.5	3.5	3.5	3.4	3.4
In Park Service campgrounds	7.9	7.1	5.9	5.8	5.7	5.4	5.2	5.0
In backcountry	1.7	2.2	1.9	1.9	1.8	1.7	1.7	1.7
Other	4.2	3.7	3.8	3.5	3.2	3.1	3.2	3.1
Land (1,000 acres): [6, 7]								
Total	76,362	77,355	78,153	78,811	79,006	79,023	79,048	78,810
Parks	46,089	49,307	49,785	49,639	49,823	49,892	49,910	49,912
Recreation areas.	3,344	3,353	3,388	3,390	3,391	3,391	3,391	3,391
Other	26,929	24,695	24,980	25,782	25,792	25,740	25,747	25,507
Acquisition, net.	21	27	186	60	138	12	17	15

[1] Financial data are those associated with the National Park System. Certain other functions of the National Park Service (principally the activities absorbed from the former Heritage Conservation and Recreation Service in 1981) are excluded. [2] Includes funds carried over from prior years. [3] For calendar year. Includes other areas, not shown separately. [4] For 1990, combined data for North Cascades National Park and two adjacent National Recreation Areas are included in National Parks total. [5] Includes military areas. [6] Federal land only, as of Dec. 31. Federal land acreages, in addition to National Park Service administered lands, also includes lands within national park system area boundaries but under the administration of other agencies. Year-to-year changes in the federal lands figures include changes in the acreages of these other lands and hence often differ from "net acquisition." [7] The decrease in the 2006 land total reflects acreage administered by Bureau of Land Management and not by the National Park Service.

Source: U.S. National Park Service, *National Park Statistical Abstract,* annual; and unpublished data. See also <http://www2.nature.nps .gov/stats/>.

Table 1226. **State Parks and Recreation Areas by State: 2005**

[For year ending June 30 (13,713 represents 13,713,000). Data are shown as reported by state park directors. In some states, park agency has under its control forests, fish and wildlife areas, and/or other areas. In other states, agency is responsible for state parks only]

State	Acreage (1,000)	Visitors (1,000) [1]	Revenue Total ($1,000)	Percent of operating expenditures	State	Acreage (1,000)	Visitors (1,000) [1]	Revenue Total ($1,000)	Percent of operating expenditures
United States. . .	13,713	725,361	847,117	39.2	Missouri	202	16,695	7,406	26.6
					Montana	55	5,671	5,214	66.4
Alabama	48	2,961	22,363	66.6	Nebraska	135	9,998	16,044	86.8
Alaska	3,353	4,678	2,511	38.9	Nevada.	133	3,178	2,565	23.9
Arizona.	64	2,224	9,188	43.3	New Hampshire . . .	232	(NA)	(NA)	(NA)
Arkansas.	53	9,751	16,174	41.6	New Jersey	397	15,791	10,176	27.6
California.	1,554	77,119	82,819	17.8	New Mexico.	93	4,157	4,097	(NA)
Colorado.	410	11,377	19,500	67.1	New York	1,367	56,405	83,000	41.3
Connecticut	204	6,235	4,611	32.0	North Carolina	187	12,674	5,132	16.5
Delaware.	24	4,557	11,366	39.3	North Dakota	18	948	1,514	47.3
Florida	696	18,202	38,179	49.3	Ohio	174	50,166	27,667	40.1
Georgia	84	10,294	32,834	55.4	Oklahoma	72	13,282	23,260	58.9
Hawaii	27	(NA)	2,111	28.2	Oregon	97	42,420	15,384	37.0
Idaho	46	(NA)	3,241	21.2	Pennsylvania	291	36,263	13,893	17.9
Illinois.	481	44,950	7,336	14.0	Rhode Island	9	5,853	3,515	39.3
Indiana	178	19,674	39,855	83.7	South Carolina	81	6,707	18,304	73.5
Iowa	68	13,580	4,070	29.6	South Dakota	103	7,399	9,951	77.4
Kansas	33	7,310	5,967	58.6	Tennessee	141	29,038	34,865	50.8
Kentucky	58	7,037	52,143	61.7	Texas	589	10,189	33,955	60.5
Louisiana	41	1,598	4,821	16.8	Utah	150	4,552	10,622	39.9
Maine	100	2,006	3,146	37.7	Vermont	69	690	6,638	98.0
Maryland.	137	11,186	13,811	38.5	Virginia	66	7,319	10,643	43.3
Massachusetts	336	33,162	13,898	22.9	Washington	106	40.026	17,627	31.2
Michigan	273	23,057	36,095	81.7	West Virginia	177	7,406	19,602	58.4
Minnesota	220	8,245	15,025	46.0	Wisconsin	135	14,964	15,773	74.5
Mississippi.	24	2,256	7,865	74.4	Wyoming.	121	2,114	1,343	8.0

NA Not available. [1] Includes overnight visitors.
Source: The National Association of State Park Directors, Raleigh, NC, *2006 Annual Information Exchange;* <http://www.naspd.org/>.

Arts, Recreation, and Travel **765**

Table 1227. National Park Service Visits and Acreage by State: 2006

State	Recreation visits [1]	Gross area acres	Federal land NPS fee acres [2]	Federal land NPS/OTFED less than fee acres [3]	Federal land Other federal fee acres [4]	Nonfederal land Other public acres	Nonfederal land Private acres
United States. .	270,587,041	84,255,120	78,084,743	254,208	438,257	1,191,515	4,286,397
Alabama	790,039	21,081	16,715	202	–	3,295	869
Alaska	2,471,970	54,638,804	51,080,429	27,889	8	188,053	3,342,425
Arizona.	10,543,205	2,962,902	2,603,150	115	92,247	56,427	210,963
Arkansas	2,556,666	104,976	98,403	3,309	6	2,736	523
California	32,906,849	8,102,836	7,558,091	150	13,061	335,219	196,314
Colorado.	5,289,308	673,296	608,160	6,859	42,451	862	14,965
Connecticut.	11,795	7,782	5,719	1,055	–	874	133
District of Columbia .	32,867,947	7,086	6,948	7	–	126	4
Florida	7,983,175	2,637,714	2,437,005	1,330	45,907	129,192	24,281
Georgia	6,462,784	62,923	39,647	43	1,461	16,775	4,997
Hawaii	5,323,425	364,999	353,661	1	11	11,228	98
Idaho	435,806	517,604	507,425	627	3,960	901	4,691
Illinois	388,887	13	12	–	–	–	1
Indiana.	2,190,492	15,317	10,516	498	–	3,280	1,022
Iowa	225,179	2,713	2,708	–	–	5	1
Kansas.	125,408	11,792	461	269	–	39	11,023
Kentucky	1,924,683	95,230	94,209	137	–	831	52
Louisiana	333,508	21,130	14,540	–	–	2,456	4,134
Maine.	2,083,588	90,256	66,768	11,119	22	10,646	1,700
Maryland	3,249,642	71,843	39,507	5,973	395	23,269	2,700
Massachusetts.	9,813,899	57,897	32,946	972	40	21,866	2,072
Michigan.	1,649,394	718,186	631,716	732	42	58,515	27,182
Minnesota.	605,606	301,333	139,508	3,213	141	98,811	59,659
Mississippi	6,016,266	117,611	103,695	5,262	–	30	8,625
Missouri	4,302,533	83,471	54,338	9,262	–	14,070	5,801
Montana.	3,897,415	1,274,374	1,214,184	1,233	6,137	1,464	51,355
Nebraska	225,937	29,379	5,434	494	–	36	23,415
Nevada	5,911,839	778,512	774,509	–	2,508	81	1,415
New Hampshire	25,858	15,856	8,362	1,556	5,772	162	5
New Jersey.	5,708,286	99,100	35,216	81	3,208	59,001	1,594
New Mexico	1,620,457	391,029	376,527	5	2,524	3,365	8,607
New York	15,154,997	72,214	33,138	3,919	164	19,812	15,181
North Carolina.	20,091,486	405,772	362,662	12,272	20,782	3,289	6,767
North Dakota.	472,986	72,581	71,252	258	151	56	865
Ohio	2,704,686	34,157	19,387	1,334	84	8,203	5,149
Oklahoma.	1,358,201	10,241	10,008	9	189	8	27
Oregon.	806,344	199,085	192,012	1,404	4,975	182	512
Pennsylvania.	8,842,235	135,734	48,426	2,511	387	18,614	65,796
Rhode Island.	52,671	5	5	–	–	–	–
South Carolina.	1,383,500	32,618	30,082	61	5	51	2,419
South Dakota.	3,703,047	307,746	141,317	122,327	–	79	44,023
Tennessee	7,758,199	382,781	352,201	1,679	9,629	3,616	15,656
Texas.	5,488,711	1,236,599	1,190,152	85	1,013	5,079	40,270
Utah	7,840,356	2,117,043	2,097,112	833	1,142	12,803	5,155
Vermont.	22,484	22,178	8,830	3,874	8,809	544	120
Virginia.	22,944,011	361,245	306,799	6,233	21,260	6,973	19,979
Washington.	6,518,791	1,965,386	1,832,272	2,099	100,187	12,691	18,136
West Virginia.	1,737,487	92,597	63,142	308	314	6,894	21,939
Wisconsin.	442,472	133,754	61,741	11,481	802	47,629	12,101
Wyoming	5,322,531	2,396,340	2,343,696	1,126	48,462	1,380	1,677

– Represents zero.   [1] See Table 1228, footnote 1.   [2] National Park Service (NPS) fee represents complete federal ownership of all rights in the land.   [3] Represents federal ownership of some rights in the land.   [4] NPS acreage lies under the jurisdiction of another federal agency (such as Bureau of Land Management).

Source: U.S. National Park Service, Statistical Abstract, and unpublished data. See also <http://www2.nature.nps.gov/stats/>.

Table 1228. National Park Service Visits and Acreage by Type of Area: 2006

[Includes data for five areas in Puerto Rico and Virgin Islands, one area in American Samoa, and one area in Guam]

Type of area	Recreation visits [1]	Gross area acres	Federal land NPS fee acres [2]	Federal land NPS/OTFED less than fee acres [3]	Federal land Other federal fee acres [4]	Nonfederal land Other public acres	Nonfederal land Private acres
Total [5]	272,623,980	84,314,832	78,099,792	254,211	456,392	1,211,586	4,292,851
National historic sites . . .	10,045,276	37,327	21,053	783	51	922	14,518
National historical parks. . .	26,030,463	171,913	122,406	3,049	360	28,510	17,588
National memorials.	29,000,276	10,585	7,961	8	149	63	2,404
National monuments. . . .	19,614,242	2,027,901	1,802,559	14,830	30,671	19,777	160,064
National parks	60,366,404	52,090,267	49,697,046	149,931	64,808	496,405	1,682,078
National recreation areas. .	47,780,735	3,696,962	3,146,335	1,331	243,101	127,902	178,293
National seashores.	15,817,043	595,013	403,187	14,890	61,226	106,131	9,579
National parkways	32,574,228	176,859	157,726	8,520	125	278	10,209

[1] Recreation visit represents the entry of a person onto lands or waters administered by the National Park Service (NPS) for recreational purposes excluding government personnel, through traffic (commuters), trades-persons, and persons residing within park boundaries.   [2] Fee represents complete federal ownership of all rights in the land.   [3] Represents federal ownership of some rights in the land.   [4] NPS acreage lies under the jurisdiction of another federal agency (such as Bureau of Land Management).   [5] Includes other areas not shown separately.

Source: U.S. National Park Service, Statistical Abstract. See also <http://www2.nature.nps.gov/stats/>.

Table 1229. Participants in Wildlife-Related Recreation Activities: 2001

[In thousands (37,805 represents 37,805,000). For persons 16 years old and over engaging in activity at least once in 2001. Based on survey and subject to sampling error; see source for details]

Participant	Number	Days of participation	Trips	Participant	Number	Days of participation
Total sportsmen [1]	37,805	785,762	636,787	Wildlife watchers [1]..	66,105	(X)
Total anglers	34,071	557,394	436,662	Nonresidential [2]	21,823	372,006
Freshwater	28,439	466,984	365,076	Observe wildlife	20,080	295,345
Excluding Great Lakes..	27,913	443,247	349,188	Photograph wildlife.....	9,427	76,324
Great Lakes	1,847	23,138	15,888	Feed wildlife	7,077	103,307
Saltwater...........	9,051	90,838	71,586			
				Residential [3]	62,928	(X)
Total hunters	13,034	228,368	200,125	Observe wildlife	42,111	(X)
Big game	10,911	153,191	114,445	Photograph wildlife.....	13,937	(X)
Small game	5,434	60,142	46,450	Feed wild birds	53,988	(X)
Migratory birds	2,956	29,310	24,155	Visit public parks	10,981	(X)
Other animals.........	1,047	19,207	15,074	Maintain plantings or natural areas	13,072	(X)

X Not applicable. [1] Detail does not add to total due to multiple responses and nonresponse. [2] Persons taking a trip of at least 1 mile for activity. [3] Activity within 1 mile of home.

Source: U.S. Fish and Wildlife Service, 2001 National Survey of Fishing, Hunting, and Wildlife Associated Recreation, May 2002. Internet links: <http://www.census.gov/prod/www/abs/fishing.html>, <http://federalaid.fws.gov/surveys/surveys.html>.

Table 1230. Tribal Gaming Revenues: 2001 to 2006

[In millions (12,821.7 represents $12,821,700,000). For year ending September 30]

Gaming operation	2001 Number of operations	2001 Revenue	2002 Number of operations	2002 Revenue	2003 Number of operations	2003 Revenue	2004 Number of operations	2004 Revenue	2005 Number of operations	2005 Revenue	2006 Number of operations	2006 Revenue
Revenue range:												
Total.........	329	12,821.7	330	14,497.0	358	16,826.1	375	19,479.1	392	22,578.8	387	25,075.8
$250 million and over .	(X)	(X)	(X)	(X)	11	5,381.2	15	7,200.9	21	9,692.0	23	11,214.8
$100 to $250 million ..	39	8,398.5	41	9,399.0	32	5,333.4	40	6,277.7	39	6,206.8	40	6,730.4
$50 to $100 million....	19	1,415.8	24	1,698.2	35	2,459.7	33	2,240.0	43	2,897.3	45	3,186.1
$25 to $50 million.....	43	1,528.6	55	1,977.8	57	2,040.7	60	2,144.5	58	2,019.7	64	2,241.0
$10 to $25 million.....	58	976.5	61	984.6	69	1,170.2	71	1,180.4	75	1,267.9	72	1,229.2
$3 to $10 million	57	385.7	59	367.8	57	350.4	58	354.1	68	411.5	66	412.7
Under $3 million.....	113	95.6	90	69.7	98	90.6	98	81.5	88	83.7	77	61.5
Revenue by region: [1]												
Total.........	329	12,821.7	330	14,497.0	358	16,826.1	375	19,479.1	392	22,578.8	387	25,075.8
Region I..........	75	1,013.5	47	1,196.2	46	1,441.5	45	1,601.7	49	1,829.3	45	2,080.3
Region II..........	48	2,891.5	51	3,594.4	54	4,699.9	54	5,822.1	57	6,992.8	56	7,675.4
Region III.........	34	1,634.0	40	1,782.3	43	1,898.5	45	2,159.9	48	2,529.1	45	2,927.7
Region IV	79	3,254.2	109	3,523.7	109	3,597.0	117	3,815.9	118	3,983.6	117	4,050.1
Region V	72	437.4	79	580.5	82	867.1	87	1,258.7	92	1,729.8	97	2,123.2
Region VI.........	21	3,591.2	22	3,819.9	24	4,322.1	27	4,820.9	28	5,514.1	27	6,219.1

X Not applicable. [1] Region 1: Alaska Idaho Oregon, and Washington. Region 2: California, and Northern Nevada. Region 3: Arizona, Colorado, New Mexico, and Southern Nevada. Region 4: Iowa, Michigan, Minnesota, Montana, North Dakota, Nebraska, South Dakota, Wisconsin, and Wyoming. Data for Montana not included for years 2004 and earlier. Region 5: Kansas, Oklahoma, and Texas. Region 6: Alabama, Connecticut, Florida, Louisiana, Mississippi, North Carolina, and New York.

Source: National Indian Gaming Commission, Tribal Gaming Revenues, Annual. See also <http://www.nigc.gov>.

Table 1231. Gaming Revenue by Industry: 2000 to 2005

[In millions of dollars (62,154,4 represents $62,154,400,000). Data shown are for gross revenue. Gross gambling revenue (GGR) is the amount wagered minus the winnings returned to players, a true measure of the economic value of gambling. GGR is the figure used to determine what an operation earns before taxes, salaries, and other expenses are paid]

Industry	2000	2001	2002	2003	2004	2005
Total [2]...............	62,154.4	65,173.5	68,783.0	73,061.9	78,863.6	84,664.1
Card rooms................	949.3	992.0	811.0	978.8	989.0	1,123.6
Commercial casinos	26,455.3	27,318.4	28,143.7	28,669.1	[1]30,608.1	[1]31,855.9
Charitable games and bingo [3] ...	2,465.9	2,590.6	2,670.6	2,330.9	2,336.0	2,337.8
Legal bookmaking	130.6	125.9	116.2	127.6	116.3	130.6
Lotteries	17,277.1	17,474.9	18,657.7	20,282.8	21,644.8	22,897.8
Parimutuel wagering	3,934.6	3,936.3	3,911.5	3,846.6	3,761.9	3,688.8

[1] Amount includes deepwater cruise ships, cruises-to-nowhere, and noncasino devises. [2] Includes some industries not shown separately. [3] Data are estimated.

Source: Christiansen Capital Advisors LLC. Prepared for the American Gaming Association (AGA). Industry Information, Fact Sheets, Gaming Revenue: Current-Year Data (copyright). See also <http://www.americangaming.org/Industry/factsheets/index.cfm> and <www.cca-i.com>.

Table 1232. Domestic Travel by U.S. Resident Households—Summary: 1998 to 2004

[In millions (656.3 represents 656,300,000). See headnote, Table 1233]

Type of trip	1998	1999	2000	2001	2002	2003	2004
All travel: [1]							
Household trips	656.3	640.8	637.7	645.6	637.0	643.5	663.5
Person trips	1,108.0	1,089.5	1,100.8	1,123.1	1,127.0	1,140.0	1,163.9
All overnight travel:							
Household trips	479.4	475.5	477.5	483.7	482.7	491.2	508.4
Person trips	800.0	804.9	822.4	839.2	855.4	871.6	893.1
Business travel:							
Household trips	195.8	192.9	184.9	179.0	166.6	163.5	168.2
Person trips	245.4	240.9	235.1	227.6	214.7	210.5	219.0
Leisure travel: [2]							
Household trips	460.5	447.9	452.8	466.6	470.4	480.0	490.1
Person trips	862.6	848.6	865.7	895.5	912.3	929.5	944.3

[1] Includes personal and other trips (e.g. medical, funerals, weddings), not shown separately. All domestic travel included. 95 percent of U.S. resident person trips are domestic. [2] Includes visiting friends/relatives, outdoor recreation, entertainment, and travel for other pleasure/personal reasons, etc.

Source: Travel Industry Association of America, Washington, DC, *TravelScope*, annual (copyright). See <http://www.tia.org /index.html>.

Table 1233. Characteristics of Domestic Overnight Leisure Trips by U.S. Resident Households: 1999 to 2004

[In millions except as indicated (331.1 represents 331,100,000). Represents household trips to destinations 50 miles or more, one-way, away from home, and including one or more overnights. "Leisure" includes visiting friends/relatives, outdoor recreation, entertainment, and travel for other pleasure/personal reasons etc. Other pleasure/personal trips are trips such as for medical reasons, funerals, weddings, etc. Based on a monthly mail panel survey of 25,000 U.S. households. For details, see source]

Overnight leisure trip characteristic	Unit	1999	2000	2001	2002	2003	2004
Total overnight leisure trips	Millions. . .	331.1	337.1	349.1	354.0	360.3	375.4
Average nights per trip	Number. . .	4.2	4.2	4.2	4.2	4.1	4.1
Traveled primarily by auto, truck, RV, or rental car.	Percent . . .	74	74	74	75	74	73
Traveled primarily by air	Percent . . .	18	18	18	17	17	19
Stayed in a hotel/motel/B&B while on trip	Percent . . .	42	43	42	43	44	44
Household income:							
Less than $50,000	Percent . . .	(NA)	48	44	45	43	42
$50,000 or more	Percent . . .	(NA)	52	56	55	57	58

NA Not available.

Source: Travel Industry Association of America, Washington, DC, *TravelScope*, annual (copyright). See <http://www.tia.org /index.html>.

Table 1234. North America Cruise Industry in the United States: 2000 to 2005

[The North American passenger cruise industry is defined as those cruise lines that primarily market their cruises in North America. These cruise lines offer cruises with destinations throughout the globe. While most of these cruises originate in ports throughout North America, cruises also originate at ports in other continents. International Council of Cruise Lines (ICCL) merged with Cruise Lines International Association (CLIA) in 2006 as CLIA]

Item	Unit	2000	2002	2003	2004	2005
Capacity Measures:						
Number of ships	Number. . .	163	176	184	192	192
Lower berths [1]	Number. . .	165,381	196,694	215,405	240,401	245,755
Passenger embarkations: [2]						
Global	1,000	8,000	9,220	9,830	10,850	11,500
United States	1,000	5,315	6,500	7,113	8,100	8,612
Florida	1,000	3,723	4,413	4,676	4,724	4,843
California	1,000	705	600	807	1,095	1,301
New York	1,000	309	326	438	547	370
Other U.S. ports	1,000	682	1,056	1,192	1,734	2,098
Canada	1,000	473	527	482	454	455
San Juan	1,000	373	298	325	450	581
Rest of world	1,000	1,839	1,895	1,910	1,846	1,852
Direct Economic Impact in the United States: [3]						
Passenger and cruise line spending [4]	Bil. dol. . . .	10.30	11.95	12.92	14.70	16.18
Cruise lines	Bil. dol. . . .	8.07	8.84	9.49	10.70	11.76
Passenger and crew	Bil. dol. . . .	1.34	2.06	2.36	2.88	3.23
Wages & taxes paid by cruise lines	Bil. dol. . . .	0.89	1.05	1.07	1.19	1.19

[1] Single beds. [2] Port of departure. [3] Consist of the expenditures made by the cruise lines and their crew and passengers during the course of providing or taking cruises. These included cruise expenditures for headquarters operations, food and beverages provided aboard cruise ships and businesses services such as, advertising and marketing. Additionally, cruise passengers and crew purchase a variety of goods and services including clothing, shore excursions, and lodging as part of their cruise vacation or as part of a pre- or post-cruise stay. [4] Includes wages and salaries paid to U.S. employees of the cruise lines.

Source: Business Research & Economic Advisors (BREA), Exton, PA. The Contribution of the North American Cruise Industry to the U.S. Economy in 2005. Prepared for the International Council of Cruise Lines, August 2006. See also <http://www.cruising.org>.

Table 1235. **Tourism Sales by Commodity Group, 2001 to 2006, and Tourism Employment by Industry Group, 2001 to 2006**

[Sales in billions of dollars, (524 represents $524,000,000,000). Employment in thousands (5,756 represents 5,756,000). Direct tourism-related sales comprise all output consumed directly by visitors.(e.g., traveler accommodations, passenger air transportation, souvenirs). Direct tourism-related employment comprises all jobs where the workers are engaged in the production of direct tourism-related output (e.g., hotel staff, airline pilots, and souvenir sellers)]

Tourism commodity group	Direct tourism sales (mil. dol.)				Tourism industry group	Direct tourism employment			
	2001	2004	2005	2006		2001	2004	2005	2006
All commodities [1]	524	608	654	700	All industries	5,756	5,679	5,771	5,841
Traveler accommodations	91	106	114	123	Traveler accommodations	1,377	1,339	1,358	1,373
Transportation	205	227	249	269	Transportation	1,327	1,115	1,119	1,111
Passenger air transportation	85	90	98	104	Air transportation services	592	465	461	449
All other transportation-related commodities	120	137	151	164	All other transportation-related industries	735	650	658	662
Food services and drinking places	84	102	110	119	Food and beverage services	1,608	1,772	1,832	1,882
Recreation, entertainment, and shopping	143	173	180	190	Recreation, entertainment, and shopping	1,190	1,204	1,205	1,213
Recreation and entertainment	60	75	79	83	Recreation and entertainment	596	625	637	646
Shopping	83	98	102	107	Shopping (Retailers)	594	579	568	567
					All other industries	254	250	257	263

[1] Commodities that are typically purchased by visitors from the producer: such as airline passenger fares, meals, or hotel services.

Source: U.S. Bureau of Economic Analysis, *"Industry Economic Accounts, Satellite Industry Accounts, Travel and Tourism;"* <http://www.bea.gov/bea/dn2/home/tourism.htm>.

Table 1236. **Travel Forecast Summary: 2004 to 2010**

[In billions of dollars (10,703.5 represents 10,703,500,000,000)]

Measurement	Unit	2004	2005	2006 [1]	2007 [2]	2008 [2]	2009 [2]	2010 [2]
Real GDP	Billions	10,703.5	11,048.6	11,415.3	11,650.2	11,976.7	12,369.7	12,748.0
Unemployment rate	Percent	5.5	5.1	4.6	4.7	4.9	4.7	4.0
Consumer price index (CPI) [3]	Percent	188.9	195.3	201.6	205.8	209.8	214.0	218.0
Travel price index (TPI) [3]	Percent	210.2	219.5	230.4	233.6	240.9	246.7	253.4
Total travel expenditures in US	Billions	606.9	653.8	699.9	733.9	762.9	791.2	821.0
U.S. residents	Billions	532.4	572.1	614.2	641.8	664.3	685.5	708.0
International visitors [4]	Billions	74.5	81.7	85.7	92.1	98.6	105.7	113.0
Total international visitors to the United States	Millions	46.1	49.2	51.1	52.8	54.8	57.0	60.0
Total domestic person trips [5]	Millions	1,953.3	1,992.4	2,000.6	2,032.3	2,069.9	2,109.5	2,147.0

[1] Projected. [2] Forecast. [3] 1982 through 1984 = 100. [4] Excludes international visitors' spending on traveling to the U.S. on U.S. flag carriers, and other misc. transportation. [5] One person on one trip 50 miles or more, one way, away from home or including one or more nights away from home.

Source: TIA's Travel Forecast Model; TravelScope/Directions (copyright); Bureau of Labor Statistics, Office of Travel and Tourism Industries, Bureau of Economic Analysis, Department of Commmerce; <http://www.tia.org/researchpubs/index.html>.

Table 1237. **Domestic Travel Expenditures by State: 2004**

[532,355 represents $532,355,000,000. Represents U.S. spending on domestic overnight trips and day trips of 50 miles or more, one way, away from home. Excludes spending by foreign visitors and by U.S. residents in U.S. territories and abroad]

State	Total (mil. dol.)	Percent distribution	Rank	State	Total (mil. dol.)	Percent distribution	Rank	State	Total (mil. dol.)	Percent distribution	Rank
U.S., total	532,355	100.0	(X)	IA	5,014	0.9	32	NC	13,253	2.5	11
				KS	4,172	0.8	37	ND	1,340	0.3	50
				KY	5,868	1.1	29	OH	13,171	2.5	12
AL	5,969	1.1	28	LA	9,539	1.8	19	OK	4,456	0.8	34
AK	1,470	0.3	48	ME	2,085	0.4	43	OR	5,835	1.1	30
AZ	9,974	1.9	16	MD	9,734	1.8	18	PA	16,175	3.0	7
AR	4,281	0.8	36	MA	10,975	2.1	15	RI	1,510	0.3	47
CA	65,700	12.3	1	MI	12,751	2.4	13	SC	7,764	1.5	24
CO	9,965	1.9	17	MN	8,494	1.6	22	SD	1,663	0.3	46
CT	7,132	1.3	27	MS	5,697	1.1	31	TN	11,164	2.1	14
DE	1,181	0.2	51	MO	9,465	1.8	20	TX	33,818	6.4	3
DC	4,776	0.9	33	MT	2,184	0.4	42	UT	4,030	0.8	38
FL	46,672	8.8	2	NE	2,982	0.6	39	VT	1,446	0.3	49
GA	15,390	2.9	9	NV	26,250	4.9	5	VA	15,041	2.8	10
HI	8,032	1.5	23	NH	2,860	0.5	40	WA	8,594	1.6	21
ID	2,404	0.5	41	NJ	15,733	3.0	8	WV	1,966	0.4	44
IL	23,010	4.3	6	NM	4,348	0.8	35	WI	7,581	1.4	25
IN	7,143	1.3	26	NY	30,458	5.7	4	WY	1,842	0.3	45

X Not applicable.

Source: Travel Industry Association of America, Washington, DC, *Impact of Travel on State Economies, 2004* (copyright); <http://www.tia.org/index.html>.

Arts, Recreation, and Travel 769

Table 1238. Top States and Cities Visited by Overseas Travelers: 2000 to 2006

[25,975 represents 25,975,000. Includes travelers for business and pleasure, international travelers in transit through the United States, and students. Excludes travel by international personnel and international businessmen employed in the United States. States and Cities are ranked by the latest overseas traveler data]

State and other area	Overseas visitors [1] (1,000)				City	Overseas visitors [1] (1,000)			
	2000	2001	2005	2006		2000	2001	2005	2006
Total overseas travelers [2, 3]...	25,975	21,833	21,679	21,668	New York City, NY	5,714	4,803	5,810	6,219
New York	5,922	5,043	6,092	6,414	Los Angeles, CA	3,533	2,816	2,580	2,514
California................	6,364	4,847	4,791	4,615	Orlando, FL	3,013	2,467	2,016	1,993
Florida	6,026	5,262	4,379	4,117	San Francisco, CA	2,831	1,965	2,124	1,993
Hawaii	2,727	2,205	2,255	2,058	Miami, FL	2,935	2,554	2,081	1,972
Nevada.................	2,364	1,572	1,821	1,690	Oahu/Honolulu, HI	2,234	1,747	1,821	1,733
Guam...................	1,325	1,113	1,127	1,170	Las Vegas, NV	2,260	1,506	1,778	1,647
Massachusetts............	1,429	1,179	867	1,105	Chicago, IL	1,351	1,070	1,084	1,062
Illinois..................	1,377	1,113	1,149	1,083	Washington, DC	1,481	1,201	1,106	1,062
Texas	1,169	939	954	975	Boston, MA	1,325	1,070	802	997
New Jersey	909	808	997	845	San Diego, CA	701	589	499	650
Pennsylvania	649	699	629	672	Atlanta, GA	701	699	564	477
Arizona.................	883	633	564	563	Houston, TX	442	415	369	455
					Philadelphia, PA	390	415	434	412
					San Jose, CA	494	415	347	412
					Dallas/Ft. Worth, TX	494	349	347	347
					Tampa/St. Petersburg, FL	519	502	455	347
					Seattle, WA	416	349	347	325

[1] Excludes Canada and Mexico.   [2] A person is counted in each area visited, but only once in the total.   [3] Includes other states and cities, not shown separately.

Source: U.S. Department of Commerce; International Trade Administration; Office of Travel and Tourism Industries and Bureau of Economic Analysis (BEA); released: March 2007; <http://www.tinet.ita.doc.gov>.

Table 1239. Impact of International Travel on States' Economies: 2004

[(74,547.0 represents $74,547,000,000)]

State	Travel expenditures (mil. dol.)	Travel generated payroll (mil. dol.)	Travel generated employment (1,000)	Travel generated tax receipts (mil. dol.)	State	Travel expenditures (mil. dol.)	Travel generated payroll (mil. dol.)	Travel generated employment (1,000)	Travel generated tax receipts (mil. dol.)
U.S., total [1]..	74,547.0	20,444.3	883.4	11,654.6	MO	134.9	40.0	2.0	24.5
AL	(NA)	(NA)	(NA)	(NA)	MT	(NA)	(NA)	(NA)	(NA)
AK	(NA)	(NA)	(NA)	(NA)	NE	(NA)	(NA)	(NA)	(NA)
AZ	1,525.4	501.2	21.7	243.3	NV	2,596.4	948.4	42.1	372.5
AR	(NA)	(NA)	(NA)	(NA)	NH	125.4	21.5	1.1	12.0
CA	11,605.3	3,312.7	134.7	1,925.3	NJ	723.9	230.0	9.2	132.1
CO	684.5	221.9	10.0	144.1	NM	(NA)	(NA)	(NA)	(NA)
CT	219.3	44.2	1.8	34.8	NY	10,507.8	3,148.3	112.8	2,126.7
DE	(NA)	(NA)	(NA)	(NA)	NC	456.7	141.1	7.1	79.1
DC	1,641.9	386.2	13.7	238.5	ND	(NA)	(NA)	(NA)	(NA)
FL	14,446.1	4,145.4	190.6	2,229.9	OH	509.8	117.3	6.2	87.3
GA	1,249.8	493.1	17.3	275.1	OK	(NA)	(NA)	(NA)	(NA)
HI	6,505.6	1,806.0	71.4	947.4	OR	362.7	92.7	4.9	53.9
ID	(NA)	(NA)	(NA)	(NA)	PA	1,192.6	363.3	15.5	201.1
IL	1,511.1	436.9	18.8	303.5	RI	(NA)	(NA)	(NA)	(NA)
IN	217.3	57.7	3.1	33.7	SC	515.7	114.1	7.4	75.1
IA	(NA)	(NA)	(NA)	(NA)	SD	(NA)	(NA)	(NA)	(NA)
KS	(NA)	(NA)	(NA)	(NA)	TN	311.9	85.5	4.3	65.5
KY	(NA)	(NA)	(NA)	(NA)	TX	3,247.2	1,049.5	46.6	582.8
LA	425.4	93.3	5.2	56.9	UT	357.7	133.3	7.5	72.5
ME	(NA)	(NA)	(NA)	(NA)	VT	(NA)	(NA)	(NA)	(NA)
MD	341.8	106.7	4.5	56.9	VA	471.7	131.6	6.6	73.2
MA	1,432.0	398.8	14.8	245.4	WA	803.5	218.3	10.0	140.2
MI	604.3	167.5	7.2	107.3	WV	(NA)	(NA)	(NA)	(NA)
MN	396.4	153.4	6.5	121.1	WI	257.2	69.4	4.2	43.6
MS	(NA)	(NA)	(NA)	(NA)	WY	(NA)	(NA)	(NA)	(NA)

NA Not available.   [1] Total of states listed with data does not equal U.S. total.

Source: Travel Industry Association of America, Washington, DC, Impact of Travel on State Economies, Annual (copyright); <http://www.tia.org/index.html>.

Table 1240. **International Travelers and Payments: 1990 to 2006**

[(47,880 represents $47,880,000,000). For coverage, see Table 1241. Some traveler data revised since originally issued]

Year	Payments by U.S. travelers		Receipts from international visitors		U.S. net travel and passenger receipts (mil. dol.)	U.S. travelers to international countries (1,000)	International travelers to the U.S. (1,000)
	Total [1]	Travel payments	Total [1]	Travel receipts			
1990	47,880	37,349	58,305	43,007	10,425	44,623	39,363
1995	59,579	44,916	82,304	63,395	22,725	51,285	43,490
1999	80,278	58,963	94,586	74,801	14,308	57,222	48,509
2000	88,979	64,705	103,087	82,400	14,108	61,327	51,238
2001	82,833	60,200	89,819	71,893	6,986	59,433	46,927
2002	78,684	58,715	83,651	66,605	4,967	58,065	43,581
2003	78,401	57,444	80,041	64,348	1,640	56,250	41,218
2004	89,473	65,750	93,398	74,547	3,925	61,809	46,086
2005 [2]	95,241	69,175	102,611	81,680	7,370	63,503	49,206
2006 [2]	100,605	73,299	107,757	85,697	7,152	63,642	50,980

[1] Includes passenger fares not shown separately.   [2] Preliminary estimates for the receipts payment figures, and U.S. travelers to International countries.

Source: U.S. Department of Commerce; International Trade Administration; Office of Travel and Tourism Industries and Bureau of Economic Analysis (BEA); released May 2007; <http://www.tinet.ita.doc.gov>.

Table 1241. **International Travel: 1990 to 2006**

[In thousands (44,619 represents 44,619,000). U.S. travelers cover residents of the United States, its territories and possessions. International travelers to the U.S. include travelers for business and pleasure, excludes travel by international personnel and international businessmen employed in the United States. Some traveler data revised since originally issued]

Item and area	1990	1995	2000	2002	2003	2004	2005	2006
U.S. travelers to international countries [1, 2]	44,619	51,285	61,327	58,066	56,250	61,809	63,503	63,642
Canada	12,252	13,005	15,188	16,168	14,232	15,088	14,391	13,835
Mexico	16,377	19,221	19,285	18,501	17,566	19,370	20,325	19,659
Total overseas	15,990	19,059	26,853	23,397	24,452	27,351	28,787	30,148
Europe	8,043	8,596	13,373	10,131	10,319	11,679	11,976	12,029
International travelers to the U.S. . . .	39,363	43,491	51,238	43,581	41,218	46,086	49,206	50,980
Canada	17,263	14,663	14,667	13,024	12,666	13,857	14,862	15,995
Mexico	7,041	8,189	10,596	11,440	10,526	11,907	12,665	13,317
Total overseas	15,059	20,639	25,975	19,117	18,026	20,322	21,679	21,668
Europe	6,659	8,793	11,597	8,603	8,639	9,686	10,313	10,136
South America	4,360	6,616	7,554	5,689	5,003	5,802	6,198	6,152
Central America	1,328	2,449	2,941	1,815	1,522	1,645	1,820	1,928
Caribbean	1,137	1,044	1,331	1,053	998	1,095	1,135	1,198
Far East	412	509	822	704	656	692	696	694
Middle East	662	588	731	529	525	660	737	756
Oceania	365	454	702	483	447	502	527	553
Africa	137	186	295	241	236	241	252	253

[1] A person is counted in each area visited but only once in the total.   [2] 2006 U.S. outbound totals are preliminary estimates.

Source: U.S. Department of Commerce; International Trade Administration; Office of Travel and Tourism Industries and Bureau of Economic Analysis (BEA); released May 2007; <http://www.tinet.ita.doc.gov>.

Table 1242. **Top 20 U.S. Gateways for Nonstop International Air Travel: 2004 and 2005**

[142,242 represents 142,242,000. International passengers are residents of any country traveling nonstop to and from the United States on U.S. and foreign carriers. The data cover all passengers arriving and departing from U.S. airports on nonstop commercial international flights with 60 seats or more]

Gateway airport	2004	2005	Percent change 2004–2005	Gateway airport	2004	2005	Percent change 2004–2005
Total	142,242	150,939	6.1	Dallas-Ft. Worth, TX	4,680	5,146	10.0
Total, top 20	124,350	131,550	5.8	Washington (Dulles), DC	4,527	4,792	5.8
Top 20, percentage of total	87.4	87.2	(X)	Honolulu, HI	4,323	4,410	2.0
				Boston, MA	3,798	3,902	2.7
New York (JFK), NY.	17,090	18,502	8.3	Detroit, MI	3,616	3,823	5.7
Los Angeles, CA	15,843	16,858	6.4	Philadelphia, PA	3,624	3,694	1.9
Miami, FL	14,565	14,621	0.4	Minneapolis-St. Paul, MN	2,523	2,599	3.0
Chicago (O'Hare), IL	10,231	11,013	7.6	Guam Island, GU	2,282	2,456	7.6
Newark, NJ	8,702	9,133	4.9	Seattle-Tacoma, WA	2,336	2,356	0.8
San Francisco, CA	7,293	7,840	7.5	Fort Lauderdale, FL	1,624	2,181	34.3
Atlanta, GA	6,843	7,453	8.9	Orlando, FL	2,027	2,161	6.6
Houston (Bush), TX	6,213	6,571	5.8	San Juan, PR	2,027	2,039	0.6

X Not applicable.

Source: U.S. Department of Transportation, Bureau of Transportation Statistics, Office of Airline Information, T-100 Segment data, February 2006. See also <http://www.bts.gov/publications/pocket_guide_to_transportation/2007/>.

Arts, Recreation, and Travel   771

Table 1243. Selected U.S.-Canadian and U.S.-Mexican Border Land—Passenger Gateways: 2006

[(30,038 represents 30,038,000)]

Item and gateway	Entering the U.S. (1,000)	Item and gateway	Entering the U.S. (1,000)
All U.S.-Canadian land gateways [1]		**All U.S.-Mexican land gateways** [1]	
Personal vehicles	30,038	Personal vehicles	88,296
Personal vehicle passengers	62,986	Personal vehicle passengers	179,255
Buses.	129	Buses.	263
Bus passengers	3,499	Bus passengers	3,187
Train passengers	245	Train passengers	22
Pedestrians	532	Pedestrians	46,251
Selected top five gateways:		**Selected top five gateways:**	
Personal vehicles		Personal vehicles	
Buffalo-Niagara Falls, NY	6,026	San Ysidro, CA	17,135
Detroit, MI.	5,634	El Paso, TX	15,603
Blaine, WA	2,597	Brownsville, TX	6,967
Port Huron, MI.	1,976	Hidalgo, TX.	6,480
Calais, ME	1,174	Calexico, CA.	6,110
Personal vehicle passengers		Personal vehicle passengers	
Buffalo-Niagara Falls, NY	13,515	San Ysidro, CA	31,869
Detroit, MI.	9,932	El Paso, TX	28,000
Blaine, WA	5,276	Laredo, TX	14,244
Port Huron, MI.	4,107	Brownsville, TX	14,023
Champlain-Rouses Point. NY	2,921	Hidalgo, TX.	12,632
Pedestrians		Pedestrians	
Buffalo-Niagara Falls, NY	346	San Ysidro, CA	7,812
Calais, ME.	29	Nogales, AZ	7,726
Sumas, WA.	22	El Paso, TX	7,500
International Falls, MN	20	Laredo, TX	4,246
Point Roberts, WA	15	Calexico, CA.	4,049

[1] Data reflect all personal vehicles, buses, passengers, and pedestrians entering the U.S.-Canadian border, and U.S.-Mexican border, regardless of nationality.

Source: U.S.Department of Transportation, Bureau of Transportation Statistics, special tabulations, June 2007. Based on the following primary data source: U.S. Department of Homeland Security, Customs and Border Protection, Office of Field Operations, Operations Management Database (Washington, D.C. 2006) <http://www.bts.gov/programs/international/border_crossing_entry_data/>.

Table 1244. Foreign Visitors for Pleasure Admitted by Country of Last Residence: 1990 to 2005

[In thousands (13,418 represents 13,418,000). For years ending September 30. Represents non-U.S. citizens (also known as nonimmigrants) admitted to the country for a temporary period of time]

Country	1990	1995	2000 [1]	2005	Country	1990	1995	2000 [1]	2005
All countries [2]	13,418	17,612	30,511	23,815	United Arab Emirates . . .	7	14	36	16
					Africa [2]	105	137	327	113
Europe [2]	5,383	7,012	11,806	9,217	Egypt.	16	16	44	17
Austria	87	146	182	103	Nigeria	11	10	27	34
Belgium	95	153	254	158	South Africa	26	59	114	62
Czech Republic	(X)	12	44	25	Oceania [2]	562	478	748	673
Denmark	75	78	150	143	Australia . . . . [5]	380	327	535	507
Finland	83	47	95	69	New Zealand [5]	153	115	170	166
France	566	738	1,113	885	North America [2]	2,463	2,240	6,501	5,820
Germany [3]	969	1,550	1,925	1,197	Canada	119	127	277	304
Greece	43	44	60	38	Mexico	1,061	893	3,972	4,095
Hungary	15	29	58	28	Caribbean [2]	963	831	1,404	946
Iceland.	10	14	27	32	Aruba	10	19	24	21
Ireland.	81	126	325	361	Bahamas, The	332	234	377	266
Italy.	308	427	626	522	Barbados	34	36	57	45
Netherlands	214	308	559	399	Cayman Islands	31	31	53	54
Norway	80	71	144	114	Dominican Republic . .	137	138	195	192
Poland	55	36	116	114	Haiti.	57	43	72	58
Portugal	30	40	86	62	Jamaica	132	130	240	144
Russia	(X)	33	74	50	Netherlands Antilles . .	31	32	43	37
Spain	183	248	370	365	Trinidad and Tobago . .	81	64	133	105
Sweden	230	142	321	237	Virgin Islands, British. .	8	9	31	26
Switzerland.	236	321	400	222	Central America [2]	320	387	792	474
United Kingdom	1,899	2,342	4,671	4,092	Costa Rica [2]	62	91	172	120
Asia [2]	3,830	5,666	7,853	5,190	El Salvador	46	63	175	148
China [4]	187	378	656	105	Guatemala	91	99	177	141
Hong Kong	111	162	195	82	Honduras	52	37	87	77
India	75	75	253	198	Nicaragua	13	28	47	35
Indonesia	28	44	62	37	Panama . . . . [2]	43	54	106	73
Israel	128	160	319	220	South America [2]	1,016	1,978	2,867	1,512
Japan	2,846	3,986	4,946	3,714	Argentina	136	320	515	152
Korea	120	427	606	474	Bolivia	14	16	48	18
Malaysia.	27	40	64	26	Brazil.	300	710	706	403
Pakistan.	27	27	47	26	Chile	54	117	194	86
Philippines	76	85	163	123	Colombia	122	174	411	269
Saudi Arabia	33	45	67	14	Ecuador	57	77	122	124
Singapore.	32	61	131	64	Peru	97	98	190	139
Thailand.	25	59	76	37	Uruguay	16	37	66	26
Turkey	20	27	93	53	Venezuela	199	400	570	295

X Not applicable. [1] Due to the temporary expiration of the Visa Waiver Program from May through October 2000, data for business and pleasure not available separately for 2000 and 2001. [2] Includes other countries and countries unknown, not shown separately. [3] Data for 1990 are for former West Germany. [4] See Table 1298, footnote 2. [5] Prior to fiscal year 1995, data for Niue are included in New Zealand.

Source: U.S. Dept. of Homeland Security, Office of Immigration Statistics, *2005 Yearbook of Immigration Statistics.* See also <http://www.dhs.gov/ximgtn/statistics/publications/yearbook.shtm>.

Section 27
Accommodation, Food Services, and Other Services

This section presents statistics relating to services other than those covered in the previous few sections (22 to 26) on wholesale and retail trade, transportation, communications, financial services, and recreation services. Data shown for services are classified by kind of business and cover sales or receipts, establishments, employees, payrolls, and other items. The principal sources of these data are from the Census Bureau and include the *2002 Economic Census*, annual surveys, and the *County Business Patterns* program. These data are supplemented by data from several sources such as the National Restaurant Association on food and drink sales (Table 1255), the American Hotel & Lodging Association on lodging (Table 1254), and Universal McCann on advertising (Table 1251).

Data on these services also appear in several other sections. For instance, labor force employment and earnings data appear in Section 12, Labor Force, Employment, and Earnings; gross domestic product of the industry (Table 648) appears in Section 13, Income, Expenditures, Poverty, and Wealth; and financial data (several tables) from the quarterly *Statistics of Income Bulletin,* published by the Internal Revenue Service, appear in Section 15, Business Enterprise.

Censuses—Limited coverage of the service industries started in 1933. Beginning with the 1967 census, legislation provides for a census of each area to be conducted every 5 years (for years ending in "2" and "7"). For more information on the most current census, see the Economic Census, *Guide to Economic Census,* found at <http://www.census.gov/econ /census02/guide/index.html>. The industries covered in the censuses and surveys of business are defined in the *North American Industry Classification System* (NAICS). For information on NAICS, see the Census Web site at <http://www .census.gov/epcd /www/naics.html>.

In general, the 2002 Economic Census has two final series of publications for these sectors: 1) subject series with reports such as product lines, and establishment and firm sizes and 2) geographic reports with individual reports for each state. For information on these series, see the Census Bureau Web site at <http: //www.census.gov/econ/census02>.

Current surveys—The Service Annual Survey provides annual estimates of nationwide receipts for selected personal, business, leasing and repair, amusement and entertainment, social and health, and other professional service industries in the United States. For selected social, health, and other professional service industries, separate estimates are developed for receipts of taxable firms and revenue and expenses for firms and organizations exempt from federal income taxes. Several service sectors from this survey are covered in other sections of this publication. The estimates for tax exempt firms in these industries are derived from a sample of employer firms only. Estimates obtained from annual and monthly surveys are based on sample data and are not expected to agree exactly with results that would be obtained from a complete census of all establishments. Data include estimates for sampling units not reporting.

Statistical reliability—For a discussion of statistical collection and estimation, sampling procedures, and measures of statistical reliability applicable to Census Bureau data, see Appendix III.

Table 1245. **Selected Service-Related Industries—Establishments, Sales, Payroll, and Employees by Kind of Business 2002**

[886,801 represents $886,801,000,000. Covers only establishments with payroll. For statement on methodology, see Appendix III]

Kind of business	2002 NAICS code [1]	Estab- lishments (number)	Sales or receipts (mil. dol.)	Annual payroll (mil. dol.)	Paid employees (1,000) [2]
Professional, scientific, and technical services	**54**	**771,305**	**886,801**	**376,090**	**7,244**
Professional, scientific and technical services	541	771,305	886,801	376,090	7,244
Legal services	5411	179,420	182,098	69,869	1,160
Accounting, tax preparation, bookeeping, & payroll services	5412	112,240	84,072	41,272	1,317
Architectural, engineering, & related services	5413	107,386	161,835	68,015	1,267
Specialized design services	5414	30,484	17,075	4,952	117
Computer systems design & related services	5415	105,710	173,414	72,368	1,107
Management, scientific and tech consulting services	5416	116,159	105,452	42,825	739
Scientific research & development services	5417	15,334	64,481	43,526	618
Advertising and related services	5418	38,047	56,681	19,484	409
Other professional, scientific, and technical services	5419	66,525	41,693	13,779	508
Management of companies and enterprises	**55**	**49,308**	**107,064**	**178,996**	**2,605**
Administrative and support and waste management and remediation services	**56**	**350,583**	**432,578**	**206,439**	**8,742**
Administrative and support services	561	331,921	381,268	194,207	8,410
Office administrative services	5611	22,611	32,081	14,578	366
Facilities support services	5612	3,568	12,957	4,915	146
Employment services	5613	41,552	128,662	94,936	4,166
Business support services	5614	34,735	43,979	17,617	770
Travel arrangement & reservation services	5615	28,470	25,535	8,051	265
Investigation & security services	5616	22,957	31,375	16,004	761
Services to buildings and dwellings	5617	156,555	75,316	29,134	1,584
Other support services	5619	21,473	31,363	8,973	353
Waste management and remediation services	562	18,662	51,309	12,232	332
Waste collection	5621	8,669	28,205	6,388	172
Waste treatment & disposal	5622	2,527	10,834	2,174	50
Remediation & other waste management services	5629	7,466	12,270	3,671	109
Accommodation and food services	**72**	**565,590**	**449,499**	**127,554**	**10,121**
Accommodation	721	60,949	128,098	34,955	1,813
Traveler accommodation	7211	50,982	123,900	33,910	1,761
RV (recreational vehicle) parks & recreational camps	7212	7,353	3,467	883	39
Rooming & boarding houses	7213	2,614	731	162	13
Food services and drinking places	722	504,641	321,401	92,599	8,308
Full-service restaurants	7221	195,659	144,650	46,064	3,905
Limited-service eating places	7222	228,789	135,324	35,442	3,526
Special food services	7223	31,337	26,525	7,729	541
Drinking places (alcoholic beverages)	7224	48,856	14,902	3,364	336
Other services (except public administration)	**81**	**537,576**	**307,049**	**82,955**	**3,475**
Repair and maintenance	811	231,043	118,306	35,118	1,285
Automotive Repair and Maintenance	8111	166,821	75,219	21,592	871
Electronic & precision equipment repair & maintenance	8112	14,567	14,983	4,965	128
Commercial and industrial machinery and equipment repair and maintenance [3]	8113	24,519	19,485	5,891	173
Personal and household goods repair and maintenance	8114	25,136	8,619	2,669	113
Personal and laundry services	812	201,019	72,220	22,908	1,297
Personal care services	8121	99,454	20,217	8,180	535
Death care services	8122	22,477	14,280	3,830	148
Drycleaning & laundry services	8123	41,906	20,444	6,667	371
Other personal services	8129	37,182	17,279	4,232	242
Religious, grantmaking, civic, professional, and similar organizations	813	105,514	116,523	24,929	893
Grantmaking & giving services	8132	14,626	46,276	5,102	137
Social advocacy organizations	8133	12,469	12,059	3,162	104
Civic & social organizations	8134	31,658	14,679	4,427	321
Business/professional/labor/political & similar organizations	8139	46,761	43,509	12,238	332

[1] North American Industrial Classification System, 2002; see text, Section 15.   [2] For employees on the payroll during the pay period including March 12.   [3] Excludes automotive and electronic equipment.

Source: U.S. Census Bureau, "2002 Economic Census, Geographic Area Series," August 2005. See also <http://www.census .gov/econ/census02/guide/02ECUS.HTM>.

Table 1246. Selected Service-Related Industries—Nonemployer Establishments and Receipts by Kind of Business: 2002 to 2005

[2,553 represents 2,553,000. Includes only firms subject to federal income tax. Nonemployers are businesses with no paid employees. Data originate chiefly from administrative records of the Internal Revenue Service; see Appendix III]

Kind of business	2002 NAICS code [1]	Establishments (1,000)			Receipts (mil. dol.)		
		2002	2004	2005	2002	2004	2005
Professional, scientific, and technical services . . .	**54**	**2,553**	**2,725**	**2,854**	**96,395**	**110,596**	**118,575**
Professional, scientific, and technical services	541	2,553	2,725	2,854	96,395	110,596	118,577
Legal services	5411	227	244	247	12,899	14,457	15,087
Accounting, tax preparation, bookeeping, and payroll services	5412	325	340	338	6,423	7,159	7,371
Offices of certified public accountants	541211	38	37	37	1,619	1,721	1,795
Tax preparation services	541213	79	83	84	1,133	1,313	1,401
Payroll services	541214	4	4	4	87	106	106
Other accounting services	541219	204	216	212	3,585	4,020	4,069
Architectual, engineering [2]	5413	209	236	231	8,560	10,206	10,807
Specialized design services	5414	146	167	166	5,073	5,944	6,356
Computer systems design [2]	5415	279	312	282	10,491	12,084	12,029
Management, scientific and technical consulting	5416	465	416	580	18,637	20,157	24,232
Scientific research and development services. . .	5417	25	29	28	799	956	987
Advertising and related services	5418	108	115	112	5,495	6,211	6,414
Other	5419	770	867	871	28,018	33,421	35,294
Administrative and support and waste management and remediation services.	**56**	**1,263**	**1,337**	**1,417**	**26,910**	**30,932**	**33,028**
Administrative and support services	561	1,244	1,319	1,398	25,826	29,685	31,666
Office administrative services	5611	127	172	180	1,886	2,517	2,667
Facilities support services	5612	21	25	25	633	730	761
Employment services.	5613	30	21	19	1,013	1,128	1,179
Business support services	5614	176	183	185	4,460	5,102	5,274
Travel arrangement and reservation services . . .	5615	33	31	31	1,433	1,510	1,543
Investigations and security services	5616	70	63	64	1,123	1,161	1,184
Services to buildings and dwellings	5617	722	750	816	13,261	15,189	16,548
Exterminating and pest control services	56171	8	8	8	315	371	398
Janitorial services	56172	428	431	470	5,899	6,433	6,895
Landscaping services	56173	209	226	249	4,811	5,749	6,387
Carpet and upholstery cleaning services	56174	22	24	25	666	745	776
Other.	56179	56	61	65	1,570	1,890	2,093
Other support services	5619	65	75	77	2,016	2,348	2,511
Waste management and remediation services	562	18	18	19	1,084	1,247	1,364
Accommodation and food services	**72**	**242**	**275**	**279**	**14,178**	**15,510**	**15,307**
Accommodation	721	52	56	56	3,766	3,976	3,823
Traveler accommodation	7211	34	36	36	3,150	3,284	3,100
RV (recreational vehicle) parks and recreational camps	7212	7	7	7	333	348	365
Rooming and boarding houses	7213	11	14	14	284	345	358
Food services and drinking places	722	190	219	223	10,412	11,534	11,483
Full-service restaurants	7221	34	37	37	3,561	3,964	3,815
Limited-service eating places.	7222	43	48	47	2,978	3,238	3,168
Special food services	7223	90	109	115	2,358	2,755	2,917
Drinking places (alcoholic beverages)	7224	23	24	25	1,515	1,576	1,583
Other services (except public administration)	**81**	**2,459**	**2,800**	**2,873**	**60,468**	**70,299**	**74,025**
Repair and maintenance	811	643	695	691	22,817	25,466	26,465
Automotive repair and maintenance	8111	271	287	289	12,182	13,266	13,706
Automotive, mechanical and electrical repair [3]	81111	135	141	143	6,214	6,771	6,972
Automotive body, paint, interior, and glass repair.	81112	74	80	78	3,401	3,660	3,736
Other automotive repair and maintenance . . .	81119	62	66	68	2,567	2,835	2,998
Electronic and precision equipment repair [3]	8112	46	47	45	1,468	1,566	1,572
Commercial and industrial machinery and equipment repair and maintenance [4] . . .	8113	52	56	55	2,335	2,651	2,790
Personal and household goods repair [3].	8114	274	305	302	6,831	7,983	8,397
Personal and laundry services	812	1,642	1,924	1,996	35,127	42,151	44,809
Personal care services.	8121	666	776	827	13,582	16,354	17,707
Hair, nail, and skin care services	81211	572	660	703	11,969	14,304	15,472
Barber shops.	812111	81	91	91	1,671	1,854	1,878
Beauty salons	812112	400	449	480	8,357	9,661	10,304
Nail salons	812113	90	120	132	1,942	2,788	3,289
Other.	812119	94	117	124	1,613	2,050	2,236
Death care services.	8122	14	15	15	746	791	816
Drycleaning and laundry services	8123	37	36	36	1,741	1,865	1,884
Other personal services	8129	925	1,097	1,118	19,057	23,141	24,401
Pet care (except veterinary) services.	81291	39	46	49	762	941	1,034
Photofinishing	81292	12	14	15	298	315	326
Parking lots and garages	81293	4	4	4	221	261	271
Other.	81299	871	1,034	1,050	17,777	21,625	22,770
Religious, grantmaking, civic, professional, and similar organizations	813	174	181	186	2,524	2,682	2,752

[1] Based on the North American Industry Classification System, 2002, see text, Section 15.   [2] Includes related services.   [3] Includes maintenance.   [4] Except automotive and electronic.

Source: U.S. Census Bureau, "Nonemployer Statistics"; <http://www.census.gov/epcd/nonemployer/index.html> (accessed 10 July 2007)

Accommodation, Food Services, and Other Services   **775**

Table 1247. Selected Service-Related Industries—Establishments, Employees, and Payroll by Industry: 2003 and 2004

[781 represents 781,000. Covers establishments with payroll. Excludes most government employees, railroad employees, and self-employed persons. Kind-of-business classification based on North American Industry Classification System, 2002 (NAICS); see text, Section 15. For statement on methodology, see Appendix III]

Kind of business	2002 NAICS code	Establishments (1,000)		Employees (1,000)[1]		Annual payroll (bil. dol.)	
		2003	2004	2003	2004	2003	2004
Professional, scientific, & technical services	54	781	805	7,340	7,570	398.2	426.7
Professional, scientific, & technical services	541	781	805	7,340	7,570	398.2	426.7
Legal services	5411	182	185	1,183	1,218	73.9	78.1
Offices of lawyers	54111	171	173	1,094	1,123	70.2	74.1
Accounting, tax preparation, bookkeeping, & payroll services	5412	114	117	1,325	1,390	43.5	46.6
Tax preparation services	541213	20	22	199	198	1.6	2.0
Architectural, engineering, & related services [2]	5413	106	109	1,235	1,265	70.8	75.9
Architectural services	54131	23	24	180	181	9.9	10.5
Engineering services	54133	54	55	835	858	52.0	56.0
Specialized design services [2]	5414	30	32	117	119	4.9	5.2
Graphic design services	54143	16	16	60	60	2.6	2.7
Computer systems design & related services [2]	5415	102	106	1,059	1,105	72.0	77.7
Custom computer programming services	541511	46	47	418	435	29.5	31.9
Computer systems design services	541512	39	43	427	458	29.1	31.7
Management, scientific, & technical consulting services [2]	5416	123	129	838	880	49.5	55.5
Management consulting services	54161	99	103	721	755	43.1	48.3
Environmental consulting services	54162	9	9	59	60	2.9	3.0
Scientific research & development services	5417	15	16	616	641	46.7	51.4
Research & development in the physical engineering & life sciences	54171	13	14	561	587	43.2	47.8
Advertising & related services [2]	5418	37	39	419	390	21.2	19.6
Advertising agencies	54181	13	13	156	139	10.2	9.3
Direct mail advertising	54186	4	4	85	71	3.3	2.7
Other professional, scientific, & tech services	5419	71	72	547	562	15.7	16.8
Veterinary services	54194	26	27	253	267	6.2	6.8
Management of companies and enterprises	55	47	46	2,879	2,825	212.5	222.5
Admin/support & waste mgmt & remediation service	56	349	359	8,511	8,708	219.2	235.5
Administrative & support services [2]	561	330	340	8,171	8,364	206.0	222.1
Employment services	5613	41	41	3,902	4,028	97.0	106.5
Temporary help services [2]	56132	27	27	2,188	2,326	49.3	54.7
Business support services [2]	5614	35	35	760	774	18.6	19.8
Telephone call centers	56142	5	5	384	392	7.1	8.0
Collection agencies	56144	5	5	140	141	4.1	4.2
Credit bureaus	56145	1	1	26	26	1.5	1.5
Travel arrangement & reservation services	5615	26	24	284	270	9.9	10.3
Travel agencies	56151	19	18	146	132	4.5	4.6
Investigation & security services	5616	23	23	747	755	16.3	17.4
Investigation, guard, & armored car services	56161	13	13	637	636	12.3	13.1
Security systems services	56162	10	10	110	118	4.0	4.2
Services to buildings & dwellings	5617	158	166	1,533	1,604	31.1	33.3
Waste management & remediation services	562	18	19	340	344	13.2	13.4
Waste collection	5621	8	9	178	179	6.7	6.9
Waste treatment & disposal	5622	3	3	62	55	2.7	2.5
Remediation & other waste mgmt services	5629	7	8	101	109	3.8	4.0
Accommodation & food services	72	575	591	10,440	10,750	139.2	147.2
Accommodation	721	61	62	1,804	1,845	37.1	39.5
Traveler accommodation	7211	51	52	1,754	1,794	36.0	38.3
Hotels (except casino hotels) & motels	72111	47	48	1,366	1,407	25.6	27.5
RV (recreational vehicle) parks & recreational camps	7212	7	7	37	38	0.9	1.0
Rooming & boarding houses	7213	3	2	13	14	0.2	0.2
Food services & drinking places	722	514	529	8,636	8,905	102.1	107.7
Full-service restaurants	7221	200	206	4,091	4,263	51.7	55.2
Limited-service eating places	7222	234	242	3,641	3,772	38.1	40.4
Special food services	7223	31	32	553	508	8.5	8.1
Drinking places (alcoholic beverages)	7224	48	48	351	361	3.7	4.0
Other services (except public administration)	81	732	735	5,367	5,416	118.0	122.5
Repair & maintenance [2]	811	229	229	1,305	1,320	37.0	38.4
Automotive repair & maintenance	8111	165	166	892	905	22.5	23.2
Personal & household goods repair & maintenance	8114	25	25	108	109	2.8	2.8
Personal & laundry services [2]	812	205	208	1,310	1,333	24.0	25.0
Personal care services	8121	101	106	552	580	8.8	9.4
Death care services	8122	22	20	147	126	3.9	3.5
Drycleaning & laundry services	8123	42	43	370	390	6.9	7.6
Religious/grantmaking/civic/professional [3]	813	299	297	2,753	2,763	57.0	59.1
Religious organizations	8131	174	171	1,655	1,649	25.8	26.4
Grantmaking & giving services	8132	15	16	138	140	5.4	5.6
Social advocacy organizations	8133	12	13	109	115	3.2	3.6
Civic & social organizations	8134	32	32	328	323	4.8	4.7
Business/professional/labor/political [3]	8139	66	66	523	535	17.8	18.8
Labor unions [3]	81393	17	16	183	179	4.5	4.6

[1] Includes employees on the payroll for the pay period including March 12. [2] Includes other kinds of business not shown separately. [3] And similar organizations.

Source: U.S. Census Bureau, "County Business Patterns." <http://www.census.gov/epcd/cbp/view/cbpview.html>.

Table 1248. **Selected Service-Related Industries—Establishments, Employees, and Annual Payroll by State: 2004**

[7,570 represents 7,570,000. Covers establishments with payroll. Excludes most government employees, railroad employees, and self-employed persons. Based on the North American Industry Classification System, 2002 (NAICS); see text, Section 15. For statement on methodology, see Appendix III]

State	Professional, scientific, & technical services (NAICS 54)			Admin./ support waste mgt./ remediation services (NAICS 56)			Accommodation and food services (NAICS 72)		
	Estab-lish-ments	Employ-ees [1] (1,000)	Annual payroll (mil. dol.)	Estab-lish-ments	Employ-ees [1] (1,000)	Annual payroll (mil. dol.)	Estab-lish-ments	Employ-ees [1] (1,000)	Annual payroll (mil. dol.)
United States. .	804,569	7,570	426,713	358,902	8,708	235,542	591,022	10,750	147,178
Alabama.........	9,036	91	4,470	3,939	108	2,352	7,292	141	1,491
Alaska..........	1,769	12	616	944	13	516	1,944	23	473
Arizona.........	14,672	116	5,716	7,234	194	5,184	10,412	223	2,962
Arkansas	5,321	35	1,368	2,357	49	910	4,765	83	828
California	104,260	1,239	70,228	40,132	982	28,448	69,774	1,240	18,669
Colorado........	20,749	147	8,653	7,476	171	5,004	11,393	214	2,945
Connecticut......	10,250	99	6,454	5,368	105	3,073	7,414	125	2,285
Delaware	2,451	27	1,815	1,249	26	631	1,670	29	420
District of Columbia . .	4,278	86	8,080	919	29	950	1,790	47	1,064
Florida	62,597	414	20,069	29,653	1,157	30,802	32,285	700	9,566
Georgia	25,359	200	10,873	10,874	299	7,940	16,592	330	4,126
Hawaii	3,215	24	1,087	1,706	37	876	3,330	95	2,028
Idaho..........	3,635	31	1,242	1,852	41	847	3,170	50	549
Illinois	37,837	344	21,160	15,383	416	10,769	25,170	439	5,904
Indiana.........	12,524	103	4,654	6,757	149	3,821	12,237	244	2,849
Iowa	6,058	42	1,677	3,301	60	1,283	6,711	107	1,091
Kansas.........	7,025	60	2,531	3,301	61	1,544	5,681	99	1,047
Kentucky	7,882	59	2,260	3,627	73	1,562	6,888	143	1,613
Louisiana	11,055	82	3,316	4,389	105	2,351	7,901	177	2,191
Maine..........	3,438	23	975	1,833	25	669	3,833	45	693
Maryland	18,717	215	12,772	7,641	158	4,624	9,875	184	2,574
Massachusetts.....	21,952	237	17,984	8,975	180	6,024	15,393	245	3,978
Michigan........	22,393	294	18,042	11,748	317	9,359	19,222	335	3,775
Minnesota.......	16,150	124	6,833	6,909	137	3,862	10,742	207	2,650
Mississippi	4,610	32	1,221	2,162	43	856	4,591	118	1,622
Missouri	13,323	131	6,266	6,998	144	3,393	11,610	230	2,754
Montana........	3,155	17	578	1,426	12	238	3,343	43	457
Nebraska........	4,023	40	1,773	2,420	58	1,454	4,097	67	680
Nevada	7,003	54	2,687	3,705	86	2,487	4,677	280	7,094
New Hampshire....	4,008	28	1,488	1,954	40	1,160	3,319	53	770
New Jersey......	31,376	293	18,556	13,126	294	8,394	18,500	270	4,781
New Mexico......	4,583	34	1,571	1,802	33	818	3,853	77	912
New York	57,075	565	36,745	23,214	476	15,608	41,383	542	9,365
North Carolina	20,319	171	8,804	10,400	223	5,282	16,601	307	3,698
North Dakota.....	1,342	12	400	818	11	195	1,791	28	281
Ohio	25,497	238	11,772	13,476	318	7,711	23,148	427	4,673
Oklahoma........	8,731	61	2,528	3,842	94	2,285	6,555	117	1,215
Oregon.........	10,650	73	3,446	4,896	85	2,062	9,329	135	1,828
Pennsylvania.....	29,279	308	17,757	13,822	290	7,364	25,749	403	4,778
Rhode Island......	3,109	24	1,082	1,658	22	552	2,865	41	597
South Carolina	8,862	71	3,267	5,080	121	2,699	8,607	167	2,022
South Dakota	1,632	10	318	870	9	184	2,203	34	362
Tennessee	10,950	103	4,961	5,977	169	4,165	10,571	215	2,580
Texas..........	54,623	515	29,851	22,904	689	18,469	38,710	774	9,690
Utah	6,996	65	2,521	3,305	81	2,018	4,344	85	946
Vermont	2,076	12	514	938	7	181	1,975	29	387
Virginia.........	24,900	341	22,020	9,723	232	6,530	14,224	281	3,719
Washington......	17,791	143	8,413	8,124	125	4,460	14,551	207	2,996
West Virginia......	2,991	24	797	1,481	28	576	3,452	58	633
Wisconsin	11,374	94	4,285	6,405	121	2,860	13,722	214	2,256
Wyoming	1,668	8	269	809	7	141	1,768	25	313

[1] For employees on the payroll for the pay period including March 12.

Source: U.S. Census Bureau, "County Business Patterns"; <http://www.census.gov/epcd/cbp/view/cbpview.html>.

Accommodation, Food Services, and Other Services 777

Table 1249. **Professional, Scientific, and Technical Services—Estimated Revenue: 2000 to 2005**

[In millions of dollars (803,527 represents $803,527,000,000). For taxable employer firms. Estimates have been adjusted to the results of the 2002 Economic Census. Based on the Service Annual Survey; see Appendix III]

Kind of business	2002 NAICS code [1]	2000	2001	2002	2003	2004	2005
Professional, scientific, and technical services (except notaries).........	54	803,527	838,374	846,056	879,725	966,645	1,058,632
Legal services (except notaries)...........	5411	160,619	171,597	180,042	199,915	209,475	221,646
Offices of lawyers..................	54111	152,834	162,958	170,808	187,819	197,385	208,038
Other legal services...............	54119	7,785	8,639	9,234	12,096	12,090	13,608
Accounting, tax preparation, bookkeeping and payroll services	5412	79,361	82,845	84,073	87,791	92,884	102,316
Offices of certified public accountants......	541211	45,773	49,635	48,498	47,835	50,679	54,339
Tax preparation services	541213	3,347	3,765	4,129	4,468	4,944	5,516
Payroll services	541214	21,394	20,149	21,418	24,366	25,359	29,499
Other accounting services	541219	8,847	9,296	10,028	11,122	11,902	12,962
Architectural, engineering, & related services...	5413	150,269	157,488	158,266	160,917	184,292	209,976
Architectural services...............	54131	25,021	26,719	25,240	26,851	28,609	31,939
Landscape architectural services	54132	(X)	(X)	(X)	(X)	4,218	4,575
Engineering services	54133	111,929	115,837	116,887	117,509	132,814	152,788
Testing laboratories................	54138	7,128	7,865	8,771	8,849	9,908	10,532
Other related services	54134,5,6,7	6,191	7,067	7,368	7,708	8,742	10,142
Specialized design services	5414	17,889	17,776	17,076	18,090	19,617	21,315
Interior design services	54141	6,798	6,897	7,018	7,497	8,061	8,807
Graphic design services..............	54143	8,962	8,796	8,096	8,269	8,528	9,132
All other design services	54142,9	(X)	(X)	(X)	(X)	3,028	3,377
Computer systems design and services	5415	186,402	183,878	173,414	171,393	173,525	189,042
Custom computer programming services....	541511	70,004	65,578	60,126	58,140	58,303	64,228
Computer systems design services	541512	82,763	80,787	78,335	76,992	77,042	84,560
Computer facilities management services ...	541513	21,816	25,435	22,279	22,518	23,422	23,807
Other computer-related services	541519	11,819	12,078	12,674	13,743	14,758	16,447
Management, scientific, and technical consulting services	5416	90,129	99,511	105,452	108,783	121,709	137,931
Management consulting services	54161	78,250	86,024	90,914	92,129	102,452	115,756
Environmental consulting services	54162	5,578	6,213	6,933	7,902	8,748	9,087
Other scientific and technical consulting services....................	54169	6,301	7,274	7,605	8,752	10,509	13,088
Scientific research and development services ..	5417	35,587	41,568	45,983	48,142	54,272	59,130
Research and development in physical, engineering, and life sciences	54171	34,029	39,870	44,089	46,104	51,994	56,655
Research and development in social sciences and humanities	54172	1,558	1,698	1,894	2,038	2,278	2,475
Advertising and related services	5418	59,680	58,634	56,681	58,629	63,585	66,865
Advertising agencies	54181	21,584	21,268	21,104	22,396	24,551	25,141
Public relations agencies	54182	6,501	6,156	6,205	6,305	6,954	7,573
Media buying agencies	54183	1,036	1,025	1,150	1,063	(S)	(S)
Media representatives	54184	3,247	3,118	2,729	2,712	(S)	(S)
Display advertising	54185	4,752	4,509	4,617	4,925	5,440	6,152
Direct mail advertising	54186	10,351	10,739	10,544	10,648	11,570	12,174
All other advertising................	54187,9	(X)	(X)	(X)	(X)	11,568	12,095
Other professional, scientific, and technical services	5419	23,591	25,077	25,069	26,065	47,289	50,411
Marketing research and public opinion polling.......................	54191	11,683	11,412	10,890	11,118	11,851	12,298
Photographic services	54192	6,613	6,760	6,538	6,758	6,984	7,257
Photography studios, portrait	541921	4,642	4,773	4,752	4,879	5,031	5,259
Commercial photography	541922	1,971	1,987	1,786	1,879	1,953	1,998
Translation and interpretation services	54193	810	850	876	968	1,093	1,121
Veterinary services	54194	(X)	(X)	(X)	(X)	19,353	20,796
All other professional, scientific, and technical service	54199	4,485	6,055	6,765	7,221	8,008	8,938

S Estimate does not meet publication standards.   X Not applicable.   [1] Based on the North American Industry Classification System, 2002; see Section 15.

Source: U.S. Census Bureau, "2005 Service Annual Survey, Professional, Scientific, and Technical Sector Services." See <http://www.census.gov/econ/www/servmenu.html> (released February 2007).

778 Accommodation, Food Services, and Other Services

Table 1250. Selected Service Industries—E-Commerce Revenue: 2004 and 2005

[83,279 represents $83,279,000,000. Includes data only for businesses with paid employees, except for accommodation and food services, which also includes businesses with and without paid employees. Except as noted, based on the Service Annual Survey]

Kind of business	2002 NAICS code [1]	E-commerce revenue (mil. dol.) 2004	E-commerce revenue (mil. dol.) 2005	E-commerce as percent of total revenue, 2005	E-commerce revenue, percent distribution, 2005
Selected service industries, total	(X)	83,279	95,696	1.6	100.0
Selected transportation and warehousing [2]	(X)	4,908	6,000	2.1	6.3
Truck transportation	484	4,249	5,240	2.5	5.5
Couriers and messengers	492	(S)	(S)	(S)	(S)
Warehousing and storage	493	616	704	3.6	0.7
Information	51	22,774	26,578	2.6	27.8
Publishing industries	511	9,456	12,066	4.5	12.6
Online information services	51811	2,212	1,898	7.3	2.0
Selected finance [3]	(X)	6,043	6,087	1.5	6.4
Securities and commodity contracts intermediation and brokerage	5231	5,817	5,814	2.0	6.1
Rental and leasing services	532	(S)	5,423	4.9	5.7
Selected professional, scientific, and technical services [4]	(X)	20,167	21,864	2.0	22.8
Computer systems design and related services	5415	(S)	(S)	(S)	(S)
Administrative and support and waste management and remediation services	56	12,794	14,365	2.7	15.0
Travel arrangements and reservation services	5615	8,473	9,864	32.5	10.3
Health care and social assistance services	62	943	1,545	0.1	1.6
Arts, entertainment, and recreation services	71	(S)	1,906	(S)	2.0
Accommodation and food services [5]	72	5,834	7,474	1.4	7.8
Selected other services [6]	(X)	3,644	4,454	1.2	4.7
Repair and maintenance	811	1,026	959	0.7	1.0
Religious, grantmaking, civic, professional, and similar organizations	813	1,786	2,203	1.5	2.3

S Data do not meet publication standards. X Not applicable. [1] North American Industry Classification System (NAICS), 2002; see text Section 15. [2] Excludes NAICS 481 (air transportation), 482 (rail transportation), 483 (water transportation), 485 (transit and good passenger transportation), 487 (scenic and sightseeing transportation), 488 (support activities for transportation) and 491 (postal service). [3] Excludes NAICS 521 (monetary authorities-central bank), 522 (credit intermediation and related activities), 5232 (securities and commodity exchanges), NAICS 52391 (miscellaneous intermediation), 52399 (all other financial investment activities), 524 (insurance carriers and related activities) and 525 (funds and trusts). [4] Excludes NAICS 54112 (offices of notaries). [5] Based on 2005 Annual Retail Trade Survey. [6] Excludes NAICS 81311 (religious organizations), 81393 (labor and similar organizations), 81394 (political organizations) and 814 (private households).

Source: U.S. Census Bureau, Internet site E-Stats (released 25 May 2007); see Internet site <http://www.census.gov/eos/www/ebusiness614.htm>.

Table 1251. Advertising—Estimated Expenditures by Medium: 1990 to 2006

[In millions of dollars (129,968 represents $129,968,000,000). See source for definitions of types of advertising]

Medium	1990	1995	2000	2001	2002	2003	2004	2005	2006 [1]
Total	129,968	165,147	247,472	231,287	236,875	245,477	263,766	271,074	285,106
National	73,638	96,933	151,664	141,797	145,429	152,482	167,096	172,797	184,696
Local	56,330	68,214	95,808	89,490	91,446	92,995	96,670	98,277	100,410
Newspapers	32,281	36,317	49,050	44,255	44,031	44,843	46,614	47,335	47,709
National	3,867	3,996	7,229	6,615	6,806	7,357	7,629	7,465	7,241
Local	28,414	32,321	41,821	37,640	37,225	37,486	38,985	39,870	40,468
Magazines	6,803	8,580	12,370	11,095	10,995	11,435	12,247	12,847	13,425
Broadcast TV	26,616	32,720	44,802	38,881	42,068	41,932	46,264	44,293	47,109
Four TV networks	9,863	11,600	15,888	14,300	15,000	15,030	16,713	16,128	16,934
Syndication	1,109	2,016	3,108	3,102	3,034	3,434	3,674	3,865	4,058
Spot (national)	7,788	9,119	12,264	9,223	10,920	9,948	11,370	10,040	11,144
Spot (local)	7,856	9,985	13,542	12,256	13,114	13,520	14,507	14,260	14,973
Cable TV	2,631	6,166	15,455	15,736	16,297	18,814	21,527	23,654	24,879
Cable TV networks	2,000	4,500	11,765	11,777	12,071	13,954	16,424	18,296	19,119
Spot (local)	631	1,666	3,690	3,959	4,226	4,860	5,103	5,358	5,760
Radio	8,726	11,338	19,295	17,861	18,877	19,100	19,581	19,640	19,614
Network	482	480	780	711	775	798	836	814	838
Spot (national)	1,635	1,959	3,668	2,956	3,340	3,540	3,540	3,469	3,573
Spot (local)	6,609	8,899	14,847	14,194	14,762	14,762	15,205	15,357	15,203
Yellow Pages	8,926	10,236	13,228	13,592	13,776	13,896	14,002	14,229	14,372
National	1,132	1,410	2,093	2,087	2,087	2,114	2,110	2,163	2,185
Local	7,794	8,826	11,135	11,505	11,689	11,782	11,892	12,066	12,187
Direct mail	23,370	32,866	44,591	44,725	46,067	48,370	52,191	55,218	59,912
Business papers	2,875	3,559	4,915	4,468	3,976	4,004	4,072	4,170	4,253
Out-of-home [2]	1,084	1,263	5,176	5,134	5,175	5,443	5,770	6,232	6,731
National	640	701	2,068	2,051	2,061	2,298	2,530	2,736	2,955
Local	444	562	3,108	3,083	3,114	3,145	3,240	3,496	3,776
Internet [3]	(NA)	(NA)	6,507	5,645	4,883	5,650	6,853	7,764	9,317
Miscellaneous [4]	16,656	22,102	32,083	29,895	30,730	31,990	34,645	35,692	37,785
National	12,074	16,147	24,418	23,042	23,414	24,550	26,907	27,822	29,742
Local	4,582	5,955	7,665	6,853	7,316	7,440	7,738	7,870	8,043

NA Not available. [1] Preliminary data. [2] Prior to 2000, represents only "outdoor" billboards. Beginning 2000, includes other forms of outdoor advertising (i.e. transportation vehicles, bus shelters, telephone kiosks, etc.) previously covered under "Miscellaneous." [3] Excludes search revenue. [4] Beginning 2000, part of miscellaneous now included under Out-of-home advertising. See footnote 2.

Source: Universal McCann, New York, N.Y. (copyright). See also <http://www.universalmccann.com>.

Table 1252. **Administrative and Support and Waste Management and Remediation Services—Estimated Revenue: 2000 to 2005**

[In millions of dollars (396,499 represents $396,499,000,000). For taxable and tax-exempt employer firms. Estimates have been adjusted to results of the 2002 Economic Census. Based on the Service Annual Survey; see Appendix III]

Kind of business	2002 NAICS code [1]	2000	2001	2002	2003	2004	2005
Administrative & support waste and management and remediation services...	56	396,499	390,683	397,408	414,988	484,242	530,083
Administrative and support services..........	561	345,302	339,028	346,099	360,434	425,600	436,215
Office administrative services.............	5611	26,288	29,523	32,081	34,556	38,014	43,059
Facilities support services...............	5612	13,211	12,878	12,957	12,158	12,520	14,005
Employment services...................	5613	144,242	129,471	128,662	133,833	145,717	160,318
Employment placement agencies	56131	4,985	5,355	5,940	5,874	6,513	6,855
Temporary help services	56132	79,622	68,658	68,190	69,910	77,660	84,838
Professional employer organizations	56133	59,635	55,458	54,532	58,049	61,544	68,625
Business support services...............	5614	41,203	43,983	43,981	46,111	48,166	50,760
Document preparation services...........	56141	1,920	2,121	2,419	2,500	2,483	2,642
Telephone call centers	56142	14,805	15,116	13,394	13,273	13,843	14,528
Telephone answering services..........	561421	2,135	2,323	2,109	1,897	1,783	1,804
Telemarketing bureaus...............	561422	12,670	12,793	11,285	11,376	12,060	12,724
Business service centers...............	56143	8,257	8,342	8,234	8,335	8,469	8,425
Private mail centers...............	561431	1,692	1,830	1,957	2,187	2,274	2,279
Other business service centers (including copy shops)...............	561439	6,565	6,512	6,277	6,148	6,195	6,146
Collection agencies	56144	7,300	8,092	8,852	9,830	10,860	11,416
Credit bureaus......................	56145	3,741	4,243	4,591	5,230	5,516	6,332
Other business support services	56149	5,180	6,069	6,491	6,943	6,995	7,417
Repossession services	561491	418	467	552	549	534	(S)
Court reporting and stenotype services....	561492	1,250	1,407	1,638	1,715	1,792	1,847
All other business support services	561499	3,512	4,195	4,301	4,679	4,669	5,027
Travel arrangement and reservation services ...	5615	26,119	25,622	25,535	26,594	28,200	30,334
Travel agencies......................	56151	11,639	10,220	9,387	9,759	10,101	10,944
Tour operators......................	56152	3,564	3,266	3,190	3,212	3,515	3,685
Other travel arrangement and reservation services	56159	10,916	12,136	12,958	13,623	14,584	15,705
Convention and visitors bureaus	561591	1,020	1,124	1,128	1,227	1,256	1,314
All other travel arrangement and reservation services.............	561599	9,896	11,012	11,830	12,396	13,328	14,391
Investigation and security services	5616	27,594	28,549	31,375	32,325	33,723	37,118
Investigation, guard, and armored car services.......................	56161	17,581	17,471	19,468	20,920	21,754	24,456
Investigation services...............	561611	2,350	2,413	2,586	3,090	3,345	3,593
Security guards and patrol services	561612	13,393	13,037	14,763	15,551	16,321	18,487
Armored car services...............	561613	1,838	2,021	2,119	2,279	2,088	2,376
Security systems services	56162	10,013	11,078	11,907	11,405	11,969	12,662
Security systems services (except locksmiths)	561621	8,683	9,765	10,592	9,987	10,488	11,083
Locksmiths	561622	1,330	1,313	1,315	1,418	1,481	1,579
Services to buildings and dwellings..........	5617	35,790	38,168	40,144	43,697	85,946	93,680
Exterminating and pest control services	56171	5,723	6,067	6,597	7,206	7,673	8,118
Janitorial services..................	56172	24,593	26,220	27,009	29,303	30,288	32,059
Landscaping services	56173	(X)	(X)	(X)	(X)	40,317	44,651
Carpet and upholstery cleaning services ..	56174	2,463	2,541	2,719	2,808	2,964	3,427
Other services to buildings and dwellings	56179	3,011	3,340	3,819	4,380	4,703	5,424
Other support services	5619	30,855	30,834	31,364	31,160	33,315	36,940
Packaging and labeling services	56191	4,432	4,804	4,916	5,021	(S)	(S)
Convention and trade show organizers	56192	8,410	8,362	8,562	9,083	9,517	10,641
All other support services	56199	18,013	17,668	17,886	17,056	18,207	19,813
Waste management and remediation services	562	51,197	51,655	51,309	54,554	58,643	63,868
Waste collection	5621	28,820	28,649	28,206	30,272	32,430	34,350
Solid waste collection	562111	27,032	26,827	26,416	28,363	30,436	32,146
Hazardous waste collection	562112	1,249	1,308	1,325	1,445	1,565	1,720
Other waste collection.................	562119	539	514	465	464	429	484
Waste treatment and disposal	5622	11,025	11,290	10,834	11,173	11,398	13,092
Hazardous waste treatment and disposal	562211	3,155	3,270	3,642	3,351	3,264	3,894
Solid waste landfill	562212	5,965	5,841	5,272	5,802	6,168	6,658
Solid waste combustors and incinerators	562213	1,261	1,532	1,365	1,442	1,303	1,760
Other nonhazardous waste treatment and disposal	562219	644	647	555	578	663	780
Remediation and other waste management services..........................	5629	11,352	11,716	12,269	13,109	14,815	16,426
Remediation services	56291	6,750	7,246	7,640	7,745	8,834	9,938
Materials recovery facility..............	56292	1,593	1,546	1,800	2,222	2,633	2,749
All other waste management services	56299	3,009	2,924	2,829	3,142	3,348	3,739
Septic tank and related services	562991	2,197	2,055	1,973	2,049	2,132	2,374
All other miscellaneous waste management services	562998	812	869	856	1,093	1,216	1,365

S Data do not meet publication standards.   X Not applicable.   [1] North American Industry Classification System, 2002; see text, Section 15.

Source: U.S. Census Bureau, "2005 Service Annual Survey, Administrative & Support, and Waste Management and Remediation Services." See <http://www.census.gov/econ/www/servmenu.html> (released February 2007).

Table 1253. **Estimated Accommodation and Food Services Sales by Kinds of Business: 1995 to 2005**

[In millions of dollars (322,818 represents 322,818,000,000). Estimates are based on data from the Annual Retail Trade Survey and administrative records and have been adjusted to the results of the 2002 Economic Census]

Kind of business	2000 NAICS code[1]	1995	2000	2001	2002	2003	2004	2005
Accommodation and food services, total ..	72	322,818	443,642	451,300	463,678	484,174	516,580	547,799
Accommodation	721	89,193	138,181	133,448	131,864	134,481	144,604	153,198
Traveler accommodation...........	7211	85,526	133,582	128,591	127,050	129,610	139,731	148,155
RV parks and recreational camps......	7212	2,749	3,608	3,838	3,799	3,884	3,863	3,978
Rooming and boarding houses........	7213	918	991	1,019	1,015	987	1,010	1,065
Food services and drinking places[2]	722	233,625	305,461	317,852	331,814	349,693	371,976	394,601
Full service restaurants.............	7221	99,430	134,204	140,682	148,211	155,085	163,834	172,241
Limited service eating places.........	7222	103,143	127,879	132,924	138,302	147,087	158,699	169,684
Drinking places	7224	12,515	15,415	15,769	16,417	17,580	18,168	19,033

[1] North American Industry Classification System, 2002; see text, Section 15. [2] Includes other kinds of business not shown separately.

Source: U.S. Census Bureau, "Annual Accommodation and Food Services-2005" See Internet site <http://www.census.gov /svsd/www/artstbl.html> (accessed 25 April 2007).

Table 1254. **Lodging Industry Summary: 1990 to 2005**

Year	Average occupancy rate (percent)	Average room rate (dol.)	Room size of property	2005 Establishments	2005 Rooms (mil.)	Item	2005 Business traveler	2005 Leisure traveler
1990	63.3	57.96	Total	47,590	4.4	Typical night:		
1995	65.5	66.65				Made reservations		
2000	63.7	85.89	Percent:			(percent)	85	85
2001	60.3	88.27	Under 75 rooms ..	57.6	26.4	Amount paid (dol).....	99.00	94.00
2002	59.1	83.54	75–149 rooms ...	30.3	34.8	Length of stay (percent):		
2003	61.6	82.52	150–299 rooms ..	8.8	19.0	One night	40	45
2004	61.3	86.24	300–500 rooms ..	2.2	9.0	Two nights	25	28
2005	63.1	90.88	Over 500 rooms ..	1.0	10.8	Three or more	35	27

Source: American Hotel & Lodging Association, Washington, DC Lodging Industry Profile, annual (copyright). See also <http://www.ahla.com>.

Table 1255. **Commercial and Noncommercial Groups—Food and Drink Establishments and Sales: 1990 to 2007**

[(238,149 represents $238,149,000,000). Excludes military. Data refer to sales to consumers of food and alcoholic beverages. Sales are estimated. For details, see source]

Type of group	Establishments, 2004	Sales (mil. dol.) 1990	1995	2000	2004	2005	2006	2007[1]
Total	906,022	238,149	294,631	377,652	461,815	485,012	509,350	534,976
Commercial restaurant services[2,3]	705,195	211,606	265,910	345,345	421,753	443,667	466,747	491,200
Eating places[2]	443,866	155,552	198,293	259,743	312,024	328,379	345,124	363,340
Full-service restaurants.	197,303	77,811	96,396	133,834	156,857	165,013	172,769	181,580
Limited-service restaurants[4]	193,116	69,798[5]	92,901[5]	107,147	129,521	135,997	142,932	150,079
Snack and nonalcoholic beverage bars	38,995	(5)	(5)	12,867	15,742	17,064	18,532	20,162
Bars and taverns[6]	48,856	9,533	9,948	12,412	14,438	14,857	15,303	15,793
Managed services[2]	20,693	14,149	18,186	24,841	30,215	31,942	34,000	36,013
Manufacturing and industrial plants...	(NA)	3,856	4,814	6,223	6,281	6,570	6,905	7,099
Colleges and universities	(NA)	2,788	3,989	5,879	8,595	9,207	10,034	10,897
Lodging places	14,785	13,568	15,561	19,438	22,526	23,723	25,444	26,837
Retail hosts[2,7]	133,971	9,513	12,589	14,869	21,372	23,527	23,788	25,053
Department store restaurants.......	4,014	876	1,038	903	480	(NA)	(NA)	(NA)
Grocery store restaurants[7]	61,115	5,432	6,624	7,116	11,525	(NA)	(NA)	(NA)
Gasoline service stations	52,982	1,718	2,520	4,693	5,817	(NA)	(NA)	(NA)
Recreation and sports	26,874	2,871	3,866	4,772	10,907	10,882	11,916	12,627
Noncommercial restaurant services[2]	200,827	26,543	28,722	32,307	40,062	41,345	42,603	43,777
Employee restaurant services	4,048	1,864	1,364	986	623	541	470	479
Industrial, commercial organizations ..	1,117	1,603	1,129	717	335	(NA)	(NA)	(NA)
Educational restaurant services	104,515	7,671	9,059	9,977	10,831	10,548	11,083	11,081
Elementary and secondary schools...	100,342	3,700	4,533	5,039	5,206	5,103	5,383	5,362
Hospitals.....................	5,736	8,968	9,219	9,982	11,886	12,041	12,634	12,963
Miscellaneous	49,595	2,892	3,673	4,898	9,174	(NA)	(NA)	(NA)
Clubs	26,689	1,993	2,278	3,164	7,115	(NA)	(NA)	(NA)

NA Not available. [1] Projection. [2] Includes other types of groups, not shown separately. [3] Data for establishments with payroll. [4] Fast-food restaurants. [5] Snack and nonalcoholic beverage bars included in limited service restaurants, prior to 1997. [6] For establishments serving food. [7] Includes a portion of delicatessen sales in grocery stores.

Source: National Restaurant Association, Washington, DC, *Restaurant Numbers: 25 Year History, 1970–1995*, 1998; *Restaurant Industry in Review*, annual; and *National Restaurant Association Restaurant Industry Forecast*, December 2006, (copyright).

Accommodation, Food Services, and Other Services 781

Table 1256. Other Services—Estimated Revenue for Employer Firms: 2000 to 2005

[In millions of dollars (302,783 represents $302,783,000,000). For employer firms. Estimates have been adjusted to the results of the 2002 Economic Census. Based on the Service Annual Survey; see Appendix III]

Kind of business	2002 NAICS code [1]	2000	2003	2004	2005
Other services	81	302,783	317,363	338,022	359,798
Repair and maintenance [2]	811	112,719	123,164	127,939	136,011
Automotive repair and maintenance	8111	73,219	78,565	81,116	85,462
Automotive mechanical and electrical repair and maintenance . . .	81111	37,879	40,445	42,154	44,011
General automotive repair.	811111	30,988	33,778	35,547	37,233
Automotive body, paint, interior, and glass repair	81112	25,766	27,178	27,693	29,152
Automotive body, paint, and interior repair and maintenance . . .	811121	22,018	23,531	24,283	25,477
Other automotive repair and maintenance.	81119	9,574	10,942	11,269	12,299
Electronic and precision equipment repair and maintenance	8112	14,419	15,103	16,514	17,599
Commercial and industrial machinery and equipment (except automotive and electronic) repair and maintenance	8113	16,687	20,735	21,231	23,389
Personal and household goods repair and maintenance	8114	8,394	8,761	9,078	9,561
Home and garden equipment and appliance repair and maintenance	81141	3,866	4,209	4,285	4,625
Personal and laundry services [2].	812	67,140	72,053	76,169	80,559
Personal care services	8121	18,264	21,093	23,178	25,013
Hair, nail, and skin care services.	81211	15,553	17,081	18,932	20,301
Barber shops.	812111	479	499	522	521
Beauty salons.	812112	14,445	15,448	17,191	18,210
Nail salons.	812113	629	1,134	1,219	1,570
Other personal care services	81219	2,711	4,012	4,246	4,712
Death care services	8122	13,707	15,334	15,080	15,667
Funeral homes and funeral services.	81221	10,279	12,016	11,705	12,142
Cemeteries and crematories.	81222	3,428	3,318	3,375	3,525
Drycleaning and laundry services	8123	19,950	19,545	20,040	20,995
Coin-operated laundries and drycleaners	81231	3,359	3,238	3,235	3,241
Drycleaning and laundry services (except coin-operated)	81232	7,846	7,282	7,581	7,904
Linen and uniform supply.	81233	8,745	9,025	9,224	9,850
Other personal services	8129	15,219	16,081	17,873	18,885
Pet care (except veterinary) services	81291	(X)	(X)	1,689	1,947
Photofinishing	81292	3,809	3,678	3,173	2,609
Parking lots and garages.	81293	6,389	7,041	7,121	7,673
All other personal services	81299	5,021	5,362	5,890	6,656
Religious, grantmaking, civic, professional, and similar organizations (except religious, labor, and political organizations) [3]	813	122,924	122,146	133,913	143,228
Grantmaking and giving services	8132	57,465	47,131	56,408	61,726
Social advocacy organizations	8133	10,852	13,358	13,424	13,960
Civic and social organizations	8134	13,703	15,951	16,694	17,104
Business, professional, and other organizations (except labor and political organizations)	8139	40,904	45,706	47,387	50,438

X Not applicable.   [1] Based on the North American Industry Classification System, 2002; see Section 15.   [2] For taxable firms only.   [3] For tax-exempt firms only.

Source: U.S. Census Bureau, "2005 Service Annual Survey, Other Services." See <http://www.census.gov/econ/www/servmenu .html> (released February 2007).

Table 1257. National Nonprofit Associations—Number by Type: 1980 to 2006

[Data compiled during last few months of year previous to year shown and the beginning months of year shown]

Type	1980	1990	1995	2000	2001	2002	2003	2004	2005	2006 [1]
Total	14,726	22,289	22,663	21,840	22,449	22,141	22,464	22,659	22,720	23,772
Trade, business, commercial.	3,118	3,918	3,757	3,880	3,922	3,883	3,818	3,812	3,789	3,942
Agriculture and environment	677	940	1,122	1,103	1,120	1,125	1,137	1,140	1,170	1,286
Legal, governmental, public admin., military	529	792	776	790	807	814	832	839	868	887
Scientific, engineering, technical . . .	1,039	1,417	1,355	1,302	1,317	1,309	1,326	1,354	1,354	1,396
Educational	2,376[2]	1,291	1,290	1,297	1,346	1,307	1,301	1,313	1,318	1,365
Cultural.	(2)	1,886	1,918	1,786	1,812	1,766	1,749	1,735	1,733	1,782
Social welfare	994	1,705	1,885	1,829	1,925	1,917	1,941	1,972	2,072	2,218
Health, medical	1,413	2,227	2,348	2,495	2,574	2,601	2,808	2,921	2,982	3,089
Public affairs	1,068	2,249	2,148	1,776	1,857	1,808	1,836	1,881	1,854	1,938
Fraternal, nationality, ethnic	435	573	552	525	537	529	557	547	550	567
Religious.	797	1,172	1,230	1,123	1,160	1,154	1,155	1,157	1,147	1,162
Veteran, hereditary, patriotic	208	462	686	835	834	785	802	803	774	790
Hobby, avocational	910	1,475	1,549	1,330	1,408	1,380	1,435	1,449	1,433	1,525
Athletic sports	504	840	838	717	762	730	760	755	762	863
Labor unions	235	253	245	232	233	218	211	213	208	209
Chambers of Commerce [3]	105	168	168	143	142	141	139	136	135	137
Greek and non-Greek letter societies	318	340	336	296	312	301	309	305	303	302
Fan clubs	(NA)	581	460	381	381	373	348	327	314	314

NA Not available.   [1] The increase in the number of associations comes from the increase in newly discovered and established associations.   [2] Data for cultural associations included with educational associations.   [3] National and binational. Includes trade and tourism organizations.

Source: Gale Group, Farmington Hills, MI. Compiled from *Encyclopedia of Associations*, annual (copyright).

Section 28
Foreign Commerce and Aid

This section presents data on the flow of goods, services, and capital between the United States and other countries; changes in official reserve assets of the United States; international investments; and foreign assistance programs.

The Bureau of Economic Analysis publishes current figures on U.S. international transactions and the U.S. international investment position in its monthly *Survey of Current Business*. Statistics for the foreign aid programs are presented by the Agency for International Development (AID) in its annual *U.S. Overseas Loans and Grants and Assistance from International Organizations*.

The principal source of merchandise import and export data is the U.S. Census Bureau. Current data are presented monthly in *U.S. International Trade in Goods and Services* report Series FT 900. The *Guide to Foreign Trade Statistics*, found on the Census Bureau Web site at <http://www.census.gov/foreign-trade /guide/index.html>, lists the Bureau's monthly and annual products and services in this field. In addition, the International Trade Administration and the Bureau of Economic Analysis present summary as well as selected commodity and country data for U.S. foreign trade on their Web sites: <http://ita.doc.gov/td /industry/otea/> and <http://www.bea .gov/international/index>, respectively. The merchandise trade data published by the Bureau of Economic Analysis in the *Survey of Current Business* and on the Web include balance of payments adjustments to the Census Bureau data. The U.S. Treasury Department's *Monthly Treasury Statement of Receipts and Outlays of the United States Government* contains information on import duties. The International Trade Commission, U.S. Department of Agriculture (agricultural products), U.S. Department of Energy (mineral fuels, like petroleum and coal), and the U.S. Geological Survey (minerals) release various reports and specialized products on U.S. trade.

International accounts—The international transactions tables (Tables 1258 to 1260) show, for given time periods, the transfer of goods, services, grants, and financial assets and liabilities between the United States and the rest of the world. The international investment position table (Table 1261) presents, for specific dates, the value of U.S. investments abroad and of foreign investments in the United States. The movement of foreign and U.S. capital as presented in the balance of payments is not the only factor affecting the total value of foreign investments. Among the other factors are changes in the valuation of assets or liabilities, including changes in prices of securities, defaults, expropriations, and write-offs.

Direct investment abroad means the ownership or control, directly or indirectly, by one person of 10 percent or more of the voting securities of an incorporated business enterprise or an equivalent interest in an unincorporated business enterprise. Direct investment position is the value of U.S. parents' claims on the equity of and receivables due from foreign affiliates, less foreign affiliates' receivables due from their U.S. parents. Income consists of parents' shares in the earnings of their affiliates plus net interest received by parents on intercompany accounts, less withholding taxes on dividends and interest.

Foreign aid—Foreign assistance is divided into three major categories—grants (military supplies and services and other grants), credits, and other assistance (through net accumulation of foreign currency claims from the sale of agricultural commodities). *Grants* are transfers for which no payment is expected (other than a limited percentage of the foreign currency "counterpart" funds generated by the grant), or which at most involve an obligation on the part of the receiver to extend aid to the United States or other countries to achieve a

common objective. *Credits* are loan disbursements or transfers under other agreements which give rise to specific obligations to repay, over a period of years, usually with interest. All known returns to the U.S. government stemming from grants and credits (reverse grants, returns of grants, and payments of principal) are taken into account in net grants and net credits, but no allowance is made for interest or commissions. *Other assistance* represents the transfer of U.S. farm products in exchange for foreign currencies (plus, since enactment of Public Law 87-128, currency claims from principal and interest collected on credits extended under the farm products program), less the government's disbursements of the currencies as grants, credits, or for purchases. The net acquisition of currencies represents net transfers of resources to foreign countries under the agricultural programs, in addition to those classified as grants or credits.

In 1952, economic, technical, and military aid programs were combined under the Mutual Security Act, which in turn was followed by the Foreign Assistance Act passed in 1961. Appropriations to provide military assistance were also made in the Department of Defense Appropriation Act (rather than the Foreign Assistance Appropriation Act) beginning in 1966 for certain countries in Southeast Asia and in other legislation concerning programs for specific countries (such as Israel). Figures on activity under the Foreign Assistance Act as reported in the *Foreign Grants and Credits* series differ from data published by AID or its immediate predecessors, due largely to differences in reporting, timing, and treatment of particular items.

Exports—The Census Bureau compiles export data primarily from Shipper's Export Declarations required to be filed with customs officials for shipments leaving the United States. They include U.S. exports under mutual security programs and exclude shipments to U.S. Armed Forces for their own use.

The value reported in the export statistics is generally equivalent to a free alongside ship (f.a.s.) value at the U.S. port of export, based on the transaction price, including inland freight, insurance, and

other charges incurred in placing the merchandise alongside the carrier at the U.S. port of exportation. This value, as defined, excludes the cost of loading merchandise aboard the exporting carrier and also excludes freight, insurance, and any other charges or transportation and other costs beyond the U.S. port of exportation. The country of destination is defined as the country of ultimate destination or country where the merchandise is to be consumed, further processed, or manufactured, as known to the shipper at the time of exportation. When ultimate destination is not known, the shipment is statistically credited to the last country to which the shipper knows the merchandise will be shipped in the same form as exported.

Effective January 1990, the United States began substituting Canadian import statistics for U.S. exports to Canada. As a result of the data exchange between the United States and Canada, the United States has adopted the Canadian import exemption level for its export statistics based on shipments to Canada.

Data are estimated for shipments valued under $2,501 to all countries, except Canada, using factors based on the ratios of low-valued shipments to individual country totals.

Prior to 1989, exports were based on Schedule B, Statistical Classification of Domestic and Foreign Commodities Exported from the United States. Beginning in 1989, Schedule B classifications are based on the Harmonized System and coincide with the Standard International Trade Classification, Revision 3. This revision will affect the comparability of most export series beginning with the 1989 data for commodities.

Imports—The Census Bureau compiles import data from various customs forms required to be filed with customs officials. Data on import values are presented on two valuations bases in this section: The c.i.f. (cost, insurance, and freight) and the customs import value (as appraised by the U.S. Customs Service in accordance with legal requirements of the Tariff Act of 1930, as amended). This latter valuation, primarily used for collection of

import duties, frequently does not reflect the actual transaction value. Country of origin is defined as country where the merchandise was grown, mined, or manufactured. If country of origin is unknown, country of shipment is reported.

Imports are classified either as "General imports" or "Imports for consumption." *General imports* are a combination of entries for immediate consumption, entries into customs bonded warehouses, and entries into U.S. Foreign Trade Zones, thus generally reflecting total arrivals of merchandise. *Imports for consumption* are a combination of entries for immediate consumption, withdrawals from warehouses for consumption, and entries of merchandise into U.S. customs territory from U.S. Foreign Trade Zones, thus generally reflecting the total of the commodities entered into U.S. consumption channels.

Beginning in 1989, import statistics are based on the Harmonized Tariff Schedule of the United States, which coincides with import Standard International Trade Classification, Revision 3. This revision will affect the comparability of most import series beginning with the 1989 data.

Area coverage—Except as noted, the geographic area covered by the export and import trade statistics is the United States Customs area (includes the 50 states, the District of Columbia, and Puerto Rico), the U.S. Virgin Islands (effective January 1981), and U.S. Foreign Trade Zones (effective July 1982). Data for selected tables and total values for 1980 have been revised to reflect the U.S. Virgin Islands' trade with foreign countries, where possible.

Statistical reliability—For a discussion of statistical collection and estimation, sampling procedures, and measures of statistical reliability applicable to Census Bureau data, see Appendix III.

U.S. Census Bureau, Statistical Abstract of the United States: 2008

Table 1258. U.S. International Transactions by Type of Transaction: 1990 to 2006

[In millions of dollars (706,975 represents $706,975,000,000). Minus sign (−) indicates debits. N.i.e. = Not included elsewhere]

Type of transaction	1990	1995	1998	1999	2000	2001	2002	2003	2004	2005	2006
Exports of goods and services and income receipts	**706,975**	**1,004,631**	**1,194,993**	**1,259,809**	**1,421,515**	**1,295,693**	**1,255,936**	**1,338,325**	**1,559,191**	**1,788,557**	**2,096,165**
Exports of goods and services	535,233	794,387	933,174	965,884	1,070,597	1,004,896	974,721	1,017,757	1,157,250	1,283,070	1,445,703
Goods, balance of payments basis [1]	387,401	575,204	670,416	683,965	771,994	718,712	682,422	713,415	807,516	894,631	1,023,109
Services [2]	147,832	219,163	262,758	281,919	298,603	286,184	292,299	304,342	349,734	388,439	422,594
Transfers under U.S. military agency sales contracts [3]	9,932	14,643	17,405	15,928	13,790	12,539	11,943	13,315	15,781	19,539	17,112
Travel	43,007	63,395	71,325	74,801	82,400	71,893	66,605	64,359	74,546	81,799	85,694
Passenger fares	15,298	18,909	20,098	19,785	20,687	17,926	17,046	15,891	18,851	20,970	22,187
Other transportation	22,042	26,081	25,604	26,916	29,803	28,442	29,195	31,416	36,957	41,334	46,297
Royalties and license fees [4]	16,634	30,289	35,626	39,670	43,233	40,696	44,508	46,988	54,490	59,409	62,378
Other private services	40,251	65,048	91,774	103,934	107,904	113,857	122,207	131,563	148,149	164,301	187,771
U.S. government miscellaneous services	668	818	926	885	786	831	795	810	959	1,087	1,155
Income receipts	171,742	210,244	261,819	293,925	350,918	290,797	281,215	320,568	401,942	505,488	650,462
Income receipts on U.S.-owned assets abroad	170,570	208,065	259,382	291,177	348,083	287,918	278,404	317,755	399,120	502,598	647,582
Direct investment receipts	65,973	95,260	103,963	131,626	151,839	128,665	145,590	186,641	239,008	269,346	310,224
Other private receipts	94,072	108,092	151,818	156,354	192,398	155,692	129,511	126,641	157,114	230,537	334,958
U.S. government receipts	10,525	4,713	3,601	3,197	3,846	3,561	3,303	4,697	2,998	2,715	2,400
Compensation of employees	1,172	2,179	2,437	2,748	2,835	2,879	2,811	2,813	2,822	2,890	2,880
Imports of goods and services and income payments	**−759,290**	**−1,080,124**	**−1,356,868**	**−1,511,011**	**−1,780,296**	**−1,629,097**	**−1,651,990**	**−1,789,819**	**−2,114,926**	**−2,454,871**	**−2,818,047**
Imports of goods and services	−616,097	−890,771	−1,099,314	−1,230,974	−1,450,432	−1,370,022	−1,398,446	−1,514,672	−1,769,341	−1,997,441	−2,204,225
Goods, balance of payments basis [1]	−498,438	−749,374	−918,637	−1,031,784	−1,226,684	−1,148,231	−1,167,377	−1,264,307	−1,477,094	−1,681,780	−1,861,380
Services [2]	−117,659	−141,397	−180,677	−199,190	−223,748	−221,791	−231,069	−250,365	−292,247	−315,661	−342,845
Direct defense expenditures	−17,531	−10,043	−12,185	−13,335	−13,473	−14,835	−19,101	−25,296	−29,299	−30,075	−31,054
Travel	−37,349	−44,916	−56,483	−58,963	−64,705	−60,200	−58,715	−57,447	−65,750	−68,970	−72,029
Passenger fares	−10,531	−14,663	−19,971	−21,315	−24,274	−22,633	−19,969	−20,989	−24,718	−26,149	−27,503
Other transportation	−24,966	−27,034	−30,363	−34,139	−41,425	−38,682	−38,407	−44,705	−54,161	−61,929	−65,282
Royalties and license fees [4]	−3,135	−6,919	−11,235	−13,107	−16,468	−16,538	−19,353	−19,033	−23,274	−24,632	−26,432
Other private services	−22,229	−35,199	−47,591	−55,510	−60,520	−66,021	−72,604	−79,764	−91,267	−99,927	−116,524
U.S. government miscellaneous services	−1,919	−2,623	−2,849	−2,821	−2,883	−2,882	−2,920	−3,131	−3,778	−3,979	−4,021
Income payments	−143,192	−189,353	−257,554	−280,037	−329,864	−259,075	−253,544	−275,147	−345,585	−457,430	−613,823
Income payments on foreign-owned assets in the U.S.	−139,728	−183,090	−250,560	−272,082	−322,345	−250,989	−245,164	−266,635	−336,621	−448,139	−604,410
Direct investment payments	−3,450	−30,318	−38,418	−53,437	−56,910	−12,783	−43,244	−73,750	−99,600	−116,834	−136,010
Other private payments	−95,508	−97,149	−127,988	−138,120	−180,918	−159,825	−127,012	−119,051	−154,485	−227,431	−334,645
U.S. government payments	−40,770	−55,623	−84,154	−80,525	−84,517	−78,381	−74,908	−73,834	−82,536	−103,874	−133,755
Compensation of employees	−3,464	−6,263	−6,994	−7,955	−7,519	−8,086	−8,380	−8,512	−8,963	−9,290	−9,412
Unilateral current transfers, net	**−26,654**	**−38,074**	**−53,187**	**−50,428**	**−58,645**	**−51,295**	**−63,587**	**−70,607**	**−84,414**	**−88,535**	**−89,595**
U.S. government grants [3]	−10,359	−11,190	−13,270	−13,774	−16,714	−11,517	−17,097	−22,173	−23,634	−33,039	−27,142
U.S. government pensions and other transfers	−3,224	−3,451	−4,305	−4,406	−4,705	−5,798	−5,125	−5,341	−6,264	−6,303	−6,508
Private remittances and other transfers [5]	−13,070	−23,433	−35,612	−32,248	−37,226	−33,980	−41,365	−43,093	−54,516	−49,193	−55,945

See footnotes at end of table.

Table 1258. U.S. International Transactions by Type of Transaction: 1990 to 2006—Con.

[See headnote, page 786]

Type of transaction	1990	1995	1998	1999	2000	2001	2002	2003	2004	2005	2006
Capital account transactions, net	-6,579	-927	-766	-4,939	-1,010	-1,270	-1,470	-3,480	-2,369	-4,054	-3,913
U.S. assets abroad, net (increase/financial outflow (–))	**-81,234**	**-352,264**	**-353,829**	**-504,062**	**-560,523**	**-382,616**	**-294,646**	**-325,424**	**-905,024**	**-426,875**	**-1,055,176**
U.S. official reserve assets, net	-2,158	-9,742	-6,783	8,747	-290	-4,911	-3,681	1,523	2,805	14,096	2,374
Special drawing rights	-192	-808	-147	10	-722	-630	-475	601	-393	4,511	-223
Reserve position in the International Monetary Fund	731	-2,466	-5,119	5,484	2,308	-3,600	-2,632	1,494	3,826	10,200	3,331
Foreign currencies	-2,697	-6,468	-1,517	3,253	-1,876	-681	-574	-572	-623	-615	-734
U.S. government assets, other than official reserve assets, net	2,317	-984	-422	2,750	-941	-486	345	537	1,710	5,539	5,346
U.S. credits and other long-term assets	-8,410	-4,859	-4,678	-6,175	-5,182	-4,431	-5,251	-7,279	-3,044	-2,255	-2,992
Repayments on U.S. credits and other long-term assets [6]	10,856	4,125	4,111	9,559	4,265	3,873	5,701	7,981	4,716	5,603	8,329
U.S. foreign currency holdings and U.S. short-term assets, net	-130	-250	145	-634	-24	72	-105	-165	38	2,191	9
U.S. private assets, net	-81,393	-341,538	-346,624	-515,559	-559,292	-377,219	-291,310	-327,484	-909,539	-446,510	-1,062,896
Direct investment	-37,183	-98,750	-142,644	-224,934	-159,212	-142,349	-154,460	-149,564	-279,086	7,662	-235,358
Foreign securities	-28,765	-122,394	-130,204	-122,236	-127,908	-90,644	-48,568	-146,722	-146,549	-197,098	-289,422
U.S. claims on unaffiliated foreigners reported by U.S. nonbanking concerns	-27,824	-45,286	-38,204	-97,704	-138,790	-8,520	-50,022	-18,184	-124,137	-39,603	-83,531
U.S. claims reported by U.S. banks, n.i.e.	12,379	-75,108	-35,572	-70,685	-133,382	-135,706	-38,260	-13,014	-359,767	-217,471	-454,585
Foreign-owned assets in the United States, net (increase/financial inflow (+))	**141,571**	**438,562**	**423,569**	**740,210**	**1,046,896**	**782,859**	**797,813**	**864,352**	**1,461,766**	**1,204,231**	**1,859,597**
Foreign official assets in the U.S., net	33,910	109,880	-19,903	43,543	42,758	28,059	115,945	278,069	397,755	259,268	440,264
U.S. government securities	30,243	72,712	-3,589	32,527	35,710	54,620	90,971	224,874	314,941	213,334	380,734
Other U.S. government liabilities	1,868	-105	-3,326	-2,863	-1,825	-2,309	137	-723	-134	-421	3,133
U.S. liabilities reported by U.S. banks, n.i.e.	3,385	34,008	-9,501	915	5,746	-29,978	21,221	48,643	69,245	26,260	22,040
Other foreign official assets	-1,586	3,265	-3,487	12,964	3,127	5,726	3,616	5,275	13,703	20,095	34,357
Other foreign assets in the U.S., net	107,661	328,682	443,472	696,667	1,004,138	754,800	681,868	586,283	1,064,011	944,963	1,419,333
Direct investments in U.S.	48,494	57,776	179,045	289,444	321,274	167,021	84,372	63,750	145,812	108,996	180,580
U.S. Treasury securities	-2,534	91,544	28,581	-44,497	-69,983	-14,378	100,403	91,455	93,608	132,300	-35,931
U.S. securities other than U.S. Treasury securities	1,592	77,249	156,315	298,834	459,889	393,885	283,299	220,705	381,493	450,386	591,951
U.S. currency flows	18,800	12,300	16,622	22,407	5,315	23,783	21,513	16,640	14,829	18,969	12,571
U.S. liabilities to unaffiliated foreigners reported by U.S. nonbanking concerns	45,133	59,637	23,140	76,247	170,672	66,110	95,871	96,526	93,522	31,804	235,769
U.S. liabilities reported by U.S. banks, n.i.e.	-3,824	30,176	39,769	54,232	116,917	118,379	96,410	97,207	334,747	202,508	434,393
Financial derivatives, net	(NA)	(NA)	(NA)	(NA)	(NA)	(NA)	(NA)	(NA)	(NA)	(NA)	**28,762**
Statistical discrepancy	*25,211*	*28,196*	*146,088*	*70,421*	*-67,937*	*-14,274*	*-42,056*	*-13,348*	*85,775*	*-18,454*	*-17,794*
Balance on goods	-111,037	-174,170	-248,221	-347,819	-454,690	-429,519	-484,955	-550,892	-669,578	-787,149	-838,271
Balance on services	30,173	77,786	82,081	82,729	74,855	64,393	61,230	53,977	57,487	72,778	79,749
Balance on income	28,550	20,891	4,265	13,888	21,054	31,722	27,671	45,421	56,357	48,058	36,640
Balance on current account [7]	-78,968	-113,567	-215,062	-301,630	-417,426	-384,699	-459,641	-522,101	-640,148	-754,848	-811,477

NA Not available. [1] Excludes exports of goods under U.S. military agency sales contracts identified in census export documents, excludes imports of goods under direct defense expenditures identified in census import documents, and reflects various other adjustments (for valuation, coverage, and timing) of census statistics to balance of payments basis. [2] Includes some goods: Mainly military equipment; major equipment, other materials, supplies, and petroleum products purchased abroad by U.S. military agencies; and fuels purchased by U.S. airline and steamship operators. [3] Includes transfers of goods and services under U.S. military grant programs. [4] These lines are presented on a gross basis. The definition of exports is revised to exclude U.S. affiliates' payments to foreign affiliates and to include U.S. affiliates' receipts from foreign parents. The definition of imports is revised to include U.S. parents' payments to foreign affiliates and to exclude U.S. affiliates' receipts from foreign parents. [5] The "other transfers" includes taxes paid by U.S. private residents to foreign governments and taxes paid by private nonresidents to the U.S. government. [6] Includes sales of foreign obligations to foreigners. [7] Conceptually, "Balance on current account" is equal to "net foreign investment" in the national income and product accounts (NIPAs). However, the foreign transactions account in the NIPAs (a) includes adjustments to the international transactions accounts for the treatment of gold, (b) includes adjustments for the different geographical treatment of transactions with U.S. territories and Puerto Rico, and (c) includes services furnished without payment by financial pension plans except life insurance carriers and private noninsured pension plans.

Source: U.S. Bureau of Economic Analysis, *Survey of Current Business,* July 2007, and <http://www.bea.gov/bea/international/bp_web/list.cfm?anon=71&registered=0> (released 15 June 2007).

Table 1259. U.S. Balances on International Transactions by Area and Selected Country: 2005 and 2006

[In millions of dollars (–787,149 represents –$787,149,000,000). Minus sign (–) indicates debits]

Area or country	2005, balance on—				2006, balance on—			
	Goods [1]	Services	Income	Current account	Goods [1]	Services	Income	Current account
All areas	–787,149	72,778	48,058	–754,848	–838,271	79,749	36,640	–811,477
Europe	–147,508	14,904	1,559	–139,823	–142,538	16,859	7,238	–125,735
European Union	–125,512	12,537	–7,827	–125,000	–120,213	14,267	1,668	–106,200
Euro Area	–93,520	3,326	14,007	–83,992	–93,166	2,518	15,371	–79,747
Germany	–51,383	–5,141	–473	–58,906	–48,494	–7,014	–2,405	–57,903
Italy	–19,730	–48	3,323	–16,848	–20,388	254	4,779	–15,777
Netherlands	11,462	1,173	10,407	23,827	13,587	1,138	7,100	21,951
United Kingdom	–13,231	8,346	–21,447	–22,146	–8,972	9,841	–15,531	–11,092
Canada	–81,889	11,234	23,070	–47,913	–75,085	15,524	18,469	–40,705
Latin America, other Western Hemisphere	–103,533	10,368	18,991	–97,285	–112,579	12,180	18,885	–110,640
Mexico	–52,770	6,417	815	–56,669	–67,303	7,540	243	–70,655
Venezuela	–27,567	2,173	272	–25,124	–28,157	2,673	1,162	–24,406
Asia and Pacific	–371,192	30,728	–25,725	–379,561	–409,765	32,075	–38,897	–431,734
Australia	8,005	3,086	3,642	14,553	9,004	4,663	6,145	19,578
China [2]	–202,087	2,437	–17,106	–218,607	–233,087	3,639	–26,695	–258,207
Hong Kong	6,978	–1,083	2,436	8,488	9,589	–1,155	2,239	10,641
India	–10,846	174	377	–12,179	–11,855	62	917	–12,951
Japan [3]	–85,110	18,730	–29,005	–94,178	–90,966	16,509	–35,663	–108,314
Korea, South	–16,656	3,373	–230	–14,086	–14,393	4,193	–100	–10,851
Singapore	5,128	2,058	8,574	15,739	6,543	2,587	8,771	17,874
Taiwan [2]	–13,650	902	–2,696	–15,842	–15,769	809	–3,696	–18,983
Middle East	–32,702	673	452	–49,097	–36,112	–164	–2,531	–51,534
Africa	–50,325	4,598	4,894	–48,411	–62,192	4,606	5,243	–58,183
International and unallocated	(X)	274	24,817	7,240	(X)	–1,333	28,233	7,051

X Not applicable. [1] Adjusted to balance of payments basis; excludes exports under U.S. military sales contracts and imports under direct defense expenditures. [2] See footnote 2, Table 1298. [3] Includes Ryukyu Islands.
Source: U.S. Bureau of Economic Analysis, Survey of Current Business, July 2007, and <http://www.bea.gov/bea /international/bp_web/list.cfm?anon=71&registered=0> (released June 15, 2007).

Table 1260. Private International Service Transactions by Selected Type of Service and Selected Country: 2000 to 2006

[In millions of dollars (284,027 represents $284,027,000,000). For all transactions, see Table 1258]

Type of service and country	Exports				Imports			
	2000	2004	2005	2006	2000	2004	2005	2006
Private services, total	284,027	332,994	367,813	404,327	207,392	259,170	281,607	307,770
TYPE OF SERVICE								
Travel	82,400	74,546	81,799	85,694	64,705	65,750	68,970	72,029
Passenger fares	20,687	18,851	20,970	22,187	24,274	24,718	26,149	27,503
Other transportation	29,803	36,957	41,334	46,297	41,425	54,161	61,929	65,282
Freight	12,547	15,479	16,470	17,266	27,388	39,225	43,920	45,700
Port services	17,256	21,478	24,865	29,031	14,037	14,936	18,009	19,582
Royalties and license fees	43,233	54,490	59,409	62,378	16,468	23,274	24,632	26,432
Affiliated	30,479	40,848	43,880	44,477	12,536	17,881	20,373	20,963
Unaffiliated	12,754	13,642	15,528	17,901	3,932	5,393	4,260	5,469
Industrial processes	4,662	5,657	6,733	7,510	1,692	2,881	2,834	3,017
Other	8,093	7,984	8,795	10,390	2,241	2,513	1,428	2,453
Other private services	107,904	148,149	164,301	187,771	60,520	91,267	99,927	116,524
Affiliated	34,970	44,943	50,108	57,638	27,176	33,861	39,847	48,201
Unaffiliated	72,934	103,206	114,193	130,133	33,344	57,406	60,080	68,323
Education	10,348	13,634	14,076	14,550	2,032	3,543	3,962	4,403
Financial services	16,026	27,766	31,039	37,114	4,840	5,486	6,720	8,497
Insurance services	3,631	7,314	7,787	9,276	11,284	29,090	28,540	33,582
Telecommunications	3,884	4,651	5,231	6,257	5,429	4,602	4,527	4,557
Business, professional, & technical services . .	25,319	34,546	41,874	47,400	9,130	13,640	14,824	15,845
Other unaffiliated services	13,730	15,295	14,187	15,515	632	1,050	1,508	1,441
AREA AND COUNTRY								
Europe	107,650	137,222	148,727	163,566	89,825	111,162	123,583	137,097
European Union	94,232	118,731	128,845	140,482	77,876	97,014	106,506	117,291
Euro Area	56,735	69,148	73,625	80,439	45,625	56,279	61,945	69,747
France	10,553	13,101	13,239	14,934	10,642	11,581	12,546	15,069
Germany	15,928	19,245	20,327	20,635	12,400	17,652	18,825	20,876
Italy	5,459	6,251	7,157	7,527	5,061	5,552	6,251	6,380
Netherlands	7,057	8,359	9,087	9,945	5,698	6,906	7,837	8,875
United Kingdom	31,973	41,545	44,864	47,886	28,304	33,184	35,588	36,818
Canada	24,559	29,722	33,827	39,308	17,711	20,706	22,326	23,542
Latin America and Other Western Hemisphere . .	54,417	57,526	62,312	69,238	38,092	53,483	52,182	57,249
Mexico	14,334	17,921	20,889	22,443	11,023	13,580	14,318	14,755
Asia and Pacific	79,386	88,470	100,604	109,053	51,798	59,592	69,116	75,160
Australia	5,575	6,910	7,580	9,108	3,494	3,974	4,686	4,789
China [1]	5,211	7,577	9,070	10,899	3,259	5,784	6,630	7,248
India	2,546	4,472	5,159	6,660	1,892	2,829	5,024	6,612
Japan	33,411	35,625	40,248	41,253	17,405	19,778	22,506	23,884
Korea, South	7,287	9,237	10,366	11,454	4,617	5,450	6,089	6,431
Taiwan [1]	4,856	5,661	6,365	7,137	4,221	5,653	6,563	6,979
Middle East	6,852	8,578	9,681	11,262	3,310	5,238	5,299	5,124
Africa	4,957	6,554	7,448	8,083	2,710	3,747	3,946	4,325
International organizations and unallocated	6,206	4,923	5,217	3,817	3,946	5,243	5,156	5,276

[1] See footnote 2, Table 1298.
Source: U.S. Bureau of Economic Analysis, Survey of Current Business, July 2007.

Table 1261. **International Investment Position by Type of Investment: 2000 to 2006**

[In billions of dollars (–1,381 represents –$1,381,000,000,000). Estimates for end of year; subject to considerable error due to nature of basic data. Unless otherwise specified, types below refer to current-cost method. For information on current-cost method and market value, see article cited in source]

Type of investment	2000	2001	2002	2003	2004	2005	2006
Net international investment position	**–1,381**	**–1,919**	**–2,088**	**–2,140**	**–2,294**	**–2,238**	**–2,540**
Financial derivatives, net [1]	(X)	(X)	(X)	(X)	(X)	58	59
Net international investment position, excluding financial derivatives	–1,381	–1,919	–2,088	–2,140	–2,294	–2,296	–2,599
U.S.-owned assets abroad	**6,239**	**6,309**	**6,652**	**7,643**	**9,257**	**11,576**	**13,755**
Financial derivatives, gross positive fair value [1] . .	(X)	(X)	(X)	(X)	(X)	1,190	1,238
U.S.-owned assets abroad, excluding financial derivatives	6,239	6,309	6,652	7,643	9,257	10,386	12,517
U.S. official reserve assets	128	130	159	184	190	188	220
Gold	72	72	91	109	114	134	165
Special drawing rights	11	11	12	13	14	8	9
Reserve position in the International Monetary Fund	15	18	22	23	20	8	5
Foreign currencies	31	29	34	40	42	38	41
U.S. government assets, other	85	86	85	85	83	78	72
U.S. credits and other long-term assets	83	83	83	82	80	77	72
U.S. foreign currency holdings and U.S. short-term assets	3	3	3	3	3	1	1
U.S. private assets	6,025	6,093	6,408	7,375	8,984	10,121	12,225
Direct investment at current cost	1,532	1,693	1,867	2,054	2,464	2,535	2,856
Foreign securities	2,426	2,170	2,080	2,954	3,553	4,346	5,432
Bonds	573	557	705	874	993	1,028	1,181
Corporate stocks	1,853	1,613	1,375	2,079	2,560	3,318	4,252
U.S. claims on unaffiliated foreigners [2]	837	839	902	594	738	734	848
U.S. claims reported by U.S. banks [3]	1,232	1,391	1,559	1,773	2,230	2,506	3,089
Foreign-owned assets in the United States	**7,620**	**8,228**	**8,740**	**9,784**	**11,551**	**13,815**	**16,295**
Financial derivatives, gross negative fair value [1] . .	(X)	(X)	(X)	(X)	(X)	1,132	1,179
Foreign-owned assets in the United States, excluding financial derivatives	7,620	8,228	8,740	9,784	11,551	12,683	15,116
Foreign official assets in the United States	1,031	1,109	1,251	1,563	2,012	2,306	2,770
U.S. government securities	756	847	970	1,187	1,510	1,725	2,105
U.S. Treasury securities	640	720	812	986	1,252	1,341	1,521
Other	116	127	158	200	258	385	584
Other U.S. government liabilities	19	17	17	16	16	16	19
U.S. liabilities reported by U.S. banks [3]	153	135	156	201	270	297	297
Other foreign official assets	102	110	108	159	215	269	350
Other foreign assets	6,589	7,119	7,489	8,221	9,540	10,376	12,346
Direct investment at current cost	1,421	1,518	1,500	1,581	1,742	1,868	2,099
U.S. Treasury securities	382	375	474	527	562	644	594
U.S. securities other than U.S. Treasury securities	2,623	2,821	2,779	3,423	3,996	4,353	5,229
Corporate and other bonds	1,069	1,343	1,531	1,711	2,035	2,243	2,690
Corporate stocks	1,554	1,478	1,248	1,712	1,960	2,110	2,539
U.S. currency	256	280	301	318	333	352	364
U.S. liabilities to unaffiliated foreigners [2]	739	798	897	451	508	558	740
U.S. liabilities reported by U.S. banks [3]	1,169	1,326	1,538	1,921	2,399	2,602	3,319
Memoranda:							
Direct investment abroad at market value	2,694	2,315	2,023	2,729	3,336	3,570	4,378
Direct investment in the United States at market value	2,783	2,560	2,022	2,455	2,717	2,806	3,222

X Not applicable.   [1] A break in series in 2005 reflects the introduction of U.S. Department of the Treasury data on financial derivatives.   [2] Reported by U.S. nonbanking concerns.   [3] Not included elsewhere.

Source: U.S. Bureau of Economic Analysis, *Survey of Current Business*, July 2007.

Table 1262. **U.S. Reserve Assets: 1990 to 2006**

[In billions of dollars ($83.3 represents $83,300,000,000). As of end of year, except as indicated]

Type	1990	1995	2000	2001	2002	2003	2004	2005	2006
Total	83.3	85.8	67.6	68.7	79.0	85.9	86.8	65.1	65.9
Gold stock	11.1	11.1	11.0	11.0	11.0	11.0	11.0	11.0	11.0
Special drawing rights	11.0	11.0	10.5	10.8	12.2	12.6	13.6	8.2	8.9
Foreign currencies	52.2	49.1	31.2	29.0	33.8	39.7	42.7	37.8	40.9
Reserve position in IMF [1]	9.1	14.6	14.8	17.9	22.0	22.5	19.5	8.0	5.0

[1] International Monetary Fund.

U.S. Department of the Treasury, *Treasury Bulletin*, quarterly. For latest issue, see <http://www.fms.treas.gov/bulletin/index.html>.

Table 1263. **Foreign Direct Investment Position in the United States on a Historical-Cost Basis by Selected Country, 2000 to 2006, and by Industry, 2006**

[In millions of dollars (1,256,867 represents $1,256,867,000,000)]

Country	2000	2003	2004	2005	2006 Total [1]	2006 Manufac-turing	2006 Whole-sale	2006 Finance [2] and insurance
All countries	1,256,867	1,395,159	1,520,316	1,594,488	1,789,087	593,759	252,028	257,677
Canada	114,309	95,707	125,276	154,180	158,979	31,315	14,204	51,775
Europe [3]	887,014	1,001,237	1,078,782	1,128,161	1,270,570	454,879	121,169	173,087
Austria	3,007	3,606	3,572	2,416	2,367	1,360	(D)	1
Belgium.	14,787	11,239	12,581	10,387	12,590	2,977	1,817	1,156
Denmark.	4,025	4,531	5,064	6,121	7,209	5,573	269	(Z)
Finland	8,875	5,300	5,639	5,970	7,289	3,958	2,956	−1
France	125,740	136,434	137,927	120,272	158,830	69,857	7,788	28,941
Germany	122,412	160,691	164,921	180,339	202,581	77,510	12,284	20,425
Ireland	25,523	23,346	16,446	18,594	28,551	11,132	241	3,851
Italy	6,576	6,944	6,889	8,009	11,883	986	1,174	(D)
Luxembourg.	58,930	109,212	116,479	116,729	130,925	30,153	1,186	(D)
Netherlands	138,894	146,601	159,601	165,366	189,293	69,775	15,208	54,290
Norway	2,665	4,203	2,862	5,204	7,835	1,721	(D)	–
Spain	5,068	5,670	5,818	7,504	14,942	2,663	143	1,285
Sweden	21,991	20,156	22,292	22,247	22,287	10,591	7,037	245
Switzerland	64,719	124,247	122,165	131,342	140,259	78,843	(D)	37,454
United Kingdom	277,613	217,841	267,209	296,277	303,232	76,805	61,287	(D)
Latin America and other								
Western Hemisphere . . . . [3]	53,691	84,134	76,268	70,789	79,845	23,520	11,732	11,612
South and Central America [3] . .	13,384	22,910	25,001	22,868	29,341	3,084	8,988	(D)
Brazil.	882	548	1,195	2,051	2,122	23	(D)	(D)
Mexico	7,462	9,022	7,592	3,806	6,075	3,032	1,790	10
Panama.	3,819	8,874	10,408	11,109	12,994	−253	(D)	(D)
Venezuela	792	4,349	5,009	5,304	7,246	26	(D)	(D)
Other Western Hemisphere [3]	40,307	61,224	51,268	47,921	50,504	20,436	2,744	(D)
Bermuda	18,336	9,854	6,626	−471	2,757	2,186	−508	−6,729
Netherlands Antilles	3,807	3,597	3,532	5,424	6,179	−319	(D)	(D)
U.K.Islands, Caribbean	15,191	26,202	21,702	23,932	24,572	(D)	1,394	5,322
Africa [3]	2,700	2,196	1,859	2,734	2,244	−38	(D)	(D)
Middle East [3]	6,506	7,177	7,899	8,396	17,639	(D)	(D)	(D)
Israel	3,012	3,316	3,921	4,308	(D)	(D)	458	(D)
Saudi Arabia	(D)	(D)	(D)	(D)	(D)	(D)	(D)	2
Asia and Pacific [3]	192,647	204,708	230,231	230,228	259,810	(D)	99,974	21,074
Australia	18,775	37,059	40,107	22,411	25,727	5,721	1,974	2,610
Hong Kong	1,493	1,984	2,744	3,658	3,524	1,714	1,090	(D)
Japan.	159,690	157,176	174,490	188,687	210,996	65,866	86,977	16,799
Korea, South	3,110	1,409	5,270	5,771	8,609	591	7,148	152
Singapore	5,087	2,166	1,733	2,183	2,412	(D)	158	(D)
Taiwan [4]	3,174	2,888	3,209	3,652	4,199	1,664	1,138	16

– Represents or rounds to zero.   D Suppressed to avoid disclosure of data of individual companies.   Z Less than $500,000.   [1] Includes other industries not shown separately.   [2] Excludes depository institutions.   [3] Includes other countries not shown separately.   [4] See footnote 2, Table 1298.
Source: U.S. Bureau of Economic Analysis, *Survey of Current Business,* July 2007, and previous issues. For most recent copy and previous issues, see <http://www.bea.gov/bea/pubs.htm>.

Table 1264. **U.S. Majority-Owned Affiliates of Foreign Companies—Assets, Sales, Employment, Value, Exports, and Imports by Industry: 2004**

[(5,539,810 represents $5,539,810,000,000) Preliminary. A U.S. affiliate is a U.S. business enterprise in which one foreign owner (individual, branch, partnership, association, trust, corporation, or government) has a direct or indirect voting interest of 10 percent or more. Estimates cover the universe of nonbank affiliates]

Industry	2002 NAICS code	Total assets (mil. dol.)	Sales [2] (mil. dol.)	Employ-ment [3] (1,000)	Employee compen-sation (mil. dol.)	Gross book value P & E [4] (mil. dol.)	Mer-chandise exports [5] (mil. dol.)	Mer-chandise imports [5] (mil. dol.)
All industries.	(X)	5,539,810	2,303,543	5,116.4	324,523	1,060,181	153,902	378,111
Manufacturing [6]	31–33	1,075,992	927,115	2,039.9	150,103	484,306	88,956	141,628
Petroleum and coal products.	324	(D)	(D)	32.5	4,776	(D)	(D)	7,528
Chemicals	325	259,269	179,413	299.2	30,154	103,371	17,600	22,844
Computers and electronic products .	334	80,269	70,893	163.8	13,878	27,762	(D)	18,753
Transportation equipment.	336	240,107	214,749	375.9	25,183	109,684	27,380	55,703
Wholesale trade.	42	469,393	719,566	528.4	41,018	197,837	60,107	225,944
Retail trade	44–45	61,116	129,662	613.6	17,550	41,960	212	4,187
Information	51	266,387	84,391	220.0	18,369	40,971	988	624
Finance (except depository	52, exc.							
institutions) and insurance	521,522	3,046,258	172,743	200.7	32,022	28,070	–	–
Real estate and rental and leasing . . .	53	91,511	21,350	38.5	2,378	75,167	(D)	418
Professional, scientific, and technical								
services	54	70,403	52,078	171.4	14,017	10,240	(D)	279
Other industries		458,749	196,639	1,303.9	49,067	181,630	3,125	5,031

– Represents or rounds to zero.   D Withheld to avoid disclosure of data of individual companies.   [1] North American Industry Classification System, 2002.   [2] Excludes returns, discounts, allowances, and sales and excise taxes.   [3] Average number of full-time and part-time employees.   [4] Plant and equipment (P & E). Includes mineral rights and minor amounts of property other than land.   [5] F.a.s. value at port of exportation. Goods shipped by/to affiliates.   [6] Includes industries not shown separately.
Source: U.S. Bureau of Economic Analysis, *Survey of Current Business,* August 2006 and *Foreign Direct Investment in the United States: Operations of U.S. Affiliates of Foreign Companies,* annual.

Table 1265. **Foreign Direct Investment in the United States—Gross Book Value and Employment of U.S. Affiliates of Foreign Companies by State: 2000 to 2004**

[1,175,628 represents $1,175,628,000,000. A U.S. affiliate is a U.S. business enterprise in which one foreign owner (individual, branch, partnership, association, trust corporation, or government) has a direct or indirect voting interest of 10 percent or more. Estimates cover the universe of nonbank U.S. affiliates. Beginning 2002, data are on a majority-owned basis and not strictly comparable with 2000 data]

State and other area	Gross book value of property, plant, and equipment (mil. dol.)				Total employment				
								2004	
	2000	2002	2003	2004	2000 (1,000)	2002 (1,000)	2003 (1,000)	Total (1,000)	Percent of all businesses
Total	1,175,628	1,024,364	1,047,010	1,060,181	6,524.6	5,425.4	5,244.4	5,116.4	(X)
United States	1,070,422	913,611	(D)	931,238	6,498.3	5,398.6	5,214.4	(NA)	4.5
Alabama	16,646	15,520	15,704	16,857	77.9	75.1	72.6	70.6	4.4
Alaska.	28,964	30,052	30,526	31,121	12.0	12.6	11.7	11.3	4.9
Arizona	10,716	9,252	9,720	9,333	73.2	57.5	58.0	62.9	3.1
Arkansas	4,613	4,872	4,779	4,913	40.9	35.7	32.2	32.0	3.2
California	121,040	87,509	86,133	90,622	749.4	612.6	558.0	547.0	4.3
Colorado	15,319	13,026	13,721	16,115	102.6	77.7	72.3	71.4	3.8
Connecticut	13,604	12,790	12,113	12,517	118.0	111.0	105.5	102.7	7.1
Delaware	6,114	6,211	5,733	4,508	31.8	22.4	28.1	26.1	7.0
District of Columbia . . .	4,247	5,132	4,052	4,518	17.1	17.4	15.8	15.7	3.4
Florida.	38,755	28,662	27,431	26,819	312.1	252.1	247.8	238.4	3.6
Georgia	29,510	24,941	26,089	23,574	227.9	191.2	183.9	175.9	5.2
Hawaii.	10,369	7,720	7,496	6,948	44.8	36.7	35.2	31.6	6.6
Idaho	2,749	2,131	2,171	2,187	14.2	12.5	11.6	12.9	2.6
Illinois	48,425	40,300	40,719	39,276	325.8	262.9	252.5	235.6	4.6
Indiana	30,179	27,985	29,977	30,904	168.2	133.2	134.7	132.5	5.2
Iowa	7,186	5,776	6,109	6,391	40.9	36.6	38.7	36.2	2.9
Kansas	9,036	5,238	5,143	5,322	61.0	34.9	31.4	32.2	2.9
Kentucky	22,091	24,091	25,852	26,919	106.0	88.4	87.9	84.7	5.6
Louisiana.	31,160	26,993	28,927	27,962	61.3	50.5	49.2	49.9	3.1
Maine	5,087	5,511	5,910	5,313	33.9	31.7	29.4	29.0	5.6
Maryland	13,157	10,339	10,667	11,172	112.9	105.4	102.9	101.1	4.8
Massachusetts	23,875	24,109	23,243	22,834	226.8	196.9	188.4	182.9	6.3
Michigan	39,238	37,814	38,683	38,886	249.9	202.9	204.6	201.0	5.3
Minnesota	13,472	9,805	10,355	10,926	106.2	88.1	85.5	83.2	3.6
Mississippi	4,121	5,097	5,874	6,777	24.2	25.8	21.7	25.5	2.8
Missouri.	15,773	14,484	14,375	16,027	107.4	91.5	87.2	84.2	3.6
Montana	3,099	1,824	2,097	2,233	6.8	5.9	5.5	6.4	1.9
Nebraska.	2,737	1,840	1,699	2,021	21.7	18.7	19.0	20.0	2.6
Nevada	10,128	6,726	5,580	6,530	36.3	25.8	26.1	27.0	2.6
New Hampshire	5,124	4,488	(D)	4,693	46.5	41.1	41.7	41.0	7.4
New Jersey	35,115	30,866	32,426	33,846	272.2	228.3	224.0	219.7	6.4
New Mexico	5,801	4,557	3,963	3,792	16.7	12.8	11.6	12.6	2.1
New York	68,522	64,016	59,904	60,572	479.1	386.8	384.2	377.0	5.3
North Carolina	29,931	24,045	25,088	23,917	264.8	214.8	203.8	198.0	6.0
North Dakota	1,824	1,100	1,512	1,416	7.7	7.4	7.8	(¹)	(D)
Ohio	37,530	32,124	32,759	32,898	260.3	214.2	208.0	203.6	4.3
Oklahoma	7,635	7,434	8,297	8,222	41.9	33.9	34.5	31.7	2.7
Oregon	13,178	10,241	10,029	11,749	62.1	50.9	47.9	47.6	3.5
Pennsylvania	34,106	29,118	31,248	30,237	283.4	235.8	233.1	225.6	4.5
Rhode Island	3,394	3,037	3,279	3,381	24.2	27.5	26.1	26.1	6.1
South Carolina	23,563	21,570	20,520	21,844	138.4	133.0	126.8	121.7	7.9
South Dakota	1,011	685	743	750	6.9	7.6	6.5	5.5	1.7
Tennessee	20,842	16,790	17,919	19,890	153.2	130.1	128.5	126.9	5.4
Texas	110,032	88,107	83,192	83,739	445.2	352.8	340.3	341.2	4.2
Utah	14,340	10,612	11,837	11,402	38.1	32.3	34.0	30.9	3.3
Vermont	2,146	1,286	1,321	1,357	11.5	11.1	10.3	10.8	4.1
Virginia	23,570	17,331	16,607	16,422	181.9	141.9	138.9	133.7	4.5
Washington	22,257	16,414	17,378	17,477	106.8	84.5	83.7	83.4	3.7
West Virginia	7,061	7,388	6,092	5,716	28.1	22.7	21.4	19.0	3.3
Wisconsin	13,961	16,103	15,882	15,949	110.3	107.1	95.6	86.9	3.6
Wyoming	8,072	10,551	10,956	12,444	7.8	8.5	8.4	8.5	4.3
Puerto Rico.	2,169	2,338	2,684	2,613	17.9	16.6	16.6	16.6	(NA)
Other territories and offshore	34,105	39,746	39,142	36,125	7.9	9.9	12.9	(²)	(NA)
Foreign ¹	2,406	2,328	(D)	1,515	0.5	0.3	0.4	(³)	(NA)
Unspecified ⁴	66,526	66,341	86,645	88,688	(NA)	(NA)	(NA)	(NA)	(NA)

D Data withheld to avoid disclosure. NA Not available. X Not applicable. ¹ 5,000 to 9,999 employees. ² 10,000 to 24,999 employees. ³ 1,000 to 2,499 employees. ⁴ Covers property, plant, and equipment not located in a particular state, including aircraft, railroad rolling stock, satellites, undersea cable, and trucks engaged in interstate transportation.

Source: U.S. Bureau of Economic Analysis, *Survey of Current Business*, August 2006, and *Foreign Direct Investment in the United States, Operations of U.S. Affiliates of Foreign Companies*, annual.

Foreign Commerce and Aid   791

Table 1266. U.S. Businesses Acquired or Established by Foreign Direct Investors—Investment Outlays by Industry of U.S. Business Enterprise and Country of Ultimate Beneficial Owner: 1990 to 2006

[In millions of dollars (65,932 represents $65,932,000,000). Foreign direct investment is the ownership or control directly or indirectly, by one foreign individual branch, partnership, association, trust, corporation, or government of 10 percent or more of the voting securities of a U.S. business enterprise or an equivalent interest in an unincorporated one. Data represent number and full cost of acquisitions of existing U.S. business enterprises, including business segments or operating units of existing U.S. business enterprises and establishments of new enterprises. Investments may be made by the foreign direct investor itself, or indirectly by an existing U.S. affiliate of the foreign direct investor. Covers investments in U.S. business enterprises with assets of over $1 million, or ownership of 200 acres of U.S. land]

Industry and country	1990	2000	2001	2002	2003	2004	2005	2006, prel.
Total [1]	65,932	335,629	147,109	54,519	63,591	86,219	91,390	161,533
By type of investment:								
U.S. businesses acquired	(NA)	322,703	138,091	43,442	50,212	72,738	73,997	147,827
U.S. businesses established	(NA)	12,926	9,017	11,077	13,379	13,481	17,393	13,706
By type of investor:								
Foreign direct investors	(NA)	105,151	23,134	13,650	27,866	34,184	40,304	50,906
U.S. affiliates	(NA)	230,478	123,975	40,869	35,725	52,035	51,086	110,627
INDUSTRY [2]								
Manufacturing	(NA)	143,285	37,592	16,446	10,750	18,251	34,036	56,582
Wholesale trade	(NA)	8,561	3,982	871	1,086	(D)	3,489	8,002
Retail trade	(NA)	1,672	1,913	551	941	3,073	1,262	1,158
Information	(NA)	67,932	27,599	14,181	9,236	4,315	8,487	9,503
Depository institutions	(NA)	2,636	5,709	613	4,864	(D)	7,973	9,270
Finance (except depository institutions) and insurance	(NA)	44,420	40,780	4,344	23,511	26,234	5,529	25,347
Real estate and rental and leasing	(NA)	4,526	3,572	5,266	2,817	6,335	8,756	15,669
Professional, scientific, and technical services	(NA)	32,332	7,044	4,012	1,955	(D)	6,407	4,821
Other industries	(NA)	30,264	18,917	8,234	8,429	10,121	15,453	31,181
COUNTRY [3]								
Canada [1]	3,430	28,346	16,646	4,333	9,157	31,502	13,640	12,012
Europe [1]	36,011	249,167	78,328	39,644	39,024	43,815	56,416	109,858
France	10,217	26,149	5,772	15,196	2,955	6,415	5,608	19,682
Germany	2,363	18,452	12,733	3,067	8,830	4,788	7,239	22,683
Netherlands	2,247	47,686	14,879	3,476	1,077	461	2,609	5,463
Switzerland	3,905	22,789	16,468	2,656	649	6,505	2,332	14,625
United Kingdom	13,096	110,208	17,095	12,188	20,373	23,288	30,420	21,880
Latin America and other Western Hemisphere	796	15,400	15,274	3,487	1,607	2,629	5,042	9,130
South and Central America	399	5,334	431	373	182	1,382	980	1,215
Other Western Hemisphere	397	10,066	14,843	3,144	1,425	1,247	4,062	7,916
Africa	(D)	(D)	(D)	(D)	(D)	(D)	(D)	(D)
Middle East	472	947	(D)	(D)	1,738	1,318	5,068	12,436
Asia and Pacific [1]	23,170	40,282	11,383	5,131	11,469	6,015	10,924	17,526
Australia	1,412	(D)	4,869	1,565	9,032	3,850	4,713	6,866
Japan	19,933	26,044	5,345	3,275	1,544	1,027	4,245	8,719

D Suppressed to avoid disclosure of data of individual companies.   NA Not available.   [1] Includes other countries not shown separately   [2] Based on 1997 North American Industry Classification System (NAICS); beginning 2002, based on 2002 NAICS; see text, Section 15.   [3] For investments in which more than one investor participated, each investor and each investor's outlays are classified by country of each ultimate beneficial owner.
Source: U.S. Bureau of Economic Analysis, *Survey of Current Business*, June 2007. For most recent copy and historical issues, see <http://www.bea.gov/bea/pubs.htm>.

Table 1267. U.S. Direct Investment Position Abroad, Capital Outflows, and Income by Industry of Foreign Affiliates: 2000 to 2006

[In millions of dollars (1,316,247 represents $1,316,247,000,000). See footnote 2, Table 1266 and headnote, Table 1268]

Industry	Direct investment position on a historical-cost basis			Capital outflows (inflows (–))			Income [1]		
	2000	2005	2006	2000	2005	2006	2000	2005	2006
All industries, total [2]	1,316,247	2,135,492	2,384,004	142,627	−27,736	216,614	133,692	247,472	291,480
Mining	72,111	115,956	136,145	2,174	12,518	15,419	13,164	24,108	31,543
Manufacturing [2]	343,899	449,202	503,495	43,002	36,638	60,022	42,230	48,422	59,243
Food	23,497	30,540	32,517	2,014	2,041	2,981	2,681	3,684	3,773
Chemicals	75,807	116,075	129,778	3,812	6,364	13,577	(D)	14,295	16,144
Primary and fabricated metals	21,644	23,441	23,220	1,233	−850	3,690	1,536	2,270	2,619
Machinery	22,229	27,330	32,172	2,659	2,909	3,825	2,257	2,827	3,821
Computer and electronic products	59,909	62,074	76,660	17,303	7,718	18,428	8,860	8,430	11,992
Electrical equipment, appliances, and components	10,005	13,837	15,765	2,100	1,880	1,467	1,079	1,229	1,462
Transportation equipment	49,887	48,968	55,526	7,814	−974	4,555	4,107	1,677	4,304
Wholesale trade	93,936	139,444	164,290	11,938	15,518	22,703	14,198	25,701	29,271
Information	52,345	65,439	74,368	16,531	5,338	4,797	−964	10,467	11,069
Depository institutions	40,152	65,798	67,550	−1,274	−4,168	−4,214	2,191	213	−826
Finance and insurance	217,086	452,726	484,840	21,659	15,745	24,847	15,210	29,778	32,617
Professional, scientific, and technical services	32,868	48,834	57,429	5,441	6,546	6,813	3,548	5,974	7,542
Holding companies (nonbank)	(NA)	620,765	710,336	(NA)	−132,169	73,929	(NA)	85,602	100,387

D Withheld to avoid disclosure of individual company data.   NA Not available.   [1] Prior to 2006, income is shown net of withholding taxes. For 2006 income is shown gross of withholding taxes.   [2] Includes other industries not shown separately.
Source: U.S. Bureau of Economic Analysis, *Survey of Current Business*, July 2007. For most recent copy and historical issues, see <http://www.bea.gov/bea/pubs.htm>.

792   Foreign Commerce and Aid

Table 1268. U.S. Direct Investment Position Abroad on a Historical-Cost Basis by Selected Country: 1990 to 2006

[In millions of dollars (430,521 represents $430,521,000,000). U.S. investment abroad is the ownership or control by one U.S. person of 10 percent or more of the voting securities of an incorporated foreign business enterprise or an equivalent interest in an unincorporated foreign business enterprise. Negative position can occur when a U.S. parent company's liabilities to the foreign affiliate are greater than its equity in and loans to the foreign affiliate]

Country	1990	2000	2001	2002	2003	2004	2005	2006
All countries.........	430,521	1,316,247	1,460,352	1,616,548	1,769,613	2,124,775	2,135,492	2,384,004
Canada[1]................	69,508	132,472	152,601	166,473	187,953	213,012	233,474	246,451
Europe[1]...............	214,739	687,320	771,936	859,378	976,889	1,169,620	1,109,950	1,250,508
Austria	1,113	2,872	3,964	4,011	6,366	9,038	10,982	17,405
Belgium...............	9,464	17,973	22,589	25,727	27,415	39,254	48,409	52,054
Czech Republic.........	(X)	1,228	1,179	1,264	1,668	2,035	2,394	3,090
Denmark..........	1,726	5,270	5,160	6,184	5,597	5,438	5,655	5,753
Finland	544	1,342	1,686	1,722	1,677	2,088	2,070	2,592
France	19,164	42,628	40,125	43,348	51,229	61,362	60,127	65,933
Germany...........	27,609	55,508	63,396	61,073	72,262	77,731	90,574	99,253
Greece	282	795	835	981	1,431	1,559	1,858	2,073
Hungary............	(NA)	1,920	2,033	2,503	2,856	3,140	3,299	4,014
Ireland.............	5,894	35,903	39,541	51,598	60,604	81,987	71,255	83,615
Italy	14,063	23,484	22,883	23,771	23,092	26,063	24,845	28,936
Luxembourg..........	1,697	27,849	50,771	62,181	68,298	84,930	69,746	82,588
Netherlands	19,120	115,429	147,687	158,415	186,366	218,906	184,614	215,715
Norway	4,209	4,379	4,446	6,045	7,511	7,715	8,819	10,280
Poland	(NA)	3,884	4,573	4,231	4,382	6,330	6,125	7,190
Portugal............	897	2,664	2,746	3,093	2,402	2,275	2,391	3,033
Russia..............	(X)	1,147	883	1,135	2,511	3,860	8,562	10,064
Spain	7,868	21,236	28,174	38,001	41,119	47,969	46,528	49,413
Sweden	1,787	25,959	26,374	30,114	27,004	32,813	33,219	35,938
Switzerland	25,099	55,377	63,768	74,229	92,750	109,481	81,048	90,085
Turkey..............	522	1,826	1,641	1,869	2,213	2,115	2,010	2,088
United Kingdom	72,707	230,762	228,230	247,952	277,246	330,897	333,497	364,084
Latin America and other Western Hemisphere	71,413	266,576	279,611	289,413	297,222	341,480	365,895	403,284
South America[1]	22,933	84,220	76,809	64,603	66,256	64,949	70,316	79,146
Argentina..........	2,531	17,488	15,535	11,288	10,663	9,691	11,019	13,086
Brazil..............	14,384	36,717	32,027	27,598	29,553	28,574	29,619	32,601
Chile	1,896	10,052	10,526	8,928	9,021	9,788	9,623	10,243
Colombia	1,677	3,693	3,122	2,622	2,773	2,950	4,192	4,897
Ecuador...........	280	832	579	809	975	696	730	461
Peru	599	3,130	3,197	3,310	3,401	3,241	4,245	4,979
Venezuela	1,087	10,531	10,069	8,671	8,438	8,750	9,568	11,556
Central America[1]	20,415	73,841	60,716	65,395	64,647	75,240	84,125	93,995
Costa Rica	251	1,716	1,835	1,803	840	1,049	1,278	1,573
Honduras	262	399	227	181	272	352	367	517
Mexico.............	10,313	39,352	52,544	56,303	56,851	66,428	75,106	84,699
Panama	9,289	30,758	5,141	5,842	5,409	5,944	5,777	5,728
Other Western Hemisphere[1]..	28,065	108,515	142,086	159,416	166,319	201,291	211,453	230,143
Bahamas, The..........	4,004	3,291	5,533	7,645	8,643	11,985	15,659	26,130
Barbados	252	2,141	2,240	1,817	984	3,146	3,865	4,756
Bermuda	20,169	60,114	84,969	89,473	84,508	99,016	103,454	108,462
Dominican Republic	529	1,143	1,116	983	816	962	770	896
Jamaica	625	2,483	2,957	3,097	3,406	3,586	1,006	884
Netherlands Antilles	-4,501	3,579	5,695	4,753	2,926	3,892	3,572	3,840
Trinidad and Tobago......	485	1,550	2,025	2,326	2,392	2,450	2,883	3,846
U.K. Islands, Caribbean ...	5,929	33,451	36,443	48,305	61,882	75,710	79,728	80,604
Africa[1].................	3,650	11,891	15,574	16,040	19,835	21,708	23,018	25,556
Egypt	1,231	1,998	2,557	2,682	3,524	4,644	5,354	5,911
Nigeria	-401	470	260	901	1,100	2,012	1,195	339
South Africa	775	3,562	3,070	3,334	3,580	3,397	3,558	3,818
Middle East[1]............	3,959	10,863	13,212	15,158	16,885	19,088	22,631	26,487
Israel	746	3,735	5,690	5,726	7,020	6,601	8,350	9,964
Saudi Arabia..........	1,899	3,661	3,570	4,930	3,140	3,718	3,770	4,346
United Arab Emirates	409	683	834	1,087	1,934	2,468	3,324	4,547
Asia and Pacific[1]...........	64,716	207,125	227,418	270,086	270,830	359,866	380,523	431,718
Australia	15,110	34,838	27,778	39,074	48,447	(D)	115,623	122,587
China[2]	354	11,140	12,081	10,570	11,261	15,736	17,033	22,228
Hong Kong...........	6,055	27,447	32,494	40,329	36,426	27,847	32,577	38,118
India...............	372	2,379	2,496	4,232	4,868	6,764	6,634	8,852
Indonesia...........	3,207	8,904	10,511	(D)	(D)	(D)	9,487	10,585
Japan	22,599	57,091	55,651	66,468	57,794	69,076	79,280	91,769
Korea, South	2,695	8,968	9,977	11,856	13,063	15,890	18,188	22,280
Malaysia	1,466	7,910	7,489	7,101	7,057	8,171	10,344	12,450
New Zealand	3,156	4,271	4,273	3,926	3,859	4,432	4,897	5,721
Philippines	1,355	3,638	5,436	5,964	6,390	5,852	6,377	7,034
Singapore	3,975	24,133	40,764	50,955	51,053	60,773	54,500	60,417
Taiwan[2]	2,226	7,836	9,301	10,144	11,983	(D)	14,602	16,126
Thailand	1,790	5,824	6,176	7,774	6,886	6,922	6,573	8,217

D Suppressed to avoid disclosure of data of individual companies.   NA Not available.   X Not applicable.   [1] Includes other countries not shown separately.   [2] See footnote 2, Table 1298.

Source: U.S. Bureau of Economic Analysis, *Survey of Current Business*, July 2007. For most recent copy and historical issues, see <http://www.bea.gov/bea/pubs.htm>.

Table 1269. U.S. Government Foreign Grants and Credits by Country: 1990 to 2006

[In millions of dollars (14,396 represents $14,396,000,000). See text, this section. Negative figures (–) occur when the total of grant returns, principal repayments, and/or foreign currencies disbursed by the U.S. government exceeds new grants and new credits utilized and/or acquisitions of foreign currencies through new sales of farm products]

Country	1990	2000	2001	2002	2003	2004	2005	2006
Total, net	**14,396**	**17,878**	**12,602**	**17,213**	**23,131**	**22,335**	**31,729**	**23,304**
Investment in financial institutions.	1,304	1,500	1,704	1,486	1,434	1,994	1,263	2,024
Western Europe [1]	–103	183	220	104	345	153	142	–35
Ireland	2	–	–	44	50	–	–	30
Spain.	–122	–19	–19	–19	–19	–19	–19	–205
Yugoslavia [2]	–39	1	–	–51	231	13	4	–73
Former Yugoslavia [2]:								
Bosnia and Herzegovina	(X)	52	115	64	47	66	72	49
Macedonia	(X)	50	29	15	58	42	67	30
Former Yugoslavia—Regional [2]. . . .	(X)	74	87	128	66	38	66	120
Eastern Europe [1]	973	1,830	1,300	1,464	1,299	1,196	–169	202
Albania	–	26	38	40	42	43	53	31
Romania	79	38	43	48	66	34	57	41
Newly independent states:								
Armenia	(X)	20	52	54	74	66	85	61
Azerbaijan.	(X)	8	15	32	35	47	74	52
Georgia	(X)	36	49	97	66	113	169	74
Kazakhstan.	(X)	42	58	52	50	56	69	40
Kyrgyzstan	(X)	15	32	36	35	39	60	50
Moldova	(X)	32	60	28	23	27	38	26
Russia	(X)	797	280	266	192	251	–681	–920
Tajikistan.	(X)	8	34	18	25	40	61	35
Ukraine.	(X)	138	195	118	96	114	145	119
Former Soviet Union—Regional [3] . .	(X)	501	295	510	364	372	456	470
Near East and South Asia [1]	6,656	7,658	2,520	5,656	10,003	11,876	21,623	14,414
Afghanistan	57	5	6	140	555	1,222	2,076	3,560
Bangladesh	181	43	89	45	29	50	48	45
Egypt.	4,976	3,091	1,296	1,689	2,055	2,689	2,827	149
Greece	282	–169	–153	–218	–287	–457	–114	–103
India	13	–64	–56	–122	–150	–40	–70	61
Iraq.	–7	–	1	–	3,235	5,011	10,481	8,794
Israel.	4,380	3,932	589	3,061	2,761	2,163	4,953	390
Jordan	155	317	298	483	1,420	800	582	462
Lebanon.	9	22	60	28	24	30	37	45
Nepal	20	15	27	28	43	37	50	57
Pakistan.	531	366	170	445	223	230	530	702
Turkey	367	–86	–5	–138	–322	–299	–228	–194
Yemen	43	16	7	5	17	31	24	30
UNRWA [4]	7	97	77	71	124	27	48	137
West Bank–Gaza.	1	64	115	143	195	171	179	128
Other and unspecified [3]	29	30	15	14	23	118	107	116
Africa [1]	1,883	1,042	1,562	2,015	2,801	2,143	1,979	1,103
Algeria.	59	–53	182	–73	–123	–146	–173	–1,324
Burundi	18	3	6	3	18	27	6	37
Congo (Kinshasa)	242	9	16	33	1,078	229	118	130
Ethiopia	57	142	98	87	138	234	308	233
Ghana	14	40	86	48	50	67	53	54
Guinea.	16	19	45	41	30	33	36	29
Kenya	115	44	108	50	58	82	91	186
Liberia	32	19	19	10	13	50	40	61
Madagascar	34	21	63	36	31	34	35	44
Malawi.	35	45	41	46	42	54	46	61
Mali.	31	50	9	49	50	45	55	52
Mozambique	83	119	133	105	107	105	64	92
Nigeria.	156	–17	17	45	472	41	67	–178
Rwanda	13	26	57	32	36	35	47	55
Senegal	61	27	51	42	45	53	39	34
Somalia.	80	7	1	6	10	16	7	33
South Africa	20	68	119	98	115	332	103	106
Sudan	150	17	13	11	41	120	130	390
Tanzania	51	15	50	44	49	66	62	75
Uganda	43	92	55	71	86	120	148	154
Zambia	63	44	42	34	52	56	90	89
Zimbabwe.	10	23	24	21	23	31	27	32
Other and unspecified [3]	157	168	200	168	269	368	469	552
Far East and Pacific [1]	39	550	725	331	705	–186	–9	–127
Cambodia.	5	23	42	35	32	44	58	56
Hong Kong.	–8	–15	–24	–20	–23	–28	–28	–28
Indonesia	46	270	488	221	821	–157	–8	–71
Korea, South.	–192	–132	–215	–134	–137	–110	–43	–43
Malaysia.	–1	134	184	11	2	–45	–46	–45
Pacific Islands,								
Trust Territory of the [5]	220	145	206	193	103	204	190	174
Philippines	557	20	–17	–46	–35	–15	–36	–28
Thailand.	–19	–102	–118	–27	–37	11	4	–67
Other and unspecified [3]	38	26	12	16	–60	–145	–137	–119

See footnotes at end of table.

794 Foreign Commerce and Aid

No. 1269. U.S. Government Foreign Grants and Credits by Type and Country: 1990 to 2006—Con.

[In millions of dollars. See headnote, p. 794]

Country	1990	2000	2001	2002	2003	2004	2005	2006
Western Hemisphere [1]	2,025	1,173	1,380	710	912	1,538	1,723	1,154
Bolivia	114	136	189	152	212	217	159	142
Brazil	261	195	119	106	-78	-136	-93	-344
Colombia	-30	33	71	76	328	467	598	613
Ecuador	61	14	38	75	39	36	59	80
El Salvador	303	27	78	45	56	104	52	27
Guatemala	98	49	106	54	42	40	21	34
Haiti	54	63	106	66	64	83	118	154
Honduras	226	100	258	85	51	84	70	60
Mexico	140	-123	14	-13	5	14	40	30
Nicaragua	105	53	152	60	41	28	36	53
Peru	93	87	133	109	93	167	127	71
Other [6] and unspecified [3]	236	652	292	40	161	397	407	172
Other international organizations and unspecified areas [3]	1,619	3,942	3,191	5,447	5,632	3,621	5,177	4,569

– Represents or rounds to zero. X Not applicable. [1] Includes other countries not shown separately. [2] In 1992, some successor countries assumed portions of outstanding credits of the former Yugoslavia (assignment of the remaining portions is pending). Subsequent negative totals reflect payments to the United States on these assumed credits which were greater than the extension of new credits and grants to these countries. [3] In recent years, significant amounts of foreign assistance have been reported on a regional, interregional, and worldwide basis. Country totals in this table may understate actual assistance to many countries. [4] United Nations Relief and Works Agency for Palestine refugees. [5] Excludes transactions with Commonwealth of the Northern Mariana Islands; includes transactions with Federated States of Micronesia, Republic of the Marshall Islands, and Republic of Palau. [6] Includes Andean Development Corporation, Caribbean Development Bank, Central American Bank for Economic Integration, Eastern Caribbean Central Bank, Inter-American Institute of Agricultural Science, Organizations of American States, and Pan American Health Organization.

Source: U.S. Bureau of Economic Analysis, press releases, and unpublished data.

Table 1270. U.S. Foreign Economic and Military Aid Programs: 1980 to 2005

[In millions of dollars (9,694 represents $9,694,000,000). For years ending September 30. Economic aid shown here represents U.S. economic aid—not just aid under the Foreign Assistance Act. Major components in recent years include AID, Food for Peace, Peace Corps, and paid-in subscriptions to international financial institutions. Annual figures are gross unadjusted program figures]

Year and region	Total foreign assistance	Military assistance	Economic assistance, by funding agency					
			Total	U.S. Agency for International Development	U.S. Department of Agriculture	State Department	Other U.S. agencies	Multilateral organizations
1980	9,694	2,122	7,572	4,062	1,437	459	137	1,478
1985	18,128	5,801	12,327	8,132	2,052	431	164	1,548
1990	16,015	4,971	11,044	6,964	1,643	590	377	1,469
1991	17,048	4,949	12,099	7,667	1,698	707	408	1,619
1992	16,442	4,461	11,981	6,819	2,434	769	411	1,549
1993	18,152	4,958	13,195	7,059	3,140	745	668	1,583
1994	17,627	4,420	13,206	7,330	2,623	769	1,004	1,480
1995	16,520	4,121	12,398	7,281	1,517	763	1,056	1,781
1996	14,972	4,730	10,241	6,233	1,400	760	751	1,097
1997	14,023	4,011	10,012	5,922	1,107	944	1,109	930
1998	15,069	3,799	11,270	6,504	1,380	969	1,014	1,402
1999	17,990	3,997	13,993	7,420	3,085	772	1,265	1,451
2000	16,771	4,838	11,933	5,907	1,941	1,578	1,395	1,110
2001	17,727	3,837	13,890	6,747	2,071	2,438	1,488	1,146
2002	20,119	4,610	15,509	8,578	1,433	2,334	1,573	1,591
2003	27,930	6,569	21,360	11,941	2,676	2,179	3,834	730
2004	32,946	6,125	26,821	11,061	2,226	3,781	6,868	2,885
2005, total	34,360	7,147	27,213	10,106	2,306	4,593	8,493	1,715
Asia	5,068	1,062	4,006	2,812	256	267	572	99
Central Asia	2,419	55	2,364	699	53	96	1,516	–
Eastern Europe	722	171	551	371	1	22	47	112
Latin America and Caribbean	2,386	128	2,258	685	178	782	594	19
Middle East and North Africa	12,559	5,188	7,371	2,175	34	354	4,807	–
Oceania	162	1	161	–	–	–	161	–
Sub-Saharan Africa	5,171	262	4,908	1,487	1,735	1,262	300	124
Western Europe	143	39	103	82	–	16	5	–
Canada	21	–	21	–	–	–	21	–
World not specified	5,709	240	5,469	1,796	49	1,795	469	1,361

– Represents or rounds to zero.

Source: U.S. Agency for International Development, *U.S. Overseas Loans, Grants, Obligations, and Loan Authorizations*, annual. See also <http://qesdb.cdie.org/gbk/index.html>.

Table 1271. U.S. Foreign Economic and Military Aid by Major Recipient Country: 2000 to 2005

[In millions of dollars (16,771 represents $16,771,000,000), except as indicated. For years ending Sept. 30]

Recipient country	2000	2002	2003	2004	2005 Total	2005 Economic aid	2005 Military aid
Total ¹	16,771	20,119	27,930	32,946	34,360	27,213	7,147
Afghanistan	43	583	1,090	2,130	2,416	1,752	663
Albania	69	50	60	63	46	41	5
Angola	105	126	161	115	63	63	–
Armenia	104	98	105	97	95	86	9
Azerbaijan	54	60	73	69	76	67	9
Bangladesh	78	101	103	92	87	84	3
Bolivia	241	188	210	141	120	120	–
Bosnia and Herzegovina	170	86	95	90	51	42	9
Bulgaria	49	61	61	50	50	40	10
Burundi	7	26	45	49	63	63	–
Cambodia	27	54	63	93	93	92	1
Chad	4	5	7	58	78	75	3
Colombia	1,160	537	682	630	699	598	101
Congo (Kinshasa)	31	82	112	117	126	126	–
Ecuador	77	88	89	76	71	71	–
Egypt	2,076	2,202	1,758	1,957	1,542	251	1,291
El Salvador	35	144	63	69	58	55	3
Eritrea	37	31	106	86	133	133	–
Ethiopia	278	143	603	435	692	685	8
Georgia	111	203	122	154	130	116	14
Ghana	67	64	80	73	70	69	1
Guatemala	72	91	91	72	68	68	–
Haiti	88	62	85	154	224	223	–
Honduras	41	50	71	65	273	270	3
India	185	214	178	176	190	184	6
Indonesia	242	201	203	158	589	584	5
Iraq	5	39	3,944	8,110	6,981	5,695	1,286
Israel	3,791	2,788	3,686	2,708	2,684	482	2,202
Jamaica	22	26	26	41	54	53	1
Jordan	448	329	1,681	609	684	376	307
Kazakhstan	53	71	81	83	71	65	6
Kenya	90	107	127	186	209	207	2
Kosovo	198	85	92	116	124	124	–
Kyrgyzstan	47	58	79	51	56	53	3
Liberia	14	16	44	138	158	130	28
Macedonia	60	81	79	53	50	44	6
Madagascar	27	35	48	46	155	154	1
Malawi	44	54	44	49	79	78	1
Mali	44	47	53	55	52	52	–
Marshall Islands	41	50	47	42	44	44	–
Mexico	44	98	75	94	168	166	1
Micronesia, Federated States of	81	99	99	95	94	94	–
Morocco	51	29	38	34	52	35	17
Mozambique	88	72	94	102	114	113	1
Namibia	16	15	32	34	49	49	–
Nepal	22	65	55	55	61	60	2
Nicaragua	34	54	68	62	67	67	1
Nigeria	113	111	94	126	155	154	1
Pakistan	19	1,084	371	240	766	454	313
Peru	204	286	231	183	135	135	–
Philippines	82	212	223	223	167	124	43
Poland	85	44	33	37	81	3	79
Romania	46	63	72	54	65	50	16
Russia	719	522	781	946	1,545	1,543	2
Rwanda	38	45	49	60	77	75	2
Senegal	37	44	51	52	46	44	2
Serbia and Montenegro	354	277	257	256	225	225	–
South Africa	55	89	90	121	178	178	–
Sri Lanka	9	31	40	39	164	159	5
Sudan	51	122	188	481	1,073	915	157
Tajikistan	36	77	65	54	71	70	1
Tanzania	43	48	80	101	135	134	1
Turkey	5	278	1,030	50	54	16	37
Uganda	76	100	179	225	275	273	2
Ukraine	199	106	86	159	174	166	8
Uzbekistan	34	241	168	50	44	44	–
West Bank/Gaza	122	187	191	136	348	348	–
Zambia	35	70	66	102	142	142	–
Zimbabwe	21	48	34	32	46	46	–

– Represents or rounds to zero.   ¹ Includes other countries not shown separately.

Source: U.S. Agency for International Development, U.S. Overseas Loans, Grants, Obligations, and Loan Authorizations, annual. See also <http://qesdb.cdie.org/gbk/index.html>.

Table 1272. **U.S. International Trade in Goods and Services: 1999 to 2006**

[In millions of dollars (–265,090 represents –$265,090,000,000). Data presented on a balance of payments basis and will not agree with the following merchandise trade Tables 1273 to 1283]

Category	1999	2000	2001	2002	2003	2004	2005	2006
TRADE BALANCE								
Total..............	–265,090	–379,835	–365,126	–423,725	–496,915	–612,091	–714,371	–758,522
Goods.................	–347,819	–454,690	–429,519	–484,955	–550,892	–669,578	–787,149	–838,271
Services	82,729	74,855	64,393	61,230	53,977	57,487	72,778	79,749
Travel	15,838	17,695	11,693	7,890	6,912	8,796	12,029	13,665
Passenger fares	–1,530	–3,587	–4,707	–2,923	–5,098	–5,867	–5,179	–5,316
Other transportation	–7,223	–11,622	–10,240	–9,212	–13,289	–17,204	–20,595	–18,985
Royalties, license fees	26,563	26,765	24,158	25,155	27,955	31,216	34,777	35,946
Other private services.....	48,424	47,384	47,836	49,603	51,799	56,882	64,374	71,247
Other [1].................	2,593	317	–2,296	–7,158	–11,981	–13,518	–10,536	–13,942
U.S. govt misc. services ...	–1,936	–2,097	–2,051	–2,125	–2,321	–2,819	–2,892	–2,866
EXPORTS								
Total..............	965,884	1,070,597	1,004,896	974,721	1,017,757	1,157,250	1,283,070	1,445,703
Goods.................	683,965	771,994	718,712	682,422	713,415	807,516	894,631	1,023,109
Services	281,919	298,603	286,184	292,299	304,342	349,734	388,439	422,594
Travel	74,801	82,400	71,893	66,605	64,359	74,546	81,799	85,694
Passenger fares	19,785	20,687	17,926	17,046	15,891	18,851	20,970	22,187
Other transportation	26,916	29,803	28,442	29,195	31,416	36,957	41,334	46,297
Royalties, license fees	39,670	43,233	40,696	44,508	46,988	54,490	59,409	62,378
Other private services.....	103,934	107,904	113,857	122,207	131,563	148,149	164,301	187,771
Other [1].................	15,928	13,790	12,539	11,943	13,315	15,781	19,539	17,112
U.S. govt misc. services ...	885	786	831	795	810	959	1,087	1,155
IMPORTS								
Total..............	1,230,974	1,450,432	1,370,022	1,398,446	1,514,672	1,769,341	1,997,441	2,204,225
Goods.................	1,031,784	1,226,684	1,148,231	1,167,377	1,264,307	1,477,094	1,681,780	1,861,380
Services	199,190	223,748	221,791	231,069	250,365	292,247	315,661	342,845
Travel	58,963	64,705	60,200	58,715	57,447	65,750	68,970	72,029
Passenger fares	21,315	24,274	22,633	19,969	20,989	24,718	26,149	27,503
Other transportation	34,139	41,425	38,682	38,407	44,705	54,161	61,929	65,282
Royalties, license fees	13,107	16,468	16,538	19,353	19,033	23,274	24,632	26,432
Other private services.....	55,510	60,520	66,021	72,604	79,764	91,267	99,927	116,524
Other [1].................	13,335	13,473	14,835	19,101	25,296	29,299	30,075	31,054
U.S. govt misc. services ...	2,821	2,883	2,882	2,920	3,131	3,778	3,979	4,021

[1] Represents transfers under U.S. military sales contracts for exports and direct defense expenditures for imports.

Source: U.S. Census Bureau, *U.S. International Trade in Goods and Services, Annual Revision for 2006,* Series FT–900(07–04) and previous reports. See also <http://www.census.gov/foreign-trade/Press–Release/2006pr/final_revisions/06final.pdf> (released 08 June 2007).

Table 1273. **U.S. International Trade in Goods by Related Parties: 2000 to 2006**

[In millions of dollars (1,205,339 represents $1,205,339,000,000). "Related party trade" is trade by U.S. companies with their subsidiaries abroad as well as trade by U.S. subsidiaries of foreign companies with their parent companies. Based on the North American Industry Classification System (NAICS), 2002; see text, Section 15]

Country and commodity	2002 NAICS code	2000	2003	2004	2005	2006
IMPORTS FOR CONSUMPTION						
Total imports................ [1]	(X)	1,205,339	1,250,097	1,460,160	1,662,380	1,845,053
Related party trade, total [1]..................	(X)	563,084	593,833	697,561	775,730	862,657
Canada	(X)	100,689	96,969	116,261	127,719	139,490
Japan	(X)	108,290	93,716	102,207	108,322	116,690
Mexico	(X)	89,068	88,029	94,716	99,709	114,504
China [2]...................	(X)	18,061	34,839	53,172	62,716	70,701
Germany	(X)	37,781	44,279	46,959	30,792	54,972
Transportation equipment	336	161,150	170,822	181,805	188,445	200,855
Computer & electronic products	334	166,279	143,692	168,554	176,719	189,046
Chemicals..................	325	45,452	66,835	76,268	84,459	96,919
Machinery, except electrical	333	39,918	40,959	50,013	56,804	62,975
Oil & gas	211	13,241	17,926	31,694	48,725	61,758
EXPORTS						
Total exports................	(X)	780,418	723,743	817,936	904,380	1,037,143
Related party trade, domestic exports, total [1].....	(X)	196,596	204,543	218,688	245,712	279,832
Canada	(X)	64,133	64,641	69,029	76,331	80,687
Mexico	(X)	34,249	33,865	38,602	44,570	49,801
Japan	(X)	20,313	16,518	16,200	17,427	18,332
Netherlands	(X)	6,845	7,305	8,064	9,308	13,835
Germany	(X)	6,751	9,654	8,778	9,250	13,779
Transportation equipment	336	46,288	47,564	48,687	52,513	58,379
Chemicals..................	325	26,376	36,095	42,495	48,121	55,349
Computer & electronic products	334	51,210	42,570	39,309	41,863	47,140
Machinery, except electrical	333	19,831	19,300	23,061	25,492	27,627
Electrical equipment, appliances & components.......	335	7,575	7,647	8,675	9,888	11,642

X Not applicable. [1] Includes other countries and other commodities, not shown separately. [2] See footnote 2, Table 1298.

Source: U.S. Census Bureau, "Related Party Trade—2006"; published 10 May 2007; <http://www.census.gov/foreign-trade /Press–Release/2006pr/aip/related_party/>.

Table 1274. U.S. Exports and Imports for Consumption of Merchandise by Customs District: 2000 to 2006

[In billions of dollars (780.0 represents $780,000,000,000). Exports are f.a.s. (free alongside ship) value all years; imports are on customs-value basis. These data may differ from those in Tables 1273, 1278, and 1279. For methodology, see Foreign Trade Statistics in Appendix III]

Customs district	Exports					Imports for consumption				
	2000	2003	2004	2005	2006	2000	2003	2004	2005	2006
Total [1]	780.0	723.7	817.9	904.4	1,037.1	1,205.6	1,250.1	1,460.2	1,662.4	1,845.1
Anchorage, AK	5.9	8.4	8.7	12.1	14.9	13.4	9.2	10.5	10.2	11.4
Baltimore, MD	6.2	6.0	7.2	9.0	10.0	18.6	22.7	26.7	29.5	29.6
Boston, MA	7.0	7.0	9.7	9.9	10.5	18.7	16.4	19.2	21.4	22.6
Buffalo, NY	38.2	28.8	33.6	34.7	37.8	38.4	35.9	40.9	42.1	44.3
Charleston, SC [2]	12.6	13.6	15.4	16.1	16.2	16.9	21.0	26.0	30.9	32.4
Chicago, IL	21.7	21.3	25.9	30.0	32.2	51.1	58.3	69.1	78.5	88.5
Cleveland, OH	22.7	17.2	19.0	20.8	21.4	36.5	36.1	44.6	51.2	59.0
Dallas/Fort Worth, TX	11.5	12.3	16.4	17.8	20.6	18.8	22.4	27.8	32.0	38.3
Detroit, MI	79.4	87.6	93.4	105.7	112.6	97.6	98.8	112.2	122.8	126.0
Duluth, MN	1.5	1.7	1.8	1.9	2.0	7.0	7.6	9.0	9.4	7.0
El Paso, TX	18.0	17.5	19.3	19.9	22.0	24.1	25.3	27.8	27.7	29.5
Great Falls, MT	5.0	5.4	6.1	9.7	12.4	14.3	17.5	21.5	26.8	27.8
Honolulu, HI	0.7	2.5	1.8	2.4	3.2	2.9	2.0	2.2	2.9	4.2
Houston/Galveston, TX	29.7	32.1	39.5	46.7	58.1	40.9	48.4	64.4	89.4	104.9
Laredo, TX	57.7	48.6	56.0	60.3	67.3	62.7	66.1	74.4	78.2	88.8
Los Angeles, CA	77.6	67.7	70.8	78.4	90.4	150.1	165.4	191.0	213.5	236.0
Miami, FL	31.0	26.3	30.0	34.1	39.6	23.3	25.0	27.8	30.4	30.8
Milwaukee, WI	0.1	0.2	0.1	0.2	0.2	1.5	1.8	1.5	1.5	1.7
Minneapolis, MN	1.4	1.5	1.7	2.3	2.5	4.3	5.4	5.8	6.9	12.0
Mobile, AL [2]	4.0	4.6	5.0	4.9	6.0	7.9	8.9	11.0	13.7	16.7
New Orleans, LA	35.9	33.6	36.8	32.4	39.9	54.0	59.2	76.2	94.2	110.0
New York, NY	79.5	71.9	80.8	90.8	106.3	145.6	147.5	163.6	176.3	188.4
Nogales, AZ	7.3	5.0	5.9	6.9	8.3	14.1	11.6	12.5	13.6	17.0
Norfolk, VA [2]	12.4	12.3	13.4	16.7	18.1	13.6	17.7	20.0	23.5	26.4
Ogdensburg, NY	12.4	10.4	11.9	13.2	14.3	23.7	21.3	24.2	27.8	30.1
Pembina, ND	8.7	9.2	11.0	13.6	16.1	11.0	9.6	11.1	12.8	14.1
Philadelphia, PA	6.0	7.3	9.0	10.1	13.1	28.3	29.8	38.6	47.5	55.5
Port Arthur, TX	1.2	1.4	2.0	2.1	3.0	10.9	13.7	18.0	21.3	23.9
Portland, ME	2.6	2.8	2.8	2.8	3.1	8.7	8.8	9.3	10.9	10.9
Portland, OR	7.2	6.2	6.7	6.3	7.6	12.5	11.8	13.9	14.2	16.3
Providence, RI	(Z)	0.1	0.1	0.1	0.1	1.3	3.1	3.3	4.4	5.8
San Diego, CA	12.7	12.7	14.0	15.0	16.0	22.2	22.8	25.4	28.2	34.5
San Francisco, CA	58.3	33.1	38.2	36.6	41.4	68.6	46.2	54.9	61.8	69.2
San Juan, PR	4.8	8.9	9.7	9.7	11.8	11.8	19.0	19.1	19.4	20.5
Savannah, GA	15.9	17.0	21.6	24.6	27.9	26.1	30.8	38.4	47.6	54.2
Seattle, WA	40.4	39.8	43.5	48.9	65.2	40.5	35.7	43.2	51.0	54.1
St. Albans, VT	4.5	3.0	3.6	4.2	3.6	9.4	9.8	10.5	12.6	11.3
St. Louis, MO	1.3	0.6	0.7	1.3	1.7	7.9	7.9	9.1	10.1	11.1
Tampa, FL	4.8	6.2	7.5	10.0	12.7	14.7	14.6	15.4	19.7	25.5
Virgin Islands, U.S.	0.3	0.4	0.5	0.5	0.6	4.8	5.0	6.8	9.0	10.3
Washington, DC	2.8	2.4	2.8	3.7	5.2	2.6	2.4	3.3	3.7	7.3
Wilmington, NC	2.5	1.7	1.9	2.2	2.3	10.6	13.2	13.9	15.5	16.4

Z Less than $50 million.   [1] Totals shown for exports reflect the value of estimated parcel post and Special Category shipments, and adjustments for undocumented exports to Canada, which are not distributed by customs district. The value of bituminous coal exported through Norfolk, VA; Charleston, SC; and Mobile, AL is reflected in the total but not distributed by district.   [2] Excludes exports of bituminous coal, which are included in the "Total" line.

Source: U.S. Census Bureau, 2000–2004, *U.S. Export History* and *U.S. Import History* on compact disc; beginning 2005, *U.S. Merchandise Trade: Selected Highlights*, December issues, series FT920. See also <http://www.census.gov/foreign-trade/Press-Release/ft920_index.html>.

Table 1275. Export and Import Unit Value Indexes—Selected Countries: 2002 to 2006

[Indexes in U.S. dollars, 2000 = 100. A unit value is an implicit price derived from value and quantity data]

Country	Export unit value					Import unit value				
	2002	2003	2004	2005	2006	2002	2003	2004	2005	2006
United States	98.2	99.7	103.6	106.9	110.7	94.1	96.9	102.3	110.0	115.4
Australia	100.0	109.9	129.1	152.9	174.3	94.5	103.8	111.1	116.6	119.8
Belgium	103.5	120.4	134.9	142.0	149.2	102.2	119.8	136.1	142.8	150.5
Canada	93.2	103.8	114.9	129.0	137.9	98.2	101.9	107.9	115.9	124.3
France	109.0	130.7	141.4	140.4	126.7	98.9	118.7	127.6	127.0	123.9
Germany	101.5	118.3	128.9	129.7	134.8	97.2	110.4	120.3	123.2	139.5
Greece	111.5	133.4	154.1	160.1	168.2	(NA)	(NA)	(NA)	(NA)	(NA)
Ireland [1]	103.2	114.7	115.4	119.1	(NA)	101.1	111.1	119.6	120.7	(NA)
Italy	107.3	129.6	148.6	158.7	(NA)	104.4	124.8	143.8	157.0	(NA)
Japan	87.6	90.9	96.0	96.1	95.3	86.8	93.1	103.9	115.4	127.2
Korea, South	83.1	85.1	91.5	92.7	(NA)	87.5	95.6	107.3	117.3	(NA)
Netherlands	99.4	115.9	126.3	133.1	(NA)	101.1	117.5	130.9	132.8	(NA)
Norway	93.3	104.3	126.8	160.9	(NA)	102.8	116.1	126.5	132.4	(NA)
Spain	101.7	120.1	133.4	139.9	147.8	98.0	115.9	130.6	137.4	142.8
Sweden	93.8	110.3	121.1	124.1	130.8	98.6	116.2	131.2	138.4	148.4
Switzerland	107.1	123.5	137.2	139.4	143.2	104.8	121.5	135.3	142.1	148.4
United Kingdom	97.4	108.0	121.5	126.0	131.2	95.8	103.6	115.6	119.6	125.4

NA Not available.

Source: International Monetary Fund, Washington, DC, *International Financial Statistics*, monthly, (copyright).

798   Foreign Commerce and Aid

Table 1276. **U.S. Exports of Goods by State of Origin: 2000 to 2006**

[In millions of dollars (782,429 represents $782,429,000,000), except as indicated. Exports are on a f.a.s. value basis. Exports are based on origin of movement]

State and other area	2000	2005	2006 Total	2006 Rank	State and other area	2000	2005	2006 Total	2006 Rank
Total	782,429	904,289	1,037,320	(X)	Montana	541	711	887	48
					Nebraska	2,511	3,004	3,625	40
United States	712,055	853,765	982,193	(X)	Nevada	1,482	3,937	5,493	32
					New Hampshire	2,373	2,548	2,811	43
Alabama	7,317	10,796	13,878	23					
Alaska	2,464	3,592	4,044	36	New Jersey	18,638	21,080	27,002	9
Arizona	14,334	14,950	18,287	17	New Mexico	2,391	2,540	2,892	42
Arkansas	2,599	3,862	4,265	35	New York	42,846	50,492	57,369	3
California	119,640	116,819	127,746	2	North Carolina	17,946	19,463	21,218	15
Colorado	6,593	6,784	7,956	29	North Dakota	626	1,185	1,509	46
Connecticut	8,047	9,687	12,238	26	Ohio	26,322	34,801	37,833	8
Delaware	2,197	2,525	3,890	37	Oklahoma	3,072	4,314	4,375	34
District of Columbia	1,003	825	1,040	(X)	Oregon	11,441	12,381	15,288	21
Florida	26,543	33,377	38,545	7	Pennsylvania	18,792	22,271	26,334	10
					Rhode Island	1,186	1,269	1,531	45
Georgia	14,925	20,577	20,073	16					
Hawaii	387	1,028	706	50	South Carolina	8,565	13,944	13,615	24
Idaho	3,559	3,260	3,721	39	South Dakota	679	942	1,185	47
Illinois	31,438	35,868	42,085	5	Tennessee	11,592	19,070	22,020	14
Indiana	15,386	21,476	22,620	13	Texas	103,866	128,761	150,888	1
Iowa	4,466	7,348	8,410	28	Utah	3,221	6,056	6,798	31
Kansas	5,145	6,720	8,626	27	Vermont	4,097	4,240	3,817	38
Kentucky	9,612	14,899	17,232	18	Virginia	11,698	12,216	14,104	22
Louisiana	16,814	19,232	23,503	12	Washington	32,215	37,948	53,075	4
Maine	1,779	2,310	2,627	44	West Virginia	2,219	3,147	3,225	41
					Wisconsin	10,508	14,924	17,169	19
Maryland	4,593	7,119	7,598	30	Wyoming	503	669	830	49
Massachusetts	20,514	22,043	24,047	11					
Michigan	33,845	37,584	40,405	6	Puerto Rico	9,735	13,264	15,196	(X)
Minnesota	10,303	14,705	16,309	20	Virgin Islands	174	539	624	(X)
Mississippi	2,726	4,008	4,674	33	Other [1]	60,810	36,740	39,456	(X)
Missouri	6,497	10,462	12,776	25	Timing adjustments	-346	-19	-148	(X)

X Not applicable.   [1] Includes unreported, not specified, special category, estimated shipments, and re-exports.

Source: U.S. Census Bureau, *U.S. International Trade in Goods and Services*, series FT-900, December issues. For most recent release, see <http://www.census.gov/foreign-trade/Press-Release/2006pr/12/> (released 13 February 2007).

Table 1277. **U.S. Agricultural Exports by State: 2000 to 2006**

[In millions of dollars (50,744 represents $50,744,000,000). For years ending Sept. 30]

State	2000	2003	2004	2005	2006	State	2000	2003	2004	2005	2006
U.S.	50,744	56,014	62,409	62,516	68,721	NE	2,977	3,259	2,997	2,836	3,261
						NV	40	36	41	48	44
AL	393	473	561	574	572	NH	9	15	19	18	20
AK	1	3	3	3	4	NJ	125	173	189	194	219
AZ	394	450	468	447	520						
AR	1,235	1,563	1,765	1,733	1,912	NM	128	139	185	215	248
CA	6,685	7,462	8,649	9,405	10,475	NY	481	512	541	583	671
CO	964	851	840	712	852	NC	1,294	1,512	1,791	1,804	2,045
CT	119	75	91	88	98	ND	1,121	1,741	1,756	1,726	1,882
DE	114	116	130	143	145	OH	1,160	1,496	1,624	1,588	1,716
FL	1,289	1,470	1,607	1,572	1,699	OK	553	610	867	839	754
GA	859	1,047	1,113	1,136	1,356	OR	682	790	908	910	1,000
HI	73	81	89	95	96	PA	914	1,100	1,099	1,168	1,354
ID	772	816	820	878	911	RI	3	8	11	11	11
IL	2,843	3,254	3,767	3,322	3,787	SC	266	365	430	381	482
IN	1,412	1,614	1,976	1,867	2,044						
IA	3,124	3,170	3,931	4,031	4,211	SD	1,065	952	1,270	1,231	1,157
KS	3,175	2,928	3,311	2,787	3,221	TN	489	773	839	820	924
KY	737	923	952	1,082	1,091	TX	3,063	3,393	3,881	3,696	3,805
LA	432	545	561	569	641	UT	247	260	235	245	304
ME	64	67	70	78	96	VT	28	35	42	42	42
MD	223	276	302	288	313	VA	454	486	594	589	588
						WA	1,557	1,802	1,803	2,019	2,227
MA	117	139	173	162	167	WV	33	36	38	41	42
MI	857	912	942	1,009	1,161	WI	1,293	1,257	1,172	1,320	1,500
MN	2,286	2,427	2,542	2,770	2,977	WY	52	44	43	48	53
MS	617	866	1,027	926	950						
MO	1,038	1,181	1,555	1,298	1,461	Unallo-					
MT	352	393	465	534	590	cated	2,536	2,118	2,326	2,638	3,022

Source: U.S. Dept. of Agriculture, Economic Research Service, "State Export Data"; published 29 June 2007; <http://www.ers.usda.gov/data/stateexports/>.

Foreign Commerce and Aid   799

Table 1278. U.S. Exports, Imports, and Merchandise Trade Balance by Country: 2002 to 2006

[In millions of dollars (693,103 represents $693,103,000,000). Includes silver ore and bullion. Country totals include exports of special category commodities, if any. Data include nonmonetary gold and include trade of Virgin Islands with foreign countries. For methodology, see Foreign Trade Statistics in Appendix III. Minus sign (–) denotes an excess of imports over exports]

Country [1]	Exports, domestic and foreign					General imports					Merchandise trade balance				
	2002	2003	2004	2005	2006	2002	2003	2004	2005	2006	2002	2003	2004	2005	2006
Total	693,103	724,771	818,775	905,978	1,036,635	1,161,366	1,257,121	1,469,704	1,673,455	1,853,938	-468,263	-532,350	-650,930	-767,477	-817,304
Afghanistan	80	61	150	262	417	3	56	25	67	45	77	5	126	195	372
Albania	15	10	20	19	28	6	4	11	37	24	9	5	9	-19	4
Algeria	984	487	972	1,167	1,102	2,360	4,748	7,410	10,446	15,456	-1,376	-4,261	-6,438	-9,279	-14,354
Angola	374	491	594	929	1,550	3,123	4,267	4,521	8,484	11,719	-2,749	-3,776	-3,927	-7,555	-10,169
Anguilla	20	22	21	32	43	1	1	4	4	6	19	20	20	28	39
Antigua and Barbuda	81	127	126	190	194	4	13	4	4	6	78	115	121	186	188
Argentina	1,585	2,437	3,388	4,112	4,776	3,187	3,170	3,746	4,584	3,979	-1,602	-733	-357	-462	797
Armenia	112	103	91	66	80	31	38	46	46	47	81	65	45	19	34
Aruba	465	355	384	559	511	774	955	1,776	2,920	2,845	-309	-600	-1,392	-2,361	-2,335
Australia	13,085	13,088	14,225	15,828	17,779	6,479	6,414	7,546	7,342	8,204	6,606	6,674	6,680	8,486	9,575
Austria	2,427	1,768	1,946	2,593	2,986	3,815	4,492	5,798	6,103	8,304	-1,388	-2,724	-3,853	-3,510	-5,318
Azerbaijan	70	120	159	133	231	34	10	38	45	716	35	110	121	87	-485
Bahamas, The	975	1,075	1,186	1,787	2,282	450	479	638	700	453	526	595	548	1,087	1,830
Bahrain	419	508	302	351	475	395	378	405	432	632	24	130	-104	-81	-158
Bangladesh	269	226	289	320	333	2,134	2,074	2,303	2,693	3,271	-1,865	-1,848	-2,013	-2,373	-2,938
Barbados	268	300	348	395	443	34	43	37	32	34	233	257	312	363	409
Belarus	19	84	33	35	75	126	215	336	345	539	-106	-131	-303	-310	-465
Belgium	13,326	15,236	16,871	18,691	21,340	9,807	10,141	12,446	13,023	14,405	3,519	5,095	4,425	5,668	6,935
Belize	138	199	152	218	239	78	101	107	98	147	60	97	45	119	92
Benin	35	30	46	72	116	–	1	2	1	1	35	30	44	72	115
Bermuda	415	401	472	491	638	23	15	25	87	16	392	386	447	403	622
Bolivia	192	183	194	220	215	160	185	260	293	362	32	-2	-67	-74	-147
Bosnia and Herzegovina	32	21	28	18	52	16	12	11	71	26	16	9	17	-53	26
Botswana	32	26	54	67	27	29	14	74	178	252	3	12	-19	-111	-225
Brazil	12,376	11,211	13,897	15,372	19,231	15,781	17,910	21,160	24,436	26,367	-3,405	-6,699	-7,263	-9,064	-7,136
Brunei	46	38	48	50	48	287	423	406	563	550	-241	-385	-358	-513	-502
Bulgaria	101	156	172	268	293	310	441	507	454	458	-209	-286	-335	-186	-165
Cambodia	29	58	59	70	75	1,071	1,262	1,497	1,787	2,188	-1,042	-1,204	-1,439	-1,697	-2,114
Cameroon	156	91	100	117	120	172	214	308	158	273	-16	-123	-209	-41	-153
Canada	160,923	169,924	189,880	211,899	230,656	209,088	221,595	256,360	290,384	302,438	-48,165	-51,671	-66,480	-78,486	-71,782
Cayman Islands	232	309	400	681	632	9	12	13	54	15	223	297	387	627	617
Chad	127	64	41	54	61	6	23	756	1,498	1,918	122	42	-715	-1,444	-1,857
Chile	2,609	2,715	3,606	5,223	6,786	3,785	3,705	4,732	6,664	9,565	-1,176	-990	-1,126	-1,442	-2,779
China [2]	22,128	28,368	34,744	41,925	55,186	125,193	152,436	196,682	243,470	287,774	-103,065	-124,068	-161,938	-201,545	-232,589
Colombia	3,583	3,756	4,505	5,462	6,709	5,604	6,385	7,256	8,849	9,266	-2,022	-2,629	-2,751	-3,387	-2,557
Congo (Brazzaville)	52	79	66	182	138	182	433	858	1,623	3,097	-130	-354	-792	-1,519	-2,959
Congo (Kinshasa)	28	31	67	65	71	204	175	124	264	85	-176	-144	-57	-199	-14
Costa Rica	3,117	3,414	3,306	3,599	4,132	3,142	3,364	3,333	3,415	3,844	-25	49	-27	183	288
Cote d'Ivoire	76	103	118	124	148	376	490	715	1,198	702	-300	-387	-597	-1,074	-554
Croatia	78	197	130	159	147	146	181	291	364	353	-68	16	-161	-206	-207
Cuba	146	259	404	369	341	–	–	–	–	–	145	259	400	369	340
Cyprus	193	212	96	84	240	26	25	26	31	51	168	187	70	54	189
Czech Republic	654	672	827	1,054	1,123	1,233	1,394	1,756	2,193	2,349	-580	-722	-929	-1,139	-1,227

See footnotes at end of table.

Table 1278. U.S. Exports, Imports, and Merchandise Trade Balance, by Country: 2002 to 2006—Con.

[See headnote, page 800]

Country	Exports, domestic and foreign					General imports					Merchandise trade balance				
	2002	2003	2004	2005	2006	2002	2003	2004	2005	2006	2002	2003	2004	2005	2006
Denmark	1,496	1,548	2,147	1,918	2,269	3,237	3,708	3,876	5,144	5,540	-1,741	-2,161	-1,730	-3,226	-3,272
Djibouti	59	32	44	48	48	2	1	1	1	3	57	31	43	47	44
Dominica	45	34	36	62	68	5	5	3	-	3	40	29	33	58	65
Dominican Republic	4,250	4,205	4,358	4,719	5,351	4,169	4,455	4,527	4,604	4,532	81	-250	-169	115	818
Ecuador	1,606	1,447	1,669	1,964	2,727	2,143	2,722	4,283	5,759	7,094	-538	-1,275	-2,615	-3,795	-4,367
Egypt	2,868	2,607	3,078	3,159	4,133	1,356	1,143	1,284	2,091	2,396	1,512	1,464	1,794	1,068	1,737
El Salvador	1,664	1,821	1,868	1,854	2,152	1,982	2,020	2,052	1,989	1,857	-318	-199	-185	-135	295
Equatorial Guinea	109	336	215	282	552	502	904	1,170	1,561	1,733	-393	-568	-955	-1,280	-1,182
Estonia	82	121	134	145	221	164	182	393	511	526	-82	-61	-259	-366	-305
Ethiopia	61	409	355	510	137	26	31	41	62	81	35	379	314	448	56
Fiji	17	20	25	28	33	156	175	214	170	146	-139	-156	-188	-141	-113
Finland	1,535	1,713	2,069	2,254	2,648	3,447	3,602	3,887	4,342	4,974	-1,912	-1,889	-1,818	-2,088	-2,326
France	19,016	17,053	21,263	22,410	24,217	28,240	29,219	31,606	33,842	37,040	-9,224	-12,166	-10,342	-11,432	-12,822
French Guiana	250	156	27	27	33	8	3	-	-	1	242	152	228	27	33
French Polynesia	79	92	93	112	108	44	48	67	60	58	35	44	26	52	50
Gabon	66	63	93	99	135	1,588	1,970	2,467	2,816	1,361	-1,522	-1,907	-2,374	-2,717	-1,226
Georgia	99	131	227	214	264	18	54	67	194	105	81	77	149	20	158
Germany	26,630	28,832	31,416	34,184	41,319	62,506	68,113	77,266	84,751	89,082	-35,876	-39,281	-45,850	-50,567	-47,763
Ghana	193	209	310	337	290	116	82	145	158	192	76	127	164	179	97
Gibraltar	26	14	138	163	286	1	3	2	-	1	25	11	136	159	285
Greece	1,152	2,507	2,063	1,192	1,555	546	614	724	884	966	606	1,893	1,340	309	589
Grenada	56	68	70	82	74	11	8	5	6	5	50	61	65	77	70
Guadeloupe	40	46	38	55	65	7	3	3	-	3	29	43	35	52	63
Guatemala	2,044	2,263	2,551	2,835	3,511	2,796	2,947	3,154	3,137	3,102	-752	-683	-603	-302	409
Guinea	63	36	59	94	65	72	69	64	75	94	-9	-33	-5	19	-29
Guyana	128	117	138	177	179	116	119	122	120	125	13	-2	16	57	54
Haiti	573	639	673	710	817	255	332	371	447	496	318	307	302	262	321
Honduras	2,571	2,826	3,078	3,254	3,687	3,261	3,313	3,640	3,749	3,718	-690	-486	-562	-495	-30
Hong Kong	12,594	13,521	15,827	16,351	17,776	9,328	8,851	9,314	8,892	7,947	3,266	4,669	6,514	7,459	9,829
Hungary	688	933	1,143	1,023	1,188	2,637	2,701	2,573	2,561	2,584	-1,950	-1,767	-1,430	-1,538	-1,397
Iceland	219	242	309	512	366	297	282	274	269	228	-78	-40	35	243	138
India	4,101	4,980	6,109	7,998	10,056	11,818	13,055	15,572	18,804	21,831	-7,717	-8,076	-9,463	-10,815	-11,775
Indonesia	2,556	2,516	2,671	3,054	3,079	9,643	9,515	10,811	12,014	13,425	-7,088	-6,999	-8,139	-8,960	-10,346
Iran	32	99	85	96	86	156	161	152	175	157	-125	-62	-67	-79	-71
Iraq	32	310	857	1,374	1,491	3,548	4,585	8,514	9,054	11,546	-3,517	-4,275	-7,657	-7,680	-10,055
Ireland	6,745	7,696	8,167	9,336	8,516	22,438	25,747	27,448	28,733	28,526	-15,693	-18,051	-19,281	-19,397	-20,010
Israel	7,027	6,892	9,169	9,737	10,965	12,416	12,769	14,552	16,831	19,167	-5,389	-5,877	-5,382	-7,093	-8,202
Italy	10,057	10,561	10,685	11,524	10,546	24,220	25,414	28,097	31,009	32,655	-14,164	-14,854	-17,413	-19,485	-20,109
Jamaica	1,420	1,470	1,431	1,701	2,036	396	423	320	376	528	1,024	1,047	1,111	1,325	1,508
Japan	51,449	52,004	54,243	55,485	59,613	121,429	118,037	129,805	138,004	148,181	-69,979	-66,032	-75,562	-82,519	-88,568
Jordan	404	492	552	644	650	412	674	1,093	1,267	1,422	-8	-181	-542	-623	-772
Kazakhstan	605	168	320	538	646	335	393	539	1,101	961	270	-224	-218	-563	-314
Kenya	32	197	394	633	526	189	249	352	348	354	83	-53	42	285	172
Korea, South	22,576	24,073	26,413	27,765	32,442	35,572	37,229	46,168	43,781	45,804	-12,996	-13,157	-19,755	-16,016	-13,362

See footnotes at end of table.

Table 1278. U.S. Exports, Imports, and Merchandise Trade Balance, by Country: 2002 to 2006—Con.

[See headnote, page 800]

Country	Exports, domestic and foreign					General imports					Merchandise trade balance				
	2002	2003	2004	2005	2006	2002	2003	2004	2005	2006	2002	2003	2004	2005	2006
Kuwait	1,015	1,507	1,519	1,975	2,087	1,940	2,277	3,231	4,335	3,981	-926	-770	-1,712	-2,360	-1,894
Kyrgyzstan	31	39	29	31	71	5	11	11	5	4	26	28	19	27	67
Latvia	91	124	121	178	246	197	377	365	362	299	-106	-254	-244	-185	-53
Lebanon	317	314	464	466	931	62	92	75	86	89	256	222	390	379	842
Lesotho	2	5	6	4	4	322	393	467	404	408	-320	-388	-461	-400	-404
Liberia	28	33	61	69	68	46	60	84	91	140	-18	-26	-23	-22	-72
Libya	18	-	39	84	435	-	-	332	1,590	2,472	18	-	-292	-1,507	-2,037
Liechtenstein	15	16	11	20	16	238	262	286	296	324	-223	-246	-276	-276	-309
Lithuania	103	162	295	390	567	300	347	482	634	570	-197	-185	-187	-244	-3
Luxembourg	480	279	705	782	581	300	265	290	389	534	180	14	414	394	47
Macau	79	55	86	102	200	1,232	1,356	1,487	1,249	1,230	-1,153	-1,301	-1,401	-1,147	-1,030
Macedonia	19	26	21	32	22	73	61	78	48	42	-55	-35	-57	-17	-20
Madagascar	15	46	36	28	45	216	384	470	324	281	-200	-337	-434	-295	-236
Malawi	30	17	22	28	46	71	77	61	116	60	-41	-60	-39	-88	-14
Malaysia	10,344	10,914	10,921	10,461	12,544	24,009	25,440	28,179	33,685	36,533	-13,665	-14,526	-17,258	-23,224	-23,989
Mali	11	31	31	32	43	3	2	4	4	8	8	29	27	28	35
Malta	210	202	181	194	163	310	373	383	283	371	-100	-171	-202	-89	-208
Martinique	24	22	28	35	32	1	1	2	22	42	22	21	26	13	-9
Mauritania	23	35	34	86	90	1	2	7	1	51	22	33	27	85	39
Mauritius	28	32	28	31	36	281	298	270	222	219	-253	-266	-242	-191	-183
Mexico	97,470	97,412	110,835	120,365	133,979	134,616	138,060	155,902	170,109	198,253	-37,146	-40,648	-45,067	-49,744	-64,274
Moldova	31	25	40	40	30	39	43	49	50	37	-8	-18	-10	-10	-7
Monaco	11	11	18	17	34	15	22	23	38	32	-4	-11	-5	-21	2
Mongolia	66	21	28	22	23	162	183	239	144	114	-95	-163	-211	-122	-91
Morocco	565	469	526	525	878	392	385	515	446	521	173	83	11	79	357
Mozambique	95	62	77	63	64	9	8	11	12	16	86	54	66	51	49
Namibia	58	28	75	112	127	57	123	238	130	116	1	-95	-164	-17	11
Nepal	20	16	25	25	17	152	171	143	111	99	-132	-155	-118	-87	-83
Netherlands	18,311	20,695	24,289	26,485	31,129	9,849	10,953	12,451	14,862	17,342	8,462	9,742	11,839	11,623	13,787
Netherlands Antilles	741	747	824	1,138	1,485	362	632	435	922	1,119	380	115	390	215	366
New Caledonia	37	43	45	38	44	10	13	19	27	51	27	30	26	11	-7
New Zealand	1,813	1,848	2,073	2,652	2,929	2,262	2,403	2,968	3,155	3,116	-469	-555	-895	-503	-188
Nicaragua	437	502	592	626	752	680	770	990	1,181	1,526	-243	-268	-398	-555	-774
Niger	41	34	34	79	129	1	4	27	66	66	40	30	7	13	63
Nigeria	1,058	1,017	1,554	1,621	2,234	5,945	10,394	16,249	24,239	27,863	-4,888	-9,377	-14,694	-22,618	-25,630
Norway	1,407	1,466	1,604	1,942	2,394	5,843	5,232	6,509	6,776	7,085	-4,436	-3,766	-4,904	-4,834	-4,691
Oman	356	322	330	595	829	401	695	418	555	909	-45	-372	-88	40	-80
Pakistan	693	843	1,814	1,252	1,989	2,305	2,531	2,875	3,253	3,672	-1,612	-1,688	-1,061	-2,002	-1,683
Panama	1,407	1,849	1,835	2,162	2,701	303	301	316	327	379	1,104	1,547	1,519	1,835	2,322
Papua New Guinea	23	30	43	55	44	90	66	59	59	84	-67	-36	-12	-3	-40
Paraguay	433	484	623	896	911	44	53	59	52	58	389	430	564	844	853
Peru	1,563	1,699	2,101	2,309	2,927	1,939	2,409	3,702	5,119	5,880	-377	-710	-1,601	-2,810	-2,954
Philippines	7,276	7,987	7,087	6,895	7,617	10,980	10,059	9,137	9,250	9,694	-3,704	-2,072	-2,050	-2,355	-2,077
Poland	686	758	929	1,268	1,961	1,109	1,324	1,822	1,949	2,253	-422	-566	-892	-681	-292
Portugal	861	863	1,046	1,132	1,471	1,673	1,967	2,243	2,329	3,060	-811	-1,105	-1,197	-1,197	-1,590
Qatar	314	408	455	987	1,279	485	331	387	448	262	-171	76	68	539	1,017
Romania	248	367	525	609	554	695	730	853	1,208	1,119	-447	-363	-328	-599	-565

See footnotes at end of table.

U.S. Census Bureau, Statistical Abstract of the United States: 2008

Table 1278. U.S. Exports, Imports, and Merchandise Trade Balance, by Country: 2002 to 2006—Con.

[See headnote, page 800]

Country	Exports, domestic and foreign					General imports					Merchandise trade balance				
	2002	2003	2004	2005	2006	2002	2003	2004	2005	2006	2002	2003	2004	2005	2006
Russia	2,397	2,447	2,961	3,962	4,701	6,870	8,618	11,891	15,307	19,828	-4,473	-6,171	-8,930	-11,344	-15,127
Saudi Arabia	4,781	4,596	5,257	6,813	7,640	13,150	18,069	20,959	27,193	31,689	-8,369	-13,473	-15,702	-20,380	-24,050
Senegal	75	102	89	159	97	4	5	3	4	21	71	97	86	155	76
Serbia and Montenegro	78	50	143	133	147	10	15	92	55	68	68	35	51	78	79
Sierra Leone	26	28	41	38	39	4	7	11	9	36	22	22	30	29	3
Singapore	16,218	16,560	19,609	20,642	24,684	14,802	15,138	15,370	15,110	17,768	1,416	1,422	4,238	5,532	6,916
Slovakia	93	115	132	150	510	260	1,009	1,211	961	1,405	-168	-894	-1,080	-811	-895
Slovenia	131	140	192	234	239	307	484	510	413	483	-176	-345	-318	-179	-244
South Africa	2,526	2,819	3,179	3,907	4,462	4,034	4,624	5,945	5,886	7,501	-1,509	-1,805	-2,766	-1,979	-3,039
Spain	5,298	5,930	6,638	6,914	7,426	5,733	6,677	7,350	8,615	9,778	-435	-747	-712	-1,701	-2,352
Sri Lanka	172	155	164	198	237	1,810	1,808	1,957	2,083	2,146	-1,639	-1,653	-1,793	-1,885	-1,909
St. Kitts and Nevis	50	59	60	94	127	49	45	42	50	50	1	14	19	44	77
St. Lucia	100	120	105	135	149	20	13	14	32	30	80	107	91	103	119
St. Vincent and the Grenadines	40	46	46	45	58	16	4	5	16	2	24	42	41	30	56
Sudan	11	26	68	108	77	2	3	3	14	6	9	23	65	95	71
Suriname	125	193	179	246	259	133	140	141	166	165	-8	53	38	80	94
Swaziland	12	8	12	12	12	115	162	198	199	156	-103	-154	-186	-187	-144
Sweden	3,153	3,223	3,267	3,715	4,126	9,216	11,119	12,683	13,821	13,870	-6,063	-7,896	-9,416	-10,106	-9,745
Switzerland	7,783	8,656	9,280	10,720	14,375	9,382	10,685	11,628	13,000	14,230	-1,600	-2,029	-2,348	-2,280	145
Syria [2]	274	214	213	155	224	161	246	268	324	214	113	-32	-55	-169	11
Taiwan [2]	18,382	17,448	21,744	22,069	23,047	32,148	31,599	34,624	34,826	38,212	-13,766	-14,152	-12,879	-12,757	-15,165
Tajikistan	33	50	56	29	43	1	7	7	241	61	32	43	48	-212	-18
Tanzania	63	65	128	96	161	25	24	24	34	35	38	41	103	63	126
Thailand	4,860	5,835	6,368	7,257	8,147	14,793	15,179	17,579	19,890	22,466	-9,933	-9,343	-11,211	-12,633	-14,320
Togo	14	15	24	28	108	3	6	2	6	4	11	9	22	22	105
Trinidad and Tobago	1,020	1,063	1,208	1,417	1,615	2,440	4,334	5,842	7,891	8,362	-1,420	-3,271	-4,635	-6,474	-6,748
Tunisia	195	171	258	261	363	93	102	209	264	470	102	68	49	-3	-107
Turkey	3,113	2,900	3,362	4,269	5,724	3,516	3,788	4,934	5,182	5,359	-403	-888	-1,572	-913	365
Turkmenistan	47	34	295	237	113	60	76	81	135	76	-13	-42	214	102	37
Turks and Caicos Islands	54	72	137	238	366	–	6	7	9	12	54	66	130	228	354
Uganda	24	42	63	63	51	15	35	25	26	22	9	7	38	37	29
Ukraine	255	231	399	533	756	362	262	800	1,098	1,640	-108	-32	-400	-565	-884
United Arab Emirates	3,593	3,508	4,086	8,482	11,648	923	1,128	1,143	1,468	1,385	2,670	2,380	2,943	7,014	10,263
United Kingdom	33,205	33,828	36,000	38,588	45,410	40,745	42,795	46,274	51,033	53,513	-7,540	-8,967	-10,274	-12,445	-8,103
Uruguay	209	327	326	357	482	193	256	580	732	512	16	71	-254	-376	-30
Uzbekistan	139	256	230	74	54	77	84	88	96	152	61	173	142	-22	-98
Venezuela	4,430	2,831	4,767	6,421	9,002	15,094	17,136	24,921	33,978	37,134	-10,664	-14,305	-20,153	-27,557	-28,132
Vietnam	580	1,324	1,164	1,193	1,100	2,395	4,555	5,275	6,631	8,567	-1,815	-3,231	-4,111	-5,438	-7,466
Virgin Islands, British	67	71	97	125	217	40	35	18	34	26	27	36	79	91	191
Yemen	366	191	232	219	255	246	66	61	279	447	120	125	171	-60	-193
Zambia	36	20	26	29	52	8	13	19	22	29	28	7	7	7	23
Zimbabwe	49	42	47	46	48	103	57	62	61	103	-54	-15	-15	-15	-56

– Represents or rounds to zero. [1] Includes timing adjustment and unidentified countries, not shown separately. [2] See footnote 2, Table 1298.

Source: U.S. Census Bureau, U.S. International Trade in Goods and Services, Series FT–900(07-04), and previous final reports. See also <http://www.census.gov/foreign-trade/Press–Release/2006pr/final_revisions/> (released 8 June 2007).

Table 1279. U.S. Exports and General Imports by Selected SITC Commodity Groups: 2000 to 2006

[In millions of dollars (781,918 represents $781,918,000,000). SITC = Standard International Trade Classification. For methodology, see Foreign Trade Statistics in Appendix III. N.e.s. = not elsewhere specified]

Selected commodities	Exports [1]				General imports [2]			
	2000	2004	2005	2006	2000	2004	2005	2006
Total	781,918	818,775	905,978	1,036,635	1,218,022	1,469,704	1,673,455	1,853,938
Agricultural commodities [3]	51,296	61,383	63,139	70,912	39,186	54,222	59,530	65,459
Animal feeds	3,780	3,808	4,029	4,534	597	778	699	828
Cereal flour	1,310	1,802	2,015	2,339	1,753	2,730	3,010	3,357
Corn	4,695	6,132	5,062	7,251	160	127	125	179
Cotton, raw and linters	1,893	4,251	3,929	4,514	28	18	20	15
Meat and preparations	7,004	5,203	6,669	7,257	3,841	5,707	5,747	5,231
Soybeans	5,284	6,680	6,282	6,949	31	53	63	56
Vegetables and fruits	7,477	8,890	10,259	11,071	9,286	12,787	14,082	15,455
Wheat	3,734	5,148	4,410	4,205	229	162	174	311
Manufactured goods [3]	625,894	623,961	685,398	785,599	1,012,855	1,174,788	1,287,376	1,416,302
ADP equipment, office machinery	46,595	28,241	29,800	31,091	92,133	93,762	98,584	106,416
Airplane parts	15,062	15,295	17,538	20,515	5,572	4,824	5,592	6,771
Airplanes	24,777	24,493	30,291	43,933	12,412	11,389	10,734	10,604
Alcoholic beverages, distilled	424	684	726	844	2,946	4,022	4,360	4,912
Aluminum	3,780	3,807	4,483	5,596	6,949	9,547	11,931	14,919
Artwork/antiques	1,387	1,322	1,858	3,250	5,864	5,307	5,512	6,633
Basketware, etc	3,309	5,084	5,612	6,200	4,840	8,435	8,585	9,093
Chemicals, cosmetics	5,292	7,441	8,059	9,100	3,539	6,948	7,922	8,333
Chemicals, dyeing	4,089	4,569	4,901	5,337	2,667	2,667	2,971	3,054
Chemicals, fertilizers	2,249	2,595	2,990	2,941	1,684	2,536	3,701	3,438
Chemicals, inorganic	5,359	6,196	7,698	9,074	6,108	8,276	10,165	11,414
Chemicals, medicinal	12,893	23,433	25,012	28,431	14,685	34,937	39,176	45,746
Chemicals, n.e.s.	12,264	14,563	15,846	17,860	5,725	7,982	8,939	9,477
Chemicals, organic	17,990	25,852	26,765	29,839	28,578	35,447	38,009	42,212
Chemicals, plastics	19,519	25,202	28,861	32,617	10,647	14,222	17,385	18,813
Clothing	8,191	4,423	4,129	3,849	64,296	72,316	76,383	79,149
Copper	1,425	1,918	2,118	3,266	4,471	4,754	7,040	12,888
Cork, wood, lumber	4,320	3,857	4,038	4,273	8,227	10,605	10,939	10,386
Crude fertilizers	1,724	1,724	1,702	1,947	1,401	1,471	1,698	1,825
Electrical machinery	89,917	73,320	74,286	83,228	108,747	93,290	99,121	109,721
Fish and preparations	2,806	3,517	3,864	4,012	9,907	11,177	11,915	13,176
Footwear	663	453	508	572	14,842	16,506	17,932	19,160
Furniture and bedding	4,744	4,058	4,415	4,877	18,923	27,737	30,633	32,788
Gem diamonds	1,289	939	2,578	3,884	12,068	14,661	16,238	17,285
General industrial machinery	33,094	34,824	38,902	44,089	34,667	45,632	52,333	59,710
Glass	2,502	2,651	2,696	3,041	2,248	2,711	2,782	2,956
Gold, nonmonetary	5,898	4,430	5,533	8,790	2,657	3,996	4,430	5,633
Iron and steel mill products	5,715	8,022	10,430	11,799	15,807	22,400	24,632	32,904
Jewelry	1,574	2,566	3,029	4,033	6,459	8,557	9,696	11,222
Lighting, plumbing	1,384	1,476	1,694	1,868	5,104	6,811	7,591	8,069
Metal manufactures, n.e.s.	13,453	12,121	13,510	15,860	16,204	21,777	24,777	27,893
Metal ores; scrap	4,234	7,766	11,057	16,617	3,817	4,583	5,335	6,533
Metalworking machinery	6,191	5,983	6,457	8,228	7,726	6,262	7,530	8,644
Nickel	401	511	752	1,038	1,425	1,897	2,178	3,348
Optical goods	3,246	2,556	3,076	3,173	4,019	3,534	3,789	4,378
Paper and paperboard	10,640	10,689	11,457	12,337	15,185	16,581	17,561	18,503
Photographic equipment	4,236	3,534	3,343	3,590	6,896	4,905	4,481	4,506
Plastic articles, n.e.s.	7,607	7,390	8,036	8,915	8,034	11,776	13,633	14,823
Platinum	888	548	610	1,739	5,566	3,508	3,916	5,833
Power generating machinery	32,743	36,177	41,296	44,036	33,773	35,981	41,263	44,742
Printed materials	4,776	4,910	5,445	5,748	3,680	4,508	4,917	5,142
Pulp and waste paper	4,576	4,488	5,093	5,738	3,381	2,949	3,049	3,181
Records/magnetic media	5,395	4,757	5,142	4,912	5,172	6,799	7,258	7,095
Rubber articles, n.e.s.	1,673	1,520	1,598	1,787	1,962	2,733	2,925	3,039
Rubber tires and tubes	2,379	2,532	2,778	3,007	4,785	6,305	7,725	8,662
Scientific instruments	30,984	33,049	34,544	39,278	22,007	28,449	30,242	32,297
Ships, boats	1,070	1,649	1,913	2,575	1,178	2,084	1,719	1,548
Specialized industrial machinery	30,959	28,842	33,144	37,469	22,711	26,417	31,076	33,010
Television, VCR, etc.	27,921	20,072	20,974	22,515	70,468	87,885	104,079	115,327
Textile yarn, fabric	10,534	11,516	11,830	12,106	15,171	19,505	21,249	22,184
Toys/games/sporting goods	3,609	3,403	3,756	4,172	20,011	22,479	25,069	26,547
Travel goods	351	312	379	461	4,430	5,655	6,183	6,882
Vehicles	57,421	65,217	71,747	83,472	161,544	187,723	195,926	211,946
Watches/clocks/parts	348	272	256	304	3,481	3,790	3,939	4,082
Wood manufactures	1,842	1,796	1,818	2,007	7,228	12,309	12,847	12,539
Mineral fuel [3]	13,179	18,642	26,488	34,711	135,367	206,660	289,723	332,500
Coal	2,162	2,758	3,471	3,663	805	2,416	2,418	2,639
Crude oil	463	277	595	853	89,876	136,030	182,944	225,156
Petroleum preparations	5,746	9,726	14,782	22,078	25,673	37,988	59,698	66,197
Liquified propane/butane	663	426	587	805	1,508	2,899	4,371	4,419
Natural gas	411	2,125	3,094	2,226	12,594	23,908	34,911	28,268
Mineral fuels, other mineral	3,734	2,701	3,191	4,435	4,911	2,349	3,055	3,942
Reexports	68,203	89,662	101,125	108,070	(X)	(X)	(X)	(X)

X Not applicable. [1] F.a.s. basis. Exports by commodity are only for domestic exports. [2] Customs value basis. [3] Includes other commodities not shown separately.

Source: U.S. Census Bureau, U.S. International Trade in Goods and Services, Series FT-900(07-04), and previous final reports. See also <http://www.census.gov/foreign-trade/Press-Release/2006pr/final_revisions/> (released 8 June 2007).

Table 1280. United States Total and Aerospace Foreign Trade: 1990 to 2005

[In millions of dollars (–101,718 represents –$101,718,000,000), except percent. Data are reported as exports of domestic merchandise, including Department of Defense shipments and undocumented exports to Canada, f.a.s. (free alongside ship) basis, and imports for consumption, customs value basis. Minus sign (–) indicates deficit]

Year	Merchandise trade			Aerospace trade						
						Exports				
								Civil		
	Trade balance	Imports	Exports	Trade balance	Imports	Total	Percent of U.S. exports	Total	Transports	Military
1990	–101,718	495,311	393,592	27,282	11,801	39,083	9.9	31,517	16,691	7,566
1991	–66,723	488,453	421,730	30,785	13,003	43,788	10.4	35,548	20,881	8,239
1992	–84,501	532,665	448,164	31,356	13,662	45,018	10.0	36,906	22,379	8,111
1993	–115,568	580,659	465,091	27,235	12,183	39,418	8.5	31,823	18,146	7,596
1994	–150,630	663,256	512,626	25,010	12,363	37,373	7.3	30,050	15,931	7,322
1995	–158,801	743,543	584,742	21,561	11,509	33,071	5.7	25,079	10,606	7,991
1996	–170,214	795,289	625,075	26,602	13,668	40,270	6.4	29,477	13,624	10,792
1997	–180,522	869,704	689,182	32,239	18,134	50,374	7.3	40,075	21,028	10,299
1998	–229,758	911,896	682,138	40,960	23,110	64,071	9.4	51,999	29,168	12,072
1999	–328,821	1,024,618	695,797	37,381	25,063	62,444	9.0	50,624	25,694	11,820
2000	–436,104	1,218,022	781,918	26,734	27,944	54,679	7.0	45,566	19,615	9,113
2001	–411,899	1,140,999	729,100	26,035	32,473	58,508	8.0	49,371	22,151	9,137
2002	–468,263	1,161,366	693,103	29,533	27,242	56,775	8.2	47,348	21,661	9,427
2003	–532,350	1,257,121	724,771	27,111	25,393	52,504	7.2	44,060	19,434	8,445
2004	–650,930	1,469,704	818,775	31,002	25,815	56,817	6.9	47,325	18,577	9,492
2005	–767,477	1,673,455	905,978	39,784	27,649	67,433	7.4	57,225	21,888	10,207

Source: Aerospace Industries Association of America, Washington, DC, *Aerospace Facts and Figures*, annual.

Table 1281. U.S. High Technology Exports by Industry and Selected Major Country: 2000 to 2005

[In billions of dollars (222.5 represents $222,500,000,000)]

Selected industries	2000	2004	2005	Selected countries	2000	2004	2005
Total exports	222.5	191.4	199.1	Total exports	222.5	191.4	199.1
Computers and office equipment...	57.8	44.4	47.4	Canada	34.4	27.6	29.6
Consumer electronics	10.0	9.1	10.2	China [1]	4.6	8.8	10.0
Communications equipment	26.9	22.5	24.1	Japan	19.9	13.2	13.1
Electronic components	22.1	15.9	15.6	Korea, South	12.1	9.1	9.9
Semiconductors	60.0	48.1	47.2	Malaysia	7.8	7.6	7.4
Industrial electronics	30.5	33.7	34.7	Mexico	30.0	28.1	27.1
Electromedical equipment	8.1	12.2	13.8	Taiwan [1]	10.4	8.6	8.0
Photonics	7.1	5.6	6.2	European Union 25	51.5	40.9	42.6

[1] See footnote 2, table 1298.

Source: AeA (formerly the American Electronics Association), *Cyberstates 2006*, annual (copyright). See <http://www.aeanet.org>.

Table 1282. U.S. Exporting Companies Profile by Employment–Size Class: 2000 and 2005

(668,310 represents $668,310,000,000). Based on data from export trade documents and the Business Register. For information on data limitations, see the Techical Documentation in the source]

Employment–size class	Number of exporters		Known export value [1] (mil. dol.)		Percent of—			
					Number of exporters		Known export value	
	2000	2005	2000	2005	2000	2005	2000	2005
All companies, total ...	246,452	239,094	668,310	784,536	100.0	100.0	100.0	100.0
No employees	74,772	69,988	47,024	44,922	30.3	29.3	7.0	5.7
1 to 19 employees	96,268	99,677	45,272	55,582	39.1	41.7	6.8	7.1
20 to 49 employees	31,362	30,371	21,262	25,990	12.7	12.7	3.2	3.3
50 to 99 employees	16,988	15,955	19,711	24,883	6.9	6.7	2.9	3.2
100 to 249 employees	13,685	12,077	32,192	42,920	5.6	5.1	4.8	5.5
250 to 499 employees......	5,454	4,544	27,397	34,196	2.2	1.9	4.1	4.4
500 or more employees.....	7,923	6,482	475,453	556,042	3.2	2.7	71.1	70.9

[1] Known export value is defined as the value of exports by known exporters, i.e., those export transactions that could be matched to specific companies. Export values are on f.a.s. or "free alongside ship basis."

Source: U.S. Census Bureau, *A Profile of U.S. Exporting Companies, 2000* and *2004–2005*. See also <http://www.census.gov/foreign–trade/Press–Release/edb/2005/edbrel–0405.pdf> (released 10 January 2007).

Foreign Commerce and Aid   805

[In millions of dollars (712,285 represents $712,285,000,000). Includes nonmonetary gold. For methodology, see Foreign Trade Statistics in Appendix III. NAICS = North American Industry Classification System; see text, Section 15]

Product category	2000	2002	2003	2004	2005	2006
Domestic exports, total	712,285	629,599	651,713	729,425	803,920	929,811
Agricultural, forestry, and fishery products	29,153	30,068	34,699	37,830	37,013	41,503
Agricultural products, total	23,596	24,827	29,194	31,949	30,611	34,770
Livestock and livestock products.............	1,255	1,020	1,177	963	1,123	1,283
Forestry products, not elsewhere specified	1,644	1,419	1,462	1,653	1,667	1,698
Fish, fresh or chilled; and other marine products ...	2,658	2,802	2,866	3,265	3,612	3,753
Mining, total	6,187	5,585	6,117	8,677	12,550	13,970
Oil and gas.........................	1,706	1,725	2,143	3,001	4,453	4,229
Minerals and ores	4,481	3,860	3,973	5,676	8,098	9,741
Manufacturing, total.....................	644,440	562,834	577,789	645,104	711,420	821,855
Food and kindred products	24,966	25,175	26,795	25,952	28,849	32,201
Beverages and tobacco products	5,568	3,559	3,648	3,644	3,400	3,847
Textiles and fabrics....................	7,010	7,397	7,557	8,363	8,471	8,520
Textile mill products	2,236	1,875	1,881	2,072	2,343	2,561
Apparel and accessories	8,104	5,462	4,923	4,350	4,069	3,789
Leather and allied products	2,322	2,049	2,035	2,190	2,295	2,450
Wood products	4,854	3,777	3,818	4,249	4,445	4,913
Paper products	15,539	13,640	13,965	15,168	16,565	17,985
Printed, publishing, & similar products	4,869	4,509	4,706	4,983	5,495	5,798
Petroleum and coal products	8,862	7,897	9,349	12,579	17,788	25,959
Chemicals	77,649	78,049	88,384	105,238	114,214	129,504
Plastics and rubber products	16,970	15,383	15,661	17,316	18,787	20,575
Nonmetallic mineral products	7,830	6,025	6,069	6,596	6,911	7,766
Primary metal products	20,126	15,371	17,877	21,159	27,423	37,079
Fabricated metal products	21,737	18,893	18,848	20,821	23,296	27,238
Machinery, except electrical	85,038	70,178	69,285	86,264	96,760	109,364
Computers and electronic products	161,449	116,243	115,883	122,161	123,926	135,025
Electrical equipment, appliances and components	25,401	20,587	20,632	23,606	26,551	31,360
Transportation equipment	121,701	123,970	122,246	129,907	147,244	177,990
Furniture and fixtures	2,882	2,158	2,349	2,633	2,829	3,158
Miscellaneous manufactured commodities	19,327	20,640	21,591	24,795	29,831	34,449
Special classification provisions	32,505	31,112	33,109	37,814	42,936	52,482
Waste and scrap	4,948	5,081	6,456	8,548	10,357	15,843
Used or second-hand merchandise	1,950	1,562	1,808	2,108	2,742	4,359
Goods returned or reimported	333	241	205	152	62	55
Special classification provision, not elsewhere specified.............	25,274	24,228	24,640	27,006	29,776	32,225
Imports for consumption, total	1,205,339	1,154,811	1,250,097	1,460,161	1,662,380	1,845,053
Agricultural, forestry, and fishery products	24,378	24,327	26,197	27,814	30,751	34,641
Agricultural products, total	11,771	11,773	13,035	14,356	15,803	17,342
Livestock and livestock products.............	3,085	3,455	2,782	2,498	3,276	4,104
Forestry products, not elsewhere specified	1,409	1,288	1,612	2,019	2,250	2,771
Fish, fresh or chilled; and other marine products ...	8,113	7,811	8,768	8,942	9,422	10,424
Mining, total	79,841	76,288	105,662	138,427	188,942	222,412
Oil and gas.........................	76,166	72,830	101,800	133,606	182,473	214,738
Minerals and ores	3,675	3,458	3,862	4,821	6,469	7,674
Manufacturing, total.....................	1,040,329	995,103	1,060,349	1,231,005	1,373,160	1,512,175
Food and kindred products	18,944	21,110	23,769	27,740	29,759	31,802
Beverages and tobacco products	8,350	9,772	10,925	11,652	12,845	14,611
Textiles and fabrics....................	7,042	6,778	6,791	7,387	7,453	7,361
Textile mill products	7,347	8,643	9,857	11,707	13,508	14,680
Apparel and accessories	62,928	62,313	66,499	70,533	74,473	77,010
Leather and allied products	21,463	22,104	22,627	24,541	26,554	28,473
Wood products	15,388	15,720	16,581	22,869	23,652	22,730
Paper products	19,080	17,528	18,414	20,645	22,120	23,461
Printed, publishing, & similar products	4,197	4,432	4,699	5,148	5,601	5,806
Petroleum and coal products	40,156	31,976	39,161	54,544	81,402	92,968
Chemicals	76,606	87,311	102,078	115,246	132,031	146,751
Plastics and rubber products	17,362	18,554	20,504	24,085	28,087	30,564
Nonmetallic mineral products	14,740	13,547	14,428	16,531	18,455	20,285
Primary metal products	43,833	34,356	34,065	56,498	64,642	88,616
Fabricated metal products	27,974	28,607	30,068	35,976	41,065	45,963
Machinery, except electrical	79,366	68,645	77,344	94,402	109,589	121,285
Computers and electronic products	250,694	205,564	212,201	248,033	269,986	295,375
Electrical equipment, appliances and components	39,567	39,707	41,914	48,781	55,179	62,252
Transportation equipment	213,110	219,186	223,304	239,565	252,199	269,390
Furniture and fixtures	15,607	17,492	19,636	22,560	25,096	27,020
Miscellaneous manufactured commodities	56,577	61,759	65,484	72,563	79,465	85,775
Special classification provisions	60,791	59,093	57,889	62,915	69,526	75,826
Waste and scrap	1,875	1,613	1,810	3,054	3,206	4,788
Used or second-hand merchandise	6,345	5,668	4,752	5,710	6,013	7,155
Goods returned or reimported	33,851	34,981	33,605	34,223	37,057	38,586
Special classification provision, not elsewhere specified.............	18,750	16,831	17,723	19,928	23,250	25,298

Source: U.S. Census Bureau, *U.S. International Trade in Goods and Services*, series FT-900, December issues. For most recent, see <http://www.census.gov/foreign-trade/Press-Release/2006pr/12/#exhibits> (released 13 February 2007) and previous December or final reports.

U.S. Census Bureau, Statistical Abstract of the United States: 2008

Section 29
Puerto Rico and the Island Areas

This section presents summary economic and social statistics for Puerto Rico, the U.S. Virgin Islands, Guam, American Samoa, and the Northern Mariana Islands. Primary sources are the decennial censuses of population and housing, county business patterns, and the censuses of agriculture, business, manufactures, and construction (taken every 5 years) conducted by the U.S. Census Bureau; the annual *Vital Statistics of the United States*, issued by the National Center for Health Statistics; and the annual *Income and Product* of the Puerto Rico Planning Board.

Jurisdiction—The United States gained jurisdiction over these areas as follows: the islands of *Puerto Rico* and *Guam*, surrendered by Spain to the United States in December 1898, were ceded to the United States by the Treaty of Paris, ratified in 1899. Puerto Rico became a commonwealth on July 25, 1952, thereby achieving a high degree of local autonomy under its own constitution. The *U.S. Virgin Islands*, comprising 50 islands and cays, was purchased by the United States from Denmark in 1917. *American Samoa*, a group of seven islands, was acquired by the United States in accordance with a convention among the United States, Great Britain, and Germany, ratified in 1900 (Swains Island was annexed in 1925). By an agreement approved by the Security Council and the United States, the Northern Mariana Islands, previously under Japanese mandate, was administered by the United States between 1947 and 1986 under the United Nations trusteeship system. The Northern Mariana Islands became a commonwealth in 1986.

Censuses—Because characteristics of the Puerto Rico and the Island Areas differ, the presentation of census data for them

is not uniform. The 1960 Census of Population covered all of the places listed above except the Northern Mariana Islands (their census was conducted in April 1958 by the Office of the High Commissioner), while the 1960 Census of Housing also excluded American Samoa. The 1970, 1980, 1990, and 2000 Censuses of Population and Housing covered all five areas. The 1959, 1969, and 1978 Censuses of Agriculture covered Puerto Rico, American Samoa, Guam, and the U.S. Virgin Islands; the 1964, 1974, and 1982 censuses covered the same areas except American Samoa; and the 1969, 1978, 1987, 1992, and 1997 censuses included the Northern Mariana Islands. Beginning in 1967, Congress authorized the economic censuses, to be taken at 5-year intervals, for years ending in "2" and "7." Prior economic censuses were conducted in Puerto Rico for 1949, 1954, 1958, and 1963 and in Guam and the U.S. Virgin Islands for 1958 and 1963. In 1967, the census of construction industries was added for the first time in Puerto Rico; in 1972, the U.S. Virgin Islands and Guam were covered; and in 1982, the economic census was taken for the first time for the Northern Mariana Islands.

Information in other sections—In addition to the statistics presented in this section, other data are included as integral parts of many tables showing distribution by states in various sections of the *Abstract*. See "Puerto Rico and the Island Areas" in the Index. For definition and explanation of terms used, see Section 1, Population; Section 4, Education; Section 17, Agriculture; Section 20, Construction and Housing; Section 21, Manufactures; and Section 22, Wholesale and Retail Trade.

U.S. Census Bureau, Statistical Abstract of the United States: 2008

Fig. 29.1
Selected Island Areas of the United States

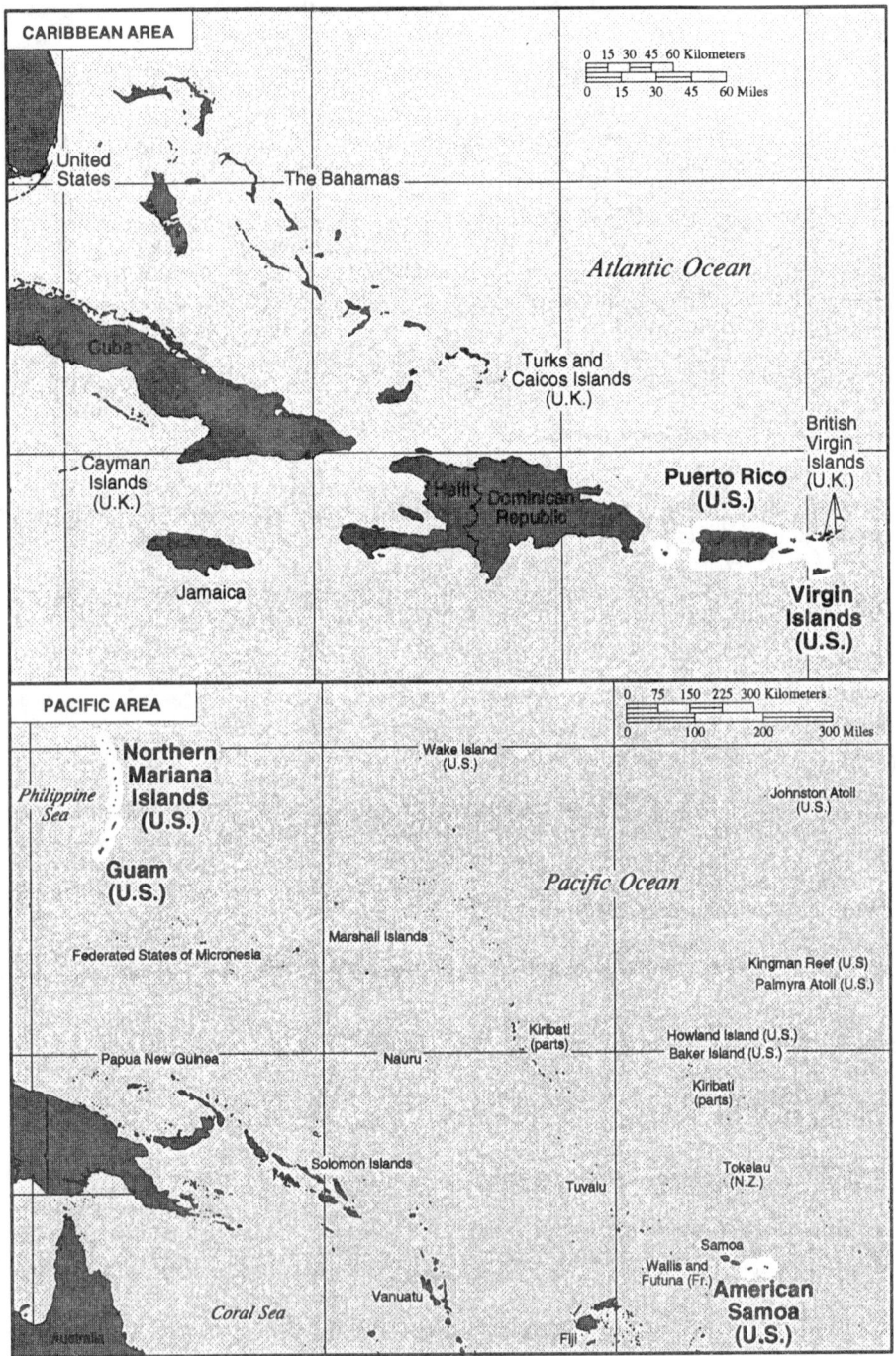

U.S. Census Bureau, Statistical Abstract of the United States: 2008

Table 1284. **Estimated Resident Population With Projections: 1980 to 2025**

[In thousands (3,210 represents 3,210,000). Population as of July 1. Population data generally are de-facto figures for the present territory. Data for 1990 to 2000 are adjusted to the 2000 Census of Population for Puerto Rico only. See text, Section 30, for general comments regarding the data. For details of methodology, coverage, and reliability, see source]

Area	1980	1990	2000	2005	2006	2007	Projected			
							2010	2015	2020	2025
Puerto Rico...............	3,210	3,537	3,816	3,911	3,928	3,944	3,988	4,046	4,083	4,096
American Samoa...........	32	47	57	58	58	58	57	56	54	52
Guam	107	134	155	169	171	173	181	192	203	213
Virgin Islands.............	98	104	109	109	109	108	108	107	107	108
Northern Mariana Islands	17	44	70	80	82	85	91	100	109	116

Source: U.S. Census Bureau, International Data Base. See Internet site: <http://www.census.gov/ipc/www/idb/.

Table 1285. **Vital Statistics—Specified Areas: 1980 to 2005**

[Births, deaths, and infant deaths by place of residence. Rates for 1980, 1990, and 2000 based on population enumerated as of April 1; for other years, on population estimated as of July 1]

Area and year	Births		Deaths		Infant deaths	
	Number	Rate [1]	Number	Rate [1]	Number	Rate [2]
Puerto Rico:						
1980.............	72,986	22.8	20,413	6.4	1,351	18.5
1990.............	66,417	18.8	25,957	7.3	888	13.4
2000.............	59,333	15.2	28,369	7.2	574	9.7
2004.............	51,127	13.1	28,922	7.4	409	8.0
2005 [3]	50,572	12.9	(NA)	(NA)	(NA)	(NA)
Guam:						
1980.............	2,945	27.8	393	3.7	43	14.6
1990.............	3,839	28.6	520	3.9	31	8.1
2000.............	3,766	24.4	648	4.2	22	5.8
2004.............	3,410	20.5	683	4.1	40	11.7
2005 [3]	3,187	29.3	(NA)	(NA)	(NA)	(NA)
Virgin Islands:						
1980.............	2,504	25.9	504	5.2	61	24.4
1990.............	2,267	21.8	480	4.6	33	14.6
2000.............	1,564	12.9	641	5.3	21	13.4
2004.............	1,574	14.5	626	5.8	13	(NA)
2005 [3]	1,599	14.7	(NA)	(NA)	(NA)	(NA)
American Samoa:						
1997.............	1,634	27.1	257	4.3	17	(B)
2002.............	1,627	28.2	294	5.1	25	(NA)
2005 [3]	1,720	29.7	(NA)	(NA)	(NA)	(NA)
Northern Marianas:						
1998.............	1,462	21.9	162	2.4	13	(B)
2002.............	1,290	17.4	163	2.2	9	(NA)
2005 [3]	1,332	16.6	(NA)	(NA)	(NA)	(NA)

B Base figure too small to meet statistical standards of reliability.   NA Not available.   [1] Per 1,000 population.   [2] Rates are infant deaths (under 1 year) per 1,000 live births.   [3] Data for 2005 are preliminary.

Source: U.S. National Center for Health Statistics, *Vital Statistics of the United States*, annual; and *National Vital Statistics Reports (NSVR)* and unpublished data; <http://www.cdc.gov/nchs/nvss.htm>.

Table 1286. **Public Elementary and Secondary Schools by Area: 2004**

[For school year ending in year shown, unless otherwise indicated. (2,425,372 represents $2,425,372,000)]

Item	Puerto Rico	Guam	Virgin Islands	American Samoa	Item	Puerto Rico	Guam	Virgin Islands	American Samoa
Enrollment, fall	575,648	30,605	16,429	16,126	Teachers..........	43,054	1,672	1,545	945
Elementary (kindergarten grade 8)........	408,607	21,686	11,650	11,873	Student support staff..........	3,927	62	85	206
Secondary (grades 9–12 and post graduates)	167,041	8,919	4,779	4,253	Other support services staff.....	18,833	235	480	103
Staff, fall	76,865	3,318	2,977	1,813	Current expendi-				
School district staff .	2,320	287	230	163	tures [1] ($1,000)	2,425,372	182,506	128,250	55,519
School staff	51,785	2,734	2,182	1,341	Per pupil [2] (dol.) ...	4,147	5,781	7,239	3,493

[1] Public elementary and secondary day schools.   [2] Per pupil expenditures include current expenditures, capital expenditures, and interest on school debt and excludes "other current expenditures" such as community services, private school programs, adult education, and other programs not allocable to expenditures per pupil in public schools.

Source: U.S. National Center for Education Statistics, *Digest of Education Statistics*, annual; and unpublished data. See Internet site <http://nces.ed.gov/annuals>.

Puerto Rico and the Island Areas **809**

[The Occupational Employment Survey (OES) program conducts a semiannual mail survey designed to produce estimates of employment and wages for specific occupations. For more details on the survey, see <http://www.bls.gov/oes/oesemp.htm#scope>]

Selected occupations	SOC code [1]	Guam	Puerto Rico	Virgin Islands
Total, all occupations [2, 3]	(X)	54,670	1,031,650	44,270
Management	11	4,150	40,040	1,920
Business and financial operations	13	1,980	38,060	1,520
Computer and mathematical	15	360	9,420	340
Architecture and engineering	17	860	13,740	(NA)
Life, physical, and social science	19	270	9,910	250
Community and social services	21	570	17,940	410
Legal	23	190	4,620	490
Education, training, and library	25	4,390	71,620	3,170
Arts, design, entertainment sports	27	580	7,110	280
Healthcare practitioner and technical	29	1,460	44,270	1,210
Healthcare support	31	560	11,020	350
Protective service	33	2,250	65,130	2,520
Food preparation and serving related	35	5,860	71,340	4,100
Buildings and grounds cleaning and maintenance	37	3,050	44,570	2,840
Personal care and service	39	1,730	16,640	1,100
Sales and related occupations	41	5,200	110,250	4,700
Office and administrative support	43	9,990	193,730	8,180
Farming, fishing, and forestry	45	(NA)	1,710	(NA)
Construction and extraction	47	3,670	66,250	3,320
Installation, maintenance, and repair	49	2,770	37,660	2,490
Production	51	1,450	87,890	2,120
Transportation and material moving	53	(NA)	68,750	2,530

NA Not available. X Not applicable. [1] Office of Management and Budget's Standard Occupational Classification (SOC) is used to define occupations. SOC categorizes workers into 1 of 801 detailed occupations and aggregates the detailed occupations into 23 major occupational groups. [2] Estimates for detailed occupations do not sum to the totals because the totals include occupations not shown separately. [3] Estimates do not include self-employed workers.

Source: U.S. Department of Labor, Bureau of Labor Statistics; *Occupational Employment and Wages*, May 2006; Bulletin 2585; See also <http://www.bls.gov/oes/home.htm>.

Table 1288. **Prisoners in Custody of Correctional Authorities in U.S. Territories and Commonwealths: 2004 and 2005**

[As of December 31. Minus sign (–) indicates decrease]

Jurisdiction	Total inmates			Sentenced to more than 1 year			
	2004	2005	Percent change 2004–2005	2004	2005	Percent change 2004–2005	Incarceration rate, 2005 [1]
Total	15,757	15,735	–0.1	12,185	12,399	1.8	287
American Samoa	258	222	–14.0	165	174	5.5	301
Guam	393	505	28.5	122	238	95.1	141
Northern Mariana Islands	150	149	–0.7	98	83	–15.3	103
Puerto Rico	14,380	14,263	–0.8	11,374	11,469	0.8	293
U.S. Virgin Islands	576	596	3.5	426	435	2.1	400

[1] The number of prisoners with a sentence of more than 1 year per 100,000 persons in the resident population.

Source: U.S. Department of Justice, Office of Justice Programs, Bureau of Justice Statistics, *Prisoners in 2005*, November 2006, NCJ 215092. See also <http://www.ojp.usdoj.gov/bjs/abstract/p05.htm>.

Table 1289. **Federal Direct Payments: 2004**

[In thousands of dollars (5,667,797 represents $5,667,797,000). For fiscal years ending September 30]

Selected program payments	Puerto Rico	Guam	Virgin Islands	American Samoa	Northern Mariana Islands
Direct payments to individuals for retirement and disability [1]	5,667,797	221,055	155,075	43,973	24,090
Social Security:					
Retirement insurance	2,341,320	69,584	89,762	11,191	5,750
Survivors' insurance	1,028,104	29,500	23,803	11,580	4,558
Disability insurance	1,506,016	15,796	18,678	9,905	1,310
Federal retirement and disability:					
Civilian [2]	223,124	56,249	14,908	1,756	5,812
Military	110,554	35,393	4,824	4,022	1,890
Veterans' benefits:					
Service-connected disability	250,964	11,384	1,698	4,376	606
Other	178,185	2,195	659	1,076	82

[1] Includes other payments, not shown separately. [2] Includes retirement and disability payments to former U.S. Postal Service employees.

Source: U.S. Census Bureau, *Consolidated Federal Funds Report for Fiscal Year, 2004* (issued December 2005). See also <http://www.census.gov/govs/www/cffr04.html>.

Table 1290. Puerto Rico—Summary: 1980 to 2006

[3,184.0 represents 3,184,000]

Item	Unit	1980	1990	1995	2000	2003	2004	2005	2006
POPULATION									
Total [1]	1,000	3,184.0	3,512.4	3,641.1	3,808.0	3,869.0	3,886.7	3,903.5	3,919.9
Persons per family	Number	4.3	3.7	3.5	3.4	3.3	3.3	3.3	3.2
EDUCATION [2]									
Enrollment, total	1,000	941.4	953.0	932.7	971.5	1,172.3	(NA)	(NA)	(NA)
Public (except public colleges or universities)	1,000	716.1	651.2	621.4	612.3	596.3	584.9	575.9	(NA)
College and university	1,000	130.1	156.0	165.4	175.5	199.8	207.1	208.0	(NA)
Expenses	Mil. dol.	825.0	1,686.4	2,555.8	4,254.1	4,962.3	5,534.8	6,017.3	(NA)
As percent of GNP	Percent	7.5	7.8	9.0	10.3	10.5	10.9	11.2	(NA)
Public	Mil. dol.	612.2	1,054.2	1,689.4	3,160.4	3,617.0	3,945.5	4,389.5	(NA)
Private	Mil. dol.	212.8	644.2	866.4	1,093.7	1,345.3	1,589.3	1,627.8	1,687.3
LABOR FORCE [3]									
Total [4]	1,000	907	1,124	1,219	1,303	1,352	1,360	1,385	1,420
Employed [5]	1,000	753	963	1,051	1,159	1,188	1,206	1,238	1,253
Agriculture [6]	1,000	38	36	34	24	24	25	26	22
Manufacturing	1,000	143	168	172	159	134	136	138	136
Trade	1,000	138	185	211	239	252	253	261	271
Government	1,000	184	222	232	249	269	268	274	278
Unemployed	1,000	154	161	168	143	164	155	147	167
Unemployment rate [7]	Rate	17.0	14.0	14.0	11.0	12.1	11.4	10.6	11.7
Compensation of employees	Mil. dol.	7,200	13,639	17,773	23,504	26,183	27,769	29,361	30,347
Average compensation	Dollar	9,563	14,854	16,911	20,280	22,039	23,026	23,716	24,220
Salary and wages	Mil. dol.	7,200	13,639	17,773	23,504	22,670	24,016	25,421	26,190
INCOME [8]									
Personal income:									
Current dollars	Mil. dol.	11,002	21,105	27,378	38,856	44,216	45,566	48,268	50,949
Constant (1954) dollars	Mil. dol.	3,985	5,551	6,547	8,491	9,155	9,289	9,536	9,609
Disposable personal income:									
Current dollars	Mil. dol.	10,403	19,914	25,591	36,239	41,120	42,476	45,749	48,008
Constant (1954) dollars	Mil. dol.	3,768	5,238	6,119	7,919	8,514	8,659	9,038	9,055
Average family income:									
Current dollars	Dollar	14,858	22,232	26,316	34,693	37,716	38,688	40,806	41,592
Constant (1954) dollars	Dollar	5,381	5,847	6,293	7,581	7,809	7,887	8,062	7,845
BANKING [9]									
Assets	Mil. dol.	10,223	27,902	39,859	58,813	74,315	94,427	109,292	112,658
TOURISM [8]									
Number of visitors	1,000	2,140	3,426	4,087	4,566	4,402	4,889	5,073	5,022
Visitor expenditures	Mil. dol.	619	1,366	1,828	2,388	2,677	3,024	3,239	3,369
Average per visitor	Dollar	289	399	447	523	608	619	638	671
Net income from tourism	Mil. dol.	202	383	499	615	678	735	771	806

NA Not available. [1] 1980, 1990, and 2000 enumerated as of April 1; all other years estimated as of July 1. [2] Enrollment for the first school month. Expenses for school year ending in year shown. Public includes: Public Preschool, Public Elementary, Public Intermediate, Public High School, Public Post-High School, Public Technological, Public Adult Education, Public Vocational Education, and Public Special Education. College and university includes both public and private colleges and universities. [3] Annual average of monthly figures. For fiscal years. [4] For population 16 years old and over. [5] Includes other employment not shown separately. [6] Includes forestry and fisheries. [7] Percent unemployed of the labor force. [8] For fiscal years. [9] As of June 30. Does not include federal savings banks and international banking entities.

Source: Puerto Rico Planning Board, San Juan, PR, *Economic Report of the Governor*, annual; <http://www.gobierno.pr/gprportal/inicio>.

Table 1291. Puerto Rico—Economic Summary by Industry: 2004

[In thousands of dollars, (15,376,735 represents $15,376,735,000). Covers establishments with payroll. Employees are for the pay period including March 12. See headnote, Table 735. Based on the County Business Patterns (CBP). This annual series is used as a benchmark for statistical series, surveys, and databases between economic censuses. For a description of CBP; see Appendix III. Starting with the 2003 CBP series, the data are tabulated using the 2002 North American Industial Classification System (NAICS)]

Industry	2002 NAICS code [1]	Total number of establishments	Number of employees	Annual payroll (1,000)
Establishments, total [2]	(X)	46,595	722,529	15,376,735
Construction	23	2,778	62,443	1,048,082
Manufacturing	31–33	2,111	114,998	3,309,031
Wholesale trade	42	2,260	34,503	1,051,787
Retail trade	44–45	10,928	126,692	1,898,784
Transportation and warehousing	48–49	1,046	14,219	383,189
Information	51	517	20,676	772,263
Finance and insurance	52	1,977	37,924	1,403,673
Real estate and rental and leasing	53	1,745	13,334	266,632
Professional, scientific, and technical services	54	3,972	26,705	830,251
Management of companies and enterprises	55	96	5,084	171,461
Admin/support waste mgt/remediation services	56	1,716	59,517	911,490
Educational services	61	721	33,716	586,447
Health care and social assistance	62	6,419	69,697	1,308,535
Accommodation and food services	72	3,989	68,136	833,811

X Not Applicable. [1] See text, Section 12 for more information on NAICS. [2] Includes other industries not shown separately.

Source: U.S. Census Bureau, "County Business Patterns"; annual. See <http://www.census.gov/epcd/cbp/view/cbppr.html>.

Puerto Rico and the Island Areas **811**

Table 1292. **Puerto Rico—Gross Product and Net Income: 1990 to 2006**

[In millions of dollars (21,619 represents $21,619,000,000). For fiscal years ending June 30. Data for 2006 are preliminary. Minus sign (–) indicates decrease]

Item	1990	1995	2000	2003	2004	2005	2006
Gross product	**21,619**	**28,452**	**41,419**	**47,479**	**50,709**	**53,601**	**56,688**
Agriculture	434	318	529	333	414	360	333
Manufacturing	12,126	17,867	24,079	31,532	33,267	34,363	36,556
Contract construction and mining [1] . . .	720	1,006	1,875	1,772	1,905	1,874	1,821
Transportation & other public services [2] . . .	2,468	3,276	4,237	5,178	5,343	5,353	5,508
Trade.	4,728	5,989	8,340	9,150	9,802	10,260	10,717
Finance, insurance, real estate	3,896	5,730	9,977	12,508	13,029	14,016	14,733
Services.	3,015	4,724	6,603	7,261	7,646	8,023	8,164
Government	3,337	4,440	5,478	6,948	7,389	8,151	8,424
Commonwealth.	2,884	3,793	4,601	5,947	6,362	7,032	7,204
Municipalities	453	647	877	1,000	1,026	1,118	1,220
Rest of the world	–8,985	–14,195	–20,283	–27,348	–28,501	–29,049	–29,776
Statistical discrepancy.	*–121*	*–703*	*585*	*146*	*415*	*251*	*209*
Net income	**17,941**	**23,653**	**32,610**	**38,045**	**40,517**	**43,431**	**46,244**
Agriculture	486	442	669	604	697	670	654
Manufacturing	11,277	16,685	22,348	29,761	31,405	32,570	34,709
Mining	26	30	41	40	42	45	48
Contract construction	679	903	1,691	1,593	1,706	1,676	1,627
Transportation & other public services [2] . . .	1,778	2,360	2,968	3,542	3,649	3,654	3,761
Trade	3,420	4,108	5,752	6,289	6,804	7,219	7,655
Finance, insurance, and real estate	3,280	4,735	8,264	10,411	10,787	11,608	12,179
Services	2,643	4,146	5,682	6,208	6,539	6,888	6,964
Commonwealth government [3]	3,337	4,440	5,478	6,948	7,389	8,151	8,424
Rest of the world	–8,985	–14,195	–20,283	–27,348	–28,501	–29,049	–29,776

[1] Mining includes only quarries.   [2] Includes other public utilities, and radio and television broadcasting.   [3] Includes public enterprises not elsewhere classified.

Source: Puerto Rico Planning Board, San Juan, PR, *Economic Report of the Governor*, annual; <http://www.gobierno.pr/gprportal /inicio>.

Table 1293. **Puerto Rico—Transfer Payments: 1990 to 2006**

[In millions of dollars (4,871 represents $4,871,000,000). Data represent transfer payments between federal and state governments and other nonresidents. Data for 2006 are preliminary. Minus sign (–) indicates decrease]

Item	1990	1995	2000	2003	2004	2005	2006
Total receipts	**4,871**	**6,236**	**8,659**	**10,451**	**10,087**	**10,551**	**10,918**
Federal government.	4,649	5,912	7,966	9,742	9,273	9,673	10,064
Transfers to individuals [1].	4,577	5,838	7,868	9,619	9,161	9,547	9,921
Veterans benefits	349	440	491	517	521	491	463
Medicare.	368	661	1,196	1,929	1,844	1,825	1,805
Old age, disability, survivors (social security)	2,055	2,912	3,863	4,739	4,810	5,118	5,501
Nutritional assistance	880	1,063	1,193	1,237	1,241	1,306	1,374
Industry subsidies	72	74	98	123	112	127	143
U.S. state governments	18	18	15	19	16	15	13
Other nonresidents	205	307	679	690	797	863	841
Total payments	**1,801**	**2,301**	**2,763**	**3,229**	**3,471**	**3,583**	**3,677**
Federal government.	1,756	2,132	2,693	3,085	3,350	3,516	3,614
Transfers from individuals	817	1,052	1,326	1,548	1,700	1,792	1,832
Contribution to Medicare	97	162	191	227	258	303	280
Employee contribution for social security. . .	720	888	1,133	1,317	1,438	1,483	1,547
Transfers from industries.	16	49	51	58	49	74	62
Unemployment insurance	247	184	234	240	219	221	224
Employer contribution for social security. . . .	675	847	1,081	1,240	1,382	1,429	1,496
Other nonresidents [2]	45	164	70	144	121	67	63
Net balance.	**3,070**	**3,935**	**5,897**	**7,222**	**6,616**	**6,968**	**7,242**
Federal government.	2,893	3,780	5,273	6,657	5,923	6,157	6,450
U.S. state governments	16	13	10	–56	–21	10	10
Other nonresidents	162	143	614	621	714	801	781

[1] Includes other receipts and payments not shown separately.   [2] Includes U.S. state governments.

Source: Puerto Rico Planning Board, San Juan, PR, *Economic Report of the Governor*, annual; <http://www.gobierno.pr/gprportal /inicio>.

Table 1294. **Puerto Rico—Merchandise Imports and Exports: 1980 to 2006**

[In millions of dollars (9,018 represents $9,018,000,000). Imports are imports for consumption; see text, Section 28]

Item	1980	1985	1990	1995	1999	2000	2001	2002	2003	2004	2005	2006
Imports.	9,018	10,162	16,200	18,969	26,697	27,199	27,690	30,511	35,945	37,252	40,418	42,462
From U.S.	5,345	6,130	10,792	12,213	15,949	15,171	14,718	15,675	16,949	18,124	20,994	21,982
From other. . .	3,673	4,032	5,408	6,756	10,754	11,834	12,972	14,824	18,996	19,128	19,424	20,480
Exports	6,576	11,087	20,402	23,573	37,779	43,191	46,689	50,641	55,814	54,982	56,843	59,218
To U.S.	5,643	9,873	17,915	20,986	33,173	38,335	40,981	44,907	46,880	45,311	47,121	47,452
To other	933	1,214	2,487	2,587	4,785	4,856	5,708	5,734	8,934	9,671	9,722	11,766

Source: U.S. Census Bureau, *Foreign Commerce and Navigation of the United States*, annual; *U.S. Trade with Puerto Rico and U.S. Possessions, FT 895*; and, through 1985, *Highlights of U.S. Export and Import Trade, FT990*; thereafter, *FT920*; <http://www.census.gov/foreign-trade/statistics/index.html>.

Section 30
Comparative International Statistics

This section presents statistics for the world as a whole and for many countries on a comparative basis with the United States. Data are shown for population, births and deaths, social and industrial indicators, finances, agriculture, communication, and military affairs.

Statistics of the individual nations may be found primarily in official national publications, generally in the form of yearbooks, issued by most of the nations at various intervals in their own national languages and expressed in their own or customary units of measure. (For a listing of selected publications, see Guide to Sources.) For handier reference, especially for international comparisons, the United Nations Statistics Division compiles data as submitted by member countries and issues a number of international summary publications, generally in English and French. Among these are the *Statistical Yearbook*; the *Demographic Yearbook*; *International Trade Statistics Yearbook*; *National Accounts Statistics: Main Aggregates and Detailed Tables*; *Population and Vital Statistics Reports* (quarterly); the *Monthly Bulletin of Statistics*; and the *Energy Statistics Yearbook*. Specialized agencies of the United Nations also issue international summary publications on agricultural, labor, health, and education statistics. Among these are the *Production Yearbook* and *Trade Yearbook* issued by the Food and Agriculture Organization, the *Yearbook of Labour Statistics* issued by the International Labour Office, *World Health Statistics* issued by the World Health Organization, and the *Statistical Yearbook* issued by the Educational, Scientific, and Cultural Organization.

The U.S. Census Bureau presents estimates and projections of basic demographic measures for countries and regions of the world in the *World Population Reports* (WP) series. The *International Population Reports* (Series IPC), and *International Briefs* (Series IB) also present population figures for many foreign countries. Detailed population statistics are also available from the Census Bureau's International Data Base (http://www.census.gov/ipc/www/idb/>.

The International Monetary Fund (IMF) and the Organization for Economic Cooperation and Development (OECD) also compile data on international statistics. The IMF publishes a series of reports relating to financial data. These include *International Financial Statistics, Direction of Trade*, and *Balance of Payments Yearbook*, published in English, French, and Spanish. The OECD publishes a vast number of statistical publications in various fields such as economics, health, and education. Among these are *OECD in Figures, Main Economic Indicators, Economic Outlook, National Accounts, Labour Force Statistics, OECD Health Data*, and *Education at a Glance*.

Statistical coverage, country names, and classifications—Problems of space and availability of data limit the number of countries and the extent of statistical coverage shown. The list of countries included and the spelling of country names are based almost entirely on the list of independent nations, dependencies, and areas of special sovereignty provided by the U.S. Department of State.

In recent years, several important changes took place in the status of the world's nations. In 1991, the Soviet Union broke up into 15 independent countries: Armenia, Azerbaijan, Belarus, Estonia, Georgia, Kazakhstan, Kyrgyzstan, Latvia, Lithuania, Moldova, Russia, Tajikistan, Turkmenistan, Ukraine, and Uzbekistan.

In the South Pacific, the Marshall Islands, Micronesia, and Palau gained full independence from the U.S. in 1991.

Following the breakup of the Socialist Federal Republic of Yugoslavia in 1992, the United States recognized Bosnia and Herzegovina, Croatia, Slovenia, and Macedonia as independent countries.

The Treaty of Maastricht created the European Union (EU) in 1992 with 12 member countries. The EU is not a state intended to replace existing states, but it is more than just an international organization. Its member states have set up common institutions to which they delegate some of their sovereignty so that decisions on specific matters of joint interest can be made democratically at a European level. This pooling of sovereignty is also called "European integration." The EU has grown in size with successive waves of accessions in 1995, 2004, and 2007. The 27 current members of the EU are: Austria, Belgium, Bulgaria, Cyprus, Czech Republic, Denmark, Estonia, Finland, France, Germany, Greece, Hungary, Ireland, Italy, Latvia, Lithuania, Luxembourg, Malta, the Netherlands, Poland, Portugal, Romania, Slovakia, Slovenia, Spain, Sweden, and the United Kingdom.

In 1992, the EU decided to go for economic and monetary union (EMU), involving the introduction of a single European currency managed by a European Central Bank. The single currency—the euro— became a reality on 1 January 2002, when euro notes and coins replaced national currencies in 12 of the then 15 countries of the European Union (Belgium, Germany, Greece, Spain, France, Ireland, Italy, Luxembourg, the Netherlands, Austria, Portugal, and Finland). Since then, 12 countries have become members of the EU, but Slovenia has been the only new member to adopt the euro as its national currency.

On January 1, 1993, Czechoslovakia was succeeded by two independent countries: the Czech Republic and Slovakia. Eritrea announced its independence from Ethiopia in April 1993 and was subsequently recognized as an independent nation by the United States. In May of 2002, East Timor won independence from Indonesia.

Serbia and Montenegro, both former republics of Yugoslavia, became independent of one another on May 31, 2006. This separation is seen in the population estimates tables (Tables 1298, 1300, and 1305), but some tables still show both countries as combined.

The population estimates and projections used in Tables 1295–1298, 1300, and 1305 were prepared by the Census Bureau. For each country, the data on population, by age and sex, fertility, mortality, and international migration were evaluated and, where necessary, adjusted for inconsistencies and errors in the data. In most instances, comprehensive projections were made by the component method, resulting in distributions of the population by age and sex and requiring an assessment of probable future trends of fertility, mortality, and international migration.

Economic associations—The Organization for European Economic Co-Operation (OEEC), a regional grouping of Western European countries established in 1948 for the purpose of harmonizing national economic policies and conditions, was succeeded on September 30, 1961, by the Organization for Economic Cooperation and Development (OECD). The member nations of the OECD are Australia, Austria, Belgium, Canada, Czech Republic, Denmark, Finland, France, Germany, Greece, Hungary, Iceland, Ireland, Italy, Japan, Luxembourg, Mexico, the Netherlands, New Zealand, Norway, Poland, Portugal, Slovakia, South Korea, Spain, Sweden, Switzerland, Turkey, the United Kingdom, and the United States.

Quality and comparability of the data—The quality and comparability of the data presented here are affected by a number of factors:

(1) The year for which data are presented may not be the same for all subjects for a particular country or for a given subject for different countries, though the data shown are the most recent available. All such variations have been noted. The data shown are for calendar years except as otherwise specified.

(2) The bases, methods of estimating, methods of data collection, extent of coverage, precision of definition, scope of territory, and margins of error may vary for different items within a particular country, and for like items for different countries. Footnotes and headnotes to the tables give a few of the major time-periods and coverage qualifications attached to the figures; considerably

814   Comparative International Statistics

more detail is presented in the source publications. Many of the measures shown are, at best, merely rough indicators of magnitude.

(3) Figures shown in this section for the United States may not always agree with figures shown in the preceding sections. Disagreements may be attributable to the use of differing original sources, a difference in the definition of geographic limits (the 50 states, conterminous United States only, or the United States including certain outlying areas and possessions), or to possible adjustments made in the United States' figures by other sources in order to make them more comparable with figures from other countries.

International comparisons of national accounts data—In order to compare national accounts data for different countries, it is necessary to convert each country's data into a common unit of currency, usually the U.S. dollar. The market exchange rates, which are often used in converting national currencies, do not necessarily reflect the relative purchasing power in the various countries. It is necessary that the goods and services produced in different countries be valued consistently if the differences observed are meant to reflect real differences in the volumes of goods and services produced. The use of purchasing power parities (see Table 1316) instead of exchange rates is intended to achieve this objective.

The method used to present the data shown in Table 1316 is to construct volume measures directly by revaluing the goods and services sold in different countries at a common set of international prices. By dividing the ratio of the gross domestic products of two countries expressed in their own national currencies by the corresponding ratio calculated at constant international prices, it is possible to derive the implied purchasing power parity (PPP) between the two currencies concerned. PPPs show how many units of currency are needed in one country to buy the same amount of goods and services that one unit of currency will buy in the other country. For further information, see *National Accounts, Main Aggregates, Volume I,* issued annually by the Organisation for Economic Cooperation and Development, Paris, France.

International Standard Industrial Classification—The original version of the International Standard Industrial Classification of All Economic Activities (ISIC) was adopted in 1948. Wide use has been made both nationally and internationally in classifying data according to kind of economic activity in the fields of production, employment, national income, and other economic statistics. A number of countries have utilized the ISIC as the basis for devising their industrial classification scheme.

Substantial comparability has been attained between the industrial classifications of many other countries, including the United States and the ISIC by ensuring, as far as practicable, that the categories at detailed levels of classification in national schemes fitted into only one category of the ISIC. The United Nations, the International Labour Organization, the Food and Agriculture Organization, and other international bodies have utilized the ISIC in publishing and analyzing statistical data. Revisions of the ISIC were issued in 1958, 1968, and 1989.

International maps—A series of regional world maps is provided on pages 816–822. References are included in Table 1298 for easy location of individual countries on the maps. The Robinson map projection is used for this series of maps. A map projection is used to portray all or part of the round Earth on a flat surface, but this cannot be done without some distortion. For the Robinson projection, distortion is very low along the Equator and within 45 degrees of the center but is greatest near the poles. For additional information on map projections and maps, please contact the Earth Science Information Center, U.S. Geological Survey, 507 National Center, Reston, VA 22092.

U.S. Census Bureau, Statistical Abstract of the United States: 2008

World

S5 (Asia and Russia)

S6 (Australia, Southeast Asia, and Pacific Islands)

S3 (Europe)

S4 (Africa)

S1 (North and Central America)

S2 (South America)

S6 (Australia, Southeast Asia, and Pacific Islands)

816 Comparative International Statistics

S1 (North and Central America)

INSET

Atlantic Ocean

Turks and Caicos Islands (U.K.)

British Virgin Islands (U.K.)

Virgin Islands (U.S.)

Anguilla (U.K.)

Antigua & Barbuda

Dominica

St. Lucia

Barbados

Trinidad & Tobago

Grenada

St. Vincent & The Grenadines

Martinique (France)

Guadeloupe (France)

Montserrat (U.K.)

St. Kitts and Nevis

Puerto Rico (U.S.)

Dominican Republic

Netherlands Antilles (Neth.)

Aruba (Neth.)

Haiti

Cuba

Jamaica

Cayman Islands (U.K.)

The Bahamas

Gulf of Mexico

Caribbean Sea

Atlantic Ocean

Bermuda (U.K.)

SEE INSET

St. Pierre and Miquelon (France)

Greenland (Denmark)

Canada

United States

Gulf of Mexico

Mexico

Belize

Honduras

Nicaragua

Panama

Guatemala

El Salvador

Costa Rica

Arctic Ocean

United States

Pacific Ocean

United States

Comparative International Statistics 817

U.S. Census Bureau, Statistical Abstract of the United States: 2008

S2 (South America)

Caribbean Sea

Venezuela

Guyana
Suriname
French Guiana
(France)

Colombia

Galapagos Islands
(Ecuador)

Ecuador

Peru

Brazil

Bolivia

Paraguay

Pacific Ocean

Atlantic Ocean

Uruguay

Chile

Argentina

Falkland Islands
(United Kingdom)

U.S. Census Bureau, Statistical Abstract of the United States: 2008

Svalbard
(Norway)

Jan Mayen
(Norway)

Arctic Ocean

Iceland

Faroe Islands
(Denmark)

Finland

Norway

Sweden

Denmark

Estonia

Latvia

Russia Lithuania

Ireland

Netherlands

Belarus

Isle of Man
(U.K.)

United
Kingdom

Germany

Poland

Guernsey
(U.K.)

Luxembourg

Jersey
(U.K.)

Belgium

Czech
Republic

Slovakia

Moldova

Ukraine

France

Switzerland

Austria

Slovenia

Hungary

Romania

Atlantic
Ocean

Liechtenstein

Croatia

Bosnia &
Herzegovina

Black Sea

San Marino

Serbia

Montenegro

Andorra

Monaco

Italy

Albania

Bulgaria

Spain

Corsica
(France)

Holy
See

Sardinia
(Italy)

Greece

Portugal

Balearic Islands
(Spain)

Sicily
(Italy)

Macedonia

Malta

Mediterranean Sea

U.S. Census Bureau, Statistical Abstract of the United States: 2008

Atlantic Ocean

Azores
(Portugal)

Madeira Islands
(Portugal)

Canary Islands
(Spain)

Western
Sahara

Cape
Verde

The Gambia

Guinea-Bissau

Sierra Leone

Liberia

Ascension
(United Kingdom)

St. Helena
(United Kingdom)

Atlantic Ocean

Tristan da Cunha Islands
(United Kingdom)

Morocco

Mauritania

Senegal

Guinea

Cote
d'Ivoire

Mali

Burkina
Faso

Ghana

Togo

Sao Tome &
Principe

Equatorial
Guinea

Angola

Algeria

Tunisia

Benin

Nigeria

Cameroon

Gabon

Niger

Chad

Central African
Republic

Congo
(Brazzaville)

Rwanda

Congo
(Kinshasa)

Angola

Zambia

Namibia

Botswana

Zimbabwe

Swaziland

Lesotho

South Africa

Libya

Egypt

Mediterranean Sea

Red Sea

Sudan

Eritrea

Djibouti

Ethiopia

Somalia

Uganda

Kenya

Burundi

Tanzania

Malawi

Mozambique

Comoros

Bassas
de India
(France)

Europa
Island
(France)

Madagascar

Indian Ocean

Seychelles

Mayotte
(France)

Mauritius

Reunion
(France)

Prince Edward Islands
(South Africa)

French Southern and
Antarctic Lands
(France)

Heard Island and
McDonald Islands
(Australia)

820 Comparative International Statistics

Pacific Ocean

Arctic Ocean

Japan

North Korea

South Korea

Taiwan

Macau

Hong Kong

China

Mongolia

Russia

Bhutan

Nepal

Bangladesh

India

Sri Lanka

Indian Ocean

Kyrgyzstan

Kazakhstan

Uzbekistan

Tajikistan

Turkmenistan

Afghanistan

Pakistan

Maldives

Oman

Socotra (Yemen)

Caspian Sea

Azerbaijan

Iran

United Arab Emirates

Georgia

Armenia

Iraq

Kuwait

Bahrain

Qatar

Saudi Arabia

Yemen

Black Sea

Turkey

Cyprus

Syria

Jordan

Red Sea

Lebanon

West Bank

Gaza Strip

Israel

S6 (Australia, Southeast Asia, and Pacific Islands)

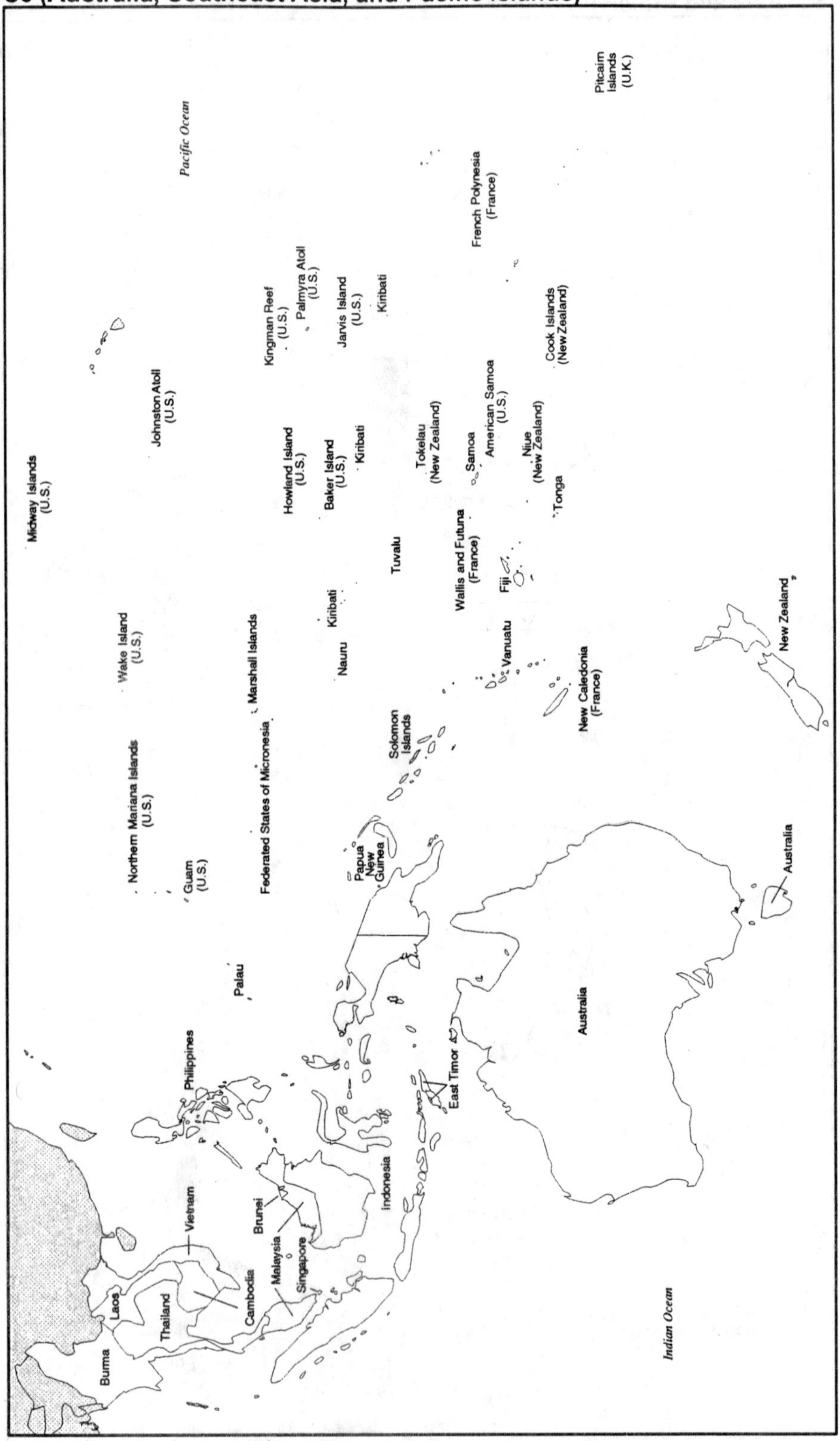

Figure 30.1
Net Additions to the World: 2007
In 2007, the world gained 2.5 people per second

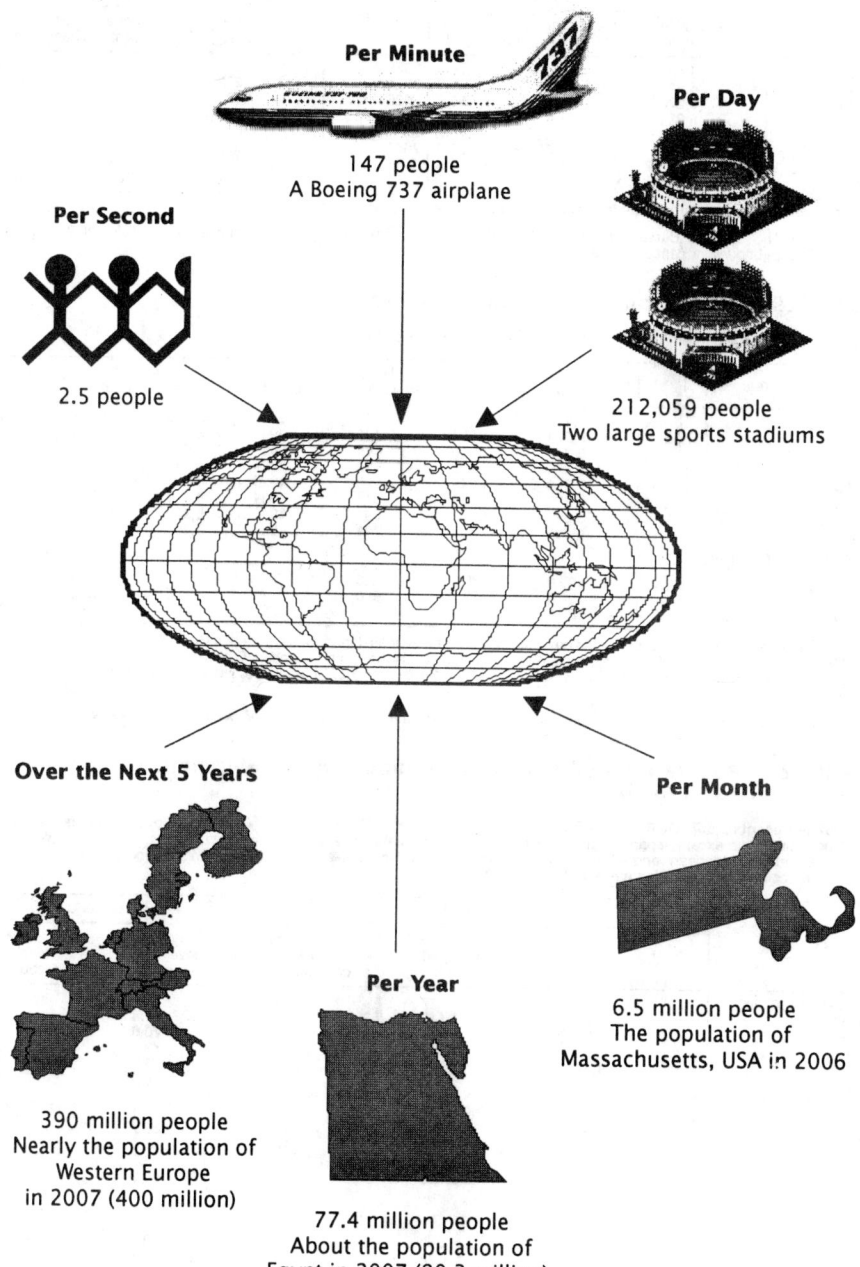

Per Minute

147 people
A Boeing 737 airplane

Per Day

Per Second

2.5 people

212,059 people
Two large sports stadiums

Over the Next 5 Years

Per Month

Per Year

6.5 million people
The population of
Massachusetts, USA in 2006

390 million people
Nearly the population of
Western Europe
in 2007 (400 million)

77.4 million people
About the population of
Egypt in 2007 (80.3 million)

Source: U.S. Census Bureau, International Programs Center, International Database and
unpublished tables.

Comparative International Statistics   823

Table 1295. **Total World Population: 1980 to 2050**

[As of midyear (**4,447** represents 4,447,000,000)]

Year	Population (mil.)	Average annual [1] Growth rate (percent)	Average annual [1] Population change (mil.)	Year	Population (mil.)	Average annual [1] Growth rate (percent)	Average annual [1] Population change (mil.)
1980......	4,447	1.7	75.4	2015......	7,226	1.1	76.9
1985......	4,844	1.7	83.0	2020......	7,603	1.0	72.9
1990......	5,273	1.6	83.8	2025......	7,959	0.9	68.1
1995......	5,682	1.4	79.9	2030......	8,290	0.8	63.8
2006......	6,526	1.2	76.7	2035......	8,601	0.7	59.8
2007......	6,602	1.2	77.3	2040......	8,892	0.6	55.4
2008......	6,680	1.2	77.5	2045......	9,159	0.6	50.5
2010......	6,835	1.1	78.3	2050......	9,402	(NA)	(NA)

NA Not available. [1] Represents change from year shown to immediate succeeding year.

Source: U.S. Census Bureau, International Data Base, "Total Midyear Population for the World: 1950–2050," updated 16 July 2007; <http://www.census.gov/ipc/www/idb/>.

Table 1296. **Population by Continent: 1980 to 2050**

[In millions, except percent (**4,447** represents 4,447,000,000). As of midyear]

Year	World	Africa [1]	North America [1]	South America [1]	Asia	Europe [1]	Oceania
1980	4,447	472	371	242	2,645	695	23
1990	5,273	624	423	296	3,180	723	27
2000	6,072	800	485	348	3,676	731	31
2010	6,835	997	539	393	4,143	729	35
2020	7,603	1,219	593	432	4,601	720	38
2030	8,290	1,461	644	463	4,978	702	41
2040	8,892	1,723	691	484	5,272	679	43
2050	9,402	2,001	733	494	5,480	649	45
PERCENT DISTRIBUTION							
1980	100.0	10.6	8.3	5.4	59.5	15.6	0.5
2000	100.0	13.2	8.0	5.7	60.5	12.0	0.5
2050	100.0	21.3	7.8	5.3	58.3	6.9	0.5

[1] Estimates and projections for France now include the four overseas departments of French Guiana, Guadeloupe, Martinique, and Reunion in the national total. These areas will now be included in the same regions as France (Europe) and not in the regions where they were included in prior releases (French Guiana in South America, Guadeloupe and Martinique in North America, and Reunion in Africa).

Source: U.S. Census Bureau, "International Data Base" (as of 16 July 2007); <http://www.census.gov/ipc/www/idb/>.

Table 1297. **Population and Population Change, by Development Status: 1950 to 2050**

[(**2,557** represents 2,557,000,000). As of midyear. Minus sign (–) indicates decrease. The "less developed" countries include all of Africa, all of Asia except Japan, the Transcaucasian and Central Asian republics of the New Independent States, all of Latin America and the Caribbean, and all of Oceania except Australia, New Zealand, and Hawaii. This category matches the "less developed country" classification employed by the United Nations]

Year	Number (mil.) World	Number (mil.) Less developed countries	Number (mil.) More developed countries [1]	Percent of world Less developed countries	Percent of world More developed countries
POPULATION					
1950	2,557	1,749	807	68.4	31.6
1960	3,041	2,129	911	70.0	30.0
1970	3,708	2,704	1,004	72.9	27.1
1980	4,447	3,365	1,082	75.7	24.3
1990	5,273	4,129	1,144	78.3	21.7
2000	6,072	4,877	1,195	80.3	19.7
2010	6,835	5,611	1,224	82.1	17.9
2020	7,603	6,362	1,242	83.7	16.3
2030	8,290	7,043	1,247	85.0	15.0
2040	8,892	7,648	1,244	86.0	14.0
2050	9,402	8,168	1,233	86.9	13.1
POPULATION CHANGE					
1950–1960	484	380	104	78.5	21.5
1960–1970	667	574	93	86.1	13.9
1970–1980	739	661	78	89.5	10.5
1980–1990	826	764	62	92.4	7.6
1990–2000	798	748	50	93.7	6.3
2000–2010	763	734	29	96.1	3.9
2010–2020	768	751	17	97.7	2.3
2020–2030	687	681	6	99.2	0.8
2030–2040	601	605	–3	100.5	–0.5
2040–2050	510	521	–11	102.1	–2.1

[1] Includes the four overseas departments of France. See footnote 1, Table 1296.

Source: U.S. Census Bureau, "International Data Base" (as of 16 July 2007); <http://www.census.gov/ipc/www/idb/>.

824   Comparative International Statistics

Table 1298. Population by Country or Area: 1990 to 2010

[5,273,415 represents 5,273,415,000. Population data generally are de facto figures for the present territory. Population estimates were derived from information available as of winter 2006–07. See text of this section for general comments concerning the data. For details of methodology, coverage, and reliability, see source. Minus sign (–) indicates decrease]

Country or area	Map refer-ence	Midyear population (1,000)				Popu-lation rank, 2006	Annual rate of growth, 2000-2010 (percent)	Popula-tion per sq. mile, 2006	Area (sq. mile)
		1990	2000	2006	2010, proj.				
World	S0	5,273,415	6,071,711	6,525,559	6,834,935	(X)	1.2	129	50,464,407
Afghanistan	S5	14,669	23,898	31,057	34,505	38	3.7	124	250,000
Albania	S3	3,251	3,474	3,582	3,660	130	0.5	339	10,579
Algeria	S4	25,093	30,409	32,930	34,555	37	1.3	36	919,591
Andorra	S3	53	67	71	74	200	1.0	409	174
Angola	S4	8,297	10,377	11,993	13,068	70	2.3	25	481,351
Antigua and Barbuda	S1	63	66	69	71	201	0.6	404	171
Argentina	S2	33,022	37,498	39,922	41,405	30	1.0	38	1,056,637
Armenia	S5	3,377	3,043	2,976	2,967	136	-0.3	271	10,965
Australia	S6	17,022	19,165	20,264	20,925	54	0.9	7	2,941,285
Austria	S3	7,723	8,113	8,193	8,214	90	0.1	257	31,832
Azerbaijan	S5	7,200	7,809	8,066	8,304	92	0.6	243	33,243
Bahamas, The	S1	257	290	304	311	175	0.7	78	3,888
Bahrain	S4	500	634	699	737	161	1.5	2,721	257
Bangladesh	S5	109,897	130,407	147,365	159,765	7	2.0	2,850	51,703
Barbados	S1	263	273	280	284	178	0.4	1,686	166
Belarus	S3	10,201	10,034	9,766	9,613	81	-0.4	122	80,154
Belgium	S3	9,969	10,264	10,379	10,423	76	0.2	888	11,690
Belize	S1	191	248	288	314	177	2.4	33	8,803
Benin	S4	4,676	6,628	7,863	8,731	93	2.8	184	42,710
Bhutan	S5	1,598	2,005	2,280	2,476	141	2.1	126	18,147
Bolivia	S2	6,574	8,153	8,989	9,499	87	1.5	21	418,683
Bosnia and Herzegovina	S3	4,424	4,035	4,499	4,622	117	1.4	228	19,741
Botswana	S4	1,263	1,639	1,788	1,893	147	1.4	8	226,012
Brazil	S2	151,084	175,553	188,078	195,580	5	1.1	58	3,265,061
Brunei	S6	253	325	368	395	173	1.9	181	2,035
Bulgaria	S3	8,894	7,818	7,385	7,149	95	-0.9	173	42,683
Burkina Faso	S4	8,336	11,309	13,903	15,667	62	3.3	132	105,714
Burma	S5	39,243	44,301	46,986	48,511	25	0.9	185	253,954
Burundi	S4	5,505	6,621	8,090	9,281	91	3.4	817	9,903
Cambodia	S5	9,345	12,396	13,758	14,753	63	1.7	202	68,154
Cameroon	S4	11,884	15,343	17,658	19,294	57	2.3	97	181,251
Canada	S1	27,791	31,278	33,099	34,253	36	0.9	9	3,511,006
Cape Verde	S1	349	401	421	431	170	0.7	271	1,556
Central African Republic	S4	3,084	3,935	4,303	4,567	121	1.5	18	240,533
Chad	S4	5,841	7,943	9,649	10,543	83	2.8	20	486,178
Chile	S2	13,128	15,153	16,134	16,720	60	1.0	56	289,112
China [2]	S5	1,148,364	1,268,853	1,313,974	1,347,563	1	0.6	365	3,600,930
Colombia	S2	32,957	39,817	43,742	46,271	28	1.5	109	401,042
Comoros	S4	429	579	691	773	163	2.9	825	838
Congo (Brazzaville) [3]	S4	2,265	3,102	3,702	4,124	128	2.8	28	131,853
Congo (Kinshasa) [3]	S4	39,048	52,299	63,605	72,681	20	3.3	73	875,521
Costa Rica	S2	3,027	3,711	4,075	4,306	124	1.5	208	19,560
Cote d'Ivoire	S4	11,981	15,563	17,655	19,093	58	2.0	144	122,780
Croatia	S3	4,508	4,411	4,495	4,487	118	0.2	206	21,781
Cuba	S1	10,513	11,106	11,362	11,477	72	0.3	265	42,803
Cyprus	S5	681	758	784	801	159	0.5	220	3,568
Czech Republic	S3	10,310	10,270	10,235	10,202	77	-0.1	343	29,836
Denmark	S3	5,141	5,337	5,451	5,516	109	0.3	333	16,368
Djibouti	S4	366	431	487	526	166	2.0	57	8,486
Dominica	S1	70	71	72	73	199	0.3	249	290
Dominican Republic	S1	7,083	8,410	9,226	9,794	85	1.5	494	18,680
East Timor	S6	746	847	1,063	1,153	156	3.1	188	5,641
Ecuador	S2	10,318	12,505	13,548	14,245	64	1.3	127	106,888
Egypt	S4	56,683	70,512	78,950	84,440	15	1.8	205	384,344
El Salvador	S1	5,100	6,126	6,830	7,304	99	1.8	854	8,000
Equatorial Guinea	S4	368	473	540	585	165	2.1	50	10,830
Eritrea	S4	2,996	4,357	4,787	5,278	114	1.9	102	46,842
Estonia	S3	1,569	1,380	1,324	1,291	152	-0.7	79	16,684
Ethiopia	S4	48,197	64,690	74,778	81,754	16	2.3	173	432,310
Fiji	S6	738	832	906	958	157	1.4	128	7,054
Finland [4]	S3	4,986	5,169	5,231	5,255	111	0.2	45	117,557
France [4]	S3	58,203	61,172	63,329	64,806	21	0.6	256	247,125
Gabon	S4	937	1,235	1,425	1,543	151	2.2	14	99,486
Gambia, The	S4	949	1,368	1,642	1,831	148	2.9	425	3,861
Georgia	S5	5,426	4,777	4,661	4,601	115	-0.4	173	26,911
Germany [5]	S3	79,380	82,188	82,422	82,283	14	(Z)	611	134,835
Ghana	S4	15,414	19,736	22,479	24,279	49	2.1	252	89,166
Greece	S3	10,130	10,559	10,688	10,750	74	0.2	212	50,502
Grenada	S2	92	89	90	91	195	0.2	675	133
Guatemala	S1	8,966	11,085	12,455	13,550	67	2.0	297	41,865
Guinea	S4	6,279	8,639	9,690	10,758	82	2.2	102	94,927
Guinea-Bissau	S4	996	1,279	1,443	1,565	149	2.0	133	10,811
Guyana	S2	751	755	767	774	160	0.2	10	76,004
Haiti	S1	6,131	7,444	8,498	9,386	89	2.3	799	10,641
Honduras	S1	4,792	6,348	7,326	7,944	96	2.2	170	43,201
Hungary	S3	10,372	10,137	9,981	9,880	80	-0.3	280	35,653
Iceland	S1	255	281	299	309	176	0.9	8	38,707
India	S5	838,159	1,004,124	1,111,714	1,184,090	2	1.6	968	1,147,950
Indonesia	S6	181,770	213,829	231,820	242,968	4	1.3	329	705,189

See footnotes at end of table.

Comparative International Statistics 825

Table 1298. Population by Country or Area: 1990 to 2010—Con.

[See headnote, page 825]

Country or area	Map refer- ence	Mid-year population (1,000) 1990	2000	2006	2010 proj.	Popu- lation rank, 2006	Annual rate of growth, 2000- 2010 (percent)	Popula- tion per sq. mile, 2006	Area (sq. mile)
Iran	S5	56,669	63,273	65,025	67,038	18	0.6	103	631,660
Iraq	S5	18,135	22,676	26,783	29,672	44	2.7	161	166,858
Ireland	S3	3,508	3,792	4,062	4,250	125	1.1	153	26,598
Israel	S4	4,512	5,842	6,352	6,645	102	1.3	809	7,849
Italy	S3	56,743	57,719	58,134	58,091	23	0.1	512	113,521
Jamaica	S1	2,348	2,615	2,758	2,843	138	0.8	660	4,181
Japan	S5	123,537	126,729	127,515	126,804	10	(Z)	881	144,689
Jordan	S4	3,262	4,999	5,907	6,486	104	2.6	166	35,510
Kazakhstan	S5	16,398	15,032	15,233	15,460	61	0.3	15	1,030,811
Kenya	S4	23,354	30,508	35,891	40,047	34	2.7	163	219,788
Kiribati	S6	71	92	105	115	192	2.3	337	313
Korea, North	S5	20,019	21,648	23,113	23,802	47	0.9	497	46,490
Korea, South	S5	42,869	47,351	48,847	49,568	24	0.5	1,288	37,911
Kuwait	S5	2,142	1,974	2,418	2,788	140	3.5	352	6,880
Kyrgyzstan	S5	4,382	4,851	5,214	5,509	112	1.3	71	73,861
Laos	S5	4,210	5,498	6,368	6,994	101	2.4	71	89,112
Latvia	S3	2,664	2,376	2,275	2,218	142	-0.7	93	24,552
Lebanon	S4	3,150	3,581	3,878	4,061	127	1.3	982	3,950
Lesotho	S4	1,721	2,068	2,122	2,133	143	0.3	181	11,718
Liberia	S4	2,117	2,695	3,044	3,534	135	2.7	82	37,189
Libya	S4	4,140	5,115	5,901	6,447	105	2.3	9	679,359
Liechtenstein	S3	29	32	34	35	210	0.8	547	62
Lithuania	S5	3,695	3,654	3,586	3,545	129	-0.3	142	25,174
Luxembourg	S3	383	439	474	498	167	1.3	475	998
Macedonia	S3	1,861	2,015	2,051	2,072	144	0.3	214	9,597
Madagascar	S4	11,633	15,742	18,872	21,282	56	3.0	84	224,533
Malawi	S4	9,536	11,560	13,284	14,613	65	2.3	366	36,324
Malaysia	S6	17,504	21,793	24,386	26,144	46	1.8	192	126,853
Maldives	S5	216	301	359	400	174	2.8	3,099	116
Mali	S4	8,085	10,049	11,681	13,025	71	2.6	25	471,042
Malta	S4	359	390	400	407	171	0.4	3,280	122
Marshall Islands	S6	46	53	60	66	204	2.2	865	70
Mauritania	S4	1,984	2,668	3,177	3,561	133	2.9	8	397,838
Mauritius	S4	1,074	1,179	1,241	1,280	153	0.8	1,583	784
Mexico	S1	84,914	99,927	107,450	112,469	11	1.2	145	742,486
Micronesia, Federated States of	S6	109	108	108	107	191	-0.1	398	271
Moldova	S5	4,394	4,391	4,334	4,317	120	-0.2	333	13,012
Monaco	S3	30	32	33	33	211	0.4	42,143	1
Mongolia	S5	2,218	2,664	2,908	3,087	137	1.5	5	603,906
Montenegro	S3	583	732	692	667	162	-0.9	130	5,333
Morocco	S4	24,686	30,122	33,241	35,301	35	1.6	193	172,317
Mozambique	S4	12,667	18,125	20,530	22,061	53	2.0	68	302,737
Namibia	S4	1,471	1,906	2,044	2,077	145	0.9	6	318,694
Nauru	S6	9	12	13	14	220	1.9	1,639	8
Nepal	S5	19,325	24,702	28,287	30,758	41	2.2	512	55,282
Netherlands	S3	14,952	15,908	16,491	16,783	59	0.5	1,261	13,082
New Zealand	S6	3,360	3,820	4,076	4,228	123	1.0	39	103,483
Nicaragua	S2	3,684	4,932	5,570	5,990	107	1.9	120	46,430
Niger	S4	7,945	10,516	12,525	14,054	66	2.9	26	489,073
Nigeria	S4	88,510	114,307	131,860	145,032	9	2.4	375	351,649
Norway	S3	4,242	4,492	4,611	4,676	116	0.4	39	118,865
Oman	S5	1,773	2,533	3,102	3,523	134	3.3	38	82,031
Pakistan	S5	114,452	143,959	161,744	173,814	6	1.9	538	300,664
Palau	S6	15	19	21	22	217	1.4	116	177
Panama	S2	2,390	2,889	3,191	3,393	132	1.6	109	29,340
Papua New Guinea	S6	3,825	4,927	5,671	6,171	106	2.3	32	174,849
Paraguay	S2	4,244	5,592	6,509	7,162	100	2.5	42	153,398
Peru	S2	21,511	25,980	28,303	29,758	40	1.4	57	494,208
Philippines	S6	64,318	79,740	89,469	95,868	12	1.8	777	115,124
Poland	S3	38,119	38,654	38,537	38,464	33	(-Z)	328	117,554
Portugal	S3	9,923	10,336	10,606	10,736	75	0.4	299	35,502
Qatar	S5	481	744	885	970	158	2.6	200	4,416
Romania	S5	22,866	22,452	22,304	22,181	50	-0.1	251	88,934
Russia	S5	147,973	146,710	142,069	139,390	8	-0.5	22	6,562,083
Rwanda	S4	6,982	8,278	9,638	10,769	84	2.6	1,001	9,633
Saint Kitts and Nevis	S1	41	39	39	40	209	0.4	388	101
Saint Lucia	S1	140	156	168	177	187	1.3	720	234
Saint Vincent and the Grenadines	S1	107	115	118	119	188	0.3	785	150
Samoa	S0	172	197	212	223	182	1.3	187	1,133
San Marino	S3	23	27	29	31	212	1.3	1,263	23
Sao Tome and Principe	S4	119	160	193	219	185	3.1	500	386
Saudi Arabia	S4	16,061	23,153	27,020	29,222	43	2.3	33	829,996
Senegal	S4	7,846	10,332	12,191	13,516	69	2.7	164	74,131
Serbia	S3	9,348	10,118	10,140	10,173	79	0.1	297	34,116
Seychelles	S4	73	79	82	83	197	0.4	463	176
Sierra Leone	S4	4,221	4,809	6,005	6,580	103	3.1	217	27,653
Singapore	S6	3,047	4,037	4,492	4,701	119	1.5	17,060	263
Slovakia	S3	5,263	5,400	5,439	5,470	110	0.1	289	18,842
Slovenia	S3	1,991	2,011	2,010	2,003	146	(-Z)	258	7,780
Solomon Islands	S6	335	466	552	610	164	2.7	52	10,633
Somalia	S4	6,675	7,253	8,863	9,922	88	3.1	37	242,216

See footnotes at end of table.

U.S. Census Bureau, Statistical Abstract of the United States: 2008

Table 1298. **Population by Country or Area: 1990 to 2010**—Con.

[See headnote, page 825]

Country or area	Map reference	Mid-year population (1,000) 1990	2000	2006	2010, proj.	Population rank, 2006	Annual rate of growth,[1] 2000-2010 (percent)	Population per sq. mile, 2006	Area (sq. mile)
South Africa	S4	38,391	44,066	44,188	43,333	27	−0.2	94	471,008
Spain	S3	39,351	40,016	40,398	40,549	29	0.1	209	192,873
Sri Lanka	S5	17,365	19,436	20,718	21,514	52	1.0	829	24,996
Sudan	S4	26,050	34,194	38,574	41,980	31	2.1	42	917,375
Suriname	S2	395	432	466	487	168	1.2	7	62,344
Swaziland	S4	885	1,110	1,136	1,119	154	0.1	171	6,641
Sweden	S3	8,601	8,924	9,017	9,074	86	0.2	57	158,662
Switzerland	S3	6,837	7,267	7,524	7,623	94	0.5	490	15,355
Syria	S4	12,436	16,306	18,881	20,606	55	2.3	266	71,062
Tajikistan	S5	5,272	6,230	6,944	7,487	97	1.8	126	55,097
Tanzania	S4	25,214	33,712	38,569	41,893	32	2.2	113	342,100
Thailand	S5	55,197	61,863	64,632	66,303	19	0.7	327	197,595
Togo	S4	3,505	4,712	5,549	6,185	108	2.7	264	20,998
Tonga	S0	92	102	115	123	189	1.8	414	277
Trinidad and Tobago	S2	1,198	1,118	1,066	1,029	155	−0.8	538	1,980
Tunisia	S4	8,207	9,564	10,175	10,583	78	1.0	170	59,985
Turkey	S5	56,085	65,667	70,414	73,322	17	1.1	237	297,591
Turkmenistan	S5	3,659	4,520	5,015	5,345	113	1.7	27	188,456
Tuvalu	S6	9	11	12	13	221	1.5	1,176	10
Uganda	S4	17,456	23,956	29,207	33,399	39	3.3	379	77,108
Ukraine	S5	51,622	49,005	46,620	45,416	26	−0.8	200	233,089
United Arab Emirates	S5	1,826	3,219	4,266	4,976	122	4.4	133	32,000
United Kingdom	S3	57,493	59,522	60,609	61,285	22	0.3	650	93,278
United States	S1	250,132	282,339	298,444	309,163	3	0.9	84	3,537,421
Uruguay	S2	3,110	3,328	3,443	3,510	131	0.5	51	67,035
Uzbekistan	S5	20,624	24,756	27,307	29,280	42	1.7	166	164,247
Vanuatu	S6	154	190	209	221	183	1.5	44	4,710
Venezuela	S2	19,325	23,493	25,641	27,223	45	1.5	75	340,560
Vietnam	S5	67,283	79,060	84,403	87,814	13	1.1	672	125,622
Yemen	S5	12,416	17,495	21,474	24,658	51	3.4	105	203,849
Zambia	S4	7,978	10,205	11,288	12,057	73	1.7	39	285,994
Zimbabwe	S4	10,153	11,751	12,237	12,516	68	0.6	82	149,293
OTHER									
Taiwan [2]	S5	20,278	22,183	22,782	23,025	48	0.4	1,829	12,456
AREAS OF SPECIAL SOVEREIGNTY AND DEPENDENCIES									
American Samoa	S0	47	57	58	57	205	(−Z)	752	77
Anguilla	S1	8	12	13	14	219	1.8	342	39
Aruba	S1	63	90	98	105	193	1.5	1,322	75
Bermuda	S1	58	63	66	67	202	0.7	3,214	20
Cayman Islands	S1	26	38	45	50	208	2.7	453	100
Cook Islands	S0	18	20	22	22	215	0.9	232	93
Faroe Islands	S3	47	45	47	48	207	0.6	87	541
French Polynesia	S0	202	249	275	291	179	1.6	195	1,413
Gaza Strip [6]	S4	643	1,132	1,429	1,651	150	3.8	10,279	139
Gibraltar	S3	29	28	28	28	213	0.2	12,056	2
Greenland	S1	56	56	56	56	206	(−Z)	(Z)	131,931
Guam	S6	134	155	171	181	186	1.5	819	209
Guernsey	S3	63	64	65	66	203	0.3	2,172	30
Hong Kong	S5	5,688	6,659	6,940	7,090	98	0.6	17,251	402
Isle of Man	S3	69	73	75	77	198	0.5	342	221
Jersey	S3	84	89	91	92	194	0.3	2,016	45
Macau	S6	352	431	453	468	169	0.8	41,914	11
Mayotte	S4	90	156	201	231	184	3.9	1,386	145
Montserrat	S1	11	6	9	10	222	4.3	244	39
Netherlands Antilles	S2	189	210	222	229	180	0.8	598	371
New Caledonia	S6	168	202	219	230	181	1.3	31	7,172
Northern Mariana Islands	S6	44	70	82	91	196	2.6	448	184
Puerto Rico	S1	3,537	3,816	3,928	3,988	126	0.4	1,147	3,425
Saint Helena	S4	7	7	8	8	223	0.6	47	159
Saint Pierre and Miquelon	S1	6	7	7	7	224	0.2	76	93
Turks and Caicos Islands	S1	12	18	21	24	216	3.0	127	166
Virgin Islands	S1	104	109	109	108	190	−0.1	813	134
Virgin Islands, British	S1	16	20	23	25	214	2.0	399	58
Wallis and Futuna	S6	14	15	16	17	218	0.9	153	106
West Bank [6]	S4	1,255	2,020	2,460	2,765	139	3.1	1,130	2,178
Western Sahara	S4	221	309	372	417	172	3.0	4	102,703

X Not applicable. Z Less than 0.05 percent or less than one person per square mile. [1] Computed by the exponential method. For explanation of average annual percent change, see Guide to Tabular Presentation. [2] With the establishment of diplomatic relations with China on January 1, 1979, the U.S. government recognized the People's Republic of China as the sole legal government of China and acknowledged the Chinese position that there is only one China and that Taiwan is part of China. [3] "Congo" is the official short-form name for both the Republic of Congo and the Democratic Republic of the Congo. To distinguish one from the other the U.S. Dept. of State adds the capital in parentheses. This practice is unofficial and provisional. [4] Data for France now include the overseas departments of French Guiana, Guadeloupe, Martinique, and Reunion. [5] Data for 1990 are for former West Germany and East Germany combined. [6] The Gaza Strip and West Bank are Israeli occupied with interim status subject to Israeli/Palestinian negotiations. The final status is yet to be determined.

Source: U.S. Census Bureau, "International Data Base" (as of 16 July 2007); <http://www.census.gov/ipc/www/idb/>.

Comparative International Statistics   827

Table 1299. Foreign or Foreign-Born Population, Labor Force, and Net Migration in Selected OECD Countries: 1995 and 2004

[24,648 represents 24,648,000. In Australia and the United States the data refer to people present in the country who are foreign born. In the European countries and Japan they generally refer to foreigners and represent the nationalities of residents]

Country	Foreign population [1]				Foreign labor force [2]				Average net migration 1991– 2004 [3] (per 1,000 population)
	Number (1,000)		Percent of total population		Number (1,000)		Percent of total labor force		
	1995	2004	1995	2004	1995	2004	1995	2004	
United States	24,648	37,592	9.3	12.8	12,900	(NA)	9.7	(NA)	4.5
Australia.	4,164	4,751	23.0	23.6	2,139	(NA)	23.9	(NA)	4.9
Austria	677	777	8.5	9.5	325	403	9.9	11.9	3.4
Belgium	910	871	9.0	8.4	364	428	8.3	9.1	1.5
Denmark.	223	268	4.2	4.9	84	107	3.0	3.9	2.2
France	(NA)	(NA)	(NA)	(NA)	1,573	1,541	6.2	5.6	1.2
Germany [4]	7,174	6,739	8.8	8.9	(NA)	3,701	(NA)	9.1	3.8
Italy	729	(NA)	1.7	(NA)	332	(NA)	1.7	(NA)	3.1
Japan	1,362	1,974	1.1	1.5	88	192	0.1	0.3	–
Luxembourg	138	177	33.4	39.0	112	188	52.4	62.0	8.3
Netherlands	725	699	4.7	4.3	282	299	4.0	3.8	2.8
Spain.	500	1,977	1.3	4.6	139	1,077	0.8	5.4	5.0
Sweden	532	463	5.2	5.1	220	216	5.1	4.8	2.5
Switzerland	1,331	1,495	18.9	20.2	729	817	20.9	20.6	3.9
United Kingdom	1,948	2,857	3.4	4.9	862	1,445	3.4	5.2	1.4

– Represents zero.   NA Not available.   [1] Data are from population registers of foreigners except for France, Greece, Mexico, and Poland (census), Ireland and the United Kingdom (Labour Force Survey), Portugal (residence permits), Australia (inter-and post-censal estimates), and the United States (Current Population Survey).   [2] Includes unemployed except for Belgium, Greece, Norway, Luxembourg, Netherlands, and the United Kingdom. Germany, Luxembourg, and Netherlands include cross-border workers. Belgium and Italy include the self-employed. Data for Austria, Germany, and Luxembourg are from social security registers, and for Denmark, from the register of population. Data for Italy, Spain, and Switzerland are from residence and work permits. Figures for Japan and Netherlands are estimates. Data for other countries are from labor force surveys.   [3] Or latest period available.   [4] Labor force data are for western Germany only.
Source: Organization for Economic Cooperation and Development, Paris, France, *International Migration Outlook* (2007 Edition) (copyright).

Table 1300. Age Distribution by Country or Area: 2006 and 2010

[In percent. Covers countries with 11 million or more population in 2006]

Country or area	2006		2010, proj.		Country or area	2006		2010, proj.	
	Under 15 years old	65 years old and over	Under 15 years old	65 years old and over		Under 15 years old	65 years old and over	Under 15 years old	65 years old and over
World	27.6	7.4	26.7	7.7	Madagascar	44.1	3.1	43.3	3.0
					Malawi.	46.3	2.7	45.6	2.7
Afghanistan	44.6	2.4	44.4	2.4	Malaysia	32.6	4.7	31.0	5.1
Algeria	28.1	4.8	24.8	5.0	Mali.	48.1	3.1	48.3	3.0
Angola.	43.8	2.8	43.4	2.7	Mexico.	30.6	5.8	28.7	6.4
Argentina	25.2	10.6	24.1	11.0	Morocco.	31.6	5.0	29.6	5.2
Australia.	19.6	13.1	18.7	13.9	Mozambique	44.8	2.8	44.1	2.9
Bangladesh	32.9	3.5	33.8	3.7	Nepal	38.7	3.7	37.3	3.9
Bolivia	35.0	4.6	32.1	4.9	Netherlands	18.0	14.2	17.2	15.2
Brazil.	25.8	6.1	24.0	6.8	Niger.	46.9	2.4	46.9	2.4
Burkina Faso	46.8	2.5	46.3	2.4	Nigeria.	42.3	3.1	42.1	3.2
Burma	26.5	5.2	24.9	5.5	Pakistan.	37.5	4.3	35.1	4.4
Cambodia.	35.0	3.5	32.2	3.7	Peru	30.9	5.3	28.5	5.8
Cameroon	41.5	3.2	40.7	3.3	Philippines	35.0	4.1	33.2	4.4
Canada	17.6	13.3	16.7	14.2	Poland.	15.9	13.3	14.8	13.5
Chile	24.7	8.2	22.7	9.2	Romania	15.7	14.7	15.5	14.7
China [1]	20.8	7.7	19.6	8.3	Russia	14.6	14.2	15.0	13.3
Colombia	30.3	5.3	28.5	5.8	Saudi Arabia	38.2	2.4	38.0	2.5
Congo (Kinshasa) [2] . .	47.7	2.5	47.1	2.6	Senegal	42.2	3.0	41.6	3.1
Cote d'Ivoire	40.8	2.8	40.1	3.0	South Africa	29.7	5.3	27.6	5.8
Cuba	19.2	10.4	18.1	11.6	Spain	14.4	17.7	14.5	18.4
Ecuador.	33.0	5.0	31.0	5.4	Sri Lanka	24.6	7.6	23.6	8.3
Egypt	32.6	4.5	31.0	4.9	Sudan	42.1	2.4	40.2	2.5
Ethiopia.	43.7	2.7	42.5	2.8	Syria	37.0	3.3	35.5	3.4
France [3]	18.6	16.2	18.6	16.5	Taiwan [1]	18.3	10.0	16.2	10.8
Germany	14.1	19.4	13.5	20.4	Tanzania	44.3	2.8	42.5	2.9
Ghana	38.7	3.5	36.9	3.6	Thailand.	22.0	8.0	20.4	8.9
Guatemala	41.5	3.6	38.7	3.8	Turkey	25.5	6.8	23.5	7.3
India	32.1	5.0	30.7	5.4	Uganda	50.3	2.2	50.0	2.1
Indonesia	29.1	5.6	27.7	6.1	Ukraine	14.3	16.4	13.7	15.5
Iran	24.3	5.3	21.3	5.4	United Kingdom.	17.5	15.8	16.5	16.4
Iraq	39.7	3.0	38.5	3.0	United States.	20.4	12.5	20.0	13.0
Italy.	13.8	19.7	13.4	20.3	Uzbekistan	32.9	4.8	31.7	4.3
Japan	13.9	20.4	13.3	22.6	Venezuela	32.1	5.0	30.0	5.3
Kazakhstan	23.0	8.2	21.6	7.6	Vietnam	27.0	5.8	24.3	5.7
Kenya	42.0	2.6	42.3	2.7	Yemen	46.4	2.7	46.1	2.5
Korea, North	23.8	8.2	22.2	9.5	Zambia	46.0	2.4	44.8	2.3
Korea, South	18.9	9.2	16.6	10.4	Zimbabwe	37.4	3.5	36.8	3.6

[1] See footnote 2, Table 1298.   [2] See footnote 3, Table 1298.   [3] See footnote 4, Table 1298.
Source: U.S. Census Bureau, "International Data Base" (as of 16 July 2007); <http://www.census.gov/ipc/www/idb/>.

Table 1301. Births to Unmarried Women by Country: 1980 to 2005

[Percent of all live births. For U.S. figures, marital status is inferred from a comparison of the child's and parents' surnames on the birth certificate for those states that do not report on marital status. No estimates are included for misstatements on birth records or failures to register births]

Country	1980	1990	2000	2005
United States	18.4	28.0	33.2	36.8
Canada	12.8	24.4	28.3	(NA)
Japan	0.8	1.1	1.6	(NA)
Denmark	33.2	46.4	44.6	45.7
France	11.4	30.1	43.6	48.4
Germany [1]	(NA)	15.1	23.4	29.2
Ireland	5.9	14.6	31.5	32.0
Italy	4.3	6.5	9.7	13.8
Netherlands	4.1	11.4	24.9	34.9
Spain	3.9	9.6	17.7	26.6
Sweden	39.7	47.0	55.3	55.4
United Kingdom	11.5	27.9	39.5	42.9

NA Not available.   [1] Data are for 1991 instead of 1990.
Source: U.S. Bureau of Labor Statistics, updated and revised from "Families and Work Transition in 12 Countries 1980–2001," *Monthly Labor Review*, September 2003, with unpublished data.

Table 1302. Marriage and Divorce Rates by Country: 1980 to 2005

[Per 1,000 population aged 15–64 years]

Country	Marriage rate				Divorce rate			
	1980	1990	2000	2005 [1]	1980	1990	2000	2005 [2]
United States [3]	15.9	14.9	12.5	11.2	7.9	7.2	6.2	5.4
Canada	11.5	10.0	7.5	6.8	3.7	4.2	3.4	(NA)
Japan	9.8	8.4	9.3	8.4	1.8	1.8	3.1	3.1
Denmark	8.0	9.1	10.8	10.1	4.1	4.0	4.0	4.3
France [4]	9.7	7.7	7.9	7.1	2.4	2.8	3.0	3.5
Germany [4,5]	(NA)	8.2	7.6	7.0	(NA)	2.5	3.5	4.0
Ireland [4]	10.9	8.3	7.6	7.2	(6)	(6)	1.0	1.2
Italy [4]	8.7	8.2	7.3	6.5	0.3	0.7	1.0	1.2
Netherlands	9.6	9.3	8.2	6.7	2.7	2.8	3.2	2.9
Spain [4]	9.4	8.5	7.9	7.0	(NA)	0.9	1.4	1.7
Sweden	7.1	7.4	7.0	7.5	3.7	3.5	3.8	3.4
United Kingdom [7]	11.6	10.0	8.0	8.0	4.1	4.1	4.0	3.9

NA Not available.   [1] Provisional marriage rates for the United States and Canada. U.S. marriage rate may be understated because of incomplete reporting in Oklahoma.   [2] Provisional divorce rates for the United States, Germany, Ireland, Spain, France, and Italy. U.S. divorce rate may be understated because of incomplete reporting in Oklahoma.   [3] Divorce rates for 2000–2005 are estimated by the Bureau of Labor Statistics; includes unlicensed marriages in California.   [4] Divorces for 2005 are estimated by Eurostat.   [5] Date are for 1991 instead of 1990.   [6] Divorce not allowed by law prior to 1997.   [7] Marriages for 2005 are estimated by Eurostat.
Source: U.S. Bureau of Labor Statistics, updated and revised from "Families and Work in Transition in 12 Countries, 1980–2001," *Monthly Labor Review*, September 2003, with unpublished data.

Table 1303. Single-Parent Households: 1980 to 2006

[In thousands (6,061 represents 6,061,000). For the United Kingdom in 1981, children are defined as those under 15 and those who are 15, 16, or 17 and attended school full-time; for later years, children are defined as those under 16 and those who are 16 or 17 and attend school full-time. For Ireland, children are defined as those under 15. For all other countries, children are defined as children living at home, or away at school, under the age of 18. Data are generally for the entire year, but in some instances they are only for a particular month within the year]

Country and year	Number	Percent of all households with children	Country and year	Number	Percent of all households with children
United States:			Germany:		
1980	6,061	19.5	1991	1,429	15.2
1990	7,752	24.0	1995	2,496	18.8
1995	9,055	26.4	2000 [2]	2,274	17.6
2005	10,339	28.3	2005	2,525	20.1
Canada:			Ireland: [1]		
1981	437	12.7	1981	30	7.2
1991	572	16.2	1991	44	10.7
1996	690	18.7	1996	56	13.8
2001	707	19.3	2006	78	22.6
Japan:			Netherlands:		
1980	796	4.9	1988	179	9.6
1990	934	6.5	1995 [2]	208	11.7
1995	884	6.9	2000	240	13.0
2005	1,102	9.8	2006	297	15.3
Denmark: [1]			Sweden:		
1980	99	13.4	1985	117	11.2
1990	117	17.8	1990	151	14.8
1995	120	18.6	1995 [2]	189	17.4
2006	138	20.5	2004 [3]	208	19.6
France:			United Kingdom: [4]		
1988	761	11.9	1981	1,010	13.9
1990	755	11.9	1991	1,344	19.4
1995	874	14.0	1994–95	1,617	21.9
2000	1,039	17.1	2006	1,694	24.1

[1] Data are from family-based, rather than household-based, statistics.   [2] Break in series.   [3] Bureau of Labor Statistics estimates.   [4] Great Britain only (excludes Northern Ireland).
Source: U.S. Bureau of Labor Statistics, updated and revised from "Families and Work in Transition in 12 Countries, 1980–2001," *Monthly Labor Review*, September 2003, with unpublished data.

U.S. Census Bureau, Statistical Abstract of the United States: 2008

Table 1304. **Percent Distribution of Households by Type and Country: 1980 to 2006**

[Data are generally for the entire year, but in some instances they are only for a particular month within the year]

Year	Total	Married-couple households [1]			Single parent [2]	One-person	Other [3]
		Total	With children [2]	Without children [2]			
United States:							
1980	100.0	60.8	30.9	29.9	7.5	22.7	9.0
1990	100.0	56.0	26.3	29.8	8.3	24.6	11.0
1995	100.0	54.4	25.5	28.9	9.1	25.0	11.5
2000	100.0	52.8	24.1	28.7	8.9	25.5	12.7
2005	100.0	51.4	23.1	28.2	9.1	26.4	13.1
Canada:							
1981	100.0	66.8	36.3	30.5	5.3	20.3	7.6
1991	100.0	62.8	29.6	33.2	5.7	22.9	8.6
1996	100.0	60.5	27.8	32.7	6.4	24.2	8.9
2001	100.0	59.4	25.6	33.8	6.1	25.7	8.8
Japan:							
1980	100.0	68.4	42.9	25.6	2.2	19.8	9.5
1990	100.0	65.2	33.1	32.1	2.3	23.1	9.4
1995	100.0	62.8	27.4	35.4	2.0	25.6	9.6
2000	100.0	60.3	23.6	36.7	2.1	27.6	10.0
2005 . . [4]	100.0	59.1	21.0	38.1	2.3	27.6	11.0
Denmark: [4]							
1980	100.0	50.3	25.0	25.3	3.9	44.9	1.0
1990	100.0	45.6	19.5	26.1	4.2	49.6	0.6
1995	100.0	44.9	18.2	26.6	4.2	50.4	0.5
2001	100.0	45.7	18.5	27.2	4.2	49.6	0.6
2006	100.0	45.1	18.4	26.7	4.7	49.6	0.6
France:							
1982	100.0	67.0	39.7	27.3	4.3	24.6	4.1
1990	100.0	64.9	38.6	26.2	6.6	26.1	2.5
1995	100.0	62.2	35.9	26.3	6.7	28.9	2.3
2000	100.0	60.0	32.8	27.1	7.2	30.8	2.0
Germany:							
1991	100.0	55.3	31.6	23.7	7.1	33.6	4.0
1995	100.0	53.3	29.2	24.0	6.8	34.9	5.1
2000 [5]	100.0	56.8	28.0	28.8	6.0	36.1	1.2
2004	100.0	55.3	26.1	29.2	6.3	37.2	1.2
2005	100.0	54.7	25.5	29.1	6.4	37.5	1.4
Ireland:							
1981	100.0	(NA)	(NA)	(NA)	(NA)	16.9	(NA)
1991	100.0	61.6	47.9	13.7	10.6	20.2	7.6
1996	100.0	59.6	44.5	15.1	11.2	21.5	7.7
2002	100.0	59.2	41.4	17.7	11.7	21.6	7.6
2006	100.0	57.3	37.4	20.0	11.6	22.4	8.7
Netherlands:							
1988	100.0	64.7	37.3	27.4	5.4	28.7	1.2
1993 [5]	100.0	63.1	33.3	29.9	5.0	30.9	1.0
1995 [5]	100.0	61.2	32.6	28.5	5.6	32.6	0.7
2000	100.0	60.2	30.6	29.6	5.6	33.4	0.7
2006	100.0	58.0	29.1	28.9	6.3	35.0	0.7
Sweden:							
1985	100.0	54.8	23.8	31.0	3.2	36.1	5.9
1990	100.0	52.1	21.9	30.2	3.9	39.6	4.4
1995 [5]	100.0	50.7	21.2	29.4	4.6	42.3	2.4
2000 [6]	100.0	45.8	19.1	26.7	5.3	46.5	1.9
2004	100.0	46.3	18.9	27.3	4.7	46.4	2.1
United Kingdom: [7]							
1981	100.0	65.0	31.0	34.0	5.0	22.0	8.0
1991	100.0	61.0	25.0	36.0	6.0	27.0	6.0
1994-95	100.0	58.0	25.0	33.0	7.0	27.0	8.0
2000	100.0	58.0	23.0	35.0	6.0	29.0	7.0
2006	100.0	57.0	22.0	35.0	7.0	28.0	8.0

NA Not available.   [1] May include unmarried cohabiting couples. Such couples are explicitly included under married couples in Canada, Denmark, Ireland, France, the Netherlands, and Sweden. In Germany, cohabitants are grouped with married couples beginning in 2000. In other countries, some unmarried cohabitants are included as married couples, while some are classified under "other households."   [2] Children are defined as unmarried children living at home according to the following age limits: under 18 years old in the United States, Canada, Japan, Denmark, Sweden, and the United Kingdom, except that the United Kingdom includes 15-, 16-, and 17-year-olds in 1981, and 16- and 17-year-olds thereafter only if they are attending school full-time; under 25 years old in France; and children of all ages in Germany, Ireland, and the Netherlands.   [3] Includes both family and nonfamily households not elsewhere classified. These households comprise, for example, siblings residing together, other households composed of relatives, and households made up of roommates. Some unmarried cohabitating couples may also be included in the "other" group. See footnote 1.   [4] From family-based statistics. However, one person living alone constitutes a family in Denmark. In this respect, the Danish data are closer to household statistics.   [5] Break in series.   [6] Bureau of Labor Statistics estimates for single-parent households.   [7] Great Britain only (excludes Northern Ireland).

Source: U.S. Bureau of Labor Statistics, updated and revised from "Families and Work in Transition in 12 Countries, 1980–2001," *Monthly Labor Review*, September 2003 with unpublished data.

Table 1305. Vital Statistics, by Country or Area: 2006 and 2010

[Covers countries with 12 million or more population in 2006]

Country or area	Crude birth rate [1] 2006	Crude birth rate [1] 2010, proj.	Crude death rate [2] 2006	Crude death rate [2] 2010, proj.	Expectation of life at birth (years) 2006	Expectation of life at birth (years) 2010, proj.	Infant mortality rate [3] 2006	Infant mortality rate [3] 2010, proj.	Total fertility rate per woman [4] 2006	Total fertility rate per woman [4] 2010, proj.
United States......	14.1	14.2	8.3	8.3	77.9	78.4	6.4	6.2	2.09	2.11
Afghanistan	46.6	45.1	20.3	18.8	43.3	45.1	160.2	149.3	6.69	6.47
Algeria...........	17.1	16.7	4.6	4.7	73.3	74.3	29.9	25.7	1.89	1.76
Argentina.........	16.7	15.8	7.6	7.5	76.1	76.9	14.7	13.1	2.16	2.03
Australia.........	12.1	11.7	7.5	7.7	80.5	81.0	4.6	4.4	1.76	1.75
Bangladesh	29.8	27.8	8.3	7.7	62.5	63.9	60.8	54.3	3.11	3.04
Brazil...........	16.6	15.5	6.2	6.3	72.0	73.0	28.6	24.9	1.91	1.81
Burkina Faso	45.6	44.2	15.6	14.5	48.9	50.2	91.4	85.2	6.47	6.21
Burma	17.7	16.7	9.4	9.1	62.1	63.8	52.3	46.2	1.98	1.86
Cambodia.........	25.4	25.8	8.3	8.0	60.9	62.5	60.4	53.0	3.16	3.00
Cameroon	35.6	33.6	13.0	12.0	52.3	54.0	67.2	62.2	4.58	4.25
Canada	10.8	10.7	7.8	8.0	80.2	80.7	4.7	4.5	1.61	1.62
Chile	15.2	14.5	5.8	6.1	76.8	77.5	8.6	7.7	2.00	1.90
China [5]	13.3	14.3	7.0	7.1	72.6	73.8	23.1	19.4	1.73	1.80
Colombia	20.5	19.3	5.6	5.5	72.0	73.1	20.8	18.3	2.54	2.44
Congo (Kinshasa) [6] ..	43.4	41.7	10.6	9.7	56.8	58.4	67.0	61.2	6.45	6.11
Cote d'Ivoire	35.1	33.3	14.8	14.5	48.8	49.5	89.1	82.4	4.50	4.20
Ecuador..........	22.3	20.8	4.2	4.2	76.4	77.2	22.9	19.9	2.68	2.50
Egypt	22.9	21.3	5.1	5.1	71.3	72.4	30.7	26.2	2.83	2.61
Ethiopia..........	38.0	35.6	14.9	14.1	49.0	49.8	93.6	86.9	5.22	4.76
France [7]	13.1	12.4	8.4	8.7	80.7	81.1	3.4	3.3	1.99	1.97
Germany	8.3	8.2	10.6	11.0	78.8	79.4	4.1	4.0	1.39	1.42
Ghana...........	30.5	27.9	9.7	9.1	58.8	60.2	54.9	49.9	3.99	3.57
Guatemala	29.6	27.4	5.4	5.0	69.4	70.6	30.8	26.9	3.82	3.36
India	23.2	21.3	6.8	6.1	67.9	70.5	37.1	28.1	2.85	2.67
Indonesia........	20.1	18.5	6.3	6.3	69.9	71.1	33.3	28.9	2.41	2.28
Iran............	16.3	17.3	5.6	5.8	70.3	71.4	39.3	34.7	1.72	1.70
Iraq............	32.0	29.4	5.4	4.9	69.0	70.3	48.6	42.2	4.18	3.76
Italy............	8.7	8.0	10.4	10.8	79.8	80.3	5.8	5.4	1.28	1.32
Japan	8.3	7.4	8.7	9.8	82.0	82.2	2.8	2.8	1.24	1.20
Kazakhstan	16.0	16.7	9.4	9.4	66.9	68.2	28.3	24.9	1.89	1.87
Kenya	39.8	35.1	11.5	9.3	54.2	58.8	59.0	53.5	4.91	4.38
Korea, North......	15.5	13.8	7.1	7.5	71.7	72.7	23.3	20.5	2.10	1.90
Korea, South	10.0	9.5	5.9	6.4	77.0	77.8	6.2	5.7	1.27	1.31
Madagascar	38.8	37.9	8.7	8.0	61.8	63.3	58.5	52.8	5.29	5.09
Malawi	42.4	41.2	18.7	17.4	42.4	44.1	93.7	87.6	5.82	5.51
Malaysia	22.9	22.1	5.1	5.1	72.5	73.6	17.2	15.0	3.04	2.92
Mexico..........	20.7	19.4	4.7	4.8	75.4	76.3	20.3	17.8	2.42	2.31
Morocco..........	22.0	20.6	5.6	5.4	70.9	72.1	40.2	34.7	2.68	2.46
Mozambique.......	39.0	37.8	20.7	19.8	40.8	41.4	112.1	103.8	5.35	5.13
Nepal	31.0	28.8	9.3	8.7	60.2	61.7	65.3	58.7	4.10	3.73
Netherlands	10.9	10.3	8.7	8.8	79.0	79.6	5.0	4.7	1.66	1.66
Niger...........	50.7	48.6	20.9	19.6	43.8	44.8	118.3	112.6	7.46	7.11
Nigeria..........	40.4	39.5	16.9	15.9	47.1	48.6	97.1	90.9	5.49	5.33
Pakistan.........	28.1	25.7	8.2	7.5	63.4	64.9	70.8	63.4	3.84	3.32
Peru	20.5	18.9	6.2	6.2	69.8	71.0	30.9	27.2	2.51	2.32
Philippines	24.9	23.2	5.4	5.2	70.2	71.4	22.8	20.2	3.11	2.89
Poland	9.9	10.0	9.9	10.1	75.0	75.9	7.2	6.7	1.25	1.29
Romania	10.7	10.4	11.8	11.9	71.6	72.7	25.5	22.1	1.37	1.40
Russia	10.8	11.1	16.0	16.0	65.8	66.2	11.3	10.3	1.38	1.41
Saudi Arabia......	29.3	28.2	2.6	2.5	75.7	76.5	12.8	11.3	4.00	3.77
Senegal	38.3	34.7	11.2	10.3	56.3	57.9	61.4	56.6	5.13	4.60
South Africa	18.2	17.3	22.0	22.7	42.7	42.7	60.7	56.2	2.20	2.02
Spain	10.1	9.5	9.7	10.1	79.7	80.2	4.4	4.2	1.28	1.32
Sri Lanka	17.3	15.9	6.0	6.2	74.6	75.3	19.9	18.1	2.08	1.96
Sudan	35.3	33.3	15.2	12.3	47.9	52.5	96.8	78.1	4.79	4.37
Syria	27.8	25.2	4.8	4.6	70.3	71.5	28.6	25.0	3.40	3.02
Taiwan [5].........	9.0	9.0	6.4	6.9	77.4	78.2	5.6	5.3	1.11	1.15
Tanzania	36.8	33.4	14.0	12.3	49.7	52.5	73.0	68.1	4.93	4.31
Thailand.........	13.9	13.2	7.0	7.3	72.3	73.4	19.5	17.1	1.64	1.65
Turkey..........	16.6	15.6	6.0	6.1	72.6	73.7	39.7	34.3	1.92	1.82
Uganda	48.1	47.6	13.0	11.9	51.0	53.0	68.5	63.7	6.88	6.73
Ukraine	9.3	9.6	16.3	15.7	67.7	68.5	9.7	8.7	1.24	1.27
United Kingdom.....	10.7	10.7	10.1	10.0	78.5	79.2	5.1	4.8	1.66	1.66
Uzbekistan	26.4	26.1	7.8	7.4	64.6	66.2	70.0	65.6	2.91	2.80
Venezuela	21.5	20.3	5.1	5.1	73.1	73.8	23.0	21.1	2.59	2.45
Vietnam.........	16.9	16.1	6.2	6.2	70.9	71.9	25.1	22.2	1.91	1.80
Yemen	42.9	41.8	8.3	7.4	62.1	63.6	59.5	53.2	6.58	6.23
Zimbabwe	28.0	26.6	21.8	21.6	39.3	40.2	51.7	49.6	3.13	2.93

[1] Number of births during 1 year per 1,000 persons (based on midyear population). [2] Number of deaths during 1 year per 1,000 persons (based on midyear population). [3] Number of deaths of children under 1 year of age per 1,000 live births in a calendar year. [4] Average number of children that would be born if all women lived to the end of their childbearing years and, at each year of age, they experienced the birth rates occurring in the specified year. [5] See footnote 2, Table 1298. [6] See footnote 3, Table 1298. [7] France now includes the overseas departments of French Guiana, Guadeloupe, Martinique, and Reunion.

Source: U.S. Census Bureau, "International Data Base" (as of 16 July 2007); <http://www.census.gov/ipc/www/idb/>.

Comparative International Statistics 831

Table 1306. Life Expectancy at Birth and at Age 65, by Sex—Selected Countries: 1980 and 2004

Country	Life expectancy at birth Females 1980	Females 2004	Males 1980	Males 2004	Life expectancy at age 65 Females 1980	Females 2004	Males 1980	Males 2004
United States [1]	77.4	80.4	70.0	75.2	18.3	20.0	14.1	17.1
Australia	78.1	83.0	71.0	78.1	17.9	21.1	13.7	17.8
Austria	76.1	82.1	69.0	76.4	16.3	20.3	12.9	16.9
Belgium	76.8	(NA)	70.0	(NA)	16.9	(NA)	13.0	(NA)
Canada	78.9	(NA)	71.7	(NA)	18.9	(NA)	14.5	(NA)
Czech Republic	73.9	79.0	66.8	72.6	14.3	(NA)	11.2	(NA)
Denmark	77.3	79.9	71.2	75.2	17.6	(NA)	13.6	(NA)
Finland	77.6	82.3	69.2	75.3	16.5	(NA)	12.5	(NA)
France	78.4	83.8	70.2	76.7	18.2	(NA)	13.6	(NA)
Germany	76.1	81.4	69.6	75.7	16.7	(NA)	13.0	(NA)
Greece	76.8	81.4	72.2	76.6	16.8	(NA)	14.6	(NA)
Hungary	72.7	76.9	65.5	68.6	14.6	16.9	11.6	13.1
Iceland	79.7	82.7	73.7	79.2	19.1	20.5	15.8	17.9
Ireland	75.6	(NA)	70.1	(NA)	15.7	(NA)	12.6	(NA)
Italy	77.4	(NA)	70.6	(NA)	17.1	(NA)	13.3	(NA)
Japan	78.8	85.6	73.4	78.6	17.7	23.3	14.6	18.2
Luxembourg	75.9	(NA)	69.1	(NA)	16.0	(NA)	12.3	(NA)
Mexico	70.2	77.6	64.1	72.7	17.0	18.6	15.4	17.1
Netherlands	79.2	81.4	72.5	76.9	18.0	19.8	13.7	16.3
New Zealand	76.3	81.3	70.0	77.0	17.0	20.1	13.2	17.1
Norway	79.2	82.3	72.3	77.5	18.0	(NA)	14.3	(NA)
Poland	74.4	79.2	66.0	70.7	15.5	18.4	12.0	14.2
Portugal	75.2	(NA)	67.7	(NA)	16.5	(NA)	12.9	(NA)
Slovakia	74.3	77.8	66.8	70.3	15.4	(NA)	12.3	(NA)
Spain	78.6	83.8	72.5	77.2	17.9	(NA)	14.8	(NA)
Sweden	78.8	82.7	72.8	78.4	17.9	20.6	14.3	17.4
Switzerland	79.6	83.7	72.8	78.6	(NA)	(NA)	(NA)	(NA)
Turkey	60.3	73.6	55.8	68.8	12.8	14.9	11.7	13.1
United Kingdom	76.2	(NA)	70.2	(NA)	16.6	(NA)	12.6	(NA)

NA Not available. [1] Source of 2004 data: U.S. National Center for Health Statistics, *Vital Statistics of the United States,* annual.
Source: Organization for Economic Cooperation and Development, Paris, France, *OECD Health Data 2006* (copyright). See also <http://www.oecd.org/health/healthdata>.

Table 1307. People Infected With HIV and AIDS-Related Deaths, by Region: 2004 and 2006

[In thousands (36,900 represents 36,900,000). Estimates are based on ranges, called 'plausibility bounds,' which reflect the certainty associated with each estimate and define the boundaries within which the actual numbers lie]

Region	Adults and children living with HIV 2004	2006	Adults and children newly infected with HIV 2004	2006	Adult prevalence (percent) 2004	2006	Adult and child deaths due to AIDS 2004	2006
Total	36,900	39,500	3,900	4,300	1.0	1.0	2,700	2,900
Sub-Saharan Africa	23,600	24,700	2,600	2,800	6.0	5.9	1,900	2,100
North Africa and Middle East	400	460	59	68	0.2	0.2	33	36
South and South-East Asia	7,200	7,800	770	860	0.6	0.6	510	590
East Asia	620	750	90	100	0.1	0.1	33	43
Oceania	72	81	8	7	0.3	0.4	3	4
Latin America	1,500	1,700	130	140	0.5	0.5	53	65
Caribbean	240	250	25	27	1.1	1.2	21	19
Eastern Europe and Central Asia	1,400	1,700	160	270	0.7	0.9	48	84
Western and Central Europe	700	740	22	22	0.3	0.3	12	12
North America	1,200	1,400	43	43	0.7	0.8	18	18

Source: Joint United Nations Programme on HIV/AIDS (UNAIDS) and World Health Organization (WHO), *AIDS Epidemic Update: December 2006* (copyright). See also <http://www.unaids.org/en/HIV_data/epi2006/default.asp>.

Table 1308. Percentage of the Adult Population Considered to be Obese: 2004

[Obesity rates are defined as the percentage of the population with a Body Mass Index (BMI) over 30 kg/m^2. The BMI is a single number that evaluates an individual's weight status in relation to height (weight/height^2, with weight in kilograms and height in meters). For Australia, the United Kingdom, and the United States, figures are based on health examinations, rather than self-reported information. Obesity estimates derived from health examinations are generally higher and more reliable than those coming from self-reports because they preclude any misreporting of people's height and weight. However, health examinations are only conducted regularly in a few countries. For more information on methods by country, see <http://www.irdes.fr/EspaceAnglais/home.htm>]

Country	2004	Country	2004	Country	2004
United States	[1]30.6	France	9.5	Luxembourg	18.7
Australia	[2]21.7	Germany	[4]12.9	Mexico	[3]24.2
Austria	[2]9.1	Greece	[4]21.9	New Zealand	[4]20.9
Belgium	12.7	Hungary	[4]18.8	Norway	[1]8.3
Canada	22.4	Ireland	[1]13.0	Spain	[4]13.1
Czech Republic	[1]14.8	Italy	[4]9.0	Sweden	9.8
Denmark	[3]9.5	Japan	[4]3.2	Switzerland	[1]7.7
Finland	14.0	Korea, South	[5]3.2	United Kingdom	23.0

[1] 2002 data. [2] 1999 data. [3] 2000 data. [4] 2003 data. [5] 2001 data.
Source: Organization for Economic Cooperation and Development, Paris, France, *OECD Health Data,* 2006 (copyright). See also <http://dx.doi.org/10.1787/341527146806>.

Table 1309. Tobacco Consumption by Country and Sex: 1980 and 2004

Country	Daily cigarette consumption per smoker (number)		Daily tobacco consumption (percent)					
			Total		Females		Males	
	1980	2004	1980	2004	1980	2004	1980	2004
United States.	13.4	16.8	33.5	17.0	29.3	15.1	37.6	19.0
Australia.	20.3	14.1	36.0	17.7	31.1	16.5	41.1	18.9
Canada	(NA)	15.2	(NA)	15.0	(NA)	13.0	(NA)	17.0
Denmark.	12.0	13.2	60.5	26.0	44.0	23.0	57.0	29.0
Finland.	15.9	14.2	26.1	23.0	16.6	19.5	35.2	27.1
France	19.1	(NA)	30.0	23.0	16.0	19.0	44.0	28.0
Greece.	(NA)	(NA)	(NA)	38.6	(NA)	31.3	(NA)	46.0
Iceland	(NA)	(NA)	(NA)	20.2	(NA)	18.9	(NA)	21.5
Ireland	25.0	15.0	(NA)	(NA)	34.1	(NA)	(NA)	(NA)
Italy	(NA)	(NA)	35.5	(NA)	16.7	(NA)	54.3	(NA)
Japan	(NA)	(NA)	42.3	29.4	14.4	13.2	70.2	46.9
Luxembourg	(NA)	(NA)	(NA)	27.0	(NA)	23.0	(NA)	30.0
Netherlands	21.0	11.4	43.0	30.0	34.0	26.0	52.0	34.0
New Zealand.	(NA)	12.0	(NA)	22.0	(NA)	21.0	(NA)	23.0
Norway.	12.2	13.3	36.0	26.0	30.0	25.0	42.0	27.0
Poland	(NA)	16.7	(NA)	26.3	(NA)	19.3	(NA)	33.9
Sweden	13.9	(NA)	32.4	16.2	28.7	17.5	36.3	15.0
United Kingdom	16.1	14.0	39.0	25.0	37.0	23.0	42.0	26.0

NA Not available.

Source: Organization for Economic Cooperation and Development, Paris, France, OECD Health Data 2006 (copyright).

Table 1310. Medical Doctors and Inpatient Care—Selected Countries: 1990 to 2004

Country	Medical doctors per 1,000 population			Inpatient care					
				Beds per 1,000 population			Average length of stay (days)		
	1990	2000	2004	1990	2000	2004	1990	2000	2004
United States	1.8	2.3	2.4	4.9	3.5	3.3	9.1	6.8	6.5
Australia.	2.2	2.5	(NA)	(NA)	4.0	(NA)	(NA)	16.0	(NA)
Austria.	2.2	3.1	3.5	10.1	8.6	7.7	12.8	8.6	(NA)
Belgium	3.3	3.9	4.0	8.1	7.1	6.8	13.8	(NA)	(NA)
Canada	2.1	2.1	2.1	6.0	3.8	(NA)	13.0	(NA)	(NA)
Czech Republic	2.7	3.4	3.5	(NA)	8.8	8.7	15.4	11.4	10.7
Denmark.	2.5	2.8	(NA)	5.6	4.3	(NA)	8.2	6.0	5.2
Finland.	2.0	2.3	2.4	(NA)	(NA)	(NA)	18.2	10.3	10.0
France	3.1	3.3	3.4	9.7	8.1	7.5	15.1	13.2	13.4
Germany	(NA)	3.3	3.4	(NA)	9.1	8.6	(NA)	11.4	10.4
Greece.	3.4	4.3	4.9	(NA)	4.7	(NA)	9.9	8.4	(NA)
Hungary	2.8	(NA)	3.3	(NA)	8.1	7.8	12.6	8.9	8.2
Iceland	2.8	3.4	3.6	(NA)	(NA)	(NA)	18.3	(NA)	(NA)
Ireland	(NA)	2.2	2.8	6.1	4.7	4.2	7.9	7.4	7.5
Italy	(NA)	4.1	4.2	7.2	4.7	(NA)	11.7	7.7	(NA)
Japan	1.7	1.9	2.0	(NA)	14.7	14.2	50.5	39.1	36.3
Korea, South.	0.8	1.3	1.6	3.1	6.1	7.3	13.0	14.0	(NA)
Luxembourg	2.0	2.5	2.8	11.7	6.9	6.7	17.6	(NA)	(NA)
Mexico	1.0	1.5	1.6	1.6	1.9	1.9	(NA)	4.2	(NA)
Netherlands	2.5	3.2	3.6	5.9	5.2	(NA)	16.0	12.9	(NA)
New Zealand.	1.9	2.2	(NA)	(NA)	(NA)	(NA)	9.4	8.0	(NA)
Norway.	(NA)	2.9	3.5	4.6	3.8	3.7	(NA)	8.9	8.2
Poland	2.1	2.2	(NA)	(NA)	(NA)	(NA)	12.5	8.9	(NA)
Portugal	2.8	3.2	3.4	4.1	3.8	3.7	10.8	9.2	8.9
Slovakia	(NA)	3.1	3.1	(NA)	7.8	(NA)	(NA)	10.4	8.6
Spain	(NA)	3.2	3.4	4.6	3.7	(NA)	12.2	9.0	(NA)
Sweden	2.9	3.1	(NA)	(NA)	(NA)	(NA)	18.0	6.4	(NA)
Switzerland.	3.0	3.5	3.8	6.5	4.1	3.8	(NA)	12.8	11.9
Turkey	0.9	1.3	(NA)	2.4	2.6	2.6	6.9	5.9	5.7
United Kingdom	1.6	1.9	2.3	(NA)	3.8	4.1	17.6	8.4	7.2

NA Not available.

Source: Organization for Economic Cooperation and Development, Paris, France, OECD Health Data 2006 (copyright).

U.S. Census Bureau, Statistical Abstract of the United States: 2008

Table 1311. Health Expenditures as Percent of GDP by Country: 1980 to 2004

[In percent. GDP = gross domestic product; for explanation, see text, Section 13]

Country	Total health expenditures					Public health expenditures				
	1980	1990	2000	2003	2004	1980	1990	2000	2003	2004
United States	8.8	11.9	13.3	15.2	15.3	3.6	4.7	5.8	6.8	6.9
Australia	6.8	7.5	8.8	9.2	(NA)	4.3	5.1	6.0	6.2	(NA)
Austria	7.5	7.0	9.4	9.6	9.6	5.1	5.1	6.6	6.8	6.8
Belgium	6.3	7.2	8.6	10.1	(NA)	(NA)	(NA)	6.5	7.2	(NA)
Canada	7.1	9.0	8.9	9.9	9.9	5.4	6.7	6.3	6.9	6.9
Czech Republic	(NA)	4.7	6.7	7.5	7.3	(NA)	4.6	6.1	6.7	6.5
Denmark	8.9	8.3	8.3	8.9	8.9	7.9	6.9	6.8	(NA)	(NA)
Finland	6.3	7.8	6.7	7.4	7.5	5.0	6.3	5.0	5.7	5.7
France	7.0	8.4	9.2	10.4	10.5	5.6	6.4	7.0	8.2	8.3
Germany [1]	8.7	8.5	10.4	10.9	(NA)	6.8	6.5	8.2	8.5	(NA)
Greece	6.6	7.4	9.9	10.5	10.0	3.7	4.0	5.2	5.6	5.3
Hungary	(NA)	(NA)	7.1	8.3	8.3	(NA)	(NA)	5.0	6.0	6.0
Iceland	6.2	7.9	9.2	10.5	10.2	5.5	6.9	7.6	8.8	8.5
Ireland	8.3	6.1	6.3	7.2	7.1	6.8	4.4	4.6	5.6	5.7
Italy	(NA)	7.7	7.9	8.2	8.4	(NA)	6.1	5.8	6.2	6.4
Japan	6.5	5.9	7.6	8.0	(NA)	4.6	4.6	6.1	6.5	(NA)
Korea, South	(NA)	4.4	4.8	5.5	5.6	(NA)	1.7	2.2	2.8	2.9
Luxembourg	5.2	5.4	5.8	7.7	8.0	4.8	5.0	5.2	7.0	7.3
Mexico	(NA)	4.8	5.6	6.3	6.5	(NA)	2.0	2.6	2.8	3.0
Netherlands	7.2	7.7	7.9	9.1	9.2	5.0	5.2	5.0	5.8	5.7
New Zealand	5.9	6.9	7.7	8.0	8.4	5.1	5.7	6.0	6.3	6.5
Norway	7.0	7.7	8.5	10.1	9.7	5.9	6.4	7.0	8.5	8.1
Poland	(NA)	4.9	5.7	6.5	6.5	(NA)	4.5	4.0	4.5	4.5
Portugal	5.6	6.2	9.4	9.8	10.0	3.6	4.1	6.8	7.1	7.2
Slovakia	(NA)	(NA)	5.5	5.9	(NA)	(NA)	(NA)	4.9	5.2	(NA)
Spain	5.3	6.5	7.2	7.9	8.1	4.2	5.1	5.2	5.5	5.7
Sweden	9.0	8.3	8.4	9.3	9.1	8.3	7.5	7.1	7.9	7.7
Switzerland	7.4	8.3	10.4	11.5	11.6	(NA)	4.3	5.8	6.7	6.8
Turkey	3.3	3.6	6.6	7.6	7.7	1.0	2.2	4.2	5.4	5.5
United Kingdom	5.6	6.0	7.3	7.9	8.3	5.0	5.0	5.9	6.8	7.1

NA Not available.   [1] Data prior to 1991 are for West Germany.

Source: Organization for Economic Cooperation and Development, Paris, France, *OECD Health Data 2006* (copyright).

Table 1312. Educational Performance: 2002 and 2003

[Tertiary-type A includes education leading to a BA, Master's, or equivalent degree, and advanced research programs. Performance figures were gathered from the Program for International Student Assessment (PISA), an internationally standardized assessment jointly developed by participating countries, which takes place in three-yearly cycles. To implement PISA, each of the participating countries selects a nationally representative sample of 15-year-olds, regardless of grade level. In the United States, 5,456 students from public and private schools took the PISA assessment in 2003. Tests are typically administered to between 4,500 and 10,000 students in each country]

Country	Student performance on the combined reading, scientific, and mathematical literacy scales, (2003)			Educational attainment of adult population and current graduation rates, (2002) (percent)	
	Mean score on the combined reading literacy scale [1]	Mean score on the mathematical literacy scale [2]	Mean score on the scientific literacy scale [3]	Upper secondary or higher attainment (25-64 year-olds) [4]	Tertiary-type A attainment (25-64 year-olds)
Australia	525.4	524.3	525.1	60.9	20.0
Austria	490.7	505.6	491.0	77.9	7.0
Canada	527.9	532.5	518.7	82.6	[5]21.0
Czech Republic	488.5	516.5	523.3	87.9	[5]11.9
Finland	543.5	544.3	548.2	74.8	15.6
France	496.2	510.8	511.2	64.8	12.4
Germany	491.4	503.0	502.3	83.0	13.4
Greece	472.3	444.9	481.0	50.5	12.7
Italy	475.7	465.7	486.5	44.4	[5]10.4
Japan	498.1	534.1	547.6	83.7	20.1
Korea	534.1	542.2	538.4	70.8	18.5
Luxembourg	479.4	493.2	482.8	56.6	11.6
Mexico	399.7	385.2	404.9	12.6	2.5
Poland	496.6	490.2	497.8	47.0	[5]12.1
Spain	480.5	485.1	487.1	41.3	17.3
Sweden	514.3	509.0	506.1	81.6	17.7
Switzerland	499.1	526.6	513.0	82.4	16.2
United Kingdom	(NA)	(NA)	(NA)	64.3	18.6
United States	495.2	482.9	491.3	87.3	29.0
Country mean	494.2	500.0	499.6	64.9	15.5

NA Not available.   [1] Reading literacy is understanding, using, and reflecting on written texts in order to achieve one's goals, to develop one's knowledge and potential, and to participate in society.   [2] Mathematical literacy is an individual's capacity to identify and understand the role that mathematics plays in the world, to make well-founded judgements, and to use and engage with mathematics in ways that meet the needs of that individual's life.   [3] Scientific literacy is the capacity to use scientific knowledge to identify questions and to draw evidence-based conclusions in order to understand and help make decisions about the natural world and the changes made to it through human activity.   [4] Excluding ISCED 3C short programs.   [5] All tertiary levels: type A and type B (focus on practical, technical, or occupational skills).

Source: Organization for Economic Cooperation and Development, Paris, France, *OECD in Figures*, 2005 (copyright). See also <http://www.oecd.org/document/62/0,2340,en_2649_34489_2345918_1_1_1_1,00.html>.

[In degrees Fahrenheit, except as noted. Data are generally based on a standard 30-year period; for details, see source. For data on U.S. cities, see Tables 377–381. Minus sign (–) indicates degrees below zero]

City	January Average high	January Average low	January Warm-est	January Coldest	January Average precipitation (inches)	July Average high	July Average low	July Warm-est	July Coldest	July Average precipitation (inches)
Amsterdam, Netherlands . . .	41	34	57	3	3.1	69	55	90	39	2.9
Athens, Greece	55	44	70	28	1.9	89	73	108	61	0.2
Baghdad, Iraq	58	38	75	25	1.1	110	78	122	61	–
Bangkok, Thailand	89	71	95	54	0.4	90	78	99	72	6.2
Beijing, China	34	17	54	1	0.2	86	72	104	63	8.8
Berlin, Germany	35	26	58	–11	(NA)	73	56	95	41	(NA)
Bogota, Colombia	66	43	84	27	1.9	64	47	82	32	1.8
Brasilia, Brazil	81	64	95	54	(NA)	79	52	97	37	(NA)
Buenos Aires, Argentina . . .	85	64	104	44	4.2	58	41	88	23	2.3
Cairo, Egypt	65	49	86	32	0.2	93	72	108	63	–
Frankfurt, Germany	38	30	56	–4	1.8	75	57	97	38	2.4
Geneva, Switzerland	39	29	57	–2	2.2	77	56	96	41	2.8
Hong Kong, China	67	58	79	43	1.1	89	81	97	70	14.3
Istanbul, Turkey	46	37	64	16	3.7	82	66	100	50	0.7
Jakarta, Indonesia	83	75	92	72	(NA)	88	74	92	67	(NA)
Karachi, Pakistan	76	55	93	39	0.3	89	83	109	68	3.5
Lagos, Nigeria	82	79	93	64	(NA)	79	76	88	70	(NA)
London, England	45	36	61	15	2.4	72	56	93	45	1.8
Madrid, Spain	51	32	68	14	1.8	90	61	104	46	0.4
Manila, Philippines	86	71	95	61	0.8	88	76	99	70	15.9
Mexico City, Mexico	70	45	86	26	0.3	74	56	86	37	5.1
Montreal, Canada	21	7	52	–31	2.8	79	61	93	43	3.4
Moscow, Russia	21	11	46	–33	1.4	71	55	95	41	3.2
Nairobi, Kenya	77	58	88	45	1.8	71	54	85	43	0.5
New Delhi, India	68	48	85	32	0.9	93	81	111	70	7.9
Paris, France	43	34	59	1	(NA)	75	58	95	41	(NA)
Rio De Janeiro, Brazil. . . .	91	74	109	64	5.3	81	64	102	52	1.8
Rome, Italy	55	39	64	19	3.2	83	66	100	55	0.6
Seoul, Korea	33	21	55	–1	(NA)	82	71	97	55	(NA)
Singapore, Singapore	85	73	100	66	9.4	86	76	99	70	5.9
Sydney, Australia	79	65	109	49	4.0	62	44	80	32	2.5
Tel Aviv, Israel	62	46	84	32	(NA)	87	69	100	50	(NA)
Tokyo, Japan	48	35	66	25	2.0	82	71	95	55	5.3
Toronto, Canada	28	15	59	–24	1.9	79	60	99	45	2.8

– Represents zero.   NA Not available.

Source: U.S. National Oceanic and Atmospheric Administration, *Climates of the World*.

Table 1314. **Carbon Dioxide Emissions From Consumption of Fossil Fuels by Country: 1990 to 2004**

[In million metric tons of carbon equivalent (5,843 represents 5,843,000,000). Includes carbon dioxide emissions from the consumption of petroleum, natural gas, and coal, and the flaring of natural gas]

Country	1990	1995	1998	1999	2000	2001	2002	2003	2004
World, total	5,843	6,009	6,232	6,325	6,505	6,578	6,668	6,999	7,376
Australia	72	78	91	96	96	100	102	101	105
Brazil	61	79	88	91	94	96	96	87	92
Canada	131	138	148	152	155	151	154	162	160
China [1]	611	784	801	791	827	869	902	1,063	1,284
France	101	102	111	109	109	110	109	111	111
Germany	(NA)	239	235	227	231	237	230	235	235
India	160	236	246	255	273	278	279	284	304
Indonesia	41	58	65	72	75	81	85	86	84
Iran	55	71	80	86	87	91	99	105	110
Italy	113	117	119	119	121	120	122	128	132
Japan	277	293	301	313	325	319	323	339	344
Korea, South	65	107	103	116	121	120	127	130	135
Mexico	82	87	100	98	104	103	105	107	105
Netherlands	56	60	65	64	68	75	70	70	73
Poland	90	83	85	88	79	75	74	78	78
Russia	(NA)	434	399	419	424	422	422	437	460
Saudi Arabia	57	64	70	71	79	82	84	94	100
South Africa	81	94	99	101	103	106	102	112	117
Spain	61	66	75	81	86	87	92	94	99
Taiwan	32	49	60	60	68	67	73	78	84
Thailand	23	43	44	46	44	47	51	56	60
Turkey	35	41	50	49	55	50	53	56	58
Ukraine	(NA)	122	90	88	88	86	88	96	99
United Kingdom	163	151	152	150	150	154	151	154	158
United States	1,367	1,443	1,523	1,543	1,586	1,566	1,570	1,584	1,612

NA Not available.   [1] See footnote 2, Table 1298.

Source: U.S. Energy Information Administration, *International Energy Annual, 2004*. See also <http://www.eia.doe.gov/pub/international/iealf/tableh1.xls> (accessed 11 July 2007).

Comparative International Statistics   835

Table 1315. Gross National Income (GNI) by Country: 2000 and 2005

[48 represents $48,000,000,000. GNI (gross national product, or GNP, in the terminology of the 1968 United Nations System of National Accounts) measures the total domestic and foreign value added claimed by residents. GNI comprises GDP plus net receipts of primary income (compensation of employees and property income) from nonresident sources]

Country	Gross national income [1]				GNI on purchasing power parity basis [2]			
	Total (bil. dol.)		Per capita (dol.)		Total (bil. dol.)		Per capita (dol.)	
	2000	2005	2000	2005	2000	2005	2000	2005
Algeria	48	90	1,580	2,730	157	[3]222	5,150	[3]6,770
Argentina	276	173	7,690	4,470	438	539	11,820	13,920
Australia	385	673	20,080	33,120	488	622	25,430	30,610
Bangladesh	50	67	380	470	211	296	1,610	2,090
Belarus	14	27	1,380	2,760	48	77	4,810	7,890
Belgium	255	379	24,900	36,140	277	342	26,990	32,640
Brazil	621	662	3,650	3,550	1,220	1,534	7,170	8,230
Bulgaria	13	27	1,580	3,450	50	67	6,070	8,630
Burkina Faso	3	5	250	400	11	[3]16	1,010	[3]1,220
Cambodia	4	6	290	430	21	[3]35	1,770	[3]2,490
Cameroon	9	16	580	1,000	26	35	1,750	2,150
Canada	668	1,053	21,720	32,590	836	1,041	27,180	32,220
Chile	73	96	4,810	5,870	135	187	8,890	11,470
China [4]	1,064	2,270	840	1,740	4,817	[5]8,610	3,810	[5]6,600
Colombia	87	105	2,050	2,290	252	[3]338	5,960	[3]7,420
Congo (Kinshasa) [6]	2	7	510	120	2	[3]41	680	[3]720
Cote d'Ivoire	11	16	690	870	23	27	1,480	1,490
Czech Republic	54	115	5,250	11,220	140	206	13,620	20,140
Ecuador	16	35	1,330	2,620	38	54	3,060	4,070
Egypt	95	93	1,490	1,260	229	329	3,580	4,440
Ethiopia	7	11	110	160	45	[3]71	700	[3]1,000
France	1,453	[7]2,169	23,990	[7]34,600	1,503	1,859	25,530	30,540
Germany	2,067	2,876	25,150	34,870	2,133	2,409	25,950	29,210
Ghana	6	10	330	450	37	[3]52	1,910	[3]2,370
Greece	124	220	11,700	19,480	178	262	16,860	23,620
Guatemala	19	30	1,700	2,400	45	[3]56	3,920	[3]4,410
Hong Kong	179	192	26,830	27,670	175	241	26,310	34,670
Hungary	48	102	4,770	10,070	120	171	11,930	16,940
India	456	804	450	730	2,439	[3]3,787	2,400	[3]3,460
Indonesia	118	282	570	1,280	585	821	2,840	3,720
Iran	105	177	1,650	2,600	378	549	5,940	8,050
Iraq	(NA)	(NA)	(NA)	[8]	(NA)	(NA)	(NA)	(NA)
Italy	1,164	1,773	20,170	30,250	1,427	1,690	24,730	28,840
Japan	4,492	4,977	35,400	38,950	3,337	4,013	26,300	31,410
Kazakhstan	19	45	1,250	2,940	65	117	4,310	7,730
Kenya	11	18	350	540	30	40	990	1,170
Korea, South	423	756	9,010	15,840	712	1,055	15,140	21,850
Madagascar	4	5	250	290	13	16	810	880
Malawi	2	2	170	160	6	8	590	650
Malaysia	79	126	3,390	4,970	191	262	8,210	10,320
Mexico	500	753	5,100	7,310	852	1,034	8,690	10,030
Morocco	34	53	1,180	1,740	97	132	3,390	4,360
Mozambique	4	6	210	310	15	[3]25	820	[3]1,270
Nepal	5	7	230	270	31	42	1,330	1,530
Netherlands	403	642	25,330	39,340	435	530	27,340	[3]32,480
Niger	2	3	180	240	8	[3]11	740	[3]800
Nigeria	34	74	270	560	100	137	790	1,040
Pakistan	62	107	450	690	260	366	1,880	2,350
Peru	53	74	2,050	2,650	120	163	4,620	5,830
Philippines	79	110	1,030	1,320	319	440	4,170	5,300
Poland	164	273	4,230	7,160	381	515	9,850	13,490
Portugal	112	181	11,090	17,190	171	208	16,930	19,730
Romania	38	85	1,680	3,910	127	193	5,670	8,940
Russia	250	638	1,720	4,460	1,027	1,523	7,050	10,640
Saudi Arabia	168	289	8,120	12,510	261	[3]341	12,610	[3]14,740
Senegal	5	8	500	700	14	[3]21	1,460	[3]1,770
Singapore	92	120	22,780	27,580	96	129	23,780	29,780
South Africa	131	224	2,980	4,770	406	[3]568	9,220	[3]12,120
Spain	599	1,096	14,790	25,250	800	1,121	19,760	25,820
Sri Lanka	16	23	890	1,160	63	89	3,400	4,520
Sudan	11	23	340	640	49	[3]73	1,560	[3]2,000
Sweden	254	369	28,680	40,910	216	284	24,340	31,420
Switzerland	284	411	39,610	55,320	222	276	30,910	37,080
Syria	16	[9]26	960	[9]1,380	52	71	3,190	3,740
Tanzania	9	[9]13	270	[9]340	17	28	510	730
Thailand	122	175	2,010	2,720	381	542	6,270	8,440
Turkey	201	342	2,980	4,750	425	[3]607	6,300	8,420
Uganda	6	8	270	270	29	[3]43	1,240	[3]1,500
Ukraine	34	72	690	1,520	197	317	3,980	6,720
United Kingdom	1,485	2,273	25,220	37,740	1,462	1,969	24,840	32,690
United States	9,697	12,913	34,360	43,560	9,791	12,434	34,690	41,950
Uzbekistan	9	14	360	520	37	53	1,490	2,020
Venezuela	104	128	4,310	4,820	135	171	5,580	6,440
Vietnam	30	51	380	620	156	250	1,990	3,010
Yemen	7	13	420	600	13	19	760	920
Zimbabwe	6	5	440	350	32	25	2,500	1,940

NA Not available.   [1] Gross national income calculated using the World Bank Atlas method; for details, see source.   [2] See footnote 1, Table 1316.   [3] The estimate is based on regression; others are extrapolated from the latest International Comparison Program benchmark estimates.   [4] See footnote 2, Table 1298.   [5] Estimate based on bilateral comparison between China and the United States.   [6] See footnote 3, Table 1298.   [7] GNI and GNI per capita estimates include the French overseas departments of French Guiana, Guadeloupe, Martinique, and Reunion.   [8] Estimated to be lower middle income ($876–$3,465).   [9] Data refer to mainland Tanzania only.

Source: The World Bank, Washington, DC, World Development Indicators CD-ROM, annual (copyright).

Table 1316. Gross Domestic Product (GDP) by Country: 1995 to 2004

[20,673 represents $20,673,000,000,000. PPP stands for purchasing power parity. Except as noted, based on the System of National Accounts, 1993; for details, see source]

Country	Current price levels and PPPs [1] (bil. dol.)					Constant (2000) price levels [2] and PPPs [1] (bil. dol.)					GDP per capita, 2004 based on—	
	1995	2000	2002	2003	2004	1995	2000	2002	2003	2004	Current prices and PPPs [1]	Constant (2000) prices [2] and PPPs [1]
OECD, total [3,4]	20,673	26,492	28,536	29,598	31,353	22,509	26,493	27,202	27,735	28,665	28,502	26,058
OECD Europe [3]	8,180	10,295	11,223	11,509	12,079	8,922	10,296	10,598	10,732	11,013	25,696	23,428
Australia	393	525	586	621	655	434	525	562	585	598	32,409	29,600
Austria	185	230	242	250	266	199	230	234	237	243	32,520	29,752
Belgium	226	273	303	312	327	240	273	280	283	290	31,323	27,850
Canada	657	860	925	963	1,017	702	860	902	920	947	31,828	29,640
Czech Republic	133	150	169	176	190	139	150	156	157	168	18,643	16,493
Denmark	119	154	162	165	174	134	154	156	157	160	32,141	29,578
Finland	98	134	146	150	160	106	134	138	141	147	30,594	28,028
France [5]	1,247	1,575	1,720	1,749	1,838	1,366	1,575	1,627	1,640	1,678	29,554	26,993
Germany	1,803	2,102	2,238	2,281	2,360	1,903	2,102	2,129	2,125	2,160	28,605	26,182
Greece	138	178	210	226	239	150	178	193	202	211	21,596	19,111
Hungary	96	124	147	153	161	102	124	134	138	145	15,948	14,325
Iceland	6	8	8	9	10	6	8	8	8	9	32,528	30,809
Ireland	65	109	130	136	148	69	109	123	129	134	36,341	33,133
Italy	1,190	1,443	1,528	1,542	1,588	1,312	1,443	1,474	1,478	1,496	27,312	25,731
Japan	2,832	3,302	3,466	3,582	3,775	3,100	3,302	3,299	3,342	3,432	29,567	26,875
Korea, South	578	768	879	924	993	620	768	853	880	921	20,644	19,148
Luxembourg	13	22	23	25	27	15	22	22	23	24	60,188	53,301
Mexico	627	897	951	984	1,054	688	897	904	917	957	10,139	9,200
Netherlands	349	453	505	516	537	377	453	460	460	467	32,996	28,726
New Zealand [6]	64	80	89	95	100	71	80	87	90	94	24,608	22,987
Norway	104	163	166	170	186	136	163	169	171	176	40,568	38,317
Poland	291	397	428	442	474	310	397	407	423	445	12,409	11,661
Portugal	132	178	195	184	190	147	178	181	179	181	18,098	17,194
Slovakia	44	58	68	71	74	48	58	63	66	70	13,752	12,915
Spain	631	849	981	1,042	1,105	694	849	902	929	958	25,875	22,439
Sweden	190	241	253	264	280	206	241	248	253	262	31,139	29,148
Switzerland [6]	186	219	239	246	260	198	219	222	221	226	34,710	30,169
Turkey [6]	343	459	454	478	543	379	459	459	485	529	7,562	7,364
United Kingdom	1,152	1,506	1,719	1,763	1,843	1,285	1,506	1,571	1,610	1,661	30,806	27,765
United States	7,342	9,765	10,418	10,919	11,679	7,973	9,765	9,998	10,269	10,704	39,732	36,414

[1] The goods and services produced in different countries should be valued consistently if the differences observed are meant to reflect real differences in the volumes of goods and services produced. The use of purchasing power parities (PPPs) instead of exchange rates is intended to achieve this objective. PPPs show how many units of currency are needed in one country to buy the same amount of goods and services which one unit of currency will buy in the other country. See text of this section. [2] Based on constant (2000) price data converted to U.S. dollars using 2000 PPPs. [3] Excluding Czech Republic, Hungary, Poland, and Slovakia. [4] OECD Europe: Austria, Belgium, Denmark, Finland, France, Germany, Greece, Iceland, Ireland, Italy, Luxembourg, Netherlands, Norway, Portugal, Spain, Sweden, Switzerland, Turkey, United Kingdom. [5] Based on System of National Accounts, 1968. [6] Includes overseas departments.

Source: Organization for Economic Cooperation and Development, Paris, France, "National Accounts of OECD Countries annual, Vol. 1"; published July 2006.

Comparative International Statistics   837

Table 1317. Average Annual Percent Changes in International Economic Composite Indexes by Country: 1990 to 2006

[Change from previous year; derived from indexes with base 2000 = 100. The coincident index changes are for calendar years and the leading index changes are for years ending June 30 because they lead the coincident indexes by about 6 months, on average. The G-7 countries are United States, Canada, France, Germany, Italy, United Kingdom, and Japan. Minus sign (−) indicates decrease]

Country	Leading index						Coincident index					
	1990	2000	2003	2004	2005	2006	1990	2000	2003	2004	2005	2006
Total, 13 countries	2.1	6.3	2.9	7.5	4.6	5.7	4.5	5.0	0.4	3.7	2.4	4.2
12 countries, excluding U.S.	3.8	7.7	1.7	7.4	5.7	6.2	6.8	5.4	0.8	3.6	2.1	4.6
G-7 countries	2.0	6.0	2.8	7.5	4.6	5.7	4.5	4.8	0.1	3.5	2.2	4.1
North America	−0.9	4.1	4.9	7.4	2.8	4.9	−0.2	4.8	0.0	3.9	2.7	3.4
United States	−1.0	3.9	5.1	7.8	2.8	4.9	−0.1	4.4	−0.7	3.8	2.7	3.3
Canada	−1.1	7.1	2.0	3.1	3.1	4.9	−1.7	9.7	2.8	4.8	3.5	3.6
Four European countries	1.8	4.4	−1.3	4.7	5.0	4.9	5.9	9.8	0.2	2.5	1.4	6.1
France	1.5	1.5	−2.3	5.0	6.8	5.9	5.7	14.4	−1.1	1.4	2.0	4.7
Germany	4.5	6.2	−1.5	6.8	6.7	6.7	7.2	7.9	−3.0	1.2	−1.3	6.2
Italy	0.2	7.2	0.1	1.6	2.7	4.5	9.3	16.2	4.8	5.0	4.2	10.5
United Kingdom	−0.3	2.5	−0.6	3.3	1.8	1.1	0.9	4.0	4.1	4.8	3.3	3.8
Seven Pacific region countries . .	6.1	11.2	4.7	10.5	6.5	7.6	8.1	1.2	1.2	4.5	2.7	3.2
Australia	−1.4	8.2	3.0	4.5	3.1	1.1	−0.4	5.1	6.0	7.9	4.7	4.4
Taiwan [1]	4.9	8.5	6.8	11.5	6.7	4.9	5.1	4.9	3.2	8.3	4.3	3.3
Thailand	12.1	9.5	6.7	13.8	5.7	5.2	11.6	9.4	8.9	8.2	6.5	2.7
Japan	6.6	11.3	4.5	11.1	6.8	8.1	8.6	−0.5	0.5	4.0	2.3	3.0
Korea, South	6.5	15.9	6.6	8.9	7.1	12.3	9.9	13.7	1.9	4.6	4.3	5.9
Malaysia	−0.8	12.7	6.2	4.6	1.6	0.4	1.5	3.5	−2.3	−1.2	−4.1	−2.7
New Zealand	0.8	4.6	−0.4	5.5	2.7	2.1	−1.2	2.7	6.2	9.3	5.1	1.1

[1] See footnote 2, Table 1298.

Source: Foundation for International Business and Economic Research, New York, NY, *International Economic Indicators*, monthly.

Table 1318. Sectoral Contributions to Gross Value Added: 1994 and 2004

[In percent. According to the 1993 System of National Accounts (SNA) and the International Standard Industrial Classification (ISIC), Revision 3. Value added is estimated at basic prices and includes financial intermediation services indirectly measured (FISIM). It represents an industry's contribution to national GDP and is calculated as the difference between production and intermediate inputs. Value added comprises labor costs, consumption of fixed capital, indirect taxes less subsidies, and net operating surplus and mixed income]

| Country | Agriculture | | Industry | | | | | |
| | | | Total | | Manufacturing | | Services | |
	1994	2004	1994	2004	1994	2004	1994	2004
United States [1]	1.9	1.3	[2]26.4	[2]22.0	[3]17.5	[3]13.2	[4]71.7	[4]76.7
Australia	3.4	3.3	28.9	27.0	15.1	12.4	67.6	69.7
Austria	3.0	1.9	30.2	29.7	19.0	20.0	66.8	68.4
Belgium	1.7	1.0	27.7	24.8	[5]20.2	17.3	70.5	74.2
Canada	2.7	[6]2.2	30.0	[6]30.9	17.1	[6]17.6	67.3	[6]67.0
Czech Republic	4.9	3.3	38.8	37.9	[5]23.2	25.9	56.1	58.8
Denmark.	3.2	1.9	24.6	24.1	16.9	13.6	72.2	74.0
Finland.	5.1	3.1	31.0	30.2	[5]25.0	22.1	63.9	66.7
France	3.3	2.5	24.7	21.3	(NA)	13.8	73.1	76.3
Germany	1.2	1.1	32.9	29.1	23.1	22.7	65.9	69.8
Greece	10.3	5.7	22.9	21.3	[5]13.1	11.1	66.3	73.1
Hungary	6.4	3.9	30.0	30.9	(NA)	22.5	63.7	65.2
Iceland	10.5	6.7	27.9	24.8	[7]16.0	12.8	61.6	68.4
Ireland	7.9	2.5	36.2	37.5	[5]30.1	27.0	55.9	60.0
Italy	3.3	2.5	30.1	27.3	21.7	19.0	66.6	70.2
Japan [8]	2.1	1.6	33.9	29.0	[9]22.4	20.2	64.0	69.4
Korea	6.7	3.8	41.6	40.7	27.2	28.6	51.7	55.6
Luxembourg	1.0	0.6	22.3	16.7	[5]13.7	9.4	76.7	82.7
Mexico	5.6	3.8	26.0	26.0	18.2	17.8	68.4	70.2
Netherlands	3.4	2.1	26.6	23.9	(NA)	14.0	69.7	74.0
New Zealand [10]	7.3	[11]9.1	26.7	[11]24.1	18.6	[11]16.0	66.0	[11]66.8
Norway.	3.0	1.5	32.9	39.2	12.8	[12]10.8	64.1	59.2
Poland	6.4	2.9	26.2	32.1	22.2	20.2	57.4	65.0
Portugal	6.1	3.3	27.6	25.0	18.6	[12]15.8	66.3	71.7
Slovakia	6.7	3.9	38.1	32.1	22.3	21.0	55.2	64.0
Spain	4.8	3.5	28.9	29.2	(NA)	16.3	66.3	67.3
Sweden	2.7	1.8	28.7	27.7	20.4	[12]19.7	68.7	70.5
Switzerland	2.0	[12]1.2	30.4	[12]26.4	20.4	[12]18.5	67.6	[12]72.3
Turkey [10, 13]	15.4	11.5	32.9	29.0	21.9	20.7	51.7	59.6
United Kingdom	1.7	1.0	30.6	24.3	20.7	14.4	67.7	74.7

NA Not available.   [1] Value added is estimated at factor cost.   [2] Sanitary and similar services are included under industry.   [3] Contribution to GDP instead of value added.   [4] Includes government enterprises.   [5] 1995.   [6] 2002.   [7] 1997.   [8] Value added is estimated approximately at market prices.   [9] 1996.   [10] Value added is estimated at producer's prices.   [11] 2001.   [12] 2003.   [13] According to 1968 SNA (System of National Accounts).

Source: Organization for Economic Cooperation and Development, Paris, France, *OECD in Figures*, 2006–07 (copyright). See also <http://www.oecd.org/document/43/0,3343,en_2649_201185_37806443_1_1_1,00.html>.

Table 1319. Index of Industrial Production by Country: 1980 to 2005

[Annual averages of monthly data. Industrial production index measures output in the manufacturing, mining, and electric, gas, and water utilities industries. Minus sign (–) indicates decrease]

Country	Index (2000 = 100)								Annual percent change				
	1980	1990	1995	2000	2002	2003	2004	2005	2000–2001	2001–2002	2002–2003	2003–2004	2004–2005
OECD, total. . . .	62.1	78.1	83.4	100.0	97.9	99.4	102.8	105.1	–2.4	0.3	1.5	3.4	2.2
Australia	61.9	80.4	87.0	100.0	103.3	103.4	103.7	104.9	0.1	3.2	0.1	0.3	1.2
Austria . [1]	52.6	60.0	74.5	100.0	103.6	105.6	112.3	117.3	2.8	0.8	1.9	6.3	4.5
Belgium [1]	70.6	85.9	86.5	100.0	100.3	101.1	104.3	103.9	–1.0	1.3	0.8	3.2	–0.4
Canada . . . . . . [1] . .	55.8	69.1	78.6	100.0	97.5	98.1	100.1	101.4	–4.0	1.6	0.6	2.0	1.3
Czech Republic [1] . .	(X)	119.9	90.6	100.0	108.7	114.7	125.7	134.0	6.7	1.9	5.5	9.6	6.6
Denmark.	57.5	75.8	86.5	100.0	103.0	103.2	103.2	104.9	1.6	1.4	0.2	–	1.6
Finland.	45.5	60.3	69.1	100.0	102.0	103.2	108.4	105.8	–0.2	2.2	1.2	5.0	–2.4
France . . [1]	75.9	86.5	87.0	100.0	100.0	99.6	102.1	102.3	1.2	–1.2	–0.4	2.5	0.2
Germany [2]	75.2	90.7	87.4	100.0	99.1	99.6	102.6	106.1	0.2	–1.1	0.5	3.0	3.4
Greece. . [1]	75.6	83.2	81.7	100.0	99.0	99.3	100.2	99.5	–1.8	0.8	0.3	0.9	–0.7
Hungary [1]	69.3	67.6	59.4	100.0	106.4	113.2	121.5	129.9	3.6	2.7	6.4	7.3	6.9
Ireland	16.8	30.9	49.6	100.0	117.9	123.5	123.8	127.6	10.0	7.2	4.7	0.2	3.1
Italy . . [1]	76.6	86.4	93.0	100.0	97.4	96.9	96.3	95.5	–1.0	–1.6	–0.5	–0.6	–0.8
Japan [1]	66.8	98.5	95.5	100.0	92.6	95.4	100.5	101.7	–6.3	–1.2	3.0	5.3	1.2
Korea, South [1] . . .	14.3	43.1	64.9	100.0	108.8	114.6	126.3	134.1	0.7	8.0	5.3	10.2	6.2
Luxembourg	55.4	79.5	81.3	100.0	105.2	110.7	117.8	125.2	3.1	2.0	5.2	6.4	6.3
Mexico [3]	56.6	67.3	70.4	100.0	96.4	96.3	100.3	101.9	–3.5	–0.1	–0.1	4.2	1.6
Netherlands	76.3	83.9	90.9	100.0	101.5	100.1	102.6	101.4	0.6	0.9	–1.4	2.5	–1.2
New Zealand.	(NA)	83.1	94.9	100.0	105.8	108.2	111.6	108.7	–0.4	6.2	2.3	3.1	–2.6
Norway.	46.3	71.5	90.3	100.0	99.6	95.5	97.4	96.9	–1.3	0.9	–4.1	2.0	–0.5
Poland	(NA)	61.0	69.7	100.0	101.8	110.7	124.8	129.9	0.4	1.4	8.7	12.7	4.1
Portugal	54.7	87.2	84.7	100.0	102.7	102.7	102.6	100.0	3.1	–0.4	–0.1	–2.5	0.3
Spain . . [4]	66.9	80.6	83.7	100.0	98.7	100.1	101.6	102.4	–1.4	0.1	1.4	1.5	0.8
Sweden [4] [5]	51.7	69.1	83.4	100.0	98.8	100.2	105.4	107.3	–1.1	–0.1	1.4	5.2	1.8
Switzerland	64.9	79.1	82.2	100.0	94.2	94.5	98.4	101.0	–0.7	–5.1	0.3	4.1	2.6
Turkey	(NA)	70.5	82.5	100.0	99.9	108.7	119.3	125.7	–8.7	9.4	8.8	9.8	5.4
United Kingdom . . .	71.5	87.7	93.2	100.0	96.6	96.3	97.1	95.3	–1.5	–1.9	–0.3	0.8	–1.9
United States	54.2	66.3	77.0	100.0	96.5	97.6	100.0	103.2	–3.5	–	1.1	2.5	3.2

– Represents or rounds to zero.   NA Not available.   X Not applicable.   [1] Not adjusted for unequal number of working days in the month.   [2] Data prior to 1991 are for former West Germany.   [3] Including construction.   [4] Mining and manufacturing. [5] Annual figures correspond to official annual figures and differ from the average of the monthly figures.

Source: Organization for Economic Cooperation and Development, Paris, France, *Main Economic Indicators*, monthly (copyright).

Table 1320. Annual Percent Change in Labor Productivity and Hours Worked by Country: 1995 to 2006

[Change for period shown. For OECD countries and Eastern Europe, labor productivity growth refers to the growth in gross domestic product per hour worked. Data are derived from an annual database maintained by the Groningen Growth and Development Centre at the University of Groningen, Netherlands, in association with The Conference Board. Growth for regional aggregates is calculated based on the sum of gross domestic product divided by the sum of total hours worked. Gross domestic product for each country was converted based on the 2002 OECD benchmark for purchasing power parities and updated to 2006 using the aggregate inflation rate for each country relative to U.S. inflation. Minus sign (–) indicates decrease]

Country	Labor productivity		Total hours worked		Country	Labor productivity		Total hours worked	
	1995–2000	2000–2006	1995–2000	2000–2006		1995–2000	2000–2006	1995–2000	2000–2006
All OECD	2.0	1.9	1.2	0.4	European Union (EU-10, new) [3]	3.6	3.9	–0.4	0.4
All OECD, excl. United States	1.8	1.7	1.0	0.5	Bulgaria	0.8	2.7	–1.6	2.3
United States	2.3	2.3	1.8	0.2	Cyprus	1.8	(Z)	2.0	3.3
					Czech Republic	2.4	3.9	–0.9	(Z)
European Union (EU-25, enlarged) [1] . .	2.1	1.5	0.8	0.6	Estonia	8.4	6.9	–2.1	1.7
					Hungary	2.4	3.8	1.6	0.3
European Union (EU-15, old) [2]	1.8	1.1	1.1	0.6	Latvia	6.1	7.0	–0.7	1.5
Austria	3.0	1.7	–0.1	(Z)	Lithuania	5.3	6.6	–0.6	1.1
Belgium	1.8	1.2	0.9	0.5	Malta	4.4	(Z)	0.7	0.7
Denmark.	1.1	1.2	1.7	0.5	Poland	5.5	3.3	–0.1	(Z)
Finland.	2.8	2.3	2.0	0.6	Slovakia	5.3	4.7	–1.5	0.5
France	2.1	1.7	0.7	–0.1	Slovenia	4.7	3.6	–0.3	0.1
Germany.	2.0	1.4	(Z)	–0.5	Romania	–0.6	5.6	–0.7	0.4
Greece.	2.0	3.0	1.4	1.3	Other OECD members. .	1.5	2.0	1.2	0.5
Ireland	6.3	2.6	3.8	2.5	Japan	1.7	2.3	–0.7	–0.6
Italy	1.0	(Z)	0.9	0.8	Australia	2.3	1.5	1.6	1.7
Luxembourg	2.4	1.5	3.6	1.8	Canada	1.7	1.3	2.4	1.3
Netherlands	1.8	1.4	2.3	0.1	Iceland	2.2	3.5	2.5	0.6
Portugal	3.4	0.3	0.7	0.4	Mexico	1.4	1.2	4.0	1.1
Spain	–0.1	–0.3	4.2	3.7	New Zealand	1.4	0.8	1.1	2.5
Sweden	2.5	2.6	0.8	0.1	Norway	2.3	1.9	1.3	0.3
U.K.	2.2	1.9	1.0	0.5	South Korea	3.7	3.7	0.6	0.9
					Switzerland	1.5	1.4	0.5	(Z)
					Turkey	2.7	4.3	1.2	0.3

Z Less than .05 percent.   [1] Referring to all members of the European Union as of 1 May 2004, and including Bulgaria and Romania, who joined on 1 January 2007.   [2] Referring to membership of the European Union until 30 April 2004.   [3] Referring to new membership of the European Union as of 1 May 2004, and including Bulgaria and Romania, who joined on 1 January 2007.

Source: The Conference Board, New York, NY, *Performance 2007: Productivity, Employment, and Income in the World's Economies*, by Bart van Ark, Catherine Guillemineau and Robert H. McGuckin, 2007 (copyright). See also <http://www.conference-board.org/economics/research.cfm>.

Comparative International Statistics   839

Table 1321. Annual Percent Changes in Consumer Prices, by Country: 2000 to 2006

[Change from previous year. See text of this section for general comments concerning the data. For additional qualifications of the data for individual countries, see source. Minus sign (–) indicates decrease]

Country	2000	2003	2004	2005	2006	Country	2000	2003	2004	2005	2006
United States	3.4	2.3	2.7	3.4	3.2	Kenya	10.0	9.8	11.6	10.3	14.5
Argentina	-0.9	13.4	4.4	9.6	10.9	Korea, South	2.2	3.5	3.6	2.8	2.2
Australia	4.5	2.8	2.3	2.7	3.5						
Austria	2.4	1.4	2.1	2.3	1.5	Malaysia	1.5	1.1	1.5	3.0	3.6
Bangladesh	2.4	5.7	9.2	7.0	6.8	Mexico	9.5	4.6	4.7	4.0	3.6
Belgium	2.5	1.6	2.1	2.8	1.8	Netherlands	2.5	2.1	1.2	1.7	1.1
Bolivia	4.6	3.3	4.4	5.4	4.3	Nigeria	14.5	14.1	19.4	13.5	(NA)
Brazil	7.0	14.7	6.6	6.9	4.2	Norway	3.1	2.5	0.5	1.5	(NA)
Canada	2.7	2.8	1.8	2.2	2.0	Pakistan	4.4	2.9	7.4	9.1	7.9
Chile	3.8	2.8	1.1	3.1	3.4	Peru	3.8	2.3	3.7	1.6	2.0
Colombia	9.2	7.1	5.9	5.1	4.3	Philippines	4.4	3.5	6.0	7.6	6.2
Egypt	2.7	4.5	11.3	4.9	7.6	Portugal	2.8	3.3	2.4	2.3	2.7
France	1.7	2.1	2.2	1.7	1.7	Romania	45.7	15.3	11.9	9.0	6.6
Germany	1.5	1.1	1.7	2.0	1.7	Russia	20.8	13.7	10.9	12.7	9.7
Ghana	25.2	26.7	12.6	15.1	10.9	South Africa	5.4	5.9	1.4	3.4	4.6
Greece	3.1	3.5	2.9	3.6	3.2	Spain	3.4	3.0	3.0	3.4	3.5
Guatemala	6.0	5.5	7.4	8.4	6.5	Sri Lanka	6.2	6.3	7.6	11.6	13.7
India	4.0	3.8	3.8	4.3	5.8	Sweden	0.9	1.9	0.4	0.5	1.4
Indonesia	4.5	6.6	6.2	10.5	13.1	Switzerland	1.5	0.6	0.8	1.2	1.1
Iran	14.5	16.5	14.8	13.4	(NA)	Thailand	1.6	1.8	2.8	4.5	4.6
Israel	1.1	0.7	-0.4	1.3	2.1	Turkey	54.9	25.3	8.6	8.2	9.5
Italy	2.5	2.7	2.2	2.0	2.1	United Kingdom	2.9	2.9	3.0	2.8	3.2
Japan	-0.7	-0.3	0.0	-0.3	0.2	Venezuela	16.2	31.1	21.8	16.0	(NA)

NA Not available.

Source: International Monetary Fund, Washington, DC, *International Financial Statistics*, monthly (copyright).

Table 1322. Comparative Price Levels—Selected OECD Countries: 2007

[Purchasing power parities (PPPS) are the rates of currency conversion that eliminate the differences in price levels between countries. Comparative price levels are defined as the ratios of PPPs to exchange rates. The PPPs are given in national currency units per U.S. dollar. The table is to be read vertically. Each column shows the number of specified monetary units needed in each of the countries listed to buy the same representative basket of consumer goods and services. In each case, the representative basket costs a hundred units in the country whose currency is specified. Example of data: An item that costs $1.00 in the United States would cost $1.18 (U.S. dollars) in Japan]

Country	United States (U.S. dollar)	Canada (Canadian dollar)	Mexico (Mexican peso)	Japan (yen)	France (euro)	Germany (euro)	Italy (euro)	United Kingdom (pound)
United States	100	91	143	85	82	82	88	85
Australia[1]	115	105	165	98	95	94	102	98
Austria	121	110	172	102	99	99	106	103
Belgium	118	108	169	100	97	97	104	100
Canada	110	100	157	93	90	90	97	93
Czech Republic	69	63	99	59	57	57	61	59
Denmark	155	141	221	131	127	127	136	131
Finland	138	126	197	117	114	113	122	117
France	121	111	173	103	100	99	107	103
Germany	122	111	174	104	101	100	108	104
Greece	101	92	144	86	83	83	89	86
Hungary	76	69	108	64	62	62	67	64
Iceland	165	151	236	140	136	135	146	141
Ireland	151	138	215	128	124	123	133	128
Italy	114	104	162	96	93	93	100	96
Japan	118	108	169	100	97	97	104	100
Korea, South	94	86	134	79	77	77	83	80
Luxembourg	120	110	172	102	99	99	106	102
Mexico	70	64	100	59	58	57	62	60
Netherlands	120	109	171	102	99	98	106	102
New Zealand[1]	111	102	159	94	92	91	98	95
Norway	155	142	222	132	128	127	137	132
Poland	69	63	99	59	57	57	61	59
Portugal	92	84	131	78	75	75	81	78
Slovakia	76	70	109	65	63	63	67	65
Spain	104	95	148	88	86	85	92	88
Sweden	134	122	191	113	110	109	118	114
Switzerland	145	132	207	123	119	118	127	123
Turkey	73	66	104	62	60	59	64	62
United Kingdom	118	107	168	100	97	96	104	100

[1] Estimates based on quarterly consumer prices.

Source: Organization for Economic Cooperation and Development, Paris, France, *Main Economic Indicators*, April 2007 (copyright). See also <http://www.oecd.org/dataoecd/48/18/18598721.pdf>.

Table 1323. Percent of Household Final Consumption Expenditures Spent on Food, Alcohol, and Tobacco Consumed at Home by Selected Countries: 2004

Country/Territory	Food [1]	Alcoholic beverages and tobacco	Country/Territory	Food [1]	Alcoholic beverages and tobacco
United States	7.5	2.2	Saudi Arabia	22.0	1.2
Ireland	7.5	6.2	Latvia	22.7	9.2
United Kingdom	9.1	3.9	Estonia	23.1	9.5
Canada.	9.7	3.8	Vietnam	24.2	6.1
Australia	10.6	4.5	Taiwan [2]	24.2	2.1
Netherlands	10.8	3.1	Mexico	24.9	2.6
Switzerland	11.1	3.6	Colombia.	26.2	4.6
United Arab Emirates. . .	11.2	0.7	China [2]	26.4	2.3
Germany.	11.9	4.0	Turkey	27.0	4.8
Korea, South	11.9	2.0	Russia	28.5	10.2
Belgium	12.0	3.2	Lithuania	28.6	7.3
Brazil	12.7	3.3	Ecuador	29.0	6.1
Sweden	12.7	4.0	Thailand	29.2	7.4
Austria	12.8	3.0	Chile	29.6	2.4
Singapore	12.8	1.8	Bolivia	29.9	2.6
Finland	12.8	5.9	Tunisia	30.8	3.4
Hong Kong	13.0	0.7	Romania	31.0	8.4
New Zealand	13.5	4.7	Peru.	31.3	2.6
Norway.	13.9	4.5	Morocco	34.9	2.3
Japan.	14.4	3.2	Croatia	35.3	5.9
France	14.9	3.5	Algeria	37.6	3.1
Italy	14.9	2.4	Bulgaria	37.6	8.3
Spain	17.1	3.4	Philippines.	37.7	1.6
Venezuela.	17.3	2.8	Egypt	39.1	0.9
Slovenia	17.9	4.6	Ukraine.	40.7	7.0
Czech Republic	18.0	8.5	Kazakhstan	44.2	4.3
South Africa.	18.7	8.7	Belarus	46.1	7.5
Portugal	19.6	4.4	Jordan	46.2	5.1
Hungary	19.8	8.5	Turkmenistan	47.8	2.5
Israel	20.2	1.8	Nigeria	54.3	2.9
Poland	21.0	7.1	Indonesia	55.1	4.8
Malaysia	21.5	2.6	Pakistan	57.2	3.1
Slovakia	21.8	5.3	Azerbaijan	57.3	3.0
Kuwait	21.9	1.3			

[1] Includes nonalcoholic beverages. [2] See footnote 2, Table 1298.
Source: U.S. Department of Agriculture, Economic Research Service; Food, CPI, Prices and Expenditures: Expenditure Tables; <http://www.ers.usda.gov/Briefing/CPIFoodAndExpenditures/Data/>.

Table 1324. Gross Public Debt, Expenditures, and Receipts by Country: 1990 to 2006

[Percent of nominal gross domestic product. Gross debt includes one-off revenues from the sale of the mobile telephone licenses. Expenditures and receipts refer to the general government sector, which is a consolidation of accounts for the central, state, and local governments plus social security. Expenditures, or total outlays, are defined as current outlays plus capital outlays. Receipts cover current receipts, but exclude capital receipts. Nontax receipts consist of property income (including dividends and other transfers from public enterprises), fees, charges, sales, fines, capital transfers received by the general government, etc.). Minus sign (–) indicates deficit]

Country	Gross debt			Expenditures			Receipts		
	1990	2000	2006	1990	2000	2006	1990	2000	2006
United States [1]	-4.2	1.6	-2.3	37.1	34.2	36.5	32.8	35.8	34.2
Australia.	-2.1	[2]0.9	2.5	35.7	[2]34.8	34.0	33.6	35.7	36.5
Austria	-2.5	[2]-1.6	-1.3	51.5	[2]51.4	49.1	48.9	49.7	47.8
Belgium	-6.7	(Z)	(Z)	52.2	49.0	49.0	45.5	49.1	49.0
Canada.	-5.8	2.9	0.9	48.8	41.1	39.5	43.0	44.1	40.5
Czech Republic	(X)	-3.7	-3.7	(X)	41.7	42.9	(X)	38.0	39.2
Denmark.	-1.3	2.3	3.4	55.9	53.9	51.8	54.6	56.2	55.2
Finland	5.4	6.9	2.5	48.0	48.3	48.9	53.4	55.2	51.4
France	-2.3	-1.5	-2.7	49.4	51.6	53.8	47.1	50.1	51.1
Germany.	-1.9	[2]1.3	-2.3	43.6	[2]45.1	45.9	41.7	46.4	43.5
Greece.	-15.4	-4.1	-2.6	49.2	51.2	45.6	33.8	47.1	42.9
Hungary	(NA)	-3.0	-8.7	(NA)	46.6	50.5	(NA)	43.6	41.8
Iceland	-3.3	2.4	4.1	41.5	42.1	43.3	38.3	44.5	47.5
Ireland	-2.8	4.6	1.0	43.1	31.6	[2]34.6	40.3	36.2	35.6
Italy	-11.4	[2]-0.9	-4.8	52.9	[2]46.1	[3]49.6	41.5	45.3	44.9
Japan [4]	2.1	-7.7	-4.6	31.8	39.2	36.3	33.9	31.5	31.7
Korea, South.	3.1	5.4	2.2	20.0	[2]39.9	29.8	23.1	29.3	31.9
Netherlands	-5.1	[2]2.0	-0.4	52.9	[2]44.0	46.7	47.8	46.0	46.3
New Zealand.	-4.6	[2]1.6	3.5	53.2	[2]39.6	40.0	48.7	41.2	43.4
Norway.	2.2	15.6	19.3	54.0	42.7	41.8	56.2	58.2	61.1
Portugal	-6.3	[2]-3.0	-4.6	40.3	[2]43.1	47.5	34.0	40.2	42.8
Spain	-3.9	[2]-0.9	1.4	42.6	[2]39.0	38.0	38.7	38.1	39.4
Sweden	3.4	5.0	2.9	61.3	56.8	55.9	64.7	61.8	58.8
United Kingdom	-1.8	[2]4.0	-3.0	42.4	[2]37.5	45.3	40.6	41.5	42.3

NA Not available.   X Not applicable.   Z Less than 0.05.   [1] Receipts exclude the operating surpluses of public enterprises, while expenditures include them.   [2] Includes substantial one-off revenues from the sale of the mobil telephone licenses.   [3] Outlays include a one-off refund of VAT receipts amounting to 0.9 percentage points of GDP.   [4] The 2000 expenditures include capital transfers to the Deposit Insurance Company. Receipts include deferred tax payments on postal savings accounts in 2000.
Source: Organization for Economic Cooperation and Development, Paris, France, *OECD Economic Outlook*, December 2006 (copyright).

Table 1325. Percent Distribution of Tax Receipts by Country: 1990 to 2005

Country	Total [1]	Income and profits taxes [2]			Social security contributions			Taxes on goods and services [5]		
		Total [3]	Individual	Corporate	Total [4]	Employees	Employers	Total [3]	General consumption taxes [6]	Taxes on specific goods and services [7]
United States:										
1990.........	100.0	45.4	37.7	7.7	25.9	11.0	13.4	17.3	8.0	7.1
2000.........	100.0	50.7	41.9	8.7	23.2	10.4	11.6	16.1	7.6	6.3
2005.........	100.0	46.7	35.8	10.9	24.7	10.9	12.6	17.2	8.1	6.6
Canada:										
1990.........	100.0	48.6	40.8	7.0	12.2	4.4	7.6	25.8	14.1	10.3
2000.........	100.0	50.1	36.8	12.2	13.6	5.5	7.8	24.2	14.3	8.5
2005.........	100.0	47.9	36.1	10.5	14.6	5.9	8.2	25.3	14.9	9.0
France:										
1990.........	100.0	17.2	11.8	5.3	44.1	13.2	27.2	28.4	18.8	8.7
2000.........	100.0	24.9	18.0	6.9	36.0	8.9	24.8	25.7	16.9	8.2
2005.........	100.0	23.5	17.2	6.3	36.9	9.3	25.0	25.5	17.1	7.8
Germany:										
1990.........	100.0	32.4	27.6	4.8	37.5	16.2	19.1	26.7	16.6	9.2
2000.........	100.0	30.1	25.3	4.8	39.0	17.2	19.2	28.1	18.4	8.8
2005.........	100.0	28.2	23.0	5.2	39.9	17.4	19.2	29.0	18.0	9.9
Italy:										
1990.........	100.0	36.5	26.3	10.0	32.9	6.3	23.6	28.0	14.7	10.6
2000.........	100.0	33.2	24.9	6.8	28.6	5.4	19.9	27.8	15.4	9.7
2005.........	100.0	31.5	25.6	6.9	30.8	5.6	21.6	26.4	14.7	9.3
Japan:										
1990.........	100.0	48.5	26.9	21.6	29.0	11.0	15.0	13.2	4.3	7.3
2000.........	100.0	34.8	21.1	13.8	35.1	14.7	16.4	19.3	9.1	8.0
2005.........	100.0	52.9	28.4	24.4	(NA)	(NA)	(NA)	31.3	15.3	12.4
United Kingdom:										
1990.........	100.0	38.3	27.1	11.2	16.7	6.5	9.7	30.5	16.4	12.4
2000.........	100.0	39.1	29.3	9.7	16.9	6.8	9.5	32.0	18.3	12.3
2005.........	100.0	38.5	29.2	9.3	18.9	7.8	10.5	30.3	18.6	10.5

NA Not available. [1] Includes property taxes, employer payroll taxes other than Social Security contributions, and miscellaneous taxes, not shown separately. [2] Includes taxes on capital gains. [3] Includes other taxes not shown separately. [4] Includes contributions of self-employed not shown separately. [5] Taxes on the production, sales, transfer, leasing, and delivery of goods and services and rendering of services. [6] Primary value-added and sales taxes. [7] For example, excise taxes on alcohol, tobacco, and gasoline.

Source: Organization for Economic Cooperation and Development, Paris, France, *Revenue Statistics of OECD Member Countries,* annual (copyright).

Table 1326. Income Tax and Social Security Contributions as Percent of Labor Costs: 2004

[Data are for a single individual at the income level of the average production worker]

Country	Labor costs per worker [1] (dol.)	Percent of labor costs		Social security contributions	
		Total [2]	Income tax	Employee	Employer [3]
Belgium	46,261	54	27	14	14
Germany	42,543	51	20	21	10
Australia.............	40,630	29	24	–	4
Netherlands	39,614	44	9	26	9
Switzerland	38,213	29	10	11	8
Norway..............	37,550	37	21	8	8
Denmark.............	37,788	41	31	11	–
Luxembourg	35,767	32	9	14	9
Canada	37,856	32	18	7	8
Korea, South	36,125	17	2	7	7
Finland..............	37,174	44	24	6	13
United States	**37,606**	**30**	**17**	**8**	**5**
Italy................	35,005	46	19	9	18
France	35,443	47	13	14	21
Austria	34,356	45	11	18	16
United Kingdom	36,159	31	16	9	7
Japan	35,103	27	6	12	9
Sweden	34,606	48	24	7	17
Iceland..............	32,194	30	25	–	4
New Zealand.........	28,228	21	21	–	–
Ireland..............	30,236	24	11	5	8
Spain...............	29,382	38	13	6	19
Czech Republic	19,395	44	11	13	20
Greece..............	22,138	35	1	16	18
Turkey	20,003	43	15	15	12
Poland..............	17,319	43	6	25	12
Portugal.............	16,128	33	6	11	16
Hungary.............	13,229	46	12	14	20
Mexico..............	10,278	15	3	2	11

– Represents or rounds to zero. [1] Adjusted for purchasing power parities, see text of this section. Labor costs include gross wages plus employers' compulsory social security contributions. [2] Due to rounding, total may differ one percentage point from aggregate columns for income tax and social security contributions. [3] Includes reported payroll taxes.

Source: Organization for Economic Cooperation and Development, Paris, France, *Taxing Wages, 2003–2004* (copyright).

Table 1327. Household Tax Burden by Country: 2005

[Percent of gross wage earnings of the average production worker. The tax burden reflects income tax plus employee social security contributions less cash benefits]

Country	Single person without children	One-earner family with two children	Country	Single person without children	One-earner family with two children
Australia	24.0	10.9	Korea, South	9.9	8.6
Austria	32.1	16.7	Luxembourg	26.5	0.3
Belgium	41.9	22.2	Mexico	7.9	7.9
Canada	23.5	12.3	Netherlands	32.2	21.7
Czech Republic	24.1	1.5	New Zealand	20.5	14.5
Denmark	41.0	29.2	Norway	29.0	20.4
Finland	31.3	23.6	Poland	32.0	30.3
France	29.0	17.1	Portugal	21.1	9.1
Germany	41.7	22.3	Slovakia	22.1	3.0
Greece	21.6	22.1	Spain	20.3	13.0
Hungary	32.9	18.4	Sweden	31.0	23.7
Iceland	24.9	5.9	Switzerland	21.7	9.6
Ireland	17.7	-1.8	Turkey	30.4	30.4
Italy	27.3	13.7	United Kingdom	26.5	19.4
Japan	18.5	15.3	United States	23.6	5.0

Source: Organization for Economic Cooperation and Development, Paris, France, *Taxing Wages, 2004–2005*, (copyright).

Table 1328. Civilian Labor Force, Employment, and Unemployment by Country: 1990 to 2006

[125,840 represents 125,840,000. Data based on U.S. labor force definitions (see source) except that minimum age for population base varies as follows: United States, Canada, France, Sweden, and United Kingdom, 16 years; Australia, Japan, Netherlands, Germany, and Italy (beginning 1993), 15 years; and Italy (prior to 1993) 14 years]

Year	United States	Canada	Australia	Japan	France	Germany[1]	Italy	Netherlands	Sweden	United Kingdom
Civilian labor force (1,000):										
1990	125,840	14,043	8,440	63,050	24,159	29,410	22,670	6,767	4,594	28,766
2000	[2]142,583	15,632	9,590	66,990	26,099	39,302	23,361	8,011	4,489	28,952
2004	[2]147,401	16,956	10,244	65,770	26,954	39,711	24,084	8,279	4,576	29,775
2005	149,320	17,114	10,524	65,850	27,071	[2]40,760	24,179	8,291	[2]4,693	30,087
2006	151,428	17,351	10,714	65,956	(NA)	(NA)	24,362	8,353	4,745	30,525
Labor force participation rate:[3]										
1990	66.5	67.3	64.7	62.6	55.7	55.3	47.2	57.0	67.3	64.3
2000	[2]67.1	65.8	64.4	62.0	56.6	56.7	48.1	63.1	63.8	62.9
2004	[2]66.0	67.3	64.7	60.0	56.7	56.4	49.1	63.6	63.7	63.0
2005	66.0	67.0	65.4	60.0	56.6	[2]57.6	48.7	63.4	[2]64.9	63.1
2006	66.2	67.4	65.7	60.0	(NA)	(NA)	48.8	63.7	65.0	63.5
Civilian employment (1,000):										
1990	118,793	12,956	7,877	61,700	22,075	27,950	21,080	6,251	4,513	26,713
2000	[2]136,891	14,676	8,989	63,790	23,714	36,236	20,973	7,781	4,229	27,368
2004	[2]139,252	15,864	9,677	62,640	24,330	35,604	22,124	7,847	4,276	28,358
2005	141,730	16,087	9,987	62,910	24,392	[2]36,185	22,290	7,860	[2]4,333	28,628
2006	144,427	16,393	10,190	63,206	(NA)	(NA)	22,701	7,979	4,413	28,859
Employment-population ratio:[4]										
1990	62.8	62.1	60.4	61.3	50.9	52.6	43.9	52.7	66.1	59.8
2000	[2]64.4	61.9	60.3	59.0	51.4	52.2	43.2	61.3	60.1	59.4
2004	[2]62.3	63.4	61.2	57.1	51.2	50.6	45.1	60.3	59.5	60.0
2005	62.7	63.4	62.1	57.3	51.0	[2]51.2	44.9	60.1	[2]59.9	60.0
2006	63.1	63.6	62.5	57.5	(NA)	(NA)	45.5	60.8	60.4	60.0
Unemployment rate:										
1990	5.6	7.7	6.7	2.1	8.6	5.0	7.0	7.6	1.8	7.1
2000	[2]4.0	6.1	6.3	4.8	9.1	7.8	10.2	2.9	5.8	5.5
2004	[2]5.5	6.4	5.5	4.8	9.7	[2]10.3	8.1	5.1	6.6	4.8
2005	5.1	6.0	5.1	4.5	9.9	[2]11.2	7.8	5.2	[2]7.7	4.8
2006	4.6	5.5	4.9	4.2	9.2	10.3	6.8	4.5	7.0	5.5
Under 25 years old	10.5	10.6	10.3	8.1	(NA)	(NA)	21.6	7.5	21.7	14.2
Teenagers[5]	15.4	14.8	15.1	9.6	(NA)	(NA)	32.4	10.1	31.4	20.2
20 to 24 years old	8.2	8.2	6.9	7.8	(NA)	(NA)	19.3	5.4	16.8	10.5
25 years old and over	3.6	4.6	3.6	3.8	(NA)	(NA)	5.5	3.9	5.0	3.8

NA Not available. [1] Unified Germany for 1991 onward. Prior to 1991, data relate to the former West Germany. [2] Break in series. Data not comparable with prior years. [3] Civilian labor force as a percent of the civilian working-age population. Germany and Japan include the institutionalized population as part of the working-age population. [4] Civilian employment as a percent of the civilian working-age population. Germany and Japan include the institutionalized population as part of the working-age population. [5] 16- to 19-year-olds in the United States, Canada, France, Sweden, and the United Kingdom; 15- to 19-year-olds in Australia, Japan, Germany, Italy, and the Netherlands.

Source: U.S. Bureau of Labor Statistics, *Comparative Civilian Labor Force Statistics, Ten Countries, 1960–2006*, 19 March 2007. See also <http://www.bls.gov/fls/lfcompendium.pdf>.

Comparative International Statistics 843

Table 1329. Percent of Persons Not in Education or at Work by Age Group and Sex: 2004

[Represents those persons not in education and either unemployed or not in the labor force]

Country	15 to 19 years old			20 to 24 years old		
	Total	Male	Female	Total	Male	Female
Australia	7.5	7.6	7.4	12.3	9.8	14.8
Belgium	4.9	5.8	3.9	16.9	15.2	18.5
Canada.	7.5	8.4	6.6	13.0	14.1	11.9
Czech Republic	5.7	5.0	6.4	18.5	15.3	21.9
Denmark.	1.5	0.7	2.3	8.5	7.1	9.8
Finland	5.3	5.1	5.5	13.4	13.6	13.3
France	5.4	6.2	4.5	17.6	16.0	19.1
Germany	3.6	3.5	3.7	17.5	17.3	17.7
Greece	9.2	7.6	10.7	22.3	15.5	29.2
Hungary	6.2	6.6	5.8	18.6	15.3	21.8
Italy	9.7	9.1	10.3	21.1	18.3	23.8
Luxembourg	2.6	2.1	3.1	10.0	7.2	13.0
Mexico	17.0	7.6	26.3	27.4	7.1	46.1
Netherlands.	3.3	2.5	2.2	9.1	7.4	8.3
Poland	2.6	3.0	2.1	24.1	24.5	23.7
Portugal	10.4	9.7	11.0	13.6	12.4	14.8
Spain	10.4	10.0	10.8	16.2	13.6	19.0
Sweden	5.9	7.8	4.0	13.7	14.4	12.9
Switzerland	7.2	7.6	6.8	11.0	10.3	11.7
United States	6.9	6.5	7.3	16.9	13.2	20.6

Source: Organization for Economic Cooperation and Development, Paris, France, *Education at a Glance 2006* (copyright).

Table 1330. Unemployment Rates by Country: 2000 to 2005

[Annual averages. The standardized unemployment rates shown here are calculated as the number of unemployed persons as a percentage of the civilian labor force. The unemployed are persons of working age who, in the reference period, are without work, available for work, and have taken specific steps to find work]

Country	2000	2003	2004	2005	Country	2000	2003	2004	2005
OECD, total	6.2	7.1	6.9	6.6	Ireland	4.3	4.7	4.5	4.4
EU-15 [1]	7.6	8.0	8.1	7.9	Italy	10.1	8.4	8.0	7.7
					Japan	4.7	5.3	4.7	4.4
United States	4.0	6.0	5.5	5.1	Korea, South	4.4	3.6	3.7	3.7
Australia	6.3	6.1	5.5	5.1	Luxembourg	2.3	3.7	5.1	4.5
Austria	3.6	4.3	4.9	5.2	Netherlands	2.8	3.7	4.6	4.7
Belgium	6.9	8.2	8.4	8.4	New Zealand	6.0	4.6	3.9	3.7
Canada.	6.8	7.6	7.2	6.8	Norway	3.4	4.5	4.4	4.6
Czech Republic . . .	8.7	7.8	8.3	7.9	Poland	16.1	19.6	19.0	17.7
Denmark.	4.3	5.4	5.5	4.8	Portugal	4.0	6.2	6.7	7.6
Finland	9.7	9.0	8.9	8.4	Spain	11.1	11.1	10.6	9.2
France	9.1	9.5	9.6	9.9	Sweden	5.6	5.6	6.4	(NA)
Germany	7.2	9.1	9.5	9.4	Switzerland	2.7	4.2	4.4	4.5
Hungary	6.4	5.9	6.1	7.2	United Kingdom . . .	5.4	4.9	4.7	4.8

NA Not available. [1] For list of EU-15 countries, see Table 1320.

Source: Organization for Economic Cooperation and Development, Paris, France, *Main Economic Indicators*, April 2007 and earlier releases.

Table 1331. Female Labor Force Participation Rates by Country: 1980 to 2005

[In percent. Female labor force of all ages divided by female population 15-64 years old]

Country	1980	1990	2000	2005	Country	1980	1990	2000	2005
Australia	52.7	62.1	66.4	69.6	Korea, South	(NA)	51.2	54.3	58.1
Austria	48.7	55.4	62.2	65.7	Luxembourg	39.9	50.7	68.8	89.2
Belgium	47.0	52.4	59.2	60.1	Mexico	33.7	(NA)	42.4	44.6
Canada.	57.8	67.6	70.4	72.8	Netherlands.	35.5	[1]53.1	65.2	68.8
Czech Republic	(X)	69.1	64.3	63.0	New Zealand	44.6	[1]63.0	67.6	72.3
Denmark.	(NA)	78.5	75.9	76.2	Norway	62.3	71.2	76.3	75.4
Finland	70.1	73.8	72.2	73.3	Poland	(NA)	(NA)	59.7	57.8
France	54.4	57.8	62.0	64.5	Portugal	54.3	62.9	67.2	71.7
Germany [2].	52.8	56.7	64.0	67.4	Slovakia	(NA)	(NA)	63.0	61.3
Greece	33.0	43.6	50.2	53.4	Spain	32.2	41.2	50.7	58.4
Hungary	(NA)	(NA)	52.5	54.7	Sweden	74.1	[1]80.4	75.0	76.0
Iceland	(NA)	65.6	82.8	80.5	Switzerland	54.1	65.7	70.6	77.6
Ireland	36.3	43.8	56.2	60.9	Turkey	(NA)	36.7	26.9	27.2
Italy	39.6	45.9	46.8	50.7	United Kingdom	58.3	66.5	67.8	68.8
Japan	54.8	60.3	64.2	65.3	United States	59.7	[1]68.5	71.7	69.9

NA Not available. X Not applicable. [1] Break in series. Data not comparable with prior years. [2] Prior to 1991, data are for former West Germany.

Source: Organization for Economic Cooperation and Development, Paris, France, *OECD in Figures*, annual (copyright). See also <http://www.oecdobserver.org/news/fullstory.php/aid/1988/OECD_in_Figures_2006-2007.html>.

Table 1332. Civilian Employment-Population Ratio: 1990 to 2006

[Civilian employment as a percent of the civilian working-age population. See headnote, Table 1328]

Country	Women					Men				
	1990	1995	2000	2005	2006	1990	1995	2000	2005	2006
United States [1]...	54.3	55.6	57.5	56.2	56.6	72.0	70.8	71.9	69.6	70.1
Canada	54.1	52.6	56.0	58.3	58.9	70.5	66.0	68.1	68.6	68.6
Australia	49.5	50.5	52.5	55.0	55.6	71.4	68.2	68.4	69.4	69.6
Japan	48.0	47.7	46.4	45.7	46.0	75.4	75.0	72.5	69.7	69.8
France	41.5	41.9	44.6	45.5	(NA)	61.4	57.4	59.1	57.0	(NA)
Germany [1,2,3]	40.9	42.7	44.4	44.9	(NA)	65.6	63.1	60.6	57.9	(NA)
Italy [1]	29.2	29.1	31.6	34.1	34.7	60.0	56.2	55.8	56.8	57.3
Netherlands [1]	39.4	44.4	51.5	52.9	53.5	66.5	66.7	71.3	67.5	68.1
Sweden	[3]61.8	54.7	56.1	56.0	56.4	70.6	62.1	64.3	63.9	64.6
United Kingdom..	50.3	49.8	52.5	53.7	53.8	70.0	64.7	66.9	66.7	66.6

NA Not available.   [1] Break in series between 1990 and 1995 for women in United States, Germany, Italy, and Netherlands; and for men, in United States, Germany, and Italy.   [2] Unified Germany for 1991 onward. Prior to 1991, data relate to the former West Germany. Break in series between 1995 and 2000.   [3] Break in series between 2000 and 2005.

Source: U.S. Bureau of Labor Statistics, *Comparative Civilian Labor Force Statistics, Ten Countries, 1960-2006*. 19 March 2007. See also <http://bls.gov/fls/lfcompendium.pdf>.

Table 1333. Civilian Employment by Industry and Country: 2000 and 2006

[136,891 represents 136,891,000. Civilian employment as a percent of the civilian working-age population. See headnote, Table 1328]

Industry	United States [1,2]	Canada [1]	Aus- tralia	Japan	France	Ger- many	Italy	Sweden [2]	United Kingdom
TOTAL EMPLOYMENT (1,000)									
2000, total	136,891	14,764	8,989	63,790	23,714	36,238	20,973	4,217	27,058
Agriculture, forestry, fishing [3]	2,464	487	446	3,070	922	952	1,120	122	419
Industry [4]	30,050	3,220	1,901	19,710	5,508	11,898	6,635	999	6,637
Manufacturing.............	19,644	2,249	1,129	13,180	4,079	8,647	4,944	761	4,612
Services [5]................	104,377	11,057	6,642	41,010	17,284	23,388	13,218	3,096	20,002
2006, total	144,427	16,484	10,190	63,206	(NA)	(NA)	22,701	4,392	(NA)
Agriculture, forestry, fishing [3]	2,206	436	358	2,581	(NA)	(NA)	965	102	(NA)
Industry [4]	28,813	3,428	2,107	17,158	(NA)	(NA)	6,746	938	(NA)
Manufacturing.............	16,377	2,118	1,062	11,582	(NA)	(NA)	4,817	658	(NA)
Services [5]................	113,408	12,620	7,725	43,467	(NA)	(NA)	14,990	3,352	(NA)
PERCENT DISTRIBUTION									
2000, total	100.0	100.0	100.0	100.0	100.0	100.0	100.0	100.0	100.0
Agriculture, forestry, fishing [3]	1.8	3.3	5.0	4.8	3.9	2.6	5.3	2.9	1.5
Industry [4]	22.0	21.8	21.1	30.9	23.2	32.8	31.6	23.7	24.5
Manufacturing.............	14.4	15.2	12.6	20.7	17.2	23.9	23.6	18.0	17.0
Services [5]................	76.2	74.9	73.9	64.3	72.9	64.5	63.0	73.4	73.9
2006, total	100.0	100.0	100.0	100.0	(NA)	(NA)	100.0	100.0	(NA)
Agriculture, forestry, fishing [3]	1.5	2.6	3.5	4.1	(NA)	(NA)	4.3	2.3	(NA)
Industry [4]	19.9	20.8	20.7	27.1	(NA)	(NA)	29.7	21.4	(NA)
Manufacturing.............	11.3	12.8	10.4	18.3	(NA)	(NA)	21.2	15.0	(NA)
Services [5]................	78.5	76.6	75.8	68.8	(NA)	(NA)	66.0	76.3	(NA)

NA Not available.   [1] Data for the United States and Canada are based on the 2002 North American Industry Classification System (NAICS).   [2] Break in series between 2000 and 2006.   [3] Includes hunting.   [4] Includes manufacturing, mining, and construction.   [5] Transportation, communication, public utilities, trade, finance, public administration, private household services, and miscellaneous services.

Source: U.S. Bureau of Labor Statistics, *Comparative Civilian Labor Force Statistics, Ten Countries, 1960–2006*, 19 March 2007. See also <http://bls.gov/fls/lfcompendium.pdf>.

U.S. Census Bureau, Statistical Abstract of the United States: 2008

Table 1334. **World Supply and Utilization of Major Crops, Livestock, and Products: 1995 to 2006**

[In millions of units (214.3 represents 214,300,000). For major crops, data ending in year shown. For meat and dairy, calendar year data, selected countries]

Commodity	1995	1999	2000	2001	2002	2003	2004	2005	2006 [1]
Wheat									
Area (hectares)	214.3	225.1	215.4	217.6	214.7	214.6	209.9	218.9	218.1
Production (metric tons)	523.1	590.0	585.8	581.5	581.1	567.7	554.6	628.8	618.9
Exports (metric tons) [2] ... [3]	101.5	102.0	112.7	104.1	110.8	110.1	104.5	113.1	113.7
Consumption (metric tons) [3]	545.0	579.0	585.0	583.9	585.0	604.8	588.5	610.1	623.3
Ending stocks (metric tons) [4]	160.2	208.1	208.9	206.5	202.7	166.6	132.7	151.4	147.1
Coarse grains									
Area (hectares)	323.6	308.5	299.7	296.7	301.4	293.3	307.3	300.3	301.2
Production (metric tons)	869.7	890.9	877.6	862.3	893.7	875.8	916.7	1,014.6	975.2
Exports (metric tons) [2] ... [3]	98.6	96.7	104.8	104.4	102.7	104.7	102.7	102.1	108.9
Consumption (metric tons) [3]	858.8	869.2	882.4	884.5	906.6	903.0	946.7	975.5	987.1
Ending stocks (metric tons) [4]	190.8	237.4	232.2	210.0	197.0	169.9	139.9	179.0	167.1
Rice, milled									
Area (hectares)	147.4	152.7	155.2	151.5	150.5	145.8	148.1	149.6	152.2
Production (metric tons)	363.6	394.6	408.8	398.7	399.1	377.5	391.8	400.5	415.5
Exports (metric tons) [2] ... [3]	20.7	24.8	22.8	24.4	27.9	27.6	27.2	29.0	28.0
Consumption (metric tons) [3]	365.2	388.1	398.0	394.5	412.0	407.4	412.9	407.7	413.0
Ending stocks (metric tons) [4]	118.3	134.3	145.1	149.2	136.4	106.5	85.4	78.1	80.6
Total grains [5]									
Area (hectares)	685.3	686.3	670.3	665.8	666.6	653.7	665.3	668.8	671.5
Production (metric tons)	1,756.4	1,875.5	1,872.2	1,842.5	1,873.9	1,820.9	1,863.1	2,043.9	2,009.6
Exports (metric tons) [2] ... [3]	220.8	223.5	240.3	232.9	241.4	242.4	234.4	244.2	250.6
Consumption (metric tons) [3]	1,769.0	1,836.3	1,865.4	1,862.9	1,903.6	1,914.2	1,948.1	1,993.3	2,023.4
Ending stocks (metric tons) [4]	469.3	579.8	586.2	565.7	536.1	443.0	358.0	408.5	394.8
Oilseeds									
Crush (metric tons)	238.3	278.4	247.3	254.4	264.9	268.9	278.5	302.1	317.9
Production (metric tons)	299.5	346.0	303.9	314.2	325.2	330.3	335.2	381.3	389.0
Exports (metric tons)	47.5	63.5	59.9	66.9	62.7	70.0	67.1	74.6	77.5
Ending stocks (metric tons)......	28.1	32.9	35.1	38.9	41.2	47.5	43.9	56.3	60.8
Meals									
Production (metric tons)	166.2	194.6	168.5	175.0	182.8	185.3	189.7	206.0	215.5
Exports (metric tons)	61.5	71.6	47.2	49.2	52.5	53.6	58.3	60.1	65.2
Oils									
Production (metric tons)	73.4	87.7	86.4	90.0	92.7	95.8	101.6	111.2	117.0
Exports (metric tons)	27.3	32.4	29.0	31.0	31.6	35.6	38.4	42.3	44.9
Cotton									
Area (hectares)	32.2	32.9	32.2	32.0	33.7	30.5	32.2	35.8	34.4
Production (bales) [6]	85.9	85.5	87.7	88.9	98.8	88.3	95.3	120.3	114.1
Exports (bales) [6]	28.4	23.5	27.2	26.4	29.0	30.3	33.2	35.0	44.2
Consumption (bales) [6]	84.4	84.8	91.1	92.2	94.3	98.3	98.0	108.8	117.4
Ending stocks (bales) [6]	29.9	52.2	50.2	48.1	53.7	44.2	43.1	54.0	52.2
Beef and Pork									
Production (metric tons)	124.2	131.4	132.1	133.2	139.3	140.6	144.1	148.6	153.3
Consumption (metric tons)	123.2	131.1	131.2	132.2	138.1	139.3	142.0	146.0	150.4
Exports (metric tons) [2]	7.6	9.2	8.9	8.9	10.2	10.6	11.4	12.3	12.2
Broilers and Turkeys									
Production (metric tons)	43.6	52.3	55.3	57.1	59.2	59.2	60.8	63.9	64.9
Consumption (metric tons)	43.1	51.6	54.1	55.5	57.6	57.7	58.9	62.1	63.6
Exports (metric tons) [2]	5.0	4.9	5.4	6.1	6.3	6.6	6.6	7.4	7.0
Dairy									
Milk production (metric tons)	(NA)	376.7	381.6	384.8	392.5	396.6	403.8	414.9	425.9

NA Not available. [1] Forecast for crops, preliminary for meat and dairy. [2] Excludes intra-EU (European Union) trade but includes intra-FSU (Former Soviet Union) trade. [3] Where stocks data are not available, consumption includes stock changes. [4] Stocks data are based on differing marketing years and do not represent levels at a given date. Data not available for all countries. [5] Wheat, coarse grains and rice. [6] 480 pound bales.

Source: U.S. Dept. of Agriculture, Economic Research Service, "Agricultural Outlook: Statistical Indicators" (published December 2006); <http://www.ers.usda.gov/publications/agoutlook/aotables/>.

Table 1335. World Crop Production Summary: 2005 to 2007

[In millions of metric tons, (622.3 represents 622,300,000), except as indicated]

Country	Wheat 2005–2006	Wheat 2006–2007, prel.	Coarse Grains 2005–2006	Coarse Grains 2006–2007, prel.	Rice (milled) 2005–2006	Rice (milled) 2006–2007, prel.	Oilseeds [1] 2005–2006	Oilseeds [1] 2006–2007, prel.	Cotton [2] 2005–2006	Cotton [2] 2006–2007, prel.
World	622.3	594.1	978.6	976.0	418.0	416.6	390.4	404.3	114.3	116.7
United States	57.3	49.3	298.8	280.1	7.1	6.2	95.5	96.6	23.9	21.6
Canada	26.8	27.3	26.0	23.5	(3)	(3)	12.9	12.8	(3)	(3)
Mexico	3.0	3.2	25.8	28.7	0.2	0.2	0.7	0.6	0.6	0.7
EU-25 [4]	123.0	116.9	132.6	127.0	1.7	1.7	20.9	21.3	2.5	1.6
Russia	47.7	44.9	27.6	30.2	0.4	0.4	7.4	8.0	(3)	(3)
Ukraine	18.7	14.0	18.1	19.2	0.1	0.1	5.6	6.8	(3)	(3)
China	97.5	103.5	147.7	151.6	126.4	128.0	55.9	57.5	26.2	30.9
India	68.6	69.4	34.0	32.2	91.8	91.1	30.6	29.9	19.1	21.5
Indonesia	(3)	(3)	6.5	6.7	35.0	33.3	7.7	7.9	–	–
Pakistan	21.6	21.7	1.8	2.0	5.5	5.2	5.1	5.3	10.2	9.9
Thailand	(3)	(3)	4.1	3.9	18.2	18.3	0.5	0.6	0.1	–
Argentina	14.5	14.2	19.2	27.5	0.8	0.7	45.0	50.9	0.6	0.8
Brazil	4.9	2.2	44.2	52.6	7.9	7.7	59.1	61.8	4.7	6.5
Australia	25.0	10.5	13.7	6.4	0.7	0.1	2.5	1.0	2.8	1.1
South Africa	1.9	2.1	7.3	6.9	(3)	(3)	1.1	0.6	0.1	0.1
Turkey	18.5	17.5	11.9	11.1	0.4	0.4	2.0	2.2	3.6	4.0
All others	93.3	97.4	159.2	166.5	121.9	123.2	37.8	40.7	20.0	18.0

– Represents zero. [1] Includes soybean, cottonseed, peanut (in shell), sunflower seed, rapeseed for individual countries. Copra and palm kernel are added to world totals. [2] In millions of 480 pound bales. [3] Indicates no reported or insignificant production. [4] See footnote 3, Table 1339.

Source: U.S. Department of Agriculture, Foreign Agricultural Service, *World Agricultural Production*, June 2007. See also <http://www.fas.usda.gov/wap/circular/2007/07-06/wapfull0607.pdf>.

Table 1336. Wheat, Rice, and Corn—Exports and Imports of Leading Countries: 2000 to 2006

[In thousands of metric tons (28,027 represents 28,027,000). Wheat data are for trade year beginning in July of year shown; rice data are for calendar year; corn data are for trade year beginning in October of year shown. Countries listed are the ten leading exporters or importers in 2006]

Leading exporters	Exports 2000	Exports 2005	Exports 2006	Leading importers	Imports 2000	Imports 2005	Imports 2006
WHEAT				**WHEAT**			
United States	28,027	27,424	24,500	Brazil	7,453	6,194	7,500
Canada	17,351	15,644	20,500	Egypt	6,050	7,771	7,000
EU-25 [1]	16,792	15,032	15,000	EU-25 [1]	4,694	7,609	6,800
Australia	16,682	15,213	12,000	India	45	118	6,000
Russia	696	10,664	10,000	Japan	5,885	5,469	5,500
Argentina	11,396	8,301	10,000	Indonesia	4,069	4,981	4,800
Kazakhstan	3,972	3,000	5,000	Algeria	5,600	5,469	4,800
Ukraine	78	6,461	2,800	Nigeria	1,913	3,656	3,600
China [2]	623	1,397	2,500	Mexico	3,066	3,549	3,600
Turkey	1,601	2,900	2,000	Korea, South	3,127	3,884	3,600
RICE				**RICE**			
Thailand	7,521	7,411	8,700	Philippines	1,175	1,900	1,850
Vietnam	3,528	4,694	4,900	Indonesia	1,500	600	1,800
India	1,936	3,800	4,300	Nigeria	1,906	1,600	1,700
United States	2,541	3,300	3,400	Iraq	959	1,200	1,200
Pakistan	2,417	3,000	3,000	EU-25 [1]	1,189	1,100	1,100
China [2]	1,847	1,216	1,200	Saudi Arabia	1,053	1,000	1,000
Egypt	705	1,000	900	Iran	765	1,200	900
Uruguay	806	812	625	Senegal	874	750	850
Argentina	368	450	500	Malaysia	633	850	850
Cambodia	–	350	450	South Africa	572	800	800
CORN				**CORN**			
United States	48,329	56,181	56,000	Japan	16,340	16,619	16,500
Argentina	12,229	10,707	13,000	Korea, South	8,743	8,483	8,800
Brazil	3,741	2,826	5,000	Mexico	5,928	6,787	7,500
China [2]	7,276	3,727	4,000	Egypt	5,268	4,397	4,800
Serbia and Montenegro	50	1,274	1,200	Taiwan [2]	4,924	4,464	4,500
Ukraine	397	2,464	1,000	EU-25 [1]	3,800	3,138	4,000
Romania	50	271	600	Colombia	1,857	3,151	3,300
South Africa	1,415	1,406	500	Malaysia	2,588	2,517	2,600
Paraguay	386	1,314	500	Iran	1,265	2,300	2,500
Bulgaria	15	400	450	Algeria	1,265	1,989	2,100

– Represents zero. [1] See footnote 3, Table 1339. [2] See footnote 2, Table 1298.

Source: U.S. Department of Agriculture, Economic Research Service, unpublished data from the PS&D (Production, supply, and distribution) database.

Comparative International Statistics 847

Table 1337. Fisheries—Commercial Catch by Country: 1990 to 2004

[In thousands of metric tons, live weight (97,852 represents 97,852,000). Catch of fish, crustaceans, mollusks (including weight of shells). Includes aquaculture (the farming of aquatic organisms), but not marine mammals and aquatic plants]

Country	1990	2000	2003	2004	Country	1990	2000	2003	2004
World [1]	97,852	130,957	133,187	140,506	Vietnam	939	1,949	2,794	3,078
					Russia	7,604	4,048	3,390	3,051
China [2]	31,136	41,568	45,642	47,508	Philippines.	2,209	2,291	2,626	2,724
Peru.	6,874	10,665	6,100	9,635	Bangladesh	846	1,661	1,998	2,102
India.	3,800	5,609	6,025	6,088	Burma	743	1,169	1,596	1,987
Indonesia	3,022	4,909	5,623	5,856	Korea, South	2,843	2,118	2,031	1,981
Chile	5,195	4,692	4,176	5,610	Iceland	1,508	1,986	1,984	1,737
United States	5,871	5,174	5,483	5,566	Mexico	1,383	1,369	1,540	1,539
Japan	10,361	5,751	5,494	5,178	Malaysia	1,005	1,441	1,454	1,507
Thailand	2,790	3,736	3,914	4,018	Canada	1,685	1,125	1,261	1,319
Norway.	1,754	3,191	3,132	3,160	Taiwan [2]	1,444	1,338	1,486	1,226

[1] Includes other countries, not shown separately.   [2] See footnote 2, Table 1298.

Source: U.S. National Oceanic and Atmospheric Administration, National Marine Fisheries Service, *Fisheries of the United States*, annual. Data from Food and Agriculture Organization of the United Nations, Rome, Italy.

Table 1338. Meat Production by Type and Country: 2004 and 2005

[In thousands of metric tons (51,327 represents 51,327,000). Carcass weight basis for beef, veal, and pork. Excludes offals and rabbit]

Country	Beef and veal 2004	Beef and veal 2005, prel.	Country	Pork [1] 2004	Pork [1] 2005, prel.	Country	Poultry meat 2004	Poultry meat 2005, prel.
World [2]	51,327	52,374	World [2]	90,678	94,215	World [2]	55,952	59,092
United States . . .	11,261	11,317	China [3]	47,016	50,106	United States . . .	15,286	15,869
Brazil	7,975	8,592	European Union [4].	20,851	21,102	China [3]	9,998	10,200
European Union [4] .	8,007	7,770	United States. . .	9,312	9,392	Brazil.	8,408	9,350
China [3]	6,759	7,115	Brazil.	2,600	2,800	European Union [4].	7,627	7,736
Argentina	3,130	3,200	Canada	1,936	1,914	Mexico.	2,389	2,498
India	2,130	2,250	Russia	1,725	1,735	India	1,650	1,900
Mexico	2,099	2,125	Japan	1,271	1,245	Japan	1,124	1,166
Australia	2,081	2,102	Mexico.	1,150	1,195	Argentina	910	1,030
Russia	1,590	1,525	Philippines	1,145	1,175	Canada	946	977
Canada.	1,496	1,523	Korea, South . . .	1,100	1,036	Thailand.	900	950

[1] Includes edible pork fat, but excludes lard and inedible greases (except United States).   [2] Includes other countries, not shown separately.   [3] See footnote 2, Table 1298.   [4] See footnote 3, Table 1339.

Source: U.S. Department of Agriculture, National Agricultural Statistics Service, *Agricultural Statistics*, annual.

Table 1339. Meat Consumption by Type and Country: 2005 and 2006

[In thousands of metric tons (12,663 represents 12,663,000). Carcass weight basis for beef, veal, and pork. Broiler (chicken, 16-week-old) weight based on ready-to-cook equivalent]

Country	Beef and veal 2005	Beef and veal 2006 [1]	Country	Pork 2005	Pork 2006 [1]	Country	Poultry meat 2005	Poultry meat 2006 [1]
United States . . .	12,663	12,830	China [2]	49,703	51,809	United States. . .	13,430	13,754
European Union [3].	8,194	8,270	European Union [3].	19,768	20,015	China [2]	10,088	10,371
China [2]	7,026	7,395	United States. . .	8,669	8,640	European Union [3].	7,596	7,380
Brazil	6,774	6,939	Russia	2,476	2,637	Brazil.	6,612	6,853
Argentina	2,443	2,550	Japan	2,507	2,450	Mexico.	2,871	3,005
Mexico	2,419	2,509	Brazil.	1,949	2,191	Russia	2,139	2,382
Russia	2,503	2,370	Mexico.	1,556	1,580	India	1,899	2,000
India [4]	1,623	1,625	Korea, South . . .	1,305	1,402	Japan	1,880	1,908
Japan	1,200	1,173	Philippines	1,198	1,240	Argentina	949	1,124
Canada.	1,106	1,140	Taiwan [2]	950	932	South Africa	1,010	1,062
Australia	735	719	Canada	978	(NA)	Saudi Arabia	1,011	972
Other Countries . .	4,165	4,205	Other Countries. .	3,540	3,542	Other Countries. .	8,933	8,141

NA Not available.   [1] Preliminary data.   [2] See footnote 2, Table 1298.   [3] European Union-25: Austria, Belgium, Cyprus, Czech Republic, Denmark, Estonia, Finland, France, Germany, Greece, Hungary, Ireland, Italy, Latvia, Lithuania, Luxembourg, Malta, Netherlands, Poland, Portugal, Slovakia, Slovenia, Spain, Sweden, and United Kingdom.   [4] Includes buffalo.

Source: U.S. Department of Agriculture, Foreign Agricultural Service, *Livestock and Poultry: World Markets and Trade*, annual. See also <http://www.fas.usda.gov/dlp/circular/2007/livestock_poultry_04-2007.pdf>.

Table 1340. EU and U.S. Organic Land, Farm Sector, and Sales: 2005

[EU numbers for land and farms include those certified organic and in-conversion; U.S. numbers include only certified organic farms and land. For definition of "certified organic" in the United States, see headnote, Table 804. 1 hectare = 2.47 acres]

Country	Total organic land (hectares)	Organic farms (number)	Farms under organic production (percent)	Farmland under organic production (percent)	Retail sales (mil. Euros)[1]	Per capita spending on organic food (Euros)[2]
Austria	360,972	20,310	11.5	14.2	450	70.3
Belgium	22,996	693	1.4	1.7	201	25.0
Denmark.	145,636	2,892	6.0	5.6	401	84.0
Finland	147,587	4,296	6.1	6.5	250	61.2
France	560,838	11,402	2.0	2.0	1,700	37.4
Germany.	807,406	17,020	4.4	4.7	3,900	59.3
Greece	288,255	14,614	1.2	3.2	21	2.4
Ireland	35,266	978	0.7	0.8	45	15.2
Italy	1,067,102	44,733	2.6	8.4	1,700	36.0
Luxembourg	3,243	72	3.0	2.5	(NA)	(NA)
Netherlands.	48,765	1,377	1.7	2.5	467	37.9
Portugal	233,458	1,577	0.5	6.3	(NA)	(NA)
Spain	807,569	15,693	1.5	3.2	144	3.8
Sweden	200,010	2,951	3.9	6.3	433	63.2
United Kingdom	619,852	4,285	1.7	3.9	2,200	48.7
European Union	5,348,955	142,893	2.3	4.2	11,912	40.2
United States	1,642,044	8,493	0.5	0.4	11,065	51.4

NA Not available. [1] U.S. dollars converted using average exchange rate for 2005, 0.80 euro per dollar. Retail sales for Greece, Ireland, and Spain are from 2003. [2] U.S. per capita is based on population 18 years and older; EU per capita is based on population 20 years and older.

Source: U.S. Department of Agriculture, Economic Research Service, "Market-Led Versus Government-Facilitated Growth: Development of the U.S. and EU Organic Agricultural Sectors," August 2005; and unpublished data. See also <http://www.ers.usda.gov/Publications/WRS0505/>.

Table 1341. World Production of Major Mineral Commodities: 1990 to 2005

[5,348 represents 5,348,000,000]

Commodity	Unit	1990	2000	2004	2005	Leading producers, 2004
MINERAL FUELS						
Coal.	Mil. short tons . . .	5,348	4,935	6,079	(NA)	China [3], United States, India
Dry natural gas	Tril. cu. ft..	73.6	88.3	98.5	101.5	Russia, United States, Canada
Natural gas plant liquids [1] . . .	Mil. barrels [2]	4,640	6,608	7,631	(NA)	United States, Saudi Arabia, Canada
Petroleum, crude	Mil. barrels [2]	22,079	24,955	26,362	(NA)	Saudi Arabia, Russia, United States
NONMETALLIC MINERALS						
Cement, hydraulic	Mil. metric tons . .	1,160	1,600	2,190	2,310	China [3], India, United States
Diamond, gem and industrial .	Mil. carats	111	(NA)	182	183	Australia, Botswana, Russia
Nitrogen in ammonia.	Mil. metric tons . .	97.5	109.0	117.0	121.0	China [3], India, Russia
						United States, China [3], Morocco and
Phosphate rock, marketable. .	Mil. metric tons . .	162	133	141	147	Western Sahara
Potash, marketable.	Mil. metric tons . .	28.0	25.3	29.0	31.0	Canada, Russia, Belarus
Salt	Mil. metric tons . .	183	214	229	238	United States, China [3], Germany
Sulfur, elemental basis	Mil. metric tons . .	58.0	57.2	64.0	66.0	United States, Canada, China [3]
METALS						
Aluminum [4]	Mil. metric tons . .	19.3	24.0	30.0	32.0	China [3], Russia, Canada
Bauxite, gross weight	Mil. metric tons . .	113	135	159	169	Australia, Brazil, Guinea
Chromite, gross weight.	1,000 metric tons.	13,200	14,400	17,000	19,300	South Africa, Kazakhstan, India
Copper, metal content [5]	1,000 metric tons.	8,950	13,200	14,600	15,000	Chile, United States, Peru
Gold, metal content	Metric tons	2,180	2,550	2,430	2,470	South Africa, Australia, United States
Iron ore, gross weight [6]	Mil. metric tons . .	983	1,060	1,340	1,540	China [3], Brazil, Australia
Lead, metal content [5]	1,000 metric tons.	3,370	3,100	3,150	3,270	China [3], Australia, United States
Nickel, metal content [5]	1,000 metric tons.	974	1,250	1,400	1,480	Russia, Canada, Australia
Tin, metal content [5]	1,000 metric tons.	220	238	264	290	China [3], Indonesia, Peru

NA Not available. [1] Excludes China. [2] 42-gallon barrels. [3] See footnote 2, Table 1298. [4] Unalloyed ingot metal. [5] Mine output. [6] Includes iron ore concentrates and iron ore agglomerates.

Source: Mineral fuels, U.S. Energy Information Administration, *International Energy Annual, 2004 and 2005* (accessed 11 July 2007); nonmetallic minerals and metals, 1990, U.S. Bureau of Mines, thereafter, U.S. Geological Survey, *Minerals Yearbook; Annual Reports;* and *Mineral Commodity Summaries, 2006.*

Comparative International Statistics 849

Table 1342. **World Primary Energy Production by Region and Type: 1980 to 2004**

[In quadrillion Btu (287.6 represents 287,600,000,000,000,000). Btu = British thermal unit. For Btu conversion factors, see source]

Region and type	1980	1985	1990	1995	1999	2000	2001	2002	2003	2004 [1]
World total [2]	287.6	307.2	349.7	364.2	385.3	397.1	404.3	406.1	421.7	443.1
North America	83.3	87.7	91.9	96.0	98.4	98.8	99.5	100.0	98.5	99.3
United States	67.3	67.8	70.8	71.1	71.7	71.3	71.9	70.9	70.1	70.4
Central and South America	12.1	13.7	16.7	21.1	24.5	26.0	26.0	25.3	25.7	27.2
Europe	40.2	47.6	46.9	49.1	51.0	50.8	51.4	51.2	50.7	50.6
Eurasia [3]	56.5	65.3	72.1	52.2	53.2	55.7	57.7	59.5	63.2	66.7
Middle East	42.3	25.8	41.0	48.3	53.8	57.5	56.2	54.3	57.6	62.1
Africa	17.4	18.4	21.6	24.2	26.7	27.8	28.1	28.0	30.1	32.0
Asia and Oceania.	35.9	48.7	59.4	73.3	77.7	80.5	85.5	87.9	95.9	105.2
Petroleum	133.1	121.2	136.2	141.9	150.3	156.4	155.6	153.6	159.0	166.3
Dry natural gas	54.7	64.2	75.9	80.2	87.9	91.3	93.7	96.7	98.9	102.2
Coal	71.2	82.2	90.9	88.9	90.4	91.4	96.9	97.1	104.6	113.3
Hydroelectric power . . .	17.9	20.4	22.4	25.3	26.6	27.0	26.4	26.4	26.8	27.5
Nuclear electric power. . .	7.6	15.3	20.4	23.3	25.1	25.7	26.4	26.7	26.4	27.5
Geothermal, solar, wind, wood, and waste . .	0.5	0.8	1.7	2.2	2.8	3.0	3.1	3.4	3.7	3.9

[1] Preliminary. [2] Includes geothermal, solar, and wood and waste energy produced in the United States and not used for generating electricity, not shown separately by type. [3] Prior to 1995, data were for the former U.S.S.R.
Source: U.S. Energy Information Administration, *International Energy Annual, 2004*. See also <http://www.eia.doe.gov/emeu /iea/contents.html> (accessed 11 July 2007).

Table 1343. **World Primary Energy Consumption by Region and Type: 1980 to 2004**

[In quadrillion Btu (283.6 represents 283,600,000,000,000,000). Btu = British thermal unit. For Btu conversion factors, see source]

Region and type	1980	1985	1990	1995	1999	2000	2001	2002	2003	2004 [1]
World total [2]	283.6	308.6	347.3	365.6	389.1	399.6	403.5	409.7	425.7	446.4
North America	91.8	91.3	100.9	108.9	115.8	118.4	115.6	117.4	118.3	120.6
United States	78.3	76.6	84.7	91.2	96.8	99.0	96.5	98.0	98.3	100.4
Central and South America	11.5	12.4	14.5	17.6	20.3	20.9	21.2	21.2	21.7	22.5
Europe	71.7	73.1	76.2	76.6	80.2	81.3	82.5	82.2	84.0	85.6
Eurasia [3]	46.7	55.7	60.9	42.4	39.8	40.6	41.0	41.7	43.4	45.2
Middle East	5.9	8.6	11.3	13.9	16.8	17.3	18.1	19.1	19.9	21.1
Africa	6.8	8.5	9.5	10.6	11.5	12.0	12.6	12.7	13.3	13.7
Asia and Oceania.	49.2	59.1	74.1	95.6	104.7	109.1	112.6	115.5	125.0	137.6
Petroleum	131.0	123.1	136.2	142.4	153.4	155.4	156.8	158.1	161.5	167.5
Dry natural gas	54.0	63.6	75.2	81.0	88.2	91.4	92.8	96.1	99.6	103.4
Coal.	70.2	82.4	89.4	89.1	90.9	94.9	96.1	97.0	105.6	114.5
Hydroelectric power	17.9	20.4	22.4	25.3	26.6	27.0	26.4	26.4	26.8	27.5
Nuclear electric power. . .	7.6	15.3	20.4	23.3	25.1	25.7	26.4	26.7	26.4	27.5
Geothermal, solar, wind, wood, and waste	0.5	0.8	1.7	2.2	2.8	3.0	3.1	3.4	3.7	3.9

[1] Preliminary. [2] See footnote 2, Table 1342. [3] See footnote 3, Table 1342.
Source: U.S. Energy Information Administration, *International Energy Annual, 2004*. See also <http://www.eia.doe.gov/emeu /iea/contents.html> (accessed 11 July 2007).

Table 1344. **World Energy Consumption by Region and Energy Source, 1990 to 2003, and Projections, 2010 to 2025**

[In quadrillion Btu (347.3 represents 347,300,000,000,000,000). Btu = British thermal units. For Btu conversion factors, see source. Energy totals include net imports of coal coke and electricity generated from biomass in the United States. Totals may not equal sum of components due to independent rounding. The electricity portion of the national consumption values consists of generation for domestic use plus an adjustment for electricity trade based on a fuel's share of total generation in the exporting country]

Region and energy source	1990	2002	2003	Projections			
				2010	2015	2020	2025
World, total	347.3	410.3	420.7	509.7	563.4	613.0	665.4
North America	100.8	117.5	118.3	131.4	139.9	148.4	157.0
United States [1]	84.6	98.1	98.1	107.9	114.2	120.6	127.0
Western Europe.	69.9	77.9	78.9	84.4	87.2	88.7	91.3
Industrialized Asia.	26.7	36.5	37.1	40.3	42.8	44.4	46.1
Eastern Europe and former Soviet Union . . .	67.2	46.9	48.5	56.5	62.8	68.7	74.0
Developing Asia.	47.5	78.4	83.1	126.2	149.4	172.8	197.1
Middle East	11.3	19.1	19.6	25.0	28.2	31.2	34.3
Africa	9.5	12.8	13.3	17.7	20.5	22.3	24.3
Central and South America.	14.5	21.3	21.9	28.2	32.5	36.5	41.2
Oil.	136.1	158.7	162.1	185.6	199.1	210.8	224.3
Natural gas	75.2	95.9	99.1	121.1	139.8	156.1	172.5
Coal.	89.4	96.8	100.4	128.8	144.4	160.1	176.7
Nuclear.	20.4	26.7	26.5	28.9	31.0	32.9	34.0
Other	26.3	32.2	32.7	45.2	49.1	53.1	57.8

[1] Includes the 50 states and the District of Columbia.
Source: U.S. Energy Information Administration (EIA), *International Energy Outlook 2006*. See also <http://www.eia.doe.gov/oiaf /ieo/ieorefcase.html>.

850   Comparative International Statistics

Table 1345. Energy Consumption by Country: 2000 and 2004

[399.6 represents 399,600,000,000,000,000. See text of this section for general comments about the data. For data qualifications for countries and Btu conversion factors, see source]

Country	Total (quad. Btu) 2000	Total (quad. Btu) 2004, prel.	Per capita (mil. Btu) 2000	Per capita (mil. Btu) 2004, prel.	Country	Total (quad. Btu) 2000	Total (quad. Btu) 2004, prel.	Per capita (mil. Btu) 2000	Per capita (mil. Btu) 2004, prel.
World total	399.6	446.4	65.7	70.1	Japan	22.4	22.6	177.2	177.7
United States	99.0	100.4	350.6	342.7	Korea, North	0.9	0.9	39.7	39.2
Algeria	1.2	1.2	40.7	38.6	Korea, South	7.9	9.0	167.3	185.5
Argentina	2.7	2.8	71.1	71.2	Kuwait	0.9	1.1	460.1	470.0
Australia	4.8	5.3	252.2	264.5	Libya	0.6	0.7	122.9	133.0
Austria	1.4	1.5	170.3	178.1	Malaysia	1.9	2.5	85.9	107.1
Bahrain	0.4	0.4	575.0	611.5	Mexico	6.3	6.6	63.3	63.0
Bangladesh	0.5	0.7	3.9	4.7	Morocco	0.4	0.4	14.8	13.8
Belarus	1.1	1.0	101.4	93.7	Netherlands	3.8	4.1	238.5	251.4
Belgium	2.7	2.8	262.4	269.0	New Zealand	0.9	0.9	226.4	221.4
Brazil	8.6	9.1	48.9	49.3	Nigeria	0.8	1.0	7.1	8.1
Bulgaria	0.9	0.8	111.1	112.6	Norway	2.0	1.9	435.2	424.2
Burma	0.2	0.2	3.7	4.4	Pakistan	1.9	2.0	12.7	12.5
Canada	13.0	13.6	417.2	418.4	Peru	0.5	0.6	20.3	20.9
Chile	1.0	1.2	66.9	74.6	Philippines	1.3	1.3	15.7	15.2
China[1]	38.8	59.6	30.6	45.9	Poland	3.6	3.7	93.9	95.1
Colombia	1.2	1.2	29.9	28.2	Portugal	1.1	1.1	103.6	105.5
Congo (Kinshasa)[2]	0.1	0.1	1.8	1.5	Romania	1.6	1.6	70.6	73.5
Cuba	0.5	0.5	41.0	41.5	Russia	27.5	30.1	187.1	208.8
Czech Republic	1.7	1.8	162.4	172.7	Saudi Arabia	4.8	6.1	209.2	236.5
Denmark	0.9	0.9	164.1	159.6	Serbia and Montenegro[3]	0.6	0.8	57.8	71.3
Ecuador	0.3	0.4	27.5	29.0	South Africa	4.6	5.1	103.3	115.2
Egypt	2.0	2.5	28.5	33.1	Spain	5.5	6.4	138.2	158.9
Finland	1.2	1.3	235.9	258.1	Sweden	2.2	2.3	246.5	257.9
France	10.9	11.2	183.0	186.1	Switzerland	1.3	1.3	177.2	172.0
Germany	14.3	14.7	173.5	178.3	Syria	0.8	0.8	48.5	45.7
Greece	1.3	1.4	126.7	135.8	Taiwan[1]	3.8	4.4	170.1	193.3
Hong Kong	0.8	1.1	120.8	159.1	Thailand	2.6	3.4	41.7	53.7
Hungary	1.0	1.1	101.3	106.1	Trinidad and Tobago	0.4	0.6	376.0	546.8
India	13.6	15.4	13.5	14.5	Tunisia	0.3	0.3	31.4	33.4
Indonesia	4.1	4.7	18.2	19.7	Turkey	3.2	3.5	48.1	51.3
Iran	5.0	6.4	76.2	95.5	Ukraine	5.8	6.5	117.4	137.1
Iraq	1.1	1.2	47.7	47.5	United Arab Emirates	1.8	2.3	757.9	925.4
Ireland	0.6	0.6	157.4	160.6	United Kingdom	9.7	10.0	162.6	166.5
Israel	0.8	0.9	144.5	140.8	Venezuela	2.8	2.9	117.5	115.3
Italy	7.6	8.3	132.2	142.3	Vietnam	0.7	0.9	9.5	11.5

[1] See footnote 2, Table 1298. [2] See footnote 3, Table 1298. [3] As of June 2006, Serbia and Montenegro are separate countries.
Source: U.S. Energy Information Administration, *International Energy Annual*. See also <http://www.eia.doe.gov/emeu/iea/contents.html> (accessed 11 July 2007).

Table 1346. World Daily Crude Oil Production by Major Producing Country: 1980 to 2004

[In thousands of barrels per day (59,558 barrels represents 59,558,000 barrels)]

Country	1980	1990	1995	1999	2000	2001	2002	2003	2004
World, total[1]	59,558	60,492	62,333	65,848	68,369	67,984	66,967	69,235	72,224
Saudi Arabia	9,900	6,410	8,231	7,833	8,404	8,031	7,634	8,775	9,101
Russia	(X)	(X)	5,995	6,079	6,479	6,917	7,408	8,132	8,805
United States	8,597	7,355	6,560	5,881	5,822	5,801	5,746	5,681	5,419
Iran[2]	1,662	3,088	3,643	3,557	3,696	3,724	3,444	3,743	4,001
China[2]	2,114	2,774	2,990	3,195	3,249	3,300	3,390	3,409	3,485
Mexico	1,936	2,553	2,618	2,906	3,012	3,127	3,177	3,371	3,383
Norway	486	1,630	2,766	3,019	3,222	3,226	3,131	3,042	2,954
Venezuela	2,168	2,137	2,750	2,826	3,155	3,010	2,604	2,335	2,557
United Arab Emirates	1,709	2,117	2,233	2,169	2,368	2,205	2,082	2,348	2,478
Canada	1,435	1,553	1,805	1,907	1,977	2,029	2,171	2,306	2,398
Kuwait	1,656	1,175	2,057	1,898	2,079	1,998	1,894	2,136	2,376
Nigeria	2,055	1,810	1,993	2,130	2,165	2,256	2,118	2,275	2,329
Iraq	2,514	2,040	560	2,508	2,571	2,390	2,023	1,308	2,011
United Kingdom	1,622	1,820	2,489	2,684	2,275	2,282	2,292	2,093	1,845
Algeria	1,106	1,175	1,202	1,202	1,254	1,310	1,306	1,611	1,677
Libya	1,787	1,375	1,390	1,319	1,410	1,367	1,319	1,421	1,515
Brazil	182	631	695	1,132	1,269	1,295	1,455	1,496	1,477
Indonesia	1,577	1,462	1,503	1,472	1,428	1,340	1,249	1,155	1,096
Angola	150	475	646	745	746	742	896	903	1,052
Kazakhstan	(X)	(X)	362	530	610	721	818	893	1,014
Qatar	472	406	442	665	737	714	679	715	783
Malaysia	283	619	682	693	690	659	698	738	755
Oman	282	685	851	910	970	913	897	819	751
Argentina	491	483	715	802	761	802	799	783	733
India	182	660	703	653	646	642	665	660	683
Egypt	595	873	920	852	748	698	631	618	594
Colombia	126	440	585	816	691	625	577	541	529
Ecuador	204	285	392	373	395	412	393	411	528
Australia	380	575	562	539	722	657	626	512	436
Yemen	–	193	345	409	440	438	443	448	424

– Represents zero. X Not applicable. [1] Includes countries not shown separately. [2] See footnote 2, Table 1298.
Source: U.S. Energy Information Administration, *International Energy Annual, 2004*. See also <http://www.eia.doe.gov/pub/international/iealf/table22.xls> (accessed 11 July 2007).

Comparative International Statistics 851

Table 1347. **World Dry Natural Gas Production by Major Producing Country: 1980 to 2005**

[In trillion cubic feet (53.35 represents 53,350,000,000,000)]

Country	1980	1990	1995	2000	2001	2002	2003	2004	2005
World, total [1]	53.35	73.57	77.96	88.30	90.45	92.21	95.39	98.53	101.53
Russia	(X)	(X)	21.01	20.63	20.51	21.03	21.77	22.39	22.62
United States	19.40	17.81	18.60	19.18	19.62	18.93	19.10	18.59	18.07
Canada	2.76	3.85	5.60	6.47	6.60	6.63	6.45	6.48	6.56
Iran	0.25	0.84	1.25	2.13	2.33	2.65	2.86	2.96	3.56
Algeria	0.41	1.79	2.05	2.94	2.79	2.80	2.85	2.83	3.11
United Kingdom	1.32	1.75	2.67	3.83	3.69	3.66	3.63	3.39	3.10
Norway	0.92	0.98	1.08	1.87	1.95	2.41	2.70	2.95	3.07
Netherlands	3.40	2.69	2.98	2.56	2.75	2.68	2.57	3.04	2.78
Indonesia	0.63	1.53	2.24	2.36	2.34	2.48	2.61	2.66	2.61
Saudi Arabia	0.33	1.08	1.34	1.76	1.90	2.00	2.12	2.32	2.52
Malaysia	0.06	0.65	1.02	1.50	1.66	1.71	2.01	2.20	2.24
Turkmenistan.	(X)	(X)	1.14	1.64	1.70	1.89	2.09	2.07	2.22
Uzbekistan	(X)	(X)	1.70	1.99	2.23	2.04	2.03	2.11	2.11
China [2]	0.51	0.51	0.60	0.96	1.07	1.15	1.21	1.44	1.76
United Arab Emirates	0.20	0.78	1.11	1.36	1.39	1.53	1.58	1.63	1.66
Qatar	0.18	0.28	0.48	1.03	0.95	1.04	1.11	1.38	1.62
Argentina	0.28	0.63	0.88	1.32	1.31	1.28	1.45	1.58	1.61
Mexico	0.90	0.90	0.96	1.31	1.30	1.33	1.40	1.46	1.52
Egypt	0.03	0.29	0.44	0.65	0.87	0.88	1.06	1.15	1.50
Australia	0.31	0.72	1.03	1.16	1.19	1.23	1.27	1.31	1.42
Pakistan	0.29	0.48	0.65	0.86	0.77	0.81	0.89	0.97	1.09
Trinidad and Tobago	0.08	0.18	0.27	0.49	0.54	0.61	0.87	0.99	1.07
India	0.05	0.40	0.63	0.79	0.85	0.93	0.96	1.00	1.06
Venezuela	0.52	0.76	0.89	0.96	1.12	1.00	0.86	0.96	1.01
Kazakhstan	(X)	(X)	0.17	0.31	0.36	0.46	0.49	0.72	0.93
Thailand	–	0.21	0.37	0.66	0.66	0.71	0.77	0.79	0.84
Nigeria	0.04	0.13	0.18	0.44	0.53	0.50	0.72	0.77	0.79
Germany	(X)	(X)	0.74	0.78	0.79	0.79	0.78	0.73	0.70
Oman	0.03	0.10	0.15	0.32	0.49	0.53	0.56	0.61	0.70
Ukraine	(X)	(X)	0.62	0.64	0.64	0.65	0.69	0.68	0.69

– Represents or rounds to zero.   X Not applicable.   [1] Includes countries not shown separately.   [2] See footnote 2, Table 1298.

Source: U. S. Energy Information Administration, *International Energy Annual, 2005.* See also <http://www.eia.doe.gov/pub /international/iealf/table24.xls> (accessed 11 July 2007).

Table 1348. **World Coal Production by Major Producing Country: 1980 to 2004**

[In millions of short tons (4,181.8 represents 4,181,800,000)]

Country	1980	1990	1995	1999	2000	2001	2002	2003	2004
World, total	4,181.8	5,347.5	5,095.8	4,941.2	4,935.0	5,232.9	5,265.3	5,648.3	6,078.6
China [1]	683.6	1,190.4	1,537.0	1,364.9	1,314.4	1,458.7	1,521.2	1,837.6	2,156.4
United States	829.7	1,029.1	1,033.0	1,100.4	1,073.6	1,127.7	1,094.3	1,071.8	1,112.1
India	125.8	247.6	320.6	356.3	370.0	388.7	404.9	428.9	443.7
Australia	116.1	225.8	266.5	320.8	338.2	362.9	376.8	377.3	391.0
Russia	(X)	(X)	270.9	259.2	264.9	273.4	261.9	283.3	308.9
South Africa	131.9	193.2	227.3	243.0	248.9	250.8	245.8	263.8	267.7
Germany	(X)	(X)	274.2	226.1	226.0	227.1	232.6	229.1	232.7
Poland	253.5	237.1	221.2	188.6	179.5	180.3	178.5	180.6	177.7
Indonesia	0.6	11.6	45.4	81.3	84.4	102.0	113.9	127.1	142.3
Kazakhstan	(X)	(X)	93.1	65.9	81.5	93.0	89.2	98.1	95.7
Greece	25.6	57.2	63.6	68.4	70.4	73.1	77.7	75.3	79.5
Canada	40.4	75.3	82.7	79.9	76.2	77.6	73.3	68.5	72.7
Ukraine	(X)	(X)	94.6	69.6	69.1	68.0	68.3	70.8	69.3
Czech Republic	(X)	(X)	82.6	65.2	71.8	72.9	69.8	70.4	68.1
Colombia	4.5	22.6	28.4	36.1	42.0	47.9	43.6	55.1	59.2
Turkey	20.2	52.3	60.6	73.9	69.6	68.3	59.4	53.1	51.1
Serbia and Montenegro [2] . . .	(X)	(X)	44.7	36.5	40.8	40.0	42.3	44.4	44.9
Romania	38.8	42.1	45.3	25.2	32.3	36.7	33.5	36.4	34.8
Korea, North	48.6	51.0	34.5	30.6	32.8	33.7	31.9	32.5	33.8
Bulgaria	33.3	34.9	30.6	27.9	29.1	29.4	28.7	30.1	29.1
United Kingdom	143.8	104.1	52.5	39.9	33.7	34.7	32.6	30.6	27.0
Spain	31.2	39.6	31.4	26.8	25.9	25.0	24.3	22.7	22.6
Thailand	1.6	13.7	20.3	20.1	19.6	21.6	21.6	20.8	22.1
Vietnam	5.8	5.1	9.2	10.6	12.8	14.3	17.5	18.4	18.1
Estonia	(X)	(X)	13.7	11.8	12.9	13.0	13.7	16.4	15.4
Mexico	4.0	8.6	10.3	11.4	12.5	12.5	12.1	10.6	12.5
Hungary	28.3	19.7	16.1	16.0	15.5	15.3	14.4	14.7	12.4
Venezuela	0.0	2.4	4.5	7.7	8.7	8.4	8.1	7.3	9.0
Mongolia	5.3	7.9	5.5	6.6	6.4	6.6	7.1	7.2	7.2
Macedonia	(X)	(X)	8.0	8.1	8.3	8.9	8.4	8.1	6.8

X Not applicable.   [1] See footnote 2, Table 1298.   [2] As of June 2006, Serbia and Montenegro are separate countries.

Source: U.S. Energy Information Administration, *International Energy Annual, 2004.* See also <http://www.eia.doe.gov/pub /international/iealf/table25.xls> (accessed 11 July 2007).

Table 1349. Net Electricity Generation by Type and Country: 2003

[15,883.5 represents 15,883,500,000,000. kWh = kilowatt hours]

Country	Total [1] (bil. kWh)	Percent distribution Ther-mal [2]	Hydro	Nuclear	Country	Total [1] (bil. kWh)	Percent distribution Ther-mal [2]	Hydro	Nuclear
World, total [3]	15,883.5	65.7	16.5	15.9	Norway	105.6	0.4	98.9	–
United States	3,891.7	70.9	7.1	19.6	Netherlands	91.1	90.0	0.1	4.2
China [4]	1,806.8	82.1	15.4	2.3	Venezuela	89.4	32.8	67.2	–
Japan	982.8	65.1	9.5	23.2	Argentina	88.2	52.8	38.0	8.0
Russia	869.1	65.6	18.0	16.2	Egypt	87.1	85.0	14.7	–
India	598.8	83.9	12.5	2.7	Finland	80.0	48.9	11.9	27.0
Canada	569.4	27.1	58.7	12.5	Belgium	79.1	40.7	0.3	56.9
Germany	561.6	63.2	3.4	27.9	Czech Republic	78.2	66.2	1.8	31.4
France	535.5	9.8	10.9	78.3	Pakistan	77.5	63.2	34.4	2.3
United Kingdom	373.3	74.5	0.9	22.6	Malaysia	74.0	92.3	7.7	–
Brazil	358.6	7.4	84.4	3.7	Switzerland	63.1	1.5	54.6	41.4
Korea, South	325.7	60.1	1.5	37.8	Kazakhstan	60.4	85.9	14.1	–
Italy	268.2	83.2	12.5	–	Austria	59.3	35.5	60.7	–
Spain	245.2	53.4	16.6	24.0	Greece	54.7	89.2	8.6	–
South Africa	215.9	93.7	0.4	5.9	Romania	52.4	66.3	25.0	8.7
Australia	215.0	91.7	7.4	–	Paraguay	51.3	(Z)	100.0	–
Mexico	206.7	81.6	9.5	4.8	Philippines	50.2	65.9	15.5	–
Ukraine	170.0	49.5	5.4	45.1	Chile	47.0	49.0	47.6	–
Taiwan [4]	166.0	73.4	4.1	22.5	Uzbekistan	46.8	86.6	13.4	–
Saudi Arabia	143.8	100.0	–	–	United Arab Emirates. .	46.6	100.0	–	–
Iran	142.9	92.3	7.7	–	Colombia	46.1	21.1	77.7	–
Poland	141.1	98.2	1.2	–	Portugal	44.5	60.0	34.9	–
Turkey	133.9	73.7	26.1	–	Israel	44.2	99.9	0.1	–
Sweden	130.8	6.2	40.3	49.0	Denmark	43.6	80.8	(Z)	–
Thailand	110.4	91.2	6.5	–	Bulgaria	39.9	51.8	8.0	40.2
Indonesia	106.6	86.0	8.4	–					

– Represents zero. Z Less than 0.05 percent. [1] Includes thermal, hydro, nuclear, and geothermal, solar, wind, and wood and waste generation. [2] Electricity generated from coal, oil, and gas. [3] Includes countries not shown separately. [4] See footnote 2, Table 1298.

Source: U.S. Energy Information Administration, *International Energy Annual 2004*. See also <http://www.eia.doe.gov /pub/international/iea2004/table63.xls> (accessed 11 July 2007).

Table 1350. Commercial Nuclear Power Generation by Country: 1990 to 2006

[Generation for calendar years; other data as of December (1,743.9 represents 1,743,900,000,000). kWh = kilowatt hours. kW = kilowatts]

Country	Reactors 1990	2004	2005	2006	Gross electricity generated (bil. kWh) 1990	2004	2005	2006	Gross capacity (1,000 kW) 1990	2004	2005	2006
Total	368	436	446	446	1,743.9	2,707.1	2,690.4	2,688.7	301,745	382,875	391,366	393,893
United States . .	112	104	104	104	606.4	828.2	815.8	822.9	105,998	104,015	104,235	104,997
Argentina	2	2	2	2	7.0	7.9	6.9	7.7	1,005	1,005	1,005	1,005
Armenia	(NA)	1	1	1	(NA)	2.4	2.7	2.6	(NA)	408	408	408
Belgium	7	7	7	7	42.7	47.3	47.6	46.6	5,740	6,101	6,101	6,101
Brazil	1	2	2	2	2.0	11.5	9.8	13.8	657	2,007	2,007	2,007
Bulgaria	(NA)	4	4	4	(NA)	16.8	18.7	19.5	(NA)	2,880	2,880	2,880
Canada	19	21	21	21	74.0	90.9	92.5	98.4	13,855	15,426	15,341	15,341
China [1]	(NA)	2	9	9	(NA)	13.9	53.1	11.5	(NA)	1,968	7,014	7,014
Czech Republic .	(NA)	6	6	6	(NA)	26.2	24.7	25.9	(NA)	3,760	3,760	3,760
Finland	4	4	4	4	18.9	22.7	23.3	22.9	2,400	2,760	2,760	2,800
France	58	59	59	59	314.1	448.2	451.5	450.2	58,862	66,042	66,042	66,130
Germany	22	18	18	17	147.2	167.1	163.0	167.4	23,973	21,693	21,723	21,366
Great Britain . . .	42	24	23	23	68.8	77.2	(NA)	(NA)	15,274	14,000	13,760	13,760
Hungary	4	4	4	4	13.6	11.9	13.8	13.5	1,760	1,866	1,866	1,866
India	6	14	15	16	6.0	16.9	17.6	17.6	1,330	2,770	3,310	3,900
Italy	2	(NA)	(NA)	(NA)	–	(NA)	(NA)	(NA)	1,132	(NA)	(NA)	(NA)
Japan	40	52	54	55	191.9	281.9	287.9	303.2	31,645	45,742	48,222	49,580
Korea, South . . .	9	19	20	20	52.8	129.6	145.6	148.7	7,616	16,768	17,768	18,393
Lithuania	(NA)	2	1	1	(NA)	14.1	10.9	8.6	(NA)	3,000	1,500	1,500
Mexico	1	2	2	2	2.1	9.2	10.8	10.9	675	1,350	1,350	1,350
Netherlands . . .	2	1	1	1	3.4	3.8	3.9	3.5	540	480	480	512
Pakistan	1	2	2	2	0.4	2.1	2.6	2.7	137	462	462	462
Romania	(NA)	1	1	1	(NA)	5.5	5.5	5.6	(NA)	706	706	706
Russia	(NA)	30	31	31	(NA)	142.9	146.8	154.5	(NA)	22,266	23,266	23,266
Slovakia	(NA)	6	6	6	(NA)	17.0	17.7	12.4	(NA)	2,640	2,640	2,640
Slovenia	1	1	1	1	4.6	4.0	5.9	5.5	664	707	707	707
South Africa . . .	2	2	2	2	8.9	14.9	12.8	10.6	1,930	1,930	1,930	1,930
Spain	10	9	9	9	54.3	63.7	57.5	60.1	7,984	7,895	7,895	7,895
Sweden	12	11	11	10	68.2	77.3	72.5	67.7	10,344	9,852	9,852	9,241
Switzerland	5	5	5	5	23.6	26.8	23.2	27.6	3,079	3,352	3,352	3,352
Taiwan [1]	6	6	6	6	32.9	39.5	39.9	39.9	5,146	5,144	5,144	5,144
Ukraine	(NA)	15	15	15	(NA)	85.4	88.8	90.2	(NA)	13,880	13,880	13,880

– Represents zero. NA Not available. [1] See footnote 2, Table 1298.

Source: Platts Energy. A Division of The McGraw-Hill Companies Inc., New York, NY, *Nucleonics Week*, February issue (copyright).

Comparative International Statistics 853

Table 1351. **Selected Indexes of Manufacturing Activity by Country: 1990 to 2005**

[1992 = 100. Data relate to employees (wage and salary earners) in Belgium, and to all employed persons (employees, self-employed workers, and unpaid family workers) in the other countries. Minus sign (–) indicates decrease. For explanation of average annual percent change, see Guide to Tabular Presentation]

Index	United States	Can- ada	Japan	Bel- gium	France	Ger- many	Italy	Nether- lands	Nor- way	Swe- den	United King- dom
Output per hour:											
1990	93.5	93.4	94.4	96.8	92.7	(NA)	97.3	98.7	98.3	94.6	90.1
1995	112.1	112.4	111.0	112.7	116.0	110.2	111.1	117.3	98.7	125.1	105.0
2000	147.7	131.9	131.7	125.7	148.2	132.0	116.0	138.5	105.9	176.8	119.4
2003	175.5	130.7	142.3	134.5	164.2	141.6	111.3	146.4	121.6	204.5	132.3
2004	187.8	130.8	150.4	141.0	170.0	146.6	112.4	153.7	128.8	227.9	139.7
2005	194.0	135.6	154.1	144.9	176.7	154.8	112.5	160.0	132.4	241.9	143.3
Average annual percent change:											
1995–2000	5.7	3.3	3.5	2.2	5.0	3.7	0.9	3.4	1.4	7.2	2.6
2003–2004	7.0	0.1	5.7	4.9	3.6	3.5	0.9	5.0	5.9	11.5	5.6
2004–2005	3.3	3.7	2.4	2.8	3.9	5.6	0.2	4.1	2.8	6.2	2.6
Compensation per hour, national currency basis: [1]											
1990	90.5	88.5	90.6	90.1	88.5	(NA)	87.7	89.8	92.3	87.8	88.7
1995	107.3	106.5	108.3	108.6	110.7	117.0	112.0	112.1	109.2	106.8	107.9
2000	134.7	120.9	114.9	120.1	127.0	136.3	128.7	132.8	140.5	136.8	136.1
2003	158.2	133.0	114.6	135.8	141.4	147.2	140.6	152.8	164.3	159.2	156.8
2004	161.4	134.6	115.1	138.8	144.7	148.0	145.1	158.0	169.7	163.5	164.2
2005	168.8	139.8	117.0	144.6	148.7	149.7	149.5	163.2	175.6	167.2	171.7
Average annual percent change:											
1995–2000	4.7	2.6	1.2	2.0	2.8	3.1	2.8	3.5	5.2	5.1	4.8
2003–2004	2.0	1.2	0.5	2.2	2.3	0.5	3.2	3.5	3.3	2.7	4.7
2004–2005 [2]	4.6	3.9	1.6	4.2	2.7	1.1	3.0	3.3	3.5	2.3	4.6
Real hourly compensation: [2]											
1990	96.1	94.9	95.2	95.2	93.8	(NA)	98.1	95.6	97.7	97.6	97.4
1995	100.1	102.1	106.4	101.7	104.8	107.3	98.0	104.2	102.8	97.9	100.2
2000	112.0	106.2	111.2	103.6	113.2	117.4	99.7	110.9	118.0	120.1	110.7
2003	123.2	108.4	113.0	110.7	119.2	121.3	100.8	116.0	129.1	130.5	119.8
2004	122.3	107.7	113.5	110.8	119.5	120.0	101.8	118.7	132.7	133.5	121.8
2005	123.8	109.3	115.7	112.4	120.6	119.0	102.9	120.4	135.1	136.2	123.8
Average annual percent change:											
1995–2000	2.3	0.8	0.9	0.4	1.6	1.8	0.3	1.3	2.8	4.2	2.0
2003–2004	–0.7	–0.6	0.4	0.1	0.3	–1.1	1.0	2.3	2.8	2.3	1.7
2004–2005	1.2	1.5	1.9	1.4	0.9	–0.8	1.1	1.4	1.8	2.0	1.6
Unit labor costs, national currency: [1]											
1990	96.8	94.8	95.9	93.0	95.5	(NA)	90.2	91.1	93.9	92.9	98.5
1995	95.7	94.7	97.6	96.4	95.4	106.2	100.8	95.6	110.7	85.3	102.7
2000	91.2	91.7	87.3	95.6	85.7	103.3	110.9	95.9	132.7	77.4	114.0
2003	90.2	101.8	80.5	101.0	86.1	104.0	126.3	104.3	135.1	77.9	118.6
2004	85.9	102.9	76.5	98.4	85.1	100.9	129.2	102.8	131.7	71.7	117.6
2005	87.0	103.1	75.9	99.8	84.1	96.7	132.9	102.0	132.6	69.1	119.8
Average annual percent change:											
1995–2000	–0.9	–0.7	–2.2	–0.2	–2.1	–0.5	1.9	0.1	3.7	–1.9	2.1
2003–2004	–4.7	1.1	–5.0	–2.6	–1.2	–2.9	2.3	–1.5	–2.5	–7.9	–0.8
2004–2005	1.3	0.2	–0.8	1.5	–1.2	–4.2	2.9	–0.8	0.7	–3.6	1.9
Unit labor costs, U.S. dollar basis: [1,3]											
1990	96.8	98.1	83.9	89.5	92.8	(NA)	92.7	87.9	93.3	91.3	99.5
1995	95.7	83.4	131.7	105.2	101.3	115.8	76.2	104.8	108.6	69.6	91.8
2000	91.2	74.6	102.6	70.3	63.8	76.2	65.1	70.7	93.6	49.1	97.8
2003	90.2	87.8	88.1	91.1	78.7	94.0	91.0	94.3	118.6	56.2	109.7
2004	85.9	95.5	89.7	97.5	85.5	100.2	102.2	102.1	121.4	56.9	122.0
2005	87.0	102.8	87.4	99.0	84.5	96.1	105.3	101.3	128.0	53.9	123.5
Average annual percent change:											
1995–2000	–0.9	–2.2	–4.9	–7.7	–8.8	–8.0	–3.1	–7.6	–2.9	–6.7	1.3
2003–2004	–4.7	8.8	1.9	7.0	8.6	6.6	12.4	8.3	2.4	1.3	11.2
2004–2005	1.3	7.6	–2.6	1.5	–1.1	–4.1	3.0	–0.7	5.4	–5.2	1.2
Employment:											
1990	105.4	113.2	97.5	102.5	105.2	(NA)	104.2	100.0	105.1	117.2	115.0
1995	102.8	104.8	90.1	91.9	92.6	86.1	94.6	92.1	107.0	98.0	100.9
2000	102.5	116.6	81.4	89.3	91.3	82.7	93.5	92.5	107.9	98.1	95.1
2003	86.3	114.8	73.7	84.3	88.1	79.1	94.7	86.7	98.6	93.9	82.3
2004	85.2	114.7	72.1	82.5	85.3	77.9	93.7	83.1	95.2	91.5	78.7
2005	84.8	112.9	71.6	81.7	83.3	76.6	92.4	81.2	94.4	89.5	75.9
Average annual percent change:											
1995–2000	–0.1	2.2	–2.0	–0.6	–0.3	–0.8	–0.2	0.1	0.2	–	–1.2
2003–2004	–1.3	–0.1	–2.1	–2.2	–3.1	–1.5	–1.1	–4.2	–3.5	–2.6	–4.3
2004–2005	–0.5	–1.6	–0.7	–0.9	–2.3	–1.7	–1.4	–2.3	–0.8	–2.2	–3.6
Aggregate hours:											
1990	105.0	113.5	102.9	104.3	105.5	(NA)	103.3	100.3	103.4	116.4	116.9
1995	104.6	106.4	89.1	92.4	91.6	85.3	98.2	92.3	106.6	105.9	102.7
2000	103.4	120.9	79.8	92.1	86.8	79.4	97.3	91.9	106.4	107.3	96.3
2003	85.4	117.0	72.2	84.3	80.6	74.3	96.8	85.9	94.5	99.6	83.7
2004	84.9	119.2	71.5	83.6	79.1	74.2	96.6	83.2	94.2	98.5	80.9
2005	84.0	115.8	70.5	80.9	77.2	72.6	94.5	80.0	93.9	96.5	78.0
Average annual percent change:											
1995–2000	–0.2	2.6	–2.2	–0.1	–1.1	–1.4	–0.2	–0.1	–	0.3	–1.3
2003–2004	–0.5	1.9	–1.0	–0.9	–1.8	–0.1	–0.2	–3.2	–0.2	–1.1	–3.4
2004–2005	–1.1	–2.8	–1.3	–3.2	–2.4	–2.2	–2.2	–3.8	–0.3	–2.0	–3.6

– Represents or rounds to zero. NA Not available. [1] In Canada, France, Sweden, and the United Kingdom, compensation adjusted for employment taxes and government subsidies to estimate the actual labor cost to employers. [2] Index of hourly compensation divided by the index of consumer prices to adjust for changes in purchasing power. [3] Indexes in national currency adjusted for changes in prevailing exchange rates.

Source: U.S. Bureau of Labor Statistics, *International Comparisons of Manufacturing Productivity and Unit Labor Cost Trends 2005*, Revised, 22 February 2007. See also <http://www.bls.gov/news.release/pdf/prod4.pdf>.

Table 1352. Indexes of Hourly Compensation Costs for Production Workers in Manufacturing by Country: 1980 to 2005

[United States = 100. Compensation costs include pay for time worked, other direct pay (including holiday and vacation pay, bonuses, other direct payments, and the cost of pay in kind), employer expenditures for legally required insurance programs and contractual and private benefit plans, and for some countries, other labor taxes. Data adjusted for exchange rates. Area averages are trade-weighted to account for difference in countries' relative importance to U.S. trade in manufactured goods. The trade weights used to compute the average compensation cost measures for selected economic groups are based on the relative dollar value of U.S. trade in manufactured commodities (exports plus imports) with each country or area in 2004; see source for detail]

Area or country	1980	1985	1990	1994	1995	1996	1997	1998	1999	2000	2001	2002	2003	2004	2005
United States	100	100	100	100	100	100	100	100	100	100	100	100	100	100	100
Total [1]	67	52	80	83	87	83	77	72	73	70	65	65	73	79	80
OECD [2,3]	73	56	85	88	92	88	81	77	78	74	69	70	79	85	86
Europe [3]	99	61	113	111	123	119	107	105	102	90	87	91	107	117	116
EU-15 [4]	98	60	112	110	123	119	107	106	103	91	87	92	107	118	116
Asian newly industrializing economies [5] . . .	12	13	25	35	39	40	39	32	35	36	33	33	34	36	39
Brazil	(NA)	(NA)	(NA)	(NA)	(NA)	32	32	30	18	18	14	12	12	14	17
Canada	92	88	110	97	96	96	93	86	85	84	79	78	88	95	101
Mexico	23	12	11	16	10	9	10	9	10	11	11	12	11	11	11
Australia	88	64	88	84	89	96	92	82	84	73	65	72	89	102	105
Hong Kong [6]	16	14	22	27	28	29	30	29	28	28	28	27	25	24	24
Israel	35	29	52	49	55	57	59	59	56	58	59	52	52	53	53
Japan	57	49	85	125	137	115	104	95	108	112	94	87	91	96	92
Korea, South	10	10	25	38	42	46	43	31	39	42	38	41	44	49	57
New Zealand	56	36	57	54	60	64	62	51	50	43	39	43	53	60	63
Singapore	16	20	25	37	44	46	44	40	37	37	34	31	32	32	32
Sri Lanka.	2	2	2	3	3	3	3	3	2	2	2	2	2	2	(NA)
Taiwan [7]	11	12	26	33	35	34	33	29	31	32	30	26	26	26	27
Austria	92	60	121	128	147	139	120	119	114	97	93	97	115	125	124
Belgium.	122	65	121	131	149	142	122	122	117	102	97	102	120	132	130
Czech Republic.	(X)	(X)	(X)	(NA)	15	17	15	16	16	14	15	18	21	24	26
Denmark	112	64	124	126	147	143	129	130	129	111	108	114	136	151	150
Finland	86	65	143	114	142	133	118	118	114	99	97	102	122	134	135
France	92	59	104	102	112	107	94	94	90	79	76	80	95	105	104
Germany	(X)	(X)	(X)	151	175	167	143	136	130	115	109	114	134	142	140
Greece	39	29	46	46	53	53	50	48	(NA)	(NA)	(NA)	(NA)	(NA)	(NA)	(NA)
Hungary	(NA)	(NA)	(NA)	16	16	15	15	15	15	14	15	18	21	25	26
Ireland	63	47	79	75	80	80	76	74	73	65	66	72	86	96	96
Italy	84	60	117	92	91	96	88	85	82	70	66	69	82	90	89
Luxembourg.	120	59	108	119	137	127	109	106	104	89	84	88	104	116	117
Netherlands	125	69	121	124	140	130	114	115	113	98	97	104	124	135	135
Norway	123	82	147	128	145	143	133	132	131	115	115	131	147	160	166
Poland	(NA)	(NA)	(NA)	(NA)	(NA)	(NA)	15	16	15	14	16	15	16	17	19
Portugal	21	12	24	26	30	30	28	28	27	23	22	24	28	31	31
Spain	61	36	76	68	74	75	66	64	63	54	53	56	68	75	75
Sweden.	129	76	140	111	126	137	122	119	114	103	90	95	113	125	121
Switzerland	114	75	139	147	168	157	131	130	123	107	105	111	125	132	129
United Kingdom	78	49	85	77	80	86	92	92	86	82	86	86	96	109	109

NA Not available.   X Not applicable.   [1] For 1980–1990, the trade-weighted measure includes all 32 foreign economies except for Brazil, the Czech Republic, Hungary, and Poland. For 1994, it includes all but Brazil, the Czech Republic, and Poland. For 1995, it includes all but Brazil and Poland. For 1996, it includes all but Poland. For 1998 onward, the measure includes all 32 economies.   [2] Organization for Economic Cooperation and Development; see text of this section.   [3] Data for the Czech Republic 1980–1994, for Hungary 1980–1990, and for Poland 1980–1996 are not included.   [4] European Union-15 refers to European Union member countries prior to the expansion of the European Union to 25 countries on May 1, 2004, and to 27 countries on January 1, 2007. For a list of EU-15 countries, see Table 1320.   [5] Hong Kong, South Korea, Singapore, and Taiwan.   [6] Hong Kong Special Administrative Region of China.   [7] See footnote 2, Table 1298.

Source: U.S. Bureau of Labor Statistics, *International Comparisons of Hourly Compensation Costs for Production Workers in Manufacturing, 2005*, 30 November 2006. See also <http://www.bls.gov/news.release/pdf/ichcc.pdf>.

Comparative International Statistics **855**

Table 1353. Key Global Telecom Indicators for the World Telecommunication Service Sector: 1995 to 2004

[In billions U.S. dollars (779 represents $779,000,000,000), except as indicated. All data were converted by annual average exchange rates. Country fiscal year data was aggregated to obtain calendar year estimates]

Indicators	1995	1999	2000	2001	2002	2003	2004
Telecom market total revenue (bil. dol.)	779	1,123	1,210	1,232	1,314	1,426	(NA)
Telecom telephone services revenue [1] (bil. dol.)	428	476	477	479	478	475	552
Other statistics:							
Main telephone lines (mil.) [2]	689	905	983	1,053	1,086	1,140	1,207
Mobile cellular subscribers (mil.)	91	490	740	955	1,166	1,414	1,758
International telephone traffic minutes [3] (bil.)	63	100	118	127	131	142	145
Personal computers (mil.).....................	235	435	500	555	615	650	775
Internet users (mil.)........................	40	277	399	502	619	724	863

NA Not available. [1] Revenue from installation, subscription and local, trunk and international call charges for fixed telephone service. [2] See footnote 1, Table 1354. [3] Including traffic between countries of former Soviet Union.

Source: International Telecommunication Union, Geneva Switzerland, 2005; <http://www.itu.int/ITU-D/ict/statistics/at_glance /KeyTelecom99.html>. Reproduced with the kind permission of ITU.

Table 1354. Telephones, Cellphones, and Computers by Country: 2005

[Rates per 100 persons. For data qualifications for countries, see source]

Country	Telephone main lines [1]	Cellular phone subscribers	Personal computers [2]	Country	Telephone main lines [1]	Cellular phone subscribers	Personal computers [2]
Afghanistan	0.33	4.02	0.28	Lebanon	17.75	27.78	11.45
Argentina......	24.47	57.41	9.07	Malaysia	16.79	75.17	21.54
Australia	50.21	91.39	76.61	Mexico	18.23	44.04	13.08
Austria	45.74	105.81	61.12	Netherlands	46.63	97.15	85.55
Bahamas......	41.19	70.50	12.38	New Zealand ...	42.91	87 61	51.55
Belgium.......	45.35	90.00	37.62	Nigeria	0.93	14.13	0.91
Brazil	21.38	46.25	16.09	Norway	46.08	102.90	59.41
Canada.......	64.12	52.51	87.31	Pakistan	3.40	8.30	0.52
China [3].......	26.63	29.90	4.22	Peru	8.05	19.96	10.01
Colombia......	16.84	47.92	4.15	Poland	30.72	75.70	23.99
Cuba	7.60	1.20	3.35	Portugal	40.34	109.08	13.40
Czech Republic..	31.48	115.22	27.40	Russia........	27.94	83.62	12.13
Egypt	14.57	19.10	3.78	Saudi Arabia ...	15.64	57.64	48.46
Finland	40.39	100.40	50.01	Singapore	42.39	100.76	68.02
France	55.72	79.49	57.86	South Africa	9.97	71.60	8.36
Germany	66.15	95.78	60.47	Spain	42.17	100.01	28.11
Greece	56.75	92.27	9.17	Sudan........	1.62	5.21	9.26
Hungary	33.24	92.30	14.90	Sweden.......	70.56	100.70	83.49
India	4.55	8.17	1.54	Switzerland	69.02	91.60	86.18
Indonesia.....	5.73	21.06	1.47	Syria	15.24	15.49	4.20
Iran	27.31	10.39	12.51	Thailand	10.95	48.47	6.86
Ireland	49.47	102.94	52.99	Turkey........	25.93	59.58	5.56
Israel	42.56	112.42	122.52	United Kingdom .	57.10	109.73	76.52
Italy	43.12	124.28	36.99	United States ..	58.74	71.50	(NA)
Japan	45.32	75.33	67.45	Venezuela	13.65	46.71	9.25
Korea, South ..	55.93	79.39	53.18	Vietnam.......	18.81	11.39	1.39

NA Not available. [1] Fixed telephone lines refer to telephone lines connecting a customer's terminal equipment (e.g. telephone set, facsimile machine) to the public switched telephone network (PSTN) and which have a dedicated port on a telephone exchange. Fixed telephone lines per 100 inhabitants is calculated by dividing the number of fixed telephone lines by the population and multiplying by 100. [2] In many countries mainframe computers are used extensively, and thousands of users can be connected to a single mainframe computer; thus the number of PCs understates the total use of computers. [3] See footnote 2, Table 1298.

Source: International Telecommunications Union, Geneva, Switzerland, World Telecommunication Indicators, (copyright). See also <http://www.itu.int/ITU-D/ict/statistics/at_glance/main05.pdf>. Reproduced with the kind permission of ITU.

Table 1355. Patents by Country: 2006

[Includes only U.S. patents granted to residents of areas outside of the United States and its territories. See also Table 753]

Country	Total [1]	Inventions	Designs	Country	Total [1]	Inventions	Designs
Total	94,165	83,948	9,274	Netherlands	1,647	1,323	107
				Sweden	1,537	1,325	160
Japan	39,411	36,807	2,405	Switzerland.......	1,388	1,201	182
Germany	10,889	10,005	773	Australia........	1,360	1,243	112
Taiwan [2].......	7,919	6,360	1,553	Israel	1,325	1,218	64
Korea, South.....	6,509	5,908	589	Finland.........	1,005	950	53
United Kingdom....	4,328	3,585	664	Belgium	720	625	69
Canada	4,094	3,572	501	Austria	625	577	48
France	3,856	3,431	395	Denmark........	546	439	33
Italy	1,899	1,480	416	Other countries	5,107	3,899	1,150

[1] Includes patents for botanical plants and reissues, not shown separately. [2] See footnote 2, Table 1298.

Source: U.S. Patent and Trademark Office, Technology Assessment and Forecast Database.

Table 1356. Dow-Jones World Stock Index by Country and Industry: 2000 to 2006

[Index figures shown are as of December 31. Based on share prices denominated in U.S. dollars. Stocks in countries that impose significant restrictions on foreign ownership are included in the world index in the same proportion that shares are available to foreign investors]

Country and industry	2000	2004	2005	2006	Country and industry	2000	2004	2005	2006
World, total. . . .	210.9	214.0	234.1	277.5	Asia/Pacific	93.0	108.6	132.0	146.2
Americas.	299.1	289.0	307.3	351.7	Australia	156.0	280.7	312.5	400.6
United States	306.9	289.4	302.4	343.2	Hong Kong.	245.6	255.8	273.6	378.0
Canada	225.3	291.2	369.4	425.7	Indonesia	31.2	72.5	79.0	128.0
Mexico	132.2	257.3	360.1	501.0	Japan	88.3	90.6	113.5	115.8
Europe	241.2	246.7	267.4	349.7	Malaysia	88.5	120.7	119.5	158.9
Austria	86.2	277.5	335.5	400.6	New Zealand	96.7	235.1	227.3	259.5
Belgium	196.9	310.9	321.2	427.5	Singapore	135.2	158.6	176.3	249.4
Denmark	220.1	307.8	375.1	505.7	Thailand	27.2	73.0	76.7	81.3
Finland	1,537.8	834.0	948.5	1,206.6					
France	252.9	250.5	273.3	365.7	Basic materials.	117.6	179.4	213.8	273.5
Germany	219.1	206.8	224.3	302.8	Consumer goods	183.8	226.4	241.9	290.4
Ireland.	312.3	470.8	470.4	672.0	Consumer services	192.8	209.8	214.4	245.3
Italy	192.2	218.1	213.8	280.6	Oil and gas	230.7	298.2	383.3	450.7
Netherlands	335.7	279.4	309.6	401.8	Financial	207.1	236.3	259.8	314.2
Norway	151.8	228.2	276.1	402.4	Healthcare.	329.9	287.0	310.6	340.5
Spain	193.5	279.7	288.6	422.1	Industrial.	167.1	171.2	192.4	226.4
Sweden.	339.0	348.9	378.3	542.6	Technology	552.7	355.3	375.1	412.7
Switzerland	388.8	393.8	452.5	577.6	Telecommunications . . .	273.3	217.8	201.6	260.1
United Kingdom	199.8	207.3	217.6	278.3	Utilities	156.0	159.3	176.9	233.0

Source: Dow Jones & Company, Inc., New York, NY, *Dow Jones Indexes*, (copyright).

Table 1357. Foreign Stock Market Activity—Morgan Stanley Capital International Indexes: 2000 to 2006

[Index figures shown are as of December 31. January 1, 1970 = 100, except as noted. Minus sign (–) indicates decrease. Based on share prices denominated in U.S. dollars. EM = Emerging Markets]

Index and country	Index			Percent change [1]		Index and country	Index			Percent change [1]	
	2000	2005	2006	2005	2006		2000	2005	2006	2005	2006
ALL COUNTRY (AC) INDEXES						Sweden.	4,240	4,868	6,839	8.1	40.5
						Switzerland	2,695	3,241	4,079	14.9	25.9
AC World index [2]	289.8	309.6	367.8	8.8	18.8	United Kingdom	1,146	1,206	1,522	3.7	26.2
AC World index except USA [2]	195.4	236.4	292.7	13.9	23.8	Hong Kong	5,475	5,742	7,250	4.8	26.3
AC Asia Pacific [2]	92.7	122.7	140.5	21.0	14.5	Japan	2,552	3,053	3,208	24.1	5.1
AC Europe [2]	376.5	407.8	531.5	7.3	30.3	Singapore	2,081	2,396	3,400	10.8	41.9
European Union [2]	361.5	378.2	494.1	5.6	30.6						
						EMERGING MARKETS					
DEVELOPED MARKETS						EM Far East index [4] . . .	123.8	256.4	327.1	22.1	27.6
World index [3]	1,221	1,258	1,484	7.6	18.0	India [6]	114.5	262.3	390.6	35.4	48.9
EAFE index [3]	1,492	1,680	2,074	10.9	23.5	Indonesia.	78.2	264.9	449.3	12.6	69.6
Europe index	1,378	1,548	1,912	6.5	30.2	Korea, South	78.7	302.8	336.7	54.3	11.2
Pacific index	1,832	2,333	2,577	20.6	10.5	Malaysia [6]	160.9	216.9	288.6	-1.5	33.1
Far East index	2,583	3,061	3,287	22.4	7.4	Pakistan [6]	44.3	143.6	141.2	56.5	-1.7
United States	1,250	1,181	1,336	3.8	13.1	Philippines	142.2	169.4	263.2	19.9	55.4
Canada	832.5	1,302	1,513	26.6	16.2	Sri Lanka [6]	36.3	128.3	183.2	30.7	42.8
Australia	317.7	629.0	799.0	12.6	27.0	Taiwan [7]	191.7	239.8	278.8	3.3	16.3
New Zealand [4]	56.4	134.0	147.9	-3.8	10.4	Thailand	56.9	177.7	189.7	4.9	6.7
Austria	708.3	2,411	3,249	23.0	34.8	EM Latin America. . .	1,002	2,150	2,996	44.9	39.3
Belgium	1,222	1,696	2,261	5.6	33.3	Argentina.	1,233	1,857	3,084	59.7	66.1
Denmark	2,201	3,551	4,859	22.5	36.8	Brazil	870	1,569	2,205	50.0	40.5
Finland [4]	921.8	534.0	679.3	14.0	27.2	Chile.	605	1,181	1,492	18.4	26.4
France	1,509	1,558	2,052	7.8	31.7	Colombia [6]	42.1	495.7	549.8	102.3	10.9
Germany	1,436	1,430	1,902	7.7	33.0	Mexico	1,197	3,944	5,483	45.2	39.0
Greece [4]	475.8	609.0	801.7	12.6	31.6	Peru [6]	125.0	441.3	671.4	28.5	52.1
Ireland [4]	308.4	393.0	565.4	-4.8	43.9	Venezuela [6]	106.1	107.4	174.1	-28.9	62.1
Italy	447.2	497.0	636.0	-1.2	28.0	Czech Republic [8] . . .	79.9	421.5	546.5	43.5	29.7
Luxembourg [5]	491.9	(NA)	(NA)	(NA)	(NA)	Hungary [8]	233.6	765.0	1,003	15.6	31.1
Netherlands	2,177	1,939	2,487	10.6	28.3	Jordan [8]	55.1	309.8	209.1	71.7	-32.5
Norway	1,181	2,392	3,386	20.0	41.6	Poland [8]	499.0	903.9	1,223	21.0	35.3
Portugal [4]	127.8	135.0	193.3	-4.3	43.2	Russia [8]	155.2	813.4	1,250	69.5	53.7
Spain	347.1	494.4	716.0	1.6	44.8	South Africa [8]	157.6	377.9	443.1	24.0	17.3
						Turkey. [8]	247.7	486.6	441.7	51.6	-9.2

NA Not available. [1] Percent change during calendar year (e.g. December 31, 2005 through December 31, 2006). Adjusted for foreign exchange fluctuations relative to U.S. dollar. [2] January 1, 1988 = 100. [3] Europe, Australasia, Far East Index. Comprises all European and Far East countries listed under developed markets plus Australia and New Zealand. [4] January 1, 1988 = 100. [5] MSCI Luxembourg Index discontinued as of March 29, 2002. [6] January 1, 1993 = 100. [7] See footnote 2, Table 1298. [8] January 1, 1995 = 100.

Source: Morgan Stanley Capital International, New York, NY, <http://www.mscibarra.com/about/indexdata_tou.jsp?/products /indices/stdindex/performance.jsp> (copyright). This information may not be reproduced or redisseminated in any form without prior written permission from Morgan Stanley Capital International. This information is provided on an "as is" basis. Neither Morgan Stanley nor any other party makes any representation or warranty of any kind either express or implied, with respect to this information (or the results to be obtained by the use thereof) and Morgan Stanley expressly disclaims any and all warranties of originality, accuracy, completeness, merchantability, and fitness for any particular purpose. The user of this information assumes the entire risk of any use made of the information. In no event shall Morgan Stanley or any other part be liable to the user for any direct or indirect damages, including without limitation, any lost profits, lost savings, or other incidental or consequential damages arising out of use of this information.

Table 1358. **Foreign Stock Market Indices: 1980 to 2006**

[As of year end. The DAX-30 index is a total return index which includes dividends, whereas the other foreign indices are price indices which exclude dividends]

Year	London FTSE 100	Tokyo Nikkei 225	Hong Kong Hang Seng	Germany DAX-30	Paris CAC-40	Dow Jones Europe STOXX 50
1980	647	7,116	1,477	481	(X)	(X)
1985	1,413	13,113	1,752	1,366	(X)	(X)
1990	2,144	23,849	3,025	1,398	1,518	835
1992	2,847	16,925	5,512	1,545	1,858	1,058
1993	3,418	17,417	11,888	2,267	2,268	1,429
1994	3,066	19,723	8,191	2,107	1,881	1,299
1995	3,689	19,868	10,073	2,254	1,872	1,538
1996	4,119	19,361	13,452	2,889	2,316	1,850
1997	5,136	15,259	10,723	5,002	2,999	2,634
1998	5,883	13,842	9,507	5,002	3,943	3,320
1999	6,930	18,934	16,962	6,958	5,958	4,742
2000	6,223	13,786	15,096	6,434	5,926	4,557
2001	5,217	10,543	11,397	5,160	4,625	3,707
2002	3,940	8,579	9,321	2,893	3,064	2,408
2003	4,477	10,677	12,576	3,965	3,558	2,660
2004	4,814	11,489	14,230	4,256	3,821	2,775
2005	5,619	16,111	14,876	5,408	4,715	3,349
2006	6,221	17,226	19,965	6,597	5,542	3,697

X Not applicable.

Source: Global Financial Data, Los Angeles, CA, <http://www.globalfinancialdata.com>, unpublished data (copyright).

Table 1359. **United States and Foreign Stock Markets—Market Capitalization and Value of Shares Traded: 2000 to 2006**

[In billions of U.S. dollars (15,104.0 represents $15,104,000,000,000). Market capitalization is the market value of all domestic listed companies at the end of the year. The market value of a company is the share price times the number of shares outstanding. Value of shares traded is the annual total turnover of listed company shares]

Country	Market capitalization				Value of shares traded			
	2000	2004	2005	2006	2000	2004	2005	2006
United States	15,104.0	16,323.7	16,970.9	19,425.9	31,862.5	19,354.9	21,510.0	33,267.6
Argentina	166.1	46.4	61.5	79.7	6.0	7.6	16.4	4.5
Australia	372.8	776.4	804.1	1,095.9	226.3	514.2	616.1	826.3
Austria	29.9	85.8	124.4	191.3	9.4	23.8	45.9	79.6
Belgium	182.5	768.4	288.5	396.2	38.0	70.3	125.7	165.9
Brazil	226.2	330.3	474.6	711.1	101.3	93.6	154.2	254.5
Canada	841.4	1,177.5	1,480.9	1,700.7	634.7	653.9	845.0	1,290.2
Chile	60.4	117.1	136.4	174.6	6.1	11.6	18.9	28.8
China [1]	581.0	639.8	780.8	2,426.3	721.5	748.3	586.3	1,635.1
Denmark	107.7	151.3	178.0	231.0	91.6	97.5	152.0	176.7
Egypt	28.7	38.5	79.7	93.5	11.1	5.6	25.4	47.5
Finland	293.6	183.8	209.5	265.5	206.6	220.0	273.5	356.8
France	1,446.6	1,857.2	1,758.7	2,428.6	1,083.3	1,311.7	1,526.1	2,504.7
Germany	1,270.2	1,194.5	1,221.3	1,637.8	1,069.1	1,406.1	1,763.2	2,486.7
Greece	110.8	125.2	145.0	208.3	95.1	43.5	65.3	107.5
Hong Kong	623.4	861.5	1,055.0	1,715.0	377.9	439.0	460.1	830.7
India	148.1	387.9	553.1	818.9	509.8	379.1	433.9	638.5
Indonesia	26.8	73.3	81.4	138.9	14.3	27.6	41.9	48.8
Iran	34.0	47.0	38.7	37.9	5.0	13.3	8.2	4.9
Ireland	81.9	114.1	114.1	163.4	14.4	44.3	64.7	79.9
Israel	64.1	95.5	120.1	173.3	23.4	46.2	59.9	88.8
Italy	768.4	789.6	798.2	1,026.6	778.4	804.3	1,115.2	1,366.1
Japan	3,157.2	3,678.3	4,736.5	4,726.3	2,693.9	3,430.4	4,997.4	6,252.5
Korea, South	171.6	428.6	718.2	835.2	1,067.7	638.9	1,203.0	1,340.1
Luxembourg	34.0	50.1	51.3	79.5	1.2	0.4	0.2	0.2
Malaysia	116.9	190.0	181.2	235.4	58.5	59.9	50.0	66.9
Mexico	125.2	171.9	239.1	348.3	45.3	42.8	52.7	80.1
Morocco	10.9	25.1	27.2	49.4	1.1	1.7	4.1	13.5
Netherlands	640.5	622.3	592.9	779.6	677.2	604.2	835.8	1,096.1
New Zealand	18.6	43.7	43.4	44.9	10.8	15.4	17.4	19.8
Norway	65.0	141.4	191.0	281.1	60.1	135.5	194.8	351.0
Philippines	51.6	28.9	40.2	68.4	8.2	3.7	7.0	11.2
Poland	31.3	71.1	93.9	149.1	14.6	16.6	30.0	55.0
Portugal	60.7	73.4	67.0	104.2	54.4	34.6	41.6	70.2
Russia	38.9	268.0	548.6	1,057.2	20.3	130.8	159.3	514.4
Saudi Arabia	67.2	306.2	646.1	326.9	17.3	473.0	1,103.5	1,403.0
Singapore	152.8	171.6	316.7	276.3	91.5	81.3	119.8	184.4
Sweden	328.3	376.8	403.9	573.3	390.0	412.4	464.0	677.1
Switzerland	792.3	825.8	938.6	1,212.5	609.1	727.1	883.3	1,286.8
Taiwan [1]	247.6	441.4	516.0	654.9	983.5	718.6	716.5	894.6
Thailand	29.5	115.4	124.9	141.1	23.3	109.9	89.3	100.8
Turkey	69.7	98.3	161.5	162.4	179.2	147.4	201.3	227.6
United Kingdom	2,580.0	2,815.9	3,058.2	3,794.3	1,835.3	3,707.2	4,167.0	4,242.1

[1] See footnote 2, Table 1298.

Source: Standard and Poor's, New York, NY, Standard & Poor's Emerging Stock Markets Factbook 2007 (copyright).

858 Comparative International Statistics

Table 1360. Foreign Exchange Rates: 2006

[Foreign currency units per U.S. dollar. Rates shown include market, official, principal, and secondary rates]

Country	Currency	2006	Country	Currency	2006
Afghanistan[1]	Afghanis	46.00	Laos	Kip	10,235.0
Albania	Leks	98.38	Latvia	Lats	0.56
Algeria	Algerian dinars	72.65	Lebanon	Lebanese pounds	1,507.50
Antigua and Barbuda	E.Caribbean dollars	2.70	Lesotho	Maloti	6.85
Argentina	Argentine pesos	3.05	Liberia	Liberian dollars	59.43
Armenia	Drams	414.69	Libya[1]	Libyan dinars	1.31
Aruba	Aruban florins	1.79	Lithuania[2]	Litai	2.75
Australia	Australian dollars	1.33	Luxembourg[2]	Euro	0.80
Austria[2]	Euro	0.80	Macedonia	Denars	48.98
Bahamas, The	Bahamian dollars	1.00	Madagascar	Malagasy ariary	2,161.40
Bahrain	Bahrain dinars	0.38	Malaysia	Ringgit	3.67
Bangladesh	Taka	69.03	Mali	CFA francs	522.59
Barbados	Barbados dollars	2.00	Malta	Maltese liri	0.37
Belarus[2]	Belarusian rubel	2,144.60	Mauritania	Ouguiyas	271.30
Belgium[2]	Euro	0.80	Mauritius	Mauritian rupees	31.66
Belize	Belize dollars	2.00	Mexico	Mexican pesos	10.90
Benin	CFA francs	522.59	Moldova	Lei	13.13
Bolivia	Bolivianos	8.02	Mongolia	Togrogs	1,179.60
Botswana	Pula	5.84	Morocco	Dirhams	8.77
Brazil	Reals	2.18	Mozambique	Meticais	25.40
Bulgaria	Leva	1.56	Namibia	Namibia dollars	6.76
Burkina Faso	CFA francs	522.59	Nepal	Nepalese rupees	72.45
Burma[1]	Kyats	(NA)	Netherlands[2]	Euro	0.80
Cambodia	Riel	4,103.00	Netherlands Antilles	Guilders	1.79
Cameroon	CFA francs	522.59	New Zealand	New Zealand dollars	1.54
Canada	Canadian dollars	1.13	Nicaragua	Cordobas	17.58
Central African Republic	CFA francs	522.59	Niger	CFA francs	522.59
Chad	CFA francs	522.59	Nigeria	Naira	127.38
Chile	Chilean pesos	530.29	Norway	Norwegian kroner	6.41
China[3]	Yuan	7.97	Oman	Rials omani	0.38
Colombia	Colombian pesos	2,358.60	Pakistan	Pakistan rupees	60.35
Comoros	Comorian francs	392.03	Panama	Balboas	1.00
Congo (Brazzaville)[4]	CFA francs	522.59	Papua New Guinea	Kina	3.06
Costa Rica	Colones	511.30	Paraguay	Guaranies	5,672.80
Cote d'Ivoire	CFA francs	522.89	Peru	Nuevos soles	3.27
Croatia	Kunas	5.86	Philippines	Philippine pesos	51.25
Cyprus	Cyprus pounds	0.46	Poland	Zlotys	3.10
Czech Republic	Koruny	22.60	Portugal[2]	Euro	0.80
Denmark	Kroner	5.95	Qatar	Qatar riyals	3.64
Djibouti	Djibouti francs	174.75	Romania	Lei	2.81
Dominica	E.Caribbean dollars	2.70	Russia	Russian rubles	27.20
Dominican Republic	Dominican pesos	33.41	Rwanda	Rwanda francs	560.00
Ecuador	U.S. dollars	(NA)	Saint Kitts and Nevis	E. Caribbean dollars	2.70
Egypt	Egyptian pounds	5.73	Saint Lucia	E. Caribbean dollars	2.70
El Salvador	Colones	(NA)	Saint Vincent and the		
Equatorial Guinea	CFA francs	522.40	Grenadines	E. Caribbean dollars	2.70
Estonia	Krooni	12.47	Saudi Arabia	Saudi A. riyals	3.75
Ethiopia[1]	Birr	8.69	Senegal	CFA francs	522.89
Euro area (EMU-11)[2]	Euro	0.80	Sierra Leone	Leones	2,961.70
Fiji	Fiji dollars	1.73	Singapore	Singapore dollar	1.59
Finland[2]	Euro	0.80	Slovakia	Koruny	29.61
France[2]	Euro	0.80	Slovenia	Tolars	190.85
Gabon	CFA francs	522.89	South Africa	Rand	6.76
Georgia[2]	Lari	1.78	Spain[2]	Euro	0.80
Germany[2]	Euro	0.80	Sri Lanka	Sri Lanka rupees	103.99
Greece[2]	Euro	0.80	Sudan	Sudanese dinars	217.20
Guatemala	Quetzales	7.60	Suriname[1]	Suriname dollar	(NA)
Guyana	Guyana dollars	200.28	Swaziland	Emalangeni	6.85
Haiti	Gourdes	40.23	Sweden	Swedish kronor	7.37
Honduras	Lempiras	18.90	Switzerland	Swiss francs	1.25
Hong Kong	Hong Kong dollars	7.77	Syria	Syrian pounds	51.69
Hungary	Forint	210.39	Tanzania	Tanzania shillings	1,251.90
Iceland	Kronur	70.20	Thailand	Baht	37.88
India	Indian rupees	45.30	Togo	CFA francs	522.59
Indonesia	Rupiah	9,159.30	Trinidad and Tobago	Tt dollars	6.31
Iran	Rials	9,227.10	Tunisia	Tunisian dinars	1.33
Iraq	Dinars	1,466.00	Turkey	Liras	1.43
Ireland[2]	Euro	0.80	Uganda	Uganda shillings	1,834.90
Israel	New sheqalim	4.46	Ukraine	Hryvnias	5.05
Italy[2]	Euro	0.80	United Arab Emirates	Dirhams	3.67
Jamaica	Jamaica dollars	65.77	United Kingdom	Pounds sterling	0.54
Japan	Yen	116.18	Uruguay	Uruguayan pesos	24.05
Jordan	Jordinian dinars	0.71	Vanuatu	Vatu	111.93
Kazakhstan	Tenge	126.09	Venezuela	Bolivars	2,147.00
Kenya	Kenya shillings	72.10	Yemen	Yemeni rials	197.18
Korea, South	Won	955.30	Zambia	Zambian kwacha	3,601.50
Kuwait	Kuwaiti dinars	0.29	Zimbabwe	Zimbabwe dollar	162.07
Kyrgyzstan	Soms	40.15			

NA Not available. [1] End-of year values were used if annual averages were unavailable. Some values were estimated using partial year data. [2] The euro became the official currency of the 11 Euro Area (EMU) nations on January 1, 1999, Greece in 2001, and Slovenia in 2007. [3] See footnote 2, Table 1298. [4] See footnote 3, Table 1298.

Source: Central Intelligence Agency, The World Factbook, 2007. See also <https://www.cia.gov/library/publications/the-world-factbook/fields/2076.html/>.

Comparative International Statistics 859

Table 1361. Reserve Assets and International Transaction Balances by Country: 2000 to 2006

[In millions of U.S. dollars (56,600 represents $56,600,000,000). Assets include holdings of convertible foreign currencies, special drawing rights, and reserve position in International Monetary Fund and exclude gold holdings. Minus sign (−) indicates debits]

Country	Total reserve assets		2006 Total	2006 Currency holdings[1]	Current account balance			Merchandise trade balance		
	2000	2005			2000	2005	2006	2000	2005	2006
United States	56,600	54,080	54,850	40,940	−415,150	−791,510	(NA)	−449,780	−778,940	(NA)
Algeria	12,024	56,303	77,914	77,781	(NA)	(NA)	(NA)	(NA)	(NA)	(NA)
Argentina	25,147	27,179	30,903	30,421	−8,981	5,395	(NA)	2,452	12,805	(NA)
Australia	18,118	41,941	53,448	52,821	−14,763	−40,977	(NA)	−4,862	−13,372	(NA)
Austria	14,319	6,839	7,010	6,573	−4,864	4,252	(NA)	−2,737	3,427	(NA)
Bangladesh	1,486	2,767	3,806	3,804	−306	−132	(NA)	−1,654	−3,106	(NA)
Belgium[2]	9,994	8,241	8,783	7,619	11,381	(NA)	(NA)	2,591	(NA)	(NA)
Brazil	32,488	53,574	85,561	85,553	−24,225	14,199	(NA)	−698	44,757	(NA)
Burma	223	771	1,236	1,235	−212	(NA)	(NA)	−504	(NA)	(NA)
Cameroon	212	949	1,716	1,711	−249	(NA)	(NA)	502	(NA)	(NA)
Canada	32,102	32,962	34,994	33,198	19,622	26,555	21,441	45,047	53,791	47,780
Chile	15,035	16,929	19,392	19,225	−898	703	(NA)	2,119	10,180	(NA)
China[3]	168,278	821,514	1,068,493	1,066,344	20,518	160,818	(NA)	34,474	134,189	(NA)
Colombia	8,916	14,787	15,296	14,673	764	−1,886	(NA)	2,633	1,595	(NA)
Congo (Brazzaville)[4]	222	732	1,841	1,840	648	903	(NA)	2,037	3,374	(NA)
Cote d'Ivoire	668	1,322	1,798	1,796	−241	−12	(NA)	1,486	2,394	(NA)
Denmark	15,108	[5]32,930	29,724	29,160	2,262	9,731	6,696	6,641	7,417	2,906
Ecuador	947	1,714	1,490	1,456	921	−59	(NA)	1,395	712	(NA)
Egypt	13,118	20,609	24,462	24,341	−971	2,103	(NA)	−8,321	−7,745	(NA)
Finland	7,977	10,521	6,494	6,135	10,526	9,517	(NA)	13,684	9,562	(NA)
France	37,039	27,753	42,652	40,287	18,580	−33,290	(NA)	−3,620	−32,140	(NA)
Germany	56,890	45,140	41,687	37,719	−31,960	116,030	(NA)	55,460	189,270	(NA)
Ghana	232	1,753	2,090	2,089	−387	−812	(NA)	−830	−2,543	(NA)
Greece	13,424	506	566	408	−9,820	−17,879	(NA)	−20,239	−34,253	(NA)
Hungary	11,190	18,539	21,527	21,316	−4,004	−7,451	(NA)	−2,913	−1,795	(NA)
India	37,902	131,924	170,738	170,187	−4,601	(NA)	(NA)	−10,640	(NA)	(NA)
Indonesia	28,502	32,989	40,934	40,697	7,992	929	(NA)	25,042	22,323	(NA)
Ireland	5,360	779	720	494	−516	−5,331	(NA)	25,010	36,809	(NA)
Israel	23,281	28,059	29,153	29,011	−854	3,756	(NA)	−3,540	−3,768	(NA)
Italy	25,567	25,515	25,662	24,413	−5,781	−27,724	(NA)	9,549	60	(NA)
Japan	354,902	834,275	879,682	874,936	119,660	165,780	(NA)	116,720	93,960	(NA)
Kenya	898	1,799	2,415	2,395	−199	−495	(NA)	−1,262	−2,168	(NA)
Korea, South	96,131	210,317	238,882	238,388	12,251	16,559	(NA)	16,954	33,473	(NA)
Kuwait	7,082	8,863	12,566	12,178	14,679	32,634	(NA)	13,027	31,203	(NA)
Malaysia	28,330	69,850	82,133	81,724	8,488	19,980	(NA)	20,827	33,156	(NA)
Mexico	35,509	74,054	76,271	75,448	−18,707	−5,054	(NA)	−8,337	−7,587	(NA)
Morocco	4,823	16,187	20,341	20,182	−501	1,018	(NA)	−3,235	−8,204	(NA)
Nepal	945	1,499	(NA)	(NA)	−299	1	(NA)	−814	−1,374	(NA)
Netherlands	9,643	8,986	10,802	9,327	7,264	48,936	(NA)	17,800	46,460	(NA)
Nigeria	9,911	28,280	(NA)	(NA)	7,429	24,202	(NA)	10,415	30,781	(NA)
Norway	27,597	46,986	56,842	56,181	25,851	46,560	(NA)	25,975	49,689	(NA)
Pakistan	1,513	10,033	11,543	11,328	−85	−3,608	(NA)	−1,157	−6,341	(NA)
Peru	8,374	13,599	16,733	16,732	−1,526	1,030	(NA)	−411	5,163	(NA)
Philippines	13,090	15,926	20,025	19,891	−2,225	2,338	(NA)	−5,971	−7,546	(NA)
Poland	26,562	40,864	46,371	46,107	−9,981	−5,105	(NA)	−12,307	2,766	(NA)
Portugal	8,909	3,479	2,064	1,835	−11,748	−17,000	(NA)	−14,532	−20,855	(NA)
Romania	2,470	19,872	28,066	28,066	−1,355	−8,621	(NA)	−1,684	−9,618	(NA)
Saudi Arabia	19,585	26,530	27,523	25,971	14,317	87,131	(NA)	13,956	37,890	(NA)
Singapore	80,132	115,794	136,717	136,270	10,728	33,212	(NA)	4,698	−1,204	(NA)
South Africa	6,083	18,579	23,057	22,720	−191	−9,142	(NA)	−37,087	−85,592	(NA)
Spain	30,989	9,678	10,822	10,088	−23,155	−83,136	(NA)	−1,044	−1,630	(NA)
Sri Lanka	1,039	2,651	2,837	2,762	−1,044	−740	(NA)	440	−1,122	(NA)
Sudan	138	1,869	1,660	1,657	−557	3,013	(NA)	15,215	19,701	(NA)
Sweden	14,863	22,090	24,778	24,074	6,617	23,643	(NA)	2,071	5,886	(NA)
Switzerland	32,272	36,297	38,094	37,364	33,562	60,973	(NA)	1,423	−1,940	(NA)
Syria	(NA)	(NA)	(NA)	(NA)	1,061	−1,065	(NA)	(NA)	(NA)	(NA)
Thailand	32,016	50,691	65,291	65,147	9,313	−7,857	(NA)	11,701	3,204	(NA)
Trinidad and Tobago	1,386	4,856	(NA)	(NA)	544	(NA)	(NA)	969	(NA)	(NA)
Turkey	22,488	50,579	61,074	60,892	−9,822	−23,155	(NA)	−21,959	−32,926	(NA)
United Kingdom	38,770	38,470	40,700	38,890	−37,360	−53,350	(NA)	−49,850	−125,070	(NA)
Venezuela	13,088	23,919	29,417	28,933	11,853	25,533	27,167	16,664	31,780	32,984

NA Not available. [1] Holdings of convertible foreign currencies. [2] Balance of payments current account and trade balance data for 2000 are for Belgium-Luxembourg. Thereafter, data is for Belgium only. [3] See footnote 2, Table 1298. [4] See footnote 3, Table 1298. [5] Break in series. Data not comparable to earlier years.

Source: International Monetary Fund, Washington, DC, International Financial Statistics, monthly, (copyright).

Table 1362. Foreign Trade—Destination of Exports and Source of Imports for Selected Countries: 2004

[In billions of dollars (4.1 represents $4,100,000,000)]

Country	United States Imports (source)	United States Exports (destination)	Canada Imports (source)	Canada Exports (destination)	Australia Imports (source)	Australia Exports (destination)	Japan Imports (source)	Japan Exports (destination)	France Imports (source)	France Exports (destination)	Germany Imports (source)	Germany Exports (destination)	Italy Imports (source)	Italy Exports (destination)	United Kingdom Imports (source)	United Kingdom Exports (destination)
Argentina	4.1	3.4	0.2	0.1	0.1	0.1	0.5	0.4	0.5	0.7	1.2	1.1	1.2	0.7	0.5	0.3
Australia	7.9	14.3	1.4	1.2	0.4	–	19.5	11.8	1.2	2.9	1.5	5.7	1.4	3.1	3.3	4.4
Austria	5.9	2.0	1.0	0.2	0.6	(Z)	1.3	1.3	4.0	4.4	28.7	47.9	8.9	8.3	4.3	2.0
Belgium	12.8	16.9	1.0	1.7	0.9	0.5	2.1	7.2	31.6	31.7	34.9	50.4	15.4	8.5	23.2	18.6
Brazil	22.7	13.9	1.8	0.7	0.4	0.4	3.7	2.3	3.1	2.3	5.7	5.7	3.3	2.2	2.8	1.5
Canada	259.7	189.1	2.7	(NA)	1.4	1.4	8.4	7.6	2.2	3.0	2.9	5.9	1.7	3.0	6.7	6.1
China	210.5	34.7	18.5	5.1	13.2	8.1	94.3	73.9	20.5	6.6	40.2	25.8	14.7	5.4	26.4	4.4
Colombia	7.8	4.5	0.3	0.3	(Z)	(Z)	0.3	0.7	0.3	0.3	0.6	0.7	0.6	0.3	0.5	0.2
Czech Republic	1.8	2.1	0.8	0.1	0.1	0.1	0.3	1.2	2.5	2.8	21.0	21.6	2.1	3.2	2.3	1.8
Denmark	4.0	3.1	0.8	0.2	0.7	0.1	0.3	0.8	3.5	3.2	10.9	13.5	1.6	2.6	5.6	3.7
Egypt	1.4	2.1	0.2	0.2	(Z)	0.5	0.1	0.8	0.4	1.3	0.6	1.7	1.9	2.6	0.9	1.2
Finland	4.1	3.1	0.7	0.2	0.7	0.4	1.4	1.7	2.7	2.2	7.5	9.1	1.9	1.8	4.3	2.5
France	32.6	21.2	4.1	1.8	3.1	0.7	8.3	8.4	(NA)	(NA)	64.6	92.2	38.0	42.7	36.9	33.7
Germany	79.1	31.4	7.2	2.1	6.0	1.0	17.1	19.0	75.4	62.2	(NA)	(NA)	62.2	47.2	63.8	39.4
Hungary	2.6	1.1	0.2	(Z)	0.1	(Z)	0.5	1.5	2.7	2.5	16.6	15.4	2.9	3.3	2.8	1.7
India	16.4	6.1	1.2	0.7	0.8	4.0	2.6	3.0	2.1	1.6	3.6	3.9	2.5	1.5	4.3	4.1
Indonesia	11.7	2.7	0.7	0.5	2.7	2.4	18.7	9.1	1.4	0.5	2.8	2.0	1.5	0.6	1.9	0.7
Ireland	27.6	8.2	1.3	0.4	1.3	0.1	3.8	2.0	8.0	3.2	18.7	5.3	5.3	1.7	18.6	25.5
Israel	14.8	9.2	0.5	0.3	0.4	0.1	0.8	1.2	1.0	1.2	1.1	2.9	1.1	1.7	1.6	2.6
Italy	29.4	10.7	3.5	1.3	3.3	1.0	6.9	6.5	39.0	38.6	43.2	63.3	(NA)	(NA)	22.2	15.3
Japan	133.3	54.4	10.3	6.6	12.3	16.3	(NA)	(NA)	13.3	6.6	26.0	15.4	6.9	5.4	15.1	6.9
Luxembourg	0.3	0.7	0.1	0.1	(Z)	(Z)	0.1	0.2	2.0	2.3	2.7	4.0	1.4	0.7	1.2	0.5
Mexico	157.8	110.8	10.3	2.3	0.5	0.3	2.2	5.2	0.8	1.9	2.0	6.0	0.4	2.2	3.2	1.1
Netherlands	13.2	24.3	1.2	1.6	0.9	1.1	2.0	13.4	19.1	16.4	55.7	53.5	19.9	8.1	33.0	21.9
Norway	6.9	1.6	3.8	1.2	0.2	0.1	1.2	0.8	8.6	1.6	9.3	6.3	4.4	1.4	15.4	3.7
Poland	2.0	0.9	0.3	0.2	0.2	(Z)	0.2	3.1	3.9	5.3	19.7	22.9	8.1	6.1	7.0	2.6
Russia	12.6	3.0	1.1	0.3	(Z)	0.1	5.7	2.9	9.1	3.9	14.5	18.3	16.0	6.2	5.6	2.7
South Africa	6.2	3.2	0.5	0.3	0.9	1.2	4.6	5.0	1.3	2.1	3.8	7.2	1.5	1.4	16.1	3.4
Spain	7.9	6.6	1.0	0.9	0.9	0.5	1.7	2.2	32.0	41.4	21.4	45.1	14.9	24.9	9.4	16.6
Sweden	13.1	3.3	1.7	0.3	1.3	0.2	2.1	0.9	5.6	5.6	12.5	19.4	4.7	3.5	4.8	7.9
Switzerland	11.8	9.3	1.3	0.5	1.0	0.3	4.8	0.9	9.9	12.7	25.6	33.4	11.6	14.6	3.2	5.4
Thailand	18.6	6.4	1.6	0.4	2.8	2.3	14.1	20.3	1.8	1.0	3.0	2.5	1.5	0.9	5.4	1.2
United Kingdom	47.7	36.0	7.4	6.0	4.2	3.7	6.7	15.0	28.1	38.7	42.1	74.3	14.9	24.0	(NA)	(NA)
United States	(NA)	(NA)	160.8	267.8	15.1	7.0	62.6	127.0	27.9	28.7	48.3	79.2	12.3	27.7	41.8	52.1

– Represents zero. NA Not available. Z Less than 50,000,000. [1] See footnote 2, Table 1298.

Source: Organization for Economic Cooperation and Development, Paris, France, OECD International Trade by Commodities Statistics, 2005.

Table 1363. International Tourism Arrivals, Expenditures, and Receipts—Leading Countries: 2000 to 2006

[Expenditures and receipts in millions of dollars; arrivals in thousands of nonresident tourists at national borders, excluding same-day visitors (77,190 represents 77,190,000). Receipts are dollars spent by foreign tourists on travel inside the country shown. Expenditures are dollars visitors (same-day visitors and tourists) from a given country of origin spend on travel outside their country of residence. Excludes international transport receipts]

Country	Arrivals 2000	Arrivals 2003	Arrivals 2004	Arrivals 2005	Arrivals 2006[1]	Expenditures 2000	Expenditures 2004	Expenditures 2005	Expenditures 2006[1]	Receipts 2000	Receipts 2003	Receipts 2004	Receipts 2005	Receipts 2006[1]
France	77,190	75,048	75,121	75,908	79,083	17,800	28,800	30,500	31,200	30,757	36,617	45,289	44,018	46,342
Spain	47,898	50,854	52,430	55,916	58,451	6,000	12,200	15,100	16,700	29,968	41,770	45,248	47,970	51,115
United States	51,238	41,218	46,086	49,206	51,063	64,700	65,800	69,000	72,000	82,400	83,254	74,546	81,799	85,694
China[2]	31,229	32,970	41,761	46,809	49,600	13,100	19,100	21,800	24,300	16,231	17,406	25,739	29,296	33,949
Italy[2]	41,181	39,604	37,071	36,513	41,058	15,700	20,500	22,400	23,100	27,493	31,247	35,656	35,398	38,129
United Kingdom[3]	23,211	24,715	25,677	28,038	30,092	38,400	56,500	59,600	62,600	21,857	22,668	28,221	30,675	33,458
Germany[4]	18,992	18,399	20,137	21,500	23,569	53,000	71,600	74,400	74,800	18,693	23,125	27,668	29,173	32,760
Mexico	20,641	18,665	20,618	21,915	21,353	5,500	7,000	7,600	8,100	8,294	9,362	10,796	11,803	12,177
Austria[4]	17,982	19,078	19,373	19,952	20,261	8,800	8,300	8,500	9,300	9,931	13,842	15,582	16,012	16,658
Russia	(NA)	20,443	19,892	19,940	20,199	8,800	15,700	17,800	18,800	3,429	4,502	5,225	5,564	7,025
Turkey	9,586	13,341	16,826	20,273	18,916	1,700	2,500	2,900	2,700	7,636	13,203	15,888	18,152	16,853
Canada	19,627	17,534	19,145	18,771	18,245	12,400	15,900	18,400	20,800	10,778	10,602	12,871	13,584	14,487
Malaysia	10,222	10,577	15,703	16,431	17,547	2,100	3,100	3,700	3,700	5,011	5,901	8,198	8,543	9,630
Hong Kong	8,814	9,676	13,655	14,773	15,821	12,500	13,300	13,300	14,000	5,907	7,106	8,999	10,292	11,630
Poland	17,400	13,720	14,290	15,200	15,700	4,600	3,800	4,300	5,700	5,677	4,069	5,833	6,274	7,239
Greece	13,096	13,969	13,313	14,276	(NA)	2,800	2,800	3,000	3,000	9,219	10,766	12,872	13,731	14,259
Thailand	9,579	10,082	11,737	11,567	13,882	500	4,500	3,800	4,600	7,468	7,856	10,034	9,591	12,423
Ukraine	6,341	12,514	(NA)	17,631	(NA)	2,200	2,800	2,800	2,800	394	935	2,560	3,125	3,485
Portugal	12,097	11,707	10,639	10,612	11,282	12,200	2,800	3,100	3,300	5,243	6,580	7,707	7,712	8,349
Netherlands[4]	10,003	9,181	9,646	10,012	10,739	(NA)	16,400	16,200	17,100	7,217	9,249	10,333	10,475	11,516
Macao[5]	5,197	6,309	8,324	9,979	10,683	1,700	(NA)	(NA)	(NA)	3,205	5,303	7,344	(NA)	(NA)
Hungary[4]	(NA)	(NA)	12,212	9,014	9,259	568	2,900	2,900	2,600	3,757	4,061	4,061	4,271	4,519
Croatia[4]	5,831	7,409	7,912	8,467	8,659	1,100	839	(NA)	(NA)	2,782	4,584	6,848	7,463	7,902
Egypt	5,116	5,746	7,795	8,244	8,641	2,100	1,300	1,600	1,800	4,345	6,377	6,125	6,851	7,591
Saudi Arabia[6]	5,872	6,505	8,599	8,396	8,396	(NA)	4,300	3,400	3,400	2,675	(NA)	6,282	7,327	7,875
South Africa	6,585	7,332	6,678	7,369	(NA)	2,500	(NA)	(NA)	(NA)	2,633	3,862	6,486	5,177	(NA)
Ireland	6,646	6,764	6,953	7,333	8,002	6,300	8,800	3,800	6,800	5,142	9,169	4,398	4,744	5,242
Switzerland[7]	7,835	6,530	(NA)	7,229	7,863	4,500	9,200	6,100	10,100	7,777	(NA)	10,556	11,040	11,843
Singapore	6,062	5,705	6,553	7,080	7,588	31,900	9,200	9,900	10,400	3,373	3,790	5,221	5,908	7,061
Japan	4,757	5,212	6,138	6,747	7,334	9,400	38,200	27,300	26,900	6,592	8,849	11,269	6,630	8,469
Belgium[4]	6,457	6,690	5,710	6,378	6,995	426	14,000	14,900	17,200	2,039	8,163	9,233	9,868	11,535
Morocco	4,278	4,761	5,998	5,843	6,558	263	575	(NA)	(NA)	1,682	3,221	3,924	4,621	5,967
Tunisia	5,058	5,114	6,061	6,378	6,550	1,300	340	(NA)	(NA)	2,973	1,583	1,970	2,124	2,227
Czech Republic[4]	4,773	5,076	5,818	6,336	6,435	7,100	2,300	2,400	2,700	6,834	3,556	4,172	4,668	5,007
Korea, South[3]	5,322	4,753	(NA)	6,023	6,155	3,000	12,400	15,400	18,200	1,063	5,358	6,069	5,806	(NA)
United Arab Emirates[5,7]	3,907	5,871	4,774	5,020	(NA)	6,400	4,500	5,300	(NA)	9,274	1,439	1,594	(NA)	17,840
Australia	4,530	4,354	4,794	5,499	(NA)	3,900	5,300	4,700	11,700	1,810	10,312	15,191	16,866	4,316
Brazil	5,313	4,133	5,321	5,020	5,019	3,200	2,900	3,600	5,800	4,975	2,479	3,222	3,861	4,448
Indonesia	5,064	4,467	5,321	5,002	4,871	3,200	3,500	3,600	3,600	4,975	4,037	4,798	4,521	9,081
Sweden	2,746	(NA)	3,003	3,133	3,270	8,000	10,200	10,800	11,500	4,064	5,304	6,196	7,405	9,081

NA Not available. [1] Preliminary. [2] See footnote 2, Table 1298. [3] Arrivals are of nonresident visitors at national borders, including tourists and same-day visitors. [4] Arrivals are of nonresident tourists in all types of accommodation establishments. [5] Expenditures and receipts include both travel and passenger transport. [6] Receipts include both travel and passenger transport. [7] Arrivals are of nonresident tourists in hotels and similar establishments.

Source: World Tourism Organization. Madrid, Spain. World Tourism Barometer, June 2007 (copyright).

Table 1364. Net Flow of Financial Resources to Developing Countries and Multilateral Organizations: 1995 to 2005

[165,182 represents $165,182,000,000. Net flow covers loans, grants, and grant-like flows minus amortization on loans. Military flows are excluded. Developing countries are designated by Development Assistance Committee as developing. GNI = gross national income. For explanation of GNI, see headnote, Table 1315. Minus sign (−) indicates net inflow]

Type of aid and country	Amount (mil. dol.)					Percent of GNI		
	1995	2000	2003	2004	2005	1995	2000	2005
Total net flows	165,182	134,485	125,551	160,356	305,019	0.75	0.56	0.94
United States	46,984	25,252	37,860	32,283	104,410	0.65	0.25	0.84
Australia............	2,536	1,961	3,010	2,466	5,366	0.76	0.53	0.79
Austria..............	906	1,135	1,445	1,352	4,215	0.39	0.61	1.40
Belgium.............	−234	2,281	1,221	816	3,142	−0.09	1.00	0.84
Canada.............	5,724	6,483	4,949	5,986	13,373	1.04	0.95	1.20
Denmark............	1,799	2,176	1,896	2,634	2,215	1.07	1.39	0.85
Finland.............	604	1,087	−44	1,338	1,642	0.50	0.91	0.84
France..............	12,477	5,557	6,936	12,599	15,744	0.81	0.41	0.74
Germany	21,197	12,331	5,224	15,251	30,059	0.87	0.66	1.07
Greece.............	−	229	403	328	709	−	0.20	0.32
Ireland..............	247	740	2,334	3,851	5,298	0.46	0.93	3.09
Italy................	2,800	10,846	4,218	3,239	4,103	0.26	1.01	0.23
Japan..............	42,295	11,423	6,335	11,368	23,259	0.82	0.24	0.50
Luxembourg	72	129	201	242	265	0.40	0.75	0.84
Netherlands..........	6,795	6,947	15,196	14,106	22,781	1.71	1.85	3.65
New Zealand.........	166	142	208	271	401	0.31	0.32	0.40
Norway.............	1,670	1,437	3,306	2,785	2,791	1.16	0.87	0.94
Portugal............	395	4,622	1,145	676	1,109	0.38	4.45	0.62
Spain..............	2,025	23,471	6,667	12,762	6,801	0.37	4.25	0.61
Sweden.............	2,224	3,952	1,255	2,954	3,545	1.00	1.76	0.99
Switzerland..........	1,118	2,054	3,225	1,372	7,474	0.35	0.80	1.87
United Kingdom........	13,382	10,230	18,561	31,680	46,318	1.19	0.72	2.03

− Represents zero.

Source: Organization for Economic Cooperation and Development, Paris, France, *Annual Reports of the Development Assistance Committee* (copyright).

Table 1365. External Debt by Country: 1990 to 2005

[In millions of dollars (28,149 represents $28,149,000,000). Total external debt is debt owed to nonresidents repayable in foreign currency, goods, or services. Total external debt is the sum of public, publicly guaranteed, and private nonguaranteed long-term debt, use of IMF credit, and short-term debt. Short-term debt includes all debt having an original maturity of one year or less and interest in arrears on long-term debt]

Country	1990	2000	2004	2005	Country	1990	2000	2004	2005
Algeria	28,149	25,272	21,987	16,879	Mexico	104,442	150,314	138,689	167,228
Angola	8,592	9,410	9,521	11,755	Morocco	25,004	20,721	17,672	16,846
Argentina	62,233	145,879	169,247	114,335	Nigeria	33,439	31,355	35,890	22,178
Bangladesh	12,439	15,682	20,344	18,935	Pakistan	20,663	32,779	35,687	33,675
Brazil	119,964	238,793	222,026	187,994	Panama	6,493	7,046	9,469	9,765
Bulgaria	(NA)	10,188	15,661	16,786	Peru	20,044	28,710	31,296	28,653
Cameroon.	6,431	9,277	9,496	7,151	Philippines	30,580	57,429	60,550	61,527
Chile	19,226	37,048	44,058	45,154	Poland	49,364	63,259	99,190	98,821
China [1]	55,301	145,706	248,934	281,612	Romania	1,140	10,498	30,034	38,694
Colombia	17,222	33,934	37,732	37,656	Russia [3]	(NA)	160,027	197,335	229,042
Congo (Kinshasa) [2] .	10,259		11,841	10,600	Serbia and Montenegro [4,5] . . .	(NA)	11,851	15,882	16,295
Cote d'Ivoire	17,251	12,138	11,739	10,735	Slovakia	(NA)	12,140	22,068	23,654
Croatia	(NA)	11,344	31,548	30,169	South Africa	(NA)	24,861	28,500	30,632
Czech Republic	(NA)	21,526	45,561	(NA)	Sri Lanka	5,863	9,155	10,887	11,444
Ecuador	12,107	13,717	16,868	17,129	Sudan	14,762	15,741	19,332	18,455
Egypt	33,017	29,187	30,291	34,114	Syria	17,259	21,657	21,521	6,508
Ghana	3,734	6,625	7,035	6,739	Tanzania	6,454	7,394	7,799	7,763
Hungary	21,201	29,520	63,159	66,193	Thailand	28,094	79,716	51,307	52,266
India	83,628	99,098	122,723	123,123	Tunisia	7,688	10,629	18,700	17,789
Indonesia	69,872	144,407	140,649	138,300	Turkey	49,424	117,431	161,595	171,059
Iran	9,020	7,982	13,622	21,260	Ukraine	(NA)	12,190	21,652	33,297
Jordan	8,333	7,354	8,175	7,696	Uruguay	4,415	8,196	12,376	14,551
Kazakhstan.	(NA)	11,805	32,310	43,354	Venezuela.	33,171	38,152	35,570	44,201
Lebanon	1,779	9,856	22,177	22,373	Vietnam	23,270	12,822	17,825	19,287
Malaysia	15,328	41,941	52,145	50,981					

NA Not available. [1] See footnote 2, Table 1298. [2] See footnote 3, Table 1298. [3] The debt of the former Soviet Union is included in Russia's data after 1990 on the assumption that 100 percent of all outstanding external debt as of December 1991 has become a liability of Russia. Beginning in 2000, the data for Russia has also been revised to include obligations to members of the former Council for Mutual Economic Assistance and other countries in the form of trade-related credits amounting to $15.4 billion as of the end of 1996. [4] External debt obligations, excluding IBRD, IMF, and short-term, of Bosnia and Herzegovina before 2000 are included under Serbia and Montenegro. Data from 2000 onwards are estimates and also reflect borrowing by the former Yugoslavia that are not yet allocated to the successor republics. [5] As of June 2006, Serbia and Montenegro are separate countries (formerly Yugoslavia).

Source: The World Bank, Washington, DC, *2007 World Development Indicators CD–ROM* (copyright).

Table 1366. Foreign Direct Investment Flows in OECD Countries: 1994 to 2003

[In billions of dollars (1,288.0 represents $1,288,000,000,000). Data are converted to U.S. dollars using the yearly average exchange rate]

Country	Inflows				Outflows			
	2000	2002	2003 [1]	Cumulative, 1994–2003	2000	2002	2003 [1]	Cumulative, 1994–2003
OECD, total....	1,288.0	535.0	384.4	5,194.2	1,235.8	566.7	576.3	6,081.0
Australia........	13.2	16.5	7.8	82.3	0.7	7.6	14.3	57.4
Austria.........	8.8	1.0	6.9	41.2	5.7	5.3	7.1	33.6
Belgium........	(NA)	13.1	31.3	44.4	(NA)	11.0	39.0	49.9
Canada........	66.8	21.0	6.6	208.3	44.7	26.4	21.6	237.5
Czech Republic...	5.0	8.5	2.6	37.9	(Z)	0.2	0.2	1.2
Denmark.......	33.8	6.6	2.6	91.8	26.5	5.7	1.2	82.1
Finland........	8.8	7.9	2.8	45.9	24.0	7.6	-7.4	72.7
France........	43.3	48.9	47.0	351.9	177.5	49.5	57.3	653.3
Germany.......	198.3	36.0	12.9	387.4	56.6	8.6	2.6	453.1
Greece........	1.1	0.1	0.7	8.7	2.1	0.7	(Z)	3.7
Hungary........	2.8	2.8	2.5	32.4	0.6	0.3	1.6	3.9
Iceland........	0.2	0.1	0.1	1.0	0.4	0.2	0.2	1.5
Ireland........	25.8	24.4	25.5	120.1	4.6	3.1	1.9	26.7
Italy..........	13.4	14.6	17.0	86.6	12.3	17.1	9.1	112.5
Japan.........	8.3	9.2	6.3	50.5	31.5	32.3	28.8	268.3
Korea, South....	9.3	2.4	3.2	41.0	5.0	2.6	3.4	37.6
Luxembourg.....	(NA)	117.1	73.2	190.4	(NA)	126.2	81.8	208.2
Mexico........	16.4	14.4	10.7	138.4	(NA)	1.0	(NA)	[2]5.4
Netherlands.....	63.9	25.6	19.7	286.7	75.6	34.6	36.1	383.1
New Zealand.....	1.3	-0.6	0.8	19.9	0.6	-1.0	-0.1	2.9
Norway........	6.9	0.7	2.2	35.5	7.6	4.2	2.6	37.7
Poland........	9.3	4.1	4.2	52.0	(Z)	0.2	0.4	1.1
Portugal.......	6.8	1.8	1.0	25.8	7.5	3.3	0.1	29.2
Spain.........	37.5	35.9	25.6	183.6	54.7	31.5	23.4	230.1
Sweden........	23.2	11.6	3.4	168.4	40.7	10.7	10.6	150.3
Switzerland.....	19.3	5.7	12.2	82.0	44.7	7.6	10.9	190.6
Turkey........	1.0	1.0	0.6	10.6	0.9	0.2	0.5	3.6
United Kingdom..	118.8	27.8	14.6	463.5	233.5	35.2	55.3	879.5
United States...	321.3	72.4	39.9	1,366.4	159.2	134.8	173.8	1,354.6

NA Not available. Z Less than $50 million. [1] Preliminary. [2] Based on outflow data for 2001 and 2002 only.

Source: Organization for Economic Cooperation and Development, Paris, France, *Financial Market Trends*, June 2005.

Table 1367. Military Expenditures and Manpower, by Country: 2005

[5,172 represents 5,172,000. Manpower covers males and females deemed fit for military service, ages 15–49]

Country	Expenditures (percent of GDP [1])	Manpower (1,000)	Country	Expenditures (percent of GDP [1])	Manpower (1,000)
Afghanistan..........	[2]1.9	5,172	Israel...............	[2]7.3	2,468
Albania.............	1.5	1,317	Italy................	1.8	21,416
Algeria.............	[2]3.3	13,301	Japan..............	[2]0.8	43,730
Argentina...........	1.3	14,759	Kazakhstan.........	[5]0.9	5,642
Australia............	[2]2.4	8,076	Korea, North........	(NA)	9,664
Austria.............	0.9	3,066	Korea, South........	[2]2.7	19,838
Bahrain.............	[2]4.5	287	Kuwait.............	[2]5.3	1,142
Belarus.............	1.4	3,761	Laos...............	[2]0.5	1,961
Belgium............	1.3	3,939	Lebanon............	3.1	1,688
Bolivia.............	[2]1.9	2,814	Libya..............	3.9	2,522
Bosnia and Herzegovina...	[2]2.6	71,199	Malaysia...........	2.0	9,188
Brazil..............	4.5	1,792	Mexico.............	[2]0.5	41,025
Bulgaria............	2.6	2,667	Morocco............	[6]5.0	13,161
Burma..............	2.1	16,490	Netherlands.........	1.6	5,643
Cambodia...........	3.0	4,004	New Zealand........	1.0	1,612
Canada.............	[2]2.7	13,321	Nicaragua..........	[2]0.6	2,181
Chile [3]............	[2]3.8	6,252	Nigeria............	[2]1.5	28,914
China [3]...........	3.4	550,266	Norway............	1.9	1,628
Colombia...........	[2]3.1	15,781	Oman..............	[1]1.4	1,017
Congo (Brazzaville) [4]....	1.6	801	Pakistan............	[2]3.2	57,821
Cote d'Ivoire.........	2.4	3,885	Peru...............	[2]1.5	10,217
Croatia.............	[2]3.8	1,550	Philippines..........	0.9	32,101
Cuba...............	1.8	4,839	Poland.............	1.7	15,599
Czech Republic.......	1.5	3,920	Russia.............	(NA)	50,106
Denmark............	[2]2.8	1,891	Saudi Arabia........	10.0	11,252
Ecuador............	3.4	4,719	Singapore..........	4.9	(NA)
Egypt..............	[2]5.0	30,480	South Africa........	[2]1.7	9,537
El Salvador..........	[2]3.0	2,271	Spain..............	1.2	15,058
Ethiopia............	2.0	15,975	Sudan.............	[2]3.0	11,077
Finland.............	2.6	1,789	Sweden............	1.5	2,935
France.............	1.5	22,342	Switzerland.........	1.0	2,719
Germany............	4.3	29,702	Syria..............	5.9	6,875
Greece.............	[2]0.6	4,019	Thailand...........	1.8	21,884
Honduras...........	1.8	2,223	Turkey.............	5.3	27,242
Hungary............	[2]2.5	3,645	Ukraine............	1.4	16,689
India..............	3.0	429,390	United Arab Emirates.....	3.1	947
Indonesia...........	[2]2.5	98,940	United Kingdom......	2.4	23,602
Iran...............	[2]8.6	30,671	United States........	4.1	109,306
Iraq...............	0.9	9,701	Venezuela..........	1.2	10,060
Ireland.............		1,629	Vietnam............	2.5	33,954

NA Not available. [1] GDP calculated on an exchange rate basis. [2] 2006 data. [3] See footnote 2, Table 1298. [4] See footnote 3, Table 1298. [5] 2002 data. [6] 2003 data.

Source: Central Intelligence Agency, *The World Factbook, 2007*. See also <https://www.cia.gov/cia/publications/factbook/fields/2025.html> (accessed 26 July 2007).

Appendix I
Guide to Sources of Statistics, State Statistical Abstracts, and Foreign Statistical Abstracts

Alphabetically arranged, this guide contains references to important primary sources of statistical information for the United States and other countries. Secondary sources have been included if the information contained in them is presented in a particularly convenient form or if primary sources are not readily available. Nonrecurrent publications presenting compilations or estimates for years later than 2000, or types of data not available in regular series, are also included. Data are also available in press releases.

Valuable information may also be found in state reports, foreign statistical abstracts, which are included at the end of this appendix, and in reports for particular commodities, industries, or similar segments of our economic and social structures, many of which are not included here.

Publications listed under each subject are divided into two main groups: "U.S. Government" and "Nongovernment." The location of the publisher of each report is given except for federal agencies located in Washington, DC. Most federal publications may be purchased from the Superintendent of Documents, U.S. Government Printing Office, Washington, DC, tel. 202-512-1800, (Web site <http://bookstore.gpo.gov>). In some cases, federal publications may be obtained from the issuing agency.

Title	Frequency	Paper	Internet PDF	Internet Other formats
U.S. GOVERNMENT				
Administrative Office of the United States Courts <http://www.uscourts.gov>				
Calendar Year Reports on Authorized Wiretaps (state and federal)	Annual	X	X	X
Federal Court Management Statistics	Annual	X	X	X
Federal Judicial Caseload Statistics	Annual	X		
Judicial Business of the United States Courts	Annual	X		
Statistical Tables for the Federal Judiciary	Semiannual	X	X	X
Agency for International Development <http://www.usaid.gov>				
U.S. Overseas Loans and Grants and Assistance From International Organizations	Annual	X	X	
Army Corps of Engineers <http://www.usace.army.mil>				
Waterborne Commerce of the United States (in five parts)	Annual	X		X
Board of Governors of the Federal Reserve System <http://www.federalreserve.gov>				
Assets and Liabilities of Commercial Banks in the United States H.8	Weekly	X	X	X
Consumer Credit G.19	Weekly	X	X	X
Federal Reserve Bulletin	Annual	X	X	X
Foreign Exchange Rates H.10	Weekly	X	X	X
Flow of Funds Accounts of the United States Z.1	Quarterly	X	X	X
Industrial Production and Capacity Utilization G.17	Monthly	X	X	X
Money Stock and Debt Measures H.6	Weekly	X	X	X
Statistical Supplement to the Federal Reserve Bulletin	Monthly	X	X	X
Bureau of Economic Analysis <http://www.bea.gov>				
Survey of Current Business	Monthly	X	X	X
Preliminary 2004 Estimates	Periodic			X
Revised 2003 Estimates	Periodic			X
Revised 2002 Estimates	Periodic		X	X
Revised 2001 Estimates	Periodic		X	X
Revised 2000 Estimates	Periodic		X	X
Revised 1999 Estimates	Periodic		X	X
Revised 1998 Estimates	Periodic		X	X
U.S. Direct Investment Abroad: 1999 Benchmark Survey, 2004	Periodic	X	X	X
Bureau of Justice Statistics <http://www.ojp.usdoj.gov/bjs>				
American Indians and Crime: A BJS Statistical Profile, December 2004	Periodic	X	X	X
Background Checks for Firearm Transfers	Annual	X	X	X
Capital Punishment	Annual	X	X	X

Title	Frequency	Paper	PDF	Other formats
Bureau of Justice Statistics—Con.				
Carjacking, 1993–2002, July 2004	Periodic		X	X
Census of Publicly Funded Forensic Crime Laboratories, 2002, February 2005	Periodic	X	X	X
Census of State and Federal Correctional Facilities, 2000, August 2003	Periodic		X	X
Civil Rights Complaints in U.S. District Courts, July 2002	Periodic	X	X	X
Civil Trial Cases and Verdicts in Large Counties, 2001, April 2004	Periodic	X	X	X
Compendium of Federal Justice Statistics, 2004	Annual	X	X	X
Contacts Between Police and Public: Findings from the 2002 National Survey	Periodic	X	X	X
Contract Trials and Verdicts in Large Counties, 2001, February 2005	Periodic	X	X	X
Crime and the Nation's Households, 2004, April 2006	Annual	X	X	X
Crimes Against Persons Age 65 or Older, 1993–2002, January 2005	Periodic	X	X	X
Criminal Victimization in the United States	Annual	X	X	X
Cross-National Studies in Crime and Justice, September 2004	Periodic	X	X	X
Defense Counsel in Criminal Cases, November 2000	Periodic	X	X	X
Education and Correctional Populations, January 2003	Periodic	X	X	X
Family Violence Statistics	Periodic	X	X	X
Federal Criminal Case Processing	Annual		X	X
Federal Law Enforcement Officers, 2004, July 2006	Biennial		X	X
Felony Defendants in Large Urban Counties, 2002, February 2006	Biennial	X	X	X
Felony Sentences in State Courts, 2002, December 2004	Biennial		X	X
Firearm Use by Offenders, November 2001	Periodic	X	X	X
Hepatitis Testing and Treatment in State Prisons, April 2004	Periodic	X	X	X
Hispanic Victims of Violent Crime, 1993–2000, April 2002	Periodic	X	X	X
HIV in Prisons and Jails	Annual	X	X	X
Homicide Trends in the United States	Annual	X	X	X
Identity Theft, 2004, April 2006	Periodic	X	X	X
Immigration Offenders in the Federal Criminal Justice System, August 2002	Periodic	X	X	X
Incarcerated Parents and Their Children, August 2000	Periodic	X	X	X
Indicators of School Crime and Safety	Annual	X	X	X
Intimate Partner Violence in the United States, December 2006	Periodic	X	X	X
Jails in Indian Country, 2004, November 2006	Annual	X	X	X
Justice Expenditure and Employment in the United States, 2004, December 2006	Periodic	X	X	X
Juvenile Offenders and Victims	Periodic	X	X	X
Juvenile Victimization and Offending, 1993–2003	Periodic	X	X	X
Law Enforcement Management and Administrative Statistics 2000: Data for Individual State and Local Agencies with 100 or More Officers	Periodic	X	X	X
Local Police Departments, 2003, May 2006	Periodic	X	X	X
Medical Malpractice Trials and Verdicts in Large Counties, April 2004	Periodic	X	X	X
Money Laundering Offenders, 1994–2001, July 2003	Periodic	X	X	X
Prevalence of Imprisonment in the U.S. Population, 1974–2001, August 2003	Periodic	X	X	X
Prison and Jail Inmates at Midyear	Annual	X	X	X
Prisoners in 2005	Annual	X	X	X
Probation and Parole in the United States	Annual	X	X	X
Profile of Jail Inmates, 2002, July 2004	Periodic	X	X	X
Prosecutors in State Courts, 2001, May 2002	Biennial		X	X
Rape and Sexual Assault: Reporting to Police and Medical Attention, August 2002	Periodic	X	X	X
Reentry Trends in the United States Current Data Electronic	Periodic		X	X
Sheriff's Offices, 2003, April 2006	Periodic	X	X	X
Sourcebook of Criminal Justice Statistics	Annual	X	X	X
State Court Prosecutors in Large Districts, December 2001	Periodic	X	X	X
State Court Prosecutors in Small Districts, 2001, January 2003	Periodic		X	X
State Court Sentencing of Convicted Felons, 2000, June 2003	Biennial		X	X
State Prison Expenditures, 2001, June 2004	Periodic		X	X
Summary of State Sex Offender Registries, 2001, March 2002	Periodic		X	X
Survey of DNA Crime Laboratories, 2001, January 2002	Periodic		X	X
Survey of State Criminal History Information Systems, September 2003	Biennial	X	X	X
Survey of State Procedures Related to Firearm Sales	Annual		X	X
Tort Trials and Verdicts in Large Counties, November 2004	Periodic		X	X
Traffic Stop Data Collection Policies for State Police, 2004, June 2005	Periodic	X	X	X
Violent Victimization of College Students, 1995–2002, January 2005	Periodic		X	X
Weapon Use and Violent Crime, 1993–2001, September 2003	Periodic	X	X	X
Bureau of Labor Statistics				
<http://www.bls.gov>				
100 Years of U.S. Consumer Spending: Data for the Nation, New York City, and Boston, Report 991	Periodic	X	X	
College Enrollment and Work Activity of High School Graduates	Annual	X		
Comparative Labor Force Statistics, Ten Countries	Annual	X	X	X
Compensation and Working Conditions	Quarterly	X	X	X
Consumer Expenditure Survey, Integrated Diary and Interview Survey data	Annual	X	X	X
Consumer Prices: Energy and Food	Monthly	X	X	X
CPI Detailed Report	Monthly	X	X	X
Employee Benefits in Private Industry	Annual	X	X	X
Employer Costs for Employee Compensation	Annual	X	X	X
Employment and Earnings	Monthly	X	X	X
Employment and Wages	Annual	X	X	X
Employment Characteristics of Families	Annual	X	X	X
Employment Cost Index	Quarterly	X	X	X
Employment Cost Indexes and Levels	Annual	X	X	X
The Employment Situation	Monthly	X	X	X
Geographic Profile of Employment and Unemployment	Annual	X	X	X
International Comparisons of Hourly Compensation Costs for Production Workers in Manufacturing	Annual	X	X	X
International Comparisons of Manufacturing Productivity and Unit Labor Cost Trends	Annual	X	X	X
Metropolitan Area Employment and Unemployment	Monthly	X	X	X
Monthly Labor Review	Monthly	X	X	X
Occupational Injuries and Illnesses in the United States by Industry	Annual	X	X	X
Occupational Projections and Training Data	Biennial	X	X	X

866   Appendix I

Title	Frequency	Paper	PDF	Other formats
Bureau of Labor Statistics—Con.				
Producer Price Indexes Detailed Report	Monthly	X	X	X
Productivity and Costs by Industry	Periodic	X	X	X
Selected Service-Providing and Mining Industries, 2005	Annual	X	X	X
Manufacturing, 2005	Annual	X	X	X
Wholesale Trade, Retail Trade, and Food Services and Drinking Places, 2005	Annual	X	X	X
Real Earnings	Monthly	X	X	X
Regional and State Employment and Unemployment	Monthly	X	X	X
Relative Importance of Components in the Consumer Price Indexes	Annual	X	X	X
Union Members	Annual	X	X	X
U.S. Import and Export Price Indexes	Monthly	X	X	X
Usual Weekly Earnings of Wage and Salary Workers	Quarterly	X	X	X
Work Experience of the Population	Annual	X	X	X
Bureau of Land Management <http://www.blm.gov/wo/st/en.html>				
Public Land Statistics	Annual	X	X	
Census Bureau <http://www.census.gov>				
2002 Economic Census				
Comparative Statistics	Quinquennial	X	X	X
Bridge Between NAICS and SIC	Quinquennial	X	X	X
Business Expenses	Quinquennial	X		X
Industry/Geography	Quinquennial			X
2002 Economic Census, Company Statistics Series, Survey of Business Owners	Quinquennial	X		X
American Indian- and Alaska Native-Owned Firms	Quinquennial	X		X
Asian-Owned Firms	Quinquennial	X		X
Black-Owned Firms	Quinquennial	X		X
Hispanic-Owned Firms	Quinquennial	X		X
Native Hawaiian- and Other Pacific Islander-Owned Firms	Quinquennial	X		X
American Community Survey Annual Earnings and Poverty Report, 2005	Annual	X		
American Community Survey Reports Series ACS	Annual		X	
Annual Revision of Monthly Retail and Food Services: Sales and Inventories	Annual		X	
Annual Revision of Monthly Wholesale Distributors: Sales and Inventories	Annual	X	X	X
Annual Survey of Manufactures	Annual	X	X	
Census of Governments	Quinquennial	X	X	
Volume 3, No. 2 Compendium of Public Employment	Quinquennial	X	X	
Volume 4, No. 6 Employee-Retirement Systems of State and Local Governments	Quinquennial	X	X	
Volume 3, No. 1 Employment of Major Local Governments	Quinquennial	X	X	
Volume 3, No. 3 Finances of County Governments	Quinquennial	X	X	
Volume 1, No. 1 Government Organization	Quinquennial	X	X	
Volume 4, No. 1 Public Education Finances	Quinquennial	X	X	
Census of Housing Decennial (2000, most recent)	Decennial	X	X	
Census of Population Decennial (2000, most recent)	Decennial	X	X	X
CFFR Consolidated Federal Funds Report	Annual	X	X	X
State and County Areas	Annual	X	X	X
County Business Patterns	Annual	X	X	X
Current Construction Reports:				
New Residential Construction and New Residential Sales	Annual	X	X	
Value of Construction Put in Place, C30	Monthly	X	X	
Residential Improvements and Repairs, C50	Monthly	X	X	
Current Housing Reports:				
Housing Vacancies, H111	Quarterly		X	X
Who Can Afford to Buy a House, H121	Occasional	X	X	X
Market Absorption of Apartments 2005, H130	Quarterly	X	X	X
Characteristics of Apartments Completed, H131	Annual	X	X	X
American Housing Survey for the United States, H150	Biennial	X	X	X
American Housing Survey for Selected Metropolitan Areas, H170	Biennial	X	X	X
Current Industrial Reports			X	
Current Population Reports (Series P20 and P23)		X	X	X
Consumer Income and Poverty, P60, and Household Economic Studies, P70		X	X	
Alternative Poverty Estimates in the United States: 2003	Periodic	X	X	
Alternative Income Estimates in the United States: 2003	Periodic	X	X	
Income, Poverty, and Health Insurance Coverage in the United States, 2006	Annual	X	X	X
Economic Census of Outlying Areas	Quinquennial	X	X	
Federal Aid to States for Fiscal Year	Annual	X	X	
Global Population Profile: 2002 (Series WP)		X	X	X
International Briefs (Series IB)		X	X	X
International Data Base				X
International Population Reports (Series P95)		X	X	
Manufacturer's Shipments, Inventories, and Orders	Monthly	X	X	
Manufacturer's Shipments, Inventories, and Orders: 1992–2005	Annual	X	X	
New York City Housing and Vacancy Survey, 2005	Every 3 years			X
Nonemployer Statistics	Annual		X	X
Population Estimates and Projections				X
Quarterly Financial Report for Manufacturing, Mining, and Trade Corporations	Quarterly	X	X	
Residential Finance Survey, 2001	Every 10 years	X	X	X
Service Annual Survey Report	Annual	X	X	
Survey of Plant Capacity Utilization (Current Industrial Reports MQ-C1): includes cumulative data	Annual	X	X	
U.S. International Trade in Goods and Services: 2003	Annual	X	X	X
U.S. Trade with Puerto Rico and U.S. Possessions (FT 895)	Monthly	X	X	
Vehicle Inventory and Use Survey	Quinquennial	X	X	
Centers for Disease Control and Prevention, Atlanta, GA <http://www.cdc.gov>				
Injury Fact Book, 2001–2002		X	X	X
Morbidity and Mortality Weekly Report	Annual	X	X	X
Centers for Medicare and Medicaid Services (CMS) <http://www.cms.hhs.gov>				

Census Bureau, Statistical Abstract of the United States: 2008

Title	Frequency	Paper	PDF	Other formats
Centers for Medicare and Medicaid Services (CMS)—Con.				
CMS Statistics	Annual	X	X	
Data Compendium	Annual	X	X	
Health Care Financing Review Medicare and Medicaid Statistical Supplement	Quarterly	X	X	
Health Care Financing Review	Quarterly	X	X	
Trustees' Report	Annual	X	X	
Central Intelligence Agency <http://www.cia.gov>				
World Factbook	Annual	X	X	X
Coast Guard (See Department of Homeland Security)				
Comptroller of the Currency <http://www.occ.treas.gov>				
Quarterly Journal	Quarterly		X	X
Office of the Clerk U.S. House of Representatives <http://clerk.house.gov>				
Statistics of the Presidential and Congressional Election	Biennial		X	X
Council of Economic Advisers <http://www.whitehouse.gov>				
Economic Indicators	Monthly	X	X	X
Economic Report of the President	Annual	X	X	
Department of Agriculture, Economic Research Service <http://www.ers.usda.gov>				
Agricultural Income and Finance (Situation and Outlook Report)	Quarterly	X	X	X
Agricultural Price Reports	Annual	X	X	X
Amber Waves	Periodic	X	X	X
America's Diverse Family Farms: Structure and Finances	Periodic	X	X	
Cotton Ginnings	Periodic	X	X	X
Cotton and Wool Yearbook	Annual	X	X	
Dairy Yearbook	Annual	X	X	
Feedgrains Yearbook	Annual	X	X	
Floriculture and Nursery Yearbook	Annual	X	X	
Food Spending in American Households (Statistical Bulletin No. 824)	Annual	X	X	X
Food Marketing Review, (Agricultural Economic Report No. 743)	Annual	X	X	
Fruit and Tree Nut Yearbook	Annual	X	X	
Income, Wealth, and the Economic Well-Being of Farm Households	Periodic	X	X	X
Oil Crops Yearbook	Annual	X	X	
Poultry Yearbook	Annual	X	X	
Red Meat Yearbook	Annual	X	X	
Rice Yearbook	Annual	X	X	
Rural Development Perspectives	3 times per year	X	X	
Sugar and Sweeteners Yearbook	Annual	X	X	
Situation and Outlook Reports Issued for agricultural exports, cotton and wool, dairy, feed, fruit and tree nuts, agricultural resources, livestock and poultry, oil crops, rice, aquaculture, sugar and sweeteners, tobacco, vegetables, wheat, and world agriculture	Periodic	X	X	
Structure and Finances of U.S. Farms: Family Farm Report, 2007 edition	Periodic	X	X	
Tobacco Yearbook	Annual	X	X	
Vegetable and Melons Yearbook	Annual	X	X	
World Agricultural Supply and Demand Estimates	Monthly	X	X	X
Department of Agriculture, Foreign Agricultural Service <http://www.fas.usda.gov>				
Livestock and Poultry World Markets and Trade	Biannual	X	X	
Department of Agriculture, National Agricultural Statistics Service <http://www.nass.usda.gov>				
Agricultural Chemical Usage	Periodic	X	X	X
Agricultural Land Values and Cash Rents	Annual	X	X	
Agricultural Statistics	Annual	X	X	X
Catfish Production	Annual	X	X	X
Cattle	Biennial	X	X	
Census of Agriculture	Quinquennial	X	X	
Cherry Production	Annual	X	X	X
Chickens and Eggs	Annual	X	X	X
Citrus Fruits	Annual	X	X	X
Cranberries	Annual	X	X	X
Crop Production Reports	Monthly	X	X	X
Crop Values Report	Annual	X	X	X
Dairy Products	Annual	X	X	X
Farm Labor	Quarterly	X	X	X
Farms, Land in Farms, and Livestock Operations	Annual	X	X	X
Floriculture Crops	Annual	X	X	X
Livestock Slaughter	Annual	X	X	X
Meat Animals: Production, Disposition, and Income	Annual	X	X	X
Milk Production	Annual	X	X	X
Noncitrus Fruits and Nuts	Biennial	X	X	X
Poultry: Production and Value Summary	Annual	X	X	X
Stock Reports. Stocks of grain, peanuts, potatoes, and rice	Periodic	X	X	X
Trout Production	Annual	X	X	X
Turkeys: Hatchery and Raised	Annual	X	X	X
Usual Planting and Harvesting Dates	Periodic	X	X	X
Vegetable Reports	Periodic	X	X	X
Weekly Weather and Crop Bulletin Report	Weekly	X	X	
Winter Wheat Seedlings	Monthly	X	X	X
Department of Agriculture, Food and Nutrition Service <http://www.fns.usda.gov/fns/default.htm>				
Characteristics of Food Stamp Households	Annual	X	X	

868   Appendix I

Title	Frequency	Internet Paper	Internet PDF	Internet Other formats
Department of Agriculture, Food and Nutrition Service—Con.				
Food and Consumer Service Programs	Monthly			X
Department of Agriculture, Natural Resources and Conservation Service <http://www.nrcs.usda.gov>				
National Resources Inventory	Periodic	X		X
Department of Defense <http://www.defenselink.mil/pubs>				
Foreign Military Sales and Military Assistance Facts	Annual			X
Personnel Statistics	Annual		X	
Department of Education <http://www.ed.gov/index.jhtml>				
Department of Education, Rehabilitation Services Administration				
Caseload Statistics of State Vocational Rehabilitation Agencies in Fiscal Year	Annual	X	X	X
Department of Health and Human Services <http://www.os.hhs.gov>				
Annual Report	Annual	X		
Department of Homeland Security (DHS) <http://www.dhs.gov/index.shtm>				
Budget in Brief	Annual	X	X	
Department of Homeland Security, Coast Guard <http://www.uscg.mil/default.asp>				
Fact File		X	X	X
Department of Homeland Security, Office of Immigration Statistics <http://www.dhs.gov/ximgtn/statistics/>				
Yearbook of Immigration Statistics	Annual	X	X	
Department of Housing and Urban Development <http://www.hud.gov>				
Survey of Mortgage Lending Activity	Monthly	X		X
Department of Labor <http://www.dol.gov>				
Annual Report of the Secretary	Annual	X	X	X
Department of State <http://www.state.gov>				
United States Contribution to International Organizations	Annual			X
Department of Transportation <http://www.dot.gov>				
Air Travel Consumer Report	Monthly	X	X	X
Airport Activity Statistics of Certified Route Air Carriers	Annual	X		X
Transportation Safety Information Report	Quarterly	X		X
U.S. International Air Travel Statistics	Quarterly	X	X	X
Wage Statistics of Class I Railroads in the United States	Annual	X	X	
Department of the Treasury, Alcohol and Tobacco Tax and Trade Bureau <http://www.atf.treas.gov>				
Alcohol and Tobacco Summary Statistics	Annual	X		
Tobacco Products Monthly Statistical Releases		X		
Department of the Treasury, Bureau of Public Debt <http://www.publicdebt.treas.gov>				
Monthly Statement of the Public Debt of the United States	Monthly	X	X	X
Department of the Treasury, Financial Management Services <http://www.fms.treas.gov>				
Active Foreign Credits of the United States Government	Quarterly	X		
Combined Statement of Receipts, Outlays, and Balances	Annual	X	X	X
Monthly Treasury Statement of Receipts and Outlays of the United States Government	Monthly	X	X	X
Treasury Bulletin	Quarterly	X	X	X
Financial Report of the United States Government	Annual	X	X	
Department of Veterans Affairs <http://www.va.gov>				
Disability Compensation, Pension, and Death Pension Data	Annual	X		X
Government Life Insurance Programs for Veterans and Members of the Service	Annual	X		X
Selected Compensation and Pension Data by State of Residence	Annual	X		X
Veterans Affairs Annual Accountability Report	Annual	X	X	X
Drug Enforcement Administration <http://www.whitehousedrugpolicy.gov>				
Drug Abuse and Law Enforcement Statistics	Irregular	X		X
Employment and Training Administration <http://www.doleta.gov>				
Unemployment Insurance Claims	Weekly			X
Energy Information Administration <http://www.eia.doe.gov>				
Annual Energy Outlook	Annual	X	X	X
Annual Energy Review	Annual	X	X	X
Annual Coal Report	Annual		X	X
Electric Power Annual	Annual		X	X
Electric Power Monthly	Monthly		X	X
Electric Sales, Revenue and Retail Price	Annual			X
Emissions of Greenhouse Gases in the U.S.	Annual		X	X
International Energy Annual	Annual			X
International Energy Outlook	Annual	X	X	X
Monthly Energy Review	Monthly		X	X
Performance Profiles of Major Energy Producers	Annual		X	X
Petroleum Marketing Annual	Monthly		X	X

U.S. Census Bureau, Statistical Abstract of the United States: 2008

Title	Frequency	Paper	Internet PDF	Internet Other formats
Energy Information Administration—Con.				
Petroleum Supply Annual Volume 1	Annual		X	X
Petroleum Supply Annual Volume 2 (Web only)	Annual		X	X
Petroleum Supply Monthly	Monthly		X	X
Quarterly Coal Report	Quarterly		X	X
Renewable Energy Annual	Annual		X	
Residential Energy Consumption Survey	Quadrennial		X	X
State Electricity Profiles	Annual		X	X
State Energy Data Report	Annual		X	X
State Energy Price and Expenditure Report	Annual		X	X
U.S. Crude Oil, Natural Gas, and Natural Gas Liquids Reserves	Annual		X	X
Weekly Coal Production, 2005 (Web only)	Weekly		X	X
Environmental Protection Agency <http://www.epa.gov/>				
Air Quality Data	Annual			X
Drinking Water Infrastructure Needs Survey	Periodic	X	X	
Needs Survey, Conveyance and Treatment of Municipal Wastewater Summaries of Technical Data	Biennial		X	
Toxics Release Inventory	Annual		X	X
National Water Quality Inventory: 2000 Report (EPA-841-T-01-001)	Biennial	X	X	
Export-Import Bank of the United States <http://www.exim.gov/>				
Annual Report	Annual	X	X	
Report to the U.S. Congress on Export Credit Competition and the Export-Import Bank of the United States	Annual	X	X	
Farm Credit Administration <http://www.fca.gov/FCA-HomePage.htm>				
Annual Report on the Work of the Cooperative Farm Credit System	Annual	X	X	
Loans and Discounts of Farm Credit Banks and Associations	Annual	X		
Production Credit Association: Summary of Operations	Annual	X		
Report to the Federal Land Bank Associations	Annual	X		
Federal Bureau of Investigation <http://www.fbi.gov/ucr/ucr.htm>				
Bomb Summary	Annual			
Crime in the United States	Annual	X	X	X
Hate Crime Statistics	Annual	X	X	X
Law Enforcement Officers Killed and Assaulted	Annual	X	X	X
Federal Communications Commission <http://www.fcc.gov/>				
Annual Report	Annual	X	X	
Statistics of Communications Common Carriers	Annual	X	X	
Federal Deposit Insurance Corporation <http://www.fdic.gov/>				
Annual Report	Annual	· X	X	
Bank and Thrift Branch Office Data Book	Annual	X	X	X
FDIC Quarterly	Quarterly	X	X	
Historical Statistics on Banking	Annual			X
Quarterly Banking Profile	Quarterly	X	X	
Statistics on Banking	Quarterly			X
Summary of Deposits	Annual			X
Trust Assets of Financial Institutions	Annual	X		X
Federal Highway Administration <http://www.fhwa.dot.gov>				
Highway Statistics	Annual	X	X	
Federal Railroad Administration <http://www.fra.dot.gov> <http://safetydata.fra.dot.gov/officeofsafety>				
Accident/Incident Bulletin Summary, statistics, and analysis of accidents on railroads in the United States	Annual	X	X	
Rail-Highway Crossing Accident/Incident and Inventory Bulletin	Annual	X	X	
Railroad Safety Statistics	Annual	X	X	X
Fish and Wildlife Service <http://www.fws.gov/>				
Federal Aid in Fish and Wildlife Restoration	Annual	X	X	
National Survey of Fishing, Hunting, and Wildlife Associated Recreation	Quinquennial	X	X	
Forest Service <http://www.fs.fed.us/>				
An Analysis of the Timber Situation in the United States 1996–2050	Periodic			X
Land Areas of the National Forest System	Annual	X		X
The 1993 RPA Timber Assessment Update	Periodic			
U.S. Timber Production, Trade, Consumption, and Price Statistics 2001	Biennial	X	X	
General Services Administration, Federal Real Property Council <http://www.gsa.gov/Portal/gsa/ep/home.do?tabId=5>				
Federal Real Property Profile	Annual		X	X
Geological Survey <http://ask.usgs.gov>				
A Statistical Summary of Data from the U.S. Geological Surveys National Water Quality Networks (Open-File Report 83-533)		X		
Estimated Use of Water in the United States in 2000	Quinquennial	X	X	X
Mineral Commodity Summaries	Annual	X		X
Mineral Industry Surveys	Monthly	X	X	X
Minerals Yearbook	Monthly	X	X	X
Internal Revenue Service <http://www.irs.gov>				
Corporation Income Tax Returns	Annual	X	X	X

870 Appendix I

Title	Frequency	Paper	PDF	Other formats
Internal Revenue Service—Con.				
Individual Income Tax Returns	Annual	X	X	X
IRS Data Book	Annual	X	X	X
Statistics of Income Bulletin	Quarterly	X	X	X
International Trade Administration, Office of Travel and Tourism Industries <http://www.tinet.ita.doc.gov>				
Travel Data reports		X		
International Trade Commission <http://www.usitc.gov>				
Recent Trends in U.S. Services	Periodic	X	X	
Synthetic Organic Chemicals, U.S. Production and Sales	Annual	X	X	
Library of Congress <http://www.loc.gov/index.html>				
Annual Report	Annual	X	X	
Maritime Administration <http://www.marad.dot.gov>				
Annual Report	Annual	X	X	
Cargo-Carrying U.S. Flag Fleet by Area of Operation	Semiannual	X	X	X
Merchant Fleet Ocean-Going Vessels 1,000 Gross Tons and Over	Quarterly			X
Seafaring Wage Rates	Biennial	X	X	
Mine Safety and Health Administration <http://www.msha.gov>				
Informational Reports by Mining Industry: Coal; Metallic Minerals; Nonmetallic Minerals (except stone and coal); Stone, Sand, and Gravel	Annual			X
Mine Injuries and Worktime (Some preliminary data)	Quarterly	X		X
National Aeronautics and Space Administration <http://ifmp.nasa.gov>				
Annual Procurement Report	Annual	X	X	
The Civil Service Work Force		X	X	
National Center for Education Statistics <http://nces.ed.gov>				
Characteristics of the 100 Largest Public Elementary and Secondary School Districts in the United States	Annual	X	X	X
College and University Library Survey				X
Computer and Internet Use by Children and Adolescents	Biennial	X	X	
The Condition of Education	Annual	X	X	
Digest of Education Statistics	Annual	X	X	
Earned Degrees Conferred	Annual		X	X
Elementary and Secondary Education	Annual	X	X	X
Faculty Salaries, Tenure, and Benefits	Annual	X		
Fall Enrollment in Degree-Granting Institutions	Annual	X	X	X
Fall Staff in Postsecondary Institutions	Biennial	X		
Federal Support for Education	Annual		X	
Financial Statistics of Higher Education	Annual	X	X	
Indicators of School Crime and Safety	Annual	X	X	
National Assessment of Educational Progress	Annual	X	X	
National Education Statistics Quarterly (last edition 4th quarter 2005)	Quarterly			X
National Household Education Survey:	Annual	X	X	
Early Childhood Program Participation Survey	Periodic	X	X	
The Nation's Report Card: Mathematics Highlights 2003	Periodic	X	X	
The Nation's Report Card: Reading Highlights 2003	Periodic	X	X	
The Nation's Report Card: Geography 2004	Periodic	X	X	
The Nation's Report Card: Science 2000	Periodic	X	X	
The Nation's Report Card: History 2001	Periodic	X	X	
The Nation's Report Card: Writing 2002	Periodic	X	X	
Private School Survey	Biennial	X		X
Projections of Education Statistics	Annual	X	X	X
Revenues and Expenditures for Public Elementary and Secondary Education	Annual	X	X	X
School and Staffing Survey:	Quadrennial			X
Characteristics of Schools, Districts, Teachers, Principals, and School Libraries in the United States	Annual	X	X	
Statistics of Public Elementary and Secondary School Systems Fall	Annual	X	X	X
Status and Trends in the Education of Blacks		X	X	
National Center for Health Statistics <http://www.cdc.gov/nchs/>				
Ambulatory Care Visits to Physician Offices, Hospital Outpatient Departments, and Emergency Departments	Annual	X	X	
Health: United States	Annual	X	X	
Health Characteristics of Adults 55 Years of Age and Over	Periodic	X	X	
Fertility, Family Planning, and Reproductive Health of U.S. Women:				
Data from the 2002 National Survey of Family Growth	Periodic		X	X
National Hospital Discharge Survey: Annual Summary	Annual		X	
National Vital Statistics Reports (NVRS)	Monthly		X	
Vital and Health Statistics			X	
Series 10: Health Interview Survey Statistics	Annual	X	X	
Series 11: Health and Nutrition Examination Survey Statistics	Irregular	X	X	
Series 13: Data from National Health Care Survey	Irregular	X	X	
Series 14: Data on Health Resources: Manpower and Facilities	Irregular	X	X	
Series 20: Mortality Data	Irregular	X	X	
Series 21: Natality, Marriage, and Divorce Data	Irregular	X	X	
Series 23: Data from the National Survey of Family Growth	Irregular	X	X	
National Credit Union Administration <http://www.ncua.gov>				
Annual Report	Annual	X	X	

Title	Frequency	Paper	Internet PDF	Internet Other formats
National Credit Union Administration—Con.				
Yearend Statistics	Annual		X	
National Endowment for the Arts				
<http://www.nea.gov>				
National Endowment for the Arts, Annual Report	Annual			X
The Performing Arts in the GDP, 2002	Periodic	X	X	
Artist Labor Force by State, 2000	Periodic	X	X	
Artist Employment, 2000–2002	Periodic	X	X	
The Arts in the GDP	Periodic	X	X	
Demographic Characteristics of Art Attendance, 2002	Periodic	X	X	
2002 Survey of Public Participation in the Arts	Periodic	X	X	
National Endowment for the Humanities				
<ttp://www.neh.gov>				
Budget Request	Annual	X		X
National Guard Bureau				
<http://www.ngb.army.mil/default.aspx>				
Annual Review of the Chief	Annual	X	X	
National Highway Traffic Safety Administration				
<http://www.nhtsa.dot.gov>				
Traffic Safety Facts	Annual	X	X	
National Oceanic and Atmospheric Administration				
<http://www.lib.noaa.gov>				
Climates of the World, HCS 6-4	Monthly	X		
Climatological Data Issued in sections for states and outlying areas	Monthly	X		X
Comparative Climatic Data	Annual	X		X
Daily Normals of Temp, Precip, HDD, & CDD/Clim 84	Periodic			X
Fisheries of the United States	Annual	X	X	
General Summary of Tornadoes	Annual			X
Hourly Precipitation Data Monthly with annual summary; for each state	Monthly			X
Local Climatological Data Monthly with annual summary; for major cities	Monthly			X
Monthly Climatic Data for the World	Monthly			X
Monthly Normals of Temp, Precip, HDD, & CDD/Clim 84	Periodic		X	
Our Living Oceans	Periodic	X	X	
Storm Data	Monthly			X
U.S. Climate Normals	Daily	X	X	X
Weekly Weather and Crop Bulletin National Summary	Weekly	X	X	
National Park Service				
<http://www.nps.gov/>				
Federal Recreation Fee Report	Annual	X		
National Park Statistical Abstract	Annual	X	X	
National Science Foundation				
<http://www.nsf.gov>				
Academic Research and Development Expenditures	Annual	X	X	X
Academic Science and Engineering: Graduate Enrollment and Support	Annual	X	X	X
Characteristics of Doctoral Scientists and Engineers in the United States	Biennial	X	X	
Characteristics of Recent Science/Engineering Graduates	Biennial	X	X	
Federal Funds for Research and Development	Annual	X	X	
Federal R&D Funding by Budget Function Report	Annual	X	X	X
Federal Science and Engineering Support to Universities, Colleges, and Nonprofit Institutions: Detailed Statistical Tables	Annual	X	X	X
Federal Support to Universities, Colleges, and Nonprofit Institutions	Annual		X	
Graduate Science and Engineering Students and Post Doctorates	Annual		X	X
Graduate Students and Postdoctorates in Science and Engineering	Annual	X	X	X
Immigrant Scientists, Engineers, and Technicians	Annual	X		
International Science and Technology Data Update Report	Annual		X	
National Patterns of Research & Development Resources Report	Annual	X	X	
Research and Development in Industry	Annual	X	X	X
Science and Engineering Degrees	Annual	X	X	
Science and Engineering Degrees, by Race/Ethnicity of Recipients: Detailed Statistical Tables	Annual	X	X	X
Science and Engineering Doctorate Awards	Annual	X	X	
Science and Engineering Indicators Report	Biennial		X	X
Science and Engineering Personnel: A National Overview Report	Biennial		X	X
Science and Engineering Profiles	Annual	X	X	X
Science and Technology Pocket Data Book Report	Annual	X	X	X
Science Resources Studies Data Brief	Frequent			X
Scientific and Engineering Research Facilities at Universities and Colleges	Biennial		X	X
Scientists, Engineers, and Technicians in the United States: Detailed Statistical Tables	Triennial	X	X	X
U.S. Scientists and Engineers	Biennial	X	X	X
Women, Minorities in Science and Engineering Report	Biennial	X	X	
National Transportation Safety Board				
<http://www.ntsb.gov>				
Accidents; Air Carriers	Annual	X	X	
Accidents; General Aviation	Annual	X	X	
Office of Juvenile Justice and Delinquency Prevention				
<http://ojjdp.ncjrs.org/>				
Highlights of the 2002 National Youth Gang Survey (FS-200401)	Annual		X	X
Juvenile Arrests 2002 (Bulletin, NCJ 204608)	Annual	X	X	X
Victims of Violent Juvenile Crime (Bulletin, NCJ 201628)	Periodic	X	X	X
Office of Management and Budget				
<http://www.whitehouse.gov/omb>				
The Budget of the United States Government	Annual	X	X	
Office of Personnel Management				
<http://www.opm.gov>				

Title	Frequency	Paper	PDF	Other formats
Office of Personnel Management—Con.				
Civil Service Retirement and Disability Fund Report	Annual	X		
Demographic Profile of the Federal Workforce	Biennial	X	X	X
Employment and Trends	Bimonthly	X	X	X
The Fact Book	Annual	X	X	X
Federal Employment Statistics	Annual			X
Statistical Abstract for the Federal Employee Benefit Programs	Annual			X
Work Years and Personnel Costs	Annual	X	X	
Patent and Trademark Office				
<http://www.uspto.gov>				
Technology Assessment and Forecast Reports		X	X	X
All Technologies (Utility Patents)	Annual	X	X	X
Patent Counts by Country/State and Year, Utility Patents Report	Annual	X	X	X
Patenting Trends in the United States	Annual	X		
Railroad Retirement Board, Chicago, IL				
<http://www.rrb.gov/default.asp>				
Annual Report	Annual	X	X	
Monthly Benefit Statistics	Monthly	X	X	
Statistical Supplement to the Annual Report	Annual	X	X	
Securities and Exchange Commission				
<http://www.sec.gov/about.shtml>				
Select SEC and Market Data, Fiscal 2006	Annual			X
Small Business Administration				
<http://www.sba.gov>				
Annual Report	Annual	X		X
Handbook of Small Business Data		X	X	
Quarterly Indicators	Annual	X	X	X
Small Business and Micro Business Lending	Annual	X	X	X
State and Territory Small Business Profiles	Annual	X	X	X
The Small Business Economy	Annual	X	X	X
The State of Small Business	Annual	X	X	
Social Security Administration				
<http://www.ssa.gov>				
Annual Statistical Report on the Social Security Disability Insurance Program	Annual	X	X	X
Annual Statistical Supplement to the Social Security Bulletin	Annual	X	X	X
Children Receiving SSI	Annual	X	X	X
Congressional Statistics	Annual	X	X	X
Income of the Population 55 and over	Biennially	X	X	X
SSI Annual Statistical Report	Annual	X	X	X
SSI Disabled Recipients Who Work	Annual	X	X	X
SSI Recipients by State and County	Annual	X	X	X
OASDI Beneficiaries by State and County	Annual	X	X	X
Social Security Bulletin	Quarterly	X	X	X
State Assistance Programs for SSI Recipients	Annual	X	X	X
Fast Facts & Figures about Social Security	Annual	X	X	X
Substance Abuse and Mental Health Services Administration				
<http://www.samhsa.gov>				
National Survey on Drug Use and Health	Annual	X	X	X
National Survey on Substance Abuse Treatment Services (N-SSATS)	Annual	X	X	X

NONGOVERNMENT

Title	Frequency	Paper	PDF	Other formats
Aerospace Industries Association, Washington, DC				
<http://www.aia-aerospace.org>				
Aerospace Facts and Figures	Annual	X	X	
Aerospace Industry Year-End Review and Forecast	Annual	X	X	X
Commercial Helicopter Shipments	Triennial	X	X	
Employment in the Aerospace Industry	Monthly		X	
Exports of Aerospace Products	Quarterly	X	X	
Imports of Aerospace Products	Quarterly	X	X	
Manufacturing Production, Capacity, and Utilization in Aerospace and Aircraft and Parts	Monthly	X	X	
Orders, Shipments, Backlog, and Inventories for Aircraft, Missiles, and Parts	Monthly	X	X	
Air Transport Association of America, Inc., Washington, DC				
<http://www.airlines.org>				
Air Transport Association, Annual Report	Annual	X	X	
The Alan Guttmacher Institute, New York, NY				
<http://www.guttmacher.org>				
Perspectives on Sexual and Reproductive Health	Bimonthly	X	X	X
American Bureau of Metal Statistics, Inc., Secaucus, NJ				
<http://www.abms.com>				
Non-Ferrous Metal Yearbook	Annual	X		X
American Council on Education, Washington, DC				
<http://www.acenet.eduAM/Template.cfm?Section=Home>				
A Fact Book on Higher Education	Quarterly	X		
National Norms for Entering College Freshmen	Annual	X		
American Council of Life Insurers, Washington, DC				
<http://www.acli.com/ACLI/DefaultNotLoggedIn.htm>				
Life Insurers Fact Book	Annual	X	X	
American Dental Association, Chicago, IL				
<http://www.ada.org>				
Dental Students Register	Annual	X		
Distribution of Dentists in the United States by Region and State	Triennial	X		

Title	Frequency	Paper	PDF	Internet Other formats
American Dental Association, Chicago, IL—Con.				
Survey of Dental Practice	Annual	X		
American Forest & Paper Association, Washington, DC				
<http://www.afandpa.org>				
Annual Statistical Summary of Recovered Paper Utilization	Annual	X	X	
Statistical Roundup..	Monthly	X	X	
Statistics of Paper, Paperboard, and Wood Pulp	Annual	X	X	
American Frozen Food Institute, Burlingame, CA				
<http://www.affi.com>				
Frozen Food Pack Statistics................................	Annual	X		
American Gas Association, Washington, DC				
<http://www.aga.org>				
Gas Facts..	Annual	X		X
America's Health Insurance Plans, Washington, DC				
<http://www.ahip.org>				
Source Book of Health Insurance Data........................	Annual	X		
American Iron and Steel Institute, Washington, DC				
<http://www.steel.org/AM/Template.cfm?Section=Home>				
Annual Statistical Report	Annual	X		
American Jewish Committee, New York, NY				
<http://www.ajc.org/site/c.ijITI2PHKoG/b.685761/k.CB97/Home.htm>				
American Jewish Year Book................................	Annual	X		
American Medical Association, Chicago, IL				
<http://www.ama-assn.org>				
Physician Characteristics and Distribution in the U.S.	Annual	X		
Physician Marketplace Statistics	Annual	X		
U.S. Medical Licensure Statistics, and License Requirements.	Annual	X		
American Metal Market, New York, NY				
<http://www.amm.com>				
Metal Statistics	Annual	X		
American Osteopathic Association, Chicago, IL				
<http://www.osteopathic.org/index.cfm>				
American Osteopathic Association Fact Sheet	Biennial	X	X	
American Petroleum Institute, Washington, DC				
<http://www.api.org>				
The Basic Petroleum Data Book (online subscription)	Annual	X		
Joint Association Survey on Drilling Costs (JA5).	Annual	X		
Petroleum Industry Environmental Report	Annual	X		X
Quarterly Well Completion Report (online subscription)	Quarterly	X		
American Public Transportation Association, Washington, DC				
<http://www.apta.org>				
Public Transportation Fact Book	Annual	X	X	
Association for Manufacturing Technology, McLean, VA				
<http://www.amtonline.org>				
Economic Handbook of the Machine Tool Industry 2003–2004 (online version by subscription only)	Annual		X	
Association of American Railroads, Washington, DC				
<http://www.aar.org>				
Analysis of Class I Railroads	Annual	X	X	X
Cars of Revenue Freight Loaded	Weekly		X	X
Freight Commodity Statistics, Class I Railroads in the United States	Annual	X	X	X
Yearbook of Railroad Facts	Annual	X	X	
Association of Racing Commissioners International, Inc., Lexington, KY				
<http://www.arci.com>				
Statistical Reports on Greyhound Racing in the United States	Annual	X		
Statistical Reports on Horse Racing in the United States................	Annual	X		
Statistical Reports on Jai Alai in the United States	Annual	X		
Book Industry Study Group, Inc., New York, NY				
<http://www.bisg.org>				
Book Industry Trends	Annual	X		
Used-Book Sales	Periodic	X		
Boy Scouts of America, Irving, TX				
<http://www.scouting.org>				
Annual Report	Annual	X		
The Bureau of National Affairs, Inc., Washington, DC				
<http://www.bna.com>				
Basic Patterns in Union Contracts............................	Annual	X		
BNA's Employment Outlook	Quarterly	X		
BNA's Job Absence and Turnover.............................	Quarterly	X		
Directory of U.S. Labor Organizations	Annual	X		
National Labor Relations Board Election Statistics	Annual	X		
Union Membership & Earnings Data Book	Annual	X		
Source Book on Collective Bargaining	Annual	X		
Carl H. Pforzheimer & Co, New York, NY				
Comparative Oil Company Statistics Annual	Annual	X		
Chronicle of Higher Education, Inc., Washington, DC				
<http://chronicle.com>				
Almanac...	Annual	X		
College Board, New York, NY				
<http://www.collegeboard.com>				
National Report on College-Bound Seniors	Annual	X	X	

			Internet	
Title				Other
	Frequency	Paper	PDF	formats
Commodity Research Bureau, Logical Systems, Inc., Chicago, IL				
<http://www.crbtrader.com>				
Commodity Year Book Update CD.	Quarterly			
CRB Commodity Index Report	Weekly	X		
CRB Commodity Year Book	Annual	X		
CRB Futures Perspective.	Weekly	X	X	
Electronic Futures Trend Analyzer.	Daily			X
Final Markets-End-of-Day Data.	Daily			X
Futures Market Service	Weekly		X	
The Conference Board, New York, NY				
<http://www.conference-board.org>				
<http://www.conference-board.org/economics/bci>				
Business Cycle Indicators	Monthly	X	X	
Corporate Contributions.	Annual	X	X	
Productivity, Employment, and Income, in the World's Economies	Annual	X	X	
CQ Press, Washington, DC				
<http://www.cqpress.com/gethome.asp>				
America Votes.	Biennial	X		
Consumer Electronics Association (Electronic Industries Alliance), Arlington, VA				
<http://www.ce.org>				
Consumer Electronics Association (CEA) Sales and Forecasts	Semiannual	X	X	
The Council of State Governments, Lexington, KY				
<http://www.csg.org>				
The Book of the States	Annual	X	X	
State Administrative Officials Classified by Function	Annual	X		
State Elective Officials and the Legislatures	Annual	X		
State Legislative Leadership, Committees, and Staff.	Annual	X		
Credit Union National Association, Inc., Madison, WI				
<http://www.cuna.org>				
The Credit Union Ranking Report	Annual	X		
Credit Union Services Profile	Annual	X		
Operating Ratios and Spreads	Semiannual	X		
Dow Jones & Co., New York, NY.				
<http://online.wsj.com/public/us>				
Wall Street Journal	Daily	X		
Edison Electric Institute, Washington, DC				
<http://www.eei.org>				
Statistical Yearbook of the Electric Power Industry	Annual	X	X	X
Editor & Publisher Co., New York, NY				
<http://www.editorandpublisher.com/eandp/index.jsp>				
Editor & Publisher	Monthly	X		
International Year Book	Annual	X		X
Market Guide.	Annual	X		
Euromonitor International, London, England				
<http://www.euromonitor.com>				
Consumer Asia	Annual	X		
Consumer China	Annual	X		
Consumer Eastern Europe.	Annual	X		
Consumer Europe	Annual	X		
Consumer International	Annual	X		
Consumer Latin America	Annual	X		
European Marketing Data and Statistics	Annual	X		
International Marketing Data and Statistics	Annual	X		
Latin America Marketing Data and Statistics	Annual	X		
World Consumer Expenditure Patterns.	Annual	X		
World Consumer Income Patterns.	Annual	X		
World Economic Factbook	Annual	X		
World Retail Data and Statistics	Annual	X		
Federal National Mortgage Association, Washington, DC				
<http://www.fanniemae.com>				
Annual Report	Annual	X		
Food and Agriculture Organization of the United Nations, Rome, Italy				
<http://www.fao.org>				
Fertilizer Yearbook	Annual	X		
Production Yearbook.	Annual	X		
Trade Yearbook	Annual	X		
Yearbook of Fishery Statistics.	Annual	X		
Yearbook of Forest Products	Annual	X		
The Foundation Center, New York, NY				
<http://www.foundationcenter.org>				
Foundation Yearbook	Annual	X		
General Aviation Manufacturers Association, Washington, DC				
<http://www.gama.aero/home.php>				
Shipment Report	Quarterly	X		X
Statistical Databook	Annual	X	X	
Girl Scouts of the USA, New York, NY				
<http://www.girlscouts.org>				
Annual Report	Annual	X	X	
Giving Institute (previously AAFRC), Indianapolis, IN				
<http://www.aafrc.org>				
Giving USA.	Annual	X		

Title	Frequency	Internet Paper	Internet PDF	Internet Other formats
Health Forum, an American Hospital Association Company, Chicago, IL <http://www.healthforum.com>				
Annual Report	Annual	X		
AHA Hospital Statistics .	Annual	X		X
Independent Petroleum Association of America, Washington, DC <http://www.ipaa.org>				
Domestic Oil and Gas Trends	Monthly	X		
Oil & Natural Gas Production in Your State	Annual	X		X
U.S. Petroleum Statistics	Annual	X		X
Information Today, Inc., Medford, NJ <http://www.infotoday.com>				
American Library Directory	Annual	X		
Bowker Annual Library and Book Trade Almanac	Annual	X		
Institute for Criminal Justice Ethics, New York, NY <http://www.lib.jjay.cuny.edu/cje>				
Criminal Justice Ethics	Semiannual	X		
Insurance Information Institute, New York, NY <http://www.iii.org>				
The I.I.I. Insurance Fact Book	Annual	X		
Inter-American Development Bank, Washington, DC <http://www.iadb.org>				
Annual Report	Annual	X	X	
Economic and Social Progress in Latin America.	Annual	X		
International Air Transport Association <http://www.iata.org/index.htm>				
World Air Transport Statistics	Annual	X	X	X
International City Management Association, Washington, DC <http://www.icma.org>				
Compensation: An Annual Report on Local Government Executive Salaries and Fringe Benefits.	Annual			X
Municipal Year Book	Annual	X		
International Labour Organization, Geneva, Switzerland <http://www.ilo.org/global/lang—en/index.htm>				
Yearbook of Labour Statistics	Annual	X		
International Monetary Fund, Washington, DC <http://www.imf.org>				
Annual Report	Annual	X	X	X
Balance of Payments Statistics	Monthly	X		
Direction of Trade Statistics	Monthly	X		
Government Finance Statistics Yearbook	Annual	X		
International Financial Statistics	Monthly	X		
International Telecommunication Union, Geneva, Switzerland <http://www.itu.int/home/index.html>				
ITU Yearbook of Statistics	Annual	X		
World Telecommunication Indicators	Annual	X		
Investment Company Institute, Washington, DC <http://www.ici.org>				
Mutual Fund Fact Book	Annual	X	X	
Jane's Information Group, Coulsdon, UK, and Alexandria, VA <http://www.janes.com>				
Jane's Air-Launched Weapons	Monthly			X
Jane's All the World's Aircraft	Annual			X
Jane's Armour and Artillery.	Annual			X
Jane's Avionics	Annual			X
Jane's Fighting Ships	Annual			X
Jane's Infantry Weapons	Annual			X
Jane's Merchant Ships	Annual			X
Jane's Military Communications	Annual			X
Jane's Military Logistics	Annual			X
Jane's Military Training Systems	Annual			X
Jane's NATO Handbook	Annual			X
Jane's Spaceflight Directory	Annual			X
Joint Center for Housing Studies of Harvard University, Cambridge, MA <http://www.jchs.harvard.edu/>				
The State of the Nation's Housing	Annual	X	X	X
Joint Center for Political and Economic Studies, Washington, DC <http://www.jointcenter.org>				
Black Elected Officials: A Statistical Summary	Annual	X	X	
McGraw-Hill Construction Dodge, a Division of the McGraw-Hill Companies, New York, NY <http://www.construction.com> <http://www.dodge.construction.com/Analytics/>				
Dodge Construction Potential (online subscription)	Monthly	X	X	
National Academy of Sciences, Washington, DC <http://www.pnas.org>				
Summary Report Doctorate Recipients from United States' Universities	Annual	X		
National Academy of Social Insurance, Washington, DC <http://www.nasi.org>				
Workers' Compensation, Benefits, Coverage, and Costs	Annual	X	X	
National Association of Home Builders, Washington, DC <http://www.nahb.org>				
Home Builders Forecast (online subscription)	Monthly			X
Housing Economics (online subscription)	Monthly			X

Title	Frequency	Paper	Internet PDF	Internet Other formats
National Association of Home Builders, Washington, DC—Con.				
Housing Market Statistics (online subscription)...................	Monthly			X
National Association of Latino Elected and Appointed Officials, Washington, DC <http://www.naleo.org>				
National Directory of Latino Elected Officials	Annual		X	X
National Association of Realtors, Washington, DC <http://www.realtor.org> <http://realtor.org/reinsights.nsf/pages/home?openDocument>				
Real Estate Outlook: Market Trends & Insights. (discontinued)	Monthly	X		X
Real Estate Insights	Monthly		X	X
National Association of State Budget Officers, Washington, DC <http://www.nasbo.org>				
State Expenditure Report..	Annual	X	X	
Fiscal Survey of the States	Semiannual	X	X	
National Association of State Park Directors, Raleigh, NC <http://www.naspd.org>				
Annual Information Exchange.....................................	Annual		X	X
National Catholic Educational Association, Washington, DC <http://www.ncea.org>				
Catholic Schools in America......................................	Annual		X	X
United States Catholic Elementary and Secondary Schools Staffing and Enrollment.	Annual	X		X
U.S. Catholic Secondary Schools and Their Finances...................	Biennial	X		
National Center for State Courts, Williamsburg, VA <http://www.ncsconline.org>				
State Court Caseload Statistics...................................	Annual	X	X	
National Council of Churches USA, New York, NY <http://www.ncccusa.org>				
Yearbook of American and Canadian Churches	Annual	X		X
National Education Association, Washington, DC <http://www.nea.org/index.html>				
Rankings of the States and Estimates of School Statistics	Annual	X	X	
Status of the American Public School Teacher, 2000–2001	Quinquennial	X	X	
National Fire Protection Association, Quincy, MA <http://www.nfpa.org>				
NFPA Journal	Bimonthly			X
National Golf Foundation, Jupiter, FL <http://www.ngf.org/cgi/home.asp>				
Golf Consumer Profile...	Annual		X	
Golf Facilities in the U.S..	Annual	X	X	
National Marine Manufacturers Association, Chicago, IL <http://www.nmma.org>				
Boating (A Statistical Report on America's Top Family Sport)	Annual	X		X
U.S. Recreational Boat Registration Statistics	Annual	X	X	
National Restaurant Association, Washington, DC <http://www.restaurant.org>				
Quick-Service Restaurant Trends	Annual	X		
Restaurant Economic Trends (online subscriptions)	Monthly			X
Restaurant Industry Forecast	Annual	X		
Restaurant Industry in Review	Annual	X	X	X
Restaurant Industry Operations Report............................	Annual	X		
Restaurant Industry Pocket Factbook..............................	Annual			
Restaurant Industry 2015, 2005	Annual	X		
Restaurant Performance Index	Monthly	X		X
Restaurant Spending	Annual	X		
State of the Restaurant Industry Work Force........................	Annual	X		
Tableservice Restaurant Trends	Annual	X		
The Economic Impact of the Nation's Eating and Drinking Places	Annual	X		
Hourly Wages for Food Service Occupations........................	Annual	X		
Research News and Numbers	Monthy	X		
National Safety Council, Itasca, IL <http://www.nsc.org>				
Injury Facts...	Annual	X		X
National Sporting Goods Association, Mt. Prospect, IL <http://www.nsga.org/public/pages/index.cfm?pageid=1096>				
The Sporting Goods Market in 2006	Annual	X	X	
Sports Participation in 2005	Annual	X	X	
New York Stock Exchange, Inc., New York, NY <http://www.nyse.com>				
Fact Book (online subscription)...................................	Annual	X	X	
The New York Times Almanac, 2006	Annual	X		
Organisation for Economic Cooperation and Development, Paris, France <http://caliban.sourceoecd.org/vl=2166835/cl=28/nw=1/rpsv/home.htm>				
OECD-FAO Agricultural Outlook	Annual	X		X
Bank Profitability: Financial Statements of Banks, 1924–2003	Biannual	X		X
Central Government Debt: Statistical Yearbook, 1996–2005...............	Annual	X		X
Coal Information..	Annual	X		X
CO2 Emissions From Fuel Combustion, 1971–2004	Annual	X		X
Communications Outlook...	Biannual	X		X
DAC Journal	Quarterly	X	X	
Education at a Glance: OECD Indicators	Annual	X		X
Electricity Information	Annual	X		X
Energy Balances of Non-OECD Countries	Annual	X		X

Title	Frequency	Paper	PDF	Other formats
Organisation for Economic Cooperation and Development, Paris, France—Con.				
Energy Balances of OECD Countries	Annual	X		X
Energy Prices and Taxes	Quarterly	X	X	
Energy Statistics of Non-OECD Countries	Annual	X	X	X
Energy Statistics of OECD Countries	Annual	X	X	X
Environmental Data Compendium	Annual	X		X
Environmental Outlook	Sporadic	X	X	
Financial Market Trends	Triennial	X	X	
Geographical Distribution of Financial Flows to Aid Recipients	Annual	X		
Historical Statistics, 1970–2000. 2001 Edition (discontinued as of 2001)		X	X	X
Information Technology Outlook, 2002 Edition	Biennial	X	X	X
Insurance Statistics Yearbook	Annual	X	X	X
International Development Statistics	Annual			X
Internal Migration Outlook	Annual	X	X	
International Trade by Commodity Statistics	Annual	X	X	
Iron and Steel Industry in 2002, 2004 Edition	Annual			
Labor Force Statistics	Annual	X	X	
Main Economic Indicators	Monthly	X	X	
Main Science and Technology Indicators, Vol. 2003	Biennial	X	X	
Measuring Globalisation: The Role of Multinationals in OECD Countries	One time			
Monthly Statistics of International Trade	Monthly	X	X	
National Accounts of OECD Countries	Annual			
Volume I: Main Aggregates		X	X	X
Volume II: Detailed Tables		X	X	X
Volume IIIa: Financial Accounts	Annual		X	X
Volume IIIb: Financial Balance Sheets	Annual		X	X
Volume IV: Summary of General Aggregates and Balances			X	X
Natural Gas Information	Annual	X	X	X
Nuclear Energy Data	Annual	X		
OECD Economic Outlook	Biennial	X		X
OECD Economic Studies	Annual	X		X
OECD Economic Surveys	Annual	X		X
OECD Employment Outlook	Annual	X		X
OECD Factbook	Annual	X	X	X
OECD Health Data	Annual	X	X	X
OECD Science, Technology, and Industry Outlook	Biennial	X	X	X
OECD Territorial Reviews	Quarterly	X		
Organisation for Economic Cooperation and Development (OECD) in Figures	Bimonthly	X		
Oil Information 2003 Edition	Annual	X	X	
Oil, Gas, Coal, and Electricity Quarterly Statistics	Quarterly	X	X	
Quarterly Labour Force Statistics (discontinued as of 4th quarter 2004)	Quarterly	X	X	
Quarterly National Accounts	Quarterly	X	X	
Research and Development Statistics	Annual	X	X	X
Revenue Statistics 1965–2005, 2006 Edition	Annual	X	X	
Review of Fisheries in OECD Member Countries	Annual	X	X	
Structural Statistics for Industry and Services	Annual	X	X	
Taxing Wages	Annual	X	X	
Trends in International Migration 2004 Edition	Annual	X	X	
Trends in the Transport Sector	Annual	X	X	
Uranium Resources Production and Demand, 2001	Biennial	X	X	
World Energy Outlook	Annual	X	X	
Pan American Health Organization, Washington, DC <http://www.paho.org>				
Health Conditions in the Americas	Quadrennial	X	X	X
PennWell Corporation, Tulsa, OK <http://www.pennwell.com>				
Offshore (online subscription)	Monthly	X	X	
Oil and Gas Journal (online subscription)	Weekly	X	X	
Population Association of America, Washington, DC <http://www.popassoc.org>				
Demography	Quarterly	X	X	X
Puerto Rico Planning Board, San Juan, PR <http://www.jp.gobierno.pr>				
Balance of Payments Puerto Rico	Annual	X		
Selected Statistics on External Trade	Annual	X		
Selected Statistics on Construction Industry	Annual	X		
Activity Index	Monthly	X		X
Projections	Annual	X		
Economic Report to the Governor	Annual	X		
Statistical Appendix-Economic Report to the Governor	Annual	X		X
Income and Product	Annual	X		
Radio Advertising Bureau, New York, NY <http://www.rab.com>				
Media Facts	Biennial	X		
Radio Marketing Guide and Fact Book	Annual	X		
Reed Business Information, New York, NY <http://www.reedbusiness.com/index.html>				
Library Journal	Semimonthly	X		X
Publishers Weekly	Weekly	X		X
School Library Journal	Monthly	X		X
Regional Airline Association, Washington, DC <http://www.raa.org>				
Statistical Report	Annual	X		X
Securities Industry Association, New York, NY <http://www.sia.com>				

Title	Frequency	Paper	Internet PDF	Internet Other formats
Securities Industry Association, New York, NY—Con.				
Foreign Activity Report	Quarterly	X		
Securities Industry Trends	Periodic	X		
Securities Industry Yearbook	Annual	X		X
Standard and Poor's Corporation, New York, NY				
<http://www.standardandpoors.com>				
Analysts' Handbook	Monthly	X		
Corporation Records.	Daily	X		
Daily Stock Price Records	Quarterly	X		
Standard and Poor's Global Stock Market Factbook	Annual	X		
United Nations Statistics Division, New York, NY				
<http://unstats.un.org/unsd/default.htm>				
Compendium of Human Settlements Statistics (Series N)	Annual	X		
Demographic Yearbook (Series R).	Annual	X	X	X
Energy Balances and Electricity Profiles (Series W)	Annual	X	X	
Energy Statistics Yearbook (Series J).	Annual	X	X	
Industrial Statistics Yearbook (Series P)				
Commodity Production Statistics	Annual	X		
International Trade Statistics Yearbook (Series G)	Annual	X		
Monthly Bulletin of Statistics (Series Q)	Monthly	X		
National Accounts Statistics (Series X)				
Main Aggregates and Detailed Tables.	Annual	X		
Analysis of Main Aggregates.	Annual	X		
Population and Vital Statistics Report (Series A)	Quarterly	X		
Social Statistics and Indicators (Series K)	Occasional	X		X
The World's Women: Progress in Statistics, 2005.		X	X	X
Statistical Yearbook (Series; also available in CD-ROM, Series S/CD)	Annual	X		X
World Statistics Pocketbook (Series V).	Annual	X		
United Nations Conference on Trade and Development, Geneva, Switzerland				
<http://www.unctad.org/Templates/StartPage.asp?intItemID=2068&lang=1>				
Development and Globalization: Facts and Figures.	Annual	X	X	X
Handbook of Statistics	Annual	X	X	X
United States Telecom Association, Washington, DC				
<http://www.usta.org>				
Statistics of the Local Exchange Carriers	Annual	X		
University of Michigan, Center for Political Studies, Institute for Social Research, Ann Arbor, MI				
<http://www.umich.edu>				
National Election Studies Cumulative Datafile	Biennial	X		X
Warren Communications News, Washington, DC				
<http://www.warren-news.com>				
Cable and Station Coverage Atlas.	Annual			X
Television and Cable Action Update.	Weekly			X
Television and Cable Factbook	Annual	X		X
World Almanac, New York, NY				
<http://www.worldalmanac.com>				
The World Almanac and Book of Facts.	Annual	X		
The World Bank Group, Washington, DC				
<http://www.worldbank.org>				
Global Development Finance, 2006	Annual	X	X	
The Little Data Book.	Annual	X	X	
World Bank Atlas, 2004.	Annual	X	X	
World Development Indicators	Annual	X	X	
World Health Organization, Geneva, Switzerland				
<http://www.who.int/en/>				
Epidemiological and Vital Statistics Report	Monthly	X		
World Health Statistics	Quarterly	X		
World Trade Organization				
<http://www.wto.org>				
International Trade Statistics	Annual	X	X	X

Guide to State Statistical Abstracts

This bibliography includes the most recent statistical abstracts for states published since 2000, plus those that will be issued in late 2007. For some states, a near equivalent has been listed in substitution for, or in addition to, a statistical abstract. All sources contain statistical tables on a variety of subjects for the state as a whole, its component parts, or both. Internet sites also contain statistical data.

Alabama
University of Alabama, Center for Business and Economic Research, Box 870221, Tuscaloosa, AL 35487-0221. 205-348-6191. Fax: 205-348-2951. Internet site <http://cber.cba.ua.edu/>.
Economic Abstract of Alabama, 2000.
Alabama Economic Outlook, 2007. Revised annually.

Alaska
Department of Commerce, Community, and Economic Development, Division of Community Advocacy, P.O. Box 110809, Juneau, Alaska 99811-0809. 907-465-4750. Fax 907-465-4761. Internet site <http://www.dced.state .ak.us/dca/home.htm>.
The Alaska Economic Performance Report, 2005. Online.

Arizona
Economic and Business Research Center, University of Arizona, 1130 East Helen Street, McClelland Hall, Rm. 103, P.O. Box 210108, Tucson, AZ 85721-0108. 520-621-2155. Fax: 520-621-2150. Internet site <http://www.ebr.eller .arizona.edu/>.
Arizona Statistical Abstract, 2003.
Arizona's Economy. Quarterly newsletter.
Arizona Economic Indicators Databook. Semiannual. Online.

Arkansas
University of Arkansas at Little Rock, Institute for Economic Advancement, Economic Research, 2801 South University Avenue, Little Rock, AR 72204-1099. 501-569-8519. Fax: 501-569-8538. Internet site <http://www.aiea.ualr.edu/default .html>.
Arkansas State and County Economic Data, 2006.
Arkansas Personal Income Handbook, 2006.
Arkansas Statistical Abstract, 2006. Revised biennially.

California
Department of Finance, 915 L Street, Sacramento, CA 95814. 916-445-3878. Internet site <http://www.dof.ca.gov /default.asp>.
California Statistical Abstract, 2005. Annual. Online only.

Colorado
University of Colorado, University Libraries, 184 UCB, 1720 Pleasant St., Boulder, CO 80309-0184. 303-492-8705. Internet site <http://www.colorado.edu/libraries/govpubs /online.htm>.
Colorado by the Numbers. Online only.
Colorado Office of Economic Development and International Trade, 1625 Broadway, Suite 2700, Denver, CO 80202. 303-892-3840. Fax: 303-892-3848. Internet site <http://www.state.co.us/oed/index.cfm>.
Colorado Data Book. Online only.

Connecticut
Connecticut Department of Economic & Community Development, 505 Hudson St., Hartford, CT 06106-7106. 860-270-8000. Internet site <http://www.ct.gov/ecd/site/default.asp>.
Connecticut Town Profiles, 2007.

Delaware
Delaware Economic Development Office, 99 Kings Highway, Dover, DE 19901-7305. 302-739-4271. Fax: 302-739-5749. Internet site <http://dedo.delaware.gov>.
Delaware Statistical Overview. Online only.

District of Columbia
Business Resource Center, John A. Wilson Building, 1350 Pennsylvania Avenue, NW, Washington, DC 20004. 202-727-1000. Internet site <http://brc.dc.gov/resources /facts.asp>.
Market Facts and Statistics. Online only.

Florida
University of Florida, Bureau of Economic and Business Research, P.O. Box 117145, 221 Matherly Hall, Gainesville, FL 32611-7145. 352-392-0171, ext. 378. Internet site <http://www.bebr.ufl.edu/>.
Florida Statistical Abstract, 2006. Annual. Also available on CD-ROM.
Florida County Perspective, 2006. One profile for each county. Annual. Also available on CD-ROM.
Florida County Rankings, 2006. Annual. Also available on CD-ROM.

Georgia

University of Georgia, Selig Center for Economic Growth, Terry College of Business, Athens, GA 30602. 706-542-8100. Internet site <http://www.selig.uga.edu/>.

Georgia Statistical Abstract, 2006–07.

University of Georgia, Center for Agribusiness and Economic Development, 301 Lumpkin House, Athens, GA 30602-7509. 706-542-2434. Fax: 706-542-0770. Internet site <http://www.georgiastats.uga.edu/>.

The Georgia County Guide, 2007. Annual.

Hawaii

Hawaii State Department of Business, and Economic Development & Tourism, Research and Economic Analysis Division, Statistics and Data Support Branch, P.O. Box 2359, Honolulu, HI 96804. 808-586-2423. Fax. 808-587-2790. Internet site <http://www.hawaii.gov/dbedt/>.

The State of Hawaii Data Book 2005. Annual. Periodically updated.

Idaho

Idaho Commerce & Labor, 700 West State St., P.O. Box 83720, Boise, ID 83720-0093. 208-334-2470. Fax. 208-334-2631. Internet site <http://cl.idaho.gov/DNN/Default.aspx?alias=cl.idaho.gov/dnn/idcl>.

County Profiles Idaho. Online.

Idaho Community Profiles. Online.

Profile of Rural Idaho, 2005.

Illinois

Institute of Government and Public Affairs, 1007 W. Nevada Street, Urbana, IL 61801. 217-333-3340. Internet site <http://www.igpa.uiuc.edu/abstract/>.

Illinois Statistical Abstract, 2004. Online only.

Indiana

Indiana University, Indiana Business Research Center, Kelley School of Business, Ste 3110, 1275 E. 10th Street, Bloomington, IN 47405. 812-855-5507. Internet site <http://www.stats.indiana.edu/>.

STATS Indiana. Online only.

Iowa

Office of Social and Economic Trend Analysis, 303 East Hall, Ames, IA 50010-1070. 515-294-9903. Fax: 515-294-0592. Internet site <http://www.seta.iastate.edu/>.

Iowa by the Numbers, 2005. CD-ROM and online.

State Library of Iowa, State Data Center, Ola Babcock Miller Building, 1112E Grand, Des Moines, IA 50319-0233. 800-248-4483. Fax: 515-242-6543. Internet site <http://www.iowadatacenter.org>.

Kansas

University of Kansas, Policy Research Institute, 1541 Lilac Lane, 607 Blake Hall, Lawrence, KS 66044-3171. 785-864-3701. Fax: 785-864-3683. Internet site <http://www.ipsr.ku.edu/>.

Kansas Statistical Abstract, 2005. 40th ed. Online only.

Kentucky

Kentucky Cabinet for Economic Development, Division of Research, 300 West Broadway, Frankfort, KY 40601. 800-626-2930. Internet site <http://www.thinkkentucky.com/>.

Kentucky Deskbook of Economic Statistics. Online only.

Louisiana

Louisiana State Census Data Center, Office of Electronic Services, P.O. Box 94095, Baton Rouge, LA 70804. 225-219-5987. Fax: 225-219-4027. Internet site <http://www.louisiana.gov/wps/wcm/connect/louisiana.gov/home/>.

Maine

Maine State Planning Office, 38 State House Station, 184 State Street, Augusta, ME 04333. 800-662-4545. Fax: 207-287-6489. Internet site <http://www.maine.gov/spo/>.

Maryland

RESI, Towson University, 8000 York Road, Towson, MD 21252-0001. 410-704-7374. Fax 410-704-4115. Internet site <http://wwwnew.towson.edu/>.

Maryland Statistical Abstract, 2006.

Massachusetts

MassCHIP, Massachusetts Department of Public Health, 250 Washington Street, Boston, MA 02108-4619. 617-624-6000. Internet site <http://masschip.state.ma.us/>.

Instant Topics. Online only.

Michigan

Michigan Economic Development Corporation, 300 North Washington Square, Lansing, MI 48913. 1-888-522-0103. Internet site <http://www.michigan.org/medc/miinfo>.

Economic Profiler. Online only.

Minnesota

Minnesota Department of Employment and Economic Development, 1st National Bank Building, 332 Minnesota Street Suite E200, Saint Paul, MN 55101-1351. 800-657-3858. Internet site <http://www.deed.state.mn.us/facts/index.htm>.

Compare Minnesota: Profiles of Minnesota's Economy & Population. Online only.

Minnesota State Demographic Center, 658 Cedar Street, Saint Paul, MN 55155. Room 300. 651-296-2557. Internet Site <http://www.demography.state.mn.us/>.

Mississippi
Mississippi State University, College of Business and Industry, Office of Business Research and Services, P.O. Box 5288, Mississippi State, MS 39762. 662-325-3817. Internet site <http://www.cbi.msstate.edu/dept/bizserv/abstract/>.
Mississippi Statistical Abstract, 2006. 39th ed. Also available on CD-ROM.

Missouri
University of Missouri, Economic and Policy Analysis Research Center, 10 Professional Building, Columbia, MO 65211. 573-882-4805. Fax: 573-882-5563. Internet site <http://econ.missouri.edu/eparc/>.
Statistical Abstract for Missouri, 2003. 13th ed. Biennial. Online only.

Montana
Census and Economic Information Center, Montana Department of Commerce, 301 S. Park Ave., P.O. Box 200505, Helena, MT 59620-0505. 406-841-2740. Fax: 406-841-2731. Internet site <http://ceic.commerce.state.mt.us/>.

Nebraska
Nebraska Department of Economic Development, P. O. Box 94666, 301 Centennial Mall South, Lincoln, NE 68509-4666. 800-426-6505. Fax 402-471-3778. Internet site <http://info.neded.org/>.
Nebraska Data Book. Online only.

Nevada
Department of Administration, Budget and Planning Division, 209 East Musser Street, Room 200, Carson City, NV 89701. 775-684-0222. Fax: 775-684-0260. Internet site <http://www.budget.state.nv.us/>.
Nevada Statistical Abstract. Online only.

New Hampshire
New Hampshire Office of Energy and Planning, 57 Regional Drive, Suite 3, Concord, NH 03301-8519. 603-271-2155. Fax 603-271-2615. Internet site <http://www.nh.gov/oep/index.htm>.

New Jersey
New Jersey State Data Center, NJ Department of Labor and Workforce Development, P.O. Box 388, Trenton, NJ 08625-0388. 609-984-2595. Fax: 609-984-6833. Internet site <http://www.state.nj.us/labor/lra/>.
Labor Market Information. Online only.

New Mexico
University of New Mexico, Bureau of Business and Economic Research, MSC02 1720, 1 University of New Mexico, Albuquerque, NM 87131-0001. 505-277-6626. Fax 505-277-2773. Internet site <http://www.unm.edu/~bber/>.
New Mexico Business, Current Economic Report Monthly.
FOR-UNM Bulletin. Quarterly.

New York
Nelson A. Rockefeller Institute of Government, 411 State Street, Albany, NY 12203-1003. 518-443-5522. Fax: 518-443-5788. Internet site <http://www.rockinst.org/>.
New York State Statistical Yearbook, 2006. 31st ed.

North Carolina
Office of State Budget and Management, 116 West Jones Street, Raleigh, NC 27603-8005. 919-807-4700. Fax 919-733-0640. Internet site <http://www.osbm.state.nc.us/osbm/>.
How North Carolina Ranks, 2004. Online only.

North Dakota
University of North Dakota, Bureau of Business and Economic Research, P.O. Box 8369, Grand Forks, ND 58202. 800-225-5863. Fax 701-777-3365. Internet site <http://business.und.edu/bber/>.
North Dakota Statistical Abstract. Online only.

Ohio
Office of Strategic Research, Ohio Department of Development, 77 S. High Street, 27th Floor, Columbus, OH 43215-6130. 614-466-2116. Internet site <http://www.odod.state.oh.us/research>.
Research products and services. Updated continuously.
Ohio County Profiles, 2005.
Ohio County Indicators. Updated periodically.

Oklahoma
University of Oklahoma, Center for Economic and Management Research, Michael F. Price College of Business, 307 West Brooks, Suite 4, Norman OK 73019. 405-325-2931, Fax: 405-325-7688. Internet site <http://cemr.ou.edu/academics/cntremrcontact.aspx>.
Statistical Abstract of Oklahoma, 2005.

Oregon
Secretary of State, Archives Division, Archives Bldg., 800 Summer Street, NE, Salem, OR 97310. 503-373-0701. Fax: 503-373-0953. Internet site <http://www.sos.state.or.us/bbook>.
Oregon Blue Book. 2007–2008. Biennial.

Pennsylvania
Pennsylvania State Data Center, Institute of State and Regional Affairs, Penn State Harrisburg, 777 West Harrisburg Pike, Middletown, PA 17057-4898. 717-948-6336. Fax: 717-948-6754 Internet site <http://pasdc.hbg.psu.edu>.
Pennsylvania Statistical Abstract, 2006.

Rhode Island

Rhode Island Economic Development Corporation, 315 Iron Horse Way, Suite 101, Providence, RI 02908. 401-278-9100. Fax 401-273-8270. Internet site <http://www.riedc.com/r/index.html>. *RI Databank.* Online only.

South Carolina

Budget and Control Board, Office of Research and Statistics, 1919 Blanding Street, Columbia 29201. 803-898-9949. Internet site <http://www.ors2.state.sc.us/abstract/index.asp>. *South Carolina Statistical Abstract, 2007.* Also available on CD-Rom.

South Dakota

South Dakota State Data Center, Business Research Bureau, The University of South Dakota, 414 E. Clark Street, Vermillion, SD 57069. 605-677-5287. Fax: 605-677-5427. Internet site <http://www.usd.edu/brbinfo/>. *2006 South Dakota Community Abstracts.*

Tennessee

College of Business Administration, The University of Tennessee, Temple Court, Suite 100, 804 Volunteer Blvd., Knoxville, Tennessee 37996-4334. 865-974-5441. Fax: 865-974-3100. Internet site <http://cber.bus.utk.edu/Default.htm>. *Tennessee Statistical Abstract, 2003.* Last printed edition.

Texas

Dallas Morning News, Communications Center, P.O. Box 655237, Dallas, TX 75265-5237. 214-977-8262. Internet site <http://www.texasalmanac.com/>. *Texas Almanac, 2006-2007.* 63rd ed.

Texas State Data Center and Office of the State Demographer, Institute for Demographic and Socioeconomic Research, University of Texas at San Antonio, One UTSA Circle, San Antonio, TX 78249-0704. 210-458-6543. Fax: 210-458-6541. Internet site <http://txsdc.utsa.edu/>.

Utah

Governor's Office of Planning and Budget, Demographic & Economic Analysis, E-210 State Capitol Complex, Salt Lake City, UT 84114. 801-538-1027. Fax: 801-538-1547. Internet site <http://www.governor.utah.gov/dea/. *2007 Economic Report to the Governor.* Annual.

Utah Data Guide Newsletter. Quarterly.

Vermont

Department of Labor, Labor Market Information, P.O. Box 488, Montpelier, VT 05601-0488. 802-828-4202. Fax: 802-828-4050. Internet site <http://www.vtlmi.info/>. *Vermont Economic-Demographic Profile, 2006.* Annual.

Virginia

Weldon Cooper Center for Public Service, P.O. Box 400206, Charlottesville, VA 22904-4206. 434-982-5582. Fax: 434-982-5536. Internet site <http://www.coopercenter.org/>. *VaStat.* Online only.

Washington

Washington State Office of Financial Management, Forecasting Division, P.O. Box 43113, Olympia, WA 98504-3113. 360-902-0555. Internet site <http://www.ofm.wa.gov/>. *Washington State Data Book, 2005.* Online only.

West Virginia

West Virginia University, College of Business and Economics, Bureau of Business and Economic Research, P.O. Box 6025, Morgantown, WV 26506-6025. 304-293-4092. Fax: 304-293-5652. Internet site <http://www.be.wvu.edu/bber/index.htm>. *2006 West Virginia County Data Profiles.* *West Virginia Economic Outlook, 2006.* Annual.

Wisconsin

Wisconsin Legislative Reference Bureau, One East Main Street, Suite 200, Madison, WI 53701-2037. 608-266-3561. Internet site <http://www.legis.state.wi.us/lrb/pubs/bluebook.htm/>. *2005–2006 Wisconsin Blue Book.* Biennial.

Wyoming

Department of Administration and Information, Economic Analysis Division, 1807 Capitol Avenue, Suite 206, Cheyenne, WY 82002-0060. 307-777-7504. Fax: 307-632-1819. Internet site <http://eadiv.state.wy.us/>. *The Equality State Almanac, 2006.*

Guide to Foreign Statistical Abstracts

This bibliography presents recent statistical abstracts for member nations of the Organization for Economic Cooperation and Development and Russia. All sources contain statistical tables on a variety of subjects for the individual countries. Many of the following publications provide text in English as well as in the national language(s). For further information on these publications, contact the named statistical agency which is responsible for editing the publication.

Australia
Australian Bureau of Statistics, Canberra. <http://www.abs.gov.au>.
Year Book Australia. Annual. 2007. With CD-ROM. (In English.)

Austria
Statistik Austria, A-1033 Wien. <http://www.statistik.at/index.shtml>.
Statistisches Jahrbuch Osterreichs. Annual. 2007. With CD-ROM. (In German.) With English translations of table headings.

Belgium
Institut National de Statistique, Rue de Louvain; 44-1000 Bruxelles. <http://statbel.fgov.be/info/linksen.asp>.
Annuaire statistique de la Belgique. Annual. 1995. (In French.)

Canada
Statistics Canada, Ottawa, Ontario, K1A OT6. <http://www.statcan.ca/start.html>.
Canada Yearbook: A review of economic, social and political developments in Canada. 2001. Irregular. (In English.)

Czech Republic
Czech Statistical Office, Sokolovska 142, 186 04 Praha 8; <http://www.czso.cz/>.
Statisticka Rocenka Ceske Republiky 2006. With CD-ROM. (In English and Czech.)

Denmark
Danmarks Statistik, Sejrogade 11, 2100 Kobenhavn O. <http://www.dst.dk/665>.
Statistisk ARBOG. 2007. Annual. English version available only on internet and is free of charge at: <www.dst.dk/yearbook>. (Printed version—in Danish only.)

Finland
Statistics Finland, Helsinki. <http://www.stat.fi/tk/tilastotietoaen.html>.
Statistical Yearbook of Finland, Annual. 2005. With CD-ROM. (In English, Finnish, and Swedish.)

France
Institut National de la Statistique et des Etudes Economiques, Paris 18, Bld. Adolphe Pinard, 75675 Paris (Cedex 14). <http://www.insee.fr/fr/home/homepage.asp>.
Annuaire Statistique de la France. Annual. 2003. (In French.) 2005 CD-ROM only.

Germany
Statistische Bundesamt, D-65180 Wiesbaden. <http://www.destatis.de>.
Statistisches Jahrbuch fur die Bundesrepublic Deutschland. Annual. 2006. (In German.)
Statistisches Jahrbuch fur das Ausland. 2006. *Statistisches Jahrbuch 2006 Fur die Bundesreublik Deutschland und fur das ausland—CD-ROM.*

Greece
National Statistical Service of Greece, Athens. <http:// www.statistics.gr/>.
Concise Statistical Yearbook 2005. (In English and Greek.)
Statistical Yearbook of Greece. Annual. 2005. (In English and Greek.)

Hungary
Hungarian Central Statistical Office, 1024 Budapest. <http://www.ksh.hu>.
Statistical Yearbook of Hungary, 2005. With CD-ROM. (In English and Hungarian.)

Iceland
Hagstofa Islands/Statistics Iceland; <http://www.hagstofa.is/template41.asp?PageID=251>.
Statistical Yearbook of Iceland. 2006 with CD-ROM. Irregular. (In English and Icelandic.)

Ireland
Central Statistics Office, Skehard Road, Cork. <http://www.cso.ie>.
Statistical Yearbook of Ireland. Annual. 2005. (In English.)

Italy
Istituto Nazionale Statistica; <http://www.istat.it>. Via Cesare Balbo 16 Roma.
Annuario Statistico Italiano. Annual. 2006. With CD-ROM. (In Italian.)

Japan
Statistics Bureau, Ministry of Internal Affairs and Communications, Statistical Research and Training Institute, Ministry of Internal Affairs and Communications, Japan. <http://www.stat.go.jp/english/data/index.htm>.
Japan Statistical Yearbook. Annual. 2007. (In English and Japanese.)

Korea, South
National Statistical Office, Government Complex, #920 Dunsan-dong Seo-gu Daejeon 302-701. <http://www.nso.go.kr/>.
Korea Statistical Yearbook. Annual. 2006. (In Korean and English.)

Luxembourg
Statec Centre Administratif Pierre Werner, 13 rue Erasme, B.P. 304, L-2013, Luxembourg. <www.statec.public.iu/>.
Annuaire Statistique du Luxembourg. 2006. (In French.) (Alphabetical numbering system).

Mexico
Instituto Nacional de Estadistica Geografia e Informatica, Av. Heroe Nacozari Num. 2301 Sur Fracc. Jardines del Parque, CP 20270 Aguascalientes, Ags. <http://www.inegi.gob.mx/difusion/ingles/fiest.html>.
Anuario estadistico de los Estados Unidos Mexicanos. Annual. 1998. Also on disc. (In Spanish.) *Agenda Estadistica 1999.*

Netherlands
Statistics Netherlands, R L Vellekoop. Prinses Beatrixlaan 428, 2273 X Z Voorburg; <http://www.cbs.nl/en/>.
Statistical Yearbook 2007 of the Netherlands. (In English.)
Statistisch Jaarboek 2006.

New Zealand
Department of Statistics, Wellington. <http://www.stats.govt.nz/>.
New Zealand Official Yearbook. Annual. 2006. (In English.)

Norway
Statistics Norway, Oslo/Kongsvinger. <http://www.ssb.no/english/subjects/>.
Statistical Yearbook. Annual. 2005. (In English.)

Poland
Central Statistical Office al. Niepodleglosci 208, 00-925 Warsaw. <http://www.stat.gov.pl/english/index.htm>.
Concise Statistical Yearbook 2005. CD-ROM only. (In Polish and English.) *Statistical Yearbook of the Republic of Poland 2004.* CD-ROM only. (In Polish and English.)

Portugal
INE (Instituto Nacional de Estatistica.) <http://www.ine.pt/indexeng.htm>. Avenida Antonio Jose de Almeida P-1000-043 Lisboa.
Anuario Estatistico de Portugal. 2001. (In Portuguese and English.)

Russia
State Committee of Statistics of Russia, Moscow. <http://www.gks.ru/eng/>.
Statistical Yearbook. 2006. (In Russian with CD-ROM.)

Slovakia
Statistical Office of the Slovak Republic, Bradacova 7, 852 86 Bratislava. <http://www.statistics.sk/webdata/english/index2a.htm>.
Statisticka Rocenka Slovenskej Republiky. 2006. (In English and Slovak.) With CD-ROM.

Spain
INE (Instituto Nacional de Estadistica); Paseo de la Castellana, 183, Madrid 16. <http://www.ine.es/welcoing.htm>.
Anuario Estadistico de Espana. 2006. CD-ROM only. (In Spanish.)

Sweden
Statistics Sweden, S-11581 Stockholm. <http://www.scb.se/indexeng.asp>.
Statistisk Arsbok for Sverige. Annual. 2006. With CD-ROM. (In English and Swedish.)

Switzerland
Bundesamt fur Statistik, Hallwylstrasse 15, CH-3003, Bern.
Statistisches Jahrbuch der Schweiz. Annual. 2007. With CD-ROM. (In French and German.)

Turkey
State Institute of Statistics, Prime Ministry, Necatibey Cad/Ankara. No. 114 06100.
Statistical Yearbook of Turkey. 2004. With CD-ROM. (In English and Turkish.)
Turkey in Statistics. 1999. (In English only.)

United Kingdom
The Stationary Office; P.O. Box 29, Norwich, NR3 1GN. <http://www.statistics.gov.uk/>.
Annual Abstract of Statistics. Annual. 2002. (In English.)

Metropolitan and Micropolitan Statistical Areas: Concepts, Components, and Population

The United States Office of Management and Budget (OMB) defines metropolitan and micropolitan statistical areas according to published standards that are applied to U.S. Census Bureau data. The general concept of a metropolitan or micropolitan statistical area is that of a core area containing a substantial population nucleus, together with adjacent communities having a high degree of economic and social integration with that core. Currently defined metropolitan and micropolitan statistical areas are based on application of 2000 standards (which appeared in the Federal Register on December 27, 2000) to 2000 decennial census data. Current metropolitan and micropolitan statistical area definitions were announced by OMB effective June 6, 2003, and subsequently updated as of December 2003, November 2004, December 2005, and December 2006.

Standard definitions of metropolitan areas were first issued in 1949 by the then Bureau of the Budget (predecessor of OMB), under the designation "standard metropolitan area" (SMA). The term was changed to "standard metropolitan statistical area" (SMSA) in 1959 and to "metropolitan statistical area" (MSA) in 1983. The term "metropolitan area" (MA) was adopted in 1990 and referred collectively to metropolitan statistical areas (MSAs), consolidated metropolitan statistical areas (CMSAs), and primary metropolitan statistical areas (PMSAs). The term "core-based statistical area" (CBSA) became effective in 2000 and refers collectively to metropolitan and micropolitan statistical areas.

OMB has been responsible for the official metropolitan areas since they were first defined, except for the period 1977 to 1981, when they were the responsibility of the Office of Federal Statistical Policy and Standards, U.S. Department of Commerce. The standards for defining metropolitan areas were modified in 1958, 1971, 1975, 1980, 1990, and 2000.

Defining Metropolitan and Micropolitan Statistical Areas—The 2000 standards provide that each CBSA must contain at least one urban area of 10,000 or more population. Each metropolitan statistical area must have at least one urbanized area of 50,000 or more inhabitants. Each micropolitan statistical area must have at least one urban cluster of at least 10,000 but less than 50,000 population.

Under the standards, the county (or counties) in which at least 50 percent of the population resides within urban areas of 10,000 or more population, or that contain at least 5,000 people residing within a single urban area of 10,000 or more population, is identified as a "central county" (counties). Additional "outlying counties" are included in the CBSA if they meet specified requirements of commuting to or from the central counties. Counties or equivalent entities form the geographic "building blocks" for metropolitan and micropolitan statistical areas throughout the United States and Puerto Rico.

If specified criteria are met, a metropolitan statistical area containing a single core with a population of 2.5 million or more may be subdivided to form smaller groupings of counties referred to as "metropolitan divisions."

As of December 2006, there are 363 metropolitan statistical areas and 576 micropolitan statistical areas in the United States. In addition, there are eight metropolitan statistical areas and five micropolitan statistical areas in Puerto Rico.

Principal Cities and Metropolitan and Micropolitan Statistical Area Titles—The largest city in each metropolitan or micropolitan statistical area is designated a "principal city." Additional cities qualify if specified requirements are met concerning population size and employment. The title of each metropolitan or micropolitan statistical area consists of the names of up to three of its principal cities and the

U.S. Census Bureau, Statistical Abstract of the United States: 2008

name of each state into which the metropolitan or micropolitan statistical area extends. Titles of metropolitan divisions also typically are based on principal city names, but in certain cases consist of county names.

Defining New England City and Town Areas—In view of the importance of cities and towns in New England, the 2000 standards also provide for a set of geographic areas that are defined using cities and towns in the six New England states. The New England city and town areas (NECTAs) are defined using the same criteria as metropolitan and micropolitan statistical areas and are identified as either metropolitan or micropolitan, based, respectively, on the presence of either an urbanized area of 50,000 or more population or an urban cluster of at least 10,000 but less than 50,000 population. If the specified criteria are met, a NECTA containing a single core with a population of at least 2.5 million may be subdivided to form smaller groupings of cities and towns referred to as New England city and town area divisions.

Changes in Definitions Over Time—Changes in the definitions of these statistical areas since the 1950 census have consisted chiefly of (1) the recognition of new areas as they reached the minimum required city or urbanized area population and (2) the addition of counties (or cities and towns in New England) to existing areas as new decennial census data showed them to qualify.

In some instances, formerly separate areas have been merged, components of an area have been transferred from one area to another, or components have been dropped from an area. The large majority of changes have taken place on the basis of decennial census data. However, Census Bureau data serve as the basis for intercensal updates in specified circumstances.

Because of these historical changes in geographic definitions, users must be cautious in comparing data for these statistical areas from different dates. For some purposes, comparisons of data for areas as defined at given dates may be appropriate; for other purposes, it may be preferable to maintain consistent area definitions. Historical metropolitan area definitions are available for 1999, 1993, 1990, 1983, 1981, 1973, 1970, 1963, 1960, and 1950.

Excluding Tables 20 through 24 in the Population section; Table 576 in the Labor Force section; Table 661 in the Income section, and the tables that follow in this appendix, the tables presenting data for metropolitan areas in this edition of the *Statistical Abstract* are based on the 1999 or earlier metropolitan area definitions. For a list of component counties according to the 1999 definition, see Appendix II in the 2002 edition of the *Statistical Abstract* or <http://www.census.gov /population /www/estimates/pastmetro .html>.

U.S. Census Bureau, Statistical Abstract of the United States: 2008

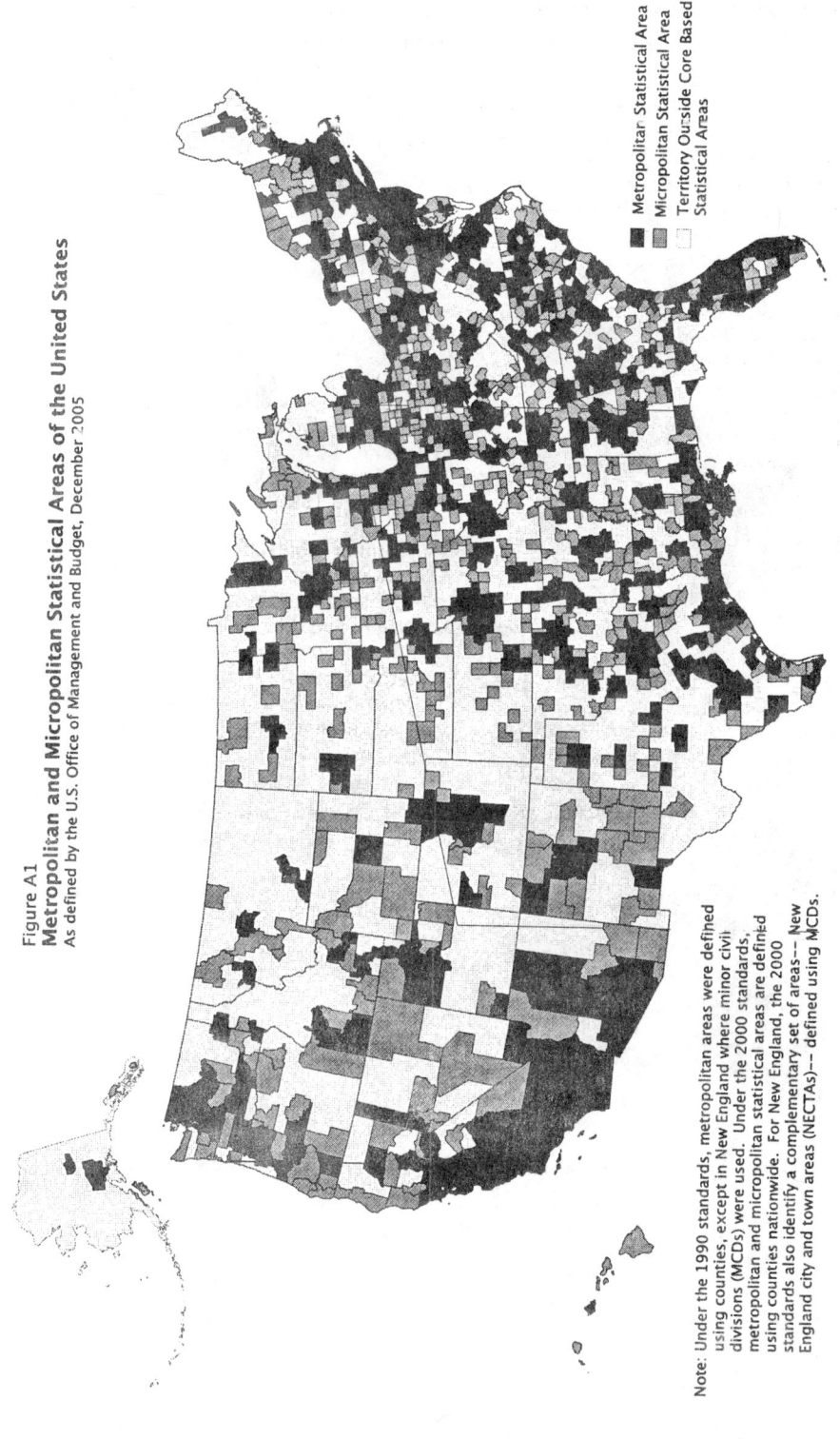

Figure A1
Metropolitan and Micropolitan Statistical Areas of the United States
As defined by the U.S. Office of Management and Budget, December 2005

- Metropolitan Statistical Area
- Micropolitan Statistical Area
- Territory Outside Core Based Statistical Areas

Note: Under the 1990 standards, metropolitan areas were defined using counties, except in New England where minor civil divisions (MCDs) were used. Under the 2000 standards, metropolitan and micropolitan statistical areas are defined using counties nationwide. For New England, the 2000 standards also identify a complementary set of areas— New England city and town areas (NECTAs)— defined using MCDs.

U.S. Census Bureau, Statistical Abstract of the United States: 2008

Metropolitan and Micropolitan New England City and Town Areas (NECTAs)
As defined by the U.S. Office of Management and Budget, December 2005

■ Metropolitan NECTA

▨ Micropolitan NECTA

▫ Territory Outside NECTAs

Note: Under the 2000 standards, metropolitan and micropolitan statistical areas are defined using counties nationwide. For New England, the 2000 standards also identify a complementary set of areas-- New England city and town areas (NECTAs) -- defined using MCDs.

Table A. **Metropolitan Statistical Areas and Components as of December 2005**

[Population as of **July 2006. 158** represents 158,000. All metropolitan areas are arranged alphabetically]

Metropolitan statistical area / Metropolitan division / Component county	Population, 2006 (1,000)	Metropolitan statistical area / Metropolitan division / Component county	Population, 2006 (1,000)	Metropolitan statistical area / Metropolitan division / Component county	Population, 2006 (1,000)
Abilene, TX..............	158	Madison County, NC ...	20	Ascension Parish, LA...	97
Callahan County, TX ...	13	**Athens-Clarke County, GA** .	185	**Baton Rouge, LA—Con.**	
Jones County, TX	20	Clarke County, GA.....	113	East Baton Rouge	
Taylor County, TX	125	Madison County, GA	28	Parish, LA...........	429
Akron, OH	701	Oconee County, GA....	31	East Feliciana Parish,	
Portage County, OH....	155	Oglethorpe County, GA .	14	LA................	21
Summit County, OH....	546			Iberville Parish, LA.....	33
Albany, GA	164	**Atlanta-Sandy Springs-Marietta, GA**	5,138	Livingston Parish, LA ...	115
Baker County, GA	4	Barrow County, GA	64	Pointe Coupee Parish,	
Dougherty County, GA .	95	Bartow County, GA	91	LA................	23
Lee County, GA........	32	Butts County, GA......	24	St. Helena Parish, LA ..	11
Terrell County, GA	11	Carroll County, GA.....	107	West Baton Rouge	
Worth County, GA	22	Cherokee County, GA ..	195	Parish, LA..........	22
		Clayton County, GA	271	West Feliciana Parish,	
Albany-Schenectady-Troy, NY	851	Cobb County, GA	679	LA................	16
Albany County, NY	298	Coweta County, GA....	115	**Battle Creek, MI**	138
Rensselaer County, NY .	155	Dawson County, GA....	21	Calhoun County, MI....	138
Saratoga County, NY...	215	DeKalb County, GA	724	**Bay City, MI**	108
Schenectady County, NY	150	Douglas County, GA ...	120	Bay County, MI.......	108
Schoharie County, NY ..	32	Fayette County, GA	107	**Beaumont-Port Arthur, TX**..	380
		Forsyth County, GA....	151	Hardin County, TX.....	51
Albuquerque, NM	817	Fulton County, GA.....	960	Jefferson County, TX ...	244
Bernalillo County, NM...	615	Gwinnett County, GA...	757	Orange County, TX	84
Sandoval County, NM ..	114	Haralson County, GA...	29	**Bellingham, WA**	186
Torrance County, NM ...	18	Heard County, GA	11	Whatcom County, WA ..	186
Valencia County, NM ...	70	Henry County, GA	178	**Bend, OR**	149
		Jasper County, GA	14	Deschutes County, OR..	149
Alexandria, LA	150	Lamar County, GA	17	**Billings, MT**	148
Grant Parish, LA......	20	Meriwether County, GA .	23	Carbon County, MT	10
Rapides Parish, LA	130	Newton County, GA....	91	Yellowstone County, MT.	138
Allentown-Bethlehem-Easton, PA-NJ..........	800	Paulding County, GA ...	122	**Binghamton, NY**	248
Warren County, NJ	111	Pickens County, GA....	30	Broome County, NY....	196
Carbon County, PA.....	63	Pike County, GA	17	Tioga County, NY	51
Lehigh County, PA.....	336	Rockdale County, GA...	80	**Birmingham-Hoover, AL** ...	1,100
Northampton County, PA	291	Spalding County, GA...	62	Bibb County, AL......	21
		Walton County, GA	79	Blount County, AL.....	56
Altoona, PA	126	**Atlantic City, NJ**	272	Chilton County, AL.....	42
Blair County, PA	126	Atlantic County, NJ	272	Jefferson County, AL...	657
Amarillo, TX	242	**Auburn-Opelika, AL**	126	St. Clair County, AL....	75
Armstrong County, TX ..	2	Lee County, AL........	126	Shelby County, AL.....	178
Carson County, TX	7	**Augusta-Richmond County, GA-SC**	523	Walker County, AL.....	70
Potter County, TX	121	Burke County, GA	23	**Bismarck, ND**	101
Randall County, TX	111	Columbia County, GA ..	107	Burleigh County, ND ...	75
Ames, IA	80	McDuffie County, GA ...	22	Morton County, ND	26
Story County, IA	80	Richmond County, GA . .	194	**Blacksburg-Christiansburg-Radford, VA**	152
Anchorage, AK	359	Aiken County, SC	152	Giles County, VA......	17
Anchorage Municipality, AK................	279	Edgefield County, SC...	25	Montgomery County, VA.	85
Matanuska-Susitna Borough, AK	80	**Austin-Round Rock, TX**....	1,514	Pulaski County, VA	35
		Bastrop County, TX	72	Radford city, VA	15
Anderson, IN	131	Caldwell County, TX....	37	**Bloomington, IN**	179
Madison County, IN....	131	Hays County, TX......	130	Greene County, IN.....	33
Anderson, SC	178	Travis County, TX	921	Monroe County, IN.....	123
Anderson County, SC...	178	Williamson County, TX..	354	Owen County, IN......	23
Ann Arbor, MI...........	344	**Bakersfield, CA**.........	780	**Bloomington-Normal, IL** ...	161
Washtenaw County, MI..	344	Kern County, CA......	780	McLean County, IL.....	161
Anniston-Oxford, AL	113	**Baltimore-Towson, MD**	2,658	**Boise City-Nampa, ID**	568
Calhoun County, AL....	113	Anne Arundel County, MD................	509	Ada County, ID.......	359
Appleton, WI	217	Baltimore County, MD..	787	Boise County, ID......	8
Calumet County, WI....	45	Carroll County, MD	170	Canyon County, ID	173
Outagamie County, WI..	173	Harford County, MD....	241	Gem County, ID	17
Asheville, NC	398	Howard County, MD....	272	Owyhee County, ID	11
Buncombe County, NC..	222	Queen Anne's County, MD................	46	**Boston-Cambridge-Quincy, MA-NH**	4,455
Haywood County, NC...	56	Baltimore city, MD	631	**Boston-Quincy, MA**.....	1,836
Henderson County, NC .	99	**Bangor, ME**.............	147	Norfolk County, MA	655
		Penobscot County, ME..	147	Plymouth County, MA...	494
		Barnstable Town, MA	225		
		Barnstable County, MA..	225		
		Baton Rouge, LA	767		

U.S. Census Bureau, Statistical Abstract of the United States: 2008

Metropolitan statistical area / Metropolitan division / Component county	Population, 2006 (1,000)
Boston-Cambridge-Quincy, MA-NH—Con.	
Boston-Quincy, MA—Con.	
Suffolk County, MA	688
Cambridge-Newton-Framingham, MA	1,467
Middlesex County, MA	1,467
Essex County, MA	736
Essex County, MA	736
Rockingham County-Strafford County, NH	416
Rockingham County, NH	296
Strafford County, NH	120
Boulder, CO	282
Boulder County, CO	282
Bowling Green, KY	113
Edmonson County, KY	12
Warren County, KY	101
Bremerton-Silverdale, WA	241
Kitsap County, WA	241
Bridgeport-Stamford-Norwalk, CT	900
Fairfield County, CT	900
Brownsville-Harlingen, TX	388
Cameron County, TX	388
Brunswick, GA	101
Brantley County, GA	16
Glynn County, GA	74
McIntosh County, GA	11
Buffalo-Niagara Falls, NY	1,138
Erie County, NY	921
Niagara County, NY	216
Burlington, NC	143
Alamance County, NC	143
Burlington-South Burlington, VT	206
Chittenden County, VT	150
Franklin County, VT	48
Grand Isle County, VT	8
Canton-Massillon, OH	410
Carroll County, OH	29
Stark County, OH	381
Cape Coral-Fort Myers, FL	571
Lee County, FL	571
Carson City, NV	55
Carson City, NV	55
Casper, WY	70
Natrona County, WY	70
Cedar Rapids, IA	249
Benton County, IA	27
Jones County, IA	21
Linn County, IA	202
Champaign-Urbana, IL	217
Champaign County, IL	186
Ford County, IL	14
Piatt County, IL	17
Charleston, WV	306
Boone County, WV	26
Clay County, WV	10
Kanawha County, WV	192
Lincoln County, WV	22
Putnam County, WV	55
Charleston-North Charleston, SC	603
Berkeley County, SC	152
Charleston County, SC	332
Dorchester County, SC	119
Charlotte-Gastonia-Concord, NC-SC	1,583
Anson County, NC	25
Cabarrus County, NC	156
Gaston County, NC	199
Mecklenburg County, NC	827
Union County, NC	175
York County, SC	199
Charlottesville, VA	190
Albemarle County, VA	92
Fluvanna County, VA	25
Greene County, VA	18
Nelson County, VA	15
Charlottesville city, VA	40
Chattanooga, TN-GA	497
Catoosa County, GA	62
Dade County, GA	16
Walker County, GA	65
Hamilton County, TN	313
Marion County, TN	28
Sequatchie County, TN	13
Cheyenne, WY	85
Laramie County, WY	85
Chicago-Naperville-Joliet, IL	9,506
Chicago-Naperville-Joliet, IL	7,930
Cook County, IL	5,289
DeKalb County, IL	100
DuPage County, IL	933
Grundy County, IL	46
Kane County, IL	494
Kendall County, IL	88
McHenry County, IL	312
Will County, IL	668
Gary, IN	701
Jasper County, IN	32
Lake County, IN	494
Newton County, IN	14
Porter County, IN	160
Lake County-Kenosha County, IL-WI	875
Lake County, IL	713
Kenosha County, WI	162
Chico, CA	216
Butte County, CA	216
Cincinnati-Middletown, OH-KY-IN	2,104
Dearborn County, IN	50
Franklin County, IN	23
Ohio County, IN	6
Boone County, KY	110
Bracken County, KY	9
Campbell County, KY	87
Gallatin County, KY	8
Grant County, KY	25
Kenton County, KY	155
Pendleton County, KY	15
Brown County, OH	44
Butler County, OH	355
Clermont County, OH	193
Hamilton County, OH	823
Warren County, OH	202
Clarksville, TN-KY	241
Christian County, KY	67
Trigg County, KY	13
Montgomery County, TN	147
Stewart County, TN	13
Cleveland, TN	109
Bradley County, TN	94
Polk County, TN	16
Cleveland-Elyria-Mentor, OH	2,114
Cuyahoga County, OH	1,314
Geauga County, OH	96
Lake County, OH	233
Cleveland-Elyria-Mentor, OH—Con.	
Lorain County, OH	302
Medina County, OH	169
Coeur d'Alene, ID	132
Kootenai County, ID	132
College Station-Bryan, TX	192
Brazos County, TX	159
Burleson County, TX	17
Robertson County, TX	16
Colorado Springs, CO	599
El Paso County, CO	577
Teller County, CO	22
Columbia, MO	156
Boone County, MO	146
Howard County, MO	10
Columbia, SC	704
Calhoun County, SC	15
Fairfield County, SC	24
Kershaw County, SC	57
Lexington County, SC	240
Richland County, SC	348
Saluda County, SC	19
Columbus, GA-AL	289
Russell County, AL	50
Chattahoochee County, GA	14
Harris County, GA	29
Marion County, GA	7
Muscogee County, GA	189
Columbus, IN	74
Bartholomew County, IN	74
Columbus, OH	1,726
Delaware County, OH	157
Fairfield County, OH	141
Franklin County, OH	1,096
Licking County, OH	156
Madison County, OH	41
Morrow County, OH	35
Pickaway County, OH	54
Union County, OH	47
Corpus Christi, TX	416
Aransas County, TX	25
Nueces County, TX	321
San Patricio County, TX	70
Corvallis, OR	79
Benton County, OR	79
Cumberland, MD-WV	100
Allegany County, MD	73
Mineral County, WV	27
Dallas-Fort Worth-Arlington, TX	6,004
Dallas-Plano-Irving, TX	4,019
Collin County, TX	699
Dallas County, TX	2,346
Delta County, TX	6
Denton County, TX	584
Ellis County, TX	139
Hunt County, TX	83
Kaufman County, TX	93
Rockwall County, TX	69
Fort Worth-Arlington, TX	1,984
Johnson County, TX	149
Parker County, TX	106
Tarrant County, TX	1,671
Wise County, TX	58
Dalton, GA	134
Murray County, GA	41
Whitfield County, GA	93
Danville, IL	82
Vermilion County, IL	82

Metropolitan statistical area Metropolitan division Component county	Population, 2006 (1,000)	Metropolitan statistical area Metropolitan division Component county	Population, 2006 (1,000)	Metropolitan statistical area Metropolitan division Component county	Population, 2006 (1,000)
Danville, VA	107	El Centro, CA	160	Fort Wayne, IN—Con.	
Pittsylvania County, VA. .	62	Imperial County, CA. . . .	160	Whitley County, IN.	33
Danville city, VA	46				
		Elizabethtown, KY.	111	Fresno, CA	892
Davenport-Moline-Rock		Hardin County, KY.	97	Fresno County, CA	892
Island, IA-IL	377	Larue County, KY	14		
Henry County, IL	50			Gadsden, AL.	103
Mercer County, IL	17	Elkhart-Goshen, IN	198	Etowah County, AL	103
Rock Island County, IL. . .	148	Elkhart County, IN	198		
Scott County, IA	163			Gainesville, FL	244
		Elmira, NY	89	Alachua County, FL	227
Dayton, OH.	839	Chemung County, NY . .	89	Gilchrist County, FL. . . .	17
Greene County, OH	152				
Miami County, OH	102	El Paso, TX.	736	Gainesville, GA	173
Montgomery County,		El Paso County, TX	736	Hall County, GA	173
OH.	542				
Preble County, OH.	42	Erie, PA	280	Glens Falls, NY.	129
		Erie County, PA.	280	Warren County, NY	66
Decatur, AL.	150			Washington County, NY .	63
Lawrence County, AL. . .	34	Eugene-Springfield, OR. . . .	338		
Morgan County, AL	115	Lane County, OR.	338	Goldsboro, NC	114
				Wayne County, NC	114
Decatur, IL	109	Evansville, IN-KY	350		
Macon County, IL	109	Gibson County, IN	33	Grand Forks, ND-MN	97
		Posey County, IN	27	Polk County, MN	31
Deltona-Daytona Beach-		Vanderburgh County, IN .	173	Grand Forks County,	
Ormond Beach, FL	497	Warrick County, IN.	57	ND.	65
Volusia County, FL.	497	Henderson County, KY. .	46		
		Webster County, KY. . . .	14	Grand Junction, CO	134
Denver-Aurora, CO	2,409			Mesa County, CO	134
Adams County, CO	414	Fairbanks, AK.	87		
Arapahoe County, CO . .	537	Fairbanks North Star		Grand Rapids-Wyoming, MI.	774
Broomfield County, CO. .	45	Borough, AK	87	Barry County, MI	60
Clear Creek County, CO.	9			Ionia County, MI	65
Denver County, CO. . . .	567	Fargo, ND-MN.	187	Kent County, MI	600
Douglas County, CO . . .	264	Clay County, MN	54	Newaygo County, MI . . .	50
Elbert County, CO	23	Cass County, ND.	133		
Gilpin County, CO	5			Great Falls, MT	79
Jefferson County, CO. . .	527	Farmington, NM	126	Cascade County, MT. . .	79
Park County, CO	17	San Juan County, NM . .	126		
				Greeley, CO	237
Des Moines-West Des		Fayetteville, NC	341	Weld County, CO.	237
Moines, IA	534	Cumberland County, NC.	299		
Dallas County, IA.	55	Hoke County, NC.	42	Green Bay, WI.	299
Guthrie County, IA	11			Brown County, WI	240
Madison County, IA	16	Fayetteville-Springdale-		Kewaunee County, WI . .	21
Polk County, IA	409	Rogers, AR-MO.	421	Oconto County, WI	38
Warren County, IA	44	Benton County, AR	196		
		Madison County, AR . . .	15	Greensboro-High Point, NC.	685
Detroit-Warren-Livonia, MI. .	4,469	Washington County, AR .	187	Guilford County, NC. . . .	452
Detroit-Livonia-Dearborn,		McDonald County, MO. .	23	Randolph County, NC . .	140
MI	1,972			Rockingham County,	
Wayne County, MI	1,972	Flagstaff, AZ.	125	NC.	93
Warren-Troy-Farmington		Coconino County, AZ . . .	125		
Hills, MI.	2,497			Greenville, NC	166
Lapeer County, MI	94	Flint, MI	442	Greene County, NC	20
Livingston County, MI. . .	185	Genesee County, MI . . .	442	Pitt County, NC	146
Macomb County, MI. . . .	833				
Oakland County, MI. . . .	1,214	Florence, SC.	199	Greenville, SC.	602
St. Clair County, MI	172	Darlington County, SC . .	68	Greenville County, SC . .	417
		Florence County, SC . . .	131	Laurens County, SC. . . .	70
Dothan, AL	138			Pickens County, SC. . . .	114
Geneva County, AL	26	Florence-Muscle Shoals,			
Henry County, AL	17	AL	143	Gulfport-Biloxi, MS	228
Houston County, AL. . . .	96	Colbert County, AL.	55	Hancock County, MS . . .	40
		Lauderdale County, AL. .	88	Harrison County, MS . . .	172
Dover, DE	148			Stone County, MS	16
Kent County, DE	148	Fond du Lac, WI	99		
		Fond du Lac County, WI.	99	Hagerstown-Martinsburg,	
Dubuque, IA	92			MD-WV.	258
Dubuque County, IA. . . .	92	Fort Collins-Loveland, CO. .	276	Washington County, MD.	144
		Larimer County, CO. . . .	276	Berkeley County, WV. . .	98
Duluth, MN-WI	274			Morgan County, WV. . . .	16
Carlton County, MN. . . .	34	Fort Smith, AR-OK	289		
St. Louis County, MN. . .	196	Crawford County, AR . . .	59	Hanford-Corcoran, CA.	146
Douglas County, WI. . . .	44	Franklin County, AR . . .	18	Kings County, CA	146
		Sebastian County, AR . .	120		
Durham, NC	464	Le Flore County, OK . . .	50	Harrisburg-Carlisle, PA	525
Chatham County, NC. . .	60	Sequoyah County, OK . .	41	Cumberland County, PA .	226
Durham County, NC. . . .	247			Dauphin County, PA. . . .	254
Orange County, NC	120	Fort Walton Beach-		Perry County, PA.	45
Person County, NC	37	Crestview-Destin, FL	180		
		Okaloosa County, FL . . .	180	Harrisonburg, VA	113
Eau Claire, WI.	155			Rockingham County, VA.	73
Chippewa County, WI. . .	60	Fort Wayne, IN	408	Harrisonburg city, VA . . .	41
Eau Claire County, WI . .	95	Allen County, IN	347		
		Wells County, IN	28		

Metropolitan statistical area / Metropolitan division / Component county	Population 2006 (1,000)
Hartford-West Hartford-East Hartford, CT	**1,189**
Hartford County, CT..	877
Middlesex County, CT ..	164
Tolland County, CT	148
Hattiesburg, MS	**135**
Forrest County, MS	76
Lamar County, MS.....	46
Perry County, MS	12
Hickory-Lenoir-Morganton, NC	**360**
Alexander County, NC ..	36
Burke County, NC	90
Caldwell County, NC ...	80
Catawba County, NC ...	154
Hinesville-Fort Stewart, GA.	**74**
Liberty County, GA	63
Long County, GA......	11
Holland-Grand Haven, MI ..	**258**
Ottawa County, MI.....	258
Honolulu, HI	**910**
Honolulu County, HI....	910
Hot Springs, AR	**95**
Garland County, AR....	95
Houma-Bayou Cane-Thibodaux, LA	**203**
Lafourche Parish, LA ...	94
Terrebonne Parish, LA ..	109
Houston-Sugar Land-Baytown, TX	**5,540**
Austin County, TX......	26
Brazoria County, TX....	288
Chambers County, TX .	29
Fort Bend County, TX ..	493
Galveston County, TX ..	284
Harris County, TX	3,886
Liberty County, TX.....	76
Montgomery County, TX.	398
San Jacinto County, TX .	25
Waller County, TX	35
Huntington-Ashland, WV-KY-OH	**285**
Boyd County, KY.....	49
Greenup County, KY ...	37
Lawrence County, OH ..	63
Cabell County, WV	94
Wayne County, WV	42
Huntsville, AL	**377**
Limestone County, AL ..	72
Madison County, AL....	304
Idaho Falls, ID	**117**
Bonneville County, ID...	95
Jefferson County, ID ...	22
Indianapolis-Carmel, IN....	**1,666**
Boone County, IN	54
Brown County, IN	15
Hamilton County, IN....	251
Hancock County, IN....	65
Hendricks County, IN ..	131
Johnson County, IN	133
Marion County, IN	866
Morgan County, IN.....	70
Putnam County, IN.....	37
Shelby County, IN	44
Iowa City, IA	**140**
Johnson County, IA	118
Washington County, IA..	22
Ithaca, NY.	**100**
Tompkins County, NY...	100
Jackson, MI	**164**
Jackson County, MI....	164

Metropolitan statistical area / Metropolitan division / Component county	Population 2006 (1,000)
Jackson, MS.	**529**
Copiah County, MS	29
Hinds County, MS	249
Madison County, MS ...	87
Rankin County, MS	136
Simpson County, MS ...	28
Jackson, TN	**112**
Chester County, TN....	16
Madison County, TN ...	96
Jacksonville, FL	**1,278**
Baker County, FL	25
Clay County, FL	179
Duval County, FL......	838
Nassau County, FL	67
St. Johns County, FL ...	169
Jacksonville, NC.	**151**
Onslow County, NC....	151
Janesville, WI	**159**
Rock County, WI	159
Jefferson City, MO	**145**
Callaway County, MO...	43
Cole County, MO......	73
Moniteau County, MO .	15
Osage County, MO	13
Johnson City, TN	**191**
Carter County, TN	59
Unicoi County, TN	18
Washington County, TN .	114
Johnstown, PA	**147**
Cambria County, PA....	147
Jonesboro, AR	**113**
Craighead County, AR ..	88
Poinsett County, AR....	25
Joplin, MO	**169**
Jasper County, MO	113
Newton County, MO....	56
Kalamazoo-Portage, MI	**320**
Kalamazoo County, MI .	241
Van Buren County, MI ..	79
Kankakee-Bradley, IL	**109**
Kankakee County, IL ...	109
Kansas City, MO-KS	**1,967**
Franklin County, KS....	27
Johnson County, KS ...	517
Leavenworth County, KS.	74
Linn County, KS	10
Miami County, KS	31
Wyandotte County, KS..	156
Bates County, MO	17
Caldwell County, MO ...	9
Cass County, MO	96
Clay County, MO	207
Clinton County, MO	21
Jackson County, MO ...	664
Lafayette County, MO ..	33
Platte County, MO	83
Ray County, MO	24
Kennewick-Richland-Pasco, WA	**226**
Benton County, WA....	159
Franklin County, WA ...	67
Killeen-Temple-Fort Hood, TX	**351**
Bell County, TX.......	258
Coryell County, TX.....	73
Lampasas County, TX ..	21
Kingsport-Bristol-Bristol, TN-VA.	**302**
Hawkins County, TN ...	57
Sullivan County, TN	153

Metropolitan statistical area / Metropolitan division / Component county	Population 2006 (1,000)
Kingsport-Bristol-Bristol, TN-VA—Con.	
Scott County, VA......	23
Washington County, VA .	52
Bristol city, VA........	17
Kingston, NY	**183**
Ulster County, NY	183
Knoxville, TN	**667**
Anderson County, TN...	74
Blount County, TN.....	118
Knox County, TN......	412
Loudon County, TN	45
Union County, TN	19
Kokomo, IN	**101**
Howard County, IN	85
Tipton County, IN......	16
La Crosse, WI-MN	**129**
Houston County, MN ...	20
La Crosse County, WI ..	109
Lafayette, IN	**186**
Benton County, IN.....	9
Carroll County, IN	21
Tippecanoe County, IN..	156
Lafayette, LA	**254**
Lafayette Parish, LA ...	203
St. Martin Parish, LA ...	51
Lake Charles, LA	**192**
Calcasieu Parish, LA ...	185
Cameron Parish, LA ...	8
Lakeland, FL.	**562**
Polk County, FL.......	562
Lancaster, PA	**494**
Lancaster County, PA...	494
Lansing-East Lansing, MI ..	**454**
Clinton County, MI.....	70
Eaton County, MI......	107
Ingham County, MI	277
Laredo, TX	**231**
Webb County, TX	231
Las Cruces, NM	**194**
Dona Ana County, NM ..	194
Las Vegas-Paradise, NV ...	**1,778**
Clark County, NV......	1,778
Lawrence, KS	**112**
Douglas County, KS....	112
Lawton, OK	**109**
Comanche County, OK..	109
Lebanon, PA.	**127**
Lebanon County, PA ...	127
Lewiston, ID-WA	**60**
Nez Perce County, ID ..	38
Asotin County, WA.....	21
Lewiston-Auburn, ME	**108**
Androscoggin County, ME.	108
Lexington-Fayette, KY.	**437**
Bourbon County, KY ...	20
Clark County, KY......	35
Fayette County, KY	271
Jessamine County, KY .	45
Scott County, KY......	42
Woodford County, KY...	24
Lima, OH	**106**
Allen County, OH......	106
Lincoln, NE.	**284**
Lancaster County, NE ..	267

U.S. Census Bureau, Statistical Abstract of the United States: 2008

Metropolitan statistical area / Metropolitan division / Component county	Population, 2006 (1,000)
Lincoln, NE—Con.	
Seward County, NE....	17
Little Rock-North Little Rock, AR	653
Faulkner County, AR ...	101
Grant County, AR	17
Lonoke County, AR ...	63
Perry County, AR.....	10
Pulaski County, AR....	367
Saline County, AR.....	94
Logan, UT-ID.	111
Franklin County, ID....	12
Cache County, UT.....	99
Longview, TX	203
Gregg County, TX......	117
Rusk County, TX......	48
Upshur County, TX....	38
Longview, WA.	100
Cowlitz County, WA....	100
Los Angeles-Long Beach-Santa Ana, CA	12,950
Los Angeles-Long Beach-Glendale, CA. ...	9,948
Los Angeles County, CA.	9,948
Santa Ana-Anaheim-Irvine, CA	3,002
Orange County, CA....	3,002
Louisville-Jefferson County, KY-IN	1,222
Clark County, IN	104
Floyd County, IN	73
Harrison County, IN ...	37
Washington County, IN..	28
Bullitt County, KY.....	73
Henry County, KY	16
Jefferson County, KY...	702
Meade County, KY.....	28
Nelson County, KY	42
Oldham County, KY	55
Shelby County, KY.....	40
Spencer County, KY ...	16
Trimble County, KY	9
Lubbock, TX.	261
Crosby County, TX	7
Lubbock County, TX....	255
Lynchburg, VA	240
Amherst County, VA....	32
Appomattox County, VA .	14
Bedford County, VA	67
Campbell County, VA...	53
Bedford city, VA.......	6
Lynchburg city, VA.....	68
Macon, GA	229
Bibb County, GA	155
Crawford County, GA...	13
Jones County, GA	27
Monroe County, GA....	24
Twiggs County, GA	10
Madera, CA.	146
Madera County, CA....	146
Madison, WI.	543
Columbia County, WI...	55
Dane County, WI.......	464
Iowa County, WI	24
Manchester-Nashua, NH ...	403
Hillsborough County, NH..................	403
Mansfield, OH.	127
Richland County, OH ...	127
McAllen-Edinburg-Mission, TX	701
Hidalgo County, TX	701
Medford, OR.	197
Jackson County, OR ...	197
Memphis, TN-MS-AR.	1,275
Crittenden County, AR ..	52
DeSoto County, MS....	145
Marshall County, MS ...	30
Tate County, MS	27
Tunica County, MS	10
Fayette County, TN	36
Shelby County, TN.....	911
Tipton County, TN	57
Merced, CA.	246
Merced County, CA....	246
Miami-Fort Lauderdale-Miami Beach, FL	5,464
Fort Lauderdale-Pompano Beach-Deerfield Beach, FL. ...	1,788
Broward County, FL....	1,788
Miami-Miami Beach-Kendall, FL	2,402
Miami-Dade County, FL .	2,402
West Palm Beach-Boca Raton-Boynton Beach, FL.	1,274
Palm Beach County, FL .	1,274
Michigan City-La Porte, IN.	110
La Porte County, IN	110
Midland, TX	124
Midland County, TX....	124
Milwaukee-Waukesha-West Allis, WI	1,510
Milwaukee County, WI ..	915
Ozaukee County, WI ...	86
Washington County, WI .	128
Waukesha County, WI ..	381
Minneapolis-St. Paul-Bloomington, MN-WI	3,175
Anoka County, MN	327
Carver County, MN	88
Chisago County, MN ...	50
Dakota County, MN	388
Hennepin County, MN .	1,122
Isanti County, MN	39
Ramsey County, MN ...	493
Scott County, MN	124
Sherburne County, MN .	85
Washington County, MN.	225
Wright County, MN	115
Pierce County, WI	39
St. Croix County, WI ...	80
Missoula, MT	101
Missoula County, MT ...	101
Mobile, AL	404
Mobile County, AL	404
Modesto, CA.	512
Stanislaus County, CA ..	512
Monroe, LA.	172
Ouachita Parish, LA....	149
Union Parish, LA......	23
Monroe, MI.	155
Monroe County, MI	155
Montgomery, AL	362
Autauga County, AL....	50
Elmore County, AL.....	76
Lowndes County, AL ...	13
Montgomery County, AL.	224
Morgantown, WV	115
Monongalia County, WV.	85
Preston County, WV ...	30
Morristown, TN.	133
Grainger County, TN ...	22
Hamblen County, TN ...	61
Jefferson County, TN ...	49
Mount Vernon-Anacortes, WA.	116
Skagit County, WA.....	116
Muncie, IN	115
Delaware County, IN ...	115
Muskegon-Norton Shores, MI.	175
Muskegon County, MI ..	175
Myrtle Beach-Conway-North Myrtle Beach, SC	238
Horry County, SC	238
Napa, CA	134
Napa County, CA	134
Naples-Marco Island, FL ..	315
Collier County, FL	315
Nashville-Davidson–Murfreesboro, TN	1,455
Cannon County, TN....	13
Cheatham County, TN ..	39
Davidson County, TN...	579
Dickson County, TN....	47
Hickman County, TN ...	24
Macon County, TN.....	22
Robertson County, TN ..	62
Rutherford County, TN ..	229
Smith County, TN	19
Sumner County, TN ...	149
Trousdale County, TN ..	8
Williamson County, TN..	161
Wilson County, TN.....	104
New Haven-Milford, CT ...	845
New Haven County, CT .	845
New Orleans-Metairie-Kenner, LA	1,025
Jefferson Parish, LA	431
Orleans Parish, LA	223
Plaquemines Parish, LA .	23
St. Bernard Parish, LA..	16
St. Charles Parish, LA ..	53
St. John the Baptist Parish, LA............	49
St. Tammany Parish, LA.	231
New York-Northern New Jersey-Long Island, NY-NJ-PA	18,819
Edison, NJ	2,309
Middlesex County, NJ ..	787
Monmouth County, NJ ..	635
Ocean County, NJ	562
Somerset County, NJ ...	324
Nassau-Suffolk, NY	2,795
Nassau County, NY	1,326
Suffolk County, NY	1,470
Newark-Union, NJ-PA ...	2,153
Essex County, NJ	786
Hunterdon County, NJ ..	131
Morris County, NJ	493
Sussex County, NJ	153
Union County, NJ	531
Pike County, PA	58
New York-White Plains-Wayne, NY-NJ	11,562
Bergen County, NJ	904
Hudson County, NJ	601
Passaic County, NJ	497
Bronx County, NY	1,361
Kings County, NY	2,509
New York County, NY...	1,612
Putnam County, NY	101
Queens County, NY....	2,255
Richmond County, NY ..	477
Rockland County, NY...	295

Appendix II 895

Metropolitan statistical area / Metropolitan division / Component county	Population, 2006 (1,000)
New York-Northern New Jersey-Long Island, NY-NJ-PA—Con.	
New York-White Plains-Wayne, NY-NJ—Con.	
Westchester County, NY.	949
Niles-Benton Harbor, MI ...	162
Berrien County, MI.....	162
Norwich-New London, CT ..	263
New London County, CT..............	263
Ocala, FL	316
Marion County, FL.....	316
Ocean City, NJ	98
Cape May County, NJ ..	98
Odessa, TX	127
Ector County, TX......	127
Ogden-Clearfield, UT.	498
Davis County, UT	276
Morgan County, UT	8
Weber County, UT.....	213
Oklahoma City, OK	1,172
Canadian County, OK ..	101
Cleveland County, OK ..	229
Grady County, OK.....	50
Lincoln County, OK	33
Logan County, OK.....	37
McClain County, OK ..	31
Oklahoma County, OK..	691
Olympia, WA.	235
Thurston County, WA...	235
Omaha-Council Bluffs, NE-IA	823
Harrison County, IA ...	16
Mills County, IA......	16
Pottawattamie County, IA..............	90
Cass County, NE......	26
Douglas County, NE ...	492
Sarpy County, NE	143
Saunders County, NE..	20
Washington County, NE.	20
Orlando-Kissimmee, FL.	1,985
Lake County, FL	290
Orange County, FL	1,044
Osceola County, FL....	244
Seminole County, FL ...	407
Oshkosh-Neenah, WI	161
Winnebago County, WI..	161
Owensboro, KY.	112
Daviess County, KY....	94
Hancock County, KY ...	9
McLean County, KY....	10
Oxnard-Thousand Oaks-Ventura, CA	800
Ventura County, CA....	800
Palm Bay-Melbourne-Titusville, FL.	534
Brevard County, FL	534
Panama City-Lynn Haven, FL.	164
Bay County, FL.......	164
Parkersburg-Marietta-Vienna, WV-OH	162
Washington County, OH.	62
Pleasants County, WV ..	7
Wirt County, WV	6
Wood County, WV	87
Pascagoula, MS	152
George County, MS....	22
Jackson County, MS ...	131
Pensacola-Ferry Pass-Brent, FL	440
Escambia County, FL...	295
Santa Rosa County, FL .	145
Peoria, IL	370
Marshall County, IL	13
Peoria County, IL......	182
Stark County, IL	6
Tazewell County, IL	131
Woodford County, IL ...	38
Philadelphia-Camden-Wilmington, PA-NJ-DE-MD.	5,827
Camden, NJ	1,250
Burlington County, NJ ..	451
Camden County, NJ....	517
Gloucester County, NJ ..	282
Philadelphia, PA	3,885
Bucks County, PA	623
Chester County, PA	482
Delaware County, PA...	556
Montgomery County, PA.	776
Philadelphia County, PA .	1,448
Wilmington, DE-MD-NJ ..	652
New Castle County, DE .	526
Cecil County, MD.....	100
Salem County, NJ	67
Phoenix-Mesa-Scottsdale, AZ	4,039
Maricopa County, AZ ..	3,768
Pinal County, AZ	271
Pine Bluff, AR	104
Cleveland County, AR ..	9
Jefferson County, AR ...	81
Lincoln County, AR	14
Pittsburgh, PA	2,371
Allegheny County, PA...	1,223
Armstrong County, PA ..	70
Beaver County, PA	176
Butler County, PA	183
Fayette County, PA	146
Washington County, PA .	206
Westmoreland County, PA..............	366
Pittsfield, MA	131
Berkshire County, MA ..	131
Pocatello, ID	86
Bannock County, ID....	78
Power County, ID	8
Portland-South Portland-Biddeford, ME.	514
Cumberland County, ME.	275
Sagadahoc County, ME .	37
York County, ME	202
Portland-Vancouver-Beaverton, OR-WA	2,138
Clackamas County, OR .	374
Columbia County, OR ..	49
Multnomah County, OR .	681
Washington County, OR.	514
Yamhill County, OR	95
Clark County, WA	413
Skamania County, WA ..	11
Port St. Lucie-Fort Pierce, FL.	392
Martin County, FL	139
St. Lucie County, FL ...	253
Poughkeepsie-Newburgh-Middletown, NY.	672
Dutchess County, NY...	295
Orange County, NY	376
Prescott, AZ	208
Yavapai County, AZ	208
Providence-New Bedford-Fall River, RI-MA.	1,613
Bristol County, MA.....	545
Bristol County, RI......	52
Kent County, RI.......	170
Newport County, RI	82
Providence County, RI ..	636
Washington County, RI..	128
Provo-Orem, UT.	474
Juab County, UT......	9
Utah County, UT	465
Pueblo, CO.	153
Pueblo County, CO	153
Punta Gorda, FL.	154
Charlotte County, FL ...	154
Racine, WI	196
Racine County, WI.....	196
Raleigh-Cary, NC	995
Franklin County, NC....	56
Johnston County, NC...	152
Wake County, NC	787
Rapid City, SD	119
Meade County, SD	24
Pennington County, SD .	94
Reading, PA	401
Berks County, PA	401
Redding, CA.	180
Shasta County, CA	180
Reno-Sparks, NV	401
Storey County, NV.....	4
Washoe County, NV....	396
Richmond, VA.	1,194
Amelia County, VA.....	13
Caroline County, VA....	27
Charles City County, VA.	7
Chesterfield County, VA .	297
Cumberland County, VA .	9
Dinwiddie County, VA. ..	26
Goochland County, VA .	20
Hanover County, VA ...	99
Henrico County, VA	284
King and Queen County, VA	7
King William County, VA.	15
Louisa County, VA	31
New Kent County, VA. ..	17
Powhatan County, VA ..	28
Prince George County, VA	36
Sussex County, VA	12
Colonial Heights city, VA.	18
Hopewell city, VA	23
Petersburg city, VA	32
Richmond city, VA	193
Riverside-San Bernardino-Ontario, CA	4,026
Riverside County, CA...	2,027
San Bernardino County, CA.	1,999
Roanoke, VA.	295
Botetourt County, VA ...	32
Craig County, VA......	5
Franklin County, VA.....	51
Roanoke County, VA ...	90
Roanoke city, VA	92
Salem city, VA........	25
Rochester, MN	180
Dodge County, MN	20
Olmsted County, MN...	138
Wabasha County, MN ..	22

U.S. Census Bureau, Statistical Abstract of the United States: 2008

Metropolitan statistical area / Metropolitan division / Component county	Population, 2006 (1,000)
Rochester, NY	1,035
Livingston County, NY	64
Monroe County, NY	731
Ontario County, NY	104
Orleans County, NY	43
Wayne County, NY	93
Rockford, IL	348
Boone County, IL	53
Winnebago County, IL	296
Rocky Mount, NC	146
Edgecombe County, NC	54
Nash County, NC	92
Rome, GA	95
Floyd County, GA	95
Sacramento–Arden–Arcade–Roseville, CA	2,067
El Dorado County, CA	178
Placer County, CA	326
Sacramento County, CA	1,375
Yolo County, CA	188
Saginaw-Saginaw Township North, MI	206
Saginaw County, MI	206
St. Cloud, MN	183
Benton County, MN	39
Stearns County, MN	144
St. George, UT	126
Washington County, UT	126
St. Joseph, MO-KS	122
Doniphan County, KS	8
Andrew County, MO	17
Buchanan County, MO	85
DeKalb County, MO	12
St. Louis, MO-IL [1]	2,796
Bond County, IL	18
Calhoun County, IL	5
Clinton County, IL	37
Jersey County, IL	23
Macoupin County, IL	49
Madison County, IL	265
Monroe County, IL	32
St. Clair County, IL	261
Franklin County, MO	100
Jefferson County, MO	216
Lincoln County, MO	50
St. Charles County, MO	339
St. Louis County, MO	1,001
Warren County, MO	30
Washington County, MO	24
St. Louis city, MO	347
Salem, OR	385
Marion County, OR	311
Polk County, OR	73
Salinas, CA	410
Monterey County, CA	410
Salisbury, MD	118
Somerset County, MD	26
Wicomico County, MD	92
Salt Lake City, UT	1,068
Salt Lake County, UT	979
Summit County, UT	35
Tooele County, UT	54
San Angelo, TX	106
Irion County, TX	2
Tom Green County, TX	104
San Antonio, TX	1,942
Atascosa County, TX	44
Bandera County, TX	20
Bexar County, TX	1,556
Comal County, TX	101
Guadalupe County, TX	108
San Antonio, TX—Con.	
Kendall County, TX	30
Medina County, TX	44
Wilson County, TX	39
San Diego-Carlsbad-San Marcos, CA	2,941
San Diego County, CA	2,941
Sandusky, OH	78
Erie County, OH	78
San Francisco-Oakland-Fremont, CA	4,180
Oakland-Fremont-Hayward, CA	2,482
Alameda County, CA	1,457
Contra Costa County, CA	1,024
San Francisco-San Mateo-Redwood City, CA	1,698
Marin County, CA	249
San Francisco County, CA	744
San Mateo County, CA	705
San Jose-Sunnyvale-Santa Clara, CA	1,787
San Benito County, CA	56
Santa Clara County, CA	1,731
San Luis Obispo-Paso Robles, CA	257
San Luis Obispo County, CA	257
Santa Barbara-Santa Maria, CA	400
Santa Barbara County, CA	400
Santa Cruz-Watsonville, CA	250
Santa Cruz County, CA	250
Santa Fe, NM	142
Santa Fe County, NM	142
Santa Rosa-Petaluma, CA	467
Sonoma County, CA	467
Sarasota-Bradenton-Venice, FL	683
Manatee County, FL	313
Sarasota County, FL	370
Savannah, GA	320
Bryan County, GA	30
Chatham County, GA	241
Effingham County, GA	49
Scranton–Wilkes-Barre, PA	551
Lackawanna County, PA	210
Luzerne County, PA	313
Wyoming County, PA	28
Seattle-Tacoma-Bellevue, WA	3,263
Seattle-Bellevue-Everett, WA	2,497
King County, WA	1,827
Snohomish County, WA	670
Tacoma, WA	767
Pierce County, WA	767
Sebastian-Vero Beach, FL	130
Indian River County, FL	130
Sheboygan, WI	115
Sheboygan County, WI	115
Sherman-Denison, TX	118
Grayson County, TX	118
Shreveport-Bossier City, LA	387
Bossier Parish, LA	107
Caddo Parish, LA	253
De Soto Parish, LA	26
Sioux City, IA-NE-SD	143
Woodbury County, IA	103
Dakota County, NE	21
Dixon County, NE	6
Union County, SD	14
Sioux Falls, SD	213
Lincoln County, SD	35
McCook County, SD	6
Minnehaha County, SD	163
Turner County, SD	9
South Bend-Mishawaka, IN-MI	318
St. Joseph County, IN	267
Cass County, MI	51
Spartanburg, SC	271
Spartanburg County, SC	271
Spokane, WA	447
Spokane County, WA	447
Springfield, IL	206
Menard County, IL	13
Sangamon County, IL	194
Springfield, MA	686
Franklin County, MA	72
Hampden County, MA	461
Hampshire County, MA	153
Springfield, MO	407
Christian County, MO	71
Dallas County, MO	17
Greene County, MO	255
Polk County, MO	30
Webster County, MO	36
Springfield, OH	142
Clark County, OH	142
State College, PA	141
Centre County, PA	141
Stockton, CA	673
San Joaquin County, CA	673
Sumter, SC	104
Sumter County, SC	104
Syracuse, NY	650
Madison County, NY	70
Onondaga County, NY	457
Oswego County, NY	123
Tallahassee, FL	337
Gadsden County, FL	47
Jefferson County, FL	15
Leon County, FL	246
Wakulla County, FL	30
Tampa-St. Petersburg-Clearwater, FL	2,698
Hernando County, FL	165
Hillsborough County, FL	1,158
Pasco County, FL	450
Pinellas County, FL	924
Terre Haute, IN	168
Clay County, IN	27
Sullivan County, IN	22
Vermillion County, IN	17
Vigo County, IN	103
Texarkana, TX-Texarkana, AR	135
Miller County, AR	43
Bowie County, TX	91

U.S. Census Bureau, Statistical Abstract of the United States: 2008

Metropolitan statistical area / Metropolitan division / Component county	Population, 2006 (1,000)	Metropolitan statistical area / Metropolitan division / Component county	Population, 2006 (1,000)	Metropolitan statistical area / Metropolitan division / Component county	Population, 2006 (1,000)
Toledo, OH	654	**Virginia Beach-Norfolk-Newport News,**		**Weirton-Steubenville,**	
Fulton County, OH	43	**VA-NC—Con.**		**WV-OH—Con.**	
Lucas County, OH	445	York County, VA	62	Brooke County, WV	24
Ottawa County, OH	41	Chesapeake city, VA	221	Hancock County, WV	31
Wood County, OH	124	Hampton city, VA	145		
		Newport News city, VA	178	**Wenatchee, WA**	107
Topeka, KS	229	Norfolk city, VA	229	Chelan County, WA	71
Jackson County, KS	14	Poquoson city, VA	12	Douglas County, WA	36
Jefferson County, KS	19	Portsmouth city, VA	101		
Osage County, KS	17	Suffolk city, VA	81	**Wheeling, WV-OH**	147
Shawnee County, KS	173	Virginia Beach city, VA	436	Belmont County, OH	69
Wabaunsee County, KS	7	Williamsburg city, VA	12	Marshall County, WV	34
				Ohio County, WV	45
Trenton-Ewing, NJ	368	**Visalia-Porterville, CA**	420		
Mercer County, NJ	368	Tulare County, CA	420	**Wichita, KS**	592
				Butler County, KS	63
Tucson, AZ	946	**Waco, TX**	226	Harvey County, KS	34
Pima County, AZ	946	McLennan County, TX	226	Sedgwick County, KS	471
				Sumner County, KS	24
Tulsa, OK	898	**Warner Robins, GA**	128		
Creek County, OK	69	Houston County, GA	128	**Wichita Falls, TX**	146
Okmulgee County, OK	40			Archer County, TX	9
Osage County, OK	46	**Washington-Arlington-**		Clay County, TX	11
Pawnee County, OK	17	**Alexandria, DC-VA-MD-WV.**	5,290	Wichita County, TX	125
Rogers County, OK	82	**Bethesda-Gaithersburg-**			
Tulsa County, OK	578	**Frederick, MD**	1,155	**Williamsport, PA**	118
Wagoner County, OK	66	Frederick County, MD	223	Lycoming County, PA	118
		Montgomery County,			
Tuscaloosa, AL	199	MD	932	**Wilmington, NC**	326
Greene County, AL	9	**Washington-Arlington-**		Brunswick County, NC	95
Hale County, AL	18	**Alexandria, DC-VA-MD-**		New Hanover County,	
Tuscaloosa County, AL	171	**WV**	4,135	NC	183
		District of Columbia, DC	582	Pender County, NC	49
Tyler, TX	195	Calvert County, MD	89		
Smith County, TX	195	Charles County, MD	140	**Winchester, VA-WV**	119
		Prince George's County,		Frederick County, VA	71
Utica-Rome, NY	297	MD	841	Winchester city, VA	25
Herkimer County, NY	63	Arlington County, VA	200	Hampshire County, WV	22
Oneida County, NY	234	Clarke County, VA	15		
		Fairfax County, VA	1,010	**Winston-Salem, NC**	457
Valdosta, GA	126	Fauquier County, VA	66	Davie County, NC	40
Brooks County, GA	16	Loudoun County, VA	269	Forsyth County, NC	332
Echols County, GA	4	Prince William County,		Stokes County, NC	46
Lanier County, GA	8	VA	358	Yadkin County, NC	38
Lowndes County, GA	98	Spotsylvania County, VA	120		
		Stafford County, VA	120	**Worcester, MA**	785
Vallejo-Fairfield, CA	412	Warren County, VA	36	Worcester County, MA	785
Solano County, CA	412	Alexandria city, VA	137		
		Fairfax city, VA	22	**Yakima, WA**	233
Victoria, TX	114	Falls Church city, VA	11	Yakima County, WA	233
Calhoun County, TX	21	Fredericksburg city, VA	21		
Goliad County, TX	7	Manassas city, VA	37	**York-Hanover, PA**	416
Victoria County, TX	86	Manassas Park city, VA	12	York County, PA	416
		Jefferson County, WV	50		
Vineland-Millville-Bridgeton,				**Youngstown-Warren-**	
NJ	155	**Waterloo-Cedar Falls, IA**	162	**Boardman, OH-PA**	587
Cumberland County, NJ	155	Black Hawk County, IA	126	Mahoning County, OH	251
		Bremer County, IA	24	Trumbull County, OH	217
Virginia Beach-Norfolk-		Grundy County, IA	12	Mercer County, PA	119
Newport News, VA-NC	1,649				
Currituck County, NC	24	**Wausau, WI**	130	**Yuba City, CA**	162
Gloucester County, VA	38	Marathon County, WI	130	Sutter County, CA	91
Isle of Wight County, VA	35			Yuba County, CA	70
James City County, VA	60	**Weirton-Steubenville,**			
Mathews County, VA	9	**WV-OH**	125	**Yuma, AZ**	188
Surry County, VA	7	Jefferson County, OH	70	Yuma County, AZ	188

[1] The portion of Sullivan city in Crawford County, Missouri, is legally part of the St. Louis, MO-IL MSA. The estimate shown here for the St. Louis, MO-IL Metropolitan Statistical Area does not include this area.

Source: U.S. Census Bureau, "CBSA-EST2006-alldata: Population Estimates and Estimated Components of Change for Metropolitan and Micropolitan Statistical Areas and Their Geographic Components: April 1, 2000 to July 1, 2006" <http://www.census.gov/population/estimates/metrogeneral/2006/CBSA-EST2006-alldata.csv>; and unpublished data.

Table B. Micropolitan Statistical Areas and Components as of December 2005

[Population as of July 2006. 56 represents 56,000. All micropolitan areas are arranged alphabetically]

Micropolitan statistical area Component county	Popu- lation, 2006 (1,000)	Micropolitan statistical area Component county	Popu- lation, 2006 (1,000)	Micropolitan statistical area Component county	Popu- lation, 2006 (1,000)
Abbeville, LA	56	**Astoria, OR.**	37	**Big Rapids, MI**	42
Vermilion Parish, LA	56	Clatsop County, OR.	37	Mecosta County, MI.	42
Aberdeen, SD.	39	**Atchison, KS**	17	**Big Spring, TX**	32
Brown County, SD.	35	Atchison County, KS	17	Howard County, TX.	32
Edmunds County, SD	4	**Athens, OH.**	62	**Bishop, CA.**	18
Aberdeen, WA.	72	Athens County, OH	62	Inyo County, CA	18
Grays Harbor County, WA .	72	**Athens, TN**	52	**Blackfoot, ID.**	44
Ada, OK	35	McMinn County, TN.	52	Bingham County, ID	44
Pontotoc County, OK.	35	**Athens, TX**	80	**Bloomsburg-Berwick, PA** . .	83
Adrian, MI.	102	Henderson County, TX. . . .	80	Columbia County, PA.	65
Lenawee County, MI	102	**Auburn, IN**	42	Montour County, PA	18
Alamogordo, NM.	63	De Kalb County, IN	42	**Bluefield, WV-VA.**	106
Otero County, NM.	63	**Auburn, NY.**	81	Tazewell County, VA	45
Albany-Lebanon, OR.	111	Cayuga County, NY.	81	Mercer County, WV	61
Linn County, OR	111	**Augusta-Waterville, ME.** . . .	121	**Blytheville, AR**	48
Albemarle, NC	59	Kennebec County, ME. . . .	121	Mississippi County, AR . . .	48
Stanly County, NC.	59	**Austin, MN**	39	**Bogalusa, LA**	45
Albert Lea, MN	32	Mower County, MN	39	Washington Parish, LA . . .	45
Freeborn County, MN	32	**Bainbridge, GA.**	29	**Bonham, TX**	33
Albertville, AL.	87	Decatur County, GA	29	Fannin County, TX	33
Marshall County, AL	87	**Baraboo, WI**	58	**Boone, IA.**	27
Alexander City, AL	52	Sauk County, WI.	58	Boone County, IA	27
Coosa County, AL.	11	**Barre, VT**	60	**Boone, NC**	43
Tallapoosa County, AL. . . .	41	Washington County, VT . . .	60	Watauga County, NC.	43
Alexandria, MN	35	**Bartlesville, OK.**	49	**Borger, TX**	22
Douglas County, MN	35	Washington County, OK. . .	49	Hutchinson County, TX . . .	22
Alice, TX.	41	**Bastrop, LA**	30	**Bozeman, MT**	81
Jim Wells County, TX	41	Morehouse Parish, LA. . . .	30	Gallatin County, MT.	81
Allegan, MI	114	**Batavia, NY.**	59	**Bradford, PA.**	44
Allegan County, MI	114	Genesee County, NY.	59	McKean County, PA	44
Alma, MI.	42	**Batesville, AR.**	35	**Brainerd, MN**	90
Gratiot County, MI.	42	Independence County, AR .	35	Cass County, MN	29
Alpena, MI	30	**Bay City, TX**	38	Crow Wing County, MN . . .	61
Alpena County, MI.	30	Matagorda County, TX. . . .	38	**Branson, MO**	75
Altus, OK	26	**Beatrice, NE**	23	Stone County, MO.	31
Jackson County, OK	26	Gage County, NE	23	Taney County, MO	44
Americus, GA.	37	**Beaver Dam, WI**	89	**Brenham, TX.**	32
Schley County, GA	4	Dodge County, WI.	89	Washington County, TX . . .	32
Sumter County, GA	32	**Beckley, WV**	79	**Brevard, NC**	30
Amsterdam, NY.	49	Raleigh County, WV	79	Transylvania County, NC . .	30
Montgomery County, NY . .	49	**Bedford, IN.**	46	**Brigham City, UT**	47
Andrews, TX.	13	Lawrence County, IN.	46	Box Elder County, UT	47
Andrews County, TX	13	**Beeville, TX**	33	**Brookhaven, MS**	34
Angola, IN	34	Bee County, TX	33	Lincoln County, MS.	34
Steuben County, IN.	34	**Bellefontaine, OH**	46	**Brookings, OR**	22
Arcadia, FL.	35	Logan County, OH	46	Curry County, OR	22
DeSoto County, FL	35	**Bemidji, MN**	43	**Brookings, SD**	28
Ardmore, OK	57	Beltrami County, MN	43	Brookings County, SD. . . .	28
Carter County, OK.	48	**Bennettsville, SC**	29	**Brownsville, TN**	19
Love County, OK.	9	Marlboro County, SC.	29	Haywood County, TN.	19
Arkadelphia, AR	23	**Bennington, VT.**	37	**Brownwood, TX**	39
Clark County, AR	23	Bennington County, VT . . .	37	Brown County, TX.	39
Ashland, OH.	55	**Berlin, NH-VT**	40	**Bucyrus, OH.**	45
Ashland County, OH	55	Coos County, NH	33	Crawford County, OH	45
Ashtabula, OH	103	Essex County, VT	7	**Burley, ID.**	40
Ashtabula County, OH. . . .	103			Cassia County, ID.	21

U.S. Census Bureau, Statistical Abstract of the United States: 2008

Micropolitan statistical area Component county	Popu- lation, 2006 (1,000)	Micropolitan statistical area Component county	Popu- lation, 2006 (1,000)	Micropolitan statistical area Component county	Popu- lation, 2006 (1,000)
Burley, ID—Con.		**Clarksburg, WV**	93	**Cullman, AL**	80
Minidoka County, ID	19	Doddridge County, WV . . .	7	Cullman County, AL.	80
		Harrison County, WV . . .	69		
Burlington, IA-IL	49	Taylor County, WV	16	**Culpeper, VA.**	45
Henderson County, IL	8			Culpeper County, VA	45
Des Moines County, IA . . .	41	**Clarksdale, MS**	28		
		Coahoma County, MS	28	**Danville, KY**	54
Butte-Silver Bow, MT	33			Boyle County, KY	28
Silver Bow County, MT . . .	33	**Clearlake, CA**	66	Lincoln County, KY	25
		Lake County, CA.	66		
Cadillac, MI.	47			**Daphne-Fairhope, AL**	169
Missaukee County, MI. . . .	15	**Cleveland, MS.**	38	Baldwin County, AL.	169
Wexford County, MI.	32	Bolivar County, MS	38		
				Decatur, IN	34
Calhoun, GA.	51	**Clewiston, FL**	40	Adams County, IN.	34
Gordon County, GA.	51	Hendry County, FL	40		
				Defiance, OH	39
Cambridge, MD.	32	**Clinton, IA**	50	Defiance County, OH.	39
Dorchester County, MD . . .	32	Clinton County, IA. . . . ,. . .	50		
				Del Rio, TX.	48
Cambridge, OH.	41	**Clovis, NM**	46	Val Verde County, TX	48
Guernsey County, OH	41	Curry County, NM	46		
				Deming, NM	27
Camden, AR	32	**Coffeyville, KS**	35	Luna County, NM	27
Calhoun County, AR	6	Montgomery County, KS . .	35		
Ouachita County, AR.	27			**De Ridder, LA.**	35
		Coldwater, MI	46	Beauregard Parish, LA . . .	35
Campbellsville, KY	24	Branch County, MI	46		
Taylor County, KY	24			**Dickinson, ND.**	23
		Columbia, TN	78	Billings County, ND	1
Canon City, CO.	48	Maury County, TN.	78	Stark County, ND	22
Fremont County, CO	48				
		Columbus, MS	60	**Dillon, SC.**	31
Canton, IL.	37	Lowndes County, MS.	60	Dillon County, SC	31
Fulton County, IL.	37				
		Columbus, NE	32	**Dixon, IL.**	36
Cape Girardeau-Jackson,		Platte County, NE	32	Lee County, IL	36
MO-IL	93				
Alexander County, IL.	9	**Concord, NH.**	148	**Dodge City, KS.**	34
Bollinger County, MO.	12	Merrimack County, NH. . . .	148	Ford County, KS.	34
Cape Girardeau County,					
MO	72	**Connersville, IN**	25	**Douglas, GA.**	48
		Fayette County, IN	25	Atkinson County, GA.	8
Carbondale, IL	58			Coffee County, GA	40
Jackson County, IL.	58	**Cookeville, TN**	100		
		Jackson County, TN	11	**Dublin, GA.**	57
Carlsbad-Artesia, NM	52	Overton County, TN.	21	Johnson County, GA	10
Eddy County, NM	52	Putnam County, TN.	68	Laurens County, GA	47
Cedar City, UT	41	**Coos Bay, OR.**	65	**DuBois, PA.**	82
Iron County, UT	41	Coos County, OR	65	Clearfield County, PA.	82
Cedartown, GA.	41	**Corbin, KY**	38	**Dumas, TX**	21
Polk County, GA.	41	Whitley County, KY	38	Moore County, TX.	21
Celina, OH	41	**Cordele, GA.**	22	**Duncan, OK**	43
Mercer County, OH	41	Crisp County, GA	22	Stephens County, OK	43
Central City, KY	32	**Corinth, MS**	36	**Dunn, NC**	106
Muhlenberg County, KY . . .	32	Alcorn County, MS	36	Harnett County, NC.	106
Centralia, IL	40	**Cornelia, GA.**	41	**Durango, CO.**	48
Marion County, IL	40	Habersham County, GA. . .	41	La Plata County, CO	48
Centralia, WA	74	**Corning, NY**	98	**Durant, OK**	38
Lewis County, WA.	74	Steuben County, NY	98	Bryan County, OK	38
Chambersburg, PA	140	**Corsicana, TX.**	49	**Dyersburg, TN**	38
Franklin County, PA.	140	Navarro County, TX.	49	Dyer County, TN.	38
Charleston-Mattoon, IL	62	**Cortland, NY.**	48	**Eagle Pass, TX**	52
Coles County, IL.	51	Cortland County, NY	48	Maverick County, TX.	52
Cumberland County, IL . . .	11				
		Coshocton, OH.	37	**East Liverpool-Salem, OH** . .	111
Chester, SC	33	Coshocton County, OH . . .	37	Columbiana County, OH . .	111
Chester County, SC.	33				
		Crawfordsville, IN	38	**Easton, MD.**	36
Chillicothe, OH	76	Montgomery County, IN . . .	38	Talbot County, MD.	36
Ross County, OH	76				
		Crescent City, CA	29	**East Stroudsburg, PA**	166
City of The Dalles, OR.	24	Del Norte County, CA	29	Monroe County, PA.	166
Wasco County, OR	24				
		Crossville, TN.	52	**Edwards, CO**	57
Claremont, NH	43	Cumberland County, TN. . .	52	Eagle County, CO.	49
Sullivan County, NH	43			Lake County, CO	8
		Crowley, LA	60		
		Acadia Parish, LA.	60		

900   Appendix II

Micropolitan statistical area / Component county	Population, 2006 (1,000)	Micropolitan statistical area / Component county	Population, 2006 (1,000)	Micropolitan statistical area / Component county	Population, 2006 (1,000)
Effingham, IL	34	Fort Leonard Wood, MO	44	Great Bend, KS	28
Effingham County, IL	34	Pulaski County, MO	44	Barton County, KS	28
El Campo, TX	41	Fort Madison-Keokuk,		Greeneville, TN	66
Wharton County, TX	41	IA-MO	44	Greene County, TN	66
El Dorado, AR	44	Lee County, IA	36		
Union County, AR	44	Clark County, MO	7	Greensburg, IN	25
				Decatur County, IN	25
Elizabeth City, NC	61	Fort Morgan, CO	28		
Camden County, NC	9	Morgan County, CO	28	Greenville, MS	58
Pasquotank County, NC	40			Washington County, MS	58
Perquimans County, NC	12	Fort Payne, AL	68		
		DeKalb County, AL	68	Greenville, OH	53
Elk City, OK	19			Darke County, OH	53
Beckham County, OK	19	Fort Polk South, LA	47		
		Vernon Parish, LA	47	Greenwood, MS	46
Elko, NV	49			Carroll County, MS	10
Elko County, NV	47	Fort Valley, GA	25	Leflore County, MS	36
Eureka County, NV	1	Peach County, GA	25		
				Greenwood, SC	68
Ellensburg, WA	37	Frankfort, IN	34	Greenwood County, SC	68
Kittitas County, WA	37	Clinton County, IN	34		
				Grenada, MS	23
Emporia, KS	38	Frankfort, KY	69	Grenada County, MS	23
Chase County, KS	3	Anderson County, KY	21		
Lyon County, KS	35	Franklin County, KY	48	Guymon, OK	20
				Texas County, OK	20
Enid, OK	57	Freeport, IL	47		
Garfield County, OK	57	Stephenson County, IL	47	Hammond, LA	113
				Tangipahoa Parish, LA	113
Enterprise-Ozark, AL	94	Fremont, NE	36		
Coffee County, AL	46	Dodge County, NE	36	Hannibal, MO	38
Dale County, AL	48			Marion County, MO	28
		Fremont, OH	62	Ralls County, MO	10
Escanaba, MI	38	Sandusky County, OH	62		
Delta County, MI	38			Harriman, TN	53
		Gaffney, SC	54	Roane County, TN	53
Espanola, NM	41	Cherokee County, SC	54		
Rio Arriba County, NM	41			Harrisburg, IL	26
		Gainesville, TX	39	Saline County, IL	26
Eufaula, AL-GA	31	Cooke County, TX	39		
Barbour County, AL	28			Harrison, AR	45
Quitman County, GA	2	Galesburg, IL	70	Boone County, AR	36
		Knox County, IL	53	Newton County, AR	8
Eureka-Arcata-Fortuna, CA	128	Warren County, IL	17		
Humboldt County, CA	128			Hastings, NE	40
		Gallup, NM	72	Adams County, NE	33
Evanston, WY	20	McKinley County, NM	72	Clay County, NE	7
Uinta County, WY	20				
		Garden City, KS	39	Havre, MT	16
Fairmont, MN	21	Finney County, KS	39	Hill County, MT	16
Martin County, MN	21				
		Gardnerville Ranchos, NV	46	Hays, KS	27
Fairmont, WV	57	Douglas County, NV	46	Ellis County, KS	27
Marion County, WV	57				
		Georgetown, SC	61	Heber, UT	20
Fallon, NV	25	Georgetown County, SC	61	Wasatch County, UT	20
Churchill County, NV	25				
		Gettysburg, PA	101	Helena, MT	71
Faribault-Northfield, MN	62	Adams County, PA	101	Jefferson County, MT	11
Rice County, MN	62			Lewis and Clark County,	
		Gillette, WY	39	MT	59
Farmington, MO	62	Campbell County, WY	39		
St. Francois County, MO	62			Henderson, NC	44
		Glasgow, KY	51	Vance County, NC	44
Fergus Falls, MN	58	Barren County, KY	41		
Otter Tail County, MN	58	Metcalfe County, KY	10	Hereford, TX	19
				Deaf Smith County, TX	19
Fernley, NV	51	Gloversville, NY	55		
Lyon County, NV	51	Fulton County, NY	55	Hilo, HI	171
				Hawaii County, HI	171
Findlay, OH	74	Granbury, TX	57		
Hancock County, OH	74	Hood County, TX	49	Hilton Head Island-	
		Somervell County, TX	8	Beaufort, SC	164
Fitzgerald, GA	28			Beaufort County, SC	142
Ben Hill County, GA	18	Grand Island, NE	70	Jasper County, SC	22
Irwin County, GA	10	Hall County, NE	56		
		Howard County, NE	7	Hobbs, NM	57
Forest City, NC	64	Merrick County, NE	8	Lea County, NM	57
Rutherford County, NC	64				
		Grants, NM	27	Homosassa Springs, FL	138
Forrest City, AR	28	Cibola County, NM	27	Citrus County, FL	138
St. Francis County, AR	28				
		Grants Pass, OR	82	Hood River, OR	22
Fort Dodge, IA	39	Josephine County, OR	82	Hood River County, OR	22
Webster County, IA	39				

Appendix II   901

U.S. Census Bureau, Statistical Abstract of the United States: 2008

Micropolitan statistical area / Component county	Population, 2006 (1,000)
Hope, AR	33
Hempstead County, AR	23
Nevada County, AR	9
Houghton, MI	38
Houghton County, MI	35
Keweenaw County, MI	2
Hudson, NY	63
Columbia County, NY	63
Humboldt, TN	48
Gibson County, TN	48
Huntingdon, PA	46
Huntingdon County, PA	46
Huntington, IN	38
Huntington County, IN	38
Huntsville, TX	63
Walker County, TX	63
Huron, SD	16
Beadle County, SD	16
Hutchinson, KS	64
Reno County, KS	64
Hutchinson, MN	37
McLeod County, MN	37
Indiana, PA	88
Indiana County, PA	88
Indianola, MS	32
Sunflower County, MS	32
Iron Mountain, MI-WI	32
Dickinson County, MI	27
Florence County, WI	5
Jackson, WY-ID	27
Teton County, ID	8
Teton County, WY	19
Jacksonville, IL	41
Morgan County, IL	36
Scott County, IL	5
Jacksonville, TX	49
Cherokee County, TX	49
Jamestown, ND	21
Stutsman County, ND	21
Jamestown-Dunkirk-Fredonia, NY	135
Chautauqua County, NY	135
Jasper, IN	54
Dubois County, IN	41
Pike County, IN	13
Jennings, LA	31
Jefferson Davis Parish, LA	31
Jesup, GA	29
Wayne County, GA	29
Juneau, AK	31
Juneau City and Borough, AK	31
Kahului-Wailuku, HI	141
Maui County, HI	141
Kalispell, MT	85
Flathead County, MT	85
Kapaa, HI	63
Kauai County, HI	63
Kearney, NE	51
Buffalo County, NE	44
Kearney County, NE	7
Keene, NH	77
Cheshire County, NH	77
Kendallville, IN	48
Noble County, IN	48
Kennett, MO	32
Dunklin County, MO	32
Kerrville, TX	47
Kerr County, TX	47
Ketchikan, AK	13
Ketchikan Gateway Borough, AK	13
Key West-Marathon, FL	75
Monroe County, FL	75
Kill Devil Hills, NC	34
Dare County, NC	34
Kingsville, TX	31
Kenedy County, TX	(Z)
Kleberg County, TX	30
Kinston, NC	58
Lenoir County, NC	58
Kirksville, MO	29
Adair County, MO	24
Schuyler County, MO	4
Klamath Falls, OR	66
Klamath County, OR	66
Kodiak, AK	13
Kodiak Island Borough, AK	13
Laconia, NH	62
Belknap County, NH	62
La Follette, TN	41
Campbell County, TN	41
La Grande, OR	24
Union County, OR	24
LaGrange, GA	63
Troup County, GA	63
Lake City, FL	67
Columbia County, FL	67
Lake Havasu City-Kingman, AZ	193
Mohave County, AZ	193
Lamesa, TX	14
Dawson County, TX	14
Lancaster, SC	64
Lancaster County, SC	64
Laramie, WY	30
Albany County, WY	30
Las Vegas, NM	29
San Miguel County, NM	29
Laurel, MS	85
Jasper County, MS	18
Jones County, MS	67
Laurinburg, NC	37
Scotland County, NC	37
Lawrenceburg, TN	41
Lawrence County, TN	41
Lebanon, MO	35
Laclede County, MO	35
Lebanon, NH-VT	172
Grafton County, NH	85
Orange County, VT	29
Windsor County, VT	58
Levelland, TX	23
Hockley County, TX	23
Lewisburg, PA	43
Union County, PA	43
Lewisburg, TN	29
Marshall County, TN	29
Lewistown, PA	46
Mifflin County, PA	46
Lexington, NE	27
Dawson County, NE	25
Gosper County, NE	2
Lexington Park, MD	99
St. Mary's County, MD	99
Liberal, KS	23
Seward County, KS	23
Lincoln, IL	30
Logan County, IL	30
Lincolnton, NC	72
Lincoln County, NC	72
Lock Haven, PA	37
Clinton County, PA	37
Logansport, IN	40
Cass County, IN	40
London, KY	57
Laurel County, KY	57
Los Alamos, NM	19
Los Alamos County, NM	19
Lufkin, TX	83
Angelina County, TX	83
Lumberton, NC	129
Robeson County, NC	129
Macomb, IL	32
McDonough County, IL	32
Madison, IN	33
Jefferson County, IN	33
Madisonville, KY	47
Hopkins County, KY	47
Magnolia, AR	24
Columbia County, AR	24
Malone, NY	51
Franklin County, NY	51
Manhattan, KS	106
Geary County, KS	24
Pottawatomie County, KS	19
Riley County, KS	63
Manitowoc, WI	82
Manitowoc County, WI	82
Mankato-North Mankato, MN	90
Blue Earth County, MN	58
Nicollet County, MN	31
Marinette, WI-MI	68
Menominee County, MI	25
Marinette County, WI	43
Marion, IN	70
Grant County, IN	70
Marion, OH	66
Marion County, OH	66
Marion-Herrin, IL	64
Williamson County, IL	64

902   Appendix II

Micropolitan statistical area Component county	Population, 2006 (1,000)	Micropolitan statistical area Component county	Population, 2006 (1,000)	Micropolitan statistical area Component county	Population, 2006 (1,000)
Marquette, MI	65	**Mineral Wells, TX**	28	**Newberry, SC**	38
Marquette County, MI	65	Palo Pinto County, TX	28	Newberry County, SC	38
Marshall, MN	25	**Minot, ND**	63	**New Castle, IN**	47
Lyon County, MN	25	McHenry County, ND	5	Henry County, IN	47
Marshall, MO	23	Renville County, ND	2	**New Castle, PA**	92
Saline County, MO	23	Ward County, ND	55	Lawrence County, PA	92
Marshall, TX	64	**Mitchell, SD**	23	**New Iberia, LA**	76
Harrison County, TX	64	Davison County, SD	19	Iberia Parish, LA	76
Marshalltown, IA	40	Hanson County, SD	4	**New Philadelphia-Dover, OH**	92
Marshall County, IA	40	**Moberly, MO**	25	Tuscarawas County, OH	92
Marshfield-Wisconsin Rapids, WI	75	Randolph County, MO	25	**Newport, TN**	35
Wood County, WI	75	**Monroe, WI**	36	Cocke County, TN	35
Martin, TN	33	Green County, WI	36	**Newton, IA**	37
Weakley County, TN	33	**Montrose, CO**	39	Jasper County, IA	37
Martinsville, VA	71	Montrose County, CO	39	**New Ulm, MN**	26
Henry County, VA	56	**Morehead City, NC**	64	Brown County, MN	26
Martinsville city, VA	15	Carteret County, NC	64	**Nogales, AZ**	43
Maryville, MO	22	**Morgan City, LA**	52	Santa Cruz County, AZ	43
Nodaway County, MO	22	St. Mary Parish, LA	52	**Norfolk, NE**	49
Mason City, IA	52	**Moscow, ID**	35	Madison County, NE	35
Cerro Gordo County, IA	44	Latah County, ID	35	Pierce County, NE	8
Worth County, IA	8	**Moses Lake, WA**	83	Stanton County, NE	7
Mayfield, KY	38	Grant County, WA	83	**North Platte, NE**	37
Graves County, KY	38	**Moultrie, GA**	45	Lincoln County, NE	36
Maysville, KY	31	Colquitt County, GA	45	Logan County, NE	1
Lewis County, KY	14	**Mountain Home, AR**	41	McPherson County, NE	(Z)
Mason County, KY	17	Baxter County, AR	41	**North Vernon, IN**	28
McAlester, OK	45	**Mountain Home, ID**	28	Jennings County, IN	28
Pittsburg County, OK	45	Elmore County, ID	28	**North Wilkesboro, NC**	67
McComb, MS	54	**Mount Airy, NC**	73	Wilkes County, NC	67
Amite County, MS	13	Surry County, NC	73	**Norwalk, OH**	60
Pike County, MS	40	**Mount Pleasant, MI**	66	Huron County, OH	60
McMinnville, TN	40	Isabella County, MI	66	**Oak Harbor, WA**	81
Warren County, TN	40	**Mount Pleasant, TX**	30	Island County, WA	81
McPherson, KS	29	Titus County, TX	30	**Oak Hill, WV**	47
McPherson County, KS	29	**Mount Sterling, KY**	43	Fayette County, WV	47
Meadville, PA	89	Bath County, KY	12	**Ocean Pines, MD**	49
Crawford County, PA	89	Menifee County, KY	7	Worcester County, MD	49
Menomonie, WI	42	Montgomery County, KY	25	**Ogdensburg-Massena, NY**	111
Dunn County, WI	42	**Mount Vernon, IL**	49	St. Lawrence County, NY	111
Meridian, MS	104	Hamilton County, IL	8	**Oil City, PA**	55
Clarke County, MS	18	Jefferson County, IL	41	Venango County, PA	55
Kemper County, MS	10	**Mount Vernon, OH**	59	**Okeechobee, FL**	40
Lauderdale County, MS	77	Knox County, OH	59	Okeechobee County, FL	40
Merrill, WI	30	**Murray, KY**	35	**Olean, NY**	82
Lincoln County, WI	30	Calloway County, KY	35	Cattaraugus County, NY	82
Mexico, MO	26	**Muscatine, IA**	55	**Oneonta, NY**	63
Audrain County, MO	26	Louisa County, IA	12	Otsego County, NY	63
Miami, OK	33	Muscatine County, IA	43	**Ontario, OR-ID**	54
Ottawa County, OK	33	**Muskogee, OK**	71	Payette County, ID	23
Middlesborough, KY	30	Muskogee County, OK	71	Malheur County, OR	31
Bell County, KY	30	**Nacogdoches, TX**	61	**Opelousas-Eunice, LA**	92
Midland, MI	84	Nacogdoches County, TX	61	St. Landry Parish, LA	92
Midland County, MI	84	**Natchez, MS-LA**	52	**Orangeburg, SC**	91
Milledgeville, GA	55	Concordia Parish, LA	19	Orangeburg County, SC	91
Baldwin County, GA	45	Adams County, MS	33	**Oskaloosa, IA**	22
Hancock County, GA	10	**Natchitoches, LA**	39	Mahaska County, IA	22
Minden, LA	41	Natchitoches Parish, LA	39	**Ottawa-Streator, IL**	154
Webster Parish, LA	41	**New Bern, NC**	118	Bureau County, IL	35
		Craven County, NC	95	La Salle County, IL	113
		Jones County, NC	10		
		Pamlico County, NC	13		

U.S. Census Bureau, Statistical Abstract of the United States: 2008

Micropolitan statistical area Component county	Population, 2006 (1,000)	Micropolitan statistical area Component county	Population, 2006 (1,000)	Micropolitan statistical area Component county	Population, 2006 (1,000)
Ottawa-Streator, IL—Con.		**Plattsburgh, NY**	82	**Rolla, MO**	42
Putnam County, IL	6	Clinton County, NY	82	Phelps County, MO......	42
Ottumwa, IA	36	**Plymouth, IN.**	47	**Roseburg, OR.**	105
Wapello County, IA	36	Marshall County, IN......	47	Douglas County, OR	105
Owatonna, MN	36	**Point Pleasant, WV-OH**	57	**Roswell, NM**	62
Steele County, MN	36	Gallia County, OH.......	31	Chaves County, NM	62
Owosso, MI	73	Mason County, WV	26	**Ruidoso, NM.**	21
Shiawassee County, MI ...	73	**Ponca City, OK.**	46	Lincoln County, NM......	21
Oxford, MS	41	Kay County, OK	46	**Russellville, AR**	80
Lafayette County, MS	41	**Pontiac, IL**	39	Pope County, AR	58
Paducah, KY-IL	98	Livingston County, IL.....	39	Yell County, AR.	22
Massac County, IL	15	**Poplar Bluff, MO.**	42	**Ruston, LA**	57
Ballard County, KY	8	Butler County, MO.......	42	Jackson Parish, LA	15
Livingston County, KY	10	**Portales, NM.**	18	Lincoln Parish, LA.	42
McCracken County, KY ...	65	Roosevelt County, NM....	18	**Rutland, VT**	64
Pahrump, NV	43	**Port Angeles, WA**	70	Rutland County, VT......	64
Nye County, NV	43	Clallam County, WA	70	**Safford, AZ.**	41
Palatka, FL	74	**Portsmouth, OH**	76	Graham County, AZ.	34
Putnam County, FL......	74	Scioto County, OH	76	Greenlee County, AZ.	8
Palestine, TX	57	**Pottsville, PA**	147	**St. Marys, GA**	45
Anderson County, TX	57	Schuylkill County, PA.....	147	Camden County, GA	45
Palm Coast, FL.	83	**Price, UT**	19	**St. Marys, PA**	33
Flagler County, FL.	83	Carbon County, UT	19	Elk County, PA	33
Pampa, TX	23	**Prineville, OR**	23	**Salina, KS.**	60
Gray County, TX........	22	Crook County, OR.	23	Ottawa County, KS	6
Roberts County, TX......	1	**Pullman, WA.**	40	Saline County, KS.......	54
Paragould, AR	40	Whitman County, WA.	40	**Salisbury, NC**	136
Greene County, AR......	40	**Quincy, IL-MO.**	77	Rowan County, NC	136
Paris, TN	32	Adams County, IL	67	**Sanford, NC**	57
Henry County, TN	32	Lewis County, MO.......	10	Lee County, NC	57
Paris, TX	50	**Raymondville, TX**	21	**Sault Ste. Marie, MI.**	39
Lamar County, TX........	50	Willacy County, TX	21	Chippewa County, MI	39
Parsons, KS	22	**Red Bluff, CA**	62	**Sayre, PA**	62
Labette County, KS	22	Tehama County, CA	62	Bradford County, PA	62
Payson, AZ.	52	**Red Wing, MN.**	46	**Scottsbluff, NE**	37
Gila County, AZ	52	Goodhue County, MN	46	Banner County, NE	1
Pecos, TX.	11	**Rexburg, ID**	44	Scotts Bluff County, NE ...	37
Reeves County, TX	11	Fremont County, ID......	12	**Scottsboro, AL.**	54
Pella, IA	33	Madison County, ID......	31	Jackson County, AL.	54
Marion County, IA.......	33	**Richmond, IN**	69	**Scottsburg, IN**	24
Pendleton-Hermiston, OR ..	85	Wayne County, IN.......	69	Scott County, IN	24
Morrow County, OR.	12	**Richmond-Berea, KY.**	96	**Seaford, DE**	180
Umatilla County, OR	73	Madison County, KY	79	Sussex County, DE	180
Peru, IN	36	Rockcastle County, KY ...	17	**Searcy, AR**	73
Miami County, IN	36	**Rio Grande City-Roma, TX** .	62	White County, AR	73
Phoenix Lake-Cedar Ridge,		Starr County, TX........	62	**Sebring, FL.**	98
CA	57	**Riverton, WY**	37	Highlands County, FL	98
Tuolumne County, CA	57	Fremont County, WY.....	37	**Sedalia, MO**	41
Picayune, MS	57	**Roanoke Rapids, NC**	77	Pettis County, MO.......	41
Pearl River County, MS ...	57	Halifax County, NC	56	**Selinsgrove, PA**	38
Pierre, SD	20	Northampton County, NC..	21	Snyder County, PA	38
Hughes County, SD......	17	**Rochelle, IL**	55	**Selma, AL.**	44
Stanley County, SD......	3	Ogle County, IL.........	55	Dallas County, AL	44
Pierre Part, LA	23	**Rockingham, NC.**	47	**Seneca, SC.**	71
Assumption Parish, LA ...	23	Richmond County, NC....	47	Oconee County, SC	71
Pittsburg, KS	38	**Rockland, ME**	41	**Seneca Falls, NY.**	35
Crawford County, KS.	38	Knox County, ME	41	Seneca County, NY.	35
Plainview, TX	36	**Rock Springs, WY.**	39	**Sevierville, TN**	81
Hale County, TX	36	Sweetwater County, WY ..	39	Sevier County, TN.	81
Platteville, WI	49				
Grant County, WI	49				

U.S. Census Bureau, Statistical Abstract of the United States: 2008

Micropolitan statistical area / Component county	Population, 2006 (1,000)
Seymour, IN	42
Jackson County, IN	42
Shawnee, OK	69
Pottawatomie County, OK	69
Shelby, NC	98
Cleveland County, NC	98
Shelbyville, TN	43
Bedford County, TN	43
Shelton, WA	56
Mason County, WA	56
Sheridan, WY	28
Sheridan County, WY	28
Sidney, OH	49
Shelby County, OH	49
Sierra Vista-Douglas, AZ	128
Cochise County, AZ	128
Sikeston, MO	41
Scott County, MO	41
Silver City, NM	30
Grant County, NM	30
Silverthorne, CO	25
Summit County, CO	25
Snyder, TX	16
Scurry County, TX	16
Somerset, KY	60
Pulaski County, KY	60
Somerset, PA	79
Somerset County, PA	79
Southern Pines-Pinehurst, NC	83
Moore County, NC	83
Spearfish, SD	23
Lawrence County, SD	23
Spencer, IA	17
Clay County, IA	17
Spirit Lake, IA	17
Dickinson County, IA	17
Starkville, MS	42
Oktibbeha County, MS	42
Statesboro, GA	63
Bulloch County, GA	63
Statesville-Mooresville, NC	146
Iredell County, NC	146
Staunton-Waynesboro, VA	116
Augusta County, VA	71
Staunton city, VA	23
Waynesboro city, VA	21
Stephenville, TX	34
Erath County, TX	34
Sterling, CO	21
Logan County, CO	21
Sterling, IL	60
Whiteside County, IL	60
Stevens Point, WI	67
Portage County, WI	67
Stillwater, OK	74
Payne County, OK	74
Storm Lake, IA	20
Buena Vista County, IA	20
Sturgis, MI	63
St. Joseph County, MI	63
Sulphur Springs, TX	33
Hopkins County, TX	33
Summerville, GA	26
Chattooga County, GA	26
Sunbury, PA	92
Northumberland County, PA	92
Susanville, CA	35
Lassen County, CA	35
Sweetwater, TX	15
Nolan County, TX	15
Tahlequah, OK	45
Cherokee County, OK	45
Talladega-Sylacauga, AL	80
Talladega County, AL	80
Tallulah, LA	12
Madison Parish, LA	12
Taos, NM	32
Taos County, NM	32
Taylorville, IL	35
Christian County, IL	35
The Villages, FL	69
Sumter County, FL	69
Thomaston, GA	28
Upson County, GA	28
Thomasville, GA	45
Thomas County, GA	45
Thomasville-Lexington, NC	156
Davidson County, NC	156
Tiffin, OH	57
Seneca County, OH	57
Tifton, GA	42
Tift County, GA	42
Toccoa, GA	25
Stephens County, GA	25
Torrington, CT	190
Litchfield County, CT	190
Traverse City, MI	142
Benzie County, MI	18
Grand Traverse County, MI	85
Kalkaska County, MI	17
Leelanau County, MI	22
Troy, AL	30
Pike County, AL	30
Truckee-Grass Valley, CA	99
Nevada County, CA	99
Tullahoma, TN	99
Coffee County, TN	52
Franklin County, TN	41
Moore County, TN	6
Tupelo, MS	132
Itawamba County, MS	23
Lee County, MS	80
Pontotoc County, MS	29
Tuskegee, AL	23
Macon County, AL	23
Twin Falls, ID	92
Jerome County, ID	20
Twin Falls County, ID	72
Ukiah, CA	88
Mendocino County, CA	88
Union, SC	28
Union County, SC	28
Union City, TN-KY	39
Fulton County, KY	7
Obion County, TN	32
Urbana, OH	40
Champaign County, OH	40
Uvalde, TX	27
Uvalde County, TX	27
Valley, AL	35
Chambers County, AL	35
Van Wert, OH	29
Van Wert County, OH	29
Vermillion, SD	13
Clay County, SD	13
Vernal, UT	28
Uintah County, UT	28
Vernon, TX	14
Wilbarger County, TX	14
Vicksburg, MS	49
Warren County, MS	49
Vidalia, GA	37
Montgomery County, GA	9
Toombs County, GA	28
Vincennes, IN	38
Knox County, IN	38
Wabash, IN	34
Wabash County, IN	34
Wahpeton, ND-MN	24
Wilkin County, MN	7
Richland County, ND	17
Walla Walla, WA	58
Walla Walla County, WA	58
Walterboro, SC	39
Colleton County, SC	39
Wapakoneta, OH	47
Auglaize County, OH	47
Warren, PA	42
Warren County, PA	42
Warrensburg, MO	51
Johnson County, MO	51
Warsaw, IN	77
Kosciusko County, IN	77
Washington, IN	30
Daviess County, IN	30
Washington, NC	46
Beaufort County, NC	46
Washington, OH	28
Fayette County, OH	28
Watertown, SD	32
Codington County, SD	26
Hamlin County, SD	6
Watertown-Fort Atkinson, WI	80
Jefferson County, WI	80
Watertown-Fort Drum, NY	114
Jefferson County, NY	114

U.S. Census Bureau, Statistical Abstract of the United States: 2008

Micropolitan statistical area Component county	Popu- lation, 2006 (1,000)	Micropolitan statistical area Component county	Popu- lation, 2006 (1,000)	Micropolitan statistical area Component county	Popu- lation, 2006 (1,000)
Wauchula, FL	29	**Willimantic, CT**	117	**Winona, MN**	49
Hardee County, FL	29	Windham County, CT	117	Winona County, MN	49
Waycross, GA.	53	**Williston, ND.**	19	**Woodward, OK**	19
Pierce County, GA	17	Williams County, ND	19	Woodward County, OK . . .	19
Ware County, GA	36	**Willmar, MN**	41	**Wooster, OH.**	114
West Helena, AR.	23	Kandiyohi County, MN	41	Wayne County, OH	114
Phillips County, AR	23	**Wilmington, OH**	43	**Worthington, MN.**	20
West Plains, MO	39	Clinton County, OH	43	Nobles County, MN	20
Howell County, MO	39	**Wilson, NC**	77	**Yankton, SD**	22
West Point, MS	21	Wilson County, NC	77	Yankton County, SD	22
Clay County, MS.	21	**Winfield, KS**	35	**Yazoo City, MS**	28
Whitewater, WI	101	Cowley County, KS	35	Yazoo County, MS	28
Walworth County, WI	101			**Zanesville, OH**	86
				Muskingum County, OH. . .	86

Z Less than 500.

Source: U.S. Census Bureau, "CBSA-EST2006-alldata: Population Estimates and Estimated Components of Change for Metropolitan and Micropolitan Statistical Areas and Their Geographic Components: April 1, 2000 to July 1, 2006" <http://www.census.gov/population/estimates/metrogeneral/2006/CBSA-EST2006-alldata.csv>; and unpublished data.

U.S. Census Bureau, Statistical Abstract of the United States: 2008

Limitations of the Data

Introduction—The data presented in this *Statistical Abstract* came from many sources. The sources include not only federal statistical bureaus and other organizations that collect and issue statistics as their principal activity, but also governmental administrative and regulatory agencies, private research bodies, trade associations, insurance companies, health associations, and private organizations such as the National Education Association and philanthropic foundations. Consequently, the data vary considerably as to reference periods, definitions of terms and, for ongoing series, the number and frequency of time periods for which data are available.

The statistics presented were obtained and tabulated by various means. Some statistics are based on complete enumerations or censuses while others are based on samples. Some information is extracted from records kept for administrative or regulatory purposes (school enrollment, hospital records, securities registration, financial accounts, social security records, income tax returns, etc.), while other information is obtained explicitly for statistical purposes through interviews or by mail. The estimation procedures used vary from highly sophisticated scientific techniques, to crude "informed guesses."

Each set of data relates to a group of individuals or units of interest referred to as the *target universe* or *target population*, or simply as the *universe* or *population*. Prior to data collection the target universe should be clearly defined. For example, if data are to be collected for the universe of households in the United States, it is necessary to define a "household." The target universe may not be completely tractable. Cost and other considerations may restrict data collection to a *survey universe* based on some available list, such list may be inaccurate or out of date. This list is called a *survey frame* or *sampling frame*.

The data in many tables are based on data obtained for all population units, *a census*, or on data obtained for only a portion, or *sample*, of the population units. When the data presented are based on a sample, the sample is usually a scientifically selected *probability sample*. This is a sample selected from a list or sampling frame in such a way that every possible sample has a known chance of selection and usually each unit selected can be assigned a number, greater than zero and less than or equal to one, representing its likelihood or probability of selection.

For large-scale sample surveys, the probability sample of units is often selected as a multistage sample. The first stage of a multistage sample is the selection of a probability sample of large groups of population members, referred to as primary sampling units (PSUs). For example, in a national multistage household sample, PSUs are often counties or groups of counties. The second stage of a multistage sample is the selection, within each PSU selected at the first stage, of smaller groups of population units, referred to as secondary sampling units. In subsequent stages of selection, smaller and smaller nested groups are chosen until the ultimate sample of population units is obtained. To qualify a multistage sample as a probability sample, all stages of sampling must be carried out using probability sampling methods.

Prior to selection at each stage of a multistage (or a single stage) sample, a list of the sampling units or sampling frame for that stage must be obtained. For example, for the first stage of selection of a national household sample, a list of the counties and county groups that form the PSUs must be obtained. For the final stage of selection, lists of households, and sometimes persons within the households, have to be compiled in the field. For surveys of economic entities and for

the economic censuses, the Bureau generally uses a frame constructed from the Bureau's Business Register. The Business Register contains all establishments with payroll in the United States including small single establishment firms as well as large multi-establishment firms.

Wherever the quantities in a table refer to an entire universe, but are constructed from data collected in a sample survey, the table quantities are referred to as *sample estimates*. In constructing a sample estimate, an attempt is made to come as close as is feasible to the corresponding universe quantity that would be obtained from a complete census of the universe. Estimates based on a sample will, however, generally differ from the hypothetical census figures. Two classifications of errors are associated with estimates based on sample surveys: (1) *sampling error*—the error arising from the use of a sample, rather than a census, to estimate population quantities and (2) *nonsampling error*—those errors arising from nonsampling sources. As discussed below, the magnitude of the sampling error for an estimate can usually be estimated from the sample data. However, the magnitude of the nonsampling error for an estimate can rarely be estimated. Consequently, actual error in an estimate exceeds the error that can be estimated.

The particular sample used in a survey is only one of a large number of possible samples of the same size which could have been selected using the same sampling procedure. Estimates derived from the different samples would, in general, differ from each other. The *standard error* (SE) is a measure of the variation among the estimates derived from all possible samples. The standard error is the most commonly used measure of the sampling error of an estimate. Valid estimates of the standard errors of survey estimates can usually be calculated from the data collected in a probability sample. For convenience, the standard error is sometimes expressed as a percent of the estimate and is called the relative standard error or *coefficient of variation* (CV). For example, an estimate of 200 units with an estimated standard error of 10 units has an estimated CV of 5 percent.

A sample estimate and an estimate of its standard error or CV can be used to construct interval estimates that have a prescribed confidence that the interval includes the average of the estimates derived from all possible samples with a known probability. To illustrate, if all possible samples were selected under essentially the same general conditions, and using the same sample design, and if an estimate and its estimated standard error were calculated from each sample, then: 1) approximately 68 percent of the intervals from one standard error below the estimate to one standard error above the estimate would include the average estimate derived from all possible samples; 2) approximately 90 percent of the intervals from 1.6 standard errors below the estimate to 1.6 standard errors above the estimate would include the average estimate derived from all possible samples; and 3) approximately 95 percent of the intervals from two standard errors below the estimate to two standard errors above the estimate would include the average estimate derived from all possible samples.

Thus, for a particular sample, one can say with the appropriate level of confidence (e.g., 90 percent or 95 percent) that the average of all possible samples is included in the constructed interval. Example of a confidence interval: An estimate is 200 units with a standard error of 10 units. An approximately 90 percent confidence interval (plus or minus 1.6 standard errors) is from 184 to 216.

All surveys and censuses are subject to nonsampling errors. Nonsampling errors are of two kinds—*random* and *nonrandom*. Random nonsampling errors arise because of the varying interpretation of questions (by respondents or interviewers) and varying actions of coders, keyers, and other processors. Some randomness is also introduced when respondents must estimate. Nonrandom nonsampling errors result from total nonresponse (no usable data obtained for a sampled unit), partial or item nonresponse (only a portion of a response may be usable), inability or unwillingness on the part of respondents to provide correct information, difficulty interpreting questions, mistakes

U.S. Census Bureau, Statistical Abstract of the United States: 2008

in recording or keying data, errors of collection or processing, and coverage problems (overcoverage and undercoverage of the target universe). Random nonresponse errors usually, but not always, result in an understatement of sampling errors and thus an overstatement of the precision of survey estimates. Estimating the magnitude of nonsampling errors would require special experiments or access to independent data and, consequently, the magnitudes are seldom available.

Nearly all types of nonsampling errors that affect surveys also occur in complete censuses. Since surveys can be conducted on a smaller scale than censuses, nonsampling errors can presumably be controlled more tightly. Relatively more funds and effort can perhaps be expended toward eliciting responses, detecting and correcting response error, and reducing processing errors. As a result, survey results can sometimes be more accurate than census results.

To compensate for suspected nonrandom errors, adjustments of the sample estimates are often made. For example, adjustments are frequently made for nonresponse, both total and partial. Adjustments made for either type of nonresponse are often referred to as *imputations*. Imputation for total nonresponse is usually made by substituting for the questionnaire responses of the nonrespondents the "average" questionnaire responses of the respondents. These imputations usually are made separately within various groups of sample members, formed by attempting to place respondents and nonrespondents together that have "similar" design or ancillary characteristics. Imputation for item nonresponse is usually made by substituting for a missing item the response to that item of a respondent having characteristics that are "similar" to those of the nonrespondent.

For an estimate calculated from a sample survey, the *total error* in the estimate is composed of the sampling error, which can usually be estimated from the sample, and the nonsampling error, which usually cannot be estimated from the

sample. The total error present in a population quantity obtained from a complete census is composed of only nonsampling errors. Ideally, estimates of the total error associated with data given in the *Statistical Abstract* tables should be given. However, due to the unavailability of estimates of nonsampling errors, only estimates of the levels of sampling errors, in terms of estimated standard errors or coefficients of variation, are available. To obtain estimates of the estimated standard errors from the sample of interest, obtain a copy of the referenced report which appears at the end of each table.

Source of Additional Material: The Federal Committee on Statistical Methodology (FCSM) is an interagency committee dedicated to improving the quality of federal statistics <http://fcsm.ssd.census.gov>.

Principal data bases—Beginning below are brief descriptions of 35 of the sample surveys and censuses that provide a substantial portion of the data contained in this *Abstract*.

U.S. DEPARTMENT OF AGRICULTURE, National Agriculture Statistics Service

Basic Area Frame Sample

Universe, Frequency, and Types of Data: June agricultural survey collects data on planted acreage and livestock inventories. The survey also serves to measure list incompleteness and is subsampled for multiple frame surveys.

Type of Data Collection Operation: Stratified probability sample of about 11,000 land area units of about 1 sq. mile (range from 0.1 sq. mile in cities to several sq. miles in open grazing areas). Sample includes 42,000 parcels of agricultural land. About 20 percent of the sample replaced annually.

Data Collection and Imputation Procedures: Data collection is by personal enumeration. Imputation is based on enumerator observation or data reported by respondents having similar agricultural characteristics.

Estimates of Sampling Error: Estimated CVs range from 1 percent to 2 percent for regional estimates to 3 percent to 6 percent for state estimates of major crop acres and livestock inventories.

Other (nonsampling) Errors: Minimized through rigid quality controls on the collection process and careful review of all reported data.

Sources of Additional Material: U.S. Department of Agriculture, National Agricultural Statistics Service, USDA's National Agricultural Statistics Service: The Fact Finders of Agriculture, March 2007.

Multiple Frame Surveys

Universe, Frequency, and Types of Data: Surveys of U.S. farm operators to obtain data on major livestock inventories, selected crop acreage and production, grain stocks, and farm labor characteristics, farm economic data, and chemical use data.

Type of Data Collection Operation: Primary frame is obtained from general or special purpose lists, supplemented by a probability sample of land areas used to estimate for list incompleteness.

Data Collection and Imputation Procedures: Mail, telephone, or personal interviews used for initial data collection. Mail nonrespondent follow-up by phone and personal interviews. Imputation based on average of respondents.

Estimates of Sampling Error: Estimated CV for number of hired farm workers is about 3 percent. Estimated CVs range from 1 percent to 2 percent for regional estimates to 3 percent to 6 percent for state estimates of livestock inventories and crop acreage.

Other (nonsampling) Errors: In addition to above, replicated sampling procedures used to monitor effects of changes in survey procedures.

Sources of Additional Material: U.S. Department of Agriculture, National Agricultural Statistics Service), USDA's National Agricultural Statistics Service: The Fact Finders of Agriculture, March 2007.

Objective Yield Surveys

Universe, Frequency, and Types of Data: Surveys for data on corn, cotton, potatoes, soybeans, and wheat to forecast and estimate yields.

Type of Data Collection Operation: Random location of plots in probability sample. Corn, cotton, soybeans, spring wheat, and durum wheat selected in June from Basic Area Frame Sample (see above). Winter wheat and potatoes selected from March and June multiple frame surveys, respectively.

Data Collection and Imputation Procedures: Enumerators count and measure plant characteristics in sample fields. Production measured from plots at harvest. Harvest loss measured from post harvest gleanings.

Estimates of Sampling Error: CVs for national estimates of production are about 2 to 3 percent.

Other (nonsampling) Errors: In addition to above, replicated sampling procedures used to monitor effects of changes in survey procedures.

Sources of Additional Material: U.S. Department of Agriculture, National Agricultural Statistics Service), USDA's National Agricultural Statistics Service: The Fact Finders of Agriculture, March 2007.

U.S. BUREAU OF JUSTICE STATISTICS (BJS)

National Crime Victimization Survey

Universe, Frequency, and Types of Data: Monthly survey of individuals and households in the United States to obtain data on criminal victimization of those units for compilation of annual estimates.

Type of Data Collection Operation: National probability sample survey of about 42,000 interviewed households in 203 PSUs selected from a list of addresses from the 1990 census, supplemented by new construction permits and an area sample where permits are not required.

Data Collection and Imputation Procedures: Interviews are conducted every 6 months for 3 years for each household in the sample; 7,000 households are interviewed monthly. Personal interviews are used in the first interview; the intervening interviews are conducted by telephone whenever possible.

Estimates of Sampling Error: CVs for 2005 estimates are: 4.1 percent for personal crimes (includes all crimes of violence plus purse snatching crimes),

4.2 percent for crimes of violence; 16.2 percent for estimate of rape/sexual assault counts; 9.7 percent for robbery counts; 4.4 percent for assault counts; 15.1 percent for purse snatching/pocket picking; 2.2 percent for property crimes; 4.2 percent for burglary counts; 2.5 percent for theft (of property); and 6.6 percent for motor vehicle theft counts.

Other (nonsampling) Errors: Respondent recall errors which may include reporting incidents for other than the reference period; interviewer coding and processing errors; and possible mistaken reporting or classifying of events. Adjustment is made for a household noninterview rate of about 9 percent and for a within-household noninterview rate of 16 percent.

Sources of Additional Material: U.S. Bureau of Justice Statistics, *Criminal Victimization in the United States,* annual.

U.S. Bureau of Labor Statistics

Consumer Expenditure Survey (CE)

Universe, Frequency and Types of Data: Consists of two continuous components: a quarterly interview survey and a weekly diary or recordkeeping survey. They are nationwide surveys that collect data on consumer expenditures, income, characteristics, and assets and liabilities. Samples are national probability samples of households that are representative of the civilian noninstitutional population. The surveys have been ongoing since 1980.

Type of Data Collection Operation: The Interview Survey is a panel rotation survey. Each panel is interviewed for five quarters and then dropped from the survey. About 7,500 consumer units are interviewed each quarter. The Diary Survey sample is new each year and consists of about 7,500 consumer units. Data are collected on an ongoing basis in 102 areas of the country.

Data Collection and Imputation Procedures: For the Interview Survey, data are collected by personal interview with each consumer unit interviewed once per quarter for five consecutive quarters. Designed to collect information that respondents can recall for 3 months or longer, such as large or recurring

expenditures. For the Diary Survey, respondents record all their expenditures in a self-reporting diary for two consecutive 1-week periods. Designed to pick up items difficult to recall over a long period, such as detailed food expenditures. Missing or invalid attributes, expenditures, or incomes are imputed. Assets and liabilities are not imputed. The U.S. Census Bureau collects the data for the Bureau of Labor Statistics.

Estimates of Sampling Error: Standard error tables are available since 2000.

Other (nonsampling) Errors: Includes incorrect information given by respondents, data processing errors, interviewer errors, and so on. They occur regardless of whether data are collected from a sample or from the entire population.

Sources of Additional Material: Bureau of Labor Statistics, see Internet site <http://www.bls.gov/cex>.

Consumer Price Index (CPI)

Universe, Frequency, and Types of Data: A monthly survey of price changes of all types of consumer goods and services purchased by urban wage earners and clerical workers prior to 1978, and urban consumers thereafter. Both indexes continue to be published.

Type of Data Collection Operation: Prior to 1978, and since 1998, sample of various consumer items in 87 urban areas; from 1978–1997, in 85 PSUs, except from January 1987 through March 1988, when 91 areas were sampled.

Data Collection and Imputation Procedures: Prices of consumer items are obtained each month from about 23,000 retail outlets and from about 4,000 housing units in 87 areas. Prices of food, fuel, and a few other items are obtained monthly; prices of most other commodities and services are collected every month in the three largest geographic areas and every other month in others.

Estimates of Sampling Error: Estimates of standard errors are available.

Other (nonsampling) Errors: Errors result from inaccurate reporting, difficulties in defining concepts and their operational implementation, and introduction of product quality changes and new products.

Sources of Additional Material: U.S. Bureau of Labor Statistics, Internet site <http://www.bls.gov/cpi/home.htm> and *BLS Handbook of Methods,* Chapter 17, see Internet site <ttp://www.bls.gov/opub/hom/pdf/homch17.pdf>.

Current Employment Statistics (CES) Program

Universe, Frequency, and Types of Data: Monthly survey drawn from a sampling frame of over 8 million unemployment insurance tax accounts in order to obtain data by industry on employment, hours, and earnings.

Type of Data Collection Operation: In 2006, the CES sample included about 160,000 businesses and government agencies, which represent approximately 400,000 individual worksites.

Data Collection and Imputation Procedures: Each month, the state agencies cooperating with BLS, as well as BLS Data Collection Centers, collect data through various automated collection modes and mail. BLS Washington staff prepares national estimates of employment, hours, and earnings while states use the data to develop state and area estimates.

Estimates of Sampling Errors: The relative standard error for total nonfarm employment is 0.1 percent. From April 2002 to March 2003, the cumulative net birth/death model added 469,000.

Other (nonsampling) Errors: Estimates of employment adjusted annually to reflect complete universe. Average adjustment is 0.2 percent over the last decade, with an absolute range from less than 0.05 percent to 0.6 percent.

Sources of Additional Material: U.S. Bureau of Labor Statistics, Employment and Earnings, monthly, Explanatory Notes and Estimates of Errors, Tables 2-A through 2-F. See <http://www.bls.gov/web/cestntab.htm>.

National Compensation Survey (NCS)

Universe, Frequency, and Types of Data: NCS collects data from establishments of all employment-size classes in private industries as well as state and local governments. The survey stratifies its data by geographic area and industry. NCS collects data on work schedules, wages, salaries, and employer costs for employee benefits. For approximately 80 metropolitan areas and the nation, NCS produces information on workers' earnings and benefits in a variety of occupations at different work levels. NCS is also responsible for two quarterly releases: the Employment Cost Index (ECI), which measures percent changes in the cost of employment, and the Employer Costs for Employee Compensation (ECEC), which measures costs per hour worked for individual benefits. The survey provides data by industry sector, industry division, occupational group, bargaining status, metropolitan area status, census region, and census division. ECEC also provides data by establishment-size class.

Type of Data Collection Operation: Establishments are selected for the survey based on a probability-proportionate-to-employment technique. NCS replaces its sample on a continual basis. Private industry establishments are in the survey for approximately 5 years.

Data Collection and Imputation Procedures: A personal visit to the establishment is the initial source for collecting data. Communication via mail, fax, and telephone provide quarterly updates. Imputation is done for individual benefits.

Estimates of Sampling Error: NCS uses standard errors to evaluate published series. These standard errors are available at <http://www.bls.gov/ncs/ect/home.htm>.

Other (nonsampling) Errors: Nonsampling errors have a number of potential sources. The primary sources are (1) survey nonresponse and (2) data collection and processing errors. Nonsampling errors are not measured. The use of quality assurance programs reduces the potential for nonsampling errors.

These programs include the use of rein-terviews, interview observations, and the systematic professional review of reports. The programs also serve as a training device that provides feedback on errors for field economists (or data collectors). Quality assurance programs also provide information on sources of error. This information is used to improve procedures that result in fewer errors. NCS also conducts extensive training of field economists to maintain high standards in data collection.

Sources of Additional Material: Bureau of Labor Statistics, *BLS Handbook of Methods*, Chapter 8 <http://www.bls .gov/opub/hom/pdf/homch8.pdf>.

Producer Price Index (PPI)

Universe, Frequency, and Types of Data: Monthly survey of producing companies to determine price changes of all com-modities and services produced in the United States for sale in commercial transactions. Data on agriculture, for-estry, fishing, manufacturing, mining, gas, electricity, construction, public utilities, wholesale trade, retail trade, transportation, healthcare, and other services.

Type of Data Collection Operation: Prob-ability sample of approximately 30,000 establishments that result in about 100,000 price quotations per month.

Data Collection and Imputation Proce-dures: Data are collected by mail and facsimile. If transaction prices are not supplied, list prices are used. Some prices are obtained from trade publica-tions, organized exchanges, and govern-ment agencies. To calculate index, price changes are multiplied by their relative weights taken from the Census Bureau's 1997 shipment values from their Census of Industries.

Estimates of Sampling Error: Not appli-cable.

Other (nonsampling) Errors: Not available at present.

Sources of Additional Material: U.S. Bureau of Labor Statistics, *BLS Handbook of Methods*, Chapter 14, Bulletin 2490. U.S. Bureau of Labor Statistics Internet site <http://stats.bls.gov/ppi>.

BOARD OF GOVERNORS OF THE FEDERAL RESERVE SYSTEM

Survey of Consumer Finances

Universe, Frequency, and Types of Data: Periodic sample survey of families. In this survey a given household is divided into a primary economic unit and other economic units. The primary economic unit, which may be a single individual, is generally chosen as the person or couple who either holds the title to the home or is listed on the lease, along with all other people in the household who are financially dependent on that person or couple. The primary economic unit is used as the reference family. The survey collects detailed data on the composition of family balance sheets, the terms of loans, and relationships with financial institutions. It also gathers information on the employment history and pension rights of the survey respon-dent and the spouse or partner of the respondent.

Type of Data Collection Operation: The survey employs a two-part strategy for sampling families. Some families are selected by standard multistage area probability sampling methods applied to all 50 states. The remaining families in the survey are selected using statistical records derived from tax returns, under the strict rules governing confidentiality and the rights of potential respondents to refuse participation.

Data Collection and Imputation Proce-dures: National Opinion Research Center (NORC) at the University of Chicago has collected data for the survey since 1992. Since 1995, the survey has used computer-assisted personal interview-ing. Adjustments for nonresponse are made through multiple imputation of unanswered questions and through weighting adjustments based on data used in the sample design for families that refused participation.

Estimates of Sampling Error: Because of the complex design of the survey, the estimation of potential sampling errors is not straightforward. A replicate-based procedure is available.

Other (nonsampling) Errors: The survey aims to complete 4,500 interviews, with about two thirds of that number deriv-ing from the area-probability sample.

The response rate is typically about 70 percent for the area-probability sample and about 35 percent over all strata in the tax-data sample. Proper training and monitoring of interviewers, careful design of questionnaires, and systematic editing of the resulting data were used to control inaccurate survey responses.

Sources of Additional Material: Board of Governors of the Federal Reserve System, "Recent Changes in U.S. Family Finances: Evidence from the 2001 and 2004 Survey of Consumer Finances," *Federal Reserve Bulletin,* 2006, <http://www.federalreserve.gov/Pubs/Bulletin>.

U.S. CENSUS BUREAU

2002 Economic Census
(Industry Series, Geographic Area Series and Subject Series Reports) (for NAICS sectors 22, 42, 44-45, 48-49, and 51-81).

Universe, Frequency, and Types of Data: Conducted every 5 years to obtain data on number of establishments, number of employees, total payroll size, total sales/receipts/revenue, and other industry-specific statistics. In 2002, the universe was all employer and nonemployer establishments excluding agriculture, forestry, fishing and hunting, and government.

Type of Data Collection Operation: All large employer firms were surveyed (i.e., all employer firms above payroll-size cutoffs established to separate large from small employers) plus a 5 percent to 25 percent sample of the small employer firms. Firms with no employees were not sent a census return.

Data Collection and Imputation Procedures: Mail questionnaires were used with both mail and telephone follow-ups for nonrespondents. Businesses also had the option to respond electronically. Data for nonrespondents and for small employer firms not mailed a questionnaire were obtained from administrative records of other federal agencies or imputed. Nonemployer data were obtained exclusively from IRS 2002 income tax returns.

Estimates of Sampling Error: Not applicable for basic data such as sales, revenue, receipts, payroll, etc. Other (nonsampling) errors: establishment response rates by NAICS sector in 2002 ranged from 80 percent to 89 percent. Item response rates generally ranged from 50 percent to 90 percent with lower rates for the more detailed questions. Nonsampling errors may occur during the collection, reporting, and keying of data, and due to industry misclassification.

Sources of Additional Material: U.S. Census Bureau, *2002 Economic Census: Industry Series, Geographic Area Series* and *Subject Series Reports* (by NAICS sector), Appendix C and <http://www.census.gov/econ/census02/guide/index.html>.

American Community Survey (ACS)

Universe, Frequency, and Types of Data: Nationwide survey to obtain data about demographic, social, economic, and housing characteristics of people, households, and housing units. Covers household population and excludes the population living in institutions, college dormitories, and other group quarters.

Type of Data Collection Operation: First-phase sampling is performed during both Main and Supplemental sampling for approximately 3,000,000 housing units in the U.S. and 36,000 in Puerto Rico (PR). First stage sampling defines the universe for the second stage of sampling through two steps. First, all addresses that were in a first-stage sample within the past four years are excluded from eligibility. This ensures that no address is in sample more than once in any 5-year period. The second step is to select a 20 percent systematic sample of "new" units, i.e. those units that have never appeared on a previous Master Address File (MAF) extract. Each new address is systematically assigned to either the current year or to one of four back-samples. This procedure maintains five equal partitions of the universe.

Data Collection and Imputation Procedures: The American Community Survey is conducted every month on independent samples. Each housing unit in the

independent monthly samples is mailed a prenotice letter announcing the selection of the address to participate, a survey questionnaire package, and a reminder postcard. These sample units receive a second (replacement) questionnaire package if the initial questionnaire has not been returned by a scheduled date. In the mail-out/mail-back sites, sample units for which a questionnaire is not returned in the mail and for which a telephone number is available are defined as the telephone nonresponse follow-up universe. Interviewers attempt to contact and interview these mail nonresponse cases. Sample units from all sites that are still unresponsive two months after the mailing of the survey questionnaires and directly after the completion of the telephone follow-up operation are subsampled at rates between 1 in 2 and 1 in 3. The selected nonresponse units are assigned to Field Representatives (FRs), who visit the units, verify their existence or declare them nonexistent, determine their occupancy status, and conduct interviews. After data collection is completed, any remaining incomplete or inconsistent information was imputed during the final automated edit of the collected data.

Estimates of Sampling Error: The data in the ACS products are estimates of the actual figures that would have been obtained by interviewing the entire population using the same methodology. The estimates from the chosen sample also differ from other samples of housing units and persons within those housing units.

Other (nonsampling) Errors: Nonsampling Error—In addition to sampling error, data users should realize that other types of errors may be introduced during any of the various complex operations used to collect and process survey data. An important goal of the ACS is to minimize the amount of nonsampling error introduced through nonresponse for sample housing units. One way of accomplishing this is by following up on mail nonrespondents.

Sources of Additional Material: U.S. Census Bureau, American Community Survey Web site available on Internet, <http://www.census.gov/acs/www

/index.html>, U.S. Census Bureau, American Community Survey Accuracy of the Data documents available on the Internet, <http://www.census.gov/acs /www/UseData/Accuracy/Accuracy1.htm>.

American Housing Survey

Universe, Frequency, and Types of Data: Conducted nationally in odd numbered years to obtain data on the approximately 121 million occupied or vacant housing units in the United States (group quarters are excluded). Data include characteristics of occupied housing units, vacant units, new housing and mobile home units, financial characteristics, recent mover households, housing and neighborhood quality indicators, and energy characteristics.

Type of Data Collection Operation: The national sample was a multistage probability sample with about 57,000 units eligible for interview in 2005. Sample units, selected within 394 PSUs, were surveyed over a 4-month period.

Data Collection and Imputation Procedures: For 2005, the survey was conducted by personal interviews. The interviewers obtained the information from the occupants or, if the unit was vacant, from informed persons such as landlords, rental agents, or knowledgeable neighbors.

Estimates of Sampling Error: For the national sample, illustrations of the Standard Error (SE) of the estimates are provided in Appendix D of the 2003 report. As an example, the estimated CV is about 0.2 percent for the estimated percentage of owner-occupied units with two persons.

Other (nonsampling) Errors: Response rate was about 92 percent. Nonsampling errors may result from incorrect or incomplete responses, errors in coding and recording, and processing errors. For the 2005 national sample, approximately 2.2 percent of the total housing inventory was not adequately represented by the AHS sample.

Sources of Additional Material: U.S. Census Bureau, *Current Housing Reports,* Series H-150 and H-170, *American Housing Survey* see <http://www.census.gov /hhes/www/ahs.html>.

Annual Survey of Government Employment and Payroll

Universe, Frequency, and Types of Data: The survey measures the number of state, local, and federal civilian government employees and their gross payrolls for the pay period including March 12, 2005. The survey is conducted annually. The survey provides data on full-time and part-time employment, part-time hours worked, full-time equivalent employment, and payroll statistics by governmental function (elementary and secondary education, higher education, police protection, fire protection, financial administration, central staff services, judicial and legal, highways, public welfare, solid waste management, sewerage, parks and recreation, health, hospitals, water supply, electric power, gas supply, transit, natural resources, correction, libraries, air transportation, water transport and terminals, other education, state liquor stores, social insurance administration, and housing and community development).

Type of Data Collection Operations: The survey sample is taken from the 2002 Census of Governments and contains approximately 11,000 local government units. These units were sampled from a sampling frame that contained 83,767 local governments (county, city, township, special district, school districts) in addition to 50 state governments and the District of Columbia. This frame was slightly different from the Annual Finance Survey sampling frame. Thirty-nine of the state governments provided data from central payroll records for all or most of their agencies/institutions. Data for agencies and institutions for the remaining state governments were obtained by mail canvass questionnaires. Local governments were also canvassed using a mail questionnaire. However, elementary and secondary school system data in Florida, North Dakota, and Washington were supplied by special arrangements with the state education agency in each of these states. All respondents receiving the mail questionnaire had the option of responding using the Employment Web site developed for reporting data. Approximately 22.6 percent of the state agency and local government respondents chose to respond on the Web.

Editing and Imputation Procedures: Editing: Editing is a process that ensures survey data are accurate, complete, and consistent. Efforts are made at all phases of collection, processing, and tabulation to minimize errors. Although some edits are built into the Internet data collection instrument and the data entry programs, the majority of the edits are performed after the case has been loaded into the Census Bureau's database. Edits consist primarily of two types: consistency and a ratio of the current year's reported value to the prior year's value. The consistency edits check the logical relationships of data items reported on the form. For example, if a value exists for employees for a function, then a value must exist for payroll also. If part-time employees and payroll are reported then part-time hours must be reported and vice versa. The current year/prior year edits compare data for the number of employees, the function reported for the employees, and the average salary between reporting years. If data falls out of acceptable tolerance levels, the item is flagged for review. Some additional checks are made comparing data from the Annual Finance Survey to data reported on the Annual Survey of Government Employment and Payroll to verify that employees reported on the Annual Survey of Government Employment and Payroll at a particular function have a corresponding expenditure on the Finance Survey. For both types of edits, the edit results are reviewed by analysts and adjusted when needed. When the analyst is unable to resolve or accept the edit failure, contact is made with the respondent to verify or correct the reported data.

Imputation: Not all respondents answer every item on the questionnaire. There are also questionnaires that are not returned despite efforts to gain a response. Imputation is the process of filling in missing or invalid data with reasonable values in order to have a complete data set. For general purpose governments and for schools, the imputations were based on recent historical

U.S. Census Bureau, Statistical Abstract of the United States: 2008

data from either a prior year annual survey or the most recent Census of Governments, if it was available. These data were adjusted by a growth rate that was determined by the growth of units that were similar (in size, geography, and type of government) to the nonrespondent. If there was no recent historical data available, the imputations were based on the data from a randomly selected donor that was similar to the nonrespondent. This donor's data was adjusted by dividing each data item by the population (or enrollment) of the donor and multiplying the result by the nonrespondent's population (or enrollment). For special districts, if prior year data are available, the data are brought forward with a national level growth rate applied. Otherwise, the data are imputed to be zero. In cases where good secondary data sources exist, the data from those sources were used.

Estimates of Sampling Error: Estimated relative standard errors for all variables are given in tabulations on the Web site. For U.S. and state-and-local government-level estimates of total full-time equivalents and total payroll, most relative standard errors are generally less than 1 percent, but vary considerably for detailed characteristics.

Other (nonsampling) Errors: Although every effort is made in all phases of collection, processing, and tabulation to minimize errors, the sample data are subject to nonsampling errors such as inability to obtain data for every variable from all units in the sample, inaccuracies in classification, response errors, misinterpretation of questions, mistakes in keying and coding, and coverage errors. These same errors may be evident in census collections and may affect the Census of Governments data used to adjust the sample during the estimation phase and used in the imputation process.

Sources of Additional Material:
<http://www.census.gov/govs/www /apes.html> and <http://www.census .gov/govs/www/apesstl05.html>.

Annual Survey of Government Finances

Universe, Frequency, and Types of Data: The United States Census Bureau conducts an Annual Survey of Government Finances, as authorized by law under Title 13, United States Code, Section 182. Alternatively, every five years, in years ending in a '2' or '7,' a Census of Governments, including a Finance portion, is conducted under Title 13, Section 161. The survey coverage includes all state and local governments in the United States. For both the census and annual survey, the finance detail data is equivalent, encompassing the entire range of government finance activities—revenue, expenditure, debt, and assets.

Type of Data Collection Operations: The data collection phase for the annual survey made use of two methods to obtain data: mail canvass and central collection from state sources. In 28 states, all or part of the general purpose finance data for local governments was obtained from cooperative arrangements between the Census Bureau and a state government agency. These usually involved a data collection effort carried out to meet the needs of both agencies—the state agency for purposes of audit, oversight, or information, and the Census Bureau for statistical purposes. Data for the balance of local governments in this annual survey were obtained via mail questionnaires sent directly to county, municipal, township, special district, and school district governments. School district data were collected via cooperative arrangements with state education agencies. Data for state governments were compiled by analysts of the Census Bureau, usually with the cooperation and assistance of state officials. The data were compiled from state government audits, budgets, and other financial reports, either in printed or electronic format. The compilation generally involved recasting the state financial records into the classification categories used for reporting by the Census Bureau.

Data Collection and Imputation Procedures: Survey is conducted by mail with mail follow-ups of nonrespondents.

U.S. Census Bureau, Statistical Abstract of the United States: 2008

Imputation for all nonresponse items is based on previous year reports or, for new governments, on data from similar donors.

Estimates of Sampling Error: The local government statistics in this survey are developed from a sample survey. Therefore, the local totals, as well as national or state and local aggregates, are considered estimated amounts subject to sampling error. State government finance data are not subject to sampling. Consequently, state-local aggregates shown here are more reliable (on a relative standard error basis) than the local government estimates they include. Estimates of major United States totals for local governments are subject to a computed sampling variability of less than one-half of 1 percent. State and local government totals are generally subject to sampling variability of less than 3 percent.

Other (nonsampling) Errors: The estimates are also subject to the inaccuracies in classification, response, and processing. Efforts were made at all phases of collection, processing, and tabulation to minimize errors. However, the data are still subject to errors from estimating for missing data, errors from misreported data, errors from miscoding, and difficulties in identifying every unit that should be included in the report. Every effort was made to keep such errors to a minimum through care in examining, editing, and tabulating the data reported by government officials.

Sources of Additional Material:
<http://www.census.gov/govs/www /financegen.html> and <http://www .census.gov/govs/www /05censustechdoc.html>.

Annual Survey of Manufactures (ASM)

Universe, Frequency, and Types of Data: The Annual Survey of Manufactures is conducted annually, except for years ending in 2 and 7 for all manufacturing establishments having one or more paid employees. The purpose of the ASM is to provide key intercensal measures of manufacturing activity, products, and location for the public and private sectors. The ASM provides statistics on employment, payroll, worker hours,

payroll supplements, cost of materials, value added by manufacturing, capital expenditures, inventories, and energy consumption. It also provides estimates of value of shipments for 1,800 classes of manufactured products.

Type of Data Collection Operation: The ASM includes approximately 50,000 establishments selected from the census universe of 346,000 manufacturing establishments. Approximately 24,000 large establishments are selected with certainty, and the remaining 26,000 other establishments are selected with probability proportional to a composite measure of establishment size. The survey is updated from two sources: Internal Revenue Service (IRS) administrative records are used to include new single-unit manufacturers and the Company Organization Survey identifies new establishments of multiunit forms.

Data Collection and Imputation Procedures: Survey is conducted by mail with phone and mail follow-ups of nonrespondents. Imputation (for all nonresponse items) is based on previous year reports, or for new establishments in survey, on industry averages.

Estimates of Sampling Error: Estimated relative standard errors for number of employees, new expenditures, and for value added totals are given in annual publications. For U.S. level industry statistics, most estimated relative standard errors are 2 percent or less, but vary considerably for detailed characteristics.

Other (nonsampling) Errors: The unit response rate is about 85 percent. Nonsampling errors include those due to collection, reporting, and transcription errors, many of which are corrected through computer and clerical checks.

Sources of Additional Material: U.S. Census Bureau, *Annual Survey of Manufactures,* and Technical Paper 24.

Census of Population

Universe, Frequency, and Types of Data: Complete count of U.S. population conducted every 10 years since 1790. Data obtained on number and characteristics of people in the U.S.

Type of Data Collection Operation: In the 1990 and 2000 censuses, the 100 percent items included: age, date of birth,

sex, race, Hispanic origin, and relationship to householder. In 1980, approximately 19 percent of the housing units were included in the sample; in 1990 and 2000, approximately 17 percent.

Data Collection and Imputation Procedures: In 1980, 1990, and 2000, mail questionnaires were used extensively with personal interviews in the remainder. Extensive telephone and personal follow-up for nonrespondents was done in the censuses. Imputations were made for missing characteristics.

Estimates of Sampling Error: Sampling errors for data are estimated for all items collected by sample and vary by characteristic and geographic area. The coefficients of variation (CVs) for national and state estimates are generally very small.

Other (nonsampling) Errors: Since 1950, evaluation programs have been conducted to provide information on the magnitude of some sources of nonsampling errors such as response bias and undercoverage in each census. Results from the evaluation program for the 1990 census indicated that the estimated net undercoverage amounted to about 1.5 percent of the total resident population. For Census 2000, the evaluation program indicated a net overcount of 0.5 percent of the resident population.

Sources of Additional Material: U.S. Census Bureau, The Coverage of Population in the 1980 Census, PHC80-E4; *Content Reinterview Study: Accuracy of Data for Selected Population and Housing Characteristics as Measured by Reinterview,* PHC80-E2; *1980 Census of Population,* Vol. 1, (PC80-1), Appendixes B, C, and D. *Content Reinterview Survey: Accuracy of Data for Selected Population and Housing Characteristics as Measured by Reinterview,* 1990, CPH-E-1; Effectiveness of Quality Assurance, CPH-E-2; Programs to Improve Coverage in the 1990 Census, 1990, CPH-E-3. For Census 2000 evaluations, see <http://www.census.gov/pred/www>.

County Business Patterns

Universe, Frequency, and Types of Data: County Business Patterns is an annual tabulation of basic data items extracted from the Business Register, a file of all known single- and multilocation employer companies maintained and updated by the U.S. Census Bureau. Data include number of establishments, number of employees, first quarter and annual payrolls, and number of establishments by employment-size class. Data are excluded for self-employed individuals, private households, railroad employees, agricultural production workers, and most government employees.

Type of Data Collection Operation: The annual Company Organization Survey provides individual establishment data for multilocation companies. Data for single establishment companies are obtained from various Census Bureau programs, such as the Annual Survey of Manufactures and Current Business Surveys, as well as from administrative records of the IRS, the Social Security Administration, and the Bureau of Labor Statistics.

Estimates of Sampling Error: Not applicable.

Other (nonsampling) Errors: The data are subject to nonsampling errors, such as inability to identify all cases in the universe; definition and classification difficulties; differences in interpretation of questions; errors in recording or coding the data obtained; and estimation of employers who reported too late to be included in the tabulations and for records with missing or misreported data.

Sources of Additional Materials: U. S. Census Bureau, County Business Patterns

Current Population Survey (CPS)

Universe, Frequency, and Types of Data: Nationwide monthly sample designed primarily to produce national and state estimates of labor force characteristics of the civilian noninstitutionalized population 16 years of age and older.

Type of Data Collection Operation: Multistage probability sample that currently includes 72,000 households from 824 sample areas. Oversampling in some states to improve data reliability for those areas on an annual average basis. A continual sample rotation system is

used. Households are in sample 4 months, out for 8 months, and in for 4 more. Month-to-month overlap is 75 percent; year-to-year overlap is 50 percent.

Data Collection and Imputation Procedures: For first and fifth months that a household is in sample, personal interviews; other months, approximately 85 percent of the data collected by phone. Imputation is done for both item and total nonresponse. Adjustment for total nonresponse is done by a predefined cluster of units, by MSA size and residence; for item nonresponse imputation varies by subject matter.

Estimates of Sampling Error: The national total estimates of the civilian labor force and of employment have monthly CVs of about .2 percent and annual average CVs of about .125 percent. Unemployment is a much smaller characteristic and consequently has substantially larger CVs than the civilian labor force or employment. The national unemployment rate, the most important CPS statistic, has a monthly CV of about 2 percent and an annual average CV of about 1 percent. The CVs for states vary since more populous states have larger samples (and smaller CVs) than states with smaller populations. Assuming a 6 percent unemployment rate, the smallest states have monthly CVs of about 17 percent and annual average CVs of about 8 percent. The estimated CVs for family income and poverty rate for all persons in 2005 are .4 percent and 1.2 percent, respectively. CVs for subnational areas, such as states, tend to be larger and vary by area.

Other (nonsampling) Errors: Estimates of response bias on unemployment are available. Estimates of unemployment rate from reinterviews range from −2.4 percent to 1.0 percent of the basic CPS unemployment rate (over a 30-month span from January 2004 through June 2006). Eligible CPS households are approximately 82 percent of the assigned households, with a corresponding response rate of 91 percent.

Sources of Additional Material: U.S. Census Bureau and Bureau of Labor Statistics, Current Population Survey: Design and Methodology, (Technical Paper 66),

available on the Internet <http://www.census.gov/prod/2006pubs/tp-66.pdf> and the Bureau of Labor Statistics, <http://www.bls.gov/cps/> and the *BLS Handbook of Methods*, Chapter 1, available on the Internet at <http://www.bls.gov/opub/hom/homch1_a.htm>.

Foreign Trade—Export Statistics

Universe, Frequency, and Types of Data: The export declarations collected by U.S. Bureau of Customs and Border Protection are processed each month to obtain data on the movement of U.S. merchandise exports to foreign countries. Data obtained include value, quantity, and shipping weight of exports by commodity, country of destination, district of exportation, and mode of transportation.

Type of Data Collection Operation: Shipper's Export Declarations (paper and electronic) are generally required to be filed for the exportation of merchandise valued over $2,500. U.S. Bureau of Customs and Border Protection officials collect and transmit the documents to the Census Bureau on a flow basis for data compilation. Data for shipments valued under $2,501 are estimated, based on established percentages of individual country totals.

Data Collection and Imputation Procedures: Statistical copies of Shipper's Export Declarations are received on a daily basis from ports throughout the country and subjected to a monthly processing cycle. They are fully processed to the extent they reflect items valued over $2,500. Estimates for shipments valued at $2,500 or less are made, based on established percentages of individual country totals.

Estimates of Sampling Error: Not applicable.

Other (nonsampling) Errors: The goods data are a complete enumeration of documents collected by the U.S. Bureau of Customs and Border Protection and are not subject to sampling errors; but they are subject to several types of nonsampling errors. Quality assurance procedures are performed at every stage of collection, processing and tabulation;

however the data are still subject to several types of nonsampling errors. The most significant of these include reporting errors, undocumented shipments, timeliness, data capture errors, and errors in the estimation of low-valued transactions. Additional information on errors affecting export data can be found at <http://www.census.gov /foreign-trade/Press-Release/current _press_release/explain.pdf>.

Sources of Additional Material: U.S. Census Bureau, FT 900 U.S. International Trade in Goods and Services, FT 925 (discounted after 1996), U.S. Merchandise Trade, FT 895 U.S. Trade with Puerto Rico and U.S. Possessions, FT 920 U.S. Merchandise trade: selected highlights, and Information Section on Goods and Services at <http://www.census.gov/ft900>.

Foreign Trade—Import Statistics

Universe, Frequency, and Types of Data: The import entry documents collected by U.S. Bureau of Customs and Border Protection are processed each month to obtain data on the movement of merchandise imported into the United States. Data obtained include value, quantity, and shipping weight by commodity, country of origin, district of entry, and mode of transportation.

Type of Data Collection Operation: Import entry documents, either paper or electronic, are required to be filed for the importation of goods into the United States valued over $2,000 or for articles which must be reported on formal entries. U.S. Bureau of Customs and Border Protection officials collect and transmit statistical copies of the documents to the Census Bureau on a flow basis for data compilation. Estimates for shipments valued under $2,001 and not reported on formal entries are based on estimated established percentages for individual country totals.

Data Collection and Imputation Procedures: Statistical copies of import entry documents, received on a daily basis from ports of entry throughout the country, are subjected to a monthly processing cycle. They are fully processed to the extent they reflect items valued at $2,001 and over or items which must be reported on formal entries.

Estimates of Sampling Error: Not applicable.

Other (nonsampling) Errors: The goods data are a complete enumeration of documents collected by the U.S. Bureau of Customs and Border Protection and are not subject to sampling errors; but they are subject to several types of nonsampling errors. Quality assurance procedures are performed at every stage of collection, processing and tabulation; however the data are still subject to several types of nonsampling errors. The most significant of these include reporting errors, undocumented shipments, timeliness, data capture errors, and errors in the estimation of low-valued transactions. Additional information on errors affecting import data can be found at <http://www.census.gov /foreign-trade/Press-Release/current _press_release/explain.pdf>.

Sources of Additional Material: U.S. Census Bureau, FT 900 U.S. International Trade in Goods and Services, FT 925 (discounted after 1996), U.S. Merchandise Trade, FT 895 U.S. Trade with Puerto Rico and U.S. Possessions, FT920 U.S. Merchandise Trade: selected highlights, and Information Section on Goods and Services at <http://www.census.gov/ft900>.

Monthly Retail Trade and Food Service Survey

Universe, Frequency, and Types of Data: Provides monthly estimates of retail and food service sales by kind of business and end of month inventories of retail stores.

Type of Data Collection Operation: Probability sample of all firms from a list frame. The list frame is the Bureau's Business Register updated quarterly for recent birth Employer Identification (EI) Numbers issued by the IRS and assigned a kind of business code by the Social Security Administration. The largest firms are included monthly; a sample of others is included every month also.

Data Collection and Imputation Procedures: Data are collected by mail questionnaire with telephone follow-ups and

U.S. Census Bureau, Statistical Abstract of the United States: 2008

fax reminders for nonrespondents. Imputation is made for each nonresponse item and each item failing edit checks.

Estimates of Sampling Error: For the 2006 monthly surveys, CVs are about 0.4 percent for estimated total retail sales and 0.7 percent for estimated total retail inventories. Sampling errors are shown in monthly publications.

Other (nonsampling) Errors: Imputation rates are about 22 percent for monthly retail and food service sales, and 29 percent for monthly retail inventories.

Sources of Additional Material: U.S. Census Bureau, Current Business Reports, Annual Revision of Monthly Retail and Food Services: Sales and Inventories.

Monthly Survey of Construction

Universe, Frequency, and Types of Data: Survey conducted monthly of newly constructed housing units (excluding mobile homes). Data are collected on the start, completion, and sale of housing. (Annual figures are aggregates of monthly estimates.)

Type of Data Collection Operation: A multistage probability sample of approximately 900 of the 20,000 permit-issuing jurisdictions in the U.S. was selected. Each month in each of these permit offices, field representatives list and select a sample of permits for which to collect data. To obtain data in areas where building permits are not required, a multistage probability sample of 70 land areas (census tracts or subsections of census tracts) was selected. All roads in these areas are canvassed and data are collected on all new residential construction found. Sampled buildings are followed up until they are completed (and sold, if for sale).

Data Collection and Imputation Procedures: Data are obtained by telephone inquiry and/or field visit. Nonresponse/ undercoverage adjustment factors are used to account for late reported data.

Estimates of Sampling Error: Estimated CV of 3 percent to 4 percent for estimates of national totals of units started,

but may be higher than 20 percent for estimated totals of more detailed characteristics, such as housing units in multiunit structures.

Other (nonsampling) Errors: Response rate is over 90 percent for most items. Nonsampling errors are attributed to definitional problems, differences in interpretation of questions, incorrect reporting, inability to obtain information about all cases in the sample, and processing errors.

Sources of Additional Material: All data are available on the Internet at <http://www.census.gov/starts>, <http://www.census.gov/newhomesales> or <http://www.census.gov/const /www/newsresconstindex.html>. Further documentation of the survey is also available at those sites.

Nonemployer Statistics

Universe, Frequency, and Types of Data: Nonemployer statistics are an annual tabulation of economic data by industry for active businesses without paid employees that are subject to federal income tax. Data showing the number of firms and receipts by industry are available for the U.S., states, counties, and metropolitan areas. Most types of businesses covered by the Census Bureau's economic statistics programs are included in the nonemployer statistics. Tax-exempt and agricultural-production businesses are excluded from nonemployer statistics.

Type of Data Collection Operation: The universe of nonemployer firms is created annually as a byproduct of the Census Bureau's Business Register processing for employer establishments. If a business is active but without paid employees, then it becomes part of the potential nonemployer universe. Industry classification and receipts are available for each potential nonemployer business. These data are obtained primarily from the annual business income tax returns of the IRS. The potential nonemployer universe undergoes a series of complex processing, editing, and analytical review procedures at the Census Bureau to distinguish nonemployers from employers, and to correct and complete data items used in creating the data tables.

Estimates of Sampling Error: Not applicable.

Other (nonsampling) Errors: The data are subject to nonsampling errors, such as industry misclassification as well as errors of response, keying, nonreporting, and coverage.

Sources of Additional Material: U. S. Census Bureau, Nonemployer Statistics <http://www.census.gov/epcd/nonemployer/index.html>.

Service Annual Survey

Universe, Frequency, and Types of Data: The U.S. Census Bureau conducts the Service Annual Survey to provide nationwide estimates of revenues and expenses for selected service industries. Estimates are summarized by industry classification based on the 2002 North American Industry Classification System (NAICS). Selected service industries covered by the Service Annual Survey include all or part of the following NAICS sectors: Transportation and Warehousing (NAICS 48–49); Information (NAICS 51); Finance and Insurance (NAICS 52); Real Estate and Rental and Leasing (NAICS 53); Professional, Scientific, and Technical Services (NAICS 54); Administrative and Support and Waste Management and Remediation Services (NAICS 56); Health Care and Social Assistance (NAICS 62); Arts, Entertainment, and Recreation (NAICS 71); and Other Services, except Public Administration (NAICS 81). Data collected include total revenue, total expenses, detailed expenses, revenue from e-commerce transactions; and for selected industries, revenue from detailed service products, revenue from exported services, and inventories. For industries with a significant nonprofit component, separate estimates are developed for taxable firms and firms and organizations exempt from federal income taxes. Questionnaires are mailed in January and request annual data for the prior year. Estimates are published approximately 12 months after the initial survey mailing.

Type of Data Collection Operation: The Service Annual Survey estimates are developed from a probability sample of employer firms and administrative records for nonemployers. Service Annual Survey questionnaires are mailed

to a probability sample that is periodically reselected from a universe of firms located in the United States and having paid employees. The sample includes firms of all sizes and covers both taxable firms and firms exempt from federal income taxes. Updates to the sample are made on a quarterly basis to account for new businesses. Firms without paid employees, or nonemployers, are included in the estimates through imputation and/or administrative records data provided by other federal agencies. Links to additional information about confidentiality protection, sampling error, nonsampling error, sample design, definitions, and copies of the questionnaires may be found on the Internet at <http://www.census.gov/econ/www/servmenu.html>.

Estimates of Sampling Error: CVs for the 2005 Service Annual Survey estimates range from 0.4 percent to 1.8 percent for total revenue estimates computed at the NAICS sector (two-digit NAICS code) level. The full 2005 Service Annual Survey results, including coefficients of variations (CVs), can be found at <http://www.census.gov/econ/www/servmenu.html>. Links to additional information regarding sampling error may be found at: <http://www.census.gov/svsd/www/cv.html>.

Other (Nonsampling) Errors: Data are imputed for unit nonresponse, item nonresponse, and for reported data that fails edits. The percent of imputed data for total revenue for the 2005 Service Annual Survey is approximately 9 percent.

Sources of Additional Material: U.S. Census Bureau, Current Business Reports, Service Annual Survey, Census Bureau Web site: <http://www.census.gov/econ/www/servmenu.html>.

Survey of Business Owners (SBO)

Universe, Frequency, and Types of Data: The Survey of Business Owners (SBO), formerly known as the Surveys of Minority- and Women-Owned Business Enterprises (SMOBE/SWOBE), provides statistics that describe the composition of U.S. businesses by gender, Hispanic

or Latino origin, and race. Data are presented for businesses owned by American Indians and Alaska Natives, Asians, Blacks, Hispanics, Native Hawaiians and Other Pacific Islanders, and Women. All U.S. firms operating during 2002 with receipts of $1,000 or more, which are classified by the North American Industry Classification System (NAICS) codes 11 through 99, are represented, except for the following: NAICS 111, 112, 4811 (part), 482, 491, 525 (part), 813, 814, and 92. The lists of all firms (or sample frames) are compiled from a combination of business tax returns and data collected on other economic census reports. The published data include the number of firms, gross receipts, number of paid employees, and annual payroll. Data are presented by industry classifications and/or geographic area (states, metropolitan and micropolitan statistical areas, counties, and corporate municipalities (places) including cities, towns, townships, villages, and boroughs), and size of firm (employment and receipts).

Type of Data Collection Operation: The survey is based on a stratified probability sample of approximately 2.3 million firms from a universe of approximately 23 million firms. There were 5.5 million firms with paid employees and 17.4 million firms with no paid employees. The data are based on the entire firm rather than on individual locations of a firm.

Data Collection and Imputation Procedures: Data were collected through a mailout/mailback operation. Compensation for missing data is addressed through reweighting, edit correction, and standard statistical imputation methods.

Estimates of Sampling Error: Sampling error is present in these estimates because they are based on the results of a sample survey and not on an enumeration of the entire universe. Since these estimates are based on a probability sample, it is possible to estimate the sampling variability of the survey estimates. The standard error (SE) provides a measure of the variation. The relative SE or CV provides a measure of the magnitude of the variation relative to the estimate and is calculated as 100 multiplied by the ratio of the estimate to the

SE. The CVs for number of firms and receipts at the national level typically range from 0 to 4 percent.

Other (nonsampling) Error: Nonsampling errors are attributed to many sources: inability to obtain information for all cases in the universe, adjustments to the weights of respondents to compensate for nonrespondents, imputation for missing data, data errors and biases, mistakes in recording or keying data, errors in collection or processing, and coverage problems. Explicit measures of the effects of these nonsampling errors are not available. However, it is believed that most of the important operational and data errors were detected and corrected through an automated data edit designed to review the data for reasonableness and consistency. Quality control techniques were used to verify that operating procedures were carried out as specified.

Sources of Additional Materials: U.S. Census Bureau, Guide to the 2002 Economic Census and Related Statistics.

U.S. DEPARTMENT OF EDUCATION National Center for Education Statistics

Higher Education General Information Survey (HEGIS), Degrees and Other Formal Awards Conferred. Beginning 1986, Integrated Postsecondary Education Data Survey (IPEDS), Completions

Universe, Frequency, and Types of Data: Annual survey of all institutions and branches listed in the Education Directory, Colleges and Universities to obtain data on earned degrees and other formal awards, conferred by field of study, level of degree, sex, and by racial/ethnic characteristics (every other year prior to 1989, then annually).

Type of Data Collection Operation: Complete census.

Data Collection and Imputation Procedures: Data are collected through a Web-based survey in the fall of every year. Missing data are imputed by using data of similar institutions.

Estimates of Sampling Error: Not applicable.

Other (nonsampling Errors: For 2004–05, approximately 99.9 percent response rate for degree-granting institutions.

Sources of Additional Material: U.S. Department of Education, National Center for Education Statistics, *Postsecondary Institutions in the United States: Fall 2005 and Degrees and Other Awards Conferred: 2004–05.* See <http://www.nces.ed.gov/ipeds/>.

National Household Education Surveys (NHES) Program

Universe, Frequency, and Types of Data: The National Household Education Surveys Program is a system of telephone surveys of the noninstitutionalized civilian population of the United States. Surveys in NHES have varying universes of interest depending on the particular survey. Specific topics covered by each survey are at the NHES Web site <http://nces.ed.gov/nhes>. A list of the surveys fielded as part of NHES, each universe, and the years they were fielded is provided below. 1) Adult Education—Interviews were conducted with a representative sample of civilian, noninstitutionalized persons age 16 and older who were not enrolled in grade 12 or below (1991, 1995, 1999, 2001, 2003, 2005). 2) After-School Programs and Activities—Interviews were conducted with parents of a representative sample of students in grades K through 8 (1999, 2001, 2005). 3) Civic Involvement—Interviews were conducted with representative samples of parents, youth, and adults (1996, 1999). 4) Early Childhood Program Participation—Interviews were conducted with parents of a representative sample of children from birth through grade 3, with the specific age groups varying by survey year (1991, 1995, 1999, 2001, 2005). 5) Household and Library Use—Interviews were conducted with a representative sample of U.S. households (1996). 6) Parent and Family Involvement in Education—Interviews were conducted with parents of a representative sample of children age three through grade 12 or in grades K through 12 depending on the survey year (1996, 1999, 2003, and 2007 forthcoming). 7) School Readiness—Interviews were conducted with parents of a representative sample of 3- to 7-year old children

(1993, 1999, and 2007 forthcoming). 8) School Safety and Discipline—Interviews were conducted with a representative sample of students in grades 6–12, their parents, and the parents of a representative sample of students in grades 3–12 (1993).

Type of Data Collection Operation: NHES uses telephone interviews to collect data.

Data Collection and Imputation Procedures: Telephone numbers are selected using random digit dialing (RDD) techniques. Approximately 45,000 to 64,000 households are contacted in order to identify persons eligible for the surveys. Data are collected using computer-assisted telephone interviewing (CATI) procedures. Missing data are imputed using hot-deck imputation procedures.

Estimates of Sampling Error: Unweighted sample sizes range between 2,250 and 55,708. The average root design effects of the surveys in NHES range from 1.1 to 1.5, except for the Adult Education survey of 1991. In 1991, average root design effects for the Adult Education survey ranged from 2.3 to 4.5.

Other (nonsampling) Errors: Because of unit nonresponse and because the samples are drawn from households with telephone instead of all households, nonresponse and/or coverage bias may exist for some estimates. However, both sources of potential bias are adjusted for in the weighting process. Analyses of both potential sources of bias in the NHES collections have been studied and no significant bias has been detected.

Sources of Additional Material: Please see the NHES Web site at <http://nces.ed .gov/nhes>.

Schools and Staffing Survey (SASS)

Universe, frequency, and Types of Data: NCES designed the SASS survey system to emphasize teacher demand and shortage, teacher and administrator characteristics, school programs, and general conditions in schools. SASS also collects data on many other topics, including principals' and teachers' perceptions of school climate and problems in their schools; teacher compensation;

U.S. Census Bureau, Statistical Abstract of the United States: 2008

district hiring practices and basic characteristics of the student population. The SASS has had four core components: the School Questionnaire, the Teacher Questionnaire, the Principal Questionnaire, and the School District Questionnaire. For the 2003–04 SASS, a sample of public charter schools is included in the sample as part of the public school questionnaire. Since 1987–88, the SASS is the largest, most extensive survey of K through 12 school districts, schools, teachers, and administrators in the U.S. Surveys have been conducted every 3 to 4 years depending on budgetary constraints. The SASS includes data from public, private, and Bureau of Indian Affairs school sectors. Therefore, the SASS provides a multitude of opportunities for analysis and reporting on elementary and secondary educational issues

Type of Data Collection Operation: The U.S. Census Bureau performs the data collection and begins by sending advance letters to the sampled Local Education Agencies (LEAs) and schools in August and September of collection years. Beginning in October, questionnaires are delivered by U.S. Census Bureau field representatives. The sampling frame for the public school sample is the most recent Common Core of Data (CCD) school file. CCD is a universe file that includes all elementary and secondary schools in the United States. Schools operated by the Department of Defense or those that offered only kindergarten or pre-kindergarten or adult education were excluded from the SASS sample. The list frame used for the private school sample is the most recent Private School Universe Survey (PSS) list, updated with association lists. An area frame supplement is based on the canvassing of private schools within specific geographical areas. A separate universe of schools funded by the Bureau of Indian Affairs (BIA) is drawn from the Program Education Directory maintained by the BIA. To avoid duplicates in the BIA files, BIA schools in the CCD school file are treated as public schools.

Estimates of Sampling Error: Sample errors can be calculated using replicate weights and Balanced Repeated Replication complex survey design methodology. Errors depend on cell sizes and range from less than 1 percent to over 5 percent (for reasonable cell sizes).

Other (nonsampling) Errors: Because of unit nonresponse, bias may exist in some sample cells. However, bias has been adjusted for in the weighting process. Analysis of bias has been studied and no significant bias has been detected.

Sources of Additional Material: Please see the SASS web site at <http://nces.ed.gov/surveys/sass/>.

U.S. FEDERAL BUREAU OF INVESTIGATION

Uniform Crime Reporting (UCR) Program

Universe, Frequency, and Types of Data: Monthly reports on the number of criminal offenses that become known to law enforcement agencies. Data are also collected on crimes cleared by arrest or exceptional means; by age, sex, and race of arrestees and for victims and offenders for homicides, number of law enforcement employees, on fatal and nonfatal assaults against law enforcement officers, and on hate crimes reported.

Type of Data Collection Operation: Crime statistics are based on reports of crime data submitted either directly to the FBI by contributing law enforcement agencies or through cooperating state UCR programs.

Data Collection and Imputation Procedures: States with UCR programs collect data directly from individual law enforcement agencies and forward reports, prepared in accordance with UCR standards, to FBI. Accuracy and consistency edits are performed by FBI.

Estimates of Sampling Error: Not applicable.

Other (nonsampling) Errors: The coverage is 94 percent of the population (95 percent in MSAs, 87 percent in "cities outside of metropolitan areas," and 88 percent in nonmetropolitan counties) by UCR Program, through varying number of agencies reporting.

U.S. Census Bureau, Statistical Abstract of the United States: 2008

Sources of Additional Material: U.S. Federal Bureau of Investigation, *Crime in the United States*, annual, *Hate Crime Statistics*, annual, *Law Enforcement Officers Killed & Assaulted*, annual, <http://www.fbi.gov/ucr/ucr.htm>.

U.S. INTERNAL REVENUE SERVICE

Corporation Income Tax Returns

Universe, Frequency, and Types of Data: Annual study of unaudited corporation income tax returns, Forms 1120, 1120-A, 1120-F, 1120-L, 1120-PC, 1120-REIT, 1120-RIC, and 1120S, filed by corporations or businesses legally defined as corporations. Data provided on various financial characteristics by industry and size of total assets, and business receipts.

Type of Data Collection Operation: Stratified probability sample of approximately 146,000 returns for Tax Year 2004, allocated to sample classes which are based on type of return, size of total assets, size of net income or deficit, and selected business activity. Sampling rates for sample classes varied from .25 percent to 100 percent.

Data Collection and Imputation Procedures: Computer selection of sample of tax return records. Data adjusted during editing for incorrect, missing, or inconsistent entries to ensure consistency with other entries on return and to comply with statistical definitions.

Estimates of Sampling Error: Estimated CVs for Tax Year 2004: Returns with assets over $10 million are self-representing. Coefficients of variation are published in the 2004 Statistics of Income Corporation Income Tax Returns, Table 1, by industry group.

Other (nonsampling) Errors: Nonsampling errors include coverage errors, processing errors, and response errors.

Sources of Additional Material: U.S. Internal Revenue Service, *Statistics of Income, Corporation Income Tax Returns*, annual.

Individual Income Tax Returns

Universe, Frequency, and Types of Data: Annual study of unaudited individual income tax returns, Forms 1040, 1040A, and 1040EZ, filed by U.S. citizens and residents. Data provided on various financial characteristics by size of adjusted gross income, marital status, and by taxable and nontaxable returns. Data by state, based on the population of returns filed, also include returns from 1040NR, filed by nonresident aliens plus certain self employment tax returns.

Type of Data Collection Operation: Annual 2004 stratified probability sample of approximately 201,000 returns broken into sample strata based on the larger of total income or total loss amounts, the size of business plus farm receipts, and other criteria such as the potential usefulness of the return for tax policy modeling. Sampling rates for sample strata varied from 0.05 percent to 100 percent.

Data Collection and Imputation Procedures: Computer selection of sample of tax return records. Data adjusted during editing for incorrect, missing, or inconsistent entries to ensure consistency with other entries on return.

Estimates of Sampling Error: Estimated CVs for tax year 2004: Adjusted gross income less deficit 0.11 percent; salaries and wages 0.21 percent; and tax exempt interest received 1.76 percent. (State data not subject to sampling error.)

Other (nonsampling) Errors: Processing errors and errors arising from the use of tolerance checks for the data.

Sources of Additional Material: U.S. Internal Revenue Service, *Statistics of Income, Individual Income Tax Returns*, annual, (Publication 1304).

Partnership Income Tax Returns

Universe, Frequency, and Types of Data: Annual study of unaudited income tax returns of partnerships, Form 1065. Data provided on various financial characteristics by industry.

Type of Data Collection Operation: Stratified probability sample of approximately 44,000 partnership returns from a population of 2.9 million filed during calendar year 2006 The sample is classified based on combinations of gross

U.S. Census Bureau, Statistical Abstract of the United States: 2008

receipts, net income or loss, total assets, and on industry. Sampling rates vary from 0.09 percent to 100 percent.

Data Collection and Imputation Procedures: Computer selection of sample of tax return records. Data are adjusted during editing for incorrect, missing, or inconsistent entries to ensure consistency with other entries on return. Data not available due to regulations are not imputed.

Estimates of Sampling Error: Estimated CVs for tax year 2005 (latest available): For number of partnerships, 0.32 percent; business receipts, 0.18 percent; Net income, 0.57 percent; net loss; 1.31 percent.

Other (nonsampling) Errors: Processing errors and errors arising from the use of tolerance checks for the data.

Sources of Additional Material: U.S. Internal Revenue Service, *Statistics of Income, Partnership Returns and Statistics of Income Bulletin*, Vol. 26, No. 2 (Fall 2006).

Sole Proprietorship Income Tax Returns

Universe, Frequency, and Types of Data: Annual study of unaudited income tax returns of nonfarm sole proprietorships, Form 1040 with business schedules. Data provided on various financial characteristics by industry.

Type of Data Collection Operation: Stratified probability sample of approximately 63,000 sole proprietorships for tax year 2004. The sample is classified based on presence or absence of certain business schedules; the larger of total income or loss; size of business plus farm receipts, and other criteria such as the potential usefulness of the return for tax policy modeling. Sampling rates vary from 0.05 percent to 100 percent.

Data Collection and Imputation Procedures: Computer selection of sample of tax return records. Data adjusted during editing for incorrect, missing, or inconsistent entries to ensure consistency with other entries on return.

Estimates of Sampling Error: Estimated CVs for tax year 2004 are available. For sole proprietorships, business receipts, 0.64 percent; depreciation 1.35 percent.

Other (nonsampling) Errors: Processing errors and errors arising from the use of tolerance checks for the data.

Sources of Additional Material: U.S. Internal Revenue Service, *Statistics of Income, Sole Proprietorship Returns* (for years 1980 through 1983) and *Statistics of Income Bulletin*, Vol. 26, No. 1 (Summer 2006, as well as bulletins for earlier years).

U.S. NATIONAL CENTER FOR HEALTH STATISTICS (NCHS)

National Health Interview Survey (NHIS)

Universe, Frequency, and Types of Data: Continuous data collection covering the civilian noninstitutional population to obtain information on demographic characteristics, conditions, injuries, impairments, use of health services, health behaviors, and other health topics.

Type of Data Collection Operation: Multistage probability sample of 49,000 households (in 198 PSUs) from 1985 to 1994; 36–40,000 households (358 design PSUs or 449 effective PSUs when divided by state boundaries) from 1995 to 2005; an estimated completed 35,000 households (428 effective PSUs) beginning in 2006.

Data Collection and Imputation Procedures: Some missing data items (e.g., race, ethnicity) are imputed using a hot deck imputation value. Sequential regression models are used to create multiple imputation files for family income. Unit nonresponse is compensated for by an adjustment to the survey weights.

Estimates of Sampling Error: For 2004 medically attended injury episodes rates in the past 12 months by falling for: females 46.38 (3.50), and males 36.87 (3.24) per 1,000 population; for 2004 injury episodes rates during the past 12 months inside the home—29.72 (2.11) per 1,000 population.

Other (nonsampling) Errors: The response rate was 93.8 percent in 1996; in 2006, the total household response rate was 87.3 percent, with the final family response rate of 87.0 percent, and the final sample adult response rate of 70.8

percent. (Note: the NHIS questionnaire was redesigned in 1997, and a new sample design was instituted in 2006).

Sources of Additional Material: National Center for Health Statistics, Summary Health Statistics for the U.S. Population: National Health Interview Survey, 2005, Vital and Health Statistics, Series 10 #233; National Center for Health Statistics, Summary Health Statistics for U.S. Children: National Health Interview Survey, 2005, Vital and Health Statistics, Series 10 #231; National Center for Health Statistics, Summary Health Statistics for U.S. Adults: National Health Interview Survey, 2005, Vital and Health Statistics, Series 10 #232; U.S. National Center for Health Statistics, Design and Estimation for the National Health Interview Survey, 1995–2004, Vital and Health Statistics, Series 2 #130.

National Survey of Family Growth (NSFG)

Universe, Frequency, and Types of Data: Periodic survey of men and women 15–44 years of age in the household population of the United States. Interviews were conducted in 2002 in person by trained female interviewers. Interview topics covered include births and pregnancies, marriage, divorce, and cohabitation, sexual activity, contraceptive use, and medical care. For men, data on father involvement with children were collected. The most sensitive data—on sexual behavior related to HIV and Sexually Transmitted Disease risk—were collected in a self-administered form in which the data are entered into a computer.

Type of Data Collection Operation: In the 2002 (Cycle 6) NSFG, the sample was a multistage area probability sample of men and women 15–44 years of age in the household population of the United States. Only one person 15–44 was selected from households with one or more persons 15–44. Data were collected and entered into laptop (notebook) computers. In the self-administered portion, the respondent entered his or her own answers into the computer. Sample included 12,571 interviews. The response rate was 79 percent. Hispanic and Black persons, as well as those 15–19 years of age, were

sampled at higher rates than White adults. All percentages and other statistics shown for the NSFG are weighted to make national estimates. The weights adjust for the different rates of sampling for each group, and for nonresponse.

Data Collection and Imputation Procedures: When interviews are received, they are reviewed for consistency and quality, and analysis variables (recodes) are created. Missing data on these recodes were imputed using multiple regression techniques and checked again for consistency. Variables indicating whether a value has been imputed ("imputation flags") are included on the data file.

Estimates of Sampling Error: Sampling error codes are included on the data file so that users can estimate sampling errors for their own analyses. Sampling error estimates for nine illustrative analyses are shown on the NSFG Web site at <http://www.cdc.gov/nchs/nsfg.htm>. Sampling error estimates are also shown in most NCHS reports.

Other (nonsampling) Errors: In any survey, errors can occur because the respondent (the person being interviewed) does not recall the specific fact or event being asked about. The NSFG questionnaire in 2002 was programmed to check the consistency of many variables during the interview, so that the interviewer and respondent had a chance to correct any inconsistent information. Further checking occurred after the interview and during recoding and imputation. Typically, less than 1 percent of cases need imputation because of missing data.

Sources of Additional Material: The following references can be found at <http://www.cdc.gov/nchs/nsfg.htm>. "National Survey of Family Growth, Cycle 6: Sample Design, Weighting, and Variance Estimation." Vital and Health Statistics, Series 2, Number 142, July 2006. "Plan and Operation of Cycle 6 of the National Survey of Family Growth." Vital and Health Statistics, Series 1, No. 42. August 2005. "Sexual Behavior and Selected Health Measures: Men and Women 15–44 Years of Age, United States, 2002." *Advance Data from Vital and Health Statistics*, No. 362, Sept 15, 2005.

National Vital Statistics System

Universe, Frequency, and Types of Data: Annual data on births and deaths in the United States.

Type of Data Collection Operation: Mortality data based on complete file of death records, except 1972, based on 50 percent sample. Natality statistics 1951–1971, based on 50 percent sample of birth certificates, except a 20 percent to 50 percent sample in 1967, received by NCHS. Beginning 1972, data from some states received through Vital Statistics Cooperative Program (VSCP) and complete file used; data from other states based on 50 percent sample. Beginning 1986, all reporting areas participated in the VSCP and are providing complete files of birth certificates.

Data Collection and Imputation Procedures: Reports based on records from registration offices of all states, District of Columbia, New York City, Puerto Rico, Virgin Islands, Guam, American Samoa, and Northern Marianas.

Estimates of Sampling Error: For recent years, there is no sampling for these files; the files are based on 100 percent of events registered.

Other (nonsampling) Errors: Data on births and deaths believed to be at least 99 percent complete.

Sources of Additional Material: U.S. National Center for Health Statistics, *Vital Statistics of the United States*, Vol. I and Vol. II, annual, and the *National Vital Statistics Reports*. See the NCHS Web site at, <http://www.cdc.gov/nchs/nvss.htm>.

National Highway Traffic Safety Administration (NHTSA)

Fatality Analysis Reporting System (FARS)

Universe, Frequency, and Types of Data: FARS is a census of all fatal motor vehicle traffic crashes that occur throughout the United States including the District of Columbia and Puerto Rico on roadways customarily open to the public. The crash must be reported to the state/jurisdiction and at least one directly related fatality must occur within thirty days of the crash.

Type of Data Collection Operation: One or more analysts, in each state, extract data from the official documents and enter the data into a standardized electronic database.

Data Collection and Imputation Procedures: Detailed data describing the characteristics of the fatal crash, the vehicles and persons involved are obtained from police crash reports, driver and vehicle registration records, autopsy reports, highway department, etc. Computerized edit checks monitor the accuracy and completeness of the data. The FARS incorporates a sophisticated mathematical multiple imputation procedure to develop a probability distribution of missing blood alcohol concentration (BAC) levels in the database for drivers, pedestrians, and cyclists.

Estimates of Sampling Error: Since this is census data, there are no sampling errors.

Other (nonsampling) Errors: FARS represents a census of all police reported crashes and captures all data reported at the state level. FARS data undergo a rigorous quality control process to prevent inaccurate reporting. However, these data are highly dependent on the accuracy of the police accident reports. Errors or omissions within police accident reports may not be detected.

Sources of Additional Material: The FARS Coding and Validation Manual, ANSI D16.1 Manual on Classification of Motor Vehicle Traffic Accidents (Sixth Edition).

Appendix IV
Weights and Measures

[For assistance on metric usage, call or write:

Elizabeth J. Gentry
NIST
Weights and Measures Division
100 Bureau Drive – Mail Stop 2600
Gaithersburg, MD 20899-2600

Telephone: 301-975-3690 or 4004   FAX: 301-975-8091

E-mail: TheSI@nist.gov

Internet site <http://www.nist.gov/metric>

Symbol	When you know conventional	Multiply by	To find metric	Symbol
in	inches	2.54	centimeters	cm
ft	feet	30.48	centimeters	cm
yd	yards	0.91	meters	m
mi	miles	1.61	kilometers	km
in^2	square inches	6.45	square centimeters	cm^2
ft^2	square feet	0.09	square meters	m^2
yd^2	square yards	0.84	square meters	m^2
mi^2	square miles	2.59	square kilometers	km^2
	acre	0.41	hectare	ha
oz	ounces [1]	28.35	grams	g
lb	pounds [1]	.45	kilograms	kg
oz (troy)	ounces [2]	31.10	grams	g
	short tons (2,000 lb)	0.91	metric tons	t
	long tons (2,240 lb)	1.02	metric tons	t
fl oz	fluid ounces	29.57	milliliters	mL
c	cups	0.24	liters	L
pt	pints	0.47	liters	L
qt	quarts	0.95	liters	L
gal	gallons	3.78	liters	L
ft^3	cubic feet	0.03	cubic meters	m^3
yd^3	cubic yards	0.76	cubic meters	m^3
F	degrees Fahrenheit (subtract 32)	0.55	degrees Celsius	C

Symbol	When you know metric	Multiply by	To find conventional	Symbol
cm	centimeters	0.39	inches	in
cm	centimeters	0.03	feet	ft
m	meters	1.09	yards	yd
km	kilometers	0.62	miles	mi
cm^2	square centimeters	0.15	square inches	in^2
m^2	square meters	10.76	square feet	ft^2
m^2	square meters	1.20	square yards	yd^2
km^2	square kilometers	0.39	square miles	mi^2
ha	hectares	2.47	acre	
g	grams	.035	ounces [1]	oz
kg	kilograms	2.21	pounds [1]	lb
g	grams	.032	ounces [2]	oz (troy)
t	metric tons	1.10	short tons (2,000 lb)	
t	metric tons	0.98	long tons (2,240 lb)	
mL	milliliters	0.03	fluid ounces	fl oz
L	liter	4.24	cups	c
L	liters	2.13	pints (liquid)	pt
L	liters	1.05	quarts (liquid)	qt
L	liters	0.26	gallons	gal
m^3	cubic meters	35.32	cubic feet	ft^3
m^3	cubic meters	1.32	cubic yards	yd^3
C	degrees Celsius (after multiplying, add 32)	1.80	degrees Fahrenheit	F

[1] For weighing ordinary commodities.   [2] For weighing precious metals, jewels, etc.

U.S. Census Bureau, Statistical Abstract of the United States: 2008

Index

NOTE: Index citations refer to **table** numbers, not page numbers.

U.S. Census Bureau, Statistical Abstract of the United States: 2008

NOTE: Index citations refer to **table** numbers, not page numbers.

NOTE: Index citations refer to **table** numbers, not page numbers.

U.S. Census Bureau, Statistical Abstract of the United States: 2008

NOTE: Index citations refer to **table** numbers, not page numbers.

NOTE: Index citations refer to **table** numbers, not page numbers.

U.S. Census Bureau, Statistical Abstract of the United States: 2008

NOTE: Index citations refer to **table** numbers, not page numbers.

NOTE: Index citations refer to **table** numbers, not page numbers.

U.S. Census Bureau, Statistical Abstract of the United States: 2008

NOTE: Index citations refer to **table** numbers, not page numbers.

NOTE: Index citations refer to **table** numbers, not page numbers.

U.S. Census Bureau, Statistical Abstract of the United States: 2008

NOTE: Index citations refer to **table** numbers, not page numbers.

NOTE: Index citations refer to **table** numbers, not page numbers.

U.S. Census Bureau, Statistical Abstract of the United States: 2008

NOTE: Index citations refer to **table** numbers, not page numbers.

NOTE: Index citations refer to **table** numbers, not page numbers.

NOTE: Index citations refer to **table** numbers, not page numbers.

NOTE: Index citations refer to **table** numbers, not page numbers.

U.S. Census Bureau, Statistical Abstract of the United States: 2008

NOTE: Index citations refer to **table** numbers, not page numbers.

U.S. Census Bureau, Statistical Abstract of the United States: 2008

NOTE: Index citations refer to **table** numbers, not page numbers.

U.S. Census Bureau, Statistical Abstract of the United States: 2008

NOTE: Index citations refer to **table** numbers, not page numbers.

NOTE: Index citations refer to **table** numbers, not page numbers.

U.S. Census Bureau, Statistical Abstract of the United States: 2008

NOTE: Index citations refer to **table** numbers, not page numbers.

NOTE: Index citations refer to **table** numbers, not page numbers.

U.S. Census Bureau, Statistical Abstract of the United States: 2008

NOTE: Index citations refer to **table** numbers, not page numbers.

NOTE: Index citations refer to **table** numbers, not page numbers.

U.S. Census Bureau, Statistical Abstract of the United States: 2008

NOTE: Index citations refer to **table** numbers, not page numbers.

NOTE: Index citations refer to **table** numbers, not page numbers.

U.S. Census Bureau, Statistical Abstract of the United States: 2008

NOTE: Index citations refer to **table** numbers, not page numbers.

NOTE: Index citations refer to **table** numbers, not page numbers.

NOTE: Index citations refer to **table** numbers, not page numbers.

NOTE: Index citations refer to **table** numbers, not page numbers.

U.S. Census Bureau, Statistical Abstract of the United States: 2008

NOTE: Index citations refer to **table** numbers, not page numbers.

NOTE: Index citations refer to **table** numbers, not page numbers.

U.S. Census Bureau, Statistical Abstract of the United States: 2008

NOTE: Index citations refer to **table** numbers, not page numbers.

NOTE: Index citations refer to **table** numbers, not page numbers.

U.S. Census Bureau, Statistical Abstract of the United States: 2008

NOTE: Index citations refer to **table** numbers, not page numbers.

NOTE: Index citations refer to **table** numbers, not page numbers.

NOTE: Index citations refer to **table** numbers, not page numbers.

NOTE: Index citations refer to **table** numbers, not page numbers.

U.S. Census Bureau, Statistical Abstract of the United States: 2008

NOTE: Index citations refer to **table** numbers, not page numbers.

NOTE: Index citations refer to **table** numbers, not page numbers.

NOTE: Index citations refer to **table** numbers, not page numbers.

NOTE: Index citations refer to **table** numbers, not page numbers.

U.S. Census Bureau, Statistical Abstract of the United States: 2008

NOTE: Index citations refer to **table** numbers, not page numbers.

NOTE: Index citations refer to **table** numbers, not page numbers.

NOTE: Index citations refer to **table** numbers, not page numbers.

NOTE: Index citations refer to **table** numbers, not page numbers.

U.S. Census Bureau, Statistical Abstract of the United States: 2008

NOTE: Index citations refer to **table** numbers, not page numbers.

982   Index

NOTE: Index citations refer to **table** numbers, not page numbers.

U.S. Census Bureau, Statistical Abstract of the United States: 2008

NOTE: Index citations refer to **table** numbers, not page numbers.

NOTE: Index citations refer to **table** numbers, not page numbers.

U.S. Census Bureau, Statistical Abstract of the United States: 2008

NOTE: Index citations refer to **table** numbers, not page numbers.

NOTE: Index citations refer to **table** numbers, not page numbers.

U.S. Census Bureau, Statistical Abstract of the United States: 2008

NOTE: Index citations refer to **table** numbers, not page numbers.

NOTE: Index citations refer to **table** numbers, not page numbers.

NOTE: Index citations refer to **table** numbers, not page numbers.

NOTE: Index citations refer to **table** numbers, not page numbers.

U.S. Census Bureau, Statistical Abstract of the United States: 2008

NOTE: Index citations refer to **table** numbers, not page numbers.

NOTE: Index citations refer to **table** numbers, not page numbers.

U.S. Census Bureau, Statistical Abstract of the United States: 2008

NOTE: Index citations refer to **table** numbers, not page numbers.